CONNECT FEATURES

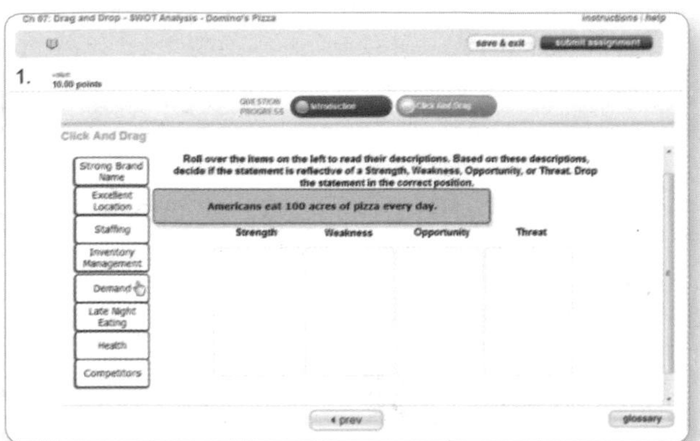

Interactive Applications

Interactive Applications offer a variety of automatically graded exercises that require students to apply key concepts. Whether the assignment includes a *click and drag*, *video case*, or *decision generator*, these applications provide instant feedback and progress tracking for students and detailed results for the instructor.

eBook

Connect Plus includes an eBook that allows you to share your notes with your students. Your students can insert and review their own notes, highlight the text, and search for specific information. Using an eBook with Connect Plus gives your students a complete digital solution that allows them to access their materials from any computer.

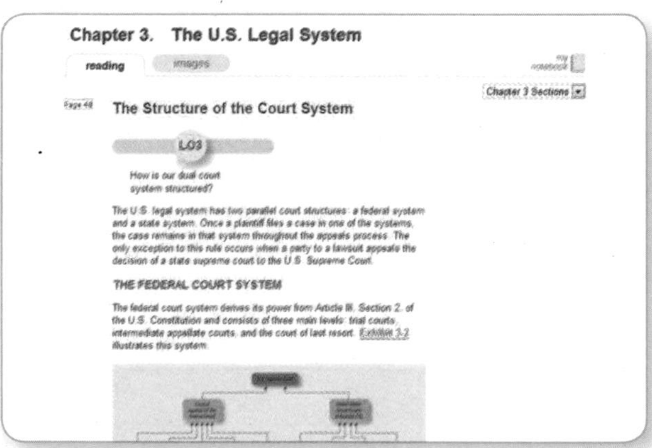

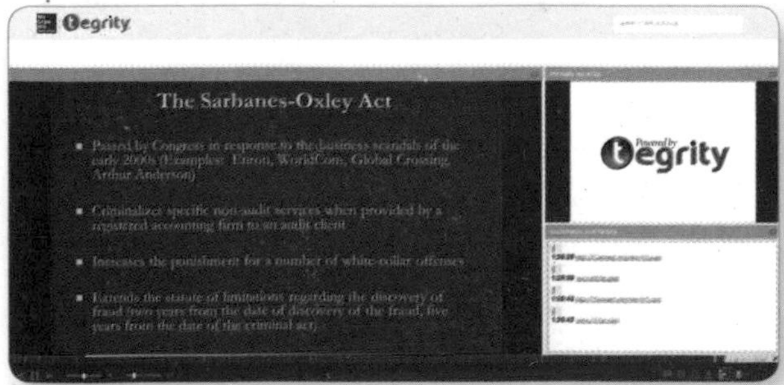

Tegrity

Make your classes available anytime, anywhere. With simple, one-click recording, students can search for a word or phrase and be taken to the exact place in your lecture that they need to review.

EASY TO USE

Learning Management System Integration

McGraw-Hill Campus is a one-stop teaching and learning experience available to use with any learning management system. McGraw-Hill Campus provides single sign-on to faculty and students for all McGraw-Hill material and technology from within the school website. McGraw-Hill Campus also allows instructors instant access to all supplements and teaching materials for all McGraw-Hill products.

Blackboard users also benefit from McGraw-Hill's industry-leading integration, providing single sign-on to access all Connect assignments and automatic feeding of assignment results to the Blackboard grade book.

POWERFUL REPORTING

Connect generates comprehensive reports and graphs that provide instructors with an instant view of the performance of individual students, a specific section, or multiple sections. Since all content is mapped to learning objectives, Connect reporting is ideal for accreditation or other administrative documentation.

Dynamic Business Law

Dynamic Business Law

THIRD EDITION

NANCY K. KUBASEK
Bowling Green State University

M. NEIL BROWNE
Bowling Green State University

LUCIEN J. DHOOGE
Scheller College of Business, Georgia Institute of Technology

DANIEL J. HERRON
Miami University

LINDA L. BARKACS
University of San Diego

CARRIE WILLIAMSON
*DLA Piper US LLP
East Palo Alto, California*

DYNAMIC BUSINESS LAW, THIRD EDITION
Published by McGraw-Hill Education, 2 Penn Plaza, New York, NY 10121.

Some ancillaries, including electronic and print components, may not be available to customers outside the United States.

This book is printed on acid-free paper.

1 2 3 4 5 6 7 8 9 0 DOW/DOW 1 0 9 8 7 6 5 4

ISBN 978-0-07-802378-1
MHID 0-07-802378-5

Senior Vice President, Products & Markets: *Kurt L. Strand*
Vice President, Content Production & Technology Services: *Kimberly Meriwether David*
Managing Director: *Tim Vertovec*
Executive Director of Development: *Ann Torbert*
Development Editor II: *Rebecca Mann*
Director of Digital Content: *Patricia Plumb*
Digital Development Editor: *Julie Hankins*
Senior Marketing Manager: *Michelle Nolte*
Director, Content Production: *Terri Schiesl*
Content Project Manager: *Emily Kline*
Senior Buyer: *Carol A. Bielski*
Design: *Matt Diamond*
Lead Content Licensing Specialist: *Keri Johnson*
Typeface: *10/12 Times LT Std Roman*
Compositor: *Laserwords Private Limited*
Printer: *R. R. Donnelley*

Library of Congress Cataloging-in-Publication Data

Kubasek, Nancy, author.
Dynamic business law / Nancy K. Kubasek, Bowling Green State University; M. Neil Browne, Bowling Green State University; Lucien J. Dhooge, Scheller College of Business, Georgia Institute of Technology; Daniel J. Herron, Miami University; Linda L. Barkacs, University of San Diego; Carrie Williamson, DLA Piper US LLP, East Palo Alto, California.—Third edition.
pages cm
Includes index.
ISBN 978-0-07-802378-1 (alk. paper)—ISBN 0-07-802378-5 (alk. paper)
1. Commercial law—United States. I. Browne, M. Neil, 1944- author. II. Dhooge, Lucien J., author. III. Herron, Daniel J., author. IV. Williamson, Carrie, author. V. Barkacs, Linda L., author. VI. Title.
KF889.K83 2015
346.7307—dc23

2013042896

www.mhhe.com

About the Authors

Nancy K. Kubasek received her J.D. from the University of Toledo College of Law in 1981 and her B.A. from Bowling Green State University in 1978. She joined the BGSU faculty in 1982, became an associate professor in 1988, and became a full professor in 1993.

During her tenure at Bowling Green State University, she has primarily taught courses in business law, legal environment of business, environmental law, health care law, and moral principles. She has published over 75 articles, primarily in law reviews and business journals. Most of her substantive articles focus on environmental questions. She has helped get students involved in legal research, and a number of her articles have been coauthored with students. She has also published a number of pedagogical articles in teaching journals, focusing primarily on the teaching of critical thinking and ethics.

She wrote the first environmental law text for undergraduate students, *Environmental Law,* and coauthored *The Legal Environment of Business: A Critical Thinking Approach.* She has written supplemental materials, such as study guides, test banks, and instructors' manuals.

Active in many professional organizations, she has served as president of the Academy of Legal Studies in Business, the national organization for professors of legal studies in colleges of business. She has also served as president of the Tri-State Academy of Legal Studies in Business, her regional professional association.

In her leisure time, she and her husband, Neil Browne, fish for halibut and salmon in Alaska, as well as largemouth bass in Florida. In addition, they are regular participants in polka, waltz, zydeco, and Cajun dance festivals in Europe and the United States. For almost 30 years, they have been successful tournament blackjack players. Both are avid exercisers—lifting weights, doing yoga, and running almost every day.

M. Neil Browne is a senior lecturer and research associate and a Distinguished Teacher professor emeritus at Bowling Green State University. He received his B.A. in history and economics at the University of Houston, his Ph.D. in economics at the University of Texas, and his J.D. from the University of Toledo. He has been a professor at Bowling Green for more than four decades.

Professor Browne teaches courses in economics and law, legal research, jurisprudence, ethical reasoning, critical thinking, and economics at both the undergraduate and graduate levels. He has received recognition as the Silver Medalist National Professor of the Year, the Ohio Professor of the Year, and Distinguished Teacher and Master Teacher at Bowling Green State University, as well as numerous research awards from his university and from professional organizations. His consulting activities with corporate, governmental, and educational institutions focus on improving the quality of critical thinking in those organizations. In addition, he serves as a Rule 26 expert with respect to the quality of the reasoning used by expert witnesses called by the party opponent in legal actions.

Professor Browne has published 25 books and over 140 professional articles in law journals, as well as in economics, sociology, and higher-education journals. His current research interests focus on the relationship between orthodox economic thinking and legal policy. In addition, he is in the midst of writing books about the power of questionable assumptions in economics, the usefulness of asking questions as a learning strategy, and the deficiencies of legal reasoning.

Lucien J. Dhooge is the Sue and John Staton Professor of Law at the Scheller College of Business at the Georgia Institute of Technology, where he teaches international business law and ethics and serves as the area coordinator in law and ethics. Prior to his tenure at the Georgia Institute of Technology, Professor Dhooge practiced law for 11 years and served on the faculty of the University of the Pacific in California for 12 years. He has authored more than 50 scholarly articles, coauthored and contributed to 13 books, and is a past editor in chief of the *American Business Law Journal* and the *Journal of Legal Studies Education.* Professor Dhooge has presented courses and research throughout the United States, as well as in Asia, Europe, and Central and South America, and has received numerous research and teaching awards, including seven Ralph C. Hoeber Awards for excellence in published research. After completing an undergraduate degree in history at the University of Colorado, Professor Dhooge earned his J.D. from the University of Denver College of Law and his LL.M. from the Georgetown University Law Center.

Daniel J. Herron is a professor of business legal studies in the Richard T. Farmer School of Business at his undergraduate alma mater, Miami University in Oxford, Ohio, where he earned a bachelor's degree in English. He earned his law degree from Case Western Reserve University School of Law in Cleveland and is a member of the Ohio and federal bars. His research includes articles on business ethics plus a variety of "business and law" topics. In addition to his teaching and scholarly publications, he founded in 1994, and since then has been coaching, the James Lewis Family Mock Trial Program at Miami, a consistent top-10 program in a field of more than 300 mock trial programs nationwide. Before coming to Miami in 1992, he taught at Bowling Green State University, the University of Wyoming, the University of North Carolina–Wilmington, and Western Carolina University. He has been married for over 35 years to Deborah, and they have two children, Christopher (married to Amanda) and Elisabeth (married to Mark). They have four grandchildren—Jack, Nate, Samantha, and Wesley—plus two rambunctious beagles, Max and Missy.

Linda L. Barkacs received her J.D. from the University of San Diego in 1993. She also has a B.A. in political science from San Diego State University and an A.A. in accounting from Irvine Valley College.

Upon graduating from law school and passing the California bar exam, Professor Barkacs became an associate at a downtown San Diego law firm. During that time she was involved in a number of high-profile trials, including a sexual harassment case against the City of Oceanside that resulted in a $1.2 million verdict. In 1997, Professor Barkacs and her husband Craig (also a professor at USD) started their own law firm specializing in business and civil litigation (in both federal and state courts), employment law cases, and appeals. They were also involved in numerous mediations and arbitrations.

Professor Barkacs began teaching at USD in 1997 and went full-time in Spring 2002. She is now a tenured Associate Professor of Business Law. As an educator, she has designed and taught numerous courses on law, ethics, and negotiation. She teaches in USD's undergraduate and graduate programs, including the Master of Science in Executive Leadership (a Ken Blanchard program), the Master of Science in Global Leadership, the Master of Science in Real Estate, and the Master of Science in Supply Chain Management. Professor Barkacs often teaches in USD's study-abroad classes and has traveled extensively throughout Europe, Asia, and South America.

Professor Barkacs has received numerous awards for her teaching at USD, including the 2008 USD Outstanding Undergraduate Business Educator; 2008 and 2007 Professor of the Year, USD Senior Class (universitywide); 2007 Creative and Innovative Teaching Award, Academy of Education Leadership (national); and 2009 and 2010 nominee for U.S. Professor of the Year (Carnegie Foundation).

She and her husband are principals in The Barkacs Group (www.tbgexecutivetraining.com), a consulting firm that provides negotiation, ethics, and team training for the private sector. Professor Barkacs has published numerous journal articles in the areas of law, ethics, and negotiation. She and her husband are coauthoring a book on negotiation. She has been the president, vice president, conference chair, and treasurer of the Pacific Southwest Academy of Legal Studies in Business (www.pswalsb.net).

Professor Barkacs currently spends her time teaching, publishing, consulting for The Barkacs Group, and doing volunteer work for various civic causes. She enjoys walking, weight lifting, and spending her free time with her husband Craig and their three cats, Phoenix, Violet, and Vanessa.

Carrie Williamson is an associate in the intellectual property litigation group at DLA Piper US LLP. She has participated in three patent infringement trials. She earned her J.D. from Boalt Hall, University of California at Berkeley, and her B.A. from Bowling Green State University. She has coauthored *Practical Business Ethics: A Guide for a Busy Manager,* and six legal journal articles. Her research interests include critical thinking, ethics, the use of expert testimony, women's legal issues, and patent litigation issues.

Preface

We wrote this book because our primary sense of who we are as professionals is that we are teachers. We play various roles in our careers, but we are especially dedicated to our students. We want them to listen, read, create, and evaluate more effectively as a result of their experience in a business law class.

We have constructed a book that is both comprehensive and readable. But the features integrated into the chapters provide its distinctive worth. Each feature stands by itself as an aid to the kind of learning we hope to encourage. Yet the features are also a cohesive unit, contributing both to the liberal education of the students who use this book and to their skills as decision makers in a market economy.

Specifically, we provide a comprehensive examination of all the relevant questions, concepts, and legal rules of business law. Our text addresses the power and authority of constitutions, statutes, case law, and treaties as sources of law. Together the various elements of what we call "the law" make up the foundation and structure of the market exchange process.

Decisions to trade and produce require trust—trust that consumers, firms, workers, financial institutions, and asset owners will do as they promise and that violations of such promises will be unacceptable in the marketplace. Without guarantees that promises will be kept, market exchanges would grind to a halt. Business law provides these guarantees and the boundaries within which certain promises can be made and enforced.

Market decisions are made in a context—a persistently changing context. The law, in turn, is dynamic in response. New technologies and business practices bring new disputes over rights and responsibilities in a business setting. Future business leaders need knowledge of existing business law, as well as a set of skills permitting them to adjust efficiently and effectively to new legal issues that arise over the course of their careers.

We are excited about the contents of our features and want to explain the function of each of them in preparing our students for leadership in business.

BUT WHAT IF . . .

WHAT IF THE FACTS OF THE CASE OPENER WERE DIFFERENT?

Let's say, in the Case Opener, that Hooters and Phillips had settled through arbitration. The arbitrator awarded Hooters a sum of money yet did not give any reasons or cite any laws to support the decision. Is the lack of justification legal? What could Phillips do in response to the decision?

A. BUT WHAT IF . . .

NEW to the third edition, the But What If feature is designed to promote critical thinking by providing students with hypothetical variations on the fact patterns outlined in real cases. This feature takes advantage of what we were taught so regularly in law school: Change the factual context and the legal conclusion may well shift along with the fact pattern. The But What If hypotheticals should heighten students' sensitivity to the importance of details in legal reasoning.

B. COMPARING THE LAW OF OTHER COUNTRIES BOXES

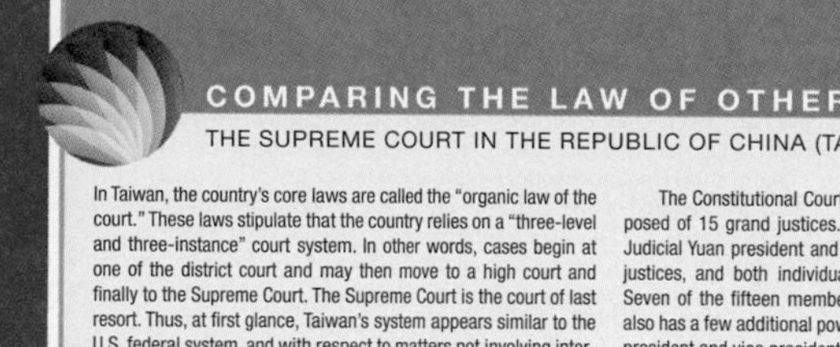

COMPARING THE LAW OF OTHER COUNTRIES

THE SUPREME COURT IN THE REPUBLIC OF CHINA (TAIWAN)

In Taiwan, the country's core laws are called the "organic law of the court." These laws stipulate that the country relies on a "three-level and three-instance" court system. In other words, cases begin at one of the district court and may then move to a high court and finally to the Supreme Court. The Supreme Court is the court of last resort. Thus, at first glance, Taiwan's system appears similar to the U.S. federal system, and with respect to matters not involving interpretation of the the country's constitution, it is. But Taiwan's system also has an additional court that is absent from the U.S. system.

While Taiwan's Supreme Court is the court of last resort for civil and criminal cases, the Supreme Court is not responsible for interpreting the country's constitution. This responsibility falls to the Constitutional Court of the Judicial Yuan.

The Constitutional Court of the Judicial Yuan is a council composed of 15 grand justices. The president of Taiwan chooses the Judicial Yuan president and vice president from among the active justices, and both individuals serve terms that last four years. Seven of the fifteen members serve eight-year terms. This court also has a few additional powers, such as the ability to impeach the president and vice president of the republic.

Cases heard by the Supreme Court are presented to five judges, including a Supreme Court president who not only attends to administrative concerns but also acts as a presiding judge over the fellow members of the court.

This feature highlights the emerging, interconnected market. Each chapter contains multiple Comparing the Law of Other Countries boxes. Because so many market decisions are made in an international context, learners need to familiarize themselves with the likelihood that a particular legal principle essential to doing business in one country may not be appropriate in other countries. The Comparing the Law of Other Countries boxes provide heightened awareness of this likelihood by illustrating how unique the law in a certain country often is. After reading dozens of these "stories of difference," readers will certainly better understand the need to discover relevant law in all jurisdictions where their market decisions have legal implications.

We believe that students learn innumerable valuable lessons about U.S. business law by contrasting the concepts of our business law system with those of our primary trading partners. We typically use Canada, Japan, China, Russia, Mexico, and the European Union for our comparisons because modern business managers will more likely be interacting with the law in those particular jurisdictions.

C. E-COMMERCE BOXES

WWW E-COMMERCE AND THE LAW

THE SLIDING-SCALE STANDARD FOR INTERNET TRANSACTIONS

Does a business that has Internet contact with a plaintiff in a different state satisfy the minimum-contact standard? Anyone who engages in transactions over the Internet should be concerned about this question.

A federal district court established the following "sliding-scale" standard in the 1997 case *Zippo Mfg. Co. v. Zippo Dot Com, Inc.*:*

> [T]he likelihood that personal jurisdiction can be constitutionally exercised is directly proportionate to the nature and quality of commercial activity that an entity conducts over the Internet. This sliding scale is consistent with well developed personal jurisdiction principles.

At one end of the spectrum are situations in which a defendant clearly does business over the Internet. If the defendant enters into contracts with residents of a foreign jurisdiction that involve the knowing and repeated transmission of computer files over the Internet, personal jurisdiction is proper.

At the opposite end are situations in which a defendant has simply posted information on an Internet website that is accessible to users in foreign jurisdictions. A passive website that does little more than make information available to those who are interested in it is not grounds for the exercise of personal jurisdiction.

The middle ground is occupied by interactive websites at which a user can exchange information with the host computer. In such cases, the exercise of jurisdiction is determined by examining the level of interactivity and commercial nature of the exchange of information that occurs on the website.

* 952 F. Supp. 1119, 1124 (W.D. Pa. 1997).

A central feature of modern business decisions is new technology, specifically the rapid spread of electronic commerce. This development has created new challenges and opportunities that were unforeseeable until very recently.

Our initial approach was to construct an e-commerce chapter that stood by itself. But the more we thought about that approach and listened to our reviewers, we decided to place E-Commerce boxes in most of our chapters, as well as to integrate the e-commerce material throughout relevant chapters. By this infusion approach, we think we can best convince students of the pervasive influence of this new, complicating aspect of business decisions.

gaming activities on the Internet and discovered that a Costa Rican company, Rio International Interlink (RII), was operating an online, international sports book that allegedly infringed on Rio Properties' registered trademark. When the court attempted to serve RII at its U.S. address, the court found that it was only an address for an international courier that was not authorized to accept service on behalf of the company, and the court could not find any address for the company in Costa Rico. Rio Properties then filed a motion for alternative service of process with the court for permission to serve RII via its e-mail address, and the motion was granted by the district court. The court of appeals upheld the validity of the district court's order, noting that the Constitution does not require any specific means of service, only a means of service "reasonably calculated to provide notice and an opportunity to respond."[1] Because the method seemed to be the method of service most likely to reach RII, the court found that it clearly met the standard.

If the defendant is a corporation, courts generally serve either the president of the corporation or an agent that the corporation has appointed to receive service. Most states require that corporations appoint an agent for service when they incorporate. Corporations are subject to *in personam* jurisdiction in three locations: the state of their incorporation, the location of their main offices, and the geographic areas in which they conduct business.

To read more about how the choice of where to incorporate relates to jurisdiction, please see the **Connecting to the Core** activity on the text website at www.mhhe.com/kubasek3e.

Courts have *in personam* jurisdiction only over persons within a specific geographic region. In the past, a state court could not acquire *in personam* jurisdiction over out-of-state defendants unless it served the defendants within the court's home state. Thus, defendants who injured plaintiffs could evade legal action by leaving the state and remaining outside its borders. To alleviate this problem, most

[1] *Rio Properties, Inc. v. Rio International Interlink,* 284 F.3d 1007 (2002).

D. CONNECTING TO THE CORE

The business curriculum, as experienced by students, can easily be seen as a collection of silos, with each silo, or academic department, walled off from the others with its own special language and issues. But successful business decisions start with the recognition that decision makers should take advantage of the interrelatedness of the various subject areas.

The purpose of the Connecting to the Core feature is to drive home the point that concepts from finance, accounting, marketing, management, and economics are closely linked to concepts and dilemmas in business law. The study of business law is best seen as a foundational component of the larger study of business administration. This feature for the third edition has been placed on the website assigned to *Dynamic Business Law.*

E. CRITICAL THINKING

After each case in the book, we have provided critical-thinking questions to highlight the need to think critically about the reasoning used by the court. In addition, we include in every chapter a Point / Counterpoint problem that encourages the reader to evaluate the conflicting reasoning surrounding a key issue in the chapter.

But we do much more than just ask a lot of critical-thinking questions at particular locations throughout the chapters. We encourage the use of a step-by-step critical-thinking approach that has been developed and used in classrooms in many countries. We do not just repeatedly urge students to "think critically." Instead, we describe for them what is meant by that phrase in the context of business law. We include this step-by-step approach in Appendix 1A at the end of Chapter 1. Instructors who want to emphasize critical thinking can use that appendix as a structured approach for learning how to evaluate legal reasoning.

state-law rules that stand as an obstacle to the accomplishment of the FAA's objectives. The FAA's overarching purpose is to ensure the enforcement of arbitration agreements according to their terms so as to facilitate informal, streamlined proceedings. Parties may agree to limit the issues subject to arbitration, to arbitrate according to specific rules, and to limit with whom they will arbitrate.

d. Class arbitration, to the extent it is manufactured by Discover Bank rather than consensual, interferes with fundamental attributes of arbitration. The switch from bilateral class arbitration greatly increases risks to defendants. The absence of multilayered review makes it more likely that errors will go uncorrected. That risk of error may become unacceptable when damages allegedly owed to thousands of claimants are aggregated and decided at once. Arbitration is poorly suited to these higher stakes. In litigation, a defendant may appeal a certification decision and a final judgment, but 9 U. S. C. §10 limits the grounds on which courts can vacate arbitral awards.

REVERSED and REMANDED.

CRITICAL THINKING

Do you think AT&T was being dishonest when it linked its stipulation for arbitration to ensuring a smooth and streamlined resolution process? Are there rival reasons that the company was hiding?

ETHICAL DECISION MAKING

Why would companies favor arbitration over class action lawsuits? Is it fair for a company to ban resolution practices just because they could be more expensive for the company, among other problems?

F. ETHICAL REASONING

After each case in the book, we have provided ethical reasoning questions to highlight the need to think ethically about the reasoning used by the court. Throughout, our book emphasizes consideration of all stakeholder interests in every market decision. Business ethics should never be an afterthought or something firms consider because they think they must.

Instead, business ethics is what provides the social legitimacy for markets, what distinguishes markets from the life of the jungle. While market decisions are calculating and purposeful, they must at the same time reflect awareness that the good and the right provide social borders that elevate those decisions above simple greed and egoism.

Ethical discussion focuses on the basic observation that we are socially and globally interdependent as entrepreneurs, asset owners, workers, businesspeople, and consumers. Our inescapable contact with one another requires that our aspirations be defined, at least in part, by their impact on others.

Our text has several ethical reasoning possibilities in each chapter. But for the reader to make use of this emphasis requires a practical step-by-step approach. In other words, students need more than just a discussion about values or ethics. They need to have some sense that the discussion is headed somewhere. They want to know, "How will my behavior be any more ethical after I have read the chapter and participated in the class discussions?" Our text answers their question.

Chapter 2 provides a clear explanation of our approach—an approach that students can use on a regular basis. The language and organization of our model of ethical reasoning leans implicitly on standard ethical theories. But it meets the challenge of a fast-paced business world. It pushes stakeholders to the forefront of market decisions, where they belong, and does so in a manner that is both powerful and doable without becoming tedious.

Business ethics are the guidelines we use to shape the world we want to create. As such, they provide guidance for the kind of business behavior we want to reinforce. After each case excerpt, under the heading "Ethical Decision Making," we pause to think about the ethics of business law by asking a question or questions derived from the practical approach to business ethics developed in Chapter 2. Because we want students to see stakeholder interests as having numerous ethical dimensions, we have included frequent references to the ethical questions arising in modern business enterprises throughout *Dynamic Business Law*.

Learn with Adaptive

SMARTBOOK™

Fueled by LearnSmart—the most widely used and intelligent adaptive learning resource—SmartBook is the first and only adaptive reading experience available today.

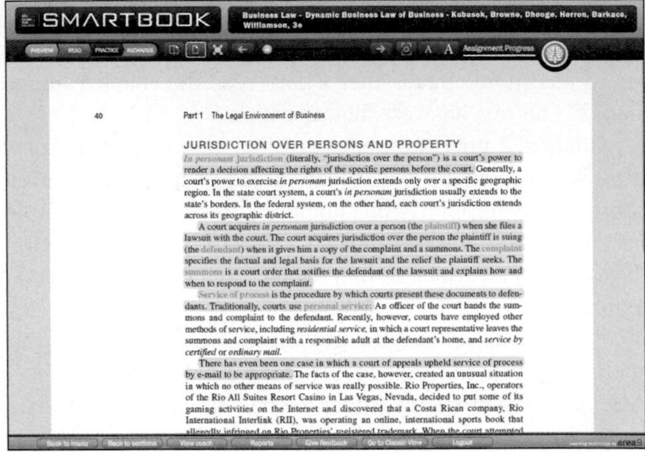

Distinguishing what students know from what they don't, and honing in on concepts they are most likely to forget, SmartBook personalizes content for each student in a continuously adapting reading experience. Reading is no longer a passive and linear experience, but an engaging and dynamic one in which students are more likely to master and retain important concepts, coming to class better prepared. Valuable reports provide instructors insight as to how students are progressing through textbook content, and they are useful for shaping in-class time or assessment. As a result of the adaptive reading experience found in SmartBook, students are more likely to retain knowledge, stay in class, and get better grades.

This revolutionary technology is available only from McGraw-Hill Education and for hundreds of course areas as part of the LearnSmart Advantage series.

How Does SmartBook Work?

Each SmartBook contains four components: Preview, Read, Practice, and Recharge. Starting with an initial preview of each chapter and key learning objectives, students read the material and are guided to topics that need the most practice on the basis of their responses to a continuously adapting diagnostic. Read and practice continue until SmartBook directs students to recharge important material they are most likely to forget to ensure concept mastery and retention.

Technology

LEARNSMART®

LearnSmart is one of the most effective and successful adaptive learning resources available on the market today. More than 2 million students have answered more than 1.3 billion questions in LearnSmart since 2009, making it the most widely used and intelligent adaptive study tool that's proven to strengthen memory recall, keep students in class, and boost grades. Students using LearnSmart are 13 percent more likely to pass their classes and 35 percent less likely to drop out.

Distinguishing what students know from what they don't, and honing in on concepts they are most likely to forget, LearnSmart continuously adapts to each student's needs by building an individual learning path so that students study smarter and retain more knowledge. Turnkey reports provide valuable insight to instructors, so precious class time can be spent on higher-level concepts and discussion.

This revolutionary learning resource is available only from McGraw-Hill Education, and because LearnSmart is available for most course areas, instructors can recommend it to students in almost every class they teach.

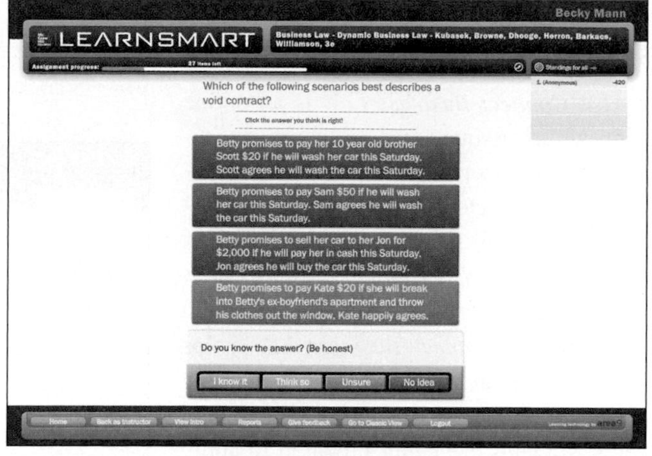

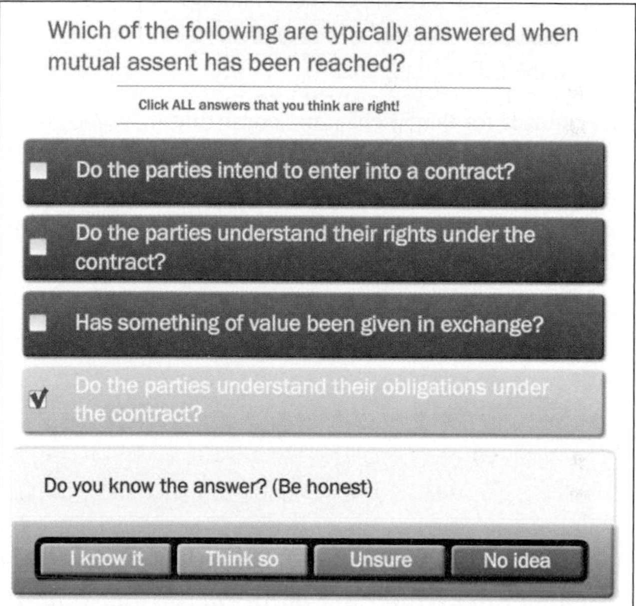

Leading Technology Extends Learning

MCGRAW-HILL *CONNECT BUSINESS LAW*

Get *Connect Business Law.* Get Results.

McGraw-Hill *Connect Business Law* is an online assignment and assessment system that gives students the means to better connect with their coursework, with their instructors, and with the important concepts that they will need to know for success now and in the future. With *Connect Business Law,* instructors can deliver assignments, quizzes, and tests easily online. *Connect Business Law* helps students master critical conceptual material in the course. By using *Connect Business Law* to master concepts, students are better prepared to apply those concepts to higher-level discussions and topics in the business law course. *Connect Business Law* offers you the following features:

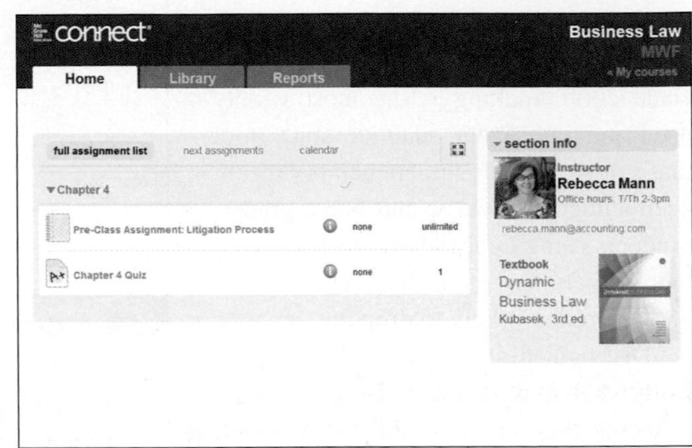

- Chapter quizzes for the 52 chapters, consisting of 15 to 25 multiple-choice questions, testing students' overall comprehension of concepts presented in the chapter.
- At least two specially crafted interactive applications for each of the 52 chapters that drill students in the use and application of the concepts and tools of strategic analysis.
- Automatic grading for the majority of the *Connect* exercises, which simplifies the tasks of evaluating each class member's performance and monitoring the learning outcomes.

> *As a student I need to interact with course material in order to retain it, and Connect offers a perfect platform for this kind of learning. Rather than just reading through textbooks, Connect has given me the tools to feel engaged in the learning process.*
>
> —*Jennah Epstein Kraus, Student, Bunker Hill Community College*

Beyond the Classroom

Interactive Applications

Interactive Applications offer a variety of automatically graded exercises that require students to **apply** key concepts. Whether the assignment includes a *click & drag, video case,* or *decision generator,* these applications provide instant feedback and progress tracking for students and detailed results for the instructor.

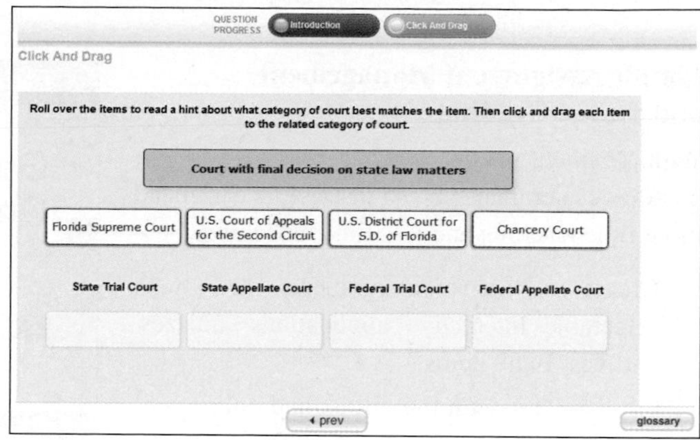

Click and Drag Interactive Applications–These fun and interactive click and drag exercises motivate students to apply concepts within the context of a scenario or case allowing them to think about legal issues.

Comprehensive Case Interactive Applications–These cases generate deeper understanding of the core concepts by applying chapter concepts in an open-ended question format. They are the most difficult Interactive Applications in Connect and are the only exercises that are manually graded.

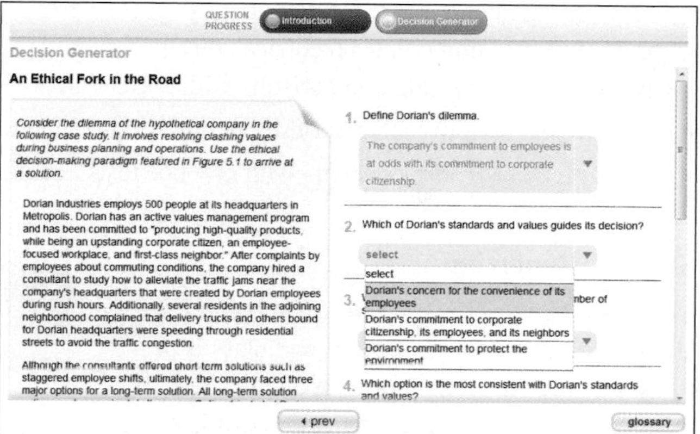

Decision Generator Interactive Applications–These exercises ask students to apply critical thinking skills and allow students to see the interdependencies of their decisions in a mini case scenario.

Video Case Interactive Applications–These case study videos include pop-up questions that appear as the video plays to test concept and/or terminology comprehension.

But What If Interactive Applications–These exercises, only available with Dynamic Business Law, ask students to apply critical thinking skills and allow students to see how changing the factual context may change the legal conclusion.

Student Library

The *Connect Business Law* Student Library gives students access to additional resources such as recorded lectures, online practice materials, an eBook, and more.

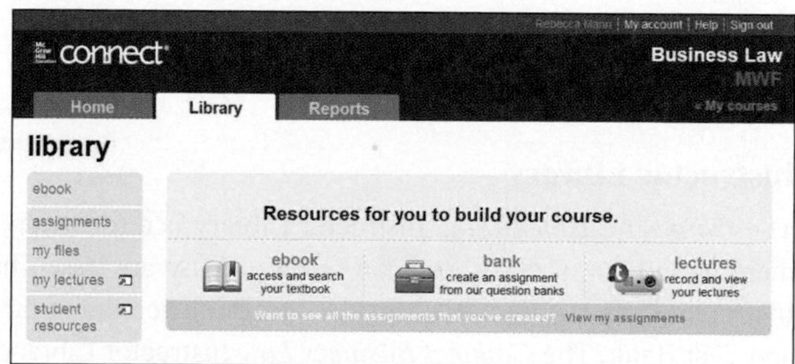

MCGRAW-HILL *CONNECT BUSINESS LAW* FEATURES

Connect Business Law offers a number of powerful tools and features to make managing assignments easier, so faculty can spend more time teaching.

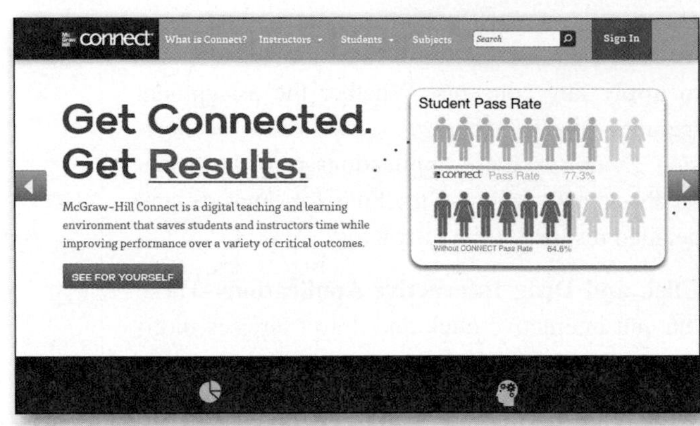

Simple Assignment Management and Smart Grading

With *Connect Business Law,* creating assignments is easier than ever, so instructors can spend more time teaching and less time managing.

- Create and deliver assignments easily with selectable interactive applications, quizzes, and Test Bank items.
- Go paperless with the eBook and online submission and grading of student assignments.
- Have assignments scored automatically, giving students immediate feedback on their work and side-by-side comparisons with correct answers.
- Access and review each response; manually change grades or leave comments for students to review.
- Reinforce classroom concepts with practice tests and instant quizzes.

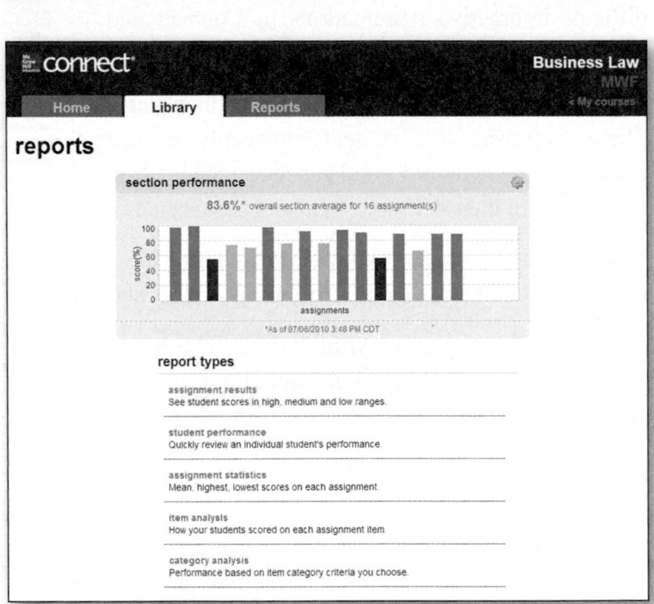

Student Reporting

Connect Business Law keeps instructors informed about how each student, section, and class is performing, allowing for more productive use of lecture and office hours. The progress-tracking function enables you to:

- View scored work immediately and track individual or group performance with assignment and grade reports.
- Access an instant view of student or class performance relative to learning objectives.
- Collect data and generate reports required by many accreditation organizations, such as AACSB.

Instructor Library

The *Connect Business Law* Instructor Library is a repository for additional resources to improve student engagement in and out of class. You can select and use any asset that enhances your lecture. The *Connect Business Law* Instructor Library includes access to the eBook version of the text, videos, slide presentations, Instructor's Manual, and Test Bank. The *Connect Business Law* Instructor Library also allows you to upload your own files.

MCGRAW-HILL *CONNECT PLUS BUSINESS LAW*

McGraw-Hill reinvents the textbook learning experience for the modern student with *Connect Plus Business Law.* A seamless integration of an eBook and *Connect Business Law, Connect Plus Business Law* provides all of the *Connect Business Law* features plus the following:

- An integrated eBook, allowing for anytime, anywhere access to the textbook.
- Media-rich capabilities like, highlighting and sharing notes.
- Dynamic links between the problems or questions you assign to your students and the locations in the eBook where the concepts are covered.
- A powerful search function to pinpoint key concepts for review.

In short, *Connect Plus Business Law* offers students powerful tools and features that optimize their time and energy, enabling them to focus on learning.

jump to pg go book contents search ebook go

Chapter 3. The U.S. Legal System

reading images my notebook

Chapter 3 Sections

Page 48 The Structure of the Court System

LO3

How is our dual court system structured?

The U.S. legal system has two parallel court structures: a federal system and a state system. Once a plaintiff files a case in one of the systems, the case remains in that system throughout the appeals process. The only exception to this rule occurs when a party to a lawsuit appeals the decision of a state supreme court to the U.S. Supreme Court.

THE FEDERAL COURT SYSTEM

The federal court system derives its power from Article III, Section 2, of the U.S. Constitution and consists of three main levels: trial courts, intermediate appellate courts, and the court of last resort. Exhibit 3-2 illustrates this system.

Exhibit 3-2
The Federal Court System

For more information about *Connect Plus Business Law,* go to **www.mcgrawhillconnect.com,** or contact your local McGraw-Hill sales representative.

TEGRITY CAMPUS: LECTURES 24/7

Tegrity Campus is a service that makes class time available 24/7 by automatically capturing every lecture. With a simple one-click start-and-stop process, you capture all computer screens and corresponding audio in a format that is easily searchable, frame by frame. Students can replay any part of any class with easy-to-use browser-based viewing on a PC, Mac, iPod, or other mobile device.

Educators know that the more students can see, hear, and experience class resources, the better they learn. In fact, studies prove it. Tegrity Campus's unique search feature helps students efficiently find what they need, when they need it, across an entire semester of class recordings. Help turn your students' study time into learning moments immediately supported by your lecture. With Tegrity Campus, you also increase intent listening and class participation by easing students' concerns about note-taking. Tegrity Campus will make it more likely you will see students' faces, not the tops of their heads.

To learn more about Tegrity, watch a two-minute Flash demo at **http://tegritycampus.mhhe.com.**

MCGRAW-HILL CAMPUS

Campus

McGraw-Hill Campus™ is a new one-stop teaching and learning experience available to users of any learning management system. This institutional service allows faculty and students to enjoy single sign-on (SSO) access to all McGraw-Hill Higher Education materials, including the award-winning McGraw-Hill Connect platform, directly from within the institution's website. McGraw-Hill Campus provides faculty with instant access to teaching materials (e.g., eTextbooks, Test Banks, PowerPoint slides, animations, and learning objects), allowing them to browse, search, and use any ancillary content in McGraw-Hill's vast library. Students enjoy SSO access to a variety of free products (e.g., quizzes, flash cards, and presentations) and subscription-based products (e.g., McGraw-Hill *Connect*). With McGraw-Hill Campus, faculty and students will never need to create another account to access McGraw-Hill products and services.

CUSTOM PUBLISHING THROUGH CREATE

McGraw-Hill Create™ is a self-service website that allows instructors to create custom course materials by drawing upon McGraw-Hill's comprehensive, cross-disciplinary content. Instructors can add their own content quickly and easily and tap into other rights-secured third-party sources as well, and then arrange the content in a way that makes the most sense for their course. Instructors can even personalize their book with the course name and information and choose the best format for their students—color print, black-and-white print, or an eBook.

Through Create, instructors can:

- Select and arrange the content in a way that makes the most sense for their course.
- Combine material from different sources and even upload their own content.
- Choose the best format for their students—print or eBook.
- Edit and update their course materials as often as they'd like.

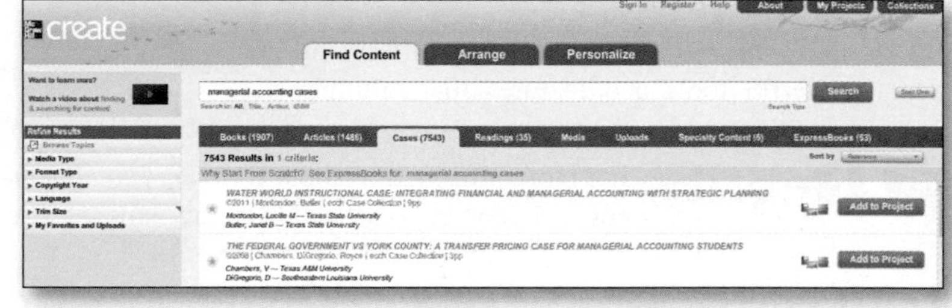

Begin creating now at www.mcgrawhillcreate.com.

COURSESMART

Learn Smart. Choose Smart.

CourseSmart is a way for faculty to find and review eTextbooks. It's also a great option for students who are interested in accessing their course materials digitally and saving money.

CourseSmart offers thousands of the most commonly adopted textbooks across hundreds of courses from a wide variety of higher education publishers. It is the only place for faculty to review and compare the full text of a textbook online, providing immediate access without the environmental impact of requesting a print exam copy.

With the CourseSmart eTextbook, students can save up to 45 percent off the cost of a print book, reduce their impact on the environment, and access powerful web tools for learning. CourseSmart is an online eTextbook, which means users access and view their textbook online when connected to the Internet. Students can also print sections of the book for maximum portability. CourseSmart eTextbooks are available in one standard online reader with full text search, notes and highlighting, and e-mail tools for sharing notes between classmates. For more information on CourseSmart, go to www.coursesmart.com.

What's New in the Third Edition?

We received an incredible amount of feedback prior to writing the third edition of *Dynamic Business Law.* The following list of changes and improvements is a testament to our users and their commitment to making *Dynamic Business Law* the best book of its kind.

Chapter 1 An Introduction to Dynamic Business Law

- Revised the critical-thinking model to reflect the importance of curiosity.

Chapter 2 Business Ethics

- Replaced previous Case Opener, Wrap-Up, and Case 2-1 with more recent legal cases to reflect current issues in business ethics.
- Updated example of value conflicts in the "What Are the Ultimate *Purposes* of the Decision?" section.
- Revised "Public Disclosure Test" section to include a more recent example of violation of the public disclosure test.
- Inserted Case Nugget about Tyson Foods in the "Universalization Test" section.
- Included information about the AIG bailout to provide a more recent example of corporate violations of business ethics.
- Replaced E-Commerce and the Law topic "Computer Use and Ethics" with "Technological Records and Ethics" to reflect ongoing ethical issues.
- Revised Questions & Problems to reflect changes made throughout the chapter

Chapter 3 The U.S. Legal System

- Inserted new case, *Hertz Corp. v Friend* to illustrate the potential difficulty of determining whether a case falls under concurrent jurisdiction.
- Repositioned E-Commerce and the Law box for better clarity and relevance to the chapter.
- Inserted paragraph to explain the E-Commerce and the Law topic and its significance.
- Added Case Nugget about *Wachovia Bank N.A. v. Schmidt* to demonstrate diversity of citizenship.
- Updated Questions & Problems to match changes made throughout the chapter.

Chapter 4 Alternative Dispute Resolution

- Inserted *A.T. & T. Mobility LLC v. Concepcion* to demonstrate the court's refusal to uphold arbitration agreements when federal statutory rights are at issue.
- Improved Questions & Problems to reflect the changes in the chapter.

Chapter 5 Constitutional Principles

- Refurbished Case Opener to demonstrate more recent issues concerning constitutionality of laws.
- Inserted paragraph explaining *Bronkala v. Morrison* and the Affordable Care Act's relevance to the commerce clause and, thereby, Congress's scope of regulating commerce.
- Replaced Case 5-2 with *Family Winemakers of California v. Jenkins* to model current developments in the scope of the state's power to restrict interstate commerce.
- Revised Case Nugget to include *Trunk v. City of San Diego* to exhibit conflicts between freedom of speech and California's no preference clause.
- Removed E-Commerce and the Law "Is Computer Code Speech" due to the outdated nature of the case.
- Replaced Case Opener Wrap-Up.
- Updated Questions & Problems to mirror changes made in the chapter.

Chapter 6 International and Comparative Law

- Updated membership in the World Trade Organization.
- Provided information regarding U.S. free trade agreements.
- Updated minimum-wage laws in the United States and other countries.
- Added new Case Nugget addressing personal jurisdiction and the Internet.
- Added new U.S. Supreme Court case regarding personal jurisdiction.
- Revised Questions & Problems to include new cases concerning personal jurisdiction, forum selection agreement, choice-of-law clauses, and international sales contracts.

Chapter 7 Crime and the Business Community

- Revised Case Opener to reflect more recent examples of insider trading.
- Edited content to ensure consistency throughout the chapter.
- Replaced Case 7-1 with *U.S. v. Ruiz* to include a more recent case illustrating fraud.
- Refurbished Case Opener Wrap-Up to mimic the Case Opener.
- Added text to clarify the Racketeer Influenced and Corrupt Organizations Act (RICO).
- Improved Questions & Problems to mirror changes made throughout the chapter.

Chapter 8 Tort Law

- Added text to "Intentional Infliction of Emotional Distress" section to explain the role of the intentional infliction of emotional distress tort in business.
- Replaced *Cindy R. Lourcey et al. v. Estate of Charles Scarlett* with *Aaron Olson, Appellant v. CenturyLink, Respondent.*
- Refurbished Questions & Problems to reflect more recent issues in tort law.

Chapter 9 Negligence and Strict Liability

- Revamped Case Opener and Case Opener Wrap-Up with a more recent case.
- Enhanced "Duty" subsection of "Elements of Negligence" to include content relevant to the Case Opener.
- Revised content in the "Duty," "Breach of Duty," "Causation," "Damages," and "*Res Ipsa Loquitur*" subsections to better explain the text of each subsection.
- Replaced Case 9-2, *Barbara Debusscher v. Sam's East, Inc.*, with *District of Columbia v. Wayne Singleton, et al.*, to provide a more recent example of *res ipsa loquitur.*
- Inserted Case Nugget to explain the application of assumption of the risk.
- Updated Questions & Problems to mirror changes made in the chapter.

Chapter 10 Product Liability

- Added Case Nugget regarding application of product liability theories to intangible products.
- Enhanced discussion of duty to warn.
- Added discussion of the "sophisticated-user" defense that acts as a complete defense to failure-to-warn claims.
- Updated discussion of Toyota's settlements of loss-of-economic-value claims in "Damages" section.

- Added discussion regarding seller's exception statutes.
- Enhanced discussion of the risk-utility and consumer expectations tests.
- Added case problems regarding failure to warn, evidence necessary for design defect claims, and manufacturing defects.

Chapter 11 Liability of Accountants and Other Professionals

- Replaced Case Nugget topic *Lee v. Ernst & Young, L.L.P.*, with *In re Century Aluminum Company Securities Litigation* to echo recent violations of the Securities Act of 1933.
- Updated Case 11-3 with *Matrixx Initiatives, Inc., et al. v. Siracusano et al.* to illustrate a recent example of liability under Section 10(b) of the Securities Exchange Act and SEC Rule 10b-5.
- Updated Questions & Problems to mirror changes made throughout the chapter.

Chapter 12 Intellectual Property

- Revised Case Opener to introduce intellectual property issues in the context of smartphone wars.
- Updated Case Nugget regarding registering a color as a trademark with Second Circuit decision in the context of the fashion industry.
- Added *Grokster* Supreme Court case and discussion regarding fair-use defense and peer-to-peer file sharing in the music industry.
- Included section discussing the America Invents Act (AIA).
- Enhanced discussion of trade secrets by adding issues business managers will want to consider, such as having a company policy regarding marking information as confidential and trade secret.
- Added case problems regarding copyrights, trademarks, and trade secrets in popular culture.

Chapter 13 Introduction to Contracts

- Added text to subsections "Common Law" and "Bilateral versus Unilateral Contracts."
- Removed case example *D.L. Peoples Group, Inc. v. Hawley* due to outdated nature of the case.
- Refurbished Questions & Problems to reflect changes made throughout the chapter.

Chapter 14 Agreement

- Updated Case 14-3 with *Alexander v. Lafayette Crime Stoppers, Inc.*, to provide a more recent interpretation of the provisions specifying the means of acceptance.
- Replaced E-Commerce and the Law "When Clicking 'OK' Might Not Be OK" with "Disclosure of Definite and Certain Terms."
- Updated Questions & Problems, including more recent cases relevant to the chapter.

Chapter 15 Consideration

- Added Comparing the Law of Other Countries box on contract enforcement in China relative to other countries.
- Deleted learning objective and text related to Uniform Commercial Code (covered in another chapter).

- Revised and enhanced Exhibits 15-1 and 15-2.
- Enhanced discussion of past consideration through addition of a case regarding a dispute in the NBA.
- Deleted Case Nugget on discussion of requirements contracts (related to UCC).
- Updated Questions & Problems.

Chapter 16 Capacity and Legality

- Refurbished Case Opener and Case Opener Wrap-Up to include a newer case involving contracts.
- Discarded *Swalberg v. Hannegan* case to be more concise.
- Added *King v. Riedl* to demonstrate the effect of licensing statutes on contracts.
- Inserted E-Commerce and the Law "Observing Sabbath Days Online."
- Improved Questions & Problems by adding more current problems and questions relevant to the material in the chapter.

Chapter 17 Legal Assent

- Replaced *Ronald Jackson and Willa Jackson, Appellant v. Robert R. Blanchard, Helen M. Blanchard, Maynard L. Shellhammer, and Philip Schlemmer, Appellee* with *Simkin v. Blanki* to provide a more recent example of a mutual mistake.
- Revamped Questions & Problems with more recent problems concerning contracts.

Chapter 18 Contracts in Writing:

- Revised Case Opener and Case Opener Wrap-Up to include a more recent case involving oral contracts made after the creation of a written contract.
- Inserted E-Commerce and the Law "The Statute of Frauds and Legally Binding Electronic Transactions."
- Improved Questions & Problems to echo recent developments relevant to contracts.

Chapter 19 Third-Party Rights to Contracts

- Updated Case 19-3 to include *Allan v. Nersesova,* to better illustrate a case involving a creditor beneficiary.
- Added new exhibits to illustrate the assignment of the same right to two parties and legal recourse of third-party beneficiaries.
- Refurbished Questions & Problems to include recent issues with third-party rights to contracts.

Chapter 20 Discharge and Remedies

- Replaced Case 20-1, *Miller v. Mills Constriction, Inc.,* with *Hamilton v. State Farm Fire & Casualty Insurance Company* to better illustrate the potential analysis used to determine whether a defendant's behavior forms a material breach.
- Updated Questions and Problems to include more recent court cases and problems.

Chapter 21 Introduction to Sales and Lease Contracts

- Expanded coverage and application of the CISG.
- Explored in detail the nature of UCC Article 2 offers: Are trade names covered and do "quotes" constitute an offer?

Chapter 22 Title, Risk of Loss, and Insurable Interests

- Introduced the United Nation's Law of the Seas (UNCLOS) and its application to transactional activity.
- Included debate about the wisdom of application of the rule regarding passing of title and "entrustment."

Chapter 23 Performance and Obligations under Sales and Leases

- Added comparison of the U.S. Restatements with the innovative European "restatement" known as *PECL,* "Principles of European Contract Law."
- Expanded discussion of contractual remedies such as whether "cure" should be mandatory under the UCC.

Chapter 24 Remedies for Breach of Sales and Lease Contracts

- Introduced discussion of "hot damages."
- Added Case Nugget that explores the expanding doctrine of consequential damages.
- Inserted comparison of the U.S. approach to liquidated damages with the approach taken by the People's Republic of China.

Chapter 25 Warranties

- Inserted Case Nugget that examines how far the implied warranty of title extends and should extend with subsequent purchasers.
- Added Case Nugget that discusses when the statue of limitations tolls.

Chapter 26 Negotiable Instruments: Negotiability and Transferability

- Inserted Case 26-1 *Reger Development, LLC v. National City Bank* to demonstrate the use of a promissory note as a demand instrument.
- Added E-Commerce and the Law "Can All Negotiable Instruments Be in Electronic Format?"
- Replaced Comparing the Law of Other Countries "Formation of a Negotiable Instrument in Dutch Commercial Law" with "Negotiable Instruments in South African Law."
- Removed case *New Wave Technologies, Inc. v. Legacy Bank of Texas.*
- Revamped "Questions & Problems, adding questions and problems that reflect more recent issues.

Chapter 27 Negotiation, Holder in Due Course, and Defenses

- Swapped Comparing the Law of Other Countries "The Evolution of Bills of Exchange in Russia" with "Bills of Exchange Act in Australia" to provide a better of example of the use of bills of exchange.
- Repositioned Case 27-3 and replaced *Buckeye Check Cashing, Inc. v. Camp* with *Wawel Savings Bank v. Jersey Tractor Trailer Training, Inc.*
- Improved Questions & Problems, removing outdated questions and adding relevant and recent problems.

Chapter 28 Liability, Defenses, and Discharge

- Revised E-Commerce and the Law with new information concerning electronic signatures.
- Updated Case 28-1 *Start Bank v. Theodore Jackson, Jr.,* with *Heartland State Bank v. American Bank & Trust.*
- Replaced Comparing the Law of Other Countries "Negotiability and Forgery in Japan" with "Negotiable Instruments Law of the People's Republic of China."
- Refurbished Questions & Problems to include more recent cases and problems relevant to the chapter.

Chapter 29 Checks and Electronic Fund Transfers

- Replaced Case Opener and Case Opener Wrap-Up with a recent example of fraudulent electronic fund transfers.
- Inserted Comparing the Law of Other Countries box about money orders in India to contrast them to money orders in the United States.
- Revised Case 29-3 with *Merister v. Bank of America* to illustrate liability in cases involving fraud.
- Added paragraph in subsection "Unauthorized Transfers," tying the section to the Case Opener.
- Updated Questions & Problems with newer questions that reflect recent developments in cases involving checks and electronic fund transfers.

Chapter 30 Secured Transactions

- Added new Case Opener addressing secured transactions, motor vehicles, and repossession.
- Revised material concerning security agreements.
- Added new case on the distinction between consumer goods and business equipment.
- Revised material relating to perfection of security interests in movable collateral.
- Updated material on the disposition of collateral by a creditor after default.
- Revised Questions & Problems to include new cases concerning perfection of security interests, repossession, and disposition of collateral by creditors after default and lien searches.

Chapter 31 Other Creditors' Remedies and Suretyship

- Added new Case Opener addressing compliance with mortgage foreclosure procedures.
- Added new case describing qualifications to be considered a mechanic or artisan entitled to lien rights.
- Updated material on exemptions from writs of execution.
- Added new case addressing proceeds subject to garnishment.
- Updated material concerning the amount of homestead exemptions.
- Revised Questions & Problems to include new cases concerning entitlement to artisan liens, garnishment of pension funds, and the consequences of abusive residential real estate lending practices.

Chapter 32 Bankruptcy and Reorganization

- Updated Case Opener.
- Provided new bankruptcy filing statistics.
- Updated discussion of bankruptcy laws in Spain.
- Added new Case Nugget discussing bankruptcy and requirements for credit counseling.
- Updated procedures relating to involuntary bankruptcy proceedings.
- Updated values of property subject to bankruptcy exemptions.
- Revised list of largest corporate bankruptcy filings.
- Revised Questions & Problems to include new cases concerning determination of the proper bankruptcy chapter to utilize in a filing, effect of discharge, undue hardship as a means of discharging student loan debt, and fraudulent prepetition transfers of property.

Chapter 33 Agency Formation and Duties

- Changed text in the "Introduction to Agency Law" section to explain the relationship between agency laws and the states, especially agency laws concerning athletes.
- Inserted exhibits to help explain agency laws.
- Replaced Comparing the Law of Other Countries "Formation of Power of Attorney under Civil Law in France" with "Formation of Power of Attorney in Luxembourg" to better explain agency by implied authority.
- Updated Case 33-1 by replacing *Thomas & Linda Genovese v. Theresa Bergeron* with *Ackerman v. Sobol Family Partnership, LLP,* a more recent case that focuses on the actions of the principal in an agency issue.
- Revamped Point / Counterpoint to address the topic "Should sports agents be held personally accountable for NCAA violations involving signing college athlete clients?" and updated the responses.
- Improved Questions & Problems to include more recent issues concerning agency law.

Chapter 34 Liability to Third Parties and Termination

- Updated Case Opener and Case Opener Wrap-Up with a more recent example of vicarious liability.
- Replaced case *Sharon D. Jones v. Renee S. Brandt* with *In re Estate of Kurrelmeyer* to demonstrate the extent of power of attorney.
- Enhanced footnotes to include further explanation and clarification concerning the liability of agency.
- Swapped Comparing the Law of Other Countries "Termination in the Netherlands" for "Termination in the United Arab Emirates."
- Revised Point / Counterpoint, replacing the question with "Should attorneys and agents be required to pass mental fitness assessments before being given roles in power-of-attorney circumstances?" and replacing the responses with new answers that correspond to the new question.
- Refurbished Questions & Problems to include more recent issues.

Chapter 35 Forms of Business Organization

- Swapped Comparing the Law of Other Countries "Sole Traders in Germany" with "Limited Liability Partnerships in Japan" to better compare and contrast partnerships in other countries with partnerships in the United States.
- Updated Case 35-1 with *Meyer v. Christie* to illustrate joint ventures.
- Revised Exhibit 35-8, updating the list of "The Top 10 Global Franchises, 2013."
- Improved Questions & Problems, including more recent issues and cases concerning termination, franchisees, and trusts.

Chapter 36 Partnerships: Nature, Formation, and Operation

- Revised Case Opener and Case Opener Wrap-Up to demonstrate potential liability of a partnership.
- Swapped Case 36-1, *Ingram v. Deere,* with *Leoff v. S&J Land Co.* to illustrate whether a partnership relationship exists.
- Enhanced text in subsection "Liability to Third Parties" to include information from the new Case Opener.
- Replaced Comparing the Law of Other Countries "Silent Partnerships in Germany" with "Duties of Partnerships in Japan" to contrast partnerships in Japan with partnerships in the United States.
- Inserted E-Commerce and the Law "Partnerships: An Essential Part of Online Business" to explain the benefits of an e-company having a partner.
- Updated Questions & Problems to include newer issues and cases relating to the chapter.

Chapter 37 Partnerships: Termination and Limited Partnerships

- Replaced Case 37-1, *Liem Phan Vu v. Davis Ha et al.,* with *Miller v. Bill & Carolyn Ltd. P'Ship* to illustrate the dissolution of a partnership due to a court decision.
- Revised Comparing the Law of Other Countries with "Dissolution of Partnerships in India" to explain the cause for dissolution of a firm in India.
- Removed Comparing the Law of Other Countries "Effects of Dissolution in Scotland."
- Improved Questions & Problems to include more recent cases and issues.

Chapter 38 Corporations: Formation and Financing

- Added Comparing the Law of Other Countries "Corporate Structure in China" to compare and contrast forms of centralized management in the United States and in China.
- Inserted E-Commerce and the Law "Nonprofit Corporations" to explain the role of technology and the Internet in the operation of nonprofits.
- Updated Case 38-2 with *King v. American Family Mutual Insurance Company* to describe the process of authorization.
- Refurbished Questions & Problems to include issues concerning age discrimination and the termination of contracts.

Chapter 39 Corporations: Directors, Officers, and Shareholders

- Updated Case Opener and Case Opener Wrap-Up to provide a recent example of the power of shareholders in a company.
- Replaced Case 39-1, *Frieda H. Rabkin v. Philip A. Hunt Chemical Corp.,* with *McCann v. McCann* to illustrate the duties of majority shareholders.

- Revamped Comparing the Law of Other Countries, including "Criminal Liability in France" to contrast the criminal liability in France with that in the United States.
- Refurbished Point / Counterpoint, replacing the question with "Should shareholder and stock information be permitted as discussion topics on social media websites?"
- Improved Questions & Problems, including recent cases and issues relating to corporations.

Chapter 40 Corporations: Mergers, Consolidations, Terminations

- Changed Case Opener and Case Opener Wrap-Up to "Acquisitions as Horizontal Mergers."
- Swapped Case 40-2, *Charland v. Country View Golf Club, Inc.*, with *Shiftan v. Morgan Joseph Holdings, Inc.*
- Added E-Commerce and the Law "Hostile Takeovers Online" to demonstrate possible measures taken to prevent hostile takeovers.
- Improved Point / Counterpoint by replacing the question with "Should the SEC require early disclosure of major cash tender stock purchases for publicly traded stock?" and updating the responses.
- Replaced Questions & Problems that were outdated.

Chapter 41 Corporations: Securities and Investor Protection

- Revised Case 41-1, *Securities and Exchange Commission v. Life Partners, Inc.*, with *Securities and Exchange Commission v. Mutual Benefits Corp.* to provide a more recent example of how courts apply the Howey test.
- Updated Questions & Problems to include more recent issues related to securities and investor protection.

Chapter 42 Employment and Labor Law

- Added case related to privacy of e-mails sent between attorney and client.
- Updated Questions & Problems.

Chapter 43 Employment Discrimination

- Enhanced discussion of age discrimination including a new Case Nugget on the topic.
- Added new case on the Equal Pay Act.
- Revised and updated discussion of discrimination based on sexual orientation, including same-sex marriage laws and the 2013 U.S. Supreme Court decisions on both the Defense of Marriage Act and California's Proposition 8.
- Updated Questions & Problems.

Chapter 44 Administrative Law

- Enhanced discussion of the Freedom of Information Act (FOIA) through addition of a case regarding the National Security Administration (NSA).
- Revised and updated discussion of California's request for a waiver from the Environmental Protection Agency (EPA) under the Clean Air Act.
- Updated Questions & Problems.

Chapter 45 Consumer Law

- Replaced Case Opener and Case Opener Wrap-Up with "Deceptive Advertising and the Ultimate Weight Loss Cure" to provide an example of misrepresentation.
- Improved E-Commerce and the Law by replacing "Consumers on the Net" with "Deceptive Ads Could Lead to Computer Consequences" to explain "bait and click."
- Updated Comparing the Law of Other Countries with "Advertising in China" to explain the Chinese definition of false advertising.
- Revamped Questions & Problems to include updated issues related to consumer law.

Chapter 46 Environmental Law

- Changed Case 46-1 to *Brodsky v. United States Nuclear Regulatory Commission* to demonstrate a case concerning whether an EIS is required.
- Added Comparing the Law of Other Countries "An Alternative Approach to Cleaner Air: Germany's Shift to Renewable Energy."
- Revised Questions & Problems to include recent environmental law issues and cases.

Chapter 47 Antitrust Law

- Replaced Case 47-1 with *California v. Safeway,* a more recent case involving a violation of the Sherman Act.
- Inserted E-Commerce and the Law "Is Google a Monopoly?" to illustrate the difficulty in determining monopolies in e-commerce.
- Added E-Commerce and the Law "Making Bid-Rigging Easy" to explain the problem of bid rigging online.
- Refurbished Questions & Problems to include updated cases concerning antitrust law.

Chapter 48 The Nature of Property, Personal Property, and Bailments

- Revamped Case 48-2, replacing the original case with *Campbell v. Robinson* to illustrate a conditional contract.
- Updated Questions & Problems, including recent cases and disputes involving property.

Chapter 49 Real Property

- Replaced Case Opener and Case Opener Wrap-Up with an example of riparian water rights.
- Inserted Case Nugget "The Importance of Knowing Types of Tenancies" to illustrate the differences in tenancies.
- Enhanced Case Opener Wrap-Up to include more details about the case.
- Improved Questions & Problems to include more recent examples of issues concerning real property.

Chapter 50 Landlord-Tenant Law

- Updated Case 50-1 with *Choices in Cmty. Living, Inc. v. Petkus* to demonstrate a recent example of a potential violation of the Housing Act.
- Added Comparing the Law of Other Countries "Eviction in Japan" to contrast the eviction rates in Japan and the United States.

- Revamped Point / Counterpoint to include a new question: "Should landlords be permitted to screen potential tenants for criminal background checks?" and provided new answers to correspond with the question.
- Revised Questions & Problems to include current developments in landlord-tenant law.

Chapter 51 Insurance Law

- Added updated Case Opener addressing insurance coverage for Chinese drywall claims.
- Revised list of interesting insurance policies.
- Added new case addressing the types of interests protected by insurance policies.
- Added new case on interpretation of automobile insurance policies.
- Revised Questions & Problems to include new cases concerning coverage for flooding, differences between commercial and noncommercial policies, the interpretation of automobile policies, liability for injuries occurring as a result of an accident involving a loaned vehicle, and insurable interests in life insurance policies.

Chapter 52 Wills and Trusts

- Added new Case Opener addressing problems arising from the use of preprinted wills.
- Included new case concerning the determination of heirs under state law in the context of modern science.
- Added new case concerning undue influence and fraud in the context of preparation of a will.
- Added new Case Nugget addressing tortious interference with the expectancy of inheritance or gift.
- Updated material on organ donation in Japan.
- Revised Questions & Problems to include new cases addressing the enforceability of unsigned wills and *in terrorem* clauses, the recognition of holographic wills, competency to make a will, and interpretation of vague clauses.

Acknowledgments

This element of the Preface contains a palpable tone of gratitude and humility. Any project the scope of *Dynamic Business Law* is a collective activity; the authors are but the visible component of a remarkably large joint effort. We want to thank several contributors by name, but there are doubtlessly many other students, colleagues, and friends who made essential contributions to these pages.

Our largest gratitude goes to the dozens of business law colleagues who saved us from many embarrassing errors, while tolerating our stubborn reluctance to adhere to certain of their suggestions. Many thanks go to our manuscript reviewers and focus group participants:

Patricia Sanchez Abril
University of Miami

Joan P. Alexander
Nassau Community College

Wayne Anderson
Missouri State University

Curtis J. Bell
Western Michigan University

Dr. Jon D. Bible
Texas State University–San Marcos

Robert W. Bing
William Patterson University

Joyce Birdoff
Nassau Community College

Bonnie Bolinger
Ivy Tech Community College of Indiana

Eli Bortman
Babson College

Daniel R. Cahoy
Pennsylvania State University

Anita Cava
University of Miami–Coral Gables

Michael Chikeleze, JD
Cincinnati State College

Wade Chumney
Georgia Institute of Technology

Mark Conrad
Fordham University

Angelo J. Corpora
Palomar College

Mark A. Crawford
Charleston Southern University

Richard E. Custin
University of San Diego

Dr. Raven Davenport
Houston Community College System

Howard Davidoff
Brooklyn College

Peter Dawson
Collin County Community College–Plano

Mary Elena Ellison
Florida Atlantic University

Joseph L. Flack. Jr.
Washentaw Community College

Darrell G. Ford
University of Central Oklahoma

Joan Gabel
Florida State University

Gary S. Gaffney
Florida Atlantic University

Christopher Giles
Virginia Tech

Robert Gonzalez
American River College

Dale Arrison Grossman
Cornell University

Francine Guice
Indiana Purdue University–Fort Wayne

William Harwood
Dutchess Community College

Norman Hawker
Western Michigan University

Lynda F. Hodge
Guilford Technical Community College

Karen A. Holmes
Hudson Valley Community College

Russell Holmes
Des Moines Area Community College

Jennifer Barger Johnson
University of Central Oklahoma

Catherine Jones-Rikkers
Grand Valley State University

Steve Kaber
Baldwin-Wallace College

Brian Keliher
Grossmont College

Cheryl Kirschner
Babson College

Gordon Klein
University of California–Los Angeles

Patricia Laidler
Massasoit Community College

Elizabeth W. Lane
Columbia College

Konrad S. Lee
Utah State University

Erin LeGrand
Wayne Community College

Laurie A. Lucas
Oklahoma State University
James Mac Donald
Weber State University
Bruce Mather
State University of New York–New Paltz
Catherine McKee
Mt. San Antonio College
James L. Molloy
University of Wisconsin–Whitewater
Sandra Mullings
Bernard M. Baruch College
George A. Nation III
Lehigh University
Jan Novak
Chabot College
Ann Morales Olazábal
University of Miami
Gary Patterson
University of California–Riverside
Mark Patzkowski
Northwestern Oklahoma
George A. Redmond
Franklin University
Linda Reid
University of Wisconsin–Whitewater
Bruce Rich
California State University–San Marcos
Keith Roberts
University of Redlands
Thomas Rossi
Broome Community College
Don Sanders
Texas State University–San Marcos
Dr. Martin Segal
University of Miami
Lou Ann Simpson
Drake University
George Swan
North Carolina A & T University
John Swenson
University of Missouri–Columbia
Robert Scott Taylor
Moberly Area Community College
Cheryl Thomas
Fayetteville Technical Community College
David W. Tiffany
California State University–San Marcos
Carol A. Vance
University of South Florida–Tampa
Russell A. Waldon
College of the Canyons
Curt M. Weber
University of Wisconsin-Whitewater
Norman Young
California State Poly University–Pomona
Thomas Young
Lone Star College Tomball
Mary-Kathryn Zachary
University of West Georgia
Bruce Zucker
California State University–Northridge

In addition, the third edition of the book could not have been written without the competent and dedicated research assistance we received from Chelsea Brown, Lauren Biksacky, and Cassandra Baker. Special thanks to Micayla Beuley for assistance in improving the design of the exhibits.

Finally, a book is but a raw, unsold manuscript until the talent team at a publishing house starts to refine it. Our manuscript benefited immeasurably from the guidance of the multiple levels of skill provided to us by McGraw-Hill Education. We respect and honor our Managing Director, Tim Vertovec; our Development Editor, Rebecca Mann; the book's Senior Marketing Manager, Michelle Nolte; its Senior Digital Product Analyst, Xin Lin; and its Content Project Manager, Emily Kline.

Brief Contents

Part One
THE LEGAL ENVIRONMENT OF BUSINESS

Part Two
CONTRACTS

Part Three
DOMESTIC AND INTERNATIONAL SALES LAW

Part Four
NEGOTIABLE INSTRUMENTS AND BANKING

Part Five
CREDITORS' RIGHTS AND BANKRUPTCY

Part Six
AGENCY

Part Seven
BUSINESS ORGANIZATIONS

Part Eight
EMPLOYMENT AND LABOR RELATIONS

Part Nine
GOVERNMENT REGULATION

Part Ten
PROPERTY

Appendixes

Contents

Part Two
CONTRACTS

Part Nine
GOVERNMENT REGULATION

CHAPTER 44

CHAPTER 45

CHAPTER 46

CHAPTER 47

Part Ten
PROPERTY

CHAPTER 48

List of Cases

CHAPTER 15: CONSIDERATION

CHAPTER 16: CAPACITY AND LEGALITY

CHAPTER 17: LEGAL ASSENT

CHAPTER 18: CONTRACTS IN WRITING

CHAPTER 19: THIRD-PARTY RIGHTS TO CONTRACTS

CHAPTER 20: DISCHARGE AND REMEDIES

CHAPTER 21: INTRODUCTION TO SALES AND LEASE CONTRACTS

CHAPTER 22: TITLE, RISK OF LOSS, AND INSURABLE INTEREST

CHAPTER 23: PERFORMANCE AND OBLIGATIONS UNDER SALES AND LEASES

CHAPTER 24: REMEDIES FOR BREACH OF SALES AND LEASE CONTRACTS

CHAPTER 25: WARRANTIES

CHAPTER 26: NEGOTIABLE INSTRUMENTS: NEGOTIABILITY AND TRANSFERABILITY

CHAPTER 27: NEGOTIATION, HOLDER IN DUE COURSE, AND DEFENSES

CHAPTER 28: LIABILITY, DEFENSES, AND DISCHARGE

CHAPTER 29: CHECKS AND ELECTRONIC FUND TRANSFERS

CHAPTER 30: SECURED TRANSACTIONS

CHAPTER 31: OTHER CREDITORS' REMEDIES AND SURETYSHIP

CHAPTER 32: BANKRUPTCY AND REORGANIZATION

CHAPTER 33: AGENCY FORMATION AND DUTIES

CHAPTER 34: LIABILITY TO THIRD PARTIES AND TERMINATION

CHAPTER 35: FORMS OF BUSINESS ORGANIZATION

CHAPTER 36: PARTNERSHIPS: NATURE, FORMATION, AND OPERATION

CHAPTER 37: PARTNERSHIPS: TERMINATION AND LIMITED PARTNERSHIPS

CHAPTER 38: CORPORATIONS: FORMATION AND FINANCING

CHAPTER 39: CORPORATIONS: DIRECTORS, OFFICERS, AND SHAREHOLDERS

CHAPTER 40: CORPORATIONS: MERGERS, CONSOLIDATIONS, TERMINATIONS

CHAPTER 41: CORPORATIONS: SECURITIES AND INVESTOR PROTECTION

CHAPTER 42: EMPLOYMENT AND LABOR LAW

CHAPTER 43: EMPLOYMENT DISCRIMINATION

CHAPTER 44: ADMINISTRATIVE LAW

CHAPTER 45: CONSUMER LAW

CHAPTER 46: ENVIRONMENTAL LAW

CHAPTER 47: ANTITRUST LAW

CHAPTER 48: THE NATURE OF PROPERTY, PERSONAL PROPERTY, AND BAILMENTS

CHAPTER 49: REAL PROPERTY

CHAPTER 50: LANDLORD-TENANT LAW

CHAPTER 51: INSURANCE LAW

CHAPTER 52: WILLS AND TRUSTS

CHAPTER 1

An Introduction to Dynamic Business Law

LEARNING OBJECTIVES

After reading this chapter, you will be able to answer the following questions:

1 What is business law?

2 How does business law relate to business education?

3 What are the purposes of law?

4 What are alternative ways to classify the law?

5 What are the sources of the law?

6 What are the various schools of jurisprudence?

LO1 What is business law?

This book is for future business managers, especially those who wish to be leaders. The preparation for that career requires, in part, an awareness of the legal issues arising in business. Businesses need to finance capital growth, purchase inputs, and hire and develop employees. They must sell to consumers, please owners, and comply with government rules. All these activities are full of potential legal conflicts. Appendix 1A explains the role of critical thinking in resolving these conflicts.

LO2 How does business law relate to business education?

Business law consists of the enforceable rules of conduct that govern commercial relationships. For example, a firm is required by law to obey the antitrust laws when it considers merging with another firm. In other words, buyers and sellers interact in market exchanges within the rules that specify the boundaries of legal business behavior. Constitutions, legislatures, regulatory bodies, and courts spell out what market participants may and may not legally do. These rules and responsibilities provide the stability required in a thriving market economy.

Business activities must follow legal guidelines. All contracts, employment decisions, and payments to a supplier are constrained and protected by business law. Each of the six functional areas of business—management, production and transportation, marketing, research and development, accounting and finance, and human resource management—sits on a foundation of business law, as Exhibit 1-1 illustrates.

Law and Its Purposes

LO3 What are the purposes of law?

As individuals, few of us can impose rules on others, but a majority of citizens in a democracy can agree to permit certain authorities to make and enforce rules of behavior in their community. These rules are the *law,* and they are enforceable in the courts the community maintains. Exhibit 1-2 lists just a few of the many purposes fulfilled by the law.

Each is important, but taken together they remind us why we are proud to say we are a society of laws. The respect we give the law as a source of authority is in part our recognition that in its absence, we would rely solely on the goodwill and dependability of one another. Most of us greatly prefer the law.

Classification of the Law

LO4 What are alternative ways to classify the law?

There are many ways of dividing laws into different groups. Some include national versus international law, federal versus state law, and public versus private law. **Private law** regulates disputes between private individuals or groups. If a store owner is delinquent in paying rent to the landlord, the resulting dispute is governed by private law. **Public law** controls disputes between private individuals or groups and their government. If a store dumps waste behind its building in violation of local, state, or federal environmental regulations, public law will resolve the dispute.

Another distinction we make is between civil and criminal law. (See Exhibit 1-3.) **Civil law** delineates the rights and responsibilities implied in relationships between persons and between persons and their government. It also identifies the remedies available when someone's rights are violated. For example, in 1993 the restaurant chain Jack-In-the-Box was ordered to pay civil damages after a two-year-old child died of food poisoning and several other people became ill from eating meat tainted with *E. coli* bacteria.

Criminal law, in contrast, regulates incidents in which someone commits an act against the public as a whole, such as by conducting insider trading on the stock exchange. Insider trading occurs when an individual uses insider, or secret, company information to increase her or his own finances or those of family or friends. Several years ago an IBM secretary allegedly told her husband, who in turn told several other people, that the company was

Exhibit 1-1
Business Law and the Six Functional Areas of Business

FUNCTIONAL AREA OF BUSINESS	RELEVANT AREAS OF BUSINESS LAW
Corporate management	International and comparative law White-collar crime Contracts Corporate law Antitrust law Administrative law Agency law Insurance law Employment law
Production and transportation	Tort law Contracts Environmental law Consumer law
Marketing	Tort law Contracts Antitrust law Consumer law Intellectual property
Research and development	Product liability Intellectual property Property law Consumer law
Accounting and finance	Liability of accountants Contracts Negotiable instruments and banking Bankruptcy White-collar crime
Human resource management	Agency law Contracts Employment and labor law Employment discrimination

Exhibit 1-2
Purposes of the Law

- Providing order such that one can depend on a promise or an expectation of obligations
- Serving as an alternative to fighting
- Facilitating a sense that change is possible, but only after a rational consideration of options
- Encouraging social justice
- Guaranteeing personal freedoms
- Serving as a moral guide by indicating minimal expectations of citizens and organizations

Exhibit 1-3
Civil versus Criminal Law

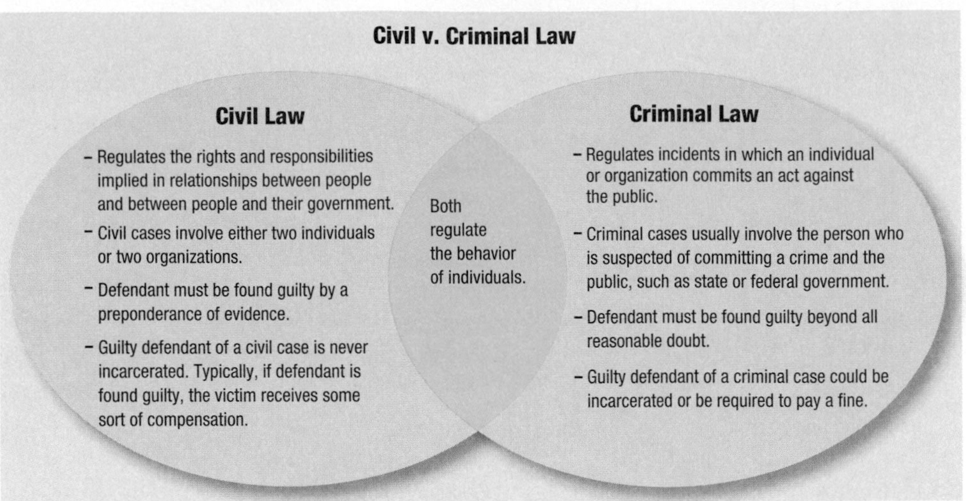

going to take over operations of Lotus Development. The leaked information spread among a number of individuals, 25 of whom bought stock that increased greatly in value following IBM's public announcement of the takeover. The Securities and Exchange Commission filed charges against them for creating an unfair trading environment for the public. Criminal law cases are prosecuted not by individuals but by the state, federal, or local government.

While some new laws have been adopted to regulate the kinds of activities businesses can now conduct online, **cyberlaw** is based primarily on existing laws. Laws governing contracts, for instance, are essentially the same in all situations, yet adaptations are necessary because contracts can now be made and signed online through retailers such as Amazon and eBay. Activities by companies such as Napster and YouTube have raised the question of whether and when the copying of certain intellectual property, such as music and video, constitutes theft.

Sources of Business Law

How is law created, and where do we look to find the laws? The sources of law are discussed below.

LO5
What are the sources of the law?

CONSTITUTIONS

The United States Constitution and the constitution of each state establish the fundamental principles and rules by which the United States and the individual states are governed. The term **constitutional law** refers to the general limits and powers of these governments as stated in their written constitutions. The U.S. Constitution is the supreme law of the land, the foundation for all laws in the United States. It is the primary authority to study when trying to identify the relationship between business organizations and government.

STATUTES

The assortment of *statutes,* or rules and regulations put forth by legislatures, is what we call **statutory law.** These legislative acts are written into the United States Code when they are passed by Congress or into the appropriate state codes when they are enacted by state legislatures. The codes are a collection of all the laws in one convenient location.

Business managers must also be familiar with the local city and county ordinances that govern matters not covered by federal or state codes. These ordinances address important business considerations such as local taxes, environmental standards, zoning, and building codes. If you wish to open a Krispy Kreme franchise in Santa Fe, New Mexico, you must follow local guidelines regarding where you may build your store, the materials you may use, and the state minimum wage you must pay employees making donuts. The regulations will be different if you wish to open your franchise in Toledo, Ohio, or Seattle, Washington.

While they are not a source of law in the same sense as constitutions and statutory law, **model** or **uniform laws** serve as a basis for some statutory law at the state level. Business activity is made more difficult when laws vary from state to state. To prevent such problems, a group of legal scholars and lawyers formed the National Conference of Commissioners on Uniform State Laws (NCC). The NCC regularly urges states to enact model laws to provide greater uniformity. The response is entirely in the hands of the state legislatures. They can ignore a suggestion or adopt part or all of the proposed model law.

The proposals of the NCC, while not laws themselves, have been adopted on more than 200 occasions by state legislatures. The NCC is an especially important influence on business law. Paired with the publications of the American Law Institute, it became the source of the *Uniform Commercial Code (UCC).* The UCC is a body of law so significant for business activities that it will be the focus of intensive study in several chapters of this text. The UCC laws include sales laws and other regulations affecting commerce, such as bank deposits and collections, title documents, and warranties. For example, these laws govern the different types of warranties that companies such as Microsoft, Sony, and Honda provide with their products.

CASES

Constitutions, legislatures, and administrative agencies encourage certain behaviors and prevent others. But laws are seldom self-explanatory and often require interpretation. **Case law,** also called **common law,** is the collection of legal interpretations made by judges. These interpretations are law unless revoked later by new statutory law.

Case law is especially significant for businesses that operate in multiple legal jurisdictions. Courts in two different business locations may interpret similarly worded statutes differently.

Courts issue judicial decisions that often include interpretations of statutes and administrative regulations, as well as the reasoning they used to arrive at a decision. Such reasoning depends heavily on **precedent,** past decisions in similar cases that guide later decisions, thereby providing greater stability and predictability to the law.

Business managers must pay attention to changes in the law and cases in which new precedents are set and take them into account when making business decisions. After a woman was severely burned by very hot coffee, McDonald's was found negligent for failing to provide a warning label on its hot-beverage cups. Now many retailers provide warning labels on their beverage cups because of the precedent set by this case.

When courts rely on precedent, they are obeying the principle of **stare decisis** ("standing by their decision"), in which rulings made in higher courts become binding precedent for lower courts. When an issue is brought before a state court, the court will determine whether the state supreme court has made a decision on a similar issue, which creates a binding precedent or pattern of law the lower court must follow. If there is no binding decision, both state courts need to look for other rulings on similar cases.

They are not bound by each other's decisions and might decide differently on the same issue. Decisions in lower courts can be appealed to the state appeals court, however, and the appeals court's decision can be appealed to the state supreme court. If the state supreme court rules on the case, its decision is binding for the state in that and future cases but does not affect earlier decisions made by state courts.

Perhaps the most well-known case associated with stare decisis is *Roe v. Wade.*[1] This landmark case, decided in 1973, made a decision on the issue of abortion. The U.S. Supreme Court decided that until a fetus is "viable," a woman may terminate her pregnancy for any reason. The Court went on to define *viable* as the ability of the fetus "to live outside the mother's womb, albeit with artificial aid." The Court added that such a capability could occur around 24 weeks, although usually around 7 months. The decision in *Roe v. Wade* has been upheld in cases since. The precedent still stands today, despite attempts to overturn it. In 1992, *Planned Parenthood of Southeastern Pennsylvania v. Casey*[2] used the decision to determine that a woman has a constitutional right to have an abortion, although the standard for restricting abortions was lowered.

Another case that has been used in accordance with stare decisis as a binding precedent is *Brown v. Board of Education,*[3] which abolished discriminatory policies for individuals of different racial backgrounds. In *Regents of the University of California v. Bakke,*[4] the plaintiff, a white male, had applied to the University of California at Davis medical school two years in a row and been denied admittance. He alleged the admissions process was discriminatory because 16 of 100 slots were reserved for members of minority races. The U.S. Supreme Court found the school's admissions policy was not lawful, referencing *Brown* and stating that the basic principle behind it and similar cases was that individuals could not be excluded on the basis of race or ethnicity. The Court wrote, "Preferring members of any one group for no reason other than race or ethnic origin is discrimination for its own sake."

Another U.S. Supreme Court case that relied in part on *Brown v. Board of Education* was *Wygant v. Jackson Board of Education.*[5] The Board of Education and teachers' union

[1] 410 U.S. 113 (1973).
[2] 505 U.S. 833 (1992).
[3] 347 U.S. 483 (1954).
[4] 438 U.S. 265 (1978).
[5] 476 U.S. 267 (1986).

in Jackson, Michigan, had agreed that if teachers were laid off, those with more seniority would be retained and the minority teachers' percentage of the layoffs would not be higher than their percentage of all teachers employed by the school district at the time of the layoffs. When layoffs did occur, nonminority teachers were laid off and minority teachers with less seniority were retained. The nonminority teachers sued. When the case was brought before the Supreme Court, the Court ruled that the layoff policy was not lawful because "[c]arried to the logical extreme, the idea that black students are better off with black teachers could lead to the very system the Court rejected in *Brown v. Board of Education.*" Again in accordance with *Brown,* the Court ruled that singling people out on the basis of race was not lawful.

However, the case *Plessy v. Ferguson*[6] is an interesting circumstance in regard to stare decisis. In this case, the court decided that separate accommodations for blacks and whites were acceptable as long as such separation was "separate but equal." This case essentially made the legal acknowledgment of a difference between blacks and whites, and different treatment, acceptable. Interestingly, in 1954, *Brown v. Board of Education* did not follow the precedent established by *Plessy v. Ferguson.* In fact, the ruling established in *Plessy* was overturned. The Supreme Court determined that segregation of blacks and whites violated the equal protection clause of the Fourteenth Amendment of the Constitution. Thus, the court overturned the precedent and created a new one, one that has been used in decisions made by courts ever since.

Just as state statutes have been strongly influenced by the suggestions of the NCC, common law evolves with the assistance of a mechanism called **Restatements of the Law.** These are summaries of the common law rules in a particular area of the law that have been enacted by most states. The American Law Institute prepares these Restatements for contracts, agency, property, torts, and many other areas of law that affect business decisions. While the Restatements are not themselves a source of business law, judges frequently use them to guide their interpretations in a particular case.

In addition to the Restatements, many influences are at work in the minds of judges when they interpret constitutions, statutes, and regulations. Their own values and social backgrounds function as lights and shadows, moving the judges toward particular legal decisions.

Courts in one jurisdiction need not obey precedents in other jurisdictions, but they may be influenced by them. At least two current Supreme Court justices are using law in other countries as a basis for rethinking certain laws in the United States. The logic of this reliance on precedent is based on respect for those who have already wrestled with the issue and provided us guidance with their earlier decision.

ADMINISTRATIVE LAW

Constitutions and statutes never cover all the detailed rules that affect relationships between government and business. The federal, state, and local governments have dozens of administrative agencies whose task is to perform a particular government function. For example, the Environmental Protection Agency (EPA) has broad responsibilities to enforce federal statutes in the area of environmental protection. The Occupational Safety and Health Administration (OSHA) oversees health and workplace safety and makes sure working conditions are not hazardous. In 1994, OSHA settled a complaint that United Parcel Service (UPS) was not providing adequate safety measures and equipment for workers who handled hazardous waste by making sure UPS adapted its practices to follow federal safety guidelines.

[6] 163 U.S. 537 (1896).

Exhibit 1-4
Major Federal Administrative Agencies

INDEPENDENT AGENCIES	EXECUTIVE AGENCIES
• Commodity Futures Trading Commission (CFTC) http://www.cftc.gov/	• Federal Deposit Insurance Corporation (FDIC) http://www.fdic.gov/
• Consumer Product Safety Commission (CPSC) http://www.cpsc.gov/	• Occupational Safety and Health Administration (OSHA) http://www.osha.gov/
• Equal Employment Opportunity Commission (EEOC) http://www.eeoc.gov/	• General Services Administration (GSA) http://www.gsa.gov/
• Federal Trade Commission (FTC) http://www.ftc.gov/	• National Aeronautics and Space Administration (NASA) http://www.nasa.gov/
• Federal Communications Commission (FCC) http://www.fcc.gov/	• Small Business Administration (SBA) http://www.sba.gov
• National Labor Relations Board (NLRB) http://www.nlrb.gov/	• U.S. Agency for International Development (USAID) http://www.usaid.gov/
• National Transportation Safety Board (NTSB) http://www.ntsb.gov/	• National Science Foundation (NSF) http://www.nsf.gov/
• Nuclear Regulatory Commission (NRC) http://www.nrc.gov/	• Veterans Administration (VA) http://www.va.gov/
• Securities and Exchange Commission (SEC) http://www.sec.gov/	• Office of Personnel Management (OPM) http://www.opm.gov/

Administrative law is the collection of rules and decisions made by all these agencies. Just glance at Exhibit 1-4 to get a sense of the scope of a few of the major federal administrative agencies.

TREATIES

A **treaty** is a binding agreement between two states or international organizations. It may be an international agreement, a covenant, an exchange of letters, a convention, or protocols. In the United States, a treaty is generally negotiated by the executive branch. To be binding, it must then be approved by two-thirds of the Senate.

A treaty is similar to a contract in two important ways. Both treaties and contracts are attempts by parties to determine rights and obligations among themselves, and when a party fails to obey a treaty or a contract, international law imposes liability on it.

EXECUTIVE ORDERS

The president and state governors can issue directives requiring that officials in the executive branch perform their functions in a particular manner. The Code of Federal Regulations (CFR) contains all the executive orders created by the president. (It is online at www.gpoaccess.gov/cfr/index.html.) Presidents claim the power to issue such orders on the basis of their Article II, Section 1, constitutional power to "take care that the laws be faithfully executed." President George W. Bush issued 284 executive orders during the eight years of his presidency.

An especially controversial executive order is Order 9066, issued by President Franklin Roosevelt during World War II, which sent Japanese-Americans on the West Coast, as well as thousands of Italian-American and German-American families, to internment camps for the duration of the war.

Exhibit 1-5 summarizes the various locations where you can find particular laws.

Exhibit 1-5 Where to Locate the Law

	Source by Level of Government		
TYPE OF LAW	**FEDERAL**	**STATE**	**LOCAL**
Statutes	United States Code (USC) United States Code Annotated (USCA) United States Statutes at Large	State code	Municipal ordinances
Administrative law	Code of Federal Regulations (CFR) *Federal Register*	State administrative code	Municipality administrative regulations
Common law	United States Reports (U.S.) United States Supreme Court Reporter (S. Ct.) Federal Reporter (F. F.2d) Federal Supplement (F.Supp.)	Regional reporters State reporters	Check the clerk's office at the local courthouse
Executive order	Title 3 of Code of Federal Regulations Codification of Presidential Proclamations and Executive Orders	See state government website	n/a
Treaty	See http://www.asil.org/treaty1.cfm	n/a	n/a

SCHOOLS OF JURISPRUDENCE

L06 What are the various schools of jurisprudence?

When legislators or courts make law, they do so guided by certain habits of mind and specific beliefs about human nature. Beliefs are deeply rooted within a person's emotions and habits, and thus they are sure to guide one's opinions and decisions. Such beliefs may be commonly held and thus create various larger schools of thought. Once one determines what schools of thought influence certain types of decisions and opinions, one is sure to better understand such decisions. This section briefly describes several of the more common guides to legal interpretation.

Natural Law. The term **natural law** describes certain ethical laws and principles believed to be morally right and "above" the laws devised by humans. Under natural law individuals have not only basic human rights but also the freedom to disobey a law enacted by people if their conscience goes against it and they believe it is wrong. Dow Chemical wants its suppliers to conform to U.S. environmental and labor laws, not just the local laws in the supplier's country, where regulations may not be as stringent. This policy reflects the beliefs that people have a right to be treated fairly in their jobs and a right as human beings to have a clean environment.

Legal Positivism. The concept of **legal positivism** sees our proper role as obedience to duly authorized law. That law is quite distinct from morality, and moral questions about the law should not interfere with our inclination to obey it. A judge with leanings in the direction of legal positivism might write that she is deciding to enforce the law in question but that her decision does not necessarily mean she sees the law as the morally correct rule.

Identification with the Vulnerable. Closely linked to pursuing legal change through natural law is pursuing change through **identification with the vulnerable,** on the grounds that some higher law or body of moral principles connects all of us in the human community. Some members of our society are able to take care of themselves in terms of most life situations. Others, especially the ill, children, the aged, the disabled, and the poor, require assistance to meet their fundamental needs of life, health, and education.

This guide to legal change is tied closely to the pursuit of fairness, a "level playing field," in our society. We might look at a particular employment contract and feel outrage that "it is just not fair." That outrage can be a stimulus for legal change. Minimum-wage laws reflect the belief that workers should receive a minimum hourly wage and that employers should not be allowed to pay them less.

Historical School: Tradition. One of the guidelines most often used for shaping the law is tradition, or custom. Stare decisis is rooted in this *historical school.* When we follow tradition, instead of reinventing the wheel, we link our behavior to the behavior of those who faced similar problems in earlier periods. We assume past practice was the product of careful thought.

Legal Realism. **Legal realism** is based on the idea that, when ruling on a case, judges need to consider more than just the law; they also weigh factors such as social and economic conditions, since legal guidelines were designed by humans and exist in an ever-changing environment. Judges who follow this school of thought are more likely to depart from past court decisions to account for the fact that our society is constantly shifting and evolving. They believe the law can never be enforced with complete consistency and argue that because judges are human, they will bring different methods of reasoning to very similar cases.

One law enacted to reflect social changes is the Family and Medical Leave Act. This act mandates that businesses employing more than 50 people provide their workers with up to 12 weeks' unpaid leave every year to take care of family-related affairs, including caring for oneself or ill parents and adopting or having a child. The law also protects pregnant women who take time off work, as their employers must provide them with the same pay and the same or an equivalent job when they return to work. More mothers are working outside the home, and more women are returning to work soon after they have a child. The act protects them against some types of discrimination that might occur after they return.

Cost-Benefit Analysis. Suppose we could attach a monetary figure to the benefits of a particular law or legal decision. We would next need to examine all its costs and place a monetary value on it. If we possessed these figures, we could use **cost-benefit analysis** as a guide to legal change, choosing the alternatives that maximized benefits and minimized costs.

This approach is tied closely to the pursuit of efficiency. If the law to be applied yields more benefits than costs, then we have saved resources that we can, in turn, use to obtain more goods and services. Our economy is thus more efficient because it produces more with less.

Polluted land is an economic loss as it cannot be used for farming or recreation. Polluted water can be toxic for fish and cannot be used for drinking. Polluted air can cause health problems and result in higher health care costs. While complying with EPA pollution controls may cost companies more initially, the price of environmental cleanup and lost productivity in the economy as a whole may be even greater.

Global and Comparative Law

Advances in technology and transportation make trade with other countries far easier today than in the past. Boeing Co. can make hundreds of components for the same airliner all over the world and then assemble them in the United States. An antique store can operate in Poughkeepsie but sell to customers in Moscow or Taipei through a website.

This ease in trade means business managers must be familiar with laws that regulate business practices between nations. The United States has entered into trade agreements, such as the North American Free Trade Agreement (NAFTA) with Canada and Mexico and the General Agreement on Tariffs and Trade (GATT) with about 150 other countries, that help establish the conditions of global trade.

Future managers should also understand comparative law, which studies and compares the laws in different countries. The European Union (EU) regulates taxes on Internet sales and the amount of pollution firms can release differently than does the U.S. government. Companies doing business in the EU must take these standards into account. The Chinese government does not want its citizens to have access to certain information and websites. To do business in China, Google had to conform to Chinese standards by restricting the content of searches performed on Google.cn. Some felt that by thus restricting access to information, Google had violated its own mission statement to "do no evil."

Business law tells managers the basic rules of the business game. Play any game without having first studied the rules, and you will probably fail. But unlike an ordinary game, business has a rule book that is changing dynamically. So modern business managers must have an ongoing fascination with the law to function effectively.

KEY TERMS

APPENDIX 1A CRITICAL THINKING AND BUSINESS LAW

Success in business requires the development of **critical-thinking skills** and attitudes—the ability and desire to understand the structure of what someone is saying and then apply a set of criteria to evaluate its worth. In other words, businesspeople need to be able to sort sense from nonsense by developing critical attitudes and abilities. There is no better context in which to develop these skills than the study of the laws that affect business.

Legal reasoning is like other kinds of reasoning in some ways. The stimulus that gets us thinking is an *issue,* stated as a question that requires us to *do* something, to think about answers.

We may be interested in such issues as the following:

- When are union organizers permitted under the National Labor Relations Act to trespass on an employer's property?
- Do tobacco manufacturers have liability for the deaths of smokers?
- Must a business fulfill a contract with an unlicensed contractor in a state requiring that all contractors be licensed?

These questions have several potential answers, but which best accomplishes a particular business objective? Which is consistent with the law? Here is where critical thinking is essential to business success. Some answers can get the decision maker into trouble; others will advance the intended purpose. Each answer is called a *conclusion.*

Business firms are both consumers of and contributors to legal conclusions. As they learn about and react to decisions or conclusions made by courts, businesspeople can respond in two ways:

1. Understand the conclusions in the case, and use this understanding as a guide for future business decisions.
2. Make judgments about the quality of the conclusions.

This book encourages you to do both. Critical thinking is active; it challenges each of us to form judgments about the quality of the link between a set of reasons and the conclusion derived from them. In particular, we will be focusing on the link between a court's reasons and its conclusions.

The following structure for critical thinking is a thoroughly tested method used by successful market decision makers. Every time you read a case, try to follow it.

1. Find the *facts.*

   Here we are looking for the most basic building blocks in a legal decision or argument. They provide the environment or context in which the legal issue is to be resolved. Certain events occurred; certain actions were or were not taken; particular persons behaved or failed to behave in specific ways. We always want to know, What happened in this case?

2. Look for the *issue.*

   The issue is the question that caused the lawyers and their clients to enter the legal system.

3. Identify the judge's *reasons and conclusion.*

   We want a world rich with opinions so that we can have a broad field of choice. But we should agree with only those legal opinions that have convincing reasons supporting the conclusion. Asking "Why?" is our respectful way of saying, "I want to believe you, but you have an obligation to help me by sharing the reasons for your conclusion."

4. Locate in the decision the *rules of law* that govern the judge's reasoning.

   Judges cannot offer just any reasoning that they please. They must always look back over their shoulders at the laws and previous court decisions that together provide an anchor for current and future decisions. What makes legal reasoning so complex is that statutes and legal findings are never crystal clear. They may seem very clear, but judges and businesspeople have room for interpretive flexibility in their reasoning.
5. Apply *critical thinking* to the reasoning.

   A judge's reasoning, once we have laid it out by following the steps discussed here, is a message we may either accept or reject. *Critical thinking in the legal context* consists of examining the legal opinion in search of potential problems in the reasoning.

One of the most exciting things about our legal system is its potential for change. Listed below is a small sample of some especially useful critical-thinking tools for business managers to use when thinking about business law. (See Exhibit 1-6.)

- Look for potential ambiguity in the reasoning. *Ambiguity* is a lack of clarity in a word or phrase. Many words have multiple meanings; until we know the intended one, we cannot tell whether we agree or disagree with the reasoning.
- Ask whether the analogies used in the decision are strong. When judges follow precedents, they are saying the facts in the precedent and those in the case at hand are so similar that it makes sense to apply the same rule of law in both. Are there key differences in the facts that raise questions about the quality of that analogy?
- Check the quality of the judge's reasoning. Is the judge's supporting evidence both abundant enough and reliable enough that we should agree with the reasoning?

Exhibit 1-6

Critical-Thinking Tools for Business Managers

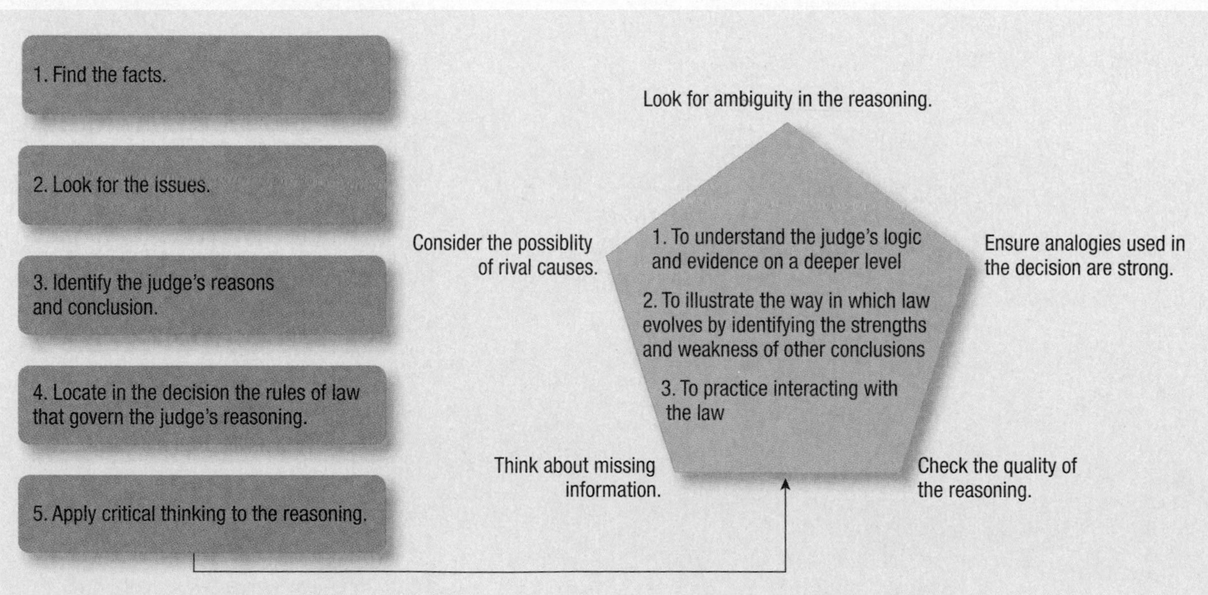

- Think about the extent to which missing information prevents you from being totally confident about the judge's reasoning. Is there information you would need to have before making up your mind?
- Consider the possibility of rival causes. When the judge claims one action caused another, think about whether some alternative cause may have been responsible.

Working through these steps accomplishes several things. First, walking through this process familiarizes you at a deeper level with what the judge is saying. You have to wrestle with the judge's logic and use of evidence to complete the critical-thinking activity. Second, the critical thinking provides a sense that the law evolves as we put together the strengths and weaknesses of previous thinking by judges and legal scholars. Most importantly, critical thinking enables us to practice interacting with the law, always with an eye to considering ways to improve our legal system.

This chapter has enabled you to understand several important things. First, you should now be acquainted with what business law is and how business law and business education are intertwined. Second, you should understand the purposes of law, be acquainted with different kinds of law, and have a basic understanding of how different courts and agencies cooperate with one another. You should also now know about the interplay between case law and stare decisis, or binding precedent. You should also be able to pinpoint where various kinds of laws come from.

More importantly, however, you should realize that all of our courts and legal documents are thought to be just and that justice is an idea based on other ideas. Different schools of thought arise from deep-rooted, commonly held beliefs, and these schools guide decisions about what is fair and just and why. Finally, you should be able to critically evaluate a judge's or court's opinion. Only by doing so can you sort through the logic of the decision and pinpoint all the factors that went into the decision, including not only precedent and case law but the perspective flowing from schools of legal thought, rooted in personal beliefs and opinions.

KEY TERM

critical-thinking skills 12

Business Ethics

CHAPTER

2

LEARNING OBJECTIVES

After reading this chapter, you will be able to answer the following questions:

1 What are business ethics and the social responsibility of business?

2 How are business law and business ethics related?

3 How can we use the WPH framework for ethical business decisions?

CASE OPENER

Acne Medication and Gastrointestinal Injury

Since 1999, Kamie Kendall had experienced ongoing abdominal pain, and she was eventually diagnosed with ulcerative colitis and irritable bowel syndrome (IBD). Although Kendall had been taking an acne medication, Accutane, since 1997, the medication's warnings did not mention IBD or ulcerative colitis and, therefore, Kendall had never suspected that her ongoing illness was a result of the medication. Then, in April 2004, Kendall's grandmother informed her of a lawyer's television advertisement linking Accutane to ongoing IBD. On December 21, 2005, Kendall filed a lawsuit against Hoffman-LaRoche, the manufacturer of Accutane, alleging that the company was liable for her injuries because the medication's warnings failed to disclose the risk of developing IBD.

Kendall argued that, instead, the medication's warnings focused on pregnancy and suicide. Further, although the medication warned against "abdominal pain," there were no specific warnings, or mention on the consent form, of risk of IBD or colitis.

Hoffman-LaRoche moved to dismiss this lawsuit, arguing that the statute of limitations had expired and that Kendall's suit was untimely.

1. When is it usually considered untimely for plaintiffs to file failure-to-warn lawsuits?
2. If you were in charge of manufacturing acne medication, would you consider it your ethical obligation to list all potential illnesses that may result from your product?

The Wrap-Up at the end of the chapter will answer these questions.

What a business manager in the situation described in the opening scenario should do is not altogether clear. Ethical conversation is less about finding the one and only right thing to do than it is about finding the better thing to do. Whatever you choose to do, some stakeholders will be hurt and others will benefit. Business ethics requires a weighing of the benefits of a decision compared to their harm.

This chapter provides some assistance for thinking systematically about issues of right and wrong in business conduct. Initially, we need to sort through the meaning of key terms like *business ethics* and *social responsibility*. Then, because it is helpful to have a useful approach to ethical decision making, we provide a practical method by which future business managers can think more carefully about the ethical dilemmas they will face during their careers.

Business Ethics and Social Responsibility

L01

What are business ethics and the social responsibility of business?

Ethics is the study and practice of decisions about what is good, or right. Ethics guides us when we are wondering what we should be doing in a particular situation. **Business ethics** is the application of ethics to the special problems and opportunities experienced by businesspeople. For example, as a business manager, you might someday make a decision that you think is best for your company, as did the advertisers for Accutane, described in the Case Opener. Is a company doing the right thing when it attempts to reduce the costs of advertising by not listing all possible complications of the medicine for the consumer?

Such questions present businesses with ethical choices, each of which has advantages and disadvantages. An **ethical dilemma** is a problem about what a firm should do for which no clear, right decision is available.

For example, imagine yourself in the position of a business manager at Wells Fargo Bank. You know that providing bank accounts for customers has costs attached to it. You want to cover those costs by charging the customers the cost of their checking accounts. By doing so, you can preserve the bank's revenue for shareholders and employees of Wells Fargo. So far, the decision seems simple. But an ethical dilemma soon appears.

To see how ethics relates to accounting, please see the **Connecting to the Core** activity on the text website at www.mhhe.com/kubasek3e.

You learn from recent government reports that 12 million families cannot afford to have bank accounts when they are charged a fee to maintain one. You want to do the right thing in this situation. But what would that be? The study of business ethics can help you resolve this dilemma by suggesting approaches you can use that will show respect for others while maintaining a healthy business enterprise.

Making these decisions would be much easier if managers could focus only on the impact of decisions on the firm. If, for example, a firm had as its only objective the maximization of profits, the "right thing" to do would be the option that had the largest positive impact on the firm's profits.

But businesses operate in a community. Communities have expectations for behavior of individuals, groups, and businesses. Different communities have different expectations of businesses. Trying to identify what those expectations are and deciding whether to fulfill them complicate business ethics. The community often expects firms to do much more for it than just provide a useful good or service at a reasonable price. For example, a community may expect firms to resist paying bribes, even when the payment of such fees is an ordinary cost of doing business in certain global settings. The **social responsibility of business** consists of the expectations that the community imposes on firms doing business inside its borders. These expectations must be honored to a certain extent, even when a firm wishes to ignore them, because firms are always subject to the implicit threat that legislation will impose social obligations on them. So, if the community expects businesses to obey certain standards of fairness even when the standards interfere with profit maximization, firms that choose to ignore that expectation do so at their peril. See Exhibit 2-1 for a brief look at Pacific Gas and Electric's approach to social responsibility.

Consider also the financial meltdown of the largest insurance company in the United States, American International Group (AIG). In late October 2011, an investigation by the Government Accountability Office raised questions about the 2008 bailout of AIG by the Federal Reserve. In 2008, the company suddenly collapsed because of risky bets it made insuring mortgage-backed securities. AIG became the source of widespread public outrage after the media revealed that the company had paid $165 million in bonuses two days before its bailout; the public was especially distraught because these paid bonuses were even distributed to some members of the trading unit that had caused the company's collapse. The Federal Reserve spent $85 billion bailing out the company, but losses

Exhibit 2-1

Good Citizenship and Profits

Source: Code of Conduct from www.pgecorp.com/aboutus/corp_gov/coce.shtml.

Given the number of corporate accounting scandals that have been revealed in the past few years, many corporations are making a point of assuring their investors that their corporate goals are not focused solely on profit. As investors lost millions of dollars during the collapse of companies such as WorldCom and Enron, some corporations have been placing increased emphasis on promoting themselves not only as profitable but as conscientious and ethical in their treatment of consumers, employees, and shareholders.

Whereas in years past companies may have focused solely on their profitability in an attempt to gain new investors, today many business managers realize that corporate honesty has become just as important to those who are seeking to buy stock. Tony Early, Chairman, CEO, and President of PG&E Corporation and Chris Johns, President of Pacific Gas and Electric Company, emphasize this in their message to employees in PG&E's Code of Conduct:

"... all of us at PG&E are working hard to ensure that our company is on a solid foundation for the future. Strong performance is critical to our success, but just as important is how we go about achieving results - with honesty and respect, without taking shortcuts, and by operating ethically and with integrity in all that we do.

[Our Employee Code of Conduct] supports our continuing commitment to honest and ethical conduct and compliance with both the letter and the spirit of all laws, rules, and regulations, and our company's policies, standards, and procedures."

continued to grow. Later, the government paid a total of $182 billion, setting the record as the largest federal bailout in U.S. history.

Business Law and Business Ethics

LO2

How are business law and business ethics related?

Before business managers consider the social responsibilities of firms in their communities, they need to gather all relevant facts.

The legality of the decision in choosing a method of production, how to compete with competing firms, and the social responsibilities of the firm is the minimal standard that must be met for the firm to be an ethical business. But the existence of that minimum standard is essential for the development of business ethics. To make this point, let's take a look at the growing practice of bribery in the absence of such legal standards. In some countries businesses must pay bribes to receive legitimate supplies. Though the businessperson may be morally opposed to paying the bribes, the supplies are necessary to stay in business and there may be no other means of obtaining them.

Thus, multinational companies face an ethical dilemma: They must decide whether to pay bribes or find alternative sources of supplies. For instance, when McDonald's opened its doors in Moscow, it made arrangements to receive its supplies from foreign providers. These arrangements ensured that the franchise did not have to engage in questionable business practices.

Regardless of the ethical and legal implications, there are still multinational corporations that choose to use bribes as a means of doing business in foreign markets. For example, in December 2008, multinational giant Siemens AG was ordered to pay the largest Foreign Corrupt Practices Act (FCPA) fine in history after admitting to acts of bribery worldwide. The company had been using off-the-book slush funds, middlemen posing as agents or company consultants, and even money-filled briefcases to bribe government officials and secure contracts overseas. An FBI agent involved in the Siemens investigation went so far as to say that executives for Siemens used bribery as "standard operating procedure" and "a business strategy." As a result, $1.6 billion later, Siemens AG is now forced to restructure itself to do business ethically and legally.

Future business professionals ought to consider not just the moral and monetary costs of engaging in unethical business practices but also the cost of lost business. A tarnished reputation could mean losing contracts, sales, and partnerships in the future.

Look at Case 2-1 as an exercise in comparing what is legal with what is ethical.

CASE 2-1 UNITED STATES OF AMERICA v. ALFRED CARONIA
U.S. DISTRICT COURT FOR THE EASTERN DISTRICT OF NEW YORK
576 F. SUPP. 2D 385 (2008)

The defendant, Alfred Caronia, was a sales representative for a pharmaceutical company named Orphan when he was charged for "off-label" promotion of a drug. The company, now called Jazz Pharmaceutical, had produced a drug named Xyrem, which was a depressant that induced sleep. The main active ingredient in the drug was gamma-hydroxybutyrate, also known as "GHB." At the time, the FDA reviewed the drug and stipulated that the drug was a safe way to treat only one condition: cataplexy, which is a narcoleptic condition. Several severe problems had been associated with Xyrem, including dependence and withdrawal symptoms. Other side effects included death, coma, or seizures. The FDA regulations regarding the drug stated that children under 16 should be kept from using the drug, as positive effects had not been observed. Additionally, elderly patients were advised not to use the drug, as limited observations linked positive effects with elderly patients. Caronia was discovered to be marketing Xyrem to physicians for an extra purpose: to combat excessive daytime sleepiness. This use had certainly not been approved by the FDA.

The ethical ramifications of off-label promoting can be severe. In fact, promoting a drug for purposes not approved by the government has been a growing problem with both doctors and pharmaceutical sales representatives. These cases cast a light on the questionable financial partnerships between pharmaceutical companies and doctors who not only prescribe the drug but also advocate use of the drug. Having medicines prescribed for unapproved uses greatly increases the sales of the medicine and therefore the profits of the company. Unfortunately, the effects of these deals can lead to harm and even death to the patients taking the prescriptions. In this case, Caronia moved to dismiss the charges against him, and the court had to consider his argument about his right to free speech and the FDA's argument about its job to protect public safety.

JUDGE VITALIANO: Pursuant to the FDCA, manufacturers are restricted from marketing so-called "off-label" (i.e., non-FDA approved) uses of a drug. . . . Count one of the instant information alleges that, between March 2005 and March 2006, defendant Alfred Caronia, an Orphan sales representative, knowingly and intentionally conspired with others to misbrand a drug by marketing Xyrem for off-label uses in violation of 21 U.S.C. §§ 331(a), (k), 333(a)(1), and 18 U.S.C. § 371.

. . . In particular, the information alleges that, on October 26, 2005, Carona promoted Xyrem to a physician "John Doe" for fibromyalgia, EDS, muscle disorders, chronic pain and fatigue, which uses were for off-label indications. The information further alleges that, on November 2, 2005, Caronia introduced another physician, who was paid by Orphan, to "John Doe," and that the other physician promoted Xyrem for off-label indications, including fibromyalgia, EDS, sleepiness, weight loss and chronic fatigue.

The information supersedes a prior felony indictment against Caronia and Dr. Peter Gleason, who is the physician allegedly paid by Orphan to promote Xyrem for off-label uses. That indictment charged that Gleason and Caronia participated in a conspiracy with others to introduce a misbranded drug into interstate commerce with intent to defraud and mislead, and to make false statements in connection with the delivery of and payment for health care benefits. The indictment also charged a conspiracy to defraud public and private health care plans.

Caronia . . . argues that, assuming the lawful reach of the FDCA, he did not misbrand Xyrem within the meaning of 21 U.S.C. § 352(f) because he administered adequate warnings to the cooperating physician in October and November 2005. Somewhat confusingly, Caronia claims that no matter whether Xyrem is prescribed for on- or off-label indications, it is administered in the same manner and in the same dosage, and, therefore, the potential dangers are identical for all. Accordingly, Caronia says, his duty to provide adequate directions was satisfied when he provided the cooperating physician with the black box warning outlining the dangers and side effects of Xyrem, even if he was promoting it for off-label uses.

This argument is utterly without merit. It is well established that under the FDA's "intended use" regulations, the promotion of a drug for an off-label use by the manufacturer or its representative is prohibited regardless of what directions the manufacturer or representative may give for that use.

. . . He [also] claims (without any support whatsoever) that warnings were unnecessary because the physician to whom he promoted off-label uses of Xyrem was a confidential informant who was not going to be a user or prescriber of the drug. Yet . . . it is the mouth of the promoter not the ear or intent of the audience that controls. Promotion of off-label uses by a drug manufacturer's representative clearly falls within the broad statutory definition of the offense. On this challenge, too, count two must be sustained.

. . . Caronia's [next] argument is that the government cannot restrict truthful, non-misleading promotion by a pharmaceutical manufacturer (or its employees) to a physician of the off-label uses of an FDA-approved drug. The government rejoins that the First Amendment does not apply to Caronia's activities as alleged in the information and that, if the First Amendment does apply, the FDCA's restrictions on promotion of off-label uses are constitutional.

. . . Caronia's instant motion to dismiss appropriates an alternative First Amendment argument advanced by Gleason prior to his guilty plea. Because he was a doctor expressing his opinions about a drug he could and did prescribe, Gleason argued that his promotional activities amounted to scientific and academic speech, which resides at the core of the First Amendment and, therefore, should receive the highest constitutional protection as pure speech. Caronia, perhaps recognizing that such an argument would be of little help to him as a sales representative of the manufacturer, does not press the argument that his own speech was "pure" speech. He advances instead the alternate argument Gleason advanced that such promotional activities, if not "pure" speech, are protected at minimum as commercial speech.

. . . To determine whether a promotional activity is protectable as "commercial speech," a court must look to (1) whether the expression is an advertisement; (2) whether it refers to a specific product; and (3) whether the speaker has an economic motivation for speaking.

Regardless what else might have been covered in his discussions, Caronia's alleged speech was made on behalf of the manufacturer and clearly (1) encouraged physicians to prescribe Xyrem, (2) referred to a specific product, and (3) was economically motivated. Any such promotion by Caronia to physicians on behalf of Xyrem's manufacturer of the drug's off-label uses would be commercial speech and be "entitled to the qualified but nonetheless substantial protection accorded to commercial speech."

Finding that Caronia's alleged promotional activities in marketing Xyrem constitute commercial speech, the Court

[continued]

must now address his argument that his speech specifically is constitutionally protected. First, as a threshold matter, the Court must determine whether Caronia's commercial speech "concerns unlawful activity or is misleading." If so, then the speech is not protected. Id. If the speech concerns lawful activity and is not misleading, then the Court asks: (2) "whether the asserted government interest is substantial"; (3) whether the restriction "directly advances the government interest asserted"; and (4) whether the restriction is "not more extensive than necessary to serve that interest."

. . . Under prong one of Central Hudson, the Court finds, in harmony with the analysis in Friedman and the district court's opinion in Caputo, that promotion of the off-label uses of an FDA-approved drug concerns lawful activity and is not inherently misleading. . . . Second, the Court finds that the alleged speech is not misleading.

In line with these authorities, this Court holds that the FDCA's prohibitions on commercial speech of the kind charged in the information filed against Caronia directly advance the government's interest in subjecting off-label uses of a drug like Xyrem to the FDA's evaluation process. Central Hudson's third prong is satisfied here as well.

. . . Enter on stage the essential question—can the government satisfy the fourth prong of Central Hudson? . . . Simply put, Caronia asks this Court to extend Western States to undermine the delicate balance between ensuring the integrity of the new drug approval process while allowing patients to continue to have unfettered access to new and potentially life-saving uses for drugs and devices approved only for other purposes. As the Seventh Circuit recognized, such a result could very well leave the FDA only with options that would injure the very audience that would purportedly benefit most from the speech at issue. The Court is disinclined to do so. Quite to the contrary, the Court concludes . . . that the prohibitions on the speech which underlie the two counts in which Caronia is charged pass constitutional muster under the fourth prong of Central Hudson. Any right Caronia had as Xyrem's sales representative to express as commercial speech the truthful promotion of Xyrem's off-label uses is not unconstitutionally restricted by the misbranding provisions of the FDCA. On this ground, Caronia's motion is also denied.

SO ORDERED

CRITICAL THINKING

The Caronia case highlights a problematic relationship between pharmaceutical companies and the physicians who prescribe the medications. How could such interactions be dangerous to patients?

How, at first, did Caronia's speech fit under the umbrella of protected free speech? What reason, then, did Judge Vitaliano give for why Caronia's speech was not protected due to fulfilling the prongs of the Central Hudson test?

ETHICAL DECISION MAKING

The case mentions a physician named Gleason. Gleason was convicted in association with Orphan Pharmaceuticals prior to Caronia's case. How was Gleason acting unethically?

Business managers must sometimes decide whether to hire and fire particular employees. Their decisions will be guided by legal rules that have both ethical foundations and implications for needed legal reform.

In addition, the definition of business ethics refers to *standards* of business conduct. *It does not result in a set of correct decisions.* Business ethics can improve business decisions by serving as a reminder not to choose the first business option that comes to mind or the one that enriches us in the short run. But business ethics can never produce a list of correct business decisions that all ethical businesses will make.

At the same time that business ethics guides decisions within firms, ethics helps guide the law. Law and business ethics serve as an interactive system—informing and assessing each other. For example, our ethical inclination to encourage trust, dependability, and efficiency in market exchanges shapes many of our business laws. See Exhibit 2-2, for instance. The principles of contract law facilitate market exchanges and trade because the

COMPARING THE LAW OF OTHER COUNTRIES

BUSINESS GIFTS AND FAVORS IN CHINA

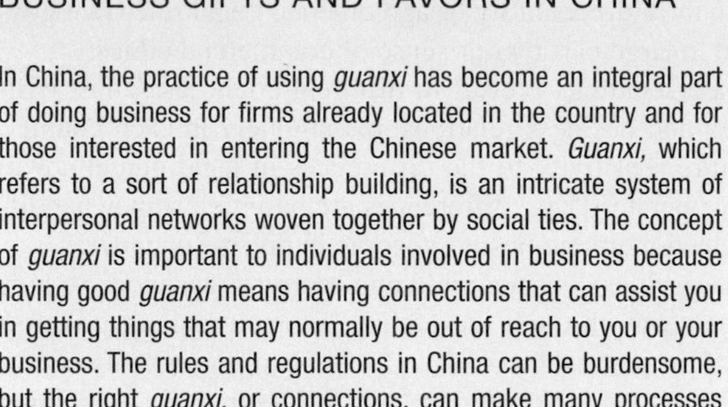

In China, the practice of using *guanxi* has become an integral part of doing business for firms already located in the country and for those interested in entering the Chinese market. *Guanxi,* which refers to a sort of relationship building, is an intricate system of interpersonal networks woven together by social ties. The concept of *guanxi* is important to individuals involved in business because having good *guanxi* means having connections that can assist you in getting things that may normally be out of reach to you or your business. The rules and regulations in China can be burdensome, but the right *guanxi,* or connections, can make many processes much easier. The *guanxi* system is built on reciprocity, and if someone does a favor for you, you'll be expected to return that favor in the future. A favor could technically be any number of things, from access to partnerships, contacts, and government officials to special consideration or useful information.

The process of creating and maintaining *guanxi* may seem somewhat taboo to westerners because businesses in the United States often have strict rules about accepting gifts, doing favors and offering preferential treatment or consideration to clients. However, Dan Mintz, a Brooklyn native with no college degree, who is now the CEO of one of the largest advertising agencies in China, claims *guanxi* is a necessity when doing business in China. After moving to Beijing with no contacts and little experience, Mintz established his own business (Dynamic Marking Group) with two Chinese partners, Peter Xiao and Wu Bing. Both Xiao and Bing had extensive *guanxi,* networks that extended into high levels of Chinese government and banking. The trio spent their time targeting potential clients, delivering gifts, and hosting dinners as means to strengthen their *guanxi* and improve their business opportunities. Through their hard work and strong *guanxi* Mintz, Xiao, and Bing were eventually able to secure deals with some of the biggest brands in the world: Budweiser, Kraft, Audi, Volkswagen, and Nike.

Source: Flora F. Gu, Kineta Hung, and David K. Tse, "When Does Guanxi Matter? Issues of Capitalization and Its Dark Sides," *Journal of Marketing* 72 (July 2008), pp. 12–28; www.fastcompany.com/magazine/104/open_mintz.html?page=0%2C0; and www.chinasuccessstories.com/2008/02/07/dmg-chinese-advertising/.

Exhibit 2-2

Enron, WorldCom, and Shifts in Business Regulation

During the past several years, ethics violations have been uncovered in the accounting practices of a number of large companies. Enron and WorldCom were two of the perpetrators in these scandals. Both companies failed to report or record billions of dollars in profit losses, which resulted in stockholders' believing that the companies were in a much better financial state than actually was the case.

Enron's tangled web involved the company's creating multiple subsidiaries and related companies. These businesses were often treated as companies independent of Enron and not shown on the accounting books. Enron used the subsidiaries to conceal debts and losses in a very complex fraud scheme. When the company went bankrupt, employees who had based their retirement plans around Enron stock lost almost everything. Additionally, Enron auditor Arthur Andersen was found guilty of shredding documents about Enron's audits.

In June 2002, shortly after the Enron bankruptcy was announced, WorldCom revealed that it also had engaged in unethical accounting practices. WorldCom's violations included counting profits twice and concealing billions of dollars in expenses when making reports to the SEC. The company thereby made itself appear profitable when it was actually losing money. In total, WorldCom had more than $7 billion in misreported debt.

These two cases, among others, left investors understandably concerned about the truthfulness of individuals who were in charge of operating large corporations. Those in charge of these companies had been awarded million-dollar bonuses while completely disregarding stockholders and employees, who lost millions of dollars when the companies collapsed.

The revelations of Enron and WorldCom suggested quite blatantly that the business world could not be allowed to regulate itself ethically. Their downfall in part led to many federal regulations designed to promote truthfulness and ethical practices among business managers. In this new business environment, there is a much greater degree of government oversight to ensure that companies maintain high standards of ethical behavior. Companies are required to make their accounting records far more transparent, to satisfy not only the federal government but their understandably wary investors.

parties to an exchange can count on the enforceability of agreements. Legal rules that govern the exchange have been shaped in large part by our sense of commercial ethics.

Of course, different ethical understandings prevail in different countries. Thus, ethical conceptions shape business law and business relationships uniquely in each country. Increasingly, business leaders require sensitivity to the differences in legal guidelines in the various countries in which they operate. These differences are based on somewhat different understandings of ethical behavior among businesspeople in diverse countries.

As we mentioned above, business ethics does not yield one "correct" decision. So how are business managers to chart their way through the ethical decision-making process? One source of assistance consists of the general theories and schools of thought about ethics. Each ethical system provides a method for resolving ethical dilemmas by examining duties, consequences, virtues, justice, and so on. A detailed look at each of these ethical systems can be found in Appendix 2A.

Exhibit 2-2 reminds us that unethical behavior by businesses has huge costs. In the interest of providing future business managers with a practical approach to business ethics *that they can use to avoid these costs,* we suggest a three-step approach: the **WPH process of ethical decision making.** This approach offers future business managers some **ethical guidelines,** or practical steps, that provide a dependable stimulus to ethical reasoning in a business context. Appendix 2A provides the theoretical basis for the WPH approach used in this book.

The WPH Framework for Business Ethics

LO3

How can we use the WPH framework for ethical business decisions?

A useful set of ethical guidelines requires recognition that managerial decisions must meet the following primary criteria:

- The decisions affect particular groups of stakeholders in the operations of the firm. The pertinent question is thus, *Whom* would this decision affect?
- The decisions are made in pursuit of a particular *purpose.* Business decisions are instruments toward an ethical end.
- The decisions must meet the standards of action-oriented business behavior. Managers need a doable set of guidelines for *how* to make ethical decisions.

The remainder of this chapter explains and illustrates this framework. See Exhibit 2-3 for a summary of the key WPH elements.

Exhibit 2-3

The WPH Process of Ethical Decision Making

1. **W—WHO (Stakeholders):**
   Consumers
   Owners or investors
   Management
   Employees
   Community
   Future generations
2. **P—PURPOSE (Values):**
   Freedom
   Security
   Justice
   Efficiency
3. **H—HOW (Guidelines):**
   Public disclosure
   Universalization
   Golden Rule

WHO ARE THE RELEVANT STAKEHOLDERS?

The **stakeholders** of a firm are the many groups of people affected by the firm's decisions. Any given managerial decision affects, in varying degrees, the following stakeholders:

1. Owners or shareholders.
2. Employees.
3. Customers.
4. Management.
5. The general community where the firm operates.
6. Future generations.

Exhibit 2-4 gives a portrait of General Mills' commitments to its primary stakeholders and demonstrates that General Mills is aware of the people involved in its various decisions.

When you consider the relevant stakeholders, try to go beyond the obvious. In the Case Nugget (next page), Maria's encounter with her company's vice president clearly highlights certain common interests of management and its employees. However, a useful exercise for all of us is to force ourselves to think more broadly about additional stakeholders who may be affected just as much in the long run. Then we will be less likely to make decisions that have unintended negative ethical impacts.

Maria's ethical dilemma is complex. Many of the issues in the dilemma pertain to her career and the welfare of her firm. But consider the many stakeholders whose interests were not introduced into the conversation. When we overlook important, relevant stakeholders, we are ignoring a significant component of ethical reasoning.

Consider the negative impact that results when a firm fails to show adequate respect for a major stakeholder. On December 3, 1984, a horrible catastrophe occurred at a chemical plant in Bhopal, India. The plant was a subsidiary of Union Carbide. Damage to some

Exhibit 2-4

Commitments to General Mills' Stakeholders

We share a common purpose and a common responsibility with our stakeholders. We want them to know that they can depend on us—and that they can trust us. We know too that we must depend on them. We want every stakeholder of General Mills to feel they are part of something special.

Our Consumers

Our consumers trust General Mills to deliver quality and value when they are shopping for the most important people in their lives—their families.

Our Customers

Our customers trust General Mills to deliver quality and value for their customers—the consumers of our products—and they look to us to help them grow.

Our Partners

We treat our suppliers, vendors, and other partners with respect—conducting ourselves with integrity in every aspect of every relationship.

Our Team

We are diverse, talented, committed individuals of integrity—constantly learning and growing and contributing to our communities.

Our Shareholders

Our shareholders trust General Mills to deliver superior performance and superior total investment returns.

Our Communities

We are committed to making a positive difference in people's lives by making a positive difference in our communities.

Source: www.generalmills.com/corporate/commitment/stakeholders.aspx (accessed October 30, 2008).

HYPOTHETICAL CASE NUGGET

THE MANY STAKEHOLDERS IN A BUSINESS DECISION

Maria Lopez

Maria recently became the purchasing manager of a small lawn-mower manufacturing firm. She is excited about the opportunity to demonstrate her abilities in this new responsibility. She is very aware that several others in the firm are watching her closely because they do not believe she deserves the purchasing manager position.

Her new job at the firm requires that she interact with several senior managers and leaders. One vice president in particular, Brian O'Malley, is someone she admires because he has earned the respect of the CEO on the basis of his success at making profits for the firm. Again and again, he just seems to know how to discover and take advantage of competitive opportunities that end up paying off royally for the firm.

Maria's first responsibility is to buy the motors for the assembly line. The motors constitute 30 percent of the total construction cost of the lawn mowers. Consequently, even a small error on Maria's part would have huge implications for the firm's profitability. The bids from the motor suppliers are required to be secret in order to maximize competition among the suppliers. The bids are due at 5 p.m. today.

At 3 p.m., Maria accidentally sees Brian returning the submitted bids to the locked safe where they are to be stored, according to company policy, until all bids have been submitted at 5 p.m. Then at 4:45 p.m., she notices a postal delivery of a bid from Stein's Motor Company. Her head buzzes as it hits her that Stein's president is one of Brian O'Malley's cousins.

She has no idea what to do. However, she knows she has to decide quickly.

equipment resulted in the emission of a deadly gas, methyl isocyanate, into the atmosphere. The emission of the gas caused injuries to more than 200,000 workers and other people in the neighborhood of the chemical plant. Several thousand people died.

Many factors, including worker error, faulty management decisions, equipment failures, and poor safety standards combined to cause the accident. Union Carbide was accused of not demanding the same rigorous safety standards in India as it had in the United States. Citizens of both India and the United States demanded that the corporation be held responsible for its evident neglect of safety. Union Carbide argued that it could not operate the plant if it were required to obey rigid Indian safety standards and that the economic benefits of the plant to India outweighed the risks of not following these standards. After years of litigation in both U.S. and Indian courts, Union Carbide was eventually ordered to monetarily compensate the victims of the accident. Among other factors, Union Carbide's failure to respect the interests of a major stakeholder resulted in a disaster for the firm and for the community.

After we consider stakeholders, the next step in the WPH framework is to consider the purpose of business decisions. In the next section, we look first at the parties involved, and then we explore the purposes that bring these various parties together in a common effort.

WHAT ARE THE ULTIMATE *PURPOSES* OF THE DECISION?

When we think about the ultimate reason or purpose for why we make decisions in a business firm, we turn to the basic unit of business ethics—values. **Values** are positive abstractions that capture our sense of what is good or desirable. They are *ideas* that underlie conversations about business ethics. We derive our ethics from the interplay of values. Values represent our understanding of the purposes we will fulfill by making particular decisions.

For example, we value honesty. We want to live in communities where the trust that we associate with honesty prevails in our negotiations with one another. Business depends on the maintenance of a high degree of trust. No contract can protect us completely against every possible contingency. So we need some element of trust in one another when we buy and sell.

When that trust is lacking, businesses fall apart. In August 2011, Maryland and Connecticut sued 16 banks for alleged rate manipulation. In the following weeks, additional banks in New York were served subpoenas, under the Martin Act, which allows investigation of businesses in New York "that may have committed deceitful practices contrary to the plain rules of common honesty." Robert Schapiro, the undersecretary of commerce for economic affairs in the Clinton administration, stated, "So long as big finance will do almost anything to goose its own profits and bonuses, self-regulation is a dangerous myth."

If we think about the definition of values for a moment, we realize two things immediately. First, there are a huge number of values that pull and push our decisions. For example, the banks mentioned above may have thought of honesty as an important value, but perhaps their desire for personal success weighed more heavily on their decision making than the need for honesty did. Second, to state that a value is important in a particular situation is to start a conversation about what is meant by that particular value. For example, some people may consider success a measure of one's character, whereas one may presume from the banks' actions that their definition of success was largely based on financial achievement.

To help make WPH useful to you as a manager, Exhibit 2-5 outlines an efficient way to apply this second step in the WPH framework. The exhibit identifies four of the most important values influencing business ethics and presents alternative meanings for each. Exhibit 2-5 should not only help clarify the importance of values in your own mind but also enable you to question others who claim to be acting in an ethical fashion.

For instance, a manager might be deciding whether to fire an employee whose performance is less than impressive. In making this decision, the manager explores alternative visions of key values such as justice and efficiency and then makes choices about which action to take. Values and their alternative meanings are often the foundation for different ethical decisions.

To avoid ambiguity, many companies summarize their values in brief statements.

Nortel Networks' statement of core values, shown in Exhibit 2-6, identifies for Nortel's stakeholders which positive abstractions guide its business decisions.

Exhibit 2-5
Primary Values and Business Ethics

VALUE	ALTERNATIVE MEANINGS
Freedom	1. To act without restriction from rules imposed by others
	2. To possess the capacity or resources to act as one wishes
	3. To escape the cares and demands of this world entirely
Security	1. To possess a large-enough supply of goods and services to meet basic needs
	2. To be safe from those wishing to interfere with your property rights
	3. To achieve the psychological condition of self-confidence to such an extent that risks are welcome
Justice	1. To receive the products of your labor
	2. To treat all humans identically, regardless of race, class, gender, age, and sexual preference
	3. To provide resources in proportion to need
	4. To possess anything that someone else is willing to grant you
Efficiency	1. To maximize the amount of wealth in society
	2. To get the most from a particular output
	3. To minimize costs

Exhibit 2-6

Core Values: A Guide to Ethical Business Practice

NORTEL NETWORKS' CORE VALUES

1. We create superior value for our customers.
2. We work to provide shareholder value.
3. Our people are our strength.
4. We share one vision. We are one team.
5. We have only one standard—excellence.
6. We embrace change and reward innovation.
7. We fulfill our commitments and act with integrity.

New ways of organizing people and work within the corporation are giving each of us more decision-making responsibility. Given the complexity and constantly changing nature of our work and our world, no book of hard-and-fast rules—however long and detailed—could ever adequately cover all the dilemmas people face. In this context, every Nortel Networks' employee is asked to take leadership in ethical decision making.

In most situations, our personal values and honesty will guide us to the right decision. But in our capacity as employees and representatives of Nortel Networks, we must also always consider how our actions affect the integrity and credibility of the corporation as a whole. Our business ethics must reflect the standard of conduct outlined in this document—a standard grounded in the corporation's values and governing Nortel Networks' relationships with all stakeholders.

HOW DO WE MAKE ETHICAL DECISIONS?

Making ethical decisions has always been one of our most confusing *and* important human challenges. In the process of meeting this challenge, we have discovered a few general, ethical guidelines to assist us. An *ethical guideline* provides one path to ethical conduct. Notice that all three ethical guidelines below reflect a central principle of business ethics: consideration for stakeholders.

The Golden Rule. The idea that we should interact with other people in a manner consistent with the way we would like them to interact with us has deep historical roots. Both Confucius and Aristotle suggested versions of that identical guideline. One scholar has identified six ways the Golden Rule can be interpreted:

1. Do to others as you want them to gratify you.
2. Be considerate of others' feelings as you want them to be considerate of yours.
3. Treat others as persons of rational dignity like you.
4. Extend brotherly or sisterly love to others, as you would want them to do to you.
5. Treat others according to moral insight, as you would have others treat you.
6. Do to others as God wants you to do to them.

Regardless of the version of the Golden Rule we use, this guideline urges us to be aware that other people—their rights and needs—matter.

Let's return to the ethical problem outlined at the beginning of this chapter. Using the Golden Rule as your ethical guideline, how would you behave? Would you hide the information about the chemicals used to make your medications, or would you disclose the information? Put yourself in the consumer's position. As a consumer, would you want to know that your medications contained a potentially toxic chemical? Are there other

CASE NUGGET

TYSON FOODS' BRIBERY CHARGES

In 2004, memos containing information regarding illegal bribes were sent from a Tyson Foods plant manager in Mexico to corporate officials in the United States. Basically, company officials in Mexico were sending roughly $2,700 a month to the wives of two veterinarians involved in the safety and quality of the food produced at the plant. At the time, Tyson Foods was attempting to increase its national exports. However, countries involved in the importation of its products required that experts certify that the food products met certain safety and sanitary standards. Essentially, the two veterinarians were being sent extra payments so that they would sign off on the "quality" of the products produced at the plant regardless of whether the products were actually up to par with the standards imposed. This act was especially dangerous considering the relationship between poultry products and their reputation of passing on disease, including salmonella, to consumers.

The company officials in Arkansas, including the president of Tyson International and the vice president of operations, realized that bribing foreign officials, the biggest issue at hand, was a felony according to the Foreign Corrupt Practices Act. Faced with the option of investigating the allegations and bringing the illegal activities to light, the company officials instead found a way to keep sending the bribes but make the payments look legal. Two years later, Tyson officials finally hired a law firm to do an internal investigation of the bribery. In 2011, Tyson was charged with conspiracy and violating the Foreign Corrupt Practices Act. To avoid trial, Tyson was forced to pay $4 million as a criminal penalty and $1.2 million to the Securities and Exchange Commission to settle charges of maintaining illegal records.

stakeholders in the organization whose interests should be the focus of your application of the Golden Rule? The focus on others that is the foundation of the Golden Rule is also clearly reflected in a second ethical guideline: the public disclosure test.

Public Disclosure Test. We tend to care about what others think about us as ethical agents. Stop for a moment and think of corporations that failed to apply the public disclosure test and generated negative reactions as a result. For example, in December 2012, Walgreens was ordered to pay $16.47 million to settle a lawsuit alleging that over 600 California stores had illegally handled and dumped pesticides, bleach, paint, pharmaceutical waste, and other items. Walgreens was also charged because of improper disposal of confidential medical records of customers. Walgreens denied all charges.

Walgreens would likely have behaved differently had it considered the public disclosure test before dumping toxic waste inappropriately. The company may have realized that the community would be outraged by Walgreen's disregard for the well-being of thousands of people, and the company may even have considered that its decision would cost far more money than it would save. Presumably, Walgreens would have chosen a different waste disposal option, one that would have saved its reputation, its money, and the lives of others.

Another way to think of the public disclosure test is to view it as a ray of sunlight that makes our actions visible, rather than obscured. As Exhibit 2 7 suggests, the issue of transparency of behavior is often seen as a method of improving ethical behavior. The public disclosure test is sometimes called the "television test," for it requires us to imagine that our actions are being broadcast on national television. The premise behind the public disclosure test is that ethics is hard work, labor that we might resist if we did not have frequent reminders that we live in a community. As a member of a community, our self-concept is tied, at least in part, to how that community perceives us.

Universalization Test. A third general guideline shares with the other two a focus on the "other"—the stakeholders whom our actions affect. Before we act, the universalization test asks us to consider what the world would be like were our decision copied by everyone else. Applying the universalization test causes us to wonder aloud: "Is what I am about to do the kind of action that, *were others to follow my example,* makes the world a better place

E-COMMERCE AND THE LAW

TECHNOLOGICAL RECORDS AND ETHICS

Journalists use different technological mediums to contact and store information about confidential sources, including government whistle-blowers. One of the most important aspects of journalism is to protect confidential informants so that news sources can still enlighten the public with important and sensitive information. Here, ethical issues come up. Documents containing information about informants' identities may not be collected by the government without permission from the deputy attorney general. In other words, the First Amendment protects the privacy and individual ownership of these e-mail and phone records.

For example, in 2004, the FBI illegally obtained phone records related to the confidential informants of *The New York Times*' and *Washington Post*'s bureaus in Indonesia. The executive editors of both newspapers were called by the FBI, and both received apologies. The Justice Department looked into the illegal investigation by the FBI after the FBI went ahead with what it called "emergency" gathering of private information related to an alleged terrorist investigation. The editors were never told why their records were needed.

Now news corporations are putting numerous security barriers and encryptions around their records so that nobody can gain access to them. In fact, Wikileaks, the organization that publicizes secret government documents on its website, has probably the strongest security procedures protecting its sources. Instant messages are expertly encrypted, as are all files passed between people. Also, the Tor Project, a tool that enables users to communicate anonymously, completely hides all servers. Other news companies are attempting to mimic such standards and adjust privacy policies to not reserve the right to release any information about a source "to law enforcement authorities or to a requesting third party, without notice."

for me and those I love?" Apply the universalization test to the Case Nugget on the previous page to get a sense of how valuable it is as an ethical guide.

In summary, business managers can apply the WPH approach to most ethical dilemmas. The WPH framework provides a practical process suited to the frequently complex ethical dilemmas that business managers must address quickly in today's society.

Exhibit 2-7

A Mandate for Ethical Behavior

THE SARBANES-OXLEY ACT

The Corporate and Criminal Fraud Accountability Act, also known as the Sarbanes-Oxley Act, was signed by President Bush in 2002 in the wake of several corporate accounting scandals. The act is intended to promote high ethical standards among business managers and employees through a series of stringent requirements and controls that regulate several different facets of corporate operation.

Among other things, the act created the Public Company Accounting Oversight Board. This board is responsible for ensuring that auditors and public accounting firms compile accurate and truthful financial reports for the companies they audit. The act also requires that companies devise a system that allows employees to report suspicions of unethical behavior within the company. The act also protects these whistle-blowers from being fired or from retaliation by their employer for reporting a possible problem within the company.

Additionally, the chief executive officer (CEO) or chief financial officer (CFO) must personally vouch that the company's financial statements are correct, meet all SEC requirements for disclosure, and represent company finances accurately. The act provides for very harsh penalties in the case of violations. If the CEO or CFO knows that the company's financial reports are incorrect but claims they are truthful, or if he or she destroys or changes financial documents, the imposed fine can run into the millions of dollars.

CASE OPENER WRAP-UP

Acne Medication and Gastrointestinal Injury

Acne medication manufacturers, as well as other firms, affect the lives of many stakeholders. A manufacturer's owners, workers, and customers are perhaps the most obvious stakeholders in decisions the manufacturer makes about its production and labeling policies. It is clear that the manufacturer's questionable decisions have potentially detrimental consequences for customers who use its acne medication, but the manufacturer's decisions may also affect the business climate among other manufacturers, which may be tempted to engage in similarly questionable business practices to increase profits. All of the manufacturer's decisions have ethical implications.

For example, in the case at hand, the courts were divided on whether Hoffman-LaRoche was responsible for listing potential illnesses such as IBD or whether it was acceptable to list only common symptoms of IBD that may occur. Issues such as these are not black and white, and often the rulings regarding these issues vary among courts.

Although, as this book was being written, no final decision had been made regarding Kendall's initial lawsuit, the court had addressed the defendant's movement to dismiss the lawsuit on the basis of untimeliness. On February 27, 2012, the court found that given that Kendall's dermatologist was unaware of, and therefore did not warn her of, the risk of IBD resulting from Accutane, a reasonable person in the plaintiff's situation would not have been aware of the potential for the medication to cause her illness. Thus, given that the plaintiff was not made aware of the connection between her illness and the medication until the 2004 lawyer's advertisement, her lawsuit against Hoffman-LaRoche was timely.

KEY TERMS

business ethics 16
ethical dilemma 16
ethical guidelines 22
ethics 16
social responsibility of business 16
stakeholders 23
values 24
WPH process of ethical decision making 22

SUMMARY OF KEY TOPICS

Business Ethics and Social Responsibility

Business ethics is the application of ethics to the special problems and opportunities experienced by businesspeople.

The *social responsibility of business* consists of the expectations that the community imposes on firms doing business with its citizens.

Business Law and Business Ethics

Business ethics builds on business law. The law both affects and is affected by evolving ethical patterns. But business law provides only a floor for business ethics, telling business leaders the minimally acceptable course of action.

The WPH Framework for Business Ethics

Who are the relevant stakeholders? This question determines which interests (consumers, employees, managers, owners) are being pushed and prodded.

What are the ultimate purposes of the decision? This question determines which values (freedom, efficiency, security, and justice) are being upheld by the decision.

How do we make ethical decisions? This question leads us to apply general ethical guidelines:

- *Golden Rule:* Do unto others as you would have them do unto you.
- *Public disclosure test:* If the public knew about this decision, how would you decide?
- *Universalization test:* What would the world be like were our decision copied by everyone else?

POINT / COUNTERPOINT

Sarbanes-Oxley Act of 2002

Are the Costs Associated with the Sarbanes-Oxley Act Reason for Reform?	
NO	**YES**
Corporate and accounting scandals, such as Enron, were the reason the Sarbanes-Oxley Act of 2002 was drafted. The act promotes honesty and accountability in financial reporting, thus bringing increased security to investors. For example, corporations must now ensure the segregation of all duties related to accounting procedures.	Corporations need incentives to remain or go public. The Sarbanes-Oxley Act of 2002 is not an incentive. Although there may have been ample motivation for the development of an act that addresses accounting scandals, the costs associated with Sarbanes-Oxley are much too high. Simply purchasing and learning to use the materials needed for compliance with the act would cost approximately $3.5 million.
Although critics assert that the financial burden associated with the act is reason for reform, the compliance costs about which they speak are beginning to fall as individuals become familiar with the new systems. In addition, the Dow Jones Industrial Average is rising as a result of increased investor confidence. This confidence is the direct result of the requirement that corporations disclose information and allow for investigations by the Public Company Accounting Oversight Board.	Those who argue that the act should not be reformed often focus on the idea that every corporation is now being held to the same standards. However, as a result of the substantial economic costs associated with implementation of the guidelines, smaller businesses that would like to go public are forced to remain private to avoid the costs. Among small businesses that are already public, many are not able to gather the resources necessary to comply with the act.
Since the passing of the Sarbanes-Oxley Act, there have not been any known major accounting scandals. Without public disclosure, corporations would have little incentive to engage in rigorous evaluation of their own accounting practices. By forcing corporations to disclose information, they are being held to higher ethical standards than they were previously.	In addition to the costs associated with the act, corporations are now monitored by commissions that are appointed rather than elected. These commissions lack the accountability that is necessary to make decisions about how to regulate, tax, and punish companies and individuals that may violate the provisions of the act. Thus, the act as it is currently written does not provide an equal opportunity to all corporations and businesses.

QUESTIONS & PROBLEMS

1. How do business ethics and business law interact with each other? Is one highly ethical and the other less ethical?
2. If business ethics does not offer guidance about what is always the right thing to do, is one behavior as good as the next?
3. How does the WPH approach to ethics approach an ethical problem?
4. In December 2010, the Equal Employment Opportunity Commission filed a nationwide hiring discrimination lawsuit against the Kaplan Higher

Education Corporation. Kaplan was requiring access to applicants' credit reports and credit histories and took such information into consideration when hiring. Not only did the EEOC believe that such a requirement was discriminating against black applicants, but it also felt that during a time of financial woes for most Americans, people with damaged credit histories would have a hard time getting back into the workforce. Apparently, research showed that the reliance on credit histories significantly hurt the hiring of blacks as opposed to white applicants. The EEOC noted that the credit histories were not necessarily connected with the performance the applicant would show at the particular job being applied for. Surveys show that credit histories are required by almost half of all employers. However, states including Washington, Oregon, and Illinois have severely limited or completely banned the reliance of employers on credit histories. Because of the recession, Congress has considered imposing such restrictions or even a ban. How do you think the court ruled in this case? Do you think it is fair not only to black applicants but to all applicants that their employer bases a hiring decision on credit history? Do you think other companies will change their use of credit histories on the basis of the outcome of this case? [Civil Action No. 1:10-cv-02882 (2010).]

5. In 2011 Walmart was hit with the largest employment discrimination lawsuit in history, and the lawsuit was brought to the Supreme Court. The problems began when a female employee named Stephanie Odle found out that a male employee with the same title as hers yet less experience was earning $10,000 a year more than she was. Subsequently, she was fired when she complained about the discovery. In fact, her boss defended the salary difference, saying that the male employee should make more because he was supporting a family, even though Odle was pregnant and thus trying to save up for her family as well. The lawsuit is so large because it contains complaints from 1.5 million female Walmart employees with similar stories. However, Walmart argues that there are too many significant differences among the 1.5 million cases and that the complaints may not be brought under a single-action lawsuit. On the other hand, a group of 31 civil procedure professors created a brief saying that the women have the core point in common: Walmart discriminated against the women. In addition, because Walmart is a large corporation with an extensive litigation team and a huge amount of resources, the women need to bring their complaints to court together to stand a chance. How do you think the Supreme Court will decide? Do you think the cases among the women will be similar enough to stand under one action because there is a core ultimate problem? Do you think Walmart will win because of the resources it has as a huge corporation? [*Wal-Mart Stores, Inc. v. Betty Dukes et al.,* 131 S. Ct. 2541 (2011).]

6. Entertainment Network, Inc. (ENI), a business that provided news, entertainment, and information via the Internet, sued government officials who prohibited the company from filming the execution of Oklahoma City bomber Timothy McVeigh and selling the footage of the execution online. The government officials argued that a Justice Department regulation prohibiting audio and visual recording devices at federal executions applied in the case at hand. ENI, however, argued that the regulation violated the company's First Amendment right to free speech. How do you think the court should have ruled in this case? Do you think ENI might have altered its decision to broadcast the execution if it had applied the Golden Rule? [*Entm't Network, Inc. v. Lappin,* 134 F. Supp. 2d 1002 (2001).]

7. Ernest Price went to a doctor in 1997, seeking Oxycontin to treat pain related to sickle cell anemia. Between November 1999 and October 2000, Price sought Oxycontin prescriptions from at least ten different doctors at ten different clinics in two cities, filling the prescriptions at seven pharmacies in three cities. The doctors were notified of Price's medication-seeking behavior, and the doctors discontinued Price's treatment. Price then filed suit, claiming his doctors, pharmacies, and the pharmaceutical companies that manufactured Oxycontin had breached their duty by failing to adequately warn Price of the addictive nature of Oxycontin. How do you think the court responded to Price's claims? Think about all the stakeholders involved in such a case; how would those parties be affected by a ruling in favor of Price? In favor of the doctors and pharmaceutical companies? [*Ernest Price v. The Purdue Pharma Co.,* 920 So. 2d 479; 2006 Miss. LEXIS 67 (2006).]

8. Javier Galindo, the husband of Richard Clark's housekeeper, was sitting in his car, parked in the driveway of Clark's house, waiting to pick up his wife. While he was waiting, a leaning 80-foot tree located on an adjacent property fell on Galindo's car and killed him. Galindo's wife sued Clark, alleging that Clark

was liable for failing to notify Galindo about the danger posed by the leaning tree. Do you think that Clark had a legal responsibility to tell Galindo about the tree? Do you think Clark had an ethical responsibility to tell Galindo about the tree? Why might the answer to these questions be different? [*Galindo v. Town of Clarkstown,* 2 N.Y.3d 633 (2004).]

9. Mr. Caperton was the owner of a coal company that operated Harman mine. He sued Massey, which is a very large and powerful energy company. The suit was brought against Massey for a number of reasons. First, Massey bought another coal company called Wellmore Coal. Prior to the takeover, Wellmore Coal had bought Caperton's high-grade coal and blended that coal with its own, later selling the product to a steel company called LTV. After the takeover, Massey cut Caperton's high-quality coal out of the mix and tried to sell the cheaper product to LTV. However, LTV refused the new, low-grade coal. Thus, Massey took steps not only to make Caperton's land and business look undesirable but to ruin his business completely so that LTV had no opportunity to work with Caperton or Harman mine unless Massey owned it. Massey pushed LTV to alter contracts in ways that would financially hurt Caperton's business, and then Massey bought land around the mine to make the area unappealing to potential buyers of the mine. Massey finally offered to buy Caperton's business and mine at a huge discount. Massey told Caperton not to sue, as Massey had the resources to spend $1 million a month to fight the bankrupt company. When Caperton did sue, the lower court found Massey liable for $50 million in damages. In 2008, Massey appealed to the supreme court of appeals of West Virginia; however, the judge had special ties with the CEO of Massey. Specifically, the CEO had donated $3 million to secure Justice Benjamin's seat when he had campaigned for the supreme court of appeals. Caperton immediately motioned for Justice Benjamin to excuse himself from the case, but the court dismissed the motion, with Benjamin voting for the majority. The court then moved to dismiss the $50 million and reverse the case. Caperton finally appealed to bring the case to the Supreme Court. What do you think the Supreme Court decided? Do you think it believed that the involvement of Justice Benjamin in the case was unethical? Do you think the CEO of Massey was contributing to the campaigns of high justices to create political ties and thus garner political support? [*Caperton v. A.T. Massey Coal Co., Inc.,* 225 W. Va. 128; 690 S.E.2d 322 (2008).]

10. Brazos Higher Education Service Corporation, Inc., was a nonprofit student loan company. Brazos allowed one of its employees to store customers' personal financial information on a laptop with an unencrypted hard drive. The laptop was subsequently stolen from the employee's home during a robbery. Brazos had no way of knowing which customers' information was contained on the laptop's hard drive or whether the information would be accessed by a third party. As a precaution, Brazos notified all of its customers that their information may have been accessed by a third party and offered each customer six months of identity-theft monitoring. One customer, Guin, brought suit against Brazos for negligence, claiming that Brazos had failed to adequately protect his financial information, thereby causing Guin harm. Guin's information was never accessed by a third party, and Guin never suffered identity theft. How might other businesses be affected if Guin's lawsuit succeeded? Do you think Brazos was wrong to store its customers' financial information on an unencrypted laptop hard drive? [*Stacy Lawton Guin v. Brazos Higher Education Service Corporation, Inc.,* 2006 U.S. Dist. LEXIS 4846 (2006).]

Looking for more review material?

The Online Learning Center at **www.mhhe.com/kubasek3e** contains this chapter's "Assignment on the Internet" and also a list of URLs for more information, entitled "On the Internet." Find both of them in the Student Center portion of the OLC, along with quizzes and other helpful materials.

APPENDIX 2A THEORIES OF BUSINESS ETHICS

Ethical Relativism and Situational Ethics

An ethical school of thought that may seem appealing on the surface is ethical relativism. **Ethical relativism** is a theory of ethics that denies the existence of objective moral standards. Rather, according to ethical relativism, individuals must evaluate actions on the basis of what they feel is best for themselves. Ethical relativism holds that when two individuals disagree over a question about morality, both individuals are correct because no objective standard exists to evaluate their actions. Instead, morality is relative, and thus no one can criticize another's behavior as immoral. Many people find ethical relativism attractive because it promotes tolerance.

Ethical relativism may appear attractive at first glance, but very few people are willing to accept the logical conclusions of this theory. For example, ethical relativism requires that we see murder as a moral action as long as the murderer believes that the action is best for himself or herself. Once a person accepts the appropriateness of criticizing behavior in some situations, the person has rejected ethical relativism and must develop a more complex ethical theory.

Situational ethics is a theory that at first appears similar to ethical relativism but is actually substantially different. Like ethical relativism, **situational ethics** requires that we evaluate the morality of an action by imagining ourselves in the position of the person facing the ethical dilemma. But unlike ethical relativism, situational ethics allows us to judge other people's actions. In other words, situational ethics holds that once we put ourselves in another person's shoes, we can evaluate whether that person's action was ethical.

While situational ethics provides a useful rule of thumb to use when thinking about the ethical decision-making process, it does not offer specific-enough criteria to be useful in many real-world situations. Once we imagine ourselves in the position of a person facing an ethical dilemma, situational ethics does not tell us *how* to evaluate that person's actions. An alternative school of ethical thought, however, provides a much more judgmental approach to ethical dilemmas.

Absolutism

Absolutism, or *ethical fundamentalism,* requires that individuals defer to a set of rules to guide them in the ethical decision-making process. Unlike ethical relativism and situational ethics, absolutism holds that whether an action is moral does not depend on the perspective of the person facing the ethical dilemma. Rather, whether an action is moral depends on whether the action conforms to the given set of ethical rules.

Of course, people disagree about which set of rules to follow. Why should we accept and act on any one absolutist set of rules? Absolutism cannot tell us, for example, why we ought to follow the doctrines set forth in the Koran and not Hindu doctrines.

Moreover, the unquestionable nature of the rules in most absolutist repositories seems overly inflexible when applied to different situations. For instance, "Thou shalt not kill" seems to be an absolute rule, but, in practice, killing in self-defense seems to be an acceptable exception to this rule.

Consequentialism

In contrast to absolutism, consequentialism does not provide a rigid set of rules to follow regardless of the situation. Rather, as the word *consequentialism* suggests, this ethical approach "depends on the consequences." **Consequentialism** is a general approach to ethical dilemmas that requires that we inquire about the consequences to relevant people of our making a particular decision.

Utilitarianism is one form of consequentialism that business managers may find useful. Like many consequentialist theories of ethics, **utilitarianism** urges managers to take those actions that provide the greatest pleasure after having subtracted the pain or harm associated with the action in question.

Utilitarianism has two main branches: act utilitarianism and rule utilitarianism. **Act utilitarianism** tells business managers to examine all the potential actions in each situation and choose the action that yields the greatest amount of pleasure over pain for all involved. For example, according to act utilitarianism, a business manager who deceives an employee may be acting morally if the act of deception maximizes pleasure over pain for everyone involved.

Rule utilitarians, on the other hand, see great potential for the abuse of act utilitarianism. Instead of advocating the maximization of pleasure over pain in each individual situation, **rule utilitarianism** holds that general rules that *on balance* produce the greatest amount of pleasure for all involved should be established and followed in each situation. Thus, even if the business manager's decision to deceive an employee maximizes pleasure over pain in a given situation, the act probably would not be consistent with rule utilitarianism because deception does not generally produce the greatest satisfaction.

Rule utilitarianism underlies many laws in the United States. For example, labor laws prohibit employers from hiring children to do manufacturing work, even though in some situations the transaction would maximize pleasure over pain.

One form of utilitarianism commonly applied by firms and government is **cost-benefit analysis.** When a business makes decisions based on cost-benefit analysis, it is comparing the pleasure and pain of its optional choices, as that pleasure and pain are measured in monetary terms.

As we have shown, consequentialism is not altogether helpful because of the extreme difficulty in making the required calculations about consequences. Another issue raises an important additional objection to consequentialist thinking: Where does the important social value of justice fit into consequentialist reasoning? Many business decisions could be beneficial in their consequences for a majority of the population, but is it fair to require that a few be harmed so that the majority can be improved? Consequentialism does not provide definite answers to these questions, but an alternative ethical theory does.

Deontology

Deontology is an alternative theoretical approach to consequentialism. When you see references to *Kantian ethics*, the analysis that follows the reference will be a discussion of the most famous of the deontological approaches to business ethics. Unlike a person espousing consequentialism, a person using a deontological approach will not see the relevance of making a list of harms and benefits that result from a particular decision. Instead, **deontology** consists of acting on the basis of the recognition that certain actions are right or wrong, regardless of their consequences. For example, a business leader might consider it wrong to terminate a person whose spouse has terminal cancer because a firm has an obligation to support its employees when they are vulnerable, *period.*

But how are business managers to decide whether an action is right or wrong? The German deontological philosopher Immanuel Kant proposed the categorical imperative to determine whether an action is right. According to the **categorical imperative,** an action is moral only if it would be consistent for everyone in society to act in the same way.

Thus, for example, applying the categorical imperative would lead you to conclude that you should not cheat on a drug test, because if everyone acted in the same way, the drug test would be meaningless.

From the deontological viewpoint, the duties or obligations that we owe one another as humans are much more ethically significant than are measurements of the impacts of business decisions. For example, a person using a deontological theory of ethics may see any business behavior that violates our duty of trust as being wrong. To sell a car that one knows will probably not be usable after four years is, from this perspective, unethical. No set of positive consequences that might flow from the production decision can overcome the certainty of the deontological recognition that the sale is wrong.

The duties that we owe others imply that human beings have fundamental rights based on the dignity of each individual. This **principle of rights** asserts that whether a business decision is ethical depends on how the decision affects the rights of all involved. This principle is foundational to Western culture: The Declaration of Independence, for example, asserts that everyone has the right to "life, liberty, and the pursuit of happiness."

But just as consequentialism is incredibly complicated, deontology is difficult to apply because people disagree about what duties we owe to one another and which duties are more important than others when they conflict. For example, imagine the dilemma of a scientist working for a tobacco firm who discovers that cigarettes are carcinogenic. She owes a duty of trust to her employer, but she also has a conflicting duty to the community to do no harm. Where would a business manager find a list of relevant duties under the deontological framework, and why should we accept and act on any particular list?

In addition, as with absolutism, the absolute nature of many deontological lists of duties and rights seems overly rigid when applied to a wide variety of contexts. For instance, saying that we owe a duty to respect human life sounds absolute. In application, however, we might be forced to harm one life to preserve other life. An alternative theory of ethics, called *virtue ethics,* avoids this rigidity problem by providing us with abstract goals to pursue continually.

Virtue Ethics

Virtue ethics is an ethical system in which the development of virtues, or positive character traits such as courage, justice, and truthfulness, is the basis for morality. A morally excellent (and thus good) person develops virtues and distinguishes them from vices, or negative character traits, such as cowardice and vanity. This development of virtues occurs through practice. Virtues are the habits of mind that move us toward excellence, the good life, or human flourishing.

As a guide to business ethics, virtue ethics requires that managers act in such a way that they will increase their contributions to the good life. Virtue ethics tells them to follow the character traits that, upon introspective reflection, they see as consistent with virtue. Identifying the relevant virtues and vices requires reasoning about the kind of human behavior that moves us toward the good, successful, or happy life.

A difficulty with the application of virtue ethics is the lack of agreement about the meaning of "the good life." Without that agreement, we are not able to agree about what types of behavior are consistent with our achievement of that goal. Even so, virtue ethics is useful in reminding us that ethics is grounded in a sense of what it means to be virtuous—we need some moral beacon to call us toward a more morally excellent condition. An alternative theory of business ethics, the ethics of care, offers a clear conception of what is virtuous.

Ethics of Care

The **ethics of care** holds that the right course of action is the option most consistent with the building and maintaining of human relationships. Those who adhere to an ethic of care argue that traditional moral hierarchies ignore an important element of life: relationships. Care for the nurturing of our many relationships serves as a reminder of the importance of responsibility to others.

According to someone who adheres to an ethic of care, when one person cares for another person, the first person is acting morally. When other ethical theories emphasize different moral dimensions as a basis for resolving ethical dilemmas, they rarely consider the harm they might do to relationships; thus, from the perspective of the ethics of care, alternative theories of business ethics often encourage unethical behavior.

Ethics-of-care theorists argue that when one individual, the *caregiver,* meets the needs of one other person, the *cared-for* party, the caregiver is actually helping to meet the needs of all the individuals who fall within the cared-for party's *web of care.* Thus, by specifically helping one other individual, the caregiver is assisting numerous people.

The strength of this theoretical approach is that it focuses on the basis of ethics in general: the significance of the interests of other people. The urging to care for relationships speaks to the fundamental basis of why we are concerned about ethics in the first place. Most of us do not need any encouragement to think about how a decision will affect us personally. But ethical reasoning requires that we weigh the impact of decisions on the larger community.

Let's examine how these ethical theories are applied in real-world firms. Exhibit 2A-1 is an abridged version of the Johnson & Johnson Credo, or statement of shared corporate

Exhibit 2A-1
Johnson & Johnson's Credo

The Credo

We believe our first responsibility is to the doctors, nurses and patients, to mothers and fathers and all others who use our products and services. In meeting their needs everything we do must be of high quality. We must constantly strive to reduce our costs in order to maintain reasonable prices. Customers' orders must be serviced promptly and accurately. Our suppliers and distributors must have an opportunity to make a fair profit.

We are responsible to our employees, the men and women who work with us throughout the world. Everyone must be considered as an individual. We must respect their dignity and recognize their merit. They must have a sense of security in their jobs. Compensation must be fair and adequate, and working conditions clean, orderly and safe. We must be mindful of ways to help our employees fulfill their family responsibilities. Employees must feel free to make suggestions and complaints. There must be equal opportunity for employment, development and advancement for those qualified. We must provide competent management, and their actions must be just and ethical.

We are responsible to the communities in which we live and work and to the world community as well. We must be good citizens—support good works and charities and bear our fair share of taxes. We must encourage civic improvements and better health and education. We must maintain in good order the property we are privileged to use, protecting the environment and natural resources.

Our final responsibility is to our stockholders. Business must make a sound profit. We must experiment with new ideas. Research must be carried on, innovative programs developed and mistakes paid for. New equipment must be purchased, new facilities provided and new products launched. Reserves must be created to provide for adverse times. When we operate according to these principles, the stockholders should realize a fair return.

values. General Robert Wood Johnson, who guided Johnson & Johnson from a small, family-owned business to a worldwide enterprise, believed the corporation had social responsibilities beyond the manufacturing and marketing of products. In 1943, he wrote and published the Johnson & Johnson Credo, a document outlining those responsibilities. Does the credo depend more on ethical relativism, situational ethics, absolutism, consequentialism, deontology, virtue ethics, or the ethics of care for its ethical vision?

Exhibit 2A-2 summarizes the ethical theories discussed in this appendix.

Exhibit 2A-2
At a Glance

Theories of Business Ethics

ETHICAL APPROACH	DESCRIPTION
Ethical relativism	Asserts that morality is relative.
Situational ethics	Requires that when we evaluate whether an action is ethical, we imagine ourselves in the position of the person facing the ethical dilemma.
Consequentialism	Considers the consequences (i.e., harms and benefits) of making a particular decision.
Deontology	Recognizes certain actions as right or wrong regardless of the consequences.
Virtue ethics	Encourages individuals to develop virtues (e.g., courage and truthfulness) that guide behavior.
Ethics of care	Holds that ethical behavior is determined by actions that care for and maintain human relationships.

KEY TERMS

absolutism 33
act utilitarianism 34
categorical imperative 34
consequentialism 34
cost-benefit analysis 34
deontology 34
ethical relativism 33
ethics of care 36
principle of rights 35
rule utilitarianism 34
situational ethics 33
utilitarianism 34
virtue ethics 35

CHAPTER

3 The U.S. Legal System

LEARNING OBJECTIVES

After reading this chapter, you will be able to answer the following questions:

1. What are the different types of jurisdiction a court must have before it can render a binding decision in a case?
2. What is venue?
3. How is our dual court system structured?
4. What are the threshold requirements that must be met before a court will hear a case?
5. What are the steps in civil litigation?

CASE OPENER

Questionable Jurisdiction over Caterpillar

James Lewis, a resident of Kentucky, sustained an injury while operating a Caterpillar bulldozer. He filed suit against Caterpillar, a company incorporated in Delaware but with its principal place of business in Illinois. Lewis also filed suit against the supplier of the bulldozer, Whayne Supply Company, whose principal place of business was Kentucky. Lewis filed his case in a Kentucky state court, alleging defective manufacture, negligence, failure to warn, and breach of warranty. Lewis and Whayne Supply Company agreed to settle out of court. Caterpillar then filed a motion to exercise its right of removal (its right to move the case from the state to the federal court system), arguing that the federal court had jurisdiction over the case because Caterpillar and Lewis were from different states. Lewis disagreed with Caterpillar's contention, claiming that because he had not completed his settlement with Whayne, the case still included a defendant (Whayne) from Lewis's state, Kentucky. Thus, Lewis argued, federal courts did not have jurisdiction over the case.

The court agreed with Caterpillar's argument and moved the case to a federal district court. Shortly thereafter, Lewis and Whayne finalized their settlement agreement, and the district court dismissed Whayne from the lawsuit. The federal district court granted Caterpillar a favorable judgment. Lewis, however, appealed the district court's decision, renewing his argument that the district court did not have jurisdiction over the case. The court of appeals agreed with Lewis, holding that because Whayne was a defendant in the case at the time that Caterpillar moved the case from state to federal court, the diversity of citizenship necessary to give the federal court jurisdiction over the case was absent. Thus, a state court should have resolved the dispute. Consequently, the appellate court vacated the district court's decision. Caterpillar then appealed to the U.S. Supreme Court.

1. What factors determine whether the state or federal court system hears a case?
2. If you were a businessperson with Caterpillar, why might you prefer a federal court to hear the dispute with Lewis instead of a state court?

The Wrap-Up at the end of the chapter will answer these questions.

As the opening scenario illustrates, when a dispute arises, parties in this country do not simply "go to court." They often must choose between federal and state court systems. This chapter examines these systems, as well as the trial procedures that apply in civil cases.

Jurisdiction

LO1 What are the different types of jurisdiction a court must have before it can render a binding decision in a case?

The word **jurisdiction** comes from the Latin terms *juris,* meaning "law," and *diction,* meaning "to speak." A useful way to understand jurisdiction is to think of it as referring to courts' power to hear cases and render decisions that bind the parties before them. A court must have several types of jurisdiction to decide any particular case.

ORIGINAL VERSUS APPELLATE JURISDICTION

Trial courts, or **courts of original jurisdiction,** have the power to hear and decide cases when they first enter the legal system. In these courts, the parties present evidence and call witnesses to testify. Most state court systems refer to trial courts as *courts of common pleas* or *county courts.* The federal system calls them *district courts.*

Courts of appellate jurisdiction, or **appellate courts,** have the power to review previous judicial decisions to determine whether trial courts erred in their decisions. Appellate courts do not hold trials. Rather, appellate judges review transcripts of trial court proceedings and occasionally consider additional oral and written arguments from each party.

Appellate courts handle primarily questions of law, not questions of fact. A *question of law* is an issue concerning the interpretation or application of a law. In contrast, a *question of fact* is a question about an event or characteristic in a case. For example, whether a student yelled racial slurs on a college campus is a question of fact. On the other hand, whether the First Amendment protects the student's right to utter racial slurs is a question of law.

Only judges can decide questions of law. Questions of fact are determined in the trial court. In a *bench trial* (a trial with no jury), the judge decides questions of fact; in a *jury trial,* the jury decides questions of fact. Appellate courts can, however, overrule trial courts' decisions on questions of fact, but only when the trial court's finding was clearly erroneous or when no trial evidence supports the trial court's finding.

Legal Principle: The court in which a case is first heard is called the *court of original jurisdiction,* and the court to which a decision made by that court is appealed is called the *court of appellate jurisdiction.*

JURISDICTION OVER PERSONS AND PROPERTY

***In personam* jurisdiction** (literally, "jurisdiction over the person") is a court's power to render a decision affecting the rights of the specific persons before the court. Generally, a court's power to exercise *in personam* jurisdiction extends only over a specific geographic region. In the state court system, a court's *in personam* jurisdiction usually extends to the state's borders. In the federal system, on the other hand, each court's jurisdiction extends across its geographic district.

A court acquires *in personam* jurisdiction over a person (the **plaintiff**) when she files a lawsuit with the court. The court acquires jurisdiction over the person the plaintiff is suing (the **defendant**) when it gives him a copy of the complaint and a summons. The **complaint** specifies the factual and legal basis for the lawsuit and the relief the plaintiff seeks. The **summons** is a court order that notifies the defendant of the lawsuit and explains how and when to respond to the complaint.

Service of process is the procedure by which courts present these documents to defendants. Traditionally, courts use **personal service:** An officer of the court hands the summons and complaint to the defendant. Recently, however, courts have employed other methods of service, including *residential service,* in which a court representative leaves the summons and complaint with a responsible adult at the defendant's home, and *service by certified* or *ordinary mail.*

There has even been one case in which a court of appeals upheld service of process by e-mail to be appropriate. The facts of the case, however, created an unusual situation in which no other means of service was really possible. Rio Properties, Inc., operators of the Rio All Suites Resort Casino in Las Vegas, Nevada, decided to put some of its gaming activities on the Internet and discovered that a Costa Rican company, Rio International Interlink (RII), was operating an online, international sports book that allegedly infringed on Rio Properties' registered trademark. When the court attempted to serve RII at its U.S. address, the court found that it was only an address for an international courier that was not authorized to accept service on behalf of the company, and the court could not find any address for the company in Costa Rico. Rio Properties then filed a motion for alternative service of process with the court for permission to serve RII via its e-mail address, and the motion was granted by the district court. The court of appeals upheld the validity of the district court's order, noting that the Constitution does not require any specific means of service, only a means of service "reasonably calculated to provide notice and an opportunity to respond."[1] Because the method seemed to be the method of service most likely to reach RII, the court found that it clearly met the standard.

> To read more about how the choice of where to incorporate relates to jurisdiction, please see the **Connecting to the Core** activity on the text website at www.mhhe.com/kubasek3e.

If the defendant is a corporation, courts generally serve either the president of the corporation or an agent that the corporation has appointed to receive service. Most states require that corporations appoint an agent for service when they incorporate. Corporations are subject to *in personam* jurisdiction in three locations: the state of their incorporation, the location of their main offices, and the geographic areas in which they conduct business.

Courts have *in personam* jurisdiction only over persons within a specific geographic region. In the past, a state court could not acquire *in personam* jurisdiction over out-of-state defendants unless it served the defendants within the court's home state. Thus, defendants who injured plaintiffs could evade legal action by leaving the state and remaining outside its borders. To alleviate this problem, most

[1] *Rio Properties, Inc. v. Rio International Interlink,* 284 F.3d 1007 (2002).

states have enacted **long-arm statutes,** which enable the court to serve defendants outside the state as long as the defendant has sufficient minimum contacts within the state and it seems fair to assert long-arm jurisdiction over him or her. The U.S. Supreme Court established this "minimum-contacts" standard in the 1945 case *International Shoe Co. v. State of Washington.*[2]

Each state has its own minimum-contact requirements, but most state statutes hold that acts like committing a tort or doing business in the state are sufficient to allow the state to serve a defendant. In the opening scenario, the company sold products in Kentucky, and its products caused an injury in that state. These two facts were sufficient minimum contacts to allow the Kentucky court to serve Caterpillar, even though it was an out-of-state company.

BUT WHAT IF . . .

WHAT IF THE FACTS OF THE CASE OPENER WERE DIFFERENT?

Recall that in the Case Opener, the company sold products in Kentucky and its products caused an injury in that state. Let's say, in the Case Opener, that Caterpillar did not sell products in the state of Kentucky, but its products did cause an injury in that state. Could a Kentucky court still exercise *in personam* jurisdiction over Caterpillar and serve the company? Why or why not?

In contrast to the situation in the opening scenario, the Florida appellate court did not find minimum contacts with that state to enable a foreign corporation to sue Columbia University, located in New York City, for a tort that allegedly occurred in New York. The court found that the fact that Columbia had alumni associations in Florida, owned some interactive classrooms in that state, and offered some online classes to residents did not constitute sufficient minimum contacts for a lawsuit in which none of the tortious acts were alleged to have occurred in the state.[3]

As the E-Commerce and the Law box (next page) illustrates, the Internet has created complications for the courts in determining when an Internet presence creates in-person jurisdiction over a website operator. There is a need to protect companies from being dragged to an infinite number of courts even though their customer bases may be nationwide; at the same time, there is a need to not impinge on the sovereignty of states by curtailing the conditions under which defendants may be commanded to appear in a state's court.

If a defendant has property in a state, a plaintiff may file suit against the defendant's property instead of the owner. For example, suppose a Utah resident had not paid property taxes on a piece of land she owned in Idaho. Idaho courts have ***in rem* jurisdiction** (Latin for "jurisdiction over the thing") over the property. Thus, an Idaho state court has the power to seize the property and sell it to pay the property taxes in an *in rem* proceeding.

Courts can also gain **quasi *in rem* jurisdiction,** or *attachment jurisdiction,* over a defendant's property *unrelated* to the plaintiff's claim. For example, suppose Charlie, a Massachusetts resident, ran a red light while he was vacationing in California and collided with Jessica's car. Suppose further that Jessica suffered extensive injuries from the accident

[2] 326 U.S. 310.

[3] *Trustees of Columbia University v. Ocean World, SA,* 2009 WL 1212229, Ct. App. Fla.

E-COMMERCE AND THE LAW

THE SLIDING-SCALE STANDARD FOR INTERNET TRANSACTIONS

Does a business that has Internet contact with a plaintiff in a different state satisfy the minimum-contact standard? Anyone who engages in transactions over the Internet should be concerned about this question.

A federal district court established the following "sliding-scale" standard in the 1997 case *Zippo Mfg. Co. v. Zippo Dot Com, Inc.*:*

> [T]he likelihood that personal jurisdiction can be constitutionally exercised is directly proportionate to the nature and quality of commercial activity that an entity conducts over the Internet. This sliding scale is consistent with well developed personal jurisdiction principles.

At one end of the spectrum are situations in which a defendant clearly does business over the Internet. If the defendant enters into contracts with residents of a foreign jurisdiction that involve the knowing and repeated transmission of computer files over the Internet, personal jurisdiction is proper.

At the opposite end are situations in which a defendant has simply posted information on an Internet website that is accessible to users in foreign jurisdictions. A passive website that does little more than make information available to those who are interested in it is not grounds for the exercise of personal jurisdiction.

The middle ground is occupied by interactive websites at which a user can exchange information with the host computer. In such cases, the exercise of jurisdiction is determined by examining the level of interactivity and commercial nature of the exchange of information that occurs on the website.

* 952 F. Supp. 1119, 1124 (W.D. Pa. 1997).

and successfully sued Charlie for $200,000 in a California state court. The California court can exercise quasi *in rem* jurisdiction over Charlie's California vacation home by seizing it, selling it, and transferring $200,000 to Jessica to satisfy her judgment against Charlie. If Charlie's vacation home is worth more than $200,000, however, the court must return the excess proceeds to Charlie.

SUBJECT-MATTER JURISDICTION

Subject-matter jurisdiction is a court's power to hear certain kinds of cases. Most industrialized countries have a single court system, with courts that have the power to hear both national law cases and local law cases. In contrast, the United States has both a state and a federal court system. Subject-matter jurisdiction determines which court system may hear a particular case. Cases may fall under state jurisdiction, exclusive federal jurisdiction, or concurrent jurisdiction. Exhibit 3-1 illustrates the subject-matter-jurisdiction divisions.

Exhibit 3-1

Subject-Matter-Jurisdiction Divisions

Exclusive Federal Jurisdiction. The federal court system has exclusive jurisdiction over very few cases: admiralty cases, bankruptcy cases, federal criminal prosecutions, lawsuits in which one state sues another state, claims against the United States, and cases involving federal copyrights, patents, or trademarks. Additionally, federal courts have exclusive jurisdiction over claims arising under federal statutes that specify exclusive federal jurisdiction.

State Jurisdiction. The state court system has a broad range of jurisdiction; state courts have the power to hear all cases not within the exclusive jurisdiction of the federal court system. State courts also have exclusive jurisdiction over certain cases, such as cases concerning adoption and divorce. Most cases, therefore, fall under state court jurisdiction.

The Caterpillar case fell under state court jurisdiction because its subject matter—product liability and negligence—did not place the case under the exclusive jurisdiction of the federal court system.

Concurrent Federal Jurisdiction. Concurrent federal jurisdiction means that both state and federal courts have jurisdiction over a case. Concurrent jurisdiction covers two types of cases: federal-question and diversity-of-citizenship cases. *Federal-question* cases require an interpretation of the United States Constitution, a federal statute, or a federal treaty. For example, suppose a plaintiff alleges that a Florida campaign financing law violates his First Amendment free speech rights. Because this case raises a federal question, it falls under concurrent jurisdiction, and both state and federal courts have the power to hear it.

A *diversity-of-citizenship* case must satisfy two conditions: (1) The plaintiff(s) does (do) not reside in the same state as the defendant(s), and (2) the controversy concerns an amount in excess of $75,000. Courts use the location of a party's residence to determine whether diversity of citizenship exists. Most federal court cases are based on diversity of citizenship.

A business may reside in two states: the state of its incorporation and the state of its principal place of business. Thus, in the opening scenario, Caterpillar was a resident of Delaware, the state where it incorporated, and of Illinois, the state of its primary place of business.

Diversity must be complete, however, for a case to fall under concurrent jurisdiction. In the Caterpillar case, Lewis argued that diversity was not complete because both he and the supply company, the second defendant he originally sued, were residents of Kentucky. The appellate court agreed with his argument and overturned the district court's decision because the district court lacked subject-matter jurisdiction.

BUT WHAT IF . . .

WHAT IF THE FACTS OF THE CASE OPENER WERE DIFFERENT?

Recall that in the Case Opener, Caterpillar was a resident of Delaware, the state where it incorporated, and of Illinois, the state of its primary place of business. Let's say that Whayne was not a defendant in the case. How would Whayne's absence affect the diversity of the case? What court, or courts, would have jurisdiction over the case?

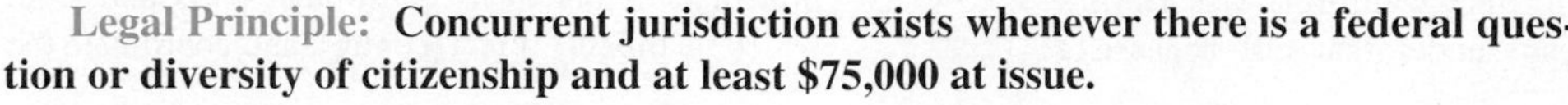

Legal Principle: **Concurrent jurisdiction exists whenever there is a federal question or diversity of citizenship and at least $75,000 at issue.**

When a case falls under concurrent jurisdiction, the plaintiff initially chooses which court will hear the case by filing in whichever court system the plaintiff wishes the case to be heard in. If a plaintiff files the case in a state court, however, the defendant has a *right of removal.* This right entitles the defendant to transfer the case to the federal court system. Thus, either party to a case involving concurrent jurisdiction has the ability to ensure that the case will be heard in the federal court system: The plaintiff can file the case in federal court initially, or the defendant can transfer the case to federal court by exercising her right of removal if the case is initially filed in state court. In the opening scenario, Caterpillar exercised its right of removal, and the state trial court moved the case to a federal district court.

Sometimes it is not easy to determine whether a case falls under concurrent jurisdiction, as Case 3-1 illustrates.

CASE 3-1 UNITED STATES SUPREME COURT 130 S. CT. 1181 (2010)

HERTZ CORP. v. FRIEND

Two residents of California filed a lawsuit against Hertz Corporation on behalf of a group of people arguing that the company's labor practices were illegal. The corporation was labeling workers as managers and thereby exempting them from receiving overtime pay for overtime hours worked. Hertz had the case removed to a federal court, which is allowed due to the Class Action Fairness Act. The act allows such a move when there is diversity among the parties of a class action lawsuit and the monetary amount in question is over $5 million. The plaintiffs argued that while Hertz had its headquarters in New Jersey and was incorporated in Delaware, it was still a citizen of California and thus was not diverse from any of the plaintiffs. The district court in California applied the "total activity/place of operations" test, a test that considered a huge number of factors relating to a company to try to determine its principal place of business. Some of these factors include where most "business functions" take place, where most of the company executives work, where most of the sales take place, and where most of the workers are employed. Eventually, the district court determined that Hertz's principal place of business was California, because much of its business took place there, and remanded the case to the state court. The Ninth Circuit affirmed, and Hertz appealed to the United States Supreme Court.

JUSTICE BREYER: The District Court concluded that it lacked diversity jurisdiction because Hertz was a California citizen under Ninth Circuit precedent, which asks, *inter alia,* whether the amount of the corporation's business activity is "significantly larger" or "substantially predominates" in one State. Finding that California was Hertz's "principal place of business" under that test because a plurality of the relevant business activity occurred there, the District Court remanded the case to state court. The Ninth Circuit affirmed. . . .

2. The phrase "principal place of business" in §1332(c)(1) refers to the place where a corporation's high level officers direct, control, and coordinate the corporation's activities, *i.e.,* its "nerve center," which will typically be found at its corporate headquarters.

   a. A brief review of the legislative history of diversity jurisdiction demonstrates that Congress added §1332(c)(1)'s "principal place of business" language to the traditional state-of-incorporation test in order to prevent corporations from manipulating federal-court jurisdiction as well as to reduce the number of diversity cases.

   b. However, the phrase "principal place of business" has proved more difficult to apply than its originators likely expected. After Congress' amendment, courts were uncertain as to where to look to determine a corporation's "principal place of business" for diversity purposes. If a corporation's headquarters and executive offices were in the same State in which it did most of its business, the test seemed straightforward. The "principal place of business" was in that State. But if those corporate headquarters, including executive offices, were in one State, while the corporation's plants or other centers of business activity were located in other States, the answer was less obvious. Under these circumstances, for corporations with "far-flung" business activities, numerous Circuits have looked to a corporation's "nerve center," from which the corporation radiates out to its constituent parts and from which its officers direct, control, and coordinate the corporation's activities. However, this test did not go far enough, for it did not answer what courts should do when a corporation's operations are not far-flung but rather limited to only a few States. When faced with this question, various courts have focused more heavily on where a corporation's actual business activities are located, adopting divergent and increasingly complex tests to interpret the statute.

c. In an effort to find a single, more uniform interpretation of the statutory phrase, this Court returns to the "nerve center" approach: "[P]rincipal place of business" is best read as referring to the place where a corporation's officers direct, control, and coordinate the corporation's activities. In practice it should normally be the place where the corporation maintains its headquarters—provided that the headquarters is the actual center of direction, control, and coordination, *i.e.,* the "nerve center," and not simply an office where the corporation holds its board meetings.

   i. Three sets of considerations, taken together, convince the Court that the "nerve center" approach, while imperfect, is superior to other possibilities. First, §1332(c)(1)'s language supports the approach. The statute's word "place" is singular, not plural. Its word "principal" requires that the main, prominent, or most important place be chosen. And the fact that the word "place" follows the words "State where" means that the "place" is a place *within* a State, not the State itself. A corporation's "nerve center," usually its main headquarters, is a single place. The public often considers it the corporation's main place of business. And it is a place within a State. By contrast, the application of a more general business activities test has led some courts, as in the present case, to look, not at a particular place within a State, but incorrectly at the State itself, measuring the total amount of business activities that the corporation conducts there and determining whether they are significantly larger than in the next-ranking State. Second, administrative simplicity is a major virtue in a jurisdictional statute. A "nerve center" approach, which ordinarily equates that "center" with a corporation's headquarters, is simple to apply *comparatively speaking*. By contrast, a corporation's general business activities more often lack a single principal place where they take place. Third, the statute's legislative history suggests that the words "principal place of business" should be interpreted to be no more complex than an earlier, numerical test that was criticized as too complex and impractical to apply. A "nerve center" test offers such a possibility. A general business activities test does not.

   ii. While there may be no perfect test that satisfies all administrative and purposive criteria, and there will be hard cases under the "nerve center" test adopted today, this test is relatively easier to apply and does not require courts to weigh corporate functions, assets or revenues different in kind, one from the other. And though this test may produce results that seem to cut against the basic rationale of diversity jurisdiction, accepting occasionally counterintuitive results is the price the legal system must pay to avoid overly complex jurisdictional administration while producing the benefits that accompany a more uniform legal system.

   iii. If the record reveals attempts at jurisdictional manipulation—for example, that the alleged "nerve center" is nothing more than a mail drop box, a bare office with a computer, or the location of an annual executive retreat—the courts should instead take as the "nerve center" the place of actual direction, control, and coordination, in the absence of such manipulation.

d. Although petitioner's unchallenged declaration suggests that Hertz's "nerve center" and its corporate headquarters are one and the same, and that they are located in New Jersey, not in California, respondents should have a fair opportunity on remand to litigate their case in light of today's holding.

Judgment in favor of Hertz, with decision of Circuit Court of Appeals VACATED and REMANDED.

CRITICAL THINKING

The Supreme Court decided that the previous test used to determine a company's principal state of residency was too open to different interpretations by different courts. Do you think the new test solves that problem? Why or why not?

ETHICAL DECISION MAKING

How does this decision affect the future of class action lawsuits between corporations and employees? Which party benefits from the new test designed by the Supreme Court?

CASE NUGGET

CITIZENSHIP OF A NATIONAL BANK

Wachovia Bank N.A. v. Schmidt
United States Supreme Court
126 S. Ct. 941 (2006)

When plaintiff Schmidt and other citizens of South Carolina sued Wachovia National Bank, an institution with its headquarters in North Carolina and branches in many states, including South Carolina, in a state court of South Carolina, the bank immediately attempted to exercise its right of removal to have the case moved to the federal court system. Ultimately, the United States Supreme Court had to decide which state a federally chartered bank was considered a citizen of for purposes of diversity jurisdiction. The Court noted that corporations are deemed citizens of the state in which they are incorporated and the state that is their principal place of business. Federally chartered banks, however, are slightly different from corporations in that they are not incorporated in any state. Congress, therefore, deemed that these banks would be considered citizens of states in which they are "located." The high court agreed with the bank that "located" must refer to the state in which its main office, as specified in its articles of incorporation, is located. To agree with the plaintiffs—that banks were located in every state in which they have branches—would dramatically reduce the availability of federal jurisdiction to federally chartered banks, making the federal court system dramatically less accessible to these banks than it is to state banks and state incorporated corporations, which the Court felt would not be what Congress had intended.

The Case Nugget illustrates how the courts have had to struggle with determining the citizenship of another entity that has a presence in many states: federally chartered banks.

While the question of which court system will hear a case is a matter that we think of as arising once a dispute has occurred, sometimes companies' decisions about where to locate are influenced by their knowledge about the court system in a state they are considering. And some organizations actually encourage companies to take a state's court system into account. As you already know, companies take into account the laws of the states where they are considering locating and doing business. Another factor some businesses consider is whether a state's courts seem hospitable to businesses. The American Tort Reform Association (ATRA), a national organization based in Washington, D.C., attempts to eliminate some of the "legal guesswork" for businesses by creating a list of the nation's top "Judicial Hellholes" each year. ATRA identifies its top hellholes as places where the law is applied in an "inequitable manner, generally against defendants in civil lawsuits."[4] One state in particular, West Virginia, continues to top the ATRA charts and was named the number-one Judicial Hellhole in the United States for both 2007 and 2008. ATRA mentions that one of West Virginia's major legal shortcomings is that it happens to be only one of two states in the country that does not "guarantee the right to appeal a civil verdict."[5]

Also crippling West Virginia's ability to offer a favorable business environment is its reputation as being a lawsuit- and plaintiff-friendly state. For example, a judge in West Virginia recently ordered the DuPont company to pay $196 million in punitive damages and $55 million for site cleanup and to commit $130 million to medical monitoring and testing after several West Virginia citizens filed suit against the company, claiming one of its plants contaminated their city and posed serious health risks, even though at the time of the verdict none of the residents were ill or showed health effects. High-profile and high-award cases like the DuPont case, coupled with an arguably flawed judicial system, could be enough to deter businesses from locating in West Virginia in the future. The DuPont case demonstrates that, as with any business decision, the costs and benefits of doing business in a particular state and legal climate need to be evaluated before moving forward.

Venue

L02
What is venue?

Once a case is in the proper court system, **venue** determines which trial court in the system will hear the case. Venue is a matter of geographic location determined by each state's

[4] www.atra.org/reports/hellholes/.
[5] Ibid.

statutes. Usually, the trial court where the defendant resides is the appropriate venue. If a case involves property, the trial court where the property is located is also an appropriate venue. Finally, if the focus of the case is a particular incident, the trial court where the dispute occurred is an appropriate venue. The plaintiff initially chooses from among the appropriate venues when she files the case.

If the location of the court where the plaintiff filed the case is an inconvenience to the defendant or if the defendant believes it will be difficult to select an unbiased jury in that venue, he may request that the judge move the case by filing a motion for a change of venue. The judge has the discretion to grant or deny the motion.

For example, one particular reason a defendant might choose to request a change of venue is negative pretrial publicity. In May 2008, Sholom Rubashkin, the manager of the nation's largest kosher slaughterhouse, was arrested in an immigration raid, and he now faces roughly 100 charges ranging from document fraud and identity theft to child-labor and minimum-wage violations. The scale of the raid, which led to the arrest of approximately 400 of Rubashkin's employees, and the severity of Rubashkin's charges attracted national media attention. Fearing that he would not be able to receive a fair trial or an unbiased jury,[6] Rubashkin filed a request to have his trial moved from Iowa to either Minneapolis or Chicago. A federal district court judge disagreed with Rubashkin, and denied his initial request for a new venue. However, the judge did acknowledge that publicity may increase even more as the trial draws near and mentioned that she may allow Rubashkin to renew his argument for a new venue at that time.

Legal Principle: **Venue is appropriate in the county where the defendant resides or where the incident took place over which the lawsuit arose.**

The Structure of the Court System

LO3 How is our dual court system structured?

The U.S. legal system has two parallel court structures: a federal system and a state system. Once a plaintiff files a case in one of the systems, the case remains in that system throughout the appeals process. The only exception to this rule occurs when a party to a lawsuit appeals the decision of a state supreme court to the U.S. Supreme Court.

THE FEDERAL COURT SYSTEM

The federal court system derives its power from Article III, Section 2, of the U.S. Constitution and consists of three main levels: trial courts, intermediate appellate courts, and the court of last resort. Exhibit 3-2 on the next page illustrates this system.

Federal Trial Courts. In the federal court system, the trial courts, or courts of original jurisdiction, are U.S. district courts. The United States has 94 districts; each district has at least one trial court of general jurisdiction. Courts of general jurisdiction have the power to hear a wide range of cases and can grant almost any type of remedy. Almost every case in the federal system begins in one of these courts.

A small number of cases, however, do not begin in trial courts of general jurisdiction. For cases concerning certain subject matter, Congress has established special trial courts of limited jurisdiction. The types of cases for which Congress has established these special trial courts include bankruptcy cases, claims against the U.S. government, international trade and customs cases, and disputes over certain tax deficiencies.

In an extremely limited number of cases, the U.S. Supreme Court functions as a trial court of limited jurisdiction. These cases include controversies between states and lawsuits against foreign ambassadors.

[6] www.nytimes.com/2008/10/31/us/31immig.html?hp; and seattletimes.nwsource.com/html/businesstechnology/2008881497_apkosherslaughterhousetrial.html.

Exhibit 3-2 The Federal Court System

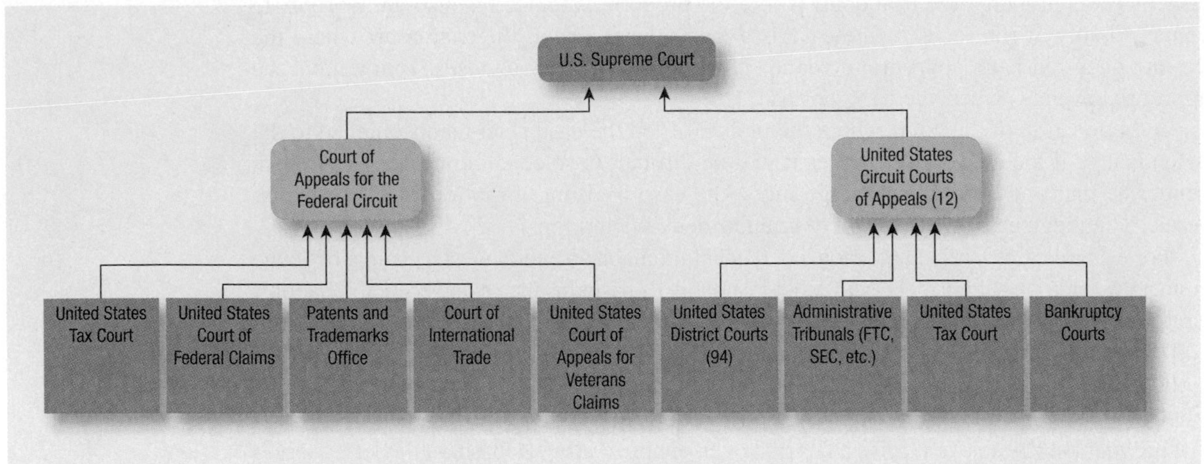

Intermediate Courts of Appeal. The U.S. circuit courts of appeal make up the second level of courts in the federal system. The United States has 12 circuits, including a circuit for the District of Columbia. Each circuit court hears appeals from district courts in its geographic area. Additionally, a federal circuit court of appeals hears appeals from government administrative agencies. Exhibit 3-3 illustrates the geographic circuit divisions.

Exhibit 3-3 The Circuits of the Federal Court System

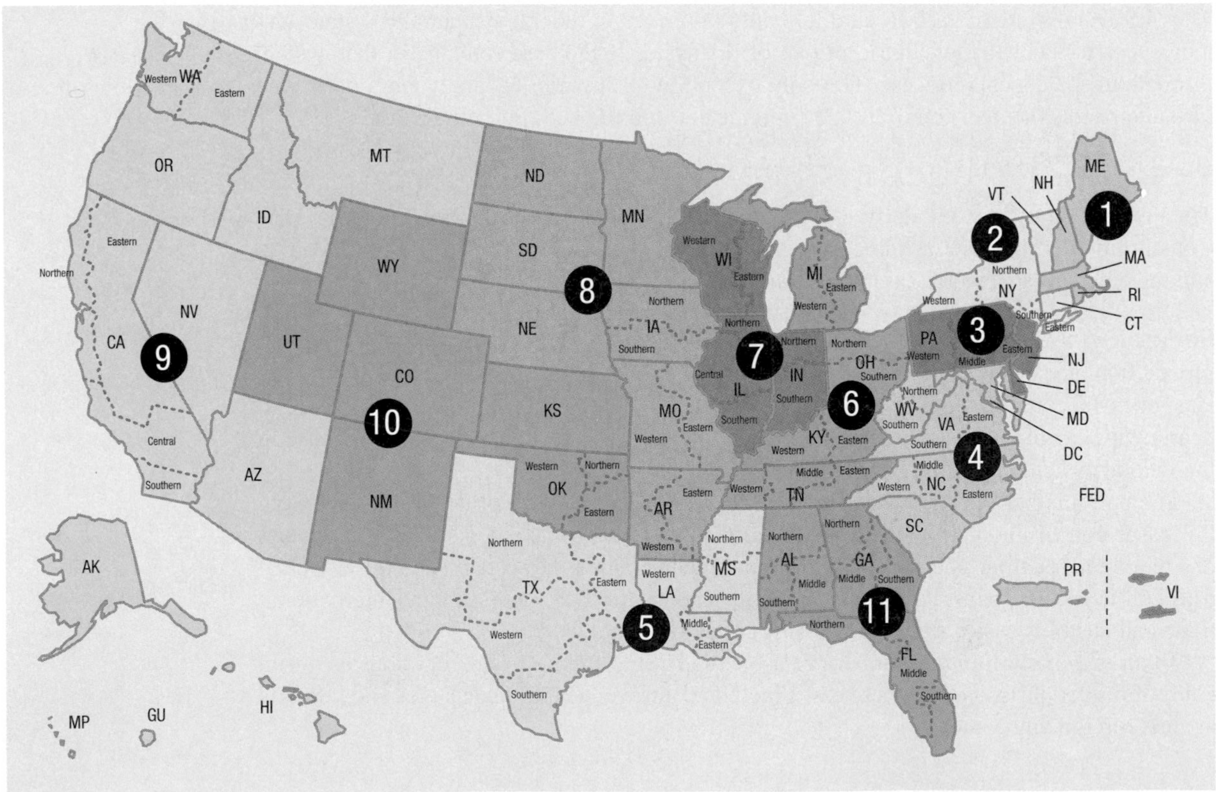

The Court of Last Resort. The U.S. Supreme Court is the final appellate court in the federal system. Nine justices, who have lifetime appointments, make up the high court. Exhibit 3-4 shows the nine justices on the U.S. Supreme Court in 2010.

The U.S. Supreme Court hears appeals of cases from the court of last resort in a state system. The Court will not, however, hear cases considering questions of pure state law. The Court also functions as a trial court in rare occasions. The structure and functioning of the U.S. Supreme Court system differ from those of similar courts in other countries, as the Comparing the Law of Other Countries box illustrates.

STATE COURT SYSTEMS

No uniform state court structure exists because each state has devised its own court system. Most states, however, have a structure similar to the federal court system's structure.

State Trial Courts. In state court systems, most cases begin in a trial court of general jurisdiction. As in the federal system, state trial courts of general jurisdiction have

Exhibit 3-4
U.S. Supreme Court Justices, 2010

COMPARING THE LAW OF OTHER COUNTRIES

THE SUPREME COURT IN THE REPUBLIC OF CHINA (TAIWAN)

In Taiwan, the country's core laws are called the "organic law of the court." These laws stipulate that the country relies on a "three-level and three-instance" court system. In other words, cases begin at one of the district court and may then move to a high court and finally to the Supreme Court. The Supreme Court is the court of last resort. Thus, at first glance, Taiwan's system appears similar to the U.S. federal system, and with respect to matters not involving interpretation of the the country's constitution, it is. But Taiwan's system also has an additional court that is absent from the U.S. system.

While Taiwan's Supreme Court is the court of last resort for civil and criminal cases, the Supreme Court is not responsible for interpreting the country's constitution. This responsibility falls to the Constitutional Court of the Judicial Yuan.

The Constitutional Court of the Judicial Yuan is a council composed of 15 grand justices. The president of Taiwan chooses the Judicial Yuan president and vice president from among the active justices, and both individuals serve terms that last four years. Seven of the fifteen members serve eight-year terms. This court also has a few additional powers, such as the ability to impeach the president and vice president of the republic.

Cases heard by the Supreme Court are presented to five judges, including a Supreme Court president who not only attends to administrative concerns but also acts as a presiding judge over the fellow members of the court.

the power to hear all cases over which the state court system has jurisdiction except those cases for which the state has established special trial courts of limited jurisdiction. Most states have a trial court of general jurisdiction in each county. The names of these courts vary by state, but most states refer to them as *courts of common pleas* or *county courts*. In some states, these courts have specialized divisions: domestic relations, probate, and so on.

Most states also have trial courts of limited jurisdiction. Usually, these courts can grant only certain remedies. For example, small claims courts, a common type of court of limited jurisdiction in most states, may not grant damage awards larger than a specified amount. Other courts of limited jurisdiction have the power to hear only certain types of cases. For example, probate courts hear only cases about asset and obligation transfers after an individual's death.

Intermediate Courts of Appeal. Intermediate courts of appeal, analogous to federal circuit courts of appeal, exist in approximately half the states. These courts usually have broad jurisdiction, hearing appeals from courts of general and limited jurisdictions, as well as from state administrative agencies. The names of these courts also vary by state, but most states call them *courts of appeal* or *superior courts.*

Courts of Last Resort. Appeals from the state intermediate courts of appeal lead cases to the state court of last resort. Most states call this court the *supreme court,* although some states refer to it as the *court of appeals.* Because approximately half the states lack intermediate courts of appeal, appeals from trial courts in these states go directly to the state court of last resort.

L04

What are the threshold requirements that must be met before a court will hear a case?

Threshold Requirements

Before a case makes it to court, it must meet three *threshold requirements.* These requirements ensure that courts hear only cases that genuinely require adjudication. The three requirements are standing, case or controversy, and ripeness.

STANDING

A person who has the legal right to bring an action in court has **standing** (or *standing to sue*). For a person to have standing, the outcome of a case must personally affect him or her. For example, if you hire a landscaper to mow your lawn every week and she fails to show up every other week, you have standing to sue your landscaper. But if your friend hired the landscaper to mow his lawn, you lack the standing to sue on your friend's behalf because you do not have a personal stake in the outcome of the case. The American legal system requires that a plaintiff have a personal stake in the outcome of the case because, the theory goes, the plaintiff's personal stake stimulates her to present the best possible case.

Standing requirements are subject to frequent litigation when citizen groups sue to enforce environmental laws. For example, the standing of the plaintiff, Friends of the Earth (FOE), was a central issue in the 2000 U.S. Supreme Court case *FOE v. Laidlaw Environmental Services.*[7] In the case, FOE filed a lawsuit against Laidlaw, alleging that it had violated the Clean Water Act by discharging excessive amounts of pollutants into a river.

Writing for the majority, Justice Ginsburg cited three factors plaintiffs need for standing: (1) The plaintiff must have an injury in fact that is concrete and actual or imminent; (2) the injury must be fairly traceable to the challenged action of the defendant; and (3) it must be likely that the injury will be redressed by a favorable decision.[8] In applying those criteria to the Laidlaw case, the Supreme Court found that FOE members' testimony that they were afraid to fish and swim in a river they previously enjoyed satisfied the first two criteria. The Court held that although the FOE members would not directly receive money from a penalty against Laidlaw, they would benefit because the penalties would deter Laidlaw and other companies from polluting the river in the future.[9] The Court ruled in FOE's favor and assessed Laidlaw a $405,800 penalty payable to the U.S. Treasury.

CASE OR CONTROVERSY

The **case or controversy** (or *justiciable controversy*) requirement ensures that courts do not render advisory opinions. Three criteria are necessary for a case or controversy to exist. First, the relationship between the plaintiff and the defendant must be adverse. Second, actual or threatened actions of at least one of the parties must give rise to an actual legal dispute. Third, courts must have the ability to render a decision that will resolve the dispute. In other words, courts can give final judgments that solve existing problems; they cannot provide rulings about hypothetical situations.

RIPENESS

The case or controversy requirement is closely linked to the **ripeness** requirement. A case is *ripe* if a judge's decision is capable of affecting the parties immediately. Usually the issue of ripeness arises when one party claims that the case is moot—in other words, there is no point in the court's hearing the case because no judgment can affect the situation between the parties.

In the Laidlaw case cited previously, Laidlaw also argued that the case was moot because by the time the case went to trial, the company had complied with the requirements of its discharge permits. Thus, Laidlaw argued, the only remedy left to the courts—a penalty Laidlaw must pay to the government—would not affect the plaintiffs. The Supreme Court

[7] 120 S. Ct. 923 (2000).

[8] Ibid.

[9] Ibid.

disagreed, ruling that the fact that a defendant voluntarily ceases a practice once litigation has commenced does not deprive a federal court of its power to determine the legality of the practice, because such a ruling would leave the defendant free to return to his old unlawful practices. Thus, the Court found the case was not moot because imposing a penalty on the defendant would have an important deterrent effect.[10]

Legal Principle: **Before a case can be heard, it must meet the three threshold requirements of standing, case or controversy, and ripeness.**

Steps in Civil Litigation

L05

What are the steps in civil litigation?

The U.S. litigation system is an adversary system: a neutral fact finder—a judge or jury—hears evidence and arguments that opposing sides present and then decides the case on the basis of the facts and law. Strict rules govern the types of evidence fact finders may consider. Theoretically, fact finders make informed and impartial rulings because each party has an incentive to find all relevant evidence and make the strongest possible arguments on behalf of her or his position.

Critics of the adversary system, however, point out several drawbacks: the time and expense each lawsuit requires, the damage a suit may cause to the litigating parties' relationship, and the unfair advantage to those with wealth and experience using the court system.

THE PRETRIAL STAGE

The *rules of civil procedure* govern civil case proceedings. The Federal Rules of Civil Procedure apply in all federal courts. Each state has its own set of rules, but most states' rules are very similar to the Federal Rules of Civil Procedure. In addition, each court usually has its own set of local court rules.

Informal Negotiations. The initial attempt to resolve a business dispute is usually informal: a discussion or negotiation among the parties to try to find a solution. If the parties are unable to resolve their dispute, one party often seeks an attorney's advice. Together, the attorney and client may be able to resolve the dispute informally with the other party.

Pleadings. The first formal stage of a lawsuit is the *pleading stage.* The plaintiff's attorney initiates a lawsuit by filing a *complaint* in the appropriate court. The complaint states the names of the parties to the action, the basis for the court's subject-matter jurisdiction, the facts on which the plaintiff bases his claim, and the relief the plaintiff seeks. The pleadings prevent surprises at trial; they allow attorneys to prepare arguments to counter the other side's claims. Exhibit 3-5 shows a typical complaint.

Service of Process. To obtain *in personam* jurisdiction over a defendant and to satisfy due process, a court must notify the defendant of the pending lawsuit. Service of process occurs when the defendant is given a copy of the complaint and summons by a process server or by certified or ordinary mail.

[10] Ibid.

EXHIBIT 3-5
Typical Complaint

THE COURT OF COMMON PLEAS OF CLARK COUNTY, NEVADA

Bob Lyons and Sue Lyons, Plaintiffs

v.

Christine Collins, Defendant

COMPLAINT FOR NEGLIGENCE

Case No.

Now come the plaintiffs, Bob Lyons and Sue Lyons, and, for their complaint, allege as follows:

1. Plaintiffs, Bob Lyons and Sue Lyons, both of 825 Havercamp Street, are citizens of Clark County, in the state of Nevada, and defendant, Christine Collins, 947 Rainbow Ave., is a citizen of Clark County in the state of Nevada.
2. On May 1, 2001, the Defendant built a wooden hanging bridge across a stream that runs through the plaintiffs' property at 825 Havercamp Street.
3. Defendant negligently used ropes in the construction of the bridge that were not thick enough to sustain human traffic on the bridge.
4. At approximately 4:00 p.m., on May 20, 2001, the plaintiffs were attempting to carry a box of landscaping stones across the bridge when the ropes broke, and the bridge collapsed, causing plaintiffs to fall seven feet into the stream.
5. As a result of the fall, plaintiff, Bob Lyons, suffered a broken arm, a broken leg, and a skull fracture, incurring $160,000 in medical expenses.
6. As a result of the fall, plaintiff, Sue Lyons, suffered two broken cervical vertebrae, and a skull fracture, incurring $300,000 in medical expenses.
7. As a result of the fall, the landscaping stones, which had cost $1,200, were destroyed.
8. As a result of the foregoing injuries, plaintiff, Bob Lyons, was required to miss eight weeks of work, resulting in a loss of $2,400 in wages.
9. As a result of the foregoing injuries, plaintiff, Sue Lyons, was required to miss twelve weeks of work, resulting in a loss of $3,600 in wages.

WHEREFORE, Plaintiffs demand judgment in the amount of $467,200, plus costs of this action.

Harlon Elliot
Attorney for Plaintiff
824 Sahara Ave.
Las Vegas, Nevada 89117

JURY DEMAND

Plaintiff demands a trial by jury in this matter.

The complaint explains the basis of the lawsuit to the defendant. The summons tells the defendant that if he or she does not respond to the lawsuit within a certain period of time, the plaintiff will receive a default judgment. A **default judgment** is a judgment in favor of the plaintiff that occurs when the defendant fails to answer the complaint and the plaintiff's complaint alleges facts that would support such a judgment.

Defendant's Response. The defendant responds to the complaint with an **answer.** In this document, the defendant denies, affirms, or claims no knowledge of the accuracy of the plaintiff's allegations.

A defendant uses an *affirmative defense* when her or his answer admits that the facts contained in the complaint are accurate but also includes additional facts that justify the defendant's actions and provide a legally sound reason to deny relief to the plaintiff.

For example, if a woman sued a man for battery because he punched her in the face, he might claim that he hit her only because she aimed a gun at him and threatened to shoot. His claim that he was acting in self-defense is an affirmative defense.

If the defendant plans to raise an affirmative defense, he must raise it in his answer to give the plaintiff adequate notice. If he fails to raise an affirmative defense in the answer, the judge will likely not allow him to raise it during the trial.

Upon receiving the complaint, if the defendant believes that even though all the plaintiff's factual allegations are true, the law does not entitle the plaintiff to a favorable judgment, the defendant may file a **motion to dismiss,** or *demurrer.* (A **motion** is a request by a party for the court to do something; in this instance, the request is to dismiss the case.) In deciding whether to grant a motion to dismiss, a judge accepts the facts as stated by the plaintiff and rules on the legal issues in the case. Judges generally grant a motion to dismiss only when it appears beyond a doubt that the plaintiff cannot prove any set of facts to justify granting the judgment she seeks.

If the defendant believes he has a claim against the plaintiff, he includes this **counterclaim** with the answer. As Exhibit 3–6 shows, the form of a counterclaim is identical to the form of a complaint. The defendant states the facts supporting his claim and asks for relief.

EXHIBIT 3-6
Defendant's Answer and Counterclaim

THE COURT OF COMMON PLEAS OF CLARK COUNTY, NEVADA

Bob Lyons and Sue Lyons, Plaintiffs v. Christine Collins, Defendant ANSWER AND COUNTERCLAIM FOR BREACH OF CONTRACT Case No.

Now comes the defendant, Christine Collins, and answers the complaint of plaintiff herein as follows:

First Defense

1. Admits the allegations in paragraphs 1 and 2.
2. Denies the allegation in paragraph 3.
3. Is without knowledge as to the truth or falsity of the allegations contained in paragraphs 4, 5, 6, 7, 8, and 9.

Second Defense

4. If the court believes the allegations contained in paragraph 3, which the defendant expressly denies, plaintiffs should still be denied recovery because they were informed prior to the construction of the bridge that there should be no more than one person on the bridge at one time and that no individual weighing more than 200 pounds should be allowed to walk on the bridge.

Counterclaim

5. On April 15, the parties agreed that Defendant would build a wooden hanging bridge across a stream that runs through the defendants' property at 825 Havercamp Street, in exchange for which plaintiffs would pay defendant $2,000 upon completion of construction.
6. On May 1, 2001, the Defendant built the agreed upon ornament, wooden, hanging bridge across a stream that runs through the defendants' property at 825 Havercamp Street, but Plaintiffs failed to pay the agreed upon price for the bridge.
7. By their failure to pay, plaintiffs breached their contract and are liable to defendant for the contract price of $2,000.

WHEREFORE, defendant prays for a judgment dismissing the plaintiffs' complaint, and granting the defendant a judgment against plaintiff in the amount of $2,000 plus costs of this action.

Melissa Davenport
Attorney for Defendant
777 Decatur Ave.
Las Vegas, Nevada 89117

If the defendant files a counterclaim, the plaintiff generally files a reply. A **reply** is an answer to a counterclaim. In the reply, the plaintiff admits, denies, or claims a lack of knowledge as to the accuracy of the facts of the defendant's counterclaim. If the plaintiff plans to use an affirmative defense, she must raise it in the reply.

Pretrial Motions. The early pleadings establish the legal and factual issues of the case. After the pleadings, the plaintiff or defendant may file a motion to conclude the case early, eliminate some claims, or gain some advantage. A party may move, or request, that the court do almost anything pertaining to the case. For example, if the plaintiff files a suit about the right to a piece of property, she may move that the court prohibit the current possessor of the land from selling it. Courts may grant or deny such motions at their discretion.

When a party files a motion with the court, the court sends a copy to the opposing attorney, who may respond to the motion, usually by requesting that the judge deny the motion. In many cases, the judge rules on the motion immediately. In other cases, the judge holds a hearing at which the attorneys for both sides argue how the judge should decide the motion.

Two primary pretrial motions are a motion for judgment on the pleadings and a motion for summary judgment. Once the parties file the pleadings, either party can file a **motion for judgment on the pleadings.** The motion is a request for the court to consider that all the facts in the pleadings are true and to apply the law to those facts. The court grants the motion if, after this process, it finds that the only reasonable decision is in favor of the moving party.

Either party can file a **motion for summary judgment** after the discovery process (described below). The motion asserts that no factual disputes exist and that if the judge applied the law to the undisputed facts, her only reasonable decision would be in favor of the moving party. The difference between this motion and a motion for judgment on the pleadings is that in a motion for summary judgment, the moving party may use affidavits (sworn statements from the parties or witnesses), relevant documents, and depositions or interrogatories (a party's sworn answers to written questions) to support his motion. The judge grants the motion if, after examining the evidence, she finds no factual disputes. If, however, she finds any factual issues about which the parties disagree, she denies the motion and sends the case to trial.

Discovery. After filing the initial pleadings and motions, the parties gather information from each other through **discovery.** The discovery process enables the parties to learn about facts surrounding the case so that they are not surprised in the courtroom. Three common discovery tools are interrogatories, requests to produce documents, and depositions.

Interrogatories are written questions that one party sends to the other to answer under oath. Frequently, a *request to admit certain facts* accompanies interrogatories. Attorneys work with their clients to answer interrogatories and requested admissions of facts.

A **request to produce documents** (or other items) forces the opposing party to produce (turn over) certain information unless it is privileged or irrelevant to the case. Parties may request documents such as photographs, contracts, written estimates, medical records, tax forms, and other government documents. In tort cases, the defendant frequently asks the plaintiff to submit a mental- or physical-examination report.

Finally, the parties may obtain testimony from a witness before trial through a deposition. At a **deposition,** attorneys examine a witness under oath. A court reporter (stenographer) records every word the witnesses and attorneys speak. Both parties receive a copy of the testimony in document form. Depositions provide information and may also set up inconsistencies between a witness's testimony at the deposition and his testimony at trial. If a party discovers an inconsistency in the testimony of one of the other party's witnesses, she can bring the inconsistency to the fact finder's attention to diminish the witness's credibility. The parties may also use depositions when a witness is elderly, moving, or ill such that he may be unavailable at the time of the trial.

If a party does not comply with requests for discovery, the court may admit the facts the other party sought to discover. Attorneys who feel that certain material is outside the scope of the case often argue that the material is irrelevant to the case. If the court disagrees, however, the party must supply the requested information. Although these discovery tools are important in the United States, not all countries have a discovery process.

In discovery, as in other areas, technology is having an impact. It is estimated that 90 percent of all documents and communications are created and maintained in electronic formats. In December 2006, the Federal Rules of Civil Procedure were amended to reflect changes in technology. Parties are now required to "make provisions for disclosure or discovery of electronically stored information"[11] at the start of the litigation process, and they must develop a discovery plan during their pretrial conferences. Once it appears that litigation is imminent, litigants have an obligation not to delete or destroy electronic files that may be discoverable. However, "absent exceptional circumstances, a court may not impose sanctions . . . on a party for failing to provide electronically stored information lost as a result of the routine, good-faith operation of an electronic information system."[12]

Parties who might become embroiled in litigation, however, probably should not count on using the good-faith exception because the consequences of destroying electronic data can be significant. For example, in the sex discrimination case of *Zubulake v. UBS Warburg LLC,*[13] the judge found that the company's employees had intentionally deleted e-mail messages, lost a number of backup tapes, and failed to produce files as requested. As a sanction, she issued an *adverse-inference* instruction to the jury, basically telling them that they could assume that any documents not produced would have been harmful to the company's case. The jury ultimately awarded the woman $29.3 million in damages.

Morgan Stanley had to pay an even bigger price for its failure to meet its obligations for electronic discovery of relevant e-mail messages and documents. In *Coleman Holdings Inc. v. Morgan Stanley & Co.,*[14] the firm produced more than 1,300 pages of e-mail messages but failed to reveal in a timely fashion the existence of 1,423 backup tapes. In that case, the court also issued an adverse-inference instruction, stating that Morgan Stanley would have to bear the burden of proving that it lacked knowledge of the fraud. The jury found in favor of the plaintiff and awarded damages in the amount of $1.6 billion. Morgan Stanley also had to pay the U.S. Securities and Exchange Commission $15 million in fines for failure to comply with discovery requirements in a related commission investigation.

What organizations can learn from these cases is that as soon as they reasonably anticipate that litigation will occur, they must suspend their routine policy for retaining and destroying documents and put in place a "litigation hold" to make sure that documents that might be relevant to the lawsuit are preserved. Some plaintiffs' lawyers are now sending *litigation-hold demand* letters to potential defendants, making it almost impossible for a firm to claim that relevant documents were innocently deleted.

[11] Rule 16(B), Federal Rules of Civil Procedure.

[12] Rule 37(F), Federal Rules of Civil Procedure.

[13] 231 F.R.D. 159, 2005 U.S. Dist. LEXIS 1525 (S.D.N.Y., Feb. 2, 2005).

[14] 2005 WL 679071 (Fla. Cir. Ct., Mar. 1, 2005).

Pretrial Conference. A pretrial conference precedes the trial. A **pretrial conference** is an informal meeting of the judge with the attorneys representing the parties. During this conference, the parties try to narrow the legal and factual issues and possibly work out a settlement. If the parties cannot reach a settlement, the attorneys and the judge discuss the administrative details of the trial: its length, witnesses, and any pretrial stipulations of fact or law to which the parties agree.

THE TRIAL

If a plaintiff seeks at least $20 in monetary damages, the Seventh Amendment to the U.S. Constitution entitles the parties to a jury trial. The plaintiff must, however, demand a jury trial in his or her complaint. Following the English tradition, most civil trials have 12 jurors; however, in many jurisdictions the number of required jurors has been reduced by the legislature. In some jurisdictions, fewer than 12 jurors may be allowed if both parties consent. If the plaintiff seeks an equitable remedy (an injunction or other court order) or if the parties have waived their right to a jury, a judge serves as the fact finder in the case.

Trials have six stages: jury selection, opening statements, examination of witnesses, closing arguments, conference on jury instructions, and posttrial motions. The following sections describe these stages.

Jury Selection. The jury selection process begins when the clerk of the courts randomly selects a number of potential jurors from the citizens within the court's jurisdiction. Once the potential jurors have reported for jury duty, the **voir dire,** or jury selection, process begins. The voir dire process selects the jurors who will decide the case, as well as two or three "alternate jurors" who will watch the trial and be available to replace any juror who, for some legitimate reason, must leave jury duty before the trial ends.

During voir dire, the judge and/or attorneys question potential jurors to determine whether they are able to render an unbiased opinion in the case. If a potential juror's response to a question indicates that she or he may be biased, either attorney may challenge, or ask the court to remove, that potential juror "for cause." For example, a lawyer could challenge for cause a potential juror who was a college roommate of the defendant. In most states, each party has a certain number of **peremptory challenges.** These peremptory challenges allow a party to challenge a certain number of potential jurors without giving a reason.

Peremptory challenges, however, may lead to abuse. For example, in the past, attorneys have used peremptory challenges to eliminate a certain class, ethnic group, or gender from the jury. In the 1986 case *Batson v. Kentucky,*[15] the U.S. Supreme Court ruled that race-based peremptory challenges in criminal cases violate the equal protection clause of the Fourteenth Amendment to the U.S. Constitution. (Chapter 5 discusses the amendments to the Constitution in more detail.) The Supreme Court later extended the ban on race-based challenges to civil cases. In Case 3-2, the U.S. Supreme Court addressed the issue of whether the equal protection clause covers gender-based challenges.

The voir dire process has become more sophisticated over time. In cases involving significant amounts of money, rather than relying on their instinct or experience during jury selection, attorneys use professional jury selection services to identify demographic data to help select ideal jurors.

[15] 476 U.S. 79 (1986).

Jury selection firms also provide additional services, including mock trials and shadow juries. Jury selection firms set up **mock trials** by recruiting individuals who match the demographics of the real jury to listen to attorneys' arguments and witnesses' testimony. These mock trials give attorneys a sense of how their approach to the case will appear to the actual jurors. If the mock jury is not receptive to a particular argument or witness's testimony, the attorneys can modify their approach before trial.

Parties also often hire jury selection firms to provide shadow juries. Like a mock trial, a **shadow jury** uses individuals whose demographics match the demographics of a trial's real jurors. A shadow jury, however, sits inside the courtroom to watch the actual trial. At the end of each day of the trial, the shadow jury deliberates, giving the attorneys an idea of how the real jurors are reacting to the case. If the shadow jury finds the opposing side to be winning, the attorneys can modify their strategy.

Many attorneys believe that these services increase their clients' chances of winning cases. Critics argue, however, that jury selection services give an unfair advantage to one side when only one party can afford these services.

CASE 3-2 UNITED STATES SUPREME COURT 114 S. CT. 1419 (1994)

J.E.B. v. ALABAMA, *EX. REL. T.B.*

The State of Alabama filed a complaint for paternity and child support against J.E.B. on behalf of T.B., the unwed mother of a minor child. The court called a panel of twelve males and twenty-four females as potential jurors. Only ten males remained after three individuals were removed for cause. The state used its peremptory challenges to remove nine male jurors, and J.E.B. removed the tenth, resulting in an all female jury. The trial court rejected J.E.B.'s objection to the gender-based challenges, and the jury found J.E.B. to be the father. J.E.B. appealed, and the court of appeals affirmed the trial court's ruling that the Equal Protection Clause does not prohibit gender-based challenges. The Alabama Supreme Court declined to hear the appeal, and J.E.B. appealed to the U.S. Supreme Court.

JUSTICE BLACKMUN: Discrimination in jury selection, whether based on race or on gender, causes harm to the litigants, the community, and the individual jurors who are wrongfully excluded from participation in the judicial process. The litigants are harmed by the risk that the prejudice which motivated the discriminatory selection of the jury will infect the entire proceedings. The community is harmed by the State's participation in the perpetuation of invidious group stereotypes and the inevitable loss of confidence in our judicial system that state-sanctioned discrimination in the courtroom engenders.

As with race-based *Batson* claims, a party alleging gender discrimination must make a prima facie showing of intentional discrimination before the party exercising the challenge is required to explain the basis for the strike. When an explanation is required, it need not rise to the level of a "for cause" challenge; rather, it merely must be based on a juror characteristic other than gender and the proffered explanation may not be pretextual.

Equal opportunity to participate in the fair administration of justice is fundamental to our democratic system. It reaffirms the promise of equality under the law—that all citizens, regardless of race, ethnicity, or gender, have the chance to take part directly in our democracy. When persons are excluded from participation in our democratic processes solely because of race or gender, this promise of equality dims, and the integrity of our judicial system is jeopardized.

REVERSED and REMANDED in favor of J.E.B.

CRITICAL THINKING

The defendant was contesting the removal of males from the jury. Does this fact weaken the Court's reasoning? Explain.

ETHICAL DECISION MAKING

Which values does this decision tend to emphasize?

Opening Statements. Once the attorneys have impaneled, or selected, a jury, the case begins with opening statements. Each party's attorney explains to the judge and jury which facts he or she intends to prove, the legal conclusions to which these facts lead, and how the fact finder should decide the case based on those facts.

The Examination of Witnesses and Presentation of Evidence. Following opening statements, the plaintiff and defendant, in turn, present their cases-in-chief by examining witnesses and presenting evidence. The plaintiff has the burden of proving the case, meaning that if neither side presents a convincing case, the fact finder must rule in favor of the defendant. Thus, the plaintiff presents her case first.

The procedure for each witness is the same. First, the plaintiff's attorney questions the witness in *direct examination.* The plaintiff's attorney asks the witness questions to elicit facts that support the plaintiff's case-in-chief. Questions must relate to matters about which the witness has direct knowledge. Attorneys cannot elicit "hearsay" from the witnesses. *Hearsay* is testimony about what a witness heard another person say. Hearsay is impermissible because the opposing attorney cannot question the person who made the original statement to determine the statement's veracity.

The federal rules of evidence also prohibit attorneys from asking leading questions. Leading questions are questions that imply a specific answer. For example, an attorney cannot ask a witness, "Did the defendant come to your office and ask you to purchase stock from him?" Instead, attorneys must ask questions such as, "When did you first encounter the defendant?"

After direct examination, opposing counsel may *cross-examine* the witness. Opposing counsel, however, may ask only questions related to the witness's direct examination. On cross-examination, attorneys can ask leading questions. Attorneys try to show inconsistencies in the witness's testimony, cast doubt on the claims of the plaintiff's case, and elicit information to support the defendant's case.

After cross-examination, the plaintiff's attorney may conduct a *redirect examination,* a series of questions to repair damage done by the cross-examination. At the judge's discretion, opposing counsel has an opportunity to *re-cross* the witness to question his testimony on redirect examination. The parties follow this procedure for each of the plaintiff's witnesses.

Immediately following the plaintiff's presentation of her case, the defendant may move for a **directed verdict.** This motion is a request for the court to direct a verdict for the defendant because even if the jury accepted all the evidence and testimony presented by the plaintiff as true, the jury would still have no legal basis for a decision in favor of the plaintiff. The federal court system refers to a motion for a directed verdict as a *motion for a judgment as a matter of law.* Courts rarely grant motions for a directed verdict because plaintiffs almost always present at least *some* evidence to support each element of the cause of action.

If the court denies the defendant's motion for a directed verdict, the defendant then presents his case. The parties question the defendant's witnesses in the same manner as they questioned the plaintiff's witnesses, except that the defendant's attorney conducts direct and redirect examination and the plaintiff's attorney conducts cross-examination and re-cross-examination.

Closing Arguments. After the defendant's case, the attorneys present closing arguments. In the *closing argument,* each attorney summarizes evidence from the trial in a manner consistent with his or her client's case. The plaintiff's attorney presents her closing

COMPARING THE LAW OF OTHER COUNTRIES

TRIALS IN JAPAN

Civil procedure in Japan differs significantly from American civil procedure. The Japanese legal system has no juries and no distinct pretrial stage. Instead, a trial is a series of discrete meetings between the parties and the judge. At the first meeting, the parties identify the most critical and contested issues. They choose one and recess to gather evidence and marshal arguments on the issue.

At the next meeting, the judge rules on the chosen issue. If the judge decides against the plaintiff, the case is over. If the plaintiff wins, the process continues with the next issue. The process continues until the plaintiff loses an issue or until the judge decides all issues in the plaintiff's favor, resulting in a verdict for the plaintiff.

In addition, the discovery process in the Japanese court system is not as simple as it is in the United States. To obtain evidence, parties must convince the judge to order others to testify or produce documents. The judge can fine or jail parties who refuse to comply with such orders. Additionally, if a party does not comply with the judge's requests for discovery, the judge may admit the facts the other party sought to discover.

argument first, followed by the defendant's attorney, and the plaintiff has the option to present a rebuttal of the defendant's closing argument.

Jury Instructions. In a jury trial, the judge "charges the jury" by instructing the jurors how the law applies to the facts of the case. Both sides' attorneys submit statements to the judge explaining how they believe he should charge the jury. The judge's instructions are usually a combination of both sides' suggestions.

Different types of cases require different standards of proof. In most civil cases, the plaintiff must prove her case by a *preponderance of the evidence;* in other words, she must show that her claim is more likely to be true than the defendant's claim. In some civil cases, particularly cases involving fraud or oral contracts, the plaintiff must prove her case by *clear and convincing evidence,* a higher standard of proof. Criminal cases have an even higher burden of proof: The prosecution must prove its case *beyond a reasonable doubt.*

After the judge charges the jury, the jurors retire to the jury room to deliberate. Once they reach a decision, they return to the courtroom, where the judge reads their verdict and discharges them from their duty.

Trial procedures in the United States are quite different from trial procedures in other countries, as the Comparing the Law of Other Countries box illustrates.

Posttrial Motions. Once the trial ends, the party who received the favorable verdict files a *motion for a judgment in accordance with the verdict.* Until the judge enters the judgment, the court has not issued a legally binding decision for the case.

The party who loses at trial has a number of available options. One option is to file a *motion for a judgment notwithstanding the verdict,* or *judgment non obstante verdicto,* asking the judge to issue a judgment contrary to the jury's verdict. To grant the motion, the judge must find that, when viewing the evidence in the light most favorable to the nonmoving party, a reasonable jury could not have found in favor of that party. In other words, as a matter of law, the judge must determine that the trial did not produce sufficient evidence to support the jury's verdict. This motion is similar to a motion for a directed verdict, except the parties cannot make this motion until *after* the jury issues a verdict. The federal court system refers to this motion as a *motion for judgment as a matter of law.*

The losing party can also file a *motion for a new trial.* Judges grant motions for a new trial only if they believe the jury's decision was clearly erroneous but they are not sure that the other side should necessarily have won the case. A judge often grants a motion for a new trial when the parties discover new evidence, when the judge made an erroneous ruling, or when misconduct during the trial may have prevented the jury from reaching a fair decision.

APPELLATE PROCEDURE

Either party may appeal the judge's decision on posttrial motions or on her or his final judgment. Sometimes, both parties appeal the same decision. For example, if a jury awarded the plaintiff $10,000 in damages, the plaintiff and the defendant may both appeal the amount of the judgment. Appellate courts, however, reverse only about 1 out of every 10 trial court decisions on appeal.

To be eligible for appeal, the losing party must argue that a prejudicial error of law occurred during the trial. A **prejudicial error of law** is a mistake so significant that it likely affected the outcome of the case. For example, a prejudicial error could occur if the judge improperly admitted hearsay evidence that allowed the plaintiff to prove an element of her case.

To appeal a case, the attorney for the appealing party (the appellant) files a notice of appeal with the clerk of the trial court within a prescribed time. The clerk then forwards the record of appeal to the appeals court. The record of appeal typically contains a number of items: the pleadings, a trial transcript, copies of the trial exhibits, copies of the judge's rulings on the parties' motions, the attorneys' arguments, jury instructions, the jury's verdict, posttrial motions, and the judgment order.

The appellant then files a **brief**, or written argument, with the court. Appellants file briefs to explain why the judgment in the lower court was erroneous and why the appeals court should reverse it. The attorney for the party who won in the lower court (the appellee) files an answering brief. The appellant may then file a reply brief in response to the appellee's brief. Generally, however, appellants do not file reply briefs.

The appeals court then usually allows the attorneys to present oral arguments before the court. The court considers these arguments, reviews the record of the case, and renders a decision.

An appellate court may render four basic decisions. The court can accept the lower court's judgment by *affirming* the decision of the lower court. Alternatively, if the appellate court concludes that the lower court's decision was correct but the remedy was inappropriate, it *modifies* the remedy. If the appellate court decides that the lower court was incorrect in its decision, it *reverses* the lower court's decision. Finally, if the appeals court thinks the lower court committed an error but does not know how that error affected the outcome of the case, it *remands* the case to the lower court for a new trial.

An appellate court usually has a bench with at least three judges. Appellate courts do not have juries; rather, the judges decide the case by majority vote. One of the judges who votes with the majority records the court's decision and its reasons in the *majority opinion.* These decisions have precedential value—that is, judges use these prior appellate court decisions to make decisions in future cases. Also, these decisions establish new guidelines in the law that all citizens must follow. If a judge agrees with the majority's decision, but for different reasons, she may write a *concurring opinion,* stating the reasons she used to reach the majority's conclusion. Finally, judges disagreeing with the majority may write a *dissenting opinion,* giving their reasons for reaching a contrary conclusion. Attorneys arguing that a court should change the law frequently cite dissenting opinions from previous cases in their briefs. Likewise, appellate judges who change the law often cite dissenting opinions from past cases.

For most cases, only one appeal is available. In states with both an intermediate and a final court of appeals, a losing party may appeal from the intermediate appellate court to the state supreme court. In a limited number of cases, the losing party can appeal the decision of a state supreme court or a federal circuit court of appeals to the U.S. Supreme Court.

Appeal to the U.S. Supreme Court. Every year thousands of individuals file appeals with the U.S. Supreme Court. The Court, however, hears, on average, only 80 to 90 cases each year. To file an appeal to the U.S. Supreme Court, a party files a petition asking the Court to issue a **writ of certiorari,** an order to the lower court to send to the Supreme Court the record of the case. The Court issues very few writs.

The justices review petitions and issue a writ only when at least four justices vote to hear the case (the *rule of four*). The court is most likely to issue a writ in four instances: (1) The case presents a substantial federal question that the Supreme Court has not yet addressed; (2) multiple circuit courts of appeal have decided the issue of the case in different ways; (3) a state court of last resort has ruled that a federal law is invalid or has upheld a state law that may violate federal law; or (4) a federal court has ruled that an act of Congress is unconstitutional. If the Supreme Court does not issue a writ of certiorari, the lower court's decision stands.

CASE OPENER WRAP-UP

Questionable Jurisdiction over Caterpillar

The timing of events was crucial to the outcome of the Caterpillar case. At the time Lewis filed the case in the state court system, one of the defendants and the plaintiff were from the same state, so the state court system had jurisdiction. Once the supply company reached an agreement with Lewis, the other defendant, Caterpillar, filed a motion to exercise its right of removal because diversity of citizenship existed in the absence of the Kentucky defendant. But the agreement was not final at the time of the motion because the agreement was subject to the insurer's approval. Thus, the appellate court ruled that because the supply company was still a party to the agreement, the federal court system could not exercise jurisdiction over the case.

The U.S. Supreme Court, however, overruled the appellate court. The Supreme Court ruled that the state court should not have granted Caterpillar's initial motion to remove the case because at the time of removal, the insurer had not accepted the settlement agreement, the supply company remained a party in the case, and, therefore, the diversity of citizenship was not complete. The Supreme Court held further, however, that the district court's error in hearing the case was not fatal because the settlement agreement was approved and the case satisfied the jurisdictional requirements by the time the federal court issued its decision. The Court ruled that to require the district court to send the case back to the state system would be an undue waste of judicial resources.

Why might Caterpillar have wanted to move the case to the federal court system? First, the case involved product liability claims. Data suggest that average damage awards in product liability cases tend to be higher in state courts than in federal courts. Second, Caterpillar may have feared local prejudice. While all judges must strive for neutrality, out-of-state defendants may fear that state judges are slightly biased in favor of in-state parties.

KEY TERMS

answer 53
appellate court 39
brief 61
case or controversy 51
complaint 40
counterclaim 54
court of appellate jurisdiction 39
court of original jurisdiction 39
default judgment 53
defendant 40
deposition 55
directed verdict 59
discovery 55
in personam jurisdiction 40
in rem jurisdiction 41
interrogatories 55
jurisdiction 39
long-arm statute 41
mock trial 58
motion 54
motion for judgment on the pleadings 55
motion for summary judgment 55
motion to dismiss 54
peremptory challenge 57
personal service 40
plaintiff 40
prejudicial error of law 61
pretrial conference 57
quasi *in rem* jurisdiction 41
reply 55
request to produce documents 55
ripeness 51
service of process 40
shadow jury 58
standing 51
subject-matter jurisdiction 42
summons 40
trial court 39
venue 46
voir dire 57
writ of certiorari 62

SUMMARY OF KEY TOPICS

Jurisdiction

In personam jurisdiction is the power of a court to render a decision affecting a person's legal rights. *Subject-matter jurisdiction* is the power of a court to render a decision in a particular type of case. The three forms of subject-matter jurisdiction are state, exclusive federal, and concurrent.

Venue

Venue is the geographic location of the trial.

The Structure of the Court System

The U.S. has two parallel court structures: the state and federal systems. The federal structure has *district courts* (trial courts), *circuit courts of appeal,* and the *U.S. Supreme Court.* The state court structure varies by state, but generally includes courts of common pleas (trial courts), state courts of appeal, and a state supreme court.

Threshold Requirements

Standing: For a person to have the legal right to file a case, the outcome of the case must personally affect that person.

Case or controversy: There must be an issue before the court that a judicial decision is capable of resolving. Parties cannot ask the judge for an "advisory opinion."

Ripeness: The case cannot be moot; it must be ready for a decision to be made.

Steps in Civil Litigation

The stages of a civil trial include the pretrial, trial, posttrial, and appellate stages.

Pretrial includes consultation with attorneys, pleadings, the discovery process, and the pretrial conference.

The *trial* begins with jury selection, followed by opening statements, the plaintiff's case, the defendant's case, closing arguments, jury instructions, jury deliberations, the jury's verdict, and the judgment.

After the trial, parties may file *posttrial motions.*

The parties may then file *appeals* to the appropriate appellate court and, in some cases, to the U.S. Supreme Court.

POINT / COUNTERPOINT

Is the Adversarial System the Most Effective Approach to Justice?

YES

Proponents of the adversarial system argue that justice is best served when each individual's rights and freedoms are protected. The adversarial system requires that the fact finder remain a neutral and objective party, free from bias. The parties are responsible for developing their own individual theories of the case. By allowing individuals to decide what information they wish to present as a part of their case, the system allows them to take a more active role in the legal process.

In addition to promoting individual rights, the adversarial system also helps prevent the abuse of power by the finder of fact. Proponents argue that excluding finders of fact from question asking and evidence collection prevents them from reaching a premature decision or abusing their power.

In response to critics who argue that the adversarial system is more about resolving a dispute than finding the truth, proponents argue that by pitting the two sides against one another, the truth will emerge. The parties involved in the litigation have a stronger motivation to uncover and disclose the facts relevant to the case than does any neutral party (such as the judge in the inquisitorial system). Individual rights and zealous advocacy will best lead to the administration of justice.

NO

Critics of the adversarial system argue that the quest for truth should be central to the administration of justice. By pitting parties against one another in the courtroom, the adversarial system becomes more interested in solving controversies than discovering the truth. Since the parties are allowed to decide what evidence they do and do not wish to present to the fact finder, it is likely that a decision will be rendered on the basis of incomplete and biased information.

In addition to overemphasizing controversy, the adversarial system creates a wealth disparity between parties. For example, if Suzie the secretary decides to sue her employer, Giant Corporate Entity, the sheer size and financial strength of her opponent puts her at an immediate disadvantage. While Suzie may be able to afford an attorney, it is likely that her employer will be able to afford a team of attorneys, paralegals, and support staff. The adversarial system quickly goes from a "system designed to protect individual rights" to a system that primarily protects the rights of the wealthy few who can afford better attorneys and fund a lengthy litigation.

Rather than having the adversarial system, the country would be better served by an inquisitorial system. In the inquisitorial system, the finder of fact, not the parties, is responsible for gathering evidence and investigating. The finder of fact has the opportunity to gather as much information as necessary before rendering an opinion. In the inquisitorial system, the truth, not the controversy, guides the way.

QUESTIONS & PROBLEMS

1. Explain the two types of jurisdiction that a court must have to hear a case and render a binding decision over the parties.
2. Explain the differences between trial courts and appellate courts.
3. Identify and define the alternative tools of discovery.
4. Explain the three threshold requirements a plaintiff must meet before he or she can file a lawsuit.
5. Missouri was International Shoe Corporation's principal place of business, but the company employed between 11 and 13 salespersons in the state of Washington who exhibited samples and solicited orders for shoes from prospective buyers in Washington. The state of Washington assessed the company for contributions to a state unemployment fund. The state served the assessment on one of International Shoe Corporation's sales representatives in Washington and sent a copy by registered

mail to the company's Missouri headquarters. International Shoe's representative challenged the assessment on numerous grounds, arguing that the state had not properly served the corporation. Is the corporation's defense valid? Why or why not? [*International Shoe Co. v. Washington,* 326 U.S. 310 (1945).]

6. Nicastro, the plaintiff, was using a metal-shearing machine in New Jersey when he hurt his hand. The machine was produced by J. McIntyre Machinery, Ltd., which manufactured the machine in England, where the company is based. However, Nicastro brought the company to court in New Jersey because that is where the injury occurred. The company argued that it could not be brought to court in New Jersey because the court did not have personal jurisdiction over it due to the company's lack of minimum contacts in the state. Nicastro said that the company's distributor for the United States sold the equipment in the country, company officials attended trade shows in the country, even if they were not in New Jersey, and the record shows that one machine ended up in New Jersey. Ultimately, the company knew that its U.S. distributor could potentially sell its products in any state and that any product could somehow end up in any state. On the other hand, the company did not travel to, advertise, or contact any residents of New Jersey. Do you think the company is subject to personal jurisdiction in the state of New Jersey? How do you believe the Supreme Court ruled in this case? Why? [*J. McIntyre Machinery, Ltd. v. Nicastro,* 131 S. Ct. 2780 (2011).]

7. The plaintiff, a Texas resident, and the defendants, Colorado residents, were cat breeders who met at a cat show in Colorado. Subsequently, the plaintiff sent two cats to the defendants in Colorado for breeding and sent a third cat to them to be sold. A dispute over the return of the two breeding cats arose, and the plaintiff filed suit against the defendants in Texas. The defendants alleged that the Texas court lacked personal jurisdiction over them because they did not have minimum contacts within the state of Texas.

The Texas statute provides that the Texas court could exercise jurisdiction over an out-of-state defendant only if (1) the defendant has purposefully established minimum contacts with the forum state and (2) the exercise of jurisdiction comports with traditional notions of fair play and substantial justice. The defendants were not residents of Texas and had no business in Texas. The only contact the defendants had with Texas was a single trip they made to Texas to pick up two other cats, not related to the litigation, that they were going to take to a cat show. During that same visit, the defendants took a cat unrelated to the lawsuit to see a Texas veterinarian, and the plaintiff's husband assisted the defendants with a web page for their business. The trial court found that sufficient minimum contacts had been established. The defendants appealed. How do you believe the appellate court would rule in this case, and why? [*Hagan v. Field,* Court of Appeals of Texas, Fifth District, Dallas, 2006 Tex. App. LEXIS 393.]

8. Gucci America discovered that Wang Huoqing, a man living in China, was running multiple websites selling counterfeit Gucci products. Huoqing was selling intellectual property that was protected in Gucci's registered trademarks without permission. Gucci decided to hire a private investigator to order counterfeit Gucci merchandise from Huoqing's sites. Once the investigator received the merchandise at his address in California, Gucci filed a lawsuit against Huoqing for copyright infringement in a federal district court in California. Huoqing was notified of the lawsuit in an e-mail. However, he never appeared in court, so Gucci asked the court to make a default judgment. In turn, the court needed to decide whether it had the personal jurisdiction over the case involving Huoqing since he lived in China and his only contact with the United States was through sales over the Internet. The court decided that it would have jurisdiction over a person who had sufficient minimum contact with residents within the state. Courts have to apply a three-prong test to decide whether someone has had sufficient minimum contact with their forum: (1) Did Huoqing purposefully direct his activities and transactions with the forum or resident thereof or engage in an act whereby he was purposefully benefited by engaging in the activities in the forum, subsequently receiving the benefits and protections of its laws? (2) Did the lawsuit claim relate to Huoqing's forum-related activities? (3) If the court exercised jurisdiction, would doing so be reasonable? [*Gucci America v. Wang Huoqing,* F. Supp. 3d (2011).]

9. Jones lived in California, and for four years received weekly psychotherapy and dream counseling over the telephone from Williams, a licensed therapist living in New Mexico. Williams made several trips to California at Jones's request to provide additional treatment. For one year, Jones also received shamanic counseling over the phone from Williams's wife, Ritzman. Jones eventually ceased treatment and decided to sue Williams and Ritzman for medical malpractice. However, he filed the suit in California. Subsequently, the defendants moved to have the complaint dismissed for lack of personal jurisdiction. How do you think the court decided? [*Jones v. Williams,* 660 F.Supp.2d 1145 (2009).]

10. The plaintiffs, parents of underage children, sued the Advanced Brands and Importing Co., an importer of alcoholic beverages, seeking an injunction prohibiting advertisers from advertising its beers and damages in the form of compensation for the money spent by their children on illegal purchases of beer. The parents argued that the advertising campaign of the defendant causes underage children, like theirs, to illegally purchase the defendant's beer. The trial court dismissed the claim, in part, based on lack of standing, and the parents appealed. Do you think the appellate court found that they had standing? Why or why not? [*Alston v. Advanced Brands and Importing Co.,* 494 F.3d 562 (6th Cir. 2007).]

Looking for more review materials?

The Online Learning Center at **www.mhhe.com/kubasek3e** contains this chapter's "Assignment on the Internet" and also a list of URLs for more information, entitled "On the Internet." Find both of them in the Student Center portion of the OLC, along with quizzes and other helpful materials.

Alternative Dispute Resolution

CHAPTER 4

LEARNING OBJECTIVES

After reading this chapter, you will be able to answer the following questions:

1 What are the primary forms of alternative dispute resolution?

2 What are other ADR methods?

3 What is court-annexed ADR?

4 How is ADR used in international disputes?

CASE OPENER

Mandatory Arbitration at Hooters

Hooters Restaurant in Myrtle Beach, South Carolina, used an alternative dispute resolution program, a program to resolve disputes outside the traditional court system. Employees of Hooters had to sign an "agreement to arbitrate employment-related disputes" to be eligible for raises, transfers, and promotions. Under the agreement, both Hooters and the employee agreed to resolve all disputes arising out of employment, including "any claim of discrimination, sexual harassment, retaliation, or wrongful discharge, whether arising under federal or state law," through arbitration. *Arbitration* is a type of alternative dispute resolution where a neutral third party makes a decision that resolves the dispute.

In a separate policy document not shared with employees until after they had signed the agreement, Hooters set forth the rules and procedures of its arbitration program:

- The employee had to provide notice of the specifics of the claim, but Hooters did not need to file any type of response to these specifics or notify the employee of what kinds of defenses the company planned to raise.
- Only the employee had to provide a list of all fact witnesses and a brief summary of the facts known to each.
- While the employee and Hooters could each choose an arbitrator from a list, and the two arbitrators chosen would then select a third to create the arbitration panel that would hear the dispute, Hooters alone selected the arbitrators on the list.

- Only Hooters had the right to widen the scope of arbitration to include any matter, whereas the employee was limited to the matters raised in his or her notice.
- Only Hooters had the right to record the arbitration.
- Only Hooters had the right to sue to vacate or modify an arbitration award if the arbitration panel exceeded its authority.
- Only Hooters could cancel the agreement to arbitrate or change the arbitration rules.

Annette Phillips had worked as a bartender at the Hooters restaurant in Myrtle Beach for about five years before Hooters adopted its arbitration policy. Ms. Phillips was given a copy of the agreement to arbitrate to review for five days and then sign. Approximately two years later, a Hooters official grabbed and slapped her buttocks. After appealing to her manager for help and being told to "let it go," she quit her job. When she threatened to file a lawsuit for sexual harassment, Hooters filed an action in federal district court to compel arbitration of Phillips's claims.[1]

1. Should Phillips be forced to settle her claim through arbitration?
2. Assume your company's arbitration policy was exactly like Hooters'. Which aspects would you retain, and which might you change?

The Wrap-Up at the end of the chapter will answer these questions using the legal principles discussed in this chapter.

[1] *Hooters of America, Inc. v. Phillips,* 173 F.3d 933 (4th Cir. 1999).

Many companies, like Hooters Restaurant, are finding that using **alternative dispute resolution (ADR)** to resolve their legal problems offers many benefits. The term *ADR* refers to the resolution of legal disputes through methods other than litigation, such as negotiation, mediation, arbitration, summary jury trials, minitrials, neutral case evaluations, and private trials. Organizations often use ADR to resolve disputes involving contracts, insurance, labor, the environment, securities, technology, and international trade.

Some organizations have created internal mediation systems for resolving disputes within the organization. For example, United Parcel Service (UPS) has a five-step dispute resolution program:

1. *Open door:* The employees are encouraged to bring their problems to their supervisors.
2. *Facilitation:* The regional managers ensure that the open-door options are explored.
3. *Peer review:* The employee and the company representative communicate the differing perspectives of the dispute before a panel of three employees (two selected by the complainant and one by the employer), which recommends a nonbinding solution.
4. *Mandatory mediation.*
5. *Optional binding arbitration.*[2]

Why might a business prefer to resolve a dispute through ADR rather than litigation? First, ADR methods are generally faster and cheaper than litigation. According to the National Arbitration Forum, the average time from filing a complaint to receiving a

[2] F. Peter Phillips, "Mediation Is Alternative to Adjudicating Disputes: Internal Employment Dispute Management Programs Are New Trend," *National Law Journal,* June 14, 2004, p. S4.

judgment through litigation is 25 months.[3] Because ADR is faster, it is usually cheaper. According to the American Intellectual Property Law Association, for litigation of patent cases valued in the $1 million to $25 million range, the average cost to each party from the filing of the complaint through the close of discovery is $1.9 million.[4] Through the end of trial, the average cost to each party is $3.5 million. Thus, if a party can resolve a dispute in the early stages of the case through alternative dispute resolution, this may save significant money. Second, a business may wish to avoid the uncertainty associated with a jury decision; many forms of ADR give the participants more control over the resolution of the dispute. Specifically, the parties can select a neutral third party, frequently a person with expertise in the area of the dispute, to help facilitate resolution of the case. Third, a business may wish to avoid setting a precedent through a court decision. Thus, many businesses prefer ADR because of its confidential nature. Fourth, because many forms of ADR are less adversarial than litigation, the parties are able to preserve a business relationship.

Not only are businesses increasingly turning to ADR, but courts are generally quite supportive of ADR methods, which alleviate some of the pressure on the overwhelming court dockets. Congress has recognized the benefits of ADR methods through its enactment of the Alternative Dispute Resolution Act of 1998. This act requires that federal district courts have an ADR program along with a set of rules regarding the program. Congress also passed the Administrative Dispute Resolution Act, which mandates that federal agencies create internal ADR programs. This chapter explains the various ADR methods, as well as the advantages and disadvantages of each. Because ADR is becoming more favored internationally, the latter portion of this chapter discusses its use in other countries.

Primary Forms of Alternative Dispute Resolution

NEGOTIATION

L01 What are the primary forms of alternative dispute resolution?

Many business managers make frequent use of **negotiation,** a bargaining process in which disputing parties interact informally, either with or without lawyers, to attempt to resolve their dispute. A neutral third party, such as a judge or jury, is not involved. Thus, negotiation differs from other methods of dispute resolution because the parties maintain high levels of autonomy. Some courts require that parties negotiate before they bring their dispute to trial.

Before negotiation begins, each side must determine its goals for the negotiation. Moreover, each side must identify the information it is willing to give the other party. A party can enter negotiations with one of two approaches: adversarial or problem solving. In **adversarial negotiation,** each party seeks to maximize its own gain. In contrast, in **problem-solving negotiation,** the parties seek joint gain. Typically, however, to reach a successful settlement, each party must give up something in exchange for getting something from the other side. Because negotiation generally occurs in every case before a more formal dispute resolution method is chosen, negotiation is not necessarily considered an alternative to litigation.

MEDIATION

An extension of negotiation is mediation. In **mediation,** the disputing parties select a neutral party to help facilitate communication and suggest ways for the parties to solve their

[3] National Arbitration Forum, *Business-to-Business Mediation/Arbitration vs. Litigation: What Courts, Statistics, & Public Perceptions Show about How Commercial Mediation and Commercial Arbitration Compare to the Litigation System,* January 2005, p. 3.

[4] AIPLA, *Report of the Economic Survey,* 2005, pp. 1-109–1-110.

dispute. Therefore, the distinguishing feature of mediation is that the parties voluntarily select a neutral third party to help them work together to resolve the dispute. The neutral third party frequently has expertise in the area of the dispute.

Mediation begins when parties select a mediator. Typically, a week before the mediation, each party provides the mediator with a short brief explaining why it should win. Attorneys, along with client representatives, then meet with the mediator. The mediator first assures the parties that the proceedings are confidential, and the parties take turns explaining the dispute to the mediator.

One of the mediator's main goals is to help each party listen carefully to the opposing party's concerns. The mediator asks the parties to identify any additional concerns. This discussion is an attempt to identify underlying circumstances that might have contributed to the dispute. A dispute typically arises after various problematic incidents; mediation permits the parties to address the various incidents, as well as the underlying circumstances leading to those incidents. After concerns have been highlighted, the mediator emphasizes areas of agreement and reframes the disputed points.

The parties then begin generating alternatives or solutions for the disputed points. The mediator helps the parties evaluate the alternatives by comparing the alternatives with the disputed points and interests identified earlier. Finally, the mediator helps the parties create a solution. Because the mediator's role is to facilitate an agreement, the mediator will often need to be persuasive to help the parties concede certain points so that agreement can be reached.

The mediation concludes when an agreement between the parties is reached. The agreement is then usually put into the form of a contract and signed by the parties. The mediator may participate in the drafting of the contract. If one of the parties does not follow the agreement, that party can be sued for breach of contract. However, parties typically abide by the agreement because they helped create it.

If mediation is not successful, the parties can turn to litigation or arbitration to resolve their dispute. However, nothing said during the mediation can be used in another dispute resolution method; the mediation process is confidential.

There are more than 2,500 state and federal rules regarding mediation. Lawmakers have recognized that with such a large number of different laws governing ADR, conducting business in different states is difficult and unduly complicated. In an attempt to create uniformity in mediation procedures, the American Bar Association committee helped draft the Uniform Mediation Act (UMA), which provides for a mediation privilege, which protects communications made during mediation as privileged and requires that mediators identify any conflicts of interest. Thus far, nine states have enacted the UMA.[5]

Mediation at work.

Selecting a Mediator. Mediators are available through nonprofit sources as well as private companies, such as Judicial Arbitration and Mediation Services (JAMS). JAMS has more than 200 full-time neutrals specializing in complex, multiparty business cases.[6] When selecting a mediator, parties should be aware that mediators come from a variety of backgrounds: experts in the area of the dispute, lawyers, judges, psychologists, and sociologists.

[5] "A Few Facts about the Uniform Mediation Act," www.nccusl.org/Update/uniformact_factsheets/uniformacts-fs-uma2001.asp.

[6] "JAMS: The Resolution Experts: Fact Sheet," www.jamsadr.com/press/kit.asp.

Advantages and Disadvantages of Mediation. For disputes in which the parties must maintain a working relationship, mediation is popular because it allows parties to preserve their relationship throughout the dispute. Mediation helps parties work together to reach a consensus. Because parties are encouraged to communicate openly, they usually do not experience bitterness toward the opposing party. Furthermore, each party typically leaves mediation with a better understanding of the opposing party; consequently, this understanding may actually facilitate a better working relationship between the parties. Therefore, the first advantage of mediation is that it helps disputing parties preserve their relationships.

The second advantage to mediation is the potential for creative solutions. The parties are responsible for offering alternatives to solve problems. A party to mediation is often not necessarily looking for a money award. Instead, that party may be trying to find a solution so that both parties can benefit from the resolution of the dispute.

In addition, parties to mediation have a high level of autonomy. Unlike litigation or arbitration, where a neutral third party makes a decision that resolves the dispute, mediation allows parties to take control of the process and resolve the dispute together. The parties generally have more dedication to the agreement because they helped make the decision. Finally, mediation, like other methods of alternative dispute resolution, is less costly, less time-consuming, and less complicated than litigation.

These benefits can obviously be very worthwhile. However, critics of mediation argue that its informal process improperly creates an image of equality between the parties. Consequently, we improperly assume that the resulting agreement between the parties is also equal. However, if one party has more power than the other, the agreement is not necessarily fair or equal. Thus, the image of equality in mediation can be misleading. Furthermore, a party who knows that he or she has no chance of winning a case could enter the mediation process in bad faith, with no intention of making an agreement. Therefore, some people may abuse the mediation process in an attempt to simply draw out the dispute.

To see how ADR relates to resolving conflicts that arise in the workplace, please see the **Connecting to the Core** activity on the text website at www.mhhe.com/kubasek3e.

Uses of Mediation. Mediation is used to resolve collective bargaining disputes. Because workers and employers must continue to work together, mediation typically helps preserve the relationship between the workers and the employers. Under the National Labor Relations Act (NLRA), a union must contact the Federal Mediation and Conciliation Services to attempt to mediate its demands before beginning a strike to achieve higher wages or better working hours.

Similarly, the Equal Employment Opportunity Commission (EEOC) encourages the mediation of employment discrimination claims. The EEOC has a mediation program that uses mediators employed by the EEOC, as well as external mediators trained in mediation and discrimination law. Between 1999 and 2008, the EEOC mediation program held almost 111,000 mediations.[7] Approximately 69 percent of these mediations (over 76,000 charges) were successfully resolved in an average of 85 days.[8]

Mediation is also commonly used in environmental disputes. For example, Japan has created a committee, the Environmental Pollution Disputes Committee, devoted solely to the resolution of environmental disputes. This committee may use mediation or arbitration. Why is mediation particularly useful for environmental disputes? First, mediation allows for creative solutions and compromises, which are often needed in environmental

[7] "History of the EEOC Mediation Program," www.eeoc.gov/mediate/history.html.

[8] Ibid.

disputes. Suppose an endangered species makes its home on land that an entrepreneur recently purchased with the intention of building a bed-and-breakfast facility. Because the Endangered Species Act prohibits landowners from destroying an endangered species' habitat, the entrepreneur cannot build on the land. Mediation can help the landowner come to some kind of compromise to use the land. For example, there might be a way to preserve a portion of the land so that the species may thrive while the landowner can operate the bed-and-breakfast in perhaps a smaller facility.

Second, multiple parties are often involved in environmental disputes. While most dispute resolution methods limit the participation of parties, numerous parties can participate in mediation. Third, those involved in environmental disputes will often become involved in future disputes. Thus, it is important that the parties maintain a good relationship, and mediation helps them do so.

In Germany, mediation has a special use by the parliamentary groups, the Bundestag and the Bundesrat, similar to Congress. These two groups must reach a majority consensus on all pieces of federal legislation in Germany. The Mediation Committee was formed for the purpose of reaching such consensus on bills being debated by the two groups. The Mediation Committee is composed of 16 members from each group. The meetings of the committee are confidential to prevent outside political pressures from barring consensus. Free of unwanted pressures, the committee creates a proposal for the disputed bill. The frequency of the meetings of the Mediation Committee depends on the political atmosphere of the time. Between 1972 and 1976, when rival majorities held the Bundestag and the Bundesrat, the Mediation Committee convened 96 times. Yet between 1983 and 1987, the committee met only six times.

Mediation and Litigation. While mediation is one of the more common alternatives to litigation, a primary purpose of mediation is to keep disputes out of the court system. However, sometimes litigation results from mediation.

ARBITRATION

One of the most frequently used methods of dispute resolution is **arbitration,** the resolution of a dispute by a neutral third party outside the judicial setting. Arbitration is often a voluntary process in that parties typically have a contractual agreement to arbitrate any disputes. This agreement may stipulate how the arbitrator will be selected and how the hearing will be administered.

If a party wants to begin arbitration, it sends the other party a written demand for arbitration. This demand identifies the parties involved, the dispute issue, and the type of relief claimed. The opposing party typically responds to the demand in writing, indicating agreement or disagreement with the claim that the dispute is arbitrable.

Selecting an Arbitrator. If the contract does not specify how the parties will select an arbitrator, they typically use either the Federal Mediation and Conciliation Services (FMCS), a government agency, or the American Arbitration Association (AAA), a private, nonprofit organization. The AAA has more than 7,000 arbitrators and mediators worldwide, over 1,000 of whom are bilingual or multilingual.[9] In 2008, more than 138,477 cases were filed with the AAA.[10]

When a party contacts one of the agencies, the party receives a list of potential arbitrators. This list includes biographical information about the potential arbitrators, and

[9] American Arbitration Association, "Arbitration and Mediation," www.adr.org/arb_med.

[10] American Arbitration Association, "American Arbitration Association Provides Neutral Evaluation for Complex Insurance Disputes" (press release), April 6, 2009.

both parties examine the list and agree on an arbitrator. While most arbitrations are conducted by one arbitrator, panels of three arbitrators are becoming more frequent. Typically, each party chooses one arbitrator, and then those two arbitrators select an additional arbitrator.

Lawyers, professors, or other professionals typically serve as arbitrators. The general qualifications for being an arbitrator are honesty, impartiality, and subject-matter competence. Additionally, arbitrators are expected to follow the Arbitrator's Code of Ethics.

The parties must determine whether they will select one arbitrator or a panel of arbitrators. Selecting a panel may reduce the risk of error or prejudice in the arbitration decision. However, selecting a panel would also increase the costs associated with the arbitration.

Once the parties agree on an arbitrator, the parties and the arbitrator agree on the location and time of the arbitration. The parties may or may not have a discovery period. Additionally, they determine which procedural and substantive rules will be followed during the arbitration.

The Arbitration Hearing. The arbitration hearing is quite similar to a trial. Both parties present their case to a neutral third party; they may represent themselves or use legal counsel. During this presentation, the parties may introduce witnesses and documentation, may cross-examine the witnesses, and may offer closing statements. The fact finder offers a legally binding decision. In these ways, a trial and an arbitration hearing are similar.

However, arbitration is also different in several ways. First, the arbitrator often takes a much more active role in an arbitration hearing, in the sense that the arbitrator is more likely than a judge to question a witness. Second, no official written record of the hearing is kept. Third, the rules of evidence applicable in a trial are typically relaxed in arbitration. Fourth, the arbitrator is not as constrained by precedent as are judges.

The Arbitrator's Award. The arbitrator typically provides a decision within 30 days of the arbitration hearing. The arbitrator's decision is called an *award,* even if no monetary compensation is awarded. The arbitrator's decision differs from a judge's decision in several ways. The arbitrator does not have to state any findings of fact, conclusions of law, or reasons to support the award, and he or she is not as bound by precedent as a judge is. Also, because the arbitrator was hired to resolve a dispute between two parties, the arbitrator is more likely to make a compromise ruling instead of a win-lose ruling. After all, if the parties are satisfied with the ruling, they will probably be more likely to use that arbitrator again to resolve future disputes.

The arbitrator's decision is legally binding. In certain cases, a decision may be appealed to the district court. However, few of these cases are appealed. The courts give extreme deference to arbitrators' decisions. Unless a party can clearly demonstrate that an arbitrator's decision was contrary to law or that there was a defect in the arbitration process, the decision will be upheld. The Federal Arbitration Act (FAA), the federal law enacted to encourage the use of arbitration, explicitly lists four grounds on which an arbitrator's award may be set aside:

1. The award was the result of corruption, fraud, or other undue means.
2. The arbitrator displayed bias or corruption.
3. The arbitrator refused to postpone the hearing despite sufficient cause, refused to hear relevant evidence, or otherwise misbehaved to prejudice the rights of one of the parties.
4. The arbitrator exceeded his or her authority or failed to use that authority to make a mutual, final, and definite award.

The U.S. Supreme Court has held that these four grounds are the exclusive grounds for vacating, modifying, or correcting an arbitrator's award, and parties cannot expand on these grounds in contract.[11] Consequently, in the United States, arbitration decisions are generally upheld. Other countries are taking actions to increase the number of arbitrations, while reducing the need to appeal the arbitration decisions. For example, Brazilian lawmakers reformed several articles in the Brazilian Civil Code to increase the practice of arbitration. These reforms mandate that parties sign an "arbitration commitment" during arbitration proceedings. This commitment states the disputed issue, the venue of the arbitration, and the parties involved. The arbitration commitment renders the outcome of the arbitration comparable to a decision handed down by the judiciary branch. Consequently, parties no longer need to appeal to the judiciary branch after an arbitration hearing.

Legal Principle: **An arbitration award can be set aside for only four reasons: (1) the award resulted from fraud or corruption; (2) the arbitrator is biased or corrupt; (3) the arbitrator misbehaved in a way that prejudiced the rights of a party; and (4) the arbitrator misused his authority in the making of the award.**

BUT WHAT IF . . .

WHAT IF THE FACTS OF THE CASE OPENER WERE DIFFERENT?

Let's say, in the Case Opener, that Hooters and Phillips had settled through arbitration. The arbitrator awarded Hooters a sum of money yet did not give any reasons or cite any laws to support the decision. Is the lack of justification legal? What could Phillips do in response to the decision?

Advantages and Disadvantages of Arbitration. Arbitration may be preferable to litigation for several reasons. First, arbitration is more efficient and less expensive than litigation. For example, on May 11, 2005, Google filed a complaint with the National Arbitration Forum because another party had registered the following Internet domain names: googkle.com, ghoogle.com, gfoogle.com, and gooigle.com.[12] Less than two months later, an arbitration panel concluded that these domain names were confusingly similar to the google.com trademark and that they had been registered in bad faith. Consequently, the panel determined that the googkle.com, ghoogle.com, gfoogle.com, and gooigle.com domain names be transferred to Google.

Second, parties have more control over the process of dispute resolution through arbitration. They choose the arbitrator and determine how formal the process will be. Third, the parties can choose someone to serve as the arbitrator who has expertise in the specific subject matter. Because the arbitrator has expertise, the parties believe that the arbitrator will be able to make a better decision. Fourth, the arbitrator has greater flexibility in decision making than a judge has. Unlike judges, who are bound by precedent, arbitrators generally do not have to offer reasons for their decisions.

However, arbitration is not without its critics. First, arbitration panels are being used more frequently, resulting in a loss of some of the prior advantages of arbitration. For example, using a panel, as opposed to one arbitrator, causes greater scheduling difficulties

[11] *Hall Street Assoc., L.L.C. v. Mattel, Inc.,* 128 S. Ct. 1396 (2008).

[12] *Google Inc. v. Sergey Gridasov,* Claim Number: FA0505000474816, National Arbitration Forum (2005), www.arb-forum.com/domains/decisions/4_7_4816.htm.

because of the number of people involved, consequently negating some of the efficiency associated with arbitration. Along the same lines, paying an arbitration panel is more costly than paying one arbitrator.

Second, because appealing an arbitration award is so difficult, some scholars argue that injustice is more likely to occur. Third, some individuals are concerned that by agreeing to give up one's right to litigate, one may be losing important civil rights or giving up important potential remedies without really understanding which rights are being given up. Especially in an employment context, people may not really want to give up such rights, but they have no choice if they want the job.

Fourth, some scholars are afraid that if more and more employers and institutions turn to mandatory arbitration, it will become more like litigation. An increasing number of people will be forced to arbitrate their disputes; consequently, the efficiency associated with arbitration will start to erode.

Fifth, some scholars are concerned about the privacy associated with arbitration. Companies and employers are able to "hide" their disputes through arbitration. Suppose a credit card company is charging greater amounts of money than its posted finance charge. If an individual arbitrates her claim, other customers might not learn about the problem and therefore won't know to check their credit card statements to ensure that they are being charged the correct amount. If the claim went to court, the publicity surrounding the case would probably better educate people to pay more attention to their statements. Thus, the confidentiality associated with an arbitration proceeding may be harmful in some cases.

If you applied the ethical principle of universalization to arbitration, would you be able to justify its use in spite of these disadvantages? Why might the application of the universalization principle cause one to become hesitant to use arbitration?

BUT WHAT IF . . .

WHAT IF THE FACTS OF THE CASE OPENER WERE DIFFERENT?

Let's say, in the Case Opener, that when Phillips read the arbitration clause in her employment contract, she took issue with it. Phillips went to her manager to talk about her issues not only with the binding arbitration clause presented to her but with arbitration as a method of dispute resolution in general. What are some issues she might raise about the process of arbitration where she might be able to claim some support from scholars who have studied the process?

Methods of Securing Arbitration. Given the benefits associated with arbitration, parties may voluntarily submit their cases to arbitration. The primary method of securing arbitration is through a **binding arbitration clause,** a provision in a contract that mandates that all disputes arising under the contract must be settled by arbitration. The clause also typically states how the arbitrator will be selected. Exhibit 4-1 shows an example of a binding arbitration clause that could be included in almost any business contract.

If a contract does not contain a binding arbitration clause, parties may secure arbitration by entering into a **submission agreement,** a contract providing that a specific dispute will be resolved through arbitration. The submission agreement typically states the following: the nature of the dispute, how the arbitrator will be selected, the place of the arbitration, and any limitations on the arbitrator's authority to remedy the dispute.

If parties have a binding arbitration agreement or have entered into a submission agreement, the parties *must* resolve the dispute through arbitration. Both federal and state courts

Exhibit 4-1
Sample Binding Arbitration Clause

Any controversy, dispute, or claim of whatever nature arising out of, in connection with, or in relation to the interpretation, performance, or breach of this agreement, including any claim based on contract, tort, or statute, shall be resolved, at the request of any party to this agreement, by final and binding arbitration conducted at a location determined by the arbitrator in (City, State) administered by and in accordance with the existing Rules of Practice and Procedure of Judicial Arbitration and Mediation Services (JAMS), Inc., and judgment upon any award rendered by the arbitrator may be entered by any state or federal court having jurisdiction thereof.

must uphold agreements to arbitrate. In 2003, the Ninth Circuit joined all other circuits in concluding that Title VII does not bar compulsory arbitration of claims.[13]

Like the law in general, however, the law governing arbitration agreements is not a fixed set of rules or precedents. Rather, it changes as new and unforeseen issues arise. In many cases, lawmakers and courts do not fully understand the consequences of the laws they enact and the decisions they issue. Thus, although federal and state courts originally upheld all arbitration agreements, more recently they have not upheld certain types of arbitration clauses. For example, courts do not uphold arbitration agreements when federal statutory rights are at issue if the agreement is not "clear and unmistakable."

In Case 4-1, the Supreme Court considered whether contract provisions requiring the arbitration of claims on an individual basis, and prohibiting the joinder of such claims in a class action–type arbitration, would be upheld.

[13] *EEOC v. Luce, Forward, Hamilton, & Scripps,* 345 F.3d 742 (9th Cir. 2003).

CASE 4-1 A.T. & T. MOBILITY LLC v. CONCEPCION
UNITED STATES SUPREME COURT
U.S. 20110 LEXIS 3367 (2011)

When the Concepcions went to AT&T to get a phone, they were confused as to why they were paying money for the phone when it was advertised as being free. They had to pay sales tax on the full normal price of the phone. When the couple sued the company, their lawsuit was added to a class action suit that argued the company had engaged in fraud and false advertising. However, the contract the couple had signed with the company stipulated that the parties must settle through arbitration and a class action suit was off limits. However, the first court rejected the company's motion, saying that the contract could not ban class action suits and thus was unconscionable under California law. The company appealed.

JUSTICE SCALIA: [The contract] "stands as an obstacle to the accomplishment and execution of the full purposes and objectives of Congress."...

a. Section 2 reflects a "liberal federal policy favoring arbitration," and the "fundamental principle that arbitration is a matter of contract." Thus courts must place arbitration agreements on an equal footing with other contracts, and enforce them according to their terms. Section 2's saving clause permits agreements to be invalidated by "generally applicable contract defenses," but not by defenses that apply only to arbitration or derive their meaning from the fact that an agreement to arbitrate is at issue.

b. In *Discover Bank,* the California Supreme Court held that class waivers in consumer arbitration agreements are unconscionable if the agreement is in an adhesion contract, disputes between the parties are likely to involve small amounts of damages, and the party with inferior bargaining power alleges a deliberate scheme to defraud.

c. The Concepcions claim that the Discover Bank rule is a ground that "exist[s] at law or in equity for the revocation of any contract" under FAA §2. When state law prohibits outright the arbitration of a particular type of claim, the FAA displaces the conflicting rule. But the inquiry is more complex when a generally applicable doctrine is alleged to have been applied in a fashion

[continued]

that disfavors or interferes with arbitration. Although §2's saving clause preserves generally applicable contract defenses, it does not suggest an intent to preserve state law rules that stand as an obstacle to the accomplishment of the FAA's objectives. The FAA's overarching purpose is to ensure the enforcement of arbitration agreements according to their terms so as to facilitate informal, streamlined proceedings. Parties may agree to limit the issues subject to arbitration, to arbitrate according to specific rules, and to limit with whom they will arbitrate.

d. Class arbitration, to the extent it is manufactured by Discover Bank rather than consensual, interferes with fundamental attributes of arbitration. The switch from bilateral to class arbitration sacrifices arbitration's informality and makes the process slower, more costly, and more likely to generate procedural morass than final judgment. And class arbitration greatly increases risks to defendants. The absence of multilayered review makes it more likely that errors will go uncorrected. That risk of error may become unacceptable when damages allegedly owed to thousands of claimants are aggregated and decided at once. Arbitration is poorly suited to these higher stakes. In litigation, a defendant may appeal a certification decision and a final judgment, but 9 U. S. C. §10 limits the grounds on which courts can vacate arbitral awards.

REVERSED and REMANDED.

CRITICAL THINKING

Do you think AT&T was being dishonest when it linked its stipulation for arbitration to ensuring a smooth and streamlined resolution process? Are there rival reasons that the company was hiding?

ETHICAL DECISION MAKING

Why would companies favor arbitration over class action lawsuits? Is it fair for a company to ban resolution practices just because they could be more expensive for the company, among other problems?

In 2013, the U.S. Supreme Court continued to strengthen its support for enforcing binding arbitration agreements in the case of *American Express Co. v. Italian Colors Restaurant.* In that case, Justice Scalia wrote that the courts must "rigorously enforce" arbitration agreements in keeping with their terms, even for claims alleging a violation of a federal statute, unless the FAA's mandate has been "overridden by a contrary congressional command." In that case, several merchants had signed a binding arbitration agreement, as well an agreement to not pursue class action arbitration. The retailers subsequently filed a class action arbitration claim against American Express, arguing that it would be too expensive to pursue these claims individually, and so therefore the intent of the statute would be defeated if they were not allowed to pursue class action arbitration. Ultimately, however, the high court agreed with American Express that the parties should be held to the agreements they had signed, even if costs of individually pursuing those claims might be extremely expensive. Thus, with respect to the question of "whether the Federal Arbitration Act permits courts, invoking the Federal substantive law of arbitrability, to invalidate arbitration agreements on the ground that they do not permit class arbitration of a federal law claim," the answer, at least for now, is no.

Another constraint on binding arbitration clauses is that they must be drafted in such a way as to ensure that the courts do not see them as being unconscionable. An *unconscionable contract provision* has been defined as one in which the terms are "manifestly unfair or oppressive and are dictated by a dominant party."[14] The doctrine has been used most often to strike down binding arbitration clauses in consumer and employment contracts.

For example, in the Hooters illustration at the beginning of the chapter, the court refused to uphold the contract because of a number of provisions it found to be unconscionable,

[14] *Farris v. County of Camden,* 61 F. Supp. 2d 307, 341 (D.N.J. 1999).

including requiring that employees provide notice of the specifics of the claim but not making the company file any type of response to these specifics or notify the employee of what kinds of defenses the company planned to raise; making only the employee provide a list of all fact witnesses and a brief summary of the facts known to each; allowing the company to widen the scope of arbitration to include any matter, whereas the employee was limited to the matters raised in his or her notice; giving only the company the right to record the arbitration; allowing only the company to sue to vacate or modify an arbitration award because the arbitration panel exceeded its authority; and allowing only the company to cancel the agreement to arbitrate or change the arbitration rules. Provisions found to be unconscionable in other binding arbitration clauses included provisions that mandated cost sharing for hiring a three-member arbitration panel,[15] limited available damages,[16] adopted unreasonably short time periods for filing claims, and limited the amount of discovery available.[17]

Exhibit 4-2 offers tips on creating a binding arbitration clause.[18]

Common Uses of Arbitration. Arbitration is used in a variety of situations. It is commonly used in labor disputes. And just like the management of Hooters, employers

Exhibit 4-2

Tips for Creating a Binding Arbitration Clause

OVERALL, MAKE SURE THE CLAUSE TREATS BOTH PARTIES FAIRLY

1. *Be clear and unmistakable.* If you wish to arbitrate employment disputes or discrimination claims, make sure that you explicitly state "employment disputes and discrimination claims" in the binding arbitration clause.
2. *The arbitration clause must be bilateral.* If the arbitration clause requires one party only to arbitrate but does not spell out the same requirement for the other party, the clause will probably not be upheld. This agreement would be asking one party to give up its right to have a claim before a jury while the other party retains that right. The courts are concerned about fairness. This bilateral consideration must extend to damages. For example, both parties must be able to get the same damages.
3. *State explicitly which party will pay the arbitrator's fees, and make sure that it will not cost the employee more to arbitrate than it would have cost to litigate.* Courts have refused to enforce arbitration agreements that require that the plaintiff pay the costs of the arbitration. Some courts have refused to enforce agreements requiring that the employee pay a pro rata share of arbitration expenses. Furthermore, a court recently refused to enforce an agreement that did not specify who would pay the arbitrator's fees along with other costs. For ease and assurance that the agreement will be enforced, companies might consider stating that they will pay the costs of the arbitration.
4. *Specify how the arbitrator will be selected.*
5. *Spell out the costs associated with the arbitration.*
6. *Avoid limitations on the remedies available to the parties.* Limitations on punitive damages or attorney fees are likely to be causes for refusing to uphold cases.
7. *Consider other potential parties when determining where to hold the arbitration.* If a credit card company states in its arbitration clause that all disputes will be arbitrated in its state of incorporation, a court might be more likely to not enforce the agreement. Requiring that consumers travel far distances may be perceived as an unfair burden on the consumer.

[15] *Maciejewski v. Alpha Systems Lab Inc.*, 87 Cal. Rptr. 2d 390 (Cal. Ct. App. 1999).

[16] *Johnson v. Circuit City Stores, Inc.*, 203 F.3d 821 (4th Cir. 2000).

[17] *Geiger v. Ryan's Family Steak House and Employment Dispute Services Inc.*, 2001 WL 278120 (S.D. Ind. 2001).

[18] See, e.g., *Shubin v. William Lyon Homes, Inc.*, 84 Cal. App. 4th 1041 (2000), and *Cole v. Burns Internal Security Services*, 105 F.3d 1465 (D.C. Cir. 1997).

are often eager to resolve all employment-related disputes through arbitration. However, before *Gilmer,* discussed in Case 4-2, employers and employees were extremely uncertain as to whether employees could be required to resolve all employment disputes through arbitration, especially those involving discrimination claims.

CASE 4-2 ROBERT GILMER v. INTERSTATE/JOHNSON LANE CORPORATION
UNITED STATES SUPREME COURT
500 U.S. 20 (1991)

Plaintiff Robert Gilmer filed a charge with the Equal Employment Opportunity Commission (EEOC) and sued his employer, defendant Interstate/Johnson Lane Corporation. Gilmer alleged that his employer violated the Age Discrimination in Employment Act (ADEA). When the defendant hired him as a registered securities dealer, Gilmer had signed an agreement to settle by arbitration any disputes arising out of that employment. The employer therefore filed a motion to compel arbitration. The trial court denied the defendant's motion, and the defendant appealed to the circuit court. The circuit court reversed in favor of the defendant, and the plaintiff appealed to the U.S. Supreme Court.

JUSTICE WHITE: The question presented in this case is whether a claim under the Age Discrimination in Employment Act of 1967 (ADEA) can be subjected to compulsory arbitration pursuant to an arbitration agreement in a securities registration application.

. . . It is by now clear that statutory claims may be the subject of an arbitration agreement, enforceable pursuant to the FAA. . . . In [recent] cases we recognized that "by agreeing to arbitrate a statutory claim, a party does not forgo the substantive rights afforded by the statute; it only submits to their resolution in an arbitral, rather than a judicial, forum."

Although all statutory claims may not be appropriate for arbitration, "[h]aving made the bargain to arbitrate, the party should be held to it unless Congress itself has evinced an intention to preclude a waiver of judicial remedies for the statutory rights at issue." The burden is on Gilmer to show that Congress intended to preclude a waiver of a judicial forum for ADEA claims. . . . Throughout such an inquiry, it should be kept in mind that "questions of arbitrability must be addressed with a healthy regard for the federal policy favoring arbitration."

Gilmer concedes that nothing in the text of the ADEA or its legislative history explicitly precludes arbitration. He argues, however, that compulsory arbitration of ADEA claims pursuant to arbitration agreements would be inconsistent with the statutory framework and purposes of the ADEA. Like the Court of Appeals, we disagree.

We also are unpersuaded by the argument that arbitration will undermine the role of the EEOC in enforcing the ADEA. An individual ADEA claimant subject to an arbitration agreement will still be free to file a charge with the EEOC, even though the claimant is not able to institute a private judicial action. Indeed, Gilmer filed a charge with the EEOC in this case.

Gilmer also argues that compulsory arbitration is improper because it deprives claimants of the judicial forum provided for by the ADEA. Congress, however, did not explicitly preclude arbitration or other nonjudicial resolution of claims, even in its recent amendments to the ADEA. Moreover, Gilmer's argument ignores the ADEA's flexible approach to resolution of claims. The EEOC, for example, is directed to pursue "informal methods of conciliation, conference, and persuasion," which suggests that out-of-court dispute resolution, such as arbitration, is consistent with the statutory scheme established by Congress.

In arguing that arbitration is inconsistent with the ADEA, Gilmer also raises a host of challenges to the adequacy of arbitration procedures. Such generalized attacks on arbitration "res[t] on suspicion of arbitration as a method of weakening the protections afforded in the substantive law to would-be complainants," and as such, they are "far out of step with our current strong endorsement of the federal statutes favoring this method of resolving disputes."

It is also argued that arbitration procedures cannot adequately further the purposes of the ADEA because they do not provide for broad equitable relief and class actions. As the court below noted, however, arbitrators do have the power to fashion equitable relief. Indeed, the NYSE rules applicable here do not restrict the types of relief an arbitrator may award, but merely refer to "damages and/or other relief."

AFFIRMED in favor of Defendant, Interstate/Johnson Lane Corp.

[continued]

CRITICAL THINKING

What are the primary facts in *Gilmer v. Interstate/Johnson Lane Corporation?*

What missing facts should be called for when evaluating the judge's reasoning?

What ambiguities are present in the reasoning?

ETHICAL DECISION MAKING

Which group of stakeholders would be most happy with the outcome of this case? Which would be the least happy?

Gilmer upheld the validity of the National Association of Securities Dealers' policy of requiring all employees who execute, buy, or sell orders at brokerages or investment banks to arbitrate all employment disputes as a condition of their employment. Immediately following this case, the use of mandatory arbitration agreements in employment contracts increased significantly.

However, the EEOC became concerned about whether arbitration agreements that had to be accepted as a condition of employment were actually voluntary. In July 1997, the EEOC issued a statement regarding arbitration agreements; the statement indicated that arbitration of discrimination claims as a condition of employment was in conflict with the fundamental principles of employment laws. What values are involved in the EEOC's protection of workers against employers forcing employees into arbitration?

While the EEOC strongly supported agreements to arbitrate once a dispute has arisen, they did not support inclusion of arbitration agreements as an unconditional element of employment. In response to the EEOC's statement, the National Association of Securities Dealers created a policy that allowed employees to choose between entering into a private arbitration agreement with the employer and reserving the right to file suit in a federal or state court for discrimination claims.

Gilmer did not end the questions about whether binding arbitration contracts in the employment area should be enforced. Two subsequent U.S. Supreme Court decisions, however, have clarified the impact of the Federal Arbitration Act on binding arbitration clauses in employment contracts. Perhaps the most significant ruling was that in the 2001 case of *Circuit City v. Saint Clair Adams.*[19] In that case, the plaintiff, an employee of Circuit City, had signed a binding arbitration agreement that had specifically included claims based on discrimination, but two years later he brought an employment discrimination case against his employer in state court. Circuit City filed suit in federal district court to enjoin the state case and compel arbitration. The district court issued the order.

On appeal of the district court's order, the circuit court of appeals held that the Federal Arbitration Act did not apply to employment contracts. This ruling was contrary to all other appellate rulings, and the U.S. Supreme Court heard the case. The high court overruled the circuit court's ruling, clearly setting forth the rule that the Federal Arbitration Act does apply to employment contracts, thereby making binding arbitration agreements in employment contracts enforceable, a decision giving much relief to employers. Many commentators forecast that this decision will lead to an even greater number of employers putting binding arbitration clauses in their employment contracts.

A subsequent decision by the high court, however, was not viewed quite so favorably by many employers. As discussed in Case 4-3, the Court went back to a situation similar to that in *Gilmer,* but in this case, it was not the employee seeking to bring a discrimination claim—it was the EEOC. While this case involved the ADA, the high court stated that the

[19] 532 U.S. 105 (2001).

analysis was applicable to all the civil rights statutes used to eradicate discrimination in the workplace.

Arbitration is also used in medical malpractice cases, environmental disputes, commercial contract disputes, and insurance liability claims. However, no area uses arbitration in as great a percentage of cases as does the employment area.

CASE 4-3 EQUAL EMPLOYMENT OPPORTUNITY COMMISSION v. WAFFLE HOUSE, INC.
UNITED STATES SUPREME COURT
534 U.S. 279 (2002)

All employees of Waffle House had to sign an agreement requiring employment disputes to be settled by binding arbitration. After Eric Baker suffered a seizure and was fired by Waffle House, he filed a discrimination charge with the Equal Employment Opportunity Commission (EEOC) alleging that his discharge violated the Americans with Disabilities Act of 1990 (ADA) under Title VII. The EEOC subsequently filed an enforcement suit, to which Baker was not a party, alleging that Waffle House's employment practices, including Baker's discharge "because of his disability," violated the ADA. The EEOC sought the following: an injunction to "eradicate the effects of [Waffle House's] past and present unlawful employment practices"; specific relief designed to make Baker whole, including back pay, reinstatement, and compensatory damages; and punitive damages.

Waffle House sought to dismiss the EEOC's suit and compel arbitration because of the binding arbitration clause signed by Baker. The District Court denied Waffle House's motion to dismiss. The Fourth Circuit agreed with the District Court that the arbitration agreement between Baker and Waffle House did not foreclose the enforcement action because the EEOC was not a party to the contract, but had independent statutory authority to bring an action to enforce the statute. However, the appellate court held that the EEOC was limited to injunctive relief and precluded from seeking victim-specific relief because the FAA policy favoring enforcement of private arbitration agreements outweighs the EEOC's right to proceed in federal court when it seeks primarily to vindicate private, rather than public, interests. The EEOC appealed to the United States Supreme Court.

JUSTICE STEVENS: In 1972, Congress amended Title VII to authorize the EEOC to bring its own enforcement actions; indeed, we have observed that the 1972 amendments created a system in which the EEOC was intended "to bear the primary burden of litigation. . . ." In 1991, Congress again amended Title VII to allow the recovery of compensatory and punitive damages by a "complaining party." The term includes both private plaintiffs and the EEOC. . . . Thus, these statutes unambiguously authorize the EEOC to obtain the relief that it seeks in its complaint if it can prove its case against respondent.

The Court of Appeals based its decision on its evaluation of the "competing policies" implemented by the ADA and the FAA . . . It recognized that the EEOC never agreed to arbitrate its statutory claim . . . and that the EEOC has "independent statutory authority" to vindicate the public interest, but opined that permitting the EEOC to prosecute Baker's claim in court "would significantly trample" the strong federal policy favoring arbitration, because Baker had agreed to submit his claim to arbitration. To effectuate this policy, the court distinguished between injunctive and victim-specific relief, and held that the EEOC is barred from obtaining the latter, because any public interest served when the EEOC pursues "make whole" relief is outweighed by the policy goals favoring arbitration.

If it were true that the EEOC could prosecute its claim only with Baker's consent, or if its prayer for relief could be dictated by Baker, the court's analysis might be persuasive. But once a charge is filed, the exact opposite is true under the statute—the EEOC is in command of the process. The EEOC has exclusive jurisdiction over the claim for 180 days. During that time, the employee must obtain a right-to-sue letter from the agency before prosecuting the claim. If, however, the EEOC files suit on its own, the employee has no independent cause of action, although the employee may intervene in the EEOC's suit. In fact, the EEOC takes the position that it may pursue a claim on the employee's behalf even after the employee has disavowed any desire to seek relief. The statute makes the EEOC the master of its own case and confers on the agency the authority to evaluate the strength of the public interest at stake. Absent textual support for a contrary view, it is the public agency's province—not that of the court—to determine whether public resources should be committed to the recovery of victim-specific relief. And if the agency makes that determination, the statutory text unambiguously authorizes it to proceed in a judicial forum.

The Court of Appeals . . . simply sought to balance the policy goals of the FAA against the clear language of Title VII and the agreement. While this may be a more coherent approach, it is inconsistent with our recent arbitration cases.

[continued]

The FAA directs courts to place arbitration agreements on equal footing with other contracts, but it "does not require parties to arbitrate when they have not agreed to do so." . . . Here there is no ambiguity. No one asserts that the EEOC is a party to the contract, or that it agreed to arbitrate its claims. It goes without saying that a contract cannot bind a nonparty.

[T]he statutory language is clear; the EEOC has the authority to pursue victim-specific relief regardless of the forum that the employer and employee have chosen to resolve their disputes. Rather than attempt to split the difference, we are persuaded that, pursuant to Title VII and the ADA, whenever the EEOC chooses from among the many charges filed each year to bring an enforcement action in a particular case, the agency may be seeking to vindicate a public interest, not simply provide make-whole relief for the employee, even when it pursues entirely victim-specific relief.

The only issue before this Court is whether the fact that Baker has signed a mandatory arbitration agreement limits the remedies available to the EEOC. The text of the relevant statutes provides a clear answer to that question. They do not authorize the courts to balance the competing policies of the ADA and the FAA, or to second-guess the agency's judgment concerning which of the remedies authorized by law that it shall seek in any given case.

REVERSED in favor of petitioner, EEOC.

CRITICAL THINKING

How are previous rules of law and precedents used in Justice Stevens's reasoning? Is sufficient evidence provided to support the extension of these precedents to this case?

The EEOC filed the claim because of the damages suffered by Baker as a result of Waffle House's actions. Are there potential alternative causes for the damages suffered by Baker?

ETHICAL DECISION MAKING

What is the purpose of the decision that Waffle House made in the facts leading to this case?

Other ADR Methods

L02

What are other ADR methods?

Several other methods of ADR are used less frequently than those discussed above. Some of these methods are similar to negotiation, involving the assistance of a neutral third party. It will be clear after finishing this section that today's manager really does have a variety of options to choose from when a dispute arises. Exhibit 4-3 provides some key questions for a manager to consider when choosing from among this array of dispute resolution options.

MED-ARB

Med-arb is a dispute resolution process in which the parties agree to start out in mediation and, if the mediation is unsuccessful on one or more points, also agree to move on to arbitration. In some cases, the same neutral third party may participate in both the mediation

Exhibit 4-3

Questions to Ask When Selecting a Dispute Resolution Method

If you are a party in a dispute, ask yourself the following questions to determine which dispute resolution method would be best.

1. How concerned am I about keeping costs low?
2. How quickly do I want to resolve the dispute?
3. Do I want to keep the dispute private?
4. Do I want to protect the relationship between the disputing parties?
5. Am I concerned about vindication?
6. Do I want to set a precedent with the resolution of my dispute?

and the arbitration. However, some critics argue that if parties know that the mediator may become the ultimate decision maker, they will be less likely to disclose information during the mediation stage. In contrast, others argue that having the same neutral mediator-arbitrator offers faster resolution because the third party is familiar with the facts of the case.[20]

BUT WHAT IF . . .

WHAT IF THE FACTS OF THE CASE OPENER WERE DIFFERENT?

Let's say that, in the Case Opener, Hooters and Phillips decided to settle through mediation. However, mediation did not work out. Phillips wanted to then try another form of ADR, but Hooters said that only one form of alternative dispute resolution could be used in a dispute. Is Hooters correct? Why or why not?

SUMMARY JURY TRIAL

The summary jury trial began in 1983 when a court in Cleveland attempted to relieve pressure on an overloaded docket. A **summary jury trial** is an abbreviated trial that leads to a nonbinding jury verdict. Two advantages are inherent in this method of dispute resolution. First, it is quick; a summary jury trial lasts only a day. Second, because the jury offers a verdict, both parties get a chance to see how their case would fare before a jury of their peers.

The process of the summary jury trial is similar to that of a regular trial, but there are some important differences. Each judge can set his or her own rules. At the start of the summary trial, the judge advises the jury on the law. Then, each party's lawyer presents an opening statement along with a limited amount of evidence before the jury. Two key differences here are that the lawyers have a limited amount of time for this presentation and there are generally no witnesses. All the evidence is presented by the lawyers. The jury then reaches a verdict. Although this verdict is only advisory, the jury is not aware that the verdict is not binding. After the jury provides the verdict, the parties participate in a settlement conference, where they decide either to accept the jury verdict, to reject the verdict, or to settle on some compromise. Approximately 95 percent of cases are settled at this time. However, if the case is not settled, it will go to a regular trial. At that trial, nothing from the summary jury trial is admissible as evidence.

MINITRIAL

A **minitrial** is similar to arbitration and mediation because it involves a neutral third party. Disputing businesses generally use minitrials. Business representatives of the disputing businesses participate and have settlement authority. Lawyers for each side present their arguments before these representatives and the neutral adviser, who then offers an opinion as to what the verdict would be if the case went to trial. The neutral adviser's opinion, like the jury's verdict in the summary jury trial, is not binding. Next, the business representatives discuss settlement options. If they reach an agreement, they enter into a contract that reflects the terms of the settlement.

A minitrial may be preferred to arbitration for three reasons. First, a minitrial is less costly than arbitration. Second, in the typical minitrial, the business representatives, who presumably understand the complex matters of the dispute better than an outside arbitrator,

[20] See Gerald F. Phillips, "Same Neutral Med-Arb: What Does the Future Hold?" *Dispute Resolution Journal* 60 (May–July 2005), p. 24.

E-COMMERCE AND THE LAW

ADR IN CYBERSPACE

Increasingly, litigants are using arbitration and mediation to resolve disputes in e-commerce cases. The National Arbitration Forum (NAF) is one of the world's most active organizations in the ADR field, and it is helping more and more litigants resolve e-commerce disputes. This chapter has already discussed one example of NAF's work: the conflict involving Google over which domain names rightfully belong to that company. Another example involves a dispute between Sigma Two Group LLC and Avenstar.

Sigma Two Group manufactures simulated firefly lights for residential and consumer use. It sells its goods using the domain name fireflymagic.com. Avenstar, a competitor, registered the domain name magicalfireflies.com and used this site to sell competing goods. Sigma Two Group asked NAF to step in to resolve the domain-name conflict. NAF considered the "magical fireflies" case on the basis of its authority under the Uniform Domain Name Dispute Resolution Policy (UDRP) of the Internet Corporation for Assigned Names and Numbers, known as ICANN. NAF determined that the domain names magicalfireflies.com and fireflymagic.com were confusingly similar. It also ruled that Avenstar had no rights or legitimate interest in the domain name magicalfireflies.com and that, in fact, the company had registered and used the domain name in bad faith. The result was that Avenstar was required to transfer the domain name magicalfireflies.com to Sigma Two.

An important advantage of using the ADR policy outlined in ICANN is that it is faster and cheaper than pursuing litigation based on trademark law. NAF relies on its panel of legal experts, who apply their knowledge of trademark, copyright, and e-commerce law. In ruling on the magical fireflies case, an attorney for Sigma Two pointed out that "[i]t's important for businesses with similar problems to know there is a speedy and relatively inexpensive dispute resolution process that may resolve their problem short of litigating in federal court."

Source: "Christie, Parker & Hale, LLP Wins Favorable Ruling for Client Sigma Two Group LLC in Domain Name Dispute," *Business Wire,* July 9, 2008.

have settlement authority. Third, the procedures of the minitrial can be modified to meet more precisely the needs of the parties. For example, parties may give the neutral adviser the authority to settle the case if the representatives cannot come to a settlement agreement after a certain period of time.

EARLY NEUTRAL CASE EVALUATION

With *early neutral case evaluation,* the parties select a neutral third party and explain their respective positions to this neutral, who then evaluates the strengths and weaknesses of the case. The parties use this evaluation to reach a settlement. Eighteen federal district courts currently use early neutral case evaluation.[21]

PRIVATE TRIALS

Several states now allow **private trials,** an ADR method in which a referee is selected and paid by the disputing parties to offer a legally binding judgment in a dispute. The referees do not have to have any specific training; however, because retired judges often serve as referees, this method is often referred to as "rent-a-judge."

Generally, a private trial occurs after a case has been filed in district or state court. After the parties have engaged in discovery and developed their positions, the parties may choose to participate in a private trial. The parties would typically notify the trial judge overseeing their case that they are participating in a private trial. The disputing parties determine the time and place of the trial and conduct the trial in private to ensure confidentiality. The referee writes a report stating the findings of fact and the conclusions of the law. This report is filed with the trial judge; however, if any party is dissatisfied with the resolution of the case, the party can request a trial before a trial court judge. If this request is denied, the party can appeal the decision of the referee.

[21] Michael H. Diamant et al., "Strategies for Mediation, Arbitration, and Other Forms of Alternative Dispute Resolution," SK074 ALI-ABA 205 (2005), citing the CPR Institute for Dispute Resolution, www.cprador.org.

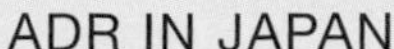

COMPARING THE LAW OF OTHER COUNTRIES

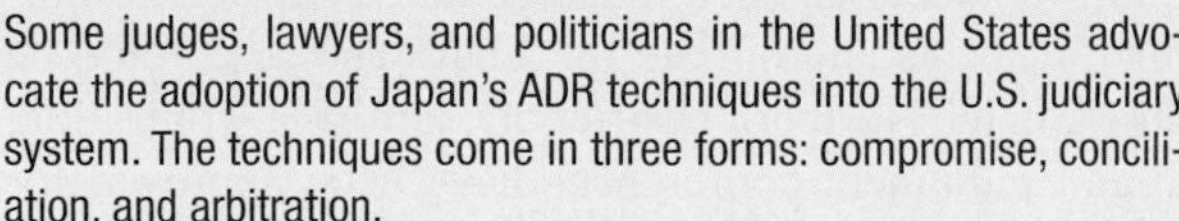

ADR IN JAPAN

Some judges, lawyers, and politicians in the United States advocate the adoption of Japan's ADR techniques into the U.S. judiciary system. The techniques come in three forms: compromise, conciliation, and arbitration.

Compromise (wakai) is defined as a contractual agreement between parties that becomes the basis for a voluntary settlement. Due to the voluntary nature, no compromise is possible if one party does not wish to settle. Compromise may be proposed at three distinct times. First, a simple compromise may be reached before the initiation of a suit. Second, after initiation, but before litigation, the parties may appear in court and present a compromise. Such a compromise is legally binding on both parties. Third, parties may compromise during litigation, which is when most compromises occur. It has been estimated that nearly one-third of all disputes are settled using compromise.

The second ADR technique used in Japan is *conciliation (chotei).* Conciliation, reaching compromise through a third party's intervention, has been a part of Japanese culture for hundreds of years. In modern times, conciliation committees consist of one judge and two appointed members of the community. Acceptance of the committee's recommendation is not necessary, but if the parties wish to concede, the recommendation has the force of a judgment.

The final type of ADR is *arbitration (chusai).* The arbitration procedure in Japan is markedly similar to that in the United States. A two- or three-judge panel reaches a recommendation that is a binding decision.

The success and popularity of all three types of ADR in Japan are attributed to the attitudes of the citizens. People in Japan are reluctant to bring a lawsuit against a fellow citizen. To them, using ADR is a less brash way to resolve a dispute than suing someone outright. Obviously, this attitude is quite distinct from that of the American legal culture.

Recently, private firms have started to offer private jury trials. The jurors are hired by the private firms and are often better educated than typical jurors and have served in multiple private jury trials. Many scholars criticize the typical jury because they believe that such a jury is unable to accurately fulfill its role as fact finder. Thus, offering a better-educated, experienced jury helps assuage criticisms of the jury yet offers the advantage of judgment by a jury of peers.

The private trial has been criticized for several reasons. First, scholars argue that use of the private trial could lead to a two-tiered system of justice. Those who have financial resources can afford a private trial that is much faster than litigation, while those who are lacking resources are forced to use the slower public system. Second, private trials, like arbitration, have been criticized because they allow disputing parties to "hide" the dispute from the public.

Court-Annexed ADR

L03 What is court-annexed ADR?

The 1998 Alternative Dispute Resolution Act required that in all district courts, civil litigants must "consider the use of an alternative dispute resolution process at an appropriate stage in the litigation." However, each district court can decide whether to *require* ADR. Some courts mandate certain forms of ADR, while other courts make ADR completely voluntary. Some simply mandate that all potential litigants be informed about alternatives to litigation. Some courts refer almost all civil cases to ADR, while others refer cases according to subject matter.

Mediation is the primary ADR process used in federal district courts. In the federal system, most of the district courts and almost all the circuit courts have mediation programs using judges or lawyers as mediators. Mediation programs are also under way in more than one-third of the state courts and in many bankruptcy courts. The Fourth Circuit Court of Appeals held at least one mediation conference in 675 cases in fiscal year 2002, 600 cases in fiscal year 2003, and 623 cases in fiscal year 2004.[22]

[22] Robert J. Niemic, *Mediation & Conference Programs in the Federal Courts of Appeals: A Sourcebook for Judges and Lawyers,* 2nd ed. (Ann Arbor: University of Michigan Library, 2006), p. 40.

The district courts vary greatly in terms of which ADR methods are approved. For example, in the Northern District Court of Alabama, each judge conducts an ADR evaluation conference to determine whether a case is appropriate for ADR. The case could be either arbitrated or mediated. In contrast, in the Northern District of California, arbitration, mediation, early neutral evaluation, and settlement conferences have been approved for use, and approximately 43 percent of parties choose mediation.[23] The ADR staff of the Northern District of California also works with parties to structure a nonbinding summary bench or jury trial. The judicial officer may order a nonbinding arbitration to all simple contract and tort cases under $100,000.

Moreover, some courts use ADR to resolve particular disputes within a case. For example, some judges appoint special masters or discovery masters to assist in resolving complex disputes. The special master may mediate discovery disputes within the case and make discovery rulings if the parties cannot resolve the disputes. A judge may also be creative in employing ADR methods to resolve discovery disputes. When the parties could not agree to a location for a deposition, a Florida district court judge created a new form of ADR technique by ordering the parties to "convene at a neutral site agreeable to both parties. If counsel cannot agree on a neutral site, they shall meet on the front steps of the [courthouse]. Each lawyer shall be entitled to be accompanied by one paralegal who shall act as an attendant and witness. At that time and location, counsel shall engage in one (1) game of 'rock, paper, scissors.' The winner of this engagement shall be entitled to select the location for the 30(b)(6) deposition. . . ."[24]

Appellate courts also use ADR techniques. All 13 appellate courts have created programs to help parties resolve issues on appeal. These programs typically encourage mediation. For example, the Tenth Circuit's mediation office may schedule a mandatory settlement conference for any civil case on its docket. Once the conference is scheduled, the parties are required to participate. The purpose of the conference is to explore the possibility of settlement.

Use of ADR in International Disputes

LO4

How is ADR used in international disputes?

Think, for a moment, how difficult litigation would be for an international dispute. Where would the case be heard? Who would decide the case? What kinds of awards would be offered? Because these questions are difficult to answer in the global context, ADR is favored over litigation. For example, the European Union has been considering a directive that would offer mediation as a dispute resolution option for companies doing business in Europe.[25]

Currently, 144 countries belong to the United Nations Convention on the Recognition and Enforcement of Foreign Arbitral Awards, otherwise known as the New York Convention. This treaty ensures that an arbitration award will be enforced by countries that are parties to the treaty. There are three defenses to lack of enforcement of the arbitration award. First, the arbitrator acted outside the scope of her or his authority when making the decision. Second, one of the parties to the agreement did not have the authority to enter into a legal contract. Third, the losing party did not receive notice of the arbitration.

Various organizations offer dispute resolution methods for international companies. These organizations include the American Arbitration Association, the International

[23] Justin Scheck, "The Option to Be Heard," *The Recorder,* January 2, 2007, p. 7.

[24] *Avista Management, Inc. v. Wausau Underwriters Ins. Co.,* Case No. 6:05-cv-1430-Orl-31JGG, District Court for the Middle District of Florida (Order of June 6, 2006).

[25] C. Mark Baker and Aníbal M. Sabater, "Continental Drift: The European Union Tries to Warm Up to ADR, but Its Embrace Is Tentative, at Best," *National Law Journal,* November 27, 2006, p. 14.

CASE NUGGET

PREFERENCE FOR ARBITRATION

Mitsubishi Motors Corp. v. Soler Chrysler-Plymouth
473 U.S. 614 (1985)

Plaintiff Mitsubishi Motors was a joint-venture company formed by a Swiss and a Japanese firm to engage in the worldwide distribution of motor vehicles manufactured in the United States and bearing Mitsubishi and Chrysler trademarks. Defendant Soler Chrysler-Plymouth, a dealership incorporated in Puerto Rico, entered into a distributorship agreement with Mitsubishi that included a binding arbitration clause. Defendant Soler began to have difficulty selling the requisite number of cars, so it asked Mitsubishi to delay shipment of several orders. The defendant refused to accept liability for its failure to sell vehicles under the contract. In accordance with a binding arbitration clause in the distribution agreement, plaintiff Mitsubishi filed an action to compel arbitration. The district court ordered arbitration of all claims, including the defendant's allegations of antitrust violations. The court of appeals reversed in favor of Soler Chrysler-Plymouth. Plaintiff Mitsubishi appealed to the U.S. Supreme Court.

The Supreme Court considered whether an American court could enforce an agreement to resolve antitrust claims by arbitration when that agreement arises from an international transaction. The Supreme Court found that the liberal policy favoring arbitration agreements in the Arbitration Act "creates a body of federal substantive law establishing and regulating the duty to honor an agreement to arbitrate." The Supreme Court concluded that "concerns of international comity, respect for the capacities of foreign and transnational tribunals, and sensitivity to the need of the international commercial system for predictability in the resolution of dispute" required that the Court enforce the parties' agreement.

The Supreme Court decided in favor of Mitsubishi, requiring "this representative of the American business community to honor its bargain" by holding the agreement to arbitrate enforceable.

Chamber of Commerce, the United Nations Commission of International Trade Law, and the London Court of International Arbitration. The number of arbitration cases they hear each year is not insubstantial; the International Chamber of Commerce Commission on Arbitration alone heard 541 arbitration cases in 2000.[26]

The United States favors arbitration for resolution of international disputes. The Mitsubishi case illustrates this U.S. policy (see the Case Nugget). Similarly, given that arbitration in Japan and China has become increasingly popular, the Japan Commercial Arbitration Association (JCAA) and the China International Economic and Trade Arbitration Commission (CIETAC) have revised their rules to encourage the filing of international arbitration cases in Japan.[27]

BUT WHAT IF . . .

WHAT IF THE FACTS OF THE CASE OPENER WERE DIFFERENT?

Let's say, in the Case Opener, that Phillips was an American citizen suing an international branch of Hooters. Which form of resolution would be easiest, litigation or ADR? What are three reasons why one might be favored over the other?

[26] Emmanuel Gaillard, "The New ADR Rules of the International Chamber of Commerce," *New York University Law Journal,* October 10, 2001, p. 3.

[27] Melanie Ries and Bryant Woo, "International Arbitration in Japan & China: A Review of the Revised Arbitration Rules of the JCAA and CIETAC," *Dispute Resolution Journal* 61 (November 2006–January 2007), p. 63.

CASE OPENER WRAP-UP

Mandatory Arbitration at Hooters

The District Court of Virginia denied Hooters' petition to compel arbitration. Hooters appealed to the Fourth Circuit Court of Appeals, which likewise refused to enforce the arbitration agreement. The court held that although an agreement to arbitrate sexual harassment claims is generally enforceable, the employer in this particular case promulgated "egregiously unfair" arbitration rules that called into question its contractual obligation to draft the arbitration rules in good faith.[28] The court found the arbitration rules so one-sided that it concluded, "Their only possible purpose is to undermine the neutrality of the proceeding." Thus, when employers create mandatory arbitration agreements, they should consider the principles of fairness when drafting these agreements.

Although the procedures that turned the arbitration proceeding into a one-sided affair clearly need to be redrafted, Hooters did do some things well. For example, it clearly stipulated in the agreement exactly which claims were going to be arbitrated, thereby giving employees full notice of the rights they were giving up. It also gave employees five days to think about signing the agreement. Had Hooters provided full details of the arbitration procedures, employees would have had time to review and consider the contents of the agreement.

KEY TERMS

adversarial negotiation 69
alternative dispute resolution (ADR) 68
arbitration 72
binding arbitration clause 75
med-arb 82
mediation 69
minitrial 83
negotiation 69
private trial 84
problem-solving negotiation 69
submission agreement 75
summary jury trial 83

SUMMARY OF KEY TOPICS

Primary Forms of Alternative Dispute Resolution

Negotiation: An informal bargaining process, with or without lawyers, to try to solve a dispute.

Arbitration: An ADR method in which a neutral third party (known as the arbitrator) hears both parties' cases and renders a binding decision.

Summary jury trial: An abbreviated trial that leads to a nonbinding jury verdict.

Minitrial: An ADR method in which a neutral adviser oversees presentation of the dispute, with the settlement authority residing with the senior executives of the disputing corporations.

Other ADR Methods

Early neutral case evaluation: An ADR method in which parties independently explain their positions to a neutral third party who evaluates the strengths and weaknesses of the case. This evaluation guides them in their settlement.

Private trial: A trial in which the disputing parties select and pay a referee to provide a legally binding judgment in a dispute.

[28] *Hooters of America, Inc. v. Phillips,* 173 F.3d 933 (4th Cir.1999).

Court-Annexed ADR

Programs whereby courts encourage or mandate that parties use some form of ADR before they bring a dispute to trial.

Use of ADR in International Disputes

ADR is favored in international disputes.

POINT / COUNTERPOINT

Binding arbitration clauses are often included in consumer contracts and even in consumer bills. For example, if you open a credit card account, the terms and conditions of the credit application will likely require that you submit any dispute you have to binding arbitration.

Should Companies Be Permitted to Include Binding Arbitration Clauses in Consumer Contracts?

YES	NO
Arbitration is a much faster way to resolve a likely small dispute. Through the discovery process, a defendant could draw out a case for two to three years before the case would actually go to trial. Thus, the consumer benefits from the binding arbitration clause because it forces the defendant to resolve the dispute quickly. According to a recent study by Ernst & Young, 55 percent of consumer arbitrations were resolved in the consumer's favor.* Another study suggested that 93 percent of people who participated in arbitration thought that they were treated fairly.† Consumers receive fair and fast treatment through mandatory arbitration. Consumers have a choice as to whether to purchase a good or service, and in some cases the purchase may include a requirement on how disputes will be resolved. If a consumer is opposed to a mandatory arbitration clause, the consumer can purchase the good or service from another provider. In conclusion, companies should be permitted to include binding arbitration clauses in their consumer contracts.	Arbitration may require that the consumer pay more upfront costs to begin the dispute resolution process. For example, the consumer may have to pay for the costs of the arbitrator. To file a complaint, a consumer has to pay filing fees only, which cost around $150. To file a claim through the American Arbitration Association, a consumer has to pay between $500 and $1,000, and the consumer is required to advance the arbitrator's fees. Many consumers are not likely to read all the fine print when applying for a credit card or purchasing a service. A consumer has no bargaining power to remove a mandatory arbitration clause from the contract; consequently, the consumer has no choice. It is unfair to force a consumer to submit a dispute to arbitration when she or he has no power to bargain regarding that aspect of the sales or service contract. Finally, because arbitration is secret, a company can "hide" its disputes from the general public. The public exposure associated with lawsuits encourages companies to better respond to and resolve disputes. In conclusion, consumers are harmed more than helped by binding arbitration clauses in consumer contracts.

* Ernst & Young, "Outcomes of Arbitration: An Empirical Study of Consumer Lending Cases," www.adrforum.com/rcontrol/documents/ResearchStudiesAndStatistics/2005ErnstAndYoung.pdf.

† "Report to the Securities and Exchange Commission Regarding Arbitrator Conflict Disclosure Requirements in NASD and NYSE Securities Arbitrations," www.nyse.com/pdfs/arbconflict.pdf.

QUESTIONS & PROBLEMS

1. What are the advantages and disadvantages of ADR?
2. When will a court overturn an arbitrator's decision?
3. What type of ADR is preferred for resolving international disputes?
4. Unity Communications Corp. resold phone services provided by Cingular pursuant to a reseller agreement that included an arbitration clause. Unity sued Cingular in federal district court, alleging breach of contract. The parties engaged in pretrial activity, and Cingular filed a motion for summary judgment regarding a letter agreement between Unity and Cingular. The district court denied the motion for summary judgment, and on appeal the Fifth Circuit affirmed the district court's decision. On remand before the district court, Cingular moved the court to compel arbitration. The district court ruled that Cingular had waived its right to arbitration by participating in the litigation and waiting three years to raise the arbitration argument. Do you think the appellate court agreed? Why? [*Unity Communications Corp. v. Cingular Wireless,* 256 Fed. App. 679 (5th Cir. 2007).]
5. General Dynamics sent out a companywide e-mail to its employees announcing a policy requiring arbitration of employment disputes. Some time after the e-mail was sent, an employee filed a lawsuit arguing that he was fired because of a disability. General Dynamics argued that the employee should be required to arbitrate his claim under the new company policy. Do you think the court required that the employee arbitrate his claim? Why? [*Campbell v. General Dynamics* (D. Mass. 2004).]
6. The plaintiffs, members of the International Brotherhood of Teamsters, Local 30, sued the Turnpike Commission, arguing that the commission was violating the Fair Labor Standards Act (FLSA) by imposing a fluctuating-hours method of compensation on the plaintiffs. The grievance first went to mediation; when this process was unsuccessful, the lawsuit was filed. The plaintiffs sought to introduce evidence of statements made by one of the commission's attorneys during depositions taken for and introduced in the mediation. They sought to introduce the evidence on the grounds that it was necessary for them to establish their retaliation claim under the FLSA. The defendants argued that the statements, which were made for the purpose of furthering the mediation process, should not be admissible in court. How do you believe the court ruled in this case? Why? [*Patsy B. Sheldone et al. v. Pennsylvania Turnpike Commission,* 48 Fed. R. Serv. 3d 943 (2001).]
7. In 2007, an employee of Citigroup named Anthony Orefice was let go from the company and given a severance package of $900,000. The award was filed with the Financial Industry Regulatory Authority (FINRA), a Wall Street organization that mediates arbitration issues. In January 2008, Citigroup paid Orefice $900,000. However, Orefice also received a second payment of $900,000 from the company. To support the payments, Citigroup created two separate and enforceable contracts for the release of both payments to the former executive. Yet Citigroup went to FINRA claiming that one payment was in error and that, as part of the severance package, Orefice was supposed to receive only one payment of $900,000. Thus, the company wanted $900,000 back from Orefice. How do you think FINRA decided? Should the contracts be upheld in light of the initial severance agreement? [FINRA Arbitration 09-02278 (July 1, 2011).]
8. When Matthew Shankle was hired by B-G Maintenance Management, he signed an employment agreement that included a binding arbitration clause. This clause stated that any disputes between Shankle and B-G were to be resolved through arbitration and that Shankle would "be responsible for one-half of the arbitrator's fees, and the company is responsible for the remaining half." Shankle was fired, and he brought suit against B-G for employment discrimination. B-G moved to mandate arbitration. The arbitrator required a $6,000 deposit. The district court ruled in Shankle's favor, refusing to compel arbitration because the fee-splitting requirement was held to be unenforceable. B-G appealed. Did the appellate court agree with Shankle? Why or why not? [*Shankle v. B-G Maintenance Management of Colorado,* 163 F.3d 1230 (10th Cir. 1999).]
9. When Chuck Lorre, the producer of *Two and a Half Men,* and Warner Brothers fired Charlie Sheen

from the popular sitcom, Sheen set out to sue both parties in court. However, Sheen petitioned for a temporary restraining order, which would have blocked the issue from being settled through arbitration rather than in court. Warner Brothers fought to send the matter to an arbitrator, stating that matters between cast or crew and production must be settled through arbitration according to contractual agreements. Sheen and his lawyer were denied a temporary restraining order in one court because the court in which he was suing Lorre and Warner must also be the same court in which he can be granted a restraining order. Sheen and his lawyer subsequently planned to file for the order in the correct court. Alternatively, JAMS, the mediation firm, said it would put an arbitrator on Sheen's case within days if he refused to choose one. How do you think the court decided? Did the court approve Sheen's request for a temporary restraining order so that he might avoid arbitration? [Los Angeles Superior Court Case No. SC111794 (March 10, 2011).]

10. After Joel Varela died due to a work-related accident, his spouse and children filed a wrongful death action against his employee, Igloo Products Corp. Igloo filed a motion to compel arbitration under the terms of the arbitration agreement that Varela had signed in connection with his participation in an employee injury benefit plan. The trial court denied the motion to compel arbitration. What do you think happened on appeal? Why? [*In re Igloo Products Corp.,* 238 S.W.3d 574 (Tex. App. 2007).]

Looking for more review material?

The Online Learning Center at **www.mhhe.com/kubasek3e** contains this chapter's "Assignment on the Internet" and also a list of URLs for more information, entitled "On the Internet." Find both of them in the Student Center portion of the OLC, along with quizzes and other helpful materials.

CHAPTER

5 Constitutional Principles

LEARNING OBJECTIVES

After reading this chapter, you will be able to answer the following questions:

1 What is federalism?

2 How does the U.S. government's system of checks and balances operate?

3 What effects does the commerce clause have on the government's regulation of business?

4 How does the Bill of Rights protect the citizens of the United States?

CASE OPENER

The Constitutionality of the Affordable Care Act

In 2010, in an attempt to increase the number of Americans covered by health insurance and reduce the cost of health care, Congress passed the Patient Protection and Affordable Care Act. A key provision of the act was the "individual mandate," a provision requiring that most Americans obtain "minimum essential" health insurance. By 2014, those not exempt or covered by insurance provided by their employer or a government program would have to buy insurance from a private insurer, or they would be assessed a "shared responsibility payment" by the Internal Revenue Service. This penalty would be assessed and collected in the same manner as any other tax penalty.

Twenty-six states, several individuals, and the National Federation of Independent Business brought an action challenging the constitutionality of the individual mandate, among other provisions. The 11th Circuit Court of Appeals upheld the other challenged provisions of the act but found that Congress lacked the authority to pass the individual mandate. The appellate court went on to hold that the individual mandate was severable from the rest of the act, despite the argument that the framework of the act was dependent on the individual mandate, and so upheld the rest of the act.[1]

[1] Florida ex,rel Atty. Gen, v. U.S. Dept. of Health and Human Services, 648 F.3d. 1235 (2011)

1. Is the individual mandate severable from the rest of the act, or is it integral to the effectiveness of the law, thereby requiring that the entire law be struck down if this provision is unconstitutional?
2. Does Congress have the authority to enact the individual mandate under either the commerce clause or the taxing clause?

The Wrap-Up at the end of the chapter will answer these questions.

The U.S. Constitution sets forth the framework of our nation's government; it establishes a system of government that divides power between the federal government and the states. This system of government provides the focus for this chapter.

In this chapter we examine the constitutional provisions that affect business. Then we turn our focus to the primary source of the federal government's authority to regulate business: the commerce clause. We next examine the federal government's authority to tax and spend. Finally, in the last part of the chapter, we focus on how several amendments to the Constitution affect business.

The U.S. Constitution

LO1 What is federalism?

The U.S. Constitution establishes a system of government based on the principle of **federalism**, according to which the authority to govern is divided between federal and state governments. According to the Tenth Amendment to the Constitution, all powers that the Constitution neither gives exclusively to the federal government nor takes from the states are reserved for the states. Because the federal government has only those powers granted to it by the Constitution, federal legislation that affects business must be based on an expressed constitutional grant of authority.

LO2 How does the U.S. government's system of checks and balances operate?

In addition to allocating authority between state and federal governments, the Constitution allocates the power of the federal government among the three branches of government. The first three articles of the Constitution establish three independent branches of the federal government: the legislative, executive, and judicial branches. The Constitution ensures that each branch maintains a separate sphere of power to prevent any one branch from obtaining undue power and monopolizing control of government.

The Constitution also establishes a system of *checks and balances.* Each branch's powers keep the other branches from dominating the government. For example, Congress, the legislative or lawmaking branch, has the power to enact legislation, but the president can veto a law that Congress passes. The legislature, however, can overturn a presidential veto with a two-thirds vote of the members of Congress. And if Congress passes a bill and the president signs it, the judiciary can strike it down as unconstitutional. Exhibit 5-1 illustrates the system of checks and balances in more detail.

To see how the system of checks and balances relates to the checks and balances taught in internal controls in accounting, please see the **Connecting to the Core** activity on the text website at www.mhhe.com/kubasek3e.

Legal Principle: Under the current system of checks and balances, each branch of government has its own distinct responsibilities, and each one has its powers checked by the other two branches to ensure that no branch has enough unchecked power to take control of the government.

JUDICIAL REVIEW

Although the Constitution does not explicitly allow courts to review legislative and executive actions to determine whether they are constitutional, early common law established

Exhibit 5-1

The System of Checks and Balances

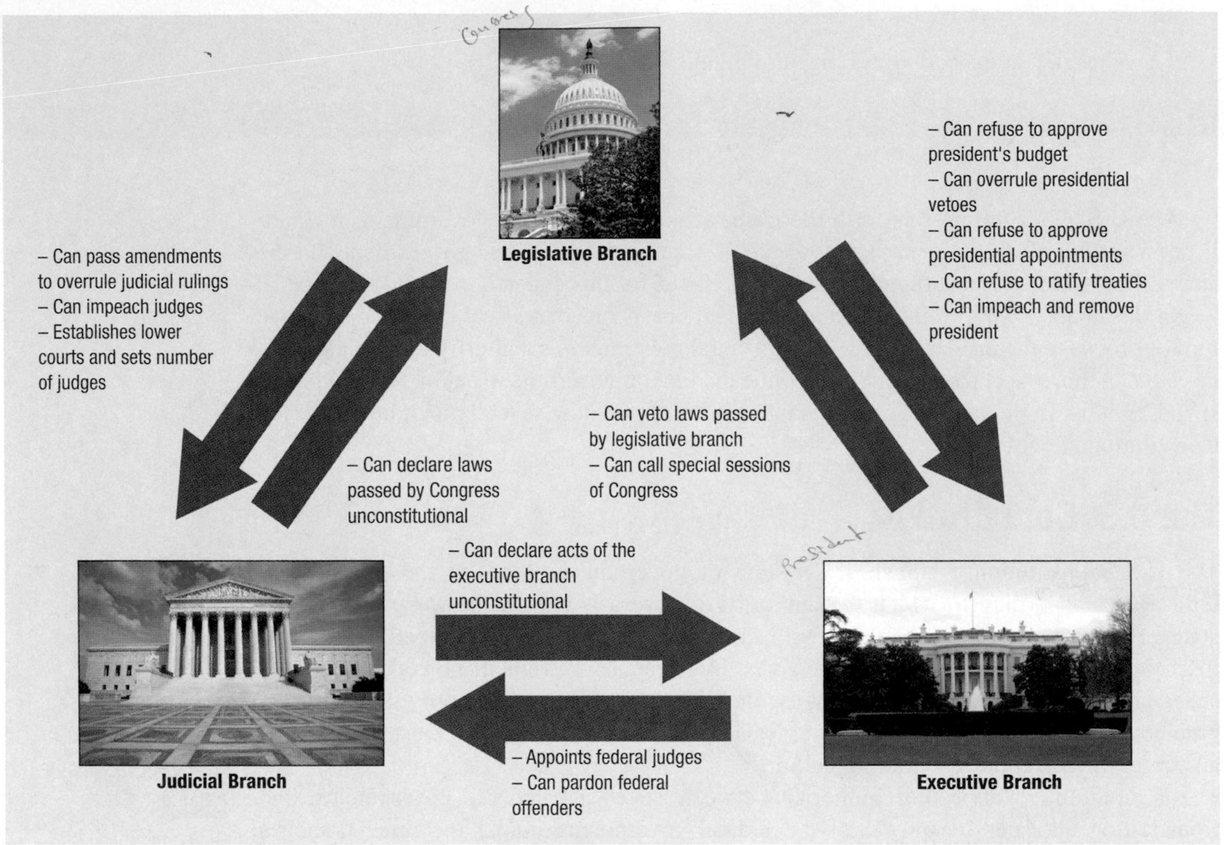

this process, which is known as **judicial review.** In the landmark 1803 U.S. Supreme Court case *Marbury v. Madison,*[2] Chief Justice John Marshall wrote for the majority:

> [I]f a law be in opposition to the constitution; if both the law and the constitution apply to a particular case, so that the court must either decide that case [conforms] to the law, disregarding the constitution; or [conforms] to the constitution, disregarding the law; the court must determine which of these conflicting rules governs the case. This is of the very essence of judicial duty.

Judicial review also allows courts to review the constitutionality of lower courts' decisions. Notice that in the Case Opener, the high court is being asked to review the constitutionality of a major piece of legislation passed by Congress.

The Supremacy Clause and Federal Preemption

The **supremacy clause,** located in Article VI of the Constitution, provides that the Constitution, laws, and treaties of the United States constitute the supreme law of the land, "any Thing in the Constitution or Laws of any State to the Contrary notwithstanding."

[2] 5 U.S. 137 (1803).

Any state or local law that directly conflicts with the Constitution, federal laws, or treaties is void. Federal laws include rules passed by federal administrative agencies. For example, the Federal Aviation Administration has banned the use of cell phones on airplanes. If a Missouri law permitted cell phone usage on airplanes, it would be unconstitutional according to the supremacy clause. In this case we say that the federal law has preempted the state law.

In some areas, the state and federal governments have **concurrent authority;** that is, both governments have the power to regulate the same subject matter. In such cases, the states may regulate in the area as long as a person's compliance with the state regulation would not cause him or her to be in violation of a federal regulation. For example, Congress has established a number of environmental standards, but some states have passed even more protective standards.

Sometimes, however, in areas where the state and federal governments have concurrent authority, the federal government can decide to regulate that area exclusively. In such a situation, according to the doctrine of **federal preemption,** the state law is unconstitutional. This form of preemption is sometimes referred to as *field preemption.* To determine whether Congress intended to provide exclusive regulation, courts look to the language of the statute and transcripts of congressional hearings.

The two forms of preemption we previously described are often referred to as implied preemption. Congress can also engage in express preemption by including a provision in a statute expressing this intention.

The Commerce Clause

The primary source of authority for federal regulation of business is the **commerce clause,** located in Article I, Section 8, of the Constitution. This clause states that the U.S. Congress has the power to "regulate Commerce with foreign Nations, and among the several States, and with the Indian Tribes." This allocation of authority simultaneously empowers the federal government and restricts the power of state governments.

LO3 What effects does the commerce clause have on the government's regulation of business?

THE COMMERCE CLAUSE AS A SOURCE OF AUTHORITY FOR THE FEDERAL GOVERNMENT

Today, most federal regulations are exercises of congressional authority under the commerce clause. As long as a law affects commerce among the states, or interstate commerce, in some way, the regulation is generally constitutional. The phrase "among the several states" has been subject to changing interpretations throughout U.S. history. Prior to the 1930s, courts interpreted the clause very strictly, requiring that the regulated activity actually involve trade between states. This interpretation limited federal regulation of business.

In the 1930s, however, the Supreme Court began to interpret the commerce clause more broadly. The 1937 case *NLRB v. Jones & Laughlin Steel Corp.* was a turning point in the Supreme Court's interpretation of the commerce clause. In that case, the Court ruled that Congress could regulate labor relations at a manufacturing plant because a work stoppage at the plant would seriously affect interstate commerce. The Court stated, "Although activities may be intrastate in character when separately considered, if they have such a close and substantial relationship to interstate commerce that their control is essential or appropriate to protect that commerce from burdens or obstructions, Congress cannot be denied the power to exercise that control."[3] Since that case, Congress has regulated a broad

[3] *NLRB v. Jones & Laughlin Steel Corp.*, 301 U.S. 1 (1937).

range of business activities according to the commerce clause, through legislation such as the Federal Mine Safety and Health Act, which sets standards for safety in coal mines; the Americans with Disabilities Act, which prohibits firms from discriminating against employees and potential employees who have disabilities; and the Consumer Protection Act, which criminalizes certain loan-sharking activities. Although businesses have challenged statutes like these as being beyond the scope of congressional power, courts have upheld the statutes as valid exercises of congressional authority according to the commerce clause.[4]

The 1995 case *United States v. Lopez,*[5] however, marked another significant change in the Supreme Court's interpretation of the commerce clause. In *Lopez,* the Court ruled that Congress had exceeded its commerce clause authority when it passed the Gun-Free School Zone Act, a law banning the possession of guns within 1,000 feet of any school. In its ruling, the Court said that Congress could not regulate in an area that had "nothing to do with commerce, or any sort of economic enterprise."

Case 5-1 illustrates how the Supreme Court applies the commerce clause to determine the constitutionality of congressional regulations.

Even with cases like Lopez and *Brzonkala v. Morrison* limiting the scope of activities Congress can regulate under the commerce clause, many commentators thought that the Affordable Care Act's individual mandate would be seen as a regulation affecting

[4] See *U.S. v. Lake,* 985 F.2d 265 (1995); *International House of Pancakes v. Theodore Pinnock,* 844 F. Supp. 574 (1993); and *Perez v. United States,* 402 U.S. 146 (1971).

[5] 514 U.S. 549 (1995).

CASE 5-1 CHRISTY BRZONKALA v. ANTONIO J. MORRISON ET AL.
UNITED STATES SUPREME COURT
120 S. CT. 1740 (2000)

Petitioner Christy Brzonkala met respondents Antonio Morrison and James Crawford at a campus party at Virginia Polytechnic Institute (Virginia Tech), where they were all students. At the party, the respondents allegedly assaulted and raped her. According to Brzonkala, during the months following the rape, Morrison made boasting, debasing, and vulgar remarks in the dormitory's dining room about what he would do to women. Brzonkala alleged she become severely emotionally disturbed and depressed as a result of this attack and Morrison's subsequent behavior. Consequently, she had to seek assistance from a university psychiatrist, who prescribed antidepressant medication. Shortly thereafter, she stopped attending classes and withdrew from the university.

Brzonkala filed a complaint against the respondents under the university's Sexual Assault Policy. Morrison was initially found guilty and suspended for two semesters, but his punishment was ultimately set aside.

She then sued Morrison, Crawford, and Virginia Tech in federal court, alleging, among other claims, that Morrison's and Crawford's attack violated the Violence Against Women Act. The respondents moved to dismiss the complaint on the grounds that it failed to state a claim and that the Act's (§ 13981's) civil remedy was unconstitutional.

The District Court found that Brzonkala's complaint stated a claim against the respondents under § 13981, but dismissed the complaint because it concluded that Congress lacked constitutional authority to enact § 13981's civil remedy. The United States Court of Appeals, by a divided vote, affirmed the District Court's conclusion. Brzonkala appealed.

CHIEF JUSTICE REHNQUIST: . . . Section 13981 was part of the Violence Against Women Act of 1994. . . . It states that "[a]ll persons within the United States shall have the right to be free from crimes of violence motivated by gender." To enforce that right, subsection (c) declares:

"A person . . . who commits a crime of violence motivated by gender and thus deprives another of the right declared in subsection (b) of this section shall be liable to the party injured, in an action for the recovery of compensatory and punitive damages, injunctive and declaratory relief, and such other relief as a court may deem appropriate." . . .

Every law enacted by Congress must be based on one or more of its powers enumerated in the Constitution. . . . [W]e turn to the question whether § 13981 falls within Congress' power under Article I, § 8, of the Constitution. Brzonkala and the United States rely upon the third clause of the Article, which gives Congress power "[t]o regulate Commerce with foreign Nations, and among the several States, and with the Indian Tribes."

As we discussed at length in Lopez, our interpretation of the Commerce Clause has changed as our Nation has developed. . . . Lopez emphasized, however, that even under our modern, expansive interpretation of the Commerce Clause, Congress' regulatory authority is not without effective bounds.

. . . [M]odern Commerce Clause jurisprudence has "identified three broad categories of activity that Congress may regulate under its commerce power." . . . "First, Congress may regulate the use of the channels of interstate commerce." . . . "Second, Congress is empowered to regulate and protect the instrumentalities of interstate commerce, or persons or things in interstate commerce, even though the threat may come only from intrastate activities." . . . "Finally, Congress' commerce authority includes the power to regulate those activities having a substantial relation to interstate commerce, . . . i.e., those activities that substantially affect interstate commerce."

Petitioners . . . seek to sustain § 13981 as a regulation of activity that substantially affects interstate commerce. Given § 13981's focus on gender-motivated violence wherever it occurs . . . we agree that this is the proper inquiry.

Since Lopez most recently canvassed and clarified our case law governing this third category of Commerce Clause regulation, it provides the proper framework for conducting the required analysis of § 13981. In Lopez, we held that the Gun-Free School Zones Act of 1990, which made it a federal crime to knowingly possess a firearm in a school zone, exceeded Congress' authority under the Commerce Clause. Several significant considerations contributed to our decision.

First, we observed that § 922(q) was "a criminal statute that by its terms has nothing to do with 'commerce' or any sort of economic enterprise, however broadly one might define those terms." . . . [T]he pattern of analysis is clear. "Where economic activity substantially affects interstate commerce, legislation regulating that activity will be sustained."

Both petitioners and Justice Souter's dissent downplay the role that the economic nature of the regulated activity plays in our Commerce Clause analysis. But a fair reading of Lopez shows that the noneconomic, criminal nature of the conduct at issue was central to our decision in that case. . . . Lopez's review of Commerce Clause case law demonstrates that in those cases where we have sustained federal regulation of intrastate activity based upon the activity's substantial effects on interstate commerce, the activity in question has been some sort of economic endeavor.

The second consideration that we found important in analyzing § 922(q) was that

> the statute contained "no express jurisdictional element which might limit its reach to a discrete set of firearm possessions that additionally have an explicit connection with or effect on interstate commerce." Such a jurisdictional element may establish that the enactment is in pursuance of Congress' regulation of interstate commerce.

Third, we noted that neither § 922(q) "nor its legislative history contain[s] express congressional findings regarding the effects upon interstate commerce of gun possession in a school zone." . . . While "Congress normally is not required to make formal findings as to the substantial burdens that an activity has on interstate commerce," the existence of such findings may "enable us to evaluate the legislative judgment that the activity in question substantially affect[s] interstate commerce, even though no such substantial effect [is] visible to the naked eye."

Finally, our decision in Lopez rested in part on the fact that the link between gun possession and a substantial effect on interstate commerce was attenuated. The United States argued that the possession of guns may lead to violent crime, and that violent crime "can be expected to affect the functioning of the national economy in two ways. First, the costs of violent crime are substantial, and, through the mechanism of insurance, those costs are spread throughout the population. Second, violent crime reduces the willingness of individuals to travel to areas within the country that are perceived to be unsafe." The Government also argued that the presence of guns at schools poses a threat to the educational process, which in turn threatens to produce a less efficient and productive workforce, which will negatively affect national productivity and thus interstate commerce.

We rejected these "costs of crime" and "national productivity" arguments because they would permit Congress to "regulate not only all violent crime, but all activities that might lead to violent crime, regardless of how tenuously they relate to interstate commerce." We noted that, under this but-for reasoning: "Congress could regulate any activity that it found was related to the economic productivity of individual citizens: family law (including marriage, divorce, and child custody), for example. Under the[se] theories . . ., it is difficult to perceive any limitation on federal power, even in areas such as criminal law enforcement or education where States historically have been sovereign. Thus, if we were to accept the Government's arguments, we are hard pressed to posit any activity by an individual that Congress is without power to regulate."

With these principles underlying our Commerce Clause jurisprudence as reference points, the proper resolution of the present cases is clear. Gender-motivated crimes of violence are not, in any sense of the phrase, economic activity. While we need not adopt a categorical rule against aggregating the effects of any noneconomic activity in order to decide these cases, thus far in our Nation's history our cases have upheld Commerce Clause regulation of intrastate activity only where that activity is economic in nature.

Like the Gun-Free School Zones Act at issue in Lopez, § 13981 contains no jurisdictional element establishing that the federal cause of action is in pursuance of Congress' power to regulate interstate commerce.

In contrast with the lack of congressional findings that we faced in Lopez, § 13981 is supported by numerous findings regarding the serious impact that gender-motivated violence has on victims and their families. . . . But the existence of congressional findings is not sufficient, by itself, to sustain the constitutionality of Commerce Clause legislation. As we stated in Lopez, "[S]imply because Congress may conclude that a particular activity substantially affects interstate commerce does not necessarily make it so." . . . Rather, "[w]hether particular operations affect interstate commerce sufficiently to come under the constitutional power of Congress to regulate them is ultimately a judicial rather than a legislative question, and can be settled finally only by this Court."

In these cases, Congress' findings are substantially weakened by the fact that they rely so heavily on a method of reasoning that we have already rejected as unworkable if we are to maintain the Constitution's enumeration of powers. Congress found that gender-motivated violence affects interstate commerce "by deterring potential victims from traveling interstate, from engaging in employment in interstate business, and from transacting with business, and in places involved in interstate commerce; . . . by diminishing national productivity, increasing medical and other costs, and decreasing the supply of and the demand for interstate products." Given these findings and petitioners' arguments, the concern that we expressed in Lopez that Congress might use the Commerce Clause to completely obliterate the Constitution's distinction between national and local authority seems well founded.

The reasoning that petitioners advance seeks to follow the but-for causal chain from the initial occurrence of violent crime (the suppression of which has always been the prime object of the States' police power) to every attenuated effect upon interstate commerce. If accepted, petitioners' reasoning would allow Congress to regulate any crime as long as the nationwide, aggregated impact of that crime has substantial effects on employment, production, transit, or consumption. Indeed, if Congress may regulate gender-motivated violence, it would be able to regulate murder or any other type of violence since gender-motivated violence, as a subset of all violent crime, is certain to have lesser economic impacts than the larger class of which it is a part.

We accordingly reject the argument that Congress may regulate noneconomic, violent criminal conduct based solely on that conduct's aggregate effect on interstate commerce. The Constitution requires a distinction between what is truly national and what is truly local. . . . In recognizing this fact we preserve one of the few principles that has been consistent since the Clause was adopted. The regulation and punishment of intrastate violence that is not directed at the instrumentalities, channels, or goods involved in interstate commerce has always been the province of the States.

AFFIRMED in favor of respondents.

Dissent

JUSTICE SOUTER, with whom Justice Stevens, Justice Ginsberg, and Justice Breyer join:

. . . Congress has the power to legislate with regard to activity that, in the aggregate, has a substantial effect on interstate commerce. The fact of such a substantial effect is not an issue for the courts in the first instance, but for the Congress, whose institutional capacity for gathering evidence and taking testimony far exceeds ours. By passing legislation, Congress indicates its conclusion, whether explicitly or not, that facts support its exercise of the commerce power. The business of the courts is to review the congressional assessment, not for soundness but simply for the rationality of concluding that a jurisdictional basis exists in fact. Any explicit findings that Congress chooses to make, though not dispositive of the question of rationality, may advance judicial review by identifying factual authority on which Congress relied.

One obvious difference from United States v. Lopez is the mountain of data assembled by Congress, here showing the effects of violence against women on interstate commerce. Passage of the Act in 1994 was preceded by four years of hearings, which included testimony from physicians and law professors; from survivors of rape and domestic violence; and from representatives of state law enforcement and private business. The record includes reports on gender bias from task forces in twenty-one states, and we have the benefit of specific factual findings of the eight separate Reports issued by Congress and its committees over the long course leading to enactment.

Having identified the problem of violence against women, Congress may address what it sees as the most threatening manifestation. . . . Congress found that "crimes of violence motivated by gender have a substantial adverse effect on interstate commerce, by deterring potential victims from traveling interstate, from engaging in employment in interstate business, and from transacting with business, and in places involved, in interstate commerce . . . [,] by diminishing national productivity, increasing medical and other costs, and decreasing the supply of and the demand for interstate products. . . ."

Congress thereby explicitly stated the predicate for the exercise of its Commerce Clause power. Is its conclusion irrational in view of the data amassed? True, the methodology of particular studies may be challenged, and some of the figures arrived at may be disputed. But the sufficiency of the evidence before Congress to provide a rational basis for the finding cannot seriously be questioned. . . . Indeed, the legislative record here is far more voluminous than the record compiled by Congress and found sufficient in two prior cases upholding Title II of the Civil Rights Act of 1964 against Commerce Clause challenges.

The fact that the Act does not pass muster before the Court today is therefore proof, to a degree that Lopez was not, that the Court's nominal adherence to the substantial effects test is merely that. Although a new jurisprudence has not emerged with any distinctness, it is clear that some congressional conclusions about obviously substantial, cumulative effects on commerce are being assigned lesser values than the once-stable doctrine would assign them. These devaluations are accomplished not by any express repudiation of the substantial effects test or its application through the aggregation of individual conduct, but by supplanting rational basis scrutiny with a new criterion of review.

Thus, the elusive heart of the majority's analysis in these cases is its statement that Congress's findings of fact are "weakened" by the presence of a disfavored "method of reasoning." This seems to suggest that the "substantial effects" analysis is not a factual enquiry, for Congress in the first instance with subsequent judicial review looking only to the rationality of the congressional conclusion, but one of a rather different sort, dependent upon a uniquely judicial competence.

This new characterization of substantial effects has no support in our cases (the self-fulfilling prophecies of Lopez aside), least of all those the majority cites.

CRITICAL THINKING

Explain why you find the reasoning in either the majority or minority opinion more persuasive.

ETHICAL DECISION MAKING

Explain how different stakeholders would be the primary beneficiaries of the majority and minority decisions.

interstate commerce, as the implementation of the act would certainly lead to an increase in purchases of health care insurance, thereby significantly affecting the market for health care insurance and also for health care, as more people would be able to avail themselves of additional health care with their new insurance. However, Justice Roberts disagreed, making a new distinction between regulating existing activity and creating activity, with the former being seen as affecting interstate commerce and the latter being outside the scope of congressional power to regulate.

BUT WHAT IF . . .

WHAT IF THE FACTS OF THE CASE OPENER WERE DIFFERENT?

Recall that, in the Case Opener, Obama's mandate was spurring people into actions that could affect interstate commerce. What if Obama's act imposed certain rules only on those who already had health care insurance and, in other words, imposed rules on preexisting actions? Why might people be more open to this scenario than to the real facts?

THE COMMERCE CLAUSE AS A RESTRICTION ON STATE AUTHORITY

The federal government's authority to regulate interstate commerce sometimes conflicts with the states' authority to regulate intrastate commerce. Courts have attempted to resolve this conflict by distinguishing between regulations of commerce and regulations under states' police power. **Police power** consists of the residual powers retained by each state to safeguard the health and welfare of its citizenry. Typical exercises of a state's police power include state criminal laws, building codes, zoning laws, sanitation standards for restaurants, and regulations for the practice of medicine.

Sometimes a state's use of its police power affects interstate commerce. If the purpose of a state law is to regulate interstate commerce or to discriminate against interstate commerce, the law is usually unconstitutional. Likewise, if a law substantially interferes with interstate commerce, it is generally unconstitutional. This restriction on states' authority to pass laws that substantially affect interstate commerce is called the **dormant commerce clause.**

Most cases are not so simple, however, and courts must balance the states' interest in protecting their citizens against the impact on interstate commerce. In balancing these competing interests, a court generally asks whether the state regulation is rationally related to a legitimate state end. If it is, the court then asks whether the regulatory burden imposed on interstate commerce is outweighed by the state's interest in enforcing the legislation. The court may also inquire whether there is a less drastic alternative available to attain the legitimate state purpose.

Although the supremacy clause establishes the sovereignty of federal law, courts generally presume that laws passed in accordance with states' police power are valid. For example, the city of Chicago passed an ordinance banning spray paint in the city as a means to reduce graffiti. Paint manufacturers challenged the legislation as a violation of the dormant commerce clause, but the U.S. court of appeals upheld the legislation.[6] The legislation did not treat paint from out-of-state manufacturers any differently than paint from in-state manufacturers; it had been demonstrated that limiting the availability of spray paint would decrease the amount of graffiti; and it is within the states' police power to determine that graffiti is not good for the public welfare.

Case 5-2 illustrates how the United States Supreme Court responded to an attempt to challenge a state regulation on grounds that it places an undue burden on interstate commerce.

[6] *Nat'l Paint & Coatings Ass'n v. Chi.*, 803 F. Supp. 135 (1992).

CASE 5-2 FAMILY WINEMAKERS OF CALIFORNIA v. JENKINS
U.S. COURT OF APPEALS, FIRST CIRCUIT
592 F.3D 1 (2010)

A group of winemakers from California challenged a Massachusetts law that distinguished how "large" and "small" winemakers may distribute their wines in the state of Massachusetts. The law defined wineries that produced over 30,000 gallons of wine as "large" and allowed large wineries to either sell directly to consumers or sell through wholesalers, but not both. On the other hand, "small" wineries could use both distribution methods. Conveniently, all wineries in Massachusetts were below the 30,000-gallon cap. Thus, the only wineries being blocked from certain forms of distribution were wineries from outside the state. Thus, out-of-state winemakers decided to sue, claiming that the state's laws on this matter were violating the Commerce Clause by giving in-state businesses an unfair advantage over out-of-state businesses. The district court enjoined enforcement of the law and the state appealed.

CHIEF JUDGE LYNCH: Massachusetts officials appeal from an injunction against a 2006 Massachusetts statute establishing differential methods by which wineries distribute wines in Massachusetts. The district court enjoined enforcement of § 19F on the ground that the law discriminates against interstate commerce in violation of the Commerce Clause of the United States Constitution.

The primary question before us is whether § 19F unconstitutionally discriminates against interstate commerce. We

[continued]

hold that § 19F violates the Commerce Clause because the effect of its particular gallonage cap is to change the competitive balance between in-state and out-of-state wineries in a way that benefits Massachusetts's wineries and significantly burdens out-of-state competitors. Massachusetts has used its 30,000 gallon grape wine cap to expand the distribution options available to "small" wineries, including all Massachusetts wineries, but not to similarly situated "large" wineries, all of which are outside Massachusetts. The advantages afforded to "small" wineries by these expanded distribution options bear little relation to the market challenges caused by the relative sizes of the wineries. Section 19F's statutory context, legislative history, and other factors also yield the unavoidable conclusion that this discrimination was purposeful. Nor does § 19F serve any legitimate local purpose that cannot be furthered by a non-discriminatory alternative.

We further hold that the Twenty-first Amendment cannot save § 19F from invalidation under the Commerce Clause. Section 2 of the Twenty-first Amendment does not exempt or otherwise immunize facially neutral but discriminatory state alcohol laws like § 19F from scrutiny under the Commerce Clause. We affirm the grant of injunctive relief.

. . . When drafting the Wilson and Webb-Kenyon Acts, Congress was presumably aware that these types of facially neutral but discriminatory state laws were subject to invalidation under the Commerce Clause. Yet Congress made no reference to the notion that the Wilson and Webb-Kenyon Acts would permit states to enact liquor laws with a discriminatory effect or motive. Although "Congress may authorize the States to engage in regulation that the Commerce Clause would otherwise forbid," courts can "exempt state statutes from the implied limitations of the Clause only when the congressional direction to do so has been unmistakably clear." The Wilson and Webb-Kenyon Acts do evince an unmistakably clear intention to permit states to regulate alcohol which traveled in interstate commerce the same way as they regulated in-state alcohol. But the two Acts cannot be construed to authorize anything more.

Contemporaneous treatises on liquor law likewise concluded that the Wilson Act did not immunize any kind of discriminatory state law from scrutiny under the non-discrimination rule.

Against this background, we hold that the Twenty-first Amendment does not exempt facially neutral state alcohol laws with discriminatory effects from the non-discrimination rule of the Commerce Clause. Nor, of course, are such laws exempt when they also discriminate by design.

We also reject Massachusetts's alternate contention that the Twenty-first Amendment lessens the degree of Commerce Clause scrutiny for facially neutral but discriminatory state alcohol laws to mere rational basis review. The Supreme Court implicitly rejected this argument in Granholm when it applied the usual, searching degree of scrutiny to invalidate the facially discriminatory laws at issue. And there is nothing in the text, legislative history, or contemporaneous understandings of the Wilson or Webb-Kenyon Acts that supports Massachusetts's argument, let alone yields an unambiguous indication of congressional intent to reduce Commerce Clause scrutiny. In the absence of such evidence, Massachusetts's interpretation of the Twenty-first Amendment fails.

Finally, we need not address whether § 19F could escape invalidation on the ground that, despite its discriminatory effect and design, the "core purposes" of the Twenty-first Amendment "are sufficiently implicated . . . to outweigh the Commerce Clause principles that would otherwise be offended." Those purposes include "promoting temperance, ensuring orderly market conditions, and raising revenue." Massachusetts does not present any argument as to why § 19F serves any of these purposes. In any event, it is unclear that this balancing test survives Granholm.

Judgment AFFIRMED in favor of Plaintiffs.

CRITICAL THINKING

Do you think the Massachusetts state government was manipulating the definitions of "large" and "small" wineries to purposefully aid in-state wineries? Could the outcome have been different if its definition of small wineries excluded many in-state wineries as well as those out of state?

ETHICAL DECISION MAKING

Do you think it could be important to give certain advantages to small wineries to even the playing field between wineries with many resources and much financial backing and small, family wineries? Do you think there should be a difference in how different wineries are treated? Why or why not?

Although the dormant commerce clause does impose many restrictions on state authority, the power to offer tax credits to businesses within the state, which might be seen by some as "affecting" interstate commerce, is not prohibited. Therefore, individual states have the ability to provide tax credits for companies that locate in or do business within their boundaries. Tax credits for businesses are important because individual states may use them to lure or keep businesses within their state's limits. For businesses, the tax credits offered by the states may be extremely important. The value of tax credits can reach well into the millions, and this is often a source of cost savings for businesses. Thus, tax credits can be the deciding factor for a business when selecting where to invest and set up operations.

In recent years, the states' ability to provide tax credits to businesses has been challenged, most notably in *Daimler Chrysler v. Cuno.* In the Cuno case, a group of plaintiffs alleged that $280 million in tax credits, offered to Daimler Chrysler by the state of Ohio, was in violation of the commerce clause. However, in 2006 the U.S Supreme Court heard the case and ruled that the challenges brought by the plaintiffs had no standing in federal court. The case was then dismissed, and the states were free to continue offering tax credits to businesses.[7]

Taxing and Spending Powers of the Federal Government

No government can function without a source of revenue. Article I, Section 8, of the Constitution gives the federal government the "Power to lay and collect Taxes, Duties, Imports and Excises." The taxes laid by Congress, however, must be uniform across the states. In other words, the government cannot impose higher taxes on residents of one state than another.

Although tax collection allows the government to provide essential services, the government can also use taxes for other purposes. For example, to encourage the development of certain industries and discourage the development of others, the government can provide tax credits for firms entering favored industries. As long as the "motive of Congress and the effect of its legislative action are to secure revenue for the benefit of the general government,"[8] the tax is constitutional. The fact that it also has a regulatory impact does not affect the constitutionality of the tax.

While we may all think we know what a tax is, sometimes we may be surprised by what the courts call a tax. For example, many were surprised by the Supreme Court's determination that the penalty imposed under the Affordable Care Act on those who do not obtain medical insurance is a tax. In explaining that finding, Justice Roberts explained that while the payment was intended to encourage the purchase of insurance, there was nothing in the mandate that made the failure to purchase insurance unlawful; the law could be read as simply imposing a tax, collected by the IRS like other taxes, on those choosing not to purchase health insurance. The chief justice found no problem with the fact that the statute referred to the payment as a "penalty" and not a tax.

BUT WHAT IF . . .

What if the facts had been different and the language of the statute had explicitly stated that even though the payment was to be made through the IRS, this payment was a penalty and not a tax? Would that language have affected the constitutionality of the provision as an exercise of congressional taxing authority?

Article I, Section 8, also grants Congress spending power by authorizing it to "pay the Debts and provide for the common Defence and general Welfare of the United States." As with its power to tax, Congress can use its spending power to achieve social welfare

[7] www.supremecourtus.gov/opinions/05pdf/04-1704.pdf; and www.law.duke.edu/publiclaw/supremecourtonline/certGrants/2005/daivcun.

[8] *J. W. Hampton Co. v. United States,* 276 U.S. 394 (1928).

E-COMMERCE AND THE LAW

SALES TAXES ON INTERNET TRANSACTIONS?

Due to the rapid rise in Internet commerce in recent years, many states have become concerned about their ability to collect sales tax on Internet transactions. Sales taxes are a large source of revenue for state governments, but states can require that a business submit sales tax payments only if the business has a store or distribution center in the state. Otherwise, states cannot collect sales taxes, although residents are supposed to keep track of their out-of-state purchases (including those made over the Internet) and self-report the taxes on these purchases. The tax is known as a use tax, but the reality is that very few residents actually pay such taxes.

Bills have been unsuccessfully proposed in the past to allow for sales tax of purchases made over the Internet. Congress has been unenthusiastic about enacting enabling legislation that would allow states to ask Internet companies to collect sales taxes. Also, state laws vary regarding what gets taxed. For example, New Jersey has a separate sales tax for fur coats. California offers a partial exemption for sales tax on farm equipment. The variety in state laws means it would be complicated for Internet retailers to collect state sales taxes. If states adopted uniform rules, it would be easier to collect sales taxes. In the meantime, as e-commerce sales grow, states are missing out on tax revenue.

Source: Joshua Zumbrun, "A Flat Sales Tax?" *Forbes,* December 28, 2009; and 2009 WLNR 25303357.

objectives. For example, in the 1987 case *South Dakota v. Dole,*[9] the Supreme Court upheld a federal statute that grants federal funds for state highways to only those states in which 21 is the legal drinking age.

Other Constitutional Restrictions on Government

THE PRIVILEGES AND IMMUNITIES CLAUSE

Article IV, Section 2, of the Constitution states that "Citizens of each State shall be entitled to all Privileges and Immunities of Citizens in the several States." This provision, called the **privileges and immunities clause,** prohibits states from discriminating against citizens of other states when those nonresidents engage in ordinary and essential activities. These activities include buying and selling property, seeking employment, and using the court system. States may treat residents and nonresidents differently only when they have substantial reason for doing so.

For example, according to the privileges and immunities clause, a state cannot prohibit nonresidents from opening restaurants in the state. States can, however, allow state universities to charge higher tuition to out-of-state students because residents pay taxes that fund state universities, while out-of-state students do not.

THE FULL FAITH AND CREDIT CLAUSE

Article IV, Section 1, of the Constitution contains the **full faith and credit clause.** This clause states, "Full Faith and Credit shall be given in each State to the public Acts, Records, and judicial Proceedings of every other State." This provision requires that courts in all states uphold contracts and public acts established in other states. For example, this clause protects wills, marriage and divorce decrees, and judgments in civil courts. Courts have held, however, that states do not have to give full faith and credit to laws that violate their "public policy." Thus, for example, although Massachusetts permits same-sex marriage, the full faith and credit clause does not require that other states recognize such marriages.

THE CONTRACT CLAUSE

Article I, Section 9, contains the **contract clause,** which states that government may not pass any "Law impairing the Obligation of Contract." In application, courts interpret

[9] 483 U.S. 203 (1987).

this clause to mean that no law can be passed that will unreasonably interfere with existing contracts. For example, in the 1934 U.S. Supreme Court case *Home Building & Loan Association v. Blaisdell,*[10] the Home Building & Loan Association challenged Minnesota's Mortgage Moratorium Act as a violation of the contract clause. The act, implemented temporarily during the Great Depression, authorized courts to extend the redemption periods of mortgages to delay foreclosures of mortgages on real estate. The Court ruled that the act's provisions were within the state's police power to protect its citizens and did not violate the contract clause. Although the act impaired contractual obligations between lenders and borrowers, the Court held that courts must balance even substantial contractual impairments against states' interest in protecting the welfare of their citizens.

The Amendments to the Constitution

L04

How does the Bill of Rights protect the citizens of the United States?

The first 10 amendments to the U.S. Constitution, known as the *Bill of Rights,* substantially affect government regulation of business. These amendments prohibit the federal government from infringing on individual freedoms. Moreover, the Fourteenth Amendment extends most of the provisions in the Bill of Rights to the states, prohibiting state interference in citizens' exercise of their rights. Thus, the federal and state governments cannot deprive individuals of the freedoms protected by the Bill of Rights.

Many other countries do not have constitutional provisions to protect citizens from the government. The Australian constitution, for example, creates the framework for government in Australia. In many of the countries that do have individual protections in their constitutions, these protections have emerged recently, as the Comparing the Law of Other Countries box on Canada's constitution (see page 106) illustrates. Some other countries' constitutions provide rights that American citizens do not have. The constitution of Belarus, for example, featured later in this chapter, guarantees citizens' right to health care.

Courts apply many amendments to corporations because corporations are treated, in most cases, as "artificial persons." The remainder of this chapter describes the amendments that most significantly affect the regulatory environment of business. Exhibit 5-2 summarizes the first 10 amendments.

THE FIRST AMENDMENT

Freedom of Speech and Assembly. The First Amendment guarantees freedom of speech, including gestures and other forms of expression, and of the press. It prohibits abridgment of the right to assemble peacefully and to petition the government for redress of grievances. Finally, it prohibits the government from aiding the establishment of religion and from interfering with the free exercise of religion.

Like other rights, First Amendment rights are not absolute. For example, a person does not have the right to yell "Fire!" in a crowded theater. Nor does the First Amendment protect false statements about another that are injurious to that person's reputation. Due to the difficulty of determining the boundaries of individual rights, courts hear a large number of First Amendment cases.

Political Speech. The First Amendment protections also apply to corporations. Courts do not, however, treat all corporate speech the same. Sometimes corporations engage in **political speech;** that is, they support political candidates or referenda. At one time, states

[10] 290 U.S. 398.

AMENDMENT	PROVISIONS
First	• Protects freedom of religion, press, speech, and peaceable assembly
	• Ensures that citizens have the right to ask the government to redress grievances
Second	• Finds that in light of the need for a well-regulated militia for security, government cannot infringe on citizens' right to bear arms
Third	• Provides that government cannot house soldiers in private residences during peacetime, or during war except for provisions in the law
Fourth	• Protects citizens from unreasonable search and seizure
	• Ensures that government issues warrants only with probable cause
Fifth	• Ensures that government does not put citizens on trial except by the indictment of a grand jury
	• Gives citizens the right to not testify against themselves
	• Prevents government from trying citizens twice for the same crime
	• Creates the right to due process
	• Provides that government cannot take private property for public use without just compensation
Sixth	• Provides the right to a speedy public trial with an impartial jury, the right to know what criminal accusations a citizen faces, the right to have witnesses both against and for the accused, and the right to have an attorney
Seventh	• States that in common law suits where the monetary value exceeds $20, citizens have the right to a trial by jury
Eighth	• Provides that government will not set bail at excessive levels
	• Prohibits government imposition of excessive fines
	• Prohibits cruel and unusual punishment
Ninth	• Provides that although the Bill of Rights names certain rights, such naming does not remove other rights retained by citizens
Tenth	• Provides that powers that the Constitution does not give to the federal government are reserved to the states

EXHIBIT 5-2

Summary of the Bill of Rights

restricted firms' political advertising because they feared that corporations, with their large assets, would drown out other voices. However, in 2010, the United States Supreme Court struck down as unconstitutional federal campaign financing legislation that had prohibited corporations and unions from spending money to elect or defeat candidates for Congress or the White House. In *Citizens United v. Federal Election Commission,*[11] the court described corporations not as the "creatures of the law" that some previous courts had considered them, but rather as "associations of citizens" deserving the same free speech rights as individuals. Justice Scalia wrote: "To exclude or impede corporate speech is to muzzle the principal agents of the modern economy. . . . We should celebrate rather

[11] 130 S. Ct. 876 (2010).

COMPARING THE LAW OF OTHER COUNTRIES

CONSTITUTION ACT OF CANADA

The United States is not the only country to hold that a national constitution is the supreme law of the land. Section 52(1) of the Constitution Act of Canada, passed in 1982, states, "[T]he Constitution of Canada is the supreme law of Canada, and any law that is inconsistent with the provisions of the Constitution is, to the extent of the inconsistency, of no force or effect."

The Constitution Act established the Canadian Charter of Rights and Freedoms, which superseded the 1960 Canadian Bill of Rights. The Bill of Rights had applied only to the Canadian national government, not to the provincial governments. Like the Fourteenth Amendment of the U.S. Constitution, Section 32(1) of the Canadian Charter states that the charter applies to Canada's Parliament and national government and to the legislature and government of each province of Canada. Like the U.S. Bill of Rights, the Canadian Charter protects rights and fundamental freedoms, including freedom of conscience and religion, freedom of peaceful assembly and association, freedom from unreasonable searches and seizures, and the right to equal protection of the law. These rights and freedoms, however, are qualified. The charter states, in Section 1, "The Canadian Charter of Rights and Freedoms guarantees the rights and freedoms set out in the subject only to such reasonable limits prescribed by law as can be demonstrably justified in a free and democratic society."

This photo may look like an exercise of free speech, but the Court ultimately ruled that the suspension of the maker of the banner was not a violation of his free speech rights in *Morse v. Frederick,* better known as the "Bong Hits for Jesus" case.

than condemn the addition of this speech to the public debate."[12] The effect of this case on corporate behavior remains to be seen.

Commercial Speech. Not all corporate speech is political speech. **Commercial speech** is speech that conveys information related to the sale of goods and services. Courts analyze government restrictions on commercial speech according to a four-part test established in *Central Hudson Gas & Electric Corp. v. Public Service Commission of New York.*[13] The Central Hudson test is illustrated in Exhibit 5-3.

In Case 5-3, the Supreme Court applied this test to several New York regulations.

Unprotected Speech. The First Amendment right to free speech is not absolute. In the 1942 case *Chaplinsky v. New Hampshire,*[14] the U.S. Supreme Court held:

> There are certain well-defined and narrowly limited classes of speech, the prevention and punishment of which have never been thought to raise any Constitutional problem. These include the lewd and obscene, the profane, the libelous, and the insulting or fighting words—those which by their very utterance inflict injury or tend to incite an immediate breach of the peace.

Thus, for example, the First Amendment does not protect *defamation,* or speech that harms the reputation of another. As you will learn in Chapter 6, moreover, courts may require that an individual who uses such speech compensate the person whose reputation was harmed by the speech.

The First Amendment does not protect *obscenity* either, although in many cases courts find it difficult to determine whether particular speech constitutes obscenity.

[12] Id.

[13] 447 U.S. 557 (1980).

[14] 315 U.S. 568 (1942).

Exhibit 5-3 The Central Hudson Test for Commercial Speech

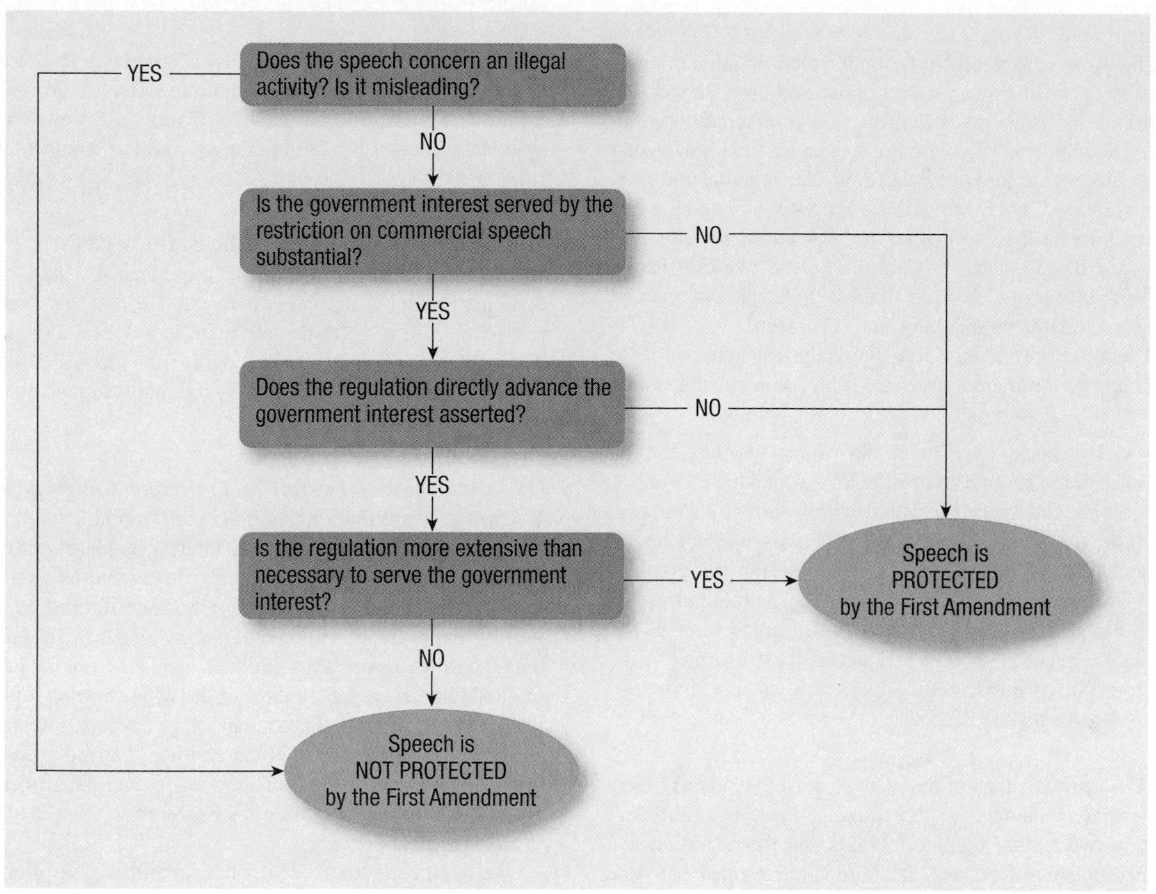

CASE 5-3 BAD FROG BREWERY v. NEW YORK STATE LIQUOR AUTH.

U.S. COURT OF APPEALS FOR THE SECOND CIRCUIT 134 F.3D 87 (1998)

Bad Frog, a Michigan corporation, manufactures and markets alcoholic beverages under its "Bad Frog" trademark. Each label prominently features an artist's rendering of a frog holding up its middle "finger." Versions of the label feature slogans such as "He just don't care," "An amphibian with an attitude," "Turning bad into good," and "The beer so good . . . it's bad."

In May 1996, Bad Frog's New York distributor applied to the New York State Liquor Authority for brand label approval and registration pursuant to section 107-a(4)(a) of New York's Alcoholic Beverage Control Law. NYSLA denied the application in July. Explaining its rationale for the rejection, the Authority found that the label "encourages combative behavior" and that the gesture and the slogan, "He just don't care," placed close to and in larger type than a warning concerning potential health problems, foster a defiance to the health warning on the label, entice underage drinkers, and invite the public not to heed conventional wisdom and to disobey standards of decorum.

In addition, the Authority said that it considered that approval of this label means that the label could appear in grocery and convenience stores, with obvious exposure on the shelf to children of tender age, and that it is sensitive to the label's adverse effects on a youthful audience.

Bad Frog filed suit against the NYSLA in October 1996 and sought a preliminary injunction barring NYSLA from taking any steps to prohibit the sale of beer by Bad Frog under the controversial labels.

JON O. NEWMAN, CIRCUIT JUDGE: Bad Frog's label attempts to function, like a trademark, to identify the source of the product. The picture on a beer bottle of a frog behaving badly is reasonably to be understood as attempting to identify to consumers a product of the Bad Frog Brewery. In addition, the label serves to propose a commercial transaction. Though the label communicates no information beyond the source of the product, we think that minimal information, conveyed in the context of a proposal of a commercial transaction, suffices to invoke the protections for commercial speech, articulated in Central Hudson. We thus assess the prohibition of Bad Frog's labels under the commercial speech standards outlined in Central Hudson.

Central Hudson sets forth the analytical framework for assessing governmental restrictions on commercial speech:

> At the outset, we must determine whether the expression is protected by the First Amendment. For commercial speech to come within that provision, it at least must concern lawful activity and not be misleading. Next, we ask whether the asserted government interest is substantial. If both inquiries yield positive answers, we must determine whether the regulation directly advances the government interest asserted, and whether it is not more extensive than is necessary to serve that interest.

The last two steps in the analysis have been considered, somewhat in tandem, to determine if there is a sufficient "'fit' between the [regulator's] ends and the means chosen to accomplish those ends." The burden to establish that "reasonable fit" is on the governmental agency defending its regulation, though the fit need not satisfy a least-restrictive-means standard.

A. Lawful Activity and Not Deceptive

We agree with the District Court that Bad Frog's labels pass Central Hudson's threshold requirement that the speech "must concern lawful activity and not be misleading." The consumption of beer (at least by adults) is legal in New York, and the labels cannot be said to be deceptive, even if they are offensive.

B. Substantial State Interests

NYSLA advances two interests to support its asserted power to ban Bad Frog's labels: (i) the State's interest in "protecting children from vulgar and profane advertising," and (ii) the State's interest "in acting consistently to promote temperance, i.e., the moderate and responsible use of alcohol among those above the legal drinking age and abstention among those below the legal drinking age."

Both of the asserted interests are "substantial" within the meaning of Central Hudson. States have "a compelling interest in protecting the physical and psychological well-being of minors," and "this interest extends to shielding minors from the influence of literature that is not obscene by adult standards."

The Supreme Court also has recognized that states have a substantial interest in regulating alcohol consumption. We agree with the District Court that New York's asserted concern for "temperance" is also a substantial state interest.

C. Direct Advancement of the State Interest

To meet the "direct advancement" requirement, a state must demonstrate that "the harms it recites are real and that its restriction will in fact alleviate them to a material degree." A restriction will fail this third part of the Central Hudson test if it "provides only ineffective or remote support for the government's purpose."

(1) Advancing the Interest in Protecting Children from Vulgarity. A prohibition that makes only a minute contribution to the advancement of a state interest can hardly be considered to have advanced the interest "to a material degree."

NYSLA endeavors to advance the state interest in preventing exposure of children to vulgar displays by taking only the limited step of barring such displays from the labels of alcoholic beverages. In view of the wide currency of vulgar displays throughout contemporary society, including comic books targeted directly at children, barring such displays from labels for alcoholic beverages cannot realistically be expected to reduce children's exposure to such displays to any significant degree.

We appreciate that NYSLA has no authority to prohibit vulgar displays appearing beyond the marketing of alcoholic beverages, but a state may not avoid the criterion of materially advancing its interest by authorizing only one component of its regulatory machinery to attack a narrow manifestation of a perceived problem. If New York decides to make a substantial effort to insulate children from vulgar displays in some significant sphere of activity, at least with respect to materials likely to be seen by children, NYSLA's label prohibition might well be found to make a justifiable contribution to the material advancement of such an effort, but its currently isolated response to the perceived problem, applicable only to labels on a product that children cannot purchase, does not suffice. We do not mean that a state must attack a problem with a total effort or fail the third criterion of a valid commercial speech limitation. Our point is that a state must demonstrate that its commercial speech limitation is part of a substantial effort to advance a valid state interest, not merely the removal of a few grains of offensive sand from a beach of vulgarity.

The valid state interest here is not insulating children from these labels, or even insulating them from vulgar displays on labels for alcoholic beverages; it is insulating children from displays of vulgarity.

(2) Advancing the State Interest in Temperance. We agree with the District Court that NYSLA has not established that its rejection of Bad Frog's application directly advances the state's interest in "temperance."

NYSLA maintains that the raised finger gesture and the slogan "He just don't care" urge consumers generally to defy authority and particularly to disregard the Surgeon General's warning, which appears on the label next to the gesturing frog. NYSLA also contends that the frog appeals to youngsters and promotes underage drinking.

The truth of these propositions is not so self-evident as to relieve the state of the burden of marshalling some empirical evidence to support its assumptions. All that is clear is that the gesture of "giving the finger" is offensive. Whether viewing that gesture on a beer label will encourage disregard of health warnings or encourage underage drinking remain matters of speculation.

NYSLA has not shown that its denial of Bad Frog's application directly and materially advances either of its asserted state interests.

D. Narrow Tailoring

Central Hudson's fourth criterion, sometimes referred to as "narrow tailoring," requires consideration of whether the prohibition is more extensive than necessary to serve the asserted state interest. Since NYSLA's prohibition of Bad Frog's labels has not been shown to make even an arguable advancement of the state interest in temperance, we consider here only whether the prohibition is more extensive than necessary to serve the asserted interest in insulating children from vulgarity.

In this case, Bad Frog has suggested numerous less intrusive alternatives to advance the asserted State interest in protecting children from vulgarity, short of a complete statewide ban on its labels. Appellant suggests "the restriction of advertising to point-of-sale locations; limitations on billboard advertising; restrictions on over-the-air-advertising; and segregation of the product in the store." Even if we were to assume that the state materially advances its asserted interest by shielding children from viewing the Bad Frog labels, it is plainly excessive to prohibit the labels from all use, including placement on bottles displayed in bars and taverns where parental supervision of children is to be expected. Moreover, to whatever extent NYSLA is concerned that children will be harmfully exposed to the Bad Frog labels when wandering without parental supervision around grocery and convenience stores where beer is sold, that concern could be less intrusively dealt with by placing restrictions on the permissible locations where the appellant's products may be displayed within such stores. Or, with the labels permitted, restrictions might be imposed on placement of the frog illustration on the outside of six-packs or cases, sold in such stores.

NYSLA's complete statewide ban on the use of Bad Frog's labels lacks a "reasonable fit" with the state's asserted interest in shielding minors from vulgarity, and NYSLA gave inadequate consideration to alternatives to this blanket suppression of commercial speech.

REVERSED and REMANDED.

CRITICAL THINKING

Suppose an editorial writer read the Bad Frog case and concluded that the Supreme Court is apparently uninterested in temperance. Explain how the editorial writer has misunderstood the Court's reasoning.

ETHICAL DECISION MAKING

What values are competing with freedom of speech in this case?

How do the standards in the *Central Hudson* decision give us a strong sense about how important freedom of speech is to the Court as a value?

In the 1973 case *Miller v. California,*[15] the U.S. Supreme Court established a three-part standard to determine whether speech is obscene:

1. Would the average person, applying contemporary community standards, find that the speech, taken as a whole, appeals to the prurient (marked by or arousing an immoderate or unwholesome interest or desire) interest?
2. Does the speech depict or describe, in a patently offensive way, sexual conduct specifically defined by law?
3. Does the speech, taken as a whole, lack serious literary, artistic, political, or scientific value?

[15] 413 U.S. 15 (1973).

If the answer to all three questions is yes, then the First Amendment does not protect the speech in question. You may note that there are significant ambiguities in the Miller standard.

Fighting words are a third class of unprotected speech. In *Chaplinsky v. New Hampshire,* a man protesting the government called the city marshal a "damned racketeer" and a "damned Fascist." The city arrested him for violating a statute prohibiting the use of offensive, derisive, or annoying words toward another in a public place. The U.S. Supreme Court held: "The English language has a number of words and expressions which by general consent are 'fighting words' when said without a disarming smile. . . . Such words, as ordinary men know, are likely to cause a fight." The Court further held that "'damned racketeer' and 'damned Fascist' are epithets likely to provoke the average person to retaliation, and thereby cause a breach of the peace."[16] Thus, the Court determined that the First Amendment did not protect the man's speech.

Many universities believe that "hate speech," or derogatory speech directed at members of another group, such as another race, satisfies the definition of fighting words. Thus, 60 percent of universities have banned verbal abuse and verbal harassment, and 28 percent of universities have banned advocacy of an offensive viewpoint.[17] State and federal appellate courts have struck down almost every one of these hate-speech codes and codes of conduct that have been challenged, usually on grounds of being overbroad or vague. For example, in 2008, the Third Circuit Court of Appeals struck down Temple University's sexual harassment policy that provided, in part, that "all forms of sexual harassment are prohibited, including . . . expressive, visual, or physical conduct of a sexual or gender-motivated nature, when . . . such conduct has the purpose or effect of unreasonably interfering with an individual's work, educational performance, or status; or (d) such conduct has the purpose or effect of creating an intimidating, hostile, or offensive environment."[18] The policy was challenged by a student who felt that by expressing his opinions in class about the role of women in combat, he would be risking violating the policy, thus indicating the policy could have a chilling effect on speech in the classroom. The appellate court agreed, finding the policy facially overbroad.[19] A student group was granted a preliminary injunction on overbreadth grounds against enforcement of San Francisco State University's speech code that gave the school permission to punish students for behavior that was not "civil" or was inconsistent with the university's goals.[20] No cases have reached the Supreme Court yet. The international community, however, is less protective of hate speech. For example, a United Nations declaration and a number of foreign laws state that hate speech is not a protected form of expression.[21]

Freedom of Religion. The First Amendment contains two provisions that protect citizens' freedom of religion. The **establishment clause** maintains that government "shall make no law respecting an establishment of religion." In the 1971 case

[16] See note 12.

[17] Timothy C. Shiell, *Campus Hate Speech on Trial* (Lawrence: University Press of Kansas, 1998), pp. 2, 49.

[18] *Christian M. Dejohn v. Temple University,* 537 F.3d 301 (2008).

[19] Id.

[20] *College Republicans of San Francisco State Univ. v. Reed,* 523 F. Supp. 2d 1005 (2007).

[21] Ibid., p. 32.

CASE NUGGET

WHEN DO RELIGIOUS DISPLAYS ON PUBLIC LANDS VIOLATE THE FIRST AMENDMENT?

Trunk v. City of San Diego
U.S. Court of Appeal, Ninth Circuit
629 F.3d 1099 (2011)

For over a century, a memorial Latin Cross had been present at Mount Soledad, but in 1989 the city of San Diego was sued on grounds that the presence of the cross violated the no-preference clause of the California constitution and the First Amendment. In response to a court ruling that the cross had to be removed and sold to the highest bidder, the city simply sold the land to a nonprofit association, which then spent around $1 million making the towering 43-foot Latin Cross the centerpiece of a Korean War memorial. A decade of litigation followed, and the act of the city was seen as a ruse to avoid the judgment that maintaining the cross did establish a preference for a religion. For years, the city sought to find a way to prevent the court-ordered removal of the cross.

Finally, in 2006, a federal judge ordered the city to remove the cross within 90 days. However, Congress obtained the land through eminent domain to preserve it in its original state. In response, the Jewish War Veterans of the United States of America and other individuals represented by the American Civil Liberties Union then brought a lawsuit challenging Congress's taking of the memorial and the presence of the cross on federal property under the establishment clause. The parties alleged that congressional preservation of the cross denoted an unfair advancement of a religion and an excessive entanglement with a religion.

The district court ruled the cross constitutional because, instead of promoting a religion, it was there to promote the service of veterans. However, the Ninth Circuit Court of Appeals, after conducting an inquiry into the purpose and history of the memorial, learned that "the Memorial has a long history of religious use and symbolism that is inextricably intertwined with its commemorative message. This history, combined with . . . the prominence of the Cross in the Memorial, leads us to conclude that a reasonable observer would perceive the Memorial as projecting a message of religious endorsement, not simply secular memorialization," and therefore violates the establishment clause. In its opinion, the court applied the Lemon test of asking whether the action or policy at issue (1) has a secular purpose, (2) has the principal effect of advancing religion, or (3) causes excessive entanglement with religion, in conjunction with the suggestion from the Van Orden case that analysis of a case involving a monument must also take into consideration "the nature of the monument and . . . our Nation's history."

The U.S Supreme Court refused to hear an appeal of the case, so the Ninth Circuit's grant of summary judgment to the Jewish War Veterans Association appears to be the final judgment in this long-standing dispute.

Lemon v. Kurtzman,[22] the U.S. Supreme Court codified the following three tests to determine whether a particular government statute violates the establishment clause:

1. Does the statute have a secular legislative purpose?
2. Does the statute's principal or primary effect either advance or inhibit religion?
3. Does the statute foster an excessive government entanglement with religion?

To determine whether the statute fosters an excessive government entanglement with religion, courts examine the character and purposes of the institutions benefited, the nature of the aid that the government provides, and the resulting relationship between the government and the religious authority.

Legal Principle: A state statute will not violate the establishment clause if it has a secular legal purpose, has a primary effect of neither advancing nor inhibiting religion, and does not foster an excessive government entanglement with religion.

The **free-exercise clause** states that government cannot make a law "prohibiting the free exercise" of religion. Although government must remain neutral in matters of religion, determining whether a government action advances religion or merely allows free exercise of religion is often difficult. Likewise, determining whether a government action establishes religion or simply avoids interference with free exercise of religion is also difficult.

[22] 403 U.S. 602 (1971).

COMPARING THE LAW OF OTHER COUNTRIES

FREE SPEECH IN CHINA

The Chinese constitution does not guarantee freedom of speech or assembly, nor does it recognize any form of natural rights or human rights. Instead, it recognizes citizens' rights, which are specifically enumerated in the Chinese constitution or laws. Not only does the Chinese constitution not provide protections for expressive activity, but numerous Chinese laws prohibit citizens from engaging in political acts directed against the regime—acts that are protected in the United States. For example, Article 25 of China's Publishing Control Act prohibits the publication of any material that opposes the basic rules of the constitution. Articles 7 and 12 of the Law on Assemblies, Processions, and Demonstrations prohibit assemblies, processions, and demonstrations that oppose those basic rules.

Issues concerning the establishment clause and the free-exercise clause often arise in workplace settings. In government workplaces, this conflict sometimes raises difficult issues. For example, in 1966, Tucker, an employee of the California Department of Education, insisted on signing office memos with his name and the letters "SOTLJC," an abbreviation for "Servant of the Lord Jesus Christ." In an attempt to avoid workplace disruptions and the appearance of government support for religion, Tucker's supervisor prohibited all displays of religious symbols in the workplace. The supervisor suspended Tucker for refusing to comply with the restrictions. When Tucker challenged the suspension on grounds that the rules interfered with his free exercise of religion, the appellate court agreed.[23]

In private workplaces, issues related to free exercise of religion most often arise under Title VII, the federal law prohibiting employment discrimination. We discuss this important legislation in greater detail in Chapter 42.

THE FOURTH AMENDMENT

Freedom from Unreasonable Searches and Seizures. The Fourth Amendment guarantees citizens the right to be "secure in their persons, their homes, and their personal property." Thus, it prohibits government from conducting unreasonable searches of individuals and seizing their property to use as evidence against them.

A search is unreasonable if the government official conducting the search does not first obtain a search warrant from a court. A **search warrant** is a court order that authorizes law enforcement agents to search for or seize items specifically described in the warrant. Government officials can obtain search warrants only if they can show *probable cause* to believe that the search will uncover specific evidence of criminal activity. In other words, the government officials must have a sufficient reason based on known facts to obtain a warrant.

The Supreme Court has ruled, however, that in certain circumstances, government officials do not need a search warrant. For example, when law enforcement officials believe it is likely that the items sought will be removed before they can obtain a warrant, they may conduct a search without a warrant. Law enforcement officials frequently conduct automobile searches without a warrant according to this rule.

In most other cases, though, law enforcement officials must obtain a warrant before conducting a search. For example, an Ohio law required that buyers of five or more beer kegs provide the beer distributor with the address of the party where the kegs would be consumed. Additionally, the law required that the buyers sign a form allowing police and liquor agents to enter their property without a warrant to search the premises to enforce

[23] *Tucker v. State of Cal. Dep't of Ed.*, 97 F.3d 1204 (9th Cir. 1996).

E-COMMERCE AND THE LAW

TECHNOLOGY AND THE FOURTH AMENDMENT

Technological improvements have raised new issues in the application of the Fourth Amendment. New technologies have made eavesdropping and other covert activities easier. For example, in a 2001 U.S. Supreme Court case, police had information suggesting that Danny Kyllo grew marijuana in his home. Growing marijuana indoors requires heat lamps that use large amounts of electricity, and Kyllo had unusually high electric bills. The police used a thermal imager, an instrument that detects heat emissions, to provide them with the evidence necessary to obtain a warrant to physically search his house.

The Court addressed the issue of whether the use of thermal-imaging instruments on private property constituted a "search." Judges analyze cases by comparing them to past cases to see how other judges determined similar cases. Thus, in this case, the Court asked whether using thermal-imaging instruments is more like going through someone's garbage or more like using a high-powered telescope to look through someone's window. Previous Supreme Court cases held that the former behavior does not constitute a search but the latter scenario does constitute a search and therefore requires a warrant. The appellate court, examining the use of this technology for the first time, ruled that using thermal imaging was not a search prohibited by the Fourth Amendment without a warrant.

On appeal, however, the U.S. Supreme Court ruled that police use of thermal-imaging devices to detect heat patterns emanating from private homes constitutes a search that requires a warrant. The Court held, further, that the warrant requirement applies not only to the relatively crude thermal-imaging device but also to any "more sophisticated systems" that give the police knowledge that in the past would have required physical entry into the home. In explaining the Court's decision, Justice Scalia wrote that in the home, "all details are intimate details, because the entire area is held safe from prying government eyes." He added that the Court's precedents "draw a firm line at the entrance to one's house."

This case, however, is not necessarily the final word on the use of technology. The Court relied heavily on the fact that police used thermal imaging to see inside Kyllo's home. Thus, courts may in the future uphold thermal imaging of other locations.

state liquor laws. In 2001, a college professor challenged the law on grounds that it infringed on citizens' Fourth Amendment rights.[24] Before the court decided the case, Ohio repealed the law.[25]

Drug sniffing dogs had a surprisingly prominent role in the Supreme Court's holdings in 2013. In the most recent case, *Florida v. Jardines*[26], the high court held that bringing a drug sniffing dog onto someone's front porch without a warrant does violate the Fourth Amendment's protection against warrantless searches. Justice Scalia wrote that a person's minimal expectation of privacy extends not only to his house but to its immediate surroundings such as the porch.

The outcome is somewhat different, however, if the drug sniffing dog is accompanying an officer to a person's vehicle for a routine traffic stop. In *Florida v. Harris,*[27] an officer made a routine traffic stop of a truck, and when he walked up to the vehicle with the drug sniffing dog, the dog, through its behavior, indicated the presence of illegal drugs in the door of the truck. The officer treated the dog's behavior as giving him probable cause to go ahead and search the interior of the door of the truck, where he subsequently found 200 pseudoephedrine pills and other methamphetamine precursors. In this case, the high court upheld the search.

In addition to protecting individuals and their homes, the Fourth Amendment also protects corporations and places of business. This protection generally applies in criminal cases, but Fourth Amendment issues also arise when government regulations authorize administrative agencies to conduct warrantless searches.

Although administrative searches usually require search warrants, courts have established an exception to this rule: If an industry has a long history of pervasive regulation, a

[24] Robert Ruth, "Lawsuit Challenges Restrictions on Beer Buyers," *Columbus Dispatch,* May 26, 2001, p. 1B.
[25] *Hooper v. Morkle,* 219 F.R.D. 120 (2003).
[26] 569 U. S. _____ (2013).
[27] 568 U. S. _____ (2013).

warrantless search is not unreasonable. In such industries, administrative agencies can use warrantless searches to ensure that firms uphold regulations.

This *pervasive-regulation exception,* however, is not always easy to interpret. Courts have ruled that warrantless searches authorized by the Federal Mine Safety and Health Act are legal because the federal regulatory presence is comprehensive and well defined. Thus, reasonable commercial-property owners ought to know that their property is subject to periodic inspections.[28] A warrantless search based on the Occupational Safety and Health Act, however, may violate the Fourth Amendment because no significant legislation of working conditions existed before Congress passed that act in 1970. Hence, businesspeople covered by the law cannot reasonably anticipate warrantless searches.

For example, in the 1988 U.S. Supreme Court case *Braswell v. United States,*[29] the Court distinguished between the rights of corporate-record custodians and sole proprietors. Braswell was both the operator and the sole shareholder of his business. When a grand jury issued a subpoena requiring that he produce corporate books and records, Braswell argued that the subpoena violated his Fifth Amendment privilege against self-incrimination. The Court denied Braswell's claim, writing that "subpoenaed business records are not privileged, and as a custodian for the records, the act of producing the records is in a representative capacity, not a personal one, so the records must be produced."[30] The Court held that the subpoena would have violated Braswell's privilege against self-incrimination if his business had been a sole proprietorship.

THE FIFTH AMENDMENT

The Fifth Amendment protects individuals in several important ways. First, it protects against *self-incrimination,* meaning that in a criminal case, the defendant does not have to testify in court as a witness against herself or himself. The Fifth Amendment also protects against *double jeopardy.* Thus, government cannot try a person more than once for the same crime. It also contains the important protections of the due process clause.

Due Process. For businesspeople and corporations, the Fifth Amendment's **due process clause** provides extensive protection. This clause states that government cannot deprive a person of life, liberty, or property without *due process* of law.

The due process clause guarantees two types of due process: procedural and substantive. **Procedural due process** requires that the government use fair procedures when taking the life, liberty, or property of an individual or corporation. At a minimum, procedural due process entitles a person to notice of any legal action against her and to a hearing before an impartial tribunal. Originally, courts interpreted the due process clause as protecting an individual's right of procedural due process only in federal criminal proceedings. The subsequent passage of the Fourteenth Amendment extended the requirement of due process to criminal proceedings by state governments. Today, courts apply the due process clause to diverse situations, including the termination of welfare benefits, food stamps, or Social Security benefits; the suspension of a driver's license; the discharge of a public employee from his job; and the suspension of a student from school.

The procedures that government must follow when taking an individual's life, liberty, or property vary according to the nature of the taking. Generally, more procedures are necessary as the magnitude of potential deprivation increases.

[28] *Raymond J. Donovan, Secretary of Labor, United States Department of Labor v. Douglas Dewey et al.,* 452 U.S. 594, 101 S. Ct. 2534 (1981).

[29] 487 U.S. 99 (1988).

[30] Ibid.

CASE NUGGET

UNITED STATES v. WINDSOR

United States Supreme Court
569 U.S. __ (2013)

One of the most awaited Supreme Court decisions in 2013 was the case of *United States v. Windsor,* in which the high court ultimately struck down the Defense of Marriage Act (DOMA), an act which had said that for purposes of all federal laws, a marriage must be between opposite sex partners. Even if a state recognized a marriage for same-sex partners, those partners were not considered married under federal laws. Obviously, this statute imposed a tremendous burden on same-sex couples, but it also made things more complicated for business, because there are both state and federal laws imposing certain obligations on employers to married employees, so in terms of their treatment of married employees, firms had to ensure that they treated some employees one way under state law and another under federal law.

As the constitutionality of DOMA was being debated, many thought that it would be struck down on grounds of federalism, that the state always has been and should be the one to define marriage. However, the court instead found that DOMA denies same-sex couples the dignity that the states intended them to have and sets them apart in a way that violates the due process and equal protection principles guaranteed under the Constitution.

As Justice Kennedy explained in his majority opinion, "DOMA singles out a class of persons deemed by a State entitled to recognition and protection to enhance their own liberty. It imposes a disability on the class by refusing to acknowledge a status the State finds to be dignified and proper. DOMA instructs all federal officials, and indeed all persons with whom same-sex couples interact, including their own children, that their marriage is less worthy than the marriages of others. The federal statute is invalid, for no legitimate purpose overcomes the purpose and effect to disparage and to injure those whom the State, by its marriage laws, sought to protect in personhood and dignity. By seeking to displace this protection and treating those persons as living in marriages less respected than others, the federal statute is in violation of the Fifth Amendment."

This ruling will have a significant impact on how businesses must now treat a significant number of employees, bringing them under the umbrella of several federal statutes.

Substantive due process refers to the basic fairness of laws that may deprive an individual of her life, liberty, or property. To satisfy the substantive due process requirement, government must have a proper purpose for enacting laws that restrict individuals' liberty or the use of their property. The standard for determining whether a law violates substantive due process depends on the nature of the potential deprivation. Laws affecting fundamental rights must bear a substantial relationship to a compelling government purpose. These fundamental rights generally include the rights protected in the Constitution: the right to vote, the right to travel freely from state to state, the right to privacy, and so on. Compelling state interests include, for example, public safety and national security. The Case Nugget illustrates the continuing importance of substantive due process.

Not all laws, however, affect fundamental rights. To show that laws that do not affect fundamental rights satisfy the substantive due process requirement, government must prove only that the law bears a rational relationship to a legitimate state interest. Courts uphold most government regulations according to this *rational-basis test.* For example, courts have upheld minimum-wage laws, rent control laws, banking regulations, environmental laws, and regulations prohibiting unfair trade practices according to the rational-basis test.

The Prohibition against Uncompensated Takings. The Fifth Amendment also provides that when government takes private property for public use, it must pay the owner *just compensation,* or fair market value, for his property. This provision is called the **takings clause,** and it applies to corporations. Several significant issues have arisen with respect to the takings clause. For example, what constitutes a "public use" for which government can take private property?

Kelo v. City of New London is a U.S Supreme Court case that specifically addressed the issue of what constitutes "public use." In 1998, the Pfizer pharmaceutical company decided to build a new research facility in the city of New London, Connecticut. The city of New London was excited about the corporate addition and believed that the new Pfizer facility would bring business, revenue, and job creation to the area. In an effort to further economic development, the city of New London wished to supplement the new Pfizer facility with additional construction. The city, with the help of private developers, created a plan for a new conference center, hotel, and housing and retail units in the area surrounding the Pfizer facility.

Complications in the city's plan occurred because the land surrounding the Pfizer facility was privately held. Consequently, before the city could move forward with development, it had to first use its power of eminent domain to obtain the privately held land. When the city of New London attempted to seize the homes and land around the Pfizer facility, several citizens filed suit. In court, the citizens alleged that the city's plan did not constitute "public use" and was thus unconstitutional and in violation of their Fifth Amendment rights. However, the U.S Supreme Court, in a 5-4 decision, found that the use of eminent domain for the purpose of economic development was constitutional. The citizens of New London were therefore required to surrender their land.[31]

The takings clause has prompted other issues as well. What happens, for instance, when a government regulation interferes so substantially with an individual's use of her property that it effectively "takes" her property? For example, environmental regulations often affect the way landowners can use their property. In many cases, property owners have challenged the constitutionality of these regulations. While the courts have not drawn a clear line as to when a regulation is so extensive that it constitutes a taking, it is clear that if the regulation prohibits the owner from deriving any economic benefit from the land, a taking has occurred and the owner must be compensated.

The classic case in which such a regulatory taking occurred was *Lucas v. South Carolina Coastal Commission,*[32] which arose out of a dispute between a beachfront-property owner and the state of South Carolina over a law prohibiting permanent construction on any eroding beach. Lucas had bought two beachfront lots for $975,000 in 1986, before the passage of the law in question. Lucas, who had not yet begun construction on his property when the law was passed, lost the right to use his property for condominiums, so he challenged the law as constituting a taking without just compensation. The state court agreed with Lucas that the regulation denied him full value of his property and thus constituted a taking, so it awarded him $1.2 million in damages. The South Carolina Supreme Court disagreed and overturned the lower court's decision.

Lucas appealed the decision to the U.S. Supreme Court, which reversed the state supreme court, holding that a state regulation that deprives a private property owner of all economically beneficial uses of property constitutes a taking of private property for which the Fifth Amendment's takings clause requires payment. This total deprivation of the value of the property is referred to as a *regulatory taking*. While we know that total deprivation constitutes a taking, we do not know the minimum that might be arguably a taking.

Legal Principle: **A regulatory taking, entitling a property owner to just compensation, occurs when a regulation deprives the property owner of all economically beneficial uses of the land.**

[31] 545 U.S. 469; 125 S. Ct. 2655; and www.law.cornell.edu/supct/html/04-108.ZO.html.

[32] 112 U.S. 2886 (1992).

The Privilege against Self-Incrimination. Although most provisions of the Fifth Amendment apply to corporations, corporations do not enjoy the Fifth Amendment's protection against self-incrimination. Sole proprietors, however, are entitled to this protection. Thus, different businesses have different constitutional rights depending on their form of business organization.

THE NINTH AMENDMENT

Privacy Rights. The Ninth Amendment states, "The enumeration in the Constitution, of certain rights, shall not be construed to deny or disparage others retained by the people." Although this amendment does not expressly guarantee the right to privacy, courts have interpreted the Ninth Amendment, together with the First, Third, Fourth, and Fifth amendments, as providing individuals with a right to privacy.

In the 1965 case *Griswold v. Connecticut,*[33] the Supreme Court ruled that a Connecticut law prohibiting the use of contraceptives was unconstitutional because it violated individuals' right to privacy. Justice Douglas wrote:

> [S]pecific guarantees in the Bill of Rights have penumbras [fringes]. . . . Various guarantees create zones of privacy. The right of association contained in the penumbra of the First Amendment is one. . . . The Third Amendment in its prohibition against the quartering of soldiers "in any house" in time of peace without the consent of the owner is another facet of that privacy. The Fourth Amendment explicitly affirms the "right of the people to be secure in their persons, houses, papers, and effects, against unreasonable searches and seizures." The Fifth Amendment in its Self-Incrimination Clause enables the citizen to create a zone of privacy which government may not force him to surrender to his detriment.

The right to privacy has since been used in a broad variety of contexts.

THE FOURTEENTH AMENDMENT

Equal Protection. The Fourteenth Amendment contains the **equal protection clause,** which prevents states from denying "the equal protection of the laws" to any citizen. This clause combats discrimination because it applies whenever government treats certain individuals differently than other similarly situated individuals, usually through a classification scheme.

As with the due process clause, to determine whether a law violates the equal protection clause, courts use different standards based on the nature of the rights the classification affects. Three different standards of scrutiny apply: strict scrutiny, intermediate scrutiny, and the rational-basis test.

If a law prevents individuals from exercising a fundamental right, or if the law's classification scheme involves suspect classifications, the action will be subject to **strict scrutiny.** *Suspect classifications* include classifications based on race, national origin, and citizenship. Courts uphold suspect classifications only if they are necessary to promote a compelling state interest. In cases involving suspect classifications, courts do not begin their analysis with a presumption that the classification is constitutional, so few laws pass the strict-scrutiny standard. For example, in the 1954 case *Brown v. Board of Education,*[34] the U.S. Supreme Court ruled that the classification scheme used to racially segregate public schools violated the equal protection clause.

[33] 381 U.S. 479 (1965).

[34] 347 U.S. 483 (1954).

COMPARING THE LAW OF OTHER COUNTRIES

THE CONSTITUTION OF THE REPUBLIC OF BELARUS

The constitution of Belarus, adopted in 1994, provides Belarusian citizens with an exhaustive set of rights that surpasses most other nations' constitutions. The Belarusian constitution guarantees the following rights to citizens:

- Citizens accused of crimes are presumed innocent until proven guilty (Article 26).
- The defendant in a criminal case enjoys protection from providing evidence against herself or close family relations (Article 27).
- Citizens can move freely and choose their place of residence within the Republic of Belarus. They can leave Belarus and return without hindrance (Article 30).
- Citizens have the right to profess any religion individually or jointly with others or to profess none at all. They also have the right to express and spread beliefs connected with their attitudes toward religion and to participate in religious rituals (Article 31).
- Citizens have freedom of thought and belief and may freely express their thoughts and beliefs (Article 33).
- Citizens may organize assemblies, rallies, street marches, demonstrations, and pickets that do not disturb law and order or violate other citizens' rights (Article 35).
- Citizens have the right to choose a profession, type of occupation, and work in accordance with their capabilities, education, and vocational training. Moreover, they have the right to healthy and safe working conditions.
- The constitution binds the Belarusian government to create the conditions necessary for full employment of the population. For citizens who are unemployed for reasons beyond their control, the constitution guarantees training in new specializations, an upgrade of their qualifications, and unemployment benefits (Article 41).
- The constitution limits the workweek to 40 hours. It guarantees annual paid leave, weekly rest days, and shorter working hours for citizens who work at night (Article 43).
- Citizens have the right to health care, including free treatment at all government health care establishments (Article 45).

Several courts have held, however, that in some cases, remedying past discrimination against a group is a compelling state interest. Chapter 42 discusses this issue in greater detail.

If the law's classification scheme is based on gender or on the legitimacy of children, courts use **intermediate scrutiny.** According to this standard, the law is constitutional only if it is substantially related to an important government objective.

When a classification scheme involves other matters, courts apply a **rational-basis test.** According to this test, courts ask whether there is any justifiable reason to believe that the classification scheme advances a legitimate government interest. Because courts begin their analysis with a strong presumption that the government action is constitutional, almost all laws pass this test.

CASE OPENER WRAP-UP

The Constitutionality of the Affordable Care Act

In a decision that surprised many, the United States Supreme Court upheld the individual mandate of the Affordable Care Act (ACA).[35] However, it did so on the ground that it was a valid exercise of congressional power under the taxing clause.

The high court did not agree with the federal government's argument that the mandate was a lawful exercise of commerce clause authority. In rejecting this argument, Chief Justice Roberts said that the power to regulate presupposes the existence of the commercial activity to be regulated. The act was not regulating existing activity but, rather, was trying to require people to become active. Roberts feared that extending the reach of regulation under the commerce clause to individuals because they were doing nothing would open a

[35] National Federation of Independent Business v. Sebelius, 132 S. Ct. 25666 (2012).

[continued]

new and potentially vast domain to congressional authority. He noted that the Constitution gave Congress the authority to regulate commerce, not compel it.

In her opinion, Justice Ginsburg disagreed with the chief justice's contention that the ACA was not a regulation of commerce. She pointed out that the uninsured are in fact very active in the market for health care services and that it is the legislature that should determine the borders of the market that it is attempting to regulate. She also pointed out that the high court has upheld the authority of Congress to direct the conduct of individuals today because of their prophesied conduct tomorrow, noting that as far back in the history of commerce clause interpretation as *Wickard v. Filburn,* the court upheld prohibiting a farmer's growing wheat for home consumption because in the future he might grow wheat for sale in the market. And in *Raisch,* home-grown marijuana could be regulated because at some point in the future, the price of marijuana in the market may lead the individual growing for home consumption to enter the market as a seller, just as the uninsured in the future might need medical care. And, in fact, the need for medical care at some future date is much more certain than entry in the market in either *Filburn* or *Raisch.*

Because the high court upheld the constitutionality of the individual mandate, it did not have to address the issue of whether it was severable from the rest of the act.

KEY TERMS

commerce clause 95
commercial speech 106
concurrent authority 95
contract clause 103
dormant commerce clause 100
due process clause 114
equal protection clause 117
establishment clause 110
federal preemption 95
federalism 93
free-exercise clause 111
full faith and credit clause 103
intermediate scrutiny 118
judicial review 94
police power 100
political speech 104
privileges and immunities clause 103
procedural due process 114
rational-basis test 118
search warrant 112
strict scrutiny 117
substantive due process 115
supremacy clause 94
takings clause 115

SUMMARY OF KEY TOPICS

The U.S. Constitution

Federalism: The authority to govern is divided between two sovereigns, or supreme lawmakers: the federal government and the states.

Checks and balances: The Constitution divides power among the legislative, executive, and judicial branches of government. The system of checks and balances allocates specific powers to each branch to keep the other branches from dominating government.

The Supremacy Clause and Federal Preemption

Federal supremacy: Any state or local law that directly conflicts with the U.S. Constitution or federal laws or treaties is void.

Concurrent authority: Both state and federal governments have the power to regulate certain matters; generally, the federal government defers to the state.

Federal preemption: The federal government uses this doctrine to strike down laws that do not directly conflict with a federal law but attempt to regulate an area within federal legislative jurisdiction.

The Commerce Clause

This clause grants the federal government the authority to pass regulations that significantly affect interstate commerce. Today, it provides the basis for most federal government regulations.

Police powers are the residual powers retained by states to pass laws to safeguard the health and welfare of their citizens.

The *dormant commerce clause* prohibits states from passing laws that significantly interfere with interstate commerce.

Taxing and Spending Powers of the Federal Government

Congressional taxes must be uniform across all states. Congress can use taxes and spending for purposes other than generating revenue; e.g., it can use them to indirectly promote social goals.

Other Constitutional Restrictions on Government

The *privileges and immunities clause* prohibits states from discriminating against citizens of other states.

The *full faith and credit clause* states that in civil matters, courts in all states must uphold rights established by legal documents.

The *contract clause* states that Congress cannot pass laws that unreasonably interfere with existing contracts.

The Amendments to the Constitution

First Amendment:

- Protects corporate speech in certain circumstances. It protects corporate political speech to the same extent that it protects individuals' political speech. The Central Hudson test determines whether the First Amendment protects particular corporate commercial speech.
- Contains the *establishment clause,* which states that Congress may not make laws respecting an establishment of religion, and the *free-exercise clause,* which states that Congress may not make laws prohibiting the free exercise of religion.

Fourth Amendment:

- Protects both corporations and individuals from unreasonable government searches and seizures. Although administrative searches generally require a warrant, administrative agencies may inspect some industries without a warrant to ensure compliance with industry regulations.

Fifth Amendment:

- States that government cannot take an individual's life, liberty, or property without due process of law. There are two types of due process: *procedural due process,* which focuses on rules for enforcing laws and entitles individuals to notice of legal action against them, and *substantive due process,* which requires that government have a proper purpose for enacting laws that restrict individuals' liberty or the use of their property.
- States that if government takes private property for public use, it must compensate the owner. The extent to which some government regulations constitute takings, however, generates much litigation.

- Includes a privilege against self-incrimination, although the provision does not apply to corporations. Only individual citizens and sole proprietorships may exercise this right.
- Guarantees individuals equal protection under the law. Courts use three different standards of scrutiny in equal protection cases: (1) *strict scrutiny,* to analyze government actions that abridge fundamental rights or that include suspect classifications; (2) *intermediate scrutiny,* to analyze classifications based on gender or on legitimacy of children; (3) the *rational-basis test,* to analyze classifications involving other matters.

Fourteenth Amendment:

- Applies the due process clause, except parts of the Fifth Amendment, to the states and contains the equal protection clause.

POINT / COUNTERPOINT

Should Warrantless Wiretapping Be Allowed under the Fourth Amendment ?

YES

Warrantless wiretapping differs from standard wiretapping procedures only in the lack of a court-ordered warrant. In matters of national security and cases in which secrecy is of paramount importance, the acquisition of intelligence information must come before the procedural formalities of the legal system. Valuable surveillance necessary for the protection of U.S. citizens is conducted by warrantless wiretapping and should not be prevented because of a lack of a warrant.

The Internet has spawned an expanded realm of communications that creates new risks to national security. Technologies such as e-mail, instant messaging, and websites allow individuals or nations to communicate in ways that are difficult to monitor in real time while still trying to obtain a warrant. Internet technology has accelerated the pace of communication, and the methods for surveillance must accelerate as well to match. Some terrorist attacks have been planned not through traditional channels, for which it is reasonable to obtain warrants in advance, but through the Internet. New situations require new methods of surveillance.

The events of recent years demand a reexamination of the traditional intent of the Fourth Amendment. The rise in terrorist attacks and the new dynamics of conflict have shifted the nature of the conflict from that of conflict between nations to that of conflict among factions within one nation or several. Traditional conceptions of how wiretapping was applied in a different time must be replaced to preserve the overall intent of the Fourth Amendment: to keep people "secure in their persons."

NO

The Fourth Amendment was designed to protect the right to privacy of all U.S. citizens. Breaching that privacy without a court-ordered warrant sets a dangerous precedent for the powers given to the federal government. The act of wiretapping without a warrant from the court violates the separation of powers doctrine by placing full authority for search and seizure in the hands of the executive branch of the federal government.

Moreover, the Internet has brought forth a wide array of additional methods of communication that can potentially be "wiretapped." E-mail, instant messaging, websites, and other forms of electronic communication compound the problem by rendering private citizens even more vulnerable to surveillance by the federal government. Because electronic wiretaps are easier to obtain, monitor, and record than traditional wiretaps, the volume of information that the federal government can gather and use is significantly larger than it was before the advent of the Internet.

Questions have been raised as to the efficacy of the warrantless wiretapping program. Since the program remains shrouded in secrecy, it is hard to demonstrate a reasonable benefit from the wiretapping. The program was initially designed for monitoring communications into and out of other countries, not within the borders of the United States. Nevertheless, the program has recently been applied to U.S. citizens communicating within U.S. borders. This marks a vast expansion of the power of the federal government regarding surveillance of the civilian population.

QUESTIONS & PROBLEMS

1. Explain how each branch of the government checks the power of the other branches.
2. How can both Sue and Sam be correct when Sue claims the commerce clause increases government's power and Sam claims the commerce clause reduces government's power?
3. What is the purpose of the contract clause?
4. How does the First Amendment protection of corporate political speech differ from the protection of corporate commercial speech?
5. In 2007, the Prescription Confidentiality Law was passed in the state of Vermont. One of the key measures of the law was that it stipulated that without a doctor's consent, any documents containing information about prescribing practices could not be sold or used for marketing. The law was in response to some companies' practice of using doctors' personal prescribing histories without the doctors' knowledge. Subsequently, pharmaceutical and data companies argued that the law violated their First Amendment rights by restricting their speech without good reason. Are the companies right? How did the court decide? [*Sorrell v. IMS Health Inc.*, 131 S. Ct. 2653 (2011).]
6. Arizona uses a three-tier system for regulation of wine sales in the state. Suppliers sell to wholesalers, who sell to retailers, who sell to the public. However, an exception is provided for small wineries that produce no more than 20,000 gallons of wine annually; they may sell an unlimited amount of wine directly to the public and directly to retailers, regardless of where the small winery is located. A second exception allows any winery to ship up to two cases of its wine per year directly to a consumer, but only if the consumer is physically at the winery when the order is placed. Black Star Farms, a winery that produces 40,000 gallons of wine annually and thus cannot take advantage of the small-winery exception, sued to have the exceptions struck down on grounds that they violated the dormant commerce clause. The district court found that there was no violation of the dormant commerce clause because the law treated both in-state and out-of-state wineries the same. How do you think the appellate court ruled on Black Star Farm's appeal and why? [*Black Star Farms v. Oliver,* 600 F.3d 1225 (2010).]
7. During a legal search of Alvin Smith's house, police discovered a large amount of child pornography. A subsequent police investigation revealed that Smith had taken 1,768 sexually explicit pictures of girls below the age of 18. The investigation also revealed that the children depicted in the pictures were Florida residents and that Smith, a Florida resident, took the pictures in his house. The paper on which the photographs were printed, however, came from Rochester, New York, and the photographs were processed by equipment made in California. The government prosecuted Smith for violating a federal statute prohibiting child pornography. Smith challenged his conviction on grounds that Congress overstepped its commerce clause authority because his production of child pornography did not involve or substantially affect interstate commerce. Do you think the court agreed with Smith's argument? Why or why not? [*United States v. Smith,* 402 F.3d 1303 (2005).]
8. Robert Stevens maintained a website through which he sold videos that showed pit bulls engaging in dogfights. He was convicted of violating a federal statute, 18 U.S.C.S. § 48, that made it a criminal offense to sell depictions of animal cruelty, defined as the maiming, mutilation, torture, wounding, or killing of an animal, that violated the law of the state where the creation, sale, or possession of the depiction of the cruelty occurred. The defendant argued that his conviction should be overturned because the statute was facially invalid under the First Amendment. The United States Supreme Court ultimately agreed with Stevens and overturned his conviction. Explain the reasoning that you believe supports this outcome. [*United States v. Robert Stevens,* 130 S. Ct. 1577 (2010).]
9. The Glendale Traffic Code prohibited any cars parked on public streets from having for-sale signs on them. Cars with for-sale signs could be parked only on private driveways or private property. When Pagan was ordered by police to remove the for-sale sign in his car that was parked on the public street in front of his house, he challenged the

ordinance as violating his First Amendment rights. Do you think the court agreed or disagreed with him? Why? [*Pagan v. Fruchey,* 492 F.3d 766 (6th Cir. 2007).]

10. In 2004, the Oklahoma state legislature amended laws that previously forbade employees from bringing firearms onto company property. Under the amended laws, employers could be held criminally liable if they prohibited employees from storing firearms inside their locked vehicles while located on company property. Multiple Oklahoma business owners filed a suit to challenge the constitutionality of the amendments. The owners argued, among other things, that the Occupational Safety and Health Act was passed to establish standards for worker safety and, therefore, that the states were preempted from passing a law that might interfere with the creation of a safe workplace. The district court found that the amended state laws created an obstacle to the creation of a safe workplace in accordance with the Occupational Safety and Health Act and therefore ruled in favor of the employers. The case was appealed to the 10th U.S. Circuit Court of Appeals. Do you believe the court of appeals agreed that OSHA preempted the state law? Why or why not? [*Ramsey Winch Inc. et al. v. C. Brad Henry et al.,* No. 07-5166, 2009 WL 388050 (10th Cir., Feb. 18, 2009).]

Looking for more review material?

The Online Learning Center at **www.mhhe.com/kubasek3e** contains this chapter's "Assignment on the Internet" and also a list of URLs for more information, entitled "On the Internet." Find both of them in the Student Center portion of the OLC, along with quizzes and other helpful materials.

CHAPTER

6 International and Comparative Law

LEARNING OBJECTIVES

After reading this chapter, you will be able to answer the following questions:

1. What is international law?
2. How is business transacted in the international marketplace?
3. What ethical considerations impact business in the international marketplace?
4. What is the General Agreement on Tariffs and Trade, and what are its important provisions?
5. What are regional trade agreements?
6. What is comparative law?
7. How does contract law differ among states?
8. How does employment law differ among states?
9. How are disputes settled in the international marketplace?

CASE OPENER

Resolving a Breach of Contract under the CISG

Chicago Prime Packers, Inc., is a Colorado corporation with its principal place of business in Avon, Colorado. Northam Food Trading Company is a Canadian corporation with its principal place of business in Montreal, Quebec, Canada. Chicago Prime and Northam are wholesalers of meat products. On March 30, 2001, Chicago Prime contracted with Northam to sell 1,350 boxes (40,500 pounds) of government-inspected fresh, blast-frozen pork back ribs, which Chicago Prime purchased from Brookfield Farms, a meat processor. The agreed-on price for the ribs was $178,200, and payment was required within seven days of the date of shipment. The ribs were stored at three different locations en route to Northam's customer Beacon Premium Meats, but at all times they were stored at or below acceptable temperatures. The ribs ultimately proved to be spoiled and were condemned by the U.S. Department of Agriculture. Nevertheless, Chicago Prime continued to demand payment from Northam. Chicago Prime brought a breach-of-contract action against Northam in U.S. federal court after Northam refused to pay for the ribs.

1. What law will the court apply to this transaction?
2. Could the parties have selected the law for the court to apply before the occurrence of their dispute?

The Wrap-Up at the end of this chapter will answer these questions.

LO1 What is international law?

The terms *international law* and *comparative law* are often used interchangeably, but they are quite different. **International law** governs the conduct of states and international organizations and their relationships with one another and with natural and juridical persons.[1]

A *state,* for purposes of international law, is an entity possessing territory, a permanent population, a government, and the legal capacity to engage in diplomatic relations.[2] We generally think of *international organizations* as consisting of states. The United Nations, the International Monetary Fund, the International Bank for Reconstruction and Development (World Bank), and the World Trade Organization are international organizations. The term *natural and juridical persons* refers to individuals as well as business organizations.

In contrast, **comparative law** is the study of the legal systems of different states. For example, a comparative legal theorist might study contracts in the American, Chinese, and French legal systems by identifying and contrasting applicable national laws. Comparative legal studies start with the examination of national sources of law embodied in constitutions, legislative enactments, administrative rules and regulations, and the decisions of judicial bodies. But where do we find principles of international law? Article 38 of the Statute of the International Court of Justice, a part of the United Nations system, identifies four sources of international law: customs, international agreements, general principles of law recognized by legal systems throughout the world (such as equity and elementary considerations of humanity), and secondary sources (such as decisions of the International Court of Justice, resolutions of the U.N. General Assembly, and scholarly writings).[3]

Legal Principle: International law governs the conduct of states and international organizations and their relationships with one another and natural and juridical persons, while comparative law is the study of legal systems of different states.

Most important for our purposes are customs and international agreements. *Customary international law* has two characteristics. First, in order to be deemed a custom, a practice must be general and consistent among states. Second, states must accept this general and consistent practice as binding law. The U.S. Supreme Court has held that in the absence of a governing international agreement or controlling executive or legislative act or judicial decision, U.S. courts must rely on customary international law.[4]

[1] Restatement (Third) of the Foreign Relations Law of the United States, § 101 (1987).

[2] Montevideo Convention on the Rights and Duties of States, December 26, 1933, art. 1, 165 L.N.T.S. 19, reprinted in *American Journal of International Law* 28 (Supp. 1934), p. 75.

[3] Statute of the International Court of Justice, June 26, 1945, art. 38, 59 Stat. 1055, 1060.

[4] *Paquete Habana,* 175 U.S. 677, 700 (1900).

By contrast, an *international agreement* is a written agreement made between states governed by international law that relates to an international matter.[5] International agreements can be bilateral (between two states) or multilateral (between three or more states). Regardless of their form, they do not take effect until ratified. Ratification occurs in many different ways. In the United States, it requires the advice and consent of two-thirds of the Senate after the president submits the agreement for consideration.[6]

Doing Business Internationally

LO2

How is business transacted in the international marketplace?

The simplest method of entering a foreign market is through the *export* of the company's product to the foreign marketplace. A **foreign sales representative** is an agent who distributes, represents, or sells goods on behalf of a foreign seller and forwards orders directly to the company. The representative is usually compensated through commissions on completed transactions. Companies may also engage **distributors** for their products, who purchase goods from a seller for resale in a foreign market. Distributors are responsible for supporting and servicing the products they sell. Unlike the foreign sales representative, the distributor takes title to the goods and assumes the risk of being unable to resell them at a profit.

BUT WHAT IF . . .

What if the facts of the Case Opener were different?

Recall, in the Case Opener, that both Northam and Chicago Prime were wholesalers. Let's say that Northam bought Chicago Prime meat from a distributor. The distributor picked up the meat from Chicago Prime and then made a deal with Northam to sell Northam the meat. When Northam received the meat, inspectors discovered that it was rancid. It turned out that the meat had been bad when the distributor picked it up from Chicago Prime. Who has to absorb the cost of the bad meat—Chicago Prime or the distributor?

To see how economics and trade deficits relate to international business, please see the **Connecting to the Core** activity on the text website at www.mhhe.com/kubasek3e.

Companies seeking to enter foreign markets may also do so through franchise and licensing agreements. A **franchise agreement** is a contract whereby a company (known as the *franchisor*) grants permission (a license) to a foreign entity (known as a *franchisee*) to utilize the franchisor's name, trademark, or copyright in the operation of a business and associated sale of goods in a foreign state. In return for this license, the franchisee pays the franchisor, usually a percentage of the franchisee's gross or net sales. In a **licensing agreement,** the foreign company (known as the *licensor*) grants permission to a company in the targeted market (known as the *licensee*) to utilize the licensor's intellectual property, consisting of patents, trademarks, copyrights, or trade secrets. In return, the licensor receives royalty payments from the licensee, usually based on the licensee's gross or net sales.

Companies seeking a more permanent presence in a foreign jurisdiction have several options. A company may establish a *representative office* for limited purposes, such as market analysis or product promotion. An even more significant presence arises from a **joint venture** with a company in the host state, wherein the parties share profits and management responsibilities for a specific project. Companies may also establish a

[5] Vienna Convention on the Law of Treaties, May 23, 1969, art. 2, 1155 U.N.T.S. 331.

[6] U.S. Const., art. II, § 2, cl. 2.

foreign subsidiary, or **affiliate.** An affiliate is a business enterprise located in one state that is directly or indirectly owned and controlled by a company located in another state. The affiliate is usually established in conformity with the laws of the foreign state and is subject to that state's regulation.

Ethical Considerations

LO3 What ethical considerations impact business in the international marketplace?

International businesspersons must take ethical considerations into account in the decision-making process. A company considering exporting its product for ultimate consumption by overseas consumers must resolve usage and safety issues. Foreign consumers may not fully understand risks associated with use of the product, or national safety standards may offer less protection than those applicable in the United States. Although tobacco products, for example, are subject to stringent regulation in the United States with respect to advertising, health warnings, and availability to minors, that is the exception rather than the global norm.

Ethical considerations are not limited to products. Companies must also carefully consider the location of their operations. Ethical considerations also arise from how a company does business overseas. For example, the **Foreign Corrupt Practices Act (FCPA)** prohibits U.S. companies from offering or paying bribes to foreign government officials, political parties, and candidates for office for the purpose of obtaining or retaining business.[7] The direct trigger for the FCPA was an investigation launched by the U.S. Securities and Exchange Commission in the 1970s that discovered 450 U.S. companies had engaged in bribery overseas totaling more than $400 million. For example, aircraft manufacturer Lockheed paid $12.6 million to Japanese officials and $10 million to Dutch, Italian, and German officials in its efforts to convince these officials to purchase Lockheed aircraft on behalf of their respective governments. The FCPA also requires that firms maintain records to fairly and accurately reflect transactions and the disposition of assets. Exhibit 6-1 summarizes recently settled cases involving alleged violations of the FCPA.

The General Agreement on Tariffs and Trade

LO4 What is the General Agreement on Tariffs and Trade, and what are its important provisions?

There are two primary types of barriers to international trade. **Tariffs** are taxes levied on imported goods. They can be calculated as a percentage of the value of the imported good *(ad valorem tariff),* on the basis of the number or weight of the imported units or a flat per-unit charge *(specific tariff),* or as a combination of the two *(compound tariff).* A **nontariff**

[7] 15 U.S.C. §§ 78dd-1–78ff (2010).

Exhibit 6-1 Summary of Recent Settlements of FCPA Cases

COMPANY	STATE	CONTRACT	FINE (MILLIONS)
Baker Hughes	Kazakhstan	Oil and gas	$ 44.0
Kellogg, Brown & Root	Nigeria	Natural gas	579.0
Siemens	China, Russia, and 7 other states	Equipment, service, and construction	$1,600.0
Titan Corporation	Benin	Telecommunications	28.5
Willbros Group	Nigeria	Oil services	32.0

barrier is any impediment to trade other than tariffs, including quotas, embargoes, and indirect barriers. *Quotas* are limits on imported goods, usually imposed for national economic reasons or for the protection of domestic industry. An *embargo* is a ban on trade with a particular state or on the sale of specific products, usually on the basis of foreign policy or national security. *Indirect barriers* are laws, practices, customs, and traditions that limit or discourage the sale and purchase of imported goods.

The **General Agreement on Tariffs and Trade (GATT)** is a comprehensive multilateral trading system designed to achieve distortion-free international trade by minimizing tariffs and removing artificial barriers. GATT is a legacy of the Great Depression and World War II. Originally conceived as a temporary measure, it became effective on January 1, 1948, and included the United States as one of 23 signing countries. Since then it has undergone numerous changes as a result of eight different negotiating rounds. The most recently completed round is the Uruguay Round, which was completed in 1994 and took effect on January 1, 1995. Thus, the most recent version of GATT is known as *GATT 1994*. The most recent round of GATT, the Doha Development Agenda, has been under negotiation for several years, and negotiations for its completion are presently stalled.

The Uruguay Round established the **World Trade Organization (WTO)**. The WTO facilitates international cooperation in opening markets and provides a forum for future trade negotiations and the settlement of international trade disputes. WTO membership presently consists of 157 states, thereby making the WTO the most comprehensive trading system in world history.

GATT established several general principles of trade law. Article I addresses the principle of *most-favored-nation* relations, a principle now known as **normal trade relations.** This principle requires that WTO member states treat like goods coming from other WTO member states on an equal basis. WTO member states are specifically prohibited from discriminating against like products on the basis of their country of origin. **National treatment** is set forth in Article III. It prohibits WTO member states from regulating, taxing, or otherwise treating imported products any differently from domestically produced products. Article XI prohibits **quantitative restrictions** that limit the importation of certain products on the basis of number of units, weight, or value, for national economic reasons, or for the protection of domestic industry.

Legal Principle: As a general rule, GATT and the WTO prohibit discrimination against imported goods on the basis of their country of origin and also prevent quantitative restrictions on such imports.

BUT WHAT IF . . .

What if the facts of the Case Opener were different?

Let's say, in the Case Opener, that Northam, the Canadian company, was trying to sell products to Chicago Prime, the American company. To import the products, Chicago Prime had to pay an extra .06 percent tax on the products. Also, Chicago Prime could purchase only 200 pounds of Northam's meat products. Which impediment is a tariff, and which is a nontariff barrier? What is the reasoning behind imposing such barriers?

Article VI relates to dumping and subsidies. **Dumping** is the practice wherein an exporter sells products in a foreign state for less than the price charged for the same or comparable goods in the exporter's home market. Article VI condemns dumping if it causes or threatens to cause material injury to an established industry. Government authorities usually make this determination by examining the volume of imports, their effect on prices, and their impact on the industry. After investigation, the remedy for dumping is the assessment of *antidumping duties,* tariffs equal to the difference between the export and domestic prices.

A **subsidy** is a government payment to a specific industry or enterprise. Subsidies can be direct transfers of funds, such as loans and grants; loan guarantees; tax credits; government procurement; and price supports. There are three basic types. *Actionable subsidies* are illegal under Article VI. They include subsidies payable to domestic manufacturers either on the basis of export performance or for the use of domestic, rather than imported, input in the manufacturing process. Actionable subsidies are remedied through the imposition of countervailing duties, special tariffs imposed on subsidized goods to offset the benefit of the illegal subsidy. *Nonactionable subsidies* are expenditures on research and development, aid to underdeveloped regions within a state, and aid to foster compliance with environmental standards. *Domestic subsidies* are generally not actionable unless they are not part of the government's legitimate responsibility of directing industrial growth and funding social programs and they cause material injury to other WTO member states.

Legal Principle: As a general rule, GATT and the WTO prohibit dumping and subsidies that are based on export performance or the use of domestic rather than imported input in the manufacturing process.

The **Dispute Settlement Understanding** allows recognized governments of WTO member states to bring an action alleging a violation. After an aggrieved state files a complaint, the states that are parties to the dispute consult with one another in an attempt to resolve the dispute. The states may also ask a trade expert to mediate. If these efforts are unsuccessful, the WTO Secretariat establishes a panel of three to five trade experts to hear oral arguments and review the written submissions of the parties. The panel then drafts and ultimately adopts a report determining the merits of the claims. Aggrieved states have the right to contest the panel's decision before the WTO's appellate body. The panel and the appellate body may only recommend that a state found in violation of its obligations cease and desist from such practices within a reasonable time. Failure to comply may lead to the imposition of sanctions, usually consisting of the suspension of concessions by the injured state. Such sanctions may impose only an equivalent burden on the noncomplying state and can be imposed only for as long as the trade barrier remains in place.

Regional Trade Agreements

LO5 What are regional trade agreements?

There are three basic types of regional trade agreements: multilateral free trade agreements, customs unions, and bilateral free trade agreements. In a multilateral **free trade agreement,** three or more states agree to reduce and gradually eliminate tariffs and other trade barriers. The **North American Free Trade Agreement (NAFTA)** between the United States, Canada, and Mexico is a multilateral free trade agreement. In effect since January 1, 1994, NAFTA mirrors many of the provisions set forth in GATT but accords favorable treatment only to goods of "North American origin." NAFTA also reduces barriers to direct foreign investment and ensures the free flow of capital. Disputes between NAFTA members are resolved through a dispute resolution process coordinated by the Free Trade Commission. This process includes attempts to reach a negotiated settlement, the convocation of dispute resolution panels to hear evidence and determine the existence of a violation, and enforcement of orders through the authorization of retaliation in the event of noncompliance. Unlike the WTO system, NAFTA addresses environmental and workers' rights issues. Its three members pledge to cooperate in protecting the environment and developing common environmental standards. They also recognize basic labor rights, including freedom of association, the right to engage in collective bargaining and strikes, prohibitions on forced labor and child labor, freedom from employment discrimination, the right to receive equal pay for work of equal value, and the right to minimum acceptable working conditions and occupational safety and health. The United States is also a party to the Central American Free Trade Agreement (CAFTA) with El Salvador, Guatemala, Nicaragua, Honduras, Costa Rica, and the Dominican Republic.

A *customs union* is a free trade area with the additional feature of a common external tariff on products originating outside the union. The European Union (EU) is a customs union. It is a loose association of states with a basis in international law formed for the purpose of forging closer ties among the peoples of Europe. The modern EU had its inception in three treaties between Belgium, France, Italy, Luxembourg, the Netherlands, and West Germany (now Germany) in the 1950s. These treaties integrated industrial sectors within the states, eradicated internal tariffs, created a common external tariff for goods originating in nonmember states, and strove to create a common market through the free movement of people, services, goods, and capital. Subsequent rounds of expansion added Austria, Denmark, Finland, Greece, Ireland, Portugal, Spain, Sweden, and the United Kingdom. Expansion in 2004 added 10 more states: Cyprus, the Czech Republic, Estonia, Hungary, Latvia, Lithuania, Malta, Poland, Slovakia, and Slovenia. This expansion created the largest regional trading bloc in the world, containing more than 500 million people. The most recent expansions in 2007 and 2013 added Bulgaria, Romania, and Croatia.

States may also enter into **bilateral free trade agreements,** which relate to trade between two states. The United States has several bilateral free trade agreements, including those with Australia, Bahrain, Chile, Colombia, Israel, Jordan, Korea, Morocco, Oman, Panama, Peru, and Singapore.

Comparative Law

LO6 What is comparative law?

What are the benefits of comparing the laws and legal systems of different states? First, we gain a better understanding of the general purpose of law by studying other legal systems and their goals. Second, we can better develop a critical viewpoint on our own legal system as just one of many alternatives. Third, the specific laws you will encounter will likely be different from U.S. laws. After thinking critically about alternative laws, you might decide your own state should adopt the other state's law or method of resolving a dispute.

What do comparative legal scholars actually study? What kinds of questions do they ask? Generally they ask two types: questions about the system and its procedures and questions about substantive law. Below we look at different legal systems and procedures. Then we consider substantive law by comparing contract law and employment law in a variety of states. The chapter concludes with a look at dispute resolution between private parties.

Legal Systems and Procedures

CIVIL LAW SYSTEMS

Many *civil law systems* are derived from Roman law. Other civil law systems were strongly influenced by the French Civil Code of 1804 and the German Civil Code of 1896. Other legal systems fashioned their own laws around a mixture of these. The codes generally covered areas of private law such as property, contracts, torts, and family law and tended to reflect preferences for the protection of private property, individual freedom, and freedom of contract.

Today, codes in civil law systems serve as the sole official source of law. Secondary sources include custom and general principles of law; precedent is not an important source of civil law. The civil law system is the most common legal system in the world. We find examples in most European nations, the People's Republic of China, and Japan. Louisiana, because of its French roots, has a "mixed" legal system.

Civil law systems assume a separation of powers, but it is unlike the U.S. system of checks and balances. In civil law systems, the legislative branch has ultimate authority. Remember, the ultimate source of law in a civil law system is the code. The judicial branch interprets the code and applies it to resolve disputes. However, the judicial branch cannot create its own law. Thus, the separation of powers refers to the limitations on the judicial branch and the superiority of the codes.

Judges in the civil law system typically assume the role early in their careers, following a training period and examination. At the highest judicial levels they are typically professors or experienced practitioners.

After the pleadings have entered the legal system, the evidence period—a series of meetings and hearings—begins. The judge is primarily responsible for developing evidence by asking witnesses questions and introducing legal theories. Neither the parties nor the judge is required to formally admit evidence to the court, and hearsay and opinion are acceptable.

Judges in the civil law system have primary responsibility for determining and applying the correct legal principles. However, the judge responsible for deciding the case may not be the same one who helped gather evidence. In fact, several judges might serve on a panel to decide the case.

COMMON LAW SYSTEMS

Common law systems originated in the English legal system. English common law began in 1066, when William the Conqueror assumed the English throne. The centralization of government that followed paved the way for a centralized court system.

In the common law system, the courts develop rules governing areas of law. In addition to relying on constitutions, legislation, and regulations, they are guided by precedent, or *stare decisis;* thus, if a higher court has created a precedent, a lower court is bound by that precedent. However, if a court cannot find a precedent to guide its reasoning, it may offer its own rule. Both the emphasis on precedent and the judge's ability to create rules are important characteristics of common law systems. Common law systems exist in Australia, India, the United Kingdom, and the United States.

Unlike civil law judges who are trained and tested, judges in the common law system are typically appointed. In the United States, some judges are elected.

Because common law judges have opportunities to make law through their decisions, they are relatively well known and the public perceives them as powerful. Some in the United States have been criticized for being "activists" and going beyond the bounds of their roles.

The common law system is an *adversarial system,* in which two opposing sides present their arguments before a neutral fact finder who determines which side has presented the most credible evidence or met its burden of proof. The adversarial method leads to procedures that differ from those in civil law systems. First, after the advocates enter pleadings in the common law system, there is a period in which discovery is conducted. Second, the judge typically does not become significantly involved in the case until trial. Third, in the common law system, the judge is not responsible for gathering any evidence; the parties themselves bear this responsibility. Fourth, common law systems often rely on juries as fact finders; civil law systems do not use juries. Fifth, as a consequence of the use of juries, common law systems have extensive rules governing admissibility of evidence.

OTHER LEGAL SYSTEMS

Although the civil and common law systems are predominant, other legal systems deserve mention. *Socialist legal systems,* such as exist in Cuba and North Korea, are based on the premise that the rights of society as a whole outweigh the rights of the individual. In such systems, law does not act as a limit on the exercise of government power. Traditionally, the state owns the means of production and property in a socialist legal system.

An *Islamic legal system* is based on the fundamental tenet that law is derived from and interpreted in harmony with *Shari'a* ("God's law") and the Koran. The preeminent concern is moral conduct, such as honoring agreements and acting in good faith. However, there are many interpretations of Islamic law, as evidenced by the differences between the legal systems in Iran, Pakistan, and Saudi Arabia and that practiced by the former Taliban regime in Afghanistan.

Substantive Law

COMPARATIVE CONTRACT LAW

LO7

How does contract law differ among states?

The U.S. businessperson in the global marketplace should give careful thought to the question of what law may be applicable to the interpretation and enforcement of his or her contracts. Anyone who assumes all applicable laws are identical, or similar enough that differences do not matter, is likely to be unpleasantly surprised. This section reviews the sources of contract law in the international marketplace and notes some of the similarities and differences between these sources.

The Lex Mercatoria and National Contract Codes. One potential source of contract law is the *lex mercatoria,* literally the "law of merchants." This is the body of customs or trade usages merchants developed to facilitate business transactions. Its sources are public international law, uniform laws, general principles of contract law, rules of international organizations, custom and usage, standard form contracts, and arbitral decisions.

Another source of law applicable to international contracts is *national laws.* In the United States, these laws are embodied in the common law of contracts and, for contracts relating to the sale of goods, in the Uniform Commercial Code. Given the predominance of the civil law system, most nations' contract laws are set forth in codes. These codes have many similarities to U.S. law. For example, Section 2-615 of the Uniform Commercial Code excuses delays in the delivery of goods or nondelivery in the event performance has been rendered "impracticable by the occurrence of a contingency the nonoccurrence of which was a basic assumption on which the contract was made." In a similar fashion, the Civil Code of the Russian Federation excuses nonperformance if it is the result of an unanticipated "essential change of circumstances" that could not be avoided through the exercise of reasonable care. A similar excuse for nonperformance exists in the Unified Contract Law of the People's Republic of China and in the Principles of European Contract Law. Under China's national contract code, a nonperforming party is excused from liability if its inability to perform was the result of *force majeure* ("superior force"). Force majeure is a "situation which, on an objective view, is unforeseeable, unavoidable and is not able to be overcome." The Principles of European Contract Law excuse nonperformance if it is due to an impediment that is not "reasonably expected" and is beyond the control of the nonperforming party.

BUT WHAT IF . . .

What if the facts of the Case Opener were different?

Let's say that products from Northam were being shipped to Russia, China, and the United States. The plane was to make a stop in all three countries and had delivery contracts with all three stating the shipment would arrive no later than the following week. However, the plane encountered an unforeseeable tropical storm and was unable to deliver the products by the date stated in the contracts. According to clauses in the contract laws of the countries, how would China, Russia, and the United States respond?

Despite their similarities, the differences between U.S. law and national contract codes may be very pronounced. The Principles of European Contract Law provide that a contract is concluded only when the acceptance reaches the offeror. The principles further require that the parties give reasons for terminating contract negotiations. In the United States, parties do not owe one another a duty to negotiate in good faith and may terminate negotiations in bad faith without liability unless the other party relied on the likelihood of a final agreement. Furthermore, the European Principles do not require that the contract be in writing. Rather, a contract can be proved by any means. Contracts are subject to interpretation utilizing the totality of the circumstances surrounding the transaction, including statements made by the parties before entering into the contract.

Even in the areas where U.S. law and national contract codes converge, international businesspeople must be aware of differences. Despite having writing requirements like those in the United States, China's Unified Contract Law provides, in addition, that all written contracts must state the name and residence of each party, subject matter of the contract, quantity and quality of the subject matter, price, time, place and methods of contractual performance, liability for breach, and methods of dispute resolution.

Legal Principle: **Despite numerous similarities among contract laws, international businesspersons must be aware of significant differences between U.S. and other national contract laws.**

The Convention on the International Sale of Goods. The Convention on the International Sale of Goods (CISG) applies to the commercial sale of goods. A *commercial sale of goods* is the exchange of tangible personal property between merchants in return for consideration. A *merchant* is a person engaged in the transfer of goods in the ordinary course of business.

The CISG was adopted in 1980 and has been ratified by the majority of states in the developed world, including Australia, Canada, China, Korea, Mexico, Russia, most nations of Western Europe, and the United States, where it became effective in 1988. Notable states that have not adopted the CISG include Brazil, India, Pakistan, Saudi Arabia, and the United Kingdom.

Two sets of laws govern the sale of goods in the United States, the CISG and the Uniform Commercial Code (UCC). The UCC applies when both parties to the sales transaction are residents of the United States. The CISG is applicable when one party is a U.S. resident and the other is a resident of a jurisdiction that has ratified the CISG. Nevertheless, the parties are always free to opt out of the CISG and select another law to apply to their transaction. In the absence of such a selection, the CISG applies to the sale of goods between merchants residing in different states that have ratified the CISG. The CISG also applies if national conflict-of-law rules direct the court or arbitral body to apply the law of a state that has ratified the CISG. Finally, the CISG may serve as evidence of trade usage and customs. National contract law applies in areas not covered by the CISG, such as services, real estate, and intellectual property.

How do U.S. businesspeople determine which set of rules they want to apply to their international contracts? There are numerous similarities between the UCC and CISG. For example, both recognize express warranties and implied warranties of merchantability and fitness for a particular purpose arising from the sale of goods.[8] Both the UCC and the CISG limit damages to those that were foreseeable at the time of the formation of the contract. Furthermore, only damages that can be proved with some degree of certainty may be awarded. The nonbreaching party has a duty to mitigate damages, and damage awards can be reduced to the extent that the loss could have been prevented or minimized through mitigation.

However, the differences between the UCC and CISG are substantial in many areas. Exhibit 6-2 summarizes some of these differences.

COMPARATIVE EMPLOYMENT LAW

LO8

How does employment law differ among states?

The employment relationship in the United States is governed by the *employment-at-will standard.* This standard means either the employer or the employee may terminate the employment relationship at any time. Furthermore, both parties are free to determine the conditions of employment. If an express employment agreement exists, however, and either party breaks it, the other can sue for breach of contract.

Although the employment-at-will doctrine remains predominant in the United States, the nature of the employment relationship has changed. Federal, state, and local government restrictions protect workers in the areas of minimum wages, unemployment and workers' compensation, occupational health and safety, employment discrimination, and termination. These restrictions vary significantly when a U.S. firm seeks to hire employees outside the United States where the employment-at-will standard does not apply.

This section discusses two such differences, minimum-wage laws and termination. We conclude with a look at the effect of international labor standards on the employment relationship.

Exhibit 6-2

Some Differences between the UCC and the CISG

RULE OR DOCTRINE	UCC PROVISION	CISG PROVISION
Mailbox rule	Acceptance is generally effective upon mailing.	Acceptance is generally effective only upon receipt.
Statute of frauds	Requires that contracts for the sale of goods in excess of $500 be in writing.	No required writing.
Parol evidence rule	Prevents introduction of preliminary negotiations to alter an unambiguous written contract.	No parol evidence rule.
Notice of nonconforming goods	Specific description of nonconformity is generally not required.	Specific description of nonconformity is required.
Additional time to perform contract	None unless specified in contract.	*Nachfrist*—allows additional time for performance of a contract upon notice to the other party.

[8] Compare UCC §§ 2-313–316 with CISG art. 35.

National Regulation of the Employment Relationship

Minimum-Wage Laws. Under the Fair Labor Standards Act (FLSA), all U.S. employers are required to pay a minimum wage to employees.[9] The current federal minimum wage under the act is $7.25 per hour, as of summer 2013. States are free to adopt minimum-wage laws in excess of the federal rate, and many have done so.[10]

The U.S. businessperson seeking to hire employees overseas will find a wide variety of frequently changing laws relating to the payment of minimum wages. Some states, such as the People's Republic of China, have no national minimum-wage laws. Minimum wages are established by provincial and municipal government officials. A similar method of regulation exists in Canada, which also lacks a national minimum-wage law. Minimum wages are established individually by the provinces. Thus, the hourly minimum wage is C$11 (Canadian dollars) in Nunavut, C$10.25 in Ontario, but only C$9.75 in Alberta. In other states that lack national minimum-wage laws, such as Denmark, Finland, Germany, Italy, and Sweden, industrial collective agreements establish minimum wages.

Some states with minimum wages vary them depending on the age of the worker. In Ireland, employers are required to pay no less than €8.65 (euros) per hour. However, employers are permitted to reduce this amount by 30 percent for employees under the age of 18. A 20 percent reduction is permitted for employees over the age of 18 but in their first year of employment since turning 18. The permitted reduction is 10 percent for workers in their second year of employment since turning 18.

Other states calculate minimum wages on the basis of weekly earnings. Australia requires that employers pay at least A$606.40 (Australian dollars) per week. States may also require the payment of minimum wages calculated on the basis of monthly earnings. In the Russian Federation, national law establishes the minimum wage as R4,330 (rubles) per month. Some states have a combination of minimum-wage requirements. For example, in January 2012, Taiwan adopted a law raising the minimum monthly wage to NT$18,780 (new Taiwan dollars) and the minimum hourly wage to NT$103. Other states use different combinations. For example, Greece has a monthly minimum wage of €683.76, but this amount may vary depending on whether the worker is employed in a white- or blue-collar position, the length of the worker's service, and his or her marital status.

Employment Termination Laws. The employment-at-will doctrine has been modified over the years by federal and state laws prohibiting the termination of employment on the basis of certain statuses such as race, gender, age, and disability.[11] Termination for whistle-blowing is also prohibited.[12] Finally, the ability to terminate employment may be impacted by statements contained within employment manuals.[13]

The employment-at-will doctrine has been rejected in many states throughout the world. In some states, employment is viewed as a property right or a lifetime entitlement. These jurisdictions sharply restrict the ability of the employer to terminate the relationship. The German Termination Protection Act of 2004 provides that, in the absence of detrimental behavior, employees of "works" with more than 10 employees can be terminated

[9] 29 U.S.C. § 206(a)(1) (2010).

[10] The states are Alaska, Arizona, California, Colorado, Connecticut, Florida, Illinois, Maine, Massachusetts, Michigan, Missouri, Montana, Nevada, New Mexico, Ohio, Oregon, Rhode Island, Vermont, and Washington. Washington currently has the highest minimum wage in the United States, $9.19 per hour.

[11] 29 U.S.C. § 623(a)(1) (2010) (age discrimination); 42 U.S.C. § 2000e-2(a)(1) (2010) (race, national origin, gender, and religion); Americans with Disabilities Act of 1990, Pub. L. No. 101-336, 104 Stat. 327.

[12] Whistleblower Protection Act of 1989, Pub. L. No. 101-12, 103 Stat. 16.

[13] See, e.g., *Litton v. Maverick Paper Co.*, 354 F. Supp. 2d 1209 (D. Kan. 2005); *Continental Airlines, Inc. v. Keenan*, 731 P.2d 708 (Colo. 1987); *Gaudio v. Griffin Health Servs. Corp.*, 733 A.2d 197 (Conn. 1999); *O'Brien v. New England Tel. & Tel. Co.*, 664 N.E.2d 843 (Mass. 1996); *Bobbitt v. The Orchard, Ltd.*, 603 So. 2d 356 (Miss. 1992); *Wuchte v. McNeil*, 505 S.E.2d 142 (N.C. App. 1998); *Thompson v. St. Regis Paper Co.*, 685 P.2d 1081 (Wash. 1984).

for operational reasons only if the termination is "socially justified." Social justification depends on the worker's age, years of service, disability, and number of dependents. The employer must provide notice of four weeks to seven months, depending on the employee's years of service. Termination also must be coordinated with the appropriate works councils. Employers must pay severance equal to one-half month's gross salary for every year of service.

Termination laws are similar in other jurisdictions. France's Labor Code states that termination of employment by companies with more than 20 employees on economic grounds other than *faute grave* (serious fault or gross negligence on the part of the employee) or elimination or transformation of the job requires written notice in French, a pretermination meeting with the employee, consultation with the appropriate works committee, and a required waiting period. Redundancies (layoffs for economic reasons) require the existence of severe economic constraints and notice to the government. China's Labor Contract Law recognizes three separate grounds for termination. First, the occurrence of certain events such as expiration of the term, death of the employee, or bankruptcy of the employer may cause termination of the employment agreement. Second, the employee may terminate the agreement upon 30 days' written notice unless the termination occurs under "extreme circumstances." Third, the employer may terminate the agreement for the employee's failure to satisfy the conditions of employment during any probationary period, material breach of contract, serious dereliction of duty, corruption, conflict of interest, criminal activity, or inability to perform the work due to a nonwork-related injury or illness or for a major change in the employer's circumstances (upon 30 days' notice or payment of one month's wages). Mass layoffs are defined as termination of 20 or more employees or 10 percent of the total number of employees. Such layoffs are only permitted in the event of bankruptcy, "serious difficulties" in production or operations, changes that require layoffs (such as technological innovation), or "major change in objective economic circumstances." The employer must explain the circumstances to affected labor unions and workers no less than 30 days in advance. Such employers may also be required to retain "priority persons" such as employees with long fixed-term or open-ended contracts and those who are the only employed members of a family containing elderly persons or minors.

International Labor Standards. Employers must ensure that their employment practices conform to international labor standards. This concern is particularly acute in the developing world, where national labor protections are lax or nonexistent, enforcement attitudes vary widely, and the temptation to exploit local populations is significant.

International labor standards arise from general human rights instruments that apply across a broad spectrum of areas and from specialized documents that focus exclusively on labor. The Universal Declaration of Human Rights of 1948, often referred to as the basis for modern human rights law, prohibits slavery and grants everyone the right to free choice of employment, just and favorable conditions of work, reasonable limitation of working hours, and compensation adequate to provide for the worker's health and that of his or her family.[14] The International Covenant on Economic, Social and Cultural Rights also recognizes these rights, as well as fair wages and safe and healthy working conditions.[15]

Many of the specialized instruments that focus exclusively on labor rights are based on norms developed by the International Labor Organization (ILO). Established in 1919 by the Treaty of Versailles, the ILO operates under the principle that "labor should not

[14] Universal Declaration of Human Rights, G.A. Res. 217A (III), U.N. GAOR, 3d Sess., at 71, arts. 4, 23–25, U.N. Doc. A/810 (1948).

[15] International Covenant on Economic, Social and Cultural Rights, G.A. Res. 2200A (XXI), 21 U.N. GAOR, 21st Sess., Supp. No. 16, arts. 6–7, 11, U.N. Doc. A/6316 (1966).

CASE NUGGET

PERSONAL JURISDICTION AND THE INTERNET

Pebble Beach Company v. Caddy
453 F.3d 1151 (9th Cir. 2006)

Pebble Beach Company is a well-known golf course and resort located in Monterey County, California. The golf resort has used "Pebble Beach" as its trade name since 1956. Caddy ran a three-room bed and breakfast, restaurant, and bar located on a cliff overlooking the pebbly beaches of England's south shore, in a town called Barton-on-Sea. The name of Caddy's operation was "Pebble Beach." Caddy advertised his services, which did not include a golf course, at his website, www.pebblebeach-uk.com. Caddy's website included information about the accommodations, lodging rates, a menu, and a wine list. The website did not have a reservation system and did not allow potential guests to book rooms or pay for services online. Pebble Beach sued Caddy for infringement and dilution of its "Pebble Beach" trademark in the U.S. District Court for the Central District of California. Caddy moved to dismiss the complaint for lack of personal jurisdiction. The district court granted Caddy's motion, and Pebble Beach appealed to the U.S. Court of Appeals for the Ninth Circuit.

The court of appeals affirmed the dismissal of the lawsuit for lack of personal jurisdiction. Pebble Beach failed to identify any conduct by Caddy that took place in California or in the United States that could be considered purposeful availment. All of Caddy's actions identified by Pebble Beach took place in the United Kingdom. Alternatively, Pebble Beach claimed that Caddy expressly aimed conduct at California through his website and domain name. The court rejected this contention as the website was passive in nature. The court held that an Internet domain name and passive website alone are not enough to subject a party to jurisdiction. The fact that the name "Pebble Beach" was a famous mark known worldwide was of little practical consequence to the determination of whether an action was directed at a particular forum via the Internet. Such aiming also could not be supported by the fact that Caddy's business was located in an area frequented by Americans and that Americans often were guests at the establishment. Although vacationing Americans may have stopped at Caddy's business, there was no evidence that this patronage was related to Caddy's choice of a domain name or the posting of a passive website.

be regarded merely as a commodity or article of commerce." In 1998, the ILO issued its Declaration on Fundamental Principles and Rights at Work. This statement enumerated a number of "core labor standards," including freedom of association, the right to engage in collective bargaining, and the elimination of all forms of forced or compulsory labor, child labor, and employment discrimination.[16] Many of the ILO's instruments relate to specific labor practices. For example, the Convention Concerning Forced or Compulsory Labor and the Abolition of Forced Labor Convention obligate states to prohibit the utilization of forced or compulsory labor, including labor for the benefit of private individuals, companies, or associations.[17]

Dispute Settlement in an International Context

Disputing parties to international transactions can resolve their differences in two ways. Assuming settlement negotiations, mediation, conciliation, or some other form of nonadversarial dispute resolution fails, they can resort to litigation or arbitration. However, each of these methods has disadvantages of which an international businessperson must be aware.

L09 How are disputes settled in the international marketplace?

LITIGATION

The first step in litigation is determining whether the selected court has **jurisdiction,** specifically, the power to hear the case and resolve the dispute. Judgments entered by a court without jurisdiction are null and void. There are two primary types of jurisdiction. A court must possess **subject-matter jurisdiction,** which is power over the type of case presented to it. In the United States, subject-matter jurisdiction is based on the type of case (such as civil, criminal, probate, or domestic relations) or the amount of money at issue.

[16] ILO, Declaration on Fundamental Principles and Rights at Work, art. 2(a–d) (1998).

[17] Abolition of Forced Labor Convention (ILO No. 105), art. 1, 320 U.N.T.S. 291 (1957); Convention Concerning Forced or Compulsory Labor (ILO No. 29), arts. 1–2, 4–5, 39 U.N.T.S. 55 (1930).

In contrast, **personal jurisdiction** is the power of the court over the persons appearing before it. **General personal jurisdiction** permits adjudication of any claims against a defendant regardless of whether the claim has anything to do with the forum, or location, where the claim is filed. To obtain general personal jurisdiction, the defendant must maintain some presence in the forum. For a court to exercise **specific personal jurisdiction,** the defendant must have purposefully availed itself of the protections of the forum, and the selected forum must be reasonable.[18] Merely placing a product into the stream of commerce is not sufficient unless the product was designed specifically for the forum or the defendant provided regular advice to customers or maintained a distributor in the forum.

Case 6-1 demonstrates the application of these jurisdictional rules.

[18] *Asahi Metal Indus. v. Superior Court,* 480 U.S. 102, 109, 113 (1987).

CASE 6-1 GOODYEAR DUNLOP TIRES OPERATIONS, S.A. v. BROWN
UNITED STATES SUPREME COURT
131 S. CT. 2846 (2011)

Two North Carolina teenagers were fatally injured when the bus upon which they were riding overturned on a roadway outside Paris, France. The parents of the decedents brought a lawsuit in North Carolina state court against Goodyear Tire and Rubber Company and its subsidiaries based in Luxembourg, Turkey, and France, alleging that the accident was caused by negligent design and production of the bus tires. The plaintiffs alleged that the subsidiaries placed their tires into the stream of commerce and some of these tires ended up in North Carolina. The subsidiaries alleged that there was no personal jurisdiction as the mere placement of a product in the stream of commerce is an insufficient basis for the assertion of personal jurisdiction especially when the accident had no connection with the forum other than the residence of the decedents. Additionally, the mere placement of tires into the stream of commerce did not constitute a continuous and systematic presence in North Carolina as to subject the subsidiaries to personal jurisdiction. The North Carolina state courts disagreed and exercised personal jurisdiction over the subsidiaries. The subsidiaries appealed to the U.S. Supreme Court.

ASSOCIATE JUSTICE GINSBURG: This case concerns the jurisdiction of state courts over corporations organized and operating abroad. We address, in particular, this question: Are foreign subsidiaries of a United States parent corporation amenable to suit in state court on claims unrelated to any activity of the subsidiaries in the forum State?

A state court's assertion of jurisdiction exposes defendants to the State's coercive power, and is therefore subject to review for compatibility with the Fourteenth Amendment's Due Process Clause. *International Shoe Co.* v. *Washington,* 326 U.S. 310, 316 (1945). Opinions in the wake of the pathmarking *International Shoe* decision have differentiated between general or all-purpose jurisdiction, and specific or case-linked jurisdiction. *Helicopteros Nacionales de Colombia, S. A.* v. *Hall,* 466 U.S. 408 (1984).

A court may assert general jurisdiction over foreign (sister-state or foreign-country) corporations to hear any and all claims against them when their affiliations with the State are so "continuous and systematic" as to render them essentially at home in the forum State. See *International Shoe,* 326 U.S., at 317. Specific jurisdiction, on the other hand, depends on an "affiliatio[n] between the forum and the underlying controversy," principally, activity or an occurrence that takes place in the forum State and is therefore subject to the State's regulation. In contrast to general, all-purpose jurisdiction, specific jurisdiction is confined to adjudication of issues deriving from, or connected with, the very controversy that establishes jurisdiction.

We granted certiorari to decide whether the general jurisdiction the North Carolina courts asserted over petitioners is consistent with the Due Process Clause of the Fourteenth Amendment.

The Due Process Clause of the Fourteenth Amendment sets the outer boundaries of a state tribunal's authority to proceed against a defendant. The canonical opinion in this area remains *International Shoe* in which we held that a State may authorize its courts to exercise personal jurisdiction over an out-of-state defendant if the defendant has "certain minimum contacts with [the State] such that the maintenance of the suit does not offend traditional notions of fair play and substantial justice." *Id.* at 316.

Endeavoring to give specific content to the "fair play and substantial justice" concept, the Court in *International Shoe* classified cases involving out-of-state corporate defendants. First, as in *International Shoe* itself, jurisdiction unquestionably could be asserted where the corporation's in-state activity is "continuous and systematic" and *that activity gave rise to the episode-in-suit.* Further, the Court observed, the commission of certain "single or occasional acts" in a State may be sufficient to render a corporation answerable in that State with respect to those acts, though not with respect to matters unrelated to the forum connections. The heading courts today use to encompass these two *International Shoe* categories is "specific jurisdiction." Adjudicatory authority is "specific" when the suit arises out of or relates to the defendant's contacts with the forum.

International Shoe distinguished from cases that fit within the "specific jurisdiction" categories, "instances in which the continuous corporate operations within a state [are] so substantial and of such a nature as to justify suit against it on causes of action arising from dealings entirely distinct from those activities." Adjudicatory authority so grounded is today called "general jurisdiction." For an individual, the paradigm forum for the exercise of general jurisdiction is the individual's domicile; for a corporation, it is an equivalent place, one in which the corporation is fairly regarded as at home.

In only two decisions postdating *International Shoe* has this Court considered whether an out-of-state corporate defendant's in-state contacts were sufficiently "continuous and systematic" to justify the exercise of general jurisdiction over claims unrelated to those contacts: *Perkins* v. *Benguet Consol. Mining Co.,* 342 U.S. 437 (1952) (general jurisdiction appropriately exercised over Philippine corporation sued in Ohio, where the company's affairs were overseen during World War II); and *Helicopteros,* 466 U.S. 408 (helicopter owned by Colombian corporation crashed in Peru; survivors of U.S. citizens who died in the crash, the Court held, could not maintain wrongful-death actions against the Colombian corporation in Texas, for the corporation's helicopter purchases and purchase-linked activity in Texas were insufficient to subject it to Texas court's general jurisdiction).

To justify the exercise of general jurisdiction over petitioners, the North Carolina courts relied on the petitioners' placement of their tires in the "stream of commerce." The stream-of-commerce metaphor has been invoked frequently in lower court decisions permitting "jurisdiction in products liability cases in which the product has traveled through an extensive chain of distribution before reaching the ultimate consumer." Typically, in such cases, a nonresident defendant, acting *outside* the forum, places in the stream of commerce a product that ultimately causes harm *inside* the forum.

The North Carolina court's stream-of-commerce analysis elided the essential difference between case-specific and all-purpose (general) jurisdiction. Flow of a manufacturer's products into the forum, we have explained, may bolster an affiliation germane to *specific* jurisdiction. But ties serving to bolster the exercise of specific jurisdiction do not warrant a determination that, based on those ties, the forum has *general* jurisdiction over a defendant.

Helicopteros concluded that "mere purchases [made in the forum State], even if occurring at regular intervals, are not enough to warrant a State's assertion of [general] jurisdiction over a nonresident corporation in a cause of action not related to those purchase transactions." *Id.* at 418. We see no reason to differentiate from the ties to Texas held insufficient in *Helicopteros,* the sales of petitioners' tires sporadically made in North Carolina through intermediaries. Under the sprawling view of general jurisdiction urged by respondents and embraced by the North Carolina Court of Appeals, any substantial manufacturer or seller of goods would be amenable to suit, on any claim for relief, wherever its products are distributed.

Measured against *Helicopteros* and *Perkins,* North Carolina is not a forum in which it would be permissible to subject petitioners to general jurisdiction. Petitioners are in no sense at home in North Carolina. Their attenuated connections to the State fall far short of "the continuous and systematic general business contacts" necessary to empower North Carolina to entertain suit against them on claims unrelated to anything that connects them to the State.

For the reasons stated, the judgment of the North Carolina Court of Appeals is reversed.

CRITICAL THINKING

What were the factual and legal grounds for the Court's refusal to find personal jurisdiction in this case? Was the Court correct in its conclusion? Should it be foreseeable to any modern multinational corporation engaged in manufacturing that its products may end up anywhere in the world and thus become the subject matter of litigation? What policy reasons may underlie the Court's decision in this case?

ETHICAL DECISION MAKING

The result in this case requires the plaintiffs to proceed in a court outside the United States with respect to claims against Goodyear Dunlop's foreign subsidiaries despite the fact that some of their tires entered the U.S. marketplace and, in particular, the North Carolina marketplace. Does this result strike you as fair and reasonable? Should non-U.S. companies that place their goods into the U.S. stream of commerce be responsible under all circumstances when those products cause harm in the United States?

The reasonableness of the selected forum is determined by balancing the burden on the defendant, the interest of the forum in resolving the dispute, the plaintiff's interest in obtaining relief in the forum, and foreign policy concerns. For example, the forum may be unreasonable if the majority of the evidence and witnesses are located outside the forum or the case involves an occurrence that is of little relevance to the jurors that might decide the case. The Case Nugget on page 137 addresses the issue of asserting personal jurisdiction over a foreign defendant on the basis of the defendant's presence in the jurisdiction through the Internet.

Legal Principle: **For a U.S. court judgment to be fully enforceable, the court must possess power over the type of case (subject-matter jurisdiction) and the people appearing before it (personal jurisdiction), which may be obtained by the defendant's presence in the forum (general personal jurisdiction) or purposeful availment of the protection of the forum (specific personal jurisdiction).**

There are numerous defenses available to the exercise of jurisdiction. The Foreign Sovereign Immunities Act is a federal statute that denies subject-matter jurisdiction and grants immunity from civil actions to foreign states and their political subdivisions, agencies, and instrumentalities.[19] One important exception to foreign sovereign immunity is a situation in which the immune entity engages in a commercial activity. A commercial activity is defined as a regular course of commercial conduct or a particular commercial transaction with a U.S. nexus.

There are also several instances when a court may refuse to exercise existing jurisdiction. *The act of state doctrine* has been defined as "a nonjurisdictional, prudential doctrine based on the notion that the courts of one country will not sit in judgment on the acts of the government of another state done within its own territory."[20] The *political question doctrine* may be invoked when there has been a demonstrable constitutional commitment of an issue to a coordinate political department; there is a lack of judicially discoverable and manageable standards; it is impossible to decide the case without resolving an issue appropriate for nonjudicial discretion or without demonstrating lack of respect for coordinate branches of government; there is an unusual need for unquestioning adherence to a political decision already made; and there is the potential of embarrassment from multiple pronouncements by various departments on one question.[21] *Comity* has been defined as the "recognition which one nation allows within its territory to the legislative, executive or judicial acts of another nation."[22]

Forum non conveniens is a doctrine that permits courts to decline to exercise jurisdiction where there is a more convenient forum to hear the case.[23] This determination is based on judicial analysis of the adequacy of the alternative forum and the balance of private- and public-interest factors. Public-interest factors include court congestion, the unfairness of imposing jury duty on a community with no relation to the litigation, the interest of the community in having localized controversies decided at home, and the avoidance of problems associated with conflict of laws and the application of foreign law. Private-interest factors include ease of access to evidence, the cost for witnesses to attend trial, and the availability of compulsory process.

Case 6-2 demonstrates the application of the doctrine of forum non conveniens in the context of product liability litigation.

[19] 28 U.S.C. §§ 1602–1611 (2010).

[20] *Underhill v. Hernandez,* 168 U.S. 250, 252 (1897).

[21] *Baker v. Carr,* 369 U.S. 186, 217 (1962).

[22] *Hilton v. Guyot,* 159 U.S. 113, 164 (1895).

[23] *Piper Aircraft Co. v. Reyno,* 454 U.S. 235, 254 n.22 (1981); and *Gulf Oil Corp. v. Gilbert,* 330 U.S. 501, 507 (1947).

CASE 6-2 GONZALES v. CHRYSLER CORP.
U.S. COURT OF APPEALS FOR THE FIFTH CIRCUIT

In 1995, while in Houston, the plaintiff, Jorge Luis Machuca Gonzalez ("Gonzalez") saw several magazine and television advertisements for the Chrysler LHS. The advertisements sparked his interest, and Gonzalez visited Houston car dealerships. Convinced by these visits that the Chrysler LHS was a high-quality and safe car, Gonzalez purchased a Chrysler LHS upon returning to Mexico.

On May 21, 1996, Gonzalez's wife was involved in a collision with another moving vehicle while driving the Chrysler LHS in Atizapan de Zaragoza, Mexico. The accident triggered the passenger-side air bag. The force of the air bag's deployment instantaneously killed Gonzalez's three-year-old son, Pablo.

CIRCUIT JUDGE E. GRADY JOLLY: Gonzalez brought suit in Texas district court against (1) Chrysler, as the manufacturer of the automobile; (2) TRW, Inc. and TRW Vehicle Safety Systems, Inc., as the designers of the front sensor for the air bag; and (3) Morton International Inc., as designer of the air bag module. Gonzalez asserted claims based on products liability, negligence, gross negligence, and breach of warranty. Texas, however, has a tenuous connection to the underlying dispute. Neither the car nor the air bag module was designed or manufactured in Texas. The accident took place in Mexico, involved Mexican citizens, and only Mexican citizens witnessed the accident. Moreover, Gonzalez purchased the Chrysler LHS in Mexico (although he shopped for the car in Houston, Texas). Because of these factors, the district court granted the defendants' motions for dismissal on the ground of forum non conveniens. Gonzalez now appeals.

The primary question we address today involves the threshold inquiry in the forum non conveniens analysis: Whether the limitation imposed by Mexican law on the award of damages renders Mexico an inadequate alternative forum for resolving a tort suit brought by a Mexican citizen against a United States manufacturer.

The forum non conveniens inquiry consists of four considerations. First, the district court must assess whether an alternative forum is available. An alternative forum is available if the entire case and all parties can come within the jurisdiction of that forum. Second, the district court must decide if the alternative forum is adequate. An alternative forum is adequate if the parties will not be deprived of all remedies or treated unfairly, even though they may not enjoy the same benefits as they might receive in an American court. If the district court decides that an alternative forum is both available and adequate, it next must weigh various private interest factors. If consideration of these private interest factors counsels against dismissal, the district court moves to the fourth consideration in the analysis. At this stage, the district court must weigh numerous public interest factors. If these factors weigh in the moving party's favor, the district court may dismiss the case.

The heart of this appeal is whether the alternative forum, Mexico, is adequate.

The jurisprudential root of the adequacy requirement is the Supreme Court's decision in *Piper Aircraft Co. v. Reyno,* 454 U.S. 235 (1981). The dispute in *Piper Aircraft* arose after several Scottish citizens were killed in a plane crash in Scotland. A representative for the decedents filed a wrongful death suit against two American aircraft manufacturers. The Court noted that the plaintiff filed suit in the United States because U.S. laws regarding liability, capacity to sue, and damages are more favorable to her position than are those of Scotland. The Court further noted that Scottish law does not recognize strict liability in tort. The Court held that although the relatives of the decedent may not be able to rely on a strict liability theory, and although their potential damage award may be smaller, there is no danger that they will be deprived of any remedy or treated unfairly in Scotland. Thus, the Court held that Scotland provided an adequate alternative forum for resolving the dispute, even though its forum provided a significantly lesser remedy.

Gonzalez contends that a Mexican forum would provide a clearly unsatisfactory remedy because (1) Mexican tort law does not provide for a strict liability theory of recovery for the manufacture or design of an unreasonably dangerous product and (2) Mexican law caps the maximum award for the loss of a child's life at approximately $2,500 (730 days' worth of wages at the Mexican minimum wage rate). Thus, according to Gonzalez, Mexico provides an inadequate alternative forum for this dispute.

Gonzalez's first contention may be quickly dismissed based on the explicit principle stated in *Piper Aircraft.* There is no basis to distinguish the absence of a strict products liability cause of action under Mexican law from that of Scotland. Accordingly, we hold that the failure of Mexican law to allow for strict liability on the facts of this case does not render Mexico an inadequate forum.

Gonzalez's second contention—that the damage cap renders the remedy available in a Mexican forum "clearly unsatisfactory"—is slightly more problematic. We start from basic principles of comity. Mexico, as a sovereign nation, has made a deliberate choice in providing a specific remedy for this tort cause of action. In making this policy choice, the Mexican government has resolved a trade-off among the competing objectives and costs of tort law, involving interests of victims, of consumers, of manufacturers, and of various other economic and cultural values. In

[continued]

resolving this trade-off, the Mexican people, through their duly-elected lawmakers, have decided to limit tort damages with respect to a child's death. It would be inappropriate—even patronizing—for us to denounce this legitimate policy choice by holding that Mexico provides an inadequate forum for Mexican tort victims. In short, we see no warrant for us, a United States court, to replace the policy preference of the Mexican government with our own view of what is a good policy for the citizens of Mexico.

Having concluded that Mexico provides an adequate forum, we now consider whether the private and public interest factors nonetheless weigh in favor of maintaining this suit in Texas. The district court found that almost all of the private and public interest factors pointed away from Texas and toward Mexico as the appropriate forum. It is clear to us that this finding does not represent an abuse of discretion. After all, the tort victim was a Mexican citizen, the driver of the Chrysler LHS (Gonzalez's wife) is a Mexican citizen, and the plaintiff is a Mexican citizen. The accident took place in Mexico. Gonzalez purchased the car in Mexico. Neither the car nor the air bag was designed or manufactured in Texas. In short, there are no public or private interest factors that would suggest that Texas is the appropriate forum for the trial of this case.

For the foregoing reasons, the district court's dismissal of this case on the ground of forum non conveniens is affirmed.

CRITICAL THINKING

Given the cap on damages in Mexican law for the loss of a child and the cost of litigation, is it likely that Gonzales will file a lawsuit in Mexico? Does Mexico offer an inadequate forum because it does not make economic sense for Gonzalez to file his lawsuit in Mexico? Why or why not?

ETHICAL DECISION MAKING

Would the universalization principle or the Golden Rule provide any strong argument against the ruling made by Judge Jolly?

Businesses can minimize some of the uncertainties associated with personal jurisdiction by carefully selecting the forum and inserting choice-of-law clauses in international agreements. A **forum selection agreement** allows the parties to choose where disputes between them will be resolved. In the United States, such clauses are presumptively valid and will be disregarded only if they are unreasonable.[24] Grounds for ignoring a forum selection clause include fraud or coercion in its procurement, unconscionability, lack of notice, or serious inconvenience posed by the selected forum. A **choice-of-law clause** lets the parties to a contract choose the law of a certain state to apply to the interpretation of the contract or in the event of a dispute. Choice-of-law clauses are generally enforceable as long as there is a reasonable relation between the transaction and the law of the selected jurisdiction.

Legal Principle: The parties to an international contract may select the forum in which disputes are to be resolved and the applicable law within the terms of their agreement.

The plaintiff must also select the proper **venue** for the litigation. Proper venue is the court with subject-matter and personal jurisdiction that is the most appropriate geographic location for the resolution of the dispute. With respect to federal litigation in the United States, the Alien Venue Statute provides that aliens may be sued in any federal judicial district but makes an exception for suits against foreign sovereigns, which may be initiated only in the U.S. District Court for the District of Columbia.[25]

There are other problems with litigation as a method of international dispute resolution. Methods of discovery used in civil litigation in the United States may be ineffective if used to obtain evidence located abroad. Although the **Hague Evidence Convention,** a

[24] *M/S Bremen v. Zapata Off-Shore Co.,* 407 U.S. 1, 15 (1972).

[25] 28 U.S.C. § 1391(d) (2010).

multilateral convention establishing procedures for transnational discovery between private persons in different states, attempts to resolve such problems, it has been ratified by only 47 states. Furthermore, judgments obtained in foreign courts may not be enforceable in other states. For example, in the United States, foreign judgments are not entitled to full faith and credit but are only evidence of the justice of the plaintiff's claims.[26] U.S. courts may ignore the results of foreign proceedings under numerous circumstances, including lack of fairness, jurisdiction, or timely notice; fraud; and inconsistency with U.S. public policy. Foreign states take similar views with respect to U.S. judgments. Courts in such states may refuse to enforce U.S. civil judgments deemed to be criminal or penal in nature (such as taxes and fines) and awards of punitive damages.

ARBITRATION

Arbitration is a type of alternative dispute resolution by private, nonofficial persons selected in a manner provided by law or the agreement of the parties. The **New York Convention,**[27] an international agreement governing the arbitration of private international disputes, has been ratified by 148 states to date, including the United States. The convention applies when an award is made and one party seeks enforcement in the territories of the contracting states. It requires that each state recognize written arbitration agreements and recognize arbitral awards as enforceable in its national courts.

Arbitration as a means of dispute resolution has many advantages over litigation. It is cheaper and faster, and it is a nonpublic procedure. Arbitration also permits the parties to select the forum and the presiding party. Concerns regarding the enforceability of a judicial decision entered in one state but sought to be enforced in another state are also minimized. However, the ability of parties in arbitration to conduct discovery of the opposing party's case may be limited, as well as the ability to appeal an adverse decision. Furthermore, arbitrators' decisions may not serve as precedent in future cases. Any company contemplating the use of arbitration as a means of dispute resolution must carefully balance these disadvantages with the benefits of the arbitral process.

[26] Restatement (Third) of the Foreign Relations Law of the United States, § 481 (1987).

[27] Convention on the Recognition and Enforcement of Foreign Arbitral Awards, June 10, 1958, 21 U.S.T. 2517, 330 U.N.T.S. 38.

CASE OPENER WRAP-UP

Resolving a Breach of Contract under the CISG

In the case of *Chicago Prime Packers, Inc. v. Northam Food Trading Co.,*[28] the district court held that the transaction was governed by the CISG. The CISG was applicable as Chicago Prime was a U.S. resident and Northam Food Trading was a resident of a jurisdiction that had ratified the CISG. The court held that because the contract did not contain an inspection provision, the requirement under Article 38 of the CISG that the buyer examine the goods, or cause them to be examined, "within as short a period as is practicable in the circumstances" was controlling. Decisions under the CISG indicated that the buyer bears the burden of proving that the goods were inspected within a reasonable time. Northam did not present any evidence as to why the ribs, or a portion of the ribs, were not and could

[28] 320 F. Supp. 2d 702 (N.D. Ill. 2004).

not have been examined by Northam, Beacon, or someone acting on their behalf when the shipment was delivered to Beacon or within a few days thereafter.

Northam also failed to prove that it gave notice to Chicago Prime within a reasonable time after it ought to have discovered the alleged lack of conformity. Article 39 of the CISG states that "[a] buyer loses the right to rely on a lack of conformity of the goods if he does not give notice to the seller specifying the nature of the lack of conformity within a reasonable time after he has discovered it or ought to have discovered it." A buyer bears the burden of showing that notice of nonconformity has been given within a reasonable time. The court further noted that when defects are easy to discover by a prompt examination of the goods, the time of notice must be reduced. The putrid condition of the meat was apparent even in its frozen state. Because the court found that Northam failed to examine the shipment of ribs in as short a period of time as was practicable, it followed that Northam also failed to give notice within a reasonable time after it should have discovered the alleged nonconformity.

As a result, the court entered a judgment in favor of Chicago Prime Packers, Inc., and against Northam Food Trading Company in the amount of $178,200 plus $27,242.63, representing prejudgment interest calculated at a rate of 5 percent from May 1, 2001, for a total payment of $205,442.63.

Before their dispute arose, the parties could have selected the law for the court to apply through a choice-of-law clause, which permits the parties to a contract to choose the law of a certain state to apply to the interpretation of the contract in the event of a dispute. Choice-of-law clauses are generally enforceable as long as there is a reasonable relation between the transaction and the law of the selected jurisdiction. The same rules apply with respect to the CISG. The parties are always free to opt out of the CISG and select another law to apply to their transaction. Thus, the parties could have selected U.S. or Canadian sales law to apply to the resolution of disputes arising from their transaction. In the absence of such a selection, the CISG applied to this transaction.

KEY TERMS

affiliate 127
arbitration 143
bilateral free trade agreement 130
choice-of-law clause 142
comparative law 125
Convention on the International Sale of Goods (CISG) 133
Dispute Settlement Understanding 129
distributor 126
dumping 128
Foreign Corrupt Practices Act (FCPA) 127
foreign sales representative 126
foreign subsidiary 127
forum selection agreement 142
franchise agreement 126
free trade agreement 129
General Agreement on Tariffs and Trade (GATT) 128
general personal jurisdiction 138
Hague Evidence Convention 142
international law 125
joint venture 126
jurisdiction 137
lex mercatoria 132
licensing agreement 126
national treatment 128
New York Convention 143
nontariff barrier 127
normal trade relations 128
North American Free Trade Agreement (NAFTA) 129
personal jurisdiction 138
quantitative restriction 128
specific personal jurisdiction 138
subject-matter jurisdiction 137
subsidy 129
tariff 127
venue 142
World Trade Organization (WTO) 128

SUMMARY OF KEY TOPICS

Doing Business Internationally

International law refers to the laws governing the conduct of states and international organizations and their relations with one another and natural and juridical persons.

Ethical Considerations

Firms participating in international markets have special ethical considerations, including whether to do business with repressive governments, whether to provide products for the poor at reduced prices, and whether to treat workers according to local custom or to international standards of humane treatment.

The General Agreement on Tariffs and Trade

GATT is a comprehensive multilateral trading system designed to achieve distortion-free international trade through the minimization of tariffs and removal of artificial barriers. It established several general principles of trade law:

- *Article I:* Addresses the principle of *most-favored-nation relations,* now known as *normal trade relations;* requires that WTO member states treat like goods coming from other WTO member states on an equal basis, specifically prohibiting member states from discriminating against like products on the basis of their country of origin.
- *Article III:* Sets forth the principle of *national treatment,* which prohibits WTO member states from regulating, taxing, or otherwise treating imported products any differently than domestically produced products.
- *Article VI:* Prohibits certain types of *dumping* and *subsidies.*
- *Article XI:* Prohibits *quantitative restrictions* on imports (e.g., limits on importation of certain products on the basis of number of units, weight, or value for national economic reasons or the protection of domestic industry).

Regional Trade Agreements

Free trade agreement: Two or more states agree to reduce and gradually eliminate tariffs and other trade barriers [e.g., North American Free Trade Agreement (NAFTA)].

Customs union: States in a free trade area agree on a common external tariff on products originating outside the union (e.g., European Union).

Bilateral trade agreement: Two states agree on issues relating to trade between them (e.g., United States–Australia agreement).

Comparative Law

Comparative law is the study of the legal systems of different states. This study provides a better understanding of the general purpose of law, assists in the development of a critical viewpoint of one's own legal system, and demonstrates that one's own legal system is only one of many alternatives. After thinking critically about alternative laws, one might decide that one's own state should adopt the other state's law or method of resolving a dispute.

Legal Systems and Procedures

Civil law systems constitute the majority of the world's legal systems and are based on detailed national legal codes, which serve as the sole official source of law. *Common law* systems derive from the British and American models and are based on constitutions, legislation, regulations, and their interpretation by courts of law. *Socialist law* systems are based on the premises that the rights of society as a whole outweigh individual rights and that the state owns the means of production and property. *Islamic law* systems are based on the tenet that law is derived from and interpreted in conformance with *Shari'a* ("God's Law") and the Koran.

Dispute Settlement in an International Context

If the parties to international transactions are unable to resolve their dispute through nonadversarial methods, the parties may use litigation or arbitration to resolve their differences.

POINT / COUNTERPOINT

Should U.S. Courts Refer to Foreign Law in Their Decisions?

NO

Reference to foreign law fails to recognize the exceptional nature of the U.S. legal system and experience. Such reference is an unnecessary surrender of sovereignty and abdication of the judiciary's responsibility to interpret and apply the national laws of the land. The U.S. Constitution and statutes enacted in accordance with it should be interpreted according to the framers' original intent and congressional intent. Reference to foreign law in U.S. courts fails to recognize that only domestic law should serve the American people. Additionally, foreign legislative bodies that adopt laws and the courts that interpret them are not accountable to the American people. Utilization of such laws and decisions expands judicial discretion in the United States beyond that which is desirable. Finally, there is little need for uniformity in many areas of the law.

YES

Reference to foreign law in U.S. court decisions recognizes that the United States is a member of the family of nations and demonstrates respect for the legal systems of other states. Foreign law may serve as a source of inspiration for U.S. courts, enriches legal thinking, enhances judicial creativity, and strengthens democratic ties and the foundations of different legal systems. U.S. judges could learn from their brethren in other states. Reference to foreign law promotes uniformity and predictability, which is extremely important in international business transactions. State courts already reference foreign law when they cite the decisions of courts in other states, the results of which are persuasive authority at best. In any event, foreign law is not binding on U.S. courts, and there is no danger that such law could serve as precedent or mandate an outcome in a particular case.

QUESTIONS & PROBLEMS

1. Spain divided unroasted nondecaffeinated coffee into five separate classifications. A 7 percent tariff was imposed on three of these classifications. The other two classifications were duty-free. Brazil, the principal supplier of the coffee subject to the tariff, alleged that the Spanish classification regime failed to extend most-favored-nation treatment to like products originating from Brazil, thus violating GATT. Spain defended the classifications on the basis that the products were not like products due to differences resulting from geographic factors, cultivation methods, processing, and genetics. The GATT panel rejected these arguments. The panel noted that most coffees are blends, coffee is universally regarded as a well-defined and single product intended for drinking, and no other state maintained a similar classification scheme. The panel thus concluded that the classification system discriminated against like products in violation of GATT's most-favored-nation requirement. Do you agree with this decision? Is coffee a single universal product regardless of where it is grown, how it is processed, or what the cost is to consumers? [*Spain—Tariff Treatment of Unroasted Coffee,* 1981 GATTPD LEXIS 5 (1981).]

2. Italy adopted a law that permitted the government to extend credit to Italian farmers in order to finance the purchase of agricultural machinery. Farmers purchasing machinery manufactured in Italy were entitled to a loan of up to 75 percent of the value of the machinery for a term of five years at a 3 percent interest rate. Farmers purchasing machinery not manufactured in Italy were also entitled to loans but at an interest rate of 10 percent. The United Kingdom claimed that the Italian loan program violated GATT's national treatment obligation by modifying the conditions of sale between imported and domestically produced machinery. Italy defended the loan program on the basis that national treatment applied only to sales in the context of international trade and not to internal conditions of sale. Italy also claimed that national treatment was not applicable to economic development initiatives such as the loan program. The GATT panel disagreed and held that the national treatment requirement applied to internal conditions impacting domestic sales. The panel also concluded that economic development initiatives were required to be consistent with the principle of national treatment.

Based on this decision, are there any limits to the concept of national treatment? How might a state undertake an economic development initiative without violating national treatment? [*Italy—Imported Agricultural Machinery,* GATT Report L/833-7S/60 (1958).]

3. Nicastro was severely injured at his workplace in New Jersey by an industrial metal-shearing machine manufactured by J. McIntyre Machinery, Ltd., an English company. Nicastro filed a product liability claim against McIntyre in New Jersey state court. McIntyre denied that the New Jersey state courts had personal jurisdiction. McIntyre had no office in New Jersey, and it did not pay taxes, own property, advertise, or maintain employees in New Jersey. McIntyre's only contact with New Jersey was the presence of the metal-shearing machine at Nicastro's workplace. The New Jersey Supreme Court held that state courts could exercise personal jurisdiction with respect to Nicastro's claim. McIntyre appealed this decision to the U.S. Supreme Court. Do the New Jersey courts have personal jurisdiction over McIntyre arising from Nicastro's injuries? [*J. McIntyre Machinery, Ltd. v. Nicastro,* 131 S. Ct. 2780 (2011).]

4. In *Asahi Metal Industries v. Superior Court,* the U.S. Supreme Court held that the mere placement of a product in the stream of commerce is not sufficient to subject the manufacturer to the personal jurisdiction of a California state court in the absence of "purposeful availment," such as designing a product specifically for the forum, maintaining a distributor in the forum, or providing regular advice to customers in the forum. Is this reasoning still valid in the modern global marketplace, where goods routinely cross international boundaries? Why or why not? [*Asahi Metal Industries v. Superior Court,* 480 U.S. 102 (1987).]

5. Seung was a passenger on the M/S *Paul Gauguin* cruise ship owned by Regent Seven Seas Cruises. The cruise ship operated exclusively in French Polynesia. Seung's ticket contained a forum selection clause that designated Paris, France, as the sole location for any lawsuit that might be filed arising from passenger injuries on cruises that did not include a U.S. port. Seung was injured on her cruise and filed a lawsuit in the U.S. District Court for the Southern District of Florida. Regent Seven Seas Cruises moved to dismiss the lawsuit on the basis of the forum selection clause. Seung claimed that the clause was unfair as she was financially and medically unable to bring a lawsuit in Paris and that Paris was a "remote alien forum" designated for the sole purpose of discouraging passengers from bringing legitimate claims. The district court dismissed Seung's lawsuit, and she appealed to the U.S. Court of Appeals for the 11th Circuit. Is the forum selection clause as drafted enforceable against Seung barring her lawsuit in the United States? Why or why not? [*Seung v. Regent Seven Seas Cruises, Inc.,* 2010 U.S. App. LEXIS 17449 (11th Cir., August 19, 2010).]

6. Juliette Shulof Furs (JSF) was a New York corporation that had been in the fur-dealing business for 15 years. George Shulof, an officer of JSF, attended two auctions conducted by Finnish Fur Sales (FFS) in Finland in 1987. He purchased more than $1.2 million worth of skins at the auctions. Shulof attended each auction and was the actual bidder. The conditions of sale were listed in the auction catalog in English. Section 4 of "Conditions of Sale" provided that "[a]ny person bidding at the auction shall stand surety as for his own debt until full payment is made for purchased merchandise. If he has made the bid on behalf of another person, he is jointly and severally liable with the person for the purchase." Section 15 of "Conditions of Sale" provided that "[t]hese conditions are governed by Finnish law." JSF paid for the majority of the skins purchased, leaving an unpaid balance of $202,416.85. FFS brought an action to recover the contract price of the skins from Shulof, claiming he was personally liable for payment under Finnish law. Shulof responded that he was acting only as the agent for JSF and that under New York law he was not personally responsible for the contracts of the corporation he represented at the auction. He also claimed that the choice of Finnish law was invalid, and its application would lead to a result contrary to the public policy of the state of New York. Is the choice-of-law clause valid? Would the imposition of personal liability upon Shulof be in violation of New York public policy? What are the reasons for your answers? [*Finnish Fur Sales Co., Ltd. v. Juliette Shulof Furs, Inc.,* 770 F. Supp. 139 (S.D.N.Y. 1991).]

7. In an interview published in the *New York Times* in February 1976, former Lockheed president A. Carl Kotchian defended the payment of bribes by the company as follows:

> Some call it gratuities. Some call them questionable payments. Some call it extortion. Some call it grease. Some call it bribery. I look at these payments as necessary to sell a product. I never felt I was doing anything wrong.

More than 30 years later, Reinhard Siekaczek, an accountant employed by Siemens who oversaw an annual budget for questionable payments in excess of $50 million, stated:

> I never thought I would go to jail for my company. . . . We thought we had to do it. Otherwise, we'd ruin the company. . . . People will only say about Siemens that they were unlucky and that they broke the Eleventh Commandment. The Eleventh Commandment is "Don't get caught."

Given these attitudes, is the Foreign Corrupt Practices Act likely to result in a change in corporate culture at multinational businesses? Is the FCPA a success or a failure to the extent that its prohibitions are not taken seriously, as demonstrated by the above statements?

8. A construction company submitted a bid to build a municipal swimming pool in the Netherlands. The mayor and his municipal councilors found this bid to be the best and to be within the municipality's budget for the project. However, the town council rejected the bid and awarded the contract to another firm. The construction company sued the town for expenses incurred in preparing the bid and damages suffered as a result of loss of the contract. The court held that, under Dutch law, there are three stages of contract negotiation. In the initial stage, either party may break off negotiations without incurring liability. In the second or continuing stage, either party may break off the negotiations but is liable to the other party for expenses. In the final stage, the parties are prohibited from terminating negotiations without incurring liability for damages resulting from loss of the contract. Parties enter the third stage of negotiations when they have a mutual and reasonable expectation that a contract will result from the negotiations. In this case, the court concluded the parties were in the continuing-negotiation stage and awarded the construction company the expenses incurred in preparing its bid proposal. Is such an approach to contract negotiations realistic? How would you define the different stages of negotiation created by the court? [*Plas v. Valburg,* 18-6 Netherlandse Jurisprudentie 723 (1983).]

9. A U.S. software manufacturer sold software for processing credit card charges to a U.S. limited liability company that was a wholly-owned subsidiary of a German corporation. The software did not function properly. The U.S. buyer and its German parent sued the software manufacturer for breach of contract. The plaintiffs asserted that the CISG was applicable to the transaction as the head of the German parent company signed the purchase and sales contract. The software manufacturer alleged that the CISG was inapplicable as the contract was addressed to the U.S. limited liability company and the purchase price was paid with a check tendered by the U.S. purchaser. Is the CISG applicable to this transaction? Why or why not? [*American Mint LLC v. GOSoftware, Inc.,* 2006 U.S. Dist. LEXIS 1569 (M.D. Pa. 2006).]

Looking for more review material?

The Online Learning Center at **www.mhhe.com/kubasek3e** contains this chapter's "Assignment on the Internet" and also a list of URLs for more information, entitled "On the Internet." Find both of them in the Student Center portion of the OLC, along with quizzes and other helpful materials.

CHAPTER 7

Crime and the Business Community

LEARNING OBJECTIVES

After reading this chapter, you will be able to answer the following questions:

1 What are the basic elements of a crime?

2 What are some of the common crimes affecting businesses, and how do we prove them?

3 When a crime is committed to benefit a corporation, who can be held liable?

4 What are the basic constitutional safeguards for a person accused of a crime?

5 What are the basic steps of a criminal proceeding?

6 How can we prevent white-collar crimes?

CASE OPENER

Untenable Trading

Mathew Martoma, a portfolio manager for Steven Cohen's SAC Capital Advisors LP, was accused of illegal insider trading by the U.S. Securities and Exchange Commission (SEC). Subsequently, Martoma, his former hedge fund, and the doctor accused of giving Martoma insider information were all sued by the SEC. Allegedly, the companies Wyeth LLC and Elan Corp. had been developing an Alzheimer drug that ended up showing poor performance. When one of the doctors involved in the drug trials called Martoma, he gave Martoma this information. Martoma then told Cohen to sell his company's shares of the two drug companies to avoid losses. The results of the drug tests and trials had not been released to the public before Martoma was informed of them and passed the information on.

Ultimately, the SEC could not prove that Cohen knew that the advice Martoma received was illegal; thus he was excluded from the lawsuit. However, Martoma's tips netted the company a record-breaking $276 million. Thus, the SEC charged Martoma with two counts of insider trading and conspiracy.

1. Do you believe Martoma did anything illegal?
2. If a person has inside information and does not trade on it himself but passes it on to another who uses it to trade, is the person who passed on the information guilty of insider trading?

The Wrap-Up at the end of the chapter will answer these questions.

Crime comes in many forms, and sometimes the number of people affected can quickly grow. Although some crimes might at first seem victimless, there is always a victim. While SAC Capital Advisors, made large sums of money, they did so at the expense of other investors. It is important to remember that crime always has a victim, even if the victim is not readily identifiable.

In this chapter, we explain the elements of criminal law, common business crimes, and how liability can be assessed to corporations and corporate executives. We introduce common criminal defenses and constitutional safeguards, describe the criminal justice process, and identify some primary laws for combating business crime.

Elements of a Crime

LO1

What are the basic elements of a crime?

The purpose of criminal law is to punish an offender for causing harm to public health, safety, or morals. Thus, in a criminal trial, society is seen as the victim, and the *government* files charges against the defendant. In contrast, in a civil trial there is an individual victim or victims, and an individual person or corporation can file a suit.

Criminal laws usually define criminal behavior and set guidelines for punishment. To punish an individual for criminal behavior, the government must demonstrate the two elements of a crime:

1. Wrongful behavior, that is, ***actus reus*** or a guilty act.
2. Wrongful state of mind, also known as ***mens rea*** or a guilty mind.

The government thus must show that a defendant committed a prohibited act with a wrongful intent.

To prove the first element, *actus reus,* the government must establish the nonmental elements of the crime and demonstrate that a prohibited act or consequence resulted because of the defendant's actions.

To prove the second element, *mens rea,* the government must prove that the defendant acted with purpose, knowledge, recklessness, or negligence, depending on which of these states of mind is required by the law defining the relevant offense. The defendant's type of wrongful state of mind helps determine the seriousness of the punishment. First, a defendant can *purposefully* commit a crime by engaging in a specific wrongful behavior to bring about a specific wrongful result. Second, a defendant can *knowingly* commit a wrongful act if the person knows the act is wrongful or believes so yet does nothing to confirm or disconfirm this belief. Third, a defendant is *reckless* if a criminal act occurs when the individual consciously ignores substantial risk. Finally, a defendant is *negligent* if he or she does not meet the standard of care a reasonable person would use under the circumstances.

Only certain crimes, typically violations of regulatory statutes, allow punishment without proof of guilty mind. This **liability without fault,** or **strict liability,** applies to actions that, regardless of the care taken, are specifically prohibited, such as selling cigarettes or alcohol to a minor. Although a business might not have intended to sell to a minor (thus lacking a guilty mind), the statutory violation still allows liability to be assessed.

BUT WHAT IF . . .

WHAT IF THE FACTS OF THE CASE OPENER WERE DIFFERENT?

Recall that, in the Case Opener, Martoma advised Cohen to buy and sell securities on the basis of his tip. Instead, what if Martoma believed he was discussing the poor performance of the new drugs with a close friend and did not believe this friend would ever financially benefit from such information? How would such a change affect *mens rea?*

Classification of Crimes

Crimes are divided into categories based on the seriousness of the offense. Today, the categories used are felonies, misdemeanors, and petty crimes. **Felonies** include serious crimes, such as murder, that are punishable by imprisonment for more than one year or death. **Misdemeanors** are less serious crimes punishable by fines or imprisonment for less than one year. **Petty offenses,** such as violating a building code, are minor misdemeanors usually punishable by a jail sentence of less than six months or a small fine. The statute defining the crime usually establishes whether the crime is a felony, misdemeanor, or petty offense.

Crimes may also be federal or state, depending on whether they are enacted by the state or federal legislature.

Common Crimes Affecting Business

When people hear the word *crime,* they often think of homicide. In this section, however, we examine not violent offenses but crimes that occur in a business context. As a future business manager, you should become familiar with the following crimes, which could affect your company.

LO2
What are some of the common crimes affecting businesses, and how do we prove them?

PROPERTY CRIMES AGAINST BUSINESS

We now examine four criminal acts: robbery, burglary, larceny, and arson. Certainly, these crimes do not occur solely in the business context; however, they are crimes that could be committed against your future business. We distinguish these crimes from white-collar crimes for three reasons. First, nonemployees often commit these four crimes, while employees usually commit white-collar crimes. Second, these crimes are committed against the business, while white-collar crimes are usually committed against society. Third, these crimes may provoke violence, while white-collar crimes usually do not.

Robbery. Most states define **robbery** as the forceful and unlawful taking of personal property. If force or fear is absent, the crime is theft. Someone who steals your wallet undetected while you are walking down the street has committed theft. Someone who tackles you, pins you down, and wrests your wallet from you has committed robbery. Someone who threatens you with a deadly weapon while taking your property would likely be charged with *aggravated robbery,* which carries a more severe penalty.

Burglary. A **burglary** occurs when someone unlawfully enters a building with the intent to commit a felony. Although burglary is commonly referred to as *breaking and entering,* the requirement for burglary is met whenever a person enters a building without the owner's consent and with intent to commit a wrongful act.

Larceny. Although the definition may vary slightly state by state, **larceny** is the secretive and wrongful taking and carrying away of the personal property of another with the intent to permanently deprive the rightful owner of its use or possession. Unlike robbery, larceny does not require force or fear. In the business context larceny occurs, for example, when an employee takes office supplies, such as paper or blank CDs, for personal use.

States generally make a distinction between *grand larceny* and *petty larceny.* Grand larceny involves items of greater value; thus, it is a felony and carries more severe penalties than does petty larceny. As the Comparing the Law of Other Countries box reveals, other nations distinguish degrees of larceny in different ways that sometimes reflect their culture.

COMPARING THE LAW OF OTHER COUNTRIES

LARCENY IN SPAIN

The common legal definition of larceny in the United States is the fraudulent intent to deprive an owner *permanently* of property without threat or force. Someone who intends to return the property cannot be convicted of larceny. In Spain, however, larceny occurs if the property is merely taken without the owner's consent, without respect to a time period.

Punishment for larceny in Spain is relatively minor with one exception. If the stolen property is something (1) used in religious services, (2) stolen during a religious service, or (3) stolen from a religious building, the fine and potential jail time immediately increase. In U.S. law, location is immaterial except as it may dictate whether the crime is tried in federal or state court. A crucifix stolen from a church and a rake stolen from a garage are treated equally under U.S. law.

Arson. **Arson** is the intentional burning of another's dwelling. The definition is typically expanded to include other real property beyond dwellings, as well as destruction by means other than burning, such as the use of explosive devices.

WHITE-COLLAR CRIME

Originally, white-collar crimes were distinguished from other crimes by the social status of the offender. The more modern approach is to define **white-collar crime** as a variety of nonviolent illegal acts against society that most often occur in the business context. Clearly, the crimes in the opening scenario fall under this broad definition.

Mail fraud, bribery, embezzlement, and computer crimes are typically classified as white-collar crimes. These occur more frequently than you might think. According to some estimates, one in three U.S. households is the victim of white-collar crime every year.

The consequences of white-collar crimes are far-reaching. First, the cost can be tremendous. Fraud in the health care industry alone costs society an estimated $100 billion each year. And Bernie Madoff, perpetrator of what has been called the largest investor fraud scheme ever committed by a single person, cost his clients alone an estimated $65 billion in losses. Second, when company employees commit the crime, many companies fail to report it to avoid publicity and the offense goes unpunished. Third, white-collar crimes can be costly to the environment. For example, improper disposal of chemicals in a stream has long-term repercussions for marine life, the surrounding ecosystem, and any humans who come in contact with the contaminated water source.

It turns out "creative accounting" is a creative term for "white collar crime."

LO3

When a crime is committed to benefit a corporation, who can be held liable?

Money collected in fines from corporate executives engaged in criminal activity has not been insignificant. In 2012, the government won over $4.1 billion in fines, judgments, and settlements from health care fraud cases alone.[1] And in 2009, repeat offender Pfizer Drug Company was assessed a record-breaking $2.3 billion in criminal fines.[2] However, fines are only one way those found guilty of white-collar crimes might be punished; there are at least four others.

First is incarceration. As the prevalence of white-collar crime has increased, so has the number of white-collar offenders in jail. Bernie Madoff, an atypical criminal because of the magnitude of his crime, received the maximum sentence possible, 150 years. A second punishment is mandated community service. Junk-bond king Michael Milliken was required to give speeches on corporate crime after being convicted of insider trading. Third, the judge may prohibit the offender from engaging in an occupation where the same or a similar criminal act could occur again. Fourth, the offender can be placed under house arrest and wear a monitoring device.

Bribery. One of the better-known white-collar crimes is bribery. **Bribery** is the offering, giving, soliciting, or receiving of money or any object of value for the purpose of influencing the judgment or conduct of a person in a position of trust. *Bribery of a public official* is a statutory offense under federal law, which also covers bribes offered to witnesses in exchange for testimony. The Salt Lake City Olympics Bid Committee allegedly gave International Olympic Committee (IOC) members between $4 million and $7 million in cash and other benefits like college tuition payments, shopping trips for bathroom fixtures and doorknobs, and trips to the Super Bowl.

To demonstrate bribery under the federal statute, the government must show three elements: (1) Something of value was offered, given, or promised to (2) a federal public official with (3) intent to influence that person's judgment or conduct. The "thing of value" has been construed very liberally; actual commercial value is not necessary. Had the Salt Lake City Olympics Bid Committee given a member of the IOC stock shares in a start-up company that was never established, this act may constitute bribery even though the stock is commercially worthless. In the actual case, ultimately, the Department of Justice was unable to prove any of the 15 charges of bribery filed against two members of the Salt Lake City committee. Several members of the committee resigned, however; and 10 members of the IOC were fired, and another 10 were sanctioned.

The statute defines *public officials* broadly, as members of Congress, government officers and employees, and anyone "acting for or on behalf of" the federal government "in any official function, under or by authority of" a federal government department or agency. Private employees responsible for carrying out federal programs or policies are considered public officials.

Another offense is *commercial bribery,* a bribe in exchange for information or payoffs. Suppose Comdac Computers is looking for a company that manufactures a certain part. Jane Devlon owns such a company and realizes that if Comdac gets its parts from her, she will make a lot of money. She offers Comdac's contractor $500,000 in exchange for his promise that Comdac will buy all such parts from only her factory for the next year. Devlon might also bribe the contractor to disclose the dollar amounts of any competing bids so that she can offer a better bid to win the contract.

The Foreign Corrupt Practices Act (FCPA) serves to combat *bribery of foreign officials.* You might think of it as an extension of the law to prevent bribery of a public official. Multinational organizations often pressure the United States to conform its law to certain international standards. To conform to the antibribery convention adopted by the Organization for Economic Cooperation and Development (OECD), Congress amended the FCPA by broadening the scope of actions covered and the definition of a public official.

[1] HHS.gov, http://www.hhs.gov/news/press/2012pres/02/20120214a.html, February 2, 2012.

[2] Devlin Barrett, "Pfizer to Pay Record $2.3B Penalty over Promotions," September 2, 2009, www.texaslawyers.com/coomer/pharmaceuticalmarketingfraudlawsuits.htm.

Unfortunately, however, many of the world's leading exporting countries are failing to enforce the OECD antibribery convention. According to the Transparency International (TI) "2009 Progress Report," only 4 of the 36 countries TI evaluated are actively enforcing the convention. Enforcement was moderate in 11 countries, and there was little or no enforcement in 21 countries.[3]

Extortion. **Extortion,** otherwise known as *blackmail,* is the making of threats for the purpose of obtaining money or property. Whereas bribery is offering someone something to obtain a desired result, extortion is the threat of doing something if the victim does not relinquish money or a specific piece of property.

Many celebrities have been victims of extortion and attempted extortion. Most recently, David Letterman went public with allegations that a CBS producer was attempting to force him to pay $2 million to keep the producer from revealing Letterman's affair with a young staff member. In 1997, the famous family man Bill Cosby was the victim of an extortion attempt by 23-year-old Autumn Jackson, who requested $40 million from Cosby in exchange for not telling the press that she was the star's illegitimate daughter. In that case, Cosby had given the girl and her mother over $100,000 in the past, and he admitted that he had had an affair with her mother but denied being the girl's father. Jackson, who was convicted along with two accomplices, received a 26-month prison sentence.

In 1993, comedian Louie Anderson paid $100,000 to Richard John Gordon to keep him from selling the tabloids a story stating that Anderson had propositioned a man in Las Vegas. Seven years later, Gordon sought an additional payment of $250,000 to keep the story under wraps, but this time Anderson went to the police, and his blackmailer ended up going to prison.

Fraud. Criminal **fraud** encompasses a variety of means by which an individual intentionally uses misrepresentation to gain an advantage over another. Fraud generally requires the following three elements: (1) a material false representation made with intent to deceive *(scienter),* (2) a victim's reasonable reliance on the false representation, and (3) damages. Under both federal and state statutes, schemes to defraud include credit card fraud, insurance fraud, and securities fraud. Exhibit 7-1 summarizes fraudulent acts in the corporate setting, many of which we discuss below.

When these fraudulent schemes are uncovered and successfully prosecuted, there are generally several individuals involved; if the government can secure cooperation of at least one of the defendants, a number of significant sentences are handed down. For example, in 2009, when a $2.8 billion fraudulent scheme led to the bankruptcy of National Century Financial Enterprises, its CEO and owner was sentenced to 30 years in prison, and its co-owner to 25 years, for conspiracy, fraud, and money laundering. A former vice chairman was sentenced to 25 years for conspiracy, securities fraud, wire fraud, and money laundering, but she fled after the conviction. The defendants were also ordered to pay $2.3 billion in restitution.[4] The executive vice president for compliance was sentenced to 48 months in prison for securities fraud but was released for testifying against the others. Also convicted were the former director of compliance and the former chief financial officer.[5]

In June 2000, the FBI achieved the largest *securities fraud* crackdown in its history when it arrested a group of Mafia leaders for a series of scams that cost investors an estimated $25 million. Government officials claimed the Mob bought large stakes in small

[3] "2009 Progress Report on the OCED Anti-bribery Convention," June 23, 2009, www.financialtaskforce.org/2009/06/23/2009-progress-report-on-the-oecd-anti-bribery-convention/.

[4] Dept. of Justice, "Former National Century Financial Enterprises CEO Sentenced to 30 Years in Prison," www.usdoj.gov/usao/ohs.

[5] Ibid.

Exhibit 7-1
Selected Types of Fraudulent Crimes

1. *Forgery:* The fraudulent making or altering of any writing in a way that changes the legal rights and liabilities of another.
2. *Defalcation:* The misappropriation of trust funds or money held in a fiduciary capacity.
3. *False entry:* An entry in the books of a bank or corporation designed to represent funds that do not exist.
4. *False token:* A false document or sign of existence used to perpetrate a fraud, such as counterfeit money.
5. *False pretenses:* A designed misrepresentation of existing facts or conditions by which a person obtains another's money or goods, such as the writing of a worthless check.
6. *Fraudulent concealment:* The suppression of a material fact that a person is legally bound to disclose.
7. *Mail fraud:* The use of mail to defraud the public.
8. *Health care fraud:* Any fraudulent act committed in the provision of health care products or services.
9. *Telemarketing fraud:* Any scheme, including cramming and slamming, that uses the telephone to commit a fraudulent act.
10. *Ponzi scheme:* An investment swindle in which high profits are promised from fictitious sources and early investors are paid off with funds raised from later ones.
11. *Check kiting:* Drawing checks on an account in one bank and depositing them in an account in a second bank when neither account has sufficient funds to cover the amounts drawn. Just before the checks are returned for payment to the first bank, the kiter covers them by depositing checks drawn on the account in the second bank. The brief delay in transferring funds from one bank to the other, known as the "float" time, creates an artificial balance in the account.
12. *Pretexting:* Using fraudulent means to obtain information about someone's phone use.
13. *Mortgage and real estate fraud:* Any fraudulent act committed by anyone involved in a real estate transaction, including sellers, buyers, mortgage brokers, title closers, land developers, and real estate lawyers.

companies and then bribed and coerced brokers to promote the stocks to other investors at inflated prices.

The Enron scandal also included securities fraud, with Enron's top executives allegedly overstating its earnings to maintain high stock prices and using complex accounting methods to hide debt. These executives and other big investors sold their overvalued stock while encouraging employees to continue buying it. When the company's value plummeted, many Enron employees lost all their retirement investments.

Another specific type of securities fraud in the Enron case, as well as in the chapter's opening scenario, is insider trading. **Insider trading** is generally the buying or selling of a security, in breach of a fiduciary duty or other relationship of trust and confidence, while in possession of material, nonpublic information about the security. Insider-trading violations may also include "tipping" such information and trading on it by the person "tipped."[6] Enron's big investors and top executives knew the stock prices were inflated due to overstated earnings. They used this information, which was not public knowledge, to sell off their stock before the price fell. In the opening scenario, Martoma passed information to Cohen, who then traded on the basis of that information. Cohen's profits were a direct result of Martoma's tip. How might insider trading violate each of the ethical norms we have discussed?

[6] U.S. Securities and Exchange Commission, www.sec.gov/answers/insider.htm.

Stock-option backdating occurs when an employee falsifies documents to make it appear as if the company had granted options on certain dates. The employee selects dates after the fact by looking for past dates on which the stock price was low, thereby falsely inflating the company's net profits. In 2007, Myron F. Olesnyckyj, the former general counsel of Monster Worldwide, Inc., pleaded guilty to securities fraud for participating in a multiyear scheme with other Monster executives to backdate stock options granted to thousands of Monster officers, directors, and employees, including himself. Monster thus granted undisclosed compensation to its employees, failed to recognize compensation expenses, and overstated its net income by $340 million from 1997 through 2005. Olesnyckyj personally made $381,000 from the scheme, which he forfeited.

False pretenses, another type of fraud, is the illegal obtaining of property belonging to another through materially false representations of an existing fact, with knowledge of their falsity and intent to defraud. Suppose Jim goes door-to-door selling vacuum cleaners at an amazing discount. To obtain the discount, the customers must pay immediately for delivery in three to five business days. However, Jim has no vacuum cleaners and does not plan on delivering any. He has committed the crime of false pretenses.

In July 2009, New York City lawyer Marc S. Dreier, whom prosecutors called a "Houdini of impersonation and false documents,"[7] was sentenced to 20 years in prison for selling over $700 million worth of bogus promissory notes to investors. Five months later, ex-SEC lawyer Robert Miller pleaded guilty to helping Dreier defraud hedge funds by impersonating a representative of both a Canadian pension plan and an Icelandic hedge fund in a scheme to sell a fictitious $44.7 million note.[8]

Forgery is the fraudulent making or altering of any writing in a way that changes the legal rights and liabilities of another. If you sign your colleague's name to the back of a check made out to her, you have committed forgery.

One of the most frequently prosecuted frauds is *mail fraud,* the use of mail to defraud the public, which is a federal crime under the Mail Fraud Act of 1990. To prove mail fraud, the government must demonstrate (1) an intent to defraud and (2) the use of or causing the use of mail to further the fraudulent scheme. Case 7-1 demonstrates the consideration of these two elements.

[7] "Marc S. Dreier," *New York Times,* November 18, 2009, http://topics.nytimes.com/top/reference/timestopics/people/d/marc_s_dreier/index.html?inline=nyt-per.

[8] "Dreier Fraud Case Leads to Guilty Plea by Ex-SEC Lawyer Miller," *Bloomberg.com,* November 18, 2009, www.bloomberg.com/apps/news?pid=20601103&sid=awYs1J0cYkL4.

CASE 7-1 U.S. v. RUIZ
10TH CIRCUIT COURT OF APPEALS
589 F.3D 1310 (10TH CIR. 2009)

Mr. Ruiz was a deputy superintendent in New Mexico's insurance division. He was primarily responsible for enforcing the state's insurance code, which requires, among other things, that insurance adjusters doing business in the state be licensed by the state. Prior to Mr. Ruiz's assuming his position, the insurance division rarely assessed fines against companies that employed unlicensed adjusters. Mr. Ruiz revived the licensing requirement and perpetrated a quid pro quo scheme through his enforcement of it.

Under Mr. Ruiz's scheme, he would detect licensing violations by insurers and threaten them with the maximum possible fines. Then, he would tell them that they could avoid paying the fines if they contributed 10 to 20 percent of the fine amount to two charities to which he and his supervisor were connected.

Insurers who agreed to contribute to one or both of the charities were not fined and were placed in good standing with the insurance department, and no record of their violations was ever made. Insurers who rejected the charitable-contribution option ended up paying a fine lower than the threatened one but higher than the requested charitable contribution. Plus, their licensing violations were made public

[continued]

and forwarded to the National Association of Insurance Commissioners.

Mr. Ruiz, who had been informed on at least three occasions that the insurance division was not authorized to solicit any type of charitable contribution in lieu of a fine, succeeded in soliciting over $150,000 for the two charities and consequently received over $1,500 in royalties from books purchased with funds "donated" by insurance companies during the course of the scheme.

Mr. Ruiz was convicted of multiple counts of honest services mail and wire fraud, corrupt solicitation, extortion, and aiding and abetting on each count. He appealed.

CIRCUIT JUDGE TACHA: Mail fraud requires the use of the mail to execute a fraudulent scheme or artifice. . . . To establish this necessary element of federal mail fraud, the government must prove that the defendant "set forces in motion which . . . would involve mail uses." . . . In other words, "[t]he only causation required by the mail fraud statute is whether the defendant could reasonably foresee the occurrence of mailings."

Mr. Ruiz's two mail fraud convictions are based on his requests that two insurance companies make contributions directly to Con Alma or SAI, and those companies' subsequent uses of the mail to deliver their contribution checks. Mr. Ruiz claims that he did not cause the use of the mail because he had no meaningful control over these companies' method of delivering their contribution checks. This argument places a much higher burden on the government to prove causation than our case law has previously imposed. The evidence that Mr. Ruiz directed two insurance companies to make charitable donations directly to the charities, alone, establishes that he set forces in motion, the reasonably foreseeable result of which would be the use of the mail to further his fraudulent scheme. Accordingly, we conclude that there was sufficient evidence to support this necessary element of Mr. Ruiz's mail fraud conviction.

All but one of Mr. Ruiz's claims on appeal are based on a flawed and unreasonable interpretation of New Mexico law. Contrary to Mr. Ruiz's claims, the New Mexico insurance code does not permit a deputy insurance superintendent to solicit donations to charities in which he and his superior have personal interests instead of collecting fines for the state. Furthermore, there was ample evidence that Mr. Ruiz caused the use of the mail to further his fraudulent scheme.

AFFIRMED in favor of the United States.

CRITICAL THINKING

Suppose Mr. Ruiz had supplemented his request for charitable contributions with the warning "Do Not Use the Mail." Would this warning provide him good reason for saying the convictions were improper?

ETHICAL REASONING

Does this case raise ethical questions about law and justice similar to those raised in the play, movie, and novel *Les Misérables?* Does the universalization test serve as a helpful way to answer that question?

The statute also bans the use of wire, radio, and television transmissions to defraud the public, and in 1994 Congress amended it to include commercial carriers and courier services such as FedEx and UPS. Internet mail has not been explicitly legislated into the mail fraud law. However, in response to the growing threat of fraud from this source, the Postal Inspection Service formed the Internet Mail Fraud Initiative, which trains postal inspectors across the country in specialized techniques and strategies that target cyber scammers. Postal inspectors also work with analysts at the Internet Fraud Complaint Center, the Federal Trade Commission's Consumer Sentinel, and the Postal Inspection Service's Fraud Complaint System (FCS), soliciting and receiving fraud referrals for investigative attention. A major outcome of the Internet Mail Fraud Initiative was that the FCS was enhanced to receive online complaints directly from Internet users.[9]

The Department of Justice recently named *health care fraud* its top priority after violent crime. Submitting false claims to insurance plans such as Medicare or Medicaid is health care fraud, as is prescribing unneeded equipment to patients for kickbacks from the equipment manufacturers.

[9] For more about Internet crime, see https://postalinspectors.uspis.gov/radDocs/pubs/ar01_03.pdf.

There are a variety of different techniques that are used to commit telemarketing fraud. For example, *cramming* is a scheme in which companies bill consumers for optional services they did not order. Another scheme is *slamming,* in which consumers are tricked into changing their phone service to another carrier.

The elderly, more susceptible to telemarketing fraud, are often the specific targets of such schemes. Thus, the Department of Justice and the FBI have been collaborating on various undercover operations, such as Operation Senior Sentinel, to investigate and prosecute fraudulent telemarketers.

In 2012, 1,181,016 debtors filed for bankruptcy to be relieved of oppressive debt. Yet claims need to be carefully reviewed to prevent *bankruptcy fraud* by either party. A debtor might hide assets so that they will not be considered during the proceedings, or a creditor might file a false claim against a debtor. One debtor in Illinois filed a bankruptcy claim and failed to list the fact that he had just filed his state and federal tax returns prior to filing bankruptcy and was expecting to receive significant tax refunds. The most common bankruptcy fraud techniques involve lying under oath, providing false documentation during bankruptcy, or concealing or transferring financial assets. The Department of Justice estimates that 10 percent of all bankruptcy petitions contain elements of fraud.

Some cases encompass multiple types of fraud. A Beverly Hills lawyer was recently convicted of three counts of mail fraud, seven counts of wire fraud, and five counts of lying to a court hearing. In an elaborate fraud, the lawyer had purchased a yacht for $1.9 million, sold it to two partners to drive up its insurance value, and had a company he owned repurchase it and insure it for $3.5 million. Finally, he and his partners sank the yacht and tried to collect the insurance.

BUT WHAT IF . . .

Former Mets outfielder Lenny Dykstra went to court for fraud in 2012. While Dykstra owned a mansion formerly owned by Wayne Gretzky, he claimed that he was over $31 million in debt and his total assets amounted to only $50,000. Thus, he was seeking to file for bankruptcy. If Dykstra secretly hid and sold $400,000 worth of possessions yet on the stand said he had only a few items put into his storage unit, would he be accountable for only bankruptcy fraud or other types of fraud as well? Alternatively, if Dykstra had reviewed the sold, stored, and destroyed items with a bankruptcy trustee, would he be liable for fraud at all?

Pretexting is using or causing others to use false pretenses, fraudulent statements, fraudulent or stolen documents, or other misrepresentations, including posing as an account holder or employee of a telecommunications carrier, to obtain telephone records of another. Pretexting entered the national lexicon in 2006 when news broke that the investigators hired by Hewlett-Packard's board of directors to locate the source of several leaks to the media were engaging in this practice. Under the federal Telephone Records and Privacy Protection Act of 2006, anyone convicted of employing fraudulent tactics to persuade phone companies to hand over confidential data about a customer's calling habits can be jailed for up to 10 years. Some states also have statutes outlawing pretexting.

To minimize the chances that your firm will be a victim of fraud, review Exhibit 7-2, "Fraud Prevention Tips."

Exhibit 7-2
Fraud Prevention Tips

RED FLAGS SUGGESTING POSSIBLE FRAUD

When an investment opportunity seems too good to be true, it may indeed be less good than it seems, especially if it contains these red flags of fraud:

- No independent proof, such as names and addresses of specific companies in which the fund invests.
- Control by a single person.
- No audited financial statements and no evidence of internal controls.
- Rates of return that are significantly higher than those for other funds with a similar investment strategy.
- New investors' reliance primarily on existing investors in deciding to invest.

Investors should also be wary of these false "assurances" that an investment opportunity is not fraudulent:

- *Long-time existence of investment opportunity:* A Ponzi scheme can operate for a long time. As long as the company keeps getting new investors, it can continue to use them to pay off the few who insist on collecting their returns. Many investors may be content to accumulate paper profits, especially if there is a financial incentive to reinvest them. The Financial Advisory Fund had been in business for almost 20 years before its fraudulent foundation was uncovered.
- *A list of names and addresses of satisfied investors you can contact:* All such schemes will have some satisfied investors who have received payments from the new investors' money.
- *Membership in the Better Business Bureau:* Any company can pay to join.
- *A report of profitability from Dun & Bradstreet:* Dun & Bradstreet does not do an independent financial audit of a company's profits. As stated on its website, it simply provides information companies send it about profits.
- *Acceptance of money rolled over from IRAs:* There is no government check on the soundness of firms that roll over IRAs.
- *Bank references:* If a firm has a large sum in a checking account and has never sought a loan from the bank, the bank will have no reason to do any due diligence on it, particularly if the owner of the firm is personable and the account has never been overdrawn.
- *Glossy brochures and television ads:* All you need for both is some money and the knowledge that many people are impressed by a fancy brochure or ad campaign.

These tips come from Barry Minkow, who started a carpet-cleaning business at age 16, took his multimillion-dollar company public at age 20, and faced a 23-year prison sentence and a $26 million victim restitution payment at age 21 for massive fraud and theft. His fascinating story of building a company through Ponzi schemes, check kiting, and theft is told in his book, *Cleaning Up.* Minkow is now a pastor and the cofounder of the Fraud Discovery Institute.

Embezzlement. Suppose Kathleen gives Devin, her attorney, $5,000 to put in escrow, an account where Devin will have access to the money although it is not his to use as he pleases. Devin takes some of that money out and uses it to gamble, fixing the records to cover himself. Devin has committed the crime of **embezzlement,** the wrongful conversion of another's property by one lawfully in possession of it. Embezzlement is distinguished from larceny because the embezzler does not take property from another; he is already in possession of it.

COMPARING THE LAW OF OTHER COUNTRIES

EMBEZZLEMENT AND BRIBERY IN CHINA

Between 1981 and 1982, the People's Republic of China witnessed a dramatic rise in white-collar crimes, including embezzlement, extortion, and bribery. Chinese officials were alarmed by the increase and sought to severely punish all offenders regardless of political or social rank. On March 8, 1982, a resolution entitled "Severely Punishing Criminals Who Do Great Damage to the Economy" was added to the Chinese Criminal Code. It targeted top-ranking officials by stating that any state functionaries who extort, accept bribes, or exploit their office would no longer receive the standard fixed-term punishment (usually 10 years). Instead, they would be sentenced to life imprisonment or put to death.

Bank fraud is another white-collar crime that may be punishable by death. In 2004, China executed four people, including employees of two of its Big Four state banks, for fraud totaling $15 million. Three cases involved China Construction Bank, where a former accounting officer worked with others to steal 20 million yuan ($2.4 million) using fake papers. The officer and an accomplice were executed, along with another Construction Bank employee found to have taken 20 million yuan from the bank in an unrelated case.

The precise number of people executed in China is a secret, but estimates range from 5,000 to 10,000 a year for crimes including murder, corruption, and on occasion even bottom-pinching. Such punishment may seem extreme, but the reaction of the Chinese to the increase in white-collar crime reflects their culture's unusually great concern for social harmony.

It is often employees in banks who commit embezzlement. As the recent embezzlement of $6.9 million from the American Cancer Society demonstrates, even nonprofit organizations are vulnerable. The Chinese government, which has been focusing on economic crimes, caught employees in two major Chinese banks altering deposit slips and bank orders to direct money to personal accounts throughout China. Those employees received death sentences, as discussed in the Comparing the Law of Other Countries box.

Even though Ponzi schemes have been around for a long time, and there has been significant publicity surrounding a number of them, people still continue to fall for them. For example, in mid-2009, the Securities and Exchange Commission and the Commodity Futures Trading Commission charged two California men, Peter Son and Jin Chung, of luring about 500 investors, primarily Korean-Americans, into a scam in which the money from the new investors was used to pay the old ones.[10] Many of those who fell for Bernie Madoff's massive Ponzi scheme were highly intelligent and sophisticated individuals who one would normally not think would be victims of such fraud.

Computer Crimes. The term **computer crime** refers broadly to any wrongful act that (1) is directed against computers, (2) uses computers to commit a crime, or (3) involves computers. Computer crime is not necessarily a new kind of crime but is, instead, a new way of committing traditional crimes. Consider fraud, a crime that has existed for centuries. Today, online auctions such as eBay are a common location of fraud in the United States. Indeed, some statistics suggest that using computers is simply a more profitable method of committing crimes. According to the FBI, the cost of online scams and fraud for Americans more than doubled from 2008 to 2009, reaching nearly $560 million.[11]

Computer crimes are often difficult to prosecute, largely because they are difficult to detect. They can be committed by an insider, such as an employee, or by an outsider, such as a **hacker**—a person who illegally accesses a computer system to obtain information or steal money. Computer systems are also quite open to attack. The American Society for Industrial Security has reported that U.S. companies experienced losses from computer crimes of more than $250 billion in a single year. Attacks are also frequent. The IRS alone detects 800 to 1,200 cases of computer system misuse annually.

[10] "Two California Men Charged in Ponzi Scheme," *USA Today,* June 10, 2009, p. B1.

[11] Victor Godinez, "Experts At Dallas Cyber Summit Say Speed Essential In Fight Against High-Tech Crime," *Dallas News,* June 1, 2010, *Available at* http://www.dallasnews.com/sharedcontent/dws/bus/stories/050610dnbuscybersec.3f79f2c.html.

A **cyber terrorist** is a hacker who intends to exploit a target computer or network to create a serious impact, such as crippling a communications network or sabotaging a business or organization. A successful cyber-terrorist attack can affect millions of people if it strikes a major stock exchange, any bank, or any federal agency or government.

To aid prosecutions of computer crimes, Congress passed the Counterfeit Access Device and Computer Fraud and Abuse Act of 1984 (also know as the Computer Fraud and Abuse Act, or CFAA). The act prohibits six broad categories of computer crimes:

1. Unauthorized use of or access to a computer to obtain classified military or foreign policy information with the intent to harm the United States or to benefit a foreign country.
2. Unauthorized use of a computer to collect financial or credit information protected under federal privacy law.
3. Unauthorized access to a federal computer and the use, modification, destruction, or disclosure of data it contains or the prevention of authorized persons' use of such data.
4. Alteration or modification of data in financial computers causing a loss of $1,000 or more.
5. Modification of data that impedes medical treatment to individuals.
6. Fraudulent transfer of computer passwords or other similar data that could aid unauthorized access that either (a) affects interstate commerce or (b) permits access to a government computer.

Computer crimes in the first category are felonies, whereas the others are misdemeanors.

The National Information Infrastructure Protection Act of 1996 amended the Computer Fraud and Abuse Act to extend protection to any computer attached to the Internet. The Justice Department also formed the Computer Crime and Intellectual Property Section (CCIPS) in its Criminal Division. Attorneys in this division prosecute only federal computer crimes. They also coordinate their activities with numerous government entities, the private sector, scholars, and foreign representatives to develop a global response to computer crime.

BUT WHAT IF . . .

In 2009, a group of hackers attacked a user named Cyxymu through various websites. To attack this user, they not only bombarded his Facebook, Twitter, and Live journal accounts with spam messages but used previously infected personal computers to have other accounts bombarded with junk e-mails that appeared to be coming from his accounts. While the attack was aimed at Cyxymu, other users were affected as well as the websites involved. In fact, the website Twitter was down for several hours. In accordance with the above cyber-terrorism definition and categories, were the damages from this prank sufficient enough to qualify these hackers as cyber terrorists?

Destruction of Computer Data. Destruction of data is one of the most serious problems facing companies today. A **virus** is a computer program that rearranges, damages, destroys, or replaces computer data. The most economically destructive computer crime to date was the creation of the "love bug" virus, which spread rapidly throughout the world by e-mail in May 2000. Once the e-mail was opened, the virus destroyed files on the user's computer and then sent itself to every address in that computer's e-mail address book. In the end, the love bug caused over $10 billion in damages and halted computers in major companies and government agencies worldwide.

Companies can try to prevent the destruction of data by installing virus detection programs on their computers, installing firewalls, and adopting procedures such as the use of confidential passwords and encryption keys. However, virus detection programs recognize only previously existing harmful files. If someone creates a new virus, the detection program is useless. To counter this drawback, all antivirus providers offer a subscription service by which users can get automatic updates that provide as much protection as possible against newly created viruses for which cures have been developed.

Unlawful Appropriation of Data or Services. An employee who uses his or her computer in a manner not authorized by the employer, such as to run a personal business on the side, has committed a crime, most often theft of company assets (the computer). Employers must clearly communicate with employees about authorized versus unauthorized behavior. As a business manager, you will want to explicitly list acceptable computer uses and penalties for unauthorized use.

Liability for Crimes

An individual or a corporation can be charged with and convicted of a crime. However, there has been much debate over whether corporations should be held criminally responsible.

CORPORATE CRIMINAL LIABILITY

Under the common law, a corporation could not be considered a criminal because it was not an actual person and thus did not have a "mind." Consequently, it could not meet the *mens rea* (guilty-mind) requirement for a crime. Slowly, however, courts began to impose liability on corporations for **strict-liability offenses,** those offenses that do not require state of mind. Next, courts imposed liability on corporations by imputing the state of mind of the employee to the corporation. Currently, corporations can be held criminally accountable for almost any crime except those punishable only by a prison sentence.

The first case in which criminal liability was assigned to a corporation for a crime other than a strict-liability offense was decided by the Supreme Court in 1909.[12] Courts have since refined the standards required for finding a corporation criminally liable for the acts of one of its employees or agents. Today, it must be shown that (1) the individual was acting within the scope of her or his employment; (2) the individual was acting with the purpose of benefiting the corporation; and (3) the act was imputed to the corporation.

LIABILITY OF CORPORATE EXECUTIVES

Corporate executives may also be personally liable for a business crime, regardless of whether it was committed for their personal benefit or that of the corporation. Under the "responsible corporate officer" doctrine, a court may assess criminal liability even on a corporate executive or officer who did not engage in, direct, or know about a specific criminal violation. As Case 7-2 demonstrates, corporate executives sometimes have the responsibility and power to ensure the company's compliance with the law. One who fails to do so can be held criminally liable.

Since *United States v. Park* (Case 7-2), the general rule that corporate executives may be held accountable for crimes arising from their failure to meet their responsibility has remained intact. In fact, it has broadened; now executives can be held criminally liable for

[12] *New York Central & Hudson River Railroad Company v. United States,* 212 U.S. 481 (1909).

CASE 7-2 UNITED STATES v. PARK
UNITED STATES SUPREME COURT
421 U.S. 658 (1975)

Defendant Park, the president of a national food-chain corporation, was charged, along with the corporation, with violating the Federal Food, Drug, and Cosmetic Act by allowing food in the warehouse to be exposed to rodent contamination. Park conceded that his responsibility for the "entire operation" included warehouse sanitation but claimed he had delegated the responsibility for sanitation to dependable subordinates. He admitted at trial that he had received a warning letter from the Food and Drug Administration about unsanitary conditions at one of the company's warehouses. The trial court found him guilty, the court of appeals reversed, and the case was appealed to the U.S. Supreme Court.

CHIEF JUSTICE BURGER: The question presented was whether "the manager of a corporation, as well as the corporation itself, may be prosecuted under the Federal Food, Drug, and Cosmetic Act of 1938 for the introduction of misbranded and adulterated articles into interstate commerce." In Dotterweich, a jury had disagreed as to the corporation, a jobber purchasing drugs from manufacturers and shipping them in interstate commerce under its own label, but had convicted Dotterweich, the corporation's president and general manager.

Central to the Court's conclusion that individuals other than proprietors are subject to the criminal provisions of the Act was the reality that "the only way in which a corporation can act is through the individuals who act on its behalf."

The rationale of the interpretation given the Act in Dotterweich, as holding criminally accountable the persons whose failure to exercise the authority and supervisory responsibility reposed in them by the business organization, resulted in the violation complained of, has been confirmed in our subsequent cases. . . . In order to make "distributors of food the strictest censors of their merchandise," the Act punishes "neglect where the law requires care, and inaction where it imposes a duty." " The accused, if he does not will the violation, usually is in a position to prevent it with no more care than society might reasonably expect and no more exertion than it might reasonably extract from one who assumed his responsibilities."

Thus, Dotterweich and the cases which have followed reveal that in providing sanctions which reach and touch the individuals who execute the corporate mission—and this by no means necessarily confined to a single corporate agent or employee—the Act imposes not only a positive duty to seek out and remedy violations when they occur, but also, and primarily, a duty to implement measures that will insure that violations will not occur. The requirements of foresight and vigilance imposed on responsible corporate agents are beyond question, demanding, and perhaps onerous, but they are not more stringent than the public has a right to expect of those who voluntarily assume positions of authority in business enterprises whose services and products affect the health and well-being of the public that supports them.

The Act does not, as we observed in Dotterweich, make criminal liability turn on "awareness of some wrongdoing" or "conscious fraud." The duty imposed by Congress on responsible corporate agents is, we emphasize, one that requires the highest standard of foresight and vigilance, but the Act, in its criminal aspect, does not require that which is objectively impossible. The theory upon which responsible corporate agents are held criminally accountable for "causing" violations of the Act permits a claim that a defendant was "powerless" to prevent or correct the violation to "be raised defensively at a trial on the merits."

. . . [I]t is equally clear that the Government established a prima facie case when it introduced evidence sufficient to warrant a finding by the trier of the facts that the defendant had, by reason of his position in the corporation, responsibility and authority either to prevent in the first instance, or promptly to correct, the violation complained of, and that he failed to do so. The failure thus to fulfill the duty imposed by the interaction of the corporate agent's authority and that statute furnishes a sufficient causal link. The considerations, which prompted the imposition of this duty, and the scope of the duty, provide the measure of culpability.

REVERSED in favor of the Government.

CRITICAL THINKING

The Court relied heavily on the *Dotterweich* decision in coming to its present conclusion. Why? Do you think the Court should have relied so much on this case?

ETHICAL DECISION MAKING

Suppose you were in Park's position and allowed food in your warehouse to be exposed to rodent contamination. If you were guided by the public disclosure test, what would you decide to do?

offenses we generally do not think of as crimes. In *United States v. Iverson,*[13] a corporate officer of a waste treatment facility was convicted and sentenced for violating the Clean Water Act after he ordered employees to illegally dispose of wastewater. This case demonstrates that corporate executives can be sentenced not only for committing common law crimes we have traditionally understood to be criminal offenses but also for violating provisions of regulatory statutes that permit criminal sanctions. Using the idea of **vicarious liability,** courts have held employers liable for the wrongful acts of their employees if the employer directed, partook in, or authorized the wrongful act.

Legal Principle: As a general rule, when a lower-level employee commits a crime, she or he will be individually liable for the crime, and under the responsible corporate officer doctrine, the employee's manager, and any other corporate official who could have prevented the crime, can also be held vicariously liable for the crime.

Defenses to Crimes

In addition to claiming the defendant is innocent or the prosecution did not follow proper procedures, the defense may use several **affirmative defenses,** which are excuses for unlawful behavior. Some of the most common are infancy, mistake of fact, intoxication, insanity, duress, and entrapment.

INFANCY

By law, persons under the age of majority (the age at which someone becomes a legal adult) are considered **infants.** They are typically judged as lacking the mental capabilities of an adult, and thus infancy can be a partial defense to defuse the guilty-mind requirement of a crime. However, for some offenses a defendant under the age of majority can be determined by a judge to be a legal adult and be tried as such.

MISTAKE OF FACT

A **mistake-of-fact** defense tries to prove the defendant made an honest and reasonable mistake that negates the guilty-mind element of a crime. Proving that a mistake of fact was reasonable, however, is often difficult.

In contrast, *mistake of law* is generally not a legitimate defense. For example, Martoma could not have escaped conviction by claiming to have not known insider trading is against the law. While initially these two rules may seem contradictory (because in both cases the defendant seems to lack a guilty mind), the mistake-of-law rule serves a policy goal. Courts have refused to recognize mistake of law as a defense because they fear creating a disincentive for people to learn basic tenets of law.

BUT WHAT IF . . .

What if, in the opening scenario, Cohen thought that the information Martoma gave him about the Alzheimer drug was public knowledge? What defense could he use to defend himself against an insider-trading sentence? Alternatively, is there any way that Martoma could argue that he didn't know that what he was doing constituted insider trading and was punishable by law?

[13] 162 F.3d 1015 (1998).

INTOXICATION

A person who was forced to ingest or involuntarily ingested an intoxicating agent can claim **involuntary intoxication.** This defense applies only if intoxication left the person unable to understand that the act committed was wrong. In most states, a defendant who knowingly chose to become intoxicated cannot claim intoxication as a defense.

INSANITY

Although insanity is a well-known criminal defense, it is not used as often as the public believes. A person cannot simply claim he or she is or was crazy; psychiatrists usually testify to the defendant's mental state at the time of the crime. Standards vary from state to state, but in general defendants can claim **insanity** if their mental condition when the crime was committed was so impaired that they could not (1) understand the wrongful nature of the act or (2) distinguish between right and wrong in a general sense.

The insanity defense often creates a "battle of the experts." The psychiatrist for the defense claims the accused was insane, and the psychiatrist for the prosecution refutes that diagnosis. The complexity of the insanity standards almost guarantees that experts will disagree. Further, legal scholars debate whether psychiatrists *can* determine whether an individual is or was insane at the time of the criminal act.

Adding to the difficulty, the test used to establish the defendant's mental state varies by jurisdiction. Approximately one-third of the states still apply the *M'Naghten test,* also known as the "right-wrong test." This allows a defendant to be found not guilty if she did not understand the nature of the act.

The *irresistible-impulse test* allows a verdict of not guilty by reason of insanity even if the accused knew a criminal act was wrong, as long as some "irresistible impulse" resulting from a mental deficiency drove the person to commit the crime.

A third test for establishing criminal insanity is recognized in the Model Penal Code, Section 4.01, which states, "A person is not responsible for criminal conduct if at the time of such conduct as a result of mental disease or defect he lacks substantial capacity either to appreciate the wrongfulness of his conduct or to conform his conduct to the requirements of the law." While this standard is easier to meet than the first two, it is still extremely difficult to prove criminal insanity.

In raising the insanity defense for Andrea Yates, accused of the murder of her five children, Yates's lawyer argued that his client believed killing them was the right thing to do. In support, he offered evidence that she had said her children were "going to be tormented the rest of their lives, and they were going to perish in the fires of hell," so she killed them to save them. This defense was not successful in her first trial. However, that verdict was overturned on appeal due to erroneous testimony, and in retrial the defense was successful.

DURESS

If Greg threatened Bill with immediate bodily harm or loss of life unless Bill performed a wrongful act, Bill can use the **duress** defense. However, to claim duress, Bill must establish the following three elements:

1. Greg threatened Bill with *serious bodily harm or loss of life.* Threatening to take Bill's money would not be considered duress.
2. Greg's threat of harm must be *more serious* than the harm caused by Bill's crime. If Greg threatened to seriously injure Bill's daughter unless Bill handed over the $5,000 in the company cash register, duress would apply.

3. Greg's threat of harm must be *immediate* and *inescapable.* If Greg threatened to kill Bill in a year if Bill did not comply with Greg's order, Bill could not use the duress defense.

ENTRAPMENT

The **entrapment** defense applies if the idea for a crime originated with a police officer or some other government official who suggested it to the defendant, who would not otherwise have committed the crime. The purpose of this defense, common in white-collar cases, is to prevent law enforcement officials from instigating crime. To refute the defense, the prosecution must demonstrate that the defendant either was not induced by government agents to commit the crime or was predisposed to commit it. A long-time drug dealer could not use the entrapment defense to claim that an undercover agent who offered to buy the dealer's drugs was the one who gave her the idea to sell drugs.

NECESSITY

One possible defense is to say a crime was necessary to prevent a more severe crime from occurring. Section 3.01 of the Model Penal Code allows for the **necessity** defense when "the harm or evil sought to be avoided by such conduct is greater than that sought to be prevented by the law defining the offense charged." A person could use the necessity defense if he or she broke into a store to prevent arson from occurring at night.

JUSTIFIABLE USE OF FORCE

Although not typical in white-collar crime cases, one defense in cases of physical violence is **justifiable use of force.** The best-known example is self-defense in protection of your life. However, in many jurisdictions, justifiable use of force can apply to defense of your dwelling or other property and to the prevention of a crime. The force used must be reasonable, which is understood in the law to be enough to make an adequate defense but not more than necessary for protection. Deadly force (sufficient to kill or cause serious bodily harm) is unjustifiable where the threat of deadly force does not exist, and it can never be used to protect property, as the law values life over property.

Constitutional Safeguards

LO4
What are the basic constitutional safeguards for a person accused of a crime?

The state obviously has vast resources that it can use to try to obtain a guilty verdict. To reduce this imbalance of power, constitutional safeguards are built into the system that protect defendants during criminal proceedings. Most, but not all, are contained within the Bill of Rights, the first 10 amendments to the Constitution.

FOURTH AMENDMENT PROTECTIONS

> *The right of the people to be secure in their persons, houses, papers, and effects, against unreasonable searches and seizures, shall not be violated, and no warrants shall issue, but upon probable cause, supported by oath or affirmation, and particularly describing the place to be searched, and the persons or things to be seized.*

The Fourth Amendment contains two important safeguards: protection from unreasonable search and seizure, and restrictions on warrants. The prohibition against unreasonable search and seizure is fairly straightforward. Government officials are not allowed to perform any searches without a proper warrant or without probable cause for a search. The Fourth Amendment therefore protects an individual's privacy.

The restriction on warrants requires that warrants be specific about who is to be arrested and on what cause or what objects are to be sought and in which locations. The Fourth Amendment thus prevents law enforcement officials from searching anywhere they wish for anything illegal they might find.

Fourth Amendment protections extend to businesses as well. Government inspectors may not legally enter a business to conduct an inspection without a warrant, except to search highly regulated industries such as food, liquor, or firearms. General manufacturing is *not* a highly regulated industry; thus a warrant is required for an agent to inspect a manufacturing plant.

FIFTH AMENDMENT PROTECTIONS

> *. . . nor shall any person be subject for the same offense to be twice put in jeopardy of life or limb; nor shall be compelled in any criminal case to be a witness against himself, nor be deprived of life, liberty, or property, without due process of law.*

The three main provisions of the Fifth Amendment are the prohibition on double jeopardy, the right not to incriminate yourself, and the right to due process.

Double jeopardy occurs when a person is retried for the same criminal offense after being declared not guilty. The Constitution expressly forbids this, but only for criminal offenses. A person found not guilty of a criminal offense may still face a civil charge, decided independently of the verdict in the criminal case and entailing a lower burden of proof. Such was the case with O. J. Simpson, who was acquitted of murder charges in the deaths of Nicole Brown Simpson and Ron Goldman but found civilly liable for their deaths. To "take the fifth" is to invoke your constitutional right not to testify against yourself. A criminal defendant does not have to, and cannot be forced to, testify against himself or herself. This right applies *not* to corporations but only to natural persons (remember, corporations are legal entities, not natural persons, in the eyes of the law). Nonetheless, sole proprietorships that have not been incorporated may be considered natural persons embodied in the person of the owner, who may therefore use the Fifth Amendment protection against self-incrimination.

The guarantee of due process of law ensures that a defendant may not be stricken of life, liberty, or property without first going through the appropriate legal actions (typically a trial or plea bargaining). Unlike the right not to incriminate oneself, the guarantee of due process of law does extend to corporations.

SIXTH AMENDMENT PROTECTIONS

> *In all criminal prosecutions, the accused shall enjoy the right to a speedy and public trial, by an impartial jury . . . and to be informed of the nature and cause of the accusation; to be confronted with the witnesses against him; to have compulsory process for obtaining witnesses in his favor, and to have the assistance of counsel for his defense.*

Sixth Amendment protections are crucial to ensuring fair proceedings in a criminal trial. These rights are:

1. The right to a speedy and public trial.
2. The right to a trial by an impartial jury.
3. The right to be informed of the accusations against you.
4. The right to confront witnesses.
5. The right to have witnesses on your side.
6. The right to counsel at various stages of the proceedings.

EIGHTH AMENDMENT PROTECTIONS

Excessive bail shall not be required, nor excessive fines imposed, nor cruel and unusual punishments inflicted.

While the explicit meanings of "excessive bail," "excessive fines," and "cruel and unusual punishment" are open to judicial interpretation, the protections embodied in the Eighth Amendment are easy to grasp.

FOURTEENTH AMENDMENT PROTECTIONS

No state shall make or enforce any law which shall abridge the privileges or immunities of citizens of the United States; nor shall any state deprive any person of life, liberty, or property, without due process of law; nor deny to any person within its jurisdiction the equal protection of the laws.

While not part of the Bill of Rights, the Fourteenth Amendment does contain important constitutional safeguards that extend the federal guarantee of due process—and most constitutional protections—to all states.

THE EXCLUSIONARY RULE

The *exclusionary rule,* not stated in any specific amendment, holds that all evidence obtained in violation of the constitutional rights spelled out in the Fourth, Fifth, and Sixth amendments is normally not admissible at trial. Such evidence is considered "fruit of the poisonous tree" because it is the result of an illegal procedure.

Under the *good-faith exception,* however, evidence found when an official acts in good faith is admissible. Evidence gathered by a law enforcement official who uses an incorrect search warrant to obtain evidence but acts in good faith, believing the search warrant to be correct and valid, is admissible. The *inevitability exception* holds that illegally obtained evidence may be used at trial if it would have been obtained "inevitably" by law enforcement officials using lawful means.

Criminal Procedure

LO5

What are the basic steps of a criminal proceeding?

Criminal procedure differs from civil procedure in several key ways. First, the government, as *prosecutor,* always brings the criminal case, whereas in a civil case the plaintiff filing the case can be an individual, business, or government entity. Second, in a criminal case the objective is punishment, so the defendant may be fined or imprisoned. In a civil case the objective is to remedy a wrong done to the plaintiff, so the defendant will have to compensate the plaintiff or be subject to an equitable remedy, such as an injunction or order for specific performance. Other differences will become clear as you read the following sections describing the pretrial, trial, and posttrial procedures in a criminal case. Exhibit 7-3 illustrates the complete criminal procedure.

PRETRIAL PROCEDURE

Before an arrest, grand juries may conduct criminal investigatory proceedings or issue a grand jury subpoena for company records. Criminal proceedings generally begin when an individual is **arrested** by a law enforcement officer for a crime. The arresting agent is often a police officer but may also be part of another government agency, such as the Bureau of Alcohol, Tobacco, Firearms and Explosives; the Federal Bureau of Investigation; or the Immigration and Naturalization Service. Ordinarily, to obtain the necessary arrest warrant, the agent must demonstrate that there is **probable cause,** or likelihood, that a suspect

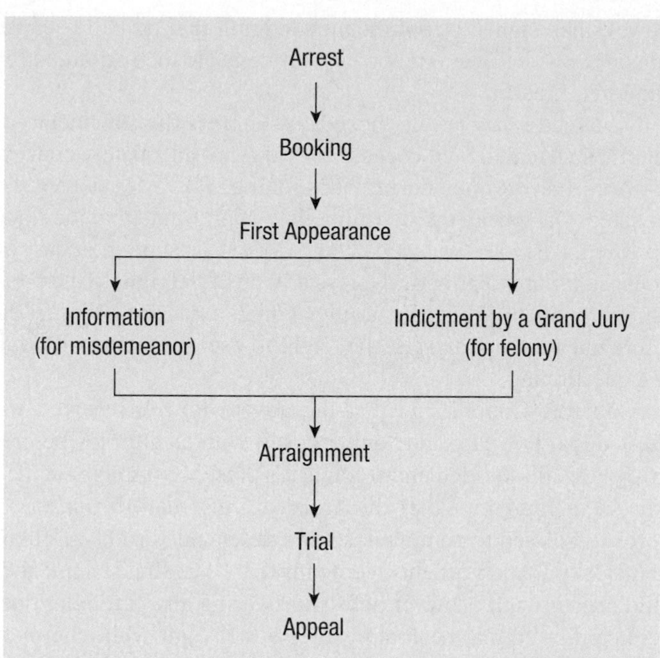

Exhibit 7-3
Steps in a Criminal Procedure

committed or is planning to commit a crime. A *magistrate,* the lowest-ranking judicial official, issues the arrest warrant. In certain circumstances, however, law enforcement agents can arrest a suspect without a warrant if they believe there is probable cause but not enough time to obtain the warrant.

To comply with the Supreme Court's requirements for protecting a citizen's rights, law enforcement officers must inform any individual they arrest of his or her **Miranda rights.** If the officers fail to do so, any information a defendant offers at the time of the arrest is not admissible at trial. The Miranda rights and warnings are these:

1. "You have the right to remain silent and refuse to answer any questions."
2. "Anything you say may be used against you in a court of law."
3. "You have the right to consult an attorney before speaking to the police and have an attorney present during any questioning now or in the future."
4. "If you cannot afford an attorney, one will be appointed for you before the questioning begins."
5. "If you do not have an attorney available, you have the right to remain silent until you have had an opportunity to consult with one."
6. "Now that I have advised you of your rights, are you willing to answer any questions without an attorney present?"

The Supreme Court, however, in 2010, showed that it is not rigid in terms of exactly how the defendant must be told of his rights.[14] In a case in February, Powell, the defendant, was taken down to police headquarters and told, "You have the right to remain silent. If you give up the right to remain silent, anything you say can be used against you in court. You have the right to talk to a lawyer before answering any of our questions. If you cannot afford to hire a lawyer, one will be appointed for you without cost and before any questioning. You have the right to use any of these rights at any time you want during this

[14] *Florida v. Powell,* 130 S. Ct. 1195.

interview."[15] Powell then signed a form acknowledging that he had been read his rights, understood them, and was willing to talk to the officers. He then admitted to being in possession of a prohibited firearm.

Once Powell obtained a lawyer, he moved to suppress the statement on grounds that the Miranda warnings were deficient because they did not adequately convey the suspect's right to the presence of an attorney during questioning. The court denied the motion, and Powell was convicted. On appeal, the state appellate court found that the statements should have been suppressed. The case was appealed to the state supreme court on the specific question of "Does the failure to provide express advice of the right to the presence of counsel during questioning vitiate Miranda warnings which advise of both (A) the right to talk to a lawyer 'before questioning' and (B) the 'right to use' the right to consult a lawyer 'at any time' during questioning?"[16]

The Florida Supreme Court found that the advice Powell received was misleading because it suggested that Powell could "only consult with an attorney before questioning" and did not convey Powell's entitlement to counsel's presence throughout the interrogation.

However, the U.S. Supreme Court disagreed, saying that *Miranda* does not require any specific words to be used to communicate the defendant's rights. Looking at what the police said, the majority found no rights were omitted: "The first statement communicated that Powell could consult with a lawyer before answering any particular question, and the second statement confirmed that he could exercise that right while the interrogation was underway. In combination, the two warnings reasonably conveyed [the suspect's] right to have an attorney present, not only at the outset of interrogation, but at all times."[17]

While Justice Stevens, in dissent, argued that the separate and distinct right "to have counsel present during any questioning" was not provided by the police, it is clear from the outcome of the case that in the future the court is not going to be looking for precise language in determining whether *Miranda* has been satisfied.

Case 7-3 presents the seminal case of *Miranda v. Arizona* in which these rights were spelled out. Notice the points of law from which the Miranda rights are derived.

[15] Ibid.

[16] Ibid.

[17] Ibid.

CASE 7-3 MIRANDA v. ARIZONA
UNITED STATES SUPREME COURT
384 U.S. 436 (1966)

On March 13, 1963, Ernesto Miranda was arrested for kidnapping and rape and taken to a Phoenix police station. After being identified by the complaining witness, he was questioned by two police officers, who emerged from the interrogation room two hours later with a written and signed confession. At the top of the statement was a typed paragraph stating the confession was made voluntarily, without threats or promises of immunity, and "with full knowledge of my legal rights, understanding any statement I make may be used against me."

At trial, the officers admitted Miranda had not been advised he had a right to have an attorney present, and the written confession was admitted into evidence over the objection of defense counsel. The officers testified to a prior oral confession made by Miranda during the interrogation. Miranda was found guilty and sentenced to 20 to 30 years' imprisonment. On appeal, the Supreme Court of Arizona held that Miranda's constitutional rights were not violated and affirmed the conviction. Miranda appealed to the Supreme Court, which joined his case with the cases of three other defendants making similar constitutional arguments regarding a violation of rights.

JUSTICE WARREN: The cases before us raise questions which go to the roots of our concepts of American criminal jurisprudence: the restraints society must observe consistent

[continued]

with the Federal Constitution in prosecuting individuals for crime. More specifically, we deal with the admissibility of statements obtained from an individual who is subjected to custodial police interrogation and the necessity for procedures which assure that the individual is accorded his privilege under the Fifth Amendment to the Constitution not to be compelled to incriminate himself.

This case is but an explication of basic rights enshrined in our Constitution—that "No person . . . shall be compelled in any criminal case to be a witness against himself," and that "the accused shall . . . have the Assistance of Counsel"—rights which were put in jeopardy in this case through official overbearing. These precious rights were fixed in our Constitution only after centuries of persecution and struggle. And in the words of Chief Justice Marshall, they were secured "for ages to come, and . . . designed to approach immortality as nearly as human institutions can approach it."

Our holding . . . briefly stated is this: the prosecution may not use statements, whether exculpatory or inculpatory, stemming from custodial interrogation of the defendant unless it demonstrates the use of procedural safeguards effective to secure the privilege against self-incrimination. By custodial interrogation, we mean questioning initiated by law enforcement officers after a person has been taken into custody or otherwise deprived of his freedom of action in any significant way. As for the procedural safeguards to be employed, unless other fully effective means are devised to inform accused persons of their right of silence and to assure a continuous opportunity to exercise it, the following measures are required.

Prior to any questioning, the person must be warned that he has a right to remain silent, that any statement he does make may be used as evidence against him, and that he has a right to the presence of an attorney, either retained or appointed. The defendant may waive effectuation of these rights, provided the waiver is made voluntarily, knowingly and intelligently. If, however, he indicates in any manner and at any stage of the process that he wishes to consult with an attorney before speaking there can be no questioning. Likewise, if the individual is alone and indicates in any manner that he does not wish to be interrogated, the police may not question him. The mere fact that he may have answered some questions or volunteered some statements on his own does not deprive him of the right to refrain from answering any further inquiries until he has consulted with an attorney and thereafter consents to be questioned.

From the testimony of the officers and by the admission of respondent, it is clear that Miranda was not in any way apprised of his right to consult with an attorney and to have one present during the interrogation, nor was his right not to be compelled to incriminate himself effectively protected in any other manner. Without these warnings the statements were inadmissible. The mere fact that he signed a statement which contained a typed-in clause stating that he had "full knowledge" of his "legal rights" does not approach the knowing and intelligent waiver required to relinquish constitutional rights.

Therefore, in accordance with the foregoing, the judgment of the Supreme Court of Arizona is reversed.

REVERSED.

CRITICAL THINKING

What is the reasoning structure in the Miranda case?

Does Justice Warren offer a logically powerful argument for giving defendants' rights greater protection than was customary at the time?

ETHICAL DECISION MAKING

In arguing for greater protection of the rights of the accused, what values is Justice Warren upholding?

With what values might Justice Warren's values be in contention?

The Miranda rights are not absolute. In fact, the Supreme Court has several times allowed for exceptions. In *New York v. Quarles,*[18] the Court created a "public safety" exception that allows statements to be used at trial, even if a person was not informed of his or her Miranda rights, if the need to protect the public is served by the admissibility of the statements in question. In *Arizona v. Fulminante,*[19] the Court held that a coerced confession can be ignored and treated as nonprejudicial at trial if the other evidence is sufficient to obtain a conviction.

[18] 467 U.S. 649 (1984).

[19] 499 U.S. 279 (1991).

In a third exception to the Miranda rights, *Davis v. United States*[20] held that defendants must "unequivocally and assertively" state their right to counsel in order to activate it. The phrase "Maybe I should talk to a lawyer" or a similar utterance made during an interrogation does not affirmatively signal that an accused desires to activate his or her right to counsel.

Despite being recognized for over 40 years, Miranda rights are still applied with limitations; a ruling by the U.S. Supreme Court is often necessary. For example, in the second term of 2004 alone, the high court made three rulings clarifying applications of the warnings. In *Missouri v. Seibert,*[21] the Court held that a confession made after receipt of the Miranda warnings was inadmissible if the police had asked for it before giving the warnings. In *United States v. Patane,*[22] the Court ruled that physical evidence discovered as a result of statements made without the Miranda warnings was admissible in court as long as the statements were not forced by police, even though the statements themselves were not admissible. In the third case, *Yarborough v. Alvarado,*[23] the Court clarified that a person was "in custody" and therefore entitled to receive Miranda warnings when a reasonable person of the defendant's age and educational background would not feel free to leave or terminate the questioning.

The current Supreme Court, a more conservative court, has been narrowing *Miranda* the last few years. The nearby Case Nugget highlights a controversial 5-4 decision interpreting *Miranda.*

After being arrested and read their Miranda rights, defendants are taken to the police station for **booking,** a procedure during which the name of the defendant and the alleged crime are recorded in the investigating agency's or police department's records. After the prosecutor files the complaint, the defendant makes the **first appearance** before a magistrate, who determines whether there was probable cause for the arrest. If not, the individual is freed.

If the defendant committed a minor offense and pleads guilty, the magistrate sentences the individual. However, if the defendant claims innocence, the magistrate ensures that the defendant has a lawyer or appoints one, if necessary for an indigent defendant, and sets bail. **Bail** is the amount of money defendants pay the court on release from custody as security that they will return for trial.

Next, the prosecutor has a choice: Should the case be prosecuted? The *Principles of Federal Prosecution,* established by the U.S. Department of Justice, suggest that at the federal level the decision to prosecute depends on two primary factors: (1) whether the evidence is sufficient to obtain a conviction, and (2) whether prosecuting the case serves a federal interest. If the prosecutor decides not to go forward with the case, the defendant may still be liable for his or her actions in civil court.

A prosecutor who chooses to proceed with a criminal action must demonstrate the likelihood that the defendant's actions and intent meet the elements of a crime by charging the defendant with a crime through an *information* or an *indictment.* For a misdemeanor, the prosecutor must present the magistrate with evidence sufficient to justify prosecution through an **information,** a formal written accusation stating the facts and specifying the violation of criminal law. However, for a felony, the prosecutor must present a grand jury with evidence adequate to justify bringing the defendant to trial. If the grand jury agrees

[20] 512 U.S. 452 (1994).

[21] 542 U.S. 600 (2004).

[22] 542 U.S. 630 (2004).

[23] 541 U.S. 652 (2004).

CASE NUGGET

IS SILENCE A WAIVER OF *MIRANDA* RIGHTS?

Berghuis v. Thompkins
United States Supreme Court 130 S. Ct. 2250 (2010)

The facts of the case are simple. Thompkins, a murder suspect, was read his rights, but refused to sign a statement saying he understood his rights. He remained silent for almost three hours as police continued to question. After two hours and 45 minutes of questioning, Mr. Thompkins said yes in response to each of three questions: "Do you believe in God?" "Do you pray to God?" and, "Do you pray to God to forgive you for shooting that boy down?" His yes to the third question was used to convict him of murder.

The appellate court ruled that the statement should have been excluded because prosecutors could not prove that Mr. Thompkins had knowingly and voluntarily waived his right to remain silent. But the high court disagreed, even though Justice Kennedy wrote that "some language in *Miranda* could be read to indicate that waivers are difficult to establish absent an explicit written waiver or a formal, express oral statement." The majority still held that absent an explicit invocation of the right to remain silent, police may continue to interrogate a suspect, and what he says may be used against him in court.

As the dissent pointed out, the original *Miranda* decision said that you cannot presume a defendant has waived his rights just because he remains silent; a lengthy interrogation that results in a confession usually means the confession is coerced. But Kennedy said that decisions since *Miranda* had undercut that decision's language and that a more sensible decision put the burden on the suspect to exercise his rights. "A suspect who has received and understood the Miranda warnings, and has not invoked his Miranda rights, waives the right to remain silent by making an uncoerced statement to the police."

that the evidence is adequate, it issues an **indictment,** a written accusation against the defendant. Note that the grand jury does not determine guilt. It is simply a group of citizens who consider evidence of criminal conduct presented by the prosecutor and then determine whether there is enough evidence to try the defendant for the crime.

In early December 2001, Enron Corp., once a multibillion-dollar energy trader, filed for bankruptcy. The U.S. Securities and Exchange Commission (SEC) then stated it would widen its investigation into Enron by considering whether Arthur Andersen, the accounting firm that was Enron's chief auditor, destroyed documents while the investigation was under way—in fact, until November 8, 2001, when the SEC issued Andersen a subpoena. On March 14, 2002, the U.S. Justice Department issued an indictment against the accounting firm, and a grand jury indicted Andersen for ordering its employees to intentionally destroy documents that included information about official proceedings and criminal investigations.

In federal cases, a defendant accused of a felony has a constitutional right to a grand jury indictment. However, a felony prosecution may proceed by information if the defendant waives that right. For instance, in a high-profile case in which the defense attorney is trying to work out a deal with the prosecution, the defendant may ask that the case proceed by information. Federal misdemeanor cases may proceed by indictment or information.

If the criminal trial takes place in state court, the defendant may or may not have access to a grand jury. The U.S. Supreme Court has held that a grand jury trial is not a fundamental right, and thus states are not required to offer grand juries. About half the states still require that felony prosecutions be initiated by grand jury indictments; most of the rest use information to commence prosecution.

The defendant appears in court to answer the indictment in an appearance called the **arraignment.** At this time, the defendant enters a plea of guilty or not guilty. A defendant may also plead **nolo contendere,** not admitting guilt but agreeing not to contest the charges. The advantage of a nolo contendere plea over a plea of guilty is that the former cannot be used against the defendant in a civil suit. If the defendant pleads not guilty, his case will be heard before a **petit jury,** a fact-finding jury.

At any time, the prosecutor and defendant can make a **plea bargain,** an agreement in which the prosecutor agrees to reduce charges, drop charges, or recommend a certain sentence if the defendant pleads guilty. Plea bargaining benefits both parties: The defendant gets a lesser sentence, and the prosecution saves time and resources by not trying the case. Businesspeople who commit crimes that affect business often engage in plea bargaining to avoid the publicity associated with a trial and the risk of a severe sentence.

TRIAL PROCEDURE

If the case goes to trial and the crime is a felony or a misdemeanor punishable by six months or more in prison, the defendant has a constitutional right to a jury trial. In most states, if the defendant waives the right to a jury trial, a judge will hear the case and act as fact finder in a **bench trial.**

In a criminal trial, the prosecutor has the burden of proof, and the defendant does not have to prove anything. The **burden of proof** has two elements. To meet the *burden of production of evidence,* the prosecution must produce any tangible evidence and testimony that prove the elements of the crime the defendant allegedly committed. To meet the *burden of persuasion,* the prosecutor must persuade the jury *beyond reasonable doubt* that the defendant committed the crime. The burden of proof, then, is higher in a criminal case than in a civil case, because in a civil case the burden of persuasion requires only that the claim be supported by a preponderance of the evidence.

As noted above, the defendant in a criminal trial need not testify, and her refusal to testify cannot be held against her. However, if she does choose to testify, then like all other witnesses, she must swear to tell the truth. In Italy, all witnesses except the defendant testify under oath.

After the jury hears the case, it deliberates and tries to reach a verdict. If the jury finds the defendant not guilty, he or she is acquitted and released. If the jury returns a guilty verdict, the judge will set a date for sentencing the criminal. A jury unable to reach a verdict is a "hung jury."

If a person has inside information and does not trade on it himself but passes it on to another who uses it to trade, the person who passed on the information is guilty of insider trading.

POSTTRIAL PROCEDURE

If the petit jury returns a verdict of not guilty, the government cannot appeal the acquittal. However, if the verdict is guilty, the defendant may appeal by claiming that a prejudicial error of law occurred at the original trial.

If there is no appeal, the defendant will be sentenced after the judge has received additional relevant information. Before 1991, sentencing was *indeterminate,* with judges allowed but not required to engage in free-form fact finding before selecting the appropriate punishment within broad statutory ranges. In 1991, however, there was a shift to *determinate sentencing,* under which federal sentences are determined largely by sentencing guidelines prescribing a specific range of possible penalties for each crime.

Judges are given certain factors to consider in sentencing, such as the defendant's criminal record. Guidelines have also been established for white-collar crimes, once again allowing judges to consider individual factors such as the company's history of past violations and cooperation with federal investigators. Many states have adopted similar state sentencing guidelines.

The role of the federal sentencing guidelines has been sharply curtailed by two significant Supreme Court cases. The first, *Blakely v. Washington,*[24] used a Sixth Amendment challenge to the procedure for imposing an aggravated penalty above the standard range set by the guidelines. In *Blakely,* the Court held that in cases relying on state laws for determinate sentencing, judges are bound by facts consistent with the verdict or admitted by the defendant. Blakely pleaded guilty to a lower offense than the one with which he was originally charged. The prosecutor recommended that Blakely be sentenced to the statutorily mandated maximum of 53 months, but the judge expanded his sentence to three years beyond that recommendation. The Court found that the extension violated Blakely's Sixth Amendment rights because he did not admit to the facts the judge took into consideration nor did a jury find them relevant to a verdict. Note that *Blakely* does not hold determinate sentencing to be unconstitutional but, rather, requires that it comply with Sixth Amendment protections.

The second case, *U.S. v. Booker,*[25] had far more radical effects, extending the *Blakely* holding to the federal sentencing guidelines. Moreover, *Booker* found that the two sections of federal law mandating determinate sentences were unconstitutional and struck them from the statute, effectively making the act advisory. With sentencing no longer mandatory, judicial fact finding is not "legally essential to punishment" and does not pose any Sixth Amendment problem.

Tools for Fighting Business Crime

LO6 How can we prevent white-collar crimes?

Three federal crime-fighting laws are RICO, the False Claims Act, and the Sarbanes-Oxley Act of 2002. RICO and the False Claims Act were originally created with different purposes in mind. Sarbanes-Oxley, however, was created specifically to combat white-collar crime.

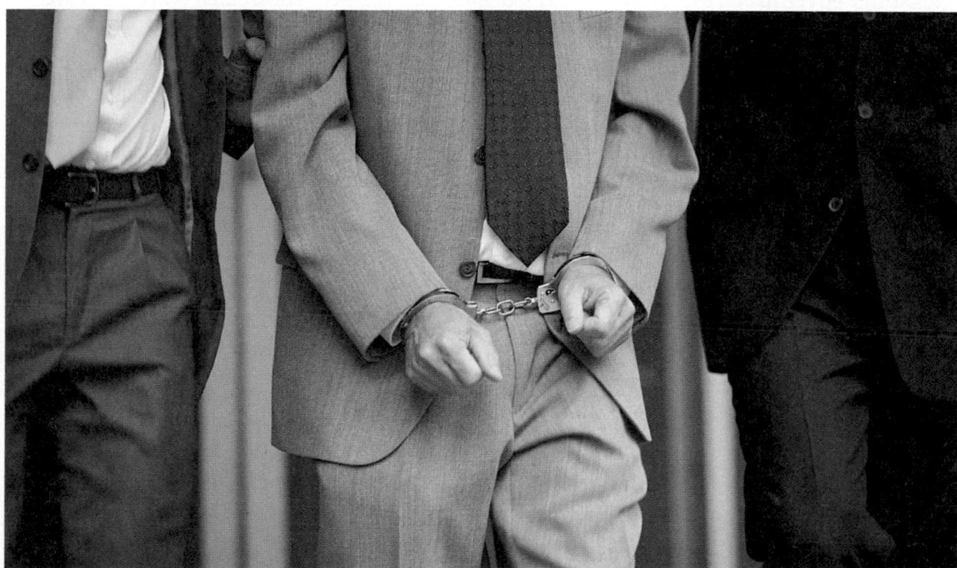

Some people argue that there might be a lot less white-collar crime if we saw more white-collar criminals in handcuffs.

[24] 124 S. Ct. 2531 (2004).

[25] 125 S. Ct. 738 (2005).

THE RACKETEER INFLUENCED AND CORRUPT ORGANIZATIONS ACT

One of the most important tools for fighting white-collar crime is in Title IX of the Organized Crime Control Act of 1970: the *Racketeer Influenced and Corrupt Organizations (RICO) Act,* originally enacted to combat organized crime. In effect it prevents legitimate businesses from serving as covers for racketeering. Anyone whose business or property has been damaged by racketeering activity can sue to recover treble damages and attorney fees in a civil action. This statute makes it a federal crime to (1) use income obtained from racketeering activity to purchase any interest in an enterprise, (2) acquire or maintain an interest in an enterprise through racketeering activity, (3) conduct or participate in the affairs of an enterprise through racketeering activity, or (4) conspire to do any of the three preceding activities.

Demonstrating a claim under RICO thus requires proof of a *pattern* of racketeering—that is, more than one action. Some courts have also found that a pattern requires continued criminal activity over a "substantial" period of time. *Racketeering* includes almost all criminal actions, such as acts of violence, fraud, bribery, securities fraud, and the provision of illegal goods and services, making RICO an extremely effective tool in combating white-collar crimes.

The enterprise that the statute refers to does not have to be a formal enterprise, such as a corporation or partnership, but may be an informal association. This association may be any collection of persons united for a common objective.

In addition to being held civilly liable under RICO, a violator may be subject to criminal penalties—a fine of up to $25,000 per violation, imprisonment for up to 20 years, or both.

THE FALSE CLAIMS ACT

Since 1986 private citizens have been using the *False Claims Act* to sue employers for fraud against the government. An employee in a health care facility who realizes his employer is submitting fraudulent claims to Medicare can bring a suit for fraud against the employer on behalf of the government. The employee must first notify the government of intent to file the case. If the government chooses to intervene and prosecute the case itself with the employee's help, the employee can receive 25 percent of the amount recovered. If the government opts not to act, an employee who pursues the case on behalf of the government receives 30 percent.

Certainly, an employee who brings a suit against an employer might be worried about retaliation, such as being fired or demoted. Thus, the act provides protection for employees who use it. An employer found guilty of retaliation may be forced to pay the employee twice the amount of lost back pay plus special damages.

The biggest settlement under the act as of 2010 was $1 billion with Pfizer in September 2009.[26] Previously, the record was the more than $900 million that Tenet Health Corporation settled for in 2006 regarding improper billing to Medicare and other federal health programs. The whistle-blowers stood to recover $135 million to $225 million for their efforts under the False Claims Act. The reward in this case was far above the norm. The estimated mean award in all *qui tam* cases (cases filed by private individuals on behalf of the government) that included government involvement and were settled between the act's inception and the close of fiscal year 2008 was around $3,460,000. Between the law's amendment in 1986 to encourage private whistle-blowers and the end of 2009, the government has recovered $2,399,854,364 under this act. As of September 30, 2009, the U.S. government had a total of 996 qui tam cases under investigation.[27]

[26] The False Claims Act Legal Center, "Top False Claims Act Cases," www.taf.org/top100fca.htm (accessed June 2, 2010).

[27] The False Claims Act Legal Center, www.taf.org/statistics.htm (accessed May 1, 2010).

Some critics of the False Claims Act argue that whistle-blowers are receiving money that should belong to taxpayers, while others say that the act prompts people not to report fraud right away but to wait until the value of the case grows. Still others complain that the act results in frivolous lawsuits as employees try to find an "easy" way to make money.

Defenders of the act say that it has uncovered significant cases of fraud that might have cost the government millions of dollars. They also point out how difficult it is for an employee reporting fraud to get a job in that field in the future, and thus a significant incentive must be offered for employees to act.

A number of False Claims Act cases have been filed against universities, including an interesting 2006 case against Chapman University. Three faculty members alleged that the institution had for years encouraged early dismissals, resulting in many students' not getting the minimum classroom training required in several subjects. If the college had admitted it engaged in this practice, it would never have been accredited or have received millions of dollars in federal grants and student aid, which the lawsuit claimed it took under false pretenses.[28] The U.S. District Court for the Central Division of California granted summary judgment for Chapman University in 2007. The court argued that the credit-hour requirements were guidelines for independent evaluators that, when applied to Chapman University, revealed no fraudulent misrepresentation by the university. Also, the court stated that the plaintiffs failed to offer evidence that the early dismissal policy was as widespread as they claimed it was.[29] The plaintiffs appealed to the Ninth Circuit, but ultimately the summary judgment was upheld.

THE SARBANES-OXLEY ACT

Congress passed the Sarbanes-Oxley Act in 2002 largely in response to the business scandals of the early 2000s that implicated firms such as Enron, WorldCom, Global Crossing, and Arthur Andersen. While much of the act consists of new rules and regulations for accounting firms, part of it specifically addresses white-collar crime.

Sarbanes-Oxley Section 201 makes it illegal for registered public accounting firms to provide these nonaudit services to an audit client:

1. Bookkeeping or other services related to the accounting records or financial statements of the audit client.
2. Financial information systems design and implementation.
3. Appraisal or valuation services, fairness opinions, or contribution-in-kind reports.
4. Actuarial services.
5. Internal audit outsourcing services.
6. Management functions or human resources.
7. Broker or dealer, investment adviser, or investment banking services.
8. Legal services and expert services unrelated to the audit.
9. Any other service the board determines, by regulation, is impermissible.

To see how the disallowance provisions of the IRS relate to the fight against white-collar crime, please see the **Connecting to the Core** activity on the text website at www.mhhe.com/kubasek3e.

Also under Sarbanes-Oxley, it is now a felony to willfully fail to maintain proper records of audits and work papers for at least five years, and the punishment is up to 10 years' imprisonment. The destruction of documents in a federal bankruptcy investigation is now a felony with possible sentences of up to 20 years' imprisonment. The punishment for securities fraud has been increased to 25 years' imprisonment.

[28] Martin Van Der Werf, "Lawsuit U.: The Growing Reach of the False Claims Act Has Lawyers Fearing Trouble Everywhere," *Chronicle of Higher Education,* August 4, 2006, http://chronicle.com/weekly/v52/i48/48a02301.htm.

[29] *U.S. v. Chapman University,* 2007 U.S. Dist. LEXIS 98166.

In addition, Sarbanes-Oxley extended the statute of limitations regarding the discovery of fraud to two years from the date of discovery of the fraud and five years from the criminal act. It has also taken affirmative steps toward further protecting whistle-blowers.

CASE OPENER WRAP-UP

Untenable Trading

At the time this book went to press, Martoma's case had not yet been decided. You may want to look up this case to see how it ultimately turned out, but before you do, ask yourself how you think the court decided. In an interesting twist, new charges have been filed in the case against Martoma, alleging that he had tried to make contact with other doctors who might have been able to provide inside information by e-mailing an expert networking firm a list of 20 doctors who were serving as investigators in the Alzheimer's drug trial and asking for consultations with them. All refused to talk with him, however. The doctor who originally gave Martoma the information ultimately cooperated with prosecuters and agreed to pay a $186,781 disgorgement,

If a person has inside information and does not trade on it himself but passes it on to another who uses it to trade, the person who passed on the information is still guilty of insider trading.

KEY TERMS

actus reus 150
affirmative defense 164
arraignment 173
arrest 168
arson 152
bail 172
bench trial 174
booking 172
bribery 153
burden of proof 174
burglary 151
computer crime 160
cyber terrorist 161
duress 165
embezzlement 159
entrapment 166
extortion 154
false pretenses 156
felony 151
first appearance 172
forgery 156
fraud 154
hacker 160
indictment 172
infant 164
information 172
insanity 165
insider trading 155
involuntary intoxication 165
justifiable use of force 166
larceny 151
liability without fault 150
mens rea 150
Miranda rights 169
misdemeanor 151
mistake of fact 164
necessity 166
nolo contendere 173
petit jury 173
petty offense 151
plea bargain 173
probable cause 168
robbery 151
strict liability 150
strict-liability offense 162
vicarious liability 164
virus 161
white-collar crime 152

SUMMARY OF KEY TOPICS

Elements of a Crime

Actus reus is wrongful behavior (guilty act).

Mens rea is a wrongful state of mind or intent (guilty mind).

Classification of Crimes

Felonies are serious crimes punishable by imprisonment for more than one year or death.

Misdemeanors are less serious crimes punishable by fines or imprisonment for less than one year.

Petty offenses are minor misdemeanors punishable by small fines or short jail sentences.

Common Crimes Affecting Business

Property crimes against business:

1. *Robbery:* The forceful and unlawful taking of personal property.
2. *Burglary:* The unlawful entry into a building with the intent to commit a felony.
3. *Larceny:* The secretive and wrongful taking and carrying away of the personal property of another with the intent to permanently deprive the rightful owner of its use or possession.
4. *Arson:* The intentional burning of another's dwelling.

White-collar crimes:

1. *Bribery:* The offering, giving, soliciting, or receiving of money or any object of value for the purpose of influencing the judgment or conduct of a person in a position of trust.
2. *Extortion:* The making of threats for the purpose of obtaining money or property.
3. *Fraud:* An individual's intentional use of misrepresentation to gain an advantage over another. Fraud generally requires the following three elements: (1) a material false representation made with intent to deceive *(scienter),* (2) a victim's reasonable reliance on the false representation, and (3) damages.
4. *Embezzlement:* The wrongful conversion of another's property by one lawfully in possession of it.
5. *Computer crime:* Any wrongful act that (1) is directed against computers, (2) uses computers to commit a crime, or (3) involves computers. Examples are the destruction of computer data and the unlawful appropriation of data or services.

Liability for Crimes

Both corporations, as legal entities, and the corporate officers and managers can be held liable for crimes committed on behalf of the corporation.

Defenses to Crimes

Infancy: The person is not of legal age and lacks the mental capabilities of an adult. It is a partial defense used to defuse the guilty-mind requirement.

Mistake: The defendant made an honest and reasonable mistake that negates the guilty-mind element of a crime.

Involuntary intoxication: The defendant was forced to ingest or involuntarily ingested an intoxicating agent that left him unable to understand that the act committed was wrong.

Insanity: The defendant's mental condition when the crime was committed was so impaired that she could not (1) understand the wrongful nature of the act or (2) distinguish between right and wrong in a general sense.

Duress: The crime was committed in response to a threat of immediate bodily harm.

Entrapment: The idea for the crime was put into the defendant's head by a law enforcement official.

Necessity: Committing the crime was necessary to prevent a more severe crime from occurring.

Justifiable use of force: The defendant used reasonable force in self-defense to protect his life. In many jurisdictions, this defense also applies to the defense of the defendant's dwelling or other property and to the prevention of a crime.

Constitutional Safeguards

Fourth Amendment:

1. Protection from unreasonable search and seizure.
2. Restrictions on warrants.

Fifth Amendment:

1. Prohibition of double jeopardy.
2. Right not to incriminate oneself.
3. Right to due process.

Sixth Amendment:

1. Right to a speedy and public trial.
2. Right to a trial by an impartial jury of one's peers.
3. Right to be informed of the accusations against oneself.
4. Right to confront witnesses.
5. Right to have witnesses on one's side.
6. Right to counsel at various stages of the proceedings.

Eighth Amendment:

1. Freedom from excessive bail.
2. Freedom from excessive fines.
3. Freedom from cruel and unusual punishment.

Fourteenth Amendment:

1. Extension of the right to due process to all state matters.
2. Extension of most constitutional rights to defendants at the state level.

Exclusionary rule:

Illegally obtained evidence is inadmissible in court.

Criminal Procedure

Pretrial procedure: The arrest, booking, first appearance, indictment, and arraignment.

Trial procedure: Jury selection, trial with burden of proof on prosecution, jury deliberations, jury verdict, and (if guilty) sentencing hearing.

Posttrial procedure: Appeal.

Tools for Fighting Business Crime

RICO: Prohibits persons employed by or associated with an enterprise from engaging in a pattern of racketeering activity. Anyone whose business or property has been damaged by this pattern of activity can sue under RICO to recover treble damages and attorney fees in a civil action.

False Claims Act: Allows employees to sue employers on behalf of the federal government for fraud against the government. The employee retains a share of the recovery as a reward for his or her efforts.

Sarbanes-Oxley Act: Criminalizes specific nonaudit services when provided by a registered accounting firm to an audit client; also increases the punishment for a number of white-collar offenses.

POINT / COUNTERPOINT

How Severely Should the Law Punish Individuals Convicted of White-Collar Crime?

As you are considering this issue, you might want to think about statistics that would help you resolve it.

LESS SEVERELY THAN VIOLENT CRIMINALS

Street crimes are different in kind than white-collar crimes. Whereas white-collar crime affects only individuals' property, street crime threatens individuals' lives and health. The law ought to recognize that protecting lives is more important than protecting property.

Moreover, white-collar crime tends to affect higher-income individuals, whereas street crime tends to affect lower-income individuals who lack the resources to protect themselves. Street crime disproportionately affects lower-income individuals who cannot afford the private security measures that higher-income individuals use to protect their persons and their property. The law ought to protect those who lack the power to protect themselves.

A third reason to punish white-collar crime less heavily than street crime is that white-collar criminals are more likely to engage in careful cost-benefit analysis when determining whether to commit white-collar crime. If the severity of the punishment, discounted by the chance they will get caught, is not less than the expected payoff from the white-collar crime, rational individuals will not see the crime as a profitable enterprise. It seems less likely that street criminals engage in the same kind of careful cost-benefit analysis before deciding, for example, whether to use illegal drugs. Thus, the most effective punishment for undeterrable street crime is likely to be severe punishment that incapacitates the criminals so that they are unable to commit more street crime. White-collar crime, on the other hand, can effectively be curbed by setting the punishment just high enough to make the crime unprofitable.

MORE SEVERELY THAN VIOLENT CRIMINALS

It is far from clear that white-collar crime has less serious consequences than street crime. For example, individuals who defraud the government in effect steal taxes paid by all members of society, whereas individuals in possession of small amounts of marijuana may never adversely affect other members of society.

Indeed, white-collar crime affects all groups in society in both direct and indirect ways. Companies victimized by white-collar crime often must raise the prices of their goods to recoup the costs of the crime. Everyone in society feels the effects of the higher prices. Street crime, while by no means negligible, tends to affect smaller circles of people. Thus, to get the biggest bang for our buck, we should punish white-collar crime more heavily than street crime.

Another reason to punish white-collar crime more heavily than street crime focuses on the underlying causes of crime. Much street crime has its roots in other social problems. Often, individuals commit street crime because of the poor environments in which they were raised. Much white-collar crime, however, is committed by well-off individuals out of avarice. The law ought to dole out more severe punishments for crimes caused by individual responsibility, and society ought to use other mechanisms to address crime caused by aleatory factors.

QUESTIONS & PROBLEMS

1. How does criminal law differ from civil law, both in terms of their purposes and in terms of the procedures used in each type of case.
2. Explain how crimes are classified.
3. List and define the primary affirmative defenses used in criminal cases.
4. Explain the federal laws that are currently being used to fight white-collar crime.
5. Robert Morris, a PhD student in computer science at Cornell University, designed a computer program known as a "worm" and released it onto the Internet. The worm spread and multiplied and

eventually caused computers at various educational and military institutions to crash. Morris argued that he released the worm to demonstrate to fellow graduate students the lack of security protecting computer networks. With what crime was he most likely charged? Was this prosecution successful? [*United States v. Robert Tappen Morris,* 928 F.2d 504 (1991).]

6. The Pasquantinos, while in New York, ordered liquor over the telephone from discount package stores in Maryland. They employed Hilts and others to drive the liquor over the Canadian border, without paying the required excise taxes. The drivers avoided paying taxes by hiding the liquor in their vehicles and failing to declare the goods to Canadian customs officials. During the time of the Pasquantinos' smuggling operation, between 1996 and 2000, Canada heavily taxed the importation of alcoholic beverages. The Pasquantinos and Hilts were indicted for charges of federal wire fraud. They contest no wire fraud existed because the federal government cannot enforce the revenue laws of Canada and this therefore prevents the existence in the United States of a fraud charge. How did the Supreme Court rule? Should the Pasquantinos and Hilts be able to succeed in their legal argument? [*Pasquantino v. United States,* 125 S. Ct. 1766 (2005).]

7. Each year the Cook County, Illinois, Treasurer's Office holds a public auction at which it sells tax liens it has acquired on the property of delinquent taxpayers. Prospective buyers bid on the liens. The winning bidder obtains the right to purchase the lien in exchange for paying the outstanding taxes on the property. Cook County awards the liens on a rotating basis when there are tie bids, spreading the property among the bidders. To prevent people from using multiple bidders to increase their odds, the county adopted the "Single, Simultaneous Bidder Rule," which requires each "tax buying entity" to submit bids in its own name and prohibits it from using "apparent agents, employees, or related entities" to submit simultaneous bids for the same parcel. Upon registering for an auction, each bidder must submit a sworn affidavit affirming that it complies with the Single, Simultaneous Bidder Rule.

A group of regular participants in Cook County's tax sales filed a complaint contending that Sabre Group, LLC, had fraudulently obtained a disproportionate share of liens by violating the Single, Simultaneous Bidder Rule at the auctions held from 2002 to 2005. As a result, when the county allocated liens on a rotating basis, it treated the firms related to Sabre Group as independent entities, allowing them collectively to acquire a greater number of liens than would have been granted to a single bidder acting alone. The related firms then purchased the liens and transferred the certificates of purchase to Sabre Group. The group of regular bidders sued, alleging that Sabre Group violated and conspired to violate RICO by conducting its affairs through a pattern of racketeering activity involving numerous acts of mail fraud. The bidders assert that Sabre Group sent mail to the property owners, which thus furthered its scheme. The district court dismissed the RICO claim, arguing that while the bidders were financially harmed, they did not rely on the alleged fraudulent mail and thus could not sue under RICO. The court of appeals reversed because the fraudulent mail harmed the bidders, even if they did not directly rely on this mail. Sabre Group appealed to the Supreme Court. Did Sabre Group's actions violate RICO, and could the bidders sue? What would the bidders need to prove to succeed with their claims? [*Bridge v. Phoenix Bond & Indemnity Co.,* 128 S. Ct. 2131 (2008).]

8. Toby Scammel's girlfriend was briefly involved in Disney's acquisition of Marvel in 2009. Scammel bought 659 Marvel options for $5,465 in the days prior to the announcement of the acquisition. Within the nine days following the announcement, Scammel sold all his Marvel shares, amounting to a total of $192,496.61. While Scammel's girlfriend had mentioned general facts about a "big project" she was working on, the couple claimed that she never gave him details about the acquisition. However, he had access to her electronic documents related to the acquisition and had begun piecing together the companies involved and the timing of the acquisition. Although Marvel's shares had never closed for over $42, Scammel was purchasing the shares at $50. Scammel claimed that his girlfriend had told him nothing and he had done nothing wrong; he had frequently been involved in the stock market and was simply normally trading shares as he had done before. What crime do you believe Scammel's actions led to his being charged with? Do you think there was enough evidence to warrant his conviction for that crime? [*S.E.C. v. Scammel,* 2011 WL 3506153 (C.A.C.D., Aug. 11, 2011).]

9. Throughout the 1990s, Morteza Eghbal and Marilyn Trujillo purchased Housing and Urban Development (HUD) foreclosed homes and resold them for profit to buyers with mortgage-secured loans insured by HUD. Eghbal and Trujillo sold to buyers who lacked sufficient assets to cover the down payment on the properties, and they provided the down payment for the buyers. HUD would not insure a loan for a home for which the down payment was paid by the seller. To that end, HUD required that a seller of a home sign a document called "Addendum to the HUD-1 Settlement Statement." By signing the addendum, the seller certified that he had not, and would not, pay the buyer for any part of the down payment and that he did not have knowledge of any loans made to the buyer for purposes of financing the transaction other than those described in the sales contract. HUD would not insure a loan without a validly signed addendum. For each instance in which they provided the down payment, Eghbal and Trujillo fraudulently signed the addendum, falsely stating that they provided no funds toward the down payment. HUD ultimately paid out about $2.8 million for the balances owing on 27 defaulted mortgages for properties Eghbal and Trujillo sold.

The government sued Eghbal and Trujillo under the False Claims Act (FCA). The government argued that without the false statements on the addendum, HUD would not have insured the mortgage loans. Eghbal and Trujillo contend that the government failed to show that their false statements set in motion a false claim. Eghbal and Trujillo sought only to fraudulently induce HUD to insure the mortgage, not to have the buyers default or cause the mortgage holders to make claims on HUD. Eghbal and Trujillo were not parties to the actual claims presented to HUD, made after the buyers defaulted, that resulted in monetary payments by the government. The district court granted summary judgment in favor of the government, and Eghbal and Trujillo appealed. Did the addendums constitute a false claim helping to defraud the government? Why? [*U.S. v. Eghbal,* 548 F.3d 1281 (9th Cir. 2008).]

10. At Boyle's trial, the state demonstrated that Boyle and others had committed a series of bank robberies in four states during the 1990s. There was a core group involved in all the robberies, but sometimes others would also assist them. The group would meet together before each crime to plan the robbery, assign everyone's tasks, and assemble the tools. After each heist, they would divide the proceeds. There was no clear leader, and no overall master plan for a series of robberies.

At the trial the judge told jurors that to establish the existence of an enterprise, the government had to prove that "(1) there [was] an ongoing organization with some sort of framework, formal or informal, for carrying out its objectives; and (2) the various members and associates of the association function[ed] as a continuing unit to achieve a common purpose." The judge also told the jury that it could "find an enterprise where an association of individuals, without structural hierarchy, [was] form[ed] solely for the purpose of carrying out a pattern of racketeering acts" and that "[c]ommon sense suggests that the existence of an association-in-fact is oftentimes more readily proven by what it does, rather than by abstract analysis of its structure."

The judge did not give the jury Boyle's requested instruction that the government was required to prove that the enterprise "had an ongoing organization, a core membership that functioned as a continuing unit, and an ascertainable structural hierarchy distinct from the charged predicate acts."

After Boyle was convicted of 11 of 12 counts against him, including the RICO counts, and was sentenced to prison, he appealed on grounds that the instructions as to what would constitute proof of an enterprise incorrectly set forth the law. The circuit court affirmed his convictions, and he appealed to the U.S. Supreme Court. How do you think the high court ruled and why? [*Boyle v. United States,* 129 S. Ct. 2237 (2009).]

Looking for more review materials?

The Online Learning Center at **www.mhhe.com/kubasek3e** contains this chapter's "Assignment on the Internet" and also a list of URLs for more information, entitled "On the Internet." Find both of them in the Student Center portion of the OLC, along with quizzes and other helpful materials.

CHAPTER

8 Tort Law

LEARNING OBJECTIVES

After reading this chapter, you will be able to answer the following questions:

1. How do we classify torts?
2. What are some of the most common intentional torts, and what are the elements needed to prove these torts?
3. What types of damages are available in tort cases?

CASE OPENER

Plastic Surgeon Defamation

Dr. Walter Sullivan was one of several plastic surgeons in Las Vegas visited by Julie Jones. Jones, an exotic dancer, sought plastic surgery to improve her ability to make money in her profession. After visiting Sullivan for a consultation, she then visited Dr. Joseph Bongiovi, Jr. During her consultation with Bongiovi, Jones mentioned her earlier visit with Sullivan. Bongiovi then told her that Sullivan had a patient die the previous week during the same procedure Jones sought. Bongiovi told her the death was the direct result of Sullivan's negligence.

Despite Bongiovi's allegations, Jones saw Sullivan again and scheduled the surgery with him. Jones did, however, attend a prescheduled appointment with Bongiovi. During the appointment, at Jones's prompting, Bongiovi confirmed what he had said before—that Sullivan had recently been responsible for a patient's death during the same procedure Jones sought.

On the basis of the confirmation from Bongiovi, Jones called to cancel her surgical appointment with Sullivan. When Sullivan's office manager asked why she was canceling the appointment, Jones said she had been told that Sullivan was under investigation for a patient's death. When Sullivan learned of the cancellation, he called Jones to find out who had made the statements; he was unsuccessful in obtaining a name. After speaking with Sullivan, Jones again called Bongiovi's office to receive confirmation about the allegation. Bongiovi's assistant confirmed that the statements were true.

When Sullivan eventually learned the identity of Bongiovi, he filed suit for defamation. According to Sullivan, Bongiovi's statements were slanderous per se. At the conclusion of a trial, a jury found in favor of Sullivan and awarded him $250,000 in compensatory damages and $250,000 in punitive damages. Bongiovi appealed, arguing that the jury should have been instructed that actual malice was the standard because Sullivan was a public figure. Furthermore, Bongiovi argued that the compensatory and punitive damages awarded were exorbitant.

1. What defenses, if any, could Bongiovi have presented to prevent the damage awards?
2. Under which ethical system, if any, should Bongiovi be required to pay damages to Sullivan? Why?

The Wrap-Up at the end of the chapter will answer these questions using the legal principles discussed in this chapter.

As a business manager, you may encounter one party who believes he or she has been injured by the actions of another, as Dr. Sullivan believed he had been injured by Dr. Bongiovi. A **tort** (from a French word meaning "wrong") is a wrong or injury to another, other than a breach of contract. This chapter first examines the goals of tort law and the three primary classifications of torts. It next explains a variety of intentional torts and concludes by discussing damages available in tort cases.

Introduction to Tort Law

The preceding chapter showed that the state always brings suit in a criminal case, but crime victims may be able to bring a tort action against the criminal because the same actions that constitute a criminal offense often constitute a tort.

While the primary objectives of criminal law are to punish wrongdoers and preserve order in society, tort law's primary objective is to provide compensation for injured parties. Tort law also contributes to maintaining order because it discourages private retaliation by injured persons and their friends. After all, we do not want a community where vigilantes roam about righting some harm they believe they have suffered.

A third objective of tort law is to satisfy our collective sense of right and wrong by providing that someone who creates harm should make things right by compensating those harmed. The recognition that offenders will have to pay for personal injuries they cause may also deter the commission of torts. Exhibit 8-1 summarizes the purposes of tort law and the types of torts.

Although this chapter discusses torts as if they were the same everywhere, tort law is primarily state law, so states may have slightly different definitions of each tort. This chapter uses definitions common in most states, noting significant differences where they exist.

Despite the public impression of a litigation explosion, tort litigation has been declining gradually since 1990.[1] The National Center for State Courts' statistics on tort filings in 15 states showed a general downward trend each year from 1995 to 2004. In 2003, the last year for which detailed data are available, there were 198,377 cases.[2] However, potential tort liability should still concern a competent business manager.

[1] National Center for State Courts, www.ncsconline.org/D_Research/csp/2002_Files/2002_Tables_10-16.pdf (accessed September 9, 2005). Unfortunately, this oft-cited data is the most current data available.

[2] *Examining the Work of State Courts, 2005: A National Perspective from the Court Statistics Project,* 2006, p. 27. (The Court Statistics Project is a joint project of the National Center for State Courts, the State Justice Institute, and the Bureau of Justice Statistics of the Department of Justice.)

Exhibit 8-1
Tort Law

Definition: The body of law that concerns torts. A tort is a civil wrong that gives the injured party the right to bring a lawsuit against the wrongdoer to recover compensation for injuries.

Purposes of Tort Law:

1. To compensate innocent persons who are injured
2. To prevent private retaliation by injured parties
3. To reinforce a vision of a just society
4. To deter future wrongs

Types of Torts:

1. *Intentional tort:* Occurs when the defendant acts with the intention of engaging in a specific act that ultimately results in an injury.
2. *Negligent tort:* Occurs when the defendant fails to act in a responsible way and thereby subjects other people to an unreasonable risk of harm.
3. *Strict-liability tort:* Occurs when the defendant takes an action that is inherently dangerous and cannot be undertaken safely.

Classification of Torts

LO1
How do we classify torts?

In the United States torts are classified as intentional, negligent, or strict liability. The categories differ in terms of the elements needed to prove the tort, available damages, available defenses, and degree of willfulness of the actor. **Intentional torts** occur when the defendant takes an action intending certain consequences or knowing they are likely to result. **Negligent torts** occur when the defendant acts in a way that subjects other people to an unreasonable risk of harm. In other words, the defendant is careless to someone else's detriment. Finally, **strict-liability torts** occur when the defendant takes an action that is inherently dangerous and cannot ever be undertaken safely, no matter what precautions the defendant takes. Not all countries share the same definitions, however. The Chinese legal system, for example, more narrowly defines the activities actionable under tort law.

This chapter focuses on intentional torts. Negligence and strict liability are discussed in Chapter 9.

As you think about the opening scenario, which category of tort do you think Bongiovi's actions would fall under?

BUT WHAT IF . . .

WHAT IF THE FACTS OF THE CASE OPENER WERE DIFFERENT?

Recall, in the Case Opener, that Bongiovi knew Jones was contemplating going to Sullivan for treatment, and because he wanted her business, he told her negative stories about Sullivan. What if Bongiovi had no idea Jones had ever heard of Sullivan and was telling her the story just as a reminder that no surgery is completely risk-free?

Intentional Torts

LO2
What are some of the most common intentional torts, and what are the elements needed to prove these torts?

Intentional torts, the most "willful" of torts, share the common element of intent. This intent is not to harm but, rather, to engage in a specific act, which ultimately results in an injury, physical or economic, to another. In fact, motive is not required to prove liability in an intentional tort case. Moreover, tort law assumes people intend the normal consequences of their actions. For example, if Rob threw a rock toward a group of people, we assume under the law that he intended to hit someone with the rock and that the person hit would be hurt, regardless of Rob's intention merely to scare the group.

Not all harms intentionally committed will fall neatly into an existing category of torts. Therefore, a general theory of intentional tort liability has been created to aid judges in their decision making. Section 870 of the Restatement (Second) of Torts explains the general theory:

> One who intentionally causes injury to another is subject to liability to the other for that injury, if his conduct is generally culpable and not justifiable under the circumstances. This liability may be imposed although the actor's conduct does not come within a traditional category of tort liability.

Intentional torts are divided into (1) torts against persons, (2) torts against property, and (3) torts against economic interests.

INTENTIONAL TORTS AGAINST PERSONS

Torts against persons are intentional acts that harm an individual's physical or mental integrity. As you might imagine, there are a significant number. Those a businessperson is most likely to either commit or be a victim of are assault and battery, defamation, privacy torts, false imprisonment, intentional infliction of emotional distress, and misuse of legal procedure.

Assault and Battery. Imagine that, after searching for a parking space for 20 minutes, you finally pull into a spot. However, as soon as you turn off your engine, a large man pounds on your car window, yelling angrily, "You just took my spot! If you don't move your car now, I'm going to hit you so hard you won't remember what your car looks like!" The man has just assaulted you.

An assault occurs when one person places another in fear or apprehension of an immediate, offensive bodily contact. If you think the man pounding your window is just joking and you start laughing, no assault has taken place because the element of apprehension is missing. However, apprehension and fear are not the same thing when it comes to assault. A person may be in apprehension of physical harm but be too courageous to be afraid. An assault occurs if apprehension exists, regardless of fear.

Someone who is overly fearful is not assaulted every time he or she experiences apprehension. The test for assault is *reasonable* apprehension. If a reasonable person would experience apprehension in a given situation, and the person in that situation does experience apprehension (not necessarily fear), an assault occurs.

Likewise, if someone called you on the telephone and threatened to come over and break your nose, this is not an assault because there is no question of *immediate* bodily harm. Immediacy is also the reason that words, however violent, are not typically considered enough to establish an assault. Words without a sign of action do not usually imply immediacy. Moreover, words, in most situations, are not enough to create reasonable apprehension of harm. Without immediacy or reasonable apprehension, they do not constitute an assault.

Regardless, if words *are* enough to establish a reasonable apprehension of immediate harm, they constitute an assault, typically when combined with what might otherwise be an innocent movement. Pat has had a few too many beers and starts an argument with Sam. Sam tries to calm Pat down, at which point Pat screams "I'm going to cut you" and starts to reach toward his pocket, causing Sam to become apprehensive. Together, Pat's words and actions constitute an assault, as reasonable apprehension of immediate physical bodily harm has been established by a threat and what can be construed as a motion toward grabbing a knife.

An assault is often, but not always, followed by a **battery,** an intentional, unwanted, offensive bodily contact. Almost any unwanted intentional contact constitutes a battery, even if harmless, and intent is irrelevant for establishing liability. If the touch was intended as a joke but a reasonable person would be offended, the contact is deemed "offensive."[3] If the man in the parking lot actually hit you, his action constitutes a battery. But if you both happened to be getting out of your cars at the same time and bumped into each other, no battery has occurred because there was no *intentional* bodily contact.

Legal Principle: **An assault occurs when a person is placed in fear or apprehension of an offensive bodily contact; if the contact actually occurs, it constitutes a battery.**

BUT WHAT IF . . .

WHAT IF THE FACTS OF THE CASE OPENER WERE DIFFERENT?

Recall, in the Case Opener, that Sullivan sued Bongiovi because of the false statement Bongiovi made. What if, instead of calling a lawyer, Sullivan had called Bongiovi and said, "If you ever tell a potential client a lie like that about me again, I will slit your throat"? Would Sullivan have committed an assault or battery? Why or why not?

A limited number of defenses are available to an action for a battery (see Exhibit 8-2). *Consent* mitigates the element of unwanted. A person cannot commit a battery if the other party consented to the contact.

The most common defense is *self-defense,* responding to the force of another with comparable force to defend yourself. If the man in the parking lot took a swing at you and, to try to keep him from hitting you, you shoved him, causing him to fall backward and hit his head on the street, you could escape liability for battery by arguing you were acting in self-defense. You cannot respond with greater force than is being used against you. You may use deadly force only against another's deadly force.

A third defense, *defense of others,* is just what it sounds like. If the parking lot man is pummeling you, your brother could use his fists and try to hit the man in an attempt to make him stop hitting you. The degree of force your brother can use in defending you is limited to the degree of force you could use yourself.

A final defense to a claim of battery is *defense of property.* You can use *reasonable force* to defend your property from an intruder. The use of deadly force in defense of property is rarely, if ever, considered justified.

Defamation. The tort alleged in this chapter's opening case was **defamation,** the intentional publication (or communication to a third party) of a false statement harmful to an individual's reputation.[4] In addition to the person who publishes a false statement, anyone who republishes, or in any manner repeats, a defamatory statement is also liable for defamation, even if he or she cites the original source of the defamation.

If the defamation is published in a permanent form, such as in a magazine or newspaper, it is known as *libel.*[5] Television and radio broadcasts are also considered libel, since

[3] Restatement (Second) of Torts, sec. 19.

[4] Restatement (Second) of Torts, sec. 558.

[5] Restatement (Second) of Torts, sec. 568.

COMPARING THE LAW OF OTHER COUNTRIES

DEFAMATION IN CHINA

Chinese law treats defamation similarly to U.S. law. First, the Chinese courts determine whether there is a defamatory statement. Second, the statement must be published in writing, made orally, or communicated by gestures or signs. Third, the statement must clearly identify a particular person. However, in China, defamation can be either a civil or a criminal action.

Exhibit 8-2
Defenses to Battery

Consent	Battery did not occur because the other party agreed to the contact.
Self-defense	You responded to the unwanted contact with comparable force to defend yourself.
Defense of others	You tried to defend another from the unwanted contact with a force comparable to what you could use to defend yourself.
Defense of property	You used reasonable force to defend your property from an intruder.

they are permanently recorded. In the case of libel, "general damages" are presumed. Thus, the victim is entitled to compensation for damages that are presumed to flow from defamation but are hard to prove, such as humiliation.

If the defamation is made orally, it is *slander.*[6] Because slander lacks permanence, to recover damages the plaintiff must prove "special damages," or specific monetary loss. If the people who heard the slander do not act in a way to cause harm to the slandered person, there is no cause for compensation, which is one of the main goals of tort law.

In most states, an exception to the requirement of special damages occurs if the defamation constitutes *slander per se,* statements so inherently harmful that general damages are presumed. While the exact wording of the categories of slander per se varies slightly among the states, slander per se generally includes claims that the plaintiff (1) has a loathsome, communicable disease (traditionally venereal disease or leprosy); (2) has committed a crime for which imprisonment is a possibility; (3) is professionally incompetent; or (4) if a woman, is unchaste (although in most states today where this category is still recognized, it usually applies only to underage girls).

BUT WHAT IF . . .

WHAT IF THE FACTS OF THE CASE OPENER WERE DIFFERENT?

Recall, in the Case Opener, that Jones chose not to go to Sullivan for treatment because of the story that Bongiovi told her. What if Jones had never considered going to Sullivan and had already scheduled an appointment with Bongiovi, so the story did not affect Sullivan? Would slander have occurred? If slander had occurred, could Sullivan receive damages?

Case 8-1 illustrates how a plaintiff attempted to use defamation per se. As you read the decision, think of how it might be applicable to the case described in the opening scenario.

[6] Restatement (Second) of Torts, sec. 568A.

CASE 8-1 STEVEN J. HATFILL v. THE NEW YORK TIMES COMPANY AND NICHOLAS KRISTOF
FOURTH CIRCUIT COURT OF APPEALS
416 F.3D 320 (4TH CIR. 2005)

In the fall of 2001, shortly after the terrorist attacks on the World Trade Center and the Pentagon, someone mailed letters laced with anthrax to several news organizations and members of Congress. Nicholas Kristof wrote a regular column for the editorial page of The New York Times. *During the spring and the summer of 2002, Kristof wrote several columns criticizing the FBI's investigation of the anthrax mailings. From May through July 2002, Kristof focused his attention on the FBI's handling of information pertaining to a man he called "Mr. Z." In August of 2002, Kristof identified Mr. Z as Dr. Steven J. Hatfill, a research scientist employed by the Department of Defense. Kristof wrote:*

> *[T]rained bloodhounds were given scent packets preserved from the anthrax letters and were introduced to a variety of people and locations. This month, they responded strongly to Dr. Hatfill, to his apartment, to his girlfriend's apartment and even to his former girlfriend's apartment, as well as to restaurants that he had recently entered. . . .*

On July 13, 2004, Hatfill filed suit asserting a claim for defamation. Hatfill alleged, among other things, that "[d]efendants' false and reckless public identification of Dr. Hatfill with the anthrax mailings, both directly and by implication from the manner in which his personal and professional background were presented in the 'Mr. Z' columns, constituted a false factual allegation of terrorist and homicidal activity and impugned Dr. Hatfill's good name as a citizen, a physician and a biomedical researcher to a reasonable reader." The district court dismissed Hatfill's suit on grounds that it failed as a matter of law because Kristof's columns, when read in their entirety and in context, could not reasonably be read as accusing Hatfill of being responsible for the anthrax attacks. Hatfill appealed.

JUDGE SHEDD: Count One alleges that The Times' publication of Kristof's columns defamed Hatfill by implying that Hatfill was involved in the anthrax mailings. Under Virginia law, a plaintiff seeking to recover for defamation *per se* must allege a publication of false information concerning the plaintiff that tends to defame the plaintiff's reputation. *See Chapin v. Knight-Ridder, Inc.*, 993 F.2d 1087, 1092 (4th Cir. 1993). . . .

Under Virginia law, the following kinds of statements are actionable as defamation *per se:* (1) statements that "impute to a person the commission of some criminal offense involving moral turpitude, for which the party, if the charge is true, may be indicted and punished," (2) statements that "impute that a person is infected with some contagious disease, where if the charge is true, it would exclude the party from society," (3) statements that "impute to a person unfitness to perform the duties of an office or employment of profit, or want of integrity in the discharge of duties of such an office or employment," and (4) statements that "prejudice such person in his or her profession or trade." *Carwile v. Richmond Newspapers, Inc.,* 196 Va. 1 82 S.E.2d 588, 591 (Va. 1954).

It is not always clear whether particular words actually charge a person with a crime of moral turpitude or unfitness for employment or the like, but the general rule of interpretation is that "allegedly defamatory words are to be taken in their plain and natural meaning and to be understood by courts and juries as other people would understand them, and according to the sense in which they appear to have been used." *Id.* At 591-92. A defamatory charge may be made expressly or by "inference, implication or insinuation." *Id.* At 592. . . .

Hatfill contends that Krisof's columns defamed him by imputing to him the commission of crimes of moral turpitude, namely, the murders of five people who were exposed to the anthrax letters. If the columns fairly can be read to make such a charge, then they are defamatory *per se*. . . .

Hatfill's complaint adequately alleges that Kristof's columns, taken together, are capable of defamatory meaning. The columns did not describe any other actual or potential target of investigation, and they recounted detailed information pertaining to Hatfill alone. Once Kristof named Hatfill as Mr. Z (and perhaps even before that time), a reasonable reader of his columns could believe that Hatfill had the motive, means, and opportunity to prepare and send the anthrax letters in the fall of 2001; that he had particular expertise with powder forms of anthrax, the type used in the mailings; that his own anthrax vaccinations were current; that he was the prime suspect of the biodefense community as well as federal investigators; that he had failed numerous polygraph examinations; that specially trained bloodhounds had "responded strongly" to Hatfill, his apartment, and his girlfriend's apartment but not to anyone else or any other

[continued]

location; and that Hatfill was probably involved in similar anthrax episodes in recent years. Based on these assertions, a reasonable reader of Kristof's columns likely would conclude that Hatfill was responsible for the anthrax mailings in 2001.

. . . Because Krisof's columns, taken together, are capable of defamatory meaning under Virginia law, the district court erred in dismissing Count One.

REVERSED and REMANDED.

CRITICAL THINKING

Why did the court conclude that Kristof's columns were capable of defamatory meaning? Do you agree with the reasons that led to the ruling? Why or why not?

What fundamental issue does this case address? Does the court's decision seem to prefer one value over another? If so, do you see this preference as justified? Why or why not?

ETHICAL DECISION MAKING

Which set of stakeholders would you weigh the heaviest in deciding a case of this type? Why would you raise their interests above those of other relevant parties?

If you say your boss is a tyrant or your roommate is a slob, are you in danger of being sued for defamation? Probably not, because such statements are really subjective opinions not capable of being proved. As such they are generally not actionable.

One of the important elements of defamation is that the defamatory statement must be damaging to someone's reputation, as the nearby Case Nugget illustrates.

The increase in communication over the Internet has presented new questions for the law of defamation to answer. First, does a false statement made over the Internet constitute defamation? Second, if it does, who can be held liable?

The court first attempted to answer these issues in the case of *Cubby v. CompuServ,*[7] in which CompuServ was sued because of defamatory statements published on one of the forums available through its online information service. In holding CompuServ not liable, the court made an analogy between an online information service provider and a bookstore, saying, "CompuServ's CIS product is in essence an electronic, for-profit library." The court went on to say that once CompuServ decides to carry a given publication such as a news forum, it has little or no editorial control over that forum. It would therefore be no more feasible for CompuServ to examine every publication it carries for defamatory material than it would be for libraries or booksellers to do so.

Since *Cubby* was decided, the Communications Decency Act of 1996[8] was passed. One section gives immunity to providers of interactive computer services for liability they might otherwise incur on account of material disseminated by them but created by others. This immunity is illustrated in the E-Commerce box later in this chapter.

Another situation that addresses the issues surrounding communication over the Internet is that of Whole Foods chairman and CEO John Mackey and his anonymous postings on Yahoo Finance. For almost eight years, Mackey made postings on Yahoo Finance message boards under the pseudonym "Rahodeb" (an anagram of his wife Deborah's name). In his postings, Mackey often talked about how great Whole Foods, its stock, and even the company's CEO (himself) were. However, on the message boards Mackey also made several negative comments about Whole Foods' rival, Wild Oats. Mackey criticized Wild Oats' management and even went so far as to mention that he couldn't understand why any company would want to acquire the Wild Oats business "at its then-current stock

[7] 77b F. Supp. 135 (1991).
[8] 47 U.S.C. § 230.

CASE NUGGET

CAN YOU DEFAME A PERSON WHO HAS NO GOOD REPUTATION TO BE HARMED?

Thomas P. Lamb v. Tony Rizzo
U.S. Court of Appeals for the Tenth Circuit
391 F.3d 1133 (2004)

The state of Kansas incarcerated Thomas P. Lamb over 30 years ago. He is serving three consecutive life sentences for two counts of first-degree kidnapping and one count of first-degree murder. In July 2001, newspaper reporter Tony Rizzo wrote two articles about Lamb's convictions and upcoming parole hearing. When Lamb's request for parole was subsequently denied, he sued Rizzo in Kansas state court, asserting, among other things, that Rizzo's articles contained "lies and false information" that caused Lamb to be denied parole.

Rizzo filed a motion to dismiss, attaching to it numerous newspaper articles chronicling Lamb's criminal history. In the motion, Rizzo contended that Lamb was libel-proof as a matter of law; in other words, Lamb's public reputation at the time the articles were published was so diminished with respect to a specific subject (his kidnapping and murder convictions) that he could not be further injured by allegedly false statements on that subject. Because damage to reputation is the heart of a defamation action in Kansas, argued Rizzo, Lamb's claims must be dismissed.

The district court dismissed Lamb's complaint for failure to state a claim on which relief could be granted. Lamb appealed.

In upholding the dismissal, the appellate court said:

> [T]he facts surrounding Mr. Lamb's case fit within the Kansas Supreme Court's description of when the [libel-proof] doctrine might apply. Mr. Lamb . . . was convicted long before Mr. Rizzo's allegedly defamatory articles were published. Thus, Mr. Lamb had already suffered from a lowered reputation in the community due to his prior convictions for the crime alleged in the publication or for a similar crime.

Clearly, a plaintiff's reputation is an important factor in determining whether a defamation case will be successful.

price." The CEO's negative comments were particularly shocking because in February 2007, Whole Foods made a bid to purchase Wild Oats.

The Federal Trade Commission opposed the acquisition, fearing that the merger would create a monopoly in the organic grocer sector. Thus, in an effort to halt Whole Foods' purchase of Wild Oats, the FTC launched an investigation into the acquisition. It was during the FTC investigation that officials uncovered Mackey's double-life as online poster Rahodeb. People began to question whether Mackey had been purposely trying to talk down Wild Oats and its stock, and wondered if there was an agenda behind his constant boasting about Whole Foods. Concerns about the legality of Mackey's behavior led to further examination by the Securities and Exchange Commission. In the end, Mackey was cleared of any wrongdoing. However, Whole Foods did change its code of conduct policy, and the company now prohibits officials from posting business-related information on Internet message boards.[9]

A person accused of defamation can raise two defenses: truth and privilege. *Truth* is frequently considered an absolute defense. That is, the defendant cannot be held liable for defamation, regardless of whether damages result, if the statement made was true. If I say Bill is a convicted felon and he is, I have not committed defamation. Under ordinary circumstances, the fact that I *thought* a statement was true is not a defense. If I honestly believe Bill is a convicted felon and I tell others he is but he is not, then I have committed slander, despite my sincere belief in the truth of what I have said.

Privilege is an affirmative defense in a defamation action. An affirmative defense, you may recall from Chapter 7, occurs when the defendant admits to the accusation but argues there is a reason he should not be held liable.

A privilege is either absolute or conditional. A person with **absolute privilege** cannot be sued for defamation for any false statements made, regardless of intent or knowledge of their falsity. Absolute privilege arises in only a limited number of circumstances. The speech and debate clause of the U.S. Constitution gives absolute privilege to individuals

[9] Heather Havenstein, "Whole Foods Handcuffs Execs on Web Postings," *ComputerWorld,* November 12, 2007; Lev Grossman, "The Price of Anonymity," *Time* 170, no. 5, pp. 47–49; and Mark Hamstra, "Investor Calls for Mackey to Leave," *Supermarket News* 55, no. 31, p. 6.

COMPARING THE LAW OF OTHER COUNTRIES

LIABILITY OF ONLINE SERVICE PROVIDERS IN CANADA

In Canada, there have not yet been any landmark cases or any legislation to clearly establish the liability of online service providers (OSPs) for content they disseminated but did not originate. Currently, an OSP being sued under such circumstances in Canada would have to rely on the existing Canadian libel code's defense of innocent dissemination, which will succeed if the defendant demonstrates all the following:

a. The defendant does not know of the libel contained in the work published or authored by him or her.
b. There was no reason for the defendant to suppose the work he or she authored or published would be libelous.
c. It was not negligence on the defendant's part that he or she did not know the work contained libelous material.

speaking on the House and Senate floors during congressional debate because Congress wants to get to the truth of matters before it, and if people testifying had to fear being sued, they might be afraid to testify.

Absolute privilege also arises in the courtroom during a trial. Again, we do not want people to fear testifying in court, so we prohibit their being sued for whatever occurs within the courtroom.

Conditional privilege is the second type. Under conditional privilege, a party will not be held liable for defamation unless the false statement was made with **actual malice,**[10] that is, with *either* knowledge of its falsity or reckless disregard for its truth.[11]

Businesspersons should be most concerned about the conditional privilege that arises with respect to job recommendations. To encourage honest assessments of former employees, this privilege protects an employer who makes a false statement about a former worker: The employer will not be held liable as long as the statement was made in good faith and only to those with a legitimate interest in the information.

BUT WHAT IF . . .

WHAT IF THE FACTS OF THE CASE OPENER WERE DIFFERENT?

Recall, in the Case Opener, that Bongiovi's false story about Sullivan hurt Sullivan's business. But what if Bongiovi thought the story about Sullivan was actually true and was telling his friends about an interesting story in his field? Would conditional privilege be an applicable defense for Bongiovi? If the story were actually true, would Bongiovi have committed slander at all?

Another conditional privilege is the **public figure privilege.** Public figures are those in the public eye, typically politicians and entertainers. Because they have a significant impact on our lives, we want to encourage free discussion about them, so we do not hold people liable for making false statements about them as long as the statements were not made with malice. This privilege does not unfairly burden public figures, because their position lets them easily respond publicly to any false claims through appropriate outlets. In the opening scenario, Bongiovi argued on appeal that Sullivan was a public figure by nature of his profession. If Bongiovi could establish that Sullivan was a public figure, Sullivan would have to show that Bongiovi acted with actual malice while making the statements to the patient.

A third conditional privilege recognized in some states is the *fair report privilege.* This privilege protects the media if defamatory material is published in an article based on an

[10] Restatement (Second) of Torts, sec. 580A.
[11] *New York Times Co. v. Sullivan,* 376 U.S. 254 (1964).

official report. For the media to use the privilege, two conditions must exist: (1) The report must be of an official proceeding, and (2) the report must be complete and accurate or a fair abridgment of the official proceeding.

Some believe a conditional privilege should apply when the defamatory statement is posted on the Internet, because the person defamed can respond in the same forum with minimal effort. Thus, there is less need for the stronger legal protection we ordinarily give. Relaxing defamation standards on the Internet can encourage people to speak their minds freely. Thus far, however, no such privilege has been established. When a person is found to have committed defamation on an online bulletin board or website, damages can be significant. For example, a jury awarded a university professor $3 million when a former student accused him of being a pedophile on a website she maintained.[12]

Privacy Torts. The fact that truth is an absolute defense to a defamation action does not mean people are free to reveal everything they know. Four distinct torts, collectively called *invasion of privacy,* protect the individual's right to keep certain things out of public view even if they are true. The four privacy torts are (1) false light, (2) public disclosure of private facts, (3) appropriation for commercial gain, and (4) intrusion on an individual's affairs or seclusion.

False light is closely related to defamation and occurs when publicity about a person creates an impression about that individual that is not valid. It could involve attributing characteristics or beliefs to a person that she does not possess or creating the impression that an individual has taken certain actions he has not taken. Sometimes tabloids publish articles that may lead to false-light claims, like the one that was filed by Nellie Mitchell when a newspaper published a story about a 101-year-old Australian newspaper-delivery woman who had to quit her job when she became pregnant. The problem was that they illustrated the story with a picture of 96-year-old Nellie Mitchell, a woman living in a small town in Arkansas, who had spent most of her adult life as a newspaper carrier, She sued for, among other claims, false light, and recovered $650,000 in compensatory damages and $850,000 in punitive damages.[13]

A false-light claim can be defended against using public figure privilege; however, that defense is not absolute. The creators (World Wrestling Enterprises, Inc., Vincent McMahon, and Titan Sports, Inc.) of a DVD documentary about a professional wrestler known as "Warrior" believed they were safe against his lawsuit, which alleged defamation and false light. However, because some of the statements on the DVD were about Warrior's personal life, specifically his relationship with his father, the court found that the false-light claims could not all be dismissed. The court decided that statements that presented Warrior's private life in a false light should be treated as if they were statements about a private person rather than a public figure.[14]

Public disclosure of private facts occurs when someone publicizes a private fact about another that a reasonable person would find highly offensive.[15] The individual must have not waived his or her right to privacy. Publication of information about someone's sex life or failure to pay debts would fall under this tort.

Appropriation for commercial gain occurs when someone uses another person's name, likeness, voice, or other identifying characteristic for commercial gain without that person's permission.[16] Many businesses may choose to use celebrities in their

[12] See Paul J. Martin, "North Dakota Jury Awards $3M for Internet Defamation," *Lawyers Weekly USA,* www.lawyersweeklyusa.com/usanews040802a.cfm (accessed April 8, 2002).

[13] *Nellie Mitchell v. Globe Inc. D/B/A "Sun,"* U.S. District Court, W. D. Arkansas, 786 F. Supp. 791 (1992).

[14] *Ultimate Creations, Inc. v. McMahon,* 515 F. Supp. 2d 1060 (D. Ariz. 2007).

[15] Restatement (Second) of Torts, sec. 652D.

[16] Restatement (Second) of Torts, sec. 652C.

advertisements as a way to appeal to consumers. However, when companies use a celebrity's likeness or image without his or her consent, they open themselves up to potential litigation and liability. For example, Woody Allen believed that American Apparel appropriated his image when they used an image of him from the movie *Annie Hall* in their billboards. Allen sued for $20 million, but ended up settling the day before the case was to go to trial for $5 million.[17]

Another illustration occurred in April 2008, when Disney star Brenda Song, of the television show *The Suite of Zack & Cody,* sued Vibe Media, Inc., and its owner after discovering that the company had used her image in an advertisement without her consent. The advertisement in question was for an escort service and featured Brenda's picture next to a caption that read "Hawaiin[sic] beauty. Come get lei'd." In the text of the advertisement, Brenda's name was never mentioned; however, the image was undoubtedly hers. The lawsuit filed by Brenda Song thus alleged emotional distress and commercial misappropriation of her image. In March 2009, Song won her suit, and Vanessa Sean, the woman accused of actually taking Brenda's image from the Internet, was ordered to pay the young actress $16,000.[18]

The final privacy tort is **intrusion on an individual's affairs or seclusion,** which occurs when someone invades a person's solitude, seclusion, or personal affairs when the person has the right to expect privacy.[19] Examples include wiretapping and using people's passwords to gain access to their e-mail messages. Installing two-way mirrors in a women's dressing room at a gym or store constitutes an invasion of privacy because people should be able to expect a certain degree of privacy in a dressing room.

Entertainers often allege invasion-of-privacy claims. For example, Actress Joan Collins sued the *Globe* for invasion of privacy when it took pictures of her and a male friend. However, editors and owners often claim that the public "demands" these invasions of privacy. As evidence they point out the higher circulation that results from sensational pictures.

To see how the use of celebrities in advertising relates to tort liability, please see the Connecting to the Core activity on the text website at www.mhhe.com/kubasek3e.

BUT WHAT IF . . .

A patient of the famous Mayo Clinic in Minnesota sued the clinic and a news station for not only filming her surgery but airing it on a local news channel. Subsequent to the airing, the patient sued for invasion of privacy. However, the patient had signed a form giving the clinic permission to release materials involving her surgery, including films for the purposes of releasing important health information to the general public. How do you believe this release affected the outcome of the lawsuit?

False Imprisonment. **False imprisonment** occurs when an individual is confined or restrained against his or her will for an appreciable period of time. The imprisonment may occur by (1) physical restraint, such as tying someone to a chair, (2) physical force, such as forcibly pinning someone against a wall, (3) a threat to use immediate physical force, or (4) refusal to release the plaintiff's property. The use of moral pressure is not enough to establish a false imprisonment. Suppose the Pushy Toy Company is holding a "training session" for new moms, really a thinly veiled demonstration of new products, in a

[17] http://cityroom.blogs.nytimes.com/2009/05/18/american-apparel-settles-lawsuit-with-woody-allen/?scp=1&sq=%22woody%20allen%22&st=cse.

[18] http://news.yahoo.com/s/eonline/20090305/en_celeb_eo/80799> (accessed March 5, 2009); and www.gantdaily.com/news/12/ARTICLE/45490/2009-03-05.html (accessed March 5, 2009).

[19] Restatement (Second) of Torts, sec. 652B.

COMPARING THE LAW OF OTHER COUNTRIES

DEFAMATION OF PUBLIC FIGURES IN THE UNITED KINGDOM

As you know from your reading, the media in the United States can print false information about public figures without being liable if they can demonstrate they did so without malice. In the United Kingdom, public figures about whom false statements have been made have a much easier time winning a libel case.

All a public figure, or any other libel plaintiff, must do to win a case against the media in the United Kingdom is demonstrate that the defamatory statement was communicated in the United Kingdom and his or her reputation was damaged as a result. The only defenses are (1) the statements are true or (2) the statements were made in Parliament or court. The burden of proving truth is on the defendant.

If a statement was originally broadcast by a U.S. company and rebroadcast in the United Kingdom without the consent of the originator, the U.S. company may still be held liable in the U.K. court.

conference room. People are told they are free to leave at any time. Once Hillary realizes what is going on, she decides to go. As she approaches the exit, the CEO of Pushy Toys tells her that only a terrible mother would leave early but she is free to leave if she wants to be a terrible mother. The moral pressure the CEO is using, although ethically repugnant, does not constitute false imprisonment as Hillary is still free to leave.

Because retailers and security guards are the usual defendants in false-imprisonment cases as a result of their need to sometimes detain and question a suspected shoplifter, this tort is known as the "shopkeeper's tort." Retailers are protected under "shopkeeper's privilege," but the suspect cannot be held an unreasonable length of time, and questioning must be reasonable.

Claims of false imprisonment are not limited to suits against retailers or security guards. For example, three ambulance drivers recently filed a false-imprisonment suit against a local psychiatric center because the crisis center locked them in and would not allow them to leave. The center claimed that the drivers had committed certain improprieties when delivering a violent girl to the crisis center.

Proving damages in a false-imprisonment case is not easy. If the physical restraint caused harm requiring medical treatment, such damages would be clear, but most cases do not include physical harm. Typically, plaintiffs request compensation for time lost from work and for pain and suffering from mental distress and humiliation.

Intentional Infliction of Emotional Distress. Sometimes called the "tort of outrage," **intentional infliction of emotional distress** occurs when someone engages in outrageous, intentional conduct likely to cause extreme emotional distress to another party. For example, if a person calls his former employer and falsely says her son was just arrested for a double homicide after a botched robbery attempt, most courts would find that behavior outrageous enough to satisfy the first element of the tort.

Before damages are awarded in some jurisdictions, the plaintiff must demonstrate injury through physical symptoms directly related to the emotional distress. For instance, in the above example, if the employer fainted upon hearing the news, hitting her head on the table and cutting it as she passed out, she would have physical symptoms sufficient to justify a recovery. Other physical symptoms from emotional distress include headaches, a sudden onset of high blood pressure, hives, chills, inability to sleep, and inability to get out of bed.

Businesses frequently find themselves sued for this type of tort when they terminate someone's employment or fail to provide a service that a consumer expected. Many of these actions, like the one in Case 8-2 below, are unsuccessful, primarily because the bar for what is considered outrageous is high, as are the standards for emotional distress.

CASE 8-2 AARON OLSON, APPELLANT, v. CENTURYLINK, RESPONDENT
COURT OF APPEALS OF MINNESOTA
NO. A12–0884 (UNPUBLISHED OPINION), FEBRUARY 4, 2013

On December 14, 2011, appellant Aaron Olson contracted to receive telephone service from respondent CenturyLink and also applied for reduced-rate service that CenturyLink provides through Minnesota's Telephone Assistance Plan (TAP), a statewide program established to reduce telephone rates for low-income households.

CenturyLink did not apply the reduced rate to Olson's first bill but had attached a blank copy of the TAP application. Olson completed the application and mailed it to CenturyLink, but his next bill also did not reflect a reduced rate. Olson called CenturyLink and learned that the company had not received his application. Olson then faxed another application to CenturyLink. A few days later, he contacted CenturyLink but could not confirm whether his application had been received. On January 31, 2012, CenturyLink disconnected his telephone service. When Olson called CenturyLink to resolve the dispute, the company representatives repeatedly hung up on him.

In April 2012, Olson filed suit, claiming that CenturyLink violated the Minnesota Human Rights Act (MHRA), was negligent, and committed intentional infliction of emotional distress. Because he did not have the money for filing fees, Olson also filed a petition to proceed in forma pauperis (IFP). The district court denied the petition, determining that the action was frivolous because the claims had no basis in law. Olson appealed.

JUDGE BJORKMAN: . . . Olson argues that the district court improperly denied his IFP petition because his claims are legally sound. . . .

Finally, Olson claims that CenturyLink is liable in tort for intentional infliction of emotional distress. To prevail on this tort, a plaintiff must establish the defendant's conduct (1) was extreme and outrageous, (2) was intentional or reckless, (3) caused emotional distress, and (4) the distress was severe. . . . Extreme and outrageous conduct is behavior "so atrocious that it passes the boundaries of decency and is utterly intolerable to the civilized community. . . . Furthermore, the emotional distress must be so severe "that no reasonable man could be expected to endure it." . . .

The conduct alleged in the amended complaint does not approach this standard. First, CenturyLink's acts of failing to process Olson's application, disconnecting his telephone service, and hanging up on him during telephone conversations are not so atrocious that they pass the boundaries of decency. See *Langeslag v. KYMN* Inc., . . . (holding that insults, indignities, annoyances, petty oppressions, and other trivialities do not constitute extreme and outrageous conduct); see also *Venes v. Prof'l Serv. Bureau, Inc.* (concluding a jury could reasonably find that a debt collector engaged in extreme and outrageous conduct by repeatedly threatening a debtor in light of the debtor's medical problems). Second, Olson does not allege that he experienced severe emotional distress as a result of CenturyLink's conduct. See *Covey v. Detroit Lakes Printing Co.* . . . (determining plaintiff's distress was not severe where he had sought no psychiatric, psychological, or other treatment); see also *Wenigar v. Johnson*, . . . (concluding that plaintiff's distress was severe when he suffered from nightmares, crying spells, physical illness, and post-traumatic stress disorder).

Because Olson's claims lack any reasonable basis in law, the district court did not abuse its discretion by determining that his action is frivolous and denying his IFP petition.

AFFIRMED in favor of Defendant CenturyLink.

CRITICAL THINKING

Notice that case law can, as in this case, serve as a restriction on our emotional response to a case. Many of us have had trouble with our phone carrier. The alleged behavior of CenturyLink is at minimum annoying. But case law lays out standards that determine the availability of remedies in cases like these. Reading the case law, describe behavior that CenturyLink would have had to have engaged in for the plaintiff to have prevailed.

ETHICAL REASONING

What value is the court upholding in finding against the plaintiff?

Misuse of Legal Procedure. Three separate torts protect those unreasonably subjected to litigation—malicious prosecution, wrongful civil proceedings, and abuse of process. These torts serve two functions. They proactively limit frivolous litigation, and they try to rectify harm done to a party through inappropriate litigation.

The first two of these torts, **malicious prosecution** and **wrongful civil proceedings**, serve similar functions. Both seek to compensate those wrongfully charged with either criminal or civil matters. Successful plaintiffs are entitled to damages for legal fees related to the improperly brought litigation; harm to reputation, credit, or standing caused by the false claims; and any emotional distress caused by the improper litigation.

Abuse of process is more general and applies to both criminal and civil matters in which a legal procedure is misused to achieve a different goal than it intends. For example, Ben and Jennifer are recently divorced; Ben owes Jennifer alimony as part of the divorce settlement. As retaliation, he sues her for slandering him to his business partners. Ben's attorney offers to settle out of court if Jennifer will drop the alimony requirement from the divorce settlement. Regardless of whether Ben wins in court, Jennifer can file abuse-of-process charges against him in civil court because legal proceedings for slander are not intended to be used as mitigating devices for divorce disputes.

Exhibit 8-3 summarizes the intentional torts against persons.

Exhibit 8-3
Intentional Torts against Persons

Assault	Placing another in fear or apprehension of an immediate, offensive bodily contact. Assault occurs if reasonable apprehension exists, regardless of fear.
Battery	Making an intentional, unwanted, and reasonably offensive bodily contact.
Defamation	Intentionally publicizing or communicating to a third party a false statement harmful to an individual's reputation. Defamation is referred to as *slander* if oral and *libel* if written.
Public disclosure of private facts	Publicizing a private fact about another that a reasonable person would find highly offensive; a type of privacy tort.
False light	Creating an impression that is not valid, such as attributing to a person characteristics or beliefs he or she does not hold; a type of privacy tort.
Appropriation for commercial gain	Using another person's name, likeness, voice, or other identifying characteristic for commercial gain without that person's permission; a type of privacy tort.
Intrusion on an individual's affairs or seclusion	Invading a person's solitude, seclusion, or personal affairs when the person has the right to expect privacy; a type of privacy tort.
False imprisonment	Confining or restraining a person against his or her will for an appreciable period of time. The imprisonment may occur by physical restraint, physical force, threats to use immediate physical property, or refusal to release the plaintiff's property.
Intentional infliction of emotional distress	Engaging in outrageous, intentional conduct likely to cause extreme emotional distress to another party.
Misuse of legal procedure	Misusing a legal procedure to achieve a goal other than the one for which the process was intended to be used; includes the torts of malicious prosecution, wrongful civil proceedings, and abuse of process.

INTENTIONAL TORTS AGAINST PROPERTY

Trespass to Realty. The tort of **trespass to realty,** also called *trespass to real property,* occurs when a person intentionally (1) enters the land of another without permission; (2) causes an object to be placed on the land of another without the landowner's permission; (3) stays on the land of another when the owner tells him to depart; or (4) refuses to remove something he placed on the property that the landowner asked him to remove.[20]

It is no defense to argue that you thought you had a legal right to be on the property or you thought it belonged to someone else. The intent refers to intentionally being on that particular piece of land.[21] In a recent unusual case heard in a small claims court in Westchester County, a plaintiff sued for trespass to realty when the defendant entered the plaintiff's property, from which he had previously been barred, to serve a reply affidavit for another legal action. Arguing that the defendant could not dictate how legal papers are served, the plaintiff sued for $3,000 in compensatory, nominal, and punitive damages. While the court ruled that the defendant committed trespass to realty, it awarded only nominal damages in the sum of $1.

Because guests are welcome, they are not considered trespassers. However, a guest who is asked to leave and refuses immediately becomes a trespasser with no right to be on the property. If charges are brought, the person cannot raise the defense of being a guest.

A trespasser is also liable for damages she might cause to the property and cannot hold an owner liable for damages she sustained while on the property. However, courts now typically maintain that owners owe a reasonable duty to anyone who may end up on their property. The specifics of the duty vary by jurisdiction and by the status of the parties. In some jurisdictions (although this is rare), owners may be liable to trespassers injured while trying to steal from them.

Private Nuisance. A **private nuisance** occurs when a person uses her property in an unreasonable manner that harms a neighbor's use or enjoyment of his property.[22] Examples include subjecting a neighbor to flooding, vibrations, excessive noise, or smoke.

Trespass to Personal Property. A person commits trespass to personal property, also called **trespass to personalty,** by temporarily exerting control over another's personal property or interfering with the owner's right to use it. The trespasser is responsible for damages to the property and to the owner.[23] If I take Eloy's bike from his garage and use it for a week, I have committed trespass to personalty. If I return the bike with a flat tire, I must compensate Eloy for the cost of repairing the tire and any other expenses that resulted from my actions. If the bike was Eloy's only way to get to work, I would be responsible for his lost wages.

Conversion. **Conversion** occurs when a person permanently removes personal property from the owner's possession and control.[24] The owner usually recovers damages for the full value of the converted item, plus any additional damages resulting from the loss. It is not a defense to argue that you believed you had a legal claim to the goods. For example, if Brittany accidentally takes Melvin's suitcase believing it to be hers and then loses it, she is still liable for conversion.

Moreover, the possession of stolen goods also makes a person liable for conversion. Therefore, buying goods in good faith without knowledge of any impropriety also is not a

[20] Restatement (Second) of Torts, sec. 158.
[21] Restatement (Second) of Torts, sec. 164.
[22] Restatement (Second) of Torts, sec. 821D.
[23] Restatement (Second) of Torts, sec. 218.
[24] Restatement (Second) of Torts, sec. 222A.

E-COMMERCE AND THE LAW

TORT LAW VERSUS CRIMINAL LAW TO IMPROVE THE ONLINE PERSONALS INDUSTRY

Suppose your ex-boyfriend posed as you on a number of online personals sites, such as iwantu.com. He posted what he described as your rape fantasies and listed your name and address. He then encouraged men to act out your fantasies in person. Would you be afraid? How might criminal law respond? Could tort law also help you? In a real case in 1992, Gary Dellapenta, the ex-boyfriend, was sentenced to six years in prison for violating California's then new cyberstalking law.

If someone were threatening you as Dellapenta threatened his ex-girlfriend, you might want the creator of the website and/or an Internet service provider to assist you in pulling the posts before harm occurs. Unfortunately, Internet service providers are exempt from liability under tort law if they fail to respond to your concerns. The Communications Decency Act of 1996 outlined this exemption.

You might be able to pursue the creator of the website, depending on how the facts play out and on your state's law. You might be able to sue for defamation, false-light invasion of privacy, negligence, and/or intentional infliction of emotional distress. You will face an uphill battle, though, in meeting your burden of proof. In the mid-1990s, Ken Zeran brought tort claims against a radio station that broadcast untrue information suggesting he was selling T-shirts and other items with insensitive remarks about the Oklahoma City bombing of a federal building. Zeran was unable to prove any of the torts he alleged. Perhaps as cyberstalking becomes more prevalent, and more frightening, tort law will change to provide more protection to victims.

defense. Even a person who bought the goods believing the purchase was legal is liable to the legal owner.

An illustration of conversion comes from a recent case heard in Westchester County Supreme Court. An amateur race-car driver left her race car at a service station. While it was in the service station's possession, an employee with a known drinking problem apparently drove the car, got into an accident, and totally destroyed it. The car could never be returned to the condition it was in when brought to the station. The owner sued for conversion and recovered the value of the car in damages.

Legal Principle: When a person temporarily deprives another of the use and enjoyment of his personal property, a trespass to property occurs; if that deprivation becomes permanent, conversion has occurred.

INTENTIONAL TORTS AGAINST ECONOMIC INTERESTS

All businesspersons should be familiar with the torts against economic interest. The five most common torts against economic interests, frequently referred to as "business torts," are disparagement, intentional interference with contract, unfair competition, misappropriation, and fraudulent misrepresentation. The first, **disparagement,** is similar to defamation, because both torts involve the making of a false statement, but it is different because it is a tort designed to protect one's property interests, whereas defamation is designed to protect one's reputational interests.

The plaintiff in a disparagement case must prove that the defendant published a false statement of a material fact about the plaintiff's product or service that resulted in a loss of sales. When such statements are criticisms of the quality, honesty, or reputation of the business or product, the tort is sometimes called **slander of quality** (if spoken) or **trade libel** (if printed). If the statements relate to ownership of the business property, it is **slander of title.**

Damages for disparagement are ordinarily based on a decrease in profits linked to the publication of the false statement. A less common method is to demonstrate that the plaintiff had been negotiating a contract with a third party who lost interest shortly after publication of the false statement. The profits the plaintiff would have made on the contract are the damages.

Some interesting variations of the tort of disparagement have developed. For example, in 2007, California became the 13th state to recognize the tort of **food disparagement,** which critics call "veggie libel." Such laws provide ranchers and farmers with a cause of action when someone knowingly makes false, damaging statements about a food product. The California law was drafted in response to an incident during 2006 in which Taco Bell executives wrongly identified green onions grown at Boskovich Farms in Oxnard as the source of an *E. coli* outbreak that sickened 70 of the fast-food chain's customers.

The most famous veggie-libel lawsuit was filed by a cattle rancher against talk-show host Oprah Winfrey and one of her guests. During the broadcast at issue, Oprah said the conversation they were having about the possibility of contracting disease from meat had caused her to give up eating hamburgers. Shortly after the show aired, the price of cattle futures fell. Oprah and her guest were sued under the Texas veggie-libel law, which says anyone who knowingly makes a false claim that a perishable food product is unsafe may be required to pay damages to the producer of the product. The jury decided there was no liability, because the statements were merely the parties' opinions, not knowingly false statements of fact.

With the growing use of technology, it seemed inevitable that a computer-related disparagement tort would evolve, and it has. *Disparagement by computer* occurs when (1) erroneous information from a computer about a business's credit standing or reputation impairs the business's ability to obtain credit and (2) the computer information's owner fails to correct the incorrect information in a timely manner.

Intentional Interference with Contract. Another tort against economic interests is the tort of **intentional interference with contract.** To successfully bring this claim, the plaintiff must prove (1) a valid and enforceable contract between the two parties existed; (2) the defendant knew of the existence of the contract and its terms; (3) the defendant intentionally undertook steps to cause one of the parties to breach the contract; and (4) the plaintiff was injured as a result of the breach.[25]

Clear liability is placed on third parties for inducing a party to an existing contract to breach it. However, a third party might also be liable for inducing a party to pull out of a prospective contract before it is formed. Because the essence of business is competition, simply offering a better deal is not enough to create liability. However, using illegal means to cause another party not to enter into a contract does create liability for interfering with contractual relations.[26]

Liability for intentional interference with a contract is most common in recruitment, when one employer knows that an employee has a contract for a set period of time with another employer, yet tries to lure that employee away anyway.

Several damage remedies are available when a third party interferes with a contract. Injured parties may recover for what was directly lost through the breached contract and any losses suffered related to the breached contract, in addition to damages for emotional distress and harm to reputation.[27]

Unfair Competition. The tort of **unfair competition** exists because U.S. law protects businesses acting on the profit motive. Thus, when someone enters an industry with the sole intent of driving another firm out of business, the law punishes this act as unfair competition. For example, if Ali's is the only jewelry store in town, Mark cannot set up a store that makes no profits just to drive Ali out of business so that Mark's friend can open a legitimate jewelry store once Ali's has been eliminated. The line between unfair competition and legitimate competition can be hard to determine. In a recent case,

[25] Restatement (Second) of Torts, sec. 766.

[26] Restatement (Second) of Torts, sec. 766B.

[27] Restatement (Second) of Torts, sec. 774A.

Overstock.com believed that pop-up advertisements from a competing website, SmartBargains, were unfair competition. SmartBargains had pop-ups that appeared when users went to Overstock.com. However, because the pop-ups were in separate browser windows, and did not contain any deception or attempt to confuse consumers between Overstock.com and SmartBargains, the court ruled in favor of SmartBargains. Having pop-up advertisements for a competing business appear on your website constitutes legitimate competition rather than unfair competition.[28]

Fraudulent Misrepresentation. **Fraudulent misrepresentation** occurs when a party uses intentional deceit to facilitate personal gain. To prove this tort occurred, the injured party must demonstrate all the following:

1. Someone knowingly, or with reckless disregard for the truth, misrepresented material facts and conditions.
2. The defendant intended to have other parties rely on the misrepresentations.
3. The injured party reasonably relied on the misrepresentations.
4. The injured party suffered damages because of this reliance.
5. A direct link exists between the injuries suffered and a reliance on the misrepresentations.[29]

As in the criminal act of fraud, in the civil act of fraudulent misrepresentation a party materially misrepresents something and thereby causes another party to suffer damages. Typically, fraudulent misrepresentation applies only to the misrepresentation of material facts. However, when a party with expert knowledge regarding a specific matter states an opinion, any party reasonably relying on the statement, although it is an opinion and not fact, may recover damages under the tort of fraudulent misrepresentation.

Exhibit 8-4 summarizes the intentional torts against economic interest.

Exhibit 8-4
Intentional Torts against Economic Interest

Disparagement	Publishing a false statement of a material fact about a business's product or service that results in a loss of sales; includes the torts of slander of quality, slander of title, trade libel, and food disparagement.
Intentional interference with contract	Inducing a party to a contract to breach it. The plaintiff must prove that a valid and enforceable contract between the two parties existed; the defendant knew of the existence of the contract and its terms; the defendant intentionally undertook steps to cause one of the parties to breach the contract; and the plaintiff was injured as a result of the breach.
Unfair competition	Entering an industry with the sole intent of driving another firm out of business.
Misappropriation	Using another person's name, likeness, voice, or other identifying characteristic for commercial gain without that person's permission.
Fraudulent misrepresentation	Intentionally using a false statement to deceive another who reasonably relies on the deception to facilitate personal gain.

[28] Overstock.com, *Inc. v. SmartBargains, Inc.*, 192 P.3d 858 (Utah 2008).

[29] Restatement (Second) of Torts, sec. 525.

Damages Available in Tort Cases

LO3 What types of damages are available in tort cases?

Three types of damages are available in tort cases: compensatory, nominal, and punitive (see Exhibit 8-5). You will see this system of classifying damages again when we talk about damages in other contexts, such as in cases of breach of contract.

COMPENSATORY DAMAGES

Because the primary objective of tort law is to compensate victims, the primary type of damages is **compensatory damages,** designed to compensate the victim for all the harm caused by the person who committed the tort, often called the **tortfeasor.** While we seem to hear a lot about "runaway jury" awards, the median jury award for personal injury cases from 1998 to 2004 was $35,298. That amount actually fell from $37,086 in 2003 to $35,000 in 2004.[30]

Compensatory damages are typically rewarded for pain and suffering, costs of repairing damaged property, medical expenses, and lost wages. For example, in the opening scenario, Sullivan won compensatory damages because he lost a client, and the related monies from the surgery, as a result of Bongiovi's defamatory statement. Surprisingly, attorney fees are *not* recoverable as compensatory damages, despite the fact that most plaintiffs could not bring an action against the tortfeasor without hiring an attorney. Because the plaintiffs in personal injury cases must usually pay their attorneys anywhere from one-third to one-half of their recovery, some argue that compensatory damages fail to meet the intended goal of properly compensating victims. Others point out that one way plaintiffs can, in essence, recover their attorney fees is by increasing their pain and suffering damages enough to cover these expenses.

NOMINAL DAMAGES

Nominal damages are a small amount of money given to recognize that a defendant did indeed commit a tort in a case where the plaintiff suffered no compensable damages. A plaintiff may receive nominal damages by simply failing to prove actual damages. Nominal damages, however, can sometimes be important because if a party is awarded nominal damages, the court may also require that the losing party pay all the court costs, which may include attorney fees (if allowed), as well as the costs of discovery and expert-witness fees.

Exhibit 8-5
Types of Tort Damages

TYPE	PURPOSE	AMOUNT
Compensatory	To make the plaintiff whole again	An amount equivalent to all losses caused by the tort, including compensation for pain and suffering, but not attorney fees
Nominal	To recognize that the defendant committed a tort against the plaintiff	A trivial amount, typically $1 to $5
Punitive	To punish the defendant and deter future wrongdoers	An amount based on two factors: the severity of the wrongful conduct and the wealth of the defendant

[30] JVR news release, www.juryverdictresearch.com/Press_Room/Press_releases/Verdict_study/verdict_study41.html (accessed October 10, 2006).

PUNITIVE DAMAGES

Punitive damages are awarded both to punish conduct that is extremely outrageous and to deter similar activity by the defendant and others. Juries usually consider the egregiousness or willfulness of the tort and the wealth of the defendant. Obviously, the more wrongful the nature of the defendant, the greater the desire to send a message that such behavior will not be tolerated; and the greater the defendant's wealth, the higher the damages must be in order to be significant.

While many groups, including consumer advocates, see the threat of large punitive damages against manufacturers as a good method for encouraging them to produce the safest possible products, others disagree. They believe that no threat beyond compensatory damages is required and that the main effect of punitive damages is to discourage innovation by manufacturers who fear the risk of producing a defective product that could cost them millions in punitive damages.

Since the late 1970s, insurance companies and tort reform groups have been trying to limit punitive damages and get the courts to strike them down as unconstitutional violations of defendants' due process rights. The 1994 Supreme Court case of *Honda Motor Company v. Oberg*[31] provided their first judicial victory. It was a limited victory, however, because of two aspects of the case. First, the punitive damages were over 500 times the compensatory damages, extraordinarily rare. Second, the state law under which the damages were awarded was the only one in the country with no provision for judicial review of the amount of punitive-damage awards, and it was the denial of this safeguard that violated the due process clause. Thus, *Oberg* did not provide much guidance about when punitive damages were so excessive as to violate due process.

A few years later, however, in *BMW v. Gore,*[32] the Supreme Court set forth a test that a number of commentators thought would substantially curb punitive-damage awards. The Court said three factors should be considered in determining whether an award was grossly excessive: "the degree of reprehensibility of the nondisclosure; the disparity between the harm or potential harm suffered by [the plaintiff] and his punitive damages award; and the difference between this remedy and the civil penalties authorized or imposed in comparable cases." However, a 1999 study found that the year after *BMW v. Gore,* punitive-damage awards across the country were not reduced any more frequently than the year before.[33] (Exhibit 8-6 lists several cases that resulted in major punitive-damage awards.)

Since *BMW v. Gore,* the Supreme Court has continued to encourage the courts to carefully scrutinize punitive-damage awards. In the 2001 case of *Cooper Industries, Inc. v. Leatherman Tool Group, Inc.,*[34] the high court ruled that appellate courts must review the trial court's decision on the constitutionality of an award *de novo,* meaning they should no longer give deference to the trial court's determination that the jury award was not unconstitutionally excessive and uphold it, unless there was a clear abuse of discretion on the part of the trial court judge.

In the 2003 case *State Farm v. Campbell,*[35] the Supreme Court once again addressed the issue of how to properly determine punitive damages. The Campbells had won a jury verdict for $1 million in compensatory damages and $145 million in punitive damages after State Farm failed to settle what was clearly a valid claim. The high court ruled that punitive-damage awards should bear some relationship to the actual harm caused and not

[31] 114 S. Ct. 2331 (1994).

[32] *BMW of North America v. Ira Gore, Jr.,* 116 S. Ct. 1589 (1995).

[33] James Dam, "Large Punitives Mostly Upheld, but $5B Award Overturned," *Lawyer's Weekly USA,* November 12, 2001, p. A1.

[34] 532 U.S. 424 (2001).

[35] 123 S. Ct. 1513 (2003).

Exhibit 8-6 Some Major Punitive-Damage Awards

CASE	JURY AWARD	ULTIMATE RESOLUTION
Romo v. Ford Motor Co., 99 Cal. App. 4th 1115 (2002)	The Romo family was in an accident in which their 1978 Ford Bronco rolled over. The top of the Bronco collapsed and shattered, killing three family members and seriously injuring the other three. The jury awarded the Romos more than $6 million in compensatory damages and $290 million in punitive damages.	After several appeals, the jury verdict was lowered to under $3 million.
Liebeck v. McDonald's, 787 A.2d 443 (1994)	A jury awarded Stella Liebeck $2.9 million in damages, including $2.7 million in punitive damages, for extensive burns she received when she spilled 170-degree coffee on her legs. Part of the reason for the high punitive-damage award was the fact that McDonald's had prior knowledge of other customers receiving burns from the excessively hot coffee.	The trial court reduced the original jury award to $640,000. Subsequently, the parties settled out of court for an undisclosed amount.
Gober v. Ralphs Grocery Company, 128 Cal. App. 4th 648 (2005)	In the largest sexual harassment jury verdict in the United States, the jury awarded six plaintiffs $30.6 million in damages, approximately $30 million of which was punitive damages.	The judge reduced the verdict to approximately $8 million, in light of *State Farm v. Campbell.* Both parties appealed to the supreme court of California, but the court denied review.
Robinson v. State Farm Idaho, 2000 WL 1877745	A plaintiff's insurance company, State Farm, was found to have acted in bad faith when it refused to cover injuries she sustained in an auto accident by claiming they must have been caused by something else. The company's refusal was ostensibly based on a recommendation from an independent company that reviewed the plaintiff's medical records, but she demonstrated that State Farm had a practice of referring claims to that company, knowing no payment would be recommended. The jury awarded punitive damages of $9.5 million, 95 times the amount of the compensatory damages.	The award was appealed and subsequently upheld by the Idaho Supreme Court.
Williams v. Philip Morris, Inc., 2002 U.S. Dist. LEXIS 13522 (2002)	Williams's estate brought a fraud and negligence suit against Philip Morris after Williams died of lung cancer. The jury awarded Williams's estate $820,000 in compensatory damages and $79.5 million in punitive damages.	The trial judge reduced the damages to $32 million. The Oregon court of appeals affirmed the original $79.5 million verdict. The state supreme court vacated the decision and remanded the case to be decided in light of *State Farm v. Campbell.* The Oregon court of appeals subsequently ruled the $79.5 million award was lawful under *State Farm.*
In re Exxon Valdez, 9th Cir. Court of Appeals, 2009	In 1989, one of the worst oil spills in our nation's history occurred due to the negligence of the captain of the *Exxon Valdez.* When the ship ran into ice, the hull burst and leaked 10.8 million gallons of oil into Prince William Sound. Cleanup costs ultimately totaled $2.5 billion. The jury awarded $5 billion in punitive damages to a class of 32,000 fishermen, Alaska natives, business owners, and other litigants in 1996.	The court of appeals ordered Exxon Mobil Corp. to pay $507.5 million in punitive damages, plus 5.9 percent interest running from the 1996 trial judgment. The amount is equal to the compensatory damages provided in the settlement agreement of the case, consistent with an earlier U.S. Supreme Court ruling that in maritime cases, punitive damages should be no more than the compensatory, or actual, damages. That 1-to-1 ratio was a new legal standard for punitive awards in maritime cases.

CASE 8-3 CLARK v. CHRYSLER CORPORATION
U.S. COURT OF APPEALS FOR THE SIXTH CIRCUIT
2006 U.S. APP. LEXIS 2435

Charles Clark was fatally injured in an automobile accident when he pulled into an intersection in front of an oncoming vehicle and collided with it. He was not wearing a seat belt and was consequently ejected from his vehicle. His wife sued Chrysler, claiming that its pickup truck was defectively and negligently designed.

After a three-day trial, the jury rendered a unanimous verdict in favor of Mrs. Clark on claims of strict liability, negligence, and failure to warn. The jury found Chrysler and Mr. Clark each 50% at fault, returning a verdict of $471,258.26 in compensatory damages and $3,000,000 in punitive damages. The court entered a judgment against Chrysler for $3,235,629.13, reflecting 50% of the compensatory damages plus the $3 million punitive damages award. After a series of appeals, the last being an appeal of the trial court's motion to deny the defendant's motion for remittitur, the case finally landed at the Circuit Court of Appeals on the issue whether the jury verdict was constitutionally excessive.

JUDGE JANE A. RESTANI: . . . The Court in *State Farm* elaborated on the three *Gore* guideposts that courts must consider when reviewing punitive damage awards. Namely, (1) the degree of reprehensibility of the defendant's misconduct; (2) the disparity between the actual or potential harm suffered by the plaintiff and the punitive damage award; and (3) the difference between the punitive damages awarded by the jury and the civil penalties authorized or imposed in comparable cases. . . . In light of *State Farm* . . . we conclude that the $3 million award here is constitutionally excessive. An application of the *Gore* guideposts to the facts of this case reveals that a punitive damage award approximately equal to twice the amount of compensatory damages, or $471,258.26, would comport with the requirements of due process.

With respect to the first *Gore* guidepost, *State Farm* emphasized that the degree of reprehensibility is the most important indicium of the reasonableness of a punitive damages award. . . . The Court laid out a list of five criteria that lower courts must consider in determining the reprehensibility of a defendant's conduct: the harm caused was physical as opposed to economic; the tortious conduct evinced an indifference to or a reckless disregard of the health or safety of others; the target of the conduct had financial vulnerability; the conduct involved repeated actions or was an isolated incident; and the harm was the result of intentional malice, trickery, or deceit, or mere accident. The existence of any one of these factors weighing in favor of a plaintiff may not be sufficient to sustain a punitive damages award; and the absence of all of them renders any award suspect. . . . [T]he physical harm suffered by Mr. Clark weighs strongly in favor of finding Chrysler's conduct reprehensible. After considering the four other factors, however, we conclude that the factors as a whole show that Chrysler's conduct was not sufficiently reprehensible to warrant a $3 million punishment.

. . . The second guidepost is the disparity between the actual or potential harm inflicted on the plaintiff and the punitive damage award. . . . [B]ecause the compensatory damage award here is not particularly large, a 1:1 ratio is inappropriate. . . . But due to the lack of several of the reprehensibility factors, any ratio higher than 2:1 is unwarranted. Accordingly, we conclude that a ratio of approximately 2:1 would comport with the requirements of due process.

The third guidepost is the difference between the punitive damage award and the civil or criminal penalties that could be imposed for comparable misconduct. . . . Given *State Farm*'s focus on civil penalties, however, we now conclude that a $3 million punitive damage award is excessive in light of comparable civil penalties.

Denial of Chrysler's motion for remittitur REVERSED and REMANDED with instructions to enter a punitive damage award of $471,258.26.

CRITICAL THINKING

The decision that the punitive-damage award was excessive in this case was primarily based on the interpretation of several ambiguous words in the judge's opinion. What are they? Would different interpretations of these words change the court's ruling?

ETHICAL DECISION MAKING

What values are guiding the judge's decision that the punitive-damage award was excessive? Do you think the values promoted by the decision are appropriate for the situation? Why or why not?

COMPARING THE LAW OF OTHER COUNTRIES

PUNITIVE DAMAGES IN CANADA

Those who believe the United States tort system is in need of reform with respect to its treatment of punitive damages may look to their Canadian neighbors with envy. Punitive-damage awards in Canada are both rare and small. A 1990 study of punitive-damage awards in Ontario found that the highest was $50,000 and the majority less than $25,000; the median award was approximately 20 percent of the compensatory-damage award in the case.

Following English common law, Canadian courts have traditionally restricted punitive damages to two situations: cases of oppressive, arbitrary, or unconstitutional actions by government servants and cases in which the defendant's conduct was calculated to have made a profit in excess of compensatory damages. In 1989, the Canadian Supreme Court recognized that punitive damages could also be awarded for conduct deserving punishment because of its "harsh, vindictive, reprehensible, and malicious manner."

Two reasons seem to explain the differences between Canadian and U.S. treatment of punitive damages. First, Canadians see something undignified about the flamboyant punitive-damage awards in the United States. Second, civil juries are less common in Canada, and, in general, judges tend to be more conservative than juries in making punitive-damage awards.

focus on the wealth of the defendants. While refusing to say what ratio of compensatories to punitives was acceptable, the Court did say that "in practice, few awards exceeding a single-digit ratio between punitive and compensatory damages, to a significant degree, will satisfy due process."[36] The Court also stated that damages should not focus on deterrence based on wealth, or on actions unrelated to the case at hand. Case 8-3 demonstrates how the courts are applying these guidelines today.

Even though we now have more guidance from the Supreme Court as to when punitive damages will be allowed, it is not always easy to predict what a court will do in any given case. For example, the appellate court in California upheld a $28 million punitive-damage award against Philip Morris in a case where compensatory damages were only $850,000. The court acknowledged that under *State Farm,* a presumption exists that a ratio of punitives to compensatories significantly greater than 9 to 1 violates due process, but in this case the "extreme reprehensibility" of Philip Morris's conduct in marketing its cigarettes and the "scale and profitability" of its misconduct justified the 33-to-1 ratio.[37]

Legal Principle: **In general, in deciding whether to strike down a punitive-damage award as unconstitutional, the court will look at (1) the degree of reprehensibility of the defendant's misconduct; (2) the disparity between the actual or potential harm suffered by the plaintiff and the punitive-damage award; and (3) the difference between the punitive damages awarded by the jury and the civil penalties authorized or imposed in comparable cases.**

Attempts to curb punitive-damage awards are being made not only in the courts but also in the legislatures with so-called tort reform legislation. The one successful piece of tort reform legislation at the national level is the Class Action Fairness Act (CAFA), signed into law by President Bush in February 2005 to limit the conditions under which class action suits can be brought, as opposed to limiting damage awards. CAFA grants original jurisdiction to the federal courts over any civil action in which (1) the amount in controversy is in excess of $5 million, (2) the action is brought as a "class action" with at least 100 class members, and (3) any one of the plaintiffs is a citizen of a state different from that of any defendant, and two-thirds or more of the class members and the primary defendant are not citizens of the state in which the action was filed.

[36] Ibid., p. 1524.

[37] "$28M Punitive Award Upheld in Cigarette Smoker, Recent Decisions," *Lawyer's Weekly USA,* May 8, 2006, p. 6.

Therefore, even actions originated as state actions will fall into the original jurisdiction of the federal courts if all the above criteria are met. Once there, CAFA deems that all cases failing to meet federal requirements for class action suits will be immediately dismissed, even if previously accepted under state law. As such, CAFA is designed to limit the number of large, interstate class action suits.

Whether CAFA will fulfill its purpose is not yet certain. According to the Federal Judicial Courts Center, as recently as four months after the act went into force, the number of federal tort and contract class actions sharply increased from an average of 10.48 per day to 11.96, and the number of cases removed from state court increased from 18 percent of all class actions to 23 percent.[38]

[38] Marcia Coyle, "Class Action Changes Bring Quick Impact," *National Law Journal,* October 2, 2006, p. 6.

CASE OPENER WRAP-UP

Plastic Surgeon Defamation

On appeal, Dr. Bongiovi argued that Dr. Sullivan was a public figure and as a result the jury should have been instructed that actual malice had to be shown. The supreme court of Nevada held that Sullivan did not qualify as a public figure because he "did not voluntarily interject himself into a public [medical] controversy." Additionally, the court found that the awarded compensatory and punitive damages were proper. Sullivan had lost income as the result of Bongiovi's statement, and the compensatory damages were equivalent to the income lost. According to the court, the punitive-damage award was "reasonable and proportionate to the amount of harm to Sullivan" and would adequately serve as a deterrent. The district court ruling was affirmed.

KEY TERMS

absolute privilege 192
abuse of process 198
actual malice 193
appropriation for commercial gain 194
assault 187
battery 188
compensatory damages 203
conditional privilege 193
conversion 199
defamation 188
disparagement 200
false imprisonment 195
false light 194
food disparagement 200
fraudulent misrepresentation 202
intentional infliction of emotional distress 196
intentional interference with contract 201
intentional torts 186
intrusion on an individual's affairs or seclusion 195
malicious prosecution 198
negligent torts 186
nominal damages 203
private nuisance 199
public disclosure of private facts 194
public figure privilege 193
punitive damages 204
slander of quality 200
slander of title 200
strict-liability torts 186
tort 185
tortfeasor 203
trade libel 200
trespass to personalty 199
trespass to realty 199
unfair competition 201
wrongful civil proceedings 198

SUMMARY OF KEY TOPICS

Introduction to Tort Law

Tort: A civil wrong giving the injured party the right to bring a lawsuit against the wrongdoer to recover compensation for injuries.

Goals of tort law:

1. Compensate innocent persons who are injured.
2. Prevent private retaliation by injured parties.
3. Reinforce a vision of a just society.
4. Deter future wrongs.

Classification of Torts

Intentional torts occur when the defendant takes an action intending that certain consequences will result or knowing they are likely to result.

Negligent torts occur when the defendant fails to act in a responsible way and thereby subjects other people to an unreasonable risk of harm.

Strict-liability torts occur when the defendant takes an action that is inherently dangerous and cannot be undertaken safely.

Intentional Torts

Intentional torts against persons:

- *Assault* is the placing of another in fear or apprehension of an immediate, offensive bodily contact.
- *Battery* is an intentional, unwanted, offensive bodily contact.
- *Defamation* is the intentional publication (or communication to a third party) of a false statement harmful to an individual's reputation.
- *Public disclosure* of private facts is the publicizing of a private fact about another that a reasonable person would find highly offensive.
- *False light* is the creation of an impression that is not valid, such as attributing to a person characteristics or beliefs he or she does not hold.
- *Appropriation for commercial gain* is the use of another person's name, likeness, voice, or other identifying characteristic for commercial gain without that person's permission.
- *Intrusion on an individual's affairs or seclusion* is the invasion of a person's solitude, seclusion, or personal affairs when the person has the right to expect privacy.
- *False imprisonment* is confining or restraining a person against his or her will for an appreciable period of time.
- *Intentional infliction of emotional distress* is engaging in outrageous, intentional conduct that is likely to cause extreme emotional distress to another party.
- *Misuse of legal procedure* is the misuse of a legal procedure to achieve a goal other than the one for which the process was intended to be used.

Intentional torts against property:

- *Trespass to realty* is the temporary exertion of control over another's personal property or interference with the owner's right to use it.
- *Private nuisance* is the use of one's property in an unreasonable manner that harms a neighbor's use or enjoyment of his property.
- *Trespass to personalty* occurs when one person deprives another of the temporary possession of his personal property.
- *Conversion* is the permanent removal of personal property from the owner's possession.

Intentional torts against economic interest:

- *Disparagement* is the publishing of a false statement of a material fact about a business's product or service that results in a loss of sales.

- *Intentional interference with a contract* occurs when a valid and enforceable contract between two parties exists; the perpetrator knows of the existence of the contract and its terms; the perpetrator intentionally undertakes steps to cause one of the parties to breach the contract; and the other party is injured as a result of the breach.
- *Unfair competition* occurs when a business enters an industry with the sole intent of driving another firm out of business.
- *Misappropriation* is the use of another person's name, likeness, voice, or other identifying characteristic for commercial gain without that person's permission.
- *Fraudulent misrepresentation* is the intentional use of a false statement to deceive another who reasonably relies on the deception to facilitate personal gain.

Damages Available in Tort Cases

Compensatory damages are an award that puts the plaintiff in the position he or she would have been in had the tort not occurred.

Nominal damages are a minimal amount that signifies the defendant's behavior was wrongful but caused no harm.

Punitive damages are damages that punish the defendant and deter such conduct in the future.

POINT / COUNTERPOINT

Should Punitive Damages Be More Strictly Limited?

YES

Excessive punitive damages are fundamentally unfair. Tort law is supposed to be a way to compensate victims; punitive damages are not a normal part of this system. They are quasi-criminal in nature, designed to punish the defendant. And they reward a plaintiff with, in some cases, riches far beyond what any reasonable person would see as compensation. The possibility of huge punitive-damage awards has turned tort cases into litigation lotteries over lawsuits brought in hopes of striking it rich.

If punitive damages were more reasonable, patients could not sue the phone company for publishing false information about a physician that led to a botched liposuction or sue NBC because a *Fear Factor* episode about eating rats made a viewer "dizzy and lightheaded and caused him to vomit and run into a doorway." Sure, damage awards have fallen since the BMW and State Farm cases, but they were so exorbitant that they could hardly have gone any higher! Besides, the fact that they have fallen does not mean that they have fallen to reasonable levels.

Further, juries get so emotionally caught up in some of these cases that it is often impossible for them to be objective or fair.

Unfair punitive-damage awards can also ruin a defendant's good name and run target companies out of business. We need more stringent standards for punitive damages to bring predictability, efficiency, and fairness to our civil justice system.

NO

The BMW standard strikes a fair balance, protecting the interests of consumers and firms. In the 20 years before the BMW case, courts handed down huge punitive-damage awards, some exceeding $100 million. But we have since seen the court's three-pronged test result in much lower awards, generally below a 9-to-1 ratio of punitive to compensatory damages.

In the top 10 jury verdicts of 2005, awards were significantly lower than those in 2004 and earlier. There is no need to further limit punitive damages; they are now reasonably related to the harm caused and still large enough to deter behavior.

Punitive damages now fill two important functions. First, they allow a significantly harmed plaintiff to recover costs and attorney fees. Without the possibility of large punitive-damage awards, the plaintiff may not actually be compensated for losses because so much of the recovery goes to attorneys and litigation costs.

Second, punitive damages perform a necessary deterrence function without posing unreasonable risk to potential defendants. If corporations no longer fear punitive-damage awards, they will lose some of their motivation to produce safe products and behave as responsible citizens.

QUESTIONS & PROBLEMS

1. Distinguish the three types of damages available in tort cases.

2. Explain why some people see punitive damages as a necessary aspect of our tort system, while others want to restrict their availability.

3. List five intentional torts, and explain the elements needed to prove each.

4. Randy Senna owned Wildwood Fascination parlor, an arcade game on the boardwalk in Wildwood. His rival, Walter Florimont, owned Olympic Enterprises, located nearby on the boardwalk in North Wildwood. To keep his client base, Senna promised that prize tickets won at his Seaside Heights parlor would be honored at the Wildwood location. Soon afterward, Senna learned that staff members at Florimont's Olympic Enterprises were telling Olympic's boardwalk customers that Senna would not honor the prize tickets that he had issued. Senna asked Florimont to restrain his employees from "bad-mouth[ing]" him and his business with false and derogatory comments. According to Senna, however, Florimont's employees continued to verbally assail his business.

   Within a few months, Senna closed his Wildwood Fascination parlor, only to resurrect it in 2000 under the name of Flipper's Fascination. On dates in July, August, and September 2003, Florimont's employees broadcast over a public address system to his boardwalk customers that Senna was "dishonest" and "a crook," charging that he "'ran away and screwed all of his customers in Seaside.'" As they had done several years earlier, Florimont's employees accused Senna of having left his Seaside Heights customers with worthless prize tickets—tickets he would not honor in Wildwood—and warned that he would cheat his customers again.

   Senna filed a civil complaint alleging that Florimont and his employees defamed Senna and tortiously interfered with his ability to conduct business at Flipper's Fascination. Senna demanded compensatory and punitive damages. The trial court granted summary judgment in favor of Florimont. Senna appealed. Were Florimont's comments enough to defame Senna's business? Why or why not? [*Senna v. Florimont,* 958 A.2d 427 (N.J. 2008).]

5. Former Major League Baseball player and radio game announcer Bob Uecker sought an injunction against Ann Ladd, alleging a six- or seven-year pattern of harassment. Ladd, who claimed to be a "devoted fan," was charged with felony stalking. An injunction was issued against her bothering Uecker, but the stalking charge was dropped when she agreed to cooperate. Later, Ladd sued Uecker for defamation, claiming that Uecker defamed her in the material he filed in support of his application for the injunction. The trial court dismissed her suit, and she appealed. What do you think the outcome of her appeal was and why? [*Ladd v. Uecker,* 780 N.W.2d 216 (Ct. App. Wisc. 2010).]

6. Anthony Caruso lived in Mohican Historic Housing from 1998 to 2001, when he died. The Mohican Historic Housing Association was aware Margherita Del Core was Caruso's next of kin, his sister. Although Mohican had been informed that Del Core was Caruso's next of kin, it did not respond to efforts by the hospital to obtain that information after his death. In the absence of that information, the hospital arranged for Caruso's burial in a pauper's grave. Four months later, Mohican informed Del Core of the death. Del Core filed suit against Mohican for, among other things, inflicting extreme emotional distress upon her by not informing her in a timely manner about her brother's death so that she could have arranged a proper funeral. The trial court granted Mohican's motion to dismiss, and Del Core appealed. Is Mohican liable for an intentional infliction of emotional distress? Should Mohican have informed Del Core sooner regarding her brother's death? [*Del Core v. Mohican Historic Housing Assocs.,* 81 Conn. App. 120 (2004).]

7. Dr. Timothy Brown is a licensed medical doctor certified in dermatology and anatomic and clinical pathology. Brown started a dermatology practice and thereafter maintained an advertisement in Dex's Yellow Pages directory, under the subheading "Dermatology (skin)." Brown later began to offer liposuction in his office, after receiving some limited informal training in how to perform that procedure. Brown placed a second advertisement in Dex's Yellow Pages—this time under the subheading "Surgery, Plastic and Reconstructive." The new

advertisement stated that Brown was "Board Certified"—without specifying any area of certification. Brown added the new advertisement at the urging of a Dex sales representative, Mueller. Mueller said that the "plastic and reconstruction surgery" subheading in the Yellow Pages would be the best place to reach the desired target market. Mueller also said that the advertisement should identify Brown as "board certified," because "patients were expecting a [board-certified] plastic surgeon to do these techniques."

Knepper was considering cosmetic liposuction surgery. She consulted the "Surgery, Plastic and Reconstructive" subheading in the Yellow Pages and saw Brown's advertisement, believing him to be a plastic surgeon because of the location of his ad and the board-certified designation that appeared after his name. Knepper decided to retain Brown, and he performed a liposuction procedure on her. After the procedure, Knepper contacted Brown's office to report continuing pain and "misshapenness," and Brown performed two more liposuction procedures in an unsuccessful attempt to repair the damage. Knepper eventually sued Brown and Dex. Brown later settled with Knepper, leaving her fraud claim against Dex for intentional misrepresentation. The jury returned a $1.58 million verdict for the plaintiff, which the trial court reduced by the amount of Knepper's settlement with Brown. Dex appealed, arguing that Knepper failed to prove her claims. How did the court rule on appeal? What does Knepper need to demonstrate to win her claim for intentional misrepresentation? [*Knepper v. Brown*, 345 Or. 320 (2008).]

8. At 2:08 A.M. on Friday, December 29, 2006, Northwest Herald Newspapers received via e-mail the Lake in the Hills police department "Daily Bulletin," which reported that Carolene Eubanks had been charged with theft and obstruction of justice. As it normally does, the newspaper placed the information from the report in an article and then placed the article in line for publication in the upcoming issue of the paper. The article was eventually printed before 6 A.M. on January 2, 2007, and appeared in the newspaper on the same date.

The Lake in the Hills police department had sent a second e-mail, on December 29 at 10:25 P.M., in which it said to remove the name Carolene Eubanks and replace it with the name Barbara Bradshaw. The employee who posted the article had already gone home, and because it was a long holiday weekend, and no one was in the office when the second e-mail arrived, it wasn't read until January 2, 2007, at 10:17 A.M.

Consequently, the January 2 edition of the newspaper included the article indicating that Carolene Eubanks had been arrested and charged with theft and attempted obstruction of justice. The newspaper published a retraction of the article in its January 3 paper, stating that Eubanks was not the one charged with those crimes.

On June 15, 2007, Eubanks filed her complaint against Northwest Herald for defamation and false-light invasion of privacy based on the January 2 publication. The trial court granted the defendant's motion for summary judgment based on its exercise of a privilege. The plaintiff appealed. What privilege do you think the court relied on? What do you think the outcome of the appeal was and why? [*Eubanks v. Northwest Herald Newspapers, 397 Ill. App. 3d 746, 922 N.E.2d 1196 (2010).*]

9. Plaintiff Wilspec, a U.S. company, and defendant DunAn, a Chinese corporation, design, produce, and sell parts for air-conditioning (AC) units. They entered into a three-year contract under which DunAn would make specified parts for AC units with the Wilspec name on them. The defendant knew that these parts were to be sold in North America under the Wilspec name and that Wilspec would be the exclusive distributor for the products to AC manufacturers in North America. Wilspec alleged that while the contract was in force, DunAn engaged in intentional interference with contractual relations by soliciting the sale of the same kind of AC parts to Wilspec's customers in North America and by making disparaging remarks to those same customers regarding Wilspec's ability to perform. Wilspec sued Dun An for intentional interference with contractual relations, seeking both compensatory and punitive damages. Do you believe Wilspec is entitled to such damages? Why or why not? [*Wilspec Technologies, Inc. v. DunAn Holding Group Co.*, 204 P.3d 69 (Sup. Ct. Okla. 2009).]

10. Michael Buchanan went shopping in Maxfield Enterprises Inc.'s store, which is located on Melrose Avenue in Los Angeles. Buchanan did not know, at the time he entered the store, that celebrities Jennifer Lopez and Ben Affleck were also in the store, shopping. Less than 20 minutes after Buchanan entered the store, Maxfield store manager Jacqueline Sassoon asked Buchanan to leave the store. When Buchanan asked Sassoon for an explanation, she refused to give a reason. When Buchanan became angered, Maxfield store security placed him under a citizen's arrest. Two local sheriff's deputies, on hand because of Affleck and Lopez, handcuffed Buchanan and escorted him into the Maxfield parking lot. Because of the presence of Lopez and Affleck, the parking lot was "thronged" with TV and other media reporters and film crews. Buchanan was led, handcuffed, straight into the media circus. After Buchanan was walked around the store parking lot, Sassoon told the deputies she did not want Buchanan arrested after all. The deputies removed the handcuffs and Buchanan was free to leave. Excerpts from television and print media purported to report that a stalker had shadowed Lopez and Affleck in the Maxfield store and the stalker was removed from the scene by police officers who had responded to a call from the store about the stalker. Buchanan sued Maxfield for invasion of privacy, alleging that the defendant invaded his right to privacy by parading him, handcuffed, before the media and, as a result of this, that he suffered injury to his reputation, as well as mental anguish and emotional distress. Buchanan also sued for false imprisonment and intentional infliction of emotional distress. Maxfield filed a motion to dismiss, which was granted by the trial court. Buchanan appealed. Was Buchanan successful on appeal? What must he prove to be successful in his claims? [*Buchanan v. Maxfield Enterprises, Inc.,* 130 Cal. App. 4th 418 (2005).]

Looking for more review materials?

The Online Learning Center at **www.mhhe.com/kubasek3e** contains this chapter's "Assignment on the Internet" and also a list of URLs for more information, entitled "On the Internet." Find both of them in the Student Center portion of the OLC, along with quizzes and other helpful materials.

CHAPTER

9 Negligence and Strict Liability

LEARNING OBJECTIVES

After reading this chapter, you will be able to answer the following questions:

1. What are the elements of negligence?
2. What are the doctrines that help a plaintiff establish a case of negligence?
3. What are the defenses to a claim of negligence?
4. What are the elements of strict liability?

CASE OPENER

The Case of the Collapsing Dock

Defendants Jack and Claire Lein owned and lived on Willow Creek Farm from 1980 through 2004. The farm manager, Stewart, and his girlfriend, plaintiff Tambra Curtis, also lived on the farm during this time.

While Curtis was walking across a wooden dock located on the farm, the dock collapsed, and she fell, suffering a hairline fracture to her tibia. Consequently, Curtis brought a personal injury suit against the Leins, hoping to collect damages for her personal injury. After Curtis's injury, the defendants destroyed the dock, claiming that the soon-to-be new owners of the farm planned to build a school on the property and, thus, there was no reason to replace the broken dock. Because there was no longer any evidence of the condition of the dock, the plaintiff invoked the doctrine of *res ipsa loquitur* to support her case of negligence. Curtis asserted that a wooden dock does not give way unless the creators were negligent in their creation and maintenance of the structure. The trial court granted the defendants summary judgment and ruled that the doctrine of *res ipsa loquitur* did not apply. According to the court, *res ipsa loquitur* did not apply because the dock could have collapsed for reasons other than negligence. The plaintiff appealed.

The Washington Court of Appeals affirmed the lower court's ruling, both courts concluding that *res ipsa loquitur* did not apply, but for different reasons. In contrast to the trial court, the court of appeals reasoned that the doctrine of *res ipsa loquitur* could be applied as evidence of negligence but that the plaintiff still had the burden of proving that the flaws in the dock's construction were discoverable by the defendants.

After the court of appeals affirmed the ruling of the trial court, the plaintiff sought review.[1]

1. Suppose you are the judge in this case. Do you think that Jack and Claire had a duty of care to protect Curtis? Why or why not?
2. How do you think the court ruled on review? Why?

The Wrap-Up at the end of the chapter will answer these questions.

[1] *Curtis v. Lein,* 169 Wn. 2d 884, 239 P.3d 1078, 2010 Wash. LEXIS 809 (2010).

Introduction to Negligence and Strict Liability

In the previous chapter we discussed intentional torts, wrongs in which an individual took an action that he or she should have known would harm another person. In this chapter, we consider two other types of torts: negligent and strict-liability torts. These torts are generally committed when an individual fails to maintain a duty of care to another individual.

Suppose Ross uses a piece of wood to smack Joey, the mailman, on the face. Ross has committed battery. If Ross is building a tree house in his yard, however, and accidentally drops a piece of wood on Joey, who is delivering Ross's mail, Ross's action lacks intent, so there is no battery. Yet he might be negligent.

Allegations of negligence are made in a wide variety of circumstances. For example, people have alleged negligence when incidents of teenage violence occurred. The parents of Marcos Delgado, Jr., filed a claim of negligence against a movie theater when it admitted 13-year-old Raymond Aiolentuna without an adult to the R-rated movie *Dead Presidents.* After the movie, Aiolentuna emerged from the theater, walked one block, and shot Delgado. Delgado's parents argued that the movie theater was negligent because it did not enforce the movie ratings system. The court, however, ruled in favor of the movie theater.[2] In another instance, the families of the victims of the 1999 Columbine school shootings in Colorado sued the two alleged shooters and the gun manufacturer for negligence. What exactly is required to establish a successful negligence claim?

In this chapter, we begin by examining the elements of negligence. Then we consider the methods that courts have adopted to help plaintiffs make successful negligence claims. Next, we examine the defenses that defendants to negligence claims can raise. Finally, we consider strict-liability torts.

Elements of Negligence

LO1 What are the elements of negligence?

Negligence is behavior that creates an unreasonable risk of harm to others. In contrast to intentional torts, which result from a person's willfully taking actions that are likely to cause injury, negligent torts involve the failure to exercise reasonable care to protect another's person or property.

Sometimes, however, harm occurs because an individual suffers an **unfortunate accident,** an incident that simply could not be avoided, even with reasonable care. For example, suppose Jonathan is driving on the highway when he suffers a stroke. Because of the stroke, he crashes into two other vehicles. He is not, however, liable for damages

[2] *Delgado v. American Multi-Cinema Inc.,* 99 C.D.O.S. 4772, Los Angeles Superior Court (1999).

caused by the accident. Yet if Jonathan had some type of warning that the stroke was going to occur, he might be liable for the accident.

To win a negligence case, the plaintiff must prove four elements: (1) duty, (2) breach of duty, (3) causation, and (4) damages. (See Exhibit 9-1.) A plaintiff who cannot establish all four of these elements will be denied recovery.

DUTY

The plaintiff must first establish that the defendant owes a *duty* to the plaintiff. In some particular situations, the law specifies the duty of care one individual owes to another. In most cases, however, the courts use the reasonable person standard to determine the defendant's duty of care. The **reasonable person standard** is a measurement of the way members of society expect an individual to act in a given situation. To determine the defendant's duty of care, the judge or jury must determine the degree of care and skill that a reasonable person would exercise under similar circumstances. The judge or jury then uses this standard to evaluate the actions of the individual in the case.

Let's return to the personal injury case in the opening scenario. What duty of care do you think a reasonable person in the position of the farm owners would owe Curtis?

When courts attempt to determine whether a reasonable person would have owed a duty to others, they consider four questions:

1. How likely was it that the harm would occur?
2. How serious was the harm?
3. How socially beneficial was the defendant's conduct that posed the risk of harm?
4. What costs would have been necessary to reduce the risk of harm?

BUT WHAT IF. . .

WHAT IF THE FACTS OF THE CASE OPENER WERE DIFFERENT?

Let's say, in the Case Opener, that the farm owners knew that the dock was extremely dangerous but figured no one would ever make it out to the dock because it was out of the way. What standard would a court apply to this case? What would be the likely outcome?

In many situations, it is far from clear what a reasonable person would do. For example, if a reasonable person saw an infant drowning in a shallow swimming pool, what would she do? In most situations like this one, the law holds that individuals have no duty to rescue strangers from perilous situations.

Exhibit 9-1
Elements of Negligence

To prove negligence, a plaintiff must demonstrate:

1. *Duty:* The standard of care a reasonable person owes another.
2. *Breach of duty:* Failure to live up to the standard of care.
3. *Causation:* (a) Actual cause (cause in fact)—the determination that the plaintiff's harm was a direct result of the defendant's breach of duty; and (b) proximate cause (legal cause)—the extent to which, as a matter of policy, the defendant will be held liable for the consequences of his actions.
4. *Damages:* A compensable loss suffered by the plaintiff.

In some cases, however, the courts hold that individuals have a duty to aid strangers in certain types of peril. For example, if Sam negligently hits Janice with his car and, as a result, Janice is lying in the street, Sam has a duty to remove her from that dangerous position. Similarly, employers have a special duty to protect their employees from dangerous situations.

The courts generally hold that landowners have a duty of care to protect individuals on their property. Similarly, businesses have a duty of care to customers who enter business property. It is important, therefore, for future business managers to be knowledgeable about this duty. Businesses should warn customers about risks they may encounter on business property. Some risks, however, are obvious, and businesses need not warn customers about them. For example, a business need not inform customers that they could get a paper cut from the pages of a book.

The courts generally hold that businesses have a duty of care to protect their customers against foreseeable risks about which the owner knew or reasonably should have known. For example, in *Haywood v. Baseline Construction Company,* a woman who tripped over lumber on the front porch of the House of Blues restaurant in Los Angeles sued for negligence. The business's attempt to warn customers by marking the lumber with yellow construction tape was insufficient to avoid the determination of negligence; the woman was awarded $91,366 in damages. Similar to *Haywood,* the Case Opener at the beginning of this chapter raises the question of the duty of care that landowners owe to individuals who are on their property with their permission.

Businesses and corporations are also obligated to provide products to consumers that are safe from foreseeable harm or injury. Failure to care for customers' safety can mean serious legal and financial repercussions for business owners and CEOs, especially if a company knowingly offers products or services that contain defects. For example, in early 2009, the Centers for Disease Control (CDC) traced hundreds of reported cases of salmonella-related sickness back to food products containing peanut substances manufactured by Peanut Corporation of America. Upon further investigation by the Food and Drug Administration (FDA), documents revealed that Peanut Corporation knew that its products tested positive for salmonella, on multiple occasions, over a time period of nearly two years. Rather than taking preventive measures to guarantee that its tainted peanut products didn't reach the public, Peanut Corporation instead decided to ship the contaminated goods.

So far, Peanut Corporation of America's bad judgment has resulted in 9 deaths and over 600 reported cases of illness. Many families of those who died or fell ill from the salmonella outbreak caused by Peanut Corporation are now filing suit and claiming negligence on the part of the company for turning a blind eye to laboratory results that confirmed salmonella's existence in its products. Other companies, such as Kellogg and King Nut, which manufactured products using peanut substances provided by Peanut Corporation, are finding themselves included in the lawsuits. Peanut Corporation has since shut down all its manufacturing plants and has filed for Chapter 7 bankruptcy. The FDA and the FBI have launched a criminal investigation and are looking into the activities of Peanut Corporation of America.[3]

Sometimes it can be difficult to tell when there is a duty of care between a business and its customers. For example, a man brought a negligence suit against AT&T, his cellular phone provider, for not providing information about the cell phone's calls when he was searching for his missing mother. Ernest Frey had bought the cell phone for his mother

[3] http://minnesota-lawyer.com/death-attorney/pritzker-law-firm-files-lawsuit-against-peanut-corporation-of-america/; "FDA Investigates PCA Plant for Salmonella Contamination," *Candy Industry* 174, no. 2 (February 2009), p. 12; and www.newsinferno.com/archives/4793.

E-COMMERCE AND THE LAW

NEGLIGENCE ON THE INTERNET

A commonly offered explanation for the increasing occurrence of violence is the increased violence portrayed in the media. Some plaintiffs try to hold owners of certain websites liable under negligence theories for violent acts committed by teenagers. For example, in *James v. Meow Media,* a 14-year-old boy took six guns to school and shot three of his classmates to death. The parents of the deceased classmates brought suit against several Internet websites and the creators and distributors of various video games. The parents argued that these defendants had a duty of ordinary care to the slain girls.

The courts have been consistent, however, in finding that it was not foreseeable that a boy who played certain video games and viewed certain websites would murder three of his classmates. In similar cases, courts have ruled that defendants (such as website owners, creators and distributors of video games, and directors and producers of movies) do not have a duty to protect a person from the criminal acts of a third party unless there is a special relationship that requires that the defendant act with that duty.

Although it appears that website owners, manufacturers, and producers will not be held liable, plaintiffs continue to bring suits against these groups of people. Can you think of an argument for why these groups of people might owe a duty of care to these plaintiffs?

after seeing an advertisement about the enhanced safety brought about by carrying a cell phone. When his mother went missing, he contacted the police and then AT&T to find out the location of any recent calls made from her phone. A call had been made, but AT&T refused to give Ernest Frey the location of the call without a subpoena. By the time Ernest's mother was found, after a subpoena had been issued for the cellular tower location, she was dead from a fatal injury. The U.S. district court refused to dismiss the case and found that there might be both a contractual duty of care to Ernest and his mother and a common law duty of care because the representative from AT&T was made aware of the urgency of the situation and the danger to Ernest's mother. Although previous cases involving landline telephone companies were found to lack a duty of care, the district court decided that there were enough important differences between landline and cellular telephones, as well as between the specifics of this case and the previous cases, to merit review by a trial court.[4]

Professionals have more training than ordinary people. Thus, when professionals are serving in their professional capacity, courts generally hold that they have a higher duty of care to clients than does the ordinary person. A professional cannot defend against a negligence suit by claiming ignorance of generally accepted principles in her or his field of expertise. Clients who feel that they have suffered damages as a result of a professional's breach of her duty of care can bring a negligence case against her. These actions are referred to as *malpractice cases,* and they are discussed in greater detail in Chapter 11.

BREACH OF DUTY

Once the plaintiff has established that the defendant owes her a duty of care, she must prove that the defendant's conduct violated that duty. This violation is called a *breach of duty.* For example, the driver of an automobile owes the other passengers in his car a duty of care to obey traffic signs. If he fails to stop at a stop sign, he has violated his duty to follow traffic signs and has therefore breached his duty of care. Once a duty of care has been established, it seems as if determining whether a breach of that duty occurred would be a simple task. Kathleen Turner believed that when she was hit by a foul ball at a baseball game there had been a clear breach of duty by the stadium. The Nevada Supreme Court found that Mandalay Sports Entertainment and the Las Vegas 51s had a limited duty of care to their patrons, which they fulfilled by putting up barriers in areas of high

[4] *Frey v. AT&T Mobility, Inc.,* 2008 U.S. Dist. LEXIS 72335 (N.D. Okla. 2008).

risks and providing written and audio announcements about the danger of foul balls. So, although there was a duty of care, that duty of care was fulfilled and the defendants were not negligent.[5] Looking back at the Case Opener, one can see the challenges of proving breach of duty when evidence of the breach is lacking. Because the defendants in the Case Opener destroyed the wooden dock that allegedly caused the plaintiff's personal injury, the plaintiff had to invoke the doctrine of *res ipsa loquitur* to try to prove breach of duty. The doctrine of *res ipsa loquitur* is discussed later in this chapter.

CAUSATION

Causation is the third element of a successful negligence claim, and it has two separate elements: actual cause and proximate cause. The plaintiff must prove both elements of causation to be able to recover damages.

The first element, **actual cause** (also known as *cause in fact*), is the determination that the defendant's breach of duty resulted directly in the plaintiff's injury. The courts commonly determine whether a breach of duty actually caused the plaintiff's injury by asking whether the plaintiff would have been injured if the defendant had fulfilled his or her duty. If the answer is no, then the actual cause of the plaintiff's injury was the defendant's breach. Actual cause is sometimes referred to as "but-for" causation because the plaintiff argues that the damages she suffered would not have occurred *but for* (except because of) the actions of the defendant. For example, in the personal injury case in the opening scenario, Curtis argued that *but for* the flawed construction and maintenance of the wooden dock, she would not have injured her tibia.

Proximate cause, sometimes referred to as *legal cause,* refers to the extent to which, as a matter of policy, a defendant may be held liable for the consequences of his actions. In most states, proximate cause is determined by foreseeability. Proximate cause is said to exist only when both the plaintiff and the plaintiff's damages were reasonably foreseeable at the time the defendant breached his duty to the plaintiff. Thus, if the defendant could not reasonably foresee the damages that the plaintiff suffered as a result of his action, the plaintiff's negligence claim will not be sustained because it lacks the element of proximate causation.

For example, if a defective tire on a vehicle blows out, it is foreseeable that the driver may lose control and hit a pedestrian. It is not foreseeable, however, that the pedestrian may be a scientist carrying a briefcase full of chemicals that may explode on impact, causing a third-floor window to shatter and injuring an accountant at his desk. In most states, the accountant would not succeed if he sued the tire manufacturer for negligence. The tire failure is not considered a proximate cause of the accountant's injury because the contents of the pedestrian's briefcase were highly unusual. The pedestrian, however, would be eligible to recover damages from the tire manufacturer because hitting a pedestrian is a foreseeable consequence of tire failure. Thus, the defect in the tire is a proximate cause of the pedestrian's injury.

Palsgraf v. Long Island Railroad Company is one of the most well-known cases addressing the issue of proximate cause (see Case 9-1).

BUT WHAT IF. . .

WHAT IF THE FACTS OF THE CASE OPENER WERE DIFFERENT?

Let's say, in the Case Opener, that the dock looked extremely rickety and looked as if it hadn't been touched for years. Would this alone have been enough for Curtis to foreseeably know that the dock was unsafe and would most likely collapse?

[5] *Turner v. Mandalay Sports Entertainment, LLC,* 180 P.3d 1172 (Nev. 2008).

CASE 9-1 PALSGRAF v. LONG ISLAND RAILROAD COMPANY
NEW YORK COURT OF APPEALS
248 N.Y. 33 (1928)

Mrs. Palsgraf was waiting for a train on a platform of a railroad. When a different train came into the station, two men ran to get on that train before it left the station. While one of the men safely reached the train, the other man, who was carrying a package, jumped on the already moving train but seemed as though he was going to fall off the train. The guard on the moving train tried to help pull the man onto the train, while another guard off of the train pushed the man from behind. Consequently, his small package wrapped in newspaper, which contained fireworks, fell upon the rails, causing the fireworks to explode. The shock of the explosion dislodged scales at the other end of the platform, and the falling scales hit Mrs. Palsgraf, causing injuries for which she brought suit against the railroad.

JUDGE CARDOZO: Nothing in the situation gave notice that the falling package had in it the potency of peril to persons thus removed. Negligence is not actionable unless it involves the invasion of a legally protected interest, the violation of a right. "Proof of negligence in the air, so to speak, will not do." If no hazard was apparent to the eye of ordinary vigilance, an act innocent and harmless, at least to outward seeming, with reference to her, did not take to itself the quality of a tort because it happened to be a wrong, though apparently not one involving the risk of bodily insecurity, with reference to someone else. "In every instance, before negligence can be predicated of a given act, back of the act must be sought and found a duty to the individual complaining, the observance of which would have averted or avoided the injury." "The ideas of negligence and duty are strictly correlative" (Bowen, L. J., in *Thomas v. Quartermaine,* 18 Q. B. D. 685, 694).

The argument for the plaintiff is built upon the shifting meanings of such words as "wrong" and "wrongful," and shares their instability. What the plaintiff must show is "a wrong" to herself, i.e., a violation of her own right, and not merely a wrong to someone else, nor conduct "wrongful" because unsocial, but not "a wrong" to any one. We are told that one who drives at reckless speed through a crowded city street is guilty of a negligent act and, therefore, of a wrongful one irrespective of the consequences. Negligent the act is, and wrongful in the sense that it is unsocial, but wrongful and unsocial in relation to other travelers, only because the eye of vigilance perceives the risk of damage. If the same act were to be committed on a speedway or a race course, it would lose its wrongful quality. . . . [W]rong is defined in terms of the natural or probable, at least when unintentional (*Parrot v. Wells-Fargo Co.* [The Nitro-Glycerine Case], 15 Wall. [U.S.] 524). . . . Here, by concession, there was nothing in the situation to suggest to the most cautious mind that the parcel wrapped in newspaper would spread wreckage through the station. If the guard had thrown it down knowingly and willfully, he would not have threatened the plaintiff's safety, so far as appearances could warn him. His conduct would not have involved, even then, an unreasonable probability of invasion of her bodily security. Liability can be no greater where the act is inadvertent.

Negligence, like risk, is thus a term of relation. Negligence in the abstract, apart from things related, is surely not a tort, if indeed it is understandable at all. . . . Negligence is not a tort unless it results in the commission of a wrong, and the commission of a wrong imports the violation of a right, in this case, we are told, the right to be protected against interference with one's bodily security. But bodily security is protected, not against all forms of interference or aggression, but only against some. One who seeks redress at law does not make out a cause of action by showing without more, that there has been damage to his person. If the harm was not willful, he must show that the act as to him had possibilities of danger so many and apparent as to entitle him to be protected against the doing of it, though the harm was unintended. Affront to personalty is still the keynote of the wrong.

The law of causation, remote or proximate, is thus foreign to the case before us. The question of liability is always anterior to the question of the measure of the consequences that go with liability. If there is no tort to be redressed, there is no occasion to consider what damage might be recovered if there were a finding of a tort.

REVERSED and COMPLAINT DISMISSED.

CRITICAL THINKING

Why does the court believe that Mrs. Palsgraf should not be awarded damages? Are you persuaded by these reasons? Why or why not?

ETHICAL DECISION MAKING

Think about the WPH process of ethical decision making. It may seem unfair that Mrs. Palsgraf was unable to collect damages for her injuries. Study the list of values or purposes for a decision. Which value do you think the court was upholding through its decision? Which value is in conflict with this favored value? With which value do you most agree?

The decision in *Palsgraf* set out the rule of foreseeability that is followed by most states today. However, a different definition of proximate cause is followed in a small minority of states. Courts in a few states do not distinguish actual cause from proximate cause. In these states, if the defendant's action constitutes an actual cause, it is also considered the proximate cause. Therefore, in these few states, both the pedestrian-scientist and the third-floor accountant would be able to recover damages from the tire manufacturer in the previous example.

Legal Principle: Proximate cause is defined in the majority of states as foreseeability of both the plaintiff and his or her injury, whereas in the minority of states proximate cause is the same as actual cause.

DAMAGES

Damages are the final required element of a negligence action. The plaintiff must have sustained compensable injury as a result of the defendant's actions. Because the purpose of tort law is to compensate individuals who suffer injuries as a result of another's action or inaction, a person cannot bring an action in negligence seeking only nominal damages. Rather, a person must seek **compensatory damages,** or damages intended to reimburse a plaintiff for her or his losses. In the opening case scenario, Curtis sought compensatory damages for her personal injury.

In typical negligence cases, courts rarely award **punitive damages,** or *exemplary damages,* which are imposed to punish the offender and deter others from committing similar offenses. Instead, courts usually award punitive damages in cases in which the offender has committed **gross negligence,** an action committed with extreme reckless disregard for the property or life of another person.

Plaintiff's Doctrines

The plaintiff has the burden of proving all four elements of a negligence case. Direct evidence of negligence by the defendant, however, is not always available. For example, there may have been no witnesses to the negligent conduct and other evidence may have been destroyed. Therefore, two doctrines have been adopted by courts to aid plaintiffs in establishing negligence claims: *res ipsa loquitur* and negligence per se.

LO2
What are the doctrines that help a plaintiff establish a case of negligence?

RES IPSA LOQUITUR

Res ipsa loquitur literally means "the thing speaks for itself." The plaintiff uses this doctrine to allow the judge or jury to infer that more likely than not, the defendant's negligence was the cause of the plaintiff's harm, even though there is no direct evidence of the defendant's lack of due care. To establish *res ipsa loquitur* in most states, the plaintiff must demonstrate that:

1. The event was a kind that ordinarily does not occur in the absence of negligence.
2. Other responsible causes, including the conduct of third parties and the plaintiff, have been sufficiently eliminated.
3. The indicated negligence is within the scope of the defendant's duty to the plaintiff.

Proof of these three elements does not require a finding of negligence, however; it merely permits it. Once the plaintiff has demonstrated these three elements, the burden of proof shifts to the defendant, who must prove that he was not negligent to avoid liability.

COMPARING THE LAW OF OTHER COUNTRIES

NEGLIGENCE IN GERMANY

German law is concerned with the defendant's ability to foresee, understand, and avoid danger. Both mental and physical capabilities are taken into account. For example, the duty-of-care standard stipulates that "physical and mental disabilities or defects, panic, or confusion" exempt the defendant from being found negligent. Also, although the distinction is not recognized by a statute, the courts distinguish between conscious and unconscious negligence. *Conscious negligence* requires knowledge that the offense is about to occur and that it is an actual offense. *Unconscious negligence* occurs when the defendant is either unaware that the act constitutes an offense or unaware that the act is occurring at all. In such cases, the defendant is found not guilty by reason of unconscious negligence.

One of the earliest uses of *res ipsa loquitur* was the case of *Escola v. Coca Cola.*[6] In that case, the plaintiff, a waitress, was injured when a bottle of Coca-Cola that she was removing from a case exploded in her hand. From the facts that (1) bottled soft drinks ordinarily do not spontaneously explode and (2) the bottles had been sitting in a case, undisturbed, in the restaurant for approximately 36 hours before the plaintiff simply removed the bottle from the case, the jury reasonably inferred that the defendant's negligence in the filling of the bottle resulted in its explosion. The plaintiff therefore recovered damages without direct proof of the defendant's negligence. Plaintiffs in numerous accident cases have subsequently used the doctrine where there has been no direct evidence of negligence. The defendant's best response to this doctrine is to demonstrate other possible causes of the accident. Think back to the opening case scenario: The plaintiff, Curtis, chose to invoke the doctrine of *res ipsa loquitur* because the wooden dock, which allegedly caused her personal injury, had been destroyed. Without the necessary evidence of negligence, Curtis had to rely on *res ipsa loquitur.*

Case 9-2 illustrates a plaintiff's attempt to use *res ipsa loquitur.*

[6] 24 Cal. 2d 453, 150 P.2d 436 (1944).

CASE 9-2 DISTRICT OF COLUMBIA v. WAYNE SINGLETON, ET AL.

COURT OF APPEALS OF MARYLAND

NO. 77 WITH 425 MD. 398, 41 A.3D 717 (2012)

In 2008, Wayne Singleton and his eight-year-old son, Jaron, were traveling on a bus for a school field trip to Six Flags. Wayne fell asleep on the way, and while he was asleep, the bus became "airborne" and drove off the road into a wooded area. The bus eventually collided with a tree. Singleton was asleep when the bus went off the road but woke up for the collision. Jaron was awake the whole time but did not understand the situation. Wayne sued the District of Columbia, due to the negligence of its employee. At the trial, only Wayne and his son were presented as witnesses. They did not call the bus driver or any other passenger or driver as a witness to provide evidence for why the bus went off the road. Due to this lack of evidence, Wayne invoked res ipsa loquitur *to infer evidence for the negligence of the driver. The trial court disagreed and granted the District's motion for judgment.*

JUSTICE HARRELL: With regard to a negligence action based on a perceptually single-vehicle accident, res ipsa loquitur ("res ipsa" or "the doctrine") will be available "if the accident or injury is one which ordinarily would not occur without negligence on the part of the operator of the vehicle" and "the facts are so clear and certain that the inference [of negligence] arises naturally from them." Res ipsa loquitur (literally, "the thing speaks for itself") allows generally a plaintiff to establish a prima facie case of negligence when direct evidence of the cause of the accident is unavailable and the circumstantial evidence permits the drawing of an inference by the fact-finder that the defendant's negligence was the cause. "The rule is not applied by the courts except where the facts and circumstances and the demand of justice make its application essential, depending upon the facts and circumstances in each particular case." Nonetheless, the plaintiff retains his or her burden to prove the defendant's negligence. A defendant confronted properly with a res ipsa inference is obliged to go forward with his case, shouldering what has been described as the "risk of non-persuasion." In effect, res ipsa loquitur allows the plaintiff to present the question of negligence to the fact-finder, notwithstanding a lack of direct evidence bearing on causation.

To invoke successfully the doctrine, the plaintiff must establish that the accident was "(1) of a kind that does not ordinarily occur absent negligence, (2) that was caused by an instrumentality exclusively in the defendant's control, and (3) that was not caused by an act or omission of the plaintiff." Additionally, although not an indispensable requirement of res ipsa, "one of the circumstances which calls for the application of the doctrine is when the facts surrounding the accident are more within the knowledge of the defendant than within the knowledge of the plaintiff."

To satisfy the exclusive-control requirement, the evidence adduced must demonstrate that no third-party or other intervening force contributed more probably than not to the accident. We iterated in Holzhauer that a res ipsa inference of the defendant's negligence is not permissible where an intervening force may have precipitated the accident. The existence of that potentiality "weakens the probability that the injury is attributable to the defendant's [negligent] act or omission." In proving the absence of other, more-probable causes of the accident, the plaintiff "is not required to exclude every possible cause for [his] injuries other than that of negligence; [he] is only required to show a greater likelihood that [his] injury was caused by the defendant's negligence than by some other cause."

In sum, res ipsa loquitur requires the conclusion that, "by relying on common sense and experience, the incident more probably resulted from the defendant's negligence rather than from some other cause."

Respondents failed to show that negligence attributable to the District more probably caused the accident than other potential causes. This deficiency stems from their inability to recount personally the events leading to the bus leaving the travel-portion of Route 50 and their apparent decision not to adduce other reasonably available evidence that could have cast light on that inquiry (e.g., testimony from the bus driver, other bus passengers, motorists who witnessed the accident, emergency responders, or possibly the police accident report, if admissible in whole or in part). Respondents' attorney stated during oral argument before this Court that he spoke with witnesses, indicating that obviously some of these witnesses were known and accessible. Nonetheless, Respondents envisage that the nature of the accident entitled them merely to prove that the bus left the road and rest, taking advantage of res ipsa loquitur to plug the hole in the doughnut. Their position, however, belies the doctrine's requirement that plaintiffs' evidence must show that the defendant's negligence, and not a third-party causation or force, more probably than not caused the accident, given the particular circumstances of the accident.

In Hanes v. State ex rel. Lamm, we said that "[w]here a motor vehicle leaves the roadway without a prior collision and thereby causes injury or damage, the courts, as a general rule, are prepared to draw an inference of negligence from the occurrence, assuming, of course, that all the other conditions of applicability are met." Requiring plaintiffs to show that a motor vehicle left the roadway, without an antecedent collision, is not an absolute threshold condition for applying res ipsa loquitur. Rather, it represents one conception of the exclusive-control element of res ipsa whereby plaintiffs must demonstrate that the defendant's negligence, and not an intervening act such as another vehicle, more likely than not caused the accident.

We are persuaded also by the Supreme Court of Connecticut's case of Chasse v. Albert, where a sleeping passenger in a vehicle that left the road sued, on a negligence theory, the administratrix of the deceased driver's estate. The only evidence regarding the accident came from another driver, who was 150 yards away and uninvolved in the accident. The Supreme Court of Connecticut affirmed the trial court's directed verdict against the passenger, noting that the paucity of evidence did not warrant an inference of negligence: "[M]any possibilities, other than negligence on the part of the operator, existed as to the cause of the accident here. The doctrine of res ipsa loquitur was not available to the plaintiff in this situation."

Here, Respondents' perhaps unnecessarily bare-bones case-in-chief failed to eliminate sufficiently other causes of the accident, and failed to evince that the bus driver's negligence was the most probable causative factor. Respondents point out that their testimony established that the driving conditions were dry and that there were tire marks on Route 50 where the bus "jumped the median." This evidence, however, is ambiguous. Tire marks do not demonstrate necessarily that the speed of the bus was excessive relative to the ambient physical conditions or even the posted limit on that section of the road (there was no evidence of the latter or the speed of the bus as it crossed the median). "Tire-skid" marks, if that is what Singleton observed, could indicate also a sudden emergency, such as a tire blowout, avoiding another vehicle or other moving obstacle, an unforeseen medical emergency, or a mechanical failure unrelated to inadequate maintenance. Although plaintiffs are not required to exclude all other potential causes of the accident, Respondents' limited evidence here established only that "the probabilities are at best evenly divided between negligence and its absence," in which case "it becomes the duty of a court to direct a jury that there is no sufficient proof." Therefore, the trial court granted properly the District's motion for judgment.

Respondents' evidence failed to evince that the District's bus driver's negligence more probably than not caused the bus to leave the road because other potential causes were

[continued]

not explored or excluded sufficiently. Thus, we cannot say their evidence is "so clear and certain that the inference [of negligence] arises naturally."

Our conclusion that res ipsa loquitur is inapplicable in the present case is buoyed by Respondents' apparent tactical decision to avoid reasonably available witnesses. Application of res ipsa loquitur is justified, in some circumstances, by a defendant's superior access to identification of the facts surrounding the accident. Failing to produce reasonably available and likely probative witnesses, where substantive and direct evidence is otherwise lacking, leads to the inference that the facts surrounding the happening of the accident were equally accessible to the plaintiff and the defendant.

Here, Respondents failed to produce apparently reasonably accessible witnesses that might have supplemented their limited evidence with additional direct or circumstantial evidence of negligence. Although it is understandable that Respondents may have been loathe to call the bus driver, a listed defense witness and inferentially hostile to Respondents' case, Respondents' testimony established the existence of other potential witnesses: the other passengers on the bus, motorists "who actually saw the accident" and pulled over to help the accident victims, and emergency responders; nor did Respondents offer a copy of the police accident report. It may be inferred that Respondents had equal access as the defendant to the facts surrounding the accident. Therefore, Respondents may not rely upon res ipsa loquitur to satisfy their burden to adduce a prima facie case of negligence and thus defeat the District's motion for judgment.

. . . Respondents' inferred equal access to a fuller presentation of the facts of the accident cements our conclusion that the Circuit Court granted properly the District's motion for judgment.

REVERSED in favor the Defendant.

CRITICAL THINKING

What evidence does the judge say the defendants ought to have brought to court? Do you think this evidence would have helped them?

ETHICAL DECISION MAKING

Suppose you were a representative for the District of Columbia. The plaintiff's attorney has contacted you, claiming that the district was liable for the employee's negligence in this case. What would your response to the plaintiff's attorney be?

Business owners need to be mindful when selecting employees to work for their companies. When an employee engages in unlawful actions, it is the business owner who may actually end up in costly litigation. For example, when trash collector Christopher McCowen was found guilty for the murder and rape of well-known fashion writer Christa Worthington, the family of the deceased filed a $10 million lawsuit against his employer, Cape Cod Disposal. Worthington's family alleged that Donald Horton, the owner of Cape Cod Disposal, failed to use reasonable care when hiring McCowen and negligently sent the former criminal to collect Worthington's trash at her home. A background check after the murder revealed that McCowen had a violent past that included burglary, grand theft, felony assault, and trafficking of stolen property. Additionally, McCowen had been issued several restraining orders for threats against women. In 2007, Horton and the Worthington family settled for an undisclosed amount. Business owners may avoid negligent hiring and wrongful-death claims by using proper preemployment screening techniques. Many companies utilize background checks, call references, and verify previous employment to safeguard themselves and their employees against potential injury and liability.[7]

To see how paying and receiving a negligence judgment relates to income taxation, please see the **Connecting to the Core** activity on the text website at www.mhhe.com/kubasek3e.

NEGLIGENCE PER SE

Negligence per se (literally, "negligence in or of itself") is another doctrine that helps plaintiffs succeed in negligence cases. Negligence per se applies to cases in which the defendant has violated a statute enacted to prevent a certain type

[7] www.nytimes.com/2006/11/17/us/17cape.html; www.boston.com/news/local/articles/2005/05/18/cape_writers_family_sues_over_death/; and www.entrepreneur.com/tradejournals/article/161024244.html (all accessed March 3, 2009).

of harm from befalling a specific group to which the plaintiff belongs. If the defendant's violation causes the plaintiff to suffer from the type of harm that the statute intends to prevent, the violation is deemed negligence per se. The plaintiff does not have to show that a reasonable person would exercise a certain duty of care toward the plaintiff. Instead, the plaintiff can offer evidence of the defendant's violation of the statute to establish proof of the negligence.

For example, if Ohio passes a statute prohibiting the sale of alcohol to minors, and a minor runs a red light and kills two pedestrians while driving under the influence of alcohol sold to him illegally, the liquor store's violation of the statute prohibiting the sale of alcohol to minors establishes negligence per se on the part of the store. The families of the pedestrians do not need to establish that a reasonable person would have a duty not to sell alcohol to a minor.

A defendant who complies with legislative statutes, however, can still be held liable if a reasonable person would have exercised a more stringent duty of care toward the plaintiff. The legislative statutes are minimum, not sufficient, standards for behavior.

Before examining the defenses against negligence claims, compare the definition of negligence in the United States with its definition in South Africa, as described in the Comparing the Law of Other Countries box on the next page.

SPECIAL PLAINTIFF'S DOCTRINES AND STATUTES

In addition to recognizing *res ipsa loquitur* and negligence per se, some states have established other doctrines or statutes to aid plaintiffs in negligence suits. For example, suppose an airplane taxiing at Reagan National Airport in the winter runs off the runway and into the Potomac River due to the negligence of the airline. Some bystanders observe the crash and jump into the water to rescue the crash survivors. If any of the bystanders are injured while attempting to rescue the survivors, many courts will hold the airline liable for their injuries under what is known as the *danger invites rescue* doctrine.

Many states have also enacted statutes to aid plaintiffs in successfully establishing specific kinds of negligence claims. For instance, many states have **dram shop acts,** which allow bartenders and bar owners to be held liable for injuries caused by individuals who become intoxicated at the bar. Other states have passed laws that hold hosts liable for injuries caused by individuals who became intoxicated at the hosts' homes.

BUT WHAT IF. . .

WHAT IF THE FACTS OF THE CASE OPENER WERE DIFFERENT?

Let's say, in the Case Opener, that Curtis was a guest on the farm and became intoxicated at a gathering held on the farm. She wandered to the dock and improperly used it, causing it to collapse. Who is liable for the collapse of the dock and Curtis's injuries?

Defenses to Negligence

LO3 What are the defenses to a claim of negligence?

The courts' doctrines of *res ipsa loquitur* and negligence per se help the plaintiff in a negligence case, but the courts permit certain defenses that relieve the defendant from liability even when the plaintiff has proved all four elements of negligence. Defendants can successfully rebut negligence claims with contributory negligence, comparative negligence, assumption of the risk, and other special negligence defenses.

COMPARING THE LAW OF OTHER COUNTRIES

NEGLIGENCE IN SOUTH AFRICAN LAW

South Africa's legal system is a combination of selected legal traditions—from Roman to Dutch to German. The Roman *actiones legis Aquiliae* influences South Africa's statutes concerning liability. Under this Roman tradition, certain cases concerning liability mandate the presence of *culpa,* or negligence. South African law dictates that individuals can be found negligent in three different ways.

Negligence is first defined as failure to observe an accepted standard of conduct. In other words, individuals must exercise care and foresight with regard to others. A failure to do so indicates negligent behavior. Second, negligence is determined by whether the defendant could have prevented the consequent damages. The law expects individuals to take precautions to avoid harm or damage. Finally, South African law outlines the extent to which one can be found negligent in a crisis situation. In such instances, individuals have a duty to do what is "reasonably" expected. Because of the obvious ambiguity associated with this definition, South African law cites the American "doctrine of sudden emergency" as a standard for determining negligence in crisis situations. Encompassing all three of these definitions is an implicit duty of the individual to take precautions to prevent harm.

CONTRIBUTORY NEGLIGENCE

Contributory negligence, a defense once available in all states but replaced today in some states by the defense of comparative negligence (discussed in the next section), applies in cases in which the defendant and the plaintiff were both negligent. The defendant must prove that (1) the plaintiff's conduct fell below the standard of care needed to prevent unreasonable risk of harm and (2) the plaintiff's failure was a contributing cause to the plaintiff's injury. How can defendants use contributory negligence in a case? Some defense lawyers argue that if a plaintiff involved in a car accident failed to wear her seat belt, that failure constitutes contributory negligence because her action contributed to her injuries.

If the defendant successfully proves contributory negligence, no matter how slight the plaintiff's negligence, the plaintiff will be denied any recovery of damages. Because this defense seems unfair, many states have adopted the **last-clear-chance doctrine.** This doctrine allows the plaintiff to recover damages despite proof of contributory negligence as long as the defendant had a final clear opportunity to avoid the action that injured the plaintiff.

For example, suppose that Samantha and Nicole, in their cars, are facing each other while stopped at a red light. The light turns green, and Nicole starts to turn left at the intersection. Samantha sees Nicole start to turn, but she still continues to travel straight through the intersection and crashes into Nicole's car. Although Samantha had the right-of-way at the intersection, she could have avoided hitting Nicole's car by braking or swerving. Thus, according to the last-clear-chance doctrine, Nicole could recover damages.

Legal Principle: If the court finds that (1) the plaintiff's conduct fell below the standard of care needed to prevent unreasonable risk of harm and (2) the plaintiff's failure was a contributing cause of the plaintiff's injury, the defendant will not be liable for the plaintiff's injuries unless the plaintiff can prove that the defendant had the last opportunity to avoid the accident.

COMPARATIVE NEGLIGENCE

The adoption of the last-clear-chance doctrine, however, leaves many situations in which an extremely careless defendant can cause a great deal of harm to a plaintiff who is barred from recovery due to minimal contributory negligence. Thus, most states have replaced the contributory negligence defense with either pure or modified comparative negligence.

According to a **pure comparative negligence** defense, the court determines the percentage of fault of the defendant. The defendant is then liable for that percentage of the plaintiff's damages.

Courts calculate damages according to **modified comparative negligence** in the same manner, except that the defendant must be more than 50 percent at fault before the plaintiff can recover.

Twenty-eight states have adopted modified comparative negligence, thirteen have adopted pure comparative negligence, and nine have adopted contributory negligence. Every state has adopted one of these three defenses. Thus, the parties to a negligence suit cannot choose among them.

ASSUMPTION OF THE RISK

Another defense available to defendants facing negligence claims is called **assumption of the risk.** To use this defense successfully, a defendant must prove that the plaintiff voluntarily and unreasonably encountered the risk of the actual harm the defendant caused. In other words, the plaintiff willingly assumed as a risk the harm she suffered. There are two types of this defense. *Express assumption of the risk* occurs when the plaintiff expressly agrees (usually in a written contract) to assume the risk posed by the defendant's behavior. In contrast, *implied assumption of the risk* means that the plaintiff implicitly assumed a known risk.

The most difficult part of establishing this defense is showing that the plaintiff assumed the risk of the *actual* harm she suffered. A 1998 case against the Family Fitness Center illustrates an unsuccessful attempt to use assumption of the risk as a defense against a negligence claim.[8] In that case, the plaintiff was injured when a sauna bench on which he was lying collapsed beneath him at the defendant's facility. The trial court granted summary judgment in favor of the defendant on the basis of assumption of the risk. The plaintiff had signed a contract that included the following provision: "Buyer is aware that participation in a sport or physical exercise may result in accidents or injury, and Buyer assumes the risk connected with the participation in a sport or exercise and represents that Member is in good health and suffers from no physical impairment which would limit their use of FFC's facilities." The appellate court overturned the trial court's decision because the type of injury the plaintiff suffered was not the type of risk he had assumed. The court held that anyone signing a membership agreement could be deemed to have waived any hazard known to relate to the use of the health club facilities, such as the risk of a sprained ankle due to improper exercise or overexertion, a broken toe from a dropped weight, injuries due to malfunctioning exercise or sports equipment, or injuries from slipping in the locker-room shower. No patron, however, could be charged with realistically appreciating the risk of injury from simply reclining on a sauna bench. Because the collapse of a sauna bench, when properly used, is not a "known risk," the court concluded that the plaintiff did not assume the risk of this incident as a matter of law.

Case 9-3 illustrates the successful use of assumption of the risk as a defense. Compare this case to the action against the Family Fitness Center to see whether you agree with the different outcomes in the two cases.

[8] *Leon v. Family Fitness Center, Inc.*, 61 Cal. App. 4th 1227 (1998).

CASE 9-3 EX PARTE EMMETTE L. BARRAN III
SUPREME COURT OF ALABAMA
730 SO. 2D 203 (1998)

When Jason Jones enrolled at Auburn University in 1993, he chose to become a pledge of the Kappa Alpha fraternity. Within two days, Jones began to experience hazing by fraternity members. Hazing activities included the following: (1) digging a ditch and jumping into it after it was filled with water, urine, feces, dinner leftovers, and vomit; (2) receiving paddlings to his buttocks; (3) eating foods such as peppers, hot sauce, and butter; (4) being pushed and kicked; (5) doing chores for fraternity members; (6) appearing at 2 a.m. "meetings" where pledges would be hazed for several hours; and (7) "running the gauntlet," in which pledges would run down a hallway and flight of stairs while fraternity members would push, kick, and hit them. Although Jones was aware that 20–40% of the pledges dropped out of the pledge program, Jones remained in the program until he was suspended from the university for poor academic performance. In 1995, Jones sued the national and local Kappa Alpha organization, alleging negligence, assault and battery, negligent supervision, and various other claims. He argued that he suffered "mental and physical injuries" as a result of the hazing. For the negligence claims, the trial court granted summary judgment for Kappa Alpha. The trial court argued that Jones assumed the risk of hazing because he voluntarily entered the organization and could have quit at any time. Jones appealed, and the Court of Civil Appeals reversed the negligence ruling, reasoning that the peer pressure associated with fraternity life prevented Jones from voluntarily withdrawing from the pledge class. Kappa Alpha appealed.

JUSTICE SEE: Assumption of the risk has two subjective elements: (1) the plaintiff's knowledge and appreciation of the risk; and (2) the plaintiff's voluntary exposure to that risk. . . . [I]n order to find, as a matter of law, that Jones assumed the risk, this Court must determine that reasonable persons would agree that Jones knew and appreciated the risks of hazing and that he voluntarily exposed himself to those risks.

First, KA and its members argue that Jones knew and appreciated the risks inherent in hazing. . . . Jones's deposition indicates that before he became a KA pledge he was unfamiliar with the specific hazing practices engaged in at KA, but that the hazing began within two days of his becoming a pledge; that despite the severe and continuing nature of the hazing, Jones remained a pledge and continued to participate in the hazing activities for a full academic year; that Jones knew and appreciated that hazing was both illegal and against school rules; and that he repeatedly helped KA cover up the hazing by lying about its occurrence to school officials, his doctor, and even his own family. Given Jones's early introduction to the practice of hazing and its hazards, and in light of his own admission that he realized that hazing would continue to occur, the trial court correctly determined that reasonable people would conclude that Jones knew of and appreciated the risks of hazing.

Second, in addition to establishing that Jones both knew of and appreciated the risk, KA and the individual defendants argue that Jones voluntarily exposed himself to the hazing. Jones responds by arguing that a coercive environment hampered his free will to the extent that he could not voluntarily choose to leave the fraternity. The Court of Civil Appeals, in reversing the summary judgment as to KA and the individual defendants, stated that it was not clear that Jones voluntarily assumed the risk of hazing, because, that court stated:

> In today's society, numerous college students are confronted with the great pressures associated with fraternity life and . . . compliance with the initiation requirements places the students in a position of functioning in what may be construed as a coercive environment.

With respect to the facts in this case, we disagree. . . . The record indicates that Jones voluntarily chose to continue his participation in the hazing activities. After numerous hazing events, Jones continued to come back for more two o'clock meetings, more paddlings, and more gauntlet runs, and did so for a full academic year. Auburn University officials, in an effort to help him, asked him if he was being subjected to hazing activities, but he chose not to ask the officials to intervene. Jones's parents, likewise acting in an effort to help him, asked him if he was being subjected to hazing activities, but he chose not to ask his parents for help.

Moreover, we are not convinced by Jones's argument that peer pressure created a coercive environment that prevented him from exercising free choice. Jones had reached the age of majority when he enrolled at Auburn University and pledged the KA fraternity. We have previously noted: "College students and fraternity members are not children. Save for very few legal exceptions, they are adult citizens, ready, able, and willing to be responsible for their own actions." Thus, even for college students, the privileges of liberty are wrapped in the obligations of responsibility.

Jones realized that between 20% and 40% of his fellow pledges voluntarily chose to leave the fraternity and the hazing, but he chose to stay. See Prosser & Keeton, The Law of Torts 491 ("Where there is a reasonably safe alternative open, the plaintiff's choice of the dangerous way is a free one, and

[continued]

may amount to assumption of the risk. . . ."). As a responsible adult in the eyes of the law, Jones cannot be heard to argue that peer pressure prevented him from leaving the very hazing activities that, he admits, several of his peers left.

Jones's own deposition testimony indicates that he believed he was free to leave the hazing activities:

> *Q:* You didn't have to let this [hazing] happen to you, did you?
> *A:* No.
> *Q:* And you could have quit at any time?
> *A:* Yes.
> *Q:* But yet you chose to go through with what you have described here in your complaint with the aspirations that you were going to become a brother in the Kappa Alpha Order? You were willing to subject yourself to this for the chance to become a member of the brotherhood . . . were you not?
> *A:* Yes.

We conclude that Jones's participation in the hazing activities was of his own volition. The trial court correctly determined that reasonable people could reach no conclusion other than that Jones voluntarily exposed himself to the hazing.

REVERSED and REMANDED.

CRITICAL THINKING

Is there any important missing information that might influence your thinking about the court's conclusion that Jones participated in the hazing activities of his own volition? Why is this missing information important?

ETHICAL DECISION MAKING

Return to the WPH process of ethical decision making. Which stakeholders are affected by the court's decision? Why are these people affected?

Compare the defendant's use of the assumption-of-the-risk defense in Case 9-3 with the Kansas City Royals' attempt to use the defense in the Case Nugget on the next page.

Legal Principle: **If the plaintiff voluntarily and unreasonably encountered the risk of the actual harm the defendant caused, the defendant may raise the defense of assumption of the risk to avoid liability.**

SPECIAL DEFENSES TO NEGLIGENCE

Many states have additional ways to defend against a claim of negligence. For example, laws in some states hold that people in peril who receive voluntary aid from others cannot hold those offering aid liable for negligence. These laws, commonly called **Good Samaritan statutes,** attempt to encourage selfless and courageous behavior by removing the threat of liability.

The defendant in a negligence suit can also avoid liability by establishing a superseding cause. A *superseding cause* is an unforeseeable event that interrupts the causal chain between the defendant's breach of duty and the damages the plaintiff suffered. For example, suppose Jennifer is improperly storing ammonia in her garage when a meteor strikes her garage, spilling the ammonia into a stream nearby. Will, living downstream, drinks water from the stream and becomes dangerously ill. Because the meteor was unforeseeable, Jennifer is not liable for Will's injuries, even though she breached her duty of care to Will.

Superseding causes allow the defendant to avoid liability because they are evidence that the defendant's breach of duty was not the proximate cause of the plaintiff's injuries. In other words, superseding causes disprove the causation element necessary to sustain a negligence claim.

Strict Liability

Strict liability is liability without fault. The law holds an individual liable without fault when the activity in which she engages satisfies three conditions: (1) It involves a risk of serious harm to people or property; (2) it is so inherently dangerous that it cannot ever be

L04 What are the elements of strict liability?

CASE NUGGET

ASSUMING THE RISK OF A FLYING HOTDOG?

John Coomer v. Kansas City Royals Baseball Team
__S.W.3d ---, 2013 WL 150838 (Mo. App. W.D. 2013)

Coomer and his father were sitting in open seats six rows behind the third-base dugout. Between the third and fourth innings, the Royals had its promotional event, the "Hotdog Launch," during which Shores, the team mascot, shot a number of hot dogs into the stands with an air gun and then began tossing hot dogs into the stands by hand. Shores was in the third-base dugout, in front of Coomer and his father, and people behind them were cheering and yelling for Shores to throw hot dogs to them. Coomer saw Shores turn his back and make a motion with his arm behind his back; Coomer then looked away to the scoreboard and "a split second later" felt something hit him in the face and knock off his hat. Coomer assumed he had been hit with a line drive.

Two mornings later, Coomer had difficulty seeing, and he was subsequently diagnosed with a tearing and detached retina, requiring surgery. He lost vision for three weeks, and he developed a cataract, for which he had surgery, and now has an artificial lens in his eye.

Coomer sued the baseball team for negligence, but the jury found the plaintiff 100 percent at fault, applying jury instructions including the defense of primary assumption of the risk. Coomer appealed on grounds (among others) that a "mascot throwing hotdogs directly at business invitees is not an inherent or unavoidable risk of the game of baseball," which was the basis for the primary-assumption-of-risk defense.

To prove a claim for negligence, Coomer was required to show that (1) the Royals had a duty to conform to a standard of conduct to protect him from unreasonable risks, (2) that duty was breached, (3) the breach resulted in proximately causing him injury, and (4) he suffered damages.

The defendant raised the defense of assumption of the risk, which was successful at the trial court level. On appeal, however, the court overturned the trial court decision, ruling that the jury had been improperly instructed on the assumption-of-the-risk defense. The appellate judge stated that everyone who attends a baseball game assumes the risk of being hit by a ball, making that a risk inherent in the game. However, being hit by a hotdog is not a well-known incidental risk of attending a baseball game, even though the "Hotdog Launch" promotion had been a long-running event. Consequently, it could not be said that the plaintiff had consented to, and voluntarily assumed, the risk merely by attending the game. That tossing out promotional items is a customary activity does not equate to a fan's consent to the risk of being hit by a promotional item. According to the court, inherent risks are those that inure in the nature of the sport itself, not the general experience of enjoying the game.

safely undertaken; and (3) it is not usually performed in the immediate community. Instead of banning these activities, the law allows people to engage in such activities but holds them liable for all resulting harm.

Inherently dangerous activities include dynamite blasting in a populated area and keeping animals that have not been domesticated. If an animal has shown a "vicious propensity," strict liability applies and the owner of the animal is responsible for any injuries suffered in an attack by the animal.[9] If an individual keeps an animal that has not shown vicious propensity, he has a duty to warn and protect individuals who come into contact with the animal. As you will see in the next chapter, in today's society, strict liability has had an enormous impact on cases involving unreasonably dangerous products.

BUT WHAT IF. . .

WHAT IF THE FACTS OF THE CASE OPENER WERE DIFFERENT?

Let's say, in the Case Opener, that the farm owners spend a little time each day trying to knock down the dock so that they can be rid of it. Eventually the dock is extremely unsafe, but they leave it up, deciding to completely take it apart at a later time. What three conditions would this situation have to satisfy to result in strict liability? Does this situation meet the three conditions?

[9] *Schwartz v. Armand ERPF Estate,* 688 N.Y.S.2d 55 (Sup. Ct., App. Div., N.Y. 1999).

CASE OPENER WRAP-UP

The Case of the Collapsing Dock

The appellate court affirmed the decision of the trial court, which claimed that the doctrine of *res ipsa loquitur* did not apply. The plaintiff then sought review of the appellate court's decision. On review the court ruled that the plaintiff could in fact rely on the doctrine of *res ipsa loquitur* to fill the evidentiary gaps of the case. According to the court, the plaintiff showed all the necessary elements to rely on the doctrine to prove negligence: (1) the accident would not ordinarily happen in the absence of negligence because properly maintained wooden docks do not give way under foot; (2) there was no evidence before the court that the dock was not in the exclusive control of the defendants; and (3) the plaintiff herself did not contribute in any way to the accident.

In conclusion, the court reversed the appellate court's ruling that the doctrine of *res ipsa loquitur* did not apply and remanded the case to trial by jury. Whether the plaintiff's injury was caused by negligence on the part of the defendants is to be decided by the future jury.

KEY TERMS

actual cause 219
assumption of the risk 227
compensatory damages 221
contributory negligence 226
dram shop acts 225
Good Samaritan statutes 229
gross negligence 221
last-clear-chance doctrine 226
modified comparative negligence 227
negligence 215
negligence per se 224
proximate cause 219
punitive damages 221
pure comparative negligence 226
reasonable person standard 216
res ipsa loquitur 221
strict liability 229
unfortunate accident 215

SUMMARY OF KEY TOPICS

Introduction to Negligence and Strict Liability

When an individual fails to maintain a duty of care to protect other individuals, negligence and strict liability may occur.

Elements of Negligence

Duty: The standard of care that the defendant (i.e., a reasonable person) owes the plaintiff.

Breach of duty: The defendant's lack of maintaining the standard of care a reasonable person would owe the plaintiff.

Causation: The defendant's conduct (breach of duty) that led to the plaintiff's injury.

Damages: Compensable injuries suffered by the plaintiff.

Plaintiff's Doctrines

Res ipsa loquitur: Doctrine that permits the judge or jury to *infer* that the defendant's negligence was the cause of the plaintiff's harm in cases in which there is no direct evidence of the defendant's lack of due care.

	Negligence per se: Doctrine that permits a plaintiff to prove negligence by offering evidence of the defendant's violation of a statute that has been enacted to prevent a certain type of harm.
Defenses to Negligence	*Contributory negligence:* A defense that allows the defendant to entirely escape liability by demonstrating any degree of negligence on the part of the plaintiff that contributed to the plaintiff's harm.
	Comparative negligence: A defense that allows the liability to be apportioned between plaintiff and defendant in accordance with the degree of responsibility each bears for the harm suffered by the plaintiff.
	Assumption of the risk: A defense that allows the defendant to escape liability by establishing that the plaintiff engaged in an activity fully aware that the type of harm he or she suffered was a possible consequence of engaging in that activity.
Strict Liability	Persons who engage in activities that are so inherently dangerous that no amount of due care can make them safe are strictly liable, regardless of the degree of care they used when undertaking the activity.

POINT / COUNTERPOINT

Should Negligence Law Hold All Individuals to the Reasonable Person Standard?

NO

One major problem with the reasonable person standard is that it fails to set up clear rules to which individuals can conform their behavior. "Reasonableness" varies tremendously from one person to another; what one person considers reasonable, another considers unnecessary. Unclear laws also discourage efficiency because both the plaintiff and the defendant may believe they are likely to be victorious in court and thus have little incentive to settle. When the law is clear, individuals have a better idea of the strength of their case, and those with poor chances of victory have an incentive to settle and thereby avoid costly litigation expenses.

In addition, the reasonable person standard holds all individuals to the same duty of care, regardless of their individual characteristics. This standard is unfair to individuals who exercise all the possible care of which they are capable yet whose level of care still does not meet the reasonable person standard. Alternatively, individuals can exercise levels of care that they know create a substantial likelihood of harm to others yet the care satisfies the reasonable person standard. Thus, the reasonable person standard functions like a regressive tax. To promote fairness to all defendants, tort law ought to take into account individualized factors. Instead of asking whether the defendant has behaved reasonably, the law ought to ask whether the defendant has behaved reasonably given his or her individual characteristics, including age, education, gender, wealth, and so on.

YES

The law should certainly concern itself with fairness to defendants, but that concern is only half the story. The law also ought to concern itself with fairness to plaintiffs. A plaintiff who gets run over by a high school dropout is no less injured than a plaintiff who gets run over by a professor. Yet an individualized negligence standard might allow the second plaintiff to recover but not the first. Civil society requires a certain absolute level of care from all its members, regardless of their individual predispositions.

Moreover, a more individualized standard in negligence law would tend to decrease, not increase, the clarity of the law. An injured defendant would have to ascertain the plaintiff's individual characteristics to determine the likelihood of victory in court, and more variables mean more uncertainty. Who owes a higher standard of care: a college-educated yet poor defendant or a high school–educated yet rich defendant? If the law wants to promote uniformity, consistency, and stability, it ought to use a uniform standard, not a more individualized one.

Finally, it is not clear how individualized characteristics of a defendant would count. How does a defendant's gender affect the standard of care to which the law will hold him or her? If women are held to a different standard of care than men, is the law making a statement about the relative reasonableness of men and women?

QUESTIONS & PROBLEMS

1. Explain the differences between contributory and comparative negligence.
2. Explain the relationship between negligence per se and *res ipsa loquitur.*
3. Explain the purpose of Good Samaritan statutes.
4. List and describe the elements that must be proved for a successful strict-liability claim.
5. The plaintiff's father collapsed near the racquetball courts of a Bally's health club. While an ambulance was being called, a Bally's employee trained in cardiopulmonary resuscitation and the use of the club's automatic external defibrillator (AED) assessed the man's medical condition. The employee decided that neither life-saving measure was appropriate given that the heart attack victim was breathing and had a pulse. He left the man to check on the status of the 911 response, and when he returned to the plaintiff's father, two club members, a doctor and a medical student, were administering CPR.

   Upon arrival, the paramedics shocked the father with an AED, but he never recovered. The plaintiff submitted the affidavit of a board-certified cardiologist, who opined that the father's "chances of survival would have been significantly higher if the AED had been used within the first few minutes after his collapse" rather than upon arrival of the ambulance.

   At the time of the incident, the state had a law that required all health clubs in the state to provide on the premises an AED and a person in attendance at the club who was properly certified to operate an AED and perform CPR.

   The trial court initially dismissed the case on grounds that the state law requiring health clubs to have AEDs on the premises did not impose a duty on health clubs to use the devices in cardio emergencies. On appeal, the court overturned the dismissal, saying that the plaintiff should have an opportunity to present his case not based on the statutory duty of defendants but based on a different duty. What duty do you think that, according to the court, the plaintiff should have a chance to prove the defendant breached? *Miglino v. Bally Total Fitness of Greater New York,* [New York State Court of Appeals No. 10. Feb. 7, 2013. Lawyers USA No. 993–3800.]
6. Mary Dobsa owned a home in Biloxi, Mississippi, in which she and Neil Paul resided. Countrywide Home Loans, Inc., was the mortgage lender on the home. Before financing and in accordance with the National Flood Insurance Act, Countrywide selected Landsafe to determine whether Dobsa's home was located in a federal flood zone. Dobsa paid for Landsafe's services. Landsafe indicated that the home was not situated in a flood-hazard area. Accordingly, Countrywide provided financing without requiring Dobsa to obtain flood insurance through the National Flood Insurance Program. Unfortunately, Hurricane Katrina struck and caused substantial damage to this residence for which no flood insurance coverage existed. It was then learned that the home was actually located in a flood-hazard area. Dobsa and Paul sued Landsafe, alleging negligence and negligent misrepresentation. The district court granted Landsafe's motion for summary judgment. Dobsa appealed. How did the court rule on appeal? Why? [*Paul v. Landsafe Flood Determination, Inc.,* 550 F.3d 511 (5th Cir. 2008).]
7. Plaintiff Caruso was gambling at the Foxwoods Casino, which was owned by defendant Mashantucket Pequot Gaming Enterprise. When he went to use the restroom, Caruso noticed an attendant holding a mop in his hand. Almost immediately thereafter, Caruso slipped and fell on the floor in an area that had just been mopped. To gain compensation for the injuries he suffered from the fall, he sued the casino for negligence for failing to place warning signs or cones around the just-mopped area. The casino argued that contributory negligence on the part of Caruso in failing to pay attention to his surroundings in light of the obviousness of the danger should bar him from recovering. How do you believe the court ruled in this case and why? [*Caruso v. Mashantucket Pequot Gaming Enterprise,* 2010 WL 323079 (Mash. Pequot Tribal Ct. 2010).]
8. Mashantucket Pequot Gaming Enterprise owned a casino that Scanlon was patronizing. Scanlon was viewed on a security camera standing on a box on a balcony. Two security guards went to investigate because they were concerned for the customer's safety. Scanlon told the guards that he was fine and had just talked another patron out of

committing suicide on that very spot. The guards still did not want him standing on the box, so they walked Scanlon out of that area and into the main mall area of the casino. After they left him, Scanlon evidently went back to where he had been and jumped, killing himself. His heirs sued the casino for negligently causing the death of Scanlon by not taking steps to prevent him from committing suicide. The casino filed a motion to dismiss. How do you think the court ruled in this case and why? [*Scanlon v. Mashantucket Pequot Gaming Enterprise,* 2009 WL 4188488 (Mash. Pequot Tribal Ct. 2009).]

9. David Glenn Koch and Roderick Cook were employees of International Tentnology Corporation (InTents), a company that provides and installs equipment for events and parties. InTents set up a tent for the Chile Pepper Festival that is held in an open field at the University of Arkansas. Koch and Cook, as well as four other employees of InTents, were moving a large, fully assembled hexagonal tent across the field. To avoid a temporary mesh fence in their path, they attempted to lift the tent over it. The aluminum center support pole of the tent hit an energized overhead power line and three of the men, including Koch and Cook, were fatally electrocuted. Three others were severely injured. The administrators of the estates of Koch and Cook sued Southwestern Electric Power Company (SWEPCO). SWEPCO maintains and operates the power line traversing the field. The line is at least 25 feet above the ground and complies with National Electric Safety Code clearance requirements. The line was installed at a time when the area was much more rural than it is today, and the estates contend that SWEPCO was negligent in not elevating, burying, or insulating the line now that the field is occasionally used for major public events. The district court granted SWEPCO's motion for summary judgment on the ground that it had had no legal duty because it had not received written notification that work would be occurring near the power line. The estates appealed, conceding that no notification was sent to the utility but arguing that SWEPCO owed the decedents a duty of care. Did SWEPCO owe any duty of care to anyone using the field for public events? Was the failure to change the line enough to constitute negligence? Why? [*Koch v. Southwestern Electric Power Co.,* 544 F.3d 906 (8th Cir. 2008).]

Looking for more review materials?

The Online Learning Center at **www.mhhe.com/kubasek3e** contains this chapter's "Assignment on the Internet" and also a list of URLs for more information, entitled "On the Internet." Find both of them in the Student Center portion of the OLC, along with quizzes and other helpful materials.

Product Liability

CHAPTER 10

LEARNING OBJECTIVES

After reading this chapter, you will be able to answer the following questions:

1 What are the theories of liability in product liability cases?

2 What is market share liability?

CASE OPENER

Is Human Sperm Subject to Product Liability Laws?

Many single women and married couples use donated sperm to conceive children each year. Pennsylvania resident Donna Donovan decided to use donated sperm from Idant Laboratories, a New York sperm bank that emphasized (1) its screening process far exceeded mandated standards and (2) its rigorous screening process ensured that donors had a good genetic history. After using sperm from Idant Laboratories, Donovan gave birth to a girl, Brittany. Donovan began noticing abnormalities in Brittany's development, and Brittany was soon diagnosed as a Fragile X baby. Fragile X is a genetic mutation that causes a range of mental and physical impairments, such as learning disabilities, mental retardation, and behavior disorders. A genetic test for Fragile X was developed two years before Donovan used the sperm from Idant Laboratories. Two years after Brittany's birth, genetic tests showed that the sperm from Idant Laboratories was the carrier of the Fragile X defect. Donovan and Brittany brought suit against Idant Laboratories for selling defective sperm.

1. What do you think the outcome of Donovan's case was?
2. Should the sale of sperm be considered the sale of a product?
3. How do product liability issues affect you?

The Wrap-Up at the end of the chapter will answer these questions.

Breast implants, Ford Explorers, cigarettes, pet food, fast food, fingers in fast food—all of these topics have been the subject of product liability suits. According to the U.S. Department of Justice's Bureau of Justice Statistics, approximately 5 percent of state tort trials in 2005 involved product liability issues.[1] Approximately 25 percent of these trials addressed toxic substances, such as asbestos, tobacco, chemicals, and other toxic substances. The median award to plaintiffs in state court product liability cases that went to trial was $500,000. Each year, juries award hundreds of millions of dollars to plaintiffs bringing suit against companies offering products. If a company manufactures or sells a product, it should expect to be a party to a product liability lawsuit.

In this chapter, we examine the legal theories commonly used by plaintiffs in product liability cases, along with some of the defenses that are used against these cases. By understanding the law of product liability, you may be less likely to take actions that would lead you and your company into costly litigation.

Theories of Liability for Defective Products

L01

What are the theories of liability in product liability cases?

Product liability law is based primarily on tort law. There are three commonly used theories of recovery in product liability cases: negligence, strict product liability, and breach of warranty. A plaintiff may bring a lawsuit based on as many of these theories of liability as apply to the plaintiff's factual situation. While a plaintiff must establish different elements under each of these theories, the plaintiff must generally show two common elements: (1) that the product is defective, and (2) that the defect existed when the product left the defendant's control.

How might a product be defective? Suppose you select a glass bottle of Diet Coke at the grocery store. When you grab the bottle, it shatters in your hand and severely cuts your thumb. Most bottles of soda do not shatter when touched; thus, there must have been a problem in the manufacture of this particular bottle. When an individual product (e.g., the shattered Diet Coke bottle) has a defect making it more dangerous than other identical products (the 200 other Diet Coke bottles at the grocery store), this individual product has a **manufacturing defect.**

Given your severe cut from the Diet Coke bottle, you get into your car to drive to the hospital. Unfortunately, someone rear-ends your car; the crash causes your driver's seat to bend backward such that you hit your head on the backseat and suffer a serious neck injury. The design of the driver's seat allowed the seat to bend backward, and all driver's seats in this type of car have the same design. When all products of a particular design are defective and dangerous, these products have a **design defect.**

Because of the pain associated with your neck injury and lacerated thumb, you take a new over-the-counter pain reliever. You read and follow the instructions on the box and take two pills. However, you begin to feel incredibly ill. You rush to the hospital and discover that you are experiencing negative side effects from the pain reliever because it has interacted with some of your other medications. You had carefully read the instructions and warnings, but you did not see anything about drug interactions. A product may be defective as a result of the manufacturer's **failure to provide adequate warnings** about potential dangers associated with the product.

The product examples above (Diet Coke bottle, driver's seat in a car, pain reliever) are tangible items. However, can an intangible "product" be subject to product liability claims? See the Case Nugget "What Is a Product?"

[1] Bureau of Justice Statistics, "Civil Justice Survey of State Courts: Tort Breach and Jury Trials in State Courts, 2005," November 2009, http://bjs.ojp.usdoj.gov/content/pub/pdf/tbjtsc05.pdf.

CASE NUGGET

WHAT IS A PRODUCT?

Radford v. Wells Fargo Bank
2011 WL 1833020 (D. Haw. 2011)

Plaintiff Richard Radford brought a suit against Wells Fargo Bank alleging that he was enticed into purchasing a defective product and claiming an intentional or negligent failure to warn of a defective product (i.e., his mortgage loan). The district court held that a mortgage is not a "product" that can be subject to product liability claims for at least three reasons. First, "[p]roducts liability covers products that are reasonably certain to place life and limb in peril and may cause bodily harm if defective. The language of products liability law reflects its focus on tangible items." Second, the Restatement (Second) of Torts provides examples of items covered by product liability claims, and a mortgage loan does not appear on the list. Finally, there was no case law in Hawaii supporting Radford's contention that a loan is a product.

In summary, a product may be defective because of a manufacturing defect, a design defect, or inadequate warnings. As you read the chapter, think about how these types of defects fit in with the three theories of liability: negligence, strict liability, and breach of warranty.

NEGLIGENCE

To win a case based on negligence, the plaintiff must prove the four elements of negligence explained in Chapter 9: (1) The defendant manufacturer or seller owed a duty of care to the plaintiff; (2) the defendant breached that duty of care by supplying a defective product; (3) this breach of duty caused the plaintiff's injury; and (4) the plaintiff suffered actual injury.

Prior to the landmark 1916 case of *MacPherson v. Buick Motor Co.,* negligence was rarely used as a theory of recovery for an injury caused by a defective product because of the difficulty of establishing the element of duty. Until that case, the courts said that a plaintiff who was not the purchaser of the defective product could not establish a duty of care, because one could not owe a duty to someone with whom one was not "in privity of contract." Being *in privity of contract* means being a party to a contract. Because most consumers do not purchase goods directly from the manufacturers, product liability cases against manufacturers were rare before the *MacPherson* case.

Following *MacPherson,* any foreseeable plaintiff can sue a manufacturer for its breach of duty of care. Foreseeable plaintiffs include users, consumers, and bystanders. Moreover, foreseeable plaintiffs can bring a case against retailers, wholesalers, and manufacturers. However, retailers and wholesalers can satisfy their duty of care by making a cursory reasonable inspection of a product when they receive it from the manufacturer.

Negligent Failure to Warn. To bring a successful case based on negligent failure to warn, the plaintiff must demonstrate that the defendant knew or should have known that without a warning, the product would be dangerous in its ordinary use, or in any *reasonably foreseeable* use, yet the defendant still failed to provide a warning. For example, the 10th Circuit recently affirmed a trial court decision in which a smoker was awarded approximately $200,000 from R. J. Reynolds Tobacco, which before 1969 had negligently failed to warn smokers of the harm associated with smoking cigarettes. No duty to warn exists for dangers arising either from unforeseeable misuses of a product or from obvious dangers. A producer of razor blades, for example, need not give a warning that a razor

Prior to these required warning labels on cigarette packages, one basis for suing the tobacco industry was failure to warn.

CASE NUGGET

MCDONALD'S COFFEE IS HOT!

Liebeck v. McDonald's Corp.
No. D-202 CV-93-02419

One of the most famous product liability cases is the McDonald's coffee-cup case. Stella Liebeck, a 79-year-old woman, spilled a cup of McDonald's coffee in her lap. She sued McDonald's, and in 1994, a jury awarded her almost $3 million in damages. Many people cite the case as an example of the need for product liability law reform; however, they either intentionally or inadvertently omit a discussion of the facts of the case:

- Liebeck spilled the entire cup of coffee in her lap. McDonald's required that its franchises serve coffee at 180 to 190 degrees Fahrenheit. Liquid at this high temperature causes third-degree burns in two to seven seconds. Liebeck suffered third-degree burns on her skin that required skin grafting. She was in the hospital for eight days and required two years of treatment for the burns.
- Liebeck asked McDonald's to cover her medical costs and settle the case for $20,000; McDonald's offered $800. She filed the lawsuit after McDonald's refused to raise its offer from $800.
- Through documents produced by McDonald's, Liebeck discovered that between 1982 and 1992, McDonald's had received over 700 complaints about the temperature of the coffee. Some of these complaints discussed burns in varying degrees of severity, and McDonald's had previously received claims arising from burn complaints for over $500,000.
- Before the beginning of the jury trial, a retired judge, who was serving as a mediator, recommended that the parties settle the case for $225,000. McDonald's refused.
- While the jury awarded Liebeck $200,000 in compensatory damages and $2,700,000 in punitive damages, the court reduced the damages award to $160,000 in compensatory damages (finding Liebeck 20 percent at fault in the spill) and $480,000 in punitive damages. The parties ultimately settled the case for an undisclosed amount under $600,000.

How do these facts affect your thinking about product liability law?

blade may cut someone. For example, in *Ward v. Arm & Hammer,*[2] after being convicted on criminal charges for distribution of crack cocaine, the plaintiff brought suit against Arm & Hammer, arguing that the company should have included a warning on its package of baking soda of the criminal consequences of using the baking soda to make cocaine. The court emphasized that the manufacturer of a raw component that is not in itself dangerous has no duty to warn the public of the dangers associated with combining that component in a dangerous or criminal manner. Courts often consider the likelihood of the injury, the seriousness of the injury, and the ease of warning when deciding whether a manufacturer was negligent in failing to warn. To the extent that a company is aware of potential harm associated with reasonably foreseeable uses of its products, the safest course of action for the company is to identify this harm to the consumers as a warning.

When providing a warning, the manufacturer must ensure that the warning will reach those who are intended to use the product. For example, if parties other than the original purchaser will be likely to use the product, the warning should be placed directly on the product itself, not just in a manual that comes with the product. Picture warnings may be required if children, or those who are illiterate, are likely to come into contact with the product and risk harm from its use.

Products such as drugs and cosmetics are often the basis for actions based on negligent failure to warn because the use of these products frequently causes adverse reactions. When the user of a cosmetic or an over-the-counter drug has a reaction to that product, many courts find that there is no duty to warn unless the plaintiff proves that (1) the product contained an ingredient to which an appreciable number of people would have an adverse reaction; (2) the defendant knew or should have known, in the exercise of ordinary care, about the existence of this group; and (3) the plaintiff's reaction was due to his or her membership in this abnormal group.

[2] 341 F. Supp. 2d (D.N.J. 2004).

CASE NUGGET

FAILURE TO WARN ABOUT FOOD

Pelman v. McDonald's
237 F. Supp. 2d 512 (S.D.N.Y 2003)

Consumers have recently been bringing cases that attempt to hold others liable for their health problems allegedly caused by unhealthy food. In *Pelman v. McDonald's,* the plaintiffs alleged that McDonald's failed to warn customers of the "ingredients, quantity, qualities and levels of cholesterol, fat, salt and sugar content and other ingredients in those products, and that a diet high in fat, salt, sugar and cholesterol could lead to obesity and health problems." Judge Sweet originally dismissed the plaintiffs' claims, stating his decision was guided by the principle that legal consequences should not attach to the consumption of hamburgers and other fast-food fare unless consumers are unaware of the dangers of eating such food. He determined that consumers know, or should reasonably know, the potential negative health effects associated with eating fast food. The plaintiffs filed an amended complaint, asserting that McDonald's engaged in a scheme of deceptive advertising that in effect created the impression that McDonald's food products were nutritionally beneficial and part of a healthy lifestyle. In September 2006, Judge Sweet refused to dismiss the plaintiffs' claims, and as of February 2010, the case was still moving forward as a class action.

Similarly, in *Gorran v. Atkins Nutritionals, Inc.,* Jody Gorran argued that he developed heart disease by following the Atkins diet, which encourages dieters to limit carbohydrates such as bread, rice, and pasta while increasing meat, cheese, eggs, and other high-protein (and high-fat) foods.* According to Gorran's complaint, Atkins Nutritionals promoted the health benefits of its diet while knowing that some people were "fat-sensitive" and subject to adverse health effects, yet Atkins failed to warn the public. The court determined that as long as the food was sold in a condition anticipated by the consumer, it was not a defective product simply because it could negatively affect the consumer's health.

* "Judge Rebuffs Atkins' Second Bid to Dismiss Dieter's Lawsuit," *Andrews Product Liability Litigation Reporter* 16, no. 1 (2005), p. 2.

Other courts, however, use a balancing test to determine negligence in such cases. They weigh the degree of danger to be avoided with the ease of warning. For example, in 1994, a jury awarded over $8.8 million to a man who suffered permanent liver damage as a result of drinking a glass of wine with a Tylenol capsule (the award was reduced to $350,000 due to a statutory cap). As early as 1977, the company knew that combining a normal dose of Tylenol with a small amount of wine could cause massive liver damage in some people, but the company failed to put a warning to that effect on the label because such a reaction was rare. Through the balancing test, the court found that the degree of potential harm was substantial and that it would have been relatively easy to place a warning on the product label.

Furthermore, some courts have permitted a "sophisticated-user" defense, which acts as a complete defense to failure-to-warn claims. For example, in a 2008 case, the Supreme Court of California adopted the sophisticated-user defense, noting that a user's knowledge of certain dangers is equivalent to notice. In that case, the plaintiff was a trained and certified heating, ventilation, and air-conditioning (HVAC) technician who alleged that he suffered harm from exposure to a certain gas frequently used in air-conditioning systems. Because the training and certification for HVAC taught about the harm related to this gas, the court determined that the technician, as a sophisticated or educated user, could not recover.

Negligence Per Se. As you know from Chapter 9, a statute violation that causes the harm that the statute was enacted to prevent constitutes *negligence per se.* This doctrine is also applicable to product liability cases based on negligence. When a law establishes labeling, design, or content requirements for products, the manufacturer has a duty to meet these requirements. Failure by the manufacturer to meet those standards means that the manufacturer has breached its duty of reasonable care. If the plaintiff can establish that the failure to meet such a standard caused injury, the plaintiff can recover under negligence per se.

Damages. Damages that are recoverable in negligence-based product liability cases are the same as those in any action based on negligence: compensatory damages and punitive damages. As you should recall from Chapter 8, *compensatory damages* are those designed to make the plaintiff whole again; they cover items such as medical bills, lost wages, and compensation for pain and suffering. While this list of recoverable harms may seem "obvious" to us, not all countries allow such extensive recovery. For example, in German product liability cases, consumers do not have a right to recover damages for pain and suffering or for emotional distress. *Punitive damages* are meant to punish the defendant for extremely harmful conduct. The amount of the punitive-damage award is determined by the wealth of the defendant and the maliciousness of the action.

In 2009–2011, Toyota announced that millions of its cars would be recalled due to acceleration and braking problems. As of February 2010, dozens of product liability lawsuits had been filed against Toyota. In many of these cases, plaintiffs were seeking damages for personal injuries or wrongful death due to the alleged acceleration and braking problems. Some of these cases were claims against Toyota to recover damages for the reduced value of their cars. Specifically, before the recall, Toyota owners claim that they could resell their cars at a certain price; after the recall, this price was several thousand dollars lower. In fact, the *Kelley Blue Book* reported that the resale value of Toyota models fell 1 to 3 percent in just one week following certain recalls.[3]

In December 2012, Toyota agreed to pay over $1 billion to settle the class action litigation regarding the loss-of-economic-value claims related to the recalls.[4] The National Highway Traffic Safety Administration fined Toyota more than $60 million for failing to inform regulators of internal information Toyota had regarding the sudden acceleration.

Legal Principle: **The plaintiff in a product liability case may recover compensatory damages, designed to provide compensation for provable losses, and punitive damages, an amount awarded to punish the defendant.**

Defenses to a Negligence-Based Product Liability Action. The defenses to negligence discussed in the previous chapter are available in product liability cases based on negligence. A common defense in such cases is that the plaintiff's own failure to act reasonably contributed to the plaintiff's own harm. This negligence on the part of the plaintiff allows the defendant to raise the defense of *contributory, comparative,* or *modified comparative negligence,* depending on which defense is accepted by the state where the case arose. Remember, in a state that allows the contributory negligence defense, proof of any negligence by the plaintiff is an absolute bar to recovery. In a state where the defense of pure comparative negligence is allowed, the plaintiff can recover for only that portion of the harm attributable to the defendant's negligence. In a modified comparative negligence state, the plaintiff can recover the percentage of harm caused by the defendant as long as the jury finds the plaintiff's negligence responsible for less than 50 percent of the harm.

A closely related defense is *assumption of the risk.* This defense arises when a consumer knows that a defect exists but still proceeds unreasonably to make use of the product, creating a situation in which the consumer has voluntarily assumed the risk of injury from the defect and thus cannot recover. To decide whether the plaintiff did indeed assume the risk, the trier of fact may consider such factors as the plaintiff's age, experience, knowledge, and understanding, as well as the obviousness of the defect and the danger it poses. When a plaintiff knows of a danger but does not fully appreciate the magnitude of the risk, the applicability of the defense is a question for the jury to determine.

Another common defense is *misuse* of the product. The misuse must be unreasonable or unforeseeable. When a defendant raises the defense of product misuse, the defendant is really arguing that the harm was caused not by the defendant's negligence but by the plaintiff's failure to properly use the product.

[3] Nick Bunkley, "Some Toyota Owners Voice an Eroding Loyalty," *The New York Times,* February 7, 2010.

[4] Bill Vlasic, "Toyota Agrees to Settle Lawsuit Tied to Accelerations," *New York Times,* December 26, 2012.

COMPARING THE LAW OF OTHER COUNTRIES

PRODUCT MISUSE IN JAPAN

Like the United States, Japan also addresses situations in which the consumer misuses a defective product. In Japan, such a situation is called *comparative negligence.* The negligence of both the defendant and the plaintiff is taken into account when determining the distribution of damages. The leading case of comparative negligence is that of *Miyahara v. Matsumoto Gas Company.* In this case, the defendant purchased a gas stove from Matsumoto. A faulty rubber nose valve caused the stove to start a fire, resulting in extensive damage to Miyahara's home. An investigation after the fire, however, showed that Miyahara had failed to close the valve before going to sleep the evening of the fire. Consequently, both he and the gas company were found negligent. The cost of the damages was split between the two parties.

The *state-of-the-art defense* is used by a defendant to demonstrate that his alleged negligent behavior was reasonable, given the available scientific knowledge existing at the time the product was sold or produced. If a case is based on the defendant's negligent defective design of a product, the state-of-the-art defense refers to the technological feasibility of producing a safer product at the time the product was manufactured. In cases of negligent failure to warn, the state-of-the-art defense refers to the scientific knowability of a risk associated with a product at the time of its production. This is a valid defense in a negligence case because the focus is on the reasonableness of the defendant's conduct. However, the state of scientific knowledge at the time of production, and the lack of a feasible way to make a safer product, does not always preclude liability. The court may find that the defendant's conduct was still unreasonable because even in its technologically safest form, the risks posed by the defect in the design so outweighed the benefits of the product that the reasonable person would not have produced a product of that design.

Suppose a defendant designs a product to comply with federal safety regulations regarding that product. That defendant may attempt to argue that *compliance with federal laws* is a defense to state tort law because the state tort law is preempted by a federal statute designed to ensure the safety of a particular class of products. The Supreme Court recently issued a ruling on whether a state tort claim was preempted because the FDA had approved the drug label (see Case 10-1).

Each preemption case requires careful scrutiny of the purpose of the statute. For example, in *Tebbetts v. Ford Motor Co.,* the plaintiff argued that the 1988 Ford Escort was defectively designed because it did not have a driver's side air bag. Ford raised the preemption defense, arguing that it had complied with federal safety regulations under the National Traffic and Motor Vehicle Safety Act (NTMVSA). Consequently, Ford argued that its compliance preempted recovery under state product liability laws. After considering the legislative history and the law, the court discovered a clause in the law stating that "[c]ompliance with any Federal motor vehicle safety standard issued under this act does not exempt any person from any liability under common law." Thus, the court ruled that the Tebbetts were not preempted from bringing their product liability action.

Similarly, oil companies have argued that their compliance with the Clean Air Act should not subject them to tort liability for MTBE contamination in groundwater. Through the Clean Air Act, Congress required that oil companies include an oxygenate in gasoline to allow the gasoline to burn more cleanly and thus to improve air quality. MTBE, or methyl tertiary butyl ether, is one type of oxygenate. While everyone expected MTBE to help improve air quality, widespread use of this oxygenate had a negative consequence: It contaminated water. A very small amount of MTBE affects the smell and taste of water. Given these extreme negative consequences, numerous states banned MTBE. Moreover, cities and individuals have sued oil companies to pay for the costs, in the millions of dollars, that will be incurred to clean the drinking water. While a few courts have agreed with

CASE 10-1 WYETH v. LEVINE
UNITED STATES SUPREME COURT
555 U.S. 555, 2009, 129 S. CT. 1187 (2009)

Diana Levine, a professional musician, sought treatment for her migraine headaches and was given an injection of Wyeth's antinausea drug, Phenergan. While the drug was supposed to be injected directly into Levine's vein through a method called the IV-push method, the drug entered an artery instead. Consequently, Levine developed gangrene and had to have her right hand and entire forearm amputated. She incurred substantial medical expenses and could no longer perform as a professional musician. At trial, Levine argued that Wyeth's labeling was defective because although it warned of the danger of gangrene and amputation following inadvertent intra-arterial injection, it failed to instruct clinicians to use the IV-drip method of intravenous administration instead of the higher-risk IV-push method. The jury agreed with Levine. Wyeth argued that the judge should overturn the jury verdict because Levine's claim was preempted because the drug's label had been approved by the Food and Drug Administration. The judge rejected Wyeth's argument, and the Vermont Supreme Court upheld that ruling, holding that the federal regulations created a floor and not a ceiling and Wyeth could have warned against IV-push administration. Wyeth appealed to the U.S. Supreme Court, making 2 arguments: (1) it was impossible to comply with both its state and federal law obligations and (2) Levine's common-law claims stand as an obstacle to the accomplishment of Congress' purposes in the Food, Drug and Cosmetic Act (FDCA).

JUSTICE STEVENS: The . . . question presented is whether federal law preempts Levine's claim that Phenergan's label did not contain an adequate warning about using the IV-push method of administration. Wyeth first argues that Levine's state-law claims are preempted because it is impossible for it to comply with both the state-law duties underlying those claims and its federal labeling duties. The FDA's premarket approval of a new drug application includes the approval of the exact text in the proposed label. Generally speaking, a manufacturer may only change a drug label after the FDA approves a supplemental application. There is, however, an FDA regulation that permits a manufacturer to make certain changes to its label before receiving the agency's approval. Among other things, this "changes being effected" (CBE) regulation provides that if a manufacturer is changing a label to "add or strengthen a contraindication, warning, precaution, or adverse reaction" or to "add or strengthen an instruction about dosage and administration that is intended to increase the safe use of the drug product," it may make the labeling change upon filing its supplemental application with the FDA; it need not wait for FDA approval.

Wyeth argues that the CBE regulation is not implicated in this case because a 2008 amendment provides that a manufacturer may only change its label "to reflect newly acquired information." Resting on this language, Wyeth contends that it could have changed Phenergan's label only in response to new information that the FDA had not considered.

Wyeth could have revised Phenergan's label even in accordance with the amended regulation. As the FDA explained in its notice of the final rule, "newly acquired information" is not limited to new data, but also encompasses "new analyses of previously submitted data." The rule accounts for the fact that risk information accumulates over time and that the same data may take on a different meaning in light of subsequent developments. Levine . . . present[ed] evidence of at least 20 incidents prior to her injury in which a Phenergan injection resulted in gangrene and an amputation. After the first such incident came to Wyeth's attention in 1967, it notified the FDA and worked with the agency to change Phenergan's label. In later years, as amputations continued to occur, Wyeth could have analyzed the accumulating data and added a stronger warning about IV-push administration of the drug.

[A]bsent clear evidence that the FDA would not have approved a change to Phenergan's label, we will not conclude that it was impossible for Wyeth to comply with both federal and state requirements.

Impossibility preemption is a demanding defense. On the record before us, Wyeth has failed to demonstrate that it was impossible for it to comply with both federal and state requirements. The CBE regulation permitted Wyeth to unilaterally strengthen its warning, and the mere fact that the FDA approved Phenergan's label does not establish that it would have prohibited such a change.

Wyeth also argues that requiring it to comply with a state-law duty to provide a stronger warning about IV-push administration would obstruct the purposes and objectives of federal drug labeling regulation. Levine's tort claims, it maintains, are preempted because they interfere with "Congress's purpose to entrust an expert agency to make drug labeling decisions that strike a balance between competing objectives." We find no merit in this argument, which relies on an untenable interpretation of congressional intent and an overbroad view of an agency's power to preempt state law.

Wyeth contends that the FDCA establishes both a floor and a ceiling for drug regulation. Wyeth relies . . . on the preamble to a 2006 FDA regulation governing the content and format of prescription drug labels. In that preamble, the FDA declared that the FDCA establishes "both a 'floor' and a 'ceiling,'" so that "FDA approval of labeling . . . preempts conflicting or contrary State law." It further stated that

[continued]

certain state-law actions, such as those involving failure-to-warn claims, "threaten FDA's statutorily prescribed role as the expert Federal agency responsible for evaluating and regulating drugs." . . .

[T]he FDA's 2006 preamble does not merit deference. When the FDA issued its notice of proposed rulemaking in December 2000, it explained that the rule would "not contain policies that have federalism implications or that preempt State law." In 2006, the agency finalized the rule and, without offering States or other interested parties notice or opportunity for comment, articulated a sweeping position on the FDCA's preemptive effect in the regulatory preamble. The agency's views on state law are inherently suspect in light of this procedural failure.

In short, Wyeth has not persuaded us that failure-to-warn claims like Levine's obstruct the federal regulation of drug labeling. Congress has repeatedly declined to preempt state law, and the FDA's recently adopted position that state tort suits interfere with its statutory mandate is entitled to no weight. Although we recognize that some state-law claims might well frustrate the achievement of congressional objectives, this is not such a case.

We conclude that it is not impossible for Wyeth to comply with its state and federal law obligations and that Levine's common-law claims do not stand as an obstacle to the accomplishment of Congress' purposes in the FDCA. Accordingly, the judgment of the Vermont Supreme Court is affirmed.

AFFIRMED.

CRITICAL THINKING

What are the reasons for the Court's conclusion that Levine's product liability claims are not preempted?

ETHICAL DECISION MAKING

Recall the WPH process for ethical decision making. Who are the relevant stakeholders affected by this decision?

the oil companies, most cases have held that the Clean Air Act does not preempt tort cases because the oil companies had a choice of oxygenates to use. Moreover, the courts state that the problem of water contamination is too far removed from the problem that Congress was trying to address through the Clean Air Act regulations; thus, there is no preemption.

Certain statutory defenses are also available in negligence-based product liability cases. To ensure that there will be sufficient evidence from which a trier of fact can make a decision, states have *statutes of limitations* that limit the time within which all types of civil actions may be brought. In most states, the statute of limitations for tort actions, and thus for negligence-based product liability cases, varies between one and four years from the date of injury.

Statutes of repose provide an additional statutory defense by barring actions arising more than a specified number of years after the product was purchased. Statutes of repose are usually much longer than statutes of limitations, generally running at least 10 years.

STRICT PRODUCT LIABILITY

The requirements for proving strict product liability can be found in Section 402A of the Restatement (Second) of Torts. This section reads as follows:

1. One who sells any product in a defective condition, unreasonably dangerous to the user or consumer or his family is subject to liability for physical harm, thereby, caused to the ultimate user or consumer, or to this property, if
   a. the seller is engaged in the business of selling such a product, and
   b. it is expected to and does reach the consumer or user without substantial change in the condition in which it was sold.
2. The rule stated in Subsection (1) applies although
   a. the seller has exercised all possible care in the preparation and sale of his product, and
   b. the user or consumer has not bought the product from or entered into any contractual relation with the seller.

Under **strict product liability,** courts may hold liable the manufacturer, distributor, or retailer to any reasonably foreseeable injured party. Any reasonably foreseeable injured party includes the buyer; the buyer's family, guests, and friends; and foreseeable bystanders. The actions of the manufacturer or seller are not relevant; rather, strict product liability focuses on the *product.* Thus, duty is irrelevant. Courts focus on whether the product was in a "defective condition, unreasonably dangerous" when sold. To succeed in a strict-liability action, the plaintiff must prove three things:

1. The product was defective when sold.
2. The product was so defective that the product was unreasonably dangerous.
3. The product was the cause of the plaintiff's injury.

As stated earlier, a product may be defective because of (1) a flaw in its manufacturing that led to its being more dangerous; (2) a defective design; or (3) missing or inadequate instructions or warnings that could have reduced or eliminated foreseeable risks posed by the product.

Plaintiffs usually prove that a defect exists by means of (1) experts who testify as to the type of flaw in the product that led to the plaintiff's injury and/or (2) evidence of the circumstances surrounding the accident that would lead the jury to infer that the accident must have been caused by a defect in the product. Exhibit 10-1 describes how expert opinion is used in product liability cases. Case 10-2 illustrates how circumstances can provide a reasonable basis for such an inference.

Exhibit 10-1
The Battle of the Experts

EXPERT OPINION IN PRODUCT LIABILITY CASES

Plaintiffs use experts in product liability cases to show the existence of a flaw or to show that a flaw caused the plaintiff's injuries. To rebut the plaintiff's expert opinion, the defense usually hires an expert to show that there is no defect or that the product did not cause the plaintiff's injuries. These experts frequently battle over the scientific evidence regarding causation.

Expert testimony is used in various types of litigation: drugs, breast implants, automobile accidents, and pollution. Expert opinion is generally admissible in a trial if two conditions are met:

1. The subject matter is one in which scientific, technical, or other specialized knowledge would help the finder of fact, and the knowledge is relevant and reliable.
2. The expert offering the testimony is qualified as an expert.

Juries, or even judges, have sometimes been persuaded by an "expert" advocating "junk science." Junk science may be "biased data, spurious inferences, and logical legerdemain, patched together by researchers whose enthusiasm for discovery and diagnosis outstrips their skill. It is a catalog of every conceivable kind of error: data dredging, wishful thinking, truculent dogmatism, and now and again, outright fraud."* In an attempt to reduce the use of junk science in the courtroom, the Supreme Court, in *Daubert v. Merrell Dow Pharmaceutical,* determined that judges are responsible for assessing expert opinion. It identified four considerations for relevant and reliable opinions:

1. Did the expert use the scientific method?
2. Has the expert's theory or technique been subjected to peer review and publication?
3. Does the particular technique have a significant rate of error?
4. Is the methodology generally accepted in the scientific community?

Expert-witness fees may range from $100 to $1,000 an hour. Experts are usually deposed during litigation, so their time preparing for depositions and trial can easily run into hundreds of hours, which can be quite costly for clients.

* Peter Huber, *Galileo's Revenge: Junk Science in the Courtroom* (New York: Basic Books, 1991).

CASE 10-2 WELGE v. PLANTERS LIFESAVERS CO.
COURT OF APPEALS FOR THE SEVENTH CIRCUIT

17 F.3D 209 (7TH CIR. 1994)

Richard Welge, who boarded with Karen Godfrey, liked peanuts on his ice cream sundaes. Godfrey bought a 24-ounce vacuum-sealed plastic-capped jar of Planters peanuts for Welge at K-Mart. To obtain a $2 rebate, Godfrey needed proof of her purchase from the jar of peanuts. She used an Exacto knife to remove the part of the label that contained the bar code and placed the jar on top of the refrigerator for Welge. A week later, Welge removed the plastic seal from the jar, uncapped it, took some peanuts, replaced the cap, and returned the jar to the top of the refrigerator. A week after that, he took down the jar, removed the plastic cap, spilled some peanuts into his left hand to put on his sundae, and replaced the cap with his right hand. As he pushed the cap down on the open jar, the jar shattered. His hand was severely cut, and became permanently impaired.

Welge filed product liability actions against K-Mart, the seller of the product; Planters, the manufacturer of the peanuts; and Brockway, the manufacturer of the glass jar. Defendants filed a motion for summary judgment after discovery. The district judge granted the motion on the ground that the plaintiff had failed to exclude possible causes of the accident other than a defect introduced during the manufacturing process. The plaintiff appealed.

JUSTICE POSNER: No doubt there are men strong enough to shatter a thick glass jar with one blow. But Welge's testimony stands uncontradicted that he used no more than the normal force that one exerts in snapping a plastic lid onto a jar. So the jar must have been defective. No expert testimony and no fancy doctrine are required for such a conclusion. A nondefective jar does not shatter when normal force is used to clamp its plastic lid on. The question is when the defect was introduced. It could have been at any time from the manufacture of the glass jar by Brockway (for no one suggests that the defect might have been caused by something in the raw materials out of which the jar was made) to moments before the accident. But testimony by Welge and Godfrey . . . excludes all reasonable possibility that the defect was introduced into the jar after Godfrey plucked it from a shelf in the K-Mart store. From the shelf she put it in her shopping cart. The checker at the check out counter scanned the bar code without banging the jar. She then placed the jar in a plastic bag. Godfrey carried the bag to her car and put it on the floor. She drove directly home, without incident. After the bar code portion of the label was removed, the jar sat on top of the refrigerator except for the two times Welge removed it to take peanuts out of it. Throughout this process it was not, so far as anyone knows, jostled, dropped, bumped, or otherwise subjected to stress beyond what is to be expected in the ordinary use of the product. Chicago is not Los Angeles; there were no earthquakes. Chicago is not Amityville either; no supernatural interventions are alleged. So the defect must have been introduced earlier, when the jar was in the hands of the defendants.

. . . [I]t is always possible that the jar was damaged while it was sitting unattended on the top of the refrigerator, in which event they are not responsible. Only if it had been securely under lock and key when not being used could the plaintiff and Karen Godfrey be certain that nothing happened to damage it after she brought it home. That is true—there are no metaphysical certainties—but it leads nowhere. Elves may have played ninepins with the jar of peanuts while Welge and Godfrey were sleeping; but elves could remove a jar of peanuts from a locked cupboard. The plaintiff in a product liability suit is not required to exclude every possibility, however fantastic or remote, that the defect which led to the accident was caused by someone other than one of the defendants. The doctrine of *res ipsa loquitur* teaches that an accident that is unlikely to occur, unless the defendant was negligent, is itself circumstantial evidence that the defendant was negligent. The doctrine is not strictly applicable to a product liability case because, unlike an ordinary accident case, the defendant in a products case has parted with possession and control of the harmful object before the accident occurs. . . . But the doctrine merely instantiates the broader principle, which is as applicable to a products case as to any other tort case, that an accident can itself be evidence of liability. . . . If it is the kind of accident that would not have occurred but for a defect in the product, and if it is reasonably plain that the defect was not introduced after the product was sold, the accident is evidence that the product was defective when sold. The second condition (as well as the first) has been established here, at least to a probability sufficient to defeat a motion for summary judgment. Normal people do not lock up their jars and cans lest something happens to damage these containers while no one is looking. The probability of such damage is too remote. It is not only too remote to make a rational person take measures to prevent it; it is too remote to defeat a product liability suit should a container prove dangerously defective.

. . . [I]f the probability that the defect which caused the accident arose after Karen Godfrey bought the jar of Planters peanuts is very small—and on the present state of the record we are required to assume that it is—then the probability that the defect was introduced by one of the defendants is very high.

. . . The strict-liability element in modern product liability law comes precisely from the fact that a seller, subject to that law, is liable for defects in his product even if those defects were introduced, without the slightest fault of his own for failing to discover them, at some anterior stage of production. . . . So the fact that K-Mart sold a defective jar of peanuts to Karen Godfrey would be conclusive of K-Mart's

[continued]

liability, and since it is a large and solvent firm there would be no need for the plaintiff to look further for a tortfeasor.

. . . Here we know to a virtual certainty (always assuming that the plaintiff's evidence is believed, which is a matter for the jury) that the accident was not due to mishandling after purchase, but to a defect that had been introduced earlier.

REVERSED and REMANDED in favor of the plaintiff.

CRITICAL THINKING

What are Justice Posner's reasons for reversing the decision? Do you find his reasons compelling?

ETHICAL DECISION MAKING

Suppose that the defect had been introduced by Brockway and that corporate management had been aware of the defect but believed the chances of someone's being hurt were small enough to be negligible. Therefore, Brockway did not inform Planters of the defect. Should it have informed Planters?

In Case 10-2, the product had a manufacturing defect, which was fairly straightforward to prove. However, it is sometimes more difficult to prove that a design is defective. States are not in agreement as to how to establish a design defect, and two different tests have evolved to determine when a product is so defective as to be unreasonably dangerous. The first test, set out in the Restatement (Second) of Torts, is the *consumer expectations test:* Did the product meet the standards that would be expected by the reasonable consumer? This test relies on the experiences and expectations of the ordinary consumer, and thus it is not answered by the use of expert testimony about the merits of the design. See Exhibit 10-2 for an analysis of the difference between the second and third Restatement of Torts.

Exhibit 10-2

Impact of the Restatement (Third) of Torts

Section 402A of the Restatement (Second) of Torts is generally the foundation of modern product liability law, but that section has been subject to considerable criticism. In 1998, the criticisms led the American Law Institute to adopt the "Restatement of the Law (Third), Torts: Product Liability," which is intended to replace Section 402A.

Under the Restatement (Third):

> [O]ne engaged in the business of selling or otherwise distributing products who sells or distributes a defective product is subject to liability for harm to persons or property caused by the defect.

The section departs from the Restatement (Second) by holding the seller to a different standard of liability, depending on whether the defect in question is a manufacturing defect, a design defect, or a defective warning.

> It is only a manufacturing defect that results in strict liability. A manufacturing defect arises when "the product departs from its intended design," and liability is imposed regardless of the care taken by the manufacturer.

The Restatement (Third) applies a reasonableness standard to design defects, stating:

> [A] product is defective in design when the foreseeable risks of the harm posed by the product could have been reduced or avoided by the adoption of a reasonable alternative design by the seller . . . and the omission of the alternative design renders the product not reasonably safe.

Comments in the Restatement (Third) list a number of factors the court can use to determine whether a reasonable alternative design renders the product not reasonably safe, including:

(continued)

Exhibit 10-2
Continued

> the magnitude and probability of the foreseeable risks of harm, the instructions and warnings accompanying the product, and the nature and strength of consumer expectations regarding the product, including expectations arising from product portrayal and marketing, . . . the relative advantage and disadvantages of the product as designed and as it alternatively could have been designed, . . . the likely effects of the alternative design on product longevity, maintenance, repair and esthetics, and the range of consumer choice among products.

Thus, the Restatement (Third) has in effect shifted to a risk-utility test.

The Restatement (Third) has likewise adopted a reasonableness standard for defective warnings:

> A product is defective because of inadequate instructions or warnings when the foreseeable risks of harm posed by the product could have been reduced or avoided by the provision of reasonable instructions or warnings by the seller . . . and the omission of the warnings renders the product not reasonably safe.

The potential effects of changes brought about by the newest Restatement have yet to be fully felt. As of 2001, the Restatement (Third) had not been widely adopted by the states.

The second is the *feasible alternatives test,* sometimes referred to as the *risk-utility test.* In applying this test, the court focuses on the usefulness and safety of the design and compares it to an alternative design. The exact factors that the court examines are detailed in Case 10-3, which makes explicit the differences between the two tests.

CASE 10-3 SPERRY–NEW HOLLAND, A DIVISION OF SPERRY CORPORATION v. JOHN PAUL PRESTAGE AND PAM PRESTAGE

SUPREME COURT OF MISSISSIPPI

617 SO. 2D 248 (1993)

Mr. Prestage's foot and lower leg were caught in a combine manufactured by defendant Sperry–New Holland. He and his wife sued defendant for damages arising out of the accident. Their first cause of action was based on the theory of strict product liability. A jury awarded John $1,425,000 for his injuries and Pam $218,750 for loss of consortium (the ability to engage in sexual relations with one's spouse). Defendant appealed.

JUDGE PRATHER: . . . Two competing theories of strict liability in tort can be extrapolated from our case law. While our older decisions applied a "consumer expectations" analysis in products cases, recent decisions have turned on an analysis under "risk-utility." We today apply a "risk-utility" analysis and write to clarify our reasons for the adoption for that test.

Section 402A is still the law in Mississippi. How this Court defines the phrases "defective conditions" and "unreasonably dangerous" used in 402A dictates whether a "consumer expectations" analysis or a "risk-utility" analysis will prevail. Problems have arisen because our past decisions have been unclear and have been misinterpreted in some instances.

"Consumer Expectations" Analysis

. . . In a "consumer expectations" analysis, "ordinarily the phrase 'defective condition' means that the article has something wrong with it, that it did not function as expected." Comment g of Section 402A defines "defective condition" as "a condition not contemplated by the ultimate consumer, which will be unreasonably dangerous to him." Thus, in a "consumer expectations" analysis, for a plaintiff to recover, the defect in a product which causes his injuries must not be one which the plaintiff, as an ordinary consumer, would know to be unreasonably dangerous to him. In other words, if the plaintiff, applying the knowledge of an ordinary consumer, sees a danger and can appreciate that danger, then he cannot recover for any injury resulting from that appreciated danger.

"Risk-Utility" Analysis

In a "risk-utility" analysis, a product is "unreasonably dangerous" if a reasonable person would conclude that thedanger-in-fact, whether foreseeable or not, outweighs the utility of the product. Thus, even if a plaintiff appreciates the danger of a product, he can still recover for any injury resulting from the danger, provided that the utility of the product is

[continued]

outweighed by the danger that the product creates. Under the "risk-utility" test, either the judge or the jury can balance the utility and danger-in-fact, or risk, of the product.

A "risk-utility" analysis best protects both the manufacturer and the consumer. It does not create a duty on the manufacturer to create a completely safe product. Creating such a product is often impossible or prohibitively expensive. Instead, a manufacturer is charged with the duty to make its product reasonably safe, regardless of whether the plaintiff is aware of the product's dangerousness. . . . In balancing the utility of the product against the risk it creates, an ordinary person's ability to avoid the danger by exercising care is also weighed.

Having here reiterated this Court's adoption of a "risk-utility" analysis for product liability cases, we hold, necessarily, that the "patent danger" bar is no longer applicable in Mississippi. Under a "risk-utility" analysis, the "patent danger" rule does not apply. In "risk-utility," the openness and obviousness of a product's design is simply a factor to consider in determining whether a product is unreasonably dangerous.

There is sufficient evidence to show that Prestage tried his case under a "risk-utility" analysis. It is also clear from the record that the trial court understood "risk-utility" to be the law in Mississippi and applied that test correctly.

AFFIRMED in favor of plaintiff.

CRITICAL THINKING

Why was the risk-utility test viewed as the best method of evaluating this case?

ETHICAL DECISION MAKING

The risk-utility test allows products to pose a danger to consumers as long as they are reasonably safe. Under which ethical theory would producing such a product be ethical? Under which theory would such production not be ethical?

Some states require that one of these tests must be used. For example, in South Carolina, the risk utility test is the exclusive test.[5] Other states permit use of either the consumer expectations test or the risk utility test (e.g., Illinois).[6]

Legal Principle: **A product liability case based on the theory of strict product liability may be brought when a person is injured by a product with a manufacturing defect that caused that product to be unreasonably dangerous.**

Liability to Bystanders. We have been looking thus far at liability to those who are in lawful possession of the defective product. The question arises as to whether strict product liability can be used by someone other than the owner or user of the product. The Bystanders Case Nugget provides the rationale of one court that chose to allow recovery by a bystander.

Various companies involved in manufacturing and selling products may be named as defendants in product liability cases. However, some states restrict which companies may be named as defendants. See the Case Nugget "Who Is the Proper Defendant?"

Defenses to a Strict–Product Liability Action. Most of the defenses to a negligence-based product liability claim are available in a strict–product liability case. These defenses include product misuse, assumption of the risk, and the lapse of time under statutes of limitations and statutes of repose.

One defense that may not be available in all states, however, is the state-of-the-art defense. Courts have rejected the use of this defense in most strict-liability cases, reasoning

[5] *Peters-Martin v. Navistar Intern. Transp. Corp.*, 2011 WL 462657 (4th Cir. 2011).

[6] 659 F.3d 584 (7th Cir. 2011).

CASE NUGGET

STRICT LIABILITY FOR BYSTANDERS

James A. Peterson, Adm'r of the Estate of Maradean Peterson et al. v. Lou Backrodt Chevrolet Co.
Appellate Court of Illinois
307 N.E.3d 729 (1974)

A car dealer sold an automobile with a defective brake system. When the defective brakes failed, the driver struck two minors, killing one and injuring the other. The deceased minor's estate brought a product liability action against the car dealer. The court relied on a statement by the California Supreme Court in *Elmore v. American Motors Corp.* to allow recovery by bystanders:

If anything, bystanders should be entitled to greater protection than the consumer or user where injury to bystanders from the defect is reasonably foreseeable. Consumers and users, at least, have the opportunity to inspect for defects and to limit their purchases to articles manufactured by reputable manufacturers and sold by reputable retailers, whereas the bystander ordinarily has no such opportunities. In short, the bystander is in greater need of protection from defective products which are dangerous, and if any distinction should be made between bystanders and users, it should be made . . . to extend greater liability in favor of the bystanders.

that the issue in such cases is not what the producers knew at the time the products were produced but whether the product was defective and whether the defect caused it to be unreasonably dangerous. For example, the supreme court of Missouri, in a case involving an asbestos claim, said that the state of the art has no bearing on the outcome of a strict-liability claim because the issue is the defective condition of the product, not the manufacturer's knowledge, negligence, or fault.

The refusal of most courts to allow the state-of-the-art defense in strict-liability cases is consistent with the social policy reasons for imposing strict liability. A reason for imposing strict liability is that the manufacturers or producers are best able to spread the cost of the risk; this risk-spreading function does not change with the availability of scientific knowledge. The counterargument is that if the manufacturer has indeed done everything as safely and carefully as available data allow, it seems unfair to impose liability on the defendant. After all, how else could the company have manufactured the product?

WARRANTY

Another theory of liability for defective products is *breach of warranty.* Unlike negligence and strict-liability theories, breach of warranty stems from contract theory rather than tort theory. This theory of liability is established through the Uniform Commercial Code (UCC). A **warranty** is a guarantee or a binding promise regarding a product. Generally, the product (or the product's performance) does not meet the manufacturer's or seller's promises.

To see how total quality management relates to prevention of product liability cases, please see the **Connecting to the Core** activity on the text website at www.mhhe.com/kubasek3e.

Warranties may be either *express* (clearly stated by the seller or manufacturer) or *implied* (automatically arising out of a transaction). Either type may give rise to liability. Two types of implied warranties may provide the basis for a product liability action: warranty of merchantability and warranty of fitness for a particular purpose.

Express Warranty. When a seller makes an affirmative representation about a product, this representation—an **express warranty**—becomes part of the bargain. The representation may be a written or verbal guarantee about the product. For example, a car dealer may make an express statement that the car will work perfectly for the first 30,000 miles. In contrast, a car dealer may engage in vague sales talk (e.g., "This car runs well") that does not constitute an express warranty.

Determining whether a statement is a warranty may be a difficult task. In one case, for example, the court considered whether advertising statements constituted a warranty:

CASE NUGGET

WHO IS THE PROPER DEFENDANT?

Block v. Toyota Motor Corporation
2011 WL 6306689 (8th Cir. 2011)

Angela Block filed a strict-liability suit after her son was killed and her daughter was seriously injured in a collision with a Toyota vehicle that allegedly improperly suddenly accelerated. Block filed suit in Minnesota state court against Toyota (the manufacturer of the vehicle), its affiliates, and Brooklyn Park Motors, the automobile dealership that had originally sold the Toyota vehicle 10 years earlier. The defendants removed the case to federal court, and the plaintiff argued that removal of the case to federal court was improper because the automobile dealership was a Minnesota resident. Minnesota has a "seller's exception statute" that requires the dismissal of strict-liability claims against nonmanufacturers when the nonmanufacturer provides the identity of the manufacturer unless the plaintiff shows that the nonmanufacturer falls into one of three exceptions:

1. The defendant has exercised some significant control over the design or manufacture of the product or provided instruction or warnings to the manufacturer.
2. The defendant had actual knowledge of the defect in the product that caused the injury, death, or damage.
3. The defendant created the defect in the product that caused the injury, death, or damage. The district court concluded that the auto dealership fell under the seller's exception statute and dismissed all claims with prejudice against the dealership. On appeal, the Eighth Circuit upheld the dismissal.

When a consumer was deciding whether to buy a luxury yacht, the seller gave him a brochure with a picture of the yacht along with the following caption: "Offering the best performance and cruising accommodations in its class, the 3375 Esprit offers a choice of either stern drive or inboard power, superb handling and sleeping accommodations for six." The buyer argued that on the basis of express representations about the yacht in this brochure, he chose to purchase the $150,000 yacht. Later, the yacht had mechanical and electrical problems. The supreme court of Utah concluded that an express warranty is a promise or affirmation of fact. "[T]he photograph and caption contained in Cruisers' brochure are not objective or specific enough to qualify as either facts or promises; the statements made in the caption are merely opinions, and the photograph makes no additional assertions with regard to the problems of which Boud has complained." Thus, the court ruled there was no express warranty.

To establish a claim for breach of express warranty, the plaintiff must show that (1) the representation was the basis of the bargain and (2) there was a breach of the representation. Generally, the plaintiff simply has to demonstrate a breach of warranty; she does not have to prove that the occurrence of the breach was the defendant's fault.

Implied Warranty of Merchantability. When a seller sells a particular kind of goods, there is an implied warranty of merchantability. *Merchantability* means that the particular goods would be accepted by others who deal in similar goods. Thus, an **implied warranty of merchantability** means that the goods are fit for the purpose for which they are sold and used. This warranty is found in Article 2, Section 314(2), of the UCC. Under the UCC, for goods to be merchantable, they must meet six conditions:

a. Pass without objection in the trade under the contract description.
b. In the case of fungible goods, be of fair average quality within the description.
c. Be fit for the ordinary purposes for which such goods are used.
d. Run, within the variations permitted by the agreement, of even kind, quality and quantity within each unit and among all units involved.
e. Be adequately contained, packaged, and labeled as the agreement may require.
f. Conform to the promises or affirmations of fact made on the container or label, if any.

E-COMMERCE AND THE LAW

USER GUIDES ON THE INTERNET

In a footnote in the Sperry–New Holland case, the court relied on Professor John Wade's article "On the Nature of Strict Tort Liability for Products"* to list seven factors a trial court may find helpful when balancing a product's utility against the risk the product creates:

1. The usefulness and desirability of the product—its utility to the user and to the public as a whole.
2. The safety aspects of the product—the likelihood that it will cause injury and the probable seriousness of the injury.
3. The availability of a substitute product that would meet the same need and not be as unsafe.
4. The manufacturer's ability to eliminate the unsafe character of the product without impairing its usefulness or making it too expensive to maintain its utility.
5. The user's ability to avoid danger by the exercise of care in the use of the product.
6. The user's anticipated awareness of the dangers inherent in the product and their avoidability, because of general public knowledge of the obvious condition of the product or of the existence of suitable warnings or instructions.
7. The feasibility, on the part of the manufacturer, of spreading the loss by setting the price of the product or carrying liability insurance.

With regard to factor 6, the court's analysis considered whether warnings included in an owner's manual were suitable to warn Prestage of the danger of the combine. One of Sperry's expert witnesses testified: "Warnings are a third-rate way of preventing accidents. . . . [W]arnings are something that . . . operators read once, and forget."

Query: Is it possible that as owner's and user's manuals become available online, judges and experts will be less sympathetic to the owner or user who says he read the warnings once but then forgot about them? Have you ever misplaced an owner's or user's manual and later looked for it online when you needed information about a product? If so, are you more likely to review safety information than you may have been in the past, when it was easy to misplace manuals?

* *Mississippi Law Journal* 44 (1973), p. 825.

For example, a consumer purchased an "unbreakable" baseball bat that developed cracks after the repeated use of hitting baseballs. The consumer brought suit against the retailer that sold the bat. Given that the bat could not be used for the purpose for which it was intended (i.e., hitting baseballs), the judge relied on the implied warranty of merchantability to determine that the consumer was entitled to a refund.[7]

One of the requirements of this provision is that the seller of the good must be a "merchant with respect to goods of that kind" [UCC Section 2–314(1)]. Thus, the seller must deal with the goods in question on a regular or continuous basis. For example, a private individual who places an advertisement in the paper to sell her personal car is not a seller of goods under this section of the UCC.

Contracts for sales of goods frequently contain numerous disclaimers, and one of these disclaimers includes the implied warranty of merchantability. If the disclaimer uses the word *merchantability,* the disclaimer will be upheld for economic losses but not personal injuries.

Here's a dilemma. Should the disclaimer for our client's new sleeping pill read, "May cause drowsiness" or "May not cause drowsiness"?

Implied Warranty of Fitness for a Particular Purpose. When a customer purchases a product for a particular purpose and the seller is aware of this purpose, an **implied warranty of fitness for a particular purpose** arises. This warranty is found in Article 2, Section

[7] *Dudzik v. Klein's All Sports,* 158 Misc. 2d 72 (N.Y. Just. Ct. 1993).

CASE NUGGET

WHEN MIGHT YOUR COMPANY UNEXPECTEDLY BE CONSIDERED A SELLER OF GOODS?

Nutting v. Ford Motor Company
180 A.D.2d 122 (N.Y.A.D. 1992)

Catherine Nutting was driving her 1984 Mercury Marquis station wagon when the engine stalled, and the car collided with another vehicle. Nutting brought suit against Ford Motor Company, the car manufacturer, and Hewlett-Packard (HP), a manufacturer and seller of computer products. Why HP? HP had purchased the car at issue in this case from Ford through a program where HP purchased approximately 3,200 cars for use by HP employees. After about one and a half years, HP disposed of the cars through an auction conducted by its agent. Hi-Way Motors, a used-car dealership owned by Nutting's father, purchased the car at auction and transferred titled to Nutting. When Nutting brought suit against HP for breach of implied warranty of merchantability, HP argued that it was an occasional seller of surplus vehicles. The court disagreed, finding that HP was in the regular business of a used-car dealer and thus was a seller and merchant within the meaning of UCC Section 2-314. You may want to examine the way that your business regularly disposes of surplus equipment or other products to consider whether you could unexpectedly be considered a seller of goods.

315, of the UCC. The buyer is relying on the seller's skill and judgment to select the particular goods. Thus, to succeed on a claim for breach of implied warranty of fitness for a particular purpose, the plaintiff would need to show (1) knowledge—the seller had knowledge of the customer's specific purpose; and (2) reliance—the customer relied on the seller's skill and judgment. Unlike the implied warranty of merchantability, which requires that the seller be a merchant of the goods involved, the implied warranty of fitness for a particular purpose applies to a sale of goods regardless of whether the seller qualifies as a merchant.

Exhibit 10-3 summarizes the three theories of product liability.

Exhibit 10-3 Summary of Product Liability Theories

THEORIES OF LIABILITY	WHO CAN SUE	WHO CAN BE LIABLE	DEFENSES	DAMAGES
Negligence	Any foreseeable plaintiff	Any commercial supplier in the distribution chain (Retailers and sellers can satisfy their duty by a cursory reasonable inspection.)	Assumption of the risk Comparative/contributory negligence	Personal injuries Property damages No recovery solely for economic damages
Strict liability	Anyone harmed (buyer, user, bystander)	Any commercial supplier in the distribution chain	Assumption of the risk Product misuse	Personal injuries Property damages No recovery solely for economic damages
Warranty	Privity required (Injured party must be the buyer, the buyer's family, or the buyer's guest.)	Any seller	Assumption of the risk Product misuse Disclaimer	Recovery solely for economic damage

Market Share Liability

LO2

What is market share liability?

In most cases, the plaintiff can identify the manufacturer of a defective product that caused the injury at issue. Sometimes, however, some plaintiffs may not learn of their injuries until years after the injury occurs. By this time, plaintiffs cannot trace the product to any particular manufacturer. Often, a number of manufacturers produced the same product, and the plaintiff would have no idea whose product had been used. A plaintiff may have even used more than one manufacturer's product.

Before the 1980s, plaintiffs in this situation would have been unable to gain any sort of recovery for their injuries. However, recovery may be possible today because of the **market share theory,** created by the California Supreme Court in the case of *Sindell v. Abbott Laboratories.*

In *Sindell,* the plaintiffs' mothers had all taken a drug known as diethylstilbestrol (DES) during pregnancies that had occurred before the drug was banned in 1973. Because DES had been produced 20 years before the plaintiffs suffered any effects from the drug their mothers had taken, it was impossible to trace the defective drug back to each manufacturer that had produced the drug causing each individual's problems. To balance the competing interests of the victims, who had suffered injury from the drug, and the defendants, who did not want to be held liable for a drug they did not produce, the court allowed the plaintiffs to sue all the manufacturers that had produced the drug at the time that the plaintiffs' mothers had used the drug. Then the judge apportioned liability among the defendant-manufacturers on the basis of the share of the market they had held at the time that the drug had been produced.

This theory has since been used by some other courts, primarily in drug cases. Courts using the market share theory generally require that the plaintiff prove that (1) all defendants are tortfeasors; (2) the allegedly harmful products are identical and share the same defective qualities; (3) the plaintiff is unable to identify which defendant caused her injury, through no fault of her own; and (4) the manufacturers of substantially all the defective products in the relevant area and during the relevant time are named as defendants.

Some states have modified the approach of *Sindell.* At least one court has held that the plaintiff need sue only one maker of the allegedly defective drug. If the plaintiff can prove that the defendant manufactured a drug of the type taken by the plaintiff's mother at the time of the mother's pregnancy, that defendant can be held liable for all damages. However, the defendant may join other defendants, and the jury may apportion liability among all defendants.

While the utility of this theory for drug cases is evident, plaintiffs have not been as successful in extending the theory to products other than drugs. For example, in 2001, plaintiffs who were unable to identify the maker of the guns that were used to kill their family members were unsuccessful in their attempt to sue a group of manufacturers for negligent marketing under the theory of market share liability. However, at least one court has extended the theory to lead carbonate to permit market share liability for lead poisoning.

A related issue is product liability insurance. Start-up companies often have difficulty obtaining product liability insurance because they frequently cannot meet the insurance company's requirements, such as sales totaling a certain amount per year. The cost of the insurance will depend on the purpose of the product. If the product is related to safety or product performance, the product will be more expensive to insure than a product related to a decorative function. Insurance premiums for start-up products could range from $2,500 to $10,000 per year.[8]

[8] Karen Klein, "When You Can't Secure Product Liability Insurance," *BusinessWeek,* June 9, 2009, www.businessweek.com/smallbiz/content/jun2009/sb2009069_307233.htm.

COMPARING THE LAW OF OTHER COUNTRIES

COLLECTIVE INSURANCE IN SCANDINAVIA

The Scandinavian countries of Sweden, Finland, Denmark, and Norway share a unique feature: the role of collective insurance groups in product liability. Manufacturers, producers, and importers of similar products form cooperative groups and obtain an insurance policy. For example, in Finland, a voluntary insurance policy group headed by the Finnish Pharmaceutical Insurance Pool enlists pharmaceutical companies as members. To hear the appeals of those seeking damages, the pool appoints a board. The board follows the basic liability principle of insurance groups, which is that causation, rather than fault or defectiveness, determines compensation.

Pharmaceutical companies find this principle especially appealing because they can admit liability without damaging the name of their products as a whole. Supporters of the insurance system also point out that elimination of the defectiveness requirement enables product developers to concentrate on improving their products, as opposed to being tied up with product liability cases.

CASE OPENER WRAP-UP

Is Human Sperm Subject to Product Liability Laws?

Donovan's case was the first decision to hold that a sperm bank could be sued under product liability theories for the sperm it provides.[9] One of the issues was whether Pennsylvania or New York law applied to the sale of the sperm. (Donovan and Brittany were Pennsylvania residents, and the sperm came from New York.) Many states, including Pennsylvania and New York, have enacted "blood shield" statutes that prohibit product liability suits based on donated blood. Pennsylvania's blood shield statute included human tissue other than blood, but New York's statute shielded blood and its derivatives only. Therefore, Donovan could have a product liability claim in New York but not in Pennsylvania. The court decided that because the screening of the sperm and the formation of the contract occurred in New York, New York law would apply in Donovan's case and thus, under New York law, the suit could move forward. Another issue was whether Idant provided a service or a product. The court again referred to the blood shield statute and stated that "[u]nder New York law, the sale of sperm is a product and is subject to strict liability."

The court's decision did not find that the sperm actually was defective; it simply found that a New York sperm bank could be sued under product liability laws. However, the case raises some interesting questions: Should a laboratory be held responsible for genetic diseases for which there are no tests? Do the same standards apply to donated eggs? Suppose Brittany Donovan had children who had the same genetic effects. Would they have any claim against the sperm bank?

[9] *Donovan v. Idant Laboratories,* Case No. 08-4075, Memorandum and Order (E.D. Pa., Mar. 31, 2009).

KEY TERMS

design defect 236
express warranty 249
failure to provide adequate warnings 236
implied warranty of fitness for a particular purpose 251
implied warranty of merchantability 250
manufacturing defect 236
market share theory 253
strict product liability 244
warranty 249

SUMMARY OF KEY TOPICS

Theories of Liability For Defective Products

Negligence: Plaintiff must show that (1) the defendant manufacturer or seller owed a duty of care to the plaintiff; (2) the defendant breached that duty of care by supplying a defective product; (3) this breach of duty caused the plaintiff's injury; and (4) the plaintiff suffered actual injury.

Strict product liability: Plaintiff must show that (1) the product was defective when sold; (2) the product was so defective that the product was unreasonably dangerous; and (3) the product was the cause of the plaintiff's injury.

Express warranty: The plaintiff must show that (1) the representation was the basis of the bargain and (2) there was a breach of the representation.

Implied warranty of merchantability: The plaintiff must show that the goods are fit for the purpose for which they are sold and used.

Implied warranty of fitness for a particular purpose: The plaintiff must show that the customer purchased a product for a particular purpose and the seller was aware of this purpose.

Market Share Liability

When plaintiffs cannot trace a product to any particular manufacturer and a number of manufacturers produced the same product, a court may use the theory of market share liability to impose a portion of fault on a number of manufacturers.

POINT / COUNTERPOINT

Should Companies Be Held Strictly Liable for Their Products?	
YES	**NO**
Companies, rather than individual consumers, are in the best position to absorb the risk of their products. The manufacturer is in the best position to anticipate the harm the product might cause and has more information regarding the product. If a company manufactures and sells a product that seriously harms large numbers of individuals (both consumers and bystanders), the company, rather than the individuals should be responsible for these costs. The company receives all the rewards of selling the product (i.e., the profit) and should thus bear the risks associated with selling the product.	The cost of product liability insurance is so high that companies need to add this cost to the price of the product. Consequently, consumers have to pay unnecessarily higher prices for products, and this creates inefficiency in the market. Similarly, manufacturers waste time and resources creating unnecessary warnings on labels (e.g., "Do not eat" warnings on nonfood products). Furthermore, strict liability discourages companies from developing and testing new products because of the fear that the product could be faulty. Finally, strict–product liability law incentivizes consumers to improperly use products.

QUESTIONS & PROBLEMS

1. Explain the elements one would have to prove to bring a successful product liability case based on negligence, and identify the available defense.
2. Why would a defendant prefer to be found to have produced a product that was defectively manufactured rather than defectively designed?
3. Explain the defenses available in a case based on a theory of strict product liability.
4. The plaintiff suffered a carotid artery tear that left him partially paralyzed after being tackled during a high school football scrimmage. While he was on the field, his coaches removed his helmet, which was then lost. The plaintiff's mother filed suit against the helmet manufacturers, alleging that the helmet's liner and foam padding were defectively designed. The district court granted summary judgment to the defendants because the plaintiff could not produce the specific helmet at issue and thus could not prove the helmet was defective. The plaintiff appealed, arguing that the fact that she could not produce the specific helmet was irrelevant as she was arguing that all of the helmets were defective due to their design. Do you think the appellate court agreed that the specific helmet need not be produced?

[*A.K.W. v. Easton-Bell Sports, Inc., et al.*, No. 11-60293, 2011 U.S. App. LEXIS 21108 (5th Cir. 2011).]

5. The plaintiff's son was given St. Joseph's Aspirin for Children when he had the flu. The aspirin triggered Reye's syndrome, leaving the child a quadriplegic, blind, and mentally retarded. The aspirin contained a warning, approved by the Food and Drug Administration, about the dangers of giving aspirin to children with the flu. The product was advertised in Spanish in the Los Angeles area, but the warning was not in Spanish. The child's guardians could not read English. Do you believe the court imposed liability on the company for failure of its duty to warn? Why or why not? [*Ramirez v. Plough, Inc.*, 25 Cal. Rptr. 2d (1993).]

6. Plaintiff Darren Traub was playing a pickup game of basketball on his college campus and tried to dunk the ball, but his hand hit the rim and he fell down, hurting both wrists. He sued the basketball hoop manufacturer and the university, claiming that the rigid rim caused his injury or made it worse. The defendants filed a motion for summary judgment. Do you think it should have been granted? [*Traub v. Cornell*, 1998 WL 187401 (N.D.N.Y. 1998).]

7. In 1991, three-year-old Douglas Moore was playing with one of BIC's lighters. While playing with the lighter, he started a fire that severely injured his 17-month-old brother. BIC Manufacturers Inc. included several child-safety warning labels on their lighters. These labels identified the risk of fire or injury as a result of misusing the product. The lighter provided warnings to adults to "keep out of reach of children" or "keep away from children." The BIC Corporation had knowledge that its lighters could be manipulated by children, but it felt that including safety features would significantly increase the cost of the lighter. The Moore family brought a strict-liability suit against BIC. Explain why strict liability should or should not be applicable in this case. [*Price v. BIC Corp.*, 702 A.2d 330 (Sup. Ct. N.H. 1997).]

8. The federal Organic Foods Production Act and National Organic Program create uniform federal standards for organic labeling. Under these federal programs, producers of products can become certified as organic. Aurora's Milk, sold by Aurora Dairy Corp., was certified as organic under these programs. In 2007, the USDA produced a report regarding alleged violations in Aurora's organic operations, but Aurora's organic certification was not revoked. The plaintiffs brought suit against Aurora Dairy Corp. for false certification. The defendants argued that the plaintiffs' claims were preempted. Do you think the defendants were successful in their preemption argument? [Aurora Dairy Corp. Organic Milk Marketing and Sales Practices Litigation, Case No. 08-md-01907 (E.D. Mo. 2009).]

9. Three men were riding in a pickup truck when the tire tread separated on a rear wheel. The driver lost control of the truck, which rolled over. The two passengers in the truck were killed, and the estate of one of the passengers brought suit against Cooper Tire, the manufacturer of the tire. The plaintiff argued that the tire was defective in design and had a manufacturing defect. During the discovery portion of the case, the plaintiff sought information regarding all tires manufactured by the defendant; specifically, the plaintiff was seeking information to show that Cooper Tire had notice of a tread separation problem in its other tires. Cooper Tire refused to produce that information, arguing that information regarding other tires that it manufactured but were not at issue in the case was irrelevant. What arguments, if any, could the plaintiff use to establish that the information regarding other tires is relevant? [*Mario Alvarez v. Cooper Tire & Rubber Co.*, 75 So. 3d 789 (Fla. Dist. Ct. App., 4th Dist. 2011).]

10. Chris Hill ran a red light while talking on his cell phone. He crashed into a car driven by Linda Doyle, who was killed in the collision. Doyle's estate brought suit against Sprint/Nextel Corp., arguing that Sprint was negligent in failing to warn Hill that it was dangerous to use a cell phone while driving. Sprint moved to dismiss the case, arguing that it had no duty to noncustomer automobile drivers to warn customers of the dangers of talking on the phone while driving. Do you think the court agreed with Sprint? [*Estate of Doyle v. Sprint/Nextel Corp.*, 248 P.3d 947 (Okla. Civ. App. 2010).]

Looking for more review materials?

The Online Learning Center at **www.mhhe.com/kubasek3e** contains this chapter's "Assignment on the Internet" and also a list of URLs for more information, entitled "On the Internet." Find both of them in the Student Center portion of the OLC, along with quizzes and other helpful materials.

CHAPTER 11

Liability of Accountants and Other Professionals

LEARNING OBJECTIVES

After reading this chapter, you will be able to answer the following questions:

1. Under common law, what is the duty of an accountant to his or her clients?
2. Under common law, what is the duty of an accountant to third parties?
3. What is the impact of federal securities law on accountant liability?
4. What is the extent of liability of professionals other than accountants?

CASE OPENER

Questionable Accounting at WorldCom

Bert C. Roberts, Jr., was chairman of WorldCom's board of directors. Immediately before that, he had been chairman of MCI, which WorldCom acquired on September 14, 1998, in a transaction valued at $40 billion. The acquisition made WorldCom the second-largest telecommunications company in the world.

Roberts signed a number of required documents filed by WorldCom with the Securities and Exchange Commission (SEC). These included Form 10-K for 1999, 2000, and 2001 and the registration statements for the 2000 and 2001 stock offerings, as well as registration statements filed in connection with WorldCom's acquisition of SkyTel Communications, Inc., in 1999 and of Intermedia Communications, Inc., in 2001.

On June 25, 2002, WorldCom announced a massive restatement of its financial statements for 2001 and the first quarter of 2002. Several weeks later, it entered bankruptcy. WorldCom ultimately made approximately $76 billion in financial adjustments for 2000 and 2001, reducing the company's net equity from approximately $50 billion to approximately minus $20 billion. It is undisputed that beginning at least as early as 2001, WorldCom executives engaged in a secret scheme to misrepresent WorldCom's financial condition in the company's filings with the SEC.

The facts underlying WorldCom's June 25 announcement spurred numerous lawsuits. A consolidated class action was brought on behalf of a class of all persons and entities, excluding defendants and certain others affiliated with them or with WorldCom, who were financially injured after they acquired publicly traded WorldCom securities between April 29, 1999, and June 25, 2002. Roberts faced charges under a number of different federal acts regulating securities.[1]

1. Who should be liable for the massive loss investors suffered due to the restatement of WorldCom's financial records?
2. What could Roberts have done to avoid the catastrophe that ensued when WorldCom had to restate its financial statements?

The Wrap-Up at the end of the chapter will answer these questions.

[1] *In re WorldCom, Inc., Sec. Litig.*, 2005 U.S. Dist. LEXIS 4193 (2005).

Just as manufacturers and sellers of defective products may be liable for harm caused by their products, professionals who provide substandard services may likewise be liable for the harm they cause. Actions brought against attorneys, lawyers, real estate brokers, doctors, architects, and other professionals are referred to as **malpractice actions.** Just as product liability cases are based on different legal theories, so are malpractice actions. Most malpractice cases are based on theories of negligence, breach of contract, or fraud.

Because most businesspersons require accounting services, they are more likely to encounter malpractice by an accountant than by other professionals, and so we focus here on accountant liability. Indeed, after a significant amount of responsibility for the bankruptcy of the Enron Corporation was placed on the firms that provided its accounting services, accountants' role and accountability became a matter of significant public interest.

Currently, there are a number of professional malpractice cases stemming from the recent economic downturn. After people became aware of the role that banks and other financial institutions played in creating artificial assets, many lawsuits were filed in an attempt to punish those seen as responsible. These lawsuits were also an attempt to recoup lost assets. As bank failures continue to occur, cases are being brought against banks' officers and directors, as well as their outside professionals. For example, in April of 2013, claims were filed against the CEO and a former loan clerk of the recently failed City Bank of Lynwood, Washington, seeking damages of "not less than $41 million," for negligence, gross negligence and breaches of fiduciary duties, That same day a complaint was filed against eight former officers and directors of the failed Riverside National Bank of Ft. Pierce, Florida, for alleged breaches of duties, gross negligence and negligence "based on defendants' permitting an excessive number of poorly underwritten loans to be made that were secured solely or largely by the stock of affiliates of the bank's holding company."[2]

Common Law Accountant Liability to Clients

L01

Under common law, what is the duty of an accountant to his or her clients?

Three primary types of liability are assessed to accountants under the common law: negligence, breach of contract, and fraud.

ACCOUNTANT LIABILITY FOR NEGLIGENCE

An accountant is liable for negligence if he or she fails to exercise the care of a competent, reasonable professional and that failure causes loss or injury to the client. To prove

[2] "No Getting Away from Bank Failures and Bank Failure Lawsuits," *Securities Law Blog*, April 22, 2013.

negligence by the accountant, the plaintiff establishes the basic elements of negligence as discussed in Chapter 9: duty, breach of duty, causation, and damages.

At minimum, the duty of care of the accountant entails compliance with the *generally accepted accounting principles (GAAP),* established by the Financial Accounting Standards Board (FASB), and the *generally accepted auditing standards (GAAS),* established by the American Institute of Certified Public Accountants (AICPA). While failure to comply with GAAP and GAAS will almost certainly constitute a breach of duty, compliance does not automatically mean the duty of care has been met. In some circumstances, a reasonable, competent accountant would do more than GAAP or GAAS requires. Also, sometimes a state statute or judicial opinion may impose additional legal requirements on accountants beyond GAAP and GAAS.

Generally, unless engaged to detect fraud, an accountant is not a fraud detector unless the fraud is uncovered in the course of exercising reasonable care and skill. An accountant is, likewise, not required to have perfect judgment; she or he will not be held liable simply for errors in judgment that were made in good faith while operating in accordance with GAAP and GAAS. Nonetheless, an accountant who fails to meet these standards or to detect fraud or misconduct that a normal audit would uncover may be held liable for negligence.

Failure to adhere to GAAS can have serious professional repercussions for accountants. For example, John Goldberger, an accountant in Pennsylvania, lost the privilege of practicing before the SEC because he negligently performed an audit, failing to live up to professional standards and identify fraud. The SEC argued that Goldberger (1) failed to obtain sufficient competent evidence to afford a reasonable basis for his firm's opinion on the issuer's financial statements; (2) failed to properly assess whether the issuer's financial statements were fairly presented in conformity to generally accepted accounting principles; and (3) failed to exercise due professional care in the performance of an audit.[3]

To see how internal controls relate to accountant liability, please see the **Connecting to the Core** activity on the text website at www.mhhe.com/kubasek3e.

When faced with a charge of negligence, an accountant has several defenses. First, the accountant can deny failing to meet the professional standards. Second, regardless of such failure, an accountant can argue that the failure is not the cause of the client's loss. Third, in a few states an accountant may argue contributory or comparative negligence (as discussed in Chapter 9, under "Defenses to Negligence").

In addition to asserting a defense to a charge of negligence, accountants can also try to limit their liability. After completing an audit, they issue an opinion letter stating their assessment of the audited firm. Usually, an *unqualified* opinion letter is issued. To avoid potential liability, the accountant may make a qualification or issue a disclaimer as part of the letter, expressing, for instance, doubt about the accuracy of the papers the client presented. Any qualifications or disclaimers must be specific, because broad, general qualifications or disclaimers do not grant protection. Nor does a qualification or disclaimer protect an accountant from liability based on failure to discover fraudulent financial transactions that one properly applying GAAP and GAAS would have discovered.

To see how state codes of ethics relate to accountant liability, please see the **Connecting to the Core** activity on the text website at www.mhhe.com/kubasek3e.

On occasion, a business may hire an accountant to create an unaudited financial statement for some purpose. A financial statement is considered unaudited if no, or insubstantial, accounting procedures were used in the compilation of the document. Accountants are not liable for the contents of an unaudited financial statement. Nonetheless, an accountant can still be held liable if he or she fails to clearly mark the financial statement as being unaudited.

[3] *Goldberger v. State Board of Accountancy,* 833 A.2d 815 (2003).

BUT WHAT IF . . .

WHAT IF THE FACTS OF THE CASE OPENER WERE DIFFERENT?

Let's say, in the Case Opener, that Roberts had earnestly thought he filled out all of the companies' financial forms correctly and thoroughly and he had records of his compilations of documents that he used for information. However, let's also say that he missed some small signs of a big fraud scheme within the company that he was not involved in. What would Roberts most likely be charged with?

ACCOUNTANT LIABILITY FOR BREACH OF CONTRACT

When hired to perform a task, the accountant enters into a contract called an *engagement letter* with the client that makes certain explicit and implicit promises. Explicitly, the accountant agrees to perform the contractual tasks. Implicitly, the accountant agrees to complete the work in a competent and professional manner according to professional standards (GAAP and GAAS). Failure to fulfill these explicit and implicit agreements can subject an accountant to liability based on breach of contract. (See Chapter 20 for discussion of breach of contract.)

When an accountant breaches a contract, the client is entitled to recovery for damages that include the cost of obtaining a different accountant and any reasonable and foreseeable damages related to the breach. Suppose Collin, an accountant, breaches his contract to perform an audit for Isis, and as a result her business's assets drop in value. Isis is entitled to recovery for the cost of hiring another accountant as well as for the loss in value of her assets, which occurred because Collin breached his contract with her.

An accountant who engages in a material breach of contract is not entitled to compensation for work completed. However, if the contract is substantially performed and the breach is therefore immaterial, the accountant may be entitled to the full amount of the contractually agreed-on fee minus the amount of damages caused by the breach.

ACCOUNTANT LIABILITY FOR FRAUD

An accountant is liable to his or her client for fraud when all the following have occurred:

1. The accountant misrepresented a material fact.
2. The accountant acted with the intent to deceive.
3. The client justifiably relied on the misrepresentation.
4. The client suffered an injury by relying on the fraudulent information.

An accountant who commits fraud is liable to those parties he or she reasonably should have foreseen would be injured through a justifiable reliance on the fraudulent information.

Accountants may be held liable for actual fraud or constructive fraud, depending on the circumstances. *Actual fraud* exists when the accountant's actions meet the above criteria. *Constructive fraud* is fraud without fraudulent intent—a plaintiff must prove that the accountant was grossly negligent in performing his or her duties. Evidence of reckless disregard for duty and professional standards can help establish gross negligence and, thus, constructive fraud. Accountants found liable for fraud can be assessed compensatory, as well as punitive, damages. Over the last few years, plaintiffs have been successful in bringing fraud suits against accountants under the Racketeer Influenced and Corrupt Organizations (RICO) Act, discussed in Chapter 7.

COMPARING THE LAW OF OTHER COUNTRIES

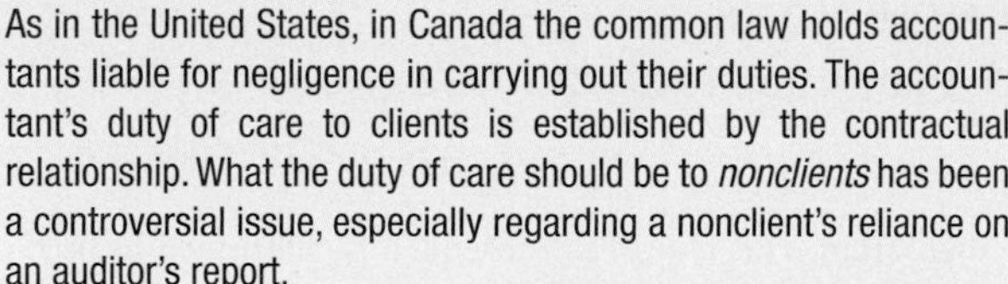

LIABILITY OF ACCOUNTANTS TO THIRD PARTIES IN CANADA

As in the United States, in Canada the common law holds accountants liable for negligence in carrying out their duties. The accountant's duty of care to clients is established by the contractual relationship. What the duty of care should be to *nonclients* has been a controversial issue, especially regarding a nonclient's reliance on an auditor's report.

Under common law in Canada, plaintiffs must prove they reasonably relied on an auditor's report to their detriment. However, in some provinces, securities laws are now providing an important exception for misrepresentations made in a prospectus distributed by an issuer of securities. The Ontario Securities Act gives purchasers of securities in the primary market a right of action for damages against auditors for misrepresentations in their reports, opinions, or statements included in or referred to in the prospectus with the auditors' filed consent. Purchasers need not prove they relied on the misrepresentation. In 2005, the Ontario Securities Act was amended to expand auditors' statutory liability to include misrepresentations in secondary-market disclosures made with the auditors' written consent.

In Quebec, a plaintiff who can prove fault, damage, and a causal link between the two has sufficient grounds for a court to hold the accountant liable.

Legal Principle: **An accountant can be held liable for malpractice under any of three different theories of liability: negligence, breach of duty, or fraud.**

Common Law Accountant Liability to Third Parties

L02 Under common law, what is the duty of an accountant to third parties?

An important issue in accountant liability that varies by state is whether third parties have any claim against an accountant on the basis of their reliance on negligently prepared financial statements. Third-party liability, as decided by the states, falls into three general groupings: (1) privity or near-privity (the Ultramares rule), (2) foreseen users and classes of users (the Restatement rule), and (3) reasonably foreseeable users. Third-party liability was the focus of the most famous case of accountant legal liability, *Ultramares v. Touche,*[4] discussed below.

LIABILITY BASED ON PRIVITY OR NEAR-PRIVITY (THE ULTRAMARES RULE)

In *Ultramares v. Touche,* Justice Benjamin Cardozo, writing for the highest state court in New York, took a narrow view of which third parties were permissible plaintiffs. Concerned that a more liberal rule would subject accountants to a liability of "an indeterminate amount, for an indeterminate time, to an indeterminate class," Cardozo held an accountant liable in negligence only to those with whom he or she had *privity of contract,* meaning the client and anyone for whose "primary benefit" the accounting statements were prepared.

The New York courts have fundamentally continued the *Ultramares* approach by requiring the accountant's awareness of the particular use for his or her work product, known reliance on the work product by an identified third party, and conduct by the accountant recognizing his or her awareness of such reliance. This is the *near-privity,* or *primary-benefit, test,* and only a few states utilize it because it is viewed as too restrictive. The near-privity requirement was appended to the original privity requirement in the 1985 New York case *Credit Alliance Corp. v. Arthur Andersen & Co.* (see Case 11-1).

Legal Principle: **Under the *Ultramares rule,* an accountant will be held liable for negligence only to those with whom he or she had *privity of contract,* meaning the client and anyone for whose "primary benefit" the accounting statements were prepared.**

[4] 255 N.Y. 170 (1931).

CASE 11-1 CREDIT ALLIANCE CORP. v. ARTHUR ANDERSEN & CO.
COURT OF APPEALS FOR NEW YORK
65 N.Y.2D 536; 483 N.E.2D 110; 493 N.Y.S.2D 435; 1985 N.Y. LEXIS 15157 (1985)

Before 1978, Credit Alliance had provided financing to L. B. Smith, Inc., of Virginia, a capital-intensive enterprise that regularly required financing. During 1978, Credit Alliance advised Smith that as a condition to extending additional major financing, it would insist upon examining an audited financial statement. Accordingly on two separate occasions Smith provided Credit Alliance with its consolidated financial statements, covering itself and its subsidiaries. These statements contained an auditor's report prepared by Arthur Andersen, stating it had examined the statements in accordance with generally accepted auditing standards ("GAAS") and found them to fairly reflect the financial position of Smith in conformity with generally accepted accounting principles ("GAAP"). In reliance upon the statements, Credit Alliance provided substantial amounts in financing to Smith.

In 1980, Smith filed a petition for bankruptcy. By that time, Smith had already defaulted on several millions of dollars of obligations to Credit Alliance. In August 1981, Credit Alliance sued for damages lost on its outstanding loans to Smith, claiming both negligence and fraud by Andersen in the preparation of its audit reports. The complaint alleges Andersen knew, should have known, or was on notice that the certified statements were being utilized by Smith to induce companies such as Credit Alliance to make credit available. It is also alleged Andersen knew or recklessly disregarded facts that indicated the certified statements were misleading.

Andersen filed a motion to dismiss the complaint. The court concluded Credit Alliance fell within the exception to the general rule that requires privity to maintain an action against an accountant for negligence. Andersen appealed.

JUDGE JASEN: In the seminal case of *Ultramares Corp. v Touche* (255 NY 170), this court, speaking through the opinion of Chief Judge Cardozo more than 50 years ago, disallowed a cause of action in negligence against a public accounting firm for inaccurately prepared financial statements which were relied upon by a plaintiff having no contractual privity with the accountants. This court distinguished its holding from *Glanzer v Shepard* (233 NY 236), a case decided in an opinion also written by Cardozo nine years earlier. We explained that in *Glanzer,* an action in negligence against public weighers had been permitted, despite the absence of a contract between the parties, because the plaintiff's intended reliance, on the information *directly transmitted* by the weighers, created a bond so closely approaching privity it was, in practical effect, virtually indistinguishable there from. This court has subsequently reaffirmed its holding in *Ultramares* which has been, and continues to be, much discussed and analyzed by the commentators and by the courts of other jurisdictions. This appeal now provides us with the opportunity to re-examine and delineate the principles enunciated in both *Ultramares* and *Glanzer.* Inasmuch as we believe a relationship "so close as to approach that of privity" (255 NY, at pp 182–183) remains valid as the predicate for imposing liability upon accountants to noncontractual parties for the negligent preparation of financial reports, we restate and elaborate upon our adherence to that standard today.

The critical distinctions between the two cases were highlighted in *Ultramares* where we explained:

> In *Glanzer v. Shepard* . . . [the certificate of weight], which was made out in duplicate, one copy to the seller and the other to the buyer, *recites that it was made by order of the former for the use of the latter.* . . . Here was something more than the rendition of a service in the expectation that the one who ordered the certificate would use it thereafter in the operations of his business as occasion might require. Here was a case where *the transmission of the certificate to another was* not merely one possibility among many, but *the "end and aim of the transaction,"* as certain and immediate and deliberately willed as if a husband were to order a gown to be delivered to his wife, or a telegraph company, contracting with the sender of a message, were to telegraph it wrongly to the damage of the person expected to receive it. . . . The *intimacy of the resulting nexus* is attested by the fact that after stating the case in terms of legal duty, we went on to point out that . . . we could reach the same result by stating it in terms of contract. . . . The bond was *so close as to approach that of privity, if not completely one with it.* Not so in the case at hand [i.e., *Ultramares*]. No one would be likely to urge that there was a contractual relation, *or even one approaching it,* at the root of any duty that was owing from the [accountants] now before us to the indeterminate class of persons who, presently or in the future, might deal with the [accountants' client] in reliance on the audit. In a word, the service rendered by the defendant in *Glanzer v. Shepard* was primarily for the information of a third person, *in effect, if not in*

> *name, a party to the contract,* and only incidentally for that of the formal promisee. (*Ultramares Corp. v Touche, supra,* at pp. 182–183 [emphasis added].)

Upon examination of *Ultramares* and *Glanzer* and our recent affirmation of their holdings in *White,* certain criteria may be gleaned. Before accountants may be held liable in negligence to noncontractual parties who rely to their detriment on inaccurate financial reports, certain prerequisites must be satisfied: (1) the accountants must have been aware that the financial reports were to be used for a particular purpose or purposes; (2) in the furtherance of which a known party or parties was intended to rely; and (3) there must have been some conduct on the part of the accountants linking them to that party or parties, which evinces the accountants' understanding of that party or parties' reliance. While these criteria permit some flexibility in the application of the doctrine of privity to accountant liability, they do not represent a departure from the principles articulated in *Ultramares, Glanzer* and *White,* but, rather, they are intended to preserve the wisdom and policy set forth therein.

In the appeals we decide today, application of the foregoing principles presents little difficulty. The facts as alleged by Credit Alliance fail to demonstrate the existence of a relationship between the parties sufficiently approaching privity. Though the complaint and supporting affidavit do allege Andersen specifically knew, should have known or was on notice that Credit Alliance was being shown the reports by Smith, Andersen's client, in order to induce their reliance thereon, nevertheless, there is no adequate allegation of either a particular purpose for the reports' preparation or the prerequisite conduct on the part of the accountants. While the allegations state Smith sought to induce plaintiffs to extend credit, no claim is made Andersen was being employed to prepare the reports with that particular purpose in mind. Moreover, there is no allegation Andersen had any direct dealings with Credit Alliance, had specifically agreed with Smith to prepare the report for Credit Alliance's use or according to Credit Alliance's requirements, or had specifically agreed with Smith to provide Credit Alliance with a copy or actually did so. Indeed, there is simply no allegation of any word or action on the part of Andersen directed to Credit Alliance, or anything contained in Andersen's retainer agreement with Smith which provided the necessary link between them. We therefore dismiss the charges against Arthur Andersen.

REVERSED.

CRITICAL THINKING

Think about the judge's reasoning leading to the conclusion that the relationship between Arthur Andersen & Co. and Credit Alliance was not enough to establish privity. Is there any additional information that you would have liked to know to help decide whether Andersen acted negligently?

ETHICAL DECISION MAKING

What are the values associated with requiring that the relationship between Andersen and Credit Alliance be enough to establish privity? What values would have been in conflict when making the decision? Do you think the values promoted by the decision are appropriate for the situation? Why or why not?

LIABILITY TO FORESEEN USERS AND FORESEEN CLASS OF USERS (THE RESTATEMENT RULE)

About half the states have adopted a more expansive approach to accountant liability for negligence to third parties. The *Restatement test* was codified in the Restatement (Second) of Torts. It holds an accountant liable to known third-party users of the accountant's work product and also to those in the limited class whose reliance on the work the accountant specifically foresaw.

The rationale behind the Restatement test is simple: Much of what accountants do is prepare work for parties who are not their clients; therefore, it makes sense for them to owe a duty to these intended receivers. The test extends liability to those people, or the class of people, the accountant foresaw or should have foreseen as being the recipients of and relying on his or her work. Despite the expansion, as Section 552 of the Restatement of Torts explains, accountant liability is not extended to potential investors and the general public.

Assume a client has an accountant certify financial statements as part of a loan application of Third State Bank. The accountant, aware of this purpose, negligently audits the statements, which overvalue inventory and undervalue liabilities. The client uses the financials not only at Third State Bank but also at Federal State Bank, which makes the loan. When the client defaults on the loan because of too much indebtedness, Federal State can properly sue the accountant for negligence because the bank's use of the financial statements for loan considerations was foreseeable, even if the specific institution was not. The Restatement test is a middle-ground test between the very restrictive, pro-accountant primary-benefit test represented by *Ultramares* and the liability-expanding reasonably foreseeable users test discussed next.

Legal Principle: **Under the *Restatement rule,* an accountant is liable to known third-party users of the accountant's work product and also to those in the limited class whose reliance on the work the accountant specifically foresaw.**

BUT WHAT IF . . .

WHAT IF THE FACTS OF THE CASE OPENER WERE DIFFERENT?

Let's say that Roberts was commissioned to do some outside accounting work for a bank. He was paid for a month to approve loan applications. He negligently approved some loans. As a result, the bank tried to sue him when the applicants defaulted on their loans. Additionally, one of the applicants, Bob, lost his home, and his live-in girlfriend Stacey attempted to sue Roberts for losing her home. Which party may actually sue Roberts? Why can the other party not sue Roberts?

LIABILITY TO REASONABLY FORESEEABLE USERS

Very few states have adopted the general negligence standard of accountant third-party liability called the *reasonably foreseeable users test.* This test holds an accountant liable to any third party who was or should have been foreseen as a possible user of the accountant's work product and who did in fact use and rely on that work product for a proper business purpose. The justification for this expanded accountant liability was succinctly stated by the New Jersey Supreme Court in a case subsequently overruled by statute:

> The responsibility of a public accountant is not only to the client who pays his fee, but also to investors, creditors, and others who may rely on the financial statements which he certifies. . . . The auditor's function has expanded from that of a watchdog for management to an independent evaluator of the adequacy and fairness of financial statements issued by management to stockholders, creditors and others.[5]

The court justified its protection of reasonably foreseeable users on the policy grounds that this approach would encourage accountants to be more careful and thorough and the cost of the increased liability risk, through insurance or otherwise, could be spread among all the accountant's clients. Courts used similar reasoning as justification for imposing strict product liability.

Legal Principle: **Under the *reasonably foreseeable users test,* an accountant is liable to any third party who was or should have been foreseen as a possible user of the accountant's work product and who did in fact use and rely on that work product for a proper business purpose.**

The *Bily* decision excerpted in Case 11-2 contains a good discussion of the three theories of the accountant's legal liability to third parties.

[5] *Rosenbloom, Inc. v Adler,* 461 A.2d 138 (1983).

CASE 11-2 BILY v. ARTHUR YOUNG & CO.
SUPREME COURT OF CALIFORNIA
834 P.2D 745 (1992)

Plaintiffs purchased stock warrants (rights to purchase) for blocks of Osborne Computer Corp., the manufacturer of the first mass-market portable personal computer. Because of inability to produce a new product line with sufficient speed and the entry of IBM-compatible software into the personal computer market, Osborne filed for bankruptcy shortly after the warrants were issued. Plaintiffs thus received nothing for their investment.

Arthur Young had audited Osborne's financial statements for the two years preceding the issuance of the warrants and had issued unqualified opinions on their fairness and compliance with Generally Accepted Accounting Principles. Plaintiffs sued Arthur Young for fraud, negligence, and negligent misrepresentation. After a thirteen-week trial in which the plaintiffs' expert witness alleged forty deficiencies in Arthur Young's audit and its noncompliance with Generally Accepted Auditing Standards, the jury found Arthur Young liable for professional negligence. Arthur Young appealed based on the jury instructions regarding its liability to third parties.

CHIEF JUSTICE LUCAS: The AICPA's professional standards refer to the public responsibility of auditors:

> A distinguishing mark of a profession is acceptance of its responsibility to the public. The accounting profession's public consists of clients, credit grantors, governments, employers, investors, the business and financial community, and others who rely on the objectivity and integrity of certified public accountants to maintain the orderly functions of commerce. This reliance imposes a public interest responsibility on certified public accountants. [2 AICPA Professional Standards (CCH 1988) §53.01]

[The court then discussed different states' approaches to the issue of accountant liability to third parties.]

A. Privity of Relationship

The New York Court of Appeals restated the law in light of *Ultramares, White v. Guarente,* and other cases in *Credit Alliance v. Arthur Andersen & Co.* (1985) 65 N.Y. 2d 536 [493 N.Y.S. 2d 435, 483 N.E. 2d 110]. *Credit Alliance* subsumed two cases with different factual postures: in the first case, plaintiff alleged it loaned funds to the auditor's client in reliance on audited financial statements which overstated the client's assets and net worth; in the second, the same scenario occurred, but plaintiff also alleged the auditor knew plaintiff was the client's principal lender and communicated directly and frequently with plaintiff regarding its continuing audit reports. The court dismissed plaintiff's negligence claim in the first case, but sustained the claim in the second.

The New York court promulgated the following rule for determining auditor liability to third parties for negligence:

> Before accountants may be held liable in negligence to noncontractual parties who rely to their detriment on inaccurate financial reports, certain prerequisites must be satisfied: (1) the accountant must have been aware that the financial reports were to be used for a particular purpose or purposes; (2) in the furtherance of which a known party or parties was intended to rely; and (3) there must have been some conduct on the part of the accountants linking them to party or parties, which evinces the accountants' understanding of that party or parties reliance. (*Credit Alliance v. Arthur Andersen & Co.,* supra, 483 N.E. 2d at p. 118)

Discussing the application of its rule to the cases at hand, the court observed the primary, if not exclusive, "end and aim" of the audits in the second case was to satisfy the lender. The auditor's direct communications and personal meetings [with the lender] result[ed] in a nexus between them sufficiently approaching privity. In contrast, in the first case, although the complaint did not allege the auditor knew or should have known of the lender's reliance on its reports: "There was no allegation of either a particular purpose for the reports' preparation or the prerequisite conduct on the part of the accountants . . . [nor] any allegation [the auditor] had any direct dealings with plaintiffs, and agreed with [the client] to prepare the report for plaintiffs' use or according to plaintiffs' requirements, or had specifically agreed with [the client] to provide plaintiffs with a copy [of the report] or actually did so."

B. Foreseeability

Arguing that accountants should be subject to liability to third persons on the same basis as other tortfeasors, Justice Howard Wiener advocated rejection of the rule of *Ultramares* in a 1983 law review article. In its place, he proposed a rule based on foreseeability of injury to third persons. Criticizing what he called the "anachronistic protection" given to accountants by the traditional rules limiting third person liability, he concluded:

> Accountant liability based on foreseeable injury would serve the dual functions of compensation for injury and deterrence of negligent conduct.

> Moreover, it is a just and rational judicial policy that the same criteria govern the imposition of negligence liability, regardless of the context in which it arises. The accountant, the investor, and the general public will in the long run benefit when the liability of the certified public accountant for negligent misrepresentation is measured by the foreseeability standard.

Under the rule proposed by Justice Wiener, "[f]oreseeability of the risk would be a question of fact for the jury to be disturbed on appeal only where there is insufficient evidence to support the finding."

C. The Restatement: Intent to Benefit Third Persons

Section 552 of the Restatement Second of Torts covers "Information Negligently Supplied for the Guidance of Others." It states a general principle that one who negligently supplies false information "for the guidance of others in their business transactions" is liable for economic loss suffered by the recipients in justifiable reliance on the information. But the liability created by the general principle is expressly limited to loss suffered: "(a) by the person or one of a limited group of persons for whose benefit and guidance he intends to supply the information or knows that the recipient intends to supply it, and (b) through reliance upon it in a transaction that he intends the information to influence or knows that the recipient so intends or in a substantially similar transaction." To paraphrase, a supplier of information is liable for negligence to a third party only if he or she indents to supply the information for the benefit of one or more third parties in a specific transaction or type of transaction identified to the supplier.

The authors of the Restatement Second of Torts offer several variations on the problem before us as illustrations of section 552. For example, the auditor may be held liable to a third party lender if the auditor is informed by the client that the audit will be used to obtain a $50,000 loan, even if the specific lender remains unnamed or the client names one lender then borrows from another. However, there is no liability where the auditor agrees to conduct the audit with the express understanding the report will be transmitted only to a specified bank and it is then transmitted to other lenders. Similarly, there is no liability when the client's transaction (as represented to the auditor) changes so as to increase materially the audit risk, e.g., a third person originally considers selling goods to the client on credit and later buys a controlling interest in the client's stock, both in reliance on the auditor's report.

Under the Restatement rule, an auditor retained to conduct an annual audit and to furnish an opinion for no particular purpose generally undertakes no duty to third parties. Such an auditor is not informed

> of any intended use of the financial statements; but . . . knows that the financial statements, accompanied by an auditor's opinion, are customarily used in a wide variety of financial transactions by the [client] corporation, and that they may be relied upon by lenders, investors, shareholders, creditors, purchasers, and the like, in numerous possible kinds of transactions. [The client corporation] uses the financial statements and accompanying auditor's opinion to obtain a loan from [a particular] bank. Because of [the auditor's] negligence, he issues an unqualifiedly favourable opinion upon a balance sheet that materially misstates the financial position of [the corporation] and through reliance upon it [the bank] suffers pecuniary loss.

Consistent with the text of section 552, the authors conclude: "[The auditor] is not liable to [the bank]."

Analysis of Auditor's Liability to Third Persons for Audit Opinions

D. Negligence

In permitting negligence liability to be imposed in the absence of privity, we outlined the factors to be considered in making such a decision: "The determination whether in a specific case the defendant will be held liable to a third person not in privity is a matter of policy and involves the balancing of various factors, among which are the extent to which the transaction was intended to affect the plaintiff, the foreseeability of harm to him, the degree of certainty that the plaintiff suffered injury, the moral blame attached to the defendant's conduct, and the policy of preventing future harm."

Viewing the problem before us in light of the factors set forth above, we decline to permit all merely foreseeable third party users of audit reports to sue the auditor on a theory of professional negligence. Our holding is premised on three central concerns: (1) Given the secondary "watchdog" role of the auditor, the complexity of the professional opinions rendered in audit reports, and the difficult and potentially tenuous causal relationships between audit reports and economic losses from investment and credit decisions, the auditor exposed to negligence claims from all foreseeable third parties faces potential liability far out of proportion to its fault; (2) the generally more sophisticated class of plaintiffs in auditor liability classes (e.g., business lenders and investors) permits the effective use of contract rather than tort liability to control and adjust the relevant risks through "private ordering"; and (3) the asserted advantages of more accurate auditing and more efficient loss spreading relied upon by those who advocate a pure foreseeability approach are unlikely to occur; indeed, dislocations of resources, including increased expense and decreased availability of

[continued]

auditing services in some sectors of the economy, are more probable consequences of expanded liability.

For the reasons stated above, we hold that an auditor's liability for general negligence in the conduct of an audit of its client's financial statements is confined to the client, i.e., the person who contracts for or engages the audit services. Other persons may not recover on a pure negligence theory.

There is, however, a further narrow class of persons who, although not clients, may reasonably come to receive and rely on audit reports and whose existence constitutes a risk of audit reporting that may fairly be imposed on the auditor. Such persons are specifically intended beneficiaries of the audit report who are known to the auditor and for whose benefit it renders the audit report. While such persons may not recover on a general negligence theory, we hold they may . . . recover on a theory of negligent misrepresentation.

REVERSED.

CRITICAL THINKING

If you were a justice on the supreme court of a state that had yet to decide which of the three rules to follow in determining the extent of auditors' liability to third parties, which would you adopt? Why?

ETHICAL DECISION MAKING

Which stakeholders would primarily benefit from each of the three alternatives?

Accountants' and Clients' Rights

When an accountant and a client are engaged in a contract, certain legal rights and issues arise. Two of the most salient rights issues are working papers and accountant-client privilege.

WORKING PAPERS

Legal issues involving rights to documents may arise when the audit is complete and a new set of documents, the working papers, has been created. **Working papers** are the various documents used and developed during an audit, including notes, calculations, copies, memorandums, and other papers constituting the accountant's work product.

After an audit, the accountant is the legal owner of the working papers. Accountants are advised to maintain all working papers because they can be used as evidence in negligence cases (to show competency of work product). Not only is it wise to keep working papers, but the Sarbanes-Oxley Act of 2002 requires keeping them for five years starting with the end of the fiscal period in which the audit was conducted. Willful violation results in a fine, imprisonment up to 10 years, or both.

Although the accountant is the legal owner of the working papers, the information contained within them belongs to the client. Accordingly, the client has a right to access working papers on request. Also, because of the sensitive nature of their contents, an accountant may not disclose working papers unless (1) the client consents or (2) the court orders the documents. Improper disclosure of a client's working papers is unethical.

BUT WHAT IF . . .

WHAT IF THE FACTS OF THE CASE OPENER WERE DIFFERENT?

Let's say that one of Roberts's audits was called into question. The SEC asked for the documents and notes related to Roberts's audit, but Roberts had not kept them. What, if anything, could happen to Roberts for not having these papers anymore? Why?

ACCOUNTANT-CLIENT PRIVILEGE

An **accountant-client privilege,** the right of an accountant to refuse to reveal any information given to him during the course of providing accounting services to a client, is not recognized by the common law or by federal law. However, a number of states have adopted statutes granting some form of accountant-client privilege, but when a federal law is at issue, state protection does not apply. Accountant-client privilege is typically granted to the client, although some states extend it, or some form of it, to the accountant. Under the IRS Restructuring and Reform Act, accountants authorized by federal law to practice before the IRS have privilege of confidentiality when giving tax advice to clients with respect to the Internal Revenue Code.

Even where privilege does not exist, it is unethical for an accountant to willfully disclose the contents of confidential communications with a client unless the disclosure is done in accordance with the American Institute of Certified Public Accountants (AICPA) or GAAS requirements, as part of a court order, or on the client's request.

Federal Securities Law and Accountant Liability

L03

What is the impact of federal securities law on accountant liability?

Several federal acts have been critical in assessing criminal and civil liability to accountants. Among these are the Securities Act of 1933, the Securities Exchange Act of 1934, the Private Securities Litigation Reform Act of 1995, and the Sarbanes-Oxley Act of 2002. Also, as mentioned above and in Chapter 7, RICO has been useful in bringing suits against accountants for their wrongdoings.

THE SECURITIES ACT OF 1933

Under Section 11 of the Securities Act of 1933, accountants are civilly liable for misstatements and omissions of material facts made in registration statements the SEC requires. When a person buys a security covered by a registration statement that contains false information or is missing information, the accountant who helped prepare and file the statement may be liable for damages. A recent court case found that an accounting firm, Todman & Co., CPAs, could be held liable for failing to correct audits once it was aware that the information in the audits was wrong, as well as for recklessly ignoring warning flags that information in the audits was probably incorrect. The federal appeals court had previously assumed that these actions could be included under Section 10(b) of the Securities Exchange Act and SEC Rule 10b-5, but it had never directly stated that failing to correct information or recklessly ignoring warning flags could constitute liability. This ruling seems to expand the responsibility of accountants. The appeals court vacated the district court's decision to dismiss the case and remanded the case back to the lower court.[6]

To recover damages, a plaintiff—someone who purchased a security covered by a flawed registration statement—does not need to prove reliance on the statement or to establish privity. The purchaser may recover damages without knowing about or relying on the flawed information or even being a party to the contractual agreement. Originally liable only to those who purchased securities in an initial public offering (IPO), accountants are now liable to subsequent purchasers as well, as the Case Nugget illustrates.

Accountants are liable when they do not perform their jobs according to the generally accepted standards and practices of their profession. Under Section 11 of the Securities Act, accountants have a duty to perform their tasks with due diligence. This includes the creation of financial statements filed with the SEC as part of registration statements. Under Section 11, an accountant is not liable if "after reasonable investigation, [he or she has]

[6] *Overton v. Todman & Co.*, 478 F.3d 479 (2d Cir. 2007).

CASE NUGGET

ATTEMPTED EXPANSION OF LIABILITY TO SUBSEQUENT PURCHASERS

In re Century Aluminum Company Securities Litigation
2013 U.S. App. LEXIS 7759 (9th Cir., Jan. 2, 2013)

In *In re Century Aluminum Company Securities Litigation,* purchasers bought shares of the Century Aluminum Company around the time of a secondary offering of 24.5 million shares. Before this offering, 49 million shares of the company already existed in the market. The purchasers of the secondary-offering shares argued that there were misrepresentations of the shares in the statements released regarding the secondary offering. The claims of the purchasers were filed in accordance with Section 11 of the Securities Act of 1933. This section gives purchasers a cause of action if there are misrepresentations in statements about registration to buy securities. If purchasers can trace their aftermarket shares back to the statements, Section 11 gives them cause of action as well. Since the Supreme Court, in *Twombly* and *Iqbal,* abolished notice pleading and instead set plausibility pleading as the standard, a plaintiff has been required to show "factual content that allows the court to draw the reasonable inference that the defendant is liable for the misconduct alleged." In this case, the court determined that it would be "often impossible" for purchasers of aftermarket shares to have claims based on Section 11 because their purchasing is normally done through brokers that don't acknowledge the source of the shares. Thus, the court affirmed the dismissal of the lawsuit.

reasonable ground to believe and did believe, at the time such part of the registration statement became effective, that the statements therein were true and that there was no omission to state a material fact required to be stated therein or necessary to make the statements therein not misleading."[7] An accountant's failure to fulfill obligations under GAAP and GAAS is prima facie evidence of a failure of due diligence.

Under the Securities Act an accountant can prove due diligence by showing that he or she did not act fraudulently or negligently in preparing the registration statements in question or that no misstatements or omissions exist. An accountant can also acknowledge misstatements or omissions but contest liability on the ground that they do not involve material facts or had no causal connection to the purchaser's loss or that the purchaser invested in the securities knowing of the misstatements or omissions.

The final defense available to an accountant is to argue that the misstatements or omissions did not occur as a result of the financial statement created by the accountant but were made by another party. For example, if two accounting firms provided information to the SEC about the same public company and one set of paperwork contained misstatements, only the firm that filed that set would be liable. An accountant cannot be held liable for something he or she did not do. In the WorldCom case in the opening scenario, Roberts was charged with, among other things, violation of Section 11 of the Securities Act for the statements he filed with the SEC. He asserted the affirmative defense of due diligence and argued that he "relied and was entitled to rely on the integrity of WorldCom's officers and the work of WorldCom's auditor in connection with the contents of the Registration Statements."[8] Should Roberts's alleged reliance on his employees enable him to claim that he acted with due diligence? According to the SEC, directors must perform "a due diligence inquiry" regardless of whether another expert compiles the statement.[9] Courts have also held that a director may not use a defense of reliance when red flags about the questionable quality of an audit exist.[10]

For willful violations of the Securities Act, the U.S. Department of Justice can seek fines up to $10,000, imprisonment up to five years, or both. To prevent future fraud, the SEC may seek an injunction against willful violators to prevent their engaging in similar practices in the future and may ask the court to impose other forms of relief.

[7] U.S.C. § 77(b)(3).

[8] See footnote 1.

[9] "New High Risk Ventures," SEC Release No. 5275, 1972 WL 125474, p. 6.

[10] *WorldCom,* 346 F. Supp. 2d, p. 672.

Another relevant and related section of the Securities Act is Section 15. Under Section 15, "[E]very person who, by or through stock ownership, agency, or otherwise . . . controls any person liable under section 11 or 12, shall also be liable jointly and severally with and to the same extent as such controlled person to any person to whom such controlled person is liable."[11] Section 15 is typically used to charge executive board members or other high-level officials who fail to use a reasonable standard of care when running their business. To establish liability, a plaintiff must prove control on the part of the defendant and an underlying claim under Section 11 or 12.

Section 15 does contain an affirmative defense. A controlling person will not be liable if he or she "had no knowledge of or reasonable ground to believe in the existence of the facts by reason of which the liability of the controlled person is alleged to exist."[12] Roberts of WorldCom was charged with violations under Section 15 as well as Section 11. He asserted the affirmative defense available to him. However, the court determined that as chairman of the board of directors for WorldCom, he clearly was a controlling person. The question remains, Did Roberts have reasonable ground to believe in the financial statements he signed? If he did believe he signed accurate documents, should he still be held liable for his failure to review the documents thoroughly?

THE SECURITIES EXCHANGE ACT OF 1934

Liability under Section 18 of the Securities Exchange Act of 1934. The Securities Exchange Act of 1934, Section 18, states:

> Any person who shall make or cause to be made any statement in any application, report, or document . . ., which statement was at the time and in the light of the circumstances under which it was made false or misleading with respect to any material fact, shall be liable to any person (not knowing that such statement was false or misleading) who, in reliance upon such statement, shall have purchased or sold a security at a price which was affected by such statement, for damages caused by such reliance, unless the person sued shall prove that he acted in good faith and had no knowledge that such statement was false or misleading.

According to Section 18, accountants are liable for fraudulent statements made to the SEC in documents filed with it. Section 18 contains a built-in statute of limitations for recovery requiring that the action be brought within one year of discovering the fraud and within three years of its occurrence.

While the Securities Act imposes liability for negligence in performing an audit or constructing a financial statement, the Securities Exchange Act imposes liability for making fraudulent statements to the SEC. It requires a higher burden of proof to recover damages than does the Securities Act. It requires that a plaintiff prove two things. First, the false or misleading statement in question actually affected the price of the security. Second, reliance was placed on the false or misleading statement without knowledge of its inaccuracy. Like the Securities Act, the Securities Exchange Act does not require privity, but it now requires demonstration of reliance on the false or misleading statement. (The Securities Act did not require demonstration of reliance.)

Another difference between the Securities Act and the Securities Exchange Act is the duty imposed on accountants. Instead of requiring due diligence, the Securities Exchange Act uses a "good-faith" requirement. Under Section 18, an accountant is not liable if he or she acted in good faith. *Good faith* means the accountant did not know the financial statement was false or misleading and did not intend to use the falsity to gain an unfair advantage over another person. Without knowledge and intent, the accountant cannot be

[11] 15 U.S.C. § 770.

[12] Ibid.

found liable. To prove the absence of good faith on the part of the accountant, the plaintiff must establish three things: *scienter* (the accountant knowingly committed an illegal act), reckless conduct, and gross negligence in the accountant's actions. Without all three elements, a plaintiff will not succeed with a claim under the Securities Exchange Act.

As a second defense, the accountant can prove that the plaintiff knew the statements in question were false. The reasoning behind this defense is that a plaintiff who knows a statement is false places no reliance on it, and reliance must be proved to establish a claim. Therefore, without reliance on the falsity, the accountant would not be liable to the plaintiff.

Liability under Section 10(b) of the Securities Exchange Act and SEC Rule 10b-5. Section 10(b) of the act is an antifraud provision that makes it unlawful for accountants, or anyone, to use "any manipulative or deceptive device or contrivance in contravention of such rules and regulations as the [SEC] may prescribe as necessary or appropriate in the public interest or for the protection of investors." Accountants are thus liable to buyers and sellers for fraudulent statements made to the SEC, as well as for written or oral fraudulent statements made in the process of selling any security.

To recover under Section 10(b) and the corresponding SEC Rule 10b-5, a buyer or seller of a security must prove each of the following six elements:

1. Status as purchaser or seller (privity not required).
2. Scienter.
3. Fraudulent act or deception.
4. Reliance on the fraudulent statement.
5. Statement in regard to a material fact.
6. Reliance on the statement as the cause of the plaintiff's loss.

Once the buyer or seller establishes all six elements, he or she is eligible for recovery of damages from the liable accountant. Case 11-3 discusses the circumstances under which an accounting firm is liable under Section 10(b) and Rule 10b-5.

CASE 11-3 MATRIXX INITIATIVES, INC., ET AL. v. SIRACUSANO ET AL.

UNITED STATES SUPREME COURT NO. 09–1156, CERTIORARI TO THE U.S. COURT OF APPEALS FOR THE NINTH CIRCUIT (2011)

Matrixx is a pharmaceutical company that manufactures medicines and sells them through its subsidiary Zicam, LLC. Zicam Cold Remedy was one medicine produced and distributed through the company, and it took the form of a nasal spray or gel and contained zinc gluconate, an active ingredient. In 2004, plaintiffs filed a lawsuit against the company alleging that the company did not release studies that the product had been known to result in a loss of smell, which was a violation of §10(b) of the Securities Exchange Act and SEC Rule 10b-5. The district court granted the company's motion to dismiss the claim, saying that the complaints were not material or statistically significant. The plaintiffs then appealed to the Court of Appeals for the Ninth Circuit, which reversed and remanded the decision. In 2010, the company filed a petition for a writ of certiorari to the Ninth Circuit with the United States Supreme Court.

JUSTICE SOTOMAYOR: Respondents filed this securities fraud class action, alleging that petitioners (hereinafter Matrixx) violated §10(b) of the Securities Exchange Act of 1934 and Securities and Exchange Commission Rule 10b–5 by failing to disclose reports of a possible link between Matrixx's leading product, Zicam Cold Remedy, and loss of smell (anosmia), rendering statements made by Matrixx misleading. Matrixx moved to dismiss the complaint, arguing that respondents had not pleaded the element of a material misstatement or omission and the element of scienter. The District Court granted the motion, but the Ninth Circuit reversed. It held that the District Court erred in requiring an allegation of statistical significance to establish materiality, concluding instead that the complaint adequately alleged information linking Zicam and anosmia that would have been significant to a reasonable investor. It also held that Matrixx's withholding of information about reports of adverse effects and about pending lawsuits by Zicam users gave rise to a strong inference of scienter.

Held: Respondents have stated a claim under §10(b) and Rule 10b–5.

a. To prevail on their claim, respondents must prove, as relevant here, a material misrepresentation or omission by Matrixx and scienter. See Stoneridge Investment Partners, LLC v. Scientific-Atlanta, Inc., 552 U. S. 148. Matrixx contends that they failed to plead these required elements because they did not allege that the reports Matrixx received reflected statistically significant evidence that Zicam caused anosmia.

b. Respondents have adequately pleaded materiality.

   1. Under Basic Inc. v. Levinson, §10(b)'s materiality requirement is satisfied when there is "a substantial likelihood that the disclosure of the omitted fact would have been viewed by the reasonable investor as having significantly altered the 'total mix' of information made available." The Court declined to adopt a bright-line rule for determining materiality in Basic, observing that "[a]ny approach that designates a single fact or occurrence as always determinative of an inherently fact-specific finding such as materiality, must necessarily be overinclusive or underinclusive." Here, Matrixx's bright-line rule—that adverse event reports regarding a pharmaceutical company's products are not material absent a sufficient number of such reports to establish a statistically significant risk that the product is causing the events—would "artificially exclud[e]" information that "would otherwise be considered significant to [a reasonable investor's] trading decision." Matrixx's premise that statistical significance is the only reliable indication of causation is flawed. Both medical experts and the Food and Drug Administration rely on evidence other than statistically significant data to establish an inference of causation. It thus stands to reason that reasonable investors would act on such evidence. Because adverse reports can take many forms, assessing their materiality is a fact-specific inquiry, requiring consideration of their source, content, and context. The question is whether a reasonable investor would have viewed the nondisclosed information "as having significantly altered the 'total mix' of information made available." Something more than the mere existence of adverse event reports is needed to satisfy that standard, but that something more is not limited to statistical significance and can come from the source, content, and context of the reports.

   2. Applying Basic's "total mix" standard here, respondents adequately pleaded materiality. The complaint's allegations suffice to "raise a reasonable expectation that discovery will reveal evidence" satisfying the materiality requirement, Bell Atlantic Corp. v. Twombly, and to "allo[w] the court to draw the reasonable inference that the defendant is liable." Assuming the complaint's allegations to be true, Matrixx received reports from medical experts and researchers that plausibly indicated a reliable causal link between Zicam and anosmia. Consumers likely would have viewed Zicam's risk as substantially outweighing its benefit. Viewing the complaint's allegations as a whole, the complaint alleges facts suggesting a significant risk to the commercial viability of Matrixx's leading product. It is substantially likely that a reasonable investor would have viewed this information "as having significantly altered the 'total mix' of information made available." Assuming the complaint's allegations to be true, Matrixx told the market that revenues were going to rise 50 and then 80 percent when it had information indicating a significant risk to its leading revenue-generating product. It also publicly dismissed reports linking Zicam and anosmia and stated that zinc gluconate's safety was well established, when it had evidence of a biological link between Zicam's key ingredient and anosmia and had conducted no studies to disprove that link.

c. Respondents have also adequately pleaded scienter, "a mental state embracing intent to deceive, manipulate, or defraud." This Court assumes, without deciding, that the scienter requirement may be satisfied by a showing of deliberate recklessness. Under the Private Securities Litigation Reform Act of 1995, a complaint adequately pleads scienter "only if a reasonable person would deem the inference of scienter cogent and at least as compelling as any opposing inference one could draw from the facts alleged." Matrixx's proposed bright-line rule requiring an allegation of statistical significance to establish a strong inference of scienter is once

[continued]

again flawed. The complaint's allegations, "taken collectively," give rise to a "cogent and compelling" inference that Matrixx elected not to disclose adverse event reports not because it believed they were meaningless but because it understood their likely effect on the market. "[A] reasonable person" would deem the inference that Matrixx acted with deliberate recklessness "at least as compelling as any [plausible] opposing inference."

AFFIRMED.

CRITICAL THINKING

What words or phrases in this decision could be considered ambiguous? How might the outcome of this case change if different meanings were given to those words or phrases?

ETHICAL DECISION MAKING

Why do you think each court disagreed with the prior court's decision? What is compelling about each side?

Under Section 32 an accountant guilty of violating the Securities Exchange Act can be punished with a fine of not more than $5 million, imprisonment for not more than 20 years, or both. An accounting firm (but not an individual) may be fined up to $25 million.

BUT WHAT IF . . .

WHAT IF THE FACTS OF THE CASE OPENER WERE DIFFERENT?

Let's say, in the Case Opener, that Roberts had released financial statements regarding the success of the company and that the statements were false. However, these statements had led purchasers to buy many company shares. The purchasers tried to sue Roberts for liability under Section 10(b) of the Securities Exchange Act and SEC Rule 10b-5. What six elements would they have to prove?

Liability under Section 20(a) of the Securities Exchange Act. Like Section 15 of the Securities Act, Section 20(a) of the Securities Exchange Act is a controlling-person provision. It states:

> Every person who, directly or indirectly, controls any person liable under any provision of this chapter or of any rule or regulation thereunder shall also be liable jointly and severally with and to the same extent as such controlled person to any person to whom such controlled person is liable, unless the controlling person acted in good faith and did not directly or indirectly induce the act or acts constituting the violation or cause of action.[13]

Similarities between Section 15 of the Securities Act and Section 20(a) of the Securities Exchange Act should be immediately obvious. Both seek to apply liability to high-level officials for their direct misdeeds or their negligence in running their corporations.

Also similar is the method of proving liability. Under Section 20(a), to establish liability, the plaintiff must show (1) there was a primary violation by a controlled person; (2) the defendant controlled the primary violator; and (3) the defendant participated in a meaningful way in the primary violation. The first two requirements directly echo Section 15 of the Securities Act, but the third provides an additional step the plaintiff must complete.

Another similarity is provision of an affirmative defense. Section 20(a) allows defendants to avoid liability when "the controlling person acted in good faith and did not directly

[13] 15 U.S.C. § 78t.

or indirectly induce the act or acts constituting the [underlying] violation or cause of action."[14]

Roberts, from the opening scenario, also faced charges under Section 20(a). Once again, he asserted his affirmative defense. Since the Second Circuit held in *Marbury Mgmt. v. Kohn*[15] that Section 20(a) of the Securities Exchange Act parallels Section 15 of the Securities Act, we know Roberts meets the first two criteria for establishing liability. If he were not at all involved in the primary act, or were he to establish that he acted in good faith, he would not be held liable for losses suffered by the crash of WorldCom's stock.

THE PRIVATE SECURITIES LITIGATION REFORM ACT OF 1995

The Private Securities Litigation Reform Act (PSLRA) placed new statutory obligations on accountants by requiring that they use adequate procedures when performing an audit so that they can detect any illegal acts committed by the audited company. It also lists a specific set of actions and guidelines an accountant must follow after identifying a potentially illegal activity. Depending on the circumstances, the accountant must immediately notify the board of directors, the audit committee, or the SEC.[16]

PSLRA makes accountants liable for the portion of damages for which they are responsible.[17] It also amends the Securities Exchange Act of 1934 by making it a violation to in any way aid and abet a violation of that act, which includes keeping silent after discovering a potential fraud. For willful violation of PSLRA, the SEC can seek an injunction against the accountant and/or monetary fines. It is important to note that, under PSLRA, an accountant's silence when the accountant thinks he or she might have discovered fraud is enough to constitute aiding and abetting.

THE SARBANES-OXLEY ACT OF 2002

As explained in Chapter 7, the Sarbanes-Oxley Act was enacted in 2002 by Congress as a response to the business scandals of the early 2000s. The act consists largely of new rules and regulations for public accounting firms in an attempt to reduce fraud in accounting practices. It also created the Public Company Accounting Oversight Board, whose four members and chairperson report to the SEC. Titles I and II, the key provisions of the act, outline the duties of the board and establish new requirements and greater government oversight for public accounting firms, to protect investors from another Enron–Arthur Andersen type of scandal. The board has the power to oversee audit procedures for public companies and to ensure compliance with securities law, including Sarbanes-Oxley.

The board is also responsible for registering public accounting firms that prepare audit reports for issuers. It establishes standards and rules for audit reports, as well as quality control and ethics standards for registered public accounting firms. Third, the board is responsible for inspecting, investigating, and enforcing compliance on registered public accounting firms and anyone associated with them.

Sarbanes-Oxley also establishes rules for auditor independence by prohibiting registered public accounting firms (RPAFs) from engaging in the following nonauditing acts for their auditing clients:

- Bookkeeping.
- Financial information systems design and implementation.

[14] 15 U.S.C. § 78t(a).
[15] 629 F.2d 705 (1980).
[16] 15 U.S.C. § 78j–1.
[17] 15 U.S.C. § 78-4(g).

- Appraisal or valuation services.
- Actuarial services.
- Internal-audit outsourcing services.
- Management functions or human resources.
- Broker or dealer, investment adviser, or investment banking services.
- Legal or expert services unrelated to the audit.
- Any additional service the board deems impermissible.

Three additional rules provided by Title II help ensure auditor independence: (1) The lead or coordinating partners of audits of issuers of securities may not provide audit services to one particular issuer for more than five consecutive years; (2) any audit service an RPAF provides to an issuer must go through a preapproval process, and any nonaudit function performed must be disclosed in financial statements; and (3) an RPAF may not perform audit services for an issuer if the issuer's CEO, controller, CFO, chief accounting officer, or equivalent executive was employed by that RPAF and participated in any capacity in the audit of that issuer during the one-year period preceding the date of the initiation of the (current) audit.

The act also prohibits the destruction or falsification of records with the intent to obstruct or influence federal investigations or bankruptcy proceedings. The consequences of violating this prohibition can be a fine, imprisonment for up to 20 years, or both.

Liability of Other Professionals

LO4 What is the extent of liability of professionals other than accountants?

By no stretch of the imagination are accountants the only professionals likely to be sued for malpractice. As people become more aware of the legal requirements placed on professionals, they also become more alert to a lack of quality in some services and more ready to file suit against injurious professionals to hold them accountable for substandard work.

Most people have heard horror stories of doctors' failing to notice an obvious suspicious lump or amputating the wrong limb. It is over incidents like these that patients may sue doctors and other health practitioners for malpractice. Such suits award the victim just compensation, as well as deter professionals from failing to perform to the standards of their profession.

Attorneys, lawyers, real estate brokers, architects, and other professionals may also be liable for breach of contract or negligence if they fail in their contractual obligations or do not perform their duty according to the standards of their professions and another person is harmed. They may be liable for fraud if their actions were intentional. Exhibit 11-1 summarizes the elements of proof and common defenses in cases of professional liability.

Professionals can also be on the receiving end. An attorney misled by an accountant who provides fraudulent information is the victim of malpractice. If the same attorney provides fraudulent information to a client, the attorney could face a malpractice suit. Thus, the attorney could be the plaintiff in one malpractice case and the defendant in another.

In *Gulf Ins. Co. v. Jones*[18] we see an attorney malpractice suit arising out of a medical malpractice suit. Donald R. Blum, a podiatrist, performed a procedure on Sonia Y. Jones. After her surgery, Jones suffered excruciating pain in her feet and required corrective surgery to alleviate it. She sued Blum for malpractice, claiming he was negligent in performing the original procedure. Blum's insurer, Gulf Insurance, retained Cowles & Thompson, PC, to represent him. Due to conflicts at the law firm, a less experienced associate named

[18] 2005 U.S. App. LEXIS 16228 (2005).

Exhibit 11-1
Liability for Professionals

THEORY OF LIABILITY	ELEMENTS OF PROOF	COMMON DEFENSES
Negligence	The professional failed to live up to the standard of care of his or her profession, and this breach of duty caused compensable damage to the client.	Contributory or comparative negligence.
Breach of contract	The professional failed to perform his or her responsibilities under the contract for professional services within the agreed-on time.	The client's own actions or inactions were the cause of the professional's failure to perform.
Fraud	The professional made a misstatement of a material fact that the client relied on to his or her detriment.	No real defenses, other than showing that the elements of fraud were not proved.

Paula Shiroma-Bender represented Blum. After being found liable, Blum sued Cowles & Thompson, as well as Shiroma-Bender, for legal malpractice. Blum also sued his insurer for failing to settle out of court. The court determined that Blum did not meet his burden of proof. Nonetheless, the case serves as an example of how insurers, doctors, and attorneys may all end up being the target of malpractice suits.

Increasingly, computer and software professionals have to worry about liability for professional malpractice. For example, a firm may hire a software consultant to develop a software program that will allow the firm to better track significant data about its customers. Due to an error in the design by the consultant, significant amounts of data are lost. Or a consultant may enter into a contract to develop a software system, and the contract contains benchmarks for speed and other requirements, but due to the consultant's negligence, the benchmarks are never met, resulting in a suit for lost profits based on negligence or breach of contract.

PROTECTION FROM CLAIMS OF PROFESSIONAL MALPRACTICE

Today, most professionals who might be subject to malpractice claims, including architects, quality surveyors, home inspectors, lawyers, physicians, computer consultants, and accountants, will purchase professional indemnity insurance, which provides coverage for them in the event that they are sued for failing to live up to their professional responsibilities. Usually, the policies pay for claims that arise while the policy is in effect, meaning that the policyholder must be insured at the time the claim arose as well as at the time the claim is filed. These insurance policies are sometimes referred to as "errors and omissions" policies, as they are covering a person for errors or omissions made in the course of carrying out her or his professional responsibilities.

CASE OPENER WRAP-UP

Questionable Accounting at WorldCom

Roberts faced charges of liability under Sections 11 and 15 of the Securities Act and Sections 10(b) and 20(a) of the Securities Exchange Act. He raised an affirmative defense against all the claims against him and moved for summary judgment. In March 2005, Judge Cote denied Roberts's motion on all counts, claiming Roberts did not meet his burden of proof for any of the affirmative defenses. Roberts was then scheduled to go to trial; before the beginning of the trial, Roberts agreed to pay $4.5 million from his own pocket to settle the claims against him. Additionally, WorldCom's former CEO, Bernard J. Ebbers, was convicted around the start of Roberts's trial in the same district.

KEY TERMS

accountant-client privilege 268

malpractice actions 258

working papers 267

SUMMARY OF KEY TOPICS

Common Law Accountant Liability to Clients

There are three primary types of common law accountant liability to clients:

1. *Accountant liability for negligence:* An accountant is liable for negligence if the accountant fails to exercise the care of a competent, reasonable professional and that failure causes loss or injury to the client. At a minimum, an accountant has a duty to perform his or her task according to generally accepted accounting principles (GAAP) and generally accepted auditing standards (GAAS).
2. *Accountant liability for breach of contract:* Whenever an accountant is hired to perform a specific task, he or she enters into a contract with the client. Explicitly, the accountant agrees to perform the contractual agreed-on tasks. Implicitly, the accountant agrees to complete the work in a competent and professional manner according to professional standards (GAAP and GAAS). Accountants may be held liable for violating their explicit or implicit agreements.
3. *Accountant liability for fraud:* Accountants who commit fraud are liable to those parties the accountant reasonably should have foreseen as being injured through a justifiable reliance on the fraudulent information. Actual fraud exists when the accountant's actions meet the criteria necessary to prove fraud. Constructive fraud is fraud without fraudulent intent. To establish constructive fraud, a plaintiff must prove that the accountant was grossly negligent in performing his or her duties.

Common Law Accountant Liability to Third Parties

Third-party liability, as decided by the states, falls into three general categories:

1. *Privity or near-privity (the Ultramares rule):* Requires that the third party be in privity of contract with the accountant or be substantially close enough to the accountant to constitute near-privity.

2. *Foreseen users and class of users (the Restatement rule):* Requires that the third party be a known recipient or be of a class of known recipients of the accountant's work for liability to be established.
3. *Reasonably foreseeable users:* Allows any third party that should have been reasonably foreseen as using the product of an accountant's work to bring suit against the accountant for liability.

Accountants' and Clients' Rights

Working papers are the various documents used and developed during an audit, including notes, calculations, copies, memorandums, and other papers constituting the accountant's work product. The accountant is the legal owner of the working papers, but the material is the data of the client, who may access the working papers at any time upon request.

Accountant-client privilege exists only under some states' laws. It typically gives the client the right to confidentiality, whereas the accountant has fewer protections.

Federal Securities Law and Accountant Liability

Securities Act of 1933:

- Under Section11, accountants are civilly liable for misstatements and omissions of material facts made in registration statements filed with the SEC.
- Section 15 applies liability to controlling persons when a violation under Section 11 occurs.

Securities Exchange Act of 1934:

- According to Section 18, accountants are liable for fraudulent statements made in documents filed with the SEC.
- Section 10(b) and SEC Rule 10b-5 make it unlawful for accountants, or anyone, to use "any manipulative or deceptive device or contrivance in contravention of such rules and regulations as the [SEC] may prescribe as necessary or appropriate in the public interest or for the protection of investors."
- Section 20(a) (similar to Section 15 of the Securities Act) is a controlling-person provision. When a person is in control of a primary violator of the act and the person significantly partook in the illegal activity, he or she may be liable.

Private Securities Litigation Reform Act of 1995:

- The act requires that accountants use adequate procedures when performing an audit so that they can detect any illegal acts of the company being audited. Also under the act is a specific set of actions and guidelines an accountant must follow after identifying a potentially illegal activity when conducting an audit.

Sarbanes-Oxley Act of 2002:

- The act consists largely of new rules and regulations for public accountant firms in an attempt to reduce fraud in accounting practices. To limit fraud, the act created the Public Company Accounting Oversight Board. Titles I and II outline the duties of the board, as well as establish new requirements for public accounting firms.

Liability of Other Professionals

Many professionals who provide services, including attorneys, lawyers, real estate brokers, doctors, architects, and other professionals, are potential targets for professional liability. These professionals are liable under the same theories as accountants.

POINT / COUNTERPOINT

Is Sarbanes-Oxley Helping or Harming the Business Climate?

HARMING

While Congress may have had the best intentions in passing Sarbanes-Oxley, the law's unintended consequences have seriously hurt U.S. corporations and financial markets without increasing investor confidence.

One unintended consequence may be that more companies will choose to remain private, rather than going public, and consequently will be subject to much less regulation than public companies. Some small public companies have gone back to being privately held. In a 2003 survey of CEO readers of *Chief Executive Magazine,* 82 percent of the respondents believed it is better to remain a private company than to go public.[a]

The law disproportionately affects small businesses, imposing unfair costs on them. According to California congressman Brad Sherman, "The Government Accountability Office found that, proportionately, small public companies were spending considerably more on implementing Sarbanes-Oxley than large companies. Firms with less than $75 million in market capitalization were spending $1.14 in audit fees per $100 of revenue, the congressional researchers calculated, compared to just 13 cents per $100 of revenue for firms with greater than $1 billion in market capitalization."[b] A law that imposes such disparate costs clearly is not working.

While the act was supposed to eliminate conflicts of interest by prohibiting firms from providing nonauditing functions for their audit clients, it did not abolish what many consider the major conflict-of-interest problem: that auditing firms are paid by the companies they audit.

What are we getting for these unintended consequences? According to an editorial in *The New York Times,* we are not even getting increased consumer confidence: "[T]he best measure of investor confidence is the price-earnings ratio—the price that investors are willing to pay for each dollar of a company's reported earnings. The overall price-earnings ratio for the Standard & Poor's 500 stock index, however, has declined continuously since the Sarbanes-Oxley Act was being drafted in the spring of 2002."[c]

One last argument for significantly rolling back this onerous regulation is that foreign firms may be reluctant

HELPING

Like any law, Sarbanes-Oxley could perhaps be improved by some minor tinkering, but it is a sound piece of legislation that should not be rolled back.

Just think about what the law does. It forces companies to implement tough internal controls that ensure that the financial information they provide investors is honest and accurate, not false as in the Enron and WorldCom cases. It eliminates conflicts of interest that previously led major Wall Street firms to recommend that their clients buy stocks the firms themselves thought were worthless.

Opponents argue that the law should be abolished because the percentage of IPOs filed in the United States has fallen since Sarbanes-Oxley's enactment. In fact, the U.S. share of IPOs began falling six years before Sarbanes-Oxley was passed, declining from approximately 60 percent in 1996 to 8 percent in 2001. And it was approximately 15 percent in 2005, actually higher than in 2001.[e]

The U.S. financial markets still attract more money than any other markets in the world. Why? Primarily because of their reputation for fairness and transparency, which Sarbanes-Oxley has strengthened.

The two main groups behind the movement to roll back the law are the Chamber of Commerce and Wall Street insiders—those whose behavior is being scrutinized.

We should not let memories of Enron fade. The public needs the protections of Sarbanes-Oxley. They may impose some costs, but they are less onerous to society than the fraudulent profits some firms are making from innocent members of the investing public.

to make initial public offerings in U.S. markets because they fear Sarbanes-Oxley requirements. In 2005, 23 of 24 firms that had raised more than $1 billion in capital chose not to register their security offerings in U.S. markets, according to the New York Stock Exchange.[d]

Given all the negative consequences of the act, and its limited benefits, the law should be abolished or significantly reformed.

[a] "Getting Real about Sarbanes-Oxley" (Editorial), *Chief Executive Magazine,* July 2003, http://findarticles.com/p/articles/mi_m4070/is_190/ai_107204657.

[b] Brad Sherman, "Making Sarbanes-Oxley Work Better for Small Public Companies," October 18, 2006, www.house.gov/list/speech/ca27_sherman/op_061018.html.

[c] William A. Niskanen, "Enron's Latest Victims—American Markets," *The New York Times,* January 3, 2007, www.nytimes.com/2007/01/03/opinion/03niskanen.html?ex=1325480400&en=5b590f938ab3ba85&ei=5088&partner=rssnyt&emc=rss.

[d] Mallory Factor, "Cox and Sarbox: For the Good of Business and the American Shareholder, Sarbanes-Oxley Must Be Repealed or Radically Reformed," *National Review Online,* http://article.nationalreview.com/?q=OTIlNGE4MjMxYmRiMGQ1ZGU4Y2U2MDZlZDczNTY3M2E=.

[e] Reynolds Holding, "Plugging the IPO Drain," *Time,* March 19, 2007, www.time.com/time/magazine/article/0,9171,1587282,00.html.

QUESTIONS & PROBLEMS

1. What are the fundamental differences between the three theories of third-party accountant negligence?
2. When would an accountant-client privilege arise?
3. For what do *GAAP* and *GAAS* stand, and what function do they serve in the accounting profession?
4. In 2012, multiple producers of the 1990s television series *Sister, Sister* filed suit against the show's former accounting firm, Green Hasson Janks. The lawsuit alleged the accounting firm's professional negligence regarding the auditing and calculation of the show's profits. Specifically, the producers discovered that a full audit had never been performed for the show's production finances after several years of the show's television run. The producers claimed that because of this error, they lost around $5 million in profits. How did the court decide based on the evidence that the producers brought to the case? [*DePasse Jones et al. v. Green Hasson Janks et al.,* (Sup. Ct. L.A. 2012).]
5. A nonprofit organization called the Free Enterprise Fund filed a lawsuit claiming that Title I of the Sarbanes-Oxley Act was unconstitutional. Specifically, it alleged that the act's mandatory creation of the Public Company Accounting Oversight Board kept the president from having enough control over the board. Therefore, the lawsuit alleged, the act violated the appointments clause. However, the board is under the supervision of the Securities and Exchange Commission (SEC), and the president appoints and can remove the commissioners of the SEC. The D.C. court of appeals determined that the creation of the Public Company Accounting Oversight Board did not infringe on the separation-of-powers principle or violate the appointments clause. The court argued that the members of the board were under the supervision of the SEC, giving them much less power than other government officials. Does the Sarbanes-Oxley Act in fact violate the separation-of-powers doctrine because it gives extensive powers to the board and, at the same time, disallows the president the power to appoint or remove board members? [*Free Enterprise Fund v. Public Company Oversight Board,* 561 U.S. ___ (2010).]
6. Friede Goldman International and Halter Marine Group, Inc., merged to form Friede Goldman Halter, Inc. (FGH). FGH constructed large maritime equipment. Shortly after the merger, FGH hired Ernst & Young (E&Y) to audit its year-end financial statements and provide the audit opinion for its 10-K filing with the SEC. E&Y did not qualify its

opinion with any disclaimers or raise any concerns about FGH's ongoing viability, although the report did mention two problematic construction projects.

FGH shortly thereafter attempted to obtain surety bonds from Travelers Insurance and two other companies. Only Travelers agreed to issue the bonds, after FGH undertook a liquidity campaign that would ensure that the firm could cover the expected losses on the problematic projects. Shortly after Travelers issued the bonds, FGH ran out of money and filed for bankruptcy. Travelers was required to pay out approximately $58 million to complete the projects covered by its bonds. Travelers sued E&Y for negligence, arguing that E&Y had been negligent in failing to conduct the necessary inquiries and perform the proper audit tests to confirm and substantiate potential loss estimates, thereby leading to an understatement of the company's ongoing viability. Travelers had relied on the accuracy of the audit statement in issuing its bond. The jury, finding that Travelers had reasonably relied on the audit statements, allocated 15 percent of the loss to E&Y. E&Y appealed. Do you think that Travelers' reliance on the statements of E&Y should have been considered sufficient to form the basis for the imposition of liability on E&Y? [*Travelers Casualty and Surety Co. v. Ernst & Young,* 542 F.3d 475 (5th Cir. 2008).]

7. KGA is a public accounting firm that performed audits for Webb Cooley Company. KGA performed its audits after the calendar year in question. Thus, KGA issued its report on the 1998 financial statement in May 1999; KGA issued its report on the 1999 financial statement in April 2000. Compass Bank was Webb Cooley's lender. In April 1999, before KGA completed the 1998 audit, Compass loaned Webb Cooley $1.5 million pursuant to a term loan and extended Webb Cooley an additional $3.5 million revolving credit line. Compass increased Webb Cooley's credit line by $1 million in March 2000 and by an additional $500,000 in May 2000. Shortly after the May 2000 credit-line increase, Webb Cooley defaulted on its loans, and it eventually filed for bankruptcy. Compass then filed an action against KGA, claiming that KGA negligently misrepresented Webb Cooley's finances in the 1998 and 1999 audits, causing Compass to extend additional credit to Webb Cooley. Is KGA liable to Compass for the losses suffered by Webb Cooley's defaulting on its loans, and if so, for how much is KGA liable? [*Compass Bank v. King Griffin & Adamson P.C.,* 2004 U.S. App. LEXIS 21593 (2004).]

8. In 2012, Peregrine Financial Group (PFG) founder and CEO Russell Wasendorf, Sr., was accused of lying to regulators. Wasendorf had previously signed a confession in which he described bilking customers of his firm for almost 20 years. Specifically, Wasendorf "overstated the value of PFG's customer segregated funds by at least tens of millions of dollars" to the Commodity Futures Exchange Commission. Wasendorf had used home printers and photoshop computer software to intercept and forge financial statements from U.S. Bank, where his firm's customer money was held in different accounts, and from the firm's auditors—the National Futures Association. The newest complaint argued not that Wasendorf was using customer money but that he misrepresented the value of customer funds for two years. How did the court decide the 2012 case against Wasendorf? [*United States v. Russell R. Wasendorf, Sr.,* 12-CR-2021 LRR (2013).]

9. Todman & Co. audited the financial statements of Direct Brokerage, a broker-dealer, for several years. In his audit statements, he claimed that the statements accurately reflected the financial condition of the company when, in fact, the statements did not reflect payroll tax liabilities. Overton sued Todman & Co., claiming that he had invested $500,000 in Direct and loaned it $1.5 billion based on the audited statements. The district court dismissed the suit, and Overton appealed. What do you think the legal basis for Overton's claim was? On what grounds do you believe the appellate court affirmed or overturned the dismissal? [*Overton v. Todman & Co.,* 478 F.3d 479 (2d Cir. 2007).]

10. Colonial Bank failed in 2009. The Federal Deposit Insurance Corporation (FDIC) argued that the failure was a result of wire and securities fraud by the bank's biggest mortgage customer, Taylor Bean & Whitaker. The ex-chairman of Taylor Bean, Farkas, was arrested in 2011 for both types of fraud. Two top Colonial Bank executives pleaded guilty to being involved in the Taylor Bean fraud scheme as well. The FDIC decided to sue the accounting firms hired by the companies—Pricewaterhouse

Coopers LLP and Crowe Horwath LLP. The FDIC's lawsuit sought $1 billion for negligence. The complaint argued that had the accountants done their job accurately, they could not have missed the extensive fraud that was going on within the two companies and Colonial Bank never would have had to close. How do you think the court decided? [*Federal Deposit Insurance Corporation v. Pricewaterhouse Coopers LLP et al.,* Docket No. 2:12-cv-00957 (M.D. Ala., 2012).]

Looking for more review materials?

The Online Learning Center at **www.mhhe.com/kubasek3e** contains this chapter's "Assignment on the Internet" and also a list of URLs for more information, entitled "On the Internet." Find both of them in the Student Center portion of the OLC, along with quizzes and other helpful materials.

Intellectual Property

CHAPTER 12

LEARNING OBJECTIVES

After reading this chapter, you will be able to answer the following questions:

1. What are trademarks, and how do we protect them?
2. What are copyrights, and how do we protect them?
3. What are patents, and how do we protect them?
4. What are trade secrets, and how do we protect them?
5. How do treaties expand protection of intellectual property?

CASE OPENER

Smartphone Wars: Focus on Intellectual Property Rights

In the past five years, there have been significant innovations in technology such as smartphones and tablets. Technology companies rely on intellectual property (IP) rights, such as patents, trademarks, copyrights, and trade secrets, to protect their innovations. For example, Apple and Samsung, the two largest smartphone companies, have filed various patent infringement suits against each other in courts around the world. Apple and Samsung are strong competitors, so if one company were able to obtain an injunction preventing the other company from selling certain phones and tablets, this injunction could be devastating to the losing company. In one of these cases that proceeded to a jury trial, Apple argued that Samsung copied Apple's design of the iPhone and iPad—specifically, that Samsung copied the rounded-rectangle shape of the iPhone in violation of Apple's design patent and the iPhone's trade dress. Steve Jobs, the former CEO of Apple, emphasized the importance of neat, clean design for Apple products, and Apple has sought and received hundreds of design patents along with trademarks protecting its products. Similarly, Samsung has asserted a number of its own patents against Apple, including a patent covering the e-mailing of photos from a camera phone.

Critics argue that these patents and trademarks are too broad (i.e., that something as simple as a "rounded rectangle" or the sending of a photo from a phone should not be protected by patents or trademarks). Critics further argue that such broad IP rights stifle innovation and prevent smaller players from entering the market, as they cannot withstand the costs of litigation associated with competing in the smartphone and tablet markets. In response, the patent owners argue that they have expended significant resources in creating their products and deserve to avail themselves of the protection afforded by IP rights. Critics further argue that technology companies spend millions of dollars on litigation rather than on developing and improving products. Technology companies respond that they have no choice but to seek enforcement of their intellectual property rights through the legal system.

Furthermore, in January 2013, Apple Computer was granted a trademark for its retail store design and layout.[1] Specifically, the trademark covers the storefront design, the shelves in the store, and the location of the tables displaying products. One of the main reasons that this trademark was important to Apple was that fake Apple stores in China confuse customers.

1. Do you think that technology companies should be able to receive protection for allegedly "basic" ideas (e.g., store design or shape or color of a product) and functionalities?
2. How does intellectual property litigation between competitors (such as Apple and Samsung) affect you?

[1] Erin Geiger Smith, "Apple Trademarks Design of Its Retail Stores," *Reuters*, January 29, 2013.

Types of Intellectual Property

Intellectual property consists of the fruits of someone's mind. The laws of intellectual property protect property that is primarily the result of mental creativity rather than physical effort. Protection for various forms of intellectual property comes from trademarks, trade secret protection, patents, and copyrights, all of which we discuss in this chapter. Different types of intellectual property rights can apply to the same product. For example, certain aspects of the iPhone or the iPad could be protected by either a patent or a trade secret, and Apple would need to decide whether to apply for patent protection or keep the information a trade secret.

Trademarks

L01

What are trademarks, and how do we protect them?

A **trademark** is a distinctive mark, word, design, picture, or arrangement used with a product that helps consumers identify the product with the producer. Even the shape of a product or package may be a trademark if it is nonfunctional. For example, Papa John's has registered trademarks such as the name "Papa John's," as well as "Papa John's Pizza," and the phrase "Better Ingredients. Better Pizza." Other well-known trademarks include the Nike "swoosh" or the McDonald's Golden Arches. In addition to owning a trademark on the design of the Apple stores, Apple also owns the trademarks on iTunes, iPad, iPod, Facetime, and Mac.

To see how trademarks relate to marketing, please see the **Connecting to the Core** activity on the text website at www.mhhe.com/kubasek3e.

Even though the description of a trademark is very broad, there has still been substantial litigation over precisely what features can and cannot serve as a trademark. In one case, discussed in the Case Nugget, the U.S. Supreme Court grappled with the issue of whether a color can be a trademark.

A trademark used *intrastate* is protected under state common law. To be protected in *interstate* use, the trademark must be registered with the U.S. Patent and Trademark Office (USPTO) under the Lanham Act of 1947. Several types of marks are protected under this act (see Exhibit 12-1 for a list).

If a mark is registered, the holder of the mark may recover damages from an infringer who uses it to pass off goods as being those of the mark owner. The owner may also obtain an injunction prohibiting the infringer from using the mark. (Only the latter remedy is available for an unregistered mark.)

CASE NUGGET

COLOR AS A TRADEMARK?

Qualitex Co. v. Jacobson Products Co. 514 U.S. 159 (1995)
Christian Louboutin S.A. et al. v. Yves Saint Laurent America, Inc. et al. 696 F.3d 206 (2d Cir. 2012)

For years, plaintiff Qualitex Co. had colored the dry-cleaning press pads it manufactured a special shade of green-gold. When Jacobson Products, a competitor, started coloring its pads the same shade, Qualitex sued it for trademark infringement. The defendant argued that color alone should not qualify for registration as a trademark.

The district court found in favor of the plaintiff, but the Ninth Circuit reversed, holding that color alone could not be registered as a trademark. The plaintiff appealed to the Supreme Court.

Justice Breyer said the basic underlying principles of trademark law would seem to include color within the universe of things that could qualify as a trademark. He noted that the broad language used to describe trademarks included "any word, name, symbol, or device, or any combination thereof." Justice Breyer noted that a particular shape (of a Coca-Cola bottle), a particular sound (of NBC's three chimes), and even a particular scent (of plumeria blossoms on sewing thread) could be trademarked and thus, if a shape, a sound, and a fragrance can act as symbols, it made sense that so could a color.

He also noted that a color, if unusual enough in the context, could in fact come to identify goods with their source, just as descriptive words on a product could. The Court concluded the green-gold color acts as a symbol that has developed secondary meaning (customers identified it as Qualitex's) and identifies the press pads' source. The high court therefore reversed the decision in favor of the plaintiff.

Seventeen years later, courts considered whether a color can serve as a trademark in the fashion industry. Christian Louboutin designs and sells high-fashion shoes with red lacquered soles, and the red lacquered sole was registered as a trademark in 2008. In 2011, Yves Saint Laurent America, Inc. (YSL), planned to offer a line of monochromatic shoes in which the upper part of the shoe matched the color of the sole, and one of these shoes had a red upper portion along with a red sole. When Louboutin learned of the red YSL shoe, Louboutin sued YSL for trademark infringement.

Relying on *Qualitex,* the district court held that a single color could never serve as a trademark in the fashion industry because single-color marks are inherently functional. On appeal, the Second Circuit determined that there was nothing about the fashion industry that should warrant treatment different from other industries. However, the Second Circuit determined that Louboutin had put the color red "in a place that seemed unusual." Based on the evidence in the record, Louboutin's trademark should be limited to a red lacquer sole that *contrasts* with the upper portion of the shoe. Thus, YSL was permitted to sell its monochromatic shoe.

* *Qualitex,* 514 U.S. at 162.

Once the mark has been registered, the registration must be renewed between the fifth and sixth years. After that renewal, the mark holder must renew every 10 years. (If the mark was initially registered before 1990, however, renewal is necessary only every 20 years.)

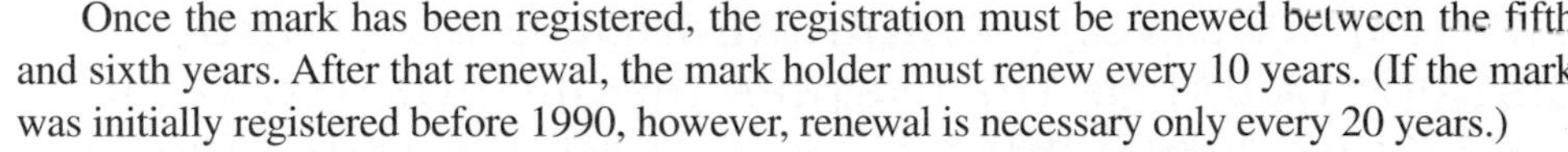

To register a mark with the USPTO, the holder must submit a drawing of it and indicate when it was first used in interstate commerce and how it is used. The USPTO conducts an

Exhibit 12-1
Types of Marks

1. *Service mark:* A mark used in conjunction with a service, such as the name "AT&T" painted on a vehicle that provides repair services for AT&T phone users.
2. *Product trademark:* A mark affixed to a good, its packaging, or its labeling, such as the Nike "swoosh."
3. *Collective mark:* A mark identifying the producers as belonging to a larger group, such as a trade union.
4. *Certification mark:* A mark licensed by a group that has established certain criteria for use of the mark, such as "U.L. Tested" or "Good Housekeeping Seal of Approval."

Diet Coke has a trademark familiar to most students.

investigation to verify those facts and will register a trademark as long as it is not generic, descriptive, immoral, deceptive, the name of a person whose permission has not been obtained, or substantially similar to another's trademark. For example, in May 2009, Ozzy Osbourne brought suit against former Black Sabbath bandmate Anthony Iommi, claiming that Iommi wrongfully registered the Black Sabbath trademark in the United States, the United Kingdom, and the European Union.[2] Osbourne argued that Iommi made false statements to the USPTO by claiming that Iommi had exclusive rights to the Black Sabbath trademark. Osbourne argued that his name was synonymous with the name "Black Sabbath" and that he had handled the licensing of Black Sabbath products for many years. Iommi argued that Osbourne gave up any rights to the name "Black Sabbath" when Osbourne left the group in 1980. In July 2010, the parties settled the dispute but did not disclose the terms of the settlement.

It is sometimes difficult to determine whether a trademark will be protected. Also, once a trademark is registered, it is not always easy to predict whether a similar mark will be found to infringe on the registered trademark. The primary issue is whether consumers are likely to be confused by the two marks. This decision is based on factors such as "the similarity of the marks; the similarity of the products or services in issue; . . . the sophistication of consumers"; and even the "intent of the defendant to palm off its product as that of another."[3]

Case 12-1 demonstrates a typical analysis used in a trademark infringement suit.

Legal Principle: **A trademark is a nonfunctional design, shape, color, symbol, or word that has come to identify the product with its producer.**

[2] *Osbourne v. Iommi,* Case No. 1:09-cv-04947 (S.D.N.Y. 2009).

[3] *Papa John's Int'l, Inc. v. Rezko,* 446 F. Supp. 2d 801 (N. D. Ill. 2006).

CASE 12-1 TOYS "R" US, INC. v. CANARSIE KIDDIE SHOP, INC.
DISTRICT COURT OF THE EASTERN DISTRICT OF NEW YORK
559 F. SUPP. 1189 (1983)

Beginning in 1960, plaintiff Toys-R-Us, Inc., sold children's clothes in stores across the country. The firm obtained a registered trademark and service mark for Toys "R" Us in 1961 and aggressively advertised and promoted their products using these marks. In the late 1970s, defendant Canarsie Kiddie Shop, Inc., opened two kids' clothing stores within two miles of a Toys "R" Us Shop, and contemplated opening a third. The owner of Canarsie Kiddie Shop, Inc., called the stores Kids "r" Us. He never attempted to register the name. Toys "R" Us sued for trademark infringement in the federal district court.

JUDGE GLASSER: In assessing the likelihood of confusion and in balancing the equities, this Court must consider the now classic factors. . . .

1. Strength of the Senior User's Mark

A mark can fall into one of four general categories which, in order of ascending strength, are: (1) generic; (2) descriptive; (3) suggestive; and (4) arbitrary or fanciful. A generic term "refers, or has come to be understood as referring to the genus of which the particular product is a species." A generic term is entitled to no trademark protection whatsoever, since any manufacturer or seller has the right to call a product by its name. A descriptive mark identifies a significant characteristic of the product, but is not the common name of the product. To achieve trademark protection a descriptive term must have attained secondary meaning, that is, it must have "become distinctive of the applicant's goods in commerce." . . . A suggestive mark is one that "requires imagination, thought and perception to reach a conclusion as to the nature of the goods." These marks fall short of directly describing the qualities or functions of a particular product or service, but merely suggest such qualities. If a term is suggestive, it is entitled to protection without proof of secondary meaning. . . . Arbitrary or fanciful marks require no extended definition. They are marks which in no way describe or suggest the qualities of the product.

. . . Because I find that through the plaintiff's advertising and marketing efforts the plaintiff's mark has developed strong secondary meaning as a source of children's products, it is sufficient for purposes of this decision to note merely that the plaintiff's mark is one of medium strength, clearly entitled to protection, but falling short of the protection afforded an arbitrary or fanciful mark.

2. Degree of Similarity between the Two Marks

. . . [T]he key inquiry is . . . whether a similarity exists which is likely to cause confusion. This test must be applied from the perspective of prospective purchasers. Thus, it must be determined whether "the *impression* which the infringing [mark] makes upon the consumer is such that he is likely to believe the product is from the same source as the one he knows under the trade-mark."

Turning to the two marks involved here, various similarities and differences are readily apparent. The patent similarity between the marks is that they both employ the phrase, "R Us." Further, both marks employee the letter "R" in place of the word "are," although the plaintiff's mark uses an inverted capitalized "R," while the defendants generally use a non-inverted lower case "r" for their mark. . . . The most glaring difference between the marks is that in one the phrase "R Us" is preceded by the word "Toys," while in the other it is preceded by the word "Kids." Other differences include the following: plaintiff's mark ends with an exclamation point, plaintiff frequently utilizes the image of a giraffe alongside its mark, plaintiff's mark is set forth in stylized lettering, usually multi-colored, and plaintiff frequently utilizes the words, "a children's bargain basement" under the logo in its advertising. . . . While the marks are clearly distinguishable when placed side by side, there are sufficiently strong similarities to create the possibility that some consumers might believe that the two marks emanated from the same source. The similarities in sound and association also create the possibility that some consumers might mistake one mark for the other when seeing or hearing the mark alone.

3. Proximity of the Products

Where the products in question are competitive, the likelihood of consumer confusion increases.

. . . [B]oth plaintiff and defendants sell children's clothing; . . . the plaintiff and defendants currently are direct product competitors.

4. The Likelihood That Plaintiff Will "Bridge the Gap"

. . . "[B]ridging the gap" refers to two distinct possibilities; first, that the senior user presently intends to expand his sales efforts to compete directly with the junior user, thus creating the likelihood that the two products will be directly competitive; second, that while there is no present intention to bridge the gap, consumers will assume otherwise and conclude, in this era of corporate diversification, that the parties are related companies. . . . I find both possibilities present here.

5. Evidence of Actual Confusion

Evidence of actual confusion is a strong indication that there is a likelihood of confusion. It is not, however, a prerequisite for the plaintiff to recover.

6. Junior User's Good Faith

The state of mind of the junior user is an important factor in striking the balance of the equities. In the instant case, Mr. Pomeranc asserted at trial that he did not recall whether he was aware of the plaintiff's mark when he chose to name his store Kids 'r' Us in 1977. . . . I do not find this testimony to be credible. In view of the proximity of the stores, the overlapping of their products, and the strong advertising and marketing effort conducted by the plaintiff for a considerable amount of time prior to the defendants' adoption of the name Kids 'r' Us, it is difficult to believe that the defendants were unaware of the plaintiff's use of the Toys "R" Us mark.

7. Quality of the Junior User's Product

If the junior user's product is of a low quality, the senior user's interest in avoiding any confusion is heightened. [T]here is no suggestion that the defendants' products are inferior, and this factor therefore is not relevant.

8. Sophistication of the Purchasers

The level of sophistication of the average purchaser also bears on the likelihood of confusion. The goods sold by both plaintiff and defendants are moderately priced clothing articles, which are not major expenditures for most purchasers. Consumers of such goods, therefore, do not exercise the same degree of care in buying as when purchasing more expensive items.

9. Junior User's Goodwill

[A] powerful equitable argument against finding infringement is created when the junior user, through concurrent use of an identical trademark, develops goodwill in their mark. Defendants have not expended large sums advertising their store or promoting its name. In light of this lack of development of goodwill, I find that the defendants do not have a strong equitable interest in retaining the Kids 'r' Us mark.

[continued]

Conclusion on Likelihood of Confusion

[T]he defendants use of the Kids 'r' Us mark does create a likelihood of confusion for an appreciable number of consumers. . . . In reaching this determination, I place primary importance on the strong secondary meaning that the plaintiff has developed in its mark, the directly competitive nature of the products offered by the plaintiff and defendants, the plaintiff's substantially developed plans to open stores similar in format to those of the defendants', the lack of sophistication of the purchasers, the similarities between the marks, the defendants' lack of good faith in adopting the mark, and the limited goodwill the defendants have developed in their mark.

Judgment for the plaintiff.

CRITICAL THINKING

How does this depend to a large extent on the definitions of a few particular terms? How good are the definitions used? What standard are you using in determining whether the definitions are good?

ETHICAL DECISION MAKING

If you were the owner of Canarsie Kiddie Shop, Inc., how would your decision to refer to your store as Kids "r" Us change if you were to act in accordance with the Golden Rule?

What values are in conflict when considering the decisions of the owner of Canarsie Kiddie Shop, Inc., and one who follows the Golden Rule?

TRADE DRESS

The term **trade dress** means the overall appearance and image of a product. For example, as described in the Case Opener, the shape and design of Apple's iPhone are an example of trade dress. Trade dress is entitled to the same protection as a trademark. To succeed on a claim of trade-dress infringement, a party must prove three elements: (1) The trade dress is primarily nonfunctional; (2) the trade dress is inherently distinctive or has acquired a secondary meaning; and (3) the alleged infringement creates a likelihood of confusion.

The main focus of a case of trade-dress infringement is usually on whether there is likely to be consumer confusion. For example, in a recent case,[4] Tour 18, Ltd., a golf course, copied golf holes from famous golf courses without permission of the course owners. Tour 18 even copied the Harbour Town lighthouse, a distinctive feature of one of the most famous courses in the country, and featured it prominently in its advertising. The operator of the Harbour Town course sued Tour 18 for trade-dress infringement. The court found there was infringement and made Tour 18 remove the lighthouse and disclaim in its advertising any affiliation with the owner of the Harbour Town course.

Two different examples of trade-dress infringement were at issue in *Two Pesos v. Taco Cabana*[5] and *Heart Attack Grill v. Heart Stoppers Sports Grill.* In the first case, Taco Cabana's trade dress consisted of "a festive eating atmosphere having interior dining and patio areas decorated with artifacts, bright colors, paintings and murals; . . . a patio that has interior and exterior areas with the interior patio capable of being sealed off from the outside patio by overhead garage doors;" a stepped exterior of the building that has "a festive and vivid color scheme using top border paint and neon stripes;" and "bright awnings and umbrellas." When Two Pesos opened a series of competing Mexican restaurants that mimicked those features almost perfectly, the court found the company guilty of trade-dress infringement. In the second case, in Florida, the Heart Stoppers Sports Grill features waitresses dressed as nurses who serve "Chili Chest Pain Fries," "Nacho Intense Chips Unit" (NICU), "The Heart Attacker" burger, and the "Heart Attack Jack" patty melt. After the

[4] *Pebble Beach Co. v. Tour 18 Ltd.*, 942 F. Supp. 1513 (S.D.Tex. 1996).

[5] 112 S. Ct. 2753 (1994).

E-COMMERCE AND THE LAW

TRADEMARKS AND DOMAIN NAMES

If you have a very strong trademark, what better domain name to have than that trademark? Unfortunately, the same trademark may be owned by two companies selling noncompeting goods, yet there can be only one user of any single domain name. For example, *Apple* is a trademark owned by both a computer company and the company that produces the Beatles' records. Both cannot establish a website identified as apple.com.

Domain names are important because they are the way people and businesses are located on the web. Most websites have two domains. The first-level domain, the one the address ends with, generally identifies the type of site. For example, if it is a government site, it will end in *gov.* An educational site will end in *edu,* a network site in *net,* an organization in *org,* and a business in *com.* These top-level domain names are the same worldwide.

The second-level domain is usually the name of whoever maintains the site. For a college, for example, it would be an abbreviation of the college name, as in *bgsu.* Businesses generally want to use their company name or some other trademark associated with their product, because that makes it easiest for their customers to find them.

Network Solutions, Inc. (NSI), which is funded by the National Science Foundation, is responsible for registering domain names. Anyone seeking to register a domain name must now state in the application that the name will not infringe on anyone else's intellectual property rights and that the registrant intends to use it on a regular basis on the Internet.

A registrant may lose registration of a domain name by not using it for more than 90 days, or the domain name may be canceled if the registrant lied on the registration application. If you have a registered trademark and find that someone is using your trademark as a domain name, and that person does not also have ownership of that mark, you may give written notice to the NSI; under its Domain Dispute Policy, the NSI will most likely put the name "on hold," meaning no one can use that name until the dispute is resolved. Of course, if that person had registered the domain name before you had obtained the trademark, there is probably nothing you can do. The person will be entitled to retain the domain name.

Some firms have tried to get the domain name they desire by going to another country. However, many countries require that a firm be incorporated within their borders before it can gain the right to the domain name there. And trademark law relating to domain names is even more unclear abroad than it is in the United States.

For the new entrepreneur, the best advice is to try to simultaneously apply for federal trademark protection and register the domain name. For those not yet on the web, the sooner you register your domain name, the more likely you are to get the name you want. If you feel that your mark is being violated by someone else's domain name, you may want to sue the person for infringement, because the unauthorized use of another's trademark in a domain name has been found to be illegal. You may be in for quite a fight, however, because this is a new area of the law.

Heart Stoppers Sports Grill was featured on the *Today* show in January 2010, the Heart Attack Grill in Arizona filed suit against the Heart Stopper Sports Grill for trade-dress infringement and trademark infringement.[6] The Heart Attack Grill sells "medically themed" food that has a "Taste Worth Dying For," such as the "Quadruple Bypass Burger" (a burger with four hamburger patties), "Flatliner" fries, and "Jolt" cola. Heart Attack Grill waitresses also dress as nurses and use wheelchairs to seat patrons. According to the complaint filed by Heart Attack Grill, owners of the Heart Stoppers Sports Grill contacted the owner of the Heart Attack Grill to inquire about franchising and licensing but the parties could not reach agreement. How do you think the court will resolve this dispute?

Legal Principle: **Trade dress, the overall appearance and image of a product that have acquired secondary meaning, is entitled to the same legal protection as a trademark.**

BUT WHAT IF . . .

WHAT IF THE FACTS OF THE CASE OPENER WERE DIFFERENT?

What if Samsung had presented evidence at the trial that half of the phones on the market at the time of the trial that were made by companies other than Apple or Samsung also shared the iPhone's design of being rectangular with rounded corners?

[6] *HAC, LLC v. B & I Enterprises, LLC,* Case No. 10-CV-80127 (S.D. Fla., Jan. 26, 2010) (complaint).

FEDERAL TRADEMARK DILUTION ACT OF 1995

Under the Lanham Act, trademark owners were protected from the unauthorized use of their marks on only competing goods or related goods, where the use might lead to consumer confusion. Consequently, a mark might be used without permission on completely unrelated goods, potentially diminishing the value of the mark. In response, a number of states passed **trademark dilution** laws, which prohibited the use of "distinctive" or "famous" trademarks, such as "McDonald's," even without a showing of consumer confusion.

In 1995, Congress made similar protection available at the federal level by passing the Federal Trademark Dilution Act. In one of the first cases under the act, Ringling Brothers–Barnum & Bailey was challenging Utah's use of the slogan "The Greatest Snow on Earth" as diluting the circus's famous "The Greatest Show on Earth." In denying Utah's motion to dismiss on the ground that the slogans were not identical, the court said that the marks need not be identical, only similar.

Legal Principle: Two key differences between trademark dilution and trademark infringement are that (1) dilution additionally requires that the mark be famous and (2) dilution does not require a showing of consumer confusion, as required by infringement.

Copyrights

L02 What are copyrights, and how do we protect them?

Copyrights protect the *expression* of creative ideas. That is, they do not protect the ideas themselves but only the fixed form of expressing them, such as books, periodicals, musical compositions, plays, motion pictures, sound recordings, lectures, works of art, and computer programs. Titles and short phrases may not be copyrighted. It is only the expression of the idea that is protected by copyright law, and not the underlying idea.

There are three criteria for a work to be copyrightable. First, it must be *fixed,* which means set out in a tangible medium of expression. Second, it must be *original.* Third, it must be *creative.*

A copyright automatically arises under common law when the idea is expressed in tangible form. However, if the work is freely distributed without notice of copyright, it falls into the public domain. A copyrighted work reproduced with the appropriate notice affixed is protected for the life of its creator plus 70 years.

Under the common law of copyright, an infringer may be enjoined only from reproducing a copyrighted work. For the creator to be able to also recover damages arising from the infringement, the copyrighted work must be registered via a form filed with the Register of Copyright and two copies of the copyrighted materials sent to the Library of Congress. Whenever the work is reproduced, the appropriate notice of copyright *should* accompany it, although such notice is no longer required by law. Printed works, for example, should be published with the word *copyright* and the symbol © or the abbreviation *copr.,* followed by the first date of publication and the name of the copyright owner. Once the work is registered, the holder of the copyright has the additional right to sue an infringer for damages caused by the infringer's use of it and to recover any profits the infringer has made from it.

Legal Principle: A copyright will be granted when a work is set out in a tangible medium of expression, is original, and is creative.

It is not always easy to determine whether a copyright has been infringed, even when two works are similar. After all, if we are talking about creative works, such as photographs of a famous scene, two people might independently take very similar pictures at completely different times and without even knowing of each other's work.

The original AP photo is on the left, and the poster is on the right.

From Dave Itzkoff, Associated Press files, "Countersuit over Obama Poster," *The New York Times,* March 11, 2009, http://artsbeat.blogs.nytimes.com/2009/03/11/associated-press-files-countersuit-over-obama-poster/?scp=2&sq=fairey&st=cse (accessed June 8, 2009).

For example, in 2009, Shepard Farley, who created a poster based on an Associated Press (AP) photograph taken by Mannie Garcia in 2006, sued the Associated Press for a declaratory judgment that the poster did not infringe on the AP copyright and for an injunction prohibiting AP from suing either him or his firm for infringement. AP counterclaimed, seeking damages and injunctive relief for copyright infringement.

Case 12-2 illustrates the court's reasoning in a successful copyright infringement case.

CASE 12-2 CROWN AWARDS, INC. V. DISCOUNT TROPHY & CO., INC.
U.S. COURT OF APPEALS, SECOND CIRCUIT
2009 U.S. APP. LEXIS 8540 (2009)

Crown Awards is a retailer of trophies, awards and other similar items sold through mail order catalogs and over the Internet. Crown designed and sold a diamond-shaped spinning trophy ("Spin Trophy") for which it owned two copyright registrations. Discount Trophy is one of Crown's competitors. Discount sold a trophy that was strikingly similar to Crown's Spin Trophy. When Discount refused Crown's requests that it discontinue the sale of the alleged copy, Crown filed suit in the Southern District of New York.

After a two-day bench trial, the court found in favor of Plaintiff. The court reasoned that Discount's infringing copy and Crown's Spin Trophy shared an unusual number of characteristics. Discount appealed.

JUDGES STRAUB, POOLER, AND RAGGI: To prevail on a claim of copyright infringement, a plaintiff must demonstrate both ownership of a valid copyright and infringement. "To establish infringement, the copyright owner must demonstrate that (1) the defendant has actually copied the plaintiff's work; *and* (2) the copying is illegal because a substantial similarity exists between the defendant's work and the protectable elements of plaintiff's.". . . Actual copying may be proved directly or indirectly. "[I]ndirect evidence of copying includes proof that the defendants had access to the copyrighted work and similarities that are probative of copying between the works."

[continued]

. . . If a plaintiff cannot demonstrate a reasonable possibility of access, its infringement claim will fail absent proof of a "striking" similarity between the original and infringing works." . . . The court must "analyze the two works closely to figure out in what respects, if any, they are similar, and then determine whether these similarities are due to protected aesthetic expressions original to the allegedly infringed work, or whether the similarity is to something in the original that is free for the taking." . . .

. . . Here, the district court found that Crown owned a valid copyright in its diamond-shaped spinning trophy and that Discount had access to Crown's design through its receipt of Crown's 2006 catalog and its monitoring of Crown's products. The district court found, however, that Crown had failed to demonstrate that Xiamen Xihua Arts and Crafts ("Xiamen"), the manufacturer of the allegedly infringing trophy, also had access to Crown's design because there was no record evidence (1) that Discount asked Xiamen to manufacture a trophy that looked like Crown's copyrighted trophy, or (2) that Xiamen ever received a Crown catalog. While acknowledging that Crown's design could be viewed on the Internet after January of 2006, the district court noted that "there is no evidence in the record about the Internet habits" of Xiamen's principal. The district court nevertheless inferred access on the part of Xiamen from the "striking" similarity between the diamond-shaped spinning trophies sold by Crown and Discount. The court further found that the two products were "substantially similar and shared the same "total concept and feel."

. . . Discount principally challenges the district court's findings of both "striking" and "substantial" similarity. In urging affirmance, Crown submits that though there was no error in the district court's finding of striking similarity, the district court erred in requiring proof that Xiamen *actually* viewed Crown's copyrighted design. Crown argues that the proper standard required only proof of a "reasonable possibility" that Xiamen had access to Crown's design combined with similarities probative of copying and substantial similarity between the products in question. . . . We agree with Crown both as to the standard of proof and its satisfaction of that standard.

. . . First, while we identify no error in the district court's detailed and thorough factual findings, we conclude that Crown was not required to prove Xiamen's *actual* access to Crown's trophy design.

. . . Second, the district court's factual findings, as a matter of law, establish a "reasonable possibility" that Xiamen had access to Crown's design. The district court found that the nature of Xiamen's business, the timing of Discount's orders from Xiamen, and Mr. Lin's failure to offer any credible account of independent creation of the allegedly infringing design made it "absolutely impossible to believe" that Xiamen created the infringing design without coordinating with Discount in advance. . . . These facts, together with the district court's finding that Discount had direct access to Crown's trophy design through its receipt of the Crown catalog and its monitoring of Crown's products, compel a conclusion of a "reasonable possibility" that through Discount, Xiamen had access to Crown's work prior to creating Discount's infringing product. And in light of the similarities between the works, we agree with the district court's determination that Crown established actual copying.

Third, for substantially the reasons stated by the district court in its detailed analysis of the issue, we agree that Discount unlawfully appropriated Crown's protected expression. . . . On *de novo* examination of both Crown's copyrighted trophy and Discount's allegedly infringing copy, we conclude, as the district court did, that Discount's product while not identical to Crown's mimics Crown's protectable aesthetic decisions in the arrangement of the trophy's elements to an extent that their "total concept and feel" are the same.

AFFIRMED in favor of the plaintiff.

CRITICAL THINKING

What type of information could the defendant, Discount Trophy, have submitted in the case that might have led the court to rule in its favor?

ETHICAL DECISION MAKING

Which value does this decision tend to emphasize?

FAIR-USE DOCTRINE

One source of controversy for copyrighted works is the application of the **fair-use doctrine.** This doctrine provides that others may reproduce a portion of a copyrighted work for purposes of "criticism, comment, news reporting, teaching (including multiple copies for classroom use), scholarship, and research."

E-COMMERCE AND THE LAW

INTELLECTUAL PROPERTY WATCHDOG

Widespread copyright violations against the movie, music, and book industries have prompted the U.S. Justice Department to form an intellectual property task force. The primary goal of the task force is to put a stop to copyright piracy. Copyright piracy costs the movie, music, and book industries to lose billions of dollars a year.

Federal, state, and international watchdogs are weighing in on the most effective strategies for protecting companies' intellectual property rights. Leaders from both companies (e.g., Walt Disney Co.) and industry associations (e.g., the Recording Industry Association of America) agree that it is important to go after companies rather than individuals. Of particular concern are Chinese DVD and CD factories.

It is important to remember that piracy violates American intellectual property rights. It also costs people their jobs. For instance, in February 2010, Sony Pictures cut 550 positions from its home entertainment and information technology divisions.

Source: "U.S. Announces Intellectual Property Watchdog," *Thomson Financial News,* February 12, 2010, p. 59; Ben Fritz, "Company Town Facetime," *Los Angeles Times,* February 18, 2010, p. 3.

In determining whether the fair-use doctrine provides a valid defense to a claim of copyright infringement, Section 107 of the Copyright Act requires that the court weigh the following four factors:

1. The purpose and character of the use, including whether such use is of a commercial nature or is for nonprofit educational purposes.
2. The nature of the copyrighted work.
3. The amount and substantiality of the portion used in relation to the copyrighted work as a whole.
4. The effect of the use on the potential market for or value of the copyrighted work.

In 1994, the Supreme Court decided that commercial parody may be fair use. In that case, 2 Live Crew, a rap group known for its explicit lyrics, recorded and released a song called "Pretty Woman," which was a parody of Roy Orbison's "Oh, Pretty Woman." The Supreme Court considered the four factors listed above. With respect to the purpose and character of the use, the more "transformative" the new work is, the less courts will need to focus on the other three factors.

In the 1970s, Sony developed a format for videotaping called *Betamax.* Film studios brought suit against Sony in 1976, arguing that taping a television show was copyright infringement. The district court concluded that recording a show for personal, noncommercial use was fair use, but the appellate court disagreed and found Sony liable. The Supreme Court ultimately ruled on this issue in 1984, agreeing that recording a television program for the noncommercial purpose of time shifting is fair use.[7]

As technology has continued to develop, copyright enforcement has remained an important concern. For example, Napster was a peer-to-peer file-sharing network through which one user could download a file from another user for free. Files that were typically transferred were digital music files. The record industry brought suit against Napster and received a preliminary injunction to stop the exchange of digital music files. Napster appealed to the Ninth Circuit Court of Appeals, which affirmed the preliminary injunction.[8] Napster made several arguments regarding fair use. As with the time-sharing purpose in the Betamax case, Napster argued that users were engaging in space sharing (i.e., transferring music files from CDs they had purchased to their computers). However, the court found that although the user may have been transferring the format (from CD to computer file) for personal use, the user was necessarily sharing the files with other users, which was not a fair use. Case 12-3 shows the Supreme Court's reasoning regarding peer-to-peer file sharing.

[7] *Sony Corp. of America v. Universal City Studios, Inc.,* 464 U.S. 417 (1984).

[8] *A&M Records, Inc. v. Napster, Inc.,* 239 F.3d 1004 (2001).

CASE 12-3 METRO-GOLDWYN-MAYER STUDIOS, INC. v. GROKSTER, LTD.
UNITED STATES SUPREME COURT
545 U.S. 913 (2005)

Like Napster, Grokster was software that allowed users to share digital files directly, and these digital files were typically music files. Billions of files were shared each month, and Grokster was aware that the primary use for the software was to download copyrighted music files.

The district court and appellate court acknowledged that the users were engaging in copyright infringement but concluded that a distributor of a product with substantial noninfringing uses could not be liable for contributory infringement unless it had actual knowledge of specific instances of copyright infringement and failed to act to stop that infringement.

JUSTICE SOUTER: MGM and many of the amici fault the Court of Appeals' holding for upsetting a sound balance between the respective values of supporting creative pursuits through copyright protection and promoting innovation in new communication technologies by limiting the incidence of liability for copyright infringement. The more artistic protection is favored, the more technological innovation may be discouraged; the administration of copyright law is an exercise in managing the trade-off. . . . The tension between the two values is the subject of this case, with its claim that digital distribution of copyrighted material threatens copyright holders as never before, because every copy is identical to the original, copying is easy, and many people (especially the young) use file-sharing software to download copyrighted works.

The argument for imposing indirect liability in this case is, however, a powerful one, given the number of infringing downloads that occur every day using StreamCast's and Grokster's software. When a widely shared service or product is used to commit infringement, it may be impossible to enforce rights in the protected work effectively against all direct infringers, the only practical alternative being to go against the distributor of the copying device for secondary liability on a theory of contributory or vicarious infringement. One infringes contributorily by intentionally inducing or encouraging direct infringement . . . and infringes vicariously by profiting from direct infringement while declining to exercise a right to stop or limit it.

MGM advances the argument that granting summary judgment to Grokster and StreamCast as to their current activities gave too much weight to the value of innovative technology, and too little to the copyrights infringed by users of their software, given that 90% of works available on one of the networks was shown to be copyrighted. Assuming the remaining 10% to be its noninfringing use, MGM says this should not qualify as "substantial," and the Court should quantify Sony to the extent of holding that a product used "principally" for infringement does not qualify.

[We hold] that one who distributes a device with the object of promoting its use to infringe copyright, as shown by clear expression or other affirmative steps taken to foster infringement, is liable for the resulting acts of infringement by third parties.

Here, the summary judgment record is replete with other evidence that Grokster and StreamCast, unlike the manufacturer and distributor in Sony, acted with a purpose to cause copyright violations by use of software suitable for illegal use. . . . Three features of this evidence of intent are particularly notable. First, each company showed itself to be aiming to satisfy a known source of demand for copyright infringement, the market comprising former Napster users. StreamCast's internal documents made constant reference to Napster, it initially distributed its Morpheus software through an OpenNap program compatible with Napster, it advertised its OpenNap program to Napster users, and its Morpheus software functions as Napster did except that it could be used to distribute more kinds of files, including copyrighted movies and software programs. Grokster's name is apparently derived from Napster, it too initially offered an OpenNap program, its software's function is likewise comparable to Napster's, and it attempted to divert queries for Napster onto its own Web site. Grokster and StreamCast's efforts to supply services to former Napster users, deprived of a mechanism to copy and distribute what were overwhelmingly infringing files, indicate a principal, if not exclusive, intent on the part of each to bring about infringement.

Second, this evidence of unlawful objective is given added significance by MGM's showing that neither company attempted to develop filtering tools or other mechanisms to diminish the infringing activity using their software. While the Ninth Circuit treated the defendants' failure to develop such tools as irrelevant because they lacked an independent duty to monitor their users' activity, we think this evidence underscores Grokster's and StreamCast's intentional facilitation of their users' infringement.

Third, there is a further complement to the direct evidence of unlawful objective. It is useful to recall that StreamCast and Grokster make money by selling advertising space, by directing ads to the screens of computers employing their software. As the record shows, the more the software is used, the more ads are sent out and the greater the advertising revenue becomes. Since the extent of the software's use determines the gain to the distributors, the commercial sense of their enterprise turns on high-volume use, which the record shows is infringing. This evidence alone would not justify an inference of unlawful intent, but viewed in the context of the entire record its import is clear.

The unlawful objective is unmistakable.

In sum, this case is significantly different from Sony and reliance on that case to rule in favor of StreamCast and Grokster was error. Sony dealt with a claim of liability based solely on distributing a product with alternative lawful and unlawful uses, with knowledge that some users would follow the unlawful course. The case struck a balance between the interests of protection and innovation by holding that the product's capability of substantial lawful employment should bar the imputation of fault and consequent secondary liability for the unlawful acts of others.

MGM's evidence in this case most obviously addresses a different basis of liability for distributing a product open to alternative uses. Here, evidence of the distributors' words and deeds going beyond distribution as such shows a purpose to cause and profit from third-party acts of copyright infringement. If liability for inducing infringement is ultimately found, it will not be on the basis of presuming or imputing fault, but from inferring a patently illegal objective from statements and actions showing what that objective was.

VACATED and REMANDED.

CRITICAL THINKING

How are the facts in the Grokster case different from those in the Sony Betamax case? Does this decision create a desirable precedent?

ETHICAL DECISION MAKING

What value does this decision emphasize?

In May 2012, Dish Network offered a feature called AutoHop that allows customers to skip past commercials during prime-time television. The "Hopper DVR" automatically records the prime-time broadcasts for ABC, CBS, NBC, and Fox. The next day, the user can watch the broadcast without commercials. Television networks brought suit against Dish Network, arguing copyright infringement. Dish Network has argued that the copies are fair use. While the district court has refused to issue a preliminary injunction, the networks have appealed to the Ninth Circuit Court of Appeals. How do you think the court will resolve this dispute?

NO ELECTRONIC THEFT ACT

Before 1997, it was not a criminal act to infringe on someone's copyright if the infringement were not for financial gain. But in 1997, Congress passed the No Electronic Theft Act, which makes it illegal for a person not only to infringe a copyright for commercial purposes or financial gain but also to reproduce or distribute, for no financial gain, the copyrighted work of another. Criminal penalties for violating the act include fines of up to $250,000 and imprisonment for up to five years.

DIGITAL MILLENNIUM COPYRIGHT ACT

Computers and the Internet have made it much easier for people to illegally copy and distribute copyrighted material. To protect their copyrighted materials, software manufacturers and entertainment companies have developed antipiracy protections and methods of encryption to make it more difficult for people to steal digital copyrighted materials. As soon as these copyright owners developed these protective technologies, however, copyright "pirates" began developing the technology to crack the encryption and other antipiracy technology. To attempt to protect the owners of digital intellectual property, in 1998 Congress passed the Digital Millennium Copyright Act (DMCA).

The main provisions of the act make it illegal to circumvent the encryption and other antipiracy technology that protects commercial software and outlaw the manufacture, sale, or distribution of encryption-breaking devices that can be used to illegally copy software. It also requires that "webcasters" pay licensing fees to record companies.

The act, however, does allow the cracking of copyright protection devices to conduct encryption research, assess product interoperability, and test computer security systems. It also limits liability of Internet service providers from copyright infringement liability for simply transmitting information over the Internet, but it does require that they remove material from users' websites when that material appears to constitute copyright infringement. Nonprofit institutions of higher education, when they serve as online service providers, are given limited liability for copyright infringement by faculty and graduate students.

Under the act, if someone's computer is found to have copyrighted materials on it, the copyright holder could sue the owner to recover damages and costs, and even if there is no proof of actual damages, statutory damages of up to $30,000 may be awarded or up to $150,000 for willful infringement. And in some cases of infringement for "commercial advantage" or "private financial gain," the government may seek criminal penalties of fines up to $500,000 and imprisonment for up to 5 years for a first offense and fines of up to $1 million and imprisonment of up to 10 years for repeat offenses.

Patents

LO3

What are patents, and how do we protect them?

A **patent** protects a product, process, invention, machine, or plant produced by asexual reproduction. For this protection to be granted, four criteria must be satisfied. First, the subject matter of the patent must be *patentable.* Second, the object of the patent must be *novel,* or new. No one else must have previously made or published the plans for this object. Third, the object must be *useful,* unless it is a design. It must provide some utility to society. Fourth, the object must be *nonobvious.* The invention must not be one that a person of ordinary skill in the trade could have easily discovered. When a patent is issued for an object, it gives its holder the exclusive right to produce, sell, and use the object of the patent for 20 years from the date of application. The holder of the patent may *license,* or allow others to manufacture and sell, the patented object. In most cases, patents are licensed in exchange for the payment of *royalties,* a sum of money paid for each use of the patented process.

The only restrictions on the patent holder are that he or she may not use the patent for an illegal purpose such as a tying arrangement or a cross-licensing. A **tying arrangement** occurs when the holder issues a license to use the patented object *only* if the licensee agrees to buy some nonpatented product from the holder. **Cross-licensing** occurs when two patent holders license each other to use their patents *only* on the condition that neither licenses anyone else to use his or her patent without the other's consent. Both activities are unlawful because they tend to reduce competition.

To obtain a patent, the inventor generally contacts an attorney licensed to practice before the U.S. Patent and Trademark Office (USPTO). The attorney does a *patent search* to make sure no similar patent exists. If none exist, the attorney fills out a patent application and files it with the USPTO. As part of the application process,

COMPARING THE LAW OF OTHER COUNTRIES

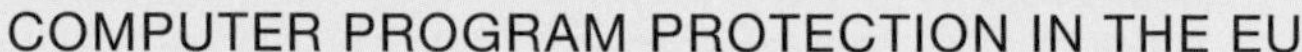

COMPUTER PROGRAM PROTECTION IN THE EU

In May 1991, the Council of European Communities adopted a directive to protect computer programs by equating them with literary works under the Berne Convention standards (see page 299). The protection is inclusive of all "preparatory design material," and the only criteria is that the program must be the intellectual creation of the author. If a program is developed by a group of individuals, they jointly hold the rights. If an employee creates a program while fulfilling an employer's instructions, the employer has exclusive rights over the program. These protections are guaranteed for life and 70 years after the author's death. Specific remedies against violators of the directive are left to the jurisdiction of each member state.

In October 1998, the Data Protection Directive was added, requiring that each member state legally regulate the processing of personal data within the European Union. Most importantly, personal data can travel outside the EU only if the destination country has an adequate level of protection for the subject of the data. This stipulation may affect the EU's trading relations. The United States, Canada, Japan, and Australia, for example, do not have comprehensive statutes that regulate information within the private sector. Other countries have even less adequate protection for certain data. If these countries wish to receive the same amount of information from European countries as they have in the past, they may have to consider altering their regulations.

the inventor has a duty to disclose any *prior art* he or she is aware of that is related to the invention, including other patents. The Patent Office evaluates the application, and if the object meets the criteria already described, a patent is issued within approximately two years. While two years may seem like a long time, it is short compared to the six years it typically takes to secure a patent in Japan.

Once the patent has been issued, the holder may bring a patent infringement suit in a federal court against anyone who uses, sells, or manufactures the patented invention without the patent holder's permission. A successful action may result in an injunction prohibiting further sale or use of the infringing product by the infringer and also an award of damages. Sometimes, however, the result of a patent infringement case is that the holder loses the patent because the court finds that the patent is *invalid.* For example, the alleged infringer may prove that the USPTO should not have issued the patent in the first place because the ideas in the patent were already in existence before the patent application was filed. A patent can be invalid if the alleged infringer shows that the patent holder sold or offered for sale a product that performed the patent more than a year before the patent application was filed. Thus, companies need to be very diligent about filing patent applications within a year after selling or offering for sale products that perform patents.

Another way in which a potential patent infringer may attempt to challenge a patent is to ask the USPTO to "reexamine" the patent. Through the reexamination process, a party presents what it argues is invalidating prior art (i.e., patents, articles, or products that disclosed all features of the invention *before* the patent at issue was granted). The USPTO then considers whether the patent should have in fact been issued. Reexamination requests are frequently granted, and it may take several years for the USPTO to reconsider whether a patent should have been issued. Thus, reexaminations are tools frequently used by defendants to slow down or even pause litigation, as a court may prefer the USPTO to complete the reexamination before litigation may proceed.

Legal Principle: It is unlawful for a patent holder to enter into a tying arrangement, whereby the holder issues a license to use the patented object *only* if the licensee agrees to buy some nonpatented product from the holder, or to engage in cross-licensing, which occurs when two patent holders license each other to use their patents *only* on the condition that neither licenses anyone else to use his or her patent without the other's consent.

BUT WHAT IF . . .

WHAT IF THE FACTS OF THE CASE OPENER WERE DIFFERENT?

What if Samsung had been able to bring in evidence that, in fact, it had sold a phone with a design similar to the iPhone's before the iPhone had come out? Would that fact have affected the outcome of the case with respect to Apple's claim of infringement on its design patent?

ANATOMY OF PATENT LITIGATION

While a patent owner may file a patent infringement case in any federal court, patent owners tend to file in certain district courts: the Northern District of California, the District of Delaware, and the Eastern District of Texas. Patent holders prefer to file in these courts for at least two reasons: (1) The judges in these district courts have more experience with technical issues in patent cases; and (2) juries in these courts have tended to give large damage awards to patent holders. These districts typically have a special set of rules called *patent local rules* that set out the procedures for patent litigation.

First, after the initial pleadings (i.e., complaint and answer) are filed, the patent holder must file patent infringement contentions that explain in detail how the defendant infringes the patent. Typically, at that time, the patent holder must provide copies of all documents relating to the conception of the patent. Second, the defendant must file invalidity contentions that explain why the ideas in the patent already existed in the public domain and must provide copies of all the publications that contain those ideas. Third, the parties identify all the terms in the patent that have special definitions and provide their proposed definitions of these terms. This step is very important because a party may or may not infringe a patent depending on the definition of certain words in the patent. Fourth, the court considers the proposed definitions and decides how the terms will be defined for the purpose of the litigation. At this point, the patent case generally proceeds as any other litigation would.

THE AMERICA INVENTS ACT

In 2011, Congress passed the America Invents Act, which changed the U.S. patent system in several important ways. First, the first person to file a patent application in the United States for an invention will be deemed to have rights to the invention. This is a change from the previous policy, where the first person to *invent* had the rights to the invention. This change is important because in the past, employees could keep diligent records and take their time applying for the patent. The European and Japanese patent systems also have a first-to-file rule. Second, the act expands the types of prior art that may be considered by the USPTO when granting a patent, thereby arguably making it more difficult to obtain a patent. Third, the act makes changes to the reexamination process, making the process more like litigation by allowing discovery requests during the process. Fourth, the act prohibits a plaintiff from filing one suit against many unrelated defendants, a practice that typically increases the number of patent infringement cases filed. Finally, the act makes it easier and more affordable for small businesses and sole entrepreneurs to apply for patents.

Trade Secrets

LO4

What are trade secrets, and how do we protect them?

A **trade secret** is a process, product, method of operation, or compilation of information that gives a businessperson an advantage over his or her competitors. Inventions and designs such as Papa John's dough and sauce recipes might be considered trade secrets.

Furthermore, a company's client list (or an employee's contact list) could be considered a trade secret. A trade secret is protected by the common law from unlawful appropriation by competitors as long as it is kept secret and consists of elements not generally known in the trade. Most states now have statutes that prevent the misappropriation of confidential information. Unlike patents or trademarks, there is no "registration" of trade secrets. The key issue is whether the information has been kept secret.

Competitors may discover a trade secret by any lawful means, such as by doing reverse engineering or by going on a public plant tour and observing its use. Lawful discovery of a secret means there is no longer a trade secret to be protected.

If a competitor acquires a trade secret by unlawful means, the originator of the secret can take legal action. To enjoin such a competitor from continuing to use a trade secret and/or to recover damages caused by the use of the secret, a plaintiff must prove that:

1. A trade secret actually existed.
2. The defendant acquired it through unlawful means, such as breaking into the plaintiff's business and stealing it or securing it through misuse of a confidential relationship with the plaintiff or one of the plaintiff's present or former employees.
3. The defendant used the trade secret without the plaintiff's permission.

A common dilemma facing an inventor is whether to protect an invention through patent or trade-secret law. An inventor who successfully patents an invention and defends the patent has a guaranteed monopoly on the use of the invention for 20 years, a substantial period of time. Once this period is over, however, the patented good goes into the public domain and everyone has access to it. There is also the risk that the patent may be successfully challenged and the protection lost prematurely. Trade-secret law, on the other hand, could protect the invention in perpetuity. But once someone discovers the secret lawfully, the protection is lost.

When an employee leaves a company to work for a competing company, the original company frequently investigates whether the employee has taken any trade secrets to the competitor. According to one study, 59 percent of departing employees take confidential information from the employer when leaving.[9] To ensure that confidential information is protected, companies should consider creating a policy mandating that any trade-secret information be labeled "confidential" or "trade secret" by employees (this would help the employer maintain a trade-secret claim) and should limit access to this confidential information within the company.

International Protection of Intellectual Property

LO5 How do treaties expand protection of intellectual property?

Because many U.S. companies operate worldwide, they need to be able to protect their intellectual property abroad as well as at home. The primary international protection for intellectual property is offered through multilateral conventions. These treaties are generally administered by the World Intellectual Property Organization, a specialized agency of the United Nations.

THE BERNE CONVENTION OF 1886

As of September 2013, there are 167 states that are signatories of the Berne Convention of 1886, the oldest treaty designed to protect artistic rights. Four basic principles underlie their obligations under the treaty:

1. The *national treatment principle* requires that each member nation protect artists of all signatory nations equally.

[9] "Protecting Trade Secrets When Employees Depart," *Law 360,* September 18, 2009, http://www.law360.com/articles/116377/protecting-trade-secrets-when-employees-depart.

2. The *nonconditional protection principle* requires that protection not be conditioned on the use of formalities, although the country of origin may require registration or a similar formality.
3. The *protection independent of protection in the country of origin principle* allows nationals of nonsignatory countries to protect works if they are created in a member country.
4. The *common rules principle* establishes minimum standards for granting copyrights that all nations must meet.

THE UNIVERSAL COPYRIGHT CONVENTION OF 1952, AS REVISED IN 1971

The Universal Copyright Convention (UCC) was developed by the United Nations as an alternative for countries that wanted to participate in some form of multilateral protection of copyrights but did not want to agree to the terms of the Berne Convention. The United States, China, and the Soviet Union are among the nations that are now signatories.

The primary way the UCC differs from the Berne Convention is that the UCC allows members to establish formalities for protection and make exceptions to common rules as long as they are not inconsistent with the essence of the treaty. The UCC also does not require signatory countries to protect author's rights. However, the UCC has lost some of its importance as almost all countries are conforming to the 1994 Agreement on Trade-Related Aspects of Intellectual Property Rights discussed below.

THE PARIS CONVENTION OF 1883

The Paris Convention's 174 members have agreed to protect so-called industrial rights, such as inventions and trademarks. Unfair competition is also restricted under this treaty.

The treaty has been revised several times, and not all members have signed all versions. While it is highly complex, it has three basic principles: (1) *national treatment,* as defined under the Berne Convention; (2) *the right of priority,* which allows a national of a member state 12 months after filing in his or her home nation to file an application in any other member state and have the date of application be the date of the filing in the home nation; and (3) *common rules,* which set out minimum standards of protection in all states. These common rules include such items as outlawing false labeling and protecting trade names of companies from member states even without registration.

The Patent Cooperation Treaty of 1970 was open to signatories of the Paris Convention. It contains a provision for making a patent application filed in any member state an international application as effective as individually filed applications in all member states. When the application is filed in any member state, it is then forwarded to an international search authority.

Despite the existence of such agreements, enforcement in foreign countries is often very lax. In 1994, problems with blatant trademark infringement in China were so severe that President Clinton threatened to impose trade sanctions if enforcement were not improved.

THE 1994 AGREEMENT ON TRADE-RELATED ASPECTS OF INTELLECTUAL PROPERTY RIGHTS

Over 100 nations are signatories to the 1994 Agreement on Trade-Related Aspects of Intellectual Property Rights (TRIPS). Each must establish broad intellectual property protections and effective means for enforcing these protections. The agreement also provides that no country can give its own citizens better intellectual property protections than it grants to citizens of other signatories.

COMPARING THE LAW OF OTHER COUNTRIES

SOFTWARE PIRACY IN CHINA

An ongoing source of tension between the United States and China has been China's lax enforcement of intellectual property laws. A study released in July 1999 found that 95 percent of the business software installed in China during 1998 was pirated. Software piracy was estimated to have cost China $1.2 billion that year, more than the cost in any other Asian nation, according to one study.*

The first indication that China is attempting to crack down on the piracy of software occurred in July 1999, when China handed down its first criminal sentence for software piracy. Wang Antao was sentenced to four years in prison, fined 20,000 yuan ($2,400), and required to pay the software owner 280,000 yuan ($33,800) for selling a slightly modified version of the company's software without permission.

Since then, progress has been made, albeit slowly. According to the Business Software Alliance, the percentage of pirated software in computers in 2009 in China was 79 percent, down from 93 percent in 2003. In April 2007, a senior vice president and general counsel for Microsoft reported that the previous year had been encouraging, with more personal computers sold in the country with legitimate software installed. He expressed a belief that the Chinese government had indeed taken action to curb software piracy in the region, although the Chinese remain one of the biggest pirates of the company's software.

* The study was conducted by the U.S. Business Software Alliance and the Software and Information Industry Association.

CASE OPENER WRAP-UP

Smartphone Wars: Focus on Intellectual Property Rights

In August 2012, Apple and Samsung participated in a four-week jury trial regarding patent infringement and trademark claims. Both Apple and Samsung asserted patents in this trial; however, the jury found that (1) Samsung infringed Apple's patents, (2) Apple did not infringe Samsung's patents, and (3) the trade dress of Apple's iPhone was diluted by some of Samsung's products. The jury awarded Apple over $1 billion in damages, which was one of the highest patent infringement awards in history. Prior to the trial, the judge issued a preliminary injunction that prevented Samsung from selling one of its tablets. However, following the trial, the injunction was lifted.

KEY TERMS

copyrights 290
cross-licensing 296
fair-use doctrine 292
intellectual property 284
patent 296
trade dress 288
trade secret 298
trademark 284
trademark dilution 290
tying arrangement 296

SUMMARY OF KEY TOPICS

Intellectual Property

Intellectual property is property that is the result of one's intellectual and creative efforts, rather than physical efforts.

Trademarks

A *trademark* is a distinctive mark, word, design, picture, or arrangement that is used by a producer in conjunction with a product and that tends to cause the consumer to identify the product with the producer. Trademarks used in interstate commerce can be protected under the Lanham Act.

Copyrights

A *copyright* protects the fixed form of the *expression* of an original, creative idea. The most common defense to an allegation of copyright infringement is the *fair-use doctrine,* which provides that a portion of a copyrighted work may be reproduced for purposes of "criticism, comment, news reporting, teaching (including multiple copies for classroom use), scholarship, and research."

Patents

A *patent* protects a product, process, invention, machine, or plant that is produced by asexual reproduction and that meets the criteria of being novel, useful, and nonobvious. Obtaining a patent under the Lanham Act allows the holder to license the use of his or her patented idea for royalties as long as the holder does not enter into a tying arrangement or engage in cross-licensing.

Trade Secrets

An alternative to using a patent is to protect information as a trade secret. This allows the holder of the trade secret to sue one who illegally takes the trade secret if the owner of the secret can prove that:

1. A trade secret actually existed.
2. The defendant acquired it through unlawful means, such as breaking into the plaintiff's business and stealing it or securing it through misuse of a confidential relationship with the plaintiff or one of the plaintiff's present or former employees.
3. The defendant used the trade secret without the plaintiff's permission.

International Protection of Intellectual Property

Intellectual property is protected internationally primarily by the use of treaties. Such treaties include the Universal Copyright Convention, the Berne Convention, the Paris Convention of 1883, and the TRIPS agreement.

POINT / COUNTERPOINT

The process of applying for a patent and keeping a patent can be difficult and costly. As you know, an alternative to patenting an invention is to protect it through trade-secret law.

Should Inventors Avoid the Hassles of Patent Protection and Protect Their Inventions through Trade-Secret Law?

YES	NO
Inventors should choose to protect their inventions through trade-secret law. Trade-secret protection does not require registration with government agencies. Unlike patent protection, whereby the owner of the patent has exclusive rights to produce, sell, and use the object of the patent only for a limited time, trade-secret protection offers the owner of the trade secret exclusive rights indefinitely. For example, the unique process by which Coca-Cola makes its soft drink has been protected as a trade secret for over 100 years. This approach has prevented competitors from duplicating Coca-Cola's product. Patent holders also risk the chance of losing their patent if a challenger is able to show that the patent should not have been issued. Because trade-secret protection is not limited by registration requirements, inventors should use trade-secret law to protect their products.	Inventors should not choose to protect their inventions through trade-secret law. Protection through trade-secret law is risky. It is the responsibility of the owner of the trade secret to take precautionary measures to maintain the privacy of the secret. With technological advances, the chance of competitors' using legal methods such as reverse engineering to discover the trade secret is likely. An owner of a patent may bring a patent infringement suit if the patent has been used without permission. If a trade secret is discovered through lawful means, it is no longer a secret and the owner cannot bring actions against those using the product or process. Through patent protection the owner can decide whether to license the patent and can earn a profit from those who choose to use the product. The risks associated with trade-secret protection are too great to make it a desirable choice.

QUESTIONS & PROBLEMS

1. List and define the classic factors that a court must weigh when determining whether there has been trademark infringement that warrants an award of damages and an injunction.
2. What is the relationship between copyright infringement and the fair-use doctrine?
3. Identify the factors one would look at when deciding whether to protect intellectual property either with a patent or through trade-secret law.
4. Miller Brewing produced a reduced-calorie beer called "Miller Lite," which it began selling in the 1970s and spent millions of dollars advertising. In 1980, Falstaff Brewing Corporation started marketing a reduced-calorie beer called "Falstaff Lite." Miller filed an action seeking an injunction against Falstaff to prevent it from using the term *Lite.* What was the outcome of the case? [*Miller Brewing Co. v. Falstaff Brewing Corporation,* 655 F.2d 5 (1987).]
5. Securities brokerage firm Charles Schwab filed suit against a former employee who left the company and started his own wealth management firm. Charles Schwab claimed that the names of its clients, along with information regarding their accounts and assets, were trade secrets and the employee misappropriated these trade secrets when he contacted the clients to ask them to transfer their accounts to his new firm. Charles Schwab argued that the employee could not have learned of these individuals but for his work at Charles Schwab. Do you think that this customer information will be treated as trade secrets? What factors do you think the court will consider when determining whether the customer information is trade secrets? [*Charles Schwab & Co. Inc. v. Douglas Castro,* Case No. 650053/2013 (E.D.N.Y., Jan. 7, 2013).]
6. The Stop & Shop Supermarket and Big Y Foods are supermarkets offering the same services and competing for the same customers. In an advertisement introducing their new, easy-to-use scan saver cards, Stop & Shop Supermarket used the slogan "It's that Simple." The supermarket used the slogan in radio, television, and print advertisements. The service mark was licensed to the supermarket by plaintiff Fullerton, who owns the right to the service mark. After Stop & Shop started using the slogan, Big Y Foods began to use a similar slogan, "We Make Life Simple." Both service marks are always accompanied by the name of the store. Fullerton and Stop & Shop Supermarket brought an action alleging infringement of the service mark. Do you think that the court granted the injunction? Why or why not? [*The Stop & Shop Supermarket Company and Fullerton Corp. v. Big Y Foods Inc.,* 943 F. Supp. 120 (1996).]
7. Nike and Michael Jordan created the Air Jordan line in the 1980s. Jordan filed suit in China against a Chinese sportswear company, Qiaodan Sports. Jordan is known in China as "Qiaodan," and Qiaodan Sports uses a logo of a silhouette of a tall man holding a basketball, along with the number "23." The company registered "Qiaodan" as a trademark in China. Qiaodan also filed applications for trademarks on Jordan's sons' names. According to the complaint, Qiaodan had sales of approximately $450 million per year. Do you think that Jordan will be successful in his suit against Qiaodan? Why? [http://www.globalpost.com/dispatch/news/regions/americas/united-states/120223/michael-jordan-lawsuit-filed-against-qiaodan-spo (accessed 9/23/2013); and http://www.therealjordan.com/en/Facts-of-the-case.aspx (accessed 9/23/2013).]
8. Plaintiff Pfizer manufactures and sells the prescription drug Viagra, for which it holds two registered trademarks: Viagra and Viva Viagra. As a result of the significant amount of money spent advertising the drugs with the trademark, the mark has become extremely well known. Sachs, the defendant, has a website, JetAngeel.com, on which he sells outdoor advertising that he places on decommissioned military equipment. Sachs placed a 20-foot-tall missile bearing the word *Viagra* on it in front of Pfizer's headquarters in New York and was using the attention that the missile was generating to get media coverage for his business. Pfizer sent Sachs a letter demanding that he immediately quit using the Viagra mark on his missile. Sachs not only ignored Pfizer's demand but announced he was taking the missile on a national tour. Pfizer sued and obtained a temporary restraining order prohibiting Sachs from displaying the Viagra or Viva Viagra marks in conjunction with any goods or services. Should

Pfizer be entitled to a permanent injunction? Why or why not? [*Pfizer, Inc. v. Sachs,* 652 F. Supp. 2d 512, 2009 WL 2876255 (S.D.N.Y. 2009).]

9. Plaintiff Bourne owns the copyright for the song "When You Wish Upon a Star," which he wrote for the Walt Disney film *Pinocchio.* Bourne heard the song "I Need a Jew" on Fox Cartoon Network's show *Family Guy* and recognized the melody of the song as being that of "When You Wish Upon a Star," although all the words were completely different. Bourne sued for copyright infringement. What defense do you think the defendant was able to raise in this case? Do you think the defense was successful? [*Bourne Co. v. Twentieth Century Fox Film Corp.,* 602 F. Supp. 2d 499, 2009 WL 700400 (S.D.N.Y. 2009).]

10. Universal City Studios owns the movie rights to the book *Fifty Shades of Grey* and was in the process of making a movie version of the book when a company called Smash Pictures announced that it was making a pornographic film titled *Fifty Shades of Grey: A XXX Adaption.* An executive at Smash Pictures was quoted as saying that the pornographic version "will stay very true to the book." Universal brought suit against Smash Pictures, asking for an injunction and damages. Do you think that Smash Pictures will be able to release its film? [*Fifty Shades Ltd. and Universal City Studios LLC v. Smash Pictures, Inc.,* Case No. 12-cv-10111 (C.D. Cal.), complaint filed December 2012.]

Looking for more review materials?

The Online Learning Center at **www.mhhe.com/kubasek3e** contains this chapter's "Assignment on the Internet" and also a list of URLs for more information, entitled "On the Internet." Find both of them in the Student Center portion of the OLC, along with quizzes and other helpful materials.

Introduction to Contracts

CHAPTER

13

LEARNING OBJECTIVES

After reading this chapter, you will be able to answer the following questions:

1 What is a contract?

2 What are the sources of contract law?

3 How can we classify contracts?

4 What are the rules that guide the interpretation of contracts?

CASE OPENER

A Questionable Contract

Mary Kay Morrow began working for Hallmark in 1982. At the beginning of 2002, Hallmark adopted the "Hallmark Dispute Resolution Program," which required, among other things, that claims against the company be resolved in binding arbitration rather than litigation. Hallmark assumed that employees who remained at Hallmark after the policy became effective were bound by the new company policy. Additionally, Hallmark reserved the right to modify the program at any time and excluded claims it brought from the arbitration requirement.

Fifteen months after the policy became effective, Hallmark terminated Morrow's employment. Morrow filed a claim against Hallmark, claiming that she had not been fired for just cause but, rather, had been terminated because of age discrimination and retaliation resulting from her earlier complaints about company policies. In response to the suit, which was filed in the circuit court of Jackson County, Hallmark filed a motion to stay the litigation and compel arbitration in accordance with its Dispute Resolution Program. The court granted Hallmark's motion.

After several additional failed attempts to get the circuit court to hear the case, Morrow proceeded with the only route she had left—arbitration. The arbitrator dismissed Morrow's claims for lack of timeliness and ruled that the program constituted a valid contract and was not unconscionable. In yet another effort to have the case heard, Morrow went back to the trial court with a motion to vacate the arbitrator's ruling. The motion was denied. Morrow appealed the case to the Missouri Court of Appeals on the grounds that the Dispute Resolution Program did not constitute an enforceable contract.

1. By what standard would the courts determine whether a contract existed?
2. Did each party to the supposed contract make a valid promise that would support the existence of the contract?

The Wrap-Up at the end of the chapter will answer these questions.

The Definition of a Contract

LO1

What is a contract?

This part of the text focuses on contracts, but what is a contract? The Restatement (Second) of Contracts defines a **contract** as "a promise or set of promises for the breach of which the law gives a remedy or the performance of which the law in some way recognizes a duty."[1] Another way to think of a contract is as a set of legally enforceable promises. Contracts play a fundamental role in business; after all, almost all business relationships are created by contracts.

One of the most important business relationships, the relationship that exists between employers and employees, is often created through contracts. Typically, during the hiring process, an employer will establish an employment contract, which lists the terms and obligations a new employee must agree to before starting work. One particular type of employment contract is a **covenant not to compete.** Covenants not to compete restrict what an employee may do after leaving a company, and they often dictate where, when, and with whom an employee may work. Employers justify the use of covenants not to compete by saying they are necessary to protect their trade secrets, talent, and proprietary information.

Noncompete contracts are especially common in industries such as technology and sales, where possession of cutting-edge information or client lists can greatly affect the competition between companies. For example, in 2008, IBM and Apple found themselves in a court battle over employee Mark Papermaster. Apple had hired Papermaster away from his high-level position at IBM and wished to put him in charge of Apple's iPhone and iPod division. In turn, IBM argued that Papermaster's move to Apple violated his covenant not to compete, which stated that he would not work for a competitor during the year after he left IBM. Former employer IBM also argued that because Papermaster had been a top executive at IBM, he was in possession of confidential and proprietary information that could be valuable to Apple. The court agreed with IBM and thus issued an injunction barring Papermaster from starting work at Apple until after a trial had taken place. Apple and IBM opted to reach an agreement out of court, and Papermaster was cleared to start work at his new position in April 2009.[2] Covenants not to compete are discussed in greater detail in Chapter 16 of this text.

ELEMENTS OF A CONTRACT

We can flesh out the definition of a contract by examining the four elements that are necessary for it to exist. These elements are the agreement, the consideration, contractual capacity, and a legal object. The **agreement** consists of an **offer** by one party, called the *offeror,* to enter into a contract and an **acceptance** of the terms of the offer by the other party, called the *offeree* (see Exhibit 13-1). This first element is discussed in detail in Chapter 14.

The second element of the contract is the **consideration,** the bargained-for exchange or what each party gets in exchange for his or her promise under the contract. We discuss consideration in Chapter 15.

[1] Restatement (Second) of Contracts, sec. 1.

[2] See www.networkworld.com/community/node/37835 and http://library.findlaw.com/2003/Feb/5/132530.html.

BUT WHAT IF . . .

WHAT IF THE FACTS OF THE CASE OPENER WERE DIFFERENT?

To fulfill the element of consideration, both parties to a contract must make promises to the other. Recall that, in the Case Opener, Hallmark made no promises to the employees who had to agree to the program. In fact, Hallmark stipulated that it could "modify or discontinue" the program at any time. But what if Hallmark promised raises to each employee who agreed to abide by the rules of the program? Do you see any potential problems with such an agreement?

Exhibit 13-1 The Formation of a Contract

This exhibit illustrates the first element of the contract, the agreement. For a contract to exist, the parties also must have legal capacity to enter into a contract, exchange valid consideration, and be entering into a contract with a legal purpose. The contract is formed as soon as the second party makes his or her promise.

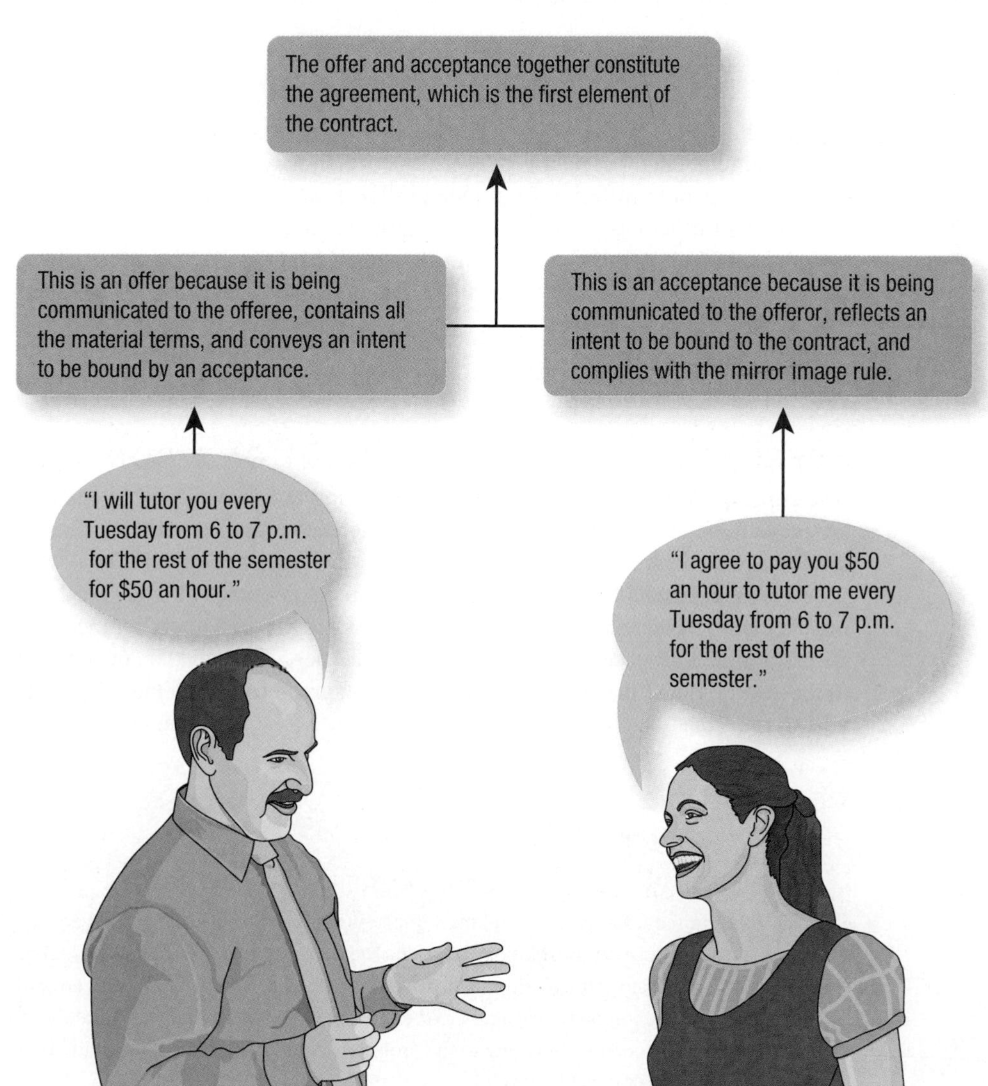

E-COMMERCE AND THE LAW

CONTRACT FORMATION AND E-COMMERCE

Contract law operates on the Internet, with adjustments for special issues that range from jurisdiction to payment. Which state's or country's laws apply if the parties to an e-contract end up in a dispute? What happens if an online company engages in fraud by using a customer's credit card information in ways the customer never intended?

Contract formation via the Internet is especially important. Issues regarding contract formation range from timing to contract terms. For instance, given the speed with which e-mails go back and forth between parties, it is sometimes difficult to know when the parties have created a contract. Once a contract is formed, additional questions arise: What specific terms does the contract include? Can a company post standard terms on a website rather than in a document or on a ticket?

Fortunately, legislators have drafted and implemented key pieces of legislation that clarify issues related to contract formation and e-commerce. Two examples of e-commerce legislation are the Electronic Signatures in Global and National Commerce (ESIGN) Act and the Uniform Electronic Transactions Act (UETA).

Congress passed ESIGN to facilitate the use of electronic records and signatures in e-commerce. The federal law affirms e-contracts as legally valid. This law makes it clear that documents produced electronically are as valid as documents produced on paper. Congress did not write or pass UETA. Instead, the National Conference of Commissioners on Uniform State Laws proposed this piece of legislation, which almost every state has adopted. UETA's intent was similar to Congress's intent regarding ESIGN. In addition to affirming electronic contracts as legally valid, UETA attempts to make state laws consistent regarding topics such as the validity of signatures created online.

The third element is **contractual capacity.** Capacity is the legal ability to enter into a binding agreement. Most adults over the age of majority have capacity; those under the age of majority, people suffering from mental illness, and intoxicated persons do not. Chapter 16 explains further cases that limit or prohibit capacity.

Chapter 16 also discusses the fourth element of a binding legal contract, legal object. This means that to be enforceable, the contract cannot be either illegal or against public policy.

Legal Principle: **A legally binding contract requires four elements: agreement, consideration, capacity, and legal object.**

DEFENSES TO THE ENFORCEMENT OF A CONTRACT

Sometimes a contract appears to be legally binding because all four elements of a contract are present, but one of the parties may have a defense to its enforcement. Such defenses fall into two categories. The first is a **lack of genuine assent** (Chapter 17). A contract is supposed to be entered into freely by both parties, but sometimes the *offeror* (the party proposing the contract) secures acceptance of the agreement through improper means such as fraud, duress, undue influence, or misrepresentation. In these situations, there is no genuine assent to the contract, and the *offeree* (the person who agreed to or accepted the contract) may be able to raise that lack of genuine assent as a defense to enforcement of the agreement.

BUT WHAT IF . . .

WHAT IF THE FACTS OF THE CASE OPENER WERE DIFFERENT?

Recall that, in the Case Opener, Hallmark made it company policy for employees to participate in the dispute Resolution Program when a dispute arose. Employees were bound to the program through employment documents. But what if the facts were different? Let's say that company managers told employees they would be immediately terminated if they did not sign a contract agreeing to the program. Would the contract be valid? If not, on what grounds would the contract be invalid?

The second defense, discussed in Chapter 18, is that the contract lacks the *proper form,* which typically means it lacks a writing. As Chapter 18 will explain, the contract itself does not have to be in writing, but a writing meeting certain criteria that confirms the existence of the contract must exist.

Exhibit 13-2 summarizes the requirements of an enforceable contract.

Legal Principle: **Two defenses to the enforcement of a contract are lack of genuine assent and lack of proper form.**

THE OBJECTIVE THEORY OF CONTRACTS

Contract law is based on an *objective theory of contracts,* which means we base the existence of a contract on the parties' outward manifestations of intent and we base its interpretation on how a reasonable person would interpret it. Thus, the subjective intent of the parties is not usually relevant; what matters is how they represented their intent through their actions and words.

The subjective intent may be relevant, however, under a limited number of circumstances. As Chapter 17 explains in its discussion of mistake, if a mutual misunderstanding between the parties exists, and if as a result they did not really come to a meeting of the minds, there is no contract. The courts may then look at how each party subjectively interpreted the situation to determine whether the parties really reached an agreement.

Legal Principle: **In determining whether parties intended to enter into a contract, the courts look at their objective words and behavior and do not try to figure out what they might have been secretly intending.**

Sources of Contract Law

L02 What are the sources of contract law?

The two most important sources of contract law are case law and the Uniform Commercial code (UCC). A third source of law, which has become more important with increasing globalization, is the Convention on Contracts for International Sales of Goods (CISG). In this part of the book we focus primarily on the law of contracts as established by common law. (Part Three, "Domestic and International Sales Law," focuses more on the law as set out by the UCC and CISG.)

COMMON LAW

Today's law of contracts actually originated in judicial decisions in England, later modified by early courts in the United States. Since then, contract law has been further modified by U.S. legislatures and court rulings. The law of contracts is primarily common law. Therefore, to find out what the law is, we could go to the Reporters and read the decisions,

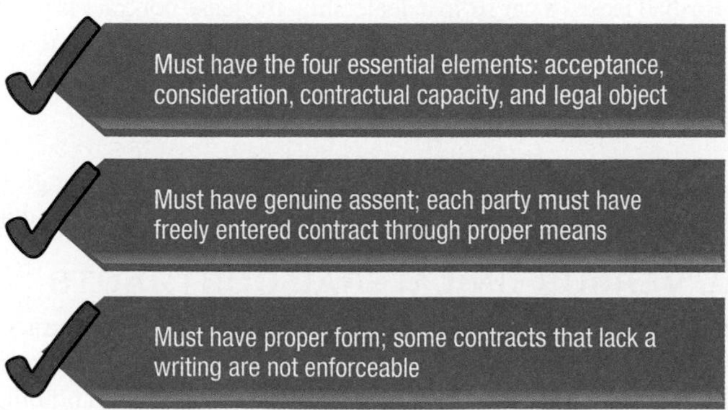

Exhibit 13-2
Requirements of an Enforceable Contract

COMPARING THE LAW OF OTHER COUNTRIES

CHINA

Countries outside the United States have slightly different laws for different types of contracts. China, for example, has seven chapters of general provisions for contracts but also has chapters with special provisions for 15 different types of contracts governing sales, leases, loans, donations, construction projects, storage, and transportation.

but it is easier to go to the Restatement (Second) of the Law of Contracts. Prominent legal scholars, recruited by the American Law Institute, organized the principles of the common law of contracts into the original *Restatement of the Law, Contracts.* The compilation has been revised and published as *Restatement of the Law Second, Contracts.* The case in the opening scenario is governed by common law.

The Restatement (Second) is not actually the law itself, although judges frequently cite it because it is an authoritative statement of what the law is. As the common law of contracts evolved, not all states interpreted all aspects of it in the same way, so while we can make generalizations about the law of contracts, you will always want to know exactly what the law at issue is in your own state. In the Restatement (Second), the drafters often explain what the law about a particular matter is in the majority of states and then provide alternative approaches other states have adopted.

UNIFORM COMMERCIAL CODE

Having different laws governing contracts in different states did not make interstate commerce flow smoothly. To remedy some of the difficulties created by a patchwork of different laws governing commercial transactions, the National Conference of Commissioners on Uniform State Laws and the American Law Institute drafted a set of commercial laws that could be applicable to all states. This effort was called the **Uniform Commercial Code (UCC).** The UCC became law in each state that adopted it in whole or in part as an element of its state code. Thus, if a firm enters into a contract governed by the Uniform Commercial Code in Ohio, it will be operating under the Ohio Uniform Commercial Code.

Legal Principle: **All contracts are governed by either common law or the Uniform Commercial Code (UCC). If the contract is for the sale of a good, it falls under Article 2 of the UCC; if it is for anything else, it falls under common law.**

The part of the Uniform Commercial Code relevant to contracts is Article 2, which governs contracts for the sale (exchange for a price) of goods (tangible, movable objects). In this part of the book we will sometimes point out important differences between the UCC and common law, but we discuss contracts governed by the UCC primarily in Part Three. Also relevant to contract law is UCC Article 2A, which governs contracts for the lease of goods. For instance, if Rashad leases a car from a dealership, the lease contract is governed by Article 2A. If Rashad purchases the car, the purchase contract is governed by Article 2 of the UCC.

Classification of Contracts

L03

How can we classify contracts?

Contracts are classified in a number of different ways. Different classifications are useful for different purposes. This section describes the primary ways by which we classify contracts.

BILATERAL VERSUS UNILATERAL CONTRACTS

All contracts are either unilateral or bilateral. Knowing whether a contract is unilateral or bilateral is important because that classification determines when the offeree is legally bound to perform. Exhibit 13-3 highlights the difference between unilateral and bilateral contracts.

A PROMISE + A PROMISE = A *BILATERAL* CONTRACT

A PROMISE + A REQUESTED ACTION = A *UNILATERAL* CONTRACT

Exhibit 13-3
Bilateral vs. Unilateral Contracts

If the offeror wants a promise from the offeree to form a binding contract, the contract is a **bilateral contract,** commonly defined as a promise in exchange for a promise. As soon as the promises are exchanged, a contract is formed and the parties' legal obligations arise. When Shannon promises to pay Gary $1,000 in exchange for his promise to paint her car on July 1, they have a bilateral contract. If either party fails to perform, the other may sue for breach. In the opening scenario, Hallmark wanted its employees to promise to submit any claims against it to arbitration rather than litigation. At issue in this case is, among other things, the question of whether Hallmark promised anything in return.

Another example of a bilateral contract can be found in the bidding process used by eBay. When an auction on eBay's website has closed, a bilateral contract exists between the seller and the individual who made the highest bid. The seller has promised to send the item (which needs to be comparable to the item described in the listing) to the bidder. The bidder has promised to make payment to the seller in the full amount of his or her bid. Should either party fail to perform, the other party may seek legal remedy according to the terms and conditions set forth by eBay's seller-bidder agreements.

In a bilateral contract, it is crucial that both parties are in fact making binding promises. In Case 13-1, you can see that one party wanted to argue that there was a bilateral agreement, when in fact that party was not binding itself to anything.

CASE 13-1 IN RE ZAPPOS.COM INC., CUSTOMER DATA SECURITY BREACH LITIGATION

2012 WL 4466660 (D. NEV., SEPT. 27, 2012)

Zappos.com is a popular website known mainly for its discounted shoe sales. In 2012, a hacker hacked into the Zappos website in an effort to obtain the personal account information of Zappos shoppers. After releasing news of the breach, Zappos faced numerous lawsuits from unhappy customers. Subsequently, Zappos moved to compel arbitration as mandated in its terms of use listed on its website. Zappos argued that it and its customers were in a bilateral agreement stating that arbitration must be used in the event of a dispute between the two parties, as supported by its customer terms of use. However, also in the terms of use, Zappos stipulated that it could change its terms of use and all of its agreements anytime at its own discretion. Hence, customers argued that the agreement was not bilateral and was in fact unfairly unilateral. Specifically, customers argued that Zappos was not actually agreeing to anything and made no promise to its customers regarding dispute resolution. Therefore, customers argued that they should not have to use arbitration and instead should be able to file their class action lawsuit against Zappos.

JUDGE JAMES: . . . The first paragraph of the Terms of Use provides [a] relevant part: "We reserve the right to change this Site and these terms and conditions at any time." The Priera Plaintiffs argue that because the Terms of Use grants Zappos the unilateral right to revise the Arbitration Clause, the contract is illusory and therefore unenforceable. In other words, Plaintiffs argue that the Arbitration Clause is illusory because Zappos can avoid the promise to arbitrate simply by amending the provision, while Zappos.com users are simultaneously bound to arbitration.

Most federal courts that have considered this issue have held that if a party retains the unilateral, unrestricted right to terminate the arbitration agreement, it is illusory and unenforceable, especially where there is no obligation to receive consent from, or even notify, the other parties to the contract.

. . .The Terms of Use gives Zappos the right to change the Terms of Use, including the Arbitration Clause, at any time without notice to the consumer. On one side, the Terms of Use purportedly binds any user of the Zappos.com website to mandatory arbitration. However, if a consumer sought

[continued]

to invoke arbitration pursuant to the Terms of Use, nothing would prevent Zappos from unilaterally changing the Terms and making those changes applicable to that pending dispute if it determined that arbitration was no longer in its interest. In effect, the agreement allows Zappos to hold its customers and users to the promise to arbitrate while reserving its own escape hatch. By the terms of the Terms of Use, Zappos is free at any time to require a consumer to arbitrate and/or litigate anywhere it sees fit, while consumers are required to submit to arbitration in Las Vegas, Nevada. Because the Terms of Use binds consumers to arbitration while leaving Zappos free to litigate or arbitrate wherever it sees fit, there exists no mutuality of obligation. We join those other federal courts that find such arbitration agreements illusory and therefore unenforceable.

A court cannot compel a party to arbitrate where that party has not previously agreed to arbitrate. The arbitration provision found in the Zappos.com Terms of Use purportedly binds all users of the website by virtue of their browsing. However, the advent of the Internet has not changed the basic requirements of a contract, and there is no agreement where there is no acceptance, no meeting of the minds, and no manifestation of assent. A party cannot assent to terms of which it has no knowledge or constructive notice, and a highly inconspicuous hyper link buried among a sea of links does not provide such notice. Because Plaintiffs did not assent to the terms, no contract exists, and they cannot be compelled to arbitrate. In any event, even if Plaintiffs could be said to have consented to the terms, the Terms of Use constitutes an illusory contract because it allows Zappos to avoid arbitration by unilaterally changing the Terms at any time, while binding any consumer to mandatory arbitration in Las Vegas, Nevada. We therefore decline to enforce the arbitration provision on two grounds: there is no contract, and even if there was, it would be illusory and therefore unenforceable.

IT IS, THEREFORE, HEREBY ORDERED that Defendant Zappos.com, Inc.'s Motion to Compel Arbitration and Stay Action (#3) is DENIED.

CRITICAL THINKING

Is there enough ambiguity with the word *agreement* that Zappos could argue that it had an agreement with its customers? If Zappos could change any rule or promise it made to a customer at any time, how could Zappos argue that it was agreeing to anything?

ETHICAL DECISION MAKING

When a court makes a decision in a contract case, what values is it elevating? In other words, the court is anchoring its reasoning on a preference for a particular value or set of values. What is that value or set of values in a contract case?

In a **unilateral contract,** the offeror wants the offeree to *do* something, not to promise to do something. Perhaps the most common kind of unilateral offer is a reward. If Jim loses his dog, he may post a sign saying, "$50 reward for the safe return of my Poodle, Frenchie." When Michiko calls Jim and says, "Don't worry, I'll find your dog," she is not making a contract because the unilateral offer calls for an action, not a promise.

Just as the offeree is under no obligation to actually perform the act called for by the offeror, the offeror may revoke the offer at any time before performance. Initially this situation created problems because a person could be halfway through the performance and the offeror could revoke the offer. Because of the unfairness of such a scenario, today the courts hold that once an offeree begins performance, the offeror must hold the offer open for a reasonable time to allow the offeree to complete it.

BUT WHAT IF . . .

WHAT IF THE FACTS OF THE CASE OPENER WERE DIFFERENT?

Recall that, in the Case Opener, Hallmark's contract with its employees involved an employee promise to settle disputes with the company through arbitration. What if, instead, the contract said that if employees settled disputes with the company through arbitration, all fees resulting from the dispute would be covered by Hallmark? Which scenario is bilateral? Which is unilateral?

EXPRESS VERSUS IMPLIED CONTRACTS

We can classify contracts as express or implied depending on how they are created. The terms of **express contracts** are all clearly set forth in either written or spoken words. In the opening scenario, Hallmark contended that the Dispute Resolution Program constituted an express contract because it had laid out the terms for the contract in a writing received by its employees. **Implied contracts,** in contrast, arise not from words but from the conduct of the parties. If you have a dental emergency and the dentist pulls your severely infected tooth without prior negotiation about payment, or even any mention of payment, you have an implied contract for payment for her services. However, if you go to the dentist's office, ask how much it will cost to whiten your teeth, and sign a written agreement that stipulates exactly what the process will entail and how much you will pay, you have an express contract.

Apple's iTunes store provides another example of express contracts. Apple has several express contracts with music labels and television stations to sell music and television shows online. As a result of each sale, Apple retains a percentage of the profit and submits the remainder to the music label or television station. Should Apple, or the label, not receive the appropriate percentage of the sale, a breach-of-contract suit could be filed.

As a general rule, three conditions must be met for the courts to find an implied, or *implied-in-fact,* contract. First, the plaintiff provided some property or service to the defendant. Second, the plaintiff expected to be paid for such property or service, and a reasonable person in the position of the defendant would have expected to pay for it. Third, the defendant had an opportunity to reject the property or service but did not. In Case 13-2, the court had to decide whether the facts gave rise to an implied-in-fact contract.

CASE 13-2 PACHE v. AVIATION VOLUNTEER FIRE CO.
SUPREME COURT OF NEW YORK, APPELLATE DIVISION, THIRD DEPARTMENT
20 A.D.3D 731, 800 N.Y.S.2D 228 (2005)

Mr. Pache was the fire chief of the Aviation Volunteer Fire Company, which serves several neighborhoods in the Bronx. Mr. Pache suffered a fatal heart attack at the scene of a fire. His widow applied for Workers' Compensation, and was ultimately granted benefits by the Workers' Compensation Board. The decision was based on a finding that there was an implied contract between Aviation and the City of New York giving rise to the City's liability pursuant to the Volunteer Fireman's Benefit Law. The City appealed.

MERCURE, J.: . . . The City initially contended that claimant was not a covered employee within the meaning of Volunteer Firefighters' Benefit Law because the City had no written contract with Aviation. In relevant part, Volunteer Firefighters' Benefit Law § 30(2) provides:

> If at the time of injury the volunteer fire[fighter] was a member of [an incorporated] fire company . . . and located in a city, . . . protected under a contract by the fire department or fire company of which the volunteer fire[fighter] was a member, any benefit under this chapter shall be a city . . . charge.

Having conceded at oral argument that an implied contract against the City is a legal possibility, the City argues that it was error to find an implied contract in this case because there was no evidence that the Commissioner of the Fire Department of the City of New York (hereinafter FDNY) ever approved such a contract and there was insufficient proof of the elements of formation of an implied contract. We find both contentions to be unavailing.

In general, "it is well settled that a contract may be implied in fact where inferences may be drawn from the facts and circumstances of the case and the intention of the parties as indicated by their conduct." . . . However, there cannot be a valid implied contract with a municipality when the Legislature has assigned the authority to enter into contracts to a specific municipal officer or body or has prescribed the manner in which the contract must be approved, and there is no proof that the statutory requirements have been satisfied.

Here, the City relies on several provisions of the City Charter for the proposition that the Commissioner of the FDNY has the exclusive authority to enter into contracts on behalf of the FDNY (New York City Charter §§ 16-389, 17-394, 19-487). To the extent that this argument—explicitly

[continued]

asserted for the first time before this Court—is properly before us, it is unpersuasive because these provisions, individually and in conjunction, do not include an express assignment of exclusive contracting authority to the Commissioner.

The City further contends that there was insufficient evidence to support the Board's finding of an implied-in-fact contract because there was no evidence of assent by the City to the alleged contract. While acknowledging the absence of direct evidence on the issue of assent, we conclude that the Board's finding of an implied contract between the City and Aviation should not be disturbed. The Board was presented with evidence that Aviation had been in existence since 1923, and that it worked "hand in hand" with the local FDNY company to fight fires. There was evidence that the local fire company occasionally called Aviation to request its assistance. A representative of the City provided evidence that the City was aware of Aviation, and knew that it fought fires in conjunction with the FDNY. If Aviation arrived at the scene of a fire before the local FDNY company, Aviation would be in charge of a fire scene until the FDNY company arrived and would thereafter continue working under its supervision. There was no evidence that City officials or the local fire company ever objected to or rejected the services of Aviation. Moreover, although the City was directed to produce an employee from the local FDNY company with knowledge of the relationship between the local fire company and Aviation as well as other facts relevant to the implied contract issue, it failed to do so. . . . Inasmuch as the Board was entitled to draw reasonable and adverse inferences from the City's failure to produce a knowledgeable employee, we are satisfied that substantial evidence supports the Board's determination that an implied-in-fact contract existed between the City and Aviation.

AFFIRMED in favor of Plaintiff.

CRITICAL THINKING

Do you agree that enough evidence has been considered in establishing an implied-in-fact contract? If so, what makes the evidence strong; and if not, what further evidence do you feel is necessary to make a confident claim?

Can you find an appreciable body of evidence in this case in support of an opposite contention? What is it?

ETHICAL DECISION MAKING

Justify the decision reached by the court by using different guidelines for ethical decision making. Which guideline fits most strongly with the case data? Why?

What values might the court be attempting to uphold with this ruling? What values are necessarily sacrificed to these interests? Can you justify this preference, and if so how?

QUASI-CONTRACTS

Quasi-contracts are sometimes called *implied-in-law contracts,* but they are not actually contracts. Rather, in order to prevent one party from being unjustly enriched at the expense of another, the courts impose contractual obligations on one of the parties *as if* that party had entered into a contract.

Assume Diego hears a noise in his driveway. He looks out and sees a group of workers apparently getting ready to resurface it. The doorbell rings, but he does not answer it. He goes down to his basement office and stays there until the workers have gone and he has a resurfaced driveway. When he receives a bill from the paving company, Diego refuses to pay on the grounds that he did not ask to have the driveway paved. In such a case, where the defendant knew the company was getting ready to bestow on him a benefit to which he was not entitled, the court will probably impose a quasi-contract, requiring that Diego pay the paving company the fair market value of the resurfacing. Imposing such a duty prevents him from being unjustly enriched at the expense of the paving company.

There are limits to the doctrine, however; specifically, the enrichment must be unjust. Sometimes a benefit may be conferred on you simply because of a mistake by the other party, and the courts will not make people pay for others' mistakes. Had Diego been out of town when his driveway was repaved, he would have just gotten lucky. The courts are not going to make him pay for the pavers' mistake when he could have done nothing to prevent the benefit from being bestowed on him.

A defendant, however, does not need to acknowledge the subcontractor's role, as was the case in Case 13-3, for a quasi-contract to exist.

CASE 13-3 REISENFELD & CO. v. THE NETWORK GROUP, INC.; BUILDERS SQUARE, INC.; KMART CORP.

U.S. COURT OF APPEALS FOR THE SIXTH CIRCUIT 277 F.3D 856 U.S. APP. (2002)

Network Group ("Network") was contracted by BSI to assist in selling or subleasing closed Kmart stores in Ohio. A few years later, Network entered into a commission agreement with Reisenfeld, a real estate broker for Dick's Clothing and Sporting Goods ("Dicks"). Dicks then subleased two stores from BSI. According to executed assignment and assumption agreements signed in November of 1994, BSI was to pay a commission to Network. Network was then responsible, pursuant to the commission agreement with Reisenfeld, to pay a commission of $1 per square foot to Reisenfeld. There was no direct agreement made between BSI and Reisenfeld.

During this time, Network's sole shareholder was defrauding BSI. This shareholder was convicted of several criminal charges stemming from his fraudulent acts. Network was ordered by the district court to disgorge any commissions received from BSI, and BSI was relieved of any duty to pay additional commissions to Network. As such, Reisenfeld never received his commission related to the Dicks sublease.

Reisenfeld sued in state court for the $160,320 in commissions he had not been paid. In addition to suing Network, Reisenfeld also named BSI as a defendant. The suit alleged, among other things, that based on a theory of quasi-contracts, BSI was jointly and severally liable for the commission.

JUDGE BOOGS: . . . A contract implied-in-law, or "quasi-contract," is not a true contract, but instead a liability imposed by courts in order to prevent unjust enrichment. . . . Under Ohio law, there are three elements for a quasi-contract claim. There must be: (1) a benefit conferred by the plaintiff upon the defendant; (2) knowledge by the defendant of the benefit; and (3) retention of the benefit by the defendant under circumstances where it would be unjust to do so without payment. . . .

There is no disagreement as to the first two requirements. It is clear that Reisenfeld's work as broker benefited BSI and that BSI was aware of the work Reisenfeld was doing. The disagreement rests on the third requirement—whether it would be unjust for BSI to retain the benefit it received without paying Reisenfeld for it. . . . Unreported Ohio Court of Appeals cases support the proposition that, in the contractor/subcontractor context, when the subcontractor is not paid by the contractor and the owner has not paid the contractor for the aspect of the job at issue, the subcontractor can look to the owner for payment under a theory of unjust enrichment. . . . Further, another Ohio case, in dicta, supports the proposition that nonpayment by the owner would make payment on an unjust enrichment theory appropriate. . . .

[H]ere, BSI has not paid Network on this contract, and the losses suffered by BSI at Network's hands were "soft" losses of additional profits Network might have made, rather than quantifiable losses (due, for example, to theft) that might be held to constitute payment. . . . Therefore, though not controlling of this matter, the Ohio contractor/subcontractor cases involving property owners who have not paid the contractors provide persuasive support for the proposition that Reisenfeld may hold BSI accountable on a theory of quasi-contract for the benefits it provided to BSI, and for which it was not compensated by Network. . . .

Of course, liability under quasi-contract does not necessarily imply liability for the amount of money promised Reisenfeld under its contract with Network. Instead, the proper measure of liability is the reasonable value of the services Reisenfeld provided to BSI. We must therefore vacate the district court's order and remand the case for a determination of value.

REMANDED for consideration of damages.

CRITICAL THINKING

What words or phrases important to the reasoning of this decision might be ambiguous? What alternate definitions are possible? How does this ruling appear to be defining the words or phrases? Would another choice affect the acceptability of the conclusion?

Provide an example of one piece of new evidence that might lead Judge Boggs to a different conclusion, and explain how this information changes the consideration.

ETHICAL DECISION MAKING

Does this ruling establish a positive precedent in terms of the potential effect on future participants in disputes of this sort?

Does this decision appear to follow the Golden Rule guideline? Why or why not? How is this question particularly relative to the person making the judgment, and what sorts of interpersonal differences might lead to a variety of responses?

Legal Principle: **Recovery in quasi-contract may be obtained when (1) a benefit is conferred by the plaintiff upon the defendant; (2) the defendant has knowledge of the benefit that is being bestowed upon her; and (3) the defendant retains the benefit under circumstances in which it would be unjust to do so without payment.**

VALID, VOID, VOIDABLE, AND UNENFORCEABLE CONTRACTS

What everyone hopes to enter into, of course, is a **valid** contract, one that contains all the legal elements set forth in the beginning of this chapter. As a general rule, a valid contract is one that will be enforced. However, sometimes a contract may be valid yet **unenforceable** when a law prohibits the courts from enforcing it. The statute of frauds (Chapter 18) requires that certain contracts must be evidenced by a writing before they can be enforced. Similarly, the statute of limitations mandates that an action for breach of contract must be brought within a set period of time, thereby limiting enforceability.

A **void** contract is in effect not a contract at all. Either its object is illegal or it has some defect so serious that it is not a contract. If you entered into a contract with an assassin to kill your business law professor, that contract would be void because it is obviously illegal to carry out its terms.

A contract is **voidable** if one or both parties has the ability to either withdraw from the contract or enforce it. If the parties discover the contract is voidable after one or both have partially performed, and one party chooses to have the contract terminated, both parties must return anything they had already exchanged under the agreement so that they will be restored to the condition they were in at the time they entered into it.

Certain types of errors in the formation of a contract can make it voidable. Typically, the person who can void the contract is the person the court is attempting to protect, or the party the court believes might be taken advantage of by the other. For example, contracts by minors are usually voidable by the minor (Chapter 16). Contracts entered into as a result of fraud, duress, or undue influence, as described in Chapter 17, may be voided by the innocent party. In the opening scenario, Morrow attempted to prove that the Dispute Resolution Program was a voidable contract because it did not include mutual promises, could be changed at any time without approval, and lacked genuine assent from the employees.

EXECUTED VERSUS EXECUTORY CONTRACTS

Once all the terms of the contract have been fully performed, the contract has been **executed.** As long as some of the terms have not yet been performed, the contract is **executory.** If Randolph hires Carmine to paint his garage on Saturday for $800, with $200 paid as a down payment and the balance due on completion of the job, the contract becomes executory as soon as they reach agreement. When Randolph makes the down payment and Carmine's work is half complete, it is still executory. Once the painting has been finished and the final payment made, the contract is an executed contract. In the opening scenario, Hallmark assumed that any employee who remained at the company had executed the contract.

FORMAL VERSUS INFORMAL CONTRACTS

Contracts can be formal or informal. **Formal contracts** have a special form or must be created in a specific manner. The Restatement (Second) of Contracts identifies the following

COMPARING THE LAW OF OTHER COUNTRIES

A SPECIAL KIND OF CONTRACT IN IRAQ

While most foreign states recognize the marriage contract, a different kind of marriage contract, sanctioned by Shiite clerics, is legal in Iraq. Called *muta'a* ("contract for a pleasure marriage"), it can last anywhere from an hour to 10 years and is renewable. Under the contract, the male typically receives sexual intimacy, in exchange for which the woman receives money. For a one-hour contract, she can generally expect the equivalent of $100; for a longer-term arrangement, $200 a month is typical, although she might receive more. The couple agrees to not have children, and if the woman does get pregnant, she can have an abortion but then must pay a fine to a cleric. The male can usually void the contract before the term ends, but the female can do so only if such a provision is negotiated when the contract is formed. *Muta'as* originally developed as a way for widows and divorced women to earn a living and for couples whose parents would not allow a permanent marriage to be together. Many women's rights advocates, however, see these contracts as exploiting women and are opposed to their increased popularity after the fall of Saddam Hussein in 2003. But as the aftermath of the war in Iraq continues to produce greater numbers of widows, increasing numbers of them are turning to this method of putting food on the table for themselves and their children.

Source: Rick Jervic, "'Pleasure Marriages' Regain Popularity in Iraq," *USA Today,* May 5, 2005, p. 8A; Bobby Caina Calvin, "In Shiite Iraq, Temporary Marriage May Be Rising," *McClatchy News,* www.mcclatchydc.com/103/story/21584.html (accessed June 9, 2009).

four types of formal contracts: (1) contracts under seal, (2) recognizances, (3) letters of credit, and (4) negotiable instruments.

When people hear the term *formal contract,* what often comes to mind is a *contract under seal,* named in the days when contracts were sealed with a piece of soft wax into which an impression was made. Today, sealed contracts may still be sealed with wax or some other soft substance, but they are more likely to be simply identified with the word *seal* or the letters *L.S.* (an abbreviation for *locus sigilli,* which means "the place for the seal") at the end. Preprinted contract forms with a printed seal can be purchased today, and parties using them are presumed, without evidence to the contrary, to be adopting the seal for the contract.

U.S. states today do not require that contracts be under seal. However, 10 states still allow a contract without consideration to be enforced if it is under seal.

A **recognizance** arises when a person acknowledges in court that he or she will perform some specified act or pay a price upon failure to do so. A bond used as bail in a criminal case is a recognizance. The person agrees to return to court for trial or forfeit the bond.

A **letter of credit** is an agreement by the issuer to pay another party a sum of money on receipt of an invoice and other documents. The Uniform Commercial Code governs letters of credit.

Negotiable instruments (discussed in detail in Chapters 26 and 27) are unconditional written promises to pay the holder a specific sum of money on demand or at a certain time. The most common negotiable instruments are checks, notes, drafts, and certificates of deposit. They are governed primarily by the UCC.

Any contract that is not a formal contract is an **informal contract,** also called a **simple contract.** Informal contracts may in fact be quite complex, but they are called "simple" because no formalities are required in making them. Even though informal, or simple, contracts may appear less official, they are just as important and legally binding as their more formal counterparts. One particular case, *Baum v. Helget Gas Products, Inc.,* proved that something as basic as handwritten notes can be considered an enforceable employment contract in a court of law.

In *Baum v. Helget Gas Products, Inc.,*[3] Robert Baum alleged that a series of handwritten notes, which were compiled during his interview with Helget Gas Products, constituted a three-year employment contract with the company. The notes Baum took during the interview process outlined three years' worth of salary, bonuses, benefits, and vacation time as discussed in the meetings. After being hired by the company, Baum also added "contract with Helget Gas Products St. Louis Mo. Market" to the top of the notes and had a Helget executive sign the document. Helget countered by saying that Baum, a salesman for the company, knew that he must meet certain performance goals each month or risk being fired. Thus, Helget's decision to fire Baum, based on his poor performance only a year after being hired, was legitimate. Helget further said that the itemizations produced by Baum in his notes were simply specifications of what Baum would receive if he remained employed by the company for the duration of three years and were not the components of an employment contract.

BUT WHAT IF . . .

In 2012, a hospital in Pennsylvania communicated with Republic Bank through e-mails about purchasing medical equipment from the bank. In the series of e-mails, the hospital agreed to purchase the equipment for stipulated prices. The bank agreed to the terms. However, the hospital never followed through with the deal. The bank sued the hospital, claiming there was a breach of contract. What kind of contract could the e-mails be labeled as?

Initially, the district court agreed with Helget Gas Products and ruled against Baum on his breach-of-contract claim. However, Baum appealed, and the U.S Court of Appeals for the Eighth Circuit reversed the district court's judgment on the breach-of-contract claim. For business students, *Baum v. Helget Gas Products, Inc.,* demonstrates the importance of being aware of what you are agreeing to when you sign a document, regardless of how informal, or simple, it may seem.

For a summary of contract classification, see Exhibit 13-4.

Interpretation of Contracts

LO4

What are the rules that guide the interpretation of contracts?

Perhaps the best-known rule of interpretation is the **plain-meaning rule,** which states that if a writing, or a term in question, appears to be plain and unambiguous on its face, we must determine its meaning from just "the four corners" of the document, without resorting to outside evidence, and give the words their ordinary meaning.

Although parties try to draft contracts as clearly as possible, sometimes they disagree about exactly what their obligations are under the agreement. Over time, the courts have developed some general guidelines to aid them in interpreting contracts and ascertaining the intentions of the parties:

- A judge should interpret a contract so as to give effect to the parties' intentions at the time they entered into the contract and to ensure the agreement makes sense as a whole. If possible, the court should ascertain the parties' intentions from the writing.

[3] 440 F.3d 1019; 2006 U.S. App. (accessed on Lexis Nexis, April 4, 2009).

Exhibit 13-4 Classification of Contracts

BILATERAL	or	UNILATERAL
Consists of a promise in exchange for a promise		Requires a performance by the offeree to form a contract
EXPRESS	or	**IMPLIED**
The terms of the contract are clearly formed either in written or spoken words		Arises from the conduct of the parties rather than their words
EXECUTED	or	**EXECUTORY**
A contract whose terms have been fully performed		A contract in which not all the duties have been performed
FORMAL	or	**INFORMAL**
Contracts created in a specific manner: contracts under seal, recognizances, letters of credit, and negotiable instruments		Simple contracts that require no formalities in making them; payment can be demanded by the payee at any time (e.g., checks)

VALID	or	VOID	or	UNENFORCEABLE	or	VOIDABLE
A contract that has all the legal elements of a contract and thus can be enforced		Not a contract because either its object is illegal or it has a serious defect		A valid contract that can't be enforced because some law prohibits it		A contract in which one or both parties has the ability to either withdraw from or enforce the contract

- If multiple interpretations are possible, the court should adopt the interpretation that makes the contract lawful, operative, definite, reasonable, and capable of being carried out.
- If the contract contains ambiguity, the judge should interpret it against the interests of the drafter. After all, the drafter is the one who could have prevented the ambiguity in the first place.
- If there is a conflict between preprinted and handwritten terms, the handwritten ones prevail. If numerals and numbers written out in words conflict, the written words prevail. If there is a conflict between general terms and specific ones, the specific terms apply.
- The court should interpret technical words in a contract as they are usually understood by persons in the profession or business to which they relate, unless clearly used in a different sense.

The Case Nugget on page 320 illustrates how some of these principles can be important in determining the outcome of a case.

CASE NUGGET

A QUESTION OF INTERPRETATION

Davco Holding Co. v. Wendy's International
2008 U.S. Dist. LEXIS 27108

Plaintiff Davco Holding Co., a franchisee of Wendy's, sued the company for breach of the franchise agreement for refusing to allow Davco to sell Pepsi from an unapproved supplier. The franchise agreement permits franchisees desiring to purchase products from an unapproved supplier to submit a written request to Wendy's for approval to do so. In response to Davco's written request to obtain beverage syrup from unapproved Pepsi, Wendy's informed Davco that CCF was the only approved supplier for fountain beverages and, further, that Pepsi syrup was not even an equivalent to Coke syrup because the drinks were made from two different secret formulas. The plaintiff alleged that Wendy's failed to adequately consider its request to solicit bids from Pepsi or to investigate Pepsi as a potential supplier and that this failure resulted in a breach by Wendy's of the franchise agreement.

The paragraph discussing the request for using an unapproved supplier contained the following language:

> Franchisor shall have the right to require that Franchisor be permitted to inspect the supplier's facilities, and that samples from the supplier be delivered, either to Franchisor or to an independent laboratory designated by Franchisor for testing. . . . Franchisor reserves the right to reinspect the facilities and products of any such approved supplier and to revoke its approval upon the supplier's failure to continue to meet any of Franchisor's then-current criteria. Nothing in the foregoing shall be construed to require Franchisor to approve any particular supplier, nor to require Franchisor to make available to prospective suppliers, standards and specifications for formulas that Franchisor, in its sole discretion, deems confidential.

The plaintiff claimed that Wendy's breached the agreement because it didn't inspect the facilities of Pepsi, request samples, or make its criteria available to Pepsi.

In interpreting the contract, the court said that where the terms of an existing contract are clear and unambiguous, the court "cannot create a new contract by finding an intent not expressed in the clear and unambiguous language of the written contract," and that a written agreement that appears complete and unambiguous on its face will not be given a construction other than that which the plain language of the contract provides.

As the court pointed out in dismissing the plaintiff's claims, the clause gives Wendy's the right to inspect a potential supplier, but giving someone a right to do something is not imposing a duty to do so. Thus, Wendy's failure to inspect cannot be a breach. Likewise, the terms of the clause clearly state that approval of another supplier lies within the sole discretion of Wendy's and that Wendy's does not have to share its criteria with the potential supplier.

CASE OPENER WRAP-UP

A Questionable Contract

The main issue in the Hallmark case was whether a valid contract existed. Hallmark argued that by staying with the company beyond the effective date of the program, employees were agreeing to the terms of the contract. To Hallmark, the bargained-for exchange was continued employment in exchange for a promise to submit to arbitration in lieu of litigation. The circuit court sent the case to arbitration, where the arbitrator found that the program constituted a valid contract.

The appellate court, however, using the objective standard for determining whether a contract existed, found that there was not a valid contract. For a valid, bilateral contract to exist, both sides would have to be making a valid promise. Hallmark was not binding itself to anything. The program did not require Hallmark to submit its claims to arbitration or in any way bind the company to keep any other promise mentioned in the Dispute Resolution Program (DRP). Further, Hallmark had reserved the right to "modify or discontinue the DRP at any time."

In response to the claim that continued employment was given to the employees in exchange for their promise to submit all disputes to arbitration, the court found that no such promise had been made by Hallmark. The employees to be bound by the program were at-will employees. As such, employment could be terminated at any time by Hallmark. Thus, the employees were receiving no rights in regard to employment that they did not already have. Because no mutually binding promises were exchanged, the appellate court ruled that the trial court had erred in accepting the arbitrator's award. In other words, because there was no consideration from Hallmark, there was no binding contract to submit disputes to arbitration. The case was remanded for further proceedings on Morrow's discrimination and retaliation claims.[4]

KEY TERMS

acceptance 306
agreement 306
bilateral contract 311
consideration 306
contract 306
contractual capacity 308
covenant not to compete 306
executed 316
executory 316
express contracts 313
formal contracts 317
implied contracts 313
informal contract 317
lack of genuine assent 308
letter of credit 317
negotiable instruments 317
offer 306
plain-meaning rule 318
quasi-contracts 313
recognizance 317
simple contract 317
unenforceable 316
Uniform Commercial Code (UCC) 310
unilateral contract 311
valid 316
void 316
voidable 316

SUMMARY OF KEY TOPICS

The Definition of a Contract

Contracts at their simplest level are legally enforceable agreements. A *valid contract* is generally one that has the following elements:

- *Agreement,* which is made up of the offer and the acceptance.
- *Consideration,* which is the bargained-for exchange.
- *Legal object,* which means that the subject matter does not violate the law or public policy.
- *Parties with contractual capacity,* which means they are at least the age of majority and do not suffer from any defect that renders them unable to understand the nature of the contract or their obligations under it.

Sources of Contract Law

The two most important sources of contract law are state common law and the Uniform Commercial Code. The Uniform Commercial Code, in Article 2, governs contracts for the sale of goods. All other contracts are also governed by the UCC.

Classification of Contracts

Contracts may be classified in a number of ways. Every contract is either unilateral or bilateral; express or implied; valid, voidable, void, or enforceable; executed or executory; and formal or informal.

- A *unilateral contract* requires a performance in order to form a contract.
- A *bilateral contract* consists of a promise in exchange for a promise.
- An *express contract* has all the terms clearly set forth in either written or spoken words.
- An *implied contract* arises from the conduct of the parties rather than their words.

[4] *Mary Kaye Morrow v. Hallmark Cards,* 273 S.W.3d 15, 2008 Mo. App. LEXIS 908.

- A *valid contract* is one that contains *all* the legal elements of a contract (agreement, consideration, contractual capacity, and legal object).
- A contract is *void* when either its object is illegal or it has some defect so serious that it is not actually a contract.
- A contract is *unenforceable* when some law prohibits the court from enforcing an otherwise valid contract.
- A contract is *voidable* if one or both of the parties has the ability to withdraw from the contract or to enforce it.
- *Executed contracts* are those whose terms have been fully performed.
- A contract is considered *executory* when some of the duties have not yet been performed.

Interpretation of Contracts

Courts have established rules to help interpret contracts so that they can ascertain and enforce the intent of the agreement.

The *plain-meaning rule* requires that if a writing, or a term in question, appears to be plain and ambiguous, its meaning must be determined from the instrument itself, with the words given their ordinary meaning.

POINT / COUNTERPOINT

Should the Distinction between Sealed and Unsealed Contracts Be Abolished?

NO

The distinction between sealed and unsealed contracts was drawn for several reasons, many of which are still relevant. As such, the distinction should remain intact despite the many attempts to have it abolished.

Sealed contracts, at common law, did not require consideration. In many instances today, consideration is not a necessary part of the agreement. These instances include releases, modifications and discharges, promises to keep offers open, promises based on past consideration, and promises to make gifts. In these instances, one party is offering to give something without consideration. For example, an individual wishing to make a charitable donation could enter into a binding agreement to make the donation without receiving any consideration in return. By sealing the contract, the charitable organization receiving the donation would be protected against lawsuits arising from a lack of consideration. In this instance, the distinction between a sealed and unsealed contract would be the difference between a judgment in favor of the charitable organization despite the lack of consideration and an outright dismissal.

Additionally, sealed contracts are often accompanied by an increased statute of limitations. In instances when there are potentially long-term ramifications tied to the signing of a contract, a sealed contract would provide a much longer period in which the parties could sue than would be the case if the contract were left unsealed.

YES

Advocates of abolishing the distinction between sealed and unsealed contracts argue that the distinction has become unnecessary and outdated. Sealed contracts can be dated back to medieval England when a substantial portion of the population was illiterate and many people were unable to sign their own names. As a result, each party to a sealed contract was responsible for impressing on the physical document a wax seal or some other mark bearing his or her individual sign of identification. The seals, in place of signatures, became proof of the parties' identities as well as the authenticity of the document.

The practice of actually affixing a seal to a document is no longer necessary. Today, the parties to a sealed contract need only write the words "under seal" or "sealed" or the letters "L.S" (*locus sigilli*) for the document to be given the privileged status of a sealed document.

In response to those who argue that sealed contracts are necessary to bind contracts that do not contain consideration, abolishment advocates argue that there are other, and perhaps more meaningful, methods of accomplishing this. Instead of sealing a contract, one could (1) require that the promise without consideration be explicitly referenced and agreed to in the text itself; or (2) require that witnesses be present at the signing of the contract (as is the practice with regard to wills); or (3) simply rewrite the contract to provide for consideration.

(Continued)

Given the protections offered by sealed contracts, abolishing them would be irresponsible. Moreover, the elimination of the sealed-unsealed distinction would necessarily result in the creation of another method of enforcement. Why should we abolish a technique that provides protection to the parties involved in the making of a contract only to turn around and create a similar distinction under a different name?

The practice of sealing contracts is outdated and irrelevant. Parties to contracts lacking consideration could be more protected from lawsuits by using different methods of enforcement. The sealed contract should be abolished in all states (as has already been done in several states).

QUESTIONS & PROBLEMS

1. What are the elements of a valid contract?
2. What is the difference between an offer for a unilateral contract and an offer for a bilateral contract? Why might that difference be important to understand?
3. Explain how a valid contract differs from one that is void or voidable.
4. What is the objective theory of contracts?
5. What must a party prove to recover under the theory of quasi-contract?
6. What is the difference between a formal and an informal contract?
7. What is the plain-meaning rule?
8. AES was formed in 1996 and hired eight employees. At a meeting in 1997, these employees expressed concern that the company might not survive as it was using outdated equipment. At that meeting, a company executive asked the employees to remain with the firm and stated that the company was likely to merge with another firm and, if it did, the original eight employees would receive 5 percent of the value of the sale or merger as a reward for staying. In 2001, the firm was bought by another firm, and the seven employees who had stayed sought to collect their 5 percent. The company refused to pay on grounds there was no contract. Did the company and employees have a bilateral or a unilateral contract? Explain. [*Vanegas v. American Energy Services,* 302 S.W.3d 299, 2009 WL 4877734 (Sup. Ct. Tex., 2009).]
9. R.J. Reynolds Tobacco Company (RJR) operated a customer rewards program, called Camel Cash, from 1991 to 2007. Under the terms of the program, RJR urged consumers to purchase Camel cigarettes, to save Camel Cash certificates included in packages of Camel cigarettes, to enroll in the program, and, ultimately, to redeem their certificates for merchandise featured in catalogs distributed by RJR.

   The plaintiffs were 10 individuals who joined the Camel Cash program by purchasing RJR's products and filling out and submitting signed registration forms to RJR. RJR sent each plaintiff a unique enrollment number that was used in communications between the parties. These communications included catalogs RJR distributed to the plaintiffs containing merchandise that could be obtained by redeeming Camel Cash certificates.

   From time to time, RJR issued a new catalog of merchandise offered in exchange for Camel Cash, which it either sent on request or mailed to consumers enrolled in the program. The number of Camel Cash certificates needed to obtain merchandise varied from as few as 100 to many thousands, and this encouraged consumers to buy more packages of Camel cigarettes and also to save Camel Cash certificates to redeem them for more valuable items.

   RJR honored the program from 1991 to 2006, and during that time Camel's share of the cigarette market nearly doubled, from approximately 4 percent to more than 7 percent. In October 2006, however, RJR mailed a notice to program members announcing that the program would terminate on March 31, 2007. The termination notice stated: "As a loyal Camel smoker, we wanted to tell you our Camel Cash program is expiring. C–Notes will no longer be included on packs, which means whatever Camel Cash you have is among the last of its kind. Now this isn't happening overnight—there'll be plenty of time to redeem your C–Notes before the program ends. In fact, you'll have from OCTOBER '06 though MARCH '07 to go to camelsmokes.com to redeem your C–Notes. Supplies will be limited, so it won't hurt to get there before the rush."

Beginning in October 2006, however, RJR stopped printing and issuing catalogs and told consumers that it did not have any merchandise available for redemption. Several of the plaintiffs attempted, without success, to redeem C–Notes or obtain a catalog during the final six months of the program. The plaintiffs had saved hundreds or thousands of Camel Cash certificates that they were unable to redeem.

In November 2009, the plaintiffs filed a class action complaint against RJR. They alleged breach of contract and promissory estoppel, among other claims, because RJR's actions had made the plaintiffs' unredeemed certificates worthless.

The Defendant argued that it had no bilateral contract to breach because the plaintiffs had not promised to do anything. The trial court agreed and dismissed the complaint. The plaintiffs appealed. How do you think the appellate court ruled, and why? [*Sateriale v. R.J. Reynolds Tobacco Co., 697* F.3d 777, C.A.9 (Cal. 2012).]

10. An oral agreement was made among multiple parties to put together some money and open a bar and restaurant. The men had to first create a joint company. However, one potential owner was not able to provide his share of the funding at the time of the company formation and was subsequently pushed out of the deal by the other owners, who formed the company without him. The man then sued the owners. In response, the defendants argued that the plaintiff had no documentation to support a cause of action. The court had to decide whether the plaintiff's complaint and statement of fact could support a breach-of-contract claim when no contract seemed to exist. Furthermore, the court considered the idea that a theory of quasi-contract could maintain a cause of action that could consist of the theft of ownership opportunity and/or breach of fiduciary duty. How do you think the court ultimately decided? [*Don v. Broger,* Index No. 6826/12 (Sup. Ct. Kings Cnty., Oct. 10, 2012).]

Looking for more review materials?

The Online Learning Center at **www.mhhe.com/kubasek3e** contains this chapter's "Assignment on the Internet" and also a list of URLs for more information, entitled "On the Internet." Find both of them in the Student Center portion of the OLC, along with quizzes and other helpful materials.

Agreement

LEARNING OBJECTIVES

After reading this chapter, you will be able to answer the following questions:

1 What are the elements of a valid offer?

2 How may an offer terminate?

3 What are the elements of an acceptance?

CASE OPENER

The Problematic Promotion

A Pepsi promotion encouraged consumers to collect "Pepsi points" and redeem them for merchandise. If they did not have quite enough points for the prize they wanted, they could buy additional points for 10 cents each; however, at least 15 original Pepsi points had to accompany each order.

In an early commercial for the promotion, which can be viewed on the web at www.youtube.com/watch?v=U_n5SNrMaL8, three young boys are sitting in front of a high school, one reading his Pepsi Stuff catalog while the others drink Pepsi. All look up in awe at an object rushing overhead as the military march in the background builds to a crescendo. A Harrier Jet swings into view and lands by the side of the school building, next to a bicycle rack. Several students run for cover, and the velocity of the wind strips one hapless faculty member down to his underwear. The voice-over announces: "Now, the more Pepsi you drink, the more great stuff you're gonna get."

A teenager opens the cockpit of the fighter and can be seen, without a helmet, holding a Pepsi. He exclaims, "Sure beats the bus," and chortles. The military drumroll sounds a final time as the following words appear: "Harrier Fighter 7,000,000 Pepsi Points." A few seconds later, the following appears in more stylized script: "Drink Pepsi—Get Stuff."

A 21-year-old student named John Leonard decided to accept what he believed was Pepsi's offer of the Harrier fighter jet for 7 million Pepsi points. He quickly realized it would be easier to raise the money to buy points than to collect 7 million points. In early March 1996, he filled out an order form requesting the jet and submitted it to Pepsi, along with 15 Pepsi points and a check for $700,000.

The plaintiff in the opening scenario hoped to obtain a jet like this one.

In response, Pepsi sent him a letter saying, "The item that you have requested is not part of the Pepsi Stuff collection. It is not included in the catalogue or on the order form, and only catalogue merchandise can be redeemed under this program." Leonard sued for breach of contract.

1. Did Pepsi offer to sell the Harrier jet for 7 million points?
2. Did Leonard's submission of the order form constitute an acceptance of an offer?

The Wrap-Up at the end of the chapter will answer these questions.

Elements of the Offer

L01

What are the elements of a valid offer?

The first element of a contract is the agreement, which is made up of an offer and an acceptance, as shown in Exhibit 14-1. Formation of the agreement begins when the party initiating the contract, called the *offeror,* makes an offer to another party, called the *offeree.* The elements of an offer are (1) serious intent by the offeror to be bound to an agreement, (2) reasonably definite terms, and (3) communication to the offeree. Remember, this chapter focuses on the elements of a contract under the common law. Some of these elements have been modified under the UCC for contracts for the sale of goods, and we discuss these changes in Chapter 21.

BUT WHAT IF . . .

WHAT IF THE FACTS OF THE CASE OPENER WERE DIFFERENT?

Recall that, in the Case Opener, the Pepsi commercial shows a fighter jet jokingly dropping a boy off at school. But what if the Pepsi commercial featured a man fully capable of owning and operating a fighter jet who turned in an appropriate and realistic number of Pepsi points and Pepsi Company officials subsequently handed him the keys and deeds to such a prize? What if the commercial announcer turned to the viewers and seriously announced that such a prize was included in the prize catalog and could be theirs? Do both scenarios constitute a realistic offer, or does neither scenario, or only the second scenario constitute such an offer?

INTENT

The first element of the offer is **intent.** The offeror must show intent to be bound by the offeree's acceptance. As explained in Chapter 13, we interpret contracts using an objective standard, meaning the courts are concerned only with the party's outward manifestations of intent, not internal thought processes. The courts interpret the parties' words and actions the way a reasonable person would interpret them.

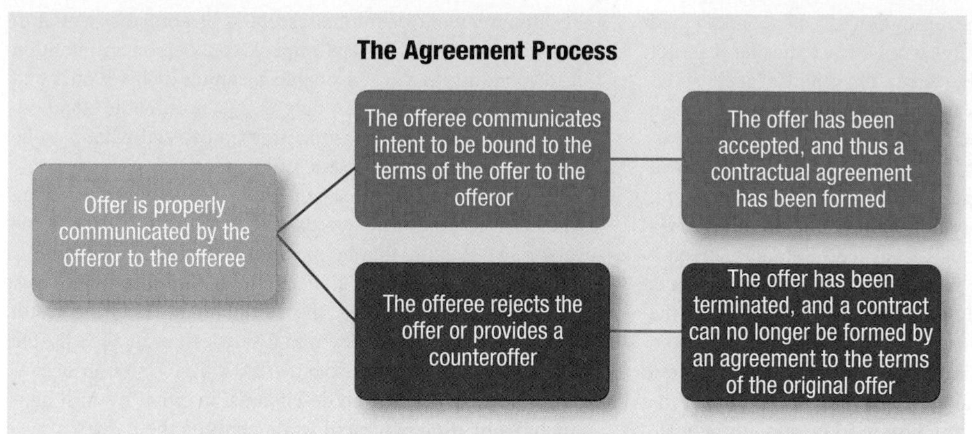

Exhibit 14-1
The Formation of an Agreement

Thus, if Jude is clearly joking or speaking in anger, a reasonable person would not think Jude seriously intended to make an offer and the courts will not treat his words as an offer. If someone tries to accept Jude's offer, the courts will find a contract has not been made.

Sometimes an offeror may try to avoid being bound to a contract by later claiming she was only joking when she made the offer, but the courts are not interested in her hidden intent. As Case 14-1 demonstrates, if you joke too well, you may find yourself in an unwanted contract.

CASE 14-1 LUCY v. ZEHMER
SUPREME COURT OF APPEALS OF VIRGINIA
196 VA. 493, 84 S.E.2D 516 (1954)

Plaintiffs W. O. and J. C. Lucy had wanted to purchase Ferguson Farm from the Zehmers for at least eight years. One night, Lucy stopped by the establishment the Zehmers operated and said that he bet Zehmer wouldn't accept $50,000 for the place. Zehmer replied that he would, but he bet that Lucy wouldn't pay $50,000 for it. Over the course of the evening, the parties drank whiskey and engaged in casual conversation, with the talk repeatedly returning to the sale of Ferguson Farm. Eventually Lucy got Zehmer to draw up a contract for the sale of the farm for $50,000.

When Lucy later attempted to enforce the agreement, Zehmer refused to complete the sale, arguing that he had been drunk, and that the agreement to sell the property had been made in jest. Lucy sued to enforce the agreement. The trial court found for the defendants and the plaintiffs appealed.

JUSTICE BUCHANAN: If it be assumed, contrary to what we think the evidence shows, that Zehmer was jesting about selling his farm to Lucy and that the transaction was intended by him to be a joke, nevertheless the evidence shows that Lucy did not so understand it but considered it to be a serious business transaction and the contract to be binding on the Zehmers as well as on himself. The very next day he arranged with his brother to put up half the money and take a half interest in the land. The day after that he employed an attorney to examine the title. The next night, Tuesday, he was back at Zehmer's place and there Zehmer told him for the first time, Lucy said, that he wasn't going to sell, and he told Zehmer, "You know you sold that place fair and square." After receiving the report from his attorney that the title was good, he wrote to Zehmer that he was ready to close the deal.

Not only did Lucy actually believe, but the evidence shows he was warranted in believing, that the contract represented a serious business transaction and a good faith sale and purchase of the farm.

In the field of contracts, as generally elsewhere, "We must look to the outward expression of a person as manifesting his intention rather than to his secret and unexpressed intention. 'The law imputes to a person an intention corresponding to the reasonable meaning of his words and acts.'"

[continued]

At no time prior to the execution of the contract had Zehmer indicated to Lucy by word or act that he was not in earnest about selling the farm. They had argued about it and discussed its terms, as Zehmer admitted, for a long time. Lucy testified that if there was any jesting it was about paying $50,000 that night. The contract and the evidence show that he was not expected to pay the money that night. Zehmer said that after the writing was signed he laid it down on the counter in front of Lucy. Lucy said Zehmer handed it to him. In any event there had been what appeared to be a good faith offer and a good faith acceptance, followed by the execution and apparent delivery of a written contract. Both said that Lucy put the writing in his pocket and then offered Zehmer $5 to seal the bargain. Not until then, even under the defendants' evidence, was anything said or done to indicate that the matter was a joke. Both of the Zehmers testified that when Zehmer asked his wife to sign he whispered that it was a joke so Lucy wouldn't hear and that it was not intended that he should hear.

The mental assent of the parties is not requisite for the formation of a contract. If the words or other acts of one of the parties have but one reasonable meaning, his undisclosed intention is immaterial except when an unreasonable meaning which he attaches to his manifestations is known to the other party.

The law, therefore, judges of an agreement between two persons exclusively from those expressions of their intentions which are communicated between them.

An agreement or mutual assent is of course essential to a valid contract but the law imputes to a person an intention corresponding to the reasonable meaning of his words and acts. If his words and acts, judged by a reasonable standard, manifest an intention to agree, it is immaterial what may be the real but unexpressed state of his mind.

So a person cannot set up that he was merely jesting when his conduct and words would warrant a reasonable person in believing that he intended a real agreement. . . .

Whether the writing signed by the defendants and now sought to be enforced by the complainants was the result of a serious offer by Lucy and a serious acceptance by the defendants, or was a serious offer by Lucy and an acceptance in secret jest by the defendants, in either event it constituted a binding contract of sale between the parties.

Defendants contend further, however, that even though a contract was made, equity should decline to enforce it under the circumstances. These circumstances have been set forth in detail above. They disclose some drinking by the two parties but not to an extent that they were unable to understand fully what they were doing. There was no fraud, no misrepresentation, no sharp practice and no dealing between unequal parties. The farm had been bought for $11,000 and was assessed for taxation at $6,300. The purchase price was $50,000. Zehmer admitted that it was a good price. There is in fact present in this case none of the grounds usually urged against specific performance.

REVERSED and REMANDED in favor of Plaintiff.

CRITICAL THINKING

How can someone be held to have made a contract when the necessary acceptance was "in secret jest"? In other words, why must a joke be visibly a joke to a reasonable observer for there to be no acceptance?

ETHICAL DECISION MAKING

What stakeholders are being protected by this ruling? What value is playing the largest role in shaping this ruling?

Legal Principle: **In determining intent to enter into a contract, the court looks at the person's objective manifestation of intent and does not try to interpret what the person may have been secretly thinking.**

Preliminary Negotiations. An invitation to negotiate or an expression of possible interest in an exchange is not an offer because it does not express any willingness to be bound by an acceptance. For example, if Rachael asked Bill whether he would sell his car for $5,000, she is not making an offer; she is just inquiring about his potential willingness to sell. Likewise, when a firm or government entity requests bids for a construction project, the request is just an invitation for contractors to make offers. The bids, however, would be offers.

While it may seem easy to distinguish an offer from an invitation to negotiate, whether an offer in fact existed is a question of fact and sometimes ends up being litigated. When

CASE NUGGET

WHEN IS AN AD AN OFFER?

Lefkowitz v. Great Minneapolis Surplus Store, Inc.
251 Minn. 188, 86 N.W.2d 689 (1957)

Great Minneapolis Surplus Store published a newspaper announcement stating: "Saturday 9 AM Sharp, 3 Brand New Fur Coats, Worth up to $1,000.00, First Come First Served $1 Each." Morris Lefkowitz arrived at the store, dollar in hand, but was informed that under the defendant's "house rules," the offer was open to ladies but not gentlemen. The court ruled that because the plaintiff had fulfilled all the terms of the advertisement, and the advertisement was specific and left nothing open for negotiation, a contract had been formed.

From this case came the often-quoted exception to the rule that advertisements do not create any power of acceptance in potential offerees: an advertisement that is "clear, definite, and explicit, and leaves nothing open for negotiation." In that circumstance, "it constitutes an offer, acceptance of which will complete the contract." Unlike the illustration of the invitation for an offer in the text (below), where the store obviously could not give every person who came to the store a rocking chair, in the Lefkowitz case, it was very clear that there were three new fur coats and the first three people who showed up with $1 would receive them. There was nothing indefinite or unclear about how to accept the offer.

you are either making an offer or attempting to begin negotiations about a possible contract, you should use very precise language that clearly expresses your intent.

Advertisements. Another illustration of an offer to make an offer is the advertisement. If a custom furniture maker places an advertisement in the paper that reads, "Old-fashioned, hand-crafted cedar rocking chairs only $250 the first week in May," the store is merely inviting potential customers to come to the store and offer $250 for a rocker. Because no reasonable person would expect the store to be able to sell a rocking chair to every person who might see the ad, the court will interpret the intent of the store as being to invite readers to make an offer.

Under limited circumstances, however, an ad can be treated as an offer. If it appears from the wording that the store did, in fact, intend to make an offer, that is, the ad specifies a limited quantity and provides a specific means by which the offer can be accepted, the courts will treat the ad as an offer, as demonstrated by the Case Nugget at top of this page.

John Leonard, the plaintiff in the case described in the opening scenario, tried to rely on the *Lefkowitz* decision to argue that the Pepsi commercial was an offer because it was "clear, definite, explicit, and left nothing to negotiation." After all, the commercial clearly stated that 7 million points earned a Harrier jet, and the catalog provided an additional means of buying the points for cash.

The court, however, found that the commercial could not be regarded as sufficiently definite because it specifically reserved the details of the offer to a separate writing, the catalog. Also, the commercial itself made no mention of the steps a potential offeree would be required to take to accept the alleged offer of a Harrier jet.

The court further found that the only offer in this scenario was the plaintiff's letter of March 27, 1996, along with the order form and appropriate number of Pepsi points. Since Pepsi rejected this offer with its letter, there is no contract.

Sometimes, however, unlike in the opening scenario, the advertiser's intent does appear to be to enter into a contract, even though that is not what the advertiser subjectively had in mind. A good example of such a situation occurred when Cathy McGowan called in to a U.K. radio station to enter a contest and win the advertised prize: a brand new car. The radio DJ told McGowan that to win the new car, a Renault Clio, she would have to identify a scrambled version of a song. McGowan did correctly identify the song and was told that she could come down to the radio station to collect her prize. It was not until she arrived at the radio station that McGowan became aware that she was going to receive not an actual new car but, instead, a toy version of the Renault Clio.

An upset McGowan took her case to court and argued that the radio station broadcasters gave no indication to their listeners the contest prize was actually a toy version of the car. A Derby crown court judge agreed with McGowan and ruled that the radio station had a legal contract to provide the contest winner with a new car. The judge further said that after reviewing the broadcast, he saw nothing that suggested the radio DJ was joking or intended to award contest winners with toy cars. Cathy McGowan was thus awarded £8,000, the cost of a new Renault Clio. The case, although from the United Kingdom, still has important implications for U.S. business students. In many respects U.K. contract laws are very similar to those of the United States, and had this case occurred on U.S. soil, a similar outcome would have been reached.[1]

To prevent possible "bait-and-switch" advertising that would appear as offers, some states have consumer protection laws requiring advertisers to state in their ads either that quantities of the item are limited to the first *X* number of people or that rain checks will be available if the item sells out.

Auctions. Another situation in which what seems to be an offer may not be is the auction. When Janine places a good with an auctioneer for sale by auction, is she making an offer, or is Kevin, who bids on it? It depends on what kind of auction is taking place.

If nothing is stated to the contrary in the terms of the auction, an auction is presumed to be *with reserve,* which means that the seller is merely expressing intent to receive offers. The auctioneer may withdraw the item from auction at any time before the hammer falls, signaling the acceptance of the bid. The bidder may also revoke the bid before that point.

In an auction *without reserve,* the seller is treated as making an offer to accept the highest bid and therefore must accept it. Not surprisingly, very few auctions are without reserve.

Legal Principle: If an auction is without reserve, the auctioneer must accept the lowest bid; if it is with reserve, the auctioneer may refuse to sell the item if he or she is not satisfied with the size of the highest bid.

DEFINITE AND CERTAIN TERMS

Under the common law, the terms of the offer must be **definite and certain.** In other words, all the material terms must be included.[2] The **material terms** allow a court to determine damages in the event that one of the parties breaches the contract. They include the subject matter, price, quantity, quality, and parties.

Sometimes an offer contains not the material term itself but a method for determining it. For example, Hampton's Construction Company is building a new garage for Jones, and the parties want to make it possible for Jones to pay one-third of the price of the garage in advance, one-third upon completion, and one-third in 12 monthly payments, with interest, beginning a month after completion. Rather than stipulating an interest rate to be charged on the monthly payments, the contract might specify an external standard according to which the interest rate would be set through the course of the 12-month payment period.

The question of whether the terms of an alleged offer were adequate for the formation of a valid contract often arises when one party believes a contract has been formed and the other believes the terms were not definite enough. That issue is the focus of Case 14-2.

[1] www.dailymail.co.uk/news/article-40153/8-000-Clio-winner-handed-toy.html.

[2] See UCC § 2-204 or Chapter 21 of this text for the modification of this element for sale-of-goods contracts.

CASE 14-2 ANDRUS v. STATE, DEPARTMENT OF TRANSPORTATION, AND CITY OF OLYMPIA
WASHINGTON STATE APPELLATE COURT
117 P.3D 1152 (WASH. APP. 2005)

Scott Andrus applied for a position as a building inspector with the city of Olympia. He received a call from Tom Hill, an engineering supervisor with the city. Hill stated, "You're our number one choice, and I'm offering you the job." Andrus responded "Great" and "Yes." Hill did not discuss the specifics of the job, so Andrus asked Hill to fax him those details. The city never sent such a fax or a written job offer and request for acceptance.

On the same day that Andrus received the call from Hill, the city checked Andrus's employment references, including his current employer (the Washington Department of Transportation), which proved unsatisfactory. Hill called Andrus the next day, informing him that the city had withdrawn the job offer because of further reference checks.

Andrus sued the city and the DOT, claiming wrongful discharge and arguing that the phone call from Hill offering the position was an employment contract. He also alleged the DOT was liable for defamation for providing a bad employment reference to the city. The superior court granted the city's request to dismiss his claims without a trial, and he appealed only the breach of contract claim against the city.

JUSTICE QUINN-BRINTNALL: An enforceable contract requires, among other things, an offer with *reasonably certain* terms. Restatement (Second) of Contracts §33 (1979) ("The fact that one or more terms of a proposed bargain are left open or uncertain may show that a manifestation of intention is not intended to be understood as an offer or as an acceptance"). Hill's "job offer" contained no starting date, salary, or benefit information. Moreover, it was to be followed by a written offer and request for acceptance. Under these facts, the July 13 phone conversation did not form an employment contract.

AFFIRMED in favor of the city.

CRITICAL THINKING

How could the original phone call from Hill be considered an employment contract? What would have to be included in the conversation? What could be left out? How different do you think the call would have needed to be to qualify as an employment contract between the plaintiff and the city? Why?

ETHICAL DECISION MAKING

How well does this decision hold up under examinations of ethicality, such as the public disclosure test and the universalization test? Do you think Justice Quinn-Brintnall took such examinations into account in reaching this decision? Why or why not?

COMMUNICATION TO THE OFFEREE

The third element of the offer is **communication.** The offer must be communicated to the offeree or the offeree's agent. Only the offeree (or his agent acting on his behalf) can accept the offer. If Bill overhears Sam offer to sell his car to Helen for $5,000, Bill cannot walk over and form a contract with Sam by accepting the offer to Helen. If he says to Sam, "I'll give you $5,000 for your car," he is not accepting the offer but, rather, is making a new offer.

Legal Principle: To have a valid offer under the common law, you need (1) the intent to be bound by an acceptance, (2) definite and certain terms, and (3) communication to the offeree.

Termination of the Offer

L02 How may an offer terminate?

Offers, once made, do not last forever. At some point in time they terminate. When an offer is terminated, the offeree can no longer accept it to form a binding contract. **Termination** of an offer can occur in one of five ways: revocation by the offeror, rejection or counteroffer by the offeree, death or incapacity of the offeror, destruction or subsequent illegality of the subject matter of the offer, or lapse of time or failure of other conditions stated in the offer. Each method is discussed below and summarized in Exhibit 14-2.

REVOCATION BY THE OFFEROR

To see how the six components of communication relate to the making of an agreement, please see the **Connecting to the Core** activity on the text website at www.mhhe.com/kubasek3e.

The offeror is said to be the "master of his or her offer" and, as such, can revoke it at any time, even if the offer states it will be open for a specified period of time. If Jim sends Carol a letter offering to mow her yard every week during the summer for the price of $20 per week as long as she responds to his offer within the next month, he can still change his mind and tell her at any time before she responds that he is no longer interested in working for her, thereby revoking his offer.

As a general rule, a **revocation** is effective when the offeree receives it. If it is really important to the offeror that the offeree know the offer has been revoked, the offeror should deliver the revocation personally.

Exceptions to the Revocability of the Offer. An offeree who wishes to ensure that an offer will in fact be held open for a set period of time may do so by entering into an option contract with the offeror. In an **option contract** the offeree gives the offeror a piece of consideration in exchange for holding the offer open for the specified period of time.

There is no requirement as to the value of the consideration. If it is money, the parties may agree that if the offer is eventually accepted and a contract is formed, the consideration will become part of the offeree's payment under the contract. This situation frequently arises in real estate contracts. Jose may be considering opening a restaurant and would like to have the option of purchasing a lot owned by Simone, so he gives her $1,000 for a 30-day option to purchase, with the provision that she will deduct the $1,000 from the purchase price if Jose purchases the property. If he does not, Simone will keep the $1,000.

Detrimental reliance on the offer may also form the basis for the court's not allowing the offeror to revoke an offer. If the offeree had reasonably relied on the offeror's promise to hold the offer open and had taken action in reliance on the offer, the courts may use the doctrine of promissory estoppel to estop, or prevent, the offeror from revoking his offer.

Detrimental reliance also comes into play to prevent a party who made a unilateral offer from revoking the offer once the offeree has begun performance of the action necessary to accept the unilateral offer. While the contract cannot be considered formed until the action requested has been completed, most courts recognize that to allow the offeror to revoke her offer after the offeree has expended significant amounts of time or money in

Exhibit 14-2
Ways an Offer Can Be Terminated

Revocation	The offeror can revoke the offer at any time unless the offeree entered into an option contract with the offeror.
Rejection	The offeree can reject the offer.
Counteroffer	If the offeree offers a counteroffer, the original offer is terminated.
Death or incapacity	If the offeror becomes incapacitated or dies, the offer immediately terminates.
Illegality	If the subject matter of the offer becomes illegal, the offer immediately terminates.
Lapse of time	The offer will expire after a reasonable amount of time, which depends on the subject matter of the offer, unless a specific time condition is given.

reliance on the offer would be to allow an unjustifiable injustice to occur. Therefore, once significant partial performance in reliance has begun, most courts require that the offeror give the offeree a reasonable amount of time to complete performance.

BUT WHAT IF . . .

In 1985, two New York couples went to court over an adopted two-year-old girl. The girl's adopted parents had reared the girl since she was five days old, yet when the girl was 15 weeks old her biological parents decided they wanted her back. In other words, the biological parents wanted to revoke their offer for their baby to be adopted. The biological parents argued that a revocation time frame for revocation had not been made sufficiently clear. However, New York State adoption law clearly stipulates that parents have only 30 days to revoke their consent for adoption, and the parents in this case had signed an "irrevocable consent" form. Would the parents be able to get their biological daughter back? Why or why not?

REJECTION OR COUNTEROFFER BY THE OFFEREE

The second means by which an offer can be terminated is **rejection** by the offeree. Regardless of how long the offer was stated to be open, once the offeree rejects it, it is terminated. In our earlier illustration, if Carol calls Jim and says she is not interested in his working for her this summer or any summer because of the poor quality of his work but then she calls him back an hour later to say she has changed her mind and would like to hire him in accordance with his proposed terms, it is too late. There is no offer for her to accept because her rejection terminated it.

In the same illustration, if Carol tells Jim she would indeed like him to cut her grass every week this summer but will pay him only $15 each week, she has made a **counteroffer,** defined by the Restatement as "an offer made by an offeree to his offeror relating to the same matter as the original offer and proposing a substituted bargain differing from that proposed by the original offer."[3] A counteroffer terminates the original offer, and so Carol's counteroffer terminates Jim's original offer. Thus, if you receive an offer that you might want to accept but you are wondering whether you can get better terms, you should inquire about how set the offeror is on the terms proposed before you make a counteroffer. For example, Carol might have simply asked Jim whether he would consider doing the job at any other price.

DEATH OR INCAPACITY OF THE OFFEROR

An offer terminates immediately if the offeror dies or loses the legal capacity to enter into the contract, even if the offeree does not know of the terminating event. If the parties had already entered into an option contract to hold the offer open for a set period of time, however, the administrator of the offeror's estate or the guardian of the offeror must hold the offer open until it expires in accordance with the option contract.

DESTRUCTION OR SUBSEQUENT ILLEGALITY OF THE SUBJECT MATTER

If the subject matter of the offer is destroyed or becomes illegal, the offer immediately terminates. For example, if Jamie offers Mercedes a job managing the riverboat casino he plans to open on January 1 but, before Mercedes accepts the offer, the state decides to no longer allow riverboat casinos to operate, the offer of employment terminates.

[3] Restatement (Second) of Contracts, sec. 39 (1981).

CASE NUGGET

THE IMPORTANCE OF CONDITIONS IN OFFERS

Adone v. Paletto
2005 NY Slip Op 50196U; 6 Misc. 3d 1026A; 800 N.Y.S.2d 341

On July 26, 2004, the defendants' counsel made an "Offer to Compromise" and settle the action in the amount of $500,000, plus costs accrued to that date, which represented the entire available coverage under the defendants' insurance policy. Part of the offer stated:

> If within ten days thereafter the claimant serves a written notice that he accepts the offer, either party may file the summons, complaint, and offer, with proof of acceptance, and thereupon the clerk shall enter judgment accordingly. If the offer is not accepted and the claimant fails to obtain a more favorable judgment, he shall not recover costs from the time of the offer, but shall pay costs from that time. An offer of judgment shall not be made known to the jury.

On August 9, 2004, the parties appeared before the court for a settlement conference in which the plaintiffs' counsel made a demand of $700,000 to settle the case. This demand was clearly not an acceptance of the offer to compromise; instead, it was a counteroffer that rejected that $500,000 offer.

The plaintiffs' $700,000 demand was not acceptable to the defendants, and the case was not settled. On September 24, 2004, the plaintiffs' counsel sent a letter to the defendants accepting the $500,000 judgment offered two months earlier, which was to include interest from the date of the summary judgment and costs. On September 28, the defendants rejected the acceptance in writing because it was not within 10 days of the offer.

The plaintiffs' motion for a judgment to enforce the offer to compromise was denied because the acceptance was not within the 10-day time frame.

LAPSE OF TIME OR FAILURE OF ANOTHER CONDITION SPECIFIED IN THE OFFER

We've noted that the offeror has the power to revoke the offer at any time, even if the offer states that it will be held open for a set period. But if the offer states that it will be held open for only a certain time, it terminates when that time expires. In the absence of such a time condition, the offer will expire after the lapse of a reasonable amount of time. What constitutes a reasonable amount of time varies, depending on the subject matter of the offer. An offer by a retailer to purchase seasonal goods from a wholesaler would lapse sooner than an offer to purchase goods that could be easily sold all year long. The Case Nugget above illustrates the consequences of not paying attention to the time or other limiting conditions specified in an offer, and see again a summary of the ways a contract can be terminated can be found in Exhibit 14-2.

The Acceptance

L03
What are the elements of an acceptance?

Once an offer has been made, the offeree has the power to accept that offer and form a contract. Under the common law, the basic requirements for a valid **acceptance** parallel those for a valid offer. There should be a manifestation of intent to be bound by the acceptance to the contract, agreement to the definite and certain terms of the offer, and communication to the offeror.

MANIFESTATION OF INTENT TO BE BOUND TO THE CONTRACT

In general, there are two ways an offeree can manifest intent to enter into the contract: by performance or by a return promise. The offeree must either do or say something to form the contract.

Recall, from Chapter 12, the distinction between a bilateral and a unilateral contract. If the offer is for a unilateral contract, the offeree can accept only by providing the requested performance. If Bill offered to pay $500 to anyone who returned his lost dog to him, Mary could accept the offer only by returning the dog. Bill did not want her promise, and if she called and promised to return the dog to him, that promise would have no legal effect because the only way to accept a unilateral offer is by performance.

BUT WHAT IF . . .

WHAT IF THE FACTS OF THE CASE OPENER WERE DIFFERENT?

Recall that, in the Case Opener, PepsiCo required that a customer mail in Pepsi points before the company would mail the customer a prize. But what if the Pepsi-points contract required that the customer only send in a signed statement that they had the requisite number of points and would be subsequently sending in the Pepsi points on a certain date and that PepsiCo would send the prize upon receipt of the statement? Would this scenario create a unilateral or a bilateral contract?

Remember from the previous section that the offeror has the right to revoke the offer at any time before it has been accepted. This rule is slightly modified with respect to unilateral offers so that if one party has begun performance, the offeror must give the offeree a reasonable time to complete it.

In a bilateral contract, what the offeror wants is not performance but, rather, a return promise. Sometimes, however, it is not clear what the offeror wants. Then the offeree has the option of either performing or making a return promise.

Silence as a Form of Acceptance. Silence, as a general rule, cannot be used to form a contract. Lisa and Marie both work at a local diner where the manager is very flexible about their hours and lets them trade shifts. Marie leaves Lisa a voice-mail message saying, "I can't work my three night shifts this week. If you can cover them for me, I'll pay you an extra $40 on top of the money you'll receive from the boss for working my shifts. If I don't hear from you by 7 p.m. tomorrow, I'll assume we have a deal. Thanks so much!" If Lisa does not call back, no contract has been formed because silence under these circumstances will not constitute acceptance.

There are, however, a few situations in which silence *can* mean acceptance. In the most common, the parties, by their previous course of dealing with each other, have established a pattern of behavior whereby it is reasonable to assume silence communicates acceptance. If a wholesaler and a retailer have a long-standing relationship in which the retailer will reject a shipment that does not meet his needs, when a shipment is not sent back it is reasonable for the wholesaler to assume that the retailer means to accept it.

Silence can also be acceptance when the offeree receives the benefits of the offered services with reasonable opportunity to reject them and knowledge that some form of compensation is expected yet remains silent. In this case, an implied-in-fact contract is created. Because many unscrupulous businesspersons once took advantage of this rule and sent unordered merchandise to people, stating the goods could be returned or be kept on payment of a set price, most states have passed laws providing that unsolicited merchandise does not have to be returned and the recipient may keep it as a gift, with no contract being formed.

A third situation occurs when the parties agree that silence will be an acceptance. For example, a person may join a book club whose contract provides that a new book will be sent every month if the member does not send notification rejecting the month's selection.

COMPARING THE LAW OF OTHER COUNTRIES

CONTRACTS IN JAPAN

The Japanese tend to view contracts as ongoing relationships in which parties work with each other to smooth out any problems that arise in performance of the contract. Often suspicious of long, detailed contracts, they have a distinct preference for short, flexible agreements that leave a number of terms to be decided later.

ACCEPTANCE OF DEFINITE AND CERTAIN TERMS: THE MIRROR-IMAGE RULE

When a bilateral contract is being formed under the common law, the mirror-image rule applies to the acceptance. The **mirror-image rule** says that the terms of the acceptance must mirror the terms of the offer. If they do not, no contract is formed. Instead, the attempted acceptance is a counteroffer.[4]

COMMUNICATION TO THE OFFEROR

An offeror has the power to control the means by which the acceptance is communicated, so if the offeror specifies that only a certain means of communication will be accepted, then only an acceptance by that means forms a valid contract. Suppose Jennifer offers to paint Rashad's car for $500 but says he must accept the offer by telephone before midnight on Thursday. If Rashad sends Jennifer an e-mail Thursday morning accepting her offer, there is no contract. Even though e-mail might be a valid means of accepting a contract offer if no means is specified, when the offer is limited to a specific means of communicating the acceptance, only that means results in a valid contract. Thus, Rashad's attempted acceptance was simply a new offer.

BUT WHAT IF . . .

WHAT IF THE FACTS OF THE CASE OPENER WERE DIFFERENT?

Recall that, in the Case Opener, PepsiCo stipulated that customers must mail in Pepsi points. What if, instead, the company required that contestants fax in photos of their collected Pepsi points. If Leonard mailed his Pepsi points to the company, would that count as a valid acceptance of the offer?

If no means of communicating the acceptance is specified, any reasonable means is generally acceptable. Telephone, mail, fax, and e-mail are all valid means of accepting an offer, as is accepting it in person. When drafting an offer, if a person wishes acceptance to be only by a particular means, the offer must make it clear that only certain means are allowed. As Case 14-3 illustrates, courts will carefully interpret provisions specifying the means of acceptance.

The Mailbox Rule. Because not all acceptances are made in person, the courts needed a rule to determine the point at which an acceptance made through the mail became effective. They settled on the **mailbox rule,** which provides that an acceptance is valid when the offeree places it in the mailbox, whereas a revocation is effective only when the offeree receives it. The mailbox rule is not applicable when there is instantaneous communication, such as over the phone, in person, or by telex.

[4] See UCC § 2-207 and Chapter 21 for an explanation of how the UCC modifies the mirror-image rule for contracts for the sale of goods.

CASE 14-3 ALEXANDER v. LAFAYETTE CRIME STOPPERS, INC.
COURT OF APPEALS OF LOUISIANA, THIRD CIRCUIT
28 SO. 3D 1253 (LA. APP. 3 CIR., 2010)

In the summer of 2002, after several South Louisiana women had been murdered, the Multi Agency Homicide Task Force (Task Force) was established to investigate these murders, which they believed were being committed by the individual referred to as the South Louisiana Serial Killer. In April 2003, the Baton Rouge Crime Stoppers (BRCS) began publicizing a reward offer in newspapers, television stations, and billboards around the Baton Rouge area regarding the South Louisiana Serial Killer. A short time later, Lafayette Crime Stoppers (LCS) also publicized a reward offer. Both reward offers included an expiration date of August 1, 2003.

On July 9, 2002, Dianne Alexander was attacked in her home in St. Martin Parish. Her son came home during the attack and chased the attacker away. Ms. Alexander reported the attack to local police, and, later, both Ms. Alexander and her son described the attacker to the St. Martin Sheriff's Department.

The lead investigator on Ms. Alexander's attack began to suspect that Ms. Alexander's attacker could be the South Louisiana Serial Killer, so in May 2003, he shared information regarding Ms. Alexander's attack with the Lafayette Sheriff's Department, which then shared it with the Task Force.

On May 22, 2003, Ms. Alexander was interviewed by an FBI agent assisting the Task Force. Based upon that interview, a composite sketch was drawn and released to the public on May 23, 2003. Investigators believed the composite sketch matched the description of a possible suspect in an investigation being handled by the Louisiana Attorney General's Office and the Zachary Police Department. On May 25, 2003, Ms. Alexander, in a photo lineup, identified her attacker as the same man suspected in the Zachary investigation.

Around August 14, 2003, Ms. Alexander contacted LCS and sought to collect the advertised award, but was told she was ineligible to receive the award. In 2006, Ms. Alexander and her son sued BRCS and LCS, alleging that the defendants owed them $100,000 and $50,000, respectively, for the information they provided to the defendants. The defendants filed motions for summary judgment asserting there was no genuine issue of material fact because the plaintiffs would be unable to prove that a contract ever existed between the parties. The trial court granted the motions. The plaintiffs appealed, asserting that there is a genuine issue of material fact over whether LCS and BRCS offers contained a requirement that acceptance of the reward must be done through the Crime Stoppers' tip line.

JUDGE AMY: . . . The defendants filed motions for summary judgment asserting that a valid contract never existed between the parties. Specifically, the defendants argued that the plaintiffs never provided information to Crime Stoppers via the tipster hotline and thus did not comply with the "form, terms, or conditions required by the Crime Stoppers offers[.]" The trial court granted the defendants' motions for summary judgment, finding that the offer from Crime Stoppers was conditioned on the information being provided to the defendant entities rather than law enforcement. . . .

Louisiana Civil Code Article 1927 provides:

> A contract is formed by the consent of the parties established through offer and acceptance.
>
> Unless the law prescribes a certain formality for the intended contract, offer and acceptance may be made orally, in writing, or by action or inaction that under the circumstances is clearly indicative of consent.
>
> Unless otherwise specified in the offer, there need not be conformity between the manner in which the offer is made and the manner in which the acceptance is made.

"Louisiana jurisprudence has recognized that an advertisement may constitute an offer susceptible of giving rise to a binding contract upon acceptance in instances where a prize is offered or where the terms of a contest are announced." . . . Once a plaintiff performs all of the requirements of the offer in accordance with the published terms, it creates a valid and binding contract, under which one is entitled to the promised rewards. . . . '68 So. 2d (1953)

The offer made by LCS in a May 14, 2003, press release, reads as follows:

> The Greater Lafayette Chamber of Commerce has joined with Lafayette Crime Stoppers to offer a reward of $50,000 for information relating to the murders of five south Louisiana women. A $25,000 reward offer by Lafayette Crime Stoppers has been matched through commitments from Chamber members.
>
> In order to qualify for the reward, the tipster must provide information which leads to the arrest, DNA match, and the formal filing of charges against a suspect through grand jury indictment or Bill of Information. In addition, the qualifying tip must be received prior to midnight, August 1, 2003. Investigators with the Serial Killer Task Force have expressed optimism that a large enough reward might provide the impetus for someone with knowledge of the killings to come forward. By stipulating a deadline, investigators hope to expedite receipt of the information.
>
> All callers the Crime Stoppers Tips line remain anonymous. A code number is issued as the only means of identification. Tips can be submitted 24 hours a day at 232–TIPS or toll free at 1–800–805–TIPS.

[continued]

The offer from BRCS, as published in the *Morning Advocate,* reads as follows:

> Crime Stoppers, Inc. $100,000 reward for information on the South Louisiana Serial Killer. A $100,000 reward will be given for information leading to the arrest and indictment of the South Louisiana Serial Killer. Call today and help make Baton Rouge a safer place for you and your family. All calls remain anonymous. 334–STOP or 1–877–723–7867. Reward expires August 1, 2003.

Both LCS and BRCS offers were irrevocable offers because they specified a period of time for acceptance. La. Civil Code Article 1934 provides that "acceptance of an irrevocable offer is effective when received by the offeror." Acceptance is received when it comes into the possession of a person authorized by the offeror to receive it, or when it is deposited in a place the offeror has indicated as the place where communications of that kind are to be deposited for him.

The plaintiffs argue that there is a genuine issue of material fact as to whether they accepted the Crime Stoppers' reward offers; however, the plaintiffs admit that they did not contact either Crime Stopper organization before August 1, 2003. The plaintiffs argue that they accepted the offers by performance when they provided information about the serial killer to law enforcement. Further, the plaintiffs contend that this performance is a customary manner of accepting reward offers from Crime Stopper organization.

In the present matter, the plaintiffs' acceptance of the reward offers must have been received by the defendants (offerors) by the time prescribed in the offer (August 1, 2003) in the place where communications of that kind were to be deposited (the phone number cited in the offers). The record contains no evidence indicating the defendants were notified by the plaintiffs in the time and manner indicated in the offer. While the plaintiffs may have provided information related to the arrest or indictment of Derrick Todd Lee to local law enforcement and the Task Force, there is no indication in the offer that either of those parties were the offerors of the reward or persons authorized to receive acceptance on their behalf.

The plaintiffs argue that they accepted the offers by performance when they provided information about the serial killer to law enforcement. Further, the plaintiffs contend that this performance is a customary manner of accepting reward offers from Crime Stopper organization. While acceptance may be valid if customary in similar transactions, according to La.Civ.Code art. 1936, it must be "customary in similar transactions at the time and place the offer is *received.*" As indicated above, there is no evidence in the record that the defendants received any acceptance of the offer. Accordingly, no contract was formed between the parties.

Summary Judgment in favor of Defendants, AFFIRMED.

CRITICAL THINKING

What is ambiguous about the concept of acceptance? How does the law act to clarify the potential liability?

ETHICAL DECISION MAKING

How might the public disclosure test give false guidance to the ethics of this decision? Do you think that the public's attitude toward the interaction between Crime Stoppers and the people who helped solve a crime might have resulted in a different decision had the public disclosure principle been used to resolve the case?

Since the mailbox rule does not apply to instantaneous communications, when are faxes, text messages, and e-mail effective? Are these instantaneous forms of communication? Text messages seem the easiest to answer yes to. There is still some disagreement among jurisdictions as to whether faxes and e-mail should be effective on dispatch or receipt. The majority rule with respect to faxes appears to be that faxes are instantaneous transmissions and therefore effective on receipt, but some jurisdictions have applied the mailbox rule to them. There seems to be greater split among the jurisdictions over how to treat e-mail transmissions. The Uniform Electronic Transactions Act seems to create an electronic version of the mailbox rule, providing that an e-mail is sent when properly addressed to an information processing system designated by the recipient, in a form capable of being processed by that system, and enters an information processing system out of

E-COMMERCE AND THE LAW

DISCLOSURE OF DEFINITE AND CERTAIN TERMS

Many people would like to know what sort of terms they are going to be held to when buying a product. Unfortunately, many people aren't aware of the importance of receiving prior disclosures and also don't realize that online businesses commonly refrain from giving full disclosure of terms about a product until they receive the customer's payment information. If e-businesses do happen to provide these certain terms before a customer agrees to buy a product, the link to the terms themselves may be hard to find. Another aspect of the terms (if given) is that the language in which the contract is written is dense legal language, which may be hard for the ordinary person to understand fully. These e-business practices in regard to disclosure of terms can be very deceptive. A customer may inadvertently agree to a contract when the customer is only given some information about it. This situation would be similar to one in which a student were given a page of text that appeared to be whole and complete, and the student had completed an entire report on the text before being given an additional 50 pages that were also a part of the text. Customers who shop online should be aware of the potential for deception with online sellers and should use caution when making purchases.

Source: http://digitalcorpora.org/corp/nps/files/govdocs1/021/021056.pdf.

the control of the sender. It is considered received when it enters the information processing system designated by the recipient.

Authorized Means of Acceptance. The means by which the offeree can communicate acceptance to the offeror may either be expressly stated in the offer, which is called an *express authorization,* or be implied from the facts and circumstances surrounding the communication of the offer to the offeree. If the offer specifies that acceptance must be communicated by a specific mode, that mode is the only means for accepting the offer, and once the acceptance is dispatched, the contract has been formed. If any other attempted means of acceptance is used, there is no valid contract. For example, if the offer says acceptance must be by certified mail, then as soon as the acceptance is taken to the post office, there is a valid contract. If the offeree instead faxes an acceptance, there is no contract.

According to the Restatement, if no mode of communication is specified in the offer, any reasonable means of acceptance is valid. To determine the reasonableness of the means, courts look at such factors as the means by which the offer was communicated and the surrounding circumstances.

Effect of an Unauthorized Means of Acceptance. As noted above, when an offer specifies that acceptance must be communicated by a particular mode, no other form of acceptance is valid. However, if the offer merely authorizes certain modes of acceptance but does not condition acceptance on the use of those modes, use of an unauthorized means of acceptance is acceptable but the contract is not formed until the acceptance is received by the offeror. For example, if Beth sends an offer to Joe via a fax, saying in the offer that acceptance may be via fax or e-mail, and Joe accepts her offer by overnight mail, his acceptance is valid but it is effective only on receipt.

If the offeree makes a mistake and sends the acceptance to the wrong address, there is no acceptance on dispatch. However, if a correction is made and the letter eventually reaches the offeror, the acceptance is valid on receipt, assuming the offer was still open.

The Effect of an Acceptance after a Rejection. We've seen that if an acceptance is received after a rejection, the acceptance is not valid because the rejection terminated the offer. However, sometimes a rejection is dispatched, but before it is received, the acceptance is communicated to the offeror. In that case, a valid contract has been formed because the rejection is not effective until it is received. Suppose Brenda e-mails an offer to Harry, and he puts a rejection in the mail; then, before it is received, Harry calls Brenda and tells her he accepts. A valid contract has been formed, and the rejection will have no effect when Brenda receives it. However, if Harry telephoned after Brenda had received the rejection, there could be no contract.

BUT WHAT IF . . .

WHAT IF THE FACTS OF THE CASE OPENER WERE DIFFERENT?

What if Leonard had sent in a certain number of Pepsi points to receive a corresponding prize but at the last minute e-mailed the company to reject the prize because he wanted to save his points for a bigger prize. If the company receives his mailed points before his e-mailed rejection, is his rejection valid?

CASE OPENER WRAP-UP

The Problematic Promotion

Much to the plaintiff's dismay, the court in the Pepsi case found that the commercial could not be regarded as sufficiently definite to be an offer, because it specifically reserved the details of the offer to a separate writing, the catalog.[5] Also, the commercial itself made no mention of the steps a potential offeree would be required to take to accept the alleged offer of a Harrier jet. As in most cases where a consumer attempts to place an order for an advertised item, the court regarded the plaintiff's purported acceptance as an offer. And it was an offer that Pepsi obviously rejected. And while the court did not specifically mention this factor, common sense should have indicated to the plaintiff and his family that Pepsi did not really intend to give a harrier jet as one of the promotional prizes.

KEY TERMS

acceptance 334
communication 331
counteroffer 333
definite and certain terms 330
intent 326
mailbox rule 336
material terms 330
mirror-image rule 336
option contract 332
rejection 333
revocation 332
termination 331

SUMMARY OF KEY TOPICS

Elements of the Offer A valid offer requires (1) the manifestation of the offeror's intent to be bound, (2) definite and certain terms, and (3) communication to an offeree.

Termination of the Offer An offer can be terminated by revocation by the offeror; rejection or counteroffer by the offeree; death or incapacity of the offeror; destruction or subsequent illegality of the subject matter of the offer; or lapse of time or failure of other conditions stated in the offer.

The Acceptance An acceptance is valid when a manifestation of intent to be bound to the terms of the offer is communicated to the offeror by the offeree.

[5] *Leonard v. Pepsico*, 210 F.3d 88, 2000 U.S. App. LEXIS 6855.

POINT / COUNTERPOINT

Should Internet Click-Wrap and Browse-Wrap Agreements Be Treated as Legally Binding Contacts?

YES

Nearly all computer users have, at some point, encountered form contracts while browsing the Internet. Whether they pertain to downloading software, signing up for a free e-mail service, or making an online purchase, many online forms are designed to protect the host company or retail store's interests. To protect these companies and ensure continued online commerce, these contracts *must* be viewed as legally binding.

The two types of Internet contracts are click-wrap and browse-wrap contracts. A click-wrap contract requires that users read all terms and conditions before clicking an "I Agree" button. Such contracts give users the ability to *choose* whether to accept the conditions and proceed or decline and withdraw. This process includes an offer by the offeror (the terms and conditions as listed) and acceptance by the offeree (clicking the "I Agree" button). The contract includes a clear manifestation of the offeree's intent to be bound when he or she clicks the accept button.

In the second type of Internet contract, the browse-wrap agreement, the user is not required by the site to click any button but is seen under the law as having accepted the terms by viewing the website. In such instances, the site provides its terms and conditions via a hyperlink at the top of a web page. By posting the link, the website has provided users with notice that there are terms and conditions associated with the site and that users who continue making use of the site should be bound by those terms. By viewing the site (the performance), the user is bound to the terms (the offer).

Given the large quantity of transactions occurring over the Internet, browse-wrap and click-wrap agreements offer an efficient means for governance. In an effort to protect companies and ensure compliance by consumers, these agreements *must* be treated as legally binding contracts.

NO

Nearly all computer users have agreed to and proceeded beyond click-wrap agreements. Many of these computers users have used websites that have browse-wrap agreements embedded within their pages. But the mere existence of these agreements does not mean that they are valid contracts under existing contract laws; they should not.

In both click-wrap and browse-wrap agreements, the terms are decided prior to the user even installing the software or visiting the site. The user is not given an opportunity to negotiate the terms; in essence, there is no meeting of the minds. If the user wishes to use the website, software, or e-mail system, he or she must accept the prewritten terms.

Click-wrap agreements have become so prevalent throughout recent years that Internet users often ignore the text of the agreement and simply click the "I Agree" box. Without reading and understanding the terms of the agreement, lawyers, consumers, and companies are left to wonder whether the user lacked genuine assent.

Browse-wrap agreements, unlike click-wrap agreements, are not even located on the general web page. In order to view the terms and conditions of use, the user must find the hyperlink on a page, click on it, read the terms, and then decide whether or not to continue reading the web page. The site owners cannot be certain that users will find, read, or understand the terms and conditions of use before they browse the site. Without knowledge, Internet users should not be bound to the terms and conditions.

Finally, when paper contracts are signed, one can be certain whom the relevant parties are. With electronic contracts, that certainty quickly dissipates. Even though a click-wrap agreement is offered and accepted, without proper verification, one cannot be certain who was using the computer at the time the contract was formed. If, for example, a friend uses your computer while visiting your dorm room and enters into a click-wrap agreement, which you later violate unknowingly, who is accountable? Can you prove you were not the one who agreed to the terms? Identifying the parties associated with electronic contracts would be more difficult than identifying those associated with paper contracts.

QUESTIONS & PROBLEMS

1. What is the mirror-image rule?
2. What is the mailbox rule?
3. In July 2012, the six adult cast members of the hit television show *Modern Family* filed a joint lawsuit against Twentieth Century Fox Television in an attempt to void their contracts. The lawsuit claimed that their contracts were illegal, in that the contracts broke California's "7-year rule." The 7-year rule stipulates that contracts regarding personal services may not span longer than seven years. Yet the actors' contracts guaranteed their services from 2009 to 2016. A big incentive for the actors to file the lawsuit was to increase the amount they each were paid per episode, which for most of them was $65,000 an episode. If a contract is illegal, may it be voided even if the actors knowingly signed to the terms of the contract? How do you think the judge should have decided this case, and why? [*Vergara et al. v. Twentieth Century Fox International Television, Inc.* BC488786 (Sup. Ct. L.A. 2012).]
4. Michael and Laurie Montgomery negotiated with Norma English with regard to the potential sale of the Montgomerys' home. English submitted a bid for $272,000, but she included a request to purchase some of the Montgomerys' personal property and expressed that an "as-is" provision was not applicable to the sale. When the Montgomerys received the offer, they deleted the personal property provision, deleted provisions related to latent defects and a building inspection, and added a specific as-is rider. English's agent then delivered the counteroffer to English, who initialed many, but not all, of the Montgomerys' modifications, such as the deletion of the personal property provision. The Montgomerys refused to proceed with the sale, so English filed suit for specific performance of the contract. Under the mirror-image rule, did a contract exist between the Montgomerys and English? Why or why not? [*Montgomery v. English,* 2005 Fla. App. LEXIS 4704.]
5. Nutritional Sciences LLC sponsored the "Quarter Million Dollar Challenge," a contest requiring contestants to use the company's nutritional products and training plans to lose weight and get in shape during a 13-week period. A panel of judges would select a number of winners based on their success in the program. Contest rules stipulated that "all winners must agree to the regulations outlined specifically for winners before claiming championship or money." Next to this statement was an asterisk. The note linked to the asterisk reserved the right of Nutritional Sciences to cancel the contest or alter its terms at any time. Donna Englert learned that she was chosen female runner-up in her age group, and she expected to receive the advertised prize of $1,500 cash and $500 worth of products. When she went to sign the agreement to claim her prize, she found that the company had changed the cash prize to $250, so she refused to sign and sued for breach of contract. The trial court initially dismissed her case, and she appealed. How do you think the court of appeals decided the case and why? [*Englert v. Nutritional Sciences, LLC,* 2008 WL 44 4416597 (Ohio App. 2008).]
6. The Pennsylvania Department of Transportation (PennDOT) issued a Request for Bid Proposal for Vending Machine Services for rest areas on highways in the state. ATI submitted the lowest bid for the sites. PennDOT selected ATI for a contract for 35 vending sites. Enclosed with the notice of award sent to ATI was a service purchase contract to be executed by ATI, by PennDOT, by the commonwealth comptroller, and by PennDOT's attorney. Also, "if required," signature lines for the Office of General Counsel and the Attorney General's Office were provided. The award notice indicated that the contract would become effective "after all approvals have been received from the administrative and fiscal personnel in Harrisburg" and further stated that no activities may be performed until the contract is fully executed. ATI returned an executed contract to PennDOT. PennDOT's director of the Bureau of Maintenance and Operations and a representative from its legal department executed the agreement. The comptroller and Office of General Counsel subsequently signed the contract; however, the Attorney General's Office refused to execute the agreement. The Attorney General's Office subsequently filed criminal charges, related to sales tax issues, against ATI's president. As a result, the Attorney General's Office notified PennDOT it would not approve the contract.

PennDOT never returned an executed contract to ATI or provided a notice-to-proceed to ATI. Instead, PennDOT notified ATI it would not enter into the contract because it determined ATI is not a responsible contractor. ATI filed a complaint alleging PennDOT breached a valid contract. After the hearing, the board determined that PennDOT never delivered an acceptance of the offer to ATI and, as a result, a contract was never formed. ATI appealed, arguing that the board erred in finding a contract did not exist because PennDOT's representatives, who signed the contract, intended to bind PennDOT to the terms of the contract. How did the court rule on appeal? Did the documents contain a proper acceptance? [*Makoroff v. DOT,* 938 A.2d 470 (Pa. Commw. Ct. 2007).]

7. Plaintiff Business Systems Engineering, Inc., was one of several subcontractors that agreed to provide technical consultants for defendant IBM's work on a transit project. In a "plan of utilization" provided by IBM to the transit authority, IBM had listed Business Systems as one of its intended subcontractors, with $3.6 million listed on that document under the heading "contract amount." The terms of the arrangement between IBM and its subcontractors for the job were that when IBM needed technical consultants for a part of the project, the subs would submit bids and when the subcontractor's bid was accepted, the subcontractor would receive a specific statement of work detailing the scope of the specific project, the time frame, the conditions under which the task would be deemed complete, and the hourly wage, followed by a work authorization. The transit authority retained the authority to reject any individual consultant who was selected by the subcontractor, and the contract between the subcontractors and IBM incorporated by reference the contract between IBM and the transit authority. Work was not to begin until a final work authorization was issued. At the end of the project, 38 work authorizations had been issued to the plaintiff by the defendant for a total of $2.2 million, rather than the $3.6 million that had been projected in the original estimate IBM had provided to the transit authority. IBM had paid the plaintiff the $2.2 million for the work done on the work authorizations, but the plaintiff argued that it should have been entitled to the full $3.6 million contained in the estimate that was incorporated by reference in the contracts between IBM and the subcontractors. The plaintiff argued that it had a contract with IBM for the full $3.6 million. The district court granted summary judgment for the defendant. What do you think the plaintiff's argument was on appeal? What do think the outcome of the appeal was and why? [*Business Systems Engineering, Inc. v. International Business Machines Corp.,* 547 F.3d 883, 2008 U.S. App LEXIS 23682.]

8. Plaintiff VanHierden injured his thumb and finger at work and had it surgically repaired. He later developed a persistent pain at the base of his thumb. He went to see the defendant about having a sympathectomy to alleviate his pain. The defendant told the plaintiff, "We're going to get rid of your pain and get you back to work." The plaintiff then signed a written consent form to have the surgery, which included the following:

> The procedure listed under paragraph 1 has been fully explained to me by Dr. Swelstad and I completely understand the nature and consequences of the procedure(s). I have further had explained to me and discussed available alternatives and possible outcomes, and understand the risk of complications, serious injury or even death that may result from both known and unknown causes. I have been informed that there are other risks that are adherent to the performance of any surgical procedure. I am aware that the practice of medicine and surgery is not an exact science and I acknowledge that no guarantees have been made to me concerning the results of the operation or procedure(s).

The defendant performed the sympathectomy, but it did not alleviate the plaintiff's pain; nor was he able to return to work, so he sued the defendant for breach of a contract to cure the pain. The district court granted summary judgment for the defendant, finding that no contract had been formed as a matter of law. On appeal, do you believe the court found a valid agreement between the parties? Why or why not? [*Ronald VanHierden v. Jack Swelstad, MD,* 2010 Wis. App. 16, 2009 Wis. App. LEXIS 1013.]

9. In 2008, a lawyer for Mutual Life Insurance e-mailed Dr. Miles regarding the settlement of a lawsuit that he had filed against the insurance company. The e-mail that the attorney sent contained proposed settlement terms. Dr. Miles's attorney sent an e-mail back explicitly stating that Dr. Miles accepted the terms the company was offering. After the trial was canceled in light of the settlement, the company's attorney sent Dr. Miles a written settlement that was different from the terms contained in the e-mail. Thus, Dr. Miles rejected the offer, and the company subsequently claimed that there was no settlement. Dr. Miles then took the company to court a second time regarding whether a contract was created through the e-mail that proposed specific settlement terms. If the e-mail seemed to contain all the essential terms of an offer, how do you think the judge decided? [*Miles v. Northwestern Mutual Life Insurance Company,* 677 F. Supp. 2d 1312, U.S. Dist. LEXIS 123597 (2009).]

10. Sarah and Eddie Hogan wanted to sell 2.5 acres of land through their real estate agent, Darita Richardson. On December 10, 2001, Warren Kent offered to purchase the land for $52,500. An "Agreement to Buy or Sell" was created, which Kent signed right away. One term of the agreement was that the offer would expire on December 11, 2001, at 3 p.m., and it stated additionally, "Time is of the essence and all deadlines are final except where modifications, changes, or extensions are made in writing and signed by all parties." Although Richardson scheduled a meeting on December 11, 2001, at 2 p.m. with the Hogans, the Hogans failed to appear. However, the parties agreed to a two-day extension, lasting until December 13, 2001, at 3 p.m., and the extension was binding and irrevocable according to the "Addendum to Agreement to Purchase or Sell." The Hogans signed both documents at 9 a.m. on December 13, 2001. At about 11 a.m., Kent also signed the addendum. However, neither Kent's agent nor Richardson contacted the Hogans before 3 p.m. about Kent's acceptance. After 3 p.m., Richardson realized that the Hogans had not placed the date and time next to their signatures. When she met with the Hogans, the Hogans placed the date and the time as 4:48 p.m., informing Richardson that they, the Hogans, had changed their minds about the sale. Kent sued for specific performance of the contract. What effect, if any, did the failure to communicate the acceptance of the offer before 3 p.m. have in terms of whether a contract was formed? What was the appellate court's reasoning? [*Kent v. Hogan,* 2004 La. App. LEXIS 2539.]

Looking for more review material?

The Online Learning Center at **www.mhhe.com/kubasek3e** contains this chapter's "Assignment on the Internet" and also a list of URLs for more information, entitled "On the Internet." Find both of them in the Student Center portion of the OLC, along with quizzes and other helpful materials.

Consideration

LEARNING OBJECTIVES

After reading this chapter, you will be able to answer the following questions:

1. What is consideration?
2. What are the rules regarding consideration?
3. What is promissory estoppel, and when can it be used?
4. What is an illusory promise?
5. What is the difference between a liquidated debt and an unliquidated debt?
6. What is an accord and satisfaction?

CASE OPENER

Upper Deck—Contract Liability or Gift?

In 1988 the Upper Deck Company was a company with an idea for a better baseball card: one that had a hologram on it. By the 1990s the firm was a major corporation worth at least a quarter of a billion dollars.

In 1988, however, its outlook hadn't been so bright. Upper Deck lacked the funds for a $100,000 deposit it needed to buy some special paper by August 1. Without that deposit its contract with the Major League Baseball Players Association would have been jeopardized.

Upper Deck's corporate attorney, Anthony Passante, Jr., loaned the company the money. That evening, the directors of the company accepted the loan and, in gratitude, agreed to give Passante 3 percent of the firm's stock. Passante never sought to collect the stock, and later the company reneged on its promise. Passante sued for breach of oral contract.[1]

1. If you were on the jury, how would you decide the case? Was the offer of 3 percent of the firm's stock legal consideration for the loan? Or was it a mere gift?
2. Does Upper Deck have a moral obligation to give Passante the stock? If so, is this obligation legally enforceable?

The Wrap-Up at the end of the chapter will answer these questions.

[1] *Passante v. McWilliam,* 53 Cal. App. 4th 1240 (1997).

What is Consideration?

LO1

What is consideration?

Consideration is required in every contract. It is what a person will receive in return for performing a contract obligation. Suppose Dan agrees to purchase Marty's car for $1,000. Dan's payment of $1,000 is the consideration Marty will receive for the car. Title to and possession of the car are the consideration Dan will receive in exchange. Consideration can be anything, as long as it is the product of a bargained-for exchange. In a business context it is often (but not always) money. Exhibit 15-1 provides other examples of consideration.

Rules of Consideration

LO2

What are the rules regarding consideration?

The key to understanding consideration is understanding the rules that govern it and their exceptions. We explore them below.

LACK OF CONSIDERATION

A court will enforce one party's promise only if the other party promised some consideration in exchange. For example, in a bilateral contract (a promise for a promise), the consideration for each promise is a return promise. Suppose Nicole promises to pay Mike $2,000 tomorrow for his car. Mike promises to sell Nicole his car tomorrow for $2,000. There is an oral contract between them. Nicole's promise is her consideration to Mike. Mike's promise is his consideration to Nicole. There has been a mutual exchange of something of value.

An example of a bilateral contract, or a promise for a promise, occurred when the U.S. government seized control of insurance giant American International Group (AIG). The government agreed to lend AIG up to $85 billion in exchange for nearly 80 percent of AIG's stock. The consideration AIG received was the promise of up to $85 billion in U.S. government loans. The consideration the government received was a promise of almost 80 percent of AIG's stock.[2]

In a unilateral contract (a promise for an act), one party's consideration is the promise and the other party's consideration is the act. Suppose your professor made the following statement in class: "If any student shows up at my house on Saturday and does the gardening, I will pay that student $100." You show up and do the gardening. The professor's consideration to you is the promise of the payment of $100 on completion of the gardening, and your consideration to the professor is the act of completing the gardening. Once again, there has been a mutual exchange of something of value.

Exhibit 15-1

Examples of Consideration

TYPE OF CONSIDERATION	EXAMPLE
A benefit to the promisee	A promise to stay in a job until a particular project is complete (this is a benefit to the employer)
A detriment to the promisor	A promise to your football coach to refrain from riding your motorcycle during football season even though you love riding it
A promise to do something	A promise to cook dinner for your roommate for the next six months
A promise to refrain from doing something	A promise to stop staying out late at night during exam week

[2] "U.S. Seizes Control of AIG with $85 Billion Emergency Loan," *Washington Post*, September 17, 2008, www.washingtonpost.com/wp-dyn/content/article/2008/09/16/AR2008091602174 (accessed May 25, 2009).

Exhibit 15-2
Type of Consideration Based on Type of Contract

TYPE OF CONTRACT	PROMISOR	PROMISEE
Bilateral	A promise	A promise
Unilateral	A promise	An act

See Exhibit 15-2 for an explanation of bilateral and unilateral contracts.

Legal Principle: **For a promise to be enforced by the courts, there must be consideration.**

LO3
What is promissory estoppel, and when can it be used?

One exception to the rule requiring consideration is **promissory estoppel**. Promissory estoppel occurs when three conditions are met:

- One party makes a promise and either knows or should know that the other party will reasonably rely on it.
- The other party does reasonably rely on the promise.
- The only way to avoid injustice is to enforce the promise.

How does promissory estoppel work? Suppose upon graduation from college, Amanda receives a job offer across the country. She gives up her apartment, cancels all her other job interviews, and moves all her possessions. Upon arriving, she rents a new apartment and shows up for work. Amanda is then told there is no job! May she sue the employer? The answer in most states is yes, under the theory of promissory estoppel. Amanda may be able to recover her *reliance damages* (money she spent in "reliance" on the job offer). Promissory estoppel is not awarded regularly, but in the right case it can provide a remedy where no other remedy exists.

In a recent case, the Ninth Circuit Court of Appeals held that Yahoo's promise to remove a nude photo from its website was subject to a claim of promissory estoppel. In that case, the plaintiff learned that her ex-boyfriend, pretending to be her, had posted nude photos of her on Yahoo. He also included all her contact information and an invitation for men to contact her for sexual purposes.[3] The plaintiff contacted Yahoo (in accordance with its established policies) and requested that the photo be removed. Yahoo agreed but, despite repeated requests, did not remove the photo for six months. The court held that Yahoo's promise to depost the profile meant that Yahoo had a duty to the plaintiff. As such, the plaintiff's claim of promissory estoppel could be maintained. If the plaintiff is able to prove that she reasonably relied on Yahoo's promise to her detriment, she may well prevail on her claim for damages.

BUT WHAT IF . . .

WHAT IF THE FACTS OF THE CASE OPENER WERE DIFFERENT?

Recall, in the Case Opener, that the attorney for the Upper Deck Company was a very wealthy attorney who invested $100,000 in the company for a 3 percent share. But what if the attorney was not very wealthy, invested in the company at extreme financial risk to himself, and was promised a quick return on the money, which did not get returned. If the attorney could prove that he reasonably relied on the promise of the company to his detriment, could promissory estoppel be awarded?

[3] "Do Interactive Websites Have a Legal Duty to Remove Malicious Content?" http://writ.news.findlaw.com/scripts/printer_friendly.pl?page5/ramasastry/20090519.html (accessed May 25, 2009) [discussing *Barnes v. Yahoo, Inc.*, 2009 U.S. App. LEXIS 10940 (9th Cir. 2009)].

CASE NUGGET

PROMISSORY ESTOPPEL

Double AA Builders, Ltd. v. Grand State Construction L.L.C.
114 P.3d 835 (Ariz. Ct. App. 2005)

In anticipation of submitting a bid for the construction of a Home Depot Store in Mesa, Arizona, Double AA solicited bids from subcontractors for various portions of the work. Grand State faxed a written but unsigned bid to Double AA in the amount of $115,000 for installation of the exterior insulation finish system (EIFS) on the project. The proposal stated: "Our price is good for 30 days." Double AA relied on several subcontractor bids, including Grand State's, in preparing its overall price for the project.

On December 21, 2001, Home Depot advised Double AA it was the successful bidder for the project. On January 11, 2002, within the 30-day "price is good" period, Double AA sent a subcontract for the EIFS work to Grand State to be signed and returned. Grand State advised Double AA it would not sign the subcontract or perform on the project. Double AA subsequently entered into a subcontract with a replacement subcontractor to install the EIFS at a cost of $131,449, which exceeded Grand State's quoted price by $16,449. Double AA demanded that Grand State pay the difference between its bid and Double AA's ultimate cost to perform the same work. After Grand State refused, Double AA filed suit based on promissory estoppel.

When a general contractor prepares an overall bid for a competitively bid construction project, it receives bids and quotes from subcontractors for portions of the work. The general contractor uses the bids in preparing its overall price for the project. A subcontractor's refusal to honor its bid can be financially disastrous for the general contractor, because the general contractor will typically be bound by the bid price it submitted to the project owner.

Promissory estoppel may be used to require that the subcontractor perform according to the terms of its bid to the contractor if the contractor receives the contract award, because the contractor has detrimentally relied on the subcontractor's bid and must perform for a price based on that reliance. Double AA prevailed. Nonperformance by the subcontractor resulted in damages equal to the difference between what the contractor had to pay and what it would have paid had the subcontractor performed.

A second exception to the rule requiring consideration is a *contract under seal.* In the past, contracts were sealed with a piece of soft wax into which an impression was made. Today, sealed contracts are typically identified with the word *seal* or the letters *L.S.* (an abbreviation for *locus sigilli,* which means "the place for the seal") at the end. Consumers may also purchase contract forms with a preprinted seal. The parties using them are presumed, without evidence to the contrary, to be adopting the seal for the contract. States in the U.S. no longer require that contracts be under seal. However, 10 states still allow a contract without consideration to be enforced if it is under seal.

Legal Principle: **Promissory estoppel and contracts under seal are two exceptions to the common law rule requiring consideration.**

ADEQUACY OF CONSIDERATION

The court does not weigh whether you made a good bargain. Suppose Donna purchases a flat-screen TV from Celia, a friend in her business law class. Donna pays $500 for the TV but later realizes it is worth less than $100! May Donna sue Celia? Typically, the answer is no. It is Donna's responsibility to do her research and determine what price she should pay. The court will not set aside the sale because she made a bad deal. Conversely, if the court believes fraud or undue influence occurred, the court may look at adequacy of consideration. (For example, suppose a person divests himself of all his assets for pennies on the dollar and then declares bankruptcy—the court would likely review the consideration paid to determine whether there was fraud by the debtor against the creditors.)

BUT WHAT IF . . .

WHAT IF THE FACTS OF THE CASE OPENER WERE DIFFERENT?

Recall, in the Case Opener, that the company attorney Passante invested $100,000 into the Upper Deck Company so that it could produce hologram baseball cards. In return, Passante received a 3 percent share of the company. What if the hologram baseball cards were not successful and the company filed for bankruptcy? If Passante made a bad investment and did not receive a return on his money, could he sue the company for damages?

Legal Principle: **The court seldom considers adequacy of consideration.**

Is a promise to refrain from something you are legally entitled to do appropriate consideration for a contract? See Case 15-1.

CASE 15-1 HAMER V. SIDWAY
COURT OF APPEALS OF NEW YORK
124 N.Y. 538 (1891)

Plaintiff sought to enforce against the defendant estate a promise made by his now-deceased uncle to pay plaintiff a sum of money if plaintiff refrained from the use of alcohol and tobacco for a period of years. Plaintiff so refrained and sought recovery of the sum promised.

J. PARKER: In 1869, William Story, 2d, promised his nephew that if he refrained from drinking liquor, using tobacco, swearing, and playing cards or billiards for money until he was 21 years of age, then he would pay him the sum of $5,000. William Story, the nephew, agreed and fully performed.

The defendant (the deceased uncle's estate) now contends that the contract was without consideration to support it, and, therefore, invalid. He asserts that the nephew, by refraining from the use of liquor and tobacco, was not harmed but benefited; that that which he did was best for him to do independently of his uncle's promise, and insists that it follows that unless the nephew was benefited, the contract was without consideration. This contention, if well founded, would seem to leave open for controversy in many cases whether that which the promisee did or omitted to do was, in fact, of such benefit to him as to leave no consideration to support the enforcement of the promisor's agreement.

Such a rule could not be tolerated, and is without foundation in the law. Consideration means not so much that one party is profiting as that the other abandons some legal right in the present or limits his legal freedom of action in the future. Now, applying this rule to the facts before us, the promisee used tobacco, occasionally drank liquor, and he had a legal right to do so. He abandoned that right for a period of years based upon the promise of his uncle that for such forbearance he would give him $5,000. We need not speculate on the effort which may have been required to give up the use of those stimulants. It is sufficient that he restricted his lawful freedom of action within certain prescribed limits upon the faith of his uncle's agreement. Now, having fully performed the conditions imposed, it makes no difference whether such performance was actually a benefit to the promisor, and the court will not inquire into it. Even if it were a proper subject of inquiry, we see nothing in this record that would permit a determination that the uncle was not benefited in a legal sense. It is deemed established for the purposes of this appeal, that on January 31, 1875, defendant's testator was indebted to William E. Story, 2d, in the sum of $5,000. All concur.

The order reversing the trial court judgment in favor of plaintiff is reversed on the grounds that plaintiff's promise to abandon his legal right to use tobacco and alcohol was sufficient consideration to enforce the contract.

CRITICAL THINKING

What difference would it have made in this case had the nephew not had the legal right to drink or smoke? Why is this question crucial to the decision?

ETHICAL DECISION MAKING

William Story, 2d, may well have thought that he should win the case on moral grounds. He is applauding his nephew's behavior in recognition that the behavior the nephew stopped was behavior that was harming his nephew. So, since his nephew is now in better condition than he was before their exchange of views, why does the court put itself in the position of requiring William Story, 2d, to pay the $5,000?

In Case 15-2, the court had to consider whether $1 plus "love and affection" was adequate consideration for the transfer of property.

CASE 15-2 THELMA AGNES SMITH V. DAVID PHILLIP RILEY

COURT OF APPEALS OF TENNESSEE, EASTERN SECTION, AT KNOXVILLE

2002 TENN. APP. LEXIS 65 (2002)

The plaintiff, Thelma Agnes Smith, lived with the defendant out of wedlock for several years. When the relationship ended, she sued the defendant, seeking to enforce two written agreements with him regarding the sale and assignment of property to her. The trial court enforced the agreements and divided the parties' property. The defendant appealed, arguing the agreements lacked consideration and were void as against public policy.

JUDGE CHARLES D. SUSANO: . . . Thelma Agnes Smith and David Phillip Riley, both of whom then resided in Florida, separated from their respective spouses in 1997 and began a romantic relationship. In early 1998, the two moved to Tennessee and began cohabitating. . . . Smith and Riley opened a joint checking account in March, 1998. Over time, Smith deposited into that account $9,500—the proceeds from an insurance settlement and monies received when her divorce later became final; she also deposited her monthly social security check of $337 into the same account. Smith continued to deposit her social security check in the joint account until December, 1998, when she opened her own checking account. Riley also contributed to the joint account. He placed a settlement of $84,000 from the Veteran's Administration into the account. In addition, he deposited his monthly pension check of $2,036 into the same account. . . .

On July 31, 1998, Riley entered into a lease with Jerry Strickland and Wanda Strickland with respect to a residence owned by them; the lease was accompanied by an option to purchase. Almost four months later, on November 20, 1998, Smith and Riley returned to their attorney's office, at which time the attorney prepared a bill of sale and an assignment. In the bill of sale, Riley transferred [to Smith] a one-half undivided interest in seven items of personal property. . . . Riley also assigned to Smith a one-half undivided interest in the lease and option to purchase with the Stricklands, which interest included a right of survivorship in the one-half interest retained by Riley as well. The property Riley sold and assigned to Smith in the two agreements was stated in each to be "for and in consideration of the sum of One Dollar ($1.00) and other and good and valuable consideration, the sufficiency of which is hereby acknowledged. . . ."

When Smith and Riley separated in April, 1999, Smith filed suit against Riley in the trial court, seeking the dissolution of their "domestic partnership." Smith alleged that she and Riley had been living together for several years without the benefit of marriage and had acquired both real and personal property, some of which Riley had assigned to her. As a result, she asked the court to award her 50 percent of the "partnership" assets, leaving the other 50 percent to Riley. . . . [The trial court ruled in favor of Smith and Riley appealed.]

Riley first argues that the trial court erred in finding that the bill of sale and assignment are supported by valid consideration. Specifically, Riley relies on Smith's statements at trial that she considered their pending engagement and the funds she deposited into their joint account to be consideration for their agreements.

It is a well-settled principle of contract law that in order for a contract to be binding, it must, among other things, be supported by sufficient consideration. [Citations omitted.] In expounding on the adequacy of consideration, the Tennessee Supreme Court has stated that it is not necessary that the benefit conferred or the detriment suffered by the promisee shall be equal to the responsibility assumed. Any consideration, however small, will support a promise. In the absence of fraud, the courts will not undertake to regulate the amount of the consideration. The parties are left to contract for themselves, taking for granted that the consideration is one valuable in the eyes of the law. . . .

Quoting the United States Supreme Court, the Tennessee Supreme Court went on to state that "[a] stipulation in consideration of $1 is just as effectual and valuable a consideration as a larger sum stipulated for or paid." [Citations omitted.] Indeed, the consideration of love and affection has been deemed sufficient to support a conveyance. . . .

Both the bill of sale and the assignment recite that they are undertaken "for and in consideration of the sum of One Dollar ($1.00) and other and good and valuable consideration, the sufficiency of which is hereby acknowledged. . . ." Facially, the documents are therefore supported by sufficient consideration, as clearly recognized by the Supreme Court. . . . Moreover, Smith's "society and consortium"—a concept comparable to the love and affection . . . is further evidence of sufficient consideration to support these conveyances.

Riley calls our attention to Smith's statement at trial that she considered the funds she deposited into their joint

[continued]

account to be consideration for the conveyances. If this were the only consideration involved in this case, Riley's argument regarding past consideration supporting a present transaction might have some merit. However, the recitals of nominal consideration that are present in both agreements, as well as the consideration of Smith's love and affection, are adequate consideration and will support the conveyances represented by the assignment and bill of sale. . . .

Judgment affirmed in favor of Plaintiff.

CRITICAL THINKING

What is the reasoning of the appellant in terms of why the consideration was not adequate to cause the contracts to be enforceable? What key rule of law did this reasoning overlook?

ETHICAL DECISION MAKING

What values are being advanced by the logic of the relevant rule of law in this case? In other words, what values prevent the rule of law from being that "consideration must be in an amount similar in value to the item or services being transferred in order for the contract to be enforceable"?

ILLUSORY PROMISE

LO4 What is an illusory promise?

What is an illusory promise? Suppose Shawn offers to sell Molly his skis for $300. Molly responds, "I'll look at them in the morning, and if I like them, I'll pay you." At this point, Molly has not committed to doing anything. The law considers this an **illusory promise**—it is not a promise at all.

Legal Principle: An illusory promise is not consideration.

BUT WHAT IF . . .

WHAT IF THE FACTS OF THE CASE OPENER WERE DIFFERENT?

Let's say that, in the Case Opener, Passante was approached by executives of the Upper Deck Company and they asked him to invest money into their company so that they could purchase hologram baseball cards. In response, Passante told them, "That sounds like a good idea. I'll have my financial adviser call you for more details." Is Passante making a contractual promise to the company? What is the term for his type of response in this situation?

PAST CONSIDERATION

For a court to enforce a promise, both sides must offer consideration. Imagine you graduate from college and get a great job. After five years, your boss says to you, "Because you have done such a great job the last five years, I am going to give you 5 percent of the company stock." Six months later, you still have not received the stock. May you sue your boss to enforce the promise? The answer is no. For a promise to be enforceable, there must be bargaining and an exchange. Because your work has already been performed, you have given nothing in exchange, and the court will not enforce the promise. A promise cannot be based on consideration provided before the promise was made. You are at the mercy of your boss's goodwill.

Legal Principle: Past consideration is no consideration at all.

As you have probably guessed by now, there is an exception to this rule. Under the Restatement (Second) of Contracts (a persuasive, though not binding, authority), promises

COMPARING THE LAW OF OTHER COUNTRIES

CONTRACT ENFORCEMENT IN CHINA

Every year the World Bank publishes its Doing Business rankings, which rate 181 countries by ease of doing business (the rankings can be found at **www.doingbusiness.org/rankings**). In the category "Enforcing Contracts," China is rated number 10. This means that China has one of the best systems in the world for enforcement of contracts. Compare that with India, which is rated 180 out of 181 countries, or Brazil, which is rated at 100. China is actually rated better than the United Kingdom, which comes in at 23, and better than Japan, which comes in at 21. It is therefore a serious mistake to place China in the same category as some of its developing country competitors.

Source: Dan Harris, "Enforcing Contracts in China: Way, Way Better Than You Think," July 13, 2009, www.chinalawblog.com/2009/07/enforcing_contracts_in_china_w.html.

based on past consideration may be enforceable "to the extent necessary to avoid injustice." In some cases, if past consideration was given with expectation of future payment, the court may enforce the promise.

In Case 15-3, the court must decide whether the promise to pay a friend for coming up with a merchandising idea is compensable when the promise to pay was made after the idea was given.

CASE 15-3 JAMIL BLACKMON V. ALLEN IVERSON

U.S. DISTRICT COURT FOR THE EASTERN DISTRICT OF PENNSYLVANIA

324 F. SUPP. 2D 602 (2003)

The defendant, Allen Iverson, was a professional basketball player. The plaintiff, Jamil Blackmon, was a family friend. In July of 1994, Mr. Blackmon suggested that Mr. Iverson use "The Answer" as a nickname in the summer league basketball tournaments in which Mr. Iverson would be playing. Mr. Blackmon told Mr. Iverson that Mr. Iverson would be "The Answer" to all of the National Basketball Association's ("NBA's") woes. Mr. Blackmon and Mr. Iverson also discussed the fact that the nickname "The Answer" had immediate applications as a label, brand name, or other type of marketing slogan for use in connection with clothing, sports apparel, and sneakers. The parties also discussed using "The Answer" as a logo. Later that evening, Mr. Iverson promised to give Mr. Blackmon twenty-five percent of all proceeds from the merchandising of products sold in connection with the term "The Answer." The parties understood that in order to "effectuate Mr. Iverson's agreement to compensate" Mr. Blackmon, Mr. Iverson would have to be drafted by the NBA.

Mr. Blackmon thereafter began to invest significant time, money, and effort in the refinement of the concept of "The Answer." Mr. Blackmon continued to develop and refine the marketing strategy for the sale of merchandise, such as athletic wear and sneakers, in connection with the term "The Answer." He retained a graphic designer to develop logos bearing "The Answer" as well as conceptual drawings for sleeveless T-shirts, adjustable hats, and letterman jackets for sale in connection with "The Answer." In 1994 and 1995, during Mr. Iverson's freshman year at Georgetown University and the summer thereafter, there were numerous conversations between Mr. Blackmon and Mr. Iverson regarding Mr. Blackmon's progress in refining the marketing concept for "The Answer." In 1996, just prior to the NBA draft, during which Mr. Iverson was drafted by the Philadelphia 76ers, Mr. Iverson advised Mr. Blackmon that Mr. Iverson intended to use the phrase "The Answer" in connection with a contract with Reebok for merchandising of athletic shoes and sports apparel. Mr. Iverson repeated his promise to pay Mr. Blackmon twenty-five percent of all proceeds from merchandising goods that incorporated "The Answer" slogan or logo. . . . Despite repeated requests and demands from Mr. Blackmon, Mr. Iverson has never compensated Mr. Blackmon and continues to deny Mr. Blackmon twenty-five percent of the proceeds from the merchandising of products incorporating "The Answer."

Mr. Blackmon is now suing Mr. Iverson, seeking damages for claims alleging [among others] . . . breach of contract . . . arising out of the basketball player's use of "The Answer," both as a nickname and as a logo or slogan. The defendant filed a motion to dismiss this complaint.

JUDGE MARY A. MCLAUGHLIN: . . . The essence of . . . the plaintiff's claim is that the defendant took and used the plaintiff's ideas without compensating the plaintiff.

. . . The plaintiff claims that he entered into an express contract with the defendant pursuant to which he was to receive twenty-five percent of the proceeds that the defendant received from marketing products with "The Answer" on them. The defendant argues that there was not a valid contract because the claim was not timely filed under the Pennsylvania

[continued]

statute of limitations, the terms of the contract were not sufficiently definite, and there was no consideration alleged. Because the Court has determined that the claim should be dismissed for failure to allege proper consideration, the Court need not address the defendant's other arguments about the statute of limitations and definiteness of terms. . . .

According to the facts alleged by the plaintiff, he made the suggestion that the defendant use "The Answer" as a nickname and for product merchandising one evening in 1994. This was before the defendant first promised to pay; according to the plaintiff, the promise to pay was made later that evening. The disclosure of the idea also occurred before the defendant told the plaintiff that he was going to use the idea in connection with the Reebok contract in 1996, and before the sales of goods bearing "The Answer" actually began in 1997. Regardless of whether the contract was formed in 1994, 1996, or 1997, the disclosure of "The Answer" idea had already occurred and was, therefore, past consideration insufficient to create a binding contract.

Motion granted in favor of Defendant.

CRITICAL THINKING

What key fact would have had to be different for Mr. Blackmon to have received a favorable ruling in this case?

ETHICAL DECISION MAKING

Most people reading this case probably feel some sympathy for Mr. Blackmon. He put in a lot of time in reliance on a promise he was made by Iverson. He received nothing for that time even though Iverson benefited from some of it. What stakeholders in a contract are being protected by strict adherence to the need for consideration that the court used to form its conclusion?

PREEXISTING DUTY

There are two parts to the **preexisting duty** rule. *Performance of a duty you are obligated to do under the law is not good consideration.* Part of a police officer's sworn public duty is catching suspected criminals. If someone offers a reward for the capture of a suspect, the police officer may not collect it, as he or she was already obligated to apprehend the suspect. Moreover, *performance of an existing contractual duty is not good consideration.* Gene decides to have a pool built in his backyard. Under the existing contract, the pool is to be completed by June 1, just in time for summer. The pool contractor then explains that due to a shortage of workers, the completion date cannot be met; however, if Gene were to pay an extra $5,000, additional workers could be hired and the pool completed on time. Gene tells the contractor he will pay the $5,000. On June 1, the pool is completed and the contractor asks for the additional payment. Is Gene legally obligated to pay? The answer is no. The pool contractor had a preexisting contractual duty to complete the pool by June 1. Gene is under no obligation to pay the additional money.

Legal Principle: A promise to do something that you are already obligated to do is not valid consideration.

BUT WHAT IF . . .

WHAT IF THE FACTS OF THE CASE OPENER WERE DIFFERENT?

Recall that, in the Case Opener, Passante agreed to invest $100,000 in the Upper Deck Company so that he could own 3 percent of it. But what if the company told Passante that its sales were sinking and that if he didn't agree to invest another $50,000, the company would go bankrupt and Passante would receive no return on his investment? Suppose Passante agrees. If a month later the company came to collect the $50,000, does Passante legally have to pay the extra money because he told the company he would?

Exceptions to the Preexisting Duty Rule. There are exceptions to the preexisting duty rule: unforeseen circumstances, additional work, and UCC Article 2 (sale of goods).

If *unforeseen circumstances* cause a party to make a promise regarding an unfinished project, that promise is valid consideration. Suppose the pool contractor has been building pools in Gene's neighborhood for the last 20 years and has never had any problem with rocks—until now. While bulldozing the hole for the pool in Gene's backyard, the pool contractor hits solid rock. It will cost an additional $5,000 to clear the rock with jackhammers, possibly even dynamite. The contractor says unless Gene agrees to pay the additional money, he will not be able to finish the pool. Gene agrees to pay. When the pool is completed, the contractor asks for the additional $5,000. Will a court enforce Gene's promise? The answer is yes. Even though the contractor is completing only what he was obligated to do under the contract, neither party knew of the solid rock. The contractor has given additional consideration (removal of the rock) and Gene will be held to his promise to pay the additional money.

If a party to a contract agrees to do *additional work* (more than the contract requires), the promise to do it is valid consideration. If the contractor asks Gene for an additional $10,000 but agrees to add a waterfall and a deck to the pool, the promise to do the additional work is consideration. If Gene agrees to pay the $10,000, that is his consideration. Both parties are now bound.

Partial Payment of a Debt

LO5

What is the difference between a liquidated debt and an unliquidated debt?

Partial payment of a debt may or may not be valid consideration, depending on whether the debt is liquidated or unliquidated. In a **liquidated debt**, there is no dispute that money is owed or how much. Natalie calls her credit card company and explains she is a poor student and cannot afford to pay the entire $3,000 she owes. The credit card company agrees to accept $2,000 as payment in full. The following month, Natalie receives her new credit card statement showing she owes the remaining $1,000. May the credit card company collect the additional $1,000? Yes! A creditor's promise to accept less than owed, when the debtor is already obligated to pay the full amount, is not binding.

The exception to the rule regarding liquidated debt occurs when the debtor offers different performance. Suppose Natalie offered the credit card company her car in full settlement of the $3,000 debt. If the credit card company accepts, regardless of the value of the car, the debt is paid in full and the credit card company may not sue Natalie for any additional money.

LO6

What is an accord and satisfaction?

In an **unliquidated debt**, the parties either disagree about whether money is owed or dispute the amount. They can settle for less than the full amount if they enter into an **accord and satisfaction**, which must meet three requirements to be enforceable:

1. The debt is unliquidated (the amount or existence of the debt is in dispute).
2. The creditor agrees to accept as full payment less than it claims is owed.
3. The debtor pays the amount they have agreed on.

Under these circumstances, the debt is fully discharged. The *accord* is the new agreement to pay less than the creditor claims is owed. The *satisfaction* is the debtor's payment of the reduced amount. It pays to keep your word: If the debtor fails to pay the new amount, the creditor may sue for the full amount of the original debt. Exhibit 15-3 clarifies the accord-and-satisfaction process.

Legal Principle: **When a debt is unliquidated, the parties may enter into an accord and satisfaction.**

Debtors sometimes attempt to create an accord and satisfaction by sending the creditor a check with "paid in full" written on it. Under the common law, in many states this did

Exhibit 15-3 Accord and Satisfaction

DEBT DISPUTED?	STATUS OF DEBT	PAYMENT?	CREATE AN ACCORD?	CREATE A SATISFACTION?
Yes—*amount* of debt in dispute	Unliquidated	Debtor offers to pay less money than creditor believes is owed as full payment, and creditor agrees.	Yes	Yes. Once debtor pays the money agreed to, the debt is satisfied and the creditor may not collect any additional money.
Yes—*existence* of debt in dispute	Unliquidated	Debtor offers to pay a sum of money as full payment when debtor does not believe anything is owed, and creditor agrees.	Yes	Yes. Once the debtor pays the money agreed to, the debt is satisfied and the creditor may not collect any additional money.
No dispute over amount of debt or existence of debt	Liquidated	Debtor offers to pay less money than is owed as full payment, and creditor agrees.	No	No. Even if the debtor pays the money agreed to, the creditor may still sue for the balance it believes is owed.
No dispute over amount of debt or existence of debt	Liquidated	Debtor offers a *different* payment (e.g., her car) as full payment.	Yes	Yes. Once the debtor makes a *different* payment, the debt is satisfied and the creditor may not collect anything else.

create an accord and satisfaction, and if the creditor cashed the check, he or she was bound to accept the lesser amount as payment in full. The UCC (introduced in Chapter 13) has reduced the scope of this rule, however. Under UCC Section 3-311, effective in 30 states, the rule has two major exceptions.

First, business organizations can receive thousands of checks each day. To protect themselves, they may notify their debtors that any offer to settle a claim for less than the amount owed must be sent to a particular address and/or person. If you check the terms printed on your credit card statement, you will likely find language directing you to send such payments to a different address and person than regular payments are sent to. This safeguard protects businesses from inadvertently creating accord-and-satisfaction agreements. Below is a typical clause you might find on any credit statement regarding conditional payments:

> *Conditional Payments:* Any payment check or other form of payment that you send us for less than the full balance that is marked "paid in full" or contains a similar notation, or that you otherwise tender in full satisfaction of a disputed amount, must be sent to [address omitted]. We reserve all rights regarding these payments (e.g., if it is determined that there is no valid dispute or if any such check is received at any other address, we may accept the check and you will still owe any remaining balance).[4]

In the second exception, if a business does inadvertently cash a "paid-in-full" check, it has 90 days to offer the debtor repayment in the same amount. For example, if John owed his credit card company $3,000 and sent a $2,000 check marked "paid in full" to the correct address and person, the credit card company has 90 days to offer to repay John the $2,000. Once the business has made that offer, no accord and satisfaction exists.

To see how an accord and satisfaction relates to income taxation, please see the **Connecting to the Core** activity on the text website at www.mhhe.com/kubasek3e.

[4] From Chase Visa statement.

CASE NUGGET

ACCORD AND SATISFACTION

Thomas v. CitiMortgage, Inc.
2005 U.S. Dist. LEXIS 14641 (Dist. Ct. Ill. 2005)

In November 1979, Thomas assumed an existing mortgage, which CitiMortgage now holds, that required him to make a payment on the first of each month. Beginning in April 1996, his payments became sporadic. On December 16, 1996, Thomas sent a letter to CitiMortgage. He wrote:

> My primary concern is the effect on my credit rating and the fact that I have an application to refinace [*sic*] the mortgage which cannot be finalized, at great cost to me, unless this matter is resolved and my credit cleared up. I have enclosed a check in the amount of the monthly payment on condition that it be applied to tha [*sic*] May payment and that it will allow you to remove the negative material relative to my credit rating.

CitiMortgage cashed the check enclosed with the December 16 letter and credited it to Thomas's account. At CitiMortgage as of 1996, mail was sorted in a central mail room. The persons processing checks lacked the authority either to accept conditions on payments or to change credit reports. In his breach-of-contract claim, Thomas asserted that he and CitiMortgage had entered an agreement whereby he would make a payment on his mortgage in exchange for CitiMortgage's agreement to "remove the negative material" from his credit rating. He further claimed that CitiMortgage accepted the contract when it cashed the check he enclosed with his December 16 letter. Whether Thomas's claim was considered an accord and satisfaction or a simple contract, he could not prevail unless he established that consideration supported the agreement.

Consideration can consist of a promise, an act, or a forbearance. The preexisting duty rule provides, however, that when a party does what it is already legally obligated to do, there is no consideration because there has been no detriment. Thomas claimed that the payment he made with his December 16 letter constituted consideration for the agreement. As of that date, however, he was already two months in arrears on his mortgage payment. Thus, he was already legally obligated—under the terms of the mortgage—to make the payment he enclosed with the letter. Accordingly, that payment could not be consideration for an additional agreement to "remove the negative material" from his credit rating.

CASE OPENER WRAP-UP

Upper Deck—Contract Liability or Gift?

As you know from the Case Opener, Passante sued Upper Deck for breach of oral contract. At trial, the jury awarded him close to $33 million—the value of 3 percent of Upper Deck's stock at the time of the trial in 1993. Upper Deck appealed.

As a matter of law, any claim by Passante for breach of contract is necessarily based on the rule that consideration must result from a bargained-for exchange. In this case, the appellate court held that if the stock promised was truly bargained for, then Passante had an obligation to give Upper Deck the opportunity to have separate counsel represent it in the course of that bargaining. The legal profession has certain rules regarding business transactions with clients. Bargaining between the parties might have resulted in Passante's settling for just a reasonable finder's fee.

All Passante's services in arranging the $100,000 loan for Upper Deck had already been rendered (even though the board had not formally accepted the loan) before the idea of giving him stock came up. There was no evidence he had any expectation of receiving stock in return. If there is no expectation of payment by either party when services are rendered, the promise is a mere promise to make a gift and not enforceable. The promise of 3 percent of the stock represented a moral obligation but was legally unenforceable.

KEY TERMS

accord and satisfaction 354
consideration 346
illusory promise 351
liquidated debt 354
preexisting duty 353
promissory estoppel 347
unliquidated debt 354

SUMMARY OF KEY TOPICS

What Is Consideration?

Consideration is something of value given in exchange for something else of value; it must be the product of a mutually bargained-for exchange.

Rules of Consideration

The key to understanding consideration is understanding the various rules:

- For a promise to be enforced by the courts, there must be consideration.
- *Exception: Promissory estoppel* occurs when one party makes a promise knowing the other party will rely on it, the other party does rely on it, and the only way to avoid injustice is to enforce the promise even though it is not supported by consideration.
- The court seldom considers adequacy of consideration.
- An *illusory promise* is not consideration.
- Past consideration is no consideration at all.
- A promise to do something you are already obligated to do is not valid consideration. (This is the *preexisting duty rule.*)

Partial Payment of a Debt

In a *liquidated debt,* there is no dispute that money is owed or the amount. In an *unliquidated debt,* the parties dispute either the fact that money is owed or the amount.

To be enforceable, an *accord and satisfaction* must meet three requirements: (1) The debt is unliquidated (the amount or existence of the debt is in dispute); (2) the creditor agrees to accept as full payment less than the creditor claims is owed; and (3) the debtor pays the amount they agree on.

POINT / COUNTERPOINT

Should the Courts Require Consideration to Create a Binding Contract?

YES	NO
The rules of consideration have been established for many years and precedent should be followed. Requiring consideration gives the court a way to distinguish between binding and nonbinding promises, or between a promise made as a gift and a promise made as part of a contract. We have enough exceptions to the rule requiring consideration to make enforcement fair. If a promise was made and there was expectation of economic benefit, some courts will permit enforcement under the moral-obligation exception. If we suddenly did not require consideration to create binding contracts, the courts would fill with civil cases of people trying to enforce all kind of promises.	All promises should be enforced, eliminating the need to distinguish between binding and nonbinding promises. If a person makes a promise, its timing should not make a difference. If Barbara's grandmother promises her $50,000 for "all you have done for me these last five years," why should Barbara be denied the money because it was based on acts she did in the past? The right thing, ethically and morally, is to enforce this promise whether or not Barbara acted with expectation of payment. Under current law, some states can use the moral-obligation exception to reward those who expect something when they do good and punish those who do the right thing with no expectation of reward.

QUESTIONS & PROBLEMS

1. List the four types of consideration described in the text.
2. What is required to prove promissory estoppel when consideration is missing?
3. Can $1 be adequate consideration? Why or why not?
4. List and describe the three exceptions to the preexisting duty rule.
5. List the three elements of accord and satisfaction.
6. The plaintiff is Amir Peleg, a gay Jewish male of Israeli national origin. He worked at the Neiman Marcus store in Beverly Hills from December 28, 2005, to February 21, 2008. The store is owned by the defendant, Neiman Marcus Group, Inc. Peleg worked in the fragrances department and performed his duties in an exemplary manner. Peleg alleges that on February 21, 2008, he was discharged because of his national origin, religion, and sexual orientation in violation of the California Fair Employment and Housing Act (FEHA). Neiman Marcus responded to the complaint with a motion to compel arbitration of the entire case. The company established that, at the time of hire, Peleg was given its "Mandatory Arbitration Agreement." Peleg asserted that the agreement was illusory and unenforceable in light of the following provision:

   > This Agreement to arbitrate shall survive the termination of the employer-employee relationship between the Company and any Covered Employee, and shall apply to any covered Claim whether it arises or is asserted during or after termination of the Covered Employee's employment with the Company or the expiration of any benefit plan. This Agreement can be *amended, modified, or revoked in writing by the Company at anytime,* but only upon thirty (30) days' advance notice to the Covered Employee of that amendment, modification, or revocation. However, any amendment, modification, or revocation will have *no effect on any Claim that was filed for arbitration prior to the effective date* of such amendment, modification, or revocation.

   Plaintiff alleges that the arbitration agreement is illusory. Do you agree? Why or why not? [*Peleg v. Neiman Marcus Group, Inc.*, 204 Cal. App. 4th 1425 (2012).]
7. Joana Perez began working for Datamark in January 2005. She received two booklets at orientation, the "Non-Staff Employee Handbook" and the "Summary Plan Description." She did not read either one of them. According to the human resource director, Perez also received the "Problem Resolution Program" booklet (the PRP) that described company dispute resolution policies and procedure. Perez denied receiving it, but she did sign the "Receipt and Arbitration Acknowledgment," which was maintained in her personnel file. Her signature acknowledged that she had received and read (or had the opportunity to read) both the "Summary Plan Description" and the PRP. She also acknowledged that an arbitration policy required the submission of all employee-related disputes to an arbitrator in accordance with the procedures described in the PRP. Datamark reserved the right to revoke or modify the PRP in writing at any time as long as the writing was signed by an officer of the company and articulated an intent to revoke or modify a policy. Perez learned she was pregnant in August 2005. While employed full-time, she began to miss work due to pregnancy difficulties. She was discharged on October 21, 2005, and she filed suit alleging unlawful discrimination because of her gender and/or pregnancy. Perez also alleged that Datamark intentionally or recklessly engaged in extreme and outrageous behavior that caused her severe emotional distress. Datamark filed a motion to compel arbitration. In her response to the motion, Perez alleged that the arbitration agreement was illusory because Datamark could unilaterally change or terminate the agreement without prior notice to the employees. Do you believe the agreement to arbitrate is illusory? Why or why not? [*In re Datamark, Inc., Relator,* 296 S.W.3d 614, 2009 Tex. App. LEXIS 794 (2009).]
8. On February 1, 2004, Zhang entered into a contract to buy former realtor Frank Sorichetti's Las Vegas home for $532,500. The contract listed a March closing date and a few household furnishings as part of the sale. On February 3, Sorichetti told Zhang that he was terminating the sale "to stay in the house a little longer" and that Nevada law allows the rescission of real property purchase agreements within three days of contracting. Sorichetti stated that he would sell the home, however, if Zhang paid more

money. Zhang agreed. Another contract was drafted, reciting a new sales price, $578,000. This contract added to the included household furnishings drapes that were not listed in the February 1 agreement, and it set an April, rather than March, closing date. The primary issue before the court was whether a real property purchase agreement is enforceable when it is executed by the buyer only because the seller would not perform under an earlier purchase agreement for a lesser price. Should the court enforce the second contract? Why or why not? [*Zhang v. The Eighth Judicial District Court of the State of Nevada,* 103 P.3d 20 (Sup. Ct. Nev. 2004).]

9. Charles Houser began working for the appellee, 84 Lumber Company, L.P., in 1985. In 1998, Houser became an outside salesman with 84 Lumber, and his compensation changed from a set salary to commission based on his sales. At that time, Houser signed a noncompete agreement, which prohibited him from engaging in sales activities with a competitor of 84 Lumber within a 25-mile radius of 84 Lumber's Macedonia store for a two-year period following the conclusion of his employment with 84 Lumber. In June 2008, Houser signed a contract providing a set weekly draw and yet another noncompete agreement. In March 2009, Houser left 84 Lumber and, almost immediately thereafter, began working for Carter Lumber, a competitor of 84 Lumber. 84 Lumber filed a lawsuit alleging that Houser had violated the noncompete agreement. The essential question is whether the 2008 noncompete agreement was supported by adequate consideration. "[A] restrictive covenant is enforceable if supported by new consideration, either in the form of an initial employment contract or a change in the conditions of employment." 84 Lumber Company argued that Houser's continued employment was adequate consideration for the new noncompete agreement. Do you agree? Why or why not? [*84 Lumber Co., L.P. v. Houser,* 2011 Ohio 6852 (2011).]

10. Five employees of American Electric Power (AEP) Service Corp. invented a new product. "In consideration of the sum of One Dollar (1.00), and of other good and valuable consideration paid to the undersigned Assignor," each employee signed an agreement giving AEP exclusive patent rights to the invention. Some of the employees sued, alleging that there was no contract because AEP never paid the one dollar. How do you think the court ruled? Explain your reasoning. [*Bennett et al. v. American Electric Power Service Corporation,* 2001 Ohio App. LEXIS 4357 (Ohio Ct. App. 2001).]

Looking for more review materials?

The Online Learning Center at **www.mhhe.com/kubasek3e** contains this chapter's "Assignment on the Internet" and also a list of URLs for more information, entitled "On the Internet." Find both of them in the Student Center portion of the OLC, along with quizzes and other helpful materials.

CHAPTER

16 Capacity and Legality

LEARNING OBJECTIVES

After reading this chapter, you will be able to answer the following questions:

1. What is the legal effect of a lack of capacity on a person's ability to enter into a contract?
2. Under what circumstances would a party have limited capacity to enter into a contract?
3. What is the legal effect of entering into a contract for an illegal purpose?

CASE OPENER

Apple's Questionable Contracts

Parents of minors took Apple to court in 2012 for supplying game applications, on iPhones, that were "free" but through which users could purchase in-game currencies. Apparently, parents would log on to the games, but within a subsequent 15-minute time frame, the minors using the game would rack up bills ranging from $99.99 to $338.72 "at a time."

Apple stated that while minors were downloading these applications and in-game currency, the contract in question was actually the Terms of Service between the parents and Apple. According to the Terms of Service, any unauthorized log-in on one's account or unauthorized purchases by anyone on the account were the responsibility of the account holder. On the other hand, the parents argued that all in-game purchases made by minors were separate contracts that may be disaffirmed by a parent or guardian. Apple also argued that a "contract" as the parents were describing it could not legally exist in that, as the parents described the scenario, the contractual offer was made to parents in the Terms of Service, yet accepted by the children, and consideration was provided by the parents (the original offerees).[1]

1. Do the individual purchases made by the minors indeed qualify as separate contracts between Apple and the minors?
2. Even if the purchases were contracts between the minors and Apple, could the parents void these contracts?

The Wrap-Up at the end of the chapter will answer these questions.

[1] *In re Apple In-App Purchase Litigation,* 5:11-CV-1758 (N.D. Cal., Mar. 31, 2012).

Capacity

LO1 What is the legal effect of a lack of capacity on a person's ability to enter into a contract?

Capacity is the third element of a legally binding contract. A person who has legal capacity has the mental ability to understand his or her rights and obligations under a contract and therefore presumably to comply with the terms. *Incapacity,* or *incompetence* as it is sometimes called, is the possession of a mental or physical defect that prevents a natural person from being able to enter into a legally binding contract. Depending on the nature and extent of the defect, a person may have either no capacity, the complete inability to enter into contracts, or limited capacity, the ability to form only voidable contracts.

Historically, people with limited or no capacity included married women, minors, and insane persons. Other categories were added by statutes, such as people for whom guardians had been appointed, including habitual drunkards, narcotic addicts, spendthrifts, the elderly, and convicts. Today, married women have been removed from the category of those lacking contractual capacity, although in a few states their capacity to enter into certain kinds of contracts is still limited. In this section of the chapter, we explain the current law limiting the capacity of some categories of persons to enter into legally binding agreements.

MINORS

LO2 Under what circumstances would a party have limited capacity to enter into a contract?

One of the oldest limitations on capacity is the fact that minors may enter into only voidable contracts. Today, in all but three states, a *minor* is someone under the age of 18.[2] In most states, however, a person is given full legal capacity to enter into contracts when he or she becomes emancipated before reaching the age of majority. *Emancipation* occurs when a minor's parents or legal guardians give up their right to exercise legal control over the minor, typically when the minor moves out of the parents' house and begins supporting himself or herself. Often the minor will petition the court for a declaration of emancipation. In most cases, when a minor marries, she or he is considered emancipated.

Legal Principle: **As a general rule, any contract entered into by a minor is voidable by the minor until he or she reaches the age of majority or a reasonable time thereafter.**

Disaffirmance of the Contract. Because their contracts are voidable, minors have the right, until a reasonable time after reaching the age of majority, to disaffirm or void their contracts. Note that it is only the minor who has the right to disaffirm, never the adult with whom the minor entered into the agreement. No formalities are required to disaffirm the contract; the minor need only show an intention to rescind it, either by words or actions. However, the minor must void the entire contract; he or she cannot choose to disaffirm only a portion of it.

BUT WHAT IF . . .

WHAT IF THE FACTS OF THE CASE OPENER WERE DIFFERENT?

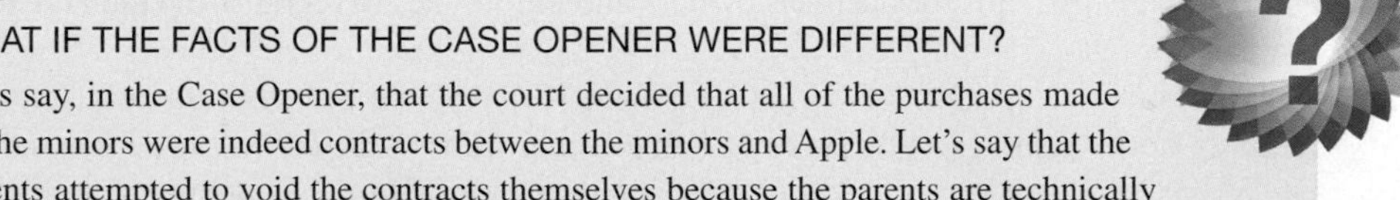
Let's say, in the Case Opener, that the court decided that all of the purchases made by the minors were indeed contracts between the minors and Apple. Let's say that the parents attempted to void the contracts themselves because the parents are technically the minors' legal guardians. Would such a move be effective? Why or why not?

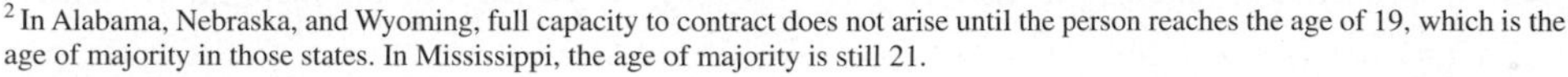
[2] In Alabama, Nebraska, and Wyoming, full capacity to contract does not arise until the person reaches the age of 19, which is the age of majority in those states. In Mississippi, the age of majority is still 21.

COMPARING THE LAW OF OTHER COUNTRIES

THE AGE OF MAJORITY IN GREAT BRITAIN

People in the United States take the idea of an "age of majority" for granted; the only question is whether it should be 18, 19, or 21. Yet in Great Britain there is no magical age at which a young person suddenly acquires the legal capacity to enter into a contract. British courts will not enforce contracts with immature minors. However, they make the decision of whether a person is too immature to enter into a contract on a case-by-case basis. If the courts consider a person under 18 to be able to look out for his or her own interests, the contract will be enforced. If not, it will be void. A key factor is often the fairness of the agreement. If the agreement is one-sided and favors the adult, the young person is usually considered to lack the maturity to enter into it.

The minor's obligations on disaffirmance vary from state to state. Traditionally, most states simply required the minor to notify the competent party and return any consideration received, regardless of its condition. If the consideration had been damaged or destroyed, the other party had no recourse against the minor. For instance, if William, a minor, purchased a flat-screen TV from Sound Systems, Inc., under a six-month contract and dropped the TV a week after he took it home, he could return it in its broken condition and tell the store owner he wished to rescind the contract. He would be entitled to the return of his down payment and would owe no further obligations to the store.

The traditional rule makes sense if we view minors as innocents in need of protection from competent adults who would otherwise take advantage of them. However, it is not going to encourage competent parties to enter into contracts with minors, and some argue that it allows a knowledgeable and unethical minor to take advantage of a competent party. Thus, a number of states have modified the duty of the minor on disaffirmance, holding that the minor has a duty of restitution, requiring that she or he place the competent party back in the position that party was in at the time the contract was made. In these states, William would have a duty of restoration that would require him to compensate the store owner for the difference between the value of the TV when he got it and its value when he returned it.

The disaffirmance must occur before or within a reasonable time of the minor's reaching the age of majority. What constitutes a reasonable time is determined on a case-by-case basis. But even when the courts scrutinize the cases individually, the laws created to protect minors from being victimized by competent adults do not necessarily protect competent adults from being taken advantage of by knowledgeable and unethical minors. Thus, individuals operating or working in businesses subject to laws requiring that their customers be the age of majority or older must familiarize themselves with the laws pertaining to minors, because often the responsibility of making sure that a business is dealing with people who are of legal age falls on the employees and the owner. However, since some minors use false identification or misrepresent themselves as adults, it is difficult for business owners and employees to recognize which customers are truly of age.

For example, as CEO of Girls Gone Wild (GGW), Joe Francis runs a business that requires he be familiar with the laws surrounding minors. In fact, Francis has said that GGW has very specific procedures in place to prevent filming underage girls and even teaches its camera crew ways to ensure that the girls the crew is selecting to appear in GGW spring break videos are of age. During the selection procedure, the GGW camera crew is required to check the IDs of girls wanting to be filmed, obtain signed written

GGW has very specific procedures in place to prevent filming underage girls and even teaches its camera crew ways to ensure that the girls the crew is selecting to appear in GGW spring break videos are of age. During the selection procedure, the GGW camera crew is required to check the IDs of girls wanting to be filmed, obtain signed written release forms in which the girls give their consent to be filmed, and videotape the girls' IDs as well as the actual process of signing the release forms. Regardless of his company's strict policies, Francis found himself in the middle of a heated legal battle in 2003 when seven girls claimed that they were underage when the GGW camera crew filmed them on vacation in Panama City, Florida. Francis fought back, saying that the girls misrepresented themselves, knowingly sought out the GGW crew and wanted to exploit the company in order to obtain a monetary settlement. After four years of court proceedings and intense media coverage, Francis reached an undisclosed settlement with the women, who reportedly wanted a total of $70 million.[3]

Exceptions to the Minor's Right to Disaffirm the Contract. The minor's right to disaffirm is designed to protect the minor from competent parties who might otherwise take advantage of him or her. But primarily for public policy reasons, in most states, courts or state legislatures have determined that the minor should *not* have the right to disaffirm contracts for life insurance, health insurance, psychological counseling, the performance of duties related to stock and bond transfers and bank accounts, education loan contracts, child support contracts, marriage contracts, and enlistment in the armed services.

Most of these exceptions apply in most, but not all, states. Another issue on which the states disagree is what should happen when a minor misrepresents his or her age. While the majority rule is that a minor's misrepresentation of age does not affect the minor's right to disaffirm the contract, some states hold that when a minor who appears to be of the age of majority misrepresents his or her age and a competent party relies on that misrepresentation in good faith, the minor gives up the right to disaffirm the agreement and can be treated as an adult. One justification for this rule is that any minor who is going to misrepresent his or her age does not need the protection that disaffirmance is designed to provide.

Other states have compromised, either by requiring that the minor restore the competent party to that party's precontract position before allowing the disaffirmance or by allowing the minor to disaffirm but then giving the competent party the right to sue the minor in tort and recover damages for fraud.

To see how marketing research relates to the legal system's protection of minors, please see the **Connecting to the Core** activity on the text website at www.mhhe.com/kubasek3e.

Liability of Minors for Necessaries. A necessary is a basic necessity of life, generally including food, clothing, shelter, and basic medical services. Technically, minors can disaffirm contracts for necessaries, but they will still be held liable for the reasonable value of the necessary. The purpose of this limitation on the minor's right to disaffirm is to ensure that sellers will not be reluctant to provide minors the basic necessities of life when their parents will not provide them.

Food, clothing, shelter, and basic medical services are clearly necessaries, but it is sometimes difficult to determine whether something is in fact a necessary. Some courts define a necessary as what a minor needs to maintain his or her standard of living and financial and social status, but this can lead to a problem when an item considered a necessary for a child of upper-income parents is a luxury to a child of lower-income parents. Whether an item is considered a necessary also depends on whether the minor's parents are

[3]www.meetjoefrancis.com/legalstory/; www.associatedcontent.com/article/280397/two_florida_women_sue_girls_gone_wild.html?cat=17; and www.usatoday.com/life/people/2007-06-13-joe-francis_N.htm.

willing to provide it. Clearly, the games in the opening scenario would not be considered necessaries!

Ratification. Once a person reaches the age of majority, he or she may ratify, or legally affirm, contracts made as a minor. Once ratified, the contract is no longer voidable. Ratification may be either express or implied (see Exhibit 16-1).

An *express ratification* occurs when, after reaching the age of majority, the person states orally or in writing that he or she intends to be bound by the contract entered into as a minor. For example, when she is 17, Marcy enters into an agreement to purchase an automobile from Sam for 10 monthly payments of $1,000. After making the fifth payment, Marcy turns 18 and decides to move out of state. She e-mails Sam and tells him not to worry because even though she is moving, she still intends to make her monthly payments to purchase the car. Marcy has expressly ratified the contract.

An *implied ratification* occurs when the former minor takes some action after reaching the age of majority consistent with intent to ratify the contract. Going back to the previous example, if the day after she turns 18 Marcy enters into an agreement with Joe to sell him the car in six months, that action is obviously consistent with intent to finish purchasing the car, so she has impliedly ratified the contract with Sam. Most courts find that continuing to act in accordance with the contract, such as continuing to make regular payments after reaching the age of majority, constitutes ratification. So, if (without the agreement with Joe) Marcy continued using the car and making payments on it for several months after reaching the age of majority, the courts would probably find that she had ratified the contract.

Parents' Liability for their Children's Contracts, Necessaries, and Torts. As a general rule, parents are not liable for contracts entered into by their minor children. Thus, merchants are often reluctant to enter into contracts with minors unless some competent person is willing to cosign and become legally bound to perform if the minor no longer wishes to live up to the terms of the contract. Parents do, however, have a legal duty to provide their children with the basic necessities of life, such as food, clothing, and shelter. Thus, they may be held liable in some states for the reasonable value of necessaries for which their children enter into contracts.

In most states, minors, not their parents, are liable for a minor's personal torts. In many states, however, parents may be liable when a child causes harm if it can be proved that the parent failed to properly supervise the child, thereby subjecting others to an unreasonable risk of harm.

Exhibit 16-1
Ratifying a Contract

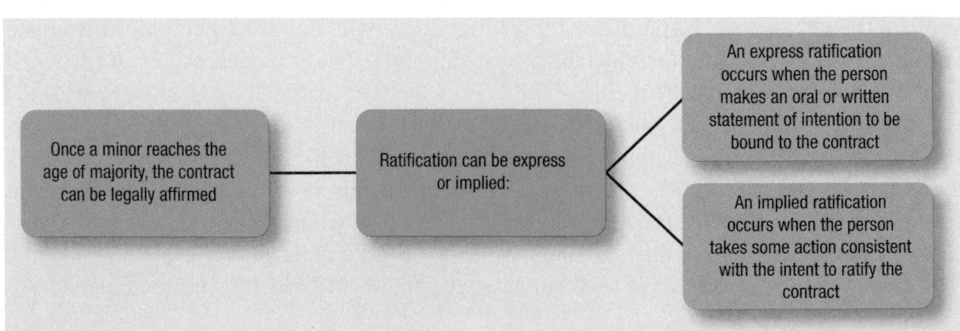

MENTALLY INCAPACITATED PERSONS

Persons suffering from a mental illness or deficiency may have full, limited, or no legal capacity to enter into a binding contract, depending on the nature and extent of their deficiency. If a person suffers from mental problems yet still understands the nature of the contract and the obligations it imposes, that person may enter into a binding, legal agreement. Suppose Gina suffers from the delusion that she is a rock star. When an encyclopedia salesperson comes to her door, she buys a set from him because she believes it is important to be knowledgeable to set a good example for her fans. As long as she understands that she is binding herself through a contract to make monthly payments for two years, Gina is bound to the contract. If, after making a year of payments, she no longer suffers from her delusions and wishes to disaffirm the contract, she will not be able to do so because her delusions had not affected her understanding of what she was legally agreeing to do when she entered into the contract.

However, a person has only limited capacity to enter into a contract if she suffers from a mental illness or deficiency that prevents her from understanding the nature and obligations of the transaction. If, in the above scenario, Gina's delusions persuaded her that she was giving the salesperson her autograph when she signed the contract, the contract is voidable. She may disaffirm it at any time until a reasonable time after she no longer suffers from the mental deficiency. Once the deficiency has been removed, Gina may also choose to ratify the contract.

As with contracts of minors, a contract for necessaries by a person suffering from a mental deficiency can be enforced for the reasonable value of the necessary.

If a person has been adjudicated insane and has a guardian appointed, that person has no capacity to enter into contracts and any contract he does attempt to enter into is void. Guardians may also be appointed for persons who have been adjudicated habitual drunkards and for those whose judgment has been impaired because of a condition such as Alzheimer disease. The guardian has the sole legal capacity to enter into contracts on such a person's behalf.

Legal Principle: **Contracts of a person with limited mental capacity can be valid, voidable, or void, depending on the extent of the mental incapacity. If a person suffers from delusions that may impair his judgment but he can still understand that he is entering into a contract and understand his obligations under the contract, his contract is valid; if his delusions prevent him from understanding that he is entering into a contract or the nature and extent of his obligations under the contract, his contract is voidable; and if he has been adjudicated insane, his contract is void.**

BUT WHAT IF . . .

WHAT IF THE FACTS OF THE CASE OPENER WERE DIFFERENT?

Let's say, in the Case Opener, that it was not children making a purchase but a mentally disabled person named Chloe, who was convinced that she owned a dog even though she didn't. And let's say that instead of purchasing in-game currencies on an iPhone, she ordered $1,000 worth of dog food. How would you describe Chloe's legal capacity? Could she avoid liability under her contract if she were subsequently treated by a therapist, no longer had her delusions, and realized that she had no need for the dog food? What if Chloe had been adjudicated insane and committed to a mental institution, but was staying with her sister on a weekend visitation pass when she made the purchase using her sister's computer?

The degree of intoxication is crucial when determining the capacity to agree to a legal contract.

INTOXICATED PERSONS

For purposes of determining capacity, intoxicated persons include those under the influence of alcohol or drugs. Most states follow the Restatement of Contracts, Section 16, which provides that contracts of an intoxicated person are voidable if the other party had reason to know that intoxication rendered the person unable to understand the nature and consequences of the transaction or unable to act in a reasonable manner in relation to the transaction. If the intoxication merely causes someone to exercise poor judgment, the person's capacity is not affected unless the other party unfairly capitalizes on this impaired judgment. Exhibit 16-2 presents the key points regarding contracts made by intoxicated persons.

Recall the case of *Lucy v. Zehmer,* discussed in Chapter 14. Another argument Zehmer tried to make in that case was that he was "high as a Georgia pine" when he signed the agreement and that the transaction was "just a bunch of two doggoned drunks bluffing to see who could talk the biggest and say the most."[4] Lucy, however, testified that while he felt the drinks, he was not intoxicated and that, from the way Zehmer handled the transaction, he did not think Zehmer was either. Zehmer's discussion of the terms of the agreement made it clear that he did in fact understand the nature of the transaction and thus could not claim a lack of capacity due to intoxication.

Similarly, if one party had no way of knowing that the other was intoxicated and if the agreement is a fair one, most courts will uphold it. Suppose Lisa e-mails Rob and offers to buy his antique car for $8,000. Rob has been drinking all day and immediately responds with a yes. Lisa has no way of knowing Rob is intoxicated, so they would have a valid contract in most states.

Exhibit 16-2
Intoxicated Individuals

Generally, contracts made by intoxicated persons are voidable. However, there are exceptions:

1. If the intoxication just causes the person to exercise poor judgment, the contract is not voidable unless the other party unfairly capitalized on the impaired judgment.
2. When the intoxicated person becomes sober, the contract can be ratified or disaffirmed; however, the courts will fairly liberally interpret behavior that seems like ratifying the contract once the intoxicated person becomes sober.

[4] *Lucy v. Zehmer,* 84 S.E.2d 516 (1954).

Once sober, the previously intoxicated person has the ability to either ratify or disaffirm the contract. Because public policy does not favor intoxication, the courts tend to not be sympathetic to intoxicated parties and will fairly liberally interpret behavior that seems like ratification as ratifying the contract. If Jim became intoxicated at a bar one evening and Randi took advantage by getting him to sign a contract to sell her his 2010 SUV for $8,000, any act Jim takes consistent with ratification after becoming sober will result in a binding contract. If Randi appears at his house the next morning with the cash, shows him the contract drafted on a napkin he signed, and asks for the keys and the title, by giving her the keys and saying, "I knew I shouldn't have drunk that much," Jim has entered into a binding contract.

If the contract is disaffirmed on the basis of intoxication, each party must return the other to the condition he or she was in at the time they entered into the contract. And, just as with contracts of minors and mentally incapacitated persons, the courts will enforce an intoxicated person's contract for necessaries for their reasonable value.

Exhibit 16-3 summarizes the general rules on incapacity and contracts.

Exhibit 16-3

The Three *I*'s of Incapacity: General Rules

TYPE OF INCAPACITY	CONSIDERATIONS	IF THE ANSWER IS YES, THE GENERAL RULE IS:
*I*nfancy	Is the person under the age of majority (a minor)?	The contract is voidable.
*I*nsanity	Is the person suffering from mental deficiencies that prevent him from understanding his legal obligations under the contract he is entering into?	The contract is voidable.
	Does the person's mental deficiency simply impair her judgment about the desirability of the contract but not prohibit her from understanding her obligations under it?	The contract is valid.
	Is the person adjudicated insane?	The contract is void.
*I*ntoxication	Is the sober party aware that the intoxicated person is so impaired that he is unable to understand his legal obligations under the contract he is entering into?	The contract Is voidable.
	Is the intoxication such that it impairs only the intoxicated person's judgment but not her understanding of her contractual obligations?	The contract is valid.
	Has the intoxicated person been adjudicated a habitual drunkard?	The contract is void.

Legality

LO3

What is the legal effect of entering into a contract for an illegal purpose?

To be enforceable, contracts must have legal subject matter and must be able to be performed legally. They cannot violate either state or federal law. A contract overturned for illegal subject matter or for being illegal to perform is generally declared void. A contract need not be in violation of a statute to be illegal; agreements against generally accepted public policy are also illegal and unenforceable.

Contracts that are made for an illegal purpose or that cannot be carried out by legal means are made void for two main reasons: First, making them void clearly indicates that such agreements are not socially acceptable, and, second, doing so prevents the legal system's being used to promote agreements that are harmful to society.

CONTRACTS THAT VIOLATE STATE OR FEDERAL STATUTES

There are any number of ways in which contracts can violate a state or federal statute. Some of the more common ones are discussed below and summarized in Exhibit 16-4.

Agreements to Commit a Crime or Tort. Again, contracts cannot be for illegal purposes or require illegal acts for performance. Any agreement to commit a crime or tort is illegal and unenforceable. However, should a legal contract be formed and its subject later become illegal under a new statute, the contract is considered to be discharged by law. Suppose Jim agrees to paint Hiroki's house and, in exchange, Hiroki agrees to be a poker dealer at Jim's casino, starting in two weeks. Before Hiroki can begin work, however, the state amends its gaming statute, making all games of chance other than slot machines illegal. Because it is now illegal for Jim's casino to offer poker, it would be illegal for Hiroki to perform the contract. Because a change in the law has made the subject matter of the contract illegal, both parties are discharged from their obligations under the contract.

Licensing Statutes. All 50 states have statutes requiring that people in certain professions obtain a license before practicing their craft. For example, doctors of all varieties, plumbers, cosmetologists, lawyers, electricians, teachers, and stockbrokers are all required to obtain a license before practicing. While this list is far from exhaustive, it demonstrates how widespread the licensing requirement can be. For most of these licensed professions, licenses are typically issued only after extensive schooling, training, and/or demonstrating some degree of competence. These requirements reflect the value society places on proper performance of duties in the licensed professions.

Licensing statutes have three main purposes in addition to indicating this value. The first is to give the government some control over which people, and how many people, can perform certain jobs. Second, by charging for licenses, the government can obtain revenue.

Exhibit 16-4

Contracts That Violate State or Federal Statutes

Agreements to commit a crime or tort are illegal in all states.

Agreements made for the purpose of protecting the public's health, safety, or welfare by a party unlicensed to do so are typically illegal in all states.

Agreements regarding usurious loans may be illegal in some states.

Agreements regarding gambling are illegal in most states.

Agreements that violate Sabbath or Sunday laws are illegal in some states.

The third purpose of licensing statutes, the protection of the public's health, safety, and welfare, is related to the public interest. By imposing legal standards on a profession, the government can try to prevent harm to public health, safety, and welfare due to substandard work. For instance, it is not in the public's best interest to allow an unqualified person to perform the delicate and complicated process of medical surgery. To limit the number of people who might be harmed during surgery, the government requires that prospective surgeons, even after extensive schooling, obtain a license.

Given these different reasons for licensing various professionals, different outcomes can result when someone enters into an agreement with a person who is unlawfully unlicensed, depending on the purpose of the licensing statute. The state in which the unlicensed person is practicing is relevant, because many licensing statutes occur at the state level and thus vary from state to state. In some states the rule is "no license, no contract." These states will not enforce any agreement with an unlawfully unlicensed professional.

However, in other states the courts typically consider the purpose of licensing. If it is to provide government control over the profession or generate revenue, most states allow enforcement of the contract. Although the unlicensed professional is acting in violation of the law and is usually required to pay a fine for working without a license, there are no grave reasons the contract should not be carried out.

If the licensing statute is intended to protect the public's health, safety, and welfare, however, the agreement is typically deemed illegal and unenforceable. For example, the public would not be made safer if the government allowed unlicensed people to perform surgery. Therefore, a person cannot enter into a contract for professional service with an unlicensed professional when the law requires a license out of intent to protect the public.

Case 16-1 illustrates how failure to obtain a license can preclude a party from suing to enforce a contract.

CASE 16-1 KING v. RIEDL
ALABAMA CIVIL COURT OF APPEALS
58 SO. 3D 190 (2010)

Roseann and Bryan Riedl entered into a contract with Jim King d/b/a King Home Services to make improvements to the Riedls' house. The improvements entailed work throughout the entire property, including work to the yard and demolition and installation work to the house. The Riedls paid King a total of $14,075 for some, but not all, of the work specified in the contract. King was not at any time a licensee of the Alabama Home Builders Licensure Board.

The Riedls were unsatisfied with the work contracted for and performed by King. Consequently, Roseann filed a small-claims complaint in the small-claims division of the Madison District Court, alleging that King had damaged her house. Roseann sought compensation for repair work performed by other parties. In response, King filed an action in the Madison Circuit Court against the Riedls, alleging a number of claims, including breach of contract. In the district court, King requested that the district-court action be consolidated with the circuit-court action. After the Riedls also requested consolidation, the district-court action was transferred to the circuit court, and the two actions were consolidated.

The Riedls filed a motion for a summary judgment in the circuit court, asserting that King lacked standing to institute the circuit-court action against them because he was an unlicensed home builder. In response, King claimed that he did not need a license in order to enforce his contract with the Riedls. After a hearing, the circuit court entered a summary judgment in favor of the Riedls, dismissing all King's claims against them. King filed an appeal of the summary judgment entered in the circuit-court action.

JUDGE THOMAS:

I. Breach of Contract Claim

Section 34–14A–5, Ala.Code 1975, requires all home builders to be licensed by the Alabama Home Builders Licensure Board. A residential home builder is defined by § 34–14A–2(10), Ala.Code 1975, as follows:

> (10) Residential home builder. One who constructs a residence or structure for sale or who, for a fixed price, commission, fee, or wage, undertakes or offers to undertake the construction or superintending of the construction, or who manages,

> supervises, assists, or provides consultation to a homeowner regarding the construction or superintending of the construction, of any residence or structure which is not over three floors in height and which does not have more than four units in an apartment complex, or the repair, improvement, or reimprovement thereof, to be used by another as a residence *when the cost of the undertaking exceeds ten thousand dollars ($10,000).* Nothing herein shall prevent any person from performing these acts on his or her own residence or on his or her other real estate holdings. Anyone who engages or offers to engage in such undertaking in this state shall be deemed to have engaged in the business of residential home building.

. . . Thus, whether a license is required depends on the cost of the undertaking.

King argues that the cost of the undertaking in the present case was less than $10,000 because, he contends, work done to the Riedls' porch, "doggie doors," and fence should not be included in calculating the cost of the undertaking. King further argues that the Riedls had full control over the subcontractors and, thus, that he is exempted from obtaining a license by § 34–14A–6(5). Also, King contends that he did not have sufficient control over the subcontractors and materials for the amounts paid to those subcontractors and for those materials to contribute toward the cost of the undertaking. Finally, King argues that he was compensated for his work by periodic payments of less than $10,000 each, and, thus, he argues, he was not required to have a license.

Two of King's arguments are raised for the first time on appeal: King's argument that work done to the porch, "doggie doors," and fence should be considered separately from work performed on the house in calculating the total cost of the undertaking and his argument that he did not have sufficient control over the subcontractors and, thus, falls within an exemption to the licensing scheme. . . . Arguments not presented to the trial court are not proper arguments for appeal. . . . Accordingly, we consider all the work performed by King to be work performed on a house, which requires a license if the cost of the undertaking is greater than $10,000.

King argues that there remains a genuine issue of fact regarding whether the cost of the undertaking was more than $10,000. The Riedls note that King's admission that the costs of the undertaking exceeded $10,000 in his response to an interrogatory is in conflict with his affidavit filed in response to the Riedls' motion for a summary judgment. King's contradictory assertions in his response to an interrogatory and in his affidavit filed in response to the motion for a summary judgment do not create a genuine issue of a material fact regarding the cost of the undertaking. The Riedls' seventh interrogatory to King stated:

> Regarding the contract alleged to have been breached by [the Riedls] within [King's] Complaint, provide the total amount to be paid for said work and services under the terms of said contract, including any and all estimated or fixed costs for materials provided.

King answered that the cost of the undertaking, under the terms of the contract, was "[i]n excess of $10,000.00." However, King submitted affidavit testimony in opposition to the motion for a summary judgment that stated that "at no time was I contracted to receive in excess of $10,000.00 as payment for my services." This contradiction cannot be used to create a genuine issue of material fact. . . .

King argues on appeal that payments made through him for the countertop and carpet were ultimately controlled by the Riedls. Contrary to his argument on appeal, however, the evidence submitted in support of and in opposition to the motion for a summary judgment does not indicate that King was hired to install carpet or to install the countertop. King produced no evidence indicating that the payments he received were intended to pay for either of those tasks, or for the materials involved in those tasks. The evidence indicates that King provided "turnkey" construction and supervision to the Riedls for an amount over $10,000.

The Riedls made periodic payments to King as he worked on the property, which, King contends, represent separate transactions. Thus, King argues, the contracted amount never exceeded $10,000. We have rejected this argument before, albeit in a case concerning a licensing statute pertaining to general contractors that is similar to § 34–14A–14. . . . "[A] contrary holding would encourage unscrupulous contractors to avoid the requirements of the licensing statute by designating payments to subcontractors and suppliers incident to 'separate contracts.' ". . . Similarly, allowing King to avoid licensure requirements by classifying a series of periodic payments as pertaining to separate contracts would render the residential home builder licensing statute meaningless. Thus, we conclude that there is no genuine issue of material fact on this issue and that the cost of the undertaking was over $10,000.

King violated § 34–14A–14 because he performed work, under his direct control and supervision, for more than $10,000. A residential home builder who fails to maintain a license with the Alabama Home Builders Licensure Board is statutorily barred from bringing or maintaining "any action to enforce the provisions of any contract for residential home building which he or she entered into in violation of this chapter." . . . King admitted that he was not a licensed residential home builder before, during, or after the construction work on the Riedls' house. Furthermore, the cost of the undertaking was more than $10,000. Therefore, King violated § 34–14A–14, and, thus, he has no standing to bring his breach-of-contract claim.

Summary Judgment affirmed in favor of the Reidls.

CRITICAL THINKING

When a judge or judicial panel makes a decision, the judge or panel must do so on the basis of the information available. What is an illustration of a fact that, were it true, would have caused this case to have provided King standing with respect to his breach-of-contract action? What fact was especially important in moving the decision in the direction of summary judgment?

ETHICAL DECISION MAKING

The statute spelling out the need for a residential home builder license has an exemption for small contracts. What stakeholders are being especially advantaged by the exemption?

Legal Principle: **If the licensing statute is intended simply to generate revenue, then the contract of an unlicensed person is valid; if the purpose of the licensing statute is to protect the public's health, safety, and welfare, however, the agreement of an unlicensed person is typically deemed illegal and unenforceable.**

Usury. Almost as widespread as licensing statutes, statutes prohibiting usury are found on the books of nearly every state. Usury occurs when a party gives a loan at an interest rate exceeding the legal maximum. The legal maximum interest rate varies from state to state, but it is easy to determine the rate of any given state.

While usury statutes act as a ceiling on rates, there are a few legal exceptions whereby loans may exceed the predetermined maximum. To facilitate business transactions and keep the economy healthy, for example, most states with usury statutes allow corporations willing to pay more to lend and borrow at rates exceeding the maximum. The rationale behind the corporation exception is that if a business needs money to expand and is willing to pay the higher interest rate, the corporation should be afforded the opportunity to borrow. The converse is that if a corporation is willing to borrow at a high interest rate, parties should be allowed to lend at that rate for corporations only. The intent is to facilitate business transactions in order to keep the economy in a healthy state.

Many states also allow parties to make small loans at rates above the maximum to parties that cannot obtain a needed loan at the statutory maximum. The belief is that if people need money and the statutory maximum is not inducing others to lend, certain parties will make the necessary loans at a higher rate as long as the loan is "small." This exception allows cash advance institutions to operate.

If no exception allows a usurious loan, the legal outcome varies by state. A few states declare all usurious loans void, which means the lender is not entitled to recover either interest or principal from the borrower. A larger number of states allow lenders to recover the principal but no interest. States most favorable toward lenders allow recovery of the principal as well as interest up to, but not exceeding, the statutory maximum.

Gambling. All states regulate gambling. As used in this chapter, the term gambling refers to agreements in which parties pay consideration (money placed during bets) for the chance, or opportunity, to obtain an amount of money or property. Industry officials, however, prefer to use the term *gaming.*

While gambling is illegal in most states, some allow casino gambling, notably Nevada, New Jersey, and Louisiana. Some allow certain other types of gambling, either intentionally or through legal loopholes. For example, given California's definition of gambling, betting on draw poker is legal. Some states make other exceptions, such as for horse tracks, casinos on Native American reservations, or state-run lotteries, which, although most people do not consider them to be such, are a form of gambling.

E-COMMERCE AND THE LAW

OBSERVING SABBATH DAYS ONLINE

Sabbath days stem from the religious traditions that were so widespread in America's early days. Among the religions that still practice observing Sabbath days today is Judaism, which has very strict laws in relation to refraining from conducting business on the Sabbath. This prohibition even extends to the online realm. Not only are those of the Jewish faith told to abstain from conducting online transactions on the day of the Sabbath, but it is also prohibited to make transactions online on the Sabbath even if the individual in question has no awareness of doing so. For example, if an individual schedules to pay for an item when it ships and the item happens to be shipped on the day of the Sabbath, it is considered that the individual has broken Sabbath law. Laws against conducting certain types of business are still active even today, though they may not be rigidly enforced.

Source: http://belogski.blogspot.com/2008/03/must-your-online-shop-shut-on-shabbat.html.

Sabbath Laws. A large number of states still have *Sabbath, Sunday,* or *blue* laws on the books. **Sabbath laws** limit the types of business activities in which parties can legally engage on Sundays. In Colonial times, these laws prohibited store operations and all work on the "Lord's day" (Sunday). Today these laws vary by state. Most prohibit the sale of all alcohol, or specific types, either all day or at particular times on Sundays. Some Sabbath laws also make it illegal to enter into any contract on a Sunday. However, an executed, or fully performed, contract created on a Sunday cannot be rescinded.

There are exceptions to Sabbath laws. Most states allow the performance of charity work on Sundays. In addition, the laws typically do not apply to contracts for obtaining "necessities," including prescription medication, food, and anything else related to health or survival.

Regardless of how widespread Sabbath laws are, the vast majority of states do not enforce some or all of their Sabbath laws. In fact, some have been held to violate the First Amendment. If they are on the books, however, they can be applied, and some states do apply them. Prudent businesspersons should always find out whether Sabbath laws exist in their state and whether authorities enforce them.

AGREEMENTS IN CONTRADICTION TO PUBLIC POLICY

Some types of agreements are not illegal per se, as they are not in violation of any statute or legal code, but are nevertheless unenforceable because courts have deemed them to be against public policy. Public policy involves both the government's concern for its citizens and the beliefs people hold regarding the proper subject of business transactions. The focus is what is "in society's best interest."

Contracts in Restraint of Trade. It is a widely held belief in economics, and in U.S. culture in general, that competition drives down prices, which is good for consumers. Thus, agreements that restrain trade, called *anticompetitive agreements,* are viewed as being harmful to consumers and against public policy. They also frequently violate antitrust laws. See Chapter 47 for an in-depth discussion of antitrust law.

When courts determine a restraint on trade is reasonable, however, and the restraint is part of a subordinate, or ancillary, clause in the contract, the restraint is typically allowed. Such restraints are known as **covenants not to compete,** or *restrictive covenants.* There are two types.

The first enforceable type of restrictive covenant is one made in conjunction with the sale of an ongoing business. The public policy argument in favor of supporting restrictions regarding the sale of a business involves the fairness of the sale, as illustrated by the following hypothetical: Suppose you purchase a jewelry store from Ann, a well-respected member of the community, whose business has been around for many years. The people in the community know the store, and they trust Ann to provide fair exchanges. As a well-informed businessperson, you know about Ann's good reputation and it made the purchase more appealing.

Now suppose a month later Ann opens another jewelry store a block away. Ann's loyal customers are likely to go to her new store because they still trust her. In the meantime, Ann's good name is no longer associated with your store, and your business suffers accordingly. You entered into the sales agreement thinking you would benefit from Ann's good name, but in the end you overpaid for a business that lacks that benefit, because Ann took her name with her when she went into competition with your store. In the interest of fairness, courts are willing to impose restrictions preventing Ann, or others in her position, from going into immediate competition with you, or others in your position. Public policy requires fairness in business transactions, which does not occur when people profit from the sale of a business and then start a new business that destroys the one they just sold.

Remember, if the covenant not to compete is an integral part of the main agreement, not subordinate, the agreement is typically considered unenforceable and void, because it goes against public policy by creating unreasonable restraints on trade. When the covenant is subordinate, however, the specific noncompetition clause can be removed and the agreement can go forward as planned. In Case 16-2, the court had to determine the reasonableness of a covenant not to compete that was included in a separation agreement.

CASE 16-2 WILLIAM CAVANAUGH v. MARGARET McKENNA
SUPERIOR COURT OF MASSACHUSETTS, AT MIDDLESEX
22 MASS. L. REP. 694; 2007 MASS. SUPER. LEXIS 298

Defendant entered into a separation agreement with the plaintiff at the time of their divorce. The agreement provided in part that defendant would not accept full-time employment or open her own funeral business in Wilmington so long as the plaintiff maintained his funeral business. The trial court found that plaintiff had breached the agreement by competing with defendant by working for, and later owning, Nichols Funeral Home. On appeal, the defendant argued that the covenant not to compete was unenforceable as a restraint of trade that violated public policy.

JUSTICE SMITH: A covenant to not compete must be reasonable in time and scope, serve to protect a party's legitimate business interest, be supported by consideration, and be consonant with the public interest. . . . While most covenants not to compete arise either in the context of an employment relationship or the sale of a business, there are situations which do not "fit neatly into existing standards for reviewing such covenants" which require analogy. *Boulanger v. Dunkin' Donuts, Inc.*, . . . (2004) (finding covenant in franchise agreement akin to that of covenant in sale of business). With the sale of a business, "courts look less critically at covenants not to compete because they do not implicate an individual's right to employment to the same degree as in the employment context." . . . Courts will consider whether the parties were represented by counsel in making the agreement and entered the agreement without compulsion. . . .

The reasonableness of a covenant not to compete must be determined by the facts of each case. . . . Factors considered in determining the reasonableness of a restriction as to time include: 1) the nature of the business; 2) the type of employment involved; 3) the situation of the parties; 4) the legitimate business interests; and 5) a party's right to work and earn a livelihood. . . . Legitimate business interests include trade secrets, confidential business information, and good will. *Id.*, 779–80.

[continued]

Here, the covenant not to compete contained within the separation agreement is most analogous to the sale of a business. While McKenna worked at Cavanaugh Funeral Home before her divorce, she was not considered to be an employee. Her relinquishment of the right to operate a competing funeral home is akin to her sale of an asset. As such, the covenant not to compete should be construed more liberally. Also important in this consideration is the fact that McKenna was represented by counsel when she agreed to the noncompete provision, and there is no allegation that she was in any way coerced.

The Court finds that her covenant not to compete in the funeral business in the town of Wilmington for as long as Cavanaugh operates his funeral home there is reasonable in time and space. The restriction only applies to the town of Wilmington. Nothing prevents McKenna from entering the funeral business in another town (in fact, she worked for a funeral business in the town of Newton previously). In addition, it is important to note that there are only two funeral homes in Wilmington, Cavanaugh's and Nichols Funeral Home, and the defendant's utilization of the personal relationships forged while working at the plaintiff's funeral home would, in effect, misappropriate the good will of the plaintiff's business.

As part of the separation agreement, Cavanaugh gave up his right to the marital home and assumed the mortgage, and, in the modification, agreed to make weekly support payments, obtaining protection for the good will of his business in return. Allowing McKenna to compete in the same town while soliciting his clientele can be expected to eviscerate the good will of his business, the protection of which he received in return for his contractual undertakings.

In these circumstances, the Court finds that her covenant not to compete is enforceable. . . . Accordingly, the Court grants summary judgment to the plaintiff on Count I, leaving the issue of damages for trial.

AFFIRMED in favor of Plaintiffs.

CRITICAL THINKING

Provide an example of a piece of evidence that the defendant could have provided to indicate the unreasonableness of the scope of the covenant in this case. How does your example weigh in comparison to the evidence provided to the contrary? Do you think it would or should be sufficient to change the conclusion of the court? Defend your answer.

ETHICAL DECISION MAKING

What values are in conflict in this case? Which are supported by the ruling, and which are not? How well can the ethical stance taken by the court in this area be defended, and what ethical guidelines might be used in the effort to do so?

Legal Principle: **Covenants not to compete in conjunction with the sale of a business are generally enforceable if they are for a reasonable length of time and involve a reasonable location.**

The second category of permissible restraints on trade is covenants not to compete in employment contracts. The employee is agreeing, in the event of her leaving, not to compete with her boss (by starting her own company or working for competitors) for a designated period of time within a designated geographic area. These covenants are not unusual. In fact, many middle or upper-level managers enter into them.

Covenants not to compete in employment contracts are legal in most states, but they must protect a legitimate business interest. They must also apply to a period of time and geographic area that are reasonable for that purpose and not unlawfully impinge on the employee's rights. Not surprisingly, the enforceability of covenants not to compete in employment contracts varies from state to state. California does not allow any covenants not to compete. Texas requires that the employee gain or be given a specific benefit beyond employment before its courts will enforce even a reasonable covenant not to compete.

Employers and employees may therefore attempt to file suit or have their cases heard in the location that can provide them with the most favorable legal environment given their situation. Thus, business owners who create covenants not to compete may prefer to file suit in a location that is more tolerant of covenants not to compete, and employees may wish to have their cases heard in a location, such as California, that generally prohibits the enforceability of covenants not to compete.

For example, when executive Kai-Fu Lee left his job with Microsoft to join rival Google, Microsoft filed suit in the state of Washington, alleging that Lee's decision was in violation of his noncompete contract. Google fought back by filing suit against Microsoft in California, the state where Google is based, saying that under California laws Lee's noncompete contract was unenforceable. Both companies fought one another in court to have the case heard in the state where one or the other had the best chance of winning. In the end, a district court judge ruled that the case would first be tried in Washington, and if Google wanted to pursue the case further in California, it could do so after the trial. Early decisions made by the judge in Washington state court seemed to fall in Microsoft's favor, and Lee was initially barred from doing certain tasks for Google until after the trial. However, before the trial could end, the two companies reached a private settlement agreement.[5]

Unconscionable Contracts or Clauses. When courts are asked to review contracts, fairness is not usually high on their list of things to look for. Instead, they typically assume that the contracting parties are intelligent, responsible adults who enter into contracts because they want to. Nevertheless, some agreements are so one-sided that the courts will not make the innocent party be harmed by fulfilling his or her contractual duties. These heavily one-sided agreements are known as **unconscionable** agreements. The term *unconscionable* refers to the fact that the agreement in question is so unfair that it is void of conscience.

The common law would not enforce contracts the courts deemed unconscionable. Now rules against unconscionable contracts exist in both the Restatement (Second) of Contracts and the Uniform Commercial Code. UCC Section 2-302 states:

> (1) If the court as a matter of law finds the contract or any clause of the contract to have been unconscionable at the time it was made, the court may refuse to enforce the contract, or it may enforce the remainder of the contract without the clause, or it may so limit the application of any unconscionable clause as to avoid any unconscionable result; (2) When it is claimed or appears to the court that the contract or any clause thereof may be unconscionable, the parties shall be afforded a reasonable opportunity to present evidence as to its commercial setting, purpose, and effect to aid the court in making the determination.

Every state except California and Louisiana has incorporated this section into its UCC. Section 208 of the Restatement also incorporates the above section.

There are two main types of unconscionable agreements, procedural and substantive. **Procedural unconscionability** describes conditions that impair one party's understanding of a contract, as well as the integration of terms into a contract. These conditions can be anything from tiny, hard-to-read print on the back of an agreement to excessive use of legalese (unnecessarily technical legal language) or even a person's inability to fully read a contract and ask questions before being required to sign.

Procedural unconscionability usually arises in an **adhesion contract,** an agreement presented on a take-it-or-leave-it basis or as the only chance the presented party (the *adhering party*) will have to enter into it. While adhesion contracts are legal, they do raise red flags for courts, which will try to determine how voluntary the agreement really was.

[5] http://news.cnet.com/Kai-Fu-Lees-California-case-put-on-hold/2100-1022_3-5918672.html; www.forbes.com/2005/12/23/gates-microsoft-google-cx_cn_1223autofacescan02.html; and http://news.cnet.com/Microsoft-sues-over-Google-hire/2100-1014_3-5795051.html.

Substantive unconscionability occurs when an agreement is overly harsh or lopsided. Courts would find the following, for example, to be substantively unconscionable: large differences between cost and price in a sales agreement; agreements in which one party gains vastly more than the other; agreements in which one party is prevented from having equal benefit or has little to no legal recourse; and portions of an agreement unrelated to either party's business risk.

Exculpatory Clauses. An **exculpatory clause** releases one of the contracting parties from all liability, regardless of who is at fault or what injury is suffered. Because tort law attempts to return the wronged party to a state he or she was in before the wrong occurred, anything preventing this corrective mechanism is against public policy. It does not benefit society to allow some parties to get away with not having to pay for wrongs they commit simply because they state they will not be liable in various contracts. In fact, the patently unfair nature of an exculpatory clause is closely tied to the idea of unconscionable contracts.

Exculpatory clauses frequently show up in rental agreements for commercial or residential property. It does not serve the public's interest to allow landlords, especially of residential property, to disavow in advance all liabilities for injuries due to carelessness, negligence, or other wrongdoing. If they were allowed to do so, nothing would require them to fix problems in their rental units, including potentially lethal problems like faulty wiring or the presence of lead-based paint.

A basic test to determine whether an exculpatory clause is enforceable is to see whether the enforcing party engages in a business directly related to the public interest, as does a bank, transportation provider, or public utility. Courts believe it is against the public interest to allow businesses engaging in work in the public's interest *not* to be held accountable to the public they are serving.

Businesses serving the public interest can also possess unfair bargaining power in negotiating a contract; they could simply demand that all customers accept the exculpatory clause, thereby escaping all liability. Worse, there would then be no financial motive for them to conduct operations carefully, and the potential for increased accidents would be great. Obviously, it is not in the public's interest to have unsafe businesses not be accountable to the public. Thus, these businesses cannot enforce exculpatory clauses.

Case 16-3 details a court's determination that an illegal exculpatory clause existed.

CASE 16-3 ERIC LUCIER AND KAREN A. HALEY v. ANGELA AND JAMES WILLIAMS, CAMBRIDGE ASSOCIATES, LTD., AND AL VASYS

SUPERIOR COURT OF NEW JERSEY, APPELLATE DIVISION

841 A.2D 907 (2004)

Eric Lucier and Karen A. Haley, a young married couple, were first-time home buyers. They contracted with the Williamses to purchase a single-family residence. Lucier and Haley engaged the services of Cambridge Associates, Ltd. (CAL), to perform a home inspection. Al Vasys had formed CAL and was its president. Lucier dealt directly with Vasys, and Vasys performed the inspection and issued the home inspection report on behalf of CAL.

The home inspection agreement contains a provision limiting CAL's liability to "$500, or 50% of fees actually paid to CAL by Client, whichever sum is smaller." This provision, like several others in the form agreement prepared by CAL, was followed by a line for the clients' initials. Lucier initialed this provision. The fee for the home inspection contract was $385, which Lucier paid to CAL.

Lucier claims when he began to read the agreement, in Vasys' presence, he felt some of the language was unfair and confusing. According to Lucier, Vasys stated he would not change any provisions, that it was a standard contract based upon home inspections done in New Jersey, and Lucier would have to sign the agreement "as is" or not at all. Vasys does not dispute this but relies upon Lucier's signing the agreement and initialing the limitation of liability clause. Likewise, Lucier does not deny signing the contract or initialing that clause.

Lucier and Haley obtained title to the property from the Williamses. Shortly after, they noticed leaks in the house. They engaged the services of a roofing contractor and found the roof was defective. Lucier and Haley argue Vasys should have observed and reported the problem to them. The cost of repair was about $8,000 to $10,000.

Lucier and Haley brought suit against the Williamses, CAL, and Vasys, seeking damages to compensate them for the loss occasioned by the alleged defect. CAL and Vasys moved for partial summary judgment seeking a declaration that the limit of their liability in the action, if any, was one-half the contract price, or $192.50. The motion for partial summary judgment was granted. Lucier and Haley then filed this appeal, seeking review of the partial summary judgment order.

JUDGE LISA: There is no hard and fast definition of unconscionability. As the Supreme Court explained in *Kugler v. Romain,* unconscionability is "an amorphous concept obviously designed to establish a broad business ethic." The standard of conduct that the term implies is a lack of "good faith, honesty in fact and observance of fair dealing."

In determining whether to enforce the terms of a contract, we look not only to its adhesive nature, but also to "the subject matter of the contract, the parties' relative bargaining positions, the degree of economic compulsion motivating the 'adhering' party, and the public interests affected by the contract." Where the provision limits a party's liability, we pay particular attention to any inequality in the bargaining power and status of the parties, as well as the substance of the contract.

We also focus our inquiry on whether the limitation is a reasonable allocation of risk between the parties or whether it runs afoul of the public policy disfavoring clauses which effectively immunize parties from liability for their own negligent actions. To be enforceable, the amount of the cap on a party's liability must be sufficient to provide a realistic incentive to act diligently.

Applying these principles to the home inspection contract before us, we find the limitation of liability provision unconscionable. We do not hesitate to hold it unenforceable for the following reasons: (1) the contract, prepared by the home inspector, is one of adhesion; (2) the parties, one a consumer and the other a professional expert, have grossly unequal bargaining status; and (3) the substance of the provision eviscerates the contract and its fundamental purpose because the potential damage level is so nominal that it has the practical effect of avoiding almost all responsibility for the professional's negligence. Additionally, the provision is contrary to our state's public policy of effectuating the purpose of a home inspection contract to render reliable evaluation of a home's fitness for purchase and holding professionals to certain industry standards.

This is a classic contract of adhesion. There were no negotiations leading up to its preparation. The contract was presented to Lucier on a standardized preprinted form, prepared by CAL, on a take-it-or-leave-it basis, without any opportunity for him to negotiate or modify any of its terms.

The bargaining position between the parties was grossly disparate. Vasys has been in the home inspection business for twenty years. He has inspected thousands of homes. He has an engineering degree. He has served as an expert witness in construction matters. He holds various designations in the building and construction field. He advertises his company and holds it and himself out as possessing expertise in the home inspection field. Lucier and Haley, on the other hand, are unknowledgeable and unsophisticated in matters of home construction. They are consumers. They placed their trust in this expert. They had every reason to expect he would act with diligence and competence in inspecting the home they desired to purchase and discover and report major defects. The disparity in the positions of these parties is clear and substantial.

The foisting of a contract of this type in this setting on an inexperienced consumer clearly demonstrates a lack of fair dealing by the professional. The cost of homes in New Jersey is substantial.

The limitation of liability clause here is also against public policy. First, it allows the home inspector to circumvent the state's public policy of holding professional service providers to certain industry standards. Second, it contravenes the stated public policy of New Jersey regarding home inspectors.

With professional services, exculpation clauses are particularly disfavored. The very nature of a professional service is one in which the person receiving the service relies upon the expertise, training, knowledge and stature of the professional. Exculpation provisions are antithetical to such a relationship.

In summary, the limitation of liability provision in this contract is unconscionable and violates the public policy of our State. The contract is one of adhesion, the bargaining power of the parties is unequal, the impact of the liability clause is negligible to the home inspector while potentially severe to the home buyer, and the provision conflicts with the purpose of home inspection contracts and our Legislature's requirement of accountability by home inspectors for their errors and omissions.

REVERSED and REMANDED.

[continued]

CRITICAL THINKING

In this decision, does Judge Lisa make any assumptions regarding the facts of the case without proper evidence to support them as a reasoning step? For instance, what evidence supports her characterization of Lucier? Is it possible he is significantly different from the way he has been presented? How might such differences affect the acceptability of the conclusion? Can you locate any other assumptions in this ruling? How do they affect the reasoning?

ETHICAL DECISION MAKING

Examine the actions of each party leading up to this dispute. Who behaved in a blameworthy fashion, and who in a praiseworthy fashion? What facts from the case and what ethical theories or guidelines support your claim?

Now consider each party's stance in the legal dispute. Does either one appear more or less ethical, relative to that party's earlier actions? Why or why not?

While businesses closely linked to the public interest cannot enforce exculpatory clauses, not all such clauses are unlawful. To prevail, the party seeking enforcement must be a private business or individual *not* important to the public interest. These private businesses or individuals provide nonessential services and thus do not have the same bargaining power as the previously discussed groups, such as banks, utilities, or airlines. Given their lack of huge bargaining power, courts assume such businesses and individuals will enter a contract voluntarily and on relatively equal terms.

Private businesses that *can* enforce exculpatory clauses thus include skiing facilities such as resorts or rental places, private gyms or health clubs, any business offering sky diving or bungee jumping, and amusement parks, to name a few. Because their services and those of others in this category are not related to the public interest and are not activities in which people *must* engage, these parties are allowed to deny liability if the other party agrees to the exculpatory clause. Just because these parties *might* be able to enforce an exculpatory clause, however, does not mean the clause is always automatically enforceable.

EFFECT OF ILLEGAL AGREEMENTS

When an agreement is deemed illegal, courts will usually label it void. The reason is the legal principle of ***in pari delicto,*** which means both parties are equally responsible for the illegal agreement. In that case, it does not make sense for the courts to attempt to salvage the agreement or reward either party. Therefore, neither party can enforce the agreement, and neither is entitled to recovery.

But what if both parties are *not* at fault? What if one is significantly more culpable? Then it sometimes makes sense to allow one party to an illegal agreement to recover various damages.

The first exception to the general rule occurs when a member of a protected class is party to an agreement that contradicts a statute intended to protect the specific class. That party is allowed to sue for performance. The reasoning is that a statute intended to protect a specific class should not be allowed to harm those in the class.

For example, a work agreement between Diego and his employer may specify that Diego gets paid for the number of hours he works as a truck driver. Yet certain statutes limit the number of hours truck drivers may drive in a given time period. If Diego accidentally drives more than the allowable hours, he has technically violated a statute. However, this violation does not allow his employer to refuse to pay him for the extra hours. Rather, Diego may sue his employer to enforce the work agreement.

The second exception to the voiding of illegal agreements occurs when *justifiable ignorance of facts* leaves one party unaware of a provision of the agreement that would

CASE NUGGET

DETERMINING THE LEGALITY OF AN ARBITRATION CLAUSE

Buckeye Check Cashing, Inc. v. Cardegna et al.
United States Supreme Court
126 S. Ct. 1204, 163 L. Ed. 2d 1038 (2006)

The respondents, Cardegna et al., entered into a number of deferred-payment transactions with Buckeye Check Cashing. Each agreement they signed contained a provision requiring binding arbitration to resolve disputes arising out of the agreement. The respondents filed a class action suit against Buckeye in Florida state court, alleging that Buckeye charged usurious interest rates and that the agreement violated various Florida laws, rendering it illegal on its face. The trial court denied Buckeye's motion to compel arbitration, holding that a court rather than an arbitrator should resolve a claim that a contract is illegal and void *ab initio.* A state appellate court reversed, but its decision was in turn reversed by the Florida Supreme Court, which reasoned that enforcing an arbitration agreement in a contract challenged as unlawful would violate state public policy and contract law. The case was appealed to the U.S. Supreme Court to determine whether the courts or an arbitrator should determine the legality of a potentially illegal contract containing a binding arbitration clause.

The Court answered this question by relying on three established propositions. First, as a matter of substantive federal arbitration law, an arbitration provision is severable from the remainder of the contract. Second, unless the challenge is to the arbitration clause itself, the issue of the contract's validity is considered by the arbitrator in the first instance. Third, this arbitration law applies in state as well as federal courts. Applying these propositions to the case, the high court concluded that when an agreement as a whole, but not specifically its arbitration provisions, is challenged, the arbitration provisions are enforceable apart from the remainder of the contract. The challenge to the legality of the contract itself should therefore be considered by an arbitrator, not a court.

make it illegal. While ignorance of the law does not excuse illegal behavior, not knowing that the other party intended to fulfill the agreement through illegal means does function as an excuse.

When one party is relatively innocent, the court may give back any consideration that party gave or may require exchange for partial performance such that both parties can be returned to the positions they were in before they entered into the agreement. If one party is completely innocent of any illegality and has completed his or her portion of the contract, then—depending on the reason the contract is considered illegal and which state's laws are in question—the court might enforce the entire agreement.

A third exception to the general rule occurs when one of the parties withdraws from an illegal agreement. The key to any recovery is that the party must have withdrawn before any illegality occurred. The party may then recover value for whatever partial or full performance has been completed. However, a party involved in the illegal activity in any way cannot recover at all.

Severable Contracts. **Severable contracts,** also known as *divisible contracts,* contain multiple parts that can each be performed separately and for which separate consideration is offered. In essence, a severable contract is like numerous contracts in one. An **indivisible contract,** on the other hand, requires complete performance by both parties, even if it appears to contain multiple parts.

With respect to illegality, severable contracts have a huge advantage: If they have both legal and illegal portions, the court can void only the illegal sections and enforce the rest as long as they represent the main purpose of the original agreement. Indivisible contracts must be enforced or rejected in their entirety. If declaring parts of a contract void substantially alters it, the court is not likely to enforce the remaining portions. Courts ultimately want to facilitate business transactions and enforce the legal wishes of parties, and severable contracts enable them to do so.

Legal Principle: **If the court can sever the illegal part of a contract from the legal part, it will generally do so and enforce only the legal part; if the contract is indivisible, then it generally will be unenforceable.**

CASE OPENER WRAP-UP

Apple's Questionable Contract

The U.S. District Court for the Northern District of California denied Apple's motion to dismiss the lawsuit. The court stated that the complaint could not be dismissed because no case law was provided to prove that Apple's Terms of Service served as a contract for all subsequent transactions. Apple then constructed a settlement with all the plaintiffs in the class action lawsuit that had to be court-approved.

First, Apple would have to immediately send notices to 23 million customers with iTunes accounts, notifying the customers of parental controls that can block extra purchases. Second, customers in the lawsuit were to receive a $5 credit for use at the iTunes store. Customers whose children spent $30 or more would be entitled to a cash refund instead of credits. Finally, Apple would pay $1.3 million in attorney fees.

KEY TERMS

SUMMARY OF KEY TOPICS

Capacity

Natural persons over the age of majority are presumed to have the full legal capacity to enter into binding legal contracts.

A person has only limited capacity to enter into a legally binding contract, and therefore can enter into only voidable contracts, if the person is either:

- A minor.
- Suffering from a mental deficiency that prevents the person from understanding the nature and obligations of contracts.
- Intoxicated.

A person has no capacity to enter into a contract if the person either:

- Has been adjudicated insane.
- Has been adjudicated a habitual drunkard.
- Has had a legal guardian appointed to enter into contracts on his or her behalf.

Necessaries: Even if a party has the ability to disaffirm a contract, if the contract is for a necessary—something like food, clothing, or shelter—the party cannot completely disaffirm the contract; she will be held liable for the reasonable value of the necessary.

Legality

Contracts that do not have a legal object are not valid.

Contracts that lack a legal object because they violate a statute or violate public policy are not valid.

When a contract is partly legal and partly illegal, if the illegal part can be severed, then the legal part will still be enforced, but if the contract is indivisible, it will be void and not enforced.

POINT / COUNTERPOINT

Should the Age at Which Minors Have Full Capacity to Enter into Binding Contracts Be Lowered to 16?

YES	NO
Given the rights and responsibilities currently granted to 16-year-olds, lowering the age at which minors can enter into legally binding contracts seems logical. One of the most widely argued reasons given against lowering the age requirement pertains to a teenager's ability to fully understand a contract and comprehend the consequences associated with it. In response, proponents argue that society has already given children responsibilities and rights that are associated with long-term consequences; 16-year-olds are viewed, in the eyes of the law, as being able to consent to a sexual relationship. Along with this right comes the responsibility of understanding the potential for pregnancy and/or disease (which are *extremely* long-term consequences).	Under the law, teenagers are not viewed as adults until they have reached the age of majority. In nearly every state, the age of majority is at least 18. The age at which teenagers can enter into binding contracts should *not* be lower than the age of majority. At the age of 16, teenagers are still in the process of completing high school. They have not taken courses in financial management and have not been adequately introduced to contracts through life experiences. As such, these youths lack the ability to fully understand or comprehend the nature of or consequences associated with entering into contracts.

Perhaps as a result of their ability to consent to sexual relationships, 16-year-olds are often able to marry if the female is pregnant. Marriage is, by definition, a contract. These teenagers are already able, albeit in a limited fashion, to enter into binding contracts.

Furthermore, at the age of 16, a teenager can request a work permit and begin employment. As a result of this employment, the teenager is able to earn an income and make purchases. By maintaining the current age at which teenagers are seen as having the legal capacity to enter into a contract, society is, in effect, limiting the teenager's ability to make transactions he or she would otherwise be able to make. This limitation not only restricts teenagers' freedoms but also reduces commerce in this country. Society *should* lower the age requirement to 16.

Additionally, at the age of 16, nearly all teenagers are still residing within the home of a parent and/or guardian. Parents are held liable for many actions and decisions of their children. To cite but one potential example, if a child under the age of majority entered into a cell phone contract and was eventually unable to pay the related bills, it is possible that under parental liability law the parents will be held responsible for the funds owed. In short, society could prevent this undue burden from being placed on parents by keeping the age at which youths have the capacity to enter into contracts equal to, or greater than, the age of majority. Parents should have the ability to decide whether or not they wish to sign a contract on their child's behalf if it is potentially they who will ultimately be held responsible.

QUESTIONS & PROBLEMS

1. How does the concept of the age of majority differ in Great Britain from that in the United States?
2. Explain the obligations of a minor who chooses to disaffirm a contract.
3. Go back to the discussion of contracts that cannot be disaffirmed by minors, and explain the policy reasons that support each of the exceptions. Can you make an argument for any additional kinds of contracts that should not be subject to disaffirmance by minors?
4. If all you know about a man is that his neighbors think he is crazy, you do not know whether the contract he entered into was valid, voidable, or void. Why not?
5. What factors determine whether a covenant not to compete is legal or illegal?
6. What is the relationship between contracts in restraint of trade and unconscionable contracts?
7. Three salesmen worked for Sentient Jet, a small luxury airline charter service. They signed a noncompete agreement, promising to not go to work for a competing employer within a year after working for Sentient and also agreeing to not take any confidential information with them when they left the firm. When there was a change in the CEO of their firm, and talk of the company's possibly being bought out, the employees left the firm and went to work for Apollo Jets, a competitor, and allegedly took proprietary information with them that allowed them to solicit former Sentient clients. The plaintiff sought an injunction to ban the employees from working for a competitor for a year and also sought damages. The defendants argued that material changes in circumstances should have made the agreement not to compete unenforceable. How do you think the jury decided in this case? [*Sentient Jet v. MacKenzie,* Massachusetts Superior Court, January 2013 non-reported case. Discussed at http://www.hrwlawyers.com/pdfs/MLW-Non-Compete-Article-1-21-2013-(A121154).pdf.]
8. Paul Stewart and Ellen Chalk bought a wireless LAN PC card, manufactured by Sony, to connect wirelessly to the Internet through service provided by T-Mobile. Stewart and Chalk also signed a one-year service agreement with T-Mobile. The service agreement mandated arbitration and prohibited class action lawsuits. For approximately three weeks after the purchase of the card, Stewart and Chalk were able to insert it into their IBM ThinkPad laptop and connect to the Internet without any difficulty. They then did not attempt to use the card again for a few months, at which time they were unable to insert the card into their ThinkPad. They contacted T-Mobile technical support several times and received refurbished cards on three separate occasions. None of the refurbished cards fit into the ThinkPad. After Stewart and Chalk were unable to insert the third card, staff from T-Mobile technical support informed them that they would have to pursue the issue at the T-Mobile store where they purchased the original card. At the store, a Sony representative attempted to insert the card, but he failed as well. He then promised to contact them about how to solve the problem. They never heard back from him, despite multiple e-mail inquiries.

   Ultimately, Stewart and Chalk filed a class action lawsuit against T-Mobile and Sony. The complaint alleged that Sony and T-Mobile knew or should have known that the card "was not compatible and/or did not fit into the IBM ThinkPad laptop" computers and that Sony and T-Mobile allowed customers to purchase cards and enter into long-term service contracts from which consumers would receive no benefit without a compatible card. Sony and T-Mobile filed a motion to compel arbitration. Stewart and Chalk opposed the motion, contending that the arbitration clause was unconscionable and therefore unenforceable. The district court ruled in favor of Sony and T-Mobile. Stewart and Chalk appealed. Is the arbitration agreement unconscionable? If you were an attorney for Stewart and Chalk, would you argue that the arbitration clause was procedurally unconscionable, substantively unconscionable, or both? Why? [*Chalk v. T-Mobile, USA, Inc.*, 560 F.3d 1087 (2009).]

9. Washington State resident Patty Gandee entered into a debt adjustment contract with Freedom Enterprises. She subsequently sought to file a class action against Freedom for violations of the state debt adjusting act and the Consumer Protection Act. The company sought to compel arbitration based on a binding arbitration clause she had signed. The clause provided that any disputes under the contract were to be submitted to arbitration that would take place in Orange County, California, under American Arbitration Association rules, and the prevailing party would be entitled to reasonable legal fees and costs, including attorney fees. Both the trial court and the Washington Supreme Court refused to enforce the binding arbitration clause. Explain why they would not enforce the clause. [*Patty J. Gandee v. LDL Freedom Enterprises,* Case No. 87674-6 (Wash. Sup. Ct., Feb. 7, 2013) (available at http://lawyersusaonline.com/wp-files/pdfs-5/gandee-v-ldl-freedom-enterprises.pdf).]

10. The Finches hired Inspectech to perform a home inspection of property they were purchasing. The contract they signed included a clause that read:

> It is understood and agreed that the COMPANY [Inspectech] is not an insurer and that the inspection and report are not intended to be construed as a guarantee or warranty of the adequacy, performance or condition of any structure, item or system at the property address. The CLIENT [the Finches] hereby releases and exempts the COMPANY and its agents and employees of and from all liability and responsibility for the cost of repairing or replacing any unreported defect or deficiency and for any consequential damage, property damage or personal injury of any nature. In the event the COMPANY and/or its agents or employees are found liable due to breach of contract, breach of warranty, negligence, negligent misrepresentation, negligent hiring or any other theory of liability, then the liability of the COMPANY and its agents and employees shall be limited to a sum equal to the amount of the fee paid by the CLIENT for the inspection and report.

After the inspection, which reported no significant defects, the Finches purchased the house. Within one week of closing, the Finches discovered water damage; prior repairs to correct the water damage; and water infiltration in the basement of their new home, as well as structural problems affecting the house's foundation. The Finches alleged that these defects were not obviously visible because of the location of a workbench owned by the sellers. They sued to recover the $39,000 they had to spend to repair the water and structural damage.

On the basis of the contractual language, the circuit court awarded summary judgment to Inspectech, concluding that the release prohibited the Finches from asserting their claims against Inspectech for damages they claimed were occasioned by Inspectech's failure to identify and disclose various defects in their new home. The court concluded that the clause was unambiguous and conspicuously placed in the contract and that the Finches had specifically agreed to its terms and its inclusion in the parties' Inspection Agreement contract. On what grounds do you think the West Virginia Supreme Court overturned the granting of summary judgment to Inspectech? [*David Finch and Shirley Finch v. Inspectech, LLC,* Case No. 11-0278 (W. Va. Sup. Ct. App., May 24, 2012) (available at http://lawyersusaonline.com/wp-files/pdfs-4/finch-v-inspectech.pdf).]

Looking for more review materials?

The Online Learning Center at **www.mhhe.com/kubasek3e** contains this chapter's "Assignment on the Internet" and also a list of URLs for more information, entitled "On the Internet." Find both of them in the Student Center portion of the OLC, along with quizzes and other helpful materials.

CHAPTER

17 Legal Assent

LEARNING OBJECTIVES

After reading this chapter, you will be able to answer the following questions:

1 Why is legal assent important?
2 What are the elements of mistake?
3 What are the elements of misrepresentation?
4 What are the elements of undue influence?
5 What are the elements of duress?
6 What are the elements of unconscionability?

CASE OPENER

A Disagreement over an Agreement

In spring 1989, Michael Jordan and the Chicago Bulls were in Indianapolis, Indiana, to play against the Indiana Pacers. At the same time, Karla Knafel was singing with a band at a hotel in Indianapolis. After Knafel's performance, a National Basketball Association referee approached her and introduced her to Jordan via telephone. Knafel and Jordan began a long-distance telephone relationship that continued for several months.

In December 1989, Knafel traveled to Chicago to meet with Jordan, where the couple had unprotected sex for the first time. In November 1990, the couple had unprotected sex again while in Phoenix, Arizona. Shortly after this second meeting, Knafel learned that she was pregnant. Knafel was "convinced that she was carrying Jordan's baby" despite having had sex with other male partners. Later, during spring 1991, Knafel informed Jordan "she was pregnant with his child."

As a result of several conversations about the baby, Knafel alleged that the two had agreed that Jordan would pay her $5 million when he retired from professional basketball. In return, Knafel promised she would not file a paternity suit against him and would keep their relationship a secret.

In July 1991, the baby was born. Jordan paid some hospital bills and medical costs, and he paid Knafel $250,000 for "her mental pain and anguish arising from her relationship with him." Knafel continued to keep the relationship and paternity a secret.

After Jordan retired from professional basketball, a lawsuit arose between the parties in 2000. Jordan sought declaratory judgment and an injunction against Knafel, who had been approaching him for the $5 million. Knafel filed a counterclaim for Jordan's alleged breach of contract. The trial court dismissed all claims, but the appellate court remanded Knafel's claim for breach of contract. Although Jordan had originally denied the existence of the agreement, on remand he did not contest the existence of the alleged settlement agreement. Instead, Jordan argued that the alleged agreement was not enforceable because it either was fraudulently induced or was based on a mutual mistake of fact. In support of his argument, Jordan produced the affidavit of Dr. Storm, who, after DNA testing, concluded that Jordan was not the child's father.

In response to Jordan's argument, Knafel claimed that the paternity of the child was irrelevant to the enforceability of the alleged agreement. An obstetrician had told Knafel that the baby was conceived on November 19 or 20, 1990 (while she was in Phoenix with Jordan). As a result of this information, Knafel believed that the baby was Jordan's. Additionally, Knafel asserted that the paternity was irrelevant because Jordan entered into the agreement knowing that she had been having sex with other men.

The trial court ruled in favor of Jordan, finding that "as a result of Knafel's fraudulent misrepresentation to Jordan that he was the child's father or, alternatively, as a result of a mutual mistake of fact, the alleged settlement contract is voidable and is therefore unenforceable against Jordan." Knafel appealed.

1. Imagine you are the judge in this case. Do you think that both parties were able to legally assent to the agreement?
2. Under which ethical system, if any, should Knafel be able to recover the $5 million for breach of contract?

The Wrap-Up at the end of the chapter will answer these questions.

The Importance of Legal Assent

LO1
Why is legal assent important?

When two people talk in the hope that an exchange will take place between them, all kinds of things can go wrong. Yet global business needs dependability. Imagine what transactions would be like if "Yes" meant "Maybe"! Deals would be closed only to be reopened again and again. The costs of all purchases would soar. Businesses would be forced to charge extra to pay for all the extra time they had to spend to finally get to the point where "Yes" really meant "Yes."

To make business transactions smoother and more dependable, courts have developed rules about when an assent to do something is a **legal assent,** that is, a promise the courts will require the parties to obey.

The courts see some forms of assent as more genuine or real than others. It is important for businesspeople to know the differences among the various kinds of assent. Why do the differences matter? Jamal may think he has sold his tutoring services to Harrison. However, without legal assent the contract may be **voidable,** a circumstance that can cost a business large profits when the transaction is significant. A voidable contract can be **rescinded,** or canceled, permitting the person who canceled the contract to require the return of everything she gave the other party. She must herself return whatever she has received. An enormous waste of time and an unnecessary cost of doing business may be the result.

The major theme of this chapter is that *best-practice firms aim for legal assent in their contracts*. This chapter shows you how to achieve legal assent. It explains the major obstacles to legal assent: mistake, misrepresentation, undue influence, duress, and unconscionability. By knowing about these potential problems, you will be in a good position to avoid them.

Mistake

LO2

What are the elements of mistake?

When people agree to buy or sell, they do so with a particular understanding about the nature of the good or service they are about to exchange. However, one or both parties may think they consented to exchange a particular thing only to find out later that no meeting of the minds had occurred. People may misunderstand either some fact about the deal or the value of what is being exchanged. We focus on misunderstandings about facts, because they are the only issues that raise the potential of rescission (the rescinding of a contract) in U.S. courts. Mistaken beliefs about the subjective value of an item do not affect the validity of the contract.

In contract law a **mistake of fact** is an erroneous belief about the facts of the contract *at the time the contract is concluded*. Legal assent is absent when a mistake of fact occurs. Later in this chapter, when we discuss misrepresentation, our focus will be on incorrect beliefs about the facts of the contract caused by the other party's untrue statements. Mistakes in contract law do *not* result from these untrue statements.

Mistakes can be **unilateral,** the result of an error by *one* party about a material fact, that is, a fact that is important in the context of the particular contract. Or mistakes can be **mutual,** shared by both parties to the agreement. As we see next, this distinction is important in determining which contracts are voidable.

COMPARING THE LAW OF OTHER COUNTRIES

THE EUROPEAN VIEW ABOUT MISTAKES ABOUT VALUE

European courts take a different approach to mistakes about the *value of performance* of the contract. In general, they agree with the reluctance of U.S. courts to interfere with a contract just because the value of the item in question has changed since the agreement. The parties are assumed to have accepted the risk that the value might change after they made the contract. However, European courts permit rescission of the contract for a mistake of value when the mistake involves more than 50 percent of the value at the time of the contract.

UNILATERAL MISTAKE

Because courts are hesitant to interfere when one of the parties has a correct understanding of the material facts of the agreement, a unilateral mistake does not generally void a contract. For instance, a widow seeking to rescind her and her husband's election to have his retirement benefits paid out over *his* life was not permitted to receive survivor's pension benefits. The court held that representatives of the retirement system had provided sufficient information to the plaintiff and her husband before they elected that particular form of payout.[1] The Case Nugget on the next page provides another illustration of a failed attempt to argue that a unilateral mistake was present.

On rare occasions, however, rescission *is* permitted for unilateral mistakes. Because our economic well-being depends so heavily on reliable contracts, we want to be fully aware of the circumstances under which unilateral mistakes permit rescission. Any of the following conditions would permit a court to invalidate a contract on grounds of unilateral mistake:

1. One party made a mistake about a material fact, and the other party knew or had reason to know about the mistake.
2. The mistake was caused by a clerical error that was accidental and did not result from gross negligence.
3. The mistake was so serious that the contract is unconscionable, that is, so unreasonable that it is outrageous.

These situations are rare, but it is important to be aware of them because any rescission can be costly in terms of time and lost opportunities.

MUTUAL MISTAKE

When both parties are mistaken about a current or past material fact, either can choose to rescind the contract. Rescission is fair because any agreement was an illusion: Ambiguity prevented a true meeting of the minds.

The famous story of the ship *Peerless*[2] has taught generations of students the importance of being very clear in defining material facts in any contract. The parties in the case had agreed that the vessel *Peerless* would deliver the cotton they were exchanging. Unfortunately for them, there were two ships named *Peerless.* So when the deal was made, one party had one *Peerless* in mind while the other meant the second. The times the ships sailed were materially different, so the court rescinded the contract. *Warning:* Anticipate ambiguity in material facts, and clarify them in advance to save yourself headaches later.

[1] *Ricks v. Missouri Local Government Employees Retirement System,* 1999 WL 663217 (Mo. App. WD).

[2] *Raffles v. Wichelhaus,* 159 Eng. Rep. 375 (1864).

CASE NUGGET

A QUESTIONABLE "MISTAKE"

Mary W. Scott (Respondent-Appellant) v. Mid-Carolina Homes, Inc. (Appellant-Respondent)
Court of Appeals of South Carolina
293 S.C. 191 (1987)

Mary Scott signed a contract to purchase a repossessed 1984 mobile home from Mid-Carolina Homes, Inc., for $5,644 to be paid in full before delivery. Scott gave the salesperson a check for $2,913.71, and agreed to pay the balance before the end of the month. Within the next week, the salesman called Scott and told her that according to the standards of the South Carolina Manufactured Housing Board he could not sell her the home because it had a bent frame. Scott offered to buy it as is and sign a waiver, but the salesman said that would not be legal. A few weeks later, Mid-Carolina sold the mobile home to another couple for $9,220. Scott sued and was awarded $3,600 actual damages, $6,400 punitive damages for breach of contract accompanied by a fraudulent act, and $3,000 actual damages for violation of a state consumer protection law. The appeals court upheld the award.

On appeal, Mid-Carolina argued that it was entitled to rescind the contract because the salesperson was acting under a mistake of fact when he gave Scott the sales price. In upholding the award, the state supreme court explained that a contract may be rescinded for unilateral mistake only when the mistake has been induced by fraud, deceit, misrepresentation, concealment, or imposition of the party opposed to the rescission, without negligence on the part of the party claiming rescission, or when the mistake is accompanied by very strong and extraordinary circumstances that would make it a great wrong to enforce the agreement. Mid-Carolina had not demonstrated the presence of any of these. The salesperson was in the superior bargaining position to know the price, and the buyer's reliance on a salesperson's representation of the price was reasonable.

For a mutual mistake to interfere with legal consent, all the following must be present:

1. A basic assumption about the subject matter of the contract.
2. A material effect on the agreement.
3. An adverse effect on a party who did not agree to bear the risk of mistake at the time of the agreement.

Courts will not void contracts for reason of mutual mistake if even one of these conditions is missing. (See Exhibit 17-1.) Let's see why they matter.

To rise to the level of a basic assumption, a mistake must be about the existence, quality, or quantity of the items to be exchanged. To be material, condition 2, the mistake must affect the essence of the agreement. A fact is material when it provides a basis for a person's agreeing to enter into the contract. Neither party can void the contract simply by falsely claiming that the item to be exchanged is not the one he intended.

The third condition protects those who bargain with someone who agreed, at the time of the agreement, to bear the risk of mistake but then later wishes to avoid that risk when the contract does not work out as well as he or she had planned. This situation might arise, for instance, if the adversely affected party had agreed in the contract to accept items "as is" but later felt they were not worth the price paid. In the opening scenario, had Jordan agreed to pay Knafel the $5 million regardless of the outcome of any future paternity tests, the

Exhibit 17-1
Enforceability of a Mutual Mistake

Before a contract can be voided for a mutual mistake, you must answer each of the following questions with a yes:

1. Is the mistake about a basic assumption that affects the subject matter of the contract?
2. Does the mistake have a material effect on the agreement?
3. Would enforcement of the contract have an adverse effect on the party who did not agree to bear the risk of mistake at the time of the agreement?

outcome of the case would have been very different. Instead, Jordan had allegedly agreed to pay Knafel the money on the basis of misinformation that the child was definitely his. Upon learning that the child was not his, Jordan wanted to have the contract rescinded on the basis, partly, of the mutual mistake made between himself and Knafel. Case 17-1 provides an illustration of an unsuccessful attempt to avoid a contract on the basis of mutual mistake.

CASE 17-1 SIMKIN v. BLANK
COURT OF APPEALS OF NEW YORK
19 N.Y.3D 46 (2012)

When Steven Simkin and Laura Blank divorced in 2006, they split their $13.5 million in assets. Most of Simkin's $5.4 million share of the settlement was invested in Bernie Madoff's Ponzi scheme, whereas Blank received a cash settlement. Then, in 2008, Simkin thought the terms of the divorce contract should be renegotiated because he lost almost all of his divorce proceeds when it came to light that his investment in Madoff's business turned out to be a fraud and Madoff's business turned out to be a huge Ponzi scheme. Simkin argued that both he and his ex-wife had shared in the mistake of investing funds into Madoff's project, yet only Simkin received the invested funds in the divorce settlement and Blank received cash. Simkin also argued that because his funds never existed as an "investment" as they had already vanished in the Ponzi scheme, he never really received an equal share of their existing assets. Thus, he asked Ms. Blank if the two could renegotiate the contract. When she refused, he sued. A lower court granted Simkin the right to sue, but the case moved on to the Court of Appeals of New York.

JUDGE GRAFFEO: Marital settlement agreements are judicially favored and are not to be easily set aside. Nevertheless, in the proper case, an agreement may be subject to rescission or reformation based on a mutual mistake by the parties. Similarly, a release of claims may be avoided due to mutual mistake. Based on these contract principles, the parties here agree that this appeal turns on whether husband's amended complaint states a claim for relief under a theory of mutual mistake.

We have explained that the mutual mistake must exist at the time the contract is entered into and must be substantial. Put differently, the mistake must be "so material that . . . it goes to the foundation of the agreement" ["The parties must have been mistaken as to a basic assumption of the contract. . . . Basic assumption means the mistake must vitally affect the basis upon which the parties contract"]. Court-ordered relief is therefore reserved only for "exceptional situations." The premise underlying the doctrine of mutual mistake is that "the agreement as expressed, in some material respect, does not represent the meeting of the minds of the parties."

Although we have not addressed mutual mistake claims in the context of marital settlement agreements, the parties cite a number of Appellate Division cases that have analyzed this issue. Husband relies on True v True . . . where the settlement agreement provided that the husband's stock awards from his employer would be "divided 50-50 in kind" and recited that 3,655 shares were available for division between the parties. After the wife redeemed her half of the shares, the husband learned that only 150 shares remained and brought an action to reform the agreement, arguing that the parties mistakenly specified the gross number of shares (3,655) rather than the net number that was actually available for distribution. The Second Department agreed and reformed the agreement to effectuate the parties' intent to divide the shares equally, holding that the husband had established "that the parties' use of 3,655 gross shares was a mutual mistake because it undermined their intent to divide the net shares available for division, 50-50 in kind."

Other cases relied on by husband involve marital settlement agreements that were set aside or reformed because a mutual mistake rendered a portion of the agreement impossible to perform. In Banker v Banker . . . the Third Department reformed a provision of a marital settlement that required the subdivision of a parcel of real property because the parties were unaware of a restrictive covenant against further subdivision.

Applying these legal principles, we are of the view that the amended complaint fails to adequately state a cause of action based on mutual mistake. As an initial matter, husband's claim that the alleged mutual mistake undermined the foundation of the settlement agreement, a precondition to relief under our precedents, is belied by the terms of the agreement itself. Unlike the settlement agreement in True that expressly incorporated a "50-50" division of a stated number of stock shares, the settlement agreement here, on its face, does not mention the Madoff account, much less evince an intent to divide the account in equal or other proportionate shares. To the contrary, the agreement provides that the $6,250,000 payment to wife was "in satisfaction of [her] support and marital property rights," along with her release of various claims and inheritance rights. Despite the fact that the agreement permitted husband to retain title to his "bank, brokerage and similar financial accounts" and

[continued]

enumerated two such accounts, his alleged $5.4 million Madoff investment account is neither identified nor valued. Given the extensive and carefully negotiated nature of the settlement agreement, we do not believe that this presents one of those "exceptional situations" warranting reformation or rescission of a divorce settlement after all marital assets have been distributed.

Even putting the language of the agreement aside, the core allegation underpinning husband's mutual mistake claim—that the Madoff account was "nonexistent" when the parties executed their settlement agreement in June 2006—does not amount to a "material" mistake of fact as required by our case law. The premise of husband's argument is that the parties mistakenly believed that they had an investment account with Bernard Madoff when, in fact, no account ever existed. In husband's view, this case is no different from one in which parties are under a misimpression that they own a piece of real or personal property but later discover that they never obtained rightful ownership, such that a distribution would not have been possible at the time of the agreement. But that analogy is not apt here. Husband does not dispute that, until the Ponzi scheme began to unravel in late 2008—more than two years after the property division was completed—it would have been possible for him to redeem all or part of the investment. In fact, the amended complaint contains an admission that husband was able to withdraw funds (the amount is undisclosed) from the account in 2006 to partially pay his distributive payment to wife. Given that the mutual mistake must have existed at the time the agreement was executed in 2006, the fact that husband could no longer withdraw funds years later is not determinative.

REVERSED in favor of defendant Blank.

CRITICAL THINKING

When Simkin claimed that the contract terms should be altered on the basis of a "mutual mistake" when the two entered into the divorce contract, he referenced their "mistake" being that the settlement terms allocated to him were nonexistent due to the Ponzi scheme. Should Simkin have defined his use of "nonexistent" according to a time frame? The funds were nonexistent two years after the divorce settlement, but the funds were existent in 2006 during the divorce.

ETHICAL DECISION MAKING

Could a decision in favor of Simkin's altering the terms of the marriage contract create copycat suits? Courts typically leave divorce terms intact except in rare circumstances, but many couples could attempt to claim that an outside force affected their divorce settlement assets.

Misrepresentation

L03 What are the elements of misrepresentation?

Misrepresentations are similar to mistakes in that at least one of the parties is in error about a fact material to the agreement. But a **misrepresentation** is an untruthful assertion by one of the parties about that material fact; it prevents the parties from having the mental agreement necessary for a legal contract. They only *appeared* to agree, so their contract lacked legal assent.

The courts insist on a meeting of the minds for a valid contract. Thus, they might rescind a contract even though the person making the false assertion was entirely innocent of any intentional deception.

The topic of misrepresentation should be particularly important to future business professionals, especially those interested in marketing or advertising careers, as it may one day be your job to develop promotional materials for a company's products. Marketing and advertising professionals must exercise special care when developing product labels, packaging, and advertisements because consumers often depend on the information provided by a company when deciding whether to purchase a product. Thus, if the marketing materials created by a company are seen as being inaccurate or appear to misrepresent what a product truly is or what benefits the product offers, consumers may attempt to take legal action.

For example, in 1991 a Michigan man, Richard Overton, filed suit against Anheuser-Busch, claiming that the company's commercials made untrue statements and misrepresentations that caused him to continually buy and consume the company's beer. More specifically, Overton alleged that Anheuser-Busch was liable for creating advertisements that falsely suggested drinking its beer would result in fantasies coming to life (tropical settings, beautiful women, and happiness). Overton sought to recover $10,000 in damages from Anheuser-Busch for causing him physical and mental injury as well as emotional distress and financial loss. A circuit court granted summary judgment in favor of the defendant. Richard Overton appealed, and the Michigan Court of Appeals affirmed the lower court's ruling.[3] While the company won the case, it still had the expense of defending its actions. It is always better to try to avoid being sued in the first place.

INNOCENT MISREPRESENTATION

An **innocent misrepresentation** results from a false statement about a fact material to an agreement that the person making it believed to be true. The person had no knowledge of the claim's falsity. We say he or she lacked **scienter** (from the Latin root of the word meaning "knowledge").

Innocent misrepresentations permit the misled party to rescind the contract. However, because the other party had no intent to mislead, the aggrieved party cannot sue for damages. The reasoning in these cases resembles the arguments in a mutual mistake case, as you might expect.

BUT WHAT IF . . .

WHAT IF THE FACTS OF THE CASE OPENER WERE DIFFERENT?

Let's say that, in the Case Opener, Knafel was incorrectly told by her doctor that the baby was Jordan's. She then told Jordan that she indeed was carrying his baby. Thus, Jordan signed the contract and paid Knafel a large sum of money. Later, the two found out the baby was not Jordan's. What kind of misrepresentation occurred? Can Jordan sue for damages?

NEGLIGENT MISREPRESENTATION

In some contract negotiations, one party makes a statement of material fact that he thinks is true. If he could have known the truth by using reasonable care to discover or reveal it, his statement is a **negligent misrepresentation.**

Even though he had no intent to deceive, in contract law the party is treated as if he did. If this standard seems unfair to you, remember that the courts find negligent misrepresentation only when the party making the false statement should have known the truth using the skills and competence required of a person in his position or profession. The impact of negligent misrepresentation is identical to that of fraudulent misrepresentation, discussed next.

FRAUDULENT MISREPRESENTATION

Any fraud on the part of a party to a contract provides a basis for rescission. The parties cannot be said to have assented when one of the parties was tricked into the "agreement"

[3] 205 Mich. App. 259, 517 N.W.2d 308 (case summary accessed on Lexis Nexis May 25, 2009).

by a fraudulent misrepresentation. Thus, the agreement was not voluntary and can be rescinded on the ground that there was no meeting of the minds.

Even in countries trying to encourage joint ventures and global commercial activity, such as the People's Republic of China, fraudulent claims can end the country's hospitality to agreements with outsiders.[4] In China, accusations of outsiders' fraudulent misrepresentation have resulted in heavy fines and even refusals to allow the fraudulent party to enter into any more agreements with Chinese firms. In most, if not all, cultures, little judicial sympathy exists for those who consciously mislead others in commercial activities.

A **fraudulent misrepresentation** is a consciously false representation of a material fact intended to mislead the other party. It is also referred to as **intentional misrepresentation.** Here scienter is clear: The party making the misrepresentation either knows or believes that the factual claim is false or knows there is no basis for it.

To understand the requirements for a finding of fraudulent misrepresentation, start with the two elements from the definition:

1. *A false statement about a past or existing fact that is material to the contract.*
2. *Intent to deceive,* which can be inferred from the particular circumstances.

Then add a third necessary element:

3. *Justifiable reliance on the false statement by the innocent party to the agreement:* Justifiable reliance is generally present unless the injured party knew, or should have known by the extravagance of the claim, that the false statement was indeed false. For example, a homeowner could not justifiably rely on a claim by a gardener that if she will pay him to apply a special fertilizer to her trees once a week, the trees would never die.

Finally, if damages are sought, the defrauded party must have been injured by the misrepresentation.

In the opening scenario, Jordan claimed that he had been the victim of a fraudulent misrepresentation made by Knafel. To meet the three requirements, Jordan argued that Knafel told him that he was definitely the child's father despite her knowledge that she had been having sexual relationships with other men during the same time period. According to Jordan, Knafel had reason to believe that her representation could be false and still made it with certainty in an effort to deceive him. Finally, it was based on the assertion that he was the father that Jordan allegedly agreed to pay Knafel $5 million. Hence, according to Jordan, he had proved that the statement qualified as a fraudulent misrepresentation. Does Knafel's representation that Jordan was the child's father amount to a fraudulent misrepresentation?

Each of the three aforementioned elements can become a source of debate in any attempt to rescind a contract on grounds of fraudulent misrepresentation. Thus, it is your responsibility as a person who will be involved with dozens of contracts in your business activities to know these elements. A rescinded contract is a time-consuming and expensive business opportunity that has gone wrong. And don't forget that you can collect damages only from parties you can locate.

Before we go into greater detail about the elements of fraudulent misrepresentation, please consider Case 17-2. Follow the court's reasoning as it works through the elements of the attempt to rescind a contract.

[4] Charles D. Paglee, "Contracts and Agreements in the People's Republic of China," www.qis.net/chinalaw/explan1.htm, updated March 6, 1998.

CASE 17-2 GARY W. CRUSE AND VENITA R. CRUSE v. COLDWELL BANKER/ GRABEN REAL ESTATE, INC.
SUPREME COURT OF ALABAMA
667 SO. 2D 714 (1995)

Mr. and Mrs. Cruse sued Mr. and Mrs. Harris, Coldwell Banker, and Graben Real Estate, Inc., alleging defective workmanship in the construction of a house they had bought from the Harrises and fraudulent misrepresentation and/or suppressed material facts about the condition of the house.

When the Cruses began looking for a home, they contacted Graben Real Estate, and a Graben agent took them to see the Harrises' house. Randy Harris, a building contractor, had built the house for sale, and he and his wife were occupying it at that time. Graben listed the house as "new" in its advertisements, and the agent told the Cruses it was new. She also told them it was comparable to, or even better than, other houses in the neighborhood, that it was a good buy, and that if they purchased it they could look forward to years of convenient, trouble-free living.

The Cruses signed a contract on November 11, 1992, to purchase the house from the Harrises. When they told the agent they wanted to hire an independent contractor to assess its condition, she told them it was not really necessary to do so because Randy Harris was a contractor and the house was well-built.

The Cruses signed an "Acceptance Inspection Contract," which stated that they had inspected the property or waived the right to do so, accepted it in "as-is" condition, and based their decision to purchase on their own inspection and not on any representations by the broker.

Plaintiffs took possession of the residence in mid-December 1992 and soon began noticing many defects in the structure and electrical wiring. They contacted Graben Real Estate, which sent an agent to remedy the problems. The defects continued and multiplied, so the Cruses sued. At the trial, defendants moved for summary judgment, which was granted. Plaintiffs appealed.

JUSTICE BUTTS: To establish fraudulent misrepresentations, the Cruses are required to show that Graben Real Estate made a false representation concerning a material fact and that they relied upon that representation, to their detriment. The Cruses contend that Graben Real Estate represented to them that the house was new; that, in reliance on that representation, they decided not to hire a contractor to inspect the house and discover its defects; and that reliance resulted in damage to them.

The unequivocal term "new," when applied to real estate, is not merely descriptive. It is a definite legal term that carries with it the implied warranty of habitability and prevents the realtor from invoking the protection of the doctrine of caveat emptor. Graben Real Estate marketed the house as "new," both in print and in direct response to the Cruses' queries. In so doing, Graben Real Estate made statements that went beyond the patter of sales talk and became representations of material fact. Moreover, Gary Cruse testified . . . that he relied upon this representation in failing to hire a contractor to inspect the house before he bought it.

Graben Real Estate argues that even if it did misrepresent the newness of the house, the Cruses could not have justifiably believed the misrepresentation and relied upon it to the point that they would not closely inspect the house before buying it. Graben Real Estate relies heavily on the fact that the Cruses knew that the house was being occupied by the Harrises at the time of the sale, and concludes that this alone should have proved to the Cruses that the house was not actually new. . . . We do not agree that the mere knowledge of the Harrises' prior occupancy so wholly contradicted the printed and spoken representations of Graben Real Estate that the Cruses could not, as a matter of law, have justifiably relied upon them.

Graben Real Estate also argues that, regardless of whether the house was new or was used, the Cruses cannot recover because they signed an "as-is" agreement at the time of the sale, thereby, Graben Real Estate says, accepting the condition of the house without a prior inspection. Graben Real Estate relies on Hope v. Brannan, wherein this Court held that buyers of a 58-year-old house who signed a statement accepting the house "as-is," without independently inspecting it for defects, could not maintain an action for fraud arising from the seller's statements concerning the condition of the house.

Graben Real Estate's reliance on Hope is misplaced; in Hope, the house was not new, nor was it represented to be new. A buyer's failure to inspect the premises of a 58-year-old house before signing an "as-is" agreement is hardly the equivalent of the Cruses' failure to inspect the premises of a house that their realtor had represented to be new.

The evidence establishes that Graben Real Estate misrepresented a material fact and creates a jury question as to whether the Cruses could have justifiably relied upon this misrepresentation in deciding not to closely inspect the house before buying it. The fact that the Cruses knew the house was occupied by a third party before they bought it, along with the fact that they signed an "as-is" agreement, separate from the purchase contract, for a house they claim to have regarded as new, are elements for the jury to consider.

REVERSED and REMANDED.

[continued]

CRITICAL THINKING

Several key points in the reasoning of this decision rely on personal testimony. On the basis of your life experience and any knowledge you may have accumulated through your educational career, how reliable do you think witness testimony is as a form of evidence in legal disputes? What are some of the ways that this testimonial evidence might be flawed? What are its particular strengths? In this case, do you think the testimonies are valid? Why or why not?

ETHICAL DECISION MAKING

What general values might the court be interested in protecting in this ruling? How are they similar to values upheld by other cases in this chapter? How are they different? What opposing values are less important in these rulings?

The elements of fraudulent misrepresentation become more complicated in the context of actual disagreements. Let's revisit them for more insight.

False Assertion of Fact. For fraudulent misrepresentation to be the basis for a contract rescission, the statement of fact need not be an actual assertion. It can also be an act of concealment or nondisclosure. **Concealment** is the *active* hiding of the truth about a material fact, for example, removing 20,000 miles from the odometer on your car before selling it. **Nondisclosure** is a failure to provide pertinent information about the projected contract. The courts have until recently been hesitant to use nondisclosure as a basis for rescinding a contract because it is a passive form of misleading conduct. Under ordinary situations associated with a legal bargain, it is not the obligation of one party to bring up any and all facts he or she might possess. Each individual is, to a large extent, treated as a responsible decision maker.

However, courts will now find nondisclosure as having the same legal effect as an actual false assertion under certain conditions:

1. *A relationship of trust exists between the parties to the contract.* In this situation the relationship provides a reasonable basis for one person's expectation that the other would never act to defraud him or her.
2. *There is failure to correct assertions of fact that are no longer true.* Caroline's failure to inform Vito of the recent outbreak of rust on her "rust-free" car that Vito agreed to purchase next month is nondisclosure.
3. *A statute requires the disclosure,* such as mandatory disclosures under residential real estate sales laws.
4. *The nondisclosure involves a dangerous defect,* such as bad brakes in a car that is being sold.

Nondisclosure is especially likely to provide the basis for rescission when one party has information about a basic assumption of the deal that is unavailable to the other party. Sellers thus have a special duty to disclose because they know more about the structural makeup of the item being purchased.

BUT WHAT IF . . .

WHAT IF THE FACTS OF THE CASE OPENER WERE DIFFERENT?

Let's say that, in the Case Opener, Knafel had Jordan sign a contract that stipulated he must make monthly payments to her for the baby they both believed was genetically theirs together. Then, after signing, Knafel discovered the baby was not in fact Jordan's but did not relay the information to him. What kind of misrepresentation occurred here?

E-COMMERCE AND THE LAW

FRAUDULENT MISREPRESENTATION IN SOCIAL MEDIA

Online social media create a prime opportunity for individuals to create false identities. In some cases, these false identities are then used to communicate with unsuspecting individuals, often causing the real individuals who communicate with the misrepresented identities to experience financial or emotional harm. A tragic example of this is the case of *United States v. Lori Drew,* in which Drew created the false identity of a boy on the networking site MySpace. Megan Meier, a young girl, was lured by Drew and Drew's daughter to strike up a relationship with the false identity. When the "boy" broke up with Meier, Meier unfortunately committed suicide. The prosecution of Drew was unsuccessful. A major issue with the prosecution was that there was no federal statute against cyberbullying, and the judge did not feel comfortable relying on a breach-of-contract premise that would make this case of fraudulent misrepresentation equivalent to a case of computer hacking. As the likelihood of fraudulently misrepresenting an individual increases, misrepresentation must be addressed in such a way that all possible aspects in which fraudulent misrepresentation could occur are covered by statutes.

Source: www.wired.com/threatlevel/2009/07/drew_court/.

Intent to Deceive. *Scienter* is present when the party making the fraudulent assertion believed it was false or had no regard for whether it was true or false. *Intent to deceive* occurs when the party making the false statement claims to have or implies having personal knowledge of its accuracy. Any resulting assent is not legal because the injured party was not allowed to join the mind of the deceiving party. The party with scienter or intent to deceive wanted the contract to be fulfilled on the basis of a falsehood.

Justifiable Reliance on the False Assertion. What responsibilities does the injured party have in a case of false assertion? As we've said, the injured party has no justifiable claim of fraud after relying on assertions whose falsity should have been obvious. Anyone who pays for a house in reliance on the claim that it was "built before the founding of our country" cannot later rescind the contract on grounds of fraudulent misrepresentation.

Nor can parties successfully claim they justifiably relied on a false assertion when its falsity would have been clear to anyone who inspected the item. However, the duty to inspect is declining in modern contract law, and courts are giving increasing responsibility to the person who made the erroneous assertion.

As you might infer from the foregoing discussion, the process of determining whether intentional misrepresentation has occurred can be an extremely difficult task. This process can become even more complex when the defendant believes that the other party was never misled in the first place. Such was the case when several individuals involved in the movie *Borat* filed suit against Sacha Baron Cohen and Twentieth Century Fox for fraudulent and negligent misrepresentation as well as other various claims. The plaintiffs in the case were lawyers who represented the locals of the Romanian village of Glod, where the opening scenes of the movie were filmed. In their suit, the villagers alleged that Cohen and Twentieth Century Fox convinced them that they were taking part in a documentary film about poverty in Romania, not a blockbuster movie set in Kazakhstan. Further, the lawsuit asserted that Cohen and Twentieth Century Fox "used their superior educational background, stature, influence and economic position" to exploit the villagers and that the company also encouraged villagers to sign documents that they did not understand and that had not been fully explained.

Twentieth Century Fox defended its film and claimed that the villagers of Glod knew they were participating in a movie and not a documentary. The company further defended its position by stating that the villagers were paid more than the average going wage for movie extras. Eventually, the lawsuit was thrown out by a U.S district court judge who stated that the allegations against Sacha Baron Cohen and Twentieth Century Fox needed to be more specific. The lawyers of the Glod villagers said that they intended to file a new suit in the future.[5]

[5] http://news.bbc.co.uk/2/hi/europe/7686885.stm; and http://74.125.113.132/search?q=cache:jQ0M5aR16wUJ:www.courthouse-news.com/onpoint/borat_NY.pdf+Twentieth+century+fox+v+michael+witti+and+ed+fagan&cd=1&hl=en&ct=clnk&gl=us.

COMPARING THE LAW OF OTHER COUNTRIES

CONSUMER CONTRACTS LAW IN JAPAN

In 1997, after studying the application of civil law in the country, the Japanese Social Policy Council, an advisory body to the prime minister, recognized that the consumer environment was growing more diversified and that a significant gap existed between consumers and businesses in their access to information and knowledge and their negotiating power. Because it cannot honestly be said that consumers and businesses are equal, as contracting parties are presumed to be under the country's Civil Code, the council developed a special Consumer Contracts Law. This legislation is considered to place consumers and businesses on a more equal footing in transactions.

Under the Consumer Contracts Law, a consumer may cancel the contract whenever a business (1) fails to provide information about the contents of the contract, (2) fails to provide information necessary for the consumer to decide to enter into the contract, or (3) makes misrepresentations. In many such cases, the consumer would not have been entitled to relief under the Civil Code because of its strict requirements for the application of fraud.

To see how certain aspects of marketing relate to misrepresentation, please see the **Connecting to the Core** activity on the text website at www.mhhe.com/kubasek3e.

Before we conclude this section about misrepresentation, consider what would have happened if Karla Knafel, in the opening scenario, had told Jordan there was a strong probability that the child was his. Would Jordan have been able to claim that their contract lacked assent because of Knafel's misrepresentation?

Legal Principle: The effect of both a negligent misrepresentation and a fraudulent misrepresentation is that the victim can either rescind the contract or keep the contract and sue for damages, whereas if the mistake is innocent, the victim can seek only rescission.

Undue Influence

L04

What are the elements of undue influence?

When legal assent is present, the courts assume both parties have made their own choices based on complete freedom to accept or reject the terms of the bargain. However, many factors can work to make our choices anything but free. **Undue influence** refers to those special relationships in which one person takes advantage of a dominant position in a relationship to unfairly persuade the other and interfere with that person's ability to make his or her own decision. When people bargain with their attorney, doctor, guardian, relative, or anyone else in a relationship that includes a high degree of trust, they are susceptible to being persuaded by unusual pressures unique to that relationship. Consequently, the assent that results may not be legal consent. The courts may see the undue influence of the relationship as interfering with the free choice required for an enforceable contract. Whatever contracts result from undue influence are voidable.

Are all contracts in which undue influence might arise likely to be rescinded? Not necessarily. The courts look to the mental condition of the person relying on the guidance of the dominant person. Courts look to the extent to which the dominant person used the persuasive powers of his or her dominance to secure assent.

Factors that enter into the finding of undue influence are the following:

1. Was the dominant party rushing the other party to consent?
2. Did the dominant party gain undue enrichment from the agreement?
3. Was the nondominant party isolated from other advisers at the time of the agreement?
4. Is the contract unreasonable because it overwhelmingly benefits the dominant party?

The more of these factors present, the more likely a court is to rescind the contract on grounds of undue influence. The Case Nugget on the next page provides an illustration of undue influence.

CASE NUGGET

A CASE OF UNDUE INFLUENCE

Evan Rothberg v. Walt Disney Pictures
1999 U.S. App. 1472

Robert Jahn was a senior executive at Walt Disney Pictures until he died of complications from AIDS. Within days before his death, a Disney official visited him at the hospital and convinced him to sign a release that waived his rights to approximately $2 million in employee benefits, including life insurance, stock options, bonuses, and deferred compensation. After his death, his estate sued to recover the benefits waived in the release. Disney received a motion for summary judgment, and the plaintiff appealed. In reversing the motion for summary judgment, the court ruled that the question of whether the release had been procured by undue influence was a question for a jury. The court pointed out that undue influence requires (1) undue susceptibility on the part of the weaker party and (2) application of excessive pressure by the stronger party. In this case, the first fact was self-evident. The defendant was in the hospital and was fearful that Disney would expose information that would destroy his reputation. Regarding the second element, however, the court noted that in most undue-influence cases, and this case was no exception, direct evidence is rarely obtainable and thus the jury must decide the issue on the basis of inferences drawn from all the facts and circumstances. Thus, the court said that summary judgment was improper.

Legal Principle: **The essential element of undue influence is the existence of a dominant-subservient relationship, so if you are going to enter into a contract with someone with whom you have such a relationship, to ensure that the agreement will be enforced in the future, make sure that the person in the subservient position has independent advice before entering into the contract.**

BUT WHAT IF . . .

WHAT IF THE FACTS OF THE CASE OPENER WERE DIFFERENT?

Let's say that, in the Case Opener, Jordan was married at the time of his affair with Knafel and he did not want his wife or the public to know about the affair or the baby. Furthermore, let's say that Knafel threatened to make the information public (among other information about Jordan) if he did not sign her contract. Would such a scenario constitute undue influence?

Duress

Duress is a much more visible and active interference with free will than is undue influence. Duress occurs when one party is forced into the agreement by the wrongful act of another.

L05 What are the elements of duress?

The wrongful act may come in various forms. Any of the following would trigger a successful request for rescission on grounds of duress:

- One party threatens physical harm or extortion to gain consent to a contract.
- One party threatens to file a criminal lawsuit unless consent is given to the terms of the contract. (Threats to bring civil cases against a party to a lawsuit do not constitute duress unless the suit is frivolous.)
- One party threatens the other's economic interests (this is known as *economic duress*). For instance, a person refuses to perform according to a contract unless the other person either signs another contract with the one making the threat or pays that person a higher price than specified in the original agreement.

COMPARING THE LAW OF OTHER COUNTRIES

DURESS IN AUSTRALIA

Australia recognizes a special category called *duress of goods,* which occurs whenever one party makes an illegitimate threat to hold goods unless another party makes payment or enters into an agreement. Note that this is different from a situation in which someone legitimately holds goods when money is owed on them or the goods have been used as security for a loan.

Australia also recognizes economic duress, which is the unacceptable use of economic power to leave someone with no practical alternative but to submit to the accompanying demand.

To prove economic duress, a plaintiff must establish that (1) pressure was used to procure his or her assent to an agreement or to the payment of money, (2) the pressure was illegitimate in the circumstance, (3) the pressure in fact contributed to the person's assenting to the transaction, and (4) the person's assent to the transaction was reasonable in the circumstances.

Just as with economic duress in the United States, it is often unclear when pressure is illegitimate. A threat to do something unlawful is almost always undue pressure. A threat to use the civil legal process is usually considered lawful, unless the contemplated legal action would clearly be an abuse of process. "Driving a hard bargain" or refusing to do any more business with someone in the future is generally not regarded as economic duress.

The injured party makes the case for duress by demonstrating that the threat left no reasonable alternatives and that the free will necessary for legal consent was removed by the specifics of the threat.

Legal Principle: **When one party is forced to enter into a contract by the wrongful threat of another, the contract is voidable by the innocent party due to duress.**

BUT WHAT IF . . .

In 2009, a humane society officer named William Sandstrom confiscated Miles Thomas's dog due to certain violations of the state's animal cruelty laws. Thomas signed a release form for the humane society to take ownership of the dog. Later, Thomas claimed the release form was unenforceable because he was under duress when he signed it. Specifically, he claimed he was under duress at the time because he was sad about his dog. Does Thomas's account of his signing the release form actually fulfill the requirements of duress? Is the release form unenforceable?

Unconscionability

LO6

What are the elements of unconscionability?

A final way to question the appropriateness of consent arises when one of the parties has so much more bargaining power than the other that he or she dictates the terms of the agreement. Such an agreement can be rescinded on grounds of **unconscionability** (as discussed in Chapter 4). The disproportionate amount of power possessed by one party to the contract has made a mockery of the idea of free will, a necessity for legal consent. The resulting contract is called an **adhesion contract.**

Although unconscionability has traditionally been limited to the sale of goods under the Uniform Commercial Code, many courts have not followed that tradition. When they see contracts written by one party and presented to the other with the threat to "take it or leave it," they sometimes extend the idea of unconscionability beyond the sale of goods.

Follow the judge's reasoning in Case 17-3 to review the type of reasoning that makes up a claim for unconscionability.

CASE 17-3 ORVILLE ARNOLD AND MAXINE ARNOLD, PLAINTIFFS v. UNITED COMPANIES LENDING CORPORATION, A CORPORATION, AND MICHAEL T. SEARLS, AN INDIVIDUAL, DEFENDANTS

SUPREME COURT OF APPEALS OF WEST VIRGINIA

1998 WL 8651015

On September 17, 1996, Michael Searls came to the residence of Orville and Maxine Arnold, an elderly couple, and offered to arrange a loan for them, acting as a loan broker. He procured a loan for them. From the loan proceeds, a mortgage broker fee of $940.00 was paid to Searls and/or Accent Financial Services, with which Searls was affiliated.

At the loan closing, United Lending had the benefit of legal counsel, while the Arnolds apparently did not. During the course of the transaction, the Arnolds were presented with more than twenty-five documents to sign. Among these were a promissory note, reflecting a principal sum of $19,300.00 and a yearly interest rate of 12.990%; a Deed of Trust, giving United Lending a security interest in the Arnolds' real estate; and a two-page form labeled "Acknowledgment and Agreement to Mediate or Arbitrate," which stated that all legal controversies arising from the loan would be resolved through nonappealable, confidential arbitration, and that all damages would be direct damages, with no punitive damages available. However, this agreement not to arbitrate did not limit the lender's right to pursue legal actions in a court of law relating to collection of the loan.

On July 10, 1997, the Arnolds filed suit against United Lending and Searls, seeking a declaratory judgment adjudging the arbitration agreement to be void and unenforceable. On August 11, 1997, United Lending moved to dismiss the entire action on the basis of the compulsory arbitration agreement. The circuit court certified three questions to the state supreme court.

JUSTICE McCUSKEY: We reformulate the question as follows: Whether an arbitration agreement entered into as part of a consumer loan transaction containing a substantial waiver of the consumer's rights, including access to the courts, while preserving for all practical purposes the lender's right to a judicial forum, is void as a matter of law.

The drafters of the Uniform Consumer Credit Code explained that the [basic test] of unconscionability is whether . . . the conduct involved is, or the contract or clauses involved are, so one-sided as to be unconscionable under the circumstances existing at the time the conduct occurs or is threatened or at the time of the making of the contract. . . . [T]his Court stated:

> ["W]here a party alleges that the arbitration provision was unconscionable, or was thrust upon him because he was unwary and taken advantage of, or that the contract was one of adhesion, the question of whether an arbitration provision was bargained for and valid is a matter of law for the court to determine by reference to the entire contract. . . ." A determination of unconscionability must focus on the relative positions of the parties, the adequacy of the bargaining position, the meaningful alternatives available to the plaintiff, and "the existence of unfair terms in the contract."

Applying the rule . . . leads us to the inescapable conclusion that the arbitration agreement between the Arnolds and United Lending is "void for unconscionability" as a matter of law. . . . The relative positions of the parties, a national corporate lender on one side and elderly, unsophisticated consumers on the other, were "grossly unequal." In addition, there is no evidence that the loan broker made any other loan option available to the Arnolds. In fact, the record does not indicate that the Arnolds were seeking a loan, but rather were solicited by defendant Searls. Thus, the element of "a comparable, meaningful alternative" to the loan from United Lending is lacking. Because the Arnolds had no meaningful alternative to obtaining the loan from United Lending, and also did not have the benefit of legal counsel during the transaction, their bargaining position was clearly inadequate when compared to that of United Lending.

Given the nature of this arbitration agreement, combined with the great disparity in bargaining power, one can safely infer that the terms were not bargained for and that allowing such a one-sided agreement to stand would unfairly defeat the Arnolds' legitimate expectations.

Finally, the terms of the agreement are "unreasonably favorable" to United Lending. United Lending's acts or omissions could seriously damage the Arnolds, yet the Arnolds' only recourse would be to submit the matter to binding arbitration. At the same time, United Lending's access to the courts is wholly preserved in every conceivable situation where United Lending would want to secure judicial relief against the Arnolds. The wholesale waiver of the Arnolds' rights together with the complete preservation of United Lending's rights "is inherently inequitable and unconscionable because in a way it nullifies all the other provisions of the contract."

Judgment in favor of Plaintiffs.

[continued]

CRITICAL THINKING

This case highlights the importance of language in the legal system. Phrases quoted from the law are subject to significant judicial discretion, which allows rulings like this to be possible. Using the contextual clues found in the information given, choose two descriptions in quotes and write your idea of how the judge must be defining the relevant phrase. Then come up with some other ways these phrases could have been defined. Would the use of your alternatives significantly affect the reasonableness of the conclusion?

ETHICAL DECISION MAKING

Does this case lend itself very well to considerations of ethicality? What sort of theoretical approach do you see the court taking with this ruling?

On the basis of other decisions you have encountered in this book, what do you think is probably the most common ethical framework U.S. courts use in guiding their rulings? How well does this case fit with larger trends? Support your answer.

CASE OPENER WRAP-UP

A Disagreement over an Agreement

The trial court agreed with Michael Jordan's argument regarding a mutual mistake or fraudulent misrepresentation in the contract. Knafel appealed, and the court affirmed the lower court's decision. The court held that Knafel's representation to Jordan that he was the father met the requirements of being (1) a material fact, (2) made for the purpose of inducing Jordan to act, (3) that either was known by Knafel to be false or was not actually believed by her on reasonable grounds to be true, but Jordan reasonably believed it to be true, and (4) that was relied on by Jordan to his own detriment. Thus, the appellate court found that Knafel's representation that Jordan *was* the father constituted fraud. The agreement can be rescinded because Jordan would not have entered into the agreement but for the fraudulent representation made by Knafel. Even if Knafel did not act fraudulently, at the time the agreement was created both parties believed that the child was Jordan's. After the paternity tests revealed that the baby was *not* Jordan's, the agreement could still be rescinded based on a mutual mistake of fact.

KEY TERMS

adhesion contract 398
concealment 394
duress 397
fraudulent misrepresentation 392
innocent misrepresentation 391
intentional misrepresentation 392
legal assent 385
misrepresentation 390
mistake of fact 386
mutual 386
negligent misrepresentation 391
nondisclosure 394
rescinded 385
scienter 391
unconscionability 398
undue influence 396
unilateral 386
voidable 385

SUMMARY OF KEY TOPICS

The Importance of Legal Assent

If assent is not genuine, or legal, a contract may be voidable.

Mistake

Mistakes are erroneous beliefs about the material facts of a contract at the time the agreement is made. They may be either unilateral or mutual. Only under certain rare conditions are unilateral mistakes a basis for rescinding a contract. However, if both parties to a contract are mistaken about a material fact, either can opt to rescind it. The agreement was not based on a meeting of the minds, a basic criterion for a legal assent.

Misrepresentation

Misrepresentation is an intentional untruthful assertion by one of the parties about a material fact. An innocent misrepresentation occurs when the party making the false assertion believes it to be true. The misled party may then rescind the contract. When a misrepresentation is fraudulent, any assent is gained by deceit and the courts permit rescission. In addition to requiring a false assertion and intent to deceive, fraudulent misrepresentation also requires the innocent party's justifiable reliance on the assertion.

Undue Influence

Undue influence is the persuasive efforts of a dominant party who uses a special relationship with another party to interfere with the other's free choice of the terms of a contract. Any relationship in which one party has an unusual degree of trust in the other can trigger concern about undue influence.

Duress

Duress occurs when one party threatens the other with a wrongful act unless assent is given. Such assent is not legal assent because coercion interferes with the party's free will. For the courts to rescind the agreement, the injured party must demonstrate that the duress left no reasonable alternatives to agreeing to the contract.

Unconscionability

Unconscionability may be a basis for avoiding a contract if one party has so much relative bargaining power that he or she in effect dictates the terms. The resulting agreement is an adhesion contract.

POINT / COUNTERPOINT

Are Payday Loans, and the Accompanying Interests Rates, Unconscionable?

YES

The consumers who take out payday loans are often desperate and lack other methods of obtaining a loan. For these consumers, getting a loan from a bank is impossible due to their poor credit ratings or lack of necessary collateral. The companies that offer these consumers payday loans are preying on a vulnerable population by exploiting their lack of bargaining power. Payday loans are unconscionable.

Regardless of the amount of advertising a lender may provide, consumers who find themselves in need of payday loans lack the necessary bargaining power to make these loans conscionable. For a loan to be unconscionable, one of the parties has to have so much more bargaining power than the other that he or she dictates the terms of the agreement; in payday loans it is the lender that has the power to dictate the terms. Desperate consumers often feel that they are left with no choice but accepting the terms offered by the payday lenders.

NO

The companies that supply payday loans offer short-term solutions to difficult financial situations. For consumers who find themselves strapped and in dire need of cash, payday loans provide a means to repair a broken-down car, pay the rent, or pay other accumulating bills. Although the interest rates are high, these loans do not violate any laws and the consumers' loan agreements are not unconscionable.

When consumers approach a payday lender for a loan, they are greeted by a plethora of signs indicating relevant interest rates. Before signing the loan documents, the consumer is given numerous documents containing the interest rates. Additionally, many states require that the lender verbally state the interest rates to consumers. These consumers have numerous opportunities to walk away from the lender if they are unwilling to accept the high interest rates.

Additionally, payday loans exploit the financial hardships experienced by consumers and often result in increased hardship. A typical bank loan is usually capped at an APR of 35 percent; payday loans average an APR of 530 percent. The consumers' ability to pay back the loans is often limited by the individuals' impoverished situation, and, as a result, these loans will often roll over, making it impossible for consumers to recover. As a result of the consumers' limited bargaining power, payday loans trap disadvantaged populations in high–interest rate loans they cannot afford. Thus, payday loans are *inherently unconscionable.*

In response to those who argue that these loans are unconscionable, supporters argue that consumers still have the free will to choose whether or not to enter into the loan agreement. These loans do not involve any coercion or enticing.

Furthermore, the high interest rates tied to payday loans are the reason these lenders are able to make small (often between \$100 and \$500) loans to otherwise risky consumers. Without the ability to raise interest rates, these companies would not be able to offset their own risk in providing the loans. Therefore, these loans are *not unconscionable.*

QUESTIONS & PROBLEMS

1. Explain the difference between a unilateral mistake and a mutual mistake.
2. Explain when a unilateral mistake can lead to a contract's being voidable.
3. Distinguish innocent misrepresentation from fraudulent misrepresentation.
4. Explain how nondisclosure can be treated as misrepresentation.
5. Explain the primary differences between duress and undue influence.
6. After a collision involving Alston and Alexander, Alston was diagnosed with chest problems and was prescribed a number of medications. During the time of her treatment and release on the day of the accident, she did not make note of any pain in her neck or back. Instead, she argued that she developed neck and back pain between one and two days after her original treatment. Later, Alston signed a release for her injury compensation check, which is standard insurer procedure. However, Alston later testified that she did not read the insurance release and her compensatory check and that the check from the insurance company did not contain compensation for her injuries that occurred later. Alston sued on the grounds of mutual mistake. Specifically, the check did not make light of all of her injuries, and she did not read the check release. Thus, she claimed the release was invalidated. The superior court upheld the validity of a general release signed by Alston and granted summary judgment in Alexander's favor on that basis. Alston appealed. With whom do you think the state's supreme court agreed and why? [*Alston v. Alexander,* Del. Sup. Ct. LEXIS 384 (2012).]
7. Audrey Vokes was a 51-year-old widow who wanted to become an "accomplished dancer." She was invited to attend a "dance party" at J. P. Davenports' School of Dancing, an Arthur Murray franchise. She subsequently signed up for dance classes, at which she received elaborate praise. Her instructor initially sold her eight half-hour dance lessons for \$14.50 each, to be used one each month. Eventually, after being continually told that she had excellent potential and that she was developing into a beautiful dancer—when, in fact, she was not developing her dance ability and had no aptitude for dance—she ended up purchasing a total of 2,302 hours' worth of dance lessons for a total of \$31,090.45. When it finally became clear to Vokes that she was not developing her dance skills, in part because she had trouble even hearing the musical beat, she sued Arthur Murray. What would be the basis of her argument? Her case was initially dismissed by the trial court. What do you think the result of her appeal was? [*Vokes v. Arthur Murray,* 212 So. 2d 906 (1968).]
8. In 1998, the governor of New York, George Pataki, formulated a \$185 million plan to update old Amtrak trains. The purpose of the project was to make the old trains faster than the more current Amtrak trains. Such a reconstruction would allow for a high-speed rail system between Albany and New York City. Unfortunately, Amtrak produced only one train, and although millions of dollars were poured into the company to fund the project, auditing showed that the company showed little spending on the trains. Problems stemmed in part from the lack of engineering expertise of the Steel Company that was picked to work on the

trains. Also, the state's Department of Transportation was not experienced in overseeing projects of this type, so little oversight was given to Amtrak. Additionally, unforeseen problems arose such as air-conditioning malfunctions and the removal of asbestos from train cabins. After the plan seemed as though it would never be successful and Amtrak was extremely low on money due to normal operations, the company tried to settle with the state to escape the project. However, the state filed a lawsuit against Amtrak. Amtrak's defense was that both parties made a unilateral mistake because neither party foresaw the problems or extra costs associated with the project that made it unrealistic. How do you think the court decided? [*New York v. Amtrak,* 2007 U.S. Dist. LEXIS 13045 (N.D.N.Y, Feb. 23, 2007).]

9. The Winklers were interested in purchasing a home in the Valleyview Farms housing development. They contacted the developer, Galehouse, and selected a lot that cost $57,000. They asked the developer to show them plans for houses for which the construction costs would range from $180,000 to $190,000, indicating this was the price they would be willing to spend for construction only and wasn't to include the lot price. The developer gave them several books and plans to look at.

After the Winklers had several conversations with Galehouse, the developer drafted plans for a 2,261-square-foot house and gave the Winklers a quote of $198,000 for construction. The lot price was not included. After several months of adding options and upgrades to the plan, the cost rose to $242,000, excluding the lot. The parties then engaged in a couple of weeks of negotiations regarding the price of the construction and lot. Eventually they reached a compromise price of $291,000 ($243,000 for the construction and $48,000 for the lot).

Galehouse prepared a written contract to reflect the parties' agreement, but the developer forgot to include the lot price. The Winklers paid Galehouse $48,000, the lot price, as a deposit on the contract. When the construction was completed, and the Winklers were finalizing their loan from the bank, the parties discovered the drafting error. Galehouse sued to have the contract reformed to reflect the agreed-on price. Should the contract be reformed? Why or why not? [*Galehouse v. Winkler,* 1998 WL 312527.]

10. Vincent Concepcion sued AT&T mobile in 2006, claiming that the company had deceptively advertised a free phone with a wireless plan. After the suit evolved into a class action suit, the company claimed that in accordance with their contracts, the plaintiffs must settle through individual arbitration processes. Yet the district court ruled that California law banned parties from creating contracts that excused them from an infraction based on certain clauses—specifically, clauses like the AT&T clause disallowing class action suits although the damages to the individual are small and not worth the time or money required to engage in an individual arbitration process. Thus, the district court refused to dismiss the suit. The company then appealed to the Ninth Circuit Court of Appeals and finally the Supreme Court, arguing that the Federal Arbitration Act should trump state law. However, unconscionability doctrines and substantial consumer protection laws are created under state law. Thus, the justices questioned, "Are we going to tell the State of California what it has to consider unconscionable?" How do you think the justices decided? [*AT&T Mobility LLC v. Concepcion,* 2011 U.S. LEXIS 3367.]

Looking for more review materials?

The Online Learning Center at **www.mhhe.com/kubasek3e** contains this chapter's "Assignment on the Internet" and also a list of URLs for more information, entitled "On the Internet." Find both of them in the Student Center portion of the OLC, along with quizzes and other helpful materials.

CHAPTER

18 Contracts in Writing

LEARNING OBJECTIVES

After reading this chapter, you will be able to answer the following questions:

1 What is the purpose of the statute of frauds?

2 Which kinds of contracts require a writing to satisfy the statute of frauds?

3 What must a writing contain to be sufficient to satisfy the statute of frauds?

4 What is the purpose of the parol evidence rule?

CASE OPENER

Admissibility of an Oral Contract in Court

Monroe Bradstad borrowed $100,000 from his aunt, Jeanne Garland, to purchase farmland. Both parties subsequently signed a promissory note stipulating that interest would be accrued prior to or on January 1, 1992. After that, payments and interest would be made on January 1 of each following year, with the final balance due on January 1, 2010. The land was used as security for the note; thus Branstad executed a mortgage. Branstad paid a total of $33,000 from 1993 to 1997. In 1998, Branstad and Garland had a falling out, and Garland served Branstad with a notice to pay $43,998 in past-due interest. However, Branstad and his wife claimed that they had made a subsequent oral agreement with Garland that they would manage and spend money on her other properties in lieu of paying interest. Garland argued that there was no oral agreement and that any oral evidence would be inadmissible in court due to the parol evidence rule. Branstad argued that the oral agreement was made after the written contract was created, not before or during, and thus the oral contract was a separate contract and not subject to the parol evidence rule.

1. Does it matter when the oral contract was made in relation to when the written contract was created?
2. Why might it be ethically important for the court to hear the subsequent oral agreement made between Branstad and Garland?

The Wrap-Up at the end of the chapter will answer these questions.

Written contracts provide certain advantages oral contracts lack. Disputes about the specifics of the terms in an oral contract are easier to settle when the terms are solidified in writing. The moment of writing also allows both parties to reconsider their terms and ensure that they are advocating what they desire in the contract. In general, written contracts smooth the conduct of business transactions. Some contracts thus require a writing.

Before entering into a contract one needs to know whether its subject matter requires a writing.

This idea actually comes from an English law, the Act for the Prevention of Frauds and Perjuries passed by Parliament in 1677. To correct a problem in the common law, the act required that specific types of contracts be in writing and be signed by both parties to ensure enforceability.

Although the law frequently references the *statute of frauds,* the term is somewhat misleading. There is no federal legislation entitled "Statute of Frauds." Rather, the statute exists as legislation at the state level. In fact, almost every state has created its own version of the 1677 English act, adopting it in total or in part. The exceptions are Louisiana, which has no such legislation, and New Mexico and Maryland, which follow statutes of frauds created by judicial decision and not the legislature. Interestingly enough, the English have repealed almost all their requirements for writing, while U.S. states and courts are still expanding the requirements for what falls within the statute of frauds.

In addition to the statute's not being a unitary government act, the name "statute of frauds" is misleading in another way. It does not relate to fraudulent contracts, nor does it address the issue of illegal contracts. Rather, it addresses the enforceability of contracts that fail to meet the requirements set forth in it. Furthermore, the statute serves to protect promisors from poorly considered oral contracts by requiring that certain contracts be in writing.

This chapter addresses some commonalities of the statutes of frauds of different states; in it, we refer to the "statute of frauds" as if it were a unitary law. We examine which contracts need to be in writing, as well as exceptions to the rule. Then we look at the parol evidence rule, which discusses which types of oral evidence are admissible and when, as related to contracts within the scope of the statute of frauds.

Statute of Frauds

LO1
What is the purpose of the statute of frauds?

The **statute of frauds** has three main purposes. First, it attempts to ease contractual negotiations by requiring sufficiently reliable evidence to prove the existence and specific terms of a contract. When a contract is deemed important enough that being in writing is required under the statute of frauds, the statute specifies what is considered reliable evidence.

The second main purpose of the statute of frauds is to prevent unreliable oral evidence from interfering with a contractual relationship. By requiring that a contract be in writing, the statute precludes the admittance of oral evidence denying the existence of a contract or claiming additional terms that would substantially alter the contract from its agreed-on written form. This chapter further discusses the admissibility or denial of oral evidence later, in the section on the parol evidence rule.

The third main purpose of the statute of frauds is to prevent parties from entering into contracts with which they do not agree. That is, it provides some degree of cautionary protection for the parties, who must carefully consider the terms, agree to them, write them out, and finally sign the contract. The law assumes that these steps will allow time for careful consideration. Thus, the statute works to prevent hasty, improperly considered contracts.

LO2

Which kinds of contracts require a writing to satisfy the statute of frauds?

Contracts Falling within the Statute of Frauds

As previously mentioned, only specific types of contracts are within the scope of the statute of frauds and thus required to be evidenced by a writing. They are (1) contracts whose terms prevent possible performance within one year, (2) promises made in consideration of marriage, (3) contracts for one party to pay the debt of another if the initial party fails to pay, and (4) contracts related to an interest in land. Although required to be in writing under the Uniform Commercial Code (UCC), and not the statute of frauds, a related fifth category is contracts for the sale of goods totaling more than $500.[1]

CONTRACTS WHOSE TERMS PREVENT POSSIBLE PERFORMANCE WITHIN ONE YEAR

Contracts whose performance, based on the terms of the contract, could not possibly occur within one year fall within the statute of frauds and therefore must be in writing.[2] Note that the one-year period begins the day after the contract is created, *not* when it is scheduled to begin.

For example, Roberto enters into a contract with Elise to work for her for one year starting October 1. If the contract is created on the preceding September 15, it cannot be completed in one year from September 16; therefore, it must be in writing. However, if the contract is scheduled to start immediately, it *can* be completed in one year and need not be in writing because it is not within the statute of frauds.

The test for compliance with the one-year rule does not consider the likelihood of completing the contract within one year. Rather, it considers the *possibility* of completing the contract in one year. While Roberto and Elise's contract is within the statute because, according to its terms, it cannot be performed within one year, a contract for lifetime employment does not need to be in writing.

If Roberto contracts with Elise for lifetime employment, they do not have to write and sign the agreement because it is possible for the contract to be completed within one year: Robert *could* die after two days of work. Moreover, if oral, their contract would be enforceable, because it is not within the statute of frauds. The possibility that a contract's terms could be performed within one year removes the contract from the statute's written requirements.

[1] UCC § 2-201.

[2] Restatement (Second) of Contracts, sec. 130.

CASE NUGGET

AURIGEMMA V. NEW CASTLE CARE, LLC

2006 Del. Super. LEXIS 337, June 12, 2006

Dr. Ralph M. Aurigemma filed suit against New Castle Care, LLC, alleging breach of an oral contract. New Castle Care operated the Arbors Rehabilitation Center, the facility where Aurigemma worked. Aurigemma claimed that after the medical director for the Arbors unexpectedly died, he and many other doctors expressed an interest in filling the newly vacant position. Aurigemma stated that individuals from New Castle Care made him interim medical director and, on September 4, 2003, created an oral contract under which he agreed to serve as permanent medical director from October 1, 2003, until October 1, 2004.

New Castle Care claimed that it made no such oral contract with Aurigemma and stated that even if it had, Aurigemma's oral contract would not be enforceable because the terms of the contract, which was created on September 4, 2003, and intended to go until October 1, 2004, could not possibly be completed within a year. Therefore, New Castle Care claimed that Aurigemma's alleged oral contract fell within the statue of frauds and thus required a writing to be enforceable. Additionally, New Castle Care claimed it had been clear that the company had not intended to have Aurigemma act as permanent medical director, and it cited a written contract it had created with another doctor on September 15, 2003, as proof that no oral contract existed.

Aurigemma countered by saying that because he began to assume the duties of medical director, he had already partially performed the terms of the contract. Thus, because partial performance sometimes creates an exception to the statue of frauds, Aurigemma argued that the oral contract did not need to be in writing.

On June 15, 2006, New Castle Care filed a motion for summary judgment; shortly after, a Delaware superior court granted summary judgment in favor of the company on both counts. In conclusion, the court stated that New Castle Care was correct in its argument. Because the terms of the oral contract were for a time period of more than a year, the oral contract would have had to have been in writing in order to have been valid. The court also pointed out that in Delaware the partial-performance exception to the statute of frauds does not apply to oral contracts incapable of being performed within a year. Therefore, Aurigemma's alleged oral contract was not included in the partial-performance exception to the statute of frauds and was accordingly unenforceable.

Similarly, contracts for complex construction projects need not be in writing because, theoretically, they can be completed within one year if a sufficiently large crew works around the clock every day, even if the scenario is highly unlikely.

Legal Principle: **If a contract can possibly be performed within a year, even if such performance is highly unlikely, then the contract does not need a writing to be enforceable.**

BUT WHAT IF . . .

WHAT IF THE FACTS OF THE CASE OPENER WERE DIFFERENT?

Let's say, in the Case Opener, that the promissory note was issued when Branstad had purchased a tractor for a price of $475 from Garland and both parties agreed on April 15, 2012, that Branstad would pay Garland back in full on or before March 30, 2013. Would such an agreement require a writing according to the statute of frauds?

The above Case Nugget illustrates how important the facts are when ascertaining whether a contract cannot be performed within a year.

PROMISES MADE IN CONSIDERATION OF MARRIAGE

Agreements regarding marriage in which one party is gaining something other than a return on his or her promise to marry are within the statute of frauds and must be in writing.[3] In other words, when one party promises something to the other as part of an offer of marriage, the contract must be in writing to be enforceable.

[3] Ibid., sec. 124.

For example, Ed and Jeanie want to get married. Ed promises Jeanie he will buy her a new car every other year if she will marry him. To be enforceable, Ed and Jeanie's agreement must be in writing because Jeanie stands to benefit, by way of new cars, if she marries Ed.

Mutual promises to marry do not fall within the statute of frauds. If Ed and Jeanie promise each other they will get married, this agreement does not need to be in writing because neither party is gaining anything other than a return on his or her promise to marry; thus the agreement does not fall within the statute.

While mutual promises to marry do not fall within the statute of frauds, prenuptial agreements do. A **prenuptial agreement** is an agreement two parties enter into before marriage that clearly states the ownership rights each party enjoys in the other party's property. For these agreements, writing is required, although not sufficient, to establish enforceability. Furthermore, although consideration is *not* legally required, courts tend to privilege prenuptial agreements that include it. Consideration offers evidence that both parties understand and agree to all the terms of the agreement and that the agreement is not biased in favor of one party.

Legal Principle: Contracts in which one party promises something in exchange for another's promise to marry must have a writing to be enforceable, but mutual promises to marry do not require a writing.

CONTRACTS FOR ONE PARTY TO PAY THE DEBT OF ANOTHER IF THE INITIAL PARTY FAILS TO PAY

The contracts within the statute of frauds that concern promises to pay a debt are of a very limited kind. Known as *secondary obligations,* they are also called *secondary promises, collateral promises,* or *suretyship promises.* A secondary obligation occurs when a party outside a primary agreement promises to fulfill one of the original party's (primary debtor's) obligations if the original party fails to fulfill it. For example, Helen enters into a contract with Tomas to sell him her car. Subsequently, Rina agrees to pay Tomas's debt if he fails to pay Helen the money he owes her. To be enforceable, Rina's promise needs to be in writing because it is a secondary obligation and therefore falls within the statute.

The distinction between primary and secondary obligations determines when the statute requires a written agreement. *Primary obligations* are debts incurred in an initial contract. Using our car-sale example, the primary obligation is Tomas's promise to pay Helen for the car. Primary obligations are not within the statute of frauds and, therefore, need not be in writing to be enforceable. Secondary obligations, as we've seen, are within the statute and need to be in writing.

A specific instance of a secondary obligation involves the administrator or executor of an estate. Administrators and executors of estates are responsible for paying off the debts of an estate and then dividing the remaining assets appropriately among the heirs. While an agreement to pay the estate's debts with these funds need not be in writing, promises the administrator or executor makes to do so personally are within the statute of frauds and must be in writing. Because the administrator or executor is promising to pay with his or her own money, and not the estate's, the promise must be in writing to be enforceable; the administrator or executor has assumed a secondary obligation.

There is an exception under which a secondary obligation need *not* be in writing: the *main-purpose rule.* If the main purpose for incurring a secondary obligation is to obtain a personal benefit, the promise does not fall within the statute and does not have to be in writing.[4] The assumption is that a party attempting to achieve a personal benefit will not

[4] Ibid., sec. 116.

back out of the promise, therefore eliminating the need of a written record of the promise. The court's job is to use the context surrounding the agreement to determine the third party's main purpose for entering the agreement, which will determine whether a writing is required for the agreement to be enforceable.

Legal Principle: **Primary obligations do not require a writing, but secondary obligations do unless the main reason a person makes a secondary promise is to obtain a personal benefit.**

BUT WHAT IF . . .

WHAT IF THE FACTS OF THE CASE OPENER WERE DIFFERENT?

Let's say that Branstad buys a tractor from Garland. Branstad makes an agreement to pay Garland back in full, but his father makes a promise to pay for the tractor in case Branstad fails to complete his payments. Garland says that there needs to be a written contract explaining the father's promise according to the statute of frauds. Is Garland correct?

Case 18-1 is an example of a court's consideration of a suretyship promise in its attempt to determine whether the promise falls within the statute of frauds.

CASE 18-1 POWER ENTERTAINMENT, INC., ET AL. v. NATIONAL FOOTBALL LEAGUE PROPERTIES, INC.

U.S. COURT OF APPEALS FOR THE FIFTH CIRCUIT 151 F.3D 247 (1998)

Pro Set had a licensing agreement with NFLP, which allowed Pro Set to market NFL cards bearing the statement "official card of the National Football League." Pro Set filed for bankruptcy owing NFLP approximately $800,000 in unpaid royalties from card sales. Representatives of Power Entertainment met with NFLP to discuss taking over the licensing agreement between NFLP and Pro Set. Power Entertainment alleges NFLP orally agreed to transfer Pro Set's license to Power Entertainment in return for Power Entertainment's agreement to assume Pro Set's debt to NFLP. NFLP subsequently refused to transfer the licensing agreement to Power Entertainment.

Power Entertainment then brought a breach of contract suit against NFLP seeking damages for amounts spent in reliance on the alleged agreement and for lost profits. The district court granted NFLP's motion to dismiss, holding Power Entertainment's contract claim failed as a matter of law because it was not in writing and Power Entertainment had failed to plead facts sufficient to support an estoppel claim. Power Entertainment filed timely notice of appeal.

JUDGE BENAVIDES: In granting NFLP's motion to dismiss, the district court concluded the "suretyship" statute of frauds rendered the alleged oral agreement between NFLP and Power Entertainment unenforceable because Power Entertainment promised to assume Pro Set's debt to NFLP as part of the alleged oral agreement. The relevant statute of frauds provision under Texas law provides "a promise by one person to answer for the debt, default, or miscarriage of another person" must be in writing. As the Supreme Court of Texas has explained, the suretyship statute of frauds serves an evidentiary function:

> Probably the basic reason for requiring a promise to answer for the debt of another to be in writing is the promisor has received no direct benefit from the transaction. When the promisor receives something, this is subject to proof and tends to corroborate the making of the promise. Perjury is thus more likely in the case of a guaranty where nothing but the promise is of evidentiary value. The lack of any benefit received by the promisor not only increases the hardship of his being called upon to pay but also increases the importance of being sure that he is justly charged.

These evidentiary concerns do not pertain, however, if "the promise is made for the promisor's own benefit and not at all for the benefit of the third person. . . ." Consistent with this common-sense approach, the Texas courts have

[continued]

adopted the "main purpose doctrine," which, broadly speaking, removes an oral agreement to pay the debt of another from the statute of frauds "wherever the main purpose and object of the promisor is not to answer for another, but to subserve some purpose of his own. . . ."

In applying the main purpose doctrine under Texas law, this court has articulated the three factors used by Texas courts to determine whether the main purpose doctrine applies:

(1) [Whether the] promisor intended to become primarily liable for the debt, in effect making it his original obligation, rather than to become a surety for another;
(2) [Whether there] was consideration for the promise; and
(3) [Whether the] receipt of the consideration was the promisor's main purpose or leading object in making the promise; that is, the consideration given for the promise was primarily for the promisor's use and benefit.

Applying these factors to the facts alleged by Power Entertainment, it is apparent Power Entertainment may be able to show the alleged oral agreement falls outside of the statute of frauds. Consistent with the allegations in its complaint, Power Entertainment may be able to adduce facts that would prove Power Entertainment intended to create primary responsibility on its part to pay Pro Set's $800,000 debt to NFLP, rather than merely acting as a surety for Pro Set's obligation. According to Power Entertainment's complaint, Pro Set had already declared bankruptcy and defaulted on its royalty obligations to NFLP, and there is no indication Pro Set was involved in any way in the negotiations between NFLP and Power Entertainment.

Further, the licensing agreement constituted valuable consideration for Power Entertainment's agreement to pay Pro Set's debt. Finally, Power Entertainment apparently agreed to pay Pro Set's debt to NFLP not to aid Pro Set, but to induce NFLP to transfer Pro Set's licensing agreement to Power Entertainment for Power Entertainment's use and benefit. Under these circumstances, we conclude Power Entertainment may be able to prove a set of facts that would allow a jury to find the alleged oral agreement is not barred by the statute of frauds. Thus, the district court erred in dismissing Power Entertainment's complaint based on the statute of frauds.

REVERSED and REMANDED.

CRITICAL THINKING

Why do you think that the judge describes a certain approach to verbal contracts as "common sense," and what is that approach? How strong is the argument for the commonsense approach? What assumptions are probably shared by most people who accept this argument as common sense?

ETHICAL DECISION MAKING

The judge seems to think that in some circumstances a verbal agreement could facilitate unethical behavior. What ethical theory does the judge seem to assume most people use in ethical decision making? Why might it be wise to use the judge's assumption when making business decisions?

CONTRACTS RELATED TO AN INTEREST IN LAND

Within the statute of frauds, "land" encompasses not only the land and soil itself but anything attached to the land, such as trees or buildings. Because the statute requires a writing as evidence of the contract, a claim to an oral contract for the sale of land is not enough to prove such a contract existed.

Contracts transferring other interests in land are also within the statute of frauds. Mortgages and leases are within the statute because they are considered transfers of interest in land.

Determining exactly what constitutes an "interest in land" within the statute of frauds is difficult. A number of things that seem as if they are interests in land do not fall within the statute. For example, promises to sell crops annually, agreements between parties for profit sharing from the sale of real property, and boundary disputes that have been settled through the use of land are all outside the statute of frauds and, therefore, do not require evidence in writing. The nearby Case Nugget presents a case related to land in which the parties disagreed as to whether a writing was needed.

CASE NUGGET

WHAT IS AN "INTEREST IN LAND"?

Shelby's, Inc. v. Sierra Bravo, Inc. 68 S.W.3d 604 (2002)

Shelby's, Inc., and Sierra Bravo entered into a written agreement that granted Sierra permission to use Shelby's land as a disposal site for waste and debris Sierra removed as part of the construction of a new highway. Shelby's claimed the parties also entered into an oral contract for Sierra to construct a waterway and building pad on Shelby's property. Sierra never completed the construction and denied that an oral contract existed. Shelby's sued, and the jury found in its favor.

Sierra appealed on the basis that the oral agreement was within the statute of frauds and therefore unenforceable. Sierra saw the alleged oral agreement as specifying a sale of an interest in land, which is within the statute of frauds. Therefore, the agreement, to be enforceable, would have had to be in writing. The court firmly disagreed with Sierra's argument, stating:

We agree with the well-reasoned argument of Respondent [Shelby's]. The contract in this case was not a "sale," much less a sale of an interest in lands. . . . Here, there was no transfer of ownership or title. The written agreement gave Appellant [Sierra] permission to deposit debris and soil on Respondent's land, not the right to do so. The oral contract was for the construction of a waterway and building pad and passed no interest in the land. . . . We decline to create a new category to which the statute of frauds applies, that of a contract for services for the deposit of dirt and soil on land. The trial court did not err in denying Appellant's motion for judgment notwithstanding the verdict. Appellant's point is denied and the judgment of the trial court is affirmed.

CONTRACTS FOR THE SALE OF GOODS TOTALING MORE THAN $500

Agreements for a sale in which the total price is $500 or more are required by the UCC, Section 2-201, to be recorded in a written contract or a memorandum. This writing need only state the quantity to be sold; buyer, seller, price, and method of payment do not need to be included. In fact, terms other than quantity can be inexact or left out of the writing as long as what is written does not contradict the parties' agreement about them. The contract will be enforceable for the stated quantity and not a unit more. Furthermore, for the contract to be enforceable, both the UCC and the statute of frauds require that the party against whom action is sought must have signed the written document.

Suppose Donnie and Gretchen enter into a sales contract. Donnie wrote the agreement, and Gretchen was the only party to sign. Later, Donnie attempts to enforce the agreement against Gretchen for the agreed-to quantity. Because Gretchen signed it, Donnie can bring suit against her. However, because Donnie did not sign the agreement, Gretchen can neither sue nor countersue him.

Other situations under the UCC that require contracts in writing are the lease of goods and the sale of securities[5] and personal property[6] if the price is greater than $5,000.

FURTHER REQUIREMENTS SPECIFIC TO CERTAIN STATES

Because the statute of frauds is actually state law, certain states have various requirements not found in others. In some states, under the **equal dignity rule** contracts that would normally fall under the statute and need a writing if negotiated by the principal must be in writing even if negotiated by an agent. For example, Luke appoints Sanjeev to act as his agent. Sanjeev enters into an agreement for Luke with Carrie that cannot be completed within one year according to the contractual terms. Had Luke contracted directly with Carrie, the agreement would be within the statute and require a writing. Therefore, Sanjeev's contract, which is on behalf of Luke, must also be in writing according to the equal dignity rule.

[5] UCC § 8-319.

[6] UCC § 81-206.

COMPARING THE LAW OF OTHER COUNTRIES

ENGLAND AND THE STATUTE OF FRAUDS

While the United States and other Western countries have adopted versions of the 1677 English act that gave birth to the statute of frauds, the English have gone in the opposite direction. Instead of expanding the powers and use of the 1677 act, they have severely limited the number of cases falling within their statute of frauds.

Although formal complaints were levied against the English statute of frauds as early as 1937, no action was taken until 1953. In that year, the Law Reform Committee addressed numerous 1937 arguments in favor of repeal. The 1953 committee recommended that Parliament repeal Section 4 of the 1677 act, which identifies specific types of contracts as required to be in writing. The Law Reform Act of 1954 subsequently repealed Section 4, with one cautionary exception. The 1954 act still required that promises to pay for the debt of others, what we call *suretyship* or *collateral promises,* be in writing.

A few states have special provisions in matters related to promises to pay debt. To be enforceable, a promise to pay a debt that has already been discharged because of bankruptcy must be in writing, to prevent the promisor from hiding behind the fact that the debt has been discharged. Another example is a promise to pay a debt when collection is barred by a statute of limitations. The logic here is the same as that in the first example. If the agreement is not in writing, the promisor can easily claim he or she does not need to pay. Therefore, the statute of frauds in certain states requires that both of these types of promises be in writing to be enforceable.

One last example of rules that hold only in some states occurs when the contract cannot be performed in the promisor's lifetime. For example, Heather promises to give $10,000 to Misha's charity on Heather's death. According to the terms of the promise, the agreement cannot be carried out within Heather's lifetime. In some states, Heather's promise would fall within the statute of frauds and would therefore have to be in writing. The intent here is to offer estates some protection from claims made on the basis of alleged oral contracts.

Exhibit 18-1 summarizes the contracts that fall within the statute of frauds and presents a mnemonic for remembering them.

Exhibit 18-1

A Mnemonic for Remembering Which Contracts Fall within the Statute of Frauds

Circumstances in Which the Statute of Frauds Applies (MY LEGS)		
M	Marriage	Contracts made in consideration of marriage
Y	Year	Contracts whose terms prevent possible performance within one year
L	Land	Contracts related to an interest in land
E	Executor	Contracts in which the executor promises to pay the debt of an estate with the executor's own money
G	Goods	Contracts for the sale of goods totaling more than $500
S	Suretyship	Contracts involving secondary obligations or suretyships

LO3

What must a writing contain to be sufficient to satisfy the statute of frauds?

Sufficiency of the Writing

There are no specific requirements for the form of a written contract under the statute of frauds. In fact, one or several documents can together make up the written agreement under the statute, although certain elements need to be present for a writing to constitute proper evidence of a written contract under the statute (see Exhibit 18-2).

Required elements include the identification of the parties to the contract, the subject matter of the agreement, the consideration (if any), and any pertinent terms. The contract

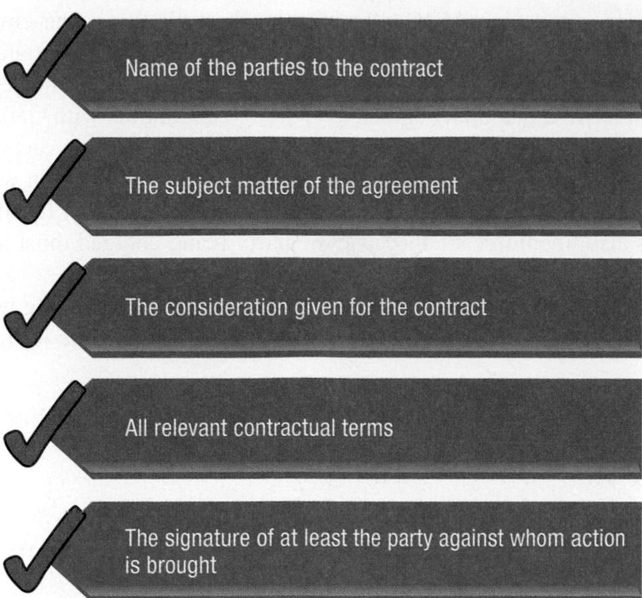

Exhibit 18-2
Requirements of a Writing Sufficient to Satisfy the Statute of Frauds under the Common Law

must be signed, but the signature need not be at the end. In fact, it need not be a full signature; a mark, such as an initial, is permissible as long as it is intended as a signature. While it is standard for both parties to sign the agreement, because the writing is being offered as proof of an agreement, only the party against whom action is sought needs to have signed it. If only one party signed, it is possible to have an agreement enforceable against that party but not the other. In some states oral testimony regarding an invoice for products sold is enough to meet the requirements under the statute if an actual invoice is not produced. The required elements in a writing can be contained in a memorandum, a document, or a compilation of several documents.

As you might gather from the information provided above, the statute of frauds can be particularly helpful to individuals involved in business transactions because it requires that certain important elements be present when a contract is in writing. In a way, the statute of frauds may help eliminate, or reduce, the ambiguity involved with contracts by requiring that certain conditions be met for a written document to constitute an enforceable contract. For example, when Medical Research Consultants (MRC) hired Michael Gallagher as a sales representative, the company required that he sign an employee handbook that outlined the terms of his employment. In signing the employee handbook, Gallagher acknowledged that he was an at-will employee of the company and could potentially be let go by MRC at any time. After Gallagher signed the handbook, a human resource representative for MRC faxed him a draft of an employment agreement which stated that Gallagher would work for a period of three years. Over the next several months, while Gallagher was working for MRC, he altered the draft that was faxed to him by MRC; Gallagher changed the number of years under the noncompete clause from two years to one year, and he wrote "3 weeks paid vacation" in a blank space on the draft (even after being told on more than one occasion that he was to receive two weeks' unpaid vacation). Then, after being employed by MRC for approximately four months, Gallagher faxed the draft with his signature back to the company. An attorney for MRC promptly responded to Gallagher and stated in an e-mail that "the draft sent to you . . . was for discussion purposes only. MRC never agreed to an employment contract with you and will not enter into one." Soon after, Gallagher was terminated from employment at MRC.

Gallagher filed suit against MRC, alleging breach of his three-year employment contract, which he maintained was created both orally during his early negotiations with MRC and also through the signed employment agreement draft. The court, however, found that even if MRC had orally agreed to a three-year contract with Gallagher, it would not have been enforceable because the statute of frauds dictates that agreements incapable of being completed within a year must be in writing. Further, according to the statute of frauds, the draft that Gallagher faxed back to MRC was also unenforceable because the party being charged must have signed the document and MRC clearly had not.[7]

To see how effective writing principles relate to contracts under the statute of frauds, please see the **Connecting to the Core** activity on the text website at www.mhhe.com/kubasek3e.

Case 18-2 demonstrates how judges go about determining what constitutes a writing and when a writing is sufficient under the statute of frauds.

[7] *Michael J. Gallagher v. Medical Research Consultants, LLP*, Civil Action No. 04-236 (case summary accessed on LexisNexis May 26, 2009).

CASE 18-2 STEWART LAMLE v. MATTEL, INC.
U.S. COURT OF APPEALS FOR THE FEDERAL CIRCUIT
394 F.3D 1355 (2005)

Steward Lamle is the inventor of Farook, a board game. Lamle obtained two patents for Farook from the United States Patent and Trademark Office and negotiated with Mattel, Inc., regarding the licensing of Farook by Mattel. Early in these negotiations, Lamle signed Mattel's standard Product Disclosure Form, which contained the following provision:

> *I understand that . . . no obligation is assumed by [Mattel] unless and until a formal written contract is agreed to and entered into, and then the obligation shall be only that which is expressed in the formal, written contract.*

The negotiations advanced, and a meeting was held on June 11 where the parties discussed the terms of a licensing agreement. Mattel and Lamle there agreed on many terms of a license including a three-year term, the geographic scope, the schedule for payment, and the percentage royalty. Mattel asked Lamle to "draft a formal document memorializing 'The Deal'" and "promised [that] it would sign a formal, written contract before January 1, 1998."

Mattel employee Mike Bucher sent Lamle an email entitled "Farook Deal" on June 26 that substantially repeated terms agreed to at the June 11 meeting. The email stated the terms "have been agreed in principal [sic] by . . . Mattel subject to contract." The salutation "Best regards Mike Bucher" appeared at the end of the email.

On October 8, Mattel notified Lamle of its decision not to go ahead with the production of Farook. Lamle filed action asserting, among other things, a claim of breach of contract. The district court granted summary judgment in favor of Mattel on all claims. The Court of Appeals vacated that grant of summary judgment and remanded the case to the district court. The district court on remand again granted summary judgment in favor of Mattel on all claims. Lamle appealed again.

JUDGE DYK: Mattel contends, and the district court held, any oral agreement made during the June 11 meeting cannot be enforced because of the California Statute of Frauds.

There is no question the alleged oral agreement for a three year license was one that, by its terms, could not be "performed within a year from the making thereof." The only question, therefore, is whether there is a writing to evidence the agreement or an applicable exception to the Statute of Frauds. To satisfy the Statute of Frauds, a writing must contain all the material terms of the contract. The writing must also be signed by the party against whom enforcement is sought. Lamle argues the June 26 email from Bucher satisfied both requirements.

The June 26 email specified the term of the license, the geographic scope, the percentage royalty, and the total advance and minimum amount to be paid under the contract. Bucher stated these terms had "been agreed in principal [sic] by [his] superiors at Mattel subject to contract" and the email message "covers the basic points."

California law is clear that "a note or memorandum under the statute of frauds need not contain all of the details of an agreement between the parties." Rather, the statute only requires "every material term of an agreement within its provisions be reduced to written form." "If the court, after acquiring knowledge of all the facts concerning the transaction which the parties themselves possessed at the time the agreement was made, can plainly determine from the memorandum the identity of the parties to the contract, the nature of its subject matter, and its essential terms, the memorandum will be held to be adequate." What is an essential term

[continued]

"depends on the agreement and its context and also on the subsequent conduct of the parties."

Mattel correctly points out the June 26 email does not contain all the terms that Lamle asserts are part of the oral contract. In particular, Mattel correctly notes Lamle alleges Mattel (1) guaranteed to sell 200,000 units of Farook each year; (2) promised to sell Farook units to Lamle at cost; and (3) promised Lamle the right to approve or disapprove the design and packaging of Farook units. None of these terms appears in the June 26 email. Again, we think there is a genuine issue of material fact as to the materiality of these terms. The Ninth Circuit, interpreting California law, has stated "the subject matter, the price, and the party against whom enforcement is sought" are the "few terms deemed essential as a matter of law by California courts." A jury could well conclude these omitted terms allegedly agreed to at the meeting but not reflected in the writing were not material.

There also remains the issue of whether an email is a writing "subscribed by the party to be charged or by the party's agent." The party to be charged in this case is Mattel, and the June 26 email was written by Bucher, an employee of Mattel, and his name appears at the end of the email, which concludes with "Best regards Mike Bucher." Mattel has not disputed the agency authority of Bucher to bind it. Therefore, the only question is whether Bucher's name on an email is a valid writing and signature to satisfy the Statute of Frauds.

California law does provide, however, typed names appearing on the end of telegrams are sufficient to be writings under the Statute of Frauds. California law also provides that a typewritten name is sufficient to be a signature. We can see no meaningful difference between a typewritten signature on a telegram and an email. Therefore, we conclude under California law the June 26 email satisfies the Statute of Frauds, assuming there was a binding oral agreement on June 11 and the email includes all the material terms of that agreement.

To prove a contract with Mattel, Lamle must prove the parties objectively intended to be immediately bound by an oral contract on June 11; the June 26 email contains the material terms of that oral contract; and Bucher had actual or apparent authority to sign for Mattel. Reviewing the record, Lamle has presented sufficient evidence to create genuine issues of material fact on these points. This is not to say Lamle should prevail at trial. Indeed, among other things, Lamle faces a difficult burden persuading the jury, despite Mattel's stating it would sign a formal contract later, the objective intention of both parties was to be immediately bound by the oral contract, and to abrogate a prior written agreement to the contrary.

Therefore, we vacate the grant of summary judgment with respect to the breach of contract claim and remand for further proceedings consistent with this opinion.

VACATED-IN-PART and REMANDED.

CRITICAL THINKING

The judge makes an argument about what constitutes a signature by referring to precedent and drawing an analogy between e-mails and telegrams. How strong is this analogy? Outline an argument against it. Explain.

ETHICAL DECISION MAKING

When Mattel's agents in charge of buying or rejecting games were negotiating with Lamle, they may have considered the ethical aspects of their decisions. If you were Mattel's agent, what ethical guidelines and values would you want to consider while evaluating the ethicality of terminating Mattel's relationship with Lamle? What ethical considerations would you find the most important?

Exceptions to the Statute of Frauds

Like most legal rules, the statute of frauds allows certain exceptions. These exceptions are (1) admission, (2) partial performance, and (3) promissory estoppel. There are also exceptions under the UCC. All these exceptions are summarized in Exhibit 18-3.

ADMISSION

An **admission** is a statement made in court, under oath, or at some stage during a legal proceeding in which a party against whom charges have been brought admits that an oral contract existed, even though the contract was required to be in writing.[8]

[8] Restatement (Second) of Contracts, sec. 133.

Exhibit 18-3
Exceptions to the Statute of Frauds

Admission	The party against whom charges have been brought admits during legal proceedings that an oral contract existed, even though the contract was supposed to be in writing.
Partial performance	A buyer of land, in alleged contract, has paid a portion of the sales price, has begun permanently improving the land, or has taken possession of it; these actions prove the existence of a contract.
Promissory estoppel	One party was detrimentally reliant on the contract, and this reliance was for seeable by the other party.
Exceptions under the UCC	1. Oral contracts between merchants selling goods to one another need not be in writing. 2. Oral contracts for customized goods are enforceable, even if they would normally have to be in writing.

Sinead enters into an agreement with Jin for the sale of a plot of land. The parties fail to write down their agreement but proceed as if it were finalized. Jin changes his mind and does not go through with the transaction. Sinead then sues him. If Jin admits during trial that there was an oral contract between him and Sinead, the courts would uphold the contract for the sale of land. Without this admission, the agreement between Sinead and Jin for the sale of interest in land would need to be in writing to be enforceable.

All states except Louisiana and California allow the admission exception. To the extent that the statute of frauds is intended to require proper evidence of agreements, the admission exception is well reasoned. However, to the extent that the statute is intended to encourage care and caution in establishing the specific details of agreements, the admission exception seems to unnecessarily punish honest parties while rewarding dishonest ones.

Like the statute of frauds, the UCC makes an exception when parties admit to the existence of an oral contract. However, it provides that a contract required to be in writing but admitted to in court will be enforceable only for the quantity admitted.[9]

BUT WHAT IF . . .

WHAT IF THE FACTS OF THE CASE OPENER WERE DIFFERENT?

Let's say that Branstad buys $1,000 worth of products from Garland. Such an agreement requires a writing, yet the two parties never made a written contract for the agreement. In court, both parties admit to making an oral agreement encompassing the same terms. Would the court be able to view such an agreement as being a valid contract?

PARTIAL PERFORMANCE

Although the statute of frauds requires a writing for sales of interests in land, under the **partial-performance** exception, if the buyer in an alleged contract for the sale of land has paid any portion of the sale price, has begun to permanently improve the land, or has taken possession of it, the courts will consider the contract partially performed and this partial performance will amount to proof of the contract.

[9] UCC § 2-201(3)(b).

Accordingly, partial performance can override the statute's requirement for a written agreement. The logic here is that the actions of both parties demonstrate the existence of their agreement, so the agreement no longer needs to be in writing to be enforceable. Under similar sections of the UCC, an oral contract is enforceable by the buyer or seller to the extent that he or she accepts payment or delivery of the goods in question.[10]

BUT WHAT IF . . .

WHAT IF THE FACTS OF THE CASE OPENER WERE DIFFERENT?

Let's say that Branstad bought land from Garland. Although such an agreement requires a writing, the two parties made only an oral agreement. Shortly after the agreement, Branstad began making payments and fixing up the land. Garland subsequently denied any agreement being made. Could some of Branstad's actions following the agreement be proof of the agreement? Could the court recognize the oral agreement as a valid contract?

PROMISSORY ESTOPPEL

Under certain circumstances, when a party relies on an oral contract that within the statute of frauds is required to be in writing, the reliance can create a situation in which the contract is nevertheless enforceable. **Promissory estoppel** is the legal enforcement of an otherwise unenforceable contract due to a party's detrimental reliance on the contract.

For promissory estoppel to be in effect, the party's reliance must be to her own detriment. Furthermore, the reliance must have been reasonably foreseeable; that is, the party who did not rely on the contract should have known the other party was going to rely on it.[11]

Suppose you enter into a contract to buy a house after having accepted an offer on your current house. The new house costs more than the price you are getting for your old house, and the person from whom you are buying knows about the sale of your old house and the difference in prices. To come up with the price difference, you sell your collection of rare coins. Unfortunately, however, you forget to create a written contract for your purchase of the new house, and the other person refuses to sell it to you. You are now homeless and have sold off your only real assets. Because the other person reasonably should have known you were relying on the contract, and because you did so to your own detriment, under promissory estoppel you could win performance of the sales contract.

This argument is not an easy one to make, however. For example, when Cheesecake Factory tried to argue that it should have been entitled to rely on a bank's oral representation that a loan would be approved, the court said that the firm's reliance on such representations was not reasonable. Further, the time between the representation and the firm's discovery that it would not receive the loan was so brief that the reliance could not have been that detrimental.[12]

EXCEPTIONS UNDER THE UCC

Exceptions also exist under the UCC. For instance, oral contracts between merchants need not be in writing to be enforceable. If one merchant agrees to sell goods to another, the contract is enforceable even if it is not in writing.

[10] UCC § 2-201(3)(c).

[11] Restatement (Second) of Contracts, sec. 139.

[12] *Classic Cheesecake Company, Inc., et al., v. JPMorgan Chase Bank, N.A.*, 546 F.3d 839, 2008 U.S. App. LEXIS 21632.

E-COMMERCE AND THE LAW

THE STATUTE OF FRAUDS AND LEGALLY BINDING ELECTRONIC TRANSACTIONS

An issue that comes up again and again in e-commerce is the lack of precedents or statutes applicable to situations arising in the new environment. Until rather recently, there weren't any statutes that specifically addressed the nature of electronic transactions. This situation requires that judges rely on their good judgment when interpreting traditional contract law and applying it to e-commerce. For some transactions to be viewed as legally valid under the statute of frauds, there must be written copies of the contract that are then signed by at least one of the parties. In 2000, the Uniform Electronic Transactions Act was proposed by the National Conference of Commissioners on Uniform State Laws. It was subsequently adopted as law in 49 states plus the District of Columbia, Puerto Rico and the U.S. Virgin Islands. This act circumvents the former requirements of the statute of frauds regarding the validity of online transactions. The act reflects the decision that particular electronic transactions may constitute a "written copy" and therefore have legal significance, despite the fact that the electronic transaction is not technically a written document. These statutory changes ensure that business owners are assured of the validity of an online contract.

Source: Uniform Electronic Transactions Act, National Conference of State Legislatures, http://www.ncsl.org/issues-research/telecom/uniform-electronic-transactions-acts.aspx.

Likewise, oral contracts for customized goods are enforceable even if they would normally have to be in writing. The reasoning is that customized goods are not likely to be salable to a general audience, so the party that did not back out of the agreement probably incurred unreasonable costs under the contract.

LO4 What is the purpose of the parol evidence rule?

Parol Evidence Rule

A problem arises with written contracts when a party asserts that the writing is in some way deficient. To smooth transactions by limiting the types of evidence admissible in such claims, the courts rely heavily on the **parol evidence rule.** This common law rule makes oral evidence of an agreement inadmissible if it is made before or at the same time as a writing that the parties intend to be the complete and final version of their agreement.[13] *Parol* in "parol evidence rule" means speech or words, specifically words outside the original writing.

The purpose of the parol evidence rule is to prevent evidence that substantially contradicts the agreement in its written form. Therefore, evidence of prior agreements and negotiations, as well as contemporaneous agreements and negotiations, is typically excluded under the parol evidence rule. A written agreement is assumed to be complete, and evidence contradicting it usually impedes business transactions, which is why the rule exists.

However, when a court determines that the written agreement does *not* represent a complete and final version of the agreement, evidence to further the court's understanding may be admissible. The additional evidence is limited to elements missing from the writing but consistent with it. These may be terms typically included in similar transactions or separate agreements in which consideration had been offered.

Note, however, that parol evidence applies first and foremost to spoken and written words extrinsic to the original writing. The parol evidence rule is also *not* a rule of evidence; rather, it relates to the substantive legal issue of what constitutes a legally binding agreement and how we know what that agreement is. Finally, the parol evidence rule is not a unitary concept or rule but an amalgamation of different rules and conditions.

Although the parol evidence rule applies to writings created at the same time as the written agreement, these writings tend to be treated differently than prior or contemporaneous oral agreements. That is, the writings are more readily admitted as part of the written agreement than is oral evidence regarding conditions or terms in the final agreement. As long as contemporaneous written documents do not substantially contradict what is in the final

[13] Restatement (Second) of Contracts, sec. 213.

writing, judges can use their discretion to deem these other writings part of that agreement. Consequently, the parol evidence rule does not usually exclude extrinsic written evidence.

Sometimes parties take the initiative and, in a **merger clause,** attempt to signal to judges that the written contract is intended to be the final and complete statement of their agreement. In essence, a merger clause seeks to blend other agreements either into the final agreement or into something explicitly identified as being outside the final agreement. Not all courts consider merger clauses to be conclusive proof of a contract. Where they are accepted, however, merger clauses greatly reduce the amount of guesswork courts must do in determining what is the final statement of the agreement.

Legal Principle: **Once a fully integrated agreement has been written, no oral evidence of any prior or contemporaneous agreement can be admitted in court to change the terms of the agreement.**

BUT WHAT IF . . .

WHAT IF THE FACTS OF THE CASE OPENER WERE DIFFERENT?

Recall that, in the Case Opener, Garland and Branstad's alleged oral agreement regarding interest payments was made after the completion of the written agreement. What if the oral agreement had been made before the two parties completed the written agreement? Would the oral agreement be admissible in court under the parole evidence rule?

Exceptions to the Parol Evidence Rule

Like the statute of frauds, the parol evidence rule admits some exceptions in which parol evidence, normally excluded, may be admissible in court. These exceptions are (1) contracts that have been subsequently modified, (2) contracts conditioned on orally agreed-on terms, (3) contracts that are not final as they are part written and part oral, (4) contracts with ambiguous terms, (5) incomplete contracts, (6) contracts with obvious typographical errors, (7) voidable or void contracts, and (8) evidence of prior dealings or usage of trade. (See Exhibit 18-4.)

Exhibit 18-4
Summary of Parol Evidence Rule

Parol Evidence Rule

Oral evidence of an agreement is inadmissible if it is made before or at the same time as a writing that the parties intend to be the complete and final version of the agreement.

Exceptions to the Rule

- Contract has been subsequently modified.
- Written agreement was based on an orally agreed-on condition.
- Contract is nonfinalized in that it is partly written and partly oral.
- Contract contains ambiguous terms that significantly affect its interpretation.
- Contract is incomplete in that it is missing critical information.
- Contract contains obvious typographical errors.
- Contract is void or voidable.
- Evidence about past business transactions will clarify missing information or ambiguities in the contract.

COMPARING THE LAW OF OTHER COUNTRIES

CIVIL LAW COUNTRIES AND THE PAROL EVIDENCE RULE

A number of our European allies, such as Germany and France, are civil law rather than common law countries and have a different approach to many of the legal doctrines the United States follows. For example, German law does not have a parol evidence rule. Instead, German courts tend to allow what U.S. courts call *parol evidence.* The logic is that such information is important for knowing the parties' intent when they entered into the contracts.

Unlike Germany, France does have a parol evidence rule, albeit a very limited one that does not apply to commercial contracts. The French court system thus attempts to facilitate business exchanges by allowing parol evidence to clarify all points related to terms of a contract or what a party thought he or she was agreeing to.

Interestingly enough, the parol evidence rule, a long-standing tradition in the common law, actually came to U.S. law by way of French law, just as the statute of frauds came through English common law. Yet the United States applies both rules to more cases than does either of the countries where these rules originated.

CONTRACTS THAT HAVE BEEN SUBSEQUENTLY MODIFIED

Although parol evidence contradictory to the final terms is inadmissible, evidence regarding a contract's subsequent modification *is* admissible. The modification must have been made after the writing, and the evidence must clearly indicate this later modification.

Despite the allowance of evidence to demonstrate modifications, not all evidence of modification is admissible. If the agreement is required to be in writing because it is within the statute of frauds, oral modifications are unenforceable. However, oral evidence of a subsequent written agreement is admissible. In addition, if the contract's terms require that modification be in writing, oral modifications are inadmissible and unenforceable.[14]

CONTRACTS CONDITIONED ON ORALLY AGREED-ON TERMS

The parol evidence rule does not prevent parties from introducing evidence proving the written agreement was conditioned on terms agreed to orally. The reason is that the evidence being elicited does not substantially modify the written agreement. Rather, what is at issue with such evidence is the enforceability of the contract as written. No terms are altered, so the parol evidence rule does not apply.

When an entire contract is conditioned on something else's occurring first, that first event is known as a **condition precedent.** Evidence of the existence of a condition precedent agreed to orally is admissible, as stated previously, because the contract is not modified by such evidence; rather, its enforceability is called into question. Since the statute of frauds is concerned primarily with the enforceability of agreements, it logically follows that the parol evidence rule does not apply to evidence of condition precedents.

NONFINALIZED, PARTIALLY WRITTEN AND PARTIALLY ORAL CONTRACTS

When a contract consists of both written and oral elements, judges tend to treat it as nonfinalized and assume that the parties do not intend to have the written part represent the entire agreement. Therefore, oral evidence related to the contract is admissible because the written document is not the complete and final representation of the agreement.

CONTRACTS CONTAINING AMBIGUOUS TERMS

A contract that contains what the court deems to be ambiguous terms presents a dilemma in interpretation. To reach the most accurate interpretation of the original agreement, the

[14] UCC § 2-209(2),(3).

court allows evidence, even if it is oral, for the sole purpose of clarifying, *not* changing, ambiguous contractual terms. As with the evidence regarding orally agreed-on condition precedents, evidence used to clarify ambiguity is believed not to modify the contract but, rather, to clarify, and therefore it is admissible.

INCOMPLETE CONTRACTS

When a contract is fundamentally flawed because it is missing critical information, typically related to essential terms, courts can allow parol evidence to fill in the missing parts while not modifying the written agreement in any substantial way. Parol evidence is here used to facilitate business transactions, not to force the parties to enter into a new, complete agreement.

CONTRACTS WITH OBVIOUS TYPOGRAPHICAL ERRORS

Whenever a written agreement under the statute of frauds contains a serious, and obvious, typographical error (typo), parol evidence is admissible to demonstrate that it was a typo, as well as to set forth the proper term. This admission does not fundamentally alter the written agreement because the typo is not an accurate reflection of the parties' agreement.

VOID OR VOIDABLE CONTRACTS

Certain conditions can make an otherwise valid contract void or voidable. (Refer to Chapter 13 for an in-depth discussion of what makes a contract void or voidable.) While the contract does not list these conditions, the courts allow parol evidence to demonstrate them. Like most exceptions to the parol evidence rule, this one does not fundamentally alter the terms of the contract but, rather, addresses its enforceability. Furthermore, evidence of a defense against a contract (discussed in Chapter 16) is admissible to prove a contract is void or voidable.

EVIDENCE OF PRIOR DEALINGS OR USAGE OF TRADE (UCC)

This final exception actually falls under the UCC and not the statute of frauds. According to the UCC, parol evidence is admissible for the sake of clarification if it addresses prior dealings between the parties or usages of trade in the business they are in.[15] Evidence related to past dealings can help clarify missing or ambiguous terms by demonstrating how the parties have previously interacted; the assumption is that they will continue to interact in a similar manner. Therefore, if a term is missing or ambiguous, the courts rely on evidence of what the parties did in the past to gauge what they intended in the contract in question.

Similarly, when a contract is ambiguous or incomplete, the courts examine standard practices in the business, assuming the parties intend to engage in these practices even if they are not included in the agreement. Once again, an exception is made to allow parol evidence to clarify a contract, as opposed to changing any material terms.

Integrated Contracts

Integrated contracts are written contracts intended to be the complete and final representation of the parties' agreement. When the courts deem a contract integrated, with the exception of the above exceptions, parol evidence is inadmissible. In partially integrated contracts, parol evidence is admissible to the extent that it clarifies part of the contract or

[15] UCC §§ 1-205 and 2-202.

CASE NUGGET

A CLEAR ILLUSTRATION OF THE NEED FOR A WRITING

Scalisi et al. v. New York University Medical Center
805 N.Y.S.2d 62 (N.Y. App. Div., 1st Dept., Dec. 6, 2005)

The plaintiffs in this breach-of-contract action learned the importance of getting guarantees in writing. They allegedly entered into an oral agreement with the Medical Center for an in vitro fertilization procedure that would not result in the birth of an autistic child. Subsequently, the parties signed a written contract stating that a certain percentage of children are born with physical and mental defects and the occurrence of such defects is "beyond the control of the physician." The document also stated that the Medical Center and its physicians would not "assume responsibility for the physical and mental characteristic or hereditary tendencies" of any child born as a result of the in vitro procedure.

When one of the twins conceived as a result of the in vitro procedure was born with "autistic traits," the parents sued for breach of the oral agreement, alleging that they had entered into it for the purpose of having offspring free of autism. The lower court granted the hospital summary judgment, holding that the written agreement signed by the parents barred the admissibility of the oral agreement. The state court of appeals affirmed, finding that even if the alleged oral promises had been made, they were inadmissible in light of the existence of the subsequent written agreement directly contradictory to them.

addresses its enforceability.[16] Therefore, the easiest test to determine the admissibility of parol evidence is to check whether the written contract, within the statute of frauds, is an integrated contract.

We've seen that one way parties can indicate their desire to create an integrated contract is through the use of a merger clause. A merger clause explicitly states that the written contract is intended to be the complete and final version of the contract between the parties and that other possible agreements between the parties, besides the one in question, are not part of the final written agreement. Most states will allow a merger clause to constitute the stated intent of the parties unless one party offers proof of a personal defense against the contract. However, some states consider merger clauses to be recommendations, not necessarily binding on the parties.

CASE OPENER WRAP-UP

Admissibility of an Oral Contract in Court

The district court found for Branstad after seeing evidence that Branstad and his wife had not only managed Garland's other properties until 1998 but had spent their own money on the properties' upkeep. Additionally, in accordance with Branstad's account of the oral agreement, the payments Branstad had made to Garland were listed in payment and tax records as noninterest payments. Such information showed that Garland had made no attempt to collect interest payments until the two had a falling out in 1998. Furthermore, the court determined that the parol evidence rule did not apply to the oral agreement in question because the agreement was made after the completion of the written contract, not before or during. Ultimately, the court determined that the oral contract existed as a separate agreement and not as part of the original written agreement.[17]

[16] Restatement (Second) of Contracts, sec. 216.

[17] *Garland v. Brandstad,* 648 NW 2d 65 (2002).

KEY TERMS

SUMMARY OF KEY TOPICS

Statute of Frauds

The term *statute of frauds* refers to various state laws modeled after the 1677 English Act for the Prevention of Frauds and Perjuries. These state laws are intended to (1) ease contractual negotiations by requiring sufficient reliable evidence to prove the existence and specific terms of a contract, (2) prevent unreliable oral evidence from interfering with a contractual relationship, and (3) prevent parties from entering into contracts with which they do not agree.

Contracts Falling within the Statute of Frauds

Contracts falling within the statute of frauds:

1. Contracts whose terms prevent possible performance within one year.
2. Promises made in consideration of marriage.
3. Contracts for one party to pay the debt of another if the initial party fails to pay.
4. Contracts related to an interest in land.
5. Under the Uniform Commercial Code, contracts for the sale of goods totaling more than $500.

Sufficiency of the Writing

A sufficient writing under the statute of frauds must clearly indicate (1) the parties to the contract, (2) the subject matter of the agreement, (3) the consideration given for the contract, (4) all relevant contractual terms, and (5) the signature of at least the party against whom action is brought.

Under the UCC, writing must clearly indicate (1) the quantity to be sold and (2) the signature of the party being sued.

Under both the statute of frauds and the UCC, a writing may consist of multiple documents as long as they explicitly reference one another.

Exceptions to the Statute of Frauds

Exceptions to the requirement of a writing under the statute of frauds:

1. Admission that an oral agreement exists.
2. Partial performance of the contract.
3. Promissory estoppel (legal enforcement due to a party's detrimental reliance on the contract).
4. Various exceptions under the UCC.

Parol Evidence Rule

The *parol evidence rule* is a common law rule stating that oral evidence of an agreement made prior to or contemporaneously with the written agreement is inadmissible when the parties intend to have a written agreement be the complete and final version of their agreement.

Exceptions to the Parol Evidence Rule

Exceptions to the parol evidence rule:

1. Contracts that are subsequently modified.
2. Contracts conditioned on orally agreed-on terms.
3. Contracts that are not final because they are partly written and partly oral.
4. Contracts with ambiguous terms.
5. Incomplete contracts.

6. Contracts with obvious typographical errors.
7. Voidable or void contracts.
8. Evidence of prior dealings or usage of trade.

Integrated Contracts *Integrated contracts* are written contracts within the statute of frauds intended to be the complete and final representation of the parties' agreement, thus precluding the admissibility of parol evidence other than in the exceptions listed above.

POINT / COUNTERPOINT

Does the United States Still Benefit from Having a Statute of Frauds?

YES

The statute of frauds provides great benefit as a social lubricant aiding U.S. business transactions. By requiring that certain types of contracts be in writing, we ensure that they either will have enough evidence to prove the existence and terms of the contract or will be unenforceable. Because only certain contracts are required to be in writing, the rule does not preclude oral contracts, but it ensures that the most important contracts can be enacted without complications.

Another way in which the statute of frauds benefits U.S. business is by preventing unreliable evidence from being used in court. Human memories are notoriously weak and faulty, and it does not make sense to base important legal decisions on what someone says he or she remembers. Furthermore, people with a vested interest can change their testimony on the basis of changed circumstances in pursuit of personal gain. However, with the requirement that certain contracts be in writing, the parties are bound by what they wrote.

Finally, the act of writing gives people time to pause for reflection. No one benefits when parties hastily rush into an agreement they later regret. Thoughtful reflection prevents parties from entering into contracts with which they do not agree, and this means fewer cases are brought due to one party's entering an unfair, or otherwise defective, agreement.

NO

The statute of frauds acts as an impediment to contractual agreements, and the states should repeal the relevant sections of their laws.

When parties agree, why should they be subjected to unnecessary formalities? The written requirements of the statute of frauds get in the way of business transactions more often than they help.

Furthermore, the required writing frequently imposes additional costs on the parties. When even simple agreements in which neither party contests the terms must be written, more time is spent *not* conducting other business. Frequently, the parties have to hire attorneys to write their contracts, imposing still more costs and helping decrease whatever benefit the parties might have gained from the original agreement before the writing took place.

In addition, although most parties enter agreements in good faith, it is not uncommon for parties to seek a way out of contracts they cannot perform. The writing requirements are not always accurately fulfilled, and unethical parties can exploit minor technicalities to have a contract declared void. In the end, the innocent party is harmed by the writing requirement, and the unethical party escapes a bad situation with little to no harm.

QUESTIONS & PROBLEMS

1. Describe the contents of a writing that would be sufficient to satisfy the statute of frauds under the common law.
2. List the kinds of contracts that require a writing under the statute of frauds.
3. Identify the exceptions to the parol evidence rule, and explain why some people might argue that the rule is not very effective.
4. The McCartheys controlled Salt Lake City's largest daily newspaper, *The Salt Lake Tribune,* through their

collective ownership of shares in the Kearns-Tribune (KT) Corporation, a holding company for the newspaper. In 1997, KT merged with Tele-Communications, Inc. (TCI). The McCartheys originally opposed the merger but later agreed to it. In 1999, TCI and AT&T merged, and AT&T sold the *Tribune* to MediaNews in 2001. The McCartheys argue that according to an oral agreement reached in 1997, at the time of the original merger that they opposed, the McCartheys have the opportunity to buy back the *Tribune* after five years (in 2002) for a fair market price but that MediaNews tried to block any attempt at a sale. The McCartheys filed suit to enforce the oral agreement. MediaNews moved for a declaratory judgment that the McCartheys have no independent rights in the *Tribune*. The district court granted the defendant's motions as to all claims. The McCartheys appealed. Under what conditions would the McCartheys' claim be successful? As a judge, what evidence would help you decide whether the oral agreement constituted a valid contract? [*MediaNews Group, Inc. v. McCarthey*, 494 F.3d 1254 (2007).]

5. Antwun Echols, a professional boxer, signed a promotional agreement with Banner Promotions Inc. The agreement gave Banner the right to be Echols's sole representative in negotiations for all fights. Banner's major obligation under the agreement was to "secure, arrange and promote" not less than three bouts for Echols during each year of the contract. Banner was to pay Echols not less than a contractually stated minimum amount for each bout in which he appeared, with the amount of the minimum depending on where the bout was televised and whether Echols appeared as a champion. However, Banner had the option to renegotiate the amounts if Echols lost a fight, which he did one month into the contract; afterward, Banner chose to negotiate Echols's compensation on a bout-by-bout basis. After several fights under the new agreement, Echols became dissatisfied with the situation, arguing that Banner had made him "take it or leave it" offers for what he believed was below-market compensation. Echols sued Banner, arguing that the variable amounts made the contract vague and therefore unenforceable. Did the agreement constitute a valid contract? Why or why not? [*Echols v. Pelullo*, 377 F.3d 272 (2004).]

6. Sunkist Growers Inc. brought Nabisco to court, claiming that under the companies' mutually agreed-on license agreement, Nabisco was causing Sunkist to engage in improper practices. Nabisco claimed that, under the license agreement, the companies had to settle the dispute through arbitration. However, Sunkist claimed that it was a nonsignatory to the contract and thus did not have to settle through arbitration. Nabisco claimed that Sunkist was legally compelled to settle through arbitration, even though Sunkist had not signed the document, because the two parties admitted to the license agreement being an agreement between them and both companies' actions had been based on the agreement. How do you think the court decided? [10 F. 3d 753 (Ga. CA 11, 1993).]

7. The plaintiff investor sued the defendant investment company for breach of an oral agreement on the part of the defendant to recommend hedge funds for the plaintiff and exercise due diligence with respect to the recommendations, in exchange for which the plaintiff would pay a 1 percent fee for every year the defendant held the fund. The suit arose when the plaintiff found out that the hedge fund the company recommended was a ponzi scheme. The district court dismissed the case on the grounds that the contract was an ongoing one that would not be completed within a year and therefore required a writing to be enforceable. The plaintiff appealed. How do you think the appellate court ruled on this issue, and why? [*South Cherry Street, LLC v. Hennessee Group LLC*, 573 F.3d 98, 2009 U.S. App. LEXIS 15467.]

8. In 1995, Schaefer was in a car accident, and his vehicle was damaged. His insurance company looked at his vehicle and gave him money to repair it. However, even with the repairs, Schaefer's vehicle's overall value dropped almost $3,000 due to the accident. Schaefer's interpretation of the insurance company's written policy was that the company would return the vehicle to its original value before the accident. On the other hand, the insurance company interpreted the written policy as meaning that the company would pay the lesser option of either replacing the vehicle with one of a similar value or paying for repairs. How do courts usually resolve cases of ambiguity in contracts? How did the court decide this case? [*Am. Mfrs. Mut. Ins. Co. v. Schaefer*, 124 S.W.3d 154, 2003 Tex. LEXIS 472, 47 Tex. Sup. Ct. J. 40 (Tex. 2003).]

9. In 2004, real estate broker Richard Davis called an A&E television executive about partnering on a

new reality show called *Flip This House.* Davis said he would undertake the financial risks of purchasing and later reselling the real estate and he and the network would split the net profits. Davis received confirmation from the network director over the phone and later with three other executives. The network never paid Davis and claimed no agreement was made. The district court found on behalf of Davis, and the network appealed. The appellate court stipulated that two facts must be true to find on behalf of Davis: first, that Davis reasonably believed that an agreement was made during the phone conversations and, second, that such a belief would be made by an objectively reasonable person. How do you think the court decided? [*Davis v. A&E Television,* 422 Fed. Appx. 199, 2011 U.S. App. LEXIS 7382.]

10. Benito Brino owned real property that he leased to Salvatore and Linda Gabriele. During the lease, the Gabrieles attempted to purchase the property from Brino. Both parties agreed on a purchase price of $565,000 with a closing date of September 15, 2001. However, the Gabrieles were not able to obtain the full amount in loan financing from the bank, so they made a counteroffer to purchase for $450,000, which Brino rejected. The Gabrieles later obtained the full $565,000 from another lending institution and drafted an addendum to the July sales agreement that altered the closing date to May 5, 2002. Brino orally accepted the terms of the agreement, but the document was not signed until May 16, 2002, after the closing date. Consequently, the bank refused to acknowledge the addendum's validity. Thereafter, the Gabrieles drafted a second sales agreement with the same terms as the July agreement, except that the second agreement did not include a closing date but stated that the effective date would be the signing date. Both parties signed the agreement on June 16, 2002, and the bank accepted the agreement and agreed to provide the loan. The Gabrieles informed Brino that they were ready to close, but Brino did not convey title of the property to the Gabrieles. The Gabrieles brought suit against Brino, seeking specific performance, but Brino argued that the agreement was not enforceable as it did not satisfy the statute of frauds, primarily because the agreement did not designate the seller. In response, the Gabrieles claimed that their obtaining financing was partial performance of the agreement. How did the court resolve this issue with regard to the statute of frauds? [*Gabriele v. Brino,* 2004 Conn. App. LEXIS 428.]

Looking for more review materials?

The Online Learning Center at **www.mhhe.com/kubasek3e** contains this chapter's "Assignment on the Internet" and also a list of URLs for more information, entitled "On the Internet." Find both of them in the Student Center portion of the OLC, along with quizzes and other helpful materials.

CHAPTER 19

Third-Party Rights to Contracts

LEARNING OBJECTIVES

After reading this chapter, you will be able to answer the following questions:

1. What is an assignment?
2. What are the rights and duties of an assignor?
3. What are the rights and duties of an assignee?
4. What is a third-party beneficiary contract?
5. What are the differences among donee beneficiaries, creditor beneficiaries, and incidental beneficiaries?

CASE OPENER

Fallout from a Unforgettable Fight

On June 28, 1997, in Las Vegas, heavyweight boxers Mike Tyson and Evander Holyfield met for what proved to be a night to remember. During the third round of the fight, a desperate Tyson illegally bit off a piece of Holyfield's ear and, moments later, bit the other ear too.[1] Tyson was disqualified. Some fans were so outraged that they decided to sue Tyson, the fight promoters, and the telecasters, seeking a refund.[2] Among other things, they claimed to be third-party beneficiaries to various contracts into which the defendants had entered.

1. Are fans entitled to refunds on the basis of third-party beneficiary rights? What type of beneficiaries would fans have to be to enforce contractual rights?
2. If you were one of the fight promoters, what sorts of contractual duties would you have to the viewers?

The Wrap-Up at the end of the chapter will answer these questions.

[1] CNN/SI, "Year in Review 1997," http://sportsillustrated.cnn.com/features/1997/yearinreview/topstories.

[2] *Castillo v. Tyson,* 268 A.D.2d 336 (2000).

As you read in Chapter 13, contracts are agreements between two parties who each agree to give to or do something for the other party. Contracts are typically private agreements in that they bind the two parties and no one else. Thus, parties not in *privity of contract* (anyone other than the contracting parties) usually do not have rights to a contract. However, as is frequently the case in the law, there are exceptions to the general rule.

A third party gains rights to a contract to which she or he is not a party in two situations. In the first, one of the contracting parties transfers rights or duties to the third party. In the second, the third party is a direct beneficiary of a contract between two other parties. This chapter examines both situations.

Assignments and Delegations

Both parties to a contract are both **obligors** (contractual parties who agreed to do something for the other party) and **obligees** (contractual parties who agreed to receive something from the other party). Contracts thus create a situation in which both parties have a duty to perform the agreed-on action and a right to be the recipient of the other party's duty. These rights and duties can be transferred to third parties. This section discusses both the transfer of rights—assignment—and the transfer of duties—delegation.

ASSIGNMENT

LO1 What is an assignment?

Assignment occurs when a party to a contract—an **assignor**—transfers her rights to receive something under the contract to a third party—an **assignee** (see Exhibit 19-1). For example, Bina agrees to sell her car to José for $8,000. She then assigns her right to receive José's payment to Kelly. Kelly, who was not part of the original contract between Bina and José, is an assignee and now has the right to receive payment from José for Bina's car.

LO2 What are the rights and duties of an assignor?

When an assignor transfers her rights to an assignee, the assignor legally gives up all rights she had to collect on the contract.[3] Now the assignee may legally demand performance from the other party to the original contract. Returning to our example, once Bina transfers her right to Kelly, Bina can no longer require that José pay her for her car; Kelly, however, can request that José pay her for Bina's car.

Exhibit 19-1
Assignment of Rights

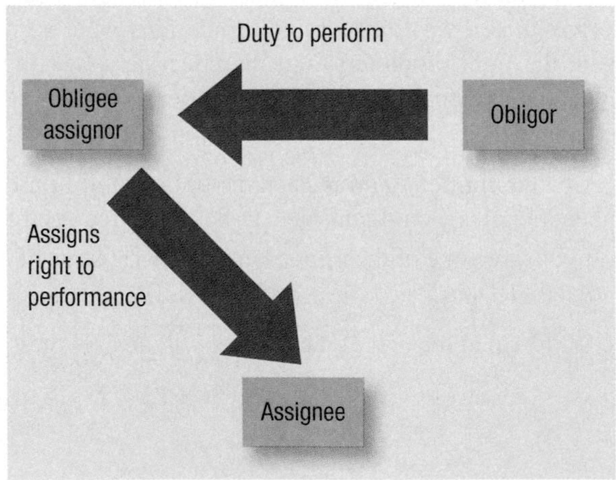

[3] Restatement (Second) of Contracts, sec. 317.

Legal Principle: A person who transfers his or her rights under a third party is an assignor, and the person who receives the transfer and is now entitled to enforce the rights is the assignee.

An assignee essentially fills in for the assignor as the legal recipient of the contractual duties and thereby acquires the same rights the assignor had. The assignee is offered no additional protections, however, and the obligor (the other party to the contract, who owes a duty to the assignee) may raise any of the same defenses for nonperformance to the assignee that he would have been able to raise against the assignor. Returning to our earlier example, if Bina failed to deliver her car to José, he can legally refuse to pay Kelly on the basis of Bina's breach of contract. It does not matter that Kelly had no duty in the original contract; she is subject to the same defense José has against Bina and therefore would not be paid in this situation.

LO3
What are the rights and duties of an assignee?

Although assignments require no special wording or forms to be valid, certain restrictions exist. First, assignments covered by the statute of frauds must be in writing.[4] Because it is difficult to prove the existence of assignments given orally, it is usually suggested they all be in writing.

Second, an assignee must agree to accept the assigned rights. An assignee may decline an assignment if he has not legally agreed to it and if he declines in a timely fashion after learning about the assignment and its terms.[5] There is no protocol for rejecting an assignment, but once rejected, it is considered rejected from the time it was first offered. Third, in some situations contractual rights cannot be assigned.[6]

Case 19-1 demonstrates the problems that can arise in business transactions when it is not clear whether something is a sale or an assignment of rights. Pay close attention to the court's discussion of assignment of rights as opposed to the transfer of business property.

[4] The UCC requires that assignments be in writing when the amount assigned is greater than $5,000.

[5] Restatement (Second) of Contracts, sec. 327.

[6] Ibid., sec. 317(2).

COMPARING THE LAW OF OTHER COUNTRIES

EXPANDING THIRD-PARTY RIGHTS IN AUSTRALIA AND THE UNITED KINGDOM

Most countries do not grant third-party rights to contracts. Rather, most countries require that a party be a direct party to a contract before he or she can recover under the contract. The logic of the doctrine of privity is that a person who is not a party to a contract does not have the right to enforce it because no consideration was offered to him or her under the contract.

One notable exception is Australia, where a third party can sue for breach of contract. In most other countries, privity must be established before a party may sue.

However, privity requirements are beginning to be relaxed in the United Kingdom, expanding third-party rights. U.K. solicitors (lawyers) who have been negligent in the creation of a will have been held liable to the will's intended beneficiaries. Privity is still required in most situations in Australia and the United Kingdom, but the number of exceptions continues to grow.

CASE 19-1 GENERAL MILLS, INC. v. KRAFT FOODS GLOBAL, INC.
U.S. COURT OF APPEALS FOR THE FEDERAL CIRCUIT
487 F.3D 1368 (2007)

General Mills sells rolled food items under the brand name Fruit by the Foot, and it owns two U.S. patents on the rolled food item. In 1995, General Mills sued Farley for infringement of these patents, a dispute that General Mills and Farley resolved through a settlement agreement. The Settlement Agreement required Farley to pay General Mills a lump sum in exchange for the grants by General Mills of a release of its patent claims and a covenant not to sue Farley for past, current, or future infringement. The Settlement Agreement includes as "Farley" any and all parent companies, subsidiaries, predecessors, and successors. The covenant not to sue also contains language defining the "Releasee" as including Farley and its "successors." The Settlement Agreement also contains two provisions that define limiting conditions to the assignment or transfer of rights under the Agreement to another party by Farley (or its successors).

Kraft became the successor to Farley. General Mills agrees that Kraft became Farley's successor. In 2002, Kraft "sold and transferred Farley assets, including the Farley trademark and goodwill, to a subsidiary of Catterton Partners." It is undisputed that Kraft retained at least some portion of the original Farley assets and of Farley's rolled food business. After a few years of what General Mills alleges to be infringing activity, Kraft sold the remainder of its rolled food business and purported to transfer whatever rights it had under the Settlement Agreement to Kellogg Company. General Mills does not claim that Kraft engaged in infringing activities after the Kellogg transaction. General Mills sued Kraft alleging infringement of the two patents in the period between the Catterton transaction and the Kellogg transaction. Kraft argues that General Mills breached the Settlement Agreement by filing suit. The district court granted Kraft's motion to dismiss. General Mills appealed.

JUDGE LINN:

II. Discussion

B. Kraft's Status as Successor to Farley

As mentioned above, General Mills concedes that Kraft became Farley's successor by virtue of the Farley transaction. General Mills does not allege infringement prior to the Farley transaction or between the Farley transaction and the Catterton transaction. Rather, General Mills argues that "[t]he Catterton Transaction divested Kraft of any rights it might have had under the Settlement Agreement, because without the Farley assets that were sold to Catterton Partners, Kraft cannot be 'Farley' under the Settlement Agreement."

The part of the Settlement Agreement from which General Mills derives this argument is Article 8.4, which requires that Farley (including its successors, under Article 1.6) "must transfer its entire rolled food business" if it wishes to assign its rights under the Settlement Agreement without General Mills' consent. Article 8.4, General Mills argues, "makes certain that the Farley Agreement remains with Farley's entire rolled-food business." However, as the district court correctly recognized, the Settlement Agreement speaks only to the assignment of rights: "[n]either article [8.3 or 8.4] addresses Farley's retention of the Settlement Agreement and sale of other assets." Because the Catterton transaction did not purport to assign Kraft's rights under the Settlement Agreement, the restrictions imposed by Article 8.4 simply do not apply.

Nor does any other provision of the Settlement Agreement bar Farley from retaining its rights under the agreement when it transfers parts of its rolled food business. As mentioned, General Mills does not dispute that pursuant to Article 8.4, Kraft became Farley's successor before the Catterton transaction. Accordingly, the question is not whether Kraft complied with the conditions necessary for it to become

Farley's successor. The question is whether the Settlement Agreement imposed conditions on Kraft's continuing entitlement to the covenant not to sue. Although General Mills and Farley could have agreed to impose on Farley or Farley's successor ongoing obligations such as the retention of specified assets, they did not do so. There is simply nothing in the contract that requires Kraft to retain all or any particular assets of the Farley business to preserve Kraft's status as successor.

General Mills nonetheless argues that general principles of successorship prevent Kraft from continuing as "Farley" or a "successor" once it had sold off assets that were part of the original Farley business in the Catterton transaction. For General Mills to prevail, Kraft's rights under the agreement must have either (1) terminated by operation of law at the time of the Catterton transaction, or (2) been transferred from Kraft to Catterton by operation of law or by the terms of the Catterton transaction. We are not persuaded that either of these eventualities has occurred. . . .

As to the second possibility—that Catterton became Farley's successor after the Catterton transaction and divested Kraft of that status—General Mills does not even make this argument. The record contains no allegations as to what law controls the Catterton transaction or what assets, aside from Farley's goodwill and trademarks, Kraft transferred to Catterton. However, we note that the general rule of corporate law is that a transaction involving a transfer of property "from one corporation to another without consolidation or merger, does not include a transfer of all the powers or immunities of the selling corporation." Here, not only did the Catterton transaction not involve a merger or consolidation, but there is not even an allegation that Catterton acquired the entirety of Farley. Indeed, had Kraft not retained at least some part of Farley's rolled food business after the transaction, General Mills could not have alleged infringement. There is simply no basis from which we might conclude that anyone other than Kraft succeeded to Farley's rights under the Settlement Agreement, at least until the Kellogg transaction.

There is also no merit to General Mills' argument that the Catterton transaction excused General Mills' obligation to perform under the Settlement Agreement pursuant to the doctrine of impossibility. It is true that after the Catterton transaction, Kraft no longer owned the Farley name and all of Farley's assets. But this fact did not prevent General Mills from affording Kraft the same rights under the Settlement Agreement that it had possessed since the Farley transaction. In the other direction, Kraft's only obligation that the Catterton transaction might possibly interfere with—the requirement in Article 8.4 that Farley "transfer its entire rolled food product business"—applies only when Farley or its successor purports to assign its rights under the Settlement Agreement. At the time of the Catterton transaction, no one alleges that this occurred.

Accordingly, we hold that at least until the Kellogg transaction, Kraft was entitled to the protection of Farley's covenant not to sue, and the district court properly dismissed General Mills' patent infringement claim against Kraft. . . .

AFFIRMED.

CRITICAL THINKING

Notice that one of the keys to the decision is whether the deal between Kraft and Catterton involved a sale of a part of a business or involved an assignment of contractual rights. In business, specific definitions can be important for determining which laws apply in a given situation. Besides the transaction between Kraft and Catterton, are there significant ambiguous words or phrases in the decision that would lead to possible confusion regarding the ruling? In what way do these ambiguities affect the ruling?

ETHICAL DECISION MAKING

Two critical events led up to this case: (1) the transaction between Kraft and Catterton and (2) General Mills' decision to sue Kraft. What ethical implications exist in each of these decisions? Can the behavior of one side or the other be deemed more ethically defensible? If so, which side, and why? What ethical theories or guidelines support your claim? Does the decision of the court reflect an agreement with your view?

Rights That Cannot Be Assigned. Exhibit 19-2 lists the four situations in which contractual rights cannot be assigned to a third party. We discuss each of them below.

First, the rights to a contract cannot be assigned when the contract is personal in nature, meaning the obligor has promised something specific to the person receiving it. Third parties cannot legally become the recipient in such situations unless the only part of a contract left to be fulfilled is the payment,[7] because rights to payment can always be assigned.

[7] Ibid., secs. 317 and 318.

COMPARING THE LAW OF OTHER COUNTRIES

ASSIGNMENT OF RIGHTS IN CHINA

Almost all developed market economies permit the free assignability of contract rights. Assignments play a crucial role in business financing because they enable banks and businesses to make loans and pay debts. Almost all developed market economies thus permit the free assignability of contract rights, while most centrally planned economies, such as China, permit only limited assignability. When a contract is with the state, approval by the proper state authority must first be obtained unless the contract allows for assignments. If the contract is with a private party, the assignor must first get the obligor's approval before an assignment can be made.

For example, when Burkhart went to work for NES, a company that rented and sold trenching equipment to Las Vegas–area contractors, he received $10,000 to sign an agreement not to compete for one year if he left the company's employ. NES was subsequently sold to Traffic Control Services. Burkhart refused to sign a noncompete agreement with the new firm and subsequently quit and went to work for a competitor. When Traffic Control Services sued to enforce the noncompete agreement Burkhard had signed with NES, the court ultimately found that the agreement could not be assigned.[8]

Second, rights cannot be assigned when the assignment increases the risk or duties the obligor would face in fulfilling the original contract. For example, Ben agrees to replace the siding on Erin's two-bedroom ranch. Erin cannot assign her right to Ben's services to Chris, who lives in a three-story, five-bedroom house, because Ben's duties would be greatly increased by the change.

Third, rights cannot be assigned when the contract expressly forbids assignments. When parties include an *antiassignment clause* in their contract, the parties are attempting to limit their ability to assign their rights under the contract. However, the wording of the antiassignment clause is determinative regarding the effectiveness of the clause. That is, if worded improperly or ambiguously, the clause does not effectively limit assignments.

Most courts consider antiassignment clauses as promises. Assignments made despite such clauses are effective, but the party who makes the assignment will still be liable for breaching the terms of the contract. Moreover, unless the clause is very specific, courts generally consider that it prevents delegation of duties, not assignment of rights.[9] A clause stating "All assignments are void under this contract" will be considered effective in prohibiting the assignment of rights. In contrast, when a contract includes a clause explicitly permitting assignments, the parties may assign rights, even when assignments would normally be considered improper because of an increased duty, risk, or burden to the obligor.[10]

Even in the presence of an antiassignment clause, there are exceptions in which assignments can still be made. For instance, antiassignment clauses do not affect assignments made by operation of law. If a law necessitates an assignment, such as in bankruptcy cases, the assignment is effective regardless of any contractual agreement to the contrary.

Exhibit 19-2

Contractual Rights That Cannot Be Assigned

1. Rights that are personal in nature.
2. Rights whose assignment would increase the obligor's risk or duties.
3. Rights whose assignment is prohibited by contract.
4. Rights whose assignment is prohibited by law or public policy.

[8] *Traffic Control Services v. United Rentals Northwest,* 87 P.3d 1054 (Sup. Ct. Nev. 2004).

[9] Restatement (Second) of Contracts, sec. 322(1) and UCC § 2-210(3).

[10] Ibid., sec. 323(1).

Likewise, as we've said above, the right to assign monetary payments cannot be denied. Therefore, even when a contract has an antiassignment clause, either party may still assign his or her right to receive payment.[11] One reason the law does not bar the right to receive payment is that companies often transfer rights to payments in the regular course of business. Preventing these transfers would have a negative impact on the business community. Also, one's duty to pay is not affected when the party receiving payment changes; that is, no added burden is placed on the obligor.

BUT WHAT IF . . .

WHAT IF THE FACTS OF THE CASE OPENER WERE DIFFERENT?

Let's say, in the Case Opener, that Tyson was performing in the match for a large sum of money. He wanted to assign his monetary rights to his mother. However, there was an antiassignment clause in the contract. Would Tyson still be able to assign his financial rights to his mother?

In addition, assignments of the right to receive damages for a breach of contract to sell goods or services are unaffected by antiassignment clauses.[12] If one party breaches the contract, the other can sue and transfer the right to recovery to a third party.

Finally, when law or public policy forbids assignments, the forbidden rights cannot be assigned. Various state and federal statutes prohibit the assigning of specific rights. If the assignment is determined to be against public policy, it is also deemed ineffective. Except as outlined in this section, all other rights are presumed assignable. Once it has been established that an assignment is valid, notice should be given to the obligor regarding the assignment.

Notice of Assignment. Although notice need not be given for a valid assignment, it is usually a good idea for the assignor or the assignee to notify the obligor. Assignments are effective immediately regardless of notice, but by providing notice the assignor can help avoid two serious complications.

The first possible complication occurs if the obligor fulfills the contract as written. Because fulfilling the contract discharges the obligor's duties, the act also discharges the assignee's claim on the assignor's right. However, once given notice, the obligor can discharge his contractual obligations only by fulfilling the contract for the assignee.

For example, suppose Stefan contracts with Latoya to purchase her speedboat. Latoya assigns her right to collect Stefan's money to Meghan. Neither Latoya nor Meghan notifies Stefan of the assignment. Accordingly, Stefan pays Latoya for the boat. His contractual duties have been discharged, and Meghan cannot request performance from him. Had Stefan been notified about the assignment, the only way he could fulfill his contractual obligations would be by paying Meghan the money owed to Latoya. If, after receiving notice, Stefan pays Latoya, Meghan may still legally request that he pay her. Giving the obligor proper notice avoids such problems with performance.

Legal Principle: **The assignee should always give notice to the obligor as soon as possible after receiving the assignment, because the obligor may satisfy his or her obligations by performing for the assignor until receiving notice of the assignment from the assignee.**

[11] UCC § 9-318(4).

[12] UCC § 2-210(2).

Exhibit 19-3
Assignment of the Same Right to Two Parties

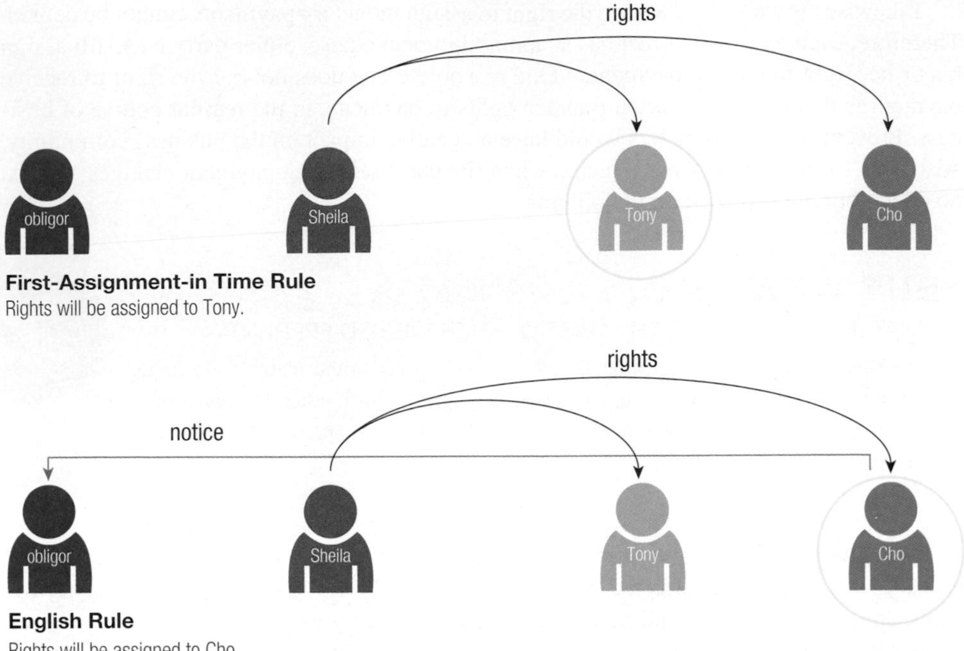

The second complication occurs when an assignor assigns two or more parties the same right, and confusion arises as to which party has the right to the contract. Most states use the **first-assignment-in-time rule,** which gives the contractual right to the first party granted the assignment. Giving proper notice can ensure that there is no confusion over when the assignment was made. Furthermore, a minority of states have adopted the **English rule,** which states that the first assignee to give notice of assignment to the obligor is the party with rights to the contract. Especially in a state using the English rule, parties are well advised to give notice of assignments to ensure that they maintain their assigned rights.

Suppose Sheila assigns her contractual rights to Tony. A week later, she assigns the same rights to Cho. As shown in Exhibit 19-3, under the first-assignment-in-time rule, Tony legally has Sheila's rights to the contract. However, if Cho gives notice first and the state in question uses the English rule, although Sheila assigned her rights to Tony first, legally Cho possesses them.

The Restatement (Second) of Contracts takes a position between the first-assignment-in-time rule and the English rule.[13] It grants legal right to the first assignee in most situations. However, if the first assignment is legally voidable or revocable by the assignor, subsequent assignments are considered evidence of the voiding or revocation of the first assignment and the later assignee has legal right to the contract. Also, the later assignee is considered the legal owner of the contractual right if she offers something to the assignor as consideration and then obtains (1) performance by the obligor on his duty, (2) judgment requiring performance by the obligor, (3) a new contract with the obligor, or (4) evidence frequently used to signify a contractual right (a writing indicating a contractual obligation).

DELEGATION

A **delegation** occurs when a party to a contract—a **delegator**—transfers her duty to perform to a third party—a **delegatee**—who is not part of the original contract. Whereas

[13] Sec. 342.

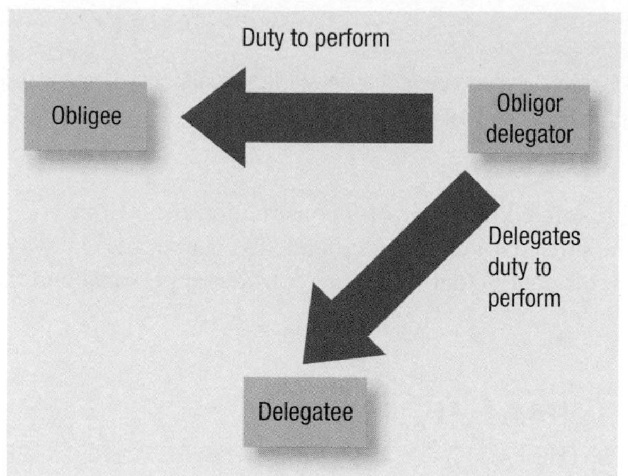

Exhibit 19-4
Delegation of Duties

assignments transfer rights to a contract, delegations transfer *duties*. (See Exhibit 19-4.) Instead of receiving something, as in an assignment, the delegatee must fulfill the delegator's contractual obligation to the obligee—the party to the contract to whom a duty is owed. For example, Johann contracts with Teresa to have her deliver machinery to his factory. Teresa then delegates her duty to Bill, who delivers the machinery to John.

One important distinction between assignments and delegations is apparent in the rights of the transferring party. After making an assignment, the assignor has no right left to the original contract. After making a delegation, however, the delegator is not relieved of his duty to perform. If the delegatee fails to fulfill the contract, the delegator is still liable to the obligee for fulfillment. Using the previous example, if Bill fails to deliver the machinery to John, Teresa is liable to Johann for damages.

Legal Principle: A party transferring her or his duties under the contract is the delegator, and the one receiving the transfer is the delegatee. After the delegation, although the delegatee is bound to perform, the delegator remains liable if the delegatee fails to perform.

Duties That Cannot Be Delegated. As with assignments, the starting assumption is that duties to a contract can be delegated. However, courts tend to examine delegations more closely than assignments. The reasoning is that assignments usually do not affect the party to the contract who is not involved in the assignment (the obligor), whereas a delegation forces the uninvolved party (the obligee) to receive performance from a party with whom he or she did not directly contract.

Also, just as with assignments, certain duties cannot be delegated (see Exhibit 19-5).[14] The first is any duty of a personal nature that requires the specific talents, skills, or expertise of the obligor. Victorine contracts with Michael, a famous artist, to paint her portrait using his skill and expertise. Michael cannot delegate his duty to paint Victorine's portrait to anyone else, not even someone of equal skill or talent.

An interesting situation arises when the initial contract bears an implicit assumption that work will be performed by others. In such situations, if supervision is important to the task, the supervision could be considered a personal duty the obligor may not delegate. Suppose you are planning to have a new office building built to specifications you have personally created. You contract

To see how delegation of duties relates to business management, please see the **Connecting to the Core** activity on the text website at www.mhhe.com/kubasek3e.

[14] Restatement (Second) of Contracts, sec. 318, and UCC § 2-210.

Exhibit 19-5
Duties That Cannot Be Delegated

1. Duties that are personal in nature.
2. Duties for which the delegatee's performance will vary significantly from the delegator's.
3. Duties in contracts that forbid delegations.

with Ian, the well-respected manager of a construction firm. Both you and Ian know that he will not build the office building single-handedly, but because he was sought out for his management skills, his contractual duties are considered personal and therefore cannot be delegated.

BUT WHAT IF . . .

WHAT IF THE FACTS OF THE CASE OPENER WERE DIFFERENT?

Assume that Mike Tyson had been hired for the match because of his fame and his enhanced skills. If Tyson tried to delegate his duties to another athlete who was neither famous nor highly skilled, would such a delegation of duties be lawful?

Delegation of personal duties is permissible where otherwise not allowed when there is an explicit contractual agreement to allow delegations. Usually, for a delegation of personal duties to be effective, the contract must state that delegations are permitted.

Any nonpersonal duties in a contract can be delegated. For example, delivering goods, mowing a lawn, paying money, and painting a house are all considered nonpersonal duties because they do not require particular skill or expertise and most people could complete them. Thus, they can all be delegated.

The second type of duty that cannot be delegated is one whose performance would vary significantly from what the obligee has a contractual right to if the performance were done by the delegatee. To protect the obligee, who is a part of the original contract, when performance would differ substantially from what the obligee contractually has the right to, courts will rule that the delegation is ineffective. The focus here is the skill or abilities of the delegatee. If the delegatee cannot perform the contract at a level comparable to that of the delegator, the obligee would be unnecessarily harmed, and thus the delegation is deemed ineffective.

The third situation in which delegations are prohibited occurs when the contract prohibits them. The courts typically treat included agreements not to delegate as indicating the parties' desire to consider the contractual obligations personal and will find otherwise-allowable delegations inappropriate. However, even if a clause prohibiting delegations exists, the courts will probably allow delegations if they are impersonal, such as the payment of money.

Case 19-2 demonstrates the problems arising from a party's failure to acknowledge a nondelegation agreement. Although the case discusses assignments of obligations, the court is treating the term *assignment* as a synonym for *delegation of duties.* Some courts use the term *assignment* to refer to a transfer of either rights *or* duties.

Assignment of the Contract

Contracts often use ambiguous language that makes it unclear what is being assigned or delegated. Examples are "I assign the contract" or "I assign all my rights under the contract," which fail to specify what is being transferred. When a court cannot clearly tell what

CASE 19-2 FOREST COMMODITY CORP. ("FCC") v. LONE STAR INDUSTRIES, INC., ET AL.

COURT OF APPEALS OF GEORGIA, THIRD DIVISION

255 GA. APP. 244 (2002)

CAL and FCC entered into a three-year contract for the "thru-putting" of aggregate stone. In the contract, FCC agreed to provide terminal space for unloading aggregate stone, which FCC would then store, reload onto trucks, and weigh for transshipment. CAL promised to unload a minimum of 150,000 tons per year, for a total of 450,000 tons over the three-year contract period. The agreement also contained a provision prohibiting the assignment or subcontracting of any portion of the obligations without the written consent of the other party.

During the contract period, CAL unloaded a total of 198,170 tons of aggregate. Soon thereafter, CAL entered into negotiations with Martin Marietta Materials, Inc., for the sale of CAL's assets. Martin Marietta agreed to accept CAL's rights and obligations under the agreement with FCC, and CAL requested FCC accept an assignment of the thru-put agreement to Martin Marietta. FCC refused. FCC and Martin Marietta eventually entered into a substantially similar contract for the thru-putting of aggregate. It is undisputed that after Martin Marietta's acquisition of CAL and its assets, and pursuant to the new contract with FCC, Martin Marietta thru-put 286,698 tons of aggregate stone at the FCC terminal during the remainder of the original contract period for the CAL thru-put agreement. When combined with the 198,170 tons shipped by CAL, a total of 484,868 tons of aggregate stone was shipped through the FCC facility, 34,868 tons more than the guaranteed minimum under the original agreement.

FCC sued CAL for breach of contract, alleging CAL failed to ship the minimum amount of aggregate stone under the contract. CAL filed a motion for summary judgment as to the breach of contract claim. The trial court granted the motion for summary judgment, finding FCC was precluded from enforcing the contract because it failed to comply with the nonassignability clause. FCC appealed.

JUDGE JOHNSON: FCC contends the trial court erred in granting summary judgment to CAL because there are genuine issues of material fact regarding whether FCC assigned the contract. However, the irrefutable evidence, even when construed in a light most favorable to FCC, points inevitably to the conclusion an assignment of the CAL thru-put agreement was effected. The numerous items of undisputed facts in this case show FCC's interests and obligations in the CAL thru-put agreement were transferred to Woodchips Export Corporation ("WEC") without the written consent of CAL, thereby violating the nonassignability clause of the agreement and extinguishing any right to recovery which FCC may have had.

The thru-put agreement obligated FCC to provide a marine terminal facility for the off-loading of aggregate and to perform both the reloading of the aggregate onto trucks and the weighing of such trucks. Yet, the evidence in the record shows the terminal facility where the CAL aggregate was off-loaded was leased by FCC to WEC. In addition, it is undisputed FCC had no employees and no equipment to perform the obligations under the CAL agreement. FCC's vice-president admits FCC had no employees and FCC entered into an unwritten agreement with WEC under which WEC agreed to perform FCC's obligations as its operations agent.

Moreover, FCC's tax returns for the years covered by the thru-put agreement show the only income received by FCC during this time period was rental income. These tax returns do not show any income for aggregate thru-putting, nor do they include any expenses for employee wages, equipment rental or maintenance, or fuel expenditures necessary to carry out its obligations under the CAL thru-put agreement. On the other hand, WEC's income statements and tax returns reveal WEC deducted the expenses incurred in conjunction with aggregate thru-putting and received income for the thru-put of aggregate in amounts that correspond to the amounts generated by the CAL thru-put agreement.

Indeed, FCC's own accountants testified such debiting and crediting could not have occurred between these two parties since FCC files separate tax returns from the tax returns of WEC and other related companies. Furthermore, the same accountants testified even if such funds had, in fact, been debited and credited between these two companies, the income would first have appeared on the company actually earning it, which in this case was WEC. As a final note, FCC has offered no documentary evidence supporting this accounting practice, such as documents memorializing such inter-company adjustments through debits and credits.

FCC next argues no assignment can be found in this case since there is no written assignment document or any other document indicating an intent to assign. However, an assignment can be inferred from the totality of the circumstances and need not be reduced to writing. In addition, Georgia courts may look to tax returns as probative evidence in ascertaining the existence of an assignment. The affirmative decision to declare the thru-put income on the tax returns of WEC and not on the tax returns of FCC is certainly evidence of an intent to assign. Moreover, FCC's vice-president testified oral agreements between FCC and WEC were entered into under his direction and supervision, showing yet another intent to assign. The trial court properly found FCC had assigned the CAL thru-put agreement to WEC.

AFFIRMED.

[continued]

CRITICAL THINKING

Do you agree with the reasoning of this decision? Is the evidence as strongly in support of the court's conclusion as the judge states? Are any pieces of evidence given unfair weight or insufficient weight?

Further, what evidence that might not be included in this decision could affect the court's conclusion? Come up with at least one fact, not included in the ruling but possible given the information provided above, that would have a significant impact on the acceptability of this reasoning.

ETHICAL DECISION MAKING

How do you think this decision would hold up under the public disclosure test? Who might react favorably, and who unfavorably? What differences in ethical standards could explain contradictory reactions? What reaction do you think the majority of the U.S. public would have? Why?

the parties intended, it usually considers the assignment to be of both rights and duties. (See Exhibit 19-6.) This interpretation removes any right the assignor had to collect under the contract, but he or she is still liable to the obligee for any duties the delegatee, who is also the assignee, fails to perform.

Third-Party Beneficiary Contracts

L04

What is a third-party beneficiary contract?

We've seen that one way third parties may obtain rights or duties to a contract is through assignments or delegations. We now move on to the other way, which is through being an intended beneficiary of the contract. A **third-party beneficiary** is created when two parties enter into a contract with the purpose of benefiting a third party, called the *intended beneficiary.* The beneficiary need not be named in the contract, as long as the terms of the contract or events occurring after its creation make it clear who he or she is.

INTENDED BENEFICIARIES

Early in the common law, courts had difficulty when contracts were written to benefit third parties, and they usually deemed that third parties had no rights to contracts to which they were not in privity. Now, however, third parties who are intended beneficiaries have the right to enforce contracts. An **intended beneficiary** is a third party to a contract whom the contracting parties intended to benefit directly from their contract. In determining whether

Exhibit 19-6

Assignment of the Contract

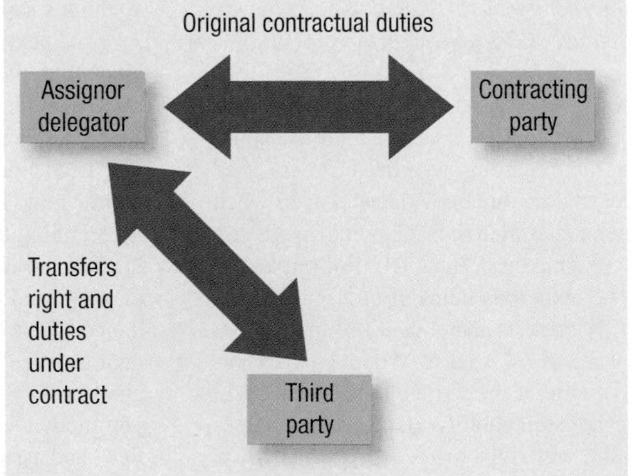

COMPARING THE LAW OF OTHER COUNTRIES

REFORMATION OF ASSIGNMENTS AND DELEGATIONS IN RUSSIA

Many industrialized nations have fairly similar laws regarding assignments and delegations. Part of this similarity is attributable to the similarity of their market-based economies. Russia, which was centrally planned under the Soviet Union, is attempting to join the industrialized nations by developing a market-based economy. To aid the transition, it has modified its Civil Code to allow the same freedom of assignments of rights and duties found in the German code, a change that may prove critical to Russia's potential for success as a market-based economy.

a third party is an intended beneficiary, courts ask whether the contracting parties intended that the third party be the "direct," "primary," or "express" beneficiary of the contract.

The **promisor** in a third-party beneficiary contract is the party who makes the promise that benefits the third party. The **promisee** is the party who owes the promisor something in exchange for the promise made to the third-party beneficiary. For example, Marissa contracts with Alex to clean his house. In exchange, Alex will pay Marissa's credit card debt. The credit card company is the third-party beneficiary, because the contract is created to benefit the company. Alex is the promisor, for he made the promise to pay the third-party beneficiary. Marissa is the promisee, because she owes a duty to the promisor, Alex.

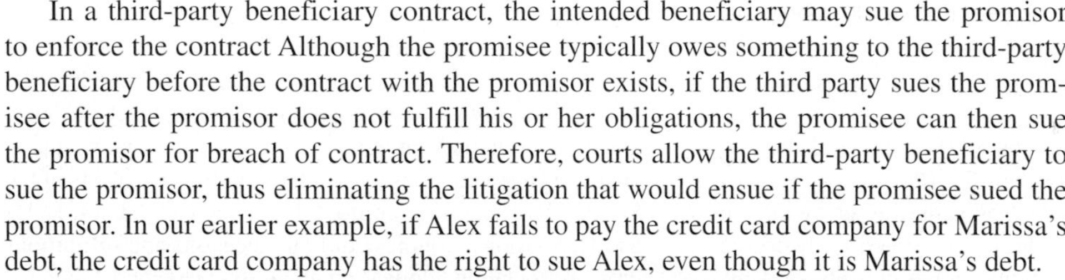

BUT WHAT IF . . .

WHAT IF THE FACTS OF THE CASE OPENER WERE DIFFERENT?

Let's say that a venue owner contacted Tyson about performing in a match at his venue. Tyson will compete in the match for free, and all of the money from the ticket sales will go to charity. Is there a third-party beneficiary in this scenario? Also, who is the promisor, and who is the promisee?

In a third-party beneficiary contract, the intended beneficiary may sue the promisor to enforce the contract Although the promisee typically owes something to the third-party beneficiary before the contract with the promisor exists, if the third party sues the promisee after the promisor does not fulfill his or her obligations, the promisee can then sue the promisor for breach of contract. Therefore, courts allow the third-party beneficiary to sue the promisor, thus eliminating the litigation that would ensue if the promisee sued the promisor. In our earlier example, if Alex fails to pay the credit card company for Marissa's debt, the credit card company has the right to sue Alex, even though it is Marissa's debt.

Let us return to the opening scenario. The fans of the Tyson fight argued that they were third-party beneficiaries and therefore had rights under several contracts that were violated when Tyson was disqualified early in the fight. Boxing matches are widely viewed events, arguably organized for the enjoyment of fans. Does the idea of boxing matches' being organized for the fans make the fans the "direct," "primary," or "express" beneficiaries of contracts involved in the fight? In other words, are the fans of the Tyson fight intended (i.e., direct, primary, or express) beneficiaries to the contracts Tyson entered into when agreeing to the fight? What else do we need to know before we can determine whether the fans have a legal right to a refund?

There are two types of intended beneficiaries: creditor beneficiaries and donee beneficiaries.

Creditor Beneficiaries. A **creditor beneficiary** is a third party that benefits from a contract in which the promisor agrees to pay the promisee's debt. In our previous example, because Alex (the promisor) agreed to pay the debt of Marissa (the promisee), Marissa's credit card company is a creditor beneficiary.

Case 19-3 illustrates the importance of being a creditor beneficiary as opposed to a donee beneficiary if you want to enforce a contract.

CASE 19-3 ALLAN v. NERSESOVA

COURT OF APPEALS OF TEXAS, DALLAS 307 S.W.3D 564, 2010 TEX. APP. LEXIS 1662

Allan and Koraev both owned condominiums in the same building. Koraev's unit was directly above Allan's. While Allan lived in her own unit, Koraev leased his. The leasing of Koraev's unit was managed by Nersesova. Between 2005 and 2007 plumbing problems in Koraev's unit damaged Allan's unit eight different times. Thus, Allan sued Nersesova and Koraev, among other building executives. The terms of the lawsuit included breach of contract and negligence. All defendants excluding Koraev and Nersesova settled with Allan before the trial. The jury found on behalf of Allan for the negligence of both Koraev and Nersesova and, additionally, breach of contract of Koraev. Both parties were found responsible for damages as third parties. However, Koraev moved for judgment notwithstanding the verdict, arguing that there was no contract between Allan and Koraev that made Koraev a third party.

JUSTICE SMITH: Having concluded a contract existed between Koraev and the Association, we next consider whether Allan could bring suit for breach of that contract. To have standing to bring a suit for breach of contract, the plaintiff must either be in privity of contract with the defendant or be a third-party beneficiary entitled to enforce the contract.

Allan's contract claim was based on the text of the governing documents. Paragraph 1 of the Declaration provided that its terms apply to "any person acquiring or owning an interest in the property." Paragraph 11 stated, "All present and future Unit Owners, tenants and occupants of Units shall be subject to and shall comply with the provisions of this Second Amended Declaration, the Amended Bylaws, and the Rules and Regulations, as they may be amended from time to time."

Privity of contract is established by proving that the defendant was a party to an enforceable contract with either the plaintiff or a party who assigned its cause of action to the plaintiff. Allan was not a party to nor an assignee of the contract between Koraev and the Association. Accordingly, Koraev and Allan were not in privity of contract. Because Allan was not in privity of contract with Koraev, she has standing to bring a breach of contract claim only if she demonstrated she was a third-party beneficiary.

A third party, such as Allan, may sue to enforce a contract as a third-party beneficiary only if the contracting parties entered into the contract directly and primarily for the third party's benefit. There is a presumption against conferring third-party-beneficiary status. There are three types of third-party beneficiaries—donee, creditor, and incidental. Donee and creditor beneficiaries may bring suit to enforce a contract; incidental beneficiaries may not. A person is a donee beneficiary if the performance of the contract inures to his benefit as a gift. A person is a donee beneficiary only if a donative intent expressly or impliedly appears in the contract. A party is a creditor beneficiary if no intent to make a gift appears from the contract, but performance will satisfy an actual or asserted duty of the promisee to the beneficiary, such as an indebtedness, contractual obligation, or other legally enforceable commitment to the third party, and the promisee must intend that the beneficiary will have the right to enforce the contract. "The intent to confer a direct benefit upon a third party 'must be clearly and fully spelled out or enforcement by the third party must be denied.' " "Incidental benefits that may flow from a contract to a third party do not confer the right to enforce the contract."

Paragraph 1 of the Declaration stated, "The Association does hereby publish and declare that the covenants, limitations, and obligations contained herein shall be deemed to run with the land and shall be a burden and a benefit to the Association and any person acquiring or owning an interest in the property." Paragraph 19 of the Declaration stated, "Each Owner shall comply strictly with the provisions of the Second Amended Declaration, the Amended Bylaws, Rules and Regulations, policies, and the decisions and resolutions of the Association adopted pursuant to the Second Amended Declaration or Amended Bylaws as the same may be lawfully amended from time to time. Failure to comply with any of the same shall be grounds for an action to recover sums due, for damages or injunctive relief or both, and for reimbursement of all attorney's fees incurred in connection therewith, which action shall be maintainable by the Managing Agent or Board of Directors in the name of the Association, in behalf of the Owners or, in a proper case, by an aggrieved owner."

Paragraph 38 of the Rules and Regulations required a unit owner to repair at his own expense any damage he (or his tenants) may cause to the condominium. Allan's testimony about the damages she suffered as a result of Koraev and his tenants' breach of the governing documents established that she was an aggrieved owner. But there must be some evidence that this is a "proper case" under Paragraph 19 of the

[continued]

Declaration for Allan as an aggrieved owner to maintain an action to recover damages and be reimbursed for attorney's fees. After reading paragraph 19 to his client, Allan's attorney elicited the following testimony from his client at trial:

Q. Did your homeowners' association take any action to recover the damages for your unit from the owner of Unit 234?

A. No.

Q. And based on their failure to act, did you have to act on your behalf?

A. Yes.

Allan then testified about having to hire attorneys to represent her in this case and stated that she had agreed to pay them a reasonable fee for their services. The Association's failure to act is some evidence that this is a proper case for the aggrieved owner herself to bring suit for damages and for reimbursement of attorney's fees, as authorized under Paragraph 19 of the Declaration.

Paragraph 1 imposed a contractual duty on Koraev to follow the requirements of the Declaration, Bylaws, and Rules and Regulations for the "benefit of the Association and any person acquiring or owning an interest in the property." Allan was such a person. The contract between the Association and Koraev "clearly and fully express[ed] an intent to confer a direct benefit to" Allan and others owning an interest in the property. Thus, Koraev's "performance will come to [Allan] in satisfaction of a legal duty owed to [her] by [Koraev]." Paragraph 19 gave authority to Allan as an aggrieved owner to bring an action against Koraev for his failure to follow the Declaration, Bylaws, and Rules and Regulations "in a proper case." Therefore, Koraev's failure to perform the contract between himself and the Association was a breach of his duty not to cause damage to Allan's unit. As an intended creditor beneficiary, Allan had standing to bring suit against Koraev for his breach of the governing documents.

We conclude the governing documents made Allan an intended creditor beneficiary of the contract between Koraev and the Association and granted her authority to bring suit for Koraev's breach of those documents. Accordingly, we conclude the trial court erred by granting Koraev's motion for judgment notwithstanding the verdict on Allan's claim for breach of contract. We sustain Allan's first issue.

AFFIRMED IN PART, REVERSED IN PART AND REMANDED

CRITICAL THINKING

Was there ambiguity in the relevant portions of the declaration quoted in the opinion that made unit owners' duties to other owners as a third party unclear? Or did Koraev simply not read the document carefully?

ETHICAL DECISION MAKING

Should each condominium owner have a duty to the other owners who own adjacent properties? Why would Koraev feel he was not liable for the damage his property caused to another?

Donee Beneficiaries. The other type of intended beneficiaries is **donee beneficiaries,** third parties who benefit from a contract in which a promisor agrees to give a gift to the third party. The most common form of donee beneficiary contract is life insurance policies. The promisee pays premiums on a life insurance plan to have the insurer (the promisor) pay a third party (the donee beneficiary) on the promisee's death.

LO5 What are the differences among donee beneficiaries, creditor beneficiaries, and incidental beneficiaries?

The fans in the Tyson case argued that they are intended beneficiaries. If the fans are correct, and we know Tyson did not have a debt to them, then they must be donee beneficiaries. Does an agreement to perform create a situation in which the audience becomes the intended beneficiaries of the performance?

Vesting of Rights. Although an intended beneficiary can enforce her rights to a contract, she cannot do so until her rights to the contract **vest,** or mature such that she can legally act on them. Before a third party's rights have vested, the original contracting parties can make changes to the original contract without her permission. For example, third-party rights in a life insurance policy do not vest until the promisee's death. Consequently, Jane (the promisee) can change the intended beneficiary of her life insurance policy from

Mercedes to Peter. Jane does not need Mercedes' permission, and Mercedes cannot sue Jane, because her rights have not vested.

Generally, one of three things must occur for a third party's right to a contract to vest.[15] First, under certain circumstances, third-party rights vest immediately even if the beneficiary does not know about the contract. When rights vest immediately, the third party can enforce the contract at any time. These rights take effect instantaneously, even if the beneficiary does not know about the contract.

Second, rights may vest when the beneficiary decides to accept them, which must sometimes be done by notifying the contracting parties of acceptance. However, in the absence of an overt act rejecting the rights to a contract, acceptance is assumed when the beneficiary becomes aware of the contract.

Third, the beneficiary must change his position based on a reliance on the contractual rights. In other words, the beneficiary must take some action he would not have otherwise taken because he is expecting to benefit from the contract. For example, when Vince finds out he is a third-party beneficiary to a contract, he decides to lease a new car because he is expecting to benefit from the contract. Obtaining the lease causes his rights to vest because doing so demonstrates a change in position based on reliance on the contract.

If a contract specifies that the original contracting parties maintain the right to alter or rescind the contract, vesting of the third party's rights does not prevent the promisor or the promisee from doing so. For instance, all life insurance policies allow the promisee to change the beneficiary.

Many states hold that donee beneficiary rights vest before creditor beneficiary rights. The rationale is that even if the contract is altered, the creditor beneficiary maintains her rights against the debtor (the promisee). Suppose your friend owes you $1,000 and enters a contract with Dagmar in which you are a creditor beneficiary. If your friend and Dagmar change the contract before your rights vest, you still have a right to the money your friend owes you, even if you cannot enforce this right against Dagmar. Donee beneficiaries do not have the same option as creditor beneficiaries, and thus many states allow their rights to vest more quickly than those of creditor beneficiaries.

Creditor versus Donee Beneficiaries. There are two main distinctions between creditor beneficiaries and donee beneficiaries (see Exhibit 19-7). The first is based on the reason the third-party beneficiary contract was created. If the promise in the contract is intended to release a party from an obligation to a third party, such as the paying of a debt, the contract creates a creditor beneficiary. Conversely, if the contract intends to grant a gift to a third party, the third party is a donee beneficiary.

Exhibit 19-7
Creditor versus Donee Beneficiaries

CREDITOR BENEFICIARY	DONEE BENEFICIARY
Purpose of the Contract	
Contractual performance fulfills an obligation to a third party.	Contractual performance gives a gift to a third party.
Enforcement of Rights	
Beneficiary can enforce rights to a contract if the contract is valid and the rights have vested.	Beneficiary has limited ability to enforce contracts, depending on the jurisdiction.
Beneficiary can enforce rights against the promisor or the promisee.	Beneficiary can enforce rights against the promisor.

[15] Restatement (Second) of Contracts, sec. 311.

The second distinction occurs when an intended beneficiary can enforce his or her rights under a contract. Creditor beneficiaries can enforce their rights under a contract whenever the contract is valid. Donee beneficiaries can enforce their rights to most contracts. However, some jurisdictions do not allow donee beneficiaries to enforce their contractual rights in all situations. For example, the state of New York does not grant them the right to enforce a contract unless they have a familial relationship to the promisee.

When a donee beneficiary may enforce rights under a contract, he or she may do so only against the promisor, because the promisee has no duty to the donee beneficiary. Conversely, creditor beneficiaries may sue the promisor or the promisee for performance, because both these parties owe him or her a duty. A creditor beneficiary who wins a judgment against one party may not seek judgment against the other party, however. In addition, if a creditor beneficiary wins judgment against the promisee, the promisee may sue the promisor to recover under a theory of breach of contract.[16]

As you might have guessed, it is not always easy to determine when someone is a creditor or a donee beneficiary. Sometimes a contract is created for reasons that are intended both to be charitable and to pay a debt. Given the lack of clear distinction, the Restatement (Second) of Contracts takes a different approach,[17] focusing on the difference between intended and incidental beneficiaries.

Legal Principle: **Both a donee beneficiary and a creditor beneficiary are intended beneficiaries of a contract and can therefore sue to enforce its performance.**

BUT WHAT IF . . .

WHAT IF THE FACTS OF THE CASE OPENER WERE DIFFERENT?

Let's say that the owner of the Las Vegas venue hosting Mike Tyson's match forms a contract with Tyson which specifies that if customers pay for the match the first night, Mike Tyson will come back to the venue a week later so that the same customers can go to a second match for free. However, Mike Tyson gets disqualified from the rest of the season during the first match. Could the fans file lawsuits as third-party beneficiaries?

INCIDENTAL BENEFICIARIES

Creditor and donee beneficiaries are both intended beneficiaries, and according to the Restatement, intended beneficiaries have the right to enforce a contract. When it is clear that the contract was created for the benefit of a third party, and performance of the contractual duties will pay off the payee's debt or give a gift as the payee intended, the third party is an intended beneficiary. When the contracting parties do not *intend* to benefit someone but unintentionally do so, that third party is an **incidental beneficiary.** (See Exhibit 19-8.)

For example, Cassandra contracts with Garrett to have him build a well-financed private high school on property she owns. The new school will raise the property values of the houses surrounding it. Although neither Cassandra nor Garrett intended to benefit these local homeowners with their contract, the homeowners did benefit. Accordingly, the local homeowners are incidental beneficiaries to Cassandra and Garrett's contract.

One significant difference between intended and incidental beneficiaries is that incidental beneficiaries maintain no rights to enforce other people's contracts. In the previous

[16] Ibid., sec. 310.

[17] Ibid., sec. 302.

Exhibit 19-8
Intended versus Incidental Beneficiaries

INTENDED BENEFICIARIES	INCIDENTAL BENEFICIARIES
Contracting parties intended to benefit the third party with their contract.	Contracting parties did not intend to benefit the third party with their contract.
Beneficiary has the right to enforce the contract.	Beneficiary does not have the right to enforce the contract.
Beneficiary benefits from direct reception of contractual performance.	Beneficiary benefits from indirect circumstances created by contractual performance.

example, if Cassandra and Garrett decide to rescind their contract, the local homeowners cannot sue to enforce it, because it was never Cassandra or Garrett's intent to benefit them.

In determining whether a party is an incidental beneficiary, the courts will take a reasonable person approach and ask whether a reasonable person in the position of the party in question would believe the contracting parties intended to benefit him or her. If so, the courts consider the party an intended beneficiary. If not, the third party is an incidental beneficiary.

Let's consider the reasonable person test in the context of the Tyson case in the opening scenario. For fans to receive refunds, a reasonable person in their position would have to believe Tyson intended to benefit his fans by entering into his contract to fight. Do the fans meet the reasonable person test? Contrast the Tyson case with the one described in the Case Nugget on the next page, in which the court found sufficient evidence that the plaintiff was an intended beneficiary.

Another thing the court considers when deciding whether a party is an incidental beneficiary is whether performance of the contract is done directly for or to the third party. For example, performance of Cassandra and Garrett's contract—payment and the building of the school—is contained wholly within the contracting parties. Nothing is explicitly done for or given to a third party, and therefore the homeowners are incidental beneficiaries.

The court also examines the third party's ability to control the specifics of performance. If a third party can provide input regarding how the contractual duties are fulfilled, he or she is probably an intended beneficiary. Suppose Dianne (the promisee) agrees to pay Charles (the promisor) to paint Hector's (the third party's) house. Hector tells Charles what color he wants the house, as well as when Charles should be there to paint. Hector's ability to control how Charles paints the house demonstrates his status as an intended beneficiary. In addition, Charles renders performance directly to Hector, so by this test also Hector is an intended beneficiary.

A third factor the courts examine in determining the type of third-party beneficiary is whether the contract directly states that the third party is the benefiting party. In the previous example, because Charles agreed in the contract to paint Hector's house, the contract lists Hector as the beneficiary. Consequently, he is an intended beneficiary. In fact Hector meets all three additional tests besides the reasonable person test, although it is not necessary to meet all three. A third party who meets at least one of the last three tests is usually an intended beneficiary.

Legal Principle: **The third-party beneficiary who is in the strongest legal position is the creditor beneficiary because he can sue both the person who made the contract on his behalf and the person who was supposed to perform for him. The donee beneficiary is in the second-strongest position because she can sue the person who is supposed to perform the contract for her. The incidental beneficiary is in the worst legal position because he cannot sue anyone.**

CASE NUGGET

INTENDED OR INCIDENTAL BENEFICIARY?

Wesley Locke v. Ozark City Board of Education
910 So. 2d 1247 (Ala. 2005)

Wesley Locke, a physical education teacher employed by the Dale County Department of Education, served as an umpire for high school baseball games. Locke was a member of the Southeast Alabama Umpires Association, which provides officials to athletic events sponsored by the Alabama High School Athletic Association (AHSAA).

One evening, Locke was serving as head umpire in a baseball game between Carroll High School and George W. Long High School. Carroll High School, where the game was being held, did not provide police protection or other security personnel for the game. After the game, the parent of one of Carroll High's baseball players attacked Locke, punching him three times in the face and causing him to sustain physical injuries to his neck and face that subjected him to pain, discomfort, scarring, and blurred vision. Locke sued the Ozark City Board of Education, alleging that the board breached its contract with the AHSAA by failing to provide police protection at the baseball game and that Locke was an intended third-party beneficiary under the contract.

While the trial court found that Locke was not an intended beneficiary and awarded summary judgment to the Board of Education, the court of appeals disagreed. It found evidence that the parties anticipated the existence of third parties by contract language stating that the purpose of the words "adequate police protection" was to provide good game administration and supervision. The court reasoned that game administration and supervision necessarily included umpires. It found further evidence of the AHSAA's and the board's intent for police protection to directly benefit the umpires in a letter from the AHSAA sanctioning one of the high schools for the incident.

The state supreme court reiterated that to recover under a third-party beneficiary theory, a complainant must show (1) that the contracting parties intended, at the time the contract was created, to bestow a direct benefit on a third party; (2) that the complainant was the intended beneficiary of the contract; and (3) that the contract was breached. Applying this standard to the facts, the court found that Locke had presented substantial evidence indicating that the board and the AHSAA intended to provide a direct benefit to umpires, that he was an intended direct beneficiary of the contract, and that the board breached the contract. It therefore overturned the summary judgment and remanded the case to the trial court for hearing on the issue of whether the board had provided adequate protection at the game.

Exhibit 19-9 summarizes third-party benefiaries' ability to sue.

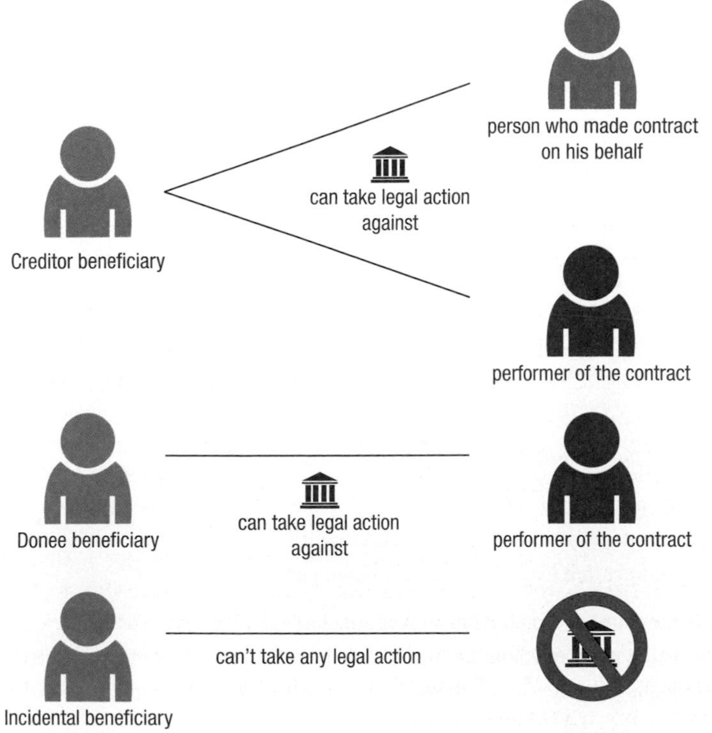

Exhibit 19-9
Legal Recourse of Third-Party Beneficiaries

CASE OPENER WRAP-UP

Fallout from a Unforgettable Fight

The court hearing the Tyson case quickly dismissed the claims. It held that the fans were in no way third-party beneficiaries to any contract into which Tyson, the promoters, or the telecasters had entered. The fans cannot meet any of the tests for an intended beneficiary. Simply put, they are incidental beneficiaries.

KEY TERMS

assignee 428
assignment 428
assignor 428
creditor beneficiary 439
delegatee 434
delegation 434
delegator 434
donee beneficiaries 441
English rule 434
first-assignment- in-time rule 434
incidental beneficiary 443
intended beneficiary 438
obligees 428
obligors 428
promisee 439
promisor 439
third-party beneficiary 438
vest 441

SUMMARY OF KEY TOPICS

Assignments and Delegations

A contract is typically an agreement between two parties. When a right or duty under that contract is transferred to a third party, we need a way to talk about the party who is not directly involved in the transfer but is one of the original parties to the contract who is now going to either perform for a third party (when there is an assignment) or receive a performance from a third party (when there is a delegation).

An *obligor* is a contractual party who owes a duty to the other party in privity of the contract and now must instead perform for a third party.

An *obligee* is a contractual party who is owed a duty from the other party in privity of the contract and now will receive performance from a third party.

An *assignment* is the transfer of rights under a contract to a third party.

The assignor is the party to a contract who transfers his or her rights to a third party.

The *assignee* is a party not in privity to a contract who is the recipient of a transfer of rights to a contract.

Contractual rights that cannot be assigned:

1. Rights that are personal in nature.
2. Rights that would increase the obligor's risks or duties.
3. Rights in a contract that expressly forbids assignment.

A *delegation* is the transfer of a duty under a contract to a third party.

A *delegator* is the party to a contract who transfers his or her duty to a third party.

A *delegatee* is the party not in privity to a contract who is the recipient of a transfer of duty to a contract.

Contractual duties that cannot be assigned:

1. Duties personal in nature.
2. Duties resulting in performance substantially different from that which the obligee originally contracted.
3. Duties in a contract that expressly forbids delegation.

Assignment of the Contract

When ambiguous language is used, courts interpret the transfer to consist of an assignment of rights and a delegation of duties.

Third-Party Beneficiary Contracts

An *intended beneficiary* is a third party to a contract whom the contracting parties intended to benefit directly from their contract.

A *promisor* is the party to a contract who made the promise that benefits the third party.

A *promisee* is the party to the contract who owes something to the promisor in exchange for the promise made to the third-party beneficiary.

A *creditor beneficiary* is a third party who benefits from a contract in which the promisor agrees to pay the promisee's debt.

A *donee beneficiary* is a third party who benefits from a contract in which a promisor agrees to give a gift to the third party.

Vesting is the maturing of rights such that a party can legally act on the rights.

An *incidental beneficiary* is a third party who unintentionally gains a benefit from a contract between other parties. That is, it was never the conscious objective of the contracting parties to benefit the third party.

POINT / COUNTERPOINT

Should Incidental Beneficiaries Be Allowed to Sue to Enforce a Contract?

YES

Suppose a major buyer places a large order for widgets from a manufacturer that employs its workers *at will* (at-will employment is discussed in Chapter 10). Suppose further that the buyer breaches its contract with the manufacturer before the manufacturer makes the widgets for the order. Because of the late notice of the buyer's breach, the manufacturer is unable to find a replacement buyer. As a result, the manufacturer is forced to lay off some workers, many of whom are unable to find replacement work. These workers are *incidental beneficiaries* of the manufacturer's contract with the buyer, and under current law they cannot sue to enforce the contract.

A number of legal scholars find this result unfair. The manufacturer's workers relied on the promises of the buyer when they made important financial decisions, such as how many hours to work and whether to look for additional employment opportunities. Moreover, at-will workers tend to have very little bargaining power. They also usually lack the resources to relocate in response to job openings in other cities, states, or countries or to obtain

NO

The difficulties facing the at-will employees in the widget manufacturing example may be compelling, but contract law is not the ideal way to address the problem. Such an approach would be expensive and slow because incidental beneficiaries could recover a remedy only after a series of lawsuits with many expensive lawyers. Instead, we ought to use the social welfare system—tax redistribution and unemployment benefits—to aid vulnerable workers.

Moreover, it is not clear that at-will workers are enormously susceptible to exploitation. A number of econometric studies have attempted to determine whether at-will employees receive higher wages than "secure" employees who provide equivalent labor. Although it is not entirely conclusive, significant evidence suggests that at-will workers receive a "bonus" for taking the risks of at-will employment (economists call these bonuses *compensating differentials*).

Permitting incidental beneficiaries to sue to enforce a contract would also establish perverse incentives. At-will employees laid off when a third party breaches a contract with their employer would know they can recover damages additional training to prepare them for other job markets. As a result, at-will employees often have difficulty finding replacement employment when buyers breach contracts with their employer. In such cases, the law fails to help the most vulnerable.

if they do not find replacement work. If they do find replacement work, however, they can recover only the difference between what they would have earned if the breach had not occurred and what they actually earned in their replacement work. This incentive would encourage them to avoid finding replacement work. (Economists call perverse incentive structures like this one *moral hazards*.)

QUESTIONS & PROBLEMS

1. Integrate the concept of assignments with the concept of delegations.
2. Explain the difference between an assignor's liability and a delegator's liability after rights have been transferred to a third party.
3. Why is it that incidental beneficiaries cannot enforce rights under a contract? Should they be able to enforce such rights?
4. Why are courts stricter with interpretations of antidelegation clauses in contracts than of antiassignment clauses?
5. An investor brought suit against an architect after the investor lost $600,000 in a failed project. To develop the real estate project in Chicago, Burnham Station, an LLC, was created by JDL. The investor arranged to buy shares of Burnham that totaled $600,000. JDL managed Burnham Station. JDL hired the architectural firm Tigerman McCurry Architects (TMA) to develop the real estate. After the investor filed suit to recover the money he had lost in the project, TMA claimed that the investor could not file that suit because the contract at issue was between TMA and JDL. TMA claimed that Burnham was never envisioned as a third party or beneficiary of the contract. If Burnham was not included in the written contract but was involved with JDL and Burnham's money was lost in the project, does this mean the investor is automatically a third party to the contract? How did the court decide? [*F. H. Paschen/S. N. Nielsen, Inc. v. Burnham Station, L.L.C.* (2007 WL 837240, 2007 Ill. App. LEXIS 245).]
6. The farmers are former customers of Ron Kaufman, the owner and operator of Southeast Implements, Inc., a Case International Harvester equipment dealership. Between 1996 and 1998, they agreed to purchase or lease various items of farm equipment from Southeast. In each instance, the farmers and Kaufman orally negotiated the terms of the purchase or lease, and Kaufman then prepared a written purchase agreement for each transaction, assigning his rights thereunder to Case. Case, in turn, after approving the assignments and agreeing to finance the purchases and leases, paid Kaufman for the equipment and looked to the farmers, as debtors, for payment. The written purchase agreements, however, were prepared and assigned without the farmers' knowledge and did not reflect the terms of the oral contracts. Kaufman inflated the purchase and lease prices and forged the farmers' signatures, thereby obtaining thousands of dollars in overpayments from Case. When Case became aware of Kaufman's fraud, it sent representatives to meet with the individual farmers. After verifying that the farmers were in possession of equipment covered by the forged purchase agreements, Case attempted to enforce the terms of the forged contracts. The farmers allege that Case's assignment was improper because the rights assigned were not the ones to which the farmers agreed. The farmers filed suit against Case and Southeast. The court found in favor of Case, and the farmers appealed. Is Kaufman's assignment made to Case binding? What defenses might the farmers have against Case? [*Day v. Case Credit Corp.*, 427 F.3d 1148 (2005).]
7. Prime Finish paints and finishes plastic parts. In 2004, Herbert–Jones became an independent sales representative responsible for developing sales for Prime Finish and formed Cameo to serve this purpose. ITW supplies automotive parts to automakers. After being contacted by Cameo, ITW expressed interest in contracting with Prime Finish

to paint and decorate ITW's automotive parts. During negotiations between Prime Finish and ITW, in which Herbert–Jones was a participant, Prime Finish explained that its financial position was not strong and its facilities were currently not capable of handling the volume of production needed by ITW. ITW, Cameo, and Prime Finish decided that ITW would guarantee a sufficient volume of business to justify the installation of a new Prime Finish paint line. Cameo offered to provide the capital for the line to facilitate this arrangement. The parties then entered into two different contracts.

The first was the Supply Agreement between ITW and Prime Finish, in which Prime Finish agreed to paint and decorate parts provided by ITW. It recognized that Prime Finish "will be investing in a new paint line to meet [ITW's] requirements," and ITW agreed to provide a sufficient number of parts to sustain certain revenue levels for Prime Finish. The Supply Agreement was to last four years and stated that ITW would have to pay a penalty if it terminated the contract early. Cameo was not a party to and is not mentioned in the Supply Agreement between Prime Finish and ITW.

The second contract was the Production Service Agreement between Prime Finish and Cameo, which stated that "Cameo will fund and place in service at Prime Finish a 2-booth paint-line and fixture painting equipment," which were both to be operated by Prime Finish. The paint line would enable Prime Finish to complete ITW's orders, and the Production Agreement stated that "all ITW projects are to run through this line." Prime Finish agreed to "pay Cameo a royalty of 7% of Prime Finish invoiced parts that are base-coated and/or clear-coated through this line." ITW was not a party to the Production Agreement, but the contract stated that "Cameo hereby agrees and acknowledges that Cameo drafted and agrees to the terms and conditions set forth in the Product Supply Agreement between Prime Finish and ITW." Herbert-Jones obtained loans on behalf of Cameo and invested his own money to arrange the $1.6 million needed to fund the new paint line.

Several months after signing the Production Agreement, Cameo and Prime Finish executed a Modification Agreement, which stated that any penalty payment received by Prime Finish pursuant to the Production Supply Agreement between Prime Finish and ITW would be paid to Cameo.

ITW terminated the Supply Agreement early. Prime Finish sued ITW, and Cameo intervened, asserting its rights under the contract to the early termination penalty. Prime Finish and ITW then moved for summary judgment against Cameo, arguing that Cameo lacked standing because it was not a party to the Supply Agreement and was not an intended creditor beneficiary. The district court agreed that Cameo lacked standing and granted summary judgment for ITW. Cameo appealed. Explain what you believe happened on appeal and why. [*Prime Finish, LLC v. Cameo, LLC,* 487 Fed. Appx. 956 (C.A.6, KY. 2012).]

8. CEI and NU were planning a multibillion-dollar merger. Among the terms and conditions of the underlying merger agreement, CEI agreed to purchase all of NU's outstanding shares for $3.6 billion to $1.2 billion over the prevailing market price. Shortly before the scheduled closing, CEI declared that NU had suffered a material adverse change that "dramatically lowered" NU's valuation, and CEI declined to proceed with the merger unless NU would agree to a lower share price. NU rejected the share price reduction, treated CEI's demand as an anticipatory repudiation and breach of the agreement, and declared that the merger was "effectively terminated." Both parties brought suit. The district court ruled that NU could sue on behalf of its shareholders for $1.2 billion. The court reasoned that the merger agreement expressly designated NU's shareholders as intended third-party beneficiaries. Due to subsequent legal actions, both parties appealed. The appellate court then decided the issue of whether any of NU's shareholders were intended third-party beneficiaries. If you were on the court, how would you have ruled? Why? [*Consol. Edison, Inc. v. Northeast Utils.,* 426 F.3d 524 (2005).]

9. Physical Distribution places long-haul and over-the-road truck drivers with parcel and freight delivery companies. Donnelley is a large printing company that purchased CTC Distribution Services and CTC's subsidiary company, Parcel Shippers Express. CTC and Parcel Shippers became subsidiary corporations of Donnelley. Parcel Shippers solicited Physical Distribution to provide drivers. Parcel Shippers and Physical Distribution entered into an agreement that included a nonassignment clause. The parties never executed a written contract, but Physical Distribution began supplying drivers to Parcel Shippers. Physical Distribution sent invoices for its services to Parcel Shippers, and Donnelley made payments on behalf of Parcel Shippers. Donnelley then sold CTC and Parcel Shippers to American Package Express. Physical Distribution continued, without complaint, to supply drivers to American Package, and American Package paid its bills. However, American Package eventually went through a period of not paying its bills before filing for bankruptcy. Physical Distribution filed suit against Donnelley, alleging breach of contract. According to Physical Distribution, it contracted with Donnelley to provide drivers to Parcel Shippers, and the sale of Parcel Shippers to American Package resulted in an assignment of the contract in violation of the antiassignment provision. Donnelley argued that the contract was between Physical Distribution and Parcel Shippers, a subsidiary corporation of CTC, which was in turn a subsidiary of Donnelley. Thus, Physical Distribution contracted with an entirely separate legal entity, and Donnelley's sale of Parcel Shippers did not result in an assignment of the contract. The district court concluded that the sale of Parcel Shippers did not breach the antiassignment language of the contract. Was Physical Distribution successful on appeal in convincing the court that Donnelley violated the antiassignment agreement? Why? [*Physical Distribution Services, Inc. v. R.R. Donnelley & Sons Co.,* 561 F.3d 792 (2009).]

10. Potential expert witnesses made an oral agreement with a plaintiff's attorney to testify on behalf of the plaintiff for $60,000. However, after receiving the money, the witnesses backed out of the agreement and said they would not testify in court or pay back the money. The witnesses claimed that the plaintiff could not sue them because their oral contract was with the attorney and not the plaintiff. Yet the plaintiff claimed she could sue because she was a third-party beneficiary to the contract. The court made a landmark decision regarding expert witnesses and third-party beneficiary case law. What was the rationale for such a surprising decision? [*Isbell v. Friedman,* U.S. App. No. 11-2113. (4th Cir. 2012).]

Looking for more review materials?

The Online Learning Center at **www.mhhe.com/kubasek3e** contains this chapter's "Assignment on the Internet" and also a list of URLs for more information, entitled "On the Internet." Find both of them in the Student Center portion of the OLC, along with quizzes and other helpful materials.

CHAPTER 20

Discharge and Remedies

LEARNING OBJECTIVES

After reading this chapter, you will be able to answer the following questions:

1 What are the primary methods of discharging a contract?

2 What are the primary legal remedies available for a breach of contract?

3 What are the primary equitable remedies available for a breach of contract?

CASE OPENER

Impossible Wine Bottles

The Anchor Glass Container Corporation and its parent company, Consumers Packaging, Inc. (CPI), entered into a series of agreements with Encore Glass, Inc., to supply glass containers of a specific type and quality for the wine industry. On June 24, 1999, Encore entered into an amended agreement with Anchor and CPI. In the amended agreement, the parties agreed that the products would be manufactured at CPI's Lavington plant. Additionally, the amended agreement gave Encore a generous rebate schedule ranging from 1 to 2.5 percent and a new discount schedule.

In May 2001, CPI filed for bankruptcy. As a result of the bankruptcy proceedings, the Lavington plant was sold in August 2001. The new owners of the Lavington plant did not assume CPI's obligations under the amended agreement. The Lavington plant could no longer be used to supply the glass containers to Encore. As a result of the sale, Anchor notified Encore on October 12, 2001, that it considered itself relieved of its obligations under the agreement due to its impossibility to perform. Encore took its business to another company, which did not offer the same rebates and discounts as had Anchor.

When Anchor filed for bankruptcy in 2002, Encore filed a claim to recover the $6,102,912.60 it lost when Anchor stopped providing it with rebates and discounts under the contract. The bankruptcy court ruled against Encore, finding that it was impossible for Anchor to perform after the Lavington plant was sold. Encore appealed.

1. Should Anchor be required to honor the contract despite the loss of the Lavington plant? Why or why not?
2. What ethical system, if any, would permit Encore to recover the lost rebates and discounts?

The Wrap-Up at the end of the chapter will answer these questions.

Methods of Discharging a Contract

LO1

What are the primary methods of discharging a contract?

The previous seven chapters focus primarily on how parties enter into a legally binding agreement. Once a party has entered into a binding agreement, how does the party terminate his or her obligation under the contract? That question is the focus of this chapter. When a party's obligations under a contract are terminated, the party is said to be discharged. There are a number of ways by which a party's contractual obligations can be terminated and the party thereby discharged. The first, and the one most parties hope to secure from the other when they enter into an agreement, is performance. The others are the happening of a condition or its failure to occur, material breach by one or both parties, agreement of the parties, and operation of law. This chapter explains each of these methods.

CONDITIONS

Under ordinary circumstances, a party's duty to perform the promise agreed to in a contract is absolute. Sometimes, however, a party's duty to perform may be affected by whether a certain condition occurs. Contracts containing conditions affecting the performance obligations of the parties are called **conditional contracts.** The conditions may be either implied by law or expressly inserted into the contract by the parties.

Discharge by Conditions Precedent, Subsequent, and Concurrent. There are three types of conditions: condition precedent, condition subsequent, and concurrent conditions (see Exhibit 20-1). A **condition precedent** is a particular event that must occur in order for a party's duty to arise. If the event does not occur, the party's duty to perform does not arise. Frequently, real estate contracts are conditioned on an event such as the buyer's being able to sell his current home by a certain date. If the home does not sell, the condition does not arise. Thus, the parties have no duty to perform and are discharged from the contract.

Another common example of a contract containing a condition precedent is an insurance contract. If Bill purchases a life insurance contract, he is obligated to pay the monthly premiums specified in the contract but the insurance company's obligation to perform arises only when he dies. His death is the condition that triggers the company's duty to pay his beneficiary.

A **condition subsequent** is a future event that terminates the obligations of the parties when it occurs. For example, Joan may enter into an agreement to lease an apartment for five years, conditioned on her not being called to active duty in the National Guard. If she is called to serve, her obligation to be bound by the lease is discharged.

Exhibit 20-1
Conditional Contracts: Types of Conditions

Condition precedent	The party's duty to perform arises after a particular event occurs; if the event never occurs, the party's duty to perform never arises and the parties are thus discharged from the contract.
Condition subsequent	The party has a duty to perform until a future event occurs that discharges the party from the obligation.
Condition concurrent	The party's duty to perform requires that each party perform for the other at the same time. If one party offers to perform his duty and the other party does not, he can sue the other for nonperformance.
Express conditions	Conditions in the contract that are usually preceded by words such as *provided that, if,* or *when.* If these conditions are not met, a party could be discharged from the contract.
Implied conditions	Conditions that are inferred from the nature and language of the contract and are not explicitly stated. If the implied conditions are met, the party could be discharged from the contract.

Legal Principle: **A condition precedent exists when a condition must occur before a party's duty to perform arises, whereas a condition subsequent exists when the occurrence of the condition extinguishes a party's duty to perform.**

Concurrent conditions occur when each party's performance is conditioned on the performance of the other. They occur only when the parties are required to perform for each other simultaneously. For example, when a buyer is supposed to pay for goods on delivery, the buyer's duty to pay is impliedly conditioned on the seller's duty to deliver the goods, and the seller's duty to deliver the goods is impliedly conditioned on the buyer's duty to pay for the goods. The legal effect of a contract's being concurrently conditioned is that each party must offer to perform before being able to sue the other for nonperformance.

Legal Principle: **Concurrent conditions exist when the parties are to perform their obligations for each other simultaneously.**

Express and Implied Conditions. Conditions in contracts are also described as being express or implied. Express conditions are explicitly stated in the contract and are usually preceded by words such as *conditioned on, if, provided that,* or *when.* For example, in a situation involving a potential sale of a house, the offer expressly required that the buyer make a deposit of $1,000 "on acceptance." The buyer wrote "accepted" on the offer and returned it but did not include the deposit. No deposit of money was ever made. The seller then canceled the transaction. Several weeks later, the buyer attempted to tender payment to the seller. The court found that under the terms of the contract, payment of the $1,000 was an express condition of acceptance and since the acceptance was incomplete, there was no contract.[1]

Implied conditions are those that are not explicitly stated but are inferred from the nature and language of the contract. For example, if one enters into a contract with a builder to replace the windows in one's house, there is an implied condition that the builder will be given access to the home so that she may fulfill her obligations under the contract.

[1] *Smith v. Holmwood,* 231 Cal. App. 2d 549 (1965).

Legal Principle: **An express condition is clearly stated, whereas an implied condition is not stated but can be inferred from the nature and language of the contract.**

BUT WHAT IF . . .

WHAT IF THE FACTS OF THE CASE OPENER WERE DIFFERENT?

Let's say, in the Case Opener, that the contract between Encore and Anchor included a clause that stated that the two companies would owe duties to each other as long as CPI was not bankrupt and was involved in the relationship. What kind of a condition would that be? Would Encore have been able to sue Anchor?

DISCHARGE BY PERFORMANCE

In most situations, parties discharge their obligations by doing what they respectively agreed to do under the terms of the contract; this is called *discharge by performance.* Parties also discharge their duty by making an offer to perform and being ready, willing, and able to perform. This offer of performance is known as a **tender.** If a painter shows up at Sam's house with his paint and ladders and is ready to start painting the garage, he has tendered performance. If Sam refuses to let him start, the painter has now discharged his duties under the contract by his tender of performance and he may sue Sam for material breach (discussed later in this chapter).

Types of Performance. There are two primary kinds of performance: complete performance and substantial performance. Performance may also be conditioned on the satisfaction of a party to the contract or of a third party.

Complete performance occurs when all aspects of the parties' duties under the contract are carried out perfectly. In many instances, complete performance is difficult, if not impossible, to attain, and courts today generally require only substantial performance.

Substantial performance occurs when the following conditions have been met: (1) completion of nearly all the terms of the agreement, (2) an honest effort to complete all the terms, and (3) no willful departure from the terms of the agreement. Substantial performance discharges the party's responsibilities under the contract, although the court may require that the party compensate the other party for any loss in value caused by the failure to meet all the standards set forth in the contract. For example, if a contract called for all bedrooms of a house to be painted blue but one was inadvertently painted green, the court may require that the contractor compensate the buyer by the amount that it will cost the buyer to have that room repainted. Of course, it is sometimes difficult to determine whether in fact there has been substantial performance, which is why there is litigation over this issue.

Performance Subject to Satisfaction of a Contracting Party. Sometimes the performance of the contract is subject to the satisfaction of one of the contracting parties. In such a case, a party is not discharged from the contract until the other party is satisfied. Satisfaction is considered an express condition that must be met before the other party's obligation to pay for the performance arises.

Satisfaction may be judged according to either a subjective or an objective standard. When the judgment involved is a matter of personal taste, such as when a woman is having a dress custom made for her, the courts apply a subjective satisfaction standard. As long as the person, in good faith, is not satisfied, the other party is deemed to have not met the condition.

If the performance is one related to a mechanical or utility standard, the objective satisfaction standard applies. Also, if the contract does not clearly specify that the satisfaction is to be personal, the objective standard applies. When an objective standard is used, the courts ask whether a reasonable person would be satisfied with the performance.

Sometimes the contract is conditioned on the satisfaction of a third party. Usually, such provisions arise in construction contracts specifying that before a buyer accepts a building, an architect must provide a certificate stating that the building was constructed according to the plans and specifications.

DISCHARGE BY MATERIAL BREACH

A *breach* occurs whenever a party fails to perform her obligations under the contract. If the breach is a minor one, it may entitle the nonbreaching party to damages but it does not discharge the nonbreaching party from the contract.

A **material breach,** however, discharges the nonbreaching party from his obligations under the contract. A material breach occurs when a party unjustifiably fails to substantially perform his obligations under the contract. It is often difficult to know when the court is going to determine that a breach is material. For example, auto racing fans thought that a contract between them and Formula One and the Indianapolis Speedway, created by their purchase of tickets to a recent car race, had been materially breached when a race that was scheduled to feature 20 cars ended up having only 6. The reduction in the number of cars occurred when it was discovered that a flaw in the tires of a number of cars made it too dangerous for those cars to be in the race and there was not enough time to find replacement vehicles. Regulations explicitly provide that races may be canceled when fewer than 12 cars are available, but the organizers chose to go ahead and hold the race. The court found that the contract was for the event and that no fan would reasonably expect that organizers were specifically guaranteeing a set number of participants.[2] Case 20-1 demonstrates the analysis a court may use to determine whether a defendant's behavior constitutes material breach.

[2] *Larry Bowers, Alan G. Symons, Carey Johnson, et al., v. Federation Internationale de l'Automobile, Formula One Administration Limited, Indianapolis Motor Speedway Corporation, et al.*, 489 F.3d 316 (2007).

CASE 20-1 HAMILTON v. STATE FARM FIRE & CASUALTY INSURANCE COMPANY

U.S. COURT OF APPEALS FOR THE FIFTH CIRCUIT

2012 U.S. APP. LEXIS 8744

When the Hamiltons' home was ruined by a hurricane, the couple moved out of the home to other residences. The couple provided their insurance company with several documents and submitted an insurance claim. However, the couple refused to allow representatives from the insurance agency to inspect their other homes and refused to give the company other vital documents proving the damage of certain assets. Thus, the insurance company denied the Hamiltons' insurance claim, saying that the couple materially breached the contract because they did not comply with the terms of the policy. The appellate court found that the couple could not recover under the insurance policy because they materially breached the contract by not complying with the cooperation clause.

JUDGES BENAVIDES, STEWART, AND HIGGINSON: Louisiana law provides that an insurance policy is a contract between the parties and should be construed by using the general rules of interpretation of contracts set forth in the Louisiana Civil Code. "If the policy wording at issue is clear and unambiguously expresses the parties' intent, the insurance contract must be enforced as written."

"In an insurance contract, the insured's duty to provide information ordinarily arises only under the express policy obligations." Cooperation clauses in insurance contracts "fulfill the reasonable purpose of enabling the insurer to obtain relevant information concerning the loss while the information is fresh." "Compliance with insurance policy provisions are conditions precedent to recovery under that policy, which must be fulfilled before an insured may proceed with a lawsuit." "[F]ailure of an insured to cooperate with the insurer has been held to be a material breach of the contract and a defense to suit on the policy." Such failure may be "manifested by a refusal to submit to an examination under oath or a refusal to produce documents."

"[T]he purpose of the oral examination of the insured is to protect the insurer against fraud, by permitting it to probe into the circumstances of the loss, including an examination of the insured[.]" The defendant must also show that it has been prejudiced by the failure of the plaintiffs to submit to examinations under oath. "The burden is on the insurer to show actual prejudice."

In this case, the Hamiltons reported the alleged theft to local law enforcement, submitted their claim to State Farm, and returned the PPIFs to State Farm as requested; the Hamiltons failed to provide most of the supporting documentation of their loss as requested by State Farm, with the exception of a few duplicate receipts. When asked for the additional documentation, the Hamiltons simply provided their sworn statements as to the losses claimed, without providing the additional supporting documentation requested.

The Hamiltons' failure to comply with State Farm's request to examine the separate residences in which they lived, while not expressly required under the policy's cooperation clause, appears from the record to have been the event which prompted State Farm to request the examinations under oath. The Hamiltons, however, failed to respond to State Farm's multiple verbal and written requests for examinations under oath. Their failure to do so was in direct violation of the policy's cooperation clause provision, Section 1 - Conditions, (2)(d)(3)(b), and is thus considered a "material breach of the contract." The Hamiltons concede in their brief that they failed to respond to State Farm's request for their examinations under oath but submit that State Farm was not prejudiced by their refusals because they would have consented to depositions to be taken later in the litigation. This argument is not persuasive. The underlying purpose of a cooperation clause is to allow the insurer to obtain the material information it needs from the insured to adequately investigate a claim of loss prior to the commencement of litigation proceedings.

Without the additional requested documentation in support of their loss or their sworn statements under oath, State Farm had nothing but the Hamiltons' original recorded statements, which often conflicted with each other factually, and several duplicated receipts to process their claim of over $120,000 in losses. Consequently, it is clear that State Farm's investigation into the claim was prejudiced from the Hamiltons' failure to comply with the terms of the cooperation clause.

Because the Hamiltons materially breached the terms of the policy by failing to comply with the terms of the cooperation clause, they were precluded from recovering under the policy. Additionally, considering that State Farm's denial of the claim was due to the Hamiltons' material breach of the policy, the Hamiltons are also precluded from recovering penalties and attorney fees.

AFFIRMED in favor of State Farm.

CRITICAL THINKING

What kind of evidence would have persuaded State Farm that the Hamiltons had a legitimate insurance claim? What is the reasoning of the court in supporting State Farm's expectations under the cooperation clause in the policy?

ETHICAL DECISION MAKING

How would the universalization principle have aided the Hamiltons in understanding the logic being used by State Farm?

BUT WHAT IF . . .

WHAT IF THE FACTS OF THE CASE OPENER WERE DIFFERENT?

Recall, in the Case Opener, that CPI manufactured Encore's products in its factory. Let's say that CPI simply stopped allowing the products in the factory. Would Encore be able to be discharged from the contract, or would Encore have to stay in the contract and find some sort of resolution?

Anticipatory Repudiation. Sometimes a contracting party may decide not to complete the contract before the actual time of performance. This situation often arises when market conditions change and one party realizes that it will not be profitable to carry out the terms of the contract. The breaching party may convey the anticipatory breach to the nonbreaching party either by making an express indication of her intent to no longer perform or by taking an action that would be inconsistent with her ability to carry out the contract when performance was due.

Once the contract has been anticipatorily repudiated, the nonbreaching party is discharged from his obligations under the contract. He is free to go ahead and sue for breach, as well as find another similar contract elsewhere. However, if the nonbreaching party wishes, he may decide to give the party who repudiated the opportunity to change her mind and still perform.

DISCHARGE BY MUTUAL AGREEMENT

Sometimes the parties to a contract agree to discharge each other from their obligations. They may do so through four primary means: discharge by mutual rescission, discharge by a substituted contract, discharge by accord and satisfaction, or discharge by novation. (See Exhibit 20-2.)

Mutual Rescission. Parties may agree that they simply wish to discharge each other from their mutual obligations and therefore rescind or cancel the contract. For example, if James had agreed to cater a graduation reception for Bill's son but it appeared that the child was not going to graduate when planned, James could agree to no longer hold Bill responsible for paying him the agreed-on cost for the catering in exchange for Bill's agreement to no longer expect James to cater a reception.

To see how techniques of group problem solving relate to mutual rescission, please see the **Connecting to the Core** activity on the text website at www.mhhe.com/kubasek3e.

Substituted Contract. Sometimes, instead of canceling the contract and terminating their relationship, the parties wish to substitute a new agreement in place of the original. The substituted contract immediately discharges the parties from their obligations under the old contract and replaces those obligations with the new obligations imposed by the substituted contract.

In the opening scenario, the amended agreement between Anchor and Encore is a substituted contract. In their original contract, the parties were silent about where the wine bottles would be produced and Anchor provided Encore with a rebate discount schedule ranging from 1 to 2.5 percent. Their substituted contract (the amended agreement) discharged the parties from the previous requirements, specified the Lavington facility as the production location, and increased the rates associated with the discount schedule.

Exhibit 20-2
Ways to Discharge by Mutual Agreement

Mutual rescission	Parties mutually agree to discharge each other from the contract.
Substituted contract	Parties mutually agree to discharge each other from the contract by substituting a new agreement.
Accord and satisfaction	Parties agree that one party will perform her or his duty differently from the performance specified in the original agreement; after the new duty is performed, the party's duty under the original contract becomes discharged.
Novation	The original parties and a third party all agree that the third party will replace one of the original parties and that the original party will then be discharged.

Accord and Satisfaction. An accord and satisfaction is used when one of the parties wishes to substitute a different performance for his or her original duty under the contract. The promise to perform the new duty is called the *accord,* and the actual performance of that new duty is called the *satisfaction.* The party's duty under the contract is not discharged until the new duty is actually performed. Thus, it is the satisfaction that discharges the party.

Novation. Sometimes the parties to the agreement want to replace one of the parties with a third party. This substitution of a party is called a **novation.** The original duties remain the same under the contract, but one party is discharged and the third party now takes that original party's place. All three parties must agree to the novation for it to be valid.

DISCHARGE BY OPERATION OF LAW

Sometimes a contract may be discharged not by anything the parties do but, rather, by operation of law. Alteration of the contract, bankruptcy, tolling of the statute of limitations, impossibility, commercial impracticability, and frustration of purpose are all situations in which a contract may be discharged by operation of law.

Alteration of the Contract. The courts wish to uphold the sanctity of contracts. Therefore, if one of the parties materially alters a written contract without the knowledge of the other party, the courts have held that such alteration allows the innocent party to be discharged from the contract. For example, if a seller, without knowledge of the buyer, changes the price of the contract, the buyer can treat the contract as terminated.

Bankruptcy. When a party files bankruptcy, the court allocates the assets of the bankrupt among the bankrupt's creditors and then issues the party a discharge in bankruptcy. Once the assets have been distributed, all of the bankrupt's debts are discharged. (Bankruptcy is discussed in detail in Chapter 32.)

Tolling of the Statute of Limitations. The tolling of the statute of limitations does not technically discharge a party's obligations under a contract. However, once the statute of limitations has tolled, neither party can any longer sue the other for breach, so for all practical purposes the parties are no longer bound to perform.

Impossibility of Performance. Sometimes an unforeseen event occurs that makes it physically or legally impossible for a party to carry out the terms of the contract. In such a situation, the party will be discharged on grounds of impossibility of performance. Courts distinguish between **objective impossibility,** meaning it is in fact not possible to lawfully carry out one's contractual obligations, and **subjective impossibility,** meaning it would be very difficult to carry out the contract. Objective impossibility, but not subjective impossibility, discharges the parties' obligations under the contract.

For example, if farmer Gray has a contract with the Hunts Corporation to provide it with 100 bushels of tomatoes on August 30 and a flood wipes out Gray's crop, it is not physically impossible for him to comply with the agreement. He has to go out on the market and purchase 100 bushels of tomatoes to ship to the Hunts Corporation. It may be inconvenient, and perhaps subjectively impossible, but it is not objectively impossible.

In contrast, suppose farmer Jones owns a historic farmhouse built in 1827 and he agrees to sell it to Smith, but the night before the parties are to exchange money for the title, lightning strikes the farmhouse and the building burns to the ground. It is now objectively impossible to comply with the terms of the contract, so the parties are discharged from their obligations. The historic farmhouse is not like tomatoes; the subject matter of the contract is forever destroyed and cannot be re-created.

There are three main situations in which the courts find objective impossibility. The first is *destruction of the subject matter*, as in the example of the historic farmhouse destroyed by fire. If we go back to the example of the tomatoes, note that we said the farmer still had to perform because it was still possible for him to obtain tomatoes elsewhere. To protect himself in the event that his crop was destroyed, farmer Gray could have drafted the contract to identify the subject matter as 100 bushels of tomatoes grown on the Gray family farm. In that case, if Gray's fields were flooded, it would be objectively impossible to comply with the contract because there would be no tomatoes from the Gray farm in existence.

The second situation of objective impossibility is the *death or incapacity of a party whose personal services are necessary* to fulfill the terms of the contract. For example, if a famous artist is commissioned to paint a portrait and the artist dies, the contract is discharged. The artist's style is unique, and there is no way for anyone to take over the artist's role.

The third situation is *subsequent illegality*. If the law changes after the contract is made, rendering the performance of the contract illegal, then the contract is discharged. For example, Bill orders a case of a nutritional supplement from Osco Drugs and Supplements. Before his order can be filled, the nutritional supplement is banned because of recently discovered harmful side effects. The parties are now discharged from their duties because to sell the banned substance would be to violate the law.

The opening scenario provides another example of impossibility of performance. The parties in the opening scenario do not dispute that the contract provided that "[t]he parties contemplate that the products (as hereinafter defined) shall be manufactured at CPI's Lavington facility" (the Lavington plant). When the Lavington plant was no longer available for production, it became impossible for Anchor to fulfill the terms of the contract. Ultimately, Anchor informed Encore that it considered itself discharged from the contract.

Legal Principle: A contract is objectively impossible, and therefore parties are discharged from their obligations under it, when the subject matter is destroyed, one of the parties whose personal services are required dies or becomes incapacitated, or the law changes, rendering performance of the contract illegal.

Commercial Impracticability. Commercial impracticability can be seen as a response to what some might interpret as a somewhat unfair harshness of the objective-impossibility standard. Commercial impracticability is used when performance is still objectively possible but would be extraordinarily injurious or expensive to one party. Commercial impracticability arises when, because of an unforeseeable event, one party would incur unreasonable expense, injury, or loss if that party were forced to carry out the terms of the agreement.

According to the Restatement (Second) of Contracts, Section 261 (1981), discharge by reason of impracticability requires that the party claiming discharge prove the following three elements:

1. That an event occurred whose nonoccurrence was a basic assumption of the contract.
2. That there is commercial impracticability of continued performance.
3. That the party claiming discharge did not expressly or impliedly agree to performance in spite of impracticability that would otherwise justify nonperformance.

It is sometimes difficult to know whether the potential harm to the party seeking to avoid the contract is sufficient to give rise to the use of commercial impracticability. The doctrine is most commonly used in situations in which raw materials needed for manufacturing goods under the contract become extraordinarily expensive or difficult to obtain because of an embargo, war, crop failure, or unexpected closure of a plant. Case 20-2 illustrates how the courts sometimes struggle to determine whether to apply the doctrine of commercial impracticability to discharge a contract.

CASE 20-2 THRIFTY RENT-A-CAR SYSTEM v. SOUTH FLORIDA TRANSPORT

U.S. DISTRICT COURT FOR THE NORTHERN DISTRICT OF OKLAHOMA

2005 U.S. DIST. LEXIS 38489

The plaintiffs, Thrifty Rent-A-Car System and its affiliates DTG and Rental Car Finance Corp., allowed South Florida Transport (SFT), the defendant, to establish a Thrifty franchise. In 2003, Thrifty and SFT entered into four agreements, which provided SFT the right to use Thrifty's trademark and business methods in exchange for payment to Thrifty of licensing and administrative fees. The agreements also provided that SFT would maintain a fleet of automobiles for rental.

In July 2004, SFT provided DTG with a check as payment, but the check was returned for insufficient funds. SFT continued to make delinquent payments, and by August, SFT owed Thrifty and DTG $1,134,819.40. Due to SFT's failure to make payments, Thrifty and DTG informed SFT that they were going to terminate the licensing agreements and repossess the vehicles, to which DTG had legal title. However, DTG agreed to postpone repossession due to predictions of severe weather, and allowed SFT to continue renting vehicles until repossession was completed.

When DTG repossessed the vehicles, DTG noticed that numerous cars were missing. In response, SFT notified DTG that it had sold 51 vehicles without authorization. By August 2005, SFT owed Thrifty and DTG $4,238,249.53. SFT claimed that several hurricanes rendered their business operations commercially impracticable. The plaintiffs filed a motion for summary judgment, seeking full reimbursement for the debts owed by SFT.

JUDGE EAGAN: Performance may become impracticable due to extreme and unreasonable difficulty, expense, injury, or loss to one of the parties involved. Impracticability does not equate to impracticality, however. "A mere change in the degree of difficulty or expense . . . unless well beyond the normal range does not amount to impracticability since it is this sort of risk that a fixed-price contract is intended to cover." The law also imposes an objective standard on the duty to perform for those seeking to invoke the defense of impracticability. A party to a contract is not discharged from his duty to perform merely by demonstrating that a supervening event prevented him from performing; he must also demonstrate that similarly situated parties were also deprived of the ability to perform.

The undisputed facts relevant to Greenstein's claim of impracticability are as follows: In August and September 2004, Hurricanes Charley, Frances, Ivan, and Jeanne hit the state of Florida. One of those storms, Hurricane Ivan, also affected the state of Alabama. Although some of SFT's rental car business locations incurred damage during the course of the storm, it is undisputed that the locations remained substantially intact, and the vehicles leased from DTG were not destroyed.

The hurricanes in late summer 2004 clearly constitute supervening events for the purposes of impracticability doctrine. However, the record suggests that the nonoccurrence of those hurricanes was not an assumption upon which the parties grounded their agreement. Hardy testified that he lived in Florida approximately ten years, during which time severe weather, including hurricanes, had hit the coast of Florida.

The doctrine of commercial impracticability is typically invoked in cases involving the sale of goods. Codified in section 2-615 of the Uniform Commercial Code (UCC), which has been adopted by the Oklahoma legislature, the doctrine of commercial impracticability provides a defense to a seller for a delay in delivery or nondelivery of promised goods if performance has been made impracticable by a contingency, the nonoccurrence of which is an assumption of the contract.

Commercial impracticability may excuse a party from performance of his obligations under a contract where performance has become commercially impracticable because of unforeseen supervening circumstances not within the contemplation of the parties at the time of contracting. UCC commentary provides that a party pleading commercial impracticability must demonstrate the "basic assumption" prong of the test also found in the impracticability of performance context, that is, that the nonoccurrence of the

[continued]

supervening event was a basic assumption of the parties at the time of contracting. A rise or a collapse in the market standing alone does not constitute a justification for failure to perform. A contract is deemed commercially impracticable when, due to unforeseen events, performance may only be obtained at "an excessive and unreasonable cost . . . or when all means of performance are commercially senseless." In applying the doctrine of commercial impracticability, the crucial question is "whether the cost of performance has in fact become so excessive and unreasonable that failure to excuse performance would result in grave injustice."

For many of the reasons already discussed, defendant is not entitled to the defense of commercial impracticability. The evidence strongly suggests that the nonoccurrence of hurricanes was not a basic assumption of the parties' agreements. Moreover, defendant provides no evidence to support a suggestion that the event of the hurricanes made the cost of performance of the terms of the agreements unduly burdensome, or even remotely more expensive. Finally, the Court observes, again, that SFT was behind on its payments to Thrifty and DTG before the arrival of the hurricanes in August 2004. No genuine issue of material fact exists, and the Court holds that the defense of commercial impracticability is unavailable to defendant.

Plaintiff's motion for summary judgment granted.

CRITICAL THINKING

What are the implications of the court's decision that commercial impracticability is not constituted by the significant hurricane damages imposed on Florida in 2004? Especially given the increased rates of severe weather and natural disasters witnessed recently around the world, to what extent can parties entering into contracts reasonably be expected to plan for the effects of a rapidly changing global climate?

ETHICAL DECISION MAKING

How might ethical theories founded in deontology and in ethics of care differ in their interpretation of the behaviors examined in this case? Which interpretation do you think is more ethically defendable? Which interpretation does Judge Eagan appear to favor? Justify your response.

What purpose does this ruling appear to support? Is there a larger ethical end implied by Judge Eagan's decision? Why or why not?

BUT WHAT IF . . .

WHAT IF THE FACTS OF THE CASE OPENER WERE DIFFERENT?

Let's say that CPI left its factory to Anchor so that Anchor could still manufacture products for Encore as stated in the contract. However, manufacturing the products as CPI did would be outrageously expensive for Anchor. Does Anchor still have to remain in the contract with Encore?

Frustration of Purpose. Closely related to impracticability is frustration of purpose. Sometimes, when a contract is entered into, both parties recognize that the contract is to fulfill a particular purpose, and the happening of that purpose is said to be a basic assumption on which the contract is made. If, due to factors beyond the control of the parties, the event does not occur, and neither party had assumed the risk of the event's nonoccurrence, the contract may be discharged.

This doctrine arose from the so-called coronation cases in England. Numerous parties had contracted for rooms along the parade route for the king's coronation, but the king became ill and the coronation was canceled. The courts held that the parties' duties under the room contracts should be discharged and that any payments made in advance should be returned as the essential purposes of the contracts could no longer be fulfilled, through no fault of any of the parties.

BUT WHAT IF . . .

WHAT IF THE FACTS OF THE CASE OPENER WERE DIFFERENT?

Let's say that Anchor and Encore had entered into the contract with the purpose of creating a certain kind of bottle that was better for the environment than normal bottles. However, the two companies tried but could not produce such a bottle. Can the contract be discharged?

This doctrine is not frequently used. For example, if you contract for an organist to play at your daughter's wedding but the groom gets cold feet at the last moment and the wedding is canceled, you cannot use frustration of purpose to discharge the contract because the groom's changing his mind was a foreseeable event, even though it was unlikely. The Case Nugget on the next page illustrates another unsuccessful attempted use of this doctrine.

Exhibit 20-3 summarizes the five methods of discharging a contract.

Exhibit 20-3
Methods of Discharging a Contract

Discharge by conditions	If precedent, concurrent, implied, and express conditions are not met or subsequent condition occurs.
Discharge by performance	If a party performs the terms of the contract or makes a tender (an offer to perform), or if the party performs to the satisfaction of the contracting party.
Discharge by material breach	If a party fails to substantially perform his obligations, thereby justifying that the nonbreaching party be discharged from the contract.
Discharge by mutual agreement	If the parties mutually agree to discharge one another, substitute a new contract, substitute a party, or substitute a different performance.
Discharge by operation of the law	If one of the following occurs: alteration of the contract, bankruptcy, tolling of the statute of limitations, impossibility, commercial impracticability, or frustration of purpose.

L02
What are the primary legal remedies available for a breach of contract?

Remedies

The fact that one party has breached a contract does not necessarily mean that the non breaching party will sue. A number of factors go into the decision of whether or not it makes sense to file suit (see Exhibit 20-4). Some of those considerations include (1) the likelihood of success, (2) the desire or need to maintain an ongoing relationship with the potential defendant, (3) the possibility of getting a better or faster resolution through some form of alternative dispute resolution, and (4) the cost of litigation or some form of ADR as compared to the value of the likely remedy.

Exhibit 20-4
Things to Consider before Filing Suit

1. The likelihood of success.
2. The desire or need to maintain an ongoing relationship with the potential defendant.
3. The possibility of getting a better or faster resolution through some form of alternative dispute resolution.
4. The cost of litigation or some form of ADR as compared to the value of the likely remedy.

CASE NUGGET

AN UNFORESEEABLE EVENT?

Liggett Restaurant Group, Inc. v. City of Pontiac
260 Mich. App. 127, 676 N.W.2d 633 (Mich. App. 2003)

Elias Brothers Restaurants, Inc., had a contract with the defendant, City of Pontiac Stadium Building Authority, to provide concessions at the Silverdome until 2000. The parties renegotiated the contract in 1990, and Elias Brothers agreed to pay additional consideration for the option to extend the contract until 2005 to coordinate with the end of the Detroit Lions' sublease. The additional consideration involved paying the city a higher percentage on profits from sales. This option was exercised on December 1, 1998, and the Detroit Lions prematurely discontinued playing in the Silverdome after the 2001 football season.

The plaintiff sought to use the frustration-of-purpose doctrine to discharge its obligations under the contract extension and therefore have returned to it the additional consideration it had paid under the extension. The plaintiff argued that the contract was made on the assumption that the Lions would play in the Silverdome until their lease ran out and thus their early departure frustrated the purpose of the extension.

The court said the doctrine was inapplicable in this case. The court first set forth the conditions under which the doctrine applied: (1) The contract must be at least partially executory; (2) the frustrated party's purpose in making the contract must have been known to both parties when the contract was made; (3) this purpose must have been basically frustrated by an event not reasonably foreseeable at the time the contract was made, the occurrence of which has not been due to the fault of the frustrated party and the risk of which was not assumed by him. Then the court noted that the situation clearly did not meet the third criterion. Far from being an unforeseeable event, the Lions' leaving prematurely was expressly addressed in the original contract by a paragraph specifying a reduction in the guaranteed minimum annual payment for each year in which the Lions did not play a minimum of eight games in the stadium.

The remedies the potential plaintiff will be thinking about can generally be classified as either *legal remedies* (also known as *monetary damages*) or *equitable remedies,* some form of court-ordered action. The distinction between legal and equitable remedies can be traced back to a time in our legal system's English roots when, instead of one unitary legal system, there were two separate courts, a court of law and a court of equity. When parties were seeking money damages, they went to the court of law; but when parties needed any remedy other than money damages, they went to the High Court of Chancery, which was a court of equity. When the United States was establishing its legal system, it combined both these types of powers in a unitary system. The reasons for this joinder are not known, but it seems likely that the primary reason was that the early colonists simply did not have the resources to support two separate systems. The courts did, however, still maintain the distinction between legal and equitable remedies. However, unlike judges in the old English courts, judges in the U.S. system have the power to award both legal and equitable remedies in the same case. This section discusses these various remedies.

LEGAL REMEDIES (MONETARY DAMAGES)

Monetary damages are also referred to as *legal damages* or *legal remedies,* and they include compensatory, punitive, nominal, and liquidated damages. Whenever possible, courts award monetary damages rather than some form of equitable relief.

Compensatory Damages. The most frequently awarded damages are **compensatory damages,** damages designed to put the plaintiff in the position he would have been in had the contract been fully performed. These damages are said to compensate the plaintiff for his loss of the benefit of the bargain. He can recover, however, only for those provable losses that were foreseeable at the time the contract was entered into. Sometimes, the plaintiff actually may have no losses. Suppose, for example, that Dr. Wilcox hires Jeremy to work exclusively as his research assistant during the fall semester, for a salary of $2,000 per month. If Wilcox breaches the contract and terminates Jeremy for no reason with two months left on the contract, and the only job Jeremy can get as a substitute pays only $500 per month, Jeremy would be entitled to compensatory damages of $3,000. However, if Jeremy gets a new job that pays $2,500 per month, he is actually better off, so no compensatory damages would be awarded. Sometimes these damages are referred to as *expectation damages* because they compensate a person for the benefit she or he expected to gain as a result of entering into the contract.

In addition to losing the benefit of the bargain, the plaintiff may suffer other losses directly caused by the breach. These losses may be compensated for as *incidental damages*. For example, because Jeremy was unfairly terminated before his contractual term was over, he may have to spend money to find another job. His job search expenditures would be considered incidental damages.

BUT WHAT IF . . .

WHAT IF THE FACTS OF THE CASE OPENER WERE DIFFERENT?

Let's say that after Anchor and Encore stopped doing business together, Encore entered into an agreement with another company whereby it received bigger discounts than those it received from Anchor. Could Encore still sue Anchor for compensatory damages for breaching the contract?

Some kinds of contracts have special rules for determining compensatory damages, namely, contracts for the sale of goods or land and construction contracts. Each of these is discussed in a little more detail below.

Contracts for the sale of goods are governed today by the Uniform Commercial Code. If the seller breaches the contract, compensatory damages are generally calculated as the difference between the contract price and the market price on the day the goods were supposed to be delivered,[3] plus any incidental damages resulting from the breach. In other words, this measure of damages is the difference between what the buyer would have paid for the goods under the contract and what he or she is now going to have to pay to obtain the goods from another seller. Occasionally, however, the buyer may have no damages because the market price of the goods is lower than the parties had anticipated it would be at the date of delivery and so the buyer can now actually purchase the goods at a lower price than the contract price.

If the buyer breaches before accepting the goods, the seller would be able to resell the goods and recover as compensatory damages the difference between the price he sold the goods for and the contract price, plus any incidental expenses associated with the sale.[4] If the seller is unable to sell the goods to another buyer, as might be the case, for example, with shirts embroidered with a company's monogram, then the seller may be entitled to the contract price as damages. If the buyer breaches before the goods are even manufactured, the seller's damages would typically be based on the profits that would have been made from the sale.

In construction contracts, contracts whereby an owner enters into an agreement to have a building constructed, damages are calculated differently depending on who the breaching party is and what stage the construction is in when the breach occurs. If the contract is breached by the owner before the construction is begun, damages are simply lost profits, which are calculated by subtracting the projected costs of construction from the contract

[3] UCC §§ 2-708 and 2-713.

[4] UCC §§ 2-706 and 2-710.

price. For example, if Cameron Construction Company anticipates building a warehouse for the Johnson Corporation with a contract price of $500,000 and the cost of raw materials and labor is $420,000, Cameron could recover $80,000 in lost profits if the Johnson Corporation were to breach the contract before performance had begun.

If, however, Cameron Construction had already expended $20,000 in materials and labor on the job when the breach occurred, the company would be able to recover $100,000 in damages because the amount of damages when construction is in progress is measured by the lost profits plus any money already invested in the project. If the breach by the owner had occurred after construction was completed, the construction company would be entitled to recover the entire contract price, plus interest from the time payment for the project was due.

If the construction company or contractor breaches the contract before or during the construction, the owner's damages are generally measured by the cost of hiring another company to complete the project, plus any incidental costs associated with obtaining a new contractor, as well as any costs arising from delays in the construction project. If the contractor completes the job but finishes after the date for completion, the owner is entitled to damages for the loss of the use of the building that she would have had if the contract had been completed in a timely manner.

Consequential Damages. It should be apparent by now that contract law requires greater certainty in the proof of damages than does tort law. Damages are not recoverable for breach of contract unless they can be proved with a high degree of certainty. One type of damages in contract cases that is often especially difficult to prove is what are called **consequential** or **special damages.** Consequential damages are foreseeable damages that result from special facts and circumstances arising outside the contract itself. These damages must be within the contemplation of the parties at the time the breach occurs.

In Case 20-3, a classic case, the court distinguishes consequential damages from the damages that arise naturally from a breach of contract.

CASE 20-3 HADLEY v. BAXENDALE
COURT OF EXCHEQUER
156 ENG. REP. 145 (1854)

Plaintiffs were millers in Gloucester. On May 11, their mill was stopped when the crank shaft of the mill broke. They had to send the shaft to Greenwich to be used as a model for a new crank to be molded. The plaintiffs' servant took the shaft to the defendant, a common carrier, and told the defendant's clerk that the mill was stopped, and that the shaft must be sent immediately. The clerk said it would be delivered at Greenwich on the following day. The defendant's clerk was told that a special entry, if required, should be made to hasten the shaft's delivery. The delivery of the shaft at Greenwich was delayed by some neglect, and consequently, the plaintiffs did not receive the new shaft for several days after they would otherwise have received it. During that time the mill was shut down, and the plaintiffs thereby lost the profits they would otherwise have received had the shaft been delivered on time. They sought to recover damages for lost profits during that time. The defendant argued that the lost profits were "too remote." The court decided for the plaintiffs and allowed the jury to consider the lost profits in awarding damages. The defendant appealed.

JUSTICE ALDERSON: We think that there ought to be a new trial in this case; but, in so doing, we deem it to be expedient and necessary to state explicitly the rule which the Judge, at the next trial, ought, in our opinion, to direct the jury to be governed by when they estimate the damages. . . .

Now we think the proper rule in such a case as the present is this: Where two parties have made a contract which one of them has broken, the damages which the other party ought to receive in respect of such breach of contract should be such as may fairly and reasonably be considered either arising naturally, i.e., according to the usual course of things, from such breach of contract itself, or such as may reasonably be supposed to have been in the contemplation of both

[continued]

parties, at the time they made the contract, as the probable result of the breach of it. Now, if the special circumstances under which the contract was actually made were communicated by the plaintiffs to the defendants, and thus known to both parties, the damages resulting from the breach of such a contract, which they would reasonably contemplate, would be the amount of injury which would ordinarily follow from a breach of contract under these special circumstances so known and communicated. But, on the other hand, if these special circumstances were wholly unknown to the party breaking the contract, he, at the most, could only be supposed to have had in his contemplation the amount of injury which would arise generally, and in the great multitude of cases not affected by any special circumstances, from such a breach of contract. For, had the special circumstances been known, the parties might have specially provided for the breach of contract by special terms as to the damages in that case; and of this advantage it would be very unjust to deprive them. . . . Now, in the present case, if we are to apply the principles above laid down, we find that the only circumstances here communicated by the plaintiffs to the defendants at the time the contract was made, were, that the article to be carried was the broken shaft of a mill, and that the plaintiffs were the millers of the mill.

But how do these circumstances show reasonably that the profits of the mill must be stopped by an unreasonable delay in the delivery of the broken shaft by the carrier to the third person? . . . But it is obvious that, in the great multitude of cases of millers sending off broken shafts to third persons by a carrier under ordinary circumstances, such consequences would not, in all probability, have occurred; and these special circumstances were here never communicated by the plaintiffs to the defendants. It follows therefore, that the loss of profits here cannot reasonably be considered such a consequence of the breach of contract as could have been fairly and reasonably contemplated by both the parties when they made this contract. For such loss would neither have flowed naturally from the breach of this contract in the great multitude of such cases occurring under ordinary circumstances, nor were the special circumstances, which, perhaps, would have made it a reasonable and natural consequence of such breach of contract, communicated to or known by the defendants.

Judgment for defendant for a new trial.

CRITICAL THINKING

What are the key terms essential to this argument? Are alternative definitions of important words or phrases possible? If so, how could the acceptability of this argument be affected by the use of these alternative meanings?

What additional information would be useful in deciding the acceptability of this argument? For instance, what do we really know about the proposed loss of profit? Does this missing information have a significant impact on the reasoning?

ETHICAL DECISION MAKING

What value preferences can be discovered in Judge Alderson's ruling? Are they properly justified? What ethical theories or guidelines might aid in their justification? Why?

Punitive Damages. Just as in tort law, **punitive damages** in contract law are designed to punish the defendant and deter him and others from engaging in similar behavior in the future. Because the primary objective of contract law, however, is to ensure that parties' expectations are met, punitive, or exemplary, damages are rarely awarded. Most jurisdictions award them only when the defendant has engaged in reprehensible conduct such as fraud. The primary factor in determining the amount of punitive damages is how much is necessary to "punish" the defendant; thus the amount depends on matters such as the wealth and income of the defendant.

Nominal Damages. In a case where no actual damages resulted from the breach of contract, the court may award the plaintiff **nominal damages.** The award is typically for $1 or $5, but it serves to signify that the plaintiff has been wronged by the defendant.

Liquidated Damages. Typically, the court determines the amount of damages to which a nonbreaching party is entitled. Sometimes, however, the parties recognize that if there is a breach of contract, it will probably be somewhat difficult for the court to determine exactly what the damages are. To prevent a difficult court battle, the parties specify in advance what the **liquidated damages** will be if there is a particular kind of breach. The parties specify these damages in what is called a *liquidated* or *stipulated-damage clause* in the contract. The damages may be specified as either a fixed amount or a formula for determining how much money is due. Such clauses are frequently used in construction contracts when the buyer needs to know the property is going to be available by a specific date so that she can make her plans for moving in. In such a case, the parties may estimate in advance what it will cost the buyer for storage and temporary housing if the property is not ready by the specified date. The courts generally enforce these clauses as long as they appear to bear a reasonable relationship to what the actual costs will be. If the amount specified is so unreasonable as to not seem to bear any logical relationship to foreseeable costs, the courts declare the clause a penalty clause and do not enforce it.

Mitigation of Damages. When a contract has been breached, the nonbreaching party is often angry at the breaching party and may want to make the breaching party "pay through the nose." However, the courts do not allow a nonbreaching party to intentionally increase his damages. In fact, to recover damages in a breach-of-contract case, the plaintiff must demonstrate that he used reasonable efforts to minimize the damage resulting from the breach. This obligation is referred to as the *duty to mitigate one's damages.*

Thus, if you are the manager of a hotel and a person who had booked 10 rooms for the week calls to cancel all the reservations, you have a duty to attempt to rent the rooms to minimize the damages. The mitigation must be reasonable, however, and no one is expected to settle for something less than what was contemplated under the contract in order to mitigate the damages.

One area where interesting mitigation issues arise is cases in which an employee is wrongfully discharged and must seek new employment to mitigate her damages. If the employee does not seek alternative employment, the amount of lost wages recovered as damages will be reduced by the amount the employee reasonably could have earned in another job. If the employee does not find another job, the court must decide whether the employee could have found comparable alternative employment with reasonable effort.

EQUITABLE REMEDIES

L03 What are the primary equitable remedies available for a breach of contract?

As noted earlier, equitable remedies grew out of the English court's authority to fashion remedies when the existing laws did not provide any adequate ones. These remedies were typically unique solutions specifically crafted to the demands of the situations. Today, the most common equitable remedies include rescission and restitution, orders for specific performance, and injunctions.

As a carryover from the days of the English courts of law and equity, a party seeking equitable relief must meet five requirements. The party must prove that (1) there is no adequate legal remedy available; (2) irreparable harm to the plaintiff may result if the equitable remedy is not granted; (3) the contract is legally valid (except when seeking relief in quasi-contract); (4) the contract terms are clear and unambiguous; and (5) the plaintiff has "clean hands," that is, has not been deceitful or done anything in breach of the contract.

Rescission and Restitution. Sometimes the parties simply want to be returned to their precontract status; they want to have the contract terminated and to have any

COMPARING THE LAW OF OTHER COUNTRIES

LIQUIDATED DAMAGES IN CHINA

Article 114 of Chapter 7, "Liability for Breach of Contracts," of the Contract Law of the People's Republic of China provides for the equivalent of the liquidated-damage clause recognized under U.S. law. The first part of the Chinese law is almost identical to our law. It provides that the parties to a contract may agree that one party shall, when violating the contract, pay breach-of-contract damages of a certain amount in light of the breach or they may agree on the calculating method of compensation for losses resulting from the breach of contract.

However, the Chinese law has an interesting twist for circumstances in which the projected damages end up being different from what the actual damages are. If the agreed breach-of-contract damages are lower than the losses caused, any party may request that the people's court or an arbitration institution increase it; if it is excessively higher than the losses caused, any party may request that the people's court or an arbitration institution make an appropriate reduction.

transferred property returned to its original owner. That is, they want rescission and restitution. **Rescission** is the termination of the contract, and **restitution** is the return of any property given up under the contract.

Restitution and rescission are most frequently awarded in situations in which there is a lack of genuine assent (discussed in Chapter 17). When a party enters into a contract because of fraud, duress, undue influence, or a bilateral mistake, the contract is voidable and the party who wants out may seek to avoid the contract or, in other words, may seek rescission and restitution.

Specific Performance. **Specific performance** is sometimes called *specific enforcement.* It is an order requiring that the breaching party fulfill the terms of the agreement. Courts are very reluctant to grant specific performance and will do so only when monetary damages simply are not adequate, typically because the subject matter of the contract is unique. If the subject matter is unique, then even if the nonbreaching party is given compensation, he cannot go elsewhere to buy the item from someone else, so this renders any kind of money damages inadequate.

Primarily for historical reasons, every piece of real property is considered unique. Therefore, an order for specific performance would often be the appropriate remedy for the breach of a contract for the sale of a piece of real estate.

Injunction. An **injunction** is an order either forcing a person to do something or prohibiting a person from doing something. Most commonly, injunctions are prohibitions against actions. Such an injunction might be used, for example, as a remedy in a contract case involving a personal service. Mandy is a lounge singer, and she has a contract to perform at JZ's Lounge every weekend night from January through June. Two months into her contract she decides to work for Bally's Lounge instead because Bally's will pay her twice as much. There is no way to adequately calculate the damages that would arise from the singer's going over to the other club to perform, so money damages would not really be an adequate remedy. Instead, the owner of JZ's may obtain an injunction prohibiting Mandy from performing in any lounge until the end of June, when her term of performance under the contract will have been completed.

Sometimes, when a party is suing another for breach of contract, one of the parties is concerned that before the court has had a chance to decide the case, the other party will do something to make it impossible for the concerned party to get the relief he would be entitled to. In such a situation, the concerned party may ask for a preliminary injunction to prohibit the other party from taking any action during the course of the lawsuit that would cause irreparable harm to any of the parties to the contract. For example, Jim agrees to sell Bob a very rare antique car for $15,000 but then says he is not going to comply with the terms of the agreement. Bob sues Jim for breach of contract, but before the case goes to trial, Bob finds out that Sara has told Jim that she would be willing to pay him $20,000 for the car. Bob may seek a preliminary injunction to prohibit Jim from selling the car to anyone else until the court decides whether Bob is entitled to an order for specific performance forcing Jim to sell the car to him. Thus, the preliminary injunction fulfills the purpose of maintaining the status quo until the case can be finally decided.

It is not always easy to predict when a court will issue a preliminary injunction, however, as Bear, Stearns & Co. recently discovered when the court refused to issue a preliminary injunction to enforce a contractual provision requiring that an employee provide 90 days' notice of termination of employment (a so-called garden-leave provision). The court's refusal was based in part on public policy concerns.[5] The company's executive director of private client services submitted his notice of resignation, effective immediately, and began working for Morgan Stanley the next day. Bear, Stearns & Co. sought to enjoin the former director from working for a competitor during the contractually specified 90-day notice period. In denying the injunction, despite a stated belief that the company would ultimately win the breach-of-contract claim, the court provided three reasons. First, the company could not establish that it would suffer irreparable harm, because its harm could be recompensed by money damages. Second, any hardship to Bear Stearns due to permitting the defendant to resume his employment with Morgan Stanley in violation of the 90-day restriction was outweighed by the risk to his "professional standing and the inability to advise his clients in times of economic turmoil." Third, the court could not order the requested relief because doing so would require the defendant to continue an at-will employment relationship against his will.[6]

Reformation. Sometimes a written contract does not reflect the parties' actual agreement, or there are inconsistencies in the contract, such as the price being listed as "$200,000 (twenty thousand dollars)." In such a case, the written document may be rewritten to reflect what the parties had agreed on.

Recovery Based on Quasi-Contract. When an enforceable contract does not in fact exist, the court may grant a recovery based on quasi-contract; that is, the court may impose a contractlike obligation on a party to prevent an injustice from occurring. Recovery in quasi-contract is often sought when a party thought a valid contract existed and thus gave up something of value in relying on the existence of a contract. To justify recovery under a theory of quasi-contract, sometimes referred to as *recovery in quantum meriut,* a plaintiff must prove that (1) the plaintiff conferred a benefit on the defendant; (2) the plaintiff had reasonably expected to be compensated for the benefit conferred on the defendant; and (3) the defendant would be unjustly enriched from receiving the benefit without compensating the plaintiff for it.

[5] "Court Declines to Issue Preliminary Injunction to Enforce Garden Leave Provision," *Labor and Employment Alert,* www.goodwinprocter.com/~/media/208D97723AA140B58BE5D0622EFEC428.ashx (accessed June 2, 2009).

[6] Ibid.

CASE OPENER WRAP-UP

Impossible Wine Bottles

Under the amended agreement between Anchor and Encore, the production of bottles was to take place at the Lavington plant. The Lavington plant was the only facility owned by CPI that was capable of producing the specific type and quality of glass container that is required by the wine industry. According to the court's ruling, when the Lavington plant was sold and the new owners did not take over CPI's obligations, the terms of the contract became impossible for Anchor to meet. As a result of the impossibility of performance, Anchor was discharged from the contract.

KEY TERMS

compensatory damages 463	consequential damages 465	monetary damages 463	restitution 468
complete performance 454	express conditions 453	nominal damages 466	special damages 465
concurrent conditions 453	implied conditions 453	novation 458	specific performance 468
condition precedent 452	injunction 468	objective impossibility 458	subjective impossibility 458
condition subsequent 452	liquidated damages 467	punitive damages 466	substantial performance 454
conditional contracts 452	material breach 455	rescission 468	tender 454

SUMMARY OF KEY TOPICS

Methods of Discharging a Contract

Contracts may be discharged in a number of different ways, including:

- The occurrence or nonoccurrence of a condition.
- Complete performance.
- Substantial performance.
- Material breach.
- Mutual agreement.
- Operation of law.

Remedies

Courts may grant parties in a breach-of-contract action legal or equitable remedies. *Legal remedies,* or money damages, include:

- *Compensatory damages:* Damages designed to put the plaintiff in the position he or she would have been in had the contract been fully performed.
- *Nominal damages:* Token damages that merely recognize that the plaintiff had been wronged.
- *Punitive damages:* Damages designed to punish the defendant.
- *Liquidated damages:* Damages specified in advance in the contract.

Equitable remedies, which are granted only when legal remedies are inadequate, include:

- *Rescission and restitution:* The termination of the contract and the return of the parties to their precontract status.
- *Specific performance:* An order requiring the defendant to perform some act.
- *Injunction:* An order prohibiting the defendant from performing some act.

POINT / COUNTERPOINT

Should Nonbreaching Parties Be Required to Mitigate Damages?

NO

Courts' requiring nonbreaching parties to mitigate damages is unfair.

Contract law is designed to reward both parties for the agreement that they have reached. If one party is irresponsible and cannot perform as agreed, why should courts then punish the nonbreaching party by requiring him or her to mitigate damages? After all, the nonbreaching party likely made decisions subsequent to the contract on the assumption that the contract terms would be carried out, and mitigating damages introduces stress regarding those decisions. For instance, if a hotel owner entered a contract with a person who agreed to rent 50 hotel rooms and a conference room for a weekend, the hotel owner would focus his time and energy on advertising for other weekends. But to require the hotel owner, after learning that the person no longer wanted the rooms, to mitigate damages places stress on the owner that he would not have otherwise experienced. Instead of completely focusing on booking rooms for other weekends, the hotel owner must now take time away from advertising those rooms so that he can try to fill the 50 vacant rooms and conference room, even if he wants to sue for breach of contract.

In addition, requiring nonbreaching parties to mitigate damages encourages irresponsible behavior on the part of contracting parties. If a party knows she can breach a contract as long as she provides enough notice, she may be able to avoid most, if not all, liability. Returning to the hotel example, if the person who contracted to rent the 50 rooms notifies the hotel owner of the breach two months before the weekend she contracted for, the hotel owner could fill the rooms and the breaching party would likely not be liable for any damages, even though the hotel owner incurred greater expense and spent additional time filling the rooms with other guests. "Mitigating damages," therefore, is just a fancy way of saying that the burden shifts back to the nonbreaching parties, rewarding the very people who should bear the costs of breaching a contract.

YES

Courts' requiring nonbreaching parties to mitigate damages provides the most equitable solution when a contract is breached.

Although a nonbreaching party could understandably be frustrated with the breaching party, such a breach does not license the nonbreaching party to force the breaching party to provide full payment for the contract, especially when many costs could have been avoided. For example, if a city contracts with a company to construct a bridge across a river and the city later learns that the roads that would connect to the bridge would disrupt a nesting bald eagle, the company should not be permitted to still build the bridge and demand full payment. The city would then have to pay for a useless bridge, even though the company could have avoided the costs of building the bridge.

In this example and similar contexts, the breaching parties would have an incentive to do nothing and still demand payment, even though damages could have been reduced. For instance, if a person entered a two-year employment contract to work for a company but the company could not honor the contract, the nonbreaching party should not be entitled to sit at home for two years and still receive compensation.

In other words, if nonbreaching parties were not required to mitigate damages—either by discontinuing performance, as in the bridge example, or by finding a reasonable replacement, such as a different job in the employment example—nonbreaching parties would run up the costs by completing performance under the contract or doing nothing. In the context of finding a reasonable alternative, nonbreaching parties would actually have an incentive to do nothing.

Finally, mitigating damages promotes better relationships between contracting parties, making both parties more willing to contract again in the future.

QUESTIONS & PROBLEMS

1. Explain the difference between legal and equitable remedies.
2. Explain how the existence of conditions subsequent and precedent affects the discharge of a contract.
3. Explain the relationship between commercial impracticability and frustration of purpose.
4. List the conditions that must be met for a court to impose a quasi-contract.

5. The Thompsons intended to buy a pickup truck from Lithia Dodge. They signed a retail installment contract which listed the annual interest rate as 3.9 percent and which stated that the contract was not binding until financing was completed and that any disputes arising under the contract would be resolved through arbitration. The Thompsons took their new truck home and left their trade-in vehicle with Lithia Dodge. A week later, the financing manager called the Thompsons and informed them that the financing rate of 3.9 had not been accepted and they would have to come in and sign a contract at a 4.9 percent rate. The Thompsons filed suit against Lithia Dodge, which by this time had already sold their trade-in vehicle. Lithia Dodge filed a motion to dismiss, arguing that the case had to go to arbitration because of the binding arbitration clause. The district court agreed. How do you believe the appellate court ruled, and why? [*Thompson v. Lithia Chrysler Jeep Dodge of Great Falls,* 185 P.3d 332 (Sup. Ct. Mt. 2008).]

6. Turner Construction entered into a contract to provide general construction of Granby Towers. Turner then entered into a subcontract with Universal to install precast concrete floors in the Granby Towers construction project. The general construction contract was incorporated by reference into the subcontract. The contract between Turner and Universal contained a "pay-when-paid provision" that conditioned any payments to Universal on Turner's first receiving payment from Universal. Due to the economic downturn, financing for the project fell through. Universal had substantially completed all its work by that time, and it sought payment of $885,507 from Turner, which refused to pay because it had not received any payment from the owner of the project. Turner asked the court for summary judgment on Universal's breach-of- contract claim. Should the court's grant of summary judgment be upheld? Why or why not? [*Universal Concrete Products v. Turner Construction Co.,* 4th Cir. Case No. 09-1569 (2010).]

7. Mantz worked for TruGreen, a lawn care company. He, along with other TruGreen employees, signed the company's noncompete, nonsolicitation, and nondisclosure agreements. Mantz quit and went to work for Mower Brothers, a competitor. Other TruGreen employees followed Mantz to Mower Brothers. TruGreen sued Mantz and the other employees for breach of the agreements and Mower Brothers for tortuous interference with contract. What do you think the Utah high court said was the proper measure of damages in such a case? [*TruGreen Companies v. Mower Brothers, Inc.,* 2008 Utah LEXIS 193 (2008).]

8. On November 7, 2005, Briarwood signed an agreement to sell Toll Brothers a planned 66-acre, 41-lot subdivision property in the Village of Pomona, New York, for $13,325,000. The agreement expressly conditioned Toll's payment obligations on Briarwood's delivery, at its sole cost and expense, of final, unappealable subdivision approval of the property in accordance with the subdivision plan and the satisfaction by Briarwood of any conditions of the final approval, such that on posting of customary security and payment of application and inspection fees by Toll Brothers, the company would be able to file the plat and commence infrastructure improvements and apply for and obtain building permits.

The agreement stated that the conditions set forth in the approval shall be subject only to "such conditions as Toll may approve at its sole discretion, which approval shall not be unreasonably withheld with respect to those modifications which do not have a material adverse effect on the proposed development." Closing was to take place 30 days following the date on which all conditions to closing set forth in the approval have been satisfied and, "[i]f on or before the date of closing all contingencies and conditions specified herein are not or cannot be satisfied, then Toll shall have the option of . . . cancelling this Agreement."

On January 12, 2006, Briarwood obtained preliminary subdivision approval of the property from the Pomona Planning Board. Final subdivision approval of the property, however, was subject to a number of conditions. By letter dated December 22, 2006, Toll notified Briarwood that five of the conditions would have a material adverse effect on the proposed development and that it would not accept them.

Toll Brothers claimed that Briarwood's December 28, 2006, response to Toll's December 22, 2006, letter was an anticipatory repudiation of the agreement.

In response to Toll's five objections, Briarwood (1) offered to post a bond to cover the potential cost of repaving Klinger Court; (2) pointed out that the steep slope condition restated the Village Code requirement to secure a site development plan permit for each lot within a subdivision; (3) agreed to pay any cost differential resulting from use of a 4 percent rather than a 10 percent grade for the cul-de-sac; (4) proposed two alternative solutions to the drainage system problem; and (5) pointed out that the landscaping plan condition, like the steep slope condition, restated a Village Code requirement.

Toll Brothers treated the letter from Briarwood as an anticipatory repudiation of the contract and refused to complete the transaction, so Briarwood sued for breach of contract. Both parties filed motions for summary judgment.

The district found that no reasonable reader could construe Briarwood's response as a positive and unequivocal repudiation of the agreement and that it did not signal that Briarwood was unwilling to comply with paragraph 16(a)(iii) or any other provision of the agreement. The court therefore granted summary judgment to Briarwood. Toll Brothers appealed. How do you believe the court of appeals ruled, and why? [*Briarwood Farms, Inc. v. Toll Bros., Inc.*, 452 Fed. Appx. 59, 2011 WL 6415185 (C.A.2, N.Y. 2011).]

9. Two companies had an agreement in which Sunrich was providing a food product to Nutrisoya. However, Sunrich allegedly did not deliver the products covered in the contract, and Nutrisoya took the company to court for material breach of contract. The seller wanted the district court to instruct the jury on the difference between a breach of a single installment and a breach of an entire installment contract, arguing that a single-installment breach did not disregard the value of the whole contract. However, the district court did not give such an instruction and left the defendant to argue the point. How do you think the jury decided? [*Nutrisoya v. Sunrich,* 641 F.3d 282, 2011 U.S. App. LEXIS 11561.]

10. The opera company was hired to perform in the outside pavilion of the Wolf Trap Foundation. The company performed the three performances without problem. Then, right before the last performance, a severe thunderstorm moved into the area and created an electrical storm. The storm cut the power on the pavilion where the performance was to have taken place. The Wolf Trap Foundation never paid the opera company for the last performance. Thus, the company took the foundation to court, demanding payment because the performers were ready and willing to perform at the event for which the company was scheduled. The foundation argued that it was dismissed from the contract due to impossibility to perform. The first court found in favor of the opera company, and the foundation appealed. How do you think the appellate court decided? [*The Opera Company of Boston, Inc., v. the Wolf Trap Foundation for the Performing Arts,* 817 F.2d 1094 (1987).]

Looking for more review materials?

The Online Learning Center at **www.mhhc.com/kubasek3e** contains this chapter's "Assignment on the Internet" and also a list of URLs for more information, entitled "On the Internet." Find both of them in the Student Center portion of the OLC, along with quizzes and other helpful materials.

CHAPTER 21

Introduction to Sales and Lease Contracts

LEARNING OBJECTIVES

After reading this chapter, you will be able to answer the following questions:

1. What is the UCC?
2. What is a sales contract?
3. What kinds of contracts fall under the UCC interpretations?
4. What is a merchant, and why is that designation significant?
5. What is a lease contract?
6. What is the CISG?

CASE OPENER

Dropped Calls, or More Appropriately, Dropped Towers: Are Cell Towers Goods or Services?

Crown Castle purchased a number of assets from a variety of cell phone providers in upstate New York between 1995 and 2000. These providers had earlier contracted with the Fred A. Nudd Corporation for the construction and placement of monopoles, more commonly known as "cell towers." However, after some time the monopoles began to collapse structurally. In fact, problems began to develop as early as 2001. In 2003, two cell towers actually collapsed. Crown Castle brought suit in 2005,[1] more than four years after the first of the monopoles began failing. This is an important timing issue: Under common law, a breach-of-contract lawsuit must be brought within six years; but, under the UCC, the lawsuit must be brought within four years. Thus, the first major legal question is whether the lawsuit can stand and not be dismissed under the statute of limitations. To decide this, the court must rule, as a matter of law, on whether the contract for the construction and placement of the monopoles was a contract created under common law or under the UCC.

1. Is the sale of monopoles a contract for the sale of goods when the contract also included installation and initial maintenance? Does this contract fall under UCC Article 2 or under common law?

[1] *Crown Castle Inc. et al. v. Fred A. Nudd Corporation et al.,* 2008 U.S. Dist. LEXIS 3416, 64 U.C.C. Rep. Serv. 2d (Callaghan) 871.

2. If this is a contract for both goods (the monopoles) and services (the installation and initial maintenance), how is the contract determined to fall under either common law or the UCC?

The Wrap-Up at the end of the chapter will answer these questions.

Businesses and organizations that purchase products need to be aware of which laws govern their purchases because the laws can differ. Three sources of laws that interpret sales contracts exist: state common law, the Uniform Commercial Code, and state statutory law. There is very little, if any, federal law that governs contracts for the buying and selling of items, and when such law does exist, it is highly specialized (e.g., the buying and selling of stock under laws created by the Securities and Exchange Commission).

This chapter introduces the Uniform Commercial Code. It explains the scope and significance of the UCC, discusses sections of the UCC that govern both sales and lease contracts, reviews how these contracts are formed, and provides a summary of the legislation that governs international sales contracts.

The Uniform Commercial Code

THE SCOPE OF THE UCC

In some areas of law, federal statutes ensure that the same law applies in all the states. Federal statutes do not govern the formation of sales and lease contracts. Instead, each state passes its own laws to outline rules in this area. Consequently, laws vary from state to state. While all states (except Louisiana) follow the English common law, over 200 years of legal precedent that has developed in each separate state can create differences in contract interpretation and application. With the development of interstate commercial activities, these differences began to pose problems for parties from different states entering into a contract with each other. What was needed was some kind of uniform law for business transactions that all the states could adopt.

LO1 What is the UCC?

In some areas of law, lawyers and law school professors have worked together to pass *uniform,* or model, state laws that states may consider adopting. Two important groups of lawyers and law school professors are the National Conference of Commissioners on Uniform State Laws (NCCUSL) and the American Law Institute (ALI), which worked together to create the **Uniform Commercial Code (UCC).** The UCC was created in 1952 and has been adopted by all 50 states, the District of Columbia, and the Virgin Islands. When a state adopts the UCC, that code becomes part of the law of that particular state; it becomes the commercial code for that state. Each state is allowed to rewrite parts of the UCC to reflect the wishes of its state legislature.

The UCC is divided into sections known as *articles.* These articles cover a wide range of topics, from sales contracts to secured transactions (see Exhibit 21-1). This book explains all the articles of the UCC, starting in this chapter and ending with Chapter 29, which explains the law that governs secured transactions. The NCCUSL and ALI work to revise the UCC as business practices change. Because, as we will learn, goods are movable from state to state, UCC Article 2 applies only to the sale of goods. Land and services contracts are still governed by common law. Therefore, the first question in any sales contract is whether common law or the UCC applies.

THE SIGNIFICANCE OF THE UCC

The UCC is significant because it clarifies sales law and makes this area of law more predictable for businesses that engage in transactions in more than one state. Essentially, the UCC facilitates commercial transactions.

Exhibit 21-1
An Outline of the UCC

ARTICLE	TOPIC
1	General provisions
2	Sales
2(A)	Leases
3	Negotiable instruments
4	Bank deposits and collections
4(A)	Wire transfers
5	Letters of credit
6	Bulk transfers
7	Documents of title
8	Investment securities
9	Secured transactions

However, it is important to emphasize that the UCC does not pertain to all business transactions. Under UCC Article 2, the subject matter of this chapter, the UCC explains the creation and interpretation of sales contracts.

Articles 2 and 2(A) of the UCC

Article 2 of the UCC governs sales contracts, while Article 2(A) governs lease contracts. Specifically, Article 2 focuses on contracts for the sale of goods; Article 2(A) focuses on contracts for the lease of goods. For the purpose of "selling something," the UCC divides all the items that can be bought and sold into three categories: goods, realty, and services (including intangible goods such as securities). Article 2 pertains only to the sale of goods. Nonetheless, Article 2 is not a comprehensive guide to sales contract formation. When Article 2 is silent on an issue of sales contract formation or interpretation, the common law rules apply. Of course, if a state has passed statutory law regarding contracts, that law always supersedes the common law. Additionally, it is important to note that under the UCC the rules for transactions involving merchants differ from those for transactions involving regular buyers and sellers. Merchants will generally be held to a higher standard of care and behavior than nonmerchants. Every state except Louisiana[2] has adopted Article 2 of the UCC.

If you are not sure whether a contract falls under common law or under the UCC, the decision-tree rubric in Exhibit 21-2 can help you make a determination. To use this rubric, consider the definitions presented in the discussion that follows of many of its terms.

BUT WHAT IF . . .

WHAT IF THE FACTS OF THE CASE OPENER WERE DIFFERENT?

Suppose that, in the Case Opener, the contract involved only the transmission of electricity. Would that fact alter the approach the court would have taken?

[2] Louisiana's civil tradition is based on the Code Napoleon, or the French Civil Code.

CASE NUGGET

ARE TRADE NAMES "GOODS" UNDER UCC ARTICLE 2?

Eureka Water Company v. Nestle Waters North America, Inc.
U.S. Court of Appeals for the 10th Circuit
690 F.3d 1139, 2012 U.S. App. LEXIS 16149, 78 U.C.C. Rep. Serv. 2d (Callaghan) 363 (Aug. 3, 2012, Filed)

In a 1975 contract Eureka was given the exclusive right to sell spring water and other products under the Ozarka trade name in 60 Oklahoma counties in exchange for $9,000 paid to Arrowhead, which owned the trade name. In 1987 Arrowhead was acquired by Perrier Group of America, which was subsequently purchased in 1992 by Nestle, making Nestle the owner of the trade name Ozarka. Nestle then began delivering spring water under the Ozarka name within Eureka's territorial claim. In 1997 this became known to Eureka, and Nestle agreed to pay Eureka royalties of 30 cents a case and 50 cents a case for bulk purchases. Eureka would receive from Nestle 67 checks totaling about $2.5 million over the next 10 years. In late 2003 Nestle unilaterally reduced the payment to 25 cents a case. Eureka invoiced Nestle for the difference but was never paid. On October 15, 2007, Eureka received a letter which stated that Nestle would no longer pay royalties.

One important legal principle here is the principle of what is a good. Goods have been defined in various legal cases as anything that was movable at the time of the contract. If a contract involves both goods and nongoods, Oklahoma uses the predominant factor to decide whether it is covered under UCC Article 2. This contract had both a right to sell under a trade name and a right to buy water at cost plus freight. A trade name has been judged by many courts to be a good, but this court said that a trade name is not movable at the time of the contract and is therefore not a good. The predominant-factor test was used, but since Eureka still has to purchase the water at cost plus freight or, if Eureka can find a different supplier, the intellectual property (i.e. the trade name) can be given to that supplier, it is a matter of financial indifference to Nestle. Therefore, the predominant factor in the $9,000 contract was the trade name. Thus the UCC was not applicable to this ruling, and Oklahoma common law was used to decide the case.

ARTICLE 2 OF THE UCC

L02 What is a sales contract?

Sale. Section 2-106(1) of the UCC states that a **sale** "consists of the passing of title from the seller to the buyer for a price." Thus, in the transaction involving Crown Castle and Fred Nudd, the sale consisted of the passing of title (right of ownership) of the monopoles to the original buyers (the various cell phone companies) and then to Crown Castle.

Goods. Section 2-105 of the UCC defines **goods** as "all [tangible] things . . . which are movable at the time of identification to the contract for sale." Items are tangible if they exist physically. The issue in our opening case is whether the delivery of "electricity" is a "good," and under the contractual interpretation of the UCC, or whether it is a "service," and under the

Exhibit 21-2
Common Law or UCC?

1. Does the transaction involve a sale or lease (as opposed to, let's say, a gift)?
   If yes → go to question 2.
   If no → apply the appropriate area of common or statutory law.
2. Is the transaction for the sale or lease of a good?
   If yes → go to question 3.
   If no → apply common law.
3. If the contract is for the sale or lease of both goods and nongoods, which type of item is predominant in the contract?
   If goods → UCC Article 2 applies; go to question 4.
   If nongoods (real estate or services) → common law applies.
4. If this is a UCC Article 2 transaction, is either party a merchant?
   If yes → pay close attention to when the special rules on merchants apply.
   If no → then only "reasonable" care applies to the parties; no "special" or heightened duty of care will apply to a party deemed to be a merchant.

contractual interpretation of the common law. Note that Section 2-105 reads "at the time of identification to the contract." Some items are not goods under Article 2. For example, corporate stocks and copyrights are not tangible, so they are not goods. Real estate cannot be moved, so it is not a good. Yet items attached to real estate that are used for business activities are known as *trade fixtures* and are treated as goods under the UCC.

BUT WHAT IF . . .

WHAT IF THE FACTS OF THE CASE OPENER WERE DIFFERENT?

Let's say, in the Case Opener, that Crown Castle had purchased an office from the New York cell phone providers. The office was poorly built and began to fall apart. Castle brought suit for breach of contract, and the court needed to determine whether common law or the UCC was applicable. If the court looked into Article 2 of the UCC, would this article be applicable to the sale of the office building? Why or why not?

Items taken from real estate may be treated as goods. Minerals, clay, and soil can all be treated as goods, with their sales contract governed by Article 2, if the owner takes these items out of the ground and then sells them to the buyer. Should the owner sell the buyer the right to come and remove the items, the contract would be governed not by the UCC but by common law for the sale of an interest in realty, in this case, an interest known as a "profit." Crops that are sold while still growing in the field are also considered goods, and their sale contracts are subject to UCC interpretation.

To see how the definition of a good relates to marketing issues, please see the **Connecting to the Core** activity on the text website at www.mhhe.com/kubasek3e.

Mixed Goods and Services Contracts. Sometimes, it is not easy to tell whether something is a good because a tangible item is tied to or mixed with something intangible, such as a service. A contract that combines a good with a service is a **mixed sale.** Article 2 applies to mixed sales if the goods are the predominant part of the transaction. This is the test that the court needed to apply to the Crown Castle case. Did the sale, installation, and initial maintenance of the monopoles constitute a contract predominantly for the sale of goods or predominantly for the sale of services? Consider Case 21-1 to determine the standard to be applied.

LO3

What kinds of contracts fall under the UCC interpretations?

In Case 21-1, the court had to decide whether a particular contract (a settlement agreement) was a contract for the sale of goods (foot-pump slippers) or a contract for something intangible (a settlement to resolve a lawsuit). The distinction was especially important to the plaintiff, Novamedix, because if the contract was for the sale of goods, the company could take advantage of other provisions of the UCC, especially implied warranties that the foot-pump slippers would serve the purpose for which they were designed.

To resolve contract issues in cases in which a tangible good is mixed with something intangible (e.g., a service or a legal settlement), most states employ some variation of the *predominant-purpose test* discussed in Case 21-1. In the Novamedix case, the court determined that the case should not be governed by Article 2 of the UCC because the settlement agreement was not predominantly a sale of goods. The predominant purpose of the agreement was to settle the patent infringement suit, not to transfer foot-pump slippers. The reader can infer from the court's analysis that the settlement agreement was more of a service contract than a goods contract, with the service component focusing on the terms of the settlement.

LO4

What is a merchant, and why is that designation significant?

Legal Principle: **When determining whether a contract falls under the UCC, first determine if the sale is for goods and then determine if the contract is predominantly for the sale of goods.**

CASE 21-1 NOVAMEDIX, LIMITED, PLAINTIFF-APPELLANT v. NDM ACQUISITION CORPORATION AND VESTA HEALTHCARE, INC., DEFENDANTS-APPELLEES

U.S. COURT OF APPEALS, FEDERAL CIRCUIT
166 F.3D 1177 (1999)

This case shows that even when a lawsuit ends through settlement, the dispute is not necessarily over. In this case, Novamedix and a competitor, NDM, resolved a patent infringement lawsuit by entering into a settlement agreement. At issue in the patent infringement lawsuit was a particular medical device—a foot-pump slipper, designed to aid in blood circulation from the feet to the heart of bedridden patients. Prior to the patent infringement lawsuit, both companies manufactured this particular foot-pump slipper. As a consequence of the patent infringement suit, NDM agreed to admit that it had infringed on Novamedix's patents, cease infringing on the patents, deliver its entire inventory of foot-pump slippers to Novamedix, grant Novamedix an exclusive license under NDM's own patents, and pay Novamedix $47,500.

When Novamedix received the inventory of foot-pump slippers, the company claimed that the slippers could not be sold because they did not meet FDA requirements for this particular medical device. Novamedix had wanted to sell NDM's inventory to NDM's former customers, but could not do so because the product failed to meet FDA requirements. Novamedix then filed suit against NDM, arguing that the settlement agreement was a contract for the sale of goods and therefore subject to the implied warranties of merchantability and fitness of New York's version of the UCC. In essence, Novamedix asked the court to declare the settlement agreement a contract for the sale of goods so it could take advantage of warranties outlined in the UCC. Novamedix asked the court to interpret the settlement agreement for NDM's inventory under Article 2 of the UCC because the foot-pump slippers were a "good" and title had passed for them from NDM to Novamedix. NDM contended that the agreement should not be interpreted under UCC Article 2. A lower court agreed with NDM, and Novamedix appealed.

SENIOR CIRCUIT JUDGE EDWARD S. SMITH: . . . Appellant [Novamedix] argues that under New York law, a "contract for the sale of goods" requires only that there be a sale (i.e., the "passing of title from the seller to the buyer for a price") . . . and that the subject of the sale be goods rather than services. Here, the argument goes, the settlement agreement was a contract for the sale of the defective slippers, because NDM passed title of the slippers (the goods) to Novamedix in exchange for a release for its patent infringement claim (the price).

We disagree. The world of commercial transactions is not limited to the binary world presented by Appellant, a world in which an agreement that passes title to Article 2 goods must either be a contract for the sale of goods or a contract for the sale of services. Many commercial transactions are not governed by Article 2 of the UCC: sale of land or securities, assignment of a contract right, or granting a license under a patent or copyright, just to name a few. The mere fact that title to Article 2 goods changed hands during one of these transactions does not by that fact alone make the transaction a sale of goods. . . . Here the mere fact that the parties' settlement agreement includes the transfer of personal property in its provisions does not make it a simple sale of goods (slippers) for a price (release of a legal claim). The settlement agreement between NDM and Novamedix is an agreement to release a legal claim for (1) binding admissions, (2) money damages of $47,500, (3) patent license rights, and (4) transfer of NDM's existing inventory to Novamedix. To elevate the inventory term over the other elements of consideration given by NDM is to distort the entire agreement through the lens of Novamedix's asserted purpose of selling the inventory when it entered into the agreement. The settlement agreement is no more a contract for the sale of slippers than it is a licensing agreement for NDM's patents. In fact, it is neither exclusively; it is a mixed contract, similar to a mixed contract for the provision of both goods and services. It should therefore be analyzed as a mixed contract.

To determine whether the UCC's implied warranties apply in a mixed goods/services contract, New York courts apply the "predominant purpose" test; if the predominant purpose of the contract was to sell goods, the contract falls within the UCC. However, "[i]f service predominates and the transfer of title to personal property is an incidental feature of the transaction, the contract does not fall within the ambit of the Code."

. . . Although the present settlement agreement is not a mixed goods/services contract, the same analysis is applicable to determine whether it should be treated as a contract for the sale of goods. Thus, the UCC's implied warranties of merchantability and fitness apply to the settlement agreement only if its predominant purpose was for the sale of slippers. We hold that it was not. The essential nature of the settlement agreement was to settle a patent infringement lawsuit. The agreement arose out of a patent infringement suit. The agreement contained multiple provisions relating to patent rights held by Novamedix and NDM. . . . Perhaps the inventory-related provisions were essential elements of the overall agreement, at least to

[continued]

Novamedix; perhaps they even support Novamedix's professed intent to sell the slippers to NDM's former customers. But those factors are simply not relevant to the question of whether the "essential nature" of the agreement was the exchange of slippers for the release of a legal claim. It was not, and cannot be construed as such with the benefit of hindsight. Therefore, the agreement was not a contract for the sale of goods, and the implied warranties of the UCC do not apply to it. . . .

AFFIRMED.

CRITICAL THINKING

Novamedix asks the court to simplify the case. How so? What rule does the court choose instead of a simple rule? Why do you suppose the court chooses a more complicated analysis than the one Novamedix prefers?

ETHICAL DECISION MAKING

In Chapter 2, you learned about the WPH framework for business ethics, which asks you to consider three questions: *Whom* would this decision affect? What is the *purpose* of the business decision? *How* should managers make decisions? When you are thinking about the purpose of a decision, it is helpful to consider values. Which value does this federal court show it prefers by ruling in NDM's favor?

Merchants. UCC Article 2 pertains to anyone buying and selling goods. However, the UCC distinguishes merchants from regular buyers and sellers (see Exhibit 21-3); thus it contains provisions that either (1) apply only to merchants or (2) impose greater duties on merchants. The drafters of the UCC assumed that merchants have a greater ability to look out for themselves than do ordinary buyers and sellers.

UCC Section 2-104(1) defines a **merchant** as "a person who deals in goods of the kind, or otherwise by his occupation, holds himself out as having knowledge or skill peculiar to the practices or goods involved in the transaction, or to whom such knowledge or skill may be attributed by his employment of an agent or broker or other intermediary who, by his occupation, holds himself out as having such knowledge or skill."

Legal Principle: **Merchants will be held to a higher standard of behavior under the UCC than will nonmerchants.**

BUT WHAT IF . . .

WHAT IF THE FACTS OF THE CASE OPENER WERE DIFFERENT?

Let's say, in the Case Opener, that Crown Castle bought land from a private citizen and the land happened to have a cell phone tower on it from the previous landowner. This private citizen didn't know anything about the cell tower and sold the land with no contract for a large cash payment from Crown Castle. Would this seller be a merchant? Depending on the answer to that question, how would he be treated by the law?

Exhibit 21-3
Determining Merchant Status under UCC Article 2

A buyer or seller is a merchant if the answer to any of these three questions is yes:

- Does the buyer or seller in question deal in goods of the kind involved in the sales contract?
- Does the buyer or seller in question, by occupation, hold himself or herself out as having knowledge and skill unique to the practices or goods involved in the transaction?
- Has the buyer or seller in question employed a merchant as a broker, an agent, or some other intermediary?

E-COMMERCE AND THE LAW

THE UCC AND THE INTERNET

The Uniform Commercial Code was designed to address the sale of tangible goods such as scooters, electric power tools, and jeans. Because the UCC was written long before the Internet and e-commerce boom, this legislation was not designed for transactions related to less tangible things, such as software and information. Not surprisingly, the UCC does not respond well to certain legal issues that arise in today's marketplace. For example, the UCC does not tell us the answers to these questions: What rules should govern computer software, which is likely to be licensed rather than sold as a good? What about downloadable software files? What rules should govern information providers like America Online (AOL), which provides a continuing service? What rules should govern the exchange of information, such as stock quotes? What rules cover travel reservations a person makes online?

The National Conference of Commissioners on Uniform State Laws (NCCUSL) has adopted the Uniform Commercial Information Transactions Act (UCITA), which answers the questions above and many more. This law promises to do for electronic contracting what the UCC did for transactions in physical goods: protect consumers by providing predictability, uniformity, and clear rules. As with the UCC, states will choose whether to adopt UCITA. In 2001, Virginia became the first state to enact UCITA, probably because major Internet-related companies (e.g., AOL, UUNET Technologies) are headquartered in northern Virginia.

Source: Robert Holleyman, "Updating Contract Law for the Digital Age," *USA Today* (magazine), March 1, 2000; and Scott W. Burt, "Controversial New Rules for Computer Contracts," *Metropolitan Corporate Counsel,* June 2000, p. 8.

Case 21-2 considers the questions of whether a particular person is a merchant and, if so, what impact this merchant status has on a dispute about who owns certain goods. In this case, the goods in question were paintings.

In Case 21-2, we see another feature of merchant status. Felix DeWeldon was a merchant because, by his occupation as an artist, he held himself out as having knowledge or skill peculiar to the paintings. Under Rhode Island's commercial code, one who entrusts goods to a merchant (DeWeldon, Ltd., entrusted the paintings to Felix DeWeldon) assumes the risk that the merchant will act unscrupulously and sell the goods to an innocent third party (McKean). The result of this entrustment was that McKean got to keep the paintings. If Felix DeWeldon had not been a merchant, DeWeldon, Ltd., would have won the case.

At this point, be thinking of questions about merchants as they relate to the transaction between Crown Castle and Fred A. Nudd. Both are businesses. Crown Castle owns and operates wireless telephone services, while Fred A. Nudd manufactures steel fabrications. There is no question, it seems, that both are merchants under any test defined by the UCC.

ARTICLE 2(A) OF THE UCC

Every state except Louisiana has adopted Article 2 of the UCC. Article 2(A) covers contracts for the lease of goods. This section of the UCC is increasingly important, as consumers (both individuals and businesses) are more likely to lease goods today than ever before. Consumers lease cars, equipment, and machines. This article does not cover leases related to real property.

L05 What is a lease contract?

Leases. UCC Section 2A-103(j) defines a **lease** as "a transfer of the right to possession and use of goods for a term in return for consideration." A **lessor** is "a person who transfers the right to possession and use of goods under a lease."[3] A **lessee** is "a person who acquires the right to possession and use of goods under a lease."[4] Thus, if you lease a car, the company that leases the car to you (the lessor) transfers the right of possession and use of the car to you (the lessee) in return for consideration (money).

Special Kinds of Leases. Two special kinds of leases are consumer and finance leases. A **consumer lease** is a lease (1) that has a value of $25,000 or less and (2) that exists

[3] UCC § 2A-103(p).
[4] UCC § 2A-103(o).

CASE 21-2 DEWELDON, LTD. v. MCKEAN
U.S. DISTRICT COURT FOR THE DISTRICT OF RHODE ISLAND
125 F.3D 24 (1997)

This case arose after Felix DeWeldon, a well-known sculptor and art collector, sold three paintings to Robert McKean in 1994.

Felix DeWeldon declared bankruptcy in 1991. In 1992, DeWeldon, Ltd., purchased all Felix DeWeldon's personal property from the bankruptcy trustee. After this purchase, the director of DeWeldon, Ltd., entrusted the paintings to Felix DeWeldon as custodian. DeWeldon, Ltd., did nothing to make it clear Felix DeWeldon did not own the paintings. For example, DeWeldon, Ltd., did not put a sign on the premises of Beacon Rock, Felix DeWeldon's home in Newport, Rhode Island, nor did DeWeldon, Ltd., tag or label the paintings themselves.

In 1993, Nancy Wardell, the sole shareholder of DeWeldon, Ltd., sold all of her DeWeldon, Ltd., stock to the Byron Preservation Trust. This trust sold Felix DeWeldon an option to repurchase the paintings and a contractual right to continue to retain possession of the paintings until the option expired.

In 1993, DeWeldon, Ltd., sued Felix DeWeldon, seeking possession of the paintings, but was unsuccessful because of the option to repurchase and right of possession. The court enjoined Felix DeWeldon from transferring or removing the paintings from Beacon Rock. The paintings that became the subject of this lawsuit never left Beacon Rock until McKean bought them in 1994.

The question in this case is whether DeWeldon, Ltd., can recover the three paintings it had entrusted to Felix DeWeldon, or, alternatively, whether the district court correctly ruled in favor of McKean, the buyer.

SENIOR CIRCUIT JUDGE HILL: As a general rule, a seller [in this case Felix DeWeldon] cannot pass better title than he has himself. Nevertheless, the Uniform Commercial Cole (UCC) as adopted by Rhode Island provides that an owner [in this case DeWeldon, Ltd.] who entrusts items to a merchant who deals in goods of that kind gives him or her the power to transfer all rights of the entruster to a buyer in the ordinary course of business. . . .

In order for McKean to be protected . . ., DeWeldon, Ltd. must have allowed Felix DeWeldon to retain possession of the paintings. McKean must have bought the paintings in the ordinary course of business. He must have given value for the paintings, without actual or constructive notice of DeWeldon Ltd.'s claim of ownership to them. Finally, Felix DeWeldon must have been a merchant as defined by R.I. Gen. Laws Sec. 6A-2-104. Under this section, a merchant is one who has special knowledge or skill and deals in goods of the kind or "otherwise by his or her occupation holds himself out as having knowledge or skill peculiar to the practices or goods involved in the transaction. . . ." . . . [The court then resolves the preceding factual issues in McKean's favor before looking at the merchant issue.]

. . . Felix DeWeldon acted as a merchant within the meaning of the Rhode Island Commercial Code. Under the Code, "merchant" is given an expansive definition. . . . The Code provides that a merchant is "one who . . . by his occupation holds himself out as having knowledge or skill peculiar to the practices . . . involved in the transaction . . ." R.I. Gen. Laws Sec. 6A-2-104. Comment 2 to this section notes that "almost every person in the business world would, therefore, be deemed to be a 'merchant.' " . . .

The entrustment provision of the UCC is designed to enhance the reliability of commercial sales by merchants who deal in the kind of goods sold. . . . It shifts the risk of resale to the one who leaves his property with the merchant. . . . The district court found that Felix DeWeldon was a "well-known" artist whose work was for sale commercially and a "collector." There was art work all over Felix DeWeldson's home. He had recently sold paintings to a European buyer. By his occupation he held himself out as having knowledge and skill peculiar to art and the art trade. McKean viewed him as an art dealer.

We conclude from these facts that Felix DeWeldon was a "merchant" within the meaning of the entrustment provision of the UCC as adopted by the Rhode Island Commercial Code.

When a person knowingly delivers his property into the possession of a merchant dealing in goods of that kind, that person assumes the risk of the merchant's acting unscrupulously by selling the property to an innocent purchaser. The entrustment provision places the loss upon the party who vested the merchant with the ability to transfer the property with apparently good title. The entrustor in this case, DeWeldon, Ltd., took that risk and bears the consequences.

DeWeldon, Ltd. entrusted three paintings to the care of Felix DeWeldon. Felix DeWeldon was a merchant who bought and sold paintings. Robert McKean was a purchaser in the ordinary course of business who paid value for the paintings without notice of any claim of ownership by another. Under the law of Rhode Island, McKean took good title to the paintings. . . .

AFFIRMED.

[continued]

CRITICAL THINKING

In Chapter 1, you learned of the importance of a particular set of facts in determining the outcome of a case. If you could change one fact in this case to make it more likely that the judge would rule in favor of DeWeldon, Ltd., which fact would you change? Explain.

ETHICAL DECISION MAKING

Apply the universalization test to the outcome of this case. Does the universalization test support Judge Hill's decision?

between a lessor regularly engaged in the business of leasing or selling and a lessee who leases the goods primarily for a personal, family, or household purpose.[5] The UCC offers protections to consumers who sign lease agreements. For example, in some situations consumers may recover attorney fees if the lessor subjects them to an unconscionable lease.

A **finance lease** is complicated by the addition of a third person—a supplier or vendor who plays a separate role from that of the lessor. In a finance lease, the lessor does not select, manufacture, or supply the goods. Rather, the lessor acquires title to the goods or the right to their possession and use in connection with the terms of the lease.[6] The UCC outlines the specific duties and rights of all three parties to finance leases.

How Sales and Lease Contracts Are Formed under the UCC

In Part Two of this textbook, you studied the common law of contracts, from the rules for agreements to the remedies for breaches. Sales and lease contracts require the same components as general contracts, but some UCC provisions that govern contracts for the sale or lease of goods are not identical to the common law requirements you learned about in Part Two. This section highlights the most important provisions of the UCC with regard to the formation of sales and lease contracts.

FORMATION IN GENERAL

Contracts for the sale or lease of goods may be made in any manner sufficient to show agreement.[7] Courts are willing to consider the conduct of the parties to determine whether a contract exists. Contracts for the sale or lease of goods may also be formed even though some terms of the contract or lease are left open.[8] A court will uphold a contract for the sale or lease of goods as long as the parties intended to make a contract and there is a reasonably certain basis for giving an appropriate remedy.[9]

OFFER AND ACCEPTANCE

Offer. Under the UCC, if certain contract terms are left open, it is acceptable to fill them in. Exhibit 21-4 indicates what generally happens under the UCC when certain terms of a contract or lease are left open. The UCC also creates a new category of offers: the firm offer. Under UCC Section 2-205, offers made by merchants are considered **firm offers** if the offer (1) is made in writing and (2) gives assurances that it will be irrevocable for up to three months despite a lack of consideration for the irrevocability. If a firm offer is silent as to time, the UCC assumes a three-month irrevocability period. This contrasts sharply with the

[5] UCC § 2A-103(1)(e).
[6] UCC § 2A-103(1)(g).
[7] UCC §§ 2-204(1) and 2A-204(1).
[8] UCC §§ 2-204(3) and 2A-204(3).
[9] Ibid.

COMPARING THE LAW OF OTHER COUNTRIES

REGULATION OF LEASES IN CHINA

In recent years, China's legislators have worked to enhance and clarify the country's commercial code. Currently, China has legislation that covers the sale of goods and the supply of services. The country does not, however, have legislation that covers leases.

Recently, China's Law Reform Commission has recommended that China regulate leasing companies. This commission believes that a statute delineating the obligations of lessors and lessees involved in lease agreements will protect Chinese consumers, who currently seek remedies through the country's common law. Legal costs in China prohibit many consumers from filing complaints.

The proposed law covers a range of business services, including home decoration and rentals of videos, cars, dinner jackets, wedding dresses, and machinery. The committee is especially concerned about the number of consumer complaints related to home renovation and wedding dress rentals.

Source: Quinton Chan, "Increased Consumer Protection Considered," *South China Morning Post,* December 18, 2000.

Exhibit 21-4
The UCC and Open Terms

TERM LEFT OPEN	INTERPRETATION UNDER UCC
Price	A "reasonable price" is supplied at the time of delivery.
Payment	Payment is due at the time and place at which the buyer is to receive the goods.
Delivery	The place for delivery is the seller's place of business.
Time	The contract must be performed within a reasonable time.
Duration	The party that wants to terminate an ongoing contract must use good faith and give reasonable notification.
Quantity	Courts generally have no basis for determining a remedy.

common law, under which an offer is revocable at any time before acceptance unless a period of irrevocability (also known as an *option*) is supported by some kind of consideration.

Acceptance. Under the UCC, an acceptance may be made by any reasonable means of communication,[10] and it is effective when dispatched. It is also important to note that the **mirror-image rule** that applies under common law does not apply under the UCC. Recall that the mirror-image rule states that an offeree's acceptance must be on the exact terms of the offer. If the acceptance includes additional terms, the acceptance becomes a counteroffer instead of an acceptance.

Under the UCC, additional terms are permitted in contracts for the sale or lease of goods. Under UCC Section 2-207(1), additional terms will not negate acceptance unless acceptance is made expressly conditional on assent to the additional terms.

Legal Principle: The intent of the parties to be bound by the contract is the overriding focus of the UCC in determining contract formation.

CONSIDERATION

Sales and lease contracts require consideration. Under the common law, when a contract is modified, it must be supported by new consideration. As explained in Chapter 15, the UCC eliminates that requirement for the modification of sales and lease contracts.[11] The UCC requires only that modifications be made in good faith.[12]

[10] UCC §§ 2-206(1) and 2A-206(1).
[11] UCC §§ 2-209(1) and 2A-208(1).
[12] UCC § 1-203.

CASE NUGGET

WHEN IS A QUOTE AN OFFER UNDER THE UCC?

Reilly Foam Corp., Plaintiff v. Rubbermaid Corp., Defendant
U.S. District Court for the Eastern District of Pennsylvania
206 F. Supp. 2d 643, 2002 U.S. Dist. LEXIS 9273, 48 U.C.C. Rep. Serv. 2d (Callaghan) 81 (May 28, 2002, Decided)

In the U.C.C. context, courts have encountered difficulty determining whether a document that quotes a seller's prices constitutes an offer. Generally, price quotes are not considered offers but rather, "mere invitations to enter into negotiations or to submit offers." The buyer's purchase order—which sets such terms as product choice, quantity, price, and terms of delivery—is usually the offer.

However, some price quotes are sufficiently detailed to be deemed offers, which turn a subsequent document containing a positive response from a buyer into an acceptance.

Reviewing Reilly Foam's March 26 correspondence and its treatment by Rubbermaid, both parties treated the price quote as an offer and not merely a price quote. First, the March 26 letter did not merely list price. The letter refers to itself as a "proposal" in its opening paragraph. The attached list also includes a number of specific terms including the identification of products, their quantities, the licensing of needed technology, and details for the special manufacture of the sponges. Rubbermaid treated the letter as an offer at least with respect to quantities and prices of "other affected products." Thus, with such an understanding the quote constitutes an offer.

REQUIREMENTS UNDER THE STATUTE OF FRAUDS

Under common law, the statute of frauds requires that all material terms to a contract be in writing. Under the UCC, contracts for the sale of goods must be in writing if they are valued at $500 or more;[13] lease contracts that require payments of $1,000 or more must be in writing to be enforceable.[14] There is a significant difference between the statute of frauds and the UCC as to what constitutes a writing that satisfies the statute. Common law requires some kind of writing created or signed by the party who is contesting the enforceability of the contract. This rule holds true under the UCC unless the parties are merchants. If two merchants have an oral agreement, a written memo from either party to the other is deemed to satisfy the statute of frauds, even if it is not acknowledged by the receiving party. If the memo is not objected to within 10 days of receipt, the oral agreement, memorialized by the memo, is binding.

The UCC outlines three exceptions to the statute of fraud's writing requirements.[15] First, the UCC recognizes an exception for *specifically manufactured* goods. If a buyer or lessee has ordered goods made to meet her specific needs, the buyer or lessee may not assert the statute of frauds if (1) the goods are not suitable for sale or lease to others in the ordinary course of the seller's or lessor's business and (2) the seller or lessor has either substantially begun the manufacture of the goods or made commitments for their procurement. Second, the UCC recognizes an exception when parties *admit* that a sales or lease contract was made. Specifically, if a party to an oral sales or lease contract admits in pleadings, testimony, or court that he agreed to a contract or lease, that party cannot assert the statute of frauds against the enforcement of the oral contract. The lease or sales contract is not enforceable beyond the quantity of goods admitted. Third, the UCC includes a *partial-performance* exception. An oral sales or lease contract is enforceable to the extent that payment has been made and accepted or goods have been received and accepted.

Legal Principle: Any kind of documentation is usually sufficient to satisfy the writing requirement of the statute of frauds.

[13] UCC § 2-201(1).
[14] UCC § 2A-201(1).
[15] UCC §§ 2-201(3) and 2A-201(4).

BUT WHAT IF . . .

WHAT IF THE FACTS OF THE CASE OPENER WERE DIFFERENT?

Let's say, in the Case Opener, that Crown Castle had a written contract with the New York cell phone providers regarding the cell towers that Castle was purchasing. The contract did not mention a price that Castle would pay for the towers or the quantity of towers that Castle would be acquiring. What are the necessary components of a contract? Do they include price and quantity?

THE PAROL EVIDENCE RULE

The **parol evidence rule** is a legal concept that aims to protect sales or lease contracts that the parties intended to be the final expression of their agreement. The UCC states that when a written agreement exists that is intended to be a final expression, neither party can provide additional evidence that alters or contradicts the written contract.[16] Courts, however, allow the parties to explain or supplement the written contract with either (1) additional terms that are consistent with the terms in the agreement or (2) evidence that helps the court interpret the agreement, including previous conduct of the parties regarding the contract in question (course of performance),[17] the way the parties have interacted in past transactions (course of dealings),[18] and the way others in a specific place, vocation, trade, or industry usually conduct business (usage of trade).[19]

When courts interpret sales and lease contracts, they look at a combination of four factors: (1) express terms, (2) course of performance, (3) course of dealing, and (4) usage of trade. If they must, courts prioritize these factors as listed. Consider the Case Nugget.

UNCONSCIONABILITY

You learned about the concept of unconscionability in Part Two. A contract or contract provision is *unconscionable* if it is so unfair that a court would be unreasonable if it enforced the contract. The UCC outlines actions a court can take if it discovers that a contract or lease provision or the contract or lease as a whole is unconscionable.[20] If a court finds that a contract or lease provision or the contract or lease as a whole was unconscionable when it was made, the court either can refuse to enforce the contract or lease or can enforce the parts of the contract or lease that are fair.

Contracts for the International Sale of Goods

LO6 What is the CISG?

THE SCOPE OF THE CISG

You read at the beginning of this chapter that lawyers and legal scholars drafted the UCC in part to facilitate increased commercial transactions across state lines. By the 1970s, it became clear that, increasingly, businesses planned to conduct commercial transactions not only across state lines but also across country borders. In 1980, the **United Nations Convention on Contracts for the International Sale of Goods (CISG)** was offered as a treaty that countries could sign, indicating their willingness to allow this treaty to govern international business-to-business sales contracts. The United Nations CISG

[16] UCC §§ 2-202 and 2A-202.
[17] UCC §§ 2-208(10) and 2A-207(1).
[18] UCC § 1-205(1).
[19] UCC § 1-205(4).
[20] UCC §§ 2-302 and 2A-108.

CASE NUGGET

COURSE OF DEALING AND USAGE OF TRADE

Loizeaux Builders Supply Co. v. Donald B. Ludwig Company

366 A.2D 721 (N.J. 1976)

When the defendant building contractor phoned the supply company about the stated price of concrete, the supply company informed the builder that the price would be "adhered to for the year." The builder then put a continuing order in that resulted in concrete being shipped to the builder from February of that year through March of the following year. The phone call had been placed in February. The supply company did not deny any of the facts stated by the builder.

On January 1 in this time period, the stated price of the concrete was increased; the builder was notified of this but did not believe the increase applied to it in light of the phone conversation from the previous February. The builder paid only the "phone call" price, and the supply company sued for the difference. The question was whether the higher price of January 1 applied to the transaction in light of the phone call stating that the lower price would be "adhered to for the year."

In finding for the supply house and awarding the higher price for deliveries after January 1, the court relied on (1) the plain meaning of "adhered to for *the* year" as opposed to "adhered to for *a* year"; (2) the customary practice in the trade for building supply products to be increased on January 1 if they were to be increased at all; and (3) the fact that the builder had had actual notice of the January 1 price increase before the deliveries after January 1.

treaty provides the legal structure for international sales. Many major trading nations, including the North American Free Trade Agreement (NAFTA) nations (Canada, the United States, and Mexico), have signed the CISG. Additionally, many South American and European countries have signed or are considering signing this treaty.

THE SIGNIFICANCE OF THE CISG

The CISG is important because if a problem arises with an international sale and a party to the transaction initiates litigation, the UCC does not provide guidance in the litigation; instead, the CISG preempts the UCC. The CISG covers the same general topics as the UCC. For instance, the CISG covers offers, acceptances, and other contract topics. However, specific provisions of the CISG differ from the UCC. For example, the CISG requirements related to the statute of frauds are more lenient than those under the UCC. In particular, the CISG does not require that contracts be in writing. Case 21-3 deals, in part, specifically with this issue.

Businesses that have chosen to operate globally see the CISG as providing the same benefits as the UCC: clarity, predictability, and uniformity. Businesses that create international contracts are increasingly careful to consider the unique context in which they operate. Exhibit 21-5 lists key questions businesses ask as they try to minimize disputes when they transact business in the global economy. However, with the United States' adopting the UCC, the question still remains as to how to apply conflicting provisions of the CISG and UCC in contract disputes between U.S. companies and companies in nations having adopted the CISG. Consider Case 21-3, regarding a contract dispute between a U.S. company and a Canadian company.

Exhibit 21-5
Conflict Avoidance in the Global Economy

Businesses that operate in the global economy try to avoid conflict by asking the following key questions as they form contracts:

- If our business ends up in a dispute with a trading partner, what *language* should govern the dispute?
- In what *forum* should our dispute be resolved?
- Which country's *laws* should apply to the dispute?

After thinking about these questions, businesses create what are known as choice-of-language, forum-selection, and choice-of-law clauses.

COMPARING THE LAW OF OTHER COUNTRIES

ISRAEL ADOPTS THE CISG AS INTERNAL ISRAELI LAW—IS THIS THE WAY TO GO?

On February 1, 2003, Israel became a signatory to the CISG, which became a part of Israeli internal law. To date, 78 nations are signatories to the CISG. The United Kingdom is not a signatory of the CISG and instead applies English common law. A debate exists in the United States as to whether the CISG should be a substitute for the UCC or remain complementary to the UCC. It is currently complementary, as the United States applies both the UCC and the CISG. The debate is a crucial one, and it is argued in the Point / Counterpoint feature at the end of this chapter. An excellent resource for following this extremely pertinent and relevant issue is the website of the United Nations Commission on International Trade Law (UNCITRAL): www.uncitral.org/uncitral/en/index.html.

CASE 21-3 THE TRAVELERS PROPERTY CASUALTY COMPANY OF AMERICA AND HELLMUTH OBATA & KASSABAUM, INC., PLAINTIFFS v. SAINT-GOBAIN TECHNICAL FABRICS CANADA LIMITED, FORMERLY KNOWN AS BAY MILLS, DEFENDANT

U.S. DISTRICT COURT FOR THE DISTRICT OF MINNESOTA 474 F. SUPP. 2D 1075 (2007)

In this case, the plaintiff Hellmuth, Obata and Kassabaum designed and oversaw the construction of an arena. Plaintiff Travelers is the Hellmuth et al. insurer. The Canadian company defendant, Saint-Gobain, provided industrial mesh for use in the construction of the arena. That mesh allegedly was not suitable for the purpose for which it was used and plaintiffs sued for breach of contract in that the mesh was defective.

Two of the issues before the trial court were:

1. *Since the contract referred to provisions in the UCC, then the CISG was preempted and the UCC would prevail.*
2. *If the UCC prevailed over the CISG, then because the contract had not been reduced to writing, it was unenforceable under the Statute of Frauds and the breach of contract suit must be dismissed pursuant to a summary judgment motion by the defendant.*

JUDGE ANN D. MONTGOMERY: . . . [U]nder the *Supremacy Clause,* the law in every state is that "the CISG is applicable to contracts where the contracting parties are from different countries that have adopted the CISG." Id. Thus, absent an express statement that the CISG does not apply, merely referring to a particular state's law does not opt out of the CISG. As the Fifth Circuit stated, "[a]n affirmative opt-out requirement promotes uniformity and the observance of good faith in international trade, two principles that guide interpretation of the CISG." *BP Oil Int'l, 332 F.3d at 337,* citing CISG art. 7(1). The Court adopts the majority position on applicability of the CISG. Therefore, the CISG governs "the formation of the contract of sale and the rights and obligations of the seller . . . and the buyer . . . arising from such a contract." CISG art. 4(a).

. . . The parties seem to assume that only their writings could have formed a contract; the CISG, however, explicitly states that "[a] contract of sale need not be concluded in or evidenced by writing and is not subject to any other requirement as to form. It may be proved by any means, including witnesses." CISG art. 11. Under the CISG, a proposal for concluding a contract is sufficiently definite . . . to constitute an offer "if it indicates the goods and expressly or implicitly fixes or makes provision for determining the quantity and price." CISG art. 14(1). Thus, oral discussions between the parties agreeing to the goods, quantity, and price may have formed a contract before any purchase orders and invoices were exchanged.

Motion by defendant for summary judgment denied on this issue.

CRITICAL THINKING

Think back to the very strict requirements of the statute of frauds, discussed in Part 2 of this text. Does the CISG approach to writing requirements in contract formation as illustrated above make more sense than the common law approach? Why or why not?

ETHICAL DECISION MAKING

Do you find it a bit odd that the Canadian company argues that the CISG should not apply while the U.S. company argues that the CISG should apply in these situations? Is this just legalistic argumentation for the purpose of "winning the case"?

CASE OPENER WRAP-UP

Dropped Calls, or More Appropriately, Dropped Towers: Are Cell Towers Goods or Services?

This case illustrates two classic issues that one has to consider when first addressing a potential UCC Article 2 case. One issue is the type of item involved. First of all, is this a contract for the sale of goods? The key concept to remember when answering this question is whether, *at the time of the contract creation,* the items being bought and sold had physical or tangible properties and were able to be moved. Then the second question is, Is the contract *predominantly* for the sale of these goods, as opposed to services and/or real estate? If the answers to these questions are yes, the case falls under Article 2 of the Uniform Commercial Code as opposed to purely common law.

In this case, the answers to these two questions are fairly clear. Yes, the purchase of cell towers or monopoles constitutes a purchase of goods. These towers have physical property and can be moved, even though once put in place they will remain stationary. Moreover, it is the monopoles that were the items being bought and sold at the time that the contract was executed. Since the monopoles were the items bought and sold under the contract and since the court found that the invoice for these items was separate and distinct from the invoice for any kind of service or maintenance, the contract was predominantly for the sale of goods, not real estate or services.

KEY TERMS

consumer lease 481
finance lease 483
firm offers 483
goods 477
lease 481
lessee 481
lessor 481
merchant 480
mirror-image rule 484
mixed sale 478
parol evidence rule 486
sale 477
Uniform Commercial Code (UCC) 475
United Nations Convention on Contracts for the International Sale of Goods (CISG) 486
writing 485

SUMMARY OF KEY TOPICS

The Uniform Commercial Code

Scope of the UCC: The UCC is a uniform or model law that governs commercial transactions, from the sale of goods to secured transactions.

Significance of the UCC: The UCC adds clarity and predictability to sales law.

Articles 2 and 2(A) of the UCC

Article 2 (Sales) covers contracts for the sale of goods.

- *Sale:* The passing of title from the seller to the buyer for a price.
- *Goods:* Tangible things that can be moved.
- *Mixed goods and services contracts:* Contracts that include both goods and services. Courts apply Article 2 if the goods are the predominant part of the transaction.
- *Merchants:* Buyers or sellers who (1) deal in goods of the kind, (2) by occupation, hold themselves out as having knowledge and skill unique to the practices or goods involved in the

transaction, or (3) employ a merchant as a broker, an agent, or some other intermediary. Various provisions of the UCC distinguish merchants from ordinary buyers and sellers.

Article 2(A)(Leases) covers contracts for the lease of goods.

- *Leases:* Transfers of the right to possession and use of goods for a term in return for consideration.
- *Special kinds of leases:* Two special kinds are consumer leases and finance leases.

The UCC outlines special rules and protections for each kind of lease.

How Sales and Lease Contracts Are Formed under the UCC

Formation in general: The UCC is more lenient than common law regarding contract formation. Courts look at the intent of the parties to a sales or lease contract.

Offer and acceptance: Offers are valid even if terms are left open. The common law mirror-image rule does not apply to contracts for the sale or lease of goods. Courts look on a case-by-case basis to determine whether to allow additional terms.

Consideration: When sales and lease contracts are modified, these modifications do not need to be supported by new consideration.

Statute of frauds: Contracts for the sale of goods must be in writing if the goods are valued at $500 or more. Lease contracts that require payments of $1,000 or more must be in writing. Exceptions exist for:

- Specifically manufactured goods.
- Contracts that parties admit exist.
- Situations in which partial performance has occurred.

Parol evidence: Courts try to enforce sales and lease contracts as written. Sometimes courts will allow parties to introduce:

- Additional terms that are consistent with contract terms.
- Information that helps interpret the agreement, including course of performance, course of dealing, and/or usage of trade.

Unconscionability: Under the UCC, a court can refuse to enforce the parts of a contract or lease that are unfair or one-sided.

Contracts for the International Sale of Goods

Scope of the CISG: The CISG is a treaty that countries can sign to allow it to govern international business-to-business sales contracts. Many major trading nations have signed the CISG.

Significance of the CISG: The CISG is important because it, rather than the UCC, governs international sales contracts. The CISG provides clarity, predictability, and uniformity for businesses that operate in the global economy.

POINT / COUNTERPOINT

Should the U.S. Adopt the CISG as a Substitute for the UCC?

YES	NO
Most global companies that do business with U.S. companies are in countries that have adopted the CISG. While similar to the UCC, the CISG does have some material differences and is not, unlike the UCC, based on common law rules of contract. For example, the CISG does not recognize the parol evidence rule, and the CISG	The common law rules of contract have a solid history and evolved for specific reasons and rationales. These rules, such as the parol evidence rule, evolved for reasons germane to the history and context of the common law. They are necessary in the context of American transactional activity. It seems that the two sets of rules are

recognizes only international trade usages, not national or local ones. However, with commercial activity becoming more and more globalized, the United States needs to "join" the rest of the world so that the rules governing transactional activities will be uniform. At the very least, the UCC should be modified to conform with the CISG.

indeed justified: When the contractual parties are from the United States, the UCC should apply as the UCC principles are relevant to domestic transactions; the CISG, with its differences, should apply to international contracts as the context is different, thus requiring a different set of rules.

QUESTIONS & PROBLEMS

1. Consider the status of being a merchant under the UCC. Should the UCC differentiate between merchants and nonmerchants?
2. In a foreclosure case involving a diner, the creditors went after the business's "real estate." However, the diner itself was a prefabricated building. The business owner claimed that the building was not realty subject to the creditors' claims but was, instead, a trade fixture. Please discuss. [*J.K.S.P Restaurant v. County of Nassau,* 513 N.Y.S. 2d 716 (N.Y. App. Div. 1987).]
3. Thomas Helvey is suing the Wabash County Rural Electrical Company for breach of contract. The electric company caused 135-volt electricity to enter Helvey's home, damaging 110-volt appliances. Helvey brought suit claiming his contract with the electric company falls under UCC Article 2 for the sale of a good. Construct an argument for the plaintiff positing that electricity is a good. Why would this position be beneficial to the plaintiff? Next, construct an argument on behalf of the defendant positing that electricity is not a good under UCC Article 2. Which argument seems more persuasive to you? [*Helvey v. Wabash County REMC,* 278 N.E.2d 608 (1972).]
4. The plaintiff, Betty Epstein, visited a beauty parlor to get her hair dyed. In the dying process, the beautician used a prebleach solution manufactured by Clairol, Inc., and then a commercial dye manufactured by Sales Affiliate, Inc. The treatment went awry, and the plaintiff suffered severe hair loss, injuries to both hair and scalp, and some disfigurement. She sued the beauty salon, Clairol, and Sales Affiliate under Article 2 of the UCC. The defendants claimed that the contract was predominantly for services rather than for the sale of a good. How would you construct arguments supporting each side? What difference does it make whether the beauty treatment is a good or a service? [*Epstein v. Giannattasio,* 197 A.2d 342 (1963).]
5. Anthony J. Ruzzo, Sr., entered into an agreement with LaRose Enterprises, which engages in business under the name Taylor Rental Center, for the use of a plumbing tool known as a "power snake." While Ruzzo was using the power snake, it malfunctioned and he was shocked severely and suffered serious personal injuries. What kind of agreement exists between Ruzzo and Taylor, and how might the kind of agreement affect the case? [*Ruzzo v. LaRose Enterprises,* 748 A.2d 261 (2000).]
6. Consider a transaction that has three parties: (1) JWCJR Corp. (JWCJR) and its owner, John W. Cumberledge, Jr., (2) Bottomline Systems, Inc., and (3) Colonial Pacific Leasing Corp. JWCJR/Cumberledge, an autobody shop and its owner, sought a computer and software package that would allow the shop to generate estimates for insurance companies and improve the way the shop was managed. Bottomline demonstrated a computer and software system to JWCJR/Cumberledge. JWCJR/Cumberledge decided to obtain the system Bottomline demonstrated and subsequently entered into an agreement with Colonial Leasing. Colonial Leasing then purchased equipment from Bottomline. JWCJR/Cumberledge agreed to make payments to Colonial Leasing. What kind of lease do these facts indicate? If the computer system does not work, why does it matter what kind of lease exists? [*Colonial Pacific Leasing Corp. v. JWCJR Corp.,* 977 P.2d 541 (1999).]
7. The purchaser, American Parts, Inc., negotiated with the seller, Deering Milliken, for the purchase of fabric. After oral negotiations, Deering Milliken forwarded to the purchaser a written confirmation of the order stating a price of $1.75 per yard. American Parts responded with a written memo

stating that it could not agree to anything more than $1.50 per yard. The seller did not respond. The seller began shipping goods to the purchaser, who accepted them. The dispute in the case is whether the contract is for $1.75 or $1.50 per yard. How could you construct an argument for each party? [*American Parts, Inc. v. American Arbitration Association,* 154 N.W.2d 5 (1967).]

8. Wisconsin Knife Works, having some unused manufacturing capacity, decided to try to manufacture spade bits for sale to its parent, Black & Decker, a large producer of tools, including drills. A spade bit is made out of a chunk of metal called a *spade bit blank,* and Wisconsin Knife Works had to find a source of supply for these blanks. National Metal Crafters was eager to supply the spade bit blanks. After some negotiating, Wisconsin Knife Works sent National Metal Crafters a series of purchase orders. On the back of each purchase order was printed "Acceptance of this Order, either by acknowledgement or performance, constitutes an unqualified agreement to the following." A list of "Conditions of Purchase" followed, of which the first was "No modification of this contract shall be binding upon Buyer [Wisconsin Knife Works] unless made in writing and signed by Buyer's authorized representative. Buyer shall have the right to make changes in the Order by a notice, in writing, to Seller." The seller met the terms of the first two purchase orders from Wisconsin Knife Works. After the first two orders, National Metal Crafters was late with the deliveries. No delivery date had been specified on the purchase orders, but the delivery dates had been communicated orally between the two parties to the contract. Wisconsin Knife Works claimed that National Metal Crafters breached the contract. National Metal Crafters claimed that it had modified the dates for delivery and that Wisconsin had accepted these dates. What could constitute a binding modification after this contract was formed? [*Wisconsin Knife Works v. National Metal Crafters,* 781 F.2d 1280 (1986).]

9. Utah International, a mining company, entered into a 35-year requirements contract with Colorado-Ute Electric Association, Inc., for the sale of coal. Utah International was to provide all the coal that Colorado-Ute would need in the operation of new electricity generators. Utah International claims that Colorado-Ute built generators that will use far more coal than Utah International is willing to supply and that this breached the contract. Utah International is asking to be released from the contract due to Colorado-Ute's alleged breach. A requirements contract is a contract in which the buyer agrees to purchase and the seller agrees to sell all or up to a stated amount of what the buyer requires. What are the limits placed on a requirements contract? Should this contract be terminated? [*Utah International v. Colorado-Ute Electric Association, Inc.,* 426 F. Supp 1093 (1976).]

10. A company contracted with a marketing firm to construct software and create a business website. A quote was requested and accepted. Sometime later the business asked for updates and revisions but failed to request a quote. The business subsequently refused to pay for the changes, claiming no contract had been formed under the requirements of the offer under the UCC. The marketing firm then took the website down because of nonpayment and subsequently sued for nonpayment of its invoice. The company countersued on the tort of conversion for the loss of the website. This intriguing case raises several questions First, does this dispute fall under UCC subject matter? Second, will the company prevail on the tort of conversion based on the improper use or interference with someone else's property? [*Dennis Conwell et al. v. Gray Look Outdoor Marketing Group, Inc.,* 906 N.E.2d 805, 2009 Ind. LEXIS 465, 69 U.C.C. Rep. Serv. 2d (Callaghan) 71 (Ind. Sup. Ct. 2009).]

Looking for more review materials?

The Online Learning Center at **www.mhhe.com/kubasek3e** contains this chapter's "Assignment on the Internet" and also a list of URLs for more information, entitled "On the Internet." Find both of them in the Student Center portion of the OLC, along with quizzes and other helpful materials.

Title, Risk of Loss, and Insurable Interest

CHAPTER 22

LEARNING OBJECTIVES

After reading this chapter, you will be able to answer the following questions:

1. What is the concept of title? How does it pass?
2. What is insurable interest?
3. What are the different kinds of sales contracts, and how does each type affect title passing, risk of loss, and insurable interest?

CASE OPENER

Keyboards Gone Astray

Silitek is a Taiwanese company. It entered into a contract FOB Taiwan with Burlington Air Express to deliver 1,000 cartons of computer keyboards to the Silitek subsidiary Lite-On in the United States. The bill of lading incorrectly stated that the goods were to be delivered to Reveal Computer Products, a California company. The mix-up occurred because once the goods were to be delivered to Lite-On, Lite-On was then going to check on Reveal Computer Products' creditworthiness and decide whether to deliver the goods to Reveal Computer Products.

The goods were delivered to Reveal Computer Products, and subsequently Reveal could not pay for them due to insolvency, thereby causing Lite-On to lose more than $100,000. Now, the catch in the whole thing is that under the delivery contract, Burlington was to collect a shipment order called a "Combined Express Bill of Lading" from Reveal Computer Products for the goods before delivery was made. Reveal did not have that bill of lading since delivery was supposed to be made to Silitek, if not for the mistake in the original bill of lading. Burlington made the delivery anyway to Reveal Computer Products. Silitek assigned its right to sue to Lite-On, which then brought a lawsuit against Burlington.

The legal question posed in light of the plaintiff's motion for summary judgment is this: Since the contract was FOB Taiwan and the seller, Silitek, is a Taiwanese firm, what kind of contract is this and what are the implications of that determination? That is, did title already pass to the buyer, Reveal, thus prohibiting Silitek's assignee, Lite-On, from suing, since it did not have title?[1]

[1] *Lite-On Peripherals, Inc. v. Burlington Air Express,* 255 F.3d 1189 (9th Cir. 2001).

1. What kind of sales contract is the one between Silitek and Burlington Air Express, and what obligations does it create between the parties?
2. What do shipping terms such as "FOB Taiwan" mean?
3. When does title pass for the computer keyboards, and what effect, if any, does that have on the transaction?

The Wrap-Up at the end of the chapter will answer these questions.

When businesses such as Burlington Air Express ship goods pursuant to UCC Article 2 sales contracts the business needs to know its rights and responsibilities. In particular, Silitek and Burlington need to know the UCC's rules regarding title, risk of loss, and insurable interest. This chapter explains these three concepts. It does so in the context of different kinds of sales contracts, including simple delivery, common-carrier delivery, goods-in-bailment, and conditional sales contracts.

The Concept of Title

LO1

What is the concept of title? How does it pass?

The UCC defines a **sale** as the passing of title from the seller to the buyer for a price. However, this definition does not indicate the relationship between *passing title* and *ownership*. Suppose, for example, that you are the owner of a computer store that wants to buy 50 keyboards from Silitek in Taiwan. The deal includes a list of keyboards with descriptions and a price for each kind of keyboard. Delivery is to be within one month.

This looks like a pretty straightforward deal—description of goods, quantity, price, time of delivery—but it is not. It does not tell the parties:

- When the buyer can resell the goods to a third party.
- When insurance on the goods can be purchased.
- When the goods become part of the buyer's inventory and can serve as collateral for a loan.

In addition, there is no indication of who takes the loss if the goods are damaged before delivery, during possession by the seller, or in transit.

Each of these issues needs to be considered before the owner of the goods can be established. Generally, the party with "good title" to the goods has ownership: You cannot own goods unless you have good title to them. This chapter discusses acquiring good title as well as the other topics listed above.

THREE KINDS OF TITLE

There are three kinds of title: good title, void title, and voidable title. First, **good title** is title that is acquired from someone who already owns the goods free and clear. Next, **void title** is not true title. Someone who purchases stolen goods, knowingly or unknowingly, has void title. Finally, **voidable title** occurs in certain situations where the contract between the original parties would be void but the goods have already been sold to a third party. The next few sections of the chapter discuss these types of title in detail.

Acquiring Good Title

The most obvious way of attaining good title is acquiring it from someone who has good title, that is, the person who owns it free and clear, without any qualifications. In contrast, someone who has come into possession of stolen goods never has good title and can never pass a good title. A person in possession of stolen goods has void title.

However, problems may arise when someone thinks he or she has good title but actually has void title. Consider Case 22-1, which concerns a large donation of goods to a charity followed by the subsequent sale of those donated items to a third party. Does that third party have a good title? Did the donee of the charitable gift have a void or voidable title? The case also talks about why that is important.

CASE 22-1 TEMPUR-PEDIC INTERNATIONAL, INC., PLAINTIFF v. WASTE TO CHARITY, INC.; BROCO SUPPLY, INC.; JACK FITZGERALD; ERIC VOLOVIC; HOWARD HIRSCH; THOMAS SCARELLO; NELSON SILVA; CLOSE OUT SURPLUS AND SAVINGS, INC.; AND ERNEST PEIA, DEFENDANTS

U.S. DISTRICT COURT FOR THE WESTERN DISTRICT OF ARKANSAS, FORT SMITH DIVISION

483 F. SUPP. 2D 766, 2007 U.S. DIST. LEXIS 54787

Tempur-Pedic International (TP) manufactures and sells mattresses, pillow cases and other bedding material. In the wake of the Hurricane Katrina disaster, Tempur-Pedic donated 15 million dollars' worth of mattresses and pillows to the Katrina disaster relief effort. It made the donation to Waste To Charity, Inc., (WTC) for distributing the mattresses to victims of the hurricane.

Waste To Charity, Inc., however, sold the donated mattresses to third parties (the other defendants named in this lawsuit). Tempur-Pedic brought this action for a temporary restraining order to stop the further sales of the mattresses and to recover the donated mattresses from the third parties. The issues are these:

1. *Did Waste To Charity, Inc., have a void title to the mattresses? If so, then any third-party purchaser has a void title, regardless of good faith.*
2. *Did Waste To Charity, Inc., have a voidable title to the mattresses? If so, then a good faith third party purchaser would get good title to the mattresses.*

HON. JAMES R. MARSCHEWSKI, U.S. MAGISTRATE: [The UCC] . . . "recognizes a legal distinction between a sale of stolen goods and a sale of goods procured through fraud." Midway Auto Sales, Inc. v. Clarkson, 71 Ark. App. 316, 318, 29 S.W.3d 788 (2000). As noted by the court in Midway Auto Sales, "[a]bsent exigent circumstances, one who purchases from a thief acquires no title as against the true owner. However, . . . the result is different when property obtained by fraud is conveyed to a bona fide purchaser." Id. [Citation omitted.]

Section 2-403 in applicable part provides as follows:

> (1) A purchaser of goods acquires all title which his transferor had or had power to transfer except that a purchaser of a limited interest acquires rights only to the extent of the interest purchased. A person with voidable title has power to transfer a good title to a good faith purchaser for value. When goods have been delivered under a transaction of purchase the purchaser has such power even though
>
> (a) the transferor was deceived as to the identity of the purchaser; or
>
> (b) the delivery was in exchange for a check which is later dishonored; or
>
> (c) it was agreed that the transaction was to be a "cash sale"; or
>
> (d) the delivery was procured through fraud punishable as larcenous under the criminal law.

The good-faith purchaser exception is designed to "promote finality in commercial transactions and thus encourage purchases and to foster commerce. It does so by protecting the title of a purchaser who acquires property for valuable consideration and who, at the time of the purchase, is without notice that the seller lacks valid and transferable title to the property." United States v. Lavin, 942 F.2d 177, 186 (3d Cir. 1991). [Citation omitted.]

. . . Here, TP voluntarily gave the donated property to WTC. There was no showing that WTC was just a sham operation. From the evidence before the court, the court believes WTC lawfully came into possession of the property. Thus, it appears clear WTC did acquire voidable title to the donated property.

After the donations were made, TP has presented evidence establishing a fair probability that at least a portion

[continued]

of the donated products were sold at various places around the country rather than put to their intended charitable use. WTC, although it claimed no knowledge of the sales, had sufficient control of the property. . . . With respect to the mattresses purchased by CSS [one of the defendants] . . . the issue therefore becomes whether CSS was a good-faith purchaser. . . . "Good faith" is defined to mean "honesty in fact in the conduct or transaction concerned." The court has given careful consideration to the documentation submitted to the court in connection with the motion for TRO and/or preliminary injunction, the response filed by CSS, the testimony of the witnesses at the hearing, and the arguments of counsel. I conclude TP has shown a probability that it will succeed on the merits of establishing that CSS is not a good faith purchaser for value of the mattresses.

A number of factors lead the court to this conclusion. First, the price of the mattresses was substantially below market value. . . . Second, the terms of the purported sale were suspicious: all tags had been removed; while the mattresses were confirmed to be TP mattresses they could not be sold as such; no sales could be made to TP dealers; and the representation was made that TP has confirmed the mattresses would not have tags on them. Third, the timing of the attempted sales . . . lends support to the conclusion that CSS was not a good faith purchaser for value. Fourth, Peia, the president of CSS, acknowledged that he knew TP did not authorize the sale of used mattresses. . . .

Request for a TRO is granted.

CRITICAL THINKING

Even though the court found that Waste To Charity, Inc., had a voidable title, it still held that no good title was passed. What would have been required to have the purchasers obtain a good title? Could these purchasers with the voidable title have transferred good title to a subsequent party? How?

ETHICAL DECISION MAKING

Should Waste To Charity be subject to any kind of legal sanctions for its behavior in this case? What public policy issues are involved in this case?

The key point to remember, which many people misunderstand, is that good faith is actually irrelevant when passing a void title. If a person has a void title (as in the best, and most frequent, example: a person has possession of stolen goods), then no matter how honorable the intentions of the seller are, that good-faith seller cannot pass anything to the buyer but another void title. The only exception to this is the entrustment situation, which is discussed later in the chapter. A good maxim to remember is that stolen goods *always* remain stolen goods.

Legal Principle: **In a title transfer, good title is passed when there is a good title held by the seller; however, if a void title is held by the seller, then a good title is never passed—a void title always begets a void title.**

BUT WHAT IF . . .

WHAT IF THE FACTS OF THE CASE OPENER WERE DIFFERENT?

Let's say, in the Case Opener, that Silitek sold the keyboards to Reveal Computer Products. The two companies had a thorough sales contract to uphold their agreement. However, it turned out that Silitek had sold stolen keyboards. What kind of contract is this called?

VOIDABLE TITLE

When a seller transfers goods to a buyer, normally the buyer gets good title. However, the buyer gets only voidable title if any of the following apply:

- The buyer has deceived the seller regarding his or her true identity.
- The buyer has written a bad check for the goods.

CASE NUGGET

VOIDABLE TITLE

Landshire Food Service, Inc. v. Coghill
709 S.W.2d 509 (Mo. App. 1986)

Coghill sold his Rolls Royce to Daniel Bellman, who paid him with a cashiers check for $94,500. Coghill transferred title over to Bellman. Bellman turned around and advertised the sale of the car and sold it to Barry Hyken for $62,000, transferring title to Hyken.

In the meantime, the cashiers check given by Bellman to Coghill turned out to be a forgery and was dishonored by the bank. Coghill then reported the car missing and stolen. Three weeks after Hyken took possession and title to the vehicle, the police arrived and seized the "stolen" car. Coghill and Hyken now both claim title to the car. The issue posed is, What kind of title did Bellman have? Did he have a good, voidable, or void title?

In answering this issue, the court ruled:

[T]he initial question is whether a bona fide purchaser for value takes good title from one who procured the automobile by a fraudulent purchase? The answer is yes. Where the original owner, although induced by fraud, has voluntarily given to another apparent ownership in the motor vehicle, a bona fide purchaser, who has relied upon that person's possession of the certificate of title and of the vehicle, is protected. . . . The person who procures title through fraud receives voidable title and is able to transfer good title to a bona fide purchaser. Although the result may seem harsh, the purpose of this rule is to promote the free transferability of property in commerce.

- The buyer has committed criminal fraud in securing the goods.
- The buyer and seller agreed that title would not pass until some later time.
- The buyer is a minor.

The first four of these situations that can create a voidable title are articulated in Section 2-403 of Article 2 of the UCC; the final one, the buyer is a minor, comes from common law. A seller who discovers any of these situations has the right to cancel the contract and reclaim the goods, even if they have already been delivered to the buyer. That is why the title is called *voidable.* The Case Nugget presents an example of a situation giving rise to a voidable title.

THIRD-PARTY PURCHASERS AND GOOD TITLE

Problems develop when a buyer with the voidable title turns around and sells the goods to a third-party purchaser. If that third-party purchaser made a good-faith purchase for value (as opposed to receiving the goods as a gift), he or she gets good title, not void or voidable title. See Exhibit 22-1.

Exhibit 22-1

Status of Title Under the UCC: Good, Bad, Voidable

Betty Buyer purchases a bicycle from Steve Seller; Betty then resells the bike to Terry, the buyer, who purchases it in good faith and for a reasonable price.

Good Title:

If Steve Seller has a good title, then he passes a good title → to Betty, who passes a good title → to Terry

Bad Title:

Let's say that Steve Seller stole the bike. Steve Seller has a bad title → Betty gets a bad title → Terry gets a bad title.

(Who has the good title? The owner from whom the bike was stolen!)

Voidable Title:*

Steve Seller has a good title → passes a voidable title to Betty; if Terry is a good-faith purchaser, then → Terry gets a good title.

*See the list in the text of the five situations in which a voidable title is created.

Here is an example of how voidable title works: Suppose a seller sells a bicycle to a buyer and the buyer pays with a bad check. Before the seller can reclaim the bike, the buyer sells the bike to a third-party good-faith purchaser for value. The buyer then takes off, never to be seen again. The seller cannot reclaim the bike from the third-party purchaser because that party has good title. Although this result may seem unfair, it upholds the philosophy of the Uniform Commercial Code itself: the facilitation of commercial activity. The code believes that good-faith purchasers should not have to look over their shoulders to determine whether a commercial transaction is valid.

ENTRUSTMENT

If an owner *entrusts* the possession of goods to a merchant who deals in goods of that kind, the merchant can transfer all rights in the goods to a buyer in the ordinary course of business. Recall that in the previous chapter, the case of *DeWeldon v. McKean* presented an example of **entrustment.** In that case, an owner had entrusted a merchant (a well-known artist) with possession of paintings. If that merchant had sold the paintings to a buyer in the ordinary course of business, then that buyer gets a good title, even though the merchant had *no* title at all. See the Point / Counterpoint at the end of this chapter to explore this issue more fully.

One form of entrustment occurs when someone entrusts the possession of a good (e.g., a car) to a merchant and asks him to repair that good. Suppose the merchant fraudulently or accidentally sells the item as if it were part of his inventory. If the purchaser is a good-faith purchaser (i.e., did not know that the item belonged to someone else and paid a fair market value, not some unreasonable discounted value), then that purchaser gets a good title. (That purchaser is a buyer in the ordinary course of business.) The original owner's only recourse is to bring suit against the merchant. Again, the rationale behind this concept is the facilitation of commercial activity regarding good-faith purchasers in the marketplace.

BUT WHAT IF . . .

WHAT IF THE FACTS OF THE CASE OPENER WERE DIFFERENT?

Let's say, in the Case Opener, that Silitek entrusted Burlington not only to ship the keyboards to Reveal Computer Products but to sell the keyboards too. Burlington drafted a sales contract for Reveal to sign. However, Reveal said that because Burlington had no title for the keyboards, Burlington could not sell them. Which side is correct in this case?

RECOURSE UNDER THE UCC

The determination of who has good title does not always result in the expected and equitable solution to a problem. For example, suppose you purchased a couch at a furniture store. It is pretty safe to say that once you identify the couch and pay for it, you have "title" to it. Now suppose that when the store attempts to deliver the couch to your home, lightning hits the store's delivery truck and destroys the couch. Is the store legally obligated to replace the couch? Most of us would intuitively answer that it is. After all, you never took possession of the couch. However, as previously noted, *you* have title. Under pre-UCC law, this loss could have fallen on whoever had title at that time—and that person would be you. Under the UCC, if the store is a merchant, the risk of loss remains with the seller until the couch is actually delivered to you.

CASE NUGGET

WHEN DOES INSURABLE INTEREST ARISE?

National Compressor Corp. v. Carrow and McGee
417 F.2d 97 (1969)

National Compressor bought a large compressor from Davis, who had bought the compressor from Carrow and McGee. Title to the compressor was not to pass to National Compressor until the compressor was removed from Carrow and McGee's property. Prior to the compressor's being moved (and title passing to National Compressor) a fire broke out at the site, destroying the compressor. National Compressor had already paid the $12,000 purchase price. The issue before the court was whether National Compressor had any kind of insurable interest since clearly title had not yet passed. The defendants claimed that National Compressor had no standing to bring the lawsuit as it had no "interest" in the property since title had yet to pass.

The court ruled otherwise, stating that National Compressor had an insurable and special interest in the good, thus giving it standing to sue. The court ruled:

Where a third party so deals with goods *which have been identified to a contract* for sale as to cause actionable injury to a party to that contract (a) a right of action against the third party is in either party to the contract for sale who has title to or a security interest or a special property or an insurable interest in the goods; and if the goods have been destroyed or converted a right of action is also in the party who either bore the risk of loss under the contract for sale or has since the injury assumed that risk as against the other. . . .

The buyer obtains a special property and an insurable interest in goods by identification of existing goods as goods to which the contract refers even though the goods so identified are nonconforming and he has an option to return or reject them. Such identification can be made at any time and in any manner explicitly agreed to by the parties. In the absence of explicit agreement identification occurs (a) when the contract is made if it is for the sale of goods already existing and identified. . . .

As a result of these kinds of dilemmas, the UCC breaks up the various issues traditionally correlated with title and treats them separately. Several different issues normally are thought of under the concept of title:

- *Ownership:* When does title actually transfer from the seller to the buyer, since the right to transfer ownership of the goods, whether through a subsequent sale or gift, is tied to title?
- *Encumbrance:* The right to encumber goods as collateral for a debt is dependent on who is holding title. When title passes is important because having title means that one can then sell or encumber the goods. In other words, having title means that one can pass title.
- *Loss:* In regard to the right to indemnification if the goods are damaged, when the risk of loss attaches is important. This is because, regardless of title passing, we need to know the seller's and buyer's responsibility to each other in the event that the goods are damaged or destroyed before the buyer takes complete possession of the goods.
- *Insurable interest:* An *insurable interest* is the right to insure the goods against any risk exposure such as damage or destruction. When an insurable interest is created in the goods is important. Both the buyer and the seller can insure themselves for potential loss, in the event that the goods are damaged or destroyed at some point in the transaction. A key point is identifying the earliest time in the transaction that the buyer can claim an insurable interest. The Case Nugget addresses that issue.

L02 What is insurable interest?

One very important point to note is that the parties are always free to create a contract that lays out and defines such issues as when title passes and when risk of loss passes. The UCC's rules are essentially the default rules for contracts that do not clearly spell out such provisions.

Let's look at each one of these issues within the context of the four kinds of sales contracts that Article 2 creates.

Types of Sales Contracts

LO3

What are the different kinds of sales contracts, and how does each type affect title passing, risk of loss, and insurable interest?

The UCC lays out essentially four broad factual scenarios for the sale of goods:

1. *Simple delivery contract:* A simple delivery contract occurs when the purchased goods are transferred to the buyer from the seller at either the time of the sale or some time later by the seller's delivery.
2. *Common-carrier delivery contract:* This type of contract occurs when the goods are delivered to the buyer via a common carrier, such as a trucking line.
3. *Goods-in-bailment contract:* This type of contract occurs when the purchased goods are in some kind of storage under the control of a third party, such as a warehouseman.
4. *Conditional sales contract:* A conditional sales contract occurs when the sale itself is contingent on approval, for example.

In the sections that follow, this chapter answers questions about ownership, encumbrance, loss, and insurable interest as they relate to these four types of sales contracts.

SIMPLE DELIVERY CONTRACT

With a **simple delivery contract,** the buyer and seller typically execute an agreement, and the buyer leaves with the goods. To most of us, it appears that title, risk of loss, and insurable interest all pass to the buyer at the moment the transaction is consummated and the buyer walks out with the goods. However, under the UCC, there are three distinct steps: (1) Title transfers to the buyer on the goods' being identified to the contract, that is, when the contract is executed; (2) risk of loss transfers to the buyer when the buyer takes possession; and (3) insurable interest is created in the buyer when the goods are identified to the contract, in other words, at the same time that title passes.

But what happens if the buyer comes back later to pick up the goods or arranges to have the seller, or an agent of the seller, deliver the goods at a later time? For the purposes of title and insurable interest, nothing really changes. The dilemma occurs with risk of loss.

Let's suppose a buyer and seller execute a contract in which the seller is going to deliver a refrigerator later in the day to the buyer. Through no fault of the seller, the refrigerator is damaged in a fire at the seller's store. Who has the risk of loss if neither party is at fault? In this case, the issue rests on the seller's status. If the seller is a merchant, as in this instance, the risk of loss remains with the seller until the goods are actually delivered to the buyer. If the seller is not a merchant, the risk of loss remains with the buyer under the rule of **tender of delivery.** Simply put, tender of delivery is the moment the goods were available for the buyer to take. Consider this example: You purchase a dresser at a garage sale, but you want to go home and get your truck so that you can get the dresser home easily. Unfortunately, a car hits the dresser and destroys it. You, the buyer, cannot get your money back because (1) the law does not consider the seller a merchant and (2) you could have taken the dresser with you when you bought it.

Note that the results are different if either party is at fault for the damage. In that case, the responsible person is liable under tort law for the damage caused. Case 22-2 considers who has the risk of loss between an innocent seller and an innocent buyer.

Legal Principle: A simple delivery contract includes the scenario in which the seller delivers the goods to the buyer via its own delivery truck. The contract becomes a shipment contract when a common carrier, not the seller's agent, is used for delivery.

With a simple delivery contract, whereby a seller transfers goods to a buyer without the middle-delivery common carrier, the various interests transfer as shown below. (*Note:* Even if the seller has its agent deliver the goods to the buyer, this is still a simple delivery.)

CASE 22-2 EMERY v. WEED
SUPERIOR COURT OF PENNSYLVANIA
343 PA. SUPER. 224, 494 A.2D 438 (1985)

In this case, Emery's son had been making down payments on a Pacer Corvette sports car sold by an automobile dealership owned by Weed Chevrolet (Weed). Emery's son died prior to paying off and taking possession of the car. In the meantime, through no negligence or fault of the automobile dealership, the car was stolen from the dealership. Emery is suing for the return of the monies paid and to cancel the contract. Weed is counterclaiming, stating that it is entitled to keep the down payments, and also to recover damages in the amount of the difference between the purchase price of the Pacer and its market value on the date Emery sought to cancel the agreement. The trial court ruled in favor of Emery, and Weed appeals.

JUDGE SPAETH: . . . With respect to several of these [UCC] provisions, there is no dispute. The parties agree that the Pacer Corvette "suffer[ed] casualty without the fault of either party," . . . and that the casualty was "total" and occurred "before the risk of loss [had] pass[ed] to the buyer." . . . We . . . agree with the trial court that risk of loss had not passed, but we base that conclusion on 13 Pa.C.S. § 2509(c) ("In any case not within subsection (a) or (b), the risk of loss passes to the buyer on his receipt of the goods if the seller is a merchant. . . .")

The item "identified when the contract was made" was the Pacer Corvette identified in the agreement of sale by its serial number. Appellant argues that it was not required by the agreement to deliver that very Pacer because, it asserts, "[e]ach such automobile was identical to all of the others manufactured, down to the details with respect to the paint job and extras." This assertion, however, is not supported by the record, which only shows that all Pacer Corvettes were painted black and silver; as will be recalled, the trial court disallowed testimony as to the effect that all Pacer Corvettes were identical. Quite apart from its identification in the agreement by serial number, the Pacer was identified by being removed from the display showroom, after the agreement was signed, and being covered and locked. From this it may be inferred that there was "a meeting of the minds as to the particular or actual goods designated." This agreement by [seller] and appellee's son that [seller] would deliver the Pacer identified in the contract was in no way affected by the seller's later apparent willingness to provide [buyer] with a different Pacer. [Seller] argues that "the parties . . . did not consider the particular automobile (the Pacer identified in the agreement by its serial number) to be unique. . . ." However, Section 2613 does not require such proof; it only requires that [buyer] establish that the "contract require[d] for its performance [the Pacer Corvette] identified when the contract [was] made." He has done so.

AFFIRMED.

CRITICAL THINKING

Is the court's decision consistent with your commonsense belief about whether risk of loss had passed? Explain how the court used the UCC to reach its conclusion.

ETHICAL DECISION MAKING

Which primary value does the court's decision show it prefers? Which primary value does Weed Chevrolet probably prefer?

Simple delivery: seller → buyer

1. Title transfers on identification of the goods to the contract.
2. If the seller is a merchant, risk of loss transfers on delivery of the goods to the buyer; if the seller is not a merchant, risk of loss transfers when the goods are made available for the buyer to possess (tender of delivery).
3. The parties may buy insurance on their goods if they hold title or have any risk of loss or other economic interest.

But what if simple delivery is not so simple. For example, what about delivery of liquid via a pipeline. Consider the nearby Case Nugget.

CASE NUGGET

WHEN DOES TITLE PASS?

City of Richmond v. Petroleum Marketers, Inc.
221 Va. 372, 269 S.E. 2d 389 (1980)

Petroleum Marketers is a wholesaler of petroleum within Henrico County, Virginia. Its offices are there, and it made all of its contracts with customers in Henrico County, not in the city of Richmond. However, the petroleum was delivered to these customers in Richmond. The city of Richmond claimed that Petroleum Marketers was liable for city taxes as a merchant doing business "in the city."

According to the Virginia Supreme Court,

> The ultimate question which we must decide is whether Petroleum's "sales" occurred where the contracts for the purchase of the oil were executed (Henrico County) or where the goods were, in fact, delivered (City). Our inquiry is whether there is a sufficient nexus between the activities of Petroleum and the City to justify the City classifying Petroleum as a wholesale merchant subject to the City's license tax.

The relevant portion of the Virginia UCC (comparable to UCC Article 2) says in part that "[a] 'sale' consists in the passing of title from the seller to the buyer for a price" and that "[u]nless otherwise explicitly agreed title passes to the buyer at the time and place at which the seller completes his performance with reference to the physical delivery of the goods."

The court found that the goods were identified to the contract when the petroleum arrived at the buyer's receptacle in the city, not when it was pumped out of the seller's holding tank in Henrico County. The obvious conclusion is that title passed when the product was pumped out of Petroleum's rented tanks and into whatever facility its customer provided.

COMMON-CARRIER DELIVERY CONTRACT

If a buyer and seller execute a contract and the seller subsequently places the goods with a common carrier for delivery to the buyer, the parties have executed a **common-carrier delivery contract.** Note that a common carrier is an independent contractor and not an agent of the seller. What makes the common carrier an independent contractor, rather than an agent, is that the carrier controls the primary aspects of performance, such as how the goods are actually delivered.

The UCC names two kinds of delivery contracts in this category: origin or shipment contracts and destination contracts. *Shipment contracts* require that the seller ship the goods to the buyer via a common carrier. The seller is required to make proper shipping arrangements and deliver the goods into the common carrier's hands. Title passes to the buyer at the time and place of shipment. Thus, the buyer bears the risk of loss while the goods are in transit. *Destination contracts* require that the seller deliver the goods to the destination stipulated in the sales contract. This may be the buyer's place of business or some other location. The seller bears the risk of loss until that time. Case 22-3 discusses the issue of who bears the risk of loss in a case in which the parties disagreed about whether the contract was an origin/shipment contract or a destination contract. See also Exhibit 22-2, which identifies shipping terms that create the conditions of transit and delivery. Remember in the opening case that the shipment term was FOB Taiwan. How is that interpreted from Exhibit 22-2?

Exhibit 22-2
Shipping Terms Specifying Requirements for Delivery

TERM	EXPLANATION
FOB (free on board)	The selling price includes transportation costs, and the seller carries the risk of loss to either the place of shipment or the place of destination.
FAS (free alongside)	The seller, at seller's expense, delivers the goods alongside the ship before the risk passes to the buyer.
CIF or C&F (cost, insurance, and freight; cost and freight)	The seller puts the goods in possession of a carrier before the risk passes to the buyer. Contracts are usually shipment contracts rather than destination contracts.
Delivery ex-ship (delivery from the carrying vessel)	Risk of loss passes to the buyer when the goods leave the ship.

COMPARING THE LAW OF OTHER COUNTRIES

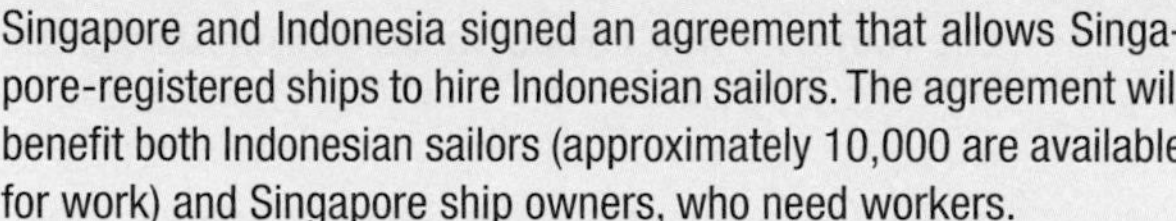

SINGAPORE TAKES STEPS TO HALT PIRACY

Singapore and Indonesia signed an agreement that allows Singapore-registered ships to hire Indonesian sailors. The agreement will benefit both Indonesian sailors (approximately 10,000 are available for work) and Singapore ship owners, who need workers.

This agreement aims to halt piracy, which occurs when sailors are out of work in a deteriorating economy. Indonesian waters are especially crime-ridden. The Straits of Malacca are a prime location for pirate attacks on ships in Indonesian waters. The agreement between Singapore and Indonesia will put Indonesian sailors on Singapore-flagged ships, where the sailors will have new, legal opportunities to support themselves.

Source: Susan Sim, "Maritime Deal Promises to Cut Piracy in Region," *The Straits Times* (Singapore), February 23, 2001.

CASE 22-3 PILERI INDUSTRIES, INC. v. CONSOLIDATED INDUSTRIES, INC.

COURT OF CIVIL APPEALS OF ALABAMA

740 SO. 2D 1108 (1999)

In this case, Pileri Industries, the seller, shipped goods via a common carrier to Consolidated Industries, Inc., the buyer. The goods were subsequently lost prior to actual delivery. Pileri claimed the sales contract was a shipping contract and thus the risk of loss had passed to the buyer, Consolidated Industries.

Consolidated Industries disagreed. Consolidated claimed the sales contract was a destination contract, and that the risk of loss remained with Pileri Industries, the seller. The trial court, through a nonjury trial, held that Pileri could not support this assertion that there was a shipping contract and thus held for Consolidated Industries, Inc.

The Court of Civil Appeals held that Pileri, the seller, was not entitled to judgment in a breach-of-contract action, and that Pileri's delivery of goods to the carrier did not entitle Pileri to recover money for the goods shipped. What follows is a portion of the dissent in the appellate case.

JUDGE CRAWLEY, DISSENTING: . . . I respectfully dissent because I believe that the trial court erred as a matter of law by entering judgment for Consolidated. . . . [E]ven if Consolidated had established that it never received the November 4 shipment, I would not thereby have proved that it was relieved of its contractual duty to pay for the goods. Under . . . the Uniform Commercial Code, a determination of whether the seller or buyer bears the risk of loss of goods in transit depends on whether the agreement of sale is a "shipment" contract or a "destination" contract.

Under [Article 2 of the Uniform Commercial Code] the "shipment" contract is regarded as the normal one and the "destination" contract as the variant type. . . . Both of these types of contracts usually employ mercantile terms or "trade symbols" specifying the requirements for delivery, such as "F.O.B. the place of shipment," . . . or "F.O.B. the place of destination." *Where no such term is employed and there has been no specific agreement otherwise, the contract for the transportation of goods by carrier will be presumed to be a shipping contract.*

Unlike the majority of this court, I believe that Pileri made a prima facie showing that the contract was a shipment contract and that Consolidated presented no evidence to the contrary. As the main opinion points out, I have, in the absence of Alabama case law on the subject, turned to the construction of the relevant UCC sections by some of our sister states.

In interpreting the UCC we must keep in mind the legislative mandate that is to be . . . applied to promote its underlying purposes and policies, one of which is to make uniform the law among various jurisdictions. . . .

At trial, Pileri introduced a bill of lading indicating that it delivered the goods on November 4, 1992, to Roadway Express for shipment to Consolidated. Mr. Pileri testified that the agreement was a "shipping contract" that required Consolidated to pay the shipping costs and to assume the risk of loss once Pileri had delivered the goods to a common carrier. Pileri stated that it made 14 shipments to Consolidated. It introduced 10 shipping invoices, 6 of which were marked "F.O.B. Farmingdale," Pileri's place of business. For the other four shipping invoices, the "F.O.B." term was left blank.

Although those invoices pertained to a prior agreement of the parties, rather than to the parties' new agreement made on March 30, 1992, they are relevant because they indicate a course of dealing between Pileri and Consolidated. . . . In the absence of any evidence from Consolidated indicating that the agreement was a "destination contract," Pileri was entitled to rely on the presumption established in § 7-2-503, Ala. Code 1975 (Comment 5), that the agreement was a "shipping contract." . . . Here, however, Pileri did more than merely rely on the presumption. Mr. Pileri testified that the "standard procedure" among Government contractors was that, unless otherwise agreed between the parties, the contract was "an F.O.B. contract." Consolidated did not object to Mr. Pileri's testimony on this point. . . . Pileri established Consolidated's liability on an account stated; it also established a breach of a shipment contract by Consolidated. . . .

[continued]

Consolidated presented no evidence either challenging the accuracy of the stated account or disputing Pileri's characterization of the agreement as a shipment contract. Consolidated neither pleaded nor proved the affirmative defense of failure of consideration. The judgment for Consolidated is erroneous as a matter of law and is due to be reversed.

The majority had affirmed; the dissent disagrees.

CRITICAL THINKING

From reading the dissent, can you make any inferences about why the majority must have ruled in favor of Consolidated? Does this case illustrate the significance of who bears the burden of proof?

ETHICAL DECISION MAKING

Which primary value does the dissent's argument show it prefers? Identify and explain a value that clashes with this value.

With a shipment contract whereby a seller transfers goods to a buyer with delivery of the goods effected by a common carrier, the various interests transfer as follows:

Shipment contract: seller → common carrier → buyer

1. If the shipment contract is an origin contract (if the contract is vague or ambiguous, an origin contract will be presumed), the title passes to the buyer when the goods are turned over by the seller to the common carrier.
2. If the shipment contract is a destination contract, the title transfers from the seller to the buyer when the common carrier delivers the goods to the buyer.
3. The risk of loss in either situation—origin or destination contract—transfers from the seller to the buyer simultaneously with the title.
4. An insurable interest is created when the buyer and/or seller holds title or retains a risk of loss.

GOODS-IN-BAILMENT CONTRACT

Goods in bailment are simply goods that are in some kind of storage (e.g., in a warehouse or on board a ship), so the seller cannot transfer physical possession of them. Instead, the seller has one of three documents indicating ownership of the goods: a negotiable document of title, a nonnegotiable document of title, or a contract or some other instrument showing ownership that is not a negotiable or nonnegotiable document of title. If the seller has a negotiable document (i.e., a document containing the words "deliver to the order of [seller]"), then both title and risk of loss transfer from the seller to the buyer as soon as that negotiable instrument is endorsed over to the buyer. On the other hand, if the document is nonnegotiable (i.e., a document lacking the words "to the order of"), then the title passes with the instrument of title but the risk of loss does not pass to the buyer until the bailee (the custodian of the goods) is notified of the transfer or a reasonable time has elapsed since the transaction. Finally, if there is neither a negotiable or nonnegotiable document of title, then the title passes at the time the sales contract is executed but the risk does not pass to the buyer until the bailee is notified of the transaction and acknowledges such notification.

E-COMMERCE AND THE LAW

WWW

THE EFFECT ON PORT OPERATORS

Globalization and the development of information technology are changing the way port operators conduct their business. According to Ernst Frankel, a professor of ocean systems at the Massachusetts Institute of Technology, ports and terminals are streamlining their management, automating their business operations and production processes, and viewing themselves as part of an integrated system that includes carrier systems.

In the future, it is likely that changes in technology will include integrated ports and shipping lines that offer door-to-door service. Frankel believes that regional and global wireless networks will bring ports, carriers, and shippers together to "maximize operating efficiencies." He states that the factor driving this change is customer need. The bottom line is that the customer wants "knowledge, speed, innovation and quality," and changes in technology are making customer wishes come true.

Source: "Technology Carriers and Operators Learn Integration Lessons," *Lloyd's List International* 6 (March 2, 2001).

With goods in bailment, the three interests—title, risk of loss, insurable interest—pass in the following way:

Seller → buyer, but the goods are elsewhere in some kind of storage and in a third party's possession and care

1. Title passes from the seller to the buyer when the document of title (e.g., a warehouse receipt or a bill of lading) is actually endorsed or signed over to the buyer. If there is no document of title, then title passes when the goods are identified to the contract and the contract is executed.
2. Risk of loss passes to the buyer simultaneously with the document of title provided that the document of title is a negotiable one. If it is nonnegotiable, the risk does not pass until the bailee (the possessor or custodian of the goods) is notified or a reasonable time elapses. If there is no document of title, risk passes to the buyer on notification and acknowledgment by the bailee.
3. Insurable interest is created when either party has title, risk of loss, or some other economic interest attached to the goods (e.g., a creditor who secures a loan by taking the goods as collateral).

CONDITIONAL SALES CONTRACT

Conditional sales contracts are either sale-on-approval contracts or sale-or-return contracts. A contract is a **sale-on-approval contract** if the seller allows the buyer to take possession of the goods before deciding whether to complete the contract by making the purchase. Title and risk of loss remain with the seller until the buyer notifies the seller about the approval of the contract.

A **sale-or-return contract** occurs when the seller and buyer agree that the buyer may return the goods at a later time. Such contracts usually occur when the buyer is buying inventory to resell. For example, suppose the seller is a dress wholesaler and the buyer is a retailer who is purchasing the dresses to sell in her store. In their sale-or-return agreement, the insurable interest is created in the buyer once the goods are identified in the contract. Title and risk of loss depend on whether the goods are in bailment, delivered by common carrier, or delivered by the seller himself. Without an agreement to the contrary, if the buyer subsequently returns the dresses, she does so at her own expense and risk.

COMPARING THE LAW OF OTHER COUNTRIES

SHIPPING ON THE SEA

The general international law regarding foreign merchant ships in internal waters has never been codified. Despite the codification efforts made by the League of Nations and the Geneva Convention on the Territorial Sea and the Contiguous Zone of 1958, the question of territorial waters was solved during the Third United Nations Conference on the Law of the Sea (UNCLOS). In addition, the right of innocent passage of foreign ships has been regulated under the 1982 convention in greater detail than ever before. Still, potential conflicts between coastal states and foreign merchant ships in internal waters and the territorial sea may well arise. The United States assisted with the development of the UNCLOS concepts but has refused to ratify the agreement despite the fact that a vast majority of the world's nations have ratified it. The United States is joined by Israel, Eritrea, Peru, Syria, Turkey, and Venezuela in not signing the treaty. For more information, see www.un.org/Depts/los/convention_agreements/convention_historical_perspective.htm.

BUT WHAT IF . . .

WHAT IF THE FACTS OF THE CASE OPENER WERE DIFFERENT?

Recall that, in the Case Opener, Silitek had Burlington deliver its products to the buyer. But what if Reveal Computer Products had come to Silitek's warehouse to pick up the goods and transport them to its own store? What kind of sales contract would this constitute?

Risk of Loss during a Breach of Contract

WHEN THE SELLER IS IN BREACH

The failure to deliver goods is the most common way a sales contract is breached. If the seller does not provide the goods that were described in the contract, the buyer may either (1) accept the nonconforming goods as is or (2) reject the goods subject to the seller's curing the deficiency in the goods. The buyer may reject the goods if no cure is possible or the seller fails to cure the deficiency within a reasonable time. In all these instances, the risk of loss remains with the seller until either the buyer accepts the goods or the seller cures the deficiency and provides the buyer with conforming goods.

If a cure is not possible or if the seller has failed to cure the deficiency within a reasonable time, the buyer has the option to revoke the contract. (The remedies will be discussed in subsequent chapters.) However, the UCC creates a disincentive for buyers who do so: If the risk of loss would have transferred to the buyer had there not been a breach, the risk transfers to the buyer to the extent of any insurance the buyer has. The loss reverts to the breaching seller only to the extent that the buyer's insurance does not cover it.

WHEN THE BUYER IS IN BREACH

Most buyer breaches occur when a buyer refuses to accept conforming goods from the seller and then the goods are subsequently lost or damaged. With an origin or shipment contract, the risk would have already transferred to the breaching buyer. However, if the contract is a destination contract, the risk remains with the seller. In order to encourage sellers to create origin contracts, the UCC requires that the risk of loss remain with the seller to the extent of the seller's insurance. If the seller does not have insurance or the loss exceeds the seller's insurance, the remainder transfers to the breaching buyer.

BUT WHAT IF . . .

WHAT IF THE FACTS OF THE CASE OPENER WERE DIFFERENT?

Let's say that, in the Case Opener, Reveal Computer Products had formed a sales contract with Silitek stating that Reveal would send its own truck to Silitek's warehouse to pick up the keyboards it had paid for. On the way back from picking up the keyboards, Reveal's truck was in an accident and the keyboards were destroyed. Reveal attempted to sue Silitek, stating that the risk remained with Silitek since Reveal had not received the products in its inventory yet. Is Reveal correct in this case?

CASE OPENER WRAP-UP

Keyboards Gone Astray

In the opening case, Lite-On Peripherals was suing Burlington Air Express for misdelivery of goods under a sales contract. The three questions posed were:

1. What kind of sales contract is the one between Silitek and Burlington Air Express, and what obligations does it create between the parties?
2. What do shipping terms such as "FOB Taiwan" mean?
3. When does title pass for the computer keyboards, and what effect, if any, does that have on the transaction?

Since the fact pattern was that the seller had engaged a common carrier to deliver goods to a buyer, the contract is a shipment contract. Moreover, since the contract terms had FOB Taiwan and the seller was in Taiwan, this is an origin contract, meaning that the title and risk of loss to the goods had transferred to the buyer when the carrier, Burlington Air Express, took possession of the goods for delivery. Burlington then argued that the seller, having neither title nor risk of loss, had no standing to sue Burlington. However, the irony is that although Burlington raised defenses related to the UCC, the court ultimately found that the controlling issue was not a UCC issue but a simple breach of contract. Burlington failed to perform the duties required under the contract, that is, to not deliver the goods until the buyer presented and turned over to Burlington the receipt. Burlington breached the express terms of its delivery obligation and thus is liable for the misdelivery.

KEY TERMS

common-carrier delivery contract 502
conditional sales contracts 505
entrustment 498
good title 494
goods in bailment 504
sale 494
sale-on-approval contract 505
sale-or-return contract 505
simple delivery contract 500
tender of delivery 500
void title 494
voidable title 494

SUMMARY OF KEY TOPICS

The Concept of Title

There are three kinds of title: good title, void title, and voidable title.

- *Good title* is title that is acquired from someone who already owns the goods free and clear.
- *Void title* is not true title. Someone who purchases stolen goods has void title.
- *Voidable title* occurs in certain situations in which the contract between the original parties would be void but the goods have already been sold to a third party.

Acquiring Good Title

Article 2 of the Uniform Commercial Code covers issues related to acquiring good title.

- The most obvious way to attain *good title* is to acquire it from someone who has good title.
- Someone who has come into possession of stolen goods never has title and can pass only *void title.*
- A buyer gets *voidable title* if he or she has deceived the seller regarding his or her true identity, written a bad check for the goods, committed criminal fraud in securing the goods, or is a minor, or if the buyer and seller agreed that title would not pass until some later time.

Third-party purchasers generally get good title. If an owner *entrusts* the possession of goods to a merchant who deals in goods of that kind, the merchant can transfer all rights in the goods to a buyer in the ordinary course of business.

The UCC provides recourse for situations in which good title may not be enough for an equitable result. The UCC responds to issues related to the following:

- *Ownership* refers to transfer of title.
- *Encumbrance* refers to when goods may be used as collateral for a debt.
- *Loss* refers to who has the risk of loss, which matters when someone is seeking indemnification for damaged goods.
- *Insurable interest* refers to the right to insure goods against any risk exposure.

Types of Sales Contracts

A *simple delivery contract* is formed when the buyer and seller execute an agreement and the buyer leaves with the goods. *Title* transfers to the buyer when the contract is executed. *Risk of loss* transfers to the buyer when the buyer takes possession. *Insurable interest* is created in the buyer at the same time title passes.

A *common-carrier delivery contract* exists when a buyer and seller execute a contract and the seller subsequently places the goods with a common carrier. There are two types of common-carrier delivery contracts: origin, or shipment, contracts and destination contracts.

- In *shipment contracts,* title transfers to the buyer at the time and place of shipment. The buyer bears the risk of loss while the goods are in transit.
- In *destination contracts,* the seller bears the risk of loss until the seller delivers the goods to the destination stipulated in the sales contract.

A *goods-in-bailment contract* is one that identifies goods that are in some kind of storage. Rules regarding passage of title, risk of loss, and insurable interest vary depending on whether the seller has a negotiable document of title, a nonnegotiable document of title, or a contract showing ownership that is neither a negotiable nor nonnegotiable document of title.

A *conditional sales contract* is either a sale-on-approval or sale-or-return contract.

- In a *sale-on-approval contract,* title and risk of loss remain with the seller until the buyer notifies the seller about the approval of the contract.
- In a *sale-or-return contract,* the insurable interest is created in the buyer once the goods are identified in the contract. Title and risk of loss depend on whether the goods are in bailment, delivered by common carrier, or delivered by the seller.

CASE NUGGET

ENTRUSTMENT AND GOODWILL

Kahr v. Markland
187 Ill. App. 3d 603, 543 N.E.2d 579

Entrustment is recognized in UCC 2-403(3). In this case, Toby Kahr gave Goodwill a bag of clothes; however, the bag also included valuable sterling silver. The court held that there had been no entrustment because Kahr intended to donate the clothes but not the silver. Its reasoning is as follows.

An entrustment requires four essential elements: (1) an actual entrustment of the goods by the delivery of possession of those goods to a merchant; (2) the party receiving the goods must be a merchant who deals in goods of that kind; (3) the merchant must sell the entrusted goods; and (4) the sale must be to a buyer in the ordinary course of business. (*Dan Pilson Auto Center, Inc. v. DeMarco* (1987), 156 Ill. App. 3d 617, 621, 509 N.E.2d 159, 162.) The court found in the Kahr case that there was no intent to transfer the sterling silver because the plaintiffs were unaware of its place in the bag of clothes.

However, the problem in the Kahr case is that Toby Kahr intended to transfer title of the bag of clothes. Usually in entrustment cases, the owner does not intend to give up title but merely possession to the initial recipient.

In light of these two cases, consider the Point / Counterpoint below.

Risk of Loss during a Breach of Contract

When the seller is in breach by failing to deliver goods, the buyer may either accept the nonconforming goods as is or reject the goods subject to the seller's curing the deficiencies in the goods. Risk of loss remains with the seller until the buyer accepts the goods or the deficiencies are corrected.

When the buyer is in breach because he or she has refused to accept conforming goods and then the goods are subsequently lost or damaged, who bears the risk of loss depends on the type of contract that exists between the buyer and the seller.

POINT / COUNTERPOINT

If a merchant (bailee) is holding goods for someone for repair or storage and sells those goods to a good-faith purchaser, that good-faith purchaser gets good title and the previous owner may recover the loss only from the bailee by suing in the tort of conversion.

Is It Right That a Bailee Who Has Only Possession, Not Title, Can Pass a Good Title to a Purchaser?

YES

The primary purpose of the Uniform Commercial Code, in addition to attempting to "uniformize" manners and methods of commercial processes, is to facilitate and enable commercial activity.

To put it succinctly, purchasers should not have to look over their shoulders, so to speak, regarding every transaction for fear that the title may not be valid. The facilitation of commercial activity requires that a good-faith purchaser can rely on the sale to validate his or her title to the goods.

We see such a perspective in other areas of the Uniform Commercial Code. As we see in Article 9, on secured transactions, if a buyer in the ordinary course of business purchases an item that is encumbered, the purchaser gets title over the creditor.

NO

The entrustment rule is an example of the Uniform Commercial Code's taking a principle to an illogical and inequitable conclusion.

There is no question that the focus of the Uniform Commercial Code is the facilitation of commerce, and the example of the buyer in the ordinary course of business that the opposing view makes is valid except that it is misplaced. A merchant who has a voidable title can pass on a good title; a merchant who has a good title can obviously pass on a good title. But a merchant who has a void or bad title or no title at all cannot pass on a good title. This is a fundamental premise regarding the ability to pass title.

This philosophy puts the greater goal of the Uniform Commercial Code ahead of any individualized inconvenience of losing title to goods in entrustment. The focus of the code is the facilitation of commerce, and, as such, parties who put goods into entrustment must exercise due care in choosing a bailee.

The entrustment rule is the exception to this title rule, and it is misplaced. First, common sense tells us that this situation occurs so infrequently as to negate the need for a special rule. Second, when it does occur, often the goods may be unique and are not replaceable. Thus, the inequity in denying possession to the true owner of unique goods truly outweighs the need to facilitate commercial activity.

QUESTIONS & PROBLEMS

1. Should entrustment apply when the entrustee is not a merchant? [See *Porter v. Wertz,* 53 N.Y.2d 696, 698 (1981), which notes that the UCC entrustment provision is "designed to enhance the reliability of commercial sales by merchants . . . while shifting the risk of loss through fraudulent transfer to the owner of the goods, who can select the merchant to whom he entrusts the property. It protects only those who purchase from the merchant to whom the property was entrusted in the ordinary course of the merchant's business."]
2. Mitchell Coach Manufacturing Company, Inc., produces motor homes and sells them to other retail dealers and directly to customers. Ronny Stephens was a customer. WW, Inc., bought and sold motor homes from Mitchell. Under their agreement, WW would pay Mitchell either a down payment on a motor home before the motor home was purchased or the entire amount due for the completed product. Under the agreement, the title of the motor home remained with WW until Stephens paid in full. WW paid Mitchell a down payment of $10,000 for the construction of the motor home. Upon completion, the motor home was to be picked up by Stephens at Mitchell. WW paid the remaining balance to Mitchell, but the check was returned for lack of sufficient funds. Stephens, through a loan, had paid for the motor home in full, but WW had not paid Mitchell. Both Mitchell and Stephens claim title to the motor home. Whom does title belong to? [*Mitchell Coach Manufacturing Company, Inc. v. Ronny Stephens,* 19 F. Supp. 2d 1277 (1998).]
3. Sture Graffman entered into a contract with Miguel Espel whereby Espel and his company (MTS) became the exclusive agent for the promotion and sale of Graffman's Picasso painting. Espel asked his brother-in-law, Michael Delecea, to help in the sale of the painting. The painting was sent to Delecea in New York, and Delecea contacted the Avanti Gallery. The gallery owners found a buyer for the painting, and the painting was sold for $875,000. Delecea sent Espel $550,000 and used $200,000 of the proceeds to pay off Espel's debts. Graffman never received any of the money. Subsequently, Graffman brought an action seeking the recovery of the painting or sufficient compensatory damages. Is the entrustment rule applicable? Was the buyer's title to the painting void? How do you think the court handled the dispute? [*Graffman v. Espel,* 96 Civ. 8247 (1998).]
4. Marilyn Thomas purchased an installed pool heater from Sunkissed. The pool heater was delivered to Marilyn's residence, but the delivery slip was signed by Nancy Thomas. Marilyn did not know of anyone by that name. She called Sunkissed to advise them to move the heater. The neighborhood was not safe, and she was worried that the heater would be taken. The heater remained in her driveway for approximately four days. When Marilyn noticed that the heater was no longer in her driveway, she again contacted Sunkissed, but she was told "not to worry." Who was responsible for the loss of the heater? Did Sunkissed actually "deliver" the heater to Marilyn? How do you think the court decided? [*In re Marilyn Thomas,* 182 B.R. 347 (1995).]
5. In 1987 R.H. Love Gallery owned the title to a painting entitled *Marlton's Cove.* The gallery sold 50 percent of the painting to Altman Fine Arts, a New York art dealer, and 50 percent to Andre Lopoukhine, a Boston art dealer. In 1989, plaintiff Morgold, Inc., purchased Altman's 50 percent of

the painting. Morgold and Lopoukhine decided to try to sell the painting. In 1990, Lopoukhine sold the painting to Mark Grossman. Lopoukhine did not pay Morgold the 50 percent due for the sale of the painting. Morgold argued that this lack of payment indicated that the title was never officially passed on to Grossman. Through an art dealer, Grossman sold the painting to Fred Keeler. In 1991, Morgold contacted Keeler and claimed to be the sole owner of the painting. Who do you believe owns title to the painting? [*Morgold, Inc. v. Keeler,* 891 F. Supp. 1361 (1995).]

6. MAN Roland agreed to sell Quantum Color Corporation a used press for $405,000. According to the contract, Quantum was supposed to pay $5,000 at the time of the contract, $265,000 at delivery, and the balance of $135,000 before the press was actually used. The first two payments were made, but MAN Roland did not receive the $135,000. MAN Roland alleged that Quantum had been using the press and, therefore, that Quantum was required to pay the balance. Quantum argued that MAN Roland breached the contract by delivering nonconforming goods. Part of the contract indicated that MAN Roland would provide standard equipment and installation, but MAN Roland did not install the equipment or provide Quantum with the standard equipment. How do you think the court settled this case? [*MAN Roland Inc. v. Color Corp.,* 57 F. Supp. 2d 576 (1999).]

7. William and Donna Hardy purchased a motor home in July 1993 for $38,989. The day after purchasing the motor home, the Hardys commenced a cross-country trip. The Hardys had noticed a small crack on the windshield, but the sellers of the motor home promised to fix the problem when the Hardys returned. Once on the road, the Hardys noticed a loud, clanking noise. They stopped at a dealership and were informed that the drive shaft needed to be replaced. The dealer told the Hardys that this replacement could be done after they completed the trip. The Hardys continued their trip but soon noticed a burning smell. They went to another dealership, and the mechanic worked on the drive shaft. The burning smell was no longer present, but the motor home continued to make loud noises. When the Hardys finally reached California, they took the Winnebago to a third dealer. The mechanic declined to perform any repairs on the motor home. The Hardys called the Winnebago hotline to see whether it was safe to continue driving the motor home. They were told that it was safe to drive the vehicle home. The Hardys returned home after putting 7,500 miles on the motor home. Hardy took the motor home to the original dealer, but he was told that it would take a few months to make the necessary repairs. Hardy demanded a refund from Winnebago. Did Hardy demonstrate revocation of acceptance? How do you think the court decided? [*Hardy v. Winnebago Industries, Inc.,* 706 A.2d 1086 (1998).]

8. Amar entered into a sales contract with the defendant, Karinol, for the purchase of electronic watches. The contract was silent as to shipping terms. However, the contract did have a notation in it stating that the goods were to be delivered to a location in Mexico. Moreover, seller Karinol put the goods into the possession of a common carrier with the instructions to deliver the goods to the plaintiff-buyer in Mexico. When the goods arrived and were opened for customs, the watches were missing. Between the buyer and the seller, who has the risk of loss? In light of these facts, is this a destination or a shipment contract? [*Pestana v. Karinol,* 367 So. 2d 1096 (1979).]

9. SMG was a frozen-poultry wholesaler, and Sanderson was one of the suppliers. SMG contracted to sell 24 containers of frozen poultry to KVADRO, a Russian company. The shipping terms were CIF (cost insurance and freight). In connection with the business, SMG acquired a one-year, open-cargo insurance policy from Lloyd's. SMG arranged for shipment to Russia though P & O Nedlloyd. In April, the Russian government suspended all previously issued permits for the import of poultry into Russia from the United States. Due to this and the change of the city to which the poultry was to be shipped, the shipment violated the 60-day rule and was subsequently seized. After the investigation ended, the shipment was released, but before it was picked up, it was seized again and SMG never received payment. SMG then filed a claim against the insurance policy with Lloyd's, which was rejected. Nedlloyd and SMG then sued each other, seeking freight charges and damages, respectively. Nedlloyd subsequently added Lloyd's to its suit, claiming to be a third-party beneficiary. Lloyd's moved for summary judgment because

Nedlloyd was not an intended third party, SMG had no insurable interest at the time, Lloyd's policy did not cover credit risk, and seizure by customs was excluded from the contract. A summary judgment was issued by the district court, claiming SMG had no insurable interest and Nedlloyd was not an intended beneficiary. The ruling was appealed by SMG. Does SMG have an insurable interest? [*Nedlloyd v. Sanderson Farms, Inc.,* 2006 U.S. App. LEXIS 22227 (2006).]

10. Marion Bottling Company bottled soft-drink beverages in Marion, Virginia, and shipped them to its warehouse in Galax for storage. The beverages were subsequently delivered from the warehouse to retailers on delivery trucks owned and operated by the bottler. Are the goods identified to the sales contract when the soft drinks are bottled in Marion or delivered from the warehouse in Galax? Which city can tax the sale? [*Marion Bottling Co. v. Town of Galax,* 195 Va. 1115, 81 S.E.2d 624 (1954).]

Looking for more review materials?

The Online Learning Center at **www.mhhe.com/kubasek3e** contains this chapter's "Assignment on the Internet" and also a list of URLs for more information, entitled "On the Internet." Find both of them in the Student Center portion of the OLC, along with quizzes and other helpful materials.

CHAPTER 23

Performance and Obligations under Sales and Leases

LEARNING OBJECTIVES

After reading this chapter, you will be able to answer the following questions:

1. What is the perfect tender rule?
2. What is the difference between conforming and nonconforming goods?
3. What is the right to cure?
4. What is a revocation of the contract as compared to rejection of nonconforming goods?
5. What is commercial impracticability?

CASE OPENER

What a Difference a Day Makes!

Founded in 1966 as a trader of oil and oil products, Vitol is a company with no external shareholders. All shareholders are also employees. It is a conglomerate company of energy companies that work in oil transportation, energy market intelligence, refining, distribution, and trading and financing.[1] It is unencumbered by external shareholders and the need to answer to analysts and investment funds. Instead, Vitol is a group of separate companies, each staffed by energy professionals with a true depth of experience in the business of oil transportation, market intelligence, refining, distribution, marketing, trading, and finance.

Vitol entered into a contract on January 13, 2000, for the delivery of oil with the defendant, Koch Petroleum Group, a component of Koch Industries, Inc., a Wichita, Kansas, private company with over $100 billion in worldwide revenues and over 70,000 employees. The sales contract required that Koch deliver 75,000 barrels of heating oil to a barge designated by Vitol within a window of time between February 3 and 5, 2000.[2] Later that January, Vitol sold the oil to a third party, Castle Oil Corporation. Castle Oil and Vitol agreed that the oil would be delivered to Castle Oil's barge on February 3, and they communicated that fact to Koch. Koch agreed. Koch was unable to deliver the oil on February 3 despite being told by Vitol that time was of the essence regarding that date for Castle Oil. Koch did deliver the oil on February 4, but that one-day difference caused

[1] See Vitol's web page at www.vitol.com/about.php.

[2] *Vitol S.A., Inc. v. Koch Petroleum Group, LP,* 2005 U.S. Dist. LEXIS 18688, 58 U.C.C. Rep. Serv. 2d (Callaghan) 2005.

Castle Oil to cancel its contract with Vitol. Castle sued Vitol for breach, and was awarded a $1.7 million arbitration judgment. Vitol then sued Koch for recovery of the $1.7 million it had to pay Castle.

The issue here is that of perfect tender. Koch claimed that it substantially complied with the contract as delivery of the oil was to be during the February 3 to 5 time window. Vitol argued that the contract was modified with Koch's acceptance to delivery specifically on February 3.

1. Did Koch's failure to deliver the oil on February 3 constitute something less than "perfect tender" and thus a breach of contract?
2. Did that one-day difference in delivery constitute a breach of the perfect tender rule?

The Wrap-Up at the end of the chapter will answer these questions.

When individuals and/or organizations like Koch Petroleum Group and Vitol enter into sales contracts or leases with others, they need to know their rights and obligations. This chapter explains the performance obligations of sellers and buyers. Additionally, it explains the performance obligations of lessors and lessees, which are similar to those of buyers and sellers. The chapter explains the perfect tender rule and exceptions to this rule. It also explains the buyer's general obligation to inspect, pay for, and accept goods, and it discusses exceptions to this general obligation.

The Basic Performance Obligation

The obligations of sellers/lessors and buyers/lessees are determined by (1) terms the parties outline in agreements, (2) custom, and (3) rules outlined by the Uniform Commercial Code (UCC). This chapter focuses on rules outlined by the UCC.

Under the UCC, sellers and lessors are *obligated to transfer and deliver conforming goods.* Buyers and lessees are *obligated to accept and pay for conforming goods in accordance with the contract.* Courts rely on UCC rules to clarify these obligations when the contract or lease the parties agreed to is unclear. In the Case Opener, Koch is obligated to deliver oil to a barge designated by Vitol. The window for such delivery is February 3 to 5, 2000. Vitol claims that it has the right to indicate within that time frame the exact date of delivery. It notifies Koch that delivery must be made on February 3. Koch does not make the delivery until February 4. Has Koch breached the contract under the perfect tender rule? Is there perhaps some kind of mistake or misunderstanding between Vitol and Koch? If so, is that material to determining breach of contract? Did Koch act in good faith? If so, does that mitigate the delay of one day? Consider the nearby Case Nugget as you think about these issues.

GOOD FAITH

UCC Section 1-203 requires **good faith** in the performance and enforcement of every contract. Good faith means *honesty in fact.* When the parties are merchants, the UCC imposes a higher standard. Between merchants, the UCC imposes not only honesty in fact but also reasonable commercial standards of fair dealing. This second requirement is often called **commercial reasonableness.** In the context of good faith, courts decide the specific

CASE NUGGET

MISTAKE AND UNCONSCIONABILITY

Donovan v. RRL Corporation
26 Cal. 4th 261 (2001)

The Donovans showed up at the defendant car dealership. After hearing the sales pitch, Mr. Donovan stated that he'd take the car at the price quoted in the newspaper, $25,995. The horrified salesman said that he could go as low as $37,995 but not $25,995. At that point, Donovan showed the salesman a copy of an ad that had been running in the local newspaper identifying the very same automobile for $25,995. The salesman responded that the advertisement had to be a mistake. Donovan said that he wanted the car at the $25,995 price. He subsequently brought an action in the municipal court in Orange County. The trial court found for RRL Corp. on mistake. However, the California court of appeals reversed, stating that all the material elements of a contract were clearly stated in the advertisement and that Donovan's acceptance of those terms constituted a good contract.

The California Supreme Court heard the case, reversing it on a combination of mistake and unconscionability. The supreme court found that a contract was indeed created but that the contract could be rescinded since the evidence showed (1) the defendant's unilateral mistake was made in good faith; (2) the defendant did not bear the risk of the mistake; and (3) the enforcement of a contract with an erroneous price would be unconscionable as a matter of law.

obligations of sellers/lessors and buyers/lessees. The next few sections of the chapter discuss these specific obligations.

Specific Obligations of Sellers and Lessors

THE PERFECT TENDER RULE

The UCC requires that sellers and lessors tender conforming goods to the buyer or lessee. UCC Sections 2-503(1) and 2A-508(1) state that **tender of delivery** requires that the seller/lessor have and hold conforming goods at the disposal of the buyer/lessee and give the buyer/lessee reasonable notification to enable him or her to take delivery. **Conforming goods** are goods that conform to contract specifications.

L01 What is the perfect tender rule?

A common law rule known as the **perfect tender rule** required that the seller deliver goods in conformity with the terms of the contract, right down to the last detail. UCC Sections 2-601 and 2A-509 embrace the perfect tender rule. These sections indicate that if goods or tender of delivery fail *in any respect* to conform to the contract, the buyer/lessee has the right to accept the goods, reject the entire shipment, or accept part and reject part. Common law usually substitutes perfect tender with the doctrine of substantial performance. *Substantial performance* occurs when all the material elements of a contract are satisfied even if some nonmaterial requirements may not be satisfied. The perfect tender rule would not recognize the distinction between material and immaterial contractual requirements.

L02 What is the difference between conforming and nonconforming goods?

To see how the concept of customized purchases is especially significant in Internet marketing, please see the **Connecting to the Core** activity on the text website at www.mhhe.com/kubasek3e.

Legal Principle: The UCC and common law differ, with the UCC requiring perfect tender and common law requiring the lesser standard of substantial performance.

BUT WHAT IF . . .

WHAT IF THE FACTS OF THE CASE OPENER WERE DIFFERENT?

Let's say, in the Case Opener, that Vitol made a delivery of barrels of oil to Castle and the time and place of the delivery were exactly as stated in the contract. However, the proper packaging that Castle stipulated was not used, even though no barrels were broken. What would the perfect tender rule say about the legality of this situation?

Consider Case 23-1, which provides an illustration of a situation in which the UCC version of the perfect tender rule was relevant when compared to the common law rule of material breach under the doctrine of substantial performance.

EXCEPTIONS TO THE PERFECT TENDER RULE

The perfect tender rule is not as inflexible as it appears. Although the rule itself demands perfection, both courts and UCC drafters have created exceptions that reduce the rule's rigidity. These exceptions limit the seller's obligation to deliver conforming goods and/or limit the buyer's power to reject goods that do not conform. This section of the chapter

CASE 23-1 ALASKA PACIFIC TRADING CO. v. EAGON FOREST PRODUCTS INC.

WASHINGTON APPELLATE DIVISION 1

933 P.2D 417 (1997)

Alaska Pacific Trading Company (ALPAC) and Eagon Forest Products, Inc. (Eagon), contracted to buy and sell raw logs. ALPAC and Eagon engaged in months of communications about a shipment of 15,000 cubic meters of logs from Argentina to Korea between the end of July and the end of August 1993. The delivery date passed without ALPAC shipping the logs. Eagon canceled the contract, alleging that ALPAC had breached the agreement by failing to deliver. ALPAC alleged that its failure to deliver was not a material breach and that the parties had modified the delivery date. Alternatively, ALPAC argued that Eagon breached the contract by failing to provide adequate assurances or repudiating the contract. The miscommunication between the parties occurred after the market for logs began to soften, making the contract less attractive to Eagon. ALPAC was reluctant to ship the goods because it was concerned that Eagon might not accept the shipment. However, Eagon never stated that it would not accept the cargo.

In the ruling below, the judge decides whether ALPAC breached the contract. ALPAC wants the court to rely on the common law doctrine of material breach under the doctrine of substantial performance, while Eagon wants the court to rely on the UCC's perfect tender rule. If the court decides to apply UCC rules, and if ALPAC failed to deliver, Eagon would be allowed to "reject the whole."

JUDGE AGID: ALPAC's first contention is that it did not breach the contract by failing to timely deliver the logs because time of delivery was not a material term of the contract. ALPAC relies on common law contract cases to support its position that, when the parties have not indicated that time is of the essence, late delivery is not a material breach which excuses the buyer's duty to accept the goods. . . . However, as a contract for the sale of goods, this contract is governed by the Uniform Commercial Code, Article II (UCC II) which replaced the common law of material breach, on which ALPAC relies, with the "perfect tender" rule. Under this rule, "If the goods or the tender of delivery fail in any respect to conform to the contract, the buyer may . . . reject the whole." . . . Both the plain language of the rule and the official comments clearly state that, if the tender of the goods differs from the terms of the contract in any way, the seller breaches the contract and the buyer is released from its duty to accept the goods. . . . ALPAC does not dispute that the contract specified a date for shipment or that the logs were not shipped by that date. Thus, under the perfect tender rule, ALPAC breached its duty under the contract and released Eagon from its duty to accept the logs.

AFFIRMED.

CRITICAL THINKING

Here, Eagon got lucky. The company got out of a contract that was unfavorable to it, given the softening market for logs. In what way did Judge Agid simplify the case? Is it fair to say the judge oversimplified the case?

ETHICAL DECISION MAKING

What ethical norm or value underlies Judge Agid's decision? Explain.

explains the six most important exceptions to the perfect tender rule. These exceptions allow sellers/lessors and buyers/lessees to ask questions such as:

- What are the norms in the particular industry and/or what past dealings have the parties had with one another?
- What does the parties' agreement say?
- Is it possible for the seller/lessor to cure or correct the problems?
- What if the goods have been destroyed?
- What if nonconformity substantially impairs the value of the goods?
- What if unforeseen circumstances make contract performance commercially impracticable?

Consider the flowchart in Exhibit 23-1 on the next page.

Norms in the Industry and Past Dealings between the Parties. The perfect tender rule will always be interpreted both in light of what is expected in the industry and within the context of past dealings between the parties. When the buyer alleges that goods failed to conform to contract specifications, the buyer does not automatically have the right to reject the goods. The UCC requires that courts consider norms in a particular trade. Sometimes, the norms for a particular trade do not permit a buyer to reject goods with minor flaws. UCC Section 1-205(2) defines **usage of trade** as any practice that members of an industry expect to be part of their dealings.

In addition to its requirement on usage of trade, the UCC requires that courts consider the ideas of course of dealing and course of performance. UCC 1-205(1) defines **course of dealing** as previous commercial transactions between the same parties. Under UCC 208(1), **course of performance** refers to the history of dealings between the parties in the particular contract at issue. This rule states that when a contract for sale involves repeated occasions for performance by either party with the other's knowledge of the nature of the performance and opportunity for objection to it, any course of performance accepted or acquiesced to without objection is relevant to determine what the parties' agreement means.

BUT WHAT IF . . .

WHAT IF THE FACTS OF THE CASE OPENER WERE DIFFERENT?

Let's say, in the Case Opener, that Castle Oil and Vitol had a long history of working together to deliver oil to various Castle locations. During these interactions Vitol had a history of using Koch to deliver the oil, and Koch was typically a day or two late delivering the oil but Castle never minded. In what way would the perfect tender rule be affected in light of this information?

Exceptions Outlined in the Parties' Agreement. Sometimes, language in the parties' agreement limits the rigidity of the perfect tender rule. For instance, parties may agree that the seller must have the opportunity to repair or replace nonconforming goods within a particular period of time. Alternatively, parties may agree with a level of performance that is less than perfect. They could indicate, by agreement, the expectation regarding performance.

LO3 What is the right to cure?

The Seller's/Lessor's Right to Cure. Under UCC Sections 2-508 and 2A-513, sellers and lessors have the right to **cure** or fix problems with nonconforming goods.

E-COMMERCE AND THE LAW

UCITA

The Uniform Computer Information Transactions Act (UCITA) is a proposed model law under review in several states. UCITA outlines a framework to govern software licenses. Software vendors such as Microsoft are generally in favor of UCITA because this model legislation protects software vendors.

One important way in which UCITA protects software vendors is that it makes sure perfect tender rules that generally apply to the sale of goods do not apply to software. UCITA's rules change when and why a consumer of software can reject a defective product. For example, if a software transaction involves a negotiated contract, UCITA eliminates customers' rights to inspect a product on delivery and reject it for any defects that do not conform to the requirements of the contract. Instead, a buyer of software must prove that the defect represents a material breach of the contract.

Source: Ed Foster, "The Gripe Line," *Info World,* July 3, 2000; and Jeff Moad, "If It Works for Microsoft, Does It Work for You?" *Eweek* (from ZD Wire), May 18, 2001.

In particular, sellers and lessors can repair, adjust, or replace defective or nonconforming goods as long as they give prompt notice of the intent to cure and go ahead and cure within the contract time for performance.

Under UCC 2-508(2) and 2A-513(2), the seller or lessor can still exercise the right to cure once the contract time for performance has passed as long as the seller or lessor has reasonable grounds to believe that the nonconforming tender would be acceptable to the buyer or lessee. In Case 23-2, the court decides whether a seller should have been allowed the right to cure and what consequence the court should impose if a buyer fails to give the seller this opportunity.

Legal Principle: **The right to cure is nearly always applicable to nonconforming goods.**

Destroyed Goods. Under UCC Sections 2-613 and 2A-221, if goods are identified at the time the parties entered into a contract and these goods are destroyed through no fault of the parties before risk passes to the buyer or lessee, the parties are excused from performance. If the goods are only partially destroyed, the buyer can inspect the goods and decide whether to (1) treat the contract as void or (2) ask the seller for a reduction of the contract price and then accept the damaged goods.

Exhibit 23-1

When Lack of Perfect Tender Is Not Fatal to the Contract

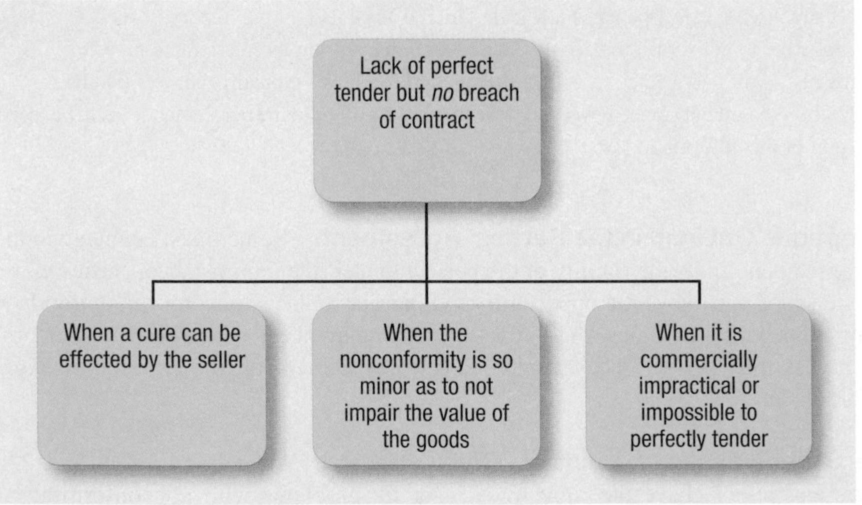

CASE 23-2 DEJESUS v. CAT AUTO TECH. CORP.
NEW YORK CITY CIVIL COURT
615 N.Y.S.2D 236 N.Y. CITY CIV. CT. (1994)

Cat Auto Tech. Corp. purchased 10,000 gift certificates from DeJesus. Cat Auto Tech. Corp., an Amoco gasoline station operator, contracted with DeJesus to make 10,000 gift certificates of various denominations, with the Amoco gasoline name and logo on them, stapled together in booklets that included approximately eight gift certificates in each. Delivery was to be within two weeks. Montefiore Hospital had wanted to give these gift certificates to their employees as a Christmas gift.

Michael DiBarro, president of Cat Auto Tech. Corp., stated that the finished product differed from the sample DeJesus had provided in two respects: the paper was different, and the sample contained a decorative border, whereas the finished product did not. Additionally, DiBarro complained that the logo colors were not within the printed borders of the Amoco logo. When the court looked at the certificates, it noted that within a book of gift certificates, two of the eight certificates had colors immediately outside the borders. On one, the problem was slightly noticeable, and on the other, the court could notice the problem only when it inspected closely. DeJesus stated that DiBarro had accepted these minor changes, and that any minor defects were insignificant.

DeJesus delivered the goods to the Cat Auto Tech. Corp. approximately two weeks after the agreed upon delivery date. DiBarro accepted the delivery and paid by check. He did not inspect the certificates at the time of delivery or before he paid. He inspected the certificates a day later, placed a stop payment order on the check without notifying DeJesus, and did not let DeJesus know why he was stopping payment on the check. DeJesus did not know of the stop payment until she eventually received a notice from her bank that she had insufficient funds in her account.

DeJesus wants Cat Auto Tech. Corp. to pay the balance due on the contract, and asks the court to clarify the seller's right to cure defects in nonconforming goods.

JUDGE LUCINDO SUAREZ: . . . UCC 2-601 provides that "if the goods . . . fail in any respect to conform to the contract, the buyer may . . . reject the whole. . . ." . . . New York subscribe[s] to the perfect tender rule, which allows a buyer to reject goods that fail to conform to the contract. UCC 2-602(1) provides the manner to accomplish an effective rejection: Rejection of goods must be within a reasonable time after their delivery or tender. It is ineffective unless the buyer seasonably notifies the seller.

An effective rejection requires the buyer to seasonably notify the seller, even though the delivery is of wholly nonconforming goods. In the case at bar delivery was made two weeks after the date called for in the contract. Defendant buyer paid for the goods by check, inspected them the next day and issued a stop payment order on the check. The time to cure a defective tender, if at all, was immediate. The buyer's notification of its rejection by a stop payment order on its draft was not seasonable, nor within a reasonable time. . . . Indeed, no reasonable attempt on the part of the buyer to notify the seller was undertaken. . . .

The purpose of notification is to afford the seller the opportunity to cure, or to permit the seller to minimize her losses, such as providing a decrease in the price. This opportunity was never afforded to the seller. The perfect tender rule is limited by the seller's ability to cure, which is conditioned upon receipt of notice. UCC 2-508 provides: (1) Where . . . tender . . . by the seller is rejected because nonconforming and the time for performance has not yet expired, the seller may seasonably notify the buyer of his intention to cure and may then, within the contract time, make a conforming delivery. (2) Where the buyer rejects a nonconforming tender which the seller had reasonable grounds to believe would be acceptable with or without the money allowance, the seller may, if he seasonably notifies the buyer, have a further reasonable time to substitute a conforming tender.

Defendant's payment for the goods without inspection on the day of delivery, approximately two weeks after the time called for by the contract, effectively waived the performance provisions of the contract regarding the time of delivery. . . . Therefore, the time within which to perform having expired, subdivision (2) must be referenced. However, subdivision (2) by implication is only applicable if there has been an effective rejection, which is not the case herein.

Defendant's payment by check for the goods upon their delivery provided the plaintiff with a measure of reliance that the same would be acceptable. Defendant's failure to properly notify plaintiff of the nonconformity effectively prevented plaintiff from an opportunity to cure any defects, within the time limitations of this case, and therefore defendant's actions cannot be considered to have effectively rejected the goods herein.

Judgment is awarded in favor of plaintiff in the amount of $1,252.00, representing the balance due and owing under the contract with interest from December 7, 1993.

Judgment for plaintiff.

[continued]

CRITICAL THINKING

In Chapter 1, you learned of the importance of a particular set of facts in determining the outcome of a case. If you could change one fact in this case to make it more likely the judge would rule in favor of Cat Auto Tech. Corp., which fact would you change? Explain.

ETHICAL DECISION MAKING

Apply the universalization test to the outcome of this case. Does the universalization test support Justice Suarez's decision?

BUT WHAT IF . . .

WHAT IF THE FACTS OF THE CASE OPENER WERE DIFFERENT?

Let's say, in the Case Opener, that Castle Oil was to inspect barrels of oil that were to be shipped to one of Castle's locations by Vitol. A representative inspected the oil purchased by Castle, which was being kept in a warehouse. The morning that the oil was to be shipped to Castle, the warehouse caught fire and the oil that had been purchased was destroyed. Is Vitol still obligated to deliver the same amount of oil to Castle's designated location that day?

LO4 What is a revocation of the contract as compared to rejection of nonconforming goods?

Substantial Impairment. Two sections of the UCC use the concept of substantial impairment to modify the perfect tender rule. The first applies when a buyer *revokes acceptance of goods.* UCC Section 2-608 indicates that the buyer who has accepted goods may later revoke the acceptance only if the buyer can show that the defects substantially impair the value of the goods. The second applies when the buyer and seller have entered into an *installment contract.* UCC Sections 2-612(2) and 2A-510(1) indicate that if a buyer/lessee rejects an installment of a particular item, that buyer/lessee may do so only if the defects substantially impair the value of the goods and cannot be cured.

LO5 What is commercial impracticability?

Commercial Impracticability. UCC Sections 2-615(a) and 2A-405(a) state that a delay in delivery or nondelivery, in whole or in part, is not a breach in circumstances in which performance has been made impracticable because a contingency has occurred that was not contemplated when the parties reached an agreement. For example, this rule would be relevant if a change in government regulation that neither party contemplated forbids the import or export of a particular item the parties had agreed would be shipped.

Specific Obligations of Buyers and Lessees

THE BASIC OBLIGATION: INSPECTION, PAYMENT, AND ACCEPTANCE

Under UCC Sections 2-301 and 2A-516(1), buyers and lessees are obligated to accept and pay for conforming goods in accordance with the contract. Before paying for and accepting the goods, buyers/lessees ordinarily inspect the goods to make sure they conform to the specifications in the parties' agreement.

EXCEPTIONS TO THE BASIC OBLIGATION

Buyers/lessees do not always end up accepting and paying for goods. Sometimes, on inspection, the buyer or lessee decides to reject the goods and refrain from paying for them. We have already seen that happen in cases earlier in the chapter. In this section, we

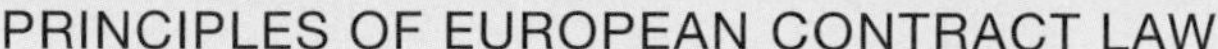

COMPARING THE LAW OF OTHER COUNTRIES

PRINCIPLES OF EUROPEAN CONTRACT LAW

For almost a century, U.S. law has been fortunate to find guidance in something known as the Restatements of the Law. The American Law Institute (ALI), created in 1923, has been publishing these "soft-law" books for nearly 100 years. The Restatements are *soft law* because they are not enacted statutorily but nonetheless influence U.S. courts, judges, and practitioners. The Restatement of Contracts has been enormously influential as soft law. "The ALI's aim is to distill the 'black letter law' from cases, to indicate a trend in common law, and, occasionally, to recommend what a rule of law should be. In essence, [the Restatements] restate existing common law into a series of principles or rules."*

In 2000, Europe began crafting its own version of the Restatement of Contracts: the Principles of European Contract Law, or PECL. The PECL aids in the current debate of whether European nations need a comprehensive statutory code beyond the CISG. The debate is ongoing, and the resolution waits to be seen.†

* See http://libguides.law.harvard.edu/content.php?pid=103327&sid=1036651.

† See Ole Lando and Hugh Beale, *Principles of European Contract Law,* Parts I and II (Commission on European Contract Law, 2000), p. xxiv; and Carlo Castronovo, "Contract and the Idea of Codification in the Principles of European Contract Law," in Ole Lando, *Festskrift,* 1997, pp. 109–124.

take a look at exceptions to the buyer's/lessee's basic obligation. These exceptions allow sellers/lessors and buyers/lessees to ask questions such as:

- What forms of payment are allowed under the UCC?
- In what circumstances can a buyer reject goods?
- Is the buyer allowed to accept part but not all of the goods?
- In what circumstances can a buyer revoke acceptance of goods?
- How and when can a buyer reject nonconforming goods?
- Are installment contracts treated differently than other kinds of contracts?

This section of the chapter answers the questions listed above in three subsections that cover (1) problems on inspection, (2) problems with acceptance, and (3) rescission or revocation of acceptance by the buyer or lessee. Note that this section asks these questions from the buyer's perspective.

Problems on Inspection. If all goes well in a transaction over the sale or lease of goods, the buyer or lessee inspects the goods and then pays by any means the parties have agreed on, including payment by cash, check, or credit card. Unless the parties have agreed otherwise, the buyer or lessee typically inspects the goods before paying. Under UCC Sections 2-513(1) and 2A-515(1), the seller or lessor must provide an opportunity for inspection before enforcing payment.

The concept of reasonableness governs the inspection process. For example, inspection must take place at a reasonable time and place, in a reasonable way. Once the buyer or lessee inspects the goods, he or she decides whether to accept the goods. Sometimes, on inspection, the buyer or lessee decides not to accept the goods. (See Exhibit 23-2 on the next page.) For instance, in Case 23-2, Cat Auto Tech. Corp. inspected the gift certificates and decided it did not want to accept the goods. When, on inspection, the buyer or lessee determines that there may be a problem with the goods, he or she wants to know what circumstances allow a buyer or lessee to reject goods. Of course, if the goods are conforming, the buyer or lessee wants to know how to communicate acceptance.

Legal Principle: **The right to inspect is seldom waived or held by courts to have been waived unless the buyer expressly waives the right.**

Problems with Acceptance. When all goes well, UCC Sections 2-606(1) and 2A-515(1b)(a) indicate that the buyer or lessee, after inspecting, signifies agreement to the seller or lessor that the goods are either (1) conforming or (2) acceptable even though they are nonconforming. UCC Sections 2-602(1), 2-606(1), and 2A-515(1)(b) allow the seller

CASE NUGGET

"WHERE'S THE BEEF?"

Chicago Prime Packers v. Northam Food Trading
U.S. Court of Appeals for the Seventh Circuit
408 F.3d 894, 2005 U.S. App. LEXIS 9355

Chicago Prime Packers, the seller, sued Northam Food Trading, the buyer, for breach of contract. At the district level, Chicago Prime was awarded the contract price plus interest. Northam appealed. Neither party was arguing that any fact found by the district court was clearly erroneous, and therefore the appeal was one based on law. On April 24, 2001, Northam had the shipping company Brown Brother's Shipping pick up 40,500 pounds of ribs from Chicago Prime. Brown Brother's signed a bill of lading indicating that the goods were in apparent good order. However, the bill of lading did state that the "contents and condition of contents of packages [were] unknown." Upon delivery, Northam signed a second bill of lading, again stating that the goods were in apparent good order, except for other issues not related to the case. The contract stated that payment was to be mailed before or on May 1, 2001. When no payment was received by May 4, Chicago Prime called Northam and demanded payment. The employee who negotiated the contract for Northam was unaware of any reason why payment would not have been made. As a result of an inspection by the U.S. Department of Agriculture, the entire shipment was deemed condemned, with no salvage value. Although this was not done until May 7, 2001, it was the opinion of the federal inspector that the shipment was contaminated when it arrived. When Chicago Prime became aware of this, it continued to demand payment.

The district court had ruled that Northam had to prove not only that the shipment was contaminated at the time it arrived but also that an inspection had been done as soon as commercially reasonable. The district court further ruled that Northam had failed in its obligation to do so and therefore lost the case and was obligated to pay. The contract was governed by CISG due to its international nature. Although CISG governed this contract, CISG is based on UCC Article 2 and therefore, although Article 2 was not per se applicable, the majority opinion still used it for guidance on the case. The appeals court cited case law in saying that the CISG does give the buyer the burden of proof. While this would have been enough to rule in favor of Northam, the court went on to say that Northam had failed to prove that the goods were contaminated at the time of delivery. Therefore, the appeals court upheld the ruling, and Northam was obligated to pay the price of the contract plus prejudgment interest.

or lessor to presume acceptance if the buyer or lessee fails to reject the goods within a reasonable period of time. Sometimes, there is confusion about whether the buyer or lessee has accepted the goods.

Exhibit 23-2

How the Concept of Reasonableness Governs the Inspection Process

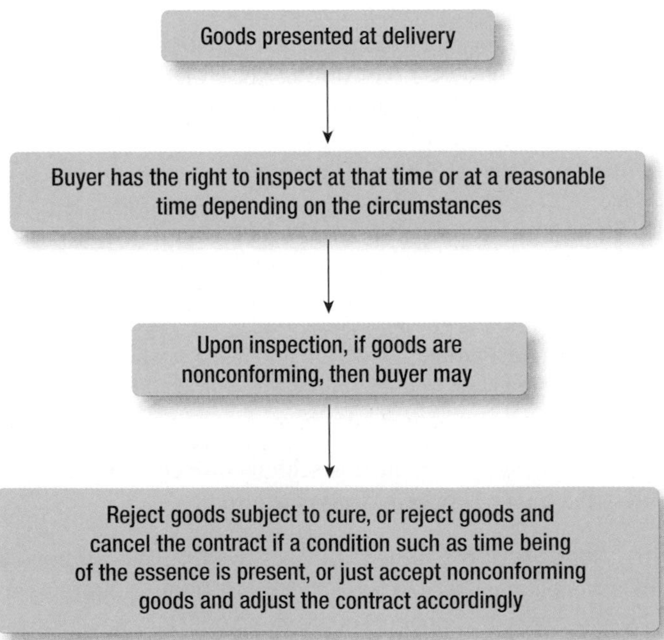

BUT WHAT IF . . .

WHAT IF THE FACTS OF THE CASE OPENER WERE DIFFERENT?

Let's say, in the Case Opener, that Castle was trying to plan an inspection of oil it wanted to buy from Vitol. Castle was attempting to plan an inspection, but the two companies could not reach an agreement regarding a time and place for the inspection. If the two companies looked into the laws surrounding inspection, what guiding framework would they come across in regard to scheduling an inspection of goods?

UCC Sections 2-601(c) and 2A-509(1) allow the buyer or lessee to make a partial acceptance when the goods are nonconforming and the seller or lessor has failed to cure the defects. When goods are nonconforming, the buyer or lessee is allowed to revoke or withdraw acceptance of the goods. The previous section on specific obligations of sellers/lessors discussed this concept under the topic of substantial impairment. From the buyer's/lessee's perspective, the buyer or lessee may revoke acceptance if the nonconformity substantially impairs the value of the goods but only if he or she had a legitimate reason for the initial acceptance.

Rescission or Revocation of Acceptance by Buyer. Cases in which a buyer decides to assert his or her right to reject nonconforming goods are often categorized under the heading "rescission or revocation of acceptance by buyer." Case 23-3 is one in which a buyer with an installment contract decided to reject nonconforming goods. Rescission or revocation of acceptance by the buyer is the primary subject of the case. The case provides a good review of a wide range of topics that fall under the subject of performance and obligation. Note how the case includes the concept of good faith. This chapter started with the concept of good faith, and it will end with the same topic. It is always good to remember the context in which courts judge the extent to which a buyer or seller has met his or her contractual obligations.

CASE 23-3 HUBBARD v. UTZ QUALITY FOODS, INC.

U.S. DISTRICT COURT (W.D.N.Y.)
903 F. SUPP. 444 (1995)

In this case, a dispute arose between a potato farmer, David Hubbard (Hubbard), and UTZ Quality Foods, Inc. (UTZ), over whether UTZ was within its legal rights when it decided to rescind or revoke acceptance of potatoes supplied by Hubbard. UTZ claims that the potatoes Hubbard supplied failed to meet the quality standards outlined in the parties' agreement.

In particular, UTZ claimed the potatoes did not meet the color standards outlined in the agreement. UTZ did not want dark potato chips, so it demanded that the potatoes had to be the whitest or lightest possible color. Potato color is defined from designation No. 1 (best or lightest) to 5 (the darkest). UTZ's contract indicated that potatoes must meet at least the No. 2 color standards. UTZ contends that the potatoes do not meet this standard, while Hubbard contends that UTZ is arbitrarily refusing to accept his potatoes. The court states that "this case turns on matters of law relating to the rights of a buyer, such as UTZ, to reject a seller's goods that are deemed to be nonconforming." In the case below, the court explores UTZ's rights.

JUDGE SPAETH: . . . The primary legal issue in this matter is whether UTZ's rejection of Hubbard's potatoes was proper or wrongful. It is clear that this transaction is a sale of goods governed by New York Uniform Commercial Code (UCC) . . . both Hubbard and UTZ are "merchants." . . . It is also clear that the contract between the parties is an "installment contract." . . . [C]oncerning payment, [the contract] states that "[b]uyer agrees to pay for all potatoes accepted within 30 days of acceptance. . . ." This language suggests paying per shipment, since each shipment is subject to inspection (and acceptance). . . .

[continued]

Clearly this is an "installment" contract as defined in UCC 2-612(1).

As an installment contract, the question of whether UTZ's rejection was wrongful or proper is governed by UCC 2-612(2) and (3). UCC 2-612(2) states that a "buyer may reject any installment which is nonconforming if the nonconformity substantially impairs the value of that installment and cannot be cured. . . ." UCC 2-612(3) states that "whenever nonconformity or default with respect to one or more installments substantially impairs the value of the whole contract there is a breach of the whole."

The purpose of this "substantial impairment" requirement is "to preclude a party from canceling a contract for trivial defects." In this case, UTZ rejected Hubbard's potatoes based upon their failure to satisfy the color standard set forth in paragraph 3(c) of the contract. Thus, the issue for me to decide is whether the failure of Hubbard's potatoes to meet the required #1 or #2 color minimum constitutes a "substantial impairment" of the installments.

Whether goods conform to contract terms is a question of fact. Moreover, in determining whether goods conform to contract terms, a buyer is bound by the "good faith" requirements set forth in NYUCC 1-203—"Every . . . duty within this Act imposes an obligation of good faith in its enforcement or performance." Thus, UTZ's determination that Hubbard's potatoes failed to satisfy the contract terms must be fairly reached.

The UTZ-Hubbard contract contains many specific requirements regarding the quality of the potatoes. In paragraph 1 the contract states that "only specified varieties as stated in contract will be accepted. . . ." Paragraph 3(a) states that "All shipments shall meet the United States Standards for Grades of Potatoes for Chipping, USDA, January 1978 . . ., in addition to other provisions enumerated in this 'Section 3,' loads that do not meet these standards may be subject to rejection. . . ." Paragraph 3(b) sets forth specific size requirements . . .; paragraph 3(c) sets forth specific gravity requirements; paragraph 3(d) contains the color requirements at issue in this case; and paragraph 3(f) sets forth a number of other defects or incidents of improper treatment or handling of the potatoes that provide UTZ with the right to reject the potatoes.

Clearly, the quality standards are of great importance to UTZ. They are the most detailed aspect of the contract—far more so than timing or even quantity specifications.

In a contract of this type, where the quality standards are set forth with great specificity, the failure to satisfy one of the specifically enumerated standards is a "substantial impairment." UTZ obviously cares the most about the specific quality specifications, as is evident from the numerous references throughout the contact.

Additionally, I find that UTZ's determination that the potatoes did not meet the required #2 color standard was made in good faith, as required by UCC 1-203. As noted above, the manner of visual testing utilized by UTZ was reasonable and customary. Further, Smith and DeGroft, the UTZ testers who rejected Hubbard's potatoes, provided credible testimony about their respective experience (Smith—30 years, DeGroft—5–6 years) and method of making such determinations. Accordingly, I find that UTZ fairly and in good faith determined that Hubbard's potatoes were nonconforming.

Thus, I find that Hubbard's failure to meet the proper color standard amounted to a "substantial impairment" of the installments (2-612(2)), substantially impairing the whole contract (2-612(3)). Accordingly, I find that UTZ's rejection of Hubbard's potatoes was proper. . . .

Judgment for defendant.

CRITICAL THINKING

The court tells us that the purpose of the substantial-impairment requirement is to preclude a party from canceling a contract for trivial defects. Then the court considers whether UTZ canceled the contract for trivial defects. Explain the relationship between the court's explanation of the purpose of the substantial-impairment requirement and the concept of good faith.

ETHICAL DECISION MAKING

Both parties probably prefer the ethical norm or value of security. How so? Which facts would each party highlight in explaining how a particular decision would enhance the value of security?

CASE NUGGET

WHAT IS "REASONABLE TIME" FOR ACCEPTANCE OF GOODS?

SCM Group, USA, Inc., v. Custom Designs & Manufacturing Co., Inc.
U.S. Court of Appeals for the Third Circuit
89 Fed. Appx. 779, 2004 U.S. App. LEXIS 2419

The plaintiff, SCM, is the manufacturer and distributor of various woodworking machinery. The defendant, Custom Designs and Manufacturing (CDM) Company, Inc., is in the business of designing and manufacturing custom kitchen cabinetry. SCM and CDM are both sophisticated businesses in the woodworking industry, having peculiar knowledge, skill, and expertise regarding the machinery and equipment attributable to merchants in that industry.

At a point in the summer of 2000, CDM expressed an interest in purchasing a computer-controlled router from SCM that could meet certain criteria. On September 21, 2000, SCM submitted its final proposal. Delivery of the router was forecast during the first half of December, and the order of confirmation was required in writing along with the down payment. The offer to sell was signed on behalf of SCM and dated September 22, 2000. It was signed on behalf of CDM and accepted on September 22, 2000, along with the initial payment of $63,600. The CDM acceptance was faxed to SCM with handwritten changes in the payment terms. The router was delivered at the end of December 2000. At the time, the Cabinet Vision software was not in place, pursuant to a separate contract CDM had with Cabinet Vision. SCM installed the router in January 2001 at CDM. At the time, the second payment of $84,800, due prior to shipment, had not been made by CDM. Thereafter, CDM refused to pay the 40 percent payment and refused to make a final payment of 30 percent that was due, depending on the judicial determination of the contract terms.

On appeal the court held that under Pennsylvania law, a reasonable time for inspection after tender or delivery for rejection or revocation of defective goods

> is generally deemed a question of fact to be resolved by the fact finder. Nevertheless, we find here that, as a matter of law, CDM has accepted the goods.
>
> First, CDM clearly had more than a reasonable opportunity to inspect and reject the goods. The Router was delivered in December 2000. By the time of the judgment in this case, CDM had had more than a reasonable amount of time for CDM to determine if the Router was satisfactory. Second, CDM never made an effective rejection of the Router. Thus, as a matter of law, it has accepted the Router and must pay the contractual price for it plus any damages that resulted from its breach of the contract.

CASE OPENER WRAP-UP

What a Difference a Day Makes!

In our opening case, *Vitol v. Koch Petroleum Group,*[3] Vitol had purchased 75,000 barrels of oil from Koch Petroleum to be delivered within the three-day window of February 3 to 5, 2000. The contract also stated that Vitol could designate the date, as long as it was in the three-day window, and location of the delivery. Before delivery of the oil, Vitol sold the oil to Castle Oil. Vitol informed Koch of this and indicated to Koch that delivery must be made on February 3 at Castle's barge in the port. Koch acknowledged this information. It was crucial that Castle receive the oil on February 3. Koch attempted delivery on February 4, but by that time Castle had "covered" its contract with Vitol and procured replacement oil. This cost Castle more than $1 million, and Castle obtained an arbitration judgment against Vitol for that amount. Vitol then sued Koch for its loss due to Koch's breach of contract with Castle. The court found that Koch had indeed violated the perfect tender rule. Since the contract allowed Vitol to set the exact date and location of the delivery, any deviation from the terms designated was indeed a breach of the perfect tender rule and a breach of contract. Koch was liable to Vitol for its loss.

[3] 58 U.C.C. Rep. Serv. 2d (Callaghan) 545 (2005).

KEY TERMS

commercial reasonableness 514	course of dealing 517	cure 517	tender of delivery 515
conforming goods 515	course of performance 517	good faith 514	usage of trade 517
		perfect tender rule 515	

SUMMARY OF KEY TOPICS

The Basic Performance Obligation

Under the UCC, sellers and lessors are obligated to *transfer and deliver conforming goods.*

Buyers and lessees are obligated to *accept and pay for conforming goods* in accordance with the contract.

The UCC requires *good faith* in the performance and enforcement of every contract.

Specific Obligations of Sellers and Lessors

The *perfect tender rule* indicates that if goods or tender of delivery fail in any respect to conform to the contract, the buyer/lessee has the right to accept the goods, reject the entire shipment, or accept part and reject part.

Exceptions to the perfect tender rule allow sellers/lessors and buyers/lessees to consider:

- Norms in the industry and past dealings between the parties.
- Exceptions outlined in the parties' agreement.
- The seller's/lessor's right to cure.
- Excuse from performance when identified goods are destroyed through no fault of the parties.
- The concept of substantial impairment as it relates to revocation of acceptance and installment contracts.
- The concept of commercial impracticability.

Specific Obligations of Buyers and Lessees

If all goes well in a transaction over the sale or lease of goods, the buyer or lessee inspects the goods and then *pays* according to the agreement.

The seller or lessor must provide an opportunity for *inspection.*

- The concept of reasonableness governs the inspection process.
- After inspection, the buyer or lessee decides whether to accept the goods.

After inspecting, the buyer/lessee signifies *acceptance* or partial acceptance.

- Sellers or lessors sometimes presume acceptance.
- Partial acceptance is allowed in some circumstances.
- Buyers or lessees are allowed to revoke or withdraw acceptance of nonconforming goods.
- Buyers or lessees must issue reasonable notice if they decide to reject goods.

Cases in which a buyer decides to assert his or her right to reject nonconforming goods are often categorized under the heading "rescission or revocation of acceptance by buyer."

POINT / COUNTERPOINT

Should "Cure" Be a Required Condition of a UCC Sale?	
YES	**NO**
Unless there are truly extenuating circumstances, such as time being of the essence, it is accepted that a breaching seller has the right to cure the defect or nonconformity in the goods before the buyer is permitted to revoke the contract. This is consistent with the UCC underlying position that every reasonable means should be taken to protect the integrity of the underlying contract and allow the agreed-on transaction to proceed to fruition. In other words, this rule or practice enforces commercial transactions. This is consistent with the thrust of the UCC in such areas as filling gaps in open contractual terms, utilizing reasonableness when a standard of care is left open, and assuming that the parties intend to be bound, even if the terms are incomplete (in direct contrast to common law). Therefore, in the absence of terms to the contrary, cure should always be allowed when reasonably practical.	When goods are delivered to the buyer and the goods are nonconforming, the option should rest with the nonbreaching buyer as to whether cure should be permitted or not. In terms of the UCC's insistence on the perfect tender rule, the UCC requires that ordered goods conform "perfectly" to the requirements of the order or else a breach is declared. If that level of exactitude is required by the UCC, why not give the buyer the option to reject goods and revoke the contract even if cure is possible? Eliminating the "right" to cure would serve as a strong incentive for sellers to get the order right in the first place instead of being able to fall back on the right to cure. Not only would this facilitate commercial activity, but it would serve as an incentive for efficient contract performance and reduce the need for litigation.

QUESTIONS & PROBLEMS

1. Think back to the *Vitol v. Koch* Case Opener. Explain how perfect tender applies not only to the nature of the actual goods themselves but to the entire contractual transaction.
2. Midwest Mobile Diagnostic Imaging (MMDI) brought suit against Ellis & Watts (E&W), a division of Dynamics Corporation of America, for breach of contract. The dispute arose when E&W delivered the first of four trailers equipped with magnetic resonance imaging (MRI) scanners that E&W had agreed to deliver pursuant to a purchase agreement. E&W designs and manufactures trailers for mobile medical uses. MMDI decided to buy the MRI scanners directly from the manufacturer, but it needed assistance from E&W. E&W needed to install the trailers subject to the manufacturer's specifications and approval. MMDI entered into an agreement with E&W for four mobile MRI units. The manufacturer subsequently delivered the first scanner to E&W in September 1995. In November, MMDI paid E&W for the first trailer. The manufacturer then completed its testing of that trailer at the end of November. The first test found that the trailer complied with all technical specifications. A second test failed because it was a "road test," meaning the MRI failed to meet requirements after the trailer was moved and parked. The problem was that the unit's side walls flexed too much, causing unacceptable "ghosting" in the MRI scans. In December, E&W installed a reinforcing brace that solved the wall-flexing problem and satisfied all of the manufacturer's specifications. Consequently, MMDI refused to accept the trailer with the brace and demanded that E&W return the full purchase price. MMDI filed suit, seeking damages. Should MMDI prevail? [*Midwest Mobile Diagnostic Imaging v. Dynamics Corp. of America,* 165 F.3d 27 C.A.6 (Mich.) 1998.]
3. Wilbur Reed operated a small greenhouse in Montana. He ordered most of his plants from McCalif Grower Supplies. Reed often supplied local Kmart and Ernst stores with his products. During the holiday season, he agreed to provide them with poinsettia

plants. Reed ordered the plants from McCalif, and McCalif had growers send the plants to Reed from Colorado. Reed's employee accepted the boxes at the airport and did not note any damages to the packaging. However, when the boxes were opened, the poinsettias appeared damaged. Reed contacted McCalif and notified it that the poinsettias were damaged as a result of poor packing. McCalif advised Reed to report the damages to the carrier, Delta Airlines. Delta paid Reed $924.66 in compensation. McCalif was not able to supply Reed with more poinsettias before the holiday season. As a result, Reed lost accounts to many of the stores. McCalif sued Reed for payment for the poinsettias, $3,223.56. Reed refused to pay and argued that McCalif had failed to deliver according to their contract. Whom did the court agree with? [*McCalif Grower Supplies, Inc. v. Wilbur Reed,* 900 P.2d 880 (1995).]

4. New furniture was delivered to the buyer, and it was badly damaged. The purchaser notified the furniture store of the damage, and the store sent a representative to the buyer. The representative explained that the furniture could be repaired and restored. After hearing the details, the buyer refused and asked for her money back. The store refused, claiming that she had accepted the goods and was required to permit the seller to cure the defects. Who prevailed? [*Clark v. Zaid, Inc.,* 263 Md. 127 (1971).]

5. Rockland Industries agreed to purchase three containers of antimony oxide at $1.80 per pound from Manley-Regan Chemicals. Rockland produces drapes, and antimony oxide is used to fireproof the drapes. A representative from Manley-Regan, David Hess, worked with Conrad Ailstock, Rockland's purchasing agent. Hess informed Ailstock of a slight delay, but he assured Ailstock that the product, which was coming from China, was "on the water." Three months after the two companies had made the agreement, Hess contacted Ailstock to report that the product was not coming. According to Hess, Manley-Regan was considering legal claims against the Chinese supplier or the Chinese government. Rockland was forced to find another supplier, but the price was substantially higher. Rockland brought suit to recover the difference between Manley-Regan's quoted price and the price of the substitute antimony oxide. Is the commercial-impracticability defense appropriate? Explain. [*Rockland Industries, Inc. v. Manley-Regan Chemicals Division,* 991 F. Supp. 468 (1998).]

6. The buyer contracted with the seller for a customized machine. The seller failed to have the machine ready by the agreed-on deadline. The buyer agreed to two extensions, both of which were not met by the seller. The buyer then terminated the contract. The seller sued for breach, claiming that it had not been given sufficient time to effect a cure. Who prevailed? [Star *Machine, Inc. v. Ford Motor Co.,* 1998 U.S. App. LEXIS 15392 (1998).]

7. David Cooper purchased a computer and software for his supermarket business. He was using a software program recommended and installed by the seller, Contemporary Computer Systems, Inc. The sales contract had a clause that stated that no refunds would be given after the 90-day warranty period. Cooper initially had problems with both the hardware and the software. Contemporary Computer Systems tried to remedy these problems. A pattern of problems and attempts to fix went on for some time, far beyond the 90-day time period expressly described in the contract. When Cooper had had enough, he decided to revoke the contract and demand his money back. Contemporary Computer Systems said the 90-day express clause in the contract precludes this action. Who won? [*David Cooper, Inc. v. Contemporary Computer Systems, Inc.,* 846 S.W.2d 777 (1993).]

8. North American Lighting (NAL) purchased a headlight aiming system from Hopkins Manufacturing Corporation. NAL produces headlamps for most major automobile manufacturers. It is important that NAL produce headlamps that meet government safety requirements, which ensure that drivers can see what they need to see without blinding oncoming motorists. Hopkins tried to sell NAL its Machine Vision System (MVS), which Hopkins believed was appropriate for the kind of testing NAL had to undertake to comply with federal guidelines. NAL decided to purchase the MVS even though it saw problems from the start. NAL based its purchase decision on Hopkins's promises that software could be added to the system to make it meet NAL's needs. After approximately two years of working with Hopkins, and the MVS still failing to meet NAL's needs, NAL informed Hopkins that it was revoking acceptance. The issue in the case is whether NAL can recover the amount it tendered Hopkins in partial payment. Hopkins wants the unpaid purchase price, as well as an amount that approximates the reasonable rental value of the equipment Hopkins had loaned to NAL. Who gets what? [*North American Lighting, Inc. v. Hopkins Manufacturing Corp.*, 37 F.3d 1253 (1994).]

9. Aubrey Reeves purchased a computer system for his business from Radio Shack Computer Center. Radio Shack is the local retailer for products sold by Tandy, its parent company. During negotiations, it became clear that Reeves needed software that Radio Shack could not provide. A Radio Shack salesperson referred Reeves to a software source book, let Reeves know he could choose compatible software from the source book, and informed him that Tandy does not support or service software from the source book. A disclaimer to this effect appears in the source book. Reeves eventually purchased computers from Tandy, some software from Tandy, and more specialized software from a company called Lizcon. The Lizcon software did not meet Reeves's needs. Reeves subsequently sent a letter to Tandy, asking for rescission of the contract and damages. Can Reeves rescind? [*Aubrey's R.V. Center, Inc. v. Tandy Corporation,* 731 P.2d 1124 (1987).]

10. The defendant, Nwabuoku, purchased $1,500 worth of furniture from the plaintiff, Y&N Furniture. Through an arrangement with the plaintiff, the defendant financed the purchase through a financing company, Beneficial. On receipt of the furniture, the defendant was to notify Beneficial that receipt was effected, and Beneficial would pay Y&N the $1,500 purchase price. Nwabuoku would then begin paying Beneficial the amount due plus interest according to their financing agreement. Nwabuoku refused to acknowledge receipt to Beneficial and eventually rejected the goods, claiming that he did not want the furniture. Is this rejection enforceable? [*Y&N Furniture Inc. v. Nwabuoku,* 734 N.Y.S.2d 392 (2001).]

Looking for more review materials?

The Online Learning Center at **www.mhhe.com/kubasek3e** contains this chapter's "Assignment on the Internet" and also a list of URLs for more information, entitled "On the Internet." Find both of them in the Student Center portion of the OLC, along with quizzes and other helpful materials.

CHAPTER 24

Remedies for Breach of Sales and Lease Contracts

LEARNING OBJECTIVES

After reading this chapter, you will be able to answer the following questions:

1. What constitutes a breach of a sales contract?
2. What is resale?
3. What money damages are available for breach?
4. What are liquidated damages?
5. What is cover?
6. When is specific performance of the contract a remedy?

CASE OPENER

Let's "See" the Damages in Defective Eye Ointment

Abbott Industries is a well-known supplier of pharmaceuticals worldwide. Founded by Dr. Wallace Abbott, the company was incorporated in 1900 after he had been developing and making pharmaceuticals since 1888. Headquartered in the greater Chicago area, Abbott had sales of nearly $30 billion in 2008 and a research and development budget of nearly $8 billion. As a supplier of pharmaceuticals, Abbott contracted with Altana, Inc., later to be purchased by NYCOMED, Inc. The contract required that Abbott provide Altana with the antibiotic erythromycin powder for Altana to use in the manufacture of ophthalmic ointment. Unfortunately, one of the shipment batches of erythromycin was bad. As a result, 1.2 million tubes of the manufactured ointment were unusable.

Abbott actually contacted Altana and admitted to the faulty batch of erythromycin powder. Altana was forced to recall from the market and destroy the 1.2 million tubes and spend a considerable amount of money in employee overtime payments to replace the destroyed tubes. Through a truly herculean effort, Altana was able to satisfy all of its outstanding contracts with buyers of the ophthalmic ointment.[1]

[1] *NYCOMED v. Abbott Laboratories*, 542 F.3d 1129 (2008).

The questions that this case raises pertain to the extent of Abbott's liability to Altana. Liability is not an issue, but the extent of the remedies is.

1. Is Abbott responsible for:
   a. The cost of the recall?
   b. The cost of the destruction of the 1.2 million tubes?
   c. The payment of overtime to Altana employees?
   d. The loss of goodwill and future sales that Altana may incur due to this incident?

The Wrap-Up at the end of the chapter will answer these questions.

This chapter explains the remedies available to sales contract parties such as Altana. The first section restates the primary goal of contract remedies. This section helps you understand the range of remedies available to sellers/lessors and buyers/lessees. The next two sections list and explain the remedies available to sellers/lessors and buyers/lessees. The first of these sections focuses on remedies available to sellers/lessors, from the right to cancel the contract to the right to reclaim goods. Then the next section looks at remedies available to buyers/lessees, from the right to recover goods to the right to accept nonconforming goods and then seek damages. The last section of the chapter provides examples of situations in which the parties' agreement modifies or limits remedies available under the UCC.

The Goal of Contract Remedies

LO1 What constitutes a breach of a sales contract?

The obligations of sellers/lessors and buyers/lessees are determined by (1) terms the parties outline in agreements, (2) custom, and (3) rules outlined by the Uniform Commercial Code (UCC). This chapter focuses primarily on rules outlined by the UCC.

The UCC adopts several common law principles, including principles that underlie remedies available under the UCC. A good way to start our analysis is to consider the following reminder of the general purpose of remedies under common law contract rules and the UCC. In *KGM Harvesting Company v. Fresh Network,*[2] the court said:

> The basic premise of contract law is to effectuate the expectations of the parties to the agreement, to give them the "benefit of the bargain" they struck when they entered into the agreement. In its basic premise, contract law therefore differs significantly from tort law. Contract actions are created to enforce the intentions of the parties to the agreement, while tort law is primarily designed to vindicate social policy. The basic object of damages is *compensation,* and in the law of contracts the theory is that the party injured by the breach should receive as nearly as possible the benefits of performance. A compensation system that gives the aggrieved party the benefit of the bargain, and no more, furthers the goal of predictability about the cost of contractual relationships in our commercial system.

Thus, as you think about the range of remedies available to sellers/lessors and buyers/lessees, think about what remedies would give the parties the benefit of the bargain they struck, and nothing more. Of course, the ultimate goal of contractual remedies is the possibility, if not probability, that a system that provides compensation will also function as a system of deterrence in which parties do not breach contracts or, if they do, will be

[2] 42 Cal. Rptr. 2d 286, 289. Quotes from and citations to cases the court cites have been omitted from the extract.

amenable to a mutually satisfied settlement. After all, remember the old adage that when disputes turn into litigation, the only winners are often the attorneys. The UCC creates a statute of limitations for bringing a lawsuit arising under a breach of contract for the sale of goods. UCC Section 2-725(1) states that four years is the time frame for a plaintiff to file suit once a cause of action accrues.

Remedies Available to Sellers and Lessors under the UCC

Sellers and lessors have various contract remedies under the UCC. These remedies are discussed below and outlined in Exhibit 24-1.

CANCEL THE CONTRACT

UCC Sections 2-703(f) and 2A-523(1)(a) allow a seller or lessor to cancel the contract if the buyer or lessee is in breach. The UCC requires that sellers/lessors notify buyers/lessees of the cancellation. Then the seller or lessor pursues remedies available under the UCC. Remember, these remedies give the seller/lessor the benefit of the bargain, and nothing more.

Legal Principle: **Canceling the contract is the remedy of last resort from the UCC's perspective. Remember: The UCC wants to maintain commercial transactions and provides remedies to keep the contract in force, even when one party has breached.**

WITHHOLD DELIVERY

Sometimes a buyer breaches the contract or lease before the seller has delivered the goods. For instance, the buyer or lessee might fail to pay according to the terms of the agreement.

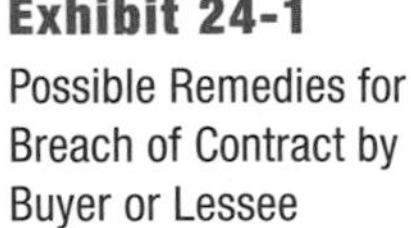

Exhibit 24-1

Possible Remedies for Breach of Contract by Buyer or Lessee

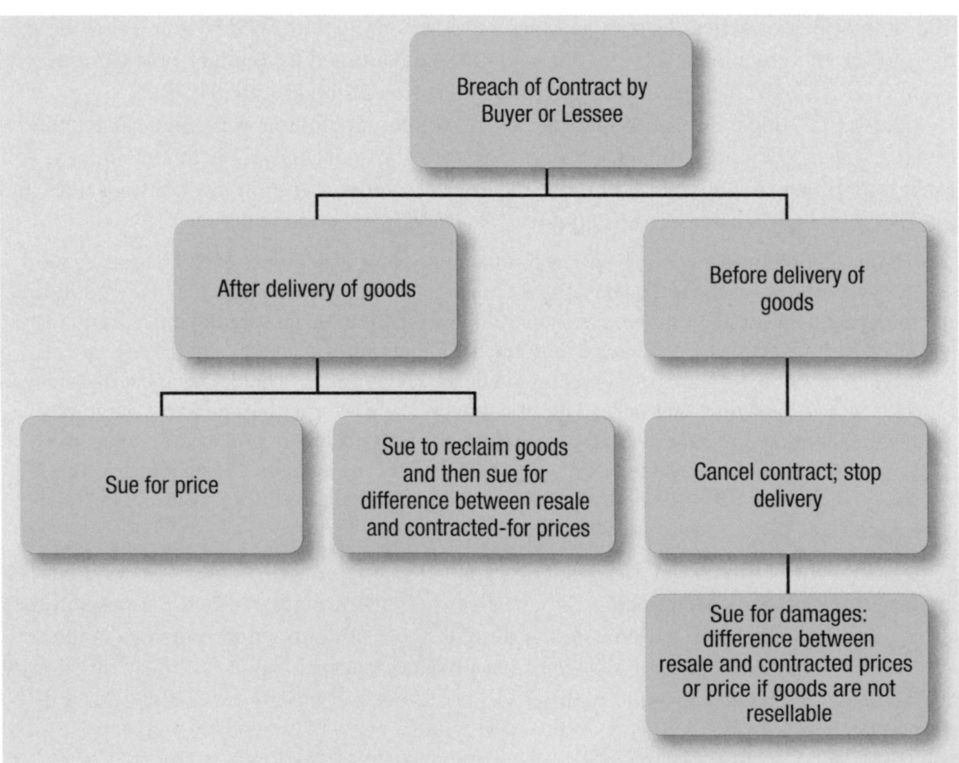

CASE NUGGET

HOW TO COMPUTE "HOT DAMAGES"

Detroit Radiant Products Company v. BSH Home Appliances Corporation
U.S. Court of Appeals for the Sixth Circuit
473 F.3d 623, 2007 U.S. App. LEXIS 300, 2007 FED App. 0005P (6th Cir.), 61 U.C.C. Rep. Serv. 2d (Callaghan) 701 (2007)

Detroit Radiant is a manufacturing company that makes gas-fired infrared heaters that are used for industrial and commercial purposes. BSH requested a price quote based on an estimated annual usage of about 30,000 units. Two purchase orders were sent from BSH to Detroit Radiant on August 10, 2001, and January 8, 2003, for 15,000 and 16,000 units, respectively. Release schedules were provided by BSH to Detroit Radiant for exact timing of the orders. By April 5, 2004, BSH had received 12,886 units, had not contested quality at any point, and had scheduled 6,000 more units to be delivered before February 2005. On April 12 a new schedule was released, slowing production schedules. On June 24 Detroit Radiant filed a suit for the profits relating to 18,114 unsold units and unsellable inventory. BSH contended both that the purchase orders were estimates and that the 2003 order superseded the 2001 order. The 2001 order was a blanket order that BSH claims was an industry standard meaning estimated order. There was an unsigned supplier agreement that stated that all scheduled orders were nonbinding forecasts. On March 1, 2006, a district court ruled in favor of Detroit Radiant, finding that the purchase orders were of a certain quantity and did not contain any language to infer that they were estimates.

Michigan, along with states except Louisiana, has adopted UCC Article 2 to regulate the sale of goods. The default measure of damages under breach of contract is contract price less the market price of items in the time and place plus any incidental damages. However, lost profits are available in two situations: One is "lost volume seller," which Detroit Radiant did not claim to be the case. The other situation is one in which the default measure does not adequately make the seller whole. This could be a result of there being no reliable market price. In this case, the units were a special order for BSH, but that does not in itself make the products unsellable. However, BSH would not have allowed the products to be sold because it considered the units to be proprietary. BSH argued in court that Detroit Radiant did not respect the proprietary nature of the items because it had listed them in a catalog. However, the court found that that did not in itself prove that Detroit Radiant did not consider the units to be proprietary property of BSH. Detroit Radiant may have simply been attempting to show the types of products that it could make. Further, BSH had no proof that Detroit Radiant had actually sold any of these units. Therefore, Detroit Radiant had shown that there was no reliable market value for the units outside BSH. Thus, Detroit Radiant was entitled to lost profits in addition to the value of the unsellable inventory that it now has.

UCC Sections 2-703(a) and 2A-523(1)(c) allow sellers or lessors to withhold delivery of goods when the buyer or lessee is in breach.

BUT WHAT IF . . .

WHAT IF THE FACTS OF THE CASE OPENER WERE DIFFERENT?

Let's say, in the Case Opener, that Abbott was set to deliver a powder to Altana in January. The contract between the two companies stipulated that Altana was supposed to make monthly payments to Abbott from November preceding the shipment to May following the shipment. Altana missed December's payment, which was scheduled right before the shipment. Could Abbott withhold the shipment even though Altana had already been paying for the powder and it had more time within the payment plan time frame?

RESELL OR DISPOSE OF THE GOODS

L02 What is resale?

Sellers or lessors are allowed to sell the goods to another buyer or dispose of the goods when the buyer is in breach and the goods have not yet been delivered. The seller/lessor then holds the buyer/lessee liable for any loss. UCC Section 2-706 allows the seller to recover the difference between the resale price and the contract price, plus incidental damages and minus expenses saved. Although the buyer is liable for these damages, the seller gets to keep any profits it makes on the resale. UCC Section 2A-527(2) outlines a similar rule for lease agreements. The lessor is allowed to lease the goods to another party and recover unpaid lease payments and any deficiency between the lease payments due under the original lease contract and those due under the new contract. The lessor can also seek incidental damages.

Legal Principle: **Resale is the preferred remedy for nonbreaching sellers (or re-lease for nonbreaching lessors) in that it provides an easy means to determine damages (resale price − contract price + resale costs = damages).**

BUT WHAT IF . . .

WHAT IF THE FACTS OF THE CASE OPENER WERE DIFFERENT?

Let's say, in the Case Opener, that Abbott and Altana had a contract laying out the terms of Altana's purchase of powder from Abbott and a payment plan for the powder. Altana breached the contract by missing a payment deadline. Because of this one missed payment, is Abbott allowed to sell the merchandise contractually obligated to go to Altana? Or are there other steps that the two companies must go through to remedy their situation?

SUE TO GET THE BENEFIT OF THE BARGAIN

LO3 What money damages are available for breach?

In trying to give the seller or lessor the benefit of the bargain, and nothing more, courts often grant damages to recover the purchase price or lease payments due. In some cases, even lost profit will be awarded, especially if the goods cannot be resold in the usual course of business.

LIQUIDATED DAMAGES

LO4 What are liquidated damages?

Liquidated damages are damages identified *before* the breach occurs. The parties are free to negotiate, as part of the contract, a liquidated-damage clause in which the parties agree in advance what the damages will be for each party should a breach occur. Generally speaking, a court will enforce a liquidated-damage clause as long as it is not so far out of reasonable range as to be punitive in nature. Liquidated-damage clauses that are deemed to be punitive in nature are not enforceable. For a perspective on the issue of liquidated-damage enforceability, see the Point/Counterpoint at the end of this chapter.

The code provides for liquidated damages if the parties have not expressly negotiated a liquidated-damage clause. UCC Section 2-718 pertains to liquidated damages and allows the nonbreaching seller to claim against a breaching buyer 20 percent of the purchase price or $500, whichever is less, as liquidated damages.

Likewise, although the UCC does not mention the availability of punitive damages, other than in its voiding of liquidated damages that are punitive in nature, an issue that remains unsettled is the awarding of punitive damages against a breaching party who intentionally or egregiously breaches the contract. You will remember from tort law that when a tort is committed either intentionally or recklessly, the court may infer legal malice and instruct a jury that it may consider the awarding of punitive damages in addition to compensatory damages. Although this concept is well settled in tort law, it has never been widely applied in contract law. Yet there are some who argue that it should be, especially to deter intentional breaches of contract.

STOP DELIVERY

UCC Sections 2-705(1) and 2A-526(1) allow a seller or lessor to stop delivery of goods that are in transit. *In transit* means that the seller or lessor has delivered the goods to a carrier or bailee but the carrier or bailee has not yet turned them over to the buyer. Of course, the

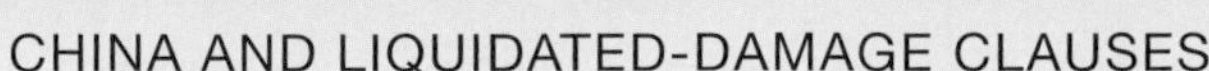

COMPARING THE LAW OF OTHER COUNTRIES

CHINA AND LIQUIDATED-DAMAGE CLAUSES

With the enactment in 1999 of the People's Republic of China (PRC) Contract Law legislation, China adopted a Western-style, relatively comprehensive legal approach to contract law. However, some differences occur between the PRC Contract Law, the CISG, and the Anglo-American common law. In Section 114.2 of the PRC Contract Law, Chinese law recognizes the existence and enforceability of liquidated-damage clauses in contracts. However, Chinese judicial interpretation of this section limits liquidated damages to no more than 30 percent above the actual damages incurred by the non-breaching party.

Source: www.wjnco.com/eng/articles show.asp?Articles_id=216.

seller/lessor must give timely notice to the carrier/bailee so that the carrier/bailee is able to stop delivery. Also, the rules are different for insolvent and solvent buyers and lessees. If the buyer/lessee is insolvent, the carrier/bailee can stop delivery regardless of the quantity shipped. If the buyer/lessee is solvent, however, the carrier or bailee can stop delivery only if the quantity shipped is a large shipment (e.g., a carload or truckload).

RECLAIM THE GOODS

Under UCC Sections 2-709(1) and 2A-529(1), if the buyer or lessee has possession of the goods and is in breach, the seller or lessor can sue for the purchase price of the goods or for the lease payments due, plus incidental damages. In some circumstances, the UCC allows the seller or lessee to reclaim the goods. UCC 2-702(2) allows a seller to reclaim goods when it discovers the buyer is insolvent. UCC 2A-525(2) allows a lessor to reclaim goods when the lessee fails to make payments according to the lease terms.

BUT WHAT IF . . .

WHAT IF THE FACTS OF THE CASE OPENER WERE DIFFERENT?

Let's say, in the Case Opener, that Abbott delivered powder to Altana that Altana was still making payments for. Altana missed a payment after already being in possession of the powder. Abbott not only went to Altana to take back the powder but additionally charged Altana for payments due and damages. Altana said that once the goods were physically transferred to Altana, they could not be taken back. Which side is correct in this instance?

Remedies Available to Buyers and Lessees under the UCC

As with sellers and lessors, buyers and lessees also have a number of contract remedies under the UCC. These remedies are explained below and outlined in Exhibit 24-2.

CANCEL THE CONTRACT

Sometimes, sellers or lessors fail to deliver the goods and thus are in breach. UCC Sections 2-711(1) and 2A-508(1)(a) allow buyers and lessees to cancel the contract and then seek remedies that give them the benefit of the bargain. In Case 24-1, a buyer of heating coils had the right to cancel a contract with the seller because the coils did not work according to the buyer's specifications. The buyer subsequently sued for damages.

OBTAIN COVER

LO5 What is cover?

Case 24-1 also explains the buyer's right to obtain cover. Under UCC Sections 2-712 and 2A-518, buyers and lessees are allowed to **cover**, or substitute, goods for those due under the sales or lease agreement.

Exhibit 24-2
Remedies for Breach by Seller or Lessor

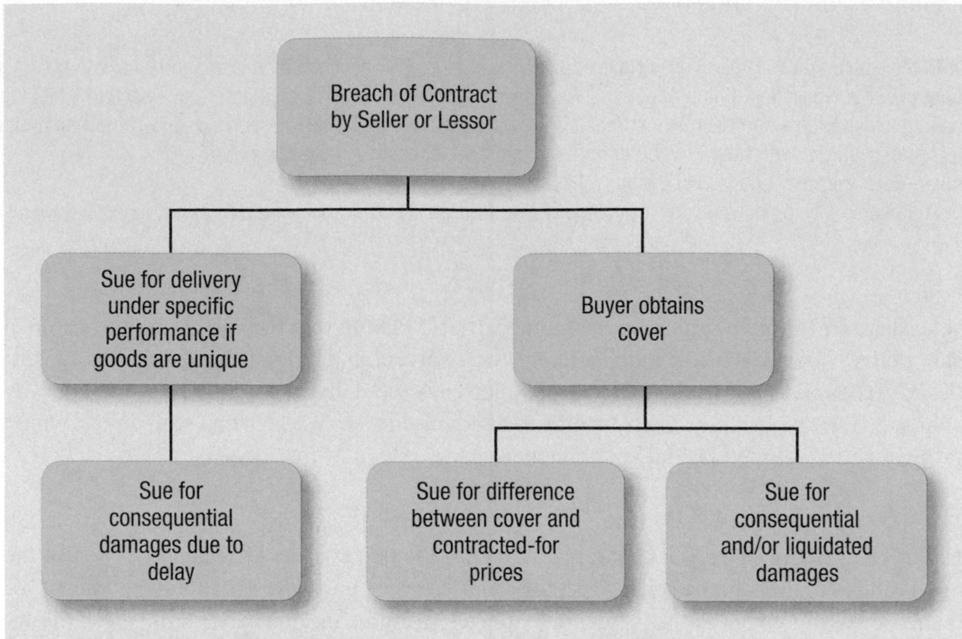

As you read Case 24-1, notice that, in obtaining cover, the buyer must (1) demonstrate good faith in obtaining the substitute goods, (2) pay a reasonable amount for the substitute goods, (3) act without unreasonable delay in purchasing the substitute goods, and (4) purchase goods that are reasonable substitutes.

CASE 24-1 U.S.A. COIL & AIR, INC. v. HODESS BUILDING CO.
WL 66582 R.I. SUPER. (1999)

U.S.A. Coil and Air, Inc. (USA), and Hodess Building Co. (Hodess) were involved in a legal dispute that arose after USA supplied cooling coils for an HVAC system, which was part of a "clean-room" project for Lockheed/Sanders. USA agreed to provide the needed coils to Hodess for $33,156.00. USA did provide the coils, but the coils failed to perform as specified.

USA subsequently sent Hodess replacement coils, but these, too, failed. USA believed the failure was related to Hodess's flawed system, not the coils. Hodess informed USA that it would replace the coils, using a different vendor to supply the coils.

USA requested to have its coils returned, and Hodess agreed, as long as USA paid for shipping or sent someone to pick up the coils. Communication between the parties broke down. Hodess never paid the contract price of $33,156.00. USA brought a breach of contract action to recover this amount. Hodess counterclaimed for breach of contract and asked for its $83,374.95 in replacement costs.

JUDGE. GIBNEY: . . . If a buyer rightfully rejects a tender of goods in a contract such as this one, he is entitled to cancel the contract. UCC 2-711(1). Once the contract is cancelled, the buyer's obligation to pay the purchase price is discharged. UCC 2-106(3).

USA does not dispute that both sets of coils it provided failed to conform to the performance specifications referenced in the contract purchase order. . . . USA blames the system design for the failure. . . . [T]his court finds that the plaintiff breached the contract purchase order when it failed to provide coils which met the performance specifications. Thus, Hodess was excused from paying the purchase price.

Moreover, with respect to USA's right to cure its breach, Hodess allowed USA the opportunity to do so. Hodess installed USA's replacement coils, carefully following USA's instructions and modifying the system at USA's suggestion. When the replacement coils failed, USA's attempts to cure the breach failed as well. . . . USA is not entitled to recover. . . .

The defendant counterclaims, arguing breach of contract and seeking recovery of the replacement costs incurred due to the breach. Generally, "where a right of action for breach exists, compensatory damages will be given for the net amount of the losses caused and gains prevented by the

[continued]

defendant's breach, in excess of savings made possible." The goal is to place the injured party in as good a position as he would have been if the contract had not been breached. . . . When a buyer justifiably revokes acceptance of goods, the measure of direct damages is the difference between the cost of cover and the contract price, less any expenses saved as a result of the seller's breach. UCC 2-711(1)(b). To cover, a buyer must "in good faith and without reasonable delay" make a "reasonable purchase or contract to purchase . . . goods in substitution for those due from the seller." UCC 2-712(1). Whether the buyer acted in good faith and in a reasonable manner is determined with reference to the conditions at the time and place the buyer attempted to cover. UCC 2-712 at comment 2. It is irrelevant that hindsight may later suggest a cheaper or more effective method. The burden of proof is on the seller of goods to prove that cover was not reasonably obtained. . . .

Having found USA breached the contract, this court also concludes that USA is liable for the resulting damages incurred by Hodess. To replace the defective coils, Hodess incurred substantial expenses for engineering, supervision of, and replacement of the coils. Hodess documented its expenditures with receipts and project expense reports, demonstrating a total reasonable replacement cost of $83,734.95. USA did not present any evidence which would tend to dispute the reasonableness of cover costs. . . . Thus, using the damages formula enunciated in UCC 2-711(1)(b), Hodess is entitled to the replacement costs less the contract price [which was $33,156.00], or $50,578.95. . . .

Judgment for defendant.

CRITICAL THINKING

Hodess appears to have had an advantage in the case because it had better evidence. How so? How could USA have increased its chances of winning?

ETHICAL DECISION MAKING

Suppose Hodess later discovers that its system design was flawed and it was not really USA's fault that the coils did not work. Which ethical test or tests would encourage Hodess's executives to come forward with that information?

Legal Principle: **Cover is the preferred remedy for nonbreaching buyers or lessees under the UCC in that it provides an easy, quantifiable means to determine damages (cost of cover − contracted price + incidental costs of cover = damages).**

SUE TO RECOVER DAMAGES

In Case 24-1, although Hodess was able to cover, it still incurred damages. Buyers such as Hodess, and lessees, are entitled to incidental and consequential damages. **Consequential damages** include damages for lost profits as long as these damages are not too speculative. These monetary damages give the injured buyer or lessee the benefit of the bargain. This is one of the contentions being argued by Altana in the Case Opener of this chapter.

RECOVER THE GOODS

UCC Sections 2-502 and 2a-522 allow buyers and lessees to recover the goods identified in the contract if the seller or lessor becomes insolvent within 10 days after receiving the first payment due under the agreement. Buyers or lessees are obligated to pay the remaining balance according to the terms of the agreement.

OBTAIN SPECIFIC PERFORMANCE

UCC Sections 2-716(1) and 2A-521(1) allow buyers and lessees to seek the remedy of specific performance when either (1) the goods are unique or (2) a remedy at law is inadequate. **Specific performance** usually requires that the seller or lessor deliver the particular goods identified in the contract. In Case 24-2, the court decides what must be shown to apply specific performance as the appropriate remedy.

LO6

When is specific performance of the contract a remedy?

CASE NUGGET

WHAT ARE CONSEQUENTIAL DAMAGES?

The Mead Corporation v. McNally-Pittsburg Manufacturing Corporation
U.S. Court of Appeals for the Sixth Circuit
654 F.2d 1197, 1981 U.S. App. LEXIS 11164, 35 U.C.C. Rep. Serv. (Callaghan) 368 (1981)

The Mead Corporation entered into a contract for the McNally-Pittsburg Manufacturing firm to build a coal-washing plant. The McNally did not get the coal-washing machinery delivered in time, and Mead sued for a wide variety of damages incurred due to the delay. The jury awarded Mead slightly over a half million dollars in damages. McNally countersued for the unpaid portion of the contracted purchase price and received a judgment for $1.3 million. McNally is appealing, claiming that the half million dollars awarded to Mead is unsubstantiated consequential damages not covered by the contract.

CASE 24-2 ALMETALS, INC., PLAINTIFF v. WICKEDER WESTFALENSTAHL, GMBH, DEFENDANT

U.S. DISTRICT COURT FOR THE EASTERN DISTRICT OF MICHIGAN 2008 U.S. DIST. LEXIS 87403

Almetals, Inc., a Michigan company, entered into a contract with the German firm Wickeder Westfalenstahl regarding the purchase of "clad metal," a specialty metal used in a variety of industries but primarily the automotive industry. Wickeder is the world's largest manufacturer of "clad metal," a bonded product of layers of different metals. Almetals, Inc., would take the clad metal from Wickeder and process it to specifications for its customers, such as BorgWarner and Dana Corporation. From an initial purchase of just a few hundred thousand dollars of clad metals, Almetals, Inc., became one of the largest suppliers of processed clad metal, a market that took Almetals nearly seven years to cultivate. The contract between Almetals and Wickeder was for seven years with a ten-year add-on for customers that Almetals had under contract. Wickeder, seeing the huge success in North America, attempted to take over Almetals, Inc. In a proposed acquisition, Almetals successfully opposed that attempt. In retaliation, Wickeder refused to renew the contract after the seven years and then demanded that Almetals pay cash for clad metal purchased from Wickeder for the customers under the contract in the ten-year add-on period. The original contract called for payment 60 days after invoicing. Almetals sued for breach of contract and asked for specific performance as the remedy. The trial court granted Almetals' request and analyzed the facts against the UCC requirements for granting specific performance and the subsequent request for a permanent injunction.

JUDGE NANCY EDMUNDS: Almetals is entitled to an order requiring Wickeder to abide by the Court's ruling as to the payment terms (60 days after invoice of the materials in exchange for a .5% price discount) for the duration of the Customer and Order Protection clause for two independent reasons: (1) Almetals has met the test for specific performance under the UCC; and (2) Almetals has met the common-law test for a permanent injunction.

1. Almetals Is Entitled to Specific Performance Under the UCC

The power to grant specific performance rests within the discretion of the court. Under Michigan law, "[t]he remedy of specific performance is an extraordinary one granted only in unusual cases to prevent irreparable harm. It is a matter of grace and not right." . . . The UCC authorizes specific performance of contracts involving unique goods or in other proper circumstances:

(i) Specific performance may be decreed where the goods are unique or in other proper circumstances.

(ii) The decree for specific performance may include such terms and conditions as to payment of the price, damages, or other relief as the court may deem just.

Michigan has also adopted Comment 2 from the 1962 official text to UCC § 2-716, which states that:

> Output and requirements contracts involving a particular or peculiarly available source or market present today the typical commercial specific performance situation. . . . [U]niqueness is not the sole basis of the remedy under this section for the relief may also be granted "in other proper circumstances" and inability to cover is strong evidence of "other proper circumstances."

The UCC is consistent with the common law in which specific performance is well-recognized as an appropriate remedy where goods are unique or scarce. Jaup v. Olmstead, 334 Mich. 614, 55 N.W.2d 119, 120 (Mich. 1952) ("Generally, specific performance is not decreed where the subject-matter of the contract is personalty. However, if the specific property is not obtainable on the market and damages will not provide adequate compensation, equity may take jurisdiction"); In re Smith Trust, 480 Mich. 19, 745 N.W.2d 754, 756

[continued]

(Mich. 2008) ("Because real property is unique . . . specific performance is the proper remedy"); 71 Am. Jur. 2d Specific Performance § 175 (2008); Bohnsack v. Detroit Trust Co., 292 Mich. 167, 290 N.W. 367 (Mich. 1940) (ordering specific performance of agreement among shareholders to buy life insurance to benefit surviving shareholders).

Indeed, under UCC § 2-716, "a more liberal test in determining entitlement to specific performance has been established than the test one must meet for classic equitable relief." Eastern Air Lines, Inc. v. Gulf Oil Corp., 415 F. Supp. 429, 442–43 (S.D. Fla. 1975) ("In the circumstances, a decree of specific performance becomes the ordinary and natural relief rather than the extraordinary one").

Specific performance under UCC § 2-716 is the appropriate remedy because the varieties of clad metal supplied by Wickeder pursuant to the parties' requirements contract are unique and there are no known alternative sources of supply, but only speculation as to a possible alternative source for .2% or .3% of the product. Sherwin Alumina L.P. v. Aluchem, Inc., 512 F. Supp. 2d 957, 960 n. 2, 970 (S.D. Tex. 2007) (applying UCC § 2-716 and ordering specific performance of a contract to supply calcined alumina, a scarce product, where the supplier had "very few competitors," "there [was] only one other manufacturer of [the product] in North America," and the buyer needed the products for its business to survive).

Order for specific performance granted.

CRITICAL THINKING

In that the defendant's actions appeared to be retaliatory and the result of an unsuccessful takeover bid, should the court have taken evidence to that effect into consideration. Why or why not?

ETHICAL DECISION MAKING

In this case, Almetals relies heavily on a single supplier for its supply chain. In this case that amount was over 40 percent. Does such an arrangement place some kind of ethical burden on the supplier who is acutely aware that such a one-sided relationship exists?

REJECT NONCONFORMING GOODS

In Chapter 23, and this chapter, several of the cases have focused on what happens when the seller or lessor delivers nonconforming goods. This section and the next two review the buyer's/lessee's remedies when the seller/lessor delivers nonconforming goods. First, UCC Sections 2-601 and 2A-519 allow the buyer or lessee to reject the goods. The buyer or lessee may then obtain cover or cancel the contract.

REVOKE ACCEPTANCE OF NONCONFORMING GOODS

UCC Sections 2-608 and 2A-517 sometimes allow the buyer or lessee to revoke acceptance of nonconforming goods. For instance, in Case 24-1, Hodess rejected acceptance of the nonconforming coils USA provided. Hodess was allowed to reject acceptance because it had made a reasonable assumption that the nonconformity would be cured but then the nonconformity was not cured within a reasonable amount of time.

ACCEPT THE NONCONFORMING GOODS AND SEEK DAMAGES

Under UCC Sections 2-607, 2-714, and 2A-519, buyers or lessees are allowed to accept nonconforming goods and then seek monetary damages to give them the benefit of the bargain. The buyer/lessee must give the seller/lessor reasonable notice of the defect.

Modifications or Limitations to Remedies Otherwise Provided by the UCC

Parties to sales and lease contracts are allowed to modify or limit remedies. Under UCC Sections 2-719 and 2A-503, parties are allowed to create agreements that make it clear the remedies outlined in the agreement are exclusive

To see how the lawmaking role of government relates to contractual agreements, please see the **Connecting to the Core** activity on the text website at www.mhhe.com/kubasek3e.

COMPARING THE LAW OF OTHER COUNTRIES

CANADA DOES NOT NEED "LEMON LAWS"

In the United States, lemon laws exist to provide remedies for buyers of defective cars when sellers have limited the remedies otherwise provided by the UCC. Lemon laws allow buyers to get a new car, seek replacement of defective parts, or obtain a refund of the consideration they have paid in situations in which a buyer has repeatedly complained about car defects and the seller has been unable to correct the defects after numerous attempts. The buyer who gets a refund of consideration gives the "lemon" back.

Canada does not have lemon laws.* Instead, each province runs an arbitration program through which a buyer can lodge complaints against a carmaker for selling a car that the consumer perceives as being damaged goods. So far, Canadian carmakers have bought back only a few vehicles. For instance, DaimlerChrysler Canada buys "very, very few" lemons, while its U.S. parent has purchased approximately 58,000 in the past eight years.† Dennis DesRosiers, an independent Toronto analyst, says the Canadian car industry does not need a lemon law because "cars are so well built these days that the chances of getting a lemon [in Canada] are very low."‡

* David Steinhart, "'Lemon' Resales Not Happening in Canada," *National Post,* March 20, 2001.

† Ibid.

‡ Ibid.

remedies. Courts uphold modifications or limitations to remedies unless the remedies fail in their essential purpose.

In Case 24-3, the court applies UCC 2-719 to rule on whether a seller could limit the buyer's remedies to repair, replace, or refund. These remedies are standard remedies in the bottling industry. Pay attention to the court's explanation of when remedies outlined in an agreement "failed of their essential purpose."

CASE 24-3 FIGGIE INTERNATIONAL, INC. v. DESTILERIA SERRALLES, INC.

U.S. COURT OF APPEALS, FOURTH CIRCUIT
190 F.3D 252 (1999)

In this case, a dispute arose between Figgie International, Inc. (Figgie), and Destileria Serralles, Inc. (Serralles), over bottle-labeling equipment Figgie sold to Serralles. Serralles is a distributor of rum and other products. It operates a bottling plant in Puerto Rico. When the bottle-labeling equipment failed to place a clear label on a clear bottle of "Cristal" Rum with a raised glass oval, Figgie attempted to repair the equipment. After several attempts to fix the equipment, Figgie returned the purchase price of the equipment and Serralles returned the equipment.

Serralles asked Figgie to pay for alleged losses caused by the equipment's failure to perform as expected. This failure caused a delay in Serralles' production of Cristal Rum. Figgie instituted a declaratory judgment action, asserting that Serralles' remedy for breach was limited to repair, replace, or refund under both the written terms and conditions of the sales agreement (which was lost) and pursuant to usage of trade in the bottle-labeling industry. In this case, the court considered the extent to which usage of trade in the bottling industry makes it clear that Serralles' remedy was limited to repair, replace, or refund. Serralles disputes that usage of trade imposes this limitation. Serralles also argues that because this limited remedy fails of its essential purpose, it is entitled to the full array of remedies the UCC provides.

CIRCUIT JUDGE TRAXLER: . . . Because the crux of this appeal centers on whether the agreement between the parties limited Serralles' remedy for breach to repair, replacement, or refund of the purchase price, we begin with the language of S.C.Code Sec. 36-2-719, which governs modifications or limitations to the remedies otherwise provided by the UCC for breach of a sales agreement. Section 36-2-719 provides that:

(1) Subject to the provisions of subsections (2) and (3) of this section and of the preceding section (Sec. 36-2-318) on liquidation of damages,

(a) the agreement may provide for remedies in addition to or in substitution for those provided in this chapter and may limit or alter the measure of damages recoverable under this chapter, as by limiting the buyer's remedies to return of the goods and repayment of the price, or to repair and replacement of nonconforming goods or parts; and

(b) resort to a remedy as provided is optional unless the remedy is expressly agreed to be exclusive, in which case it is the sole remedy.

(2) Where circumstances cause an exclusive or limited remedy to fail of its essential purpose, remedy may be had as provided in this act.

(3) Consequential damages may be limited or excluded unless the limitation or exclusion is unconscionable. Limitation of consequential damages for injury to the person in the case of consumer goods is prima facie unconscionable, but limitation of damages where the loss is commercial is not.

Under these provisions, parties to a commercial sales agreement may provide for remedies in addition to those provided by the UCC, or limit themselves to specified remedies in lieu of those provided by the UCC. An "[a]greement" for purposes in the UCC is defined as "the bargain of the parties in fact as found in their language or by implication from other circumstances, *including course of dealing or usage of trade*. . . ." . . . (emphasis added). In turn, the Code provides that "[a] course of dealing between parties and any usage of trade in the vocation, or trade in which they are engaged or of which they are or should be aware give particular meaning to and supplement or qualify terms of an agreement." . . . "Usage of trade" is defined as "any practice or method of dealing having such regularity of observance in a place, vocation or trade as to justify an exception that it will be observed with respect to the transaction in question. . . ."

. . . Serralles contends that the district court erred in concluding that usage of trade in the bottle-labeling industry supplemented the agreement between the parties with the limited remedy of repair, replacement, or refund. We disagree.

. . . Figgie submitted several affidavits of persons with extensive experience in the bottle-labeling and packaging industry, attesting that sellers in the industry always limit the available remedies in the event of a breach to repair, replacement, or return, and specifically exclude consequential damages. . . . Serralles offered no evidence to contradict the affidavits submitted by Figgie. Accordingly, the district court correctly concluded that usage of trade would limit Serralles to the exclusive remedy of repair, replacement, or return.

. . . Serralles contends that a limited remedy imposed or implied by trade usage cannot be an exclusive remedy because it is neither "expressly agreed to" nor "explicit." We disagree.

Section 36-2-719 provides that the "agreement" between the parties may limit remedies. Section 36-1-201(3) defines "[a]greement" as including terms "impli[ed] from circumstances including course of dealing or usage of trade." . . . It seems clear to us that . . . usage of trade will supplement agreements and may indeed impose an exclusive remedy in the event of a breach. . . .

Having determined that usage of trade supplemented the agreement of the parties with the exclusive remedy of repair, replacement, or return, we turn to Serralles' contention that the limited remedy "fail[ed] of its essential purpose," entitling it to nevertheless pursue the full array of UCC remedies. *See* S.C.Code Ann. Sec. 36-2-719(2). We conclude that it did not.

Section 36-2-719(1)(a) specifically contemplates that the parties to an agreement may, as they did in this case, limit remedies in the event of a breach to "return of the goods and repayment of the price or to repair and replacement of nonconforming goods or parts." Section 36-2-719(2), however, provides that the general remedies of the UCC will apply, notwithstanding an agreed-upon exclusive remedy, if the "circumstances cause [the remedy] to fail of its essential purpose." Under this provision, "where an apparently fair and reasonable clause because of circumstances fails in its purpose or operates to deprive either party of substantial value of the bargain, it must give way to the general remedy provisions of [the Code]." . . . In the instant case, however, there is no evidence that the limited remedy of repair, replacement, or return has failed of its essential purpose or that the contracting parties have been deprived of the substantial value of the bargain.

Serralles argues that Figgie, by first attempting to repair the equipment, elected to pursue repair as the exclusive remedy and, thereby, forgo enforcement of the remedy and reimbursement. From this premise, Serralles contends that Figgie's failure to repair the machines resulted in the remedy failing of its essential purpose. We find no support in the language of the UCC or in the cases interpreting it for this novel argument, and no evidence that this contemplated remedy of return and refund, once invoked, failed of its essential purpose.

. . . The district court correctly concluded that a limited remedy of repair, replacement, or return did not fail of its essential purpose.

AFFIRMED.

CRITICAL THINKING

Identify a significant ambiguous phrase that affects your ability to accept the court's conclusion. Explain the ambiguity and why it matters.

ETHICAL DECISION MAKING

Both parties probably prefer the ethical norm or value of efficiency. How so? Which facts would each party highlight in explaining how a particular decision would enhance the value of efficiency?

E-COMMERCE AND THE LAW

COMPUTER CONTRACTS

Sometimes, computer purchasers are surprised to find out they are bound to agreements that were created when sellers included contracts in the box in which the computer was delivered. Some of these agreements limit the purchaser's remedies. For instance, in *Hill v. Gateway 2000,** Hill purchased a computer from Gateway 2000 by placing a telephone order. The computer arrived through the mail. Gateway had placed a contract in the computer's shipping box that indicated that the terms sent in the box were binding on the buyer unless the buyer returned the computer within 30 days. One of the terms in this contract was a provision that stated that any disputes between the parties would be resolved through arbitration. The order taker had not read any of the terms of the contract over the telephone when Hill placed the order. When the computer arrived, Hill did not read the contract. In an effort to avoid the arbitration clause, Hill asked the court to determine that Gateway 2000 could not limit buyers' remedies or avenues through which they seek remedies (i.e., through arbitration) by bundling hardware and legal documents. The court ruled that the contract was binding on the parties. The court stated, "A contract need not be read to be effective; people who accept take the risk that the unread terms may in retrospect prove unwelcome."†

* 105 F.3d 1147 (1997).

† Ibid., p. 1148.

CASE OPENER WRAP-UP

Let's "See" the Damages in Defective Eye Ointment

When Abbott Laboratories contacted Altana about the defective erythromycin powder, the issue of liability was a foregone conclusion. Abbott had manufactured a defective product and thus is liable. But liable for what? To what extent is Abbott responsible? Some no-brainers first: Clearly the purchase price of the erythromycin would be credited back to Altana, and Abbott would be liable to Altana for the cost of manufacturing the defective batch. What about the cost to Altana of the recall and subsequent destruction of 1.2 million ointment tubes? After all, 1.2 million tubes of ointment, regardless of size, is a formidable number. The court found, fairly easily, that had it not been for Abbott's negligence, the cost of the recall and destruction would not have occurred and that it is clearly foreseeable in the pharmaceutical industry that recalls are a result of defective drug manufacture.[3] Abbott was held responsible for the costs incurred by Altana regarding the recall.

The case gets a bit more interesting regarding the last two issues of damages: employee overtime and loss of future sales due to the mistake by Abbott. Employing a test that requires the breaching party (Abbott) to put the nonbreaching party (Altana) in the position it would have been in had there not been a breach, the court found that Abbott was indeed liable to Altana for the overtime payments to employees in order to make up the lost batch and satisfy Altana's contractual customers. However, when the issue of future sales was considered, the court ruled that despite Abbott's breach, Altana was still able to fulfill all of its existing contracts. To award any money to Altana on loss of future sales would be speculative and an unfair windfall to Altana.

[3] *NYCOMED, Inc. v. Abbott Laboratories, Inc.*, 542 F.3d 1129 (2008).

KEY TERMS

consequential damages 537 | cover 535 | liquidated damages 534 | specific performance 537

SUMMARY OF KEY TOPICS

The Goal of Contract Remedies

The goal of contract remedies is to give the parties the *benefit of the bargain they struck,* and nothing more.

Remedies Available to Sellers and Lessors under the UCC

When the buyer/lessee is in breach, the seller/lessor can:

- Cancel the contract.
- Withhold delivery.
- Sell or dispose of the goods.
- Sue to recover the purchase price, lease payments due, or some other measure of damages that gives the seller or lessor the benefit of the bargain.
- Claim liquidated damages.
- Stop delivery.
- Reclaim the goods.

Remedies Available to Buyers and Lessees under the UCC

When the seller/lessor is in breach, the buyer/lessee can:

- Cancel the contract.
- Obtain cover.
- Sue to recover damages.
- Recover the goods.
- Obtain specific performance.
- Reject nonconforming goods.
- Revoke acceptance of nonconforming goods.
- Accept the nonconforming goods and seek damages.

Modifications or Limitations to Remedies Otherwise Provided by the UCC

Parties to sales and lease contracts are allowed to *modify or limit remedies.*

Courts uphold modifications or limitations to remedies unless the remedies fail in their *essential purpose.*

POINT / COUNTERPOINT

Should a Liquidated-Damage Clause Be Voided for Punitive Results?

YES	NO
The law has generally held that a liquidated-damage clause is enforceable as long as it is not punitive in nature. What is so unusual about a liquidated-damage clause is that it is a lot like a prenuptial agreement in a marriage: The parties agree how the "damages" will be allotted in the event that the relationship falls apart. Liquidated damages mirror the same concept: If the contract is breached, this contractual clause lays out how the nonbreaching party will be compensated, regardless of the actual loss incurred. However, common law throws in one condition: The liquidated damages cannot be so out of kilter with the actual damages that they become punitive in nature. When the liquidated damages are punitive, the clause is unenforceable, presumably under a fairness or public policy doctrine.	The overarching nature of contract formation is that parties may enter the marketplace and freely enter into contracts. Incorporated into this "freedom of contract" is the right and ability to negotiate and agree to liquidated-damage clauses. They are not clauses that are illegal, coerced, fraudulent, or the result of mistake. They are freely entered-into and freely executed contractual clauses. As such, the will of the parties entering into these clauses should be respected. The law negating the results of a duly negotiated liquidated-damage clause under a fairness or public policy doctrine is the kind of contract reformation that puts the entire concept of freedom to contract in doubt.

QUESTIONS & PROBLEMS

1. Define and differentiate between liquidated, consequential, and punitive damages. In your opinion, should punitive damages be permitted in intentional breaches of contracts. Explain your reasoning.

2. Are there limits to the right to cure? Does a breaching party have the right to cure the breach, or can the nonbreaching party proceed directly into a damage claim? (See *Dunleavy v. Paris Ceramics,* 47 Conn. Supp. 565 (2002), for an interesting discussion of the right to cure.)

3. A restaurant called "The Inn Between" entered into a contract to purchase a used restaurant computer system. The contract included installation and training from Remanco Metropolitan, Inc. The contract also required that Remanco keep the computer system in good operating order. The system was delivered and installed on March 29, 1995. The following day the computer malfunctioned and was down for three hours. Between March 30 and July 3, the restaurant contacted Remanco 48 times to report malfunctions. Though Remanco responded to each of the problems, the computer system continued to break down. Inn Between brought an action to revoke its acceptance of the computer system. It viewed the system as a nonconforming good. Remanco counterclaimed, seeking the unpaid price under the system maintenance agreement for nonreturn of the system. Which side gets the remedy it seeks? [*The Inn Between, Inc. v. Remanco Metropolitan, Inc.,* 662 N.Y.S.2d 1011 (1997).]

4. The defendant, Sterile Technologies, Inc., purchased a sterilizer from the plaintiff, Troy Boiler Works, on an installment payment plan. The defendant was to make installment payments charged with 1.5 percent interest per month. The sterilizer was delivered on August 23, 1996. The last payment was received on April 21, 1998. At the time of the last payment, the defendant still owed the plaintiff $112,615 as the balance due on the sterilizer; as of the time of the filing of the lawsuit, the defendant owed an additional $134,214 in finance charges. The plaintiff filed its lawsuit to collect on the account on November 20, 2002. The defendant moved to have the suit dismissed as it was filed after the four-year statute of limitations had run out (April 21, 1998, to November 20, 2002, is four years, seven months, and one day). Has the statute of limitations run? [*Troy Boiler Works, Inc. v. Sterile Technologies, Inc.,* 777 N.Y.S.2d 574 (2003).]

5. Andy and Melinda Meche purchased a car from Harvey, Inc. The Meches were interested in a low-priced car, and Harvey sold discounted program cars, which are vehicles that were previously owned by rental agencies. The sales representative explained to the Meches that program cars were usually under warranty and had relatively low mileage. The representative added that the cars were well maintained by the rental agencies and were "like new." After a short test drive, the Meches purchased a program car. The representative failed to tell them that the car had been previously wrecked and damaged. The Meches immediately noticed problems with the car and returned to Harvey to have the car inspected. On two occasions the representative told the Meches that the car had never been wrecked. A year later the Meches were involved in an accident, and the repairman noticed that the car had previously been wrecked and repaired. The Meches had put approximately 46,000 miles on the car. They brought an action to demand full rescission of the sale. Harvey, Inc., believed that the proper measure of damages should be reduction of the sales price. The company also believed that the buyers should pay for their use of the automobile. Finally, Harvey, Inc., did not agree with the trial court's finding of bad faith and subsequent award of attorney fees to the Meches. What is the appropriate remedy? [*Meche v. Harvey, Inc.,* 664 So. 2d 855 (1996).]

6. KGM Harvesting Company, the seller, had a contract to deliver 14 loads of lettuce each week to lettuce broker Fresh Network, the buyer, for 9 cents a pound. When the price of lettuce rose, KGM refused to deliver the lettuce it had promised to Fresh Network and instead sold the lettuce to others and made a profit of between $800,000 and $1,100,000. Fresh Network was angry over KGM's breach and subsequently pursued two actions. First, Fresh Network refused to pay KGM $233,000, the amount it owed the supplier for lettuce KGM had already delivered. Second, Fresh

Network purchased lettuce in the open market to fulfill its contractual obligation to Castellini/Club Chef. Fresh Network was forced to spend approximately $700,000 more for lettuce in the open market than it would have paid KGM. Castellini covered all but $70,000 of Fresh Network's extra expense. Castellini passed the extra cost along to Club Chef, which passed at least part of this cost along to its fast-food customers. KGM sought the balance due on its outstanding invoices ($233,000). Fresh Network sought damages for the difference between the price it was forced to pay to buy replacement lettuce and the price it had established through its contract with KGM ($700,000). Who prevails under this issue of cover? [*KGM Harvesting Company v. Fresh Network,* 42 Cal. Rptr. 2d 286 (1995).]

7. Maria Palomo purchased a used car from LeBlanc Hyundai Partnership. She explained to the sales representative that she needed the car to go to work and to take care of her grandchildren. The representative told her that the car would be appropriate for those purposes and that, if she took care of the car, it "would last forever." Palomo believed that this comment meant that the car would last her the rest of her life. She kept up with regular maintenance, but she began to have problems with the car. Palomo's mechanic recommended that she replace the car's engine. Palomo wanted to return the car to LeBlanc and be refunded the purchase price. The trial court awarded her $1,000 for repairs and damages. She appealed the decision. Should Palomo be allowed to revoke acceptance? What is the appropriate remedy? [*Palomo v. LeBlanc,* 665 So. 2d 414 (1996).]

8. Lupofresh, Inc., agreed to sell hops to Pabst Brewing Company. When the hops were processed and ready to be shipped to Pabst, Pabst canceled the order, claiming that the contract's pricing mechanism violated federal antitrust laws. In the subsequent lawsuit by Lupofresh for breach of contract, Pabst claimed that before Lupofresh could maintain a claim for the price, it had to attempt to resell the hops on the market since the goods had not been accepted by Pabst and had been merely identified to the contract. Did Lupofresh make a reasonable effort to resell the goods? Can Lupofresh recover the full purchase price from Pabst? [*Lupofresh, Inc. v. Pabst Brewing Company, Inc.,* 505 A.2d 37 (1985).]

9. Sherman Burrus, a printer, purchased a printing press from Itek Corporation. Itek's salesperson knew that Burrus was a job printer and even suggested various features regarding the printer that would be pertinent to Burrus's business. Burrus had continuing problems with the printer that Itek never corrected. In the subsequent lawsuit, Burrus asked the court to award consequential damages, including an amount to compensate him for lost business. Itek claimed that the defects were due to Burrus's improper maintenance and operation of the machine, but the court disagreed and ruled in favor of Burrus. What is the appropriate measure of damages? [*Burrus v. Itek Corporation,* 360 N.E.2d 1168 (1977).]

10. New Pacific Overseas Group (USA) Inc. alleged that Excal International Development Corp. and its president, Kenneth Shin-Hai King, breached a series of contracts for the sale and installation of concrete-block manufacturing equipment to New Pacific. New Pacific asked the court to issue a preliminary injunction that would require specific performance of the contracts, including the return of a computer unit taken by King from the equipment. Excal claimed that none of the goods identified in the contract were unique and that, consequently, specific performance was an inappropriate remedy. Is Excal correct? [*New Pacific Overseas Group (USA) Inc. v. Excal International Development Corp.,* 2001 WL 40822 (2001).]

Looking for more review materials?

The Online Learning Center at **www.mhhe.com/kubasek3e** contains this chapter's "Assignment on the Internet" and also a list of URLs for more information, entitled "On the Internet." Find both of them in the Student Center portion of the OLC, along with quizzes and other helpful materials.

CHAPTER

25 Warranties

LEARNING OBJECTIVES

After reading this chapter, you will be able to answer the following questions:

1 What are express warranties?

2 What is the implied warranty of title?

3 What is the implied warranty of merchantability?

4 What is the implied warranty of fitness for a particular purpose?

5 Do warranties apply to third parties?

6 Can warranties be disclaimed?

CASE OPENER

How Much Is That Doggie?

Linda Budd went searching for a new friend . . . and she found one for $400.[1] A brand new puppy. She purchased the puppy from Bernadette Vicidomine, a person who regularly sells puppies. Budd took her new friend home but realized that he was not in the best of health. Already attached to him, she did not return the puppy to Vicidomine, but instead took him to the veterinarian. Nearly $2,400 later, the puppy was medically mended. Budd then sued for the $400 purchase price and nearly $2,400 in vet bills, alleging breach of the implied warranty of merchantability. The questions raised with this simple, initially tragic but ultimately happy tale are:

1. Is this a transaction under UCC Article 2?
2. Is Vicidomine a merchant?
3. If so, does an implied warranty of merchantability attach to this sale?
4. What damages are available if this is a breach of the implied warranty of merchantability?

The Wrap-Up at the end of the chapter will answer these questions.

[1] *Linda Budd, Appellant v. Maureen Quinlan et al., Respondents,* 2008 NY Slip Op 28156, 19 Misc. 3d 66, 860 N.Y.S.2d 802, 2008 N.Y. Misc. LEXIS 2472, 66 U.C.C. Rep. Serv. 2d (Callaghan) 358 (2008).

Introduction

Chapters 21 through 24 have illustrated how the Uniform Commercial Code modified common law contract formation and execution to facilitate the ease of contracts for the buying and selling of goods and to reflect certain generally accepted business practices.

This chapter focuses on how the UCC changed the common law of **warranties,** which are assurances by one party that the other party can rely on its representations of fact. At common law, the only implied warranty is the warranty of assignability. When a party "assigns" a contract to another party, the assignor is impliedly guaranteeing that the rights being assigned are valid. However, the UCC adds to this concept. The warranties discussed in this chapter include both express and implied warranties. *Express warranties* are explicitly stated, whereas *implied warranties* are automatically, as a matter of law, injected into the contract.

After reading this chapter, you will understand what types of warranties arise with the creation of a contract. You will also understand how these warranties can be limited, as well as what role warranty law plays in protecting consumers.

Types of Warranties

Warranties generally arise in conjunction with a sale or lease. They impose certain duties on the seller or lessor, and if the seller or lessor fails to live up to these duties, he or she may be sued for breach of warranty. There are three basic categories of warranties: express warranties, implied warranties of title, and implied warranties of quality. The implied warranties of quality under the UCC include the implied warranty of merchantability, the implied warranty of particular purpose, and the implied warranty of trade usage. Each will be discussed in the following sections.

EXPRESS WARRANTIES

L01 What are express warranties?

Although the common law does not use the term *express warranty,* the concept and application does exist in the common law. It seems only fair and equitable that promises made by a seller to induce a buyer to execute a sales contract should be enforceable. An **express warranty** is any description of the good's physical nature or its use, either in general or specific circumstances, that becomes part of the contract. To use common law language, an express warranty is a material term of the sale or lease contract.

Express warranties may be found in advertisements or brochures (e.g., "This electric saw comes with a lifetime guarantee"). Such a warranty may also be part of a written sales or lease contract; or it may be a salesperson's oral promise concerning the good, made while attempting to close a deal. A sample or model may also provide an express warranty. Generally speaking, if the buyer relies on representations, those representations become part of the contract in the form of express warranties. Consider Case 25-1, which arose over the issue of whether a federally mandated label constitutes an express warranty.

Sometimes it is difficult to tell the difference between a statement of opinion and an express warranty. Statements of opinion are often salespersons' exaggerations and are known as "puffing." Puffing generally does not create an express warranty because it is not considered a representation of facts. Thus, if a salesperson says, "This is the finest piece of luggage I've ever seen," no one expects the buyer to rely on that as a promise. However, if the statement is "This suitcase is made of real crocodile," an express warranty may be created.

CASE 25-1 DONALD WELCHERT, RICK WELCHERT, JERRY WELCHERT, DEBORAH WELCHERT, APPELLEES v. AMERICAN CYANAMID INC., APPELLANT

U.S. COURT OF APPEALS FOR THE EIGHTH CIRCUIT 59 F.3D 69; 1995 U.S. APP. LEXIS 15719; CCH PROD. LIAB. REP. P14, 246 (1995)

Deborah and Jerry Welchert began commercially growing vegetables in 1989. In 1990, they leased a tract of land southeast of Blair, Nebraska, for this purpose that was also to be farmed by Jerry's brother, Rick Welchert. After they began planting vegetables, the Welcherts noticed that the vegetables were not growing properly. Deborah discovered that the herbicide Pursuit, manufactured by Cyanamid, had been applied to the land. Finding a label for Pursuit Plus, a different product, Deborah, Rick, and Jerry reviewed the label. This label claimed that crops could be planted eighteen months after application of the herbicide. Crops were again planted on the land in 1991, but continued to experience growth problems.

Meanwhile, Rick and another brother, Donald, leased another property in 1991 that had been treated with Pursuit Plus in 1989. Rick never read the Pursuit Plus label, relying on Deborah's account. Donald also did not read the label. The vegetables planted on this land experienced growth problems as well. All four Welcherts filed a suit alleging breach of express warranty for damages caused to their crops by Pursuit and Pursuit Plus.

Pursuit and Pursuit Plus are regulated by the federal government under the Federal Insecticide, Fungicide, and Rodenticide Act (FIFRA), which has specific labeling requirements. The U.S. District Court for the District of Nebraska ruled that the Welcherts' express warranty claims were not preempted by FIFRA. Cyanamid appealed.

JUDGE MCMILLIAN: Section 24 of FIFRA, as amended, provides in part:

(a) In general

A State may regulate the sale or use of any federally registered pesticide or device in the State, but only if and to the extent the regulation does not permit any sale or use prohibited by this subchapter.

(b) Uniformity

Such State shall not impose or continue in effect any requirements for labeling or packaging in addition to or different from those required under this subchapter.

At issue in the present case is the extent to which subsection (b) preempts a state law cause of action for breach of an express warranty. . . .

The express warranty claim of the Welcherts is based entirely on the label's statement with regard to the herbicide's carryover effect. They have not alleged that Cyanamid made any other statements with regard to the product which might serve as the basis for their express warranty claim. . . . [F]ederal regulation requires a pesticide manufacturer to provide labeling information about rotational crop restrictions. . . . Cyanamid's label statement on rotational crop use is thus a mandated disclosure, not a "voluntarily undertaken" promise. See Higgins v. Monsanto Co., 862 F. Supp. 751, 761 (N.D.N.Y. 1994) (Higgins) ("Express warranties have a voluntary quality, which is missing if they are mandated by EPA. The rationale that warrantors should be held to contracts that they voluntarily enter into does not apply when their actions are forced."). The determination that the challenged label statement was required by federal law was essential to the Worm court's [Worm v. American Cyanamid Co., 5 F.3d 744 (4th Cir. 1993)] decision on the preemption of the express warranty claim. The Worm court further rejected the plaintiff's argument that claims of breach of express warranty were not preempted because it "suggested that what was approved by the EPA was inadequate for purposes of establishing a state cause of action."

In the present case, like Worm, the Welcherts' express warranty claim arose solely on the basis of a labeling statement specifically required by federal law and approved by EPA. . . . Where Congress has so clearly put pesticide labeling requirements in the hands of the EPA, the Welcherts' claim challenging the accuracy of the herbicide label's federally-mandated and approved statement cannot survive. See Worm, 5 F.3d at 748 ("Because the language on the label was determined by the EPA to comply with the federal standards, to argue that the warnings on the label are inadequate is to seek to hold the label to a standard different from the federal one."). To hold otherwise would be to allow state courts to sit, in effect, as super-EPA review boards that could question the adequacy of the EPA's determination of whether a pesticide registrant successfully complied with the specific labeling requirements of its own regulations. In such case, state court consideration of the label statement would be an "additional requirement." In light of the extensive federal statutory and regulatory provisions on pesticide registration and labeling requirements, the preemptive language of §24(b) of FIFRA must be read to preclude the Welcherts' claim. Consequently, we hold that their state law claim for breach of an express warranty is preempted by FIFRA.

REVERSED in favor of defendant.

[continued]

CRITICAL THINKING

If FIFRA did not regulate Pursuit and Pursuit Plus, and Cyanamid had put the label on voluntarily, would the label then have constituted an express warranty? Why or why not?

ETHICAL DECISION MAKING

The continued problems of the Welcherts with the land where Pursuit and Pursuit Plus had been applied perhaps indicate a problem with the pesticide or with the label. Although American Cyanamid won this case, as an ethical company, should it spend money to do more research on its products to determine whether the label should be changed?

BUT WHAT IF . . .

WHAT IF THE FACTS OF THE CASE OPENER WERE DIFFERENT?

Let's say that, in the Case Opener, the breeder of the puppy said that the puppy was so energetic he would probably live forever. What kind of a statement is this? Alternatively, what if the breeder said that the puppy was in perfect health and came from a long line of dogs that never had health problems. What does this statement qualify as? Which statement is an express warranty?

Legal Principle: **An express warranty is really just another material term of the contract; it is an oral or written guarantee that is no different from any other descriptive requirement of the good being purchased, such as size, color, or weight.**

IMPLIED WARRANTIES OF TITLE

LO2 What is the implied warranty of title?

While no warranties automatically arise under the common law, the UCC assumes that the seller:

1. Has good and valid title to the goods.
2. Has the right to transfer title free and clear of any liens, judgments, or infringements of intellectual property rights of which the buyer does not have knowledge.

To see how providing warranties is a significant marketing tool, please see the **Connecting to the Core** activity on the text website at www.mhhe.com/kubasek3e.

The UCC specifically permits buyers to recover from sellers who have breached these **warranties of title.** The only exceptions to title warranties occur if they are disclaimed or modified by specific language in the contract or if the seller is obviously unable to guarantee title, as would be the case, for instance, at a sheriff's sale of seized goods. A buyer knows that goods repossessed and then resold and purchased through a sheriff's sale may have clouds on the title and unresolved liens that may surface.

Clearly, if the buyer is aware of any problem with the transfer of goods, the buyer is indeed purchasing them at her own risk. In contrast, if the buyer is unaware that the seller is transferring goods for which no good title passes or on which there are encumbrances or patent claims, the buyer may treat the contract as being in breach. Under such circumstances, the buyer may then avail himself of the remedies available under a breach situation.

IMPLIED WARRANTIES OF QUALITY

Implied warranties arise by operation of law under certain circumstances. Earlier, you read about the implied warranties of title that arise under the UCC. This section focuses on the three warranties of quality that arise under the UCC.

LO3 What is the implied warranty of merchantability?

Implied Warranty of Merchantability. Consider the following scenario: You purchase a toaster from a local discount store. When you use the toaster, all you get is either

CASE NUGGET

WHEN DOES THE TIME BEGIN TO RUN UNDER THE STATUTE OF LIMITATIONS FOR BREACH OF WARRANTY?

Lucy Mydlach, Appellee v. DaimlerChrysler Corporation, Appellant Supreme Court of Illinois
226 Ill. 2d 307, 875 N.E.2d 1047, 2007 Ill. LEXIS 1162, 314 Ill. Dec. 760, 64 U.C.C. Rep. Serv. 2d (Callaghan) 44

A buyer purchased a used car from a dealer for that brand of cars. The car was still under the car manufacturer's limited warranty. The car buyer, because of problems with the car that she alleged were not fixed, brought her claims under the Magnuson-Moss Warranty–Federal Trade Commission Improvement Act (Magnuson-Moss Act). The circuit court ruled that the claims were time-barred under the four-year statute of limitations in the Illinois Uniform Commercial Code. The state supreme court found that the car buyer could bring a breach-of-written-warranty claim under the Magnuson-Moss Act because the limitations period began to run not when the car was bought but when the repairs under the warranty were not made. However, the car buyer could not bring a revocation of acceptance claim because revocation of acceptance was unavailable under Illinois law against a car manufacturer that was not a party to the sales contract.

burnt toast or bread that is only slightly warm. You take the toaster back to the store and are met with this answer: "Well, we don't guarantee how well the toaster will work. After all, it does toast, either very, very lightly or very, very burnt." This answer, of course, is nonsense. There is a reasonable expectation of how a toaster will perform. That reasonable expectation is codified in the UCC **implied warranty of merchantability.**

To invoke this implied warranty, the purchaser must have purchased or leased the good from a merchant. Thus, a dirt bike purchased at a bicycle shop is covered by the warranty of merchantability, but a bike that is bought from a neighbor is not, unless the neighbor is a bicycle merchant.

BUT WHAT IF . . .

WHAT IF THE FACTS OF THE CASE OPENER WERE DIFFERENT?

Let's say that a woman goes to an American Kennel Club official dog breeder. She purchases a puppy and goes home. The puppy turns out to have severe physical defects resulting from genetic abnormalities. Is there an implied warranty with the dog? Can this dog be covered by the warranty of merchantability?

Under the UCC, the goods must be *merchantable,* meaning that they must:

1. Be able to pass without objection in the trade or market for similar goods.
2. In the case of fungible goods, be of fair or average quality within the description.
3. Be fit for the ordinary purposes for which such goods are used.
4. Be produced, within the variations permitted by the agreement, of even kind, quality, and quantity within each unit and among all units involved.
5. Be adequately contained, packaged, and labeled as the agreement may require.
6. Conform to the promises or affirmations made on the container or label, if any.

Given the description of the warranty of merchantability, was the puppy in the Case Opener "merchantable" when purchased? Does the implied warranty of merchantability require "good health"?

The quintessential case defining and illustrating the implied warranty of merchantability is that of the Blue Ship Tea Room and Ms. Webster (see Case 25-2). Although it is an older case, from 1964, it is one of the most enjoyable cases to read. If you read the case in its entirety, you'll find the judge giving the actual recipe for New England seafood chowder.

CASE 25-2 PRISCILLA D. WEBSTER v. BLUE SHIP TEA ROOM, INC.
SUPREME JUDICIAL COURT OF MASSACHUSETTS
347 MASS. 421, 198 N.E.2D 309 (1964)

A restaurant patron who ordered seafood chowder and choked on a fishbone brought this case. The plaintiff maintained that she would not have reasonably expected to find a bone in the chowder. At the trial, a jury found for Ms. Webster. The Blue Ship Tea Room, the defendant, appealed the case on the basis of the legal interpretation of the implied warranty of merchantability. The appellate decision below has become a classic in American jurisprudential reasoning.

JUDGE REARDON: . . . On Saturday, April 25, 1959, about 1 p.m., the plaintiff, accompanied by her sister and her aunt, entered the Blue Ship Tea Room operated by the defendant. The group was seated at a table and supplied with menus.

This restaurant, which the plaintiff characterized as "quaint," was located in Boston "on the third floor of an old building on T Wharf which overlooks the ocean."

The plaintiff, who had been born and brought up in New England (a fact of some consequence), ordered clam chowder and crabmeat salad. Within a few minutes she received tidings to the effect that "there was no more clam chowder," whereupon she ordered a cup of fish chowder. Presently, there was set before her "a small bowl of fish chowder." She had previously enjoyed a breakfast about 9 a.m. which had given her no difficulty. "The fish chowder contained haddock, potatoes, milk, water and seasoning. The chowder was milky in color and not clear. The haddock and potatoes were in chunks" (also a fact of consequence). "She agitated it a little with the spoon and observed that it was a fairly full bowl. . . . It was hot when she got it, but she did not tip it with her spoon because it was hot . . . but stirred it in an up and under motion. She denied that she did this because she was looking for something, but it was rather because she wanted an even distribution of fish and potatoes." "She started to eat it, alternating between the chowder and crackers which were on the table with . . . [some] rolls. She ate about 3 or 4 spoonfuls then stopped. She looked at the spoonfuls as she was eating. She saw equal parts of liquid, potato and fish as she spooned it into her mouth. She did not see anything unusual about it. After 3 or 4 spoonfuls she was aware that something had lodged in her throat because she couldn't swallow and couldn't clear her throat by gulping and she could feel it." This misadventure led to two esophagoscopies at the Massachusetts General Hospital, in the second of which, on April 27, 1959, a fish bone was found and removed. The sequence of events produced injury to the plaintiff which was not insubstantial.

We must decide whether a fish bone lurking in a fish chowder, about the ingredients of which there is no other complaint, constitutes a breach of implied warranty under applicable provisions of the Uniform Commercial Code, the annotations to which are not helpful on this point. As the judge put it in his charge, "Was the fish chowder fit to be eaten and wholesome? . . . [N]obody is claiming that the fish itself wasn't wholesome. . . . But the bone of contention here—I don't mean that for a pun—but was this fish bone a foreign substance that made the fish chowder unwholesome or not fit to be eaten?" The plaintiff has vigorously reminded us of the high standards imposed by this court where the sale of food is involved . . . and has made reference to cases involving stones in beans . . . , trichinae in pork . . . , and to certain other cases, here and elsewhere, serving to bolster her contention of breach of warranty.

The defendant asserts that here was a native New Englander eating fish chowder in a "quaint" Boston dining place where she had been before; that "[f]ish chowder, as it is served and enjoyed by New Englanders, is a hearty dish, originally designed to satisfy the appetites of our seamen and fishermen"; that "[t]his court knows well that we are not talking of some insipid broth as is customarily served to convalescents." We are asked to rule in such fashion that no chef is forced "to reduce the pieces of fish in the chowder to minuscule size in an effort to ascertain if they contained any pieces of bone." "In so ruling," we are told (in the defendant's brief), "the court will not only uphold its reputation for legal knowledge and acumen, but will, as loyal sons of Massachusetts, save our world-renowned fish chowder from degenerating into an insipid broth containing the mere essence of its former stature as a culinary masterpiece."

Notwithstanding these passionate entreaties we are bound to examine with detachment the nature of fish chowder and what might happen to it under varying interpretations of the Uniform Commercial Code.

Chowder is an ancient dish preexisting even "the appetites of our seamen and fishermen." It was perhaps the common ancestor of the "more refined cream soups, purees, and bisques." . . . The word "chowder" comes from the French "chaudiere," meaning a "cauldron" or "pot." "In the fishing villages of Brittany . . . 'faire la chaudiere' means to supply a cauldron in which is cooked a mess of fish and biscuit with some savoury condiments, a hodgepodge contributed by the fishermen themselves, each of whom in return receives his share of the prepared dish. The Breton fishermen probably carried the custom to Newfoundland, long famous for its chowder, whence it has spread to Nova Scotia, New

Brunswick, and New England." A New English Dictionary (MacMillan and Co., 1893) p. 386. Our literature over the years abounds in references not only to the delights of chowder but also to its manufacture. A namesake of the plaintiff, Daniel Webster, had a recipe for fish chowder which has survived into a number of modern cookbooks and in which the removal of fish bones is not mentioned at all. One old time recipe recited in the New English Dictionary study defines chowder as "A dish made of fresh fish (esp. cod) or clams, stewed with slices of pork or bacon, onions, and biscuit. 'Cider and champagne are sometimes added.'" Hawthorne, in The House of the Seven Gables . . . , speaks of "[a] codfish of sixty pounds, caught in the bay, [which] had been dissolved into the rich liquid of a chowder."

A chowder variant, cod "Muddle," was made in Plymouth in the 1890s by taking "a three or four pound codfish, head added. Season with salt and pepper and boil in just enough water to keep from burning. When cooked, add milk and piece of butter." The recitation of these ancient formulae suffices to indicate that in the construction of chowders in these parts in other years, worries about fish bones played no role whatsoever. This broad outlook on chowders has persisted in more modern cookbooks. "The chowder of today is much the same as the old chowder. . . ." The American Woman's Cook Book, supra, p. 176. The all embracing Fannie Farmer states in a portion of her recipe, fish chowder is made with a "fish skinned, but head and tail left on. Cut off head and tail and remove fish from backbone. Cut fish in 2-inch pieces and set aside. Put head, tail, and backbone broken in pieces, in stewpan; add 2 cups cold water and bring slowly to boiling point. . . ." The liquor thus produced from the bones is added to the balance of the chowder. . . .

Thus, we consider a dish which for many long years, if well made, has been made generally as outlined above. It is not too much to say that a person sitting down in New England to consume a good New England fish chowder embarks on a gustatory adventure which may entail the removal of some fish bones from his bowl as he proceeds. We are not inclined to tamper with age old recipes by any amendment reflecting the plaintiff's view of the effect of the Uniform Commercial Code upon them. We are aware of the heavy body of case law involving foreign substances in food, but we sense a strong distinction between them and those relative to unwholesomeness of the food itself, e.g., tainted mackerel . . . and a fish bone in a fish chowder. Certain Massachusetts cooks might cavil at the ingredients contained in the chowder in this case in that it lacked the heartening lift of salt pork. In any event, we consider that the joys of life in New England include the ready availability of fresh fish chowder. We should be prepared to cope with the hazards of fish bones, the occasional presence of which in chowders is, it seems to us, to be anticipated, and which, in the light of a hallowed tradition, do not impair their fitness or merchantability. While we are buoyed up in this conclusion by Shapiro v. Hotel Statler Corp. 132 F. Supp. 891 (S. D. Cal.), in which the bone which afflicted the plaintiff appeared in "Hot Barquette of Seafood Mornay," we know that the United States District Court of Southern California, situated as are we upon a coast, might be expected to share our views. We are most impressed, however, by Allen v. Grafton, 170 Ohio St. 249, where in Ohio, the Midwest, in a case where the plaintiff was injured by a piece of oyster shell in an order of friend [sic] oysters, Mr. Justice Taft (now Chief Justice) in a majority opinion held that "the possible presence of a piece of oyster shell in or attached to an oyster is so well known to anyone who eats oysters that we can say as a matter of law that one who eats oysters can reasonably anticipate and guard against eating such a piece of shell. . . ."

Thus, while we sympathize with the plaintiff who has suffered a peculiarly New England injury, the order must be . . . judgment for the defendant.

REVERSED in favor of defendant.

CRITICAL THINKING

As with most legal decisions, the critical-thinking activity that is most obvious is the need to reexamine the analogies used by the court in justifying its conclusion. The plaintiff wished the court to say that fish chowder was like what? What analogy did the defendant want the court to accept? Would the aptness of the analogy depend at all on the size of the bone in the fish chowder?

ETHICAL DECISION MAKING

The judge mainly used assumption of risk to rule against Webster, though she suffered an injury in fact. Should the restaurant have somehow compensated her? What would the WPH framework indicate should be done?

COMPARING THE LAW OF OTHER COUNTRIES

WARRANTIES IN KAZAKHSTAN

What Western law refers to as a *warranty* is called a *pledge* in Kazakhstan. Pledges serve the same function as warranties: They indicate the seller's confidence in the performance of a product and the buyer's right to compensation for nonperformance. Specifically, the Civil Code defines a pledge as "a means of securing the performance of an obligation by virtue of which the creditor (pledgeholder) has the right, in the event of the failure of the debtor to perform the obligation secured by the pledge, to receive satisfaction from the value of the pledged property preferentially before other creditors of the person to whom this property belongs."

A pledge can be given in two instances. First, and most commonly, it can arise from a contract. Second, it can be given because the situation lends itself to legislation that demands a pledge be issued.

When a pledge is violated, the concept of penalties is employed. Penalties are similar to remedies in the U.S. law. Penalties are always issued in monetary form, the amount of which is usually determined by a court. Parties may stipulate penalties for failing to fulfill a pledge in the contract, but this is not necessary for compensation to be collected. Legislation does exist that specifies penalty amounts for particular situations in an attempt to avoid excessive payments.

Implied Warranty of Fitness for a Particular Purpose. Another important UCC implied warranty is the **implied warranty of fitness for a particular purpose.** This warranty comes about when a seller or lessor knows or has reason to know (1) why the buyer or lessee is purchasing or leasing the goods in question and (2) that the buyer or lessee is relying on him or her to make the selection. Under this warranty, the seller or lessor does not have to be a merchant.

LO4 What is the implied warranty of fitness for a particular purpose?

An implied warranty of fitness for a particular purpose should not be confused with an express warranty. If the buyer walks into a store and the salesclerk says, "This saw will cut through metal," the seller has created an express warranty. However, if the buyer comes into the store and asks the salesclerk for a saw to cut through some copper tubing and the salesclerk refers the customer to a wall of different saws, it is reasonable for the buyer to assume that all the saws on the wall will satisfy the *particular purpose* that the buyer has indicated. Thus, an implied warranty of fitness for a particular purpose has been created.

Implied Warranty of Trade Usage. The UCC, always diligent in its goal to facilitate the flow and ease of commercial activity, recognizes that a well-accepted course of dealing or trade usage may create implied warranties dependent on the circumstances. For example, if it is generally accepted in the trade that a certain product is always preassembled and shrink-wrapped, the failure of the seller to deliver the goods in that condition would be a breach of the **implied warranty of trade usage.**

Warranty Rights of Third Parties

LO5 Do warranties apply to third parties?

The idea of a seller's being in breach of an implied warranty raises an entirely new issue: Is the seller liable to anyone other than the buyer? This question may initially sound peculiar. After all, the seller and the buyer are bound together by contract, and if either breaches, then the breaching party is liable to the nonbreaching party.

Consider this possible scenario: Jane buys a blender from a local store. Before using the blender, she lends it to her cousin Valerie to use at a party. While Valerie is blending drinks at the party, the blades fly off the blender and injure her. What obligation, if any, does the seller have to the injured Valerie? No contractual relationship exists between Valerie and the seller. However, it seems to be patently unfair to conclude that Valerie has no cause of action against the seller. The UCC recognizes this unfairness and clearly states that Valerie may indeed have a cause of action based on breach of warranty against

CASE NUGGET

IMPLIED WARRANTY OF MERCHANTABILITY: BLUE SHIP TEA ROOM FOLLOW-UP

Jackson v. Bumble Bee Seafoods, Inc.
2003 Mass. App. Div. 6 (2003)

Anthony Jackson ate tuna fish from two cans of tuna canned by the defendant, Bumble Bee Seafoods, Inc. The tuna had been purchased by Canteen Corporation. Small tuna fish bones were in the canned tuna and lodged in Jackson's mouth. Jackson sued Bumble Bee Seafoods, Inc., for breach of the implied warranty of merchantability (and apparently had a Massachusetts attorney who was unaware of Massachusetts case law on this issue).

The trial court granted summary judgment to the defendant, and the plaintiff appealed to the Massachusetts court of appeals.

The court of appeals cited *Phillips v. West Springfield,* which held that a cause of action would lie for the plaintiff if "the consumer reasonably should not have expected to find the injury-causing substance in the food." Yet, noting that *Phillips* goes on to cite the Blue Ship Tea Room case, the court of appeals stated:

> [A]s a matter of law, bones in fish chowder should reasonably be expected. . . . As the Supreme Judicial Court has determined as a matter of law consumers must reasonably expect to find small bones in their chowder, we must find that as a matter of law consumers must reasonably expect to find small ones in canned tuna. Therefore, there are no material facts at issue on plaintiff's claim arising out of the claimed breach of warranty of merchantability; and, the trial court was correct to grant Bumble Bee summary judgment on the portion of plaintiff's case sounding in breach of warranty.

the seller. The states are given the following three choices regarding *third-party beneficiaries of warranties:*

1. Seller's warranties extend to the buyer's household members and guests.
2. Seller's warranties extend to any reasonable and foreseeable user.
3. Seller's warranties extend to anyone injured by the good.

Most states have adopted the second option. Nevertheless, a number of questions remain concerning third-party rights, the nature of privity of contract, and the ability to maintain a lawsuit under the warranty rights of a UCC contract. Note these questions in Case 25-3.

BUT WHAT IF . . .

WHAT IF THE FACTS OF THE CASE OPENER WERE DIFFERENT?

Let's say that, in the Case Opener, the woman purchases a puppy from a registered breeder. It later turns out that the dog has genetic defects due to inbreeding that make the dog extremely aggressive. The dog attacks the owner's neighbor's child. How and why could the breeder be responsible for the attack on the child? Under what law could the neighbor file a breach of warranty against the breeder?

CASE 25-3 MELISSA KAHN v. VOLKSWAGEN OF AMERICA, INC.

SUPERIOR COURT OF CONNECTICUT, JUDICIAL DISTRICT OF STAMFORD-NORWALK AT STAMFORD

2008 CONN. SUPER. LEXIS 376 (2008)

Melissa Khan alleges that on May 27, 2004, she entered into a lease and warranty agreement with Riverbank Motors Corporation, Inc. (the Dealership), for a new, 2004 Volkswagen Toureg (the "Vehicle"), manufactured by the defendant. The Vehicle came with written "factory warranties" for any nonconformities or defects in materials or workmanship. Ms. Kahn alleges that the defendant, Volkswagen of America, Inc., and the Dealership made various other "express warranties" to the plaintiff regarding the quality of the Vehicle. After delivery, the Vehicle experienced various operating problems and malfunctions on myriad occasions during the period from February 2005 to August 2006, including multiple system monitoring lights coming on, engine stalling, problems with shifting, and the Vehicle lurching forward unexpectedly. The plaintiff returned the Vehicle to the Dealership and other Volkswagen dealerships repeatedly for repairs and service of these problems. Despite multiple attempts and a total of forty-nine days in the repair shop, the problems with the Vehicle were never rectified. She now brings this action under a variety of claims: breach of express warranties, breach of implied warranties, breach of contract, and breach of Connecticut's "lemon law." Her breach of implied warranties pertains to the fact that with all of its defects—which were confirmed—the car was undriveable and thus not merchantable. Here is the court's reasoning regarding her claim of Volkswagen's breach of the implied warranty of merchantability as it applies to the plaintiff, a third-party beneficiary of that implied warranty.

JUDGE DAVID R. TOBIN: . . . In the third count, the plaintiff asserts a claim for breach of implied warranties under the Magnuson-Moss Warranty Act, 15 U.S.C. §2301 et seq., and the Uniform Commercial Code. The defendant has moved to strike the third count on the grounds that plaintiff cannot state a legally sufficient cause of action for breach of implied warranties. The defendant makes two principal arguments in support of its motion to strike: 1) that although it made express warranties, it did not extend implied warranties to the plaintiff; and 2) that the plaintiff may not bring an action for breach of implied warranties sounding in contract against a party with whom it is not in contractual privity.

In response the plaintiff claims that the Magnuson-Moss Warranty Act guarantees that consumers who receive express warranties enjoy implied warranty protection as well, and that Connecticut law no longer enforces a privity requirement for breach of contractual implied warranty actions.

A. Implied Warranties

Contrary to the plaintiff's position, the Magnuson-Moss Warranty Act does not itself create implied warranties. It merely provides a cause of action for breach of an enforceable implied warranty. 15 U.S.C. §2310(d)(1). State law, rather than Magnuson-Moss, governs the creation and enforcement of implied warranties. . . . In her complaint the plaintiff alleges that "[t]he Vehicle was subject to implied warranties of merchantability, as defined in 15 U.S.C. §2308 and U.C.C. 2-314 and 2-318, running from the Defendants to the Plaintiff." It appears that the plaintiff's claim is that the purported implied warranty she seeks to enforce is derived from the underlying sale of the vehicle from the defendant to the Dealership (the lessor in the lease transaction), and that she is entitled to enforce such a warranty as a third-party beneficiary to that transaction. This inference may be drawn from the fact that Article 2 of the Uniform Commercial Code applies to the sale of goods and §2-318 addresses the rights of third-party beneficiaries to enforce a seller's warranties.

General Statutes §42a-2-314 establishes that a warranty of merchantability from the seller to the buyer is implied in all contracts for the sale of goods. A breach of this warranty occurs, if at all, at "the time of sale . . . or when [the goods] leave the manufacturer's control." [Citations omitted.] Criscuolo v. Mauro Motors, Inc., 58 Conn.App. 537, 546, 754 A.2d 810 (2000). However, the plaintiff was not the buyer in the sale made by the defendant manufacturer, the Dealership was. By its terms, General Statutes §42a-2-314 creates a warranty that is enforceable, if at all, by the Dealership.

The plaintiff also relies on General Statutes §42a-2-318 as a basis for her alleged right to enforce the warranty. Section 42a-2-318, however, only extends the right to enforce the seller's warranty to "any natural person who is in the family or household of his buyer or who is a guest in his home if it is reasonable to expect that such a person may use, consume, or be affected by the goods and who is injured in person by breach of warranty." The plain language explicitly limits the extension of the right of enforcement to individuals who are family members or guests in the Dealership's home and who suffer personal injuries as a result of a breach of the warranty. Therefore, the plaintiff has not pleaded facts which bring her within the application of General Statutes §42a-2-318, nor do the facts alleged give rise to any such inference.

Moreover, plaintiff has not pled any alternative theory pursuant to which she may enforce any implied warranty derived from the sale of the vehicle to the Dealership. . . . Accordingly, the court finds that plaintiff has failed to show that an implied warranty of merchantability was created between the plaintiff and the defendant, or that the plaintiff is entitled to enforce the warranty between the defendant and the Dealership as a beneficiary of that contract.

B. Privity

Even if the court were to find that the plaintiff had the right to enforce an implied warranty of merchantability against the defendant, the court would be constrained to agree with the defendant's second claim that such an action is barred by the lack of privity between the plaintiff and the defendant. The court agrees with the defendant that Connecticut law has maintained a privity requirement that prevents parties who are not in contractual privity with the warrantor from enforcing any implied warranty. See Rosenthal v. Ford Motor Co, Inc., 462 F.Sup.2d 296, 309 (D.Conn. 2006) (noting differences between common-law tortious implied warranty claim and contractual implied warranty claim include the abolition of a privity requirement in the former); Koellmer v. Chrysler Motors Corporation, 6 Conn. Cir. 478, 485, 276 A.2d 807, cert. denied, 160 Conn. 590, 274 A.2d 884 (1971). Similarly, a contractual or buyer-seller relationship between the parties is required to maintain a claim under Article 2 of the UCC which governs the sale of goods. Sylvan R. Shemitz Designs, Inc. v. Newark Corp., Superior Court, judicial district of New Haven, Docket

[continued]

No. 055001029 (May 24, 2006, Blue, J.) (41 Conn. L. Rptr. 440, 2006 Conn. Super. LEXIS 1554).

Connecticut's general rule requiring privity is subject to certain limited exceptions. For example, after reviewing developments in Connecticut law, District Judge Clarie held that the privity requirement is not etched in stone and the doctrine is only applied to situations in which alternative remedies that do not require privity are available. Utica Mutual Ins. Co. v. Denwat Corp., 778 F.Sup. 592, 595-96 (D.Conn. 1991). Courts applying Connecticut law have also recognized that it may be possible to satisfy the privity requirement by pleading facts which establish an agency relationship between a vehicle manufacturer and the Dealership. Koellmer v. Chrysler Motors Corporation., supra, 6 Conn. Cir. 485-86. "The existence of an agency relationship is one of fact." Wesley v. Schaller Subaru, Inc., 277 Conn. 526, 543, 893 A.2d 389 (2006). In Koellmer, however, a directed verdict in favor of the manufacturer was upheld due to the plaintiff's failure to prove an agency relationship where the manufacturer made express written warranties but all direct dealings surrounding the completion of the transaction were between the plaintiff and the dealer.

Other jurisdictions have liberally reduced the role of the privity requirement in breach of implied warranty actions sounding in contract. For example, some courts have found that the extension of the express warranty makes the manufacturer "a party to the retail contract and removes the privity objection as to both express and implied warranties" on the reasoning that the consumer, having received the express warranty, should be entitled to rely on the manufacturer for implied warranties absent a disclaimer. . . . Despite the trend in other jurisdictions to dispense with the privity requirement in contractual breach of implied warranty actions, Connecticut maintains the requirement except under limited circumstances which are not present in this case. There is no allegation in the complaint of an agency relationship between the Dealership and manufacturer nor is it alleged that the plaintiff has no alternative means to obtain a remedy. The no alternative remedies exception also appears particularly inapplicable in light of the plaintiff's claim of breach of express warranty set forth in the second count of her complaint.

C. Conclusion

The court finds that the plaintiff is precluded from maintaining the claim for breach of implied warranty set forth in her third count, on both grounds raised by the defendant. Accordingly, the motion to strike the third count is granted.

Defendant's motion is granted to dismiss the third count.

CRITICAL THINKING

The court emphasizes the privity-of-contract requirement to enforce an implied warranty from the car manufacturer to a subsequent purchaser (through a dealership). However, the court is clear that had certain facts been alleged, the privity requirement may have been relaxed, allowing the plaintiff to maintain her claim. What could those facts be?

ETHICAL DECISION MAKING

Do you find an ethical lapse in the court's arguments in this case regarding privity of contract? Isn't it clearly the intent of the UCC to have the implied warranties extend to foreseeable users? Why is the court so adamant in refusing to recognize this concept?

Warranty Disclaimers and Waivers

L06

Can warranties be disclaimed?

There really is no question as to whether an implied warranty may be disclaimed. The real question is *how* it is to be disclaimed. Generally speaking, if an implied warranty is to be disclaimed, the seller must do so in clear, unambiguous, conspicuous language. In order to disclaim the implied warranty of fitness for a particular purpose, the seller must disclaim the warranty in writing. The seller may disclaim the warranty of merchantability either orally or in writing; however, some states require that the term *merchantability* must be used in the disclaimer.

The buyer may also waive both implied and express warranties. A buyer may waive these rights by (1) failing to examine goods for which an express warranty was created by a sample or model or (2) failing to comply with the seller's request to inspect the goods. For example, a printer requests that the buyer come into the shop to proof letterhead and envelopes. The buyer refuses, claiming that he is too busy, and tells the printer to go ahead

COMPARING THE LAW OF OTHER COUNTRIES

WARRANTIES IN HONG KONG

An important distinction must be made between *conditions* and *warranties* in Hong Kong business contracts involving the sale of goods. In such contracts, time of payment and delivery are considered warranties unless otherwise specified. If the time of payment or delivery is not fulfilled, the procedures for breach of warranty are followed. These procedures differ from those that take place if a condition is violated. For example, if advance payment is considered a warranty and the payment is not made, the seller can sue for damages; but if the contract names payment as a condition, the seller can either recall the contract and resell the goods or sue for damages.

and run the stationery. On receipt of the stationery, the buyer discovers that the numbers in the phone number are transposed, making the stationery useless. Unfortunately, the buyer has indeed waived his rights due to his failure to inspect.

A buyer may also waive her warranty rights under the contract by failing to comply with the statute of limitations. Under the UCC, the buyer or seller must bring a lawsuit on a breached contract within four years of when the breach occurred or when the nonbreaching party became aware of it. The buyer and seller are free to negotiate contractually a shorter time period (as long as it is not less than one year), but they are not free to negotiate a longer time period than the four years.

BUT WHAT IF . . .

WHAT IF THE FACTS OF THE CASE OPENER WERE DIFFERENT?

Let's say that, in the Case Opener, the breeder of the puppy said that the puppy was so energetic he would probably live forever but that the potential buyer should take the dog to the vet to get him checked out just in case. The buyer said that she trusted the breeder and was not worried. However, when she got home, it turned out that the dog was a very sickly dog. What is the type of warranty that has been made in this scenario, and what happened to it? Could the buyer still sue the breeder for breach of warranty?

While the UCC remains the primary codification of both state and federal laws regarding sellers' warranties, there has been, in addition to the UCC, specific legislation pertaining to this issue. The 1975 federal law known as the Magnuson-Moss Act requires that if a seller decides to issue a written warranty for a consumer good (the seller is not required to do so), the seller must indicate whether that warranty is a *full* warranty or a *limited* warranty. This applies to any consumer good sold for more than $10. If the written warranty is silent, it is presumed to be a full warranty, which means that if the good fails or is defective, the good or its defective part will be replaced. If replacement cannot be timely effected, the buyer has the right to a refund or a full replacement.

CASE NUGGET

DOES THE IMPLIED WARRANTY OF TITLE EXTEND TO SUBSEQUENT PURCHASERS?

First State Bank & Trust Company of Shawnee, Appellee v. Wholesale Enterprises, Inc., Appellant/Third-Party Plaintiff v. Jim Hazelwood and Lone Star Bank, Third-Party Defendants

1994 OK CIV APP 137, 883 P.2d 207, 1994 Okla. Civ. App. LEXIS 118, 65 O.B.A.J. 3393, 25 U.C.C. Rep. Serv. 2d (Callaghan) 677 (1994)

Someone stole the Corvette in Texas from its original owner, Taylor, and later a title was issued there stating the car was a reconditioned vehicle (i.e., one with parts from other vehicles). In 1988, a Texas bank repossessed the car from a subsequent purchaser and sold it to Hazelwood (a third-party defendant in the trial court). Hazelwood somehow obtained an original vehicle title for the Corvette in Oklahoma and then traded the car to Appellant Wholesale Enterprises, Inc., as partial consideration for his purchase of another car. In October 1990, Wholesale Enterprises sold the Corvette to another individual, Gary Brown. Brown financed his purchase through appellee First State Bank & Trust Company of Shawnee, granting First State Bank a security interest to secure his loan. Brown subsequently defaulted on the loan, and First State Bank repossessed the car. Meanwhile, Brown filed bankruptcy and was relieved of any further obligation on his car loan. Shortly after repossessing the car, First State Bank tried to resell it through a local auto auction. Employees of the auction house apparently noticed that the car had an original vehicle title yet also had identifiable parts derived from other vehicles. Because of this discrepancy between the title to and the content of the car, the state of Oklahoma filed notice of forfeiture in August 1991, and First State Bank received actual notice of the forfeiture proceedings but failed to answer or defend. At the state's request, the court in the forfeiture proceeding entered a consent judgment in favor of the original owner's insurance company. Then, in September 1991, First State Bank sued Wholesale Enterprises for breach of warranty of title.

The court found for Wholesale Enterprises and ruled that the implied warranty of title did not extend to subsequent purchasers. See the Point/CounterPoint at the end of this chapter for an argument on whether the implied warranty of title should be extended to subsequent purchasers.

If the good is sold for more than $15, the written warranty must disclose a number of items of information—names and addresses of the warrantors, any limitations on the warranty, and the procedures required to activate the warranty remedies—all in readable and easily understood language, in other words, not in *legalese!*

CASE OPENER WRAP-UP

How Much Is That Doggie?

This simple case provides a wonderful template for approaching UCC Article 2 problems. The judge's reasoning lays out an approach for judges and students alike in dealing with these kinds of problems.

1. The court found that a sale of a dog was indeed a sale of a good under UCC Article 2.
2. The seller was a merchant, and as such the implied warranty of merchantability attached to any sale of goods from that merchant.
3. Usually, under a breach-of-contract theory, damages are limited to the contractual loss, in this case the $400 purchase price.
4. But, under the UCC and breach of an implied warranty, forseeable and consequential damages are not only allowed but required in the furtherance of justice.

To that end, the plaintiff was awarded reimbursement for her veterinarian bills.

KEY TERMS

SUMMARY OF KEY TOPICS

Introduction

A *warranty* is a promise on the part of the seller with respect to certain characteristics of the good.

Types of Warranties

Express warranties:

1. Description of the good's physical nature or its use.
2. Either general or specific.
3. Material term of the contract.
4. Reliance of buyer on representations.

Implied warranties of title:

1. Passage of good title.
2. Implied promise of no liens or judgments against title.
3. Implied promise that title is not subject to any copyright, patent, or trademark infringement.

Implied warranties of quality:

- *Implied warranty of merchantability:* A warranty based on a reasonable expectation of performance of the purchased good. The good must:
  1. Pass without objection.
  2. Be of fair quality within the description.
  3. Be fit for ordinary uses.
  4. Have even quality.
  5. Be adequately packaged.
  6. Conform to promises made on the label.
- *Implied warranty of fitness:* A warranty that arises when the seller knows the purpose for which the buyer is purchasing goods and the buyer relies on the seller's judgment.
- *Implied warranty of trade usage:* A warranty that arises as a result of generally accepted trade practices.

Warranty Rights of Third Parties

Third-party beneficiaries of warranties:

1. Seller's warranties may extend to the buyer's household members and guests.
2. Seller's warranties may extend to any reasonable and foreseeable user.
3. Seller's warranties may extend to anyone injured by the good.

Warranty Disclaimers and Waivers

Methods of waiving:

1. Seller does not make warranties in the first place (express warranty).
2. Seller disclaims in clear, unambiguous, conspicuous language (implied warranty).

3. Buyer fails or refuses to examine goods.
4. Buyer fails to file suit within the time of the statute of limitations.

Magnuson-Moss Act: If a seller decides to issue a written warranty for a consumer good, the seller must indicate whether the warranty is full or limited.

POINT / COUNTERPOINT

Should the Implied Warranty of Title Be Extended to Subsequent Purchasers?

YES	NO
In the Case Nugget on page 558, Oklahoma courts ruled that the implied warranty of title is not extended to subsequent purchasers. This seems to fly in the face of the logic of the general thrust of the UCC. The UCC operates under the assumption that commercial activity should be enabled and enhanced. Applying the implied warranty of title to subsequent purchasers would facilitate commercial activity by not requiring any purchasers to "look over their shoulders" to ensure that a commercial transaction is not suspect.	Title to goods is so rarely suspect that the necessity of applying the implied warranty of title to subsequent purchasers is really not a practical issue other than in situations involving financing and repossession/foreclosure, as in the Case Nugget. Further, in cases where repossession is involved, the financial institution parties are on notice to verify title. In addition, many of the applications in question deal with stolen goods, but the implied warranty of title never extends to stolen goods and thus they are not subject to its protection.

QUESTIONS & PROBLEMS

1. Poor Sarah Jane not only had a short-lived marriage but found out that her supposedly $45,000 ring was worth only half that amount. It seems that the jeweler had misrepresented the value to her now ex-husband. Sarah Jane brings an action against the jeweler for breach of an express warranty. Does she have the ability to sue even though she was not the purchaser? [*Schaurer v. Mandarin Gems of California, Inc.,*] 125 Cal. Rptr. 4th 949 (2005).]
2. Why is it even necessary to have implied warranties when the parties can and should negotiate the terms of the contracts?
3. Review Case 25-2, *Webster v. Blue Ship Tea Room.* Can you think of other situations today for which this case might serve as legal precedent?
4. Carl and Dorothy-Helen Huprich raise Arabian horses for breeding and selling. In 1989, they purchased corn from farmer David Bitto to feed to their horses after having it tested for aflatoxin, a toxin often present in horse feed. The sample tested negative, so the Huprichs purchased a large amount of feed. Soon after they began feeding their horses the corn, two died and a third soon fell ill and died as well. The Huprichs began to suspect that the corn was the culprit after another two horses died and a veterinarian confirmed that the horses had died from leukoencephalomalacia, a fatal brain disease that results from the toxin Fumonisin B-1. This toxin grows on mold known as *Fusarium moniliforme,* a mold often present on feed corn. The Huprichs sued Bitto, alleging breach of implied warranty of merchantability. Should they win on this claim? [*Huprich v. Bitto,* 667 So. 2d 685; 1995 Ala. LEXIS 307; CCH Prod. Liab. Rep. P14, 267; 28 U.C.C. Rep. Serv. 2d (Callaghan) 526.]
5. Duall Building Restoration, Inc., brought an action against the property owner of 1143 East Jersey, alleging that the owner had failed to make the necessary payments specified in the parties' painting

contract. Duall had been contracted to restore the brick walls of the property. The painting job carried a five-year guarantee against peeling or flaking. The property owners counterclaimed, stating that the paint had been defectively applied. Duall had applied Modac paint to the walls, but the paint had peeled from the walls. A brochure for the paint indicated that it was fit for the specific purpose of waterproofing brick walls. The paint manufacturer had assured Duall that the paint would adhere to the brick walls. Who was responsible for the damage? Was this a breach of the implied warranty of merchantability? How do you think the court resolved the conflict? [*Duall Bldg. v. 1143 East Jersey and Monsey Products,* 652 A.2d 1225 (1995).]

6. Kevin Scott purchased a Ford van on credit on May 14, 1987. The total cost of the van was $18,399, and Scott made a down payment of $3,406. After the van was damaged in a traffic accident, Scott failed to make the necessary installment payments required by the contract. The van was repossessed in 1998 and sold at a public auction in 1989. The credit company advised Scott that there was a deficiency of $6,452.56 that he had to pay. Ford Motor Credit Company (FMCC) filed suit for the deficiency on April 16, 1992. Scott argued that the period of limitations for FMCC's claim had passed. Maryland code required that "[a] civil action at law shall be filed within three years from the date it accrues unless another provision of the Code provides a different period of time within which an action shall be commenced." Do you agree with Scott? Why or why not? [*Scott v. Ford Motor Credit Company,* 691 A.2d 1320 (1997).]

7. After living in their home for three years, Roger Nathaniel and Sharon Diamond sold the home to the plaintiffs, Marc Copland and Joan Lund. Nathaniel and Diamond hired a pest control company to inspect the home. The company reported that there was evidence of a previously treated infestation but that no evidence of active infestation was found. This report was provided to Copland and Lund before the sale of the home. The contract specified that the purchaser had inspected the premises and agreed to purchase it "as is." A year later, the plaintiffs discovered that levels of chlordane were present on the property. The plaintiffs discovered that the home had been treated 10 years earlier for termites. At that time, chlordane was used to remove termites. Despite one toxicologist's report that the level of chlordane did not constitute a health concern, Copland and Lund spent $50,000 removing the contaminated soil from their property. They brought an action against the previous owners, Nathaniel and Diamond. How do you think the court decided? [*Copland v. Nathaniel,* 624. N.Y.S.2d 514 (1995).]

8. Knapp Shoes manufactures and distributes work shoes and sells and distributes shoes made by other shoe companies. One of Knapp's suppliers, Sylvania, produced several models of Knapp shoes. The leather Sylvania used to manufacture the soles tended to fall apart easily. There were additional problems with each line of shoe manufactured by Sylvania. Sylvania claimed that it "stood behind" its product and fully warranted its product against manufacturing defects. Knapp subsequently fell behind on its payments to Sylvania. Sylvania complained to Knapp, but Knapp contended that the defective shoes were jeopardizing important accounts. In 1990 Knapp tried to return two of the models of shoes Sylvania had produced for Knapp in 1988, but Sylvania would not accept the return. Knapp sued Sylvania for breach of express warranty and of implied warranties of merchantability and fitness for a particular purpose. Sylvania countersued for the unpaid bills. How do you think the court decided? [*Knapp Shoes Inc. v. Sylvania Shoe Mfg. Corp.,* 72 F.3d 190 (1995).]

9. Mrs. Cipollone had been a lifetime smoker, starting back in the 1940s. She subsequently died in 1984 from lung cancer. Her husband brought suit against the cigarette companies of the Liggett Group and Philip Morris, citing breach of express warranty and fraud. Mr. Cipollone based these allegations on advertisements that the defendants ran on television, particularly during the *Arthur Godfrey Show.* At trial, the court did not permit the defendants to introduce evidence to show that Mrs. Cipollone did not rely on these advertising representations in deciding whether to continue smoking. Does the plaintiff have the burden to show that the express warranties were in fact relied on? Conversely, may the defense introduce evidence to show just the opposite? [*Cipollone v. Liggett Group Inc.,* 893 F.2d 541 (1992).]

10. Does possible misuse constitute a waiver of the implied warranties? Consider the case of a lessee of a car who, after 18 months, found that the car was running roughly. When the lessee took the car back to the dealership, the lessee was told that several valves in the engine were bent due to misuse by the lessee. The lessee refused to pay the bill of over $500, claiming that the repair should be covered under the warranties. The car dealership's position was that misuse constituted a waiver of the warranties. [*LaBella v. Charlie Thomas Inc. and Mercedes-Benz of North America,* 942 S.W.2d 127.]

Looking for more review materials?

The Online Learning Center at **www.mhhe.com/kubasek3e** contains this chapter's "Assignment on the Internet" and also a list of URLs for more information, entitled "On the Internet." Find both of them in the Student Center portion of the OLC, along with quizzes and other helpful materials.

CHAPTER 26

Negotiable Instruments: Negotiability and Transferability

LEARNING OBJECTIVES

After reading this chapter, you will be able to answer the following questions:

1 Why do we need negotiable instruments?

2 What types of negotiable instruments does the UCC recognize?

3 What are the requirements of negotiability?

4 What are the words of negotiability?

CASE OPENER

Oral Agreements and Negotiable Instruments

As a gambling facility, MGM Desert Inn, Inc., regularly holds and executes negotiable instruments. During a period of two months, patron William E. Shack, Jr., entered MGM and delivered eight checks to the casino in exchange for markers. These checks, which totaled $93,400, were signed by Shack and dated at the time of transfer. When MGM sent Shack's checks to the bank for payment, they were dishonored because the funds in Shack's account were insufficient.

MGM filed an action in district court to obtain the $93,400. Shack contended that a casino host had told him he had sufficient remaining casino credit to receive the markers. The district court judge ruled in favor of MGM, affirming its argument that the checks were negotiable instruments and stating that no evidence of an oral agreement between the casino and Shack was provided. Shack was ordered to pay MGM $5,000 for attorney fees in addition to the $93,400 originally owed on the checks.[1]

1. If you were employed at MGM, what would you do to avoid future disputes with your patrons about the nature of payment agreements?
2. If Shack's claims about an oral agreement with MGM were true, would that affect your decision about whether payment on the checks was currently due?

The Wrap-Up at the end of the chapter will answer these questions.

[1] *MGM Desert Inn, Inc., dba Desert Inn Hotel & Casino v. William E. Shack,* U.S. District Court, District of Nevada, 809 F. Supp. 783 (1993).

Once a sales contract has been created and executed and the parties are aware of their respective obligations under the contract, the next phase is *payment* by the buyer to the seller for the goods purchased. Payment is usually made in one of three ways: in cash, through credit arrangements (discussed in the chapter on secured transactions), or with a *substitute for cash.* This substitute for cash is the focus of this and the next three chapters.

A substitute for cash, or a **negotiable instrument,** is a written document containing the signature of the creator that makes an unconditional promise or order to pay a certain sum of money, either at a specified time or on demand. Negotiable instruments are executed on a daily basis in the form of checks, certificates of deposit, drafts, and promissory notes in exchange for goods, services, or business financing.

Exhibit 26-1 illustrates where negotiable instruments fit in the process of market exchange for a good or service.

The Need for Negotiable Instruments

LO1

Why do we need negotiable instruments?

A currency or cash substitute has existed for centuries in Anglo-American law. England's ancient *lex mercatoria,* or law of merchants, recognized that agreements could be paid for with documents that promised payment, and these documents themselves could be circulated as a substitute for money. However, the English king's court did not at first accept the use of document paper as money. Therefore, merchants had to develop their own system and rules for using documents as payments.

It is easy to see why using documents as payments can greatly facilitate commercial transactions, especially when cash is in short supply or it is dangerous to transfer large amounts of currency or precious metals. These documents of payment were generically called *commercial paper* and under Article 3 of the UCC were specifically labeled *negotiable instruments.*

CONTRACTS AS COMMERCIAL PAPER

We've already discussed one prevalent form of commercial paper: contracts. Whether it is under common law or UCC Article 2, a contract is commercial paper and through assignment may be circulated and transferred throughout the business world. Exhibit 26-2 will help you understand the process of assignment. Follow it step-by-step as you read the following:

Exhibit 26-1

Negotiable Instruments and Market Exchange

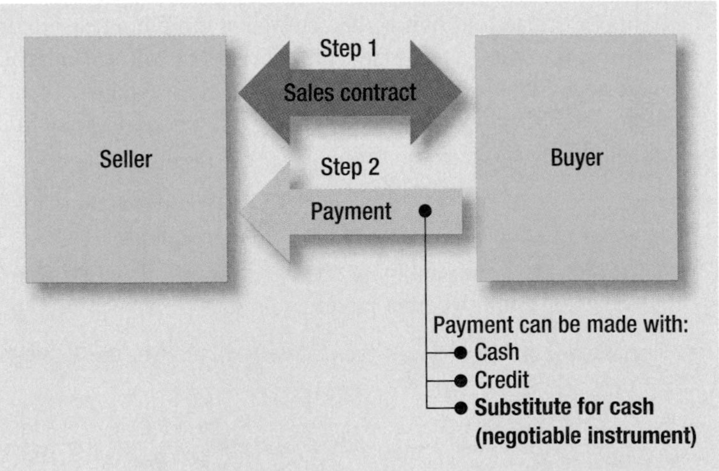

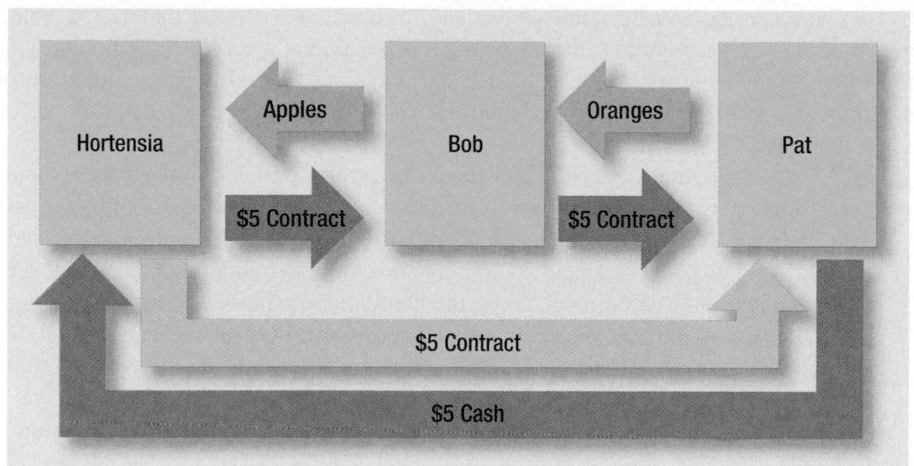

Exhibit 26-2
Negotiable-Instrument Assignment

Bob sells a bushel of apples to Hortensia; in exchange, Hortensia executes a contract to pay Bob $5 on demand. A few days later, Bob buys some oranges from Pat for $5. Instead of paying Pat $5 cash, Bob *assigns* to Pat Hortensia's obligation to pay him $5. When Pat demands the money from Hortensia, Hortensia will pay Pat and everyone will be square.

Exhibit 26-2 demonstrates that any contractual obligation, except personal and nonassignable ones, may be transferred and thus classified as commercial paper.

PROBLEMS WITH COMMERCIAL PAPER

Our example of Bob, Hortensia, and Pat is a simple one, but it still contains a potential problem. Consider the fact pattern again, but assume that unknown to Hortensia, the apples Bob sold her were rotten.

When Pat demands the $5 from Hortensia, naturally Hortensia will refuse, claiming that Bob breached their original contract by delivering defective apples. She is on legally safe ground, and all Pat can do is go back and sue Bob because the commercial paper he transferred is not acceptable. In other words, these circumstances defeat the purpose of allowing transferability of commercial paper as a substitute for currency.

Types of Negotiable Instruments

LO2
What types of negotiable instruments does the UCC recognize?

Under Article 3, the UCC recognizes four types of negotiable instruments: notes, certificates of deposit (a highly specialized type of note), drafts, and checks (a highly specialized type of draft) (UCC Section 3-104). A **note** is a promise, by the *maker* of the note, to pay a payee [UCC 3-103(a)(9)]. A **draft** is an order by a *drawer* to a drawee to pay a payee [UCC 3-103(a)(6)]; in our example, Bob could have drawn a draft ordering Hortensia to pay Pat $5, since Hortensia owed Bob $5. A note is a two-party instrument; by definition a draft is a three-party instrument.

Legal Principle: **Under the UCC, notes, certificates of deposit, checks, and drafts can be negotiable instruments.**

Notes and drafts can be either demand instruments or time instruments. The payee (or subsequent holder) of a **demand instrument** can demand payment at any time. The

UCC defines an instrument "payable on demand" as one that "(i) states that it is payable on demand or at sight, or otherwise indicates that it is payable at the will of the holder, or (ii) does not state any time of payment" [3-108(a)]. Payment on a **time instrument** can be made only at a specific future time, which the UCC says must be easily determined from the document itself [3-108(b)].

To see advantages of certificates of deposit, please see the **Connecting to the Core** activity on the text website at www.mhhe.com/kubasek3e.

Certificates of deposit and checks are specific illustrations of these distinctions. A **certificate of deposit,** or **CD,** is a promise by a bank to pay a payee a certain amount of money at a future time. The UCC defines a certificate of deposit as "an instrument containing an acknowledgment by a bank that a sum of money has been received by the bank and a promise by the bank to repay the sum of money. A certificate of deposit is a note of the bank" [3-104(j)]. Usually, a payee buys a CD from a bank and then collects the principle plus a determined amount of interest in the future.

A **check** is a specific draft, drawn by the owner of a checking account, ordering the bank to pay the payee from that drawer's account [UCC 3-104(f)]. A check is always a demand instrument and can never be a time instrument (postdating does not affect the ability of the holder to cash the check before the postdate). Types of checks include:

- *Cashier's check:* "[A] draft with respect to which the drawer and drawee are the same bank or branches of the same bank" [UCC 3-104(f)].
- *Traveler's check:* "[A]n instrument that (i) is payable on demand, (ii) is drawn on or payable at or through a bank, (iii) is designated by the term 'traveller's check' or by a substantially similar term, and (iv) requires, as a condition to payment, a countersignature by a person whose signature appears on the instrument" [UCC 3-104(i)].
- *Certified check:* "[A] check accepted by the bank on which it is drawn" [UCC 3-409(d)].

Case 26-1 addresses the question of whether a promissory note is a demand instrument.

CASE 26-1 REGER DEVELOPMENT, LLC v. NATIONAL CITY BANK
U.S. COURT OF APPEALS, SEVENTH CIRCUIT
592 F.3D 759 (2010)

Reger Development borrowed money from National City Bank, using a revolving line of credit supported by a promissory note. At the point that National City discussed the possibility of calling the note, Reger Development sued the bank for breach of contract and fraud.

Reger had met with the bank prior to using the line of credit to discuss the loan. Reger asked about changing the terms of the credit agreement. The bank representative, Duncan, responded that the National City documents were nonnegotiable. Reger then executed the contract. The main question here is whether the promissory instrument entitles National City to demand payment from Reger at will.

CIRCUIT JUDGE FLAUM: The first clause in the Note reads:

> PROMISE TO PAY: Reger Development, LLC ("Borrower") promises to pay to National City Bank ("Lender"), or order, in lawful money of the United States of America, on demand, the principal amount of Seven Hundred Fifty Thousand & 00/100 Dollars ($750,000.00) or so much as may be outstanding, together with interest on the unpaid outstanding principal balance of each advance. Interest shall be calculated from the date of each advance until repayment of each advance.
>
> PAYMENT: Borrower will pay this loan in full immediately upon Lender's demand. Borrower will pay regular monthly payments of all accrued unpaid Interest due as of each payment date, beginning July 25, 2007, with all subsequent Interest payments to be due on the same day of each month after that.

The Note proceeds to reference payment on lender's demand several times in other provisions. It also features

[continued]

a "NO COMMITMENT" clause that states: "NOTWITHSTANDING ANY PROVISION OR INFERENCE TO THE CONTRARY, LENDER SHALL HAVE NO OBLIGATION TO EXTEND ANY CREDIT TO OR FOR THE ACCOUNT OF BORROWER BY REASON OF THIS NOTE." The contract then includes integration language defining it as the final and complete agreement between parties. The Note is governed by federal and Illinois law, to the extent the former does not preempt the latter. Language above the signature line specifies in capital letters that the borrower has read and understood the terms of the document.

On August 19, 2008, National City asked the company to pay down $125,000 towards the principal of the line of credit, which appellant did the next business day. Then, on September 9, 2008, National City asked that Reger Development "term out" $300,000 of the Note by having one of Kevin Reger's other businesses agree to take out a three-year loan in that amount secured by a second mortgage on some real estate.

Kevin Reger "expressed surprise" about these developments and asked if National City would call the line of credit if Reger Development did not agree to the requests. The bank acknowledged that Reger Development was not in default but stated that "there is a possibility that we may demand payment of the line."

Reger Development then filed a complaint in Illinois state court accusing National City of breaching the terms of the Note.

While Illinois law generally holds that "a covenant of fair dealing and good faith is implied into every contract absent express disavowal," the duty to act in good faith does not apply to lenders seeking payment on demand notes. In light of this controlling law, appellant's complaint appears vacuous. Reger Development's allegations are "that National City breached the Contract Documents by arbitrarily and capriciously (1) demanding payment under the Line of Credit even though Reger Development was in good standing and (2) unilaterally changing and attempting to change the fundamental terms of the Contract Documents without Reger Development's consent." Reger Development attempts to substantiate the first part of the breach claim by pointing to several provisions in the Note that it believes to be fundamentally inconsistent with the nature of a demand instrument. These include the "INTEREST AFTER DEFAULT" provision, which reads, in relevant part, "[u]pon default, including failure to pay upon final maturity, the interest rate on this Note shall be increased by adding a 2.000 percentage point margin"; the prepayment clause, which allows the borrower to pay down "all or a portion of the amount owed earlier than it is due"; and the clause that grants National City the right to access the borrower's financial information. Reger Development describes the latter as a "financial insecurity" provision that conditions the right to demand payment on some economic cause.

We are not persuaded by the suggestion that these references to due dates and default somehow overpower the repeated, explicit contract language setting forth the lender's right to demand payment at any time. A bank that wishes to call the Note can specify some future date on which it needs payment as a "due date." Failure to pay at that point in time, as well as failure to make monthly interest payments required by the Note, would constitute default, but the mere use of the terms "due date" or "default" would not alter the nature of the agreement. Similarly, the "PREPAYMENT" provision cannot bear the interpretive load that appellant wants to place on its shoulders. The clause reads: "Borrower may pay without penalty all or a portion of the amount owed earlier than it is due. Early payments will not, unless agreed to by Lender in writing, relieve Borrower of Borrower's obligation to continue to make payments of accrued unpaid Interest." Both its content and placement (immediately following the "payment" and "variable interest rate" clauses) are innocuous. The language merely reinforces National City's right to collect scheduled monthly interest payments and does not deviate from the structure of a demand note.

For the foregoing reasons, we Affirm the district court's grant of National City's motion to dismiss the Reger Development complaint.

AFFIRMED.

CRITICAL THINKING

What is the ambiguity in the agreement with National City that Reger believes provides him with a proper basis for his cause of action against National City?

ETHICAL DECISION MAKING

What stakeholders are affected by this decision? The law is concerned with much more than the interests of the two parties in the dispute. What other parties are affected by whether Reger won this case?

Exhibit 26-3
Potential Complexity of Negotiable Instruments

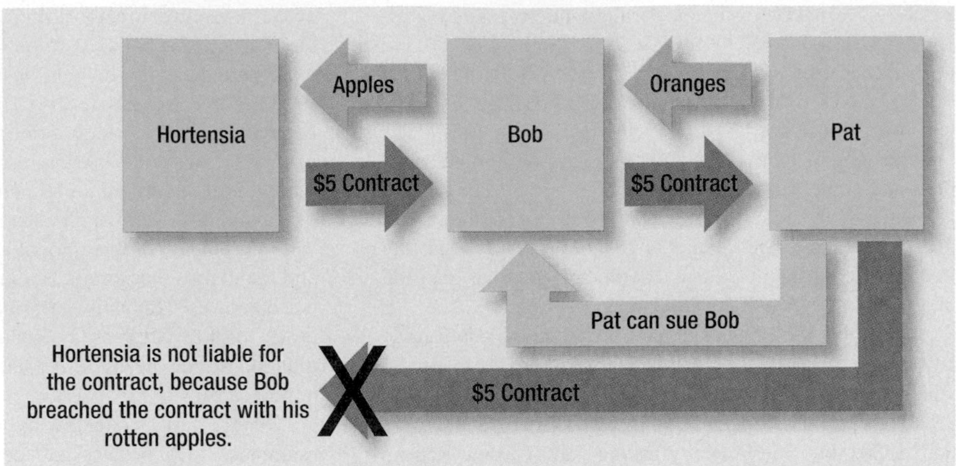

An Overview of the Law of Negotiable Instruments

LO3 What are the requirements of negotiability?

A negotiable instrument must meet specific requirements of *negotiability*. However—and this is important—if an instrument fails to qualify as a negotiable instrument, that does *not* mean it fails to be a perfectly good and enforceable contract. All it means is that the special rules regarding negotiable instruments do not apply.

A negotiable instrument confers some special rights on its possessor. Let's go back to Bob, Hortensia, and Pat. Use Exhibit 26-3 to follow the logic of the exchanges.

Hortensia buys apples from Bob and gives him a negotiable note promising to pay $5 on demand. Bob then buys oranges from Pat for $5 and properly transfers (or *negotiates*) the $5 negotiable note to Pat. Pat presents the note to Hortensia for payment, *after* Hortensia has found out that the apples she bought from Bob were bad. Hortensia refuses to pay Pat, and Bob has disappeared. Pat sues Hortensia for the $5. Under the rules of negotiable instruments, Pat could very well prevail, and Hortensia, regardless of Bob's rotten apples, might have to pay.

Here are the issues raised by this chain of events:

1. What constitutes a negotiable instrument?
2. How does someone transfer a negotiable instrument?
3. What is the status of the holder of a negotiable instrument?
4. What happens when the person who created a negotiable instrument has a good defense for not honoring it?

When the contracts for such transactions are not in breach, everything works out fine. Problems do happen, however, and have led to the evolution of the law surrounding negotiable commercial paper. Case 26-2 discusses whether a contract is a negotiable instrument or a common law contract.

CASE 26-2 SAMUEL JAMES THOMPSON v. FIRST CITIZENS BANK & TRUST CO.
COURT OF APPEALS OF NORTH CAROLINA
151 N.C. APP., 567 S.E.2D 184 (2002)

On November 5, 1998, Samuel James Thompson borrowed $10,500 from First Citizens Bank & Trust Co. As collateral for the loan First Citizens required Thompson to purchase a $10,000 certificate of deposit. Thompson met with Catherine Huggins, First Citizens' employee, to execute the documents associated with the loan and the purchase of the CD.

[continued]

Huggins gave him a CD confirmation form with her signature, acknowledging he had opened a CD account with an initial deposit of $10,000. On the same day, Thompson executed an "Assignment of Deposit Account," assigning the CD to the bank as collateral for his loan. In November 1999, Thompson paid off the $10,000 loan from First Citizens and presented the CD confirmation for payment. The bank refused to pay the amount due on the CD and claimed that, notwithstanding the signed confirmation, Thompson had not deposited $10,000 to purchase a CD.

JUDGE BIGGS: . . . Defendant argues that the trial court erred in granting summary judgment for plaintiff, and contends that the evidence raised a genuine issue of material fact regarding whether there was consideration for the CD. The resolution of this issue requires us to examine several features of the commercial transaction at issue. First, plaintiff and defendant disagree about whether the CD is a negotiable instrument as defined by the Uniform Commercial Code (UCC). We conclude that the CD at issue in the present case is not a negotiable instrument, and therefore is not governed by the negotiable instrument provisions of the UCC. The UCC applies only to negotiable instruments.

A "negotiable instrument" is "an unconditional promise or order to pay a fixed amount of money[.]" Negotiable instruments, also called simply "instruments," may include, e.g., a personal check, cashier's check, traveler's check, or CD. N.C.G.S. 25-3-104, however, provides that a financial document such as a CD "is not an instrument if, at the time it is issued or first comes into possession of a holder, it contains a conspicuous statement, however expressed, to the effect that the promise or order is not negotiable or is not an instrument governed by this Article."

In the instant case, the CD confirmation clearly states, in upper case type, "NON-TRANSFERABLE." We conclude that this qualifies as "a conspicuous statement . . . that the promise or order is not negotiable," and, thus, that the CD does not fall within the purview of the negotiable instrument provisions of the UCC.

"Because the certificate of deposit at issue does not fall under the UCC, we must turn to the common law." Holloway at 100, 423 S.E.2d at 755. The CD confirmation is a contract between plaintiff and defendant, and its interpretation is governed by principles of contract law.

. . . Notwithstanding the language of the CD confirmation, defendant contends that language in its "Deposit Account Agreement" booklet establishes that the CD confirmation was issued subject to a condition precedent. This document states that an account "is not opened or valid until we receive . . . the initial deposit in cash or collectible funds." The CD confirmation is, however, the document that verifies or acknowledges that this condition precedent (deposit of money) has already occurred. Therefore, the bank booklet does not raise an issue of fact.

Nor is evidence of a unilateral mistake admissible to contradict the terms of a contract. Goodwin v. Cashwell, 102 N.C. App. 275, 277, 401 S.E.2d 840, 840 (1991) (parol evidence rule excludes consideration of unilateral error made by one party in calculations pertaining to settlement agreement; Court notes that a "unilateral mistake, unaccompanied by fraud, imposition, undue influence, or like oppressive circumstances, is not sufficient to void a contract").

AFFIRMED in favor of defendant.
Judges GREENE and HUDSON concur.

CRITICAL THINKING

Judge Biggs gives only one reason for ruling that the contract was not a negotiable instrument. He says that it is not an instrument if, at the time it is issued or first comes into possession of a holder, it contains a conspicuous statement to the effect that the promise or order is not negotiable. What evidence from this case supports his reasoning that the agreement contains a conspicuous statement to that effect?

ETHICAL DECISION MAKING

Did First Citizens have an ethical obligation to provide further information about the negotiability of the contract? If so, what could the bank do to prevent similar cases in the future?

NEGOTIABLE INSTRUMENT VERSUS SIMPLE CONTRACT

While the Thompson case is a good example of what constitutes a negotiable instrument, it is important to note that a simple contract is very different. First, simple contracts are assigned to an assignee, while negotiable instruments are negotiated to a holder. A holder and an assignee differ because a negotiable instrument gives greater rights to the holder

E-COMMERCE AND THE LAW

CAN ALL NEGOTIABLE INSTRUMENTS BE IN ELECTRONIC FORMAT?

Electronic negotiable instruments are often preferable to traditional negotiable instruments because electronic forms foster more efficient business practices by reducing the amount of time a document must wait to be processed. However, the very nature of electronically sent information means that certain types of negotiable instruments should not be in a virtual format. An excellent illustration of this concept is found within the 2008 Kenya Communications Act, which outlines exclusions for electronic negotiable instruments. For example, the act excludes an electronically created or executed will from being upheld as a legal negotiable instrument in court. Exclusions such as this are stipulated because wills and certain other documents are legally significant and binding only if those documents have been signed in their physical form. Considering the ease with which a person could falsify an online signature, it is impractical to allow important documents such as wills to be completed in an electronic format. Specifying what is and is not legally valid in cyberspace is an important step in reducing legal ambiguities and possible conflicts.

Source: http://aitec.usp.net/Banking%20&%20Payment%20Technologies%20EA,17-19Feb2009/MichaelMurungi.pdf.

than the transferor. Second, as you will read below, negotiable instruments lack the requirements of contracts: consideration and both offer and acceptance.

REQUIREMENTS FOR NEGOTIABILITY

To be negotiable (which is *not* the same as *enforceable*) under UCC 3-104(a), the instrument must satisfy seven requirements. It must:

1. Be a written document.
2. Be signed by the creator of the instrument.
3. Have an unconditional promise or order to pay.
4. Specify a fixed sum of money.
5. Specify payment either on demand or at a fixed future time.
6. Contain the words *to the order of* or words indicating it is a bearer instrument.
7. Contain no additional promises.

As you read through the following explanation of the requirements, use Exhibit 26-4 as an example of how they apply to personal checks.

Exhibit 26-4 Requirements of Negotiability in a Check

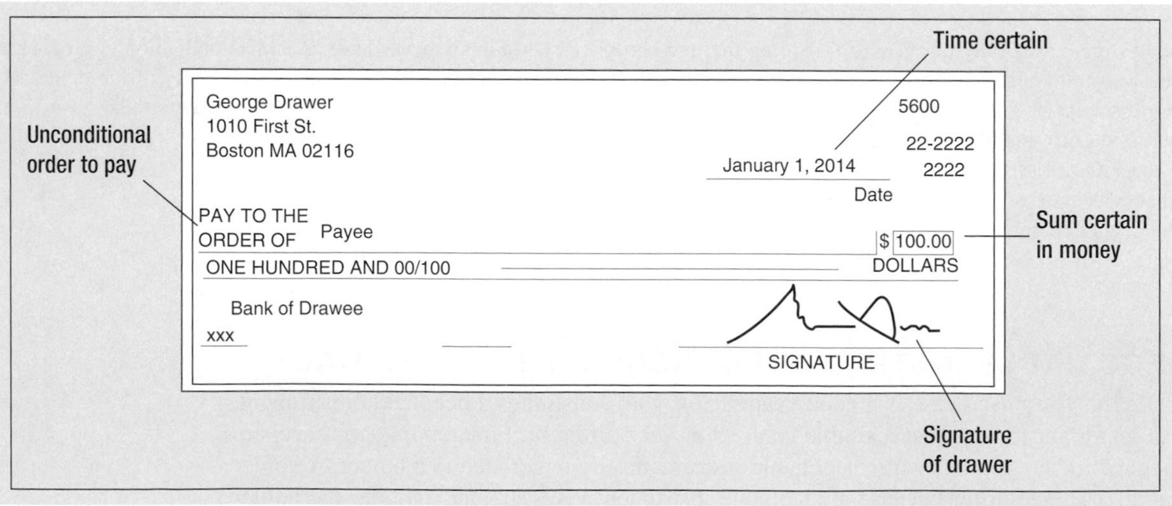

Written Document. Clearly, the law does not permit an *oral* negotiable instrument. However, under the right circumstances and when the words are provable, such a statement may be a binding, enforceable *contract.*

BUT WHAT IF . . .

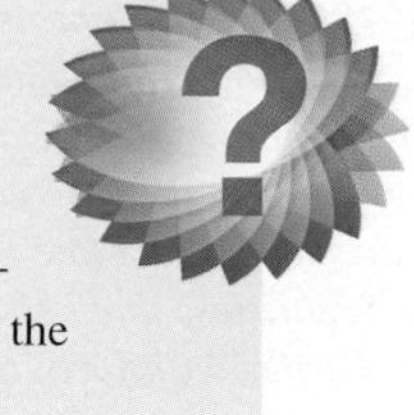

WHAT IF THE FACTS OF THE CASE OPENER WERE DIFFERENT?

Recall that, in the Case Opener, Shack contended that an oral agreement had been made between him and the plaintiff about "rolling debt." What if Shack had presented a recording of this particular oral agreement actually being made? Would the judge still rely only on the written negotiable agreement?

Recall that in the Case Opener, the judge ruled in favor of MGM partly because no evidence of an oral agreement was presented. Although Shack claimed that a conversation had occurred, this was not enough evidence for the court. Instead, the judge had to go by the written negotiable agreement. The Case Opener is just one of many examples indicating that the best business practice is to obtain written documentation of all the details pertaining to negotiable instruments.

The written document must have two characteristics: **relative permanence** and **movability.** Writing a negotiable instrument in the mud, for example, clearly lacks permanence. Thus, it is not a negotiable instrument. Likewise, mud is not something we can move about in a commercially reasonable or expected manner.

Signature of the Maker or Drawer. The UCC and precedent cases are fairly liberal in interpreting what constitutes a signature. Anyone's affirmative mark, from a full-blown *John Hancock* to an *X,* will suffice, provided the party intended that the mark be placed on the instrument and uses that mark to identify himself or herself [UCC 1-201(39)]. The UCC specifies that a signature "may be made (i) manually or by means of a device or machine, and (ii) by the use of any name, including a trade or assumed name, or by a word, mark, or symbol executed or adopted by a person with present intention to authenticate a writing" [3-401(b)]. Likewise, a duly authorized agent's signature on behalf of his or her principal binds the principal and satisfies this signature requirement [UCC 3-401(b)].

A handwritten negotiable instrument satisfies the signature requirement even without a formal signature. The handwritten statement "I, Philippe Gauchet, promise to pay Roberta Alexander or the bearer the sum of $20 on Sunday July 4, 2010" would satisfy the signature requirement because the handwriting affirms the maker's intent and, in that handwritten promise, the maker wrote his own name, Philippe Gauchet.

Case 26-3 discusses the extent to which wire transfers and electronic signatures can be governed by the laws set forth by the Uniform Commercial Code.

BUT WHAT IF . . .

WHAT IF THE FACTS OF THE CASE OPENER WERE DIFFERENT?

Let's say, in the Case Opener, that Shack bought a casino marker using a check after he told his assistant to stamp an automated "signature" at the bottom. Would he still be personally liable for the check? Alternatively, what if he signed simply an "H" at the bottom of the check? Would his check be a valid negotiable instrument?

CASE 26-3 STATE v. WARNER
SUPREME COURT OF OHIO
55 OHIO ST. 3D 31, 564 N.E.2D 18 (1990)

On December 13, 1985, defendant-appellant, Marvin L. Warner, controlling shareholder of Home State, and two former Home State Savings Bank presidents, David J. Schiebel and Burton M. Bongard, were indicted and charged with numerous felonies arising from Home State's dealings with ESM Government Securities, Inc. (ESM). The amended indictment charged Warner with forty-two counts of misapplication of funds and forty-one counts of unauthorized acts in violation of Ohio Revised Code 1153.01. Further, Warner was indicted on four counts of securities fraud. . . . The Ohio Revised Code makes it a crime to fraudulently transfer funds by means of a draft or other written instrument. Therefore, one issue before the court in this very complicated securities fraud case is whether an electronic transfer qualifies as a "draft" or "other written instrument." The Ohio Court of Appeals determined it did not and reversed.

JUSTICE HOLMES: Since this issue is one of first impression for this court, we will consider how other jurisdictions have applied laws drafted primarily to address traditional written documents, such as checks, but applied to modern wire transfers. In Richards v. Platte Valley Bank the United States Court of Appeals decided that the word "check" as used in the Uniform Fiduciaries Act could be interpreted to include wire transfers of funds. The Richards court stated:

> We believe wire transfers are analogous to checks for application of the Uniform Fiduciaries Act. The transfer of funds by cable or telegraph is in law a check. Lourie v. Chase Nat'l Bank.
>
> The transfer item must be in some form of writing, such as letter, telegram or magnetic disc. . . . Wire transfers are considered irrevocable after transmission. Delbrueck, 609 F. 2d at 1051.
>
> The wire transfer requirements are similar to the definition of a check under the Uniform Commercial Code. A check is defined as a draft drawn upon a bank and payable on demand, signed by the maker or drawer, containing an unconditional promise to pay a sum certain in money to the order of the payee. A wire transfer is a written order to pay, drawn upon a bank containing an unconditional promise to pay a sum certain in money to the order of the beneficiary. The only element missing is the maker's signature. We do not consider this element significant for purposes of excluding wire transfers from the operation of the Uniform Fiduciaries Act.

Although the Uniform Commercial Code is not directly applicable to this case due to the nature of the transfer, analogous use of its concepts supports the proposition that wire transfers are written instruments for purposes of R.C. 1153.01. Delbrueck & Co. v. Mfrs. Hanover Trust Co. ("the Uniform Commercial Code ['UCC'] is not applicable to this case because the UCC does not specifically address the problems of electronic funds transfer. However, analogous use of concepts such as the finality of checks once 'accepted' support the irrevocability of these transfers").

In Illinois, ex rel. Lignoul, v. Continental Ill. Natl. Bank & Trust Co. of Chicago, certiorari denied (1976), the United States Court of Appeals, Seventh Circuit, decided that making an electronic transfer of funds through a computer terminal was essentially the same as issuing a check. The Lignoul court observed:

> The check is merely the means used by the bank to attain the desired objective, i.e., the payment of the money to its customer. The card serves the same purpose as the check. It is an order on the bank. Any order to pay which is properly executed by a customer, whether it be check, card or electronic device, must be recognized as a routine banking function when used as here. The relationship between the bank and its customer is the same. . . .

In today's modern banking environment, electronic transfers have become commonplace. On an average day, six hundred billion dollars in funds are transferred by wire or electronic means. . . . As noted in the discussion above, under modern day conditions, transferring assets of a savings and loan association over the Fedwire is the equivalent of sending a check or issuing a draft.

Through R.C. 1553.01, the General Assembly clearly intended to criminalize the unauthorized transfers of an association's assets regardless of form. Thus, the transfer of funds through the Fedwire system qualifies as a "draft" or other "written statement" as those terms are used in R.C. 1153.01. Accordingly, the court of appeals' conclusion that the authorized transfer of Home State's assets over the Fedwire did not constitute a "writing" within the meaning of R.C. 1153.01 was erroneous.

REVERSED in favor of plaintiff.

[continued]

CRITICAL THINKING

What evidence might the court of appeals have used in its determination that an electronic transfer did not qualify as a draft?

ETHICAL DECISION MAKING

Home State Savings probably suffered negative publicity from this case. One possible safeguard for preventing further unauthorized and fraudulent electronic transfers would be to require that an accountant review all the electronic transactions the controlling shareholder makes on a monthly basis. What types of policies might the company implement to prevent such fraudulent activity in the future? Would those policies assist the relevant stakeholders?

Legal Principle: **As a general rule, the promise or order to pay must be specified and not implied.**

Unconditional Promise or Order to Pay. The promise or order to pay must be specific and not implied. The language must be affirmative in nature [UCC 3-103(a)(9)]. For example, simply acknowledging a debt does not create language for payment; therefore, a common IOU is not a promise or an order to pay and cannot be a negotiable instrument. Nevertheless, an IOU is a very strong piece of evidence for demonstrating the existence of a debt and, as such, will prove an enforceable contract. It *can* become a negotiable instrument if the language "payable on demand," or something expressing similar affirmative agreement to pay, is included. In addition, "order" or "bearer" language is required to turn an IOU into a negotiable instrument. For example, a negotiable instrument would include "payable to order or to bearer," as mandated by Section 3-104 of the UCC.

The unconditional nature of the promise or order is often the controversial variable of this requirement of negotiability. Stated as simply as possible, the promise or order to pay cannot be contingent on anything else. An instrument stating, "I promise to pay if the following occurs" is not a negotiable instrument. It may be a perfectly enforceable contract, but it fails to satisfy the terms of negotiability.

BUT WHAT IF . . .

WHAT IF THE FACTS OF THE CASE OPENER WERE DIFFERENT?

Let's say, in the Case Opener, that Shack bought a casino marker, and he, his father, and MGM signed a contract stipulating a certain payment arrangement for that marker. Let's say that the contract says that when the marker comes due, and Shack doesn't pay in cash within 48 hours, his father will pay it. In other words, his father's promise to pay is contingent on whether his son pays within a time frame. Does this document constitute a negotiable instrument? Is the document even an enforceable contract?

Legal Principle: **As a general rule, negotiable instruments must promise or order that payment be made in a national currency.**

Sum Certain in Money. Negotiable instruments must promise or order that payment be made in a national currency [UCC 3-104(a)]. For example, U.S. dollars, English pounds, Euros, and Japanese yen all satisfy the currency requirement. While promises to pay in apples or gold or stock may form a perfectly enforceable contract, these are not currencies and the resulting instrument is not a negotiable instrument. An instrument promising payment in "German marks and rare French wine" is not negotiable. Even changing the *and* to an *or* does not salvage negotiability; payment *must* be made in a currency.

BUT WHAT IF . . .

WHAT IF THE FACTS OF THE CASE OPENER WERE DIFFERENT?

Let's say, in the Case Opener, that Shack bought a casino marker, by giving MGM an IOU with the phrase "payable on demand." Would such a document classify as a negotiable instrument? What if Shack specified an amount of some payment that was payable on demand, stating "1 yacht and 1 million dollars are payable on demand"? Would this document constitute a negotiable instrument?

Payable at a Time Certain or on Demand. A negotiable instrument must be payable on demand or at a specific time that the parties can compute from the instrument itself. Obviously, if the instrument states a specific date, that is a time certain. If the instrument is dated and states "payment will be made 10 days after above date," the instrument is negotiable because we can calculate the specific date. A dated instrument that states "Payment is to be made at some future time after above date" is clearly nonnegotiable (although, again, it may be enforceable as a contract).

Likewise, an instrument that states "payment will be made 10 days after delivery of the goods" but indicates nowhere in the instrument when that delivery is to be made is not a negotiable instrument. (It might also be nonnegotiable if such a reference is construed to be a condition of payment as well.) Negotiation of an order instrument is by endorsement plus delivery, while negotiation of a bearer instrument is by delivery alone.

There are two noteworthy exceptions to the time-certain requirement. First, an instrument that permits acceleration of payment does not violate this requirement as long as there is a fixed date of payment if the acceleration clause is not satisfied. Second, an instrument that permits an extension of the payment is still negotiable if there is a fixed time for payment. The time of payment may be extended if it is at the election of the holder [UCC 3-108(b)(ii),(iii),(iv)].

Demand instruments, such as checks, are payable as soon as they are issued. If an instrument is silent as to the time of payment, the UCC presumes that it is a demand instrument and thus retains its negotiable status [3-108(a)].

Legal Principle: **For an instrument to be negotiable, the instrument must indicate that it was created for the purpose of being transferred.**

L04

What are the words of negotiability?

Words of Negotiability. Finally, for an instrument to be negotiable, the instrument must indicate it was created for the purpose of being transferred. How can the maker or drawer indicate this purpose? By writing the phrase *to the order of* or similar words near the payee's name, such as "Pay to the order of Ichiro Endo" or "Pay to Ichiro Endo on his order." When a specific payee is named, the document is an *order instrument* [UCC 3-109(b)]. Sometimes negotiable instruments have the proper words of negotiability, such as "pay to the order of," and there are still problems with receiving payment.

E-COMMERCE AND THE LAW

THE END OF THE FLOAT?

Consumers who rely on "float" (the time it takes for a check to go through the traditional check-clearing process and be paid) have a limited amount of time to enjoy the delay it affords. Businesses in many parts of the country are testing new technology that speeds the check-clearing process. Soon, float might be an outdated tradition.

Nevada State Bank, for instance, allows businesses that purchase a special service to scan checks, send them electronically, and get money for checks drawn on other banks much more quickly than they would otherwise; the delay in check processing is cut by 40 percent. Other banks are testing similar products and services. In some states, businesses can substitute electronic images of checks for the checks themselves. Here's how the process works: (1) A customer gives a business a check in payment for a product or service, (2) the business scans the check and sends it to the bank providing the new check-clearing products and services, (3) the bank sends the image to the customer's bank, (4) the customer's bank prints a substitute check, and (5) the customer's payment is quickly deposited in the business's account at that business's bank.

It remains to be seen what kinds of litigation will emerge from this expedited process.

BUT WHAT IF . . .

WHAT IF THE FACTS OF THE CASE OPENER WERE DIFFERENT?

Recall in the Case Opener that Shack contended the terms of his old marker payment agreement were not enforceable because he could acquire a new marker to "freshen" the agreement. If Shack had signed a document that simply acknowledged that Shack had acquired a marker, and not that the payment for the marker was due to MGM, would this document qualify as a negotiable instrument?

Negotiable instruments payable to whoever is bearing them are *bearer instruments* [UCC 3-109(a)] and are treated like cash. Anyone who comes into possession of a bearer instrument by any means, including theft, may claim the payment due on it. Endorsing an order instrument, such as a check, converts it into a bearer instrument that may be claimed by anyone in possession of it. Instruments payable to no one, to "X," or to "cash" are also considered bearer instruments.

The phrase *to the order of* is necessary to create a negotiable instrument. Wordings such as "Pay to bearer," "Pay to Ichiro Endo or bearer," "Pay to cash," and "Pay to the order of cash [or bearer]" all make the paper negotiable.

Until the situation moves beyond the two contractual parties, it does not really matter whether an instrument is negotiable. Consider a contractual situation such as that in Exhibit 26-5.

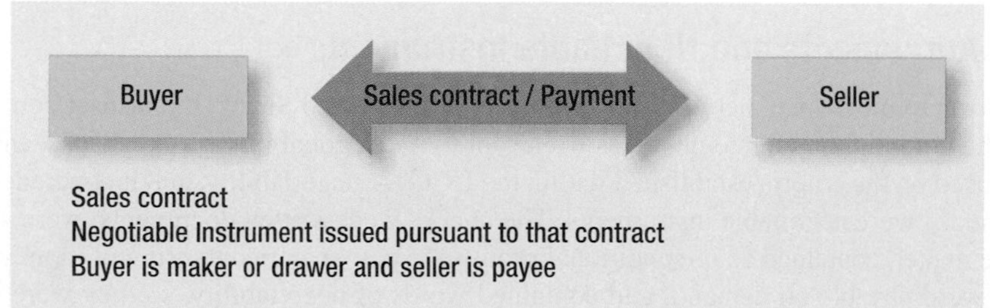

Exhibit 26-5
Illustrative Contract Situation with Two Parties

COMPARING THE LAW OF OTHER COUNTRIES

EUROPEAN UNION: NEGOTIABLE INSTRUMENTS AS DEFINED BY THE EEC

The European Economic Council's (EEC's) Contractual Obligations Convention has addressed how to characterize negotiable instruments, whose definition differs among member countries. Rather than creating one encompassing definition, however, the EEC decided to let each member country decide what types of documents to consider negotiable instruments. While this decision may prevent some problems, it could cause other problems in cross-border transactions. Thus, the convention decided to define a general concept of negotiability. If a transaction is defined as a negotiable instrument within a certain country, it must conform to certain general characteristics outlined by the EEC. These general characteristics are intended to dilute the complexities of cross-border transactions.

The relationship between the buyer and the seller is controlled by the terms of the underlying contract. The status of the negotiable instrument is really irrelevant, as it is a matter between the buyer and the seller. The instrument's being negotiable, however, becomes important when a third party comes into the situation, as in the scenario in Exhibit 26-6.

This situation leads us to the second stage of negotiable instruments: Once the negotiable instrument has been created, how is it transferred? We answer that question in Chapter 27.

Legal Principle: **Definitions of negotiable contracts may vary from country to country, which may make international transactions difficult.**

Exhibit 26-6 Effect of a Third Party

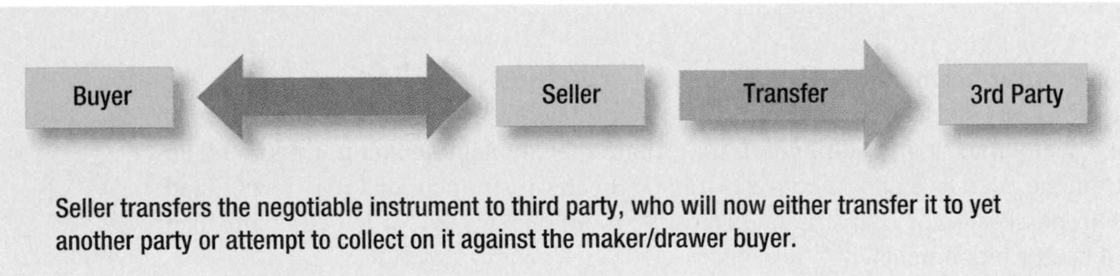

CASE OPENER WRAP-UP

Oral Agreements and Negotiable Instruments

Referring to the dispute between MGM Desert Inn, Inc., and Shack, the district court held that the potential oral agreement was irrelevant to the negotiability of the checks. Instead, it focused on the criteria established within the UCC for negotiability, and it concluded that the checks were negotiable instruments. The checks were written documents, were signed by the maker, contained an unconditional promise to pay, specified the sum of money to be paid, were payable on demand, and contained words of negotiability, so they were negotiable instruments. Hence, MGM was considered the holder of the instruments.

KEY TERMS

certificate of deposit (CD) 566
check 566
demand instrument 566
draft 565
movability 571
negotiable instrument 564
note 565
relative permanence 571
time instrument 566

SUMMARY OF KEY TOPICS

The Need for Negotiable Instruments

Negotiable Instruments are any contractual obligations, except for personal ones and nonassignable ones. They are a form of commercial paper. A breach of the contract invalidates the commercial paper.

Types of Negotiable Instruments

There are several types of negotiable instruments.

1. A *note* is a promise by a maker to pay a payee (e.g., a certificate of deposit).
2. A *draft* is an order by a drawer to a drawee to pay a payee (e.g., a check).

A *demand instrument* is one for which a payee can demand payment at any time.

A *time instrument* is one for which payment will be made only at a designated time.

An Overview of the Law of Negotiable Instruments

There are several requirements for negotiability. The following criteria must all be met:

1. Written document:
   - Relative permanence
   - Movability
2. Signature of the maker or drawer:
   - Affirmative mark
   - Duly authorized agent
   - Handwritten, even without signature
   - Automated signature
3. Unconditional promise or order to pay:
   - Must be specific, not implied
4. Sum certain in money:
   - Currency only; any currency acceptable
5. Payable at a time certain or on demand:
   - Acceleration of payment
   - Extension of payment
6. Words of negotiability:
   - To the order of
   - Order instrument

POINT / COUNTERPOINT

Should Businesses Use Contracts rather than Negotiable Instruments to Set Payment Terms?

YES

Conditional contractual agreements are preferable.

Assuming both parties abide by the stipulations in a conditional contract, payment is guaranteed. Payment will not get lost as it travels among many parties—each claiming that a previous party did not fulfill his or her obligations in the contract.

The conditional aspect of the payment contract makes the sale more appealing to the buyer, who will not have to pay for an item that does not fit the conditions agreed

NO

Unconditional negotiable instruments are a superior form of payment. They allow flexibility in payment and a much higher yield in profits.

First, negotiable instruments allow only secure monetary payment in a national currency, a restriction ideal for large businesses that cannot calculate the exact worth of gold or diamonds at a future payment date. Businesses operate nationally and internationally with cash, not gems or bottles of fine wine.

on in the payment contract. Plus, the buyer can feel confident that an unknown individual will not approach him or her to collect money for a debt the original seller transferred. Because the buyer's debt is conditional and payable to the seller *only*, the buyer will always know that his or her debt was paid properly and directly.

The conditional aspect of the contract also keeps all parties honest. The seller cannot secretly transfer the debt to another individual knowing his or her product is poor. The seller is held directly accountable for the product, and the buyer is held directly accountable for payment.

Unconditional negotiable instruments can be paid *only* in a national currency. Under a conditional agreement, which allows for more flexibility, a wine connoisseur can arrange to be paid for a shipment of fine cheese with a bottle of extremely rare 1945 Fonseca—a priceless acquisition.

Second, businesses using negotiable instruments can earn a high yield by investing their excess cash in low-risk certificates of deposit.

Negotiable instruments allow flexibility in payment, either "on demand" or "at time certain." Although these specifications seem rigid, payments can be accelerated or extended, provided a time is always set and not extended indefinitely. This flexibility allows businesses to work well together.

QUESTIONS & PROBLEMS

1. Explain the reason behind the need for negotiable instruments.
2. Are negotiable instruments more similar to money or to contracts? Explain.
3. Identify and define each of the elements of negotiability.
4. Dr. Rodrigue is an obstetrician-gynecologist who in 1989 opened her own practice. The financial support to open her new practice came from North County Women's Health Care Services P.C., which provided her with start-up and relocation assistance and a practice consultant who helped draft and publish an employee manual. In November 1990, Rodrigue missed a sponsored event due to the mishandling of postal mail addressed to the practice. She then required that all mail be given to her, unopened, for her to open personally. In May 1990, she had hired Carol Wiltshire to work as a medical receptionist and secretary. Over the nine years Wiltshire worked for Rodrigue, she held a variety of positions of increasing responsibility and authority within the office. In her position as billing specialist, Wiltshire was responsible for understanding insurance requirements and was the only person in the office trained in the Doctor's Office Management System (DOMS) when Rodrigue converted to the computerized billing system in 1992. DOMS software is used to manage accounts by tracking charges, payments, and adjustments. From 1992 until her termination in 1999, Wiltshire was solely responsible for entering charges, adjustments, and payments and closing out monthly statements for patient charges via the DOMS software. After learning how to use the software, Wiltshire began stealing checks from the doctor's mail that were sent by various insurance providers and were payable to Rodrigue. During the course of her employment at Rodrigue's office, Wiltshire stole 269 checks, totaling $372,572.18. Around 1994 to 1995, the office began to face financial troubles. Rodrigue finally discovered Wiltshire's embezzlement at the end of November 1999, after her sister-in-law, Denise Rodrigue, told her that she believed Wiltshire had been taking mail into her office, opening it, and stealing insurance checks. Which terms of negotiable instruments does this case fall under or describe? [*Rodrigue v. Olin Employees Credit Union,* 03-2470, 03-2607 (7th Cir. 2005).]
5. In 2001, Cory Babcock and Honest Air Conditioning & Heating, Inc., purchased a new 2001 Chevrolet Corvette from Cox, a car dealer. The retail installment sales contract (RISC) obligated monthly payments on the Corvette to satisfy the total indebtedness of $52,516.20 at a zero percent

interest rate. The RISC was immediately assigned to General Motors Acceptance Corp. (GMAC). On August 22, 2002, Honest Air and Babcock traded the Corvette to Florida Auto Brokers as part of the purchase of another vehicle. In September, Babcock told GMAC that he had traded the vehicle. In December 2002, GMAC was told by Babcock that the local dealership would be mailing GMAC the money due for the Corvette and the vehicle's title as a security interest. Once the check was finally sent to GMAC but not cashed yet, the security interest (the title) was returned to the dealership. However, the check was dishonored for insufficient funds. As a result, GMAC sued Honest Air and Babcock for $35,815.26 as damages resulting from the breach of the terms of the RISC. Cox argued the RISC was a negotiable instrument. What requirements must the RISC meet to be considered a negotiable instrument, and what would this mean for GMAC? [*GMAC v. Honest Air Conditioning & Heating, Inc.*, 2006 933 So. 2d 34, 2006 Fla. App. LEXIS 7255.]

6. Doseung Chung, the plaintiff, a horse player, was at Belmont Park Racetrack, which is owned by the defendant, New York Racing Association. While at the track, Chung was using a voucher to place bets on the races through an automated betting machine. After placing a bet, Chung took his betting ticket but forgot his voucher, which had thousands of dollars left on it. A few minutes later, he returned to the machine, but the voucher was gone. Chung put an electronic stop on the voucher, but the voucher had been cashed out about one minute after it was left in the machine. Chung subsequently sued the racetrack, arguing that the track was negligent in not requiring proof of identity when patrons cash out their vouchers, which constitute negotiable instruments. How did the court rule? Why? [*Doseung Chung v. New York Racing Ass'n.*, 714 N.Y.S.2d 429 (2000).]

7. In October 2006, America's Wholesale Lender (AWL) agreed to loan John Horvath $650,000. The loan was stated in an interest-only, fixed-rate note and was secured by a deed of trust on Horvath's home. In exchange for the $650,000, Horvath agreed to repay AWL in monthly installments ranging from about $3,000 to $5,000. The note allowed AWL (and any subsequent holder) to freely transfer the note. In fact, the note provided for "anyone who takes this Note by transfer" to inherit the powers of the "Note Holder," including the right to accelerate payment in the event that Horvath defaulted. Any party who took the note would have the right to enforce it. In 2009, the note was transferred to Bank of New York, and a little over a half year later, Horvath defaulted. His property was foreclosed on, and then he proceeded to sue. Was Horvath right in suing? Why or why not, based on the wording of the note? [*Horvath v. Bank of NY,* 641 F.3d 617, 2011 U.S. App. LEXIS 10152.]

8. Anthony Bango needed several short-term loans to fund a real estate closing. He contacted Dennis Mulholland of Ohio Financial Mortgage Corp. (OFMC), and Mulholland located an interested investor, James Jarvis. Jarvis was faxed a note stating, "Upon the closing of this Real Estate Transaction the lender will be repaid the principal sum of $30,000 along with the closing costs agreed upon by all parties in full by the borrower." Jarvis transferred the money to Mulholland, and Mulholland delivered the money to Bango. Bango, who had a criminal record, requested that the money be delivered in cash. After receiving the money, Bango notified Mulholland that other investors had not come through with their loans and that an additional $20,000 was needed. Again, Jarvis transferred the money to Mulholland to give to Bango. Bango verbally agreed to pay $70,000 in return for the total loan of $50,000. When Bango did not make payment, Mulholland contacted him again. Bango revealed that the real estate transaction did not exist; instead, the money was needed for his personal debts. Jarvis collected only $8,500 of the loan. Jarvis filed a motion for summary judgment against Dennis Mulholland and OFMC. He claimed that the initial fax was a negotiable instrument. The trial court determined that Mulholland's fax did not constitute a promissory note or any other type of negotiable instrument. Do you agree? How does this determination affect the outcome of the case? [*Jarvis v. Silbert,* 1999 Ohio App. LEXIS 4828.]

9. Sirius LC is a Wyoming company co-owned by William Bagley and his wife. Bagley is an attorney whose services Bryce Erickson procured for bankruptcy proceedings. Bagley agreed to represent Erickson for a Chapter 12 bankruptcy proceeding provided that Erickson sign a promissory note payable to Sirius in the amount of $29,173.38 to be secured by a mortgage on property owned by

Erickson in Caribou County, Idaho. Bagley asserts that the amount of the promissory note represented the overdue legal fees Erickson owed him for the Chapter 11 bankruptcy proceeding. Erickson then executed a promissory note payable to Sirius, which provided "[f]or value received, the undersigned Bryce H. Erickson promises to pay to SIRIUS LC . . . the sum of $29,173.38 bearing 10% interest due and payable on June 1, 2001." The case commenced when Sirius filed a complaint to foreclose on Erickson's Caribou County property after he refused to pay the note once it became due. In the proceedings, the district court held that the promissory note "clearly fell within the definition of a negotiable instrument." The case was then appealed. Do you think the decision was affirmed? Does the note have all the proper words of negotiability? [*Sirius LC v. Bryce H. Erickson,* 2007 144 Idaho 38, 156 P.3d 539, LEXIS 74.]

10. A branch of Wachovia bank in Alabama loaned $150,000 to McNamee in early 2003. In order to obtain the $150,000, McNamee was required to sign a promissory note, promising he would repay the loan. At some point, Wachovia lost, misplaced, or destroyed the original note signed by McNamee. The note ($150,000) reached maturity in late 2005, and Wachovia signed the rights of the note over to Atlantic National Trust. The trust sued for recovery of both the principal and the interest owed. However, McNamee claimed that he did not have to repay because the original documentation was lost by Wachovia. What was the result of this case? Why? [*Atlantic National Trust, LLC v. McNamee,* 984 So. 2d 375, 381 (Ala. 2007).]

Looking for more review materials?

The Online Learning Center at **www.mhhe.com/kubasek3e** contains this chapter's "Assignment on the Internet" and also a list of URLs for more information, entitled "On the Internet." Find both of them in the Student Center portion of the OLC, along with quizzes and other helpful materials.

CHAPTER

27

Negotiation, Holder in Due Course, and Defenses

LEARNING OBJECTIVES

After reading this chapter, you will be able to answer the following questions:

1. What is negotiation?
2. What is a holder in due course?
3. What requirements must be met to obtain holder-in-due-course status?
4. What is the shelter principle?
5. In what ways has the holder-in-due-course doctrine been abused?

CASE OPENER

Dishonored Check and Holder-in-Due-Course Status

In July 1993, Cigna Insurance Company issued James Mills a workers' compensation check for $484. Then Mills lied to Cigna and said he had not received the draft due to a change in his address. He requested that payment be stopped and a new draft issued. The insurer complied, stopped payment on the initial draft, and promptly issued a new check for Mills. However, Mills cashed the first check at Sun's Market before the stop-payment notation was placed on the draft. Sun's Market then presented the check for payment through its bank.

As a result of the stop payment on the initial draft, the bank dishonored the check, stamped it "Stop Payment," and returned the check to Sun's bank. After not receiving the cash for the bad check, Sun's Market tacked the check on its bulletin board. An individual, Robert Triffin, purchased the check from Sun's Market and obtained an assignment of Sun's interests in the instrument.

More than two years after the check was returned unpaid, Triffin filed a lawsuit against Cigna for payment on the check. Triffin argued that by purchasing the check from Sun's Market, he gained a special legal status, called *holder-in-due-course* status. This status entitled him to payment on the dishonored check. He argued that he received this special status under the *shelter principle* because the transfer by a holder in due course to a third party, even one with notice of the dishonor, transfers all rights of the holder in due course to the third party.

1. Who do you think should bear the dishonored check? In other words, should Cigna be required to pay Triffin for the dishonored workers' compensation check? Why or why not?
2. Suppose you are a business manager at Sun's Market. You learn that the court holds that Cigna Insurance Company does not have to pay for dishonored checks. Would you make any changes to your business policies? Would you be less likely to accept checks from insurance companies in the future?

The Wrap-Up at the end of the chapter will answer these questions.

As you can see in the Case Opener, financial transactions with negotiable instruments can be risky. A **negotiable instrument,** as we saw in the preceding chapter, is a written document signed by the maker or drawer with an unconditional promise or order to pay a certain sum of money on demand or at a specified time to the order of bearer (UCC Section 3-104). One important characteristic of negotiable instruments is the ease of transferring them to a third party through **negotiation** (UCC 3-201). A negotiation occurs when multiple parties enter into an agreement meant to resolve a conflict or another subject of interest. In the opening case, Sun's Market transferred the check through negotiation.

A party who possesses a negotiable instrument payable to the party or bearer of the instrument is a **holder** of the instrument [UCC 1-201(b)(21)]. A holder's right to an instrument may be limited, and the holder is subject to certain defenses. For example, when a party refuses to make payment on an instrument on the basis of breach of contract, the holder may not be able to collect.

A certain type of holder, however, called a **holder in due course (HDC),** has more extensive legal rights, including freedom from competing claims and defenses. (Later in the chapter, Exhibit 27-6 provides a list of the specific defenses that can and cannot be used against a holder in due course.) Basically, there are four requirements, described later, for a holder to be of HDC status. Taking a cue from the credit card industry and its platinum cards, you can think of a holder in due course as a "platinum holder."

As a business manager, you will want to know whether your business is a holder or a holder in due course, because your legal rights will vary on the basis of this status. Would Sun's Market or Triffin be considered a holder in due course of the dishonored check and thus be entitled to greater protection? Why?

In this chapter, we begin by examining the characteristics of negotiation. Next, we consider the purpose of the holder-in-due-course doctrine. Then we examine the requirements for HDC status. We also briefly discuss the shelter principle and the HDC, as well as various abuses of the HDC doctrine and their remedies.

Negotiation

LO1
What is negotiation?

The rules of negotiation are slightly different depending on whether the instrument is an order instrument (payable to a specific, named payee) or a bearer instrument (payable to cash or whoever is in possession of the instrument) (UCC Section 3-109). Bearer paper requires only delivery of the instrument to the holder by the payee; order paper requires delivery *and* an endorsement.

COMPARING THE LAW OF OTHER COUNTRIES

THE EVOLUTION OF BILLS OF EXCHANGE IN RUSSIA

The concept of bills of exchange has existed in Russia since the late 17th century. The first statutes regulating them were influenced by German and French models. In the 1930s, however, bills of exchange were outlawed in the USSR, not to reemerge until the 1990s, and then only for use in foreign trade transactions under the Decree of the Presidium, adopted June 24, 1991.

Eventually Russia recognized the benefits of lifting the ban on domestic bills of exchange. Thus, in March 1997, the Russian Federation undertook a rare act in the Russian legal system and reintroduced previously repealed legislation from 1937, declaring that bills of exchange and promissory notes are legitimate documentary transactions in accordance with language of the 1930 Geneva Convention.

DELIVERY

Delivery simply means the physical handing of an instrument from someone entitled to it to the person intended to receive it. A bearer instrument that wafts out a window and lands in someone's hand has not been properly delivered. This lucky person cannot legally demand payment of that instrument because she is not a proper holder. However, she could pass it on to someone who could legally collect on it.

A drawer who is negligent in how he or she makes the delivery may be liable for notes paid with forged or unauthorized endorsements. In *Park State Bank v. Arena Auto Auction,*[1] an Illinois court held that the drawer and not the payor bank was liable for a check cashed by an Illinois business. The drawer had mailed the check to the wrong business, an unrelated firm of the same name as the intended payee but in another state. The payor bank paid the check to the wrong corporation, its client, because the names were the same. When the drawer tried to sue the payor bank, the court ruled that the drawer had acted negligently in delivering the check to the wrong business (which cashed the check in good faith) and therefore the drawer was liable for the amount of the check.

BUT WHAT IF . . .

WHAT IF THE FACTS OF THE CASE OPENER WERE DIFFERENT?

Recall that, in the Case Opener, Triffin purchased the check in question from Sun's Market after seeing it on the bulletin board. What if Sun's Market had thrown the check away and Triffin saw it and picked it up? Would he be able to legally collect on it?

Legal Principle: **A negotiable instrument cannot be delivered if it is accidentally found or is given to the wrong person.**

ENDORSEMENT

Order paper must be *endorsed* as well as *delivered* to be negotiated. The person creating the endorsement is the **endorser;** the person receiving it is the **endorsee.** Normally, there is a place on the negotiable instrument for endorsements (such as on the back of a check). If not or if all the room has been taken by other endorsements, an **allonge,** an additional piece of paper for endorsements, can be attached (firmly, as with staples) [UCC 3-204(a)]. Three kinds of endorsements affect the legal status of a negotiable instrument: unqualified, qualified, and restrictive.

Unqualified Endorsements: Blank and Special Endorsements. There are two kinds of unqualified endorsements: blank and special. A **blank endorsement** is simply the

[1] 207 N.E.2d 158 (Ill. App. Ct. 1965).

payee's or last endorsee's signature, nothing else [UCC 3-205(b)]. See Exhibit 27-1 for an illustration. An unqualified, blank endorsement turns order paper into bearer paper that can be negotiated by delivery only.

A **special endorsement** is the endorser's signature along with a named endorsee [UCC 3-205(a)]. Exhibit 27-2 illustrates. The words "Pay to Jackie Jones" followed by the endorser's signature create a special endorsement. This type of endorsement keeps order paper as order paper that continues to require endorsement and delivery for further negotiation. The words of negotiability, *to the order of,* are not needed.

Exhibit 27-1 Blank Endorsement

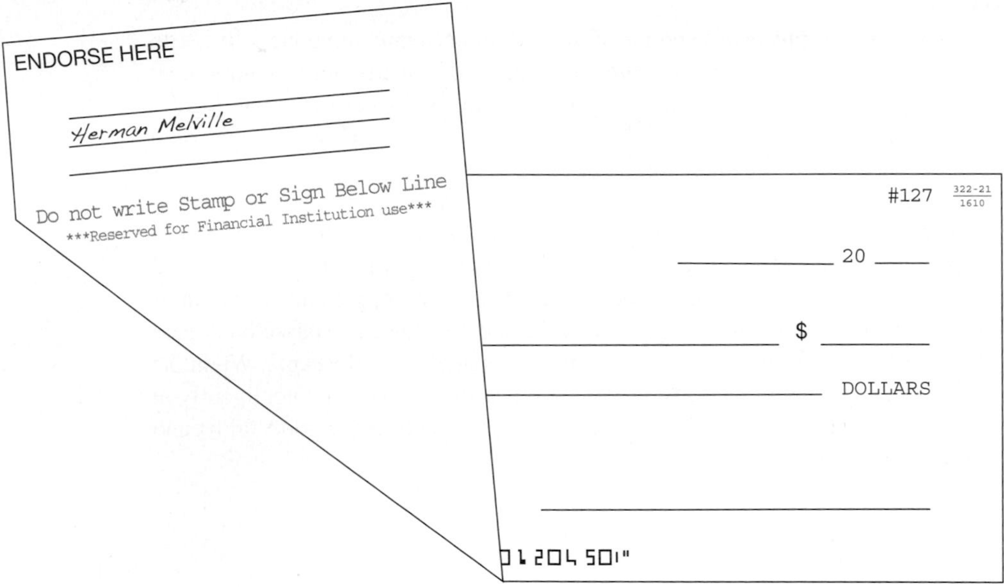

Exhibit 27-2 Special Endorsement

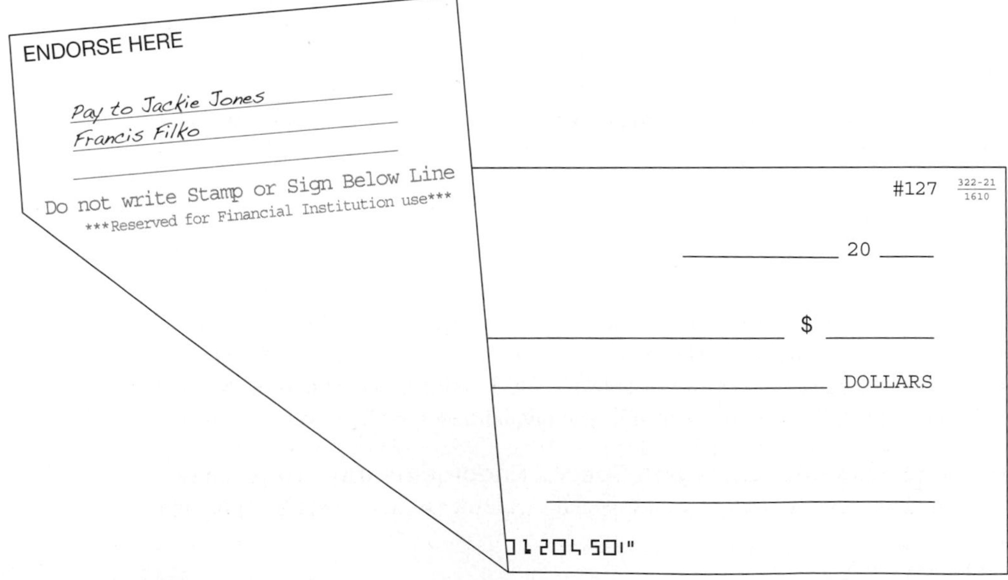

Exhibit 27-3 Blank Qualified Endorsement

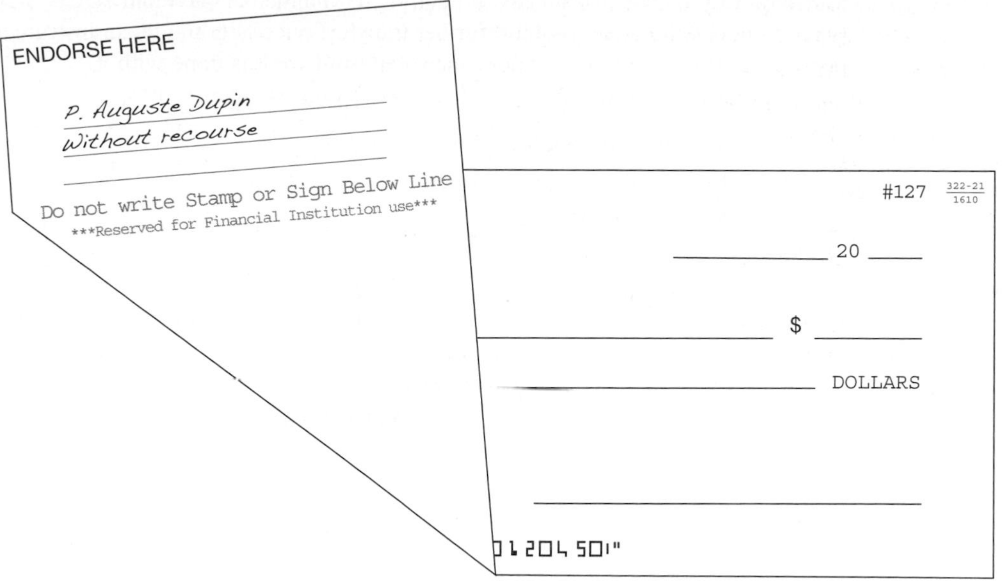

Qualified Endorsements. Qualified endorsements can also be either **blank qualified endorsements** or **special qualified endorsements.** (See Exhibit 27-3 for an illustration.) What makes them qualified is the addition of the words *without recourse.* Ordinarily, when negotiable instruments pass from one party to another, the endorser's signature guarantees payment to a subsequent holder in the event the instrument is not honored by the party who created it [UCC 3-415(a)]. The restrictive endorsement *without recourse* means the endorser does not intend to be bound by this guarantee [UCC 3-415(b)].

For example, people often mistakenly write checks to their insurance agent when the proper recipient is the insurance company. The agent can restrictively endorse the check, following his signature with the statement "without recourse," and hand it over to the agency. The agent has effectively negotiated the check to the company and is not liable for the amount if there is a problem with the check.

While any endorser is free to use them, both blank and special qualified endorsements greatly reduce the marketability and thus the transferability of an instrument. Who would accept an instrument from someone who will endorse it only with qualifications? Such an endorsement is more or less a red flag that there may be a problem with the instrument. Needless to say, it is not widely used, but it is an option for the endorser.

BUT WHAT IF . . .

WHAT IF THE FACTS OF THE CASE OPENER WERE DIFFERENT?

What if Cigna Insurance sent the workers' compensation check to the wrong James Mills? If the incorrect James Mills cashed the check, would Cigna still be liable for the check? Alternatively, let's say the incorrect James Mills signed the check with the words *without recourse* and forwarded the check to the James Mills whom the check was actually intended for. Could the incorrect James Mills be responsible for any part of the payment if there was a problem?

Restrictive Endorsements. **Restrictive endorsements** attempt to either limit the transferability of the instrument or control the manner of payment [UCC 3-206(a)]. No type of endorsement can prohibit further transfer; once negotiable, an instrument remains negotiable. But a restrictive endorsement can limit what is done with it.

The UCC gives four examples of restrictive endorsements:

1. The endorsement for deposit or collection only.
2. The endorsement to prohibit further endorsement.
3. The conditional endorsement.
4. The trust endorsement.

Endorsement for Deposit or Collection Only. The most common restrictive endorsement is the **endorsement for deposit or collection only.** The added words *for deposit only* turn an endorsement into a blank restrictive one [UCC 3-206(c)]. That check cannot be cashed; it can only be deposited into an account—*any* account. To be perfectly safe, the restrictive endorsement should read "for deposit only into National Bank Account #12345" and be signed by the endorser. Case 27-1 discusses endorsement problems.

CASE 27-1 MID-ATLANTIC TENNIS COURTS, INC. v. CITIZENS BANK AND TRUST COMPANY OF MARYLAND

U.S. DISTRICT COURT FOR THE DISTRICT OF MARYLAND 658 F. SUPP. 140 (1987)

In early 1983, Mid-Atlantic Tennis Courts, a small family-held corporation, decided to expand. It hired Loy Smith as a commissioned salesperson authorized to sell tennis court construction jobs and deliver the executed contracts and any customer deposits received directly to the business office of Mid-Atlantic in Clifton, Virginia.

In early 1984, Smith devised a scheme to defraud Mid-Atlantic. Using customer leads from the firm, he entered into eight contracts with potential customers but did not inform Mid-Atlantic of them. In all cases, he accepted deposit checks from the customers made payable either to himself only, to Mid-Atlantic only, or to himself and Mid-Atlantic jointly, and in one case, to himself and an apparently fictitious corporation named SMD. In the summer of 1984, Smith opened two checking accounts with Citizens' Bank in his own name, Loy Thompson Smith, into which he deposited 23 checks, drawn by eight different people on a number of drawees, including Citizens' Bank. For all the checks, the defendant was the depositary bank, as defined in Md. Comm. Law Code Ann. [UCC] § 4-105(a).

DISTRICT JUDGE SMALKIN: In this suit, the plaintiff requests recovery "only for those checks improperly deposited with the endorsement 'for deposit only' or no endorsement" in either one of the two personal checking accounts Smith opened with the defendant. It is undisputed from the deposition of Citizens' Vice President, Mr. Haste, that these checks (the ones that were not endorsed in any fashion with the name Mid-Atlantic) should not have been accepted by defendant for deposit in *anyone's* account other than Mid-Atlantic's.

The defendant has not answered, in its opposition affidavits, the affidavit assertions of Jim Lieberton, President of Mid-Atlantic, to the effect that Smith deposited the checks in his own account and that Mid-Atlantic has not received the proceeds of the checks, to which it was entitled as payee. Thus, it is clear that the plaintiff was the payee and "owner" of the checks in question, and that they have been converted in the common law sense, *viz.*, that Mid-Atlantic, as the true owner, has been deprived of the checks or the proceeds thereof. The U.C.C., in § 3-419, applies conversion principles to negotiable instruments.

For commercial law analysis purposes, the form of the various instruments must be examined. There are 23 checks listed. Of those, plaintiff seeks recovery for only 13. Of those 13, two were deposited having no endorsement whatever, and the remaining 11 bore "endorsements" that consisted only of the words "for deposit only." The total amount of these 13 items was $72,158.45, which appears to be all the recovery the plaintiff seeks by this lawsuit.

[continued]

It is utterly clear that the defendant did not act in conformity with the reasonable commercial standards of banking when it took in items with no endorsement at all or with no endorsement, save the restrictive language "for deposit only," that had been deposited in Smith's personal banking account, when the named payee was solely Mid-Atlantic. This was the case with every item for which the plaintiff now seeks compensation. An officer of the defendant has essentially admitted this lapse of conformity to banking standards, there is nothing disputing it in defendant's summary judgment opposition, and the legal conclusion is utterly clear. Thus, defendant, as a depositary bank, has conversion liability to plaintiff whether or not any proceeds of the checks remain in its hands.

It is axiomatic that an item is converted when it is paid on a forged endorsement, because the payment is made to one who has no good title. This is just as true in the case where an endorsement necessary to transfer title is missing, because, without the necessary endorsement, there can be no negotiation of the order paper (such as all this paper was). Although a bank is privileged in some circumstances to supply a missing endorsement, the only endorsement that it can supply is that of *its customer,* and it is clear Mid-Atlantic was not defendant's customer, because it had no account with defendant. Until the bank supplies the missing endorsement of its customer, usually with a rubber stamp, it is not a holder of the item. In this case, the missing endorsement was not that of defendant's customer, Smith, but that of the payee, Mid-Atlantic, who was not defendant's customer. Thus, the depositary bank never became the holder of the checks because of the absence of any endorsement whatever, a deficiency that it could not remedy by a stamp endorsement. Because the depositary bank never became a holder in its own right, and because it took items as to which there was no endorsement whatever, it did not have good title to these items, and, therefore, it converted them when it eventually paid the proceeds over to Smith. Although U.C.C. § 3-419(3) usually protects depositary banks which have no proceeds of the items remaining in their hands that protection is unavailable where, as here, the depositary bank has not adhered to reasonable commercial banking standards.

Thus, the Court concludes there is no genuine dispute of material fact, that plaintiff is entitled to summary judgment against the defendant for all the items deposited bearing no endorsement or the "endorsement" of "for deposit only." The damages are the face amounts of the items.

As an additional ground for recovery, the defendant is liable to the plaintiff for breach of the restrictive endorsement "for deposit only" on the items so marked, for the reason the items were never deposited to the account of Mid-Atlantic, which is the only treatment consistent with a "for deposit only" restrictive endorsement made by, or (even purportedly) on behalf of, a named payee. Thus, the plaintiff has two U.C.C. theories of recovery available with regard to the items that bore nothing more than the language "for deposit only," *i.e.,* conversion and breach of restriction, but either theory entitles it to summary judgment on these items, and the recovery is the same.

Order issued in favor of plaintiff.

CRITICAL THINKING

What reasoning supports the district judge's decision? Are there missing facts in the case that would better enable you to evaluate this reasoning if they were provided?

ETHICAL DECISION MAKING

What values does the court's decision promote? If the bank operated under the ethics-of-care philosophy, would it have forced Mid-Atlantic to court?

Endorsement to Prohibit Further Endorsement. The second kind of restrictive endorsement, the **endorsement to prohibit further endorsement,** is very rarely used. The operative word in it is *only,* as in *Pay to Oliver Twist only.* While this endorsement does not prohibit further transfer, it does provide Oliver some protection [UCC 3-206(a)]. Even if he endorses this instrument over to someone else, because of the restrictive endorsement he is not liable on the instrument until he is paid.

Conditional Endorsement. The third kind of restrictive endorsement, a **conditional endorsement,** lets the endorser put a condition on payment (one that would destroy negotiability if it were on the face of the instrument but does not affect it here) [UCC 3-204(a)]. A conditional endorsement, in effect, creates a defense for the endorser in the event that he does not live up to a preconceived promise. However, the conditional endorsement does not affect the instrument's ability to be further negotiated.

BUT WHAT IF . . .

WHAT IF THE FACTS OF THE CASE OPENER WERE DIFFERENT?

Recall that, in the Case Opener, Triffin bought a check issued by Cigna Insurance that totaled $484. Let's say Cigna and Triffin agreed that Cigna would pay Triffin $300 instead of $484 and subsequently Triffin would not sue Cigna for payment on the $484 check. Cigna would send Triffin a new check for $300 and a separate document stipulating certain terms for Triffin's cashing of the $300 check. What kind of restrictive endorsement would this qualify as? Would the check still qualify as a negotiable instrument?

Trust Endorsement. The fourth restrictive endorsement is the **trust endorsement,** used when the instrument is being transferred to an agent or trustee for the benefit of either the endorser or a third party [UCC 3-206(d)]. It might read "Pay to Jill Rogers in trust for LeBron Watkins" or "Pay to Jill Rogers as agent for LeBron Watkins" and then have either Watkins's or another endorser's signature. This endorsement gives the endorser the rights of a holder.

See Exhibit 27-4 for a summary of types of endorsements.

Exhibit 27-4
Summary of Types of Endorsements

TYPES OF ENDORSEMENTS	DEFINITION
Unqualified Endorsements	
Blank unqualified	An endorsement that is either the payee's or the last endorsee's signature; payable to whoever has possession of the instrument.
Special unqualified	An endorsement that is the endorser's signature followed by a named endorsee, who then becomes the holder of the instrument.
Qualified Endorsements	
Blank qualified	An endorsement that is either the payee's or the last endorsee's signature followed by "without recourse."
Special qualified	An endorsement that is the endorser's signature followed by a named endorsee and "without recourse."
Restrictive Endorsements	
Endorsement for deposit or collection only	An endorsement that restricts the instrument such that it must be collected by a bank for the endorser or for a particular account; the instrument cannot be cashed.
Endorsement that prohibits further endorsement	An endorsement that restricts payment to "only" the endorsee; doesn't prevent further transfer but protects the endorsee from being liable on the instrument until the endorsee receives payment
Conditional endorsement	An endorsement that is followed by a conditional statement that restricts payment; can be used as a defense for the endorser against the endorsee.
Trust endorsement	An endorsement that allows the endorser to have the rights of a holder; used when the instrument is being transferred to a trustee for the benefit of the endorser.

NONCRIMINAL ENDORSEMENT PROBLEMS

It should be no surprise that fraud and forgery create problems with endorsements, and we discuss these criminal issues in the next chapter. Here we consider noncriminal endorsement problems.

Misspelled Name. If a negotiable instrument contains a misspelled name, the holder may endorse it with the misspelled name, his or her actual name, or (as is typical practice) the misspelled name followed by the actual name.

Payable to a Legal Entity. Instruments can be made payable to a legal entity. If it is an estate, organization, partnership, or the like, any authorized representative may endorse it. If instruments are made payable to a public office, the person holding the office may endorse it. Upon filing her local taxes, Sarah, not knowing to whom her check should be payable, wrote "Pay to the order of County Tax Collector." Bill Deepockets, the county tax collector, may endorse the check, as he is the person currently holding the office named on it.

Alternative or Joint Payees. Two possibilities arise when an instrument is payable to more than one person. The first possibility is that there are *alternative payees,* as in "Pay to the order of Jones *or* Smith." Then the endorsement of any one of the listed payees is sufficient.

If, however, there are *joint payees,* the instrument reads, "Pay to the order of Smith *and* Jones." Now the endorsements of *all* listed payees are required before the instrument may be negotiated.

When an instrument is silent as to whether the listed payees are joint or alternative, courts interpret it as containing alternative payees, and the endorsement of only one listed payee is required to negotiate it.

If the instrument is negotiable and the transfer has been a proper negotiation, we can proceed to the third part of the negotiable-instrument process, in which the status and rights of the third-party holder come into play. We cover these in the next chapter. The balance of this chapter discusses the holder-in-due course status and the shelter principle.

BUT WHAT IF . . .

WHAT IF THE FACTS OF THE CASE OPENER WERE DIFFERENT?

What if Cigna Insurance sent Mills a check but misspelled his name as the payee? Would Mills still be able to cash the check, or would it need to be voided and a new check sent?

Holder-in-Due-Course Doctrine

LO2 What is a holder in due course?

Suppose you contract with a computer seller, Data Corp., to buy 50 computers for your office. As partial payment, you give Data Corp. a note for $30,000. Data Corp. negotiates the note to its landlord, Morgan, for payment of rent.

You discover that the computers are damaged. If Data Corp. still held the $30,000 note, you could refuse to honor it and claim as a defense that Data Corp. breached its contract with you. But Data Corp. negotiated the note to Morgan. If Morgan is simply a holder, you can use the defense of breach of contract against Morgan. However, if Morgan is an HDC, as defined below, you must pay Morgan, because a holder in due course has higher rights to a negotiated instrument than does an ordinary holder.

CASE NUGGET

HDC STATUS TO THE RESCUE

Watson Coatings, Inc. v. American Express Travel Services, Inc.
436 F.3d 1036 (2006)

Christine Mayfield used to work for Watson Coatings, Inc., where part of her role was to act as company treasurer. During her employment, Mayfield wrote 45 to 47 checks from Watson's account to American Express to cover her personal debts totaling $745,969.39. American Express credited each check to Mayfield's personal account. After dismissing Mayfield from her job, Watson Coatings discovered the theft and filed suit against American Express for accepting the checks from Mayfield despite their having been clearly labeled as belonging to Watson Coatings, Inc.

The district court granted American Express's motion for summary judgment, but Watson filed an appeal. Judge Smith's opinion explained that because a payee can be considered a holder in due course, American Express qualified as such a holder. However, the court also needed to decide whether this status offered American Express any protection. The appeals court found that it did, even though Watson had brought forth several common law claims, because American Express accepted the checks in good faith. Thus, the appeals court affirmed the district court's grant of summary judgment to American Express.

BUT WHAT IF . . .

WHAT IF THE FACTS OF THE CASE OPENER WERE DIFFERENT?

Recall that, in the Case Opener, Mills was the original holder of the check from Cigna Insurance Company. Cigna sent Mills the check for $484, but Mills said that he never received the check while in reality he cashed the check. So Cigna sent him a new check. Let's say, however, that Cigna realized prior to the cashing of the second check that the first check had been cashed, and due to breach of contract Cigna now attempts to deny payment on the second check. Is Mills a holder of the check or a holder in due course? Depending on his status, will Cigna be able to refuse payment or not?

REASON FOR HOLDER-IN-DUE-COURSE STATUS

Sun's Market, the check-cashing location in the Case Opener, should not be required to shoulder the transaction risks, because it was simply a financial intermediary, and the law wants to encourage companies like Sun's Market to engage in financial interactions. As you read this chapter, keep in mind the purpose of HDC status.

Requirements for Holder-in-Due-Course Status

L03

What requirements must be met to obtain holder-in-due-course status?

To be considered a *holder in due course,* a party must meet four requirements established in UCC Section 3-302:

1. The party must be a holder of a complete and authentic negotiable instrument.
2. The holder must take the instrument for value.
3. The holder must take the instrument in good faith.
4. The holder must take the instrument without notice of defects.

Meeting these requirements is very valuable, as the Case Nugget demonstrates.

Case 27-2 examines the required elements of HDC status. We consider the required elements in closer detail later in this section.

CASE 27-2 MICHAEL J. KANE, JR. v. GRACE KROLL
COURT OF APPEALS OF WISCONSIN
538 N.W.2D 605 (1995)

Michael Kane, Jr., sold Gerald Kroll, Jr., some cows. Gerald could not pay for the cows, so he arranged for his mother, Grace Kroll, to pay Kane. Gerald planned to repay his mother with $6,100, the proceeds from his expected sale of a load of hay. Grace issued a personal check to Kane in the amount of $6,100. However, the next day, Gerald told his mother he would not be able to repay her because the sale of hay fell through. Grace stopped payment on the check to Kane. When Kane presented the check to the bank, the bank refused to pay.

Kane filed suit against Grace to recover the $6,100. Grace argued that she had no legal obligation to repay Gerald's debt and thus no obligation to pay Kane. Kane argued that he was a holder in due course and not subject to Grace's defense of failure of consideration. The trial court held Kane was not a holder in due course because he did not prove he took the check in good faith and without notice of Grace's defenses. Kane appealed.

JUDGE MYSE: Whether Kane is a holder in due course is an issue involving application of § 403.302, STATS., to undisputed facts. A holder must meet three requirements to be a holder in due course under § 403.302, STATS. The holder must take the instrument (1) for value; (2) in good faith; and (3) without notice that it is overdue or has been dishonored or of any defense against or claim to it on the part of any person. We examine each of these elements in turn.

First, a holder must take the instrument for value. Section 403.302(1)(a), STATS. Under § 403.303(2), STATS., a holder takes for value when he takes an instrument in payment for an antecedent claim against *any person.* In this case, Kane took the instrument from Grace in payment of Gerald's debt and thereby satisfied the requirement of § 403.302(1)(a).

Second, a holder must take the instrument in good faith, defined in § 401.201(19), STATS., as "honesty in fact in the conduct or transaction concerned." The holder's initial burden on the issues of notice and good faith is a slight one. As one commentator has noted:

> The burden of proof of the allegations in the Complaint rests upon the plaintiff. It is not necessary, however, that the plaintiff allege in the complaint that good faith was an integral part of the transaction at each stage. That is an affirmative defense which must be raised by the defendant, if at all. [Russell A. Eisenberg, *Good Faith Under The Uniform Commercial Code—A New Look At An Old Problem,* 54 MARQ. L. REV. 1, 14 (1971) (emphasis and footnote omitted)].

In this case, Kane's affidavit supports his contention that he accepted the check in good faith for the payment of Gerald's antecedent debt. Moreover, none of the affidavits supplied by either party suggests evidence of bad faith on Kane's part. In the absence of such evidence, we conclude Kane took the check in good faith as a matter of law.

Finally, the last requirement to become a holder in due course is that the holder take the instrument without notice that it is overdue or has been dishonored or of any defense against it or claim to it on the part of any person. Section 403.302(1)(c), STATS. The knowledge of the defense for purposes of determining holder in due course status must exist at the time of issue. Therefore, we must examine whether Kane had knowledge of any defense at the time he took the check.

Because the requirement that a holder show that it did not have knowledge of a defense or claim to the instrument involves proof of a negative fact, the burden of proof is a slight one. In this case, the facts in Kane's affidavit suggest no knowledge of any claims or defenses, so the burden shifts to Grace to produce evidence that Kane had such knowledge. Grace argues that Kane was on notice that she had no preexisting obligation to pay her son's debt and that this constitutes knowledge of a defense. We disagree. Section 403.303(2), STATS., clearly allows a holder in due course to accept payment from one person for payment of the debt of another. Additionally, the fact that Grace, like any drawer, had the power to stop payment on the check does not constitute a defense that would prevent Kane from being a holder in due course. If it did, no holder would be a holder in due course because any drawer has the power to issue a stop payment order. Since Grace has not alleged that Kane had knowledge of any defense at the time he took the check, we hold that Kane met the requirement of 403.302(1)(c), STATS.

Because Kane took for value, in good faith, without knowledge of claims or defenses to the check, we conclude he was a holder in due course. As a holder in due course, Kane is not subject to Grace's claimed failure of consideration. Therefore, the fact that Gerald broke his promise to repay Grace the day after the check was issued does not affect Kane's status as a holder in due course.

Based upon the foregoing, we conclude that Kane was a holder in due course of the check and therefore not subject to Grace's asserted defenses. Thus, the trial court erred by granting judgment dismissing Kane's complaint. We reverse the judgment and remand to the trial court with directions to enter judgment in Kane's favor.

REVERSED and REMANDED.

[continued]

CRITICAL THINKING

How do rules of law play into the court's reasoning? Are there ambiguities present in these rules of law?

ETHICAL DECISION MAKING

Think about the WPH process of ethical decision making. What is the ultimate purpose of the judge's decision that Kane was a holder in due course? What value guided this conclusion?

BE A HOLDER OF A COMPLETE AND AUTHENTIC NEGOTIABLE INSTRUMENT

Party Must Be a Holder. As we mentioned earlier, a holder in due course must first be a *holder,* a party in possession of an instrument payable to the party or the bearer [UCC 1-201(20)]. If Adam Brewer possesses a check that states "Payable to Adam Brewer," Adam is a holder. Suppose Adam asked his bank for a cashier's check to buy a boat from his friend, Corey Baum. (See Exhibit 27-5.) Even though Adam possesses the cashier's check and his name appears on it, he is not a holder of it because it is payable to his friend. When Adam gives Corey the cashier's check, Corey becomes its first holder.

If someone steals a check payable to Adam Brewer and forges Adam's signature on the back, the thief is not a holder of the check because it is payable to Adam and not the thief.

Instrument Must Be Negotiable. If an instrument lacks any of the requirements for negotiability we discussed in the previous chapter, the holder cannot be a holder in due course.

Instrument Must Be Complete and Authentic. Third, the negotiable instrument must be complete and authentic [UCC 3-302(a)(1)]. What happens if it is incomplete,

Exhibit 27-5 The Relationship between Being a Payee and Being a Holder

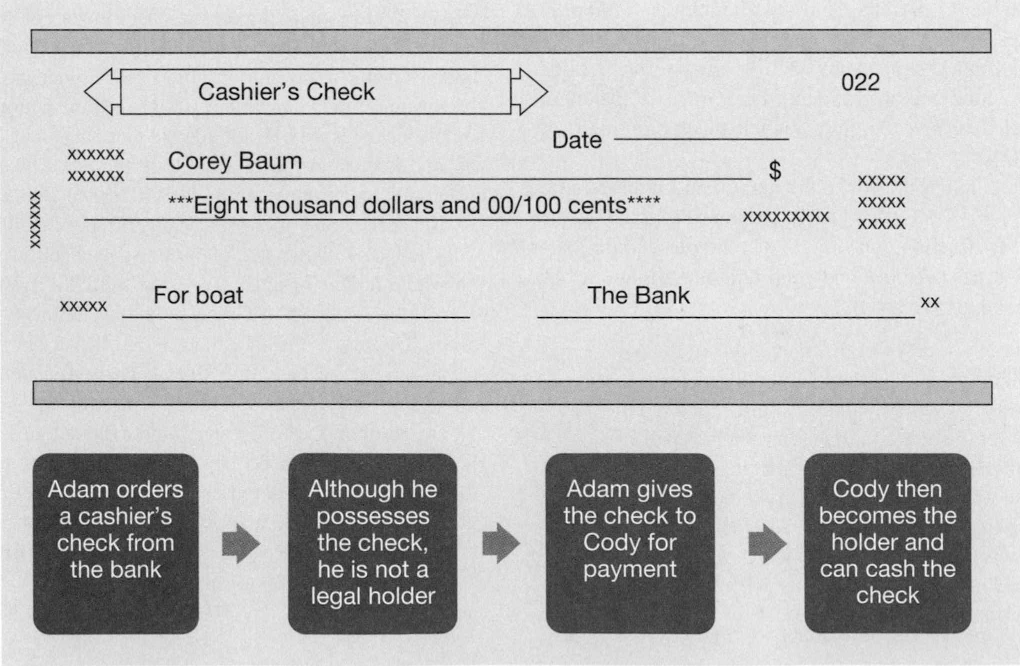

COMPARING THE LAW OF OTHER COUNTRIES

DEFINING NEGOTIABLE INSTRUMENTS IN JAPAN

The Japanese Commercial Code does not recognize the term *negotiable instruments.* In fact, the Japanese do not have any term to describe negotiable instruments. Instead, they recognize the legal concept of *yuka shoken,* which means "valuable securities" and encompasses checks, drafts, bonds, and stocks.

Japan does have separate legislation governing the same two general categories of negotiable instruments recognized in the United States, although it does not define them as such or as negotiable instruments. The first is commercial paper, or bills, notes, and checks. The formation, transfer, and defense of these are provided for in the Bills Law and the Checks Law. The second category, covered by several different statutes, is investment securities, including stocks and bonds.

The ambiguity surrounding "valuable securities" has created problems in Japan. Because there is no single definition, judges and scholars interpret *yuka shoken* on the basis of the definition they find most satisfactory at the time. The varying interpretations can lead to arbitrary exercise of judicial power.

missing the date for example? The UCC allows the holder to complete the check consistent with the intent of the issuer (3-115). However, if completion is inconsistent with the issuer's intent, the instrument is considered materially altered. If an instrument has been clearly materially altered or is so irregular or incomplete that its authenticity is called into question, the UCC bars a person taking it from becoming a holder in due course [3-302(a)(1)].

After learning about the holder-in-due-course concept, prudent businesses are often motivated to use high-security checks and change their check disbursement procedures to protect themselves. For example, American Express money orders employ intricate watermarks and seals to avoid check fraud. These security measures make it difficult for fraudulent instruments to appear complete and authentic.

TAKE INSTRUMENT FOR VALUE

How an Instrument Is Taken for Value. The holder in due course must take the negotiable instrument "for value." In other areas of the law, taking something for value usually means taking something with consideration, a bargained-for promise. However, the requirement here is more stringent: The party must take the instrument in exchange for a promise that has already been performed; the UCC explicitly excludes promises that have not yet been performed as "value." In other words, the party must suffer an out-of-pocket loss (UCC 3-303). Why? If a party has not yet performed the promise, he or she has not completely committed to the transaction financially and thus should not receive special legal protection. A party who receives a negotiable instrument as a gift or through mistake will be a holder instead of an HDC.

Legal Principle: **One characteristic of an HDC, and not a holder, is that an HDC must take a negotiable instrument for value; in other words, the HDC must take the instrument in exchange for a preexisting promise that has already been performed.**

BUT WHAT IF . . .

WHAT IF THE FACTS OF THE CASE OPENER WERE DIFFERENT?

Recall that, in the Case Opener, Cigna sent Mills a workers' compensation check. What if the check was misprinted, and the monetary amount was never printed on the check? Although Mills knew the check was supposed to be $484, he writes in the monetary amount of $1,000. Would he be able to cash this check considering Cigna made the mistake of not putting in a monetary amount?

Barbour v. Handlos Real Estate[2] offers an example of meeting the requirement of taking for value. Lucile and Alphonse Handlos accepted a note made out to their son as payment for a loan they had previously made to him. Having already given their son the loan, the Handloses had made an investment and thus had taken the note for value previously given. When the note was challenged, the Handloses were afforded holder-in-due-course status.

Legal Principle: **A holder can take an instrument for value if the holder:**

1. **Performs the promise for which the instrument was issued.**
2. **Acquires a security interest or some other lien in the instrument.**
3. **Takes the instrument for payment of a preceding claim.**
4. **Exchanges the instrument for another negotiable instrument.**
5. **Exchanges the instrument for an irrevocable obligation to a third party. [UCC 3-303(a)]**

Banking Transactions and Value. Other sections of the UCC help determine whether a commercial bank has given value for a check. Section 4-211 says that a bank has given value for the negotiable instrument to the extent it has a security interest in it. Section 4-210 identifies circumstances in which a bank has acquired a security interest in a negotiable instrument. In some of these, although the bank gives value, it does not intend to become an HDC.

Exceptions to the Value Requirement. UCC Section 3-303(3) states that a holder who takes a negotiable instrument for value does *not* become an HDC if he or she:

1. Purchases the instrument at a judicial sale or under legal process.
2. Acquires it through taking over an estate.
3. Purchases it as part of a bulk transaction not in the regular course of business of the transferor.

TAKE INSTRUMENT IN GOOD FAITH

The HDC must take the negotiable instrument in good faith [UCC 3-302(a)(2)(ii)]. What exactly is *good faith?* Historically, there has been some debate about whether it has an objective or subjective definition. Using the objective sense, some courts would decide whether the holder purchased the instrument with a proper degree of caution through a usual and ordinary manner of conducting business, doing what a reasonable holder *would have done.* However, other courts have looked at good faith in a subjective sense by asking whether the holder acted honestly when taking the instrument—in other words, considering the holder's *actual behavior.*

The UCC defines good faith somewhere between these standards, as "honesty in fact and the observance of reasonable commercial standards of fair dealing" [3-103(a)(4)]. Therefore, to act in good faith, a holder must not deviate from the reasonable commercial standards of fair dealing.

Hartford Ins. Group v. Citizens Fidelity Bank & Trust Co.[3] offers an example of a bank's being considered an HDC because it acted in good faith and within reasonable commercial standards of fair dealing. A customer of Citizens Fidelity Bank deposited a check from his insurance company. There were no

> To see how providing HDC status to banks facilitates financial transactions, please see the **Connecting to the Core** activity on the text website at www.mhhe.com/kubasek3e.

[2] 393 N.W.2d 581 (Mich. Ct. App. 1986).
[3] 579 S.W.2d 628 (Ky. Ct. App. 1979).

irregularities on the face of the check, and Citizens' manager, who had known the customer four years, credited his account in accordance with standard bank policy. Thus, the court deemed Citizens a holder in due course and not liable for the check when it was later found that the drawer had told the Citizens' customer not to negotiate it but he did so without telling Citizens about this notification.

When considering whether a holder took the negotiable instrument in good faith, the court looks only at the holder's state of mind. The transferor may have acted in bad faith. Case 27-3 shows how the court determines whether a holder has taken an instrument in good faith.

CASE 27-3 WAWEL SAVINGS BANK v. JERSEY TRACTOR TRAILER TRAINING, INC.

U.S. COURT OF APPEALS FOR THE THIRD CIRCUIT

500 F.3D 147, U.S. APP. LEXIS 19597 (2009)

Wawel Savings Bank entered into a loan agreement with Jersey Tractor Trailer Training (JTTT), Inc., for the amount of $315,000. In the agreement, JTTT pledged all capital equipment and assets of the company as collateral, and Wawel filed Uniform Commercial Code Financing Statements with the New Jersey Department of the Treasury and the Bergen County Clerk's Office. Sometime later, JTTT also entered into a factoring agreement with Yale Factors LLC whereby JTTT agreed to sell the rights to its accounts receivable in return for a 61.5% up-front payment of the amount due on the particular accounts receivable.

On April 4, 2006, JTTT filed a voluntary petition for bankruptcy, and on June 29, 2006, Wawel brought action against JTTT, seeking declaratory relief that its lien on JTTT's accounts receivable had priority over that of Yale's. The Bankruptcy Court found in favor of Wawel, stating that Wawel did not authorize JTTT's factoring agreement with Yale, and that Yale could not be considered a purchaser of instruments or a holder in due course because it did not establish that it acted in "good faith" by observing reasonable commercial standards of fair dealing. Yale appealed the decision.

JUDGE BARRY: Yale asserts that it should be considered a holder in due course, or a purchaser of instruments, and therefore should have priority over Wawel's senior security interest. Yale argues, first, that because the security agreement accompanying Wawel's loan to JTTT did not expressly prohibit the sale of collateral, Wawel waived its security interest. That argument is without merit, especially given that in its agreement with Wawel, JTTT represented that it "w[ould] not settle any account for less than its full value without your written permission," and that it would "collect all accounts until [told] otherwise." JTTT's sale of its accounts receivable, therefore, ran afoul of the security agreement.

Regardless of whether Wawel waived its security interest, Yale has priority over that interest if it is either a holder in due course or a purchaser of instruments. A holder in due course is one who takes an instrument for value, in good faith, and without notice of dishonor or any defense against or claim to it on the part of any person. "If those requirements are met, a holder in due course take[s] priority over an earlier security interest, even if perfected. . . ." U.C.C. § 9-331(a). The same is true for a purchaser of instruments. To be considered a purchaser of instruments, Yale must have "give[n] value and take[n] possession of the instrument in good faith and without knowledge that the purchase violates the rights of the secured party." "Good faith" is defined in the U.C.C. as "honesty in fact and the observance of reasonable commercial standards of fair dealing." The District Court is to remand this matter to the Bankruptcy Court to determine whether Yale qualifies as a holder in due course or a purchaser of instruments, and to resolve the good faith element of that analysis in accordance with this opinion.

REMANDED.

CRITICAL THINKING

The case entirely rested on the definition of the legal term *good faith.* Suppose that one of your classmates believes the term *good faith* as outlined by the UCC is too ambiguous to make an informed ruling. Would you agree with your classmate about the ambiguity of the term? Why or why not?

ETHICAL DECISION MAKING

Some clues supporting Judge Barry's decision and the UCC's definition of good faith include honesty, transparency, and fairness. Can you think of any value preferences at the forefront of running a business that may conflict with the values outlined by the court and its definition of good faith?

TAKE INSTRUMENT WITHOUT NOTICE

Finally, a holder must take an instrument without notice of various claims to or defects of the negotiable instrument. A holder cannot be an HDC who has notice or is aware of any of the following defects [UCC 3-302(a)]:

1. The instrument is overdue.
2. The instrument has been dishonored.
3. The instrument was issued as part of a series that is in default.
4. The instrument has been altered or contains an unauthorized signature.
5. There is a claim to the instrument. (The claims are described in Section 3-306.)
6. Another party has a defense or claim in recoupment to the instrument.

What Does It Mean to Have Notice? According to the UCC, a person has notice of a fact who either:

1. Has actual knowledge of the fact.
2. Receives notice or notification of it.
3. Has reason to know the fact exists. [UCC 1-201(25)]

For example, suppose that Sun's Market, the check-cashing business from the Case Opener, received a letter from the insurance company that listed the numbers of checks that had stop-payment orders. As long as Sun's Market received this letter *before* it accidentally accepted the dishonored check, Sun's Market would have notice of a defect and thus could not be a holder in due course. The UCC states that "to be effective, notice must be received at a time and in a manner that gives a reasonable opportunity to act on it" [3-302(f)].

Suppose a person receives an instrument that has clearly been altered but she does not notice the alteration. According to UCC requirements [3-302(a)(1)], the holder's awareness does not matter; the mere existence of such irregularities means that the holder cannot be a holder in due course. Nor can the person who has notice of a defect but still gives value for the instrument.

Overdue Instruments. Suppose you accept a check from a business associate. Unfortunately, the check falls behind your desk and is lost for the next four months. If you try to negotiate this instrument to another party, he or she will not be permitted to claim HDC status because the check is overdue. How does a holder know an instrument is overdue? The answer depends on the type of instrument. Two types of instruments—demand and time instruments—may be overdue (UCC 3-304).

Demand Instruments. A **demand instrument** becomes overdue if it has been outstanding for an unreasonably long period of time after its date [UCC 3-304(a)(3)]. If the demand instrument is a check, it is overdue 90 days after its date [UCC 3-304(a)(2)]. The date on the check gives another party notice of its overdue status; thus the party cannot be an HDC.

Legal Principle: **As a general rule, checks (a type of demand instrument) are overdue 90 days after their due date.**

Time Instruments. A **time instrument** becomes overdue at any time after the expressed due date on it. Suppose a customer tries to negotiate a promissory note to you on January 2, 2010. However, the note states that it is payable by January 1, 2010. You have notice that the note is overdue; you must have acquired it before January 1, 2010, for it to be negotiable.

Most of the rules regarding whether a time instrument is overdue depend on its payment structure. If the instrument requires payment in a lump sum rather than in installments, it is overdue if the party does not make the lump-sum payment by the due date [UCC 3-304(b)(2)]. However, overdue status of installments depends on whether payment applies to the principal or the interest. If a party misses payment of an installment of the principal, the instrument is overdue until this installment is paid [UCC 3-304(b)(1)]. If a party misses a payment of interest on this instrument, the instrument is not overdue [UCC 3-304(c)].

Sometimes, parties agree to accelerate the due date of an instrument. Thus, if a party does not make payment on either the principal *or* the interest on the instrument by the accelerated due date, the instrument is overdue [UCC 3-304(b)(3) and 304(c)]. Because it may be difficult for a holder taking an instrument to determine whether there has been an accelerated due date, the UCC permits this holder to become an HDC if he or she had no reason to know about the accelerated due date.

How might a party know that an installment payment on the principal was not made? A bank considering purchasing a consumer note from a retailer, for example, can determine whether all payments have been made on the note by looking at the consumer's credit report. If the credit report indicates an installment had not been paid, the bank would have notice that the instrument was overdue.

Dishonored Instruments. An instrument is **dishonored** when a party refuses to pay it. Suppose you deposit a check from a customer into your company's account at a Wells Fargo bank. The customer has an account at Chase Bank. Wells Fargo credits your account and later presents the check for payment at Chase.

However, Chase refuses to pay because there are insufficient funds in your customer's account. Chase has dishonored the check and will likely stamp "Insufficient funds" on it. If you then tried to negotiate this check to another party, these words would give notice that the check was dishonored. However, someone who has no reason to know a note has been dishonored (if Chase does not stamp it, for instance) can become an HDC. This hypothetical situation is parallel to the real transactions occurring in the Case Opener. However, by the time Triffin purchased the dishonored check, the words "Stop Payment" were already on it, so Triffin might have had notice that the check was dishonored. To see how this may have affected the court's ruling in this situation, see the Wrap-Up at the end of this chapter.

Legal Principle: You cannot become a holder in due course if you are aware that the negotiable instrument has been dishonored.

Claims or Defenses. A party who is aware of any claim or defense to an instrument has notice and cannot become an HDC [UCC 3-302(a)(2)(v),(vi)]. However, a party who had no reason to know various claims or defenses applied to an instrument, even though they exist, is not prevented from becoming an HDC. Exhibit 27-6 presents a summary of defenses related to holder-in-due-course status.

The Shelter Principle and HDC

Generally, if an item is transferred from one person to another, the transferee acquires all the rights the transferor had in the item. This idea is called the **shelter principle** [UCC Section 3-203(b)]. It means that even a holder who cannot attain holder-in-due-course

L04
What is the shelter principle?

Exhibit 27-6
Defenses and the Holder in Due Course

The holder in due course may be *free from* the following personal defenses:
1. Lack or failure of consideration
2. Breach of contract
3. Fraud in the inducement in the underlying contract
4. Illegality
5. Duress
6. Unauthorized completion or material alteration of the instrument
7. Unauthorized acquisition of the instrument

The HDC is *subject to* the following real defenses:
1. Fraud in the essence
2. Discharge of the party liable through bankruptcy
3. Forgery
4. Material alteration of a completed instrument
5. Infancy—a party is below the legal age of consent

status can acquire the rights and privileges of an HDC *if* the item is being transferred *from* an HDC. The instrument does not need to be transferred directly from an HDC; under the shelter principle, as long as the holder of an instrument can demonstrate that someone through the line of transfers had obtained the rights of an HDC, then all subsequent holders have these rights.

Therefore, in the Case Opener, plaintiff Triffin received the workers' compensation check from Sun's Market, a holder in due course. If Triffin did not qualify for HDC status on his own, he would have received the rights that Sun's Market, the transferor, had. In other words, Triffin is taking "shelter" in Sun's Market's status as an HDC.

One exception to the shelter principle prevents a person who engages in fraud or other illegal interference with an instrument from becoming an HDC, even if he or she obtains the instrument later from an HDC. For example, Chad and Dave devise a scheme to defraud Jenny. Jenny, unaware of the fraud, writes a check to Dave. Dave negotiates the check to Mariko. Mariko, through the negotiation, becomes an HDC and eventually negotiates the check to Chad. Although Chad should be an HDC under the shelter principle, because he was part of the original fraud against Jenny, he does not obtain the rights of an HDC.

The shelter principle may at first seem contrary to the idea of the HDC principle; however, the purpose of the shelter principle is to encourage the marketability of instruments. The greater protection offered to an HDC is very appealing; thus, allowing parties to achieve it through the shelter principle encourages financial interactions.

Legal Principle: **If an instrument is transferred from a party with holder-in-due-course status, the next party also receives HDC status.**

L05
In what ways has the holder-in-due-course doctrine been abused?

Abuse of the Holder-in-Due-Course Doctrine

While HDC status offers great protection to financial intermediaries, the intermediaries might attempt to abuse this protection. Suppose you are starting a small business and a salesperson for Office Supplies Made Easy comes to your new office to sell you high-quality office supplies. You pay for the supplies with a negotiable installment note on which you are supposed to make three installments of $1,000. When you receive your office supplies, you discover they are extremely low-quality and certainly not worth the $3,000 you agreed to pay. You call Office Supplies Made Easy, saying you want to return the supplies. However, an employee tells you that your installment note has been negotiated to a finance company, which became a holder in due course.

The finance company calls your office every day because you have refused to pay for the supplies. You later discover that it negotiates all notes of Office Supplies Made Easy, and the two firms appear to have some kind of arrangement so that the finance company can attain HDC status. Claims or defenses you have against Office Supplies Made Easy do not apply to the finance company.

When cases like this have arisen in court, judges have looked at the connection between the transferor and the transferee. If the companies are closely connected, as in our example, some judges apply the salesperson's knowledge of your claims and defenses to the finance company, preventing the finance company from achieving HDC status.

The FTC created several rules in the 1970s that help protect consumers against the kind of HDC abuse in our example. These rules require every consumer credit contract or any purchase money loan to contain the following statement in 10-point, boldface type:

> Any holder of this consumer credit contract is subject to all claims and defenses which the debtor could assert against the seller of goods or services obtained pursuant hereto or with the proceeds hereof. Recovery hereunder by the debtor shall not exceed amounts paid by the debtor hereunder.[4]

Consequently, no subsequent holder of the contract will have the rights of an HDC.

[4] FTC Holder in Due Course Regulations, 16 C.F.R. 433.2 (1978).

CASE OPENER WRAP-UP

Dishonored Check and Holder-in-Due-Course Status

In this case, the court ruled in favor of Triffin and ordered Cigna to pay him $484 plus interest for the check. Even though Triffin knew the check was dishonored when he purchased it, he still was able to receive payment under the shelter principle and holder in due course. That is, the court ruled that the transfer by a holder in due course to a third party, even one with notice of the dishonor, transfers all rights of the holder in due course to the successor in interest.

As discussed earlier in the chapter, the purpose of the holder-in-due-course doctrine is to protect financial intermediaries and encourage them to continue to engage in financial transactions. If you were a manager for Sun's Market and discovered that the insurance company would not be responsible for the dishonored check, you would probably be less likely to accept checks in the future. The holder-in-due-course doctrine and shelter principle encourage market transactions and shield businesses like Sun's Market from unnecessary risks.

KEY TERMS

allonge 583
blank endorsement 583
blank qualified endorsements 585
conditional endorsement 587
demand instrument 596
dishonored 597
endorsee 583
endorsement for deposit or collection only 586
endorsement to prohibit further endorsement 587
endorser 583
holder 582
holder in due course (HDC) 582
negotiable instrument 582
negotiation 582
restrictive endorsements 586
shelter principle 597
special endorsement 584
special qualified endorsements 585
time instrument 596
trust endorsement 588

SUMMARY OF KEY TOPICS

Negotiation

Delivery: The physical handing over of a negotiable instrument.

The two types of endorsements:

1. Unqualified endorsements
2. Qualified endorsements

Holder-in-Due-Course Doctrine

The HDC doctrine provides incentive for financial intermediaries to engage in transactions because they receive greater legal protection.

Requirements for Holder-in-Due-Course Status

The requirements for holder-in-due-course status:

1. *Be a holder of a complete and authentic negotiable instrument.*
2. *Take the instrument for value:* Holder must suffer an out-of-pocket loss.
3. *Take the instrument in good faith:* Holder must take the instrument with "honesty in fact and the observance of reasonable commercial standards of fair dealing."
4. *Take the instrument without notice:* Holder must take the instrument without notice of the following defects: It is overdue, dishonored, or part of a series in default; it has been altered or has an unauthorized signature; or it is subject to claims or defenses.

The Shelter Principle and HDC

Shelter principle: If a holder cannot attain HDC status, the holder can acquire the rights and privileges of an HDC *if* the item is being transferred *from* an HDC.

Abuse of the Holder-in-Due-Course Doctrine

FTC rule: Negotiation of consumer notes may not be subject to HDC status.

POINT / COUNTERPOINT

Should Someone Who Commits an Illegal Activity to Obtain a Negotiable Instrument Still Be Considered a Holder in Due Course?

YES	NO
Someone who commits an illegal activity to obtain a negotiable instrument should still be considered a holder in due course.	A criminal action should prevent HDC status. A person who obtains a negotiable instrument through an illegal activity does not deserve the status of holder in

Suppose a person took a misplaced betting ticket and cashed it (knowing full well the voucher was not his to cash). That person should still be awarded holder-in-due-course status.

The UCC established four requirements a holder must fulfill to be considered a holder in due course. The first requirement is that "the party must be a holder of a complete and authentic negotiable instrument." Assuming the criminal was wise enough to ensure that his recently obtained negotiable instrument is complete and authentic, a criminal can fulfill the first requirement to qualify as a holder in due course.

Another requirement established by the UCC is that "the holder must take the instrument in good faith." Especially because the definition of "good faith" is unclear, a criminal could easily obtain an instrument in good faith. Some criminals may be lucky enough to *find* a misplaced voucher. The criminal has no reason to believe that the voucher belongs to someone else. The "criminal" is fortunate, and he fulfills the good-faith requirement established by the UCC.

Additionally, to be a holder in due course, the holder also "must take the instrument without notice of defects," including notice that it is overdue, dishonored, or altered or has an unauthorized signature. As a person who does not know anything about the instrument's background, the criminal fulfills this requirement.

Meeting the requirements under the UCC should provide any holder the rights of HDC status.

due course. The criminal does not fulfill all the requirements set by the UCC to become a holder in due course.

A criminal does not fulfill two of the four requirements set by the UCC to be deemed a holder in due course. While a criminal may be in possession of a complete and authentic negotiable instrument and the instrument may have been obtained without notice of defects, fulfilling two of the four requirements is not sufficient for the criminal to be considered a holder in due course.

If obtaining the negotiable instrument through thievery, the criminal does not fulfill the second UCC requirement. The second requirement is known as both "taking the instrument for value" and "suffering an out-of-pocket loss." A criminal may "happen upon" a negotiable instrument, but he does not pay anything for the instrument. Therefore, the criminal should not be considered a holder in due course.

A criminal should not be awarded the status of holder in due course for yet another reason. The HDC doctrine was created to provide incentive for financial intermediaries to engage in transactions without fear of liability. The HDC doctrine was *not* designed to encourage or provide incentives for thieves and criminals to dishonestly obtain negotiable instruments.

Providing incentives to financial intermediaries through the holder-in-due-course doctrine is an excellent idea. A party that simply processes a payment should *not* be required to shoulder transaction risks. However, a thief or criminal does not simply process a payment. A criminal does not fulfill the role intended for the holder in due course. Therefore, a criminal should not receive the protection available to a holder in due course.

QUESTIONS & PROBLEMS

1. Evaluate the following statement: "Order paper and bearer paper must be delivered to be negotiated."
2. Explain the rationale for the following statement: "The purpose of holder-in-due-course status is to encourage parties to engage in financial transactions."
3. What are the requirements of holder-in-due-course status?
4. Todd Leparski was an assistant comptroller for Interior Crafts, Inc. Due to extremely lax accounting procedures, Leparski was allowed to both receive and deposit incoming checks from Interior's customers. Consequently, Leparski stole approximately $500,000 from Interior during his four-month employment from October 2000 to February 2001. To steal the money, Leparski took several checks from the incoming mail that were made payable to Interior by customers. He then endorsed the checks "Interior Crafts—For Deposit Only." He took the checks to an ATM machine owned by Pan American Bank and deposited the checks into his own bank account using a deposit envelope. Following the instructions on the deposit envelope, Pan American deposited the funds into Leparski's personal account at Marquette Bank. Eventually,

Marquette Bank alerted Interior to the fact that Leparski was depositing checks into his personal account that were payable to Interior. Interior was able to recover only half the money he had stolen, and it sued Leparski and Pan American Bank to seek recovery for the rest of the stolen money. What type of endorsement was on the negotiable instruments? Did the bank handle this type of endorsement properly? Can a check endorsed "for deposit only" without further limitation be deposited into any account? [*Interior Crafts, Inc. v. Leparski,* 366 Ill. App. 3d 1148, 853 N.E.2d 1244, 2006 Ill. App. LEXIS 589 (2006).]

5. Bond issued a $300,000 note to Goss in 1988. The note was secured by a deed of land. Goss later entered into an agreement to purchase commercial property owned by RAM. In lieu of partial payment, Gaetani, general partner of RAM, accepted the $300,000 note. Supanich, a trustee for Goss, endorsed the note. The note endorsement read: "For value received, the undersigned hereby assigns and transfers all right, title and interest in and to within Note to Toney E. Gaetani, Sr." The endorsement did not contain the words *without recourse.* Bond paid no principal and only partial interest on the note. Gaetani brought an action against Goss, Supanich, and Bond. At issue was whether the endorsement language allowed Gaetani to recover directly against Goss. Despite the lack of the words *without recourse,* the trial court held that Gaetani could not recover from Goss. Do you think the court allowed Gaetani to recover from Goss on appeal? [*Gaetani v. Goss-Golden,* 84 Cal. App. 4th 1118 (2000).]

6. At the end of January 2001, while cleaning out his self-storage locker, Kim Griffith found a certificate of deposit purportedly issued by Mellon Bank, N.A., of Pittsburgh, Pennsylvania, on July 3, 1975, for the amount of $530,000 plus interest to be payable to bearer on August 4, 1975. The CD was in one of several books Griffith had purchased from an unnamed buyer. On its face, the certificate of deposit had not been marked paid. On August 15, 2002, more than a year after finding the certificate of deposit, Griffith presented it for payment in person at a Mellon Bank office in Pennsylvania. Mellon refused to honor the certificate of deposit, arguing that because the bearer certificate of deposit matured 27 years earlier, the certificate was questionable on its face and thus was not genuine. On the basis of Mellon's refusal to honor the certificate of deposit, Griffith filed suit against Mellon. Mellon argues that it has no records of the CD as not being paid and that under Pennsylvania law it falls to Griffith to prove nonpayment. Griffith argues he is a holder in due course and is entitled to payment regardless of any possible defenses Mellon might raise. Is Griffith a holder in due course? Should he be able to collect on the CD? Why or why not? [*Griffith v. Mellon Bank, N.A.,* 328 F. Supp. 2d 536 (2004).]

7. Daniel DeMarais is the former chief financial officer (CFO) of Apex IT. Through a Minnesota Department of Revenue investigation it came to light that DeMarais had embezzled well over $400,000 from the company. DeMarais embezzled funds from Apex in part by using Apex's corporate checks to pay the amounts due on a personal credit card account he maintained with Chase Manhattan Bank USA, N.A. According to Apex, Chase had notice of Apex's claims to these funds because the payments were "unusual, irregular, and large" and were made using business checks from Apex's corporate accounts. Apex demanded that Chase return all funds it received from DeMarais, which Chase refused to do. Apex then sued Chase, seeking equitable relief. Chase contends that Apex's claim must fail because Chase is a holder in due course. Does Chase meet the requirements for a holder in due course? Should Chase have taken more precautions given the unusual nature of the payments? [*Apex IT v. Chase Manhattan Bank USA, N.A.,* 2005 U.S. Dist. LEXIS 3917 (2005).]

8. Delbert Williamson was driving his family home one night when they were struck by a Jeep Wrangler coming in the opposite direction. The accident was caused when the Jeep, which was being hauled by a motor home, came loose and crossed the lane of traffic, hitting the Williamsons' Mazda-MPV minivan head-on. Delbert's wife, Thanh, and their daughter Alexa were also in the car. Thanh later died at the hospital from sustained internal injuries as a result of the accident. Delbert and his daughter were wearing type 2 seatbelts, which have a lap and chest restraint. However, his wife was wearing a type 1 seatbelt, which has only the lap restraint. Williamson sued Mazda, claiming the seatbelt his wife was wearing was defective. Mazda claimed that its permit for seatbelts allows the company to install either type 1 or type 2 in the back-aisle seat of its vehicles. Do you think that Mazda was liable for the death of Thanh? Why or why not? [*Williamson v. Mazda Motor of America, Inc.,* 562 130 S. Ct. 3348, 176 L. Ed. 2d 1218, 78 U.S.L.W. 3687.]

9. Dr. Rodrigue operated a private practice as a gynecologist-obstetrician. She hired Carol Wiltshire to work as a medical receptionist and secretary, but over her nine years of employment Wiltshire held a variety of positions of increasing responsibility and authority within the office. Wiltshire was responsible for understanding insurance requirements and was the only person in the office trained in the computerized billing system. After learning how to use the billing software, Wiltshire began stealing checks that were sent by various insurance providers and were payable to Rodrigue. In sum, she stole 269 checks, totaling $372,572.18. She forged Rodrigue's endorsement on the insurance checks and deposited them in her own account at the Godfrey, Illinois, branch of Olin Employees Credit Union. Olin required that its tellers obtain a supervisor's approval before accepting third-party checks. The supervisor asked for documentation about the third-party checks, and Wiltshire provided a forged letter of authorization purporting to be from Rodrigue. The bank then began accepting the checks. When Rodrigue found out about the fraudulent checks, she alerted the authorities and brought suit against Olin Employees Credit Union. Olin argues that it did not violate reasonable commercial standards in allowing Wiltshire to cash the insurance reimbursement checks and that it used ordinary care in the negotiable-instrument transactions. Who do you think is liable for the fraudulent checks—Rodrigue or Olin? Why? [*Dr. Linda Rodrigue v. Olin Employees Credit Union,* 406 F.3d 434 (2005).]

10. Stacy and Michael Russell are residents in Harrah, Oklahoma, who live in a trailer. Oklahoma Farm Bureau Mutual Insurance Company was the insurer on the home. Within the Russells' policy a section on loss stated that Farm Bureau "will pay you unless another payee is named on the Declarations page," that "Loss shall be payable to any mortgagee named in the Declarations," and that one of Farm Bureau's responsibilities was to "protect the mortgagee's interests in the insured building." On the Declarations page of the document, Conesco Finance, which held a financial interest in the Russells' home, was named as one of the "payees." A fire completely charred the mobile home in late 2002. A $69,000 settlement amount was agreed on between Russell and Farm Bureau after an insurance claim was made. Conesco was not aware of the fire, nor did it know that a check had been made out to both Conesco and the Russells together to cover damages incurred in the fire. The Russells' deposited the check into their account, with both of their signatures and a stamp from Conesco Finance, which is believed to have been forged, at the Bank of Oklahoma (BOK). The Bank of Nichols Hills (BNH) was the banking provider for the insurance company. About a year later, Conesco learned of the fire and contacted Farm Bureau about being owed more than $50,000, which was paid in full. BNH was notified of the forgery and reimbursed the insurance company for the $50,000. BNH then proceeded to sue BOK, claiming that carelessness was the reason the forgery occurred. Who do you believe is at fault here on the basis of the information presented in the chapter? [*Bank of Nichols Hills v. Bank of Oklahoma,* 196 P.3d 984 (Okla. Civ. App. 2008).]

Looking for more review materials?

The Online Learning Center at **www.mhhe.com/kubasek3e** contains this chapter's "Assignment on the Internet" and also a list of URLs for more information, entitled "On the Internet." Find both of them in the Student Center portion of the OLC, along with quizzes and other helpful materials.

CHAPTER

28 Liability, Defenses, and Discharge

LEARNING OBJECTIVES

After reading this chapter, you will be able to answer the following questions:

1. What information is needed to determine signature liability?
2. What is warranty liability?
3. How does one avoid liability for negotiable instruments?

CASE OPENER

Bank One and the Forged Checks

Dr. Rick LaCombe practiced optometry as a sole proprietorship at LaCombe Eye Center. LaCombe's receptionist, Lana Slyfield, embezzled checks and deposited them in her own account at the bank. She did this by forging LaCombe's signature and writing her account number on the checks. She then put the checks in her account at Bank One. Slyfield successfully cashed the fraudulent checks for four years, amounting to over 500 checks totaling $70,000. When LaCombe discovered the embezzlement and fraud, he sued Bank One for negligence for accepting the forged negotiable instruments.

1. Who do you think should bear the liability for the forged checks—Bank One or LaCombe Eye Center? What values are guiding your decision?
2. As a business manager at LaCombe Eye Center, what kind of practices would you encourage to ensure that employees were not able to easily embezzle money through fraudulent checks?

The Wrap-Up at the end of the chapter will answer these questions.

As you can see from the Bank One opener, it is not always clear who should bear responsibility for the amount of a negotiable instrument. This chapter explains the various ways a party may be liable for a negotiable instrument. First, when a person signs a negotiable instrument, he or she is potentially liable for the instrument. This type of liability is called **signature liability.** In contrast, a party may be liable if the transfer of the instrument breaches a warranty associated with the instrument. This second type of liability is called **warranty liability.** After we consider both signature and warranty liability, we examine the defenses to these types of liability. Finally, we investigate how liability for a negotiable instrument may be discharged.

Signature Liability

LO1
What information is needed to determine signature liability?

UCC Section 3-401(a) imposes liability if the party or the party's agent signs the instrument. If a party does not sign, the party cannot be held liable. Thus, because the receptionist at LaCombe Eye Center forged the doctor's name on the checks, should LaCombe be liable?

Because the signature on an instrument leads to liability, it is important to know what counts as a signature. According to the UCC, a signature can be any name, word, mark, or symbol used by a party to authenticate a writing [3-401(b)]. Thus, if you wrote either your full name or an *X* with the intent to authenticate an instrument, either writing would constitute a signature.

When a party signs a negotiable instrument, he or she might be signing as a maker, acceptor, drawer, or endorser of the instrument. The signer's status as a maker, acceptor, drawer, or endorser of the note establishes the extent of the signer's liability. In other words, issuers and acceptors have a certain type of liability, while drawers and endorsers have another type of signature liability. Issuers and acceptors are primarily liable for a negotiable instrument, while drawers and endorsers are secondarily liable. If it is not possible to tell the status of the party, the general rule is that the party is considered an endorser (UCC 3-204, comment 1). Exhibit 28-1 provides a summary of the various endorsing parties and their roles.

Exhibit 28-1
Parties Signing a Negotiable Instrument

ENDORSING PARTY	DESCRIPTION	ROLE
Maker	A person promising to pay a set sum to the holder of a promissory note or certificate of deposit	Promises to pay money
Acceptor	A person (drawee) who accepts and signs the draft to agree to pay the draft when it is presented	Pays the money, or is responsible for paying the money, when it is requested
Drawer	A person ordering the drawee to pay	Orders someone (the drawee) to pay
Endorser	A person who signs an instrument to restrict payment of it, negotiate it, or incur liability	Signs an instrument at some point during negotiation

E-COMMERCE AND THE LAW

ELECTRONIC SIGNATURES

Electronic signatures are an accepted and rather standard method of authorizing payment. However, conducting business through an online payment system puts the company at potential risk. Many banking companies have policies that deem the merchant, rather than the buyer, responsible for the charge if the payment made is fraudulent. For example, Visa advises its business-account customers that make online transactions to know how to protect themselves, as the business owners could be liable if a customer's payment is fraudulent. Businesses have several options for ensuring that their online transaction system can detect fraudulent payment. One of these options is to obtain chargeback insurance to prevent liability for fraud. The second option is to increase safety measures to prevent fraud, such as having online CAPTCHA's or requiring more extensive authentication procedures when a customer makes a payment. Since online business owners are at high risk for this type of fraud, owners should always properly authenticate the customer making a payment.

Source: http://usa.visa.com/download/merchants/visa_risk_management_guide_ecommerce.pdf.

PRIMARY LIABILITY OF MAKERS AND ACCEPTORS

A party who is **primarily liable** for an instrument must pay the stated amount on the instrument when it is presented for payment. This liability for the stated amount begins as soon as the instrument is issued. Moreover, the primarily liable party must pay without resorting to any other party. For example, suppose you own a business and write a check drawing on your funds in your business account at First National Bank. First National has primary liability for the check; it must pay the stated amount when the check is presented for payment.

The UCC establishes that certain parties—makers and acceptors—are primarily liable. First, a **maker** is a party who has promised to pay. For example, the maker of a promissory note is primarily liable for the amount of the note because the party has promised to pay the amount of the instrument. Moreover, UCC Section 3-412 states that a party who signs as an issuer of an instrument is liable for the amount of the instrument as soon as it is issued. For example, a bank that issues a cashier's check is primarily liable for the amount of the check as soon as the cashier's check is created (UCC 4-412).

Second, an **acceptor,** a drawee of a draft who accepts and signs the draft to agree to pay the draft when it is presented, is primarily liable [UCC 3-413(a)]. A party who accepts a draft by signing on the face of the draft is primarily liable (UCC 3-413). For example, when a bank accepts a check, it is primarily liable for the amount of the check (UCC 3-409).

SECONDARY LIABILITY OF DRAWERS AND ENDORSERS

A party who is **secondarily liable** for an instrument must pay the amount on the instrument if the primarily liable party defaults. Return to the First National Bank example. First National has primary liability for the check; it must pay the stated amount when the check is presented for payment. However, suppose First National dishonors this check because of insufficient funds in your account. Because the primarily liable party, the bank, has defaulted, you, the issuer of the check, are now liable.

Drawers and endorsers are secondarily liable parties. An **endorser** is a party who signs an instrument to restrict payment of it, negotiate it, or incur liability [UCC 3-204(b)].

A **drawer** is a person who signs as a party ordering payment [UCC 3-103(a)(5)]. For example, if you write a check from your bank account that is payable to the electric company, you are the drawer of the check, the bank is the drawee, and the electric company is the holder of the check. The holder of the check (the electric company) presents the check to the drawee (the bank) for payment. **Presentment** is defined in the UCC as making a demand for the drawee to pay [UCC 3-501(a)]. The UCC creates specific rules that govern the time and manner of presentment.

Legal Principle: **Drawers and endorsers are secondarily liable for negotiable instruments.**

Suppose the holder (the electric company) presented your check and the bank dishonored the check because of insufficient funds in your account. The UCC states that drawers of drafts are liable for an instrument only after it has been dishonored (3-414, 3-415). Thus, you (the drawer) are now liable for the check.

By adding a disclaimer to her or his signature on a draft, a drawer might avoid liability if the instrument is dishonored [UCC 3-414(e)]. However, a drawer of a check may not include such a disclaimer of liability.

Three conditions must be met for a drawer or endorser to become liable. First, the holder of the instrument must present the instrument in a proper and timely fashion. Second, the instrument must be dishonored. Third, notice of the dishonor must be given to the drawer.

Presentment. An instrument must be presented in a proper and timely manner. Exhibit 28-2 provides a summary of the requirements for presentment of a negotiable instrument. First, the instrument must be presented to the proper party. If the instrument is a note, the holder must present the note to the maker of the note. In contrast, if the instrument is a draft, the holder must present the instrument to the drawee. Thus, continuing our electric company example, the electric company must present the check to the bank (the drawee).

Second, the instrument must be presented to the proper party in a proper way. UCC Section 3-501(b) states that an instrument can be presented (1) by any commercially reasonable means, (2) through a clearinghouse procedure, or (3) at the place designated in the instrument.

Third, the instrument must be presented to the proper party in a timely manner. Thus, if the instrument is a note, the holder must present the note to the maker on the note's due date. If the instrument is a draft, such as a check, the holder must present the instrument within a *reasonable* time. The failure to present an instrument on time is the most common reason that improper presentment occurs, which ultimately discharges unqualified endorsers from secondary liability.

The UCC states a specific timeline for presentment. If a holder does not present the instrument within a reasonable time, the drawer or endorser may not be held secondarily liable. Therefore, if the electric company waited 60 days to present your check to the bank, it probably cannot hold you secondarily liable because the UCC states that a check must be presented within 30 days of its date to hold the drawer secondarily liable [3-414(f)]. Similarly, to hold an endorser secondarily liable, a holder must present a check within 30 days of the endorsement [UCC 3-415(e)].

Exhibit 28-2

Proper Presentment of a Negotiable Instrument

1. Presented to the proper party
2. Presented in a proper way
3. Presented in a timely manner

Dishonor. When a holder presents an instrument within a timely and proper manner but acceptance or payment is refused, the instrument has been **dishonored.** The instrument must be explicitly dishonored; a refusal to pay does not necessarily mean that the instrument has been dishonored. For example, suppose you are a holder of a check that is payable to your business. You present this check for payment, but the bank refuses to pay the check because you cannot present identification [UCC 3-501(b)(2)]. Alternatively, a bank may refuse to pay on an instrument because the endorsement of the instrument is not proper. Again, this refusal to pay does not dishonor the instrument. Situations in which refusals to pay do not constitute dishonorment are found in UCC Section 3-501(b) and are listed in Exhibit 28-3. Remember, a secondarily liable party becomes liable *only* if a primarily liable party dishonors the instrument.

BUT WHAT IF . . .

WHAT IF THE FACTS OF THE CASE OPENER WERE DIFFERENT?

Recall that, in the Case Opener, LaCombe's receptionist Lana Slyfield signed LaCombe's name on the checks and went to the bank to deposit them into her account instead of his company account, where all of LaCombe's checks were legally supposed to be deposited. Slyfield did not provide evidence that this action was authorized by LaCombe. If the bank had refused to pay the checks due to Slyfield's attempting to deposit them into the wrong account, would that mean that the checks had been dishonored?

Exhibit 28-3

Refusals to Pay That Do Not Dishonor an Instrument

REASON FOR REFUSAL	UCC TEXT
Holder's failure to comply with certain requests	Upon demand of the person to whom *presentment* is made, the person making presentment must (i) exhibit the *instrument,* (ii) give reasonable identification and, if presentment is made on behalf of another person, reasonable evidence of authority to do so, and (iii) sign a receipt on the instrument for any payment made or surrender the instrument if full payment is made. [3-501(b)(2)]
Lack of proper endorsement or failure to comply with terms of the instrument	Without dishonoring the *instrument,* the *party* to whom *presentment* is made may (i) return the instrument for lack of a necessary *endorsement,* or (ii) refuse payment or *acceptance* for failure of the presentment to comply with the terms of the instrument, an agreement of the parties, or other applicable law or rule. [3-501(b)(3)]
Presentment after an established cutoff hour	The *party* to whom *presentment* is made may treat presentment as occurring on the next business day after the day of presentment if the party to whom presentment is made has established a cut-off hour not earlier than 2 p.m. for the receipt and processing of *instruments* presented for payment or *acceptance* and presentment is made after the cut-off hour. [3-501(b)(4)]

Notice of Dishonor. The UCC provides a specific timeline in which notice of dishonor of an instrument must be given to a secondarily liable party (3-503). (The process of determining secondary liability is summarized in Exhibit 28-4.) If the party that dishonors an instrument is a collection bank, it must give notice before midnight of the next day [UCC 3-503(c)]. Other parties must give notice of the dishonor within 30 days of the day on which they receive notice of dishonor. This notice can be given in any commercially reasonable manner: oral, written, or electronic communication [UCC 3-503(b)]. The notice must identify the instrument in question and state that this instrument has been dishonored. If the word *dishonored* appears on the instrument, this writing is enough to constitute notice. As long as the holder gives notice to the secondarily liable parties about the dishonor of the instrument, the holder can sue the other parties.

If all three of these conditions are met, the holder can bring suit against the secondarily liable party. However, in most cases, while a secondarily liable party may have to pay a holder the amount of the instrument, this secondarily liable party can then seek recourse against the primarily liable party. For example, suppose Angie issues a promissory note to Cesar. Cesar endorses the note on the back and transfers this note to Roopa. When the note is due, Roopa presents the note to Angie. However, Angie dishonors the note. Roopa gives notice of dishonor to Cesar and sues Cesar for the value of the instrument. Cesar will be liable; however, he can sue Angie because she was primarily liable for the amount of the promissory note.

In the event that an instrument contains more than one endorsement, each endorser is liable for the full amount to any subsequent endorser or to any holder. For example, Ron issues a note to Jenna. Jenna endorses the note and transfers it to Sally, who endorses and transfers to Bill. Bill presents the note to Ron, who refuses to honor it. Bill can then receive payment from Sally, who transferred the note to him. However, Bill can also seek repayment from Jenna, who endorsed the note before Sally did. If Bill seeks repayment from Sally, Sally can seek repayment from Jenna, who endorsed the note prior to Sally. The secondary liability established through endorsement requires that endorsers pay anyone who endorses the instrument after him or her.

Exhibit 28-4
Summary of Process of Determining Secondary Liability

	NOTE	DRAFT
To whom must the holder present the instrument?	Maker	Drawee
When should the instrument be presented?	On due date	Reasonable time; if a check, 30 days within date of check or 30 days within time of endorsement
If the instrument is presented and dishonored, who is usually now liable for the instrument?	Any endorser	Drawer or endorser
What are the requirements for an instrument to be officially dishonored so that a holder may then turn to secondarily liable parties?	1. Present to maker for payment. 2. Maker dishonors. 3. Holder gives notice of dishonor to secondarily liable parties (endorsers).	1. Present to drawee for payment. 2. Drawee dishonors. 3. Holder gives timely notice of dishonor to drawer or endorsers.

ACCOMMODATION PARTIES

Suppose that, after you graduate from college, you decide to start your own business. You need to borrow a significant amount of money from the bank, and you plan to create a promissory note. However, because you have never owned your own business and have little credit history, the bank is a little wary about whether you will be able to pay the note. Therefore, the bank decides to ask you to have a third party sign the note to ensure that the bank will be paid. Consequently, your business law professor cosigns your note. This third party is called an **accommodation party,** a party who signs an instrument to provide credit for another party who has also signed the instrument [UCC 3-419(a)].

Accommodation parties may be primarily or secondarily liable for an instrument and can sign as makers, drawers, acceptors, or endorsers. However, accommodation parties more frequently sign as makers or endorsers. As a maker, an accommodation party has primary liability; as an endorser, the party has secondary liability.

Suppose you, in the example above, cannot pay your note, and your business professor, as an accommodation party, pays the note instead. This professor has a right of reimbursement to recover the money from you, the accommodated party [UCC 3-419(e)]. If, however, you, the accommodated party, pay the note when it is due, you cannot force the professor to contribute to the amount due on the loan.

Case 28-1 highlights the importance of the timeliness of notices of dishonor from collection banks.

CASE 28-1 HEARTLAND STATE BANK v. AMERICAN BANK & TRUST

SUPREME COURT OF SOUTH DAKOTA

2010 S.D. LEXIS 122 (2010)

Heartland State Bank routed eight checks to a collections bank, Federal Reserve. Federal Reserve then delivered the checks and additional cash letters to the defendant bank, American Bank & Trust, on April 10, 2002. The defendant bank picked up the checks, and then returned them for insufficient funds before midnight on April 11, 2002. The plaintiff bank, Heartland, sued the defendant payor bank, asserting that the returns were untimely. The trial court granted the defendant's motion for summary judgment, reasoning that under the Uniform Commercial Code midnight-deadline rule for check processing, a payor bank must send notice of dishonor by midnight of the next banking day; therefore, the defendant's return of the checks to Heartland by April 11, 2002, was timely. The plaintiff bank appealed.

JUDGE KONENKAMP: When a bank returned a series of checks for insufficient funds, the returns were challenged as untimely. Under the Uniform Commercial Code midnight-deadline rule for check processing, a payor bank must, after receipt of a check presented for payment, pay the check, return it, or send notice of dishonor by midnight of the next banking day. Otherwise, the payor bank becomes "accountable" for the amount of the check.

When a payor bank receives a check, it is considered "presented," meaning a demand for payment has been made upon the party obligated to pay the check. Once a check has been provisionally settled through a Federal Reserve Bank, a payor bank upon receipt can effect final payment in several ways. But the payor bank may also revoke a provisional settlement and return the check, if the payor bank has not made final payment and returns the check before the midnight deadline. The "midnight deadline" is the "next banking day following the banking day on which [the bank] receives the relevant item or notice or from which the time for taking action commences to run, whichever is later[.]" If the midnight deadline is not met, the payor bank becomes "accountable"—strictly liable—for the amount of the check regardless of whether there were sufficient funds in the customer's account to cover payment.

American requested that the Federal Reserve Bank deliver the checks to its mailing address. The checks were so delivered on April 10, 2002. Because American had until "midnight on its next banking day following the banking day on which it" received the checks, American had until midnight April 11, 2002[,] to return the checks. As the checks were returned by that date, the circuit court properly granted summary judgment to American. We affirm the circuit court's grant of summary judgment.

JUDGMENT AFFIRMED.

[continued]

CRITICAL THINKING

The judge found the defense's evidence persuasive enough to rule that American adhered to the UCC's midnight-deadline rule for presenting notices of dishonor. What evidence seemed to convince the judge? What evidence was the plaintiff relying on to support its conclusion on appeal?

ETHICAL DECISION MAKING

Think about the WPH process of ethical decision making. What is the purpose of creating rules of timeliness for presenting notices of dishonor? Who in the business community is affected when a bank does not adhere to the midnight-deadline rule upheld by the UCC?

AGENTS' SIGNATURES

An **agent** is a party who has authority to act on behalf of and bind another party, the **principal.** The agent typically binds the principal through the agent's signature. (Agents' signatures and liability are summarized in Exhibit 28-5.) The agent's binding power through signature similarly applies to negotiable instruments (UCC 3-402). As long as the agent is *authorized* to sign a negotiable instrument on behalf of a principal, the agent's signature can create liability for the principal.

Legal Principle: **The signature of an authorized agent on behalf of the principal party is binding.**

Previously, the UCC required that the agent clearly identify the principal when signing. UCC Section 3-401, which states that a party cannot be liable unless his signature appears on the instrument, was interpreted to mean that if a principal's name was not on the instrument, he could not be held liable. This interpretation has changed. The UCC now states that if an agent signs an instrument truly on behalf of a principal, this principal *can* be held liable even if he or she is not "identified in the instrument" [3-402(a)]. This policy ensures that someone will always be held liable for the instrument. While this new interpretation serves its purpose, what values are in conflict between the old and the new interpretations? Would an ethical dilemma arise when determining whether one was "truly" signing on behalf of a principal?

Can an agent be personally liable for a negotiable instrument? Interpretation of the UCC has changed to make it easier to find that the agent was representing the principal when signing. Now it is a little more difficult to hold an agent personally liable for a negotiable instrument. The authorized agent cannot be liable if she did not sign her own name to the instrument (UCC 3-401). If the authorized agent simply signs her own name to the instrument, she might be liable. If the holder of the instrument is a holder in due course and is not aware and does not have reason to know that the agent has signed on behalf of a principal, the agent may be held personally liable. If the holder of the instrument is not a holder in due course, the agent can usually escape liability by demonstrating that it was not the intent of the principal to hold the agent personally responsible.

Exhibit 28-5
Agent Liability

AN AGENT MAY BE LIABLE IF:	AN AGENT IS NOT LIABLE IF:
The holder of the instrument has due-course status.	The agent did not sign his or her own name.
The agent is not authorized to sign on behalf of the payee.	The principal is clearly identified.

COMPARING THE LAW OF OTHER COUNTRIES

NEGOTIABLE INSTRUMENTS LAW OF THE PEOPLE'S REPUBLIC OF CHINA

The Negotiable Instruments Law in the People's Republic of China varies from its counterpart in the United States in several ways. First, the law does not address the use of promissory notes by individuals or private parties. Unlike the U.S. law, under which an individual may be an endorsing party, China's Negotiable Instruments Law addresses only banks as endorsers. Article I of the law states that the purpose of this law is to promote the development of the socialist market economy.

Second, the Negotiable Instruments Law also differs from the U.S. law in that the Chinese law mentions the role of a "prior holder," which refers to a debtor who puts his signature or seal to the negotiable instrument before it is acquired by the present signer or holder. Third, the Negotiable Instruments Law in China is very strict in requiring that monetary amounts of instruments must be written out both in Chinese characters and in numbers. The Chinese law states that if there is a conflict or discrepancy between the Chinese characters and the numbers of the instrument, the instrument is void.

There is an exception to agent liability. Even if the holder is a holder in due course and the agent simply signed his name, the agent will not be liable under specific conditions. If the instrument is a check payable from the principal's account and the principal is clearly identified on the check, the agent will not be liable on the check [UCC 3-402(c)].

Finally, the agent can be personally liable if he was not authorized to sign on behalf of the principal. This unauthorized writing falls into a broader category of unauthorized signatures.

Unauthorized Signatures and Endorsements. As a general rule, if a signature to a negotiable instrument is unauthorized, this unauthorized signature will not impose liability to the named party. This rule applies to two cases: forgery and unauthorized agents.

First, return to the accommodation party example above. Suppose you forged your business law professor's name to ensure that you would get your money to start your new business. If you could not pay on the note, your business law professor would not be forced to pay on the basis of the forged signature. Similarly, this rule applies to parties who forge the drawer's signature on a check.

Second, if an agent is not authorized to sign a negotiable instrument on behalf of a principal, the principal will generally not be liable for the instrument. Consequently, the agent would be personally liable for the instrument. However, if the principal decides to **ratify,** or approve of, the unauthorized agent's signature, the principal will then become liable for the instrument while the agent will escape personal liability [UCC 3-403(a)].

How does a principal ratify an unauthorized signature? A principal could explicitly approve the signature. For example, a Florida court held that a principal could not recover the amount of two checks he gave to his agent because the principal had ratified the signatures.[1] The agent, who was supposed to deposit two checks into the principal's account, forged the principal's signature and deposited the checks into the agent's account. The agent ultimately told the principal about the forged checks and the location of the money. The principal did nothing until the agent later ran away with the money, and the court ruled that the principal's inaction was the same as his approval of his signature.

[1] *Fulka v. Florida Commercial Banks, Inc.*, 371 So. 2d 521 (Fla. Dist. Ct. App. 1979).

Alternatively, if the principal accepts the benefits associated with an unauthorized signature, the principal in effect ratifies the signature by his or her conduct. For example, in *Rakestraw v. Rodriguez*,[2] a husband had forged his wife's signature in order to obtain a loan to start a grocery store. A few days later, the wife discovered the forgery, did nothing to correct it, and even participated in the business over the next few years. Part of running the business included sharing in the profits from the grocery store. When the business failed, the wife tried to avoid liability, claiming her husband had forged her signature. The court ruled that her actions in sharing in profits and in helping run the business effectively ratified her signature.

This ratification of an unauthorized signature does not exclusively apply to the agent-principal relationship. Your business law professor could similarly choose to ratify your unauthorized signature of his name so that he would be liable for your promissory note.

However, there are some exceptions to the general rule that an unauthorized signature is not enforceable. (See Exhibit 28-6 for a summary of the enforceability of unauthorized signatures.) Generally, the policy behind these exceptions is that courts want to place the burden on the parties who are in the best position to take a loss or take action to recover a loss. Moreover, particularly in regard to the last two rules that will be discussed here (the imposter rule and the fictitious-payee rule), the court focuses on the intent of the party who is issuing the instrument.

BUT WHAT IF . . .

WHAT IF THE FACTS OF THE CASE OPENER WERE DIFFERENT?

Recall that, in the Case Opener, several years elapsed before LaCombe discovered that his secretary had been putting checks into her account instead of the business account. Let's say that when LaCombe found out about the embezzlement, he didn't try to get the money back because he didn't want her to get in trouble but he talked to her about it. However, much later he decided he wanted the money. Would he be able to get the money back at the much later date?

Exhibit 28-6
Enforceability of Unauthorized Signatures

WHEN IS AN UNAUTHORIZED SIGNATURE ENFORCEABLE?	
If the party fails to exercise ordinary care, observing reasonable commercial standards, then the party substantially contributed to the forged signature and will be held liable.	Negligence rule
If the drawer or maker issues an instrument to an imposter who, posing as the payee, endorses the instrument, the signature is effective as the payee of the instrument and the issuing party is liable.	Imposter rule
If the party issues an instrument to a fictitious payee, an endorsement by any person in the name of the payee is effective and the party is liable and must pay the amount on the instrument when it is presented for payment.	Fictitious-payee rule

[2] 500 P.2d 1401 (Cal. 1972).

Negligence. In some cases, a party's negligence will not permit the party to escape liability for an unauthorized signature. If the party whose signature was forged behaved so negligently as to "substantially contribute to . . . the making of a forged signature," the party may be precluded from escaping liability (UCC 3-406).

For example, in *Thompson Maple Products v. Citizens National Bank,*[3] Thompson was a corporation that manufactured bowling pins from maple logs. Thompson would accept loads of logs from timber owners. When a load arrived at the mill, a Thompson employee filled out a scaling slip that listed the name of the owner, along with the quantity and grade of the logs. Thompson office employees then used these slips to prepare checks for the owner of the logs. A Thompson employee, Emery Albers, took blank scaling slips and filled them out for fictitious loads of logs. The office employees, thinking the slips represented real loads of wood, then prepared checks for payment. Albers then took the checks, forged the name of the owner of the logs, and cashed the checks or deposited them into his bank account at Citizens National Bank. The court ruled that Thompson "substantially contributed" to the forgeries because the blank scaling slips used to record loads of logs were easily accessible. In fact, office employees gave Albers two entire pads of these slips. Moreover, even though it was company policy for the slips to be initialed by authorized employees who were accepting the loads, Thompson office employees created checks for slips that were not authorized. Thus, Thompson's negligence led to the conclusion that Thompson should be liable.

BUT WHAT IF . . .

WHAT IF THE FACTS OF THE CASE OPENER WERE DIFFERENT?

Let's say that LaCombe gave Slyfield a lot of responsibility regarding his business and finances. He even let Slyfield manage his accounting and rarely checked the accounts. Then Slyfield embezzled almost all the checks sent to LaCombe's office for a month. Could LaCombe get that money back when he found out about what Slyfield embezzled?

The Imposter Rule. Suppose that Jamaar, a business manager, has been communicating through e-mail with Carlie, a potential employee. Jamaar has scheduled a meeting with Carlie. However, Samantha, without Carlie's knowledge, decides to impersonate Carlie at the interview. Samantha (as Carlie) tells Jamaar she will strongly consider signing an employment agreement if Jamaar will issue her a $200 check as a presigning bonus. Jamaar agrees and issues the check to Carlie that day. Samantha forges Carlie's name and deposits the check into her own account. Will Jamaar be liable for the amount of the check?

Jamaar's signature has not been forged; he clearly signed the check with intent to transfer money to Carlie. But he did not know Carlie was actually Samantha. Is Samantha's signature considered a forgery? No. Under the UCC's **imposter rule,** if a maker or drawer issues a negotiable instrument to an imposter, the imposter's endorsement will be effective [3-404(a)]. The court considers the intent of the drawer or maker when issuing the instrument. Because Jamaar intended for Samantha (as Carlie) to have the instrument, her endorsement of the instrument is considered valid. Moreover, it is easier for Jamaar, as maker or drawer, to identify the true identity of Carlie than it would be for a later holder of the check to do so. Perhaps some of you are surprised by the imposter rule. The UCC, as stated, places an immense responsibility on Jamaar to ensure that he is not being duped. What values are in conflict here? Should Jamaar be forced to shoulder this responsibility?

[3] 234 A.2d 32 (Pa. Super. Ct. 1967).

The Fictitious-Payee Rule. Suppose now that Jamaar, who has been authorized to write checks from the company account, draws bonus checks from the company account for five more potential employees. Unfortunately, Jamaar never actually interviewed these employees; thus these people are not entitled to the bonuses. Jamaar takes these checks that are made out to the fictitious potential employees, endorses the checks in their names, and deposits these checks into his personal bank account. These potential employees have no interest (i.e., no right to payment) in the check and are thus called **fictitious payees** (UCC 3-404, 3-405). As with the endorsement in the imposter case, Jamaar's endorsement of the fictitious payees is not considered forgery [UCC 3-404(b)(2)]. Jamaar's company will be liable for the checks.

Why is the company liable? Courts view the company as being in a better position to bear the loss of the checks. The loss has occurred because Jamaar, a company employee, has acted wrongly. Although the company is liable for the amounts of the checks, the company can recover the money from Jamaar.

Consequently, if we apply this rule to the Bank One opening case, it would seem that LaCombe Eye Center should be held liable because it is in a better position to bear the loss of the checks. Its own employee acted wrongly, and the company is in a better position to monitor the employee's behavior.

To see how a firm's employee selection process can help avoid situations in which employees mishandle checks, please see the **Connecting to the Core activity** on the text website at www.mhhe.com/kubasek3e.

Warranty Liability

LO2

What is warranty liability?

In the previous section, we explained how a party might be liable for an instrument on the basis of his or her signature on the instrument. In this section, we consider another type of liability: warranty liability. A party may be liable for an instrument because of a breach of warranty. There are two relevant types of warranties here: transfer warranties and presentment warranties.

TRANSFER WARRANTY

A negotiable instrument can be transferred from one party to another. A party who transfers a negotiable instrument to another party in good faith for consideration creates **transfer warranties** regarding the instrument and the transfer itself [UCC 3-416(a)]. Transfer warranties always apply to the party to whom the instrument is transferred (the transferee).

When a party transfers an instrument for consideration, he or she warrants:

1. The transferor is entitled to enforce the negotiable instrument.
2. Signatures on the instrument are authentic and authorized.
3. The instrument has not been altered.
4. The instrument is not subject to a defense or claim in recoupment.
5. The transferor has no knowledge of insolvency proceedings against the maker, acceptor, or drawer of the instrument. [UCC 3-416(a)]

If the transfer is through endorsement, these warranties apply to any future holders. However, if the transfer does not occur through endorsement, the warranties apply only to the transferee. For example, suppose Lisa creates a note payable to Chris. Chris endorses the note and transfers it for consideration to Yolanda. Because Chris has endorsed the instrument and transferred it for consideration, the warranties apply to Yolanda. Moreover, if Yolanda transfers the instrument to another party, the warranties Chris made would apply to this later holder.

These rules on whether the warranties apply to future holders or only to the immediate transferee are important because liability can be imposed for breach of warranty. If the warranties apply and there is a breach of one of the warranties, the parties can bring suit against the transferor, the warrantor, for damages suffered as a result of the breach [UCC

3-416(b)]. Thus, suppose Chris forges Lisa's signature on the note and then transfers the note to Yolanda, who later transfers the note to Gary. This forgery breaches one of the warranties on the instrument. Therefore, because Chris transferred the note through endorsement, Gary, the subsequent holder, can recover damages from Chris.

As soon as a transferee discovers that a breach of warranty has occurred, he or she can bring suit against the transferor. However, the transferee must give notice of the breach-of-warranty claim to the transferor within 30 days of discovering the breach [UCC 3-416(c)]. If the transferee does not give notice within 30 days of discovering the breach, the warranty will be discharged to some extent. If the transferred instrument is a check, the warranties cannot be disclaimed [UCC 3-416(c)].

While warranties on checks cannot be disclaimed, they can be disclaimed on other instruments. When parties agree to a disclaimer, an endorser can disclaim warranties by including in the endorsement the phrase *without warranties.* This endorsement is similar to the restrictive endorsement *without recourse,* which you learned about in the previous chapter. However, *without warranties* disclaims warranty liability, whereas *without recourse* disclaims contract liability.

BUT WHAT IF . . .

WHAT IF THE FACTS OF THE CASE OPENER WERE DIFFERENT?

What if Slyfield had forged LaCombe's signature on a check but, instead of depositing the check into her account, she transferred the check to another person, Bob. Bob then transferred the check to Cindy. Could Cindy recover damages from Slyfield? Also, could Cindy recover any damages if she found out about the breach of warranty a few months later?

PRESENTMENT WARRANTY

In the signature liability section, we discussed the requirements for a negotiable instrument to be properly presented for payment. Certain warranties are associated with the presentment of an instrument. Remember, presentment occurs when a party properly presents an instrument for acceptance and the party to whom it was presented accepts the instrument or pays it in good faith.

Why are presentment warranties needed? Parties who accept or pay instruments may worry that they are not paying the proper party. Thus, while transfer warranties apply to the transferee, **presentment warranties** cover parties who accept instruments for payment. The party presenting the instrument and any previous transferor of the instrument make these presentment warranties. Therefore, if there is a breach of presentment warranty, the acceptor can recover damages from the presenting party or previous transferors. As with the notice rule for transfer warranties, a party must give notice of a breach-of-presentment warranty within 30 days.

There are two types of presentment warranties. These types depend on what kind of instrument is being presented to a certain kind of party. When a party presents an unaccepted draft to a drawee, the holder guarantees:

1. The warrantor of the instrument is entitled to enforce the instrument.
2. The instrument has not been altered.
3. The warrantor has no knowledge that the drawer's signature or the draft is unauthorized. [UCC 3-417(a)]

These warranties apply only to the drawee who pays or accepts the drafts in good faith.

If the instrument is not an unaccepted draft presented to a drawee, only one presentment warranty applies. The party presenting the instrument guarantees that the warrantor is or was entitled to payment or authorized to obtain payment [UCC 3-417(d)(1)]. In other words, only warranty (1) listed above applies to presentments of instruments other than unaccepted drafts.

Case 28-2 considers whether a bank that cashed forged checks gives presentment and transfer warranties.

CASE 28-2 HALLIBURTON ENERGY SERVICES, INC. v. FLEET NATIONAL BANK

U.S. DISTRICT COURT FOR THE SOUTHERN DISTRICT OF TEXAS, HOUSTON DIVISION

334 F. SUPP. 2D 930 (2004)

On March 20, 2000, Halliburton issued a check, drawn on a Citibank account, to Arthur Andersen for $215,000.00. The check was deposited in the United States mail. An unknown person stole the check from the mail and then altered the payee to "Paul A. Schumacher."

On March 27, 2000, a person claiming to be "Paul A. Schumacher" opened a Fleet brokerage account from the bank's Internet site. The person posing as "Paul A. Schumacher" endorsed the altered check by signing the name "Paul A. Schumacher" on the back and presented it to Fleet, which honored it. Fleet then presented the check to Citibank, the drawee/payor bank. On March 30, 2000, Citibank charged Halliburton's checking account the sum of $215,000.00 because Citibank had paid the check in full.

On May 15, 2000, Arthur Andersen informed Halliburton it had not received the $215,000.00 check. A Halliburton employee working for Accounts Payable then contacted Citibank and learned that the check had been paid. On May 17, Halliburton requested the original check from Citibank. Upon receiving and examining the check, Halliburton saw that the payee's name had been altered and that the check had been endorsed by the fictitious payee, "Paul A. Schumacher" "for deposit only."

On June 26, 2000, Citibank notified Fleet that Fleet had honored a fraudulently altered check and asked for prompt reimbursement of what Citibank deemed a wrongful payment. The request was denied. Citibank then assigned any claim it may have against Fleet to Halliburton. Halliburton sued, and filed for summary judgment.

JUDGE LAKE: . . . Section 3.404 covers cases in which an instrument is payable to a fictitious or nonexistent person and in which the payee is a real person but the drawer or maker of the instrument did not intend the payee to have any interest in the instrument. The defense to which section 4.208(c) refers, by incorporating section 3.404(b), is known as the "fictitious payee" or "impostor" rule. An impostor is "one who pretends to be someone else to deceive others, esp. to receive the benefits of a negotiable instrument," or "a person who practices deception under an assumed character, identity or name."

The impostor rule applies when a bank has honored a check made out to a fictitious payee. If the impostor's endorsement is effective, the collecting bank then becomes a "holder in due course." A "holder in due course is one who takes an instrument (1) for value, (2) in good faith, and (3) without notice of any defense." Even a forger can effectively endorse an instrument. Unless the depository bank knew about the forgery, there is no breach of presentment warranty when the depository bank presents it to the drawee. Therefore, in such circumstances, the presenting bank is not liable for the drawer's or drawee's loss.

Under section 3.404(d) the drawee may override the depository/collecting/presenting bank's affirmative defense only if the collecting bank failed "to exercise ordinary care in paying or taking the instrument and that failure contributed to loss resulting from the payment of the instrument." The "ordinary care" standard is just that: It does not mandate that a depository bank engage in peculiar vigilance. In fact, the comments accompanying section 3.404(d) suggest that a collecting bank is not liable for breaching its presentment warranties unless it knew the instrument had been altered when that bank accepted it.

If the drawee bank can establish that the collecting bank failed to exercise ordinary care, the drawee may recover from the presenting bank "to the extent the failure to exercise ordinary care contributed to the loss."

Halliburton has not presented evidence that Fleet was anything other than a holder in due course. In other words, Halliburton has not offered evidence of Fleet's bad faith, e.g., that Fleet's employees connived with the forger. Nor has Halliburton provided any evidence that Fleet had reason to believe the check had been fraudulently altered. Perhaps at trial Halliburton can convince the jury that Fleet, which dealt directly with the impostor, took the forged check with notice of the forgery or accepted the instrument by failing to

[continued]

exercise ordinary care, which would have exposed the forgery. But whether Fleet could have readily ascertained that the check had been fraudulently altered is a fact issue that precludes summary judgment for Halliburton. There are too many questions that need to be answered to support Halliburton's motion for summary judgment.

MOTION DENIED.

CRITICAL THINKING

The motion for summary judgment was denied because there is too much omitted information. As a judge, what information would you deem relevant that is missing from the case? Why is the missing information relevant to this case?

ETHICAL DECISION MAKING

Think about the ethical theories you were presented with earlier. Part of the above case, and the issue of presentment warranties, is who should bear the burden for a fraudulent check. Which party would a deontologist hold responsible for the cashing of a forged check? What about a consequentialist?

Avoiding Liability for Negotiable Instruments

LO3

How does one avoid liability for negotiable instruments?

If a party tries to enforce a negotiable instrument, a defendant can try to avoid liability in two ways. First, the defendant can try to claim a defense to liability. Second, the defendant can try to claim that the liability has been discharged.

DEFENSES TO LIABILITY

In the previous chapter, we listed defenses to liability that did or did not apply to a holder in due course. Here, we return to these defenses to liability. There are two categories of defenses: real defenses and personal defenses. **Real defenses,** also called *universal defenses,* apply to all parties. **Personal defenses** do not apply to holders in due course.

Real Defenses. A party's right to enforce a negotiable instrument is subject to the following real defenses:

1. Infancy (being below the legal age of consent), to the extent that it makes a contract void.
2. Duress, to the extent that it makes a contract void.
3. Lack of legal capacity, to the extent that it makes a contract void.
4. Illegality of the transaction, to the extent that it makes a contract void.
5. Fraud in the factum.
6. Discharge through insolvency proceedings (bankruptcy).
7. Forgery.
8. Material alteration.

The first six defenses are stated explicitly in UCC Section 3-305. As we discussed earlier in this chapter, the UCC establishes forgery as a defense to liability because a party must have signed the instrument to be held liable. Finally, a material alteration of an instrument discharges a party of a liability [UCC 3-407(a)].

Fraud in the Factum. When a party signs a negotiable instrument without knowing that it is, in fact, a negotiable instrument, the party can claim **fraud in the factum** (also called *fraud in the execution* and *fraud in the essence*) as a defense. For example, suppose

CASE NUGGET

DEFENSE OF IGNORANCE?

Laborer's Pension Fund v. A & C Envtl., Inc.
301 F.3d 762 (2002)

A & C Environmental, Inc., is a corporation that transports and disposes of nonhazardous waste. In April 1999, A & C was asked to complete a job in Gary, Indiana, which prompted representatives from Laborer's Pension Fund to approach the company. Frattini of the fund asked Clark of A & C to sign a form that would guarantee the five individuals who would work in Gary, Indiana, the coverage of the local union. Clark was hesitant to sign the agreement because he feared that if someone within his company were covered under the union, the entire company would then be covered. It wasn't until after Frattini of the fund guaranteed Clark that the only employees of A & C who would be affected would be those working in Gary, Indiana, that the agreement was signed. When A & C did not pay dues for all of its employees, the fund brought suit for delinquent contributions.

The district court ruled against the fund as a result of the fraud-in-the-execution defense that was brought forth by A & C. The court had decided that any reasonable juror would believe that Clark did not know that he was agreeing to pay the fund dues for each employee of A & C. The fund appealed to the Seventh District of the U.S. Court of Appeals.

In the opinion written by Judge Ripple, the Seventh Circuit found that Clark may not have known what he was agreeing to. Unlike the district court, however, the appeals court found that Clark had a reasonable opportunity to review the document, which was written in English. Although Frattini of the fund had misrepresented the contents of the document to Clark, there was an opportunity to review the document, which established dues for all employees of A & C. Thus, the court of appeals reversed the decision of the district court.

Michael Jordan believes he is signing an autograph for a fan, but he is actually signing a promissory note. Because he did not intend to sign a negotiable instrument, he will not be held liable for the instrument.

Similarly, suppose you, a business manager, are negotiating with another company to purchase materials for your manufacturing business. After your negotiations, the company asks you to sign a document as a preorder for the materials. You hurriedly sign the document and leave. However, instead of signing a preorder, you have actually signed a note. Will you be held liable for this note? In this case, it depends.

For another illustration of these issues, see the Case Nugget.

Although fraud in the factum is a real defense, courts have held that the signer's experience may determine whether the signer should have known what he or she was actually signing. Recall the situation with Jamaar in which he was solely responsible for ensuring the identity of the individual he is signing a check to. However, that level of responsibility is not required of Michael Jordan in this situation. Can you account for the difference in the two situations, pointing out the differing values and ethical norms?

As another example, consider *Schaeffer v. United Bank & Trust Co.*[4] United Bank sued Schaeffer to collect on a promissory note Schaeffer had signed as an accommodation maker. However, the Maryland court ultimately ruled that Schaeffer was not liable due to fraud in the factum. It turns out Schaeffer barely knew how to read, did not understand the document he was signing, and was lied to by the note's maker, who had told Schaeffer that Schaeffer's signature would serve as a character witness. The court ruled that United Bank was not a holder in due course and was subject to Schaeffer's defense even if the bank were a holder in due course as the note was void due to fraud in the factum.

Material Alteration. The UCC defines a *material alteration* as "an unauthorized change in an instrument that purports to modify in any respect the obligation of a party, or an unauthorized addition of words or numbers or other change to an incomplete instrument relating to the obligation of a party" (3-407). Only unauthorized changes that affect the rights of the party are considered material alterations.

[4] 360 A.2d 461 (Md. Ct. Spec. App. 1976).

Suppose Hope creates a promissory note payable to Patrick. Patrick decides Hope should pay him $2 more. If Patrick changes the instrument to reflect the additional $2, he has made an unauthorized change that affects Hope's rights. Changes that typically fall under Section 3-407 include changes to the parties to the instrument, the amount of the instrument, the date the instrument is due, and the applicable interest rate.

If the material alteration is fraudulent, the party whose rights have been affected by the change is completely discharged from the instrument [UCC 3-407(b)]. However, if the material alteration is not fraudulent, the instrument will be enforced only under the original terms. Case 28-3 considers whether changes to a promissory note were material and fraudulent alterations.

Legal Principle: **If a material alteration is not fraudulent, the instrument will be enforced under the original terms.**

CASE 28-3 GARY DARNALL AND EMILIE DARNALL, APPELLANTS AND CROSS-APPELLEES v. BERNARD PETERSEN, APPELLEE, AND KAY PETERSEN, APPELLEE AND CROSS-APPELLANT

NEBRASKA COURT OF APPEALS

8 NEB. APP. 185, 592 N.W.2D 505 (1999)

Gary Darnall gave a business loan to Bernard and Kay Petersen to be used for the purchase of a flower shop. The parties executed a promissory note for $55,000 plus interest. The note was due on demand and provided for 13 percent interest and 18 percent default interest. Gary Darnall received only two payments in the amount of $45,000 and $2,500 for the note. The Darnalls made demand for the remainder of the money owed and wrote the Petersens a letter demanding that payment be made and threatening legal action if the note was not paid. As a result, the Darnalls brought suit to recover the remainder of the promissory note and interest.

The Petersens alleged that when they signed the note, the blanks for the interest rate and the default interest rate were not filled in. Mrs. Petersen said when the note was presented to her, no interest rate was shown on the note and that it was her understanding that no interest would be charged on the note. As a result, she argued the note had been materially altered without any authority and that no interest or due date was specified on the note she originally signed.

However, Gary Darnall, the person who loaned the Petersens the money, argued he and Bernard discussed the interest rate prior to execution of the promissory note and that at the time the Petersens signed the note, the blanks for the interest rate, the default interest rate, and the due date contained the terms agreed to by the parties.

JUDGE MUES:

1. Were Terms on Note When Petersens Signed It?

We begin by addressing the issue of whether the promissory note was altered after the Petersens signed it.

Section 3-115 addresses situations where an instrument has been altered after a party has signed it. It provides:

(1) When a paper whose contents at the time of signing show that it is intended to become an instrument is signed while still incomplete in any necessary respect it cannot be enforced until completed, but when it is completed in accordance with authority given it is effective as completed.

(2) If the completion is unauthorized the rules as to material alteration apply (Section 3-407), even though the paper was not delivered by the maker or drawer; but the burden of establishing that any completion is unauthorized is on the party so asserting.

In a bench trial of a law action, the court, as the trier of fact, is the sole judge of the credibility of the witnesses and the weight to be given their testimony. The trial court found Kay's testimony on the alteration issues to be more credible than that of the Darnalls. While we may have reached a different conclusion if we were reviewing the evidence de novo, we cannot say that the trial court's factual findings on these issues are clearly erroneous.

2. Material Alteration.

Section 3-407 provides:

(1) Any alteration of an instrument is material which changes the contract of any party thereto in any respect, including any such change in . . .

(b) an incomplete instrument, by completing it otherwise than as authorized. . . .

(2) As against any person other than a subsequent holder in due course

(a) alteration by the holder which is both fraudulent and material discharges any party whose contract is thereby changed unless that party assents or is precluded from asserting the defense;

(b) no other alteration discharges any party and the instrument may be enforced according to its original tenor, or as to incomplete instruments according to the authority given.

The trial court found that the alterations were unauthorized but determined that the changes were not done fraudulently. Kay's cross-appeal asserts that the changes were both material and fraudulent and contends that the trial court erred in not discharging her from any obligation under the note. Kay is obviously contending that the trial court's finding in this regard was clearly erroneous. We do not agree.

The changes were clearly material. As we have already determined, the changes were made after the execution of the note and without the Petersens' authority. See § 3-407(1)(b). However, a material alteration does not discharge a party from his or her obligation unless it is made for a fraudulent purpose. See § 3-407(2)(a) and (b).

> An alteration is fraudulent when the holder intends to achieve an advantage for himself to which he has reason to know he is not entitled. Thus, where the holder believes that the party has authorized or consented to the alteration or completion, the fact that no such consent or authorization actually exists does not make the alteration fraudulent. Likewise, where the holder believes that he has the right to alter the instrument to reflect the true agreement of the parties, it is not fraudulent. (William D. Hawkland & Lary Lawrence, Uniform Commercial Code Series § 3-407:07 at 741 (1994)).

Although Kay proved that the note was altered, she presented no evidence that the alteration was made for a fraudulent purpose. In fact, in her pleadings Kay did not allege that the alteration was fraudulently made and did not pray that she be discharged from her obligation. Rather, she alleged merely that the note had been materially altered and prayed that the court find that the Darnalls were entitled to collect the principal only.

Cases are heard in the state appellate courts on the theory upon which they are tried. An issue not presented to the trial court may not be raised on appeal, inasmuch as a lower court cannot commit error in resolving an issue it was never given an opportunity to resolve. Moreover, the trial court's factual finding that the alterations were not fraudulent is not clearly erroneous. Accordingly, the trial court did not err in failing to discharge Kay from her obligations under the note, and Kay's cross-appeal is without merit.

3. Effect of Nonfraudulent Material Alteration.
The Darnalls argue that the trial court's factual conclusions regarding the alteration of the interest rates rendered its usury analysis unnecessary and, as a matter of law, incorrect. We agree.

To review, the court concluded as a matter of fact that the interest "blanks" had been filled in without the authority of Kay. Under § 3-407(1)(b), this was a material alteration. The court also concluded the alteration was not a fraudulent one. Therefore, the provisions of § 3-407(2)(a) do not come into play to discharge the parties. It was at this juncture that the trial court, determining that the 18-percent default rate was usurious, found that the Darnalls could recover no interest under the note. However, as the Darnalls correctly point out, when a note is materially altered but not fraudulently so, the instrument may be enforced according to its original tenor, or as to incomplete instruments according to the authority given. § 3-407(2)(b). The trial court found that the interest figures were inserted without Kay's authorization and knowledge. However, the Darnalls were still entitled, under these findings, to enforce the note according to its "original tenor."

4. Conclusion
The trial court's finding that the promissory note was altered without any authority after Kay signed it was not clearly erroneous. However, the trial court's finding that the Darnalls did not fraudulently alter the instrument was also not clearly wrong, and therefore the Darnalls were entitled to enforce it according to its original terms.

Affirmed in part, and in part reversed and remanded with directions.

CRITICAL THINKING

Regarding whether the blanks were filled in on the note, the judge states, "The trial court found Kay's testimony on the alteration issues to be more credible than that of the Darnalls. While we may have reached a different conclusion if we were reviewing the evidence de novo [in a new trial],

ETHICAL DECISION MAKING

In a discussion about values in this case, your classmate says that "justice" was not served in this case because even though the promissory note was materially altered, it still had to be enforced by its original terms because it was not a fraudulent alteration. What might this classmate's definition

[continued]

we cannot say that the trial court's factual findings on these issues are clearly erroneous." How strong do you think this reasoning is?

If the court could hear a new case regarding the promissory note, what type of additional information might lead the judge to determine the note was entirely filled in when it was signed?

of justice be? Can you provide an alternative meaning of justice that would lead you to conclude justice was served in this case?

Personal Defenses. Personal defenses apply to holders, not holders in due course. Personal defenses can be divided into two categories. First, there are general defenses that can be asserted against the defendant on general contract theory.

Second, the UCC lists specific personal defenses created by provisions of Article 3.

DISCHARGE OF LIABILITY ON INSTRUMENTS

When a party's liability for a negotiable instrument is terminated, this party's liability has been **discharged.** In other words, the party is released from liability. Discharge can occur through a variety of ways (see Exhibit 28-7). For example, as stated earlier, discharge of endorsers can occur if a party who has a right to enforce the instrument has materially altered an instrument. Keep in mind that discharge is not effective against a holder in due course (UCC 3-601).

Discharge through Payment and Tender of Payment. Earlier in this chapter, we discussed how a party becomes liable for an instrument by signing the instrument. If a party (or another party on the first party's behalf) who has signed an instrument as

Exhibit 28-7
Ways to Be Discharged from Liability for a Negotiable Instrument

Discharge by payment or tender of payment	Once payment of the stated amount on the instrument is made to the payee, all parties who are liable will be discharged.
Discharge by cancellation or renunciation	If the holder or enforcer cancels the instrument either by mutilating the document or surrendering it to the party who was to pay, that party is no longer liable to pay the stated amount.
Discharge by reacquisition	If the instrument becomes reacquired by a former holder of the instrument, all endorsements made after the reacquirer initially became the holder are canceled and thus those endorsers are discharged from liability.
Discharge by impairment of recourse	If the endorser's ability to seek recourse has been impaired by a previous holder, the endorser is discharged from liability.
Discharge by impairment of collateral	If the holder of collateral impairs the value of the collateral, the party who posted the collateral is discharged from liability to the extent of the damage to the collateral.

an obligation to pay then pays the full amount due, all parties who are liable will be discharged (UCC 3-602).

For example, Stuart creates a note in which he promises to pay Vanessa $1,000. If Stuart pays the $1,000 on the due date, he will be discharged from liability on the note. However, if Stuart makes the payment on the note to John, knowing that John stole the note from Vanessa and is wrongfully possessing it, Stuart's obligation will not be discharged. Paying John does not discharge Stuart's liability because John, who stole the note, is not a holder and is not entitled to the amount on the note [UCC 3-602(b)(2)].

Moreover, some parties' obligations on an instrument will be discharged if the obliged party tenders full payment on the due date but the holder of the instrument refuses to accept the money [UCC 3-603(b)]. If Stuart makes a proper tender of the full amount ($1,000) to Vanessa on the note's due date but she improperly refuses to accept the money, Stuart will still be liable for the $1,000 but will not have to pay interest on the amount. However, if any endorsers or accommodation parties are liable for Stuart's note, these parties' obligation will be discharged.

Discharge by Cancellation or Renunciation. A party who is entitled to enforce an instrument may decide to cancel the instrument with or without consideration. Canceling the instrument discharges the obligation of a party who must pay the instrument (UCC 3-604). The party who decides to cancel the instrument may engage in an intentional voluntary act to cancel the instrument. For example, the party might write "Paid" on the instrument, intentionally destroy or mutilate the instrument, or give the instrument to the obliged party.

Alternatively, a party may renounce an instrument by promising not to sue to enforce the instrument. Renunciation occurs when a party agrees, in writing, not to sue the obliged party.

BUT WHAT IF . . .

WHAT IF THE FACTS OF THE CASE OPENER WERE DIFFERENT?

Let's say that a patient of LaCombe's called about a check she had given him and said she could not afford to pay the check because she had just lost her job. LaCombe decided to send her a letter saying he would not sue her to get the money from the check. If LaCombe later tells the patient he wants to deposit the check, is the patient already discharged from the obligation of paying the instrument or does she legally have to allow LaCombe to deposit the check?

Discharge by Reacquisition. Reacquisition occurs when a former holder of an instrument has the instrument transferred back to him or her by negotiation or other means. When reacquisition occurs, anyone who endorsed the instrument in between the initial acquisition and the reacquisition by the holder has his or her endorsement canceled. When an endorsement is canceled, discharge occurs. The holder who reacquired the instrument can further negotiate the instrument, but the intermediate endorsers will not be held liable (UCC 3-207).

For example, suppose Gina acquires a note through negotiation. Gina endorses and transfers the note to Jeremy. Jeremy endorses and transfers to Amanda, who endorses and transfers to Ben. Ben then endorses the note and transfers it back to Gina. When Gina endorses the note, she cancels Jeremy's, Amanda's, and Ben's endorsements. Were the note to be dishonored, Jeremy, Amanda, and Ben would all not be liable on the amount of the instrument.

Discharge by Impairment of Recourse. A right to recourse is the ability of a party to seek reimbursement. Typically, when a holder presents an instrument to an endorser, the endorser presented with the instrument can seek recourse from prior endorsers, the maker, the drawer, or accommodating parties. However, if the holder has in some way impaired the endorser's ability to seek recourse from any of these parties, the endorser is not liable on the instrument [UCC 3-605(i)].

For example, Mary is the holder of a promissory note. She presents the note to Peter, a previous endorser. Normally Peter would have to pay the note and would be entitled to collect from a number of other parties. However, Mary carelessly defaced the note in such a way as to make the note worthless. Since Peter cannot invoke his right to recourse because of Mary's actions, he is not liable on the note and does not have to pay Mary.

Discharge by Impairment of Collateral. If a party posts collateral to ensure his performance of the negotiable instrument and the holder of the collateral impairs the value of the collateral, the party to the instrument is discharged from the instrument to the extent of the damage to the collateral [UCC 3-605(d)].

CASE OPENER WRAP-UP

Bank One and the Forged Checks

The district court held for LaCombe. The bank appealed. The appellate court considered whether the bank and/or LaCombe failed to exercise ordinary care, whether either party was negligent, and whether this negligence substantially contributed to the making of the forged signatures on the checks.

The appellate court found that LaCombe was given no reason to suspect that any wrongdoing was taking place. Neither his business reports nor statements raised any "red flags." Slyfield covered her illegal activity well, choosing checks that would not be easily missed. LaCombe's accounting system was reasonable under the circumstances. Accordingly, the court found that LaCombe exercised "ordinary care" in the conduct of his practice and did not substantially contribute to the making of his forged signature on the checks.

However, Bank One failed to act in accordance with its own policies. It was the bank's policy that a check made out to a business, including a check made out to a sole proprietorship, had to be deposited into an account bearing the business's name. However, LaCombe's checks were not deposited into the business account. Therefore, Bank One failed to exercise ordinary care in taking the forged instruments. As a result, the appellate court affirmed the trial court's determination that the bank was 100 percent liable for the forged checks. This led to the conclusion that LaCombe should be reimbursed for the embezzled checks.

Several lessons can be drawn from this case. First, it emphasizes that as a business manager, you will need to carefully select your employees because hiring decisions can have an enormous impact on the financial success of your company. Second, it emphasizes the importance of paying close attention to your financial accounts. Perhaps if LaCombe had paid better attention in the first place, he would not have to deal with the stress of a lawsuit against Bank One. This case also demonstrates the importance of following proper procedures and exercising care in all business practices. The cost to LaCombe to avoid such embezzlement would have been far higher than that to the bank, which has specific procedures for check cashing of sole proprietorships.

KEY TERMS

acceptor 606
accommodation party 610
agent 611
discharged 622
dishonored 608
drawer 606
endorser 606
fictitious payees 615
fraud in the factum 618
imposter rule 614
maker 606
personal defenses 618
presentment 607
presentment warranties 616
primarily liable 606
principal 611
ratify 612
real defenses 618
secondarily liable 606
signature liability 605
transfer warranties 615
warranty liability 605

SUMMARY OF KEY TOPICS

Signature Liability

A party can be held liable for an instrument only if the party has signed the instrument.

Primary liability of makers and acceptors: They must pay the stated amount on the instrument when it is presented for payment.

Secondary liability of drawers and endorsers: They must pay the amount on the instrument if the primarily liable party dishonors the instrument and the following three conditions are met:

1. Presentment
2. Dishonor
3. Notice of dishonor

Accommodation party: An accommodation party is one who signs an instrument to provide credit for another party who has also signed the instrument.

Agent's signature: As long as the agent is *authorized* to sign a negotiable instrument on behalf of a principal, the agent's signature can create liability for the principal.

Unauthorized signature: If a signature to a negotiable instrument is unauthorized, this unauthorized signature will not impose liability to the named party.

1. Negligence
2. Imposter rule
3. Fictitious-payee rule

Warranty Liability

Transfer warranty: When a party transfers an instrument to another party for consideration, the transferring party makes certain promises or warranties regarding the instrument and the transfer itself.

Presentment warranty: When a party properly presents an instrument for acceptance, the party makes certain promises regarding the instrument and the party who is entitled to payment.

Avoiding Liability for Negotiable Instruments

1. *Defenses to liability:* The arguments as to why a party should not be held liable for an instrument include:
   a. Real defenses
   b. Personal defenses
2. *Discharge of liability:* Release from liability can occur through:
   a. Discharge by payment or tender of payment.
   b. Discharge by cancellation or renunciation.
   c. Discharge by reacquisition.
   d. Discharge by impairment of recourse.
   e. Discharge by impairment of collateral.

POINT / COUNTERPOINT

Should a Company Be Held Liable When an Employee's Work-Related Illegal Actions Include the Endorsement of Fraudulent Checks?

YES

A company should always be held liable for an employee's work-related illegal actions. The company hired the employee and put him in a position where he could commit an illegal action, so the company should be held responsible.

A company benefits from the work of each of its employees. If employees are profitable, company profits increase, shareholder stock increases, and salaries increase; everyone benefits. Thus, because the company *benefits* when the employee is *profitable,* the company should also experience *losses* when the employee is *unprofitable* or *harmful.*

One of the factors in assigning liability for fraudulent checks is the ability of a party to bear the loss of the checks. A company is better equipped to bear a loss of funds than an individual. The losses occurred because of the actions of a specific *company* employee. Therefore, a company should shoulder the blame and pay for the losses from the fraudulent checks. After the company bears the losses of the checks, the company can then assess how to penalize the employee who endorsed the fraudulent checks.

A company should be held liable for an employee's actions because the company has the ability to monitor employee activities and the company chose to use the employee to represent the company.

NO

Companies should not be held liable for an employee's fraudulent checks. The employees, not the companies, should be held liable.

Every employee is an individual who controls his or her own actions. Although a company can try to monitor employee activities, if an employee wants to commit an illegal act, she will. Most companies hire smart, well-qualified people. Smart people can always find a way around even the best company security systems.

Employees also need to feel the consequences of their own actions. If a corporation always takes the hit for an employee's poor decision, the employee cannot learn to change his behavior.

Companies should not be blamed for an employee's fraudulent checks because, sometimes, the bank responsible for paying out the fraudulent checks should be held responsible. Banks are companies as well, and as such, they should be aware of suspicious activities. When cashing large checks, the bank could easily require a verification code that would be known only by someone authorized to give checks.

Employees make their own decisions and are not forced to act against the law. Therefore, the employees should be held personally accountable.

QUESTIONS & PROBLEMS

1. What is the distinction between primary and secondary liability for a signed negotiable instrument?
2. Evaluate the following statement: "A party can never be held liable for a negotiable instrument if he or she did not sign the check."
3. What are the similarities and differences between transfer and presentment warranties?
4. Joshua Herrera found a purse in a dumpster. He contacted the owner of the purse, and it was returned to its owner. After returning the purse, Herrera returned to the dumpster. He found a check written out to "cash." Herrera testified that he thought that meant that he "could get money for the check." He presented the check at a bank, and the bank teller instructed him to put his name on the payee line next to cash. Herrera added the words "to Joshua Herrera" to the payee line and endorsed the check. The trial court found Herrera guilty of forgery. On appeal, Herrera argued that he did not alter the check because he did not change the legal efficacy of the check. Herrera claimed that the check was a bearer instrument and payable to anyone possessing the instrument. How do you think the court decided? [*State of New Mexico v. Joshua Herrera,* 2000 N.M. App. LEXIS 100 (2001).]
5. In 1992, Eric M. Schmitz executed two "Limited Power of Attorney" forms with Georgetown

Financial, a Wisconsin company that provided investment, insurance, and financial services. James O'Hearn was the sole owner and chief executive officer of Georgetown Financial. Georgetown Financial purchased mutual funds through Putnam Investments for Schmitz. Putnam issued two checks and mailed them to Schmitz, in care of Georgetown Financial, as designated in the account application. O'Hearn presented both checks to Firstar Bank for deposit into a Georgetown Financial account. The larger check did not include an endorsement by or on behalf of Schmitz. The smaller check included an endorsement bearing Schmitz's name that Schmitz claims is a forged signature. Both checks were stamped with a Georgetown Financial deposit stamp and marked "for deposit only." Firstar Bank deposited the face value of both checks into a Georgetown Financial account. Schmitz never received the funds deposited into the account. Schmitz argued that because Georgetown Financial did not have authority to endorse the larger check, Firstar Bank was liable as a matter of law for making payment on this check, which was presented by Georgetown Financial without his actual or purported signature. Should Firstar Bank be held liable for cashing both checks? How did the court decide? [*Schmitz v. Firstar Bank Milwaukee,* 2003 WI 21 (2003).]

6. Olga Ensenat, an 88-year-old woman, had substantial investment accounts. Eventually her niece, Diana Flores, moved in to take care of Ensenat. While living with her, Flores withdrew on Ensenat's accounts, forged Ensenat's signature, and deposited the money into Flores's accounts. In the end Flores embezzled $157,386.30, all of which was deposited at Hancock Bank, where Flores had an account. Ensenat alleged that she did not herself withdraw or authorize any other person to with draw retirement funds from her accounts. Ensenat sued Hancock Bank, claiming that it was responsible because it allowed the checks to be paid or deposited without her endorsement, signature, or authorization. Did the court agree with Ensenat and find Hancock Bank liable for the deposited checks? Why or why not? [*Hancock Bank v. Ensenat,* 819 So. 2d 3 (2001).]

7. Robert Carter, an employee of National Accident Insurance, intercepted insurance premium checks totaling more than $10 million that customers made payable to the insurance agency. Carter then altered those checks by adding a slash (/) and additional payees, such as "Sherman" or "Sherman Imports, Inc." These changes to the checks were made either in a different typewritten font or different handwriting than the other payee listed. After altering the checks, he endorsed and deposited the checks in his "Sherman account" at Citibank. After Citibank was taken to court for cashing the fraudulent checks, Citibank relied on the fictitious-payee rule, arguing that this is a situation in which the bank honors a check bearing the forged endorsement of a fictional payee. Thus, Citibank believes that the rule should relieve its liability and place the loss on the drawer of the checks. Do you think the fictitious-payee rule applies in this case? Would any additional information help you make your decision? [*National Accident Insurance Underwriters v. Citibank,* 243 F. Supp. 2d 763 (2002).]

8. The late Dr. Fred Clark had a bank account at Toronto Dominion Bank. Unauthorized withdrawals were made from his account to allegedly pay for outstanding balances owed by numerous unidentified customers of the various retail defendants. Somehow one or more of the defendants improperly obtained access to Clark's account and began withdrawing money through a series of electronic fund transfers. The bank is not liable for withdrawals that were not made known to the bank within one year of the withdrawals. What additional considerations would determine whether Clark or the defendant is liable for the withdrawals from Clark's account? In other words, use the "but what if" logic to show you understand this area of business law. [*Estate of Clark v. Toronto Dominion Bank,* 2013 WL 1159014 (E.D. Pa. 2013).]

9. In this strange case, Albertson has already been convicted of passing checks that were ultimately dishonored because of insufficient funds in Albertson's checking account. Both Albertson and a witness claim that the person to whom the checks were issued had an agreement with Albertson that the drawee would hold on to the checks until Albertson had sufficient funds to cover the checks. The drawee was a used-car dealer who admitted in court that he had hold-check agreements with others but could not recall whether he had one with Albertson. Naturally, Albertson does not want to be liable for the checks that were later dishonored. Given the principles of law you learned in this chapter, what facts would need to be true for Albertson to have a reasonable argument on his behalf? [*Albertson v. State,* 2013 WL 3233378 (Md. App. 2013).]

10. A Chapter 7 bankruptcy trustee is filing an action to recover funds from the wife of a debtor. The wife signed a debtor's instrument in which her husband borrowed funds to construct utility barns and fencing necessary for his horse-raising business. The debtor and his wife used the property on which the horse-raising facilities were built as their residence. The purchase of the materials to construct the barns and fence was not made with any intention of increasing the value of their residential property. What additional information would you need to determine whether the wife was an "accommodation party" for purposes of determining liability regarding the debt instrument that she signed? [*In re Simpson,* 474 B.R. 656 (Bkrtcy. S.D. Ind. 2012).]

Looking for more review materials?

The Online Learning Center at **www.mhhe.com/kubasek3e** contains this chapter's "Assignment on the Internet" and also a list of URLs for more information, entitled "On the Internet." Find both of them in the Student Center portion of the OLC, along with quizzes and other helpful materials.

CHAPTER

29

Checks and Electronic Fund Transfers

LEARNING OBJECTIVES

After reading this chapter, you will be able to answer the following questions:

1. What are the components of a check?
2. What are the differences among the various types of checks?
3. How and where are deposits accepted?
4. When may a bank charge a customer's account?
5. What are the different types of electronic fund transfers?

CASE OPENER

Fraudulent Electronic Fund Transfers

Patco Construction Company was a customer that had an account at Ocean Bank. Patco argued that its account was subject to the authorization of six fraudulent withdrawals from the account after a perpetrator supplied the correct security answers for access to Patco's account. The perpetrator successfully wired Patco's money to multiple individual accounts to which Patco had never before sent funds. Although Ocean Bank's security system flagged these transactions as "unusually high risk," given that the electronic fund transfers were inconsistent with Patco's usual payment orders, the bank still did not notify Patco and allowed the payments, totaling $588,851.26. Ocean Bank eventually recovered $243,406.83, leaving a loss of $345,444.43 with Patco.

Patco argued that the bank should bear this loss because its security system was not "commercially reasonable" under Article 4(A) of the Uniform Commercial Code. This article of the UCC is meant to govern the rights, duties, and liabilities of banks and their customers in regard to electronic fund transfers. More specifically, Patco argued that the bank's security system was not commercially reasonable because it failed to incorporate additional security measures such as monitoring high-risk transactions or immediately notifying customers of high-risk transactions.

On the other hand, the bank asserted that the security system was in fact commercially reasonable, and because Patco agreed to the security system in use, the bank was entitled to summary judgment on all six counts of the complaint by Patco.

1. Suppose that you are a business manager at a new bank. You are determining bank policy regarding your bank's security system. What additional components should you include in your policy to ensure that your bank meets the standards of the UCC in respect to electronic fund transfers?
2. Now suppose that you have created that policy. How would you decide to communicate this policy to your customers?

The Wrap-Up at the end of the chapter will answer these questions.

The relationship between a bank and its customers is quite complicated. When a customer opens an account at a bank, he or she creates a contractual relationship with the bank. Within this relationship, both the customer and the bank have certain rights and duties. This relationship is governed by Article 4 of the UCC. For example, the customer has the right to order a stop payment on a check for any or no reason. The corresponding duty of the bank is to follow this order.

As we explained in previous chapters, checks are considered negotiable instruments under Article 3 of the UCC. However, Article 4 of the UCC is also relevant; this section of the UCC governs the transfer of checks between banks. Thus, both Article 3 and Article 4 are relevant to this chapter.

Article 3 of the UCC outlines the requirements that negotiable instruments, including checks, must meet. Article 3 also establishes the rights and responsibilities pertaining to parties to negotiable instruments. Article 4 creates a framework controlling deposit and checking agreements between banks and customers. In addition, Article 4 directs the relationships between banks as checks are processed among different banks. Moreover, according to UCC Section 4-102(a), when conflicts arise between rules in Articles 3 and 4, Article 4 is to take precedence.

In 2009, Americans wrote approximately 70 billion checks. Clearly, checks are an enormous part of the bank-customer relationship. In fact, of all the negotiable instruments regulated by the UCC, checks are the most common type used. Thus, we begin this chapter by taking a closer look at different types of checks. Then we examine the process of check collection: If the bank accepts a check, how is the money from one account actually transferred to another account? Next, we consider when a bank may charge a customer's account in the context of potential problems with checks, such as stale, postdated, and forged checks. Finally, we turn to an increasingly important element of the banking process: the electronic transfer of funds.

Checks

LO1

What are the components of a check?

Although you have likely written a check, do you know what the actual characteristics of checks are? (The key terms and an illustration are provided in Exhibits 29-1 and 29-2.) According to the UCC, a check is a special kind of draft. A **draft** is an instrument that is an order. Three parties are related to an order. First, a **drawer** is the party that gives the order. Second, a **drawee** is the party that must obey the order. Finally, the **payee** is the party that receives the benefit of the order. Thus, when you write a check at the grocery store, you are the drawer ordering the drawee (your bank) to make a payment to the payee (the grocery store).

A **check** is a special draft that orders the drawee, a bank, to pay a fixed amount of money on demand [UCC Section 3-104(f)]. The UCC defines a bank as "any business

Draft	An instrument whereby one party orders a second party to pay an amount of money to the party listed on the instrument
Drawer	The party giving the order to pay on a draft
Drawee	The party ordered to pay on a draft
Payee	The party receiving the money from the draft

Exhibit 29-1
Key Terms for Checks

Exhibit 29-2 A Check

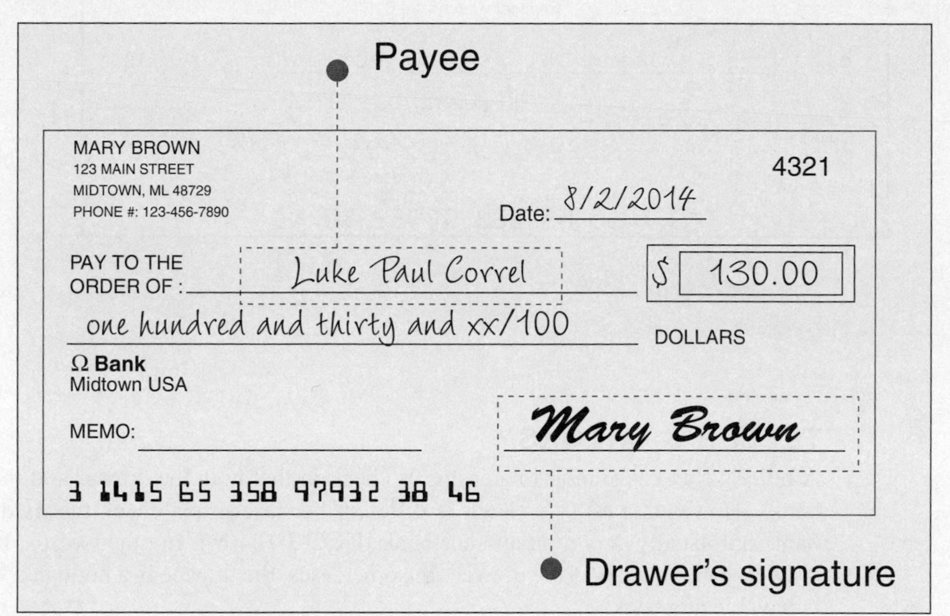

engaged in the business of banking" [4-105(1)]. Consequently, savings banks, savings and loans, credit unions, and trust companies are all considered banks. The drawer of a check writes the check and thus orders the bank to pay. The payee is the party to whom the check is written.

CASHIER'S CHECKS

LO2 What are the differences among the various types of checks?

A **cashier's check** is a check for which both the drawer and the drawee are the same bank [UCC 3-104(g)]. (See Exhibit 29-3 for an example.) The payee of the check is a specific person. In other words, the bank is drawing on itself and thus assumes the responsibility for paying the check to that specific person.

Customers often purchase cashier's checks to give to creditors who want to be sure the funds represented by the check are available. Cashier's checks are useful because they are considered by many in the business community to be the near equivalent of cash. For example, suppose Dave is buying a used car for $9,000 and wants to pay with a personal check. The seller of the car, Hudson, is not sure Dave actually has $9,000 in his checking account. Thus, Hudson asks Dave to pay for the car with a cashier's check. Dave goes to his bank and transfers the $9,000 to the bank. The bank then creates a check for $9,000 payable to Hudson.

Exhibit 29-3 A Cashier's Check

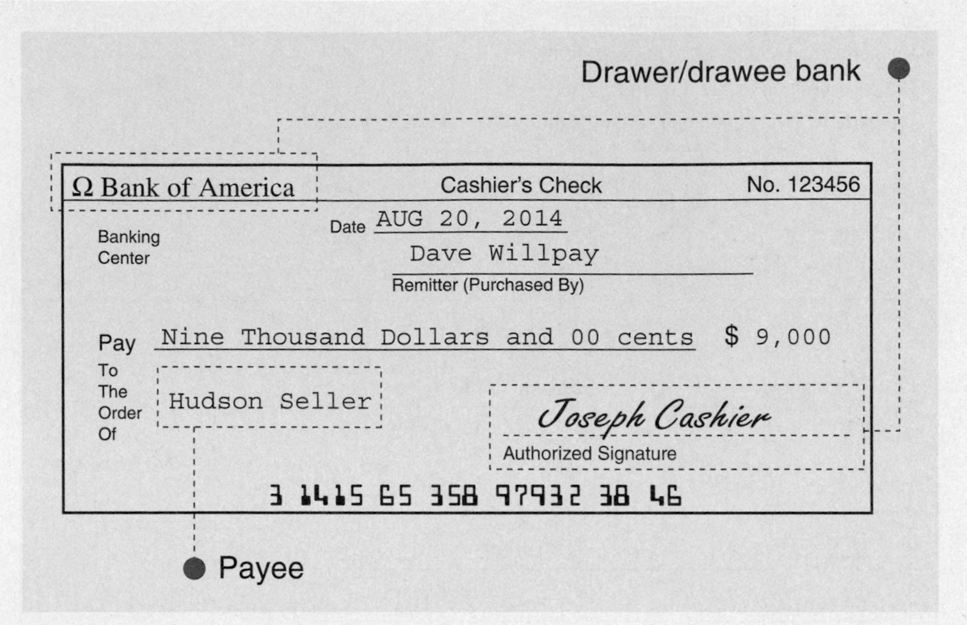

TELLER'S CHECKS

A teller's check is similar to a cashier's check in that both the drawer and the drawee are banks. However, a **teller's check** is different because it is a check that is drawn by one bank and usually drawn on another bank [UCC 3-104(h)]. In other words, bank A is the drawer, while bank B is the drawee. In some cases, the drawee is a nonbank, but the check is payable at a bank.

TRAVELER'S CHECKS

A **traveler's check** is an instrument that must have the following characteristics (see Exhibit 29-4):

1. Is payable on demand.
2. Is drawn on or through a bank.
3. Is designated by the phrase *traveler's check*.
4. Requires a countersignature by a person whose signature appears on the instrument. [UCC 3-104(i)]

The drawer of a traveler's check is usually a large financial organization, such as American Express. The person who signs the traveler's check must sign it when she buys the checks. When the person is ready to use the traveler's check to make some kind of payment, the same person must sign the traveler's check in the presence of the acceptor.

MONEY ORDERS

Money orders (see Exhibit 29-5), particularly personal money orders, are usually in the same form as personal checks and are considered checks under UCC Section 3-104. Both banks and nonbanks sell money orders. The money order states that a certain amount of

Exhibit 29-4 A Traveler's Check

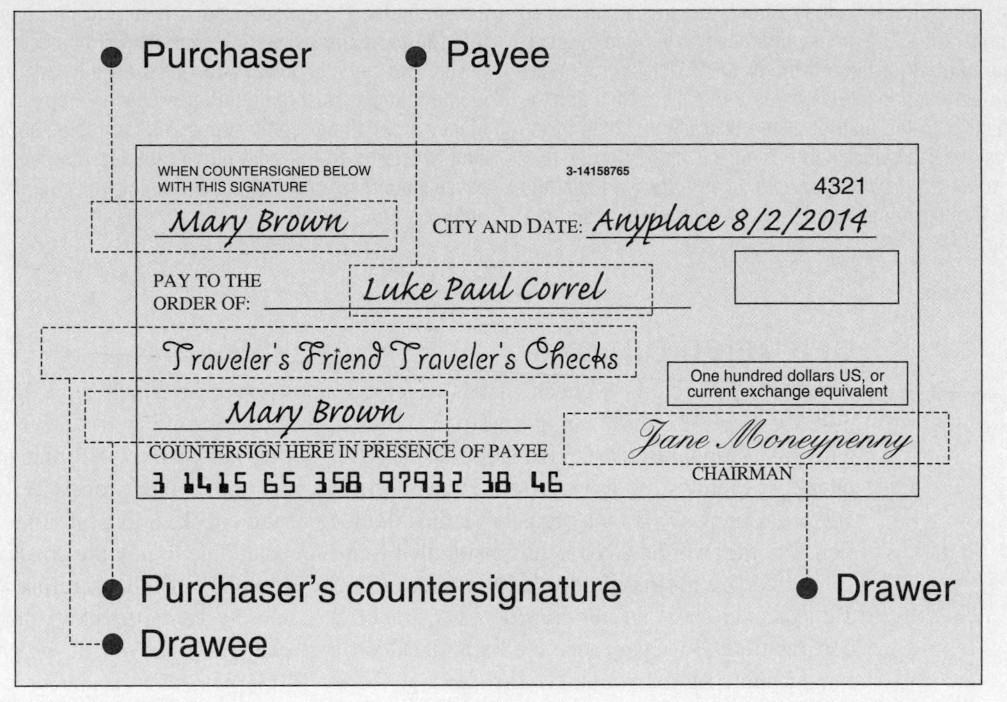

Exhibit 29-5 A Money Order

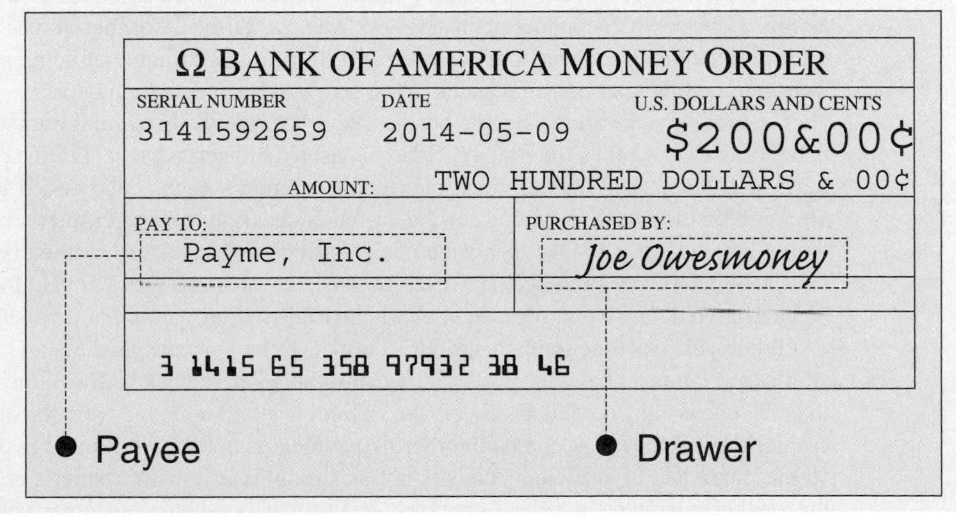

money is to be paid to a particular person. The amount of money to be paid is usually already imprinted on the money order. The person purchasing the money order signs the money order as the drawer and fills in the name of the person who is to receive the money.

Legal Principle: A bank is primarily liable for a certified check.

COMPARING THE LAW OF OTHER COUNTRIES

MONEY ORDERS IN INDIA

Unlike in the United States, in India, money orders can be issued only by the post office. The money order can be verified by a signature, a thumb mark or fingerprint, or both. Money orders can be written in various languages, such as English, Hindi, or the language specific to the district of the post office. While in the United States the individual purchasing the money order may be referred to as a *purchaser, sender,* or *remitter,* in India, the law refers to the individual who is writing the money order only as a *remitter.* The person who is receiving the money order is referred to as the *payee.* After the money has been paid to the payee, the remitter always receives acknowledgment of payment to the payee. If the remitter wishes to stop payment on the money order, there are no stipulations for doing so; the remitter simply returns to the post office, notifies the personnel of the payee's address, and offers the receipt from the issued money order.

CERTIFIED CHECKS

A **certified check** is a check that is accepted at the bank at which it is drawn [UCC 3-409(d)]. For example, suppose Hope writes a check to Jeremiah from her account at Citizens National Bank (CNB). Hope asks CNB to certify her check. CNB then accepts the check, withdraws the money from Hope's account, and places that money in its certified check account. CNB then signs or stamps the face of the check to indicate that it is certified. In other words, CNB is promising that funds are available to pay the check.

Banks are not required to certify checks [UCC 3-409(d)]. If a bank refuses to certify a check, the check is not considered dishonored; it merely lacks the extra protection of certification. However, once the bank does certify a check, the drawer of the check is no longer liable for the amount of the check [UCC 3-414(c)]. The bank has become primarily liable for the check.

WHY USE CASHIER'S, TELLER'S, OR CERTIFIED CHECKS?

There are a number of reasons to use a cashier's, teller's, or certified check as opposed to a regular check when conducting business exchanges. While all of these types of drafts are different, one thing they have in common is an increased guarantee of being paid. That is, a cashier's, teller's, or certified check is less likely to be denied by a bank.

Cashier's checks are a valuable business tool because the bank, and not the individual, is the drawer as well as the drawee. When a cashier's check is presented for payment, the bank, and not the individual, must pay for the cashier's check. The added guarantee of knowing that the bank is paying for the cashier's check makes the cashier's check a veritable guarantee to pay. One downside of the cashier's check is that it must be paid for in advance, including a small fee. However, because the cashier's check is paid for first, it can be purchased at any bank, regardless of whether one has an account at the bank.

Teller's checks function like cashier's checks. Teller's checks tend to carry with them a similar guarantee to be paid. However, because the teller's check is drawn on a bank other than the one issuing the teller's check, the process is a step removed from the one regarding cashier's checks. That is, the bank ordering payment is not the bank making the payment, so the guarantee of sufficient funds is not as strong as it is with cashier's checks. Given the weaker guarantee, a teller's check is used primarily when a customer wants to buy a cashier's check from a bank that does not currently have the funds to cover the cashier's check and thus issues a teller's check. Consequently, although a cashier's check is preferred to a teller's check, the teller's check is almost as good as the cashier's check.

Certified checks are useful in business because when a bank certifies a check, it essentially says that it cannot refuse liability on the check. A certified check is one that the bank sets aside money for and agrees to pay when the certified check is presented. Despite the

Exhibit 29-6 Relationship among Cashier's, Teller's, and Certified Checks

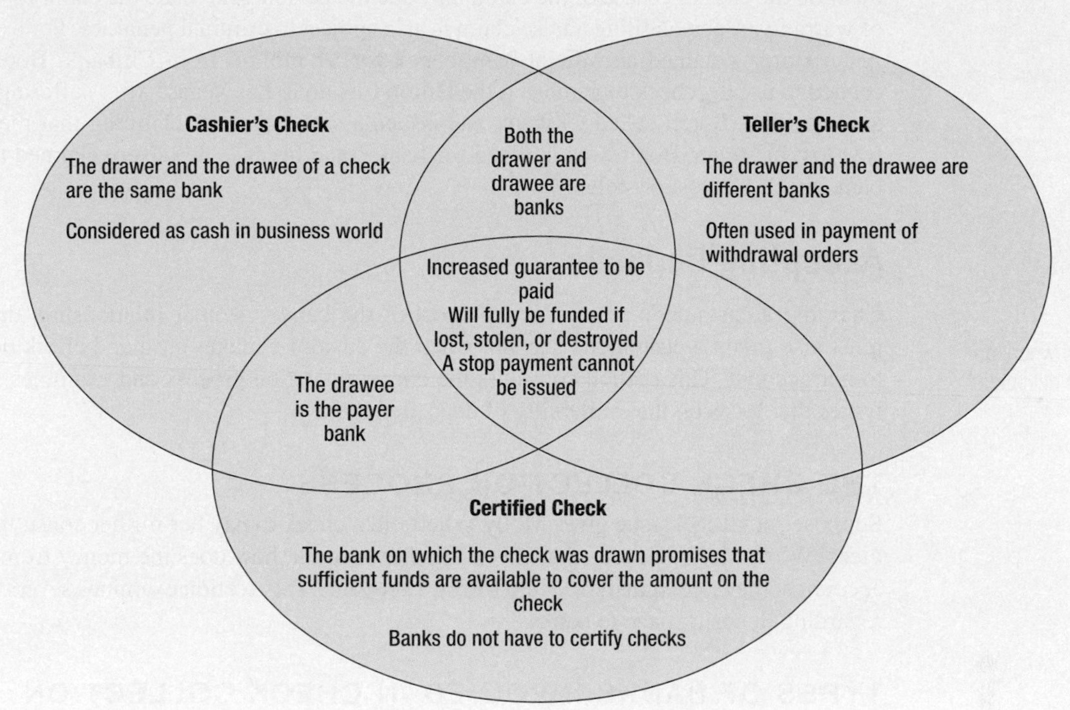

added guarantee, there are two main drawbacks to a certified check. The first is that a person must have an account at a specific bank to obtain a certified check. That is, unlike cashier's or teller's checks, if a person does not have an account at the bank, he or she cannot obtain a certified check from that bank. The second drawback is that banks do not have to certify checks. Banks may refuse to certify any check for any reason. Refusing to certify is not the same as dishonoring a check, but it does not provide the same guarantee that a certified check has. While banks do not have to certify a check, they are not allowed to refuse to sell a cashier's or teller's check as long as the payment is valid.

Exhibit 29-6 summarizes the relationship among cashier's, teller's, and certified checks.

LOST, STOLEN, OR DESTROYED CASHIER'S, TELLER'S, OR CERTIFIED CHECKS

In the event a cashier's, teller's, or certified check is lost, stolen, or destroyed, the UCC allows for recovery. According to UCC Section 3-312, the remitter (the party who purchased the check) or the payee may request a refund because the check was lost, stolen, or destroyed. With proper identification, the party should be able to obtain a full refund for the amount on the check.

The claim is enforceable when the claim is made; if it is a cashier's or teller's check, 90 days after the check was made; or if it is a certified check, 90 days after acceptance, whichever occurs last [UCC 3-312(b)(1)]. After the claim becomes enforceable, if no one presented the check for payment, a refund is issued and the bank is discharged of liability [UCC 3-312(b)(4)]. When a claim is made, the person making the claim warrants to the bank and any party who has an interest in the check that the check was really lost, stolen, or destroyed.

If the check was not lost, stolen, or destroyed, the holder barred from receiving payment on the check because of the claim may sue the person who made the claim for breach of warranty. A person filing a false claim is also subject to criminal penalties. For example, Allan Boren obtained an official bank check for $1 million from Citibank. Boren proceeded to use the check to gamble at the Hilton Casino in Las Vegas. After suffering losses at the casino, Boren called Citibank and issued a stop payment, claiming that the check was lost or stolen. Boren was indicted for bank fraud because he falsely claimed that his bank check was lost or stolen.

Accepting Deposits

LO3
How and where are deposits accepted?

Charging a customer's account is only part of the bank-customer relationship; the bank must also credit a customer's account when the customer makes cash and check deposits to her account. This section considers the check collection process and examines several issues that focus on the availability of deposited money.

THE CHECK COLLECTION PROCESS

Suppose Jack Blackstone gives Molly Whetfield a check to pay her for her consulting services. When Molly deposits that check into her account, how does the money from Jack's account actually get transferred into Molly's account? This section examines several issues regarding deposits made to banks.

TYPES OF BANKS INVOLVED IN CHECK COLLECTION

The check collection process is established by Article 4 of the UCC. Section 4-105 of the UCC defines the four types of banks that may be involved in the check collection process. Return to the Jack and Molly example. First, suppose Molly presents Jack's check to her bank for deposit in her account. Molly's bank is called the **depositary bank,** the first bank that receives a check for payment. Second, Jack's bank is called the **payor bank,** the bank on which a check is drawn. Third, any kind of bank (besides the payor bank) that handles Jack's check during the collection process is called a **collecting bank.** Finally, any bank (besides the payor bank and depositary bank) to which the check is transferred is called an **intermediary bank.**

A bank involved in the check collection process may be classified as several of these types of banks at the same time. For example, when Molly deposits Jack's check at her bank, her bank is both the depositary bank and the collecting bank.

CHECK COLLECTION WITHIN THE SAME BANK

Sometimes the depositary bank is the same bank as the payor bank. When the depositary bank is the same bank as the payor bank, the check is referred to as an "on-us item." For example, suppose Molly's and Jack's accounts are at the same bank. When Molly deposits Jack's check into her account, the check does not have to be sent to another bank because she and Jack share the same bank. Instead, the bank gives a "provisional" credit to Molly's account. If this bank does not dishonor the check on the second day, the check is paid [UCC 4-215(e)(2)]. Finally, on the third day, the provisional credit becomes an actual payment.

CHECK COLLECTION BETWEEN DIFFERENT BANKS

Suppose that Jack and Molly have accounts at different banks. Molly's account is in Los Angeles, while Jack's account is in Miami. When Molly deposits Jack's check at her bank in Los Angeles, her bank is the depositary bank. When a depositary bank receives a check, it must present the check at the payor bank or send it through intermediary banks to reach the payor bank. Once a bank receives a check, it must pass the check on before midnight of the next day [UCC 4-202(b)]. When the check finally reaches the payor bank, the payor bank must respond to the check by dishonoring it or becoming liable for the face amount of the check (UCC 4-302).

The UCC allows banks to establish cutoff hours for making entries on their books. For example, a bank may determine that 2 p.m. or later is the cutoff hour for handling checks (UCC 4-108). If the bank receives a check after this deadline, the bank will defer posting this check to its customer's account until the next day.

FEDERAL RESERVE SYSTEM FOR CLEARING CHECKS

The Federal Reserve System, consisting of 12 central banks, acts as a clearinghouse for the check collection process. (A *clearinghouse* is an institution created to facilitate banks in their exchange of checks and drafts drawn on one another, as well as to enable banks to settle their daily balances.) These 12 banks are located in the following cities: Atlanta, Boston, Chicago, Cleveland, Dallas, Kansas City, Minneapolis, New York, Philadelphia, Richmond, Saint Louis, and San Francisco. Most banks have accounts with the Federal Reserve. Thus, when Molly deposits Jack's check at her bank in Los Angeles, this bank will deposit the check in the San Francisco Federal Reserve Bank. The San Francisco Federal Reserve Bank will transfer the check to the Atlanta Federal Reserve Bank, which serves Miami. Finally, the Atlanta Federal Reserve Bank will transfer the check to Jack's bank in Miami.

ELECTRONIC CHECK PRESENTMENT

In the past, checks were physically presented to each bank in the chain of collection. Now, checks are transmitted electronically from bank to bank (UCC 4-110). Through electronic check presentment, a check can be processed on the day on which it is deposited. An item is encoded with information that is transferred from one bank's computer to another bank's computer. The person who enters the information into the computer (i.e., encodes the information) warrants that the information is correct (UCC 4-209). Alternatively, the image of a check may be transmitted for payment to other banks.

Substitute Checks. To further facilitate electronic presentment, in 2004 Congress passed the *Check Clearing for the 21st Century Act* (also known as *Check 21* or the *Check Truncation Act*). Check 21 allows banks to forgo sending original checks as part of the collection or return process and instead send a truncated version. In place of the original paper check, a bank may send (1) a substitute check or (2), by agreement, an electronic image of the check along with data from the magnetic ink character recognition (MICR) line on the original check.

A substitute check is similar to the electronic image that may be sent in lieu of the original paper check. Check 21 defines a substitute check as a paper reproduction of the original check that conforms to the following requirements:

1. Contains a clear replication of the front and back of the original paper check.
2. Bears an MICR line with all the information on the original check's MICR line.
3. Conforms with generally applicable industry standards for paper stock, dimensions, and other general qualities.
4. Is suitable for automated processing in the same manner as the original paper check.

Check 21 provides the guidelines for the issuance and use of substitute checks. The act also allows for the use of digital or paper substitutions for the original paper check.

AVAILABILITY SCHEDULE FOR DEPOSITED CHECKS

Once a check is considered deposited in a customer's account, when are the funds available to the customer? In the past, banks placed extended holds (e.g., 10 days) on deposited funds to allow for ensuring that the payor bank would not dishonor the check. If the check was from out of state, the bank might place a two-week hold on the check.

Because customers were frustrated with such extended holds on checks, Congress enacted the Expedited Funds Availability Act of 1987. This act created explicit timelines that mandate when banks must make deposited funds available to customers. If the risk of dishonor is low, the funds must be made available very quickly. For example, the first $100 of any amount deposited must be available to the depositor on the business day following the day of deposit [12 C.F.R. Section 229.10(a)–(c)]. The availability of the rest of the funds depends on whether the check is local, what the amount of the check is, and how the depositor wishes to withdraw the funds.

Legal Principle: **If the deposited check is drawn on a bank within the same Federal Reserve Bank area, the depositary bank must make the deposited funds available to the customer on the second business day following the deposit day [12 C.F.R. 229.10(b)].**

Legal Principle: **If the deposited check is outside the same Federal Reserve Bank area, the depositary bank must make the funds available on the fifth business day following the day of deposit [12 C.F.R. 229.12(c)].**

There are some exceptions to these rules. For example, if a customer makes a deposit at an ATM not owned by the bank that is receiving the deposit, the bank places a five-day hold on the deposit, including cash deposits. Moreover, if a customer makes a deposit over $5,000, the depositary bank may place an eight-day hold on the funds.

When a Bank May Charge a Customer's Account

L04

When may a bank charge a customer's account?

The following sections consider certain problems related to a bank's accepting and paying a customer's check. See Exhibit 29-7 for a summary of who bears responsibility when these problems arise.

WRONGFUL DISHONOR

When a customer opens a checking account, both the customer and the bank accept certain duties and rights. Generally, the customer assumes a duty to keep sufficient funds in her account to cover the checks written on her account. If the customer does not have enough funds to cover a check, the bank will dishonor the check and the customer becomes liable for the amount of the check.

Similarly, under the *properly payable rule,* the bank has a duty to pay checks from the customer's account as long as the check is "properly payable" [UCC Section 4-401(a)]. In other words, the check must be authorized by the drawer and must not violate the agreement between the bank and the customer. Generally, for a check to be considered properly payable, it must:

1. Have the drawer's authorized signature on the check.
2. Be paid to a person entitled to enforce the check.

Exhibit 29-7 Who Is Responsible for the Check?

The customer presents a properly payable check, and the banks fails to pay it, thus wrongfully dishonoring the check.	**The bank is responsible.**
The customer does not have enough funds in her account to cover the check, so the bank dishonors the check.	**The customer is liable.**
The customer issues a stop-payment order orally and does not submit a written stop-payment order, and the bank cashes the check 20 days later.	**The customer is responsible.**
The customer writes a postdated check and notifies the bank, but the bank processes the check early and the customer does not have sufficient funds to pay the amount.	**The bank is responsible.**
The customer presents a check for payment eight months after the draft was written.	**No one; the check is stale and nonpayable.**
The customer has been adjudicated incompetent, but the bank does not have knowledge of this.	**The bank is responsible.**
The customer dies, and a check from the deceased customer is presented for payment 11 days after his death.	**No one; the check is nonpayable.**
The bank cashes a check with an unauthorized signature of the drawer ordering payment.	**The bank is responsible.**
The bank cashes a check with an unauthorized signature of the drawer ordering payment, but the customer's negligence contributed to the forgery.	**The customer is responsible.**
The bank cashes a check with an unauthorized drawer signature, but the customer notifies the bank of this two months after the statement was made available.	**The customer is responsible.**
The bank pays a check that has been fraudulently endorsed, but the customer reports the forgery four years later.	**The customer is responsible**
The bank cashes a check that has been altered.	**The bank is responsible.**
The customer loses her ATM card and notifies the bank right away.	**The customer is liable only for the first $50.**
The customer's ATM card is stolen, and the customer does not notify the bank.	**The customer is liable for the first $500.**
The customer notifies the bank of an erroneous electronic transfer three months after the statement is made available.	**The customer is responsible.**

3. Not have been altered.
4. Not have been completed by addition of unauthorized terms if the check was incomplete.
5. Be paid on or after the date of the check.
6. Not be subject to a stop payment from the drawer.

BUT WHAT IF . . .

WHAT IF THE FACTS OF THE CASE OPENER WERE DIFFERENT?

What if Patco Construction Company had written a check to Stoneworld Masonry for $500, but the check was altered to read $5,000 and was subsequently cashed, resulting in $5,000 being taken out of Patco's account? When Patco discovered this wrongful payment, would the bank be required to redeposit the $5,000 in the Patco account?

If the bank wrongfully fails to pay a check—wrongfully dishonoring the check—the bank may be liable to the customer for damages. The UCC clearly states that banks can be held liable, but it does not cite a specific theory for recovery. Therefore, someone whose check was dishonored need prove only that the dishonoring was wrongful, and he or she will be entitled to recovery. Case 29-1 provides an example of the damages a customer may potentially recover from a bank for wrongful dishonor. The case also illustrates another important aspect of recovering damages from a wrongful dishonor. UCC 4-402 authorizes a cause of action against a bank for wrongfully dishonoring a check of a "customer." Case 29-1 illustrates the difficulty of determining who a "customer" is when corporations are involved.

CASE 29-1 PAMELA JANA v. WACHOVIA

COMMON PLEAS COURT OF PHILADELPHIA

2006 PHILA. CT. COM. PL. LEXIS 479, 61 U.C.C. REP. SERV. 2D (CALLAGHAN) 583 (2006)

Since 1991, Pamela and Jerry Jana were involved in investment opportunities which consisted of acquiring certificates of deposit ("CDs") in their own names and the name of their minor son, Jerry A. Jana. The CDs were in savings and loan and/or mutual savings banks and the Janas held the CDs until such time that the banks converted to publicly owned banks, whereupon certificate holders were entitled to purchase shares of the converting bank's stock at a favorable price. To conduct their business, the Janas formed corporations in several states to acquire the CDs because the banks preferred to deal with customers within their community.

An investment opportunity arose in September of 2003, and the Janas sought to purchase shares in a bank by three separate checks. The checks the defendant provided to the Janas did not have the account number micro-encoded on the checks but rather was written by hand. The checks at issue were made payable to the savings bank the Janas were buying stock in and were in the names of "Pamela Jana," "Jerry A. Jana" (Pamela's minor son), and "Altoona Inc." (one of the Jana's companies). The defendant subsequently dishonored the checks due to alleged micro-encoding errors. Later the defendant agreed to honor these checks, but since the deadline had passed, the Janas' investment opportunity refused to fill the stock purchase requests. As a result, the Janas claimed $306,872 in damages due to lost profits from the wrongful dishonor of the checks. The defendants motioned for summary judgment claiming that the company, not the individual members of the Jana family, were customers to the bank. Under the UCC, a person must be a "customer" to recover damages from a wrongful dishonor of checks.

JUDGE SHEPPARD: 13 Pa.C.S. § 4402(b) sets forth the liability of a bank in the event of a wrongful dishonor:

> A payor bank is liable to its customer for damages proximately caused by the wrongful dishonor of an item. Liability is limited to actual damages proved and may include damages for an arrest or prosecution of the customer or other consequential damages. Whether any consequential damages are proximately caused by the wrongful dishonor is a question of fact to be determined in each case.
>
> "Customer" is defined as "a person having an account with a bank or for whom a bank has agreed to collect items, including a bank that maintains an account at another bank." 13 Pa.C.S. § 4104.

The issue presented is whether Pamela Jana and her minor son may properly be considered "customers" for purposes of 13 Pa.C.S. § 4402(b). The account at issue was in the name of "Heronwood." Pamela and Jerry Jana were the authorized signatories on the account. Their minor son was not a signatory or otherwise named on the account.

This court is unaware of any Federal, Pennsylvania or other state decisions similar to the facts before this court. However, courts in various other jurisdictions have considered factual scenarios which are instructive. For example, in *Murdaugh Volkswagen, Inc. v. First Nat. Bank,* 801 F.2d 719 (4th Cir. 1986), an individual who was the president and sole stockholder of a corporation sought to bring an action for wrongful dishonor of a corporate check under UCC § 4-402. The bank argued that the plaintiff had no standing to assert such a claim because she did not have an account with the bank (the account was in the corporation's name). The Fourth Circuit found the bank's construction of § 4-402 to be unjustifiably narrow based on the facts presented because the evidence demonstrated a close link between the president and her corporation—the bank treated the president and the corporate depositor as one entity. The bank consistently and repeatedly looked to the president to assume the corporation's obligations by requiring her to mortgage her own home and personally borrow funds for the company's benefit. The court said that, under these facts, the president was a customer of the bank for purposes of § 4-402.

In *Parrett v. Platte Valley State Bank & Trust Co.,* 236 Neb. 139, 459 N.W.2d 371 (Neb. 1990), the Nebraska Supreme Court held that liability under UCC § 4-402 for wrongful dishonor could extend to a corporate officer who signed the check on behalf of the corporation, even though the check was written on the corporate account. The officer was the principal shareholder, president, and chief operating officer of the corporation, as well as a signatory to the corporate account. The evidence demonstrated that the officer personally participated in the business relationship between the corporation and the bank, including giving his personal guarantee to the bank for all obligations owed by the corporation to the bank. The court found that the officer was a "customer" of the bank within the meaning of § 4-402, observing that the parties' business relationship was such that it was foreseeable that dishonoring the corporation's check would reflect directly on the officer, against whom criminal charges had been brought in connection with the dishonored check.

Other courts, however, have adopted a more narrow approach. In *Loucks v. Albuquerque National Bank,* 76 N.M. 735, 418 P.2d 191 (N.M. 1966), Loucks and Martinez, as partners, had a partnership checking account at Albuquerque National. The bank dishonored the partnership's check after it had improperly charged the partnership account with a payment on a debt owed by Martinez. Loucks and Martinez individually sued the bank for wrongful dishonor of the partnership check. In determining that Loucks and Martinez, as individuals, had no cause of action against the bank for the alleged wrongful dishonor, the court stated:

> The relationship, in connection with which the wrongful conduct of the bank arose, was the relationship between the bank and the partnership. The partnership was the customer, and any damages arising from the dishonor belonged to the partnership and not to the partners individually.

However, many of the courts which adopted this strict approach seemed to leave the door open for situations where the evidence demonstrates that the corporation and the individual were one and the same or that the bank regarded the officer as its customer. See e.g., *Thrash v. Georgia State Bank,* 189 Ga. App. 21, 375 S.E.2d 112 (Ga. App. 1988) (found that the president of a corporation was not a "customer" for purposes of UCC § 4-402 where president was only a minority shareholder of the corporation who had merely joined with the other shareholders in guaranteeing the corporation's debt to the bank, and where the evidence failed to demonstrate that the president and the corporation were one and the same); *Koger v. East First Nat. Bank,* 443 So.2d 141 (Fla. App. 1983) (found that the trial court acted properly in dismissing an individual corporate stockholder's action under UCC § 4-402, since the individual was not the named customer on the account, noting that there was no allegation that the corporation was "undercapitalized" or a mere "transparent shell"); *Kesner v. Liberty Bank & Trust Co.,* 7 Mass. App. Ct. 934, 390 N.E.2d 259 (Mass. App. 1979) (held that the treasurer of a corporation could not bring an action under UCC § 4-402 since there was no ambiguity as to who had the account with the bank and where there was no suggestion that the corporation was a mere transparent shell rather than a separate and distinct legal entity with independent liability); *Farmers Bank v. Sinwellan Corp.,* 367 A.2d 180 (Del. Sup. 1976) (corporation's president was not a "customer" of the bank under plain language of statute where there was no evidence in the record supporting a finding that the bank regarded the president as its customer).

This case law suggests that where a dishonored check was drawn on the account of a small business entity, such as a closely held corporation, the wrongful dishonor can result in some actionable damage to the persons who control the corporation. In such instances, evidence may be presented to show that the person injured bore such a close relationship to the corporation that he or she should be permitted to bring an action for wrongful dishonor under the Commercial Code. Such evidence can include the failure to issue stock, undercapitalization of the business or corporation, the person's guarantee of the business' obligations, or the fact that the bank, in some way, treated the person and the business as a single entity. Such a finding would be precluded where there is evidence that the account on which the item was written carried only the corporate name and not the person's name, that the bank did not regard the person and the business as a single entity, or that the business entity was not undercapitalized.

Here, Jerry A. Jana, the minor plaintiff, has failed to satisfy this criteria. He was not a signatory or otherwise formally connected to the Account. It is admitted that he was never an officer or employee of Heronwood and never held any role in the company or had any direct dealings with the bank. As such, Jerry A. Jana, the minor plaintiff, cannot be considered a "customer" for purposes of § 4402, as a matter of law. Accordingly, summary judgment is granted in favor of defendants on this issue. Jerry A. Jana's claim is dismissed.

However, the court finds that a factual issue exists as to whether Pamela Jana can be considered a "customer." In order to survive summary judgment on this issue, Ms. Jana must produce evidence to show that she bore such a close relationship to the corporation that she should be permitted to bring an action for wrongful dishonor under § 4402 (b). This court finds that Ms. Jana has presented sufficient evidence to submit the issue to a jury, in that there is documentation to support her claim that the bank viewed she and her husband as their customers, rather than Heronwood. Based on the foregoing, summary judgment is granted in favor of defendants as to the claims of minor plaintiff Jerry A. Jana and of Heronwood, Inc. Defendants' Motion for Summary Judgment is denied with respect to the claims of Pamela Jana, individually.

Motion granted in part, denied in part.

[continued]

CRITICAL THINKING

Judge Sheppard uses several cases to make analogies with the Jana case. Do you think these analogies are effective? Are there any differences between those cases and the facts in this case that suggest that Judge Sheppard should not have relied so heavily on them?

How should the judge decide on the case when there is no clear precedent about what to do in this situation?

ETHICAL DECISION MAKING

Return to the WPH framework and ask yourself, "Who are the relevant stakeholders?" A classmate agrees with the judge and believes that the minor in the case is not a relevant stakeholder. Make an argument suggesting that the minor is a relevant stakeholder, even though he is not a legal adult.

OVERDRAFTS

Suppose you write 10 checks on your company's account to pay your employees' salaries. Unfortunately, you do not have sufficient funds to cover the full amount of the last check; you are short \$50. The bank has two options: (1) Dishonor the last check, or (2) create an **overdraft** by paying the check and charging the account the amount short [UCC 4-401(a)]. Thus, when you make your next deposit, \$50 will be deducted from that deposit.

How frequently do banks have to dishonor checks because of insufficient funds? In Europe, less than 1 percent of personal checks are returned because of insufficient funds. Approximately 1 percent of checks are returned because of insufficient funds in the United States. In contrast, 9.5 percent of personal checks bounce in Qatar, while 3.4 percent are returned in Saudi Arabia.

Many banks offer overdraft protection to their customers. In other words, some banks will promise to credit their customers' accounts if there are insufficient funds. However, these banks may charge the customers for this service. Alternatively, banks may give several options to customers to prevent overdrafts. For example, the bank may link the checking account to the customer's savings account or credit card; thus, if a customer has insufficient funds in her checking account, the bank may draw on the savings account or credit card.

If the bank chooses to dishonor the check, the holder can attempt to resubmit the check at a later date. However, as we explained in Chapter 26, once the check has been dishonored, the holder must notify the endorsers of the check of the dishonor. If the holder does not give proper notice, the endorsers will not be responsible for the amount of the check.

Legal Principle: If a bank does not honor a customer's stop-payment order, the bank is liable for any damages the customer suffers.

STOP-PAYMENT ORDER

A customer can issue a **stop-payment order,** an order by a drawer to the drawee bank not to pay a check that has been drawn on the customer's account (UCC 4-403). A customer issues a stop-payment order when she has issued a check that has not yet been accepted and she wishes the check not to be accepted. For example, Angelina orders a pair of boots from her favorite store and writes a check to cover the cost in advance. Angelina is informed the next day that the boots have been discontinued and she will not be receiving the boots. Given that Angelina has already issued the check, she can issue a stop-payment order for her check because the check is no longer covering the purchase of her boots. If the bank pays a check in violation of a stop-payment order, the bank will incur liability for the damages suffered by the customer due to the stop payment [UCC 4-403(b)].

To be effective, the stop order must meet two requirements: (1) The customer must give the order in a reasonable time, and (2) the customer must describe the item with "reasonable certainty" [UCC 4-403(a)]. For example, the stop-payment order must be given so that the bank has enough time to instruct its tellers and other employees that they should not pay the check. Moreover, the UCC states that the stop-payment order must reach the bank by a certain cutoff time. Generally, the stop-payment order should list:

1. The date of the check
2. The name of the payee
3. The amount of the check
4. The number of the check
5. The checking account number

There are several issues regarding stop-payment orders. First, how is the stop-payment order given? A stop-payment order may be given orally or in writing. If it is an oral order, it is valid for just 14 days unless the order is later confirmed in writing. If the order is given through writing, the order is valid for six months and can be extended for another six months [UCC 4-403(b)]. Note that not all states allow stop-payment orders to be delivered orally. In the event that oral stop-payment orders are not allowed, they must be given in writing.

Second, if the customer issues a stop payment and does not have a valid legal ground for this order, the holder of the instrument will likely sue the customer. Not only will the customer be liable for the value of the check, but he will also probably be liable for any damages incurred by the payee of the check because of the stop-payment order. Even with a valid legal reason, if the holder of the check is a holder in due course, the drawer's defenses will not apply and he will still be liable for the check.

Third, payment cannot be stopped on certified checks, cashier's checks, or teller's checks [UCC 3-411(b)].

BUT WHAT IF . . .

WHAT IF THE FACTS OF THE CASE OPENER WERE DIFFERENT?

Assume that Patco Construction Company had written a check to a supplier and then found out that the supplier had supplied inferior-quality materials, so Patco decided to return the materials and cancel the check. Patco immediately issued a stop-payment order over the phone, and the bank teller said the oral order was sufficient, but 21 days later the supplier cashed the check and Patco's account was debited in the amount of the check. Does Patco have any recourse against the bank?

POSTDATED CHECKS

Under previous versions of Articles 3 and 4 of the UCC, a check could not be charged to a customer's account until the date of the check. Thus, some customers attempted to hold off payment on a check by postdating the check and giving it to the payee. However, because banks generally use an automated system to process checks, checks are now frequently paid without regard to the date. If a bank pays a check before its date and thus depletes a customer's account, the bank could be liable to the customer for damages. Thus, some banks include certain clauses in their customer agreements that state they may pay checks regardless of the date.

The UCC presents a middle ground that protects a bank from liability while permitting customers to postdate checks. Section 4-401(c) states that customers can postdate checks but they must give the bank notice of the postdated check. Therefore, the bank can assume that it can pay all checks on presentment unless the bank has received notice. Most banks charge a processing fee for notice of a postdated check.

STALE CHECKS

If a check is not presented to a bank within six months of its date, the check is considered a **stale check.** If a payee presents an uncertified stale check to a bank, the bank is not required to pay the amount of the check (UCC 4-404). However, if the bank pays the check in good faith, it may charge the drawer's account. Case 29-2 explores how long a bank must honor an oral stop-payment order.

CASE 29-2 SCOTT D. LEIBLING, P.C. v. MELLON PSFS (NJ) NATIONAL ASSOCIATION

SUPERIOR COURT OF NEW JERSEY, LAW DIVISION, SPECIAL CIVIL PART, CAMDEN COUNTY

710 A.2D 1067 (1998)

Scott D. Liebling, P.C., an attorney, had an attorney trust account ("Account") at Mellon Bank (NJ) National Association. Mellon uses a computerized system to process checks for payment. Liebling represented Fredy Ramos in a personal injury case that led to a settlement.

In May 1995, Liebling issued check number 1031 for over $8,000 to Ramos as a result of the settlement. However, a few days later, Liebling mistakenly issued check number 1043 in the same amount to Ramos. Mellon honored this first check on May 26, 1995. Around May 30, 1995, Liebling called Ramos and explained that check 1043 was issued in error and should be destroyed. Moreover, Liebling called the bank and ordered an oral stop payment on the second check. On December 21, 1996, Ramos cashed check number 1043.

Liebling filed a complaint against Mellon, arguing Mellon breached their duty of good faith, payment of a stale check, and breach of contract as a result of Mellon honoring the second check, check 1043.

JUDGE RAND:

Issue

Whether the defendant bank acted in good faith when it honored a check that was presented for payment nineteen months after it was issued and subsequent to the expiration of an oral stop payment order?

Discussion

It is important to consider the relevant New Jersey statute sections before discussing what actions constitute "good faith." Under N.J.S.A. 12A:4-403(b):

> A stop payment order is effective for six months, but it lapses after 14 calendar days if the original order was oral and was not confirmed in writing within that period. A stop payment order may be renewed for additional six-month periods by a writing given to the bank within a period during which the stop-payment order is effective.

In addition, N.J.S.A. 12A:4-404 states:

> A bank is under no obligation to a customer having a checking account to pay a check . . . which is presented more than six months after its date, but it *may charge its customer's account for a payment made thereafter in good faith.*

Thus, the issue in the present case turns on whether Mellon acted in good faith when it honored Plaintiff's check. Good faith under N.J. Uniform Commercial Code has been defined in N.J.S.A. 12A:3-103(a)(4) as "honesty in fact and the observance of reasonable commercial standards of fair dealing." Since there is no New Jersey case law directly on point, it is necessary to consider alternate sources.

. . . Plaintiff's argument centers on the proposition that the bank's duty of good faith required it to inquire or consult with Plaintiff before honoring a stale check that had a previous oral stop payment order on it. This argument was upheld in the Pre-Code case of Goldberg v. Manufacturers Hanover Trust Co., 199 Misc. 167, 102 N.Y.S.2d 144 (NY Mun. Ct. 1951). In that case, the bank was held liable to the drawer for payment of a 27 month old check even though a stop payment order had expired. The Court predicated liability on the bank's payment of the check without inquiring into its own records which would have revealed the lapsed stop payment order and put the bank on notice. The [1962] N.J.

Study Comment to N.J.S.A. 12A:4-404 cites Redfield, The Law of Commercial Paper § 584, noting that the "practical way out of this dilemma is the simple expedient of making inquiry."

However, in the Uniform Commercial Code Treatise, "Hawkland § 4-404:01," Mr. Hawkland stated that the above case [is] not consistent with the Uniform Commercial Code. Specifically, "the duty [of inquiry] is inconsistent with the provisions of subsection 4-403(2) on the expiration of the 'effectiveness' of stop orders. Such a duty is hardly practical today."

Plaintiff counters that . . . this Court should give total credence to the explanatory comments drafted many years before the most recent code § 4-404 revisions. Pursuant to § 4-404, the bank may charge the customer's account for a check presented more than six months after it is dated as long as the bank acts in good faith. N.J.S.A. § 12A:3-103(a)(4) defines good faith. The definition "honesty in fact and the observance of reasonable commercial standards of fair dealings" is a revision from the 1961 version of the Code. It interjects a subjective analysis into the concept of fair dealings.

In 1990, Articles III and IV of the Code were substantially revised relating to, among other things, bank deposits and collections to become effective on June 1, 1995. The Court is satisfied as pointed out by the Defendant that those Amendments were enacted in order to address the effect of automated systems utilized by banks with the substantial increase in check usage after the original enactment of the Code. The Official Code Comment to the 1995 Amendments for § 12A:4-101, states as follows:

> 2. . . . An important goal of the 1990 revision of Article 4 is to promote the efficiency of the check collection process by making the provisions of Article 4 more compatible with the needs of an automated system and, by doing so, increase the speed and lower the cost of check collection for those who write and receive checks. [Code Comment to N.J.S.A. § 12A:4-101 (1995) (Supp. p. 157).]

The 1995 Amendments to § 12A:4-404 New Jersey Study Comment include different language than that on which the Plaintiff totally relied. Plaintiff's reliance upon the 1962 Study Comment is misplaced and outdated. The more modern and up to date approach requires a rejection of the 1962 Study Comment upon which Plaintiff's argument solely rests.

Thus, in determining whether defendant bank in the present action acted in good faith, the above cited material must be analyzed and applied. First, it appears clear that the Uniform Commercial Code acknowledges that computerized check processing systems are common and accepted banking procedures in the United States. Therefore, it can not be said that defendant bank acted in bad faith by using a computerized system when it honored Plaintiff's "stale" check. Furthermore, it appears that the test for good faith is a subjective test. Thus, based on all of the foregoing material, as long as defendant bank used an adequate computer system for processing checks (here there is no proof to the contrary), it appears to have acted in good faith even though it did not consult the Plaintiff before it honored the "stale" check that had an expired oral stop-payment order on it. [T]he obligation of a bank to stop payment on a check does not continue in perpetuity once the stop payment order expires.

The bank's conduct was fair and in accordance with reasonable commercial standards.

Judgment for defendant Mellon.

CRITICAL THINKING

What evidence does the judge rely on to come to the conclusion that the bank was not liable? Do you think the judge ignores any important evidence? Is there any missing information that would help you come to a conclusion regarding the bank's liability?

ETHICAL REASONING

What are the values associated with not holding the bank responsible to honor an expired stop-payment order? What values are in conflict? Do you think the values promoted by the decision are appropriate for the situation? Why or why not?

FORGERIES AND ALTERATIONS

In 1999, attempted check fraud in the United States rose to approximately $2.2 billion, while merchants and banks suffered actual losses approximating $679 million through check fraud. Thus, banks are clearly concerned about the acceptance of altered or forged checks.

Legal Principle: **If a bank cashes a check with a forged or fraudulent signature, the bank is liable.**

Checks Bearing Forged Signatures. Under the properly payable rule, the bank may pay a check only if it is authorized by the customer. Who is liable if a bank cashes a check signed by an unauthorized person? In other words, what happens when someone forges a drawer's signature on a check?

The UCC establishes that a forged signature has no legal effect as a signature of the drawer [3-403(a)]. Consequently, in most cases, if a bank pays a check when the drawer's signature has been forged, the bank will be liable for the amount of the check.

However, there are some exceptions to this rule. First, if the customer's negligence substantially contributed to a forged signature and the bank pays the check in good faith, the bank is not required to repay the customer [UCC 3-406(a)]. For example, if the customer is an employer who keeps a rubber stamp of his signature in an unlocked drawer, and an employee uses the signature stamp to create a check payable to the employee, the customer has substantially contributed to the forged signature and will likely not be able to recover the amount of the check.

Yet, if the bank that pays the check is also negligent, the customer may be able to recover part of the money. For example, suppose the employer-customer notified the bank of the employee's unauthorized use of the signature stamp but the bank paid the check anyway. The customer's liability for the amount of the check may be reduced by the bank's negligence in paying the check when it had been notified that the check was unauthorized.

Another exception to the forgery liability rule is related to the customer's duty to examine the bank statement. Banks make a customer's statement available to the customer approximately once a month. This statement lists or includes all the checks that have been charged against the customer's account over that past month. A customer must examine her bank statement reasonably promptly for any forgeries or unauthorized payments. If the customer discovers a forgery or unauthorized payment, she must notify the bank promptly [UCC 4-406(c)]. Under the UCC, if the customer does not notify the bank of an unauthorized signature within 30 days after the statement has been made available, she cannot hold the bank liable for the payment [4-406(d)].

The duty to examine the bank statement is particularly important in cases where there have been multiple forgeries by the same forger, or "same wrongdoer." If a customer examines a statement and does not notify the bank of the first forgery within 30 days, the customer will be liable for future forgeries on the customer's account by the same wrongdoer. For example, in one case, a customer was not aware of 17 forged checks totaling $13,000 paid on his account over a period of four months. In the fifth month, he discovered five checks forged on his account and reported these to the bank. The customer discovered his grandson had been the forger on these checks. The customer asked the bank to credit his account for the five unauthorized payments in the fifth month. When the bank refused, the customer sued. The court held that because the customer did not review his statement in the first month and all unauthorized signatures were from the same forger, the customer could not recover any of the subsequent forgeries.

Case 29-3 provides an example of alleged unauthorized electronic transfers in which the bank asserted that the consumer schemed against the bank to falsely allege unauthorized transfers.

CASE 29-3 MERISIER v. BANK OF AMERICA

U.S. COURT OF APPEALS FOR THE 11TH DISTRICT

2012 U.S. APP. LEXIS 15784 (2012)

Caroline Merisier was a customer of Bank of America. Merisier and a group of friends all opened their checking accounts with Bank of America within six months of one another. On March 5, 2010, Merisier was in Florida when her check card was rejected because of a fraud block. Merisier then completed a fraud affidavit, in which she flagged several transactions totaling $15,775.76 as unauthorized withdrawals from her account. Bank of America investigated Merisier's claim, and denied it after the investigation had verified the earliest of the withdrawals as legitimate. The bank reasoned that there were several security verifications following fraud blocks, existing security of Merisier's debit card and PIN, exclusively PIN-based transactions, and several structured deposits into the account before the alleged fraudulent withdrawals. Based on its investigation, the bank ultimately determined that Merisier was colluding with the various friends whom she had all sign up for checking accounts at the same time with the bank, and that together, they had drawn down her account and were scheming to defraud Bank of America.

On September 8, 2010, Merisier filed an instant action suit against Bank of America, asserting that the bank failed to conduct a reasonable investigation of her claim, and failed to follow the Electronic Fund Transfer Act's claim resolution procedures, consequently holding her unlawfully liable for unauthorized transactions. Merisier claimed that she was entitled to recover the damages of the unauthorized electronic funds withdrawn from her account. The District Court found that Bank of America was not liable for the amount withdrawn from Merisier's account. On appeal, Merisier contended that the District Court erred in finding that Bank of America did not violate any provision of EFTA.

JUDGE TJOFLAT: This is a case under the Electronic Fund Transfer Act ("EFTA"). A bank customer sued her bank to recover for unauthorized withdrawals from her checking account, made using her check card and personal identification number ("PIN"). EFTA requires a bank to investigate such disputed transactions, to notify the customer if it has verified the transactions as authorized, and to re-credit the account if the withdrawals were unauthorized; failure to do so renders the bank liable to the customer for up to treble damages. The bank investigated the withdrawals at issue in this case, found that they were the product of a scheme to defraud the bank, and denied liability for the withdrawals.

After a two-day bench trial, the District Court rejected the customer's EFTA claims and entered judgment for the bank. Specifically, the District Court found that the transactions were authorized because they were part of a scheme to defraud the bank. The customer appealed. Although the briefs are inartfully drawn, she appears to challenge the District Court's finding as clearly erroneous. . . . On appeal, Merisier contends that the District Court erred in finding that Bank of America did not violate any provision of EFTA. In this respect, Merisier argues that the District Court applied the wrong burden of proof to her at trial, contending that, under EFTA, Bank of America bore the burden to demonstrate the transfers were authorized. Essentially, she maintains that the District Court's finding that the subject transactions were authorized was clearly erroneous. She contends the District Court mistakenly considered the following factors because they were mischaracterized by the trial judge or irrelevant: (a) evidence of a scheme to defraud; (b) ostensible evasion of cash-deposit reporting requirements; and (c) the source of the deposits to Merisier's account.

EFTA requires banks to follow one of two paths in response to such an alleged error on an account: (1) to investigate and correct the error if an unauthorized transfer has occurred, or (2) to investigate and inform the customer that no error occurred if the transfer was authorized by the customer. The bank followed the steps of path (2) after it determined that Merisier had in fact authorized the transactions at issue. Merisier thinks the bank ought to have followed path (1) because she insists to this day that the disputed transactions were unauthorized. She thinks the District Court improperly forced her to prove the bank ought to have followed path (1) and found for the bank when she did not. . . .

On appeal, Merisier has advanced no reason to disturb the District Court's findings. That the transactions were authorized is a factual determination that we will reverse only for clear error. "A finding is clearly erroneous 'when although there is evidence to support it, the reviewing court on the entire evidence is left with the definite and firm conviction that a mistake has been committed.'" Merisier has failed to make such a showing; her arguments focus on her perception that the District Court erroneously required her to prove that the withdrawals were unauthorized. It is thus undisputed that substantial evidence supports the District Court's finding that the transactions were authorized. See id. We are thus left with no "definite and firm conviction that a mistake has been committed." The District Court therefore did not err in finding that the transactions were authorized and, consequently, that Bank of America had not violated EFTA. . . . After thorough review, we find no error and therefore affirm.

Judgment of the District Court is AFFIRMED.

[continued]

CRITICAL THINKING

The court ruled that on the basis of the evidence provided by Bank of America, the plaintiff's transactions were in fact authorized. Can you think of anything problematic about the evidence provided by Bank of America to conclude that Merisier's transactions were authorized? What evidence could Merisier have provided the court that may have changed the court's ruling in the bank's favor?

ETHICAL DECISION MAKING

Take a look at the WPH framework and attempt to think of an ethical justification for this ruling. What value do you think is at play in regard to the purpose of the Electronic Fund Transfer Act?

Again, if the bank was negligent in paying the forged checks, the customer's liability for the checks may be diminished through comparative negligence [UCC 4-406(e)]. Regardless of the 30-day requirement for multiple forgeries or the care used in cashing a check, a customer must report a forgery within one year from the date the statement is available to the customer or he will lose the right to recover this money [UCC 4-406(f)].

Finally, because a drawer is generally not liable for a forged check, the bank must credit a drawer's account for a paid forged check. The bank would likely then try to recover the money from the forger; a forged signature is effective as the signature of the forger [UCC 3-403(a)]. In other words, if Christina Simpson forges Ricky McIntyre's signature on his check, forging "Ricky McIntyre" functions to make Christina liable for the amount of the check.

Checks Bearing Forged Endorsements. If a bank pays a check that has been fraudulently endorsed, who is responsible? In the same way that a drawer is not responsible for a check that bears the drawer's forged signature, the drawer is similarly not responsible for a check that has been fraudulently endorsed. Generally, when an endorsement has been forged, the first party to accept the forged instrument is ultimately liable for the loss because a forged endorsement does not legally transfer title [UCC 4-207(a)(2)]. However, the drawer again has a duty to examine her statement for fraudulent endorsements and then notify the bank. As such, the drawer must report all forged endorsements within a three-year period after the customer was returned the forged items or given his or her statement containing the forged items. If the customer does not report the forgery within three years, the bank is no longer liable for the customer's loss (UCC 4-111).

Altered Checks. Remember, under the properly payable rule, a bank is to pay only those checks that are authorized. When a party makes an unauthorized change or alteration to a check, the check becomes unauthorized. The UCC defines **alteration** as a change (without consent) that modifies the obligation of a party to the instrument. Generally, if a bank pays a check that has been altered, the bank will be liable for the alteration.

For example, suppose a drawer writes a check for $5. The payee changes the amount paid to $55 and presents the check for payment. The bank pays $55 to the payee. The drawer discovers the alteration on his statement and reports it to the bank. The bank will then credit the drawer's account with $50; the drawer remains liable for the original amount of the check. The bank is liable for the $50 (UCC 4-111).

Again, a customer's substantial contribution to the alteration will limit the customer's ability to require that the bank credit his or her account. In other words, if the customer leaves large blank spaces open on the check so that another party may easily alter the check, the customer will likely be liable for the altered amount of the check. Similarly, suppose you, as a business manager, send an employee to purchase some supplies for a company picnic. You give the employee a check payable to the store, but you do not fill in

E-COMMERCE AND THE LAW

NEW TECHNOLOGY A WIN-WIN FOR ATM USERS AND FINANCIAL INSTITUTIONS

VSoft Corporation provides technological solutions to financial institutions. VSoft has released software that captures images at ATM locations. These images are used for processing and image exchange. The significance of this software is that it makes ATM envelopes unnecessary. Financial institutions with the VSoft technology capture a check image and related data at the ATM, and then integrate that information with validation from back-office operations. Banks can now engage in virtual sorting and deposit review. The software provides customers with a receipt that includes an image of the deposited check. This software promises service and convenience to customers. It also reduces the financial institution's operating costs and reduces opportunities for fraud.

Source: "VSoft Announces the New 5.20 Release of Its Centrum Gateway TM-ATM Software," *Business Wire*, September 17, 2008.

the dollar amount of the check. The employee then writes in an amount that is $20 more than the total cost of the goods and asks for $20 in cash back. You do not become aware of the employee's action until you receive your bank statement. Under the UCC, any drawer who leaves the dollar amount blank may not later protest paying whatever amount has been written on the check [4-401(d)(2)].

As in the case of forged signatures, the customer's duty to examine his bank statement also applies to looking for altered checks. Thus, if the customer does not discover the altered check or does not report the altered check within a reasonable time, the bank's liability for the altered check is reduced. Similarly, if both the customer and the bank are negligent in contributing to and paying an altered check, both parties will be responsible for a portion of the check.

Moreover, if a bank proves that losses from later altered checks occurred due to the customer's failure to identify and report the illegally altered checks, the bank will have a reduced liability due to the customer's contributory negligence (UCC 4-406). The bank may assert the defense of contributory negligence only if the bank exercised ordinary care (adherence to standard practices in the industry) when it cashed the altered check.

Electronic Fund Transfers

L05 What are the different types of electronic fund transfers?

The application of technology to the banking system has made the banking process more efficient and less reliant on paperwork. When money is transferred by an electronic terminal, telephone, or computer, this transfer is called an **electronic fund transfer (EFT).** Consumer fund transfers are governed by the Electronic Fund Transfer Act of 1978, while commercial electronic fund transfers are governed by Article 4(A) of the UCC. By 1996, all 50 states had adopted Article 4(A).

TYPES OF EFT SYSTEMS

The most common types of electronic fund systems are automated teller machines, point-of-sale systems, direct deposits and withdrawals, pay-by-telephone systems, and online systems. (See Exhibit 29-8.)

Automated Teller Machines. **Automated teller machines (ATMs),** machines connected to a bank's computer, are located in convenient places so that customers may conduct banking transactions without actually going into a bank. Customers may withdraw and deposit money, as well as check the balance of their savings and checking accounts. Customers use an ATM bank card and a personal identification number to access their accounts through the ATM.

Point-of-Sale Systems. A **point-of-sale system** allows a consumer to directly transfer funds from a banking account to a merchant. For example, Jay buys a CD from Best Buy

Exhibit 29-8
Types of Electronic Fund Transfer Systems

Automated teller machines (ATMs)	Convenient electronic teller machines allow customers to conduct banking transactions without going to a bank.
Point of sale	Using a debit card, customers can transfer funds directly out of their accounts to the merchant's account.
Pay by telephone	Customers can make payments or transfer funds between accounts over the phone.
Online banking	Customers can make payments or transfer funds between accounts online.
Direct deposits and withdrawals	Customers can preauthorize deposits and withdrawals performed on their accounts electronically.

and pays for the CD with his debit card. The Best Buy employee swipes Jay's debit card to determine whether there are enough funds in Jay's account to pay for the CD. Jay signs a receipt like a credit card receipt, and the amount of the sale is charged to Jay's bank account.

Direct Deposits and Withdrawals. A **direct deposit** or withdrawal is a preauthorized action performed on a customer's account through an electronic terminal. For example, an employee may now choose to have her paycheck directly deposited into her checking account instead of receiving a check from the employer. A customer can similarly authorize a direct withdrawal. For instance, a customer might have his phone bill directly withdrawn from his bank account each month.

To see the issues involved with direct-deposit employee payment, please see the **Connecting to the Core** activity on the text website at www.mhhe.com/kubasek3e.

Pay-by-Telephone Systems. Some merchants allow customers to use the telephone to make payments or transfer funds. For example, a customer may transfer money from a savings account to a checking account over the phone. Moreover, the IRS permits taxpayers to file and pay over the telephone.

Online Payments and Banking. Various banks and credit card companies allow customers to engage in banking transactions online. Customers may access their account statements and transfer funds online. Similarly, credit card companies allow customers to make monthly payments. Companies are moving toward offering more and more online services.

CONSUMER FUND TRANSFERS

Consumer fund transactions are governed by the *Electronic Fund Transfer Act of 1978 (EFTA).* This act sets out the rights and liabilities of the parties involved in electronic fund transfers. Regulation E of the act allows the Federal Reserve Board to issue rules and regulations to enforce EFTA. The following transactions are considered consumer fund transactions: transactions in which a retail customer pays for an item with a debit card that allows the customer's bank account to be instantly charged, ATM transactions, and direct deposits of paychecks.

Customer and Bank Rights and Responsibilities. EFTA requires that merchants inform customers of their rights regarding EFTs. First, if a customer's ATM card is lost or stolen, the customer must notify the bank within two days. The customer is then liable for only the first $50 stolen. If the customer does not notify the bank, the customer will then be held liable for up to $500 that is stolen. Second, the bank has a duty to provide a monthly statement that includes electronic fund transfers, and the customer has a duty to examine this bank statement for any unauthorized electronic fund transfers or errors.

Third, the customer has a duty to notify the bank of any errors in the electronic transactions within 60 days of receiving the statement. Fourth, a bank is required to provide customers with receipts for electronic transactions. Fifth, the bank must notify the customer that preauthorized payments may be stopped; however, the customer must stop the payment by notifying the bank at any time up to three days before the preauthorized payment is scheduled. While a customer may stop a preauthorized payment, a customer cannot order a stop payment on an EFT because such transfers occur instantaneously.

Unauthorized Transfers. Under EFTA, an unauthorized electronic transfer is a federal felony punishable through criminal sanctions, such as a $10,000 fine or 10-year prison sentence. An electronic transfer is unauthorized if (1) it is initiated by a person who has no authority to transfer, (2) the customer receives no benefit from the transfer, and (3) the customer did not give his personal identification number to the unauthorized party.

When banks violate EFTA, consumers may recover actual and punitive damages, where the punitive damages total between $100 and $1,000. If the consumers are part of a class action suit, the punitive damages are capped at $500,000 or 1 percent of the institution's net worth.

As suggested in the Case Opener, the relationship between a bank and its customers is quite complicated. When a customer opens an account at a bank, he or she creates a contractual relationship with the bank. Within this relationship, both the customer and the bank have certain rights and duties. This relationship is governed by Article 4 of the UCC. For example, the customer has the right to order a stop payment on a check for any or no reason. The corresponding duty of the bank is to follow this order.

COMMERCIAL FUND TRANSFERS

Because EFTA did not cover all situations in which funds may be electronically transferred, Article 4(A) of the UCC was issued to address commercial fund transfers. An important type of commercial fund transfer is a wire transfer. Funds are "wired" between two commercial parties. There are two major payment systems that coordinate wire payments: the Federal Reserve wire transfer network (Fedwire) and the New York Clearing House Interbank Payments Systems (CHIPS). These two systems account for the transfer of more than $1 trillion daily. This sum is substantially more than is transferred by any other means.

E-Money and Online Banking

With the rapid advancements in technology, the banking system is also finding itself changing rapidly. Electronic payments, or e-payments, are becoming increasingly prevalent in daily life. Increasingly, bank transactions are being conducted electronically, marking a shift away from physical currency. In fact, it is possible for electronic forms of money to completely replace physical currency such as paper and coin money. **Digital cash,** money stored electronically on microchips, magnetic strips, or other computer media, would allow for the elimination of physical currency.

Helping to lead the digital banking revolution are the various forms of **e-money** (electronic money). The most common example of e-money is **stored-value cards.** Stored-value cards are typically plastic cards that contain a magnetic strip. The magnetic strip, similar to the ones on credit cards and ATM cards, contains data regarding the value of the card. For example, suppose a new laundry facility opened up near your apartment. However, instead of your using quarters, the facility requires that you get a card and use a machine to put a balance on the card. Then, when you are ready to do your laundry, you insert the card into the washer and the cost of a load of laundry is deducted automatically from the card. Because the information regarding the amount on the card is stored in the magnetic strip on the card, the card is referred to as a *stored-value card.*

Another, newer, type of e-money is the **smart card.** Smart cards are the same size as regular check and ATM cards and look the same from the front. However, instead of having a magnetic strip, smart cards contain microchips for storing data. The advantage of the microchip over the magnetic strip is that the microchip can hold a far greater amount of data than a magnetic strip. However, because this is still a new technology, not all businesses are equipped to read smart cards yet. As the technology expands, expect to see a large influx in the use of smart cards.

Related to the expansion of technology in banking is the increase in use of online banking. With online banking, banks allow customers electronic access to their accounts so that they can check their accounts, transfer money, order payments, pay bills, check their investments, and, through some banks, even trade stock. While services vary from bank to bank, more banks are offering at least some form of online banking to their customers.

ONLINE BANKING SERVICES

There are three services most banks with online banking offer. These three services are (1) bill consolidation and payment, (2) transfer of funds from one account to another, and (3) loan applications (an appearance at the bank to sign the loan is typically required to finalize the loan process). By offering these three services, banks help cut down on their own costs as well as allow customers greater control over their funds.

Despite the number of banking services offered online, not all banking services can be conducted over the Internet. For example, depositing and withdrawing funds are two services that cannot be conducted from a computer with an Internet connection. However, the smart-card technology might allow for withdrawals and deposits from home computers hooked up to the Internet. The microchips in the smart cards could be read by devices attached to a home computer, allowing for withdrawals or deposits; but this technology has not yet been developed and marketed to consumers.

REGULATORY COMPLIANCE

In the main, banks are in favor of the increased use of online banking. Part of the reason banks like online banking is that it helps reduce the bank's operating cost and thus increase its profits. One way online banking reduces cost is through paperless billing. By not having to send paper statements to their customers, banks save on paper, ink, and envelopes, as well as postage. The bank posts all the information to the user's account online, which does not cost the bank much at all.

Another reason banks are in favor of online banking is that it decreases what is known as "float" time. *Float time* is the period between the time a check is written and the time it is presented for final payment, during which a customer can still use his or her funds. As the check does not have to transfer between banks, accounts can be credited or debited more quickly.

However, as with other areas of the Internet, it is not clear which laws apply to online banking. Part of the problem is related to the legal definition of *bank.* Banks are required by law to have a geographically defined market area, as well as to report to the proper authorities regarding their deposits and loans. These requirements are designed to ensure that all Americans have access to banks and that banks are not discriminating by choosing only certain locations for operation. The requirements are established primarily in two pieces of legislation: the Home Mortgage Disclosure Act, 12 U.S.C. Sections 2801–2810, and the Community Reinvestment Act (CRA) of 1977, 12 U.S.C. Sections 2901–2908. The CRA requires that a bank's market area surround the bank and be divided on the basis of normal divisions, such as standard metropolitan areas or county lines.

The requirement of a defined market area poses a problem for cyberbanks. How exactly would a cyberbank establish a geographic market region? Consequently, banks with online services are in a bit of a gray area when it comes to legal compliance. Not only is it hard for such banks to comply with the Home Mortgage Disclosure Act and the CRA, but it is not yet clear if these banks need to comply with these two laws.

PRIVACY PROTECTION

Are e-money institutions the same as traditional financial institutions? Do the same laws apply? These two questions hold the key to the question: How secure are e-payments and e-money? The answer is, "We do not know."

E-Money Payment Information. Which laws apply to e-money is still mostly untested legal ground. That is, there is little clarity regarding which laws do apply to e-money. The Federal Reserve has explicitly stated that Regulation E, which regulates traditional electronic fund transfers, does not apply to e-money transactions. Nonetheless, laws regarding computer files, not directly related to banking, might apply to e-money, such as laws against unauthorized access of electronic files or communication. There are several such laws regarding electronic files and communication, and it is not clear if they apply to e-money.

E-Money Issuer's Financial Records. In 1978 Congress passed the *Right to Financial Privacy Act* [12 U.S.C. Section 3401 et seq.]. Under this act, financial institutions, such as banks, may not give a federal agency information regarding a person's finances without either that person's explicit consent or a warrant. The Right to Financial Privacy Act may apply to digital cash providers if the provider is considered a legal bank or credit provider that supplies customers with a card considered to be similar to a credit or debit card. However, given the lack of a physical location for the digital cash provider, it is also possible that the Right to Financial Privacy Act does not apply, in which case digital cash providers may release your financial information freely to any federal agency.

Consumer Financial Data. In an effort to further protect people's financial privacy, Congress passed the *Financial Services Modernization Act,* also known as the *Gramm-Leach-Bliley Act* (12 U.S.C. Sections 24a, 248b, 1820a, 1828b). The act's purpose is to control how financial institutions handle customer information, ultimately providing greater privacy protections to financial institution customers. Financial institutions are prohibited from disclosing personal information about their clients to third parties unless certain requirements set forth in the act are met. In addition, financial institutions are legally required to present customers with the institution's privacy policies and practices.

CASE OPENER WRAP-UP

Fraudulent Electronic Fund Transfers

On August 4, 2011, the district court granted Ocean Bank's motion for summary judgment on all six counts of Patco's complaint and denied Patco's motion for summary judgment on Count I of liability under the UCC. On September 6, 2011, Patco appealed.

On appeal, the court found that the bank failed to introduce additional security measures, despite the fact that these additional security measures are common in the industry and are easy to implement. Further, the court ruled that this failure to implement additional security measures was especially unreasonable given that the bank was knowledgeable about ongoing fraud with electronic fund transfers. The court advised that "when Ocean Bank had warning that such fraud was likely occurring with a transaction, the bank should have monitored that transaction, and provided notice to its customers." In conclusion, the appellate court rendered Ocean Bank's security procedures commercially unreasonable under the standards of Article 4(A) of the UCC, and it reversed the district court's grant of summary judgment in favor of the bank.

However, the appellate court reversed only part of the district court's decision. In addition to the reversal of the summary judgment in favor of the bank, the appellate court also affirmed the district court's denial of Patco's motion for summary judgment. The court argued that there remained several disputed issues of fact that may be material to determining whether Patco satisfied its own obligations under the UCC. Thus, the court left these questions open for remand, especially for the purposes of mitigation of damages.

KEY TERMS

alteration 648
automated teller machines (ATMs) 649
cashier's check 631
certified check 634
check 630
collecting bank 636
depositary bank 636
digital cash 651
direct deposit 650
draft 630
drawee 630
drawer 630
electronic fund transfer (EFT) 649
e-money 651
intermediary bank 636
money orders 632
overdraft 642
payee 630
payor bank 636
point-of-sale system 649
smart card 652
stale check 644
stop-payment order 642
stored-value cards 651
teller's check 632
traveler's check 632

SUMMARY OF KEY TOPICS

Checks

Draft: An instrument that is an order.

Drawer: The party that gives the order.

Drawee: The party that must obey the order.

Payee: The party that receives the benefit of the order.

Check: A special draft that orders the drawee, a bank, to pay a fixed amount of money on demand.

Cashier's check: A check for which both the drawer and the drawee of a check are the same bank.

Teller's check: A check that is drawn by one bank and usually drawn on another bank.

Traveler's check: An instrument that is payable on demand, is drawn on or through a bank, is designated by the phrase *traveler's check,* and requires a countersignature by a person whose signature appears on the instrument.

Money order: An instrument stating that a certain amount of money is to be paid to a particular person.

Certified check: A check that is accepted at the bank at which it is drawn.

Accepting Deposits

Depositary bank: The first bank that receives a check for payment.

Payor bank: The bank on which a check is drawn.

Collecting bank: Any kind of bank (besides the payor bank) that handles a check during the collection process.

Intermediary bank: Any bank (besides the payor bank and depositary bank) to which the check is transferred.

When a Bank May Charge a Customer's Account

Properly payable rule: A bank may pay an instrument only when it is authorized by the drawer and does not violate the agreement between the bank and the customer.

Wrongful dishonor: A bank refuses to pay a properly payable check; the bank incurs liability.

Overdraft: If there are insufficient funds in the customer's account, the bank may (1) dishonor the check or (2) create an overdraft by paying the check and charging the account the amount short.

Stop-payment order: A drawer orders the drawee bank to not pay a check that has been drawn on the customer's account.

Postdated check: A customer can postdate a check but must give the bank notice of the postdated check.

Stale check: A check is not presented to a bank within six months of its date.

Forgeries and alterations:

1. *Check bearing a forged signature:* Generally, the drawer is not liable for a forged check unless the drawer substantially contributed to the forgery.
2. *Check bearing a forged endorsement:* Neither the drawer nor the drawer's bank is liable for a forged endorsement.
3. *Altered check:* If an unauthorized change modifies the obligation of a party to the instrument, the drawer is generally not liable for the altered amount unless he or she negligently contributed to the alteration.

Electronic Fund Transfers

Money is transferred by an electronic terminal, telephone, or computer.

Types of EFT systems:

ATMs (automated teller machines): Machines connected to a bank's computer, located in convenient places, that allow customers to conduct banking transactions without actually going into a bank.

Point-of-sale system: System that allows a consumer to directly transfer funds from a bank account to a merchant.

Direct deposits and withdrawals: Preauthorized actions performed on a customer's account through an electronic terminal.

Pay-by-telephone system: System whereby merchants allow customers to use the telephone to make payments or transfer funds.

Online banking: System in which banks grant customers electronic access to account data to perform banking tasks, such as transferring funds between accounts, online.

E-Money and Online Banking

Digital cash: Money stored electronically on microchips, magnetic strips, or other computer media.

Stored-value cards: Plastic cards that have magnetic strips, similar to those on credit cards or ATM cards, containing data regarding the value of the card.

Smart cards: Cards that are the same size as regular check and ATM cards but that contain microchips, instead of a magnetic strip, for storing larger amounts of data.

POINT / COUNTERPOINT

Should a Company Be Allowed to Require that Employees Receive Payment through Direct Deposit?

YES

A company should be allowed to require that employees receive payment through direct deposit because direct-deposit payment is the most efficient form of payment for both employers and employees.

Direct deposit allows employers and employees security they would not have with mailed paychecks. Companies can keep track of employee payments more accurately when employees are paid through one payment method.

Through direct deposit, employers are assured that *all employees* are paid at the same time, on the same day. Neither employees nor employers need to be concerned with lost, stolen, delayed, or damaged paychecks.

Many people have already chosen the convenience of online banking for their other banking needs; adding direct deposit only simplifies their lives. In fact, studies show that the average worker spends between 8.5 and 24 hours each year cashing and depositing payroll checks.*

Direct deposit allows for a separate payroll account and more exact bookkeeping. The losses normally associated with stolen and doubled paychecks can be reinvested in the company, eventually allowing for potential salary/wage increases for all. Furthermore, a company saves a lot of money on paper costs alone by switching to direct deposit.

Many people willingly choose to directly deposit their paychecks. A company establishing a requirement of direct-deposit payment would only streamline and simplify the process for everyone involved.

NO

A company should not be allowed to require that its employees receive payment through direct deposit. While direct deposit is a good option for employers to provide to employees, the choice of payment form should be left to the employees.

First, very few guidelines have been established regarding direct-deposit procedures. Employees would not necessarily be provided an in-depth statement discussing the details of each pay period. With direct deposit, employees have more difficulty ensuring that pay statements are accurate.

Wage-based employees, for example, need to know exactly what they are paid per hour, for how many hours, so that the employees know whether they need to be paid overtime wages. Some direct-deposit statements list only the amount of money transferred to the employee's account.

Some employees simply prefer to literally hold and personally deposit a physical check. They also have a physical copy of their pay stub for paper records. The absence of a physical receipt creates "holes" in an individual's paper records. These holes can create problems when an individual gathers documents in preparation for tax season.

Direct deposit can also cause problems with an individual's banking practices. When money is automatically (though sometimes not regularly) deposited, the individual can have difficulty keeping track of deductions and bank account balances.

While companies can and should present to employees a list of the advantages of direct deposit, the ultimate decision should be left to the employees, because the employees are most heavily affected if their paychecks are not deposited properly.

*www.msmoney.com.

QUESTIONS & PROBLEMS

1. Who are the three parties involved in the transfer of money through a check?
2. What types of banks are involved in the check collection process? How are these banks different?
3. Explain the reason for the following policy: "A customer has a duty to examine his or her bank statement."
4. Evaluate the following statement: "If a signature on a check is forged, the customer will never be responsible for the amount on the check."
5. Dustin Barwick is a resident of Arkansas who in 2009 married Lucy Sheets. Sheets then proceeded to purchase insurance from GEICO Co. GEICO is an insurance agency that issues automobile insurance to individuals along with the option of medical coverage. In applying for this insurance, Sheets waived the section including medical coverage in case of an accident. In early 2010, Barwick was hit by another car and then proceeded to submit a claim to GEICO for reimbursement in the amount of $6,284. Barwick was denied reimbursement with the reasoning that his spouse, electronically, denied medical coverage. Her signature, according to GEICO, was binding and therefore Barwick could not receive the benefit. Is an electronic signature enough to validate a document? If so, under what act or acts does this fall? [*Barwick v. GEICO,* 10-1076 (Ark. S. Ct. 2011).]
6. Mary Christelle, the mother of the president of Essential Technologies of Illinois (ETI), purchased a $50,000 cashier's check from Charter One Bank payable to ETI. Subsequently, ETI deposited the check in its MidAmerica Bank account. Four days later, Mary Christelle asked Charter One to stop payment on the check. Charter One issued a stop-payment order on the cashier's check, and it then refused to honor the check when MidAmerica presented it for payment. Charter One returned it to MidAmerica stamped with "stop payment." MidAmerica then removed $50,000 from ETI's account to recover the money from the stop-payment check. After removing the $50,000, ETI's account was closed due to a negative balance after additional deposited checks were returned for insufficient funds. In 2006, MidAmerica filed suit against Charter One to recover the value of the check. MidAmerica alleged that Charter One wrongfully stopped payment on the cashier's check. A worker for Charter One testified that Charter One permits stop-payment orders on a cashier's check only if the check is lost, destroyed, or stolen and that bank policy permits it to seek indemnification from the person who placed the stop-payment order. The bank also requires an affidavit to support the stop-payment order, but Charter One did not have an affidavit in this case. Do you think the court ruled in favor of Charter One or MidAmerica in regard to the stop payment and dishonoring of the cashier's check? Would any additional information help you reach your conclusion? [*MidAmerica Bank v. Charter One Bank,* 232 Ill. 2d 560, 905 N.E.2d 839 (2009).]
7. Casey Anthony, a Florida resident, has recently gained "fame" in the murder trial of her daughter, Kaylee. Among the charges brought against Anthony in court were check fraud and murder. The check fraud charge came about after an investigation revealed that Anthony had stolen the checkbook of her friend, Amy Huizenga, and written checks amounting to $650. She wrote the checks to pay her bills, without Huizenga's knowledge. Anthony received no additional jail time and was ordered to serve one year probation. What topics of this chapter can we apply to this case? [*Anthony v. State of Florida,* 11-2357 (Fla. Dist. Ct. App. 2012).].
8. Nicholas Fredich placed an advertisement in a newspaper seeking applications for the job of bookkeeper. He then stole the résumé and identity of one of the respondents and used the person's information to apply for a bookkeeping position at Clean World Engineering, Ltd. After two weeks of working at Clean World, he claimed he had an emergency and he took several days off. Then it was discovered that many checks were missing and Fredich had forged the checks. Fredich had complete access to the checks during his employment at Clean World. Some of these forged checks were deposited into a bank and paid by MidAmerica Bank. MidAmerica did not contest the fact that it paid the checks bearing the forged signatures, but it

argued that Clean World did not exercise ordinary care. Given these facts, who should bear the loss, MidAmerica or Clean World? [*Clean World Engineering, Ltd. v. MidAmerica Federal Savings Bank,* 341 Ill. App. 3d 992, 793 N.E.2d 110 (2003).]

9. In January 2008, $243,000 was transferred from William Ryder's account at Universal City Studios Credit Union to a bank in Hong Kong. The credit union said that someone who identified himself as Ryder called to change a telephone number supposedly associated with the account. The caller identified Ryder's date of birth, Social Security number, and mother's maiden name, as well as certain account activity. Five days later a wire transfer of funds from Ryder's line of credit to the Hong Kong account was received. After verification of the signature on the Fax, the credit union called the new telephone number to verify the request from a person who said he was Ryder. The transfer was made. The credit union submitted a claim to its insurance company for the amount of the transfer. The insurance company refused to pay because the security agreement with the credit union required that wire transfers be made through a secure telephone number that had been in place for at least 30 days prior to the transfer request. Would a court decision allowing the credit union to collect advance any values important to market exchange? [*Universal City Studios Credit Union v. CUMIS Insurance Society, Inc.*, B226868 (Cal. App. 2d 2012).]

10. On November 30, 2000, Walmart issued a check made payable to Alcon Laboratories, Inc., in the amount of $563,288.95, written on a Wachovia Bank checking account. Walmart mailed the check, but Alcon never received it. On December 7, 2000, an individual named Pit Foo Wong deposited the check in his account at Asia Bank. The payee on the check had been altered from "Alcon Laboratories, Inc." to "Pit Foo Wong." In accordance with Federal Reserve procedures, Asia Bank presented the check to the Federal Reserve Bank (FRB) of New York, which then presented the check to the FRB in Richmond. On December 8, 2000, the FRB presented the check to Wachovia, and Wachovia issued payment. Wachovia, in accordance with its internal policy, did not manually review the copy of the check presented by the FRB. However, it did review the check information through an electronic tracking system. No fraud was detected at this time. Although the employees at Asia Bank allowed Wong to deposit the check, their suspicions were aroused by his deposit of over $500,000 and a hold was placed on the funds. Asia Bank twice contacted Walmart, which informed Asia Bank that the check was "good." After Alcon determined that it had not received the check, Alcon called Walmart. Walmart indicated that the check had been paid and that its policy was to wait 30 days before tracing missing checks. When Walmart discovered that the Alcon check had been altered, it notified Wachovia, which sought reimbursement from Asia Bank. By this time the hold had expired and Wong wired the money out of his account. Asia Bank refused to reimburse Wachovia, and Wachovia brought suit against the FRB for breach of presentment and transfer warranties under the UCC and federal regulations. The FRB filed a third-party complaint against Walmart, alleging that Walmart's failure to exercise ordinary care substantially contributed to the alteration of the check. The district court granted summary judgment in favor of both Wachovia and Walmart. The parties appealed. How do you think the court ruled on appeal? Should Walmart have detected the alteration earlier? [*Wachovia Bank, N.A. v. FRB,* 338 F.3d 318 (2003).]

Looking for more review materials?

The Online Learning Center at **www.mhhe.com/kubasek3e** contains this chapter's "Assignment on the Internet" and also a list of URLs for more information, entitled "On the Internet." Find both of them in the Student Center portion of the OLC, along with quizzes and other helpful materials.

Secured Transactions

CHAPTER

30

LEARNING OBJECTIVES

After reading this chapter, you will be able to answer the following questions:

1 What are the important definitions associated with secured transactions?

2 How are secured interests created?

3 How are secured interests perfected?

4 What is the scope of a security interest?

5 How are disputes regarding priority handled?

6 What is default?

CASE OPENER

Onyx Acceptance Corporation

On July 6, 2000, Shannon Hicklin purchased a 1993 Ford Explorer under an installment sale contract. Payments under the contract were assigned to Onyx Acceptance Corporation. Hicklin fell behind in payments, and on February 11, 2004, Onyx repossessed the vehicle. Hicklin was three payments past due and owed $5,741.65 under the contract.

At the time of repossession, the fair market value of the vehicle was $2,335 after deducting $1,365 in needed repairs and accounting for mileage. The vehicle was sold for $1,500 at private auction. After deducting the sales proceeds from the costs of repossession and sale and the contract balance, there remained a deficiency of $5,018.88. Onyx sued Hicklin to collect the deficiency. Hicklin denied liability on the ground that Onyx failed to sell the vehicle in a commercially reasonable manner as required by the Uniform Commercial Code.

1. If you were the judge deciding this case, would you grant Onyx the full $5,018.88 deficiency?
2. If you were the manager of Onyx, what steps would you take to secure the rights of your company to vehicles purchased on credit, and at auction sales, to vehicles subject to repossession?

The Wrap-Up at the end of the chapter will answer these questions.

The agreement between Hicklin and Onyx regarding the automobile is a common component of business transactions. Such agreements are called *secured transactions.*

Legal Principle: A secured transaction is a transaction in which the payment of a debt is guaranteed by personal property owned by the debtor.

In the case of Hicklin, she guaranteed that she would pay the debt for the purchase of the automobile by giving Onyx rights to the vehicle, including the right to sell it on repossession. In contrast, a creditor that does not have a secured interest must file a lawsuit, obtain a judgment, and execute on the judgment to recover money for an unpaid debt.

Article 9 of the Uniform Commercial Code (UCC) governs secured transactions in personal property (as opposed to real property). Thus, throughout the chapter, we will refer to Article 9 of the UCC. The National Conference of Commissioners of Uniform State Laws approved a new version of Article 9 in 1998. This version was submitted to the states in 1999 and became effective in most states in 2001. As of 2013, with some variation, all states had enacted Article 9. Thus, while the law governing secured transactions is state law, the universal adoption of Article 9 permits us to discuss laws regarding secured transactions across state lines.

In the first section of this chapter, we examine the concepts and terms associated with secured transactions. Then, in the second section, we examine how secured transactions are created. In the third section, we consider how secured parties protect their interest in collateral through perfection, and, in the fourth section, we examine the types of collateral that can be used in secured transactions. In the fifth section, we examine the various conflicts that occur among parties who have interests in secured transactions. Finally, in the sixth section, we explain the remedies associated with a debtor's default of a loan.

Important Definitions Associated with Secured Transactions

LO1

What are the important definitions associated with secured transactions?

It is important to understand the definitions of the terms used in secured transactions to understand how the transactions are created. These definitions generally come from the UCC's definition of the terms:

1. A **secured interest** is an "interest in personal property or fixtures which secures payment or performance of an obligation." Suppose Best Buy sells you a laptop on credit. Best Buy retains a secured interest in the laptop, which means that the store can repossess the laptop if you fail to make payments.
2. A **secured party** is the person or party that holds the interest in the secured property. Thus, in the example above, Best Buy is the secured party. The secured party is also known as the *secured creditor.*
3. A **debtor** is the person or party that has an obligation to the secured party. You, the laptop owner, are the debtor because you have an obligation to make payments.
4. A **security agreement** is the agreement in which the debtor gives the secured interest to the secured party. Thus, when you made the agreement with Best Buy, you created a security agreement.
5. **Collateral** is the property that is subject to the security interest. In the Best Buy example, the laptop is the collateral. Collateral may include goods (consumer goods, farm products, inventory, and equipment), indispensable paper (documents of title, negotiable instruments, and chattel paper), intangibles (accounts, goodwill, and literary rights) and proceeds.

Creation of Secured Interests

How does a creditor become a secured party? To become a secured party, the creditor must gain a security interest in the collateral of the debtor. The secured party must take three steps to create the security interest:

LO2
How are secured interests created?

1. The two parties create a security agreement and either (a) there is a record of the security agreement (usually a written agreement that describes the collateral and is signed by the debtor) or (b) the secured party is in possession of the collateral.
2. The secured party must give value to get the security agreement.
3. The debtor has a right in or to the collateral. [UCC 9-203(b)]

Once these three criteria are met, the secured party's rights attach to the collateral. When **attachment** occurs, the creditor becomes a secured party with an interest in the collateral.

WRITTEN AGREEMENT

The written agreement, often referred to as the *security agreement,* must be signed by the debtor. Moreover, the agreement must describe the collateral. The description of the collateral must be accurate and detailed enough as to reasonably identify the collateral. For example, in a description of a laptop that is serving as collateral, the serial number of the laptop might be listed in the written agreement. Let's revisit the Case Opener. The security agreement between Hicklin and Onyx most likely included the following: (1) a statement that Hicklin was buying the automobile on credit; (2) a statement that Onyx was retaining a security interest in the automobile; (3) a description of the automobile, as well as its vehicle identification number; (4) the price of the automobile and the amount of the monthly payments; and (5) a description of the process to be utilized in the event of Hicklin's default and the subsequent repossession of the vehicle by Onyx.

It is important that the collateral be clearly described in the written agreement because the creditor could otherwise lose its rights to the collateral. For example, First Source Bank loaned money to K&K Trucking to finance its acquisition of tractors and trailers. In return, K&K granted First Source a security interest in the tractors and trailers and all present and future attachments, accessories, replacement parts, repairs, additions, documents, and certificates of title, ownership, or origin and *all proceeds thereof.* K&K also borrowed money from other lenders during this period of time, and these loans were secured, in part, with K&K's accounts and accounts receivable. First Source repossessed the tractors and trailers after K&K ceased business operations and defaulted on its loans. First Source claimed a security interest in K&K's accounts receivable when the proceeds of the sale of the tractors and trailers proved inadequate to fully repay the loans. First Source contended that K&K's accounts receivable were covered by the language in the documents creating a security interest in proceeds associated with the operation of the tractors and trailers. K&K's other lenders objected and noted that their security documents specifically identified accounts and accounts receivable as collateral. The court was required to decide whether the term "proceeds" also included "accounts receivable." The court determined that proceeds constituted whatever was substituted for the original collateral as a result of its sale, exchange, or other disposition. Proceeds did not include monies generated from the use of the collateral, which included accounts receivable. As a result, the court concluded that First Source did not have a security interest in K&K's accounts receivable on the basis of its security documents.[1]

[1] *First Source Bank v. Wilson Bank & Trust,* 2012 U.S. Dist. LEXIS 143024 (M.D. Tenn., Oct. 3, 2012).

BUT WHAT IF . . .

WHAT IF THE FACTS OF THE CASE OPENER WERE DIFFERENT?

Let's say, in the Case Opener, that Hicklin and Onyx created a written agreement regarding her car as collateral for her payments. However, the agreement simply stated that a property item of Hicklin's was being used as collateral, and there was no description of the car. Would Onyx be able to use Hicklin's car as collateral?

VALUE

The secured party must give value. What exactly does it mean to "give value"? According to the UCC, value is consideration. Thus, in the Case Opener, the use of the automobile was considered the value that Onyx gave to Hicklin. Alternatively, suppose you receive a loan from a company. The money is the value given by the company, the secured party.

DEBTOR RIGHTS IN THE COLLATERAL

The final criterion necessary for the attachment of the security interest is the debtor's rights in the collateral. Hicklin, the purchaser of the automobile, had a legal right to the vehicle (the collateral) after she signed the agreement.

PURCHASE-MONEY SECURITY INTEREST

Now that we have discussed the criteria necessary for the creation of a security interest, we briefly consider one specific type of security interest, the **purchase-money security interest (PMSI),** which is formed when a debtor uses borrowed money from the secured party to buy the collateral.

Legal Principle: A purchase-money security interest is created when a debtor uses money borrowed from the secured party to purchase the collateral.

According to the UCC, a PMSI exists when a security interest is retained or taken by (1) the seller of the collateral to secure part or all of the purchase price *or* (2) a person who gives something of value to the debtor so that the debtor can gain rights to or use of the collateral (9-103). In our laptop example, you bought the laptop on credit from Best Buy. Best Buy extended credit to you for the entire purchase price of the laptop. In other words, Best Buy is lending you the money to buy the laptop. Because the laptop is the collateral, Best Buy has a PMSI.

The examples we have used in this chapter thus far have been examples of PMSIs. What is an example of a secured transaction in which the secured party does *not* have a PMSI? Suppose your company borrows money from the bank to purchase parts that will be placed into your company's product. As collateral, the bank takes a security interest in the company's deposit accounts held at the bank.

Perfected Security Interest

LO3 How are secured interests perfected?

Suppose that you borrow money from a bank, and the bank has a secured interest in your wedding ring. You are supposed to make monthly payments to the bank, but you lose your job and cannot make the payments. When you fail to make these payments, you **default** on the loan. Because the bank has a secured interest, it can repossess your ring.

Exhibit 30-1

Summary of Methods of Perfection by Type of Collateral

Perfection by Filing

1. *Chattel paper:* Writing that indicates the debtor's monetary obligation as well as a secured interest
2. *Documents of title:* Papers that demonstrate the owner's possession of the goods (e.g., warehouse receipts)
3. *Accounts:* Rights to payments for goods sold or leased
4. *General intangibles:* Trademarks, copyrights, patents
5. *Equipment:* Goods purchased primarily for business use
6. *Farm products:* Products of livestock or crops
7. *Inventory:* Goods held for sale or lease
8. *Fixtures: Goods that have become attached to real estate*

Automatic Perfection

Purchase-money security interests in consumer goods

Perfection by Possession

1. Chattel paper
2. Documents of title
3. Instruments (stocks, bonds, checks)
4. Pawnbroker holding jewelry or other valuables

Perfection of Interests in Motor Vehicles

Notation of secured interest on certificate of title

But suppose you also borrowed money from another creditor, your boss, and you used your ring as collateral for that transaction. Your boss was unaware that you used the ring as collateral for your bank loan. Both your boss and your bank have an interest in your ring. Who gets the ring? The party that *perfects* its interest in the ring will have first claim.

Legal Principle: Perfection is a series of legal steps a secured party takes to protect its right in the collateral from other creditors that wish to have their debts satisfied through the same collateral.

We consider below the various methods of perfection. (For a summary of the methods, see Exhibit 30-1.)

PERFECTION BY FILING

The most common way to perfect an interest is to file a financing statement with a state agency. According to the UCC, a **financing statement** should list the names and addresses of all the parties involved, a description of the collateral, and the signature of the debtor (9-502). First, the names and addresses of the statement are important elements because someone looking for the financing statement may wish to contact the secured party or the debtor. Second, the financing statement must be filed under the name of the debtor whether the debtor is an individual, an unincorporated business association, or a corporation. If the statement is filed under an incorrect name, the perfection is likely not effective. Third, the financing statement must include a description of the collateral. The purpose of including a description of the collateral is to inform other potential parties who might wish to lend money to the debtor. The description of the collateral may be replicated from the description of the collateral in the security agreement.

Legal Principle: A financing statement is the document utilized to perfect a security interest by filing.

Once the financing statement is filed, the statement becomes public knowledge. Parties considering making a loan to another party are expected to search for notification of secured interests. Consequently, if you asked to borrow money from your boss, your boss should check with state agencies to ensure that you have not already used your ring as collateral. If your boss discovered that your bank has perfected its interest in your ring, your boss should not agree to loan you money with the ring as your collateral because the bank's perfection of the security interest means that the ring will go directly to the bank. Your boss would have a claim against the ring only as an unsecured creditor.

Place and Duration of Filing. Suppose you need to file a financing statement. Where should you file? For how long is the filing effective? The place of filing depends on whether the debtor is an individual or a business. If the debtor is an individual, the secured party files the financing statement in the state in which the debtor resides. The actual place of filing changes from state to state. Sometimes the statements are filed with the secretary of state. Alternatively, the statements might be filed with the county clerk. Each state must establish a central filing office.

Once you have filed the financing statement with the correct agency, for how long is the statement valid? Under the UCC, the statement is valid for five years (9-515). After five years, the statement expires, and the security interest is not protected. However, within six months of the expiration date of the financing statement, the secured party can file a continuation statement, which is valid for another five years.

PERFECTION BY POSSESSION

Sometimes a debtor gives a creditor the collateral to hold until the loan is paid off. For example, suppose that you borrow money from a bank and give the bank your diamond necklace to hold until you pay back the loan.

Legal Principle: The transfer of collateral to the secured party for the purpose of perfection is called a pledge.

When the bank takes possession of the necklace, it has perfected its interest without filing a financing statement. Once you pay off the loan, the necklace is returned to you.

There are several advantages associated with perfection by possession. First, a secured party does not have to file a financing statement. In fact, the parties do not have to even create a written security agreement. Second, there is little chance that another party will loan money to the debtor relying on the collateral that another secured party possesses. Third, if the debtor defaults on the loan, the secured party already has possession of the collateral, so there are no difficulties associated with repossession.

Despite the many advantages of perfection by possession, it is often impractical because the debtor cannot benefit from the use of the collateral. For example, if you get a loan from a bank to purchase farm equipment, you likely need the farm equipment to produce crops that will enable you to make payments on the loan.

Certain types of collateral *must* be perfected through possession. These types of collateral include **instruments**—writings that serve as evidence of rights to payment of money, such as certificates of deposit—and stocks and bonds.

BUT WHAT IF . . .

WHAT IF THE FACTS OF THE CASE OPENER WERE DIFFERENT?

Let's say, in the Case Opener, that Hicklin decided to have Onyx keep her car until she completely paid the car off. What is the name of the agreement that Onyx and Hicklin made in this case?

AUTOMATIC PERFECTION

If a retailer had to file a financing statement every time it sold a laptop, a wide-screen television, or a washer and dryer on credit, the retailer would do nothing but file statements. Moreover, it does not make sense for the retailer to possess the collateral. Thus, when a creditor sells a consumer good to a debtor on a credit basis or a creditor extends a loan to a debtor for the purchase of a consumer good, the security interest in the good perfects automatically. Under the UCC, a **consumer good** is a good used or bought for use primarily for personal, family, or household purposes [9-102(23)]. Thus, if an item is purchased for business use, the security interest would not perfect automatically; the secured party would have to file a financing statement.

The example of the sale of a consumer good in the previous paragraph is an example of a PMSI. When a PMSI in a consumer good is created, the security interest is automatically perfected; the creditor does not need to file a financing statement. However, if the PMSI is in a fixture or a motor vehicle, the security interest is *not* automatically perfected.

Clearly, the designation of property as a consumer good has important business ramifications. Case 30-1 considers whether a particular good should be classified as a consumer good or business equpment.

CASE 30-1 IN RE ROBERT O. TROUPE AND DAWN LYNN TROUPE, DEBTORS

U.S. BANKRUPTCY COURT FOR THE WESTERN DISTRICT OF OKLAHOMA

340 B.R. 86 (BANKR. W.D. OKLA. 2006)

Robert and Dawn Troupe purchased a 2001 John Deere 4300 tractor on credit from Deere's dealer in July 2001. At the time of the purchase, the Troupes lived on a ten-acre tract of land in Colorado where they raised cattle and pigs. The Troupes told the Deere dealer's salesman that they wanted to purchase the tractor for personal use on their property. The Troupes financed the $16,539 purchase price through financing extended by Deere. The Troupes and Deere executed a security agreement by which the Troupes granted to Deere a purchase money security interest in the tractor. At the top of the first page of the executed security agreement, there were boxes labeled "Personal" and "Commercial," respectively. An "x" was placed in the box labeled "Personal," while the "Commercial" box was left blank. The security agreement also contained the Troupes' certification that the transaction was a consumer credit transaction and the tractor would be used primarily for personal, family, or household purposes.

The Troupes filed for bankruptcy in September 2004. The trustee in bankruptcy filed a proceeding seeking to avoid Deere's security interest in the tractor. The trustee claimed that Deere's failure to file a financing statement rendered its purchase money security interest unperfected. The trustee asserted that the tractor was used and intended to be used for business purposes and thus was not a consumer good under Article 9 of the UCC. His contention was based upon the Troupes' tax returns in which they stated the tractor was used entirely for business and their statement at the time of the bankruptcy proceeding that their actual and intended use of the tractor was for the business purpose of farming and ranching. Deere maintained that the Troupes' primary intended and actual use of the tractor was for personal, family, and household purposes and hence was consumer goods. The issue for the court was whether the tractor was a consumer good under Article 9 such that Deere's security interest was perfected despite the absence of a filed financing statement.

CHIEF BANKRUPTCY JUDGE WEAVER: In bankruptcy proceedings, state law governs issues of validity and priority of security interests. The parties do not dispute that Colorado law applies here. Under C.R.S. § 4-9-317(a)(2), the holder of an unperfected security interest is subordinate to the rights of one who became a lien creditor before the security interest was perfected. A lien creditor includes a trustee in bankruptcy. C.R.S. §4-9-102(a)(52). Thus, Deere must have held a perfected security interest to prevail over the trustee in bankruptcy. It is not disputed that if the tractor is classified as consumer goods under the UCC, Deere held a perfected purchase money security interest despite the fact that a financing statement was not filed. C.R.S. §4-9-309(1). If the tractor is not consumer goods, however, Deere is not perfected. C.R.S. §4-9-310.

Consumer goods are "goods that are used or bought for use primarily for personal, family or household purposes." C.R.S. §4-9-102(a)(23). The other possible classification for the tractor, and the one supported by the trustee is that of equipment. Equipment is defined as "goods other than inventory, farm products or consumer goods" C.R.S. § 4-9-102(a)(33).

The classification of collateral is to be determined as of the time of the creation of the security interest. The classification does not change because of a later change in the manner in which the collateral is used. If the law were otherwise, a secured party would be required to continually monitor the use that was being made of the collateral.

From reviewing the affidavits of the debtors submitted in support of the trustee's motion for summary judgment, and their deposition testimony, it is not completely clear what oral representations the debtors may have made to Deere's dealer regarding their intended use of the collateral. . . . Yet nowhere in the debtors' sworn testimony is there any evidence that they told Deere's representative that the tractor was to be used in any type of commercial activity.

The security agreement that the debtors signed reflected that it was a "Personal" rather than a "Commercial" transaction. The body of the document stated unequivocally that it was a consumer credit transaction and that the tractor was intended to be used for personal, family or household purposes.

The case law is clear that where a debtor makes an affirmative representation in loan documents that he or she intends to use goods primarily for personal, family or household purposes, the creditor is protected even if the representation turns out to be erroneous. In *Sears, Roebuck & Co. v. Pettit (In re Pettit),* 18 B.R. 8 (Bankr. E.D. Ark. 1981), the debtor bought goods for use in his rental business. Yet the debtor did not inform the seller of his intended use. The security agreement "affirmatively and unambiguously represented" that the debtor was purchasing the collateral for personal, family or household purposes. Id. at 9. The bankruptcy court rejected the admission of extrinsic evidence to contradict the unambiguous representation in the security agreement of the debtor's intended use of the collateral. The Pettit court held that the seller's purchase money security interest was properly perfected without filing a financing statement, observing that the secured party was not required by the UCC to monitor the debtor's use of the collateral in order to determine its proper classification.

The rationale of *Pettit* is compelling. A debtor who makes representations in a security agreement regarding the intended use of the collateral should be bound by those representations. That is especially true where the debtors fail to inform the creditor that they intend to use the collateral for other than personal, family or household purposes. The classification of the collateral, for purposes of perfection of the security interest, is determined when the security interest attaches. The later use of the collateral for another purpose than as stated in the security agreement is irrelevant in determining whether the security interest is perfected.

According to the security agreement here, the debtors intended to use the tractor as consumer goods. Deere was entitled to rely on the debtors' representation. The debtors did not inform Deere of a different intended use. Therefore, Deere's purchase money security interest was perfected when it attached, and the filing of a financing statement was not required. The security interest remains perfected despite any subsequent use for purposes other than consumer, if indeed there was such other use.

The trustee argues that he should not be bound by the debtors' representations in the security agreement because the debtors did not know of the representations. However, one who signs an agreement is bound by its terms, although ignorant of them, absent fraud or false representation. As there is no allegation of fraud or false representation regarding the security agreement, this argument is without merit.

For these reasons, the court holds that Deere has a perfected purchase money security interest in the tractor. Accordingly, the defendant's motion for summary judgment is granted, and the plaintiff's motion for summary judgment is denied. The court hereby enters judgment in favor of the defendant John Deere Credit a/k/a Deere & Company and against the plaintiff Lyle R. Nelson, Trustee ("Trustee") on the Trustee's adversary complaint.

Judgment in favor of the defendant.

[continued]

CRITICAL THINKING

What was the primary issue in this case, and what reasons did the judge use to support his conclusions? Would the judge have concluded differently if he found that the tractor was not a consumer good? Why or why not?

ETHICAL DECISION MAKING

How would you analyze the Troupes' conduct in this case from an ethical standpoint? Does the Troupes' apparent change of position with respect to the primary use of the tractor raise any ethical concerns?

How would you analyze the Troupes' contention that they were unaware of the representations concerning the primary use of the tractor set forth in the security documents?

PERFECTION OF MOVABLE COLLATERAL

Suppose you borrow money from a bank in Ohio to buy farm equipment. This bank files a financing statement in Ohio and perfects its interest in the equipment. As collateral, you use your coin collection. However, after a year, you move to Indiana and bring your farm equipment with you. After you are in Indiana for a few months, you decide to take out a loan from a bank in Indiana, and you use your coin collection as collateral again. If the bank in Indiana tries to search for a financing statement in Indiana, it will obviously not find one. What happens if you default on your loans?

According to the UCC, a security interest in collateral that has been perfected in one state will generally transfer to another state for a period of four months from the date that the property is brought into the state. The secured party may reperfect the interest in the new state. However, if the interest is not reperfected, the secured party may lose its protection.

For example, Randal Reed, a resident of Kansas, purchased a boat and trailer from Sportscraft Marine in Wichita in June 1999. The purchase price was financed by Rose Hill State Bank, which took a security interest in the boat and trailer. The bank filed a financing statement with the Kansas secretary of state's office. Reed took the boat and trailer to Oklahoma for use every year for six months at a time. Reed stored the boat and trailer in Oklahoma except during the winter months, when he brought them back to Kansas for winterization and storage. Reed was advised by Sportscraft Marine that the boat was subject to Oklahoma title statutes. As a result, Reed applied for and received an Oklahoma title for the boat. The bank's lien was not noted on Sportscraft Marine's certificate of origin, the application for title, or the Oklahoma certificate of title. The trailer remained titled in Kansas.

Reed filed for bankruptcy in July 2004. The bankruptcy trustee claimed that the bank failed to perfect its security interest by the date of the filing of the bankruptcy petition, and the trustee sought to avoid the bank's lien on the boat and trailer. The court preserved the bank's lien on the trailer as the trailer had always remained titled in Kansas despite its frequent trips and extended time in storage in Oklahoma. However, the court avoided the bank's secured interest in the boat as the bank had failed to reperfect its interest in Oklahoma after the boat was retitled there and before Reed filed for bankruptcy. The court reached this conclusion despite the absence of evidence that the bank knew Reed had removed the boat from Kansas and retitled it in Oklahoma in contravention of the security agreement.[2]

PERFECTION OF SECURITY INTERESTS IN AUTOMOBILES AND BOATS

We have now discussed various methods of perfection: perfection by filing, perfection by possession, automatic possession, and perfection of movable collateral. None of these

[2] *In re Randal Steven Reed,* 2006 Bankr. LEXIS 77 (Bankr. D. Kans., Jan. 19, 2006).

methods apply to perfection of automobiles and boats. Each state has created special laws that pertain to perfection of motor vehicles.

Almost every state requires a certificate of title for any motor vehicle. Perfection of a security interest in a motor vehicle occurs when the secured party makes a notation of this interest on the certificate of title. The rationale for noting the interest on the title is that the title will follow the car owner everywhere. Thus, the title would be the best place to note a secured interest. If a creditor examines a title and discovers no notation of a secured interest in the vehicle, the creditor can assume that no other creditors have a secured interest in the vehicle. This was most apparent in the Reed case that was summarized above.

The Scope of a Security Interest

L04

What is the scope of a security interest?

Generally, once a secured party perfects its interest in collateral, the perfection is effective until the collateral is sold, exchanged, or transferred. Our examination of security interests to this point has been concerned with property the debtor currently possesses. However, a security interest can also apply to personal property that is not yet in the debtor's possession.

AFTER-ACQUIRED PROPERTY

You borrow $60,000 from your bank to start an electronics store. However, you have recently graduated from college and have only your car, valued at $3,500, as collateral. The bank will take a security interest in your car, but it will also take a security interest in the materials that you will purchase to open your store. For example, you will need to create an inventory of televisions, computers, and stereos, which are **after-acquired property,** property acquired by the debtor after the security agreement is made. After-acquired property can be inventory, livestock, equipment, or almost any other kind of property. Under the UCC, a party may agree, through a clause in the security agreement, that the security interest will attach to after-acquired property. Whenever the debtor purchases new equipment or goods, the security interest is attached to the new goods. Thus, whenever you buy a television to sell in your store, the bank's security interest in the television will attach.

PROCEEDS

When a debtor sells collateral, he or she receives **proceeds,** something that is exchanged for collateral. The secured party automatically has an interest in the proceeds. Why? If you use a good as collateral for a bank loan and then sell that good, the bank has nothing to continue to secure its loan. Consequently, the security interest in the good also applies to the proceeds from the good.

Under the UCC, the secured party's interest in the proceeds lasts only 10 days after the debtor receives the proceeds. At that time, the secured party will typically need to file a new financing statement. The parties may also agree in the security agreement that there will be extended coverage of interest in the proceeds.

Termination of a Security Interest

Suppose that rather than defaulting on the loan payment, Hicklin paid Onyx the full amount for the automobile as required under the agreement. If a secured party has filed a financing statement and the debtor has repaid the secured party, the secured party must file a termination statement with the filing office.

Legal Principle: A termination statement is an amendment to a financing statement that provides that the debtor has no obligation to the secured party [9-513(a)].

After repayment by the debtor, the secured party has one month to file the termination statement. However, if the debtor makes a written request to the secured party to file the termination statement, the secured party has 20 days to file the termination statement [9-513(b)]. If the secured party does not file a termination statement, the debtor may recover $500 from the secured party [9-625(e)].

Priority Disputes

LO5 How are disputes regarding priority handled?

We have spent much time discussing the perfection of a security interest. Why? Remember, perfection of an interest is supposed to serve as protection of the secured party's interest in collateral from other creditors. In this section, we consider various conflicts between creditors who claim interest in the same collateral (see Exhibit 30-2). A conflict may arise in many circumstances; however, priority disputes are most likely to arise when a debtor files for bankruptcy.

SECURED VERSUS UNSECURED CREDITORS

Generally, secured parties have priority over unsecured creditors. Thus, if two parties provide a loan based on the same collateral, the party with the secured interest will have priority in repossessing the collateral over the party with the unsecured interest. This priority to the collateral does not depend on the perfection of a secured interest. Rather, the priority depends on the *attachment* of the secured interest.

BUT WHAT IF . . .

WHAT IF THE FACTS OF THE CASE OPENER WERE DIFFERENT?

Let's say, in the Case Opener, that Hicklin used her car as collateral not only with Onyx but also with a bank she received a loan from. Let's say that Onyx is unsecured and the bank is secured. Who would be able to claim the vehicle if Hicklin defaults on all of her payments?

SECURED VERSUS SECURED CREDITORS

Who has priority to the collateral when both parties are secured creditors? If both parties are secured, the determination of priority to collateral moves to considerations of time and perfection.

If there is a dispute between a perfected secured party and an unperfected secured party, the creditor with the perfected interest has priority over the unperfected interest.

Exhibit 30-2 Summary of Priority of Creditors' Claims to Collateral

DISPUTE	PREVAILING PARTY
Secured vs. unsecured creditor	Secured creditor
Secured perfected creditor vs. secured unperfected creditor	Secured perfected creditor
Secured perfected creditor vs. secured perfected creditor	Party who perfected its interest first
Secured unperfected creditor vs. secured unperfected creditor	Party who attached its interest first

But what if the dispute is between two secured parties with perfected interests? The party that perfected its interest first will have priority in claim to the collateral [9-317]. Finally, if neither party has perfected its security interest, the party that attached its security interest first will have first claim to the collateral.

Consider the following example: On March 21, 1995, a debtor took out a loan from First State Bank of Newcastle, Wyoming, for the purchase of two trucks. The debtor executed a security agreement with the bank and described the two trucks as collateral. Two years earlier, the debtor had taken out a loan with Farm Credit Services of the Midlands and signed a security agreement which gave Farm Credit Services rights to after-acquired property as collateral. The debtor eventually defaulted on his loans to both creditors. Which creditor had rights to the trucks as collateral?

At first it may seem that this is a priority dispute between two secured unperfected creditors. If that were the case, then Farm Credit Services would have the right to the two trucks because it was the first to attach its agreement. However, the courts in this case found that the description of "after-acquired property" was not specific enough to grant Farm Credit Services attachment rights to the specific trucks as collateral. Consequently, this dispute was between a secured unperfected agreement and an unsecured agreement, and the secured agreement of First State Bank won.[3]

PMSI Conflicts. There is an exception to these priority rules. Generally, if a PMSI is involved, the perfected PMSI will almost always have priority over other claims to collateral. The rules regarding PMSIs depend on whether the collateral is inventory or noninventory.

First, if the PMSI is in inventory, the perfected PMSI has priority over a previously perfected non-PMSI if the following two conditions are met: (1) The PMSI party perfects its interest before or at the same time as the debtor receives her inventory; and (2) the PMSI party checks for previous secured interests and gives written notice to the holders of the PMSI [9-324(b)]. For example, General Electric Capital Commercial Automotive (GECC) Inc. entered into a security agreement with Spartan Motors, Ltd. GECC loaned Spartan over $1 million and secured this loan by attaching its rights to Spartan's entire inventory as collateral. GECC filed this agreement in New York. A few years later, Spartan signed another security agreement, but this time it was with General Motors Acceptance Corporation (GMAC). This agreement, however, was an agreement that involved a PMSI. GMAC loaned money to Spartan to purchase its inventory. Realizing that this was a PMSI, GMAC filed its agreement *and* notified GECC of its competing security interest.

The next year, Spartan filed a bankruptcy petition and went out of business. GMAC repossessed two BMWs that were purchased with the money it had loaned to Spartan and sold them in an auction for $194,500. GECC brought an action against GMAC on grounds that GECC's security interest had priority. In the end, the court found that because GMAC had a PMSI in inventory *and* notified GECC of the competing agreement, GMAC had priority to the profits from the sale of the BMWs.[4]

What happens if the collateral is *not* inventory? If the PMSI is in noninventory collateral, the PMSI has priority over any other secured perfected interests as long as the PMSI is perfected within 20 days of the debtor's possession of the collateral [9-324(a)].

[3] *Farm Credit Servs. of the Midlands v. First State Bank,* 575 N.W.2d 250 (S.D. 1998).

[4] *GE Cap. Comm. Automotive Finance v. Spartan Motors, Ltd.,* 246 A.2d 41 (N.Y. Sup. Ct. 1998).

SECURED PARTY VERSUS BUYER

If a debtor sells collateral in which a secured party has an interest, the security interest generally remains in effect. Suppose you obtain a loan from a bank and use your boat as collateral. You need more money, so you sell your boat. The bank's secured interest in the boat remains with the boat. If you default on the loan, the bank can seize the boat from the buyer. However, the UCC provides some exceptions to this general rule.

Buyer in the Ordinary Course of Business. A **buyer in the ordinary course of business** is a person who routinely buys goods in good faith from a person who routinely sells these goods. Under the UCC, a buyer in the ordinary course of business can take the goods free of any security interest created by the seller of the good *even if* the security interest is perfected [9-320(a)]. What is the rationale for this rule? Asking buyers to determine whether a security interest in inventory exists is burdensome. Thus, the purpose of this rule is to encourage commerce. For example, if your company buys products from an electronics store in the ordinary course of business, you can take possession of these products free of any security interest created by the party who originally sold the products to the electronics store.

Buyers of Consumer Goods. Suppose you buy a digital camera for $800 on credit from Best Buy. Best Buy has a security agreement for a PMSI in the digital camera. (Remember, a PMSI in a consumer good perfects automatically.) However, you discover that you do not have enough money to pay your rent. Consequently, you sell your digital camera to your neighbor, who is unaware of Best Buy's secured interest in the camera. Can Best Buy repossess the camera? Under the UCC, as long as the buyer is not aware of the security interest, purchases the good for his or her personal use, and purchases the good before the secured party files a financing statement, the buyer obtains the good free of the security interest [9-320(b)]. Even though the secured party's interest perfects automatically, the secured party must have filed a financing statement to repossess a consumer good from another buyer.

Consider Case 30-2, in which the court considers the transfer of an automobile to a third party.

CASE 30-2 IN RE GIROLAMO AFONICA, DEBTOR
U.S. BANKRUPTCY COURT FOR THE NORTHERN DISTRICT OF OHIO
174 B.R. 242 (BANKR. N.D. OHIO 1994)

First of America Bank had a security interest in a 1966 Chevrolet Chevelle owned by Girolamo Afonica. The Chevelle secured a loan of $11,276.46 made by the Bank to Afonica. Afonica transferred the Chevelle without a certificate of title for $25 to a friend who was a junk dealer. The reason for the transfer was the alleged objection to the Chevelle's continued presence on the driveway by Afonica's ex-wife.

Afonica subsequently filed for Chapter 7 bankruptcy. As a result of the prior transfer, Afonica was unable to deliver the Chevelle to the Bank as required by the security agreement. The Bank moved the bankruptcy court for an order denying Afonica a discharge or the exclusion of its debt from his discharge on the basis that Afonica willfully and maliciously injured property in which the Bank maintained a security interest.

JUDGE SPEER: To succeed [in denying Afonica a discharge], Plaintiff must establish that: (1) the debtor transferred, or permitted to be transferred; (2) property of the debtor; (3) within one year before the Petition in Bankruptcy was filed; (4) with the intent to hinder, delay or defraud the creditor. Exceptions to a discharge . . . require proof by a preponderance of the evidence.

Plaintiff's best argument . . . regards the sale and scrap of the 1966 Chevrolet Chevelle. There is no question that Defendant's actions in the transfer of the vehicle were violative of the security agreement. This Court cannot merely assume, however, that Defendant transferred this vehicle with the specific intent to hinder, delay, or defraud the Plaintiff. Rather, this intent must be demonstrated. Since it is unlikely that the

[continued]

Defendant will admit to having transferred the vehicle with the intent to hinder, delay, or defraud the Plaintiff, a finding of actual intent may be based upon circumstantial evidence or inferences drawn from a pattern of conduct.

From the facts presented in this case, the Court finds that Defendant's actions did not rise to a level necessary to deny Defendant's discharge altogether. . . . Though the Defendant's act of selling the collateral used to secure the loan was improper, the Plaintiff has failed to show that the resulting loss to be so egregious that Defendant should not be allowed a discharge as to any of his debts. Thus, this Court does not find the necessary intent to hinder, delay, or defraud creditors. . . .

To succeed [in excluding the loan made by the Bank from discharge], Plaintiff must prove the injury to the property caused by the transfer of the 1966 Chevrolet Chevelle was the result of Defendant's willful and malicious acts. The terms "willful and malicious" are not defined by statute. However, they are defined in case law "as a wrongful act done intentionally and without just cause, which necessarily leads to injury."

This Court determines that the Plaintiff has proven by a preponderance of the evidence that Defendant willfully and maliciously caused injury to the collateral pledged to Plaintiff. Without a doubt, the sale of the 1966 Chevrolet Chevelle was an intentional act. Furthermore, the sale, without notice to the lender, of a vehicle pledged as collateral to another is a wrongful act. Defendant claims that he called the scrap dealer to pick up the vehicle because his ex-wife consistently complained of the vehicle in her driveway. This explanation does not constitute "just cause." At the very least, Defendant could have notified Plaintiff of the sale. The fact that he did not offer title to the purchaser suggests he intentionally fostered the impression that the vehicle was clear of liens. Essentially, the Defendant blatantly deprived the Plaintiff of the ability to collect the collateral to recover or offset Defendant's liability in the event Defendant should default on the loan secured by the collateral. Therefore, the debt secured by the 1966 Chevrolet Chevelle is nondischargeable.

This Court agrees that in this case the amount of the debt to be held nondischargeable . . . is the lesser value of the converted property or the amount of the indebtedness. This Court is not satisfied, however, that the sale of the 1966 Chevrolet Chevelle to a scrap dealer for $25 represents the fair market value of the vehicle. Therefore, a determination as to the measure of damages will be made after both Plaintiff and Defendant provide this Court with evidence attesting to the fair market value of the 1966 Chevrolet Chevelle at the time of transfer.

The Plaintiff and Defendant are ordered to submit evidence of the fair market value at the time of the transfer of the 1966 Chevrolet Chevelle.

CRITICAL THINKING

What is the issue and conclusion in this case? What reasons does the judge use to support his argument? How convincing are they? What evidence would be needed for the judge to conclude in the opposite way?

ETHICAL DECISION MAKING

As with any disagreement over what is fair, it is relatively easy to identify the primary interests involved in the dispute. But court rulings have a responsibility to look beyond the surface interests. In this case, whose interests are affected by the ruling and need to be taken into consideration when making a determination like the one the court made?

Buyers of Chattel Paper and Instruments. If a buyer purchases **chattel paper,** a writing that indicates both a monetary obligation and a security interest in specific goods, or an *instrument,* a writing that demonstrates a right to payment of money, in the ordinary course of business, the buyer can obtain the good free of any security interest. The buyer must typically be unaware of the security interest in the good. Why is there an exception for buyers of chattel paper and instruments? Both chattel paper and instruments are easily transferable. Consequently, the UCC provides that these forms of collateral can be sold to a buyer free of the secured party's interest.

Default

L06
What is default?

Generally, when a debtor fails to make payments on a loan or declares bankruptcy, the debtor has **defaulted** on the loan. However, the UCC does not define default. Consequently, each security agreement provides the specific definition of what is considered a default.

CASE NUGGET

RIGHTS OF A SECURED PARTY

In re Tower Air, Inc.
397 F.3d 191 (3d Cir. 2005)

May a secured party recover insurance proceeds for damage to collateral that had been repaired and returned to the lender? Tower, an airline, borrowed $21 million from Finova to purchase an aircraft and four aircraft engines. As part of the security agreement, Finova received a security interest in the aircraft and four engines. The security agreement also provided that Tower would insure the collateral and that Finova would also have a security interest in the insurance proceeds. The lender perfected its security interest in the planes, engines, and insurance proceeds.

In 1997, one of the engines was damaged in an accident. Using its own funds, Tower repaired the engine for $2.25 million (while $1.91 million was attributable to the accident). Tower did not submit an insurance claim.

Tower later filed for bankruptcy. Because Finova had a secured interest, all collateral, including the repaired engine, was returned to the lender. The bankruptcy trustee then discovered the insurance policy and filed a claim for $1.91 million in repairs. The insurance company settled the claim by paying approximately $950,000. Finova objected to the settlement and argued that it was entitled to the insurance proceeds pursuant to the security agreement. The bankruptcy court ruled that the insurance proceeds should be paid to Finova, and the district court agreed.

On appeal, the trustee argued that Finova should not recover the insurance proceeds because it had already recovered the fully repaired engine. Recovering both the insurance proceeds and the repaired engine would be unfair. The court ruled that Finova was permitted to recover the collateral and insurance money to the extent of the amount of the debt. Much of the collateral was damaged; thus, Finova was permitted to recover the full value of the insurance proceeds.

Moreover, each agreement determines the procedures and consequences that occur in the event of default. Because the creditor is usually in a better bargaining position, the creditor usually determines the definition of default.

What are a secured party's remedies to recover its money when a debtor defaults on a loan? The secured party can (1) take possession of the collateral or (2) ignore its rights in the collateral and proceed to judgment. However, the party is not limited to just one of these remedies. If one method is unsuccessful, the party can attempt to pursue the other method. Note that these remedies are limited if the debtor has filed for bankruptcy.

TAKING POSSESSION OF THE COLLATERAL

If a debtor defaults on a loan, the secured party can take possession of the collateral (9-609). While the secured party may act without any court order to retain possession of the property, the secured party may not "breach the peace" in repossessing the property. What exactly is *breaching the peace?* The UCC does not define the phrase. Generally, if the secured party can repossess the collateral without using force or committing trespass, the action is not a breach of the peace. If the secured party is unable to repossess the property without breaching the peace, the party will file suit against the debtor to obtain a court order for the debtor to turn over the property. Case 30-3 demonstrates the court's consideration of breach of peace in the repossession of furniture.

CASE 30-3 LINGROSS v. HEILIG-MEYERS FURNITURE
U.S. DISTRICT COURT FOR THE NORTHERN DISTRICT OF MISSISSIPPI
1999 U.S. DIST. LEXIS 3986 (N.D. MS 1999)

On December 3, 1996, Jennifer Lingross purchased a dinette set, chairs, and a watch from Heilig-Meyers' store in Memphis, Tennessee. Heilig-Meyers retained a security interest in the merchandise in exchange for Lingross' promise to make monthly payments. The furniture was delivered to a home occupied by Patricia Lingross and Mahlon Blose.

On February 15, 1997, Lingross was in arrears totaling approximately $140, which amount represented two months *of payments. The manager of Heilig-Meyers retained three men, Michael K. Smith, Jerry Maurice Bobo, and Walter K. Roy, to repossess the merchandise. Smith and Roy traveled to Patricia Lingross' home in street clothes while Bobo arrived dressed in a black uniform, including a black ski mask, badge, handcuffs, pepper spray, mace, a knife, and a gun in a holster on his hip. The men arrived at Lingross' home at 6 a.m., pounded on the door, identified themselves as police, and demanded entry. The men refused to provide identification. A confrontation occurred during which Bobo had his hand on his gun while it was in his holster.*

Jennifer Lingross attempted to rectify the situation by paying her past due payments, but Smith rejected the offer and continued to attempt to repossess the furniture. At some point, Roy and Bobo backed Jennifer Lingross up to a wall and were shouting at her. The men continued to demand access to the house to repossess the furniture.

Ultimately, the men left upon the request of Patricia Lingross and Blose. However, they returned later in the day with a representative of the Marshall County Sheriff's Office. Patricia Lingross gave the men permission to enter the premises and remove the furniture. Blose attempted to take photographs of the repossession, but Bobo objected and a physical altercation ensued. Bobo was escorted from the home by one of the police officers. After the furniture was loaded on the truck, one of the men told Patricia Lingross "You don't know me, Lady. I've got friends in L.A., and I'll be back."

Patricia and Jennifer Lingross and Mahlon Blose subsequently filed a lawsuit against Heilig-Meyers alleging that its agents committed assault, battery, invasion of privacy, and intentional infliction of emotional distress and that the company was liable for negligence in its retention and supervision of the men.

JUDGE ALEXANDER: Defendant moves this court to dismiss plaintiffs' claims for assault. Under Mississippi law, plaintiff must prove "acts intending to cause a harmful or offensive contact with the person, or an imminent apprehension of such a contact, and the other is thereby put in such imminent apprehension. . . . Based on the evidence before the court, the undersigned finds that there are genuine issues of material fact relating to plaintiff's claim of assault. The court finds that Bobo's dress and the agent's actions could have put the plaintiffs in imminent apprehension of offensive contact. The evidence tends to show that Bobo was dressed in a manner which was intended to intimidate the plaintiffs into allowing the men to repossess the furniture without argument. Frankly, the court cannot find, and the defendants fail to explain, why their agent was dressed in this manner. The evidence also tends to show that the men advanced on Jennifer Lingross in a manner which could reasonably put her in imminent apprehension of offensive contact. The evidence also tends to show that the men verbally threatened the plaintiffs during the altercation. Finally, there is a genuine issue of material fact as to whether Bobo had his gun in his holster during the repossession. The court finds that a jury could reasonably decide, if the plaintiff proves that Bobo had his gun on his person during the repossession, that the plaintiffs were in imminent apprehension of offensive contact.

Defendant moves this court to dismiss plaintiff's claim of battery. Under Mississippi law, plaintiff must prove that "harmful contact actually occurs." However, in this case, plaintiff has failed to proffer any evidence that "harmful contact" actually occurred.

Defendant moves this court to dismiss plaintiff's trespass claim. Under Mississippi law, a creditor does have some "self help" rights to go on the debtor's property and peaceably repossess it without utilizing the judicial process. However, creditor's rights to employ "self help" are limited to those instances where the creditor can repossess the property without a "breach of the peace." Plaintiff has proffered sufficient evidence to create a genuine issue of material fact as to whether a breach of the peace occurred. The defendant's agents' dress and actions could have generated "fright or anger" on the part of the plaintiffs. Initially, the plaintiffs denied the defendant's agents access to the property in order to repossess the merchandise. This initial refusal could have been a "protest" and thus the defendant's self help rights could have terminated at this point. Therefore, when the agents returned to the property to again try and repossess the merchandise, they risked breaching the peace.

Defendant moves this court to dismiss plaintiff's claim of invasion of privacy. Under Mississippi law . . . [t]he only possibly applicable theory . . . is the intentional intrusion upon the solitude or seclusion of another. In the present case, the plaintiff's claims for invasion of privacy will turn on whether the defendants acted in bad faith when they attempted to repossess the merchandise. Plaintiff has alleged facts which would create a genuine issue of material fact as to whether defendant's agents acted in bad faith in their attempt to repossess the merchandise. Plaintiff has admitted that she was in arrears on the merchandise and that the merchandise was delivered to Patricia Lingross' property. As a result of Jennifer's deficiency, defendant had the right to peaceably repossess the merchandise. However, the actions of the defendant's agents are highly suspect once they arrived on the premises. The agents' use of intimidation, threats and scare tactics, such as dressing up in SWAT clothes and carrying a gun, could reasonably be viewed as bad faith and conduct to which a reasonable person would object.

Defendant's Motion for Summary Judgment on Plaintiffs' claims of assault, breach of peace and invasion of privacy is denied.

[continued]

CRITICAL THINKING

What is the argument that this judge is making? How good are his reasons? Is there any information that you feel he left out that would help you come to a conclusion on the issue presented in this case?

ETHICAL DECISION MAKING

Return to the WPH process of ethical decision making. Suppose you were the manager of Heilig-Meyers Furniture in this situation. How might you have behaved differently if you were following the Golden Rule?

Generally, the security agreement will state that if the debtor defaults on the loan, the debtor must turn over the collateral in a reasonable time and manner. If the debtor refuses to turn over the property, the secured party will typically hire a repossession company to obtain the collateral. Once the secured party has possession of the collateral, the party can choose to retain or dispose of the collateral.

Disposition of the Collateral. Under the UCC, the secured party can sell, lease, or transfer the collateral in any commercially reasonable method (9-610). The secured party may sell the collateral in a private or public sale. Regardless of where the collateral is sold, the secured party must strive to receive the best price for the collateral. Striving to receive the best price is part of the requirement to conduct every aspect of the sale in a "commercially reasonable manner." There is some dispute over what is commercially reasonable. A clear example of a sale that is not reasonable is the following: Suppose you, as a secured party, repossess a diamond necklace worth $10,000 and attempt to sell this necklace to recover the funds for a $10,000 loan. You give very little notice of the sale; thus, you receive only one offer to buy the necklace. You reject the offer and decide to purchase the necklace yourself for $1,000. You apply the $1,000 to the debtor's loan; the debtor still owes you $9,000. If this example actually occurred, the debtor could bring a suit against you for failing to comply with the commercially reasonable requirement established in the UCC.

Suppose you sold the necklace to a buyer for $7,500. Assuming that this sale meets the commercially reasonable requirement, the debtor would still owe you $2,500. The sale has amounted in a deficiency; consequently, the debtor is liable to the secured party for the deficiency. However, suppose that the sale of the necklace yielded $12,000. Do you, the secured party, get to keep the $2,000? If the sale of collateral leads to a surplus, the surplus must be returned to the debtor.

In addition to adhering to the commercially reasonable requirement, the secured party must also notify the debtor of the sale. Additionally, the secured party must notify any other parties who have secured interests in the collateral.

Once the collateral is sold, the proceeds must be paid in the following order: (1) paying the reasonable expenses of retaking and disposing of the collateral (including attorney fees), (2) satisfying the debt of the secured party, and (3) satisfying remaining holders of junior security interests [9-615(a)].

Retention of the Collateral. Instead of disposing of the collateral, the secured party may choose to keep the collateral in full or partial satisfaction of the debt. However, the secured party must notify the debtor of this intent by sending written notice. The debtor has 20 days to object to the secured party's retention of the collateral. If the debtor does not object to the retention, the secured party may retain the collateral (9-620). By retaining the collateral for full satisfaction of debt, the secured party gives up any claim to the debt. In other words, the secured party cannot demand additional money from the debtor. Consequently, if the collateral is not valued at the full amount of the money due to the secured party, the secured party has no right to additional money from the debtor. The 1998 version of Article 9 provides for the debtor and secured party to agree that the secured party retains the collateral for partial payment of the debt.

If the debtor objects to the secured party's retention of the collateral, the secured party must sell or dispose of the collateral. Why might a debtor object to a party's retention of the collateral? Suppose you use a Van Gogh painting as collateral for a $5,000 car loan. The Van Gogh painting could certainly be sold for more than $5,000; thus, you, the debtor, would want the sale to occur so that you can recover the surplus from the sale.

? **BUT WHAT IF . . .**

WHAT IF THE FACTS OF THE CASE OPENER WERE DIFFERENT?

Let's say, in the Case Opener, that Onyx took Hicklin's car after she defaulted on her payments, and Onyx decides to keep her car. Is Onyx free to choose to keep the collateral in satisfaction of the debt?

PROCEEDING TO JUDGMENT

Another remedy for a defaulted loan is the secured party's rejection of the right in the collateral and the party's filing of a suit against the debtor. The secured party can sue the debtor for the entire amount of the debt. Rather than taking the time to organize the sale of the collateral, the secured party may choose to file suit. In contrast, an unsecured creditor has just one option: to file suit and seek a judgment in the amount of the debt.

Could there be other reasons for rejecting the right in the collateral? Here is a real-world example. Trans World Airlines (TWA), Inc., was having major financial trouble in 1991. In fact, it had defaulted on its loans to two major creditors. Both creditors had the opportunity to repossess 10 jets and 96 spare aircraft, but the creditors continued to consistently postpone repossessing the collateral. Their reason for doing so was that they knew that the value of the aircraft was far less than what was owed to them by TWA, and they were sure that TWA would seek protection in U.S. bankruptcy court. Consequently, they chose to stick out the situation in hopes that TWA would either solve its financial problems or sell to another carrier.[5]

[5] Christopher Carey, "Creditors Unlikely to Seize TWA Jets," *St. Louis Post-Dispatch,* July 30, 1991, p. 7B.

CASE OPENER WRAP-UP

Onyx Acceptance Corporation

The Supreme Court of Delaware held that every aspect of the sale had to be commercially reasonable. Simply showing that the sale grossed more than 50 percent of the vehicle's value did not, by itself, establish that the sale was commercially reasonable. There was no evidence that a private sale, as conducted in this case, would have resulted in the sale of the vehicle to the highest bidder. Onyx failed to prove that the specific auction procedures were designed to attract the highest bidder at a highly publicized, well-attended auction run by a highly regarded auctioneer at a convenient location. Furthermore, Onyx failed to prove that its sale of the vehicle conformed with established trade practices. Onyx's good faith in selling Hicklin's vehicle did not, standing alone, establish commercial reasonableness. As a result, Onyx was barred from recovering the deficiency from Hicklin.[6]

[6] *Hicklin v. Onyx Acceptance Corp.,* 970 A.2d 244 (Del. 2009).

KEY TERMS

after-acquired property 668
attachment 661
buyer in the ordinary course of business 671
chattel paper 672
collateral 660
consumer good 665
debtor 660
default 662
defaulted 672
financing statement 663
instruments 664
perfection 663
pledge 664
proceeds 668
purchase-money security interest (PMSI) 662
secured interest 660
secured party 660
secured transaction 660
security agreement 660
termination statement 668

SUMMARY OF KEY TOPICS

Important Definitions Associated with Secured Transactions

Secured interest: An interest in personal property or fixtures that secures payment or performance of an obligation.

Secured party: The person or party that holds the interest in the secured property.

Debtor: The person or party that has an obligation to the secured party, the person who owns interest in the property.

Security agreement: The agreement in which the debtor gives the secured interest to the secured party.

Collateral: The property that is subject to the security interest.

Creation of Secured Interests

Attachment of a security interest requires these three elements:

Written agreement: An agreement that describes the collateral and is signed by the debtor.

Value: An item of value given from the creditor to the debtor.

Debtor rights in the collateral: The rights of the debtor over the collateral.

A *purchase-money security interest* is formed when a debtor uses borrowed money (e.g., buying on credit) from the secured party to buy the collateral.

Perfected Security Interest

A *perfected security interest* is a security interest in which the creditor has legally protected his or her claim to the collateral. Methods of perfection include:

1. *Perfection by filing:* Perfection of an interest by filing a financing statement with a state agency.
    - *Place and duration of filing:* Generally, the financial statements for consumer goods must be filed with the county clerk, and the statement is valid for five years.
2. *Perfection by possession:* Perfection of an interest by holding the collateral of the debtor until the loan is paid off.
3. *Automatic perfection:* Perfection that automatically occurs when a retailer sells a consumer good.
4. *Perfection of movable collateral:* Collateral that moves to another state must be "reperfected" after four months.
5. *Perfection of security interests in automobiles and boats:* An interest in an automobile or boat is perfected by noting the interest on the certificate of title.

The Scope of a Security Interest

After-acquired property: A creditor has a security interest in property acquired by the debtor after the security agreement is made if a clause to this effect is included in the agreement.

Proceeds: A creditor automatically has rights to the proceeds from the sale of collateral for 10 days.

Termination of a Security Interest

Termination statement: An amending to a financing statement stating that the debtor has no obligation to the secured party.

Priority Disputes

Priority disputes occur when two corporations or individuals claim rights to the same collateral.

Secured versus unsecured: When an individual with a secured interest is disputing with an individual with an unsecured interest, the individual with the secured interest wins.

Secured versus secured: When two individuals with secured interests are disputing, the individual who perfected his or her interest first wins.

PMSI conflicts: If a party with a perfected purchase-money security interest disputes with another party, the PMSI party will almost always have a right to the collateral—regardless of when the agreement was perfected.

Secured party versus buyer: If a debtor sells his collateral, the creditor may dispute with the buyer over the collateral.

1. *Buyers in the ordinary course of business:* If a person buys the collateral in the ordinary course of business without realizing that it is collateral, she has a right to the good.
2. *Buyers of consumer goods:* As long as the consumer does not know that the product is secured, the buyer's new product is free of any security interest.
3. *Buyers of chattel paper and instruments:* If the buyer purchases chattel paper and instruments, he is free from any security interest.

Default

Default occurs when a debtor fails to pay back her or his loan. Remedies include:

1. *Taking possession of the collateral:* If a debtor defaults on a loan, the secured party can take possession of the collateral.

   Disposition of the collateral: The creditor may sell, lease, or transfer the collateral.

   Retention of the collateral: The creditor may choose to keep the collateral as payment of the debt.
2. *Proceeding to judgment:* A secured party may sue the debtor for the entire amount of the debt instead of dealing with the collateral.

POINT / COUNTERPOINT

A secured transaction gives a creditor more assurance that it will be repaid even if the debtor is unable to pay. As you learned in this chapter, when a debtor has both secured and unsecured creditors, the secured creditors will be paid first. Some scholars have argued that secured credit unfairly transfers risk to unsecured creditors.

Should Secured Credit Be Limited?	
YES	**NO**
Suppose an unsecured creditor extended a loan to a debtor years before a secured creditor makes a loan. Later, a	Debtors and creditors are rational actors who have to make choices. An unsecured creditor makes a choice in extending

secured creditor extends credit to the debtor and gains an interest in the debtor's property. The debtor's financial situation has changed since the unsecured loan. Because of the secured creditor's interest, the likelihood that the unsecured creditor will be paid in full is now lower. The unsecured creditor's only response is to increase its interest rate; however, the unsecured creditor does not necessarily know about the secured creditor's interest in the collateral. Consequently, when the debtor is unable to pay, the unsecured creditor may get nothing.

Moreover, the availability of secured credit may force a debtor to encumber her assets to obtain credit. By limiting the availability of secured credit, both unsecured creditors and debtors will be treated more fairly.

credit to a debtor. The unsecured creditor makes money based on the interest it charges the debtor. Frequently, the interest rate on an unsecured loan is much higher than the interest rate on a secured loan. The unsecured creditor is compensated for the higher risk it may face.

Moreover, a debtor has a choice as to whether he wants to give the creditor an interest in his property. The debtor may choose a secured loan because of the lower interest rate. We should not restrict the debtor's choice.

Finally, many people who receive secured credit are economically disadvantaged. Limiting the availability of secured credit would harm these parties' ability to access credit.

QUESTIONS & PROBLEMS

1. Explain why a creditor would want a secured interest.
2. How is a security interest created?
3. What options does a secured party have if a debtor defaults?
4. Indiana Auto Sales & Repair repossessed an automobile from one of its debtors. Indiana Auto paid an independent contractor $30 to repossess the car. The contractor's 15-year-old, unlicensed employee was directed to repossess the vehicle. During the repossession, the boy exceeded the speed limit and crashed into Birrell. She sustained serious personal injuries as a result of the collision. Birrell brought a lawsuit against Indiana Auto Sales & Repair for the injuries she sustained during the repossession. The trial court found in favor of Indiana Auto Sales & Repair. Birrell appealed the decision. Do you think the court of appeals affirmed or reversed the decision? Why or why not? [*Birrell v. Indiana Auto Sales & Repair,* 698 N.E.2d 6 (Ind. Ct. App. 1998).]
5. In May 1990, Gerald Gaucher entered into a "retail installment contract and security agreement" with Cold Springs RV Corp. This agreement provided for the purchase of a travel trailer. In the agreement, Gaucher agreed to pay $320 a month for seven years and granted Cold Springs a security interest in the trailer. The agreement also stated that Gaucher's failure to make a timely payment would be considered default and would result in Cold Springs' repossession of the trailer. Gaucher's payments were not timely. After various payment failures for a year and a half, Cold Springs notified Gaucher that it was going to repossess the trailer unless it received full payment. Cold Springs repossessed the trailer and sold it without giving Gaucher notice of the sale. Gaucher brought a suit against Cold Springs for violating the Uniform Commercial Code. The trial court ruled in favor of Gaucher, ruling that the trailer was a consumer good. Cold Springs appealed. How do you think the court decided on appeal? [*Gaucher v. Cold Springs RV Corp.,* 700 A.2d 299 (N.H. 1997).]
6. On April 27, 1992, Darro and Tracy Long purchased a 1980 Ford Escort for $2,795 from Auto Credit, Inc. They made a cash down payment of $300 and financed the balance of the purchase price. The terms of the financing required that the Longs pay $38.84 a week for 84 weeks. The financing permitted Auto Credit to seize the automobile if payments became delinquent. The Longs made six timely payments but returned the automobile to Auto Credit on June 17, 1992, and made no further payments. When returned, the automobile was in the same condition it had been in when it was purchased by the Longs, with the exception of an additional 3,500 miles on the odometer. At the time of the surrender, the remaining balance due on the automobile was $2,594.02. Auto Credit informed the Longs that if they failed to pay this balance within 10 days, the automobile would be sold at a private sale. The automobile was ultimately sold by Auto Credit at the Billings Auto Auction on August 12, 1992, for $150. Auto Credit

incurred $229.47 in expenses associated with the sale. Thus, after crediting the sales price and adding the costs associated with the sale, the Longs' indebtedness was increased by $79.47. Auto Credit filed a lawsuit against the Longs, seeking recovery of the deficiency, which now totaled $2,934.15 with interest and penalties. The Longs filed a counterclaim in which they contended that the sale was unreasonable pursuant to the Uniform Commercial Code. If you were the judge deciding this case, would you grant Auto Credit the full $2,934.15 deficiency? [*Auto Credit, Inc. v. Long,* 971 P.2d 1237 (Mont. 1998).]

7. Ford Motor Credit Corporation (FMCC) hired Traciers & Associates to repossess a white 2002 Ford Expedition owned by Marissa Chapa, who was in default on the associated promissory note. Traciers assigned the job to its field manager, Paul Chambers, and gave him an address at which the vehicle could be found. Ford, Traciers, and Chambers were unaware that the address was that of Marissa's brother, Carlos Chapa. Coincidentally, Carlos and his wife, Maria Chapa, also had purchased a white Ford Expedition financed by Ford. Their vehicle, however, was a 2003 model, and the Chapas were not in default.

Chambers ultimately repossessed the wrong vehicle. At the time that repossession, Carlos and Maria Chapa's two children were in the vehicle. Chambers was unaware of their presence at the time of the he took possession of the vehicle. When Maria emerged from the house, the Expedition, with her children, was gone. Maria began screaming, telephoned 911, and called her husband at work to tell him the children were gone. In the meantime, Chambers discovered the two Chapa children. After he persuaded one of the boys to unlock the vehicle, Chambers drove the Expedition back to the Chapas' house. He returned the keys to Maria, who was outside her house, crying. By the time emergency personnel and Carlos Chapa arrived, the children were back home and Chambers had left the scene. Acting individually and on behalf of their children, Carlos and Maria Chapa sued Traciers, Chambers, and Ford. The defendants settled the children's claims but contested the individual claims of Carlos and Maria. The trial court granted summary judgment on the parents' claims in favor of Traciers, Chambers, and FMCC, and Carlos and Maria appealed. Was the mistaken repossession of the wrong vehicle a breach of the peace? How would you decide the parents' claim for emotional distress on appeal? [*Chapa v. Traciers & Associates, Inc.,* 267 S.W.3d 386 (Tex. Ct. App. 2008).]

8. Fordyce Bank & Trust Company issued several loans to Bean Timberland so that Bean could purchase timber from various landowners. Bean gave the bank security interests in the purchased timber, and the proceeds from the sale of the timber were intended to repay the loans the bank had made to Bean. The bank, intending to perfect its security interests, filed financing statements with the Arkansas secretary of state's office. However, when Bean sold the timber to the various lumber mills with which it did business, Bean failed to remit the sales proceeds to the bank. The bank filed suit against these purchasers, alleging that the purchasers had "negligently entered into contracts" with Bean for the purchase of timber and had "failed to exercise good faith" in those transactions. The bank further contended that the purchasers had been negligent in failing to request a lien search of the UCC records of the Arkansas secretary of state's office. Had the purchasers conducted a lien search, they would have discovered the bank's financing statement and security agreement. The trial court granted the purchasers' motion for a directed verdict on the basis that they were purchasers in the ordinary course of business and were not required to perform a lien search on the timber purchased from Bean. The bank filed an appeal. How would you decide this case on appeal? Do businesses have a duty to conduct lien searches with respect to firms from which they purchase goods? Should they have this duty? Why or why not? [*Fordyce Bank & Trust Co. v. Bean Timberland, Inc.,* 251 S.W.3d 267 (Ark. 2007).]

Looking for more review materials?

The Online Learning Center at **www.mhhe.com/kubasek3e** contains this chapter's "Assignment on the Internet" and also a list of URLs for more information, entitled "On the Internet." Find both of them in the Student Center portion of the OLC, along with quizzes and other helpful materials.

CHAPTER 31

Other Creditors' Remedies and Suretyship

LEARNING OBJECTIVES

After reading this chapter, you will be able to answer the following questions:

1 How can liens assist creditors?

2 What are the various kinds of statutory liens available to creditors?

3 What are the various kinds of judicial liens available to creditors?

4 How does mortgage foreclosure assist creditors?

5 What is a creditors' composition agreement for the benefit of creditors?

6 What is an assignment for the benefit of creditors?

7 What are suretyship and guaranty contracts?

CASE OPENER

Mortgage Foreclosure

Izell and Raven Reese executed a promissory note in exchange for a $650,000 loan from Provident Funding Associates, LLP, to purchase a home in Roswell, Georgia. The loan was secured by a security deed that permitted Provident to sell the home in the event of default. After Provident funded the loan, it sold and delivered the promissory note to Residential Funding Company, LLC. Provident remained as the loan servicer and retained the right to collect payments and perform all other mortgage loan servicing functions.

The Reeses defaulted on the loan, and Provident commenced foreclosure proceedings in June 2009. Provident held a nonjudicial sale of the home in July 2009 at which time it purchased the property and subsequently sought to remove the Reeses from possession. The Reeses filed a lawsuit against Provident alleging wrongful foreclosure. Specifically, the Reeses claimed that Provident was not the lender or holder of the promissory note as stated in foreclosure documents but was merely a loan servicer. The Reeses also claimed that Residential Funding was the secured creditor but that its identity was never disclosed to the Reeses. As a result, the Reeses sought to set aside the foreclosure on the basis that the foreclosure documents failed to properly reflect that they were sent by and on behalf of the proper secured creditor in violation of Georgia law.

1. If you were the judge deciding this case, would you decide that the foreclosure was wrongful?
2. If you were the manager of Provident or Residential Funding, what steps would you undertake to ensure that foreclosures such as that of the Reeses were carried out in a lawful manner?

The Wrap-Up at the end of the chapter will answer these questions.

The opening scenario presents a few of the many problems that a debtor and creditor may face when the creditor attempts to collect a debt. A debtor is a party that has an obligation to another party, while a creditor is a party that is entitled to the debtor's payment.

A creditor wants to ensure that it is repaid for money extended to or work performed for its debtors. Creditors have a variety of tools available to ensure their repayment. Some of these tools are created at the time the creditor agrees to extend money to the debtor. An example is the secured transaction, which you learned about in the previous chapter. Through an agreement between the creditor and the debtor, a creditor may take a secured interest in a debtor's personal property. If the debtor does not repay the creditor, the creditor can take possession of the personal property as repayment. Similarly, a creditor may take a secured interest in a debtor's real property in the form of a mortgage.

Moreover, a creditor may believe that extending money to a debtor alone is too risky. If the risk is too high, a creditor may require that a third party agree to pay the creditor on behalf of or in place of the debtor. Again, all parties are making an agreement regarding the creditor's right to be repaid.

However, sometimes a creditor gains an interest in a debtor's property through statute or common law rather than agreement. For example, most state legislatures have recognized that a landlord has an interest in a tenant's furniture if the tenant fails to pay rent. When signing the lease, the tenant did not make an agreement that the landlord could take possession of the tenant's property; rather, such interest is created by state statute.

Generally, laws regarding debt collection are state laws. However, if the debtor is a consumer, federal laws such as the Fair Debt Collection Practices Act may restrict the creditor's activities. For example, under the Fair Debt Collection Practices Act, the creditor may not make false statements when collecting a debt.

The purpose of this chapter is to examine the tools available to creditors for satisfying a debtor's obligation. We first consider the laws creditors may use to obtain money to satisfy a debtor's obligation, including such remedies as liens, mortgage foreclosures, creditors' composition agreements, and assignments for the benefit of creditors. In the second half of the chapter, we discuss actions that a creditor can take *before* making a loan that will ensure that the debt will be repaid, including such third-party agreements as suretyship and guaranty contracts.

Laws Assisting Creditors

LO1

How can liens assist creditors?

Generally, a **lien** is a claim to property. If you, as a creditor, have a lien on your debtor's property, you have a claim to the property or the proceeds of the sale of the property. More importantly, your claim to the property must be settled before the property (or proceeds) is distributed to other creditors. A person who holds a lien is called a *lienholder*. There are three types of liens: consensual liens, statutory liens, and judgment liens. In the previous chapter, you learned about secured interests. A secured interest is a *consensual lien:* The parties agree to the secured party's claim to the debtor's property. The following discussion will focus on statutory liens and judgment liens.

A homeowner may be surprised to find a lien against his new home if the contractor who built the home failed to pay his subcontractors.

STATUTORY LIENS

Consider the following example: Suppose that you purchase new office furniture on credit. You sign an agreement with the seller, giving the seller a secured interest in your new furniture to ensure that you will make your monthly payments. The agreement between you and the seller creates the seller's secured interest. Suppose that you hire an interior designer to reupholster your old furniture to match your new furniture. If he or she completes the job and you cannot pay, the interior designer can create a lien (and thus becomes a lienholder) on your old furniture. This lien arises under state law to ensure that the designer will be compensated for his or her work.

Legal Principle: A *statutory lien* is a lien that is created solely through statute, regardless of whether the debtor wishes the lien to be created.

L02

What are the various kinds of statutory liens available to creditors?

Suppose that one creditor has a secured interest in your furniture while another creditor has a lien on your furniture. Who has priority in obtaining your property or the proceeds of the sale of your property? By comparing the time at which the lien was created to the time at which the secured interest was perfected, you can determine which creditor has priority. If the secured interest is perfected, generally the creditor with the perfected secured interest will have priority over the lien creditor. If the secured interest is unperfected, the lien creditor will have priority over the unsecured interest. If a creditor perfects a security interest after another creditor establishes a lien on the property, the creditor with the recently perfected secured interest will not have priority over the lien creditor.

We examine below two particular kinds of statutory liens: mechanic's liens and artisan's liens.

Mechanic's Lien. When a person hires a worker to make improvements on real property but is later unable to pay the worker, the worker can create a **mechanic's lien** on the person's improved real property. What are the characteristics of the mechanic's lien? First, a mechanic's lien must be on real property, not personal property. For example, if a worker builds an addition to a house or remodels a room within the house, the worker can create a lien on the house. Second, as stated earlier, the mechanic's lien is created by statute.

BUT WHAT IF . . .

WHAT IF THE FACTS OF THE CASE OPENER WERE DIFFERENT?

Let's say that the Reeses took out a loan on the house from Provident. Let's also say that the Reeses decided to get their house remodeled. When the remodeling was finished, the Reeses could not pay the remodeling company. What can that company then create? Furthermore, does the construction company or Provident have priority on obtaining the house if the Reeses default on their payments to Provident as well?

CASE NUGGET

FORECLOSING ON A LIEN

Bend Tarp and Liner, Inc. v. Bundy
961 P.2d 857 (Or. App. 1998)

Bundy hired Bend Tarp and Liner to install a liner in a pond on his golf course. The day after the liner had been installed, Bundy discovered that a section of the wall of the pond had collapsed. At the point of the collapse, the pond liner had torn and water escaped from the pond. Bundy believed that the water loss was due to the torn liner, while Bend Tarp argued that the collapse of the wall was responsible for the tear. Bundy refused to pay Bend unless Bend agreed to repair the lining. Bend refused and filed a lien on the amount of the contract for the pond work plus interest. When Bundy still did not pay, Bend began action to foreclose its lien.

As a defense against the foreclosure, Bundy argued that Bend breached its contract because Bundy received no benefit from the liner; thus, Bend could not foreclose. The trial court ruled that Bend's installation of the liner was defective and thus Bend was not entitled to foreclose its lien. Bend appealed. The appellate court reviewed all evidence and agreed with the trial court. Thus, Bend could not foreclose on its lien.

Legal Principle: **A *mechanic's lien* attaches by operation of state statutes to real property as a result of labor or materials provided for the benefit of such property.**

What procedures must the contractor follow to create a lien? The party filing the lien must follow the requirements under the state statute, which vary from state to state. However, generally, the contractor must file, with the county clerk, a written notice of the lien on the property within a specific time period. Usually, the lien must be filed within 60 to 120 days after the delivery of materials or the last work has been completed by the contractor.

If the contractor decides to foreclose on the lien, the contractor must give the debtor notice of the foreclosure. Generally, the lien foreclosure action must be filed within 90 days of filing the lien. The foreclosure leads to a sale of the improved property. The sale must be advertised and must take place within a certain time, usually around six months to two years. The proceeds of the sale will be used to pay the debt to the contractor. If the proceeds are greater than the debt owed to the contractor, the surplus proceeds will be returned to the debtor.

However, creating a lien on property does not automatically ensure that a contractor will receive money. If a contractor performs deficient work, the mechanic's lien may not be enforced.

Compare the Bend Tarp Case Nugget to the Bates County Redi-Mix Case Nugget. While a contractor may not be entitled to foreclose on a lien when the contractor performs negligently, a supplier of goods is entitled to a lien despite a negligent performance.

Artisan's Lien. In contrast to a mechanic's lien, which is a claim on real property, an artisan's lien is a claim on personal property. Suppose that you take your television to a repair shop, and the repairman keeps your television to make extensive repairs. A week later, the repairman notifies you that the repairs are finished; unfortunately, you discover that you cannot pay for the repairs. Consequently, the repairman may keep your television until you can pay for the parts and labor used in repairing it. If you never make the payment, the repairman is permitted to foreclose and sell your television to satisfy your debt.

Legal Principle: **An *artisan's lien* attaches to personal property as a result of labor provided by a third party for the benefit of such property.**

Case 31-1 illustrates who may qualify as a mechanic or artisan and the contribution that party must make to a particular project in order to secure lien rights.

CASE NUGGET

SUPPLIERS OF GOODS AND MECHANIC'S LIENS

Bates County Redi-Mix Inc. v. Windler
162 S.W. 3d 98 (Mo. App. 2005)

Bates County Redi-Mix supplied concrete to a subcontractor hired by a general contractor, who was hired by the owner. Because the subcontractor improperly installed the concrete, the concrete had to be removed and replaced. Bates sought a mechanic's lien for the concrete it supplied. The trial court concluded that Bates was not entitled to a lien because the concrete was not incorporated in the finished property. The appellate court concluded that Bates, as a materialman, is in a special position in supplying goods to a contractor because it lost its interest in the concrete once it was delivered to the subcontractor. The court emphasized that the purpose of the lien law was to encourage suppliers such as Bates to extend credit for land improvements. Moreover, Bates was not responsible for the defective installation of the concrete. Finally, the court held that the owner is in a better position, compared to the supplier, to oversee the contractor's work and ensure that the contractor properly installs the product. Thus, despite the improper installation, the court concluded that the supplier was entitled to a mechanic's lien for the concrete it supplied.

CASE 31-1 IN RE HYDRO-ACTION, INC.

U.S. BANKRUPTCY COURT FOR THE EASTERN DISTRICT OF TEXAS 2004 BANKR. LEXIS 262 (E.D. TEX. 2004)

In August of 2000, Hydro-Action, Inc. (Hydro), began negotiating with Storagequip.com (Storagequip) for the purchase of a conveyor belt system to facilitate the movement of large fiberglass tanks at Hydro's factory. Storagequip delivered the components in late December 2000, performed on-site fabrication and welding work, and completed the installation of the system in January 2001. Hydro failed to pay Storagequip for the system and filed a Chapter 11 bankruptcy proceeding in February 2001. Hydro and Storagequip agreed that Storagequip held a secured claim of $146,383.67 in the Chapter 11 bankruptcy proceeding.

The bankruptcy proceeding was converted to a Chapter 7 liquidation in May 2003. In July 2003, Storagequip filed a motion for relief from stay in order to foreclose upon its asserted lien on the conveyor belt system. The Trustee objected to the stay motion on the ground that no such lien existed. The issue for the court's resolution was whether Storagequip qualified as a mechanic, artisan, or materialman for purposes of asserting a lien pursuant to applicable Texas law.

CHIEF UNITED STATES BANKRUPTCY JUDGE PARKER: Storagequip asserts that it is entitled to a lien pursuant to Art. XVI, § 37 of the Texas Constitution, which states as follows:

> Mechanics, artisans and material men, of every class, shall have a lien upon the buildings and articles made or repaired by them for the value of their labor done thereon, or material furnished therefore; and the Legislature shall provide by law for the speedy and efficient enforcement of said Liens.

In examining the jurisprudence interpreting the asserted Texas constitutional lien, it is clear that the constitutional lien for mechanics, artisans and materialmen "exists independently and apart from any legislative act." *First Nat'l Bank in Dallas v. Whirlpool Corp.,* 517 S.W.2d 262, 267 (Tex. 1975). Moreover, Texas courts have consistently held the Texas constitutional lien to be self-executing. This self-executing aspect of the constitutional lien is viewed as vital because it translates into the chief advantage over statutory liens: the lien-holder does not need to give notice or record his lien; his protection is automatic.

The language of Tex. Const. art. XVI, § 37 provides two clear prerequisites. First, the protection is available only to a party who qualifies as a "mechanic," an "artisan," or a "materialman." Secondly, even if a party can fulfill one of those definitions, it may obtain a constitutional lien under § 37 only if it makes or repairs an "article" or "building."

The Court must first determine whether the Claimant qualifies as either a "mechanic," an "artisan," or a "materialman" under Texas law. Texas courts have defined a mechanic as "a person skilled in the practical use of tools, a workman who shapes and applies material in the building of a house or other structure mentioned in the statutes; a person who performs manual labor." *Warner Memorial Univ. v. Ritenour,* 56 S.W.2d 236, 236–37 (Tex. Civ. App.—Eastland 1933). Similarly, Texas courts have defined an artisan as "one skilled in some kind of mechanical craft; one who is employed in an industrial or mechanic art or trade," or "one trained for manual dexterity in some mechanic art or trade; a handicraftsman; a mechanic." See *Warner Mem'l Univ.,* 56 S.W.2d at 237. As noted in *In re Enron Corp.,* "this definition suggests that an artisan is akin to a mechanic." See

295 B.R. 190, 195 (Bankr. S.D.N.Y. 2003) [stating that "the use of tools and the performance of manual labor, both hallmarks of a mechanic, are significant factors in determining whether an individual is an artisan"]. Finally, a materialman has been defined as "a person who does not follow the business of building or contracting to build homes for others, but who manufactures, purchases or keeps for sale materials which enter into buildings [or articles] and who sells or furnishes such material without performing any work or labor installing or putting them in place." See *Enron,* 295 B.R. at 196–97.

The evidence in this case establishes that approximately twenty Storagequip workers spent roughly six weeks at the Debtor's location during December 2000 and January 2001, working seven days a week to create and install the conveyor belt system for the Debtor. It is uncontested that the conveyor belt system was not merely delivered, but rather came into existence only as the Claimant's staff utilized their skill to align certain appropriated parts and to fabricate others in order to create the conveyor system. Without the utilization of its workers who were skilled in the practical use of tools in furtherance of the Claimant's business and who in this instance shaped, arranged, and applied the various components through a significant amount of skill and manual labor, the conveyor belt system would have never been constructed on the Debtor's premises.

The Claimant's activity in this instance, in which it received a project objective from the Debtor and then proceeded to craft a mechanical device through the use of its skilled and manual workforce to achieve that objective, reflects the type of skill-based enterprise which the constitutional lien provision was designed to protect. Accordingly, the Court concludes that the Claimant qualifies as a "mechanic" for purposes of art. XVI, § 37 of the Texas Constitution.

Because of the nature of the Claimant's operations, it also likely qualifies as an "artisan" under the given definitions. As has been recognized, the use of the term "handicraftsman" in the definition of an artisan further supports the proposition that a key component in determining whether an individual or an entity qualifies as such for the purposes of the Constitutional Lien is the use of manual dexterity or skill with the hands in pursuing a relevant occupation. Merriam-Webster's Collegiate Dictionary defines a handicraftsman as "a person who engages in a handicraft: artisan." Merriam-Webster's goes on to define a handicraft as, "manual skill; an occupation requiring skill with the hands." Because a higher level of "manual dexterity or skill with the hands" was required to complete this project, the evidence further supports the characterization of the Claimant as an artisan.

However, the constitutional lien is granted to such a mechanic solely if it is engaged in the manufacturing or repairing of an "article" or "building." The term "articles made" is not a technical term; hence, the Court must interpret this language according to its usual and ordinary definition. An article is commonly defined as "a member of a class of things" and as "a thing of particular and distinctive kind." See Webster's New Collegiate Dictionary 63 (1979). Similarly, Black's Law Dictionary defines an "article" as a "particular object or substance, a material thing or a class of things." Moreover, the term "made" has been defined as "produced or manufactured artificially" and as "put together of various ingredients." See Black's Law Dictionary 950 (6th ed. 1990)[,] Webster's New Collegiate Dictionary 684 (1979).

Under these usual definitions, the conveyor belt system clearly constitutes an "article made." It cannot be reasonably disputed that a conveyor belt system is a particular type of object or thing. It is uncontested that the conveyor belt system did not come into existence until such time as the Claimant appropriated the various component parts, aligned the components in the proper manner, and performed some amount of on-site fabrication, ultimately producing the conveyor system on the Debtor's worksite. The lien claimant in the present case took a substantial number of component parts and fashioned a comprehensive system where none had previously existed which was designed to facilitate the movement of large fiberglass tanks within the Debtor's factory. Thus, on its face, it appears as though the conveyor belt system constitutes an "article made" for purposes of Article XVI, § 37.

The Court therefore concludes that the Claimant, Storagequip.com, possesses a lien against the conveyor belt system owned by the Estate by virtue of Article XVI, § 37 of the Texas Constitution which is not subject to avoidance by the Trustee in this case. Accordingly, the Claimant has satisfied its ultimate burden of persuasion of establishing the existence of a secured claim against this Estate, and the Trustee's objection to that secured claim shall be denied.

Objection DENIED.

CRITICAL THINKING

What factors did the court consider most important to its determination that Storagequip was a mechanic and an artisan for purposes of the Texas lien law?

ETHICAL DECISION MAKING

What was the purpose of the court's decision in this case? What values are being upheld in this opinion? Why do you think the court upheld those values?

Now suppose the repairman gave you your television back and told you to pay the debt as soon as you could. Five months later, the repairman claims that he has an artisan's lien on your television and wants to sell your TV to cover the debt. The repairman will not be successful because an artisan's lien is possessory. As long as the repairman retains possession of the television, he or she will hold the lien. However, if the lienholder voluntarily surrenders possession, the lien is lost.

What kind of priority does the artisan's lien have in relation to other claims on property? Both artisan's and mechanic's liens have priority over other types of liens; thus, they are called *super-priority liens*. Exhibit 31-1 compares the two types of liens.

JUDICIAL LIENS

LO3 What are the various kinds of judicial liens available to creditors?

Once a debt is due but unpaid by the debtor, the creditor may bring legal action against the debtor. When a creditor, through legal action, seizes a debtor's property to satisfy the debt, the creditor has a **judicial lien.** There are three types of judicial liens: attachment, writ of execution, and garnishment. These judicial liens usually occur at different steps during the legal action against the debtor.

Attachment. **Attachment** is a court order permitting a local court officer, such as a sheriff, to seize a debtor's property. Under statute, a creditor who has an enforceable right of payment under law may obtain an attachment. A creditor typically seeks an attachment as a prejudgment remedy in a legal action. The attachment brings the debtor's property under the court's control until the legal action is complete. Typically, a creditor may ask the court to attach the debtor's checking and savings accounts, certificates of deposit, or even personal or real property.

Legal Principle: ***Attachment* is a court order permitting a local court officer to seize a debtor's property before the entry of a final judgment in the underlying case.**

Why would a creditor want to attach property? An attachment can help ensure that a debtor does not sell or hide property in an attempt to avoid paying his or her debt. An unsecured creditor typically uses attachment; secured creditors do not need to create an attachment because they usually already have the right to repossess the property. Before a creditor can attach, he or she must follow specific procedures:

1. The creditor must file a lawsuit against the debtor, alleging that the debtor owes the creditor. The creditor may then seek a right-to-attach order from the court. The process for seeking a right-to-attach order is usually very specific. The creditor must list the grounds for the attachment application.
2. Generally, the creditor must then post a bond with the court. This bond must cover the amount of the court costs associated with the attachment along with any damage associated with a wrongful attachment. The amount of the bond is usually established by statute.
3. Next, the court holds a hearing regarding the attachment. At the hearing, the creditor must prove a legal basis for the attachment, such as (1) the debtor is a foreign

Exhibit 31-1

Comparison of Mechanic's and Artisan's Liens

CHARACTERISTICS	MECHANIC'S LIEN	ARTISAN'S LIEN
Type of property	Real property	Personal property
Possession requirement	No	Yes
How created?	By statute	By statute

corporation not authorized to do business in the state; (2) the debtor has been absent from the state for an extended period of time or the debtor's whereabouts are currently unknown; (3) the debtor has concealed himself or herself; (4) the debtor has or is about to remove his or her property from the state with the intent to defraud, delay, or hinder one or more creditors; (5) the debtor has or is about to fraudulently convey, transfer, or assign his or her property so as to hinder or delay one or more creditors; or (6) the debtor has departed or is about to depart the state with the intention of removing his or her property from the state. The debtor typically makes an argument that none of the above grounds for attachment exist, the creditor will not succeed on the underlying action, or the attached property is exempt or is needed to support the debtor or his or her family.

4. The court will then consider whether to issue a right-to-attach order. An attachment order directs the county clerk to issue a *writ of attachment,* a document authorizing a law officer to seize the debtor's nonexempt property.

After the law officer seizes the property, he or she must safely hold the property. Thus, the debtor is unable to sell or otherwise dispose of the property. The debtor may have an option to post a counterbond for the release of his property. If the creditor is successful in the legal action against the debtor, the creditor will likely be permitted to sell the property to satisfy the debt. However, if the debtor is successful in the legal action, the debtor can recover damages from the creditor for any losses he suffered while deprived of the property. Moreover, if the property was wrongfully attached, the debtor may recover punitive damages from the creditor.

Writ of Execution. Suppose that as a creditor, you bring a legal action against a debtor who refuses to pay you. You successfully bring your action, yet the debtor still does not pay you. What can you do now? You can go back to the clerk of courts to ask for a **writ of execution,** a judicial order authorizing a local law officer to seize and sell any of the debtor's nonexempt real or personal property within the court's geographic jurisdiction. The purpose of this action is to enforce the judgment awarded by the court. This seized property will be sold, and you will receive the proceeds to satisfy the judgment from the legal action. If, however, the debtor pays the judgment before the sale, the court will return the property to the debtor. If there is a surplus in the sale proceeds, this money will be returned to the debtor.

Legal Principle: A *writ of execution* is a judicial order authorizing a local law officer to seize and sell any of the debtor's nonexempt real or personal property within the court's geographic jurisdiction after the entry of judgment in the underlying case.

Some states permit the debtor to designate which property will be seized under the writ of execution. However, if the debtor refuses to designate property, the law officer may take any nonexempt property.

Exempt Property. We have been discussing creditor's actions to seize property to satisfy a debtor's obligation. Some of this property is exempt from seizure. Most states create exemptions for both real and personal property. These exemptions may provide protection for a certain type of property or a certain value. However, these exemptions generally apply only to individuals.

One of these exemptions is the **homestead exemption,** which permits a debtor to retain all or a portion of the family home so that the family will have some form of shelter. If the debtor does not have a family, the exemption may not apply. The amount of the homestead exemption varies from state to state. For example, in six states, the exemption is 100 percent of the value of the home. In California, the size of the exemption depends on the status of the homeowner. A single homeowner qualifies for a $75,000 exemption, a family qualifies for $100,000, and disabled homeowners or those over the age of 65 qualify for a $175,000 exemption.

The following items are also typically exempt from seizure:

1. Household goods, appliances, and furniture (usually up to a set value).
2. Clothing.
3. Equity in a vehicle (usually up to a set value).
4. Tools and instruments needed to carry on a trade.

The debtor has the responsibility to claim property as exempt by filing a list of exempt property with the court. If the exemption is limited to a certain amount of money, an appraiser will assess the value of the property claimed by the debtor as exempt.

Garnishment. Under state law, a creditor may also ask for a **garnishment,** an order that satisfies a debt by seizing a debtor's property that is being held by a third party. A garnishment order is usually directed at a bank where the debtor has an account or at an employer who pays the debtor wages. Under a garnishment order, the bank or the employer takes part of the debtor's savings or wages and pays the creditor directly. Thus, any potential future employer should be particularly aware of garnishment procedures.

Legal Principle: ***Garnishment* is a court order that satisfies a debt by seizing a debtor's property that is being held by a third party such as a bank or an employer.**

A creditor may obtain a garnishment order as a prejudgment or postjudgment remedy. If the creditor wants a prejudgment garnishment, he or she will have to successfully argue in a hearing that the garnishment is necessary. Typically, the third party will garnish the wages, money, or property until the entire debt is paid to the creditor.

How much money, property, or wages is garnished? Both federal and state laws restrict the amount of money that can be garnished. For example, some states do not allow wage garnishment for any claim except child support, taxes, federally guaranteed student loans, and court-ordered fines and restitution.[1] Furthermore, the Federal Consumer Credit Protection Act states that a debtor must be able to keep the greater of the following two options: 75 percent of his or her weekly net income or 30 times the federal minimum wage.[2] However, these restrictions do not apply if the garnishment is for certain debts such as child support. Similarly, state laws provide dollar restrictions on the amount garnished from an employee's wages. If the debtor does not make 30 times the federal minimum wage (or another dollar amount set through state law), the debtor's wages are exempt from garnishment.

Moreover, the debtor can stop the wage garnishment by filing a notice with the court that will lead to a hearing. At the hearing, the judge will decide whether the wages are exempt. Only one wage garnishment is permissible at a time; thus, if several creditors wish to garnish a debtor's wages, the first creditor to file will usually receive the garnished wages.[3]

Case 31-2 provides a novel illustration of an attempt to garnish amounts due under a reverse mortgage.

[1] Examples include North Carolina, Pennsylvania, South Carolina, and Texas. Garnishment for child support takes priority over other types of garnishment in several states.

[2] 15 U.S.C. § 1673 (a–c) (2010).

[3] However, stacking of garnishments is permitted and allows several creditors to line up for assets and receive payment as previous judgments are paid in full.

CASE 31-2 CAMERON v. EWING
SUPERIOR COURT OF NEW JERSEY, APPELLATE DIVISION
38 A.3D 611 (SUP. CT. APP. DIV. 2012)

Cameron filed a complaint in July 2007 against Ewing seeking damages arising out of an automobile accident. Ewing was an uninsured driver. The case settled, and Ewing consented to entry of judgment against him for $400,000 in April 2009.

Two months before settling the case, Ewing entered into a reverse mortgage with Wells Fargo Bank, N.A. Ewing, then almost eighty-five years old, gave Wells Fargo a mortgage on his home in an amount "up to" $360,000. Wells Fargo agreed to pay defendant $959.01 for as long as he lived and resided in his house. Ewing's other income consisted of monthly Social Security benefits and a Pennsylvania public employee pension.

On Cameron's behalf, the Hunterdon County Sheriff served a writ of execution on Wells Fargo, levying against "monies due to defendant from a reverse mortgage from Wells Fargo Home Mortgage." After Wells Fargo refused to comply, Cameron filed a motion seeking an order compelling Wells Fargo to withhold the monies due Ewing under the reverse mortgage and pay them over to the sheriff.

Cameron argued Wells Fargo's obligation to pay Ewing was a "debt due," and therefore subject to garnishment. Wells Fargo argued its monthly payments should not be deemed property subject to garnishment. The trial court agreed the regular payments from Wells Fargo to Ewing were not subject to garnishment. The court reasoned the reverse mortgage payments to Ewing were properly characterized as loans from Wells Fargo, secured by the mortgage on the house, and repayable upon Ewing's death or other events described in the transactional documents. Cameron appealed the decision to the Superior Court.

JUDGE OSTRER: This appeal presents the novel issue whether the stream of payments due a homeowner under a home equity conversion mortgage, also known as a reverse mortgage, is subject to execution and garnishment for the benefit of judgment creditors of the homeowner.

A judgment creditor is entitled to obtain execution against a debtor's "debts" as well as earned income, trust fund income, and profits. Construing the term "debt" in the execution statute, our former Supreme Court held that "debt" should be accorded not only its ordinary legal meaning as "an obligation for the payment of money founded upon a contract, express or implied," but more broadly as "that which one person is bound to pay to another under any form of obligation." *Passaic Nat'l Bank & Trust Co. v. Eelman,* 116 *N.J.L.* 279, 281, 183 *A.* 677 (Sup. Ct. 1936).

Consistent with these principles, the monthly reverse mortgage payments due from Wells Fargo are properly deemed debts owing to defendant. Federal law defines the Home Equity Conversion Mortgage to mean "a first mortgage which provides for future payments to the homeowner based on accumulated equity." 12 *U.S.C.* § 1715z-20(b)(3). The recognized purpose of the transaction, reflected by its name, Home Equity Conversion Mortgage, is "to permit the conversion of a portion of accumulated home equity into liquid assets." 12 *U.S.C.* § 1715z-20(a)(1). Our state's law authorizing issuance of reverse mortgages characterizes the payments to the mortgagor as "income," although it exempts it from taxation as gross income. *N.J.S.A.* 46:10B-20. Although the payments are not earned income, they are a regular and recurring obligation of Wells Fargo. It is of no moment that defendant also is indebted to Wells Fargo and he or his estate is ultimately liable to repay the monies received to the extent repayment may be generated from sale of the property. Wells Fargo remains obliged to make periodic installment payments to defendant pursuant to the terms of its Loan Agreement and Mortgage.

We recognize that a debt which is uncertain and contingent, in the sense that it may never become payable, is not subject to levy and sale. However, debts may be subject to execution "if liquidated and certain in their existence." *Passaic Nat'l Bank & Trust Co., supra,* 116 *N.J.L.* at 282, 183 *A.* 677. In this case, Wells Fargo's payment obligation is certain and currently payable.

Reading "debt" to include Wells Fargo's monthly payment obligation to defendant is also consistent with the general policy favoring enforcement of judgments. "It is the general policy of the law to lend the creditor all reasonable assistance for the enforcement of his claim, especially against a debtor who, though possessed of the means to pay, seeks to evade his obligation." *Id.* at 286.

While we have found no published opinion specifically addressing whether a reverse mortgage's payment stream is subject to execution and garnishment, we find support for our conclusion in a federal appeals court's decision that a line of credit is subject to execution on behalf of judgment creditors once the credit line is exercised. *In re Southwestern Glass Co.,* 332 *F.*3d 513, 518 (8th Cir. 2003) (judgment creditor entitled to writ of garnishment against bank holding proceeds of advances against judgment debtor's line of credit). The monthly payments under defendant's reverse mortgage have some attributes of an exercised line of credit. Just as the recipient of a line of credit is indebted to the financial institution extending it, defendant is indebted to Wells Fargo as he receives payments, drawing down credit against his overall payment limit. Nonetheless, the financial institution that has agreed to provide its customer a line of credit is obligated to honor drafts against the line, making the financial institution

[continued]

indebted to its customer, and subjecting to execution the exercised line of credit. Likewise, the monthly payments Wells Fargo is obligated to make are subject to execution.

Although we find that monthly reverse mortgage payments are subject to execution and garnishment, the court on remand must determine the percentage of the payments that will be subject to execution and garnishment.

Reversed and remanded for further proceedings consistent with this opinion.

CRITICAL THINKING

What is a reverse mortgage? What factors in the reverse mortgage did the court see as most important to its determination? Do you believe the timing of Ewing's transaction with Wells Fargo had a role in the court's decision?

ETHICAL DECISION MAKING

What was the purpose of the court's decision in this case? What values are being upheld in this opinion? Why do you think the court upheld those values?

Thus far, we have discussed mechanic's liens, artisan's liens, and judicial liens. Exhibit 31-2 lists other types of liens.

MORTGAGE FORECLOSURE

L04

How does mortgage foreclosure assist creditors?

A creditor who holds an interest in real property usually has a mortgage. The creditor possessing the mortgage, the mortgagee, can foreclose on the property when the debtor (the mortgagor) defaults. Usually, the foreclosure leads to a sale of the property. However, before foreclosure and sale of property can occur, the mortgagee must follow the state procedures for foreclosing a mortgage. Basically, the mortgagee must give the debtor notice of the foreclosure. At any time before the sale of property, the debtor may recover the property by paying the debt along with additional costs and interest. In some cases, the debtor may even recover the property after the sale.

Exhibit 31-2
Other Types of Liens

TYPE OF LIEN	DESCRIPTION
Attorney's lien	A claim that allows an attorney to keep a client's money or possessions pending payment of his or her legal bill
Broker's lien	A claim to property by a real estate broker to secure payment of a commission
Common law lien	A claim to property by implication of the law rather than statute
Consummate lien	The lien of a judgment creditor that arises when a motion for a new trial has been denied
Equitable lien	A claim on property either created by a sales contract or imposed by a court in the interest of fairness
Innkeeper's lien	A claim on the baggage of guests who stay at an inn and are unable to pay their bill
Landlord's lien	A claim on a tenant's furniture and property to secure the payment of rent
Maritime lien	A claim for services rendered to a vessel
Medicare lien	A hospital's claim to benefits payable pursuant to the Medicare Act
Possessory lien	A claim to property in which the lienholder has the right to be in possession of the property until the debt is paid
Tax lien	A claim against a taxpayer's property for unpaid taxes
Vendor's lien	A vendor's claim to land for the unpaid purchase price

If the proceeds from the sale of the property are greater than the debt owed, the debtor retains the extra money. However, if the proceeds do not cover the debt, the mortgagee can seek a *deficiency judgment,* an order that permits the creditor to recover property beyond the foreclosed property.

BUT WHAT IF . . .

WHAT IF THE FACTS OF THE CASE OPENER WERE DIFFERENT?

Let's say, in the Case Opener, that Provident provided a notice of foreclosure to the Reeses. Subsequently, a date of sale of the property was scheduled for a month later. Two days before the date of the sale, the Reeses came into some money and went to Provident to pay the money they owed and stop the sale of the home. Provident refused and said the home was going to be sold. The Reeses said they were allowed to reclaim their home if they had the money. Who is correct in this situation?

CREDITORS' COMPOSITION AGREEMENTS

LO5

What is a creditors' composition agreement for the benefit of creditors?

Thus far, we have discussed rights and remedies in situations in which creditors try to force debtors to pay. However, one remedy that is more voluntary for the debtor is a *composition agreement,* a contract between creditors and a debtor in which the creditors agree to accept a lesser amount to satisfy the debts and discharge the remaining debt. However, if the debtor does not pay her debt under the composition agreement, the creditors may collect on the original debt. Unless the agreement is formed under duress, the courts usually uphold such agreements.

Why would creditors agree to a composition agreement? Generally, creditors do not have an incentive to accept a lesser amount to satisfy a debt. However, if the creditors believe that a debtor, such as a small business, could not cover the entire debt, even through bankruptcy, the creditors may agree to accept a smaller amount to permit the business to continue operating.

ASSIGNMENT FOR THE BENEFIT OF CREDITORS

LO6

What is an assignment for the benefit of creditors?

Another voluntary action the debtor can make to pay debts is to transfer, or assign, title of his or her property to a trustee or an assignee who sells the property to pay the creditors on a pro rata basis with the proceeds of the sale. This transfer of title is called *assignment for the benefit of creditors,* and it is permitted through state law. If a creditor chooses to accept the payment, this will usually discharge the debt. However, the creditor is not required to accept.

Why would a creditor accept this payment? Even though the creditor might not receive the full amount of the debt, the creditor is receiving at least part of the debt. Furthermore, the creditor is saving the time and expense of trying to force the debtor to pay through other remedies.

BUT WHAT IF . . .

WHAT IF THE FACTS OF THE CASE OPENER WERE DIFFERENT?

Let's say, in the Case Opener, that before Provident could send the Reeses a notice of foreclosure the Reeses transferred their house to a relative. The relative then sold the house so that the Reeses could use the money earned to pay Provident for what was owed on the house. What is this action called? How does Provident legally have to respond to this?

Suretyship and Guaranty Contracts

LO7 What are suretyship and guaranty contracts?

Suppose you are the business manager of a company that extends credit to consumers. You are going to sell a high-priced good to a buyer through a payment plan when you suddenly discover that the buyer has a bad credit history. You want to make the sale, yet you are worried that the debtor will default on the loan. What can you do?

One option is to have the debtor find a third party who agrees to be liable for the debt. When a third party agrees to be liable for a debtor's loan, the party creates either a *suretyship* or a *guaranty arrangement.* The third party's liability provides additional protection against loss should the debtor default on his or her loan.

SURETYSHIP

A **suretyship** is a contract between a creditor and a third party who agrees to pay another person's debt. This third party, also known as the *surety* or *cosigner,* is primarily liable for the debt. In other words, as soon as the debt is due, the surety is responsible for the payment. The suretyship is not simply an agreement in which the surety agrees to cover the loan if the debtor cannot pay. The surety must pay even if the creditor has not asked the original debtor to pay. This agreement generally does not have to be in writing.

A suretyship contract is particularly common in loans to young adults. For example, suppose you are in college and decide that you want to buy a new car. However, you need a loan to pay for the car, and the bank will not give you a loan unless you have a cosigner. If one of your parents cosigns your loan, he or she is acting as a surety. That parent is responsible for the payment.

GUARANTY

A **guaranty** is distinct from a suretyship in terms of the liability to the creditor. As you just learned, the surety is *primarily liable* to the creditor for a debtor's debt. In contrast, the third party in a guaranty contract is *secondarily liable* for the debt. Thus, in a guaranty, the third party, usually called the *guarantor,* must pay the debt *only* after the debtor has defaulted. Typically, the guarantor is not responsible until the creditors have tried unsuccessfully to collect the debt from the debtor.

Suppose that you are starting your own business and need a loan to cover some expenses. You attempt to obtain a bank loan, but the bank believes that your business may not be successful and you may not be able to pay your loan. However, the bank will offer the loan if a third party will be a guarantor and thus agree to be responsible for your loan if you cannot pay it. In this situation, both parties benefit. You receive the loan necessary to start your business, while the bank gains the safety and security that it will not lose its loaned money.

Generally, this agreement must be made in writing. This contract establishes the terms of the guaranty agreement. A guaranty may be a continuing agreement to cover numerous transactions. Alternatively, the contract can state a fixed amount of time.

Because of the distinction in liability between a surety and a guarantor, both creditors and debtors must make sure that the contract among the three parties is clear in stating whether the third party is a guarantor or surety.

DEFENSES OF THE SURETY AND THE GUARANTOR

If a creditor brings legal action against a surety or guarantor, the surety or guarantor may use several defenses to argue that he or she should not be required to pay a creditor. Generally, the defenses available to the debtor are also available to the surety and the guarantor.

As suggested in previous chapters, certain kinds of contracts must be in writing to be enforceable. A guaranty agreement to pay the debt of another is one type of contract that must be in writing. Because the third party may not receive a benefit in return for its promise to pay the debt of another, courts require that the creditor provide the writing itself when trying to enforce the agreement against the third party. If a guarantor's oral promise to pay a debt is not in writing, the guarantor can raise the statute-of-frauds defense. By requiring that the creditor produce the writing, courts provide greater protection to ensure that innocent third parties are not unfairly charged.

A surety or guarantor could argue that she has been discharged from the debt. The reasons for discharge can vary. If the debtor has paid the sum owed to the creditor, the debtor's liability, as well as the surety's or guarantor's liability, is discharged. Furthermore, if the debtor makes an agreement that materially alters the original contract without the consent of the surety or guarantor, the surety's or guarantor's liability is discharged. In Case 31-3, a material alteration of the underlying contract resulted in a discharge of the guarantors.

CASE 31-3 COOPER INVESTMENTS v. CONGER
COLORADO COURT OF APPEALS
775 P.2D 76 (COLO. APP. 1989)

On May 31, 1978, Cooper Investments, Robert C. Rifkin and Gerald Kernis (Creditors) sold to Robert L. Conger, Thomas H. Stroh, and Jack W. Welsh (Guarantors) all of the outstanding shares of stock in a corporation which owned the assets of a certain restaurant and bar. In exchange, the Creditors were given a promissory note in which the corporation promised to pay the Creditors the principal sum of $450,000 together with interest at the rate of 8% per annum. The note called for payment of principal and interest in sixty-seven monthly installments.

The Guarantors furnished the Creditors with a separate written guaranty, which provided that they jointly and severally guaranteed "the prompt payment of the note." The guaranty further provided that it was continuing and extended "to any note given in extension or renewal of this note notwithstanding the original note may have been surrendered, provided the liability of the [guarantors] shall not be increased over the amount contained in the original note."

In November 1979, the Guarantors sold the corporation to the third party and were no longer involved in operating the restaurant and bar or in the management of the corporation. In October 1981, the corporation entered into a joint venture agreement with Iona, Inc., concerning the operation of the restaurant and bar. In September 1982, the president of Iona approached the Creditors about a change in the payment terms of the note. They reached an oral agreement to reduce the monthly payments of principal and interest from $8,000 to $5,000 per month for eight months and also to increase the rate of interest from 8% to 12% per annum.

After May 1983, no further payments were made on the note. Iona later defaulted on the note and the Creditors brought suit against Guarantors. The trial court rejected the Guarantors' affirmative defenses and entered judgment jointly and severally against them. The Guarantors appealed.

JUDGE HUME: In general, when a creditor has chosen to alter materially the principal debtor's obligation to the guarantor's detriment, without the guarantor's consent, that alteration discharges the guarantor's liability. An alteration is material if it changes the nature of the principal debtor's obligation, "either by imposing some new obligation or by taking away some obligation already imposed." Accordingly, the rate of interest which the principal debtor is required to pay under a promissory note is a material term of that note.

Here, the undisputed evidence in the record establishes that, in September 1982, creditors and the president of Iona orally agreed to modify the terms of the note, by reducing the required monthly payments of principal and interest from $8,000 to $5,000, and by increasing the interest rate from 8% to 12% per annum. We conclude that as a matter of law the change in the rate of interest materially altered the principal debtor's obligation under the note, and since the change involved an increase in the rate, it was detrimental to the Guarantors.

Guarantors next urge that the alterations were not within the scope of the written guaranty agreement. We agree that the alterations were not within the scope of the written guaranty. The consent of a guarantor to an alteration is binding whether it is expressed as part of the initial obligation or is given later, either before or subsequent to the alteration. Such consent need not be evidenced by a writing.

In determining the scope of a guarantor's consent to future alterations, a guaranty agreement must be "strictly

[continued]

construed and reasonably interpreted according to the intention of the parties as disclosed by the surrounding circumstances." Further, "the liability of the guarantor is not to be extended by implication beyond the express limits or terms of the instrument, or its plain intent. It has been said a guarantor is, like a surety, a favorite of the law."

The guaranty agreement here expressly provided that it shall extend to "any note given in extension or renewal" of the original note. However, such consent to future extensions and renewals was not unlimited. The guaranty specifically provided that the guarantors did not consent to future extensions or renewals that would increase their liability over the amount contained in the original note plus accrued and unpaid interest. Here, the guaranty agreement does not expressly provide that the guarantors consented to a future increase in the rate of interest. And, the fact that guarantors consented to a future "extension" or "renewal" of the note does not necessarily imply that they also consented to an increase in the interest rate.

An "extension" or "renewal" note extends the time for payment of principal beyond the original period of the note, and necessarily increases the total amount of interest to be paid. However, such an increase in the amount of interest to be paid is dependent on the extension of time rather than a change in the interest rate to be applied to the debt. Since the guaranty must be strictly construed, we conclude that the language in the guaranty authorizing extensions and renewals neither contemplates nor authorizes an increase in the rate of interest.

The judgment is reversed and the cause is remanded to the trial court for further proceedings consistent with this opinion.

REVERSED and REMANDED.

CRITICAL THINKING

How did the judge arrive at his decision? Do you agree with the distinction the judge made between extension or renewal of the note and the alteration of the interest rate for purposes of discharge of the guarantors? Why or why not?

ETHICAL DECISION MAKING

How would you analyze the ethical behavior on both sides of this transaction? Were the creditors simply attempting to impose an interest rate increase without securing the guarantors' consent, which they knew would not be forthcoming? Were the guarantors utilizing a technicality to avoid repayment of a legitimate debt of the business?

While the surety or guarantor may assert that his or her bankruptcy or incapacity is a defense against paying the creditor, the surety or guarantor cannot use the debtor's bankruptcy or incapacity as a defense. However, if the debtor engaged in fraud to convince the surety or guarantor to enter the contract, the surety or guarantor may assert this fraud as a defense and will likely be discharged from liability.

RIGHTS OF THE SURETY AND THE GUARANTOR

If a surety or guarantor pays the debtor's obligation to the creditor, the surety or guarantor has certain rights. First, the surety or guarantor has a right to *subrogation,* which means that the surety or guarantor is entitled to all the rights that the creditor had against the debtor. If the surety or guarantor pays the debtor's loan, he or she has the right to reimbursement from the debtor. The surety or guarantor can recover the actual amount of the debt paid to the creditor as well as the expenses associated with taking legal action against the debtor for reimbursement.

If there are multiple sureties or guarantors who pay the debtor's obligation to the creditor, one surety might have paid a greater proportion of the obligation. This surety or guarantor has the *right of contribution,* which means that the other sureties or guarantors must pay their equal shares; consequently, the surety who originally paid the large amount can recover this money.

BUT WHAT IF . . .

WHAT IF THE FACTS OF THE CASE OPENER WERE DIFFERENT?

Let's say, in the Case Opener, that Mr. Reese's mom, Betty, was a guarantor on the loan agreement the Reeses had for their house. Betty decided to pay the remaining balance the Reeses owed for their house. What rights does Betty then have in regard to the house? Can she demand that the Reeses pay her back in full? What are these rights called?

CASE OPENER WRAP-UP

Mortgage Foreclosure

The Georgia Court of Appeals reversed the judgment of the trial court, which had held in favor of Provident. The appellate court held that although Georgia's foreclosure statute was ambiguous on the exact point, it nevertheless required proper identification of the secured creditor and the party on whose behalf the foreclosure was commenced. The court relied heavily on legislative history in determining that Georgia's foreclosure statute was designed to protect debtors from abusive and misleading lending practices. Although it was important for lenders to be able to foreclose on properties for nonpayment of mortgages, foreclosure was "typically a very important event for all parties involved." This "important event" required that the documents correctly identify the entities entitled to foreclose. The court of appeals reversed the trial court and found the Reeses' foreclosure to be wrongful.[4]

[4] *Reese v. Provident Funding Associates, LLP,* 730 S.E.2d 551 (Ga. Ct. App. 2012).

KEY TERMS

artisan's lien 684
attachment 687
garnishment 689
guaranty 693
homestead exemption 688
judicial lien 687
lien 682
mechanic's lien 683
suretyship 693
writ of execution 688

SUMMARY OF KEY TOPICS

Laws Assisting Creditors

Lien: A claim to property.

The principal types of liens include:

1. *Consensual lien:* A secured interest in property created by agreement of the parties.
2. *Statutory lien:* A claim to property created through statute.

- *Mechanic's lien:* A claim on real property.
- *Artisan's lien:* A claim on personal property.

3. *Judicial lien:* Legal action whereby a creditor seizes a debtor's property to satisfy the debt.
    - *Attachment:* A court-ordered judgment permitting a local court officer to seize a debtor's property.
    - *Writ of execution:* A document authorizing a law officer to seize the debtor's nonexempt property.
    - *Garnishment:* An order that satisfies a debt by seizing a debtor's property that is being held by a third party, such as a bank or an employer.

Mortgage foreclosure: The foreclosure and sale of mortgaged property to pay a debt.

Creditors' composition agreement: A contract between creditors and a debtor in which the creditors agree to accept a lesser amount to satisfy the debt and discharge the remainder of the debt.

Assignment for the benefit of creditors: The transfer of the title of property to a trustee who sells the property to pay the creditors on a pro rata basis with the proceeds of the sale.

Suretyship and Guaranty Contracts

Suretyship: A contract between a creditor and a third party who agrees to pay another person's debt and is thus primarily liable for that debt.

Guaranty: A third party, usually called the *guarantor,* who must pay the debt *only* after the debtor has defaulted and who is thus secondarily liable for that debt.

Defenses of the surety and guarantor:

1. Statute of frauds
2. Discharge from the debt
3. Bankruptcy
4. Debtor's fraud

Rights of the surety and guarantor:

1. *Right to subrogation:* Surety or guarantor is entitled to all the rights that the creditor had against the debtor.
2. *Right to reimbursement:* Surety or guarantor can recover the actual amount of the debt paid to the creditor as well as legal expenses against the debtor for reimbursement.
3. *Right of contribution:* Other sureties or guarantors must pay their equal shares.

POINT / COUNTERPOINT

As you learned in this chapter, the homestead exemption allows a debtor to retain a portion or all of the family home even though the debtor is unable to pay his or her debts. Each state has its own rules regarding the amount of the exemption. Some states, such as Florida, Iowa, Kansas, South Dakota, and Texas, have no dollar limit on the homestead exemption. Thus, if a house is worth $1 million and a debtor is unable to pay his debt, he may be permitted to keep the home and still discharge other debts. In contrast, other states have widely varying homestead exemptions. There are some states that have very high exemptions, such as Rhode Island ($500,000), Minnesota ($390,000), Montana ($250,000), and Washington ($125,000). Other states have relatively low exemptions, such as Wyoming ($20,000), Kentucky ($5,000), and Virginia ($5,000). Some states, such as New Jersey and Pennsylvania, do not have a homestead exemption.

Should Congress Create a Federal Homestead Exemption That Would Apply across All States?

YES	NO
Congress should create a federal homestead exemption. Because each state has its own exemption, a debtor is treated differently depending on the state laws. It seems unfair that a debtor in Texas can keep her entire home while a similar debtor in a different state may be forced to sell his home. When the homestead exemption is particularly high or unlimited, a debtor may be more likely to shield assets from creditors. The federal government is willing to limit the homestead exemption in certain cases. For example, under current bankruptcy law, the federal government has limited the homestead exemption to $125,000 if the debtor acquired the property within 1,215 days before filing. The federal government could set both a floor and a ceiling for the homestead exemption in other types of cases to provide more certainty for both debtors and creditors across the country.	Each state should establish its own homestead exemption. The homestead exemptions are generally found in the state statutes and even in some state constitutions. The homestead exemption is like the sales tax: Each state should be free to determine how its citizens will be treated. If a citizen is unhappy with the protections she receives in one state, she can always move to another state. Moreover, imposing a federal exemption would fail to take into account varying property values. For example, the median house price in the San Francisco Bay area is approximately $760,000. However, the median house price is $191,550 in Atlanta, Georgia, and $21,000 in Detroit, Michigan. Geography accounts for varying house values; consequently, the homestead exemption should not be uniform. Finally, unlimited homestead exemptions provide security and stability to families. Limiting the homestead exemptions would penalize and uproot children who should not be held responsible for debt problems.

QUESTIONS & PROBLEMS

1. What criterion must be satisfied for each type of lien to exist? What are the major differences between the mechanic's lien, artisan's lien, and judicial lien?
2. What is the difference between a surety and a guarantor? Why is this distinction important to business law?
3. Enterprise Products Operating L.P. entered into an agreement dated July 29, 1998, with Enron Gas Liquids, Inc. (EGLI). Enterprise agreed to perform several different types of services for EGLI, including engineering services necessary for EGLI to produce natural gas liquids, product treatment services, and the trucking and storage of certain liquids. Enterprise invoiced EGLI $888,000 for these services. On December 2, 2001, EGLI filed a voluntary petition for relief under Chapter 11 of the Bankruptcy Code. Enterprise asserted lien claims under the Texas Constitution relating to its unpaid invoices. While admitting the validity of the lien claim asserted by Enterprise for the performance of trucking and storage services in the amount of $359,572.39, EGLI denied the existence of a lien relating to engineering services and product treatment in the amount of $528,486.70. The issue for the court's resolution was whether Enterprise qualified as an artisan for purposes of asserting a lien pursuant to applicable Texas law. Is Enterprise an artisan utilizing the definition previously discussed in *In re Hydro-Action, Inc.?* Why or why not? [*In re Enron Corp.*, 295 B.R. 190 (Bankr. S.D.N.Y. 2003).]
4. On June 30, 2006, Charles Miller pleaded guilty to two counts related to a fraudulent scheme by which he obtained money from an elderly woman. Part of Miller's sentence included the obligation to pay restitution to the victim. On October 25, 2006, the district court entered a judgment against Miller for restitution in the amount of $146,938.73. Miller received a monthly benefit from the General

Motors Hourly Pension Plan of $1,715.72. Fidelity Investments was the plan administrator. On December 20, 2006, a writ of garnishment requiring Fidelity Investments to respond with information about its indebtedness to Miller was issued. Miller objected to the writ of garnishment and claimed that he had cancer and heart problems and that the garnishment would leave him homeless once he was released from prison and would prevent him from supporting himself and his wife. Miller also asserted that his pension fund was exempt from garnishment. On April 30, 2007, the magistrate judge assigned to hear Miller's objections entered a report recommending that the objections to the writ of garnishment be overruled. Miller appealed to the district court. How should the district court decide this case? What values should the court emphasize—specifically, the right of the creditor to obtain restitution or the protection of the debtor's pension earned as a result of his years of service?[*United States v. Miller,* 588 F. Supp. 2d 789 (W.D. Mich. 2008).]

5. Steven P. Cordovano entered into a contract with D'Angelo Development and Construction Company to build a house on real property purchased by Cordovano from D'Angelo. Although D'Angelo had been a home improvement contractor licensed by the state of Connecticut since 1994, D'Angelo was out of compliance with the Connecticut Home Improvement Act at the time it signed the contract with Cordovano. D'Angelo remedied the noncompliance and obtained a new certificate of registration from the state of Connecticut three days after it signed the contract with Cordovano and before it commenced construction of the home. D'Angelo completed construction of the home, but Cordovano failed to pay. As a result, D'Angelo filed a mechanic's lien against the property in July 2002 in the amount of $86,699.26. D'Angelo subsequently initiated a foreclosure action against the property, but Cordovano contended that the lien was invalid because the underlying contract was illegal due to D'Angelo's failure to possess a proper certificate of registration at the time of signing the contract. Is the mechanic's lien valid under these circumstances? Why or why not? [*D'Angelo Dev. & Constr. Co. v. Cordovano,* 897 A.2d 81 (Conn. 2006).]

6. As noted in the *Reese* opinion summarized in the Case Opener Wrap-Up, there has been considerable concern about abusive residential lending practices and mortgage foreclosures, especially since the collapse of the residential real estate market in mid-2008. Such concerns led to a series of lawsuits by the federal government and state governments against lenders that were alleged to be complicit in these practices and abuses. For example, in February 2012, the attorneys general of 49 states agreed to a settlement with Bank of America, JP Morgan Chase, Wells Fargo, Citigroup, and Ally Financial regarding their foreclosure practices of utilizing false or incomplete documentation. The amount of this settlement has been estimated at $26 billion. In January 2013, the federal government settled claims against 14 banks relating to their abusive lending practices that contributed to the 2008 financial crisis. The amount of this settlement is an estimated $18.5 billion. Conduct some research on these settlements. How are the proceeds from these settlements divided? Are these settlements sufficient to compensate all affected homeowners and dissuade lending institutions from engaging in such behavior in the future? Why or why not?

7. Wood owed DeThomas $24,160.28, which represented unpaid support for the minor child of the couple. Wood subsequently obtained a settlement in a personal injury lawsuit in the amount of $17,000. The state of Colorado served Woods's law firm in the personal injury lawsuit with a writ of garnishment. The law firm disbursed $9,830.03 to the state but withheld $6,593.22 to cover the law firm's legal fees and $576.75 for a medical lien. The state then moved the court for the remaining balance of the funds withheld by the law firm. Should the state be entitled to collect the balance from the law firm? Who has priority with respect to the balance, the state for unpaid child support or the law firm for services rendered in the personal injury lawsuit? [*In the Interest of J.W.,* 174 P.3d 315 (Colo. App. 2007).]

8. On July 1, 1994, Dressler Properties, Inc., entered into a lease agreement with Ohio Heart Care, Inc. Drs. David Utlak and Carlos Fabre signed a guaranty of performance of the rent obligations under the lease agreement. On February 14, 2003, Dressler Properties filed a complaint against Ohio Heart for unpaid rent. The court entered a default judgment against Ohio Heart Care, Utlak, and Fabre on October 17, 2003. Dressler Properties entered into a settlement agreement with Ohio Heart and Utlak and dismissed the lawsuit with prejudice in return for the execution of a promissory note from Ohio Heart and Utlak payable to Dressler Properties. On June 1, 2004, Fabre filed a motion for relief from the default judgment, claiming that the judgment had been satisfied, released, or discharged. The trial court denied the motion, and Fabre appealed. Has Fabre been discharged from his guaranty agreement and the resultant judgment as a result of the settlement between Dressler Properties, Ohio Heart, and Utlak? Why or why not? [*Dressler Props., Inc. v. Ohio Heart Care, Inc.*, 2005 Ohio App. LEXIS 1085 (Ohio App. 2005).]

Looking for more review materials?

The Online Learning Center at **www.mhhe.com/kubasek3e** contains this chapter's "Assignment on the Internet" and also a list of URLs for more information, entitled "On the Internet." Find both of them in the Student Center portion of the OLC, along with quizzes and other helpful materials.

Bankruptcy and Reorganization

LEARNING OBJECTIVES

After reading this chapter, you will be able to answer the following questions:

1. What are the goals of the Bankruptcy Act?
2. What is the basic set of procedures for bankruptcy cases?
3. What specific types of relief are available through bankruptcy?

CASE OPENER

GM Bankruptcy

After suffering five straight years of losses and market share decline, in June 2009 General Motors (GM) had $172 billion in liabilities, which far overshadowed its assets of $82 billion. As a result, General Motors filed for Chapter 11 bankruptcy, which allows a company to reorganize its structure and debt while continuing to operate during the reorganization. This reorganization led to a new legal entity, or a "new" GM. When creating its plan to restructure, GM had to make decisions about which liabilities it would keep and which liabilities it would discharge. As part of the bankruptcy plan, GM discontinued its Pontiac, Saturn, Hummer, and Saab brands and focused its resources on its Chevrolet, Cadillac, GMC, and Buick brands. The reduction in brands forced GM to lay off approximately 23,000 workers, close 13 plants, and terminate 900 dealerships. GM also decided that it would not retain responsibility for injuries that drivers suffer due to vehicle defects. Consequently, these drivers could not bring a product liability claim against the new GM but, instead, would be forced to compete with all other creditors for any assets left in the "old" GM (now known as "Motors Liquidation Company").

1. How would you handle this situation if you were one of General Motors' large creditors or, alternatively, if you were one of the company's smaller creditors who worried about being shut out by the larger lenders?
2. Suppose you were a driver injured by a defect in your GM automobile. How would you feel about GM's bankruptcy plan? Should the "new" GM be permitted to discharge liability for the "old" GM's products?

The Wrap-Up at the end of the chapter will answer these questions.

When an entity is unable to pay its debts, bankruptcy law provides various options for the entity to resolve those debts. Bankruptcy remedies are available to individuals, partnerships, and corporations. In 2011, more than 1.4 million bankruptcies were filed.[1]

Generally, a **debtor** is defined as an entity that owes money to another entity. The term *debtor* is defined differently under each type of bankruptcy remedy; thus, an individual or company that is eligible for one type of bankruptcy might not be eligible for another type of bankruptcy.

This chapter explains the various bankruptcy remedies available to debtors. We begin with a discussion of the goals of bankruptcy law and an overview of the Bankruptcy Code. We spend the rest of the chapter considering specific types of bankruptcy relief under the code.

The Bankruptcy Act and Its Goals

L01

What are the goals of the Bankruptcy Act?

Suppose that, in the opening scenario, GM decided to use all of its assets to pay its entire debt to only two of its creditors, leaving all its other creditors to receive nothing. The creditors who were not paid would have been treated unfairly; perhaps GM, the debtor, could have paid each creditor half of the debt it owed that creditor. This scenario highlights the two general goals of bankruptcy laws. First, bankruptcy laws provide protection to **creditors**—entities to which a debtor owes money. Bankruptcy laws ensure that creditors competing for a debtor's assets are treated equally and receive a fair share of the debtor's assets. Second, bankruptcy laws provide opportunities for debtors to gain a fresh financial start. In summary, bankruptcy law provides an organized method by which **insolvent debtors**—debtors who cannot pay their debts in a timely fashion—respond to their debts.

No one ever dreams they will end up in this court.

Bankruptcy law is federal law. Article I, Section 8, of the Constitution states: "The Congress shall have the power . . . To establish an uniform rule of naturalization and uniform laws on the subject of bankruptcies throughout the United States." Congress first addressed bankruptcy relief in the Bankruptcy Act of 1898. This act was replaced by the 1978 Bankruptcy Code, which was amended in 1984, 1986, and 1994.

Congress revised the Bankruptcy Code through the **Bankruptcy Abuse Prevention and Consumer Protection Act (BAPCPA) of 2005.** This act, spanning over 500 pages, took effect in October 2005. The revision includes the most comprehensive changes to bankruptcy law in over 25 years. Some of the reasons cited for these changes include:

1. Increased numbers of bankruptcy filings. In 1998, the total number of bankruptcy filings surpassed 1 million filings for the first time. In 2004, the number increased to over 1.6 million filings.
2. Significant losses associated with bankruptcy filings. According to testimony given before Senate subcommittees, in 1997, debtors discharged more than $44 billion in debt through bankruptcy relief. Furthermore, the Credit Union National Association estimated that credit unions' bankruptcy-related losses in 2004 would total approximately $900 million.

[1] Administrative Office of the U.S. Courts, "Bankruptcy Filings Slide in Calendar Year 2011" (press release), February 7, 2012.

3. "Loopholes and incentives that allow and—sometimes—even encourage opportunistic personal filings and abuse."
4. "The fact that some bankruptcy debtors are able to repay a significant portion of their debt."[2]

TITLE 11 OF THE UNITED STATES CODE

Title 11 of the United States Code (U.S.C.) contains the Bankruptcy Code, which is divided into chapters. Chapters 1, 3, and 5 provide the general definitions and provisions concerning bankruptcy case administration and debtors. These chapters apply to all types of bankruptcy relief. Chapters 7, 9, 11, 12, 13, and 15, briefly described in Exhibit 32-1, apply six specific types of bankruptcy relief.

In the following sections, we discuss bankruptcy relief under Chapters 7, 11, 12, and 13.

Exhibit 32-2 displays bankruptcy statistics in the United States for 2011. Notice the ratio between the number of filings under each chapter.

While bankruptcy law is federal law, state law applies to bankruptcy cases in the sense that state laws regarding debtor's property and creditor claims may apply. For example, states may have different laws regarding what property is subject to collection and sale through bankruptcy. Federal law also addresses what property is subject to collection and sale through bankruptcy. As you learned in previous chapters, when there is a conflict between a federal and a state law, the federal law trumps the state law and is supreme.

Legal Principle: **Bankruptcy law is federal law; however, state laws regarding property and debts may affect the bankruptcy proceeding.**

BUT WHAT IF . . .

WHAT IF THE FACTS OF THE CASE OPENER WERE DIFFERENT?

Let's say, in the Case Opener, that when General Motors filed for bankruptcy, the company lawyers had a meeting with the executives to explain the implications of having customers, debtors, and properties in multiple states and the effects of different state laws. The executives said that bankruptcy is guided by federal law and thus state law regarding the subject is nonexistent. Which party is correct? What is the true relationship between state law and bankruptcy?

Exhibit 32-1
Types of Bankruptcy Relief by Chapter

Chapter 7	Sale of debtor's assets by trustee and the distribution of money to creditors
Chapter 9	Adjustment of a municipality's debts
Chapter 11	Reorganization of the debtor's financial affairs under supervision of the bankruptcy court
Chapter 12	Reorganization of a family farmer's debts
Chapter 13	Reorganization of an individual's debts
Chapter 15	Recognition of insolvency proceedings pending in a foreign country and relief for foreign debtors

[2] "Factors Supporting Bankruptcy Reform," U.S. House of Representatives Judiciary Committee Report 109-031, 109th Congress, 1st Sess., April 8, 2005. Bankruptcy Abuse Prevention and Consumer Protection Act of 2005 Report of the Committee on the Judiciary, House of Representatives, to accompany S. 256.

Exhibit 32-2
Bankruptcy Filing Statistics, Calendar Year 2011

Total filings	1,410,653
Consumer filings	1,362,847
Business filings	47,806
Chapter 7	992,332
Chapter 11	11,529
Chapter 12	637
Chapter 13	406,084

Source: Administrative Office of the U.S. Courts, "Bankruptcy Filings Slide in 2011" (press release), February 7, 2012.

Attributes of Bankruptcy Cases

In what ways are bankruptcy cases similar to and different from other types of cases? First, while the Federal Rules of Civil Procedure set forth procedural rules for civil cases, the Bankruptcy Rules set forth procedures for bankruptcy cases. Second, like other federal cases, bankruptcy cases are filed in federal district courts. However, bankruptcy cases are then referred to bankruptcy judges, under the authority of the district courts. Bankruptcy judges are appointed to their positions, and they serve 14-year terms. These judges make decisions regarding the administration of the bankruptcy proceedings. For example, a bankruptcy judge can decide what the debtor's assets are, how the assets are to be sold, and what assets the debtor may keep. However, the judge cannot make decisions about state law claims.

As with other cases, a bankruptcy ruling can be appealed. The appeal goes to the district court judge. Moreover, a jury can hear a bankruptcy case if the district court as well as the interested parties approve.

PERCEPTIONS OF BANKRUPTCY

Historically, bankruptcy has had a negative connotation and was often associated with individuals who were not responsible with money. In the past, individuals who filed for bankruptcy were denied government licenses or permits. Moreover, creditors harassed bankrupt debtors.

During the congressional debates regarding the 2005 Bankruptcy Abuse Prevention and Consumer Protection Act, Congressman James Sensenbrenner argued: "Every day that goes by without these reforms, more abuse and fraud goes undetected. . . . America's economy should not suffer any longer from the billions of dollars in losses associated with the profligate and abusive bankruptcy filings."[3]

However, some studies suggested that most people, perhaps 80 percent, sought bankruptcy protection because an event outside their control occurred.[4] For example, an individual might file for bankruptcy because the family's home was destroyed by Hurricane Sandy or because he suffers from cancer and his insurance company refuses to cover certain treatments. Financial problems after these types of disasters are understandable; thus, bankruptcy today does not carry such a negative connotation. Moreover, Congress has recognized that denial of licenses or creditor harassment hinders a debtor's fresh start; thus, Congress has passed laws that provide greater protection for debtors.[5] For example, government units are no longer permitted to deny licenses and permits to bankrupt debtors.

[3] U.S. House Judiciary Committee, "Committee Approves Senate-Passed Bankruptcy Reform Legislation without Amendment" (press release), March 16, 2005, http://judiciary.house.gov/newscenter.aspx?A=461.

[4] See, e.g., National Association of Consumer Bankruptcy Attorneys, "Study: Controversial Bankruptcy Law Reforms Not Working" (press release), February 22, 2006, and Denise G. Callahan, "Survey Indicates New Law Punishes Debtors," *Wisconsin Law Journal,* March 15, 2006.

[5] Sec. 525(a).

Bankruptcy Proceedings

LO2 What is the basic set of procedures for bankruptcy cases?

Most bankruptcy cases share a set of procedures, or certain actions that must be taken in every bankruptcy case. These actions are as follows:

1. All bankruptcy cases begin with a filing of petition for bankruptcy.
2. Once the petition is filed, the court grants an automatic stay for creditor actions against the debtor's estate. In other words, creditors' legal actions against the debtor must cease.
3. The court determines whether an order of relief should be granted.
4. The creditors meet with the debtor.
5. Some type of payment plan is created and approved, usually by the creditors and the court.
6. The payment plan is carried out through actions of the trustee and the debtor.
7. Debts remaining after the plan is carried out are usually discharged.

We will discuss the particulars of this process as it applies to the different forms of bankruptcy throughout the chapter.

Specific Types of Relief Available

LO3 What specific types of relief are available through bankruptcy?

Before a debtor files for one specific type of relief, the clerk of courts must give the debtor written notice of the other types of relief available. This requirement helps ensure that the debtor has full information about the bankruptcy process.

Under the Bankruptcy Abuse Prevention and Consumer Protection Act of 2005, an individual may not be considered a debtor under any chapter unless within 180 days before filing, he or she receives credit counseling from a nonprofit budget- and credit-counseling agency.[6] If the individual does not fulfill the credit-counseling requirement, the bankruptcy court will dismiss the bankruptcy petition—even if the individual faces immediate home foreclosure, as in the Case Nugget on page 707, or wage garnishment.

Moreover, the 2005 bankruptcy reforms attempt to prevent "repeat filers" from filing one bankruptcy claim after another. Under BAPCPA, if an individual was a debtor in a bankruptcy case that was dismissed within 180 days of the current case, the individual is generally not eligible to be a debtor under Chapters 7, 11, or 13.[7] However, if the previous bankruptcy was completed rather than dismissed, the individual is generally permitted to file for bankruptcy again. If a party completes a Chapter 7 bankruptcy, the party is not permitted to seek a Chapter 7 bankruptcy again for eight years.

Legal Principle: **If an individual files for bankruptcy, the individual's ability to file for bankruptcy again is restricted for a particular time period depending on whether the petition was dismissed or completed.**

In the following sections we discuss the main types of relief available, including Chapter 7, 11, 12, and 13 bankruptcies.

CHAPTER 7: LIQUIDATION PROCEEDINGS

The most familiar type of bankruptcy proceeding is liquidation, which is sometimes called *straight bankruptcy.* **Liquidation** occurs when a debtor turns over all assets to a **trustee,** an individual who takes over administration of the debtor's estate. Trustees are usually

[6] BAPCPA, sec. 109(h).

[7] BAPCPA, sec. 109(f).

COMPARING THE LAW OF OTHER COUNTRIES

BANKRUPTCY LAW IN SPAIN

The primary goals of business bankruptcy laws in Spain are to ensure collection of debts by creditors, promote consensus between all parties, and enable the survival of the business if possible. Bankruptcy proceedings start in Spain with a finding of insolvency. Insolvency means that the business can no longer meet its obligations or will be unable to do so in the near future. A formal bankruptcy filing is required in a Spanish court. This filing may be done voluntarily by the debtor company, or it may be done involuntarily by the debtor's creditors in an enforced bankruptcy. Bankruptcy proceedings are administered by bankruptcy judges and an administrative body. The judge is in charge of all applicable procedures and hearings and opens and closes the process. The administrative body is appointed by the judge in each case and serves a role similar to that of a trustee in a U.S. bankruptcy case by managing the debtor's estate. However, the administrative body also defends the interests of creditors.

After appropriate notices have been published in official government publications, the administrative body has two months to submit a report to the judge determining the value of the debtor's assets, the identity of creditors, and the amounts owed to these parties. The proceedings are concluded through either an arrangement or a liquidation. An arrangement is a settlement between the debtor and the creditors in which the debtor agrees to a payment plan. The arrangement must be approved by creditors representing at least 20 percent of the debtor's liabilities and by the judge. The failure to obtain the approval of the necessary number of creditors or the judge may result in the debtor's liquidation.

attorneys in private practice who specialize in bankruptcy law. Every Chapter 7 proceeding has a trustee who sells the nonexempt assets and distributes the proceeds of the sale among the creditors. Liquidation provides an organized method of selling the debtor's property to generate cash to pay creditors.

Who Is Defined as a Debtor for Liquidation Purposes? Under Chapter 7 liquidation proceedings, individuals, partnerships, and corporations are considered debtors. Railroads, insurance companies, banks, savings and loan associations, industrial banks, credit unions, and health maintenance organizations are not eligible for Chapter 7 relief.

What Are the Liquidation Proceedings?

Petition Filing. As is the case with most bankruptcies, liquidation begins when the petition is filed. Under Chapter 7, liquidation may be voluntary or involuntary; thus, a voluntary or involuntary petition is filed. The person filing the petition is also responsible for paying filing fees.

Voluntary Liquidation Petition. When the debtor decides to file for bankruptcy, he files a voluntary petition. The debtor must state that he understands the other types of bankruptcy relief available and chooses liquidation. Once the petition is filed, all the debtor's prepetition assets form the **bankruptcy estate.** Assets that the debtor gains after filing the petition are generally not part of the bankruptcy estate unless they fall under an exemption.

A debtor does not have to be insolvent, or completely unable to pay, to file for bankruptcy under Chapter 7. Instead, the debtor must be able to demonstrate that she owes money to someone. When the debtor files the liquidation petition, she must also submit extensive information regarding her financial affairs under oath. It is a crime to conceal assets or supply false information regarding the debtor's financial affairs. Exhibit 32-3 lists the 10 schedules the debtor is responsible for filing under Chapter 7.

Involuntary Liquidation Petition. If a debtor is not paying debts as they come due, creditors can attempt to force the debtor into bankruptcy by filing an involuntary petition under Chapter 7. By filing the petition, the creditors attempt to force the debtor to surrender his or her assets so that the proceeds from the sale of the assets may be distributed among the creditors. Remember, a debtor could be a corporation; thus, creditors could force a corporation into bankruptcy.

CASE NUGGET

BANKRUPTCY AND CREDIT COUNSELING

In re Holsinger
U.S. Bankruptcy Court for the Western District of Virginia
465 B.R. 775 (Bankr. W.D. Va. 2012)

The debtor filed a Chapter 13 bankruptcy petition on December 20, 2011. The debtor also filed a request for a waiver of the prefiling debt-counseling requirement under the Bankruptcy Abuse Prevention and Consumer Protection Act of 2005. The debtor had enrolled in a credit-counseling course on December 13, 2011, but claimed that her bankruptcy petition was necessitated without completion of the course as her home was in imminent danger of foreclosure. The debtor also claimed that she could not complete the course until January 2012 due to work requirements and limited access to a computer. The debtor advised the court that she completed the course on January 30, 2012, but she was unable to present the court with a certificate evidencing completion by the time of the hearing on her requested waiver on February 1, 2012.

The court agreed with the debtor that imminent foreclosure of real property and resultant eviction qualify as exigent circumstances excusing the prefiling completion of a credit-counseling course. However, the debtor failed to satisfy other requirements in order to qualify for the waiver. Specifically, the debtor failed to provide evidence that the credit agency she contacted was unable to provide counseling within seven days of her request as required by the BAPCPA. Furthermore, regardless of the circumstances, the debtor had failed to provide proof of completing the course at the time of the February 2012 hearing. As a result, the court could not grant a deferment, no matter how compelling the case, and had no choice but to dismiss the debtor's bankruptcy petition.

What exactly is needed to force a debtor into bankruptcy? If the debtor has 12 or more creditors, 3 or more creditors who have unsecured claims that total \$14,425 must sign the petition for involuntary bankruptcy. However, if the debtor has fewer than 12 creditors, a single creditor with a claim of \$14,425 or more can file the petition for involuntary bankruptcy. These amounts are adjusted every three years. If the judge believes that creditors are using involuntary liquidation proceedings frivolously, the court may force the creditors to pay the attorney costs, fees of the debtor, and even punitive damages.

Not everyone can be forced into bankruptcy through Chapter 7. Farmers, ranchers, and nonprofit organizations are examples of debtors that cannot be forced into liquidation. Also, debtors that are ineligible to voluntarily file for Chapter 7 bankruptcy (railroads, insurance companies, banks, savings and loan associations, credit unions, and health maintenance organizations) are also excluded from forced bankruptcy.

Dismissal of Petition. A bankruptcy judge may dismiss a voluntary or involuntary bankruptcy petition. Before BAPCPA, debtors were not required to have an income below a particular level to file for Chapter 7 bankruptcy. However, under BAPCPA, a bankruptcy judge may dismiss a petition on a finding of substantial abuse. One cause for dismissal for

Exhibit 32-3
Required Schedules for Liquidation

Under Chapter 7, the debtor is required to list:
Schedule A: All real property
Schedule B: All personal property
Schedule C: Property in A & B that is exempt
Schedule D: Secured creditors and their addresses
Schedule E: Unsecured priority claims
Schedule F: Unsecured nonpriority claims
Schedule G: Executory contracts and expired leases
Schedule H: List of co-debtors
Schedule I: Statement of current income of debtor
Schedule J: Statement of current expenditures

abuse is failure of the *means test.* If an individual's debt is primarily consumer debt and if the individual's income is above the median income in his or her state,[8] the court may presume that the individual is abusing the bankruptcy provisions.[9] However, the individual may continue with the petition under the presumption. Case 32-1 provides an example of a court's consideration of what income or benefits should be included in the calculation for the means test.

[8] The court would take the debtor's current monthly income and multiply this number by 12. If the total is less than the median family income in the state, no one may file a motion to dismiss the bankruptcy petition; BAPCPA, sec. 707(b)(2).

[9] BAPCPA, sec. 707(b).

CASE 32-1 BLAUSEY v. U.S. TRUSTEE
NINTH CIRCUIT COURT OF APPEALS
552 F.3D 1124 (2009)

In 1991, Deann Blausey, a court reporter, purchased a disability insurance policy titled "Disability Income Pro-Inc Plus." After Blausey injured her elbow and was diagnosed with a permanent disability, she filed an insurance claim and began to receive benefits in December 1996. Under the policy she receives $4,000 per month in disability benefits.

In 2006, Blausey and her husband filed for Chapter 7 bankruptcy. They disclosed in their bankruptcy petition that Blausey received the $4,000 monthly payments but did not include those payments in their calculation of current monthly income ("CMI") under the statutory means test. The U.S. Trustee moved to dismiss their petition because when the disability benefits were included in the CMI, their CMI was high enough to trigger the presumption of abuse. The bankruptcy court granted the U.S. Trustee's motion. The Blauseys argued that the bankruptcy court should have interpreted the word "income" as used in the definition of CMI, based on the meaning of "gross income" under the Internal Revenue Code. Because private disability insurance benefits are excluded from gross income, Mrs. Blausey's benefits must also be excluded from CMI.

PER CURIAM: CMI is defined as "the average monthly income from all sources that the debtor receives . . . without regard to whether such income is taxable income," including "any amount paid by any entity other than the debtor . . . on a regular basis for the household expenses of the debtor or the debtor's dependents." 11 U.S.C. § 101(10A)(A), (B). The Bankruptcy Code does not define "income."

The Blauseys' chief argument is that "income" in the definition of CMI should be interpreted as consistent with "gross income" as defined in the Internal Revenue Code. "Gross income" expressly does not include "amounts received through accident or health insurance . . . for personal injuries or sickness . . ." The Blauseys reason that if the benefits are not included in gross income under the Internal Revenue Code, they likewise should not be included in income when calculating CMI.

The plain language of the Bankruptcy Code, however, does not support this interpretation. The phrase "without regard to whether such income is taxable income" in 11 U.S.C. § 101(10A)(A) reflects Congress' judgment that the Internal Revenue Code's method of determining taxable income does not apply to the Bankruptcy Code's calculation of CMI. Moreover, where Congress wishes to define a term in the Bankruptcy Code by reference to the Internal Revenue Code, it clearly knows how to do so. For example, Congress imported the Internal Revenue Service's Local and National Standards for expenses into the means test calculation.

In addition, the statute specifically excludes certain payments, such as Social Security payments and payments to victims of war crimes and terrorism, from CMI. The general rule of statutory construction is that the enumeration of specific exclusions from the operation of a statute is an indication that the statute should apply to all cases not specifically excluded. Here, the statute makes several specific exclusions from CMI but does not specifically exclude private disability insurance benefits. This indicates that Congress meant for the benefits to be included in CMI.

The Blauseys ask us to find that the disability insurance benefit payments are not "income" . . . because the benefits are not derived from labor but, instead, serve as compensation for the loss of her ability to work as a court reporter. This argument is unavailing. By the terms of her insurance policy, Mrs. Blausey's disability insurance benefits were triggered when her lost earnings exceeded twenty percent of her original monthly earnings. The monthly benefits payment under the policy is based on the amount of income lost. If Mrs. Blausey were to find a job that paid as much as her court reporter job would pay, she would no longer receive insurance benefits because she would no longer have lost income. It is thus clear that the purpose of the disability insurance plan is to replace the income that Mrs. Blausey lost due to her disability.

Finally, the history of BAPCPA indicates that excluding Mrs. Blausey's disability insurance benefits from CMI

[continued]

would contravene the purpose of the means test. The purpose of the means test is to "help the courts determine who can and who cannot repay their debts and, perhaps most importantly, how much they can afford to pay." 151 Cong. Rec. S1726-01, S1786. Excluding the $4,000 per month in replacement income from CMI would result in a figure that does not accurately reflect the Blauseys' ability to repay their debts. Congress' determination that a certain type of income should not be taxed does not reflect a determination that the income is not available to repay debts.

AFFIRMED.

CRITICAL THINKING

What reasons does the court offer for its conclusion that private disability benefits are income under the Bankruptcy Code and should have been included in the Blauseys' calculation of CMI?

ETHICAL DECISION MAKING

What values are reflected in the court's decision?

Automatic Stay. Once a petition, voluntary or involuntary, is filed, the code provides for an **automatic stay,** or moratorium, for almost all creditor litigation against the debtor. During the stay, creditors cannot bring or continue legal action against the debtor or his property. For example, creditors cannot attempt to repossess property during bankruptcy proceedings. Moreover, if a creditor received a judgment against a debtor before the bankruptcy filing, the creditor may not enforce the judgment.

There are some exceptions to the stay. First, under BAPCPA, if the debtor was a debtor in a bankruptcy case that was dismissed within a year of the current bankruptcy case filing, the stay automatically terminates 30 days after the current filing.[10] Second, legal actions to determine paternity or to collect child support or alimony payments are not subject to the stay. Third, the court may exclude secured creditors from the stay if they petition the court to show that they do not have "adequate protection" under the stay. Remember, secured creditors have an interest in property; they are therefore concerned that they will lose their interest through the stay. To provide protection for these creditors, the courts may force the debtor to make payments to these secured creditors during the stay.

If a creditor is aware of the stay and continues to engage in legal action against the debtor, the code provides that the debtor may recover damages, costs, attorney fees, and even possibly punitive damages. Again, Congress is providing protection to the debtor.

Legal Principle: Once a bankruptcy petition is filed, most litigation against the debtor is subject to a stay.

Order of Relief. After a bankruptcy petition has been filed, the next step is for the court to determine whether an order of relief is granted. An **order of relief** means that bankruptcy relief is ordered; that is, the bankruptcy proceedings can continue. If the filing of the voluntary petition is proper, the petition automatically becomes an order of relief. Similarly, if a debtor does not object to an involuntary bankruptcy, the order of relief is automatic.

Should the debtor challenge the involuntary petition for bankruptcy, a hearing will be held. At the hearing, the judge generally will grant the order of relief for involuntary bankruptcy if one of two conditions occurs:

1. The debtor is not paying debts as they become due.
2. The custodian took possession of almost all of the debtor's property within 120 days before filing the petition.

[10] BAPCPA, sec. 362(c)(3).

After the court enters the order of relief, a U.S. trustee, a government official appointed by the attorney general, selects an interim trustee. A *trustee* is the person responsible for collecting the debtor's available assets and liquidating the property into cash for the creditors. The interim trustee is responsible for organizing the creditors' meeting.

Creditors' Meeting. Between 20 and 40 days after the order of relief has been granted, the interim trustee calls a **creditors' meeting**—a meeting of all the creditors listed in the Chapter 7 required schedules for liquidation. While the debtor and the interim trustee also attend this meeting, the bankruptcy judge does not attend.

If the debtor fails to appear at the meeting, the court may refuse to grant the bankruptcy. Why is the debtor's attendance so important? The principal purpose of the creditors' meeting is to enable the creditors and trustee to examine the debtor under oath regarding her financial affairs. The debtor's filing of the Chapter 7 required schedules does not necessarily provide enough information. Creditors want to know more about the way the debtor is handling her assets and property. Moreover, they want to ensure that the debtor is not concealing property. Not only does the trustee ask the debtor questions regarding her financial status, but the trustee also ensures that the debtor is aware of the other forms of bankruptcy relief as well as the consequences of filing for bankruptcy.

Another important purpose of the creditors' meeting is the election of a permanent trustee. The interim trustee might become the permanent trustee, or the creditors might elect a different one. The creditors elect the trustee because the trustee generally represents the creditors.

The Trustee. The general duty of the trustee is to collect the debtor's available assets (i.e., the debtor's prefiling assets) and to liquidate the property to cash that will be distributed among the creditors. Thus, the trustee takes possession of the debtor's property and has it appraised. Moreover, the trustee examines the debtor's records and might even temporarily take over the debtor's business. If someone else holds the debtor's property, the trustee has the power to require that person to return the property. Next, the trustee separates the exempt property from the nonexempt property and sells the nonexempt property. (We will discuss the distinction between these two types of property shortly.) The trustee is required to keep careful records of the property and the sale of the assets during the entire liquidation process.

In addition to selling the debtor's property, the trustee has a variety of powers that assist him in fulfilling his duties. First, the trustee has the power to sue and be sued. He can initiate collection actions but must also defend against creditor actions. He has the right to assume or reject executory contracts. Moreover, he has the right to obtain credit. Finally, the trustee has the power to void certain liens against the debtor's property. For example, a debtor's ability to exempt property is hindered by any liens against such possessions; consequently, the trustee is permitted to void these liens.

Exempt Property. A debtor is not required to give up all of her property through liquidation—only the nonexempt property. As previously stated, the trustee sorts the exempt property from the nonexempt property. How does the trustee make this distinction? The exemptions are stated in the Bankruptcy Code and are adjusted every three years on the basis of the consumer price index.

There are federal exemptions as well as state exemptions. States, through legislation, can and have opted out of the federal exemptions to give debtors the option for state exemptions only. However, in some states, a debtor may choose whether to make state or federal exemptions; the debtor cannot make some state exemptions and some federal exemptions. Under BAPCPA, if a debtor purchased a home less than 1,215 days before filing for bankruptcy,

Exhibit 32-4
Federal Bankruptcy Exemptions

1. Up to $21,625 for residence
2. Interest in a motor vehicle (not necessarily an automobile) up to $3,450
3. Interest, up to $550 for a particular item, in personal and household goods and furnishings, clothing, appliances, books, animals, crops, and musical instruments (aggregate total of all items limited to $11,525)
4. Interest in jewelry up to $1,450
5. $1,150 of any property the debtor chooses (functions as a "wild-card" exemption)
6. Tools of trade and professional books up to $2,175
7. Any unmatured life insurance contract owned by the debtor
8. Professionally prescribed health aids
9. The right to receive certain personal injury awards up to $21,625
10. Retirement funds in an IRA or SEP up to $1,171,650 per person

the debtor's homestead exemption is limited to $125,000. Exhibit 32-4 lists the federal exemptions. In addition to having the exemptions in Exhibit 32-4, a debtor is entitled to 100 percent of Social Security benefits, veteran's benefits, and civil service retirement benefits.

Why did Congress create such exemptions for property? Suppose that a debtor was forced to sell all of his property through liquidation. Remember, one purpose of bankruptcy is to provide a debtor with a fresh start. If a debtor were forced to sell *all* of his property, he would likely fall right back into debt again. Thus, the exemptions are for items considered necessary to earning a living.

One of these exemptions was recently added—retirement funds in an individual retirement account (IRA). Case 32-2 provides the Supreme Court's reasoning for why funds in an IRA are exempt.

CASE 32-2 ROUSEY v. JACOWAY
UNITED STATES SUPREME COURT
544 U.S. 320 (2005)

When Richard and Betty Jo Rousey stopped working at Northrup Grumman Corp., Northrup Grumman required them to take lump-sum distributions from their employer-sponsored pension plans. The Rouseys deposited the lump sums into two IRAs, one in each of their names. Several years after forming the IRAs, the Rouseys filed a joint Chapter 7 bankruptcy petition and listed their IRAs as exempt. The trustee objected to the claim that the IRAs were exempt, and the bankruptcy court agreed with the trustee. On appeal, the Bankruptcy Appellate Panel (BAP) agreed that IRAs were not exempt. Appellate courts across the country disagreed on the issue, so the Supreme Court granted certiorari.

JUSTICE THOMAS: The question in this case is whether debtors can exempt assets in their Individual Retirement Accounts (IRAs) from the bankruptcy estate pursuant to Section 522(d)(10)(E). This exemption provides that a debtor may withdraw from the bankruptcy estate his "right to receive—(E) a payment under a stock bonus, pension, profitsharing, annuity, or similar plan or contract on account of illness, disability, death, age, or length of service, to the extent reasonably necessary for the support of the debtor and any dependent of the debtor. . . ."

Under the terms of the statute, the Rouseys' right to receive payment under their IRAs must meet two requirements to be exempted under this provision: (1) the right to receive payment must be from "a stock bonus, pension, profitsharing, annuity, or similar plan or contract" and (2) the right to receive payment must be "on account of illness, disability, death, age, or length of service."

A

We turn first to the requirement that the payment be "on account of illness, disability, death, age, or length of service." "[O]n account of" in §522(d)(10)(E) requires that the right to receive payment be "because of" illness, disability, death, age, or length of service.

[continued]

[Trustee] argues that the Rouseys' right to receive payment from their IRAs is not "because of" these listed factors. In particular, she asserts that the Rouseys can withdraw funds from their IRAs for any reason at all, so long as they are willing to pay a 10 percent penalty. Thus, [Trustee] maintains that there is no causal connection between the Rouseys' right to payment and age (or any other factor), because their IRAs provide a right to payment on demand.

We disagree. The statutes governing IRAs persuade us that the Rouseys' right to payment from IRAs is causally connected to their age. The Rouseys have a nonforfeitable right to the balance held in those accounts. That right is restricted by a 10 percent tax penalty that applies to withdrawals from IRAs made before the accountholder turns 59. Contrary to [trustee]'s contention, this tax penalty is substantial. It therefore limits the Rouseys' right to "payment" of the balance of their IRAs. And because this condition is removed when the accountholder turns age 59, the Rouseys' right to the balance of their IRAs is a right to payment "on account of" age. Accordingly, we conclude that the Rouseys' IRAs provide a right to payment on account of age.

B

In addition to requiring that the IRAs provide a right to payment "on account of" age . . . , 11 U.S.C. §522(d)(10)(E) also requires the Rouseys' IRAs to be "stock bonus, pension, profitsharing, annuity, or similar plan[s] or contract[s]." The issue is whether the Rouseys' IRAs are "similar plan[s] or contract[s]" within the meaning of §522(d)(10)(E). To be "similar," an IRA must be like, though not identical to, the specific plans or contracts listed in §522(d)(10)(E), and consequently must share characteristics common to the listed plans or contracts.

The common feature of all of these plans is that they provide income that substitutes for wages earned as salary or hourly compensation. This understanding of the plans' similarities comports with the other types of payments that a debtor may exempt under §522(d)(10)—all of which concern income that substitutes for wages.

Several considerations convince us that the income the Rouseys will derive from their IRAs is likewise income that substitutes for wages. First, the minimum distribution requirements require distribution to begin at the latest in the calendar year after the year in which the accountholder turns 70. Thus, accountholders must begin to withdraw funds when they are likely to be retired and lack wage income. Second, the Internal Revenue Code defers taxation of money held in accounts qualifying as IRAs until the year in which it is distributed, treating it as income only in such years. This tax treatment further encourages accountholders to wait until retirement to withdraw the funds: The later withdrawal occurs, the longer the taxes on the amounts are deferred. Third, absent the applicability of other exceptions discussed above, withdrawals before age 59 are subject to a tax penalty, restricting preretirement access to the funds. Finally, to ensure that the beneficiary uses the IRA in his retirement years, an accountholder's failure to take the requisite minimum distributions results in a 50-percent tax penalty on funds improperly remaining in the account. All of these features show that IRA income substitutes for wages lost upon retirement and distinguish IRAs from typical savings accounts.

In sum, the Rouseys' IRAs fulfill both of §522(d)(10)(E)'s requirements at issue here—they confer a right to receive payment on account of age and they are similar plans or contracts to those enumerated in §522(d)(10)(E).

REVERSED and REMANDED.

CRITICAL THINKING

Return to the considerations enumerated in the next to last paragraph of this case. Justice Thomas determines that these considerations all move toward the conclusion that the income the Rouseys will derive from their IRAs is income that substitutes for wages. What alternative interpretations of those considerations would lead us to believe that the considerations do not lead to that conclusion?

ETHICAL DECISION MAKING

We can certainly understand the interests advanced by the decision made by the Court in this case. But what stakeholders are potentially harmed by this decision?

A debtor must file a list of the property that she claims is exempt. Under the Bankruptcy Code and the Bankruptcy Rules, creditors may file objections to the claimed exemptions. If a debtor improperly lists property as exempt and a creditor does not timely file an objection, the debtor will likely be permitted to claim the property as exempt.

Preferential Payments. Because a major purpose of the Bankruptcy Code is to prevent debtors from making payments to one creditor and thus treating that creditor preferentially, the trustee has the power to recover **preferential payments,** or payments made by an insolvent debtor that give preferential treatment to one creditor over another. If the debtor made any payments within 90 days of the bankruptcy filing, the trustee can examine these payments as preferential payments. The trustee does not have to demonstrate the debtor's past insolvency; the debtor is assumed to be insolvent for 90 days prior to the bankruptcy. For a payment to be considered preferential, the trustee must show that the transfer gave the creditor more money than the creditor would have received through bankruptcy proceedings. Thus, other creditors are disadvantaged by the debtor's preferential payment.

If the preferred creditor is an insider, such as a relative or partner, the trustee has the power to recover payments made within two years before filing for bankruptcy. However, in such cases, the trustee must demonstrate the debtor's insolvency rather than assume insolvency. In contrast, the trustee may not recover preferential payments made for alimony or child support.

Suppose that your company has $5,000 in its checking account, but no other assets. You (i.e., your company) owe $4,000 to a credit union, $3,000 to your landlord, and $3,500 to the construction company that remodeled your offices a year ago. You pay the construction company $3,500, which leaves $1,500 for your $7,000 debt to your landlord and the credit union. A week later, you file for bankruptcy, and you have just $1,500 that will be applied to your debt to your landlord and credit union. Your landlord and credit union would have received more money through the bankruptcy proceedings if you had not paid the full amount to the construction company; thus, your $3,500 payment is a preferential payment that can be recovered from the construction company to be distributed more evenly among the creditors.

BUT WHAT IF . . .

WHAT IF THE FACTS OF THE CASE OPENER WERE DIFFERENT?

Let's say, in the Case Opener, that a few weeks before General Motors filed for bankruptcy, the company decided to pay off the creditors it preferred to pay rather than other creditors that should have been paid first. Is there any law that can fix such a situation? If so, what is the solution?

Fraudulent Transfers. A trustee can recover preferential payments because these payments are not fair to creditors. Similarly, a trustee can void **fraudulent transfers** of property. These transfers can be actually or constructively fraudulent. An actual fraudulent transfer would be made with intent to defraud creditors. Generally, there is no direct evidence of intent to defraud (e.g., an e-mail written by a debtor who states that he is transferring assets to hide them). Rather, a trustee would establish intent through circumstantial evidence.

Similarly, if a debtor transfers property for an amount significantly lower than its fair market value, he or she may have engaged in a fraudulent transfer. Suppose that you are unable to pay your debts and are preparing to file for bankruptcy. You decide to sell your $50,000 boat to your business partner for $50. The trustee of your case could recover the boat if the sale occurred within two years of your filing for bankruptcy. Furthermore, you could be subject to criminal penalties for your attempt to hide your assets. By punishing debtors who attempt to hide their assets, the Bankruptcy Code provides protection for creditors.

Suppose that, instead of selling your boat to your business partner, you sold your boat to a creditor. Because you are making a payment to a creditor, the trustee would analyze this payment as a preferential payment (assessing how the other creditors would be harmed by this payment) rather than a fraudulent transfer (assessing the reasonableness of consideration for the transfer).

Creditors' Claims. Within 90 days of the creditors' meeting, all creditors (except secured creditors) must file a proof of claim with the bankruptcy court clerk to receive a portion of the debtor's estate. This proof of claim lists the creditor's name and address and the amount of the debt owed to the creditor. If the creditor fails to file such a claim, the creditor may not receive a portion of the debt. However, the fact that the claim was filed does not mean that the creditor will automatically receive a portion of the proceeds from the sale of the debtor's assets. The trustee must permit the claim to be allowed, and there are numerous defenses to creditors' claims.

When the trustee is sorting and examining the property, the trustee must determine whether a creditor has a secured interest in the debtor's property. If a secured interest exists, the creditor has first claim to the property. The debtor may decide to surrender the property to the creditor to satisfy the debt. Alternatively, the creditor may foreclose on the property and use the proceeds of the sale to reduce the debt owed to the creditor. However, the secured party is secured only to the value of the collateral.

Distribution of Property to Creditors: Priority Claims. As suggested in the previous paragraph, all creditors do not have equal claims to the proceeds of the sale. Secured parties have priority over all unsecured parties in receiving portions of the proceeds of the liquidation. Thus, secured parties are paid first. But which unsecured parties are paid next? The code establishes classes of priority claims. One class must be completely paid before anyone in another class receives any payment. If there are insufficient funds to fully pay all the creditors in one class, one class is paid proportionately and the lower classes get nothing. The classes of priority claims among unsecured creditors are shown in Exhibit 32-5.

If there is any remaining money after the proceeds are distributed to creditors, the remaining money is returned to the debtor. If there is not enough money to cover all the debts, most of the remaining debts are discharged.

Discharge. If a debtor has honestly dealt with her creditors during bankruptcy proceedings, the debtor is likely eligible for a discharge of her remaining debts. A **discharge** is a written federal court order signed by a bankruptcy judge stating that the debtor is immune from creditor actions to collect debts. When a debt is discharged, the debtor is essentially no longer responsible for the debt.

When is a discharge of debt appropriate? Discharge of debt is a privilege, not a right. A judge determines which debts are dischargeable.

Exhibit 32-5
Classes of Priority Claims among Unsecured Creditors

Class 1	Any unpaid domestic support obligations (alimony or child support)
Class 2	Court costs, trustee fees, attorney fees, and other administrative expenses associated with the bankruptcy
Class 3	Unsecured claims in involuntary bankruptcy that arise through the debtor's ordinary business expenses from the date of filing the petition to the date of the appointment of the trustee
Class 4	Unsecured claims for unpaid wages, salaries, and commissions earned within 180 days of the filing of the petition
Class 5	Unsecured claims for contributions to employee retirement plans
Class 6	Unsecured claims by farmers and fishers against grain operators of grain storage facilities or fish storage or processing facilities
Class 7	Claims for deposits given to the debtor in connection with property or services never given
Class 8	Certain taxes and penalties due to government units
Class 9	Claims in bankruptcies related to federal depositary institutions
Class 10	Unsecured claims for personal injuries and deaths caused by the debtor's operation of a motor vehicle under the influence of alcohol or drugs

Exhibit 32-6
Nondischargeable Debts under the Bankruptcy Code

1. Claims for back taxes or government fines within three years of filing for bankruptcy
2. Claims for liabilities against the debtor for his or her obtaining money or property under false pretenses, false representation, or fraud
3. Claims by creditors who were not listed on the schedule and did not have notification of the bankruptcy proceedings
4. Claims based on fraud, embezzlement, and larceny by the debtor while she or he was acting in a fiduciary relationship
5. Alimony, child support, and some property settlements
6. Claims of willful or malicious conduct by the debtor that caused injury to another person or property
7. Specific student loans, unless payment of the loans imposes undue hardship on the debtor
8. Judgments against a debtor for claims resulting from the debtor's drinking and driving
9. Debts not discharged in previous bankruptcies
10. Claims for money borrowed to pay a tax to the United States that would be nondischargeable
11. Cash advances on a credit card

If the debtor has received a previous discharge of debt within eight years of the current filing for bankruptcy, the judge will likely refuse a new discharge of debt.

Legal Principle: **A judge has discretion in discharging debts under Chapter 7.**

Exceptions to Discharge. Generally, most debts are discharged unless there are objections to the discharge or the debts are ineligible for discharge. If a major goal for bankruptcy law is to give debtors a fresh start, why are some debts nondischargeable? Some of the debts that are not dischargeable are debts to those who are in a weak bargaining position with the debtor. For example, child support and alimony payments are nondischargeable. Children and ex-spouses often depend on payments; consequently, the court will not permit the discharge of these debts. Exhibit 32-6 lists the debts that are nondischargeable as established by the Bankruptcy Code.

BUT WHAT IF . . .

WHAT IF THE FACTS OF THE CASE OPENER WERE DIFFERENT?

Let's say, in the Case Opener, that General Motors executives were talking to their bankruptcy lawyers about being debt-free after the bankruptcy finalization. The lawyers informed the executives that the company would still owe many debts, but the executives disagreed. Which side is correct about the abolishment of debts in a bankruptcy? Which debts would General Motors still have and why?

Case 32-3 provides an example of the court's consideration of whether a debt should be discharged. In this case, the debtor was found guilty of malpractice, and the debt was therefore dischargeable.

CASE 32-3 MARGARET KAWAAUHAU ET VIR, PETITIONERS v. PAUL W. GEIGER

UNITED STATES SUPREME COURT

523 U.S. 57, 118 S. CT. 974 (1998)

In January 1983, Margaret Kawaauhau was treated by Dr. Paul Geiger for a foot injury. After examining Kawaauhau, Geiger prescribed oral penicillin to her despite his knowledge that intravenous penicillin would be more effective in fighting a potential infection. Geiger testified that he prescribed the oral penicillin because he knew that Kawaauhau was concerned about costs. Geiger then left town and placed Kawaauhau in the care of another physician, who transferred Kawaauhau to an infectious disease specialist. When Geiger returned, he canceled the transfer to the specialist and stopped Kawaauhau's antibiotic treatment. However, Kawaauhau's infection continued, and three days later, her leg was amputated below the knee.

Kawaauhau sued Geiger for malpractice and received a jury award for $355,000. Geiger, who did not carry malpractice insurance, moved to Missouri and filed for bankruptcy. Kawaauhau requested that the court refuse to discharge the malpractice judgment because the judgment was for a "willful and malicious injury" and was thus exempt from discharge. The bankruptcy court, finding that Geiger's treatment fell far below the standard of care, ruled that the debt was nondischargeable. The district court affirmed the ruling. The Eighth Circuit reversed the district court's decision, holding that malpractice was conduct that was negligent or reckless rather than intentional. Kawaauhau appealed.

JUSTICE GINSBURG: Section 523(a)(6) of the Bankruptcy Code provides:

(a) A discharge . . . does not discharge an individual debtor from any debt

. . . (6) for willful and malicious injury by the debtor to another entity or to the property of another entity.

The Kawaauhaus urge that the malpractice award fits within this exception because Dr. Geiger intentionally rendered inadequate medical care to Margaret Kawaauhau that necessarily led to her injury. According to the Kawaauhaus, Geiger deliberately chose less effective treatment because he wanted to cut costs, all the while knowing that he was providing substandard care. Such conduct, the Kawaauhaus assert, meets the "willful and malicious" specification of § 523(a)(6).

We confront this pivotal question concerning the scope of the "willful and malicious injury" exception: Does § 523(a)(6)'s compass cover acts, done intentionally that cause injury (as the Kawaauhaus urge), or only acts done with the actual intent to cause injury (as the Eighth Circuit ruled)? The words of the statute strongly support the Eighth Circuit's reading.

The word "willful" in (a)(6) modifies the word "injury," indicating that nondischargeability takes a deliberate or intentional *injury,* not merely a deliberate or intentional *act* that leads to injury. Had Congress meant to exempt debts resulting from unintentionally inflicted injuries, it might have described instead "willful acts that cause injury." . . . The Kawaauhaus' more encompassing interpretation could place within the excepted category a wide range of situations in which an act is intentional, but injury is unintended, *i.e.,* neither desired nor in fact anticipated by the debtor. Every traffic accident stemming from an initial intentional act—for example, intentionally rotating the wheel of an automobile to make a left-hand turn without first checking oncoming traffic—could fit the description.

Furthermore, "we are hesitant to adopt an interpretation of a congressional enactment which renders superfluous another portion of that same law." Reading § 523(a)(6) as the

[continued]

Kawaauhaus urge would obviate the need for § 523(a)(9), which specifically exempts debts "for death or personal injury caused by the debtor's operation of a motor vehicle if such operation was unlawful because the debtor was intoxicated from using alcohol, a drug, or another substance." 11 U.S.C. § 523(a)(9)

Finally, the Kawaauhaus maintain that, as a policy matter, malpractice judgments should be excepted from discharge, at least when the debtor acted recklessly or carried no malpractice insurance. Congress, of course, may so decide. But unless and until Congress makes such a decision, we must follow the current direction § 523(a)(6) provides.

We hold that debts arising from recklessly or negligently inflicted injuries do not fall within the compass of § 523(a)(6). For the reasons stated, the judgment of the Court of Appeals for the Eighth Circuit is affirmed.

AFFIRMED.

CRITICAL THINKING

The judge uses an analogy: traffic accidents. Does this analogy possess relevant similarities and lack relevant differences as compared to the case at hand? Does this analogy provide valuable insights that warrant the judge's conclusion?

ETHICAL DECISION MAKING

What are the consequences of this decision for the parties involved as well as other individuals who might bring similar cases? Who is benefiting from the ruling in this case?

Objections to Discharge. If a debt is not classified as a nondischargeable debt, the debt is presumably permitted to be discharged, pending the judge's approval. However, creditors or the trustee may object to discharge of debts. The objection process begins when a creditor or trustee files a complaint with the court. Any complaint must be filed within 60 days of the creditors' meeting. Once the complaint is filed, the court holds a hearing regarding the complaint. At the hearing, the court determines whether the debtor has engaged in any behavior that bars a discharge. The following behavior may cause the court to not discharge the debt:

1. The debtor has concealed or destroyed property in an attempt to defraud the creditors.
2. The debtor has concealed or destroyed financial records.
3. The debtor fails to account for a loss of assets.

Basically, if a debtor engages in dishonest behavior, the court will likely refuse to discharge the debts. Moreover, the court may sanction the debtor with a fine of up to $5,000 and/or a prison sentence of up to five years. However, if the debtor has behaved honestly, the court will generally ignore the objection and grant the discharge.

Under BAPCPA, Congress added additional reasons for denying discharge. First, if the debtor fails to complete a course in personal finance management, the court may deny a discharge. Second, if there is a proceeding against the debtor for a felony charge for (1) a securities law violation, (2) a RICO civil penalty, or (3) a personal injury or death caused by the debtor's criminal or tortious act, the court may deny a discharge.

Revocation of Discharge. While a debt might be discharged, the discharge is not necessarily permanent. If the trustee or a creditor discovers that the debtor has acted fraudulently or dishonestly during the bankruptcy proceedings, the court may revoke the discharge within one year. The revocation of discharge allows the creditors to bring action against the debtor.

Reaffirmation of Debt. Sometimes a debtor wishes to repay a debt even though the debt could be discharged. Why might the debtor wish to repay the debt? The debtor might owe money to a family member or a longtime business associate. To maintain a good relationship with these people, a debtor might choose to repay the debt instead of having the debt discharged. This repayment can occur through a **reaffirmation agreement,** an agreement in which the debtor agrees to pay the debt even though it could be discharged.

Unfortunately, creditors may attempt to pressure a debtor into reaffirming the debt. Congress was worried that debtors were unwisely surrendering their ability to discharge their debts by making reaffirmation agreements. Thus, Congress created the following extensive rules so that a decision for reaffirmation of debt cannot be an impulsive one:

1. The reaffirmation agreement must be made before the debt is discharged.
2. The debtor must be able to cancel the agreement, and the agreement must contain explicit information regarding the time frame in which the debtor may cancel the agreement.
3. The agreement should contain a statement notifying the creditor that the law does not require the agreement.
4. The agreement must be filed with the bankruptcy court. Typically, the debtor's attorney files a form along with the agreement stating that the debtor is voluntarily entering the agreement and the agreement will not result in hardship to the debtor. Unless the attorney files this form, court approval for the agreement is needed.

CHAPTER 11: REORGANIZATIONS

The largest bankruptcy in U.S. history was the 2008 Lehman Brothers Holdings, Inc., bankruptcy filing. As shown in Exhibit 32-7, Lehman Brothers, an investment bank, had over $639 billion in assets at the time of filing. Generally, the creditors and debtor agree that part of the debt will be discharged while the other part is or will be paid. Creditors generally agree to these plans because they believe that the value of the operating business is greater than the value of the business broken up and sold in pieces.

Who Is Eligible for Chapter 11 Reorganization? Corporate debtors most frequently use Chapter 11 reorganization because they are permitted to remain in business. However, the debtor does not have to be a business entity to use reorganization; the debtor can be an individual unrelated to business. Stockbrokers, commodities brokers, banks, and savings and loan companies are not permitted to file under Chapter 11.

Exhibit 32-7
Largest Bankruptcy Filings

COMPANY	FILING DATE	ASSETS PREBANKRUPTCY (BILLIONS)
Lehman Brothers Holdings, Inc.	2008	$639.0
Washington Mutual	2008	327.9
WorldCom, Inc.	2002	103.9
General Motors Corp.	2009	91.0
CIT Group	2009	71.0
Enron Corp.	2001	65.5
Conseco, Inc.	2002	61.3
MF Global Holdings	2011	40.5
Chrysler	2009	39.3

Source: "The 20 Largest Public Company Bankruptcies 1980–Present," BankruptcyData.com (New Generation Research, Inc., Boston, MA), www.bankruptcydata.com/Research/Largest_Overall_All-Time.pdf.

What Are the Reorganization Proceedings? Most of the Chapter 11 reorganization procedures are similar to Chapter 7 liquidation procedures. Like liquidation, reorganization may be voluntary or involuntary. The reorganization process begins with the filing of the reorganization petition.

When the petition is filed, an automatic stay prohibits legal action against the debtor during the reorganization process. The debtor is required to file a list of creditors. Next, the order of relief is granted, and the court appoints a trustee, who appoints a creditors' committee of unsecured creditors. Because there may be hundreds of creditors, the creditors' committee is supposed to represent the interests of the range of creditors. The Bankruptcy Code contemplates seven creditors on the committee. The members of the creditors' committee have a fiduciary duty to the other creditors, and under BAPCPA, the creditors' committee must provide the other creditors with access to information.

The debtor may continue to operate the business as a debtor in possession (DIP). However, if the court feels that the debtor has mismanaged the business, the court may ask the trustee to operate the business.

Generally, the trustee is responsible for developing the reorganization plan to handle the creditors' claims. The *reorganization plan* is a contract between a debtor and his or her creditors. The goal of the plan is to rehabilitate the debtor while preserving the assets for the creditors. Reorganization plans usually state three things:

1. The classes of claims and interests in the debtor's property.
2. The treatment for each class of creditors.
3. A description of the means for execution of the agreement.

A debtor has an exclusive right to file a plan within the first 120 days of the case. If the debtor files a plan within this period, no one else may file a plan within the first 180 days after filing. This period allows the debtor time to persuade the creditors to accept the plan. The bankruptcy court may extend these exclusive periods. However, BAPCPA limits extensions of these periods to 18 months and 20 months, respectively.

Once the plan has been developed, the creditors must vote to accept the plan. For the plan to be accepted, two-thirds of the creditors of each class of creditors must vote to approve it. If the plan is approved, it will go before the court for confirmation. The court may decide to reject the plan if it is not in the best interests of the creditors. When the court confirms a plan, the debts not under the reorganization plan are discharged.

Collective Bargaining Agreements and Reorganization. Through reorganization, a debtor can reject some contracts. In the early 1980s, legal scholars were concerned that debtors could use reorganization as a tool to avoid collective bargaining agreements. This issue became a serious concern when the Supreme Court held, in *National Labor Relations Board v. Bildisco & Bildisco,* that collective bargaining agreements are "executory contracts" and thus subject to rejection. In other words, a debtor was not required to engage in collective bargaining before rejecting part of the collective bargaining agreement through reorganization. However, in the opinion, the court stated that rejection is not permitted unless the reorganization procedures would benefit through the rejection.

After the Supreme Court decision was handed down in 1984, Congress amended the code to prevent debtors from misusing Chapter 11 to reject collective bargaining agreements. The amendments set forth procedures under which collective bargaining agreements can be rejected or modified. For instance, the code provides that a collective bargaining agreement can be rejected only if the debtor has first presented to the employees' representative the proposed changes to the agreement and the employees reject the changes without good cause. Furthermore, the debtor's financial situation under Chapter 11 must clearly benefit by the rejection of the collective bargaining agreement.

CHAPTER 13: INDIVIDUAL REPAYMENT PLANS

Chapter 13, "Adjustments of Debts for Individuals," permits individuals with regular income to pay their debts to creditors in installment plans under the supervision of the court. Repayment plans may seem similar to reorganization. Any debtor who files under Chapter 13 could also have filed under Chapter 11. However, Chapter 13 repayment plans are usually simpler and less expensive. Moreover, Chapter 13 repayment plans allow individuals the opportunity to save their houses from foreclosure. By statute, these plans last between 36 and 60 months.

BUT WHAT IF . . .

WHAT IF THE FACTS OF THE CASE OPENER WERE DIFFERENT?

Let's say, in the Case Opener, that General Motors decided to undergo a Chapter 13 loan repayment plan as a form of bankruptcy. Let's say that the company's debts were within the range eligible for the application of Chapter 13. What factor makes this scenario illegal?

Who Is Defined as a Debtor for a Chapter 13 Repayment Plan? Only individuals are permitted to file under Chapter 13; partnerships and corporations are not eligible. Individuals must have a regular income and must owe less than $336,900 for fixed unsecured debts or $1,010,650 for fixed secured debts.

Legal Principle: **Individuals, but not partnerships or corporations, may file under Chapter 13.**

What Are the Repayment Proceedings?

Filing the Petition. As with the other forms of bankruptcy relief, the repayment process begins only when the debtor files the petition. However, repayment is distinct from other types of relief because repayment is voluntary only. A debtor cannot be forced into a repayment plan.

In the petition, the debtor states that he is unable to pay his debts. The debtor might request an extension of time to pay the debt or ask that the total amount of debt be reduced. Alternatively, the debtor might request a combination of those options. As in liquidation proceedings, the debtor commonly files various schedules listing the creditors as well as the debtor's assets. Furthermore, an automatic stay on litigation against the debtor is granted when the debtor files the petition. However, one of the benefits of Chapter 13 is that this stay applies to creditors' attempts to collect from co-debtors.

Creditors' Meeting and the Repayment Plan Proceedings. After the debtor files the petition, the court calls a creditors' meeting. At this meeting, the debtor submits a plan of payment for her debts. This plan is not required to provide for the full payment of all claims. However, the plan must treat all same-class creditors equally, and the plan for repayment must not exceed a three-year period, unless the court approves otherwise.

Unlike the case with other chapters, creditors do not vote to approve a Chapter 13 plan; if the court approves of the plan, the plan is accepted. The court holds a hearing to

COMPARING THE LAW OF OTHER COUNTRIES

AN ALTERNATIVE TO BANKRUPTCY IN THAILAND

The function of bankruptcy law in Thailand is similar to that of American bankruptcy law. The law seeks to terminate the business undertakings of a failing operation, collect all assets, and compensate the creditors through redistribution of those assets. Thailand's law applies to businesses, citizens, and any person who "earns his living" within the borders of the country. Thus, foreign businesses and businesspersons operating in Thailand can petition for bankruptcy.

Thai law also offers businesses an alternative to filing for bankruptcy, which is similar to Chapter 11 bankruptcy in U.S. law. The alternative procedure is called *composition,* and its function is distinct from bankruptcy. Composition procedures allow debtors to remain in business while settling their outstanding obligations. Before the court will approve composition procedures, however, debtors must submit a clear and reliable repayment plan. Additionally, the objections of creditors are considered. Nonetheless, acceptance of this alternative is quite plausible, especially in a developing country seeking to stimulate growth.

determine whether to confirm the plan. Unsecured creditors may object to the plan at the hearing. However, the court can overrule their objections if all of the debtor's projected disposable income is used to make payments. If the court believes that the plan was created in good faith, the plan is accepted.

However, if the plan modifies a creditor's secured claim while proposing that the debtor keep the property securing the claim, the creditor may oppose the proposed plan. Court approval of an opposed plan that changes a secured claim is called a "cram down." After BAPCPA, it is harder for debtors to make changes to secured claims over the objections of creditors.

After the court approves the plan, the court then appoints a trustee to carry out the repayment plan. Every Chapter 13 case has a trustee. The debtor makes monthly payments to the trustee that are based on his or her disposable income. The trustee then disburses payments to the creditors. Moreover, as payment for services, the trustee receives a percentage of the funds distributed to creditors.

Thirty days after the debtor files the plan, the debtor must begin making payments. The trustee must ensure that the debtor is making the payments. If the debtor fails to make payments, the court may decide to transfer the case to a liquidation bankruptcy or to refuse to grant the repayment plan.

Suppose that you, a debtor, must make 12 more repayment installments to meet the terms of the repayment agreement. Suddenly you lose your job. What will happen? At any time before all payments are made in a repayment plan, the debtor, creditors, or trustee may request modification of the plan. If there are any objections to the modification, the court must hold a hearing. Thus, you and your creditors might modify the agreement such that your installments will be divided in half until you find a steady job.

Discharge of Debts under Repayment Proceedings. After a debtor makes all payments under a repayment plan, the remaining debts are discharged. However, even if all payments are not made by the expiration of the plan, the court might discharge some of the debts if the debtor has experienced a severe hardship.

Like liquidation, some debts, such as alimony and child support debts, are not dischargeable. However, some debts that are dischargeable under Chapter 13 are not dischargeable under Chapter 7.

CHAPTER 12: FAMILY-FARMER AND FAMILY-FISHERMAN PLANS

Chapter 12 provides for adjustment of debts of family farmers or family fishermen. Chapter 12 was added to the code in the midst of large numbers of farmers with severe debt in the

1980s. Many farmers had borrowed large amounts of money to increase their production; however, during that time there was a surplus of farm products. Consequently, many farmers faced serious financial problems. Congress addressed these problems with Chapter 12.

Who Is Eligible for the Chapter 12 Plan? Not all farmers or fishermen are eligible for Chapter 12 relief. A family farmer or family fisherman under Chapter 12 must have regular annual income and be either (1) an individual or individual and spouse or (2) a corporation or partnership. A family farmer's or family fisherman's gross income must be at least 50 percent farm- or fishing-dependent. Moreover, 50 percent of the family farmer's debt must be farm-related while 80 percent of the family fisherman's debt must be fishing-related. Finally, the total debt must be under $3.79 million for a family farmer and under $1.75 million for a family fisherman.

What Are the Family-Farmer and Family-Fisherman Relief Proceedings? Congress modeled Chapter 12 after Chapter 13 relief. However, Chapter 12 is less expensive and less complicated than Chapter 13. The procedure begins when the family farmer or family fisherman files a Chapter 12 petition. The debtor must file a plan for repayment with the bankruptcy petition or within 90 days after filing. Automatic stay is granted to protect the farmer or fisherman from legal action. The trustee is appointed to oversee the financial affairs and must hold a meeting of the creditors between 20 and 35 days after the petition is filed. Unsecured creditors must file claims with the court within 90 days after the first meeting of creditors. The court holds a hearing to rule on the proposed plan. Unsecured creditors are entitled to at least the liquidation value of the debt owed to them. Once the farmer or fisherman fulfills his or her adjustment plan, the individual will likely receive a discharge from debts and retain possession of the farm or fishery.

Exhibit 32-8 summarizes the types of bankruptcy relief available.

Exhibit 32-8 Summary of Bankruptcy Relief

	ELIGIBLE	PROCEDURE
Chapter 7	Individuals, partnerships, and corporations	A debtor turns over all assets to a trustee, who then sells the nonexempt assets and distributes the proceeds of the sale to the creditors.
Chapter 11	Typically, corporate debtors; can be individuals	The creditors and debtor create a plan to reorganize the debtor's financial affairs under the supervision of the bankruptcy court.
Chapter 12	Family farmer or family fisherman with regular annual income, gross income at least 50% farm- or fishing-dependent, 50% of debt farm-related or 80% of debt fishing-related, total debt under $3.79 million for farmers and under $1.75 million for fishermen	The debtor is a family farmer or family fisherman who works with creditors to adjust and discharge debt.
Chapter 13	Individuals exclusively; have regular income, owe less than $336,900 for fixed unsecured debts or $1,010,650 for fixed secured debts.	Individuals pay their debts to creditors in installment plans under the supervision of the court.

CASE OPENER WRAP-UP

GM Bankruptcy

GM argued that the new GM was not required to take responsibility for the claims because the federal bankruptcy code preempted the state laws that allowed drivers to bring product liability claims. However, in the face of significant pressure from the public and state attorneys general, GM changed its bankruptcy plan and agreed to assume some liability for injuries to drivers as a result of vehicle defects.[11] The new GM would be responsible for postbankruptcy claims even if the claims arose from vehicles manufactured prior to the bankruptcy. However, the new GM would not be responsible for lawsuits against the old GM that were pending at the time of the bankruptcy filing and any damages awarded to drivers who previously won a suit against the old GM but had not yet collected the money. These creditors were required to pursue assets of the Motor Liquidation Company that remained in bankruptcy.

KEY TERMS

automatic stay 709
Bankruptcy Abuse Prevention and Consumer Protection Act (BAPCPA) of 2005 702
bankruptcy estate 706
creditors 702
creditors' meeting 710
debtor 702
discharge 714
fraudulent transfers 713
insolvent debtors 702
liquidation 705
order of relief 709
preferential payments 713
reaffirmation agreement 718
trustee 705

SUMMARY OF KEY TOPICS

The Bankruptcy Act and Its Goals

Purpose:

1. To provide debtors with an opportunity to achieve a fresh financial start.
2. To offer protection to creditors.

Attributes of Bankruptcy Cases

1. The procedural rules are set forth in the Bankruptcy Rules.
2. Cases are filed in federal district courts and referred to bankruptcy judges.
3. Bankruptcy judges are appointed and serve 14-year terms.
4. Bankruptcy appeals go to the district court judge.

Bankruptcy Proceedings

1. The case begins with a filing of petition for bankruptcy.
2. The court grants an automatic stay for creditor actions against the debtor's estate.
3. The court determines whether an order of relief should be granted.
4. The creditors meet with the debtor.

[11] *In re General Motors Corporation,* 407 B.R. 463 (Bankr. S.D.N.Y. 2009).

5. A payment plan is created and approved, usually by the creditors and the court.
6. The payment plan is carried out through actions of the trustee and the debtor.
7. Debts remaining after the plan is carried out are usually discharged.

Specific Types of Relief Available

Chapter 7: Sale of nonexempt assets and the distribution of money to the creditors.

Chapter 11: Reorganization of the debtor's financial affairs under supervision of the bankruptcy court.

Chapter 12: Adjustment of family farmers' and family fishers' debts.

Chapter 13: Adjustment of individuals' debts.

POINT / COUNTERPOINT

Under the Bankruptcy Abuse Prevention and Consumer Protection Act of 2005, individual debtors must now complete a credit-counseling requirement before filing under Chapter 7.

Is the Credit-Counseling Requirement Helpful to Consumers?

YES	NO
Congress's intent in including the credit-counseling requirement was to provide consumers with more information. Whether the counseling takes place in person, over the telephone, or over the Internet, the consumer gains a better understanding of her debt. Generally, the consumer explains how the debt developed. A credit counselor reviews the consumer's monthly income, expenses, liabilities, and assets. The consumer reviews options for dealing with debt; not every case needs to proceed through bankruptcy. The prefiling counseling requirement succeeds in giving consumers more power by enabling them to understand their options. This requirement is helpful to consumers.	The credit-counseling requirement does not provide real information to consumers. Under BAPCPA, the credit counselors must charge a "reasonable fee" for their service. Generally, consumers have been paying $50 for the service, which is a significant amount of money to a person filing for bankruptcy. Because the debtor is required to complete the counseling before filing, the debtor may be persuaded to partake in a debt management plan. The counseling agency frequently receives part of the debts repaid in the debt management plan. The debtor may not be in a position to properly evaluate the debt management plan in relation to the bankruptcy options. Thus, the requirement is not helpful to consumers.

QUESTIONS & PROBLEMS

1. How does bankruptcy law benefit debtors and creditors?
2. Under what circumstances would Chapter 11 be used rather than Chapter 7?
3. Hall-Mark supplied electronic parts to Peter Lee. On September 23, 1992, a check that Lee had given Hall-Mark for $100,000 on September 11, 1992, was dishonored by the bank. Hall-Mark continued supplying parts to Lee, so Lee gave the company a cashier's check for $100,000 on September 25, 1992. After receiving the cashier's check, Hall-Mark supplied no more parts.

   On December 24, 1992, Lee filed a voluntary petition for bankruptcy, and the trustee attempted to have the $100,000 check to Hall-Mark set aside as a preferential payment. What were the arguments of Lee and the trustee? With whom do you believe the court would agree? [*In re Lee,* 179 B.R. 149 (1993).]

4. Carlos and Suzanne Cortez filed their petition for Chapter 7 bankruptcy on April 8, 2004. At the time of filing, Suzanne Cortez was working, but Carlos was unemployed. Suzanne had reduced her work hours so that her minimum net income per month was $750. Carlos accepted a job offer a few days after the filing of the bankruptcy petition that netted him $5,986 monthly. The Cortezes' new combined net income was $6,646 per month, which exceeded their expenses by $1,325 per month. The trustee appointed to the Cortezes' case moved to dismiss their petition on the basis that it appeared that the debtors had the means to repay a substantial portion of their debts through a Chapter 13 plan. The bankruptcy court denied this motion and ruled that it was limited to reviewing the Cortezes' financial circumstances as they existed at the time of the filing of the petition and that postpetition events could not be taken into account in determining the proper chapter under which the petition should have been filed. The trustee appealed the decision to the U.S. district court. How should this case be decided on appeal? Should postpetition events, especially those occurring within a few days of the filing, be relevant to the determination of whether a petition was properly filed? Why or why not? [*In re Cortez,* 2005 U.S. Dist. LEXIS 39778 (N.D Tex., Mar. 9, 2005).]

5. Gergely, an obstetrician, performed an amniocentesis on Jordan Lee-Brenner's mother during her pregnancy. As a result of problems with the procedure, he was blinded in one eye. After his birth, and through his guardian, Lee-Brenner brought an action against Gergely, claiming that Gergely had misrepresented the need for amniocentesis and had performed it negligently. Lee-Brenner received an award for $780,282, which he failed to collect before Gergely filed a Chapter 7 bankruptcy petition. Lee-Brenner moved to have the judgment set aside as a nondischargeable debt. The bankruptcy court dismissed his petition, so he appealed. On what grounds could he argue that the debt should not have been discharged? Do you think his argument was successful before the appellate court? [*In re Gergely,* 110 F.3d 1448 (9th Cir. 1997).]

6. Dr. Jeffrey Hall performed a colonoscopy on Hellen Nash during which he discovered a cancerous mass. Three days later, Hall performed surgery to remove the mass. However, Hall allegedly failed to remove all of the cancerous tissue, and Nash developed complications requiring additional surgery. Nash brought a medical malpractice action against Hall in federal court in Arkansas. Hall moved to Arizona and filed for Chapter 7 bankruptcy there four months later. Hall failed to list Nash as a creditor with a contingent claim and did not disclose the existence of Nash's lawsuit in his sworn statement of financial affairs. As a result, Nash never received notice of Hall's bankruptcy's pending claim and never filed a claim with the Arizona bankruptcy court. Hall obtained a discharge of his debts on June 7, 2006, five days after Nash died. Mary Waterson was appointed as the administrator of Nash's estate and pursued the malpractice action on behalf of the estate. Hall defended the action on the basis of his discharge in bankruptcy. Is the discharge that Hall received in the bankruptcy action in Arizona applicable to Nash's medical malpractice claim in Arkansas? Why or why not? [*Waterson v. Hall,* 515 F.3d 852 (8th Cir. 2008).]

7. Woodcock graduated from law school and finished his MBA in 1983. His student loans came due nine months later. Because he was a part-time student until 1990, he requested that payment be deferred, which the lender incorrectly approved. Since he was not in a degree program, payment should not have been deferred under the terms of the loan. Woodcock filed for bankruptcy in 1992, more than seven years after the loans first became due. Hence, that debt would be discharged unless there was an "applicable suspension of the repayment period." Do you feel this mistaken extension is an applicable suspension? Should his student loans be discharged through filing for bankruptcy? [*Woodcock v. Chemical Bank,* 144 F.3d 1340 (10th Cir. 1998).]

8. Nancy Polleys was a single mother living in Wyoming. She obtained federally guaranteed student loans totaling $51,000 to attend college. She ultimately obtained an accounting degree and worked for a short time in the field before losing her job. Polleys subsequently spent several years working a number of jobs that paid as much as $16,000 to as little as $3,000 annually. As a result, Polleys became unable to repay her student loans, repayment of which would have required $420 per month for over 20 years. Polleys sought to discharge her student loan indebtedness in bankruptcy on the basis of undue hardship. At the time of the filing of her petition, Polleys lived in rental property owned by her parents and paid no rent or utilities. Polleys owned a 1993 Subaru with significant body damage, but she had little other property. Polleys qualified for food stamps, and her income was below federal poverty guidelines. Polleys had no health insurance. Although in good physical health, Polleys suffered from cyclothymic disorder for which she was undergoing mental health treatment, including the use of antidepressant medication. Her mental condition resulted in a suicide attempt and involuntary commitment on one occasion. Educational Credit Management Corporation, which was charged by the U.S. Department of Education with collecting delinquent federally guaranteed student loans, objected to the discharge. The basis for the objection was Polleys' failure to prove that she could not maintain a minimal standard of living for herself and her daughter and that her current financial difficulties were most likely to continue for a significant amount of time, as well as the absence of a good-faith effort to repay the loans. Should the court grant Polleys a discharge on the basis of undue hardship? What factors are relevant to making a hardship determination? [*Educational Credit Management Corp. v. Polleys,* 356 F.3d 1302 (10th Cir. 2004).]

9. Egebjerg filed a voluntary Chapter 7 bankruptcy petition in 2006. He had been employed for 27 years, earned a gross income of $6,115.56 per month, and had unsecured consumer debt of around $31,000. About two years earlier, he took a loan from his 401(k), and he paid back this loan through automatic deductions to his paycheck in the amount of $733.90 per pay period. Egebjerg listed the 401(k) loan repayment in his bankruptcy petition as a necessary expense, leaving him with just $15.31 of disposal income per month. The U.S. trustee moved to dismiss his petition as presumptively abusive because the 401(k) loan repayment was not a necessary expense and thus his filing failed the means test. Do you think that the court agreed that the 401(k) loan repayment was a necessary expense and thus should be calculated in the debtor's monthly ability to pay? Why or why not? [*In re Egebjerg,* 574 F.3d 1074 (9th Cir. 2009).]

10. Andres Soza and his spouse transferred $30,000 into an annuity fund on October 13, 2005. The Sozas filed a Chapter 7 petition for bankruptcy the following day. The Sozas claimed that the annuity was exempt from inclusion in the bankruptcy estate. The money utilized to purchase the annuity came from an inheritance. The Sozas purchased the annuity to safeguard the inheritance from creditors pending a determination of how the proceeds were to be distributed to Soza and his siblings. The Sozas further claimed that the annuity was exempt pursuant to provisions of the Texas Insurance Code. The trustee objected to the exemption claim and alleged that the conversion of nonexempt property into an exempt annuity on the eve of bankruptcy amounted to fraud that was detrimental to the creditors and expressly prohibited by the Code. The court was required to determine whether the code prevented actual as well as constructive fraud by a debtor to the detriment of a creditor. The court focused its attention on the presence or absence of several "badges of fraud." What is a badge of fraud? What type of conduct should be considered indicative of fraud in the context of bankruptcy proceedings? [*In re Soza,* 542 F.3d 1060 (5th Cir. 2008).]

Looking for more review materials?

The Online Learning Center at **www.mhhe.com/kubasek3e** contains this chapter's "Assignment on the Internet" and also a list of URLs for more information, entitled "On the Internet." Find both of them in the Student Center portion of the OLC, along with quizzes and other helpful materials.

Agency Formation and Duties

LEARNING OBJECTIVES

After reading this chapter, you will be able to answer the following questions:

1. What is agency law?
2. How is an agency relationship created?
3. What are the different types of agency?
4. What are the different types of agency relationships?
5. What are the duties of the agent and principal?
6. What are the rights and remedies of the agent and principal?

CASE OPENER

FedEx and Independent Contractors

In July 2006, the International Brotherhood of Teamsters, Local Union 25, filed two petitions and held an election for a collective bargaining representative at two FedEx locations. However, FedEx refused to bargain with the union. FedEx did not contest the vote count of the election; instead, FedEx refused to collectively bargain because it believed that its single-route drivers were not "employees" but, rather, "independent contractors," and the rules of collective bargaining in this situation apply only to employees. However, the National Labor Relations Board concluded that FedEx committed an unfair labor practice by refusing to bargain with the union certified as the collective bargaining representative of the drivers. FedEx sought judicial review of the decision of the board, and the board cross-applied for enforcement of its order requiring that the company bargain.

1. Do you agree with the National Labor Relations Board's ruling that FedEx engaged in an unfair labor practice? Why?
2. What duties and rights would the FedEx drivers have if they were considered employees? How would their duties and rights differ if the drivers were considered independent contractors of the company?

The Wrap-Up at the end of the chapter will answer these questions.

One of the most important relationships in the business world is the agency relationship, in which the employee may be an agent of the employer and have the ability to bind that employer legally. The use of agents and independent contractors allows corporations to enter into contracts and conduct business in multiple locations simultaneously. This chapter explores the nature and creation of the agency relationship, as well as the legal obligations of the parties in such a relationship.

Introduction to Agency Law

LO1
What is agency law?

Agency is generally defined as a relationship between a principal and an agent. In the **agency relationship,** the agent is authorized to act for and on behalf of the principal, who hires the agent to represent him or her. The Restatement of Agency defines **agency** as "the fiduciary relationship that results from the manifestation of consent by one person to another that the other shall act in his behalf and subject to his control, and consent by the other so to act."[1] (A *fiduciary* is a person who has a duty to act primarily for another person's benefit. A lawyer, for example, is a fiduciary for his or her client. We discuss fiduciaries in greater depth later in this chapter.)

Agency law is primarily state law. Thus, it can vary somewhat from state to state. As of July 2010, 40 states had enacted statutes governing the behavior of sports agents. The specific legislation that regulates the conduct of athlete agents in these 40 states is the Uniform Athlete Agents Act (UAAA). There are also non-UAAA laws that regulate athlete agents in California, Michigan, and Ohio. The UAAA provides for criminal, civil, and/or administrative penalties based on the particular state's statute. Twenty-four states (including California and Florida) have established criminal penalties for sports agents who violate the state statute. In contrast, only five states have criminalized violations of the statute by the athletes themselves. In addition to state laws protecting athletes and agents, players associations' model contracts describe the nature of the services agents can perform on behalf of their principals and the duties the parties owe to one another. For example, the Major League Baseball Players Association's (MLBPA's) Regulations Governing Player Agents expressly state that agents act in a fiduciary capacity vis-à-vis their athlete clients.

Agency law is especially important for U.S. firms doing business globally. While foreign countries offer fresh markets and eager consumers, U.S. companies often run into legal difficulties due to language barriers or lack of knowledge about local laws. To avoid such problems, many companies hire agents familiar with local laws, customs, and customers to help them function smoothly in foreign markets.

Creation of the Agency Relationship

LO2
How is an agency relationship created?

Agency relationships are consensual relationships formed by informal oral agreements or formal written contracts. There are two criteria for the creation of agency relationships. First, like contracts, they can be created only for a lawful purpose; thus, a principal could not hire an agent to kill someone on his or her behalf.[2] Second, almost anyone can act as an agent; however, an individual who does not have contractual capacity, such as a minor, cannot hire an agent to make contracts on his or her behalf. (See Exhibit 33-1.)

[1] Restatement (Second) of Agency, sec. 1(1). A valuable reference that summarizes agency law, the Restatement is well respected in the legal profession and frequently cited by judges as well as attorneys and scholars in making legal arguments.

[2] Restatement (Second) of Agency, sec.19.

Exhibit 33-1
Creation of the Agency Relationship

Agency relationships can be formed if and only if:

1. They are being created for a lawful purpose.
2. The person who is to act as an agent has contractual capacity.

Agency relationships can exist as one of four types:

1. *Expressed agency,* in which parties form the agency relationship by making a written or oral agreement.
2. *Agency by implied authority,* in which the agency relationship is implied by the conduct of the parties.
3. *Apparent agency,* in which the principal falsely leads a third party to believe another individual serves as his or her agent.
4. *Agency by ratification,* in which an individual misrepresents himself as another party's agent and the principal accepts the unauthorized act.

As long as these two criteria are met, agency relationships can be created on the basis of any of the following four forms of authority:

1. By expressed agency or agency by agreement.
2. By implied authority.
3. By apparent agency, or agency by estoppel.
4. By ratification.

The following pages discuss all four forms. Agency agreements usually do not need to be in writing, with two important exceptions. First, the agreement must be in writing whenever an agent will enter into a contract that the statute of frauds requires to be in writing. Janet wants Phil to act as her agent and grants him the power to enter into contracts. The statute of frauds, or, more specifically, the equal dignities rule, mandates that the type of contracts Phil is allowed to enter into must be in writing. Therefore, Phil's agreement with Janet must also be in writing. Second, the agreement must be in writing whenever an agent is given power of attorney (discussed below).

A *gratuitous agent* is one who acts without consideration; that is, such an agent is not paid for his or her services. Gratuitous agents function much like regular agents, with a few exceptions noted later in this chapter.

Legal Principle: **Agency relationships cannot be created to conduct illegal activities.**

Types of Agency

EXPRESSED AGENCY (AGENCY BY AGREEMENT)

LO3
What are the different types of agency?

When parties form an agency relationship by making a written or oral agreement, the agency is known as an **expressed agency,** or agency by agreement. Expressed agency is the most common type of agency and gives the agent the authority to contract on behalf of the principal. While a contract is not necessary to form the agency, if there is one it must meet all the elements of a contract discussed in Chapter 13. If the principal agrees to hire no other agent for a period of time or until a particular job is done, the principal and agent have entered into an exclusive agency contract.

A *power of attorney* establishes an agency by agreement that gives an agent authority to sign legal documents on behalf of the principal. A general power of attorney grants broad authority, while a specific power of attorney gives authority only for the specific areas or purposes listed in the agreement.

CASE NUGGET

DURABLE POWER OF ATTORNEY

Penny Garrison et al. v. The Superior Court of Los Angeles et al.
132 Cal. App. 4th 253 (2005)

On Ella Needham's request, her daughter, Penny Garrison, was designated Needham's agent through a durable power of attorney. Needham was later admitted to a residential care facility. As part of the admissions process, Garrison, acting under the durable power of attorney, executed two arbitration agreements. After Needham's death, Garrison and Needham's other daughters sought to sue the facility for a number of concerns the family had regarding the care their mother had received. The facility sought to enforce the two arbitration agreements. However, the family contended that the agreements were unenforceable because Garrison could not legally enter into them.

The durable power of attorney had given Garrison power to (1) make all health care decisions for Needham according to what she believed was in Needham's best interest and (2) make decisions relating to Needham's personal care, including but not limited to determining where she lived. Therefore, Garrison was legally in charge of picking the residential care facility, and she had the power to enter into agreements regarding Needham's care.

Nowhere in the enumerated legal powers did the durable power of attorney state that Garrison could not enter into arbitration clauses. Moreover, the arbitration clauses were optional to the original contract, and they allowed a 30-day period during which Garrison could cancel them. Because the durable power of attorney was legal and enforceable, Garrison could not cancel the agreements into which she entered.

BUT WHAT IF . . .

WHAT IF THE FACTS OF THE CASE OPENER WERE DIFFERENT?

Let's say, in the Case Opener, that all FedEx delivery drivers had written employment agreements with FedEx in which the agency agreement was clearly stated. What kind of agency would this represent?

Powers of attorney are often given for business and health care purposes. Hence, an agent can make decisions about a principal's medical care if the principal cannot. Given that a principal must have the ability to enter into contracts to create an agency relationship, a principal may not enact a power of attorney after becoming incompetent. Therefore, a principal may preemptively enact a *durable power of attorney,* a written document expressing his or her wishes for an agent's authority not to be affected by the principal's subsequent incapacity. Alternatively, a durable power of attorney might become active only after a principal becomes incapacitated in any matter. (See Exhibit 33-2 for a comparison of a power of attorney and a durable power of attorney.) The Case Nugget examines the boundaries of the durable power of attorney.

Exhibit 33-2
Comparison of Powers of Attorney

Durable power of attorney— a document that states either the power of the agent is to continue to be effective if the principal becomes incapacitated or the power of the agent is to take effect after the principal has become incapacitated.

Power of attorney — a document giving an agent authority to sign legal documents on behalf of the principal; the power can be general or specific, limiting the authority of the agent.

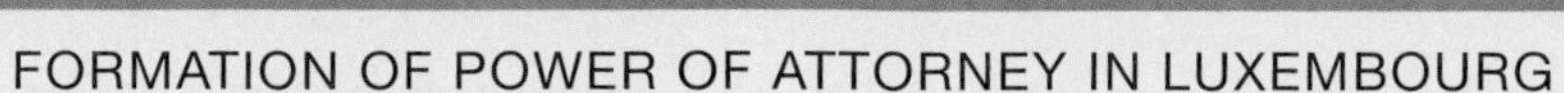

COMPARING THE LAW OF OTHER COUNTRIES

FORMATION OF POWER OF ATTORNEY IN LUXEMBOURG

In the United States and other common law jurisdictions, a power of attorney authorizes the agent only to "conduct a series of transactions" under instruction from the principal. This limitation makes the power of attorney in common law distinctly different from that provided by civil law, which authorizes the agent to do "everything and anything which the principal himself could do."

Under the law of the Grand Duchy of Luxembourg, the person on whose behalf the power of attorney is created is called a *donor,* instead of a principal. Under Luxembourg law, there are two types of power of attorney from which a donor must choose. The first type is a power of attorney that is valid until death, and the second type is a power of attorney that has unlimited validity even after death. The actions that are permitted to be performed under a power of attorney are completely determined by the law in Luxembourg.

The law in Luxembourg also requires that the power of attorney be authenticated by a public authority or a public notary by providing the donor's certified identification card or passport, as well as proof of residency.

The Restatement says, "[A]n agency relation exists only if there has been a manifestation by the principal to the agent that the agent may act on his account, and consent by the agent so to act."[3] Therefore, in addition to the above criteria, the principal must agree to have the person act as an agent, and the agent must agree to act for the principal. As noted below, the parties can reach this agreement in several ways.

AGENCY BY IMPLIED AUTHORITY

In some cases, an agency relationship is not created by an express agreement but is instead implied by the conduct of the parties. For example, if a homeowner asked a real estate broker to help sell her home, her words imply that an agency relationship has been formed. The circumstances determine the extent of an agent's ability to conduct business on behalf of the principal. However, implied authority cannot conflict with any express authority.

Legal Principle: **Agency by implied authority cannot conflict with any express authority.**

BUT WHAT IF . . .

WHAT IF THE FACTS OF THE CASE OPENER WERE DIFFERENT?

Let's say, in the Case Opener, that FedEx had released a television commercial that made it seem as though all FedEx drivers worked directly for FedEx. A month after the release of the commercial, FedEx refused to collectively bargain with a union rep for Jerry, a single-route driver. FedEx said that there was no written contract that proved an agency relationship existed and thus Jerry was not an agent of FedEx. Is FedEx correct in this argument? Why or why not?

APPARENT AGENCY (AGENCY BY ESTOPPEL)

Suppose a principal falsely leads a third party to believe another individual serves as his or her agent. Does an agency relationship exist? Yes, because by his or her conduct, the principal has created **apparent agency** or **agency by estoppel.** According to the principal's conduct, the agent has apparent authority to act; thus, the principal is estopped, or prevented, from denying that the individual is an agent.[4] An apparent agency can be created only on the acts of the principal—never on the basis of what the purported agent says or does. When a third party relies on the principal's conduct and makes an agreement with an

[3] Restatement (Second) of Agency, sec. 15.

[4] Restatement (Second) of Agency, sec. 8B.

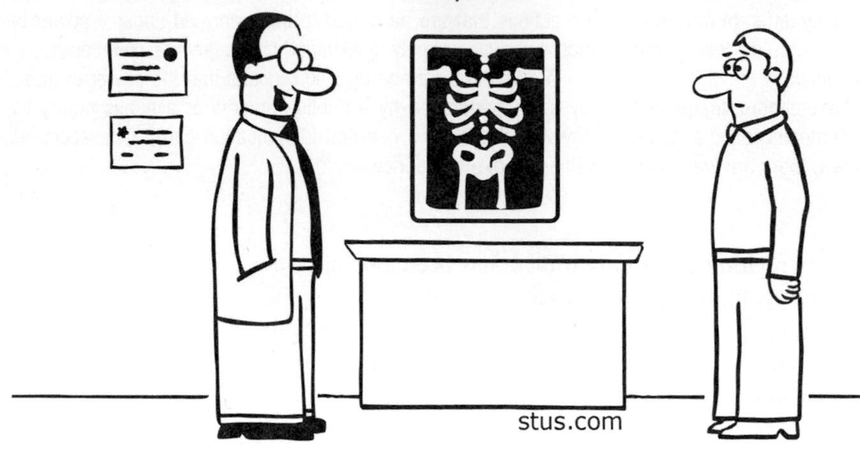

apparent agent, the principal must uphold any agreements made by the agent. If the principal attempts to deny that an agency relationship existed, the third party must demonstrate that he or she reasonably believed, on the basis of the principal's conduct, that an agency relationship existed. The court will consider the principal's conduct in determining whether an agency relationship existed.

Suppose a salesman enters the office of a third party claiming he represents a company that wants to do business. If he is really not an agent for the company and provides no evidence of a link with it, the company will not be held responsible under apparent agency because the third party had no interaction with it. The third party had no reason to believe an agency relationship existed, other than the agent's words. However, if the president of the company suggests to the third party that the salesman *is* a representative of the company, the president's conduct suggests that the salesman is an agent. Thus, the company would have to uphold any agreement the third party made with the apparent agent. In Case 33-1, pay close attention to how the court determines whether the party had apparent authority in this agency issue.

CASE 33-1 ACKERMAN v. SOBOL FAMILY PARTNERSHIP, LLP
SUPREME COURT OF CONNECTICUT
298 CONN. 495 (2010)

On May 29, 2008, the plaintiff's attorney, Glenn Coe, met the defendants for mediation. At the mediation, Coe made a detailed offer of settlement with the defendants. The defendants rejected this proposal, and afterward negotiations continued, during which Coe made an offer to settle the litigation through a series of conversations with the attorneys who represented the defendant Bank of America.

During a two-day period in June 2008, Coe expressly assured the defendants' attorneys on separate occasions, in response to direct questioning on the issue, that the settlement offer proposed by him at that time was fully authorized by his clients as well as the additional plaintiff's attorney, and that if accepted by the defendants, it would resolve the litigation.

The final settlement demand by the plaintiffs' counsel to the Bank of America was the sum of $1.1 million. The Bank of America accepted the $1.1 million settlement proposal on July 1, 2008, prior to the 5 p.m. deadline. At this time, the global settlement offer had been accepted by all defendants. At no time prior to the acceptance of the settlement proposal were the defendants or their attorneys notified that the offer had been withdrawn, unauthorized, or otherwise ineffective.

After the proposal had been accepted by the defendants, the plaintiffs sued the defendants, claiming that the plaintiffs' lead attorney, Glenn Coe, lacked the authority to make several settlement proposals or bind them to a global settlement agreement with Bank of America and the other defendants. The defendants filed motions to enforce the settlement agreement, and the Superior Court granted the defendants' motions and rendered judgments for defendants. The plaintiffs appealed.

JUDGE ZARELLA: The principal issue in this consolidated appeal . . . is whether the plaintiffs' attorney had

[continued]

apparent authority to make settlement proposals, engage in settlement discussions and bind the plaintiffs to a global settlement agreement with the defendants. The plaintiffs claim that the trial court's enforcement of a settlement agreement between the parties, based on a finding of apparent authority on the part of the plaintiffs' attorney to bind the plaintiffs to the agreement, was clearly erroneous in the absence of conduct by the plaintiffs (1) manifesting that their attorney had authority to settle the pending litigation, and (2) leading the opposing defense attorneys reasonably to believe that the plaintiffs' attorney had full and final authority to settle the litigation, as distinguished from authority only to negotiate. The plaintiffs also claim that they were denied their right to a jury trial on issues of fact under article first, § 19, of the Connecticut constitution, as amended by article four of the amendments, when the trial court, in the midst of voir dire, made findings of fact and determined that the litigants had reached a settlement of the pending litigation. The defendants respond that the trial court's finding that the plaintiffs' counsel had apparent authority to settle the litigation was not clearly erroneous and that the plaintiffs had no right to a jury trial on their equitable motions seeking to enforce the agreement. We affirm the judgment of the trial court.

Since the case of *Tomlinson v. Board of Education,* the court's inquiry as to the doctrine of apparent authority is now refined to a two part analysis. Apparent authority exists, one, where the principal held the agent out as possessing sufficient authority to embrace the act in question and knowingly permitted him to act as having such authority; and, two, in consequence thereof, the person dealing with the agent acting in good faith reasonably believed under all the circumstances that the agent had the necessary authority. . . . Based upon the court's prior findings in this matter, the court finds that [Coe] certainly did have apparent authority from his client[s]. Further . . . the court so finds, [it was] acknowledged in testimony, that the defendants' counsel reasonably believed that [Coe] was, in fact, authorized by the plaintiffs to make the settlement offer at issue, and further, that [the] defendants' counsel at all . . . relevant times were acting in good faith in their respective efforts to settle the case on the terms proposed by [Coe].

As noted earlier, [Coe] had been, in fact, engaged in settlement discussions with his client's obvious assent. [Rena Ackerman] had accompanied him to the mediation for over [one] month prior to the time the settlement was reached. [Coe] was certainly held out as being authorized to negotiate settlement on behalf of the plaintiffs and the defendants acted reasonably in believing that he had authority to do so. [Coe] acknowledged in testimony that both [Wyld] and [Schneider] acted reasonably in relying on his stated authority. Further, there was no evidence at all that [Coe's] apparent authority had been terminated at any time by [Rena] Ackerman. We affirm the judgment of the trial court.

AFFIRMED.

CRITICAL THINKING

Is any important information missing from this decision that might further clarify the nature of the issue of agency between the concerned parties? Could it change the acceptability of the judge's reasoning?

ETHICAL DECISION MAKING

Does this ruling appear to follow a coherent ethical guideline? If so, what form does it take? Who are the stakeholders in this situation? Are they awarded proper consideration under the selected ethical guideline?

AGENCY BY RATIFICATION

Francisco is driving home and sees a car with a "For Sale" sign in the window. He stops to look at it because his friend Miles wants to buy a used car. Impressed by the car's price and quality, Francisco tells the owner his friend wants to buy it. The owner claims another individual is coming to probably buy the car in an hour. To ensure that Miles gets the car, Francisco signs a contract to purchase it but notes on the contract that he is an agent of Miles. Because Francisco is not his agent, Miles is not required to uphold the contract.

However, if Miles does agree to purchase the car, he has accepted Francisco as his agent for the contract. Miles is now bound by the contract, and Francisco cannot be held liable for misrepresenting himself. This type of agency relationship is *agency by ratification.* As the example suggests, it has two requirements:

1. An individual must misrepresent himself or herself as an agent for another party.
2. The principal must accept or ratify the unauthorized act.

For ratification to be effective, two additional requirements must be met:

3. The principal must have complete knowledge of all material facts regarding the contract.
4. The principal must ratify the entirety of the agent's act. (The principal cannot accept certain parts of the agent's act and reject others.)

Agency Relationships

LO4
What are the different types of agency relationships?

Agency laws are relevant to three types of business relationships: the principal-agent relationship, the employer-employee relationship, and the employer–independent contractor relationship (see Exhibit 33-3). We discuss all three in the following sections.

PRINCIPAL-AGENT RELATIONSHIP

The *principal-agent relationship* typically exists when an employer hires an employee to enter into contracts on its behalf. This is the most basic type of agency relationship. Suppose a salesclerk at Abercrombie sells Amanda a shirt. The clerk is acting on behalf of Abercrombie's owner; consequently, any sales she makes are binding on it. Think of all the advertisements you've seen in which a professional athlete speaks on behalf of a product. The athlete usually hires an agent to find and make agreements on his or her behalf to promote products.

EMPLOYER-EMPLOYEE RELATIONSHIP

Whenever an employer hires an employee to perform some sort of physical service, the parties have created an *employer-employee relationship* in which the employee is subject to the employer's control.[5] Generally, all employees are considered agents of the employer, even those not legally authorized to enter into contracts binding their employer or to interact with third parties. However, not all agents are employees.

Legal Principle: **Employees are agents of an employer.**

EMPLOYER–INDEPENDENT CONTRACTOR RELATIONSHIP

The Restatement of Agency defines an *independent contractor* as "a person who contracts with another to do something for him but who is not controlled by the other nor subject to the other's right to control with respect to his physical conduct in the performance of the undertaking."[6] Building contractors, doctors, stockbrokers, and lawyers are types

Exhibit 33-3
Types of Agency Relationships and Their Significance

RELATIONSHIP	HOW TO IDENTIFY	SIGNIFICANT FOR WHAT ISSUES?
Principal-agent	Parties have *agreed* that agent will have power to bind principal in contract.	Contract law
Employer-employee	Employer has right to *control* conduct of employees.	Tort law, tax law, wage law, discrimination law, copyright law
Employer–independent contractor	Employer has *no control* over details of conduct of independent contractor.	Tort law, tax law, wage law, discrimination law, copyright law

[5] Restatement (Second) of Agency, sec. 2.
[6] Restatement (Second) of Agency, sec. 2.

of independent contractors. They are also agents, but not employees. However, not all independent contractors are agents. They cannot enter into contracts on behalf of the principal unless the principal authorizes them to do so.

Legal Principle: **Independent contractors cannot enter into contracts on behalf of the principal unless the contractor possesses authority from the principal.**

Employee or Independent Contractor? The question of whether a worker is an employee or an independent contractor has important implications because the employer-employee relationship is subject to the workers' compensation, workplace safety, employment discrimination, and unemployment statutes, while the employer–independent contractor relationship is not. Employers are also generally liable in tort for the actions of their employees, while they are generally not liable for the actions of independent contractors (see Chapter 34).

BUT WHAT IF . . .

WHAT IF THE FACTS OF THE CASE OPENER WERE DIFFERENT?

Let's say, in the Case Opener, that a single-route driver named Rick was an independent contractor for FedEx. He delivered a package to a woman named Sarah, but Sarah's package had been damaged at a FedEx center. Rick formed a contract for Sarah, telling her that FedEx would award her the cost of the item that was shipped. Is Rick legally correct in this scenario? Why or why not?

When courts are deciding whether a worker is an employee or an independent contractor, perhaps the most important consideration is employer control.[7] If the employer has the right to substantially control the worker's day-to-day operations, the worker is generally considered an employee. Employers will sometimes have some control over the operations of a contractor; however, this control does not always mean that the contractor is an employee. In the Case Opener, the main issue for the court to determine was whether the FedEx drivers were employees or contractors. To do so, the court relied on the standard agency principle of determining how much control the employer exerted over the agent drivers. (See Exhibit 33-4 for more criteria that distinguish employees and independent contractors.)

Exhibit 33-4 Independent Contractor or Employee?

CRITERIA	EMPLOYEE	INDEPENDENT CONTRACTOR
Does the worker engage in a distinct occupation or an independently established business?	No	Yes
Is the work done under the employer's supervision, or does a specialist without supervision complete the work?	Employer supervision	Specialist without supervision
Does the employer supply the tools?	Yes	No
What skill is required for the occupation?	No specialized skill	Great degree of skill
What is the length of time for which the worker is employed?	Long time	Varies
Is the worker a regular part of the business of the employer?	Yes	No
How is the worker paid?	Regular payments according to time	When the job is completed

[7] Restatement (Second) of Agency, sec. 2(3).

COMPARING THE LAW OF OTHER COUNTRIES

FORMATION OF AGENCY IN ITALIAN LAW

The Italian legal system has created an agency relationship that gives the agent unique powers. Although not formally recognized by the Italian Civil Code, this relationship is common in business practices and has been upheld in a number of court cases.

The agency relationship begins much like agency in the United States: The principal and agent enter into a contract under which the agent agrees to the principal's stipulations. This contract, however, also requires that the agent maintain the principal's property. Under Italian law, the agent then becomes legal owner of the property and can transfer or contract it without the principal's consent. Such autonomous powers are not granted to agents in the United States, who must maintain communication with and receive permission from principals unless otherwise specified.

The extended freedom of the agent under the Italian Civil Code results in considerably lengthy and detailed contracts between agents and principals. Both parties are looking to protect their own interests.

The IRS also must decide who is an employee and who is an independent contractor to ensure that the employer is not simply trying to lower its tax burden. The IRS has outlined 20 different criteria for its auditors to consider in determining whether someone is an independent contractor. In 1997, under advisement of the court, the IRS changed its criteria to focus on one element: how much control the employer exerts over the agent. The IRS needs to determine when people are employees and when they are independent contractors because of different tax liabilities employers face. When the IRS determines an independent contractor is really an employee, the employer becomes liable for all applicable taxes, such as Social Security and unemployment taxes.

Case 33-2 provides an illustration of the court's consideration of the criteria that establish whether a worker is an employee or an independent contractor.

CASE 33-2 CYNTHIA WALKER v. JOHN A. LAHOSKI ET AL.

COURT OF APPEALS OF OHIO, NINTH APPELLATE DISTRICT, SUMMIT COUNTY

1999 OHIO APP. LEXIS 3435 (1999)

In 1995, Cynthia Walker contracted with Genny's Home Health Care to find her employment as a home health-care worker. When Ben Lahoski contacted Genny's to obtain twenty-four-hour home health care for his wife Ann, Walker and another worker were assigned to her. Each would stay at the Lahoski's for either forty-eight or seventy-two hours, at which time the two would switch. In September 1995, while Walker was mopping the floor in the Lahoski home, the mop handle knocked a cast iron clock off the wall. Walker was hit on the head by the clock and suffered a sprain of the neck and contusions on her face, scalp, and neck. Walker filed a claim with the Ohio Bureau of Workers' Compensation, naming Ben and Ann Lahoski as her employers. The Ohio Bureau refused Walker's claim by arguing the Lahoskis were not Walker's employers.

Walker filed a claim in court against the Lahoskis for denying her workers' compensation. The trial court granted summary judgment to the Lahoskis. Walker appealed.

JUDGE BAIRD: To prevail in her workers' compensation claim, Ms. Walker would have to establish she was an employee of Ben and Ann Lahoski at the time her injury occurred. The trial court's denial of her claim is based on its finding she was not their employee, but an independent contractor.

Appellees in this matter argue Walker was an independent contractor. In support of their position they point out there was no contract between Walker and the Lahoskis, the Lahoskis did not pay Walker but paid the agency, and Walker's contract with the agency specifically stated she was an independent contractor.

Courts have distinguished an employee from an independent contractor by resolving two key questions. The first is whether the "employer" controls the "manner or means" by which the work is done or if the "employer" is interested only in the results to be achieved. In the first case, the worker would be an employee while in the second case the worker would be an independent contractor.

The second question is how the worker is paid. If the worker is paid on an hourly basis, this tends to indicate the worker was an employee, while payment by the job tends to indicate the worker was an independent contractor.

[continued]

Thus, the overriding consideration for the fact-finder in these cases is who has the right to control the manner or means of the work performed.

In the instant case, Walker signed a contract in which she acknowledged she was an independent contractor relative to Genny's and she would be an independent contractor relative to the customer, absent agreement by the customer she could be considered the customer's employee. However, such a contract provision is not necessarily controlling. The trial court must look to the substance of the relationship, not merely to a label attached to the relationship.

Appellees also assert when Walker and her coworker Peggy J. Seifert began to work for Ben Lahoski, Mr. Lahoski only briefly gave the women a tour of the house, then left it to them to perform their work as they saw fit. However, Cynthia Walker has testified otherwise, asserting Ben Lahoski was actively involved in directing her work for Mrs. Lahoski. In considering whether summary judgment was appropriate in this case, we must resolve the conflict in testimony in favor of the nonmoving party, Ms. Walker. Furthermore, the factual determination to be made in this case is who had the right to exercise control over the manner or means of the work performed.

[T]he "right to control" is agreeably the key factor in making the determination of whether an individual is an independent contractor or an employee. . . .

In the instant case, appellees merely assert "it is clear that Ben Lahoski did not reserve the right to control the manner or means of Appellant's work[.]" In point of fact, it is not clear Mr. Lahoski did not exercise such control. The statements of the two workers conflict on this point. Furthermore, even if Ben Lahoski did not exercise right to control, there is sufficient evidence to indicate he had the right to exercise that control.

The record below contains disputed facts and several indicia of employee status, such as hourly payment, control of hours worked, and control over the manner or means the work was performed. Appellees failed to meet their burden to show there was no genuine issue of material fact and reasonable minds could only decide favorably for the appellees. Thus, the trial court erred in granting summary judgment in favor of the defendants.

REVERSED.

CRITICAL THINKING

Clearly, all relevant information regarding the agreement is critical to the judge's conclusion. What missing information might be reason for the judge to form a different conclusion?

ETHICAL DECISION MAKING

The court felt that the law governing agency in this particular fact pattern was unclear enough that the lower court should not grant a summary judgment. But Walker and Seifert worked for the Lahoskis. Are there values that employers in a position like that of the Lahoskis should act on in their relationship with those who work for them? Should these values push employers beyond what they are required to do by law?

The classification as an employee or independent contractor is also important in determining who owns the output of a work project. According to the Copyright Act of 1976,[8] when an employee completes work at the request of the employer, the product is considered a "work for hire" and the employer owns the copyright. Conversely, an independent contractor normally maintains ownership of copyrights for his or her work product. Only by an agreement of both parties that a specific work is a work for hire may an employer gain copyright ownership of the work of an independent contractor.

BUT WHAT IF . . .

WHAT IF THE FACTS OF THE CASE OPENER WERE DIFFERENT?

Let's say, in the Case Opener, that single-route drivers did have agency relationships with FedEx. Although Jim, a FedEx driver, was not driving a FedEx vehicle, he had to travel to another city to perform a FedEx duty. He asked FedEx for gas money to travel, but FedEx declined. Which party is correct in this situation?

[8]17 U.S.C. §§ 101-810.

Duties of the Agent and the Principal

LO5

What are the duties of the agent and principal?

An agency relationship is a fiduciary relationship of trust, confidence, and good faith. Thus, its formation creates certain duties that the principal and agent owe each other (see Exhibit 33-5). We discuss them in the following sections.

PRINCIPAL'S DUTIES TO THE AGENT

The principal owes certain duties to the agent. If these duties are not fulfilled, the principal has violated the agent's rights and the agent can sue for contract or tort remedies. The agent can also refuse to act on behalf of the principal until the failure is remedied.

Legal Principle: The principal owes specific duties to the agent. Failure to fulfill these duties provides the basis for a tort or contract action against the principal.

Duty of Compensation. The principal has a **duty to compensate** the agent for services provided, unless the parties have agreed the agent will act gratuitously. The agency contract will usually specify the type and amount of compensation as well as the time at which it will be paid. If there is no agreement on the amount, the courts suggest compensation should be calculated according to the customary fee in the situation.[9] The Case Nugget examines which individuals are responsible under the duty to compensate.

Exhibit 33-5 Duties of Principal and Agent

PRINCIPAL DUTIES	
Compensation	The principal has a duty to compensate the agent for services provided unless the parties have agreed that the agent will act gratuitously.
Reimbursement and indemnification	The principal has a duty to reimburse or indemnify the agent for any authorized expenditures or any losses the agent incurs in the course of working on behalf of the principal.
Cooperation	The principal must assist the agent in the performance of his or her duties and cannot interfere with the reasonable conduct of the agent.
Safe working conditions	The principal has a duty to ensure safe working conditions and to warn the agent if the principal is aware of any potential danger.
AGENT DUTIES	
Loyalty	The agent has a responsibility to act in the best interest of the principal; this duty is important because the agency relationship is founded on trust.
Notification	The agent must notify the principal of any relevant information in a timely manner.
Obedience	The agent must follow the lawful instruction and direction of the principal.
Accounting	The agent must keep an accurate account of the transactions made on behalf of the principal and provide the accounting information to the principal on request.
Performance	The agent must perform the duties as specified in the agency agreement with reasonable skill, care, and professionalism.

[9] Restatement (Second) of Agency, sec. 443.

CASE NUGGET

DUTY TO COMPENSATE

Ralph T. Leonard et al. v. Jerry D. McMorris et al.
320 F.3d 1116 (2003)

NationsWay was one of the largest privately held trucking companies in the United States, with 3,200 employees operating in 43 different states. In 1999, NationsWay filed for Chapter 11 bankruptcy and terminated most of its employees. Ralph Leonard, and a number of the other employees who were terminated, sued Jerry McMorris and other NationsWay executives, arguing they were personally liable for unpaid wages under their duty to compensate arising from the employer-employee relationship.

The defendants argued they could not be held personally liable for agreements made between the employees and the corporation. As the case began, NationsWay was continuing its bankruptcy filings, under which the former employees were to receive approximately $3 million in unpaid wages. However, the plaintiffs wanted additional amounts covering accrued vacation pay, sick-leave pay, holiday pay, and other nonwage compensation, as well as a 50 percent penalty and attorney fees.

In deciding the case, the court addressed "[w]hether officers of a corporation are individually liable for the wages of the corporation's former employees under the Colorado Wage Claim Act." The court concluded, "[U]nder Colorado's Wage Claim Act, the officers and agents of a corporation are *not* jointly and severally liable for payment of employee wages and other compensation the corporation owes to its employees under the employment contract and the Colorado Wage Claim Act." Although there is a duty to compensate for the corporation, the executives who were the defendants were not individually liable to the former employees for the unpaid wages.

Duty of Reimbursement and Indemnification. The principal has a duty of reimbursement and indemnification to the agent. If an agent makes authorized expenditures in the course of working on behalf of the principal, the principal has a duty to reimburse the agent for that amount of money.[10] Thus, if an agent takes a trip on behalf of the principal, the principal must have authorized this trip if the agent is to be reimbursed.

Similarly, the principal has the duty to indemnify or reimburse the agent for any losses the agent incurs while working within the scope of authority on the principal's behalf.[11] Suppose an agent makes an agreement with a third party on behalf of the principal and the principal fails to uphold the agreement. The third party could sue the agent for damages, but the principal has a duty to indemnify the agent for the losses the third party regains.

Duty of Cooperation. The principal also owes a *duty of cooperation* to the agent and must therefore assist the agent in the performance of his or her duties. Furthermore, the principal can do nothing to interfere with the agent's reasonable conduct. If Suzi hires someone to sell her car for her, she must be willing to let the agent show the car to interested buyers.

Duty to Provide Safe Working Conditions. The principal has a *duty to provide safe working conditions* for the agent, including equipment and premises. A principal aware of unsafe working conditions has a duty to warn the agent and make necessary repairs. Federal and state statutes, such as the Occupational Safety and Health Act (OSHA), set specific standards for the working environment. Employers that violate these standards may be subject to fines.

AGENT'S DUTIES TO THE PRINCIPAL

Because the agent makes agreements on behalf of the principal in a fiduciary relationship of trust and confidence, he or she can also harm the principal. Suppose an agent makes

[10] Restatement (Second) of Agency, sec. 438.

[11] Restatement (Second) of Agency, secs. 438 and 439.

numerous contracts the principal could not possibly carry out all at once. The third parties may sue the principal for not carrying out the agreements. If the agent breaches his or her duties, the principal can sue the agent and may be entitled to a variety of contract and tort remedies beyond those stated in the contract.

Legal Principle: **When an agent fails to fulfill his duties to the principal, that failure provides the basis for a contract or tort action against the agent.**

Duty of Loyalty. Courts suggest that the **duty of loyalty** is the most important duty an agent owes to a principal. Because of their fiduciary relationship, the agent has a responsibility to act in the interest of the principal,[12] including avoiding conflicts of interest and protecting the principal's confidentiality.

An agent cannot represent both the principal and a third party in an agreement, because there could be a conflict of interest. The agent also has a duty to notify the principal of any offers from third parties. Suppose Tony has hired a real estate agent to make land purchases for him. A third party notifies the real estate agent that some of her property will soon be going up for sale and wants to know whether Tony would be interested in buying it. The real estate agent cannot decide to buy that property for himself or herself until (1) the real estate agent has communicated the offer to Tony and (2) Tony has considered and rejected the offer.

The duty of loyalty also requires that the agent keep confidential any information about the principal, during the course of agency as well as after the agency relationship has been terminated. The agent cannot disclose or misuse any information received during or after the agency relationship with the principal.

Duty of Notification. The agent has to communicate not only offers from third parties but also, under the **duty of notification,** any information he or she thinks could be important to the principal.[13] If a third party has made an agreement with a principal through an agent and fails to meet the agreement, the agent must notify the principal in a timely manner. The law typically assumes that the principal is aware of all information revealed to the agent, regardless of whether the agent shares it with the principal.

Case 33-3 pays special attention to the duties of the agent to the principal and explains what happens when an agent violates the specific duty of loyalty.

[12] Restatement (Second) of Agency, sec. 401.

[13] Restatement (Second) of Agency, sec. 381.

CASE 33-3 INTERNATIONAL AIRPORT CENTERS v. JACOB CITRIN

COURT OF APPEALS FOR THE SEVENTH DISTRICT

440 F.3D 418 (2006)

The defendant, Mr. Citrin, was employed by the plaintiffs' real estate business, IAC. In the course of their business relationship, IAC lent Citrin a laptop to use to record work data. Eventually Mr. Citrin quit his job at IAC and started his own business, which was in breach of his employment contract. Before returning the laptop to IAC, he deleted all of the business data in the computer. Ordinarily, pressing the "delete" key on a computer merely removes the index entry and such "deleted" files are easily recoverable. But Mr. Citrin loaded into the laptop a secure-erasure program to prevent the recovery of the files. Subsequently, IAC sued him for violating the Computer Fraud and Abuse Act and his duty of loyalty that agency law imposes on an employee. The district court dismissed the suit and IAC appealed.

JUDGE POSNER: [Mr. Citrin's] authorization to access the laptop terminated when, having already engaged in misconduct and decided to quit IAC in violation of his employment contract, he resolved to destroy files that incriminated himself and other files that were also the property of his employer, in violation of the duty of loyalty that agency law imposes on an employee.

Muddying the picture some, the Computer Fraud and Abuse Act distinguishes between "without authorization" and "exceeding authorized access," 18 U.S.C. § § 1030(a)(1), (2), (4), and, while making both punishable, defines the latter as "accessing a computer with authorization and . . . using such access to obtain or alter information in the computer that the accesser is not entitled so to obtain or alter." § 1030(e)(6). That might seem the more apt description of what Citrin did.

The difference between "without authorization" and "exceeding authorized access" is paper thin, but not quite invisible. In *EF Cultural Travel BV v. Explorica, Inc.*, for example, the former employee of a travel agent, in violation of his confidentiality agreement with his former employer, used confidential information that he had obtained as an employee to create a program that enabled his new travel company to obtain information from his former employer's website that he could not have obtained as efficiently without the use of that confidential information. The website was open to the public, so he was authorized to use it, but he exceeded his authorization by using confidential information to obtain better access than other members of the public.

Our case is different. Citrin's breach of his duty of loyalty terminated his agency relationship (more precisely, terminated any rights he might have claimed as IAC's agent—he could not by unilaterally terminating any duties he owed his principal gain an advantage) and with it his authority to access the laptop, because the only basis of his authority had been that relationship. "Violating the duty of loyalty, or failing to disclose adverse interests, voids the agency relationship." *(State v. DiGiulio.)* "Unless otherwise agreed, the authority of the agent terminates if, without knowledge of the principal, he acquires adverse interests or if he is otherwise guilty of a serious breach of loyalty to the principal."

Citrin points out that his employment contract authorized him to "return *or destroy*" data in the laptop when he ceased being employed by IAC. But it is unlikely, to say the least, that the provision was intended to authorize him to destroy data that he knew the company had no duplicates of and would have wanted to have—if only to nail Citrin for misconduct. The purpose of the provision may have been to avoid overloading the company with returned data of no further value, which the employee should simply have deleted. More likely the purpose was simply to remind Citrin that he was not to disseminate confidential data after he left the company's employ—the provision authorizing him to return or destroy data in the laptop was limited to "Confidential" information. There may be a dispute over whether the incriminating files that Citrin destroyed contained "confidential" data, but that issue cannot be resolved on this appeal.

REVERSED and REMANDED.

CRITICAL THINKING

Why do you think the original trial court ruled in the opposite manner? Why might you conclude that the agent in the case (Citrin) did not violate his duties to the principal (IAC)?

ETHICAL DECISION MAKING

Recall the WPH framework for ethics. A classmate argues that Citrin made the correct decision in deleting the data because he himself was a stakeholder and deleting the data bettered his own position. Do you agree? Who are the relevant stakeholders negatively affected by Citrin's decision to destroy the business data on the computer?

Duty of Performance. The *duty of performance* the agent owes the principal is twofold. First, the agent must perform the duties as specified in the agency agreement. Suppose an insurance agent contacts Bethany about purchasing a car insurance policy. Bethany agrees to purchase it, but for some reason the agent never obtains the policy for her. Bethany discovers the insurance agent's mistake when she gets into a car accident. The insurance agent did not meet the duty of performance; thus Bethany could bring a claim against the agent.

Second, the agent must perform the specified duties with the same skill, care, and professionalism as a reasonable person in the same situation would provide. An attorney who advertises he is a specialist in certain types of law will be held to the reasonable standard of care in that specialty.[14] A gratuitous agent cannot be found liable for a breach

[14] Restatement (Second) of Agency, sec. 379.

of contract for failure to perform because no contract exists between the principal and the agent. However, if a gratuitous agent begins to act as an agent and the principal affirms the relationship, a duty to perform arises insofar as the agent has begun a specific task for the principal.

Duty of Obedience. Under the *duty of obedience,* the agent must follow the lawful instruction and direction of the principal.[15] An agent who makes an unauthorized agreement has failed to meet the duty of obedience. However, if the principal gives unlawful or unethical instructions, the agent is not required to behave in accordance with them. Let us say a principal tells an agent to sell a basketball autographed by Michael Jordan and the agent knows that the principal forged the signature. The agent is not required to obey this instruction.

Duty of Accounting. Under the *duty of accounting,* the agent must keep an accurate account of the transactions of money and property made on behalf of the principal.[16] If the principal asks to see this accounting, the agent has a duty to provide it. The agent must also keep separate accounts for the principal's funds and the agent's funds and not allow them to mix.

Rights and Remedies

PRINCIPAL'S RIGHTS AND REMEDIES AGAINST THE AGENT

LO6

What are the rights and remedies of the agent and principal?

Because the agency relationship generally *is* a contractual relationship, a principal has available contract remedies, discussed in depth in Chapter 20, for breach of fiduciary duties. In addition, a principal may utilize tort remedies for an agent's misrepresentations, negligence, or other business failings causing damage to the principal. When an agent breaches his or her fiduciary duties, the principal has the right to terminate the agency relationship. Of numerous remedies available to the principal, the three main ones are constructive trust, avoidance, and indemnification.

Legal Principle: **When an agent breaches his or her duties to the principal, the principal can terminate the agency relationship and seek remedies.**

Constructive Trust. Agency relationships exist primarily for the benefit of the principal. Therefore, principals are the legal owners of anything an agent may come to possess through the employment or agency relationship. Accordingly, an agent who through deceit or other means retains such profits or goods has breached his or her fiduciary duties. Joy, an agent of Sarah's selling real estate, sells a piece of property for $2,000 more than Sarah anticipated. Joy keeps the extra $2,000 and reports the sale at the price Sarah anticipated. By law the profits belong to Sarah, and Joy has breached her fiduciary duties by keeping the money.

An agent also may not use the agency relationship to obtain goods or property for himself or herself when the principal desired to obtain the same goods or property; the principal always has right of first refusal. If Joy were to buy a piece of land for herself that she knew Sarah wanted to purchase, she again would have breached her fiduciary duties to Sarah.

[15] Restatement (Second) of Agency, secs. 383 and 385.

[16] Restatement (Second) of Agency, sec. 382.

COMPARING THE LAW OF OTHER COUNTRIES

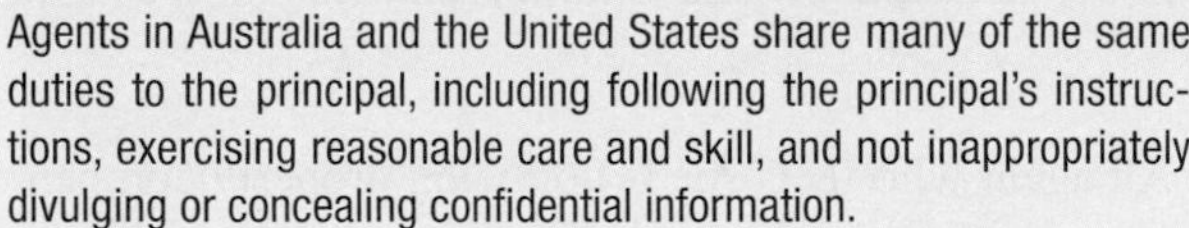

DUTIES OF THE AGENT IN AUSTRALIA

Agents in Australia and the United States share many of the same duties to the principal, including following the principal's instructions, exercising reasonable care and skill, and not inappropriately divulging or concealing confidential information.

Agents in Australia do have a unique duty, however. They are obligated to "act personally" on behalf of the principal. Suppose an agent is hired to sell apartments owned by the principal. If the agent hires an individual to sell the apartments for him, he cannot receive commission from the sale.

The basis for such a law is quite logical. The agent was hired to exercise personal skills, such as availability, in the absence of the principal. When no personal skill is demonstrated, the agent shall not be granted any compensation or reward. Specifying that duties must be performed personally may seem like an obvious and unnecessary stipulation, but this specificity is important in protecting the interests of the principal.

When an agent illegally benefits from the agency relationship, the principal may enact a **constructive trust** on the profits, goods, or property in question. A constructive trust is an equitable trust imposed on someone who wrongfully obtains or holds legal right to property he or she should not possess. The court then rules that the agent is merely holding the property or goods in trust for the principal, granting the principal legal right or possession.

Avoidance. When an agent breaches an agency contract or his fiduciary duties, the principal may use her right of *avoidance* to nullify at her discretion any contract the agent negotiated.

Indemnification. A third party who believes that an agent is acting with actual or apparent authority may sue the principal for any breach of contract. However, if the breach was caused by the agent's negligence, the principal has a right to *indemnification;* that is, when sued by a third party, a principal may sue his agent to recover the amount assessed to the third party. As Ricardo's agent, Mercedes enters into a contract with Christina knowing that Ricardo cannot possibly fulfill it. Christina sues Ricardo for breach of contract and recovers damages. Ricardo, under indemnification, is entitled to sue Mercedes to recover what he had to pay.

A principal can also recover if an agent fails to follow the principal's instructions. Ricardo tells Mercedes not to take any more orders for the widgets he produces. While Ricardo is out of town, Mercedes takes Christina's order for 1,000 widgets. When Christina sues Ricardo for breach of contract, he can recover damages from Mercedes because she did not follow his instructions. Courts have had difficulty determining when a principal gives limiting instructions and when she merely gives advice. Going against advice does not impose liability on an agent, but violating limiting instructions does. To avoid a potential lawsuit from a third party, the principal should notify the third party whenever a relationship with an agent ceases or limiting instructions are given.

AGENT'S RIGHTS AND REMEDIES AGAINST THE PRINCIPAL

While agency relationships are intended to benefit the principal, the agent is not without rights and remedies. Whenever a duty is imposed on the principal, a corresponding right exists for the agent. Agents have available tort and contract remedies, in addition to the right to demand an accounting.

Tort and Contract Remedies. Tort and contract remedies available when a principal violates an agency agreement are the standard tort and contract remedies discussed in Chapters 8 and 20, respectively.

Demand for an Accounting. An agent who feels she is not being properly compensated, especially when working on commission, may *demand an accounting* and may withhold further performance of her duties until the principal supplies appropriate accounting data. Hal is a used-car salesman working for Not a Lemon Car Dealers. When he receives his pay, he believes he has been shorted the appropriate amount he made on commission. Hal can request that Not a Lemon obtain an auditor to perform an audit and determine whether he was in fact paid the proper amount for his sales.

BUT WHAT IF . . .

WHAT IF THE FACTS OF THE CASE OPENER WERE DIFFERENT?

Let's say, in the Case Opener, that Janelle, a truck driver, was an independent contractor for FedEx. She looked at her income over the course of the prior year and was quite certain that she was not being paid her promised compensation. She demanded that FedEx hire an auditor to go over the company's records and make sure she and other independent contractors in her area had been paid fairly. Does FedEx have a duty to Janelle to do this?

Specific Performance. When a contract exists and a principal agrees to certain conditions but fails to perform, under contract remedies the agent may seek court assistance in forcing the principal to perform the contract as stipulated. However, when the agency relationship is not contractual or the contract is for personal services, an agent does not have this right. The agent may recover for services rendered and/or future damages but may not force the principal to fulfill the specific contractual agreements or even to continue to employ the agent.

CASE OPENER WRAP-UP

FedEx and Independent Contractors

Ultimately, the court ruled in favor of FedEx and found that the board's decision was unenforceable because the drivers in question were independent contractors rather than employees. To determine whether the FedEx drivers should be classified as employees or independent contractors, the court applied traditional agency law principles. It discovered that FedEx "may not prescribe hours of work, whether or when the drivers take breaks, what routes they follow, or other details of performance"; drivers "are not subject to reprimands or other discipline"; and the owners of the FedEx stores (called *contractors*) are responsible for all the costs associated with operating and maintaining their vehicles. Therefore, FedEx does not exercise the degree of control necessary for the relationship to be considered employer-employee. Rather, in this situation, the route drivers are independent contractors who have "significant entrepreneurial opportunity for gain or loss" because they can operate multiple routes, hire additional drivers and helpers, sell routes without permission, and negotiate their price to deliver the packages. Therefore, the rights and duties of employees as agents discussed throughout the chapter do not apply to FedEx drivers.

This case illustrates the importance of understanding agency relations and whether a person is an employee or independent contractor. Although FedEx was successful in the case, this case suggests that it is essential for businesses to have knowledge of the kinds of agency relationships involved in their transactions. In the future, your knowledge about agency relationships could save you or your company large amounts of time and money that would have been spent on litigation.

KEY TERMS

agency 728
agency by estoppel 731
agency relationship 728
apparent agency 731
constructive trust 743
duty of loyalty 740
duty of notification 740
duty to compensate 738
expressed agency 729

SUMMARY OF KEY TOPICS

Introduction to Agency Law

Agency: The relationship between a principal and an agent.

Agent: One authorized to act for and on behalf of a principal.

Principal: One who hires an agent to represent him or her.

Fiduciary: One with a duty to act primarily for another person's benefit.

Creation of the Agency Relationship

Agency relationships can be created only for a lawful purpose, and almost anyone can serve as an agent. Agency relationships are consensual relationships formed by informal oral agreements or formal written contracts.

Types of Agency

Expressed agency: Agency formed by making a written or oral agreement.

Power of attorney: Document giving an agent authority to sign legal documents on behalf of the principal.

Durable power of attorney: Power of attorney intended to continue to be effective or to take effect after the principal has become incapacitated.

Agency by implied authority: Agency formed by implication through the conduct of the parties.

Agency by estoppel: Agency formed when a principal leads a third party to believe that another individual serves as his or her agent but the principal had made no agreement with the so-called agent.

Agency by ratification: Agency that exists when an individual misrepresents himself or herself as an agent for another party and the principal accepts or ratifies the unauthorized act.

Agency Relationships

An *agency relationship* is a fiduciary relationship (a relationship of trust) in which an agent acts on behalf of the principal.

A *principal-agent relationship* exists when an employer hires an employee to enter into contracts on behalf of the employer.

An *employer-employee relationship* exists when an employer hires an employee to perform some sort of physical service.

An *employer–independent contractor relationship* exists when an employer hires persons, other than employees, to conduct certain tasks.

Duties of the Agent and the Principal

The duties of the principal:

- Duty of compensation
- Duty of reimbursement and indemnification
- Duty of cooperation
- Duty of safe working conditions

The duties of the agent:

- Duty of loyalty
- Duty of performance
- Duty of notification
- Duty of obedience
- Duty of accounting

Rights and Remedies

The rights and remedies of the principal:

- Constructive trust
- Avoidance
- Indemnification

The rights and remedies of the agent:

- Tort and contract remedies
- Demand for an accounting
- Specific performance

POINT / COUNTERPOINT

Should Sports Agents Be Held Personally Accountable for NCAA Violations Involving Signing College Athlete Clients?

YES

The Uniform Athlete Agents Act (2000) regulates the behavior of sports agents and their activities in representing athletes. Since the creation of the UAAA, 40 states have adopted the regulations listed in the act. While agents who violate the act can be penalized, it is more common for athletes to suffer the consequences of fines and game suspension. Likewise, it is rare for an agent to be charged at all. One of the most common violations occurs in the relationship between college athletes and agents looking to sign their principals to professional sports franchises. Moreover, it is unjust for a college athlete to be penalized for a lack of diligence on the part of the athlete's agent. Three reasons suggest the prudence of holding the agent responsible for these violations.

First, in the event of a penalty, schools and students can be punished for the actions of agents. Current college

NO

A common, yet illegal, practice of sports agents—influencing the career decisions of college athletes—has been costing universities and players their presence at important games and hundreds of thousands of dollars in civil suits. The NCAA and 40 states have passed regulations banning this practice; however, it has continued. While the outcomes may seem minor, a suspension of a player from an important game could cost the player a desirable draft position, affecting the player's salary and career prospects. While some wish to see the sports agents penalized for their involvement, three important reasons suggest against this.

First, targeting sports agents will hinder only one part of the process. To successfully conspire to secretively direct a college athlete's professional signing decision, at least three parties must be involved: the player, the agent sports rules forbid students from entering into contracts with professional agents; however, the NCAA only polices schools and student athletes. As a result, agents are infrequently held accountable, and students and schools are penalized. For example, University of Southern California (USC) running back Reggie Bush was found in violation of NCAA policies that prohibit students from receiving gifts from agents. As a result, USC was prohibited from entering lucrative bowl games for two years and was put on four years of probation, and Bush was forced to vacate and return his Heisman Trophy. Furthermore, no legal action has since been sought against the agent who presented Bush with the gifts or his agency. Because Bush's agent played an integral role in the act, he too should be held accountable. Therefore, agents should be liable for violating NCAA laws that affect their college clients.

Second, it is the responsibility of agents to represent their clients scrupulously. The core of the agent-principal relationship is trust that the agent is acting in the principal's best interest. However, violating regulations and incurring fines and suspensions are to the detriment of the principal. Furthermore, if there is likely to be no penalty for the unscrupulous agent, he or she has every incentive to use gifts and money to attract a potential athlete to the team with the highest offer. A higher standard of conduct should be expected from adult professional agents than from the college students they are wooing. Additionally, an agent-principal relationship cannot be used to conduct illegal activities, such as buying placement on a team through favors or gifts. Therefore, agents should be held to higher legal standards than those of the college-age athletes whom they represent.

Third, agents represent the only common point in an illegal conspiracy involving agents, teams, and players. While all three parties can be held responsible for their involvement in illegal recruiting, the agents not only are the common thread in most of the arrangements but, in many cases, are the sole facilitators of the deals. For example, one agent may be working with 50 players and 20 teams at any given time yet be the only common factor in each deal. To lessen the problem of illicit athletic dealings, penalizing agents would be the most effective method. Moreover, one cannot expect a player or a team to come forward, as the player's or team's career future is hanging in the balance. Thus, targeting agents and holding them personally liable is in the interest of achieving the greater goal of eliminating illegal college athletic dealings.

and a representative from the professional franchise. However, cases in the past have revealed the involvement of coaches and family members as well. While it is true that agents facilitate the relationship between the player and the future team, it is not inherently clear that the agent is most at fault. The conduct of agents, as regulated by the UAAA, requires only that all agents register and volunteer to be monitored by a state authority. Even if every state passed this regulation, athletes and team representatives could conspire to defraud the NCAA standards and practices. Additionally, an agent only facilitates the needs of clients. As a result, the agent is acting only on behalf of the will of the college athlete. Moreover, if the athlete doesn't want to be involved in any dirty dealings, the athlete is not obligated to abide by the agent's suggestion. It is therefore reasonable to assume that both athletes and professional team representatives are in favor of this widespread practice. Therefore, targeting agents would not successfully end the practice of improper college athlete agreements.

Second, agents represent an important role in the negotiation process, and their actions both protect the interests of their clients and create very few negative outcomes. College athletes work with sports agents because agents can assist them in signing to a professional team and furthering their careers. With possibly millions of dollars on the line, agents protect inexperienced athletes facing important career decisions. Targeting agents will affect the student athletes that they represent, as agents set out to find the best course of action for their respective principals. Conversely, the harm created by these inside dealings is extremely minimal. Though the practice is far from fair, aside from the rare prosecution, those involved get their desired outcomes without negatively impacting others. Thus, targeting agents will both harm the interests of the students they represent and have a small effect on harm reduction.

Third, holding sports agents personally accountable results in targeting the party with the least to gain in a deal. While initial contracts for professional athletes can be in the tens of millions of dollars, agents stand to gain only a percentage of this amount. A common amount ranges between 4 and 10 percent. Furthermore, fines levied against players who have already signed contracts pale in comparison to the potentially millions of dollars for their first-year contract. Likewise, colleges and professional sports teams profit considerably from successful teams and players. Of all those involved, agents stand to gain the least amount of money. In conclusion, targeting athletes, schools, or teams would be a more effective strategy for slowing the underhanded dealings between agents, players, and teams.

Source: Robert N. Davis, "Exploring the Contours of Agent Regulation: The Uniform Athlete Agents Act," *Villanova Sports & Entertainment Law Journal* 8 (2001), p. 1; and Alan Scher Zagier, "Laws on Sports Agents Rarely Enforced," *The Huffington Post,* August 17, 2010, www.huffingtonpost.com/2010/08/17/laws-on-sports-agents-rar_n_685000.html.

QUESTIONS & PROBLEMS

1. What are the similarities and differences between the types of agency relationships?
2. How is apparent agency, or agency by estoppel, different from expressed agency?
3. What are a principal's duties to an agent and an agent's duties to a principal?
4. William Roberts operated a McDonald's restaurant under a franchise agreement with McDonald's Corporation. Roberts hired 23-year-old David Mabin, who was just released from jail for robbery, drug use, and theft, as an hourly worker. Soon Roberts promoted Mabin to assistant manager on the night shift at the restaurant. A 15-year-old girl began working at the McDonald's, and she quickly became involved with Mabin, who provided her with free food, alcohol, and drugs (including ecstasy) and kissed her openly in the workplace. Just before the girl's 16th birthday, Mabin took her to a motel where they spent the night and engaged in sexual intercourse. The girl and her family later brought suit against McDonald's Corporation on the basis that McDonald's Corporation was the principal to Roberts through apparent agency. McDonald's Corporation was supposed to be a business with a wholesome reputation and safe workplace, but instead the minor was taken advantage of by her assistant manager. The girl argued for apparent agency with McDonald's as the principal because she claimed that as far as she was concerned, she worked for McDonald's Corporation, not just the franchise. She had a McDonald's logo on her uniform, her paycheck, and restaurant products. However, the application she filled out for employment stated, "I understand that my employer is an independent Owner/Operator of a McDonald's franchise and that I am not employed by McDonald's Corporation or any of its subsidiaries. The independent Owner/Operator of this restaurant is solely responsible for all terms, conditions and any other issues concerning my employment." Was there an apparent agency relationship between McDonald's Corporation and the franchise? Why or why not? [*D.L.S. et al. v. David Mabin et al.,* 130 Wn. App. 94, 121 P.3d 1210 (2005).]
5. Jack Kotlar was a realtor who leased commercial property on Pico Boulevard in Los Angeles. In early 1994, Kotlar leased a property to Meir Sharvit, doing business as Meir Produce. Under the lease Meir agreed to maintain liability insurance for the benefit of Kotlar.

   Meir purchased a commercial general liability insurance policy from Hartford Fire Insurance Company and named Meir and Kotlar as insureds. Subsequently, Kotlar received a certificate of insurance informing him he was named as an additional insured on the policy. The document also contained a provision in which Hartford promised it would "endeavor" to give Kotlar 30 days' advance notice of cancellation of the policy.

   The policy was to be effective from September 22, 1994, to September 22, 1995. However, at some time prior to the scheduled expiration date, Hartford canceled the policy because Meir failed to pay the premiums. Hartford sent notice of its intent to cancel the policy to Meir but not to Kotlar. The brokers who sold the policy to Meir also failed to provide notice of cancellation to Kotlar. Kotlar alleged that he was unaware the policy had been canceled and that neither Hartford nor the brokers made any effort to notify him of the cancellation before it occurred.

   After the policy was purportedly canceled, one of Meir's customers slipped and fell on the property, suffering a fractured hip. This resulted in a lawsuit in which Kotlar was named as a defendant. Kotlar tendered defense of the action to Hartford, which refused to defend or indemnify Kotlar on the ground that the policy had been canceled for nonpayment of premiums prior to the accident.

   Kotlar then brought an action against Hartford and the brokers, TriWest Insurance Services, USI Insurance Services Corp. Companies, and Max Behm and Associates. Kotlar's third amended complaint alleged causes of action for breach of contract against Hartford and negligence against the brokers. Was Kolter right in bringing the suit? Why or why not? [*Kotlar v. Hartford Fire Ins. Co.,* 83 Cal. App. 4th 1116 (2000).]
6. Jay Hellinger is a homeowner in Los Angeles County in California. He and his brother, Lee Hellinger, lived in the residence at the time. The Hellingers purchased a single homeowner's insurance policy from Farmers Insurance Exchange, Fire Insurance Exchange, and Mid-Century Insurance

Company. In 1992, the Hellinger brothers purchased a separate earthquake insurance policy for the home from Mid-Century Insurance Company. The earthquake policy provided: "We may not be sued unless there has been full compliance with all the terms of this policy. Suit on or arising out of this policy must be brought within one year after the loss occurs." In 1994, the Northridge earthquake occurred, damaging the house. Before the earthquake, Lee Hellinger had transferred his interest in the residence to his brother, Jay.

Within days of the earthquake, the Hellingers noticed cracks in interior and exterior walls, the driveway, the patio, the gazebo, and a block wall; a leak near the chimney; and electrical problems with various appliances. Farmers' agent Howard Hammer called the Hellingers within a week of the earthquake to ask about the status of their home. Lee Hellinger told Hammer about the damage to the home. After some discussion, Hammer told Lee Hellinger that he thought the losses would not exceed the deductible and that damages to the gazebo, retaining wall, sidewalk, Jacuzzi, and landscaping were not covered by the policy. Agent Hammer did not report the loss to Farmers, nor did he ask an adjuster to inspect the Hellinger home. In April 1994, the Hellingers hired a contractor to repair the visible damage caused by the earthquake, at a cost of $4,350. In July 1995, while gardening, Lee Hellinger noticed a large crack in the concrete foundation under the soil line. He reported this damage to Hammer and asked for an inspection.

Farmers sent a claims adjuster to inspect the damage in mid-September 1995. The Hellingers' claim was denied in writing on November 27, 1995, citing the policy clause which requires that suit be brought within one year of the loss. The Hellingers sued Farmers, Fire Insurance Exchange, and Mid-Century on August 26, 1996. In their original complaint, they alleged causes of action for breach of contract, breach of the implied covenant of good faith and fair dealing, and fraud. Do you think that Farmers should have paid for the damage? Also, what should have happened differently for the incident to be covered by Farmers? [*Hellinger v. Farmers Group Inc.*, 91 Cal. App. 4th 1049 (2001).]

7. Marsh &McLennan Companies is the largest provider of insurance brokerage services in the world. It holds itself out to its clients as a fiduciary that will act solely on clients' behalf in purchasing insurance policies for them. Starting in 1987, Emerson Electric Company hired Marsh to act as its fiduciary in procuring various insurance policies, such as excess liability, aircraft, and international. Emerson paid Marsh substantial amounts of money to recommend insurance policies that met its needs at the lowest possible price. Unknown to Emerson, Marsh embarked on a business plan in the early 1990s in violation of its fiduciary duties to Emerson: Marsh entered into agreements with insurance companies under which the insurers agreed to pay Marsh monies in consideration of Marsh's pledge to direct business to them. These agreements were referred to by various names such as *placement service agreements* or *market service agreements.* These documents were referred to as "kickbacks." At no time did Marsh's disclose the nature or extent of kickbacks that it was receiving. As a result of Marsh's breach of its fiduciary duties, Emerson paid an inflated price for its insurance policies. Additionally, Marsh directed Emerson to make its premium payments through Marsh itself, rather than directly to the insurance companies. The checks were made payable to Marsh. Unbeknownst to Emerson, Marsh did not immediately forward the premium payments to the insurers; instead, for a period of time before the insurance companies would be paid, Marsh would invest Emerson's premium payments to earn interest, which it retained as profit. In Marsh's 2003 Annual Report, it referred to this revenue item as "fiduciary interest income." Is this considered a breach of fiduciary duty? Why or why not? [*Emerson Electric Co. v. Marsh & McLennan Companies* (Mo. Ct. App 2011). Case No. 22054–00569, www.courts.mo.gov, accessed September 6, 2011.]

8. John Ray Lawrence, an employee of H.W. Campbell Construction Company, was killed when his head was crushed in the "pinch point" area of a crane. Coastal Marine Services of Texas, Inc., owned the crane, and Campbell employees were using it on Coastal's property when the accident occurred. Campbell took custody of the crane and began continued occupation of Coastal's property. Campbell was an independent contractor of Coastal, and no written contract existed between the two companies. Coastal employees were not directing or supervising Campbell's work on the project, nor were they on the job site when the accident occurred. Lawrence's surviving family and estate sued Campbell and Coastal,

alleging, among other things, negligence. During the trial Coastal asserted that the Lawrences had presented no evidence that Coastal retained the right to control Campbell's work, a prerequisite for finding Coastal liable under a premises liability theory. The trial court agreed and submitted an instruction precluding a finding of negligence based on the manner in which Coastal controlled the premises. The jury found no negligence on Coastal's part. At trial, in response to a series of hypothetical questions, Campbell employees testified that they would have complied with any instructions from Coastal about the movement of the crane if Coastal had given such instructions. On the basis of the Campbell employees' testimony, the court of appeals reversed the trial court's judgment, concluding that the testimony created a fact issue about Coastal's right to control the crane. Coastal appealed. What duties did Coastal owe Campbell as an independent contractor? How did the court rule on appeal? [*Coastal Marine Serv., Inc. v. Lawrence,* 988 S.W.2d 223 (1999).]

9. In 2000, Loretta Henry was pregnant and experiencing pain in her abdomen. After visiting a clinic, she was referred to Flagstaff Medical Hospital. Once there, she was examined and treated by Dr. Kraig Knoll, a physician with a physician's group providing a service for the hospital. Knoll advised her to have her gallbladder removed, and he performed the surgery. Although Henry read and signed two consent forms, she was never told that Knoll was not an employee of the hospital and was instead an independent contractor. Subsequently, Henry sued the hospital for negligence when after her child was born, both mother and child sustained injuries. She claimed there was an apparent agency relationship. The hospital argued that Henry could not establish an agency relationship between Flagstaff Hospital and Knoll. What duties did Flagstaff Hospital owe Knoll as an independent contractor? Did the court find enough evidence to establish an agency relationship? [*Loretta Henry/Charles Arnold v. Flagstaff Medical,* 212 Ariz. 365, 132 P.3d 304, 2006 Ariz. App. LEXIS 53, 476 Ariz. Adv. Rep. 11.]

10. Nu-Look Design, Inc., operated as a residential home improvement company. During calendar years 1996, 1997, and 1998, Ronald A. Stark not only was Nu-Look's sole shareholder and president but also managed the company. He solicited business, performed necessary bookkeeping, otherwise handled finances, and hired and supervised workers. Rather than pay Stark a salary or wages, Nu-Look distributed its net income during 1996, 1997, and 1998 to him "as Mr. Stark's needs arose." Nu-Look reported on its tax returns in 1996, 1997, and 1998 net incomes of $10,866.14, $14,216.37, and $7,103.60, respectively. Stark, in turn, reported the very same amounts as nonpassive income on his 1996, 1997, and 1998 tax returns. On June 8, 2001, the IRS issued to Nu-Look a "Notice of Determination Concerning Worker Classification." The notice advised that the IRS had classified an individual at Nu-Look as an employee for purposes of federal employment taxes and that such taxes "could" be assessed for calendar years 1996, 1997, and 1998. Nu-Look challenged this determination by filing a petition for redetermination in the United States Tax Court, disputing the propriety of the determination that Stark was an employee, and also sought relief from that determination. The tax court found that Stark performed more than minor services for Nu-Look and had received remuneration for those services. As a result, the court held that Stark was an employee of Nu-Look and that Nu-Look was not entitled to relief. Nu-Look appealed. Does Stark meet the requirements for an employee? Should Nu-Look be liable for a tax assessed under the assumption that Stark is an employee? [*Nu-Look Design, Inc. v. Commission of Internal Revenue,* 356 F.3d 290 (2004).]

Looking for more review materials?

The Online Learning Center at **www.mhhe.com/kubasek3e** contains this chapter's "Assignment on the Internet" and also a list of URLs for more information, entitled "On the Internet." You can find both of them in the Student Center portion of the OLC, along with quizzes and other helpful materials.

CHAPTER 34

Liability to Third Parties and Termination

LEARNING OBJECTIVES

After reading this chapter, you will be able to answer the following questions:

1 Under what circumstances might a principal be held liable to a third party on a contract negotiated by an agent?

2 Under what circumstances might a principal be held liable for the tortious behavior of its agent or independent contractor?

3 How can an agency relationship be terminated?

CASE OPENER

Vicarious Liability and Medical Malpractice Suits

In May 2001, Joann Abshure received a colonoscopy from Dr. Jeremiah Upshaw, after complaining of bloating and changes in bowel patterns. After the colonoscopy procedure, Abshure began experiencing significant discomfort in her abdominal region. Once her condition worsened, her husband called an ambulance, and Abshure was transported to Methodist Hospital. Abshure informed the emergency room doctor, Dr. Ogle, of her previous colonoscopy and of her extreme discomfort. Ogle ordered a series of lab work including CT scans and X-rays of Abshure's abdominal region. While waiting for the results of the lab work, Ogle administered several enemas to Abshure. She then began experiencing extraordinary pain. Eventually, Dr. Ogle performed a colostomy on Abshure and left her surgical incision open after packing the wound.

After time recovering in the intensive care unit, Abshure developed adult respiratory distress syndrome and sepsis. Jones eventually closed the surgical incision on May 30, 2001, and Abshure was discharged from Methodist Hospital on May 31, 2001.

Abshure initially filed a vicarious liability suit against her two treating physicians and the hospital. Later, she voluntarily dismissed the emergency room doctor from the suit. After the voluntary dismissal of the doctor, the defendant hospital filed a motion for dismissal of the plaintiff's vicarious liability claims against it. The trial court granted the defendant hospital's motion for dismissal, and upon appeal, the court affirmed the trial court's decision. Once more, the plaintiff appealed.

1. When may a principal be held vicariously liable for the negligent acts of its agent?
2. What must the plaintiff demonstrate to establish employer liability?

The Wrap-Up at the end of the chapter will answer these questions.

In the preceding chapter, we discussed how an agency relationship and its resulting authority could be created. We also introduced (1) expressed agency, or agency by agreement; (2) implied agency; and (3) agency by estoppel. Each of these avenues for creating agency includes a corresponding form of agent authority.

Contractual Liability of the Principal and Agent

L01

Under what circumstances might a principal be held liable to a third party on a contract negotiated by an agent?

When making decisions about an agency relationship's liability to third parties, courts must first identify the type of authority an agent has (see Chapter 33) and then determine the classification of the principal. Finally, the court must decide whether the principal authorized the actions of the agent. A special type of express agent authority is known as a **power of attorney.** The power of attorney is a specific form of express authority, usually in writing, granting an agent specific powers. There are two basic types of power of attorney: special and general. A **special power of attorney** grants the agent express authority over specifically outlined acts. In contrast, a **general power of attorney** allows the agent to conduct all business for the principal. While powers of attorney tend to terminate on the principal's death or incapacitation, a **durable power of attorney** specifies that the agent's authority is intended to continue beyond the principal's incapacitation.

Even with explicit instructions given through express authority, sometimes conflicts arise between principal-agent relationships in power of attorney.

Case 34-1 examines how a court determines the extent of power of attorney.

CASE 34-1 IN RE ESTATE OF KURRELMEYER
SUPREME COURT OF VERMONT
187 VT. 620, 992 A.2D 316 (2010)

After Louis H. Kurrelmeyer Sr. died in 2001, his son brought suit against the wife of Kurrelmeyer for an alleged invalid transfer of the decedent's home, into a trust. The son argued that the wife's transfer of the property into the trust was invalid because the wife did not have the authority to make the transfer under the written terms of the power of attorney. Specifically, the son asserted that the transfer was in violation of an express provision in the power of attorney prohibiting the wife from "making gifts to herself," as well as the fact that the power of attorney did not explicitly grant the wife the authority to transfer the property into the trust.

The court ruled in favor of the defendant, and the son appealed, arguing that the court erred in considering extrinsic evidence to determine the scope of the wife's authority under a power of attorney.

JUDGE REIBER: This is not the first time that this case has come to this Court on appeal. In 2006, we issued an opinion addressing challenges to wife's establishment of a trust (Kurrelmeyer I). In Kurrelmeyer I, we remanded the case to the trial court, and it is the trial court's decision on remand that is the subject of the current appeal.

On remand, the trial court held a hearing. At the hearing, the trial court allowed wife to present evidence—mainly in the form of testimony and written notes from the estate planning attorney—that the transfer of the Clearwater property carried out the intent of decedent to enhance the financial position of wife while also avoiding estate taxation through the use of trust instruments that were specifically recommended and designed by the attorney to accomplish decedent's goals. Son argues on appeal, as he argued in

[continued]

Kurrelmeyer I, that we should adopt a rule of strict construction whereby a power of attorney grants only those powers that are clearly and *explicitly delineated.* Thus, according to son, because the power of attorney did not explicitly grant wife authority to transfer the Clearwater property into the trust, wife did not have that authority. Son argues that this ends the matter and that the trial court therefore erred in considering extrinsic evidence in determining the scope of wife's authority. We disagree.

In Kurrelmeyer I, we recognized that other jurisdictions have adopted the rule of strict construction urged by son, but we rejected this approach: "we will not apply a rule of narrow construction to particular words and phrases used in the power of attorney, but will examine the express terms and the context of the instrument as a whole to give effect to the principal's intent." Although we did not explicitly state that courts could look at extrinsic evidence, such a holding was implicit in our direction to "examine the context" in which the power of attorney was created. Our remand also directed the trial court to examine "all the relevant circumstances" surrounding the creation of the trust in 2000. One of the relevant circumstances here was whether wife was acting to fulfill the intent for which decedent granted wife the power of attorney in 1996. As we stated in Kurrelmeyer I, when interpreting a document such as a power of attorney, it is a "cardinal rule that the court determine the intention of the parties." Ideally, the intention of the parties will always be apparent from the express language of the power of attorney itself. Unfortunately, that is not always the case. Thus, in an instance such as this one, where there was significant and well-documented extrinsic evidence of the reasons for which decedent created the power of attorney, the trial court did not err in taking that evidence into consideration.

The trial court had ample support for its conclusions that "[d]ecedent's overarching goal was to provide for his surviving wife" and that decedent intended that the power of attorney would allow wife to transfer the Clearwater property into the trust that she created. As the evidence indicated and as the trial court held, decedent intended the power of attorney to allow wife to take the precise actions she took here when she transferred the Clearwater property into a trust. Wife's actions were therefore in accord with decedent's intent, and there was no improper self-dealing.

AFFIRMED.

CRITICAL THINKING

What reasoning did the court use to come to the conclusion that the power of attorney did include transfers of property into trusts? If you were a judge, would you have found that the deceased's wife was authorized to transfer the property into a trust? Why or why not?

ETHICAL DECISION MAKING

What is the purpose of creating rules surrounding the extent of power of attorney? Who are the stakeholders that are affected by the conflicts that arise between principal-agent relationships in power-of-attorney cases?

CLASSIFICATION OF THE PRINCIPAL

We classify principals from the perspective of the third party's knowledge about them. The law of agency places special weight on this viewpoint of the agency relationship.

When the third party is aware that the agent is making an agreement on behalf of a principal and also knows who the principal is, the principal is a **disclosed principal.** If the third party is aware of the principal's existence but not his or her identity, we classify the principal as a **partially disclosed principal** or an **unidentified principal.** Finally, if the third party does not know that an agent is acting on behalf of a principal, we have an **undisclosed principal.** Classification of the principal is important because it helps determine the principal's liability.[1] If a principal is partially disclosed, the agent and the principal are both considered parties to the contract and each may be liable separately from the other.

[1] Restatement (Second) of Agency, sec. 4.

BUT WHAT IF . . .

WHAT IF THE FACTS OF THE CASE OPENER WERE DIFFERENT?

Let's say, in the Case Opener, that Abshure's emergency room doctor, Dr. Ogle, was working for the defendant hospital but he was a home-visit doctor and didn't work at the hospital's campus. When Ogle treated Abshure, he did so at her home and she had no idea what hospital he worked for or whether he worked for one at all. What kind of principal would the defendant hospital qualify as? Why is this distinction important?

AUTHORIZED ACTS

An agent who acts within the scope of her authority on behalf of a disclosed or partially disclosed principal is not liable for the acts of the principal.[2] The principal is liable only if the agent has authority to act on the principal's behalf. With a disclosed principal, the agent is not liable because she is not a party to the transaction. If the principal is *partially* disclosed, the agent herself can be held liable for contractual nonperformance because the courts generally treat the agent as a party to the contract.[3] Whether disclosed or partially disclosed, apart from any liability the agent might have, the principal is liable for the agreements made with the third party.

When the agent acts within her authority on behalf of an undisclosed principal, the law will likely hold her liable for the agreement. In the eyes of the third party, the agent is the only person who could be liable. Yet, if the agent is liable to the third party, then the undisclosed principal is liable to the agent. However, in certain situations the agent is the only party liable for the contract. These situations are:

1. The contract expressly excludes the principal from the contract. If the principal was not a party to the contract, he or she has no liability to the agent.
2. The agent enters into a contract that is a negotiable instrument. The Uniform Commercial Code (UCC) governs negotiable instruments and states that other parties, that is, principals, cannot be liable for them if their name is not on the instrument or if the agent's signature does not indicate that it was made in a representative capacity.[4]
3. The third party enters into a contract with the agent such that the agent's performance is required and the third party may reject the performance of the principal. For example, if the agent is a photographer and he enters into a contract for his principal without disclosing this fact, the third party may reject the principal's attempt to fulfill the contract by taking the third party's picture.
4. The principal or agent knows a third party would not enter into a contract with the principal if the principal's identity were disclosed but the agent does so anyway. The agent will be the only party liable should the third party rescind the contract.

When the third party comes to know of the undisclosed principal's identity, a judgment for the third party against the agent releases the principal from liability.[5] A judgment against a previously undisclosed principal likewise frees the agent from liability.[6]

Exhibit 34-1 summarizes contractual liability to third parties for authorized acts of the agent.

[2] Restatement (Second) of Agency, sec. 320.

[3] Restatement (Second) of Agency, sec. 321.

[4] UCC § 3-402(b)(2).

[5] Restatement (Second) of Agency, sec. 210.

[6] Restatement (Second) of Agency, sec. 337.

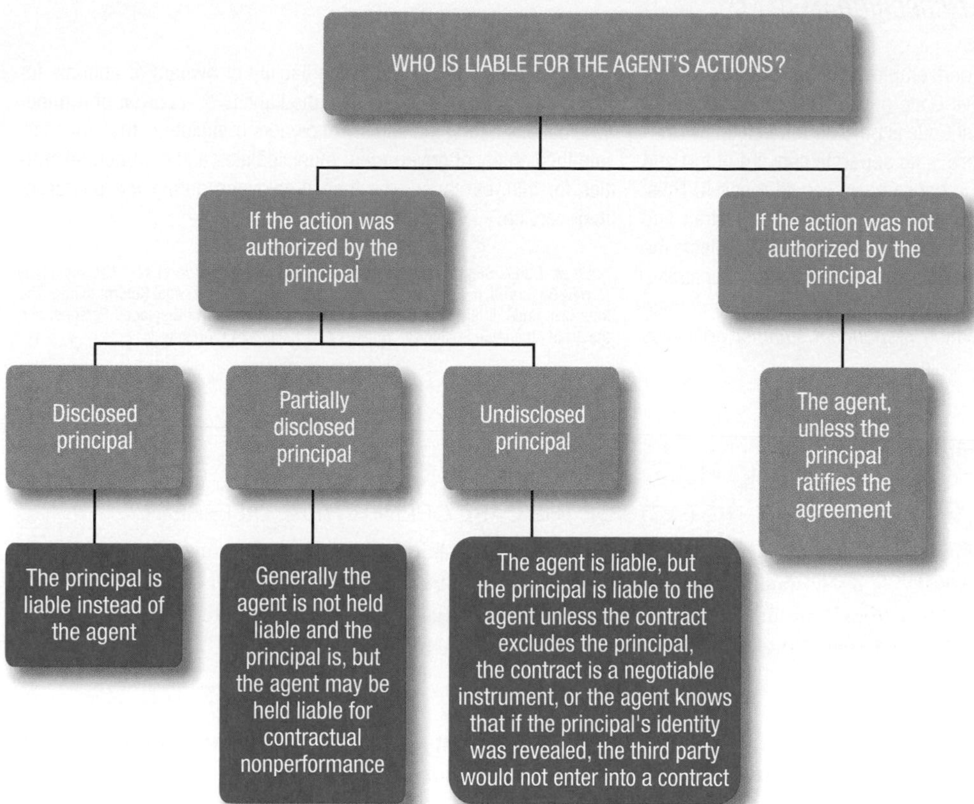

Exhibit 34-1

Contractual Liability to Third Parties for Authorized Agent Acts

In the Case Opener, one question the court must consider is whether the emergency room doctors are independent contractors or employees of the hospital. If they are employees, the hospital can be responsible for the conduct of the doctors through *respondeat superior*. However, if they are independent contractors, the hospital cannot be held liable.

UNAUTHORIZED ACTS

If an agent has no authority to act on behalf of a principal but still enters into a contract with a third party, the principal, regardless of the classification, is not bound to the contract unless the principal ratifies the agreement.

When the agent exceeds his authority to act on behalf of the principal, the agent will likely be personally liable to the third party. Yet, when the third party is aware that the agent does not represent the principal, the law does not hold the agent liable for the agreement. In almost all other cases in which the agent claims to have authority to contract on behalf of the principal, the law holds the agent liable to the third party. If an agent enters into a contract knowingly misrepresenting his alleged authority, the agent is liable to the third party in a tort action.

Agents who go beyond their authority when the principal is disclosed or partially disclosed are liable for a breach of implied warranty. They cannot be liable for breach of contract because they were never an intended party to the contract, even when exceeding their authority. The agent can breach the implied warranty intentionally, through a knowing misrepresentation, or unintentionally, through a good-faith mistake such as simply misjudging his or her authority. In either case, the agent is liable if the third party relied on the agent's alleged status.

COMPARING THE LAW OF OTHER COUNTRIES

RESPONDEAT SUPERIOR IN IRAQ

Unlike the United States' broad employment of the *respondeat superior* doctrine, the Iraqi Civil Code generally rejects the idea of *respondeat superior.* Iraq's Civil Code is partially influenced by classical Islamic law, in which there is no separate concept of tort and which suggests that those who cause harm should repair it. Thus, classical Islamic legal systems tend to follow a rule of strict and "specific" liability for torts. This notion of specific liability rejects the idea of vicarious liability of superiors and custodians and constrains liability to the actual wrongdoer. However, Iraqi law does contain some limited exceptions in which *respondeat superior* principles are permitted. These include the liability of owners of animals for damage caused by the animals, the liability of a parent of a minor who causes injury, the liability of owners of buildings that collapse, and the liability of government municipalities and commercial entities for injuries caused by their employees during the course of their service.

Sources: Dan E. Stiggal, "A Closer Look at Iraqi Property and Tort Law," *Louisiana Law Review* 68 (2008), p. 765; and Dan E. Stiggal, "Refugees and Legal Reform in Iraq: The Iraqi Civil Code, International Standards for the Treatment of Displaced Persons, and the Art of Attainable Solutions," *Rutgers Law Record* 34 (2009), p. 1.

BUT WHAT IF . . .

WHAT IF THE FACTS OF THE CASE OPENER WERE DIFFERENT?

Let's say, in the Case Opener, that Dr. Ogle had deliberately exceeded the limits his hospital had set out for him in his contract of employment. In other words, his actions were not authorized by the hospital. What would Ogle be liable for in regard to his employer? Why would Ogle not be liable for breach of contract?

Legal Principle: **As a general rule, when an agent commits an unauthorized act, the principal is neither bound to the contract nor liable.**

Tort Liability and the Agency Relationship

L02

Under what circumstances might a principal be held liable for the tortious behavior of its agent or independent contractor?

An agent who commits a tort that injures a third party is personally liable for his or her actions, regardless of both the classification and the liability of the principal.[7] The principal may also be held liable for the agent's authorized or unauthorized acts. Furthermore, tortious liability of the principal can be established directly or indirectly. Finally, if an agent is an employee and the principal/employer controls the employee's behavior, the principal can be found liable. The next section introduces these methods of establishing tortious liability.

PRINCIPAL'S TORTIOUS CONDUCT

The law holds a principal directly responsible for his or her own tortious conduct on two conditions. First, a principal who directs the agent to commit a tort is authorizing the agent's unlawful behavior and thus is liable for any damages caused by the tort.[8] Similarly, the principal who ratifies an agent's tortious act knowing that the agent acted illegally is liable, even if she does not condone the agent's conduct.[9]

Second, if the principal fails to provide proper instruments or tools or gives inadequate instructions to the agent concerning the necessity to employ competent agents, the law holds the principal liable to a third party for negligent hiring of an agent. If an agent commits a tort against a customer, the customer often argues that the principal is liable because she should have taken more care in hiring the agent.

[7] Restatement (Second) of Agency, sec. 343.
[8] Restatement (Second) of Agency, sec. 212.
[9] Restatement (Second) of Agency, sec. 218.

Respondeat Superior. The doctrine of ***respondeat superior*** (a Latin phrase meaning "let the superior speak") applies in the context of the principal/employer–agent/employee relationship. The principal/employer holds **vicarious liability,** which is liability assigned without fault, for any harm the agent/employee causes while working for the principal. In other words, the principal/employer is liable not because he was personally at fault but because he negligently hired an agent. The rationale is that if the employer is benefiting by the work of the employee, the employer should also be responsible for the harms the employee caused.

Thus, a third party injured through the negligence of an employee can sue either the employee or the employer.[10] To establish employer liability, the third party must show that the wrongful act occurred within the scope of the employment. The courts consider the following in determining this element:[11]

1. Did the employer authorize the employee's act?
2. Did the act occur within the time and space limits of employment?
3. Was the act performed, at least in part, on behalf of the employer?
4. To what extent were the employer's interests advanced by the act?
5. To what extent were the private interests of the employee involved?
6 Did the employer provide the means (tools) by which the act occurred?
7. Did the employee use force not expected by the employer?
8. Did the employer know that the act would include the commission of a serious crime?

If a delivery driver negligently injures a third party while making deliveries on behalf of the employer, both the employee and the employer will be held liable. Suppose the driver is using the company vehicle when he stops at a drive-through to get coffee. Could the employer be liable to a third party for an accident caused by the driver? If an agent makes a substantial departure from the course of the employer's business, the employer is not liable.

Courts often refer to an employee's substantial departure as a "frolic of his own." However, if the deviation from the employer's business is *not* substantial, the employer can be held liable. In Case 34-2, the court considers the scope of the employment relationship.

Legal Principle: As a general rule, a principal is vicariously liable for the actions of his or her agent.

[10] Restatement (Second) of Agency, secs. 216 and 219.

[11] Restatement (Second) of Agency, sec. 229.

CASE 34-2 IGLESIA CRISTIANA LA CASA DEL SENOR, INC., ETC. v. L.M.

COURT OF APPEAL OF FLORIDA, THIRD DISTRICT
783 SO. 2D 353 (2001)

L.M. sued Ali Pacheco, the former pastor of Iglesia Cristiana La Casa Del Senor, Inc. (the Church), as well as the Church, alleging Pacheco had sexually assaulted her in July 1991 when she was a minor. The allegation of sexual assault formed the basis of L.M.'s claims against the Church based on respondeat superior. When the criminal act occurred, L.M. was sixteen years old.

Before the criminal act took place, Pacheco visited L.M.'s residence twice when L.M. had been left home alone. On another occasion, Pacheco visited L.M. at her school. L.M. told her mother about Pacheco's visit, but did not advise anyone from the Church.

According to L.M., on July 8, 1991, Pacheco called her at work and invited her to lunch to discuss her parents' marital problems. L.M. accepted, and Pacheco picked her up from work. L.M. noticed a sandwich and soft drink in the car. Pacheco drove to a Marriott Hotel. L.M. testified Pacheco led her to a room he had rented, and told her not to worry because she would finally be cured. He then proceeded to sexually assault her. Pacheco testified L.M. consented to having sex.

[continued]

According to him, their meeting was prearranged. They had discussed the matter and had in fact been to the Marriot Hotel the previous day intending to have sexual relations but had decided against it. Pacheco testified he knew what he was doing was wrong but explained it was a great temptation in his life.

The jury returned a verdict in L.M.'s favor, finding the Church liable for Pacheco's criminal act on the grounds of respondeat superior. *The Church appealed.*

PER CURIAM: Under the doctrine of respondeat superior, an employer cannot be held liable for the tortious or criminal acts of an employee, unless the acts were committed during the course of the employment and to further a purpose or interest, however excessive or misguided, of the employer. An employee's conduct is within the scope of his employment, where (1) the conduct is of the kind he was employed to perform, (2) the conduct occurs substantially within the time and space limits authorized or required by the work to be performed, and (3) the conduct is activated at least in part by a purpose to serve the master. An exception may exist where the tort-feasor was assisted in accomplishing the tort by virtue of the employer/employee relationship.

In this case, the sexual assault did not occur on Church property, and the record does not support a finding Pacheco's criminal act against L.M. constituted the kind of conduct he was employed to perform, or he was in any way motivated by his desire to serve the Church. On the contrary, the record establishes Pacheco's purpose in arranging the meeting that day was to satisfy his personal interests, not to further the Church's objectives. Regardless of the stated reason for the meeting between Pacheco and L.M., it is undisputed no counseling occurred on the day of the crime. While Pacheco may have had access to L.M. because of his position as the Church pastor, whom L.M. and her family had become friends with over time, he was not engaging in authorized acts or serving the interests of the Church during the time he tried to seduce her or on the day he raped her. The sexual assault was an independent, self-serving act by Pacheco; an act he knew was wrong to commit and the Church would surely have tried to prevent had it known of his plans.

We agree with the Church that Pacheco's sexual assault of L.M. did not occur within the scope of his employment. Accordingly, we find, as a matter of law, the Church cannot be held vicariously liable for Pacheco's criminal act.

Therefore, we reverse the trial court's final judgment and remand with instructions to enter judgment in favor of Appellant.

REVERSED and REMANDED.

CRITICAL THINKING

Assume L.M.'s account of the crime is true. Examine the exception to the "scope of employment" criteria mentioned by the judge. How could the plaintiff make an argument, using that exception, that Pacheco's conduct was within the scope of his employment?

ETHICAL DECISION MAKING

The judge in this case outlines a doctrine for determining the liability of an employer for the actions of employees. What value preference is highlighted by that doctrine?

If the third party is able to establish employee negligence such that the employer is liable, the employer has the right to recover from the employee any damages he paid the third party as a result of the employee's negligence. The right to recover damages is referred to as the *right of indemnification.* However, if the employee is innocent of negligence, the employer is also free of liability.

Intentional Torts and *Respondeat Superior.* The agent is liable for any torts he or she commits. In the same way the principal is responsible for the negligent acts of the employee under the doctrine of *respondeat superior,* the principal may also be liable for any intentional torts of the employee. Furthermore, an employer may be responsible for any tortious acts of the employee if the employer knew or should have known that the employee had a tendency to commit such acts. Hence, a principal may be liable for negligent hiring who fails to do a background check to learn about the tendencies of potential employees.

The principal of an employee with a criminal background may be held liable for tortious acts committed by her hired agent even though the employee may not recognize the wrongfulness of his act. Therefore, employers will most likely purchase liability insurance in case particular employees engage in tortious activities.

AGENT MISREPRESENTATION

Unlike tort liability, which is based on whether the agent/employee was acting in the scope of employment, *misrepresentation liability* depends on whether the principal authorized the agent's act. If the principal authorizes the agent to engage in an act and the agent misrepresents herself intentionally or unintentionally, the principal is always liable in tort to someone who relied on the agent's misrepresentation.

If an agent has misrepresented herself, the third party has two options:

1. Cancel the contract with the principal and be compensated for any money lost.
2. Affirm the contract and sue the principal to recover damages.

Legal Principle: **As a general rule, if a principal authorizes an agent to misrepresent himself or herself, the principal is always liable.**

Principal's Liability and the Independent Contractor

As we discussed in the preceding chapter, an independent contractor is not an employee of the individual who hires him or her to do work. The individual doing the hiring does not control the details of the independent contractor's performance. Consequently, an individual who hires an independent contractor cannot be held liable for the independent contractor's tortious actions under the doctrine of *respondeat superior.*

Suppose that while working on the outside of the building he is renovating, an independent contractor accidentally injures an innocent bystander when he drops a pile of bricks. The owner of the building is not liable for the innocent bystander's injuries; the independent contractor is liable.[12]

If the independent contractor engages in extremely hazardous activities, such as blasting operations, for the principal, the principal will be responsible for any damages by the independent contractor. Certain activities are held strictly liable because of their inherently dangerous nature; an employer cannot escape this liability simply by hiring an independent contractor to complete them. Nor can the employer escape liability for an independent contractor's tort if the employer directs the contractor to commit the tort.

The Case Nugget on the next page demonstrates the role of tort principles in establishing liability.

BUT WHAT IF . . .

WHAT IF THE FACTS OF THE CASE OPENER WERE DIFFERENT?

Let's say, in the Case Opener, that Ogle, being an emergency room doctor, was an independent contractor to the hospital. When Abshure sues Ogle, she sues the hospital too because Ogle was working within the hospital when he caused her injury. Is the hospital liable for Ogle's actions in such a scenario?

[12] Restatement (Second) of Agency, sec. 250.

CASE NUGGET

LIABILITY WHEN HIRING INDEPENDENT CONTRACTORS

Larry S. Lawrence v. Bainbridge Apartments et al. Court of Appeals of Missouri, Western District 957 S.W.2d 400 (1997)

In 1989, Smart Way Janitorial offered a bid to Larry Lawrence to wash the windows of Bainbridge Apartments, two seven-story buildings and four four-story buildings. Even though Lawrence could not create a safety line for the four-story buildings, the building manager insisted he wash the windows from the outside so that the residents would not be disturbed. When Lawrence started the work, he fell from one of the shorter buildings and suffered injuries. He brought suit against Bainbridge Apartments, arguing that Bainbridge was negligent on the basis of the "inherently dangerous activity" exception to the doctrine that landowners are not vicariously liable for injuries caused by the negligence of an independent contractor or his employees.

The trial court ruled that because Lawrence had received workers' compensation benefits, the injury was not covered by the inherently dangerous activity exception. The trial court granted summary judgment to Bainbridge; however, when Lawrence appealed, the decision was reversed and remanded because the court of appeals ruled that Lawrence was not a covered employee entitled to workers' compensation benefits.

The court argued that in establishing liability in this case, it would look to which party could best avoid the harm and manage the risk of loss in the inherently dangerous activity in question. An independent contractor who knows he will not be compensated by the landowner for his injuries has a strong incentive to take additional care and avoid neglect in performing his duties. As an expert, he is in a better position to understand the risks and costs in a particular job, and he may demand sufficient remuneration and safety measures to cover what he believes the risks to be. In return for his bargained-for price, he accepts the allocation of the risk. The court held that an injured independent contractor, although uninsured, cannot recover under the inherently dangerous activity exception.

Crime and Agency Relationships

If an agent commits a crime, clearly the agent is liable for the crime. If the agent commits the crime in the scope of employment for a principal without the principal's authorization, the principal is not liable for the agent's crime. Remember, one of the elements establishing that a crime has been committed is *intent.* If a principal is unaware of or had no intent for the agent to commit a crime, there is no rationale for the principal's criminal liability. The only time the principal can be liable for the crime of an agent is when the principal has authorized the criminal act.

Legal Principle: **If an agent commits a crime in the scope of his or her employment without authorization from the principal, the principal is not liable for the crime.**

Termination of the Agency Relationship

L03

How can an agency relationship be terminated?

The parties may choose to terminate an agency relationship, or it may terminate automatically by the lapse of time, fulfillment of purpose, or operation of law. (Exhibit 34-2 lists the ways that agency relationships can be terminated.) If the relationship has ended, the agent no longer has authority to make agreements on behalf of the principal. However, the agent's apparent authority continues until the principal notifies third parties that the relationship has ended.

Notice of the termination can be actual or constructive. **Actual notice** must be given to third parties who have had business interactions with the agent; it directly informs them, orally or in writing, that the agency agreement has terminated.[13] When the agent's authority was granted in writing, actual notice also must be given in writing. Parties not directly related to an agency agreement may receive **constructive notice,** which is how the termination of an agency agreement is generally announced.[14] Constructive notice usually

[13] Restatement (Second) of Agency, sec. 136(2).

[14] Restatement (Second) of Agency, sec. 136(3).

Exhibit 34-2
Ways that an Agency Relationship Can Be Terminated

TERMINATION BY ACTS OF PARTIES	TERMINATION BY OPERATION OF LAW
1. Lapse of time	1. Death
2. Fulfillment of purpose	2. Insanity
3. Occurrence of specific event	3. Bankruptcy
4. Mutual agreement by the parties	4. Changed circumstances
5. Revocation of authority	5. Change in law
6. Renunciation by the agent	6. Impossibility
7. Agency coupled with an interest	7. Disloyalty of agent
	8. War

consists of publication in a generally circulating newspaper for the area where the agency agreement existed.

Parties forming a contract of agency in a foreign jurisdiction should include the conditions of termination within the contract. A U.S. manager conducting business in the European Union needs access to the intricacies of Chapter IV of the Agency Relationship Law that focuses on termination. Released agents in the EU receive compensation if they have brought the principal new customers from whom the principal continues to profit, if they are unable to otherwise recover costs incurred through the performance of the contract, or upon their death.

EU law prohibits the agent's receiving compensation if the principal has terminated the contract due to the agent's incapacity. EU law additionally blocks the compensation if the agent terminates the contract or assigns rights and duties under it to another person. Local legal counsel should be especially knowledgeable about such provisions and be able to help managers avoid unnecessary legal battles.

Case 34-3 highlights the potentially disastrous consequences of not understanding how an agency relationship is terminated.

CASE 34-3 ANGELA & RAUL RUIZ v. FORTUNE INSURANCE COMPANY
COURT OF APPEAL OF FLORIDA, THIRD DISTRICT
677 SO. 2D 1336 (1996)

In September 1990, Angela and Raul Ruiz purchased a homeowner's insurance policy for their mobile home from Fortune Insurance Company through Bates Hernandez Associates, an insurance broker. Bates secured the insurance through Fortune's agent, Biscayne Underwriting Management. Fortune terminated its agency relationship with Biscayne in November 1990 and notified its customers in July 1991; consequently, Fortune sent the Ruizes a notice their homeowner's insurance would not be renewed.

However, in August 1991, even though the Ruizes' insurance policy had expired, Bates sent them a renewal notice. The Ruizes paid Bates $450 to renew their insurance policy with Fortune. Bates sent this money to Biscayne, which accepted it.

In August 1992, the Ruizes' mobile home was damaged by a hurricane. When the Ruizes reported the loss to Fortune, they were told they had no current insurance policy with the company. They filed suit against Fortune. In a summary judgment, the trial court ruled for Fortune. The Ruizes appealed.

OPINION PER CURIAM: Although the Ruizes contended below they never received Fortune's notice of cancellation, Fortune produced below a copy of the notice of cancellation and proof it mailed the same to the Ruizes. The law is clear that an insurer's proof of mailing of a notice of cancellation to the insured prevails as a matter of law over the insured's denial as to its receipt.

[continued]

Fortune's actual notice of cancellation to the Ruizes was legally sufficient and binding, whether the Ruizes read or understood the import of such notice. Any lack of understanding of this written notice on the part of the Ruizes only placed a duty upon them to make further inquiry of their broker, agent and/or insurer.

We further reject the Ruizes' argument on appeal that Fortune is estopped from disclaiming coverage where Biscayne accepted the Ruizes' renewal premium after Fortune's termination of its agency relationship with Biscayne. There is no evidence that Fortune engaged in any conduct or action which would reasonably lead the Ruizes to believe Biscayne had continuing actual or apparent authority to collect such premiums on behalf of Fortune.

AFFIRMED.

CRITICAL THINKING

The judge seems to think Fortune fulfilled its obligation to the Ruizes by mailing them a notice of cancellation. Why do you think the Ruizes were confused about the cancellation? How could the plaintiffs argue that they were not properly made aware that their insurance had been canceled?

ETHICAL DECISION MAKING

Explain what you think the ethical obligations were for every party in this case: Fortune, Bates Hernandez Associates, Biscayne Underwriting Management, and the Ruizes.

TERMINATION BY ACTS OF PARTIES

The agency relationship can be terminated after certain acts, as we discuss in the following sections.

Lapse of Time. If an agency agreement specifies that the relationship will exist for a certain amount of time, it will end when that time expires.[15] An agency agreement might state that the relationship will begin on September 1 and end on September 30. While the agent and principal can agree to continue their relationship through October, they will have to make a new agreement to cover it. The agent's express authority ends when the relationship ends; thus, the principal must notify third parties that the former agent can no longer act on the principal's behalf.

Fulfillment of Purpose. Suppose John, a homeowner, enters into an agreement with Claire, a real estate agent, to sell his house. Once Claire succeeds in selling the house, she no longer has the authority to act on John's behalf. She has fulfilled the purpose of the agency relationship.[16]

Occurrence of a Specific Event. Depending on its purpose, an agency relationship can be terminated on the occurrence of a specific event. John employs Claire as an agent to sell his house. Once the sale is final, the agency relationship will terminate.

Mutual Agreement by the Parties. Agency is a consensual agreement between two parties. Consequently, if John and Claire both decide they do not wish to continue in the agency relationship, they can cancel the agreement and terminate the relationship.

Revocation of Authority. A principal can revoke an agent's authority at any time.[17] However, such revocation might constitute a breach of contract with the agent, leaving

[15] Restatement (Second) of Agency, sec. 105.

[16] Restatement (Second) of Agency, sec. 106.

[17] Restatement (Second) of Agency, sec. 119.

COMPARING THE LAW OF OTHER COUNTRIES

TERMINATION IN THE UNITED ARAB EMIRATES

After a relationship of agency ends in the United Arab Emirates (UAE), an agent is entitled to claim compensation, even if the termination occurs in accordance with the terms of the agency agreement. Whether the claim for compensation will be successful is determined by the circumstances surrounding the agent's termination.

Under the UAE Commercial Transaction Law and the UAE Civil Code, *unregistered* agents are still entitled to seek compensation in the event of termination. In the UAE, when the time comes to determine the amount of compensation to be awarded, court-appointed experts are usually the entities that are responsible for determining compensation amounts.

the principal liable for damages.[18] If the agent has somehow breached the fiduciary duty to the principal, however, the principal can revoke the agent's authority without liability.

Renunciation by the Agent. An agent can terminate the agency relationship by renouncing the authority given him or her. The agent can be liable for breach of contract if the agency agreement stated a specific amount of time that the relationship is to exist.

Agency Coupled with an Interest. An **agency coupled with an interest** is a special kind of agency relationship created for the agent's benefit, not the principal's. The principal may not terminate this relationship, which is also called *power given as security*. Rather, it is terminated when an event occurs that discharges the principal's obligation.

TERMINATION BY OPERATION OF LAW

Automatic termination of the agency relationship can occur when the agent is unable to fulfill his task, when the principal does not desire to continue the performance, or when further pursuit of the relationship's objectives would be illegal.

Death. If the principal or the agent dies, the agency relationship is automatically terminated. Even if one party is unaware of the other party's death, the relationship no longer exists. Suppose an agent has authority to buy antiques on behalf of a principal and continues to purchase items without knowing the principal has died. Those transactions are not binding on the principal's estate, because as soon as the principal died, the agent's authority to act was gone.

Insanity. If a principal or agent becomes insane, the agency relationship is finished. Some states have modified this law so that the agency contract still exists unless the person has been adjudicated insane.

Bankruptcy. If the principal or agent files a bankruptcy petition, the agency relationship is generally no longer in existence, particularly if the agent is filing for bankruptcy and his or her credit is important to the agency relationship. Insolvency, the inability to pay debts or the condition in which liabilities outweigh assets, does not necessarily result in the termination of the agency relationship.[19]

[18] Restatement (Second) of Agency, sec. 118.

[19] Restatement (Second) of Agency, sec. 113.

COMPARING THE LAW OF OTHER COUNTRIES

TERMINATION IN THE NETHERLANDS

After a relationship of agency ends in the Netherlands, the agent is entitled to compensation if his or her duties are concluded within a "reasonable" time after termination or if the agent received orders for a certain action before the termination.

In the most interesting triggering event for mandatory compensation, the agent is entitled to "goodwill compensation" if (1) the agent brought the principal new customers, (2) the agent brought new agreements with clients who are still profitable to the principal, and (3) such payment is financially reasonable for the principal (the relationship is not being terminated due to bankruptcy).

The agent must file for goodwill compensation within five years of termination. It may not exceed the equivalent of the agent's average yearly salary.

Changed Circumstances. If an unusual change in circumstances leads the agent to believe that the principal's instructions do not apply, the agency relationship terminates.[20] Suppose Danielle contracts Gregory to act as her agent to sell a painting she found in her great-aunt's attic and authorizes him to sell it for $5,000. However, in the course of showing the painting to several buyers, Gregory learns that the painting is a Van Gogh original. Because the painting is worth much more than $5,000, Gregory should infer that Danielle does not want the original agency to continue.

BUT WHAT IF . . .

WHAT IF THE FACTS OF THE CASE OPENER WERE DIFFERENT?

Let's say, in the Case Opener, that the hospital that employed Ogle had filed for bankruptcy a day before he caused injury to Abshure. What would that mean for the agency agreement between Ogle and the hospital and thus for the hospital's liability? What are the three other events that come into play in agency relationships and have the same effect as bankruptcy?

Change in Law. When a new law makes the commission of an existing agency agreement illegal, the agreement is terminated. LaToya hires Ryan to paint her house green. Then the city council passes a law making it illegal to paint houses green. The new law automatically terminates the agency agreement.

Impossibility. Suppose that while Gregory is trying to sell Danielle's painting, there is a fire in her house and the painting is destroyed. Because it is impossible for Gregory to sell the painting, the agency relationship cannot continue.[21]

If the agent loses qualifications needed to perform duties for the principal, the agency relationship also ends because of impossibility. Jackson hires a lawyer to serve as his agent who has unfortunately engaged in a series of illegal actions and is then disbarred. Because the lawyer can no longer fulfill the functions Jackson authorized him to perform, the agency relationship is terminated.

Disloyalty of Agent. An agency agreement is terminated whenever the agent, unknown to the principal, acquires interest against the principal's interest. It is also terminated if the

[20] Restatement (Second) of Agency, sec. 109.

[21] Restatement (Second) of Agency, sec. 124.

E-COMMERCE AND THE LAW

ELECTRONIC CONTRACTS IN SINGAPORE

The possibility of e-mail and electronic fraud creates certain risks in the formation of electronic contracts. Singapore passed legislation in 1997 that attempts to combat those risks and specifies the consequences of such fraud.

Agency contracts made electronically will be valid and enforceable if the principal or a principal's designated agent sent the contract. To be legally allowed to assume that the electronic record is that of the principal, the third party either follows an agreed-on procedure of clarification or is assured that the message originated from an agent endorsed by the principal.

If an agent sends an electronic record *not* approved by the principal, the third party has the right to act as a result of it. If such actions result in injuries or damages to the third party, the principal is responsible under law and cannot claim he or she was unaware of the agent's actions. While the principal may indeed not have been aware, Singapore does not recognize lack of awareness as a defense.

Singapore's legislation intends to protect third parties from the poor judgment of principals by creating this direct link between them. Making the principal answerable and liable to the third party increases the pressure to employ reliable agents.

agent breaches the duty of loyalty he or she has to the principal.[22] Marta is an attorney representing Lola in her suit against a pharmaceutical company. If the pharmaceutical company offers Marta a job and she accepts, the agency agreement terminates because Marta has acquired an interest opposed to Lola's interests.

War. A principal has an agent in Iran authorized to conduct business dealings on the principal's behalf.[23] If the United States goes to war with Iran, this agency relationship will no longer be in existence because there is no way to enforce the rights of the parties.

[22] Restatement (Second) of Agency, sec. 112.

[23] Restatement (Second) of Agency, sec. 115.

CASE OPENER WRAP-UP

Vicarious Liability and Medical Malpractice Suits

Upon Abshure's second appeal, the supreme court of Tennessee reversed the judgment of the court of appeals, which had affirmed the trial court's dismissal of the plaintiff's vicarious liability claims against the hospital. The supreme court argued that Abshure did in fact file a proper vicarious liability claim against Methodist Hospital before the claims against Dr. Ogle were voluntarily dismissed. The court reasoned that there is *not* a limitation on the plaintiff's ability to pursue a vicarious liability claim if the plaintiff had already filed an initial vicarious liability claim against a principal before dismissing any of the principal's agents from the claim.

As previously discussed in this chapter, in cases such as this one, a principal may be held vicariously liable for the negligent acts of its agent only if the plaintiff shows that the wrongful act occurred within the scope of the agent's employment. To demonstrate this element, the court considers facts such as whether the employer's interests were advanced, whether the employer provided the means by which the act occurred, and whether the employer authorized the employee's act.

KEY TERMS

actual notice 760
agency coupled with an interest 763
constructive notice 760
disclosed principal 753
durable power of attorney 752
general power of attorney 752
partially disclosed principal 753
power of attorney 752
respondeat superior 757
special power of attorney 752
undisclosed principal 753
unidentified principal 753
vicarious liability 757

SUMMARY OF KEY TOPICS

Contractual Liability of the Principal and Agent	*Classification of the principal:* The principal must be classified as either disclosed, partially disclosed, or undisclosed. *Authorized acts:* These are acts within the scope of the agent's authority. *Unauthorized acts:* These acts go beyond the scope of the agent's authority.
Tort Liability and the Agency Relationship	*Principal's tortious conduct:* The law holds a principal directly responsible for his or her own tortious conduct under two conditions: (1) The principal directs the agent to commit a tortious act, and (2) the principal fails to provide proper instruments or tools or adequate instructions. *Agent misrepresentation:* If an agent misrepresents himself or herself to a third party, the principal may be tortiously liable for the agent's misrepresentation. *Respondeat superior:* The principal/employer is liable not because he or she was personally at fault but because he or she negligently hired an agent.
Principal's Liability and the Independent Contractor	An individual who hires an independent contractor cannot be held liable for the independent contractor's tortious actions under the doctrine of *respondeat superior* unless the contractor engages in hazardous activities.
Crime and Agency Relationships	If an agent commits a crime, clearly the agent is liable for the crime.
Termination of the Agency Relationship	*Termination by acts of parties:* Termination may occur by lapse of time, fulfillment of purpose, occurrence of a specific event, mutual agreement by the parties, revocation of authority, or renunciation by the agent. *Termination by operation of law:* The agency relationship may be terminated automatically due to death, insanity, bankruptcy, changed circumstances, change in law, impossibility, disloyalty of agent, or war.

POINT / COUNTERPOINT

Should Attorneys and Other Agents Be Required to Pass Mental Fitness Assessments before Being Given Roles in Power-of-Attorney Circumstances?

YES

In cases involving the granting of power of attorney by a principal to a third party acting on the principal's interest, a high degree of trust and responsibility is put into the hands of the agent. With durable power of attorney, an agent is asked to act on the interest of a principal with a diminished mental or physical ability to represent himself. Therefore, it is reasonable to insist on the mental fitness of the agent. Three important reasons suggest the wisdom of requiring that attorneys and other agents in power-of-attorney cases pass regular mental health assessments.

First, to dutifully uphold the principal-agent relationship, an agent must be mentally sound. An agent is duty-bound to act in her client's best interest; however, mental illness or defect could severely limit her ability to do so. Therefore, when an agent is asked to represent a client who has diminished mental ability, it is rational to require proof of the agent's mental fitness. For example, durable power of attorney represents an extra-sensitive situation since agents cannot confer with clients about their desires, and it gives a dangerous amount of power to an agent with a diminished capacity of her own. Thus, regular mental fitness exams should be required of attorneys and other agents because of their duty to accurately represent the interests of their principals.

Second, discovery of an agent's insanity is grounds to terminate an agent-principal relationship. The relationship between an agent and a principal is intensified in a power-of-attorney situation in which clients cannot confer with their attorneys or other agents. Moreover, attorneys who suffer from schizophrenia or severe bouts of depression may not even be capable of upholding their legal duties to their clients. Lawyers suffering from mental disease may be unable to make court appearances or maintain necessary client communications. This is why insanity found on the part of the lawyer is cause to terminate a power-of-attorney agreement. The result of not relieving an insane attorney of his duties could mean numerous legal matters may need to be revisited and decisions rendered again to make up for any perceived impropriety. Therefore, to prevent future problems, lawyers should always be found to be of sound mind, and this is best proved through regular mental fitness exams.

NO

Requiring an attorney or another agent in a power-of-attorney agreement to take regular mental health exams is both an invasion of privacy and an unnecessarily difficult task. The U.S. Bureau of Labor Statistics estimates that there are 728,200 practicing attorneys in the United States. Cataloging their mental health would not only be difficult but also be an undue burden on an already hectic legal system. Three important explanations suggest that regular mental health exams on legal professionals present more problems than they would solve.

First, regular mental fitness exams and the discussion of their results represent a serious invasion of an attorney's privacy. Because an attorney's name and reputation has a commercial value, even informal disclosure of failure to pass a mental fitness test could negatively impact an attorney's career. Under the Medical Information Privacy and Security Act, every citizen has the right to limit the disclosure of personal health information to only his or her health professionals. Likewise, the Health Insurance Portability and Accountability Act also supports this type of privacy. With regular mental fitness exams, it would be difficult to protect this right. For example, after failing an annual checkup, a lawyer would be forced to terminate all client relationships. This would reveal to the judge, jury, opposing counsel, and clients the nature of the attorney's private health issues. Furthermore, mental health problems can be an insurmountable professional stigma. This would only be intensified if there were a new standard for the mental health of attorneys. Therefore, regular mental health exams of lawyers should be avoided to protect their right to medical privacy.

Second, enforcing and upholding a standard of regular mental fitness for attorneys would be too difficult. Because there are numerous mental health conditions and a wide range of severity, it would be hard to establish exactly what the mental health standard is. While some may agree that schizophrenia should be grounds for terminating an attorney's ability to practice, many will likely disagree on standards for depression or substance abuse.

Third, attorneys are a high-risk group for mental illness, and not building a system to check on their mental fitness means ignoring a widespread problem. In 1997, the Texas Lawyer's Assistance Program received around 300 calls a month from impaired attorneys or people concerned about an attorney's mental health. The organization estimates that 80 percent of attorneys suffer from alcohol or drug abuse. While state bar exams often require a mental fitness exam of attorneys entering the profession, little is done to ensure mental health throughout their careers. Furthermore, many of the issues stemming from stress or physical impairments can arise or worsen during one's career. Requiring regular exams would help curb this problem by ensuring annual checkups to prove consistent mental fitness. Also, problems that can be solved by therapy or medication could mean an attorney is on sabbatical for only a short time. Moreover, an attorney may not even be aware of mental issues prior to a checkup. Therefore, regular psychological checkups would ensure that attorneys are being helped and fulfilling their obligations to their principals.

Third, the administration of annual tests on 728,200 attorneys would entail a huge cost to the government. The current standard for dissolving a power-of-attorney arrangement on the grounds that the lawyer is found mentally unfit is a much better and cheaper system. Under the current arrangement, lawyers are required to disclose notice of mental disease.

These three explanations show that regular mental exams are too problematic because of the difficulty of the process and that the current method is less costly and easier to enforce.

Source: Jennifer Jolly-Ryan, "The Last Taboo: Breaking Law Students with Mental Illnesses and Disabilities Out of the Stigma Straitjacket," *University of Missouri–Kansas City Law Review* 79 (2010), p. 123; and Stephen L. Braun, "What You Should Know: Lawyers and Mental Health in a Nutshell," *The Houston Lawyer* 35, no. 6 (May–June 1998), p. 36.

QUESTIONS & PROBLEMS

1. Explain when a principal is or is not contractually liable for agreements made by an agent.
2. When might a principal be liable for torts committed by an agent?
3. What terminates an agency relationship?
4. Land Transport employed Oscar Gonzalez to operate a Land Transport tractor-trailer rig. One day while working, Robert Nichols and Gonzalez were driving west on Route 9 toward Brewer, Maine. Gonzalez tried several times to pass Nichols in no-passing zones. Angered by Gonzalez's driving, Nichols made an obscene gesture to Gonzalez on two occasions. Thereafter, Gonzalez began to tailgate Nichols for several miles and continued to try to pass him. The two trucks then stopped at a traffic light. Nichols saw Gonzalez get out of his cab, and Nichols did the same. On approaching Gonzalez, Nichols attacked Gonzalez with a rubber-coated chain-linked cable. Nichols then grabbed Gonzalez, and they fell to the ground. During the scuffle, Gonzalez got up, brandished a knife, and stabbed Nichols. Nichols sued Gonzalez and Land Transport for the injuries he suffered. Land Transport moved for summary judgment. Was Land Transport successful with its motion for summary judgment? Why? [*Nichols v. Land Transport Corp.*, 103 F. Supp. 2d 25 (1999).]
5. Mala is a citizen of the U.S. Virgin Islands, and in early 2005, he decided to take his power boat out for a cruise. He was running low on gas and decided to stop at a Crown Bay fueling station. He started fueling the boat and told the attendant to watch his boat as it was being filled up. When he returned, the tank was overflowing. Mala then proceeded to clean up the excess fuel and drive away. As he did so, the engine caught fire and exploded, throwing Mala into the water. He sustained several injuries and burns. The boat was a total loss. A year later, Mala proceeded to sue Crown Bay, claiming that it was negligent in training and supervising its attendant and that it failed to maintain its gas pump. Mala's

original complaint named "Crown Bay Marina Inc." as the sole defendant. But Mala soon amended his complaint by adding other defendants—including Crown Bay's dock attendant, Chubb Group Insurance Company, Crown Bay's attorney, and Marine Management Services Inc, a registered corporation licensed to conduct business in the state of Florida. It was determined that the only parties involved were Mala, Crown Bay, and Marine Management Services. Who was responsible for the damages incurred and why? [*Mala v. Crown Bay Marina, Inc.,* 704 F.3d 239 (2013).]

6. Genito, a licensed partnership (L.P.), was contracted to build a housing development in Chesterfield County, Virginia. The National Housing Corporation (NHC) was in charge of the builder's risk insurance for the project. The NHC in turn contracted with Acordia, an insurance broker, to obtain the actual policy that would cover the housing development. Genito, in the process of building the complex, chose fly ash to fill the ground that the development sat on. As a result, the project was compromised due to cracks in the foundation and overall structure of the complex. Genito filed suit against Acordia claiming that he would have been covered by the insurance policy, but that Acordia was negligent in failing to name Genito as insured under the policy. The L.P. claimed negligence and breach of contract as it sought to receive compensation for the now invalid housing development. Why do you think that Genito claimed negligence as a reason for bringing suit? [*Acordia of. Va. Ins. Agency, Inc. v. Genito Glenn, L.P.,* 263 Va. 377, 560 S.E.2d 246 (2002).]

7. Maria D., the plaintiff, alleged that she was raped by an on-duty security guard who worked for the Westec company. At approximately 2 a.m., she was driving along Pacific Coast Highway. The Westec security guard detained her by shining a spotlight from his patrol car into her moving vehicle. He asked, "How much have you been drinking tonight?" Maria D. thought the security guard was a police officer because the spotlight was shining in her face. The security guard ordered Maria D. to perform field sobriety tests and then told her to get her purse because he was going to take her to the station. Instead, Maria D. says he took her to another location where he raped her. The security guard denied that he had pulled the plaintiff over. He testified at his deposition that he saw her car on the side of the road and stopped to offer assistance and at no point did he rape her. At the time of the encounter, the security guard was on-duty, wearing a uniform and driving a Westec vehicle equipped with a spotlight, and he carried a gun and handcuffs on his belt and had a second firearm on the front passenger seat of his car. Maria D. sued Westec, claiming that the company was vicariously liable for the actions of the security guard under the doctrine of *respondeat superior.* Westec argues that the security guard was acting outside the scope of his employment when he allegedly detained and raped her. Do you think the court found that Westec should be held vicariously liable under *respondeat superior?* Why or why not? [*Maria D. v. Westec Residential Security, Inc.,* 85 Cal. App. 4th 125 (2000).]

8. Doug Hartmann Productions, L.L.C., and the Regal Riverfront Hotel, which was owned by Gateway Hotel Holdings, entered into an agreement for a professional boxing match to be held at the hotel. The contract contained a provision stating that a $5 million indemnity insurance policy was to be provided and Hartmann Productions was to provide a doctor at ringside for the match and an ambulance on stand-by at the hotel the night of the event. Maldonado was a professional boxer who participated in the match. The fight ended when Maldonado was knocked out and later lost consciousness in his dressing room. There was no ambulance on site. An ambulance was called, and Maldonado was taken to a hospital. He suffered severe brain damage as a result of his injury. The damage could have been less severe had an ambulance been on-site for the boxing match. Maldonado sued Gateway, asserting that Hartmann Productions was an independent contractor hired by Gateway to perform an inherently dangerous activity. As such, Gateway had a duty to take special precautions to prevent injury during the inherently dangerous activity. Therefore, Maldonado argued that Gateway should be held liable for the damages resulting from the boxing match. Should the boxing match be considered an inherently dangerous activity? Did the court find Gateway liable? [*Maldonado v. Gateway Holdings, L.L.C.,* 154 S.W.3d 303 (2003).]

9. In 1989, William Petrovich's employer, the Chicago Federation of Musicians, provided health care coverage to all of its employees by enrolling them all in Share Health Plan of Illinois. Share is an HMO and pays only for medical care that is obtained within its network of physicians. To qualify for benefits, a Share member must select a primary care physician, who will provide that member's overall care and authorize referrals when necessary. Share gives its members a list of participating physicians from which to choose. Inga Petrovich, William's wife, selected Dr. Marie Kowalski from Share's list and began seeing Kowalski as her primary care physician.

In September 1990, Mrs. Petrovich saw Kowalski because she was experiencing persistent pain in her mouth, tongue, throat, and face. She also complained of a foul mucus in her mouth. Kowalski referred her to Dr. Friedman, an ear, nose, and throat specialist who had a contract with Share. When Friedman ordered that an MRI be done, Kowalski refused and instead sent a copy of an old MRI. In June 1991, after Mrs. Petrovich had made multiple visits to both doctors, Friedman found cancerous growths in Mrs. Petrovich's mouth. He performed surgery to remove the cancer later that month.

Petrovich subsequently sued Share for medical malpractice. The complaint alleges that both Kowalski and Friedman were negligent in failing to diagnose Inga Petrovich's cancer in a timely manner and that Share is vicariously liable for their negligence. Share filed a motion for summary judgment, arguing that it cannot be held liable for the negligence of Kowalski or Friedman because they were acting as independent contractors, not as Share's agents. How should the court decide? What reasons should it give? [*Petrovich v. Share Health Plan of Illinois,* 719 N.E.2d 756 (1999).]

10. Brenda Gail Langley is a resident of Tennessee, and on October 20, 1999, she took out a $50,000 life insurance policy. In this policy, she named her three biological children—Kristin Taylor, Edward Langley, and Phillip Langley—as the three beneficiaries. The policy was taken out by Langley from Tennessee Farmers Life Reassurance Company. A clause in the policy stated that Langley reserved the right to change the beneficiaries at any time and that the beneficiaries would share the inheritance equally. In 2002, Langley created a power of attorney, naming her sister, Linda Rose, the POA. Within the document was a clause that stated: "I, Brenda Gail Langley, do hereby appoint and constitute Linda Sue Rose, my true and lawful attorney for me and in my name and on my behalf to transact all insurance business on my behalf, to apply for or continue policies, collect profits, file claims, make demands, enter into compromise and settlement agreements, file suits or actions and take any other action necessary or proper in this regard." In October 2002, Rose contacted Tennessee Farmers and changed the beneficiaries stated in the policy. Rose claims the action to change the beneficiaries was the result of Langley's frustration with her children. Then, in November of the same year, Langley executed a will, giving only $100 to her children and the rest of her assets to her sister, Rose. The following year, Langley passed away. Rose then proceeded to submit claims to collect the insurance money from the life insurance policy. Langley's children then proceeded to file their own claims. Tennessee Farmers realized there was more than one claim being made and filed suit against Rose. The original beneficiaries of the policy—the deceased's children—answered the complaint, arguing that Rose was not entitled to the proceeds because (1) the deceased's execution of the power of attorney was brought about by duress, coercion, control, and undue influence exercised by Rose or, alternatively, (2) Rose violated her fiduciary duty, as attorney in fact, by changing the beneficiary designation on the deceased's life insurance policy. Who do you think won the case and why? [*Tennessee Farmers Life Reassurance Co. v. Linda Rose et al.,* 239 S.W.3d 743 (Tenn. 2007).]

Reversed but beneficiaries are entitled to raise other defenses

Looking for more review materials?

The Online Learning Center at **www.mhhe.com/kubasek3e** contains this chapter's "Assignment on the Internet" and also a list of URLs for more information, entitled "On the Internet." Find both of them in the Student Center portion of the OLC, along with quizzes and other helpful materials.

CHAPTER 35

Forms of Business Organization

LEARNING OBJECTIVES

After reading this chapter, you will be able to answer the following questions:

1 What are the major forms of business organization, and what are the differences among them?

2 What are the specialized forms of business organization?

3 What is a franchise?

CASE OPENER

The Dunkin' Donuts Franchise Agreement

Dunkin' Donuts Corporation operates numerous restaurants worldwide, organizing many of them as franchises. Dunkin' Donuts has the exclusive license to use and to license others to use its trademarks, service marks, and trade name. These marks and trade name have been used continuously since 1960 to identify Dunkin's doughnut shops as well as the doughnuts, pastries, coffee, and other products associated with those shops. Dipak N. Bhayani operated two Dunkin' Donuts franchises in Illinois for many years. Dunkin' Donuts later notified Bhayani that his two franchises had been violating parts of the franchise license agreement. After repeated incidents and failure to cure the violations over a substantial period of time, Dunkin' Donuts (the franchisor) demanded termination of both of Bhayani's franchises.

1. Did Dunkin' Donuts lawfully revoke Bhayani's franchises?
2. What are some potential problems that a franchisor and a franchisee might experience in their relationship?

The Wrap-Up at the end of the chapter will answer these questions.

Suppose you come up with an idea to produce a novel product you think could lead to enormous profits. But what is the best way to produce this product? Should you do it yourself by creating your own business? Do you have enough money to create your own business? What are the legal ramifications if your business is not successful? What legal responsibilities do you have with respect to your business?

Perhaps you share your idea with your best friend, who suggests that the two of you become partners in the production and sale of this product. What are the benefits associated with forming a partnership? What are the disadvantages? Are there other forms of business you should consider?

Choosing the form of business to create is one of the most important decisions an enterprise makes. The extent of liability and control the owner will have depends on the form of the business. The business world is not static, however, and businesses can and do change form over time, so this chapter relates not only to new businesses but also to existing ones. The first section introduces the major types of business organizations, describing how these forms are both created and ended. The second section considers several types of business organizations that are less well known, but important nevertheless.

Major Forms of Business Organization

SOLE PROPRIETORSHIP

LO1

What are the major forms of business organization, and what are the differences among them?

If you decide to go into business on your own, you are creating a **sole proprietorship,** a business organization in which you, as the **sole proprietor,** are in sole control of the management and the profits. Thus, if you wanted to open a lawn-mowing business or a sewing shop, you would likely be creating a sole proprietorship.

Why might an entrepreneur choose to create a sole proprietorship over other forms of business organization? First, opening a sole proprietorship requires very few legal formalities. Second, a sole proprietor has complete control of the management of the organization, with freedom to hire employees, determine business hours, and expand or change the nature of the business. Third, the sole proprietor keeps all the profits from the business. These profits are taxed as the personal income of the sole proprietor.

However, sole proprietorships have disadvantages too. Suppose you are the sole proprietor of a restaurant in which a customer is injured and she sues your business. You are personally liable for any losses or obligations associated with the business. If you accrue large debts because of your business, you might have to sell your home to cover them. Moreover, because the sole proprietorship is not considered a separate legal entity, you, as the owner and sole proprietor, can be personally sued. Sole proprietorships are terminated automatically when the sole proprietor dies.

Funding for your business is limited to your personal funds and any loans you might be able to obtain. Thus, sole proprietorships often struggle in the initial stages because they have large start-up costs relative to the profits they make.

Exhibit 35-1 summarizes the advantages and disadvantages of the sole proprietorship. Sole proprietorships are by far the most popular form of business organization in the United States.

An alternative form of business organization that retains many advantages of the sole proprietorship but addresses its funding drawback is the partnership.

BUT WHAT IF . . .

WHAT IF THE FACTS OF THE CASE OPENER WERE DIFFERENT?

Recall that, in the Case Opener, Dunkin' Donuts had franchises in different locations. Let's say that, instead, there was one Dunkin' Donuts and the single location was run and managed by one person. What kind of a business would this be called?

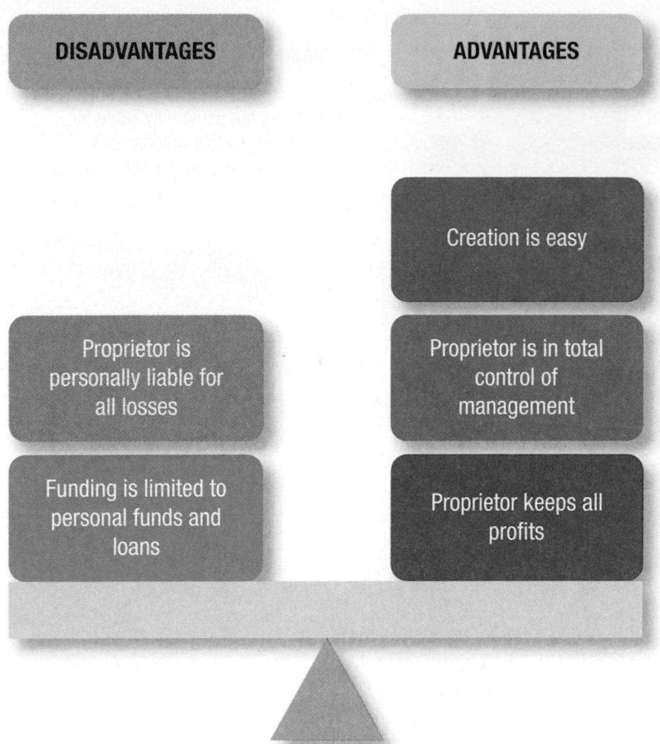

Exhibit 35-1

Advantages and Disadvantages of the Sole Proprietorship

PARTNERSHIP

Suppose you and your best friend from college decide to create a business to buy and sell used books and CDs online. Both of you agree to share control of the business and split the profits equally. According to the Uniform Partnership Act (UPA), you and your friend have created a **partnership,** a voluntary association between two or more persons who co-own a business for profit. Except in a few cases, a partnership is not considered a separate legal entity and is dissolved when any partner dies. The Uniform Partnership Act governs partnerships in most states in the absence of an express agreement.

What are the advantages of a partnership? First, formation is easy. The partners, each considered an agent of the partnership, are generally not required to create an official or even a written agreement to establish it. Second, because in most cases the partnership is not considered a separate legal entity, income from the business is taxed as individual income for each partner. For that reason, partners can also deduct business losses from their taxable income.

The major disadvantage of partnerships is that partners are personally liable for the firm's debts. If you are in a partnership with your best friend, who embezzles $50,000 through the business, you will likely be held personally liable for that $50,000. Exhibit 35-2 summarizes the advantages and disadvantages of a partnership.

There are several types of partnerships (see Exhibit 35-3). In a **general partnership** the partners divide the profits (usually equally) and the management responsibilities and share unlimited personal liability for the firm's debts. Thus, in our Internet business example, you and your best friend form a general partnership by agreeing to share management responsibilities and profits as well as assuming unlimited personal liability.

Exhibit 35-2
Advantages and Disadvantages of the Partnership

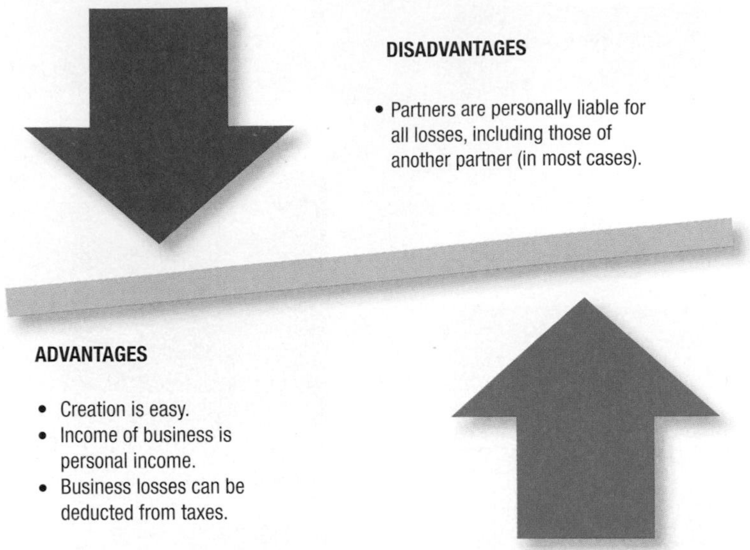

Exhibit 35-3
Types of Partnerships

General partnership	A partnership in which the partners equally divide the profits and management responsibilities and share unlimited personal liability for the partnership's debts
Limited partnership (LP)	A partnership consisting of one general partner and at least one limited partner who does not have any part in the management of the business
Limited liability partnership (LLP)	A partnership in which all partners are liable only to the extent of the partnership's assets
Cooperative	A business organization consisting of individuals who join together to gain an advantage in the market that mutually benefits all members; can be incorporated or unincorporated
Joint venture	A relationship between two or more persons or corporations that is created for a specific business undertaking
Franchise	A business organization in which a franchisee, through a contractual agreement, sells a good or service that is trademarked by a franchisor
Business trust	A business organization controlled by a group of trustees who operate the trust, according to a written agreement, for the beneficiaries; the trustees and the beneficiaries have limited liability

Now imagine that your parents want to invest in your Internet business, sharing in its profits but not assuming management responsibilities or personal liability for its debts. Your parents can join your business as limited partners, and your partnership will become a **limited partnership (LP),** an agreement between at least one general partner and at least one limited partner. The general partners, you and your best friend, assume unlimited personal liability for the partnership's debts, but your parents, the limited partners, assume no liability beyond the capital they have invested in it and no part in its management. However, as limited partners, they pay taxes on their share of the profit.

COMPARING THE LAW OF OTHER COUNTRIES

LIMITED LIABILITY PARTNERSHIPS IN JAPAN

The limited liability partnership was not introduced in Japan until 2005. Japan's LLP limits the liability of its members by their capital contribution. In regard to profits, the LLP requires that the members manage the business and negotiate among each other to determine how profits and losses should be distributed among individual members. When members are establishing the rules of the LLP, Japan requires either the agreement of all members or a majority of at least two-thirds of the members.

Japan also established additional limitations and regulations to ensure the preservation of assets of the LLPs. To ensure that members work to preserve the assets of the LLPs, Japan's Limited Liability Partnership Law puts restrictions on which types of capital contribution are permitted, as well as restrictions on the distribution of partnership assets.

If a limited partner dies, the limited partnership is usually unaffected. If a general partner dies, however, the limited partnership is usually dissolved.

A limited partnership must meet certain requirements not expected of general partnerships. First, it must use the word *limited* in its title. Second, the parties must file a certificate of partnership with a state office to create it; otherwise, it exists as a general partnership, and all parties are personally liable for all its debts.

Suppose you are an attorney and a partner in a law firm with 30 other partners. One of your partners is sued because he was negligent in his duties as an attorney. This partner has unlimited liability for professional malpractice. But will you and the other partners also be held liable?

If the partners have created a **limited liability partnership (LLP),** all the partners assume liability for one partner's professional malpractice, but only to the extent of the partnership's assets; the other partners' personal assets cannot be taken. Moreover, each partner is liable for her own negligence *and* the negligence of those that she supervises. This distinctive feature of the LLP is the reason many professionals who do business together adopt it instead of the LP form.

Legal Principle: Every partner in a limited liability partnership has liability limited to the partnership's assets.

BUT WHAT IF . . .

WHAT IF THE FACTS OF THE CASE OPENER WERE DIFFERENT?

Let's say that, in the Case opener, two women, Sara and Melissa, owned Dunkin' Donuts as a partnership. Melissa was embezzling funds from the business that made the company go $50,000 into debt. Sara had all of the documentation to prove that Melissa had embezzled the funds from the business, and she wanted only Melissa to be liable for the debt. How would the court decide in this case?

LLPs are fairly new; in 1991, Texas became the first state to enact a statute permitting their creation. Almost all states now have similar statutes. Like the limited partnership, the LLP has several special requirements. First, the business name must include the phrase *Limited Liability Partnership* or an abbreviation of the phrase. Second, the parties must file a form with the secretary of the state to create the LLP.

The LLP is not considered a separate legal entity. Each partner pays taxes on his or her share of the income of the business. An alternative form of business organization, the corporation, separates business ownership from business control.

Exhibit 35-4
Advantages and Disadvantages of the Corporation

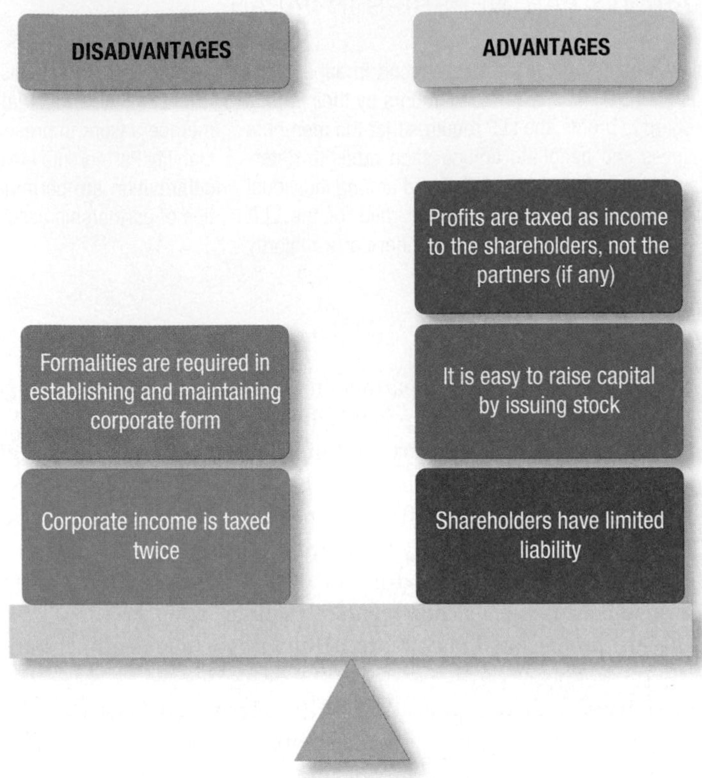

CORPORATION

When you hear the word *business,* you probably think of firms like Walmart, Kmart, McDonald's, and Nike. Perhaps the most dominant form of business organization is the **corporation,** a legal entity formed by selling shares of stock to investors, who then become **shareholders** and the owners of the company. These shareholders elect a board of directors, which is responsible for managing the business. The board of directors, in turn, hires officers to run the day-to-day business.

None of the other forms of business we have discussed are separate legal entities. How does a corporation become a separate legal entity? It must be created according to state law. (Chapter 38 discusses the laws governing the creation and functioning of the corporation.)

What are the consequences of being a separate legal entity? First, while the corporation can be sued and can be held liable for its debts, shareholders cannot. Their liability is usually limited to the amount they have invested in their share purchases, which supplies the company with capital. Second, the corporation is not dissolved when shareholders die. Third, the corporation must pay taxes on its profits, *and* its shareholders must pay taxes on the dividends (distributions of those profits) they receive from it. Exhibit 35-4 summarizes the advantages and disadvantages of the corporate form of business.

One way to avoid the double taxation is by forming an **S corporation,** which is a corporation under federal tax law but is taxed like a partnership as long as it follows certain regulations. For example, the S corporation cannot have more than 100 shareholders. Its income is taxed only when distributed to the shareholders, who must report the income on their personal income tax forms. S corporations are often, though not always, formed under federal law. Alternatively, other forms of corporation are created under state law.

Legal Principle: A corporation is a separate legal entity and can be sued.

LIMITED LIABILITY COMPANY

One of the newest forms of business organization in the United States is the **limited liability company (LLC),** an unincorporated form of business organization that many people see as combining the most advantageous features of partnerships and corporations. It combines the tax advantages and management flexibility of a partnership with the limited liability of a corporation.

First recognized in the United States in 1977 in Wyoming, the LLC is now recognized in every state, although the rules on LLCs have not evolved uniformly. To bring some uniformity to this area of law, the National Conference of Commissioners on Uniform State Laws drafted the Uniform Limited Liability Company Act (ULLCA) in 1995. In 2006, the commissioners revised the ULLCA. This act provides a model for states to follow, but it has not been uniformly adopted, so it is always necessary to check the specific requirements in the state in which you wish to create your LLC.

Key Reasons for the Rapid Acceptance of Limited Liability Companies. As previously mentioned, the LLC offers its owners (referred to as **members**) the same limited liability for business debts as that offered by the corporation. But unlike the corporation, the LLC is not required to allocate profits and losses in proportion to ownership interests; nor is it required to hold an annual meeting and draft meeting minutes, so record keeping is simpler and more flexible. Unlike the case with limited partnerships, to obtain limited liability, an LLC member does not have to give up his or her right to participate in management of the LLC. In fact, an additional advantage of the LLC is the flexibility it offers members in terms of alternative ways to structure its management.

The most frequently cited advantage of the LLC is that the IRS generally treats it like a partnership or sole proprietorship. This means that members report their share of the profits and losses of the LLC on their personal tax returns. Consequently, no separate tax is assessed on the company itself, thereby allowing its members to avoid double taxation. In contrast, members of a corporation are subjected to double taxation. However, if the LLC members prefer, they may elect to have the entity taxed like a corporation. In a situation where most of the profits are going to be reinvested in the business, this option allows the profits to be taxed at the lower corporate rate. So, while we think of the opportunity to avoid double taxation as a key benefit of the LLC, more important perhaps is the fact that the members have the choice of how they wish to be taxed.

In our global environment, an increasingly important advantage of LLCs is that members need not be citizens or permanent residents of the United States. Other organizational forms, such as the subchapter S corporation, are available only when all the owners are U.S. citizens. Finally, as with a corporation, ordinary business expenses such as salaries paid to owners can be deducted from the profits of an LLC before the LLC's income is allocated to its owners for tax purposes.

BUT WHAT IF . . .

WHAT IF THE FACTS OF THE CASE OPENER WERE DIFFERENT?

Let's say that, in the Case Opener, Dunkin' Donuts was a limited liability company. When the owners submitted their taxes for the year, the government attempted to tax the company itself. The owners said that they could be taxed only on a personal basis. Who is right in this case?

Formation and Management of Limited Liability Companies. A limited liability company is formed by filing articles of organization in the state in which members want to establish their LLC. While precise requirements vary by state, typically the articles include the name of the business, which must include the words *Limited Liability Company* or the initials *LLC,* its principal business address, the name and address of a registered agent for service, the names of the owners, and information about how the company's management will be structured.

LLCs typically want to do business in more states than just the state where they are formed, and they usually need to register in every additional state in which they intend to operate, a process referred to as *qualification.* Qualification simply entails filing a certificate of authority or some similar document, and getting a business license, in each additional state in which the business plans to operate. The LLC is usually referred to as a *foreign company* in the additional states, and under most state statutes the LLC is governed by the rules of the state where it was created, regardless of where it is transacting business.

For purposes of jurisdiction, however, an LLC is considered a citizen of every state in which its members reside. Remember that one of the reasons a party can be sued in federal court when a matter involves more than $75,000, is the existence of diversity of citizenship—no plaintiff and defendant are residents of the same state. For determining whether diversity exists, a corporation is considered a resident of the state in which it is incorporated and the state that is its primary place of business. However, this rule does not apply to LLCs, as their citizenship is determined by the residences of their members. Consequently, if parties want to increase their likelihood of having access to the federal courts, they may want to consider either limiting LLC membership to individuals of only one or a few states or using a different form of business organization.

When members form an LLC, they typically draft an operating agreement, which is the foundational contract among the entity's owners. It spells out such matters as how the company is to be managed, how the profits and losses will be allocated, how interests may be transferred, and how and when the LLC may be dissolved. Any matter not covered in the operating agreement will be resolved in accordance with the state LLC statute; if a matter is not covered by the relevant statute, the principles of partnership law are generally followed.

While there is no requirement for an LLC to have a detailed, written operating agreement, in order to ensure the smooth functioning of the company, it is a good idea to have one. Failure to have such an agreement may result in a court imposing standards on the LLC that may be very different from what the members had in mind when they formed the company.

To see an explanation of shareholder dividends and capital gains, please see the **Connecting to the Core** activity on the text website at www.mhhe.com/kubasek3e.

Exhibit 35-5 compares the standard forms of business organization discussed above.

Legal Principle: **As a general rule, an LLC is formed by filing articles of organization in the state in which members want to establish their LLC. Precise requirements for formation vary by state. Moreover, an LLC needs to register in every additional state in which it will do business.**

BUT WHAT IF . . .

WHAT IF THE FACTS OF THE CASE OPENER WERE DIFFERENT?

Let's say, in the Case Opener, that two donut shops, Dunkin' Donuts and Harry's Bagels, joined together to produce one kind of donut that turned out to be a big hit. The two companies decided to form a partnership in producing this donut together. What kind of company would this be called?

Exhibit 35-5 Traditional Forms of Business Organizations

	SOLE PROPRIETORSHIP	GENERAL PARTNERSHIP	LIMITED LIABILITY COMPANY	CORPORATION
Legal Position	Not a separate legal entity.	Not a separate legal entity in most states.	A separate legal entity.	A separate legal entity.
Creation	Creation is easy and requires very few legal formalities.	Creation is easy. The partners are generally not required to create an official or written agreement to create the partnership.	The company must file a form with a state agency and the name must include *Limited Liability Company* or an abbreviation of the phrase.	Must be created according to state law, which includes filing paperwork such as the articles of incorporation and issuing initial stock certificates to the share-holders of the corporation.
Control Considerations	Sole proprietor has total control.	Each partner is entitled to equal control.	In member-managed LLCs, all the members have control and decisions are made by majority vote. In manager-managed LLCs, the members designate a group of persons to manage the firm.	Separation of ownership and control.
Liability	Sole proprietor has unlimited personal liability.	Each partner has unlimited personal liability for partnership debts.	Each partner's liability is limited to his or her capital investments.	Liability is limited to loss of capital contribution.
Lifetime	Limited to life of proprietor.	Limited by life of partners.	Can exist beyond the illness or death of its members.	Can have unlimited life.
Taxation	Profits are taxed directly as income to the sole proprietor.	Profits are taxed as income for partners.	Profits are taxed as income for partners unless otherwise indicated on the tax form. An LLC with two or more members can choose to be taxed as a corporation or partnership.	Profits are taxed as income to the corporation and as income to the partners in the form of dividends.
Transferability of Ownership Interest	Nontransferable.	Nontransferable.	Generally unlimited transfer.	Generally unlimited transfer.
Dissolution	The business is dissolved when the proprietor dies or decides to dissolve the business.	The partnership is dissolved when one partner dies or when the partners agree to dissolve it.	The members must have a majority vote to dissolve the business. A member's dissociation does not dissolve the entire business.	The corporation is not dissolved when the share-holders die. Dissolution often involves extensive legal paperwork and approval by at least two-thirds of all voting shares.

COMPARING THE LAW OF OTHER COUNTRIES

LIMITED LIABILITY COMPANIES IN MEXICO

A limited liability company in Mexico is "an association of individuals who are exempt from individual responsibility to third parties, yet who own the stock separately from the owner." Limited liability companies are identifiable because their name must be followed by the phrase *Sociedad de Responsibilidad Limitada.* Without this phrase, courts assume that a partnership exists.

The LLC's important distinguishing factor is that members are an entity separate from the owners. Members, from 2 to 25 in number and referred to as *shareholders* or *stockholders,* invest capital in the company. While they do not have any individual responsibility, collectively they must give their consent before the company can sell shares to new members. The decision must be unanimous; generally, members have one vote for every 100-peso share.

Mexico adopted the limited liability company model from Germany, where such companies are enormously popular, in hopes of attracting more investors to small companies by limiting their responsibilities.

Specialized Forms of Business Organization

L02

What are the specialized forms of business organization?

In addition to the traditional forms of business organization we've mentioned above, some specialized forms have become important: cooperatives, joint stock companies, business trusts, syndicates, joint ventures, and franchises. (See Exhibit 35-6.)

COOPERATIVE

A **cooperative** is an organization formed by individuals who usually pool their resources to gain an advantage in the market. Farmers might pool their yields of certain crops to ensure a high market price. Usually, members of the cooperative receive dividends in proportion to how many times per year they engage in business with the cooperative.

Cooperatives may be incorporated or unincorporated. Unincorporated cooperatives are treated like partnerships, meaning members share joint liability for the cooperative's actions. Members of incorporated cooperatives, on the other hand, enjoy limited liability just as do the shareholders of a corporation.

JOINT STOCK COMPANY

A **joint stock company** is a partnership agreement in which company members hold transferable shares while all the goods of the company are held in the names of the partners. Thus, the joint stock company is a mix of corporation and partnership. As in the corporation, members who hold shares of stock own the joint stock company. As in the partnership, these shareholders have personal liability, and in most cases the company is not a separate legal entity.

Exhibit 35-6

Specialized Forms of Business Organization

Cooperative	Organization formed by individuals who pool resources to gain a market advantage
Joint stock company	Partnership agreement in which company members hold transferable shares while all the goods of the company are held in the names of the partners
Business trust	Organization governed by a group of trustees who operate the trust for beneficiaries
Syndicate	Investment group that comes together to finance a specific large project
Joint venture	Relationship between two or more persons or corporations that is created for a specific business undertaking

E-COMMERCE AND THE LAW

EXPLORING FORMS OF BUSINESS ORGANIZATION ON THE INTERNET

If you are considering starting a business, the Internet can provide much information to help you decide which form you should create. At Business Tools (http://smallbiz.findlaw.com/book), you can read more about sole proprietorships, partnerships, and corporations. You can also search online for laws that affect the forms of business within your state. At Texas Business Forms (www.sos.state.tx.us/corp/forms.shtml), you can read about and download the forms required to create various types of business in Texas. Thus, the Internet can make it easier to create your business by increasing the information available to you.

BUSINESS TRUST

A **business trust** is a business organization governed by a group of **trustees,** who operate the trust for the **beneficiaries.** A written trust agreement establishes the duties and powers of the trustees and the interests of the beneficiaries. As in a corporation, the trustees and beneficiaries enjoy limited liability, and in most states business trusts are taxed like corporations.

SYNDICATE

An investment group that comes together for the explicit purpose of financing a specific large project is a **syndicate.** Syndicates are often used to purchase professional sports teams and are quite useful for their ability to raise large amounts of money in a short time. They are usually considered a type of joint venture; thus they are almost always governed by partnership law.

JOINT VENTURE

A **joint venture** is a relationship between two or more persons or corporations created for a specific business undertaking. This relationship may entail financing, producing, and selling goods, securities, or commodities. Participants in the joint venture usually share the profits and losses equally.

Joint ventures can be agreements between small or very large businesses. For example, Penske Truck Leasing Co., L.P., is a joint venture among Penske Corporation, Penske Automotive Group, and General Electric with annual revenues of more than $4 billion. This joint venture operates more than 225,000 vehicles in North America, South America, Europe, and Asia. From a legal standpoint, partnerships and joint ventures are virtually the same. Thus, courts frequently apply partnership law to joint ventures. Joint ventures differ from partnerships, however, because they are usually created for making and selling a single product, while a partnership creates an ongoing full business. The joint venture is usually terminated when all the stock has been sold or at the discretion of the members.

Also unlike a partnership, the joint venture is not automatically terminated when one of the members dies. Members of a joint venture also have less authority than general partners because they are not agents of the other members.

Joint-venture partners usually share equal management of the task for which they have come together, but they can agree to give one party greater management responsibilities. Both (or all) parties usually assume liability for the project, and each can be held responsible for the liability of the other(s).

Like a partnership, a joint venture may be formed without drawing up a formal agreement.

COMPARING THE LAW OF OTHER COUNTRIES

TYPES OF BUSINESS ORGANIZATION IN CHINA

The concept of *legal persons* is at the root of all Chinese business law. The Civil Code of China defines a legal person as "an organization which possesses civil legal capacity for civil acts and which, according to the law, independently enjoys civil rights and assumes civil obligations." The definition goes on to describe two types of legal persons.

The first is the *enterprise legal person,* any privately, collectively, or state-owned registered enterprise that meets four criteria: (1) existence of an outlined organizational structure, (2) an organization title, (3) articles governing the structure, and (4) the necessary funds and property. A foreign-owned or foreign joint venture may also acquire enterprise legal person status by applying for approval and registration.

The second type of legal persons is *other legal persons.* These include government agencies, institutions, and associations. Government agencies need not apply for registration because they are given legal-person status on their establishment. Other institutions and associations must meet the criteria above and may also be subject to approval and registration based on State Council rules specified in 1998.

Case 35-1 provides a judicial discussion of the elements necessary for the establishment of a joint venture.

CASE 35-1 MEYER v. CHRISTIE
U.S. COURT OF APPEALS FOR THE 10TH CIRCUIT
634 F.3D 1152 (2011)

In March of 2005, David Christie and Alexander Glen met with Alan Meyer and John Pratt and allegedly entered into an "oral" joint venture agreement to purchase and manage an area for residential housing. The four agreed that they would call the joint venture "Junction City Partners," that Mr. Christie and Mr. Glen would be fifty/fifty partners with Mr. Meyer and Mr. Pratt, and that they would hire a contractor from Dovetail Builders. However, a few weeks later, Mr. Christie and Mr. Glen terminated their relationship with Mr. Meyer and Mr. Pratt, and formed a corporation, "The Bluffs, LLC." Christie and Glen then gave a fifty percent partnership interest in the The Bluffs, LLC, to two outside individuals.

At this time, plaintiffs Meyer and Pratt, joined by Dovetail Builders, filed a claim of breach of the joint venture agreement, as well as claims of breach of fiduciary duty and wrongful dissociation, against the defendants, Christie and Glen. The jury found in favor of the plaintiffs on all of these claims, and found more than $9 million in damages. The defendants appealed, asserting the lack of existence and enforceability of the alleged joint venture agreement.

JUDGE MCKAY: Defendants argue that we must find there to be insufficient evidence of a joint venture based on our interpretation of Kansas law in *Terra Venture, Inc. v. JDN Real-Estate Overland Park, L.P.* In Terra Venture, we listed five factors for determining whether a joint venture exists:

1. the joint ownership and control of property;
2. the sharing of expenses, profits, and losses, and having and exercising some voice in determining the division of net earnings;
3. a community of control over and active participation in the management and direction of the business enterprise;
4. the intention of the parties, express or implied; and
5. the fixing of salaries by joint agreement.

We then concluded there was no evidence in that case as to four of the five factors while the evidence as to the fourth factor, the intention of the parties, was insufficient to demonstrate the existence of a joint venture. Defendants argue that this holding should control in the instant case: because there is only inconclusive evidence bearing on this single factor and no evidence of the other factors, there is insufficient evidence to establish a joint venture.

We are not persuaded. Firstly, we note that these five factors are not exclusive or outcome-determinative. Moreover, the evidence regarding these factors is much stronger in the instant case than in Terra Venture. In Terra Venture, the only evidence suggesting the parties intended to form a joint venture was their agreement that they would refer to their project as a joint venture in press releases. In this case, by contrast, the evidence was that the parties agreed they would in fact form a joint venture, not just that they would refer to their project as such. The evidence also indicated that Plaintiffs and Defendants informed not just the public but also their employees and attorneys that they were jointly working on the project. Furthermore, although it is undisputed the parties did not actually share expenses, profits, and losses, the evidence introduced at trial was that they agreed they would share future profits and losses and would "true-up" expenses when the corporation paperwork had been completed.

[continued]

We likewise reject Defendants' argument that the evidence showed only an anticipatory agreement to form a joint venture in the future, not the actual formation of a joint venture. The jury was presented with ample evidence from which it could reasonably conclude the parties actually entered into a joint venture agreement in March of 2005, and "the mere existence of contrary evidence does not itself undermine the jury's findings."

Defendants then argue the entire joint venture agreement is unenforceable under the statute of frauds because it was premised on an unenforceable oral agreement to purchase and transfer land. At a minimum, they argue, the statute of frauds must prevent Plaintiffs from recovering any damages relating to D.J. Christie, Inc.'s failure to transfer the real property to the joint venture.

Although the statute of frauds would apply to a land purchase agreement as between the seller and the purchaser of the property, it does not affect the relationship between the parties to the joint venture agreement or their obligations under that agreement. We thus hold that the statute of frauds does not bar Plaintiffs' claims or limit their potential damages.

Mr. Meyers and Mr. Pratt's claims against defendants are AFFIRMED. Dovetail Builder's unjust enrichment claim against defendants is REMANDED for further consideration in light of this decision.

CRITICAL THINKING

The process of critical thinking requires that we ask critical questions to evaluate whatever reasoning we encounter, even if, as in this case, the reasoning appears very convincing. Of the five criteria Judge McKay uses to determine whether a joint venture exists, which criterion do you think he provides the least justification for?

ETHICAL DECISION MAKING

Essentially, the court ruled in favor of the plaintiffs and determined that the defendants did in fact breach a joint-venture agreement. What theory or theories of ethical decision making might lead a judge to rule in favor of the defendants instead? Who in the business community would be affected if this theory of ethical decision making was employed? Explain.

FRANCHISE

L03
What is a franchise?

When you go into McDonald's to eat lunch, what type of business are you patronizing? You are likely eating at a **franchise.** This form of business organization is a business that exists because of an arrangement between the **franchisor,** an owner of a trade name or trademark, and the **franchisee,** a person who sells goods or services under the trade name or trademark. Exhibit 35-7 summarizes the advantages and disadvantages of a franchise for the franchisor.

DISADVANTAGES	ADVANTAGES
Can become liable for the franchise if it exerts too much control	Earns increased income from the franchise
Has little control over the franchise	Takes low risk in starting a franchise

Exhibit 35-7
Starting a Franchise: Advantages and Disadvantages for the Franchisor

Franchising is one way to spread your business across the world.

Exhibit 35-8 The Top 10 Global Franchises, 2013

1. Hampton Hotels
2. Subway
3. Jiffy Lube
4. 7-Eleven
5. Supercuts
6. Anytime Fitness
7. Servpro
8. Denny's, Inc.
9. McDonald's
10. Pizza Hut

Source: Ranked by *Entrepreneur Magazine* on the basis of financial strength and stability, growth rate, and size of the system; www.entrepreneur.com/franchise500/index.html.

Generally, franchises fall into one of three categories. In a **chain-style business operation,** such as McDonald's and Burger King, the franchise operates under the franchisor's business name and is required to follow the franchisor's standards and methods of business operation.

In the second category, **distributorships,** the franchisor manufactures a product and licenses a dealer to sell it in an exclusive territory. A car dealership is an example of a distributorship.

Finally, the third category is the **manufacturing arrangement,** in which the franchisor provides the franchisee with the formula or necessary ingredient to manufacture a product. Soft-drink companies, for example, provide the syrup used to produce the final product, and then sell it, according to the franchisor's standards.

Exhibit 35-8 indicates how important franchises are for the market economy.

Look at Case 35-2 to see how the supreme court of Arkansas determined whether a franchise agreement existed between Mary Kay Cosmetics and Janet Isbell.

CASE 35-2 MARY KAY, INC., A/K/A MARY KAY COSMETICS, INC. v. JANET ISBELL

SUPREME COURT OF ARKANSAS

338 ARK. 556, 999 S.W.2D 669, 1999 ARK. LEXIS 443

In 1980, Janet Isbell signed an agreement to become a beauty consultant for Mary Kay. This agreement established that Isbell would sell products to customers at home demonstration parties, but she was prohibited from selling in retail establishments. In September 1981, Isbell signed her first agreement to become a unit sales director. She signed her second agreement in July 1991. In addition to serving as a beauty consultant, Isbell recruited other beauty consultants. She earned compensation in the form of commission on her sales as well as on the sales of the consultants she recruited. In 1994, she rented a space in a shopping mall to serve as a training center. In April 1994, Mary Kay's legal coordinator contacted Isbell, stating that the store space was not to be used to sell Mary Kay products. According to the agreement, Isbell's office could not look like a Mary Kay store. Furthermore, Isbell was told to cease all photo sessions of potential customers and to stop advertising "glamour tips."

In September 1995, the vice president of sales development notified Isbell that Mary Kay was terminating its agreements with her. Isbell filed suit against Mary Kay, *claiming she was a franchise under Arkansas' Franchise Practices Act. She argued that Mary Kay violated the Franchise Practices Act by refusing to comply with the FPA provisions for termination of a franchise. In August 1997, the trial court granted summary judgment to Isbell, but it did not explain why Isbell's relationships with Mary Kay could be considered a franchise. The trial court ruled as a matter of law that Mary Kay's termination of Isbell had violated the Act, and a jury awarded Isbell $110,583.33.*

JUDGE GLAZE: The threshold issue to be decided is whether the Arkansas Franchise Practices Act applies, because if it does, Isbell would be entitled to the designation of franchisee and permitted to invoke the protections and benefits of that Act.

To determine whether the Arkansas Franchise Practices Act applies to this case depends upon our interpretation and construction of the pertinent provisions of the Act. In this view, we turn first to Ark. Code Ann. §4-72-202 (1) (Supp. 1997), which in relevant part defines "franchise" to mean the following:

> [A] written or oral agreement for a definite or indefinite period, in which a person grants to another a license to use a trade name, trademark, service mark, or related characteristic within an exclusive or nonexclusive territory, or to sell or distribute goods or services within an exclusive or nonexclusive territory, at wholesale, retail, by lease agreement, or otherwise.

While the Act's definition of franchise is helpful, that definition alone is not dispositive of the issue as to whether Isbell, under the parties' agreement, is or is not a franchisee. The answer, however, can be found in §§ 4-72-203 and 4-72-202 (6) of the Act. Section 4-72-203 clearly provides the Act applies only to a franchise that contemplates or requires the franchise to establish or maintain a place of business in the state. Next, § 4-72-202 (6) defines "place of business" under the Act as meaning "a fixed geographical location at which the franchisee [1] displays for sale and sells the franchisor's goods or [2] offers for sale and sells the franchisor's services."

We first should note that Isbell concedes that, as a sales director, her agreements with Mary Kay provided that she could not display for sale or sell Mary Kay products from an office, whether that office was located in her home or her training center. In fact, Isbell testified that she never displayed or sold Mary Kay products from her training center, and to have done so would have been a violation of her agreement with Mary Kay.

While conceding that the parties' agreements never contemplated that Isbell would or could sell the franchisor's goods from a fixed location, she argues no such prohibition prevented her from selling Mary Kay services from her home or training center. Specifically, Isbell suggests the facial makeovers and "Glamour Shots" photo sessions that were a part of Mary Kay's demonstration and training program constituted services that the parties contemplated could be sold by Isbell from her center.

Mary Kay's Director's Guide, which was made a part of the parties' agreements, very clearly provided that a sales director's office, albeit it her home or training center, could only be used to interview potential recruits and hold unit meetings and other training events. The Guide further provided that the office or center should not give the appearance of a cosmetic studio, facial salon or retail establishment, or give the appearance of being a "Mary Kay" store. Thus, nowhere in the parties' Guide or agreements can it be fairly said that the parties ever contemplated that Isbell could use her office or center as a fixed location to display or sell Mary Kay products or services.

Even if we could agree with Isbell's contention that she was not prohibited from selling (or was otherwise authorized to sell) Mary Kay services, her argument must fail for another reason. Isbell simply never showed she sold Mary Kay services. She claims that because her contract requires her to provide motivational, counseling, and training services, such services should be considered part of the sale and commission when the product is actually sold. Isbell offered no proof as to what part of the commission, if any, was attributable to services. Neither Isbell nor Mary Kay was shown to have received any separate compensation for services provided to potential customers, but, to the contrary, evidence was presented showing these services, like the photographs taken at makeover sessions, were provided at cost with only the photographer receiving payment.

Finally, Isbell argues that her home constituted a place of business under the Act because as a consultant she occasionally displayed and sold products there. This argument, however, is not supported by the parties' agreement, since it never contemplated a fixed location for the display and sale of products. As previously stated, a Mary Kay consultant's location for selling products is her home or those of her potential customers.

In sum, we conclude that the agreements between Janet Isbell and Mary Kay did not contemplate the establishment of a fixed place of business as that term is defined in Ark. Code Ann. § 4-72-202 (6). As such, the business relationship entered into by Isbell and Mary Kay was not a franchise within the protection of the Arkansas Franchise Practices Act, and the court below erred in so holding.

REVERSED and DISMISSED.

[continued]

CRITICAL THINKING

Outline the judge's reasoning in this case. What evidence does he use to support this reasoning?

What missing information would you call for when considering the facts of this case?

Would you interpret the Arkansas Franchise Practices Act and apply it to the facts of the case differently than Judge Glaze does? Why or why not?

ETHICAL DECISION MAKING

Consider the WPH framework. What values is Isbell promoting? What values are in conflict? Was the court fair in assessing her actions in light of these values?

Franchise Law. Because franchisors are usually larger than franchisees and have more resources, they often have the upper hand in franchise relationships. However, federal and state laws have been established to protect the franchisee.

A franchise is a contractual relationship between the franchisor and the franchisee. Thus, contract law, and the Uniform Commercial Code in particular, apply. If the terms of the contract are not met, either side can sue for breach of contract.

Creation of the Franchise. In the franchise relationship, the parties make a **franchise agreement** regarding payment to the franchisor, location of the franchise, restrictions the franchisee must follow, and method of termination of the franchise.

The franchise agreement usually sets out what the franchisee pays the franchisor (a large sum) for use of the trade name or trademark and what percentage of sales income will go to the franchisor. If the franchise requires a building, the agreement will specify who pays for buying or renting it or for building it if it must be constructed.

The franchisor usually includes in the agreement business practices that are forbidden and business standards, such as for cleanliness, that must be met. The franchisor can also set sales quotas and record-keeping requirements. The franchisee might be required to purchase certain supplies from the franchisor at a set price, but the franchisor cannot establish the price at which the franchisee sells the goods.

The disagreement in the opening scenario for this chapter arose because of the third factor in franchise agreements. Because many Dunkin' Donuts restaurants are owned by franchisees, Dunkin' Donuts established guidelines and policies that promote business practices that enhance the quality of food and services at each restaurant. Dunkin' Donuts also has quality, safety, and cleanliness standards for each of its franchises. The franchise agreement stipulated that Dunkin' Donuts could inspect Bhayani's restaurant at any reasonable time.

Although the franchisor has the legal authority to ensure that the franchisee maintains the quality of goods and services associated with the franchise, it must be cautious. If it exercises too much authority in the day-to-day affairs of the business, the franchisor could be held liable for the torts of the franchisee's employees.

Termination of the Franchise. Much of the litigation associated with franchises regards wrongful termination of a franchise. The franchise agreement establishes how the franchise will be terminated. The business is usually established for a trial period, such as a year. If the franchisee does not meet the requirements in the agreement, the franchisor can terminate it but must give sufficient notice. The termination also usually must have cause. For example, good cause exists if the franchisee repeatedly violates the franchise agreement. Additionally, the franchisor needs to have documented the warnings sent to the franchisee regarding the violations. The typical agreement gives the franchisor broad authority to terminate; in recent years, however, many states have been giving the franchisee greater termination protection.

Legal Principle: **When a franchisee does not uphold the franchise agreement, the franchisor can terminate the relationship with sufficient notice.**

The courts usually rely heavily on the written agreement when determining whether a franchise was wrongfully terminated. Look at Case 35-3, which illustrates the agreement's importance.

BUT WHAT IF . . .

WHAT IF THE FACTS OF THE CASE OPENER WERE DIFFERENT?

Let's say, in the Case Opener, that the franchisee was not running his franchise with the same standards demanded by the franchiser and that one day, out of the blue, the franchiser sent a termination notice to the franchisee. The surprised franchisee said that this termination was unlawful, but the franchiser said that he could terminate a franchise at any time if it clearly broke legal standards. Who is correct in this case?

CASE 35-3 COUSINS SUBS SYSTEMS, INC. v. MICHAEL R. McKINNEY

U.S. DISTRICT COURT FOR THE EASTERN DISTRICT OF WISCONSIN

59 F. SUPP. 2D 816 (1999)

Cousins Subs Systems entered into an agreement with Michael McKinney, whose company operates a chain of gas stations, to operate several Cousins submarine sandwich shops placed in the gas stations.

In April 1998, McKinney became disillusioned with the agreement and terminated it. He claimed Cousins had guaranteed him annual sales of $250,000 to $500,000 at each of his franchises and promised to provide advertising. McKinney also claimed Cousins guaranteed it would provide assistance in recruiting other franchises. Finally, McKinney argued Cousins enforced unrealistically high prices of subs. McKinney alleges he terminated the agreement because Cousins failed to uphold its promises.

In June 1998, Cousins filed suit against McKinney for wrongfully terminating the agreement with Cousins. Later in 1998, McKinney filed a counterclaim against Cousins. Cousins filed a motion to dismiss the counterclaim.

JUDGE ADELMAN: McKinney first contends that Cousins violated Minn. Stat. § 80C.13, subd. 2, which provides:

> No person may offer or sell a franchise in this state by means of any written or oral communication which includes an untrue statement of a material fact or which omits to state a material fact necessary in order to make the statements made, in light of the circumstances under which they were made, not misleading.

McKinney does not clearly delineate his theory as to how this statute was violated. He appears to assert that Cousins violated this statute by making untrue oral representations to him about how much money he would make and about how much advertising and recruitment assistance it would provide. The main problem with this claim and, for that matter, with all of McKinney's claims is that the oral promises allegedly made by Cousins are directly contradicted by the written terms of the agreements that he signed and attached as exhibits to his pleadings. Where the allegations of a complaint are inconsistent with the terms of a written contract attached as an exhibit, the terms of the contract prevail over the averments differing therefrom. Unfortunately for McKinney, every oral representation that he alleges was made by Cousins is inconsistent with the written contracts he signed or the written circular he received.

McKinney alleges first that Cousins . . . orally guaranteed that annual sales at McKinney's franchises would be between $250,000 and $500,000, and that this level of sales was not realized. However, the Area Development Agreement states that McKinney "has not received any warranty or guaranty, express or implied, as to the potential volume, profits, or success of the business venture." The Franchise Agreement contains virtually identical language. Thus, McKinney's claim of guaranteed profits is directly contradicted by the written contracts. McKinney also claims that Cousins promised to provide "advertising . . . in excess of the amount paid by McKinney," and that Cousins failed to do so. But the Uniform Franchise Offering Circular states that "Cousins is not obligated to spend any specific amounts on advertising in the area where a particular franchisee is located. . . ." Thus, this claim too is directly contradicted by the written language of an exhibit. McKinney next alleges that Cousins "expressly guaranteed and promised to provide extensive assistance in recruitment of other franchisees in the development area," but that such assistance was not forthcoming. The Area Development Agreement, however, states, with respect to the recruitment issue, "AREA DEVELOPER shall be responsible for advertising for, recruiting and screening prospects for SHOPS within the Exclusive Area." Thus, every single oral promise that McKinney asserts was made by Cousins is inconsistent with the documents appended to his complaint. Under Seventh Circuit case law the language of the exhibits prevails.

McKinney's claims are further undermined by other language in the agreements. The area development and franchise agreements each contain integration clauses which expressly disavow any promises not included in the written agreements between the parties. The Area Development Agreement, for example, states that "this Agreement . . . constitutes the entire agreement of the parties, and there are no other oral or written understandings or agreements . . . relating to the subject matter of this agreement."

McKinney cannot prevail on his claim under the Minnesota statute unless, in offering him a franchise, Cousins made an untrue statement of material fact. Cousins offered the franchises to McKinney through the written franchise documents, not through the alleged oral promises that are inconsistent with the exhibits. And the written documents do not contain untrue statements of material fact or omissions of material facts, nor does McKinney claim that they do. Therefore, McKinney's claim that the Minnesota Franchise Act was violated fails.

In sum, McKinney is an experienced businessman who made a deal which turned out to be less favorable than he anticipated. McKinney expressly acknowledged in detailed written agreements negotiated with the assistance of counsel that his purchase of a franchise was not a risk-free endeavor. He now makes allegations that are directly contrary to the agreements he signed. For the reasons stated, his claim under the Minnesota statute fails.

DISMISSED.

CRITICAL THINKING

What are the primary facts of this case? How would you word the issue of the case in your own words?

Judge Adelman repeatedly says the written terms of the contract between Cousins and McKinney are inconsistent with any alleged oral agreements they made. Do you agree that written contracts should overrule oral agreements in most instances? Why or why not?

ETHICAL DECISION MAKING

Who are the primary stakeholders affected by the court's ruling for Cousins?

The decisions of a court have implications for business ethics. While Chapter 2 distinguishes between what the law requires of a manager and what ethics requires, the relationship between the law and ethics is reciprocal. While ethical judgments lie behind various laws, law does have impacts on business ethics. In this case, the court's decision reminds us that business ethics must pay attention to the various stakeholders who feel the impacts of any business agreement.

CASE OPENER WRAP-UP

The Dunkin' Donuts Franchise Agreement

Bhayani's Dunkin' Donuts franchises violated the license agreement on multiple levels. Financially, under the franchise agreements, Bhayani agreed to pay a franchise fee of 4.9 percent of gross sales to Dunkin' Donuts and an advertising fee of 5 percent of gross sales to the Franchise Owners Advertising and Sales promotion fund. However, Bhayani fell behind on both financial payments on numerous occasions. By the time Dunkin' Donuts sent notice of termination, Bhayani owed $33,189.38 in delinquent fees and failed to cure the financial default.

Furthermore, Bhayani's franchises were also in violation of health and safety standards from the license agreement. During its routine health inspections, Dunkin' Donuts found multiple health and sanitation violations such as pests and evidence of pests; improper storage, refrigeration, and cooking temperatures; improper food and chemical storage; unsanitized utensils; faulty faucets; unclean floors, walls, countertops, toilets, and sinks; insufficient employee hygiene; ill-kept trash areas; and various documentation deficiencies. While some of these were cured by the time of the next inspection, most were not. After each substandard inspection, Dunkin' Donuts sent a notice of default and notice to cure. On the basis of the perceived failure to cure these violations over a substantial period of time, Dunkin' Donuts sent Bhayani a supplemental notice of termination.

As a franchisor, Dunkin' Donuts Corporation is permitted to establish certain standards for franchisees. With regard to Bhayani's restaurants, Dunkin' Donuts established standards for cleanliness and also negotiated financial rates. In accordance with the provisions in the license agreement, Dunkin' Donuts terminated the franchises. Bhayani claimed that any breaches of the agreement by him—either financial breaches or health, sanitation, and safety violations—were directly caused by the bad-faith actions of Dunkin' Donuts. He argued that Dunkin' Donuts targeted him for his franchisee activism by classifying him as a "C" franchise and blocking his attempt to open another franchise. However, the court found that Bhayani did not show that his franchises were exceptional or that they were terminated on the basis of some sort of "pretext" of Dunkin' Donuts. Thus, Dunkin' Donuts was well within its legal rights to terminate the franchise agreement.

Disagreements regarding payments or health standards of franchises are examples of what could go wrong with a franchising agreement. Another example of potential problems between franchisors and franchisees is disagreement over the termination of the franchise. All of these problems existed in the Dunkin' Donuts case. Both parties probably would have benefited from a greater understanding of the responsibilities of the franchisor and franchisee.

KEY TERMS

beneficiazries 781
business trust 781
chain-style business operation 784
cooperative 780
corporation 776
distributorships 784
franchise 783
franchise agreement 786
franchisee 783
franchisor 783
general partnership 773
joint stock company 780
joint venture 781
limited liability company (LLC) 777
limited liability partnership (LLP) 775
limited partnership (LP) 774
manufacturing arrangement 784
members 777
partnership 773
S corporation 776
shareholders 776
sole proprietor 772
sole proprietorship 772
syndicate 781
trustees 781

SUMMARY OF KEY TOPICS

Major Forms of Business Organization

Sole proprietorship: The owner has total control and unlimited personal liability. Profits are taxed directly as income to the sole proprietor.

General partnership: For most purposes, the partnership is not a legal entity, and each partner has equal control and unlimited liability, with profits that are taxed as income for partners.

Limited partnership: Limited partnerships are similar to general partnerships, except that limited partners' liability is limited to the extent of their capital contributions.

Corporation: A corporation is a separate legal entity wherein the owners' liability is limited to the amount of their contributions and the profits are taxed as income to the corporation.

S Corporation: An S corporation is a corporation under federal tax law but is taxed like a partnership as long as it follows certain regulations.

Limited liability company: An LLC is an unincorporated form of business organization that combines the tax advantages and management flexibility of a partnership with the limited liability of a corporation.

Specialized Forms of Business Organization

Cooperative: A cooperative is a business organization in which the members usually pool their resources together to gain some kind of advantage in the market.

Joint stock company: A joint stock company is a partnership agreement in which company members hold transferable shares while all the goods of the company are held in the names of the partners. A joint stock company is a mixture of a corporation and a partnership.

Syndicate: A syndicate is an investment group that comes together for the explicit purpose of financing a specific large project.

Business trust: A business trust is a business organization governed by a group of trustees, who operate the trust for the beneficiaries.

Joint venture: A joint venture is a relationship between two or more persons or corporations created for a specific business undertaking.

Franchise: A franchise is a business that exists because of an arrangement between an owner of a trade name or trademark and a person who sells goods or services under the trade name or trademark.

POINT / COUNTERPOINT

Should a New Restaurateur Open a Franchise Rather than Become a Sole Proprietor?

YES	NO
A businessperson new to the restaurant business should open a restaurant as part of an existing franchise rather than encounter the substantial risks of opening a sole proprietorship. Sole proprietors have unlimited personal liability, meaning they are held solely accountable for the finances in their businesses; they often must provide their houses as collateral to obtain small-business loans.	A new restaurateur should be a sole proprietor rather than a franchisee to enjoy greater potential for long-term success. With careful research and expert advice, sole proprietors can obtain low-risk, longer-term loans that are unlikely to jeopardize their personal assets. Sole proprietors can add a full or limited business partner later and implement additional safety measures to decrease liability.

A sole proprietor can also be held personally liable for injury in the restaurant and can be sued by an employee or customer, whereas a franchisee usually is not held solely liable for an injury.

A franchisor can also provide crucial guidance and supervision to a new businessperson, including clear business practices that have already proved successful, forbidden practices that would endanger the franchise, and minimum standards of cleanliness and service. This assistance eliminates the trial-and-error period sole proprietors must experience and helps the new businessperson avoid repeating others' past errors.

A franchise must pay the franchisor a percentage of profits. After debts are repaid, a sole proprietor keeps all profits for improvements and personal income.

Franchises severely restrict creativity. A sole proprietor is truly her or his own boss and can change the look and menu of the restaurant at any time, determine which hours to be in operation, and decide whether to hire a manager or manage the restaurant directly.

Perhaps most important, a sole proprietor retains flexibility if the economy changes. If need be, she or he can simply uproot the restaurant and move to a different location.

QUESTIONS & PROBLEMS

1. What is the distinction between a general partnership and a limited partnership?
2. Explain why a cooperative could not claim to be a syndicate.
3. Suppose you were asked to review and assess a franchise agreement. What responsibilities would you expect to find included in that agreement?
4. Mike Karimi has been in the hotel management business since the 1980s. The name of Karimi's company is MAK, LLC, which manages and operates several hotels in the United States. In 2004, two brothers, the Khatris, who were friends of Karimi's, wanted him to take over the operation of one of their hotels. The problem with the hotel was that only 40 out of the 186 hotel rooms were suitable for guests to inhabit. This concerned Karimi, who nevertheless agreed to take over the hotel. Karimi received the rights to the hotel from the previous leasers. The hotel, Red Lion, wrote up a franchise agreement with Karimi. In the agreement it stated: "An 'Event of Default' will occur if you fail to satisfy or comply with any of the obligations, requirements, conditions, or terms set forth in this Agreement, the Manual, or any attachment to this Agreement. An 'Event of Default' will also occur if you make any misrepresentations to us, whether in entering into this Agreement or in the performance of your obligations to us." After the renovations were under way, a representative of Red Lion Hotels decided to tour the hotel to check on the renovations. This representative decided that the hotel looked "old and tired." In early 2008, Red Lion sent Karimi a "notice of default and termination." Did Red Lion have the right to send this notice to Karimi? [*Red Lion Hotels Franchising Inc. v. MAK, LLC,* 663 F.3d 1080 (2011).]
5. Brothers Aurelio and Hugo V. Garcia founded a trash removal business called Garcia's, Inc., in the early 2000s. Hugo served as president and director. Garcia's decided to lease trucks and equipment to United Leasing. However, United required, as a part of the agreement, that the stock of Garcia's would be collateral and that United could vote Garcia's share in the company if Garcia's defaulted. Suddenly, United claimed that Garcia's had defaulted, and United liquidated the company's assets and took control. James C. Lehner, a former employee of United, formed the Lehner Family Business Trust in 2005, and shortly thereafter Lehner offered Hugo $50,000 to assign all claims against United to the trust. Hugo executed the requested assignment, which assigned all of the legal claims, rights, and causes of action that Garcia's, "a Virginia corporation in dissolution," and Hugo, "individually and as trustee in liquidation for Garcia's, Inc.," had under the equipment leases with United and otherwise.

   The Lehner Trust sued United Leasing for breach of contract, claiming that "[b]y assignment, the Trust acquired all of Garcia's claims against [United Leasing] and all claims and rights, etc., relating to the Garcia's Leases." Also, the trust claimed that United had been secretly holding over $1 million from Garcia's, which rightfully deserved it. Was the Trust right in suing United Leasing? [*United Leasing Corp. v. Lehner Family Business Trust,* 279 Va. 510 (2010).]

6. The Garden City Boxing (GCB) Club held exclusive satellite licensing rights for a live broadcast of a boxing match between Oscar De La Hoya and Fernando Vargas. Luis Dominguez owned Antenas Enterprises, the installer of a satellite account at Mundelein Burrito restaurant. However, Antenas listed Mundelein Burrito as a residence instead of a commercial location. A commercial establishment could show the boxing match only if it was contractually authorized by GCB to do so and if it paid the appropriate fee of $20 times the maximum fire code occupancy of the establishment. Mundelein Burrito showed the event to its patrons. However, because Mundelein Burrito was classified as a residence, it did not pay the proper fee for a commercial establishment. The Garden City Boxing Club filed suit against Dominguez, the sole proprietor of Antenas, to collect the lost fees from the boxing match. As a sole proprietor, should Dominguez be held personally liable for Antenas Enterprises' actions? [*Garden City Boxing Club, Inc. v. Luis Dominguez,* 2006 U.S. Dist. LEXIS 38184 (2006).]

7. Chic Miller operated a General Motors (GM) franchise car dealership. His written franchise agreement with GM stipulated that Miller had to maintain a floor-plan financing agreement with a lender to enable him to buy new cars from GM. Initially, Miller maintained a line of credit with a GM affiliate (GMAC), but he terminated the agreement because he felt that GMAC charged him an exorbitant interest rate. Miller was able to find another line of credit from Chase Manhattan Bank, but Chase withdrew its financing agreement with Miller after one year. Miller attempted to resume the agreement with GMAC, but GMAC refused. Miller alleged *ipse dixit* (an assertion without evidence) that GMAC discouraged other lenders from providing a line of credit to Miller. GM then notified Miller that it was terminating its franchise relationship with him because he failed to satisfy the financing stipulation of the written franchise agreement. Two months after receiving this notice from GM, Miller attempted to sell his franchise to Kenneth Crowley, the owner of another car dealership. GM rejected this sale, alleging that Miller no longer had a franchise to sell because GM had terminated the franchise agreement two months earlier. Miller sued GM for failing to help his franchise obtain floor-plan financing and for rejecting the sale of his franchise to Crowley. How do you think the court ruled in this case? What requirements must GM meet to lawfully terminate a franchise? Did GM meet those requirements? [*Chic Miller's Chevrolet, Inc. v. GMC,* 352 F. Supp. 2d 251 (2005).]

8. Margaret Miller operated an H&R Block tax preparation franchise for 15 years. She hired William Hehlen as an income tax return preparer for five years, from 1997 to 2001. Each year, Miller and Hehlen signed an employment agreement drawn up by H&R Block. The 2001 agreement was between Hehlen and "Margaret Miller, doing business as H&R Block," and included stipulations prohibiting Hehlen from reproducing confidential business information and from soliciting clients away from Miller's business. Hehlen maintained on his home computer a spreadsheet of customer names that he obtained from Miller. In April 2001, H&R Block terminated its franchise agreement with Miller, and Miller subsequently operated her business as a sole proprietorship under the name "MJM & Associates." Hehlen's employment with Miller ended after the 2001 tax season. In December 2001, Miller sent advertising postcards to clients referring to Hehlen as one of her associates. When Hehlen, who went to work for another H&R Block office, learned of the postcards, he began telephoning the customers whose names he had obtained from Miller. Miller learned of the calls in February 2002 and filed a cease-and-desist action against Hehlen, arguing that Hehlen was violating his employment contract with Miller. Hehlen argued that his employment contract was with Miller's H&R Block franchise, which ceased to exist after April 2001. Do you think Hehlen's employment contract was signed with Miller's franchise or with Miller's sole proprietorship? If you think Hehlen's contract was with Miller's franchise, should Miller have the right to enforce the contract provisions after H&R Block terminated her franchise agreement? Why or why not? [*Miller v. Hehlen,* 104 P.3d 193 (2005).]

9. Tammy Duncan began working as a waitress at a diner owned by her mother Hazel Bynum and stepfather Eddie Bynum. A few weeks later, the three created an agreement in which Tammy was to assume comanager duties for her stepfather. Tammy then began doing paperwork and bookkeeping

for the diner in addition to occasionally waiting tables and performing other duties. She testified that she made no agreement to share in the diner's profits and that she understood she was going to take over her stepfather's duties as manager. The bank account for the diner was still to remain in Eddie Bynum's name and Tammy's parents did not change any business tax information. In the course of her employment, Tammy was injured when she slipped off a ladder and fell onto both knees. The diner's insurer, Cypress, paid Tammy temporary total disability benefits. However, five months later Cypress notified Tammy that it intended to controvert her claim on the basis of alleged newly discovered evidence that she was not an employee of the diner but was a co-owner under the agreement she had made with her mother and stepfather. What are the essential elements of a partnership? Was Tammy Duncan a partner in the diner? Why or why not? [*Cypress Insurance Company v. Duncan,* 281 Ga. App. 469 (2006).]

10. "1-800-Got-Junk?" is a junk removal franchise business headquartered in Vancouver, British Columbia, Canada. In late 2003, Got Junk entered into a franchise agreement with Millennium Asset Recovery, Inc. Under the agreement, the franchisee, Millennium, was to pay a percentage of its gross revenue to Got Junk on every junk removal job it performed. In 2007, Got Junk terminated Millennium's franchise on the grounds that Millennium deliberately had not reported certain jobs and the gross revenue derived from such jobs. Was Got Junk right in terminating the agreement? Why or why not? [*1-800-Got Junk? LLC v. Superior Court (Millennium Asset Recovery, Inc.),* 189 Cal. App. 4th 500 Cal. App. 4th (2010).]

Looking for more review materials?

The Online Learning Center at **www.mhhe.com/kubasek3e** contains this chapter's "Assignment on the Internet" and also a list of URLs for more information, entitled "On the Internet." Find both of them in the Student Center portion of the OLC, along with quizzes and other helpful materials.

CHAPTER

36 Partnerships: Nature, Formation, and Operation

LEARNING OBJECTIVES

After reading this chapter, you will be able to answer the following questions:

1. What is a partnership?
2. What are the different ways in which a partnership can be formed?
3. What are the rights of partners as they interact with each other?
4. Are all members of a partnership liable for interactions with third parties?

CASE OPENER

Joint-Venture Partnership and Liability

Jones Law Firm was a part of a joint venture with several other law firms. Two of the involved law firms, Barrett Law Office and Lovelace Law Firm, included individual attorneys by the names of Don Barrett and Richard Scruggs. The joint-venture agreement required that Barrett Firm's role was that of witness development, Lovelace Firm's role was that of expert retention, and Jones Firm's role was that of briefing. Additional firms held the duties of lead counsel, adjuster retention, and funding and client relations.

In March 2007, Jones Firm alleged that Richard Scruggs and Don Barrett had conspired to set Jones Firm's fee allocation at an unacceptably low percentage. Once Jones Firm refused to accept this low rate, Scruggs and Barrett allegedly removed Jones Firm from the joint venture. Consequently, Jones Firm filed claims against Scruggs and Barrett individually, as well as against their partners and co-venturers, for breach of contract, breach of fiduciary duties, intentional interference with prospective business advantage, fraud, conspiracy, and unconscionability.

Jones Firm then requested a declaratory judgment that it was entitled to 20 percent of all past and future attorney fees collected by the firms. The defendant firms appealed.

On appeal, the court found that the trial court had the authority to impose sanctions against the appellants based on the acts of a single partner that occurred in the ordinary course of a business venture.

1. What was the appellate court's reasoning for its decision on appeal?
2. When is a partnership as a whole liable for an individual attorney's actions?

The Wrap-Up at the end of the chapter will answer these questions.

In this joint-venture case, the court had to consider the laws of partnership in determining whether to find the partnership as a whole liable. The Uniform Partnership Act (UPA) is the main statute governing partnership law. If there is no express partnership agreement, UPA establishes the rules for the partnership.

This chapter discusses the creation and operation of the partnership, and the following chapter considers how partnerships are terminated as well as special types of partnerships. The first section of this chapter considers the nature of the partnership relationship, how partnerships are created, and how they function.

Nature of the Partnership

L01

What is a partnership?

What exactly is a partnership? According to UPA Section 6, a **partnership** is "an association of two or more persons to carry on as co-owners a business for profit." Let's analyze all four parts of this definition to understand their implications. (See Exhibit 36-1.)

First, by "association," UPA means that the partnership is a voluntary and consensual relationship. No one can force someone else to enter into a partnership with him or her. Second, a partnership requires "two or more persons." UPA defines *persons* as "individuals, partnerships, corporations, and other associations." Therefore, almost any individual or group of people could serve as a partner, but these persons must have the legal capacity to be partners. Although minors can serve as partners, the resulting partnership agreement is voidable.

Third, in a partnership, the partners must operate the business for a profit. This criterion is interpreted to mean that the partners must intend to make some kind of profit from the business.

Finally, the partners must serve as co-owners. Being co-owners means that they must share its profits or losses as well as share in the management of the business.

The fourth element of the definition is that the partnership be "for profit." To summarize, a partnership has the following characteristics:

- *Voluntary* and *consensual* relationship.
- Between two or more *individuals, partnerships, corporations,* or other forms of business organization.

Exhibit 36-1

Characteristics of a Partnership

A partnership is:	
An association	It is a consensual and voluntary relationship, meaning that no one was forced into the partnership.
Between two or more legal persons	It consists of two or more individuals, partnerships, corporations, or other forms of business organization.
To carry on a business for profit	Its purpose is to make several business transactions for the trade, occupation, or profession with the intention of making a profit from the business.
As co-owners	The partners share in the management and profits of the business. No party can receive a share of the profit for the purpose of payment of debt, interest, or annuity or from the sale of property.

- Who engage in *numerous business transactions* over a period of time.
- Intending *to make a profit.*
- And *sharing* the *profits* and *management* of the business.

To see a description of considerations a business manager ought to have regarding whether a partnership will result in synergy, please see the **Connecting to the Core** activity on the text website at www.mhhe.com/kubasek3e.

Courts look for these factors when parties dispute whether a partnership exists.

Probably the most important factor in determining whether a partnership exists is whether the profits from the business are shared. UPA has established several exceptions in which a sharing of profits does not constitute a partnership. For example, when an employer shares profits with an employee as payment for work, or when a landlord accepts shares of profits for payment of rent, there is no partnership. If a party receives a share of profits for any of the following reasons, there is no partnership:

- Payment of a debt.
- Payment of an annuity to a widow or representative of a deceased partner.
- Payment from the sale of goodwill of a business or some other property.
- Payment of interest on a loan.

Legal Principle: **Perhaps the most important factor in determining whether a partnership exists is whether the profits are shared. Furthermore, this sharing of profits must not meet one of the UPA exceptions.**

Case 36-1 illustrates the court's analysis of whether a partnership relationship indeed exists.

CASE 36-1 LEOFF v. S&J LAND CO.

U.S. COURT OF APPEALS FOR THE 10TH CIRCUIT

2012 U.S. APP. LEXIS 24560 (2012)

Richard Leoff and S&J Land Company entered into the condominium business together in Colorado. When their planned project fell through and was unsuccessful, Leoff filed a lien against the condominium property and sued the defendant for damages and to enforce the lien. The defendant, S&J Land Company, responded by asserting that it had formed a partnership with Leoff, and then filed a counterclaim against the plaintiff seeking damages for a wrongful filing of a lien and breach of contract. The defendant argued that under Colorado law, a partner cannot place a lien on partnership property. The district court granted the defendant's motion in June 2009 and provided Leoff with the opportunity to file an amended complaint. At that time, Leoff filed a new complaint asserting that S&J Land Company had defrauded him. The district court denied Leoff's motion, deferring it until trial. At trial, the district court filed an opinion ruling that a partnership had in fact been established between Leoff and S&J Land Company, and that S&J had dissociated as a partner by acting in a fashion that made the partnership not reasonably practical to carry out. Both parties appealed the ruling.

JUDGE HARTZ: In determining that Leoff and S&J had formed a partnership, the district court followed settled Colorado law. Colorado's version of the Uniform Partnership Act defines a partnership as "the association of two or more persons to carry on as co-owners a business for profit . . . whether or not the persons intend to form a partnership." Interpreting nearly identical language in an earlier partnership statute ("A partnership is an association of two or more persons to carry on, as co-owners, a business [*15] for profit. . . ."), the Colorado Supreme Court explained that "a partnership is a contract, express or implied, between two or more competent persons to place their money, effects, labor or skill, or some or all of them, into a business, and to divide the profits and bear the losses in certain proportions." As the final clause of the statutory definition indicates, parties can form a partnership by their conduct alone, regardless of their actual intentions.

The district court concluded that Leoff and S&J were partners because the 2006 Management Agreement provided for the sharing of profits and losses. The Agreement states that "Leoff is entitled to 30% of all profits or losses of S&J" and that "[i]f S&J suffered a loss rather than a profit, than [sic] Leoff's pro-rata share must be accounted for."

Leoff concedes that a partner cannot file a mechanic's lien against partnership property under Colorado law, but he disputes that he actually formed a partnership with S&J.

[continued]

In reviewing the district court's decision to the contrary, we must apply the same standard that the court should have applied in granting summary judgment. That is, we must view the record in the light most favorable to Leoff and ask whether it discloses any genuine issue of material fact with respect to the existence of a partnership.

Leoff argues that several facts undermine the district court's ruling. He points out that the parties never expressly designated each other as partners: the Agreement was titled "Management Agreement" rather than "Partnership Agreement," and it referred to Leoff not as a partner or owner, but as a "Manager." And he emphasizes the absence of any correspondence referring to the relationship as a partnership. But he ignores that a partnership can be created without any formalities and regardless of the parties' intentions. Similarly, Leoff's observation that the "Development Agreement and Operating Agreement of S & J Land Company, LLC," makes no mention of Leoff is irrelevant. The issue is whether Leoff and S&J became partners with each other, not whether Leoff was made a partner in S&J.

Leoff also calls attention to a Colorado statutory provision providing exceptions to the presumption that one who shares in a business's profits is a partner of that business. It states: "A person who receives a share of the profits of a business is presumed to be a partner in the business, unless the profits were received in payment . . . [f]or services as an independent contractor or of wages or other compensation to an employee. . . ." Leoff argues that his sharing in S&J's profits constituted wages for his contracting services and that the statute therefore rules out any presumption of a partnership. But Leoff was sharing in losses as well as profits. He has presented no authority that one sharing in both profits and losses can be merely an employee or an independent contractor.

Thus, we deny Leoff's challenges to the ruling of the district court that Leoff and S&J formed a partnership under Colorado law. The district court committed no error in awarding partial summary judgment to S&J.

We AFFIRM the district court's judgment regarding the formation of a partnership. We REVERSE the district court's denial of a final partnership accounting and the denial of attorney fees arising from the lien.

CRITICAL THINKING

What evidence led the court to determine that Leoff and S&J Land Company were partners? Do you think any evidence hints at suggesting that Leoff and S&J could have not been partners?

ETHICAL DECISION MAKING

Suppose for a moment that the court did not believe a partnership existed. Notice that business ethics requires that we think beyond ourselves. Use the universalization test to explain why one should not attempt to avoid partnership responsibilities.

BUT WHAT IF . . .

WHAT IF THE FACTS OF THE CASE OPENER WERE DIFFERENT?

Let's say that, in the Case Opener, Jones Law Firm and Lovelace Law Firm formed a partnership. Both firms had an equal voice when making decisions, and both firms had a single goal. However, Jones Firm did not receive profits from the partnership; it received only profits it made on its own because it was a new firm planning on getting clients through its relationship with Lovelace Firm. Which characteristics of a partnership are missing in this scenario?

In situations where there are no articles of partnership, the courts may look at other documentation to determine whether a partnership existed. Informal documentation, such as e-mails, notes, and memos, may be used to identify the existence of a partnership and/or the terms of a partnership. For example, before actress Vanessa Hudgens became famous through her recurring role in the *High School Musical* movie series, she worked with business manager Johnny Vieira. During their time together, Vieira claimed that he and Hudgens agreed to work together to launch her career and also agreed to share in the profits of her

E-COMMERCE AND THE LAW

FORMS OF PARTNERSHIPS IN THE ICT SECTOR IN DEVELOPING COUNTRIES

In the information and communication technology (ICT) sector of developing countries, businesses use partnerships between local and multinational companies to create a support structure. Three forms of partnership are especially important: (1) industrial districts, (2) *keiretsu* (a group of businesses in which each individual business has a stake in the others), and (3) offshore partnerships.

Industrial districts are loosely structured collectives of small to medium-size firms located in a specific area and highly specialized in one or more phases of a production process. Industrial districts are coordinated through both personal relationships and marketlike mechanisms. One purpose is to pool local competencies.

Keiretsus bring foreign ICT companies into a partnership and act as "hubs" served by local ICT ventures. *Keiretsus* add the strength of a competent hub, but over time this strength could make it less likely that local firms will develop strength of their own.

Offshore partnerships combine the strengths of outside firms with those of firms in developing countries. The developing-country firms use offshore partnerships to gain international exposure and technological competence. Foreign companies, such as U.S. and European Union (EU) firms, use offshore partnerships to gain (1) access to competent, low-cost workers and (2) the opportunity to enter developing markets.

success equally. However, once Hudgens became a teen star, Vieira claims that she stopped working with him and failed to pay him his portion of the profits. Consequently, Vieira filed a lawsuit against Hudgens, asking for $5 million in punitive damages. In his lawsuit, Vieira noted a signed photograph on which Hudgens wrote "Johnny, thank you for everything, without you, I would be no where, we will make it BIG—Vanessa Hudgens."[1] The case was set to go to trial; however, two weeks before trial, Hudgens and Vieira reached a settlement outside court.

Now that you know how the courts determine whether a partnership exists, what kind of legal status do partnerships have? They can be either legal entities or aggregates of the partners.

PARTNERSHIP AS A LEGAL ENTITY

In some respects, a partnership is treated as a *legal entity,* a "person" separate from the partnership with a life of its own.

First, a partnership is often considered a legal entity when it is sued or being sued. States determine when the partnership can or cannot be named in the suit. Second, under the doctrine of marshaling assets, partnership assets are arranged in a certain order to pay any outstanding debts. Partnership creditors have first priority on partnership assets, while individual personal creditors have first priority on the assets of the individual partners. Thus, partnership assets are kept separate from the individual partner assets.

Third, the partnership may hold title to property that individual partners do not hold. If the partners want to sell partnership property, all must participate in the transaction. Finally, every partner is considered an agent of the partnership, and each has a fiduciary relationship with the others.

PARTNERSHIP AS A LEGAL AGGREGATE

Sometimes a partnership is considered a legal aggregate of the partners, such as when partnership debts eventually become the debts of the individual partners. Further, the partnership is not taxed as a separate being; instead, the partners pay taxes on the income generated through the partnership. Finally, because the partnership ceases to exist when one of the partners dies (unless otherwise established by the partnership agreement), the partnership is then considered an aggregate of the individual partners.

[1] www.people.com/people/article/0,20218606,00.html.

Formation of the Partnership

LO2

What are the different ways in which a partnership can be formed?

While an explicit written agreement is not required to create a partnership, partners are advised to create one to ensure that the terms of the partnership will be upheld. Suppose that you and your partner orally agree you will receive three-fourths of the profits because you are doing significantly more management tasks. However, when you distribute the funds, your partner sues you because you give him only one-fourth of the profits. Without a written partnership agreement, the courts will have a difficult time ruling in your favor.

A written agreement that creates a partnership is called the **articles of partnership.** What kind of information do the articles usually include? First, the partners' names, as well as the name of the partnership, should be listed. Second, the agreement should address the duration of the partnership, such as the date or event that signals the agreement's expiration, or it should make the partnership's term indefinite. Third, the agreement should state the division of profits as well as losses. Fourth, it should establish the division of management duties. Fifth, the agreement should state exactly what capital contributions each partner will make.

Legal Principle: **A written agreement, although not legally mandatory, should be created when a partnership begins. This way, both parties can be protected if a dispute occurs or if an issue is brought to court.**

PARTNERSHIP BY ESTOPPEL

Parties not named in partnership agreements can sometimes be partners. How? Suppose you create a partnership agreement with your best friend. You then tell your first potential customer that your parents are also partners in the business. On the basis of your parents' participation, she decides to place an order with you. Your parents discover that you have reported they are your partners, but they do not contact the customer to tell her they are not partners. When your business cannot afford to purchase the goods to sell them to the customer, the customer sues you and your parents. Because your parents were aware of the misrepresentation but did not correct it, they will be estopped from denying they are your partners. While they will not be able to claim the rights associated with being a partner (such as sharing the profits), in many states they could be held liable for damages to the customer.

Most states recognize two situations in which a partnership by estoppel exists: (1) as in the example above, when a third party is aware of and consents to a misrepresentation of partnership, and (2) when a nonpartner has represented himself or herself as a partner and a third party *reasonably relies* on this information to his or her detriment. The nonpartner can be held liable for the third party's damages.

BUT WHAT IF . . .

WHAT IF THE FACTS OF THE CASE OPENER WERE DIFFERENT?

Let's say, in the Case Opener, that Lovelace and Jones law firms formed a partnership. To snag a potential client, they told the client that attorney John Barret was also in the partnership. Later, Lovelace and Jones reneged on their contract with the client. The client sued Lovelace, Jones, and Barret. How could Barret be liable for the faults of the Lovelace and Jones partnership?

Exhibit 36-2 summarizes how a partnership can be created.

Exhibit 36-2
Formation of a Partnership

A partnership can be formed by:	
Articles of partnership	A partnership is formed by a written agreement that states the partners' names, the name of the partnership, the duration of the partnership, the division of profits and losses, the division of management duties, and the capital contributions that will be made by each partner.
Estoppel	If a third party is aware of and consents to a misrepresentation of partnership, a partnership can be formed. Or if a nonpartner acts as a partner and a third party reasonably relies on this information, the nonpartner can be considered a partner and thus be liable for the third party's damages.

Interactions between Partners

L03 What are the rights of partners as they interact with each other?

The operation of the partnership encompasses two types of interactions: those between the partners and those between the partnership and third parties. The partners have certain rights and duties within each type.

DUTIES OF PARTNERS TO ONE ANOTHER

Most partners' duties to one another include the duty to be loyal. The duty to be loyal functions as an example of the fiduciary duty. Furthermore, most partners' duties include the duty of obedience. The duty of obedience is an example of the duty of care.

Perhaps the most important type of duty partners have toward one another is the fiduciary duty. Partners must, in good faith, work for the benefit of the partnership. They should not take any action that will undermine it, such as engaging in business that competes with it.

Partners must disclose any material facts affecting the business. A partner who derives benefit from the partnership without the consent of the other partners must notify them of this benefit. Case 36-2 considers how a partner's fiduciary duty conflicts with a partner's belief that another partner is behaving unethically.

CASE 36-2 COLETTE BOHATCH v. BUTLER & BINION
SUPREME COURT OF TEXAS
977 S.W.2D 543 (1998)

Colette Bohatch became an associate in the Washington, D.C., office of Butler & Binion in 1986. John McDonald and Richard Powers, both partners, were the only other attorneys in the office. After Bohatch was made a partner in February 1990, she became concerned that McDonald was overbilling Pennzoil, the office's main client. Bohatch met with the law firm's managing partner, Louis Paine, to report her concern. In July 1990, McDonald met with Bohatch to report that Pennzoil was dissatisfied with her work.

The next day, Bohatch spoke to Paine, as well as two other members of the law firm's management committee. Paine led an investigation of Bohatch's complaint and discussed the billed hours with the in-house counsel at Pennzoil, who concluded the bills were reasonable. In August 1990, Paine met with Bohatch, telling her that there was no basis for her claims against McDonald and that she should look for work elsewhere. The firm refused Bohatch a year-end partnership distribution for 1990. Finally, in August 1991, Bohatch was given until November to vacate her office. She filed suit in October 1991, and the firm voted to expel her from the partnership three days later.

At trial, the jury ruled the firm breached the partnership agreement and its fiduciary duty and awarded Bohatch

$57,000 for past lost wages, $250,000 for past mental anguish, $4,000,000 total in punitive damages (this amount was apportioned against several defendants), and attorney's fees. Later, the trial court reduced the punitive damages to around $237,000. The court of appeals ruled the firm's only duty to Bohatch was not to expel her in bad faith. When it found no evidence the firm had fired Bohatch for its own gain, the appeals court ruled Bohatch could not recover for breach of fiduciary duty. The case was appealed to the Supreme Court of Texas.

JUDGE ENOCH: We have long recognized as a matter of common law that "the relationship between . . . partners . . . is fiduciary in character, and imposes upon all the participants the obligation of loyalty to the joint concern and of the utmost good faith, fairness, and honesty in their dealings with each other with respect to matters pertaining to the enterprise." Yet, partners have no obligation to remain partners; "at the heart of the partnership concept is the principle that partners may choose with whom they wish to be associated." The issue presented, one of first impression, is whether the fiduciary relationship between and among partners creates an exception to the at-will nature of partnerships; that is, in this case, whether it gives rise to a duty not to expel a partner who reports suspected overbilling by another partner.

While Bohatch's claim that she was expelled in an improper way is governed by the partnership agreement, her claim that she was expelled for an improper reason is not. Therefore, we look to the common law to find the principles governing Bohatch's claim that the firm breached a duty when it expelled her.

Courts in other states have held that a partnership may expel a partner for purely business reasons. Further, courts recognize that a law firm can expel a partner to protect relationships both within the firm and with clients. Finally, many courts have held that a partnership can expel a partner without breaching any duty in order to resolve a "fundamental schism."

The fiduciary duty that partners owe one another does not encompass a duty to remain partners or else answer in tort damages. Nonetheless, Bohatch and several distinguished legal scholars urge this Court to recognize that public policy requires a limited duty to remain partners—i.e., a partnership must retain a whistleblower partner. They argue that such an extension of a partner's fiduciary duty is necessary because permitting a law firm to retaliate against a partner who in good faith reports suspected overbilling would discourage compliance with rules of professional conduct and thereby hurt clients.

While this argument is not without some force, we must reject it. A partnership exists solely because the partners choose to place personal confidence and trust in one another. Just as a partner can be expelled, without a breach of any common law duty, over disagreements about firm policy or to resolve some other "fundamental schism," a partner can be expelled for accusing another partner of overbilling without subjecting the partnership to tort damages. Such charges, whether true or not, may have a profound effect on the personal confidence and trust essential to the partner relationship. Once such charges are made, partners may find it impossible to continue to work together to their mutual benefit and the benefit of their clients.

We are sensitive to the concern expressed by the dissenting Justices that "retaliation against a partner who tries in good faith to correct or report perceived misconduct virtually assures that others will not take these appropriate steps in the future." However, the dissenting Justices do not explain how the trust relationship necessary both for the firm's existence and for representing clients can survive such serious accusations by one partner against another. The threat of tort liability for expulsion would tend to force partners to remain in untenable circumstance—suspicious of and angry with each other—to their own detriment and that of their clients whose matters are neglected by lawyers distracted with intra-firm frictions.

We emphasize that our refusal to create an exception to the at-will nature of partnerships in no way obviates the ethical duties of lawyers. Such duties sometimes necessitate difficult decisions, as when a lawyer suspects overbilling by a colleague. The fact that the ethical duty to report may create an irreparable schism between partners neither excuses failure to report nor transforms expulsion as a means of resolving that schism into a tort.

We hold that the firm did not owe Bohatch a duty not to expel her for reporting suspected overbilling by another partner.

AFFIRMED.

CRITICAL THINKING

Think about the judge's reasoning that led to the conclusion that the firm did not owe Bohatch a duty not to expel her for reporting suspected overbilling. Is there any additional information you would have liked to know to determine whether the firm should have been allowed to dismiss Bohatch?

ETHICAL DECISION MAKING

Bohatch made a decision about ethics when she chose to report what she suspected to be overbilling by a colleague. Do you think she made a good ethical decision? Would you guess she was guided by the Golden Rule, deontology, the universalization test, or some other method of ethical reasoning?

Exhibit 36-3
Duties of Partners to One Another

Fiduciary duty	The partners must work for the benefit of the partnership and not engage in any action or business that could undermine or compete with the partnership. The duty of obedience is an example of a fiduciary duty. The partners must obey the partnership agreement; if they disobey the agreement, they can be held liable for any losses.
Duty of care	The partners must perform their management functions to the best of their abilities.

The second type of duty the partners have is a duty of care to the other partners. Each partner must perform her management functions to the best of her abilities. A partner who makes an honest mistake in fulfilling responsibilities to the partnership will not be held liable for the mistake.

Exhibit 36-3 summarizes the primary duties of partners to one another.

RIGHTS OF THE PARTNERS IN THEIR INTERACTIONS WITH OTHER PARTNERS

According to the law, partners have certain rights regarding their interactions with other partners.

Right to Share in Management. Unless otherwise stated in the partnership agreement, all partners have a right to participate equally in the management of the partnership. Even if one partner has an unusually large proportion of the management duties, each partner will have one vote in determining how the partnership is managed.

While most decisions are made by majority vote, some require agreement by all partners. If the partners are voting on whether to change some element of their partnership agreement, they all must agree with the change. Other decisions that require a unanimous vote include the admission of new partners and alterations in the nature of the business.

Right to Share in Profits. If the partnership agreement does not establish another division of profits, all partners share equally in both profits and losses.

Right to Compensation. Unless otherwise agreed, no partner will receive a salary for participation in the business regardless of the amount of time and effort put in. Of course, the partners may agree to create salaries for certain partners, but no partner enters the partnership relationship with a right to compensation for performing business activities. If a partner dies during the term of the partnership, however, the surviving partners are entitled to compensation for services in closing the partnership's business affairs.

Property Rights. Partners have three property rights: (1) the right to participate in the management of the business, (2) the right to specific partnership property, and (3) the right to their partnership interest. (See Exhibit 36-4.) We've discussed the first right above; here we discuss the other two.

First, partners own the partnership property as *tenants in property,* which means they own it as a group. Any property brought into or acquired by the partnership is considered property of the partnership. Property in the name of an individual partner but purchased with partnership funds will be considered partnership property.

Exhibit 36-4
A Partner's Property Rights

Right to participate in the management of the business	All partners have a right to participate equally in the management of the partnership.
Right to specific partnership property	Partners own the partnership property as a group, and any property that is acquired by the partnership is considered property of the partnership. They have a right to this property but cannot use it to pay a personal debt and cannot sell or use the property if the purpose is outside the partnership interest. If a partner dies, the surviving partners receive the rights to the specific partnership property.
Right to partnership interest	Each partner has a right to the interest of the partner's share of the profits and a return on capital contributed by the partner. If a partner dies, the interest earned by the deceased partner is added to his or her estate and is not given back to the partnership.

One way to determine whether specific property is a partnership asset is to determine the relationship of the asset to the partnership. If the asset is closely related to the business of the partnership, it will likely be considered a partnership asset.

Each partner has the right to possess partnership property. However, a partner cannot use this property to pay a personal debt. Similarly, the partner cannot sell or use the property if the purpose is outside the partnership interest.

What happens to the partnership property if a partner dies? According to the **right of survivorship,** the rights in specific partnership property pass to the surviving partners. However, the surviving partners must account to the deceased partner's estate for the value of that partner's interest in the specific property.

Second, a partner has a right to interest in the partnership. This interest, composed of a combination of the partner's share of the profits and a return of capital contributed by the partner, is part of the partner's personal property. If necessary, a partner can sell his interest in the partnership to a creditor. A partner's personal creditor cannot seize specific items of partnership property; however, the creditor can obtain a **charging order,** which entitles the creditor to the partner's profits while the partner continues to act as a partner and engage in the partnership business.

Right to Inspect Books. Each partner has the right to receive full information regarding partnership matters. This right corresponds to the partners' fiduciary duty to disclose any information affecting the partnership. Thus, partners must have access to all partnership books and records and be allowed to make copies of them. Unless otherwise agreed, the records must be kept at the principal business office.

Right to an Account. An **accounting** is a review and listing of all partnership assets and/or profit and typically lists the distribution of assets and profit to the partners. Each partner has a right to an accounting in four circumstances:

- Whenever the partnership agreement provides for an accounting.
- Whenever the copartners wrongfully exclude a partner from the partnership or from access to the books.
- Whenever any partner fails to disclose a profit or benefit from the partnership, thus breaching his or her fiduciary duty.
- Whenever circumstances render an accounting "just and reasonable."

Legal Principle: Unless otherwise stated in the partnership agreement, a partner's rights include the right to share in management, the right to share in profits, the right to compensation, property rights, the right to inspect books, and the right to an account.

Interactions between Partners and Third Parties

LO4

Are all members of a partnership liable for interactions with third parties?

Each partner can serve as an agent for the other partners as well as for the partnership. As long as the partner has authority to act, each partner's act in performing business duties as well as making agreements with third parties is binding for the partnership. If the partner has authority to act and the partnership is bound by the act, each partner has unlimited personal liability for the obligation.

ACTUAL AUTHORITY OF THE PARTNERS

According to UPA, general agency principles establish that partners have the authority to bind a partnership in an agreement. If a partner, following normal business procedures, binds the partnership to an agreement, both the partner and the partnership are liable for the obligation in the agreement.

Suppose Brittany is a partner in a firm. While allegedly carrying on partnership business, she engages in a business transaction and binds the partnership to the agreement. Yet suppose Brittany really didn't have authority to bind the partnership to the agreement with the third party. In this case, both Brittany and the firm are liable for the obligation. However, if the third party was aware that Brittany did not have the authority to bind the partnership to the agreement, Brittany will be held liable for the obligation but the partnership will not.

IMPLIED AUTHORITY OF THE PARTNERS

Because of the nature of the partnership, partners generally have greater implied authority than do typical agents. Their implied authority is usually determined by the nature of the business, and it permits partners to enter into agreements necessary to carry on partnership business. Thus, a partner has the authority to purchase goods necessary to perpetuate the business. However, a partner does not have implied authority to sell any property without the consent of all other partners.

LIABILITY TO THIRD PARTIES

According to UPA, if a partnership is liable, each partner has unlimited personal liability. That is, all partners are **jointly liable** for the partnership's debts. To bring a claim, a party must either name all partners as defendants or simply name the partnership. If the claim is successful, each partner is liable for the judgment. If one partner pays the entire judgment, the other partners must indemnify, or reimburse, him or her. In the Case Opener, the partners of the different firms were concerned about their liability for the alleged conspiracy that occurred through their joint venture. The partners argued that they should not be held liable because they were not aware of the misconduct. How do you think the court should have ruled?

When a partner commits a tort or a breach of trust, all partners are jointly and severally liable. In fact, all partners are jointly and severally liable for the entire amount of any judgment rendered. **Joint and several liability** means that a third party can choose to sue the partners separately or all partners jointly in one action. Suppose William sues your partnership, which has four partners. William might name one of the partners in the first action. If the partner is found liable, William can sue all three other partners separately. However, if in the first claim the court ruled that the partnership was not liable in any form, William cannot bring a successful claim against a second partner on the issue of the partner's liability.

BUT WHAT IF . . .

WHAT IF THE FACTS OF THE CASE OPENER WERE DIFFERENT?

Let's say, in the Case Opener, that Lovelace and Jones law firms were in a partnership. Lovelace stipulated that it would make most of the decisions for the partnership since it was a more seasoned and successful law firm. What defense might Jones have, if any, to this seemingly unfair unilateral action?

If William brings a successful claim against a partner, he can collect the judgment only on the assets of one partner. The partner is required to reimburse the partnership for the damages it pays to William. Case 36-3 considers how other partners can be held liable for the negligence of one partner.

CASE 36-3 ERIC JOHNSON & LORI JOHNSON v. ST. THERESE MEDICAL CENTER

APPELLATE COURT OF ILLINOIS, SECOND DISTRICT

296 ILL. APP. 3D 341, 694 N.E.2D 1088, 1998 ILL. APP. LEXIS 301

In November 1990, Eric and Lori Johnson brought their 22-month-old daughter, Erica, to St. Therese Medical Center, where she was treated and released by Dr. Bruce Sands. Dr. Sands was a partner of Northern Illinois Emergency Physicians, Ltd. Drs. Richard Keller, Michael Oster, Thomas Braniff, Rodney Haenschen, and Phillip Gillespie were the other partners. The Johnsons filed suit against Dr. Sands and the partnership, arguing that Dr. Sands negligently caused the death of Erica and the partnership was liable because St. Therese acted on its behalf. A jury gave the Johnsons a $4 million award against Dr. Sands, St. Therese, and the partnership. Dr. Sands later filed for bankruptcy.

All the partners were issued citations to discover the assets of the partnership. At the citation hearings, all the partners (except Gillespie) admitted they were partners in the partnership at the time of the Johnson incident. In February 1997, the trial court judge ruled the Johnsons could proceed against the general partners individually if they were partners at the time of the incident. Consequently, the plaintiffs started motions to withhold the wages of all partners. Court proceedings ensued in which various partners argued they should not be held personally liable. Several were sentenced to jail time because they refused to testify regarding their personal assets. In June 1997, the trial court ruled that the assets of Keller, Haenschen, and Braniff be turned over to the Johnsons.

JUSTICE MCLAREN: We acknowledge that all partners are jointly and severally liable for everything chargeable to the partnership for the loss or injury of a third person due to any wrongful act or omission of any partner acting in the ordinary course of the business of the partnership. Further, "an unsatisfied judgment against a partnership in its firm name does not bar an action to enforce the individual liability of any partner." However, "[a] judgment entered against a partnership in its firm name is enforceable only against property of the partnership and does not constitute a lien upon real estate other than that held in the firm name." Therefore, where judgment is entered against a partnership, but not against the individual partners, the judgment may not be satisfied by the personal assets of the individual partners.

For example, in Cook, the Department of Revenue issued a notice of tax liability to a partnership. The Department of Revenue was unable to enforce the tax liability against the partnership because the Partnership had previously filed for bankruptcy. Therefore, the Department of Revenue attempted to enforce the partnership's tax liability against the plaintiff, a general partner. The partner received a copy and was aware of the contents of the notice of tax liability issued to the partnership. However, the Department of Revenue did not issue a notice of tax liability or a final assessment to the partner in his individual capacity.

Thus, the trial court granted the partner's motion for summary judgment.

This court affirmed, stating that, because a partnership can own property, it is a separate entity from its partners. Because the Department of Revenue issued notice of tax liability and the final assessment to the partnership, and not to the partner individually, and, because the Department of Revenue did not join the partner, the partner did not have notice that he could be liable personally for the partnership's tax debt. Thus, this court reasoned that the partner was denied due process.

The case at bar is closely analogous to Cook. The plaintiffs in the instant case named the Partnership, but not the individual Partners, in their complaint. The plaintiffs served the Partnership, but not the individual Partners. In addition, the Partners in this case, just like the partner in Cook, were aware of the contents of the plaintiffs' complaint against the Partnership. However, because the Partners were not named defendants and were not served in their individual capacities, they were not put on notice that their personal assets were at risk. Further, the plaintiffs in this case are unable to collect from Sands because he has filed for bankruptcy protection. Finally, judgment was entered against the Partnership, but not the individual Partners. Thus, the Partners were not judgment debtors and were not subject to citations proceedings to the extent that the plaintiffs had any claim upon the Partners' individual assets. Accordingly, the trial court erred when it attempted to enforce the judgment against the Partners by ordering the turnover of the Partners' assets and holding the Partners in contempt.

The plaintiffs argue that the Partners are judgment debtors because the partnership name is on the judgment order. However, the plaintiffs fail to recognize that "[a] judgment entered against a partnership in its firm name is enforceable only against property of the partnership." Because nothing in the record indicates that the Partners held assets which belonged to the Partnership, their argument fails.

Next, the plaintiffs argue that the Partners are judgment debtors because they are jointly and severally liable for the debts of the Partnership. We do not dispute this statement. However, the plaintiffs ignore the fact that judgment was entered against the Partnership, and not the Partners as individuals. Thus, until a judgment is entered against the Partners individually, the plaintiffs cannot recover from the Partners' personal assets.

The plaintiffs also argue that section 2-411(b) of the Code of Civil Procedure permits the enforcement of liability in supplementary proceedings against an individual partner. Section 2-411(b) provides, "An unsatisfied judgment against a partnership in its firm name does not bar an action to enforce the individual liability of any partner." Although "action" is not defined, the plaintiffs assert that a supplementary proceeding to collect a judgment is an "action" within the meaning of section 5/2-411(b). We disagree.

Section 12-102 of the Code of Civil Procedure provides that "[a] judgment entered against a partnership in its firm name is enforceable only against property of the partnership and does not constitute a lien upon real estate other than that held in the firm name." Under the plaintiffs' interpretation of section 2-411(b), this section has no meaning. Under the plaintiffs' interpretation, a judgment against only a partnership is enforceable against the partners individually without a judgment being entered against the partners individually. Because the plaintiffs' interpretation of section 2-411(b) renders section 12-102 ineffective, it cannot be adopted by this court.

Next, the plaintiffs assert that "a judgment against a partnership, by definition, is a judgment against each partner." However, this court's decision in Cook clearly contradicts the plaintiffs' position. In Cook, we held that, although partners are liable for the debts of the partnership, to be able to collect from the partners the plaintiff must provide the partners with notice that they will be individually liable for the partnership's debt. Since the plaintiffs failed to provide such notice, their argument fails.

REVERSED.

CRITICAL THINKING

Part of the confusion in this case was based on the ambiguity in Section 2-411(b) of the Code of Civil Procedure. Can you identify the ambiguity and explain how different interpretations of the code lead to different conclusions?

ETHICAL DECISION MAKING

Suppose you were one of the partners in this case. If you were guided by duty ethics, would any of the details of the case be altered?

COMPARING THE LAW OF OTHER COUNTRIES

DUTIES OF PARTNERSHIPS IN JAPAN

While the United States explains fiduciary duty as including a duty of "obedience" to your partner, the Japanese application of obedience and loyalty to partnerships far exceeds that of the United States. In Japan, a business partnership is expected to create a feeling of *giri* over time. *Giri* refers to feelings of honor, complete trust, and loyalty, and it is even associated with the decline of unmatched opportunities, financial or otherwise, in light of the maintenance of the relationship among the partners.

In Japan, there absolutely will not be the formation of a partnership without a nurtured and developed rapport among the partners to ensure that *giri* will be upheld throughout the partnership. Where U.S. partnerships may be separate from personal relationships, Japanese business partnerships are molded by the personal relationship of the partners. The requirement of *giri* creates a fiduciary duty of obedience and loyalty that is much more extreme than that of the United States.

Legal Principle: **As a general rule, if the partnership is liable, all partners are liable for the debts of the partnership. Furthermore, all partners are liable for a tort or breach of trust committed by a single partner.**

BUT WHAT IF . . .

WHAT IF THE FACTS OF THE CASE OPENER WERE DIFFERENT?

Let's say, in the Case Opener, that Lovelace and Jones law firms were in a partnership. They reneged on a contract with a client and were in the process of being sued by the client. At the same time, the partners joined with a new partner, Don Barrett. After the trial, Barrett realized the ordeal cut into his share of the profits too, even though the mistakes of the other partners were made long before Barrett joined the partnership. Can Barrett do anything to save himself from paying for the prior mistakes of the other firms?

LIABILITY OF INCOMING PARTNERS

When a partnership adds another partner, the new partner assumes limited liability for any obligations that occurred before he or she was added. The new partner cannot be held personally liable for them, but the capital the new partner adds can be used to pay them off. Clearly, because an incoming partner assumes limited liability, the dates of agreements, as well as the date the new partner was added, are extremely important.

The Revised Uniform Partnership Act

Just as the original Uniform Partnership Act governs partnerships in the absence of an express agreement, the Revised Uniform Partnership Act (RUPA) has significantly changed several laws that relate to partnerships. Since being approved in 1996, RUPA has been adopted in roughly half the states, so it is wise to determine whether the state in which a partnership was formed operates under UPA or RUPA. Although RUPA generally serves to expand UPA, there is some disagreement between them about the rules of partnership.

E-COMMERCE AND THE LAW

PARTNERSHIPS: AN ESSENTIAL PART OF ONLINE BUSINESS

Partnerships can be beneficial to many different businesses. Online, partnerships become almost a necessity. Unless a business owner has all the materials, technical savvy, and business sense to run an e-retail or similar business, the business owner must partner with another company to get the products and technical services the owner requires to have a functioning company. Since many online companies form such partnerships, those e-companies that don't create agreements with other businesses are likely to be much less competitive in the field of e-commerce. E-retailers that have partnered with other companies often can have more diversified product inventories. The partnered company may also have technical software that works better than the single company's software, because the partnered company's software was produced by a partner that specializes in that technical field. In the world of e-commerce, good partnerships can be one of the most powerful assets an e-company can have.

Source: www.ecommercetimes.com/story/32139.html.

CASE OPENER WRAP-UP

Joint-Venture Partnership and Liability

Under the Uniform Partnership Act (UPA) of 1997, a joint venture is liable for any penalty incurred as the result of a wrongful act or omission, or other actionable conduct, of a joint venturer acting in the ordinary course of business of the joint venture.

In this case, the appellants argued that the trial court applied an incorrect legal standard by imposing sanctions on them based on their status as joint venturers with the firms of the individual attorneys who engaged in conspiracy. However, because of the Uniform Partnership Act, the court concluded that it may in fact impose a sanction on a partnership based on its *vicarious liability* for a partner's litigation misconduct. Because a joint venture is defined as a single-purpose partnership, the court determined that a joint venture could be held liable.

KEY TERMS

accounting 803
articles of partnership 799
charging order 803
joint and several liability 804
jointly liable 804
partnership 795
right of survivorship 803

SUMMARY OF KEY TOPICS

Nature of the Partnership

The Uniform Partnership Act defines a partnership as "an association of two or more persons to carry on as co-owners a business for profit."

An essential element in a partnership is the sharing of profits from the partnership.

Formation of the Partnership

A partnership is created by the articles of partnership, which should include the name of each partner and the partnership, the duration of the partnership, how profits will be divided, the division of management duties, and the contributions to be made by each partner. A partnership can also be formed by estoppel. When a person relies to his detriment on a misrepresentation by a nonpartner that he is a partner, then the nonpartner will be held liable as if he is a partner.

Interactions between Partners

Each partner has specific duties, including:

- Duty to be loyal
- Duty of obedience
- Duty of care

Each partner has specific rights, including:

- Right to share in management
- Right to inspect books
- Right to compensation
- Rights to partnership property

Interactions between Partners and Third Parties

If a partnership has a liability, each partner has unlimited personal liability. All partners are jointly and severally liable for the commission of a tort by any partner.

There is only implied liability when purchases are made to perpetuate the partnership's business.

The Revised Uniform Partnership Act

RUPA is a revised version of UPA, and its use varies from state to state.

POINT / COUNTERPOINT

Should a Minor Be Allowed to Enter into a Business Partnership?

YES

Individuals under the age of 18 should be allowed to enter into business partnerships. If an existing business decides that a business created by a minor is a desirable partner, the minor should be able to enter into that partnership on grounds of personal liberty.

Although the United States and other countries act as if adulthood occurs at an arbitrary point in time (age 18 in the United States), research argues differently. According to Richard Fabes and Carol Lynn Martin's *Exploring Child Development,** 18 is just one year in a five-year phase called *late adolescence* or *early adulthood.* Levels of maturity and decision-making abilities vary greatly. Some individuals over 18, who may enter into contracts and partnerships, may not be as mature as other young adults a few years their junior.

Some people say minors are not accustomed to making decisions that affect the lives of others. But young adults already make life-altering decisions. In most states, the age of consent for sexual intercourse is 16, while some states (Iowa, Missouri, and South Carolina) and other developed countries (Italy and Iceland) set it as low as 14.

NO

Individuals under the age of 18 should not be allowed to enter into a business partnership. They are considered juveniles in the eyes of the law and are treated differently in court.

According to UPA, a partnership can be valid only when the relationship between partners is *voluntary* and *consensual.* Juveniles in the United States are not allowed to consent to participating in several activities because they are rightfully considered immature and inexperienced. They cannot consent to participate in a sexual relationship (in some states), marry or sign prenuptial agreements, purchase or smoke cigarettes or other tobacco products, gamble, or purchase or consume alcohol. They should also be considered too immature to make the life-altering decision of entering into a business.

A juvenile is a dependent of his or her parents. Parents decide how to invest their child's money, which schools their child should attend, and what time their child should be required home. Because parents play such a significant role in their child's life, juveniles are not accustomed to making major decisions.

Furthermore, 16- and 17-year-olds are allowed to obtain a driver's license in most states. Offenders under 18 can be tried as adults in a criminal court and be sentenced to life in prison.

If a minor has been smart and responsible enough to create a profitable business, one so successful that another business wants to create a partnership, she or he should be allowed to enter into the partnership.

It isn't fair to expect a juvenile partner to take an equal role in managing the partnership and making money when the juvenile is devoting most of his or her time to growing, developing, and learning in school.

*Informational website: http://wps.ablongman/ab_fabes_exploring_2/0,4768,225940-,00.html.

QUESTIONS & PROBLEMS

1. Explain each element of UPA's definition of a partnership.
2. What is the distinction between partnership as a legal entity and partnership as a legal aggregate?
3. What is the relationship between the obligations of a general partner and those of a limited partner?
4. Abdul Bensaid and Cynthia Brown are the sole members of Nadia's LLC, a limited liability company that owns and operates Nadia's Restaurant. After purchasing the restaurant, Bensaid discussed possible renovations for the building with the Alexander Company. Bensaid met with an architect at the restaurant several times. Brown was present at one of those meetings, but neither she nor Bensaid stated they were or were not operating as a partnership and neither disclosed that they were part of a limited liability company. Later, Bensaid entered into a contract with Alexander Company for remodeling work. Bensaid was designated in the contract as both the owner and the owner's representative. Brown did not sign the contract, but she did issue a check from her personal checking account for the initial work at the restaurant. Furthermore, when Alexander Company asked Bensaid to provide proof of financial ability before completion of the renovations, it received a letter from the bank indicating that Brown was approved for a loan in the amount of $75,000, contingent on an appraisal of her home. However, Alexander Company was not paid any additional amounts allegedly owed and subsequently filed a complaint against Bensaid and Brown. Brown rejected the notion that she should be found liable since she was not in a partnership with Bensaid. Alexander Company alleged that on the basis of its course of dealings with Bensaid and Brown, it was led to believe that the two were partners and assumed joint responsibility for payments. Did a partnership by estoppel exist between Bensaid and Brown in their dealings with Alexander Company? [*The Alexander Company, Inc. v. Abdul Bensaid and Cynthia Brown,* 2002 WI App 165, 256 Wis. 2d 693, 647 N.W.2d 467 (2002).]
5. EZ Auto is a limited liability company. The company is managed by Marks. The other party in this case, H.M. Jr. Auto Sales, is in the wholesale automobile business. In February 1999, H.M. sold three vehicles to EZ Auto via an envelope draft. In an envelope draft, the selling dealer places the title and other documents in an envelope and deposits them with his bank, which forwards the envelope and its contents to the purchasing dealer's bank. The purchasing dealer verifies the accuracy and completeness of the documents and then orders his bank to pay the selling dealer for the draft. After three unsuccessful attempts to pay for the vehicles, Marks wrote a personal check to pay for the three cars. Marks went to purchase a fourth car, which he again paid with a personal check. The fourth vehicle was noted as belonging to EZ, a third party through a title transfer. The check was returned with a note of insufficient funds, and H.M. sued EZ Auto. How could this case have been avoided? [*EZ Auto, LLC v. H.M. Jr. Auto Sales,* 04-01-00820-CV, WL 1758315 (Tex. App. 2002).]
6. Ian M. Starr was a partner in the law firm Fordham & Starrett. After Starr's first year of employment, the firm's profits were divided evenly among all partners. During his second year with the firm, Starr's relationship with the other partners began

to deteriorate, and he quit the firm on the last day of the year. Listing several negative factors relevant to Starr's performance, the firm paid him less than half an equal share. Starr brought an action to recover amounts to which he claimed he was entitled under the partnership agreement. He also claimed breach of fiduciary duty. Starr's former partners counterclaimed that Starr had violated his fiduciary duties to the partners and breached the partnership agreement. How do you think the court settled this conflict? [*Starr v. Fordham,* 648 N.E.2d 1261 (1995).]

7. The Vancouver Group is made up of five investors, Pietz, Wynne, Fordham, Indermuehle, and Smith. The group entered into a partnership with Robert Berry for the joint purchase of the Sundance Hotel and Casino. The group and Berry made an offer to purchase the hotel. Pietz agreed to supply $500,000 to the deal and post a $285,000 letter of credit. However, after receiving information that caused him to doubt Berry, Pietz withdrew his interests from the partnership. Berry threatened to sue Pietz for breach of contract, fraud, and tortious breach of the covenant of good faith. Pietz and Berry settled, and Pietz subsequently sued the group for the cost of the settlement. The trial court rejected Pietz's claim of breach of fiduciary duty. He appealed the decision. How do you think the court decided? Was there a breach of fiduciary duty? [*Pietz v. Indermuehle,* 949 P.2d 449 (1998).]

8. David Byker was an accountant working for Tom Mannes. The two talked about going into business together because they had complementary business skills—Mannes (defendant) could locate certain properties because of his real estate background and Byker (plaintiff) could raise money for the property purchases. Subsequently, the two agreed to engage in an ongoing business enterprise, to furnish capital, labor, and/or skill to the enterprise, to raise investment funds, and to share equally in the profits, losses, and expenses of the enterprise. To facilitate the investment of limited partners, Byker and Mannes created separate entities wherein they were general partners or shareholders for the purposes of operating each separate entity. After the two men encountered some financial difficulties with a venture, Byker approached Mannes with regard to equalizing payments as a result of the losses incurred with the failed business opportunity. Mannes claims that this was the first time he ever received notice about any outstanding payments. After unsuccessfully seeking reimbursement from Mannes, Byker filed suit for the recovery of the money on the basis that the two men had entered into a partnership. Specifically, Byker asserted that the obligations between him and the defendant were not limited to their formal business relationships established by the individual partnerships and corporate entities but that there was a "general" partnership underlying all their business affairs. In response, Mannes asserted that he merely invested in separate business ventures with the plaintiff and that there were no other understandings between them. Did the two businessmen form a partnership, or were their business deals all separate ventures? Was there intent to make a consensual business relationship even though Mannes argues there was not? [*Byker v. Mannes,* 465 Mich. 637, 641 N.W.2d 210 (2002).]

9. Rahemi Taghipour and Jerez, his brother, formed Taghipour and Associates, LLC, in Utah. The agreement of the LLC designated Jerez as manager of the limited liability company. The operating agreement between the LLC members stated that no loans could be made in the name of the LLC unless authorized by a resolution of all the members. Jerez obtained a loan on behalf of the LLC from Mt. Olympus without the other members' knowledge. Jerez failed to make loan payments, the LLC defaulted, and thus Mt. Olympus foreclosed on the LLC's property. The other members of the LLC sued Jerez. What should Jerez have done differently? [*Taghipour v. Jerez,* 52 P.3d 1252 (Utah S. Ct. 2002).]

10. Lyle's Plumbing was a limited liability corporation in which Dean Clegg, a shareholder of the LLC, held 51 percent of the ownership. During March 2000, the other shareholder of Lyle's Plumbing, Lyle Gehringer, met with John Warren, Warren Supply's president and CEO, to arrange for open credit for Lyle's Plumbing. Warren gave Gehringer a single-page document for Lyle's Plumbing to submit. The top of the page contained an application for credit. The bottom half contained a personal guaranty. The guaranty stated:

> In consideration of extending credit at my request by completing this new account application, I hereby personally guarantee to you, Warren Supply Co., of

any obligation and I hereby agree to bind myself to pay you on demand any sum which may become due to you by my firm whenever the firm shall fail to pay the same, plus any reasonable collection and attorney fee Warren Supply Co. incurs in collection of the debt. It is understood that this guarantee shall be a continuing and irrevocable guarantee and modification or renewal of the credit agreement hereby guaranteed.

Clegg signed the document, which designated him as the "member." Lyle's Plumbing faulted on its account, failing to pay, and Warren Supply Co. sued. Do you feel that Clegg was personally responsible for Lyle's faulting on the account? [*Warren Supply Company v. Lyle's Plumbing,* L.L.C., 74 S.W.3d 816 (Mo. Ct. App. 2002).]

Looking for more review materials?

The Online Learning Center at **www.mhhe.com/kubasek3e** contains this chapter's "Assignment on the Internet" and also a list of URLs for more information, entitled "On the Internet." Find both of them in the Student Center portion of the OLC, along with quizzes and other helpful materials.

CHAPTER 37

Partnerships: Termination and Limited Partnerships

LEARNING OBJECTIVES

After reading this chapter, you will be able to answer the following questions:

1. What are the steps in the termination of a partnership?
2. How is a limited partnership formed?
3. What are the rights and privileges of a limited partner and a general partner?

CASE OPENER

Partnership Problems of Wildmeadow Village

Christian Wyller was a partner in Wildmeadow Village partnership, which owned an office building in Juneau, Alaska. Under difficult economic circumstances, the partnership received an invitation to bid (ITB) from the state of Alaska to lease approximately 7,000 square feet of office space for five years. Wildmeadow secured the bid from the state. The partners held a partnership meeting and approved the state lease and various improvements necessary to meet the bid specifications. At the partnership meeting, it was reported that improvements of roughly $120,000 were necessary to meet the state bid. However, some of Wyller's partners authorized work on the entire building, including repairs not necessary for the state lease and not properly approved by the partnership. The total cost of repairs and improvements actually made to the building was $257,000, and the excess repairs were not authorized by the entire partnership.

After construction began, the partners discovered that their loan application to the bank was rejected and they would have to pay for the entirety of the repairs out of pocket. Wyller expressed reluctance to pledge cash or personal collateral for a loan, objected to substantial expenditures made without authorization, and said that he was at the limit of his resources. He would not pay for repairs he did not approve. Subsequently, the construction bills were not paid, and the construction company brought suit against Wildmeadow Village partnership and its individual partners. At trial, Wyller argued that he was entitled to damages because he did not authorize the repairs and he did not wrongfully cause the dissolution of the partnership. The court found Wyller partially at fault for the dissolution of the partnership and therefore not entitled to damages from the other partners. Wyller appealed to the supreme court of Alaska.

1. Should Wyller have to pay construction costs for the repairs he did not authorize?
2. How are partnerships dissolved?

The Wrap-Up at the end of the chapter will answer these questions.

Termination of the Partnership

LO1

What are the steps in the termination of a partnership?

Before any partnership can be considered completely terminated, it must go through the *dissolution stage* and the *winding-up stage.* **Dissolution** is complete when any partner stops fulfilling the role of a partner to the business (by choice or default). Partners complete the **winding-up** stage by taking account of the assets of the partner who has left and redistributing them among the other partners. The sections below explain the steps that must occur in the dissolution and winding-up stages for the termination to be complete. (Exhibit 37-1 summarizes all the stages in the life cycle of a partnership.)

Exhibit 37-1

The Life Cycle of a Partnership

The Life of a Partnership

Formation

A partnership is formed either by a written agreement (the articles of partnership) or by estoppel

Performance

Business is conducted as the partners work for the benefit of the partnership in accordance with the partnership agreement

Dissolution

A partnership dissolves either by an act of the court, an act of the partners, or an operation of the law

Winding Up

Partners complete any unfinished partnership business, collect and pay debts, collect partnership assets, and take inventory

Termination or Continuation

The partnership is terminated	The partnership continues by creating a continuation agreement

Dissolution of the Business

Section 29 of UPA defines *dissolution* as "the change in the relation of the partners caused by any partner's ceasing to be associated with the carrying on, as distinguished from the winding up"—the activity of completing unfinished partnership business, collecting and paying debts, collecting partnership assets, and taking inventory—"of the business." It is important to note that dissolution does not necessarily mean that the business cannot continue functioning; it simply means that there is a significant change in partner relations. Indeed, a partnership can continue after dissolution.

What might cause the dissolution of the partnership? The dissolution may occur by an act of the partners, an operation of the law, or an act of the court (see Exhibit 37-2). One significant issue in the case of the Wildmeadow Village partnership was whether the dissolution of the business occurred properly. As you read this section, keep the Case Opener in mind to decide for yourself how Wyller's partnership was dissolved.

ACT OF PARTNERS

The partnership is a voluntary and consensual relationship, so the partners have the power to dissolve it at almost any time. They may simply agree that it will terminate at a certain time. Suppose Soo and Geraldo, two partners in a college preparation business, are graduating from college. They both plan to accept jobs at other firms; neither expects to continue the college preparation business. When they created this business, they might have agreed to dissolve the partnership when one of them graduated from college. However, if the business is either a flop or an enormous success, they can agree to dissolve the partnership early or extend its term after graduation.

Alternatively, partners might agree to dissolve the partnership once they achieve a certain objective. Consider a partnership to sell homes in a housing development. Once all the homes have been sold, the partners may agree to dissolve the partnership.

When can a partnership be **rightfully dissolved,** meaning the dissolution does not violate the partnership agreement? We have established two circumstances above (after meeting an established objective and at the end of the term stated in the partnership agreement). Here are others:

1. *A partner withdraws from the partnership at will.* (A *partnership at will* is an agreement that does not specify the objective or duration of the partnership.)

Exhibit 37-2
Causes of a Partnership Dissolution

Act by a partner	A partner withdraws from the partnership at will. A partner withdraws or is expelled according to the partnership agreement (e.g., once the partnership has achieved a certain objective or a certain amount of time has passed).
Operation of the law	A partner dies. A partner is adjudicated bankrupt. The partnership engages in an activity that becomes illegal.
Act of the court	A partner is adjudicated insane. Continuing the partnership becomes impractical. A partner is incapable of carrying out the duties established by the agreement. The court dissolves the partnership for other reasons.

CASE NUGGET

PARTNERSHIP DISSOLUTION

In re Leah Beth Woskob, Debtor; Alex Woskob; Helen Woskob; the Estate of Victor Woskob v. Leah Beth Woskob, Appellant
U.S. Court of Appeals for the Third Circuit
305 F.3d 177 (2002)

In 1996, Leah Beth Woskob and Victor Woskob formed a partnership, the Legends Partnership, to construct, own, and operate the Legends, an apartment building. Married when they formed the partnership, the Woskobs separated and filed for divorce the following year. During the divorce proceedings, Victor prevented Leah from receiving any of the partnership proceeds. Leah was granted a petition for special relief and awarded the exclusive right to manage and derive income from the partnership. Shortly thereafter, Victor filed for bankruptcy. Leah continued to file tax returns on behalf of the partnership, each of which listed Victor as a general partner. When Victor died in a car accident in 1999, Leah gave his estate notice that she was exercising her right to buy out Victor's interest in the partnership. Victor's estate sued, claiming the partnership had already been dissolved and requesting that someone be appointed to oversee its winding up and a full accounting of the company's assets. When Leah filed for bankruptcy, the suits were moved to the bankruptcy court. The bankruptcy court ruled in favor of Leah, finding that the partnership had dissolved on Victor's death. Victor's estate appealed to the district court, which found that the partnership had dissolved two years *before* Victor's death, making Leah's attempt to buy out Victor's interest untimely. Leah appealed.

The task before the appeals court was to determine the timeliness of Leah's attempt to buy out Victor's interest in the partnership, which depended entirely on the date of the dissolution of the partnership. The court looked to the Uniform Partnership Act (UPA), which defined the dissolution of a partnership as "the change in the relation of the partners caused by any partner ceasing to be associated in the carrying on, as distinguished from the winding up, of the business." Victor's estate claimed that the dissolution occurred at any one of three points, each at least 18 months before Victor's death. First, Victor excluded Leah from the partnership after they separated; second, Leah excluded Victor from the partnership after seeking special relief from the Court of Common Pleas; third, Victor filed for bankruptcy.

The appeals court found that the exclusions of Leah and Victor from the partnership were not, in and of themselves, grounds for automatic dissolution of the partnership. Rather, they could have provided a *basis* for dissolution, had either Leah or Victor sought judicial decree of the dissolution after being excluded. In addition, bankruptcy in and of itself is not grounds for automatic dissolution of the partnership. If the nondebtor partner does not consent to continue the partnership with the debtor, bankruptcy may be grounds for dissolution. However, Leah continued to list Victor as a general partner on the tax returns she filed for the partnership, even after he filed for bankruptcy. Thus, the appeals court found that the partnership had not dissolved prior to Victor's death in 1999 and that Leah's attempt to buy out Victor's interest in the partnership was therefore timely.

BUT WHAT IF . . .

WHAT IF THE FACTS OF THE CASE OPENER WERE DIFFERENT?

Let's say, in the Case Opener, that when Wyller and his partners formed their partnership, they agreed that the partnership would be dissolved after five years. However, right around the five-year mark, the partners discussed doing construction on their properties to receive the leasing deal from the state of Alaska. At the five-year mark, Wyller decided he was not going to be a partner anymore and, further, he was not going to be financially involved in the construction. The other partners attempted to sue Wyller, arguing that he could not dissolve the partnership because the partnership responsibilities had evolved over time and the five-year agreement was now arbitrary. Which side is acting in accordance with the law?

2. *A partner withdraws in accordance with the partnership agreement.* The partnership agreement may establish specific reasons that a partner may withdraw.
3. *A partner is expelled from the partnership in accordance with the partnership agreement.* Suppose you are a partner in a law firm and you steal some type of property from the partnership. The partnership agreement will usually determine the reasons a partner may be removed from the partnership, and theft is often one of them.

If a partnership is rightfully dissolved, all partners can demand that it be wound up and can participate in that process. Moreover, if the partners unanimously agree, they can continue the business using the partnership's name.

However, a partner who dissolves the partnership in violation of the partnership agreement can be held liable for **wrongful dissolution.** That partner cannot require that the business be wound up but can be held liable for damages to the remaining partners. They can choose to continue the business under the partnership name or wind it up.

In the Case Opener, if Wyller dissolved the partnership wrongfully, he could be liable for damages resulting from the failure to pay construction costs for the renovations. Because none of the partners withdrew at will or left the partnership in accordance with the partnership agreement, it appears that the Wildmeadow Village partnership was dissolved wrongfully. Now the court must decide who was responsible for the dissolution and whether it was indeed Wyller who dissolved the partnership wrongfully. If Wyller is responsible, he cannot require the winding up of his partnership and he may be held liable for the damages to the construction company.

Legal Principle: As a general rule, the partners have the power to dissolve the partnership at almost any time.

BUT WHAT IF . . .

WHAT IF THE FACTS OF THE CASE OPENER WERE DIFFERENT?

Let's say, in the Case Opener, that while Wyller was arguing that he had no financial responsibility toward the extra construction he did not agree to, he was also trying not to pay for the construction he did approve along with the other partners. Thus, without Wyller's contribution to any construction, the partnership could not exist anymore. What kind of dissolution occurred here, and what could Wyller be liable for?

OPERATION OF LAW

Several circumstances provided by law can dissolve a partnership: if a partner dies, if a partner is adjudicated bankrupt, or if the partnership business engages in an activity that suddenly becomes illegal. Suppose Congress decides cigarettes are illegal. A partnership that manufactures and sells cigarettes will be automatically dissolved.

ACT OF THE COURT

A partner may apply to the court to dissolve the partnership for any of the following reasons:

- A partner is adjudicated insane.
- It becomes impractical to carry out the business of the partnership (continuing will result only in lost profits).
- A partner is incapable of carrying out his or her duties as established by the partnership agreement.
- Other special circumstances exist. Suppose partners begin bitterly disagreeing about how the business should be managed, preventing the cooperation necessary for a partnership to exist. In this instance, the court can dissolve the partnership.

Case 37-1 is one in which the court decides whether to dissolve a partnership.

CASE 37-1 MILLER v. BILL & CAROLYN LTD. P'SHIP
U.S. COURT OF APPEALS FOR THE 10TH CIRCUIT
593 F.3D 1155 (2010)

A family limited partnership, including Carolyn Baldwin who owned 99% limited partnership interest, was involved in a bankruptcy proceeding with a bankruptcy trustee, Miller. Following the initiation of the proceedings, Miller filed an adversary proceeding against the partnership and the general partner, seeking a declaration that Mrs. Baldwin's interest in the partnership now belonged to the bankruptcy estate. Miller then asserted that the partnership should be dissolved, due to the general partner's refusal to recognize the bankruptcy estate's interest in the partnership. The bankruptcy court ruled in favor of the trustee, and ordered the dissolution of the partnership. On appeal, the Bankruptcy Appellate Panel (BAP) reversed the court's decision regarding dissolution, and the trustee appealed the BAP's reversal of the court's decision.

JUDGE MCKAY: Oklahoma law provides that [o]n application by or for a partner[,] the district court may decree dissolution of a limited partnership whenever it is not reasonably practicable to carry on the business in conformity with the partnership agreement. The trustee argues that he is entitled to judicial dissolution of the limited partnership pursuant to this statute. Because family estate planning was the purpose of the partnership, he argues, the partnership can no longer lawfully carry on its business in conformity with the partnership agreement—it would be improper for the limited partnership to be run for family estate planning purposes now that the 99% limited partnership interest has become part of the bankruptcy estate. He also argues that the general partner's refusal to acknowledge the bankruptcy estate's interest in the partnership is grounds for judicial dissolution.

While Mrs. Baldwin's father testified at trial that the partnership was established for estate planning purposes, the partnership agreement itself expressly provides that "[t]he purpose of this Partnership shall be to engage in general business activities including but not limited to the purchasing, holding, construction, owning, operation, improving, managing, mortgaging, leasing and selling of and dealing in and with real property." Mrs. Baldwin's father testified at trial about the partnership's holding and management of real property and about various profit-seeking activities the partnership had engaged in over the past several years. He also testified that all of the partnership's profits had been put back into the partnership property. Finally, he testified that he anticipated property values to rise in the future, at which point the partnership would potentially develop a subdivision or sell some or all of its acreage for a profit. This testimony was not rebutted at trial, nor was any evidence introduced to indicate that the limited partner's bankruptcy filing had caused the partnership to deviate from its stated purpose of engaging in business activities including holding, owning, improving, and managing real property.

After reviewing the partnership agreement and the evidence introduced at trial, we agree with the BAP that the bankruptcy court clearly erred in finding the partnership could no longer carry on its business in conformity with the partnership agreement. All of the evidence in the record indicates that the partnership was continuing to carry out its business in accordance with the partnership agreement just as it had been for the past ten years. We see nothing in the Oklahoma statute permitting judicial dissolution when a partnership's business operations are continuing to be carried out in accordance with the partnership agreement, even if a new limited partner wishes to change the operation of the partnership. We note that the partnership agreement does not require any participation by or cooperation with the limited partner in the partnership's business activities, and nothing in the partnership agreement required the general partner to acknowledge or accede to the new limited partner's requests for the partnership to deviate from its long-term investment strategies. We also agree with the BAP that the general partner did not breach the partnership agreement or call its validity into question by disputing a contested issue regarding the bankruptcy trustee's interest in the partnership. We reject the trustee's argument that certain alleged improper practices by the general partner constituted grounds for dissolution. We see nothing clearly erroneous in the bankruptcy court's finding that the general partner's practices did not amount to a breach of fiduciary duty, and the trustee has cited to no legal authority indicating that the complained-of actions otherwise justified dissolution of the limited partnership under Oklahoma law.

Thus, because we see nothing in either the partnership agreement or the evidence introduced at trial to indicate that it was not reasonably practicable for the partnership to carry on its business in conformity with the partnership agreement, we affirm the BAP's reversal of the bankruptcy court's order of dissolution.

AFFIRMED.

[continued]

CRITICAL THINKING

Review the court's reasoning in this case. What evidence would the court have needed to approve an order of dissolution? The court provides hints about what that evidence would be.

ETHICAL DECISION MAKING

The text discusses the dissolution of the partnership and explains how partners can be penalized if they attempt to leave the partnership wrongfully. What is the *purpose* of the protection of the partnership? In other words, which values can you think of that support the act of protecting a partnership?

Consequences of Dissolution

A partner who intends to dissolve or withdraw from the partnership must give the other partners notice of this intent. Once the partnership is dissolved, the partner no longer has actual authority to bind the partnership. However, if the partnership does not notify third parties of the dissolution, the partner can still have implied authority to bind the partnership. Suppose one of the partners in the college preparation business intends to dissolve the partnership. Before Soo can notify Geraldo of her intent, he makes an agreement to begin working with five new students to prepare them for college. Because Soo has not yet given notice of her intent to dissolve, she is still liable for the agreement Geraldo has made.

To ensure that a dissolving partner does not create additional liability for the partnership, firms usually take active steps to notify third parties about the dissolution, often by placing an advertisement in the newspaper. However, firms must provide direct verbal or written notice to any third party that has provided credit to the partnership.

BUT WHAT IF . . .

WHAT IF THE FACTS OF THE CASE OPENER WERE DIFFERENT?

Let's say, in the Case Opener, that after first hearing about a possible construction project that the partners would have to finance, Wyller decides he is going to dissolve his partnership responsibilities. However, he does not inform the other partners of his decision, and the partners sign the construction deal. Wyller tells the other partners that he is pulling his money out of the partnership and will be in no way financially liable for the construction because he has been planning to dissolve the partnership. Is Wyller acting in accordance with the law in this scenario?

After the dissolution of the partnership, the partners' next step is either winding up the business or continuing the partnership or business. We'll discuss winding up the business first.

Winding Up the Business

Once a partnership has been liquidated, the partners begin the process of winding up, the activity of completing unfinished partnership business, collecting and paying debts, collecting partnership assets, and taking inventory. During the process, the partners must still fulfill their fiduciary duty to one another and disclose all information about the partnership assets. However, they can engage in business that competes with the partnership business. Case 37-2 examines a partner's fiduciary duty during the winding-up period of the termination of the partnership.

COMPARING THE LAW OF OTHER COUNTRIES

DISSOLUTION OF PARTNERSHIP IN INDIA

In India, the Indian Partnership Act distinguishes between "dissolution of partnership" and "dissolution of the firm." *Dissolution of the firm* refers to the dissolving of *all* partners and the termination of the partnership business. On the other hand, *dissolution of partnership* refers to the termination of the relationship between certain partners but the continuation of the partnership's business.

In India, there are several grounds for dissolution of the firm:

1. Agreement by all partners to dissolve the contract relationship and business.
2. Dissolution by notice.
3. Dissolution due to contingencies such as expiration of a fixed term, completion of the purpose of the partnership's business, or death of a partner.
4. Compulsory dissolution.
5. Dissolution by the court.

COMPARING THE LAW OF OTHER COUNTRIES

TERMINATION OF PARTNERSHIPS IN SPAIN

In Spain, full dissolution is permitted in four situations (*full dissolution* simply means that the partnership ends without litigation or a waiting period): (1) One partner dies, (2) a partner is declared insane and unfit to manage the business, (3) a partner is declared bankrupt, and (4) a partner requests that the partnership be terminated.

Spain also allows for *provisional* (temporary) *dissolution,* followed by litigation to determine the legitimacy of the termination request. Provisional dissolution occurs when (1) a partner fails to comply with provisions of the contract, (2) a partner inexplicably abandons the partnership and does not return on request, (3) a partner fails to bring the capital he or she promised, (4) a partner is accused of fraud or mismanagement, (5) a partner exceeds the limits of his or her power, and (6) a partner uses capital belonging to the partnership in his or her own name.

During partial dissolution, the accused partner is excluded from all managerial responsibilities and profits and from any liability from business conducted during this time. Provisional dissolution prevents those unfairly accused of certain behaviors from losing their position in the partnership. But the process can be a tedious and lengthy one, whether the partial dissolution moves to complete termination or the partnership resumes.

CASE 37-2 JACK A. KAHN AND DENISE W. KAHN v. STEWART MESHER AND LIESELOTTE MESHER

COURT OF APPEALS OF WASHINGTON, DIVISION ONE

2000 WASH. APP. LEXIS 2090 (2000)

Stewart Mesher and Jack "Alder" Kahn jointly invested in real estate for approximately 30 years. In October 1993, Mr. Kahn notified Mr. Mesher that he was dissolving the partnership. One year later, the parties entered into an agreement (the "SMAK Agreement") which governed the terms of the wind-down of the partnership, including the distribution of partnership properties. The SMAK Agreement specifically addressed the sale of a parcel of land called the Bothell property.

An outside party known as Sundquist wanted to make an offer on the Bothell property. Mr. Mesher arranged to sell the property secretly for $984,000 without informing Mr. Kahn of the offer. Mr. Mesher then went to Mr. Kahn to arrange for Mr. Kahn to sell him his shares in the Bothell property, still without telling him about the impending sale of the property. After the transfer of shares, Mr. Mesher signed a purchase and sale agreement for the Bothell property for $961,000 Subsequently, Mr. Kahn sued Mr. Mesher for breach of fiduciary duty to the partnership during the winding-up process. The trial court ruled in favor of Mr. Kahn. Mr. Mesher appeals.

JUDGE WEBSTER: Washington law has long held "that the relationship among partners is fiduciary in character and imposes upon the partners the obligation of candor and utmost good faith in their dealings with each other." There is no stronger fiduciary relationship known to the law than that of co-partners, and each partner is a trustee for all. The good faith obligation of a partner demands that the partner abstain from any and all concealment concerning matters pertaining to the partnership business.

Furthermore, Washington statutory and case law provides that the partners owe one another these fiduciary duties through the "winding-up" period of the partnership. The Washington statute provides in pertinent part:

> Every partner must account to the partnership for any benefit, and hold as trustee for it any profits derived by him without the consent of the other partners for any transaction connected with the formation, conduct, or liquidation of the partnership or from any use by him of its property.

Moreover, in *Bovy,* the Court of Appeals held that partners are "obligated to fully disclose any information pertaining to the winding up of partnership affairs." Thus, the obligations of good faith and full disclosure continue during the winding up of the partnership and until the partnership affairs are completely settled.

The Meshers argue that *Elmore v. McConaghy* controls, and limits the scope of fiduciary duties the parties owed to one another during the winding-up of the partnership. In *Elmore,* the Supreme Court stated that:

> Whatever fiduciary relation was imposed on the partners toward each other during the continuance of the partnership, the relation ceased when they began to negotiate between themselves as to the price to be paid by one for the other's interest.

The Meshers' reliance on *Elmore* is misplaced. *Elmore* was decided prior to this State's adoption of the Uniform Partnership Act, which explicitly defined the fiduciary duty of partners as continuing through the winding-up of the partnership.

In this case, the winding-up of the partnership was not complete, and fiduciary duties did not cease, until the Kahn/Mesher transaction closed on September 30, 1997. The closing of the real estate transaction represented the final settlement of the partnership affairs.

Indeed, the SMAK agreement, which delineated the terms of the winding-up of the partnership, specifically provided that the partnership would not terminate until all partnership accounts were settled. While Mesher argues that his fiduciary duties ceased upon the agreement of the parties on a price on August 22, 1997, the SMAK agreement required that Mesher pay Kahn and Kahn transfer the Kahns' interest to Mesher. This requirement was not met until the transaction closed on September 30. Thus, under the SMAK agreement, Mesher owed Kahn fiduciary duties until at least September 30, 1997.

Because Mesher owed Kahn a fiduciary duty after August 22, 1997, we must determine whether he breached that duty by not revealing the Sundquist offer to Kahn.

As noted above, partners are "obligated to fully disclose any information pertaining to the winding up of partnership affairs." Mesher admits that he never notified Kahn of the Sundquist offer, which is information pertaining to the winding up of partnership affairs. Moreover, when partners engage in transactions with each other, they are obligated to disclose all material facts. Here, the ability of the partnership to dispose of partnership property at a higher price is a material fact.

Instead of disclosing the Sundquist offer to Kahn, Mesher kept the offer to himself in order to keep the entire profit for himself. This was a breach of his fiduciary duty, and the Kahns were thus entitled to judgment as a matter of law.

AFFIRMED.

CRITICAL THINKING

The Meshers relied on the precedent of *Elmore v. McConaghy* to support their conclusion that Stewart Mesher did not owe a fiduciary duty to disclose information to Jack Kahn. Why was reliance on *Elmore* erroneous?

ETHICAL DECISION MAKING

Suppose a classmate argues that injustice occurred with the court's decision. Your classmate thinks that Mesher should not have been punished because he was just receiving the products of his labor. After all, he was the one negotiating the sale of the property, and he didn't *force* Mr. Kahn to sell his shares. How would you argue against your classmate?

Who can demand that the winding-up process begin? We've seen that if a partnership has been rightfully dissolved, any partner can do so. However, a partner who wrongfully dissolves a partnership has no such right. In Case 37-3, the court considers a demand for an accounting in the winding-up phase.

CASE 37-3 ROBERT M. TAFOYA v. DEE S. PERKINS, NO. 95CA0408
COURT OF APPEALS OF COLORADO, DIVISION FOUR
932 P.2D 836, 1996 COLO. APP. LEXIS 206, 20 BTR 1115

Robert Tafoya and Dee Perkins, brother and sister, entered into a partnership with Dee's husband, Eugene Perkins. Eugene bought an apartment complex in 1977; however, he did not want to manage it. He held the title to the land in his name and contributed all necessary capital. Dee was to keep the books and assist in the management of the complex. Finally, Robert Tafoya was to live at, manage, and maintain the complex. In 1979, the apartment complex was sold. The partnership took back a 10-year promissory note with a balloon payment due in 1989.

Ten years later, when the balloon payment was due, Eugene purchased the apartments again at a foreclosure sale. In December 1989, he issued a Notice of Termination of Partnership because of losses associated with the partnership. At the same time, Robert Tafoya ceased being associated with the partnership. In July 1990, Eugene Perkins died. The trial court ruled that his death, as well as Tafoya's separation from the partnership, were sufficient to dissolve the partnership. Dee continued to manage the property until January 1994, when she sold it for a profit. Tafoya filed his complaint before the sale of the property, arguing Dee had breached her fiduciary duty and requesting an accounting of the partnership's assets. The trial court found no breach of fiduciary duty yet concluded Tafoya was entitled to an accounting and awarded him a share of the proceeds from the apartment complex sale. Dee Perkins appealed, arguing Tafoya's claim was barred by a statute of limitations.

JUDGE DAVIDSON: Section 7-60-129, C.R.S (1986 Repl. Vol. 3A) of the Uniform Partnership Law (the Act) provides that:

> The dissolution of any partnership is the change in relation of the partners caused by any partner ceasing to be associated in the carrying on as distinguished from the winding up of the business.

Under this section, when a partner withdraws from the business, the partnership is dissolved as to that party. However, the remaining partners may elect to continue operating as a partnership.

Section 7-60-143, C.R.S. (1986 Repl. Vol. 3A) of the Act states as follows:

> The right to an account of his interest shall accrue to any partner or his legal representative, as against the winding up partners, the surviving partners, or the person or partnership continuing the business at the date of dissolution, in the absence of any agreement to the contrary.

Courts have reached varying conclusions, depending on the circumstances, about when a statute of limitations begins to run on a claim seeking an accounting. However, §§ 7-60-129 and 7-60-143, taken together, provide that, absent an agreement to the contrary, at least in the circumstances of a withdrawing partner seeking an accounting against any partners winding up or continuing the business, the cause of action accrues on the date the withdrawing partner ceases to be associated with the business, resulting in dissolution of the partnership. Hence, regardless of the legal effect of the husband's notice of termination or his later death, once plaintiff himself ceased to be associated with the partnership, not only did this dissolve any still-existing partnership, it also caused the statute of limitations to begin to run on his own claim for an accounting against plaintiff.

The Act does not set forth or specify the applicable statute of limitations. Nor does any statute of limitations specifically address an action for partnership accounting. We therefore conclude that the applicable statute of limitations is § 13-80-102(1)(i), C.R.S. (1987 Repl. Vol 6A), which sets forth a two-year "catch-all" period of limitations for "all other actions of every kind for which no other period of limitation is provided."

We do not agree with plaintiff's suggestion that, because the action is one to "recover . . . an unliquidated, determinable amount of money due" him, the appropriate statute of limitations for this action is six years under § 13-80-103.5. Because the amount due from the accounting was not capable of ascertainment by reference to the partnership agreement or by a simple computation derived from the agreement, that statute does not apply.

The trial court found that plaintiff ceased to be associated with the partnership in 1989, causing a dissolution of the then-existing partnership. That finding is not challenged on appeal. Plaintiff did not file his complaint until January of 1994. As a result, his claim for an accounting is not timely because it falls outside the two-year period of limitation in § 13-80-102(1)(i).

REVERSED.

CRITICAL THINKING

How do you react to the evidence in this case? Does it strike you as incomplete? What additional information would you like to have if you were deciding the case?

ETHICAL DECISION MAKING

What primary values did the court uphold in its decision? If you were the judge reviewing the case, which values would motivate your decision?

CASE NUGGET

CONTINUING PARTNERSHIP AFTER DISSOLUTION

Sanfurd G. Bluestein and Sylvia Krugman, Plaintiffs v. Robert Olden, Defendant
U.S. District Court for the Southern District of New York
2004 U.S. Dist. LEXIS 3631

In 1978, Bluestein, Krugman, and Olden formed a partnership, the principal asset of which is a building located in New York City. For 26 years, Olden operated Olden Camera and Lens Company, Inc., in part of the building. Olden Camera itself had been in the building for more than 60 years. In 2001, the plaintiffs sent a letter to Olden to terminate the partnership in accordance with the terms of the partnership agreement. After the letter was sent, the partnership continued to operate in dissolution. The partners agreed to sell the building, but they could not agree on whom to sell to and how much to charge. Olden offered $9 million for the plaintiff's combined interest in the partnership, but he wanted the plaintiffs to release any claims against him and his business, as well as any claims to profits from the partnership for 2002–2003. A competing offer from a third party contained no requirements and offered $15,400,000 for the building, to be reduced by $200,000 if Olden's business remained in the building.

The plaintiffs filed an order to show cause, requesting "1) the appointment of plaintiff Bluestein as Liquidating and/or Winding Up Partner of the general partnership; 2) a direction that Olden cooperate in the liquidation of the assets of the partnership; and 3) enjoining Olden from entering into any new leases or renewing any leases for space in the building." Because the partnership was terminated in accordance with the partnership agreement, the court ruled that Olden could not prevent maximization of the partnership's assets. Bluestein was appointed the liquidating partner and given sole authority to liquidate the partnership's assets and divide the proceeds after paying the partnership's debts. Olden was ordered to cooperate in the liquidation of the assets and enjoined from entering into or renewing any leases or agreements affecting the partnership's building in New York City. The court retained jurisdiction to ensure that the partners complied with its orders.

Once all the partnership assets have been gathered, the assets are distributed to the partners or any creditors the partnership might have. If the partnership has been successful (it has very little or no debt), the order of distribution of assets is not too important. However, if a dissolved partnership has many creditors, the order of distribution of the assets is immensely important. According to UPA, distribution of liquidated assets must take the following order:

1. Payment to creditors of the partnership.
2. Payment of refunds or loans to partners for loans made to the firm.
3. Payment to partners of the capital they invested.
4. Payment of profits distributed to partners on the basis of the partnership agreement.

To see a description of allocating income among partners, please see the **Connecting to the Core** activity on the text website at www.mhhe.com/kubasek3e.

If the partners' liabilities for the partnership are greater than their liquidated assets, the partners are liable for the losses. Each partner must contribute his or her share of the losses to pay the creditors. If one partner is unable to contribute his or her share and another partner covers the first partner's unpaid share, the second partner has a right of contribution against the partner who did not pay.

CONTINUING THE PARTNERSHIP AFTER DISSOLUTION

After a partnership has been dissolved, the remaining partners have several options, one of which is to continue the partnership. What happens to the noncontinuing partner? Regardless of why the partner is noncontinuing, this partner must receive his or her interest in the partnership. A noncontinuing partner who holds, say, 20 percent of the partnership in which the assets are valued at $10,000 must receive $2,000 after dissolution.

Legal Principle: After the dissolution of a partnership, the remaining partners may continue the partnership.

COMPARING THE LAW OF OTHER COUNTRIES

DISSOLUTION OF PARTNERSHIP IN GERMANY

In Germany, a partner who wishes to leave a partnership must give notice of his intention at least six months before the end of the business year. On receiving notification, the other partners may begin placing bids for the purchase of the leaving partner's shares. The shares do not become officially available until the end of the business year.

If the remaining partners want to continue the partnership after one leaves, declares bankruptcy, or dies, this possibility must be provided for in the contract agreement to terminate the partnership. The remaining partners may also opt to fully dissolve the relationship. Under this option, they become liquidators whose duties include concluding all current business transactions, converting all assets to money, and paying all creditors, ideally within eight months. All claims against the partnership are dismissed five years after termination.

Perhaps the best way that partners can preserve a partnership business is through a *continuation agreement.* This agreement states that continuing partners can keep partnership property and carry on the partnership business, particularly when a partner dies.

BUT WHAT IF . . .

WHAT IF THE FACTS OF THE CASE OPENER WERE DIFFERENT?

Let's say, in the Case Opener, that Wyller dissolves his partnership but the other partners want to maintain the partnership. Are they allowed to keep the partnership going without one of the original partners? After leaving the partnership, will Wyller receive any of the money he invested in the partnership over time?

Limited Partnerships

L02

How is a limited partnership formed?

Limited partnerships, introduced in Chapter 35 and also known as *special partnerships,* originated in Europe more than 500 years ago and have existed in the United States for nearly 200 years. Recall that the **limited partnership** is an agreement between at least one general partner and at least one limited partner. The general partner has management responsibility for the partnership and assumes unlimited personal liability for the debts of the partnership. In contrast, the limited partner assumes no liability for the partnership beyond the capital he or she invested in the business. Limited partnerships are attractive to potential investors because of the limited liability and tax advantages they offer.

Functioning as the equivalent of RUPA, the Revised Uniform Limited Partnership Act (RULPA) is the law governing limited partnerships. Like all law, RULPA is not static; it changes as lawmakers revise it to handle new issues that arise and to better achieve social goals. RULPA was originally drafted in 1976, revised in 1985, and revised again in 2001. About one-fourth of the states have adopted the 1976 version of RULPA, and about three-fourths have adopted the 1985 version. Only a handful of states have adopted the 2001 version. Louisiana is the only state not to have adopted any version of RULPA.

FORMATION OF THE LIMITED PARTNERSHIP

How is the limited partnership created? In contrast to the often-informal partnership agreements described in the previous chapter, the formation of a limited partnership must follow very specific statutory requirements. The general and limited partners must sign a **certificate of limited partnership** and file it with the secretary of state to receive limited liability.

E-COMMERCE AND THE LAW

HOW THE INTERNET ASSISTS BUSINESS OWNERS WHO USE LIMITED PARTNERSHIPS

The Internet is making it easier for business owners to engage in business as limited partnerships. For example, at the Michigan Corporation Division page www.michigan.gov/cis/0,1607,7-154-10557_12901-25254—,00.html, you can download a certificate of limited partnership.

The Internet also provides partnerships with an easy opportunity to advertise to the public when there is a change in the partnership. For example, a partnership in the dissolution stage that must notify third parties can simply post information on the Internet explaining the dissolution. You can see a sample partnership dissolution notice at http://smallbusiness.findlaw.com/business-forms-contracts/be28_8_1.html.

RIGHTS AND LIABILITIES OF THE LIMITED PARTNERS AND THE GENERAL PARTNERS

LO3 What are the rights and privileges of a limited partner and a general partner?

Limited partners generally have all the rights given to partners in general partnerships, as discussed in the previous chapter. Thus, the limited partner (as well as the general partner) has the right to share in the profits of the business and to receive an account of the partnership. A general partner who wants to add a partner must have the consent of all partners in the limited partnership. Finally, an additional right of limited partners is that they often recover their investment before general partners do.

However, the limited partner has a few special rights under RULPA. For example, if a general partner fails to bring a suit on behalf of the limited partnership, the limited partner can bring the suit.

What about the duties and liabilities of the partnership? The general partner has unlimited personal liability for the debts of the partnership. This broad liability is in contrast to the limited partner's liability, restricted to the amount of capital the partner has invested in the business. Thus, if you enter into a limited partnership by contributing $10,000 to it, as a limited partner you cannot be held liable for more than $10,000.

A limited partner's limited personal liability depends on the partner's maintaining three conditions:

1. The limited partner has complied in good faith with the requirement that a certificate of limited partnership is filed.
2. The limited partner does not participate in the control of the business.
3. The limited partner's surname is not part of the partnership name.

If any of these conditions are violated, the limited partner surrenders his or her limited liability. For example, the general partner typically has exclusive control and management of the limited partnership; the limited partner, in contrast, does not share in this control, so the courts will likely rule that the partner has forfeited his or her limited liability.

Exhibit 37-3 distinguishes several aspects of general partners and limited partners.

Exhibit 37-3 Comparison of General Partners and Limited Partners

	GENERAL PARTNER	LIMITED PARTNER
Control of business	Has *all* rights associated with controlling the business	Has *no* right to participate in the management and control of the business
Liability	Has unlimited personal liability for all partnership debts	Has liability limited to the amount of capital the partner has contributed to the business
Agency of partnership	Acts as an agent of the partnership	Is not an agent of the partnership

DISSOLUTION OF THE LIMITED PARTNERSHIP

Dissolution of the limited partnership is very similar to dissolution of the general partnership. The limited partner has no right or power to dissolve the partnership. While the death or bankruptcy of the limited partner rarely dissolves the partnership, the death of the general partner usually does (unless the agreement specifies otherwise). According to RULPA, a limited partnership can be dissolved for any of the following reasons:

1. The expiration of the term established in the certificate of limited partnership.
2. The completion of the objective established in the certificate.
3. The unanimous written consent of all partners (limited and general).
4. The withdrawal of the general partner (unless the certificate establishes that other general partners will continue).
5. An act of the court.

If the limited partnership is dissolved, the limited partnership's assets are distributed in the same format as described earlier in this chapter: payment to third-party creditors, payment to partners who have loaned the partnership money, payment to the partners according to their investments in the partnership, and payment to the partners on the basis of their shares of the profits.

Limited Liability Companies

Limited partnerships have been around for a number of years, but the *limited liability company (LLC)* is relatively new. An LLC is similar to a limited partnership in that each member has limited liability dependent on the investment he or she makes, while still receiving the tax breaks often afforded to those in a partnership. Like the limited partnership, the LLC is created with an agreement between members. Each member also gets a say in the management of the company, whereas in a limited partnership only the general partners make management decisions. Basically, in limited partnerships, for an LLC to obtain limited liability, the owner (referred to as a *member*) does not have to give up his right to participate in management of the LLC. In fact, an additional advantage of the LLC form is the flexibility it offers members in terms of alternative ways to structure its management.

To see how dissolution relates to a partnership's accounts, please see the **Connecting to the Core** activity on the text website at www.mhhe.com/kubasek3e.

However, because LLCs are new, the Uniform Limited Liability Company Act that has been drafted to govern them has not been accepted by many states. Until a uniform system has been adopted, managers should check the laws with regard to LLCs in each state to ensure that the liabilities, as well as rights and duties, of a company established in one state continue to apply when conducting business outside that state.

CASE OPENER WRAP-UP

Partnership Problems of Wildmeadow Village

Ultimately, the supreme court of Alaska ruled against Wyller. The court determined that he was partially at fault for the wrongful dissolution of the Wildmeadow partnership, and therefore Wyller was not entitled to damages from the other partners. Even though the other partners conducted business behind Wyller's back and approved spending that Wyller did not know about, his conduct in the situation was less than ideal. Specifically, the court observed that shortly after the bank's loan refusal, Wyller informed the other partners that he did not consider himself bound to provide financing for *any* of the improvements that by then had been made to the property. This fact is important because Wyller approved some of the renovations but refused to pay his fair share of the cost. Furthermore, Wyller refused to complete the loan application process despite having previously approved the state of Alaska as a tenant and the submission of the loan application. For these reasons, Wyller was not justified in preventing the partnership from paying for any of the improvements. Nor was he justified in denying personal or partnership responsibility for the costs.

After consideration of the facts, the court found that Wyller's failure to pay for the construction contributed to the dissolution of the partnership. Wyller wrongfully denied responsibility for any of the construction costs, and his denial of authorization to pay construction costs contributed to the course of events that precipitated the dissolution. Failure to pay construction costs brought about the suit, and that suit resulted in wrongful dissolution of the partnership. Therefore, the supreme court of Alaska affirmed the lower court's decision. To avoid such partnership problems in future scenarios, it is important to stress the importance of transparency in partnerships. Had Wyller been allowed to authorize or reject the additional construction costs, the partnership would probably not have been sued in the first place. Furthermore, an understanding of the Uniform Partnership Act and how partnerships are rightly dissolved is something all partners should have before forming a business to avoid legal problems.

KEY TERMS

certificate of limited partnership 824
dissolution 814
limited partnership 824
rightfully dissolved 815
winding up 814
wrongful dissolution 817

SUMMARY OF KEY TOPICS

Termination of the Partnership

Termination begins when a partnership dissolves. Once the partnership has been dissolved and the assets have been liquidated and distributed, the partnership has been terminated.

Dissolution of the Business

Dissolution refers to the ceasing of a partnership. Acts of partners, the operation of the law, and acts of the court can rightfully dissolve a partnership.

Consequences of Dissolution

A partner who wishes to dissolve or withdraw from the partnership must give notice of intent. Third parties should be contacted promptly to avoid creating additional liability for the partnership.

Winding Up the Business

Winding up is the activity of completing unfinished partnership business, collecting and paying debts, collecting partnership assets, and taking inventory.

Limited Partnerships

The limited partnership is governed by an agreement between at least one general partner and at least one limited partner. This partnership permits investors to share in the profits of a partnership but limits their liability to the amount they invest.

Limited Liability Companies

An LLC is formed by an agreement between members, each of whom has limited liability while receiving the tax breaks often afforded to those in a partnership. In addition, each member also gets a say in the management of the company.

POINT / COUNTERPOINT

Should a Partnership Be Allowed to Expel a Partner on the Basis of Illegal Conduct Unrelated to the Terms of the Partnership Agreement?

YES

A partnership should be able to expel a partner on the basis of illegal personal conduct even when the illegal conduct isn't specified in the partnership agreement.

It would be nearly impossible to create a partnership agreement that dictated every possible occasion for dissolving the partnership. Individuals are always expected to conduct themselves within the bounds of national, state, and local laws. Any illegal behavior should have implications for the partnership as an ongoing business enterprise.

A partner's personal behavior affects the entire partnership, its reputation, and its associated business in many ways. If one partner of a five-partner law firm is arrested for smoking marijuana, clients may associate this partner with the entire firm. If he participates in this illegal activity, in which other illegal activities does he partake? Does he keep faulty books? Will clients be overcharged?

Clients may begin to question the firm as a whole for allowing someone who partakes in illegal activities to remain a partner. Do *all* the attorneys participate in illegal activities?

While a partner may suffer personal legal consequences for his actions, the whole partnership suffers when one partner makes a poor personal choice. Therefore, the partnership should be able to determine the consequences.

NO

A partnership should not be allowed to expel an individual based on his or her involvement in illegal activity.

The partners had the opportunity when formulating the partnership agreement to include a stipulation for its dissolution in such a case. If they did not, no individual can be aware of the potential impact of her actions on her status as a partner. Had she known the possible consequences, she might have acted differently. However, she cannot be expected to abide by restrictions that were not stated in the first place.

Is it logical to revoke an individual's driver's license because she looked at pornography in a state where such activity is illegal? An individual can make a poor personal choice and still be capable of performing her expected duties.

A rule allowing partnerships to expel a partner on the basis of unrelated illegal activity could also be easily abused by partnerships that want to expel a partner for other reasons, such as convenience or the desire for additional profit. The partner already suffers personal legal consequences and should not experience additional penalties for an activity that has no impact on the partnership.

QUESTIONS & PROBLEMS

1. What stages must occur for the termination of a partnership to be complete?
2. Why is the partnership's debt particularly important in the winding-up stage?
3. What are the advantages of being a limited partner rather than a general partner?
4. In June 2001, Greenfeld, Stitely, and Karstetter negotiated to merge their practices into a partnership that would provide accounting, tax, and information technology services. The partnership was profitable every year from its inception. However, Stitely felt that Greenfeld's information technology services were not generating as much revenue as his one-third share in the partnership should. So Stitely indicated to the partners that he wanted to withdraw from the partnership. Soon after, Stitely and Karstetter agreed to instead continue as partners together after Greenfeld was out of the picture. Greenfeld did not violate his

partnership agreement, but the two partners forced Greenfeld out of the partnership without compensating him for his interest. They accomplished this by unlawful means, such as purporting to withdraw from the partnership while in reality seizing control of its assets. Furthermore, they transferred the assets of the partnership to their new company, preventing Greenfeld from having computer access to the business files, software, and client records. Was the partnership terminated properly? If the dissolution was wrongful, what potential consequences could Stitely and Karstetter face? [*Wayne I. Greenfeld v. Frank L. Stitely, et al.,* 2007 Va. Cir. LEXIS 7 (2007).]

5. Marlene Westerfeld, a resident of Missouri, filed a lawsuit against Independent Processing, LLC, a company that processed residential mortgages. She also filed suit against Independent Processing's partner: Provident Funding Associates, LP, which actually provides the mortgages. Westerfeld claims that both companies tried to charge her a "broker processing fee" and an "administrative fee." According to Westerfeld, this violated the Missouri Merchandising Practices Act. Was Westerfeld right in bringing suit to *both* the mortgage processing company and the actual lender? Why or why not? [*Westerfeld v. Independent Processing, LLC,* 621 F.3d 819 (8th Cir. 2010).]

6. Rudy and Richard Corrales, who are brothers, formed RC Electronics (RCE) in 1989, according to a written partnership agreement with an indefinite term. RCE repaired, refurbished, and sold computer tape drives. The brothers agreed that Rudy would be responsible for running the business, while Richard would supply financing and the know-how for the business. Richard already had a thriving business occupying him full-time; he became involved in RCE because Rudy could not obtain enough financing on his own to start a business. Rudy's wife, Pamela, came on board shortly after RCE started up and became the office manager. She was responsible for preparing the company's business records. The business was quite successful for several years, and Rudy and Richard obtained substantial sums from it. In 2004, however, Richard discovered that Rudy and Pamela had formed a competing business, PK Electronics (PKE), to perform the same services performed by RCE but without Richard. When Richard inquired about PKE, Rudy refused to tell him anything and cut off all communication with him. Richard sent Rudy a "Notice of Dissociation," dated April 12, 2005, in which he stated that he was withdrawing from the partnership. Richard and Rudy sued each other in 2006 in separate lawsuits. Richard sued Rudy, Pamela, their two daughters, PKE, and RCE for breach of contract, fraud, and conspiracy, misappropriation of trade secrets, and accounting. Rudy sued Richard for breach of contract, common counts, fraud, and negligent misrepresentation. Was Richard right in sending the original "Notice of Dissociation"? What evidence leads you to this answer? [*Corrales v. Corrales,* 198 Cal. App. 4th 221 (Aug. 10, 2011).]

7. Nevada Gold and Casinos Inc. develops real estate properties for the purpose of gaming. In early 2002, Nevada Gold decided it wanted to build a casino on Native American lands. However, it had to gain permission from the Native Americans to do so. American Heritage Inc. had business arrangements for building and operating casinos on tribal lands. After meeting, both companies decided to open a new casino named Route 66 in New Mexico and form a limited liability company. American Heritage was to run the casino and was to assign its rights under its agreement with the tribe to Route 66. Nevada Gold was to obtain financing of $8 million initially, for a temporary facility, and later was to obtain financing of $40 million for a permanent facility. All receipts from the casino were to be placed in a Route 66 account. Nevada Gold claims that these core obligations were memorialized in an April 2002 letter agreement and that the arrangement was finalized on June 3, 2002. The temporary casino opened on June 1, 2002. Nevada Gold claims that shortly after the agreement was signed, Gillmann (a representative of American Heritage), acting for American Heritage, stopped returning calls and eventually maintained that he was defrauded into signing the agreement and that it contained terms to which he did not agree. What determines whether the obligations in the agreement will be upheld by the court? [*Nevada Gold & Casinos v. American Heritage,* 110 P.3d 481 (2005).]

8. Carl Disotell and Earl Stiltner met in 1997. They discussed Stiltner's property and agreed to form an equal partnership to develop, construct, and operate a hotel on the property. They never entered into a written partnership agreement. They intended to convert the two-story commercial building on the property into a hotel. In May 1998, Disotell advised Stiltner that the property required a sewer line. Construction on the property had not yet begun. Stiltner disagreed that a sewer line was necessary; he thought there would be no increase in sewage from the property because Disotell had not yet commenced construction. He denied Disotell the building access needed to assess the mechanical, electrical, and other systems. He also refused to remove his personal property from the building. A complete breakdown in the relationship between Stiltner and Disotell then occurred. Subsequently, the partnership never produced a profit. Should the court, as a matter of law, dissolve the partnership and judicially supervise the winding up of the partnership affairs? Why or why not? [*Carl Disotell v. Earl Stiltner,* 100 P.3d 890 (2004).]

9. Mige Associates, a limited partnership, owned an apartment building. The building could have been developed into a housing cooperative. The projected profits for such a conversion were significant. The conversion required the signed agreement of one of Mige's general partners, Jon Meadow. Meadow's decision to sign the agreement was contingent on the promise that he receive more money from the deal than the other partners. After his request was denied, Meadow refused to sign the agreement. Two of the limited partners, Drucker and Schaffer, filed suit against Meadow. They claimed that he had breached his fiduciary responsibility to the general and limited partners of Mige Associates. The trial court found in favor of Meadow. How do you think the case was decided on appeal? Did the economic benefits of the conversion create a fiduciary obligation for Meadow to sign the agreement? [*Drucker v. Mige Associates,* 639 N.Y.S.2d 365 (1996).]

10. After the dissolution of a partnership formed to develop the Four Seasons Resort, TSA International Limited brought an action against Shimizu Corporation, alleging breach of fiduciary duty. TSA had approached Shimizu in 1986 with plans for developing the hotel. The two companies formed a partnership, and they began to make plans for several golf and hotel developments. The loans TSA and Shimizu had taken out soon became delinquent. The partners met to negotiate the payment of the hotel and golf course loans. At the request of Shimizu, the agreements were drafted in Japanese. TSA subsequently filed a complaint asserting, among other things, breach of fiduciary duty. When reaching the agreements, Shimizu had discouraged TSA from hiring its own accountants or legal counsel because of "the long-term relationship of trust between Shimizu and TSA." TSA also alleged that Shimizu arranged the agreement so that Shimizu would obtain substantial tax advantages. The circuit court found in favor of Shimizu. How do you think the case was decided on appeal? Did Shimizu breach its fiduciary duty? [*TSA Intern. Ltd. v. Shimizu Corp.,* 990 P.2d 713 (1999).]

Looking for more review materials?

The Online Learning Center at **www.mhhe.com/kubasek3e** contains this chapter's "Assignment on the Internet" and also a list of URLs for more information, entitled "On the Internet." Find both of them in the Student Center portion of the OLC, along with quizzes and other helpful materials.

Corporations: Formation and Financing

CHAPTER

38

LEARNING OBJECTIVES

After reading this chapter, you will be able to answer the following questions:

1 What are the characteristics of corporations?

2 What are the powers granted to corporations by the states?

3 How are corporations classified?

4 How are corporations formed?

5 What are some potential problems with the formation of corporations?

6 How do corporations get funding?

CASE OPENER

The Formation of the Facebook Corporation

On October 28, 2003, Mark Zuckerberg was a sophomore at Harvard University when he created a website called Facemash that was similar to an existing web service called Hot or Not. However, the following semester, in 2004, Zuckerberg began working on a new code for a new website to be called Facebook. His friends Eduardo Saverin, Dustin Moskovitz, Andrew McCollum, and Chris Hughes joined Zuckerberg to promote the new social networking site. Membership on the site quickly grew from only students at Harvard College to students at most universities in the United States. In the summer of 2004, Facebook was incorporated. As a corporation, Facebook is an "artificial person," a status with legal ramifications for both the corporate entity and its owners.

1. What are the legal implications of Facebook's status as a corporation?
2. How are corporations formed? What factors should a businessperson consider in forming a corporation?

The Wrap-Up at the end of the chapter will answer these questions.

This chapter explains the steps necessary to establish a corporate entity. Although state law generally governs corporations and each state has its own corporate regulatory statutes, the Revised Model Business Corporation Act (RMBCA) is the basis of most state statutes. More than 25 states have adopted at least part of RMBCA. This chapter refers to specific RMBCA guidelines, but remember that not all states follow them.

The first two sections of this chapter examine corporations' characteristics and powers. The third section describes different classifications of corporations. The next section explains the process of corporate formation and problems associated with it, and the final section covers corporate financing.

Characteristics of Corporations

L01 What are the characteristics of corporations?

How are corporations different from other forms of business organization? We addressed some of their characteristics in Chapter 35. Let's now take a closer look.

LEGAL ENTITY

Under U.S. law, corporations are legal entities; in other words, they exist separately from their shareholders. Thus, corporations can sue or be sued by others.

RIGHTS AS A PERSON AND A CITIZEN

Courts consider corporations to be "legal persons." For example, in 2006 in Boston, a woman was killed when the ceiling of a tunnel collapsed over her. The ceiling was fastened with bolts that were supported by a glue distributed by the corporation Powers Fasteners. Apparently the contents of this glue were known to "creep," that is, to slowly loosen. The company never informed anyone associated with the construction of the tunnel about the hazardous characteristics of the glue. The Massachusetts attorney general decided to take the corporation to court for manslaughter, just as an individual would be taken to court on such charges. Also, like natural persons, most corporations have certain rights according to the Bill of Rights. Specifically, the Fifth and Fourteenth amendments state that government cannot deprive any "person" of life, liberty, or property without due process. Courts have held that corporations are "persons" in this case and thus have a right to due process. Courts also consider corporations to be persons with respect to the Fourth Amendment and thus protected from unreasonable searches and seizures. Finally, corporations have free speech rights protected by the First Amendment. As Chapter 5 explained, however, the First Amendment protects corporate *commercial* speech to a lesser degree than corporate *political* speech.

In Case 38-1, the Supreme Court considered whether the Federal Election Commission's regulations are unconstitutional limits on speech.

CASE 38-1 FEDERAL ELECTION COMM'N v. BEAUMONT
UNITED STATES SUPREME COURT
539 U.S. 146 (2003)

In 2003, the corporation North Carolina Right to Life, Inc. (NCRL,) sued the Federal Election Commission (FEC) claiming that two FEC regulations were unconstitutional. Specifically, the first regulation challenged the one that stops corporations from making contributions, and the second regulation was the one that provides an exemption from the ban for corporate contributions for particular nonprofit corporations.

With respect to the second regulation, to be considered a "qualified nonprofit corporation," or one that is exempt from the ban, a nonprofit corporation must have the following characteristics: Its only purpose is the advancement of political ideas, it does not engage in business activities, no shareholders or other individuals receive benefits that could discourage anyone from disassociating from the corporation on the basis of that corporation's political standpoints, and it was not founded by a business corporation or labor organization and accepts no form of donations from business corporations.

NCRL said that it met this exemption except for the fact that it accepted small corporate donations and dealt in "minor business activities incidental and related to its advocacy of issues." NCRL further argued that its officers were subject to liability as criminals and thus, their First Amendment rights were suppressed.

Finally, NCRL contended that the Act's ban on corporate contributions to political candidates violated the organization's right to association.

JUDGE SOUTER: First, NCRL argues that on a class-wide basis "*[Massachusetts Citizens for Life]*-type corporations pose no potential of threat to the political system," so that the governmental interest in combating corruption is as weak as the Court held it to be in relation to the particular corporation considered in *Massachusetts Citizens for Life*. But this generalization does not hold up. For present purposes, we will assume advocacy corporations are generally different from traditional business corporations in the improbability that contributions they might make would end up supporting causes that some of their members would not approve. But concern about the corrupting potential underlying the corporate ban may indeed be implicated by advocacy corporations. They, like their for-profit counterparts, benefit from significant "state-created advantages," and may well be able to amass substantial "political" war chests. Not all corporations that qualify for favorable tax treatment under §501(c)(4) of the Internal Revenue Code lack substantial resources, and the category covers some of the Nation's most politically powerful organizations, including the AARP, the National Rifle Association, and the Sierra Club. Nonprofit advocacy corporations are, moreover, no less susceptible than traditional business companies to misuse as conduits for circumventing the contribution limits imposed on individuals.

Second, NCRL argues that application of the ban on its contributions should be subject to a strict level of scrutiny, on the ground that §441b does not merely limit contributions, but bans them on the basis of their source. This argument, however, overlooks the basic premise we have followed in setting First Amendment standards for reviewing political financial restrictions: the level of scrutiny is based on the importance of the "political activity at issue" to effective speech or political association. Restrictions on political contributions have been treated as merely "marginal" speech restrictions subject to relatively complaisant review under the First Amendment, because contributions lie closer to the edges than to the core of political expression. This is the reason that instead of requiring contribution regulations to be narrowly tailored to serve a compelling governmental interest, "a contribution limit involving 'significant interference' with associational rights" passes muster if it satisfies the lesser demand of being "'closely drawn' to match a 'sufficiently important interest.'"

It is not that the difference between a ban and a limit is to be ignored; it is just that the time to consider it is when applying scrutiny at the level selected, not in selecting the standard of review itself. But even when NCRL urges precisely that, and asserts that §441b is not sufficiently "closely drawn," the claim still rests on a false premise, for NCRL is simply wrong in characterizing §441b as a complete ban. As we have said before, the section "permits some participation of unions and corporations in the federal electoral process by allowing them to establish and pay the administrative expenses of [PACs]." The PAC option allows corporate political participation without the temptation to use corporate funds for political influence, quite possibly at odds with the sentiments of some shareholders or members, and it lets the government regulate campaign activity through registration and disclosure, without jeopardizing the associational rights of advocacy organizations' members.

NCRL cannot prevail, then, simply by arguing that a ban on an advocacy corporation's direct contributions is bad tailoring. NCRL would have to demonstrate that the law violated the First Amendment in allowing contributions to be made only through its PAC and subject to a PAC's administrative burdens. But a unanimous Court in *National Right to Work* did not think the regulatory burdens on PACs, including restrictions on their ability to solicit funds, rendered a PAC unconstitutional as an advocacy corporation's sole avenue for making political contributions. There is no reason to think the burden on advocacy corporations is any greater today, or to reach a different conclusion here.

REVERSAL.

CRITICAL THINKING

What is the assumption about advocacy corporations and traditional business corporations that Justice Souter makes? How does this assumption support his reasoning?

ETHICAL DECISION MAKING

While the FEC does not completely ban the participation of corporations in electoral processes, such participation is strictly regulated. What is the ethical basis for the explanation Justice Souter gives for the necessity of such regulation?

COMPARING THE LAW OF OTHER COUNTRIES

CORPORATE STRUCTURE IN CHINA

Chinese law establishes three tiers of corporate power. The board of directors is the lowest, the board of supervisors makes up the second, and corporate officers compose the top tier. While the corporate structure in China mirrors that in the United States, there is one important difference: In China, shareholders have more power to control the corporate structure than do shareholders in the United States.

In the United States, shareholders elect only the board of directors, and, in turn, the board of directors then hires management for the day-to-day business of the corporation. In China, shareholders elect not only the board of directors but the board of supervisors, which is the equivalent of the managers of a business in the Western corporate structure.

CREATURE OF THE STATE

State incorporation statutes establish the requirements for corporate formation. Each individual corporation's charter creates a contract between that corporation and the state.

LIMITED LIABILITY

Because corporations are legal entities separate from their shareholders, corporations assume liability for corporate actions. Shareholders' liability is therefore limited to their investment in the corporation. In 1977 Big O Tire Dealers sued Goodyear Tire & Rubber Company for copying its Bigfoot trademark on new tires. The court agreed and awarded Big O Tire several million dollars in damages, which the Goodyear corporation, and not individual Goodyear shareholders, paid. Although these damages may have reduced the dividends Goodyear shareholders received, the court did not hold the shareholders individually liable for any portion of the award.

FREE TRANSFERABILITY OF CORPORATE SHARES

Generally, shareholders can freely transfer their corporate shares. That is, they can sell their shares or give them to charity.

PERPETUAL EXISTENCE

To see why managers generally act in the interest of shareholders, please see the **Connecting to the Core** activity on the text website at www.mhhe.com/kubasek3e.

If shareholders die, corporations do not dissolve. If corporate directors or officers withdraw or die, the corporation continues to exist. The **articles of incorporation,** the document a corporation files with the state explaining its organization, may include a restriction on the duration of the corporation. Otherwise, in most states, corporations can exist indefinitely. A few states, however, set a maximum length of life for corporations, after which they must formally renew their corporate existence.

CENTRALIZED MANAGEMENT

Unless the articles of incorporation specify otherwise, shareholders do not participate in corporate management. Instead, they elect a board of directors that, in turn, selects officers to manage the day-to-day business of the corporation.

CORPORATE TAXATION

Because corporations are separate legal entities, government taxes their income directly (S corporations are an exception; we discuss them later). Corporations must pay federal and state taxes on their income, but they have control over that income. They can distribute it to shareholders in the form of **dividends,** although they do not receive tax deductions for doing so. In fact, shareholders pay taxes on dividends they receive. Since the corporation pays taxes on its income and the shareholders pay taxes on their dividends, dividends are subject to double taxation, a disadvantage for corporations. Corporations can also keep profits, or **retained earnings,** to reinvest. This can raise their stock prices, benefiting shareholders when they sell their stock.

BUT WHAT IF . . .

WHAT IF THE FACTS OF THE CASE OPENER WERE DIFFERENT?

Let's say, in the Case Opener, that after Zuckerberg had Facebook incorporated, he and the other corporate shareholders were on a private jet when it crashed, killing all the travelers. Without any of the shareholders, what would happen to Facebook? Does state or federal government put a limit on how long a corporation can exist?

LIABILITY FOR OFFICERS AND EMPLOYEES

Because the relationship between corporations and their directors, officers, and employees is an agency relationship, corporations are liable for torts and crimes committed by their agents during the scope of their employment. Courts refer to this liability as the doctrine of *respondeat superior* (Latin for "let the master answer"). Although in the past courts were reluctant to impose criminal liability on corporations, prosecutions today are much more common. Chapter 7, "Crime and the Business Community," discusses corporate sentencing guidelines and punishment.

Corporate Powers

LO2 What are the powers granted to corporations by the states?

Because corporations are creatures of the state, they have only those powers that states grant them through state incorporation statutes and each corporation's articles of incorporation. Exhibit 38-1 lists the powers of the corporation.

Legal Principle: **The only authority possessed by corporations is the powers granted to them in their articles of incorporation and through state incorporation statutes.**

EXPRESS AND IMPLIED POWERS

State incorporation statutes typically grant corporations the following express powers: the power to have perpetual existence, to sue and be sued in the corporation's name, to acquire

Exhibit 38-1 Powers of the Corporation

Express Powers

Power to have perpetual existence

Power to sue and be sued in the corporation's name

Power to acquire property; power to make contracts and borrow money

Power to lend money

Power to make charitable donations

Power to establish rules for managing the corporation

Implied Powers

Power to take whatever actions are necessary to execute express powers

Power given in the statement of corporate purpose in the articles of incorporation property, to make contracts and borrow money, to lend money, to make charitable donations, and to establish rules for managing the corporation. Corporations may take whatever actions are necessary to execute these express powers. Thus, they also have implied powers, usually given in the statement of corporate purpose in the articles of incorporation.

Classification of Corporations

LO3

How are corporations classified?

Corporations can be classified as public or private; profit or nonprofit; domestic, foreign, or alien; publicly held or closely held; an S corporation; or a professional organization.

PUBLIC OR PRIVATE

A **public corporation** is a corporation created by the government to help administer law. Public corporations, like the Federal Deposit Insurance Corporation (FDIC), often have specific government duties to fulfill. Conversely, private persons create **private corporations** for private purposes. Private corporations do not have government duties.

PROFIT OR NONPROFIT

Most corporations are **for-profit corporations.** Their objective is to operate for profit. Shareholders seeking to make a profit purchase the stock these corporations issue. Their profit if the firm prospers can take two forms. First, shareholders may receive dividends from the corporation. Second, the market price of the stock can increase, allowing shareholders to sell their stock at a higher price than they paid.

Nonprofit corporations may earn profits, but they do not distribute them to shareholders. In fact, nonprofit corporations do not have shareholders, their objective is not to earn profit, and they do not issue stock. Instead, nonprofit corporations provide services to their members (not shareholders) and reinvest most of their profits in the business. Churches and charitable organizations are examples of nonprofit corporations.

DOMESTIC, FOREIGN, AND ALIEN CORPORATIONS

A corporation is a **domestic corporation** in the particular state in which it is incorporated. Corporations that operate in more than one state must obtain a certificate of authority in each state in which they do business. A corporation is a **foreign corporation** in states in which it conducts business but is not incorporated. The McDonald's Corporation is incorporated in Delaware but does business in all 50 states. Thus, it is a domestic corporation in Delaware and a foreign corporation in the other 49 states.

An **alien corporation** is a business incorporated in another country. A U.S. corporation that wants to do business in Canada or Mexico is an alien corporation in those countries.

PUBLICLY HELD OR CLOSELY HELD

The stock of **publicly held corporations** is available to the public. Thus, if you wanted to invest in a corporation, you could purchase stock in a publicly held corporation. Most publicly held corporations have many shareholders, and managers of these corporations usually do not own large percentages of the corporation's stock. Shareholders wishing to sell their shares do not face many transfer restrictions.

In contrast, **closely held corporations** (also called *close, family,* or *privately held corporations*) generally do not offer stock to the general public. Shareholders are usually family members and friends, who often are active in or manage the business and maintain restrictions on the transfer of shares to prevent outsiders from gaining control. Although they account for only a small fraction of corporate assets and revenues, most U.S. corporations are closely held corporations. In fact, as of 2013, there was a total of 4.5 million closely held corporations in operation in the United States.

SUBCHAPTER S CORPORATION

Chapter 35 introduced **S corporations** (named after the subchapter of the Internal Revenue Code that provides for them), a particular type of closely held corporation that enjoys the tax status of partnerships. Thus, S corporation shareholders report their income from the corporation only once, as personal income.

S corporations offer two more tax advantages. First, shareholders may deduct corporate losses from their personal income, reducing their taxes in case of loss. Second, when the shareholder is part of a lower tax bracket than non-S corporations, the entirety of the corporation's income is taxed at the shareholder's lower rate, even if dividends are retained and not distributed. The lower rate applies because of the relationship between the corporation and the personal income of the shareholders.

An S corporation must meet certain requirements. First, it cannot have more than 100 shareholders. Second, only individuals, trusts, and (in certain circumstances) corporations can be shareholders (partnerships cannot be shareholders). Third, S corporations can issue only one class of shares, although they need not have identical voting rights. Fourth, all S corporations must be domestic corporations. Finally, no shareholder can be a nonresident alien.

PROFESSIONAL CORPORATION

If a group of dentists, doctors, or other professionals wants to practice as a corporation, all 50 states permit them to incorporate. Because of the nature of professional work, however, courts sometimes impose personal liability on doctors in professional corporations for medical malpractice performed under their oversight.

Formation of the Corporation

LO4 How are corporations formed?

The creation of a corporation has two steps: general organizational activities and legal activities.

ORGANIZING AND PROMOTING THE CORPORATION

Two groups of important players are responsible for the organization of the corporation: promoters and subscribers. **Promoters** begin the corporate creation and organization process by arranging for necessary capital, financing, and licenses. They raise capital for the infant corporation by making **subscription agreements** with **subscribers** (investors) who agree to purchase stock in the new corporation.

Promoters. Promoters prepare the corporation's incorporation papers. They can also enter into contracts as needed, say, to purchase or lease buildings for the corporation. Frank Seiberling was the promoter who founded the Goodyear Tire & Rubber Company. In 1898, he purchased Goodyear's first plant in Akron, Ohio, with $3,500 borrowed from his brother-in-law and established Goodyear workers' hourly wages between 13 and 25 cents.

When problems with preincorporation contracts arise, courts generally hold promoters liable and rule that these contracts do not bind infant corporations. Promoters are not agents of the infant corporation, however, because they cannot serve as such for a principal that does not yet exist.

Once incorporated, corporations can accept or reject preincorporation agreements. Even so, if a corporation accepts a preincorporation agreement, courts usually still hold promoters liable for the contract.

In two cases, however, promoters are not personally liable. They can include a clause in the contract stating that the corporation's adoption of the contract terminates their liability; or the corporation, the promoter, and a third party can enter into a **novation,** agreeing to substitute the third party for one of the two original parties in a contract and terminating the rights under it.

Case 38-2 highlights the complexity of the process of obtaining authorization and completing a certificate of authority. Notice how the process of authorization affects a court's ability to have personal jurisdiction over the business conduct of a company.

CASE 38-2 KING v. AMERICAN FAMILY MUTUAL INSURANCE COMPANY; AMERICAN STANDARD INSURANCE COMPANY OF WISCONSIN

U.S. COURT OF APPEALS FOR THE NINTH CIRCUIT
632 F.3D 570 (2011)

Defendant insurance companies had applied for certificates of authority to conduct business in the state of Montana, as they were contemplating doing business in the state. Although the companies had applied for the certificate of authority, they could not yet sell policies in Montana as they had not yet completed the process to do so. As of June 2008, the companies had not submitted and obtained approval of all insurance forms that would be used in Montana, nor had they submitted a list of sales agents and producers; both of these tasks were required to complete the process of obtaining authorization to conduct the business in Montana. In addition, the companies had no contracts, sales agents, employees, or offices in Montana. What the companies did do before completing the certificate of authority was appoint an agent for service of process in Montana. According to the defendants, they had merely "dipped their toes in the water" to test the idea of doing business in Montana.

In 2007, a couple who owned insurance under the companies in Colorado were in a motorcycle accident in Montana. The couple sued the defendant insurance companies for damages incurred after they were involved in the motorcycle accident in Montana, asserting that the companies were supposed to provide coverage for the state of Montana. The court dismissed the suit for lack of personal jurisdiction, as the authorization process was not complete. The plaintiffs appealed.

JUDGE MCKEOWN: Title 33 of the Montana Code regulates insurance companies. A foreign corporation that seeks to transact business in Montana must obtain a certificate of authority. As part of the application process to obtain this certificate, the insurer must "appoint the commissioner [of insurance] as its attorney to receive service of legal process issued against it in Montana" and file with the commissioner the name and address to which the commissioner should forward any summons or complaint received against the insurer. The appointment of this agent is "irrevocable, binds the insurer and any successor in interest or to the assets or liabilities of the insurer, and remains in effect as long as there is in force in Montana any contract made by the insurer or obligations arising from a contract." The plain language of the statute therefore does not answer the question of whether the appointment subjects the Companies to suit in Montana for business conducted elsewhere.

The Montana law regarding appointment of an agent for service of process does not, standing alone, subject foreign corporations to jurisdiction in Montana for acts performed outside of Montana, at least when the corporations transact no business in the state. Here, the Companies merely contemplated doing business in Montana; they are not amenable to suit in that state simply because they appointed the Commissioner of Insurance as their agent for service of process.

For general jurisdiction to obtain, the defendant's contacts must approximate physical presence in the forum. The Companies' contacts in Montana do not come close to meeting this standard. The Companies have no offices or employees in Montana, have made no sales in Montana, have solicited no business in Montana, and are unable to issue or sell insurance in the state. In fact, the Companies' sole contacts with Montana are their initial Certificates of Authorization and their appointments of the Insurance Commissioner as an agent for service of process. These contacts hardly approximate physical presence and are not "continuous and systematic." American Family has not set

[continued]

up a "home" in Montana. Accordingly, the court cannot exercise general personal jurisdiction over the Companies.

The Companies have dipped their toes in Montana to test the waters for doing business, but their actions do not amount to a foot planted in the state for purposes of personal jurisdiction. Under Montana law, the Companies' acts of beginning the process of applying to do business and appointing an agent for service of process provide an insufficient basis for the exercise of personal jurisdiction.

AFFIRMED.

CRITICAL THINKING

Given what you know of the facts of the case, what evidence do you think could have led the court to rule that the insurance companies did more than just dip "their toes in Montana" and were, instead, certified to do business in the state?

ETHICAL DECISION MAKING

In this case, the insurance companies were described as not having "set up a home in Montana." Who are the stakeholders that may be affected by a company's borderline authorization in a given state? What are some of the problems that can result from a company's "testing" its business in another state, without completion of authorization?

BUT WHAT IF . . .

WHAT IF THE FACTS OF THE CASE OPENER WERE DIFFERENT?

Let's say, in the Case Opener, that when Zuckerberg incorporated Facebook, he decided to set it up as a nonprofit corporation. Zuckerberg's friends and associates came forward asking to become shareholders, and Zuckerberg picked five shareholders in addition to himself. Furthermore, Zuckerberg asked his shareholders how to make the company generate money for them and provide many services for Facebook members at the same time. What part of this scenario is not a legal characteristic of a nonprofit corporation?

Subscribers. Subscribers offer to purchase stock in a corporation during the incorporation process. A subscriber becomes a shareholder once the corporation incorporates or accepts his or her purchase offer, whichever occurs first.

Courts interpret subscription agreements in two ways. In some states, subscription agreements are continuing offers to buy stock in the corporation that subscribers may revoke at any time. In other states, courts view subscription agreements as contracts among various subscribers. These contracts cannot be revoked unless all subscribers consent. RMBCA says that subscribers cannot revoke subscription agreements for six months unless the agreements provide otherwise or all subscribers consent.

SELECTING A STATE FOR INCORPORATION

Next, an infant corporation must select a state in which to incorporate. Each state has different laws governing the incorporation process and different corporate tax rates. Other factors corporations consider when selecting a state for incorporation include:

- How much flexibility does the state grant to corporate management?
- What rights do state statutes give to shareholders?
- What restrictions does the state place on the distribution of dividends?
- Does the state offer any kind of protection against takeovers?

Although most corporations incorporate in the state in which they are located and do most of their business, more than half of all publicly held corporations, including more than half of the Fortune 500 companies, are incorporated in Delaware. Decades ago, Delaware offered extremely low corporate tax rates and granted more extensive rights to management in the event of a takeover than did other states. Thus, in the 1940s and 1950s, many corporations changed their state of incorporation to Delaware. Although other states have made their corporate laws more attractive since then, many corporations remain incorporated in Delaware because its courts are highly experienced in corporate law. Closely held corporations and professional corporations, however, almost always incorporate in the state in which most of their stockholders live.

Although a corporation can incorporate in only one state, it can file a certificate of authority to do business in other states. Some states fine corporations that fail to obtain a certificate of authority before conducting business in the state. Other states fine directors and officers of these corporations directly and hold them personally liable for contracts made in the state.

Once a corporation chooses a state for incorporation, it can begin the formal legal process of incorporation.

Legal Process of Incorporation

SELECTION OF CORPORATE NAME

All states require that corporations attach *Corporation, Company, Limited, Incorporated,* or an abbreviation of one of these terms to the end of the business name to indicate the firm is incorporated. Kraft Foods Inc., The Hershey Company, Facebook Inc., and McDonald's Corporation serve as examples of corporate names. Corporations must also distinguish their names from those of all other domestic or foreign corporations licensed to do business within the state. This requirement protects third parties from confusion over similar names. Once the corporation has chosen a name, this name is subject to the approval of the state.

INCORPORATORS

An **incorporator** is an individual who applies to the state for incorporation on behalf of a corporation. RMBCA requires only one incorporator to incorporate a business, although it permits more. Although promoters frequently serve as incorporators, RMBCA does not require that incorporators be promoters or subscribers. In fact, RMBCA does not require that incorporators have an interest in the company. Generally, their only duty is to sign the articles of incorporation.

ARTICLES OF INCORPORATION

The *articles of incorporation* is a document providing basic information about the corporation. According to RMBCA, it must include (1) the name of the corporation, (2) the address of the registered office, (3) the name of the registered agent (the specific person who receives legal documents on behalf of the corporation), and (4) the names and addresses of the incorporators.

Many articles of incorporation include several additional elements, such as a clause describing the nature and purpose of the corporation. This statement of purpose grants the corporation power to engage in certain business activities. Many articles also describe the corporate capital structure and authorize the corporation to issue a certain number of shares of stock.

COMPARING THE LAW OF OTHER COUNTRIES

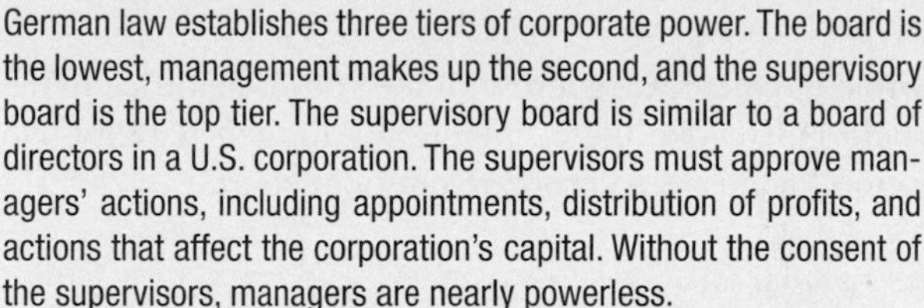

CORPORATE STRUCTURE IN GERMANY

German law establishes three tiers of corporate power. The board is the lowest, management makes up the second, and the supervisory board is the top tier. The supervisory board is similar to a board of directors in a U.S. corporation. The supervisors must approve managers' actions, including appointments, distribution of profits, and actions that affect the corporation's capital. Without the consent of the supervisors, managers are nearly powerless.

Supervisors cannot limit managerial authority to deal with third parties, however. Here managers enjoy considerable power and can act on their own discretion. Because supervisors cede considerable control in these situations, they have the power to appoint managers they feel will be reliable.

Although the board makes up the lowest tier of corporate power, it exercises considerable influence. Shareholders elect the board, a group of at least three members that acts as a mediator between shareholders and management. Because both managers and supervisors understand the importance of shareholders' interests, they listen to the board's recommendations.

The incorporators must execute and sign the articles of incorporation and file the document with the secretary of state, including the required filing fee, to legally form the corporation. Once filed, the articles govern the corporation. Next, the secretary of state usually issues a **certificate of incorporation,** a document certifying that the corporation is incorporated in the state and authorized to conduct business.

FIRST ORGANIZATIONAL MEETING

After the secretary of state issues the certificate of incorporation, the shareholders usually meet to elect the corporate board of directors, pass corporate bylaws, and carry out other corporate business. Sometimes shareholders name the board members before this first organizational meeting and list them in the articles of incorporation. In these situations, the directors usually run the meeting.

At the meeting, shareholders adopt a set of corporate **bylaws,** or rules and regulations that govern the corporation's internal management. The articles of incorporation determine who has the power to amend the corporate bylaws after the first organizational meeting: shareholders, directors, or both.

Shareholders may also authorize the corporation to issue shares of stock and approve preincorporation contracts that promoters have made in the corporation's name.

Potential Problems with Formation of the Corporation

LO5 What are some potential problems with the formation of corporations?

Most businesses incorporate to enjoy limited liability or perpetual existence. Shareholders benefit, however, only if the promoters and incorporator formally and correctly incorporate the business. If there is an error or omission during the incorporation process, courts may rule the organization is a **defective corporation.** Shareholders may be personally liable for a defective corporation's actions.

RESPONSES TO DEFECTIVE INCORPORATION

Suppose an incorporator incorrectly indicates the address of the corporate office in the articles of incorporation. Does the corporation still exist? Depending on the seriousness of the error, courts may disregard it by recognizing the firm as a *de jure* or a *de facto* corporation.

***De Jure* Corporations.** A ***de jure* corporation** (literally, "a corporation from law," or a lawful corporation) has met the substantial elements of the incorporation process. Courts usually hold that corporations that make minor errors in the incorporation process still enjoy *de jure* corporate status. Exhibit 38-2 illustrates the process for creating a *de jure* corporation.

Thus, even if the incorporator wrote the incorrect address of the corporate office in the articles of incorporation, courts would not revoke the corporation's limited liability. No party can question a *de jure* corporation's status as a corporate entity in court.

BUT WHAT IF . . .

WHAT IF THE FACTS OF THE CASE OPENER WERE DIFFERENT?

Let's say, in the Case Opener, that when filling out documents for the incorporation of Facebook, Zuckerberg's attorney became confused and wrote the company's address wrong on the documents. Later, long after Facebook was incorporated, Zuckerberg saw the incorrect company address on the documents. Should Zuckerberg worry about the clerical error? What could be the effects of having the wrong company information on such documents?

***De Facto* Corporations.** Suppose, however, that the incorporator makes a more serious mistake or omission, such as not filing the articles of incorporation with the secretary of state. In this case, courts may recognize the corporation as a ***de facto* corporation** (literally, "a corporation from the fact," or a corporation in fact). A *de facto* corporation has not substantially met the requirements of the state incorporation statute, but courts recognize it as a corporation for most purposes to avoid unfairness to third parties who believed it was properly incorporated. *De facto* corporations, regardless of whether the state has a general corporation statute, must meet the following requirements:

- The promoters, subscribers, and incorporator made a good-faith attempt to comply with the incorporation statute.
- The organization has already conducted business as a corporation.

The process for recognizing a corporation as a *de facto* corporation is depicted in Exhibit 38-3.

Only the state can challenge a *de facto* corporation's existence as a corporate entity, in a suit called an action of *quo warranto* (Latin for "by what right").

Exhibit 38-2
De Jure Corporation Formation

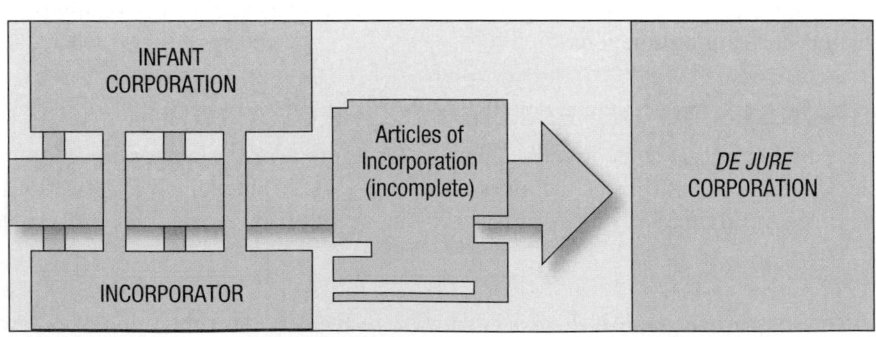

Exhibit 38-3 *De Facto* Corporation Recognition Process

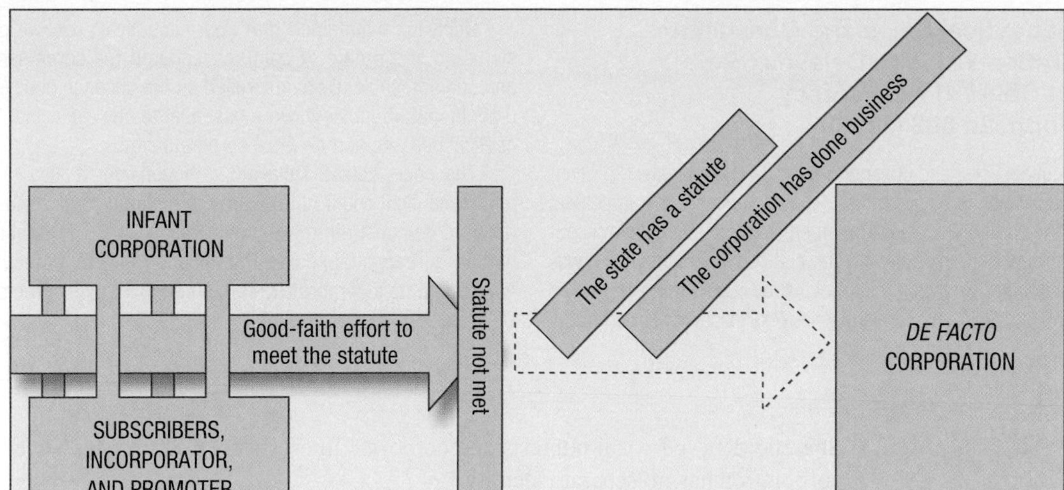

Corporation by Estoppel. Defective corporations cannot escape corporate entity status due to mistakes or omissions in their incorporation procedures. Suppose a corporation's articles of incorporation do not include the name of its registered agent and the directors, managers, and shareholders are unaware of the mistake. If the corporation conducts business with a third party who later sues for breach of contract, the corporation cannot claim it is not a corporate entity to escape liability. Courts hold that the corporation is a **corporation by estoppel;** thus, they *estop* (bar) the corporation from denying its corporate status. This ruling does not remedy the error or grant the firm corporate status for conducting future business.

If a corporation makes a significant error in the incorporation process and is not a *de jure* or *de facto* corporation, and corporation by estoppel does not apply, courts usually deny the organization corporate entity status. Thus, the organization does not enjoy limited shareholder liability.

Piercing the Corporate Veil. In some cases, courts will deny limited liability to a corporation that would normally have *de jure* or *de facto* status because shareholders have used the corporation to engage in illegal or wrongful acts. Shareholders attempt to hide behind the "corporate veil" of limited liability to protect themselves from personal liability. In these cases, courts *pierce the corporate veil,* or impose personal liability on shareholders. Shareholders of closely held and parent-subsidiary corporations frequently mix personal and corporate interests such that no separate corporate identity exists. Thus, courts often pierce the corporate veil of these corporations.

Legal Principle: **The limited liability of corporate shareholders may not exist when shareholders have acted in an illegal or wrongful manner.**

Courts are likely to pierce the corporate veil when:

- A corporation lacked adequate capital when it initially formed.
- A corporation did not follow statutory mandates regarding corporate business.

CASE NUGGET

DE FACTO INCORPORATION

Pharmaceutical Sales and Consulting Corporation v. J.W.S. Delavaux Co.
District Court of New Jersey
59 F. Supp. 2d 398 (1999)

Pharmaceutical Sales and Consulting sued J.W.S. Delavaux Co., alleging Delavaux failed to pay commissions due under a sales agreement between the parties. The sales agreement was signed by Pharmaceutical's president and on its behalf. The company had indicated it was a corporation, but Delavaux later discovered it was not a registered corporation and filed a motion to dismiss Pharmaceutical's complaint.

Delavaux maintained that Pharmaceutical's lack of corporate status as of the date of contract rendered the agreement invalid and unenforceable. Delavaux relied on the absence of several documents that, in its view, were essential to any claim that Pharmaceutical had attained *de facto* corporate status.

The court denied Delavaux's motion, but it also found that Pharmaceutical could not rely on the doctrine of *de facto* incorporation to demonstrate that it could sue Delavaux for breach of the parties' agreement, because Pharmaceutical had not made a bona fide attempt to incorporate before entering into the agreement with Delavaux.

- Shareholders' personal interests and corporate interests are commingled such that the corporation has no separate identity.
- Shareholders attempt to commit fraud through a corporation.

If a corporation does not carefully maintain separate corporate and shareholder funds and records, courts may pierce the corporate veil and impose personal liability on shareholders, as Case 38-3 illustrates.

CASE 38-3 J-MART JEWELRY OUTLETS, INC. v. STANDARD DESIGN
COURT OF APPEALS OF GEORGIA
218 GA. APP. 459 (1995)

Jim Halter, the major shareholder of J-Mart Jewelry Outlets, Inc., and several other corporations, was aware J-Mart was in financial trouble. Before the firm went out of business, Halter paid off his personal credit cards using corporate funds. He also paid the corporation $1 for a corporate car that had been purchased with corporation funds. Four of J-Mart's creditors brought suit against Halter in an attempt to recover corporate funds. The trial court jury pierced the corporate veil to hold Halter personally responsible for the debts. Halter appealed.

JUDGE BLACKBURN: The concept of piercing the corporate veil is applied in Georgia to remedy injustices which arise where a party has over extended his privilege in the use of a corporate entity in order to defeat justice, perpetrate fraud or to evade contractual or tort responsibility. Because the cardinal rule of corporate law is that a corporation possesses a legal existence separate and apart from that of its officers and shareholders, the mere operation of corporate business does not render one personally liable for corporate acts. Sole ownership of a corporation by one person or another corporation is not a factor, and neither is the fact that the sole owner uses and controls it to promote his ends. There must be evidence of abuse of the corporate form. Plaintiff must show that the defendant disregarded the separateness of legal entities by commingling on an interchangeable or joint basis or confusing the otherwise separate properties, records or control.

In deciding this enumeration of error, we are confronted with two maxims that sometimes conflict. On the one hand, we are mindful that great caution should be exercised by the court in disregarding the corporate entity. On the other, it is axiomatic that "when litigated, the issue of 'piercing the corporate veil' is for the jury[,]" unless there is no evidence sufficient to justify disregarding the corporate form. Our examination of the trial transcript convinces us that there is evidence in this case rising to such level.

Halter knew as early as late April but not later than June 1991 that J-Mart would have to cease operations as a result of its financial difficulties. There was direct evidence that the $6,902.87 balance on Halter's American Express personal account was paid by J-Mart on December 23, 1991, eight days before it ceased doing business. The check was marked "PAYMENT IN FULL: JIM'S PERSONAL[,]" indicating that a material question of fact existed as to whether Halter used corporate funds to pay a personal debt. The evidence

[continued]

also established that J-Mart, with knowledge that it would soon cease doing business, purchased a new Cadillac for Halter's use. It thereafter made three payments on the vehicle before transferring it to Halter for $1 and allowing him to assume the remaining payments, indicating the presence of further questions of material fact relative to a de facto unauthorized payment for Halter's personal benefit. In light of the evidence presented, the trial court properly denied the motion for a directed verdict upon the claim of Halter's personal liability for violation of the corporate form.

Evidence raising material questions of fact as to Halter's possible abuse of the corporate form were thus properly before the jury. On appeal, we construe all the evidence most strongly in support of the verdict, for that is what we must presume the jury did; and if there is evidence to sustain the verdict, we cannot disturb it. So viewing the evidence, we conclude that the jury's verdict was proper and must stand.

AFFIRMED.

CRITICAL THINKING

Given what you know of the facts of the case, could Halter have provided any information that would lead you to believe he was not responsible for the debts? What would it be?

ETHICAL DECISION MAKING

Describe the ethical conflict Halter was facing. For what purpose, or value, was he acting? Had Halter followed the Golden Rule, would he have acted as he did? What might have convinced Halter to refrain from using corporate funds to pay off his personal credit cards?

Corporate Financing

LO6 How do corporations get funding?

Corporations, like other businesses, need a source of funding. They most commonly obtain financing by issuing and selling corporate securities: debt securities, which represent loans to a corporation, and equity securities, which represent ownership in a corporation.

DEBT SECURITIES

Debt securities, or **bonds,** represent loans to a corporation from another party. Bonds are usually long-term loans on which the corporation promises to pay interest. They frequently list a maturity date on which the corporation must repay the face amount of the loan. Before the maturity date, however, corporations usually pay bond holders fixed-dollar interest payments on a scheduled basis. Hence, bonds are sometimes called *fixed-income securities.*

Corporations can issue the following types of bonds:

- *Unsecured bonds (debentures):* No assets support corporations' obligation to repay the face value of unsecured bonds.
- *Secured bonds (mortgage bonds):* Specific property supports corporations' obligation to repay secured bonds.
- *Income bonds:* A corporation pays interest on income bonds in proportion to its earnings.
- *Convertible bonds:* Shareholders may exchange their convertible bonds for shares of company stock.
- *Callable bonds:* Corporations may call in and repay the bonds at specific times.

EQUITY SECURITIES

While bond owners have loaned money to a corporation, stock owners actually own part of the corporation, in the form of shares of stock called **equity securities.** Stockholders

COMPARING THE LAW OF OTHER COUNTRIES

COMPANY LAW IN FRANCE

French law categorizes companies into two types: Société Anonymes (SA) and Société à Responsabilité Limitée (SARL). Several factors determine a company's category, including its relationship to shareholders, its management hierarchy, and the extent of its liabilities.

SA companies offer shares to the public and must have at least seven shareholders. SARL companies, on the other hand, sell shares exclusively to company members. They must have at least 2 but no more than 50 shareholders. Their shares are nonnegotiable and freely transferable among company members.

One managing director, with as many as 14 subordinate directors, runs SA companies; at least one director must be a shareholder. SARL companies, in contrast, have one or two managers and allow nonmembers to serve. French law also requires that all SA companies appoint an independent auditor to verify the legality of their accounts. The auditor must report to the French government any irregularities she or he suspects to be criminal in nature. French law does not require that SARL companies appoint an auditor.

Member liability is closely related to the managerial structure of SA and SARL companies. Members of SARL companies are liable only to the extent of their contributions to the company. If the manager of a SARL company makes a transaction with a third party, all members are liable for the manager's action, regardless of whether he is a member of the company. Liability to third parties does not rest on all members in SA companies. Rather, in most cases the managing director is liable for damages caused by her actions, regardless of whether she benefited personally.

thus have a voice in the firm's control. Not all corporations issue bonds, but all issue stock. Common stock and preferred stock are the two major types.

Preferred Stock. Owners of **preferred stock,** or *preferred shares,* enjoy preferences in the distribution of assets and dividends. They usually receive a percentage of dividends associated with the face value of their preferred stock, and they will receive dividends before owners of common stock do. Some corporations limit preferred stock owners' voting rights.

Cumulative preferred stock requires that if a corporation cannot pay the required dividends in a given year, it must pay them in the next year before it pays any common stock dividends. *Convertible preferred stock* allows its owner to convert shares into common stock at any time. *Redeemable preferred stock* (also known as *callable preferred stock*) permits the issuing corporation to buy shares back from shareholders in certain circumstances. *Participating preferred stock* entitles its owner to both preferred stock dividends and, after the corporation has paid common stock dividends, additional dividends.

Common Stock. Owners of **common stock,** or *common shares,* own a portion of a corporation but do not enjoy any preferences. A common stock owner is entitled to corporate dividends in proportion to the number of shares he or she owns and has the right to vote in corporate elections. Each share is usually worth one vote. Thus, if you own 20,000 common shares of a corporation, you have 20,000 votes. In some cases, however, most notably the election of the board of directors, corporations use a method called *cumulative voting* to increase the influence of shareholders who own a small number of shares. (The next chapter discusses cumulative voting in more detail.)

Common stock owners have the lowest priority when a corporation distributes dividends. Creditors and preferred stock owners receive dividends first. Once a corporation pays these groups, however, common stock owners have a claim to the remainder of the corporate earnings.

CASE OPENER WRAP-UP

The Formation of the Facebook Corporation

Zuckerberg's actions in 2004 were instrumental in creating what is now Facebook today. There are currently over 250 million users on the website from all over the world. In 2007, Microsoft bought a 1.6 percent share of the corporation for $240 million. Facebook gained another investor in November of that year, a billionaire from Hong Kong, Li Ka-shing, for $60 million. Estimates put the corporation's value around $4 billion to $5 billion. Ultimately, its corporate status allows Facebook to enjoy perpetual existence; to sue and be sued; to acquire property; to make contracts; to borrow and lend money; to make charitable donations; and to establish rules for managing the corporation. Moreover, Facebook's shareholders enjoy limited liability.

KEY TERMS

alien corporation 836
articles of incorporation 834
bonds 845
bylaws 841
certificate of incorporation 841
closely held corporations 836
common stock 846
corporation by estoppel 843
de facto corporation 842
de jure corporation 841
debt securities 845
defective corporation 841
dividends 834
domestic corporation 836
equity securities 845
for-profit corporations 836
foreign corporation 836
incorporator 840
nonprofit corporations 836
novation 838
preferred stock 846
private corporations 836
promoters 837
public corporation 836
publicly held corporations 836
retained earnings 835
S corporations 837
subscribers 837
subscription agreements 837

SUMMARY OF KEY TOPICS

Characteristics of Corporations

A corporation is a legal entity, and it has rights, just as a person and citizen has rights.

A corporation is a creature of the state.

There is limited liability of shareholders.

There is unrestricted transferability of corporate shares.

A corporation has perpetual existence and centralized management.

There is corporate taxation and liability for corporate agents.

Corporate Powers

Corporations have both express and implied powers.

Classification of Corporations

Corporations can be classified as public or private.

Corporations can be for profit or can be classified as nonprofit.

A corporation can be domestic, foreign, or alien.

A corporation can be publicly held or closely held.

A corporation can be classified as an S corporation.

A corporation can also be classified as a professional corporation.

Formation of the Corporation

Promoters organize corporate formation.

Subscribers offer to purchase stock in corporations in the formation process.

A state is selected for incorporation.

Legal Process of Incorporation

The incorporation process consists of:

- Selection of a corporate name.
- Drafting and filing of articles of incorporation.
- First organizational meeting.

Potential Problems with Formation of the Corporation

Remedies for defective incorporation include:

- *De jure* corporations
- *De facto* corporations
- Corporations by estoppel
- Piercing the corporate veil

Corporate Financing

Corporate financing can consist of:

- Debt securities (bonds)
- Equity securities (preferred stock, common stock)

POINT / COUNTERPOINT

Should Corporations Be Allowed the Status of "Legal Personhood" and Be Given Full Protection under the Bill of Rights?

YES

On May 10, 1886, in the case of *Santa Clara County v. the Southern Pacific Railroad Company,* the Supreme Court clearly decided "other corporations" deserved "equal protection of the laws," specifically the Fourteenth Amendment.

A corporation is created by and composed of natural persons directly affected by its actions. Their rights cannot be violated, and violating the rights of the corporation indirectly does that. We should not place limitations on a group of people simply because they have pooled their efforts and formed a corporation.

Logical limitations are in place to restrict corporations' existence as "persons." Corporations cannot become official citizens and cannot vote; the natural citizens involved with the corporation are expected to vote with its best interest in mind.

NO

Clearly, the creators of the Bill of Rights were aware that corporations existed at the time. Yet corporations were not mentioned as having rights independent of the natural persons associated with them, so the Bill of Rights was not designed to protect corporations as "legal persons."

Further, classifying corporations as "legal persons" and allowing them protection under the Bill of Rights, though advantageous for corporate interests, is harmful to human interests. For example, corporate money speaks much louder than one person's letter when influencing politicians.

If corporations are given rights as a natural person, the individuals making decisions behind the corporation are not being held accountable to the larger community. The corporation is punished for a poor decision rather than the individual, who used poor judgment but who may not suffer much, if any, of the consequences.

Finally, corporations deserve the same rights as natural persons because they fulfill the same obligations, only as entities separate from the natural persons associated with them. Shareholders pay taxes, for instance, and so do corporations.

Corporations also do not face the same restrictions as a natural person. A natural person's life must end, while a corporation is allowed perpetual existence.

Lastly, corporations do not face the same potential consequences as natural persons. A corporation cannot be sent to jail for its actions. It cannot be rehabilitated and changed into a profitable member of society if it breaks the law.

QUESTIONS & PROBLEMS

1. Name at least three characteristics that distinguish corporations from other forms of business organization.
2. Distinguish between a closely held corporation and a publicly held corporation.
3. Donna Leek, Larry Leonardo, John Borden, and Cindy Buschmann were all, at one point, employed by Auburn Honda in California. Auburn Honda was owned solely by one person: Jay Cooper. All of the employees, who were older in age, had worked for the company for several years. All four employees were fired; all parties claim they fell victim to age discrimination. Does Auburn Honda have the right, as a corporation, to discriminate on the basis of age? Why or why not? [*Leek v. Cooper,* 194 Cal. App. 4th 399 (2011).]
4. In 2009, Mark McEwen, a personality from the *Early Show* on CBS, brought a lawsuit against the Baltimore Washington Medical Center. McEwen went to the emergency room at the hospital with symptoms of a stroke, and a doctor told him he had the stomach flu and sent him away. On the plane heading home, McEwen suffered a stroke. Subsequently, McEwen filed a claim against the medical center, stating that his stroke could have been avoided if the doctor had prescribed aspirin and anticoagulants. How do you think the court decided the case? Do you think the court should hold the doctor responsible, or should the medical center be held accountable for the doctor's actions? [*McEwen et al. v. Baltimore Washington Medical Center, Inc., et al.* (2009).]
5. Attorney Nicholas Kepple, the president of M&K Realty, drew up a contract for the sale of a parcel of land (Lot 5) from Howard Engelsen to M&K. To establish a purchase price for the sale, Engelsen had Lot 5 appraised. The appraisers based their appraisal of Lot 5 on several facts that Kepple and Engelsen learned were incorrect after they signed the contract. These facts included the total acreage of Lot 5 and whether Lot 5 could be divided into two separate lots without the need for a subdivision approval from the planning and zoning commissioner. After learning that these facts were in error, Kepple saw that the original purchase price was well below the market price for Lot 5, and he attempted to complete the sale for the original purchase price. Engelsen informed Kepple that he would not complete the sale of Lot 5 because M&K had never legally formed as a corporation under the state incorporation statutes and thus lacked the capacity to enter the contract in the first place. Do you think the court agreed with Engelsen's argument? Why or why not? [*BRJM LLC v. Output Systems, Inc., et al.,* 2005 Conn. Super. LEXIS 1699 (2005).]
6. Richard Schoon was elected to the board of directors at the Troy Corporation, a private corporation in Delaware. There are three stock series of stock options. A series A share allows someone to elect four of five directors on the corporation's board. A series B share allows a stockholder to elect the fifth member of the board. Anyone who has a series C share has no voting rights. The CEO of Troy, Daryl Smith, owns the majority of the A shares, and thus he elected four directors of the board. Schoon was elected as the fifth director, although he owned no shares. Schoon claimed that Smith "dominated the board" because he elected the other four directors and they were

compliant to his wishes. Schoon believed that in several instances, Smith took actions that benefited him personally yet harmed the corporation's finances. In 2008, Schoon filed a derivative suit that shareholders typically file. However, Schoon was not a shareholder and owned no stock in the company. Do you think the court accepted his suit? Why or why not? [*Schoon v. Smith,* Del. Supr. No. 554 (2008).]

7. In early 2002, the president of the board of education for the East Hampton School District entered into a contract with Sandpebble Builders Inc. Sandpebble Builders would renovate certain school buildings in accordance with the requests of the school district. When the school district wanted to renegotiate its contract with the contractor, Sandpebble Builders was not in accordance. The school district voided the contract and terminated relations with Sandpebble Builders. The school district then sought to receive the money it would have put into the project from the builder. Does the school district have the right to seek the money from Sandpebble Builders? Why or why not? [*East Hampton Union Free School District v. Sandpebble Builders, Inc.,* 90 A.D.3d 820 (2011).]

Looking for more review materials?

The Online Learning Center at **www.mhhe.com/kubasek3e** contains this chapter's "Assignment on the Internet" and also a list of URLs for more information, entitled "On the Internet." Find both of them in the Student Center portion of the OLC, along with quizzes and other helpful materials.

CHAPTER

39

Corporations: Directors, Officers, and Shareholders

LEARNING OBJECTIVES

After reading this chapter, you will be able to answer the following questions:

1. Why is it important to regulate the interactions among directors, officers, and shareholders within a corporation?
2. What is the role of a director, an officer, and a shareholder?
3. What are the duties of directors, officers, and shareholders?
4. In what ways can a director, officer, and shareholder be held liable?
5. What are the rights of directors, officers, and shareholders?

CASE OPENER

A Majority Shareholder and Her Son

Stephanie Gately was the majority shareholder of Campbell Farming Corporation. Stephanie controlled 51 percent of the company's shares, while the minority shareholders controlled the remaining 49 percent. Stephanie was the director of the company, and her son, Robert Gately, was the president of the company.

Stephanie offered a bonus to her son. The minority shareholders voted their shares against the bonus, but because the majority shareholder voted her shares in favor of the bonus, the transaction was approved.

The minority shareholders sued the corporation, its majority shareholder, and her son, the president of the corporation. The plaintiff minority shareholders alleged breach of statutory and fiduciary duties.

After consideration of the business judgment rule, the district court ruled that the bonus transaction did not constitute a breach of fiduciary duties. The plaintiff minority shareholders appealed.

1. If you were a minority shareholder of Campbell Farming Corporation, would you think that the corporation's director breached her fiduciary duties?
2. What is the business judgment rule? How did this rule affect the district court's decision?

The Wrap-Up at the end of the chapter will answer these questions.

As the Case Opener demonstrates, various groups of individuals within a corporation have own their priorities and agendas. Not surprisingly, these often come into conflict. To ensure that such conflicts are equitably resolved, statutory laws delegate particular roles, duties, and rights to each group.

The statutory law governing corporations has a long and dynamic history. In 1946, the American Bar Association (ABA) drafted the first version of the Model Business Corporation Act (MBCA). Like almost all new laws, MBCA met with varying degrees of success, and over time legislatures have molded it to achieve certain objectives. The ABA has amended the act numerous times since 1946, and more than 25 states have adopted at least part of it.

When the law changes, however, it often changes at an uneven pace. A sudden reformation sometimes interrupts a trend of incremental change. Thus, after nearly 40 years of minor revisions, the ABA in 1984 discontinued its revisions of MBCA and drafted the Revised Model Business Corporation Act (RMBCA). More than half the states have adopted all or part of RMBCA. This chapter explains the duties and rights set forth in RMBCA and common law.

Importance of Regulating Interactions among Directors, Officers, and Shareholders within a Corporation

L01

Why is it important to regulate the interactions among directors, officers, and shareholders within a corporation?

The three major groups of individuals within a corporation are *directors, officers,* and *shareholders.* Each has different interests, and in many situations their interests conflict. Statutory law ensures that the directors, officers, and shareholders work together to the benefit of all.

Although directors and officers play different roles within the corporation, they share the same goal. Both attempt to ensure that their institution survives and they keep their jobs. Shareholders, on the other hand, want to raise the value of the company's stock.

These differences can lead to conflict. If a corporation has an opportunity that can quickly raise the value of its stock, shareholders will push the directors and officers to take it. But if the directors and officers believe that the decision might jeopardize their jobs, they will resist. To resolve conflicts, the law gives each group legal duties and rights.

Roles of Directors, Officers, and Shareholders

L02

What is the role of a director, an officer, and a shareholder?

The duties and rights of directors, officers, and shareholders depend on the specific roles they play. These roles are discussed below and outlined in Exhibit 39-1.

DIRECTORS' ROLES

When a corporation faces an important decision, the board of directors meets to decide what course of action it will take. Although their vital role gives directors considerable power, no one director wields much by himself or herself. A director who wants the company to move in a certain direction must solicit the approval of other directors on the board before the company will begin to shift.

Elections. Typically, shareholders use a majority vote to elect directors. The only exception occurs during incorporation. Because there are no shareholders in the beginning, either the incorporators appoint board members or the corporate articles name them. This first board serves until the first shareholder meeting, at which the shareholders elect a new board. The corporate articles or bylaws specify the number of corporate directors.

Exhibit 39-1 Roles of Directors, Officers, and Shareholders

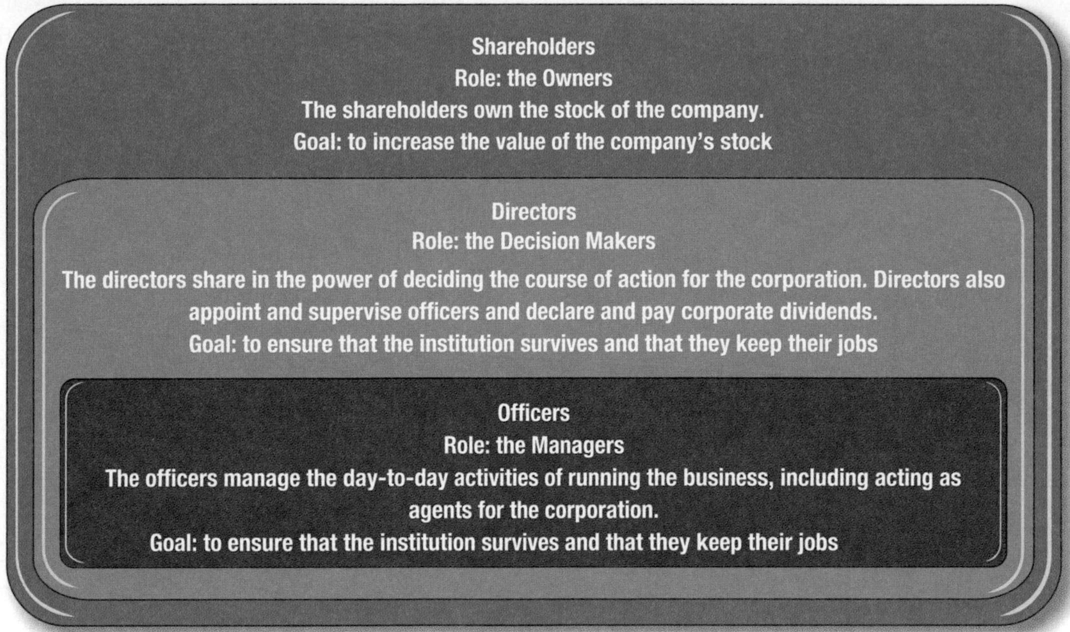

In the past, the minimum required was three, but today many states allow fewer. In fact, if a corporation has fewer than 50 shareholders, Section 7.32 of RMBCA allows companies to eliminate the board of directors altogether. This change illustrates how the need for practicality can stimulate change in the law. The benefits of the corporate form of business organization have drawn an enormous number of businesses, especially small businesses, to incorporate in recent years. The requirement of at least three directors, however, burdened small corporations that did not generate sufficient business to warrant three directors. Thus, many states eased or removed the three-director requirement.

Interestingly, almost anyone can become a director. The legal requirements are lax, and in most states directors are not even required to own stock in the corporation. In some cases, however, statutory law and corporate bylaws require not only ownership but also a minimum age.

Directors typically serve for one year, but most state statutes allow longer terms if they are staggered. Directors can be removed *for cause*—for failing to perform a required duty. Removal is typically a result of shareholder action, but in some cases directors can remove other directors for cause. Directors removed for cause can ask the courts to review the legality of their removal. Only a few states allow removal without cause, and then only if shareholders reserve that right at the board election.

Meetings and Voting. A minimum number of directors, or a *quorum,* must be present at each directors' meeting for decisions to be valid. Quorum requirements are different in each state, but most states leave the decision up to the corporation itself. Because a quorum is required at each meeting, directors are notified whenever special meetings are called. Directors vote in person, and each has one vote. While ordinary decisions require a majority vote, more important decisions sometimes require a two-thirds vote.

Although directors' meetings are usually held in a central location, Section 8.20 of RMBCA permits them to be held via telephone conference.

Directors as Managers. Although directors vote on major decisions about the corporation, they are also responsible for many day-to-day managerial activities. They appoint, supervise, and remove corporate officers as they see fit, and they declare and pay corporate dividends to shareholders. They are also responsible for making financial decisions and authorizing corporate policy decisions. Some directors are also officers or employees of the corporation; they are *inside directors.* Directors who are not officers or employees are *outside directors.* Outside directors are further divided into *affiliated directors* and *unaffiliated directors.* Affiliated directors have business contacts with the corporation, while unaffiliated directors do not.

Because the day-to-day tasks of a corporation can be overwhelming for a small board that has larger issues to address, directors often appoint an executive committee to handle day-to-day responsibilities.

OFFICERS' ROLES

Officers are executive managers whom the board of directors hires to run the day-to-day business of the corporation. Their decisions influence the corporation immensely. Officers act as agents of the corporation, and thus the rules of agency apply to their work. (Refer to Chapter 33 for the rules of agency.)

Qualifications required of officers are set forth in the corporate articles and bylaws of each corporation, but in most cases an individual may serve as both a director and an officer. Many corporations find it beneficial to include an officer on the board so that the directors can stay in touch with day-to-day operations.

SHAREHOLDERS' ROLES

Shareholders own the firm. As soon as an individual purchases the stock of a particular corporation, he or she becomes an owner of the corporation. However, there is a major division between shareholders within a corporation. There are majority shareholders and minority shareholders. A majority shareholder is a shareholder who controls more than half of the outstanding shares of a corporation, or at least 51 percent. A minority shareholder is one who controls fewer than half of the outstanding shares of a corporation.

While a shareholder is not legally recognized as an owner of corporate property, every shareholder has an *equitable,* or ownership, interest in the company. Shareholders are not directly responsible for the daily management of the corporation, but they elect the directors who are.

Power of Shareholders. The articles of incorporation established within each corporation, and general incorporation law in each state, grant shareholders certain powers. Because shareholders must approve major board decisions, they are in some sense empowered to make decisions for the corporation. Their most influential power, however, is to elect and remove directors.

For example, in 2008 and 2009, Bank of America chairman and CEO Ken Lewis approved the questionable acquisitions of two financially troubled companies, Countrywide Financial and Merrill Lynch. Many shareholders disagreed with Lewis's decisions and lost confidence in his ability to lead the company. Consequently, to remedy the situation, Bank of America shareholders voted to remove Lewis from his chairman of the board position and opted to find a new leader. Lewis was able to retain his position as CEO but was no longer permitted to head the board of directors.

Shareholders also have the power to propose ideas for the corporation. The Securities and Exchange Commission has established that any shareholder who owns more than

$1,000 worth of stock in the corporation can submit proposals to be included in *proxy materials* sent to the shareholders before their annual meeting.

Meetings. Shareholders typically meet once a year, but in emergencies they can meet more often. The board of directors, shareholders who own at least 10 percent of the corporation's outstanding shares, and others authorized in the articles of incorporation may call a special shareholder meeting.

Like directors' meetings, shareholder meetings require a quorum, generally the presence of shareholders holding more than 50 percent of the outstanding shares. A majority vote of the shares represented is then required to pass resolutions. Occasionally, however, articles of incorporation include supermajority provisions, which state that more than a majority is needed to pass major corporate proposals, such as those for corporate merger or dissolution.

Because shareholders cannot always attend shareholder meetings, they can authorize a third party to attend and vote in their place. This authorization is called a **proxy.** Under Section 7.22(c) of RMBCA, proxies last for 11 months and can be withdrawn at any time unless specifically designed to be irrevocable.

An individual shareholder can also enter a voting trust by transferring his or her share titles to a trustee in exchange for a *voting trust certificate.* The trustee is then responsible for voting for those shares, either as directed in the trust or at the trustee's discretion. The shareholder, however, retains all other shareholder rights (discussed below).

Before a meeting, shareholders can sign a *shareholder voting agreement* in which they agree to vote together in a certain manner. These agreements are usually legally enforceable.

BUT WHAT IF . . .

WHAT IF THE FACTS OF THE CASE OPENER WERE DIFFERENT?

Let's say, in the Case Opener, that after her company was incorporated, Gately decided she wanted to make her sister a director. She meets with the directors and tells them she is appointing her sister and the appointment will be effective as of the following week. The directors disapprove of the decision. Is there anything that the directors can do to stop this?

Voting. Like directors, each shareholder is entitled to one vote per share in most instances. Corporations practice unique voting processes, however, that alter the influence of each shareholder's votes and are especially important for minority shareholders. One such process required in most states, *cumulative voting,* ensures that minority shareholders have a voice in electing the board of directors. It gives each group, majority and minority shareholders, a certain number of votes to cast by multiplying the number of shares the group owns by the number of open director positions. If a company is electing eight directors and the minority shareholders own 2,000 shares, the minority shareholders get 16,000 votes to cast in the election. If the majority shareholders in the same corporation own 8,000 shares, they get 64,000 votes.

Although it may seem that minority shareholders still have little influence in the election, cumulative voting permits them to vote at least one director onto the board because they can cast all their votes for one candidate. If the majority shareholders want to elect all eight directors from their nominees, each nominee must receive more than 16,000 votes in order to beat the 16,000 votes of the minority nominee. But because the majority shareholders have only 64,000 votes to cast, they cannot cast more than 16,000 votes for each of eight candidates ($16,000 \times 8 = 128,000$). Thus, if the minority shareholders cast all their 16,000 votes for one candidate, they can guarantee that candidate's election.

Cumulative voting is more egalitarian than simple majority voting because it ensures that every voice within the corporation is heard, not just the voices of those with the most power. Without it, majority shareholders could monopolize control of the company and disregard the interests of the minority shareholders. Cumulative voting is not guaranteed in RMBCA, however; rather, it occurs only if the corporation's articles of incorporation provide for it.

Duties of Directors, Officers, and Shareholders

L03

What are the duties of directors, officers, and shareholders?

Because all individuals within a corporation depend on one another, the law gives them specific legal responsibilities called *fiduciary duties.*

DUTIES OF DIRECTORS AND OFFICERS

Shareholders have little input in the day-to-day operations of the corporation; they trust the directors and officers to run the company to the best of their ability. Thus, directors and officers have duties to the shareholders and to the corporation. Their two primary fiduciary duties are the duty of care and the duty of loyalty.

Duty of Care. The fiduciary *duty of care* means that directors and officers must exercise due care when making decisions for the corporation. The phrase *due care* is ambiguous, and various courts have interpreted it differently over time. In general, however, it requires exercising the care that an ordinary prudent person would exercise in the management of his or her own assets. In other words, a person acting with due care acts in good faith and in the best interest of the company.

Legal Principle: **The directors and officers bear liability for failure to exercise a duty of care with respect to the management of shareholder assets.**

Given their duty to act in the best interest of the company, directors and officers must supervise employees who work for the corporation to a reasonable extent. They also have a duty to attend director and corporate business meetings. Most important, however, they have a fiduciary duty to make informed and reasonable business decisions.

The directors and officers of Enron Corp. failed in their duty of care with regard to their shareholders by not acting in the best interest of the company. They continued to advocate that employees invest in the employee stock-sharing options, even though it appears that they knew the stock was drastically overpriced. Furthermore, they failed in their duty of care regarding oversight. The directors and officers either did not pay enough attention to see the collapse of their stock coming or they purposely kept the information secret. Either way, they breached their fiduciary duty of care and therefore are liable to their shareholders, many of whom were Enron employees.

In February 2009, shareholders of the company Citigroup brought action against the company's current and former directors. One of the alleged liabilities of the directors was a failure to obey fiduciary duties. Shareholders claimed that substantial risks the company faced in the subprime lending market were not properly managed or monitored. The shareholders explained that there were signs of severe problems in the credit and real estate markets beginning in 2005 that should have put the Citigroup directors on heightened alert. Essentially, what the Citigroup shareholders were claiming was that the directors failed

E-COMMERCE AND THE LAW

WWW

WHEN A B2B COMPANY COOKS THE BOOKS

When you hear the phrase "cook the books," you likely think of companies like Enron, Tyco, and Adelphia. Why did the officers and directors of these companies fail to realize that accountants were cooking company books? Were any officers or directors involved in the fraud?

E-commerce firms have cooked their books too. PurchasePro, a business-to-business software firm that gave companies access to an online marketplace, was allegedly engaged in "overstating revenues, engaging in aggressive accounting practices and mismanaging corporate assets." Basically, the company manipulated its financial records to make itself look far more successful than it really was. It went bankrupt in September 2002.

Federal prosecutors charged company officers and directors with conspiracy, securities fraud, and obstruction of justice, a breach of their duty of care. Two senior officers, Jeffrey R. Anderson and Scott H. Miller, pleaded guilty to federal crimes in 2003. Their behavior was similar to that of officers of other, more well-known companies that have cooked the books—they had secret side deals with purchasers that gave the appearance of sales that did not really exist; they misrepresented the company's financial health so that investors could not make informed decisions; and, when news of alleged fraud surfaced, they used their energy to shred incriminating documents.

in their duty of care regarding oversight. The directors did not seem to pay enough attention to problems within the subprime lending market that were going to directly affect the company.

BUT WHAT IF . . .

WHAT IF THE FACTS OF THE CASE OPENER WERE DIFFERENT?

Let's say, in the Case Opener, that the directors became upset with Gately for her decision about her son's bonus. The directors decide to make a decision that financially harms the company. What protection does Gately have against this?

Directors and officers are expected to stay abreast of all important corporate matters and obtain information about business transactions, review contracts, read reports, and attend presentations. After all, if directors and officers are uninformed, they cannot make decisions in the best interest of the company. RMBCA does allow directors to make decisions based on information gathered by other employees. Interestingly, however, most corporations do not allow directors' decisions to be based on secondhand information.

The decisions corporate directors and officers make must not only be informed; they must also be reasonable. If a director or officer is taken to court for breaching the duty of care by making an unreasonable decision, the court typically inquires whether the decision had any rational business purpose. In other words, was there good reason to think the decision *could* have helped the company?

Part of the duty of care is to voice dissent when the corporation is doing something a director or officer does not think is in its best interest. It is unusual for a dissenting director to be held personally liable for decisions made by the corporation that entail mismanagement.

Duty of Loyalty. Because directors and officers have great decision-making freedom, they have the power to make business decisions that will benefit themselves while harming the company. Thus, to protect shareholders, directors and officers have a fiduciary *duty of loyalty,* which puts the corporation's interest above their own when making business decisions.

When directors or officers violate their duty of loyalty, they are **self-dealing.** There are two types of self-dealing. The first, *business self-dealing,* occurs when a director or officer makes decisions that benefit other companies with which she has a relationship.

CASE NUGGET

DUTY OF CARE

In re Caremark Int'l
698 A.2d 959 (1996)

Caremark, a corporation headquartered in Illinois, provided patient care and managed health care services. It was indicted by a grand jury for paying a doctor to distribute a drug produced by the corporation and for making inappropriate referral payments to another doctor. Several Caremark shareholders filed a derivative suit (discussed below) alleging that Caremark's directors breached their fiduciary duty of care by allowing situations to develop that exposed the corporation to enormous legal liability.

The Court of Chancery of Delaware ruled:

> [C]ompliance with a director's duty of care can never appropriately be judicially determined by reference to the content of the board decision that leads to a corporate loss, apart from consideration of the good faith or rationality of the process employed. That is, whether a judge or jury considering the matter after the fact believes a decision substantively wrong, or degrees of wrong extending through "stupid" to "egregious" or "irrational," provides no ground for director liability, so long as the court determines that the process employed was either rational or employed in a good faith effort to advance corporate interests. To employ a different rule—one that permitted an "objective" evaluation of the decision—would expose directors to substantive second guessing by ill-equipped judges or juries, which would, in the long-run, be injurious to investor interests.

The second, called *personal self-dealing,* occurs when a director or officer makes business decisions that benefit him personally.

When Citigroup shareholders brought the company directors to court in 2009, a second complaint was that the directors and other defendants authorized a multimillion-dollar benefit and payment package for the CEO of Citigroup in 2007. Those in charge of a company are not supposed to engage in self-dealing activities that benefit them before the rest of the company.

A director or officer who is self-dealing often forces the corporation into unfair business deals. Directors and officers can also breach their fiduciary duty of loyalty, however, by *preventing* corporate opportunity. This breach usually happens when directors or officers own other companies that compete with their corporation without the consent of the board of directors or the shareholders. If a director or officer uses corporate assets to start another business, goes into the same line of business, or uses her position to develop a new business that the company might have pursued, she is preventing corporate opportunity and can be held liable for violating the fiduciary duty of loyalty.

A director or officer convicted of breaching the duty of loyalty is required to cede to the corporation all profits earned as a result of the breach. The corporation need not have been able to earn those profits in the absence of the breach. The goal of the rule is to discourage breaches of the duty of loyalty by taking all profits so made.

The fiduciary duties of care and loyalty are rooted in ethics. Without them, directors and officers could pursue their own interests at the expense of others. Think back to Chapter 2 and the different ethical guidelines used to make ethical decisions. Which ethical guideline is the legal system using when it delegates fiduciary duties?

Duty to Disclose Conflict of Interest. Because individual directors and officers can frequently benefit personally from decisions made by the board, they have a fiduciary duty to fully disclose conflicts of interest that arise in corporate transactions. If the board addresses an issue that might personally benefit a particular director, that director is required not only to disclose the self-interest but also to abstain from voting on that issue. Decisions can be made that will personally benefit one director or officer as long as (1) there is full disclosure of the interest and (2) the disinterested board members and/or disinterested shareholders approve it.

CASE NUGGET

DUTY OF LOYALTY

Patrick v. Allen
355 F. Supp. 2d 704 (2005)

RPO, a privately traded corporation, rented land to a private golf course, of which several of RPO's directors were members. The directors charged the golf course enough rent to cover only the property taxes on the land. Patrick, a shareholder of RPO, brought a suit against the directors of RPO, alleging that they breached their fiduciary duty of loyalty to the corporation by failing to maximize the value of the corporation for shareholders. The directors argued that they were exempt from liability under the business judgment rule (covered below).

The U.S. District Court for the Southern District of New York ruled against the RPO's directors, holding:

The business judgment rule will not protect a decision that was the product of fraud, self-dealing, or bad faith. Directors may benefit from the rule only if they possess a disinterested independence and do not stand in a dual relation which prevents an unprejudicial exercise of judgment. It is black-letter, settled law that when a corporate director or officer has an interest in a decision, the business judgment rule does not apply. . . . A director is considered interested in a transaction if the director stands to receive a direct financial benefit from the transaction which is different from the benefit to shareholders generally. . . . The duty of loyalty requires a director to subordinate his own personal interests to the interest of the corporation.

DUTIES OF SHAREHOLDERS

Although shareholders typically have few legal duties, in rare instances majority shareholders have fiduciary duties to the corporation and to minority shareholders. In some corporations, the majority shareholder owns such a significant portion of the corporation's stock as to essentially control the firm. When that individual sells his shares, control of the company shifts to another individual. Thus, the majority shareholder in this situation has a fiduciary duty to act with care and loyalty when selling the shares. In closely held corporations, a breach of this fiduciary duty is known as *oppressive conduct.*

More than half of U.S. publicly traded corporations are incorporated in Delaware. Thus, when Delaware courts rule on the duties of majority shareholders to minority shareholders, for example, the courts' rulings have a far-reaching impact. In Case 39-1, a minority shareholder sued the majority shareholder of a corporation for violating its fiduciary duties.

CASE 39-1 MCCANN v. MCCANN
SUPREME COURT OF IDAHO
275 P.3D 824 (2012)

McCann Ranch & Livestock Company, Inc., was a closely-held corporation created by William McCann, Sr. In the 1970s, Ron and Bill McCann, the creator's sons, were each given 36.7% of the shares of the corporation. The remaining shares were held by the creator, William, until those shares were transferred to a trust to benefit his wife, Gertrude. The trustee, Gary Meisner, was given the power and discretion to vote and sell Gertrude's shares under certain circumstances. Upon the death of the corporation's creator, William, Bill became the President and CEO of the corporation. Then, upon the death of Gertrude, Bill received her remaining shares.

In June of 2008, Ron, a minority shareholder, filed an initial complaint, alleging that the corporation breached its fiduciary duty owed to him as a shareholder by engaging in a "squeeze-out" and that such injury is grounds for a direct action. Ron's claim mentioned his treatment by the corporation as well as financial transactions of the corporation. The district court granted summary judgment in favor of the respondent, Bill. Ron appealed.

JUSTICE BURDICK: Here, Ron alleges that Respondents breached the fiduciary duty owed to Ron by engaging in a squeeze-out. Squeeze-outs, sometimes called freeze-outs, are actions taken by the controlling shareholders to deprive a minority shareholder of his interest in the business or a fair return on his investment. Because of the predicament in which minority shareholders in a close corporation are placed by a squeeze-out situation, courts have analyzed alleged "oppressive" conduct by those in control in terms

[continued]

of "fiduciary duties" owed by the majority shareholders to the minority and the "reasonable expectations" held by the minority shareholders in committing their capital and labor to the particular enterprise.

Idaho case law is clear on the fiduciary duty owed by directors. "As fiduciaries, corporate directors are bound to exercise the utmost good faith in managing the corporation. However, the 'business judgment rule' immunizes the good faith acts of directors when the directors are acting within the powers of the corporation and within the exercise of their honest business judgment." "In Idaho a director has a fiduciary responsibility to both the corporation and to shareholders." More specifically, "That the directors of a closely held corporation owe a fiduciary duty to the minority shareholders is well recognized."

Ron alleges that the Respondents engaged in a squeeze-out by: (1) not paying dividends despite sufficient cash flow; (2) not providing corporate employment to Ron; (3) not providing board membership to Ron; (4) authorizing phony transactions to Gertrude to avoid any benefit to Ron; (5) frustrating the intent of the founder of the Corporation to provide an actual financial benefit to Ron; and (6) making management decisions that allow all of the cash flow to be obtained solely for the benefit of Bill and Gertrude at the expense of Ron.

Many of the actions undertaken by the Corporation, in and of themselves, are legitimate uses of corporate power and discretion. Regardless of his ownership interest, Ron is not entitled to a seat on the board of directors. Nor is he entitled to corporate employment. Nor is there evidence he is entitled to a dividend. By themselves, any payments from the Corporation do not harm Ron any more than they harm the other shareholders. However, they may be used as facts to support a squeeze-out. Each of these actions may fall under the business judgment rule, but those are issues of fact. Even if the business judgment rule applies, it is possible for courts to find such actions harmful if the end result could have been achieved with less injury to the minority shareholder. Also, the ownership structure of the Corporation requires an additional level of analysis that places these actions beyond the scope of the business judgment rule.

Here, the Corporation used corporate funds to make payments to Gertrude, a shareholder. Since the payments were going directly to pay Gertrude's expenses, she did not experience any harm from the transactions. In this light, the actions of the Corporation and its directors have an effect on Ron above and beyond the effect of every other shareholder. Each of these transactions hurts Ron specifically. The transactions with Gertrude, coupled with the other aforementioned corporate actions, appear to be an attempt to marginalize and squeeze-out Ron. We find that there was a material question of fact as to whether the directors could be found to have engaged in a squeeze-out of the beneficiary, causing him harm beyond every other shareholder.

REVERSED and REMANDED to the district court for further proceedings.

CRITICAL THINKING

What reasons does the court give for its conclusion? Are you persuaded by those reasons?

ETHICAL DECISION MAKING

Clearly, the court emphasizes particular values in its ruling. What are these values? Which shareholders in the business community are affected by focusing on these values when assessing a corporation's fiduciary duties?

Liabilities of Directors, Officers, and Shareholders

L04

In what ways can a director, officer, and shareholder be held liable?

Because almost all individuals within a corporation have legal fiduciary duties to it, they can be held liable for harming the business by violating these duties. There are, however, certain instances in which directors, officers, and shareholders cannot be held liable for harming the business.

LIABILITY OF DIRECTORS AND OFFICERS

Liability for Torts and Crimes. Although corporations themselves are liable for the torts and crimes of their directors and officers, directors and officers can be held personally responsible for their own torts and crimes and even for those of other employees whom they have failed to adequately supervise.

According to the responsible person doctrine, a court may find a corporate officer criminally liable regardless of the extent to which the officer took part in the criminal activity. Even an officer who knew nothing about the criminal activity can be held criminally liable if the court determines that a responsible person would have known about and could have prevented it.

Directors and officers who use inside information to trade the corporation's stock for personal profit can be held liable for breaching their fiduciary duty to the shareholders from whom they purchase or to whom they sell the stock.

Legal Principle: **As a general rule, directors and officers are held liable for many of the same actions because they have nearly identical fiduciary duties to the corporation.**

BUT WHAT IF . . .

WHAT IF THE FACTS OF THE CASE OPENER WERE DIFFERENT?

Let's say that Gately's directors, all but one, were engaging in insider trading. The lone director, Jay, would have known what was going on if he had paid close attention, but he was not very observant and never knew what was happening. Eventually the directors get caught. Will Jay be liable with the others?

Business Judgment Rule. Although directors and officers are expected to make decisions in the best interest of the corporation, they are not expected to make perfect decisions all the time. Many decisions harm the corporation inadvertently. Although shareholders may want to hold their directors and officers liable for these decisions, the *business judgment rule* does not allow them to do so. This rule says that directors and officers are not liable for decisions that harm the corporation if they were acting in good faith at the time. In other words, if there was reason to believe that the decision was a good one at the time, the directors and officers are not liable for the resulting harm.

Exhibit 39-2 summarizes the liability of directors and officers.

Although the business judgment rule is not a statute, it is common law recognized by almost every court in the country. The rule is practical because it grants directors freedom

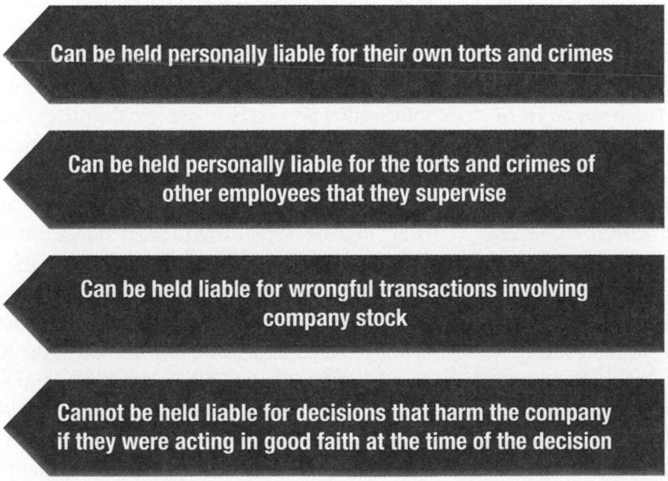

Exhibit 39-2

Liability of Directors and Officers

- Can be held personally liable for their own torts and crimes
- Can be held personally liable for the torts and crimes of other employees that they supervise
- Can be held liable for wrongful transactions involving company stock
- Cannot be held liable for decisions that harm the company if they were acting in good faith at the time of the decision

CASE NUGGET

THE BUSINESS JUDGMENT RULE

Auerbach v. Bennett
393 N.E.2d 994 (1979)

An internal audit of the GTE Corporation suggested that the corporation's management had paid more than $11 million in bribes and kickbacks both in the United States and abroad over a four-year period. Auerbach, a GTE shareholder, immediately initiated a shareholder derivative action (discussed below) against GTE's directors.

The Court of Appeals of New York, however, held that the business judgment rule exempted the GTE directors from liability for their poor business decisions. The court stated:

[The business judgment doctrine] bars judicial inquiry into actions of corporation directors taken in good faith and in the exercise of honest judgment in the lawful and legitimate furtherance of corporate purposes. Questions of policy of management, expediency of contracts or action, adequacy of consideration, lawful appropriation of corporate funds to advance corporate interests, are left solely to their honest and unselfish decision, for their powers therein are without limitation and free from restraint, and the exercise of them for the common and general interests of the corporation may not be questioned, although the results show that what they did was unwise or inexpedient.

to work without constant fear of personal liability. It also encourages individuals to serve as directors by removing the threat of personal liability for inadvertent mistakes. Case 39-2 illustrates how the courts interpret and apply the business judgment rule.

CASE 39-2 STATE OF WISCONSIN INVESTMENT BOARD v. WILLIAM BARTLETT

COURT OF CHANCERY OF DELAWARE, NEW CASTLE C.A. NO. 17727 (2000)

The State of Wisconsin Investment Board (SWIB) owned 11.5 percent of the outstanding shares of common stock in the pharmaceutical company Medco Research, Inc. In 1996, Medco began searching for a merger partner. In a proxy statement on January 5, 2000, Medco recommended shareholders vote for a merger between Medco and King Pharmaceuticals, Inc. On January 11, 2000, SWIB filed a request for injunctive relief on the grounds that the board of directors breached their fiduciary duties of care, loyalty, and disclosure in negotiating the merger. SWIB argued that the majority of Medco's directors were self-interested, and that no reasonably prudent businessperson of sound judgment would have negotiated the merger as Medco had. SWIB alleged Medco failed to disclose all information material to the shareholders, did not adequately inform themselves of all information available about the merger, and failed to adequately supervise a self-interested director. Medco refutes all claims.

JUDGE STEELE: Unless this presumption [that a board of directors acted with care, loyalty, and in good faith] is sufficiently rebutted, raising a reasonable doubt about self-interest or independence, the Court must defer to the discretion of the board and acknowledge that their decisions are entitled to the protection of the business judgment rule.

In order to require application of the entire fairness standard, the plaintiff has to show that a majority of directors has a financial interest in the transaction or a motive to entrench themselves in office through the merger. Plaintiff's allegations of self-interest do not meet the threshold necessary to rebut the presumption of the business judgment rule.

The plaintiff's allegations do not demonstrate that the Medco board failed to inform itself of all material facts concerning the proposed merger with King. I conclude that Medco's board met its duty of care in proceeding with the King merger. Despite the material disputes of fact, I am confident that Medco's board adequately informed themselves of all material information necessary to execute the merger agreement.

I cannot, on the basis of these allegations, find that the board either willfully left itself uninformed in order to serve its "self-interest" or failed to act in "good faith and in the honest belief that the merger was in the best interests of the company." It is equally apparent to me that the board sufficiently complied with the "good-faith" standard set forth by this Court in Aronson. I have also been led to conclude that the directors were acting to benefit the economic interest of the shareholders.

Plaintiff's request for preliminary injunction is hereby denied with respect to the shareholder vote and denied with respect to the merger.

Judgment for defendant.

[continued]

CRITICAL THINKING

What words or phrases in the court's argument are ambiguous? Why are these ambiguous words important?

ETHICAL DECISION MAKING

Suppose you were on the board of directors in this case. The universalization test guides your ethical decisions. Would you have made a different decision?

LIABILITY OF SHAREHOLDERS

Because shareholders are the owners of the corporation, their main liability is for the extent of their investment when the company loses money. In rare instances, however, shareholders are personally liable. For example, individuals sometimes sign stock subscription agreements before incorporation that contractually obligate them to purchase shares in the corporation. For **par-value shares,** or shares that have a fixed face value noted on the stock certificate, the shareholder must pay the corporation at least the par value of the stock. For **no-par shares,** or shares without a par value, the shareholder must pay the fair market value. A shareholder who does not buy the shares is personally liable for breach of contract.

A shareholder who receives **watered stock,** or stock issued below its fair market value, is also individually liable for the difference between the price she paid for the shares and their stated corporate value.

Finally, a shareholder can also be held personally liable for receiving illegal dividends. State statutes mandate that corporations pay dividends from only certain funds. Also, dividends are always illegal if they are paid when the corporation is insolvent or if they cause the corporation to become insolvent. A shareholder who knew that a dividend was illegal when he received it is personally liable and must return the funds to the corporation.

Exhibit 39-3 summarizes the liability of shareholders.

Rights of Directors, Officers, and Shareholders

LO5 What are the rights of directors, officers, and shareholders?

Because shareholders are in a position of limited decision-making power, they have rights that allow them to participate within the corporation. Directors and officers also have specific rights that allow them to perform their duties to the best of their abilities.

Exhibit 39-3 Liability of Shareholders

- Are liable for the debts of the corporation, to the extent of their investment
- Are liable for a breach of contract if a stock subscription agreement was signed and yet no stock was purchased
- Are liable for watered stock
- Can be held personally liable for receiving illegal dividends

COMPARING THE LAW OF OTHER COUNTRIES

CRIMINAL LIABILITY IN FRANCE

The French Penal Code does not adhere to a detailed or large list of corporate offenses but, instead, adopts what is called the *specialty principal,* which requires that corporate criminal liability is applicable only in cases that pertain to an "express mention in the law or in a French regulation."

The French system of corporate criminal liability sharply contrasts with the U.S. system in that the former has often been described as "scientific." This is because the French system requires heavy statistics outlining the frequency of a corporate officer's involvement in a crime before any criminal liability may be enforced. In contrast, in the United States the responsible person doctrine may require that a corporate officer be held criminally liable regardless of the extent of participation in a crime.

DIRECTORS' RIGHTS

The unique responsibilities of corporate directors call for unique rights. There are four: the rights of compensation, participation, inspection, and indemnification.

All corporate directors have a right to *compensation* for their work, which different corporations grant in different ways. Most directors hold other managerial positions within their companies and receive their compensation through those positions. Another common solution is to pay directors nominal sums as honorariums for their contributions. In some corporations, directors can determine their own compensation.

Because directors are required to make informed business decisions, they have the rights of *participation* and *inspection.* They can get involved in and understand every aspect of the business. A corporate director has the right to be notified of all meetings and has access to all books and records.

Finally, because of their great legal vulnerability, directors have the right to *indemnification.* In other words, they can be reimbursed for any legal fees incurred in lawsuits against them.

OFFICERS' RIGHTS

Corporate officers are technically employees of the corporation, so their rights are defined by employment contracts drawn up by the board of directors or the incorporators. Officers are in a contractual relationship with the corporation, and if they are removed in violation of the contract terms, the corporation may be liable for breach of contract.

SHAREHOLDERS' RIGHTS

Although shareholders' most powerful right is the right to vote at shareholders' meetings, they also possess many other rights.

Stock Certificates. Some corporations issue **stock certificates** to shareholders as proof of ownership in the corporation. Each certificate includes the corporation's name and the number of shares it represents. A sample stock certificate is shown in Exhibit 39-4. A shareholder's ownership in the corporation, however, does not depend on possession of the physical stock certificate. If the certificate is destroyed in a fire, the shareholder's ownership in the corporation is not destroyed. The shareholder can request a reissued certificate, although she may be required to guarantee payment to the corporation if the original certificate should reappear at a later date.

In most states, however, shares may be *uncertificated,* meaning that the corporation does not issue physical stock certificates. In this case, shareholders usually have a right to receive a letter from the corporation giving the information typically included on the face of a stock certificate.

Exhibit 39-4 Example of a Stock Certificate

Preemptive Rights. Under common law, shareholders have *preemptive rights,* which give preference to shareholders to purchase shares of a new issue of stock. Each shareholder receives preference in proportion to the percentage of stock he already owns.

Suppose Manuela owns 1,500 shares in a corporation with 5,000 outstanding shares, or 30 percent of the outstanding stock. The corporation decides to issue an additional 10,000 shares. If it does not grant preemptive rights, the degree of Manuela's control of the corporation will fall because she now owns 1,500 of 15,000 shares, or only 10 percent of its stock. With preemptive rights, if Manuela elects to purchase 3,000 shares of the newly issued stock, she owns 4,500 of 15,000 shares and retains her 30 percent control.

In most states, a corporation's bylaws can negate preemptive rights, so the corporation determines whether to grant them. Preemptive rights are especially important for individuals who own stock in close corporations due to the relatively small number of issued shares. If a close corporation issues additional shares, an individual shareholder may lose proportional control over the firm if he does not buy newly issued shares. But if preemptive rights exist, all shareholders receive **stock warrants,** which they can redeem for a certain number of shares at a specified price within a given time period. Like shares of stock, stock warrants are often traded publicly on securities exchanges.

BUT WHAT IF . . .

WHAT IF THE FACTS OF THE CASE OPENER WERE DIFFERENT?

Let's say, in the Case Opener, that after Gately, Thomas owned the most shares, at 10 percent. Another shareholder, Davis, owned 5 percent. When new shares in the company became available, both men wanted the available shares. However, Thomas said that he was getting the shares since he had more shares and more power to begin with. Is Thomas being fair and legally accurate in this instance?

To see the reasons for declaring stock dividends, please see the **Connecting to the Core** activity on the text website at www.mhhe.com/kubasek3e.

Dividends. If directors fail to declare and distribute dividends, shareholders have the right to take legal action to force them to do so. In many cases, however, directors have good reason to hold dividends for a limited amount of time to finance major undertakings such as research or expansion. Thus, shareholders must show that the directors are acting unreasonably and abusing their discretion in withholding the dividend.

Inspection Rights. All shareholders have the right to inspection in both statutory and common law. A shareholder can, moreover, appoint an agent to conduct the inspection on her behalf. To prevent abuse, however, this right has many limitations. Shareholders can inspect records and books only if they ask in advance and have a *proper purpose.* Some states allow only shareholders with a minimum number of shares to inspect; others require that shareholders own stock for a minimum amount of time before inspection. Corporations can deny shareholders the right to inspect confidential corporate information, such as trade secrets. A shareholder who feels his right of inspection has been wrongly denied can take the issue to court.

Share Transfer. The law generally permits property owners to transfer their property to another person, and in most cases stock is considered transferable property. In closely held corporations, however, transfer of stock is usually restricted so that shareholders can choose the corporation's other shareholders; they enjoy the corporate equivalent of the right of *delectus personae* (this allows partners to choose the individuals with whom they will go into business). Restrictions on transferability must be included on the face of the stock certificate.

One method of restricting stock transferability is the **right of first refusal.** If a corporation establishes this right in its bylaws, the corporation or its shareholders have the right to purchase any shares of stock offered for resale by a shareholder within a specified period of time.

Corporate Dissolution. Shareholders have the right to petition the court to dissolve their corporation if they feel that it cannot continue to operate profitably. According to Section 14.30 of RMBCA, if a corporation engages in any of the following behaviors, shareholders have a legal right to initiate dissolution:

1. Directors are deadlocked in managerial decisions and harming the corporation.
2. Directors are acting in illegal, oppressive, or fraudulent ways.
3. Assets are being wasted or used improperly.
4. Shareholders are deadlocked and cannot elect directors.

Once dissolution has taken place and the corporation has settled its debts with its creditors, shareholders have a right to receive the remaining assets of the company in proportion to the number of shares they own. Case 39-3 provides an illustration of a case seeking dissolution.

CASE 39-3 MOUZAKITIS v. PEARL NIGHTLIFE, INC., ET AL.
NEW YORK SUPREME COURT, QUEENS COUNTY
INDEX NO. 28420/08 (2009)

Marianthi and Leonidas Mouzakitis, husband and wife, own fifteen of the hundred shares that were issued in the operation of a restaurant in New York. The operator is Pearl Nightlife, Inc., and the restaurant is situated at 45-30 Bell Boulevard in Bayside, New York. The corporation's president, Nicholas Kiriakis, owns thirty shares and manages the restaurant. The Mouzakitises alleged that those in control of the corporation, including Kiriakis, did not fulfill the needs of the corporation. Specifically, Kiriakis was said to neglect paying salaries and dividends, block an inspection of corporate records and books, and mismanage and divert the corporation's funds and assets.

JUDGE KITZES: In *Leibert,* the Court of Appeals recognized a common-law right to dissolution of a corporation where the officers or directors of the corporation are engaged in conduct which is violative of their fiduciary duty to shareholders. Dissolution is appropriate if the directors or those in control of the corporation are looting the corporate assets to enrich themselves at the expense of the minority shareholders; continuing the corporation solely to benefit those in control; or that the actions of the directors or those in control have been calculated to depress the capital of the corporation in order to coerce the minority shareholders to sell their stock at a depressed price.

[The petitioners] have set forth sufficient allegations and support to raise an issue that the majority shareholders are enriching themselves at the expense of the minority. The sworn statements of the petitioners are sufficient to warrant a hearing to determine the validity of these allegations.

AFFIRMED.

CRITICAL THINKING

What reasons did the court offer to support its conclusion? What do you think about the quality of those reasons?

ETHICAL DECISION MAKING

Recall the WPH framework. Suppose that your decision is guided by the Golden Rule. Why is application of the Golden Rule more complex than it may seem at first glance? *Clue:* Are humans so similar that what one person would want to happen in a particular situation is identical to what every other person would want to happen?

Shareholder's Derivative Suit. If corporate directors fail to sue when the corporation has been harmed by an individual, another corporation, or a director, individual shareholders (who held stock at the time of the alleged wrongdoing) can file a **shareholder's derivative suit** on behalf of the corporation. Before filing, the shareholders must file a complaint with the board of directors. If there is no response, they can proceed with the suit. Enron shareholders have brought shareholder's derivative suits against various directors and officers.

It seems highly unlikely that directors will sue themselves for damages they caused. Thus, the shareholder's derivative suit is an important way for shareholders to hold directors accountable for their behavior. Because the suit is filed on the corporation's behalf, all damages recovered are given to the corporation, not the individual shareholder.

Shareholder's Direct Suit. Shareholders can also bring a direct suit against the corporation. In a *shareholder's direct suit,* the shareholder alleges damages caused by the corporation. For example, a shareholder may allege that the board of directors is improperly withholding dividends or wrongly denying the shareholder's right to inspect corporate records. However, in some instances a direct suit is not appropriate. For example, a shareholder may not file a direct suit alleging that an officer has violated a fiduciary duty.

In such a circumstance, the violation would engage all shareholders. If a court awards damages as a result of a shareholder's direct suit, they go to the shareholder personally.

Legal Principle: **Damages recovered from a derivative suit go to the corporation. In contrast, damages recovered from a direct suit go only to the shareholder.**

If more than one shareholder has suffered damages caused by the same act of the corporation, the shareholders may bring a class action suit against the corporation. A *class action suit* is brought by one shareholder on behalf of a group of shareholders to recover damages for the entire group.

CASE OPENER WRAP-UP

A Majority Shareholder and Her Son

On appeal, the court considered the district court's application of the business judgment rule. As you learned in this chapter, the business judgment rule says that directors and officers are not liable for decisions that harm the corporation if they were acting in good faith at the time. In other words, if there is reason to believe that a decision was a good one at the time, the directors and officers are not liable for the resulting harm. In this case, the district court considered the defendant shareholder's actions as director in terms of the business judgment rule and concluded that those actions satisfied the rule.

On appeal, the court also considered the district court's ruling on the plaintiff's breach-of-fiduciary-duty claim. The district court reasoned that if the controlling group in a corporation can demonstrate a legitimate business purpose for its actions, and the minority stockholders cannot demonstrate a less harmful alternative, then the disputed transaction should be upheld. The district court then ruled that the bonus transaction did not constitute a breach of fiduciary duties.

The appellate court affirmed the judgments of the district court.

KEY TERMS

no-par shares 863
par-value shares 863
proxy 855
right of first refusal 866
self-dealing 857
shareholder's derivative suit 867
stock certificates 864
stock warrants 865
watered stock 863

SUMMARY OF KEY TOPICS

Interactions among Directors, Officers, and Shareholders

The board of directors meets to decide important issues faced by the corporation. Directors also supervise officers of the corporation, as well as declare dividends for the shareholders. A corporate directors' meeting is valid only when a minimum number of directors, or a quorum, is present at the meeting.

Officers are executives hired by the directors to manage the daily actions of the corporation.

Shareholders are the owners of the firm. They elect the members of the board of directors. Usually they gather at an annual meeting to propose ideas and to listen to reports from the corporate officers. When a shareholder cannot attend, she can authorize a third party, a proxy, to vote on her behalf. Proxy materials are often sent to the shareholders before their annual meeting; these proxy materials detail shareholders' ideas for the company.

Duties of Directors, Officers, and Shareholders

The directors and officers have duties to the shareholders and to the corporation. Their primary fiduciary duties are the duty of care and the duty of loyalty. In terms of the duty of care, officers and directors must act in good faith and in a manner consistent with the best interests of the shareholders. The duty of loyalty requires that the directors and officers put the interests of the shareholders above their personal interests.

The shareholders do not generally have duties.

Liabilities of Directors, Officers, and Shareholders

Officers and directors are liable for their own actions, as well of those of employees of the firm that they had reason to be aware of. The business judgment rule provides that directors and officers are not liable for decisions that harmed the corporation if they were acting in good faith at the time of the decision.

The main liability for shareholders is the total extent of their investment in the corporation if the firm loses money.

Rights of Directors, Officers, and Shareholders

The rights of directors are the following: the rights of compensation, participation, inspection, and indemnification.

Officers' rights are determined by the terms of their employment contract.

Shareholders have many rights, including the right to vote at shareholders' meetings, occasional preferential or preemptive rights to purchase shares of a new issue of stock, the right of first refusal when shares are offered for resale by a shareholder, the right to inspect corporate books and records when they have a proper purpose, and the right to request dissolution.

Stock warrants: Vouchers issued to shareholders entitling them to a given number of shares at a specified price.

Shareholder's derivative suit: A lawsuit filed by a shareholder of a corporation when corporate directors fail to sue in a situation in which the corporation has been harmed by an individual or another corporation. Before the suit can be filed, the shareholder must file a complaint with the board of directors; the shareholder can proceed with the suit only if nothing is done in response to the complaint.

POINT / COUNTERPOINT

Should Shareholder and Stock Information Be Permitted as Discussion Topics on Social Media Websites?

YES	NO
Discussion of finances is just one of a thousand types of personal information that users of social media share on their profiles. While there are consequences for bad investment choices and ignorance of the stock market, they are wholly related to individual investment decisions and not exacerbated by social media sites. Furthermore, silencing social media is an encroachment of a fundamental American right, and that right should be	Social media has changed the way that the average person interacts with businesses. While sites like Twitter and Facebook are useful tools for advertising sales and developing targeted marketing strategies, they can play a dangerous role in the communication of stock information. Because of the volatile and reactive nature of the stock market, and the value that insider information plays, it is important that social media not be used to

protected at all costs. Three reasons suggest that limiting stockholder information on social media would be an unwise decision.

First, there is a separation between the use of social media and one's personal investment decisions. Choosing to invest or not invest in a company is comparable to gambling at a casino: Not only is losing money an ever-present possibility, but moves made in the stock market can be influenced by anything from business journalism to premonition. Likewise, social media posts can influence someone's decision, but it is ultimately the individual who makes the decision to invest or disinvest. Moreover, social media offer no greater insight into the market than do existing sources, such as the *Wall Street Journal.* Unless Twitter is used to publicize insider trading or violate a shareholder's confidentiality, no crime is being committed. In essence, the SEC must prove something illegal has taken place in order to stop it. Therefore, because there is no direct link between social media and shareholder wrongdoing, shareholder and stock information should be permitted on these sites.

Second, the policing of social media would be a nearly impossible undertaking. To prove that a shareholder violated his fiduciary duty of care or loyalty to his fellow shareholders and to the corporation, it is necessary to show that he did not act in good faith with his post. For example, the SEC would have to take a post encouraging the purchase of a stock and find that the investor in question did not agree with his post and subsequently sold off his stock once the price rose. It would also be necessary to show that he acted with the intent of defrauding other investors. Moreover, an investigation of this magnitude would be difficult with the billions of social media users and the limited resources of the SEC. Third, any social media discussion that is not in violation of these standards falls under the individual's free speech right to discuss personal finances. Likewise, since not all stock discussions are material to investors, they cannot all be limited just because some people will abuse the privilege. Thus, discussion of shareholder information should remain legal; prohibiting it would be a violation of free speech and would create a nearly insurmountable undertaking for the authorities.

In conclusion, discussion of finances on social media is too valuable a resource to outlaw.

influence public investment. The risks are far too high to ignore. Three reasons suggest the wisdom of creating an updated set of rules for shareholders and social media.

First, social media can be used to spread misleading information about a company and the value of its stock. It goes without saying that shareholders want to increase the value of their stock, and additional investment will bring about an increase in value. Moreover, when a celebrity is used to encourage the purchase of a stock on a social media site, investment will increase. For example, in 2011, rapper 50 Cent used Twitter to encourage purchase of H&H Import's stock. This resulted in an $8.7 million profit for him, as the stock value rose dramatically. Because enough fans will follow celebrity requests, it is inevitable that celebrities can manipulate investment through endorsement. However, majority shareholders have a duty to act with care for minority investors. Allowing social media investments to continue will make the policing duties of the SEC more difficult. Therefore, stockholders should not be permitted to encourage investment via social media because doing so allows major shareholders to manipulate investment at the cost of others.

Second, the potential for fraud and deceit is too high to allow stockholder information to be posted. Currently, it is not a crime for holders of any amount of stock to discuss their portfolios on the Internet, as long as they do not violate SEC regulations. However, it is difficult to know the true identity of a source of information on the Internet. For example, in 2013, a Twitter user posing as a reputable research firm erroneously posted that Audience Inc. was under investigation by the Department of Justice for fraud. Although the post was a hoax, it resulted in a hasty sell-off by stockholders and a drop in value. Similarly, someone could pose as a majority stockholder, a celebrity investor, or an employee of the SEC.

Third, given the high cost that rapid investment loss would have on a company, allowing investment information to be discussed on social media poses too large a risk.

In conclusion, because a user's identity cannot be verified on social media sites, and because fast and disastrous outcomes are possible, stock-related information should not be allowed on these sites.

Source: Carolyn Elefant, "The 'Power' of Social Media: Legal Issues & Best Practices for Utilities Engaging Social Media," *Energy Law Journal,* vol. 32 (2011), p. 1; Eleazzar David Melendez, "Twitter Stock Market Hoax Draws Attention of Regulators," *Huffington Post Business,* February 1, 2013, www.huffingtonpost.com/2013/02/01/twitterstock-market-hoax_n_2601753.html; and Kaja Whitehouse, "50 Cent Millions," *New York Post,* January 11, 2011, www.nypost.com/p/news/business/cent_millions_y5r6uquXPHX43R2NCWX6MN.

QUESTIONS & PROBLEMS

1. Explain the primary duties of officers and directors.
2. Explain the primary duties of shareholders.
3. What is the business judgment rule?
4. Julio Garcia Aguilar, M.D., Joanne E. Mortimer, M.D., and Michael W. Lew, M.D., are physicians and shareholders of California Cancer Specialists Medical Group, Inc., a professional corporation doing business as City of Hope Medical Group. This group had a relationship with a local hospital whereby any administrative duties associated with the medical group were performed by hospital employees. In 1999, the group looked for an independent company to perform its administrative and managerial tasks. It ended up hiring individuals to perform these tasks. In January 2011, when the contract between the medical group and the hospital was due to expire, both parties participated in discussions about a new contract. The hospital claimed that it should have coequal control over the administrative duties associated with the medical group. Is the hospital right in asserting that it should have coequal control? [*Aguilar v. Goldstein,* 207 Cal. App. 4th 1152 (2012).]
5. Emory B. Perry, who represents numerous shareholders, owned stock of The RAMP Corporation, a now-defunct company that developed communications technologies for the health care industry. Darryl R. Cohen and Andrew M. Brown are former directors of RAMP. Perry filed suit against Cohen and Brown in December 2004, alleging negligence, common law fraud, statutory fraud, and conspiracy. Perry claimed that Cohen and Brown made numerous misrepresentations in their original petition, and that he received false information as a result. Perry argued that both men's misrepresentations induced the stockholders to hold and refrain from selling their RAMP stock. Is this an example of a direct suit or a derivative suit? Why? [*Perry v. Cohen,* 272 S.W.3d 661 (Tex. Ct. App. 2007).]
6. Carl W. Jasper is the former CFO of Maxium Integrated Products, Inc., a semiconductor company in California. The company offered stock to shareholders, but the shareholders did not know that the stock options were backdated and were not properly expensed. The company's CFO was found guilty of the crime. Should Jasper have been held responsible? Why or why not? [*SEC v. Jasper,* 678 F.3d 1116, 1119 (9th Cir. 2012).]
7. Boston Children's Heart Foundation (BCHF) is a nonprofit corporation organized for the purposes of conducting medical research and providing medical services to patients at Boston Children's Hospital. Nadal-Ginard was the president and a member of the board of directors of BCHF. He also served as an investigator for the Howard Hughes Medical Institute (HHMI), where he was paid a substantial salary and was involved in similar research. Nadal-Ginard did not disclose his employment with HHMI to the other members of the board of directors. He determined his own salary with BCHF, established a severance benefit plan, and used BCHF funds for personal expenses. After learning that Nadal-Ginard was a salaried employee of HHMI, BCHF filed suit, claiming that Nadal-Ginard breached his fiduciary duties to the corporation. The district court agreed with BCHF and awarded damages. Nadal-Ginard appealed the court's decision, arguing that he did not breach his fiduciary duty and that no conflict of interest existed. Do you think the court affirmed the district court's decision? Why or why not? [*Boston Children's Heart Foundation, Inc. v. Bernardo Nadal-Ginard,* 73 F.3d 429 (1996).]
8. The Oakland Raiders filed suit against the National Football League. The Raiders claimed that NFL management's wrongful control of the NFL entities resulted in a breach of fiduciary duty and adverse treatment of the Raiders. As part of its investigation, the Raiders wanted to inspect the corporate documents of National Football League Properties, Inc. (NFLP). Each of the 30 NFL teams is an equal shareholder of NFLP and has a licensing agreement with it. NFLP acknowledged that the Raiders club was a shareholder but refused to produce certain documents. According to NFLP, the Raiders did not have the right to inspect corporate

documents protected by the attorney-client privilege. The court found that, as a member, director, and shareholder of NFLP, the Raiders had the right to examine privileged documents. NFLP challenged the court's decision. How do you think the court of appeals decided? Should NFLP be compelled to produce the privileged documents? Why or why not? [*National Football League Properties, Inc. v. The Superior Court of Santa Clara County,* 65 Cal. App. 4th 100 (1998).]

9. In February 2009, the SEC accused Texas billionaire P. Allen Stanford and two additional senior executives of committing a "massive Ponzi scheme," or substantial fraud. Subsequently, all of Stanford's financial operations were shut down, and a civil suit was filed against him. The SEC alleged that Stanford and the executives were pulling in investors and sold about $8 billion worth of "certificates of deposit." The certificates then seemed to be invested in real estate and other operations associated with Stanford's own personal dealings. Basically, the SEC alleged that investors were pulled in to invest in fake financial products and ventures. How do you think the court decided? Why? [*SEC v. Stanford International Bank, Ltd., et al.,* Case No. 3-09CV0298-N (N.D. Tex. 2009).]

10. Amalgamated Bank, a shareholder of UICI, a Delaware corporation, asked to inspect UICI's books and records to determine whether UICI's directors breached their fiduciary duties or otherwise harmed shareholders by acting illegally. Amalgamated also wanted to determine whether sufficient evidence existed to bring a shareholder action suit against UICI's directors, who had done business with the corporation and had profited handsomely. UICI denied Amalgamated's request for three reasons. First, the statute of limitations for bringing suit against the corporation had expired. Second, some of the meeting minutes requested by Amalgamated did not directly concern the transactions in question. Third, UICI wanted to require that Amalgamated maintain the confidentiality of the information it reviewed. The bank brought suit against UICI, alleging that it ought to be able to review the documents in question because it provided a proper purpose in its letter of request. How do you think the court ruled in this case? Why? [*Amalgamated Bank v. UICI,* 2005 Del. Ch. LEXIS 82 (2005).]

Looking for more review materials?

The Online Learning Center at **www.mhhe.com/kubasek3e** contains this chapter's "Assignment on the Internet" and also a list of URLs for more information, entitled "On the Internet." Find both of them in the Student Center portion of the OLC, along with quizzes and other helpful materials.

CHAPTER 40

Corporations: Mergers, Consolidations, Terminations

LEARNING OBJECTIVES

After reading this chapter, you will be able to answer the following questions:

1. What are mergers and consolidations?
2. What are the procedures for mergers and consolidations?
3. What are asset purchases?
4. What are stock purchases?
5. What is a takeover?
6. In what ways could the termination of mergers and consolidations occur?

CASE OPENER

Acquisitions as Horizontal Mergers

Polypore and Microporous Products both produced battery separators. Polypore primarily manufactured pure polyethylene separators for use in automotive batteries. The much smaller producer, Microporous, manufactured pure rubber battery separators for use in deep-cycle batteries. Microporous was recognized as being the industry standard for deep-cycle batteries.

In February 2008, Polypore sought to acquire Microporous, but the Federal Trade Commission issued an administrative complaint. The commission held that Polypore's acquisition of Microporous would substantially lessen competition, leading to the creation of a monopoly in the applicable market.

Polypore appealed the decision of the commission, arguing that the commission erred in labeling the acquisition as a horizontal merger.

1. How did the court rule on appeal?
2. When is an acquisition treated as a horizontal merger?

The Wrap-Up at the end of the chapter will answer these questions.

Introduction to Mergers and Consolidations

What are mergers and consolidations?

Although many people believe that mergers and consolidations are synonymous, they are in fact two legally distinct procedures. Nevertheless, in both mergers and consolidations, corporations, shareholders, and creditors have the same rights and liabilities.

MERGERS

A **merger** occurs when a legal contract combines two or more corporations such that only one of the corporations continues to exist. A useful way to understand a merger is to think of one corporation absorbing another corporation (called an *absorbed corporation* or a *disappearing corporation*), yielding a single *surviving corporation.*

The surviving entity remains a single corporation, but it changes in several ways after the merger. First, its shareholders must amend its articles of incorporation according to the specific conditions of the merger. Second, the surviving corporation becomes liable for all debts and obligations of the absorbed corporation.

The surviving corporation also grows from the merger because it obtains the absorbed corporation's property and assets. Additionally, it acquires the absorbed corporation's rights, powers, and privileges. This acquisition can be complicated if the absorbed company had a legal right to sue third parties. The surviving corporation's right to sue for debt and damages on behalf of the absorbed corporation is called a **chose in action** (*chose* is French for "thing"). Although a few states do not allow corporations to transfer their rights, powers, and privileges in a merger, most states agree that if a corporation had a right to sue third parties before a merger, then the surviving corporation retains that right.

Legal Principle: **In most states, corporations that merge may transfer their rights, powers, and privileges to the new corporation formed by the merger.**

BUT WHAT IF . . .

WHAT IF THE FACTS OF THE CASE OPENER WERE DIFFERENT?

Let's say, in the Case Opener, that Polypore did acquire Microporous. A year later, debt collectors contacted Polypore and said that it had to pay all of Microporous's debts. Polypore said that although it had acquired Microporous, it was not Microporous and did not have to pay the company's old bills. Which side was correct in this scenario?

To see a description of the general changes in day-to-day business after a consolidation occurs, please see the **Connecting to the Core** activity on the text website at www.mhhe.com/kubasek3e.

CONSOLIDATIONS

Like mergers, **consolidations** legally combine two or more corporations. In a consolidation, however, neither of the original corporations continues to exist legally. Rather, they form an entirely new corporation with its own legal status.

Because the new corporation has independent legal status, the articles of incorporation of the original companies are void. The shareholders of the new corporation create new articles of incorporation, called *articles of consolidation,* according to the details of the consolidation.

Consolidated entities assume the liabilities, debts, and obligations of the original corporations. The new corporation also acquires the original corporations' property and assets. Finally, the consolidated corporation takes on the rights, privileges, and powers of the original companies.

Today, consolidations are very rare. As Section 11.01 of RMBCA reads, "In modern corporate practice consolidation transactions are obsolete since it is nearly always advantageous for one of the parties in the transaction to be the surviving corporation."

Procedures for Mergers and Consolidations

LO2 What are the procedures for mergers and consolidations?

Whether corporations combine through merger or consolidation, the procedures governing the transition are identical. Exhibit 40-1 explains the process of mergers and consolidations.

State statutes govern mergers and consolidations. In most states, corporations can merge or consolidate with either domestic (in-state) or foreign (out-of-state) corporations. Because acquisitions between domestic corporations are very different from acquisitions between corporations from different states, different laws govern acquisitions between domestic corporations and acquisitions between foreign corporations. Although these laws vary across states, several requirements apply universally:

1. The boards of directors of all involved corporations must approve the merger or consolidation plan.
2. The shareholders of all involved corporations must approve the plan by a vote at a shareholder meeting. Most states require the approval of two-thirds of the outstanding shares of voting stock. If, however, a merger increases the number of the surviving corporation's shares by no more than 20 percent, most states do not require the approval of the surviving corporation's shareholders.
3. The involved corporations must submit the merger or consolidation plan to the secretary of state.

Exhibit 40-1 Process for Mergers and Consolidations

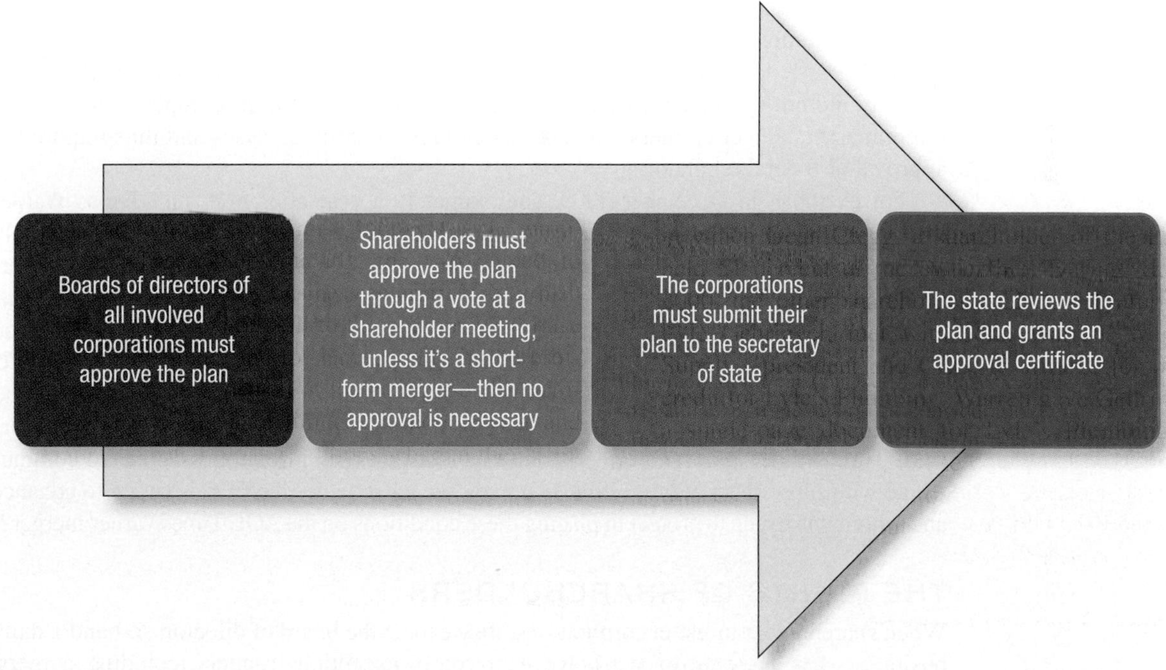

COMPARING THE LAW OF OTHER COUNTRIES

MERGER CONTROL IN FRANCE

The aim of merger control statutes in France is not to discourage mergers but to ensure that the combination of businesses does not impede competition. The creation of the Commission for Competition helps foster this goal. The commission, composed of members of the Council of State, magistrates of the administrative or judicial order, and several part-time reporters, is available to offer advice to businesses seeking to merge. The French government, specifically the minister for the economy, also uses the commission as a resource when determining whether a proposed merger will benefit the French economy or whether the resulting concentration of power will decrease competition. After learning of a proposed merger, the minister has three months to issue an opinion. During this period, the minister employs the expertise of the commission. If the commission decides that a proposed merger exceeds reasonable concentration of power, the minister for the economy must intervene with an injunctive option depending on the particular circumstances of the merger. The minister can (1) enjoin the companies from completing the merger, (2) alter the merger's value, (3) make provisions to ensure higher degrees of competition in the market, or (4) arrange compensatory contributions to social or economic welfare if the merger will necessarily reduce competition.

4. After reviewing the plan to ensure that the corporations have satisfied all legal requirements, the secretary of state issues a certificate to grant approval for the merger or consolidation.

BUT WHAT IF . . .

WHAT IF THE FACTS OF THE CASE OPENER WERE DIFFERENT?

Let's say, in the Case Opener, that Polypore shareholders met to vote on whether their company should merge with Microporous. The vote revealed that 51 percent of the outstanding shares supported the merger. Because this is the majority of the shares, does this mean that the two companies can go ahead with the merger?

In addition, the surviving or consolidated corporation issues shares or otherwise compensates shareholders of the corporation that no longer exists.

In 1998, federal regulators determined that a merger between Daimler-Benz and Chrysler did not violate antitrust laws because the two corporations competed in very different markets. Other mergers, however, often present antitrust issues and thus require the approval of federal regulators.

For example, in December 2000, approximately a year after AOL and Times Warner first announced their proposed merger, the Federal Trade Commission (FTC) unanimously approved the merger because the new company pledged to protect consumers' choice of services offered by competitors. Following the FTC's decision, the Federal Communications Commission (FCC) approved the merger in early January, imposing similar conditions on the new company to promote a competitive Internet services market. For example, the FCC required that AOL Time Warner work with EarthLink, an Internet service provider (ISP) and AOL's biggest competitor, as well as with Microsoft and Juno. The FCC also demanded that AOL Time Warner allow subscribers to use its software (i.e., instant messaging) to communicate with subscribers of other ISPs. (Can you see what values the FCC is trying to advance and whom it is trying to protect in placing these conditions on the AOL Time Warner merger?)

THE RIGHTS OF SHAREHOLDERS

When shareholders invest in corporations, they expect the board of directors to handle daily business issues. They also expect, however, to vote on exceptional matters, including mergers, consolidations, changes in partners, sales or leases of the corporation, and exchanges of assets. Because shareholders have a vested interest in the survival and prosperity of the corporation, these matters are of great significance to them. Thus, the merger and consolidation procedures require shareholder approval. In Case 40-1, the Delaware Supreme Court examined whether a shareholder vote in favor of a merger was legitimate.

CASE 40-1 HARTLEIB v. SIRIUS SATELLITE RADIO ET AL.
U.S. DISTRICT COURT, CENTRAL DISTRICT OF CALIFORNIA CASE NO. SACV 08-00790-CJC(ANx) (2008)

In 2008, the shareholders of Sirius, the satellite radio provider, sued Sirius XM after the merger between Sirius and XM. The shareholders allege that Sirius executives damaged the prices of stock for the corporation because they created and maintained agreements with XM that both companies would refrain from looking at other merger deals and canceling the merger completely. The shareholders stated that these agreements were made so that while the FCC considered approval of the merger for sixteen months, the merger would still happen with 100% certainty. Basically, the shareholders stated that Sirius executives wanted the merger to occur at "any and all costs."

JUDGE CARNEY: Although the complaint identifies alleged fraud and wrongdoing committed by Defendants, it does not state how each specific Sirius director was responsible for those actions. For instance, it would be helpful if Mr. Hartleib could show how a majority of the current directors, as individuals, approved of an allegedly fraudulent statement or action or committed some wrongdoing that would make them unable to exercise independent judgment in this case. Generalized statements alleging that "each board member" knew of some wrongdoing will not suffice to meet the heightened standards of Rule 23.1. Such generalized allegations are even more ineffective in situations, like this one, where the majority of the board was not empanelled at the time of the alleged wrongdoing. The changeover in board membership further undermines the relevance of Mr. Hartleib's argument that Sirius's lukewarm response to his shareholder activism before the merger shows that its current board cannot be trusted to exercise independent judgment. The Court also fails to see the relevance of directors' membership on the audit committee. Furthermore, Mr. Hartleib cannot escape the demand requirement simply by asserting that the majority of the board bears liability in the action because a majority of board members are named as defendants in his suit.

DISMISSED.

CRITICAL THINKING

What problems does Judge Carney have with the way that the plaintiff presented his argument?

Had the plaintiff adjusted the argument as the judge advised, do you think the judge would have ruled in his favor?

ETHICAL DECISION MAKING

If you were in the position of the Sirius executives in this case, would you have threatened the stock process in an effort to create a merger with another satellite radio corporation? If your decision was guided by the Golden Rule, how would you have behaved?

Legal Principle: **Merger and consolidation procedures require the approval of shareholders.**

SHORT-FORM MERGERS

Although most mergers require shareholder approval, short-form mergers do not. A **short-form merger,** or a **parent-subsidiary merger,** occurs when a parent corporation merges with a subsidiary corporation. The procedure for short-form mergers, detailed in Section 11.04 of RMBCA, is simpler than the procedure for mergers between unrelated corporations because short-form mergers can occur without shareholder approval.

COMPARING THE LAW OF OTHER COUNTRIES

MERGER CONTROL IN SOUTH AFRICA

South Africa, like many other countries, takes measures to secure a competitive but fair environment for mergers. Specifically, the Companies Act and the rules of the Johannesburg Stock Exchange control mergers. The Companies Act provides protection for minority shareholders. For instance, shareholders cannot approve a merger unless 90 percent of all shareholders vote to accept the offer. Additionally, minority shareholders have access to South African courts and may employ them when disputes arise. The Companies Act also establishes a panel to inquire about mergers or takeovers.

The Johannesburg Stock Exchange has established rules that govern the treatment of shareholders in mergers and takeovers. For example, if a change of corporate control takes place outside the stock exchange, the initiator of the merger must extend the offer to the shareholders and disclose all pertinent information to them within a reasonable amount of time.

Short-form mergers have other requirements, however. The parent corporation must own at least 90 percent of the outstanding shares of each class of the subsidiary's stock. If the proposed short-form merger satisfies this condition, the board of directors of the parent corporation can vote to approve the merger plan. The board must also submit the plan to the subsidiary's shareholders, even though they do not have veto power. Finally, the state must approve the merger proposition.

Although short-form mergers are legal, to protect shareholders from directors, courts often require that directors seek and adhere to shareholders' opinions.

APPRAISAL RIGHTS

The law protects shareholders as a group from corporations, but it also protects individual shareholders from one another. Suppose that although an overwhelming majority of shareholders vote to approve a merger, a single shareholder dissents. In this situation, the law does not force the dissenting shareholder to become a shareholder in a corporation different from the one in which she originally invested. Thus, the law permits dissenting shareholders to exercise their appraisal rights. An **appraisal right** is a dissenting shareholder's right to have his or her shares appraised and to receive monetary compensation from the corporation for their value.

Strict procedures govern appraisal rights. Before a shareholder vote, dissenting shareholders must submit a notification of dissent. By conveying their disapproval before the vote, the dissenting shareholders may sway other shareholders to reconsider their decision. If, however, the shareholder vote approves the transaction, the dissenting shareholders must issue another statement demanding adequate compensation for their shares.

The corporation must then present the dissenting shareholders with a document stating the value of their shares. Shareholders and corporations often clash when determining the value of these shares. Generally, however, they use the value of the shares on the day before the shareholder vote. The language of the law is of little help; it ambiguously calls for the "fair value of shares" (RMBCA 13.01). If the dissenting shareholders and the corporation cannot reach an agreement, courts intervene to establish the shares' value. Case 40-2 discusses the complexity of determining share values.

CASE 40-2 SHIFTAN v. MORGAN JOSEPH HOLDINGS, INC.
DELAWARE COURT OF CHANCERY
C.A. NO. 6424-CS (2012)

The plaintiffs in this case brought suit against Morgan Joseph Holdings, Inc., an investment bank, regarding the preferred stock they had in the bank. The plaintiffs bought the stock in 2001 when the company was first starting to provide money for the start up. In late 2010, Morgan Joseph merged with an investment bank called Tri-Artisan Capital Partners, LLC. A stock, governed by a new certificate of incorporation, was offered in place of the old stock. Instead of switching their shares, the plaintiffs decided to have their shares appraised under 8 Del. C. § 262. The new certificate of incorporation provided an automatic redemption of the new stock for $100 per share which would be allowed 6 months after the merger.

CHANCELLOR STRINE: A certificate of incorporation is a contract among the stockholders of the corporation to which the standard rules of contract interpretation apply. I must therefore take Delaware's well-established contract interpretation principles and apply them to the Certificate.

What is a bit more complicated here are some of the interpretive principles that come into play when a contract is "fairly susceptible of different interpretations," and therefore ambiguous. In that event, the court must turn to secondary methods of interpretation.

In the case of documents like certificates of incorporation or designation, the kinds of parol evidence frequently available in the case of warmly negotiated bilateral agreements are rarely available. Investors usually do not have access to any of the drafting history of such documents, and must rely on what is publicly available to them to understand their rights as investors. Thus, the subjective, unexpressed views of entity managers and the drafters who work for them about what a certificate means [have] traditionally been of no legal consequence, as it is not proper parol evidence as understood in our contract law.

Rather, in these contexts, another method of resolving ambiguity comes into play, which involves interpreting ambiguities against the drafter. Our Supreme Court has frequently invoked this doctrine of *contra proferentem* to resolve ambiguities about the rights of investors in the governing instruments of business entities. This is even true in the case of investors in preferred stock.

This use of *contra proferentem* in the context of preferred stock arguably is in tension with another principle of Delaware law. A line of precedent holds that preferences claimed by preferred stockholders must be clearly set forth in a certificate of incorporation or designation and will not be presumed or implied by the court.

With these interpretative principles in mind, I will now discuss why I believe the petitioners' interpretation is the correct one.

A review of the plain language of the Certificate demonstrates that, by relying on § B(5)(c), Morgan Joseph is straining to create an ambiguity when in fact there is none. As the petitioners point out, there was no reference to "Excess Cash" in § B(5)(a), which was the logical place in which to impose such a requirement. Such a restriction would also have been symmetrical with how the Excess Cash condition was applied to Optional Redemptions. Optional Redemptions were addressed in § B(5)(b) of the Certificate, and they were expressly and directly conditioned on the availability of Excess Cash.

The plain language of the Certificate does not indicate that the Automatic Redemption provision in § B(5)(a) would be, as Morgan Joseph contends, subject to the distribution scheme set forth in § B(5)(c). Section B(5)(c) contained instructions for redeeming the Series A Preferred Stock in the event that either an Automatic Redemption or Optional Redemption took place. The first sentence of § B(5)(c), which defined "Redemption Date," clearly and unambiguously applied to both types of redemptions. This makes sense because both an Automatic Redemption and Optional Redemptions would require an effective date. But, the sentence of § B(5)(c) that detailed the distribution scheme in the event that Morgan Joseph did not have enough Excess Cash to go around applied only to Optional Redemptions.

Further, Morgan Joseph fails to address the obvious categorical difference between the triggering events for Automatic Redemptions and for Optional Redemptions that emerges from the face of the Certificate. Under the Certificate, an Automatic Redemption would be triggered largely by strategic events—a sale of substantially all assets, an initial public offering, or a merger in which Morgan Joseph was not the survivor. These are the sort of benchmark events that commonly trigger the right of a preferred security holder to receive a preference return based on its place in the capital hierarchy. In colloquial terms, these are harvest events. It is evident that July 1, 2011[,] was also such a harvest event, and was chosen consciously. The Series A Preferred Stock was issued exactly ten years before July 1, 2011. The only reasonable way to read the Certificate was that the Series A holders were entitled to an Automatic Redemption upon the occurrence of any of the harvest triggers listed in § B(5)(a) of the Certificate, and at the latest on July 1, 2011, ten years after their investment was made. This right to an Automatic Redemption was not subject to any Excess Cash requirement; rather, payment was due to the Series A holders as the senior security holders so long as the company had legally available funds to make the redemption. In other words, the Series A holders, as holders of senior preferred securities, were entitled to harvest their investment at the latest after ten

[continued]

years were up. By contrast, the Series A holders could only exercise their right to an Optional Redemption if Morgan Joseph was sufficiently in the plush with Excess Cash.

Even if the Certificate were ambiguous, the parol evidence makes clear that the petitioners' interpretation is indisputably correct. The petitioners submitted evidence that shows the shared beliefs of the parties at the time that Morgan Joseph sold its Series A Preferred Stock: the Information Material used by Morgan Joseph to market the Series A to investors. Because Morgan Joseph drafted the Information Material and put it into circulation, it is strong evidence of what Morgan Joseph believed when it authored the Certificate. Most important, because the Information Material was used as advertising to the buyers of the Series A Preferred Stock, it speaks to the reasonable expectations of the Series A investors. For these reasons, the Information Material is very powerful parol evidence that may be properly considered by the court. Moreover, Morgan Joseph has failed to advance any contradictory parol evidence or explain through a Rule 56(f) affidavit how discovery would generate admissible parol evidence.

Under 8 *Del. C.* § 262, my task in an appraisal proceeding is to "determine the fair value *of the shares* exclusive of any element of value arising from the accomplishment or expectation of the merger or consolidation," taking into account "all relevant factors." Not only that, our Supreme Court has required this court to take into account all non-speculative information bearing on the value of the shares at issue in an appraisal.

Applied here, that means that when the court values the Series A Preferred Stock, it must take into account the economic reality that the Series A would have been entitled to a mandatory redemption on July 1, 2011, just six months after the Merger. The ability of the Series A holders to receive the full $100 per share on July 1, 2011[,] would of course have depended on whether Morgan Joseph had sufficient legally available funds to effect the redemption, but that specific, non-speculative contractual right was inarguably an important economic factor bearing on the value of the Series A as of the Merger date that any reasonable investor or market participant would have taken into account.

It is by no means unusual to recognize that the value of preferred stock often depends materially on its contractual features. As a general rule, preferred stock has the same appraisal rights as common stock, but "[u]nlike common stock, the value of preferred stock is determined solely from the contract rights conferred upon it in the certificate of designation." Therefore, when determining the fair value of preferred stock, the court must consider the contract upon which the preferred stock's value was based.

At the trial stage, therefore, this court will have to perform two related, but discrete tasks. It will have to value Morgan Joseph under the standards applicable in appraisals. This means that I will have to determine the fair value of Morgan Joseph as a going concern as of the Merger date. But the percentage of that entity value that should be awarded to the Series A Preferred Stock must, as a matter of legal and economic reality, take into account the legal right of the Series A holders to the July 1 Automatic Redemption. This works no harm to the other equity holders, as that is what you sign up for when you invest in a company with senior security holders entitled to specific preferred rights with economic value, or to Morgan Joseph, which chose to effect the Merger knowing that it had different series of stock with differing contractual claims on the company's value.

For the foregoing reasons, the petitioners' motion for partial summary judgment is granted. It is so ordered.

Motion GRANTED.

CRITICAL THINKING

Notice in the opinion that Chancellor Strine discusses the problems of the ambiguity in the contract and that the bank purposefully made elements in the contract ambiguous. Why would the bank do that?

ETHICAL DECISION MAKING

Think about what Strine says about the differences between the provisions of the stock the investors originally bought and the provisions of the new stock. Did the bank provide the investors with a fair deal after the merger?

Procedures for Appraisal Rights. The procedures governing appraisal rights are extensive. If the dissenting shareholders hope to receive compensation, they must follow the procedures accurately.

Dissenting shareholders who properly exercise their appraisal rights experience changes in their legal status as shareholders and in corresponding rights, depending on the jurisdiction. In some states, the law strips dissenting shareholders of their rights, including the right to vote and receive dividends. Shareholders who lose their legal status, however, retain the right to sue on the basis of evidence of illegal conduct associated with the merger or consolidation. Some states that revoke dissenting shareholders' legal status reinstate their status during the appraisal process. Thus, shareholders can withdraw from the appraisal process, contingent on corporate approval. Other jurisdictions do not reinstate status until after the appraisal is finished.

The issue of legal status and rights arises only if dissenting shareholders properly invoke their appraisal rights. If dissenting shareholders do not properly invoke these rights, courts force them to comply with the decision of the majority of the corporations' shareholders. If you were to operate within the WPH framework, would you find these procedures adequate, restrictive, or overly simplistic?

Purchase of Assets

LO3 What are asset purchases?

In addition to engaging in mergers and consolidations, corporations can extend their business operations by purchasing all or a substantial amount of another corporation's assets. *Assets* include intangible items (such as goodwill, a company name, and a company logo) and tangible items (such as buildings and other property). When an asset purchase occurs, the acquiring corporation (the one purchasing the assets) assumes ownership and control over tangible and intangible assets of the selling corporation.

The selling corporation needs the approval of both its board of directors and its shareholders before it can sell its assets. Shareholders of the acquired corporation who disagree with the transfer can demand appraisal rights in most states. Whether the acquiring corporation needs shareholder approval depends on the extent to which the merger alters the corporation's business position. Asset purchases normally do not change a corporation's legal status; thus, acquiring corporations do not usually need shareholder approval.

Although asset purchases seem similar to mergers and consolidations, they are significantly different because a corporation that purchases the assets of another corporation generally does not acquire its liabilities. In contrast, mergers and consolidations transfer all obligations.

In three circumstances, however, the acquiring corporation does assume the liabilities of the selling corporation. First, the contract governing the purchase may expressly or impliedly state that the acquiring corporation takes on the selling companies' liabilities in addition to its assets.

Second, although the two corporations may intend that the transaction be a purchase of assets, it may fall within the legal framework of a merger or consolidation. Thus, the acquiring corporation receives both the assets and the liabilities of the selling corporation.

Third, the purchaser does not avoid the selling corporation's liabilities if the corporations execute the sale under fraudulent circumstances. The U.S. Department of Justice and the Federal Trade Commission have stringent guidelines to ensure that the directors and shareholders of the acquired corporation have not used the asset sale to escape payment of obligations or pending lawsuits. These guidelines make it difficult, and sometimes impossible, for corporations to acquire other corporations through asset purchases. Thus, a corporation seeking to extend its business by purchasing another corporation's assets must be familiar with these guidelines to ensure that the sale is legal.

Legal Principle: **Asset purchases are significantly different from mergers and consolidations because a corporation that purchases the assets of another corporation generally does not acquire its liabilities.**

Purchase of Stock

LO4

What are stock purchases?

Besides engaging in mergers, consolidations, and asset purchases, corporations can extend their operations by purchasing another corporation's stock. As with asset purchases, an acquiring corporation, or *aggressor,* can buy any or all of another corporation's voting shares. Through such a stock purchase, the purchasing corporation gains control of the selling corporation in a corporate takeover.

The Nature of Takeovers

LO5

What is a takeover?

During the 1980s, not only did the number of corporate takeovers increase, but so too did the number of hostile takeovers. **Hostile takeovers** are takeovers to which the management of the target corporation objects. When a hostile takeover succeeds, the target corporation's management frequently compares the transition to a full-scale invasion characterized by layoffs and dramatic changes in company policy.

In the 1980s, corporations afraid of a hostile takeover concealed financial difficulties so as not to appear vulnerable to other corporations. Thus, they maintained a strong profile within the business community while their directors secretly sought a way out of their financial troubles.

TYPES OF TAKEOVERS

To initiate a stock purchase, the aggressor must appeal directly to the shareholders of the corporation it hopes to buy, known as the *target corporation.* The aggressor can offer several types of deals to the target shareholders (see Exhibit 40-2). It can make a **tender offer,** in which it offers target shareholders a price above the current market value of the stock. Aggressors, however, often require that they receive a certain number of shares within a certain time frame.

Alternatively, the aggressor may make an exchange tender offer. In an **exchange tender offer,** the aggressor offers to exchange target shareholders' current stock for stock in the aggressor's corporation. The aggressor may also make a **cash tender offer** to the target shareholders in which it pays them cash for their stock.

Other types of takeovers are more covert than these tender offers. For example, a **beachhead acquisition** occurs when an aggressor gradually accumulates the target company's shares. (The accumulated bloc of shares is analogous to a beachhead, an initial area of control from which the aggressor can launch later attacks.)

Exhibit 40-2

Types of Takeovers

Tender offer	The aggressor offers target shareholders a price above the current market value of the stock.
Exchange offer	The aggressor offers to exchange the target corporation's current stock for stock in the aggressor's corporation.
Cash tender offer	The aggressor offers to pay cash for the target corporation's stock.
Beachhead acquisition	The aggressor gradually accumulates a substantial number of the target corporation's shares and then initiates a proxy fight.
Hostile takeover	The management of the target corporation objects to the takeover.

After acquiring a substantial number of the target corporation's shares, the aggressor initiates a proxy fight by fighting for control over target shareholders' proxies. (Chapter 39 discusses proxies in more detail.) Because the holder of a proxy has the right to vote at shareholder meetings, if an aggressor can control a majority of proxies, it can outvote the other shareholders. The aggressor can then use the proxies it controls to elect a board of directors that supports the acquisition.

Before an aggressor can gain control of the target corporation through proxies, it needs a key piece of information: a list of target shareholders. Although resistant target corporations often want to conceal this information, federal securities law requires that target corporations assist aggressors in some ways. Thus, to avoid lengthy and expensive lawsuits, target corporations often provide a list of shareholders voluntarily. Providing the list does not guarantee that the aggressor will succeed, especially because federal regulations protect the target corporation. For instance, federal regulations permit the management of target companies to use corporate funds to educate shareholders on the disadvantages of a takeover.

Proxy solicitation, or fighting, doesn't always take place between an aggressor and a target corporation. In fact, proxy solicitation can occur within a company. For example, when Hewlett-Packard (HP) announced its intention to take over fellow computer company Compaq, Walter Hewlett, an HP board member and the son of HP cofounder William Hewlett, was strongly opposed. Convinced that the $22 billion HP-Compaq merger would be a failure, Walter Hewlett initiated a proxy fight within the company.

In an attempt to discourage HP voters from approving the takeover, Walter Hewlett sent out mailings to shareholders, took out advertisements in major papers, and blasted the merger, calling it a "mistake." After months of proxy fighting, HP shareholders voted to approve the merger, 838 million votes to 793 million votes. Additionally, Walter Hewlett's lawsuit was dismissed, and HP moved forward with its acquisition of Compaq.[1]

Those seeking to acquire corporations have developed tactics to overcome the law's rules encouraging cooperation from target corporations. Because contacting each individual target shareholder is expensive, aggressors often try to win the favor of a few institutional investors that own a large bloc of shares. If an aggressor can obtain the proxies of these investors, it can win control of the target corporation.

BUT WHAT IF . . .

WHAT IF THE FACTS OF THE CASE OPENER WERE DIFFERENT?

Let's say, in the Case Opener, that Polypore met with the shareholders of Microporous regarding taking over the company because of Microporous's financial troubles. Polypore aimed to take over Microporous and reduce the company's costs by implementing massive layoffs and restructuring the company. Microporous's management was against the takeover. What kind of takeover is this called?

RESPONSE TO TAKEOVERS

Once an aggressor has presented its offer to the target corporation's shareholders, the target corporation's board of directors must inform shareholders of all facts pertinent to shareholders' votes. After reviewing these material facts, the directors vote to accept or reject the offer and advise shareholders accordingly.

[1] http://news.cnet.com/Costs-mount-in-HP-proxy-fight/2100-1003_3-859261.html and www.pcworld.com/article/97944/its_official_hp_acquires_compaq.html.

If the directors conclude that a takeover is not in the company's best interest, the company may employ many methods of resistance. One common method is a **self-tender offer,** in which the target corporation offers to buy its shareholders' stock. If the shareholders accept the offer, the target corporation maintains control of the business.

Alternatively, target corporations may defend themselves using leveraged buyouts. A **leveraged buyout (LBO)** occurs when a group within a corporation (usually management) buys all outstanding corporate stock held by the public. Thus, the group gains control over corporate operations by "going private," or becoming a privately held corporation.

LBOs are usually high-risk endeavors, however, because the target corporation must borrow money to purchase the outstanding stock. It may have to borrow money from an investment bank or issue corporate bonds.

Illustrative jargon describes many methods of resistance to corporate takeovers. In Case 40-3, the Georgia court of appeals considers the legality of a "golden parachute."

CASE 40-3 ROYAL CROWN COMPANIES, INC. v. MCMAHON
COURT OF APPEALS OF GEORGIA
183 GA. APP. 543 (1987)

McMahon was the president of Arby's Inc., a subsidiary of Royal Crown Companies, Inc. It appeared that another corporation was positioning itself to buy Royal Crown. To reassure its top managers, Royal Crown enacted agreements stipulating that management would receive severance pay in the event of termination of employment or resignation after change of corporate control. McMahon resigned after the aggressor bought Royal Crown, but he did not receive his severance pay. He sued the corporation, and the trial court found in his favor. Royal Crown appealed.

JUDGE POPE: Royal Crown seeks to distinguish the agreement under consideration from the typical severance agreement because it is a special type of contract, which is commonly referred to as a "golden parachute." We are unpersuaded by Royal Crown's attempt, largely without legal support, to defeat this otherwise enforceable severance agreement simply because it is contingent upon a change in corporate control. The term "golden parachute" is not by itself legally significant. A severance contract by any other name would be just as enforceable.

Royal Crown argues that golden parachute agreements, in general, bear the taint of a conflict of interest in favor of the management beneficiaries to the detriment of the shareholders. We find no such conflict here. Plaintiff was not a member of the board of directors which approved this agreement. Moreover, the agreement was offered for the express purpose of protecting the shareholders by inducing the continued employment of plaintiff during a time of uncertainty when he might otherwise have been distracted by concerns for his own financial security to seek employment elsewhere.

Neither is the agreement void for failure of consideration. In the case at hand, plaintiff's employment was terminable at will and he was under no obligation to continue. The agreement was offered for the express purpose of inducing plaintiff to remain in his position during merger negotiations. Continued performance under a terminable-at-will contract furnishes sufficient consideration for the promise of additional severance pay. "We therefore reject any argument by the [employer] that any contract for severance pay is void as being without consideration."

AFFIRMED.

CRITICAL THINKING

Is there any missing information you would ask for when considering the facts of this case? If you were to argue to reverse the trial court's decision, what reasons would you offer? In your opinion, which of these reasons is the most persuasive? Do you find the court's reasons to affirm the trial court's decision to be equally persuasive?

ETHICAL DECISION MAKING

Think about the WPH process of ethical decision making. What is the purpose of the court's decision? In other words, which value is upheld? What value is in conflict with the reasoning of the court?

E-COMMERCE AND THE LAW

HOSTILE TAKEOVERS ONLINE

In the world of business, physical corporations are not the only ones that fear hostile takeovers. Companies such as Yahoo, the Internet web browser and e-mail hub, have recently fallen on hard times. Advertising companies have many more outlets now for their advertising, which means that advertising business is being spread thin over the online realm. This market slowdown presents a problem for Yahoo, since 90 percent of Yahoo's profits come from selling advertising space. Since Yahoo's stock prices have dropped dramatically, the company is worried about a hostile takeover. To help prevent takeover from happening, Yahoo has created a "poison pill." Under this measure, if another company, such as AOL Time Warner, owns a majority of Yahoo's stock, other stockholders with Yahoo may purchase more Yahoo stock at a significantly lower price. This bargain would drastically increase the price that a takeover company would have to pay to complete the takeover. Yahoo may then feel a little more secure about its continued independence.

Source: www.forbes.com/2001/03/02/0302ecommerce.html; http://business.yourdictionary.com/poison-pill.

Response to Termination

LO6

In what ways could the termination of mergers and consolidations occur?

The "death" of a corporation occurs in two phases: *dissolution,* the legal termination of the corporation, and *liquidation,* the process by which the board of directors converts the corporation's assets into cash and distributes them among the corporation's creditors and shareholders.

DISSOLUTION

Dissolution may be voluntary or involuntary, depending on who initiates and compels the dissolution. *Voluntary dissolution* occurs when the directors or shareholders trigger the dissolution procedures. The directors can initiate the proposal and submit it to the shareholders for a vote, or the shareholders can begin dissolution procedures. Either way, for dissolution to be successful, shareholders must unanimously vote for the proposal.

Regardless of whether the directors or shareholders initiate dissolution procedures, the corporation must follow specific procedures. First, the directors must file articles of dissolution with the secretary of state. These articles must include the company name, the date of dissolution, and the method of authorization of dissolution. Next, the directors must notify the shareholders. If shareholders or creditors have claims against the corporation, they must make them known within a stipulated time frame. Although the corporation establishes the time frame, the period must extend at least 120 days after the date of dissolution.

In an *involuntary dissolution,* the state forces the corporation to close. The state can initiate dissolution procedures, or individual shareholders can petition the state to order dissolution if they believe sufficient reason exists to terminate business operations. In some states, an individual shareholder of a closely held corporation can dissolve the corporation at will or after an event specified in the articles of incorporation occurs.

The secretary of state can compel involuntary dissolution for five reasons (RMBCA 14.20):

1. The corporation failed to pay taxes within 60 days of the due date.
2. The corporation failed to submit its annual report to the secretary of state within 60 days of the due date.
3. The corporation did not have a registered agent or office in the state for 60 days or more.
4. The corporation failed to notify the secretary of state within 60 days that its registered agent or registered office had changed.
5. The corporation's duration as specified in its articles of incorporation has expired.

In addition, courts can force involuntary dissolution for three reasons (RMBCA 14.30):

1. The corporation obtained its articles of incorporation fraudulently.

2. The directors have abused their power.
3. The corporation is insolvent.

Courts can also enforce involuntary dissolution if gridlock over an issue persists among the directors. Before ordering dissolution, however, courts usually urge shareholders to attempt to resolve the differences. If shareholders are unsuccessful, courts consider the extent to which the deadlock will result in irreversible damage to the corporation. If the disagreement will likely cause significant damage, courts will order the corporation to dissolve.

LIQUIDATION

The liquidation phase of termination begins once dissolution has occurred. In cases of voluntary dissolution, liquidation duties fall on the board of directors. The members of the board also become trustees of the corporate assets. As trustees, board members hold title to the corporation's property and become personally liable for breaches of fiduciary trustee duties.

Due to the heavy responsibilities trustees bear, some board members do not want to act as trustees. In other situations, shareholders do not want to entrust directors with the distribution of corporate assets. In these situations, the objecting party can petition the court to appoint a receiver not affiliated with the corporation to take over liquidation duties.

In cases of involuntary dissolution, courts automatically appoint a receiver to handle liquidation duties. Like the law in general, the law governing corporate terminations is dynamic; it changes in response to a host of external factors. Hence, although a company is legally terminated after it completes dissolution and liquidation, the law's view of the extent of the company's posttermination responsibilities has changed over time in response to scientific and technological developments. In the past, a corporation's liabilities dissolved when the corporation dissolved. Recently, however, scientists have discovered that companies' actions can have environmental effects that do not appear until many years later. Thus, stimulated by these scientific developments, courts have held that dissolved corporations remain responsible for their liabilities.

Exhibit 40-3 summarizes the life stages of a corporation.

Exhibit 40-3

Life Stages of a Corporation

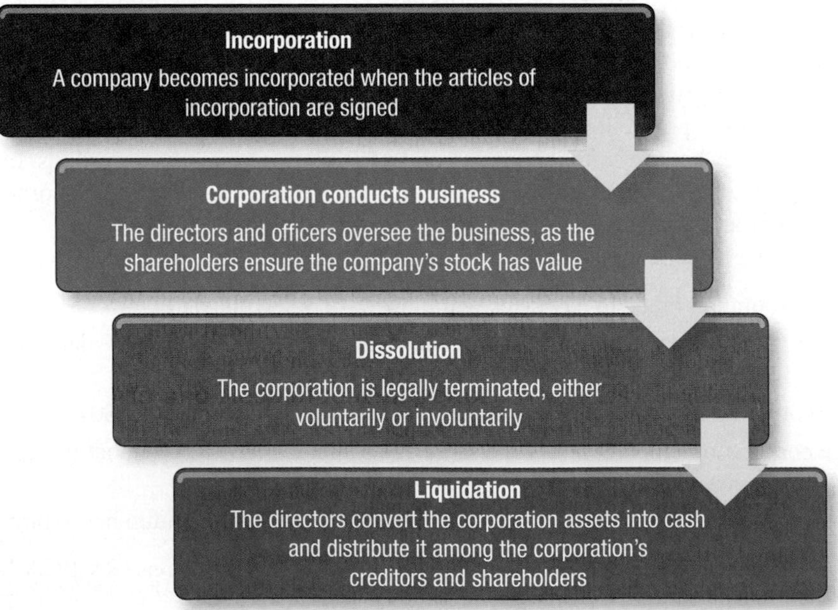

CASE OPENER WRAP-UP

Acquisitions as Horizontal Mergers

In this case, the appellate court held that the Federal Trade Commission did not err when it treated the acquisition as a horizontal merger. The court agreed that Polypore's acquisition of Microporous would substantially lessen competition in the applicable market. The court also found that the Federal Trade Commission provided ample evidence that there was only one market for deep-cycle battery separators. According to the court, the Clayton Act outlines that if a rival has already made its first sale in the monopolist's market, the merger is clearly horizontal.

KEY TERMS

appraisal right 878
beachhead acquisition 882
cash tender offer 882
chose in action 874
consolidations 874
exchange tender offer 882
hostile takeovers 882
leveraged buyout (LBO) 884
merger 874
parent-subsidiary merger 877
self-tender offer 884
short-form merger 877
tender offer 882

SUMMARY OF KEY TOPICS

Introduction to Mergers and Consolidations

Merger: A legal contract combining two or more corporations such that only one of the corporations continues to exist.

Consolidation: A legal contract combining two or more corporations and resulting in an entirely new corporation.

Procedures for Mergers and Consolidations

1. Boards of directors of all involved corporations must approve the plan.
2. Shareholders must approve the plan through a vote at a shareholder meeting.
3. The corporations must submit their plan to the secretary of state.
4. The state reviews the plan and grants an approval certificate.

Short-form merger: The parent corporation merges with a subsidiary corporation. Short-form mergers do not require shareholder approval.

Rights of shareholders: Shareholders vote only on exceptional matters regarding the corporation.

Appraisal right: An appraisal right is the shareholder's right to have his or her shares appraised and to receive monetary compensation for their value.

Purchase of Assets

One corporation can extend its business operations by purchasing the assets of another company.

Purchase of Stock

An acquiring corporation can take control of another corporation by purchasing a substantial amount of its voting stock.

The Nature of Takeovers

A corporation can expand its size and operations by purchasing the stock of another firm.

A *hostile takeover* is a takeover to which the management of the target corporation objects.

Types of takeovers:

1. Tender offers
2. Exchange offers
3. Cash tender offers
4. Beachhead acquisitions

Response to Termination

Response to takeovers: Directors declare whether they accept or reject the offer. If they object to the offer, they can engage in methods of resistance.

Dissolution is the legal death of a corporation.

In *liquidation,* a corporation sells all of its assets and distributes them to repay its outstanding debts.

POINT / COUNTERPOINT

Should the SEC Require Early Disclosure of Major Cash Tender Stock Purchases for Publicly Traded Stock?

YES

People who invest in corporations have a right to know if a potential merger or acquisition of the company they've invested in is forthcoming because such a change directly affects investors. For example, the 2012 merger of Google and Motorola Mobility significantly changed both the corporate model and the marketability of the invested products; investors in a cell phone manufacturer became investors in a website, and the price of a share rose significantly. Shareholder rights plans require that outside stock purchases over 5 percent are disclosed. Although current regulations allow for a 10-day grace period before disclosing, two important explanations suggest the wisdom of shortening this time period.

First, public investors would benefit from early disclosure. In the event that a hostile takeover is under way, shareholders would have the option to sell or buy more of their corporate stock. Moreover, if any investors decide to sell their stock, they can profit from the sale at a higher price. Likewise, their chance of profiting is increased if they know that a company is intending to continue purchasing stock. On the other hand, by buying more stock, investors will influence the outcome of a potential takeover by preventing an outsider from owning enough stock to gain a controlling interest in the company. Furthermore, if a company's shareholder rights plan includes discounting sales measures (also known as

NO

Enforcing early disclosure of major investors is an unnecessary regulation by the government that will not only stymy the stock market but also have disastrous unintended consequences. In early 2013, the SEC proposed a plan to shorten the 10-day required period before shareholders must disclose the purchase of 5 percent or more of a company's stock. Though the aim of the change is to promote transparency, it will ultimately result in preventing cash tender takeovers of companies through manipulation of the shareholders by the board of directors.

Early disclosure will trigger protection measures that will dilute the value of the stock. In the event that the purchase of 5 percent of a company's shares is disclosed, an automatic shareholder agreement measure to discount the sale of remaining stock to all other shareholders is enacted at many companies. Because current shareholders are buying up large quantities of stock, the share price will increase. If large purchases are disclosed earlier, directors can set the triggers for such measures lower.

With earlier detection of buyers, directors can set their thresholds low enough to control investors who hold small numbers of shares. Thus, early disclosure will intensify stock dilution through discounted purchases.

poison pills) to prevent hostile takeovers, the earlier the disclosure, the more likely that individual investors will be able to purchase additional stock at discounted prices. Thus, early disclosure helps investors control the outcome of their investments and profit from it.

Second, the board of directors benefits from early disclosure by learning of early intentions from outside purchasers. It is the duty of directors to vote on mergers and significant changes in corporate outcomes. The decisions of directors have a great influence on the company, and directors have a vested interest in its survival. With early detection of a hostile takeover, they are afforded the ability to manage with greater foresight for the future of their company.

Thus, in order to uphold the spirit of the Williams Act, and encourage market transparency, the period of disclosure should be shortened.

Source: Lucian A. Bebchuk, "Don't Make Posion Pills More Deadly," *New York Times,* February 7, 2013, http://dealbook.nytimes.com/2013/02/07/dont-make-poison-pills-more-deadly/; Lucian A. Bebchuk, "Don't Discourage Outside Shareholders," *New York Times,* August 15, 2012, http://dealbook.nytimes.com/2012/08/15/dont-discourage-outside-shareholders/; and John C. Coffee, Jr., "Shareholders versus Managers: The Strain in the Corporate Web," *Michigan Law Review,* vol. 85 (1986), pp. 1, 9.

QUESTIONS & PROBLEMS

1. What are the primary differences between mergers and consolidations?
2. Distinguish the various types of takeovers.
3. River Cities Investment Co.'s shareholders voted to amend the articles of incorporation to limit common stock to a total of 200 shares, reducing the existing 496,507 shares into the 200 shares. River Cities' board of directors determined that the value of the stock before the reduction was $33.23 per share, and the board offered to buy the fractions of stock the minority shareholders owned for this amount. Meanwhile, Northwest Bank Holding Company purchased River Cities and then paid the River Cities minority shareholders for their stock, in addition to notifying the stockholders of their appraisal rights. The stockholders sued, arguing that a "fair value" market price for their shares should include an additional amount per share because, by buying the shares, Northwest gains a controlling interest in the company. Does "fair value" include paying for the benefit of having a controlling interest? How would various reasonable definitions of "fair" sway the judges' opinions? [*Northwest Investment Corp. v. Wallace,* 741 N.W.2d 782 (Iowa 2007).]
4. Martin Marietta Materials Inc. and Vulcan Materials Company are the two largest providers, in the United States, of rock-mining and similar materials for infrastructure. In the mid-2000s, Vulcan approached Martin on several occasions to offer a "strategic transaction," which Martin turned down on all occasions for entrenchment reasons. When the chief operating officer of Martin became the chief executive officer, he was more willing to consider the transaction, which involved a merger between the two companies. The new CEO, however, was cautious of any transaction that might put his new position in peril and was even more wary after a failed hostile takeover attempt of his company earlier in the year. Therefore, Martin insisted on confidentiality agreements to prevent any public disclosure of the merger. A nondisclosure agreement and a joint-defense agreement were signed between the two companies. The agreements prohibited both companies from disclosing any

material from the merger other than "evaluating a transaction," and a transaction was defined as a "possible business transaction between Martin and Vulcan." The NDA permitted disclosure if required in connection with "legal proceedings, subpoena, civil investigative demand or other similar process." There was also a clause that required each company to let the other comment on any material that was to be released before the release occurred. Later on, the merger broke down due to undesirable market conditions on behalf of Vulcan. Martin launched a hostile exchange offer and a proxy contest to unseat four directors from the Vulcan board of directors. Did this act by Martin violate the proposed merger by the two companies? [*Martin Marietta Materials, Inc. v. Vulcan Materials Co.,* C.A. 7102-CS (Del. Ch., May 4, 2012).]

5. In January 2003, Motorola began a hostile tender offer to obtain the 26 percent of Next Level Communications, Inc., that it did not own. It offered Next Level shareholders $1.04 per share. After Next Level shareholders petitioned to stop the takeover, Motorola increased its offer to $1.18 per share. After four months, Motorola had acquired 88 percent of Next Level's outstanding stock. It then converted some of its preferred stock into common stock, increasing its common stock ownership of Next Level to more than 90 percent. Motorola then initiated a short-form merger with Next Level, cashing out Next Level's minority shareholders. One of these shareholders, Nick Gilliland, sued Next Level and Motorola for breach of their fiduciary duty to disclose information about Next Level's financial condition to Next Level minority shareholders. Gilliland argued that minority shareholders needed this information to decide whether to accept Motorola's cash-out offer or to exercise their appraisal rights. Motorola and Next Level argued that they sent minority shareholders information about Next Level's financial situation when Motorola made its initial tender offer. Moreover, they argued that the notice of the short-form merger they sent to minority shareholders met statutory requirements. Do you think the court sided with the corporations or with the minority shareholders in this case? Why? If you think the court sided with the shareholders, what remedies do you think should be available to them? [*Gilliland v. Motorola, Inc.,* 873 A.2d 305 (2005).]

6. H&R Block is one of the largest providers of income tax preparations and the second largest of online do-it-yourself software in the United States. In 2010, the tax preparer sought to buy out its rival, 2SS Holdings, which produced TaxAct software products for consumers. Because TaxAct is the nation's third-largest provider of tax preparation software, the proposed merger caused concern for the Justice Department. According to the department's investigation, the merger would result in fewer free tax-assistance software products and higher prices for the companies' nonfree products. H&R Block challenged by saying the merger would give it only 28 percent of the do-it-yourself tax preparation market. However, it was ultimately decided that the merger would result in an anticompetitive market; thus the merger was denied. What aspects of merger law are included in this case? [*United States v. H&R Block,* 833 F. Supp. 2d 36, 2011 U.S. Dist. LEXIS 130219 (2011).]

7. Dougherty County in Georgia is home to two hospitals, Phoebe Putney Memorial Hospital and Palmyra Medical Center, both located within 2 miles of each other. The operation of Palmyra is controlled by Hospital Corporation of America (HCA), which is a large provider, nationwide, of health care services. Memorial was owned by the county until 1990, when ownership was transferred to Phoebe Putney Health System (PPHS). In early 2010, Palmyra sought to control Memorial, which used an intermediary. Before meeting with the intermediary, HCA and Palmyra met to negotiate the terms of acquisition. In exchange for $195 million, the assets in Palmyra would be transferred to Memorial. They met with the intermediary, and the terms were agreed on without revision. In early 2011, the Federal Trade Commission issued a complaint, claiming that the merger violated certain parts of the Clayton Act and the FTC Act. The state of Georgia, along with the FTC, filed suit against PPHS, stating that the merger would lessen competition in relevant markets. Was the FTC right in asserting concern for the merger, given where the two hospitals are located? [*Federal Trade Commission and The State of Georgia v. Phoebe Putney Health System Inc., Phoebe Putney Memorial Hospital, Inc., Phoebe North, Inc., Palmyra Park Hospital Inc., and Hospital Authority of Albany-Dougherty County,* 793 F. Supp. 2d 1356 (2011).]

8. The City of Herriman, Utah, decided that it would provide water to its residents through a municipal water system. At the time, Herriman did not own any water, wells, or delivery infrastructure, but the Herriman Pipeline and Development Co. did. The city began to acquire the company's assets. It succeeded, much to the distress of a number of the company's shareholders. The shareholders sued the city, arguing that their shares entitled them to access to water and to an ownership interest in the company's assets. The court dismissed the case, and the shareholders appealed. Did the shareholders have a valid ownership interest in the company's assets? Why? [*Dansie v. City of Herriman*, 2006 UT 23.]

9. The directors of Lone Star Steakhouse & Saloon, Inc., set up a corporate provision that granted them significant retirement benefits if another company took over Lone Star and installed new directors. The corporate provision, however, held that the directors were not entitled to these golden-parachute benefits if they approved the new directors. The California Public Employees' Retirement System (CalPERS), a Lone Star shareholder, challenged the golden-parachute provision, arguing that it granted the existing directors undue voting power in director elections. Moreover, CalPERS argued that the golden-parachute provision discouraged potentially beneficial takeovers because the provision made it costly for potential aggressors to alter Lone Star's management. Lone Star argued that the provision was a legitimate defense to hostile takeovers. With whom do you think the court sided in this case? Why? [*Cal. Pub. Emples. Ret. Sys. v. Coulter*, 2005 Del. Ch. LEXIS 54 (2005).]

10. James Simmons was injured in a work-related accident at a construction site when an elevated scissorlift aerial work platform collapsed. Mark Industries designed, manufactured, and sold the scissorlift. Mark filed for bankruptcy in federal bankruptcy court and sold its assets to Terex. The agreement between Mark and Terex, which the bankruptcy court approved, included a provision stating that Terex was not responsible for any of Mark's liability. Only three Mark employees, none of whom were officers or directors, continued with Terex after Terex closed the factory it received as part of Mark's assets. Terex did not have any business relationship with Mark until purchasing its assets in the bankruptcy court auction. There has never been any commonality of officers, directors, or stockholders between Mark and Terex. Simmons sued Terex under a theory of successor liability. Was Terex a proper successor to Mark? What does Simmons need to prove to win his case? [*Simmons v. Mark Lift Industries, Inc.*, 622 S.E.2d 213 (S.C. 2005).]

Looking for more review materials?

The Online Learning Center at **www.mhhe.com/kubasek3e** contains this chapter's "Assignment on the Internet" and also a list of URLs for more information, entitled "On the Internet." Find both of them in the Student Center portion of the OLC, along with quizzes and other helpful materials.

CHAPTER

41 Corporations: Securities and Investor Protection

LEARNING OBJECTIVES

After reading this chapter, you will be able to answer the following questions:

1 What is a security?

2 What requirements are imposed by the Securities Act of 1933?

3 How does the Securities Exchange Act of 1934 regulate the trading of securities?

4 How are investment companies regulated?

5 How do states regulate securities?

CASE OPENER

The Martha Stewart Case

On December 27, 2001, Martha Stewart's stockbroker, Peter Bacanovic, informed Stewart that two of his clients, Samuel Waksal, CEO of the biopharmaceutical company ImClone, and Waksal's daughter, had just sold all of their ImClone stock. Waksal knew that the FDA was about to reject Erbitux, a key cancer drug ImClone had developed. Stewart did not know about the impending FDA rejection, and information about Waksal's sale of ImClone's stock was not available to the public. After receiving the information about Waksal's transaction, Stewart instructed her broker to sell all her shares of ImClone stock. The next day, the FDA announced its rejection of Erbitux, and ImClone's stock price plummeted 16 percent. Stewart's timely trade allowed her to avoid a $45,673 loss.

Eighteen months later, the Securities and Exchange Commission (SEC) filed charges against Stewart and her broker for illegal insider trading and securities fraud.[1]

1. Do you think Stewart violated federal securities law? Why or why not?
2. Do you think Stewart's broker violated federal securities law? Why or why not?

The Wrap-Up at the end of the chapter will answer these questions.

[1] www.sec.gov/news/press/2003-69.htm.

Companies frequently need to raise money to expand. One way to raise money is to issue securities, so corporations issue corporate **securities**—stocks and bonds—to raise capital for corporate expansion.

But a security is simply a piece of paper; it has no intrinsic value. Consequently, without securities regulations, corporations could easily commit fraud by issuing large numbers of securities and then refusing to repay them. Thus, the government heavily regulates securities issuance and trading.

Securities regulation is a relatively recent body of law. Before the Great Depression, government did not regulate securities, and fraudulent transactions occurred frequently. After the stock market crash in 1929, Congress passed several laws to regulate securities markets.

This chapter begins by defining a security. It then examines federal securities regulations. Finally, the chapter briefly discusses state securities regulation.

What Is a Security?

L01 What is a security?

Physically, a security is merely a piece of paper. But when investors buy securities, they are not buying a piece of paper. They are buying what the paper represents. The value of the security is based on what the paper represents.

Earlier, we loosely defined securities as stocks and bonds. To be more precise, securities include stocks, bonds, debentures, and warrants. Furthermore, certain items mentioned in securities acts, such as interests in oil and gas rights, are securities. In some cases, courts have even defined cosmetics, vacuum cleaners, and cemetery lots as securities. Finally, investment contracts, contracts in which individuals invest money with the expectation of making a profit, are securities. How can so many different things be securities?

The Securities Act of 1933 offers a complicated definition of *security,* and, as a result, courts have struggled when determining whether a particular instrument is a security. In an effort to provide a framework for analysis, the U.S. Supreme Court stated in the 1985 case *Landreth Timber Co. v. Landreth* that courts should presumptively treat as a security any financial instrument designated as a note, stock, bond, or other instrument named in the 1933 act.

If, however, the instrument in question does not have the characteristics of an instrument specifically named in the 1933 act, the courts apply a three-part test. In the 1946 case *SEC v. W.J. Howey Co.,*[2] the U.S. Supreme Court defined a security as an (1) investment in a common enterprise with the (2) reasonable expectation of profit gained (3) primarily or substantially from others' efforts. Anything that meets these three criteria is subject to security law.

Case 41-1 illustrates how courts apply the Howey test.

[2] 328 U.S. 293, 66 S. Ct. 1100 (1946).

CASE 41-1 SECURITIES AND EXCHANGE COMMISSION v. MUTUAL BENEFITS CORP.

U.S. COURT OF APPEALS FOR THE ELEVENTH CIRCUIT 408 F.3D 737 (2005).

From 1994 to 2004, around 30,000 investors invested more than $1 billion in viatical settlements provided by Mutual Benefits Corporation. In a viatical settlement, an insured person who is terminally ill sells the benefits of her life insurance policy to a third party in exchange for a cash payment equaling part of the policy's value. This third party will make a profit if, when the insured dies, the benefits of the policy are greater than the purchase price the third party paid. It is pivotal for one to have an accurate determination of the expected date of the insured's death. For if the insured lives longer than this expected date, the purchaser will make a lesser amount, or even lose money. Mutual Benefits Corporation (MBC) purchases these policies, and sells smaller interests to individual investors.

The Securities and Exchange Commission (SEC) filed an action against MBC based on believed violations of securities laws. First, the SEC argued that MBC lied about the life expectancy figures being produced by independent doctors, and that most of the life expectancy numbers were false. At an evidentiary hearing, the issue of whether a viatical settlement investment is an investment contract under securities laws was brought into question.

JUDGE COX: The Securities Act of 1933 and the Securities Exchange Act of 1934 both define the term "security" as including the catch-all term "investment contracts." The phrase "investment contract" is not defined in either statute. In Securities & Exchange Commission v. W.J. Howey Co., the Supreme Court provided a flexible test for determining whether a particular transaction qualified as an "investment contract." "[A]n investment contract for purposes of the Securities Act means a contract, transaction or scheme whereby a person invests his money in a common enterprise and is led to expect profits solely from the efforts of the promoter or a third party." The Court stated that this approach "embodies a flexible rather than a static principle, one that is capable of adaption to meet the countless and variable schemes devised by those who seek the use of the money of others on the promises of profits."

In Securities & Exchange Commission v. Edwards the Supreme Court reaffirmed the definition enunciated in Howey. The Court reiterated that " 'Congress' purpose in enacting the securities laws was to regulate investments, in whatever form they are made and by whatever name they are called.' To that end, it enacted a broad definition of 'security,' sufficient 'to encompass virtually any instrument that might be sold as an investment.' "

There is no genuine dispute here that there was (1) an investment of money, (2) in a common enterprise, (3) involving an expectation of profits. The only real dispute concerns whether the investor's expectation of profits is based "solely on the efforts of the promoter or a third party." MBC, relying on Securities & Exchange Commission v. Life Partners, Inc., argues that this element is "a necessarily forward-looking inquiry." MBC asks that we make a distinction between a promoter's activities prior to his having use of an investor's money and his activities after he has use of the money. This distinction was indeed made in Life Partners, a case involving facts similar to those presented here.

[W]e cannot agree that the time of sale is an artificial dividing line. It is a legal construct but a significant one. If the investor's profits depend thereafter predominantly upon the promoter's efforts, then the investor may benefit from the disclosure and other requirements of the federal securities laws. But if the value of the promoter's efforts has already been impounded into the promoter's fees or into the purchase price of the investment, and if neither the promoter nor anyone else is expected to make further efforts that will affect the outcome of the investment, then the need for federal securities regulation is greatly diminished.

We see here no "venture" associated with the ownership of an insurance contract from which one's profit depends entirely upon the mortality of the insured.

Because no significant post-purchase activity took place here, MBC argues, the expectation of profits is not based "solely on the efforts of the promoter or a third party."

We decline to adopt the test established by the Life Partners court. We are not convinced that either Howey or Edwards require such a clean distinction between a promoter's activities prior to his having use of an investor's money and his activities thereafter. The rule set forth in Howey and reiterated in Edwards directs us to broadly apply the Security Acts of 1993 and 1994 to all "schemes devised by those who seek the use of the money of others on the promise of profits."

While it may be true that the "solely on the efforts of the promoter or a third party" prong of the Howey test is more easily satisfied by post-purchase activities, there is no basis for excluding pre-purchase managerial activities from the analysis. Significant pre-purchase managerial activities undertaken to insure the success of the investment may also satisfy Howey. Indeed, investment schemes may often involve a combination of both pre- and post-purchase managerial activities, both of which should be taken into consideration in determining whether Howey's test is satisfied. Courts have found investment contracts where significant efforts included the pre-purchase exercise of expertise by promoters in selecting or negotiating the price of an asset in which investors would acquire an interest.

Furthermore, while the "solely on the efforts of the promoter or a third party" prong of the Howey test may not be met where an investment relies predominantly on market speculation, that is not the case here. The investors' expectations of profits in this case relied heavily on the pre- and post-payment efforts of the promoters in making investments in viatical settlement contracts profitable. The investors selected the "term" of their investment, and submitted completed agreement forms and money. Thereafter, MBC selected the insurance policies in which the investors' money would be placed. MBC bid on policies and negotiated purchase prices with the insureds. MBC determined how much money would be placed in escrow to cover payment of future premiums. MBC undertook to evaluate the life expectancy of the insureds—evaluations critical to the success of the venture. If MBC underestimated the insureds' life expectancy, the chances increased that the investors would realize less of a profit, or no profit at all. And, investors had no ability to assess the accuracy of representations being made by MBC or the accuracy of the life-expectancy evaluations. They could not, by reference to market trends, independently assess the prospective value of their investments in MBC's viatical settlement contracts. There were important post-purchase managerial efforts of MBC as well. Often, life-expectancy evaluations were not completed until after closing. And, after closing on a policy, MBC assumed the responsibility of making premium payments. Escrow payments were collectively managed in such

[continued]

a manner that investors were not required to pay additional premiums. Thus, investors relied on both the pre- and post-purchase management activities of MBC to maximize the profit potential of investing in viatical settlement contracts.

MBC thus offered what amounts to a classic investment contract. Investors were offered and sold an investment in a common enterprise in which they were promised profits that were dependent on the efforts of the promoters. This is true regardless of which specific MBC purchase agreement form is at issue. Whether the investors were offered a longer or shorter window in which to withdraw funds from escrow, whether the life-expectancy evaluation was actually performed before or after closing, and despite certain differences in how premiums were paid, all investors here relied on the pre- and post-purchase managerial efforts of MBC to make a profit on the investment in viatical settlement contracts. The investors here relied on MBC to identify terminally ill insureds, negotiate purchase prices, pay premiums, and perform life expectancy evaluations critical to the success of the venture. The flexible test we are instructed to apply by Howey and Edwards covers these activities, qualifying MBC's viatical settlement contracts as "investment contracts" under the Securities Acts of 1933 and 1934.

Because we conclude that these viatical settlement contracts qualify as "investment contracts" under the Securities Acts of 1933 and 1934, the district court properly denied MBC's motion to dismiss for lack of subject matter jurisdiction.

AFFIRMED.

CRITICAL THINKING

Why might the ambiguities in the definition of *security* be a problem in securities regulation?

ETHICAL DECISION MAKING

You probably have a good idea of the ethical theory you agree with most. Under that ethical theory, what is your opinion of the business of MBC? Should the SEC protect investors from such a business framework?

Securities Regulation

Congress passed two crucial acts regulating securities transactions. The Securities Act of 1933[3] regulates how companies issue corporate securities, while the Securities Exchange Act of 1934[4] oversees the purchase and sale of securities. Both acts attempt to provide greater stability to securities transaction. First, they mandate that investors have access to certain information when deciding whether to buy or sell securities. Second, they strive to curb fraudulent securities transactions.

THE SECURITIES AND EXCHANGE COMMISSION

Perhaps the most significant component of the 1934 act was the creation of the Securities and Exchange Commission (SEC), an independent agency whose function is to administer federal securities laws. The SEC is headed by five individuals appointed by the president. These five individuals serve fixed five-year terms.

The New York Stock Exchange is one of the central locations where securities are bought and sold.

[3] 15 U.S.C. §§ 77a–77aa.

[4] 15 U.S.C. §§ 78a–78mm.

COMPARING THE LAW OF OTHER COUNTRIES

SWEDEN'S SECURITIES MARKET

The Swedes divide securities into bonds and shares. Individuals invest in either the bond market or the stock market. Companies issue bonds to boost funds from sources outside their shareholders. Bondholders have a right to a fixed rate of interest regardless of whether the company earns a profit. Bondholders do not, however, have a right to take part in company decision making.

Companies issue shares to increase their equity capital. Unlike bond interest payments, shareholders' returns vary with the company's profits. Because shareholders' interests are closely tied to the success of the company, shareholders have a voice within the company. Generally, this voice comes in the form of a vote at general meetings.

Regulation of the stock and bond markets in Sweden is unique because Sweden has no equivalent of the SEC. Instead, banks themselves oversee the issuance of shares and bonds.

The SEC has a number of responsibilities. First, it is responsible for the enforcement of securities laws. Thus, in response to an allegation of violation of securities law, the SEC investigates and, if necessary, initiates an enforcement action against the violator. Enforcement actions often include penalties or injunctive remedies. If the violation is severe enough to warrant criminal prosecution, however, the Fraud Section of the Criminal Division of the Department of Justice will prosecute the alleged violator.

Second, the SEC interprets the securities acts and adopts rules to achieve the purposes of the acts. Thus, the SEC passes securities transaction regulations that have the force of law.

Third, the SEC regulates the activities of securities brokers, dealers, and advisers. All securities dealers and brokers must register with the SEC.

Fourth, the SEC regulates the trade of securities on securities exchanges. As you read about securities regulations in this chapter, remember that the SEC is responsible for their administration and enforcement.

Exhibit 41-1 outlines how the powers of the SEC were enhanced during the 1990s.

Exhibit 41-1

The Expansion of SEC Powers since 1990

Securities Enforcement Remedies and Penny Stock Reform Act of 1990

Permits the SEC to:

- Issue a cease-and-desist order against a violator of any federal securities law.
- Seek civil money penalties against any violators.
- Create rules to require that brokers and dealers provide information concerning prices and risk associated with the penny-stock market.

Market Reform Act of 1990

Allows the SEC to suspend securities trading if prices vary excessively in a short time period.

Securities Acts Amendments of 1990

Permit the SEC to seek punishment of violators of foreign securities laws.

National Securities Markets Improvement Act of 1996

Permits the SEC to exempt persons, securities, and transactions from securities regulations.

Sarbanes-Oxley Act of 2002

- Increases corporate disclosure requirements.
- Penalizes violators of securities laws more heavily.
- Holds corporate executives responsible for errors in corporate reports filed with the SEC.
- Requires earlier filing of financial and stock transaction reports.
- Creates and establishes SEC oversight over the Public Company Accounting Oversight Board to regulate public accounting firms.

COMPARING THE LAW OF OTHER COUNTRIES

MEXICAN SECURITIES MARKET

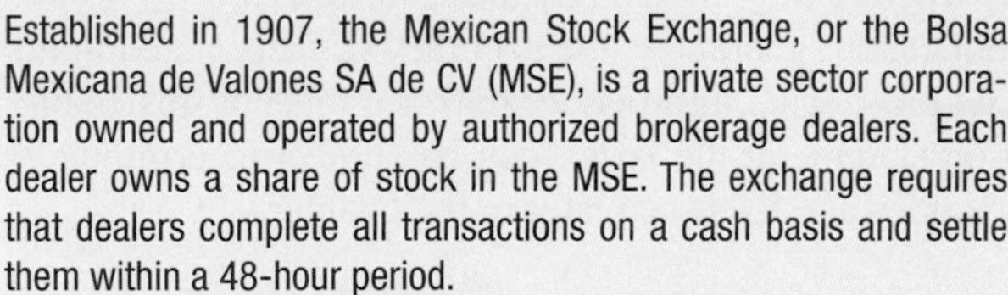

Established in 1907, the Mexican Stock Exchange, or the Bolsa Mexicana de Valones SA de CV (MSE), is a private sector corporation owned and operated by authorized brokerage dealers. Each dealer owns a share of stock in the MSE. The exchange requires that dealers complete all transactions on a cash basis and settle them within a 48-hour period.

The National Security Commission (CNV), governed by the Mexican Securities Law (MSL), regulates public offerings and securities trading. The 11-member CNV board of governors has the power to approve all applicants for listing on the MSE. These governors determine whether to accept applicants on the basis of operating history and management and asset criteria. The board of governors also has the power to investigate possible infractions of MSL, suspend trading of certain securities, and intervene in management brokerage firms when necessary.

CNV's most demanding function is the regulation of public offerings. As defined by the boards, public offerings are made "through means of mass communication or to an 'unspecified' person in order to subscribe, sell, or acquire securities." Regulation of public offerings is limited to some extent because existing laws do not permit non-Mexican entities to issue securities. Existing laws do not, however, limit investments in securities outside Mexico by Mexican individuals or companies.

Other countries have bodies that serve functions similar to those of the SEC. In Singapore, for example, the government controls securities markets through the Securities Industry Council. The council is an advisory board to the minister of finance, who, on the basis of the council's advice, issues guidelines for exchanges, mergers, and trading.

The Securities Act of 1933

LO2 What requirements are imposed by the Securities Act of 1933?

Congress passed the Securities Act of 1933 in reaction to the mistrust of securities transactions before the Great Depression. Thus, a function of the act was to legitimize security transactions by requiring the registration of securities offered to the public. Through the registration process, investors have more information to make better-informed decisions about their securities purchases.

Section 5 of the 1933 act mandates that any corporation, partnership, association, or individual that offers the sale of securities to the public through the use of mails or through any facility of interstate commerce is required to register that security unless it qualifies for an exemption (discussed later in this section). Any issuer of securities must file a written registration statement and a prospectus with the SEC.

REGISTRATION STATEMENT

Although the SEC requires that different types of companies complete slightly different registration forms, the SEC requires certain elements from all companies. The **registration statement** generally contains (1) a description of the securities offered for sale, (2) an explanation of how proceeds from the sale of the securities will be used, (3) a description of the registrant's business and properties, (4) information about the management of the company, (5) a description of any pending lawsuits in which the registrant is involved, and (6) financial statements certified by an independent public accountant.

Caution: Although the SEC requires the registration of securities, the SEC does not "approve" these securities. In other words, the SEC does not make any judgment about the worth of securities; it simply enforces the requirement that issuers provide certain information to potential buyers.

PROSPECTUS

Along with filing a registration statement, issuers of securities must also file a prospectus with the SEC. A **prospectus** is a written document that contains most of the same information as the registration statement. The prospectus is different from the registration statement, however, because it is an advertising tool that issuers distribute to potential investors who rely on the prospectus to help decide whether they should buy the securities.

The SEC requires, but cannot guarantee, the accuracy of facts stated in the registration statement and prospectus. If an issuer makes a false or misleading statement in a registration statement, the issuer can be subject to criminal or civil penalties. These penalties are discussed later in the chapter.

To be reminded of what economics teaches us about why information contained in the prospectus is so important, please see the **Connecting to the Core** activity on the text website at www.mhhe.com/kubasek3e.

PERIODS OF THE FILING PROCESS

The filing process consists of three periods: prefiling, waiting, and posteffective.

Prefiling Period. The **prefiling period** begins when an issuer begins to think about issuing securities, and it ends when the issuer files the registration statement and prospectus with the SEC. Before filing a registration statement and prospectus with the SEC, an issuer cannot make any offers to sell securities. The issuer can, however, negotiate with *underwriters,* investment banking firms that purchase securities from the issuing corporation with the intent of selling them to brokerage houses, which then sell them to the public.

Because they cannot offer to sell securities during the prefiling period, issuers, officers, directors, and underwriters usually try to avoid generating publicity about possibly issuing securities because the SEC may construe such publicity as an attempt to condition the market to generate interest in the securities. In fact, the SEC could consider speeches or press releases mentioning the potential issuance of securities to be an offer. The issuing firm is permitted, however, to publish a notice about the prospective offering, including the name of the issuer as well as a description of the potential securities, but the notice may not include the name of the underwriter.

Waiting Period. Once an issuer files a registration statement and prospectus, the **waiting period** begins. During this period, the SEC reviews the information filed by the issuing firm. Issuers must wait 20 days after the filing date to sell their securities. During the waiting period, issuers may make oral offers to sell the securities and may distribute a **red-herring prospectus**—a prospectus with a warning written in red print at the top of the page alerting investors that the registration has been filed with the SEC but not yet been approved. Moreover, the issuer may publish a **tombstone advertisement,** a brief ad with a format similar to that of a tombstone.

Posteffective Period. The **posteffective period** begins when the SEC declares the registration statement effective, and it ends when the issuer sells all securities offered or withdraws them from sale. During this time, investors may buy and sell the securities, but purchasers must receive a final prospectus, a version of the prospectus the buyer must receive at the point of sale. If an issuer does not send the purchaser a final prospectus, the issuer has violated the 1933 Securities Act.

BUT WHAT IF . . .

WHAT IF THE FACTS OF THE CASE OPENER WERE DIFFERENT?

Let's say, in the Case Opener, that Waksal had submitted his registration statement to the SEC. He went through the waiting period, and eventually the SEC declared his registration statement to be effective. Waksal thinks that he has now completed all the periods of the filing process. Is he correct? Is he missing anything?

SPECIAL REGISTRATION PROVISIONS

Amendments to the 1933 act stipulate more relaxed registration requirements for companies that have consistently satisfied applicable registration requirements. For example, shelf registrations permit certain qualified issuers to register securities that they will sell "off the shelf" on a delayed or continuous basis in the future. SEC Rule 415 requires that corporations using shelf registrations keep information in the original registration accurate and up to date.

EXEMPTIONS UNDER THE 1933 ACT

Although these complex registration requirements are standard for most securities, they do not apply to all securities in all situations. Some securities are exempt because of the nature of the securities themselves—*exempt securities*—and others are exempt when exchanged in certain ways—*exempt transactions.*

Exempt Securities. The 1933 act provides that certain securities are exempt from the registration procedures described above. These securities are *unregistered unrestricted securities,* and they include:

1. Securities issued by governments, including municipal, state, and federal governments.
2. Securities issued by nonprofit issuers, such as religious institutions or charitable organizations.
3. Securities issued by financial institutions supervised by banking associations.
4. Securities issued as a result of corporation reorganization in which one security is exchanged for another security.
5. Stock dividends and stock splits.
6. Insurance or annuity contracts issued by insurance companies.
7. Securities issued by federally regulated carriers (i.e., railways).
8. Short-term notes with a maturity date that does not exceed nine months.
9. Securities sold before July 27, 1933.
10. An issuer's offer of up to $5 million in securities in a 12-month period.

Although the last exemption permits the issuer to avoid the complex registration requirements of full registration, Regulation A[5] nevertheless requires that the issuer file certain reports with the SEC. For example, the issuer must file a notice of issue and an offering circular and provide the offering circular to investors before sale of the securities. Even with these requirements, however, the registration process under Regulation A is much less burdensome than the full registration process. For example, Regulation A permits issuers to "test the waters" for interest in their securities before preparing the offering circular, selling any securities, or gaining the commitment of interested buyers.

Exempt Transactions. If a security does not fall under one of the exempt categories described above, an issuer can nevertheless avoid registering the security by making certain exempt transactions. These securities are *unregistered restricted securities.* Issuers might want to avoid the registration process because it can be costly, complicated, and time-consuming. Exempt transactions offer an opportunity to save time and money. Consequently, many issuers sell securities through exempt transactions.

Although these transactions are exempt from registration, issuers must still provide investors with information about the securities, such as annual reports and financial statements.

[5] 17 C.F.R. §§ 230.251–230.263.

Exempt transactions include limited offers, intrastate issues, and resales of securities.

Limited Offers. Certain securities transactions, limited offers, are exempt from the registration process because they either involve small amounts of money or are offered only to sophisticated investors. The investors who participate in limited offers generally do not need the protection afforded by the registration process.

The SEC's Regulation D[6] enumerates three exemptions for limited offers (Rules 504, 505, and 506). Section 4(6) of the 1933 act contains an additional limited-offer exemption.

Rule 506: Private Placement Exemption. Issuers who make private offerings of securities are exempt from the registration process. These issuers, however, cannot advertise their private offerings to the general public. This exemption, usually referred to as the *private placement exemption,* allows firms to issue an unlimited number of securities to an unlimited number of accredited investors. Consequently, firms can easily raise large amounts of capital. Firms may not, however, issue to more than 35 unaccredited investors.

The SEC defines an **accredited investor** as:[7]

1. Any natural person who has a net worth of at least $1 million.
2. Any natural person whose annual income has been at least $200,000 for the two previous years and expects to make at least $200,000 in the current year.
3. Any corporation or partnership with total assets in excess of $5 million.
4. Insiders of the issuers, such as executive officers or directors.
5. Registered investment companies, colleges and universities, banks, and insurance companies.

The SEC assumes that accredited investors are better able to evaluate the financial risk associated with buying securities. Consequently, government protection in the form of required registration is less imperative.

The SEC also requires that firms selling to unaccredited investors under Rule 506 believe that these investors have expertise regarding securities trading. The firms must believe that the investors, or their representatives, have the reasonable ability to evaluate the financial risk associated with purchasing securities. If a firm privately offers any unaccredited investor the opportunity to purchase securities, all investors must receive the basic information contained in the registration statement (i.e., information about the issuing company and the securities). If no unaccredited investors are involved, however, the issuer does not have to disclose any information. While firms do not have to register these exempt securities with the SEC, they must notify the SEC of any sales made under the exemption.

The private placement exemption is one of the easiest ways for firms to raise capital. Instead of making a public offering, firms can simply make a private offering to investors capable of ascertaining the risk associated with buying securities. The firms cannot, however, advertise the securities to the general public.

Rule 505. Rule 505 is very similar to Rule 506, but it has two important differences. First, according to Rule 505, a firm's private offerings may not exceed $5 million in a 12-month period, while under Rule 506 a firm may issue an unlimited number of securities. Second, according to Rule 506, if a firm issues securities to unaccredited investors, it must believe that they have the knowledge to evaluate the risk associated with the security. In contrast, under Rule 505, firms need not believe that investors have the reasonable ability to evaluate the risk of purchasing securities.

[6] www.law.uc.edu/CCL/33ActRls/regD.html.

[7] SEC Rule 501.

Rule 504. Noninvestment firms—firms that do not engage primarily in the buying and selling of securities—that offer no more than $1 million in securities over a 12-month period are exempt from registration. An unlimited number of both accredited and unaccredited investors may purchase these securities; however, the firms must notify the SEC of their securities sales. Issuers need not disclose any information to investors.

Section 4(6). If a firm offers securities only to accredited investors for an amount less than $5 million, the issuer is exempt from registration. An unlimited number of accredited investors may participate in the transactions, but no unaccredited investors may buy these securities. Firms may not advertise these securities to the public. Issuers do not have to disclose any information to investors, but they must notify the SEC of any sales under this exemption. Moreover, investors who want to resell these securities must register them with the SEC.

Intrastate Issues. Under Section 3 of the 1933 act, any security offered or sold to a permanent resident of the single state where the issuer of the security resides and does business is exempt. Thus, local businesses can rely on local investors to raise an unlimited amount of capital without registration.

Courts and the SEC have interpreted this exemption very narrowly. Issuers must do at least 80 percent of their business within the state, receive at least 80 percent of their profits within the state, have at least 80 percent of their assets within the state, plan to use at least 80 percent of the profits within the state, and have their main offices in the state.

During the period of sale and for at least nine months after the period of sale, buyers of these securities under the intrastate exemption may not resell them to nonresidents. Issuers must take precautions against interstate resales.

Resales. The 1933 Securities Act created an exemption for "transactions by any person other than an issuer, underwriter, or dealer." Because another section of the act exempts dealers and brokers, only issuers and underwriters are not exempt from registering resales of securities.

Consequently, the average investor does not have to register securities when he or she wants to sell. If the investor acquired them through sales under Rule 505, 506, or Section 4(6) (e.g., intrastate issues and limited offers), they are **restricted securities.** If an investor wants to resell a restricted security, she must register the securities unless she follows Rule 144 or Rule 144a.

Rule 144. Under Rule 144, any person wanting to resell a restricted security is exempt from registration if certain criteria are met. First, the public must have access to adequate current information about the issuer. Second, the person selling the restricted security must have owned the security for at least two years. Third, the seller must sell the restricted securities in limited amounts in unsolicited broker transactions. Fourth, the seller must notify the SEC of the sale.

If a seller is not an affiliate of the issuer and has owned the securities for three years, he or she may sell the securities in unlimited amounts and is not subject to any of the criteria under Rule 144 for an exemption. An *affiliate* is a person who controls, is controlled by, or is in common control with the issuer. The 1933 act restricts sales by affiliates much more than sales by nonaffiliates. If an affiliate sells restricted or nonrestricted securities, he must meet all but one of the criteria to be exempt from registration. The affiliate does not need to hold a nonrestricted security for two years before reselling.

Legal Principle: **Exempt transactions include limited offers, intrastate issues, and resales of securities, and they do not have to be registered, but issuers must still provide investors with information about the securities, such as annual reports and financial statements.**

VIOLATIONS AND LIABILITY

If the SEC uncovers a potential violation of the 1933 act, it can (1) take administrative action, (2) take injunctive action, or (3) recommend criminal prosecution. If the SEC takes administrative action, it conducts a formal investigation of the potential violation by calling relevant witnesses to testify or produce evidence. If, through this investigation, the SEC uncovers evidence of a violation, the SEC may order an administrative proceeding before an administrative law judge, who can impose sanctions and even revoke a security's registration.

Usually the SEC takes injunctive action when it believes that a defendant is likely to continue to violate the law. Thus, the SEC may seek an injunction to prevent issuers from advertising securities by mail. In the Martha Stewart case at the beginning of the chapter, the SEC sought an injunction prohibiting Stewart and her broker from violating securities laws and limiting her activities as an officer of a public company.

Finally, if the SEC recommends criminal action, the Department of Justice prosecutes criminal charges against violators. Criminal penalties include a fine up to $10,000, imprisonment for up to five years, or both.

How might an issuing company violate the 1933 Securities Act? First, a company violates the act if it intentionally misleads investors by omitting or falsifying information on a registration statement or prospectus. Second, if a company is negligent in discovering a fraudulent statement, it can be liable. Third, an issuing company violates the act if it sells securities before the effective date of the registration statement.

Issuers charged with a violation of the 1933 act can raise several defenses. A company charged with the first or second violation described above may claim that the omitted or false statement was immaterial to the sale of the security. Similarly, if the issuer can prove that the plaintiff was aware of the omission or false statement when he bought the security, the defendant can avoid liability.

Any defendant except the issuer can assert the **due diligence defense.** This defense requires that the defendant demonstrate that she investigated the registration statement and had reasonable grounds to believe that the registration statement was accurate and had no omission of material facts.

If a defendant sold securities before the effective date of registration, however, she will almost certainly be liable because the 1933 act provides no defenses for this violation.

If an investor purchased securities and suffered damages as a result of an issuer's false or misleading statement, the investor is entitled to bring a civil suit to recover his losses. The burden of proof falls on the investor to demonstrate this incomplete or inaccurate disclosure of facts. Case 41-2 illustrates an investor's attempt to recover damages on the basis of the omission of allegedly material facts.

CASE 41-2 DAVID OVERTON AND JEROME I. KRANSDORF v. TODMAN & CO., CPAS, P.C. AND TRIEN, ROSENBERG, ROSENBERG, WEINBERG, CIULLO & FAZZARI

U.S. COURT OF APPEALS FOR THE SECOND CIRCUIT 478 F.3D 479 (2007)

Todman & Co., CPAs, audited the financial statements of Direct Brokerage, Inc. From 1999 to 2000, Todman issued its "unqualified" opinion that Direct Brokerage's financial statements accurately portrayed the company's fiscal health. Despite its certifications of accuracy, Todman allegedly made significant errors that concealed Direct Brokerage's largest liability. In 1999, Direct Brokerage's largest single line item, its certified financial statements, were listed as zero when it should have been $248,899. This same mistake was repeated until 2002. By 2003, these mistakes *had resulted in more than $3 million in unpaid taxes, interest, and penalties. Direct Brokerage sought investors without disclosing the errors. Plaintiffs were given the financial opinions prepared by Todman and based on that information invested $500,000 and loaned $1,500,000 to Direct Brokerage. Three months later Direct Brokerage collapsed. Plaintiffs filed suit to recover damages resulting from the misleading representations made by Todman. The district court granted defendant's motion to dismiss and plaintiffs appealed.*

JUDGE STRAUB: A fundamental principle of securities law is that before an individual becomes liable for his silence, he must have an underlying duty to speak.

. . . We [previously] reasoned that a duty to disclose arises only "when one party has information that the other party is entitled to know because of a fiduciary or other similar relation of trust and confidence between them. . . ."

> The concept of a duty to disclose appears to stem from the extent of reliance on the accountant's work made by the public and the expectations of the public. Clearly, in a situation in which the accountant "gives an opinion or certifies statements" about a company—statements which the accountant later discovers may not have been accurate . . .—then the accountant has a duty to disclose the fraud to the public. . . . Conversely, if an accountant does not issue a public opinion about a company, although it may have conducted internal audits or reviews for portions of the company, the accountant cannot subsequently be held responsible for the company's public statements issued later merely because the accountant may know those statements are likely untrue.

Shapiro v. Cantor, 123 F.3d 717 (2d Cir. 1997) (quoting) *In Re Cascade Int'l Sec. Litig.,* 894 F. Supp. 437, 443 (S.D. Fla. 1995).

. . . For many years we have recognized the existence of an accountant's duty to correct its certified opinions, but never squarely held that such a duty exists for the purposes of primary liability under Section 10(b) of the 1934 Act and Rule 10b-5. Presented with an opportunity to do so, we now so hold. Specifically, we hold that an accountant violates the "duty to correct" and becomes primarily liable . . . when it (1) makes a statement in its certified opinion that is false or misleading when made; (2) subsequently learns or was reckless in not learning that the earlier statement was false or misleading; (3) knows or should know that potential investors are relying on the opinion and financial statements; and (4) all the other requirements for liability are satisfied.

. . . In light of the above principles, we conclude that the District Court erred in dismissing the complaint. Plaintiffs pled that Todman's certified opinion and DBI's 2002 financial statements were misleading at the time they were issued, especially with respect to DBI's payroll tax liability; Todman, inferably through its contacts with the forensic auditor hired by DBI, subsequently learned that its opinion was false; Todman also knew that DBI was soliciting outside investors based in part on its 2002 certified financial statements and Todman's accompanying opinion; and that despite this knowledge, Todman took no action to correct or withdraw its opinion and/or DBI's financial statements.

. . . For the reasons set forth above, we VACATE the District Court's May 2, 2006, dismissal of Overton's securities claim. . . . We REMAND for further proceedings consistent with this opinion. No costs are awarded at this time. In the event that Overton prevails on the merits of his securities claim, the District Court may award plaintiffs the costs of the present appeal.

VACATED and REMANDED.

CRITICAL THINKING

What information possessed by Todman was essential to the court's holding in this case? In other words, what facts were especially controlling in producing the verdict?

ETHICAL DECISION MAKING

Which stakeholders benefit from the court's decision? Using your favorite ethical perspectives, do you think that these stakeholders deserved the benefits they derived from the court's decision? Why?

The Securities Exchange Act of 1934

While the 1933 Securities Act regulates the issuance of securities, the 1934 Securities Exchange Act regulates the subsequent trading (resale) of securities, chiefly through the required registration of securities exchanges, brokers, dealers, and national securities associations. Moreover, the act requires that certain issuers file periodic reports with the SEC.

L03

How does the Securities Exchange Act of 1934 regulate the trading of securities?

The 1934 act also permits the SEC to monitor securities markets for fraud and market manipulation.

SECTION 10(B) AND RULE 10B-5

One of the most important sections of the 1934 act is Section 10(b), which prohibits the use of manipulative and deceptive devices to bypass SEC rules. Within this section, Subsection 5 prohibits fraud associated with the purchase or sale of all securities. Thus, even though securities may be exempt from registration, they are still subject to Rule 10b-5:

> It shall be unlawful for any person, directly or indirectly, by use of any means or instrumentality of interstate commerce or of the mails, or of any facility of any national securities exchange,
>
> a) to employ any device, scheme, or artifice to defraud,
>
> b) to make any untrue statement of a material fact or to omit to state a material fact necessary in order to make the statements made, in light of circumstances under which they were made, not misleading, or
>
> c) to engage in any act, practice, or course of business that operates or would operate as a fraud or deceit upon any person, in connection with the purchase or sale of any security.

In 2009, an SEC investigation into the trading activities of investment adviser Bernard Madoff led to the discovery of numerous business violations, including failure to comply with Section 10(b) and Rule 10b-5 of the Securities Exchange Act of 1934. The SEC alleged that Madoff, a former NASDAQ chairman, had defrauded thousands of his clients, including director Stephen Spielberg and actor Kevin Bacon, by conducting a $50 billion securities trading scheme.

For several years, Madoff led his clients to believe that he was investing their money in various securities; however, rather than actually purchasing any securities or making trades, Madoff used the principal he received from new investors to pay fake returns to existing investors. To appear legitimate, Madoff sent his clientele fabricated documents with fictional returns and trades. In June 2009, Madoff was sentenced to serve 150 years in prison for his crime.[8]

Both Section 10(b) and Rule 10b-5 play an important role in preventing insider trading.

INSIDER TRADING

When a company employee or executive uses material inside information to make a profit, she or he is engaging in *insider trading.* Insider trading is illegal because it gives the violator an important advantage over the general public and shareholders.

Section 10(b) and Rule 10b-5 define *insiders* as corporate officers, directors, employees, lawyers, consultants, accountants, majority shareholders, or any other individuals who receive private information regarding the trading of securities.

A company employee or executive who has inside information may be liable depending on whether the information is material. If there is a material omission or misrepresentation during a securities transaction, the individual has violated Section 10(b) and Rule 10b-5. If the omission or misrepresentation is not material, however, the individual is not liable. Examples of material information include the following:

1. A change in the status of litigation against the company.
2. A change in dividends.

[8] www.msnbc.msn.com/id/31604191/ns/business-us_business//, www.scribd.com/doc/16495171/Bernard-Madoff-SEC-Settlement, www.scribd.com/doc/8977606/SECs-Complaint-Against-Bernard-Madoff, and www.huffingtonpost.com/2009/02/20/madoff-ponzi-scheme-stock_n_168568.html.

3. A contract for the sale of corporate assets or for the purchase of assets.
4. A new product, process, or discovery.
5. A significant change in the financial status of the company.

BUT WHAT IF . . .

WHAT IF THE FACTS OF THE CASE OPENER WERE DIFFERENT?

Let's say, in the Case Opener, that Stewart had heard on the news about the rejection of Waksal's new drug. She immediately had her agent sell her stock as fast as he could, and she beat a lot of other people to it. Is there anything wrong with Stewart's action in this case?

According to the SEC, an individual with material inside information should either refrain from using the information or disclose the information to the other parties involved in the transaction.[9] Case 41-3 is a classic example of how courts address insider trading.

[9] *Matter of Cady, Roberts & Co.*, 40 SEC 907 (1961).

CASE 41-3 SECURITIES AND EXCHANGE COMMISSION v. TEXAS GULF SULPHUR CO.

U.S. COURT OF APPEALS FOR THE SECOND CIRCUIT 401 F.2D 833 (1968)

In June 1963, Texas Gulf Sulphur acquired the option to buy land in Timmons, Ontario. A preliminary drilling in November 1963 suggested that the land held great amounts of copper and zinc. This information was supposed to be kept secret; not even officers and executives at TGS were supposed to know about the results of the drilling. TGS acquired the land and resumed drilling in March 1964. During the time from November 1963 to March 1964, certain directors, officers, and employees of TGS received "tips" and purchased TGS stock or options to buy shares at a fixed price. When drilling began in November 1963, these people had owned 1135 shares of TGS stock and possessed no calls; thereafter they owned a total of 8,235 shares and possessed 12,300 calls.

In April 1964, when rumors of a major mineral find appeared in newspapers, TGS responded by claiming that the rumors of a major find did not have factual basis. However, a few days later, TSG confirmed that the strike was expected to yield many million tons of ore. In between the days that TGS claimed the rumors were false and later confirmed the rumors, two defendants, Clayton and Crawford, ordered a combined total of 500 shares of TGS stock. The SEC brought suit against TGS and 13 of its directors, officers, and employees for violation of Section 10(b) of the Exchange Act and SEC Rule 10(b)-5, seeking an injunction to prevent TGS from publishing misleading press releases and requesting rescission of TGS's purchases and stock options. The district court dismissed the charges against all defendants but Clayton and Crawford and the SEC appealed.

JUDGE WATERMAN: Rule 10b-5 was promulgated pursuant to the grant of authority given the SEC by Congress in Section 10(b) of the Securities Exchange Act of 1934 (15 U.S.C. § 78j(b)). By that Act Congress purposed to prevent inequitable and unfair practices and to insure fairness in securities transactions generally, whether conducted face-to-face, over the counter, or on exchanges. The Act and the Rule apply to the transactions here, all of which were consummated on exchanges. Whether predicated on traditional fiduciary concepts, the Rule is based in policy on the justifiable expectation of the securities marketplace that all investors trading on impersonal exchanges have relatively equal access to material information. The essence of the Rule is that anyone who, trading for his own account in the securities of a corporation has "access, directly or indirectly, to information intended to be available only for a corporate purpose and not for the personal benefit of anyone" may not take "advantage of such information knowing it is unavailable to those with whom he is dealing," i.e., the investing public. Insiders, as directors or management officers are, of course, by this Rule, precluded from so unfairly dealing, but the Rule is also applicable to one possessing the information who may not be strictly termed an "insider" within the meaning of Sec.16(b) of the Act. Thus, anyone in possession of material inside information must either disclose it to the investing public, or, if he is disabled from disclosing it in order to protect a corporate confidence, or he chooses not to do so, must abstain from trading in or recommending the securities concerned while such inside information remains undisclosed.

[continued]

. . . As we stated in List v. Fashion Park, Inc., 340 F.2d 457, 462, "The basic test of materiality . . . is whether a reasonable man would attach importance . . . in determining his choice of action in the transaction in question." This, of course, encompasses any fact ". . . which in reasonable and objective contemplation might affect the value of the corporation's stock or securities. . . ." Such a fact is a material fact and must be effectively disclosed to the investing public prior to the commencement of insider trading in the corporation's securities. Thus, material facts include not only information disclosing the earnings and distributions of a company but also those facts which affect the probable future of the company and those which may affect the desire of investors to buy, sell, or hold the company's securities.

In each case, then, whether facts are material within Rule 10b-5 when the facts relate to a particular event and are undisclosed by those persons who are knowledgeable thereof will depend at any given time upon a balancing of both the indicated probability that the event will occur and the anticipated magnitude of the event in light of the totality of the company activity.

The core of Rule 10b-5 is the implementation of the Congressional purpose that all investors should have equal access to the rewards of participation in securities transactions. It was the intent of Congress that all members of the investing public should be subject to identical market risks—which market risks include, of course, the risk that one's evaluative capacity or one's capital available to put at risk may exceed another's capacity or capital. The insiders here were not trading on an equal footing with the outside investors. They alone were in a position to evaluate the probability and magnitude of what seemed from the outset to be a major ore strike; they alone could invest safely, secure in the expectation that the price of TGS stock would rise substantially in the event such a major strike should materialize, but would decline little, if at all, in the event of failure, for the public, ignorant at the outset of the favorable probabilities would likewise be unaware of the unproductive exploration, and the additional exploration costs would not significantly affect TGS market prices. Such inequities based upon unequal access to knowledge should not be shrugged off as inevitable in our way of life, or, in view of the congressional concern in the area, remain uncorrected.

We hold, therefore, that all transactions in TGS stock or calls by individuals apprised of the drilling results were made in violation of Rule 10b-5.

REVERSED in favor of plaintiff.

CRITICAL THINKING

Identify the reasons given by the judge for the decision. How do these reasons demonstrate the link between business law and business ethics?

ETHICAL DECISION MAKING

What values are being emphasized by the prohibition on insider trading?

THE PRIVATE SECURITIES LITIGATION REFORM ACT OF 1995

Although Rule 10b-5 was designed to encourage disclosure of accurate information, one of its unintended side effects was the deterrence of forecasts. Shareholders who purchased stock in corporations with high earnings forecasts often brought suit against the corporations' directors if actual corporate earnings fell short of forecasted earnings, alleging that the directors violated Rule 10b-5 by disclosing misleading financial information.

Congress attempted to remedy this problematic side effect by passing the *Private Securities Litigation Reform Act (PSLRA) of 1995.* Among other things, the act provides a "safe harbor" from liability for publicly held issuers who make financial forecasts as long as the forecasts are "accompanied by meaningful cautionary statements identifying important factors that could cause actual results to differ materially from those in the forward-looking statement."[10]

Although this legislation, also known as the "bespeaks caution" doctrine, protects issuers when they are making statements about the future, the Second Circuit Court of Appeals

[10] 15 U.S.C. § 77z-2 (2005).

found that it does not protect issuers when they make statements about the past or present. Smart World Technologies, LLC, a dot-com company, offered and sold "membership interests" to the P. Stolz Family Partnership in 1997. Smart World told Stolz that it had hired an investment bank for financing to take the company public and earn money through an initial public offering. Stolz alleges that Smart World, at the time of its oral statements, never planned to take the company public and knew that no money had been raised and the company was in fact insolvent. Several months after Stolz purchased the membership interests, Smart World went bankrupt. The court ruled that although the company's prospectus did have the required cautionary statements, cautionary statements could protect against only forward-looking statements. The court said that "it would be perverse indeed if an offeror could knowingly misrepresent historical facts but at the same time disclaim those misrepresented facts with cautionary language."[11]

Innovative shareholders attempted to subvert PSLRA by suing corporate directors in state courts. Congress responded to those efforts by passing the *Securities Litigation Uniform Standards Act of 1998*. This act strictly limits shareholders' ability to bring class action suits against nationally traded corporations.

OUTSIDERS AND INSIDER TRADING

Not only may insiders be liable for omitting or misrepresenting material information, but certain "outsiders" may also be liable through two theories: *misappropriation theory* and the *tipper/tippee theory*. Consider whether Martha Stewart is liable under either theory.

Misappropriation Theory. In addition to being a theory of tort (see Chapter 6), misappropriation can establish liability for insider trading. *Misappropriation theory* holds that if an individual wrongfully acquires (misappropriates) and uses inside information for trading for her personal gain, she is liable for insider trading. Because she wrongfully acquires inside information, she is essentially stealing information to use for her benefit.

Because it expands the SEC's power, application of misappropriation theory to insider trading has not gone uncontested. The 1985 case *United States v. David Carpenter*[12] was the first case in which the SEC convinced the courts to apply misappropriation theory to Rule 10b-5. The case involved a *Wall Street Journal* reporter who wrote a "Heard on the Street" column. Despite his knowledge of the *Journal*'s policy that any information acquired in the course of employment was confidential, he and a news clerk participated in a scheme with two stockbrokers in which the reporter provided the brokers with securities-related information that was going to be printed later in the column. The brokers used the information to buy or sell securities, netting the participants a profit of $690,000. The court of appeals ultimately found that the misappropriation of that confidential information and its use for the securities transactions constituted a violation of Rule 10b-5.[13] More than 10 years later, in *United States v. O'Hagan,*[14] the U.S. Supreme Court conclusively established that misappropriation theory is applicable to Rule 10b-5.

Legal Principle: **A party who wrongfully acquires and uses inside information to buy or sell securities for personal gain can be held liable for insider trading under the misappropriation theory.**

[11] *P. Stolz Family Partnership L.P. v. Daum,* 355 F.3d 92 (2d Cir. 2004).

[12] 791 F.2d 1024 (1985).

[13] 791 F.2d 1024 (1985).

[14] 117 S. Ct. 2199 (1997).

Tipper/Tippee Theory. The *tipper/tippee theory* holds that any individual who acquires material inside information as a result of an insider's breach of duty has engaged in insider trading. This individual, one who has received a "tip" from an insider, is called a **tippee.** The insider who gives the inside "tip" is called the **tipper.**

Suppose Jerry (the tipper) gives material inside information to Elaine (the tippee). Jerry is liable because he is passing on inside information. Furthermore, Elaine is liable if she makes trading decisions based on information that she should know is not public. Jerry is liable for any profits made by Elaine. Now, suppose Elaine passes the tip on to George. Elaine is now a tipper, and George is a tippee. Both Elaine and Jerry are liable for the profits made by George. George is liable for the profits of his transactions if he knew or should have known that the material information was not public.

In some business industries, such as public accounting, employees may be exposed to sensitive information when working for a client. As a preventive measure, businesses will often impose strict rules to ensure that their employees keep client information private. However, regardless of the regulations, some unethical employees may attempt to use classified client information to make money through insider trading.

For example, in 2008 two Pricewaterhouse Coopers employees were caught using their access to client information to engage in insider trading. One of the employees, Patrick Borchard, worked in PwC's Transaction Advisory Group assisting corporate clients interested in mergers or acquisitions. As a member of the Transaction Advisory Group, Borchard often heard about corporate takeovers before they were announced publicly. Rather than keeping the information private, Borchard tipped off his co-worker, Gregory Raben, to confidential client plans so that Raben could trade on the information and make a profit. Additionally, Raben tipped off two of his own acquaintances to the information provided by Borchard. Eventually PwC noticed what Raben and Borchard were doing and alerted the SEC. Both Borchard and Raben were charged by the SEC with insider trading and were required to not only pay fines but also pay back the trading profits earned with client information.[15]

SECTION 16(B)

Under Section 16(a) of the 1934 act, certain large stockholders, executive officers, and directors are considered **statutory insiders.** All statutory insiders must file a report detailing their ownership and trading of the corporation's securities.

To prevent statutory insiders from using inside information for their personal gain, Section 16(b) of the 1934 act requires that statutory insiders return all **short-swing profits,** or profits made from the sale of company stock within any six-month period by a statutory insider, to the company. Even if the insider did not use the inside information to make the transaction, all short-swing profits belong to the corporation. Section 16(b) imposes strict liability on statutory insiders who earn short-swing profits. In other words, violators cannot use lack of intent or lack of knowledge as a defense. Certain transactions, however, such as bankruptcy proceedings, are exempt from Section 16(b).

PROXY SOLICITATIONS

A **proxy** is a writing signed by a shareholder that authorizes the individual named in the writing to exercise the shareholder's votes (corresponding to his shares of stock) at a shareholders' meeting. Corporate managers often contact shareholders to request that they give a certain manager authority to vote on their behalf in an upcoming meeting. This process of obtaining authority to vote on behalf of a shareholder is called **proxy solicitation.** Because the proxy solicitation process is potentially susceptible to fraud, the SEC regulates the process.

[15] www.sec.gov/litigation/litreleases/2008/lr20429.htm.

Section 14(a) states that an issuer making proxy solicitations must also furnish a written proxy statement to shareholders. This statement must disclose to the shareholder all facts pertinent to the voting that will occur in the meeting.

VIOLATIONS OF THE 1934 ACT

The 1934 act authorizes both civil and criminal penalties. If an individual engages in insider trading, a violation of Section 10(b) or Rule 10b-5, she has committed a criminal offense punishable with a fine up to $1 million, a prison sentence up to 10 years, or both. If a defendant did not know of the rule she violated, she cannot be imprisoned. If a partnership or corporation engages in insider trading, it is subject to fines up to $2.5 million.

Both the SEC and private parties can bring civil actions against violators of the 1934 act. The SEC investigates alleged violations under the 1934 act. In the process of this investigation, the SEC can enter into consent orders with defendants or seek injunctions to stop certain actions by defendants.

Perhaps the most useful tool the SEC has for punishing those engaging in insider trading is the *Insider Trading Sanctions Act of 1984,* which permits the SEC to sue any individual who violates the 1934 act or who helps another person to engage in insider trading in violation of that act. If the SEC succeeds in demonstrating its claim, courts may assess a civil penalty up to triple the profits gained or losses avoided by the defendant.

Congress expanded the SEC's authority to punish violators of the 1934 act when it passed the *Insider Trading and Securities Fraud Enforcement Act of 1988.* This act subjects more individuals to civil liability for insider trading and grants the SEC power to award **bounty payments** (government rewards for acts beneficial to the public) to insider-trading whistle-blowers.

Private parties may also sue violators of the 1934 act. A private party may seek rescission of a contract to buy securities or may recover damages based on the violator's profits. If the court rules that an individual is liable for violations of the 1934 act, he can seek contribution from others, such as accountants or lawyers, who shared responsibility for the violation.

BUT WHAT IF . . .

WHAT IF THE FACTS OF THE CASE OPENER WERE DIFFERENT?

Let's say, in the Case Opener, that Stewart faces fines and years in jail if she is convicted of insider trading. Subsequently, Jones, who purchased a significant number of shares of ImClone stock immediately after Martha Stewart sold hers, wishes to recover the losses he suffered when the value of the stock fell the next day. Can he sue Martha Stewart?

Regulation of Investment Companies

LO4 How are investment companies regulated?

In the past century, smaller investors have become important players in securities markets. Investment companies facilitate their involvement in securities markets by purchasing a large, diverse portfolio of securities and managing it on behalf of small investor-owners. However, because small investors often lack the resources and ability to adequately supervise investment companies, they can be subject to fraud and exploitation.

To prevent exploitation of small investors, Congress passed the *Investment Company Act of 1940,* providing for SEC regulation of investment companies. Congress later expanded the SEC's power to regulate investment companies under the *Investment Company Act Amendments of 1970* and the *National Securities Markets Improvement Act of 1996.*

E-COMMERCE AND THE LAW

MARKETING SECURITIES ON THE INTERNET

Perhaps one of the most important and exciting developments in securities regulations is the explosion of the securities market on the Internet. The web permits companies to sell securities in an online initial public offering (IPO), thereby avoiding the expensive filing requirements of a traditional IPO. For example, some websites allow customers to buy and sell securities online. This technology, however, presents a greater opportunity for fraud because anyone can create a website. Several cases of securities fraud have occurred simply because a company has offered "free stock" over the Internet. The SEC has issued cease-and-desist orders against companies that illegally offered free stock on their websites because they had not registered their stocks with the SEC.

Another type of online fraud, called "pumping and dumping," occurs when an owner of a particular stock tells other investors about the virtues of the stock, artificially increasing demand for the stock and pumping up its price, only to sell (dump) it for a quick profit. Unregulated message boards on the Internet permit pumping and dumping on a fast and efficient basis. In response to the increasing use of this method of stock price manipulation, the SEC has pursued harsher and more frequent prosecution of individuals who engage in pumping and dumping online.

The web also provides potential investors with access to enormous amounts of information about securities. For example, the SEC maintains the Electronic Data Gathering, Analysis, and Retrieval (EDGAR) database to help investors access information about IPOs and other documents filed with the SEC. Visit www.sec.gov/edgar.shtml to learn more about EDGAR.

SEC regulations apply to online advertising and securities transactions. When a company delivers a paperless prospectus, it is subject to the following rules:

1. The company must provide timely and adequate notice of the delivery of information.
2. The company must use an easily accessible communication system such as the Internet.
3. The company must create evidence of the delivery of information.

The Investment Company Act defines an *investment company* as any entity (1) that is engaged primarily in the business of investing, reinvesting, or trading in securities or (2) that is engaged in such business and in which more than 40 percent of the company's assets are investment securities. The act excludes a number of institutions, however, including banks, insurance companies, savings and loans, and finance companies.

The act requires that all investment companies file a notification of registration with the SEC. Additionally, they must file annual reports with the SEC and hold all securities in the custody of a bank or member of the stock exchange. The act prohibits investment companies from purchasing securities on the margin (borrowing money to purchase securities), selling short (selling securities that the company does not yet own), and participating in joint trading accounts.

In response to the financial downturn that began in fall 2008, the SEC considered making hedge funds subject to the Investment Company Act, and the Obama administration submitted legislation to Congress to that end.[16] While the Investment Company Act was ultimately not amended, hedge funds have come under greater regulation with the passage of the Dodd-Frank Wall Street Reform Act, which no longer allows banks to own, invest, or sponsor hedge funds, private equity funds, or proprietary trading operations for their own profit, unrelated to serving their customers. Also, hedge funds of $500 million or more must register with the SEC and disclose, among other things, information for each qualifying hedge fund relating to fund exposures, portfolio liquidity, market risk, concentration of positions, and trading and financing for each such hedge fund.[17]

State Securities Laws

L05

How do states regulate securities?

Not only must issuers obey federal securities regulations, but they are also subject to state securities laws, often referred to as **blue-sky laws.** These laws regulate the offering and

[16] David Lawder, "Congress Gets Obama Hedge Funds Disclosure Bill," *Reuters,* July 15, 2009, www.reuters.com/article/GCA-Economy/idUSTRE56E7DF20090715.

[17] http://www.sec.gov/News/Speech/Detail/Speech/1365171490432#.UlM8p1CTiSo ; http://www.sec.gov/answers/hedge.htm

sale of purely intrastate securities. Hence, although certain securities are exempt from federal securities regulation, they may be subject to state securities laws.

Many state securities laws serve functions similar to those of federal securities laws. For example, many states have laws requiring registration of securities issued within the state and requiring disclosure of certain information. Moreover, state laws regulate securities brokers and dealers. Although the purposes of state and federal securities regulations overlap, the specific regulations differ. Consequently, to encourage greater coordination between federal and state securities laws, most states have adopted the Uniform Securities Act.

CASE OPENER WRAP-UP

The Martha Stewart Case

Although the SEC sought to charge Martha Stewart with illegal insider trading, a grand jury did not indict Stewart on that charge. The grand jury did, however, indict Stewart and her broker on nine criminal charges, including securities fraud, obstruction of justice, and conspiracy. Stewart pled not guilty to all charges.

The district court threw out the securities fraud charge on grounds that "no reasonable jury could find it to be accurate." A week later, however, a jury convicted her of the four remaining counts against her, all of which related to her statements to SEC investigators in their investigation of her sale of ImClone stock. The jury sentenced her to five months in a minimum-security prison. A federal appellate court upheld her sentence.[18]

KEY TERMS

accredited investor 900
blue-sky laws 910
bounty payments 909
due diligence defense 902
post effective period 898
prefiling period 898
prospectus 897
proxy 908
proxy solicitation 909
red-herring prospectus 898
registration statement 897
restricted securities 901
securities 893
short-swing profits 908
statutory insiders 908
tippee 908
tipper 908
tombstone advertisement 898
waiting period 898

SUMMARY OF KEY TOPICS

What Is a Security?

As defined by the Howey test, a security is an investment in a common enterprise with the reasonable expectation of profit gained primarily from others' efforts.

Securities Regulation

The Securities and Exchange Commission (SEC) was created in 1934 to enforce securities laws, interpret provisions of securities acts, and regulate the trade of securities as well as the activities of securities brokers, dealers, and advisers.

The Securities Act of 1933

A *registration statement* is a document containing a description of the securities offered for sale, an explanation of how proceeds from the sale will be used, a description of the registrant's business

[18] 433 F.3d 273.

and properties, information about the management of the company, a description of any pending lawsuits, and certified financial statements.

A *prospectus* is a written document that is similar to the registration statement and is used as a selling tool for potential investors.

Periods of the filing process:

1. Prefiling period
2. Waiting period
3. Post effective period

Exempt transactions:

1. *Limited offers* involve small amounts of money or are offered only to sophisticated investors. There are four possible exemptions:
    - *Private placement exemption (Rule 506):* Exempts private offerings of securities.
    - *Rule 505:* States that private offerings may not exceed $5 million in a 12-month period and firms do not have to believe that investors have a reasonable ability to evaluate risk.
    - *Rule 504:* Exempts noninvestment firms that offer no more than $1 million in securities in a 12-month period.
    - *Section 4(6):* Exempts securities offered only to accredited investors for an amount less than $5 million.
2. *Intrastate issues* exempt local investors in local businesses.
3. *Resales* exempt transactions by any person other than an issuer, underwriter, or dealer.

Restricted securities are securities acquired under Rule 505, Rule 506, or Section 4(6) that must be registered for resale unless the investor follows Rule 144 or Rule 144(a).

Violations may result in:

1. Administrative action
2. Injunctive action
3. Criminal prosecution

The Securities Exchange Act of 1934

Section 10(b) is the regulation that prohibits the use of manipulative and deceptive devices to bypass SEC rules.

Insider trading is trading in which a company employee or executive uses material inside information to make a profit.

Misappropriation theory is the theory that an individual who wrongly acquires and uses inside information for profit is liable for insider trading.

Tipper/tippee theory is the theory that an individual who receives material inside information as a result of an insider's breach of duty is guilty of insider trading.

Statutory insiders are certain stockholders, executive officers, and directors who must file a report detailing their ownership and trading of the corporation's securities.

Short-swing profits are profits made from the sale of company stock within any six-month period to a statutory insider; under Section 16(b), they must be returned to the company.

Proxy is a document that authorizes an individual to vote the shareholder's share of stocks at a shareholders' meeting.

Proxy solicitation is the process of obtaining the authority to vote on behalf of a shareholder.

Violations may result in:

1. Criminal penalties.
2. Civil penalties.

3. Suits against those involved in insider trading under the Insider Trading Sanctions Act of 1984.

Regulation of Investment Companies

Investment companies must file a notification of registration with the SEC, file annual reports with the SEC, and hold all securities in the custody of a bank or member of the stock exchange.

Investment companies are prohibited from purchasing securities on the margin, selling short, and participating in joint trading accounts.

State Securities Laws

Blue-sky laws regulate the offering and sale of securities within the state only.

POINT / COUNTERPOINT

Should the Government Increase Regulation of Securities Markets?

NO

The government currently overregulates securities markets.

Government regulation is inefficient and perpetually behind the times. For example, some securities do not provide investors with dividends or bond payments until several years after their issue date. The nature of these securities renders investors susceptible to fraud, yet they might not discover the fraud until several years later, at a point when the trail is cold and government is impotent to remedy the situation. In another infamous example, a 15-year-old in New Jersey used Internet chat rooms to "pump and dump" securities. He was able to make off with over $800,000 before the SEC discovered what he had done.

Left unregulated, securities markets will provide an efficient level of information and will punish those who commit securities fraud. Intelligent investors will refuse to purchase securities about which they have insufficient information and hence will push companies that provide insufficient information out of the market. Alternatively, if companies themselves refuse to provide information about securities they issue, investors will demand information from other sources. This investor demand will encourage the development of markets providing information about securities. Indeed, these information markets already exist in the form of publications (e.g., *The Wall Street Journal* and *The Financial Times*) and professional services (e.g., stockbrokers and financial advisers).

Moreover, as the chapter pointed out, the five leaders of the SEC are unelected. As a result, they are insulated from democratic pressure to regulate securities markets in a manner consistent with voters' goals. Thus, even if more government regulation were desirable in theory, in practice the SEC is ill-equipped to provide it.

YES

The government currently underregulates securities markets.

A common and not unfounded perception of securities markets is that small investors frequently lose everything while big investors and insiders win big. Consider, for example, the corporate accounting scandals of the early 2000s. Insiders made off with millions of dollars, while many small investors lost their retirement savings. Unless the government does more to level the playing field, these scandals will continue to occur.

Markets produce efficient results only when certain conditions exist. As the Connecting to the Core activity on the text website points out, securities markets are plagued by asymmetrical information: Investors almost always know less about securities than do issuers. If left unremedied, asymmetrical information leaves investors susceptible to many forms of securities fraud.

Even if government is unable to catch every perpetrator of securities fraud, its ability to catch high-profile perpetrators and punish them heavily still serves as an effective deterrent to other potential violators. For example, the wide publicity of the Martha Stewart case, explained at the outset of this chapter, sent a strong message to investors that the SEC will punish outsiders who use even small pieces of inside information for personal gain.

Moreover, the unelected nature of SEC board members allows the president to appoint individuals with tremendous expertise. Perhaps Congress lacks the institutional competence to regulate complex securities markets efficiently, but experts who have spent their careers working with securities are more likely to be able to regulate effectively.

Government regulation of securities markets will never be perfect, but the appropriate comparison is not between government regulation and perfect regulation but between government regulation and available alternatives.

QUESTIONS & PROBLEMS

1. What was the stimulus for the creation of securities regulation? State the purposes of the two main federal securities laws.
2. What is the function of the SEC?
3. Explain the process of registering securities.
4. Why are certain securities transactions exempt from the registration process?
5. How does the misappropriation theory apply to insider trading?
6. John A. Carley and Christopher H. Zacharias were officers and directors of Starnet Communications International, Inc. Carley and Zacharias held options to buy several hundred thousand Starnet shares. Sales to the public of shares acquired by exercise of their options would have been illegal unless a registration statement under Section 5 of the Securities Act of 1933 had been in effect. Alfred Peeper controlled seven foreign entities, collectively considered the Peeper Entities. The Peeper Entities owned several million shares in Starnet, which they had purchased and held, and which they could lawfully resell to the public. In addition, the Peeper Entities held unused warrants to several additional million shares. Carley and Zacharias did not have a registration statement filed with the SEC. Instead, they arranged with the Peeper Entities that the latter would sell several million of their original and warrant shares and would replace them with shares from Carley and Zacharias, acquired by the latter through exercise of their options. The SEC argues that because the Peeper Entities had exercised their warrants with the intention of distributing them to the public, they were underwriters and were not exempt from the registration requirements of the Securities Act of 1933. Thus, because Carley and Zacharias had sold their option shares to the Peeper Entities, the SEC concluded that they should be held liable as they committed fraud by trying to resell restricted securities through indirect and underhanded means. Carley and Zacharias argue that they should qualify for exempt status, and thus that they did nothing wrong. Did Carley and Zacharias commit securities fraud, or did they properly comply with Rule 144 and the Securities Act of 1933? Explain your reasoning. [*Zacharias v. SEC,* 569 F.3d 458 (2009).]
7. Two affiliates of a hugely successful hedge fund, SAC Capital Advisors, were charged with insider trading by the SEC. CR Intrinsic Investors and Sigma Capital Management apparently relied on "expert networks" through which, allegedly, people with information funnel it to traders. The biggest charge involved a doctor who had passed information to a trader regarding problems with a new drug that targeted Alzheimers disease. After the information was passed, around $1 billion worth of shares of two pharmaceutical companies related to the drug were sold before the drug information was released to the public. The drug was still going through scientific trials, and the results had not been finalized. The doctor was a part of that project. How do you think this case turned out? [*Securities and Exchange Commission v. Sigma Capital Management, LLC, et al.,* C.A. No. 13-civ-1740 (2013).]
8. Jon R. Marple worked as a nonemployee consultant to F10. Jon H. Marple, Marple's father, served as F10's chief executive officer. Marple signed a formal agreement with F10 in which he contracted to provide various consulting services. As part of his consulting duties, Marple introduced his father, Marple Sr., to Allen Wolfson, who orchestrated a contract between F10 and Sukumo. F10 agreed to sell Sukumo up to 10 million shares of F10 stock. Sukumo was, however, under no obligation to purchase any or all of the shares contemplated by the agreement, and Sukumo's primary objective was to sell as many of the shares as possible to overseas investors at full bid price. At F10's request and in accordance with the consulting agreement, Marple prepared draft versions of F10's quarterly and annual filings. Independent auditors reviewed Marple's drafts, and Marple Sr. certified the form's accuracy in his capacity as CEO. The final version of the quarterly filing disclosed that F10 had "issued" 10 million shares of stock to Sukumo and that F10 would receive approximately 12.5 percent of its bid price per share. It did not, however, disclose that Sukumo would keep 70 percent of the proceeds on the stock sales or that Sukumo was under no obligation to purchase any of the 10 million shares. At F10's request, Marple also drafted F10's annual filing. That filing discussed

the Sukumo arrangement and included some of the information that was omitted from the prior quarterly filing. It did not, however, disclose that Sukumo was under no obligation to purchase any F10 stock, despite the fact that Marple had agreed with F10's independent auditors to present that information in the filing. Once it learned of Sukumo's offshore operation, the SEC launched an investigation into Sukumo. The commission brought a civil enforcement action against numerous defendants, including Marple. In its complaint, the commission alleged, among other things, that Marple committed fraud in violation of Section 10(b) and Rule 10b-5. The commission and Marple both moved for summary judgment. The district court granted the commission's motion for summary judgment and denied Marple's motion for summary judgment. The district court determined that Marple was liable for F10's misstatements and omissions under Section 10(b) and Rule 10b-5. Marple appealed, arguing that he could not be primarily liable as a nonemployee without strong evidence that he made the misstatements to the SEC. How did the court rule on appeal? Why? [*SEC v. Wolfson,* 539 F.3d 1249 (2008).]

9. Under 28 U.S.C. § 1658, claims of "fraud, deceit, manipulation or contrivance" concerning the Securities Exchange Act of 1934 may be made "[two] years after the discovery of the facts constituting the violation" or "[five] years after such violation," depending on which one is earlier. In 1999 the FDA approved a painkiller by Merck named Vioxx. Merck marketed the drug using claims of safety and nonserious side effects. However, in 2001 and 2003, respectively, the *New York Times* and *Wall Street Journal* published articles regarding the connection between the drug and heart attacks. Vioxx was taken off the market voluntarily in 2004. In 2003, a lawsuit was brought against Merck claiming that the company violated securities laws by misrepresenting the side effects and risks associated with the drug. Merck argued that the two-year limitation period was already over and the case should be dismissed. How do you think the court decided? [*Merck & Co., Inc. v. Reynolds,* 559 U.S. 633 (2010)]

10. From October 2003 to February 2004, James Siracusano purchased thousands of Matrixx Initiatives Inc. shares. After purchasing the shares, Siracusano argued that the company had violated the Securities and Exchange Act of 1934 when it had sold him those shares. Specifically, he argued that before October 2003, the company had found out that one of its drugs had harmful side effects and this information was not released. The drug, Zicam, had allegedly been systematically leading to a permanent loss of smell. However, to win his case Siracusano needed to not only point out that Matrixx knew about the harmful effects of the drug before the period within which he bought his shares but also that there was a high statistical rate of the occurrence of the adverse side effect. How do you think the case turned out? [*Matrixx Initiatives v. Siracusano,* 131 S. Ct. 1309 (2011)]

Looking for more review materials?

The Online Learning Center at **www.mhhe.com/kubasek3e** contains this chapter's "Assignment on the Internet" and also a list of URLs for more information, entitled "On the Internet." Find both of them in the Student Center portion of the OLC, along with quizzes and other helpful materials.

CHAPTER 42

Employment and Labor Law

LEARNING OBJECTIVES

After reading this chapter, you will be able to answer the following questions:

1. What are wage and hour laws?
2. What are the rights of employees and obligations of employers under the Family and Medical Leave Act?
3. What is FUTA?
4. What are the rules regarding workers' compensation?
5. What is COBRA?
6. What is ERISA?
7. What is OSHA?
8. What does it mean to be an "at-will" employee?
9. What are the rights of employees and obligations of employers with regard to privacy in the workplace?
10. What are the three major pieces of labor law legislation?

CASE OPENER

Madison and Save Right Pharmacy

For the last five years, Madison has worked 20 hours per week at Save Right Pharmacy. She has always been a reliable and efficient employee. When her mother became seriously ill, Madison notified Save Right Pharmacy that under the Family and Medical Leave Act (FMLA) she planned to take up to 12 weeks off to care for her. Save Right Pharmacy denied Madison's request. When Madison left work anyway, Save Right Pharmacy terminated her employment. Madison then applied for unemployment compensation so she would have income to live on while caring for her mother. Madison also applied, under COBRA (discussed later in this chapter), for continued insurance coverage through her former employer. If you were the CEO of Save Right Pharmacy, how would you handle the employment situation with Madison?

1. Is Madison eligible for time off from work under FMLA?
2. May Save Right Pharmacy legally terminate Madison's employment?
3. Given that Madison was fired by Save Right Pharmacy, is she eligible to collect unemployment compensation?
4. May Madison continue her insurance coverage through Save Right Pharmacy even though she has been fired from her job?

The Wrap-Up at the end of the chapter will answer these questions.

Introduction to Labor and Employment Law

The employment relationship is a contractual relationship between the employer and the employee: The employer agrees to pay the employee a certain amount of money in exchange for the employee's agreement to render specific services. Until about the middle of the 20th century, workers had virtually no rights. There were no safety standards, and a worker injured on the job could be fired. Workers of all ages often toiled in unspeakable conditions.

Today, federal and state governments impose a number of conditions on the employment relationship. The first half of this chapter covers wages, benefits, health and safety standards, and employee rights, including the right to privacy. Exhibit 42-1 lists the major relevant state and federal laws. The remainder of this chapter covers labor unions.

Fair Labor Standards Act

LO1

What are wage and hour laws?

Employers may not unilaterally determine how much to pay employees or how many hours to require them to work. They must follow federal minimum-wage and hour laws. The **Fair Labor Standards Act (FLSA)**[1] covers all employers engaged in interstate commerce or the production of goods for interstate commerce.

FLSA requires that a minimum wage of a specified amount be paid to all employees in covered industries. The specified amount is periodically raised by Congress to compensate for increases in the cost of living caused by inflation. The most recent increase took effect on July 24, 2009. The federal minimum wage increased from $6.55 to $7.25.

FLSA mandates that employees who work more than 40 hours in a week be paid no less than one and one half times their regular wage for all the hours they work beyond 40 during a given week. Four categories of employees are excluded:

- Executives
- Administrative employees
- Professional employees
- Outside salespersons

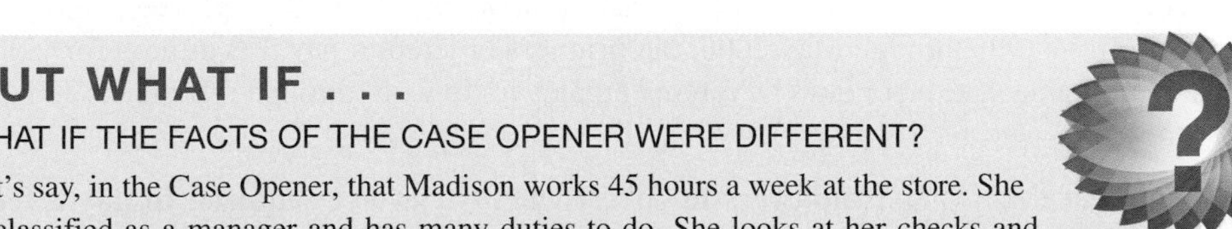

BUT WHAT IF . . .

WHAT IF THE FACTS OF THE CASE OPENER WERE DIFFERENT?

Let's say, in the Case Opener, that Madison works 45 hours a week at the store. She is classified as a manager and has many duties to do. She looks at her checks and realizes she is not being paid extra money for her time spent at work above 40 hours a week. Is Madison legally entitled to the extra money?

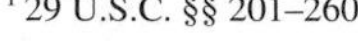

[1] 29 U.S.C. §§ 201–260.

Exhibit 42-1

Selected Laws Affecting Working Conditions in the United States

Wage and hour laws	Federal and state laws that impose minimum wage and hour requirements for employees.
Family and Medical Leave Act (FMLA)	Federal act requiring that certain employers establish a policy that provides all eligible employees with up to 12 weeks of leave during any 12-month period for several family-related occurrences (e.g., birth of a child or care of a sick spouse).
Unemployment compensation	State system, created by the Federal Unemployment Tax Act (FUTA), that provides unemployment compensation to qualified employees who lose their jobs.
Workers' compensation laws	State laws that provide for financial compensation to employees or their dependents when the covered employee is injured on the job.
Consolidated Omnibus Budget Reconciliation Act (COBRA)	Federal law ensuring that when employees lose their jobs or have their hours reduced to a level at which they would not be eligible to receive medical, dental, or optical benefits from their employer, they can continue receiving benefits under the employer's policy for up to 18 months by paying the premiums for the policy.
Employee Retirement Income Security Act (ERISA)	Federal law that sets minimum standards for most voluntarily established pension and health plans in private industry.
The Occupational Safety and Health Act of 1970 (OSHA)	Federal law that established the Occupational Safety and Health Administration, the agency responsible for setting safety standards under the act, as well as enforcing the act through inspections and the levying of fines against violators.
Employment-at-will doctrine (and wrongful discharge)	Doctrine under which an employer can fire an employee for any reason at all. The three exceptions are *implied contract, violations of public policy,* and *implied covenant of good faith and fair dealing.* In states that have adopted any of these three exceptions, employees may be able to sue for wrongful discharge.
Employee privacy laws	Federal and state laws that govern privacy policies on matters such as employer surveillance, control of and access to medical and personnel records, drug testing, and e-mail.

Employees must earn at least a minimum income and spend a certain amount of time engaged in specified activities before they become exempt. If employers try to evade the overtime rule, their employees may sue. Taco Bell felt the full impact of FLSA when several groups of its employees brought class action suits against it for allegedly shaving hours off time cards to avoid paying overtime. One suit was settled for $13 million.[2] More recently, in a class action lawsuit against Walmart by 187,000 employees who worked there from 1998 through May 2006, the firm was ordered to pay $78 million for violating Pennsylvania state labor laws by forcing employees to work through rest breaks and off the clock.[3]

Legal Principle: **Employers in covered industries are required to pay a federal minimum wage.**

[2] "Taco Bell Loses Second Big Back-Pay Case as Ore. Jury Affirms Time-Card Tampering Charge," *Nation's Restaurant News,* March 26, 2001, p. 3.

[3] "Jury Orders Pa. Walmart to Pay $78 Million," http://cbs3.com/topstories/local_story_286145532.html, October 13, 2006.

COMPARING THE LAW OF OTHER COUNTRIES

PAID VACATIONS IN OTHER COUNTRIES

In Ireland, the Holiday Act of 1973 guarantees every worker, regardless of how long he or she has been with a company, three weeks of paid vacation time and nine additional days off for public holidays. In Luxembourg, regardless of age, employees are given 25 days of holiday, 12 of which they must take in succession, as well as 10 paid public holidays. Swedish law gives employees 5 weeks of vacation time and gives them 10 weeks after five years of employment. Denmark mandates no fewer than five weeks of paid vacation a year, and Spain no fewer than 30 days in addition to the country's 14 paid public ones.

The United Kingdom is like the United States in having no laws requiring paid or even unpaid holidays. The United States does not mandate any minimum annual vacation time for employees.

Family and Medical Leave Act

L02

What are the rights of employees and obligations of employers under the Family and Medical Leave Act?

When the **Family and Medical Leave Act (FMLA)** went into effect in 1993, it was hailed by its supporters as a "breakthrough" and feared by its opponents as an unwieldy encumbrance on business. FMLA covers all public employers, as well as private employers with 50 or more employees (see Exhibit 42-2). It guarantees all eligible employees (those who have worked at least 25 hours a week for each of 12 months before the leave) up to 12 weeks of *unpaid* leave during any 12-month period for any of the following family-related occurrences:

- The birth of a child.
- The adoption of a child.
- The placement of a foster child in the employee's care.
- The care of a seriously ill spouse, parent, or child.
- A serious health condition that renders the employee unable to perform any of the essential functions of his or her job.

Madison, at the beginning of the chapter, worked for Save Right Pharmacy for five years but worked only 20 hours per week. Under FMLA, she would not be eligible to take leave to care for her mother.

Exhibit 42-2

Who Is Covered under FMLA?

	YES	NO	DEPENDS
Public employers?	√		
Private employers?	√		
Employers with 50 or more employees?	√		
Employers with fewer than 50 employees?		√	
Full-time employees for at least one year?	√		
Part-time employees for at least one year? (must work at least 25 hours per week for 12 months before taking leave)			√
The leave is paid?		√	
The leave is for up to 12 weeks in a 12-month period?	√		
The employee may take more than 12 weeks off in 12 months?		√	

FMLA is a highly complex piece of legislation, containing six titles divided into 26 sections, as well as regulations designed to guide implementation that are eight times longer than the statute itself! Many employers were still not in full compliance a year after it became effective.

To exercise rights under FMLA, an employee whose need is foreseeable (such as for childbirth) must advise the employer at least 30 days before the leave needs to begin. If the leave is unforeseeable, the employee must give notice as soon as practicable, defined as within one or two business days after the need becomes known. FMLA does not define the type of notice necessary, but the employee must state the reason for the leave and, if possible, the length of time needed. FMLA does not have to be specifically mentioned in the request.

When their FMLA leaves terminate, employees must be restored to the same position they held, or one with substantially equivalent skills, effort, responsibility, and authority. If an employee is unable to return at the end of the 12-week period, the employer need not hold the position open any longer.

While FMLA does not require that leave be paid, the employer must continue health insurance benefits. The employer may also require that an employee substitute paid time off for unpaid leave. For example, an employee with 4 weeks' accrued sick leave and 2 weeks' vacation who wishes to take a 12-week leave may be required to take the paid vacation and sick leave for that purpose, plus 6 weeks' unpaid leave.

REMEDIES FOR VIOLATIONS OF FMLA

If an employer fails to comply with FMLA, the plaintiff may recover damages for unpaid wages or salary, lost benefits, denied compensation, and actual monetary losses up to an amount equivalent to the employee's wages for 12 weeks, as well as attorney fees and court costs. If the plaintiff can prove bad faith on the part of the employer, double damages may be awarded. An employee may also be entitled to reinstatement or promotion. Although most awards under FMLA have not been large, a California worker demoted and then fired for taking time off to have surgery for a brain tumor in 1996 sued and was awarded \$313,000.[4] In 1999, a state trooper denied time off to care for his pregnant wife, and subsequently his daughter, when his wife became ill during and after the pregnancy was awarded \$375,000.[5] Many employment law specialists are now seeing FMLA as an act employers must carefully follow.

Unemployment Compensation

What is FUTA?

What happens if employees lose their jobs? The **Federal Unemployment Tax Act (FUTA)**,[6] passed in 1935, created a state system to provide **unemployment compensation** to qualified employees who lose their jobs. Under this law, employers pay taxes to the states, which deposit the money into the federal government's Unemployment Insurance Fund. Each state has an account from which it can access money in accordance with state eligibility rules. States have different minimum standards for qualifying for unemployment compensation, although most require that the applicant did not voluntarily quit or get fired for cause. Because Madison did not qualify for leave under FMLA and stopped going to work even though Save Right Pharmacy denied her request, Save Right was legally within its rights to fire her. Whether she was fired or voluntarily quit her job, she would not be entitled to unemployment compensation in most states.

[4] *Lawyer's Weekly* 6 (1996), p. 973.

[5] *Knussman v. State of Maryland et al.*, 65 F. Supp. 353 (1999).

[6] 26 U.S.C. §§ 3301–3310.

Most states fund benefits through a tax on employers; only three states require minimal employee contributions.[7] The amount of the benefit may also vary.

Workers' Compensation Laws

LO4 What are the rules regarding workers' compensation?

Workers' compensation laws came about as a result of the abuses that injured employees often suffered on the job. Before workers' compensation, an injured employee's only recourse was to sue the employer for negligence. In return for the right to recover for injuries incurred on the job, the employee gives up the right to bring negligence claims.

Unlike many other laws affecting the employment relationship, workers' compensation legislation is purely state law. Our coverage of this topic must therefore be rather generalized. Prudent businesspeople will familiarize themselves with the workers' compensation statutes of the states within which their companies operate.

Workers' compensation laws ensure that covered workers injured on the job can receive financial compensation through an administrative procedure, rather than having to sue their employer. For administrative convenience, most states exclude certain types of businesses and small firms from coverage. Some also allow businesses with sufficient resources to be self-insured, rather than participating in the state program.

Legal Principle: **Under workers' compensation laws, an employee is guaranteed the right to recover for injuries that occurred on the job without having to sue his or her employer.**

BENEFITS UNDER STATE WORKERS' COMPENSATION

To recover benefits, the injured party must demonstrate that (1) he or she is an employee, (2) both employer and employee are covered by the state workers' compensation program, and (3) the injury occurred on the job.

As a general rule, the accident leading to the injury must have taken place during the time and within the scope of the claimant's employment. Using the *premises rule,* if an employee is on company property, the courts generally find that she was on the job. If an employee who travels for work is injured on a business trip, many states will find that he is entitled to compensation for reasonable injuries suffered. A New York typist who traveled to Canada to transcribe depositions fell while showering in her hotel. She filed a successful workers' compensation claim.

An employee injured on the job must notify the employer of the injury and file a claim with the state workers' compensation board, usually within 30 to 60 days. The board will verify the claim and determine the appropriate benefits. If the employer contests the claim, a hearing takes place before the state workers' compensation board. If the claim is denied, most states provide an agency appeals process followed by a provision for appeal to the courts. Most statutes cover medical, hospital, and rehabilitation expenses and generally lost wages. In Case 42-1, the court had to decide whether workers' compensation should be the exclusive remedy for accidental injuries caused by the gross, wanton, willful, deliberate, intentional, reckless, culpable, or malicious negligence, breach of statute, or other misconduct of the employer, short of a conscious and deliberate intent to inflict an injury.

[7] U.S. Department of Labor, http://workforcesecurity.doleta.gov/unemploy/uifactsheet.asp. The states that require employee contribution are Alaska, New Jersey, and Pennsylvania.

CASE 42-1 DELGADO v. PHELPS DODGE CHINO, INC.
SUPREME COURT OF NEW MEXICO
34 P.3D 1148 (2001)

Reynaldo Delgado died following an explosion at a smelting plant in Deming, New Mexico, after a supervisor ordered him to perform a task that, according to Delgado's widow, was virtually certain to kill him or cause him serious injury. Phelps Dodge allegedly chose to subject Delgado to the risk despite knowing this. His widow brought a number of tort claims against Phelps Dodge and the individual supervisors. The trial court dismissed the case on grounds that the Workers' Compensation Act provided the exclusive remedy, leaving Phelps Dodge immune from tort liability. The Court of Appeals upheld that ruling in a memorandum opinion. The Supreme Court of New Mexico agreed to hear the case to determine whether Phelps Dodge was indeed immune.

JUDGE GENE E. FRANCHINI: In the summer of 1998, thirty-three-year-old Reynaldo Delgado resided in Deming, New Mexico, with his wife, Petitioner Michelle Delgado, and two minor children. Mr. Delgado had been working at the Phelps Dodge smelting plant in Hurley, New Mexico, for two years. The smelting plant distills copper ore from unusable rock, called "slag," by superheating unprocessed rock to a temperature in excess of 2,000 degrees Fahrenheit. During the process, the ore rises to the top, where it is harvested, while the slag sinks to the bottom of the furnace where it drains through a valve called a "skim hole." From there, the slag passes down a chute into a fifteen-foot-tall iron cauldron called a "ladle," located in a tunnel below the furnace. Ordinarily, when the ladle reaches three-quarters of its thirty-five-ton capacity, workers use a "mudgun" to plug the skim hole with clay, thus stopping the flow of molten slag and permitting a specially designed truck, called a "kress-haul," to enter the tunnel and lift and remove the ladle.

On the night of June 30, Delgado's shorthanded work crew, under the supervision of Mike Burkett and Charlie White, was being pressured to work harder in order to compensate for the loss of production and revenue incurred after a recent ten day shut down. Suddenly, the crew experienced an especially dangerous emergency situation known as a "runaway." The ladle had reached three-quarters of its capacity but the flowing slag could not be stopped because the mudgun was inoperable and manual efforts to close the skim hole had failed. To compound the situation, the consistency of the slag caused it to flow at a faster rate than ever, thus resulting in the worst runaway condition that many of the workers on the site had ever experienced. Respondents could have shut down the furnace, thereby allowing the safe removal of the ladle of slag. However, in order to avoid economic loss, Respondents chose instead to order Delgado, who had never operated a kress-haul under runaway conditions, to attempt to remove the ladle alone, with the molten slag still pouring over its fifteen-foot brim. In doing so, Respondents knew or should have known that Delgado would die or suffer great bodily harm.

When Delgado entered the tunnel, he saw that the ladle was overflowing and radioed White to inform him that he was neither qualified nor able to perform the removal. White insisted. In response to Delgado's renewed protest and request for help, White again insisted that Delgado proceed alone. Shortly after Delgado entered the tunnel, the lights shorted out and black smoke poured from the mouth of the tunnel. Delgado's co-workers watched as he emerged from the smoke-filled tunnel, fully engulfed in flames. He collapsed before co-workers could douse the flames with a water hose. "Why did they send me in there?" Delgado asked co-workers, "I told them I couldn't do it. They made me do it anyway. Charlie sent me in." Delgado had suffered third-degree burns over his entire body and died three weeks later in an Arizona hospital.

When a worker suffers an accidental injury and a number of other preconditions are satisfied, the Act provides a scheme of compensation that affords profound benefits to both workers and employers. The injured worker receives compensation quickly, without having to endure the rigors of litigation or prove fault on behalf of the employer. The employer, in exchange, is assured that a worker accidentally injured, even by the employer's own negligence, will be limited to compensation under the Act and may not pursue the unpredictable damages available outside its boundaries. The Act represents the "result of a bargain struck between employers and employees. In return for the loss of a common law tort claim for accidents arising out of the scope of employment, [the Act] ensures that workers are provided some compensation."

. . . [T]he Act limits its scope to accidents, barring both compensation and exclusivity when the worker sustains a nonaccidental injury. Because the basis for limiting exclusivity depends on the nonaccidental character of the injury, Professor Larson argues:

> [T]he common-law liability of the employer cannot, under the almost unanimous rule, be stretched to include accidental injuries caused by the gross, wanton, willful, deliberate, intentional, reckless, culpable or malicious negligence, breach of statute, or other misconduct of the employer short of a conscious and deliberate intent directed to the purpose of inflicting an injury.

We hold that when an employer intentionally inflicts or willfully causes a worker to suffer an injury that would otherwise be exclusively compensable under the Act that employer may not enjoy the benefits of exclusivity, and the injured worker may sue in tort.

REVERSED and REMANDED in favor of plaintiff.

[continued]

CRITICAL THINKING

What are the key words in determining whether an injury falls under the Workers' Compensation Act? Is it clear when anyone acts intentionally? What factors would make a court see a defendant's act as having "intentionally or willfully caused" a worker's injury?

ETHICAL DECISION MAKING

Delgado's widow and children are important stakeholders in the court's decision, as is Phelps Dodge. But ethical decisions require consideration of stakeholders who are often invisible at first glance. Who are other relevant stakeholders in this case?

ADVANTAGES AND DISADVANTAGES OF WORKERS' COMPENSATION

Employees benefit from workers' compensation laws because with very little effort they receive an almost certain recovery when injured, although the amount is less than they would have received from a successful negligence case against their employers. Employers must pay into the workers' compensation fund every year, but they thereby ensure that their employee injury costs are fixed and they will not have to pay a huge negligence award to an injured employee because workers' compensation is the employee's exclusive remedy.

To see a description of the tax treatment of workers' compensation benefits, please see the **Connecting to the Core** activity on the text website at www.mhhe.com/kubasek3e.

Consolidated Omnibus Budget Reconciliation Act of 1985

LO5 What is COBRA?

The **Consolidated Omnibus Budget Reconciliation Act (COBRA)** ensures that employees who lose their jobs or have their hours reduced to a level at which they are no longer eligible to receive medical, dental, or optical benefits can continue receiving benefits for themselves and their dependents under the employer's policy. The employee must pay the premiums for the policy, plus up to a 2 percent administration fee, to maintain coverage up to 18 months, or 29 months if disabled. Premiums are often quite expensive. An employee has 60 days after coverage would ordinarily terminate to decide whether to maintain it.

COBRA benefits do *not* arise under either of two conditions:

1. The employee is fired for gross misconduct.
2. The employer decides to eliminate benefits for all current employees.

Madison, in our opening scenario, applied to retain her insurance benefits under COBRA, but if her failure to come to work is deemed "gross misconduct," her benefits may be terminated. In most cases, however, when an employee voluntarily quits a job, or even is fired (but not for gross misconduct), insurance benefits may be continued (although the *employee* must pay the full cost). Employers who fail to comply with the law may be required to pay up to 10 percent of the annual cost of the group plan or $500,000, whichever is less.

Employee Retirement Income Security Act of 1974

LO6 What is ERISA?

The **Employee Retirement Income Security Act (ERISA)** is "a federal law that sets minimum standards for most voluntarily established pension and health plans in private industry to provide protection for individuals in these plans."[8] Under ERISA, employers must provide participants with all the following:

1. Plan information (features and funding).
2. Assurances that those in charge of managing plan assets have fiduciary responsibility.

[8] Department of Labor, Employee Retirement Income Security Act, www.dol.gov/dol/topic/health-plans/erisa.htm.

3. A grievance and appeals process for participants to get benefits from their plans.
4. The right to sue for benefits and breaches of fiduciary duty.[9]

ERISA has been amended several times. Some of the most important amendments are COBRA (discussed above) and HIPAA (Health Insurance Portability and Accountability Act), "which provides important new protections for working Americans and their families who have preexisting medical conditions or might otherwise suffer discrimination in health coverage based on factors that relate to an individual's health."[10] ERISA does not apply to health plans for government or church employees or to plans maintained to comply with disability, workers' compensation, or unemployment laws.

Legal Principle: **ERISA requires that private employers keep employees informed about voluntarily established pension and health plans.**

Occupational Safety and Health Act of 1970

LO7

What is OSHA?

The federal government regulates workplace safety primarily through the **Occupational Safety and Health Act (OSHA),** which requires that every employer "furnish to each of his employees . . . employment . . . free from recognized hazards that are likely to cause death or serious physical harm." The Occupational Safety and Health Administration (abbreviated *OSHA,* the same as the act) promulgates workplace safety standards, inspects facilities for compliance, and brings enforcement actions against violators.

Under the law, employers must prominently display in the workplace either the federal or a state OSHA poster with information about employees' safety and health rights. Employers with 11 or more employees (20 percent of the establishments OSHA covers) must keep records of work-related injuries and illnesses except in low-hazard industries such as retail, service, finance, insurance, and real estate.

PENALTIES UNDER OSHA

If OSHA inspectors find violations in the workplace, they may issue citations. Penalties for violations may range from $0 to $70,000 per violation, depending on the likelihood that the violation would lead to serious injury to an employee. Penalties may be reduced if an employer has a small number of employees, has demonstrated good faith, or has few or no previous violations. If a willful violation results in the death of a worker, criminal penalties may be imposed.

Employment-at-Will Doctrine and Wrongful Termination

LO8

What does it mean to be an "at-will" employee?

Unless an employee belongs to a union or has an employment contract with his or her employer, the employment relationship is governed by the **employment-at-will doctrine.** This doctrine provides that a contract of employment for an indeterminate period of time may be terminated at will by either party, at any time, for any reason. The traditional employment-at-will doctrine has been restricted over the past few decades, mainly by civil rights legislation (Chapter 43). States have also created exceptions that allow an employee to sue for wrongful discharge. They fall into three primary categories (not all states accept all three). The most common exception, the **implied-contract exception,** provides that an implied employment contract may arise from statements the employer makes in an employment handbook, length of service, statements by the employer

[9] Ibid.

[10] Ibid.

CASE NUGGET

OCCUPATIONAL SAFETY AND HEALTH ACT

Irving v. United States
162 F.3d 154 (1998)

Somersworth Shoe Company operated a manufacturing plant in New Hampshire. In 1979, when employee Gail Irving bent to retrieve a work glove behind her bench, her hair was drawn into the vacuum created by the high-speed rotation of a nearby drive shaft. Irving was very seriously injured. After nearly two decades of litigation, she won a $1 million judgment. The United States appealed.

At issue was whether OSHA inspectors were required to inspect every machine in a facility or could use their discretion in deciding what to inspect. OSHA's purpose is to provide a satisfactory standard of safety, not to guarantee absolute safety. The United States demonstrated that permitting inspectors discretion was grounded in its policies; therefore, it was not negligent and the award was reversed.

indicating long-term employment, or materials advertising the position. For instance, an implied contract can arise if:

1. The employment handbook contains the steps for progressive discipline leading to discharge.
2. The handbook makes no mention of the words *employment at will.*
3. The employee relies on that handbook.

If the employer does not follow the policies in its own handbook, a fired employee may sue for wrongful discharge.

The **public policy exception** prohibits employers from firing employees engaged in activities that further the public interest. Protected activities vary among states and include, but are not limited to, serving on jury duty, doing military service, filing for or testifying at hearings for workers' compensation claims, and whistle-blowing.

The least common exception to at-will employment is the **implied covenant of good faith and fair dealing exception.** This exception assumes that every employment contract contains an implicit understanding that the parties will deal fairly with one another. Because there is no clear agreement on what constitutes fair treatment of an employee, most states do not use this exception.

Exhibit 42-3 highlights some of the limits to the coverage of the employment-at-will doctrine.

BUT WHAT IF . . .

WHAT IF THE FACTS OF THE CASE OPENER WERE DIFFERENT?

Let's say, in the Case Opener, that Madison does not have any kind of written contract for employment for any set period of time and thus is an at-will employee. One day, the store fires her without any explanation. The store says it doesn't have to give her any reason, but Madison maintains that the store still needs some kind of reason or she can sue the store. Which side is correct in this case?

Legal Principle: Under the employment-at-will doctrine, a contract of employment for an indeterminate period of time may be terminated at will by either party at any time and for any reason.

Exhibit 42-3
At-Will Employment

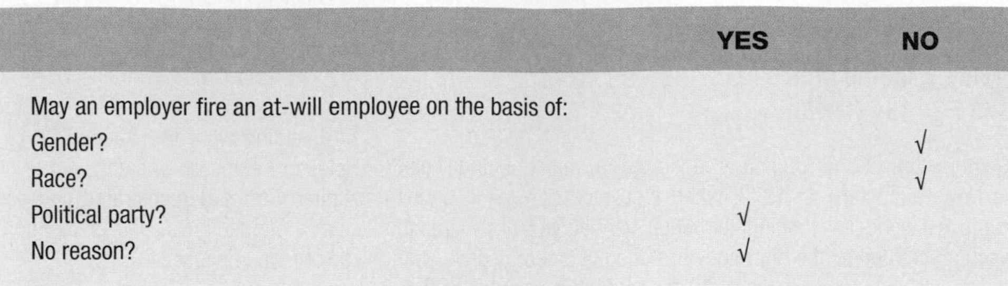

	YES	NO
May an employer fire an at-will employee on the basis of:		
Gender?		√
Race?		√
Political party?	√	
No reason?	√	

Employee Privacy in the Workplace

LO9
What are the rights of employees and obligations of employers with regard to privacy in the workplace?

Technology brings new privacy issues to the workplace. It allows employers to gather information about employees; but it also provides more temptations for employees to be "off the job" at work, thus stimulating a need for more employer monitoring.

According to a 2006 study, 93 percent of employees with Internet access at work look at nonwork-related websites.[11] Employers naturally want to monitor what employees are doing when they are supposed to be on the job, but some go too far, such as monitoring keystrokes for words such as *union* and *strike*.[12] Once employers monitor employees and discover wrongdoing, the issue of employers' right to fire at will becomes relevant.

In *Michael A. Smyth v. The Pillsbury Company*,[13] Smyth alleged that his employer, the Pillsbury Company, violated his privacy rights by reading his e-mail and then illegally firing him on the basis of the content of some of his messages. Smyth had transmitted a message to his supervisor about the company's sales management team in which he threatened to "kill the backstabbing bastards" and referred to an upcoming company party as the "Jim Jones Koolaid affair."[14]

The court granted Pillsbury's motion to dismiss, ruling that Smyth did not have a reasonable expectation of privacy in e-mail communications he made voluntarily over the company system. The court was unimpressed with Smyth's assertion that management repeatedly assured employees that it would not intercept e-mail. Ultimately, the court ruled that the employer's right to prevent inappropriate, unprofessional, and possibly illegal comments over its e-mail system outweighed an employee's privacy rights.

Legal Principle: **Employees do not have a reasonable expectation of privacy when using their employers' e-mail system, even during nonworking hours.**

BUT WHAT IF . . .

WHAT IF THE FACTS OF THE CASE OPENER WERE DIFFERENT?

Let's say, in the Case Opener, that Madison has an e-mail account provided to her by the store. She often uses the account to send personal e-mails in which she sometimes says very inappropriate things and discloses private company information. When she is fired, she says that the store had no right to go through her e-mail. Is she correct?

[11] "The Productivity Challenge: Working with the iPod Generation," http://infoacrs.com/wri/work.html, January 17, 2007.

[12] Stephen Lesavich, "Keystroke Spies: Conflicting Rights," *National Law Journal,* May 22, 2000, p. A23.

[13] 914 F. Supp. 97 (1996).

[14] Jim Jones is the cult leader whose followers committed mass suicide by drinking a poisoned drink in Jonestown, Guyana, in 1978.

ELECTRONIC MONITORING AND COMMUNICATION

Questions about employer monitoring of phone conversations, e-mail, and voice mail invoke the common law tort of invasion of privacy and the federal **Omnibus Crime Control and Safe Streets Act of 1968,**[15] as amended by the **Electronic Communications Privacy Act (ECPA) of 1986.**[16]

Under the first statute, employers cannot listen to or disclose the contents of private telephone conversations of employees. They may ban personal calls and monitor for compliance, as long as they discontinue listening to any conversation once they determine it is personal. Violators may be subject to fines of up to $10,000. Under ECPA, employees' privacy rights were extended to electronic forms of communication including e-mail and cellular phones. ECPA outlaws the intentional interception of electronic communications and intentional disclosure or use of the information so obtained.

The key question is whether the employee had a **reasonable expectation of privacy** with respect to the communication in question. The ECPA protects individuals' communications against government surveillance conducted without a court order, from third parties without legitimate authorization to access the messages, and from carriers such as Internet service providers. It provides employees little privacy protection with respect to communications conducted on the employer's equipment.

In Case 42-2, the court must determine whether plaintiff's e-mails to her attorney, sent via her workplace e-mail system, are protected by attorney-client privilege.

[15] 18 U.S.C. § 2210 et seq.

[16] 18 U.S.C. §§ 2510–2521.

CASE 42-2 HOLMES v. PETROVICH DEVELOPMENT CO., LLC
CALIFORNIA COURT OF APPEALS, THIRD APPELLATE DISTRICT
191 CAL. APP. 4TH 1047 (2011)

Gina Holmes began working for Paul Petrovich as his executive assistant in early June 2004. The employee handbook, which Holmes admitted reading and signing, contained provisions clearly spelling out the policy concerning use of the company's technology resources, such as computers and e-mail accounts. The handbook directs employees that the company's technology resources should be used only for company business and that employees are prohibited from sending or receiving personal e-mails. Moreover, the handbook warns that "[e]mployees who use the Company's Technology Resources to create or maintain personal information or messages have no right of privacy with respect to that information or message." The "Internet and Intranet Usage" policy in the handbook specifically states, "E-mail is not private communication, because others may be able to read or access the message. E-mail may best be regarded as a postcard rather than as a sealed letter. . . ." The handbook spells out further that the company may "inspect all files or messages . . . at any time for any reason at its discretion" and that it would periodically monitor its technology resources for compliance with the company's policy.

The next month, July of 2004, Holmes told Petrovich that she was pregnant and that her due date was December 7, 2004. Petrovich recalled that Holmes told him she planned to work up until her due date and then would be out on maternity leave for six weeks. Holmes did not like it when coworkers asked her questions about maternity leave; she thought such comments were inappropriate. She asked "[t]hat little group of hens" to stop, and they complied. Holmes recalled having about six conversations with Petrovich about her pregnancy, during which they discussed her belly getting big and baby names. She thought "belly-monitoring" comments were inappropriate, but never told Petrovich that he was being offensive.

In September of 2005, Holmes filed a lawsuit against defendants, asserting causes of action for sexual harassment, retaliation, wrongful termination in violation of public policy, violation of the right to privacy, and intentional infliction of emotional distress. She alleged that the negative comments in Petrovich's e-mails and his dissemination of her e-mails, which contained highly personal information, invaded her privacy, were intended to cause her great emotional distress, and caused her to quit her job to avoid the abusive and hostile work environment created by her employer. According to Holmes, Petrovich disseminated the e-mails to retaliate against her for inconveniencing him with her pregnancy and to cause her to quit. Holmes claimed she was constructively terminated in that continuing her employment with Petrovich "became untenable, as it would have been for any reasonable pregnant woman."

SCOTLAND, J.: Plaintiff Gina M. Holmes appeals from the judgment entered in favor of defendants Petrovich Development Company, LLC, and Paul Petrovich in her lawsuit for sexual harassment, retaliation, wrongful termination, violation of the right to privacy, and intentional infliction of emotional distress. She contends that the trial court erred in granting defendants' motion for summary adjudication with respect to the causes of action for discrimination, retaliation, and wrongful termination, and that the jury's verdict as to the remaining causes of action must be reversed due to evidentiary and instructional errors. We disagree and shall affirm the judgment.

Among other things, we conclude that e-mails sent by Holmes to her attorney regarding possible legal action against defendants did not constitute "confidential communication between client and lawyer" within the meaning of Evidence Code section 952. This is so because Holmes used a computer of defendant company to send the e-mails even though (1) she had been told of the company's policy that its computers were to be used only for company business and that employees were prohibited from using them to send or receive personal e-mail, (2) she had been warned that the company would monitor its computers for compliance with this company policy and thus might "inspect all files and messages . . . at any time," and (3) she had been explicitly advised that employees using company computers to create or maintain personal information or messages "have no right of privacy with respect to that information or message."

As we will explain, an attorney-client communication "does not lose its privileged character for the sole reason that it is communicated by electronic means or because persons involved in the delivery, facilitation, or storage of electronic communication may have access to the content of the communication." (Evid. Code, § 917, subd. (b).) However, the e-mails sent via company computer under the circumstances of this case were akin to consulting her lawyer in her employer's conference room, in a loud voice, with the door open, so that any reasonable person would expect that their discussion of her complaints about her employer would be overheard by him. By using the company's computer to communicate with her lawyer, knowing the communications violated company computer policy and could be discovered by her employer due to company monitoring of e-mail usage, Holmes did not communicate "in confidence by a means which, so far as the client is aware, discloses the information to no third persons other than those who are present to further the interest of the client in the consultation or those to whom disclosure is reasonably necessary for the transmission of the information or the accomplishment of the purpose for which the lawyer is consulted." (Evid. Code, § 952.) Consequently, the communications were not privileged.

The employee handbook, which Holmes admitted reading and signing, contained provisions clearly spelling out the policy concerning use of the company's technology resources, such as computers and e-mail accounts. . . .

. . . [T]he trial court correctly ruled that the attorney-client communication was not privileged.

The judgment is AFFIRMED.

CRITICAL THINKING

Why is the court so careful to explain that the attorney-client privilege is not lost simply because a communication was in electronic form?

ETHICAL DECISION MAKING

What value preferences might cause a court to rule that even within the facts of this case, the attorney-client privilege must remain valid?

Employers are in the strongest position when they have a clear policy preventing any reasonable expectation of privacy. Employment law experts advise having a written policy that employees sign. At a minimum, employer privacy policies should cover the following issues:

1. Employer monitoring of telephone conversations.
2. Employer surveillance policies.
3. Employee access to medical and personnel records.
4. Drug testing policies.
5. Lie detector policies.
6. Ownership of computers and all issues unique to the electronic workplace.
7. Workplace dating policies.

DRUG TESTING IN THE WORKPLACE

Because they can be liable for employees' actions, employers are increasingly testing employees for the use of illegal drugs. Under the Drug-Free Workplace Act, employers that receive federal financial assistance or have federal contracts worth over $25,000 must develop an antidrug policy for employees, provide drug-free awareness programs for them, and warn them of penalties for violating company drug policies.

Private employers engaged in drug testing are not limited by the U.S. Constitution as are public employers, but they still need to be aware of state statutory and constitutional limits. In most states, private companies have virtually unfettered discretion to test employees for drug usage. One exception is California, whose state constitution grants an explicit right to privacy that applies to the actions of private businesses.[17] Seven additional states have enacted at least some restrictions on drug testing in the workplace: Montana, Iowa, Vermont, Rhode Island, Minnesota, Maine, and Connecticut.[18] Some collective bargaining agreements may restrict the employer's ability to test for drugs or may mandate specific testing procedures.

Labor Law

LO10 What are the three major pieces of labor law legislation?

Workers first achieved the right to organize (join unions) during the Great Depression. During the post-World War II period, over one-third of U.S. workers were organized. Yet by 2008, only 12.4 percent were.[19] Education, training, and library occupations and protective service workers such as police and firefighters had the highest unionization rates of all occupations during 2008: 38.7 percent and 35.4 percent, respectively.[20]

Labor-management relations in the United States today are governed by three major pieces of legislation. Exhibit 42-4 summarizes this legislation.

THE WAGNER ACT OF 1935

The first major piece of federal legislation adopted explicitly to encourage the formation of labor unions and provide for **collective bargaining** between employers and unions as a means of obtaining the peaceful settlement of labor disputes was the **Wagner Act.** Collective bargaining "consists of negotiations between an employer and a group of

[17] Lectic Law Library, "Drug Testing in the Workplace," ACLU Briefing Paper No. 5, www.lectlaw.com/files/emp02.htm.

[18] Ibid.

[19] Bureau of Labor Statistics, http://www.bls.gov/news.release/pdf/union2.pdf.

[20] Ibid.

CASE NUGGET

LIE DETECTOR TESTS

Polkey v. Transtrecs Corp.
404 F.3d 1264 (11th Cir. 2005)

Polkey was a supervisor in the mailroom at Pensacola Naval Air Station run by a company called Transtrecs. After discovering that some mail had been tampered with, Polkey reported it to her supervisor. Transtrecs asked all six employees, including Polkey, to take a lie detector (polygraph) test. The employee most suspected was tested first, and the test indicated he might have been the one who tampered with the mail. Polkey and the remaining employees then refused to take the test. Transtrecs fired Polkey, who sued for violation of the Employee Polygraph Protection Act (EPPA). The district court granted summary judgment for Polkey. Transtrecs appealed.

On appeal, the district court's judgment was affirmed. The court held that Transtrecs violated EPPA by requesting and even suggesting that the employees take a polygraph test. Transtrecs had argued that it was exempt from EPPA for national security reasons, but the appellate court said that this exemption applies only to the government, for which Transtrecs was merely a contractor. Transtrecs also argued that the polygraph was part of an ongoing investigation of Polkey and that she was under suspicion. But for this exemption to apply, Transtrecs needed an articulable basis in fact to indicate that Polkey was involved in or responsible for an economic loss. Transtrecs could make no such showing, and Polkey prevailed.

employees so as to determine the conditions of employment."[21] The key sections of the Wagner Act are:

1. *Section 7,* which provides, "Employees shall have the right to self-organization, to join, form or assist labor organizations, to bargain collectively through representatives of their own choosing, and to engage in concerted activities for the purpose of collective bargaining or other mutual aid and protection."
2. *Section 8(a),* which specifies the actions that are prohibited as employer unfair labor practices.

The Wagner Act also created an administrative agency, the *National Labor Relations Board (NLRB),* to interpret and enforce the NLRA. Finally, it provides for judicial review in designated federal courts of appeal.

THE TAFT-HARTLEY ACT OF 1947

The 12 years between passage of the Wagner Act and that of the Taft-Hartley Act saw a huge growth in unionization, which resulted in an increase in workers' power. Public perception of this trend led to the passage of the **Taft-Hartley Act,** also known as the

Exhibit 42-4
Federal Labor Law Legislation

LEGISLATION	PURPOSE OF LEGISLATION
Wagner Act of 1935	Adopted explicitly to encourage the formation of labor unions and provide for collective bargaining between employers and unions
Taft-Hartley Act of 1947	Amended the Wagner Act and was designed to curtail some of the powers the unions had acquired under the Wagner Act [The Wagner Act and the Taft-Hartley Act are jointly referred to as the National Labor Relations Act (NLRA).]
Landrum-Griffin Act of 1959	Governs the internal operations of labor unions and contains "Labor's Bill of Rights" to protect employees from their own unions

[21] Legal Information Institute, www.law.cornell.edu/topics/collective_bargaining.html.

E-COMMERCE AND THE LAW

EMPLOYER MONITORING OF COMPUTER USAGE

According to the 2007 Electronic Monitoring and Surveillance Survey by the American Management Association and the ePolicy Institute, 66 percent of employers monitor website connections of employees. Of the surveyed employers, 83 percent inform employees that content, keystrokes, and time spent online are monitored, 71 percent advise of e-mail monitoring, and 84 percent tell employees their phones are monitored.

Source: http://press.amanet.org/press-releases/177/2007-electronic-monitoring-surveillance-survey/.

Labor-Management Relations Act, designed to curtail some of the powers the unions had acquired under the Wagner Act. Just as Section 8(a) of the Wagner Act designated certain employer actions as unfair, Section 8(b) of the Taft-Hartley Act designated certain union actions as unfair.

THE LANDRUM-GRIFFIN ACT OF 1959

The **Landrum-Griffin Act** primarily governs the internal operations of labor unions. This act, a response to evidence of certain undesirable internal labor union practices, requires financial disclosures by unions and establishes civil and criminal penalties for financial abuses by union officials. "Labor's Bill of Rights," contained in the act, protects employees from their own unions.

THE NATIONAL LABOR RELATIONS BOARD

The **National Labor Relations Board (NLRB)** interprets and enforces the **National Labor Relations Act (NLRA).** The NLRB's three primary functions are to:

1. Monitor the conduct of the employer and the union during an election to determine whether workers want to be represented by a union.
2. Prevent and remedy unfair labor practices by employers or unions.
3. Establish rules interpreting the act.

The NLRB has jurisdiction over all employees *except* those who work in federal, state, and local government and those covered by the Railway Labor Act (employees in the transportation industry); independent contractors; agricultural workers; household domestics; persons employed by a spouse or parent; and supervisors, managerial employees, and confidential employees.

The stimulus for forming a union is typically employee dissatisfaction with some policy of or treatment by their employer. A union representative then assists the employees in a campaign to persuade a majority of the workers to accept the union as their exclusive representative. Once a majority of workers sign authorization cards indicating an interest in being represented by the union, they present these to the employer, who decides whether to formally recognize the new local union.

If the employer refuses, the union organizers can petition the NLRB for a representation election. The NLRB will supervise the election, and if the union receives a majority of the votes in the secret-ballot election, the union will be certified as the bargaining representative. During the course of the organizing campaign, certain activities of both employers and employees are prohibited by the NLRA and by rules of conduct developed by the NLRB. The constraints on employers' behavior under the NLRA are found primarily in Section 8(a)1, which prohibits interference in employees' exercise of their Section 7 rights. If an employer engages in prohibited activity during the organizing campaign, the NLRB may set aside the results of an election and order a new election. In an extreme case where the employer's conduct was so egregious as to make it impossible to hold a fair election, and the union had previously collected authorization cards signed by a majority of the employees, the NLRB may order the employer to bargain with the union without a new election.

Employers should be sure their speech and conduct during an organizing campaign do not rise to the level of coercion, restraint, or interference. Employers may express views, arguments, or opinions as long as they do not contain any threats of reprisals or promises of benefits. Finally, employers may prohibit union solicitation and the distribution of literature during work time. However, during nonwork time, such as lunch and coffee breaks, employers may prohibit organizing activity on company property *only* if there are legitimate safety or efficiency reasons for doing so and the restraint is not manifestly intended to thwart organizing efforts. The burden of proof is on the employer to demonstrate these safety or efficiency concerns.

THE COLLECTIVE BARGAINING PROCESS

Once the union has been certified, union and management must begin to bargain in good faith about wages, hours, and other terms and conditions of work. The NLRB can order the parties only to bargain in good faith; it cannot order them to reach an agreement with respect to any contract term.

Bargaining collectively in good faith means that the parties must:

1. Meet at reasonable times and confer in good faith.
2. Sign a written agreement if one is reached.
3. When intent on terminating or modifying an existing contract, give 60 days' notice to the other party, with an offer to confer over proposals, and give 30 days' notice to the federal or state mediation services in the event of a pending dispute over the new agreement.
4. Neither strike nor engage in a lockout during the 60-day notice.

An employer who fails to bargain in good faith is committing an unfair labor practice under Section 8(a)5. The most common violation by a union is bargaining for clauses that fall outside the scope of mandatory bargaining.

Legal Principle: **The parties to a union contract must bargain collectively and in good faith.**

Strikes are one of the most powerful tools unions have.

STRIKES, PICKETING, AND BOYCOTTS

Three other activities employers may confront are strikes, picketing, and boycotts. The NLRA offers management guidance on how to respond to these activities.

A strike is a temporary, concerted withdrawal of labor. It is the most powerful weapon employees use to secure recognition and improve their working conditions, but it is also potentially the most dangerous. Delta Air Lines' Comair pilots struck in 2001 to obtain better pay.

After an eight-week work stoppage and a loss to Delta of $1.5 to $2 million per day, an agreement was reached.

A refusal to deal with, purchase goods from, or work for a business is a **boycott.** Like a strike, it is a technique for prohibiting a company from carrying on its business so that it will accede to union demands. **Primary boycotts,** against an employer with whom the union is directly engaged in a labor dispute, are lawful. However, **secondary boycotts** are illegal. These occur when employees have a labor dispute with their employer and boycott another company to force it to cease doing business with the employer.

Individuals who place themselves outside an employer's place of business for the purpose of informing passersby of the fact(s) of a labor dispute are engaged in **picketing.** Picketing may occur as part of a strike or independently. If off-duty employees picket without a strike, they can continue to work and get paid while still getting their message across. Picketing designed to truthfully inform the public of a labor dispute between an employer and the employees is called **informational picketing** and is protected by law. However, **signal picketing,** which prevents deliveries or services to the employer, is unprotected behavior.

CASE OPENER WRAP-UP

Madison and Save Right Pharmacy

By now you should be able to answer all the questions asked at the beginning of the chapter.

Madison worked for Save Right Pharmacy for five years, but she worked only 20 hours per week so she was not eligible to take leave to care for her mother. Under FMLA, an employee must work a minimum of 25 hours per week.

Because Madison did not qualify to take leave under FMLA and simply stopped coming to work, Save Right Pharmacy was legally within its rights to fire her. Moreover, whether she was fired or voluntarily quit her job, she would not be entitled to collect unemployment compensation in most states.

If Madison's failing to come to work is deemed "gross misconduct," her insurance benefits may be terminated. In most cases, however, when an employee voluntarily quits his or her job or even is fired (but not for gross misconduct), insurance benefits may be continued (although the *employee* must pay the full cost of the insurance).

KEY TERMS

National Labor Relations Board (NLRB) 931
Occupational Safety and Health Act (OSHA) 924
Omnibus Crime Control and Safe Streets Act of 1968 927
picketing 933
primary boycotts 933
public policy exception 925
reasonable expectation of privacy 927
secondary boycotts 933
signal picketing 933
strike 932
Taft-Hartley Act 930
unemployment compensation 920
Wagner Act 929
workers' compensation laws 921

SUMMARY OF KEY TOPICS

Introduction to Labor and Employment Law

Both the federal and state governments impose a number of conditions on the employment relationship. The purpose of this chapter was to explain many of the laws that created those constraints on the employer's ability to determine terms and conditions of employment and termination. The first half of this chapter covered wages, benefits, health and safety standards, and employee rights, including the right to privacy. The second half of this chapter covered labor unions.

Fair Labor Standards Act

Employers must follow federal minimum-wage and hour laws. FLSA covers all employers engaged in interstate commerce or the production of goods for interstate commerce and requires that a "minimum wage" of a specified amount be paid to all employees in covered industries. The specified amount is periodically raised by Congress to compensate for increases in the cost of living caused by inflation. The most recent increase took effect on July 24, 2009, when the minimum wage rose to $7.25 per hour.

Family and Medical Leave Act

FMLA requires that certain employers establish a policy that provides all eligible employees with up to 12 weeks of leave during any 12-month period for several family-related occurrences (birth of a child, care of a sick spouse, etc.)

Unemployment Compensation

The Federal Unemployment Tax Act (FUTA) created a state system that provides unemployment compensation to qualified employees who lose their jobs.

Workers' Compensation Laws

Workers' compensation legislation consists of state laws that provide financial compensation to employees or their dependents when a covered employee is injured on the job.

Consolidated Omnibus Budget Reconciliation Act of 1985

COBRA ensures that when employees lose their jobs or have their hours reduced to a level at which they would not be eligible to receive medical, dental, or optical benefits from their employer, the employees will be able to continue receiving benefits under the employer's policy for up to 18 months by paying the premiums for the policy.

Employee Retirement Income Security Act of 1974

ERISA is a federal law that sets minimum standards for most voluntarily established pension and health plans in private industry to provide protection for individuals in these plans.

Occupational Safety and Health Act of 1970

The Occupational Safety and Health Administration is responsible for setting safety standards under OSHA, as well as enforcing the act through inspections and the levying of fines against violators.

Employment-at-Will Doctrine and Wrongful Termination

Under the employment-at-will doctrine, the employer can fire the employee for any reason at all. The three exceptions to the doctrine are *implied contract, violations of public policy,* and *implied covenant of good faith and fair dealing.* In states that have adopted any of these three exceptions, employees may be able to sue for wrongful discharge.

Employee Privacy in the Workplace

Privacy issues are of increasing importance in the workplace. Privacy policies should cover matters such as employer surveillance, control of and access to medical and personnel records, drug testing, and e-mail.

Omnibus Crime Control and Safe Streets Act of 1968: Employers cannot listen to the private telephone conversations of employees or disclose the contents of these conversations. They may, however, ban personal calls and monitor calls for compliance as long as they discontinue listening to any conversation once they determine it is personal. Violators may be subject to fines of up to $10,000.

Electronic Communications Privacy Act (ECPA) of 1986: Under ECPA, employees' privacy rights were extended to electronic forms of communication including e-mail and cellular phones. ECPA outlaws the intentional interception of electronic communications and the intentional disclosure or use of the information obtained through such interception.

Labor Law

The Wagner Act of 1935: The Wagner Act was the first major piece of federal legislation adopted explicitly to encourage the formation of labor unions and provide for *collective bargaining* between employers and unions as a means of obtaining the peaceful settlement of labor disputes.

Collective bargaining: Collective bargaining consists of negotiations between an employer and a group of employees to determine the conditions of employment.

National Labor Relations Board (NLRB): The Wagner Act created the NLRB, an administrative agency, to interpret and enforce the National Labor Relations Act (NLRA) and to provide for judicial review in designated federal courts of appeal.

The Taft-Hartley Act of 1947: Also known as the *Labor-Management Relations Act,* the Taft-Hartley Act is designed to curtail some of the powers the unions had acquired under the Wagner Act. Just as Section 8(a) of the Wagner Act designated certain employer actions as unfair, Section 8(b) of the Taft-Hartley Act designated certain union actions as unfair.

The Landrum-Griffin Act of 1959: The Landrum-Griffin Act primarily governs the internal operations of labor unions. It requires certain financial disclosures by unions and establishes civil and criminal penalties for financial abuses by union officials. "Labor's Bill of Rights," contained in the act, protects employees from their own unions.

POINT / COUNTERPOINT

In 2007, the federal minimum wage was raised for the first time in a decade as part of a three-year series of increases.

Do You Believe It Was Time for an Increase?

YES	NO
A 2006 poll indicated that 83 percent of the U.S. public supports raising the federal minimum wage from $5.15 to $5.85 starting in 2007.* This was the first of a series of three increases. The final increase took place on July 24, 2009, when the federal minimum wage was increased to $7.25.[†] There has been strong bipartisan support for raising the federal minimum wage. The purchasing power of the pre-2007 federal minimum wage had significantly declined since 1997. Hard-working employees deserve a living wage. Everyone benefits when the lowest-paid have more spending power.	An increase in the federal minimum wage hurts business owners and lowers their profit margin. Business owners may pass the increased cost on to consumers or let workers go whom they can no longer afford. Many states have already passed laws requiring that employers pay a state minimum wage higher than the federal minimum wage. We should let each state decide what it wants to do on the basis of the cost of living in that state. Increasing the minimum wage during a recession is particularly harmful to small businesses.

*"Poll: Maximum Support for Raising the Minimum: Most Americans Now Live in States That Have Raised the Wage Floor," www.pewtrusts.org/ideas/ideas_item.cfm?content_item_id=33, April 16, 2006.

[†] www.newsitem.com/opinion/minimum_wage_hike_necessary.

QUESTIONS & PROBLEMS

1. What is required for an employee to be eligible for benefits under the Family and Medical Leave Act (FMLA)?

2. If an employee voluntarily quits his job, may the employee collect unemployment compensation? What if the employee is fired?

3. May an employee who is injured on the job collect workers' compensation and also sue the employer for negligence?

4. List and explain the exceptions to the employment-at-will doctrine.

5. What is the purpose of COBRA?

6. Safeway operates a bread-baking facility in Denver, Colorado. Safeway periodically holds company-sponsored outdoor barbecues for its employees, and it purchased a gas grill equipped with a 20-pound propane tank for the barbecues. To ensure that the grill had sufficient gas for the barbecues, Safeway purchased a 40-pound tank. The larger tanks have a warning label stating that they should not be used with a grill ordinarily equipped with a 20-pound tank. Safeway planned to hold an employee barbecue on July 17, 1998. The plant superintendent, Edward Boone, instructed the plant engineer, Jerry Lewis, to set up the grill for the barbecue. On being informed that the grill was not adequately cooking the meat, the plant manager, Jim Kirk, again summoned Lewis. Lewis and the day-shift maintenance foreman, Fred Lake, attempted to improve the flow of gas to the grill by checking the regulator and repositioning the tank. While Lewis and Lake were working on the grill, fuel escaped and a "ball of fire" erupted. Lewis suffered severe burns to his hand and Lake's facial hair was singed. After an investigation, an OSHA inspector issued a citation to Safeway. Safeway appealed the decision. Was this a workplace safety violation? Why or why not? [*Safeway, Inc. v. Occupational Safety & Health Rev. Comm.*, 382 F.3d 1189 (10th Cir. 2004).]

7. Baxter Pharmacy paid its pharmacists a salary but no overtime pay. Under the Fair Labor Standards Act (FLSA), employers must pay employees overtime for hours worked in excess of 40 hours per week. Baxter Pharmacy believes that the pharmacists are exempt under FLSA because they are "professionals." The pharmacists disagree. Is being a professional an exemption from the requirement to pay overtime under FLSA? Are pharmacists professionals? How do you think the court ruled? [*De Jesus-Rentas v. Baxter Pharmacy Services Corp.*, 400 F.3d 72 (1st Cir. 2005).]

8. Toner Plus was primarily in the business of selling toner and ink cartridges for printers to local businesses. Manuel was the president and sole stockholder of Toner Plus. He was also an employee of the company. Toner Plus made payments to the South Dakota unemployment compensation fund based on Manuel's status as a covered employee. Manuel decided to close Toner Plus on May 30, 2009. He then filed a claim for unemployment compensation benefits. At his unemployment compensation hearing, Manuel testified that he decided to close his business because sales for ink cartridges had declined over the years due to technological advances. Manuel further testified that the company doubled its advertising in an attempt to generate new business. Steps were also taken to reduce expenses. In 2007, Manuel put $35,000 into the business. Despite these efforts, Toner Plus continued to struggle financially. The administrative law judge noted that unemployed individuals who are otherwise eligible for unemployment compensation benefits may be disqualified from receiving if they "voluntarily" leave their employment and do not have "good cause" for doing so. Should Manuel receive unemployment compensation? Why or why not? [*Michael Manuel v. Toner Plus, Inc. and South Dakota Department of Labor, Unemployment Insurance Division,* 815 N.W.2d 668 (2012).]

9. Chris Blake and Achara Tanatchangsang worked on the same shift at Owens-Brockway Glass Container, Inc. Chris and Achara were also involved in a romantic relationship that ended in November 1995. In January 1996, Chris told his employer's plant superintendent that he was having difficulty coping with the breakup and that he did not want to work the same shift as Achara. The plant superintendent approached Achara and offered to transfer her to a different shift. Achara did not want to be transferred. In January 1996 and again in March

1996, she reported to her supervisor that Chris had called her derogatory names. At some point after the March 1996 incident, Chris was placed on medical leave. In April 1996, while still on medical leave, Chris entered the employer's manufacturing plant and shot and killed Achara while she was at work. He then killed himself. The personal representative of Achara's estate brought a wrongful-death action against Owens-Brockway. The company argued that it lacked notice that Chris was dangerous, and it claimed that the workers' compensation statutes provided the plaintiff's exclusive remedy. Do you believe that Achara's death was "work-related" and that workers' compensation should be the exclusive remedy? Why or why not? [*Panpat v. Owens-Brockway Glass Container, Inc.*, 334 Ore. 342 (2003).]

10. Kuhl became president of the First State Bank of Pinedale on June 1, 2007. In April 2008, Wells Fargo's human resource manager, Brad Nations, came to First State Bank to deliver written employment offers to those employees Wells Fargo wanted to retain. Kuhl was among them, and at the end of the day, Nations provided him with a letter offering him employment with Wells Fargo. The letter set forth a base salary, retention bonus payments after six months and one year of employment, and other employment details. On the second page of the letter, text inside a box setting forth "Conditions of Employment at Wells Fargo" stated that Kuhl was hired under "employment at will." Kuhl's employment with Wells Fargo was terminated on December 10, 2008 (a little over five months after he was hired). No reason was given. He sued for wrongful termination. If you were the court, how would you rule? Explain your reasoning. [*Kuhl v. Wells Fargo Bank, N.A.*, 281 P.3d 716 (2012).]

Looking for more review materials?

The Online Learning Center at **www.mhhe.com/kubasek3e** contains this chapter's "Assignment on the Internet" and also a list of URLs for more information, entitled "On the Internet." Find both of them in the Student Center portion of the OLC, along with quizzes and other helpful materials.

CHAPTER

43 Employment Discrimination

LEARNING OBJECTIVES

After reading this chapter, you will be able to answer the following questions:

1 When may an employee be legally fired?

2 What are the federal laws governing employment situations?

3 What are the legal requirements for a charge of sex discrimination?

4 What is the difference between discrimination based on disparate treatment and discrimination based on disparate impact?

5 What are the legal requirements for a charge of sexual harassment?

6 What is Title VII, and what are the employers' defenses to a charge under Title VII?

7 What are the legal requirements for a charge of age discrimination?

8 What is the Equal Pay Act?

9 May an employer discriminate on the basis of sexual orientation?

10 May employers discriminate against smokers?

CASE OPENER

Brad Gets Fired from "So Clean!"

Brad has worked in the marketing department of "So Clean!" for the last five years. So Clean is a company that produces household cleaners. Brad is an excellent employee and was recently promoted. Shortly after his promotion, Brad decided to reveal publicly that he is a homosexual. His family and most of his co-workers have been very supportive.

Soon after his promotion and announcement that he is gay, Brad began having problems with his female boss, Jennifer. She began asking Brad questions about his personal life. At first it was small things, such as asking Brad if he was a smoker (he is, although only outside the workplace). Jennifer then began asking Brad very personal questions about his sexuality and told him she did not like weak men. The final straw for Brad occurred when Jennifer announced that she would "cure" his homosexuality and told him to come home with her that night after work or be fired. Jennifer was careful that there were never any witnesses around when she asked Brad personal questions or propositioned him.

Brad refused Jennifer's advances and was fired. He filed an administrative complaint with the Equal Employment Opportunity Commission (EEOC), alleging wrongful termination, retaliation, sexual harassment, and sexual discrimination. Jennifer's response was that she fired Brad because of "creative" differences about how to run the marketing department and because he is a smoker. Jennifer has denied Brad's accusations about sexual discrimination and harassment.

1. May an employer fire an employee because that employee is gay?
2. May an employer fire an employee because the employee smokes outside the workplace?
3. May a man file a claim of sexual discrimination? Sexual harassment?
4. What rights does an employee have in the workplace?
5. What defenses does an employer have to allegations of discrimination?

The Wrap-Up at the end of the chapter will answer these questions.

When May an Employee Be Fired?

LO1 When may an employee be legally fired?

During the 18th and 19th centuries in the United States, employees had no protection in the workplace. An employee who was injured could be fired. In fact, an employer could fire a worker for no reason at all. This concept came to be known as *at-will employment.*[1] At-will employment applied in all states with no exceptions until 1959.[2]

Today, any employee who is not employed under a contract or a collective bargaining agreement[3] is considered to be an at-will employee. This means that the employee may quit at any time for any reason or no reason at all, with no required notice to the employer.[4] Similarly, an employer may fire the employee at any time, with no notice, for almost any reason. For example, your employer could decide he doesn't like the color of your shirt and fire you on the spot! The exception to the at-will rule is that an employer may not fire an employee for an illegal reason. What is an illegal reason? Broadly, any termination based on a violation of a state statute, a state constitution, a federal law, the U.S. Constitution, or public policy is illegal. (An in-depth discussion of at-will employment can be found in Chapter 42.) Exceptions to at-will employment have also been found through breaches of implied contracts with employees on the basis of employee handbooks.[5]

Federal Laws Governing Employers

LO2 What are the federal laws governing employment situations?

Employees are protected in the workplace by a number of both federal and state laws. Federal laws apply to everyone in the United States. Federal law may be described as a "minimum" level of protection for all workers. State laws may give employees more, but not less, protection than federal laws. Exhibit 43-1 is an overview of some of the most important federal employment discrimination laws.

[1] See *Toussaint v. Blue Cross & Blue Shield of Mich.*, 408 Mich. 579, 600, 292 N.W.2d 880, 885 (1980) (for an extended discussion on the at-will rule).

[2] BambooWeb Dictionary, www.bambooweb.com/articles/a/t/At-Will_Employment.html. The first judicial exception to the at-will rule was created in *Peterman v. Intl. Bhd. of Teamsters, Chauffeurs, Warehousemen, and Helpers of Am., Local 396,* 174 Cal. App. 2d 184, 344 P.2d 44 (1959).

[3] Union employees are covered by collective bargaining agreements.

[4] Most employees do give an employer notice before leaving a job as a matter of professional courtesy. Such action, however, is not required under the law.

[5] "Some challenges and exceptions to at-will employment include: breach of implied contracts through employee handbooks, public policy violations, reliance on an offer of employment, and intentional infliction of emotional distress" (Legal Database, www.legal-database.net/at-will.htm).

Exhibit 43-1
Federal Discrimination Laws

LEGISLATION	PURPOSE
Civil Rights Act of 1964 (CRA)—Title VII (as amended by the Civil Rights Act of 1991)	Protects employees against discrimination based on race, color, religion, national origin, and sex; also prohibits harassment based on the same protected categories
Pregnancy Discrimination Act of 1987 (PDA)	Amended Title VII of the CRA to expand the definition of sex discrimination to include discrimination based on pregnancy
Age Discrimination in Employment Act of 1967 (ADEA)	Prohibits employers from refusing to hire, discharging, or discriminating in terms and conditions of employment on the basis of an employee's or applicant's being age 40 or older
Americans with Disabilities Act (ADA)	Prohibits discrimination against employees and job applicants with disabilities
Equal Pay Act of 1963 (EPA)	Prohibits an employer from paying workers of one gender less than the wages paid to employees of the opposite gender for work that requires equal skill, effort, and responsibility

Civil Rights Act—Title VII

LO3
What are the legal requirements for a charge of sex discrimination?

During the 1960 presidential election, candidate John F. Kennedy (JFK) proposed that the United States pass national civil rights legislation. After winning the presidency, JFK began work with Congress on just such legislation. On November 22, 1963, JFK was assassinated. His vice president, Lyndon B. Johnson (LBJ), became president and saw JFK's quest for national civil rights legislation through to completion. The **Civil Rights Act (CRA) of 1964** was signed by LBJ and became federal law, assuring everyone in the nation of certain basic rights. The act is divided into sections, called *titles.* **Title VII** deals with discrimination in employment.

Title VII prohibits employers from hiring, firing, or otherwise discriminating in terms and conditions of employment and prohibits segregating employees in a manner that would affect their employment opportunities on the basis of their race, color, religion, sex, or national origin.

Title VII of the Civil Rights Act applies to employers who have 15 or more employees for 20 consecutive weeks within one year and who are engaged in a business that affects commerce. The U.S. government, corporations owned by the government, agencies of the District of Columbia, Indian tribes, private clubs, unions, and employment agencies are also covered by Title VII.

BUT WHAT IF . . .

WHAT IF THE FACTS OF THE CASE OPENER WERE DIFFERENT?

What if the business was a fairly new start-up firm and had only 10 employees? What if the firm was an Indian casino and Brad worked in its marketing department? Would either of these facts change the outcome of the case? Why or why not?

Exhibit 43-2
Disparate Treatment and Disparate Impact: Burden Shifting

TYPE OF DISCRIMINATION	BURDEN ON PLAINTIFF (EMPLOYEE)	BURDEN ON DEFENDANT (EMPLOYER)	BURDEN ON PLAINTIFF (EMPLOYEE)
Disparate Treatment (intentional discrimination)	Demonstrate a prima facie case of discrimination	Articulate a legitimate, non-discriminatory business reason for the action	Show that the reason given by the employer is a mere pretext
Disparate Impact (unintentional discrimination)	Establish statistically that a rule restricts employment for those in a protected class	Articulate why the policy or practice is a "business necessity"	Show that the alleged "business necessity" is a mere pretext

There are two ways to prove discrimination under Title VII: disparate treatment and disparate impact (see Exhibit 43-2). **Disparate treatment** is sometimes referred to as *intentional discrimination.* It occurs when an employee is treated differently on the basis of being a member of a protected class (i.e., race, religion, sex, national origin, or color). **Disparate impact** is often referred to as *unintentional discrimination.* It occurs when an employer sets a requirement for employment that inadvertently precludes large numbers of a protected class from employment in a particular job.

PROVING DISPARATE-TREATMENT DISCRIMINATION UNDER TITLE VII

LO4 What is the difference between discrimination based on disparate treatment and discrimination based on disparate impact?

To sue for disparate treatment under Title VII, the plaintiff must be a member of a protected class as listed in the act. In other words, the employee must have been discriminated against on the basis of race, color, national origin, religion, or sex (i.e., gender). If the employee has been hired, fired, denied a promotion, or the like, on the basis of membership in a protected class, this is a form of intentional discrimination and qualifies the employee to sue for disparate-treatment discrimination. Proving disparate-treatment discrimination in employment under Title VII is a three-step process:

1. Plaintiff (the employee) must demonstrate a prima facie case of discrimination.
2. Defendant (the employer) must articulate a legitimate, nondiscriminatory business reason for the action.
3. Plaintiff (the employee) must show that the reason given by the defendant (the employer) is a mere pretext.

To illustrate more clearly, let's break down each step. First, the plaintiff-employee has the burden of proving a prima facie case of discrimination. *Prima facie* is Latin for "at first view"[6] and means that the evidence is sufficient to raise a presumption that discrimination occurred. In the Case Opener scenario between Brad and Jennifer, Brad has alleged that Jennifer discriminated against him on the basis of sex. Brad's prima facie case may be summed up as follows: Brad was a good employee for five years. After being promoted and transferred to Jennifer's department, Jennifer began treating him differently than she did the females in the department. Jennifer told Brad that she did not like "weak males,"

[6] Lectic Law Library, www.lectlaw.com/def2/p078.htm.

In the first round, the plaintiff established a prima facie case of discrimination. In the second round, the defendant rebutted with a nondiscriminatory rationale. Now, in the third round, we'll see whether the plaintiff can show the defendant's reason to be mere pretext.

asked him to come home with her (he refused), and eventually fired him. This is likely sufficient to satisfy the prima facie requirement.

Once Brad (the employee) has set forth his prima facie case (step 1), the burden shifts to Jennifer and So Clean (the employer) to articulate a legitimate, nondiscriminatory reason for firing Brad (step 2). Jennifer and So Clean could meet this requirement by arguing that Brad was not fired on the basis of his sex (because he is a male) but rather because of his "creative" differences with Jennifer in the marketing department (remember, Brad has no contract and therefore is an at-will employee).

BUT WHAT IF . . .

WHAT IF THE FACTS OF THE CASE OPENER WERE DIFFERENT?

Let's say that Brad and his boss had gotten into several public arguments about the role of brainstorming. Brad believed the marketing team could be much more productive if there were required weekly brainstorming sessions at which everyone would subject his or her current projects to discussion by the entire department, whereas his boss saw such sessions as an excuse for people to chat and avoid serious work. She had also complained to others in the company that Brad did not seem to "know his place" ever since he had been promoted. Would her firing of Brad be more likely to be upheld under these circumstances? Why or why not?

Once Jennifer and So Clean (the employer) set forth their nondiscriminatory reason for terminating Brad (the employee), the burden shifts back to Brad one last time. Brad must demonstrate that the employer's given reason for terminating him was a mere pretext (step 3). This last step requires that Brad show that "despite his qualifications," he was fired.[7]

After all the evidence has been presented, the trier of fact (a jury in most cases)[8] must decide whether discrimination has occurred. The burden of proof in a civil case is preponderance of the evidence (i.e., more likely than not). If the jury finds in favor of the plaintiff-employee, damages must be assessed. Damages under Title VII include up to two years of back pay, compensatory damages, punitive damages (limited in some cases), attorney fees, court costs, court orders (including reinstatement), and remedial seniority. If the jury finds in favor of the defendant-employer, the plaintiff-employee receives nothing.

Legal Principle: **Under Title VII, an employer may not intentionally discriminate against an employee on the basis of race, color, national origin, sex, or religion.**

PROVING DISPARATE-IMPACT DISCRIMINATION UNDER TITLE VII

Disparate-impact cases are sometimes called unintentional-discrimination cases. While it is very difficult to prove disparate treatment, it is even more difficult to prove disparate impact. Disparate-impact cases arise when a plaintiff attempts to establish that while an employer's policy or practice appears to apply to everyone equally, its actual effect is that it disproportionately limits employment opportunities for a protected class.

The plaintiff proves a case based on disparate impact by first establishing statistically that the rule disproportionately restricts employment opportunities for a protected class. The burden of proof then shifts to the defendant, who can avoid liability by demonstrating that the practice or policy is a business necessity. The plaintiff, at this point, can still recover by proving that the "necessity" was promulgated as a pretext for discrimination.

The initial steps for proving a prima facie case of disparate impact were set forth in *Griggs v. Duke Power Co.*[9] In that case, the employer-defendant required that all applicants have a high school diploma and a successful score on a professionally recognized intelligence test for all jobs except laborer. The stated purpose of these criteria was to upgrade the quality of the workforce.

The plaintiff statistically demonstrated the discriminatory impact by showing that 34 percent of the white males in the state had high school diplomas, whereas only 12 percent of the black males did, and by introducing evidence from an EEOC study showing that 58 percent of the whites, compared to 6 percent of the blacks, had passed tests similar to the one given by the defendant. Because the defendant could not demonstrate any business-related[10] justification for either employment policy, the plaintiff was successful. Requiring a high IQ or high school or college diploma may be necessary for some jobs but not for all jobs at Duke Power.

Legal Principle: **Under Title VII, an employer may not unintentionally discriminate against an employee on the basis of race, color, national origin, sex, or religion.**

[7] *McDonnell Douglas v. Green,* 411 U.S. 792, 802 (1973).

[8] In a bench trial, the judge becomes the trier of fact as no jury is impaneled. A discrimination case could also be decided by a judge on motion for summary judgment.

[9] 401 U.S. 424 (1971).

[10] If the employer can demonstrate that the imposition of a job qualification is reasonably necessary to the legitimate conduct of the employer's business, the employer will prevail in a disparate-impact case.

SEXUAL HARASSMENT UNDER TITLE VII

LO5

What are the legal requirements for a charge of sexual harassment?

Harassment is a relatively new basis for discrimination. It first developed in the context of discrimination based on sex, and it evolved to become applicable to other protected classes. The definition of **sexual harassment** stated in the Equal Employment Opportunity Commission (EEOC) guidelines and accepted by the U.S. Supreme Court is "unwelcome sexual advances, requests for sexual favors, and other verbal or physical conduct of a sexual nature" that implicitly or explicitly makes submission a term or condition of employment; makes employment decisions related to the individual dependent on submission to or rejection of such conduct; or has the purpose or effect of creating an intimidating, hostile, or offensive work environment. Did the actions of Jennifer create a sexually hostile environment for Brad?

Two distinct forms of sexual harassment are recognized. The first, and generally easiest to prove, is *quid pro quo,* which occurs when a supervisor makes a sexual demand on someone of the opposite sex and this demand is reasonably perceived as a term or condition of employment. The basis for this rule is that the supervisor would not make similar demands on someone of the same sex. In the Case Opener, Jennifer demanded that Brad come home with her so that she could "cure" his homosexuality. When Brad refused, Jennifer fired him. Brad likely has a cause of action for quid pro quo sexual harassment.

The second form of sexual harassment involves the creation of a *hostile work environment.* Case 43-1 demonstrates the standard used by the U.S. Supreme Court to determine whether an employer's conduct has created a hostile work environment.

CASE 43-1 TERESA HARRIS v. FORKLIFT SYSTEMS, INC.
UNITED STATES SUPREME COURT
510 U.S. 17, 114 S. CT. 367 (1994)

During her tenure as a manager at defendant Forklift Systems, Inc., plaintiff Harris was repeatedly insulted by defendant's president because of her gender and subjected to sexual innuendos. In front of other employees, the president frequently told Harris, "You're just a woman, what do you know?" He sometimes asked Harris and other female employees to remove coins from his pockets and made suggestive comments about their clothes. He suggested to Harris in front of others that they negotiate her salary at the Holiday Inn. He said that he would stop when Harris complained, but he continued behaving in the same manner, so Harris quit. She then filed an action against the defendant for creating an abusive work environment based on her gender.

The district court found in favor of the defendant, holding that some of the comments were offensive to the plaintiff, but were not so serious as to severely affect Harris' psychological well-being or interfere with her work performance. The court of appeals affirmed. Plaintiff Harris appealed to the U.S. Supreme Court.

JUSTICE O'CONNOR: As we made clear in *Meritor Savings Bank* v. *Vinson,* this language [of Title VII] "is not limited to 'economic' or 'tangible' discrimination. The phrase 'terms, conditions, or privileges of employment' evinces a congressional intent 'to strike at the entire spectrum of disparate treatment of men and women' in employment," which includes requiring people to work in a discriminatorily hostile or abusive environment. When the workplace is permeated with "discriminatory intimidation, ridicule, and insult," that is "sufficiently severe or pervasive to alter the conditions of the victim's employment and create an abusive working environment."

This standard, which we reaffirm today, takes a middle path between making actionable any conduct that is merely offensive and requiring the conduct to cause a tangible psychological injury. As we pointed out in *Meritor,* "mere utterance of an . . . epithet which engenders offensive feelings in an employee," does not sufficiently affect conditions of employment to implicate Title VII. . . . Likewise, if the victim does not subjectively perceive the environment to be abusive, the conduct has not actually altered the conditions of the victim's employment, and there is no Title VII violation.

But Title VII comes into play before the harassing conduct leads to a nervous breakdown. A discriminatorily abusive work environment, even one that does not seriously affect employees' psychological well-being, can and often will detract from employees' job performance, discourage employees from remaining on the job, or keep them from

[continued]

advancing in their careers. Moreover, even without regard to these tangible effects, the very fact that the discriminatory conduct was so severe or pervasive that it created a work environment abusive to employees because of their race, gender, religion, or national origin offends Title VII's broad rule of workplace equality. The appalling conduct alleged in *Meritor,* and the reference in that case to environments "so heavily polluted with discrimination as to destroy completely the emotional and psychological stability of minority group workers," merely presents some especially egregious examples of harassment. They do not mark the boundary of what is actionable.

. . . Certainly Title VII bars conduct that would seriously affect a reasonable person's psychological well-being, but the statute is not limited to such conduct. So long as the environment would reasonably be perceived, and is perceived, as hostile or abusive, there is no need for it also to be psychologically injurious.

This is not, and by its nature cannot be, a mathematically precise test. But we can say that whether an environment is "hostile" or "abusive" can be determined only by looking at all the circumstances. These may include the frequency of the discriminatory conduct; its severity; whether it is physically threatening or humiliating, or a mere offensive utterance; and whether it unreasonably interferes with an employee's work performance. The effect on the employee's psychological well being is, of course, relevant to determining whether the plaintiff actually found the environment abusive. But while psychological harm, like any other relevant factor, may be taken into account, no single factor is required.

REVERSED and REMANDED in favor of plaintiff.

CRITICAL THINKING

Identify the Court's reasons. Do you think these reasons were sufficient to overturn the previous ruling? Why or why not?

ETHICAL DECISION MAKING

Imagine that Justice O'Connor is operating under a duty-based system of ethics. What duty is she advocating in terms of employer-employee relationships? Would this ruling serve well as a universal standard?

The definition of hostile-environment sexual harassment has evolved over the years through a series of statutes and cases. To prove such harassment, a plaintiff must demonstrate the following: (1) He or she suffered intentional, unwanted discrimination because of his or her sex; (2) the harassment was severe *or* pervasive; (3) the harassment negatively affected the terms, conditions, or privileges of his or her work environment; (4) the harassment was both subjectively and objectively unwelcome; and (5) management knew about the harassment, or should have known, and did nothing to stop it.

Sexual harassment cases were not filed in large numbers immediately after Title VII's passage, with only 10,532 sexual harassment cases filed with the EEOC or state and local agencies in the year ending on October 1, 1992. Then the number of claims increased steadily until 1995, when 15,549 cases were filed. Since 1995, the number of claims has steadily declined, with only 11,364 complaints in fiscal year 2011.[11] While the likelihood of being sued for sexual harassment is not great, once a business is sued, its reputation may be tarnished and payment of damages is a real possibility. It is therefore critically important that businesspersons be able to recognize sexual harassment and prevent its occurrence in the workplace. As a business owner or manager, how would you prevent sexual harassment claims? According to one bar association article:

> There are four essential steps that managers can take to protect their businesses from being involved in sexual harassment litigation. They are: (1) implement a policy against sexual harassment; (2) require supervisory training; (3) provide a mechanism for receiving complaints; and (4) create a method for conducting prompt and thorough investigations.[12]

[11] U.S. EEOC, "Sexual Harassment Charges: EEOC & FEPAs Combined: FY 1992–FY 2000," http://www.eeoc.gov/eeoc/statistics/enforcement/sexual_harassment.cfm., January 18, 2001 (accessed May 1, 2001); and U.S. EEOC, "Sexual Harassment Charges: EEOC & FEPAs Combined: FY 1997–FY 2006," January 31, 2007.

[12] Laura Smith, "Avoiding Sexual Harassment Lawsuits," www.dcba.org/brief/profresp/0299.htm.

Under California state law, managers are required to undergo training to prevent sexual harassment in the workplace.

Legal Principle: **Under Title VII there are two types of sexual harassment: quid pro quo and hostile environment.**

Harassment in Cyberspace. Unfortunately, new forms of technology have provided new opportunities for harassment. Consider, for example, the possibilities for online harassment. A New Jersey appellate court has ruled that employers have a duty to remedy online harassment when they have notice that employees are engaged in a pattern of retaliatory harassment using a work-related online forum.[13] Airline pilot Tammy Blakey sued her former employer, Continental Airlines, for sexual harassment, and part of her claim focused on retaliatory harassment that took place on an electronic bulletin board, the "Crew Members Forum." In particular, Blakey's fellow pilots posted information on the bulletin board that suggested that Blakey was a poor pilot and a "feminazi" and that, by filing a sexual harassment lawsuit, she was using the legal system "to get a quick buck."[14]

In ruling on the bulletin board issue, the court stated that although an electronic bulletin board did not have a physical location within an airport terminal, hangar, or aircraft, it might nonetheless have been so closely related to the workplace environment and beneficial to the employer that continuation of harassment on the forum should be regarded as part of the workplace.

This case shows that, in some situations, employers have a duty to monitor their employees' use of e-mail and the Internet. They cannot allow harassment, including retaliatory harassment on an online bulletin board. Employers can reduce their liability exposure by conducting sexual harassment training and outlining clear workplace policies that prohibit harassing behavior, including behavior that takes place in cyberspace.

Same-Sex Harassment—The Supreme Court Speaks. Initially, same-sex harassment was not covered by Title VII. By 1997, however, the courts were split on the issue. This issue was resolved in 1998 (see Case 43-2).

[13] *Blakey v. Continental Airlines,* 751 A. 2d 538 (N.J. 2000).

[14] *Blakey v. Continental Airlines, Inc.,* 2000 WL 703018.

CASE 43-2 ONCALE v. SUNDOWNER OFFSHORE SERVICES, INC.

UNITED STATES SUPREME COURT
523 U.S. 75, 118 S. CT. 998 (1998)

On several occasions, the employee was forcibly subjected to sex-related, humiliating actions against him by fellow employees in the presence of the rest of the oil-platform crew. He was also physically assaulted in a sexual manner and was threatened with rape. When his complaints to supervisory personnel produced no remedial action, the employee filed a complaint against his employer, alleging that he was discriminated against in his employment because of his sex.

The district court granted the employer's motion for summary judgment, which the appellate court affirmed, holding that the employee, who was a male, had no cause of action under Title VII for harassment by male co-workers. On certiorari, the Court held that nothing in Title VII necessarily barred a claim of discrimination because of sex merely because the plaintiff and the defendant, or the person charged with acting on behalf of the defendant, were of the same sex. In reversing the judgment, the Court concluded that sex discrimination consisting of same-sex sexual harassment is actionable under Title VII. The Court reversed the appellate court's order and remanded the case for further proceedings.

JUSTICE SCALIA: This case presents the question whether workplace harassment can violate Title VII's prohibition against "discrimination . . . because of . . . sex," *42 U.S.C. § 2000e-2*(a)(1), when the harasser and the harassed employee are of the same sex.

Title VII of the Civil Rights Act of 1964 provides, in relevant part, that "it shall be an unlawful employment practice for an employer . . . to discriminate against any individual with respect to his compensation, terms, conditions, or privileges of employment, because of such individual's race, color, religion, sex, or national origin." We have held that this not only covers "terms" and "conditions" in the narrow contractual sense, but "evinces a congressional intent to strike at the entire spectrum of disparate treatment of men and women in employment."

"When the workplace is permeated with discriminatory intimidation, ridicule, and insult that is sufficiently severe or pervasive to alter the conditions of the victim's employment and create an abusive working environment, Title VII is violated." *Harris v. Forklift Systems, Inc., 510 U.S. 17, 21, 126 L. Ed. 2d 295, 114 S. Ct. 367 (1993)*

Title VII's prohibition of discrimination "because of . . . sex" protects men as well as women . . . and in the related context of racial discrimination in the workplace we have rejected any conclusive presumption that an employer will not discriminate against members of his own race. "Because of the many facets of human motivation, it would be unwise to presume as a matter of law that human beings of one definable group will not discriminate against other members of that group."

If our precedents leave any doubt on the question, we hold today that nothing in Title VII necessarily bars a claim of discrimination "because of . . . sex" merely because the plaintiff and the defendant (or the person charged with acting on behalf of the defendant) are of the same sex.

We see no justification in the statutory language or our precedents for a categorical rule excluding same-sex harassment claims from the coverage of Title VII. As some courts have observed, male-on-male sexual harassment in the workplace was assuredly not the principal evil Congress was concerned with when it enacted Title VII. But statutory prohibitions often go beyond the principal evil to cover reasonably comparable evils, and it is ultimately the provisions of our laws rather than the principal concerns of our legislators by which we are governed. Title VII prohibits "discrimination . . . because of . . . sex" in the "terms" or "conditions" of employment. Our holding that this includes sexual harassment must extend to sexual harassment of any kind that meets the statutory requirements.

Courts and juries have found the inference of discrimination easy to draw in most male-female sexual harassment situations, because the challenged conduct typically involves explicit or implicit proposals of sexual activity; it is reasonable to assume those proposals would not have been made to someone of the same sex. The same chain of inference would be available to a plaintiff alleging same-sex harassment, if there were credible evidence that the harasser was homosexual. But harassing conduct need not be motivated by sexual desire to support an inference of discrimination on the basis of sex. A trier of fact might reasonably find such discrimination, for example, if a female victim is harassed in such sex-specific and derogatory terms by another woman as to make it clear that the harasser is motivated by general hostility to the presence of women in the workplace. A same-sex harassment plaintiff may also, of course, offer direct comparative evidence about how the alleged harasser treated members of both sexes in a mixed-sex workplace. Whatever evidentiary route the plaintiff chooses to follow, he or she must always prove that the conduct at issue was not merely tinged with offensive sexual connotations, but actually constituted "*discrimination* . . . because of . . . sex."

Because we conclude that sex discrimination consisting of same-sex sexual harassment is actionable under Title VII, the judgment of the Court of Appeals for the Fifth Circuit is reversed, and the case is remanded for further proceedings consistent with this opinion.

REVERSED and REMANDED in favor of plaintiff.

CRITICAL THINKING

What assumptions would the Court have had to make for it to rule against the plaintiff in this case? Did the reasoning explicitly reject these assumptions?

ETHICAL DECISION MAKING

What stakeholders are affected by this decision? In answering the question, push yourself to go beyond the direct and obvious stakeholders.

Harassment by Nonemployees under Title VII. Employers may be held liable for harassment of their employees by nonemployees under very limited circumstances. If an employer knows that a customer repeatedly harasses an employee yet the employer does nothing to remedy the situation, the employer may be liable. For example, in *Lockhard* *v. Pizza Hut, Inc.*,[15] the franchise was held liable for the harassment of a waitress by two male customers because no steps had been taken to prevent the harassment.

HARASSMENT OF OTHER PROTECTED CLASSES UNDER TITLE VII

Hostile-environment cases have also been used in cases of discrimination based on religion and race. For example, in a 1986 case, *Snell v. Suffolk County,*[16] Hispanic and black corrections workers demonstrated that a hostile work environment existed by proving that they had been subjected to continuing verbal abuse and racial harassment by co-workers and that the county sheriff's department had done nothing to prevent the abuse. The white employees had continually used racial epithets and posted racially offensive materials on bulletin boards, such as a picture of a black man with a noose around his neck, cartoons favorably portraying the Ku Klux Klan, and a "black officers' study guide," consisting of children's puzzles. White officers once dressed a Hispanic inmate in a straw hat, sheet, and sign that said "spic." Such activities were found by the court to constitute a hostile work environment.

PREGNANCY DISCRIMINATION ACT OF 1987—AN AMENDMENT TO TITLE VII

In 1987, Title VII was amended by the **Pregnancy Discrimination Act (PDA) of 1987.** This law expanded the definition of discrimination based on gender to include discrimination based on pregnancy. "Discrimination on the basis of pregnancy, childbirth or related medical conditions constitutes unlawful sex discrimination under Title VII."[17] Under the act, temporary disability caused by pregnancy must be treated the same as any other temporary disability.

Business owners and human resource professionals must be highly attuned to what questions may and may not be asked of potential employees. Examples of illegal questions include these: How many children do you have? Are you pregnant? What are your child care arrangements?[18] Once an employee has been hired, it is illegal to change the terms and conditions of employment on the basis of pregnancy. Moreover, an employer may not force a woman to take time off work during her pregnancy.

L06

What is Title VII, and what are the employers' defenses to a charge under Title VII?

DEFENSES TO CLAIMS UNDER TITLE VII

As a business owner or manager, how would you respond if one of your employees filed a lawsuit under Title VII? Are there any legal exceptions for discriminating against a protected class? The answer, surprising to many business owners and managers, is yes. The three most important defenses available to defendants in Title VII cases are the bona fide occupational qualification, merit, and seniority system defenses. These defenses are raised by the defendant after the plaintiff has established a prima facie case of discrimination based on either disparate treatment or disparate impact. They would obviously not be applicable to a claim based on harassment.

The Bona Fide Occupational Qualification Defense. The *bona fide occupational qualification (BFOQ)* defense allows an employer to discriminate in hiring on

[15] 162 F.3d 1062 (10th Cir. 1998).

[16] 782 F.2d 1094 (1986).

[17] EEOC, "Facts about Pregnancy Discrimination," www.eeoc.gov/facts/fs-preg.html.

[18] "Illegal Interview Questions," www.jobinterviewquestions.org/questions/illegal-questions.asp.

the basis of sex, religion, or national origin (but not race or color) when doing so is necessary for the performance of the job. Exhibit 43-3 highlights the bases for claiming a bona fide occupational qualification. Necessity must be based on actual qualifications, not stereotypes about one group's abilities. For example, being a male cannot be a BFOQ for a job because it is a dirty job. Conversely, there may be a valid requirement that an applicant be able to lift a certain amount of weight if such lifting is a part of the job. Moreover, being a female may be a BFOQ for modeling female clothing. An employer would not be required or expected to hire a male for such a job. Employer arguments about inconvenience to the employer, such as having to provide two sets of restroom facilities, have not been persuasive in the courts. Nor have customer preferences to be served by a particular gender or nationality. The only exception to customer preference is sexual privacy (e.g., female restroom attendants in the women's restroom and male attendants in the men's room).[19]

The Merit Defense. The merit defense is usually raised when hiring or promotion decisions are partially based on test scores. Professionally developed ability tests that are not designed, intended, or used to discriminate may be used. While these tests may have an adverse impact on a class, as long as they are manifestly related to job performance, they do not violate the act. Since 1978, the Uniform Guidelines on Employee Selection Procedures (UGESP) have guided government agencies charged with enforcing civil rights, and they provide guidance to employers and other interested persons about when ability tests are valid and job-related. Under these guidelines, tests must be validated in accordance with standards established by the American Psychological Association.

Three types of validation are acceptable: (1) *criterion-related validity,* which is the statistical relationship between test scores and objective criteria of job performance; (2) *content validity,* which isolates some skill used on the job and directly tests that skill; and (3) *construct validity,* wherein a psychological trait needed to perform the job is measured. A test that required a secretary to use a computer would be content-valid. A test of patience for a teacher would be construct-valid.

The Seniority System Defense. A bona fide seniority system is a legal defense under Title VII. Even though a seniority system, in which employees are given preferential

Exhibit 43-3
Bona Fide Occupational Qualification

May a BFOQ be based on:	YES	NO
Race?		√
Sex (i.e., gender)?	√	
Religion?	√	
Color?		√
National Origin?	√	
Customer preference? (exception: sexual privacy)		√

[19] *In the Matter of the Accusation of the Department of Fair Employment and Housing v. San Luis Obispo Coastal Unified School District, Respondent; Marlene Anne Mendes, Complainant,* Case No. E95-96 L-0725-00s, 98-14 (Oct. 7, 1998). See www.dfeh.ca.gov/PrecedentialD/1998-14.html.

treatment based on their length of service, may perpetuate past discrimination, such systems are considered bona fide and are thus not illegal if (1) the system applies equally to all persons; (2) the seniority units follow industry practices; (3) the seniority system did not have its genesis in discrimination; and (4) the system is maintained free of any illegal discriminatory purpose.

Legal Principle: **The three main defenses to claims under Title VII are BFOQ, merit, and seniority system.**

REMEDIES UNDER TITLE VII

A plaintiff may seek both equitable and legal remedies for violations of Title VII. Courts have ordered parties to engage in diverse activities ranging from publicizing their commitment to minority hiring to establishing special training programs for minorities. A successful plaintiff may recover back pay for up to two years from the time of the discriminatory act. *Back pay* is the difference between the amount of money the plaintiff earned since the discriminatory act and the amount of money she would have earned had the discriminatory act never occurred. For example, if one year before the case came to trial the defendant refused a promotion to a plaintiff on the basis of her sex, and the job for which she was rejected paid $1,000 more per month, she would be entitled to recover back pay in the amount of $1,000 per month multiplied by 12 months. (If the salary increased at regular increments, these are also included.) The same basic calculations are used when plaintiffs are not hired because of discrimination. Such plaintiffs are entitled to the back wages that they would have received minus any actual earnings during that time. Defendants may also exclude wages for any period during which the plaintiff would have been unable to work.

A plaintiff who was not hired for a job because of a Title VII violation may also receive remedial seniority dating back to the time when the plaintiff was discriminated against; compensatory damages, including those for pain and suffering; and, in some cases, punitive damages. In cases based on discrimination other than race, however, punitive damages are capped at $300,000 for employers of more than 500 employees; $100,000 for firms with 101 to 200 employees; and $50,000 for firms with 100 or fewer employees. An employer will not be held vicariously liable for punitive damages as long as it made "good-faith efforts" to comply with federal law.

Attorney fees may be awarded to a successful plaintiff in Title VII cases. They are typically denied only when special circumstances would render the award unjust. If it is determined that the plaintiff's action was frivolous, unreasonable, or without foundation, the courts may award attorney fees to the prevailing defendant. For more information on Title VII, visit the EEOC website at www.eeoc.gov.

PROCEDURE FOR FILING A CLAIM UNDER TITLE VII

Filing a claim under Title VII is much more complicated than simply filing a lawsuit. Failure to follow the proper procedures within the strict time framework may result in a plaintiff's losing his or her right to file a lawsuit under Title VII. Exhibit 43-4 spells out the steps for filing a claim under Title VII.

Filing a Charge with the EEOC. The first step in initiating a Title VII action is the aggrieved party's filing of a charge with the state Equal Employment Opportunity Commission or, if no such agency exists, the federal EEOC. A *charge* is a sworn statement

Exhibit 43-4 Filing a Title VII Claim of Employment Discrimination

STEP 1	STEP 2	STEP 3
File a charge with the EEOC: • Employee must file a charge with the EEOC within 180 days of the alleged discriminatory act. • Alternatively, employee may file a charge with a state agency (assuming one exists).	EEOC conciliation attempts: • EEOC notifies the employer of the charge within 10 days. • EEOC investigates and attempts to negotiate a settlement between employer and employee. • EEOC may file a lawsuit in federal court on behalf of the employee. • If no settlement is reached and no lawsuit is filed by EEOC, the commission issues a "right-to-sue" letter to the employee.	Employee may file a lawsuit.

that states the name of the charging party, the name(s) of the defendant(s), and the nature of the discriminatory act. In states that do *not* have state EEOCs, the aggrieved party must file the charge with the federal EEOC within 180 days of the alleged discriminatory act. In states that *do* have such agencies, the charge must be filed either with the federal EEOC within 180 days of the discriminatory act or with the appropriate state agency within the time limits prescribed by local law, which cannot be less than 180 days. If initially filed with the local agency, the charge must be filed with the federal EEOC within 300 days of the discriminatory act or within 60 days of receipt of notice that the state agency has disposed of the matter, whichever comes first.

EEOC Conciliation Attempts. Within 10 days of receiving the charge, the EEOC must notify the alleged violator of the charge. Then the EEOC investigates the matter to determine whether there is "reasonable cause" to believe that a violation has occurred. If the EEOC does find reasonable cause, it attempts to eliminate the discriminatory practice through conciliation, that is, by trying to negotiate a settlement between the two parties. If unsuccessful, the EEOC *may* file suit against the alleged discriminator in federal district court. Failure to file suit does not necessarily mean that the EEOC does not think the plaintiff does not have a valid claim; it may be that the EEOC simply feels that it is not the type of claim the commission wishes to use its limited resources to pursue.

The EEOC Right-to-Sue Letter. If the EEOC decides not to sue, it notifies the plaintiff of his or her right to file an action and issues the plaintiff a *right-to-sue letter,* which is not intended to be anything other than a statement that the plaintiff has followed the proper initial procedures and therefore may file a lawsuit. The plaintiff must have this letter in order to file a private action. The letter may be requested at any time after 180 days have elapsed since the filing of the charge. As long as the requisite time period has passed, the EEOC will issue the right-to-sue letter regardless of whether or not the EEOC members find a reasonable basis to believe that the defendant engaged in discriminatory behavior. In reality, due to the number of complaints, the EEOC and state EEOCs routinely issue right-to-sue letters without filing a lawsuit on the aggrieved party's behalf. Once an employee receives a right-to-sue letter, he or she is free to hire an attorney and file a lawsuit against the employer.

LO7

What are the legal requirements for a charge of age discrimination?

Age Discrimination in Employment Act of 1967

The **Age Discrimination in Employment Act (ADEA) of 1967** was enacted to prohibit employers from refusing to hire, discharging, or discriminating in terms and conditions of employment against employees or applicants age 40 or older. The language describing the prohibited conduct is virtually the same as that of Title VII, except that age is the prohibited basis for discrimination. ADEA applies to employers having 20 or more employees. It also applies to employment agencies and to unions that have at least 25 members or that operate a hiring hall. As a consequence of the Supreme Court ruling in *Kimel v. Florida Board of Regents,*[20] ADEA does not apply to state employers.

It is important that business owners understand ADEA because the number of claims under this act has increased, perhaps in response to a weakening economy since early 2000 and the aging of the baby-boomer generation. In 2012, approximately 23,000 age discrimination claims were filed.[21]

PROVING AGE DISCRIMINATION UNDER ADEA

Remember, ADEA does not protect *all* individuals from discrimination based on age but protects only those age 40 or over. Thus, an employer can refuse to promote an employee under 40 because he or she is too old or too young. Once a person is in the protected class, discrimination under ADEA may be proved in the same ways that discrimination is proved under Title VII: by the plaintiff's showing disparate treatment or disparate impact.

Termination is the most common cause of ADEA cases. To prove a prima facie case of age discrimination involving a termination, the plaintiff must establish facts sufficient to create a reasonable inference that age was a determining factor in the termination. The plaintiff raises this inference by showing that he or she:

- Belongs to the statutorily protected class (those age 40 or older).
- Was qualified for the position held.
- Was terminated under circumstances giving rise to an inference of discrimination.

The plaintiff need not prove replacement by someone outside the protected class.[22]

Once the plaintiff sets forth the facts that give rise to an inference of discrimination, the burden of proof shifts to the defendant to prove there was a legitimate, nondiscriminatory reason for the discharge. If the employer meets this standard, the plaintiff may recover only if he or she can show by a preponderance of the evidence that the employer's alleged legitimate reason is a pretext for discrimination.

[20] 120 S. Ct. 631 (2000).

[21] U.S. Equal Opportunity Commission, Age Discrimination in Employment Act, http://www.eeoc.gov/eeoc/statistics/enforcement/adea.cfm.

[22] *O'Conner v. Consolidated Caterers Corp.*, 517 U.S. 308, 116 S. Ct. 1307 (1996).

CASE NUGGET

AGE DISCRIMINATION

Danny Lambert v. Mazer Discount Home Centers, Inc. Court of Civil Appeals, Alabama 33 So. 3d 18 (2009)

Danny Lambert was employed by Mazer Discount Home Centers, Inc. ("Mazer"), a family-owned business, for almost 29 years. He was eventually promoted to the position of vice president of marketing. In 2005 Mazer's president, J.B. Mazer, retired. His son Mike Mazer took over. According to Lambert, Mike's management style differed from that of J.B. Lambert in that Mike tended to "micromanage" more than J.B. By 2006, Mike was unhappy with Lambert's performance and decided to fire him. Mike then divided and reassigned Lambert's duties to existing personnel. Lambert sued Mazer, alleging that he had been discharged from his employment in violation of the state's Age Discrimination in Employment Act. Generally, a plaintiff seeking to establish a prima facie case of age discrimination must "prove that (1) plaintiff was a member of a protected group, (2) plaintiff was discharged, (3) plaintiff was replaced with a person outside the protected group, and (4) plaintiff was qualified to do the job." The trial court determined that Lambert had not established the elements of a prima facie case of age discrimination because he had failed to produce evidence that Mazer replaced him with a younger person. Lambert also failed to present substantial evidence creating a fact question regarding whether Mazer's stated basis for Lambert's firing was a mere pretext for age discrimination. Lambert admitted having been counseled about and having been aware of Mike's dissatisfaction with the performance of at least some of his duties in the year before his discharge. The court determined that Lambert failed to establish a prima facie case of age discrimination and affirmed summary judgment entered in favor of Mazer.

DEFENSES UNDER ADEA

As under Title VII, decisions premised on the operation of a bona fide seniority system are not unlawfully discriminatory despite any discriminatory impact. Likewise, employment decisions may also be based on "reasonable factors other than age." Another defense available in both Title VII and ADEA cases is the bona fide occupational qualification (BFOQ) defense. To succeed with this defense, the defendant must establish that he or she must hire employees of only a certain age to safely and efficiently operate the business in question. The courts generally scrutinize very carefully any attempt to demonstrate that age is a BFOQ.

One example of an employer's successful use of this defense is provided by *Hodgson v. Greyhound Lines, Inc.,*[23] a case in which the employer refused to hire applicants age 35 or older. Greyhound demonstrated that its safest drivers were those between the ages of 50 and 55, with 16 to 20 years of experience driving for Greyhound. Greyhound argued that this combination of age and experience could never be reached by those who were hired at age 35 or older. Therefore, in order to ensure the safest drivers, Greyhound should be allowed to hire only applicants younger than 35. In this case, the court accepted the employer's rationale.

Even if none of the foregoing defenses are available to the employer, termination of an older employee may be legal because of the *executive exemption.* Under this exemption, an individual may be mandatorily retired after age 65 if two conditions are met:

- He or she has been employed as a bona fide executive for at least two years immediately before retirement.
- On retirement, he or she is entitled to nonforfeitable annual retirement benefits of at least $44,000.

[23] 499 F.2d 859 (7th Cir. 1974).

Remember, however, that federal laws are a minimum level of protection. If a state wishes, it may pass laws granting employees in its state more rights than those under federal law.

Americans with Disabilities Act

The goal of the **Americans with Disabilities Act (ADA)** is preventing employers from discriminating against employees and applicants with disabilities. ADA attempts to attain this objective by requiring that employers make reasonable accommodations to the known physical or mental disabilities of an otherwise qualified person with a disability unless the necessary accommodation would impose an undue burden on the employer's business.

> When the ADA was before Congress, some members predicted a flood of lawsuits that would bankrupt or at least overburden business. . . . Studies have shown, however, that businesses have adapted to the ADA much more easily—and inexpensively—than the doomsayers predicted. . . . Law Professor Peter Blanck of the University of Iowa has studied business compliance with the ADA, including Sears Roebuck and many other large businesses, and found that compliance was often as easy as raising or lowering a desk, installing a ramp, or modifying a dress code. Another survey found that three-quarters of all changes cost less than $100. Moreover, the predicted flood of lawsuits proved to be imaginary. Almost 90 percent of the cases brought before the Equal Employment Opportunity Commission are thrown out. And only about 650 lawsuits were filed in the ADA's first five years—a small number compared to 6 million businesses, 666,000 public and private employers, and 80,000 units of state and local governments that must comply. The American Bar Association recently conducted a survey and learned that, of the cases that actually go to court, 98 percent are decided in favor of the defendants, usually businesses.[24]

WHO IS PROTECTED UNDER ADA?

A disabled individual, for purposes of ADA, is defined as a person who meets one of the following criteria:

- Has a physical or mental impairment that substantially limits one or more of the major life activities of such individual.
- Has a record of such impairment.
- Is regarded as having such an impairment.

Employers often find it difficult to know how ADA applies to those who have mental disabilities. In 2012, emotional/psychiatric impairment claims (e.g., anxiety, depression, PTSD, etc.) were just over 20 percent of all claims.[25] Typical accommodations for those with mental disabilities include providing a private office, flexible work schedule, restructured job, or time off for treatment. Despite the years of experience we have had in defining covered individuals, the issue of whether someone is a disabled person under the act is still frequently litigated.

[24] Center for an Accessible Society, "Disability Issues Information for Journalists," www.accessiblesociety.org/topics/ada.

[25] National Council on Disability, "Equal Employment Opportunity Commission—Promises to Keep: A Decade of Federal Enforcement of the Americans with Disabilities Act," http://www.eeoc.gov/eeoc/statistics/enforcement/ada-receipts.cfm. June 27, 2000 (accessed September 29, 2013).

ENFORCEMENT PROCEDURES UNDER ADA

ADA is enforced by the EEOC in the same way that Title VII is enforced. To bring a successful claim under ADA, the plaintiff must show that he or she meets all of the following:

- Had a disability.
- Was otherwise qualified for the job.
- Was excluded from the job solely because of that disability.

Under ADA, the plaintiff may file a charge with the appropriate state agency or with the EEOC within 180 days of the discriminatory act. If a charge has been filed with the state agency, an EEOC charge must be filed within 300 days of the discrimination or within 30 days of receiving notice of the termination of state proceedings, whichever comes first. The charge must identify the defendant and specify the nature of the discriminatory act. On receipt of a charge, the EEOC must notify the accused and attempt to conciliate the matter. If conciliation fails, the EEOC may then bring a civil action against the violator.

REMEDIES FOR VIOLATIONS OF ADA

Remedies for ADA violations are similar to those available under Title VII. A successful plaintiff may recover reinstatement, back pay, and injunctive relief. In cases of intentional discrimination, limited compensatory and punitive damages are also available. An employer who has repeatedly violated the act may be subject to fines of up to $100,000.

Equal Pay Act of 1963

LO8 What is the Equal Pay Act?

When the **Equal Pay Act (EPA) of 1963** was passed, the average wages of women were less than 60 percent of those of men. The primary purpose of the law was to eliminate situations where women, working alongside men or replacing men, would be paid lower wages for doing substantially the same job. The EPA prohibits any employer from discriminating within any "establishment . . . between employees on the basis of sex by paying wages to employees in such establishment at a rate less than the rate at which he pays wages to employees of the opposite sex . . . for equal work on jobs the performance of which requires equal skill, effort, and responsibility, and which are performed under similar working conditions, except where payment is made pursuant to (i) a seniority system; (ii) a merit system; (iii) a system which measures earnings by quantity or quality of production; or (iv) differential based on any factor other than sex."[26]

DEFINING *EQUAL WORK* UNDER EPA

The burden of proof in an EPA claim is on the plaintiff to show that the defendant-employer pays unequal wages to men and women for doing equal work at the same establishment. The courts have interpreted *equal* to mean substantially the same in terms of all four factors listed in the act:

- Skill
- Effort
- Responsibility
- Working conditions

[26] 29 U.S.C.A. § 206(d)1.

The factors are looked at individually. If one job requires greater effort, whereas the other requires greater responsibility, and the other two factors are exactly the same, the jobs are not equal. Thus, a sophisticated employer could vary at least one duty and then pay men and women different wages or salaries. However, to warrant different pay, the differences must be real and not just some minor change added to make the jobs appear different.

The legal standard is that the jobs must be "substantially similar," not perfectly equal. A good illustration of this is the 2002 case of *Hunt v. Nebraska Public Power District.*[27] Lynda Hunt had been a clerk for 17 years in the district office, where she had various clerical duties. The office also employed two other clerks, a district supervisor, a district superintendent, and an office manager. When the district supervisor retired, Lynda Hunt was asked to take on most of his duties, in addition to her old duties, and was told she would receive a pay raise and title change. The former supervisor was earning $3,138 per month when he retired, compared to Hunt's $1,739, which did not change. The duties Hunt took on after her supervisor retired included training, disciplining, and evaluating the performance of other employees, although the actual performance forms were filled out by the remaining office manager. Other office employees testified that after the old supervisor retired, Hunt assumed the retiree's tasks and "ran the office." Hunt prevailed at trial. On appeal, the court found that the minor differences between what Hunt did and what the male supervisor had done were not significant enough to overturn the jury's finding that the jobs were substantially similar.[28]

THE IMPACT OF EXTRA DUTIES UNDER EPA

Another way to attempt to legitimize pay inequities is to give members of one sex additional duties. The courts scrutinize these duties very closely, and require that:

- The extra duties are *actually performed* by those receiving the extra pay.
- The extra duties *regularly* constitute a *significant* portion of the employee's job.
- The extra duties are *substantial,* as opposed to inconsequential.
- The extra duties are commensurate with the pay differential.
- The extra duties are available on a nondiscriminatory basis.

The courts will also make sure that different, comparable additional duties are not imposed on the parties not receiving the additional pay.

To see more on personal taxation and taxable damages, please see the **Connecting to the Core** activity on the text website at www.mhhe.com/kubasek3e.

DEFENSES UNDER EPA

As a business owner or manager, what happens if you are accused of violating EPA? There are four defenses available to the employer:

- A bona fide seniority system.
- A bona fide merit system.
- A pay system based on quality or quantity of output.
- Factors other than sex.

[27] 282 F.3d 1021 (8th Cir. 2002).
[28] Ibid.

CASE NUGGET

EQUAL PAY ACT

Crystal Dixon v. University of Toledo, et al. United States District Court for the Northern District of Ohio, Western Division 638 F. Supp. 2d 847 (2009)

Crystal Dixon worked full-time as the Acting Administrator for Human Resources at the Medical University of Ohio. In the summer of 2006, the University of Toledo merged with the Medical University of Ohio. Dixon's employment continued with the University as the Associate Vice President for Human Resources for the Medical University's campus. In July 2007, Dixon was promoted to Interim Associate Vice President for Human Resources for the entire University. Dixon then wrote an opinion piece that was published in the *Toledo Free Press*. The University took umbrage with Dixon's article and conducted an investigation that ultimately led to Dixon's termination. On May 8, 2008, the University held a hearing and, several days later, Dixon learned by mail that she was fired. The termination letter from the University stated that the reason for Dixon's termination was that her article's underlying message was in direct conflict with the "University's policies and procedures as well as its Core Values of the Strategic Plan which is mission critical." Dixon sued the University. She alleged that when she was terminated, a man who was grossly underqualified for her job replaced her and that her successor's annual salary was $40,000 more than her former salary. Moreover, she claimed that her male replacement performed substantially similar work, which required substantially equal skill, effort, responsibility, and working conditions. The University argued that Dixon's Equal Pay Act (EPA) claim should be dismissed because an EPA claim cannot be based on her successor's pay rate.

The EPA forbids employers from discriminating between employees on the basis of sex by paying wages to employees at a rate less than employees of the opposite sex. In order for a plaintiff to establish a *prima facie* case of sex-based wage discrimination, she must show that "an employer pays different wages to employees of the opposite sex 'for equal work on jobs the performance of which requires equal skill, effort, and responsibility, and which are performed under similar working conditions.'" There is no question that a plaintiff may meet her *prima facie* burden by demonstrating a wage differential between herself and her predecessor. Whether a plaintiff may meet her *prima facie* burden by demonstrating a differential between herself and her successor had not been explicitly ruled on by the Sixth Circuit.

The Court was convinced by Dixon's argument and cases in other circuits. Under the EPA, the job comparison may appropriately consider immediate predecessors or successors of the plaintiff. The Equal Pay Act does not require that jobs being compared be performed simultaneously; it also encompasses situations where an employee of one sex is hired for a particular job to replace an employee of the opposite sex. Here, the alleged difference in pay was $40,000. This was not a *de minimis* increase. Such an increase *may* serve as an indication of sex-based wage discrimination. In a situation such as this when Plaintiff's successor makes significantly more than she did, the weight of authority and logic dictate that Plaintiff may state a claim under the EPA. Dixon correctly made out her *prima facie* case by alleging the wage differential between her pay at termination and her successor's pay at the onset of his new position.

Defendant's motion to dismiss Plaintiff's EPA claim is denied.

Seniority, merit, and productivity-based wage systems must be enacted in good faith and must be applied to both men and women. At a minimum, employers should have written documentation of these policies. They should also be sure these policies are enforced. In one case, a former employee alleged that she was discriminated against because men of the same ability and ranking were consistently given higher merit raises. The employee won, despite the fact that the employer had a written merit system, because she was able to demonstrate that the merit policy was not enforced. By not considering attendance records and positions within the salary grade when giving raises, the employer had violated its own merit-raise policy.[29]

Proving that a factor other than sex resulted in the pay differential often presents great problems. The greater availability of females and their willingness to work for lower wages do *not* constitute factors other than sex. Training programs often fall into this category. A training program that requires that trainees rotate through jobs that are normally paid lower wages will be upheld as long as it is a bona fide training program and not a sham for paying members of one sex higher wages for doing the same job.

[29] *Ryduchowski v. Port Authority,* 203 F.3d 135 (2d Cir. 2000).

REMEDIES FOR VIOLATIONS OF EPA

Plaintiffs may recover back pay in the amount of the difference between what they make and what is paid to members of the opposite sex, plus attorney fees. If the employer was not acting in good faith in paying the discriminatory wage rates, the court will also award the plaintiff damages in an additional amount equal to the back pay.

LO9

May an employer discriminate on the basis of sexual orientation?

Discrimination Based on Sexual Orientation—Actionable?

There is currently no federal legislation that prohibits discrimination based on sexual orientation. What does exist are individual state laws that prohibit such discrimination. Twelve states and the District of Columbia prohibit discrimination based on both sexual orientation and gender identity: California, Colorado, Illinois, Iowa, Maine, Minnesota, New Jersey, New Mexico, Oregon, Rhode Island, Vermont, and Washington.[30] An additional nine states prohibit discrimination based solely on sexual orientation. Those states are Connecticut, Delaware, Hawaii, Maryland, Massachusetts, Nevada, New Hampshire, New York, and Wisconsin.[31]

What do these laws mean to Brad, the employee in our Case Opener? It depends on where Brad lives. If Brad lives in Texas, and he is fired for being gay, he has no legal rights and cannot sue his employer. Conversely, if Brad lives in California (or one of the above-mentioned states), Brad may sue Jennifer and So Clean, his employer, for discrimination based on sexual orientation.

Legal Principle: **Only 21 states have laws protecting against discrimination based on sexual orientation.**

When the issue is narrowed to relationship recognition (i.e., marriage licenses, civil unions, and spousal rights for unmarried couples), the number of states recognizing such rights becomes much smaller.

SAME-SEX MARRIAGE

Twelve states plus the District of Columbia now issue marriage licenses to same-sex couples: Massachusetts (2004), Connecticut (2008), Iowa (2009), Vermont (2009), New Hampshire (2010), District of Columbia (2010), New York (2011), Washington (2012), Rhode Island (2013), Delaware (2013), Minnesota (2013), Maryland (2013), and California (2013).[32]

California began issuing marriage licenses to same-sex couples on June 16, 2008, as the result of the California Supreme Court's ruling in *In re Marriage Cases,* which found that barring same-sex couples from marriage violated the state's constitution. However, in 2008, the state's residents narrowly passed California's Proposition 8 that defined marriage as only between one man and one woman. This set off a legal battle that went all the way to the U.S. Supreme Court.[33] Same-sex marriages that took place in California from June 16, 2008, to November 4, 2008, continued to be defined as marriages while the state awaited the outcome of the appeal of California's Proposition 8.

On June 26, 2013, the U.S. Supreme Court, by a 5-4 vote, held that the traditional-marriage activists who put Proposition 8 on California ballots in 2008 did not have the constitutional authority, or standing, to defend the law in federal courts after the state refused to appeal its loss

[30] "Human Rights Campaign: Statewide Employment Laws & Policies," www.hrc.org, updated February 17, 2010.

[31] Ibid.

[32] "Factbox: List of States That Legalized Gay Marriage," *Reuters,* www.reuters.com/article/2013/06/26/us-usa-court-gaymarriage-states-idUSBRE95P07A20130626, June 26, 2013.

[33] *Hollingsworth v. Perry* 133 S. Ct. 2652 (2013).

at trial.[34] Same-sex marriages resumed in California on June 28, 2013. Finally, on August 14, 2013, the California Supreme Court unanimously refused to hear one last attempt by opponents of same-sex marriage, leaving no further options to stop same-sex marriages in California.

There are currently 35 states that ban same-sex marriage and 2 states that neither ban nor legalize same-sex marriage.[35]

THE DEFENSE OF MARRIAGE ACT

The Defense of Marriage Act (DOMA) was signed by President Bill Clinton in 1996 and prevented same-sex couples whose marriages were recognized by their home state from receiving the hundreds of benefits available to other married couples under federal law. Plaintiff Edie Windsor, 84, sued the federal government after the Internal Revenue Service denied her refund request for the $363,000 in federal estate taxes she paid after her spouse, Thea Spyer, died in 2009.[36] Windsor would have received the refund had she been married to a man.[37]

Section 2 of DOMA specifies that no state "shall be required to give effect" to same-sex marriages granted by other states.[38] Section 3 limits the federal definition of *marriage* to being between one man and one woman.[39] At issue in the Windsor case was Section 3 of DOMA. On June 26, 2013, the U.S. Supreme Court held that Section 3 of DOMA was unconstitutional. The opinion, written by Justice Kennedy, holds as follows:

> The class to which DOMA directs its restrictions and restraints are those persons who are joined in same-sex marriages made lawful by the State. DOMA singles out a class of persons deemed by a State entitled to recognition and protection to enhance their own liberty. It imposes a disability on the class by refusing to acknowledge a status the State finds to be dignified and proper. DOMA instructs all federal officials, and indeed all persons with whom same-sex couples interact, including their own children, that their marriage is less worthy than the marriages of others. The federal statute is invalid, for no legitimate purpose overcomes the purpose and effect to disparage and to injure those whom the State, by its marriage laws, sought to protect in personhood and dignity. By seeking to displace this protection and treating those persons as living in marriages less respected than others, the federal statute is in violation of the Fifth Amendment. This opinion and its holding are confined to those lawful marriages.[40]

Section 2 of DOMA, stating that no state "shall be required to give effect" to same-sex marriages granted by other states, is still in effect. Because of this, same-sex couples face several major problems that arise from Section 2 of DOMA. If a same-sex couple are married in Vermont, for example, and move to Pennsylvania, their marriage is not valid in Pennsylvania.

[34] "We have never before upheld the standing of a private party to defend the constitutionality of a state statute when state officials have chosen not to," Chief Justice John Roberts wrote in the majority opinion. "We decline to do so for the first time here." Chief Justice Roberts was joined in his majority opinion by Justices Ruth Bader Ginsburg, Antonin Scalia, Stephen Breyer, and Elena Kagan. Justice Anthony Kennedy filed a dissenting opinion, joined by Justices Clarence Thomas, Samuel Alito, and Sonia Sotomayor. ("Supreme Court Rules on Prop 8, Lets Gay Marriage Resume in California," www.huffingtonpost.com/2013/06/26/supreme-court-prop-8_n_3434854.html, June 26, 2013.)

[35] *Gay Marriage,* http://gaymarriage.procon.org/view.resource.php?resourceID=004857 (retrieved August 17, 2013). States that ban same-sex marriage: Alabama (2006, 1998), Alaska (1998, 1996), Arizona (2008, 1996), Arkansas (2004, 1997), Colorado (2006, 2000), Florida (2008, 1997), Georgia (2004, 1996), Hawaii (1998, 1994), Idaho (2006, 1996), Kansas (2005, 1996), Kentucky (2004, 1998), Louisiana (2004, 1999), Michigan (2004, 1996), Mississippi (2004, 1997), Missouri (2004, 1996), Montana (2004, 1997), North Carolina (2012, 1995), North Dakota (2004, 1997), Ohio (2004, 2004), Oklahoma (2004, 1996), South Carolina (2006, 1996), South Dakota (2006, 1996), Tennessee (2006, 1996), Texas (2005, 1997), Utah (2004, 1997), Virginia (2006, 1997), Wisconsin (2006, 1979), Nebraska (2000), Nevada (2002), Oregon (2004), Illinois (1996), Indiana (1997), Pennsylvania (1996), West Virginia (2000), and Wyoming (2003). States that neither ban nor legalize gay marriage: New Jersey and New Mexico.

[36] *United States v. Windsor,* 133 S. Ct. 2675 (2013).

[37] Defense of Marriage Act, Pub. L. No. 104-199, 110 Stat. 2419 (1996), codified at 1 U.S.C. § 7 (2000); 28 U.S.C. § 1738C (2000).

[38] Defense of Marriage Act, § 2, 110 Stat. at 2419 (1996).

[39] Defense of Marriage Act, § 3, 110 Stat. at 2419 ("In determining the meaning of any Act of Congress, or of any ruling, regulation, or interpretation of the various administrative bureaus and agencies of the United States, the word 'marriage' means only a legal union between one man and one woman as husband and wife, and the word 'spouse' refers only to a person of the opposite sex who is a husband or a wife").

[40] *United States v. Windsor.*

LO10

May employers discriminate against smokers?

May an Employer Discriminate against a Smoker?

In the Case Opener Jennifer discovered that Brad was a smoker. Later, she fired him. One of Jennifer's given reasons for terminating Brad's employment was that he was a smoker. May Jennifer and So Clean legally fire an employee for smoking outside the workplace? The answer is, "It depends!"

A recent trend has been for employers to consider a potential-employee's lifestyle when deciding whether to hire that person. Employers argue that smokers have higher health care costs and miss more work, lowering productivity.

> The Centers for Disease Control and Prevention estimated that $75 billion is spent annually on medical expenses attributed to smoking. Businesses lose $82 billion in lost productivity from smokers. And smokers take about 6.5 more sick days a year than nonsmokers. About one in five Americans—or 46 million people—smoke.[41]

As a result, some companies either won't hire smokers or are threatening to fire current employees who will not or are unable to quit smoking. In 2005, Michigan-based Weyco, Inc., announced that it would terminate all workers who did not stop smoking.[42] Many states have passed laws preventing companies from engaging in such action.

> Michigan, with 1.9 million smokers and one of the highest cigarette taxes in the nation, has no "smoker's rights law" found in 29 other states, so there isn't much that employees can do. Weyco terminated four of its employees this month after they refused to submit to a smoking breath test in light of the company's new policy that bans tobacco use among its 200 employees during work and even when they are off the clock. "We are saying people can smoke if they choose to smoke. That's their choice," said Gary Climes, Weyco's chief financial officer. "But they just can't work for us."[43]

If Brad lives in Michigan, Jennifer and So Clean may legally terminate him for smoking outside the workplace. Conversely, if Brad works in a state with "smoker's rights laws," he could not be legally terminated for smoking outside the workplace.[44] Employers should be aware that giving breaks on health care plans to employees who are nonsmokers could be in violation of smoker's rights law.

Legal Principle: **Thirty states plus the District of Columbia protect a smoker's right to smoke outside the workplace.**

Employment Discrimination Internationally

With many American firms having operations overseas, the question of the extent to which the U.S. laws prohibiting discrimination apply in foreign countries naturally arises. The Civil Rights Act of 1991 extended the protections of Title VII and ADA to U.S. citizens working abroad for American employers or for foreign corporations controlled by a U.S. employer. An exception is made if enforcement of Title VII would violate foreign law. In such cases, Title VII does not apply.

It is not always easy to determine whether a multinational corporation will be considered "American" enough to be covered by U.S. antidiscrimination laws. According to guidelines issued by the EEOC in October 1993, the EEOC will first consider where the company is incorporated. If the company is not incorporated, the EEOC will evaluate

[41] "Workers Fume as Firms Ban Smoking at Home," www.detnews.com/2005/business/0501/27/A01-71823.htm.

[42] Ibid.

[43] Ibid.

[44] For a list of states with smoker protection laws, see American Lung Association, "State 'Smoker Protection' Laws," http://slati.lungusa.org/appendixf.asp, updated June 15, 2009.

COMPARING THE LAW OF OTHER COUNTRIES

LEGAL DISCRIMINATION AGAINST WOMEN IN SAUDI ARABIA

In Saudi Arabia, not only are women not entitled to pay equal to that of men, but there are actual legal statutes sanctioning discrimination against women in both public and private situations. Women, who are not even allowed to drive, constitute only 5 percent of Saudi Arabia's workforce. This number may not be surprising considering the limited labor opportunities for women. The law severely limits the industries in which women can be employed. Women are forbidden to receive business licenses if they may have to interact with males or government officials. If a woman is fortunate enough to find a job, it will probably be in education or health care. Some women can be found in various retail businesses or the banking industry.

Despite its difficulties, finding a job may be easy in comparison to the discrimination Saudi Arabian women will face at work. For instance, all places of employment are segregated by sex. The only way women can be in contact with a man is by telephone or electronic exchange. Many women complain of sexual and physical abuse while on the job. These complaints come from women at all levels in the workforce, from sweatshops to hospitals. And their situation is made worse because they have basically no legal redress. The courts have unreasonably strict evidentiary rules for harassment and discrimination cases. These rules, as well as the social shame that would arise from trying to challenge a man in public, deter women from seeking a legal solution to discriminatory treatment.

factors such as the company's principal place of business, the nationality of the controlling shareholders, and the nationality and location of management. No one factor is considered determinative, and the greater the number of factors linking the employer to the United States, the more likely the employer is to be considered "American."

To determine whether a foreign corporation is controlled by an American employer, the EEOC will again look at a broad range of factors. Some such factors include the interrelation of operations, common management, centralized labor relations, and common ownership or financial control over the two entities. A corporation that is clearly a foreign corporation and not controlled by an American entity is not subject to U.S. equal employment laws.

CASE OPENER WRAP-UP

Brad Gets Fired from "So Clean!"

At the beginning of this chapter, you were confronted with the situation between Brad and Jennifer. By now you should be able to answer all the questions presented to you.

In many states, an employee can legally be fired on the basis of sexual orientation. Discrimination in this area is based solely on state law. There is no federal protection against discrimination based on being gay. Similarly, firing an employee for smoking (including off the job) is also a state law issue. In Michigan, for example, such a firing would be legal. Many states are now passing laws preventing employers from firing those who smoke outside the workplace.

Brad is an at-will employee, but that does not mean that he can be fired for an illegal (i.e., discriminatory) reason. Laws protecting employees against sex discrimination and sexual harassment are just as applicable to men as they are to women. Anyone who is treated in a discriminatory way "based on sex" may sue under the appropriate state or federal antidiscrimination laws. Most, though not all, states have their own state laws against discrimination and harassment. States may give more protection than federal laws but not less protection. There are still a few states that have no state laws against employment discrimination.[45]

These are basic issues that every employer and employee should be familiar with. Remember, knowledge is power. The more you know, the better off you and your business will be.

[45] Alabama, Arkansas, Georgia, and Mississippi have no state employment antidiscrimination laws; see WAGE, "State-by-State Anti-Discrimination Laws," www.wageproject.org/content/statelaw/index.php).

KEY TERMS

SUMMARY OF KEY TOPICS

When May an Employee Be Fired?

At-will employment means that any employee who is not employed under a contract or a collective bargaining agreement may quit at any time for any reason or no reason at all, with no required notice to the employer. Moreover, the employer may fire the employee at any time, with no notice, for almost any reason.

Federal Laws Governing Employers

Federal employment laws provide a minimum level of protection for employees. The states may give employees more rights, but not less rights, than they have under federal law.

Civil Rights Act—Title VII

Title VII of CRA (1964, as amended by the Civil Rights Act of 1991) protects employees against discrimination based on race, color, religion, national origin, and sex. It also prohibits harassment based on the same protected categories. Defenses to a charge of discrimination under Title VII include, but are not limited to, *merit, seniority,* and *bona fide occupational qualification (BFOC).*

Disparate treatment: If the employee has been hired, fired, denied a promotion, or the like, on the basis of membership in a protected class under Title VII, this is a form of intentional discrimination and qualifies the employee to sue for disparate-treatment discrimination.

Disparate impact: Disparate-impact cases arise when a plaintiff attempts to establish that while an employer's policy or practice appears to apply to everyone equally, its actual effect is that it disproportionately limits employment opportunities for a protected class.

Sexual harassment: Sexual harassment includes unwelcome sexual advances, requests for sexual favors, and other verbal or physical conduct of a sexual nature that implicitly or explicitly makes submission a term or condition of employment; makes employment decisions related to the individual dependent on submission to or rejection of such conduct; or has the purpose or effect of creating an intimidating, hostile, or offensive work environment. Two recognized forms are *hostile-environment* and *quid pro quo* harassment.

Pregnancy Discrimination Act of 1987: PDA amended Title VII of CRA to expand the definition of sex discrimination to include discrimination based on pregnancy.

Age Discrimination in Employment Act of 1967

ADEA prohibits employers from refusing to hire, discharging, or discriminating in terms and conditions of employment on the basis of an employee's or applicant's being age 40 or older.

Americans with Disabilities Act

ADA prohibits discrimination against employees and job applicants with disabilities.

Equal Pay Act of 1963

EPA prohibits an employer from paying workers of one gender less than the wages paid to employees of the opposite gender for work that requires equal skill, effort, and responsibility.

Discrimination Based on Sexual Orientation—Actionable?

In many states, an employee can legally be fired on the basis of sexual orientation. Discrimination in this area is based solely on state law. There is no federal protection against discrimination based on sexual orientation.

May an Employer Discriminate against a Smoker?

In many states, an employer may fire or refuse to hire an employee who smokes, even outside the workplace. Approximately 30 states and the District of Columbia, however, have "smoker's rights" laws that prohibit such employment action.

Employment Discrimination Internationally

The Civil Rights Act of 1991 extended the protections of Title VII and ADA to U.S. citizens working abroad for American employers or for foreign corporations controlled by a U.S. employer (unless such enforcement would violate foreign law).

POINT / COUNTERPOINT

Should Employers Be Permitted to Fire Employees for Activities, Such as Smoking, That They Do Outside Working Hours?	
YES	**NO**
The Centers for Disease Control and Prevention estimated that $75 billion is spent annually on medical expenses attributed to smoking. Businesses lose $82 billion in lost productivity from smokers. Smokers take about 6.5 more sick days a year than nonsmokers.	Employers should have no say in what employees do outside the workplace. Forcing employees to take tests to reveal whether they are smokers is an invasion of the employees' privacy. Many employees are addicted to cigarettes and would unfairly lose badly needed employment if unable to quit smoking.

QUESTIONS & PROBLEMS

1. Name five statutes that prohibit discrimination in employment.
2. How is *equal work* defined under the Equal Pay Act?
3. Why is a disparate-impact case more difficult to establish than a disparate-treatment case?
4. Does Title VII apply to same-sex harassment?
5. List the protected classes under the Civil Rights Act of 1964 (as amended in 1991).
6. Plaintiff Vania Santiero was hired as a server at a Denny's Restaurant on August 29, 2009, and she was employed there until she voluntarily left her position on December 9, 2009. Defendant Den-Forest LLP owns the restaurant, and Assad A. Shorrosh is the managing member of Den-Forest. The plaintiff alleges that her supervisor, Shadi Hadi, began harassing her the moment she began working by "grabbing her bottom" on August 29, 2009. The following day, Hadi demanded that Santiero expose herself to him in order to be placed on the work schedule. She complied by lifting her shirt, but then Hadi allegedly assaulted Santiero by following her into a restroom where he pulled her shirt up and fondled her without her consent. The plaintiff did not report Hadi's actions until she called Assad Shorrosh on September 15, 2009. Hadi was suspended by Den-Forest on September 17, 2009, and Hadi's employment was terminated on September 21, 2009. The plaintiff worked for Den-Forest without further incident until her

voluntary resignation almost three months later. She then sued for quid pro quo sexual harassment and a hostile work environment arising under Title VII of the Civil Rights Act of 1964. Does the plaintiff have a case for quid pro quo harassment? Why or why not? Does the plaintiff have a case for hostile-environment sexual harassment? Explain your reasoning. [*Santiero v. Denny's Rest. Store*, 786 F. Supp. 2d 1228 (2011).]

7. In late 2000, Stacy Hegwine applied for a clerk/order checker position in Fibre's customer service department. The ad mentioned no lifting or other physical requirement. Hegwine interviewed for the position with Fibre employees Carlene Cox and Ron Samples on February 16, 2001. Fibre had no documented job description for the position at that time. During the interview, Samples told Hegwine that the position had a 25-pound lifting requirement. After watching a series of videos and receiving documents outlining Fibre's employment policies, Hegwine met with Cox. During this meeting, Hegwine disclosed her pregnancy. Cox called Hegwine and offered her the position on February 21, 2001, contingent on Hegwine's successful completion of a physical exam. Hegwine accepted the offer and was given a start date of March 1, 2001. Two days later, Hegwine completed her physical at the office of Dr. Ostrander, Fibre's medical director. As part of the exam, Hegwine was required to complete a medical history form that inquired as to her pregnancy status. Hegwine truthfully disclosed that she was pregnant. In response, Ostrander gave Hegwine a medical release form and told her that she must have it completed by her personal physician as a condition of her employment. Hegwine took this form to her physician, Dr. Herron, who completed it without being aware of any physical requirements related to Hegwine's prospective position at Fibre. Herron indicated on the form that Hegwine could lift between 20 and 30 pounds and could pull or push up to 40 pounds. On March 16, 2001, Cox called Hegwine and informed her that Fibre was "withdrawing [its] offer of employment" because her "availability" did not permit her "to perform the job." May an employer inquire about pregnancy status during a preemployment medical examination? Do you believe that Fibre retracted its offer of employment because Hegwine was pregnant? How should the court rule? [*Stacy L. Hegwine v. Longview Fibre Company, Inc.*, 172 P.3d 688 (2007).]

8. Exxon maintained a corporate policy that prohibited its pilots from flying corporate aircraft after they reached the age of 60 and forced such pilots to involuntarily retire at age 60. This rule mirrored a rule used by the Federal Aviation Administration that applied to pilots flying for commercial airlines. Based on the "age 60 rule," Exxon forced at least three pilots to retire in 2006 and 2007. The EEOC brought suit on behalf of these pilots and others, alleging age discrimination. Exxon argued that the requirement that pilots be under age 60 is a bona fide occupational qualification. Do you agree? Why or why not? [*EEOC v. Exxon Mobil Corp.*, 2012 U.S. Dist. LEXIS 183101 (2012).]

9. Lisa Harrison was hired by the defendant at Family House of Louisiana, a long-term residential treatment facility for chemically dependent women and their children, on November 23, 1999. She was hired as a prevention/intervention specialist, and her job included overseeing a day care program for the children of mothers staying at Family House. At the time she was hired, Harrison weighed more than 400 pounds. On September 6, 2007, Harrison was terminated from her position at Family House. At the time of her termination, she weighed 527 pounds. On October 17, 2007, Harrison filed a charge of discrimination with the EEOC, alleging that she had been terminated because the defendant regarded her as disabled due to her obesity. Is obesity a disability under the Americans with Disabilities Act? [*EEOC v. Res. for Human Dev., Inc.*, 25 Am. Disabilities Cas. (BNA) 964 (2012).]

10. Following separate lawsuits by female prisoners in Michigan and by the Civil Rights Division of the U.S. Department of Justice, both of which alleged rampant sexual abuse of female prisoners in Michigan, the Michigan Department of Corrections (MDOC) barred males from working in certain positions at its female prisons. Specifically, the MDOC designated approximately 250 correctional officer and residential unit officer positions in housing units at female prisons as "female only." A group of MDOC employees, both

males and females, sued the MDOC, alleging that the MDOC's plan violated Title VII of the Civil Rights Act of 1964. The issue before the court was whether gender was a bona fide occupational qualification for the positions in question. How do you think the court should rule? Why? [*Everson v. Michigan Dept. of Corrections,* 391 F.3d 737 (6th Cir. 2004).] BFOQ

Looking for more review materials?

The Online Learning Center at **www.mhhe.com/kubasek3e** contains this chapter's "Assignment on the Internet" and also a list of URLs for more information, entitled "On the Internet." Find both of them in the Student Center portion of the OLC, along with quizzes and other helpful materials.

CHAPTER 44

Administrative Law

LEARNING OBJECTIVES

After reading this chapter, you will be able to answer the following questions:

1. What is administrative law?
2. What is an administrative agency?
3. What types of powers do administrative agencies have?
4. How and why are administrative agencies created?
5. What is the difference between an executive agency and an independent agency?
6. What is the Administrative Procedures Act?
7. What is the *Federal Register?*
8. Describe the differences between formal and informal rule making.
9. What is hybrid rule making?
10. What are the limits on agency power?

CASE OPENER

Does the EPA Have an Obligation to Regulate Automobile Emissions?

On October 20, 1999, a group of 19 private organizations filed a rule-making petition asking the Environmental Protection Agency (EPA) to regulate "greenhouse gas emissions from new motor vehicles" under the Clean Air Act.[1] The petitioners cited the fact that 1998 was the "warmest year on record," that greenhouse gas emissions have significantly accelerated climate change, and that carbon dioxide is the most important human-made contribution to climate change. Fifteen months after the petition was filed, the EPA requested public comment on the issues. Then, on September 8, 2003, the EPA entered an order denying the rule-making petition, citing two reasons: (1) The Clean Air Act does not authorize the EPA to issue mandatory regulations to address global climate change; and

[1] *Massachusetts v. EPA*, 127 S. Ct. 1438 (2007).

(2) even if the agency had authority, it would be unwise to have done so at that time. The case, *Massachusetts v. EPA,* eventually worked its way to the U.S. Supreme Court, which had to decide whether the EPA was improperly failing to regulate carbon dioxide gas in automobile exhaust as a climate-changing pollutant.

1. What is rule making, and how does it work?
2. What limits, if any, exist on an agency's authority to regulate?
3. When may the courts review an agency decision?

The Wrap-Up at the end of the chapter will answer these questions.

Introduction to Administrative Law

WHAT IS ADMINISTRATIVE LAW?

In addition to learning about laws passed by Congress that affect your firm and industry, as a business owner you will also need to know about rules passed by **administrative agencies,** bodies of the city, county, state, or federal government that carry out specific regulatory duties. **Administrative law** consists of the substantive and procedural rules created by these bodies. It governs applications, licenses, permits, available information, hearings, appeals, and decision making.

LO1 What is administrative law?

Agencies may make rules for an entire industry, adjudicate individual cases, and investigate corporate misconduct. Because they have all three types of power traditionally placed in separate branches of government—that is, legislative, judicial, and executive—some people call administrative agencies the unofficial "fourth branch of government." Of course they are not in fact another branch, primarily because all their authority is simply delegated to them and they remain under the control of the three traditional branches.

LO2 What is an administrative agency?

The first federal administrative agency, the **Interstate Commerce Commission (ICC),** was created by Congress near the end of the 19th century as a means to better control the anticompetitive conduct of railroads. The ICC no longer exists as a separate agency,[2] but for over 100 years it regulated passenger and freight transportation. Following the crash of the stock market and the Great Depression of the 1930s, Congress saw a need for additional agencies to regulate business in the public interest. Since then, numerous agencies have been created whenever Congress believed an area required more intense regulation than Congress could provide. After the Enron scandal of 2001 there was talk that Congress might create a new agency to regulate the accounting industry. To date, no such agency has materialized.

LO3 What types of powers do administrative agencies have?

WHY AND HOW ARE AGENCIES CREATED?

When Congress sees a problem it believes needs regulation, it may create an administrative agency to deal with it. The agency can be staffed with people who have special expertise in the area and know what regulations are necessary to protect citizens. Agencies also typically act more swiftly than Congress in creating and enacting new laws. Today, administrative agencies actually create more rules than Congress and the courts combined.

LO4 How and why are administrative agencies created?

Administrative agencies are created by Congress through passage of **enabling legislation,** which is a statute that specifies the name, functions, and specific powers of the new agency. Enabling statutes grant agencies broad powers for the purpose of serving the "public interest, convenience, and necessity." These include the powers of rule making, investigation, and adjudication.

[2] The functions of the ICC were transferred to the Transportation Department by Congress as part of a cost-saving measure.

BUT WHAT IF . . .

WHAT IF THE FACTS OF THE CASE OPENER WERE DIFFERENT?

In the opening case, the EPA believed it did not have enough power to make rules regarding global climate change. Let's say that a member of the EPA argued that only Congress has the power to make this type of regulation, which would directly affect the way many businesses operate. Would the EPA member be correct?

Rule Making. Enabling statutes permit administrative agencies to issue rules that control individual and business behavior. These rules have the same effect as laws. If an individual or business fails to comply with agency rules, there are often civil, as well as criminal, penalties.

Agencies may enact three types of rules: procedural, interpretive, and legislative. *Procedural rules* govern the internal operations of the agency. *Interpretive rules* explain how the agency views the meaning of the statutes for which it has administrative responsibility. *Legislative rules* are policy expressions that have the effect of law. We discuss rule-making processes later in this chapter.

Investigation. Enabling statutes grant agencies executive power to investigate potential violations of rules or statutes. Many times, companies cooperate with agencies and voluntarily furnish information. At other times, however, agencies must use their investigative powers, defined in their enabling legislation, to gather information. Such powers typically include the power to issue a **subpoena,** an order to appear at a particular time and place and provide testimony, and a **subpoena *duces tecum*,** an order to appear and bring specified documents. Case 44-1 demonstrates the broad powers given to agencies to investigate willful violations of agency rules.

CASE 44-1 LAKELAND ENTERPRISES OF RHINELANDER, INC. v. CHAO

SEVENTH CIRCUIT COURT OF APPEALS
402 F.3D 739 (7TH CIR. 2005)

Lakeland is a northern Wisconsin sewer and water contractor. In August 2002 the company was engaged in an excavation project to install sewer and water lines on a public street in the Mill Creek Industrial Park development in Marshfield, Wisconsin. The citation at issue here arose from an August 28 impromptu inspection conducted by Chad Greenwood, an OSHA compliance officer who was driving by the industrial park project and noticed the excavation in progress. Greenwood parked his car, walked past some traffic cones blocking street traffic from the site, and observed Lakeland employee Ron Krueger excavating a trench with a backhoe. Greenwood also observed another Lakeland employee, Tony Noth, working at the bottom of the trench. The trench contained neither a ladder nor a trench box, a device used to prop up the walls and prevent collapse.

Greenwood began videotaping the scene, at which point Jim Gust, the project superintendent, asked him to step back and informed him the road was closed. Greenwood explained he was an OSHA compliance officer and indicated the nature of the inspection. While Gust and Greenwood were speaking, Noth began climbing up one of the walls of the trench. Greenwood observed loose dirt falling back into the trench, apparently unsettled by Noth's feet as he scaled the slope. Krueger later admitted he knew Noth was not supposed to be working in the trench and that he failed to remove him.

After Noth climbed out, Krueger told him he should not have been working in the trench without a trench box. Krueger then resumed the excavation. The slope of the trench walls concerned Greenwood. Sloping is "a method of protecting employees from cave-ins by excavating to form sides of an excavation that are inclined away from the excavation

[continued]

so as to prevent cave-ins." 29 C.F.R. § 1926.650(b). Eyeballing the trench, Greenwood believed the walls were too steep and there was a fair chance they could collapse. Greenwood measured the slope of the trench walls and took soil samples. . . .

Based on the soil samples and Greenwood's measurements of both the soil quality and the trench dimensions, OSHA's office in Madison, Wisconsin, issued three citations to Lakeland, including one for willfully permitting an employee to work in a trench without adequate protection.

CIRCUIT JUDGE SYKES: Lakeland argues that Greenwood's warrantless inspection violated the Fourth Amendment and that the evidence seized in the inspection should have been suppressed. The ALJ [Administrative Law Judge] denied Lakeland's suppression motion, concluding that Lakeland had no right of privacy on a jobsite on a public roadway and that the excavation site was covered by the "open fields" doctrine. The ALJ also found waiver because Lakeland did not object to the inspection and ask for a warrant at the scene . . . the ALJ correctly concluded that any Fourth Amendment objection was waived because Lakeland did not object to Greenwood's inspection and request a warrant at the scene. . . . The evidence indicates that although Gust initially told Greenwood that the road was closed, when Greenwood identified himself as an OSHA compliance officer and announced the reason for his presence, Lakeland employees acquiesced and cooperated in the inspection. Although perhaps more properly characterized as consent rather than waiver, the ALJ's conclusion that Lakeland waived any Fourth Amendment objection to the inspection is consistent with case law in this circuit.

AFFIRMED in part and remanded in part.

CRITICAL THINKING

What are the key facts responsible for Judge Sykes's opinion? What facts would have to be different for him to have overturned the administrative law judge's conclusion?

ETHICAL DECISION MAKING

This case is typical in that it rests on certain value preferences. Do you believe judges' value preferences shape which facts they tend to weight heavily in a case?

Adjudication. Enabling statutes delegate judicial power to agencies to settle or adjudicate individual disputes that an agency may have with businesses or individuals. After investigation, the agency will hold an administrative hearing before an **administrative law judge (ALJ).** The ALJ will try to convince the parties to reach a settlement via a **consent order** but also has the authority to render an **order,** which is a binding decision, after a hearing (administrative law matters are heard only by the ALJ, as there is no right to a jury trial in administrative agencies). An appeal to the full commission or the head of an agency may then be filed. That decision may then be appealed to the circuit court of appeals; decisions of the ALJ are typically upheld. If there are no appeals, the ALJ's initial order becomes the final order.

Different Types of Administrative Agencies

L05 What is the difference between an executive agency and an independent agency?

Agencies are either executive or independent. **Executive agencies** are generally located within the executive branch, under one of the cabinet-level departments. Hence, they are referred to as *cabinet-level agencies*. Examples include the Federal Aviation Agency (FAA), located within the Department of Transportation, and the Food and Drug Administration (FDA), located within the Department of Health and Human Services. The administrative head of an executive agency is appointed by the president with the advice and consent of the U.S. Senate and may be discharged by the president at any time for any reason. When elected, a new president will typically place his or her own appointees in charge of executive agencies.

CASE NUGGET

APPEAL OF ADMINISTRATIVE DECISION

Murphy et al. v. New Milford Zoning Commission et al.
402 F.3d 342 (2005)

The Murphys own a single-family home located on a cul-de-sac lined with six other single-family homes. They had been hosting Sunday afternoon prayer group meetings since 1994 and claimed that because of Robert Murphy's severe illness their home was the only acceptable location to do so. The number of people who attended varied from as few as 10 to as many as 60. In August 2000, New Milford's zoning office and the New Milford Zoning Commission received complaints about the prayer meetings from the Murphys' neighbors. The complaints cited large numbers of cars traveling to and from the Murphys' home, cars parking in the street and causing access problems, and excessive noise when meeting attendees departed. In response, the Zoning Commission directed the zoning enforcement officer (ZEO) to investigate.

The ZEO presented her findings to the Zoning Commission, which in turn issued an opinion concluding that the Murphys' sizable weekly prayer meetings were not a customary accessory use in a single-family residential area. On the basis of this opinion, on November 29, 2000, the ZEO sent the Murphys an informal letter advising them that their meetings violated zoning regulations. Two days later the Murphys sued New Milford, alleging numerous constitutional and statutory claims. On December 19, the ZEO issued a formal cease-and-desist order, charging the Murphys with violating New Milford's single-family zoning regulations. The Murphys did not appeal the order to the Zoning Board of Appeals, where they could have sought a variance from the regulations. (A *variance* is authority granted to a property owner to use his or her property in a manner ordinarily forbidden by zoning regulations.) The court held that the Murphys had prematurely commenced their lawsuit. Until the variance and appeals process was exhausted and a final, definitive decision from local zoning authorities was rendered, the dispute remained a matter of unique local import, over which the court lacked jurisdiction.

Independent agencies are governed by a board of commissioners, one of whom is the chair. The president appoints the commissioners of independent agencies with the advice and consent of the Senate, but they serve fixed terms and cannot be removed except for cause. Serving fixed terms is said to make the commissioners less accountable to the will of the executive, thus the term *independent* agency. No more than a simple majority of an independent agency can be members of any single political party (if the board consists of seven members, for instance, no more than four may be from the same party). Independent agencies are generally not located within any department. Examples include the Federal Trade Commission (FTC), the Securities and Exchange Commission (SEC), and the Federal Communications Commission (FCC).

Another difference between these two types of agencies is the scope of their regulatory authority. Executive agencies can make rules covering a broad spectrum of industries and activities and tend to focus on *social regulation.* Independent agencies, often called *commissions,* tend to have narrower authority over many facets of a particular industry, focusing on such *economic regulation* activities as rate making and licensing. Exhibit 44-1 lists the major administrative agencies.

Some **hybrid agencies** do not fall clearly into one classification or the other. Created as one type of agency, they may have characteristics of the other. The EPA, for example, was created as an independent agency, not located within any department of the executive branch. Yet it is headed by a single administrator who serves at the whim of the president. During the early 1990s, there were discussions of the need to transform the EPA into a cabinet-level executive agency. (These initiatives did not get beyond the discussion stage.) Another example is the "independent" Federal Energy Regulation Commission (FERC), which has the structure typical of an independent agency yet is located within the Department of Energy.

How Are Agencies Run?

LO6 What is the Administrative Procedures Act?

In 1946 Congress passed the **Administrative Procedures Act (APA)** as a major limitation on how agencies are run. Before its passage, agencies could decide on their own how to make rules, conduct investigations, and hold hearings and trials. Under APA, very specific

INDEPENDENT AGENCIES	EXECUTIVE AGENCIES
Commodity Futures Trading Commission (CFTC)	Federal Deposit Insurance Corporation (FDIC)
Consumer Product Safety Commission (CPSC)	General Services Administration (GSA)
Equal Employment Opportunity Commission (EEOC)	International Development Corporation Agency (IDCA)
Federal Communications Commission (FCC)	National Aeronautics and Space Administration (NASA)
Federal Trade Commission (FTC)	National Science Foundation (NSF)
Interstate Commerce Commission (ICC)	Occupational Safety and Health Administration (OSHA)
National Labor Relations Board (NLRB)	Office of Personnel Management (OPM)
Nuclear Regulatory Commission (NRC)	Small Business Administration (SBA)
Securities and Exchange Commission (SEC)	Veterans Administration (VA)

Exhibit 44-1
Major Administrative Agencies

guidelines govern rule making by agencies. The two most common types of rule making are informal and formal; these, as well as a third type known as *hybrid* and some exceptions, are discussed below.

INFORMAL RULE MAKING

LO7 What is the *Federal Register?*

The primary type of rule making used by administrative agencies is **informal rule making,** or **notice-and-comment rule making.** An agency initiates informal rule making by publishing the proposed rule in the **Federal Register,** along with an explanation of the legal authority for issuing the rule and a description of how the public can participate in the rule-making process. The *Federal Register* is the official daily publication for rules, proposed rules, and notices of federal agencies and organizations, as well as executive orders and other presidential documents.[3]

LO8 Describe the differences between formal and informal rule making.

After publication of a proposed rule, all interested parties have the opportunity to submit written comments. These comments may contain data, arguments, or other information a person believes might influence the agency in its decision making. Although the agency is not required to hold hearings, it has the discretion to receive oral testimony if it wishes. The agency is also not required to respond to all comments it receives, but it must respond to those that significantly concern the proposed rule. After considering the comments, the agency may alter the rule. It publishes the final rule, with a statement of its basis and purpose, in the *Federal Register.* This publication also includes the date on which the rule becomes effective, which must be at least 30 days after publication.

BUT WHAT IF . . .

WHAT IF THE FACTS OF THE CASE OPENER WERE DIFFERENT?

Let's say, in the Case Opener, that the EPA decides it would like to make a rule governing the carbon dioxide emissions of new vehicles. The EPA publishes the rule in the *Federal Register,* along with an explanation of the legal authority of the rule. Is this enough information for the *Federal Register?* What is the third prong that is missing?

[3] *Federal Register,* www.gpoaccess.gov/fr/.

CASE NUGGET

FORMAL RULE MAKING

Alexis Perez v. John Ashcroft
236 F. Supp. 2d 899 (2002)

Perez, a native and citizen of Venezuela, had been a member of El Buen Pastor since November 1996. Beginning in December 1996 he worked as that congregation's music director, a full-time paid position. Under the law, a limited number of visas are available to immigrants who, among other things, seek to enter the United States to work for an organization in a professional capacity in a religious vocation or occupation. The Immigration and Naturalization Service (INS) denied Perez's visa application on the basis of his lack of religious training. Perez argued that the INS adopted the requirement of religious training in violation of the Administrative Procedures Act (APA), because it is a substantive rule adopted without the use of notice and comment or other formal rule-making procedures. Perez argued that he met all the requirements specified by APA and INS regulations and, further, that the INS regulations contained no mention of a formal-religious-training requirement.

INS countered that its imposition of the formal-training requirement—and its denial of Perez's visa request because he lacked that training—simply represented a reasonable interpretation of INS regulations. There is no dispute that INS did not engage in any sort of formal rule-making process before adopting the requirement of formal religious training. The INS argued that the formal-training requirement was simply an interpretation of its regulations—more specifically, of the definition of "religious occupation"—and that therefore no formal rule making was necessary. The court disagreed. All substantive rules adopted by an agency, that is, rules that create law, must be implemented through formal rule-making procedures.

Informal rule making is most often used because it is more efficient for the agency in terms of time and cost. No formal public hearing is required, and no formal record need be established. Some people believe that informal rule making is unfair because parties interested in the proposed rule have no idea what types of evidence the agency has received from other sources. Thus, if the agency is relying on what one party might perceive as flawed or biased data, that party has no way to challenge the data.

Legal Principle: **Informal rule making applies in all situations in which the agency's enabling legislation or other congressional directives do not require another form.**

FORMAL RULE MAKING

An agency initiates formal rule making in the same manner as that for informal rule making, beginning with the agency's publication of a notice of proposed rule making in the *Federal Register*. The second step in formal rule making is a public hearing at which witnesses give testimony on the pros and cons of the proposed rule and are subject to cross-examination. An official transcript of the hearing is kept. On the basis of information received at the hearing, the agency makes and publishes formal findings. On the basis of the findings, an agency may or may not promulgate a regulation. If a regulation is adopted, the final rule is published in the *Federal Register*. Because of the expense and time needed to obtain a formal transcript and record, most enabling statutes do not require a formal rule-making procedure for promulgating regulations. If a statute is drafted in a manner that is at all ambiguous with respect to the type of rule making required, the court will *not* interpret the law as requiring formal rule making.

Legal Principle: **The APA requires formal rule making when an enabling statute or some other legislation requires that all regulations or rules be enacted by an agency as part of a formal hearing process that includes a complete transcript.**

Exhibit 44-2
Rule-Making Procedures

PROCEDURE	FORMAL RULE MAKING	INFORMAL RULE MAKING	HYBRID RULE MAKING
Public hearing	Yes	No	Yes
Formal record	Yes	No	No
Publication of proposed rule in *Federal Register*	Yes	Yes	Yes
Written comments from the public and interested parties	Yes	Yes	Yes
Oral testimony and cross-examination	Yes	No (agency discretion)	Yes (limited)
Publication of final rule in *Federal Register*	Yes	Yes	Yes

HYBRID RULE MAKING

L09 What is hybrid rule making?

After agencies began regularly making rules in accordance with the appropriate procedures, the flaws of each type of rule making became increasingly apparent. In response to these problems, a form of **hybrid rule making** became acceptable to the courts and legislature. The starting point, publication in the *Federal Register,* is the same. Publication is followed by the opportunity for submission of written comments, and then an informal public hearing with a more restricted opportunity for cross-examination than that in formal rule making. The final rule is published in the same manner as are rules in other forms of rule making.

Exhibit 44-2 lists the procedures required for formal, informal, and hybrid rule making.

Legal Principle: **Hybrid rule making contains some of the features of both formal and informal rule making.**

EXEMPTED RULE MAKING

In **exempted rule making,** the APA allows an agency to decide whether public participation will be allowed in rule-making proceedings with regard to "military or foreign affairs" and "agency management or personnel." Exemptions are also granted for rule-making proceedings relating to an agency's property, loans, grants, benefits, or contracts. Military and foreign affairs often need speed and secrecy, which are incompatible with public notice and hearings. Other exemptions are becoming more difficult to justify in the eyes of the courts unless they meet one of the exemptions of the *Freedom of Information Act* (discussed later in this chapter).

Also exempted from the rule-making procedures are interpretive rules and general policy statements. **Interpretive rules** do not create any new rights or duties but are merely detailed statements of the agency's interpretation of an existing law. They are generally very detailed, step-by-step statements of what actions a party must take to be considered in compliance with an existing law.

Policy statements are general statements about directions in which any agency intends to proceed with respect to its rule-making or enforcement activities. Again, these have no binding impact on anyone; they do not directly affect anyone's legal rights or responsibilities.

A final exemption occurs when public notice and comment procedures are "impracticable, unnecessary, or contrary to the public interest." This exemption is used most commonly either when the issue is so trivial that there would probably be little if any public input or when the nature of the rule necessitates immediate action. Whenever an agency chooses to use this exception, it must make a "good-cause" finding and include in its publication of the final rule a statement explaining why there was no public participation in the process.

REGULATED NEGOTIATION

The exceedingly high number of challenges to regulations, as well as a growing belief that structured bargaining among competing interest groups might be the most efficient way to develop rules, has stimulated interest among a number of agencies in a relatively new form of rule making, often referred to as **reg-neg.** Each concerned interest group and the agency itself sends a representative to bargaining sessions led by a mediator. After the parties achieve a consensus, that agreement is forwarded to the agency.

The agency is then expected (but is not bound) to publish the compromise as a proposed rule in the *Federal Register* and follow through with the appropriate rule-making procedures. If it does not agree with the proposal the group negotiated, the agency is free to modify it or promulgate a completely different rule. The reasoning behind reg-neg is similar to that supporting the increased use of mediation. If the parties can sit down and try to work out a compromise solution together, that solution is much more likely to be accepted than one handed down by some authority. The parties who hammered out the agreement now have a stake in making it work because they helped to create it.

PROBLEMS ASSOCIATED WITH RULE MAKING

Agency employees are not subject to the same political pressures as legislators, but they are also not unbiased. Often those with the expertise necessary to regulate specific areas come from the industry they are now regulating. Some feel it can be difficult for regulators to ignore their past ties to industry and pass regulations in the public interest, especially when the industry opposes them for cost or other reasons. While some argue that those who have been deeply engaged in an industry know it best, others refer to an agency in this situation as a "captured" agency. To prevent such actions during his administration, President Obama issued the Executive Order on Ethics Commitments by Executive Branch Personnel. The order prohibits executive branch employees from accepting gifts from lobbyists; closes the revolving door that allows government officials to move to and from private sector jobs in ways that give that sector undue influence over government; and requires that government hiring be based on qualifications, competence, and experience, not political connections.[4]

BUT WHAT IF . . .

WHAT IF THE FACTS OF THE CASE OPENER WERE DIFFERENT?

Let's say, in the Case Opener, that a large automobile manufacturer was vehemently opposed to a possible rule regulating the carbon dioxide emissions of new vehicles. An executive from the company decided to attempt to transition into an open position of power in the EPA to try to squash the rule. Is there any ethical legislation that would stop this scenario from happening, or is this legal?

[4] For a full text of the executive order, see www.whitehouse.gov/the_press_office/ExecutiveOrder-EthicsCommitments/.

CASE NUGGET

AGENCY INTERPRETATION OF STATUTES

Warner-Lambert Company v. United States
425 F.3d 1381 (2005)

Warner-Lambert imports and sells lozenges in packages under the name "Halls Defense Vitamin C Supplement Drops." The drops are composed primarily of sugar and glucose syrup, which together constitute more than 95 percent of each drop. Vitamin C constitutes just under 2 percent of each drop, with the remaining small percentage consisting of citric acid, flavors, and color. The Customs Service reclassified imported vitamin C supplement drops from their previous duty-free status as medicaments to dutiable status as sugar confectionery. As a result, the drops were subject to a duty of 6.1 percent.

Warner-Lambert sued in the Court of International Trade. On appeal, the Customs Service reclassification was upheld. In a six-page detailed letter ruling, Customs explained the reasons for its action, including that its prior classification of the drops was "based upon the belief that Vitamin C imparted therapeutic or prophylactic character to the merchandise" but that "additional research indicates that Vitamin C has not been shown in the U.S. to have substances which imbue it with therapeutic or prophylactic properties or uses."

The Court of International Trade held that Customs justifiably concluded that although the merchandise "may possess medical properties, it is being marketed as much for its flavor as for its medicinal value. Thus, it cannot be said that this merchandise is suitable only for medical purposes." The drops are marketed to provide users with their requirement of Vitamin C, not to prevent or cure disease. If a statute is ambiguous and if the implementing agency's construction is reasonable, the federal courts must accept the agency's construction of the statute, even if the agency's reading differs from what the court believes is the best statutory interpretation.

OTHER ADMINISTRATIVE ACTIVITIES

Other agency tasks include advising businesses and individuals about whether an activity is legal, conducting research, managing government property, and providing information to the public through hotlines, publications, and seminars. Agencies also conduct studies of industry and markets. For example, the FDA conducts studies to determine the safety of drugs. Agencies devote much of their time to issuing licenses or permits. The EPA, for example, helps protect the environment by requiring certain environmentally sound activities before granting permits. Local agencies issue liquor licenses and cabaret (dancing) permits to local bars and restaurants.

Case 44-2 illustrates limitations on an agency's use of its powers to issue, and in this case revoke, a driver's license.

CASE 44-2 YAN JU WANG v. GEORGE VALVERDE
CALIFORNIA COURT OF APPEALS
162 CAL. APP. 4TH 616 (2008)

The trial court granted plaintiff's petition for a writ of administrative mandate compelling the Department of Motor Vehicles (DMV) to set aside its revocation of plaintiff's class C driver's license. On appeal, the DMV argued that, as a matter of law, it had the authority to revoke plaintiff's class C license because it allegedly caught her cheating on an examination for a class B license. The DMV purported to derive its authority from Veh. Code, § 13359.

JUSTICE J. ROTHSCHILD: The facts necessary to our decision are not in dispute. The trial court provided the following useful summary: "[Wang], the holder of a valid Class C (noncommercial) driver's license, applied for a Class B (commercial) driver's license. She was given a written examination to determine whether she was qualified for a Class B license, but she was not permitted to complete that examination because she was allegedly cheating in the taking of the examination by using crib notes. [Wang] was never criminally prosecuted for using crib notes, under Vehicle Code section 14610.5, because the [DMV] determined that there was insufficient evidence to support criminal action. [Citation.] The only administrative action taken against [Wang] by the [DMV] was to order the revocation of her Class C (noncommercial) driver's license."

After exhausting her administrative remedies, Wang filed a petition for writ of administrative mandate to compel the DMV to set aside the revocation of her class C license. The parties provided the trial court with briefing and evidence, including the administrative record of the DMV proceedings.

[continued]

The trial court granted Wang's petition. The court reasoned that "[t]he issue before the court is whether, as a matter of law, the DMV can revoke [Wang's] Class C license because it caught her cheating in an examination for a Class B license." The court concluded that "[n]o such action is authorized by the Vehicle Code." The DMV timely appealed.

The DMV argues that, as a matter of law, the DMV does have authority to revoke Wang's class C license because it allegedly caught her cheating on the examination for a class B license. The DMV purports to derive that authority from the Vehicle Code as follows: (1) Section 13359 provides that the DMV "may suspend or revoke the privilege of any person to operate a motor vehicle upon any of the grounds which authorize the refusal to issue a license"; (2) section 12809, subdivision (d), provides that the DMV may refuse to issue a license to any person who has "committed any fraud in any application"; (3) an examination is part of an application; (4) the use of a crib sheet in taking an examination is a fraudulent act; so (5) by using the crib sheet, Wang committed a fraud in an application, which therefore authorized refusal to issue a class B license, which therefore authorized revocation of her class C license, because any ground for refusal to issue a license is also a ground for revocation of a license.

The DMV's argument thus depends upon the DMV's contention that under section 13359 *any* ground for refusal to issue *one* license is also sufficient to justify revocation of a *different* license. The DMV cites no authority for its construction of section 13359. We have found no case on point, but we conclude that the DMV's interpretation cannot be correct, because it would lead to untenable results. For example, if the holder of a class C license applied for a class B license, took the exam *without cheating or committing any other impropriety,* and failed the exam, then the DMV would be authorized to revoke the class C license according to the DMV's construction of section 13359, because "any of the grounds which authorize the refusal to issue" the class B license would also authorize the DMV to "suspend or revoke" the class C license. In general, the DMV's interpretation of the statute would authorize revocation of a class C license held by *any* unsuccessful applicant for a class B license. The statutory requirements for a class B license, however, are more demanding than the statutory requirements for a class C license, so statutory ineligibility for a class B license has no tendency, in itself, to show lack of statutory entitlement to a class C license. . . . Because the DMV's interpretation of section 13359 turns every unsuccessful application for a class B license into an authorization to revoke the applicant's class C license, it effectively negates the lower statutory threshold for entitlement to a class C license. For these reasons, we must reject the DMV's interpretation of section 13359. Because the DMV's argument depends upon an incorrect interpretation of section 13359, the argument fails. We therefore need not address its other steps. The judgment is affirmed. Respondent shall recover her costs of appeal.

AFFIRMED.

CRITICAL THINKING

What changes in the wording of section 13359 would have eradicated the administrative problem pointed out as the basis for the court's decision? In other words, what wording would have permitted the DMV to have acted as it did, while not providing it with excessive discretion?

ETHICAL DECISION MAKING

Who are the most relevant stakeholders in the scenario that gives rise to this decision?

Limitations on Agency Powers

LO10

What are the limits on agency power?

There are four basic limits on agency power: political, statutory, judicial, and informational (see Exhibit 44-3). These limitations are intended to keep agencies and their thousands of employees from abusing their discretion.

POLITICAL LIMITATIONS

We've seen above that administrative heads of executive agencies are particularly accountable to the executive branch. The president's politics, whether liberal or conservative, also influence the operations of these agencies.

Congress has significant control over agencies as well, since the Senate must approve presidential nominees for agencies' administrative heads. And if Congress decides a particular agency is not performing as it wishes, it can cut or even eliminate that agency's

Exhibit 44-3
Limits on Agency Power

Political	The Senate must approve nominees for agency heads, and Congress has power over agencies' budgets.
Statutory	Congress may create or eliminate agencies and amend enabling legislation (i.e., powers of agencies); Congress reviews and may override agency rules.
Judicial	Interested parties may challenge administrative rules in the courts, which may review the agency's finding of facts, its interpretation of the rule, and the scope of the agency's power in making the rule.
Informational	The Freedom of Information Act, Government in Sunshine Act, and Privacy Act of 1974 specify agencies' responsibilities regarding public access to information.

budget. Before the Enron crisis, Congress, after being heavily lobbied by the accounting industry, threatened to defund the Securities and Exchange Commission (SEC). In effect, Congress did not like the SEC's proposal that stock options be charged as expenses. Arthur Levitt, then head of the SEC, heard the warning loud and clear and decided to walk away from his firmly held position on the issue. He later said it was his biggest regret as head of the SEC.[5]

STATUTORY LIMITATIONS

Congress has the power to create or dissolve an agency and to amend its enabling legislation to limit its power. Congress also has 60 days to review proposed agency rules and may override them before they become effective. In addition, APA sets forth guidelines that all agencies must follow when engaged in rule making.

JUDICIAL LIMITATIONS

If a rule is subjected to judicial review, the court will consider the following:

1. *The facts of the case:* Courts typically defer to an agency's fact finding. The facts must be supported by **substantial evidence.**
2. *The agency's interpretation of the rule:* Once again, the courts typically defer to the expertise of the agency and uphold the agency's interpretation of the rule.
3. *The scope of the agency's authority:* Has the agency exceeded the authority granted to it by its enabling legislation?

Legal Principle: Any entity (individual or business) that believes itself harmed by an administrative rule may challenge that rule in federal court once all administrative procedures have been exhausted.[6] This is probably the biggest constraint on agency power.

INFORMATIONAL LIMITATIONS

Freedom of Information Act. The **Freedom of Information Act (FOIA),** passed in 1966, requires that federal agencies publish in the *Federal Register* places where the public can obtain information from them. The act requires similar publication of proposed rules

[5] PBS video, *Bigger Than Enron—How Greed and Politics Undercut America's Watchdogs* (1999).

[6] In a few situations, a court may not review an agency action. These include situations involving politically sensitive issues and those in which the agency's enabling legislation prohibits judicial review.

and policy statements and mandates that items such as staff manuals and interpretations of policies must be available for copying by individuals on request. Finally, all federal government agencies must publish records electronically.

Any individual or business may make a FOIA request to a federal government agency for information about how the agency gets and spends its money. Statistics and/or information collected by the agency on a given topic is also available. Perhaps most important, citizens are entitled to any records government agencies such as the Internal Revenue Service (IRS) have collected about them. FOIA does not apply to Congress, the federal courts, the executive staff of the White House, state or local governments, and private businesses. Exemptions to FOIA include, but are not limited to, national security, internal agency matters (such as human resource issues), criminal investigations, financial institutions, and an individual's private life.

BUT WHAT IF . . .

WHAT IF THE FACTS OF THE CASE OPENER WERE DIFFERENT?

Let's say, in the Case Opener, that a group of individuals were wondering whether the EPA was being monetarily influenced by any automobile manufacturers regarding the new vehicle carbon dioxide emissions rule. The individuals contacted the EPA asking for information about where the EPA gets money and how the EPA spends money. However, the EPA said its financial information was private and not to be handed out to individuals. Is the EPA legally correct in saying this?

Immediately after taking office, President Obama issued a Memorandum for the Heads of Executive Departments and Agencies indicating that FOIA should be administered with a clear presumption: In the face of doubt, openness prevails.[7] The memorandum directs that information should not be withheld simply because it is legal to do so and that if an agency cannot make full disclosure of information, it should consider making a partial disclosure.

Case 44-3 examines the limits of a FOIA request.

[7] U.S. Department of Justice, www.usdoj.gov/ag/foia-memo-march2009.pdf.

CASE 44-3 ELECTRONIC PRIVACY INFORMATION CENTER v. NATIONAL SECURITY ADMINISTRATION

UNITED STATES DISTRICT COURT FOR THE DISTRICT OF COLUMBIA 795 F. SUPP. 2D 85 (2011)

On June 25, 2009, Plaintiff EPIC submitted a FOIA request to the National Security Administration (NSA) seeking documents related to the Comprehensive National Cybersecurity Initiative (CNCI), an initiative established by former President George W. Bush that outlines federal cybersecurity goals. The plaintiff is a not-for-profit public interest research organization that reviews federal activities and policies to determine their possible impact on civil liberties and privacy interests. The NSA is an agency within the Department of Defense that is responsible for shielding our nation's coded communications from interception by foreign governments and for secretly intercepting intelligence communications from foreign nations.

President Bush established the CNCI on January 8, 2008, by issuing National Security Presidential Directive

54 (NSPD 54), also known as Homeland Security Presidential Directive 23. The contents of NSPD 54 have not been released to the public. The CNCI, as described by the Senate Committee on Homeland Security and Governmental Affairs, is a "multi-agency, multi-year plan that lays out twelve steps to securing the federal government's cyber networks." The CNCI was formed "to improve how the federal government protects sensitive information from hackers and nation states trying to break into agency networks."

On June 25, 2009, the plaintiff submitted a written FOIA request to the NSA that, in its entirety, sought the following documents: the text of the National Security Presidential Directive 54 otherwise referred to as Homeland Security Presidential Directive 23; the full text, including previously unreported sections, of the Comprehensive National Cybersecurity Initiative, as well as any executing protocols distributed to the agencies in charge of its implementation; and any privacy policies related to either the Directive, the Initiative, including but not limited to, contracts or other documents describing privacy policies for information shared with private contractors to facilitate the Comprehensive National Cybersecurity Initiative. The NSA responded to the plaintiff's request on August 14, 2009, and produced two redacted documents that had been previously released under FOIA. The NSA referred part of the plaintiff's FOIA request to the National Security Council (NSC) since a responsive document in the NSA's possession had originated with the NSC. The plaintiff brought this lawsuit against both the NSA and NSC to compel the production of documents responsive to its FOIA request.

JUDGE HOWELL: Congress enacted FOIA to promote transparency across the government. The Supreme Court has explained that FOIA is a means for citizens to know what their Government is up to. The strong interest in transparency must be tempered, however, by the legitimate governmental and private interests that could be harmed by release of certain types of information. Accordingly, Congress included nine exemptions permitting agencies to withhold information from FOIA disclosure. The text of FOIA makes clear that the statute applies to agencies only. The statutory definition of an "agency" explicitly includes any executive department, military department, Government corporation, Government controlled corporation, or other establishment in the executive branch of the Government (including the Executive Office of the President). Using legislative history as its guide, however, the Supreme Court has held that "the President's immediate personal staff or units in the Executive Office whose sole function is to advise and assist the President are not included within the term 'agency' under the FOIA." The National Security Act of 1947 established the NSC to "advise the President with respect to the integration of domestic, foreign, and military policies relating to national security." This Circuit has unambiguously held that the NSC is not an agency subject to FOIA. Organizations that are not an "agency" under FOIA are neither required to respond to a FOIA request nor subject to a FOIA lawsuit.

The plaintiff attempts to distinguish prior case law because the FOIA request in that case was made directly to the NSC, while, in this case, the NSA referred the request to the NSC. The plaintiff contends that, by referring the FOIA request to the NSC, the NSA "treat[ed] the NSC as if it were an agency subject to the FOIA," and therefore this Court should find the NSC subject to FOIA in this case. The plaintiff's argument is unpersuasive. It is true that agencies that receive FOIA requests and discover responsive documents that were created by another agency may forward, or "refer," those requests to the agency that "originated" the document. Here, however, the question is whether an entity *that is not an agency subject to FOIA* must respond to a FOIA request referred from an agency that is subject to FOIA. This question appears to be one of first impression in this Circuit, since neither the parties nor the Court have located authority that directly addresses the issue. The Court finds the answer to this question to be clear-cut: The answer is no. An entity that is not subject to FOIA cannot unilaterally be made subject to the statute by any action of an agency, including referral of a FOIA request. It would defy logic and well-settled legal norms if an agency could unilaterally expand the scope of FOIA by referring requests to entities beyond FOIA's ambit.

For the reasons stated above, the Court concludes that Counts III and IV of the plaintiff's Complaint should be dismissed and that the NSC should be dismissed from this action. Accordingly, the defendants' partial motion to dismiss is granted.

CRITICAL THINKING

What key term had to be clarified for Judge Howell to rule as he did? To what extent is the clarification he provided ambiguous itself in an important respect?

ETHICAL DECISION MAKING

What values are in tension with the transparency objective of FOIA requests?

Government in Sunshine Act. The Government in Sunshine Act requires that agency business meetings be open to the public when a quorum is present and if the agency is headed by a collegiate body. A *collegiate body* consists of two or more persons, the majority of whom are appointed by the president with the advice and consent of the Senate. The law also requires that agencies keep records of closed meetings.

Privacy Act. Under the Privacy Act of 1974, a federal agency may not disclose information about an individual to other agencies or organizations without that individual's written consent. This law guarantees three primary rights:

1. The right to see records about oneself, subject to the Privacy Act's exemptions.
2. The right to amend a nonexempt record if it is inaccurate, irrelevant, untimely, or incomplete.
3. The right to sue the government for violations of the statute, such as permitting unauthorized individuals to read your records.[8]

The Privacy Act applies only to records about individuals maintained by agencies in the executive branch of the federal government. There are 10 exemptions to the Privacy Act under which an agency can withhold certain kinds of information from you. Examples of exempt records are those containing classified information on national security and those concerning criminal investigations.[9]

Legal Principle: **Agency power is limited by the Freedom of Information Act, the Government in Sunshine Act, and the Privacy Act of 1974.**

Federal and State Administrative Agencies

More than 100 federal agencies are now in operation, as well as countless state agencies. Often, when there is a federal agency, there are also comparable state agencies to which the federal agency delegates much of its work. For example, the most important federal agency for environmental matters is the Environmental Protection Agency. Every state has a state environmental protection agency to which the federal EPA delegates primary authority for enforcing environmental protection laws. However, if at any time the state agency fails to enforce these laws, the federal EPA will step in to enforce them.

[8] FCIC, "Your Right to Federal Records," www.pueblo.gsa.gov/cic_text/fed_prog/foia/foia.htm.

[9] Ibid.

CASE OPENER WRAP-UP

Does the EPA Have an Obligation to Regulate Automobile Emissions?

Nineteen private organizations had petitioned the EPA to require that it regulate carbon dioxide from automobile emissions. After holding hearings and requesting comments from the public, the EPA declined the request to regulate, arguing that they did not have statutory authority to do so and that executive policy addressing global warming warranted their refusal to do so. The matter was appealed and eventually worked its way to the U.S. Supreme

Court. The Bush White House filed an *amicus curie* ("friend of the court") brief arguing that the EPA was attempting to get the automobile industry to voluntarily reduce emissions. The Alliance of Automobile Manufacturers also came to the EPA's defense, arguing that the agency, as well as the states, had no authority to regulate automobile emissions.

In a 5-4 decision, the U.S. Supreme Court disagreed, holding that the Clean Air Act authorizes the EPA to regulate greenhouse gas emissions from new motor vehicles in the event that it forms a "judgment" that such admissions contribute to climate change. Moreover, the Court held that the Clean Air Act's definition of *air pollutant* includes carbon dioxide.[10]

In June 2009, the EPA granted a Clean Air Act waiver of preemption to California, allowing California to implement its own, more stringent greenhouse gas emission standards for motor vehicles beginning with model-year 2009. By mid-2010, with the agreement of the auto industry, the California standard became the federal standard.[11]

[10] Kelpie Wilson, "Supreme Court Deals Win for Environment," www.alternet.org/story/50330, April 9, 2007.

[11] McAdams, Neslund, and Zucker, *Law, Business & Society,* 10th ed. (New York: McGraw-Hill, 2012) p. 745.

KEY TERMS

administrative agencies 967
administrative law 967
administrative law judge (ALJ) 969
Administrative Procedures Act (APA) 970
consent order 969
enabling legislation 967
executive agencies 969
exempted rule making 973
Federal Register 971
formal rule making 972
Freedom of Information Act (FOIA) 977
Government in Sunshine Act 980
hybrid agencies 970
hybrid rule making 973
independent agencies 970
informal rule making 971
interpretive rules 973
Interstate Commerce Commission (ICC) 967
notice-and-comment rule making 971
order 969
policy statements 973
Privacy Act 980
reg-neg 974
subpoena 968
subpoena *duces tecum* 968
substantial evidence 977

SUMMARY OF KEY TOPICS

Introduction to Administrative Law

Administrative law consists of the substantive and procedural rules created by administrative agencies (government bodies of the city, county, state, or federal government) governing applications, licenses, permits, available information, hearings, appeals, and decision making.

An *administrative agency* is a body created by the legislative branch (Congress, a state legislature, or a city council) to carry out specific duties.

Congress creates administrative agencies through *enabling legislation* that grants broad powers for the purpose of serving the "public interest, convenience, and necessity."

An *administrative law judge (ALJ)* presides over an administrative hearing. The ALJ may attempt to get the parties to settle but has the power to issue a binding decision.

Different Types of Administrative Agencies

Executive agency: The administrative head of an executive agency is appointed by the president with the advice and consent of the U.S. Senate and may be discharged by the president at any time for any reason. Executive, or cabinet-level, agencies are generally located within the executive branch, under one of the cabinet-level departments.

Independent agency: Independent agencies are governed by a board of commissioners appointed by the president with the advice and consent of the Senate. Commissioners serve fixed terms and cannot be removed except for cause. No more than a simple majority of an independent agency can be members of any single political party.

Hybrid agency: Hybrid agencies do not fall clearly into one classification or the other. The EPA, for example, was created as an independent agency, not located within any department of the executive branch, yet the head of the EPA serves at the whim of the president.

How Are Agencies Run?

In 1946 Congress passed the *Administrative Procedures Act (APA)* as a major limitation on how agencies are run. Its specific guidelines include:

- *Informal rule making:* The proposed rule is published in the *Federal Register* with opportunity for public comment.
- *Formal rule making:* All rules must be enacted by an agency as part of a formal hearing process that includes a complete transcript. It begins with publication of a notice in the *Federal Register* and a public hearing with testimony and cross-examination. The agency makes and publishes formal findings. If a regulation is adopted, the final rule is published in the *Federal Register.*
- *Hybrid rule making:* Hybrid rule making combines features of formal and informal rule making. The starting point is publication in the *Federal Register,* followed by the opportunity for submission of written comments, and then an informal public hearing with a more restricted opportunity for cross-examination than in formal rule making.
- *Exempted rule making:* APA allows an agency to decide whether public participation will occur in proceedings about military or foreign affairs, agency management or staff, and the agency's public property, loans, grants, benefits, or contracts.

Interpretive rules: Interpretive rules do not create any new rights or duties but are merely a detailed statement of the agency's interpretation of an existing law.

Reg-neg: Each concerned interest group and the agency itself sends a representative to bargaining sessions led by a mediator. If the parties achieve a consensus, the agency publishes the proposed rule in the *Federal Register* and follows the appropriate rule-making procedures. If the agency does not agree with the compromise, it can modify or replace it.

Limitations on Agency Powers

There are four basic limits on agency power: political, statutory, judicial, and informational.

Freedom of Information Act: Passed in 1966, FOIA requires that federal agencies publish in the *Federal Register* places where the public can obtain information from them about how they get and spend their money; statistics and/or information they have collected on a given topic; and any records the government has about the individual seeking information. Exemptions to FOIA include but are not limited to national security, internal agency matters, criminal investigations, financial institutions, and an individual's private life.

Government in Sunshine Act: This act requires that agency business meetings be open to the public if the agency is headed by a collegiate body and that agencies keep records of closed meetings.

Privacy Act: Under the Privacy Act, a federal agency may not disclose information about an individual to other agencies or organizations without that individual's written consent.

Federal and State Administrative Agencies

Administrative agencies exist at the federal and state levels.

POINT / COUNTERPOINT

Do Agencies Have Too Much Power?	
YES	**NO**
The U.S. government is founded on separation of powers. That is why we have three branches of government: executive, legislative, and judicial. Giving administrative agencies all three powers—executive, legislative, and judicial—grants them power to do anything they wish with virtually no oversight. Agencies also hire people who formerly worked in industry and who often view regulation skeptically.	Administrative agencies came into existence because neither Congress nor state or local governments had the expertise, time, or resources to deal with specialized problems such as air pollution, securities regulation, and banking administration. An agency employs professionals with expertise and experience in the area it regulates. These people understand the industry and the ways in which it needs to be regulated.

QUESTIONS & PROBLEMS

1. What is enabling legislation?
2. What are the three main powers given to agencies?
3. What are the limits on agency power?
4. Describe the various types of rule making.
5. John and Jacqueline Stowers are the sole owners of Manna, a limited liability company registered to do business in the state of Ohio. Manna is a family-run enterprise that sells food and other products to its members. Manna operates from the family's home, specifically from the western section of the home, where its operations occupy one main room and one overflow room (the "Manna rooms"). Manna has approximately 100 members. To become a member, one must pay a $10 initial fee, fill out an application, and complete an interview with Jacqueline Stowers. Members may order products through Manna either by mail, e-mail, or phone. The products are primarily food products, although Jacqueline Stowers testified that members may also order some cleaning or personal hygiene products. The food products available to Manna members include raw chicken, turkey, beef, and eggs. The meat is typically frozen. After receiving orders from members, Manna obtains the ordered products from various suppliers. Testimony from Jacqueline and Kathryn Stowers indicated that the primary supplier from which Manna obtains products is United Natural Foods, which delivers the products to Manna from Indiana. When ordering from other suppliers, however, the Stowers transport the products back to the Manna rooms themselves in their own unrefrigerated personal vehicles. The products are stored in refrigerators in the Manna rooms, which contain refrigerators and shelving, until members take the products from Manna. Manna has regular hours posted on the outside of the building and on its website, indicating when members may come to pick up their ordered products. Members pay Manna when they pick up their products, although the pricing is determined at the time of the order. Manna's price list is posted on its website. A search warrant was executed on the Manna rooms and the rest of the Stowers' home in December 2008. Manna's food products and other items were seized as part of an investigation of Manna as an unlicensed retail food establishment. Ohio law authorizes regulation of retail food establishments and requires that they be licensed. The Stowers did not have a retail food establishment license. Should they be forced to obtain a food license? Why or why not? [*Stowers v. Ohio Dep't of Agric.*, 2011 Ohio 2710.]

6. Morales, a native and citizen of Mexico, was arrested in 1994 for entering the United States without inspection. He was released and served with a mail-out order to show cause why he should not be sent back to Mexico. Eventually, a removal hearing was scheduled, and Morales was notified via certified mail of the time and place of the hearing. When Morales failed to attend the hearing, he was ordered removed in absentia. The INS apprehended and removed Morales from the United States in 1998. He attempted to reenter illegally in January 2001—this time using a false border-crossing card. He was apprehended at the port of entry, and was expeditiously removed. Undaunted, Morales reentered the United States undetected the following day. Sometime between his 1998 and 2001 removals, Morales had married a U.S. citizen. In March 2001, Morales' wife filed an I-130 alien relative petition based on his marriage to a U.S. citizen. When Morales and his wife met with the INS in January 2003, an immigration officer served them with a denial of the I-130 petition and a notice of intent to reinstate Morales' removal order. The case came before a three-judge panel, which held that the regulation authorizing immigration officers to issue reinstatement orders is invalid and Morales' removal order could only be reinstated by an immigration judge. Until 1997, removal orders could only be reinstated by immigration judges (i.e. not immigration officers). In 1997, the attorney general changed the applicable regulation to delegate this authority, in most cases, to immigration officers. Does the attorney general have the authority to change an INS regulation? Why or why not? [*Raul Morales-Izuierdo v. Alberto R. Gonzales, Attorney General,* 2007 U.S. App. LEXIS 10865 (9th Cir. 2007).]

7. Plaintiff *pro se* Wilfredo A. Golez filed a motion to compel the work attendance records of two former co-workers who are not parties to the litigation. Golez states that he requires their employment records to show that other employees who were late were not terminated as he was and, therefore, rebut the defendants' contention that his own attendance irregularities led to termination. He argues that he was improperly terminated during FMLA-protected absences. In addition to recognizing the rule set forth in the Privacy Act of 1974, federal courts generally recognize a privacy right that can be raised in response to discovery requests. The party whose privacy is affected may object, as the defendants have done here, or may seek a protective order. Resolution of a privacy objection or request for protective order requires a balancing of the need for the particular information against the privacy right asserted. Should Gomez be permitted to compel production of records of his co-workers over their objections? Explain your reasoning. [*Golez v. Potter,* 18 Wage & Hour Cas. 2d (BNA) 923 (2011).]

8. The county board of commissioners entered into a memorandum of understanding (MOU) with a professional baseball team. The MOU obligated the team, among other things, to relocate to the city for spring training. The MOU called for the renovation of a stadium complex. Additionally, the MOU called for renovations at the team's minor-league spring training facilities. Several informational briefings for individual members of the board were conducted privately, and e-mails were circulated among board members regarding the negotiations and agreement with the team. Sarasota Citizens for Responsible Government sued, alleging that the privately conducted meetings and e-mails by board members were a violation of the Government in Sunshine Law requiring that:

> All meetings of any board or commission of any state agency or authority or of any agency or authority of any county, municipal corporation, or political subdivision, except as otherwise provided in the Constitution, at which official acts are to be taken are declared to be public meetings open to the public at all times, and no resolution, rule, or formal action shall be considered binding except as taken or made at such meeting. The board or commission must provide reasonable notice of all such meetings.

How should the court rule? Why? [*Sarasota Citizens for Responsible Gov't v. City of Sarasota,* 48 So. 3d 755 (2010).]

9. Invention Submission Corporation (ISC) brought a lawsuit under the Administrative Procedures Act against James Rogan in his official capacity as undersecretary of commerce for intellectual property and director of the U.S. Patent and Trademark Office (PTO). The PTO started an advertising campaign to warn inventors about invention promotion scams. After a reporter saw its advertisement, he contacted the PTO about a testimonial given in

the advertisement. The reporter followed up with a story identifying ISC as the scam promoter. ISC contends that PTO's advertising campaign was both false and unauthorized, targeting ISC in order to penalize it and put it out of business. It argues that the Inventors' Rights Act of 1999 granted the PTO only limited authority to create a forum to publish complaints and responses to them and that the PTO's 2002 advertising campaign directed at ISC went beyond this stated authorization. Therefore, it asserts that the campaign was an illegal agency action and exceeded any statutory authority conferred on the PTO. Was the advertising campaign an illegal agency action? Should the court review PTO's actions? Why or why not? [*Invention Submission Corporation v. Rogan,* 357 F.3d 452 (4th Cir. 2004).]

10. Harvey is a producer and handler of organic blueberries and other crops, an organic inspector employed by USDA-accredited certifiers, and a consumer of organic foods. He alleged that multiple provisions of the National Organic Program Final Rule were inconsistent with the Organic Foods Production Act (OFPA) of 1990. The OFPA is a law passed by Congress to set national standards for organic food. The rule is the secretary of agriculture's interpretation of the law, set forth as a regulation. Harvey alleged that the portions of the rule that permitted synthetic substances to be used in organic foods was inconsistent with the law as set forth in OFPA, which states that no synthetic ingredients may be added during processing or handling. Moreover, the rule allowed dairy animals classified as "organic" to be fed 80 percent organic food for 9 months prior to their sale, while the OFPA standard is 100 percent organic food for 12 months. Must agency interpretations of a statute be consistent with congressional intent? How should the court rule? [*Arthur Harvey v. Ann Veneman, Secretary of Agriculture,* 396 F.3d 28 (1st Cir. Ct. App. 2005).]

Looking for more review materials?

The Online Learning Center at **www.mhhe.com/kubasek3e** contains this chapter's "Assignment on the Internet" and also a list of URLs for more information, entitled "On the Internet." Find both of them in the Student Center portion of the OLC, along with quizzes and other helpful materials.

CHAPTER

45 Consumer Law

LEARNING OBJECTIVES

After reading this chapter, you will be able to answer the following questions:

1. What is the purpose of the Federal Trade Commission Act?
2. How does the Federal Trade Commission determine what constitutes deceptive advertising?
3. What is the purpose of labeling and packaging laws?
4. What are the different methods of sales?
5. What are the different acts that provide credit protection?
6. What are the different acts that help ensure consumer health and safety?

CASE OPENER

Deceptive Advertising and the Ultimate Weight-Loss Cure

Defendant Trudeau acted in several infomercials promoting his product, the *Weight Loss Cure* book. Trudeau's weight-loss plan consisted of four phases. These phases included instructions on calorie intake, food restrictions, regular colonics, and skin creams. Above all else, the defendant's weight-loss plan instructed dieters to always take daily doses of coral calcium. The defendant claimed that his weight-loss method had been suppressed from the mainstream by food and restaurant companies and government agencies.

The Federal Trade Commission sought to hold Trudeau in contempt for violating a 2004 consent order which commanded that he must not misrepresent the content of his book in his infomercials. The court ruled in favor of the FTC, finding that nowhere in Trudeau's infomercials did he mention colonics, organ cleanses, consumption of organic food only, and calorie restrictions. The court found that Trudeau's statements on the infomercials misled consumers and violated the consent order.

1. What did the court look for to determine whether Trudeau misled consumers?
2. How was Trudeau sanctioned by the court?

The Wrap-Up at the end of the chapter will answer these questions

Consumers buy products and services from sellers every day. In some instances, however, consumers do not have as much power in the transaction as the seller does. The seller often has more knowledge about the product or service, how it was made, and pricing strategies than do the consumers. Because Congress has recognized the opportunities for sellers to take advantage of buyers in this way, it has created laws that regulate transactions between consumers and sellers. A *consumer law* is a statute or administrative rule serving to protect consumer interests.

Various state and federal consumer laws protect consumers from unfair trade practices of sellers as well as unsafe products. Although the laws differ among the states, many of the state laws provide consumer protection exceeding that guaranteed by federal law. This chapter explores a range of consumer laws concerning deceptive advertising, product labeling, sales procedures, health and product safety, and consumer credit. But first, it discusses a federal agency that is one of the most important creators and enforcers of consumer protection laws—the Federal Trade Commission.

The Federal Trade Commission

LO1 What is the purpose of the Federal Trade Commission Act?

Congress created the Federal Trade Commission (FTC) through the Federal Trade Commission Act (FTCA) of 1914.[1] The purpose of the act was to prevent fraud, deception, and unfair business practices. The FTC has responsibility for carrying out the act.

The FTC is an independent federal agency with five commissioners appointed by the president and confirmed by the Senate. Each commissioner serves a seven-year term. The president chooses one commissioner to serve as chair of the FTC.

How does the FTC meet its goal of protecting consumers? The FTC helps to protect consumers through two methods: (1) consumer education and (2) legal action. First, the FTC creates campaigns to educate consumers about laws that protect them. Second, the FTC educates businesses to help them comply voluntarily with consumer laws. For example, the FTC creates **industry guides**, interpretations of consumer laws, to encourage businesses to stop unlawful behavior. When businesses follow the FTC guidelines, they can cut potentially steep costs associated with violating consumer laws.

HOW THE FTC BRINGS AN ACTION

The FTC receives a variety of complaints about businesses from consumer groups and individuals. When consumers file a complaint with the FTC, they trigger a chain of events leading to an FTC action against the violator (see Exhibit 45-1). The FTC typically begins a nonpublic investigation of the company.

If, after its investigation, the FTC believes that a company violated the law, the FTC sends a complaint to the alleged violator. At that time, the FTC may settle the complaint through a consent order with the company. A **consent order** is a statement in which the company agrees to stop the disputed behavior but does not admit it broke the law. Should the company violate the consent order, it will usually be forced to pay a fine.

If the company refuses to enter into a consent agreement, the FTC may then decide to issue a formal administrative complaint. The issuing of this complaint leads to a hearing before an administrative law judge. If the judge decides that the company has violated the law, the FTC issues a **cease-and-desist order**, requiring that the company stop the illegal behavior. However, the company may appeal this decision to the five commissioners. If the commissioners uphold the ruling, the company may appeal to the U.S. court of appeals and, finally, to the Supreme Court.

[1] 15 U.S.C. §§ 41–58.

Exhibit 45-1 Federal Trade Commission Action Process

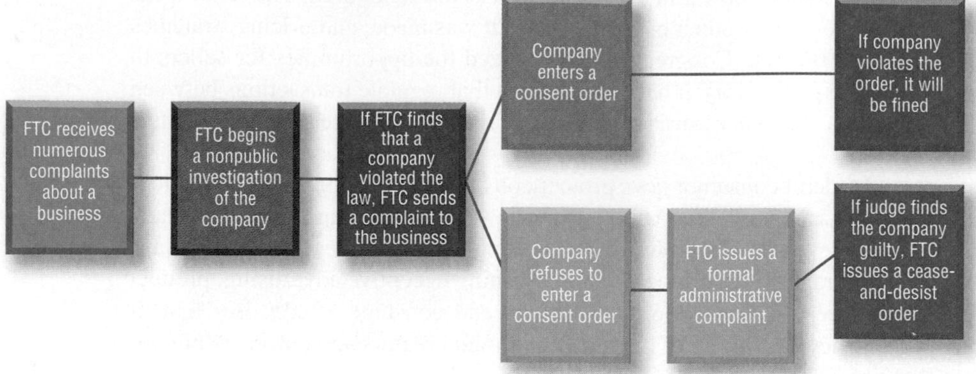

If the courts uphold the FTC's decision, the company must follow the cease-and-desist order. If the company violates the order, the FTC can seek an injunction against the company or fine the company up to $10,000 per violation.

BUT WHAT IF . . .

WHAT IF THE FACTS OF THE CASE OPENER WERE DIFFERENT?

Let's say, in the Case Opener, that the FTC investigated Trudeau and decided that he was misrepresenting his products and possibly harming people. The FTC sent him a complaint letter. What are the different options the two parties can take to resolve the issue?

TRADE REGULATION RULES

Bringing an action may be effective in protecting consumers from the activities of one company, but how can the FTC protect consumers if most companies within one industry are using the same unfair or deceptive practices? Bringing actions against all of these companies would be costly and time-consuming.

An alternative method of addressing these practices is through trade regulation rules. If the FTC finds that deception is pervasive in an industry, the FTC can recommend rule making. An administrative rule has the effect of law. Furthermore, the FTC can bring legal action against those who violate FTC rules.

Deceptive Advertising

L02

How does the Federal Trade Commission determine what constitutes deceptive advertising?

Section 5 of the Federal Trade Commission Act prohibits deceptive and unfair acts in commercial settings, including consumer purchases. This section of the chapter specifically analyzes **deceptive advertising**, in other words, those advertising claims that mislead or could mislead a reasonable consumer. **Puffing**, the use of generalities and clear exaggerations, is permissible.

The FTC decides whether an advertisement is deceptive on a case-by-case basis. Deceptive claims have three elements:[2] (1) a *material* misrepresentation, omission, or practice that is (2) *likely to mislead* a (3) *reasonable* consumer. When an advertised claim appears to be authentic but in fact is not, the advertising is deceptive. Moreover, if the advertisement is a **half-truth**—that is, the information presented is true but incomplete—the

[2] FTC's 1983 Policy Statement on Deception.

Exhibit 45-2
FTC Advertisement Regulations

Puffing is permitted.	Advertisers can use generalities and exaggerations in their advertisements.
Ad substantiation is required.	Advertisers must have a reasonable basis for the claims in their advertisements.
Deceptive advertising is prohibited.	Advertisements cannot contain a material misrepresentation or omission that is likely to mislead a reasonable consumer (such as a half-truth).

advertiser is deceiving the consumer. To combat deceptive advertisements and half-truths, the FTC mandates **ad substantiation,** requiring that advertisers have a reasonable basis for the claims made in advertisements. Exhibit 45-2 summarizes the basic concepts in the FTC's regulation of advertising.

Legal Principle: Many forms of deceptive advertising are inadmissible under Section 5 of the FTCA. However puffing, or clear exaggerations and the use of generalities, is permissible.

An illustration of an FTC claim of deceptive advertising involved Bayer HealthCare Pharmaceuticals in 2007. The FDA required Bayer to run corrective commercials that adjust assertions made in Bayer's original Yaz commercials. Federal laws state that drug advertising can promote only federally approved uses of a drug. While the agency approved Yaz as a drug for birth control with a side value of treating premenstrual dysphoric disorder, the Yaz commercials implied that Yaz was a drug for acne and general mood problems. Bayer agreed in 2009 to run a $20 million marketing campaign for the next six years that will be federally screened before being submitted for public viewing. The advertising of Yaz is a major concern because it is the leading oral contraceptive in the country. Sales of Yaz in 2008 totaled approximately $616 million.

The existence of deceptive advertisements is not enough alone to prove damages for recovery when individual civil suits are filed. For example, in *Oliveira v. Amoco Oil Co.,*[3] a class action suit was brought against Amoco for deceptive advertisements. Amoco had made many claims over a seven-year period about the superiority of its premium gasoline. However, according to the plaintiffs, no scientific evidence supported Amoco's claims. The plaintiffs then argued that the advertisements created a higher demand for Amoco gas, creating artificially high gas prices that hurt consumers regardless of specific reliance on the advertisements. The court rejected this argument, ruling that a "market theory" of causation is not enough to establish damages in an individual case. Moreover, reliance on the advertisements is a crucial element in establishing liability. Case 45-1 provides a discussion of the questions involved in deciding whether a marketing claim is materially deceptive.

[3] 201 Ill. 2d 134 (2002).

CASE 45-1 GOTLIN v. LEDERMAN
U.S. COURT OF APPEALS FOR THE SECOND CIRCUIT
483 FED. APPX. 583 (2012)

Gary D. Gotlin, an administrator of the estate of a decedent, and the deceased's surviving spouse, Giuseppe Bono, alleged the misrepresentation of a particular form of cancer treatment, Fractionated Stereotactic Radiosurgery (FSR). The plaintiffs further asserted that this deceptive marketing led the decedent to "unnecessarily undergo an ineffective and harmful form of radiation therapy." According to the plaintiffs, the marketing of the cancer treatment, which included brochures, videos, advertisements, seminars, and Internet sites, made unrealistic claims as to the treatment's success rates. Specifically, the defendants made deceiving claims that the FSR treatment had success rates of greater than ninety percent in treating pancreatic cancer. The district court dismissed the plaintiffs' claims and the plaintiffs subsequently appealed.

JUDGE KATZMANN: The New York General Business Law declares as unlawful "[d]eceptive acts and practices in the conduct of any business, trade or commerce or in the furnishing of any service in this state. . . ." Deceptive acts or practices are "those likely to mislead a reasonable consumer acting reasonably under the circumstances." The General Business Law "declare[s] unlawful" all "[f]alse advertising in the conduct of any business, trade or commerce or in the furnishing of any service in [the] state." These provisions apply "to virtually all economic activity" that occurs in New York State, including the provision of medical services, in an effort to secure "an honest market place where trust, and not deception, prevails."

Plaintiffs contend that the defendants—in their brochures, videos, advertisements, seminars, and internet sites—deceptively marketed and advertised FSR treatment by making unrealistic claims as to its success rates. Specifically, plaintiffs contend that the defendants' claims that FSR treatment had "success rates" of greater than 90% in treating pancreatic cancer were materially deceptive. In this respect, the district court correctly concluded that defendants' marketing brochures are only evidence of "what representations the defendants made" and not "whether those representations were fraudulent or misleading," Accordingly, the court concluded that it was unable to assess the relative truthfulness of the scientific and medical claims appearing in defendants' brochures without at least some evidence, expert or otherwise, indicating that those claims were false or otherwise misleading. However, the district court did not address the fact that Drs. Louis B. Harrison and Paul R. Gliedman, plaintiffs' medical experts, did offer their opinion as to the misleading nature of at least one of defendants' representations. Specifically, in their expert report, Drs. Harrison and Gliedman, in discussing the case of another plaintiff, Piera Mattaini—who, like Mrs. Bono, was diagnosed with "unresectable pancreatic carcinoma"—state that: *In our opinion, the use of [FSR] therapy, in the manner used in this patient, was not the recognized standard of care for unresectable nonmetastatic pancreatic cancer in 2002. . . . We . . . note a letter in the chart . . . claiming that "local success rate" was 94%. This data quotation seems misleading, given the universally poor outcomes for this disease.*

This claim as to FSR therapy's 94% success rate in treating pancreatic cancer is materially identical to claims made in defendants' marketing brochures. Moreover, while the brochures at one point define "success" in a relatively circumscribed manner, including cases in which the cancer stopped growing or shrunk but did not disappear altogether, at other points the brochures suggest that FSR treatment will yield much broader successes than merely arresting the growth of cancer (describing "possibilities never dreamt before," "superb results," "great effectiveness," and "superior outcomes").

In addition, Drs. Harrison and Gliedman's expert report states several times that FSR therapy was unnecessary, either because it had no "curative potential" with regard to a particular patient's circumstances or because the patient in question "presented with incurable disease" generally. Accordingly, in the opinion of Drs. Harrison and Gliedman, those patients had been "subjected to widespread radiation therapy without any chance of benefit." By making such statements, Drs. Harrison and Gliedman impliedly impugn the accuracy of defendants' brochure's representations that FSR therapy had achieved "superb results" in instances in which "normal radiation has not been successful." Importantly, Drs. Harrison and Gliedman did not merely represent that FSR treatment had not proven effective for the particular patients in question, but that defendants marketed FSR treatment as having "a very high rate of success," for "so-called 'hopeless cases,'" to patients who, in fact, had incurable cancer.

Based on the foregoing, we conclude that the summary judgment record presents genuine issues of material fact as to (a) whether defendants' marketing of FSR treatment's "success rates" was materially deceptive to a reasonable consumer in violation of New York General Business Law, and (b) whether plaintiffs suffered any legally cognizable injuries as a result of defendants' allegedly misleading marketing of FSR treatment.

VACATED and REMANDED.

CRITICAL THINKING

What are the primary facts of this case? Is there any missing information you would call for to better enable you to evaluate the court's reasoning? What evidence does the court use to support its decision? Are you persuaded by this evidence?

ETHICAL DECISION MAKING

Do you think the company's advertising for the cancer treatment in this case was ethical given the facts of the case? Review the WPH process of ethical decision making in Chapter 2. What value did the court highlight in its decision?

CASE NUGGET

BAIT-AND-SWITCH ADVERTISING

Paula E. Rossman, Individually and for All Others Similarly Situated v. Fleet Bank (R.I.) National Association et al.
U.S. Court of Appeals for the Third Circuit
280 F.3d 384 (2002)

In 1999, Paula Rossman received a credit card offer from Fleet Bank, advertising the "Fleet Platinum MasterCard" with a low annual percentage rate and no annual fee. A few months after Rossman's account was opened, Fleet imposed an annual fee. Fleet sent a letter to Rossman stating that a $35 annual fee would be charged to her account annually on the anniversary of her account's opening; however, a second letter notified Rossman that the annual fee would be charged to her account within months. Rossman sued Fleet, claiming that Fleet had violated the disclosure requirements of the Truth in Lending Act (TILA) and engaged in a bait-and-switch advertising scheme. The district court dismissed Rossman's TILA claim for failing to state a claim on which relief could be granted. Rossman appealed to the Third Circuit Court of Appeals.

The appeals court applied a two-part test to determine whether Fleet's statement that the card had no annual fee was lawful. "First, it must have disclosed all of the information required by the statute. And second, it must have been true—i.e., an accurate representation of the legal obligations of the parties at that time—when the relevant solicitation was mailed." Rossman claimed that Fleet was required to disclose all fees that were currently imposed, as well as any fees that may be imposed later. Rossman also claimed that Fleet's disclosure was misleading by suggesting that there would never be an annual fee. Additionally, Rossman claimed that Fleet engaged in a bait-and-switch scheme, using the "no annual fee" provision to lure consumers into a contract when Fleet had no intention of honoring said provision.

Fleet argued that it was not required to disclose any future fees that may be imposed, but only those that currently existed. Fleet also turned to a clause in the solicitation disclosure insert that it "reserve[d] the right to change the benefit features associated with your Card at any time." The court found that Fleet's disclosure, as placed and worded, did not adequately link itself to the no-annual-fee provision. Thus, if the annual fee was permitted to be changed within the first annual term of the agreement, then the court found that the statement "no annual fee" was an inadequate disclosure.

Turning its attention to Rossman's claim that Fleet had engaged in a bait-and-switch advertising scheme, the court did not see Fleet's behavior as resembling the classic bait-and-switch design. Ordinarily, consumers are baited with certain terms, but the switch for less enticing products or terms is made before the consumer enters into an agreement or contract. Rather, the court found Fleet's behavior to be even more egregious because Fleet actually bound the consumer in a contract before making the switch to charge an annual fee. Thus, Fleet had violated the provisions of TILA. The appeals court reversed the district court's ruling and remanded for proceedings.

Future business managers need to understand what kinds of advertising claims are permissible in our legal environment. To simplify this understanding for consumers and business owners, the FTC has classified certain types of deceptive or unfair advertising practices and created specific rules defining and prohibiting violations of these rules. The next section will examine these classifications.

BUT WHAT IF . . .

WHAT IF THE FACTS OF THE CASE OPENER WERE DIFFERENT?

Let's say, in the Case Opener, that Trudeau had customers call him to order their products. However, when they called him, he told each one that although the weight-loss book was only $20, the customer had to buy at least two. What kind of marketing is that called, and is it legal?

BAIT-AND-SWITCH ADVERTISING

When sellers advertise a low price for an item generally unavailable to the consumer and then push the consumer to buy a more expensive item, they are engaging in **bait-and-switch advertising**. The low advertised price "baits" the consumer. Then the salesperson

E-COMMERCE AND THE LAW

DECEPTIVE ADS COULD LEAD TO COMPUTER CONSEQUENCES

Deceptive advertising in the physical world usually causes consumers to waste money on a worthless product or one that does not function as advertised. On the Internet, deceptive advertising can be much more dangerous to the individual. A very popular form of online deceptive advertising is known as *bait-and-click advertising.* In bait-and-click advertising, websites attract users by having them click on ads that appear to be from well-known brands. These sites can then potentially install spyware or viruses on the individual's computer without his or her knowledge. A spyware program can access the individual's passwords or data and send them to outside sources. This could result in financial ruin for the individual if the spyware source gets bank passwords or Social Security numbers. Therefore, it's important that Internet users realize that some advertisers are attempting to deceive them online as well as in everyday life and that individuals should be cautious when clicking on advertisements on the web.

Source: www.computerworld.com/s/article/9111682/E_commerce_leaders_move_to_fight_deceptive_online_ads.

"switches" the consumer to a higher-priced item. In 1968 the FTC prohibited bait-and-switch advertising.

According to the FTC's "Guides against Bait Advertising," a seller can engage in bait-and-switch advertising in several ways. For instance, the seller might advertise a low price but have too little of the advertised good in stock or might discourage employees from selling the advertised item. These bait-and-switch advertising techniques violate FTC rules.

FTC ACTIONS AGAINST DECEPTIVE ADVERTISING

If the FTC takes action against a company and proves the advertising is deceptive, the FTC may issue a cease-and-desist order. To go a step beyond cease-and-desist orders, the FTC may also issue **multiple-product orders.** A multiple-product order is a form of cease-and-desist order issued by the FTC that applies not only to the product that was the subject of the action but also to other products produced by the same firm. Alternatively, the FTC may require that the company engage in **corrective advertising** (or *counteradvertising*), running advertisements in which the company explicitly states that the formerly advertised claims were untrue.

To see how the FTC is attempting to avoid a type of market failure, please see the **Connecting to the Core** activity on the text website at www.mhhe.com/kubasek3e.

The rationale for corrective advertising is that consumers who saw the previous ads will see the new ads; the new ads will then correct the deceptive advertising. In a commission decision regarding the deceptive advertising of Doan's Pills, Commissioner Sheila Anthony described the characteristics of a situation requiring corrective advertising:

> Requiring the dissemination of a truthful message to counteract beliefs created or reinforced by a respondent's deceptive message is an appropriate method of restoring the status quo ante and denying a respondent the ability to continue to profit from its deception. . . . Corrective advertising is an appropriate remedy if (1) the challenged ads have substantially created or reinforced a misbelief; and (2) the misbelief is likely to linger into the future.

However, some companies—and even one of the commissioners of the FTC—argued that corrective advertising is a form of compelled speech and thus violates the First Amendment right to engage in free speech.

TELEMARKETING AND ELECTRONIC ADVERTISING

Consumer law, like all law, is dynamic, and technology is often a driving force of change in consumer law. Although technological developments provide consumers with a host of benefits, these developments are often prone to abuses not covered by existing consumer law. For example, telephones and fax machines facilitate fast and inexpensive communication around the world, but telemarketers can use these technologies to deceive consumers and invade their privacy. Hence, lawmakers have passed new laws to address these issues.

E-COMMERCE AND THE LAW

CONSUMERS ON THE NET

Every year, e-commerce becomes more and more popular. In 2006, 52 million individuals shopped online, and this was up from 35 million in 2005. These consumers are likely to encounter some type of problem through e-commerce. Perhaps they will respond to an unsolicited e-mail claiming that the consumer can quickly earn money. Or perhaps they will win their bid on an item through an Internet auction but will never receive the product.

Consumers can be defrauded on the Internet in numerous ways. The anonymity associated with Internet use makes it easier for sellers to engage in deceptive business practices.

Source: Cap, Gemini, Ernst, & Young, "Global Online Retailing" (report), www.capgemini.de/sews/studien/retaking.html; and FTC, "Unsolicited Commercial E-Mail," statement before the Subcommittee on Telecommunications, Trade, and Consumer Protection of the Committee on Commerce, U.S. House of Representatives, November 3, 1999.

Two major acts regulate advertising by telephone and fax, the Telephone Consumer Protection Act (TCPA) of 1991 and the Telemarketing and Consumer Fraud and Abuse Prevention Act of 1994.[4] TCPA, which the Federal Communications Commission agency enforces, forbids phone solicitation using an automatic telephone dialing system or a prerecorded voice. TCPA also makes it illegal to transmit advertisements via fax unless the recipient agrees to the fax transmission. TCPA allows for consumers to obtain a private right to legal action. In other words, the act gives consumers the right to recover for their losses. If a telemarketer violates TCPA, the consumer can recover either monetary losses or $500 per violation. However, if the telemarketer willfully violated the act, the court can decide to triple the amount owed to the consumer.

Sometimes laws are ineffective in achieving their goals, however, so legislatures draft new laws to supplement existing law. Thus, even though the goals of consumer laws may not change, specific rules and provisions do. For example, despite the protection of TCPA, consumers still lost an estimated $40 billion in telemarketing fraud after the act went into effect.

To give consumers more protection against deceptive and abusive telemarketing practices, Congress enacted the Telemarketing and Consumer Fraud and Abuse Prevention Act of 1994.[5] Through this act Congress asked the FTC to define "deceptive and abusive" telemarketing practices and required that the FTC create and enforce rules governing telemarketing that would prohibit such practices. Consequently, the FTC created the Telemarketing Sales Rule of 1995,[6] which requires that telemarketers (1) identify the call as a sales call; (2) identify the product name and seller; (3) tell the total cost of goods being sold; (4) notify the listener or reader of whether the sale is nonrefundable; and (5) remove the consumer's name from the potential contact list if the consumer so requests.

While reviewing and amending the Telemarketing Sales Rule in 2002, the FTC created the "Do Not Call" registry. The FTC states that the purpose of the Do Not Call registry is to give consumers a choice regarding telemarketing calls. The registry makes it illegal for telemarketers to call any number that has been registered for more than 31 days. The registration lasts for five years, and can be completed online through the FTC's website. Both the FTC and the Federal Communications Commission (FCC) are responsible for maintaining the list, with help from local state law enforcement officials.

Spam is a major problem for consumers because it comprises around 90 percent of all e-mails. Over the latter portion of 2007 and the majority of 2008, the spam organization Herbalking was responsible for sending consumers billions of messages over the Internet. At one time, Herbalking was behind one-third of all Internet spam. To send such a substantial amount of e-mails, Herbalking used software that infected computers, usually without the knowledge of the owners. In fact, estimates indicate that the Herbalking spam group

[4] 47 U.S.C. § 227.

[5] 15 U.S.C. §§ 6101–6108.

[6] 16 C.F.R. § 310.

COMPARING THE LAW OF OTHER COUNTRIES

ADVERTISING LAW IN CHINA

For many years, advertising in China has been regulated by the People's Republic of China Advertising Law. However, in 2009 China's State Administration for Industry and Commerce (SAIC), the regulatory authority for advertising and marketing, released a "Draft Revised Law" for advertising regulation. This Draft Revised Law issued by the government would include heavier restrictions on permissible advertising in China.

For example, under the Draft Revised Law of China, false advertising is defined as:

1) "material inconsistencies between the representations made in the advertisement and actual fact;"
2) "concealing key information or providing misleading information" about the product being advertised;
3) "false statements concerning the prizes or awards that may be obtained upon purchasing a product or service;" and
4) "fabricating the experience of other participants with the products."

While the Draft Revised Law mirrors legislation in the United States that regulates deceptive advertising, one major difference between the two countries is that neither the Chinese Draft Revised Law nor the original People's Republic of China Advertising Law make mention of the *type of person* that a misleading or deceptive advertisement would affect. For example, as you learned earlier in this chapter, in the United States, advertisements cannot contain a material misrepresentation or omission that is likely to mislead a *reasonable consumer.* The Draft Revised Law does not contain any such specifications.

More than 50 million consumers now shop online each year.

used as many as 35,000 computers, a network capable of sending 10 billion e-mails a day. The spam group actually pulled in $400,000 from Visa charges during one month, and the group had ties to five countries. Such facts make this spam operation perhaps the most extensive spam setup the FTC has ever come across.

The Can-Spam Act of 2003 states that spammers may not send e-mail messages containing false information or provide consumers with no option concerning whether they receive messages in the future. In October 2008, the Federal Trade Commission successfully convinced a Chicago court to freeze the assets and shut down the extensive Herbalking spam network for violating the act.

TOBACCO ADVERTISING

The tobacco industry's advertising is regulated through two acts: the Public Health Cigarette Smoking Act[7] of 1970 and the Smokeless Tobacco Health Education Act[8] of 1986. The Public Health Cigarette Smoking Act prohibits radio and television cigarette advertisements, and the Smokeless Tobacco Act imposes the same restrictions for smokeless tobacco ads.

Labeling and Packaging Laws

LO3

What is the purpose of labeling and packaging laws?

When consumers examine a product to decide whether to buy it, the label often influences the decision to purchase. For example, many of us have purchased food because the label said the food was "low fat." Unfortunately, manufacturers can include or omit information on labels and thus mislead consumers.

[7] 15 U.S.C. § 1331.

[8] 15 U.S.C. §§ 4401–4408.

Exhibit 45-3

"Made in the USA" Labels and the FTC

Many companies boast that their products are "Made in the USA." But what exactly does it mean to be "Made in the USA"? The FTC is charged with setting forth standards to avoid deception and false advertising about products that are supposedly made in the USA.

In the past, the FTC stated that "Made in the USA" should not be used "unless all, or virtually all, of the components and labor are of U.S. origin." Thus, if a company assembled a product in the United States but shipped in some components from out of the country, the FTC would argue that "Made in the USA" should not be used.

The FTC's definition of the phrase was stricter than others' definitions. For example, NAFTA defines "Made in the USA" as a product for which at least 55 percent of the labor and components are from Canada, Mexico, or the United States. Customs draws the line at 50 percent.

In 1997, the FTC decided to continue enforcing the "all or virtually all" standard. Those with strong union ties had argued against any weaker definition, such as the 75 percent the FTC had been debating.

Source: Federal Trade Commission, FTC Consumer Report, "Complying with the Made in the USA Standard," www.ftc.gov/bcp/conline/pubs/buspubs/madeusa.shtm.

Consequently, federal and state governments have passed laws that regulate product labeling. These laws generally require that the manufacturer provide accurate, understandable information on the label. Furthermore, if the product is potentially harmful, the manufacturer must make the consumer aware of this harm.

Several federal laws regulate product labeling. The Wool Products Labeling Act of 1939[9] requires accurate labeling of wool products. Similarly, the Fur Products Labeling Act of 1951[10] requires the accurate labeling of fur products. The Flammable Fabrics Act of 1953[11] made it illegal to produce or distribute clothing "so highly flammable as to be dangerous when worn." The Fair Packaging and Labeling Act of 1966[12] requires that products carry labels that identify the product and provide specific information about the contents, such as the quantity of the contents and the size of a serving if the number of servings is stated. Moreover, under this act, food product labels must show the nutritional content of the product. Similarly, the Nutrition Labeling and Education Act of 1990[13] requires that standard nutrition information (i.e., calories and fat) be provided on food labels. Additionally, this act defines the words *fresh* and *low fat*. In 1994 the FTC issued a statement saying it would apply these label restrictions to food advertising to prevent deceptive advertising. Thus, not only do sellers need to be concerned about the use of *high, low,* and *light* on labels, but they are also required to use these words in particular ways in advertisements.

As Exhibit 45-3 points out, many have argued that "Made in the USA" labels are deceptive advertising.

Sales

LO4

What are the different methods of sales?

The FTC and other government agencies have the power to regulate sales. For example, the Federal Reserve Board of Governors has the power to govern credit provisions related to sales contracts through its Regulation Z.[14] The FTC has created rules that govern specific types of sales settings in which the consumer is in a more vulnerable position compared

[9] 15 U.S.C. §§ 1331–1341.

[10] 15 U.S.C. § 69.

[11] 15 U.S.C. § 1191.

[12] 15 U.S.C. §§ 1451 et seq.

[13] 21 U.S.C. § 343-1.

[14] 12 C.F.R. § 226.

COMPARING THE LAW OF OTHER COUNTRIES

RESPECTING LANGUAGES OF THE CONSUMER

U.S. consumers often purchase products that are labeled or give directions in various languages, such as Spanish and French. The United States does not require that other publications, such as billboards, restaurant menus, or television advertisements, be multilingual. However, such requirements do exist in France and Canada.

During the early 1970s, French consumers voiced concern about foreign imports. Most of those products were labeled in languages other than French, so it was difficult for consumers to read directions or determine the content and function of a product. The government responded by passing a law in 1975 that regulated the labels and advertising of imported goods. The law mandated that French and English had to be the languages used for product labels, instructions, and all forms of advertising.

Canada passed a similar decree concerning the use of the French language. The Consumer Packaging and Labeling Act of Canada requires that all goods be labeled in both French and English.

While France and Canada were legislating the inclusion of both languages, Quebec legislated the exclusion of English. The Charter of the French Language, drafted by the Quebec government, requires that all public signs and advertisements be solely in French. If a product is produced and sold in Quebec, its packaging and product instructions are also to be in French alone.

The goal of these laws is to provide consumers with specific information about product content. However, Congress has passed several laws that require information about the potential harms associated with a product. For example, the Federal Hazardous Substances Act of 1960 requires that all items containing dangerous substances carry warning labels.

Canada's cigarette labeling requirements are even more stringent than the U.S. requirements. In Canada, approximately 40 percent of cigarette packaging must be devoted to health warnings.* The Canadian Bureau of Tobacco Control, however, has proposed a new rule requiring that manufacturers dedicate 50 percent of cigarette packages to such warnings, which would include explicit pictures and images of mouth cancer or other severe diseases caused by cigarette use.†

* Tobacco Products Control Regulations, SOR/89-21.

† Action on Smoking and Health, "Majority of Canadians Want Larger Warnings on Cigarette Packages" (press release), October 2000.

to a consumer who walks into a traditional retail setting. This section examines FTC regulation of three of these uncommonly vulnerable commercial settings: door-to-door, telephone, and mail-order sales.

DOOR-TO-DOOR SALES

Imagine that you hear a knock at your door, open it, and discover a salesperson for an Internet provider. The person who knocked knows that you have just purchased a computer and are interested in learning about the Internet. The salesperson explains the price of various programs that will enable you to become familiar with the Internet. You listen but decide that you would like to get additional information from an alternative provider. However, the salesperson is extremely pushy; to get the salesperson out of your house, you decide to purchase one of his programs.

In most door-to-door sales, the consumer does not have a chance to compare products and services to find the best service for his or her money. In addition, many consumers find it difficult to escape the salesperson in their home. It is much easier to walk out of a store. Because the consumer is in a particularly vulnerable position in a door-to-door sale, the FTC has created special rules for such sales.

The FTC created the Cooling-Off Rule, giving consumers three days to cancel purchases they make from salespeople who come to their homes. Moreover, the salesperson must notify the consumer, both verbally and in writing, that the sales transaction may be canceled. The FTC rule also requires that the consumer be notified in writing in the same language in which the oral negotiations were conducted, so as to avoid unscrupulous businesses from taking advantage of non-English speakers.

The following case provides an example of the kinds of pressures that the FTC is trying to offset: Consolidated Promotions offered consumers a free gift for setting up a meeting in their home to discuss Consolidated products. This in-home meeting was in fact a sales pitch for Consolidated's photography packages, which included film and discounted photo processing.

These packages cost from $1,200 to $2,500. When Consolidated Promotions refused to cancel some of the consumers' contracts, the FTC approved a complaint and referred it to the Department of Justice. The FTC alleged that the company violated the Cooling-Off Rule by "1) failing to honor valid cancellation notices; 2) misrepresenting consumers' rights to cancel their contracts; and 3) failing to inform each buyer orally of his or her right to cancel their order."[15] The FTC proposed that Consolidated Promotions enter into a consent decree whereby Consolidated would be required to send notice to all customers who bought a photography package after July 1, 1996, giving them an opportunity to cancel their contracts.

Legal Principle: **Because consumers are particularly vulnerable during a door-to-door sale, the government provides the Cooling-Off Rule, whereby consumers have three days to cancel a purchase made during a door-to-door sale.**

TELEPHONE AND MAIL-ORDER SALES

Most consumers have purchased at least one item from a catalog. Unfortunately, telephone and mail-order purchases trigger more complaints than do traditional retail or door-to-door sales. Suppose the office manager of a small accounting firm ordered five new chairs for the office through a catalog. The writing in the catalog indicated that the chairs would arrive within two weeks. The office manager called in the chair order, but six weeks later he had heard nothing from the company. What rights does he have in this situation?

The FTC originally addressed problems with mail-order sales through the 1975 Mail-Order Rule.[16] The Mail or Telephone Order Merchandise Rule of 1993 amended the 1975 Mail-Order Rule to extend protections to consumers who purchase goods over phone lines, including through computers and fax machines.

The rule established three key guidelines. First, sellers must ship items within the time promised. If they do not specify a time, the seller is limited to 30 days from receipt of the order. Second, if the seller cannot ship the item within the promised time, the seller must notify the customer in writing and offer an opportunity to cancel. Third, if a customer decides to cancel the order, the seller must refund the customer's money within a specified period of time.

Unsolicited Merchandise. When a consumer goes to her mailbox only to discover that a company has sent her a book, must she pay for the book? Anyone who receives unsolicited merchandise may treat the item as a gift. She may keep or dispose of it without any obligation to the sender. In accordance with the Postal Reorganization Act of 1970,[17] any unsolicited merchandise sent by mail is free to be used by the recipient as he or she sees fit with no obligation by the recipient to the sender.

BUT WHAT IF . . .

WHAT IF THE FACTS OF THE CASE OPENER WERE DIFFERENT?

Let's say, in the Case Opener, that customers call Trudeau with questions about his weight-loss plan and he tells them he will send them information. He then mails the callers his weight-loss book and charges them for it. What kind of sales practice is this called? Is it legal?

[15] Federal Trade Commission, "FTC Settlement Protects Door-to-Door Sales Consumers" (press release), May 2, 2000.

[16] 16 C.F.R. §§ 435.1–435.2.

[17] 16 C.F.R. § 256.

FTC REGULATION OF SALES IN SPECIFIC INDUSTRIES

In certain industries, sellers have extensive opportunities to take advantage of customers. Thus, the FTC—and in some cases, Congress—creates special rules for certain sales practices specific to certain industries.

Used-Car Sales. Consumers who purchase a used car often have very little information about the car's history. For instance, they do not know whether the car has been in an accident or whether there are any serious problems that are just not visible.

To protect used-car buyers, Congress passed the Odometer Act of 1973, which protects against odometer fraud in used-car sales. The FTC extended its protection through the 1984 Used Motor Vehicle Registration Rule.[18] Under this rule, a dealer must attach a buyer's guide label to any used car he or she is attempting to sell. The label must state that the car is being sold "as is." This label is a warning to the customer that the seller is not guaranteeing anything at all about the performance of the car. Furthermore, the label must include a suggestion that the buyer obtain an inspection for the used car before any decision to purchase.

Consumer protections against fraud in used-car sales vary widely from state to state. During the 1960s and 1970s there was widespread pressure to reform our legislative system to protect consumers from fraud; many states responded more favorably to that pressure than did others. All states enacted the Uniform Commercial Code (UCC), but in each case the UCC was enacted with significant variations. The difference between states was also heightened in that each state had unique, nonuniform consumer protection statutes. Consequently, the consumer protection laws against used-car fraud (also known as "lemon laws") vary from state to state. Some states provide minimum protection, while others states, such as Minnesota, presume that one unsuccessful effort to repair a used car demonstrates nonrepairability. Minnesota's laws also extend statutory protection to potential buyers of returned vehicles by banning resale of automobiles returned because of major safety defects.[19]

Funeral Home Services. Consumers who must purchase goods and services for a funeral and burial are often vulnerable for several reasons. The consumer is usually preoccupied with his or her loss of a relative or friend and is unlikely to "comparison shop." Additionally, grieving consumers can be more readily persuaded to purchase unnecessary, expensive items for this last tribute to their loved ones. To prevent funeral homes from taking advantage of these customers, the FTC created the 1984 Funeral Rule and revised it in 1994. The rule requires that those who operate funeral homes provide customers itemized price information about funeral goods and services. Furthermore, funeral homes may not misrepresent legal or cemetery requirements or require that the customer buy certain funeral goods and services as a condition for receiving other funeral goods and services.

Real Estate Sales. Because real estate purchases are probably one of the largest purchases a consumer will make, Congress passed several acts requiring that sellers disclose certain information about the property. First, the Interstate Land Sales Full Disclosure Act,[20] passed in 1968, requires disclosure of information to consumers so that they can make informed decisions about real estate purchases. Under this act, anyone planning to sell or lease 100 or more lots of unimproved land through a common promotional plan must file an initial statement of record with the Department of Housing and Urban Development's (HUD's) Office of Interstate Land Sales Registration. Before the developer can offer land for sale, HUD must approve the initial statement.

[18] 16 C.F.R. §§ 455.1–455.5.

[19] David A. Rice, "Product Quality Laws and the Economics of Federalism," *Boston University Law Review* 65 (1985), p. 1.

[20] 15 U.S.C. §§ 1701–1720.

Congress provided more protection for home buyers in the Real Estate Settlement Procedures Act of 1974[21] and its 1976 amendments. This act requires the disclosure of information regarding mortgage loans to the buyer. For example, the lender must give the buyer an estimate of costs for finalizing the real estate purchase.

Online Sales. With the ever-expanding reach of the Internet, there has been an increase in business-to-consumer (B2C) sales transactions. Anyone with an Internet connection can make purchases from his or her favorite stores, from Barnes & Noble to Macy's. Most existing consumer protection laws were developed to protect consumers in their interactions with businesses face-to-face. Hence, protecting consumers online requires new approaches. Although not a specific industry, the Internet facilitates such a huge volume of commerce that additional focused protective legislation is needed.

Despite the difficulty of prosecuting online fraud, the FTC has brought a number of enforcement actions against online businesses. The federal statutes already in existence prohibiting wire fraud apply to online transactions. In addition, several states have begun to amend statutes to explicitly protect online consumers.

Legal Principle: **Certain industries can more easily take advantage of consumers than can other industries. Thus, some industries are subject to stricter advertising and labeling regulation so that consumers are protected.**

Credit Protection

The widespread use of credit to purchase goods and services means that consumer credit protection has become increasingly important. This section explores three key federal laws regulating the credit industry to protect consumers: the Truth in Lending Act, the Fair Credit Reporting Act, and the Fair Debt Collection Practices Act.

L05 What are the different acts that provide credit protection?

THE TRUTH IN LENDING ACT

One of the earliest, most significant statutes regulating credit is Title I of the Consumer Credit Protection Act (CCPA), referred to as the *Truth in Lending Act (TILA)*.[22] The purpose of the act is to require that sellers disclose the terms of the credit or loan to help consumers compare a variety of credit lines or loans. More important, consumers must be able to understand this disclosure of terms. TILA is administered, in part, by the Federal Reserve Board through the previously mentioned Regulation Z.

Suppose your business extends credit to customers. Are your credit lines through your business subject to TILA? First, TILA applies to consumer loans only. Second, TILA applies to those who lend money or arrange for credit through the ordinary course of business. Third, the credit or loan must be in the amount of $25,000 or less, unless the loan is secured by a mortgage on real estate. Fourth, the creditor must be making the loan to a natural person, not a legal entity. Fifth, the credit or loan must be subject to a finance charge or must have repayments of more than four installments.

All creditors subject to TILA must disclose the finance charge and the annual percentage rate of the credit or loan. This information must be disclosed in a meaningful way, a requirement that prevents creditors from burying the information in a large paragraph unrelated to the credit terms.

Consider the following example: In May 1999 a jury heard *Carlisle v. Whirlpool Financial National Bank*.[23] According to the case facts, Gulf Coast Electric's salespeople traveled

[21] 12 U.S.C. §§ 2601–2617.

[22] 15 U.S.C. §§ 1601–1693r.

[23] No. 97-068 (Cir. Ct., Hale Co., Ala).

door-to-door selling satellite dishes through financing. The price of the satellite dish was $1,100. However, consumers could purchase this dish for approximately $200 in stores. The consumers argued that the salespeople hid the number of payments the buyers would have to pay, thereby violating TILA. The jury found in favor of the customers and awarded them $581 million.

Types of Loans under TILA. TILA includes three categories of loans: open-end credit, closed-end credit, and credit card applications and solicitations. Each category has specific disclosure requirements. For example, an *open-end credit line* permits repeated transactions and assesses a finance charge on unpaid balances. A creditor of an open-end credit line is required to disclose information in periodic statements. In contrast, a *closed-end credit line* is one for a loan given for a specific amount of time. The creditor of a closed-end credit line must disclose the total amount financed and the number, amount, and due dates of payments. Finally, credit card applications and solicitations must include the APR, annual fees, and the grace period for paying without a finance charge.

Unauthorized Charges and Disputes. TILA establishes certain consumer protection rules regarding unauthorized charges to credit cards. If your credit card is stolen and someone makes unauthorized purchases on your account, your liability for those charges cannot exceed $50 per card if prompt notification of the theft is made to the credit card company. If you notify the credit card company before unauthorized charges are made, you cannot be held liable for any of the charges. Similarly, if a credit card company sends you an unsolicited card in the mail and the card is stolen, you cannot be held liable for any of the charges.

TILA offers another protection to consumers who unknowingly purchase damaged goods using a credit card. If three requirements are met, the consumer will not be obligated to pay for the good. First, the consumer must purchase the item near her home (i.e., the business is in the same state as the consumer's home or within 100 miles of the home). Second, the item must cost more than $50. Third, the consumer must make a good-faith effort to resolve the dispute, such as asking the store for a refund. If these requirements are met, the credit card company cannot bill the consumer for the damaged item.

Consumer Leasing Act. In 1988 the Consumer Leasing Act (CLA)[24] amended TILA to provide greater protection for people leasing automobiles and other goods. CLA applies to those who lease goods as part of their regular business. For CLA to apply, the lease must be for a minimum of four months and the price must not exceed $25,000. Under CLA, and its controlling regulation, Regulation M,[25] anyone leasing goods must disclose up front, in writing, all the material terms and conditions of the lease.

Equal Credit Opportunity Act. In the 1970s, a woman old enough to have children would have had difficulty securing credit because creditors believed that married women with children would be less likely to pay their debts. In response to this discrimination, Congress passed the Equal Credit Opportunity Act (ECOA)[26] as a 1974 amendment to TILA. This amendment makes it illegal for creditors to deny credit to individuals on the basis of race, religion, national origin, color, sex, marital status, or age. When determining the creditworthiness of a credit applicant, the creditor cannot use information about the applicant's marital status, nor can the creditor require that a spouse cosign the application. Finally, the act prohibits creditors from denying credit on the basis of whether the applicant receives public assistance benefits.

[24] 15 U.S.C. §§ 1667–1667e.

[25] 12 C.F.R. Part 213.

[26] 15 U.S.C. § 1691–1691f.

THE FAIR CREDIT REPORTING ACT

If you own a credit card, you also have a credit report. If you apply for a new credit card or a loan, the creditor will check your credit history to make a judgment about your creditworthiness by examining a copy of your credit report. This report contains information about your financial transactions, such as payments on credit, debt collection, and other financial information the creditor needs to know about if entering a business transaction with you.

Because credit bureaus influence consumers' ability to make purchases and secure loans, Congress passed the Fair Credit Reporting Act (FCRA)[27] of 1970 to ensure accurate credit reporting. FCRA regulates the issuance of credit reports for limited business purposes, such as a determination of credit or insurance eligibility, employment, and licensing. If a credit bureau issues a consumer credit report for a reason not specified by FCRA, it may be held liable for damages and additional fines. Furthermore, anyone who uses a credit report for purposes other than those specified in the act may be held liable for damages.

THE FAIR DEBT COLLECTION PRACTICES ACT

Suppose a consumer owes $3,000 on his credit card and has not been able to make monthly payments for the past six months. The credit card company will likely refer the case to a collection agency, which will notify the consumer in an attempt to get him to pay the debt. The collection agency then may start calling the consumer regularly to discuss the debt. Next, the agency might start contacting the consumer's acquaintances, telling them about the debt in an effort to pressure the consumer into paying the debt.

This type of debt-collecting behavior is prohibited by the Fair Debt Collection Practices Act (FDCPA).[28] This act applies only to debt collectors who regularly attempt to collect debts on behalf of others. The following collection behaviors are expressly prohibited by FDCPA:

1. Contacting a debtor at work if the debtor's employer objects.
2. Contacting a debtor who has notified the collection agency that he or she wants no contact with the agency.
3. Contacting the debtor before 8 a.m. or after 9 p.m.
4. Contacting third parties about the debt (exceptions: contacting the debtor's parents, spouse, or financial adviser).
5. Using obscene or threatening language when communicating with the debtor.
6. Misrepresenting the collection agency as a lawyer or a police officer.

BUT WHAT IF . . .

WHAT IF THE FACTS OF THE CASE OPENER WERE DIFFERENT?

Let's say, in the Case Opener, that some of Trudeau's customers were on payment plans. One of them fell behind in her payments, and he sent her account to a collection agency. The agency called the debtor every day at 7:30 a.m. Is this legal? What are three potential behaviors of debt collectors that are prohibited by FDCPA?

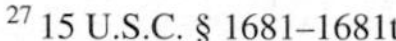

[27] 15 U.S.C. § 1681–1681t.

[28] 15 U.S.C. § 1692.

CASE NUGGET

EQUAL CREDIT OPPORTUNITY ACT

Alvin Ricciardi, Appellant, v. Ameriquest Mortgage Company
U.S. Court of Appeals for the Third Circuit
164 Fed. Appx. 221 (2006)

Alvin Ricciardi bought a home in May 2001, took out a home equity loan, and then applied for a loan to refinance the two mortgages through Ameriquest. Ricciardi closed the loan in September 2002, at which point he received the "Borrower's Acknowledgment of Final Loan Terms." The acknowledgment stated the terms of the loan that Ricciardi had originally requested, as well as the final terms of the loan. Ricciardi signed all the documents presented during the closing. Eight months later, Ricciardi filed suit against Ameriquest for violating the Equal Credit Opportunity Act, the Truth in Lending Act, and the Pennsylvania Unfair Trade Practices Act and Consumer Protection Law. The district court granted summary judgment regarding Ricciardi's ECOA claim, finding for Ameriquest. At a later nonjury trial, the court ruled in favor of Ameriquest on all counts of Ricciardi's claim as well as Ameriquest's counterclaim. Ricciardi appealed.

Ricciardi's appeal put forth three arguments. First, Ricciardi argued that the district court erred in granting summary judgment in favor of Ameriquest on his ECOA claim because Ameriquest failed to provide notice of its counteroffer before the closing of the loan. Second, Ricciardi argued that the district court erred in its adverse credibility finding. Third, Ricciardi argued that Ameriquest violated TILA by overcharging him for insurance and thereby gave him the right to rescind the loan. The appeals court rejected each of Ricciardi's arguments, affirming the ruling of the district court.

The appeals court addressed each of Ricciardi's arguments in turn. First, TILA requires that a creditor respond to an applicant within 30 days of receipt of a completed loan application. Ameriquest did respond to Ricciardi within 30 days. Contrary to Ricciardi's claim, Ameriquest was not required to respond in the form of a counteroffer. Additionally, there is no requirement that a counteroffer be received before the closing of the loan. Thus, Ricciardi's argument was without merit. Second, the appeals court found that the district court had not erred in its adverse credibility finding. Ricciardi contradicted himself numerous times on the record, in addition to committing fraud by misrepresenting his occupation and income on the loan application to Ameriquest. Third, the appeals court found that Ricciardi had not presented sufficient evidence to substantiate his claim that Ameriquest had overcharged him for insurance. In Pennsylvania, state-mandated insurance rates are published in the *Rate Manual.* The rates decrease if the property is being refinanced and was previously insured. Ricciardi failed to show that the property was previously insured; thus, the district court correctly found that there was no evidence that Ameriquest had overcharged Ricciardi.

The act states that its restrictions apply to "debt collectors." Case 45-2 considers whether individuals who write bad checks are consumer debtors or criminals.

CASE 45-2 FEDERAL TRADE COMMISSION v. CHECK INVESTORS, INC., ET AL.

U.S. DISTRICT COURT FOR THE DISTRICT OF NEW JERSEY
502 F.3D 159, 165 (3D CIR. 2007)

The Federal Trade Commission filed a complaint against National Check Control and Check Investors, Inc., in 2003. The complaint stated that the company had engaged in illegal tactics to collect debt from consumers. Such tactics included telling consumers they would be arrested and prosecuted in an effort to collect bad check charges along with other excessive and unlawful fees.

The debt collecting behavior of National Check Control violates the Fair Debt Collection Practices Act (FDCPA). Specifically, section 5 of the act stipulates that a collector may not use obscene or threatening language when communicating with the debtor.

The defense attorney stressed that the defendants were not pursuing bad debt. He further argued that the company was seeking compensation for bad checks that consumers intentionally ignored for over two years, and stated that such an act is a crime. In fact, he said that in certain states if a consumer is continuously notified of a bad check and does not make good on it in a fixed amount of time, the consumer will face criminal charges.

JUDGE BISSELL: Defendants rely on the proposition that the check writers are analogous to counterfeiters or shoplifters who, because they commit theft, are not consumers. In its Complaint, plaintiff alleges that the check writers who NCC contacts are consumers under the FDCPA and the FTCA. The FDCPA defines "consumer" as "any natural person obligated or allegedly obligated to pay any debt." The FTCA does not specifically define "consumer." While case law has made clear that persons who steal or commit fraud to attain goods or services are not consumers, there is simply no evidence before the Court that all the check writers from whom NCC collects payments purposely wrote checks on accounts with insufficient funds or on closed accounts with the intent to steal the merchandise or services they received.

Defendants, however, cannot simply assume that every check writer from whom they seek to collect a debt intended to commit a crime or is similar to persons found liable for shoplifting or cable piracy. When a person shoplifts or steals cable services, the debt incurred by such person can clearly only be attributed to a criminal act. Check writers, however, may not even know that they had insufficient funds in their accounts at the time of the consumer transaction. Thus, the debts incurred by the check writers may or may not be attributable to criminal acts. Furthermore, whether the check writers engaged in criminal conduct is not a determination for defendants to make. NCC may only attempt to collect payments on checks purchased at a discount. NCC's officers, agents and employees have no authority to determine whether the check writers are criminal and then employ law enforcement tactics to collect the payments.

AFFIRMED.

CRITICAL THINKING

What ambiguity is central to this case? Do you agree with the way the court interpreted the ambiguous word or phrase? Can you think of an alternative reasonable definition?

ETHICAL DECISION MAKING

Who are the primary stakeholders affected by the court's ruling? Does the appeals court have a stronger ethical obligation to protect the interests of some stakeholders over others? Explain.

Case 45-2 illustrates only one example of an FDCPA violation. If a debt collector violates FDCPA, the collector is liable for actual damages, attorney fees, and other fines up to $1,000. In Case 45-2, the court ordered that the defendants pay $10.2 million in restitution. The judgment was the largest that the FTC ever won for a violation of national debt collection laws.

THE CREDIT CARD FRAUD ACT

Credit card fraud is a serious problem in the United States, costing consumers millions of dollars per year. Accordingly, Congress passed the Credit Card Fraud Act of 1984[29] to close existing loopholes in federal laws that allowed credit card fraud to be pervasive. The Credit Card Fraud Act states that it is unlawful to (1) possess an unauthorized credit card; (2) counterfeit or alter a credit card; (3) use account numbers of another's credit card to perpetuate fraud; or (4) use a credit card obtained from a third party with his or her consent, if the third party conspires to report the card as stolen. The act also increases the penalty for committing credit card fraud.

THE FAIR CREDIT BILLING ACT

Did your credit card company fail to extend your credit when it informed you that your credit would be extended? Were you ever charged for merchandise you did not purchase or receive? Were you ever charged twice for one purchase? If so, you have been the victim of a credit billing error. The Fair Credit Billing Act (FCBA) of 1986[30] was created to handle such billing errors as those previously listed, as well as many others.

[29] 18 U.S.C. § 1029(a)(1–4).

[30] 15 U.S.C. § 1601.

FCBA, enforced by the FTC, creates procedures consumers are to follow in filing complaints when billing errors occur. FCBA also requires that creditors explain to the consumer and FTC why the error occurred and promptly fix any billing errors. When a complaint is filed, the creditor may not try to collect on the disputed amount, or take any action against the consumer, until the complaint is answered.

THE FAIR AND ACCURATE CREDIT TRANSACTIONS ACT

The Fair and Accurate Credit Transactions Act (FACTA) of 2003[31] was passed in response to the growing number of identity theft cases. If someone thinks she is a victim of identity theft, she may contact the FTC and an alert will be placed in her credit files. The credit files then serve as a national fraud alert system to better enable authorities to catch those who are stealing identities.

Several other requirements created by the act protect consumers. First, major credit reporting agencies are now required to provide consumers with a free copy of their credit reports every 12 months. Second, receipts from credit card purchases are now to list an abbreviated version of the card number to protect consumer accounts. Third, financial institutions must work with the FTC to "red-flag" suspicious transactions that might be a sign of identity theft. Fourth, assistance will be provided to victims of identity theft to help them rebuild their credit. Fifth, victims of identity theft may report fraud directly to creditors to protect their credit ratings.

THE CREDIT CARDHOLDERS' BILL OF RIGHTS ACT

Under FACTA, the three major agencies required to provide credit reports are Experian, Equifax, and TransUnion. Some websites or other credit bureaus have claimed to provide free credit reports, such as freecreditreport.com, but there is only one authorized site for government-required free credit reports from the three agencies: AnnualCreditReport.com. While a visitor of the site may receive one free report per year, the three agencies make money in other ways, such as providing credit numbers or additional reports in a year.

The FTC fined freecreditreport.com more than once during the Bush administration. The dishonest website claimed to give consumers a free credit report and then charged consumers who signed up for a report. Advertisements that deceive consumers about free credit reports are subject to more than mere wrist slaps now that the Credit Cardholders' Bill of Rights Act was signed by President Obama on May 22, 2009. Because of this act, the FTC may produce new rules that make free credit report advertisers affirm that only AnnualCreditReport.com provides free credit reports to consumers.

The act, also known as the *CARD Act,* has several provisions that target unfair credit card practices. The first provision mandates the adjustment of four credit practices. First, creditors are required to notify consumers of changes to fees and interest rates before such changes take place. Furthermore, contractual agreements must be made with clients if fees and interest rates are to be changed at all. Second, the limits of fees and interest rates of all credit companies will be strictly regulated by the FTC to avoid unfairly high maximums. Third, penalty fees such as late fees and over-the-limit fees must have reasonable maximums.

The second provision of the CARD Act covers notification and information. First, creditors must notify consumers about payoff timing. Second, all billing statements must conspicuously display if and when the interest rate will increase. Third, creditors must inform consumers, up front, about the dates on which payments are considered late and

[31] Pub. L. No. 108–159, 117 Stat. 1952.

the interest rates associated with late payments. Fourth, creditors must post all conditions associated with each credit arrangement option on the Internet. The last part of the provision modifies deceptive advertising associated with free credit reports.

The CARD Act's third provision prohibits credit card companies from extending credit offers to anyone under 21. Consumers under 21 may acquire credit only with a cosigner and proof of sufficient income. The third provision also blocks creditors from using tangible items to persuade college-age consumers to apply for credit. This provision also requires that creditors submit an annual report to a federal review board. Specifically, the annual report must include three pieces of information: (1) all memorandums or agreements between creditors and institutions of higher education, (2) the total number of payments and payment amounts made by creditors to institutions of higher education, (3) the number of credit accounts opened under an agreement between a credit card company and an institution of higher education per year.

The fourth provision of the CARD Act contains three directives. First, consumers will be charged fees for dormant or inactive gift cards. Second, only one fee per month may be charged to a consumer with a gift card that is inactive for 12 months. Third, gift cards, prepaid cards, and gift certificates must inform customers of three conditions before purchase: the existence of the dormancy fee, the amount of the dormancy fee, and the frequency of the dormancy charge.

Consumer Health and Safety

The legislation and rules we have examined regulate the advertising, labeling, and sale of products. Now we turn to legislation regarding product safety. The purpose of such regulations is to ensure that companies produce safe products for consumers who do not have all the information. The two main federal statutes that address product safety are the Federal Food, Drug, and Cosmetic Act and the Consumer Product Safety Act.

L06 What are the different acts that help ensure consumer health and safety?

THE FEDERAL FOOD, DRUG, AND COSMETIC ACT

In 1906 Congress created the first federal legislation regulating food and drugs, the Pure Food and Drugs Act. Subsequently, Congress amended the Pure Food and Drugs Act when it created the Federal Food, Drug, and Cosmetic Act (FFDCA)[32] in 1938 to protect consumers against misbranded or adulterated food, drugs, medical devices, or cosmetics. The U.S. Food and Drug Administration (FDA), the agency responsible for administering FFDCA, creates standards to regulate food and drugs, thus protecting consumers. Specifically, the FDA must ensure that food, drugs, cosmetics, and medical devices meet specific safety standards.

Under FFDCA, the FDA must follow a set of procedures to determine whether a drug is safe to enter the market. Recently, the Supreme Court ruled on the issue of whether the FDA has the authority to regulate tobacco (see Case 45-3). According to the FDA, it (1) has authority to regulate drugs and (2) considers nicotine a drug.

Case 45-3 demonstrates the significant influence the FDA has over the lives and health of American citizens. It also illustrates the problems with some of its regulation devices. The Food and Drug Administration Modernization Act of 1997 amended FFDCA to help improve the regulation process, particularly for drugs and medical devices. For example, the 1997 act reauthorized a drug program that cut the time required for a drug review from 30 months to 15 months. The act also increased patient access to experimental drugs and accelerated the review of important new medications.

[32] 21 U.S.C. §§ 301–393.

CASE 45-3 FOOD AND DRUG ADMINISTRATION ET AL. v. BROWN & WILLIAMSON TOBACCO CORPORATION ET AL.

UNITED STATES SUPREME COURT

120 S. CT. 1291 (2000)

Before 1995, the FDA consistently stated it did not have the power to regulate tobacco. However, in 1995, the FDA established that nicotine is a "drug" and cigarettes and smokeless tobacco are "devices" for administering the drug. The FFDCA grants the FDA authority to regulate drugs and devices. Consequently, in August 1995, the FDA published a proposed rule restricting the sale of cigarettes and smokeless tobacco to children. This rule was designed to reduce the attractiveness and availability of tobacco to young people. In August 1996, the agency issued the final rule with restrictions on sale, promotion, and labeling of tobacco products, directed at behaviors marketed to kids. Examples of these restrictions include the following: prohibiting tobacco manufacturers from distributing promotional items bearing the manufacturer's brand name as well as outdoor advertising within 1,000 feet of a school or playground.

A group of tobacco manufacturers, retailers, and advertisers filed suit against the FDA, arguing it did not have authority to regulate tobacco products and the advertising restrictions were not permissible under the Constitution. The district court ruled the FFDCA authorizes the FDA to regulate tobacco products and the labeling requirements were permitted. The Fourth Circuit Court of Appeals reversed, finding Congress did not give the FDA jurisdiction to regulate tobacco products.

JUSTICE O'CONNOR: The FDA's assertion of jurisdiction to regulate tobacco products is founded on its conclusions nicotine is a "drug" and cigarettes and smokeless tobacco are "drug delivery devices."

Because this case involves an administrative agency's construction of a statute it administers, our analysis is governed by Chevron U.S.A. Inc. v. Natural Resources Defense Council, Inc., 467 U.S. 837 (1984). Under Chevron, a reviewing court must first ask "whether Congress has directly spoken to the precise question at issue." If Congress has done so, the inquiry is at an end; the court "must give effect to the unambiguously expressed intent of Congress." But if Congress has not specifically addressed the question, a reviewing court must respect the agency's construction of the statute so long as it is permissible.

A

. . . Considering the FFDCA as a whole, it is clear Congress intended to exclude tobacco products from the FDA's jurisdiction. A fundamental precept of the FFDCA is any product regulated by the FDA—but not banned—must be safe for its intended use. Various provisions of the Act make clear this refers to the safety of using the product to obtain its intended effects, not the public health ramifications of alternative administrative actions by the FDA. That is, the FDA must determine there is a reasonable assurance the product's therapeutic benefits outweigh the risk of harm to the consumer. According to this standard, the FDA has concluded, although tobacco products might be effective in delivering certain pharmacological effects, they are "unsafe" and "dangerous" when used for these purposes. Consequently, if tobacco products were within the FDA's jurisdiction, the Act would require the FDA to remove them from the market entirely. But a ban would contradict Congress' clear intent as expressed in its more recent, tobacco-specific legislation. The inescapable conclusion is there is no room for tobacco products within the FFDCA's regulatory scheme. If they cannot be used safely for any therapeutic purpose, and yet they cannot be banned, they simply do not fit.

B

In determining whether Congress has spoken directly to the FDA's authority to regulate tobacco, we must also consider in greater detail the tobacco-specific legislation Congress has enacted over the past 35 years. Congress has enacted six separate pieces of legislation since 1965 addressing the problem of tobacco use and human health. . . .

Taken together, these actions by Congress over the past 35 years preclude an interpretation of the FFDCA that grants the FDA jurisdiction to regulate tobacco products. We do not rely on Congress' failure to act—its consideration and rejection of bills that would have given the FDA this authority—in reaching this conclusion. To the contrary, Congress has enacted several statutes addressing the particular subject of tobacco and health, creating a distinct regulatory scheme for cigarettes and smokeless tobacco. In doing so, Congress has been aware of tobacco's health hazards and its pharmacological effects. It has also enacted this legislation against the background of the FDA repeatedly and consistently asserting it lacks jurisdiction under the FFDCA to regulate tobacco products as customarily marketed. Further, Congress has persistently acted to preclude a meaningful role for any administrative agency in making policy on the subject of tobacco and health. Moreover, the substance of Congress' regulatory scheme is, in an important respect, incompatible with FDA jurisdiction. Although the supervision of product labeling to protect consumer health is a substantial component of the FDA's regulation of drugs and devices, the

FCLAA and the CSTHEA explicitly prohibit any federal agency from imposing any health-related labeling requirements on cigarettes or smokeless tobacco products.

Under these circumstances, it is clear Congress' tobacco-specific legislation has effectively ratified the FDA's previous position it lacks jurisdiction to regulate tobacco. Congress has affirmatively acted to address the issue of tobacco and health, relying on the representations of the FDA it had no authority to regulate tobacco. It has created a distinct scheme to regulate the sale of tobacco products, focused on labeling and advertising, and premised on the belief the FDA lacks such jurisdiction under the FFDCA. As a result, Congress' tobacco-specific statutes preclude the FDA from regulating tobacco products as customarily marketed.

By no means do we question the seriousness of the problem the FDA has sought to address. The agency has amply demonstrated tobacco use, particularly among children and adolescents, poses perhaps the single most significant threat to public health in the United States. Nonetheless, no matter how "important, conspicuous, and controversial" the issue, and regardless of how likely the public is to hold the Executive Branch politically accountable, an administrative agency's power to regulate in the public interest must always be grounded in a valid grant of authority from Congress. And "in our anxiety to effectuate the congressional purpose of protecting the public, we must take care not to extend the scope of the statute beyond the point where Congress indicated it would stop." Reading the FFDCA as a whole, as well as in conjunction with Congress' subsequent tobacco-specific legislation, it is plain Congress has not given the FDA the authority it seeks to exercise here. For these reasons, the judgment of the Court of Appeals for the Fourth Circuit is

AFFIRMED.

DISSENT BY JUSTICE BREYER (with whom Justice Stevens, Justice Souter, and Justice Ginsburg join, dissenting): The Food and Drug Administration (FDA) has the authority to regulate "articles (other than food) intended to affect the structure or any function of the body. . . ." Unlike the majority, I believe tobacco products fit within this statutory language.

In its own interpretation, the majority nowhere denies the following two salient points. First, tobacco products (including cigarettes) fall within the scope of this statutory definition, read literally. . . . Second, the statute's basic purpose—the protection of public health—supports the inclusion of cigarettes within its scope.

Despite the FFDCA's literal language and general purpose (both of which support the FDA's finding that cigarettes come within its statutory authority), the majority nonetheless reads the statute as excluding tobacco products for two basic reasons. . . . In my view, neither of these propositions is valid. The FFDCA does not significantly limit the FDA's remedial alternatives. And the later statutes do not tell the FDA it cannot exercise jurisdiction, but simply leave FDA jurisdictional law where Congress found it.

In short, I believe the most important indicia of statutory meaning—language and purpose—along with the FFDCA's legislative history (described briefly in Part I) are sufficient to establish the FDA has authority to regulate tobacco. The statute-specific arguments against jurisdiction the tobacco companies and the majority rely upon (discussed in Part II) are based on erroneous assumptions and, thus, do not defeat the jurisdiction-supporting thrust of the FFDCA's language and purpose. The inferences the majority draws from later legislative history are not persuasive, since one can just as easily infer from the later laws Congress did not intend to affect the FDA's tobacco-related authority at all. And the fact the FDA changed its mind about the scope of its own jurisdiction is legally insignificant because the agency's reasons for changing course are fully justified. Finally, as I explain in Part V, the degree of accountability that likely will attach to the FDA's action in this case should alleviate any concern Congress, rather than an administrative agency, ought to make this important regulatory decision.

[T]he Court today holds a regulatory statute aimed at unsafe drugs and devices does not authorize regulation of a drug (nicotine) and a device (a cigarette) the Court itself finds unsafe. Far more than most, this particular drug and device risks the life-threatening harms administrative regulation seeks to rectify. The majority's conclusion is counter-intuitive. And, for the reasons set forth, I believe the law does not require it.

CRITICAL THINKING

The first reason the majority offers for its conclusion that the FDA does not have authority to regulate tobacco is that the regulation of tobacco does not "fit" with the FDA's scheme for evaluating drugs. Consequently, the FDA would be forced to ban tobacco. What evidence does the Court offer for this reason? Are you persuaded by the evidence?

ETHICAL DECISION MAKING

Consider both the majority and the dissenting opinions. Who are the primary stakeholders affected by the decision that the FDA cannot regulate tobacco?

THE CONSUMER PRODUCT SAFETY ACT

In the Consumer Product Safety Act of 1972 Congress created the Consumer Product Safety Commission (CPSC) and directed it to "protect the public against unreasonable risks of injuries and deaths associated with consumer products."[33]

The CPSC protects the public from injuries associated with consumer products in several ways. First, the CPSC issues and enforces mandatory standards regarding product safety. Similarly, the commission works with industries to develop voluntary product standards. If the CPSC cannot establish a standard that would adequately protect the public, it can ban consumer products from the market. In addition, the CPSC can administer existing product safety legislation. Examples of such legislation include the Child Protection and Toy Safety Act of 1969[34] and the Federal Hazardous Substance Act of 1960.[35]

Second, the CPSC can arrange for a recall of products. Although the CPSC has the authority to issue product recalls on its own, usually the CPSC works with companies that are voluntarily issuing recalls for dangerous products. For example, in August 2006, both Dell and Apple issued voluntary recalls, with the help of the CPSC, for lithium ion batteries sold in their laptops. Both companies received several separate complaints about their batteries overheating, and thus the CPSC aided the companies in the battery recall.

Third, the commission conducts research regarding potentially hazardous products. The National Highway Traffic Safety Administration (NHTSA) is similar to the CPSC in that it, too, conducts investigations about the safety of potentially hazardous products. The NHTSA, however, focuses primarily on motor vehicles.

Fourth, the CPSC educates consumers about product safety. One important way the CPSC offers this education is through the National Injury Information Clearinghouse.

[33] 15 U.S.C. § 2051.

[34] Amendments to 15 U.S.C. §§ 1261, 1262, and 1274.

[35] 15 U.S.C. §§ 1261–1277.

CASE OPENER WRAP-UP

Deceptive Advertising and the Ultimate Weight-Loss Cure

To determine that Trudeau misled consumers, the court reasoned that Trudeau failed to mention a single aspect of his weight-loss protocol. Further, the court found that Trudeau painted a picture of a safe and easy diet, when in reality the diet had extreme restrictions. Trudeau's selective quotations misled consumers because they created a false image of the diet.

The FTC preferred that Trudeau reimburse all consumers who purchased his book via the infomercial—a remedy that would have resulted in over $46 million in reimbursements. Alternatively, the FTC asserted that, at the very least, Trudeau should disgorge his profits, estimated at around $12 million. In the end, the court required Trudeau to pay the FTC a little over $5.1 million.

KEY TERMS

ad substantiation 989
bait-and-switch advertising 991
cease-and-desist order 987
consent order 987
corrective advertising 992
deceptive advertising 988
half-truth 988
industry guides 987
multiple-product orders 992
puffing 988

SUMMARY OF KEY TOPICS

The Federal Trade Commission

How the FTC brings an action:

1. FTC conducts an investigation.
2. FTC sends a complaint to the violator.
3. FTC and the violator settle the complaint through a consent agreement.
4. If the company refuses to enter the consent agreement, the FTC may issue a formal administrative complaint, which leads to an administrative hearing.
5. If the company has violated the law, the FTC issues a cease-and-desist order.

If the company violates the order, the FTC can seek an injunction against the company or fine the company up to $10,000 per violation.

Deceptive Advertising

Bait-and-switch advertising: Advertising a low price to "bait" the consumer into the store only so that the salesperson can "switch" the consumer to another, higher-priced item.

FTC actions against deceptive advertising:

- *Cease-and-desist actions:* Court orders requiring that firms stop their current advertising behavior.
- *Multiple-product orders:* Court orders requiring that firms stop current advertisements on numerous products, as opposed to one specified product.
- *Corrective advertising:* Advertisements in which the company explicitly states that the formerly advertised claims were untrue.

Telemarketing and electronic advertising:

- *1991 Telephone Consumer Protection Act:* Telemarketers cannot use an automatic telephone dialing system or a prerecorded voice.
- *Telemarketing and Consumer Fraud and Abuse Prevention Act of 1994:* This act created certain requirements regarding when and how telemarketers may make calls.
- *Federal Do Not Call registry:* Telemarketers cannot call consumers who have voluntarily placed their phone numbers on the federal Do Not Call list.

Tobacco advertising: Cigarette and smokeless-tobacco advertising is restricted.

Labeling and Packaging Laws

Federal and state governments have passed laws requiring that manufacturers provide accurate, understandable information on labels. Furthermore, if a product is potentially harmful, the manufacturer must make the consumer aware of this harm.

Sales

Door-to-door sales: The *Cooling-Off Rule* gives consumers three days to cancel purchases they make from salespeople who come to their homes.

Telephone and mail-order sales: The *Mail or Telephone Order Merchandise Rule of 1993* extends protections to those who purchase over the phone or by fax.

Unsolicited merchandise: The consumer is allowed to treat any unsolicited merchandise as a gift. Thus, she is free to keep or return the merchandise as she wishes.

FTC regulation of specific industries:

1. Used-car sales
2. Funeral home services
3. Real estate sales
4. Online sales

Credit Protection

The *Truth In Lending Act* requires that sellers disclose the terms of the credit or loan to facilitate the consumer's comparison of a variety of credit lines or loans.

The *Fair Credit Reporting Act* ensures accurate credit reporting.

The *Fair Debt Collection Practices Act* regulates the actions of debt collectors that regularly attempt to collect debts on behalf of others.

The *Credit Card Fraud Act* closes loopholes in federal laws to further punish people who commit credit card fraud.

The *Fair Credit Billing Act* seeks to rectify problems and abuses associated with credit billing errors.

The *Fair and Accurate Credit Transactions Act* takes affirmative actions to control and prosecute identity theft.

Consumer Health and Safety

The *Federal Food, Drug, and Cosmetic Act* protects consumers against misbranded or adulterated food, drugs, medical devices, or cosmetics.

The *Consumer Product Safety Act* created the Consumer Product Safety Commission (CPSC) to "protect the public against unreasonable risks of injuries and deaths associated with consumer products."

POINT / COUNTERPOINT

Should Firms Be Prevented from Concealing Valuable Product Information from Consumers?

YES	NO
Consumer protection legislation should protect consumers against sellers who want to sell goods and services under cover of deception. The great benefit of markets is that they satisfy consumers. But a consumer cannot be sovereign when he is asked to purchase a tainted version of the good he thought he was buying. When firms conceal information that they well know would affect the likelihood of a sale, they are encouraging a culture of mistrust. They are saying by their behavior that it is appropriate business behavior to deceive in the interest of encouraging an exchange.	The best way to protect consumers is by placing responsibility on them to ask the right questions. They and only they know what they are seeking from a good or service. No regulatory agency understands why consumers are purchasing a particular product. To try to protect consumers against any and all possible harm is to treat them as if they were infants, incapable of watching out for themselves. A business firm should not be required to mention every attribute possessed by a product just to satisfy some utopian goal of full disclosure.

QUESTIONS & PROBLEMS

1. What is the goal of the FTC, and how does it achieve its goal? What are some pieces of legislation that enable the FTC to achieve its goal?
2. What are the elements of a deceptive advertisement, and how does the FTC prove an ad is deceptive?
3. What are the main provisions of the Truth in Lending Act, and how does it aid consumers?
4. Until 2002, the City of Bethlehem contractually retained the private law firm of Portnoff Law Associates (PLA), Ltd., to collect payment for overdue water and sewer obligations. The city notified PLA of delinquent water and sewer assessments, and PLA then contacted homeowners in attempts to collect on those claims. On February 20, 2002, the city notified PLA of a delinquent water service obligation of Bridget and Michael Piper in the amount of $252.71. PLA sent numerous letters, some on its letterhead and some on the city's letterhead, as well as made a number of telephone calls to the Piper residence in an effort to secure payment of the delinquent water service fees. PLA has never disputed that the letters it sent to the Pipers failed to include the debt verification language required by Section 1692(g) of FDCPA. PLA has likewise never disputed that its letters did not state they were sent by a debt collector, the debt collector was attempting to collect a debt, and any information obtained by PLA would be used for that purpose, as required by Section 1692(e)(11) of FDCPA. Bridget Piper filed suit against PLA and two of its attorneys in the U.S. District Court for the Eastern District of Pennsylvania. The complaint alleged that PLA's attempts to collect payment of water and sewer bills owed to the city violated FDCPA. The complaint also alleged that PLA violated this statute by failing to include statutory disclosures required for communications sent to consumers, by falsely representing or implying that the letters were from an attorney, and by collecting and attempting to collect fees not permitted by the agreement creating the debt or by law. Were the Pipers successful in their suit against PLA? Why? [*Piper v. Portnoff Law Assocs.*, 396 F.3d 227 (2005).]
5. Brenda Laramore receives federal assistance under Section 8 of the United States Housing Act. "Section [8] is a federal program designed to assist the elderly, low income, and disabled pay rent for privately owned housing." The assistance generally comes in the form of a voucher the recipient can use to pay a portion of his or her rent. On October 21, 2002, Laramore telephoned Ritchie, the company responsible for managing the apartment in question, to request an application for a lease. The woman who took the call initially told Laramore the apartment was available to rent. After Laramore informed her she intended to use a Section 8 voucher to pay a portion of the rent, however, the woman told Laramore the apartment was not available to persons using Section 8 vouchers. On February 21, 2003, Laramore filed suit, claiming that Ritchie violated ECOA by denying her a rental application because she receives public assistance. Ritchie moved to dismiss the complaint on the ground that a rental application is not a credit transaction under ECOA. The district court agreed with Ritchie and dismissed the suit. Laramore appealed. Did Ritchie violate ECOA? Should ECOA apply to rental applications? [*Laramore v. Ritchie Realty Mgmt. Co.*, 397 F.3d 544 (2005).]
6. Hewlett-Packard (HP), a U.S.-based company, is famous for its reliable laptop computers and printers. Wilson purchased an HP Pavilion Notebook computer in the summer of 2004 for approximately $1,500. In the fall of 2006, over two years after its purchase and shortly after the limited warranty expired, Wilson's laptop began to display "low power" warnings and would run on battery power even when plugged into an a/c adapter. Wilson alleged that the problem worsened to the point that he "was unable to utilize the laptop at all." When Wilson contacted HP about his laptop in or about December 2006, HP informed him that his warranty had expired on August 15, 2006, and that he could return the laptop to HP and have the motherboard replaced for over $400, plus shipping and taxes. He opted to have the battery and a/c adapter changed for $150, to no effect. Wilson then proceeded to sue, in early 2009, claiming that HP had not disclosed the defect to its consumers. The case was later dismissed after it was presented that the laptop had stopped working outside its warranty span. One day, Wilson went to use his laptop and proceeded to turn it on. It began to smoke and emit fire. When Wilson proceeded to sue again, he received the same results. Furthermore, the court stated that the "complaint's allegations were insufficient to plausibly allege a defect in the HP laptop computers that creates an unreasonable safety risk." Do you believe that HP violated consumer

safety law? Why or why not? [*Wilson v. Hewlett-Packard Co.*, 10-16249 (9th Cir. 2012).]

7. Comcast Corp. is a worldwide cable company that provides cable services to businesses and individual consumers. In Philadelphia, the company purchased some of its competitors, thereby increasing the percentage of its local ownership to about 75 percent. In early 2003, six individual customers of Comcast brought suit against the company, claiming that they paid too much for their cable service as a result of its recent acquisition. What aspects of consumer law does this case involve? [*Behrend v. Comcast Corp.*, 655 F.3d 182, 185 (3d Cir. 2011).]

8. In 2008 the Colorado Attorney General filed a complaint against the ownership of the Colorado Humane Society (CHS), a nonprofit that provided shelter, veterinarian services, and adoption outreach for surrendered and stray animals. They allegedly provided these services for Colorado Springs, Colorado, and to the general community of the relevant geographical area.

   Colorado has statutes requiring annual reporting of the financial records of firms claiming to be charities. The complaint claimed that the owners deceived, misled and financially injured consumers. They improperly solicited and spent donations made to CHS. In 2005–6, for example, they collected over $1.3 million in donations, but failed to submit financial records to the state that would enable the state to assess their compliance with consumer protection statutes. They failed repeatedly to register as a charity and collected as much as $3 million illegally. Particularly noteworthy was their effort to take advantage of the misery of pets after Katrina. They collected $66,000 in donations for Louisiana pets, but had expenses of only $16,000. In the absence of consumer protection laws such as are discussed in this chapter, how is the market process supposed to make certain that the kind of behavior alleged in this complaint would not occur? [*State of Colorado v. Colorado Humane Society,* Humane%20Society%Compaint [1].pdf (District Court, Arapahoe County, Colorado, 2008).]

9. In 2007, Andrew Cuomo, the attorney general of New York, decided to sue Dell, a computer manufacturer, after 700 complaints were made against the company to his office. In fact, a spokesperson for Cuomo stated that over 1,000 complaints were made even after the case was filed. Dell had offered a number of promotions to New York customers such as discounts, free financing, and free monitors. However, the advertisements stated that such promotions were for "well" or "best" qualified customers. What New York consumers did not know was that only 7 percent of applicants statewide qualified for the promotions. In 2008, a New York judge determined that these practices of Dell qualified as repeated deceptive advertising. Ultimately, Supreme Court Justice Teresi ordered that Dell more clearly inform consumers that most customers do not receive the benefits of next-day repair service and free financing. Dell argued that out of 6 million consumer transactions in 2007, the complaints stemmed from only a very small portion. Did Dell appeal the judge's decision? If so, was the appeal successful? [*Cuomo v. Dell.*, 514 F. Supp. 2d 397 (2007).]

10. Tobacco companies often sell tobacco products labeled as "light" or "ultra light." Labeling cigarettes as light and ultra light insinuates that the product contains lower amounts of tar and nicotine and that the consumer using the product will ingest lower amounts of nicotine and tar. However, three smokers from Maine argued that documents within the tobacco industry raised uncertainty as to whether such products actually contained lower amounts of the harmful ingredients. Furthermore, the smokers tended to take longer drags from the cigarettes, taking in more smoke. Thus, the light and ultra-light consumers were not ingesting less tar and nicotine than smokers using regular cigarettes. The three smokers determined that the Federal Trade Commission did not stop such deceptive advertising, and they sued the cigarette manufacturer, Philip Morris, and the Altria Group. The case moved beyond a federal appeals court and was ultimately brought before the Supreme Court. Did the Supreme Court allow the lawsuits to go forward on grounds of deceptive advertising? [*Altria Group Inc. v. Good.*, 555 S. Ct. 1291 (2008).]

Looking for more review materials?

The Online Learning Center at **www.mhhe.com/kubasek3e** contains this chapter's "Assignment on the Internet" and also a list of URLs for more information, entitled "On the Internet." Find both of them in the Student Center portion of the OLC, along with quizzes and other helpful materials.

Environmental Law

CHAPTER 46

LEARNING OBJECTIVES

After reading this chapter, you will be able to answer the following questions:

1. What are the alternative ways to protect the environment?
2. What are the responsibilities of the Environmental Protection Agency?
3. How does the United States regulate air quality?
4. How does the United States regulate water quality?
5. How does the United States regulate waste?
6. How does the United States regulate toxic substances?

CASE OPENER

Rogers Corporation's Hazardous Waste Debacle

Rogers Corporation is a Massachusetts company that manufactures foam products in Connecticut. During the production process, oil dripping from machinery creates hazardous wastes. Rogers collected these wastes underneath the machine and then pumped the oil into drums to sample it for excessive levels of polychlorinated biphenyls (PCBs), persistent toxic pollutants regulated under environmental laws. From 1988 through 1992, concentrations of PCBs in Rogers' drums were less than 50 parts per million (ppm), an amount in full compliance with the law.

In April 1993, another sample of the drums indicated PCBs between 50 and 170 ppm, in excess of federal standards. The testing company informed Rogers Corporation of this violation in June, and Rogers shipped the wastes off-site as required by law. In December, the Connecticut Department of Environmental Protection inspected Rogers' premises, taking a sample from underneath the machinery. This sample was found to have PCB concentrations of 170 ppm, while the drums had a level of 70 ppm. More samples from the testing company indicated the floor storage area had PCB concentrations of 110 to 140 ppm. The company cleaned this area on March 15, 1994.

1. Do you think Rogers Corporation was in violation of the law?
2. Given that Rogers Corporation was aware of exceeding PCB limitations as early as April 1993, should managers have proceeded more quickly to clean up the area?

The Wrap-Up at the end of the chapter will answer these questions.

The law is not a fixed set of statutes and rules. Once we viewed evidence of pollution, such as black smoke billowing in the air, as the sign of a productive economy, and the behavior of the Rogers Corporation's management was not only typical but lawful. Since the 1970s, however, we have recognized the dangers of some by-products of production, and we have altered the law to limit their potentially hazardous consequences and protect our air, water, and land.

This chapter begins with an examination of the alternative ways we can protect our environment, followed by an introduction to the EPA, the primary agency responsible for protecting the environment. The bulk of the chapter provides an overview of some of the major environmental laws, and the chapter concludes with a discussion of international environmental law.

While this chapter focuses on helping future managers understand the environmental laws that govern firms' operations, it is important to recognize that, rather than simply worrying about environmental compliance, firms are increasingly concerned about sustainable development, that is, "development that meets the needs of the present without compromising the ability of future generations to meet their own needs."[1] In the spirit of this new emphasis, firms are increasingly talking about the "triple bottom line," by which they mean environment, society, and economy.[2]

Alternative Means of Protecting the Environment

TORT LAW

L01

What are the alternative ways to protect the environment?

Tort law is the oldest means of protecting the environment. A tort is an injury to one's person or property. Pollution causes injury to individuals and their property, so when people started to recognize that pollution was causing them harm, they turned to tort law.

Nuisance. A nuisance arises when a person uses his or her property in a manner that unreasonably interferes with another's use and enjoyment of his or her land. When a plant emits particulates that fall on a person's property, defacing the house and making it difficult for family members to breathe, the homeowner can sue the plant's operator for nuisance. The traditional remedy, an injunction, was ordinarily granted when the nuisance could be proved, making nuisance law an ideal way to control pollution.

In the 1970 case of *Boomer v. Atlantic Cement Company,*[3] however, the court refused to issue an injunction against a company that engaged in a nuisance. Instead, the court said that such cases required a balancing of interests: If the costs of preventing the nuisance were extremely high, or the technology did not exist to prevent the harm, awarding permanent damages to the injured party was the appropriate remedy, and once damages had been paid, future landowners could not seek compensation. Thus, nuisance today plays a very minor role in environmental protection, only providing a means for victims of pollution to sometimes receive compensation.

Legal Principle: **If a person uses his or her property in a way that interferes with another's use and enjoyment of his or her land, a nuisance has occurred. The injured**

[1] World Commission on Environment and Development, "Our Common Future" (report), published as "Annex to General Assembly Document A/42/427, Development and International Co-operation: Environment," www.un-documents.net/ocf-ov.htm#I.3, August 2, 1987 (accessed August 20, 2009).

[2] Parliament of the Commonwealth of Australia, House of Representatives Standing Committee on Environment and Heritage, "Sustainability for Survival: Creating a Climate for Change" (report), www.aph.gov.au/house/committee/environ/charter/report/fullreport.pdf, September 2007, p. 11.

[3] 257 N.E.2d 870 (1970).

party may either obtain an injunction prohibiting continuation of the nuisance or receive permanent damages, depending on a balancing of the costs of preventing the nuisance and the amount of the damages.

BUT WHAT IF . . .

WHAT IF THE FACTS OF THE CASE OPENER WERE DIFFERENT?

Let's say, in the Case Opener, that Rogers Corporation was dumping PCBs into a small stream behind the plant, making the water unsafe. The stream flowed onto the properties of other individuals in the area. What kind of a tort would this be?

GOVERNMENT SUBSIDIES

Under a subsidy system, the government gives firms tax credits, low-interest loans, and/or grants if they install pollution control devices or change their production methods to reduce harmful emissions. Of course, because the subsidies rarely cover the entire cost of the new technology, the firm may still be at a slight competitive disadvantage when others in the industry make no such investment. Sometimes, however, the new technology ultimately makes firms' operations more efficient and reduces their energy costs.

MARKETABLE DISCHARGE PERMITS

The government can also determine how much of a given pollutant should be emitted during a year and issue the requisite number of permits to allow that amount, prohibiting any emissions without a permit. Firms that can cheaply reduce their emissions will do so and either sell their unused permits to other firms that need the allowance or "bank" them for future use. Each successive year the government can issue fewer permits, thereby reducing the level of pollution.

The best-known use of permits is the United States' Acid Rain Trading Program that began in 1991. The Environmental Protection Agency issued electricity-generating plants with 150,010 permits that each allow its holder to emit 1 ton of sulfur dioxide (a precursor to acid rain). By 2005, the number of permits had been reduced to 125,000 a year. The program so far has been deemed a success. By 2008, total sulfur dioxide emissions from regulated sources were down to 7.6 million tons, exceeding the program's long-term goal of 9.5 million tons long before the 2010 deadline.[4]

GREEN TAXES

An idea that is popular in Europe and gaining interest in the United States is the imposition of **green taxes** on environmentally harmful activities. Green taxes can discourage consumers and firms from engaging in these activities, while revenue from the taxes can fund environmental projects. When a province in Canada imposed a $.10 tax on each alcoholic beverage sold in a nonrefillable container, there was a dramatic shift among beer drinkers from nonrefillable containers to more environmentally friendly reusable bottles.

Green taxes are consistent with international environmental law's principle of "polluter and user pay." The ultimate goal of this approach is to phase out environmentally harmful action through the imposition of a tax.

For a better understanding of the economic principles underlying the use of marketable discharge permits, as well as green taxes, please see the **Connecting to the Core** activity on the text website at www.mhhe.com/kubasek3e.

[4] U.S. Environmental Protection Agency, "Acid Rain Program 2008 Progress Report," www.epa.gov/airmarkets/progress/ARP_1.html, January 2009.

Legal Principle: A green tax is a tax placed on environmentally harmful activities to discourage people from engaging in them.

DIRECT REGULATION

The primary approach to protecting the environment since 1970 has been direct regulation, establishing a comprehensive set of regulations to protect the environment. These regulations set specific limits on the amount of pollutants that can be discharged, and they subject violators to fines and sometimes prison terms. Most early environmental regulations in the United States were *technology forcing,* meaning that they were based primarily on health considerations, with the assumption that once standards had been established, industries would be forced to develop technology to meet them. In some cases, this approach was highly successful and impressive technological gains were made. In others, the technology was not developed, and we were unable to meet our goals.

Other standards are *technology-driven,* meaning that they are set to achieve the greatest possible improvements while taking into account existing levels of technology. These standards are easier to meet, but some observers argue that the result is that our environment is not as clean as it could be.

Environmental regulations are enforced primarily by administrative agencies through administrative proceedings. In some cases, however, agencies or citizens groups must resort to the court system to enforce the laws. The vigor with which environmental regulations are enforced often depends on how committed to them the president is, because the heads of the agencies charged with enforcing our environmental regulations are appointed by the president.

The Environmental Protection Agency

LO2 What are the responsibilities of the Environmental Protection Agency?

Environmental law consists primarily of regulations passed by a federal agency, the Environmental Protection Agency (EPA), operating under the direction of Congress. In 2010, the EPA employed 17,000 people in its headquarters, 10 regional offices, and 17 labs across the country; more than half are engineers, scientists, and environmental protection specialists.

The National Environmental Policy Act

The *National Environmental Policy Act (NEPA)* was one of the first major environmental laws enacted by the United States. It serves two primary functions: It requires that agencies take into account the environmental consequences of their actions, and it established an advisory body called the *Council on Environmental Quality (CEQ).* The CEQ prepares a report on the state of the environment every year, advises the president about environmental issues, and works with the agencies to help them prepare environmental impact statements.

ENVIRONMENTAL IMPACT STATEMENTS

NEPA requires agencies to take environmental consequences into account by mandating that an **environmental impact statement (EIS)** must be filed for (1) every federal legislative proposal or agency action (2) that is major, requiring a substantial commitment of resources, and (3) would have a significant impact on the quality of the human environment. A substantial number of such statements are filed every year. Not surprisingly, there is much litigation over whether an EIS is necessary and whether the potential environmental consequence will have a *significant* impact on the environment. Case 46-1 illustrates a typical struggle over whether an EIS is required.

CASE 46-1 BRODSKY v. UNITED STATES NUCLEAR REGULATORY COMMISSION U.S. COURT OF APPEALS FOR THE SECOND DISTRICT U.S. APP. LEXIS 339 (2013)

Richard L. Brodsky, a New York State assemblyman, asserted that the Nuclear Regulatory Commission (NRC) erred in not producing an environmental impact statement (EIS) under NEPA. The plaintiff claimed that the defendant's finding of no significant impact (FONSI) was inadequate. According to the defendant, the environmental assessment looked at increase in fire safety risk and any other adverse environmental effect. In the end, the United States District Court for the Southern District of New York concluded that the defendant agency's environmental assessment satisfied its minimal burden to justify forgoing the environmental impact statement, and granted the defendant summary judgment. The plaintiff appealed.

JUDGE SACK: Plaintiffs contend that the NRC erred in failing to produce an environmental impact statement ("EIS") under NEPA, instead producing only an environmental assessment ("EA") and a finding of no significant impact ("FONSI"). We disagree:

"Judicial review of agency decisions regarding whether an EIS is needed is essentially procedural," and "the decision not to prepare an EIS is left to the informed discretion of the agency proposing the action." "[A] reviewing court must ensure that [the agency] has taken a 'hard look' at the environmental consequences and assess whether the agency has convincingly documented its determination of no significant impact."

The NRC's EA and FONSI satisfy the agency's minimal burden to justify forgoing the EIS. The EA contains extended discussion of why the exemption does not create any fire safety risk, examines whether this exemption would have any other adverse environmental effect, and considers the alternative of not granting the exemption (and thereby requiring compliance). The NRC was not required to say more.

We have considered plaintiffs' remaining arguments and, with the exception of the public participation challenge under NEPA addressed in our related opinion issued today, conclude they are without merit. The judgment of the district court is therefore affirmed in accordance with this order.

AFFIRMED.

CRITICAL THINKING

What is the reasoning Judge Sack uses to support his argument? Is the evidence used to support the decision in this case reliable and abundant?

ETHICAL DECISION MAKING

Given the consequentialist theory of ethics, do you think the outcome of this case will yield the greatest amount of good for the greatest number of people? Who would be affected by this case?

An EIS must contain a detailed statement of:

1. The environmental impact of the proposed action.
2. Any adverse environmental effects that cannot be avoided.
3. Alternatives to the proposed action.
4. The relationship between local short-term uses of the human environment and the maintenance and enhancement of long-term productivity.
5. Any irreversible and irretrievable commitments of resources in the proposed activity should it be implemented.

While many applaud the EIS process because it forces agencies to take into account the environmental consequences of their actions and sometimes change their proposals, others are unhappy with the process. Some are concerned about how much time it takes to prepare an adequate statement. Others see the EIS requirement as "toothless" because even if it is shown that an alternative would be more benign, the agency is not required to alter its plans. All the courts can do is force agencies to prepare EISs that adequately describe the consequences and the alternatives. Despite these criticisms, many other countries have implemented similar procedures designed to reveal potential environmental consequences in advance.

Legal Principle: **An EIS must be filed whenever there is a major federal activity that has a significant impact on the environment.**

Regulating Air Quality

LO3

How does the United States regulate air quality?

As Exhibit 46-1 indicates, there are far too many environmental laws to describe in detail here, so we focus on those having the most significant impact on our environment, beginning with laws protecting the air. Air quality is better today than it was in 1970, yet 186.1 million people in the United States live in areas where the air contains excessive concentrations of at least one of six major conventional air pollutants: carbon monoxide, nitrogen oxide, sulfur dioxide, lead, ozone, and suspended particulates. Exhibit 46-2 illustrates some of the most common problems caused by these pollutants, frequently referred to as **criteria pollutants.** National air quality standards established under the Clean Air Act provide the primary basis for regulating criteria pollutants.

Exhibit 46-1

Major Environmental Laws

LAW	PURPOSE
Clean Water Act	Protect and improve the quality of surface water and preserve existing wetlands
Safe Drinking Water Act	Set drinking-water standards to ensure that the water we drink does not contain contaminants that can harm human health
Marine Protection, Research, and Sanctuaries Act	Regulate dumping of materials into the ocean
Clean Air Act	Protect and improve the quality of the air through the National Ambient Air Quality Standards, mobile-source performance standards, and new-source performance standards
Resource Conservation and Recovery Act (RCRA)	Provide cradle-to-grave regulation of hazardous waste and provide guidelines for states for regulation of non-hazardous waste
Underground Storage Tank Act	Regulate underground storage tanks to prevent and respond to leaks
Comprehensive Environmental Response, Compensation and Liability Act (CERCLA/Superfund Act)	Provide a program to respond to and ensure cleanup of contaminated sites
Federal Insecticide, Fungicide and Rodenticide Act (FIFRA)	Regulate the labeling and use of pesticides
Toxic Substances Control Act	Regulate the use of chemicals
Noise Control Act of 1972	Require that EPA establish maximum noise standards based on a best-achievable-technology standard
Oil Pollution Act of 1990	Establish liability for cleanup of navigable waters after oil spills and set tanker standards
Endangered Species Act	Protect species that are in danger of becoming extinct

Exhibit 46-2

Conventional Air Pollutants: Their Associated Health Problems and Sources

POLLUTANT	ASSOCIATED HEALTH PROBLEMS	MAIN HUMAN SOURCES
Carbon monoxide	Angina, impaired vision, lack of alertness, loss of coordination, and damage to the central nervous system of offspring of those having long-term prenatal exposure Contributes to the greenhouse effect and the formation of ozone	Automobile emissions, wood stoves, incinerators
Lead	Neurological system and kidney damage Inhibits photosynthesis and respiration in plants	Emissions from leaded gasoline, paints, leaded pipes
Nitrogen oxides	Lung and respiratory-tract damage Contributes to depletion of the ozone layer, to acid deposition, and to smog	Motor vehicle emissions, power plant and other industrial plant emissions
Ozone	Eye irritation, increased nasal congestion, asthma, reduction of lung functions, possible damage to lung tissue, and reduced resistance to infection Harms vegetation by inhibiting photosynthesis and increasing susceptibility to disease and drought	Formed when nitrogen oxides react with oxygen in the presence of sunlight, especially in the presence of hydrocarbons
Particulate matter	Reduced resistance to infection; eye, ear, and throat irritation Reduces visibility	Steel mills, power plants, cotton gins, smelters, cement plants, diesel engines, grain elevators, demolition sites, industrial roadwork, construction, wood-burning stoves, and fireplaces
Sulfur dioxide	Lung and respiratory-tract damage Contributes to the creation of acid deposition	Burning of sulfur-containing fuel, especially coal-burning electric generating plants

NATIONAL AMBIENT AIR QUALITY STANDARDS

The *Clean Air Act (CAA),* as amended, runs over 700 pages, and regulations implementing it are even longer, so this chapter provides only a basic overview of its most significant aspects. Central to the CAA are the National Ambient Air Quality Standards (NAAQS), established by the administrator of the EPA for each of the criteria pollutants.

The EPA administrator must set two types of standards. *Primary standards* are those necessary to protect the public health, including an adequate margin of safety. *Secondary standards* are limits needed to protect the public welfare (crops, buildings, and animals) from any known or anticipated adverse effect associated with a pollutant.

Legal Principle: *Primary NAAQS* protect the public health, and *secondary standards* protect the public welfare.

Before the 1970s, Americans saw smoke billowing out of smokestacks as simply a sign of progress and did not recognize the harmful effects of pollution.

The EPA is required to review the primary and secondary NAAQS every five years in the context of new scientific evidence; proposed changes in the standards are almost always controversial. The agency's new standards for particulate matter and ozone were challenged in two cases ultimately heard together by the Supreme Court. The Court was asked to address two important issues: (1) whether the delegation of authority to the EPA to establish the standards was unconstitutional and (2) whether the EPA administrator was required to consider the cost of implementation when establishing NAAQS. The high court ultimately concluded that (1) Section 109(b)(1) of the CAA does not delegate legislative power to the EPA in contravention of Article 1, Section 1, of the Constitution and (2) the EPA may not consider implementation costs in setting primary and secondary NAAQS under Section 109(b) of the CAA.

The Clean Air Act provides a mix of state and federal responsibilities. Once the administrator of the EPA establishes the NAAQS, each state has nine months to draft a state implementation plan (SIP) addressing how it will ensure that pollutants in the air within its boundaries meet the primary NAAQS within three years and the secondary standards within a reasonable time.

States did not meet the original NAAQSs within the mandated time, so the 1990 Clean Air Act amendments addressed these so-called nonattainment areas. New deadlines for meeting the primary standard for ozone ranged from 5 to 20 years. States were also required to establish or upgrade vehicle inspection and maintenance programs, as well as follow additional guidelines, depending on how far out of compliance they were.

The EPA administrator also does two other very important things with respect to air quality. First, the administrator establishes uniform national emission standards for new motor vehicles. In 2012, the administrator of the EPA finalized groundbreaking standards that will increase fuel economy to the equivalent of 54.5 miles per gallon for cars and light-duty trucks by model year 2025. When combined with previous standards set by EPA under the Obama administration, this move will nearly double the fuel efficiency of those vehicles compared to new vehicles currently on our roads. In total, the administration's national program to improve fuel economy and reduce greenhouse gas emissions will reduce U.S. oil consumption by 12 billion barrels.

Second, the EPA administrator is responsible for establishing new-source performance standards, emission standards for new stationary sources of air pollution and major expansions of existing stationary sources. The new-source performance standards are to reflect the best available control technology, limited by the costs of compliance.

COMPARING THE LAW OF OTHER COUNTRIES

AN ALTERNATIVE APPROACH TO CLEANER AIR: GERMANY'S SHIFT TO RENEWABLE ENERGY

Germany is taking a relatively novel approach to reducing carbon dioxide (CO_2) emissions. It has established a goal of producing 80 percent of the country's electricity from renewable sources by the year 2050, with an interim target of 35 percent by 2020. The country appears to be well on its way to meeting these targets, as it had increased the amount of electricity produced by renewables to 25 percent by the end of 2012.

TOXIC OR HAZARDOUS AIR POLLUTANTS

Substances that are likely to cause an increase in mortality or in serious, irreversible illness, even when emitted in small amounts, are regulated by the Air Toxics Program of the 1990 CAA amendments. To protect the public, Congress identified 189 hazardous air pollutants, including asbestos, benzene, mercury, and vinyl chloride. Industries emitting them were ordered to phase in the use of pollution control equipment that meets the maximum achievable control technology (MACT) standard. The EPA publishes guidelines as to what equipment meets this standard.

ENFORCEMENT OF THE CLEAN AIR ACT

Both the federal EPA and state environmental agencies can enforce the CAA, and citizens may file civil actions. Violations of emission limits can result in civil penalties up to $25,000 per day. Other violations, such as in record keeping, draw fines up to $5,000 per day. Parties who knowingly violate the act can be subject to criminal fines up to $1 million per day, and corporate officers risk imprisonment up to two years.

Regulating Water Quality

Two major laws protect our water quality: the Federal Water Pollution Control Act protects the quality of water in navigable waterways, while the Safe Drinking Water Act protects the quality of the water we drink.

LO4

How does the United States regulate water quality?

CLEAN WATER ACT

The 1972 amendments to the *Federal Water Pollution Control Act (FWPCA),* commonly known as the *Clean Water Act (CWA),* regulate surface waters. These amendments established two goals: (1) "fishable" and "swimmable" waters by 1983 and (2) the total elimination of pollutant discharges into navigable waters by 1985. These technology-forcing goals were to be achieved through a system of permits and effluent discharge limitations. While the country did not meet the goals, our waterways are significantly cleaner than they were in 1972, and their quality continues to improve.

Point-Source Effluent Limitations. Point-source effluent limitations are the primary tool for improving water quality. *Point sources* are distinct places from which pollutants can be discharged into water, such as factories, refineries, and sewage treatment facilities. *Effluents* are discharges from a specific source. *Effluent limitations,* therefore, are the maximum amounts of pollutants that can be discharged from a source within a given time period.

The Clean Water Act created the National Pollutant Discharge Elimination System (NPDES), which requires that every point source obtain a discharge permit from the EPA or from the state if it has an EPA-approved plan. The permits specify the types and

CASE NUGGET

SHOULD THE EPA REGULATE GREENHOUSE GASES?

Massachusetts v. EPA
128 S. Ct. 1438 (2007)

While we may think that the list of criteria pollutants has been pretty firmly established, as our understanding of the effects of various pollutants increases, the EPA is required to remain alert to the need to add new pollutants to the list. In 2007, Massachusetts led several states in a lawsuit asking that the EPA be ordered to establish vehicle emission standards for carbon dioxide and five other "greenhouse gases," gases that contribute to climate change. The high court agreed, and ruled that such standards should be set if the EPA finds that these emissions contribute to climate change. This case was considered a "landmark case" because it was the first time the EPA was ordered to recognize that global warming endangers human health.

amounts of effluent discharges allowed, based on the technology available. Most sources today must use the best-available control technology (BACT). All new sources must meet this standard, but some existing facilities are allowed to meet a slightly lower standard, best-practicable control technology (BPCT). The discharger is responsible for monitoring all discharges; administrative, civil, or criminal penalties may be issued for violations.

Enforcement is left primarily to the states, although the federal government retains authority to monitor, inspect, and enforce. Negligent violation can result in fines up to $25,000 a day; knowingly endangering someone by violating the act can result in a criminal fine up to $250,000 for an individual (and the possibility of 15 years in prison) and $1 million for an organization.

BUT WHAT IF . . .

WHAT IF THE FACTS OF THE CASE OPENER WERE DIFFERENT?

Let's say, in the Case Opener, that Rogers Corporation was leaking PCBs into a lake near the plant. However, the leakage was very minuscule. If the discharge was small, could this be ok? What legislation regulates the discharge of pollutants into bodies of water, and what does it stipulate?

Wetlands Protection. The CWA also protects wetlands, defined by the act as "areas that are inundated or saturated by surface or ground water (hydrology) at a frequency and duration sufficient to support, and that under normal circumstances do support, a prevalence of vegetation (hydrophytes) typically adapted for life in saturated soil conditions (hydric soils). Wetlands generally include swamps, marshes, bogs, and similar areas"[5] The main way we protect wetlands is through Section 404 of the CWA, which requires that any landowner seeking to add dredged or filled material to a wetland must get a permit from the Army Corps of Engineers. The permit will be issued only when the landowner demonstrates that (1) he has taken steps to avoid wetland impacts where practical, (2) he has minimized the potential impacts to wetlands, (3) he has provided compensation for any remaining unavoidable impacts through activities to restore or create wetlands, and (4) the activity is in the public interest. Some question the effectiveness of this regulation, however, as nationwide fewer than 3 percent of all requests for permits are denied and when a permit is denied, the applicant may redesign her proposal and resubmit the application.

[5] 40 CFR 232.2(r).

E-COMMERCE & THE LAW

WWW

INTECHRA MODELS HOW TO DISPOSE OF E-WASTE

Electronic waste, or e-waste, is created when consumers and companies dispose of electronics in improper ways. Today, e-waste from electronics accounts for 70 percent of the heavy metals dumped in landfills.* Consumers and companies dispose of both computers and cell phones on a regular basis. E-waste is one of the fastest-growing sectors of the waste stream.

Some businesses have responded by offering handling services. Intechra is the industry leader in the field of information technology asset disposition (ITAD).† In particular, Intechra recycles electronics throughout the United States. The company repairs and donates some equipment, making sure hard drives are wiped clean. Intechra also disassembles and recycles equipment that cannot be reused. The company employs a zero-landfill policy—it sends nothing to landfills.‡ Intechra makes sure companies dispose of equipment in ways that comply with local, state, and federal laws that protect both privacy and the environment. Intechra is part of a growing industry, one that promises to manage electronics throughout products' complete life cycles.

* http://intechra.com/html/Press_Release_042508.html.

† http://intechra.com/html/About_Intechra.html.

‡ Ibid.

SAFE DRINKING WATER ACT

The *Safe Drinking Water Act (SDWA)* regulates *public water supply systems,* which are systems having at least 15 service connections or serving 25 or more persons.

Under the act, the EPA established two levels of drinking-water standards for contaminants that could have an adverse effect on human health: maximum contaminant-level goals (MCLGs) and maximum contaminant levels (MCLs). MCLGs are nonenforceable health goals set at the level at which there would be absolutely no adverse health effects. MCLs are enforceable standards set as close as possible to the MCLGs, taking into account available technology and costs of treatment.

Legal Principle: **MCLs protect human health and must be met, whereas MCLGs are nonenforceable health goals set at the level at which there would be absolutely no adverse health effects.**

Current SDWA standards are available on the Internet. Under the "right to know" provision of the 1996 Safe Drinking Water Act amendments, drinking-water suppliers must provide every household with annual reports detailing the water contaminants in their drinking water and the health problems they may cause.

Regulating Hazardous Waste

Two primary acts focus on protection from hazardous waste: the Resource Conservation and Recovery Act and the Comprehensive Environmental Response, Compensation and Liability Act of 1980. As you read about them, try to determine with which act or acts Rogers Corporation needed to comply.

LO5
How does the United States regulate waste?

RESOURCE CONSERVATION AND RECOVERY ACT

The *Resource Conservation and Recovery Act (RCRA)* regulates hazardous and nonhazardous waste, but its primary purpose is controlling hazardous waste. The act does not explicitly reduce the amount of hazardous waste created but, instead, ensures that the waste is safely handled from creation through disposal. Some argue that making the generators pay the full costs of safe treatment, storage, transportation, and disposal of hazardous waste will provide the financial incentive to generate less.

The Manifest Program. The EPA or a generator may list a waste as hazardous, or a waste may be automatically considered hazardous if it is "garbage, refuse, or sludge or any

COMPARING THE LAW OF OTHER COUNTRIES

TAKE-BACK LAW IN GERMANY

Germany has found one effective way to help alleviate problems with trash: manufacturers must take back packing materials for their products such as crates, drums, boxes, and shrink wrap. They may not dispose of these items in the public waste disposal system. The legislation also requires that retailers take back packaging materials such as cartons and antitheft devices on CDs. Retailers must install bins into which consumers may easily deposit packaging materials. The law also imposes a mandatory deposit on nonrefillable containers for beverages, washing and cleansing agents, and water-based paints to provide an incentive for consumers to return the containers.

In response to the heavy burden placed on manufacturers under this law, a nonprofit organization, DSD, was founded to allow manufacturers, for a fee, to shift responsibility for recycling primary packing material to DSD through its green-dot program. Participating companies can mark their products with the green dot, and the packaging may then be dropped off at green-dot collection points or, in some cities, be left outside in special containers for curbside recycling.

other waste material that has any of four defining characteristics: corrosivity, ignitability, reactivity, or toxicity."

Under the manifest program, generators of hazardous waste must maintain records called **manifests** that list the amount and type of all hazardous waste produced, how it is to be transported, and how it will ultimately be disposed. Disposal must be in accordance with RCRA provisions; some wastes must receive chemical treatment to reduce toxicity or stabilize their chemistry before they can be disposed of in a landfill. A copy of the manifest accompanies the waste throughout its life cycle.

Violations of the RCRA may result in fines of up to $25,000 per violation. Criminal penalties of up to $50,000 per day of violation and up to two years in prison may also be imposed. If the defendant is a repeat violator, criminal penalties can be doubled.

RCRA Amendments of 1984 and 1986. Congress amended RCRA twice to make advanced treatment, recycling, incineration, and other forms of hazardous waste treatment the primary means of disposing of hazardous waste. Landfills are viewed as a last resort, and some wastes were banned from landfill disposal after 1988.

Nonhazardous Solid Waste. Managing nonhazardous solid waste has always been a responsibility of the states. Hence, the federal role under RCRA has been limited primarily to setting national standards for municipal solid waste landfills (those not accepting hazardous waste) and providing technical and financial assistance to the states. The law also requires that each state have a solid waste management plan with provisions for encouraging resource conservation or recovery.

Enforcement of RCRA. The EPA enforces RCRA. However, if a state sets up its own program for managing hazardous waste that is at least as stringent as the federal program, the EPA gives the state the first opportunity to prosecute violators. If the state fails to prosecute within 30 days, the EPA may issue informal warnings, seek temporary or permanent injunctions, or seek criminal penalties up to $50,000 per day and/or civil penalties up to $25,000 per violation.

COMPREHENSIVE ENVIRONMENTAL RESPONSE, COMPENSATION AND LIABILITY ACT OF 1980, AS AMENDED BY THE SUPERFUND AMENDMENT AND REAUTHORIZATION ACT OF 1986

Before the RCRA's enactment, firms were not careful about where they dumped their waste. Thousands of sites across the country were contaminated by a variety of toxic substances, and the federal government had no authority to do anything about them. But in 1980, Congress passed the *Comprehensive Environmental Response, Compensation and Liability Act (CERCLA)* to (1) clean up existing hazardous sites and (2) respond to hazardous material spills.

Under CERCLA, ultimate liability for cleanup of land contaminated by waste is placed on potentially responsible parties (PRPs). PRPs include (1) present owners or operators of a facility where hazardous materials are stored, (2) owners or operators at the time the waste was deposited there, (3) generators of the hazardous waste dumped at the site, and (4) those who transported hazardous waste to the site. Even the government can be a PRP. For example, when Atlantic Richfield cleaned up a site it leased on government property, where it retrofitted rocket motors for the government, the company was able to successfully sue the government for contribution, collecting a proportionate share of its costs based on the government's percentage of fault.[6] When the PRPs are easily identifiable and solvent, the EPA can simply order them to clean up the site. When multiple PRPs have contaminated a site, the court will allocate liability among them in accordance with how much each contributed. Case 46-2 illustrates the common problem of determining whether someone is a PRP.

[6] *U.S. v. Atlantic Research Corporation,* 127 S. Ct. 2331 (2007).

CASE 46-2 AMW MATERIALS TESTING, INC., ANTHONY ANTONIOU v. TOWN OF BABYLON & NORTH AMITYVILLE FIRE COMPANY, INC.

U.S. COURT OF APPEALS FOR THE SECOND CIRCUIT 584 F.3D 436 (2009)

Plaintiffs stored hazardous substances in their industrial facility, which caught fire and collapsed, releasing these chemicals into the atmosphere. Plaintiffs sought to hold the defendants partially liable for the cleanup, arguing that they had sufficient control of the hazardous material during the time that the fire department was responding to the fire that they could be considered "operators" of the site under CERCLA. The district court found that the defendants were not liable, as they did not discharge the hazardous substances. Plaintiffs appealed.

CIRCUIT JUDGE REENA RAGGI: . . . Although plaintiffs were undoubtedly the owners of the AMW facility from which the hazardous materials were released, they submit that defendants are liable under § 9607(a)(2) as the effective operators of the facility throughout the time they fought the fire at the site. . . .

To explain, we return to the holding in BestFoods. In that case, "the Supreme Court dismissed as 'tautolog[ical]' and 'useless' CERCLA's own definition of 'owner or operator' as 'any person owning or operating such facility.'" . . . Construing the phrase for itself, the Court concluded that it reaches broadly to encompass "the facility's owner, the owner's parent corporation or business partner, or even a saboteur who sneaks into the facility at night to discharge its poisons out of malice." With specific reference to the word "operator," the Court observed that it means "simply someone who directs the workings of, manages, or conducts the affairs of a facility." Plaintiffs submit that this definition necessarily encompasses defendants because they had "exclusive control" over the AMW facility at the time of the fire. . . . Specifically, defendants "controlled and operated the payloaders, deck guns and tower ladders" used to fight the fire.

Plaintiffs' argument, however, overlooks the very next sentence in the BestFoods opinion: "To sharpen the definition for purposes of CERCLA's concern with environmental contamination," the Supreme Court ruled that "an operator must manage, direct, or conduct operations specifically related to pollution, that is operations having to do with the leakage or disposal of hazardous waste, or decisions about compliance with environmental regulations." This "sharpen[ed]" construction, while sufficiently broad to extend beyond titular owners and day-to-day operators, nevertheless implies a level of control over the hazardous substances at issue that is simply not manifested by the evidence in this case. While defendants controlled firefighting operations at the AMW site, the hazardous materials at issue were stored in a burning building to which firefighters could not gain safe entry. These particular circumstances would not permit a conclusion as a matter of law that defendants had sufficient control over the hazardous materials to "manage, direct, or conduct operations specifically related to pollution."

AFFIRMED in favor of Defendants.

[continued]

CRITICAL THINKING

In finding for the defendants, the judge provided reasoning that permits the interpretation that firefighters or other governmental public servants called to the place of business could, under certain circumstances, be held liable as "operators" of a building where hazardous materials are housed. Explain how such an interpretation is consistent with the reasoning in this case.

ETHICAL DECISION MAKING

Make a list of the major stakeholders whose interests are affected by this decision. What important group of stakeholders are represented by the firefighters?

More commonly, the PRPs are unknown, insolvent, no longer in existence, or simply unwilling to pay. Thus, CERCLA created the *Superfund,* a pool of money funded primarily by taxing corporations in industries that create significant amounts of hazardous waste. The EPA or state and local governments use Superfund monies to clean the sites. The EPA tries to find the PRPs and collect the costs of the cleanup to replenish the fund. The Superfund can also pay for immediate responses to spills of hazardous waste other than oil. An owner who voluntarily cleans up a site before being ordered to do so is also entitled to seek contribution from other PRPs who would have been held liable if the EPA had taken the lead and cleaned up the site using Superfund money.

There are two actions under CERCLA. A *removal action* occurs when there is a spill or an immediate danger to human health or the environment posed by a hazardous waste site and removal of contaminants is necessary to provide immediate protection, not a permanent solution. Removal actions are limited to 12 months' cleanup time and a maximum of $2 million in costs. A typical removal action might occur where a neighbor notices drums sitting on an abandoned dumpsite and leaking corrosive material. The EPA would come in and remove the leaking drums. Afterward, the soil would still need to be cleaned and other hazardous materials removed, but once the immediate danger of the leaking drums is gone, the removal action is complete.

The second action is a *remedial action.* Under CERCLA, the EPA evaluates sites containing hazardous waste on a 12-point scale. Sites with the highest rankings (the most contaminated) are placed on the National Priorities List (NPL).

Once on the NPL, a site may be selected by the EPA for remediation. Before remediation begins, the EPA will go through a formal and complex process to determine the best way for cleanup to proceed, a process that includes public participation. Sites are then remediated, or cleaned up, in accordance with the plan. PRPs may be brought in at any time during the process. Superfund money is generally used at least to begin the process; then the PRPs are sued to recover the Superfund expenditures.

Regulating Toxic Substances

L06

How does the United States regulate toxic substances?

Some toxic substances are found not in waste but in products we use every day. The primary acts for regulating these substances are the Toxic Substances Control Act and the Federal Insecticide, Fungicide, and Rodenticide Act.

TOXIC SUBSTANCES CONTROL ACT

The *Toxic Substances Control Act (TSCA)* regulates any chemicals or mixtures whose manufacture, processing, distribution, use, or disposal may present an unreasonable risk of harm to human health or the environment. The act's primary role is to establish procedures for introducing a new chemical into the market. Under TSCA, every manufacturer of a new chemical must submit a premanufacturing notice (PMN) or Section Five Notice to the EPA at least 90 days before the first use of the substance in commerce. The PMN must give a significant amount of information, including the chemical name, identity, and molecular structure; trade names or synonyms; and by-products related to its manufacture. The most important information, however, is the test data related to the impact of the new chemical on human health and the environment.

The EPA then decides whether the substance presents an unreasonable risk to health or whether further testing is required to establish its safety before use. If there is no unreasonable risk or need for further testing, manufacturing may begin as proposed.

BUT WHAT IF . . .

WHAT IF THE FACTS OF THE CASE OPENER WERE DIFFERENT?

Let's say, in the Case Opener, that Rogers Corporation was beginning a new manufacturing project that would release more dangerous chemicals during the manufacturing process. The company began manufacture, tested the chemicals and amount produced, and then contacted the EPA. Did Rogers Corporation follow the proper procedures in this scenario? What is missing?

FEDERAL INSECTICIDE, FUNGICIDE, AND RODENTICIDE ACT

Pesticides, substances manufactured to prevent, destroy, repel, or mitigate any pest or to be used as a plant regulator or a defoliant, are regulated under the *Federal Insecticide, Fungicide, and Rodenticide Act (FIFRA).* Pesticides perform a wide range of functions, from killing insects that would transmit disease or destroy crops to killing pests that simply cause us discomfort. Yet they have harmful side effects and may harm species that were not their intended target. Pesticides that do not degrade quickly enough may be consumed when the crops on which they were used are eaten, potentially harming consumers' health. A pesticide may seep into the ground and contaminate the groundwater aquifer or get washed into a stream and contaminate marine life and animals that drink from that stream. Once in the food chain, it may do inestimable harm.

Under FIFRA, before it can be sold in the United States, a pesticide must be registered and properly labeled and meet three criteria: (1) Its composition warrants the claims made for it; (2) its label complies with the act; and (3) the manufacturer's data demonstrate that the pesticide can perform its intended function without unreasonable risks to human health or the environment. A pesticide that fails the third criteria may be given restricted-use registration, meaning that it can be applied by only a certified applicator with specialized knowledge or can be sold for use only during certain seasons or in certain quantities.

While pesticide registration standards are established by the federal EPA, the question of whether states can regulate federally registered pesticides through state laws, such as tort or product liability law, was not addressed by the United States Supreme Court until 2005. For the high court's reasoning on this potential preemption issue, see Case 46-3.

CASE 46-3 BATES v. DOW AGROSCIENCES, LLC

UNITED STATES SUPREME COURT
544 U.S. 541(2005)

Relying on a registered pesticide's label that claimed the use of the pesticide was safe around peanuts, farmers applied the pesticide. They believed that the pesticide not only did not destroy the weeds it was supposed to kill, but also damaged their peanut crops, so they were preparing to bring a number of state claims against Dow, including negligence, strict product liability, fraud, and breach of warranty. Dow filed suit against the farmers, seeking a declaratory judgment that the farmers' claims were preempted by FIFRA because if they were successful, the defendants would be forced to change their labels. The fact that the defendants were forced to change their labels would mean the state law conflicted with the labeling provisions of the federal law. The district court and court of appeals agreed with Dow, and the farmers appealed to the United State Supreme Court.

JUSTICE STEVENS: . . . The Court of Appeals affirmed. It read § 136v(b) to preempt any state-law claim in which "a judgment against Dow would induce it to alter its product label." . . . The court held that because petitioners' fraud, warranty, and deceptive trade practices claims focused on oral statements by Dow's agents that did not differ from statements made on the product's label, success on those claims would give Dow a "strong incentive" to change its label. Those claims were thus preempted. . . . The court also found that petitioners' strict liability claim alleging defective design was essentially a "disguised" failure-to-warn claim and therefore preempted. . . .

Under FIFRA as it currently stands, a manufacturer seeking to register a pesticide must submit a proposed label to EPA as well as certain supporting data. . . . The agency will register the pesticide if it determines that the pesticide . . . will not cause unreasonable adverse effects on humans and the environment . . . ; and that its label complies with the statute's prohibition on misbranding. . . . A pesticide is "misbranded" if its label contains a statement that is "false or misleading in any particular," including a false or misleading statement concerning the efficacy of the pesticide. . . . A pesticide is also misbranded if its label does not contain adequate instructions for use, or if its label omits necessary warnings or cautionary statements.

. . . In 1978, Congress once again amended FIFRA, . . . this time in response to EPA's concern that its evaluation of pesticide efficacy during the registration process diverted too many resources from its task of assessing the environmental and health dangers posed by pesticides. Congress addressed this problem by authorizing EPA to waive data requirements pertaining to efficacy. . . . This general waiver was in place at the time of Strongarm's registration; thus, EPA never passed on the accuracy of the statement in Strongarm's original label recommending the product's use "in all areas where peanuts are grown."

This Court has addressed FIFRA preemption in a different context. In *Wisconsin Public Intervenor* v. *Mortier*, . . . , we considered a claim that § 136v(b) preempted a small town's ordinance requiring a special permit for the aerial application of pesticides. Although the ordinance imposed restrictions not required by FIFRA or any EPA regulation, we unanimously rejected the preemption claim. In our opinion we noted that FIFRA was not "a sufficiently comprehensive statute to justify an inference that Congress had occupied the field to the exclusion of the States." . . . "To the contrary, the statute leaves ample room for States and localities to supplement federal efforts even absent the express regulatory authorization." . . .

As a part of their supplementary role, States have ample authority to review pesticide labels to ensure that they comply with both federal and state labeling requirements. Nothing in the text of FIFRA would prevent a State from making the violation of a federal labeling or packaging requirement a state offense, thereby imposing its own sanctions on pesticide manufacturers who violate federal law.

. . . For a particular state rule to be preempted, it must satisfy two conditions. First, it must be a requirement *"for labeling or packaging"*; rules governing the design of a product, for example, are not preempted. Second, it must impose a labeling or packaging requirement that is *"in addition to or different from* those required under this subchapter." A state regulation requiring the word "poison" to appear in red letters, for instance, would not be preempted if an EPA regulation imposed the same requirement.

. . . [M]any of the common-law rules upon which petitioners rely do not satisfy the first condition. Rules that require manufacturers to design reasonably safe products, to use due care in conducting appropriate testing of their products, to market products free of manufacturing defects, and to honor their express warranties or other contractual commitments plainly do not qualify as requirements for "labeling or packaging." None of these common-law rules requires that manufacturers label or package their products in any particular way. Thus, petitioners' claims for defective design, defective manufacture, negligent testing, and breach of express warranty are not preempted.

. . . Unlike their other claims, petitioners' fraud and negligent-failure-to-warn claims are premised on common-law rules that qualify as "requirements for labeling or packaging." These rules set a standard for a product's labeling that the Strongarm label is alleged to have violated by containing false statements and inadequate warnings. . . .

[continued]

Unlike the preemption clause at issue in *Cipollone,* § 136v(b) prohibits only state-law labeling and packaging requirements that are *"in addition to or different from"* the labeling and packaging requirements under FIFRA. Thus, a state-law labeling requirement is not preempted by § 136v(b) if it is equivalent to, and fully consistent with, FIFRA's misbranding provisions. Petitioners argue that their claims based on fraud and failure to warn are not preempted because these common-law duties are equivalent to FIFRA's requirements that a pesticide label not contain "false or misleading" statements, . . . or inadequate instructions or warnings. . . . We agree with petitioners insofar as we hold that state law need not explicitly incorporate FIFRA's standards as an element of a cause of action in order to survive preemption. . . . [H]owever, we leave it to the Court of Appeals to decide in the first instance whether these particular common-law duties are equivalent to FIFRA's misbranding standards.

. . . [A] state cause of action that seeks to enforce a federal requirement "does not impose a requirement that is 'different from, or in addition to,' requirements under federal law. To be sure, the threat of a damages remedy will give manufacturers an additional cause to comply, but the requirements imposed on them under state and federal law do not differ. Section 360k does not preclude States from imposing different or additional *remedies,* but only different or additional *requirements.*" . . . Accordingly, although FIFRA does not provide a federal remedy to farmers and others who are injured as a result of a manufacturer's violation of FIFRA's labeling requirements, nothing in § 136v(b) precludes States from providing such a remedy.

Judgment VACATED and case REMANDED to the Court of Appeals.

CRITICAL THINKING

Why is the Court being careful about whether the state law places responsibilities on the producer that go beyond the federal requirements? Why would it not necessarily be a good idea to impose all safety requirements on the producers regardless of who makes the rules?

ETHICAL DECISION MAKING

What value preferences are most evident in this decision? Does the Court not value safety?

Pesticide Tolerances in Food. FIFRA is not the only law to regulate pesticide use. Under the 1996 Food Quality Protection Act, the EPA was required to establish a single, health-based standard for pesticide residues on foods sold in the United States. For a level of residue to be acceptable, the EPA must conclude with reasonable certainty that no harm will result from aggregate exposure to each pesticide from dietary and other sources. When a pesticide is registered under FIFRA, tolerance levels for its residues will be established by the EPA.

International Environmental Considerations

The United States is justly proud of its system of environmental regulations, to which many countries have looked for a model. However, the most recent data from an ongoing study of 142 countries found that the United States was 49th, not first, in environmental health.[7]

To help governments become more rigorous in decision making about the environment, the study took into account 68 variables to determine *environmental sustainability,* that is, the likely environmental quality of life over the next generation. These variables included a country's approach to water and air pollution, how corrupt the government is, and how seriously it takes global climate change. The top five countries were Switzerland, Latvia, Norway, Luxembourg and Costa Rico. The five worst were South Africa, Kazakhstan,Uzbekistan, Turkmenistan, and Iraq.

[7] Environmental Performance Index and Pilot Trend Environmental Performance Index, 2012 Release (2000–2010), http://epi.yale.edu/epi2012/rankings.

Regardless of how the United States is ranked, most of its citizens recognize the real need for international cooperation on environmental issues. The interdependence of neighboring countries is obvious, but air and water patterns make our interdependence on nations all across the globe just as strong. Air pollutants emitted anywhere between 30 and 60 degrees north of the equator may ultimately end up in China or the United States, because both are located within those latitudes. The migration of animals and plants can likewise spread pollutants. If a pesticide gets into our water, migrating fish ingest it. Birds eat the contaminated fish and pass through another country during their winter migration. If they die in that other country, a pollutant from the United States may now enter the food chain in that country.

The United States can help establish global environmental policies by sharing its research on pollution prevention and cleanup, making economic aid to foreign countries contingent on compliance with environmental standards, and negotiating and signing environmental treaties.

Treaties are written agreements by nations to resolve a particular problem in an agreed-on manner. The most effective treaties spell out consequences for failure to live up to the terms. In the United States, treaties are negotiated by a representative of the executive branch and must be ratified by two-thirds of the Senate. Implementation of most environmental treaties generally requires passage of federal legislation that accomplishes the treaty's objectives. Exhibit 46-3 lists some important environmental treaties the United States has signed.

The most controversial environmental treaty today is the Kyoto Agreement, in which countries agreed to reduce their collective emissions of greenhouse gases (GHGs) by 5.2 percent, compared to 1990 levels, by 2012. The protocol, which has been ratified by 192 parties, went into force February 16, 2004, without the United States as a signatory. Interestingly, while the U.S. never ratified the treaty, it was the only country to actually meet the 2012 goal. The first committment period under the Protocol ended in 2012, and the second period is to run from 2013–2020, and reach a goal of reducing GHGs by at least 18 percent below 1990 levels during that eight-year period.

Exhibit 46-3
Environmental Treaties and Their Purposes

TREATY	PURPOSE
Montreal Protocol	Significantly reduce (and in some countries ban) the use of ozone-depleting air pollutants, namely chlorofluorocarbons and halons.
Eastern Pacific Ocean Tuna Fishing Agreement (1983)	Help regulate the harvest of tuna by granting international licenses to those who want to catch tuna within 200 miles of the coasts of the signatories to the treaty (the United States and several Latin American countries). Fees are collected and distributed to the member nations on the basis of the poundage of fish taken within the respective nations' coastal limits.
Stockholm Convention on Persistent Organic Pollutants	Require that signatory countries ban or severely restrict the use of nine of the most harmful persistent organic pesticides and work toward the ultimate goal of a total ban on their use.
Marine Pollution Prevention Protocol (MARPOL)	Require that signatory nations adopt laws to "prevent, reduce and control" any significant pollution of the marine environment.
Convention on International Trade in Endangered Species (CITES)	Prohibit international trade of endangered plants and animals.

CASE OPENER WRAP-UP

Rogers Corporation's Hazardous Waste Debacle

Rogers Corporation was indeed found to be in violation of the law. Specifically, it had violated Section 15 of TSCA and a section of the Code of the Federal Regulations by failing to clean up a hazardous area in a timely manner. A trial before the administrative law judges (ALJs) of the EPA resulted in a civil penalty of $281,400, later affirmed by the Environmental Appeals Board.

After reading this chapter, you should have a sense of the importance of understanding and following environmental regulations. Violations of environmental laws can result in jail time for the violators and anyone who had the authority to require the violators to comply with the regulations, as well as hefty fines. Regarding question 2 in the Case Opener, if you answered that Rogers Corporation did not need to clean up the area sooner, you should now realize that by taking such action regardless of whether the law required it, the firm might have escaped liability. Even without these regulations, perhaps Rogers Corporation *should have* cleaned up the area to protect the health of the workers.

KEY TERMS

criteria pollutants 1018
environmental impact statement (EIS) 1016
green taxes 1015
manifests 1024
nuisance 1014

SUMMARY OF KEY TOPICS

Alternative Means of Protecting the Environment

Tort law of nuisance: Nuisance is unreasonable interference with another's enjoyment and use of his or her land.

Government subsidies approach: Government pays polluters to reduce their emissions.

Emissions charges approach: Polluters are charged a flat fee on every unit of the pollutant they discharge.

Marketable discharge permits: Government issues a set number of permits for pollutant discharges; companies are free to sell the permits among themselves.

Green taxes: Government imposes taxes on activities that are environmentally harmful.

Direct regulation: Government regulates pollution. This is the primary approach used today.

The Environmental Protection Agency

The EPA, created in 1970, is the largest federal agency and has a mandate to address issues of pollution in the areas of air, water, solid waste, pesticides, radiation, and toxic substances. The Office of Enforcement and Compliance Assurance has been particularly successful in ensuring that companies that break environmental laws are prosecuted by the Department of Justice.

The National Environmental Policy Act

The act requires the preparation of an environmental impact statement (EIS).

- *Threshold consideration:* The activity must be federal, be major, and have a significant impact on the human environment.

- *Content of the EIS:* The statement must include the environmental impact of the proposed action; the adverse environmental effects of the action; the alternatives to the action; the relationship between the local short-term uses of the human environment and the maintenance and enhancement of its long-term productivity; and any irreversible commitments of resources.

Regulating Air Quality

National Ambient Air Quality Standards have been established for carbon monoxide, particulate matter, ozone, sulfur dioxide, nitrogen dioxide, and lead.

Primary standards are levels necessary to protect public health.

Secondary standards are levels necessary to protect public welfare.

Toxic air pollutants are pollutants that cause serious consequences even in small amounts.

Maximum achievable control technology (MACT) is the standard that must be met by industry pollution control equipment.

The *Acid Rain Control Program* is the program that allows auctioning of sulfur dioxide permits to reduce total emissions in the most efficient way possible.

Regulating Water Quality

Federal Water Pollution Control Act goals are to make all our navigable waterways fishable and swimmable and to totally eliminate all pollutant discharges into navigable waters.

Point-source effluent limitations are the maximum allowable amounts of pollutants that can be discharged from a source within a given time period.

The *Safe Drinking Water Act* sets standards for drinking water supplied by a public water supplier. "Right to know" provisions mean that utilities must provide annual reports detailing water contaminants and the harm they may possibly cause.

Regulating Hazardous Waste

The *Resource Conservation and Recovery Act* is the main act that regulates waste.

RCRA's manifest program provides "cradle-to-grave" regulation of hazardous waste by requiring that every generator of hazardous waste maintain records on the waste.

RCRA amendments of 1984 and 1986 made landfills a last resort for the disposal of many types of waste.

Enforcement of RCRA is by the EPA. States can set up their own programs, but EPA retains ultimate authority to investigate and fine violators.

The *Comprehensive Environmental Response, Compensation and Liability Act of 1980 (CERCLA), as Amended by the Superfund Amendment and Reauthorization Act of 1986,* provides money in the Superfund that is used for toxic waste cleanup. EPA may sue to recover costs expended by the fund.

Regulating Toxic Substances

Under the *Toxic Substances Control Act:*

A *toxic substance* is any chemical or mixture whose manufacture, processing, distribution, use, or disposal may present an unreasonable risk of harm to human health or the environment.

A *premanufacturing notice* is notification given to the EPA at least 90 days before the first use of a chemical; it contains information on the risk posed by the chemical.

Under the *Federal Insecticide, Fungicide, and Rodenticide Act,* registration of pesticides is required for use and selling. Registration lasts five years and can be for:

- *General use:* There are no restrictions.
- *Restricted use:* Pesticide must be used in a specific manner in order not to pose an unreasonable risk.

International Environmental Considerations

Because environmental problems know no boundaries, there is a need for international cooperation over environmental matters.

The United States plays a role in establishing global environmental policies primarily by sharing U.S. research on pollution prevention and cleanup with other nations; making economic aid to foreign countries contingent on compliance with environmental standards; and negotiating and signing environmental treaties.

POINT / COUNTERPOINT

Should the EPA Play the Primary Role in Enforcing Environmental Regulation?

As you are thinking about each argument, you may want to ask yourself which ambiguous word (or phrase) is crucial to both arguments, and how different definitions of that word affect the strength of each argument.

NO

The EPA should not be a primary instrument in enforcing environmental regulation.

EPA officials are appointed, not elected. Thus, they lack the political accountability to make legitimate decisions about environmental regulation. If EPA officials strike an unpopular or ineffective balance between environmental protection and economic development, citizens cannot vote them out of office. An institution less insulated from popular sovereignty would be better suited to make these important decisions.

Those who champion the importance of the EPA's role often point out its officials' expertise (especially relative to Congress) in environmental regulation. But expertise isn't everything; incentives matter too. Without political accountability, EPA officials lack strong incentives to vigorously enforce environmental regulation. Tort law solves this problem. When a factory's pollution infringes the rights of individuals downwind or downstream, tort law promises them restitution if they vigorously pursue their cases in court.

YES

The EPA should be the foremost instrument in enforcing environmental regulation.

Although it lacks the political accountability of the elected branches of government, the EPA is not entirely insulated from the popular will. The president appoints the administrator, the EPA's top-ranking official. If the EPA's enforcement of environmental regulation becomes sufficiently ineffective or unpopular, the appointment of a new administrator will be an important issue in the next election.

Moreover, what the EPA lacks in political accountability it makes up for in expertise. More than half its 18,000 employees are scientists or engineers. Even the most educated congressperson could master only a fraction of the EPA's knowledge. This specialization renders the EPA well suited to be the primary enforcer of environmental regulation.

Those who argue that tort law should be the primary instrument in enforcing environmental regulation overlook the constitutional requirement of *standing* (see Chapter 3). Article III of the Constitution requires that, for federal courts to hear a case, the plaintiff must have sustained an injury. Yet many violations of environmental regulations produce no measurable injury. For example, a factory that spews pollutants into the air may not result in a measurable injury to anyone. Thus, tort law is unable to redress many violations of environmental regulations.

QUESTIONS & PROBLEMS

1. Explain the common law methods of resolving pollution problems, and evaluate their effectiveness.
2. List the elements that must be contained in an environmental impact statement.
3. How does each of the primary segments of the Clean Air Act contribute to the act's overall goal of improving air quality?
4. What is erroneous about the argument that we no longer need the Superfund because the Resource Conservation and Recovery Act now ensures that all waste is properly disposed of?
5. How do we protect water quality?
6. The plaintiffs, several property owners, all owned property within a 30-square-mile area east of a nuclear weapons plant. The plaintiffs alleged that the plant released plutonium particles onto their properties. As a result, under the Price-Anderson Act (PAA), the plaintiffs filed a nuisance claim against the defendant plant owners. The jury found in favor of the plaintiffs and awarded compensatory and punitive damages. The defendants appealed. The appellate court reversed the decision of the

district court, denying the plaintiffs' nuisance claims. Identify possible reasons that would allow for a denial of the nuisance claims. [*Cook v. Rockwell Int'l Corp.,* 618 F.3d 1127 (2010).]

7. The plaintiffs, various environmental groups, sued the defendant Army Corps of Engineers for violating the Clean Water Act, the National Environmental Protection Act, and the Administrative Procedure Act by issuing two nationwide coal-mining waste-discharge permits. The defendant claimed that it had conducted the necessary cumulative-impacts analysis and environmental assessments to determine the permits' consequential environmental impacts and then determined that compensatory mitigation would reduce the adverse impacts to a "minimal level." The district court granted summary judgment in favor of the defendant, and the plaintiffs appealed. Should the judgment of the lower court be upheld or not? [*Ky. Riverkeeper, Inc. v. Midkiff,* 2013 U.S. App. LEXIS 7910 (2013).]

8. The Water District of Chicago began to voluntarily clean up property it owned that had been contaminated years before by chemical tanks, and it sued the company that had owned the tanks that were the source of the contamination. The Water District received a judgment of $8.1 million and an order for future contributions if more work was necessary to meet CERCLA cleanup standards. On appeal, the company argued that because the EPA had not ordered the cleanup, and no agreement had been reached with the EPA regarding a cleanup, the contributing party could not be required to pay. How do you believe the appellate court ruled, and why? [*Metropolitan Water Reclamation District of Greater Chicago v. North American Galvanizing & Coatings, Inc.,* 473 F.3d 824 (7th Cir. 2007).]

9. The defendants owned and operated a gas station from the mid-1930s until August 1988. During the station's operation, under management of the defendants, significant amounts of hazardous substances were disposed on the site, including oil, oil filters, gasoline, and diesel fuel. The site was thus contaminated with lead, chromium, benzene, and other highly toxic substances. Esso Standard Oil Company, the new owners of the gas station, had to pay to clean up the site. Esso sued the defendants under CERCLA to recover part of its cleanup costs from the defendants. The magistrate denied Esso's claim, and Esso appealed. Did the magistrate err in denying the claim? [*Esso Standard Oil v. Rodriguez-Perez,* 455 F.3d 1 (2006).]

10. The Medical Waste Institute and Energy Recovery Council sought review of the Environmental Protection Agency's regulation that set performance standards for new and existing hospital/medical/infectious waste incinerators (HMIWI). The petitioner argued that the EPA exceeded its authority under the Clean Air Act when it revised the HMIWI standards and that setting more stringent standards required considering additional costs. The district court dismissed the petition in part and denied it in part. Did the EPA exceed its authority in regulating HMIWI? Why or why not? [*Medical Institute and Energy Recovery Council v. EPA,* 645 F.3d 420 (2011).]

Looking for more review materials?

The Online Learning Center at **www.mhhe.com/kubasek3e** contains this chapter's "Assignment on the Internet" and also a list of URLs for more information, entitled "On the Internet." Find both of them in the Student Center portion of the OLC, along with quizzes and other helpful materials.

Antitrust Law

CHAPTER 47

PART 9 GOVERNMENT REGULATION

LEARNING OBJECTIVES

After reading this chapter, you will be able to answer the following questions:

1 What is the rationale for antitrust law?

2 What is the Sherman Act?

3 What is explored in Section 1 of the Sherman Act?

4 What is explored in Section 2 of the Sherman Act?

5 What is the Clayton Act?

6 What is the Federal Trade Commission Act?

CASE OPENER

Whole Foods Market Merger and Monopoly

Whole Foods Market, Inc., and Wild Oats Markets, Inc., operate 194 and 110 grocery stores, respectively, primarily in the United States. In February 2007, they announced that Whole Foods would acquire Wild Oats in a merger. They notified the Federal Trade Commission as required for the $565 million deal, and the FTC investigated the merger through a series of hearings and document requests. Soon after, the FTC asked for an injunction to stop the merger, and Whole Foods filed suit against the injunction.

The FTC contended that Whole Foods and Wild Oats are the two largest operators of what it called premium, natural, and organic supermarkets (PNOSs). Such stores focus on high-quality perishables including specialty and natural organic produce, generally have high levels of customer services, target affluent and well-educated customers, and are mission-driven, with an emphasis on social and environmental responsibility. The FTC asserted that in 18 cities the merger would create monopolies because Whole Foods and Wild Oats are the only PNOSs.

The FTC stated that whether the merger created an appreciable danger of anticompetitive effects depended on the relevant product and geographic markets. At the district court level, a key issue of determining whether the merger created a product monopoly was the issue of how broadly defined the "market" was for grocery stores. The court concluded that the PNOS segment was not a distinct market and that Whole Foods and Wild Oats compete within the broader market of grocery stores and supermarkets. Therefore, the court found that a monopoly would not be created in the 18 cities because other grocery stores still existed to compete with Whole Foods. The FTC appealed the ruling.

1. How does the court prove that a company holds monopoly power?
2. In addition to proving that a company holds monopoly power, what else must a court prove to find a monopoly guilty of abusing its market power?

The Wrap-Up at the end of the chapter will answer these questions.

The purpose of this chapter is to introduce you to antitrust law. First, we consider the history of and rationale for antitrust law. What exactly is antitrust law, and why do we need it? Second, we consider the major statutes regarding antitrust law. These statutes prohibit certain anticompetitive behaviors, but the courts have taken a large role in specifying how the statutes are to be enforced. As you read this chapter, think about how the Whole Foods Market case is related to the various antitrust issues and concerns.

History of and Rationale for Antitrust Law

THE NEED FOR REGULATION

LO1

What is the rationale for antitrust law?

A **trust** is a business arrangement in which stock owners appoint beneficiaries and place their securities with trustees, who manage the company and pay a share of their earnings to the stockholders. A trust is similar to a corporation in many ways; the beneficiaries of a trust are not responsible for any debt. However, a trust and a corporation are different entities and should be treated as such.

In the 1870s and 1880s, companies such as Standard Oil used trusts in an attempt to drive out their competition. In an attempt to fight such anticompetitive behavior, antitrust law was created.

Common law actions against the restraints to trade (i.e., the trusts' anticompetitive behavior) were not strong enough to stop such anticompetitive behavior. In 1887 Congress passed the Interstate Commerce Act,[1] which created the Interstate Commerce Commission, intended to regulate railroads to fight anticompetitive business behavior. Then Senator John Sherman, who was respected for his financial opinion, and others created a bill that would prohibit unfair practices and provide an action against companies that engaged in such behavior. In 1890, this bill was enacted as the Sherman Act.[2] Because the regulations were aimed at trusts engaging in anticompetitive behavior, the regulations were called *antitrust* laws.

Despite the Sherman Act, business abuses continued, and concern about antitrust policies heightened during the presidential election of 1912. As a result of this election, Congress created the Clayton Act[3] and Federal Trade Commission Act[4] in 1914.

RATIONALE FOR ANTITRUST LAWS

Before the Sherman Act was passed, several scholars argued that the prohibition of the behavior of the trusts was wrong. They argued that such behavior was natural and a result of competition. If the large trusts were successful, it was because they deserved to be successful. In contrast, others argued that the monopolies were successful through unfair

[1] 49 U.S.C. §§ 501–526.
[2] 15 U.S.C. §§ 1–7.
[3] 15 U.S.C. §§ 12–26a.
[4] 15 U.S.C. §§ 45–48A.

business practices; they did not have to compete with others because of these practices. Consequently, monopolies were not natural occurrences and needed to be regulated.

The debate about the need and purpose of antitrust law has not been quashed; in fact, Microsoft has been the target of several antitrust suits, renewing the debate and controversy over the purpose of antitrust law. Arguments regarding the purpose of antitrust law can generally be classified under one of two categories: traditional antitrust theories and Chicago School theories. Both are outlined in Exhibit 47-1.

Traditional Antitrust Theories. Traditional antitrust theorists argue that a few powerful sellers should not dominate the economy. They argue that accumulation of economic power leads to an accumulation of political power; politicians simply would not be able to ignore such economic power and would be "bought" by this power. Thus, not only do monopolies cause economic damage, but they also cause political disadvantages. Consequently, traditional antitrust theorists want many buyers and sellers in the market; they want to foster real competition.

Traditional antitrust theorists believe that efficiency is an important goal of antitrust law but is not the only goal or even the most important goal. As you will see, this idea is clearly in conflict with the Chicago School theories.

Chicago School Theories. Chicago School theorists argue that the central, and perhaps only, purpose of antitrust law is to encourage economic **efficiency**, that is, getting the most output from the least input. Unless efficiency is the sole criterion for antitrust policy, consumers will be harmed. These scholars are not persuaded by the traditional antitrust argument that concentration of economic power leads to undesirable social and political consequences.

If a company held great economic power, Chicago School theorists would determine how the company's power affected efficiency. If the concentrated power led to efficiency, Chicago theorists believe the company should be left alone. Overall, Chicago theorists tend to be more lenient regarding the enforcement of antitrust laws.

RECENT REGULATORY ATTITUDES

From the early 1960s to the early 1970s, the courts embraced a traditional antitrust theory. The courts displayed a preference for decentralizing economic power over economic efficiency. For example, the courts ruled that certain market practices were per se illegal.

Exhibit 47-1
Antitrust Law Rationale

Traditional antitrust theories	1. To foster competition, a few powerful sellers should not dominate the economy; there should be many buyers and sellers in the market.
	2. An accumulation of economic power leads to an accumulation of political power, which leads to political consequences for consumers.
	3. Efficiency should not be the only or most important goal of antitrust law.
Chicago School theories	1. Concentrated economic power does not necessarily lead to political consequences.
	2. If a company held great economic power and if the power led to efficiency, then the company should be left alone.
	3. The purpose of antitrust law is to encourage economic efficiency.

However, in the 1970s, the courts' preference changed; efficiency was given greater weight. In a landmark case in 1977, the Supreme Court stated that antitrust laws "were enacted for the 'protection of competition, not competitors.'"[5] In this case, Pueblo Bowl-O-Mat, Inc., argued that when Brunswick acquired six bowling centers, a monopoly was created and competition was substantially lessened. Thus, Pueblo claimed that such an occurrence was a violation of Section 7 of the Clayton Act. Unfortunately for Pueblo, the act states that to prove damages, one must present more than a violation of the section.

During the Reagan administration, courts and administrative agencies practiced a restricted antitrust policy; in other words, the courts and agencies permitted questionable business actions in the name of competition and efficiency. These courts and administrators gave much weight to Chicago School thought. However, in the 1990s, the courts and agencies have become more expansive in bringing more claims against companies for antitrust violations.

Some scholars, who would be more aligned with Chicago School thought, argue that antitrust law is outdated and thus damages the market. Some go so far as to argue that all antitrust laws should be repealed.[6] Opponents argue that antitrust laws need to be even more strictly enforced because large corporations are gaining too much power. They argue that the Sherman Act's strength is its flexibility and adaptability. Are proponents of traditional antitrust policies or proponents of the Chicago School more likely to find that, in the chapter opener, Whole Foods Market would violate antitrust laws?

EXEMPTIONS FROM ANTITRUST LAW

Before we start to examine the specific antitrust laws, note that certain groups and activities are exempt from antitrust regulation. These groups are listed in Exhibit 47-2. They are exempted either through federal statute or case law.

Case 47-1 provides one example of how a court determines whether a group or activity is exempt from antitrust law.

[5] *Brunswick Corp. v. Pueblo Bowl-O-Mat., Inc.*, 429 U.S. 477 (1977).

[6] See D. T. Armentano, "It's Time to Reexamine Antitrust Legislation," *CATO: This Just In*, www.cato.org/dailys/11-13-97.html, November 13, 1997; D. T. Armentano, "Myths of Antitrust Progress," *Regulation*, www.cato.org/pubs/regulation/reg20n2a.html.

CASE 47-1 CALIFORNIA v. SAFEWAY
U.S. COURT OF APPEALS FOR THE NINTH CIRCUIT
651 F.3D 1118 (2011)

In 2003, a collective-bargaining agreement among several chapters of the United Food and Commercial Workers (UFCW) and three supermarket chains in California was set to expire. In addition, another food grocery chain, Food 4 Less, had a separate contract with UFCW set to expire in the months to come. Before these contracts expired, and with the consent of the union, the defendant grocers entered into a Mutual Strike Assistance Agreement. This agreement outlined that if one party to the agreement was struck by the union, the other parties would lock out the union employees within 48 hours. The agreement also included a revenue-sharing provision (RSP) which provided that any grocer that earned revenues above its normal share during the strike period would pay 15% of the excess revenues to the other grocers to restore their pre-strike shares.

Upon a subsequent union strike, the State of California brought an action against the grocers, alleging that the RSP violated Section 1 of the Sherman Act, which prohibits any contract, combination, or conspiracy in restraint of trade or commerce. The defendant grocers moved for summary judgment on the ground that the RSP was immune from antitrust law under the non-statutory labor exemption. The district court denied the motion, holding that the exemption was inapplicable. The defendants appealed.

JUDGE GOULD: We must decide whether an agreement among competitors to share revenues during the term of a labor dispute is exempt from the antitrust laws under the non-statutory labor exemption, and if not, whether the agreement should be condemned as a per se violation of the antitrust laws or on a truncated "quick look," or whether more detailed scrutiny is required.

The grocers contend that the district court erred in holding that the RSP is not immune from the Sherman Act under the non-statutory labor exemption, and they urge that summary judgment should have been entered in their favor on the basis of the exemption.

Courts have recognized both "statutory" and "non-statutory" labor exemptions to the antitrust laws. The statutory exemption, which is not invoked here, establishes that labor unions are not combinations or conspiracies in restraint of trade and exempts certain union activities from scrutiny under the antitrust laws. However, the statutory exemption does "not exempt concerted action or agreements between unions and nonlabor parties."

The non-statutory labor exemption, invoked by the grocers as a defense in this case, has been inferred from federal labor statutes. These "set forth a national labor policy favoring free and private collective bargaining," "require good-faith bargaining over wages, hours, and working conditions," and "delegate related rulemaking and interpretive authority to the National Labor Relations Board." The implicit exemption "interprets the labor statutes . . . as limiting an antitrust court's authority to determine, in the area of industrial conflict, what is or is not a 'reasonable' practice" and "substitutes legislative and administrative labor-related determinations for judicial antitrust-related determinations" in that area. "[S]ome restraints on competition imposed through the bargaining process must be shielded from antitrust sanctions" to give effect to federal labor policy and to allow meaningful collective bargaining to occur.

"The Supreme Court has never delineated the precise boundaries of the [non-statutory labor] exemption, and what guidance it has given as to its application has come mostly in cases in which agreements between an employer and a labor union were alleged to have injured or eliminated a competitor in the employer's business or product market." The Court first elaborated on the reach of the non-statutory labor exemption in *Allen Bradley Co. v. Local Union No. 3, International Brotherhood of Electrical Workers,* involving a series of agreements between an electrical workers union and several manufacturers and contractors in which the manufacturers and contractors agreed to do business exclusively with other companies that employed union workers. Those agreements were part of "a far larger program . . . to monopolize all the business in New York City, to bar all other business men from that area, and to charge the public prices above a competitive level" and created a "situation . . . not included within the [relevant] exemptions." The Court explained that Congress did not intend to bestow on unions "complete and unreviewable authority to aid business groups to frustrate [antitrust legislation's] primary objective."

In *United Mine Workers of America v. Pennington,* the Supreme Court similarly declined to apply the exemption to insulate a wage agreement between a union of mine workers and large coal companies. The union and the large companies, to eliminate smaller coal companies and permit the larger companies to control the market, agreed to a series of terms, including increased wages for union workers. A smaller coal mine operator, unable to pay the increased wages demanded by the union under the terms of their agreement with the larger companies, filed suit claiming that the agreement violated the Sherman Act. In exploring the boundaries of the exemption, the Court observed that, had the union and employers entered into an agreement in which they collectively set prices for coal, they could not defend that agreement from antitrust attack, because "the restraint on the product market is direct and immediate, is of the type characteristically deemed unreasonable under the Sherman Act and the union gets from the promise nothing more concrete than a hope for better wages to come." The Court rejected the argument that, simply because the agreement related to wages—a subject at the heart of bargaining—rather than prices, the exemption should apply. Though "a union may conclude a wage agreement with the multi-employer bargaining unit without violating the antitrust laws," the Court explained, "there are limits to what a union or an employer may offer or extract in the name of wages." "[A] union forfeits its exemption from the antitrust laws when it is clearly shown that it has agreed with one set of employers to impose a certain wage scale on other bargaining units." The Court held that the wage agreement was not exempt from the antitrust laws.

Most recently, in *Brown v. Pro Football, Inc.,* the Supreme Court for the first time extended the non-statutory labor exemption to an agreement that was solely among employers. Brown involved an agreement among National Football League teams to restrain the salaries of certain classes of players. The collective-bargaining agreement between the players' union and the league expired, and bargaining began for a new contract. During the negotiations, the NFL adopted a plan that would permit each team to create a developmental squad of rookies who would play in practice games with the team and sometimes in regular games as substitutes for injured players, and provided that the developmental squad players would be paid $1000 per week. The players' union disagreed with these terms and insisted that developmental squad players get benefits and protections similar to those offered to regular players and that they be free to negotiate their own salaries rather than be paid the fixed rate. Two months later, bargaining reached an impasse, and the NFL unilaterally implemented the developmental squad program under its proposed terms. The developmental squad players brought an antitrust action against the league and the individual teams, claiming that the agreement to pay them $1000 per week violated the Sherman Act.

[continued]

We reject the grocers' broad reading of the exemption and hold that, under the totality of circumstances here, and in light of the history and logic of the exemption as well as the Supreme Court's guidance in Brown, application of the exemption to shield the RSP from antitrust scrutiny is not warranted.

The Court in Brown stated, as a premise of its reasoning, that the practice under examination—the unilateral imposition of terms by employers after impasse—was "unobjectionable as a matter of labor law and policy" and that it was regulated "directly, and considerably," by labor laws. In other words, post-impasse imposition of terms is not only an accepted practice in labor negotiation, but one that has been extensively regulated and "carefully circumscribed." By contrast, the use of revenue sharing as an economic weapon during a labor dispute does not enjoy any such endorsement, much less a history of careful regulation, from the realm of labor law and policy. Neither party points to a body of regulatory or judicial decisions that establishes revenue sharing among employers in a bargaining unit as an accepted economic weapon during a labor dispute. From the outset of our analysis, therefore, the RSP is on different footing than the agreement between the NFL club owners in Brown.

Addressing the practice of revenue sharing in the context of multi-employer bargaining, we conclude that the salient concerns underlying Brown and central to the history and logic of the exemption are not present here. The agreement to share revenues during and shortly after a labor dispute does not play a significant role in collective bargaining, nor is it necessary to permit meaningful collective bargaining to take place. The RSP does not relate to any core subject matter of bargaining, namely wages, hours, and working conditions, but rather relates principally to the relative revenues of the grocers in the market and the temporary, artificial maintenance of those revenues.

Although it is not an easy question, in our view the grocers cannot succeed in exempting their agreement merely by asserting its value to them and purpose as an economic weapon in the labor dispute over core bargaining subjects. If this were so, a group of employers could claim that fixing prices made them stronger and was useful as an economic weapon in a strike. Quite obviously, that could not be sufficient to gain exemption. It would be like saying "anything goes in a strike context," and we cannot read Brown so broadly. The RSP was designed to strengthen the grocers' position in negotiations with the union, but that fact alone does not entitle the agreement to antitrust immunity. Employers might undertake any number of activities to strengthen their bargaining posture and force unions to accept their terms, but the law does not necessarily exempt all such activities.

Our decision not to expand the law of non-statutory labor exemption to shield the grocers from antitrust liability in these circumstances does not place them in an untenable position or "introduce instability and uncertainty into the collective-bargaining process." The inability of grocers to enter into an RSP for fear of possible antitrust liability does not hinder the functioning of the collective-bargaining process. Grocers may continue to negotiate terms with the union without an RSP in place and may bring other potent and well-established forms of economic pressure to bear to enhance their bargaining position, including lockouts and the use of replacement workers. Although the arguments advanced by the grocers may be relevant to their position that there was no unreasonable restraint of trade, they are not sufficient to require application of a non-statutory labor exemption. The district court correctly concluded that the grocers' revenue-sharing agreement is not immune from antitrust scrutiny, and we affirm that conclusion.

AFFIRMED.

CRITICAL THINKING

One aspect of critical thinking is evaluating an argument to make sure there is adequate evidence to support the conclusion. On the basis of the evidence in this case, do you agree with the court's conclusion that the grocers' revenue-sharing agreement was not immune from antitrust scrutiny? Why or why not? Provide reasons why you believe the evidence does or does not support the court's conclusion.

ETHICAL DECISION MAKING

Who are the primary stakeholders affected by the court's ruling? Does the appeals court have a stronger ethical obligation to protect the interests of some stakeholders over others? Explain.

Exhibit 47-2
Groups and Activities Exempt from Antitrust Law

GROUP OR ACTIVITY	BASIS FOR EXEMPTION
Agricultural groups and activities and fisheries	Section 6 of the Clayton Act permits farmers to belong to cooperatives that legally set prices. In accordance with the Fisheries Cooperative Marketing Act of 1976, individuals in the fishing industry can cooperate for purposes of catching and preparing fish for market. Both farmers and fishers may set prices, as long as they do not prevent competition in their markets.
Professional baseball	The Supreme Court ruled in *Federal Baseball Club of Baltimore, Inc. v. National League of Professional Baseball Clubs* that baseball was a sport, not a trade. Furthermore, the Court ruled that baseball did not involve interstate commerce. Thus, baseball was not subject to antitrust laws. However, the case has since been amended by the Curt Flood Act of 1998, which allows players to sue team owners for anticompetitive violations if owners work together to drive certain players out of the sport or to keep wages down. Regardless, no other professional sport has been explicitly exempted.
Labor union activities	Section 6 of the Clayton Act permits labor unions to organize and bargain without violating antitrust law. Section 20 of the Clayton Act also allows unions to legally strike, as long as they do not organize with any nonunion groups.
Export activities	The Webb-Pomerene Trade Act of 1918 exempted the formation of selling cooperatives as long as this activity does not significantly enhance or depress prices in the United States. The Webb-Pomerene Trade Act was expanded by the Export Trading Company Act of 1982, which allows the DOJ to certify export-trading companies as qualified. Certified companies cannot be subjected to antitrust claims in the area of certification.
Insurance	When insurance businesses are subject to state antitrust regulation, the McCarran-Ferguson Act exempts the insurance businesses from federal antitrust law.
Regulated industries (utilities, airlines, banking, etc.)	These industries have been regulated in the public interest. The regulatory bodies have the authority to approve behaviors that might otherwise violate antitrust law.
Oil marketing	According to the Interstate Oil Compact of 1935, states can set their own quotas regarding the amount of oil to be sold in interstate commerce.
Research cooperation among businesses	The Small Business Act of 1958 allows small businesses to legally engage in cooperative research. The National Cooperative Research Act of 1984, later amended by the National Cooperative Research and Production Act of 1993, allows competitors to cooperate as joint ventures to develop new products, services, or production methods.
Federal and state exceptions	Both presidential and state actions also can be exempt from antitrust laws. For instance, activities approved by the president to defend the nation are exempt under the Defense Production Act of 1950. Also, state or city policies that are actively supervised by the state or local government often do not fall under the regulations of antitrust law.

What is the Sherman Act?

The Sherman Act

As we described earlier, the Sherman Act (or Sherman Antitrust Act) attempts to stop trusts from unfairly restricting market competition. The main thrust of the Sherman Act is contained in Sections 1 and 2. Section 1 of the Sherman Act states:

> Every contract, combination in the form of trust or otherwise, or conspiracy, in restraint of trade or commerce among the several States, or with foreign nations, is declared to be illegal. Every person who shall make any contract or engage in any combination or conspiracy hereby declared to be illegal shall be deemed guilty of a felony, and, on conviction thereof, shall be punished by fine not exceeding $10,000,000 if a corporation, or, if any other person, $350,000, or by imprisonment not exceeding three years, or by both said punishments.

BUT WHAT IF . . .

WHAT IF THE FACTS OF THE CASE OPENER WERE DIFFERENT?

Let's say, in the Case Opener, that Whole Foods attempts to monopolize the health foods market and absorb not only Wild Oats but a few other health food chains as well. According to the Sherman Act, the company could be fined. But what crime would the company technically be guilty of?

Legal Principle: **Contracts that unfairly restrict market competition in restraint of trade are illegal.**

Section 2 of the Sherman Act states:

> Every person who shall monopolize, or attempt to monopolize, or combine or conspire with any other person or persons, to monopolize any part of the trade or commerce among the several States, or with foreign nations, shall be deemed guilty of a felony, and, on conviction thereof, shall be punished by fine not exceeding $10,000,000 if a corporation, or, if any other person, $350,000, or by imprisonment not exceeding three years.

As you can see, the sections themselves are quite short. Congress did not specify which specific behaviors were prohibited under the Sherman Act. Instead, it left this task to the courts. The courts have interpreted these sections to prohibit efforts by competitors to fix prices, restrict output, and exclude rival companies.

JURISDICTION OF THE SHERMAN ACT

The Sherman Act applies to business practices that restrain trade or commerce "among the several States, or with foreign nations." Congress passed the Sherman Act through its authority to regulate interstate commerce. (Recall the discussion of the commerce clause in Chapter 5.) Therefore, to violate the Sherman Act, a business action must have directly interfered with the flow of goods in commerce. Alternatively, the action must have had an "effect on commerce." The Sherman Act also applies to foreign companies that conduct business that affects U.S. commerce.

BUT WHAT IF . . .

WHAT IF THE FACTS OF THE CASE OPENER WERE DIFFERENT?

Let's say, in the Case Opener, that instead of Whole Foods, a foreign health food company was attempting to absorb some health food chains in the United States. If the absorption would lead to a monopoly, could the Sherman Act apply to the foreign company?

COMPARING THE LAW OF OTHER COUNTRIES

ANTITRUST LAW IN JAPAN

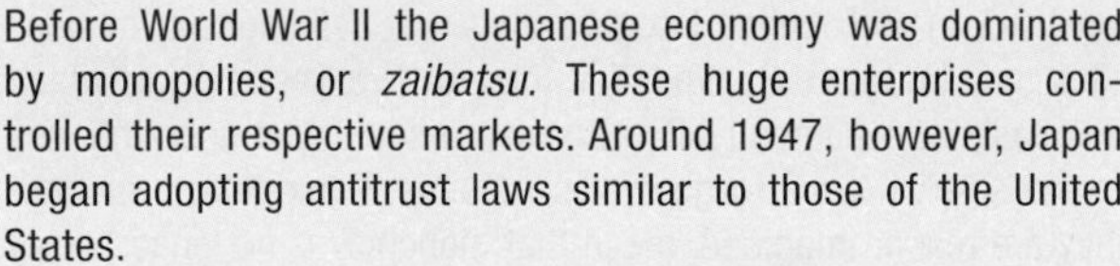

Before World War II the Japanese economy was dominated by monopolies, or *zaibatsu.* These huge enterprises controlled their respective markets. Around 1947, however, Japan began adopting antitrust laws similar to those of the United States.

The core of Japan's laws prohibits three particular practices. The first is the prohibition of private monopolization. This section, modeled after the Sherman Act, forbids businesses to set unreasonably low prices, places limits on large enterprise shareholding, and regulates mergers. In addition to these regulations, the law also deems cartels illegal if they "restrain competition substantially contrary to public interest." Cartels may try to restrain competition by fixing prices or limiting production. The Japanese law does permit depression and rationalization cartels.

The law concludes by banning "unfair" business practices. Obviously this description is riddled with ambiguity, but there are some practices generally considered unfair. Some examples of these are a refusal to deal, abuse of bargaining power, and unreasonable interference in consumer affairs.

Despite the implementation of these antitrust laws, new conglomerate businesses called *keiretsu* have sprung up in Japan. The *keiretsu* resembles an oligopoly, an enterprise that dominates a market with few competitors. Many in Japan support the huge enterprises and continue to believe that they are the most efficient way to conduct business.

SECTION 1 OF THE SHERMAN ACT

L03 What is explored in Section 1 of the Sherman Act?

To constitute a violation of Section 1 of the Sherman Act, a business act or practice must have three characteristics. The act must be (1) a combination, contract, or conspiracy (i.e., an agreement between two parties), (2) an *unreasonable* restraint on trade, and (3) a restraint that affects interstate commerce. The rationale for this violation is that consumers will be harmed if companies are permitted to combine their market power. For example, two companies that make agreements to raise prices and restrict their output harm consumers by making them pay more for a good, simply because of the two firms' unfair agreement.

However, not all agreements between firms harm consumers. Some firms enter into agreements through which they engage in joint research. This research leads to reduced costs for both firms and thus helps consumers. While the language of Section 1 states that "every contract . . . is illegal," the courts have interpreted this comment to apply to agreements that *unreasonably* restrain trade. How does a court determine whether an agreement is an unreasonable restraint on trade?

Rule-of-Reason Analysis and Per Se Violations. The Supreme Court has developed two different approaches to evaluating the reasonableness of a restraint on trade. First, the court has established the **rule-of-reason analysis,** an inquiry into the competitive effects of a company's behavior to determine whether the benefits of the behavior outweigh the harm of the anticompetitive behavior. If the court finds that certain social benefits or positive effects on competition outweigh the harm, the court will rule that the behavior was not a violation. Specifically, when engaging in rule-of-reason analysis, the court considers the following: (1) the nature and purpose of the restraint on trade, (2) the scope of the restraint, (3) the effect of the restraint on business and competition, and (4) the intent of the restraint.

However, certain business practices will always hurt consumers. These practices are called **per se violations.** To establish a per se violation, a plaintiff would simply have to prove that the prohibited conduct occurred. The defendant can offer no justification for the behavior; he or she can argue only that the behavior did not occur. Per se violations are useful in the sense that they give businesses an unambiguous guide to acceptable and unacceptable business practices. In summary, when the court establishes per se violations, it figuratively draws a line in the sand. If a company engages in behavior on the wrong side of the line, the behavior is a violation.

E-COMMERCE AND THE LAW

IS GOOGLE A MONOPOLY?

Most Internet users are probably familiar with the popular search engine known as Google. Google's control over the Internet search market is currently around 70 percent. When 70 percent of the market is controlled by a company, this usually means that the company has created a monopoly in its field. However, many argue that Google's business practices are not illegal by any means because Google has not attempted to quash its competitors. In fact, many of the companies that rival Google—such as the search engine Yelp—have reportedly had increased profits despite their looming competitor, Google. The Federal Trade Commission recently investigated Google's practices, and the FTC's interest and subsequent hesitancy in prosecuting Google shows that definitions of monopolies may be blurred online. The Internet is a vast area in which it is easy for a company, like Google, to say that a user only has to mouse-click once to go to a competitor. Competitors, whether they are real or imagined, mean that monopoly is no longer easily defined, especially online. The nature of e-commerce brings into question the tenets of antitrust law. The question of whether Google is a monopoly is therefore still open for debate.

Source: http://phys.org/news/2012-10-google-moment-truth-monopoly-probe.html; and http://news.cnet.com/8301-1023_3-57539276-93/google-is-many-things-but-not-an-illegal-monopoly/.

Both approaches have been criticized. Some scholars argue that the per se violations are too rigid, prohibiting some cases of pro-competitive behavior. Others argue that the rule-of-reason analysis is too expensive and time-consuming.

Recently, the courts have been moving away from the per se standard. At least one restraint of trade that was previously judged a per se violation is now being judged by rule-of-reason analysis. Additionally, another standard for assessing restraints of trade has emerged as an amalgamation of rule-of-reason analysis and per se violation. This new standard, called the **"quick-look" standard,** permits the defendant to offer justification for his per se violation. If the defendant can offer justification, the court then engages in rule-of-reason analysis.

While these three standards (rule of reason, per se, and quick look) are available to the courts, it is not always clear when a certain standard should be used. In *California Dental Association v. Federal Trade Commission,*[7] the Supreme Court clarified the reasons for choosing the quick-look standard over the rule of reason. However, the Court later suggested there might even be another standard—a "less quick look"—to guide analysis. In conclusion, while these standards seem quite distinct, the lines between them are actually somewhat thin. (See Exhibit 47-3 for a summary of the three standards.)

Exhibit 47-3

Restraint-of-Trade Analysis

Per Se Violations

A plantiff (consumer) need only prove the occurrence of prohibited business conduct. The defendant may not justify the behavior but may only provide proof that the behavior did not occur.

"Quick-Look" Standard

If the defendant can provide justification for the per se violation, the court then engages in rule-of-reason analysis.

Rule-of-Reason Analysis

The court inquires into the competitive effects of a company's behavior to determine whether social benefits or positive effects on competition outweigh the harm of anticompetitive behavior.
The following factors are taken into consideration:

1. Nature and purpose of the restraint on trade
2. Scope of the restraint
3. Effect of the restraint on business and competition
4. Intent of the restraint

[7] 119 S. Ct. 1604 (1999).

E-COMMERCE AND THE LAW

WWW

MAKING BID RIGGING EASY

The online auctions of e-retailers provide fertile grounds for bid rigging. Consider the online company eBay, for example. In 2004, multiple sellers on the eBay site were exploiting the website's weaknesses to drive up auction prices on many different items, including paintings and a car. The New York Attorney General prosecuted the sellers in state court. The accused e-retailers put bids on products (which were owned by the company of the bid riggers themselves) to increase the prices on the items and essentially force buyers to pay more for them. To enter their bids, the bid riggers created multiple user accounts for themselves on eBay, making it difficult to identify them as fakes.

The unsuspecting bidder may not be able to distinguish whether the other bidders are real users or not. Therefore, innocent users may be misled about certain aspects of the item, such as the value or condition of the product. Since anyone can easily create multiple user IDs on the same site, it should come as no surprise that bid rigging, especially on e-retail sites, makes easy profits for those who are willing to break the law.

Source: www.ecommercetimes.com/story/37958.html.

Courts apply these standards to two types of restraints of trade: horizontal and vertical restraints. We now consider these specific restraints.

Horizontal Restraints of Trade. When two competitors in the same market make an agreement to restrain trade, this agreement is called a **horizontal restraint of trade.** For example, two competitors make an agreement to raise the prices on their shoe lines. Types of agreements classified as horizontal restraints of trade are price fixing, horizontal division of markets, group boycotts, trade associations, and joint ventures. Some of these restraints are per se violations.

Price Fixing. When two or more competitors agree to set prices for a product or service, they are engaging in **price fixing.** Why is price fixing harmful? Such agreements simply cut out competition among companies; thus, the consumer will likely pay higher prices for goods. In *United States v. Socony-Vacuum Oil Co.,*[8] the Supreme Court ruled that any kind of horizontal price fixing is a per se violation of the Sherman Act. In this case, Justice Douglas compared free market competition and competitive pricing to the central nervous system of the economy. Justice Douglas then argued that anticompetitive actions are like diseases that attack the body's central nervous system.

Price fixing may consist of raising, lowering, fixing, or stabilizing the price of a good or service. For example, two companies might agree to set a minimum or maximum price for a certain product. Recently, two convenience-store chains filed suit against five tobacco companies, arguing that these companies met regularly to artificially inflate cigarette prices as they began the process of settling health claims against the companies.[9] In order to win their suit, however, the convenience stores must be able to prove that an agreement to fix prices existed.

A form of price fixing is **bid rigging,** an agreement among firms not to bid against one another or to submit a certain level of bid. Suppose you are accepting bids from companies that wish to perform construction work for you. You note that all the competitors submit identical bids. Alternatively, there is an unexplainable significant price difference between the winning bid and all the other bids. Your bids may have been affected by bid rigging. In the 1980s, the Department of Justice (DOJ) uncovered a bid-rigging scheme in the dairy industry. The industry was rigging its bids to supply milk and dairy products to the public school systems in Florida. As a result of its investigation, the DOJ issued almost $70 million in criminal fines against corporations and individuals for their role in the dairy bid-rigging scheme.[10]

[8] 310 U.S. 150 (1940).

[9] "Convenience Stores Level Price-Fixing Charges against Big Tobacco," *Antitrust Litigation Reporter* 7 (May 2000), p. 13.

[10] U.S. Department of Justice, "Antitrust Enforcement and the Consumer."

Horizontal Division of Markets. Suppose two shoe companies agreed to not compete with each other in California, Washington, Florida, and Georgia. They agreed that company 1 would sell shoes only in California and Washington while company 2 would sell shoes in Florida and Georgia. In another agreement, company 1 agrees to sell only men's shoes, while company 2 agrees to sell only women's shoes, in Ohio, Michigan, and Pennsylvania. These agreements would be examples of a **horizontal division of market,** an agreement between two or more competitors to divide markets among themselves by geography, customers, or products. The courts have held these divisions to be per se violations of Section 1 because they serve only to eliminate competition. Each division becomes a little monopoly.

Vertical Restraints of Trade. When two parties at different levels in the manufacturing and distribution process make an agreement that restrains trade, they have made a **vertical restraint against trade.** For example, if a manufacturer and a retailer make an agreement that restricts trade, it is likely a vertical restraint. However, if two manufacturers make an agreement, it is a horizontal restraint. Examples of vertical restraints include resale-price maintenance and territorial and customer restrictions.

Territorial and Customer Restrictions. If a manufacturer limits the territory in which a retailer may sell the manufacturer's product, the manufacturer has created a territorial restriction. Similarly, a manufacturer may mandate that a retailer can sell products only to certain customers. The manufacturer may have legitimate reasons for these territorial and customer restrictions (also called *vertical restraints on distribution* or *nonprice vertical restraints*). Some scholars argue that these restrictions can increase economic efficiency and increase competition. For example, territorial restrictions permit a manufacturer to cut costs by focusing advertising in smaller areas. However, when a manufacturer forces a retailer to agree to these restrictions on territory or resale, the manufacturer may be committing a Section 1 violation.

Historically, the courts assessed territorial restrictions and customer restrictions as per se violations;[11] however, in the landmark case presented in Case 47-2, the Supreme Court changed the standard from per se to rule-of-reason analysis.

[11] *United States v. Arnold, Schwinn & Co.*, 388 U.S. 365 (1967).

CASE 47-2 CONTINENTAL T.V., INC. v. GTE SYLVANIA INC.
UNITED STATES SUPREME COURT
433 U.S. 36 (1977)

When GTE Sylvania discovered it was losing market share to other television manufacturers, it developed a franchise plan that limited the number of retailers selling its product in each area. Moreover, it established the location in each area where the stores could be located. Sylvania required that each franchise sell only Sylvania products.

Sylvania became unhappy with its sales in San Francisco, so it established another location that would be in competition with the existing franchise, Continental T.V. Continental was upset by GTE's action, so it canceled a large order of televisions and ordered a competing brand. Sylvania terminated Continental's franchise and sued for money owed. Continental filed a cross-claim, arguing Sylvania had violated Section 1 of the Sherman Act by restricting the location of retailers that could sell its product. The district court ruled in favor of Continental, while the court of appeals reversed the decision in favor of Sylvania. Continental appealed.

JUSTICE POWELL: The [Schwinn] Court articulated the following "bright line" per se rule of illegality for vertical restrictions: "Under the Sherman Act, it is unreasonable without more for a manufacturer to seek to restrict and confine areas or persons with whom an article may be traded after the manufacturer has parted with dominion over it." But the Court expressly stated the rule of reason governs when "the manufacturer retains title, dominion, and risk with respect to the product and the position and function of the dealer in question are, in fact, indistinguishable from those of an agent or salesman of the manufacturer."

In essence, the issue before us is whether Schwinn's per se rule can be justified under the demanding standards of Northern Pac. R. Co. The Court's refusal to endorse a per se rule in White Motor Co. was based on its uncertainty as to whether vertical restrictions satisfied those standards. Addressing this question for the first time, the Court stated:

> We need to know more than we do about the actual impact of these arrangements on competition to decide whether they have such a "pernicious effect on competition and lack . . . any redeeming virtue" (Northern Pac. R. Co. v. United States, supra, p. 5) and therefore should be classified as per se violations of the Sherman Act. 372 U.S., at 263.

Only four years later the Court in Schwinn announced its sweeping per se rule without even a reference to Northern Pac. R. Co. and with no explanation of its sudden change in position.

The market impact of vertical restrictions is complex because of their potential for a simultaneous reduction of intrabrand competition and stimulation of interbrand competition. . . . Vertical restrictions reduce intrabrand competition by limiting the number of sellers of a particular product competing for the business of a given group of buyers. . . . Vertical restrictions promote interbrand competition by allowing the manufacturer to achieve certain efficiencies in the distribution of his products. These "redeeming virtues" are implicit in every decision sustaining vertical restrictions under the rule of reason. Economists have identified a number of ways in which manufacturers can use such restrictions to compete more effectively against other manufacturers.

Economists also have argued manufacturers have an economic interest in maintaining as much intrabrand competition as is consistent with the efficient distribution of their products. Although the view that the manufacturer's interest necessarily corresponds with that of the public is not universally shared, even the leading critic of vertical restrictions concedes Schwinn's distinction between sale and nonsale transactions is essentially unrelated to any relevant economic impact.

We conclude the distinction drawn in Schwinn between sale and nonsale transactions is not sufficient to justify the application of a per se rule in one situation and a rule of reason in the other. The question remains whether the per se rule stated in Schwinn should be expanded to include nonsale transactions or abandoned in favor of a return to the rule of reason. We have found no persuasive support for expanding the per se rule. As noted above, the Schwinn Court recognized the undesirability of "prohibit[ing] all vertical restrictions of territory and all franchising. . . ." And even Continental does not urge us to hold all such restrictions are per se illegal.

Accordingly, we conclude the per se rule stated in Schwinn must be overruled. In so holding we do not foreclose the possibility that particular applications of vertical restrictions might justify per se prohibition under Northern Pac. R. Co. But we do make clear that departure from the rule-of-reason standard must be based upon demonstrable economic effect rather than—as in Schwinn—upon formalistic line drawing.

In sum, we conclude the appropriate decision is to return to the rule of reason that governed vertical restrictions prior to Schwinn. When anticompetitive effects are shown to result from particular vertical restrictions they can be adequately policed under the rule of reason, the standard traditionally applied for the majority of anticompetitive practices challenged under 1 of the Act. Accordingly, the decision of the Court of Appeals is affirmed.

AFFIRMED.

CRITICAL THINKING

The Court in this case overturned the previous decision made by the Supreme Court in the Schwinn case. Why did the Court decide to overrule the *Schwinn* decision? Do you agree with the Court's overruling?

ETHICAL DECISION MAKING

Suppose you were a business manager at GTE Sylvania who wished to open a store near the Continental store. If you were guided by the universalization test, would your actions have been different? Why?

Legal Principle: **Price fixing between competitors, horizontal divisions of markets, and group boycotts are generally per se violations of the Sherman Act.**

SECTION 2 OF THE SHERMAN ACT

According to economic theory, companies with monopoly power use their economic power to limit production and raise prices, thus harming the consumer. Section 2 of the Sherman Act was designed to prohibit the unfair use of monopoly power.

L04

What is explored in Section 2 of the Sherman Act?

E-COMMERCE AND THE LAW

WEBSITES AS ANTITRUST VIOLATIONS

Antitrust law and the Internet have been clashing in several ways. For example, numerous companies are joining with their competitors to buy and sell goods over the Internet. For instance, in 1999, three automobile makers—Ford, General Motors, and DaimlerChrysler—collaborated to create a website. Their goal was to create an online marketplace for original equipment manufacturers (OEMs) that includes online catalogues, information about sourcing, and additional collaborative applications. The venture has succeeded. (To see what an online marketplace for OEMs looks like, go to www.covisint.com/web/guest/home.) Government officials were concerned that websites might provide ample opportunity for competitors to share market information in ways that would harm consumers and other competitors. For example, if a seller does not have access to this information on the Internet, will the seller be excluded from certain exchanges? Federal officials have not offered clear guidelines about acceptable business web exchanges.

Another example of the clash between antitrust law and the Internet is a recent DOJ investigation of eBay, the online auction site. Other auction sites argue that eBay is maintaining a monopoly by refusing to permit rival auction sites to scan eBay prices for price comparisons. However, eBay argues that it has a protected property right in the information; intellectual property owners are usually free from antitrust liability. Nevertheless, even if the court rules that eBay has a property right in the price information, the DOJ could decide that access to comparative information is necessary for competition.

These examples demonstrate that the application of antitrust laws to businesses' use of the Internet is far from perfect.

Monopolization. The language of Section 2 may appear to prohibit *all* monopolies; however, the courts have interpreted this section to prohibit *conduct that monopolizes.* What is the distinction? The courts permit a monopoly to exist; however, if a company *monopolizes*—that is, it (1) possesses market power and (2) unfairly achieved this market power or uses this market power for abuse—the court will rule that this company has violated the Sherman Act. The plaintiff in a monopolization case must demonstrate both elements of monopolizing.

Monopoly Power. **Monopoly power,** or **market power,** is the ability to control price and drive competitors out of the market. How do the courts determine whether a company has market power? Generally, the courts consider the company's **market share,** a firm's fractional share of the relevant market. If a company enjoys 70 percent of the relevant market, the court usually holds that the firm has monopoly power. If, however, the market share is less than 70 percent, it is questionable whether the court will consider the company to hold market power.

Before a court can determine a company's market share, the court must first identify the company's *relevant market.* The way the court defines the relevant market is immensely important in determining whether a company is monopolizing. When the court identifies the relevant market, it considers two markets: product and geographic markets. A **product market** is a market in which all products identical to or substitutes for the company's product are sold. Suppose a company is accused of monopolizing the coffee market. In its consideration of the product market, the court would identify all coffee produced by other firms. Furthermore, the court would consider tea sales because tea is considered a substitute for coffee. Recall from the case opener that the FTC and Whole Foods Market disagreed on what the exact product market was in the case. Whole Foods claimed that all grocery stores were part of the market it existed in, whereas the FTC believed that Whole Foods operated in a specialty submarket for organic and natural groceries. Which product market do you believe Whole Foods and Wild Oats belong to?

The second market a court considers while identifying the relevant market is the **geographic market,** which is the area in which the company competes with others in the relevant product market. The plaintiff usually stipulates the geographic market as local, regional, or national. For example, if the company's products are sold throughout the United States, the geographic market would be the U.S. market.

Case 47-3 provides an illustration of the court's consideration of the requirement that the plaintiff establish the relevant market.

CASE 47-3 PEPSICO, INC., PLAINTIFF v. THE COCA-COLA COMPANY, DEFENDANT
U.S. COURT OF APPEALS FOR THE SECOND CIRCUIT
315 F.3D 101 (2002)

Coca-Cola and PepsiCo, in addition to selling their famous beverages in bottles and cans, sell fountain syrup to numerous customers, including large restaurant chains, movie theater chains, and other "on-premise" accounts. PepsiCo and Coca-Cola bid for agreements to supply fountain syrup and negotiate a price directly with the customer and then pay a fee to a distributor to deliver the product. Historically, PepsiCo delivered fountain syrup primarily through bottler distributors; Coca-Cola delivered fountain syrup through bottler distributors as well as independent food distributors (IFDs), which can offer customers one-stop shopping for all of their restaurant supplies. In the late 1990s, PepsiCo decided it wanted to start delivering fountain syrup via IFDs, but when it sought to do so, Coca-Cola began to enforce the so-called "loyalty" or "conflict of interest" policy contained in its agreements with IFDs, which provides that distributors that supply customers with Coca-Cola may not "handle the soft drink products of [PepsiCo]." IFDs that breach the loyalty policy risk termination by Coca-Cola. As the district court observed, "a distributor subject to the loyalty policy can supply all its customers with either Pepsi or Coke, not both. Because distributors are given an all or nothing choice, a customer of a distributor subject to Coca-Cola's loyalty policy who wants Pepsi will have to go elsewhere to get it."

PepsiCo filed an antitrust complaint alleging the loyalty provisions constituted an illegal monopolization and attempted monopolization under Section 2 of the Sherman Act. The district court granted Coca-Cola's motion for summary judgment. PepsiCo appealed.

PER CURIAM:

II. Section 2 of the Sherman Act

As noted by the district court, in order to state a claim for monopolization under Section 2 of the Sherman Act, a plaintiff must establish "(1) the possession of monopoly power in the relevant market and (2) the willful acquisition or maintenance of that power as distinguished from growth or development as a consequence of a superior product, business acumen, or historic accident." To state an attempted monopolization claim, a plaintiff must establish "(1) the defendant has engaged in predatory or anti-competitive conduct with (2) a specific intent to monopolize and (3) a dangerous probability of achieving monopoly power."

A. The Relevant Market

As an initial matter, it is necessary to define the relevant product and geographic market Coca-Cola is alleged to be monopolizing. The parties do not dispute the relevant geographic market is the United States. A relevant product market consists of "products that have reasonable interchangeability for the purposes for which they are produced—price, use and qualities considered." Products will be considered to be reasonably interchangeable if consumers treat them as "acceptable substitutes."

In its complaint, PepsiCo defined the relevant market as the "market for fountain-dispensed soft drinks distributed through [IFDs] throughout the United States." PepsiCo sought to narrow this market definition on summary judgment by confining it to customers with certain characteristics, specifically "large restaurant chain accounts that are not 'heavily franchised' with low fountain 'volume per outlet.'" The district court rejected this definition on the grounds 1) it was not substantiated by the evidence; and 2) it was not supported by the practical indicia enunciated in Brown Shoe.

Reviewing the evidence submitted on summary judgment, the district court held fountain syrup delivered by bottler distributors was an "acceptable substitute" for fountain syrup delivered by IFDs—and thus had to be included in the relevant product market—because none of the numerous customers who were deposed or submitted affidavits for the summary judgment motion said the availability of delivery via IFDs was determinative of its choice of fountain syrup. Tellingly, in PepsiCo's own survey of 99 major customers, the availability of one-stop-shopping IFDs was ranked 35 out of 38 in importance among various factors they considered in choosing a fountain syrup.

The district court also rejected PepsiCo's argument the relevant market should be confined to certain customers, an argument the district court characterized as "PepsiCo['s attempt] to define the elements of the relevant market to suit its desire for high Coca-Cola market share, rather than letting the market define itself." The district court found, although the affidavits and exhibits submitted on the summary judgment motion showed many customers have a preference for receiving fountain syrup through IFDs because of the advantages provided by one-stop-shopping, these customers did not constitute a discrete group, but rather were included in various groups of fountain syrup customers. Indeed, franchisees, a group PepsiCo sought to exclude from the market definition, purchased 63 percent of the Coca-Cola fountain syrup delivered by IFDs. Identical types of customers expressed preferences for either IFDs or bottler distributors, and most customers stated method of delivery was simply one of several nondeterminative factors they considered in deciding which fountain syrup to stock. We agree with the district court PepsiCo failed to provide evidentiary support for its market definition restricted by distributor and customer.

AFFIRMED.

[continued]

CRITICAL THINKING

What is there about the idea of a "market" that makes it ambiguous? Why can we not all agree about what the relevant market is for antitrust purposes?

ETHICAL DECISION MAKING

Using the universalization principle, would you prefer to have markets defined broadly or narrowly? Think about who benefits and who loses from these alternatives.

In summary, when determining whether a company holds monopoly power, the court first identifies the relevant market, which includes the product and geographic markets. After the court identifies the relevant market, it determines the company's market share. If the market share is greater than or equal to 70 percent, the court will likely rule that the company in question has monopoly power. Given the geographic market requirement, it is possible for a firm that operates nationally to operate in separate, distinct markets. As such, a national firm might have a monopoly in one of the geographic markets but not in others.

The Intent Requirement. After the court determines that a company has monopoly power, it next considers the company's intent. A firm that holds monopoly power is not necessarily violating Section 2. This firm might have legitimately earned dominance in the market. For example, this firm might be manufacturing a high-quality product, or its managers may have made very wise business decisions. However, if the firm *intends* to monopolize or engages in anticompetitive activity in an attempt to maintain its monopoly power, the firm has violated Section 2. Courts look at the specific behavior of the company to determine its intent. For example, in the chapter opener, the FTC has to prove that Whole Foods had a specific intent to monopolize the organic supermarket industry when it decided to merge with Wild Oats. If intent was present, then the court can find that Whole Foods Market violated antitrust law.

Attempts to Monopolize. Suppose a company does not currently hold market power; however, this company starts to use certain business practices in the hope it will gain a greater share of the market and make more profit. If this company intended these practices to (1) exclude competitors and (2) allow the company to gain monopoly power, the courts would consider these practices as **attempts to monopolize**. (See Exhibit 47-4.) However, another important element of an attempt to monopolize is the probability of success. Only those practices that have a dangerous probability of success constitute an attempt to monopolize. For example, suppose a company that recently introduced a new soft drink

Exhibit 47-4
Attempts-to-Monopolize Analysis

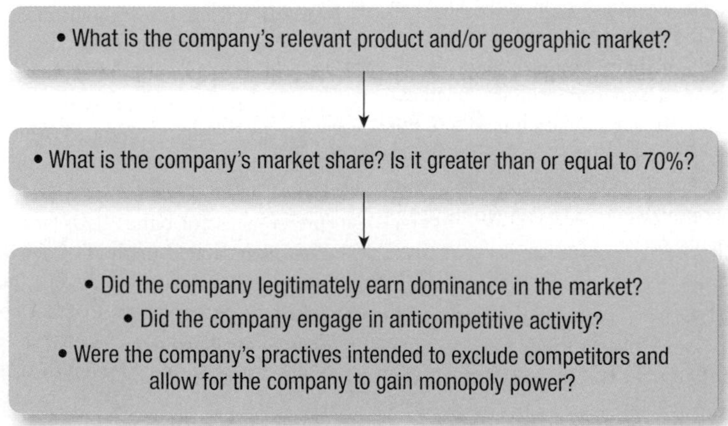

attempted to monopolize the soft-drink industry. Because it is unlikely that this company could monopolize an industry largely dominated by Coke and Pepsi, the company would likely not be found guilty of an attempt to monopolize.

Companies may use various different practices in attempts to monopolize. For example, they may steal another company's trade secrets. Alternatively, they might engage in predatory pricing. When a company prices one product below normal cost until competitors are eliminated and then sharply increases the price, the company is practicing **predatory pricing.**

Exemption for States. Some firms that monopolize are permitted to exist. Section 2 of the Sherman Act does not apply to states; consequently, the state may create monopolies.

The Clayton Act

L05 What is the Clayton Act?

During the 1912 presidential election, antitrust law was a dominant issue for the candidates. The Supreme Court had recently ruled that only those restraints on trade that were unreasonable under rule-of-reason analysis were subject to the Sherman Act. Candidate Woodrow Wilson argued that rule-of-reason analysis was not specific enough for businesspeople; he asserted that the government needed to establish specific business practices that were antitrust violations. Wilson was elected, and Congress soon enacted the Clayton Act in 1914.

The Clayton Act identifies the following four business practices not covered under the Sherman Act:

1. Price discrimination (Section 2 of the Clayton Act).
2. Exclusionary practices (Section 3).
3. Mergers (Section 7).
4. Interlocking directorates (Section 8).

These practices are considered illegal when they significantly harm competition. We will now examine these specific business practices.

SECTION 2: PRICE DISCRIMINATION

Section 2 of the Clayton Act (as amended by the Robinson-Patman Act in 1936) prohibits price discrimination by sellers. A seller engages in **price discrimination** when it sells the same goods to competing buyers for different prices. Sellers may use price discrimination to bring about monopoly power.

To demonstrate a violation of Section 2 of the Clayton Act, a plaintiff must show two basic elements. First, the seller that engaged in price discrimination must be involved in interstate commerce. Second, the seller's price discrimination must have substantially lessened competition or tended to create a monopoly.

Specifically, Section 2(a) of the act prohibits discrimination in price by sellers between two buyers of a commodity of like grade and quality. Offers to sell are not violations of this section. For example, suppose a manufacturer agrees to sell 100 pairs of jeans to a retailer for \$25 per pair. However, the manufacturer offers to sell another retailer 100 pairs of jeans for \$20 per pair. If he did not make the sale to the second retailer, he has not violated Section 2(a).

Suppose for a moment that the manufacturer did make the sale to the second retailer. However, the jeans he sold to the second retailer were of lower quality; they had slight defects in their manufacturing. If he can demonstrate a physical difference between the jeans he sold to the two retailers, he has not violated Section 2(a).

CASE NUGGET

PREDATORY PRICING

Spirit Airlines, Inc. v. Northwest Airlines, Inc.
2005 U.S. App. LEXIS 29338 (2005)

Spirit Airlines was based out of Detroit and focused its business toward "leisure or low-price-sensitive" passengers. Spirit's main flights were direct flights from Detroit to Boston and Philadelphia. Northwest Airlines, which uses Detroit as one of its main hubs, also flies direct flights from Detroit to Boston and Philadelphia. In addition, Northwest controls 64 of the 86 gates at Detroit's airport. When Spirit began selling tickets at costs far lower than those of Northwest, Northwest drastically lowered its prices and increased the number of seats available from Detroit to both Boston and Philadelphia, in addition to preventing Spirit from using any gate owned by Northwest. Spirit sued Northwest under Section 2 of the Sherman Antitrust Act, alleging predatory pricing and other predatory tactics. The district court granted summary judgment in favor of Northwest, and Spirit appealed.

At trial, Northwest alleged that it never operated below cost and therefore did not engage in predatory pricing. The district court agreed with Northwest's assertion. Furthermore, Northwest argued that the proper market included all passengers passing through Detroit to Boston or Philadelphia, not just those with direct flights. In addition, Northwest claimed that its lower price was due to a competitive response, as market logic would predict, to the entering of another firm (Spirit) into the market.

In response, Spirit argued that Northwest intentionally lowered its prices and increased capacity on the specific routes Detroit to Boston and Philadelphia. Spirit used as evidence an article an executive at Northwest wrote and published specifically explaining that the best way to drive out competition from an upstart is to undercut in price and increase seats to ensure no potential customers are turned away. Further evidence of Northwest's predatory behavior included the fact that Northwest increased its prices on both Detroit to Boston and Detroit to Philadelphia once Spirit canceled these routes, thus regaining its monopoly on flights to these two cities out of Detroit.

The appellate court, in reconsidering the evidence from the trial, determined there was sufficient evidence for a fact finder to determine that Northwest did engage in predatory pricing. The court writes:

> In sum, even if the jury were to find that Northwest's prices exceeded an appropriate measure of average variable costs, the jury must also consider the market structure in this controversy to determine if Northwest's deep price discounts in response to Spirit's entry and the accompanying expansion of its capacity on these routes injured competition by causing Spirit's departure from this market and allowing Northwest to recoup its losses and to enjoy monopoly power as a result.

The appellate court reversed and remanded the lower court's decision.

There are several reasons why a seller might legitimately engage in price discrimination. For example, the production costs associated with the products sold to the first buyer might be lower than the production costs for the products sold to the second buyer. If a seller can justify the price difference through cost difference, the seller has not violated Section 2 of the Clayton Act. Moreover, if a seller engages in price discrimination to compete in good faith with another seller's low price, the seller is not guilty of violating the Clayton Act. This defense to price discrimination is called the **meeting-the-competition defense.**

SECTION 3: EXCLUSIONARY PRACTICES

The Clayton Act spells out a large number of forbidden exclusionary practices that violate the objectives of a market economy. Section 3 of the Clayton Act provides the general basis for defining these methods of unfair competition. For instance, courts have interpreted Section 3 as prohibiting exclusive-dealing contracts and tying agreements.

If an exclusive-dealing contract or tying agreement involves services or intangibles, Section 3 does not apply to that contract. Instead, Section 3 applies only to the lease or sale of commodities. Services and intangibles in exclusive-dealing contracts or tying agreements may be tried under the Sherman Act.

Exclusive Dealing. An **exclusive-dealing contract** is an agreement in which a seller requires that a buyer buy products supplied only by that seller. This agreement prohibits a buyer from buying the seller's competitor's products. If this agreement lessens competition or tends to create a monopoly, the agreement is in violation of Section 3 of the Clayton Act.

Perhaps the most well known case that considered exclusive-dealing contracts is *Standard Oil v. United States.*[12] Standard Oil, the largest gasoline seller at the time of the case, created exclusive-dealing contracts with independent stations. Approximately half of Standard Oil's sales came from these independent stations. Six of Standard Oil's largest competitors created their own exclusive-dealing contracts. Standard Oil and its six largest competitors, through their exclusive-dealing contracts, accounted for 65 percent of the market. The court ruled that although exclusive-dealing agreements could have positive competitive effects, the exclusive-dealing contracts in this case gave Standard Oil 7 percent of the total gas sales in the area ($58 million). Furthermore, the exclusive-dealing contracts created a situation in which competitors could not freely enter into the market. Consequently, the Supreme Court ruled that these exclusive-dealing contracts were illegal under Section 3.

Consider the following case: Blockbuster Video entered into an exclusive agreement to market a Barbra Streisand concert video with an additional song not included in other versions of the video.[13] ERI Max Entertainment sued, arguing that the exclusive agreement was a violation of antitrust law. The court ruled that although Blockbuster controls a large proportion of the video market, the exclusive agreement did not cause injury to competition, particularly because the exclusive-dealing agreement applied to one song on one tape.

BUT WHAT IF . . .

WHAT IF THE FACTS OF THE CASE OPENER WERE DIFFERENT?

Let's say, in the Case Opener, that Whole Foods is simply a distributor of all kinds of orange juice. Whole Foods enters into an agreement with an orange juice manufacturing company which stipulates that Whole Foods will drop all other brands of orange juice and sell only that company's brand at all of its stores. What kind of a trade agreement is this called?

Tying Arrangements. When a seller agrees to sell a product, the tying product, to a buyer on the condition that the buyer will also purchase another product, the tied product, the seller has created a **tying arrangement.** The sale of one product is tied to the sale of another product. For example, suppose a manufacturer agrees to sell men's shoes to a retailer as long as the retailer also buys women's shoes to resell.

Like exclusive-dealing contracts, tying arrangements are not necessarily illegal. In evaluating the legality under Section 3, courts ask the following questions:

1. Are the products being tied clearly separate?
2. What is the purpose of the tying agreement?
3. Does the seller tying the products hold market power?

If the tying arrangement leads to competitive harm, the court will likely find the arrangement to be illegal.

Remember, tying arrangements apply only to commodities; therefore, arrangements tying services must be tried under the Sherman Act. For example, a plaintiff brought a suit against a funeral home for violating Section 3 of the Clayton Act by tying funeral services

[12] 37 U.S. 293 (1949).

[13] *ERI Max Entertainment Inc. d/b/a Vidi-O v. Streisand et al.,* No. 95-615-Appeal (R.I. Sup. Ct., Mar. 17, 1997).

to the purchase of a casket.[14] The court stated that for the case to be tried under the Clayton Act, both the funeral services and the casket must be a good.

SECTION 7: MERGERS

Section 7 prohibits anticompetitive mergers or acquisitions. We define **merger** as the acquisition of one company by another. Specifically, the text of the section prohibits one person or company from owning or acquiring stocks or assets in another corporation when the effect would be to lessen competition.

Given the importance placed on competition, many merger cases also focus on market concentration. Markets are considered concentrated when a few firms in the relevant market enjoy large market shares.

We restrict mergers through Section 7 because we want to ensure that competition can thrive in the market; some mergers are likely to inhibit competition because these mergers may permit companies to form monopolies. For example, suppose you are competing with another major company to sell laptop computers. Instead of trying to compete with this company, you create an offer to acquire the company. You think once you acquire the company, you will be able to increase your prices to increase your profit. Who else will compete with you?

There are three types of mergers: horizontal, vertical, and conglomerate. The classification of type of merger depends on the relationship between the acquirer and the acquired company. However, of the three types of mergers, the Department of Justice and the courts are most likely to challenge horizontal mergers.

Horizontal Mergers. A merger between two or more companies producing the same or similar products is a **horizontal merger.** Because these firms are at the same competitive level, a horizontal merger usually eliminates a competitor from the market. Historically, if a horizontal merger led to undue concentration in the market (i.e., a relatively large market share), the merger was likely to be presumed illegal.

However, in the 1970s, courts became more willing to consider certain economic factors. The FTC and DOJ created guidelines to assess the legality of mergers. Not only would the courts look at the market share of the resulting firm, but they would also look at the degree of concentration in the market. The FTC and DOJ use an index system to determine the level of concentration in the market. If the market is concentrated (i.e., a small number of companies control a large portion of the market), the FTC and DOJ will probably challenge the merger. (Remember, the goal is to preserve competition.) However, the FTC and DOJ consider a variety of other factors: the financial condition of the acquired and acquiring firm, barriers to entry in the industry, and the economic efficiency associated with the merger. Moreover, the courts might look at the history of the acquiring firm. Has this firm acquired smaller companies in the past? Is the company aggressive? The courts will also attempt to predict the success of the resulting firm from the merger.

The Case Opener considers a horizontal merger between two competing supermarkets. Before the FTC tried to stop the merger between Whole Foods and Wild Oats, it used the index system described above to determine the level of concentration in the market. The FTC found that in 18 cities the market power of Whole Foods would virtually be unchallenged. Whole Foods would have no competitors in those 18 geographic regions and, as a result, could control a large portion of the market. Because of this, the FTC opposed the horizontal merger of the two companies.

[14] *Chatelain et al. v. Mothe Funeral Homes Inc., et al.* (E.D. La., July 1, 1998).

Vertical Mergers. When one company at one level of the manufacturing-distribution system acquires a company at another level of the system, this merger is called a **vertical merger.** For example, when a manufacturer acquires a retailer, they have engaged in a vertical merger.

Unlike horizontal mergers, vertical mergers do not lead to concentration in the market. However, vertical mergers can cause other harm to competition. Most important, a vertical merger may permit one firm to foreclose competition. For example, suppose you manufacture shoes, and you decide to acquire a retail outlet for your shoes. First, you have foreclosed competition among those who were trying to purchase your products for resale. Second, when you sell the shoes through your retail outlet, you will likely not carry other brands of shoes. Thus, you have affected competition for the resale of your shoes.

Generally, courts have been most concerned with the foreclosure element associated with vertical mergers. However, the courts usually also examine the history of vertical mergers in the industry as well as by the acquiring company. If the merger does not harm competition, courts will usually permit it.

Conglomerate Mergers. When a company merges with another company that is not a competitor or a buyer or seller to the company, this merger is called a **conglomerate merger.** The two companies that are merging are unrelated in their respective businesses.

Conglomerate mergers exist in three basic forms. The first is *product extension,* which exists when a firm merges with another firm producing a related product. The purpose behind a product-extension merger is to enable the acquiring company to obtain the production of the related product and add it to the acquiring company's production of its current product. For example, if one automobile manufacturer acquires another automobile manufacturer, that would be an example of a product-extension conglomerate merger. The second type of conglomerate merger is *market extension.* Market-extension conglomerate mergers involve a firm attempting to extend the market for one of its current products by merging with a firm already active in the target market. A market-extension conglomerate merger can be seen when a company that makes air fresheners attempts to extend its product line by purchasing a company that produces fragrant candles. The third type of conglomerate merger is a *diversification merger.* Diversification mergers occur when the acquiring firm desires to spread into new markets where it currently does not have a product. The acquiring firm will merge with another firm and continue to produce the other firm's product in the target market. An example of a diversification merger is a real estate firm's acquisition of a telephone service provider.

Why might conglomerate mergers be violations of the Clayton Act? Suppose a company is planning to move into a certain industry; however, the company makes an acquisition to ease its way into the market. Instead of creating another competitor in the market (and thus benefiting consumers), the original company simply acquired its way into the market. In sum, conglomerate mergers may not encourage competitors to enter the market. Why would a company enter a new market when it can simply rely on the acquired company to carry it into the new market?

SECTION 8: INTERLOCKING DIRECTORATES

Section 8 of the Clayton Act prohibits a person from becoming a director in two or more corporations if any of the corporations (1) have capital and profits totaling more than $13.8 million or (2) are or were competitors. However, a person can serve as a director for two firms that are vertically related.

Why does Section 8 prohibit a person from serving as a director in two competing companies? If the same person exerts control over two different companies, it is possible the person will engage in some kind of anticompetitive behavior in an attempt to increase profits for both companies. This prohibition is a preventive measure; instead of waiting until anticompetitive behavior occurs, Section 8 takes steps to ensure that the behavior does not occur at all.

Legal Principle: **A person may not serve as the director of two or more horizontally related companies.**

The Federal Trade Commission Act

LO6

What is the Federal Trade Commission Act?

When Congress passed the Clayton Act, it also passed the Federal Trade Commission Act. This act prohibits unfair and deceptive methods of competition. Therefore, any anticompetitive behavior not prohibited by the Sherman Act or the Clayton Act is illegal under the Federal Trade Commission Act.

The broad language of the Federal Trade Commission Act permits the Federal Trade Commission to investigate and bring antitrust claims. For example, in May 2000, the FTC settled charges against the five largest compact-disc distributors. In the early 1990s, popular CDs were typically priced at $9.99 because of a price war among competing retailers. However, in 1995–1996, in an attempt to end the price war, the distributors adopted policies in which they required that retailers advertise popular CDs at prices at or above the distributors' set price. Consequently, CD prices increased. The FTC estimated that consumers paid approximately $480 million because of the distributors' requirement.

The Robinson-Patman Act

As originally written, the Clayton Act did not apply to buyers. Therefore, in an effort to limit buyers' power, as well as sellers', Congress adopted the Robinson-Patman Act in 1936. The Robinson-Patman Act amended Section 2 of the Clayton Act by further prohibiting price discrimination in interstate commerce, this time targeting buyers. Now, neither buyers nor sellers may engage in price discrimination. Similar to Section 2 of the Clayton Act, whenever price discrimination lessens competition or creates a monopoly, the guilty party will be subject to civil liability.

Much like the Clayton Act, when price differentials can be justified as legitimate, they do not constitute illegal practices. For example, a buyer who solicits an unreasonably low price on a product while offering the seller a portion of the profits is engaging in illegal behavior if the low price leads to a noncompetitive environment. However, if the seller offered the same price to other buyers, competition would not be affected and the activity would not be illegal.

The Robinson-Patman Act identifies three specific types of injuries. **Primary-line injuries** occur when preferential treatment is given to a competitor. **Secondary-line injuries** are those created when preferential price treatment is granted to specific buyers. Most often, large buyers are given preferential treatment at the cost of small buyers. That is, large buyers are given discounts that are subsidized by charging small buyers a higher rate. Finally, **tertiary-line injuries** exist when someone who is given an illegally low price passes her savings on to her customers. For example, Jim is a seller who supplies Erin with coats at a discounted price. Erin then sells her coats at a lower price, pulling in more business. Erin's extra business comes from customers who would have otherwise bought from Jack, who also sells coats but was not given a discount on his order of coats. The business Jack lost because of the discount Erin received and passed on to her customers is a tertiary-line injury.

E-COMMERCE AND THE LAW

MICROSOFT'S MONOPOLY

In 1998 Microsoft Corporation was charged with violating Sections 1 and 2 of the Sherman Act. According to the plaintiff, Microsoft possessed a "dominant, persistent, and increasing share of the relevant market." Microsoft's share of the market for Intel-compatible PCs was over 95 percent. To maintain its monopoly power, Microsoft convinced developers to concentrate on producing Windows-specific platforms. As a result, Microsoft's competition was unable to reach its full potential because the available technologies did not exist. Microsoft also bundled its browser, Internet Explorer, with its operating system. This action was a result of Microsoft's desire to combat competition from rival browser Netscape Navigator. The plaintiff, the U.S. DOJ, argued that Microsoft violated Section 2 of the Sherman Act by engaging in exclusionary, anticompetitive, and predatory acts to maintain a monopoly. The court ruled in favor of the plaintiff, which contended that Microsoft had violated Sections 1 and 2 of the Sherman Act by tying its browser to its operating system and attempting to monopolize the web browser market.

Enforcement of Antitrust Laws

Antitrust laws are enforced in both the public and the private sectors. The Department of Justice and the Federal Trade Commission enforce antitrust laws in the public sector. Any individual who has been injured by an illegal business practice may bring a private suit against the business.

Legal Principle: **Any individual who has been injured by an illegal business practice may bring a private suit against a business engaging in antitrust behavior.**

> To see a description of the relationship between accounting and Sherman Act fines, please see the **Connecting to the Core** activity on the text website at www.mhhe.com/kubasek3e.

PUBLIC ENFORCEMENT

Some violations of the Sherman Act are criminal acts; thus, the Antitrust Division of the DOJ can bring criminal or civil actions against violators. If a corporation commits a crime under the Sherman Act, the corporation could face a $10 million fine for each offense. Furthermore, officers and employees who are convicted under the Sherman Act face a maximum fine of $350,000 and/or jail time of up to three years.

No violations of the Clayton Act are crimes, so the DOJ or the FTC can bring a civil action against violators under the Clayton Act. Part of the DOJ's power to bring civil suits includes the ability to request divestiture or dissolution. Divestiture occurs when the DOJ requests that the court force a company to give up part of its operation procedures. For example, a court could order a firm that sells all of its products out of stores it owns to sell off the stores or allow other firms' products to be sold in the stores. The FTC has sole authority for investigating and making claims against those who violate the Federal Trade Commission Act. When either the DOJ or the FTC makes a civil claim against a potential violator, the parties may decide to settle the case by entering into a **consent decree,** an agreement that binds the violating party to cease his or her illegal behavior.

PRIVATE ENFORCEMENT

Congress wants to encourage private parties to stop anticompetitive behavior. Thus, if a party is harmed by a company's anticompetitive behavior, the party can bring a private suit under the Sherman Act or the Clayton Act. If the party successfully demonstrates its antitrust claim, the party is entitled to attorney fees and damages. More important, the Sherman Act entitles the party to receive treble damages (triple the amount of damages awarded). Treble damages serve as an incentive for private parties to bring suits; thus, treble damages also serve as an incentive for companies to ensure that they do not commit violations under the Sherman or Clayton Act. Private parties are responsible for almost all the antitrust claims brought to court in recent years.

CASE OPENER WRAP-UP

Whole Foods Market Merger and Monopoly

In the Case Opener, the FTC sought an injunction against Whole Foods to block a merger under Section 7 of the Clayton Act. The district court denied the injunction, after holding that the acquisition of Whole Foods' competitor, Wild Oats, did not create monopoly power because other supermarkets still existed in the area to compete with Whole Foods. Therefore, the district court found in favor of Whole Foods.

The case was, however, appealed. Instead of looking at the entire grocery store industry as one large market, the appellate court determined that the particular products sold by premium, natural, and organic supermarkets (PNOSs) distinguished a submarket. The court agreed with the FTC's evidence, which delineated a PNOS submarket catering to a core group of customers who have decided that "natural, organic, and ecological sustainability is important." Additionally, the FTC provided direct evidence that PNOS competition had a greater effect than conventional supermarkets on PNOS prices. For example, the opening of a new Whole Foods in the vicinity of a Wild Oats caused Wild Oats' prices to drop, while entry by non-PNOS stores had no such effect.

In addition to the creation of a monopoly, as we know from this chapter, intent is also required. In the case of Whole Foods, the FTC relied on e-mails that Whole Foods' CEO John Mackey sent to other Whole Foods executives and directors suggesting the purpose of the merger was to eliminate its major competitor in the organic foods industry. For example, in an e-mail to his company's board, Mackey explained that "[Wild Oats] is the only existing company that has the brand and number of stores to be a meaningful springboard for another player to get into this space. Eliminating them means eliminating this threat forever, or almost forever."

After the FTC made its case, the appellate court found that the district court had erred in establishing what the relevant product and geographic markets were. Indeed, the district court had defined the term "market" too broadly and had not adequately considered the special circumstances of an organic and natural submarket. As a result, the case was reversed and remanded for proceedings consistent with the appellate court's decision.

KEY TERMS

attempts to monopolize 1050
bid rigging 1045
conglomerate merger 1055
consent decree 1057
efficiency 1037
exclusive-dealing contract 1053
geographic market 1048
horizontal division of market 1046
horizontal merger 1054
horizontal restraint of trade 1045
market power 1048
market share 1048
meeting-the-competition defense 1052
merger 1054
monopoly power 1048
per se violations 1043
predatory pricing 1051
price discrimination 1051
price fixing 1045
primary-line injuries 1056
product market 1048
quick-look standard 1044
rule-of-reason analysis 1043
secondary-line injuries 1056
tertiary-line injuries 1056
trust 1036
tying arrangement 1053
vertical merger 1055
vertical restraint against trade 1046

SUMMARY OF KEY TOPICS

History of and Rationale for Antitrust Law

Regulation of business activity is necessary when firms violate certain principles of fairness and, as a result, cause harm to consumers.

The Sherman Act

The Sherman Act applies to business practices that restrain trade or commerce "among the several States, or with foreign nations." Congress passed the Sherman Act through its authority to regulate interstate commerce. Therefore, to violate the Sherman Act, a business act must have directly interfered with the flow of goods in commerce. Alternatively, the act must have had an "effect on commerce."

Section 1 of the Sherman Act: To constitute a violation of Section 1 of the Sherman Act, a business act or practice must have three characteristics. The act must be (1) a combination, contract, or conspiracy (i.e., an agreement between two parties), (2) an *unreasonable* restraint on trade, and (3) a restraint that affects interstate commerce. The rationale for this violation is that consumers will be harmed if companies are permitted to join their market power.

Horizontal restraints of trade: When two competitors in the same market make an agreement to restrain trade, this agreement is a horizontal restraint of trade.

- *Price fixing:* An agreement between two or more competitors to set prices for a product or service. Such agreements simply cut out competition among companies; thus, the consumer will likely pay higher prices for goods.
- *Horizontal division of markets:* An agreement between two or more competitors to divide markets among themselves by geography, customers, or products. The courts have held that such divisions are per se violations of Section 1 because they serve only to eliminate competition.

Vertical restraints of trade: When two parties at different levels in the manufacturing and distribution process make an agreement that restrains trade, they have made a vertical restraint against trade.

Section 2 of the Sherman Act: According to economic theory, companies with monopoly power would use their economic power to limit production and raise prices, thus harming the consumer. Section 2 of the Sherman Act was designed to prohibit the unfair use of monopoly power.

Monopolization: The courts permit a monopoly to exist; however, if a company *monopolizes,* that is, if it (1) possesses market power and (2) unfairly achieved this market power or uses this power for abuse, the court will rule that the company has violated the Sherman Act.

Attempt to monopolize: If a company intends its behavior to (1) exclude competitors and (2) allow the company to gain monopoly power, the courts would consider these practices as attempts to monopolize.

The Clayton Act

Section 2—Price discrimination: Section 2 of the Clayton Act (as amended by the Robinson-Patman Act in 1936) prohibits price discrimination by sellers. A seller engages in price discrimination when it sells the same goods to competing buyers for different prices.

Section 3—Exclusionary practices: Section 3 prohibits a number of activities that restrict the vigorous competition needed to protect consumers. For example, it prohibits exclusive dealing and tying arrangements.

Section 7—Mergers: Anticompetitive mergers and acquisitions are prohibited by Section 7.

1. *Horizontal merger:* A merger between two or more companies producing the same or similar products. Because these firms are at the same competitive level, a horizontal merger usually eliminates a competitor from the market.

2. *Vertical merger:* A merger in which one company at one level of the manufacturing-distribution system acquires a company at another level of the system.
3. *Conglomerate merger:* A merger in which a company merges with another company that is not a competitor or a buyer or seller to the company. The two companies that are merging are unrelated in their respective businesses.

The Federal Trade Commission Act This act prohibits unfair and deceptive methods of competition. Therefore, any anticompetitive behavior not prohibited by the Sherman Act or the Clayton Act is illegal under the Federal Trade Commission Act.

The Robinson-Patman Act As originally written, the Clayton Act did not apply to buyers. Therefore, in an effort to limit buyers' power, as well as sellers', Congress adopted the Robinson-Patman Act in 1936.

Enforcement of Antitrust Laws The antitrust laws are enforced by public and private means. The Justice Department and the FTC serve as public enforcement mechanisms; private individuals or firms may file court actions to enforce these laws as well.

POINT / COUNTERPOINT

Should Government Control Monopolies Aggressively?

NO

The government currently exercises too much control over large businesses when they are successful in forming monopolies. Large businesses are unfairly discriminated against solely because they are successful. Government regulation is largely not necessary—natural market competition will provide sufficient product options for the consumer. In the market, the firms that satisfy consumer desires to the greatest extent will flourish. A company goes out of business because its product isn't good enough for the consumer. Why force the most powerful company with the best product to leave 30 percent of the relevant market to companies with worse products?

Section 2 of the Sherman Act is designed to prohibit all "conduct that monopolizes." The main problem with this legislation is the focus on *intent.* According to Section 2, a monopoly is sometimes allowed to exist when formed naturally and without anticompetitive behavior. However, if a company is discovered to have the *intent* to form a monopoly, the company can be declared in violation of Section 2. Companies should not be prevented from filling consumer need because they have the best product, best advertising, and best investments. They should be rewarded for spurring continued economic growth, not restricted and prevented from expanding their business.

YES

The government currently ignores much serious social harm caused when large firms form monopolies. Current laws do not prevent large companies from forming monopolies. In fact, some monopolies are allowed to continue even after they are discovered as and labeled "monopolies." Section 2 of the Sherman Act was written in highly ambiguous language, and the act is subject to interpretation by the courts. Section 2 was designed to limit only unfair use of monopoly power, or "conduct that monopolizes," not to prevent monopolies completely.

Additionally, a company violates Section 2, and therefore can be penalized, only when it *intends* to participate in anticompetitive behavior. However, intent has little to do with the consequences of possessing a monopoly of a specific market. The mere existence of a monopoly, whether gained through "fair" or "unfair" means, is still detrimental to the consumer. The consumer needs the benefits of competition among firms whether a monopoly exists or not. When a monopoly exists, the single powerful company is able to overcharge for its product because the company does not have competition.

Additionally, society suffers when a company obtains a monopoly because competition among companies for consumer demand forces companies to continue improving their products to keep consumers purchasing their products. When a monopoly exists, the single company's product is the only, and therefore "best," option available, so demand continues even when product development stagnates. Competing ideas create better products, better music, better food, and a better standard of living.

QUESTIONS & PROBLEMS

1. What is a rule-of-reason analysis, and what is its purpose in the courts? What are the four things the courts consider when engaging in a rule-of-reason analysis?
2. What business practices can be considered illegal as a result of the Clayton Act, which Congress passed in 1914?
3. In what ways can horizontal and vertical mergers be harmful to competition?
4. Walmart Stores, Inc., one of the largest businesses in the world, had a DVDs-by-mail rental service available to its customers. Walmart's business was in close competition with Netflix. In May 2005, Walmart decided to pull out of the DVDs-by-mail rental industry and struck an agreement with Netflix. Walmart would encourage its members to transfer their service to Netflix and, in exchange, Netflix would encourage its members to buy Walmart DVDs. Walmart was expressly authorized to reenter the DVD-by-mail rental industry anytime it wanted. In 2009, a group of disgruntled Netflix users filed a lawsuit alleging that the two companies had an agreement to carve up the DVD rental and sales market and to not compete with each other in their respective markets. What areas of antitrust law does this agreement violate? [*Resnick v. Walmart.com USA LLC et al.,* 10 C 09-cv-0002 PJH (2009).]
5. Beer is one of the most important beverages in Europe. In 2007, the brewers Heineken, Grolsch, and Bavaria, all based in the Netherlands, were charged with price fixation by the European Union. All three were accused of operating a price-fixing cartel in the Netherlands. The four brewers coordinated prices and price increases of beer in the Netherlands, both in the on-trade segment of the market (in which consumption is on the premises) and the off-trade market segment (consumption is off the premises, with the beer mainly sold through supermarkets), including private-label beer. The European Commission found that in both segments the brewers had coordinated commercial conditions offered to individual customers and had allocated customers, and it found that in the on-trade market segment the companies had coordinated the rebates granted to pubs and bars. What U.S. antitrust laws would this have violated had it occurred in the United States? [*Heineken Nederland BV and Heineken NV v. European Commission,* T-240/07 (2007).]
6. The United States Postal Service (USPS) delivers millions of letters every day. Flamingo Industries, a U.S.-based company, was the sole provider of the mailbags used to carry this mail. When the USPS decided to end its contract with Flamingo, thus ending their supply of the mailbags, Flamingo sued, claiming a monopoly was created. Under the antitrust law, monopolizing an industry is illegal. The USPS defended that it was not a monopoly and that it was exempt from the law because a government-regulated agency. Do you think that USPS should be exempt from antitrust regulations and laws? Why or why not? [*USPS v. Flamingo Industries,* 02-1290 (2004).]
7. Maurice Clarett, a former running back for Ohio State University and a Big Ten Freshman of the Year, wanted to enter the NFL draft. However, Clarett was precluded under the NFL's current rules governing draft eligibility. Clarett was a season shy of the three necessary to qualify under the draft's eligibility rules. The NFL's collective bargaining group and the NFL Players Association, which is the players' union, agreed on the most recent version of the eligibility requirement. The eligibility requirement is intended to promote college attendance and has existed almost as long as the NFL. Clarett filed suit, alleging that the NFL's draft eligibility rules are an unreasonable restraint of trade in violation of Section 1 of the Sherman Act, 15 U.S.C. Section 1, and Section 4 of the Clayton Act, 15 U.S.C. Section 15. Clarett sought summary judgment on the merits of his antitrust claim. The NFL asserted that Clarett lacked "antitrust standing" and, as a matter of law, that the eligibility rules were immune from antitrust attack by virtue of the nonstatutory labor exemption. The district court granted summary judgment in favor of Clarett and ordered him eligible to enter that year's draft. The NFL appealed. How did the court rule on appeal? Why? [*Clarett v. NFL,* 369 F.3d 124 (2004).]
8. Dr. Alga Morales-Villalobos, an anesthesiologist, brought antitrust claims under Section 1 of the Sherman Antitrust Act against her former employers, the overlapping directors of an anesthesiology group and the only two hospitals in Arecibo. After arranging

an exclusive-dealing contract between their organization and the hospitals on behalf of all parties, the group eventually fired Morales-Villalobos and prevented her from working at either hospital. No patient complaints were ever filed against Morales-Villalobos. Despite doctors' requesting her services in private surgery, the group would not let Morales-Villalobos work in the hospitals. She alleged that the exclusive-dealing arrangement between the hospitals and the group prevented her from competing to offer her services. She also alleged that the defendants engaged in a group boycott to exclude her from the anesthesiology group and subsequently denied her certification to practice at those hospitals. Was Morales-Villalobos successful with her antitrust claim? Why? [*Morales-Villalobos v. Garcia-Llorens,* 316 F.3d 51 (2003).]

9. The National Football League (NFL) is an unincorporated association of separately owned and operated football teams that collectively produce an annual season of over 250 interrelated football games. In the past, the National Football League granted headwear licenses to a number of different vendors simultaneously; one of those vendors was American Needle, which held an NFL headwear license for over 20 years. However, in 2000, the NFL teams authorized the NFL to solicit bids from the vendors for an exclusive headwear license. Reebok won the bidding war, and in 2001 the NFL granted an exclusive license to Reebok for 10 years. As a result of the exclusive licensing of headwear, American Needle Inc. sued the NFL, its member football teams, and Reebok International, alleging that the teams' exclusive licensing agreement with Reebok violated the Sherman Antitrust Act. As American Needle saw it, because each of the individual teams separately owned its team logos and trademarks, the teams' collective agreement to authorize NFL Properties to award the exclusive headwear license to Reebok was, in fact, a conspiracy to restrict other vendors' ability to obtain licenses for the teams' intellectual property. American Needle also contended that, by authorizing the NFL to award the license to Reebok, the NFL teams monopolized the NFL team licensing and product wholesale markets in violation of Section 2 of the Sherman Antitrust Act. The NFL claims that it is not in violation of the Sherman Act because the sum of all the NFL teams constitutes one single entity (the NFL) when licensing intellectual property. Was the NHL in violation of the Sherman Antitrust Act? Would any additional information help you make your decision? [*American Needle Inc. v. National Football League,* 538 F.3d 736 (2008).]

10. 3M, which manufactures Scotch tape for home and office use, dominated the U.S. transparent-tape market with a market share above 90 percent until the early 1990s. LePage's sold a variety of office products including "second-brand" and private-label transparent tape, that is, tape sold under the retailer's name rather than under the name of the manufacturer. By 1992, LePage's had 88 percent of the private-label tape sales in the United States, which represented only a small portion of the transparent-tape market. LePage's brought an antitrust action asserting that 3M used its monopoly over its Scotch tape brand to gain a competitive advantage in the private-label tape portion of the transparent-tape market in the United States through the use of 3M's multitiered "bundled rebate" structure, which offered higher rebates when customers purchased products in a number of 3M's different product lines. LePage's also alleged that 3M offered to some of LePage's customers large lump-sum cash payments, promotional allowances, and other cash incentives to encourage them to enter into exclusive-dealing arrangements with 3M. If you were an executive for LePage's, which sections of the various antitrust laws would you think 3M violated? Are your claims likely to prevail in court? [*LePage's, Inc. v. 3M,* 324 F.3d 141 (2003).]

Looking for more review materials?

The Online Learning Center at **www.mhhe.com/kubasek3e** contains this chapter's "Assignment on the Internet" and also a list of URLs for more information, entitled "On the Internet." Find both of them in the Student Center portion of the OLC, along with quizzes and other helpful materials.

CHAPTER 48

The Nature of Property, Personal Property, and Bailments

LEARNING OBJECTIVES

After reading this chapter, you will be able to answer the following questions:

1 What are the classifications of property?

2 How is personal property transferred?

3 What are the rights and responsibilities of parties to a bailment?

CASE OPENER

Prisoners and Personal Property

Warner Melvin, a prisoner at a U.S. penitentiary, was required to move to a new cell. Melvin was able to move most of his belongings to his new cell before his work shift. A few items remained in his old cell: a pair of Adidas shoes, some electronic equipment, and some food. Melvin hid the property and asked the guard to deadlock the cell. The guard, Richard, looked in the cell and determined it was empty. He did not lock the cell.

When Melvin returned from work, he noticed that his property was missing. There are conflicting claims as to whether Richard knowingly allowed the other prisoners to take Melvin's property, but it is known that the cell was not locked. Melvin argued that Richard was a bailee and Richard was responsible for the lost property. Clearly the relationship between a prisoner and a prison guard is unique and different from more standard relationships, such as the relationship between a boarder and an innkeeper. However, whether this difference was strong enough to diminish any duty owed by Richard to Melvin was the question the court confronted.

Although it is often difficult for prisoners to bring litigation, several cases across the country illustrate that the loss of their personal property is not uncommon. In *Sellers v. United States,* a frequently cited case, the prison restricted the amount of personal items inmates could keep in their cells. In accordance with the restriction, the prison authorities took from Sellers an oil painting of his wife, 41 law books, an almanac, and other personal items. Sellers' items were subsequently lost. The Seventh Circuit held that once a prisoner establishes a bailment relationship and loss of property, the government is liable for conversion.[1]

[1] *Melvin v. United States,* 963 F. Supp. 1052 (1997); *Sellers v. United States,* 1996 U.S. App. LEXIS 24353. For other cases involving prisoners and lost property, see *Moore v. United States,* 1996 U.S. Dist. LEXIS 16900; *Jungerman v. City of Raytown,* 925 S.W.2d 202 (1996); and *Bacote v. Ohio Dept. of Rehabilitation and Correction,* 578 N.E.2d 565 (1988).

1. Do you think a bailment relationship existed between Richard and Melvin?
2. Pretend that Melvin was a guest at a hotel. The hotel manager asked Melvin to move to another room. Melvin was able to transfer most of his belongings to the new room, but he then had to rush to an appointment. He requested that the front-desk attendant lock his old room. Do you think this scenario is easier to resolve? Why or why not?

The Wrap-Up at the end of the chapter will answer these questions.

The Nature and Classifications of Property

LO1

What are the classifications of property?

When people hear the word *property,* they generally think of physical objects: land, houses, cars. However, this pattern of thought reflects an incomplete understanding of the concept of property. Property is a set of rights and interests in relation to others with reference to a tangible or intangible object. The essence of the concept of property is that the state provides the mechanism to allow the owner to exclude others. A less technical way to think about property is that it is anything you can own.

Those with great amounts of property have an especially significant amount of power. Because possessing property facilitates the acquisition of even more property, the identification of those who possess a disproportionate amount of property provides insight into the dynamics of influence and authority in our society.

Property is generally divided into two basic categories, real property and personal property, as shown in Exhibit 48-1. *Real property,* land and anything permanently attached to the land, is the focus of the next chapter. In this chapter, we will examine the laws governing *personal property,* which is generally defined as property that is not attached to the land, or movable property. Sometimes property is initially movable but then becomes attached to the land. In such a situation, the property is called a *fixture.* Fixtures are treated like real property, and so they are discussed in the next chapter.

Exhibit 48-1 Types of Property

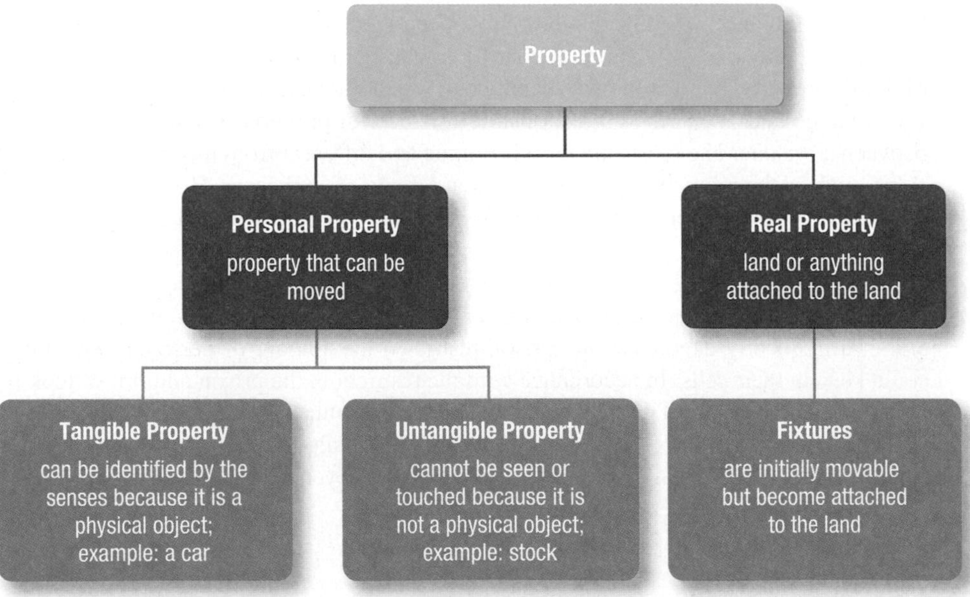

Personal Property

All property that is not land or not permanently affixed to land is **personal property.** Personal property may be either tangible or intangible. *Tangible property* is property that can be identified by the senses. It is property that you can see or touch. Tangible property includes items such as furniture, cars, and other goods.

Books are typically thought of as personal property. The owner of a book may write in it and generally do what he or she wants with it, and the law protects the owner against having the book taken by someone else. However, the growing popularity of e-books has raised questions about what rights e-book users have to their e-books. In July 2009, Amazon deleted copies of George Orwell's *1984* and *Animal Farm* directly off people's Kindles (Amazon's e-book reader) and refunded their money.[2] This action sparked massive controversy over whether Amazon has the right to remove content that customers had bought from their Kindles.[3] At least one lawsuit has already been filed as a result of this incident.[4] Much of the outrage has been due to the fact that people do not see e-books and physical books as different types of property.[5] Businesses that offer digital content should be clear about what rights customers have to the content, and they should make that information well known and visible to avoid problems related to digital content rights.

Intangible property includes such items as bank accounts, stocks, and insurance policies. Because most intangibles (with the exception of some classified as intellectual property and discussed in Chapter 12) are evidenced by writings, most of the following discussion applies to both tangible and intangible property. The primary issues that arise in conjunction with personal property involve (1) the means of acquiring ownership of the property and (2) the rights and duties arising out of a bailment. Both are discussed in this chapter in detail.

VOLUNTARY TRANSFER OF PROPERTY

LO2 How is personal property transferred?

Voluntary transfer, as a result of either a purchase or a gift, is the most common means by which property is acquired. Ownership of property is referred to as *title,* and title to property passes when the parties so intend. When transfer of the property is by purchase, the acquiring party gives some consideration to the seller in exchange for title to the property. Such a transfer of ownership usually requires no formalities, but in a few cases changes of ownership must be registered with a government agency. Sales of motor vehicles, watercraft, and airplanes are among the primary transfers requiring registration. To transfer such property, a certificate of title must be signed by the seller, taken to the appropriate government agency, and then reissued in the name of the new owner.

Gifts are another voluntary means of transferring ownership. They differ from purchases in that there is no consideration given for a gift. As you know from your previous reading, a promise to make a gift is therefore unenforceable. Once properly made, however, a gift is irrevocable.

To see how marketing decisions affect voluntary transfers of property, please see the **Connecting to the Core** activity on the text website at www.mhhe.com/kubasek3e.

Three elements are necessary for a valid gift (see Exhibit 48-2). First, there must be a *delivery* of the gift. Delivery may be actual, which is the physical presentation of the gift itself, or constructive, which entails the delivery of an

[2] Brad Stone, "Amazon Erases Orwell Books from Kindle," *NYTimes.com,* July 17, 2009, www.nytimes.com/2009/07/18/technology/companies/18amazon.html.

[3] Ibid.

[4] Alexandria Sage, "Amazon.com Sued over Deleted Digital Book Copies," *Reuters,* July 31, 2009, www.reuters.com/article/internetNews/idUSTRE56U72A20090731.

[5] Bobbie Johnson, "Why Did Big Brother Remove Paid-For Content from Amazon's Kindles?" *The Guardian,* July 22, 2009, www.guardian.co.uk/technology/2009/jul/22/kindle-amazon-digital-rights.

COMPARING THE LAW OF OTHER COUNTRIES

DISTINCTIONS IN ITALIAN PROPERTY LAW

In Italian law, there is a significant distinction between physical possession and a mental intention to possess. The term to describe the latter is *usucapione.* Instances of *usucapione* are characterized by persons having legal possession equivalent to that of the owner but only for a certain length of time.

Before a transition from legal possession to full ownership can occur, several requirements must be satisfied. These requirements differ depending on whether the property is classified as immovable or movable. For immovable property, the potential owner must possess the property for no less than 20 years. Movables require a 10-year period of possession. These periods of possession must be uninterrupted. If possession of the property is lost, the individual has one year to regain it before having to start the term of possession over.

Understanding the distinction between immovable and movable property is thus important to determining the required length of possession before ownership. Immovable property includes anything attached to the ground, such as trees, buildings, homes, and arenas. Movables, therefore, include any property not attached to the ground. Movables are further divided into those that require registration and those that do not. Registration is necessary for the transference, sale, or termination of certain movable property.

item that gives access to the gift or represents it, such as the handing over of the keys to a car. Second, the delivery must be made with *donative intent* to make an immediate gift. The donor makes the delivery with the purpose of turning over ownership at the time of delivery. Third, there must be *acceptance,* a willingness of the donee to take the gift from the donor. Usually, acceptance is not a problem, although a donee may not want to accept a gift because of a desire to not feel obligated to the donor or because of a concern that ownership of the gift may impose some unwanted legal liability.

BUT WHAT IF . . .

WHAT IF THE FACTS OF THE CASE OPENER WERE DIFFERENT?

Let's say that Melvin took his property to the inmate in the next cell for safekeeping. He then returned the next day to recover his belongings, but the inmate claimed that the items were his now because they were gifts. Which of the three elements necessary for a valid gift is missing from this scenario?

Exhibit 48-2 Proper Property Transfer by *Inter Vivos* Gifts

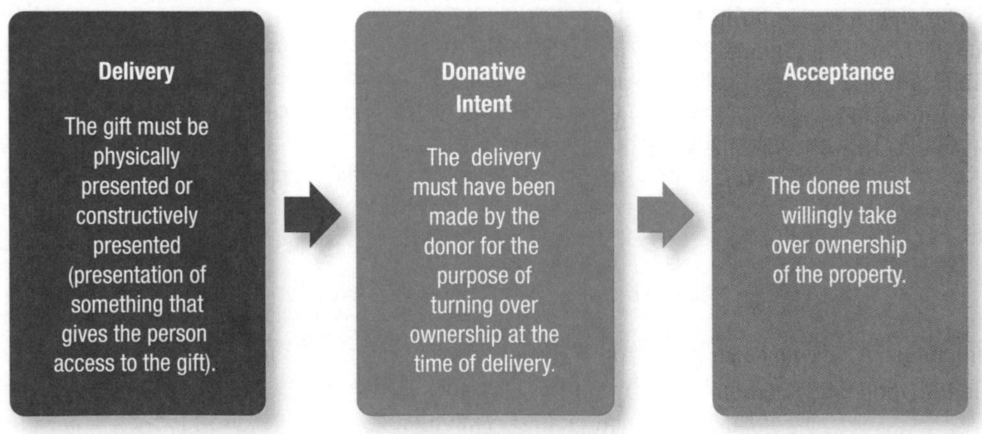

E-COMMERCE AND THE LAW

E-BUSINESSES AND THEIR CUSTOMERS BENEFIT FROM NEW LABELING AND SHIPPING OPTIONS

Within the past few years, the boom in e-commerce has inspired improvements in Internet postal technology. Now, e-businesses can use Internet postal technology to print labels and pay for shipping postage using accounts such as PayPal accounts.

For a small business that operates through eBay, for instance, this means the business can operate more efficiently. Before improvements in Internet postal technology, it was likely that a small business would print mailing labels by hand and make multiple trips to the post office. Now, it is possible for small businesses to print out labels and arrange for pickups from carriers.*

An additional benefit to both buyers and sellers is that they can track packages. Claims that the postal service "lost" a package are now less likely. Consequently, small businesses save money by not having to replace the package contents. Litigation over lost packages should go down too. Or at least the new technology will help plaintiffs determine what went wrong in the shipping process and which party was negligent.

* Beth Cox, "The Online Auction Site's New Integrated Labeling and Shipping Payment Options Can Improve Sellers' Operations—But They Are Not without Hitches," *ecommerce.internet.com,* March 25, 2004 (accessed July 29, 2005).

Sometimes, however, it can be difficult to determine whether something is a gift or a loan, especially when proper documentation is not filed at the time of the transaction. This was the scenario faced by Don Whittington when he disputed ownership of a 1979 Kremer Porsche displayed at the Indianapolis Motor Speedway Hall of Fame Museum. Whittington believed that he was the owner of the Porsche and that he had merely loaned it to the museum in 1980. The Indianapolis Motor Speedway Foundation believed that Whittington had given the car as a gift to the museum, and the foundation had even applied for and been granted a title to the car in 2001. In 2004, when Whittington requested the return of the car, he had to prove that he had a possessory interest in the car. Although the museum did not have a record of receiving the car as a gift or a loan, and Whittington had never applied for a tax reduction for giving the car as a gift and was able to produce one document in which he listed the car as an asset, the trial court found in favor of the foundation. The court determined that Whittington's behavior after the museum took possession of the car was more consistent with giving the car as a gift rather than as a loan.[6]

Legal Principle: **A gift made by a person during her or his lifetime requires delivery, donative intent, and acceptance.**

The gifts we have been discussing so far have been what are called ***inter vivos* gifts,** gifts that are made by a person during his or her lifetime. Another type of gift that can be made is a **gift *causa mortis,*** a gift that is made in contemplation of one's immediate death. It can be revoked any time before the death of the donor, and it is automatically revoked if the donor recovers.

Litigation over gifts *causa mortis* often arises because the three elements of delivery, donative intent, and acceptance still have to occur before the gift is complete and that means before the death of the donor. Case 48-1 illustrates how difficult it can sometimes be to determine whether in fact all the elements of a gift *causa mortis* have been met.

Legal Principle: **For a gift *causa mortis,* you must have the three elements of a gift: delivery, donative intent, and acceptance before the death of the donor.**

[6] *Whittington v. Indianapolis Motor Speedway Found. Inc.*, 2008 U.S. Dist. LEXIS 62760.

CASE 48-1 STEPHEN LABATT PORTER, ET AL., APPELLANT v. BLACK WARRIOR FARMS, L.L.C., ET AL.

SUPREME COURT OF ALABAMA

976 SO. 2D 984 (2006)

Donald R. Porter, Sr., and Olga Porter had seven children: Donald, Teddy, Cecil, Shari, Stephen, Marc, and Andrew. Donald Sr. died in 1976. Under his will, part of the real estate was to become subject to a trust for the life of Olga, and at her death the remainder was to pass to the seven children. Olga died on June 27, 2001. By her will, her portion of the real estate passed to the seven children. Another provision of her will addressed her children's indebtedness to her. The will states that, upon her death, any indebtedness her children or their estate have against her will be forgiven, but that amount will be subtracted from their share of the Porter Family Trust.

In March 2000, Olga sold the family beach house. Of the proceeds from the sale, Olga sent $160,000 to Stephen and $140,000 to Marc to invest for her. Stephen had invested Olga's money in land, which at the time of her death was worth $346,000. After Olga's death, Marc returned Olga's $140,000 investment to her estate. However, Stephen did not return Olga's original investment or the appreciated amount. As justification for keeping the money, he produced a handwritten letter Olga had sent to him:

> Mrs. Olga L. Porter
> Black Warrior Farms
> Gallion, AL 36742
> September 26, 2000
> Dear Steve—
> Just a note to let you know I appreciate your investing the money for me and know you will take care of it for me—
> However, should any thing happen to me I want you to keep the balance for all you have done for me in the past—
> Will check with you after October 7th—
> My love to all,
> Olga Porter

The reference to October 7 apparently related to a cruise she was taking between September 26 and October 7, 2000. Olga's other children, besides Stephen, argue that the letter related only to the cruise, and not to anything occurring after that. Olga's will was enforced, and her children created an LLC, Black Warrior Farms, for the purpose of liquidating and distributing the estate. Each of Olga's children is a member of Black Warrior Farms, except that because Stephen has disclaimed his 1/7 interest in the estate, Stephen's three children each hold a 1/21 interest in Black Warrior Farms. The funds held by Black Warrior Farms were distributed. Stephen's three children each received an amount less than their 1/21 share because of Stephen's alleged failure to pay into Olga's estate the money Olga had entrusted to him for investment. Black Warrior Farms and Marc sued Stephen, alleging that Stephen had not returned to the estate the $160,000 Olga had given him. Stephen responded that the September 26, 2000, letter from Olga entitled him to keep the $160,000. The trial court held that at the time of her death the value of the money Olga had entrusted to Stephen was $346,000 and further stated that a reasonable interpretation of the letter indicates that the money was not a gift, and that "should anything happen to me" in the letter refers only to the time of the cruise. The court ruled that Stephen owed the trust the money Olga gave him for investment, plus interest. Stephen and his children appealed.

JUSTICE PARKER: Olga's 1986 will clearly stated that her children's indebtedness to her was to be forgiven upon her death but that any indebtedness was to be offset against the share of her estate each child was to receive. When Olga entrusted $160,000 to Stephen in 2000, it is clear that it was not a gift but was an investment that Stephen was to handle on her behalf.

Stephen and his children argue that Olga's letter of September 21, 2000, clearly changed the status of the $160,000 Olga had given Stephen from an investment to a gift or bequest. . . . Rather, the trial court said: "A reasonable interpretation of the letter is that it expressed her wishes to deal with the money held by each son if she did not return from a cruise on which she was embarking." However, she did return. Although the trial court did not use the term *causa mortis,* it seems to be saying that the letter was, at most, either a gift conditioned upon Olga's failure to return from the cruise or a *gift causa mortis* that became void when she returned from the cruise. In *Smith v. Eshelman,* this Court held that "such a gift [*causa mortis*] . . . is revoked by law, if he [the donor] gets well of the sickness with which he was then afflicted."

As to whether Olga's letter constituted an *inter vivos* gift, this Court noted in *Ford v. Stinson,* the three elements that are necessary to establish an *inter vivos* gift: "(1) donative intent on the part of [the donor], (2) effective delivery to . . . the donee, and (3) acceptance by [the donee]."

The second and third elements are clearly established. Olga delivered the $160,000 to Stephen in March 2000. Stephen received, accepted, and invested the money.

The first element is more problematic. Olga did not show donative intent in March 2000 when she transferred the $160,000 to Stephen. Her purpose in transferring it to him was so that he could invest it on her behalf. The donative intent, if any, must be based on the September 26, 2000, letter. In that letter she clearly states a desire and intent that Stephen should have the money: "I want you to keep the balance for all you have done for me in the past—." But the portion of the sentence quoted above is preceded by a subordinate clause: "should any thing happen to me. . . ." This subordinate clause appears to qualify the independent clause by placing a condition on it. Furthermore, in the first paragraph of the letter Olga says: "I appreciate your investing the money *for me* and know you will take care of it *for me*" (emphasis added). The phrase "for me," especially its second appearance where it follows a future-tense verb "will take care," indicates that Olga contemplated continued ownership of the investment. Thus, the transfer of the $160,000 to Stephen, even after the September 2000 letter, cannot be considered an *inter vivos* gift, because it is conditional and to be effective only at a future time. In other words, Olga's letter does not show the requisite donative intent. . . .

We could all wish that Olga had been more explicit concerning the disposition of this property. But there are clear and legal ways to make a gift, and there are clear and legal ways to change a will or to make a new will. Olga did none of these; therefore, her 1986 will must stand as the last clear expression of her intent concerning her estate, including the $160,000 Stephen invested for her. . . .

Because we have ruled that Olga's letter to Stephen did not constitute a gift or a bequest to him of the $160,000, we conclude that the trial court's ruling that Black Warrior Farms and Stephen's siblings properly withheld that portion of the distribution of the funds in Black Warrior Farms from Stephen and his children was correct. . . .

Judgment AFFIRMED in favor of defendant.

CRITICAL THINKING

What ambiguity did the court have to decide to render a decision in this case? How did the court resolve this ambiguity?

ETHICAL DECISION MAKING

What ethical norm is being followed by the decision in this case?

BUT WHAT IF . . .

WHAT IF THE FACTS OF THE CASE OPENER WERE DIFFERENT?

Let's say that Melvin was on death row and he declared that the inmate in the next cell could have all the items he had in his cell upon his death. Would this be an *inter vivos* gift or a *causa mortis* gift? If Melvin's status changes and he is no longer on death row, is the inmate still entitled to the gift?

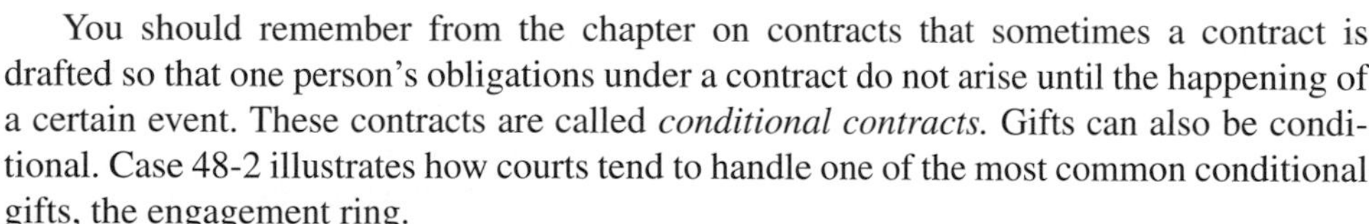

You should remember from the chapter on contracts that sometimes a contract is drafted so that one person's obligations under a contract do not arise until the happening of a certain event. These contracts are called *conditional contracts*. Gifts can also be conditional. Case 48-2 illustrates how courts tend to handle one of the most common conditional gifts, the engagement ring.

CASE 48-2 CAMPBELL v. ROBINSON

COURT OF APPEALS OF SOUTH CAROLINA

398 S.C. 12, 726 S.E.2D 221, S.C. APP. LEXIS 124 (2012)

In 2005, Campbell and Robinson became engaged. However, in 2006 the wedding was postponed and then cancelled. Robinson refused to return the engagement ring and Campbell filed a lawsuit claiming the ring was his property. Robinson countered that Campbell breached his promise to marry, and that she was entitled to repayment of her prenuptial expenses and compensation for damages to her health due to the situation. During the trial, Robinson claimed that not only had Campbell cancelled the wedding, but on two occasions he had told her to keep the ring. Campbell denied all claims. Campbell contended that an engagement ring is a gift conditioned upon marriage. The trial court ruled that the ring belonged to the party who was not "at fault" for the termination of the engagement. In other words, if Campbell reneged on his promise, Robinson could be entitled to damages. Campbell appealed.

JUDGE THOMAS: An engagement ring by its very nature is a symbol of the donor's continuing devotion to the donee.

Once an engagement is cancelled, the ring no longer holds that significance. Thus, if a party presents evidence a ring was given in contemplation of marriage, the ring is an engagement ring. As an engagement ring, the gift is impliedly conditioned upon the marriage taking place. Until the condition underlying the gift is fulfilled, the attempted gift is unenforceable and must be returned to the donor upon the donor's request.

The person challenging the assertions that the ring is an engagement ring and therefore impliedly conditioned upon marriage has the burden of presenting evidence to overcome those assertions. This burden may be satisfied by presenting evidence showing that the ring was not given in contemplation of marriage—it was not an engagement ring—or was not conditioned upon the marriage. If the parties do not dispute that the ring was originally an engagement ring conditioned upon the marriage, the burden may also be satisfied by presenting evidence establishing the ring subsequently became the challenger's property (recognizing that a conditional gift of an engagement ring could become an absolute gift after the engagement was cancelled).

Jurisdictions differ on whether ownership of an engagement ring may be based upon fault in the breakup. Courts that do consider fault generally reason that it is unfair for a person to retain the fruit of a broken promise. In contrast, courts with a "no-fault" approach often base their decision upon the abolishment of heart balm actions, adoption of no-fault divorce, desire to limit courtroom dramatics, and reduction of the difficulty in determining the issue of what constitutes fault in the decline of a relationship.

We hold that the consideration of fault has no place in determining ownership of an engagement ring. Generally, gift law will dictate who has the legal right to the ring

In other contexts, the culpability of one's conduct is determined by legal standards such as the reasonable person. "[N]egligence is the failure to use due care, i.e., that degree of care which a person of ordinary prudence and reason would exercise under the same circumstances." In contrast, no legal standard exists by which a fact finder can adjudge culpability or fault in a prenuptial breakup. ("What is fault or the unjustifiable calling off of an engagement? . . . [S]hould courts be asked to determine which of the following grounds for breaking an engagement is fault or justified? (1) The parties have nothing in common; (2) one party cannot stand prospective in-laws; (3) a minor child of one of the parties is hostile to and will not accept the other party; (4) an adult child of one of the parties will not accept the other party; (5) the parties' pets do not get along; (6) a party was too hasty in proposing or accepting the proposal; (7) the engagement was a rebound situation which is now regretted; (8) one party has untidy habits that irritate the other; or (9) the parties have religious differences. The list could be endless."); ("What fact justifies the breaking of an engagement? The absence of a sense of humor? Differing musical tastes? Differing political views? . . . They must be approached with intelligent care and should not happen without a decent assurance of success. When either party lacks that assurance, for whatever reason, the engagement should be broken. No justification is needed. Either party may act. Fault, impossible to fix, does not count.")

South Carolina's use of fault in dividing property within the family court's jurisdiction does not mandate the use of the fault approach for determining ownership of engagement rings when the marriage fails to occur.

Two of the main purposes of an engagement are to prepare the couple for marriage and test the permanency of their compatibility. In some circumstances, the fault approach may penalize a party who innocently recognizes the couple's incompatibility.

Although fault cannot determine ownership of the ring, we affirm the denial of Campbell's motions for directed verdict and JNOV on his actions for declaratory judgment and claim and delivery. Here, Campbell gave Robinson the ring during his proposal. Thus, he presented evidence that the ring was given in contemplation of marriage and therefore was an engagement ring conditioned upon the marriage occurring. Although Robinson kept the ring in a safe deposit box after the engagement was cancelled, without further evidence the ring would remain a conditional gift and Campbell would be entitled to recover it as a matter of law.

Robinson explicitly characterizes the ring as an engagement ring. However, she has presented evidence that the ring was converted into an absolute gift by testifying Campbell told her to keep the ring after the engagement was cancelled. Because Campbell disputes this contention, the evidence conflicts as to whether the ring was conditioned upon marriage (noting that a gift is complete when there is "a donative intent to transfer title to the property, a delivery by the donor, and an acceptance by the donee") . . . ("delivery" need not be "manual" but, "so far as the donor can make it so," must only be "some act which indicates a relinquishment of possession and dominion on the part of the donor in behalf of the donee.") Accordingly, ownership of the ring was a jury issue, and a directed verdict on Campbell's claims for declaratory judgment and claim and delivery were not warranted.

We also affirm the trial court's denial of Campbell's motions for directed verdict and JNOV on his restitution claim.

Here, the record does not contain evidence Campbell presented the ring to Robinson at her request. Nor does the record contain evidence Campbell permitted Robinson to keep the ring at her request or that he reasonably relied upon her to pay for the ring. Thus, Campbell was not entitled to a directed verdict or JNOV on his restitution claim.

Campbell claims the trial court erred in denying his motion for a new trial absolute because the verdict form and jury charge were erroneous. In light of our rulings above, we agree.

"An appellate court will not reverse the trial court's decision regarding jury instructions unless the trial court

[continued]

committed an abuse of discretion. An abuse of discretion occurs when the trial court's ruling is based on an error of law or is not supported by the evidence."

Here, the trial court provided an erroneous jury charge and verdict form. The evidence presented a jury issue of whether the ring was a conditional or absolute gift. While the charge instructed the jury that the gift was conditional, it did not explain that the gift could become absolute. Moreover, the jury charge and verdict form hinged ownership of the ring upon fault in the breakup.

The focus on fault in the jury charge and verdict form undoubtedly affected the verdict. Fault was the only question posed to the jury to determine ownership of the ring, and the jury's finding on the question was adverse to Campbell. Thus, his actions for declaratory judgment and claim and delivery were prejudiced by the jury charge and verdict form. He is entitled to a new trial on those claims. In contrast, no evidence shows the ring was conferred to Robinson "nongratuitously." Therefore, Campbell was not prejudiced by the verdict form or jury charge on his restitution action, and he is not entitled to a new trial on that claim.

Robinson's Appeal

Robinson argues the trial court erred in declining to grant her JNOV to award her damages, a new trial nisi additur, and a new trial as to damages because the jury's verdict was inconsistent. We affirm.

AFFIRMED in part, REVERSED in part, and REMANDED for a new trial.

CRITICAL THINKING

Do you agree that it is hard to define and distinguish fault in the case of a broken engagement as the judge explained?

ETHICAL DECISION MAKING

Do you think it is more ethical for the person who gave the engagement ring to receive it if the engagement is broken regardless of who is at fault for the broken engagement? What ethical guideline is shaping your answer?

INVOLUNTARY TRANSFER OF PERSONAL PROPERTY

Involuntary transfers of ownership occur when property has been abandoned, lost, or mislaid. The finder of such property *may* acquire ownership rights to such property through possession.

Property that the original owner has discarded is *abandoned* property. Anyone finding such property becomes its owner by possessing it. Recall the Case Opener. Assume that Richard, the prison guard, believed that Melvin had moved all of his property to the new cell. While cleaning out the cell, Richard came across the shoes, food, and electronic equipment. Does he now possess the property? The court did not address this hypothetical, but it illustrates, as does Case 48-3, that it is not always easy to determine whether property has in fact been abandoned.

CASE 48-3 OMNI HOLDING AND DEVELOPMENT CORP. v. C.A.G. INVESTMENTS, INC.

SUPREME COURT OF ARKANSAS

370 ARK. 220 (2007)

Bob Herren and Tom Papachristou met through a lawyer who represented them both. The men developed a business plan whereby Herren would provide financing and facilities for a crop-dusting service and a farm-equipment export business to be run by Papachristou. Although the business, Omni, was incorporated by Herren in Louisiana, it was to be located in Crittenden County, Arkansas. Subsequently, Herren persuaded Sherlee Despot, with whom he lived in Shreveport, to use money from her personal funds, bank loans, and Trust funds to purchase land in Crittenden

County. With Herren's assistance, Despot organized C.A.G. as a Louisiana corporation. C.A.G. purchased an 80-acre tract of land outside of Marion, Arkansas, to serve as Omni's headquarters. Additionally, C.A.G. purchased a home for Papachristou and Crockett, his girlfriend, who was also employed by Omni. Over the next several years, C.A.G. intermittently advanced funds to Omni.

To consolidate Omni's outstanding indebtedness to C.A.G., Herren, in his capacity as president of Omni, prepared and signed a promissory note in favor of C.A.G. in the sum of $175,000. The note was secured with an aircraft owned by Omni. Omni borrowed $150,000 from Textron Financial Corporation, which loan was personally guaranteed by Despot. The $150,000 note was also secured by the identical aircraft that secured the earlier $175,000 note from Omni to C.A.G.

Omni's financial difficulties continued over the next three years, resulting in the deterioration of the business relationship among the parties. In late summer 2003, Despot and Herren learned that Omni was contemplating bankruptcy and that Papachristou was out of the country, in Greece. Upon becoming aware of that information, Despot and Herren promptly traveled to Arkansas and discovered that the aircraft designated as security on both the Textron and C.A.G. notes had crashed in 2002. C.A.G. demanded that Omni immediately remove all personal property it owned or possessed from the real property owned by C.A.G. and surrender possession of the real property.

When Omni refused to comply, C.A.G. filed a complaint against Omni. Following a hearing, the court entered an order stating that Omni had committed an unlawful detainer of the property and that C.A.G. was entitled to a writ of possession of the property. In addition to its failure to vacate, equipment remained on the property, most of which had been "stripped," and Papachristou continued to reside on the premises. C.A.G. amended its complaint, seeking a judgment for the amount due and owing on the promissory note and a finding of abandonment with regard to Omni's personal property. Ultimately, the case was tried and the circuit court entered its order and judgment, finding, among other things, that Omni had abandoned all personal property it left on the premises following its failure to post the requisite bond to retain possession. Omni appealed.

JUSTICE IMBER: . . . Omni . . . asserts that the circuit court erred in ruling that Omni had abandoned personal property when the court ordered Omni to remove itself from the property. . . .

As to Omni's argument concerning the abandonment of its personal property, this court held in *Terry v. Lock* that the rights of a finder of property depend on how the found property is classified, with the character of the property determined by evaluating all the facts and circumstances present in the particular case. Additionally, we explained that,

> [p]roperty is said to be "abandoned" when it is thrown away, or its possession is voluntarily forsaken by the owner, in which case it will become the property of the first occupant; or when it is involuntarily lost or left without the hope and expectation of again acquiring it, and then it becomes the property of the finder, subject to the superior claim of the owner.

With that definition in mind, we now turn to Omni's argument that it did remove some property from the location, but was forced to leave behind a considerable number of items due to the size of the items, the number of items, the difficulty in removing the items, the absence of a suitable location to place the property, the short time involved, and the non court-ordered demands placed upon it by C.A.G.'s attorney. In sum, Omni claims that at no time did it voluntarily forsake its interest in its property, and that it never relinquished its hope or expectation of again acquiring its property as it vigorously defended its position during litigation. We disagree.

According to testimony elicited from Crockett, she removed files, furniture, computers, books, and office equipment from Omni's offices. Omni also removed several pieces of large equipment from the premises. The circuit court gave Omni a period of one week to remove all of its property, but Omni failed to take full advantage of that opportunity. Instead, Papachristou traveled to Greece when he could have stayed in Arkansas and used the time to retrieve Omni's property. Based upon the facts and circumstances as reflected in the record before us, and our standard of review, which is highly deferential to the credibility findings of the trial court, we cannot say that the circuit court clearly erred in finding that Omni abandoned the property it left on the premises after being afforded ample opportunity to accomplish its removal. In any event, with the termination of Omni's right as a lessee in a tenancy at will to remain on the property after the circuit court ordered the issuance of a writ of possession, any property left behind was abandoned. . . .

AFFIRMED in favor of appellee.

CRITICAL THINKING

What could Omni have done that would have led the court to come to a different decision?

ETHICAL DECISION MAKING

While C.A.G. had the legal right to take the property, would any ethical principle suggest that C.A.G. should not have taken it?

Lost property is property that the true owner has unknowingly or accidentally dropped or left somewhere. He or she has no way of knowing how to retrieve it. In most states, the finder of lost property has title to the lost good against all except the true owner.

Mislaid property differs from lost property in that the owner has intentionally placed the property somewhere but has forgotten its location. The person who owns the realty on which the mislaid property was placed has the right to hold the mislaid property. The reason is that it is likely that the true owner will return to the realty looking for the mislaid property.

In some states, the law requires that before becoming the owner of lost or mislaid property, a finder must place an ad in the paper that will give the true owner notice that the property has been found and/or must leave the property with the police for a statutorily established reasonable period of time.

Legal Principle: **The finder of lost or mislaid property acquires title to the property against all except the true owner.**

BUT WHAT IF . . .

WHAT IF THE FACTS OF THE CASE OPENER WERE DIFFERENT?

Let's say, in the Case Opener, that Melvin misplaced his possessions in a common area of the prison. Another inmate, John, finds the possessions. But a third inmate, Luke, tries to claim that because John is not the person who paid for the possessions he cannot claim them. Then, Luke tries to take the possessions. Is John entitled to the possessions any more than Luke?

OTHER MEANS OF ACQUIRING OWNERSHIP OF PROPERTY

There are additional means by which people acquire title to property. One such means is by creation: If a person creates a piece of property, then he or she owns that property. One exception to this rule occurs when a person is paid to create property for someone else, in which case the property is owned by the person who paid for its creation. Another means of acquiring ownership is by court order. In a number of different types of cases, the court will determine who is entitled to ownership of property. For example, in a divorce case the court may award ownership of certain property to different parties, or in a bankruptcy case the court may award ownership of certain property to a creditor.

A far less common means of acquiring ownership is confusion, which involves only fungible goods. Fungible goods are goods for which one unit of the good is essentially the same as every other unit, such as grains of wheat or gallons of oil. If two people accidentally comingle their fungible goods, or if the goods are comingled because of the actions of a third party, each party is entitled to the percentage of the fungible goods that he contributed.

However, if one of the parties was responsible for the comingling, and that person cannot prove what percentage of the comingled goods she contributed, then the innocent party acquires title to all the goods. For example, if a farmer had stored grain in a rented storage elevator, and another farmer wrongfully added his grain to the elevator, the innocent farmer would be entitled to the entire amount in the silo.

BUT WHAT IF . . .

When the Winklevoss twins were students at Harvard, they came up with the idea of creating a website at which Harvard students could create personal profiles and electronically socialize. They hired a number of other students to create the code for the website. When much of the code had been finished, they hired Mark Zuckerberg to add to the code. They did not pay him money; instead, he worked for sweat equity. However, Zuckerberg later took the code, including the portion he had created, and produced his own version of the website. If the code is a form of property, who would own the code in this case?

Bailment

A **bailment** of personal property is a relationship that arises when one party, the *bailor,* transfers possession of personalty to another, the *bailee,* to be used by the bailee in an agreed-on manner for an agreed-on time period.

The most common illustration of a bailment occurs when a woman leaves her coat in a coat-check room. She hands her coat to the clerk and is given a ticket identifying the object of the bailment so that it can be reclaimed.

The bailment may be gratuitous or for consideration and may be to benefit the bailor, the bailee, or both. Determining who benefits from the bailment is important for determining the standard of care owed by the bailee. If the bailment is intended to benefit only the bailor, the bailee is liable for damage to the property caused by the bailee's gross negligence. An example of such a bailment occurs when you agree to keep a friend's houseplants for a week for no compensation while the friend is gone on a business trip. While there would be some debate over what constitutes gross negligence, most courts would probably agree that if one of the plants died because you misunderstood the watering instructions and gave it a little too much water, you probably would not be liable. However, if you lived in Arizona, and you took the plants home and placed them in front of a south-facing window and never watered them or checked to see whether they needed watering, and they all died, a court is likely to see that behavior as gross negligence and require that you compensate the owner.

If the bailment is solely for the bailee's benefit, the bailee is responsible for harm to the property caused by even the slightest lack of due care on the part of the bailee. An illustration of this type of bailment would occur if Jim borrowed his roommate's bike to go to the library. Even if he carefully parked the bike far away from other bikes, if someone scratched the bike while he was in the library, Jim would have to compensate his roommate for the harm done to the bike.

Finally, if the bailment is for the mutual benefit of bailee and bailor, the bailee is liable for harm to the bailed property arising out of the bailee's ordinary or gross negligence. If the property is harmed by an unpreventable "act of God," there is no liability on the part of the bailee under any circumstances.

Despite the existence of these general rules, the parties to a bailment contract can limit or expand the liability of the bailee by contract. Also, conspicuous signs have been held sufficient to limit liability. For example, a health club may have lockers with a huge sign saying, "Rent a lock for a locker for $1.00. Health Club not responsible for items stolen from unlocked lockers." If a person leaves a jacket in an unlocked locker, the health club will not be liable.

RIGHTS AND DUTIES OF THE BAILOR

LO3

What are the rights and responsibilities of parties to a bailment?

The bailor has certain rights and duties in the bailment relationship (see Exhibit 48-3). Some of these rights and duties may change depending on whom the relationship primarily benefits and whether the bailment is gratuitous. This section highlights some of these important rights and duties.

In general, the bailor has the right to expect the bailee to (1) take reasonable care of the bailed property, repairing and maintaining it as necessary; (2) use the bailed property only as stipulated in the bailment agreement; (3) not alter the bailed property in any unauthorized manner; and (4) return the bailed property in good condition at the end of the bailment.

The bailor has two fundamental duties. One is the duty of compensation and reimbursement. This duty requires that the bailor provide the bailee with any agreed-on compensation for the bailment. Obviously, this aspect of the bailment has no application in a gratuitous bailment. However, in all bailments, the bailor must reimburse the bailee for any necessary costs incurred by the bailee in keeping and maintaining the bailed property, unless the bailment contract provides otherwise.

The bailor's other duty is to provide the bailee with property that is free from hidden defects that could harm the bailee. If the bailment is for the mutual benefit of both parties, the bailor must warn the bailee of any known defects or any that could have been discovered through reasonable investigation. If, however, the bailment is solely for the benefit of the bailee, the standard is slightly lower, and the bailor must warn of only known defects. If the bailor fails to live up to this duty, he may be sued for negligence by the bailee or any reasonably foreseeable third party who is injured as a result of the defect.

RIGHTS AND DUTIES OF THE BAILEE

The rights of the bailee generally complement the duties of the bailor, and the duties of the bailee complement the rights of the bailor. As with the bailor's rights and duties, those of the bailee also vary depending on the purpose of the bailment. The bailee's rights and duties are listed in Exhibit 48-4.

Foremost among the bailee's rights is the right to possess the bailed property during the term of the bailment. If anyone steals the bailed property from the bailee, the bailee may take legal action to recover the bailed property and may even seek compensation for the loss of the property or damage to it.

Exhibit 48-3

Rights and Duties of the Bailor

Rights of the Bailor

1. Right to expect that the bailee take reasonable care of the bailed property, repairing and maintaining it as necessary.
2. Right to expect that the bailee use the bailed property only as stipulated in the bailment agreement.
3. Right to expect that the bailee will not alter the bailed property in any unauthorized manner.
4. Right to expect that the bailee will return the bailed property in good condition at the end of the bailment.

Duties of the Bailor

1. Bailor must provide the bailee with any agreed-on compensation for the bailment.
2. Bailor must reimburse the bailer for any necessary costs incurred by the bailee during the bailment.

Exhibit 48-4
Rights and Duties of the Bailee

Rights of the Bailee

1. Right to possess the bailed property during the term of the bailment.
2. Right to use the property in a manner consistent with the terms and purpose of the bailment.
3. Right to receive compensation for the bailment unless the bailment is gratuitous.
4. Right to retain the bailed property until payment is received.

Duties of the Bailee

1. Bailee must take reasonable care of the bailed property, repairing and maintaining it as necessary.
2. Bailee must use the bailed property only as stipulated in the bailment agreement.
3. Bailee must not alter the bailed property in any unauthorized manner.
4. Bailee must return the bailed property in good condition at the end of the bailment.

The bailee has the right to use the property in a manner consistent with the terms and purpose of the bailment. For example, if you are borrowing your friend's car while yours is being repaired, driving to work and to the grocery store would be consistent with the bailment. However, if you own an auto repair shop and you have possession of Smith's car to repair it, you cannot use the car to go on a date.

The bailee, unless the bailment is gratuitous, has the right to be compensated in accordance with the terms of the bailment. Regardless of the type of bailment, he or she has the right to be reimbursed for expenses that were necessary to maintain the bailed property.

If the bailee is to receive compensation for the bailment, the bailee may retain possession of the bailed property until payment is made. In most states, when the bailor refuses to provide the agreed-on compensation to the bailee, the bailee may ultimately sell the property after proper notice and a hearing. To enforce this right to sell the property, the bailee is given a *bailee's lien,* or a possessory lien on the property. Then, when it is sold, the proceeds are first used to pay the bailee and to cover the costs of the sale. The remaining proceeds go to the bailor.

In the Case Opener, Melvin argued that he entered into an implied bailment relationship with Richard. Although Melvin did not explicitly ask Richard to watch his property, he argued that Richard should have known that his request was made because his property was still in the cell. As the bailee, Richard became responsible for exercising a reasonable duty of care of Melvin's personal property.

DOCUMENTS RELATED TO BAILMENTS

Bailment Agreements. Bailments may be either express or implied. When a bailment is express, there is no need for a written agreement unless the statute of frauds applies to the bailment. As you should recall from Chapter 18, the statute of frauds requires a writing for any contract that cannot be performed within a year, so any bailment relationship that will last more than a year requires a writing to be enforceable. It is probably a good idea to put all bailments in writing, especially when the property involved is valuable. If the agreement is in writing, there will be far fewer disputes over each party's responsibilities and rights.

Documents of Title. When a bailment is for the purpose of transportation or storage of goods, certain **documents of title,** governed by Article VII of the Uniform Commercial

CASE NUGGET

THE EXTENT OF A BAILEE'S LIABILITY

Ziva Jewelry, Inc. v. Car Wash Headquarters, Inc. Supreme Court of Alabama
897 So. 2d 1011, 2004 Ala. LEXIS 238

A bailee can be liable only for the property he knows he possesses. In this case, Smith left his car and his keys with a car-wash employee. A case full of jewelry was locked in the trunk, but Smith did not tell any of the car-wash employees that it was in the trunk. Smith watched the car go through the car-wash tunnel and watched the employees dry the vehicle. As he was standing at the counter waiting to pay the cashier, he saw the employee wave a flag, indicating that his car was ready to be driven away. Smith then saw the employee walk away from his vehicle. While Smith was still at the counter, someone jumped into Smith's vehicle and sped off the car-wash premises. The police were called, and Smith's car was recovered 15 minutes later. The car was not damaged, but the jewelry, valued at $851,935, was missing from the trunk and never recovered.

Smith sued for negligent failure to safeguard the jewelry, but the trial court granted the defendant a summary judgment on the grounds that a bailment for the jewelry had never been established. The Supreme Court of Alabama affirmed on grounds that a bailee is not liable for the loss of the contents of a bailed vehicle when the bailee did not have actual or implied knowledge of the contents of the vehicle. In this case, there was no evidence that the car wash knew or should have reasonably foreseen or expected that it was taking responsibility for over $850,000 worth of jewelry when it accepted Smith's vehicle for the purpose of washing it.

Code, may be issued in conjunction with the bailment. The UCC defines a document of title as one that "must purport to be issued by or addressed to a bailee and purport to cover goods in the bailee's possession which are either identified or are fungible portions of an identified mass."

The three types of documents of title governing bailments are bills of lading, warehouse receipts, and delivery orders. A **bill of lading** is a document issued by a person engaged in the business of transporting goods that verifies receipt of the goods for shipment. A **warehouse receipt** is a receipt issued by one who is engaged in the business of storing goods for compensation. A *delivery order* is a written order to deliver goods directed to a party who, in the ordinary course of business, issues warehouse receipts or bills of lading.

Negotiability of Documents of Title. As you should recall from Chapter 26, if an instrument contains the word *bearer* or the phrase *to the order of,* it is negotiable. Thus, if a document of title specifies that the goods are to be delivered to the bearer or to the order of a named person, the person who possesses that document of title is entitled to receive, hold, and dispose of the goods it covers. Further, a good-faith purchaser of such a document of title may actually have greater rights to the document and goods than the transferor had or had the right to convey.

SPECIAL BAILMENTS

Certain bailments impose additional obligations on the bailee. These bailments will be discussed in detail in the following sections.

Common Carriers. **Common carriers** are licensed to provide transportation services to the public, as opposed to private carriers, which provide transportation services to a select group. Common carriers are subject to regulation by agencies and may be limited in the scope of services they provide by geographic region or type of goods they carry, but as long as a party seeking their services does not ask them to make any deliveries outside the scope of their ordinary course of business, common carriers cannot refuse to provide the service.

CASE NUGGET

INNKEEPERS' LIABILITY

GNOC Corp. v. Powers
2006 WL 560687 (Sup. Ct. N.J. 2006)

New Jersey's State Innkeeper's Act is a law that protects hotels from being liable for losses to their guests, as Powers unfortunately discovered. He was gambling in town and staying at a Hilton Hotel. While Powers was asleep one night, the hotel issued a second key to his room to an unknown person, who allegedly entered Powers's room and stole over $75,000 in cash winnings and chips. Powers sued, claiming negligence by the hotel. The trial court ruled in favor of the Hilton Hotel, and Powers appealed. The appeals court affirmed, holding that under New Jersey law, a hotel could not be held liable for the loss of valuables that could have been deposited in the hotel safe. Both the cash and the chips fell into the category of such valuables.

When a common carrier accepts a package for transport, a mutual-benefit bailment is created. But because the bailee is a common carrier, he or she is held to a higher standard of care: the standard of strict liability in protecting the bailed property. In other words, the common carrier is absolutely liable for any harm done to the property, even if there was no negligence on the part of the common carrier.

The only situations in which the common carrier will not be liable for harm to the bailed property are those in which the injury was caused by an act of God, an act of a public enemy, an act of the shipper, or the inherent nature of the good. These exceptions are interpreted narrowly. For example, the common carrier is still liable when the harm to the property was caused by an accident or by intentional acts of a third party. Thus, if the bailed property is stolen from the common-carrier truck that was transporting it, or if the truck gets into an accident and the contents are damaged as a result, the trucking firm is liable. However, if the fragile glass property being shipped gets broken because it was improperly crated by the owner, or if a tornado picks up the truck and drops it, demolishing the truck and its contents in the process, the common carrier will not be liable.

Sometimes a party will transport property using two or more connecting carriers. In such cases, a *through bill of lading* is used, which lists all carriers. Under this document, the shipper can recover from the original carrier or any of the connecting carriers. However, there is a presumption that the last carrier received the property in good condition.

To see how management and marketing considerations affect the choice of a common carrier, please see the **Connecting to the Core** activity on the text website at www.mhhe.com/kubasek3e.

Innkeepers' Liability. At common law, **innkeepers,** as well as anyone else who provided lodging to others, were held to the same strict-liability standard of care for their guests' property as were common carriers. However, today this standard applies only to those who are regularly in the business of making lodging available to the public. The standard also applies only to guests, or travelers, as opposed to lodgers, who are defined as permanent residents of the facility.

Some states further allow that innkeepers can avoid strict liability for their guests' personal property by providing them with a safe in which they may keep their valuables. Guests must be clearly notified of the existence of the safe and the limitation on the innkeeper's liability in the event that the guests fail to take advantage of the safe. Under some statutes, failure to use the safe will merely limit the innkeeper's liability; under others, it will relieve the innkeeper from liability other than that caused by his or her ordinary negligence.

Generally, the innkeeper does not have any responsibility for a guest's automobile. However, if the innkeeper provides parking facilities, a bailment exists and the innkeeper is held to the standard of reasonable care.

CASE OPENER WRAP-UP

Prisoners and Personal Property

The court determined that a bailment relationship existed between Melvin and Richard. Further, the court explained that the relationship between an inmate and a prison official is more substantial than that between a boarder and his host. Inmates do not pay prison officials to safeguard their personal belongings; thus, the relationship cannot constitute a bailment for hire. However, the restrictions on an inmate's property and his or her ability to control access to the property are imposed for the benefit of prison officials of the United States and for the protection of inmates. Although Melvin did not tell Richard that there was property in his cell, Richard did not suggest any other reason as to why Melvin would desire to have his cell locked other than to secure his property. Once Richard agreed to lock the cell, he had the duty, as a bailee, to act with reasonable care. The court took the majority position in holding that the personal property of inmates is protected.

KEY TERMS

SUMMARY OF KEY TOPICS

The Nature and Classifications of Property

Property is a set of rights in relation to a tangible object, the most significant of which is probably the right to exclude others.

Property can be divided into three categories:

Real property: Land and anything permanently attached to it.

Personal property: Tangible movable objects and intangible objects.

Intellectual property: Property that is primarily the result of one's mental rather than physical creativity.

Personal Property

Personal property can be transferred voluntarily through a gift or sale. It may also be transferred involuntarily if it is lost or mislaid.

Bailment

A bailment is a special relationship in which one party, the *bailor,* transfers possession of personalty to another, the *bailee,* to be used by the bailee in an agreed-on manner for an agreed-on time period.

POINT / COUNTERPOINT

Barry Bonds, the San Francisco Giants slugger, stepped up to the plate in the first inning with 72 home runs for the season. With the bases empty and a full count, Bonds connected with a slow knuckleball, sending it over the right-field wall and into the baseball glove of a fan named Alex Popov. Before Popov could establish secure possession of the ball, however, a crowd of fans mobbed him, jarring the ball loose. Patrick Hayashi, a nearby fan who was not part of the crowd that mobbed Popov, picked up the ball on the ground nearby. Popov sued Hayashi for the property rights to the ball.

Should Popov Win?

YES

Popov asserted as much control over the ball as the nature of the situation permitted. If the unruly mob of fans had not descended on him as he caught the ball and jarred it loose, he likely would have been able to exercise complete and secure control over it.

The court should be wary of establishing a rule that sanctions mob rule in the stands. A ruling for Hayashi would signal to fans everywhere that a ball is fair game as long as no one exercises complete control over it. As a result, fans would have a strong incentive to assault other fans right before they could gain possession of a ball. This form of competition is not socially beneficial. Hence, the court should establish a clear rule that interference from other fans cannot deprive the original possessor of his property rights in the ball.

Allowing Popov to bring suit against the mob that jarred the ball loose from his glove is unsatisfactory for several reasons. First, it is impossible for Popov to show that but for the actions of the mob, he would have established complete control over the ball.

Second, because the mob was quite large, it is impossible to determine which fans were acting maliciously and which fans were inadvertently pulled into the mix. Hence, even though Hayashi is not guilty of any wrongdoing himself, he should not be able to profit from the wrongdoing of others.

NO

The standard rule in property law is that an individual must demonstrate full control over an object before he is deemed to have possession of that object. Popov did not have complete possession of the ball before it came loose. If the ball had been jarred loose because Popov collided with an inanimate wall, he could not argue that he had possession of the ball. This case is no different, because Hayashi did not cause the ball to fall out of Popov's glove.

A ruling for Hayashi would not tend to encourage physical fighting for the ball because Hayashi was an innocent bystander, not a part of the mob that attacked Popov. The law should not allow those who use force to take baseballs from other fans to profit from their force. But if the ball comes loose before any fan establishes certain possession of it, any other fan who did not intentionally cause the ball to come loose may capture the rights to the ball by gaining possession of it.

A ruling for Hayashi does not leave Popov without a remedy. He is free to bring suit against the fans who mobbed him and caused the ball to come loose from his glove. If he can demonstrate that they deprived him of control over the ball, he can recover the value of the ball from them. That result is the most fair because the unruly fans were the wrongdoers in this case, not Hayashi.

QUESTIONS & PROBLEMS

1. Explain which type of property each of the following is:
   a. A tree
   b. Lumber
   c. A car
   d. A built-in oven
2. What is the difference between a gift *causa mortis* and an *inter vivos* gift?
3. How is lost property different from mislaid property, and why is that distinction important?
4. What is the relationship between the rights of the bailee and the duties of the bailor?

5. A woman bought a foreclosed house at a master commissioner sale. The previous owners had left certain items on the property, which the new buyer assumed as her own. The trial court originally found in favor of the original owners; however, on appeal the court reversed. The court determined that the couple had abandoned their property because they had made no attempt to get the property back during the four years before the new buyer acquired it. The couple did not deny that they knew their items were on the foreclosed property. The couple appealed. How do you think the court decided? Did the couple abandon their property? [*Greer v. Arroz,* 330 S.W.3d 763, Ky. App. LEXIS 12 (2011).]

6. In 2011 a case arose that involved an alleged *causa mortis* gift. When Roger Hansen was alive, he owned estates that his nieces and their families were making payments on. Before he died, he wrote a draft of a will which stated that the nieces would own the properties upon his death. He delivered this draft to his attorney and was working on a final draft of his will. However, he died before the will was created. The court stated that for the debt relief to be a *causa mortis* gift, a document relieving the debts had to be delivered to the debtors themselves, not a third party. Thus, the three requirements of a valid gift were lacking. The nieces appealed. How do you think the court of appeals decided? Even though it was clear that Hansen intended to relieve the debts, would the alleged "gift" be invalid without proper delivery? [*Meegan v. Netzer,* 2012 WI App. 20, 339 Wis. 2d 460, 810 N.W.2d 358, Wis. App. LEXIS 68 (2012).]

7. Defendant Tubbs met her fiancé, Church, over the Internet. After several years of correspondence and visits, they became engaged in February 2000. Church and Tubbs planned to be married in Las Vegas in July 2000. Two months before the engagement, Church paid off $4,100 of Tubbs's credit card debt. He also gave Tubbs an engagement ring that he purchased for $7,274.42. On March 15, 2000, he deposited $194,852.56 in Tubbs's bank account to fund the purchase of land and a residential home in Michigan. Tubbs purchased the home in both of their names as joint tenants, on Church's instructions, and in April she moved in. Church moved some personal property to the residence, including a family heirloom diamond ring. On June 5, 2000, Tubbs e-mailed Church stating that their relationship was over because she was horrified after seeing his "bizarre and abnormal behavior" on the Internet and because she had discovered that he led a "risqué lifestyle as a cross-dresser and bisexual." Tubbs rejected Church's demands to repay the $4,100 and to return the engagement ring, his personal property, and her interest in the Michigan home. On July 24, 2000, Church died in England.

Church's estate subsequently filed suit to recover the property. The court entered a final judgment entitling the estate to the rings or a money judgment for their values; the real property, partitioned as a matter of law to account for its appreciation; complete right, title, interest, and possession of the land and residential home, free and clear of any claim, right, title, or interest of Tubbs; and a money judgment in the amount of $75,000 (the amount of Tubbs's home equity mortgage), less credits to Tubbs of $13,000 for property taxes she paid from 2000 through 2005, or a modified money judgment in the amount of $62,000. Tubbs appealed. What arguments might she have made on appeal? How do you think the appellate court ruled in this case, and why? [*Salens v. Tubbs,* 2008 WL 4072342 (C.A.6 Mich.).]

8. Davis and Hansen own adjacent lots. When Davis bought his lot in 1984, the warranty deed contained an easement across the lot he was purchasing to the property now owned by Hansen. The easement in the deed to Davis from the seller, Rodgers, stated that the easement on the land "shall be only for the benefit of Grantor [Rodgers], his grantees, heirs and assigns." Davis had been advised by a lawyer that the easement was not legally enforceable, so Davis put a garden on the easement area. Hansen bought his lot in 2006 and offered Davis $5,000 for an easement to access the property. Davis said no. Hansen then purchased the easement written in 1984 from Rodgers' widow, who had inherited Rodger's property.

Once he had bought the easement, Hansen told Davis he was going to use his easement and he immediately cleared the easement on Davis's property for a road and water and sewer lines. Davis then sued Hansen for trespass. Hansen countersued, seeking to prove ownership of the easement. The trial court ruled in favor of Davis, holding that Hansen had engaged in adverse possession of the easement by planting a garden over the easement, which extinguished it, and ordered Hansen to pay $13,345 in "restoration" damages.

Hansen appealed. What do you believe happened on appeal? Why? [*Hansen v. Davis,* 220 P.3d 911 (Alaska Sup. Ct. 2009).]

9. In Oregon, a man's dog scaled his fence and ran away. The man searched for his dog. He put up fliers, posted on craigslist, and alerted the local animal control by filing a report. He never saw the dog again until he saw it in a girl's car outside a café in Portland. His dog had been found by the girl who later named the dog Bear. She taught the dog how to be a service dog because she suffered from dangerous asthma attacks. The girl admitted finding the dog at the time that it ran from the man's yard. The two were supposed to meet up later so she could return the dog, but she later refused and wanted to keep the dog. The man said that the dog was his property and that because it was lost and not abandoned, he was entitled to get it back, so he filed a lawsuit. How do you think the judge decided? [*Biggs v. Hanson-Fleming,* Case No. 1207-08704 (Or. Cir. Ct. 2012).]

10. Thomas A. Carella filed for Chapter 7 bankruptcy. At the time, HSBC Bank USA held the sum of $16,540.94 on deposit in a joint bank account in the names of Carella and his father, Thomas J. Carella. The son sought to protect the money in the bank account, arguing that it was his father's account. The father had set up the joint account after finding out he needed to undergo heart bypass surgery. The father argues that he set up the joint account for convenience so that his son would have access to the money should the father pass away. The father survived the surgery and continued to manage the joint account. Only the father deposited or withdrew money from the account at any time. The son's bankruptcy trustee argued that the account was a gift *causa mortis* and thus is available as part of the bankruptcy. Did the joint account constitute a gift *causa mortis?* What are the necessary elements for establishing the joint account as a gift *causa mortis?* [*In re Thomas A. Carella,* 340 B.R. 710 (Bankr. W.D.N.Y. 2006).]

Looking for more review materials?

The Online Learning Center at **www.mhhe.com/kubasek3e** contains this chapter's "Assignment on the Internet" and also a list of URLs for more information, entitled "On the Internet." Find both of them in the Student Center portion of the OLC, along with quizzes and other helpful materials.

CHAPTER 49

Real Property

LEARNING OBJECTIVES

After reading this chapter, you will be able to answer the following questions:

1 What are the interests in real property that someone can hold?

2 How is real property voluntarily transferred?

3 How is real property involuntarily transferred?

4 How is the use of property restricted?

CASE OPENER

Groundwater and Property Rights

In 2000, Great Spring Waters of America began to create a water-bottling plant in Michigan. The company first had to procure rights to the groundwater of the property, which was just north of Osprey Lake and was called Sanctuary Springs. From January through August of 2001, four wells were installed on Sanctuary Springs to extract groundwater. In the same year, the bottling plant began to be constructed about 12 miles from Sanctuary Springs. In August of 2001 and February of 2002, the company obtained permits from the Michigan Department of Environmental Quality (DEQ) that allowed it to pump 400 gallons of the groundwater per minute. However, in September 2001, Michigan Citizens for Water Conservation (MCWC) contended that the withdrawal of water was illegal under the common law applicable to riparian rights. Furthermore, the withdrawal was unreasonable according to groundwater common law. In other words, the company's extraction of groundwater was harming the groundwater ownership rights of neighboring property owners. Thus, MCWC filed a complaint attempting to stop the company from creating the wells to extract the water.

The trial court found that the extraction of groundwater by the company was harming riparian interests. Reasonable use doctrine states that "a riparian owner may make any and all reasonable uses of the water, as long [as the owner does] not unreasonably interfere with the other riparian owners' opportunity for reasonable use." The company appealed.[1]

1. How do courts determine whether a riparian owner's groundwater rights are unreasonably interfered with?
2. Why did the MCWC think that the actions of the company in this case were harmful to other owners?

The Wrap-Up at the end of the chapter will answer these questions.

[1] *Michigan Citizens for Water Conservation v. Nestle Waters North America Inc.*, 269 Mich. App. 25, 709 N.W.2d 174 (2005).

Ownership of real property seems to be one of the goals of most people in the United States. In this chapter we examine the nature of real property, the types of interests someone can own in real property, and how those interests can be transferred.

The Nature of Real Property

Real property, commonly referred to as *realty,* is land and everything permanently attached to it. The type of ownership interest a person has in a piece of property determines his or her rights to the property. In the next section, we describe these interests in detail. They may be conveyed or transferred under legal guidelines for property rights, most often voluntarily. However, for the benefit of the public, and to protect public health, safety, and welfare, the government may require involuntary transfers of property.

The definition of real property seems straightforward, but applying it is not always easy. Many disputes over whether an item is real or personal property have revolved around whether the item really is permanently attached. The courts have generally held that a given item is attached if its removal would hinder the functioning of the structure. Because removing built-in appliances would damage a building, these are held to be part of the real property; a freestanding appliance is personal property. Items not permanently attached but essential to the use of the building have been ruled part of the real property.

FIXTURES

A **fixture** is an item that was originally a piece of personal property but became part of the realty after it was permanently attached to the real property in question. For example, if a tenant installs a built-in dishwasher in the property he is renting, the dishwasher becomes part of the real property. When he leaves, the tenant may not take the dishwasher with him. However, there are two exceptions to this rule.

The first arises when there is a written agreement between the parties that specific features will be treated as personal property. The second exception applies to personal property attached to realty for the use of a business renting the property. Such items are known as *trade fixtures* and are treated as personal property on the basis of the presumption that neither party intends such fixtures to become a permanent part of the realty. For example, if a businessperson rents a storefront for a barbershop and installs barber chairs, these chairs are trade fixtures. If the businessperson relocates, he will need the chairs at a new location, and the next tenant will have her own needs.

This exception did not hold true, however, in a case in an Arizona state appellate court. Two air service businesses, Air Commerce Center, LLP, and Airport Properties, leased public land at Scottsdale Municipal Airport. Airport Properties had built air service–related improvements that it believed were trade fixtures. However, the court found that the improvements were the property of the city. Thus, if there is any concern on the part of the tenant about how improvements will be treated, it is best to get an agreement in writing if the tenant wants to retain possession of the material used in improving the property.

Legal Principle: A fixture is created when an item that was originally a piece of personal property is permanently attached to real property, thus becoming a part of the realty.

EXTENT OF OWNERSHIP

The landowner's rights to property go beyond simply the surface of the land. The airspace above the land, extending to the atmosphere, is also part of the legal concept of real property. Rights to airspace generally do not generate much controversy, but occasionally disputes arise over aircraft flying over individuals' property. A tree's branches may hang into the airspace of the property next door, and the owner of that airspace is entitled to cut them.

In dense, commercial urban areas, airspace may actually be an asset. Owners of two commercial buildings might want to build an overhead walkway adjoining their buildings across a parking lot you own. They will have to pay you handsomely for the right to build in your airspace.

BUT WHAT IF . . .

WHAT IF THE FACTS OF THE CASE OPENER WERE DIFFERENT?

Let's say, in the Case Opener, that the bottling company had built enough wells and had enough pumping power to completely deplete a reservoir within several years. Would the property owners with water rights to this reservoir be able to block the company from operation?

The owner of real property also has *water rights,* the legal ability to use water flowing across or underneath the property. However, these rights are somewhat restricted; an owner cannot deprive landowners downstream of the use of the water by diverting it elsewhere.

Finally, ownership of real property extends to *mineral rights.* The landowner has the legal ability to dig or mine materials from the earth below the surface and may sell or give these rights to another. Ownership of these *subsurface rights* includes the right to enter onto the property to remove the underground materials.

The landowner's rights to property are illustrated in Exhibit 49-1.

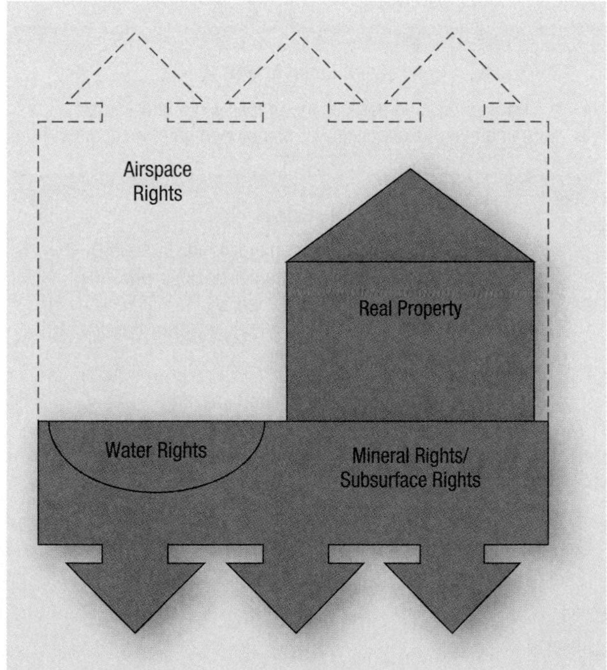

Exhibit 49-1

Extent of Real Property Rights

Interests in Real Property

LO1

What are the interests in real property that someone can hold?

Interests in land range from temporary to permanent to future. The duration of a person's ownership interest and the power he or she has over use of the land depend on the type of *estate* the person holds. We discuss the various estates below and summarize them in Exhibit 49-2.

FEE SIMPLE ABSOLUTE

A **fee simple absolute** is the most complete estate a person may have; it grants exclusive rights to ownership and possession of the land and is what most people refer to when they speak of "buying" a house or piece of land. This interest passes to the heirs when the owner dies.

CONDITIONAL ESTATE

The owner of a **conditional estate** possesses the same interest as the owner of a fee simple absolute, but it is subject to a condition. Should a prohibited event occur or a required event fail to occur, the interest will be terminated. Todd may be given property rights to a Victorian house on the condition that he preserve it in its original form. If he violates this condition by turning the house into a piano showroom or a beer hall, the house will either revert to the original owner or be transferred in accordance with the terms of the *deed,* the instrument used to convey real property.

Exhibit 49-2
Hierarchy of Estates

BUT WHAT IF . . .

WHAT IF THE FACTS OF THE CASE OPENER WERE DIFFERENT?

Let's say that the company bought the parcel of land for its factory on the condition that it would build a factory but not extract groundwater because extraction would harm the community. However, the company decided it needed to extract the groundwater because it was not going to be able to get water from the source it had originally planned to use. Could the company actually lose ownership of the land on which it built its factory because of such an action?

LIFE ESTATE

A **life estate** is granted for the lifetime of an individual. On the death of this life holder, the property will go to another party designated by the original grantor. This future owner has an interest in seeing that the life tenant does not *waste* the property; if the life holder neglects or abuses the property, or fails to make necessary repairs such that its value diminishes, the future holder can bring legal action to recover damages for waste.

Case 49-1 illustrates what the courts have found as constituting waste.

CASE 49-1 SAULS v. CROSBY

DISTRICT COURT OF APPEALS OF FLORIDA
258 SO. 2D 326 (1972)

Annie Sauls, the defendant-appellant, conveyed a future interest in certain property to plaintiff-appellees Dan and Bertha Crosby and reserved a life estate in it. She attempted to cut timber on the property to sell, and the holders of the future interest sought to enjoin her from doing so. The district court held that Sauls was not entitled to cut timber and keep the proceeds for herself. She appealed the lower court's ruling.

JUDGE RAWLS: On the 9th day of October 1968, appellant conveyed to appellees certain lands situated in Hamilton County, Florida, with the following reservation set forth in said conveyance: "The Grantor herein, reserves a life estate in said property." By this appeal appellant now contends that the trial court erred in denying her, as a life tenant, the right to cut merchantable timber and enjoy the proceeds.

The English common law, which was transplanted on this continent, holds that it is waste for an ordinary life tenant to cut timber upon his estate when the sole purpose is to clear the woodlands. American courts today as a general rule recognize that an ordinary life tenant may cut timber and not be liable for waste if he uses the timber for fuel; for repairing fences and buildings on the estate; for fitting the land for cultivation; or for use as pasture if the inheritance is not damaged and the acts are conformable to good husbandry; and for thinning or other purposes which are necessary for the enjoyment of the estate and are in conformity with good husbandry.

In this jurisdiction a tenant for life or a person vested with an ordinary life estate is entitled to the use and enjoyment of his estate during its existence. The only restriction on the life tenant's use and enjoyment is that he not permanently diminish or change the value of the future estate of the remainderman. This limitation places on the "ordinary life tenant" the responsibility for all waste of whatever character.

An instrument creating a life tenancy may absolve the tenant of responsibility for waste by stating that the life tenant has the power to consume or that the life tenant is without impeachment for waste. Thus, there is a sharp distinction in the rights of an ordinary life tenant or life tenant without impeachment for waste or life tenant who has the power to consume. An ordinary life tenant has no right to cut the timber from an estate for purely commercial reasons and so to do is tortious conduct for which the remainderman may sue immediately.

In the case before us, the trial court was concerned with the rights of an ordinary life tenant and correctly concluded that appellant does not have the right to cut merchantable timber from the land involved in this suit unless the proceeds of such cutting and sale are held in trust for the use and benefit of the remaindermen. . . .

AFFIRMED in favor of plaintiff.

[continued]

CRITICAL THINKING

What fact could you add to this case that would change the outcome?

ETHICAL DECISION MAKING

In rendering his decision, the judge gave primary weight to the interests of which stakeholders?

Legal Principle: **Waste occurs when the holder of a life estate uses the property in a way that reduces the value of the estate that the future holder will receive; it is unlawful.**

FUTURE INTEREST

The plaintiffs in Case 49-1 held a **future interest** in the estate, a present right to property ownership and possession in the future. Such an interest usually exists in conjunction with a life estate or a conditional estate. Suppose José owns a life estate in Oak Hills Apartments and on his death the property will pass to Sarah with fee-simple-absolute rights. Sarah holds a future interest in Oak Hills Apartments, and if José allows the buildings to deteriorate from neglect, she may sue to enjoin him from engaging in waste of the property.

LEASEHOLD ESTATE

The holder of a **leasehold** has a possessory but not an ownership interest. This interest is transferred by a contract known as a *lease.* Both the owner of the property (the lessor, or landlord) and the tenant (the lessee) sign the lease. The contract generally specifies the property to be leased, the amount of the rent payments and when they are due, the duration of the leasehold, and any special rights or duties of either party. A leasehold gives the lessee, or tenant, exclusive rights to the use and possession of the land, including the right to exclude the property owner under most circumstances, for the term specified by the lease.

The tenant's and landlord's rights and obligations may vary according to the lease, but some states require that landlords keep the property in good condition for the tenant's use, giving the tenant the right to withhold rent payments should the landlord fail to do so. Should the tenant fail to make the agreed-on payments *without* such grounds, the landlord may evict the tenant. The landlord is not allowed to enter the property, except in an emergency or when the tenant has given permission to make repairs. Near the end of the leasehold, the landlord may enter with notice to the tenant for the purpose of showing the property to a potential new tenant.

Subleasing of the property by the tenant to another party is permissible unless specifically prohibited by the lease. However, the initial tenant is liable throughout the entire term of the lease for payment of the rent to the landlord. We discuss leases in greater detail in Chapter 50, "Landlord-Tenant Law."

NONPOSSESSORY ESTATE

While most people think of interests in land as being possessory in nature, easements, profits, and licenses do not include the right to possess the property.

Easements and Profits. Easements and profits are similar in that they are neither ownership nor possessory interests. An **easement** is an irrevocable right to use some part of another's land for a specific purpose without taking anything from it. A **profit** is the

COMPARING THE LAW OF OTHER COUNTRIES

PROPERTY INTERESTS IN VIETNAM

In the United States, we take for granted the right to purchase a piece of property if we have the money to do so. Property is not so freely available and transferable in all nations. Vietnam's new constitution, written in 1992, provides guidelines for the allocation, transfer, and sale of private property. However, it still asserts that the people, or the state, own all the land. Thus, if individuals or private enterprises want to use land, they must pay tax on it as a form of rent and are granted a "use of right" which entitles them to extended use and the freedom to transfer the property. Technically, they are transferring not the *property,* but rather the right to use it.

Transference of property can occur only with the approval of a state official. The official ensures the new owner intends to use the land for the original, state-approved purpose. Moreover, the new owner can never be given a longer term of right or more extensive rights over the land than the original owner had. Finally, the state official determines the price that the property will be transferred for. The government has specified certain prices depending on how the land is used.

right to go onto someone's land and take part of the land or a product of it away from the land. If Rashon has the right to drive his car across Jenny's property to get to his property, he has an easement, but if he has the right to go onto her property and remove the topsoil he needs from it for his landscaping business, he has a profit.

BUT WHAT IF . . .

WHAT IF THE FACTS OF THE CASE OPENER WERE DIFFERENT?

Recall, in the Case Opener, that the company simply had groundwater rights for Sanctuary Springs. What kind of an estate is this called? What if the company actually bought the land and built offices on it? What kind of an estate would this be called, and what are the various rights that come with it?

Owners of real property with a public easement have many rights regarding the land because they still own the fee. A construction manager, Albert Taub, believed that he could remove large quantities of dirt for his construction project from a public drainage easement because his actions improved the drainage. However, the court ruled that only the fee owner or the city could alter the property to improve the drainage and that Taub had no right to alter the easement.[2]

An easement or profit is *appurtenant* when it runs with land adjacent to the property on which it exists. If Rashon's property is adjacent to Jenny's, he has an easement (or profit) appurtenant, which only he can use and which can be transferred only in conjunction with the transfer of his property.

Easements or profits *in gross* are not dependent on owning property adjacent to the land on which the nonpossessory interest exists. The gas company may obtain an easement in gross to run gas lines across someone's property.

Easements and profits can be transferred by express agreement, inheritance, necessity, implication, or prescription. Transfer by *express agreement* occurs when the landowner expressly grants the agreed-on use of the land to the holder of the easement, such as allowing a farmer to run a ditch across part of his neighbor's property to drain a field. This easement should be recorded in the appropriate county office or described on the deed to protect the holder of the easement if the property is sold. If the transfer of the interest is to be by *inheritance,* its terms are simply incorporated into the property owner's will.

[2] *Gleason v. Taub,* 180 S.W.3d 711 (Tex. App. 2005).

CASE NUGGET

THE IMPORTANCE OF KNOWING TYPES OF TENANCIES

In re Estate of Thomas,
Supreme Court of Wyoming
199 P.3d 1090 (2009)

Grantors Mike and Dorothy Thomas filed a deed with the county clerk to transfer a parcel of real estate to John Thomas and Margaret Dickson, their only children, "as tenants by the entireties with right of survivorship and not as tenants in common." They also filed a second deed with the county clerk, transferring another piece of property to John and Margaret. Years later, a dispute arose among John's heirs and Margaret as to the form of ownership of the two properties. John's heirs claimed both properties were owned as tenants in common; Margaret claimed they were owned as joint tenants. The district court held that the properties were owned as tenants in common, and Margaret appealed.

The court found that the grantors, acting without legal counsel, had attempted to create a tenancy by the entireties in John and Margaret, which was not legally possible, but the transfer stated "with right of survivorship, and not as tenants in common." In this case, the intent was to not have the transfer be as tenants in common, so a joint tenancy was created in the first property. The second property grant made no such declaration and simply transferred ownership to John and Margaret; this transfer created a tenancy in common.

An **easement by prescription** is created by state law when certain conditions are met. In most states, if someone openly uses a portion of another's property for a statutory period (usually 25 years), an easement arises by law. If a piece of property is divided and one portion is landlocked as a result, an *easement by necessity* is created. For purposes of entrance to and exit from the land, the owner of the landlocked parcel has an easement to cross the other portion.

If the land that benefits from the easement or profit is sold, the nonpossessory interest goes with the property. Thus, if Rashon sold his land to Sonny, Sonny would also receive the easement across Jenny's property. If Jenny sold her property, the new owner would have the burden of Rashon's easement as long as it had been properly recorded. Of course, just as easements and profits can be created, they can also be terminated, most often by agreement. The easement holder may simply deed the easement back to the property owner. If the easement arose by necessity and the necessity no longer exists, the easement terminates.

An *easement by implication,* sometimes called *easement by necessity,* is said to exist when a piece of property is divided into two parcels in such a way that an already existing, obvious, and continuous use of the first parcel (such as for access) is necessary for the reasonable enjoyment of the second parcel. The owner of the second parcel has an easement by implication on the first parcel.

License. A **license** is a temporary and revocable right to use another's property. Someone who purchases a theater ticket has the right to a specific use of the property for a limited time, subject to good behavior. No property interest goes to the license holder.

Co-ownership

An interest in real property may be owned by a single individual, two or more persons, or a corporation. When more than one person possesses the same property rights, **co-ownership** exists. The type of co-ownership determines the ownership rights. As the Case Nugget illustrates, it is very important when granting property rights to know what type of tenancy you intend. Otherwise, there may be unintended consequences.

TENANCY IN COMMON

Tenancy in common is the most common type of co-ownership. It gives each co-owner the right to sell his or her interest without the consent of the others, to own an unequal share of the property, and to have a creditor attach his or her interest. The heirs of a tenancy in common receive the property interest on the tenant's death.

JOINT TENANCY

Joint tenants, like tenants in common, may sell their shares without the consent of the other owners, as well as have their interest attached by creditors. However, joint tenants all own *equal* shares of the property, and on the death of one the property is divided equally among the surviving joint owners.

TENANCY BY THE ENTIRETY

Tenancy by the entirety describes co-ownership by married couples: One owner cannot sell his or her interest without the other's consent, and creditors of one owner cannot attach the property. If one owner dies, the surviving spouse assumes full ownership. If the owners divorce, the interest becomes a tenancy in common.

In each of the three types of co-ownership, all tenants have the equal right to occupy all the property. This characteristic and others are listed in Exhibit 49-3.

CONDOMINIUMS AND COOPERATIVES

Two types of joint ownership are popular in this country, especially in cities. One is the *condominium* interest. It gives the holder exclusive ownership rights of a unit within the condominium and tenancy in common with the other condominium owners over the land, buildings, and improvements of the common areas of the development. The architecture and use of common areas are regulated by a condominium association, which has the power to levy assessments against the unit owners for maintenance of these areas. This association is directed by a *Declaration of Covenants, Conditions and Restrictions (CC&Rs),* filed when the condominium is formed.

The second type of joint ownership is a *cooperative.* Here, the investor resident is a shareholder in the corporation owning (usually) an apartment building and receives a permanent lease on one unit of the facility upon acquiring stock. All the unit owners are governed by a board of directors, usually elected from among the unit owners to manage

Exhibit 49-3
Joint Ownership

TYPE OF OWNERSHIP	POSSIBLE DIVISION OF OWNERSHIP	RIGHTS OF OWNERS' CREDITORS	OWNERSHIP OF PROPERTY UPON DEATH OF AN OWNER
Tenancy in Common	Shares can be equal or unequal.	Creditors can attach any owner's interest.	Deceased owner's share is transferred to heirs.
Joint Tenancy	Shares are equal.	Creditors can attach any owner's interest.	Deceased owner's share is divided among other joint tenants.
Tenancy by the Entirety	Shares are equal.	Owner's creditors cannot attach interest.	Deceased owner's share goes to surviving spouse.

the property and establish rules for the owners. If a member violates these rules, the cooperative may evict the member and repurchase the evicted member's unit. In many cooperatives, before an apartment can be sold, the board must approve the buyer.

Voluntary Transfer of Real Property

LEGAL REQUIREMENTS

LO2

How is real property voluntarily transferred?

An owner may generally transfer any or all of his or her property to anyone for any price or no price, as the owner desires. This ability to transfer real property is part of the value of property.

The legal procedures that must be followed to effectuate such a transfer are *execution, delivery, acceptance,* and *recording,* with the last one being required to protect the recipient of the property. These procedures are outlined in Exhibit 49-4. The conveyance that results from following these procedural steps is presumed to be the conveyance of a fee simple absolute, unless the contrary is stated.

Execution. Transfer of property is initiated by the *execution* (or preparation and signing) of the deed, which is the instrument of conveyance. There are different types of deeds, but any properly drafted deed must contain the following:

1. Identification of the *grantor,* the person conveying the property, and the *grantee,* the person receiving the property.
2. An expression of the grantor's intent to convey the property.
3. A legally sufficient description of the property, including its physical boundaries and any easements.
4. Any warranties or promises made by the grantor in conjunction with the conveyance.

Exhibit 49-4 Steps in Voluntary Transfer of Property

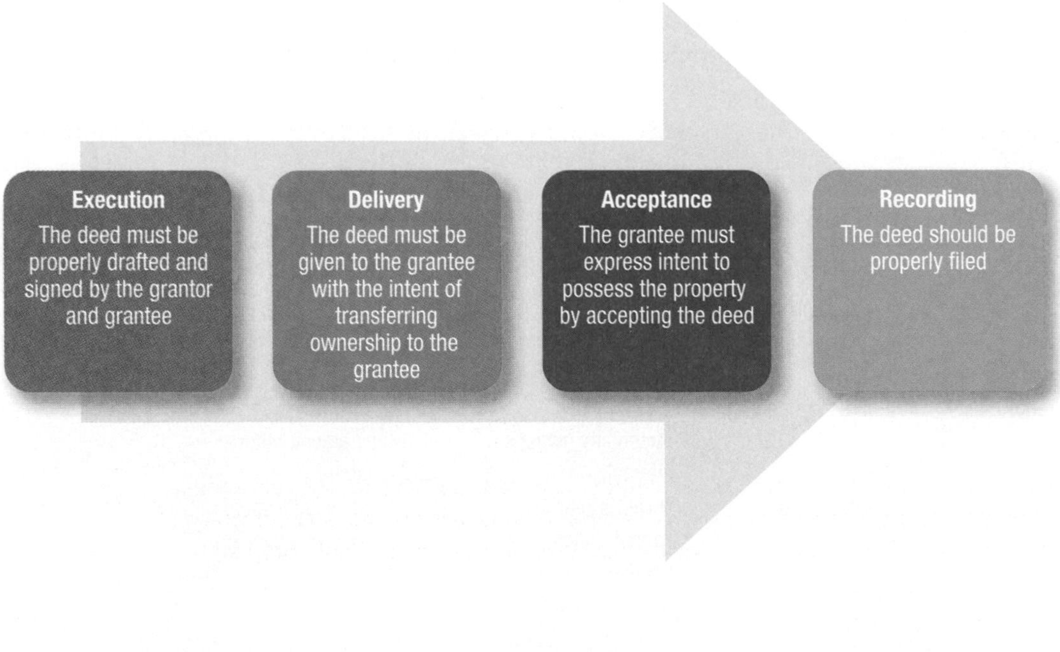

The most commonly used deed, the **general warranty deed,** contains certain warranties or promises by the grantor. Such covenants may vary slightly by state but generally promise that:

1. The grantor owns the interest he or she is conveying.
2. The grantor has the right to convey the property.
3. There are no mortgages or liens against the property unless stated in the deed.
4. The grantee will not be disturbed by anyone who has a better claim to title of the property, and the grantor will defend the grantee's title against such claims or reimburse any money spent in their defense and/or settlement.
5. The grantor will provide any additional documents the grantee needs to perfect his or her title to the property.

A grantor may not necessarily feel comfortable making all those warranties and may instead execute a **special warranty deed,** which promises only that he or she has not done anything to lessen the value of the estate.

From the grantee's perspective, the least desirable type of deed is the **quitclaim deed.** It carries no warranties; the grantor simply conveys whatever interests he or she holds. Thus, if the grantor had a defective title, the grantee receives a defective title. Because of the insecurity of such a deed, very few grantees accept it.

Once a deed of any type has been properly drafted and signed by the grantor and grantee, it has been *executed.* In many states, it must also be witnessed or notarized. *Notarization* is certification by an official of the state that she or he saw the signing of the deed and was provided evidence that the signatories were who they claimed to be.

Delivery. The next step in legal transfer of property is the *delivery* of the deed to the grantee, directly or through a third party, with the intent of transferring ownership.

Acceptance. *Acceptance* is the grantee's expression of intent to possess the property, and it is assumed if the grantee retains possession of the deed.

Recording. **Recording** is achieved by filing the deed, including any related documents such as mortgages, with the appropriate county office, thus giving the world official notice of the transfer. Although it is not a required step, recording is so important a protection of the grantee's rights that it should be part of every transfer. In fact, if two deeds allegedly convey the same piece of realty, many states give ownership to the person whose deed was recorded first.

Legal Principle: **To ensure that ownership of the property is transferred, the parties must follow the requisite steps of execution, delivery, acceptance, and recording of the deed.**

SALES TRANSACTIONS

Above we discussed the legal steps necessary for transfer of property. Now let's take a closer look at the actual sales process that generally leads to such a transfer.

Negotiation of a Sales Contract. Generally, a person seeking to sell real property will contact a real estate agent, or broker. A broker is licensed by the state in which he or she operates and is familiar with real estate law, as well as available properties.

In exchange for a commission on the sale, the broker advertises the property, shows it to potential buyers, and guides the seller through the formalities of the transfer.

In most states, a broker cannot act for both buyer and seller (given their different interests) unless both parties consent. In some states, when the buyer does not have a broker or lawyer as a representative in the transaction, the seller's broker may handle all the necessary paperwork, but the buyer must sign a statement that acknowledges that he or she knows that the broker is working exclusively for the seller.

Once the buyer finds a desired property, she makes a written offer to purchase under specified conditions and puts up *earnest money* designed to establish the seriousness of her offer. If the seller accepts the offer, the earnest money will apply toward the purchase price. If the buyer changes her mind before the seller accepts, she forfeits the earnest money. If the seller does not accept the offer, the money is returned.

Failure to accept within the time limit in the offer is considered a rejection. As with any contract, the seller may make a counteroffer at a different price or under different conditions.

Once the offer has been accepted, a sales contract is drawn up in accordance with the offer's terms. The contract will generally include a description of the property, the names and addresses of the parties, the purchase price, the type of deed, and who will bear the risk of loss if the property is destroyed before the sale has been completed.

The contract generally requires that the buyer put a deposit in an *escrow account* maintained by a neutral third party until all the preliminary steps to the transfer can be made. The deposit, which varies in size depending on the part of the country and local custom, but is often around 10 percent of the purchase price, will be turned over to the seller at the *closing,* when the transfer is completed.

Seller's Duty to Disclose. To what extent does the seller have a duty to disclose known defects to the buyer? The traditional answer was *caveat emptor,* or "Let the buyer beware," meaning that the seller had no obligation to tell the buyer about any problems. Can you tell which value is being replaced in the current move to a standard based more on reasonableness?

Today, most states require that the seller warn the buyer about any known defects that (1) the reasonable buyer could not discover through a thorough examination of the property and (2) materially affect the property's value. If the seller fails to disclose and the buyer discovers the defect only after the sales transaction has been completed, the buyer can sue the seller for fraud or misrepresentation.

Most states assume an implied warranty of habitability in the sale of a new home. With this warranty, comparable to the implied warranty of merchantability, the seller guarantees that everything in the house is of sound construction and in reasonable working order. If you purchased a new home during the winter and in warmer weather discovered the air conditioning did not run, you could sue the seller for breach of the implied warranty of habitability if he refused to fix the defective air conditioner.

Title Examination. While the buyer's deposit is in escrow, a title company or representative of the buyer or seller will search the county records to make sure the seller in fact has legal title to the property, there are no liens on it, and there are no restrictions of which the buyer is not aware. A title free of such defects is called a **marketable title.**

If a material defect is found in the search that has not been disclosed in the sales contract, the seller has breached the contract. The buyer can file an action to rescind the agreement, obtain damages, or get an order for specific performance with a price reduction. A dispute arose between Sun International and Greenlands Realty during a title examination. Sun was attempting to purchase property from Greenlands but sought to void the sale, claiming that Greenlands did not possess marketable title to the property because a different, and then-defunct, realty company held part of the title. The court granted a motion for summary judgment in Greenlands' favor, determining that the defunct company had conveyed all its title in the property and therefore Greenlands did possess marketable title.

A title search may not reveal every single defect in the title, however, so most buyers purchase title insurance or have the seller purchase it for them. Title insurance protects the buyer from losses resulting from a defect in the title.

Financing. Most buyers do not have the cash to purchase property, so most sales contracts are conditional on the buyer's being able to obtain financing within a certain period of time. In exchange for such a loan, the lender receives a security interest in the property, called a *mortgage.* While the buyer makes payments to the mortgagor or lender, the mortgagor or a third party holds title to the property and can sell it if the payments are not made.

Closing. The **closing** is the meeting at which the transfer of title actually takes place and delivery and acceptance occur. The seller signs over the deed, and the buyer gives the seller a check for the amount due. If a mortgage was necessary, it is executed at this time. Following the closing, the deed and mortgage are recorded.

Involuntary Transfer of Real Property

The transfer of the owner's interest in real property is not always voluntary. It can occur without the owner's knowledge and even, in some cases, against his or her will, by either adverse possession or condemnation.

LO3 How is real property involuntarily transferred?

ADVERSE POSSESSION

In **adverse possession,** a person takes ownership of real property by treating it as his or her own, without protest or permission from the owner. Most states have established a length of time after which such a possessor receives ownership interest in the property. The adverse possession must be *actual* (the person lives on or uses the land as an owner would), *open* (not secretive), and *notorious* (without the owner's permission). In some states, the adverse possessor must have performed certain acts such as paying real estate taxes. In other states, the adverse possessor must operate "under color of title," or the assumption that he or she actually held title to the land.

The law is similar in Japan, where adverse possession for 20 years leads to a transfer of ownership as long as the possessor began with a nonnegligent good-faith belief that he or she had legal title to the property.

Legal Principle: **Transfer by adverse possession occurs when the adverse possession is actual, open (not secretive), and notorious for the amount of time specified by the state.**

CONDEMNATION

Condemnation is the legal process by which a transfer of property is made against the protest of the property owner. As you will remember from Chapter 5's discussion of the takings clause of the Fifth Amendment, the government has a constitutional right to take private property for the use of the public, upon providing the owner fair compensation. This right is sometimes exercised on behalf of a private company operating to benefit the public.

When the government decides to exercise its power of eminent domain, it will first offer to purchase the property for what it believes is the fair market value. If the owner does not want to sell or feels the price is too low, the government will initiate a condemnation proceeding and the court will determine whether the government has a legitmate public purpose for taking the property. If it does, the court will determine the fair market value of the property, which the government will then pay to the owner, and the property will be transferred to the government.

It is sometimes difficult to determine whether the exercise of eminent domain is actually for the public's benefit when the property will be conveyed from one private individual to another private individual. Since the 1980s, businesses have increasingly appealed to cities to exercise their power of eminent domain to acquire land the owners did not want to sell, and state supreme courts have begun to address whether economic development is a public use under the constraints of the Fifth Amendment. Some courts found that job creation and expansion of the tax base did constitute public use. The U.S. Supreme Court finally settled the issue—at least for the present—in the 5–4 decision in Case 49-2.

CASE 49-2 KELO v. CITY OF NEW LONDON
UNITED STATES SUPREME COURT
126 S. CT. 326 (2005)

The city of New London approved an integrated development plan designed "to create in excess of 1,000 jobs, to increase tax and other revenues, and to revitalize an economically distressed city, including its downtown and waterfront areas." Using its development agent, the city purchased most of the property it needed for the project from willing sellers. A few property owners refused to sell, so the city initiated condemnation proceedings to take their property. The owners argued that this step would violate the "public use" restriction in the Fifth Amendment's Takings Clause. The trial court granted a permanent restraining order prohibiting the taking of some properties but allowing the taking of others. The Connecticut Supreme Court affirmed in part and reversed in part, upholding all the proposed takings. The United States Supreme Court agreed to hear the property owners' appeal.

JUSTICE STEVENS: . . . On the one hand, it has long been accepted that the sovereign may not take the property of *A* for the sole purpose of transferring it to another private party *B*, even though *A* is paid just compensation. On the other hand, it is equally clear that a State may transfer property from one private party to another if future "use by the public" is the purpose of the taking. . . . Neither of these propositions, however, determines the disposition of this case.

As for the first proposition, the City would no doubt be forbidden from taking petitioners' land for the purpose of conferring a private benefit on a particular private party. . . . Nor would the City be allowed to take property under the mere pretext of a public purpose, when its actual purpose was to bestow a private benefit. The takings before us, however, would be executed pursuant to a "carefully considered" development plan. The trial judge and all the members of the Supreme Court of Connecticut agreed that there was no evidence of an illegitimate purpose in this case. Therefore, the City's development plan was not adopted "to benefit a particular class of identifiable individuals."

. . . On the other hand, this is not a case in which the City is planning to open the condemned land . . . to use by the general public. Nor will the private lessees of the land in any sense be required to operate like common carriers, making their services available to all comers. But . . . this "Court long ago rejected any literal requirement that condemned property be put into use for the general public."

The disposition of this case therefore turns on the question whether the City's development plan serves a "public purpose." . . . [O]ur cases have defined that concept broadly, reflecting our longstanding policy of deference to legislative judgments in this field. In *Berman v. Parker* (1954), this Court upheld a redevelopment plan targeting a blighted area of Washington, D.C., in which most of the housing for the area's 5,000 inhabitants was beyond repair. Under the plan, the area would be condemned and part of it utilized for the construction of streets, schools, and other public facilities. The remainder of the land would be leased or sold to private parties for the purpose of redevelopment, including the construction of low-cost housing. The owner of a department store located in the area challenged the condemnation, pointing out that his store was not itself blighted and arguing that the creation of a "better balanced, more attractive community" was not a valid public use. Justice Douglas refused to evaluate this claim in isolation, deferring instead to the legislative and agency judgment that the area "must be planned as a whole" for the plan to be successful. The Court explained that "community redevelopment programs need not, by force of the Constitution, be on a piecemeal basis—lot by lot, building by building." The public use underlying the taking was unequivocally affirmed. . . .

In *Hawaii Housing Authority v. Midkiff,* the Court considered a Hawaii statute whereby fee title was taken from lessors and transferred to lessees in order to reduce the concentration of land ownership. We unanimously upheld the statute and rejected the Ninth Circuit's view that it was "a naked attempt on the part of the state of Hawaii to take the property of A and transfer it to B solely for B's private use and benefit." Reaffirming *Berman's* deferential approach to legislative judgments in this field, we concluded that the State's purpose of eliminating the "social and economic evils of a land oligopoly" qualified as a valid public use. . . . "[I]t is only the taking's purpose, and not its mechanics," that matters in determining public use.

. . . For more than a century, our public use jurisprudence has wisely eschewed rigid formulas and intrusive scrutiny in favor of affording legislatures broad latitude in determining what public needs justify the use of the takings power.

Those who govern the City were not confronted with the need to remove blight in the Fort Trumbull area, but their determination that the area was sufficiently distressed to justify a program of economic rejuvenation is entitled to our deference. The City has carefully formulated an economic development plan that it believes will provide appreciable benefits to the community, including—but by no means limited to—new jobs and increased tax revenue. . . . [T]he City is endeavoring to coordinate a variety of commercial, residential, and recreational uses of land, with the hope that they will form a whole greater than the sum of its parts. To effectuate this plan, the City has invoked a state statute that specifically authorizes the use of eminent domain to promote economic development. Given the comprehensive character of the plan, the thorough deliberation that preceded its adoption, and the limited scope of our review, it is appropriate for us, as it was in *Berman,* to resolve the challenges of the individual owners, not on a piecemeal basis, but rather in light of the entire plan. Because that plan unquestionably serves a public purpose, the takings challenged here satisfy the public use requirement of the Fifth Amendment.

To avoid this result, petitioners urge us to adopt a new bright-line rule that economic development does not qualify as a public use. . . . There is . . . no principled way of distinguishing economic development from the other public purposes that we have recognized.

Petitioners contend that using eminent domain for economic development impermissibly blurs the boundary between public and private takings. Again, our cases foreclose this objection. [T]he government's pursuit of a public purpose will often benefit individual private parties. . . . We cannot say that public ownership is the sole method of promoting the public purposes of community redevelopment projects.

It is further argued that without a bright-line rule nothing would stop a city from transferring citizen *A*'s property to citizen *B* for the sole reason that citizen *B* will put the property to a more productive use and thus pay more taxes. Such a one-to-one transfer of property, executed outside the confines of an integrated development plan, is not presented in this case. While such an unusual exercise of government power would certainly raise a suspicion that a private purpose was afoot, the hypothetical cases posited by petitioners can be confronted if and when they arise.

Alternatively, petitioners maintain that for takings of this kind we should require a "reasonable certainty" that the expected public benefits will actually accrue. Such a rule, however, would represent an even greater departure from our precedent. "When the legislature's purpose is legitimate and its means are not irrational, our cases make clear that empirical debates over the wisdom of takings—no less than debates over the wisdom of other kinds of socioeconomic legislation—are not to be carried out in the federal courts.". . . A constitutional rule that required postponement of the judicial approval of every condemnation until the likelihood of success of the plan had been assured would unquestionably impose a significant impediment to the successful consummation of many such plans.

Just as we decline to second-guess the City's considered judgments about the efficacy of its development plan, we also decline to second-guess the City's determinations as to what lands it needs to acquire in order to effectuate the project. . . . Once the question of the public purpose has been decided, the amount and character of land to be taken for the project and the need for a particular tract to complete the integrated plan rests in the discretion of the legislative branch.

. . . [N]othing in our opinion precludes any State from placing further restrictions on its exercise of the takings power. Indeed, many States already impose "public use" requirements that are stricter than the federal baseline. . . . This Court's authority, however, extends only to determining whether the City's proposed condemnations are for a "public use" within the meaning of the Fifth Amendment to the Federal Constitution.

AFFIRMED in favor of respondent City of New London.

JUSTICE O'CONNOR, WITH WHOM THE CHIEF JUSTICE, JUSTICE SCALIA, AND JUSTICE THOMAS JOIN, DISSENTING: Over two centuries ago, just after the Bill of Rights was ratified, Justice Chase wrote: ". . . [A] law that takes property from A. and gives it to B: It is against all reason and justice, for a people to entrust a Legislature with SUCH powers; and, therefore, it cannot be presumed that they have done it." . . .

Today the Court abandons this long-held, basic limitation on government power. Under the banner of economic development, all private property is now vulnerable to being taken and transferred to another private owner, so long as it might be upgraded—*i.e.,* given to an owner who will use it in a way that the legislature deems more beneficial to the public—in the process. To reason, as the Court does, that the incidental public benefits resulting from the subsequent ordinary use of private property render economic development takings "for public use" is to wash out any distinction between private and public use of property—and thereby effectively to delete the words "for public use" from the Takings Clause of the Fifth Amendment. Accordingly I respectfully dissent.

. . . [W]e have read the Fifth Amendment's language to impose two distinct conditions on the exercise of eminent domain: "the taking must be for a 'public use' and 'just compensation' must be paid to the owner." . . . These two limitations serve to protect "the security of Property." . . . Together they ensure stable property ownership by providing safeguards against excessive, unpredictable, or unfair use of the government's eminent domain power—particularly against those owners who, for whatever reasons, may be unable to protect themselves in the political process against the majority's will.

While the Takings Clause presupposes that government can take private property without the owner's consent, the just compensation requirement spreads the cost of condemnations and thus "prevents the public from loading upon one individual more than his just share of the burdens of government." . . . The public use requirement, in turn, imposes a more basic limitation, circumscribing the very scope of the eminent domain power: Government may compel an individual to forfeit her property for the *public's* use, but not for the benefit of another private person. This requirement promotes fairness as well as security. . . .

Where is the line between "public" and "private" property use? We give considerable deference to legislatures' determinations about what governmental activities will advantage the public. But were the political branches the sole arbiters of the public-private distinction, the Public Use Clause would amount to little more than hortatory fluff. An external, judicial check on how the public use requirement is interpreted, however limited, is necessary if this constraint on government power is to retain any meaning. . . . But "public ownership" and "use-by-the-public" are sometimes too constricting and impractical ways to define the scope of the Public Use Clause. Thus, we have allowed that, in certain circumstances and to meet certain exigencies, takings that serve a public purpose also satisfy the Constitution even if the property is destined for subsequent private use. . . .

The Court's holdings in *Berman* and *Midkiff* were true to the principle underlying the Public Use Clause. In both those cases, the extraordinary, precondemnation use of the targeted property inflicted affirmative harm on society—in *Berman* through blight resulting from extreme poverty and in *Midkiff* through oligopoly resulting from extreme wealth. And in both cases, the relevant legislative body had found that eliminating the existing property use was necessary to remedy the harm. Thus, a public purpose was realized when the harmful use was eliminated. Because each taking *directly* achieved a public benefit, it did not matter that the property was turned over to private use. Here, in contrast, New London does not claim that Susette Kelo's and Wilhelmina Dery's well-maintained homes are the source of any social harm. . . .

In moving away from our decisions sanctioning the condemnation of harmful property use, the Court today significantly expands the meaning of public use. It holds that the sovereign may take private property currently put to ordinary private use, and give it over for new, ordinary private use, so long as the new use is predicted to generate some secondary benefit for the public—such as increased tax revenue, more jobs, maybe even aesthetic pleasure. But nearly any lawful use of real private property can be said to generate some incidental benefit to the public. Thus, if predicted (or even guaranteed) positive side-effects are enough to render transfer from one private party to another constitutional, then the words "for public use" do not realistically exclude *any* takings, and thus do not exert any constraint on the eminent domain power.

[continued]

CRITICAL THINKING

When you examine the reasoning in the majority and dissenting opinions, you can see a significant conflict because of the ambiguity of a key term. Identify this term, and explain how its interpretation affects the reasoning. How do you think the courts should define the term?

ETHICAL DECISION MAKING

Who are the primary stakeholders in this case? How are they affected by the ruling? What are the implications of this ruling in terms of the distinction between public and private property? Further, this case highlights an important value conflict. Can you explain how certain values would lead someone to support the majority opinion, whereas different values support the dissenting opinion? How might your values determine how you predict the implications of this ruling?

In *Kelo,* government wanted to take property from individuals to sell to companies, but sometimes the government seeks to take property from one company for use by another. In June 2000, Costco, a large retail chain, wanted to expand its warehouse in Lancaster, California. Afraid of losing the large store, which threatened to move if it could not expand, the city considered using eminent domain to acquire an adjacent 99 Cents Only store so that Costco could obtain the property. Even businesses may be at risk of losing their property to larger, more powerful firms.

State courts had been split fairly evenly over public use, so many people were surprised that the *Kelo* ruling generated a rare congressional outcry. Within a week, some members of Congress were drafting a bill attempting to limit the use of eminent domain for economic development purposes, while others were criticizing the proposed legislation as an unconstitutional attempt to interfere with the Supreme Court's exercise of its proper role.

The response to *Kelo* was dramatic and widespread. President George W. Bush issued an executive order limiting government's taking of private property to "situations in which the taking is for public use, with just compensation, and for the purpose of benefiting the general public, and not merely for the purpose of advancing the economic interest of private parties to be given ownership or use of the property taken." During the year and a half after *Kelo,* 30 state legislatures enacted statutes limiting the use of eminent domain. By some estimates, by 2009, 43 states had enacted new laws or adopted constitutional amendments aimed at preventing Kelo-type takings, typically by restricting the definition of public use to exclude economic development.[3]

Sadly, as of 2010, the land taken in the Kelo case was a vacant field because before the development was begun, Pfizer Corporation, whose research facility was to be the centerpiece of this new development, announced that it was pulling out of New London, so plans for the development were tabled.

To see how the use of eminent domain may distort market forces, please see the **Connecting to the Core** activity on the text website at www.mhhe.com/kubasek3e.

Restrictions on Land Use

LO4

How is the use of property restricted?

No one is allowed to use land in a *completely* unrestricted manner; the doctrine of waste prohibits some uses and abuses of land. Other restrictions also exist, both voluntary and involuntary.

[3] James Ely, "A Report Card on Post-Kelo Eminent Domain Reforms," *OUPblog,* http://blog.oup.com/2009/03/eminent-domain/ (accessed October 10, 2010).

CASE NUGGET

RESTRICTIVE COVENANTS

Country Club Dist. Homes Assn. v.
Country Club Christian Church
Missouri Court of Appeals
118 S.W.3d 185 (Mo. Ct. App. 2003)

All the property in the Hampstead Gardens Subdivision was covered by a restrictive covenant providing that "none of said lots shall be improved, used nor occupied for other than private residence purposes." The Country Club Christian Church owned three lots adjacent to the lot on which its church was located. It decided to turn these lots into parking lots, but the Country Club District Homeowners Association sued to enforce the restrictive covenant and obtain a permanent injunction. The trial court upheld the agreement and granted the injunction. The appellate court affirmed the lower court's ruling, stating that the terms of a restrictive covenant will not be enforced only where a defendant can prove that (1) there has been a radical change in conditions since the covenant was entered into, (2) as a result of the change, enforcement of the restriction will work an undue hardship on the defendant, and (3) continuing enforcement of the restriction provides no substantial benefit to the plaintiff. Given this standard, it is fairly easy to see why most restrictive covenants are upheld.

RESTRICTIVE COVENANTS

Property owners may voluntarily enter into **restrictive covenants,** that is, promises to use or not use their land in particular ways. These covenants, generally included in the deeds, are binding for lawful acts related to the land. A restrictive covenant not to construct only single-story dwelling houses on property is lawful and enforceable, whereas a covenant never to convey property to a woman is unlawful and unenforceable. A restriction that the land never be used for hog farming is related to the land and therefore valid, whereas a restriction that the owner always ride a bicycle to work is not. Finally, successors to the original makers of the covenant must have notice of it.

The most common use of restrictive covenants today is in urban developments sometimes called *planned communities.* Each deed binds the grantee to abide by community rules established by the developer and a homeowners' association. Such restrictions can be substantial, although some owners enjoy the assurance that their property will maintain its value. Courts will generally uphold these restrictive covenants. The Case Nugget above illustrates a typical court's treatment of a restrictive covenant.

Restrictive covenants are sometimes used in conjunction with the sale of a business, and sometimes they contain a provision for their termination. Such a situation appears in Case 49-3.

CASE 49-3 DOUBLE DIAMOND PROPERTIES v. BP PRODUCTS
U.S. COURT OF APPEALS FOR THE FOURTH CIRCUIT
277 FED. APPX. 312 (2008)

Double Diamond Properties purchased real property from BP Products on which to operate a gas station. The purchase agreement contained a restrictive covenant prohibiting Double Diamond from selling gasoline purchased from any source other than BP. When BP assigned to Miller Oil Company its right to supply gasoline, Double Diamond sought a declaratory judgment that the restrictive covenant was no longer enforceable, as well as damages based upon the difference in cost between obtaining BP fuel from the assignee and a cheaper distributor. The defendant received a declaratory judgment that the supplier still benefitted from the covenant despite its assignment, and that the covenant specified that it terminated only if the supplier stopped selling gasoline on a direct or indirect basis, which had not occurred. Double Diamond appealed.

PER CURIUM OPINION: . . . [C]ovenants restricting the free use of land are disfavored and must be strictly construed. . . . [T]he person claiming the benefit of the restrictions must prove that the covenants are applicable to the acts of which he complains. . . .

We will also apply Virginia principles of contract interpretation and "seek to determine the intent of the parties from the language expressed in the contract". . . . Contract terms that are clear and unambiguous will be afforded their plain and ordinary meaning, but extrinsic evidence may be used to interpret vague or ambiguous terms, and substantial doubts or ambiguity about the meaning of a restrictive covenant will be resolved in favor of the unrestricted use of land. . . .

Double Diamond argues that the restrictive covenant has expired according to its terms because BP no longer benefits from the covenant as a direct supplier of fuel to the Haygood station. Double Diamond contends that the language in the covenant concerning direct or indirect supply of fuel relates only to the scope of the restriction, meaning that Double Diamond may comply with the restriction by purchasing BP fuel either directly or indirectly. Double Diamond likewise contends that BP must benefit as a direct supplier of fuel if it does not benefit as an owner or lessee of land or as a fuel retailer, because the language describing the benefit to BP from the restriction does not include the description "indirect supplier."

We find, however, that BP still benefits from the restriction as an indirect supplier of fuel to the Haygood station. Arguably, BP would still benefit as a direct supplier of retail operations even if a particular retail operator chose to obtain its BP fuel indirectly, thereby maintaining the validity of the covenant while still giving meaning to the restriction. However, the restriction could be rendered meaningless under this construction if all retail operators in the area chose to obtain BP fuel indirectly, robbing BP of its status as a direct supplier through no action of its own. We conclude that the term "supplier" in the beneficiary sentence was intended to encompass acting as either an indirect supplier or a direct supplier, because both manners of supplying are contemplated by the description of the restriction. The circumstances surrounding the covenant also indicate that BP was clearly contemplating that it would no longer own land or operate retail facilities in the area, and strongly indicate that BP contemplated phasing out its role as a direct supplier of fuel to retail operations, at the time the covenant was made. Accordingly, because BP clearly benefits from the covenant as an indirect supplier of fuel, the covenant is still enforceable according to its terms.

A restraint on alienation of property is valid if it is reasonable. . . . A court must "consider (1) whether or not the agreement in question is reasonable as between the parties; and (2) if so, whether or not the agreement is injurious to the public interest by reason of its effect upon trade and, therefore, void.". . .

Double Diamond argues that the restrictive covenant is unreasonable because the requirement that only BP fuel be sold at the Haygood station is unreasonable when applied in conjunction with Miller Oil's exclusive right to distribute BP fuel to the Haygood station, because Miller Oil competes in the retail fuel market and because BP earns the same profit on fuel it supplies regardless of whether it uses Miller or another supplier. . . .

If Double Diamond were allowed to comply with the restrictive covenant by purchasing BP fuel for the Haygood station through the supplier of its choice, the burden of the restrictive covenant on the Haygood station and its owner, Double Diamond, would be reduced, because Double Diamond could negotiate a lower price for its fuel supply. The burden is arguably no greater than it would be if BP were the sole direct supplier of its fuel, however, because Double Diamond would have no choice as to the terms of its fuel supply agreement with BP. Although Miller Oil is a potential competitor with Double Diamond in the retail market, there is evidence in the record that Miller Oil does not operate any retail gas stations within two miles of the Haygood station, and is therefore not currently in direct competition. Although this is a close issue, the standard for reasonableness established by Virginia courts does not clearly compel the invalidation of the restrictive covenant as applied to Double Diamond.

(III) Validity of the Restrictive Covenant in Changed Circumstances

A change in circumstances that is "so radical as practically to destroy the essential objects and purposes of the [covenant]" will render a restrictive covenant null and void. . . . In order to determine the extent of the restriction imposed by a covenant, a court should "look to the substance—not the label—of the activity sought to be restricted."

Double Diamond argues that the restrictive covenant has expired due to changed circumstances because BP has radically altered its business practices by discontinuing its operations as a direct supplier of fuel to retail operations, instead supplying fuel for retail operations only indirectly. We hold that the circumstances surrounding the covenant have not changed so radically as to destroy the primary purpose of the covenant for its beneficiary, BP, namely to ensure a continuing retail market for its fuel in the Virginia Beach area. Although BP now benefits from the covenant as an indirect supplier of fuel, rather than a direct supplier, the essential purpose, to ensure an ultimate retail market for BP fuel, is still being met. . . . BP's ultimate purpose in enforcing the covenant is still served.

AFFIRMED in favor of BP Products.

[continued]

CRITICAL THINKING

The facts of a case move it toward the court's conclusion. What facts, had they been true, would have caused this decision to have gone against BP Products?

ETHICAL DECISION MAKING

The court explains that the law frowns on restrictions against the free use of land. Whose interests are being protected by this legal principle?

Legal Principle: **Restrictive covenants are promises to use or not use land in particular ways, and they will be enforced as long as they are reasonable.**

ZONING

Zoning allows for the orderly growth and development of a community and protects the health, safety, and welfare of its citizens. It commonly restricts the type of use to which land may be put, such as residential, commercial, industrial, or agricultural. Zoning laws may also regulate land use on the basis of the intensity (single or multifamily dwellings), size, or placement of buildings.

There is generally a public hearing on proposed changes in zoning ordinances. Often the community allows an exception for a particular property, called a *nonconforming use,* if the zoning changes. An owner who wishes to use land in a manner prohibited by zoning laws may seek permission, called a *variance,* from the zoning board or planning commission. Variances are generally granted to prevent undue hardship.

Zoning is an exercise of police power, the power of the state to regulate to protect the health, safety, and welfare of the public. To be a valid exercise of such power, a zoning ordinance must not be arbitrary or unreasonable. It is unreasonable if (1) it encroaches on the private property rights of landowners without a substantial relationship to a legitimate government purpose such as public health, safety, or welfare or (2) there is no reasonable relationship between the ends to be obtained and the means used to attain them.

Although zoning laws typically restrict how owners of real property may use their property, they can also help protect the rights of landowners. A company, Vineyard Investments, wanted to open a wine and spirits store in Madison, Mississippi. Vineyard was in compliance with all zoning laws, but the City of Madison denied the building permit because the shopping center already had one liquor store and the city thought that having two would not convey the family-friendly atmosphere it wanted. The City of Madison told Vineyard that because it did not yet have a state permit to sell alcohol, the city could not approve the building permit. However, no zoning regulations required that Vineyard have the state permit before receiving the building permit, and Vineyard had a hearing already scheduled with the state board to receive the permit. The court ruled that because Vineyard was compliant with all the zoning regulations, the city must also abide by its zoning regulations and approve the building permit.[4]

Because zoning is intended to regulate property, not take it, it is unreasonable for a zoning ordinance to destroy the economic value of a piece of property. If it does, the zoning is considered a constructive taking of the property, and the owner is entitled to fair compensation. Frequently, but usually unsuccessfully, an owner will challenge zoning regulations on such grounds.

[4] *Vineyard Investments v. City of Madison,* 999 So. 2d 438 (Miss. App. 2009).

Legal Principle: **Zoning restricts the type of use to which land may be put, such as residential, commercial, industrial, or agricultural, or regulates land use on the basis of the intensity, size, or placement of buildings.**

OTHER STATUTORY RESTRICTIONS ON LAND USE

Another government restriction of property is the passing, in some states, of historic preservation statutes: Owners of buildings with historical importance are usually required to keep the building in good repair and obtain prior approval for any alterations to the façade.

As we are becoming more aware of environmental consequences with certain uses of land, governments are increasingly imposing restrictions on use of environmentally sensitive lands. These restrictions are often challenged in court as violating the private property owner's rights.

CASE OPENER WRAP-UP

Groundwater and Property Rights

You may have actually heard about this case because after it began, the company changed its name to Nestle Waters. In its ruling, the trial court stated, as a matter of law, that the stream connected to the groundwater at issue was not navigable and, therefore, the public trust doctrine did not apply to it. The court also determined that the plaintiffs' common law claims were governed not by riparian law but by the law applicable to groundwater withdrawals. However, the trial court ruled that diminishment of riparian flow could constitute an actionable injury under groundwater law. The plaintiffs did not appeal the summary dismissal of those two claims.

The trial court found that the defendant's pumping had harmed and would continue to harm the plaintiffs' riparian interests. The trial court concluded that these violations warranted a full injunction and ordered the defendant to terminate all water withdrawals from Sanctuary Springs within 21 days of the date of the filing of its opinion and order.

On appeal, the appellate court found that the trial court improperly applied the wrong law to the plaintiffs' groundwater claim but correctly determined that the defendant's water withdrawals from Sanctuary Springs violated the plaintiffs' riparian rights. However, the correct remedy to the violation was not a blanket injunction prohibiting all withdrawals. The case was remanded to the trial court to determine what level of water extraction from Sanctuary Springs would provide the defendant with fair participation in the common water supply while maintaining an adequate supply for the plaintiffs' water uses. Before the trial court made this ruling, the parties agreed on a pumping limit of 218 gallons per minute.

KEY TERMS

adverse possession 1095
closing 1095
condemnation 1095
conditional estate 1086
co-ownership 1090
easement 1088
easement by prescription 1090
fee simple absolute 1086
fixture 1084
future interest 1088
general warranty deed 1093
joint tenants 1091
leasehold 1088
license 1090
life estate 1087
marketable title 1094
profit 1088
quitclaim deed 1093
real property 1084
recording 1093
restrictive covenants 1100
special warranty deed 1093
tenancy by the entirety 1091
tenancy in common 1090
zoning 1102

SUMMARY OF KEY TOPICS

The Nature of Real Property

Property is land and anything permanently affixed to the land.

Interests in Real Property

A *fee simple absolute* is the right to possess property for life and devise it to heirs on death; it is the most all-encompassing interest.

A *conditional estate* is an interest comparable to a fee simple absolute, except that the interest will terminate on the happening or nonhappening of a specified condition.

A *leasehold estate* is the right to possess property for an agreed-on period of time.

An *easement* is an irrevocable right to use a portion of someone else's land for a specified purpose.

A *license* is a right to temporarily use another's property.

Co-ownership

The traditional forms of co-ownership are:

Tenancy in common: Owners hold equal or unequal shares that can be attached by creditors and that pass on to heirs at death.
Joint tenancy: Equal shares are held by all owners, and on death the shares are divided among other owners.
Tenancy by the entirety: This form is available to married couples only, with equal shares that pass to the spouse on death.

Two newer forms of co-ownership are:

Condominium ownership: The owner acquires title to a "unit" within a condominium, along with an undivided interest in the land, buildings, and improvements of the common areas of the development.
Cooperative ownership: An investor resident acquires stock in the corporation owning the facility and receives a permanent lease on one unit of the facility.

Voluntary Transfer of Real Property

For a transfer to be legal, the transferor must follow the steps of *execution, delivery, acceptance,* and, to protect the recipient of the property, *recording.*

Involuntary Transfer of Real Property

There are two forms of involuntary transfers:

Adverse possession: When a person openly treats realty as his or her own, without protest or permission from the real owner, for a statutorily established period of time, ownership is automatically vested in that person.

Condemnation: The government acquires the ownership of private property for a public use for just compensation over the protest of the owner of the property.

Restrictions on Land Use

Restrictive covenants are agreements to use or not to use land in particular ways.

Zoning is the restriction of the use of property to allow for the orderly growth and development of a community and to protect the health, safety, and welfare of its citizens.

POINT / COUNTERPOINT

Should Legislatures Be Able to Use Eminent Domain to Give Private Property to Another Private Entity in the Name of "Public Use"?

NO

The Fifth Amendment reads: "nor shall private property be taken for public use, without just compensation." This text suggests that government cannot use eminent domain unless the condemned property is available for use by the public. If the condemned property is transferred to a private corporation, the public cannot use it. Hence, this use of eminent domain does not comport with the plain meaning of the constitutional text.

Even if the constitutional text allows this use of eminent domain, the Constitution does not hold corporations accountable for their promises to create jobs and generate tax revenues. If a corporation promises 6,500 jobs and $10 million in tax revenue to a local municipality in exchange for an advantageous piece of property, and only 3,000 jobs and $800,000 in tax revenue materialize, the corporation suffers no consequences. Thus, corporations have a perverse incentive to overstate the number of jobs and amount of tax revenue they are likely to create, and legislatures might use eminent domain when, had they known the actual state of affairs, they would not.

A third strong argument against this use of eminent domain focuses on the alternative. If the private property in question is so desirable, the corporation can purchase it directly from the private owner. If the private owner is unwilling to give up her property for the price offered, the outcome is not necessarily bad. Indeed, economists would say the result is efficient because the property ends up where it is most highly valued: in the private owner's hands.

YES

Arguments emanating from constitutional text do not clearly support the position that eminent domain must yield property for use by the public. The text prohibits taking of private property for public use "without just compensation," but it says nothing about the taking of private property for *private* use. Thus, a literal reading of the constitutional text does not prohibit the use of eminent domain in question.

Moreover, even if the use of eminent domain creates perverse incentives for corporations to make unrealistic promises, the best solution is not a blanket ban on the practice. Rather, citizens can oppose the use of eminent domain at the ballot box: They can vote for local candidates who share their views. Many economic policies are unwise but not unconstitutional. As Justice Oliver Wendell Holmes wrote, the Constitution "does not enact Mr. Herbert Spencer's Social Statics." (Spencer's Social Statics was a popular economic theory during Holmes's time.) Justice Antonin Scalia once remarked that "[a] law can be both economic folly and constitutional."

Finally, the argument that society ought to use markets instead of eminent domain ignores the possibility of *positive externalities*—benefits that accrue to third parties when two individuals engage in a market transaction. If the sale of private property to corporations is likely to produce positive externalities in the form of additional jobs and increased tax revenue, legislatures may want to compel more of these sales through the use of eminent domain.

QUESTIONS & PROBLEMS

1. Explain what a fixture is and when it is not treated as a part of the real property to which it is attached.
2. Explain the five possessory interests in land.
3. List the primary characteristics of three forms of joint ownership.
4. List the steps of the voluntary transfer of ownership of real property.
5. Explain how a piece of property could be involuntarily transferred.
6. Travis Scheible was riding his bicycle and started to cross the street from behind a mature tree that overhung the sidewalk and obscured his view of oncoming traffic. As he rode into the street, Travis was struck by an oncoming car and was killed. The tree was located on residential property that Jackson had sold to Smith about six months before the accident under a contract to be paid over the course of two years. Smith began residing on the property. Travis's mother, Christine Scheible, brought a wrongful-death action against Jackson and Smith. Jackson moved for summary judgment, arguing that he had no duty to Travis because he did not own, possess, or control the property at the time of the accident. Scheible argues that Jackson controlled the property, as proved by the facts that (1) Smith needed Jackson's permission before changing the property; (2) Smith paid Jackson to continue the liability coverage for the property in Jackson's name (Smith's name was never added to the policy); and (3) Smith eventually renounced his rights and returned the property to Jackson. What type of estate did Smith have when he purchased the property from Jackson, and how does this affect who is liable for the tree on the property and thus liable for Travis's death? What evidence leads to your conclusion? [*Jackson v. Scheible,* 902 N.E.2d 807 (Ind. 2009).]
7. In Mississippi, there is a gravel road that runs between an apartment complex and private property. The 12-foot-wide road has been at the center of a five-year property dispute between Dr. Charles Scarborough and apartment complex owner Mildred Rollins. Rollins had culverts installed along the road, but Scarborough said the road was his property and removed all the culverts without returning them to Rollins. Apparently the properties were surveyed numerous times, but the results always yielded different property lines. Scarborough had originally told Rollins she had to pay him $200 a year to use the road or he would tear up the culverts, which he later ended up doing. Scarborough was arrested, and later a court stipulated that Scarborough must pay $7,500 in punitive damages, $2,150 for the culverts, and attorney fees. However, Scarborough appealed. How do you think the court of appeals decided? [*Scarborough v. Rollins,* 44 So. 3d 381 (2010).]
8. Carol Matoush owns property that grants her an easement dating back to 1901. The easement at issue here creates a right-of-way across David and Debra Lovingood's property for access between Matoush's property and an alley adjacent to the Lovingoods' property. The easement has not been used as a surface right-of-way across the Lovingoods' property since at least 1969. At some point before 1969, fences were built to enclose most of the easement area within the Lovingoods' backyard. Matoush attempted to sell her property to a buyer who inquired about using the easement as a driveway for vehicle access between Matoush's property and the alley. There is a driveway on Matoush's property that provides vehicle access to a garage located on Matoush's property. The buyer has proposed removing the driveway, relocating the garage, paving the easement area, and using the easement as a driveway for vehicle access between the alley and the new garage. Matoush brought an action against the Lovingoods to enforce her right to use the easement as a right-of-way for vehicle access between her property and the alley. The Lovingoods counterclaimed that use of the easement as a right-of-way was terminated by either abandonment, due to the lack of use, or adverse possession, due to the construction of fences obstructing the easement in 1969. Does Matoush still possess the easement across the Lovingoods' land? Why? [*Matoush v. Lovingood,* 177 P.3d 1262 (Colo. 2008).]
9. In 2004, two property owners got into an argument about the division of their property. One neighbor, Proctor, decided to hire a surveyor to establish

the true property lines. It turned out that the other neighbors, the Huntingtons, had their house and their garage on Proctor's property. The two neighbors had about 30 acres each that bordered each other. Back in 1996, the Huntingtons' surveyor marked their property line 400 feet farther west than their actual property. After receiving this information, the Huntingtons built their house. Before building the house, the Huntingtons even checked with Proctor, who verified the location. After they had been in the house for eight years, Proctor filed suit to make the Huntingtons leave his property. The family counterclaimed, arguing that they had adverse possession of the parcel of land. [*Proctor v. Huntington,* No. 82326-0 (Wash. S. Ct. 2010).]

10. Denese Welch purchased property in 1980. The adjacent property was vacant. In 1985, Welch planted a tree on what she thought was her property. As it turned out, she planted the tree across the property line, on the vacant lot. Around 1994, Welch built a woodshed behind the tree she had planted in 1985. Welch also landscaped around the shed. Before installing these improvements in 1994, Welch made some effort to locate the boundary between her lot and the vacant lot but failed to ascertain the true boundary. As a result, unbeknownst to Welch, the woodshed and the landscaping partially encroached on the vacant lot. The Harrisons purchased the vacant lot in March 2001. In June 2001, the Harrisons had the property surveyed. The survey revealed that the woodshed encroached up to 7.25 feet onto their lot and the landscaping encroached up to 9.8 feet. The total area of the encroachment amounted to 8 percent of the lot. The Harrisons sued Welch to remove the encroachment. Welch argued that she had right to the encroached land through, among other things, adverse possession. What does Welch need to prove to establish ownership through adverse possession? Was she successful? Why? [*Harrison v. Welch,* 11 Cal. Rptr. 3d 92 (Cal. Ct. App. 3d 2004).]

Looking for more review materials?

The Online Learning Center at **www.mhhe.com/kubasek3e** contains this chapter's "Assignment on the Internet" and also a list of URLs for more information, entitled "On the Internet." Find both of them in the Student Center portion of the OLC, along with quizzes and other helpful materials.

CHAPTER

50 Landlord-Tenant Law

LEARNING OBJECTIVES

After reading this chapter, you will be able to answer the following questions:

1. How is the landlord-tenant relationship created?
2. What are the rights and duties of the landlord and tenant?
3. What are landlords' liabilities for injuries on the premises?
4. How are interests in leased property transferred?
5. How are leases terminated?

CASE OPENER

Free to Choose?

Roommates.com operates a website that helps individuals find roommates. Individuals searching for roommates create profiles using questionnaires provided by the website. The questionnaires ask for information about age, sex, and sexual orientation, as well as whether the person lives with children. Roommates.com encourages users to supply additional information via profiles. Roommates.com then distributes e-mails to users after matching members on the basis of preferences. For example, if a person does not want to live with children, Roommates.com does not send that person information from potential roommates who live with children. The Fair Housing Councils of San Fernando Valley and San Diego have sued Roommates.com, alleging its business practices violate the federal Fair Housing Act and some California statutes. Roommates.com believes it enjoys immunity under the Communications Decency Act (CDA), which provides immunity from liability for providers of interactive computer services that publish information provided by others.

1. In this chapter, you will learn how the landlord-tenant relationship is created. What is "fair housing," and how does the concept of fair housing affect landlord-tenant relationships?
2. Are tenants allowed to discriminate against potential roommates?

The Wrap-Up at the end of the chapter will answer these questions.

Suppose you are a manager for a new business. One of your responsibilities is to secure office space for the business. You meet with the business owner to talk about whether you should rent or purchase the office space. If you rent the office space, you will enter into a contractual agreement with the owner such that you will be responsible for paying a specific amount of money for a specific period of time to have temporary possession of a certain space. While this agreement will name a specific piece of property (i.e., provide the street address of the property), the lease is typically an agreement for use of some structure on the property. If you will potentially be renting housing or office space for your business, you should be aware of the laws that govern the landlord-tenant relationship.

A clear understanding of the language used in the landlord-tenant relationship is essential. The owner of the property is called the **landlord** or the **lessor.** In contrast, the **lessee,** or the **tenant,** is the party who assumes temporary ownership of the property. The property in question is called the **leasehold estate.** The actual agreement between the landlord and the tenant is called the **lease.**

In the landlord-tenant relationship, the landlord grants the tenant the temporary, exclusive right to occupy and use a specific space for a specific amount of time. In turn, the tenant is obligated to pay rent to the landlord, who retains the title to the land. This entire relationship is usually established in a contractual agreement. Usually, we think of landlord-tenant relationships as private. However, sometimes landlord-tenant relationships are public-private relationships. For example, the City of Orlando is in a relationship with RP Realty Partners, a landlord to tenant Orlando Movie Co., which operates Plaza Cinema Café. The development project is a public-private one, created when the city wanted a downtown movie theater to bring people into the city.

The first part of this chapter explains how the landlord-tenant relationship is created. The next section explains the rights and responsibilities associated with the landlord-tenant relationship. The third section focuses on liability associated with injuries that occur on rental premises. The fourth section considers how landlords and tenants can transfer their interests in the rental property. The final section explains the ways a lease can be terminated.

Creation of the Landlord-Tenant Relationship

L01

How is the landlord-tenant relationship created?

How is the landlord-tenant relationship established? It is usually established by an oral or written contract. Generally, if the lease exceeds one year, it must be in writing. A landlord-tenant relationship requires the following elements: (1) the names of the tenant(s) and landlord, (2) an express or implied intent to create a landlord-tenant relationship, (3) a description of the property, (4) the specific length of the lease, and (5) the amount of rent to be paid to the landlord.

The most distinguishing factor of the landlord-tenant relationship is the tenant's right to exclusive possession of the property named in the lease. If the landlord retains control of and access to the property, the relationship is likely not a landlord-tenant relationship because the tenant does not have an exclusive right to possession of the property.

Legal Principle: Exclusive right to possession of the property is a key characteristic of the landlord-tenant relationship.

COMPARING THE LAW OF OTHER COUNTRIES

LEASES IN FRENCH LAW

Leases in France are governed by the Civil Code. Leases are under the code's jurisdiction because they engender personal contractual rights rather than property rights. The Civil Code places the rights of the tenant above the rights of the renter. Tenants are also given considerable freedom to engage in various agreements without the landlord's involvement or consent. If the lease is not renewed, the tenant has the right to collect compensation. The tenants' sovereignty, however, is a personal right. The landlord still maintains the property rights. The tenant is merely acting as his or her agent.

There are two special leases that transfer property rights to the tenant. The first is an *emphyteusis,* in which the tenant is going to be involved in extensive work on the property for anywhere between 18 and 99 years. During this period, the property rights of the land are given to the tenant, who pays a small rent fee in return. The second type of lease is a *construction lease.* It is similar to an *emphyteusis* in the sense that the tenant receives property rights for working on the land. Specifically, the tenant in a construction lease will be building and maintaining structures. If either of these leases is entered into, the property rights are ceded to the tenant for the period specified in the agreement.

BUT WHAT IF . . .

WHAT IF THE FACTS OF THE CASE OPENER WERE DIFFERENT?

Let's say, in the Case Opener, that a landlord was looking for a tenant through the Roommates.com website. The landlord found a potential tenant and e-mailed the tenant a lease to sign. The lease included the amount of rent due to the landlord, the renting duration of two years, and a description of the property. The landlord told the tenant to sign the lease and e-mail it back. Is this lease sufficient to create a landlord-tenant relationship?

TYPES OF LEASES

There are four categories of leases that can be created: definite term, period tenancy, tenancy at will, and tenancy at sufferance. Why should you understand the differences between these categories of leases? These categories are distinguishable by the duration of the agreement specified or unspecified in the lease. Some of these categories allow the landlord or tenant to terminate a lease at specific times, while other categories consider termination before the end of the term as a breach. As a future business manager, you need to be aware of the distinctions in the types of leases so that you know what kind of lease will and will not permit you to terminate the agreement.

First, a **definite-term lease,** also known as a *term for years,* automatically expires at the end of the specified term. The landlord is not required to give any notification of termination. Thus, a lease that states that the tenant has temporary possession of the property from August 1, 2015, to July 31, 2016, is an example of a definite-term lease. Second, a **periodic-tenancy lease** is created for a recurring term, such as month to month. The periodic-tenancy lease is distinct from the definite-term lease because the periodic-tenancy lease is for an indefinite time period. While either the landlord or the tenant can terminate during the recurring period, each party is required to give the other party sufficient notice. Third, parties to a **tenancy-at-will lease** may terminate the lease at any time. Fourth, if a tenant fails to leave the property after the termination of the lease, a **tenancy-at-sufferance lease** is created. The landlord may choose either to permit the tenant to remain on the property or to demand repossession of the property.

FAIR HOUSING ACT

When deciding to create a landlord-tenant relationship, the landlord has much freedom in deciding whether to accept someone as a tenant. If the individual has a history of not paying rent or severely damaging premises, the landlord does not have to enter into an agreement with this person. However, under the Fair Housing Act, the landlord may not discriminate against a prospective tenant with regard to race, color, sex, religion, national origin, familial status, or disability. Thus, if a landlord denies a rental application because of the tenant's religion (or another protected class), the prospective tenant can bring a suit against the landlord. In Case 50-1, the court considers whether the Fair Housing Act was violated.

CASE 50-1 CHOICES IN CMTY. LIVING, INC. v. PETKUS
U.S. COURT OF APPEALS FOR THE SIXTH CIRCUIT
2013 U.S. APP. LEXIS 5807 (2013)

In 2009, Celeste Boehm, an employee of Choices in Community Living (CICL), called a real estate company by the name of Real Living about finding a home for "four gentlemen who have disabilities." Real Living was owned by Michael Petkus and had several employees, including one employee by the name of Kathryn Storey. Boehm spoke directly with Storey, an employee of the real estate company, who informed Boehm that the properties were "not set up for disabilities." Boehm then clarified with Storey that the potential tenants did not have any physical disabilities that would require a special setup within the rental property, but instead, the four gentlemen had cognitive disabilities.

Storey told Boehm that she could not show the home because she was leaving for vacation, and when Boehm asked if someone else could show her the home, Storey said no because she had to research the bylaws of the real estate company in regard to tenants with disabilities.

Boehm believed that her disabled clients were being discriminated against and immediately contacted the Miami Valley Fair Housing Center (MVFHC). MVFHC informed Boehm that the bylaws of the real estate company did not prohibit the disabled clients from living at the property.

Boehm called Storey once more for a showing, and the employee again said that she still had to research the bylaws of the company. The next day, Storey received a phone call from two other prospective tenants for the property that Boehm was interested in. The callers indicated that they were looking for properties for their non-disabled, single-family households. Storey showed the home to these two callers, not knowing that they were "test renters" hired by MVFHC to investigate whether the employee was discriminating against Boehm's disabled clients.

On December 22, Storey received a letter from MVFHC implying that she had engaged in disability discrimination, threatening suit for noncompliance, and requesting a written response if her view of the facts differed from MVFHC's. One day later, Storey received a letter from the Dayton zoning office letting the employee know that three or more unrelated people living in the property, such as the circumstance of Boehm's clients, would be unlawful. The employee relayed this information to MVFHC, and advised that she would be showing the property to other potential tenants. The employee eventually leased the home to someone else on January 11, 2010.

After obtaining a ruling from the City of Dayton Human Relations Council that there was probable cause to believe that the employee of the real estate company, and the company's owner, Petkus, had engaged in discriminatory housing practices, CICL and MVFHS filed an instant suit alleging violations of the Fair Housing Act. The district court granted summary judgment to the employee and owner of the defendant real estate company. The plaintiffs appealed.

JUDGE GRIFFIN: The FHA makes it illegal to discriminate in the rental of a dwelling because of a renter's disability. It is also illegal to discriminate against anyone in the terms and conditions of a rental because of a renter's disability. Discrimination includes, inter alia, "a refusal to make reasonable accommodations in rules, policies, practices, or services, when such accommodations may be necessary to afford such person equal opportunity to use and enjoy a dwelling." The statute further prohibits a person from making a statement with respect to the rental of a dwelling "that indicates any preference, limitation, or discrimination based on [a disability] or an intention to make any such preference, limitation, or discrimination."

We analyze FHA discrimination claims using the *McDonnell Douglas* burden-shifting paradigm. The plaintiffs must first "present evidence from which a reasonable jury could conclude that there exists a prima facie case of housing discrimination." If they make this showing, the burden shifts to the defendants to proffer evidence of a legitimate, nondiscriminatory reason for the action taken. If the defendants meet their burden, plaintiffs must then present sufficient evidence from which a reasonable jury could find that the proffered reason is pretextual. "Employment discrimination case law interpreting the parties' respective burdens under *McDonnell Douglas* is fully applicable" in FHA discrimination cases.

[continued]

Courts have recognized three distinct types of FHA discrimination claims: (1) disparate treatment; (2) disparate impact; and (3) failure to make reasonable accommodations. In cases where the plaintiffs' discrimination theory does not neatly fall into one of these three categories, we find a prima facie case if "the plaintiffs have presented sufficient evidence to permit a reasonable jury to conclude [they] suffered an adverse housing action under circumstances giving rise to an inference of unlawful discrimination. . . ."

At the first step of the *McDonnell Douglas* analysis, we find that CICL and MVFHC have successfully presented a prima facie case of housing discrimination under the "catch-all" category described in Lindsay. Storey immediately expressed concern to Boehm about disabled renters. Real Living avoided showing the property to Boehm while Storey was on vacation, and Storey delayed responding to Boehm. Further, Storey treated Boehm differently compared to the test renters, determined that the zoning code "rules out" Boehm's proposed tenancy, and articulated several reasons why Boehm never saw the subject property, only one of which is relied on in this appeal. Viewing this evidence in a light most favorable to plaintiffs and considering the low threshold required to establish a prima facie case, the record justifiably permits an inference of unlawful discrimination.

However, defendants rebut this inference by offering a legitimate, nondiscriminatory reason for not showing the house to Boehm and her clients: the proposed tenancy was unlawful under the zoning code. They acknowledge this is the sole justification for not showing the property. Because Petkus and Storey have carried their burden of establishing a nondiscriminatory reason for their actions, "the mandatory presumption of discrimination created by the prima facie test drops from the case." The burden of production now returns to plaintiffs to identify the evidence in the record from which a reasonable jury could conclude that the proffered justification was a pretext for intentional disability discrimination. Plaintiffs fail to sustain that burden.

CICL and MVFHC offer three reasons why the zoning justification is pretextual, none of which warrant reversal. First, they argue that because Storey did not contemporaneously communicate the zoning justification directly to Boehm during their three phone calls, a jury could find pretext. While the lack of contemporaneous statements to support a defendant's rationale can show pretext, plaintiffs propose a definition of "contemporaneous" that is too narrow.

Next, CICL and MVFHC argue that since Storey has abandoned three justifications for not showing the house, that casts doubt on whether zoning concerns actually motivated Storey. Before plaintiffs filed suit, Storey offered four reasons why she did not show the subject property to Boehm: (1) by-laws issues; (2) lack of income; (3) lack of tenant identification; and (4) zoning problems. Storey communicated these concerns to CICL and MVFHC during her phone calls with Boehm and in her letter to MVFHC. Storey relies only on the zoning rationale in this litigation and has admitted that the other rationales became non-issues after research.

That Storey no longer relies on three of the four original justifications is not grounds for reversal because plaintiffs have failed to genuinely dispute the factual basis of the zoning justification. Storey researched zoning ordinances for five hours, contacted the Dayton zoning office about her concerns on two separate occasions, and received notice that the proposed tenancy was unlawful. CICL and MVFHC simply cannot show that the zoning justification had no basis in fact—the Dayton zoning office advised the proposed tenancy was unlawful and they admit that Storey could rely on that assessment. Moreover, it is undisputed that Storey's duty to her clients included assessment of zoning requirements.

Finally, CICL and MVFHC argue that since Storey originally had four reasons to deny the showing, and now relies only on one, her reasons are "shifting" and "inconsistent," and that shows pretext. This argument is easily rejected; Storey's zoning justification is the exact same now as it was in December 2009. "Shifting" and "inconsistent" reasons for an adverse action may create an inference of pretext when those reasons change throughout the suit. That is simply not the case here. For these reasons, we affirm the judgment of the district court.

AFFIRMED.

CRITICAL THINKING

What are the primary facts of this case? Is there any missing information you would call for to better enable you to evaluate the court's reasoning? What evidence does the court use to support its decision? Are you persuaded by this evidence?

ETHICAL DECISION MAKING

What is the purpose of upholding the Fair Housing Act in the business community? Who are the stakeholders that are affected by any adherence or lack of adherence to this act?

CASE NUGGET

WHAT TEST APPLIES UNDER THE FAIR HOUSING ACT WHEN A MENTALLY IMPAIRED TENANT SEEKS A REASONABLE ACCOMMODATION?

Douglas v. Kriegsfeld Corporation
884 A.2d 1109 (2005)

In *Douglas v. Kriegsfeld,* a tenant (Douglas) with a mood disorder asked for "reasonable accommodation" under the Fair Housing Act. In particular, she wanted time and assistance in cleaning her apartment before the landlord could succeed in an action for possession. The landlord wanted to consider the impact Douglas's unclean apartment had on other tenants. Although the trial court was willing to consider this factor, the appellate court clarified that the test for establishing a reasonable-accommodation defense focuses on the landlord-tenant relationship, not on the impact one tenant has on other tenants. In particular, the court said:

To establish a reasonable accommodation defense under the Fair Housing Act, the tenant must demonstrate that (1) she suffered from a "handicap" (or "disability"), (2) the landlord knew or should have known of the disability, (3) an accommodation of the disability may be necessary to afford the tenant an equal opportunity to use and enjoy her apartment, (4) the tenant has requested a reasonable accommodation, and (5) the landlord refused to grant a reasonable accommodation.

The court emphasized that each case should be judged on its unique facts, and it remanded the case to the lower court for consideration according to the test it had outlined.

BUT WHAT IF . . .

WHAT IF THE FACTS OF THE CASE OPENER WERE DIFFERENT?

Let's say, in the Case Opener, that a landlord was using the Roommates.com site to find a tenant, instead of roommates looking for each other. The roommates were able to select or reject potential roommates according to gender, sexual preference, disabilities, and so on. If the landlord was selecting tenants on the basis of such details, would this be illegal, or is this the right of the landlord?

RIGHTS AND DUTIES OF THE LANDLORD AND THE TENANT

LO2 What are the rights and duties of the landlord and tenant?

Both the landlord and the tenant gain certain rights and responsibilities when creating a lease. Each duty corresponds with a right: If the landlord has a duty to perform *X,* the tenant has the right to *X.* (See the examples in Exhibit 50-1.) As a future business manager, you could be either a landlord or a tenant; thus, it is important to understand what your responsibilities and rights would be as each party to the lease. These duties and rights can be classified under four main areas: possession, use, maintenance, and rent.

POSSESSION OF THE PREMISES

One of the few obligations that the landlord has to the tenant is to give the tenant possession of the premises. What exactly does *possession* mean? In the majority of states, the landlord is required to give the tenant physical possession of the premises. Suppose that you are supposed to move into your new office space tomorrow. Unfortunately, the previous tenant has refused to leave the premises. In the majority of states, the landlord is required to remove the previous tenant or break the agreement with the new tenant.

In contrast, in a minority of states, the landlord is required to simply provide legal possession of the premises. In other words, in the example above, you would be responsible for asserting your legal right to the premises and thus removing the previous tenant.

If, however, the tenant does not receive possession of the premises because of an act of the landlord, the landlord will be held liable. The tenant can bring an action for possession against the landlord.

Exhibit 50-1
Examples of Duties and Corresponding Rights of Landlord and Tenant

Because the landlord has the duty to provide the tenant with possession of the premises, the tenant has the right to possession of the premises according to the terms of the lease. An element of the tenant's right to possess the premises is the right to quietly enjoy the premises. One of the most important promises that a landlord makes in a lease is the **covenant of quiet enjoyment,** a promise that the tenant has the right to quietly enjoy the land. What exactly does this mean? The landlord promises that he or she will not interfere with the tenant's use and enjoyment of the property. If the landlord does interfere, the tenant can sue the landlord for breach of this covenant. In Case 50-2, a New York city court explores the covenant of quiet enjoyment.

CASE 50-2 JANET I. BENITEZ v. SEBASTIANO RESTIFO

CITY COURT OF NEW YORK, YONKERS

167 MISC. 2D 967, 641 N.Y.S.2D 523, 1996 N.Y. MISC. LEXIS 106 (1996)

Janet I. Benitez was a tenant in a basement apartment in New York, and Sebastiano Restifo was her landlord. On August 10, 1995, a large amount of water fell through the ceiling in Benitez's apartment, causing severe damage to much of Benitez's property (e.g., carpet, a bed, clothing, etc.). Benitez replaced the carpet, mattress, bureau, and some clothing. The source of the water was from a third floor apartment rented by Mrs. Alamar, who had previously caused flooding in Benitez's apartment. According to Restifo, Mrs. Alamar was a "problem tenant" who would intentionally fill up her kitchen sink so that the water would overflow onto the kitchen floor and eventually flood Benitez's apartment. Restifo was aware that Alamar was responsible for the floods in Benitez's apartment but did not take steps to have Alamar evicted. Benitez brought suit to recover money based on a breach of covenant of quiet enjoyment.

JUDGE DICKERSON: In this case the plaintiff seeks to recover monies expended in replacing her personal property (carpet, furniture, bedding and clothing), all of which suffered water damage. In this case the water came from a third floor apartment in which a tenant intentionally allowed water to overflow onto her kitchen floor.

[continued]

Based upon a review of the facts the court finds that plaintiff has asserted the following causes of action: (1) breach of the covenant of quiet enjoyment and (2) breach of the warranty of habitability as set forth in Real Property Law §235-b.

Breach of Covenant of Quiet Enjoyment

Implicit in the lease agreement between the landlord and tenant was a covenant of quiet enjoyment which "is an agreement on the part of the landlord that for the period of the term of the lease the tenant shall not be disturbed in his quiet enjoyment of the leased premises" (2 Rasch, New York Landlord and Tenant—Summary Proceedings 27.1 [3d ed]).

The breach of a covenant of quiet enjoyment requires actual or constructive eviction (2 Rasch, *op. cit.*, §28.1, 28.21). Constructive eviction arises when the landlord interferes with the tenant's possession of the premises to such an extent that the tenant is deprived of its beneficial enjoyment.

In this case it was the landlord's inaction and unwillingness to evict the third floor tenant, Mrs. Alamar, which directly led to the most recent flooding of the plaintiff's apartment. By failing to act, the defendant condoned and impliedly authorized Mrs. Alamar to leave the water running in her apartment, causing damage to plaintiff's apartment below (74 NY Jur 2d, Landlord and Tenant, §259-260, 265; *Brauer v Kaufman,* 72 Misc 2d 718, 721 [1972] ["It may well be that if a landlord by deliberate and affirmative action invites, encourages or permits lessees to engage in illegal and immoral conduct on the premises . . . result(s) in an endangerment to the life, health or safety of the other (tenants) . . . It should be on knowledge or upon a reckless disregard of the facts"]).

The defendant breached the covenant of quiet enjoyment in the lease agreement and is liable for all appropriate damages flowing therefrom.

JUDGMENT in favor of plaintiff.

CRITICAL THINKING

What would be the ramifications of not having a covenant of quiet enjoyment?

ETHICAL DECISION MAKING

How could the landlord have used the WPH framework to avoid this lawsuit?

EVICTION

Generally, interference with a tenant's quiet enjoyment of property is usually in the form of an eviction. Suppose you find that your landlord has changed the lock on your apartment and refuses to give you a new key for the apartment. The landlord has evicted you from the premises and has thus interfered with your use and possession of the property. When a landlord physically prevents you from entering the leased premises, this eviction is known as an **actual eviction.**

An actual eviction may be full or partial. If a landlord physically prevents you from entering any part of the premises, it is a **full eviction.** However, if the landlord prevents you from entering a part of the premises, it is a **partial eviction.** For example, if you are renting an office building and the landlord changes the locks on certain offices in the building, you have been partially evicted. In both partial and full evictions, the tenant is released from the obligation to pay rent. Furthermore, the tenant can sue for damages or bring a suit against the landlord for breach of contract.

Although a landlord might not actively prevent a tenant from using and enjoying the property, a landlord might wrongfully perform or fail to perform certain acts that cause a substantial injury to the tenant's use and enjoyment of the property. If, after a tenant notifies the landlord of a problem, the premises become unsuitable for use because of the landlord's wrongful or omitted act, a **constructive eviction** has occurred. For example, suppose your heater in your office space breaks. You notify your landlord, who then refuses to repair your heater. Clearly, in the winter, the premises are unsuitable for use without heat. Consequently, you would be permitted to abandon the premises and terminate the lease. However, you must abandon the premises within a reasonable amount of time. If a constructive eviction occurs, the tenant may bring a suit to recover damages or to attempt to move back onto the property.

E-COMMERCE AND THE LAW

USING THE INTERNET TO LAY THE FOUNDATION FOR GOOD LANDLORD-TENANT RELATIONSHIPS

Smart, tech-savvy landlords and tenants gather as much information as possible before entering into a landlord-tenant relationship. They can use the Internet to gather information. Landlords need to use a rental application to find out as much information as possible regarding the tenant, from phone numbers, to references, to emergency contacts. Landlords and tenants may want to use www.anywho.com to gather information. Landlords and tenants may also want to check out local court websites to see whether either has been sued and, if so, for what. Tenants may want to find out about pending foreclosures on property. Landlords may want to find out whether prospective tenants have ever been sued for failing to pay rent. For an example of a state website to use for this search, see Maryland's, at http://casesearch.courts.state.md.us/inquiry/inquiry-index.jsp.

Legal Principle: **Tenants have a legal expectation of quiet enjoyment of property; that is, the landlord cannot interfere with the tenant's use and enjoyment of the property by refusing to fix a major problem with the property, such as a problem with heat or water.**

USE OF THE PREMISES

Generally, the landlord is not responsible for ensuring that the leased premises are tenantable. Why? Historically, the land was the more important element being leased. Some states have modified this rule to make the landlord more responsible for the dwellings on the property.

This rule has particularly been modified in the creation of residential leases. Most states have imposed an **implied warranty of habitability** of the premises, a requirement that the premises be fit for ordinary residential purposes. These states have recognized that most people currently enter into lease agreements because they are looking for shelter. Consequently, the dwelling, not the land, is the more important element of the lease.

Tenant Use of the Premises. How may the tenant use the premises? A landlord and tenant may make an agreement to limit the uses of the premises. Obviously, if they agree that the premises will be used for certain purposes only, the tenant has a duty to abide by that agreement. If there is no agreement that limits the tenant's use of the property, the tenant may use the premises in any manner as long as the use is legal and does not impose substantial injury to the premises. However, the tenant must not use the premises in a way that creates a nuisance for surrounding tenants.

During the tenant's use of the leased property, the tenant has a duty not to commit waste. Any tenant conduct that causes permanent and substantial injury to the landlord's property is considered **waste.** For example, if a tenant cuts down several trees in the yard of the rental property without the landlord's permission, the tenant has committed waste.

Who is responsible for damages associated with use of the apartment? It depends. The tenant is not responsible for the ordinary wear and tear on the apartment. Thus, if the carpet in the rental unit becomes worn, the tenant is not responsible for replacing the carpet. If the tenant intentionally or negligently damages the apartment, however, the tenant will be responsible for paying for the damage. Consequently, if you have a party in your apartment and the guests spill drinks all over the carpet such that the carpet is permanently stained, you will likely be responsible for replacing the carpet.

COMPARING THE LAW OF OTHER COUNTRIES

EVICTION IN JAPAN

Before the year 2000, evictions were extremely uncommon in Japan because of laws intended to protect tenants. These laws provided automatic renewals of leases for tenants. In 2000, with the passing of the Law on the Promotion of Supply of Good Quality Housing, automatic renewals of lease agreements became less common. However, evictions are still fairly uncommon in Japan given that most homes are still rented using what is called *futsu shakuya keiyaku,* which is a type of lease that does not have a fixed termination date. Because most homes are rented without a fixed termination date, it is less common for landlords in Japan to engage in eviction.

Instead, when there is a conflict between a landlord and tenant in Japan, the landlord is much more likely to pay the tenant an agreed-on amount of money to vacate the property, rather than going through the eviction process, which can be quite time-consuming and expensive.

BUT WHAT IF . . .

WHAT IF THE FACTS OF THE CASE OPENER WERE DIFFERENT?

Let's say that a landlord is looking for a tenant to lease a property for residential purposes. A potential tenant e-mails the landlord, and the two sign a lease for the property to be rented as a residential residence to the tenant. Subsequently, the tenant begins to run a business from the property instead of living there. If the tenant is doing nothing illegal, is the tenant violating the lease with reason to get evicted?

Case 50-3 considers whether tobacco residue left inside an apartment constitutes ordinary wear and tear.

CASE 50-3 NANCY MCCORMICK v. ROBERT MORAN, SMALL CLAIMS #5176

JEFFERSON COUNTY CITY COURT OF WATERTOWN

699 N.Y.S.2D 273 (1999)

Nancy McCormick entered into a written lease with Robert Moran for an apartment for the period 7/13/98 to 7/12/99. McCormick brought suit against Moran to get a refund of McCormick's $375.00 security deposit. Moran responded by arguing that McCormick should pay $455.64 for the costs of the general cleaning of the apartment done after McCormick moved out. McCormick argued that such cleaning was unnecessary because she left the apartment in a better condition than when she moved in on 7/13/98. Moran argues that the extensive cleaning was necessary to remove the smoke residue from McCormick's heavy smoking.

JUDGE HARBERSON: The defendant's request for the cost to clean the floors, walls, windows, woodwork and carpets must be based on a showing such a clean-up was for conditions beyond ordinary "wear and tear" during reasonable use of the premises by the tenant. The landlord has the burden to prove such clean-up was for conditions caused by other than ordinary wear and tear due to reasonable use of the apartment by the tenant or a violation of the lease terms.

The landlord testified that the basic reason such an extensive cleaning was required was due to the excessive smoking by the tenants leaving a smelly residue of tobacco smoke throughout the leasehold on the walls, woodwork, carpets and other surfaces.

The lease provides at B (2) "Tenant shall use reasonable care to keep the premises in such condition as to prevent health and sanitation problems from arising." Paragraph 3 states "the $375.00 security deposit . . . may be used . . . at the time premises vacated by tenant toward reimbursement . . . for charges for cleaning not performed prior to vacating. . . ."

In PBN Associates v. Xerox Corp., the Court acknowledged a cause of action for breaking "provisions" of a lease.

[continued]

In this case the Court finds the plaintiff had agreed to "use reasonable care to keep the premises in such condition as to prevent health . . . problems from arising" (paragraph B [2]). The Court finds that the plaintiff's conduct of excessive smoking while in the house caused the tobacco smoke residue to collect on various surfaces of the house creating an offensive odor and a potential health risk that may arise to others who may use the premises.

There is no question that the dangers of such a situation to health due to particulate matter on surfaces left by smoke from tobacco has been recognized by the State. . . . The expression of the State's concern in this area of public health is found in Public Health Law section 1399-P(2) which allows hotel or motel operators "to implement a smoking policy for rooms rented to guests" and, if such a policy is adopted "shall post a notice . . . as to the availability . . . of rooms in which no smoking is allowed." Section 1399-q(1) provides that Article 13-E does not apply, however, "to private residences."

The Court finds that while Article 13-E does not apply to private residences, the landlord could have specifically prohibited smoking in the leased premises as part of the lease contract for the obvious health reasons outlined above. Notwithstanding the failure to specifically prohibit tobacco smoking by the plaintiff in the lease, this omission did not relieve the tenant from the obligation assumed under the lease to use reasonable care to keep the premises in such a condition as "to prevent health . . . problems from arising" (para. B[2]). The Court finds that the tenant failed to use such "reasonable care" while smoking tobacco to prevent such indoor air pollution from tobacco smoke to occur in violation of this lease term and must reimburse the plaintiff for the cost to remedy the problems since the tenant failed to do so before leaving.

The defendant is awarded as provided at paragraph 3 of the lease "reimbursement for the charges for cleaning not performed prior to vacating" the house in the amount of $455.64 to remove the tobacco smoke residue on the various surfaces of the house.

In addition the Court finds that ordinary wear and tear should not leave a leasehold in a condition that violates the warranty of habitability. When the use of tobacco by a tenant causes such a pervasive coating of tobacco smoke residue on a leasehold's surfaces, this condition results in more than ordinary wear and tear to the premises because the residue must be removed to make the rooms habitable for the protection of the health of the next tenants—a condition which if it were not corrected would be "detrimental to their life, health or safety" possibly subjecting the landlord to a violation of the warranty of habitability under Section 235-b of the Real Property Law.

The plaintiff's petition for refund of the security deposit is denied because the defendant's counterclaim damages exceed the amount remaining. The defendant is awarded $455.64 for the cost to clean the house of tobacco smoke residue. The plaintiff is entitled to an off-set for the $375.00 security deposit.

JUDGMENT in favor of defendant.

CRITICAL THINKING

There are several ambiguous phrases in this case, including "reasonable care," "health and sanitation problems," and "ordinary wear and tear." What do you think the implied definitions of these phrases are, given the context that the court uses them in? Would you define these phrases differently? How would various definitions change the validity of the court's conclusion? No evidence was provided that previous tenants of the residence did not contribute to the tobacco residue. Could there be rival causes for the presence of the residue? Can you tell from the facts provided?

ETHICAL DECISION MAKING

Suppose McCormick held the ethical theory of consequentialism. Would her decision to smoke in the apartment have been the same? Why or why not?

Suppose that you, as a tenant, want to put wallpaper in three rooms in the office space you are renting. Are you permitted to paint or wallpaper rooms in rental property? Alternatively, perhaps you want to construct a wall to divide one large room into two offices. Is construction of this wall permitted? In most states, tenants cannot make **alterations,** changes that affect the condition of the premises, without the landlord's consent. In a minority of states, tenants can make alterations as long as the alterations are necessary for the use of the property and do not reduce the value of the property.

Perhaps you want to install shelves in the offices in your rental space. Depending on the courts, you may or may not be permitted to remove these shelves later without paying for damages. Once the shelves become attached to the property, they are considered fixtures. In some states, fixtures may not be removed because they are considered the landlord's property.

MAINTENANCE OF THE PREMISES

Landlords must ensure that the premises meet certain safety and health codes. Earlier in the chapter, we discussed the implied warranty of habitability. In most states, if a landlord leases residential property, the landlord is responsible for ensuring that the property is habitable. Part of this responsibility is making certain repairs to the premises. The implied warranty of habitability generally ensures that the landlord is responsible for repairs to major defects in the rental property. For example, if there is a hole in the wall that interferes with the electricity in the rental unit, the landlord would be responsible for repairing the hole.

Moreover, the landlord is generally responsible for ensuring that the premises meet certain statutory requirements. For example, the city ordinances might have specific standards for building structures or wiring and plumbing within the premises. Thus, the landlord would be responsible for making repairs to rental units that do not meet these standards (assuming that tenant damage did not lead to the need for those repairs). For instance, a city health and safety law might require the installation of a fire hose and sprinkler system in all office buildings. The landlord would be required to pay for this change.

If you are the landlord of an office building or apartment complex, you would be responsible for repairs to **common areas,** areas such as yards, lobbies, elevators, stairs, and hallways that are used by all tenants. Thus, if certain steps in a stairway are in need of repair, you are responsible for the repairs.

The responsibility for repairs to a property in a long-term lease is a little more complicated. Suppose that you plan to rent an office space to a tenant for 10 years. Generally, when creating the lease, the parties determine who will be responsible for repairs to the rental unit. Typically, in long-term leases, the tenant is responsible for more of the repairs to the rental property. However, the tenant will usually not be required to pay for major repairs.

Pretend that you are leasing an apartment. What can you do if your landlord fails to maintain the leased property by making certain repairs? If the repairs breach the warranty of habitability or constitute constructive eviction, you have the option of terminating the lease. If you want to retain possession of the apartment, you have several options available.

First, you can withhold a rent payment. This withholding is usually justified by the landlord's breach of the implied warranty of habitability. If the tenant wishes to withhold a rent payment, he or she must usually place a specific amount of the rent due in an escrow account, an account held by an escrow agent such as the court. The funds will remain in this account until the landlord makes the repairs. However, the tenant cannot withhold all the rent; instead, the tenant can withhold only an amount associated with the defect.

Second, you might be able to have the repairs made and deduct the costs of the repairs from the rent due to your landlord. Several states have created repair-and-deduct statutes. However, the repair-and-deduct option may not be the best choice because some statutes restrict the amount of deductible rent. Furthermore, repair-and-deduct options are often restricted to essential services, such as gas, water, and electric services. However, before you attempt to repair and deduct, you must have notified the landlord, who must then refuse to make the repairs.

CASE NUGGET

HOW DOES THE THEORY OF NEGLIGENCE PER SE APPLY TO LANDLORDS?

Gradjelick v. Hance
646 N.W.2d 225 (2002)

Plaintiff Gradjelick was injured during a fire in the dwelling he rented from the Hance family. The fire was caused in part by careless smoking in another apartment, but it was allegedly exacerbated by the landlord's failure to maintain the premises. In particular, the tenant alleged that the landlord had violated several sections of the Uniform Building Code (UBC).

The court articulated the test for how the theory of negligence per se applies to landlords who allegedly violate the UBC. The court said:

[A] landlord is not negligent per se for code violations unless the following four elements are present:

(1) the landlord or owner knew or should have known of the Code violation;

(2) the landlord or owner failed to take reasonable steps to remedy the violation;

(3) the injury suffered was the kind the Code was meant to prevent; and

(4) the violation was the proximate cause of the injury or damage.

BUT WHAT IF . . .

WHAT IF THE FACTS OF THE CASE OPENER WERE DIFFERENT?

Let's say that a potential tenant, Susie, finds a landlord named Rob through a tenant-landlord matching website similar to the website in the Case Opener. Rob e-mails Susie pictures of the property. Susie sees that the front stairs to the house are completely crumbled, but she assumes there are other entrances to the house. Susie signs a lease. However, when Susie arrives at the house, she realizes the front steps are the only entrance. Rob says that because Susie was okay with the house when she viewed the pictures, he doesn't need to fix the stairs. What can Susie legally do in this situation? What repairs are landlords legally responsible to make?

Third, you can sue the landlord for damages. You can attempt to recover damages associated with the landlord's breach of the implied warranty of habitability. When deciding what to do, make sure you do not defame your landlord. Recently, a landlord sued a former tenant after the tenant created a Twitter post accusing Horizon Realty Group of Chicago of responding poorly to a complaint that there was mold in the tenant's apartment. The tweet said, "Who said sleeping in a moldy apartment was bad for you? Horizon Realty thinks it's okay."[1] Horizon sued the tenant, indicating that mold was not found in the tenant's apartment.

RENT

Rent can be defined as the compensation paid to the landlord for the tenant's right to possession and exclusive use of the premises. The tenant has a duty to pay rent to the landlord. Rent can be paid in various forms, such as money or services to the landlord. The lease usually specifies the form of the rent as well as the payment schedule.

How much rent should be paid to the landlord? In some cases, the landlord has much freedom in determining how much rent should be charged. However, in other cases, the government establishes rent ceilings.

When the lease is initially created, the landlord typically asks the tenant to pay a security deposit, usually in the amount of one month's rent. This security deposit ensures that the tenant will fulfill the duties of the lease agreement.

At the expiration of the lease, the landlord is required to return to the tenant the security deposit minus any costs for damages caused by the tenant. If the landlord retains any portion

[1] Lisa Donovan, "Landlord Suing Tenant over Tweet: She Sued Us First," *Chicago Sun-Times,* July 29, 2009.

of the security deposit, the landlord must provide the tenant with a list of the damages. Each state usually determines the amount of time that the landlord has to return the security deposit to the tenant. If the landlord exceeds this deadline, the tenant can recover the deposit, plus attorney fees. Recently, a court ruled that a landlord would have to pay a tenant $7,000 (security deposit plus attorney fees) because the landlord exceeded the deposit return deadline.

If a tenant fails to pay rent when it is due, the landlord may charge a late fee. This fee may not be excessive and must be related to the amount of rent past due. Thus, if you are two days late in paying a rent amount of $550, the landlord could not charge you $550 as a late fee. If the landlord wishes to terminate the lease because of a late payment, the landlord is generally required to give the tenant notice of the termination proceedings.

Once a lease has been signed, the landlord cannot increase the price of the rent unless there is a **rent escalation clause** included in the lease. This clause permits the landlord to increase the rent in association with increases in costs of living, property taxes, or the tenant's commercial business. A rent escalation clause would typically be found in a long-term lease.

Suppose you are a landlord, and you discover that one of your tenants has refused to pay rent. What are your options? First, you may sue the tenant to collect the unpaid rent. Second, depending on what state you live in, you might have the option of a **landlord's lien,** the right to some or all of the tenant's personal property. You would be required to initiate court proceedings so that the sheriff would seize the tenant's property. This property is often considered as security for the unpaid rent.

What can a landlord do if the tenant has vacated the premises and fails to pay rent? The tenant is responsible for paying rent to the landlord until the expiration of the lease. The landlord could choose to simply let the premises stand vacant until the expiration of the lease. Thus, the tenant would be responsible for the entire amount of rent.

Some states are requiring that landlords make a reasonable attempt to lease the property to another party. The tenant is liable for the unpaid rent for the time that it would reasonably take the landlord to find a new tenant. If a reasonable attempt to find a new tenant is made but the attempt is unsuccessful, the tenant remains responsible for the entire amount of the unpaid rent.

BUT WHAT IF . . .

WHAT IF THE FACTS OF THE CASE OPENER WERE DIFFERENT?

In New York, the Harman brothers inherited a townhouse that was already divided into one-bedroom apartments with tenants living in them. The apartments were all big luxury apartments and were all virtually the same. However, some of these apartments were rented to people for $1,000, and others were rented for $2,650. New York State rent laws allow people who have lived in the same building for decades to be subject to tight limits on how much their rent can be increased. Also, such tenants may renew their leases indefinitely. The Harmans tried to file a lawsuit to challenge these laws. What kind of clause would have been helpful to the Harmans if it had been included in the original leases for the apartments?

Liability for Injuries on the Premises

LO3 What are landlords' liabilities for injuries on the premises?

Suppose you own a building and you rent the ground floor of the building to a tenant who uses the space as a restaurant. One night, while you are watching the news, you see a story that a woman was critically injured by a large piece of ice that fell off your building. The woman was leaving the restaurant on the ground floor of your building. Will you be held responsible for the woman's injuries? Will the tenant?

COMPARING THE LAW OF OTHER COUNTRIES

LANDLORD LIABILITY IN ENGLAND

Landlords in England are not significantly restrained by common law in terms of their liability to the tenant at the time of letting. Landlords can be held liable if they violate the lease or if they are responsible for negligence or nuisance. The 1906 case of *Cavalier v. Pope* is the current precedent for the principle that the landlord owes no duty outside the contract with the tenant. For a landlord to be held liable due to negligence, he or she must have created the disputed defect. For instance, if a tenant were to injure himself on a standard feature of the rented property, the landlord could not be found guilty of negligence for letting a dangerous apartment because she did not actually create the disputed defect. The builder created the defect. A landlord may be held liable if he or she lets property without disclosing an obvious nuisance. However, if the court feels that the nuisance was not apparent, the landlord is cleared of liability. Because the statutes favor protection of the landlords, tenants need to be especially wary of any defects or nuisances on the property before signing a lease

These questions are tricky. Liability for injuries generally depends on who is in control of the area in which the injury occurred. The courts use the standard of reasonable care in deciding these cases. The person who is in control of the area must take the same precautions for safety that the reasonable person would take.

LANDLORD'S LIABILITY

When will the landlord be liable for injuries on the premises? Generally, the landlord is responsible for injuries that occur in common areas, such as elevators, hallways, and stairwells. For example, if you are a landlord for an apartment complex and an injury occurs in the elevator, you can be held responsible for the injury. The landlord is expected to inspect and repair the common areas.

Moreover, the landlord can be held responsible for injuries when he or she has a responsibility to make repairs to the premises yet wrongfully or negligently makes those repairs. Generally, the landlord has a certain amount of time to make the repairs. Thus, if a visitor to the restaurant described in the example above was injured by falling plaster from the ceiling and the landlord had assumed the responsibility for repairs to the premises, the landlord could be responsible for the visitor's injuries. However, the landlord's liability depends on the tenant's notification of need for repair.

If an injury occurs on the premises because of a condition that the landlord knew or should have known about, the landlord can be held responsible for the injury. Furthermore, if the landlord is aware of a dangerous condition but does not make the tenant aware of the condition or hides the condition from the tenant, the landlord will be responsible for the injury. Thus, if a landlord is aware that several beams within an office space are in need of repair but does not disclose this information to the tenant when signing the lease, the landlord would likely be liable if the tenant was injured by a falling beam.

If premises are used for commercial purposes, the landlord has a responsibility to ensure that the premises are in reasonably good condition before the tenant takes control of the property. However, the tenant is responsible for maintaining the premises. If injuries occur because the tenant was negligent in keeping the premises in good condition, the landlord will not be held responsible.

Legal Principle: **Tenants can expect landlords to keep common areas safe; if an injury occurs in an elevator, hallway, or stairwell, the landlord is likely to be responsible for the injury.**

TENANT'S LIABILITY

The tenant has a responsibility to keep the premises in which he or she is in control in a reasonably safe condition. For example, the tenant who runs the restaurant would be responsible for the injuries of a customer who slipped and fell on a wet floor inside the restaurant. However, if the customer slipped and fell after entering a room that said "Employees Only," the tenant would not be responsible. The tenant is responsible only for those areas in which the customer is reasonably expected to go.

Transferring Interests of Leased Property

LO4 How are interests in leased property transferred?

Unless transfers are prohibited by the lease agreement, both the landlord and the tenant may transfer their respective interests in the property. Depending on the housing market in a particular time period, landlords and tenants take turns having a superior bargaining position. In 2009, for example, retail landlords were looking for ways to attract and keep tenants.[2] In Colorado Springs, retail landlords have been supporting good tenants. For example, Kratt Commercial Properties believes that it is important to maintain retail centers well, by adding towers to increase visibility of stores such as Panera Bread, painting exteriors and adding façades for stores such as Mattress King, making sure that parking lots are striped, and enhancing landscaping.

LANDLORD TRANSFER OF INTEREST

Because the landlord is the owner of the leasehold estate, he or she can transfer that property. While the landlord can transfer ownership of the property to someone else, the lease is still legally binding. In other words, if you are renting an office space and the landlord sells the title to the leased property, the new owner could not force you to move out of your office space. The new owner becomes your landlord until your lease agreement expires.

Once a landlord provides possession of a property to a tenant, the landlord has the right to receive rent and other benefits for the property. The landlord can transfer this right to receive rent.

TENANT TRANSFER OF INTEREST

A tenant can transfer his or her interest in the leased property in two ways: assignments and subleases. Suppose you decide that you want to rent an office space to open your own business and you sign a lease that will begin next month. Unfortunately, you later discover that you don't have enough money to start your business at this time. You are still a party to the lease agreement, but you now have no use for the office space. However, your friend is interested in renting office space. You could transfer your entire interest in the leased property to your friend. A transfer of a tenant's entire interest in a leased property is an **assignment.**

Usually, a lease requires that the landlord must consent to a tenant's assignment of her interest in the lease. Why would the lease contain such a requirement? The requirement for a landlord's consent to an assignment is protection for the landlord. Perhaps the assignee, the person to whom the lease interests have been transferred, has a history of severely damaging property that he has previously rented. Consequently, if the tenant tries to assign the lease without the landlord's consent, the landlord may terminate the lease agreement. However, if the landlord knowingly accepts rent from the assignee, the landlord essentially waives the consent requirement.

Let's return to the example described above. Suppose that you make an assignment of your interest in the office space to your friend. Your friend acquires all your

[2] Becky Hurly, "Retail Landlords Getting Creative to Help, Keep, Attract Tenants," *Colorado Springs Business Journal,* July 24, 2009.

rights under the lease. However, your friend fails to make the rent payment for the first month. Who can be held liable for that rent? You can be. The assignment requires that your friend pay the rent, but it does not relieve you of your responsibility to pay the rent. You will have to pay the rent, but you have a right to be reimbursed by your friend. Thus, both you and your friend, the assignee, are liable to the landlord for failure to pay rent.

How is a sublease different from an assignment? Suppose that you are currently renting an office space but you decide to take a job that is three states away. Your lease for the office space ends in six months. You can try to find someone to sublease the office space for the six months. A **sublease** is a transfer of less than all the interest in a leased property. In essence, a sublease creates a landlord-tenant relationship between the original tenant and the sublessee. If you decided to sublease the office space to someone (with the consent of the landlord), this person would not have any legal obligations to the landlord. Instead, the legal obligations are to you, the tenant to the lease. Thus, if your sublessee does not pay rent, the landlord can hold you responsible for the rent payment.

Legal Principle: Tenants should sublease with care, as landlords can hold them responsible for rent if the sublessee does not pay.

Termination of the Lease

L05

How are leases terminated?

Generally, at the end of the term of a lease, the lease is terminated. The tenant returns possession of the premises to the landlord unless there is an option for renewal in the lease. The tenant must leave the premises.

Other than expiration of the term of the lease, there are several other ways in which a lease can be terminated. Each is discussed below and summarized in Exhibit 50-2. Remember that in almost all these cases, the termination of the lease agreement relieves the tenant from the obligation of rent.

BREACH OF CONDITION BY LANDLORD

As we discussed earlier, when a landlord interferes with a tenant's use and enjoyment of the property, the landlord has breached the covenant of quiet enjoyment. This interference usually takes place in the form of an eviction. One possible reaction to the eviction is that the tenant can choose to terminate the lease agreement.

FORFEITURE

Similarly, suppose that either the tenant or the landlord fails to perform a condition stated in the lease. That party's breach is referred to as **forfeiture** because the party is forfeiting his or her interest in the premises. For instance, if a tenant fails to pay rent by the date specified in the lease agreement, the tenant could be considered as forfeiting her interest in the property. Because forfeiture is quite severe, the courts generally do not favor upholding forfeiture.

DESTRUCTION OF THE PREMISES

If a fire or some other disaster has destroyed the subject matter of the lease, most states allow termination of the lease. The tenant is released from paying rent. If the landlord had not been able to do something to prevent the disaster, the landlord is generally not expected to restore and repair the premises.

Exhibit 50-2
Termination of a Lease

SURRENDER

Suppose that you get a job offer to manage a business in California. You have to move, but you have one month left on your lease agreement for your apartment in Ohio. You speak with your landlord, who agrees to end the lease agreement early. You are surrendering, or returning, your interest in the premises, and the landlord is agreeing to accept the return of the interest. Thus, **surrender** is a mutual agreement between a landlord and a tenant. The landlord accepts the tenant's offer to surrender the interest in the premises. Generally, a surrender of property must be in writing.

To see a discussion of Financial Accounting Standards Board (FASB) requirements regarding how companies report leases on their balance sheets, please see the **Connecting to the Core activity** on the text website at www.mhhe.com/kubasek3e.

ABANDONMENT

If a tenant moves out of leased premises before the end of the term, has no intent to return, and has defaulted on rent payments, the tenant is essentially making an offer of surrender to the landlord. This tenant behavior is called **abandonment.** If the landlord accepts the property, the tenant is usually relieved of the rent obligation and the lease is terminated.

OPENER WRAP-UP

Free to Choose?

The federal Fair Housing Act prohibits housing discrimination based on race, color, religion, sex, disability, familial status, or national origin. This law applies to landlords and also to tenants looking for roommates. In the Roommates.com case, the U.S. Court of Appeals for the Ninth Circuit ruled that the CDA did not immunize Roommates.com from potential liability for drafting and posting questionnaires that asked questions about sexual orientation of potential roommates, among other characteristics. The court held that Roommates.com was involved in categorizing, channeling, and limiting distribution of user profiles. Its involvement with the profiles made it ineligible for immunity under the CDA. The CDA protects websites that allow content created by third parties. Roommates.com was actually a content provider, creating content by creating and distributing questionnaires. The organization was enabling discrimination. How is Roommates.com different from Craigslist, Inc.? How can Roommates.com change its business practices so that it enjoys immunity under the CDA?

KEY TERMS

abandonment 1125
actual eviction 1115
alterations 1118
assignment 1123
common areas 1119
constructive eviction 1115
covenant of quiet enjoyment 1114
definite-term lease 1110
forfeiture 1124
full eviction 1115
implied warranty of habitability 1116
landlord 1109
landlord's lien 1121
lease 1109
leasehold estate 1109
lessee 1109
lessor 1109
partial eviction 1115
periodic-tenancy lease 1110
rent 1120
rent escalation clause 1121
sublease 1124
surrender 1125
tenancy-at-sufferance lease 1110
tenancy-at-will lease 1110
tenant 1109
waste 1116

SUMMARY OF KEY TOPICS

Creation of the Landlord-Tenant Relationship

The *landlord,* also known as the *lessor,* is the owner of the property.

The *tenant,* also called the *lessee,* is the party who assumes temporary ownership of the property.

A *leasehold estate* is the property in question.

A *lease* is the actual agreement between the landlord and the tenant.

Types of leases:

1. *Definite term:* The lease automatically expires at the end of a given term.
2. *Periodic tenancy:* The lease is created for a recurring term.
3. *Tenancy at will:* The lease may terminate at any time.
4. *Tenancy at sufferance:* The tenant fails to leave the property after the termination of the lease.

The *Fair Housing Act* prohibits landlords from discriminating on the basis of race, color, sex, religion, disability, national origin, or familial status.

Rights and Duties of the Landlord and the Tenant

Possession and use of the premises:

A *covenant of quiet enjoyment* is a promise that the tenant has the right to quietly enjoy the land.

Eviction:

1. *Actual eviction* occurs when a landlord physically prevents the tenant from entering the premises; it can be full (prohibited from all parts) or partial (prohibited from some parts).
2. *Constructive eviction* occurs when the premises become unsuitable for use due to the landlord.

Use of the premises:

An *implied warranty of habitability* is a requirement that the premises be fit for ordinary residential purposes.

Tenant use of the premises:

Waste is tenant conduct that causes permanent and substantial injury to the landlord's property.

Alterations are changes that affect the condition of the premises; generally, they cannot be made without the landlord's consent.

Maintenance of the premises:

Common areas are areas that are used by all the tenants and for which the landlord is responsible.

Tenants' options when repairs are not done:

1. Terminate the lease.
2. Withhold rent payment.
3. Repair and deduct costs.
4. Sue the landlord.

Rent is compensation paid to the landlord for the tenant's exclusive use of and right to possess the premises. Landlords may charge a late fee, but it must be related to the amount of rent past due.

A *rent escalation clause* is a clause included in the lease that allows the landlord to increase the rent for increases in cost of living, property taxes, or the tenant's commercial business.

A landlord's lien is a landlord's right to some or all of the tenant's property when rent is unpaid.

Liability for Injuries on the Premises

Landlord liability: A landlord can be held liable for injuries sustained in common areas and for injuries that occurred outside common areas due to repairs the landlord should have made. The landlord has the responsibility to ensure that the premises are in reasonably good condition before the tenant takes control. The foreseeability of a crime is also a factor in liability.

Tenant's liability: A tenant must keep the premises in a reasonably safe condition but is responsible only for those areas where a customer can be reasonably expected to go.

Transferring Interests of Leased Property

Landlord transfer of interest: A landlord may transfer property and the new owner becomes the landlord until the tenant's lease expires.

Tenant transfer of interest:

An *assignment* transfers the tenant's entire interest in the leased property.

A *sublease* transfers less than all of the tenant's interest in a leased property.

Termination of the Lease

Termination may occur in the following instances:

1. When the landlord *breaches a condition;* for example, the landlord interferes with the tenant's use and enjoyment of the premises.
2. Through *forfeiture,* which occurs when the tenant or landlord fails to perform conditions specified in the lease.
3. When a fire or other disaster *destroys the premises.*
4. Through *surrender,* that is, mutual agreement between landlord and tenant.
5. Through *abandonment,* which occurs when the tenant moves out of the leased premises before the end of the term.

POINT / COUNTERPOINT

Should Landlords Be Permitted to Screen Potential Tenants for Criminal Background?

YES

The modern process of securing rental housing in the United States has become a more advanced process than it used to be. Potential tenants are often asked to provide letters of recommendation and employment information, as well as submit to prescreening for credit scores and criminal background checks. Specifically, criminal background checks offer landlords the opportunity to protect their tenants and their business investments. Thus, a potential tenant's criminal history should be viewable by a landlord for two important reasons.

First, by screening potential applicants, a landlord can help protect the other tenants in his building. It is no secret that previously convicted individuals are a high-risk group for future criminal activity, and a landlord has an obligation to protect the safety of his tenants. By allowing an individual convicted of assault or burglary to live on his rental property, a landlord would be knowingly putting his other tenants at a higher risk of becoming victims of assault or burglary. Furthermore, a landlord also has a right to know if a tenant was evicted for nonpayment from her last apartment or convicted of property crimes, because this is directly related to the agreement between a landlord and a tenant. Therefore, a potential tenant's criminal history should be viewable by a potential landlord.

Second, criminal background checks will help a landlord protect his rental property. Because a landlord is usually the owner of the rental property, he has a vested interest in both the happiness of tenants and the condition of the property. If tenants believe that their neighbor is a threat to them, they will choose to live elsewhere. In many cases it is inevitable that tenants will find out about their neighbor's criminal history. For example, convicted sex offenders must register on a website. Whether neighboring tenants find out from the landlord or on their own,

NO

In the United States, citizens should always have a right to a residence. Even those citizens who have been incarcerated or convicted of a crime should be afforded the opportunity to find a dwelling place. This is the primary reason why criminal background checks on potential tenants by their landlords should be outlawed. Make no mistake: Criminal background checks serve only to exclude past offenders from housing. Convicted criminals have already paid their debt to society, and they should be given the opportunity to find work and a place to live and thus become productive members of their community. Three reasons suggest the wisdom of banning criminal background checks by landlords.

First, criminal background checks violate the privacy of potential tenants. Whether or not a person has been convicted of a crime, a personal history check by a nongovernment official is a violation of the person's privacy. When the police suspect someone of committing a crime, they must first find probable cause before they can approach a judge, obtain a warrant, and then search the suspect's belongings. However, at many rental properties, criminal background checks are done for every potential tenant without any reasonable suspicion that a crime was ever committed. Moreover, the consequences here can be severe: A criminal background check can serve to prejudice a landlord and ultimately deny a person housing. Furthermore, most convicts struggle to find work after they have been released from prison, and they are limited in available housing options. If these people were truly believed to be a threat, they would still be incarcerated and their privacy privileges would be the same as any other prisoner's. Therefore, because people with criminal histories are legally eligible to rent an apartment, their privacy should not be violated any further by a landlord's criminal background check.

they are likely to leave the property. If several tenants leave, this could force the landlord to lower his prices. Furthermore, a landlord has a legal obligation to protect his tenants. If the landlord doesn't do everything in his power to protect them, violations will hurt his business through both fines and a damaged reputation. Lastly, a tenant with a history of property crime is more likely to harm the physical makeup of a building, costing the landlord money in repairs. For these reasons, a landlord has a right to protect his business by screening the criminal histories of potential tenants.

Because the program is working, landlords should continue the practice of screening potential tenants by conducting criminal background checks.

Second, there are many discriminatory problems in the methods used for criminal background checks. Unequal race and income distributions exist in the U.S. criminal justice system, and convicted offenders, as a group, are largely minority and low-income individuals. Therefore, when landlords choose not to rent to convicted offenders, they are primarily excluding low-income minority members. Furthermore, the business of landlords has more and more become an arena dominated by corporations pushing out individual building owners. Rental property corporations are more likely to set firm policies on background checks than is an individual landowner. Moreover, it is likely that the spread of rental companies will increase, while the number of private landlords will decrease. Unless the ability to check one's criminal history is removed, the racial and income disparities in the system will only increase. Therefore, to prevent the effects of housing discrimination, landlords should no longer be allowed to check a potential tenant's criminal history.

Thus, it is in the best interest of society to eliminate criminal background checks by landlords.

Source: David Thacher, "The Rise of Criminal Background Screening in Rental Housing," *Law and Social Inquiry* 33 (2008), pp. 5, 25; and B. A. Glesner, "Landlords as Cops: Tort, Nuisance & Forfeiture Standards Imposing Liability on Landlords for Crime on the Premises," *Case Western Reserve Law Review* 42 (1992), p. 679.

QUESTIONS & PROBLEMS

1. What is the most distinguishing element of a landlord-tenant relationship?
2. As a tenant, what are the remedies available to you if the landlord breaches the implied warranty of habitability?
3. Explain the distinction between assignment and sublease.
4. In February 1998, Sutton Moore fell through a deck when he was visiting Jonathan and Kelly Hambrick. Moore was a guest of the Hambricks, who rented a house owned and maintained by Dennis Huard and his spouse. The Huards indicated that they maintained the deck regularly, having replaced rotten posts in 1995 and a broken step in 1997. The Hambricks had not noticed or reported any problems with the deck. Moore sued the Huards for negligence. What duty do the Huards, as landlords, owe to Moore, guests of the tenants? Who won? [*Moore v. Huard,* No. 31907-1-II, Slip. Op. (Wash. App. Div. 2, 2006).]
5. Hermes Reyes was injured when he was visiting his daughter at a summer rental property in 2003. When opening a sliding door and moving onto a deck, Reyes lost his balance and fell, sustaining injury. He contended that he lost his balance because there was an unexpected 6½-inch drop to the deck. Reyes brought suit against both the landlord (Egner) and the company that managed the property for the landlord (Prudential Fox & Roach Realtors). What was the result? [*Reyes v. Egner,* 962 A.2d 542 (2009).]
6. In the small village of Bellwood, Illinois, numerous African-American and white residents filed suits against Gladstone Realtors, accusing the business of "steering" white residents toward predominantly white areas and "steering" African-American people toward areas with large African-American populations. The plaintiffs further argued that as a result they were denied access to equal housing rights and the benefits of an integrated society. What areas of landlord-tenant law does this violate? [*Gladstone Realtors v. Village of Bellwood,* 441 U.S. 91, 99 (1979).]

7. On June 3, 2002, Martin Gans sent a letter to his landlord attempting to extend his lease for another five years. The original lease stated: "To exercise Tenant's options to extend, tenant must notify Landlord in writing on or before 60 days before the date of expiration of the within Lease; Notices by Tenant to Landlord shall be in writing and deposited in the United States mail, postage prepaid, certified or registered, addressed to Landlord." However, the lease term expired on July 31, 2002. The 60th day before the expiration date was Saturday, June 1, 2002. On Monday, June 3, 2002, Gans attempted to exercise the option to extend the lease by letter sent to L. C. Smull by regular mail. On June 13, 2002, the landlord wrote back, stating that Gans's request was "untimely." Smull also wrote: "Please be advised that the Landlord has elected to cancel your lease at the expiration on July 31, 2002, at which time you are to vacate the premises." Gans claimed that he waited until Monday to send the request as, according to the Code of Civil Conduct, if the last day to perform an act provided or required by law within a specified period of time is a Saturday, Sunday, or holiday, then that period is extended to the next day provided this day is not a Saturday, Sunday, or holiday. Was Smull right in evicting Gans? Why or why not? [*Gans v. Smull,* 111 Cal. App. 4th 985 (Aug. 29, 2003).]

8. Defendants John and Terry Hoffius advertised for rent a piece of residential property. The ad was answered by Kristal McCready and Keith Kerr. After learning that McCready and Kerr were unmarried, the defendants refused to rent the property to them. Another unmarried couple, Rose Baiz and Peter Perusse, were also prevented from renting the property. The couples argued that they were unfairly discriminated against because of their marital status. The defendants argued that they were motivated by a strong religious belief that unmarried couples should not live together. Do you think that this is a reasonable reason for refusing to rent the property? Why or why not? [*McCready v. Hoffius,* 586 N.W.2d 723 (Mich. 1998).]

9. In late 2011, Richard Bolmer filed a lawsuit against Connolly Properties, Inc., claiming that its rental property, in which he resided, was poorly maintained. He claimed that the property was left victim to mold, rodents, bugs, unclean common areas, and unreported theft and criminal activity. This state of disrepair was caused by the managers of the property, who allowed illegal immigrants to live in the complex. What more could Bolmer have done to ensure his safety at the rental property? [*DelRio-Mocci v. Connolly Properties, Inc.,* 672 F.3d 241 (3d Cir. 2012).]

10. Escobar, a college student, sustained injuries when he fell from a fourth-story window of the Mark Tower residence hall at the University of Southern California (USC). Before he fell, he had been sleeping on a bed that was placed against a window in Mark Tower. Escobar's friends had taken him to this residence hall so that he could sleep off the effects of excessive alcohol consumption. Escobar sued USC, alleging that the residence hall was dangerous and that USC had a duty to make the facility safe. USC sought to have the lawsuit dismissed because the fall was caused by Escobar's gross consumption of alcohol. Escobar contested USC's claim, alleging that his fall was caused by a dangerous condition in the residence hall. Specifically, when the university redesigned rooms in 1996, it created a dangerous condition by removing permanently affixed desks, which had prevented beds from being placed against the window. The university should have considered what its redesign would do to furniture arrangement and how new arrangements might place students at risk. Will Escobar get to go forward with his claim? [*Escobar v. University of Southern California,* No. B166522, Los Angeles Sup. Ct., No. BC259972, available at 2004 WL 2094602.]

Looking for more review materials?

The Online Learning Center at **www.mhhe.com/kubasek3e** contains this chapter's "Assignment on the Internet" and also a list of URLs for more information, entitled "On the Internet." Find both of them in the Student Center portion of the OLC, along with quizzes and other helpful materials.

CHAPTER

51

Insurance Law

LEARNING OBJECTIVES

After reading this chapter, you will be able to answer the following questions:

1 What is the nature of the insurance relationship?

2 What does the insurance contract include?

3 How is an insurance policy canceled?

4 What are the obligations of the insurer and the insured?

5 What is the insurer's defense for nonpayment?

6 What are the types of insurance available to consumers?

CASE OPENER

Chinese Drywall Presents Challenges for Homeowners

In May 2007, Larry Ward purchased a newly constructed home in Virginia Beach, Virginia. He obtained a homeowner's insurance policy from TravCo Insurance Company. The policy was renewed annually until May 2010. In May 2009, Ward experienced problems with the home. He retained an expert who determined that the problems were caused by Chinese drywall installed in the house during construction. Ward claimed that the drywall emitted sulfide gases and toxic chemicals that created noxious odors and caused health issues, corrosion, and damage to the home's air-conditioning system, garage door, and flat-screen television. Ward subsequently filed a claim with TravCo. TravCo denied Ward's claim on the basis that the damage caused by the Chinese drywall was excluded from coverage by the terms of the policy. Specifically, the policy excluded losses arising from latent defects; faulty, inadequate, or defective materials; rust or corrosion; and pollutants.

Ward filed a lawsuit against TravCo in federal court. The federal court certified the issue of the scope of the policy exclusions to the Virginia Supreme Court.

1. How should the Virginia Supreme Court decide this case? Is the defective drywall within the definition of losses excluded from coverage as claimed by TravCo?
2. What steps should Ward have taken prior to purchasing the house?

The Wrap-Up at the end of the chapter will answer these questions.

Insurance is a contract in which the insured party makes payments to the insurer in exchange for the insurer's promise to make payment or transfer goods to the insured or a named beneficiary in the event of injury to or destruction of the insured party's property or life. Thus, an individual interested in buying life insurance pays a certain amount of money to the insurance company in exchange for its promise to pay a specified amount of money to a designated beneficiary (such as a spouse) in the event of the insured person's death.

Millions of dollars are spent on private life, auto, and homeowner's insurance each year, while the government spends similarly large amounts on social insurance. This chapter will help you understand the role of insurance in the context of business. We first define important concepts in insurance law. Then we carefully examine the insurance contract. Finally, we consider the different types of insurance available.

The Nature of the Insurance Relationship

LO1

What is the nature of the insurance relationship?

We begin with some terminology. First, the **insured party** is the one who makes a payment, called a **premium,** in exchange for a later payment in the event of damage or injury to property or person. The **insurer,** sometimes called the **underwriter,** receives payments from the insured party and pays the **beneficiary,** the person named to receive the insurance proceeds in the event of injury or damage. The insured and insurer express their agreement in a document called a **policy.** In most insurance policies (except life insurance), the beneficiary and the owner of the policy are the same person.

RISK

The most important element of the insurance agreement is **risk,** the potential for loss. In our society, we try to identify risks and manage them by transferring and distributing them. Through the insurance agreement, the insured party *transfers* his or her risk of loss of property or life to the insurance company. The insurance company, in turn, distributes this risk among a large group of persons who share the same risk. If a loss does occur, one party is not forced to bear the entire weight of it.

You, like many other people, face the risk of your house burning down. When you and other homeowners purchase insurance to protect against the risk of fire, you each pay the insurance company a premium that is small relative to the amount you would receive if your house burned down, because the insurance company has distributed the risk of fire among all of you. This transfer and distribution of risk is known as **risk management.**

Moral hazard suggests that individuals who are insulated from risk sometimes behave differently. For instance, if a person has car insurance, she might be careless with regard to locking the car because the insurance company covers the risk of theft. If a person has health insurance, he might have very high expectations with regard to medical tests because the insurance company covers the cost. Insurance companies lessen the impact of moral hazard by requiring that individuals with insurance make co-payments or pay a deductible. These features of insurance policies create a financial incentive for individuals to refrain from making claims.

Legal Principle: Insurance plays an important role in risk management. Insurance law articulates the rules that govern the insurance relationship.

BUT WHAT IF . . .

WHAT IF THE FACTS OF THE CASE OPENER WERE DIFFERENT?

Let's say, in the Case Opener, that when Ward went to the TravCo offices to sign up for home insurance, TravCo representative Callie told Ward that TravCo chose to have few insured parties and also low monthly premiums. Ward said that such a setup did not seem logical due to risk absorption. Which party seems to have a better understanding of risk?

Exhibit 51-1
Examples of Interesting Insurance Policies

Troy Polamalu's hair—$1 million
Keith Richards's right middle finger—$1.6 million
Heidi Klum's legs—$2.2 million
Bruce Springsteen's voice—$6 million
Jennifer Lopez's buttocks—purportedly $27 million
David Beckham's entire body—$151 million

Source: *Parade Magazine,* www.parade.com/celebrity/slideshows/news/celebrity-insurance-policies.

INSURABLE INTEREST

To have an **insurable interest** in property or life, a person must be subject to economic loss if there is damage or harm to the person or property. Only individuals who have insurable interests can enter into a valid insurance agreement.

Insurable interest can exist in either a person or property. A person or company can take out an insurance policy on someone from whom that person or company expects to benefit during his or her continued life. Microsoft Corporation could insure Bill Gates's life because the corporation would likely suffer an economic loss if he were to die. If the insurable interest is in a life, the interest must exist at the time the policy is obtained. In contrast, an individual has an insurable interest in property whenever that person derives a financial benefit from its continued use. However, the interest must also exist *at the time of the loss.* If not, the person cannot collect the beneficiary payment.

Many things can be and have been insured. Exhibit 51-1 contains just a few dramatic illustrations.

Case 51-1 considers the types of interests protected by insurance policies.

CASE 51-1 ROYAL CAPITAL DEVELOPMENT LLC v. MARYLAND CASUALTY COMPANY
GEORGIA SUPREME COURT, 2012 GA. LEXIS 501 (GA., MAY 29, 2012)

Royal Capital owned an eight-story commercial building in the Buckhead area of Atlanta. In 2003, Royal Capital purchased an insurance policy from Maryland Casualty to insure the building. After construction activity on an adjacent property caused physical damage to the building, Royal Capital submitted a timely claim under the policy to Maryland Casualty, seeking both the costs of repair and the post-repair diminution in value resulting from the damage. Maryland Casualty acknowledged that the damage to the building was a covered cause of loss under the policy and paid $1,132,072.96 to compensate Royal Capital for the estimated costs of repair. However, Maryland Casualty refused to make payment on Royal Capital's claim of diminution in the value of the building.

Royal Capital filed a lawsuit against Maryland Casualty in Georgia state court. The case was removed to the U.S. District Court for the Northern District of Georgia. The district court concluded that Georgia law did not permit recovery on insurance contracts for diminution of value damages in addition to the costs of repair. Royal Capital appealed to the U.S. Court of Appeals for the Eleventh Circuit. Finding no controlling precedent from Georgia state courts, the Eleventh Circuit determined that the case raised an important unsettled question of state law. Accordingly, it certified the issue of whether state law permitted recovery of diminutions of property value as well as repair costs to the Georgia Supreme Court.

JUSTICE THOMPSON: The United States Court of Appeals asked this Court to decide the following question of law: For an insurance contract providing coverage for "direct physical loss of or damage to" a building that allows the insurer the option of paying either "the cost of repairing the building" or "the loss of value," if the insurer elects to repair the building, must it also compensate the insured for the diminution in value of the property resulting from stigma due to its having been physically damaged?

[continued]

This question stems from a dispute over the proper interpretation under Georgia law of a contract insuring real property. The primary issue presented to this Court is whether our ruling in *State Farm Mut. Auto. Ins. Co. v. Mabry,* 556 SE2d 114 (2001), a case involving an automobile insurance policy wherein we held that a provision requiring the insurer to pay for loss to the insured's car required the insurer to also pay for any diminution in value of the repaired vehicle, is applicable. As the Eleventh Circuit observed, the single question presented in this appeal is whether the Georgia courts would hold that the *Mabry* rule extends to standard insurance contracts for buildings. For the reasons which follow, we hold that our ruling in Mabry is not limited by the type of property insured, but rather speaks generally to the measure of damages an insurer is obligated to pay.

In *Mabry,* this Court determined that value, not condition, is the baseline for the measure of damages in a claim under an automobile insurance policy in which the insurer undertakes to pay for the insured's loss from a covered event, and that a limitation of liability provision affording the insurer an option to repair serves only to abate, not eliminate, the insurer's liability for the difference between pre-loss value and post-loss value. As we noted in our decision, "[r]ecognition of diminution in value as an element of loss to be recovered on the same basis as other elements of loss merely reflects economic reality."

These same principles have long been applied under Georgia law in cases involving the proper determination for measuring damages to real property. This Court has consistently held that the measure of damages in such cases is intended to place an injured party, as nearly as possible, in the same position they would have been if the injury had never occurred. Moreover, this Court has long considered diminution in value to be an element in determining the proper measure of damages to real property.

In applying these principles, this Court has recognized that under Georgia law, cost of repair and diminution in value can be alternative, although often interchangeable, measures of damages with respect to real property. Although unusual, it may sometimes be appropriate, in order to make the injured party whole, to award a combination of both measures of damages. In such cases, notwithstanding remedial measures undertaken by the injured party, there remains a diminution in value of the property, and an award of only the costs of remedying the defects will not fully compensate the injured party. Based on well-established precedent authorizing full recovery, including in some circumstances both diminution in value and cost of repair, we thus reject Maryland Casualty's contention that the contract at issue did not include coverage for post-repair diminution in value as no insurer or insured had reason to expect such coverage under a standard real property insurance policy.

Finally, we find no reason to distinguish *Mabry* from the instant case based on the alleged sophistication of the parties entering into insurance policies covering real property versus those who purchase automobile insurance policies. Although this case involves an insurance contract covering commercial property, a vast number of policies covering real property insure residential property for homeowners—a group far less sophisticated and more closely aligned to the automobile policyholders in *Mabry.*

We adhered in *Mabry* to the long-standing contract interpretation rule in Georgia that where an insurance policy, drafted by the insurer, promises to pay for the insured's loss[,] what is lost when physical damage occurs is both utility and value; therefore, the insurer's obligation to pay for the loss includes paying for any lost value. We see no reason to limit our holding in *Mabry* to automobile insurance policies and we thus answer the primary question posed by the Eleventh Circuit Court of Appeals in the affirmative: The *Mabry* rule applies to the insurance contract at issue in this case. Accordingly, whether damages for diminution of value are recoverable depends on the specific language of the contract itself and can be resolved through application of the general rules of contract construction.

Judgment overruled in favor of the Plaintiff.

CRITICAL THINKING

Was this the correct decision in this case? Are there significant differences between automobile and real property insurance policies that the court failed to recognize?

ETHICAL DECISION MAKING

What interests is the court protecting in this case? Is the court looking beyond the facts of this case and attempting to set rules that might apply when the parties are not of equal sophistication, such as in the context of a homeowner's policy? Should there be different rules regarding the interpretation of insurance contracts depending on the parties' sophistication? Why or why not?

How exactly is the insurance agreement created? What kinds of restrictions are placed on the creation and execution of the insurance agreement? The next section examines these questions.

BUT WHAT IF . . .

WHAT IF THE FACTS OF THE CASE OPENER WERE DIFFERENT?

Let's say, in the Case Opener, that Ward could not afford homeowner's insurance for his new house. In his will he stipulated that his house was to be left to his son, but his son was too young to pay the insurance premiums. Ward's cousin Rhonda ended up taking out homeowner's insurance on Ward's house since she could afford the monthly premiums. Is this scenario legal? Why or why not?

The Insurance Contract

LO2 What does the insurance contract include?

Many of the elements of contract law that you learned about in Chapters 13 to 16, such as offer, acceptance, and consideration, are relevant to the creation of an insurance contract.

APPLICATION FOR INSURANCE

The insurance relationship usually begins when the party with the insured interest makes an offer to purchase insurance by completing an insurance company application. On the basis of the application, the insurance company evaluates the risk and determines whether to accept the offer.

Applicants have a duty to reveal all significant information regarding the risk associated with the insurance policy. If the applicant makes a misleading or misrepresentative material statement and the insurance company relies on this false statement, the insurance company can void the contract. The insurance company must demonstrate two elements to void the contract: (1) The misrepresentation was material, and (2) the company's knowledge of it would have resulted in the rejection of the offer.

Legal Principle: **Insurance companies can void a contract if the insured has made a material misrepresentation in the insurance application.**

Effective Date. How does the insurance company accept the insurance agreement? Generally, it communicates to the insured party its intent to accept. The date the policy becomes effective, the **effective date,** is extremely important. What happens if someone sends in an insurance application and is injured in an accident two days later? Who is responsible for the losses associated with the accident? In some cases, insurance coverage does not begin until the company sends a formal letter to the insured party. In other cases, the insurance may begin as soon as the insured party signs the application. Let's look a little more closely at the effective date.

Suppose Ashley meets with an insurance agent to create an insurance policy. If Ashley pays a premium, signs the insurance application, and gives the application to the insurance agent, she will be covered. The insurance agent will likely write a **binder,** an agreement that gives temporary insurance until the company decides to accept or reject the insurance application.

In contrast, suppose Ashley makes an agreement with the insurance company that the policy will be issued at some later date. The insurance will not become effective until

Ashley receives the policy. If she had an accident before that date, the insurance would not cover the losses.

Case 51-2 considers whether a renewal of an insurance contract is effective and demonstrates how complicated cases that consider the effective date of the policy can be.

CASE 51-2 EQUITY FIRE & CASUALTY COMPANY v. LAURENCE TRAVER

SUPREME COURT OF ARKANSAS 953 S.W.2D 565 (ARK. 1997)

Laurence Traver received a renewal notice for his auto insurance with a due date of March 9, 1994, and an expiration date of March 14, 1994. Traver's payment was postmarked March 12, 1994, and later postmarked again March 21, 1994. Equity received the payment and reinstated the policy on March 22, 1994.

Traver was in an automobile accidence on March 19, 1994. The other party to the accident filed a claim with his own insurance carrier, which filed a suit against Traver, who filed an action against Equity. Equity refused to cover the accident because it argued that Traver's policy had lapsed on March 14 and was not effective on the date of the accident.

The trial court ruled in favor of Traver, finding that his mailing of the premium before March 14, 1994, was an effective renewal of the policy.

JUDGE ARNOLD: There is no Arkansas case directly addressing this issue. In Kempner v. Cohn, we recognized the mailbox rule for the acceptance of a contract. Once an offer has been made, a contract is completed when the acceptance is mailed if the acceptance is made in a reasonable amount of time. If a letter of withdrawal is mailed, before the mailing of the acceptance, it is effective only if the party to whom the offer was made receives the withdrawal before making the acceptance.

Despite the fact that this case was decided in the 1800s, there are few cases following it which expound upon this theory. The Kempner decision has been followed as a routine matter of contract theory, with the proviso that parties are free to dictate the terms of offers and acceptances as they deem necessary.

In the case before us, the policy language requires actual receipt of a premium payment prior to the expiration date of the policy to constitute acceptance of a renewal offer. The actual renewal notice gave the due date as a date five days before the expiration date. It does not contain the language requiring actual receipt of the premium payment; it instructs the insured to pay the amount listed as due in order to renew the policy.

In Mississippi Insurance Underwriting Association v. Maenza, 413 So. 2d 1384 (Miss. 1982), the Mississippi Supreme Court examined a situation closely analogous to the case at bar. A property and casualty policy renewal notice/offer was sent to the insured with an expiration date of September 10, 1979. The insured mailed payment on September 8, 1979, but it was not received by the insurer until September 11, 1979. A hurricane destroyed the insured's property on September 11, 1979. The insurer accepted the payment, but claimed the policy had lapsed because payment was not received on or before the due date. The insurer then treated the payment as an application for new coverage and issued a policy with the effective date of September 14, 1979.

The insured brought a claim before the Mississippi Insurance Commission, and it rendered a ruling that the renewal was effective when the premium payment was deposited in the United States mail, as long as it was deposited in time to reach the insurer on or before the expiration date. The insurance commission determined that neither party was to blame for a delay within the postal service; however, the insurer was the party that should bear the imputed burden because it adopted the postal service as its agent when allowing premiums to be transported via mail. 413 So. 2d at 1386.

The Mississippi Supreme Court affirmed the findings of the insurance commission. Specifically, that court held that the insurer's renewal notice is an offer that is accepted by the offeree/insured sending premium payments. The insurer in this instance required that payment be received before acceptance became effective; the Mississippi court rejected this notion because there was no clear language to suggest that acceptance was not effective until receipt. However, the court went on to conclude that in circumstances where an insurer invites premiums to be forwarded through the mail, it adopts the postal service as its agent and deposit of a payment with that agent constitutes acceptance of coverage. According to the Mississippi court, adopting the postal service as an agent imputed any negligence on their behalf to the insurer despite any contract language to the contrary; therefore contract language requiring receipt before acceptance was valid does not render the mailbox acceptance rule inapplicable. Id. at 1388.

In Maenza, the Mississippi court based the finding that the insurer invited the use of the postal service on several factors. First of all, the renewal notice itself indicated that payment could be made via mail, and the insurer utilized the mail to send the renewal notice. The insurer's office

[continued]

was over 100 miles from most of its insureds, so personal delivery would have been impractical. There are two other important factors to note in the Maenza decision. First, the payment was deposited with the postal service prior to the expiration date, in apt time to reach the insurer in a timely manner. Second, upon receipt of the payment it deemed late, the insurer made no attempt to refund the money, but caused a new policy to come into effect with a gap in the coverage.

In the case before us, Equity did have written language requiring receipt of the payment in order for acceptance to be effective; however, that language was in the policy and not on the actual renewal notice. Equity utilized the postal service as a carrier for its offer and expected to receive the acceptance via the mail. Traver mailed the premium payment in a timely manner where, absent negligence or mistake by the postal service, it had ample time to reach Equity prior to the termination date. Upon receipt of Traver's check, Equity did not refuse the payment, yet accepted it as an application for a new policy.

Based upon the facts of this case, it is our determination that Traver's placing the renewal premium in the mail in a timely manner constituted acceptance of Equity's renewal offer. Due to the peculiar factual scenario provided here, this holding is limited to the particular facts and circumstances of this case. We do not institute an absolute rule of applying the "mailbox rule" to all renewal premium payments, nor do we hold that parties are not free to dictate the terms of acceptance of offers. The facts before us present a unique situation where Traver was not afforded notice through the actual offer that receipt of payment was required before acceptance was effective. Given the fact that there was no fraud or negligence on behalf of Traver and the fact that Traver placed the payment in the mail with ample time for it to reach Equity prior to the expiration of the offer, we hold that in this instance there was a manifest acceptance of the renewal offer. Therefore, Traver's policy did not lapse, and it was effective beginning on March 14, 1984.

AFFIRMED in favor of defendant.

CRITICAL THINKING

Judge Arnold states that "the facts before us present a unique situation." What are these facts? How do they make the situation unique?

ETHICAL DECISION MAKING

Which party seems to benefit from the court's decision in this case? Who in the business world is likely to benefit? If the insurance company were acting under the public disclosure test, would it have behaved differently? If so, how?

IMPORTANT ELEMENTS OF THE INSURANCE CONTRACT

Generally, the insurance company fashions the insurance contract. However, most states require that such contracts contain certain clauses to give the insured a little more power, and if the company creates a confusing policy, the courts will find in favor of the insured. Case 51-3 considers the definition of "occupying a vehicle" in a motor vehicle insurance policy.

CASE 51-3 HARTFORD UNDERWRITERS INSURANCE COMPANY v. THE CINCINNATI INSURANCE COMPANY

U.S. DISTRICT COURT FOR THE DISTRICT OF VERMONT, 2011 U.S. DIST. LEXIS 2771 (D. VT., JAN. 11, 2011)

On March 7, 2007, Toby Young was participating in a five-day cross-country ski and yoga program with Elderhostel and the Craftsbury Center, Inc. Young, an active 70-year-old woman, spent the afternoon cross-country skiing. A Craftsbury employee drove a Craftsbury van to pick up Young's group at the end of their ski trail. Young was struck by a pickup truck operated by Jessie Peters as she loaded her skis into the back of the van. Peters was insured by Peerless Insurance Company. Young was pinned between the pickup and the back of the van. Young's legs and pelvis were crushed, and she sustained multiple fractures and injuries to internal organs. She ultimately incurred $422,427 in medical expenses.

Young filed a claim against Peters and Peerless and settled for the $100,000 policy limit. Young also filed claims with Hartford Underwriters Insurance Company, on the *basis of a personal automobile and umbrella policy she maintained with Hartford, and with Craftsbury's insurer, the Cincinnati Insurance Company, for under-insured motorist ("UIM") benefits. Hartford settled with Young for $750,000. Cincinnati refused coverage on the basis that Young was loading the van at the time of the accident and was not "occupying" the van as required by Craftsbury's policy in order for coverage to exist. Cincinnati's policy defined "occupying" as "in, upon, getting in, on, out or off." Hartford brought an action against Cincinnati seeking an order declaring Cincinnati to be the primary insurer and for reimbursement of amounts paid by Hartford to Young. The issue presented to the court was whether Young was "occupying" the van at the time of the accident such as to trigger coverage under Craftsbury's insurance policy with Cincinnati.*

SENIOR U.S. DISTRICT COURT JUDGE MURTHA: Cincinnati argues the policy's definition of "occupying" is clear and unambiguous. Under the policy, "occupying" means "in, upon, getting in, on, out or off." The terms comprised in this definition of "occupying" are not further defined by the policy. Terms of an insurance policy are read "according to their ordinary and popular meaning.'" *Sperling v. Allstate Indem. Co.,* 944 A.2d 210, 216 (Vt. 2007). "Any ambiguities in insurance policies are construed in favor of finding coverage. As with other contracts, the determination of ambiguity is a question of law. . . ." *DeBartolo v. Underwriters at Lloyd's of London,* 925 A.2d 1018, 1022 (Vt. 2007). "If a term is subject to more than one reasonable interpretation, 'the ambiguity must be resolved in favor of the insured.'" *Sperling,* 944 A.2d at 213.

On the undisputed facts, the issue is whether "getting in," or "getting . . . on," could encompass Toby A. Young's actions when she began the process of embarking by loading her skis at the back of the van with an intent to go around to a passenger door and climb in. An ambiguity exists in policy language "if reasonable people could differ as to the interpretation of the language at issue." *Id.* at 217.

While there is no patent ambiguity on the face of the policy, the terms comprising the definition of "occupying" are ambiguous when applied to facts of this case, because reasonable people could differ regarding whether Ms. Young was "getting into" or "getting . . . on" the van at the time of impact, depending on which point in time one believes the process of embarking began. Some could conclude "getting into" or "getting . . . on" began at the time she started loading her skis, because this was the first step in the process of entering a vehicle in which she intended to ride away, while others could conclude "getting on" should only encompass the process of getting into a passenger seat from a passenger door.

The parties agree there is no controlling Vermont precedent directly on point. A review of cases from numerous jurisdictions addressing identical policy definitions of "occupying" indicates innumerable courts have differed widely in how they interpret the definition. For example, the Texas Supreme Court has outlined at least twelve tests various state courts have used to determine whether a person was "occupying" a covered vehicle for the purpose of un- or under-insured motorist coverage given identical, or nearly identical, definitions. *U.S. Fid. & Guaranty Co. v. Goudeau,* 272 S.W.3d 603, 606-08 (Tex. 2008). That courts have differed so widely in interpreting this policy language, which is clear on its face, but is subject to competing interpretations when courts attempt to apply the definition to facts, demonstrates the latent ambiguity. Therefore, Cincinnati's definition of "occupying" contains a latent ambiguity which should be resolved in favor of Young, because Cincinnati, as an insurer, "is in a far better position to avoid latent ambiguity in the text of a policy." *Sanders v. St. Paul Mercury Ins. Co.,* 536 A.2d 914, 916 (Vt. 1987).

Even if this Court were to conclude the definition of "occupying" is not ambiguous, the plain, ordinary and popular meanings of the terms "getting on" or "getting in" would most reasonably encompass an injured party's acts as she began the process of embarking a vehicle by loading belongings at the rear doors, with an intent to proceed to a passenger door. The gerund "getting," combined with the words "on" or "in," suggests a process which could reasonably begin with loading belongings into a vehicle. A reasonable reading of the policy would include Young's claim.

Hartford Underwriters Insurance Company's Motion for Partial Summary Judgment on the issue of "Occupying" is granted. Cincinnati Insurance Company's Motion for Summary Judgment on the Issue of "Occupying" is denied. Young is entitled to UIM benefits under the Cincinnati policy. Once Cincinnati's obligations as primary insurer are determined, Hartford is entitled to recover from Cincinnati sums paid to Young that exceeded what it is obligated to pay as excess insurer.

CRITICAL THINKING

Do you agree with the court's decision in this case? The court refers to several different tests for determining whether a passenger is occupying a motor vehicle. What test would you apply in this case and why?

ETHICAL DECISION MAKING

What interests is the court protecting in this case? How does the court attempt to balance the disparate bargaining power between insurers and insured parties in order to create a more equal relationship?

COMPARING THE LAW OF OTHER COUNTRIES

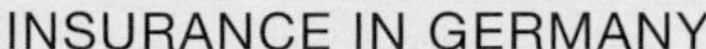

INSURANCE IN GERMANY

German manufacturers (like manufacturers in many countries) often obtain insurance that covers the risk of product liability. The policies have generally been straightforward, but as the firms expand internationally, insurance has become more complicated. When they distribute their products abroad, where should the firms buy their insurance?

Manufacturers could seek insurance through a German insurance company regardless of where their products are shipped. This is beneficial because they can establish a close, even personal, relationship with the insurer. However, German insurers may not take into consideration significant differences in product liability statutes in foreign markets. Courts generally award larger compensations for product liability cases than do German insurers. Consequently, in the United States, insurance companies offer higher settlements. Today, manufacturers are likely to have an insurance company in Spain, Japan, the United States, or wherever else they send their goods. Obviously, complications may arise from having insurance companies in several different countries. Thus far, it is unclear what option is more advantageous, and each manufacturer must consider its own situation before choosing.

Incontestability Clause. The **incontestability clause** is a state-mandated clause ensuring that after an insurance policy has existed for a specified period (usually two years), the insurance company cannot contest any statements made in the application. This clause prohibits the insurer from delaying payment because it decides to investigate the application for fraud.

Antilapse Clause. Suppose you accidentally forget to pay the premium for your insurance. Is the policy lapsed and no longer effective? Some states require that insurance companies include an **antilapse clause,** typically in life insurance policies, that provides a grace period of usually 30 days in which to make an overdue payment. During this grace period, the insurance is effective. If the insured fails to make a payment in those 30 days, the insurer is not allowed to automatically cancel the policy.

Appraisal Clause. Suppose some of your property is insured for $50,000 and is damaged in a fire. The insurance company determines you have suffered a loss of $10,000; you believe your loss is around $25,000. If you and the insurance company cannot agree, you can demand an appraisal under your policy's **appraisal clause.** Both you and the insurance company will select a disinterested appraiser. Each will evaluate the loss and state the actual value and loss of each item. If the appraisers fail to agree on the loss, they will typically submit their different appraisals to an umpire who will resolve the differences.

Arbitration Clause. Some insurance contracts include clauses that force both the insurer and the insured to submit any dispute to an arbitrator. An **arbitration clause** can help swiftly settle disputes between the parties.

Legal Principle: **Consumers of insurance need to know whether their policies include an arbitration clause.**

Canceling the Insurance Policy

LO3 How is an insurance policy canceled?

An insured party who decides to discontinue a policy at any time can simply stop paying the premiums or tell the insurance company to cancel the policy. But what happens when the insurer wants to cancel? The company must give the insured advance notice, typically including a grace period, before the policy is canceled. The insured may also be entitled to a refund of premium payments.

Exactly *when* is an insurer permitted to cancel a policy? State statutes usually govern the circumstances. If the insured misrepresented a material fact on the application or fails to pay premiums after a certain period, the insurance company may cancel. Car insurance may be canceled if the insured loses her license because of a driving violation.

BUT WHAT IF . . .

WHAT IF THE FACTS OF THE CASE OPENER WERE DIFFERENT?

Let's say, in the Case Opener, that when Ward filled out the documents to obtain his homeowner's insurance, he got confused and mistakenly wrote that there was no drywall in his house. Later, when he tried to file a claim regarding the faulty drywall, TravCo said that because Ward misrepresented the presence of drywall in his home, it could cancel the insurance contract. Is TravCo legal in doing this?

Insurer and Insured Obligations

LO4

What are the obligations of the insurer and the insured?

As parties to the insurance contract, both insurer and insured have obligations. If either does not meet its obligation, the other can usually sue for breach of contract.

INSURER DUTY TO DEFEND THE INSURED

The insurer has a duty to defend the insured from claims for which the insured is liable. Suppose Jackie runs a stop sign and crashes into Roberto's car. Jackie's insurance company has a duty to defend her against claims filed by Roberto's insurance company. To begin the defense process, Jackie must notify her insurer, which provides an attorney to defend her and assumes responsibility for the cost of the attorney and any litigation. If the insurer does not provide an attorney, it has breached the contract.

INSURER DUTY TO PAY SUMS OWED BY THE INSURED

Let's return to the stop-sign accident. If Jackie is liable to Roberto for any damages to Roberto's vehicle, her insurer has a duty to pay these compensatory damages. Most claims for damages for individuals like Roberto are settled through negotiation between the insurance company and Roberto. However, if the claim cannot be settled, the dispute will go to court.

INSURED DUTY TO DISCLOSE INFORMATION

As we saw above, the insured has a duty to disclose all material information on the application and fully and truthfully answer any questions.

INSURED DUTY TO COOPERATE WITH THE INSURER

For the insurer to meet its duty to defend, the insured must provide information regarding the incident that led to the claim. Suppose that after running the stop sign, Jackie refuses to discuss the accident with her insurer. If it does not have enough information, the company cannot defend her. Thus, Jackie has a duty to cooperate with the insurer. This duty extends into certain elements that lead to a trial. Insured individuals might be asked to provide the insurance company with a deposition or testify at the trial.

BUT WHAT IF . . .

WHAT IF THE FACTS OF THE CASE OPENER WERE DIFFERENT?

Let's say, in the Case Opener, that when the drywall in Ward's house started causing problems, he filled out a claim with his insurance company but he refused to take pictures or meet with representatives in person, stating that he didn't have enough time. Can the representatives at TravCo do anything to make Ward be more cooperative with them?

E-COMMERCE AND THE LAW

INTERNET LIABILITY PROTECTION

As courts and legislatures decide the legal rules that will govern e-commerce, insurance companies are revising the products they offer businesses engaged in e-commerce. One form of insurance, Internet liability protection, protects companies against copyright and trade infringement claims, alleged plagiarism committed via the Internet, failure to protect confidential information gathered online, and failure to stop a computer virus. It usually does not cover claims related to patents or trade secrets, which are more expensive than other intellectual property claims.

Insurance companies that offer Internet liability protection are likely to assist their customers by helping to prevent claims. One such company, Chubb, offers a handbook to help customers rethink Internet and website practices that may leave them vulnerable to litigation. This kind of interaction can also help insurance companies get to know their clients better and more accurately determine which forms of protection they need.

The Insurer's Defenses for Nonpayment

LO5 What is the insurer's defense for nonpayment?

If the insured fails to fulfill his duty to provide all material information on the insurance contract or to cooperate with the insurer, the insurer may argue that the insured has breached the contract; consequently, the insurer is not required to pay on a claim. The insurer may also use several other defenses for nonpayment.

First, if the insured did not have an insurable interest (see above), the insurance contract is void and the insurer is not required to pay. Second, some types of illegal activity, such as arson, permit the insurer to cancel the policy. Suppose a person intentionally sets fire to her business to receive the insurance benefits. The insurer, assuming it can provide evidence that the fire was intentionally set, can claim that the insured's behavior is a defense against payment of the claim.

Types of Insurance

LO6 What are the types of insurance available to consumers?

There are several ways to categorize insurance. If the insured party is the one purchasing the policy, it is **individual insurance.** If the purchaser is neither the insured nor the insurer (say, an employer), it is **group insurance.** Generally, a policy that covers an individual's life or health is **personal insurance.** If it covers some type of business risk, the policy is **commercial insurance,** such as title, contractor, or fidelity insurance.

Is the insurance property or casualty insurance? **Property insurance,** like fire, theft, homeowner's, and marine insurance, protects property from loss or damage. Insurance that protects a person or property from accidental injury is **casualty insurance.** Examples include workers' compensation, health, machine, and auto insurance.

LIABILITY AND PROPERTY INSURANCE

Liability insurance is one of the most important types of insurance you will need as a businessperson: It protects your business from tort liability to third parties. Suppose a customer is injured on your premises. Your business would probably be liable to the customer for her injuries and without insurance could suffer severe losses if the customer chooses to sue for damages. *Property insurance* protects against destruction or loss of property. The types of liability and property insurance are summarized in Exhibits 51-2 and 51-3.

A business should purchase a **commercial general liability policy** that protects against a broad range of risks that the firm can specify, including personal injury suits by customers and suits by competitors over intellectual property. This policy is subject to some exclusions, however. It does not provide protection for intentional acts, such as an

COMPARING THE LAW OF OTHER COUNTRIES

MARINE INSURANCE IN SCOTLAND

In 1906, Scotland added the Marine Insurance Act to its mercantile law to legitimize the finer points of insurance contracts related to "marine adventure." Marine insurance policies cover most marine activities, including ships under construction, ships being used on the sea, goods transported by sea, and liability to third parties in the event of difficulties while at sea. They are among the most complicated forms of insurance in Scotland.

Marine insurance policies tend to be exacting. As one example, before an insurer will sign a policy, the value of the item to be insured must be agreed on and specified in the contract. This value is nonnegotiable after the signing. Thus, if a business wants to insure a ship under construction, it can cover it only for its value as an incomplete vessel, regardless of the passage of time or a change in the nature of the ship. Once the ship has been finished, the business will have to cancel the policy and take out another one. Otherwise, the ship will not be insured for its true value.

employee's shoving a customer down a flight of steps or the firm's intentionally discharging pollutants into a river.

LIFE INSURANCE

Suppose Bill Gates had been killed within the first few years that Microsoft exploded in the technology market. Would Microsoft have been able to become so successful without him? **Life insurance** allows a business to take out a policy on a key employee and provide a payment in the event of the person's death.

There are a few types of life insurance. **Whole-life insurance** provides protection for the entire life of the insured but is distinctive because it has a cash-surrender value. If the owner decides to cancel the policy, he or she will receive a certain amount of cash back, which increases as more premiums are paid. This cash-surrender value also permits the owner of the policy to borrow money from the insurance company at a favorable interest rate.

Term-life insurance provides coverage for a specified term (say, 6 months, 1 year, or 10 years). The premiums are usually smaller than those for whole-life insurance, but the beneficiary receives payment only if the insured dies within the specified term. Therefore, the insurance company may never have to pay out on the policy. Term-life insurance usually has no cash-surrender value or loan opportunities, although it often has a guaranteed

Exhibit 51-2
Types of Liability Insurance

Type	Description
Contractors' liability insurance	Protects contractors against liability for injuries that might occur while completing a job (excluding injuries to employees)
Garage liability insurance	Protects the garage owner from liability to persons injured by the operation of the garage
Product liability insurance	Protects the producer or manufacturer of a good from loss due to damages paid to people injured using the good
Professional liability insurance	Protects members of specific professions from liability associated with their professional acts

Exhibit 51-3
Types of Property Insurance

Type	Description
Fire insurance	Protects property from loss or damage from fire
Livestock insurance	Protects the owner from loss due to injury or death of the livestock
Water, weather, and natural forces insurance	Protects against damage from flooding, water, weather (such as tornado, cyclone, hurricane, and rain), hail, lightning, etc.

CASE NUGGET

WILL STATES PROTECT THE TERMINALLY ILL FROM BEING TAKEN ADVANTAGE OF?

Life Partners, Inc. v. Miller 420 F. Supp. 2d 452 (E.D. Va. 2006)

Viatical companies are companies that buy insurance policies from terminally ill patients for a percentage of the policy's face value. A terminally ill woman, "Jane Doe," asked the state of Virginia to protect her from the unscrupulous act of a Texas investment company, Life Partners, Inc., which had paid her $29,900 for a life insurance policy worth $115,000. By state law, the Virginia Viatical Settlements Act, the minimum Jane Doe should have received was $69,000.

Life Partners, Inc., challenged Virginia's law as unconstitutional under the commerce clause but was unsuccessful. In defending Virginia's statute, the judge pointed out that the law does not discriminate against interstate commerce, its effect on interstate commerce is only incidental, and the law is an appropriate use of the state's police powers. The state is allowed to protect dying Virginians who want to sell their life insurance. The court said: "It is obvious to the court that a terminally-ill person . . . is in a particularly vulnerable position and could easily fall prey to sharp business practices and fraud."

renewability clause, which permits renewal regardless of the health of the insured. Instead of renewing, the owner might also choose to convert the policy to another type of life insurance policy at the end of the term.

Legal Principle: **When choosing a life insurance policy, consumers must decide whether they view the insurance policy as more than risk management. In addition, they must decide whether the policy is a financial investment.**

What types of situations are excluded under a life insurance policy? Generally, insurance companies do not pay if the insured died through suicide, war, or execution by the state. Almost any other type of death is covered.

Let's look at a few of the major legal issues associated with life insurance. One of the most common is misrepresentations on the application about the insured's health that might affect the insurance company's willingness to offer the policy. If you have cancer when you apply for insurance and do not make the insurance company aware of it, your insurance policy will likely be void. However, if you are unaware you have a disease when you apply for insurance, the insurance company cannot void your policy.

Another commonly misrepresented fact is the applicant's age. Generally, the older the applicant, the higher the premiums. Misrepresentation of age is not cause for cancellation of a policy. Instead, the insurance company will lower its payment to the beneficiary to reflect the premiums appropriate for the correct age.

CASE OPENER WRAP-UP

Chinese Drywall Presents Challenges for Homeowners

The Virginia Supreme Court concluded that the damage was the result of a latent defect in the drywall. As such, the policy unambiguously excluded from coverage damage caused by the Chinese drywall installed in the house. Additionally, the drywall constituted "faulty, inadequate or defective materials" within the meaning of the exclusions from coverage. The court also held that the rust and corrosion caused by emissions from the drywall were excluded from coverage, and the sulfur emissions were pollutants within the meaning of

[continued]

the exclusions. TravCo was thus correct in denying Ward coverage for damage caused by the Chinese drywall in his house.[1]

It is unclear from the court's opinion whether Ward performed an inspection of the house prior to his purchase and, if so, whether the problem with the drywall was an issue that should have been discovered through the exercise of reasonable care.

[1] *TravCo Insurance Company v. Ward,* 2012 Va., LEXIS 203 (Va., Nov. 1, 2012).

KEY TERMS

SUMMARY OF KEY TOPICS

The Nature of the Insurance Relationship

The *insured party* is the party who pays a premium in exchange for payment in the event of damage or injury.

A *premium* is a payment on a policy.

The *insurer* is the party who receives premiums from the insured party.

The *beneficiary* is the person who receives insurance proceeds.

A *policy* is a document that expresses agreement between the insured party, the beneficiary, and the insurer.

Risk:

1. Refers to potential loss.
2. Can be transferred and distributed.

Insurable interest means that:

1. A property interest must exist at the time of the loss.
2. A life interest must exist at the time the policy is obtained.

The Insurance Contract

Application for insurance:

The *effective date* for an insurance policy is the date on which the policy becomes effective.
A *binder* gives temporary insurance until a decision to accept or reject the application is made.

Important elements of the contract:

1. An *incontestability clause* ensures that the insurance company cannot contest statements made in an insurance application after a certain period of time.

2. An *antilapse clause* provides a grace period for the insured to pay the premium.
3. An *appraisal clause* allows the insured party and the insurer to select a disinterested appraiser for a second opinion on damages.
4. An *arbitration clause* provides that disputes must be submitted to an arbitrator.

Canceling the Insurance Policy

While either the insurer or the insured may cancel the insurance policy at specific times, the insurer is limited as to when it may cancel the policy. If either party breaches its duties as established in the insurance policy, the other party has some type of remedy.

Insurer and Insured Obligations

An insurer has a *duty to defend* the insured from claims for which the insured party is liable.

An insurer has a *duty to pay sums owed by the insured* to third parties.
The insured party has a *duty to disclose material information on* the insurance application; the insured party must fully and truthfully answer questions.
The insured party has a *duty to cooperate with the insurer;* the insured party must discuss claims with the insurer to be defended.

The Insurer's Defenses for Nonpayment

An insurer has a multitude of defenses, including breach of contract, lack of insurable interest, and illegal activity.

Types of Insurance

Individual insurance is purchased by the insured party.

Group insurance is purchased by a party that is neither the insured party nor the insurer.

Personal insurance covers an individual's life or health.

Commercial insurance covers business interests.

Casualty insurance protects a person or property from accidental injury.

These are types of *liability insurance:*

A *commercial general liability policy* protects a business against a broad range of risks.
Product liability insurance covers the cost of recalling and replacing products.
Professional insurance protects professionals from suits by third parties who claim that the professional was negligent in her or his job performance.

Property insurance protects property from loss or damage.

These are types of *life insurance:*

Whole-life insurance provides protection for the entire life of the insured.
Term-life insurance provides coverage for a specified term. A beneficiary is paid only if the insured party dies during this term.

POINT / COUNTERPOINT

Are Insurance Companies That Sell Policies to Homeowners to Blame for Homeowners' Confusion about Insurance Coverage?

YES*	NO
When a natural disaster such as a flood or hurricane occurs, homeowners count on private insurance companies to pay them for the damage that results. A problem arises when customers find out, too late, that they made	When a natural disaster such as a flood or hurricane strikes, private insurance companies must be careful to make payouts consistent with the terms of the insurance policies they have issued. If a policy doesn't cover a loss,

incorrect assumptions about what their insurance policy covers. For example, homeowner's insurance policies do not cover damage that occurs when a home is flooded in the aftermath of a hurricane.

Many customers find out the hard way what their homeowner's policies do *not* cover. The first floor of Paul and Julie Leonard's Pascagoula, Mississippi, home took in 5 feet of water during Hurricane Katrina, and they spent $30,000 of their own money on repairs because their insurance company denied their claim. It turned out that the Leonards were not insured for flood damage. They believed their insurance agent misled them by selling them a hurricane policy, which they assumed protected them when a hurricane caused a flood.

Customers like the Leonards are disappointed when they find out they are not covered. Homeowners are eager to rebuild and get on with their lives. It is good for the economy when individuals can rebuild.

The problem is that insurance companies have much more knowledge than their clients about the types of coverage their clients need. They should educate customers about the *gaps* in their insurance coverage so that customers can get additional forms of insurance or riders on the policies they have. Insurance companies should *suggest* extra protection that customers are likely to need. Do insurance companies benefit when their customers are confused? It seems they must. Otherwise, they would be educating customers.

insurance companies do not pay. The last thing an insurance company wants to do is take back a payment it has granted on the basis of erroneous decision making.

After Hurricane Katrina, many private insurance companies refused to pay homeowners' claims because much of the damage they suffered was caused by flooding and most homeowners did not have flood insurance. Instead, they had insurance to cover damage caused by wind.

Courts have generally ruled in favor of insurance companies in cases like the Leonards', and courts have been right. A spokesman for the Property Casualty Insurers Association of America has stated, "A healthy insurance market is absolutely key to a rejuvenated economy [on the Gulf Coast]."[†]

Insurance companies are not to blame when customers like the Leonards misunderstand what they have purchased. Homeowners need to engage in research so that they know what their policies do and do not cover. They need to ask agents questions about policies. Agents are excellent at educating customers about insurance. Unfortunately, customers often lack the willingness to consider the detailed language in policies.

For all we know, the Leonards' insurance agent did, in fact, suggest insurance to cover flood damage. Flood coverage is available through the National Flood Insurance Program.[‡] Perhaps the Leonards did not want to pay for flood insurance.

Insurance companies want their customers to be satisfied. Unfortunately, consumers are not always as careful or as rational as they should be. The good news is that disasters like Hurricane Katrina, and stories like the Leonards', help raise awareness.

* This side of the debate relies on facts from Michael Kunzelman, "Trial Begins over Katrina Insurance Payments," *St. Louis Post-Dispatch,* July 16, 2006, p. C2.
[†] Michael Kunzelman, "Insurance Company Wins Case on Katrina: Won't Have to Pay for Water Damage," *New Jersey Record,* August 16, 2006, p. A06.
[‡] "Many Homeowners Confused about Insurance," www.marcusagency.com/Homeowners%20Insurance.doc.

QUESTIONS & PROBLEMS

1. Why do states often require that insurance contracts include certain clauses?
2. When may the insurer cancel the insurance policy?
3. Why are liability policies important for businesses?
4. Sharon and Robert McNutt's residence on Kent Island in Stevensville, Maryland, caught fire on January 23, 2005. The fire burned beneath a firebox, a metal insert inside a hearth, which was part of a fireplace. The damage from the fire was extensive. The McNutts filed a claim under their homeowner's policy. The insurer was Erie Insurance Exchange. Erie sued Builder Services Group (BSG), Inc., under a theory of subrogation. Erie contended that BSG had negligently installed the firebox when the house was built in 1999. Erie did not notify BSG of its possible subrogation claim until after the fire scene had been destroyed. BSG was, in essence, deprived of access to the scene, thereby making it impossible to evaluate Erie's

contention that BSG had omitted a safety strip designed to protect the wooden framing of the firebox from burning embers. Will the court allow Erie to pursue a claim against BSG? [*Erie Insurance Exchange v. Davenport Insulation, Inc.* 659 F. Supp. 2d 701 (D. Md., 2009).]

5. In February 2008, the Washington State Department of Transportation diverted snowmelt through trenches located in the vicinity of Northwest Bedding Company's facilities. The water overflowed the trenches, inundated Northwest's building, and damaged the building and surrounding property. Northwest filed a claim with its insurer, National Fire Insurance Company. Northwest maintained an all-risk commercial-property policy and commercial general liability policy with National Fire. National Fire denied coverage and claimed that the damage was due to surface water flowage and flooding, which were excluded from coverage. Northwest sued National Fire for damages and a judicial declaration that the loss was covered. Northwest claimed that the loss was covered because the water was channeled onto its property through actions of a third party rather than an act of nature. National Fire claimed that the reason for the water on the property was irrelevant. Rather, the loss was caused by surface water and flooding, which were clearly excluded from coverage. Is the reason for the presence of water on the property relevant, or is the mere presence of the water sufficient to support a denial of coverage? [*Northwest Bedding Co. v. National Fire Insurance Co.,* 225 P.3d 484 (Wash. App. 2010).]

6. In October 1997, Auburn Flying Services participated in a "fly-in" at the airport in Auburn, Nebraska. As part of the event, attendees could pay $10 for a fifteen-minute airplane flight over the surrounding countryside. Auburn Flying's airplane crashed during one of these flights resulting in the deaths of the pilot and his three passengers. Auburn Flying was insured by Avemco Insurance Company at the time of the accident. Auburn Flying's policy was a noncommercial liability policy and excluded bodily injury and property damage when the aircraft was used for a "commercial purpose." "Commercial purpose" was defined as "any use of your insured aircraft for which an insured person receives, or intends to receive, money or other benefits." The exclusion did not include the equal sharing of the operating cost of a flight among occupants. Avemco filed a lawsuit seeking a judicial declaration that there was no coverage for the accident and resultant fatalities. Auburn Flying and representatives of the decedents claimed the exclusion was ambiguous and that Auburn Flying was not using the airplane for a commercial purpose at the time of the accident as the $10 fee was not sufficient to cover the operating expenses of the flights. Was the exclusion for "commercial purpose" ambiguous? Why or why not? [*Avemco Insurance Co. v. Auburn Flying Service, Inc.,* 242 F.3d 819 (8th Cir. 2001).]

7. On February 27, 1995, Eileen Nygaard's daughter committed suicide by driving her car into an 18-wheel tractor-trailer driven by Lonnie Odegard. As a result of the crash, Odegard developed problems that required surgery and forced him to miss work. Nygaard's insurance company, State Farm Insurance Company, refused to cover damages from the collision because Nygaard's daughter intended to commit suicide by driving into Odegard's truck. State Farm claimed the collision was not an "accident" as defined by the policy, which stated: "We will . . . pay damage which an insured becomes legally liable to pay because of bodily injury to others, and damage to or destruction of property including loss of its use, caused by accident and resulting from ownership, maintenance or use of your car." Odegard's insurance company brought suit against State Farm, and Nygaard joined the suit. The district court granted summary judgment for State Farm without any explanation. Nygaard appealed. The Minnesota Court of Appeals was required to determine whether the deceased's suicide qualified as an accident for the purpose of motor vehicle third-party coverage. Is this an accident for purposes of State Farm's insurance policy given the fact that Nygaard's suicide was an intentional act? Does the fact that Odegard was an innocent party and was not at fault for the circumstances that led to the crash influence your decision? [*Nygaard v. State Farm Insurance Co.,* 591 N.W.2d 738 (Minn. Ct. App. 1999).]

8. Amy and Wade Finley, Jr., were married in 1990. They faced fertility challenges and consequently produced and froze four embryos through an in vitro fertilization and embryo transfer program.

In July 2001, the couple was successful in their first attempt to implant an embryo, but Amy miscarried. Later in the same month, Wade Jr. was killed during the course and scope of his employment with Farm Cat, Inc. Farm Cat's workers' compensation carrier paid benefits to Amy. In June 2002, Amy went through another implantation process. This time, she became pregnant and gave birth to Wade III in March 2003. Amy then filed for workers' compensation benefits on behalf of Wade III, alleging that Wade III is the dependent child of Wade Jr. Farm Cat denied the claim. Will a court support Farm Cat's denial of the claim? [*Finley v. Farm Cat, Inc.*, 288 S.W.3d 685 (Ark. Ct. App. 2008).]

9. In June 2006, Jessica Koehler loaned her automobile to her boyfriend, Jesse Raddatz, for the purpose of driving to a convenience store. Instead, Raddatz picked up five friends and drove to a party in another town. Raddatz had an accident in which two of the occupants of the automobile were killed and the remaining four, including Jessica Seibert, suffered serious injuries. Seibert sued Wisconsin American Mutual Insurance Company, which had issued an insurance policy for the automobile in Koehler's father's name. American Mutual denied coverage on the basis that Raddatz did not qualify as an insured because he exceeded the scope of the permission for use of the automobile given to him by Koehler. Seibert claimed that Koehler knew that Raddatz did not have a valid driver's license but allowed him to use the automobile. As a result, Koehler's negligence was attributable to American Mutual. How far may one deviate from permission granted by an owner to use an automobile before insurance coverage will be extinguished? Should Koehler's poor judgment in allowing Raddatz to use the automobile be attributable to American Mutual? [*Seibert v. Wisconsin American Mutual Insurance Co.*, 542 F.3d 1060 (5th Cir. 2008).]

10. Liberte Capital Group was an Ohio-based investment company that purchased life insurance policies from policyholders who were terminally ill or who were elderly and in poor health, in exchange for payment of an up-front lump sum. When the customer/owner of the policy died, Liberte cashed in the policy for the full amount. Liberte persuaded three elderly individuals to purchase life insurance policies from Manufacturers Life Insurance Company (MLIC) and immediately assign the policies to Liberte. Liberte agreed to pay the premiums on the policies. These purchases were part of a larger scheme in which Liberte sold purchased life insurance policies to investors in return for $100 million. When the scheme failed and Liberte collapsed, MLIC sought to void the three policies in question. Liberte's receiver sued MLIC, seeking a refund of the insurance premiums paid by Liberte in an attempt to maximize the assets available to Liberte's creditors. The district court ruled in favor of the receiver, and MLIC appealed. Does Liberte have an insurable interest in this case? Why or why not? [*Wuliger v. Manufacturers Life Insurance Co.*, 567 F.3d 787 (6th Cir. 2009).]

Looking for more review materials?

The Online Learning Center at **www.mhhe.com/kubasek3e** contains this chapter's "Assignment on the Internet" and also a list of URLs for more information, entitled "On the Internet." Find both of them in the Student Center portion of the OLC, along with quizzes and other helpful materials.

Wills and Trusts

CHAPTER 52

LEARNING OBJECTIVES

After reading this chapter, you will be able to answer the following questions:

1. How does one engage in estate planning?
2. What legal issues relate to wills?
3. How are trusts used as estate planning tools?
4. What end-of-life decisions are important from a legal perspective?
5. How does international law protect wills?

CASE OPENER

The Danger of Preprinted Forms

In April 2004, Ann Aldrich wrote her will on an "E-Z Legal Form." In Article III, entitled "Bequests," Aldrich handwrote instructions stating that all of her listed possessions go to her sister Mary Jane Eaton. The list included Aldrich's house and contents, three bank accounts, an IRA, a life insurance policy, and an automobile. Aldrich also wrote that if her sister predeceased her, then all such property was devised to her brother James Aldrich. The will contained no other distributive provisions.

Mary Jane predeceased Ann in May 2007. Mary Jane's will left cash and land to Ann. Ann opened a new bank account for the cash. Ann died in October 2009 without having revised her will to account for the new bank account and land she inherited from Mary Jane. James claimed the new bank account and land upon Ann's death. However, Mary Jane's daughters (James's nieces) also claimed the new bank account and land. The nieces claimed that these assets passed to them as Ann's will did not contain a residuary clause stating that any other property in Ann's estate other than that listed under "Bequests" was to be inherited by James. The nieces claimed that the new bank account and land passed to them through intestate succession as Mary Jane's most direct relatives. James filed a lawsuit requesting that the court determine who was entitled to the new bank account and land.

1. How should the court decide this case? What was Ann's intent with respect to the disposition of her estate? Did she make this intent clear in her will?
2. What are the dangers of using preprinted forms without legal assistance?

The Wrap-Up at the end of the chapter will answer these questions.

This chapter focuses on what happens to an individual's property during his or her life and especially after life. Some people think carefully about how they want their property to be distributed; others die without expressing their wishes. State law protects the wishes individuals have outlined. Additionally, state law provides guidance for what to do with a person's property if the person did not express his or her wishes. Generally, then, this chapter focuses on state law regarding estate planning.

In particular, this chapter presents information about a wide range of topics, including a general discussion of estate planning, an overview of how to create a will, an outline of how individuals use trusts as estate planning tools, a summary of decisions individuals make at the end of life (e.g., what to do with the person's body), and an explanation of how wills are protected worldwide. This information helps individuals make informed decisions about what to do with their assets.

Estate Planning

L01

How does one engage in estate planning?

Estate planning is the process by which an individual decides what to do with his or her real and personal property during and after life. Estate planning also encourages individuals to make decisions about issues that frequently arise at the end of life, such as what to do with a person's organs and body after death.

THE UNIFORM PROBATE CODE

Laws that govern issues related to estate planning vary from state to state. As in other areas of law that this book covers, the National Conference of Commissioners on Uniform State Laws has developed uniform laws that make recommendations about what legal rules should govern a particular topic. One example of a uniform law that provides guidance in the area of estate planning is the **Uniform Probate Code,** which covers a wide range of topics, from wills to gifts to life insurance.

TOOLS OF ESTATE PLANNING

This chapter highlights wills and trusts because they are the most important tools of estate planning. A **will** is a legal document that outlines how a person wants his or her property distributed on death. As the Comparing the Law of Other Countries box explains, a **trust** allows a person to transfer property to another person, and this property is used for the benefit of a third person.

WHY INDIVIDUALS ENGAGE IN ESTATE PLANNING

Individuals engage in estate planning for a variety of reasons. Some people want to make sure they provide for their family financially after their death. Others want to arrange their property in ways that reduce taxes so that the family can preserve its wealth. Another purpose of estate planning is to promote family harmony. In other words, families fight less about assets after a loved one dies if that loved one expressed his or her wishes clearly. Finally, for nontraditional family arrangements, such as gay or lesbian couples or an unmarried heterosexual couple, careful estate planning can provide benefits that resemble those provided by marriage. For example, careful estate planning can ensure that a surviving member of a nontraditional couple can stay in the home the couple established during their life together.

Recently, courts have started to respond to issues that arise in nontraditional families. One form of nontraditional family is a family in which a surviving member of an unmarried heterosexual couple wants to conceive a child using the deceased partner's sperm.

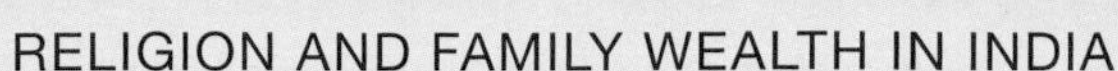

COMPARING THE LAW OF OTHER COUNTRIES

RELIGION AND FAMILY WEALTH IN INDIA

In the United States, we have developed certain legal constructs that allow families to pass assets from generation to generation in ways that help families accomplish particular goals, such as reducing taxes and making sure family assets are not mismanaged. One such construct is known as a *trust.* A trust allows a person to transfer property to another person, and this property is used for the benefit of a third person. This legal construct is consistent with our culture, which emphasizes freedom and individual decision making.

In countries such as India, legal constructs exist that are similar to trusts. However, whereas European civil law provides the underpinnings of trusts, in countries such as India religion provides the underpinnings of legal constructs that determine how families can pass wealth from generation to generation. India has a large Islamic population. Under the religious law of Islam, families can use what is known as a family *waqf* as a tool to manage family wealth.* The family *waqf* resembles a trust, although the beneficiary of a family *waqf* must have a religious, pious, or charitable purpose.

Some legal scholars have suggested that although *waqfs* and trusts are similar, the religious roots of the *waqf* have made this construct less flexible and responsive to change over time than the trust, with its secular roots.

* For additional information about the *waqf,* see Jeffrey A. Schoenblum, "The Role of Legal Doctrine in the Decline of the Islamic Waqf: A Comparison with the Trust," *Vanderbilt Journal of Transnational Law* 32 (1999), p.1191.

Case 52-1 considers the determination of heirs under state law in the context of modern science.

CASE 52-1 MATTISON v. SOCIAL SECURITY COMMISSIONER

MICHIGAN SUPREME COURT

2012 MICH. LEXIS 2222 (MICH., DEC. 21, 2012)

Pamela and Jeffery Mattison were married in 1995. In 1997, Pamela became pregnant with the aid of artificial insemination and gave birth to a daughter. Pamela and Jeffery wanted more children but were unable to conceive naturally because of Jeffery's medical conditions, which included lupus.

Because chemotherapy treatment for lupus would damage Jeffery's sperm, he interrupted his chemotherapy treatment and deposited his semen into a sperm bank, where it was frozen and stored. Soon after the birth of his daughter, Jeffery executed a general durable power of attorney that appointed Pamela as his attorney-in-fact. Included among the powers given to her was the authority to "take any and all action necessary pertaining to any sperm or embryos Jeffery may have stored including their implantation or termination."

In October 2000, Pamela and Jeffery began an in vitro fertilization program. Jeffery died unexpectedly in January 2001. Pamela continued the in vitro fertilization program after his death. Pamela's eggs were inseminated with Jeffery's sperm and transplanted into Pamela later in January 2001. As a result of the transplantation process, Pamela gave birth to twins in October 2001.

In October 2001, Pamela filed an application for social security survivors' benefits based on Jeffery's earnings records on behalf of her twins. The Social Security Administration denied the application on the basis that the twins were not entitled to inherit from Jeffery under Michigan intestacy law. Pamela filed a lawsuit against the Social Security Administration in August 2005 in the U.S. District Court for the Western District of Michigan. The district court certified the following question to the Michigan Supreme Court for determination: Whether the twins, conceived after the death of Jeffery Mattison via artificial insemination using his sperm, can inherit from Jeffery Mattison as his children under Michigan intestacy law.

JUSTICE KELLY: The Social Security Act authorizes disbursement of survivors' benefits for children who were dependent on a deceased worker before his or her death. As the United States Supreme Court has noted, the purpose of providing survivors' benefits is to protect children from a loss of support resulting from the death of a parent. However, not all children of a deceased parent are eligible for these benefits. To be eligible, an applicant must demonstrate that he or she (1) is the "child" of the deceased wage earner and (2) was dependent on that person at the time of that person's death.

The United States Supreme Court recently spoke on this subject in the case of *Astrue v Capato,* 132 S. Ct. 2021 (2012). The respondent's husband had died 18 months before she gave birth to twins conceived through in vitro fertilization using the decedent's frozen sperm. The respondent applied for social security survivors' benefits on their behalf. When the Social Security Administration denied her application, she brought an action in the courts to review the decision. . . . The United States Supreme Court . . . held that the question whether posthumously conceived children qualify for social security survivors' benefits must be determined under state intestacy law.

Michigan law has long established that the rights to intestate inheritance vest at the time of a decedent's death. They are governed by statutory provisions found in article II, part 1 of the Estates and Protected Individuals Code (EPIC).

Several EPIC provisions bear on whether plaintiff's twins can inherit from Jeffery. The first, MCL 700.2101(1), provides that "[a]ny part of a decedent's estate not effectively disposed of by will passes by intestate succession to the decedent's heirs as prescribed in this act. . . ." Next, MCL 700.2103 provides that "[a]ny part of the intestate estate that does not pass to the decedent's surviving spouse . . . passes . . . to [certain] . . . individuals who survive the decedent." MCL 700.1107(j) defines "survive" as meaning that "an individual neither predeceases an event, including the death of another individual, nor is considered to predecease an event. *Random House Webster's College Dictionary* (2001) similarly defines "survive" as, among other things, "**1.** to remain alive, as after the death of another or the occurrence of some event; continue to live . . . **4.** to continue to live or exist after the death, cessation, or occurrence of." Thus, to survive the death of another, one must be living at the time of that person's death.

Likewise, MCL 700.2106(3)(b) defines "surviving descendant" as "a descendant who neither predeceased the decedent nor is considered to have predeceased the decedent under [MCL 700.2104]." MCL 700.2104 states, "An individual who fails to survive the decedent by 120 hours is considered to have predeceased the decedent for purposes of . . . intestate succession, and the decedent's heirs are determined accordingly." Hence, an individual must be alive when the decedent dies and live more than 120 hours afterward to inherit from the decedent's estate under the laws of intestate succession.

Also relevant is MCL 700.2108 which states, "An individual in gestation at a particular time is treated as living at that time if the individual lives 120 hours or more after birth." Finally, MCL 700.2114(1)(a) provides, in pertinent part: If a child is born or conceived during a marriage, both spouses are presumed to be the natural parents of the child for purposes of intestate succession. A child conceived by a married woman with the consent of her husband following utilization of assisted reproductive technology is considered as their child for purposes of intestate succession.

On the basis of these provisions, there are two groups of people relevant to this case that may acquire intestate inheritance rights: (1) descendants alive at the moment of the decedent's death who live more than 120 hours immediately following the decedent's death and (2) descendants in gestation at the time of the decedent's death who live 120 hours after birth.

Considering these statutes, plaintiff's twins cannot inherit from Jeffery by intestate succession. The record shows that plaintiff's eggs were not inseminated with Jeffery's sperm and implanted until January 30, 2001, which was 12 days after Jeffery died. Because plaintiff's twins were not in gestation at Jeffery's death, no inheritance rights vested in them at that time pursuant to MCL 700.2108. Moreover, because the twins were not living at the time of his death, they had no inheritance rights as heirs pursuant to MCL 700.2104.

Nor does MCL 700.2114(1)(a) allow the twins to inherit from Jeffery. That statute indicates that, for purposes of intestate succession, a child is presumed to be the natural issue of both spouses if born or conceived during the marriage. It includes in that presumption children conceived by a married woman with the consent of her husband following the use of assisted reproductive technology. Applying that provision here, the twins were neither conceived nor born during plaintiff and Jeffery's marriage because marriage is a status that legally terminates upon the death of a spouse. Accordingly, the twins are not Jeffery's children for purposes of the state laws of intestate succession and, therefore, they cannot inherit from him.

In sum, nothing in EPIC or in other relevant statutory provisions contemplates intestate succession rights for plaintiff's twins. Because they were conceived and born after Jeffery's death, they did not survive him as his heirs in the eyes of the law. Therefore, we answer the certified question in the negative.

Judgment against the Plaintiff's claim that intestate succession rights extend to twins conceived after the death of the father.

CRITICAL THINKING

What was the basis for the court's determination that the twins were not Jeffery's heirs and thus could not inherit from him pursuant to applicable Michigan law? Is this the correct decision in this case given that other states would have decided this case differently on the basis of their laws? Should there be a national standard given these differences?

ETHICAL DECISION MAKING

The law has been slow to adapt to scientific and technological breakthroughs. How should courts deal with questions presented by scientific and technological developments that are far ahead of legal developments?

Legal Issues Related to Wills

LO2

What legal issues relate to wills?

In an ideal world, every person would write a legally valid will that clearly expresses the person's wishes about how his or her property should be distributed after death. Unfortunately, many people die without wills. In our rushed society, many people do not take the time to consult a lawyer about a will. Also, some people do not want to spend the money to seek legal advice about a will. Finally, a reality of life is that many people procrastinate. They simply might die before getting around to writing a will.

INTESTACY STATUTES

If a person dies without a will, state laws outline how the person's property will be distributed. These state laws are called **intestacy statutes.** When a person dies without a will, we say that the person died **intestate.** Intestacy statutes address issues such as the rights of a surviving spouse. Surprisingly, state laws vary regarding the amount a surviving spouse inherits when a spouse dies intestate. The surviving spouse usually splits real and personal property with children of the marriage, children not of the marriage (e.g., children from the deceased's previous marriage), and the deceased's parents. For instance, if a person dies intestate in the state of California, the surviving spouse receives all of the community property but only one-half of the separate property if there is only one surviving child. If there are two or more surviving children, the surviving spouse receives one-third and the children split the remaining two-thirds, regardless of whether they are children from the marriage. Parents inherit through intestate succession only if there are no surviving children. In Oregon, the surviving spouse generally receives *all* real and personal property, unless the intestate is survived by children not of the marriage, in which case the surviving spouse receives half the intestate's real and personal property.

The one legal document almost everyone will make is a last will and testament.

Legal Principle: **State law outlines what happens when an individual dies without a will.**

BUT WHAT IF . . .

WHAT IF THE FACTS OF THE CASE OPENER WERE DIFFERENT?

Let's say, in the Case Opener, that the bank account and land that Ann inherited from Mary Jane would automatically go to Mary Jane's daughters according to the laws in the daughters' state of Montana, so they said that they were entitled to the money and land. However, James argued that the law would be different under intestacy statutes in Ann's home state because intestacy is regulated by state law. Who is correct in this scenario?

REQUIREMENTS FOR A LEGALLY VALID WILL

Individuals should create legally valid wills so that their own wishes control what happens to their property and children. Otherwise, the wishes of a state legislature will control, and legislators may or may not place the same importance on the roles of particular family

Exhibit 52-1
Requirements for a Legally Valid Will

- Testamentary capacity
- Writing
- Testator's signature
- Attestation

members in a person's life. Small business owners also should create wills. They need to make some decisions in advance, such as who will inherit the business, how power and assets will be transferred, and who will run the business if the owner is incapacitated for a period of time.

A person who writes a will is called a **testator.** A will is generally valid if it meets four requirements (see Exhibit 52-1). First, the testator must have **testamentary capacity,** which means that the person must be old enough to write a will (age 18 in most states) and be of sound mind. Courts decide whether a person is of sound mind by considering whether the testator knows the extent of his or her property, understands traditions regarding who should get the property (even though the testator does not have to follow tradition), knows he or she is making a will, and is not delusional. Second, a will almost always must be in *writing* to be valid. The writing may take a variety of forms, but usually a will is typewritten on regular paper. It is possible, however, for a legally valid will to be written in handwriting on a pillowcase! One exception to the writing requirement is that a person may make a verbal will as he or she is about to die. (Exhibit 52-2 explains some special kinds of wills.) Third, the person writing the will must *sign* the will. Usually, a person signs his or her name at the end of the will and signs or initials each page to make sure no one adds or omits a page after the testator dies. Fourth, witnesses must *attest* to the will. A witness must witness the signing of the will and then sign as a witness at the end of the document. A person who will receive property under a will, a **beneficiary,** cannot be a witness. Also, witnesses must be of sound mind.

As we become more technology-dependent, small businesses have arisen to respond to our changing needs. For example, Legacy Locker makes it easy for individuals to pass along digital items upon death. For less than $30 a year, a person can set up a "digital will," giving beneficiaries access to digital assets, including photos, videos, and e-mail correspondence. Legacy Locker makes it possible to pass on log-in credentials. Without Legacy Locker, a court would have to issue an order for individuals to gain access to digital items.

GROUNDS FOR CONTESTING A WILL

When a person with *standing* (an interest in a will, such as that of a potential beneficiary) has doubts about whether a particular will is legally valid, he or she may contest the will. Usually, wills are contested in two circumstances. First, a person contests a will if she

Exhibit 52-2
Special Kinds of Wills

Oral	A will that the testator declares verbally during his or her last illness, in front of witnesses, who later write the person's wishes.
Holographic	A will that the testator writes or signs in his or her own handwriting. Usually, states do not require witnesses because when the entire will is in handwriting, there is less chance of fraud or forgery.
Mutual	A will that two or more testators execute in which they leave property to each other as long as the survivor agrees that when he or she dies, the remaining property will be distributed according to a plan created by all testators.

believes that the will does not meet the four criteria outlined in the preceding section. For instance, a person might doubt whether the testator was of sound mind when he wrote the will or might think that the will was not signed or witnessed properly.

Second, a person contests a will if she believes that although the will is technically valid, the testator was a victim of **fraud** or **undue influence.** Fraud occurs when the testator relied on false statements when he made the will. Undue influence occurs when the testator wrote the will under circumstances in which a person he trusted took advantage of his weak physical or emotional condition to persuade him to write the will in a particular way.

Case 52-2 illustrates allegations of undue influence and fraud.

CASE 52-2 MCDANIEL v. MCDANIEL

SUPREME COURT OF GEORGIA

707 S.E.2D 60 (GA. 2011)

Mary McDaniel was married to Luther McDaniel for over 60 years, until her death at age 87 in December 2006. Luther died two-and-a-half years later in June 2009 at the age of 92. The McDaniels had two sons, Charles (the caveator) and Jerry (the propounder).

In 2002, Luther and Mary, who were then in their 80s, executed wills prepared by their attorney, James Clyde Morris, Jr., leaving everything to the surviving spouse, and if there was no surviving spouse, to their two sons equally. Mary suffered from Alzheimers-related dementia and other ailments, and by 2006, Luther could no longer care for her on his own. The caveator moved in with his parents in January 2006, and for the first part of that year, the propounder and his wife stayed with Luther some weekends to alleviate the burden on the caveator. Over the course of 2006, Luther and Mary added the caveator's name to all their bank accounts so that he could manage their financial affairs for them.

Luther exhibited several common signs of dementia. After Mary died, the propounder and his wife encouraged the caveator and his wife to take a much-needed vacation to Florida. Before leaving, the caveator drove Luther to several banks to remove Mary's name from joint accounts worth several hundred thousand dollars. The caveator also closed an account at Regions Bank worth approximately $32,000 that had been held jointly in his and Mary's names and transferred the funds into a new account in his name only. This was in accordance with Mary's wishes to provide for her and Luther's funerals.

Unbeknownst to the caveator, the propounder and his wife believed that the caveator had stolen from Luther the roughly $600,000 they estimated was held in the joint bank accounts by having his name added to the accounts. They convinced Luther that the caveator had stolen all his money, that he was now "broke," and that the caveator and his wife had moved to Florida and were not coming back. The testator was confused and distraught, and he repeated these claims to other relatives, as did the propounder.

The propounder and his wife drove Luther to the banks, where he removed the caveator's name from all the joint accounts. The propounder changed the locks on Luther's house. The propounder also had Morris draft a new will in which Luther left all of his assets to the propounder other than 10% to his granddaughter and 1% to his grandson. The caveator was not included in the will. The propounder and his wife moved the testator into the basement of their home in December 2007, where he lived until his death in June 2009. The caveator was not allowed to visit Luther without first making an appointment with the propounder, and the propounder told the caveator that he was recording the visits. The propounder also attempted to make the caveator "sign in" on a register whenever he visited.

After Luther's death, the propounder filed a petition to probate the 2007 will, and the caveator objected. The probate court found that the 2007 will was not valid on the grounds of undue influence and fraud, and the propounder appealed.

JUSTICE NAHMIAS: The sole question in a proceeding to probate a will in solemn form is "whether the paper propounded is, or is not, the last will and testament of the deceased." *In re Estate of Corbitt,* 454 S.E.2d 129 (1995). The result turns on three issues: (1) whether the document was properly executed; (2) whether the testator had the mental capacity to execute a will; and (3) whether the document was the result of undue influence, fraud, duress, or mistake. The caveator conceded due execution of the will, and the jury found in favor of the propounder on the issue of testamentary capacity. The propounder contends that the probate court erred in denying his motion for directed verdict on undue influence and fraud.

"Undue influence 'may take many forms and may operate through diverse channels.'" There is no requirement that the undue influence be directly attributable to the propounder or to a single beneficiary. Although evidence which merely shows an opportunity to influence is not itself sufficient, a

[continued]

"caveat based upon the ground of undue influence may be supported by a wide range of evidence, as such influence can seldom be shown except by circumstantial evidence." *Bailey v. Edmundson,* 630 S.E.2d 396 (2006). Absent legal error on the part of the probate court, a jury's finding of undue influence will be affirmed "if there is any evidence to support the trier of fact's determination." *Trotman v. Forrester,* 279 Ga. 844, 845 (621 S.E.2d 724) (2005).

The jury in this case was clearly authorized to find that the 2007 will was the result of undue influence. When the testator could no longer care for his sick wife of over 60 years, the caveator moved in with them and provided the care his mother and father needed with little help from the propounder. After Ms. McDaniel died, the propounder and his wife encouraged the caveator and his wife to leave the state for a vacation and in their absence poisoned the testator's mind against the caveator, telling him falsely that the caveator had stolen all his money, that he was now broke, and that the caveator had abandoned him and would not return. The propounder and his wife also participated in the preparation of the 2007 will.

Furthermore, acting under the influence of the propounder and his wife, the testator secured a restraining order that prevented the caveator from seeing him for six months after the caveator returned from Florida, and the propounder made sure that the caveator was never left alone with their father again. Although the jury found that the testator had sufficient testamentary capacity, he was elderly and showing signs of declining mental acuity before the 2007 will was executed, and his symptoms had increased after his wife passed just a few weeks earlier.

Finally, the 2007 will radically changed the distribution of the estate envisioned by the testator's 2002 will, which would have divided the estate equally between the testator's two grown sons, to a scheme awarding 89% of the estate to the propounder and nothing to the caveator. We therefore conclude that evidence regarding "the circumstances and surroundings of the testator and his associations" authorized the jury's finding that the 2007 will was the product of undue influence.

There was also sufficient evidence to support the jury's finding that the will was procured by fraud. The evidence showed that after the propounder and his wife encouraged the caveator and his wife to go on vacation in Florida, they embarked on a campaign to convince the testator that the caveator had stolen all his money, left him broke, and abandoned him by moving to Florida. These were misrepresentations, but they worked; the testator changed his will to disinherit the caveator completely. As a result of these misrepresentations, the testator went into the meeting with the attorney who drafted the 2007 will intending to leave his entire estate to the propounder, and he would have done so were it not for the attorney's suggestion that he leave something to the caveator's children, who were the testator's grandchildren. Accordingly, we conclude that the evidence supports the jury's finding that the 2007 will was procured through misrepresentation and fraudulent practices upon the testator's fears, affections, or sympathies.

The evidence supports the jury's findings of undue influence and fraud, and the probate court's evidentiary rulings were not an abuse of discretion.

AFFIRMED in favor of the appellee.

CRITICAL THINKING

What were the critical factors identified by the court with respect to undue influence and fraud in this case?

ETHICAL DECISION MAKING

How far should courts go to protect the elderly and infirm from undue influence and fraud, especially in cases, such as this one, in which the testator possessed adequate mental capacity at the time of the making of the 2007 will?

Legal Principle: **Even when a will is legally valid (i.e., is signed and in writing), individuals can contest the will. For example, they can claim that the will was created under undue influence.**

CHANGING A WILL

Wills are **ambulatory,** which means testators can change them. It is not uncommon for people to change their wills several times during their life. People change their wills through **codicils,** which are separate documents with new provisions that outline changes to the will. Testators must go through the same procedures to make a valid codicil as those followed in making the original will. For instance, testators must sign the codicil in front of witnesses. After a person writes a codicil, it is read with the will as a unit that expresses the testator's wishes.

Case 52-3 illustrates problems that arise when a testator tries to change a will without the assistance of a lawyer. The case involves Charles Kuralt, the journalist known for his CBS show *On the Road.*

CASE 52-3 IN RE THE ESTATE OF CHARLES KURALT, DECEASED

SUPREME COURT OF MONTANA

981 P.2D 771 (1999)

This case arose when Charles Kuralt died, leaving behind both a wife and a secret intimate companion, with whom he had a close personal relationship for nearly thirty years. Mr. Kuralt was hospitalized on June 18, 1997, after he became suddenly ill. He died on July 4, 1997. After his death, his wife, Petie, filed proof of authority to probate certain property in Montana. Petie did not know about her husband's secret intimate companion until Patricia Elizabeth Shannon (Shannon) filed a petition for ancillary probate of will, claiming a letter Kuralt wrote on June 18, 1997, and mailed to her constituted a valid holographic will with regard to the Montana property.

At issue in the case is the language in the letter dated June 18, 1997. Mr. Kuralt had taken three actions prior to June 19, 1997, to clarify what he wanted to happen to his property upon his death. On May 3, 1989, he executed a holographic will in which he bequeathed certain Montana property to Shannon. On May 4, 1997, Kuralt executed a formal will in which he devised all his property to his wife, Petie. On April 9, 1997, Mr. Kuralt deeded his interest to certain land in Montana to Shannon. He transferred a twenty-acre parcel of land with a cabin along the Big Hole River to Shannon through a sham sale; he disguised the transaction to look like a sale even though he gave Shannon the $80,000 needed to buy the parcel. Shannon and Kuralt agreed to the "sale" of an additional ninety acres along the Black Hole River. The sale was to be consummated in September 1997. Unfortunately for Shannon, Mr. Kuralt became ill and died prior to the transaction.

Here is what the June 18, 1997, letter said:

> *Dear Pat—*
> *Something is terribly wrong with me and they can't figure out what. After cat-scans and a variety of cardiograms, they agree it's not lung cancer or heart trouble or blood clot. So they're putting me in the hospital today to concentrate on infectious diseases. I am getting worse, barely able to get out of bed, but still have high hopes for recovery . . . if only I can get a diagnosis! Curiouser and curiouser! I'll keep you informed. I'll have the lawyer visit the hospital to be sure you inherit the rest of the place in MT if it comes to that.*
> *I send love to you & [your youngest daughter,] Shannon. Hope things are better there!*
> *Love,*
> *C.*

Shannon sought to probate this letter dated June 18, 1997, as a valid holographic codicil to Mr. Kuralt's formal 1994 will. She did so because she wanted to make sure she got the ninety acres of Montana property she believed Mr. Kuralt wanted her to have.

A district court in Madison County, Montana, ruled that the estate should be granted a summary judgment regarding the June 18 letter. The district court rejected Shannon's claim that the letter was a valid holographic codicil and Shannon appealed. In the following case, the highest court of Montana decides whether the lower court was correct in granting the estate a summary judgment. If the lower court erred, Shannon will be allowed to present evidence in a trial of Kuralt's intent regarding who should get the Montana property.

JUSTICE W. WILLIAM LEAPHART: We disagree with the Estate's position that Shannon's extrinsic evidence is "immaterial" to the question of testamentary intent, and is merely "an insubstantial attempt to manufacture a material issue of fact." Rather, we agree with Shannon that the District Court improperly resolved contested issues of material fact when it found, in support of its conclusion that the letter "clearly contemplates a separate testamentary instrument not yet in existence," that: The extrinsic evidence—none of which is contested—confirms this conclusion. Petitioner herself testified during her deposition and at trial that the decedent intended to "sell"—not "will"—the Montana property to her in the fall of 1998 [*sic*]. While the extrinsic evidence substantiates a close and personal relationship between Petitioner and the decedent extending over twenty-nine years, during which she and her children were apparently entirely housed, supported, educated, and temporarily set up in business by the decedent, those facts are not sufficient to create a testamentary intent which the language of the letter clearly refutes.

When drawing all reasonable inference in favor of Shannon, as the party opposed to summary judgment, we conclude that the extrinsic evidence raises a genuine issue of material fact as to whether Mr. Kuralt intended to gift, rather than sell, the remaining ninety acres of his Madison County property to Shannon. The plain language of the letter of June 18, 1997, indicates, as Shannon points out, that Mr. Kuralt desired that Shannon "inherit" all of his property along the Big Hole River. While other language in the letter—"I'll have the lawyer visit the hospital . . . if it comes to that"—might

[continued]

suggest, as the Estate argues and as the District Court concluded, that Mr. Kuralt was contemplating a separate testamentary instrument not yet in existence, it is far from certain that this is the result Mr. Kuralt intended by the letter.

At the very least, when reading the language of the letter in light of the extrinsic evidence showing the couple's future plans to consummate the transfer of the remaining ninety acres vis-à-vis a mock "sale," there arises a question of material fact as to whether Mr. Kuralt intended, given the state of serious illness, that the very letter of June 18, 1997, effect a posthumous disposition of his ninety acres of Madison County. Nor are the parties merely arguing different interpretations of the facts here; we have, in this case, a fundamental disagreement as to a genuine material fact which would be better reconciled by trial.

. . . We hold that, because there is a genuine issue of material fact, the District Court erred in granting judgment as a matter of law. Accordingly, we reverse the court's grant of summary judgment and remand, for trial, the factual question of whether, in light of the extrinsic evidence, Mr. Kuralt intended the letter of June 18, 1997, to effect a testamentary disposition of the ninety acres in Madison County to Shannon.

REVERSED and REMANDED.

CRITICAL THINKING

As a critical thinker, you want to be able to identify strengths as well as weaknesses in arguments. What is particularly good about this court's reasoning in deciding in favor of Shannon?

ETHICAL DECISION MAKING

Compare the universalization and Golden Rule guidelines as they apply to the facts of this case. Which guideline best supports Petie Kuralt's perspective on what should happen to her husband's assets?

REVOKING A WILL

In Case 52-3, Kuralt could have clarified his intent regarding property for Shannon by clearly *revoking,* or canceling, the formal will he executed in May 1997. He could have revoked the 1997 will by physically destroying it. Then he could have executed a new will that made it clear he had revoked the 1997 will. Instead, he initiated sham sales of property so that his wife would not find out about his secret intimate companion.

SETTLEMENT OF AN ESTATE

When someone dies, a **personal representative** chosen by the testator collects the testator's property, pays debts and taxes, and makes sure the remainder of the estate is distributed. He or she makes sure that *gifts* of real and personal property go to the correct *beneficiaries,* persons who inherit under a will. The process of settling an estate is known as **probate.**

Some property a person owns does not become part of the estate. Property that is not part of the probate estate is called **nonprobate property.** The most important forms of nonprobate property are life insurance with named beneficiaries, pension plan distributions, and property held in certain kinds of trusts, which are described in the next section.

LO3 How are trusts used as estate planning tools?

Trusts as Estate Planning Tools

HOW AND WHY INDIVIDUALS CREATE TRUSTS

A person who creates a trust is called a **settlor.** A settlor delivers and transfers legal title to property to another person, called a **trustee,** who holds the property and uses it for the benefit of a third person. This third person is called the *beneficiary.* Trusts are usually created through formal, written documents.

Trusts usually have two components: income and the trust corpus. The trust corpus is the property held in trust, while the income is generated by the trust through interest or appreciation. Often, income is paid to an **income beneficiary,** who may or may not have access to the trust corpus. When the trust is terminated, a designated person called a **remainderman** gets the trust corpus.

BUT WHAT IF . . .

WHAT IF THE FACTS OF THE CASE OPENER WERE DIFFERENT?

Let's say, in the Case Opener, that Mary Jane had put the bank account and the land in a trust for her daughters many years before she died. After her death, the daughters want to find out exactly what they will be receiving when the items are taken out of the trust. What exactly will the girls receive? What are the two parts of a trust?

Individuals create trusts for a variety of reasons. Sometimes, a person creates a trust because he wants to protect another person. A settlor can even create a trust to protect an animal. For instance, a person can create a trust to provide for her beloved pet. Settlors also create trusts to prevent individuals from getting access to certain assets. For instance, the Wrigley family, known for its chewing gum, placed Wrigley Company stock in trusts and made family members income beneficiaries, not owners of the stock itself.[1] The significance of these legal actions is that when Wrigley family members marry and later divorce, the outsider who married a Wrigley family member cannot get Wrigley Company stock because it is "separately owned" property that cannot be divided on divorce. A final reason settlors create trusts is to avoid paying taxes. For instance, a person might create a charitable trust to avoid paying federal estate tax.

BASIC KINDS OF TRUSTS

Two basic kinds of trusts exist. The most common kind of trust is the **express trust.** An express trust is a trust the settlor creates either while he or she is alive **(living trust)** or by will **(testamentary trust).** Usually, express trusts are written and called trust *instruments* or *agreements.*

A second kind of trust is the **implied trust.** Implied trusts are also called *involuntary trusts* because courts, rather than settlors, create them. Courts create implied trusts in two situations. The first occurs when an express trust fails and the court can imply a trust from certain behavior. For instance, if a person pays for property and names a different person on the title, a court can infer that the person intended to create a trust. This kind of trust is a *resulting trust.* The second situation occurs when the law steps in to protect someone from fraud or other wrongdoing. A court creates a **constructive trust** to hold property in trust for its rightful owner. For instance, a court can place assets of a partnership in a constructive trust if it discovers that one partner is engaging in fraudulent or unconscionable conduct that might negatively affect the interests of another partner.

Many people who acquire a considerable amount of wealth worry about what that wealth will do to their families. They often create special kinds of trusts. They wonder: Will my family members start to fight over the family business? If I give my children money and assets, will they end up lacking character? Will my children be reluctant to work hard if I give them too much? One new kind of trust is a **family incentive trust.** This kind of trust responds to concerns raised by wealthy businesspersons, who worry about what their wealth might do to their families. With a family incentive trust, the person who

[1] For more information about the expert estate planning related to the Wrigley family, see Darryl Van Duch, "Double Wrigley Trouble," *National Law Journal,* May 31, 1999, p. A01.

E-COMMERCE AND THE LAW

DO YOU NEED A WILL IN A HURRY?

If you need a will in a hurry, what better way to create one than to do one yourself with help from forms available on the Internet? One advertisement on the web says: "Save Time and Money!! Why go to an attorney when you can make your own Will and Trust? These are easy-to-use documents that you can individually customize for your specific needs."*

Is it true? Should you avoid the time, energy, and money it takes to have a lawyer prepare a will or trust when you can write your own using forms available on the Internet?

The best answer is, "It depends." For some people, creating a will using an easy-to-use form available on the Internet is better than not having a will at all. However, the risks of making mistakes by using such forms are high. The risks of using these forms come in two varieties. First, it is risky to use the forms if your family structure is complicated. For instance, if you have a family with the standard grandparents, parents, children, and grandchildren, all of whom get along and treat one another fairly, perhaps the forms will work for you. If, however, the parents are separated or divorced, grandmother has a secret lover, and grandfather wants to disinherit unruly grandchildren, you will probably need to consult a lawyer. Second, it is risky to use the forms if family property is complicated. For example, if your family has standard assets, such as a handful of heirlooms, one large house, few investments, and little accumulated wealth, perhaps the forms will work for you. In contrast, if your family has accumulated so much wealth that estate taxes are a concern or if the family needs to create one or more trusts, you need to consult an attorney.

The primary reason you should be cautious about using forms available on the Internet is that the law of trusts and estates has its own special language and you might not know enough about legal terms to write a will or trust that expresses your wishes. Do you know the difference between personal property and tangible property? (*Personal property* is all property other than real property, while *tangible property* is any real or personal property that can be possessed physically.) Between distribution *per stirpes* and distribution *per capita?* (Distribution *per stirpes* means distributing an estate by class or representation, while distribution *per capita* means distributing an estate by the individual.) Between a devise and a behest? (A *devise* is a gift of real property by will, while a *behest* is a gift of personal property.) When you consult a lawyer, he or she will know legal terminology and have a good understanding of the law of your particular state.

* www.easylegalforms.com.

designs the trust can create incentives for certain behavior. For instance, the trust can pay "awards" to family members who make significant contributions in certain fields, such as education, science, law, or medicine. The trust can also pay a sum of money to descendants who obtain graduate degrees. By creating family incentive trusts, wealthy individuals can promote the kind of behavior that matters to them.

Legal Principle: When individuals use careful estate planning, they make their wishes clear and protect their loved ones.

HOW TRUSTS ARE TERMINATED

A settlor is not allowed to revoke a trust unless he or she reserves a right to revoke the trust. Usually, a trust includes a provision that specifies the date on which the trust will terminate. Alternatively, the trust document states that the trust will terminate when an event happens, such as when the remainderman reaches a certain age. For instance, Diana, princess of Wales, created a trust that ended when Princes William and Harry reached the age of 30.

End-of-Life Decisions

LO4

What end-of-life decisions are important from a legal perspective?

ADVANCE DIRECTIVES

In 1990, in *Cruzan v. Director, Missouri Department of Health,*[2] the U.S. Supreme Court made a decision that indicated that a person has a constitutionally protected right under the Fourteenth Amendment to refuse life-sustaining medical procedures. Since that time,

[2] 497 U.S. 261 (1990).

CASE NUGGET

TORTIOUS INTERFERENCE WITH THE EXPECTANCY OF INHERITANCE OR GIFT

Beckwith v. Dahl
141 Cal. Rptr. 3d 142 (Ca. Ct. App. 2012)

Brent Beckwith and Marc MacGinnis maintained long-standing personal and business relationships. MacGinnis's sole living relative was his sister Susan Dahl, with whom he was estranged. On his computer, MacGinnis maintained a copy of his will, which divided his estate between Beckwith and Dahl. However, MacGinnis never printed the will or signed it.

In May 2009, MacGinnis was hospitalized, awaiting surgery to repair holes in his lungs. He requested that Beckwith print a copy of the will for him to sign. Beckwith could not find the will on MacGinnis's computer but downloaded a form from the Internet and completed it to provide for equal division of MacGinnis's estate between Beckwith and Dahl. Beckwith also contacted Dahl about the will. Dahl told Beckwith that she was in favor of creating a trust and that she would contact attorneys to draw up the trust documents. Dahl requested that Beckwith not present the will to MacGinnis for signature. Beckwith obeyed these instructions, and MacGinnis never signed the will. Dahl never presented MacGinnis with trust documents to sign.

After the surgery, the doctors refused to discuss MacGinnis's health with Beckwith as he was not a family member. Dahl had MacGinnis removed from life support six days after the surgery as his condition worsened. MacGinnis died intestate and left an estate valued at more than $1 million. Beckwith subsequently sued Dahl for intentional interference with the expectation of inheritance (IIEI) after it became clear that she intended to claim the entire estate for herself.

The California court of appeals was confronted with the question of whether it should recognize the tort of IIEI, which had heretofore not been recognized in the state. The court reviewed a law review article surveying recognition of the tort as well as cases from states in which the tort was recognized, such as Tennessee and Indiana. The court identified five elements to the tort: (1) an expectation of receiving an inheritance; (2) an intentional interference with the expectation by a third party; (3) the interference was wrongful; (4) but for the interference, the plaintiff would have received the inheritance; and (5) damages. The court also concluded that public policy grounds supported recognition of IIEI. The court remanded the case to the trial court in order to give Beckwith an opportunity to present evidence indicative of the occurrence of IIEI in this case.

states have clarified the nature and extent of this liberty interest by clarifying common and statutory law related to a patient's **right to die.** The right to die refers to a person's right to place limits on other people's efforts to prolong her or his life. A person can express his or her wishes regarding these limits through **advance directives,** which include a variety of legal instruments. The most frequently used advance directives are the living will, health care proxy, and durable power of attorney. Individuals who are gravely ill may use one or more of these instruments to express their wishes.

Nearly every state has enacted statutes that allow people to express their wishes regarding the extent of medical treatment they want if an accident or illness prevents them from participating in making medical decisions. The document that allows them to express their wishes is called a **living will.** Usually, a person who writes a living will does so because he wants to make sure that he dies a natural death and that his death is not prolonged through medical or surgical treatment. A person who writes a living will must make sure that it complies with the legal requirements of his particular state. The Internet assignment at the end of the chapter provides direction about how to find the particular requirements of your state.

Some states have passed laws that allow an agent to make medical decisions for a principal who is unable to participate in medical decisions. The document that outlines this principal-agent relationship is called a **health care proxy.** Some states outline instead a **durable power of attorney,** which is similar to a health care proxy. A durable power of attorney is a written document executed when the principal is in good mental health that allows an agent to make medical decisions for the principal at some later date when the principal can no longer make decisions. For example, a patient in the early stages of Alzheimer disease could execute a durable power of attorney that allows another person, such as a spouse, to make medical decisions once that patient is no longer able to do so.

Legal Principle: The law has provided and supported mechanisms that make end-of-life decisions clearer.

CASE NUGGET

THE TERRY SCHIAVO CASE

In re Guardianship of Schiavo
851 So. 2d 182 (Fla. Dist. Ct. App. 2003)
("Schiavo IV")

In April 2005, Terry Schiavo died, 15 years after she had a heart attack and lapsed into a vegetative state. After a seven-year legal battle between her husband, Michael Schiavo, and her parents, Robert and Mary Schindler, a court granted permission to terminate life support. In the Schiavo case, life support was a feeding tube. The Schiavo case was the longest-running, most politically charged right-to-die battle in recent U.S. history.

The case is significant because it demonstrates what happens when a person fails to express her wishes with regard to end-of-life decisions. As a judge in one of many Schiavo cases stated: "It may be unfortunate that when families cannot agree, the best forum we can offer for this private, personal decision is a public courtroom and the best decision-maker we can provide is a judge with no prior knowledge of the ward, but the law currently provides no better solution that adequately protects the interests of promoting the value of life."

The judge's words in Schiavo IV make clear the extent to which, in the absence of an advance directive, judges are likely to view themselves as protectors of life. It is in everyone's best interests to write down the circumstances in which they do and do not want protection.

BUT WHAT IF . . .

WHAT IF THE FACTS OF THE CASE OPENER WERE DIFFERENT?

Let's say, in the Case Opener, that Ann became very sick toward the end of her life and she was in a lot of pain. She was stuck in a hospital with doctors administering tests and medications to her frequently. Ann decided she did not want the doctors performing the tests or any other life-sustaining activities anymore. Was that a legally permissible decision to make?

ANATOMICAL GIFTS

The Uniform Anatomical Gifts Act (UAGA) has been adopted by every state in the United States. This law provides that any individual age 18 or older may give all or any part of his or her body to a donee on death. These donations are **anatomical gifts.** Individuals may donate parts of their body or their whole body to a hospital, physician, surgeon, medical or dental school, college or university, organ bank, or any person they specify who needs a transplant.

The UAGA has made it possible for thousands of people to receive organ transplants. In the United States, surgeons use a brain-death standard rather than a heart-lung standard to determine death. The brain-death standard allows surgeons to make use of organs such as the heart, lungs, liver, and kidney. You will see in the Comparing the Law of Other Countries box that cultural and religious beliefs about the body affect individual and familial decisions about what to do with organs on death. A person may express his or her wishes regarding organ donation in more than one way. A person may donate organs by expressing this gift through language in a will. Also, a person may sign a document such as an **organ donor card** that expresses his or her desire to donate organs or tissue. Sometimes donors register with a national donor registry, such as the Living Bank. In some states, the administrative agency that registers motor vehicles creates and maintains a program that allows people to make anatomical gifts when they receive a driver's license. It is common for a person's driver's license to identify the person as an organ donor. Finally, adult members of a person's family sometimes make decisions related to anatomical gifts.

CHOICES ABOUT THE BODY AFTER DEATH

When a person dies, someone has to decide what to do with the body. The best scenario occurs when the decedent made his or her wishes about the body clear. Sometimes people

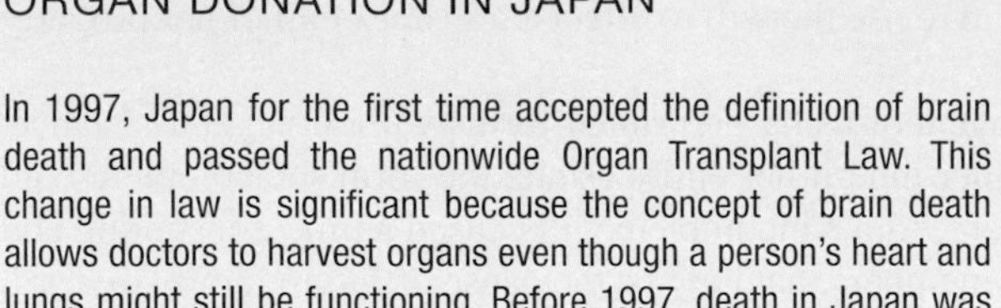

COMPARING THE LAW OF OTHER COUNTRIES

ORGAN DONATION IN JAPAN

In 1997, Japan for the first time accepted the definition of brain death and passed the nationwide Organ Transplant Law. This change in law is significant because the concept of brain death allows doctors to harvest organs even though a person's heart and lungs might still be functioning. Before 1997, death in Japan was official only when the heart stopped beating.

The law changed again in 2010 to permit organ transplants from children to address the needs of a growing number of parents who were seeking organs for their children outside Japan. The law also dropped the written consent requirement and permitted potential donors to note their consent on medical insurance cards and driver's licenses. This provision was designed to provide alternatives to the *ishihyōji kado* (donor card) which had been the only means by which to demonstrate consent. However, family members may veto organ donation in the absence of consent.

Japan has one of the lowest rates of organ transplantation in the developed world. For example, kidney transplant rates in Western Europe are 25 to 40 times the rate in Japan. The U.S. transplantation rate for kidneys is 30 times that of Japan. The waiting list for organ transplants is very long. Many Japanese patients receive transplants in the United States, United Kingdom, and other countries. Some people are concerned that the unwillingness of the Japanese to donate organs creates an unfair situation in which Japan burdens individuals in other countries by taking organs without adding organs to the pool of organs available for transplant.

Although the law has changed in Japan, it is unlikely that the Japanese will be quick to favor organ donation. Doctors will declare brain death, but the Japanese law allows families to veto this diagnosis. It is likely that many families will reject the diagnosis because of different cultural norms regarding bodies and death. In Japan, many view death as a process, not a specific point in time. Also, religious traditions in Japan shape attitudes toward brain death. Many believe that respect for the dead ensures the welfare of the living. Additionally, some cultural traditions require that a corpse be buried intact. Some religious beliefs assert that the spirit of the deceased will be content only if there is no violence to the body. Organ removal is one form of violence to the body. Perhaps most important, for the Japanese, the mind and body are one. And no matter what the law says, it is the heart, not the brain, that controls the body.

have clearly outlined wishes regarding whether the family should cremate their remains, what kind of funeral service they should have, and whether the body should be buried or be donated to a hospital or university for scientific study.

International Protection for Wills

LO5 How does international law protect wills?

In 1973, official delegates of 42 countries met in Washington, D.C., to adopt the Convention Providing for a Uniform Law on the Form of an International Will. The convention was sponsored by the International Institute for the Unification of Private Law (UNIDROIT). UNIDROIT is an independent intergovernmental organization that prepares uniform private laws that strive to promote harmony and unity in private law worldwide. Those who signed the 1973 convention for uniform law agreed to accept wills of other signatories for probate, as to matters of form, if such wills are executed with the provisions of the convention.

CASE OPENER WRAP-UP

The Danger of Preprinted Forms

The Florida court of appeals held that the nieces were entitled to the cash in the new bank account and the land inherited by Ann from Mary Jane. The court concluded that partial intestacy results when a will fails to dispose of all of the decedent's property through a residuary clause. Such property is subject to disposition pursuant to the provisions of Florida's intestacy statute. According to the court, Ann's intent was for James to inherit only the property listed in the bequest section, with rights to any additional property to be determined by applicable Florida law. Ann's will could be reasonably construed only in this manner, and the court refused to revise the will to effect a transfer of all of her property to James.[3]

This case demonstrates the dangers of using preprinted forms without legal assistance. If Ann truly intended that her brother inherit her entire estate, the form she completed did not evidence this intent. Furthermore, Ann's incomplete will caused a time-consuming and expensive lawsuit between family members that may be the cause of future family discord. The lesson to be learned from this case is that form documents are valuable but can never take the place of advice and guidance from an attorney.

KEY TERMS

advance directives 1161
ambulatory 1156
anatomical gifts 1162
beneficiary 1154
codicils 1156
constructive trust 1159
durable power of attorney 1161
estate planning 1150
express trust 1159
family incentive trust 1159
fraud 1155
health care proxy 1161
implied trust 1159
income beneficiary 1159
intestacy statutes 1153
intestate 1153
living trust 1159
living will 1161
nonprobate property 1158
organ donor card 1162
personal representative 1158
probate 1158
remainderman 1159
right to die 1161
settlor 1158
testamentary capacity 1154
testamentary trust 1159
testator 1154
trust 1150
trustee 1158
undue influence 1155
Uniform Probate Code 1150
will 1150

SUMMARY OF KEY TOPICS

Estate Planning

Estate planning is the process by which an individual decides what to do with his or her real and personal property during and after life.

The *Uniform Probate Code* guides states in developing laws related to estate planning.

Two important estate planning tools are:

- A *will,* a legal document that outlines how a person wants his or her property distributed on death.
- A *trust,* which allows a person to transfer property to another person, and this property is used for the benefit of a third person.

Individuals engage in estate planning:

- To *provide for their family* financially after their death.
- To *reduce taxes* and preserve wealth.
- To promote family *harmony.*
- To allow individuals in *nontraditional family relationships* to gain the benefits of traditional family relationships.

Legal Issues Related to Wills

Intestacy statutes outline how a person's property will be distributed if he or she dies without a will.

To have a legally valid will, a person must have:

[3] *Basile v. Aldrich,* 70 So 3d 682 (Fla. Dist. Ct. App. 2011).

- *Testamentary capacity,* which means the person must be old enough to write a will and must be of sound mind.
- A document in writing, which usually means a typed, written statement.
- A *signature,* which includes initials on each page.
- Witnesses, who *attest* to the will.

Grounds for contesting a will: The most common grounds for contesting a will are that a person believes the will fails to meet legal requirements and that a person believes that although the will is legally valid, the testator was a victim of fraud or undue influence.

Changing a will: Individuals are allowed to change wills by writing *codicils.*

Revoking a will: The most common way to revoke a will is to destroy it.

Settlement of an estate: A personal representative settles an estate through a process known as *probate.*

Trusts as Estate Planning Tools

How individuals create trusts: Trusts are created when a settlor delivers and transfers legal title to property to another person, called a *trustee,* who holds the property and uses it for the benefit of a third person. Trusts can be express or implied.

Individuals create trusts for a variety of reasons, but usually to protect another person.

Basic kinds of trusts include:

- *Express trusts,* which are created when a settlor is alive or through a will.
- *Implied trusts,* which are created by courts.

Trusts are terminated through a clause in the trust itself, which indicates the date on which the trust will be terminated.

End-of-Life Decisions

Advance directives: Individuals can express their wishes regarding medical treatment at the end of life by using advance directives. Advance directives include:

- *Living wills,* which allow individuals to express their wishes regarding the extent of medical treatment if they are in an accident or suffer from a life-threatening illness.
- *Health care proxies* or *durable powers of attorney,* which allow a person to make medical decisions for someone else.

Anatomical gifts allow individuals to donate all or any part of their body to a donee on death. *Choices about your body after death* should be made known before death.

International Protection for Wills

The *Uniform International Wills Act* protects wills written in other countries, as long as the wills follow a particular format. This act is part of the Uniform Probate Code.

POINT / COUNTERPOINT

As a Society, Should We Be Concerned about the Extent to Which Doctors Are Using Feeding Tubes on Seriously Ill Patients with Limited Cognitive Function? *	
YES	**NO**
Today, doctors are overusing feeding tubes on seriously ill patients. Often, doctors use feeding tubes at the request of family members. It is important to educate Americans about the extent to which feeding tubes truly benefit	Under current law, patients are allowed to forgo artificial nutrition and hydration by making their wishes clear or by designating a surrogate decision maker to make the decision when necessary. It is possible the law could

patients in terms of how long they live or whether they maintain a particular quality of life.

Families in situations that ask them to decide whether to use a feeding tube on a loved one often make the decision on the basis of an incorrect assumption. They assume that a relatively safe procedure that provides nutrition to the patient will help the patient recover from illness.

Studies in recent years have suggested that feeding tubes provide few benefits to patients, especially patients with dementia. Only rarely do patients and/or their families report improvement in nutrition, physical function, cognitive function, mood, pain, or quality of life. In fact, with regard to comfort, it is not uncommon for patients with feeding tubes to be restrained, either physically or via sedating drugs, so that they will not pull the feeding tube out.

Ongoing medical care for patients who will never recover and never regain their cognitive function is expensive. One reason patients or their surrogate decision makers seek feeding tubes is because a third party (such as an insurer) is usually paying for it. We should be concerned about the extent to which doctors are using feeding tubes. If doctors would discuss the issue with patients in a nonsentimental way, perhaps patients and their surrogate decision makers would make wiser decisions.

change. Legally, we could require that doctors ask some patients to comply with a *duty* to refuse feeding tubes. If this happens, vulnerable patients may become victims of abuse.

The bottom line is that, even if a person is terminally ill and lacks cognitive function, families generally do not want to hasten a loved one's death. They want to know they did everything possible to keep their loved one alive.

People who argue that doctors are overusing feeding tubes on some seriously ill patients disregard the sanctity of human life. In addition, they disregard the symbolic value of nourishment. Even if a scientist can tell us feeding tubes do not benefit some patients, it is still important for families to engage in behavior that shows a desire to keep a loved one alive. Decisions families make near the end of a loved one's life have a profound effect on their grieving process. Anyone who argues against feeding tubes denies that reality.

More practically, doctors and medical facilities have a duty to provide care to their patients, including the use of feeding tubes. If, as a society, we start asking questions about which patients "deserve" resources near the end of life, we start on a path that may lead to even more egregious decisions about the extent to which a life deserves protection.

* Information from David Orentlicher and Christopher Callahan, "Feeding Tubes, Slippery Slopes, and Physician-Assisted Suicide," *Journal of Legal Medicine* 25 (2004), p. 389.

QUESTIONS & PROBLEMS

1. Identify and describe the two most important estate planning tools.
2. What are intestacy statutes, and why are they important?
3. What is the difference between a living will and a health care proxy?
4. Thomas Chastain died in November 2009. At the time of his death, he had a will dated September 2004. However, Chastain failed to sign the will in the signature bloc on the second page. He did sign a separate one-page document, titled "Self-Proved Will Affidavit," acknowledging the unsigned will. The affidavit was signed by two of the three witnesses to the will. The question before the court was whether to give the will force and effect or refuse to accept it and declare Chastain to have died intestate. The Tennessee Probate Code required strict compliance with all statutory formalities for executing a will. Is Chastain's will effective, or did he die intestate? [*In re Estate of Chastain,* 2012 Tenn. LEXIS 816 (Tenn., Nov. 16, 2012).]
5. Dorothy Wehrheim, now deceased, signed a will on July 23, 2002. She relied on the assistance of Rebecca Fierle, a geriatric care manager, who helped her arrange her personal affairs. This will named Golden Pond Assisted Living Facility as the primary beneficiary. It also named Fierle as Wehrheim's personal representative. Wehrheim lived at this assisted living facility in 2002, and she died in the facility. After Wehrheim's death, her three children, Gary, Albert, and Debra, contested the 2002 will on the grounds of undue influence and lack of testamentary capacity. Three prior wills had not included the children as beneficiaries. Do the Wehrheim children have standing to challenge the will and ask that the state's intestacy statute be invoked? [*Wehrheim v. Golden Pond Assisted Living Facility,* 905 So. 2d 1002 (Fla. App. 5th Dist. 2005).]

6. In February 2010, Thomas Stewart died in an accident. He was survived by five adult children. In 2007, Stewart executed a will and trust that explicitly excluded one of his sons, Sean Stewart, from receiving any interest in the estate. The will and trust contained so-called *in terrorem* clauses which provided that any beneficiary who contested the will or trust or cooperated or aided another in making any such contest would forfeit his or her share. Sean sought to invalidate the will and trust. Sean also sought to invalidate the *in terrorem* clauses. Sean contended that the clauses impeded his ability to conduct discovery by prohibiting his siblings from cooperating or aiding him in contesting the will and trust. Sean also argued that such clauses violate public policy. Do such clauses violate public policy, or do they serve an important purpose by discouraging often groundless litigation by disappointed heirs? [*Stewart v. Stewart,* 286 P.3d 1089 (Ariz. App. 2012).]

7. In December 2008, Cecelia Harmon executed a holographic will leaving significant portions of her estate to Dennis Waitts, who, at the time, was serving as her primary caregiver. In January 2009, Harmon executed a will at her home in the presence of her attorney and with witnesses in which she left her entire estate to her adopted son Roger Harmon. Roger was also named as Cecelia's personal representative. The January 2009 will revoked all prior wills. When Cecelia died in March 2009, Roger presented the January 2009 will to the court for probate. Waitt challenged the January 2009 will and presented the December 2008 will for probate. Waitt claimed that the January 2009 will was invalid as a result of undue influence exercised by Roger. Specifically, Waitt contended that Cecelia's weakened condition due to pancreatic cancer rendered her vulnerable to Roger's influence. Waitt also contended that Roger abused his confidential relationship with his adopted mother to procure her preparation of the January 2009 will. Finally, Waitt claimed that Cecelia told him, shortly before her death, that Roger was "very greedy" and that she had been "hoodwinked" into signing the January 2009 will. Has Waitt met the test for undue influence to invalidate the January 2009 will? Why or why not? [*In re Estate of Harmon,* 253 P.3d 821 (Mont. 2011).]

8. Fred Berg executed a will in December 1997 in which he named one of his nephews, Roger Berg, as his sole heir. Roger was acting as Fred's attorney-in-fact at the time but was unaware that he had been named the sole heir in Fred's will. Fred had a long history of mental health issues dating back to his discharge from the U.S. Army in 1943. He had been institutionalized on several occasions, subjected to a bilateral prefrontal lobotomy in 1950, and declared incompetent by the Veterans Administration in 1967 for purposes of insurance and disbursement of benefits. Fred died in November 2006, leaving an estate totaling more than $500,000. Roger disclaimed his interest in the estate and stated that it should go to Fred's surviving sister Helen. Fred's niece Carol Opdahl objected to Fred's will and sought a declaration of intestacy. Opdahl sought an equal share of Fred's estate and claimed that he was incompetent. Her claims were based on Fred's belief that a fictitious person was his father and on the facts that he did not know the amount of his estate and had been declared incompetent by the Veterans Administration. Opdahl also claimed that Roger exercised undue influence over Fred. Roger responded that Fred's delusions never affected his testamentary capacity and that the Veterans Administration's declaration was silent as to Fred's ability to make a valid will. Furthermore, Roger claimed that he did not exert undue influence in order to gain access to Fred's estate as he had disclaimed his interest in favor of Helen. What is the standard for determining whether a person possesses testamentary capacity? What evidence would be relevant to such a determination? Can a person be declared incompetent with respect to some activities while remaining competent to make a will? Can a person be held to have exerted undue influence when he or she later disclaims any interest in the estate? [*In re Estate of Berg,* 783 N.W.2d 831 (S.D. 2010).]

9. Jesse Smith died unexpectedly at age 20 from heart problems. His driver's license indicated that he intended to make an anatomical gift of his organs. A medical examiner, Dr. Nabila Haikal, performed an autopsy. Haikal's position was funded by a nonprofit organization that researches brain disorders, Stanley Medical Research Institute (SMRI). Haikal asked Smith's mother, Nancy Adams, for permission to take Smith's brain tissue for research purposes. Adams consented. Over a year later, Adams discovered that Haikal had taken Smith's entire brain and other body samples for SMRI's use.

As a consequence, Adams suffered from grief and depression and required psychological and psychiatric treatment. Adams sued the county and SMRI, alleging violations of the Washington Uniform Anatomical Gift Act (WAGA), tortious interference with a dead body, invasion of privacy, conspiracy, and fraud. What was the result? [*Adams v. King County,* 192 P.3d 891 (2008).]

10. Joseph Goyette died in 2001. He was survived by his cousins and three sisters. Prior to his death, Goyette executed a holographic will in which he stated that he divided "my money" equally between two of his friends and neighbors, James Hayward and Vi York. At the time of his death, Goyette's estate consisted of retirement savings accounts, checking and savings accounts, certificates of deposit, a money market account, a U.S. Government Reserves Fund, and U.S. Treasury bills and savings bonds totaling more than $652,000. One of Goyette's sisters challenged the distribution of these assets to Hayward and York and claimed that the term "my money" referred only to cash or cash equivalents. Hayward and York claimed that "my money" meant all of Goyette's wealth. How would you define "my money" for purposes of deciding this case? How could Goyette have avoided this dispute between his friends and family? [*Goyette v. Harkey,* 19 Cal. Rptr. 3d 760 (Cal. App. 2004).]

Looking for more review material?

The Online Learning Center at **www.mhhe.com/kubasek3e** contains this chapter's "Assignment on the Internet" and also a list of URLs for more information, entitled "On the Internet." Find both of them in the Student Center portion of the OLC, along with quizzes and other helpful materials.

APPENDIX A

THE CONSTITUTION OF THE UNITED STATES OF AMERICA

Preamble

We the People of the United States, in Order to form a more perfect Union, establish Justice, insure domestic Tranquility, provide for the common defense, promote the general Welfare, and secure the Blessings of Liberty to ourselves and our Posterity, do ordain and establish this Constitution for the United States of America.

Article I

Section 1. All legislative Powers herein granted shall be vested in a Congress of the United States, which shall consist of a Senate and House of Representatives.

Section 2. The House of Representatives shall be composed of Members chosen every second Year by the People of the several States, and the Electors in each State shall have the Qualifications requisite for Electors of the most numerous Branch of the State Legislature.

No Person shall be a Representative who shall not have attained to the age of twenty five Years, and been seven Years a Citizen of the United States, and who shall not, when elected, be an Inhabitant of that State in which he shall be chosen.

Representatives and direct Taxes shall be apportioned among the several States which may be included within this Union, according to their respective Numbers, which shall be determined by adding to the whole Number of free Persons, including those bound to Service for a Term of Years, and excluding Indians not taxed, three fifths of all other Persons.[1] The actual Enumeration shall be made within three Years after the first Meeting of the Congress of the United States, and within every subsequent Term of ten Years, in such Manner as they shall by Law direct. The Number of Representatives shall not exceed one for every thirty Thousand, but each State shall have at Least one Representative, and until such enumeration shall be made, the State of New Hampshire shall be entitled to choose three, Massachusetts eight, Rhode-Island and Providence Plantations one, Connecticut five, New York six, New Jersey four, Pennsylvania eight, Delaware one, Maryland six, Virginia ten, North Carolina five, South Carolina five, and Georgia three.

When vacancies happen in the Representation from any State, the Executive Authority thereof shall issue Writs of Election to fill such Vacancies.

The House of Representatives shall chuse their Speaker and other Officers; and shall have the sole Power of Impeachment.

Section 3. The Senate of the United States shall be composed of two Senators from each State, chosen by the Legislature thereof,[2] for six Years; and each Senator shall have one Vote.

Immediately after they shall be assembled in Consequence of the first Election, they shall be divided as equally as may be into three Classes. The Seats of the Senators of the first Class shall be vacated at the Expiration of the second Year, of the second Class at the Expiration of the fourth Year, and of the third Class at the Expiration of the sixth Year, so that one third may

[1]Changed by the Fourteenth Amendment.

[2]Changed by the Seventeenth Amendment.

be chosen every second Year; and if Vacancies happen by Resignation, or otherwise, during the Recess of the Legislature of any State, the Executive thereof may make temporary Appointments until the next Meeting of the Legislature, which shall then fill such Vacancies.[3]

No Person shall be a Senator who shall not have attained to the Age of thirty Years, and been nine Years a Citizen of the United States, and who shall not, when elected, be an Inhabitant of that State for which he shall be chosen.

The Vice President of the United States shall be President of the Senate, but shall have no Vote, unless they be equally divided.

The Senate shall chuse their other Officers, and also a President pro tempore, in the Absence of the Vice President, or when he shall exercise the Office of President of the United States.

The Senate shall have the sole Power to try all Impeachments. When sitting for that Purpose, they shall be on Oath or Affirmation. When the President of the United States is tried, the Chief Justice shall preside: And no Person shall be convicted without the Concurrence of two thirds of the Members present.

Judgment in Cases of Impeachment shall not extend further than to removal from Office, and disqualification to hold and enjoy any Office of honor, Trust or Profit under the United States: but the Party convicted shall nevertheless be liable and subject to Indictment, Trial, Judgment and Punishment, according to Law.

Section 4. The Times, Places and Manner of holding Elections for Senators and Representatives, shall be prescribed in each State by the Legislature thereof; but the Congress may at any time by Law make or alter such Regulations, except as to the Places of chusing Senators.

The Congress shall assemble at least once in every Year, and such Meeting shall be on the first Monday in December, unless they shall by Law appoint a different Day.[4]

Section 5. Each House shall be the Judge of the Elections, Returns and Qualifications of its own Members, and a Majority of each shall constitute a Quorum to do Business; but a smaller Number may adjourn from day to day, and may be authorized to compel the Attendance of absent Members, in such Manner, and under such Penalties as each House may provide.

Each House may determine the Rules of its Proceedings, punish its Members for disorderly Behaviour, and with the Concurrence of two thirds, expel a Member.

Each House shall keep a Journal of its Proceedings, and from time to time publish the same, excepting such Parts as may in their Judgment require Secrecy; and the Yeas and Nays of the Members of either House on any question shall, at the Desire of one fifth of those Present, be entered on the Journal.

Neither House, during the Session of Congress, shall, without the Consent of the other, adjourn for more than three days, nor to any other Place than that in which the two Houses shall be sitting.

Section 6. The Senators and Representatives shall receive a Compensation for their Services, to be ascertained by Law, and paid out of the Treasury of the United States. They shall in all Cases, except Treason, Felony and Breach of the Peace, be privileged from Arrest during their Attendance at the Session of their respective Houses, and in going to and returning from the same; and for any Speech or Debate in either House, they shall not be questioned in any other Place.

No Senator or Representative shall, during the Time for which he was elected, be appointed to any civil Office under the Authority of the United States, which shall have been created, or the Emoluments whereof shall have been encreased during such time; and no Person holding any Office under the United States, shall be a Member of either House during his Continuance in Office.

[3]Changed by the Seventeenth Amendment.

[4]Changed by the Twentieth Amendment.

Section 7. All Bills for raising Revenue shall originate in the House of Representatives; but the Senate may propose or concur with Amendments as on other Bills.

Every Bill which shall have passed the House of Representatives and the Senate, shall, before it becomes a Law, be presented to the President of the United States; If he approves he shall sign it, but if not he shall return it, with his Objections to that House in which it shall have originated, who shall enter the Objections at large on their Journal, and proceed to reconsider it. If after such Reconsideration two thirds of that House shall agree to pass the Bill, it shall be sent, together with the Objections, to the other House, by which it shall likewise be reconsidered, and if approved by two thirds of that House, it shall become a Law. But in all such Cases the Votes of both Houses shall be determined by Yeas and Nays, and the Names of the Persons voting for and against the Bill shall be entered on the Journal of each House respectively. If any Bill shall not be returned by the President within ten Days (Sundays excepted) after it shall have been presented to him, the Same shall be a Law, in like Manner as if he had signed it, unless the Congress by their Adjournment prevent its Return, in which Case it shall not be a Law.

Every Order, Resolution, or Vote to which the Concurrence of the Senate and House of Representatives may be necessary (except on a question of Adjournment) shall be presented to the President of the United States; and before the Same shall take Effect, shall be approved by him, or being disapproved by him, shall be repassed by two thirds of the Senate and House of Representatives, according to the Rules and Limitations prescribed in the Case of a Bill.

Section 8. The Congress shall have Power To lay and collect Taxes, Duties, Imposts and Excises, to pay the Debts and provide for the common Defence and general Welfare of the United States; but all Duties, Imposts and Excises shall be uniform throughout the United States.

To borrow Money on the credit of the United States;

To regulate Commerce with foreign Nations, and among the several States, and with the Indian Tribes;

To establish an uniform Rule of Naturalization, and uniform Laws on the subject of Bankruptcies throughout the United States;

To coin Money, regulate the Value thereof, and of foreign Coin, and fix the Standard of Weights and Measures;

To provide for the Punishment of counterfeiting the Securities and current Coin of the United States;

To establish Post Offices and post Roads;

To promote the Progress of Science and useful Arts, by securing for limited Times to Authors and Inventors the exclusive Right to their respective Writings and Discoveries;

To constitute Tribunals inferior to the supreme Court;

To define and punish Piracies and Felonies committed on the high Seas, and Offences against the Law of Nations;

To declare War, grant Letters of Marque and Reprisal, and make Rules concerning Captures on Land and Water;

To raise and support Armies, but no Appropriation of Money to that Use shall be for a longer Term than two Years;

To provide and maintain a Navy;

To make Rules for the Government and Regulation of the land and naval Forces;

To provide for calling forth the Militia to execute the Laws of the Union, suppress Insurrections and repel Invasions;

To provide for organizing, arming, and disciplining, the Militia, and for governing such Part of them as may be employed in the Service of the United States, reserving to the States respectively, the Appointment of the Officers, and the Authority of training the Militia according to the discipline prescribed by Congress;

To exercise exclusive Legislation in all Cases whatsoever, over such District (not exceeding ten Miles square) as may, by Cession of particular States, and the Acceptance of Congress, become the Seat of the Government of the United States, and to exercise like Authority over all Places purchased by the Consent of the Legislature of the State in which the Same shall be, for the Erection of Forts, Magazines, Arsenals, dock-Yards, and other needful Buildings;—And

To make all Laws which shall be necessary and proper for carrying into Execution the foregoing Powers, and all other Powers vested by this Constitution in the Government of the United States, or in any Department or Officer thereof.

Section 9. The Migration or Importation of such Persons as any of the States now existing shall think proper to admit, shall not be prohibited by the Congress prior to the Year one thousand eight hundred and eight, but a Tax or duty may be imposed on such Importation, not exceeding ten dollars for each Person.

The Privilege of the Writ of Habeas Corpus shall not be suspended, unless when in Cases of Rebellion or Invasion the public Safety may require it.

No Bill of Attainder or ex post facto Law shall be passed.

No Capitation, or other direct, Tax shall be laid, unless in Proportion to the Census of Enumeration herein before directed to be taken.[5]

No Tax or Duty shall be laid on Articles exported from any State.

No Preference shall be given by any Regulation of Commerce or Revenue to the Ports of one State over those of another: nor shall Vessels bound to, or from, one State, be obliged to enter, clear, or pay Duties in another.

No Money shall be drawn from the Treasury, but in Consequence of Appropriations made by Law; and a regular Statement and Account of the Receipts and Expenditures of all public Money shall be published from time to time.

No Title of Nobility shall be granted by the United States: And no Person holding any Office of Profit or Trust under them, shall, without the Consent of the Congress, accept of any present, Emolument, Office, or Title, of any kind whatever, from any King, Prince, or foreign State.

Section 10. No State shall enter into any Treaty, Alliance, or Confederation; grant Letters of Marque and Reprisal; coin Money; emit Bills of Credit; make any Thing but gold and silver coin a Tender in Payment of Debts; pass any Bill of Attainder, ex post facto Law, or Law impairing the Obligation of Contracts, or grant any Title of Nobility.

No State shall, without the Consent of the Congress, lay any Imposts or Duties on Imports or Exports, except what may be absolutely necessary for executing its inspection Laws: and the net Produce of all Duties and Imposts, laid by any State on Imports or Exports, shall be for the Use of the Treasury of the United States; and all such Laws shall be subject to the Revision and Control of the Congress.

No State shall, without the consent of Congress, lay any Duty of Tonnage, keep Troops, or Ships of War in time of Peace, enter into any Agreement or Compact with another State, or with a foreign Power, or engage in War, unless actually invaded, or in such imminent Danger as will not admit of delay.

Article II

Section 1. The executive Power shall be vested in a President of the United States of America. He shall hold his Office during the Term of four Years, and, together with the Vice President, chosen for the same Term, be elected, as follows

Each state shall appoint, in such Manner as the Legislature thereof may direct, a Number of Electors, equal to the whole Number of Senators and Representatives to which the State may be entitled in Congress: but no Senator or Representative, or Person holding an Office of Trust or Profit under the United States, shall be appointed an Elector.

[5]Changed by the Sixteenth Amendment.

The Electors shall meet in their respective States, and vote by Ballot for two Persons, of whom one at least shall not be an inhabitant of the same State with themselves. And they shall make a List of all the Persons voted for, and of the Number of Votes for each; which List they shall sign and certify, and transmit sealed to the Seat of the Government of the United States, directed to the President of the Senate. The President of the Senate shall, in the Presence of the Senate and House of Representatives, open all the Certificates, and the Votes shall then be counted. The Person having the greatest Number of Votes shall be the President, if such Number be a Majority of the whole Number of Electors appointed; and if there be more than one who have such Majority, and have an equal Number of Votes, then the House of Representatives shall immediately chuse by Ballot one of them for President; and if no Person have a Majority, then from the five highest on the List the said House shall in like Manner chuse the President. But in chusing the President, the Votes shall be taken by States, the Representation from each State having one Vote; A quorum for this purpose shall consist of a Member or Members from two thirds of the States, and a Majority of all the States shall be necessary to a Choice. In every Case, after the Choice of the President, the Person having the greatest Number of Votes of the Electors shall be the Vice President. But if there should remain two or more who have equal Votes, the Senate shall chuse from them by Ballot the Vice President.[6]

The Congress may determine the Time of chusing the Electors, and the Day on which they shall give their Votes; which Day shall be the same throughout the United States.

No Person except a natural born Citizen, or a Citizen of the United States, at the time of the Adoption of this Constitution, shall be eligible to the Office of President; neither shall any Person be eligible to that Office who shall not have attained to the Age of thirty five Years, and been fourteen Years a Resident within the United States.

In Case of the Removal of the President from Office, or of his Death, Resignation, or Inability to discharge the Powers and Duties of the said Office, the Same shall devolve on the Vice President, and the Congress may by Law provide for the Case of Removal, Death, Resignation or Inability, both of the President and Vice President, declaring what Officer shall then act as President, and such Officer shall act accordingly, until the Disability be removed, or a President shall be elected.[7]

The President shall, at stated Times, receive for his Services, a Compensation, which shall neither be encreased nor diminished during the Period for which he shall have been elected, and he shall not receive within that Period any other Emolument from the United States, or any of them.

Before he enter on the Execution of his Office, he shall take the following Oath or Affirmation:—"I do solemnly swear (or affirm) that I will faithfully execute the Office of President of the United States, and will to the best of my Ability, preserve, protect, and defend the Constitution of the United States."

Section 2. The President shall be Commander in Chief of the Army and Navy of the United States, and of the Militia of the several States, when called into the actual Service of the United States; he may require the Opinion, in writing, of the principal Officer in each of the executive Departments, upon any Subject relating to the Duties of their respective Offices, and he shall have Power to grant Reprieves and Pardons for Offences against the United States, except in Cases of Impeachment.

He shall have Power, by and with the Advice and Consent of the Senate, to make Treaties, provided two thirds of the Senators present concur; and he shall nominate, and by and with the Advice and Consent of the Senate, shall appoint Ambassadors, other public Ministers and Consuls, Judges of the supreme Court, and all other Officers of the United States, whose Appointments are not herein otherwise provided for, and which shall be established by Law; but the

[6]Changed by the Twelfth Amendment.

[7]Changed by the Twenty-Fifth Amendment.

Congress may by Law vest the Appointment of such inferior Officers, as they think proper, in the President alone, in the Courts of Law, or in the Heads of Departments.

The President shall have Power to fill up all Vacancies that may happen during the Recess of the Senate, by granting Commissions which shall expire at the End of their next Session.

Section 3. He shall from time to time give to the Congress Information of the State of the Union, and recommend to their Consideration such Measures as he shall judge necessary and expedient; he may, on extraordinary Occasions, convene both Houses, or either of them, and in Case of Disagreement between them, with Respect to the Time of Adjournment, he may adjourn them to such Time as he shall think proper; he shall receive Ambassadors and other public Ministers; he shall take Care that the Laws be faithfully executed, and shall Commission all the Officers of the United States.

Section 4. The President, Vice President and all civil Officers of the United States, shall be removed from Office on Impeachment for, and Conviction of, Treason, Bribery, or other high Crimes and Misdemeanors.

Article III

Section 1. The judicial Power of the United States, shall be vested in one supreme Court, and in such inferior Courts as the Congress may from time to time ordain and establish. The Judges, both of the supreme and inferior Courts, shall hold their Offices during good Behaviour, and shall, at stated Times, receive for their Services, a Compensation, which shall not be diminished during their Continuance in Office.

Section 2. The judicial Power shall extend to all Cases, in Law and Equity, arising under this Constitution, the Laws of the United States, and Treaties made, or which shall be made, under their Authority;—to all Cases affecting Ambassadors, other public Ministers and Consuls;—to all Cases of admiralty and maritime Jurisdiction;—to Controversies to which the United States shall be a party;—to Controversies between two or more States;—between a State and Citizens of another State;[8]—between Citizens of different States;—between Citizens of the same State claiming Lands under Grants of different States, and between a State, or the Citizens thereof, and foreign States, Citizens or Subjects.

In all Cases affecting Ambassadors, other public Ministers and Consuls, and those in which a State shall be Party, the supreme Court shall have original Jurisdiction. In all the other Cases before mentioned, the supreme Court shall have appellate Jurisdiction, both as to Law and Fact, with such Exceptions, and under such Regulations as the Congress shall make.

The Trial of all Crimes, except in Cases of Impeachment, shall be by Jury: and such Trial shall be held in the State where the said Crimes shall have been committed; but when not committed within any State, the Trial shall be at such Place or Places as the Congress may by Law have directed.

Section 3. Treason against the United States, shall consist only in levying War against them, or in adhering to their Enemies, giving them Aid and Comfort. No Person shall be convicted of Treason unless on the Testimony of two Witnesses to the same overt Act, or on Confession in open Court.

The Congress shall have Power to declare the Punishment of Treason, but no Attainder of Treason shall work Corruption of Blood, or Forfeiture except during the Life of the Person attainted.

[8]Changed by the Eleventh Amendment.

Article IV

Section 1. Full Faith and Credit shall be given in each State to the public Acts, Records, and judicial Proceedings of every other State. And the Congress may by general Laws prescribe the Manner in which such Acts, Records and Proceedings shall be proved, and the Effect thereof.

Section 2. The Citizens of each State shall be entitled to all Privileges and Immunities of Citizens in the several States.

A Person charged in any State with Treason, Felony, or other Crime, who shall flee from Justice, and be found in another State, shall on Demand of the executive Authority of the State from which he fled, be delivered up, to be removed to the State having Jurisdiction of the Crime.

No Person held to Service or Labour in one State, under the Laws thereof, escaping into another, shall, in Consequence of any Law or Regulation therein, be discharged from such Service or Labour, but shall be delivered up on Claim of the Party to whom such Service or Labour may be due.[9]

Section 3. New States may be admitted by the Congress into this Union; but no new State shall be formed or erected within the Jurisdiction of any other State; nor any State be formed by the Junction of two or more States, or Parts of States, without the Consent of the Legislatures of the States concerned as well as of the Congress.

The Congress shall have Power to dispose of and make all needful Rules and Regulations respecting the Territory or other Property belonging to the United States; and nothing in this Constitution shall be so construed as to Prejudice any Claims of the United States, or of any particular State.

Section 4. The United States shall guarantee to every State in this Union a Republican Form of Government, and shall protect each of them against Invasion; and on Application of the Legislature, or of the Executive (when the Legislature cannot be convened) against domestic Violence.

Article V

The Congress, whenever two thirds of both Houses shall deem it necessary, shall propose Amendments to this Constitution, or, on the Application of the Legislatures of two thirds of the several States, shall call a Convention for proposing Amendments, which, in either Case, shall be valid to all Intents and Purposes, as Part of this Constitution, when ratified by the legislatures of three fourths of the several States, or by Conventions in three fourths thereof, as the one or the other Mode of Ratification may be proposed by the Congress; Provided that no Amendment which may be made prior to the Year One thousand eight hundred and eight shall in any Manner affect the first and fourth Clauses in the Ninth Section of the first Article; and that no State, without its Consent, shall be deprived of its equal Suffrage in the Senate.

Article VI

All Debts contracted and Engagements entered into, before the Adoption of this Constitution, shall be as valid against the United States under this Constitution, as under the Confederation.

The Constitution, and the Laws of the United States which shall be made in Pursuance thereof; and all Treaties made, or which shall be made, under the Authority of the United States,

[9]Changed by the Thirteenth Amendment.

shall be the supreme Law of the Land; and the Judges in every State shall be bound thereby, any Thing in the Constitution or Laws of any State to the Contrary notwithstanding.

The Senators and Representatives before mentioned, and the Members of the several State Legislatures, and all executive and judicial Officers, both of the United States and of the several States, shall be bound by Oath or Affirmation, to support this Constitution; but no religious Test shall ever be required as a Qualification to any Office or public Trust under the United States.

Article VII

The Ratification of the Conventions of nine States, shall be sufficient for the Establishment of this Constitution between the States so ratifying the Same.

Done in Convention by the Unanimous Consent of the States present the Seventeenth Day of September in the Year of our Lord one thousand seven hundred and eighty seven and of the Independence of the United States of America the Twelfth. In witness whereof We have hereunto subscribed our Names.

Amendments

[The first 10 amendments are known as the "Bill of Rights."]

AMENDMENT I (RATIFIED 1791)

Congress shall make no law respecting an establishment of religion, or prohibiting the free exercise thereof; or abridging the freedom of speech, or of the press; or the right of the people peaceably to assemble, and to petition the Government for a redress of grievances.

AMENDMENT 2 (RATIFIED 1791)

A well regulated Militia, being necessary to the security of a free State, the right of the people to keep and bear Arms, shall not be infringed.

AMENDMENT 3 (RATIFIED 1791)

No Soldier shall, in time of peace be quartered in any house, without the consent of the Owner, nor in time of war, but in a manner to be prescribed by law.

AMENDMENT 4 (RATIFIED 1791)

The right of the people to be secure in their persons, houses, papers, and effects, against unreasonable searches and seizures, shall not be violated, and no Warrants shall issue, but upon probable cause, supported by Oath or affirmation, and particularly describing the place to be searched, and the persons or things to be seized.

AMENDMENT 5 (RATIFIED 1791)

No person shall be held to answer for a capital, or otherwise infamous crime, unless on a presentment or indictment of a Grand Jury, except in cases arising in the land or naval forces, or in the Militia, when in actual service in time of War or public danger; nor shall any person be subject for the same offence to be twice put in jeopardy of life or limb; nor shall be compelled in any criminal case to be a witness against himself, nor be deprived of life, liberty, or property, without due process of law; nor shall private property be taken for public use, without just compensation.

AMENDMENT 6 (RATIFIED 1791)

In all criminal prosecutions, the accused shall enjoy the right to a speedy and public trial, by an impartial jury of the State and district wherein the crime shall have been committed, which district shall have been previously ascertained by law, and to be informed of the nature and cause of the accusation; to be confronted with the witnesses against him; to have compulsory process for obtaining Witnesses in his favor, and to have assistance of counsel for his defence.

AMENDMENT 7 (RATIFIED 1791)

In Suits at common law, where the value in controversy shall exceed twenty dollars, the right of trial by jury shall be preserved, and no fact tried by a jury, shall be otherwise re-examined in any Court of the United States, than according to the rules of the common law.

AMENDMENT 8 (RATIFIED 1791)

Excessive bail shall not be required, nor excessive fines imposed, nor cruel and unusual punishments inflicted.

AMENDMENT 9 (RATIFIED 1791)

The enumeration in the Constitution, of certain rights, shall not be construed to deny or disparage others retained by the people.

AMENDMENT 10 (RATIFIED 1791)

The powers not delegated to the United States by the Constitution, nor prohibited by it to the States, are reserved to the States respectively, or to the people.

AMENDMENT 11 (RATIFIED 1795)

The Judicial power of the United States shall not be construed to extend to any suit in law or equity, commenced or prosecuted against one of the United States by Citizens of another State, or by Citizens or Subjects of any Foreign State.

AMENDMENT 12 (RATIFIED 1804)

The Electors shall meet in their respective states, and vote by ballot for President and Vice-President, one of whom, at least, shall not be an inhabitant of the same state with themselves; they shall name in their ballots the person voted for as President, and in distinct ballots the person voted for as Vice-President, and they shall make distinct lists of all persons voted for as President, and of all persons voted for as Vice-President, and of the number of votes for each, which lists they shall sign and certify, and transmit sealed to the seat of the government of the United States, directed to the President of the Senate;—The President of the Senate shall, in the presence of the Senate and House of Representatives, open all the certificates and the votes shall then be counted;—The person having the greatest number of votes for President, shall be the President, if such number be a majority of the whole number of Electors appointed; and if no person have such majority, then from the persons having the highest numbers not exceeding three on the list of those voted for as President, the House of Representatives shall choose immediately, by ballot, the President. But in choosing the President, the votes shall be taken by states, the representation from each state having one vote; a quorum for this purpose shall consist of a member or members from two-thirds of the states, and a majority of all the states shall be necessary to a choice. And if the House of Representatives shall not choose a President whenever the right of choice shall devolve upon them, before the fourth day of March next following, then the Vice-President shall act as president, as in the case of the death or other constitutional disability of the President.[10]—The person having the greatest number of votes as Vice-President, shall be the Vice-President, if such number be a majority of the whole number of Electors appointed, and if no person have a majority, then from the two highest numbers on the list, the Senate shall choose the Vice-President; a quorum for the purpose shall consist of two-thirds of the whole number of Senators, and a majority of the whole number shall be necessary to a choice. But no person constitutionally ineligible to the office of President shall be eligible to that of Vice-President of the United States.

AMENDMENT 13 (RATIFIED 1865)

Section 1. Neither slavery nor involuntary servitude, except as a punishment for crime whereof the party shall have been duly convicted, shall exist within the United States, or any place subject to their jurisdiction.

Section 2. Congress shall have power to enforce this article by appropriate legislation.

AMENDMENT 14 (RATIFIED 1868)

Section 1. All persons born or naturalized in the United States, and subject to the jurisdiction thereof, are citizens of the United States and of the State wherein they reside. No State shall make or enforce any law which shall abridge the privileges or immunities of citizens of the United States; nor shall any State deprive any person of life, liberty, or property, without due process of law; nor deny to any person within its jurisdiction the equal protection of the laws.

Section 2. Representatives shall be apportioned among the several States according to their respective numbers, counting the whole number of persons in each State, excluding Indians not taxed. But when the right to vote at any election for the choice of electors for President and Vice President of the United States, Representatives in Congress, the Executive and Judicial officers of a State, or the members of the Legislature thereof, is denied to any of the male inhabitants of such State, being twenty-one[11] years of age, and citizens of the United States, or in any way abridged except for participation in rebellion, or other crime, the basis of representation therein shall be reduced in the proportion which the number of such male citizens shall bear to the whole number of male citizens twenty-one years of age in such State.

Section 3. No person shall be a Senator or Representative in Congress, or elector of President and Vice President, or hold any office, civil or military, under the United States, or under any State, who, having previously taken an oath, as a member of Congress, or as an officer of the United States, or as a member of any State legislature, or as an executive or judicial officer of any State, to support the Constitution of the United States, shall have engaged in insurrection or rebellion against the same, or given aid or comfort to the enemies thereof. But Congress may by a vote of two-thirds of each House, remove such disability.

Section 4. The validity of the public debt of the United States, authorized by law, including debts incurred for payment of pensions and bounties for services in suppressing insurrection or rebellion, shall not be questioned. But neither the United States nor any State shall assume or pay any debt or obligation incurred in aid of insurrection or rebellion against the United States, or any claim for the loss or emancipation of any slave; but all such debts, obligations and claims shall be held illegal and void.

[10]Changed by the Twentieth Amendment.

[11]Changed by the Twenty-Sixth Amendment.

Section 5. The Congress shall have power to enforce, by appropriate legislation, the provisions of this article.

AMENDMENT 15 (RATIFIED 1870)

Section 1. The right of citizens of the United States to vote shall not be denied or abridged by the United States or by any State on account of race, color, or previous condition of servitude.

Section 2. The Congress shall have power to enforce this article by appropriate legislation.

AMENDMENT 16 (RATIFIED 1913)

The Congress shall have power to lay and collect taxes on incomes, from whatever source derived, without apportionment among the several States, and without regard to any census or enumeration.

AMENDMENT 17 (RATIFIED 1913)

The Senate of the United States shall be composed of two Senators from each State, elected by the people thereof, for six years; and each Senator shall have one vote. The electors in each State shall have the qualifications requisite for electors of the most numerous branch of the State legislatures.

When vacancies happen in the representation of any State in the Senate, the executive authority of such State shall issue writs of election to fill such vacancies: *Provided,* That the legislature of any State may empower the executive thereof to make temporary appointments until the people fill the vacancies by election as the legislature may direct.

This amendment shall not be so construed as to affect the election or term of any Senator chosen before it becomes valid as part of the Constitution.

AMENDMENT 18 (RATIFIED 1919; REPEALED 1933)

Section 1. After one year from the ratification of this article the manufacture, sale, or transportation of intoxicating liquors within, the importation thereof into, or the exportation thereof from the United States and all territory subject to the jurisdiction thereof for beverage purposes is hereby prohibited.

Section 2. The Congress and the several States shall have concurrent power to enforce this article by appropriate legislation.

Section 3. This article shall be inoperative unless it shall have been ratified as an amendment to the Constitution by the legislatures of the several States, as provided in the Constitution, within seven years from the date of the submission hereof to the States by the Congress.[12]

AMENDMENT 19 (RATIFIED 1920)

The right of citizens of the United States to vote shall not be denied or abridged by the United States or by any State on account of sex.

Congress shall have power to enforce this article by appropriate legislation.

AMENDMENT 20 (RATIFIED 1933)

Section 1. The terms of the President and Vice President shall end at noon on the 20th day of January, and the terms of Senators and Representatives at noon on the 3rd day of

[12]Repealed by the Twenty-First Amendment.

January, of the years in which such terms would have ended if this article had not been ratified; and the terms of their successors shall then begin.

Section 2. The Congress shall assemble at least once in every year, and such meeting shall begin at noon on the 3rd day of January, unless they shall by law appoint a different day.

Section 3. If, at the time fixed for the beginning of the term of the President, the President elect shall have died, the Vice President elect shall become President. If a President shall not have been chosen before the time fixed for the beginning of his term, or if the President elect shall have failed to qualify, then the Vice President elect shall act as President until a President shall have qualified; and the Congress may by law provide for the case wherein neither a President elect nor a Vice President elect shall have qualified, declaring who shall then act as President, or the manner in which one who is to act shall be selected, and such person shall act accordingly until a President or Vice President shall have qualified.

Section 4. The Congress may by law provide for the case of the death of any of the persons from whom the House of Representatives may choose a President whenever the right of choice shall have devolved upon them, and for the case of the death of any of the persons from whom the Senate may choose a Vice President whenever the right of choice shall have devolved upon them.

Section 5. Sections 1 and 2 shall take effect on the 15th day of October following the ratification of this article.

Section 6. This article shall be inoperative unless it shall have been ratified as an amendment to the Constitution by the legislatures of three-fourths of the several States within seven years from the date of its submission.

AMENDMENT 21 (RATIFIED 1933)

Section 1. The eighteenth article of amendment to the Constitution of the United States is hereby repealed.

Section 2. The transportation or importation into any State, Territory, or possession of the United States for delivery or use therein of intoxicating liquors, in violation of the laws thereof, is hereby prohibited.

Section 3. This article shall be inoperative unless it shall have been ratified as an amendment to the Constitution by conventions in the several States, as provided in the Constitution, within seven years from the date of the submission hereof to the States by the Congress.

AMENDMENT 22 (RATIFIED 1951)

Section 1. No person shall be elected to the office of the President more than twice, and no person who has held the office of President, or acted as President, for more than two years of a term to which some other person was elected President shall be elected to the office of the President more than once. But this Article shall not apply to any person holding the office of President when this Article was proposed by the Congress, and shall not prevent any person who may be holding the office of President, or acting as President, during the term within which this Article becomes operative from holding the office of President or acting as President during the remainder of such term.

Section 2. This Article shall be inoperative unless it shall have been ratified as an amendment to the Constitution by the legislatures of three-fourths of the several States within seven years from the date of its submission to the States by the Congress.

AMENDMENT 23 (RATIFIED 1961)

Section 1. The District constituting the seat of Government of the United States shall appoint in such manner as the Congress may direct:

A number of electors of President and Vice President equal to the whole number of Senators and Representatives in Congress to which the District would be entitled if it were a State, but in no event more than the least populous State; they shall be in addition to those appointed by the States, but they shall be considered, for the purposes of the election of President and Vice President, to be electors appointed by a State; and they shall meet in the District and perform such duties as provided by the twelfth article of amendment.

Section 2. The Congress shall have power to enforce this article by appropriate legislation.

AMENDMENT 24 (RATIFIED 1964)

Section 1. The right of citizens of the United States to vote in any primary or other election for President or Vice President, for electors for President or Vice President, or for Senator or Representative in Congress, shall not be denied or abridged by the United States or any State by reason of failure to pay any poll tax or other tax.

Section 2. The Congress shall have power to enforce this article by appropriate legislation.

AMENDMENT 25 (RATIFIED 1967)

Section 1. In case of the removal of the President from office or of his death or resignation, the Vice President shall become President.

Section 2. Whenever there is a vacancy in the office of the Vice President, the President shall nominate a Vice President who shall take office upon confirmation by a majority vote of both Houses of Congress.

Section 3. Whenever the President transmits to the President pro tempore of the Senate and the Speaker of the House of Representatives his written declaration that he is unable to discharge the powers and duties of his office, and until he transmits to them a written declaration to the contrary, such powers and duties shall be discharged by the Vice President as Acting President.

Section 4. Whenever the Vice President and a majority of either the principal officers of the executive departments or of such other body as Congress may by law provide, transmit to the President pro tempore of the Senate and the Speaker of the House of Representatives their written declaration that the President is unable to discharge the powers and duties of his office, the Vice President shall immediately assume the powers and duties of the office as Acting President.

Thereafter, when the President transmits to the President pro tempore of the Senate and the Speaker of the House of Representatives his written declaration that no inability exists, he shall resume the powers and duties of his office unless the Vice President and a majority of either the principal officers of the executive department or of such other body as Congress may by law provide, transmit within four days to the President pro tempore of the Senate and the Speaker of the House of Representatives their written declaration that the President is unable to discharge the powers and duties of his office. Thereupon Congress shall decide the issue, assembling within forty-eight hours for that purpose if not in session. If the Congress, within twenty-one days after receipt of the latter written declaration, or, if Congress is not in session, within twenty-one days after Congress is required to assemble, determines by two-thirds vote of both Houses that the President is unable to discharge the powers and duties of his office, the

Vice President shall continue to discharge the same as Acting President; otherwise, the President shall resume the powers and duties of his office.

AMENDMENT 26 (RATIFIED 1971)

Section 1. The right of citizens of the United States, who are eighteen years of age or older, to vote shall not be denied or abridged by the United States or by any State on account of age.

Section 2. The Congress shall have power to enforce this article by appropriate legislation.

AMENDMENT 27 (RATIFIED 1992)

No law, varying the compensation for the services of the Senators and Representatives, shall take effect, until an election of Representatives shall have intervened.

APPENDIX B

UNIFORM COMMERCIAL CODE

Article 2—Sales

PART 1: SHORT TITLE, GENERAL CONSTRUCTION AND SUBJECT MATTER

§ 2-101. Short Title. This Article shall be known and may be cited as Uniform Commercial Code—Sales.

§ 2-102. Scope; Certain Security and Other Transactions Excluded from This Article. Unless the context otherwise requires, this Article applies to transactions in goods; it does not apply to any transaction which although in the form of an unconditional contract to sell or present sale is intended to operate only as a security transaction nor does this Article impair or repeal any statute regulating sales to consumers, farmers or other specified classes of buyers.

§ 2-103. Definitions and Index of Definitions.

(1) In this Article unless the context otherwise requires
  (a) "Buyer" means a person who buys or contracts to buy goods.
  (b) "Good faith" in the case of a merchant means honesty in fact and the observance of reasonable commercial standards of fair dealing in the trade.
  (c) "Receipt" of goods means taking physical possession of them.
  (d) "Seller" means a person who sells or contracts to sell goods.

(2) Other definitions applying to this Article or to specified Parts thereof, and the sections in which they appear are:

"Acceptance"	Section 2–606.
"Banker's credit"	Section 2–325.
"Between merchants"	Section 2–104.
"Cancellation"	Section 2–106(4).
"Commercial unit"	Section 2–105.
"Confirmed credit"	Section 2–325.
"Conforming to contract"	Section 2–106.
"Contract for sale"	Section 2–106.
"Cover"	Section 2–712.
"Entrusting"	Section 2–403.
"Financing agency"	Section 2–104.
"Future goods"	Section 2–105.
"Goods"	Section 2–105.
"Identification"	Section 2–501.
"Installment contract"	Section 2–612.
"Letter of credit"	Section 2–325.
"Lot"	Section 2–105.

"Merchant"	Section 2–104.
"Overseas"	Section 2–323.
"Person in position of seller"	Section 2–707.
"Present sale"	Section 2–106.
"Sale"	Section 2–106.
"Sale on approval"	Section 2–326.
"Sale or return"	Section 2–326.
"Termination"	Section 2–106.

(3) The following definitions in other Articles apply to this Article:

"Check"	Section 3–104.
"Consignee"	Section 7–102.
"Consignor"	Section 7–102.
"Consumer goods"	Section 9–109.
"Dishonor"	Section 3–502.
"Draft"	Section 3–104.

(4) In addition Article 1 contains general definitions and principles of construction and interpretation applicable throughout this Article.

As amended in 1994.

See Appendix XI for material relating to changes made in text in 1994.

§ 2–104. Definitions: "Merchant"; "Between Merchants"; "Financing Agency".

(1) "Merchant" means a person who deals in goods of the kind or otherwise by his occupation holds himself out as having knowledge or skill peculiar to the practices or goods involved in the transaction or to whom such knowledge or skill may be attributed by his employment of an agent or broker or other intermediary who by his occupation holds himself out as having such knowledge or skill.

(2) "Financing agency" means a bank, finance company or other person who in the ordinary course of business makes advances against goods or documents of title or who by arrangement with either the seller or the buyer intervenes in ordinary course to make or collect payment due or claimed under the contract for sale, as by purchasing or paying the seller's draft or making advances against it or by merely taking it for collection whether or not documents of title accompany the draft. "Financing agency" includes also a bank or other person who similarly intervenes between persons who are in the position of seller and buyer in respect to the goods (Section 2–707).

(3) "Between merchants" means in any transaction with respect to which both parties are chargeable with the knowledge or skill of merchants.

§ 2–105. Definitions: "Transferability"; "Goods"; "Future" Goods; "Lot"; "Commercial Unit".

(1) "Goods" means all things (including specially manufactured goods) which are movable at the time of identification to the contract for sale other than the money in which the price is to be paid, investment securities (Article 8) and things in action. "Goods" also includes the unborn young of animals and growing crops and other identified things attached to realty as described in the section on goods to be severed from realty (Section 2–107).

(2) Goods must be both existing and identified before any interest in them can pass. Goods which are not both existing and identified are "future" goods. A purported present sale of future goods or of any interest therein operates as a contract to sell.

(3) There may be a sale of a part interest in existing identified goods.
(4) An undivided share in an identified bulk of fungible goods is sufficiently identified to be sold although the quantity of the bulk is not determined. Any agreed proportion of such a bulk or any quantity thereof agreed upon by number, weight or other measure may to the extent of the seller's interest in the bulk be sold to the buyer who then becomes an owner in common.
(5) "Lot" means a parcel or a single article which is the subject matter of a separate sale or delivery, whether or not it is sufficient to perform the contract.
(6) "Commercial unit" means such a unit of goods as by commercial usage is a single whole for purposes of sale and division of which materially impairs its character or value on the market or in use. A commercial unit may be a single article (as a machine) or a set of articles (as a suite of furniture or an assortment of sizes) or a quantity (as a bale, gross, or carload) or any other unit treated in use or in the relevant market as a single whole.

§ 2-106. Definitions: "Contract"; "Agreement"; "Contract for Sales"; "Sale"; "Present Sale"; "Conforming" to Contract; "Termination"; "Cancellation".

(1) In this Article unless the context otherwise requires "contract" and "agreement" are limited to those relating to the present or future sale of goods. "Contract for sale" includes both a present sale of goods and a contract to sell goods at a future time. A "sale" consists in the passing of title from the seller to the buyer for a price (Section 2–401). A "present sale" means a sale which is accomplished by the making of the contract.
(2) Goods or conduct including any part of a performance are "conforming" or conform to the contract when they are in accordance with the obligations under the contract.
(3) "Termination" occurs when either party pursuant to a power created by agreement or law puts an end to the contract otherwise than for its breach. On "termination" all obligations which are still executory on both sides are discharged but any right based on prior breach or performance survives.
(4) "Cancellation" occurs when either party puts an end to the contract for breach by the other and its effect is the same as that of "termination" except that the cancelling party also retains any remedy for breach of the whole contract or any unperformed balance.

§ 2-107. Goods to Be Severed from Realty: Recording.

(1) A contract for the sale of minerals or the like (including oil and gas) or a structure or its materials to be removed from realty is a contract for the sale of goods within this Article if they are to be severed by the seller but until severance a purported present sale thereof which is not effective as a transfer of an interest in land is effective only as a contract to sell.
(2) A contract for the sale apart from the land of growing crops or other things attached to realty and capable of severance without material harm thereto but not described in subsection (1) or of timber to be cut is a contract for the sale of goods within this Article whether the subject matter is to be severed by the buyer or by the seller even though it forms part of the realty at the time of contracting, and the parties can by identification effect a present sale before severance.
(3) The provisions of this section are subject to any third party rights provided by the law relating to realty records, and the contract for sale may be executed and recorded as a document transferring an interest in land and shall then constitute notice to third parties of the buyer's rights under the contract for sale. As amended in 1972.

PART 2: FORM, FORMATION AND READJUSTMENT OF CONTRACT

§ 2-201. Formal Requirements; Statute of Frauds.

(1) Except as otherwise provided in this section a contract for the sale of goods for the price of $500 or more is not enforceable by way of action or defense unless there is some writing sufficient to indicate that a contract for sale has been made between the parties and signed

by the party against whom enforcement is sought or by his authorized agent or broker. A writing is not insufficient because it omits or incorrectly states a term agreed upon but the contract is not enforceable under this paragraph beyond the quantity of goods shown in such writing.

(2) Between merchants if within a reasonable time a writing in confirmation of the contract and sufficient against the sender is received and the party receiving it has reason to know its contents, it satisfies the requirements of subsection (1) against such party unless written notice of objection to its contents is given within 10 days after it is received.

(3) A contract which does not satisfy the requirements of subsection (1) but which is valid in other respects is enforceable

(a) if the goods are to be specially manufactured for the buyer and are not suitable for sale to others in the ordinary course of the seller's business and the seller, before notice of repudiation is received and under circumstances which reasonably indicate that the goods are for the buyer, has made either a substantial beginning of their manufacture or commitments for their procurement; or

(b) if the party against whom enforcement is sought admits in his pleading, testimony or otherwise in court that a contract for sale was made, but the contract is not enforceable under this provision beyond the quantity of goods admitted; or

(c) with respect to goods for which payment has been made and accepted or which have been received and accepted (Section 2–606).

§ 2–202. Final Written Expression: Parol or Extrinsic Evidence. Terms with respect to which the confirmatory memoranda of the parties agree or which are otherwise set forth in a writing intended by the parties as a final expression of their agreement with respect to such terms as are included therein may not be contradicted by evidence of any prior agreement or of a contemporaneous oral agreement but may be explained or supplemented

(a) by course of dealing or usage of trade (Section 1–205) or by course of performance (Section 2–208); and

(b) by evidence of consistent additional terms unless the court finds the writing to have been intended also as a complete and exclusive statement of the terms of the agreement.

§ 2–203. Seals Inoperative. The affixing of a seal to a writing evidencing a contract for sale or an offer to buy or sell goods does not constitute the writing a sealed instrument and the law with respect to sealed instruments does not apply to such a contract or offer.

§ 2–204. Formation in General.

(1) A contract for sale of goods may be made in any manner sufficient to show agreement, including conduct by both parties which recognizes the existence of such a contract.

(2) An agreement sufficient to constitute a contract for sale may be found even though the moment of its making is undetermined.

(3) Even though one or more terms are left open a contract for sale does not fail for indefiniteness if the parties have intended to make a contract and there is a reasonably certain basis for giving an appropriate remedy.

§ 2–205. Firm Offers. An offer by a merchant to buy or sell goods in a signed writing which by its terms gives assurance that it will be held open is not revocable, for lack of consideration, during the time stated or if no time is stated for a reasonable time, but in no event may such period of irrevocability exceed three months; but any such term of assurance on a form supplied by the offeree must be separately signed by the offeror.

§ 2-206. Offer and Acceptance in Formation of Contract.

(1) Unless otherwise unambiguously indicated by the language or circumstances
   (a) an offer to make a contract shall be construed as inviting acceptance in any manner and by any medium reasonable in the circumstances;
   (b) an order or other offer to buy goods for prompt or current shipment shall be construed as inviting acceptance either by a prompt promise to ship or by the prompt or current shipment of conforming or non-conforming goods, but such a shipment of non-conforming goods does not constitute an acceptance if the seller seasonably notifies the buyer that the shipment is offered only as an accommodation to the buyer.

(2) Where the beginning of a requested performance is a reasonable mode of acceptance an offeror who is not notified of acceptance within a reasonable time may treat the offer as having lapsed before acceptance.

§ 2-207. Additional Terms in Acceptance or Confirmation.

(1) A definite and seasonable expression of acceptance or a written confirmation which is sent within a reasonable time operates as an acceptance even though it states terms additional to or different from those offered or agreed upon, unless acceptance is expressly made conditional on assent to the additional or different terms.

(2) The additional terms are to be construed as proposals for addition to the contract. Between merchants such terms become part of the contract unless:
   (a) the offer expressly limits acceptance to the terms of the offer;
   (b) they materially alter it; or
   (c) notification of objection to them has already been given or is given within a reasonable time after notice of them is received.

(3) Conduct by both parties which recognizes the existence of a contract is sufficient to establish a contract for sale although the writings of the parties do not otherwise establish a contract. In such case the terms of the particular contract consist of those terms on which the writings of the parties agree, together with any supplementary terms incorporated under any other provisions of this Act.

§ 2-208. Course of Performance or Practical Construction.

(1) Where the contract for sale involves repeated occasions for performance by either party with knowledge of the nature of the performance and opportunity for objection to it by the other, any course of performance accepted or acquiesced in without objection shall be relevant to determine the meaning of the agreement.

(2) The express terms of the agreement and any such course of performance, as well as any course of dealing and usage of trade, shall be construed whenever reasonable as consistent with each other; but when such construction is unreasonable, express terms shall control course of performance and course of performance shall control both course of dealing and usage of trade (Section 1–205).

(3) Subject to the provisions of the next section on modification and waiver, such course of performance shall be relevant to show a waiver or modification of any term inconsistent with such course of performance.

§ 2-209. Modification, Rescission and Waiver.

(1) An agreement modifying a contract within this Article needs no consideration to be binding.

(2) A signed agreement which excludes modification or rescission except by a signed writing cannot be otherwise modified or rescinded, but except as between merchants such a requirement on a form supplied by the merchant must be separately signed by the other party.

(3) The requirements of the statute of frauds section of this Article (Section 2–201) must be satisfied if the contract as modified is within its provisions.
(4) Although an attempt at modification or rescission does not satisfy the requirements of subsection (2) or (3) it can operate as a waiver.
(5) A party who has made a waiver affecting an executory portion of the contract may retract the waiver by reasonable notification received by the other party that strict performance will be required of any term waived, unless the retraction would be unjust in view of a material change of position in reliance on the waiver.

§ 2–210. Delegation of Performance; Assignment of Rights.

(1) A party may perform his duty through a delegate unless otherwise agreed or unless the other party has a substantial interest in having his original promisor perform or control the acts required by the contract. No delegation of performance relieves the party delegating of any duty to perform or any liability for breach.
(2) Unless otherwise agreed all rights of either seller or buyer can be assigned except where the assignment would materially change the duty of the other party, or increase materially the burden or risk imposed on him by his contract, or impair materially his chance of obtaining return performance. A right to damages for breach of the whole contract or a right arising out of the assignor's due performance of his entire obligation can be assigned despite agreement otherwise.
(3) Unless the circumstances indicate the contrary a prohibition of assignment of "the contract" is to be construed as barring only the delegation to the assignee of the assignor's performance.
(4) An assignment of "the contract" or of "all my rights under the contract" or an assignment in similar general terms is an assignment of rights and unless the language or the circumstances (as in an assignment for security) indicate the contrary, it is a delegation of performance of the duties of the assignor and its acceptance by the assignee constitutes a promise by him to perform those duties. This promise is enforceable by either the assignor or the other party to the original contract.
(5) The other party may treat any assignment which delegates performance as creating reasonable grounds for insecurity and may without prejudice to his rights against the assignor demand assurances from the assignee (Section 2–609).

PART 3: GENERAL OBLIGATION AND CONSTRUCTION OF CONTRACT

§ 2–301. General Obligations of Parties. The obligation of the seller is to transfer and deliver and that of the buyer is to accept and pay in accordance with the contract.

§ 2–302. Unconscionable Contract or Clause.

(1) If the court as a matter of law finds the contract or any clause of the contract to have been unconscionable at the time it was made the court may refuse to enforce the contract, or it may enforce the remainder of the contract without the unconscionable clause, or it may so limit the application of any unconscionable clause as to avoid any unconscionable result.
(2) When it is claimed or appears to the court that the contract or any clause thereof may be unconscionable the parties shall be afforded a reasonable opportunity to present evidence as to its commercial setting, purpose and effect to aid the court in making the determination.

§ 2–303. Allocation or Division of Risks. Where this Article allocates a risk or a burden as between the parties "unless otherwise agreed", the agreement may not only shift the allocation but may also divide the risk or burden.

§ 2–304. Price Payable in Money, Goods, Realty, or Otherwise.

(1) The price can be made payable in money or otherwise. If it is payable in whole or in part in goods each party is a seller of the goods which he is to transfer.

(2) Even though all or part of the price is payable in an interest in realty the transfer of the goods and the seller's obligations with reference to them are subject to this Article, but not the transfer of the interest in realty or the transferor's obligations in connection therewith.

§ 2–305. Open Price Term.

(1) The parties if they so intend can conclude a contract for sale even though the price is not settled. In such a case the price is a reasonable price at the time for delivery if
 (a) nothing is said as to price; or
 (b) the price is left to be agreed by the parties and they fail to agree; or
 (c) the price is to be fixed in terms of some agreed market or other standard as set or recorded by a third person or agency and it is not so set or recorded.

(2) A price to be fixed by the seller or by the buyer means a price for him to fix in good faith.

(3) When a price left to be fixed otherwise than by agreement of the parties fails to be fixed through fault of one party the other may at his option treat the contract as cancelled or himself fix a reasonable price.

(4) Where, however, the parties intend not to be bound unless the price be fixed or agreed and it is not fixed or agreed there is no contract. In such a case the buyer must return any goods already received or if unable so to do must pay their reasonable value at the time of delivery and the seller must return any portion of the price paid on account.

§ 2–306. Output, Requirements and Exclusive Dealings.

(1) A term which measures the quantity by the output of the seller or the requirements of the buyer means such actual output or requirements as may occur in good faith, except that no quantity unreasonably disproportionate to any stated estimate or in the absence of a stated estimate to any normal or otherwise comparable prior output or requirements may be tendered or demanded.

(2) A lawful agreement by either the seller or the buyer for exclusive dealing in the kind of goods concerned imposes unless otherwise agreed an obligation by the seller to use best efforts to supply the goods and by the buyer to use best efforts to promote their sale.

§ 2–307. Delivery in Single Lot or Several Lots. Unless otherwise agreed all goods called for by a contract for sale must be tendered in a single delivery and payment is due only on such tender but where the circumstances give either party the right to make or demand delivery in lots the price if it can be apportioned may be demanded for each lot.

§ 2–308. Absence of Specified Place for Delivery. Unless otherwise agreed

 (a) the place for delivery of goods is the seller's place of business or if he has none his residence; but
 (b) in a contract for sale of identified goods which to the knowledge of the parties at the time of contracting are in some other place, that place is the place for their delivery; and
 (c) documents of title may be delivered through customary banking channels.

§ 2–309. Absence of Specific Time Provisions; Notice of Termination.

(1) The time for shipment or delivery or any other action under a contract if not provided in this Article or agreed upon shall be a reasonable time.

(2) Where the contract provides for successive performances but is indefinite in duration it is valid for a reasonable time but unless otherwise agreed may be terminated at any time by either party.

(3) Termination of a contract by one party except on the happening of an agreed event requires that reasonable notification be received by the other party and an agreement dispensing with notification is invalid if its operation would be unconscionable.

§ 2–310. Open Time for Payment or Running of Credit; Authority to Ship Under Reservation. Unless otherwise agreed

(a) payment is due at the time and place at which the buyer is to receive the goods even though the place of shipment is the place of delivery; and
(b) if the seller is authorized to send the goods he may ship them under reservation, and may tender the documents of title, but the buyer may inspect the goods after their arrival before payment is due unless such inspection is inconsistent with the terms of the contract (Section 2–513); and
(c) if delivery is authorized and made by way of documents of title otherwise than by subsection (b) then payment is due at the time and place at which the buyer is to receive the documents regardless of where the goods are to be received; and
(d) where the seller is required or authorized to ship the goods on credit the credit period runs from the time of shipment but postdating the invoice or delaying its dispatch will correspondingly delay the starting of the credit period.

§ 2–311. Options and Cooperation Respecting Performance.

(1) An agreement for sale which is otherwise sufficiently definite (subsection (3) of Section 2–204) to be a contract is not made invalid by the fact that it leaves particulars of performance to be specified by one of the parties. Any such specification must be made in good faith and within limits set by commercial reasonableness.
(2) Unless otherwise agreed specifications relating to assortment of the goods are at the buyer's option and except as otherwise provided in subsections (1)(c) and (3) of Section 2–319 specifications or arrangements relating to shipment are at the seller's option.
(3) Where such specification would materially affect the other party's performance but is not seasonably made or where one party's cooperation is necessary to the agreed performance of the other but is not seasonably forthcoming, the other party in addition to all other remedies
   (a) is excused for any resulting delay in his own performance; and
   (b) may also either proceed to perform in any reasonable manner or after the time for a material part of his own performance treat the failure to specify or to cooperate as a breach by failure to deliver or accept the goods.

§ 2–312. Warranty of Title and Against Infringement; Buyer's Obligation Against Infringement.

(1) Subject to subsection (2) there is in a contract for sale a warranty by the seller that
   (a) the title conveyed shall be good, and its transfer rightful; and
   (b) the goods shall be delivered free from any security interest or other lien or encumbrance of which the buyer at the time of contracting has no knowledge.
(2) A warranty under subsection (1) will be excluded or modified only by specific language or by circumstances which give the buyer reason to know that the person selling does not claim title in himself or that he is purporting to sell only such right or title as he or a third person may have.
(3) Unless otherwise agreed a seller who is a merchant regularly dealing in goods of the kind warrants that the goods shall be delivered free of the rightful claim of any third person by way of infringement or the like but a buyer who furnishes specifications to the seller must hold the seller harmless against any such claim which arises out of compliance with the specifications.

§ 2–313. Express Warranties by Affirmation, Promise, Description, Sample.

(1) Express warranties by the seller are created as follows:
  (a) Any affirmation of fact or promise made by the seller to the buyer which relates to the goods and becomes part of the basis of the bargain creates an express warranty that the goods shall conform to the affirmation or promise.
  (b) Any description of the goods which is made part of the basis of the bargain creates an express warranty that the goods shall conform to the description.
  (c) Any sample or model which is made part of the basis of the bargain creates an express warranty that the whole of the goods shall conform to the sample or model.

(2) It is not necessary to the creation of an express warranty that the seller use formal words such as "warrant" or "guarantee" or that he have a specific intention to make a warranty, but an affirmation merely of the value of the goods or a statement purporting to be merely the seller's opinion or commendation of the goods does not create a warranty.

§ 2–314. Implied Warranty: Merchantability; Usage of Trade.

(1) Unless excluded or modified (Section 2–316), a warranty that the goods shall be merchantable is implied in a contract for their sale if the seller is a merchant with respect to goods of that kind. Under this section the serving for value of food or drink to be consumed either on the premises or elsewhere is a sale.

(2) Goods to be merchantable must be at least such as
  (a) pass without objection in the trade under the contract description; and
  (b) in the case of fungible goods, are of fair average quality within the description; and
  (c) are fit for the ordinary purposes for which such goods are used; and
  (d) run, within the variations permitted by the agreement, of even kind, quality and quantity within each unit and among all units involved; and
  (e) are adequately contained, packaged, and labeled as the agreement may require; and
  (f) conform to the promise or affirmations of fact made on the container or label if any.

(3) Unless excluded or modified (Section 2–316) other implied warranties may arise from course of dealing or usage of trade.

§ 2–315. Implied Warranty: Fitness for Particular Purpose. Where the seller at the time of contracting has reason to know any particular purpose for which the goods are required and that the buyer is relying on the seller's skill or judgment to select or furnish suitable goods, there is unless excluded or modified under the next section an implied warranty that the goods shall be fit for such purpose.

§ 2–316. Exclusion or Modification of Warranties.

(1) Words or conduct relevant to the creation of an express warranty and words or conduct tending to negate or limit warranty shall be construed wherever reasonable as consistent with each other; but subject to the provisions of this Article on parol or extrinsic evidence (Section 2–202) negation or limitation is inoperative to the extent that such construction is unreasonable.

(2) Subject to subsection (3), to exclude or modify the implied warranty of merchantability or any part of it the language must mention merchantability and in case of a writing must be conspicuous, and to exclude or modify any implied warranty of fitness the exclusion must be by a writing and conspicuous. Language to exclude all implied warranties of fitness is sufficient if it states, for example, that "There are no warranties which extend beyond the description on the face hereof."

(3) Notwithstanding subsection (2)
  (a) unless the circumstances indicate otherwise, all implied warranties are excluded by expressions like "as is", "with all faults" or other language which in common

understanding calls the buyer's attention to the exclusion of warranties and makes plain that there is no implied warranty; and

(b) when the buyer before entering into the contract has examined the goods or the sample or model as fully as he desired or has refused to examine the goods there is no implied warranty with regard to defects which an examination ought in the circumstances to have revealed to him; and

(c) an implied warranty can also be excluded or modified by course of dealing or course of performance or usage of trade.

(4) Remedies for breach of warranty can be limited in accordance with the provisions of this Article on liquidation or limitation of damages and on contractual modification of remedy (Sections 2–718 and 2–719).

§ 2–317. Cumulation and Conflict of Warranties Express or Implied. Warranties whether express or implied shall be construed as consistent with each other and as cumulative, but if such construction is unreasonable the intention of the parties shall determine which warranty is dominant. In ascertaining that intention the following rules apply:

(a) Exact or technical specifications displace an inconsistent sample or model or general language of description.

(b) A sample from an existing bulk displaces inconsistent general language of description.

(c) Express warranties displace inconsistent implied warranties other than an implied warranty of fitness for a particular purpose.

§ 2–318. Third Party Beneficiaries of Warranties Express or Implied.
Note: *If this Act is introduced in the Congress of the United States this section should be omitted. (States to select one alternative.)*

Alternative A
A seller's warranty whether express or implied extends to any natural person who is in the family or household of his buyer or who is a guest in his home if it is reasonable to expect that such person may use, consume or be affected by the goods and who is injured in person by breach of the warranty. A seller may not exclude or limit the operation of this section.

Alternative B
A seller's warranty whether express or implied extends to any natural person who may reasonably be expected to use, consume or be affected by the goods and who is injured in person by breach of the warranty. A seller may not exclude or limit the operation of this section.

Alternative C
A seller's warranty whether express or implied extends to any person who may reasonably be expected to use, consume or be affected by the goods and who is injured by breach of the warranty. A seller may not exclude or limit the operation of this section with respect to injury to the person of an individual to whom the warranty extends.

As amended in 1966.

§ 2–319. F.O.B. and F.A.S. Terms.

(1) Unless otherwise agreed the term F.O.B. (which means "free on board") at a named place, even though used only in connection with the stated price, is a delivery term under which

(a) when the term is F.O.B. the place of shipment, the seller must at that place ship the goods in the manner provided in this Article (Section 2–504) and bear the expense and risk of putting them into the possession of the carrier; or

(b) when the term is F.O.B. the place of destination, the seller must at his own expense and risk transport the goods to that place and there tender delivery of them in the manner provided in this Article (Section 2–503);

(c) when under either (a) or (b) the term is also F.O.B. vessel, car or other vehicle, the seller must in addition at his own expense and risk load the goods on board. If the term is F.O.B. vessel the buyer must name the vessel and in an appropriate case the seller must comply with the provisions of this Article on the form of bill of lading (Section 2–323).

(2) Unless otherwise agreed the term F.A.S. vessel (which means "free alongside") at a named port, even though used only in connection with the stated price, is a delivery term under which the seller must
   (a) at his own expense and risk deliver the goods alongside the vessel in the manner usual in that port or on a dock designated and provided by the buyer; and
   (b) obtain and tender a receipt for the goods in exchange for which the carrier is under a duty to issue a bill of lading.

(3) Unless otherwise agreed in any case falling within subsection (1)(a) or (c) or subsection (2) the buyer must seasonably give any needed instructions for making delivery, including when the term is F.A.S. or F.O.B. the loading berth of the vessel and in an appropriate case its name and sailing date. The seller may treat the failure of needed instructions as a failure of cooperation under this Article (Section 2–311). He may also at his option move the goods in any reasonable manner preparatory to delivery or shipment.

(4) Under the term F.O.B. vessel or F.A.S. unless otherwise agreed the buyer must make payment against tender of the required documents and the seller may not tender nor the buyer demand delivery of the goods in substitution for the documents.

§ 2–320. C.I.F. and C. & F. Terms.

(1) The term C.I.F. means that the price includes in a lump sum the cost of the goods and the insurance and freight to the named destination. The term C. & F. or C.F. means that the price so includes cost and freight to the named destination.

(2) Unless otherwise agreed and even though used only in connection with the stated price and destination, the term C.I.F. destination or its equivalent requires the seller at his own expense and risk to
   (a) put the goods into the possession of a carrier at the port for shipment and obtain a negotiable bill or bills of lading covering the entire transportation to the named destination; and
   (b) load the goods and obtain a receipt from the carrier (which may be contained in the bill of lading) showing that the freight has been paid or provided for; and
   (c) obtain a policy or certificate of insurance, including any war risk insurance, of a kind and on terms then current at the port of shipment in the usual amount, in the currency of the contract, shown to cover the same goods covered by the bill of lading and providing for payment of loss to the order of the buyer or for the account of whom it may concern; but the seller may add to the price the amount of the premium for any such war risk insurance; and
   (d) prepare an invoice of the goods and procure any other documents required to effect shipment or to comply with the contract; and
   (e) forward and tender with commercial promptness all the documents in due form and with any indorsement necessary to perfect the buyer's rights.

(3) Unless otherwise agreed the term C. & F. or its equivalent has the same effect and imposes upon the seller the same obligations and risks as a C.I.F. term except the obligation as to insurance.

(4) Under the term C.I.F. or C. & F. unless otherwise agreed the buyer must make payment against tender of the required documents and the seller may not tender nor the buyer demand delivery of the goods in substitution for the documents.

§ 2–321. C.I.F. or C. & F.: "Net Landed Weights"; "Payment on Arrival"; Warranty of Condition on Arrival. Under a contract containing a term C.I.F. or C. & F.

(1) Where the price is based on or is to be adjusted according to "net landed weights", "delivered weights", "out turn" quantity or quality or the like, unless otherwise agreed the seller must reasonably estimate the price. The payment due on tender of the documents called for

by the contract is the amount so estimated, but after final adjustment of the price a settlement must be made with commercial promptness.

(2) An agreement described in subsection (1) or any warranty of quality or condition of the goods on arrival places upon the seller the risk of ordinary deterioration, shrinkage and the like in transportation but has no effect on the place or time of identification to the contract for sale or delivery or on the passing of the risk of loss.

(3) Unless otherwise agreed where the contract provides for payment on or after arrival of the goods the seller must before payment allow such preliminary inspection as is feasible; but if the goods are lost delivery of the documents and payment are due when the goods should have arrived.

§ 2–322. Delivery "Ex-Ship".

(1) Unless otherwise agreed a term for delivery of goods "ex-ship" (which means from the carrying vessel) or in equivalent language is not restricted to a particular ship and requires delivery from a ship which has reached a place at the named port of destination where goods of the kind are usually discharged.

(2) Under such a term unless otherwise agreed
   (a) the seller must discharge all liens arising out of the carriage and furnish the buyer with a direction which puts the carrier under a duty to deliver the goods; and
   (b) the risk of loss does not pass to the buyer until the goods leave the ship's tackle or are otherwise properly unloaded.

§ 2–323. Form of Bill of Lading Required in Overseas Shipment; "Overseas".

(1) Where the contract contemplates overseas shipment and contains a term C.I.F. or C. & F. or F.O.B. vessel, the seller unless otherwise agreed must obtain a negotiable bill of lading stating that the goods have been loaded in board or, in the case of a term C.I.F. or C. & F., received for shipment.

(2) Where in a case within subsection (1) a bill of lading has been issued in a set of parts, unless otherwise agreed if the documents are not to be sent from abroad the buyer may demand tender of the full set; otherwise only one part of the bill of lading need be tendered. Even if the agreement expressly requires a full set
   (a) due tender of a single part is acceptable within the provisions of this Article on cure of improper delivery (subsection (1) of Section 2–508); and
   (b) even though the full set is demanded, if the documents are sent from abroad the person tendering an incomplete set may nevertheless require payment upon furnishing an indemnity which the buyer in good faith deems adequate.

(3) A shipment by water or by air or a contract contemplating such shipment is "overseas" insofar as by usage of trade or agreement it is subject to the commercial, financing or shipping practices characteristic of international deep water commerce.

§ 2–324. "No Arrival, No Sale" Term. Under a term "no arrival, no sale" or terms of like meaning, unless otherwise agreed,

   (a) the seller must properly ship conforming goods and if they arrive by any means he must tender them on arrival but he assumes no obligation that the goods will arrive unless he has caused the non-arrival; and
   (b) where without fault of the seller the goods are in part lost or have so deteriorated as no longer to conform to the contract or arrive after the contract time, the buyer may proceed as if there had been casualty to identified goods (Section 2–613).

§ 2–325. "Letter of Credit" Term; "Confirmed Credit".

(1) Failure of the buyer seasonably to furnish an agreed letter of credit is a breach of the contract for sale.

(2) The delivery to seller of a proper letter of credit suspends the buyer's obligation to pay. If the letter of credit is dishonored, the seller may on seasonable notification to the buyer require payment directly from him.

(3) Unless otherwise agreed the term "letter of credit" or "banker's credit" in a contract for sale means an irrevocable credit issued by a financing agency of good repute and, where the shipment is overseas, of good international repute. The term "confirmed credit" means that the credit must also carry the direct obligation of such an agency which does business in the seller's financial market.

§ 2–326. Sale on Approval and Sale or Return; Consignment Sales and Rights of Creditors.

(1) Unless otherwise agreed, if delivered goods may be returned by the buyer even though they conform to the contract, the transaction is
   (a) a "sale on approval" if the goods are delivered primarily for use, and
   (b) a "sale or return" if the goods are delivered primarily for resale.

(2) Except as provided in subsection (3), goods held on approval are not subject to the claims of the buyer's creditors until acceptance; goods held on sale or return are subject to such claims while in the buyer's possession.

(3) Where goods are delivered to a person for sale and such person maintains a place of business at which he deals in goods of the kind involved, under a name other than the name of the person making delivery, then with respect to claims of creditors of the person conducting the business the goods are deemed to be on sale or return. The provisions of this subsection are applicable even though an agreement purports to reserve title to the person making delivery until payment or resale or uses such words as "on consignment" or "on memorandum". However, this subsection is not applicable if the person making delivery
   (a) complies with an applicable law providing for a consignor's interest or the like to be evidenced by a sign, or
   (b) establishes that the person conducting the business is generally known by his creditors to be substantially engaged in selling the goods of others, or
   (c) complies with the filing provisions of the Article on Secured Transactions (Article 9).

(4) Any "or return" term of a contract for sale is to be treated as a separate contract for sale within the statute of frauds section of this Article (Section 2–201) and as contradicting the sale aspect of the contract within the provisions of this Article on parol or extrinsic evidence (Section 2–202).

§ 2–327. Special Incidents of Sale on Approval and Sale or Return.

(1) Under a sale on approval unless otherwise agreed
   (a) although the goods are identified to the contract the risk of loss and the title do not pass to the buyer until acceptance; and
   (b) use of the goods consistent with the purpose of trial is not acceptance but failure seasonably to notify the seller of election to return the goods is acceptance, and if the goods conform to the contract acceptance of any part is acceptance of the whole; and
   (c) after due notification of election to return, the return is at the seller's risk and expense but a merchant buyer must follow any reasonable instructions.

(2) Under a sale or return unless otherwise agreed
   (a) the option to return extends to the whole or any commercial unit of the goods while in substantially their original condition, but must be exercised seasonably; and
   (b) the return is at the buyer's risk and expense.

§ 2–328. Sale by Auction.

(1) In a sale by auction if goods are put up in lots each lot is the subject of a separate sale.

(2) A sale by auction is complete when the auctioneer so announces by the fall of the hammer or in other customary manner. Where a bid is made while the hammer is falling in

acceptance of a prior bid the auctioneer may in his discretion reopen the bidding or declare the goods sold under the bid on which the hammer was falling.

(3) Such a sale is with reserve unless the goods are in explicit terms put up without reserve. In an auction with reserve the auctioneer may withdraw the goods at any time until he announces completion of the sale. In an auction without reserve, after the auctioneer calls for bids on an article or lot, that article or lot cannot be withdrawn unless no bid is made within a reasonable time. In either case a bidder may retract his bid until the auctioneer's announcement of completion of the sale, but a bidder's retraction does not revive any previous bid.

(4) If the auctioneer knowingly receives a bid on the seller's behalf or the seller makes or procures such a bid, and notice has not been given that liberty for such bidding is reserved, the buyer may at his option avoid the sale or take the goods at the price of the last good faith bid prior to the completion of the sale. This subsection shall not apply to any bid at a forced sale.

PART 4: TITLE, CREDITORS AND GOOD FAITH PURCHASERS

§ 2–401. Passing of Title; Reservation for Security; Limited Application of This Section. Each provision of this Article with regard to the rights, obligations and remedies of the seller, the buyer, purchasers or other third parties applies irrespective of title to the goods except where the provision refers to such title. Insofar as situations are not covered by the other provisions of this Article and matters concerning title become material the following rules apply:

(1) Title to goods cannot pass under a contract for sale prior to their identification to the contract (Section 2–501), and unless otherwise explicitly agreed the buyer acquires by their identification a special property as limited by this Act. Any retention or reservation by the seller of the title (property) in goods shipped or delivered to the buyer is limited in effect to a reservation of a security interest. Subject to these provisions and to the provisions of the Article on Secured Transactions (Article 9), title to goods passes from the seller to the buyer in any manner and on any conditions explicitly agreed on by the parties.

(2) Unless otherwise explicitly agreed title passes to the buyer at the time and place at which the seller completes his performance with reference to the physical delivery of the goods, despite any reservation of a security interest and even though a document of title is to be delivered at a different time or place; and in particular and despite any reservation of a security interest by the bill of lading
   (a) if the contract requires or authorizes the seller to send the goods to the buyer but does not require him to deliver them at destination, title passes to the buyer at the time and place of shipment; but
   (b) if the contract requires delivery at destination, title passes on tender there.

(3) Unless otherwise explicitly agreed where delivery is to be made without moving the goods,
   (a) if the seller is to deliver a document of title, title passes at the time when and the place where he delivers such documents; or
   (b) if the goods are at the time of contracting already identified and no documents are to be delivered, title passes at the time and place of contracting.

(4) A rejection or other refusal by the buyer to receive or retain the goods, whether or not justified, or a justified revocation of acceptance revests title to the goods in the seller. Such revesting occurs by operation of law and is not a "sale".

§ 2–402. Rights of Seller's Creditors Against Sold Goods.

(1) Except as provided in subsections (2) and (3), rights of unsecured creditors of the seller with respect to goods which have been identified to a contract for sale are subject to the buyer's rights to recover the goods under this Article (Sections 2–502 and 2–716).

(2) A creditor of the seller may treat a sale or an identification of goods to a contract for sale as void if as against him a retention of possession by the seller is fraudulent under any rule of law of the state where the goods are situated, except that retention of possession in good faith and current course of trade by a merchant-seller for a commercially reasonable time after a sale or identification is not fraudulent.

(3) Nothing in this Article shall be deemed to impair the rights of creditors of the seller
   (a) under the provisions of the Article on Secured Transactions (Article 9); or
   (b) where identification to the contract or delivery is made not in current course of trade but in satisfaction of or as security for a pre-existing claim for money, security or the like and is made under circumstances which under any rule of law of the state where the goods are situated would apart from this Article constitute the transaction a fraudulent transfer or voidable preference.

§ 2–403. Power to Transfer; Good Faith Purchase of Goods; "Entrusting".

(1) A purchaser of goods acquires all title which his transferor had or had power to transfer except that a purchaser of a limited interest acquires rights only to the extent of the interest purchased. A person with voidable title has power to transfer a good title to a good faith purchaser for value. When goods have been delivered under a transaction of purchase the purchaser has such power even though
   (a) the transferor was deceived as to the identity of the purchaser, or
   (b) the delivery was in exchange for a check which is later dishonored, or
   (c) it was agreed that the transaction was to be a "cash sale", or
   (d) the delivery was procured through fraud punishable as larcenous under the criminal law.

(2) Any entrusting of possession of goods to a merchant who deals in goods of that kind gives him power to transfer all rights of the entruster to a buyer in ordinary course of business.

(3) "Entrusting" includes any delivery and any acquiescence in retention of possession regardless of any condition expressed between the parties to the delivery or acquiescence and regardless of whether the procurement of the entrusting or the possessor's disposition of the goods have been such as to be larcenous under the criminal law.
   [*Publisher's Editorial Note: If a state adopts the repealer of Article 6—Bulk Transfers (Alternative A), subsec. (4) should read as follows:*]

(4) The rights of other purchasers of goods and of lien creditors are governed by the Articles on Secured Transactions (Article 9) and Documents of Title (Article 7).
   [*Publisher's Editorial Note: If a state adopts Revised Article 6—Bulk Sales (Alternative B), subsec. (4) should read as follows:*]

(4) The rights of other purchasers of goods and of lien creditors are governed by the Articles on Secured Transactions (Article 9), Bulk Sales (Article 6) and Documents of Title (Article 7).

As amended in 1988.

For material relating to the changes made in text in 1988, see section 3 of Alternative A (Repealer of Article 6—Bulk Transfers) and Conforming Amendment to Section 2–403 following end of Alternative B (Revised Article 6—Bulk Sales).

PART 5: PERFORMANCE

§ 2–501. Insurable Interest in Goods; Manner of Identification of Goods.

(1) The buyer obtains a special property and an insurable interest in goods by identification of existing goods as goods to which the contract refers even though the goods so identified are non-conforming and he has an option to return or reject them. Such identification can be made at any time and in any manner explicitly agreed to by the parties. In the absence of explicit agreement identification occurs

(a) when the contract is made if it is for the sale of goods already existing and identified;
(b) if the contract is for the sale of future goods other than those described in paragraph (c), when goods are shipped, marked or otherwise designated by the seller as goods to which the contract refers;
(c) when the crops are planted or otherwise become growing crops or the young are conceived if the contract is for the sale of unborn young to be born within twelve months after contracting or for the sale of crops to be harvested within twelve months or the next normal harvest season after contracting whichever is longer.

(2) The seller retains an insurable interest in goods so long as title to or any security interest in the goods remains in him and where the identification is by the seller alone he may until default or insolvency or notification to the buyer that the identification is final substitute other goods for those identified.
(3) Nothing in this section impairs any insurable interest recognized under any other statute or rule of law.

§ 2–502. Buyer's Right to Goods on Seller's Insolvency.

(1) Subject to subsection (2) and even though the goods have not been shipped a buyer who has paid a part or all of the price of goods in which he has a special property under the provisions of the immediately preceding section may on making and keeping good a tender of any unpaid portion of their price recover them from the seller if the seller becomes insolvent within ten days after receipt of the first installment on their price.
(2) If the identification creating his special property has been made by the buyer he acquires the right to recover the goods only if they conform to the contract for sale.

§ 2–503. Manner of Seller's Tender of Delivery.

(1) Tender of delivery requires that the seller put and hold conforming goods at the buyer's disposition and give the buyer any notification reasonably necessary to enable him to take delivery. The manner, time and place for tender are determined by the agreement and this Article, and in particular
   (a) tender must be at a reasonable hour, and if it is of goods they must be kept available for the period reasonably necessary to enable the buyer to take possession; but
   (b) unless otherwise agreed the buyer must furnish facilities reasonably suited to the receipt of the goods.
(2) Where the case is within the next section respecting shipment tender requires that the seller comply with its provisions.
(3) Where the seller is required to deliver at a particular destination tender requires that he comply with subsection (1) and also in any appropriate case tender documents as described in subsections (4) and (5) of this section.
(4) Where goods are in the possession of a bailee and are to be delivered without being moved
   (a) tender requires that the seller either tender a negotiable document of title covering such goods or procure acknowledgment by the bailee of the buyer's right to possession of the goods; but
   (b) tender to the buyer of a non-negotiable document of title or of a written direction to the bailee to deliver is sufficient tender unless the buyer seasonably objects, and receipt by the bailee of notification of the buyer's rights fixes those rights as against the bailee and all third persons; but risk of loss of the goods and of any failure by the bailee to honor the non-negotiable document of title or to obey the direction remains on the seller until the buyer has had a reasonable time to present the document or direction, and a refusal by the bailee to honor the document or to obey the direction defeats the tender.
(5) Where the contract requires the seller to deliver documents
   (a) he must tender all such documents in correct form, except as provided in this Article with respect to bills of lading in a set (subsection (2) of Section 2–323); and
   (b) tender through customary banking channels is sufficient and dishonor of a draft accompanying the documents constitutes non-acceptance or rejection.

§ 2–504. Shipment by Seller. Where the seller is required or authorized to send the goods to the buyer and the contract does not require him to deliver them at a particular destination, then unless otherwise agreed he must

(a) put the goods in the possession of such a carrier and make such a contract for their transportation as may be reasonable having regard to the nature of the goods and other circumstances of the case; and
(b) obtain and promptly deliver or tender in due form any document necessary to enable the buyer to obtain possession of the goods or otherwise required by the agreement or by usage of trade; and
(c) promptly notify the buyer of the shipment.

Failure to notify the buyer under paragraph (c) or to make a proper contract under paragraph (a) is a ground for rejection only if material delay or loss ensues.

§ 2–505. Seller's Shipment Under Reservation.

(1) Where the seller has identified goods to the contract by or before shipment:
   (a) his procurement of a negotiable bill of lading to his own order or otherwise reserves in him a security interest in the goods. His procurement of the bill to the order of a financing agency or of the buyer indicates in addition only the seller's expectation of transferring that interest to the person named.
   (b) a non-negotiable bill of lading to himself or his nominee reserves possession of the goods as security but except in a case of conditional delivery (subsection (2) of Section 2–507) a non-negotiable bill of lading naming the buyer as consignee reserves no security interest even though the seller retains possession of the bill of lading.
(2) When shipment by the seller with reservation of a security interest is in violation of the contract for sale it constitutes an improper contract for transportation within the preceding section but impairs neither the rights given to the buyer by shipment and identification of the goods to the contract nor the seller's powers as a holder of a negotiable document.

§ 2–506. Rights of Financing Agency.

(1) A financing agency by paying or purchasing for value a draft which relates to a shipment of goods acquires to the extent of the payment or purchase and in addition to its own rights under the draft and any document of title securing it any rights of the shipper in the goods including the right to stop delivery and the shipper's right to have the draft honored by the buyer.
(2) The right to reimbursement of a financing agency which has in good faith honored or purchased the draft under commitment to or authority from the buyer is not impaired by subsequent discovery of defects with reference to any relevant document which was apparently regular on its face.

§ 2–507. Effect of Seller's Tender; Delivery on Condition.

(1) Tender of delivery is a condition to the buyer's duty to accept the goods and, unless otherwise agreed, to his duty to pay for them. Tender entitles the seller to acceptance of the goods and to payment according to the contract.
(2) Where payment is due and demanded on the delivery to the buyer of goods or documents of title, his right as against the seller to retain or dispose of them is conditional upon his making the payment due.

§ 2–508. Cure by Seller of Improper Tender or Delivery; Replacement.

(1) Where any tender or delivery by the seller is rejected because non-conforming and the time for performance has not yet expired, the seller may seasonably notify the buyer of his intention to cure and may then within the contract time make a conforming delivery.

(2) Where the buyer rejects a non-conforming tender which the seller had reasonable grounds to believe would be acceptable with or without money allowance the seller may if he seasonably notifies the buyer have a further reasonable time to substitute a conforming tender.

§ 2–509. Risk of Loss in the Absence of Breach.

(1) Where the contract requires or authorizes the seller to ship the goods by carrier
  (a) if it does not require him to deliver them at a particular destination, the risk of loss passes to the buyer when the goods are duly delivered to the carrier even though the shipment is under reservation (Section 2–505); but
  (b) if it does require him to deliver them at a particular destination and the goods are there duly tendered while in the possession of the carrier, the risk of loss passes to the buyer when the goods are there duly so tendered as to enable the buyer to take delivery.
(2) Where the goods are held by a bailee to be delivered without being moved, the risk of loss passes to the buyer
  (a) on his receipt of a negotiable document of title covering the goods; or
  (b) on acknowledgment by the bailee of the buyer's right to possession of the goods; or
  (c) after his receipt of a non-negotiable document of title or other written direction to deliver, as provided in subsection (4)(b) of Section 2–503.
(3) In any case not within subsection (1) or (2), the risk of loss passes to the buyer on his receipt of the goods if the seller is a merchant; otherwise the risk passes to the buyer on tender of delivery.
(4) The provisions of this section are subject to contrary agreement of the parties and to the provisions of this Article on sale on approval (Section 2–327) and on effect of breach on risk of loss (Section 2–510).

§ 2–510. Effect of Breach on Risk of Loss.

(1) Where a tender or delivery of goods so fails to conform to the contract as to give a right of rejection the risk of their loss remains on the seller until cure or acceptance.
(2) Where the buyer rightfully revokes acceptance he may to the extent of any deficiency in his effective insurance coverage treat the risk of loss as having rested on the seller from the beginning.
(3) Where the buyer as to conforming goods already identified to the contract for sale repudiates or is otherwise in breach before risk of their loss has passed to him, the seller may to the extent of any deficiency in his effective insurance coverage treat the risk of loss as resting on the buyer for a commercially reasonable time.

§ 2–511. Tender of Payment by Buyer; Payment by Check.

(1) Unless otherwise agreed tender of payment is a condition to the seller's duty to tender and complete any delivery.
(2) Tender of payment is sufficient when made by any means or in any manner current in the ordinary course of business unless the seller demands payment in legal tender and gives any extension of time reasonably necessary to procure it.
(3) Subject to the provisions of this Act on the effect of an instrument on an obligation (Section 3–310), payment by check is conditional and is defeated as between the parties by dishonor of the check on due presentment.

As amended in 1994.

See Appendix XI for material relating to changes made in text in 1994.

§ 2–512. Payment by Buyer Before Inspection.

(1) Where the contract requires payment before inspection non-conformity of the goods does not excuse the buyer from so making payment unless

(a) the non-conformity appears without inspection; or
(b) despite tender of the required documents the circumstances would justify injunction against honor under this Act (Section 5–109(b)).

(2) Payment pursuant to subsection (1) does not constitute an acceptance of goods or impair the buyer's right to inspect or any of his remedies.

As amended in 1995.

See Appendix XIV for material relating to changes made in text in 1995.

§ 2–513. Buyer's Right to Inspection of Goods.

(1) Unless otherwise agreed and subject to subsection (3), where goods are tendered or delivered or identified to the contract for sale, the buyer has a right before payment or acceptance to inspect them at any reasonable place and time and in any reasonable manner. When the seller is required or authorized to send the goods to the buyer, the inspection may be after their arrival.

(2) Expenses of inspection must be borne by the buyer but may be recovered from the seller if the goods do not conform and are rejected.

(3) Unless otherwise agreed and subject to the provisions of this Article on C.I.F. contracts (subsection (3) of Section 2–321), the buyer is not entitled to inspect the goods before payment of the price when the contract provides
(a) for delivery "C.O.D." or on other like terms; or
(b) for payment against documents of title, except where such payment is due only after the goods are to become available for inspection.

(4) A place or method of inspection fixed by the parties is presumed to be exclusive but unless otherwise expressly agreed it does not postpone identification or shift the place for delivery or for passing the risk of loss. If compliance becomes impossible, inspection shall be as provided in this section unless the place or method fixed was clearly intended as an indispensable condition failure of which avoids the contract.

§ 2–514. When Documents Deliverable on Acceptance; When on Payment. Unless otherwise agreed documents against which a draft is drawn are to be delivered to the drawee on acceptance of the draft if it is payable more than three days after presentment; otherwise, only on payment.

§ 2–515. Preserving Evidence of Goods in Dispute. In furtherance of the adjustment of any claim or dispute

(a) either party on reasonable notification to the other and for the purpose of ascertaining the facts and preserving evidence has the right to inspect, test and sample the goods including such of them as may be in the possession or control of the other; and
(b) the parties may agree to a third party inspection or survey to determine the conformity or condition of the goods and may agree that the findings shall be binding upon them in any subsequent litigation or adjustment.

PART 6: BREACH, REPUDIATION AND EXCUSE

§ 2–601. Buyer's Rights on Improper Delivery. Subject to the provisions of this Article on breach in installment contracts (Section 2–612) and unless otherwise agreed under the sections on contractual limitations of remedy (Sections 2–718 and 2–719), if the goods or the tender of delivery fail in any respect to conform to the contract, the buyer may

(a) reject the whole; or
(b) accept the whole; or
(c) accept any commercial unit or units and reject the rest.

§ 2–602. Manner and Effect of Rightful Rejection.

(1) Rejection of goods must be within a reasonable time after their delivery or tender. It is ineffective unless the buyer seasonably notifies the seller.
(2) Subject to the provisions of the two following sections on rejected goods (Sections 2–603 and 2–604),
  (a) after rejection any exercise of ownership by the buyer with respect to any commercial unit is wrongful as against the seller; and
  (b) if the buyer has before rejection taken physical possession of goods in which he does not have a security interest under the provisions of this Article (subsection (3) of Section 2–711), he is under a duty after rejection to hold them with reasonable care at the seller's disposition for a time sufficient to permit the seller to remove them; but
  (c) the buyer has no further obligations with regard to goods rightfully rejected.
(3) The seller's rights with respect to goods wrongfully rejected are governed by the provisions of this Article on Seller's remedies in general (Section 2–703).

§ 2–603. Merchant Buyer's Duties as to Rightfully Rejected Goods.

(1) Subject to any security interest in the buyer (subsection (3) of Section 2–711), when the seller has no agent or place of business at the market of rejection a merchant buyer is under a duty after rejection of goods in his possession or control to follow any reasonable instructions received from the seller with respect to the goods and in the absence of such instructions to make reasonable efforts to sell them for the seller's account if they are perishable or threaten to decline in value speedily. Instructions are not reasonable if on demand indemnity for expenses is not forthcoming.
(2) When the buyer sells goods under subsection (1), he is entitled to reimbursement from the seller or out of the proceeds for reasonable expenses of caring for and selling them, and if the expenses include no selling commission then to such commission as is usual in the trade or if there is none to a reasonable sum not exceeding ten percent on the gross proceeds.
(3) In complying with this section the buyer is held only to good faith and good faith conduct hereunder is neither acceptance nor conversion nor the basis of an action for damages.

§ 2–604. Buyer's Options as to Salvage of Rightfully Rejected Goods. Subject to the provisions of the immediately preceding section on perishables if the seller gives no instructions within a reasonable time after notification of rejection the buyer may store the rejected goods for the seller's account or reship them to him or resell them for the seller's account with reimbursement as provided in the preceding section. Such action is not acceptance or conversion.

§ 2–605. Waiver of Buyer's Objections by Failure to Particularize.

(1) The buyer's failure to state in connection with rejection a particular defect which is ascertainable by reasonable inspection precludes him from relying on the unstated defect to justify rejection or to establish breach
  (a) where the seller could have cured it if stated seasonably; or
  (b) between merchants when the seller has after rejection made a request in writing for a full and final written statement of all defects on which the buyer proposes to rely.
(2) Payment against documents made without reservation of rights precludes recovery of the payment for defects apparent on the face of the documents.

§ 2–606. What Constitutes Acceptance of Goods.

(1) Acceptance of goods occurs when the buyer
  (a) after a reasonable opportunity to inspect the goods signifies to the seller that the goods are conforming or that he will take or retain them in spite of their non-conformity; or

(b) fails to make an effective rejection (subsection (1) of Section 2–602), but such acceptance does not occur until the buyer has had a reasonable opportunity to inspect them; or

(c) does any act inconsistent with the seller's ownership; but if such act is wrongful as against the seller it is an acceptance only if ratified by him.

(2) Acceptance of a part of any commercial unit is acceptance of that entire unit.

§ 2–607. Effect of Acceptance; Notice of Breach; Burden of Establishing Breach After Acceptance; Notice of Claim or Litigation to Person Answerable Over.

(1) The buyer must pay at the contract rate for any goods accepted.

(2) Acceptance of goods by the buyer precludes rejection of the goods accepted and if made with knowledge of a non-conformity cannot be revoked because of it unless the acceptance was on the reasonable assumption that the non-conformity would be seasonably cured but acceptance does not of itself impair any other remedy provided by this Article for non-conformity.

(3) Where a tender has been accepted

(a) the buyer must within a reasonable time after he discovers or should have discovered any breach notify the seller of breach or be barred from any remedy; and

(b) if the claim is one for infringement or the like (subsection (3) of Section 2–312) and the buyer is sued as a result of such a breach he must so notify the seller within a reasonable time after he receives notice of the litigation or be barred from any remedy over for liability established by the litigation.

(4) The burden is on the buyer to establish any breach with respect to the goods accepted.

(5) Where the buyer is sued for breach of a warranty or other obligation for which his seller is answerable over

(a) he may give his seller written notice of the litigation. If the notice states that the seller may come in and defend and that if the seller does not do so he will be bound in any action against him by his buyer by any determination of fact common to the two litigations, then unless the seller after seasonable receipt of the notice does come in and defend he is so bound.

(b) if the claim is one for infringement or the like (subsection (3) of Section 2–312) the original seller may demand in writing that his buyer turn over to him control of the litigation including settlement or else be barred from any remedy over and if he also agrees to bear all expense and to satisfy any adverse judgment, then unless the buyer after seasonable receipt of the demand does turn over control the buyer is so barred.

(6) The provisions of subsections (3), (4) and (5) apply to any obligation of a buyer to hold the seller harmless against infringement or the like (subsection (3) of Section 2–312).

§ 2–608. Revocation of Acceptance in Whole or in Part.

(1) The buyer may revoke his acceptance of a lot or commercial unit whose non-conformity substantially impairs its value to him if he has accepted it

(a) on the reasonable assumption that its non-conformity would be cured and it has not been seasonably cured; or

(b) without discovery of such non-conformity if his acceptance was reasonably induced either by the difficulty of discovery before acceptance or by the seller's assurances.

(2) Revocation of acceptance must occur within a reasonable time after the buyer discovers or should have discovered the ground for it and before any substantial change in condition of the goods which is not caused by their own defects. It is not effective until the buyer notifies the seller of it.

(3) A buyer who so revokes has the same rights and duties with regard to the goods involved as if he had rejected them.

§ 2-609. Right to Adequate Assurance of Performance.

(1) A contract for sale imposes an obligation on each party that the other's expectation of receiving due performance will not be impaired. When reasonable grounds for insecurity arise with respect to the performance of either party the other may in writing demand adequate assurance of due performance and until he receives such assurance may if commercially reasonable suspend any performance for which he has not already received the agreed return.
(2) Between merchants the reasonableness of grounds for insecurity and the adequacy of any assurance offered shall be determined according to commercial standards.
(3) Acceptance of any improper delivery or payment does not prejudice the aggrieved party's right to demand adequate assurance of future performance.
(4) After receipt of a justified demand failure to provide within a reasonable time not exceeding thirty days such assurance of due performance as is adequate under the circumstances of the particular case is a repudiation of the contract.

§ 2-610. Anticipatory Repudiation. When either party repudiates the contract with respect to a performance not yet due the loss of which will substantially impair the value of the contract to the other, the aggrieved party may

(a) for a commercially reasonable time await performance by the repudiating party; or
(b) resort to any remedy for breach (Section 2–703 or Section 2–711), even though he has notified the repudiating party that he would await the latter's performance and has urged retraction; and
(c) in either case suspend his own performance or proceed in accordance with the provisions of this Article on the seller's right to identify goods to the contract notwithstanding breach or to salvage unfinished goods (Section 2–704).

§ 2-611. Retraction of Anticipatory Repudiation.

(1) Until the repudiating party's next performance is due he can retract his repudiation unless the aggrieved party has since the repudiation cancelled or materially changed his position or otherwise indicated that he considers the repudiation final.
(2) Retraction may be by any method which clearly indicates to the aggrieved party that the repudiating party intends to perform, but must include any assurance justifiably demanded under the provisions of this Article (Section 2–609).
(3) Retraction reinstates the repudiating party's rights under the contract with due excuse and allowance to the aggrieved party for any delay occasioned by the repudiation.

§ 2-612. "Installment Contract"; Breach.

(1) An "installment contract" is one which requires or authorizes the delivery of goods in separate lots to be separately accepted, even though the contract contains a clause "each delivery is a separate contract" or its equivalent.
(2) The buyer may reject any installment which is non-conforming if the non-conformity substantially impairs the value of that installment and cannot be cured or if the non-conformity is a defect in the required documents; but if the non-conformity does not fall within subsection (3) and the seller gives adequate assurance of its cure the buyer must accept that installment.
(3) Whenever non-conformity or default with respect to one or more installments substantially impairs the value of the whole contract there is a breach of the whole. But the aggrieved party reinstates the contract if he accepts a non-conforming installment without seasonably notifying of cancellation or if he brings an action with respect only to past installments or demands performance as to future installments.

§ 2–613. Casualty to Identified Goods. Where the contract requires for its performance goods identified when the contract is made, and the goods suffer casualty without fault of either party before the risk of loss passes to the buyer, or in a proper case under a "no arrival, no sale" term (Section 2–324) then

(a) if the loss is total the contract is avoided; and
(b) if the loss is partial or the goods have so deteriorated as no longer to conform to the contract the buyer may nevertheless demand inspection and at his option either treat the contract as avoided or accept the goods with due allowance from the contract price for the deterioration or the deficiency in quantity but without further right against the seller.

§ 2–614. Substituted Performance.

(1) Where without fault of either party the agreed berthing, loading, or unloading facilities fail or an agreed type of carrier becomes unavailable or the agreed manner of delivery otherwise becomes commercially impracticable but a commercially reasonable substitute is available, such substitute performance must be tendered and accepted.
(2) If the agreed means or manner of payment fails because of domestic or foreign governmental regulation, the seller may withhold or stop delivery unless the buyer provides a means or manner of payment which is commercially a substantial equivalent. If delivery has already been taken, payment by the means or in the manner provided by the regulation discharges the buyer's obligation unless the regulation is discriminatory, oppressive or predatory.

§ 2–615. Excuse by Failure of Presupposed Conditions. Except so far as a seller may have assumed a greater obligation and subject to the preceding section on substituted performance:

(a) Delay in delivery or non-delivery in whole or in part by a seller who complies with paragraphs (b) and (c) is not a breach of his duty under a contract for sale if performance as agreed has been made impracticable by the occurrence of a contingency the non-occurrence of which was a basic assumption on which the contract was made or by compliance in good faith with any applicable foreign or domestic governmental regulation or order whether or not it later proves to be invalid.
(b) Where the causes mentioned in paragraph (a) affect only a part of the seller's capacity to perform, he must allocate production and deliveries among his customers but may at his option include regular customers not then under contract as well as his own requirements for further manufacture. He may so allocate in any manner which is fair and reasonable.
(c) The seller must notify the buyer seasonably that there will be delay or non-delivery and, when allocation is required under paragraph (b), of the estimated quota thus made available for the buyer.

§ 2–616. Procedure on Notice Claiming Excuse.

(1) Where the buyer receives notification of a material or indefinite delay or an allocation justified under the preceding section he may by written notification to the seller as to any delivery concerned, and where the prospective deficiency substantially impairs the value of the whole contract under the provisions of this Article relating to breach of installment contracts (Section 2–612), then also as to the whole,
    (a) terminate and thereby discharge any unexecuted portion of the contract; or
    (b) modify the contract by agreeing to take his available quota in substitution.
(2) If after receipt of such notification from the seller the buyer fails so to modify the contract within a reasonable time not exceeding thirty days the contract lapses with respect to any deliveries affected.
(3) The provisions of this section may not be negated by agreement except in so far as the seller has assumed a greater obligation under the preceding section.

PART 7: REMEDIES

§ 2–701. Remedies for Breach of Collateral Contracts Not Impaired. Remedies for breach of any obligation or promise collateral or ancillary to a contract for sale are not impaired by the provisions of this Article.

§ 2–702. Seller's Remedies on Discovery of Buyer's Insolvency.

(1) Where the seller discovers the buyer to be insolvent he may refuse delivery except for cash including payment for all goods theretofore delivered under the contract, and stop delivery under this Article (Section 2–705).

(2) Where the seller discovers that the buyer has received goods on credit while insolvent he may reclaim the goods upon demand made within ten days after the receipt, but if misrepresentation of solvency has been made to the particular seller in writing within three months before delivery the ten day limitation does not apply. Except as provided in this subsection the seller may not base a right to reclaim goods on the buyer's fraudulent or innocent misrepresentation of solvency or of intent to pay.

(3) The seller's right to reclaim under subsection (2) is subject to the rights of a buyer in ordinary course or other good faith purchaser under this Article (Section 2–403). Successful reclamation of goods excludes all other remedies with respect to them.

As amended in 1966.

§ 2–703. Seller's Remedies in General. Where the buyer wrongfully rejects or revokes acceptance of goods or fails to make a payment due on or before delivery or repudiates with respect to a part or the whole, then with respect to any goods directly affected and, if the breach is of the whole contract (Section 2–612), then also with respect to the whole undelivered balance, the aggrieved seller may

(a) withhold delivery of such goods;
(b) stop delivery by any bailee as hereafter provided (Section 2–705);
(c) proceed under the next section respecting goods still unidentified to the contract;
(d) resell and recover damages as hereafter provided (Section 2–706);
(e) recover damages for non-acceptance (Section 2–708) or in a proper case the price (Section 2–709);
(f) cancel.

§ 2–704. Seller's Right to Identify Goods to the Contract Notwithstanding Breach or to Salvage Unfinished Goods.

(1) An aggrieved seller under the preceding section may
   (a) identify to the contract conforming goods not already identified if at the time he learned of the breach they are in his possession or control;
   (b) treat as the subject of resale goods which have demonstrably been intended for the particular contract even though those goods are unfinished.

(2) Where the goods are unfinished an aggrieved seller may in the exercise of reasonable commercial judgment for the purposes of avoiding loss and of effective realization either complete the manufacture and wholly identify the goods to the contract or cease manufacture and resell for scrap or salvage value or proceed in any other reasonable manner.

§ 2–705. Seller's Stoppage of Delivery in Transit or Otherwise.

(1) The seller may stop delivery of goods in the possession of a carrier or other bailee when he discovers the buyer to be insolvent (Section 2–702) and may stop delivery of carload, truckload, planeload or larger shipments of express or freight when the buyer repudiates or fails to make a payment due before delivery or if for any other reason the seller has a right to withhold or reclaim the goods.

(2) As against such buyer the seller may stop delivery until
(a) receipt of the goods by the buyer; or
(b) acknowledgment to the buyer by any bailee of the goods except a carrier that the bailee holds the goods for the buyer; or
(c) such acknowledgment to the buyer by a carrier by reshipment or as warehouseman; or
(d) negotiation to the buyer of any negotiable document of title covering the goods.
(3) (a) To stop delivery the seller must so notify as to enable the bailee by reasonable diligence to prevent delivery of the goods.
(b) After such notification the bailee must hold and deliver the goods according to the directions of the seller but the seller is liable to the bailee for any ensuing charges or damages.
(c) If a negotiable document of title has been issued for goods the bailee is not obliged to obey a notification to stop until surrender of the document.
(d) A carrier who has issued a non-negotiable bill of lading is not obliged to obey a notification to stop received from a person other than the consignor.

§ 2–706. Seller's Resale Including Contract for Resale.

(1) Under the conditions stated in Section 2–703 on seller's remedies, the seller may resell the goods concerned or the undelivered balance thereof. Where the resale is made in good faith and in a commercially reasonable manner the seller may recover the difference between the resale price and the contract price together with any incidental damages allowed under the provisions of this Article (Section 2–710), but less expenses saved in consequence of the buyer's breach.
(2) Except as otherwise provided in subsection (3) or unless otherwise agreed resale may be at public or private sale including sale by way of one or more contracts to sell or of identification to an existing contract of the seller. Sale may be as a unit or in parcels and at any time and place and on any terms but every aspect of the sale including the method, manner, time, place and terms must be commercially reasonable. The resale must be reasonably identified as referring to the broken contract, but it is not necessary that the goods be in existence or that any or all of them have been identified to the contract before the breach.
(3) Where the resale is at private sale the seller must give the buyer reasonable notification of his intention to resell.
(4) Where the resale is at public sale
(a) only identified goods can be sold except where there is a recognized market for a public sale of futures in goods of the kind; and
(b) it must be made at a usual place or market for public sale if one is reasonably available and except in the case of goods which are perishable or threaten to decline in value speedily the seller must give the buyer reasonable notice of the time and place of the resale; and
(c) if the goods are not to be within the view of those attending the sale the notification of sale must state the place where the goods are located and provide for their reasonable inspection by prospective bidders; and
(d) the seller may buy.
(5) A purchaser who buys in good faith at a resale takes the goods free of any rights of the original buyer even though the seller fails to comply with one or more of the requirements of this section.
(6) The seller is not accountable to the buyer for any profit made on any resale. A person in the position of a seller (Section 2–707) or a buyer who has rightfully rejected or justifiably revoked acceptance must account for any excess over the amount of his security interest, as hereinafter defined (subsection (3) of Section 2–711).

§ 2–707. "Person in the Position of a Seller".

(1) A "person in the position of a seller" includes as against a principal an agent who has paid or become responsible for the price of goods on behalf of his principal or anyone who otherwise holds a security interest or other right in goods similar to that of a seller.

(2) A person in the position of a seller may as provided in this Article withhold or stop delivery (Section 2–705) and resell (Section 2–706) and recover incidental damages (Section 2–710).

§ 2–708. Seller's Damages for Non-acceptance or Repudiation.

(1) Subject to subsection (2) and to the provisions of this Article with respect to proof of market price (Section 2–723), the measure of damages for non-acceptance or repudiation by the buyer is the difference between the market price at the time and place for tender and the unpaid contract price together with any incidental damages provided in this Article (Section 2–710), but less expenses saved in consequence of the buyer's breach.
(2) If the measure of damages provided in subsection (1) is inadequate to put the seller in as good a position as performance would have done then the measure of damages is the profit (including reasonable overhead) which the seller would have made from full performance by the buyer, together with any incidental damages provided in this Article (Section 2–710), due allowance for costs reasonably incurred and due credit for payments or proceeds of resale.

§ 2–709. Action for the Price.

(1) When the buyer fails to pay the price as it becomes due the seller may recover, together with any incidental damages under the next section, the price
   (a) of goods accepted or of conforming goods lost or damaged within a commercially reasonable time after risk of their loss has passed to the buyer; and
   (b) of goods identified to the contract if the seller is unable after reasonable effort to resell them at a reasonable price or the circumstances reasonably indicate that such effort will be unavailing.
(2) Where the seller sues for the price he must hold for the buyer any goods which have been identified to the contract and are still in his control except that if resale becomes possible he may resell them at any time prior to the collection of the judgment. The net proceeds of any such resale must be credited to the buyer and payment of the judgment entitles him to any goods not resold.
(3) After the buyer has wrongfully rejected or revoked acceptance of the goods or has failed to make a payment due or has repudiated (Section 2–610), a seller who is held not entitled to the price under this section shall nevertheless be awarded damages for non-acceptance under the preceding section.

§ 2–710. Seller's Incidental Damages. Incidental damages to an aggrieved seller include any commercially reasonable charges, expenses or commissions incurred in stopping delivery, in the transportation, care and custody of goods after the buyer's breach, in connection with return or resale of the goods or otherwise resulting from the breach.

§ 2–711. Buyer's Remedies in General; Buyer's Security Interest in Rejected Goods.

(1) Where the seller fails to make delivery or repudiates or the buyer rightfully rejects or justifiably revokes acceptance then with respect to any goods involved, and with respect to the whole if the breach goes to the whole contract (Section 2–612), the buyer may cancel and whether or not he has done so may in addition to recovering so much of the price as has been paid
   (a) "cover" and have damages under the next section as to all the goods affected whether or not they have been identified to the contract; or
   (b) recover damages for non-delivery as provided in this Article (Section 2–713).
(2) Where the seller fails to deliver or repudiates the buyer may also
   (a) if the goods have been identified recover them as provided in this Article (Section 2–502); or
   (b) in a proper case obtain specific performance or replevy the goods as provided in this Article (Section 2–716).

(3) On rightful rejection or justifiable revocation of acceptance a buyer has a security interest in goods in his possession or control for any payments made on their price and any expenses reasonably incurred in their inspection, receipt, transportation, care and custody and may hold such goods and resell them in like manner as an aggrieved seller (Section 2–706).

§ 2–712. "Cover"; Buyer's Procurement of Substitute Goods.

(1) After a breach within the preceding section the buyer may "cover" by making in good faith and without unreasonable delay any reasonable purchase of or contract to purchase goods in substitution for those due from the seller.
(2) The buyer may recover from the seller as damages the difference between the cost of cover and the contract price together with any incidental or consequential damages as hereinafter defined (Section 2–715), but less expenses saved in consequence of the seller's breach.
(3) Failure of the buyer to effect cover within this section does not bar him from any other remedy.

§ 2–713. Buyer's Damages for Non-delivery or Repudiation.

(1) Subject to the provisions of this Article with respect to proof of market price (Section 2–723), the measure of damages for non-delivery or repudiation by the seller is the difference between the market price at the time when the buyer learned of the breach and the contract price together with any incidental and consequential damages provided in this Article (Section 2–715), but less expenses saved in consequence of the seller's breach.
(2) Market price is to be determined as of the place for tender or, in cases of rejection after arrival or revocation of acceptance, as of the place of arrival.

§ 2–714. Buyer's Damages for Breach in Regard to Accepted Goods.

(1) Where the buyer has accepted goods and given notification (subsection (3) of Section 2–607) he may recover as damages for any non-conformity of tender the loss resulting in the ordinary course of events from the seller's breach as determined in any manner which is reasonable.
(2) The measure of damages for breach of warranty is the difference at the time and place of acceptance between the value of the goods accepted and the value they would have had if they had been as warranted, unless special circumstances show proximate damages of a different amount.
(3) In a proper case any incidental and consequential damages under the next section may also be recovered.

§ 2–715. Buyer's Incidental and Consequential Damages.

(1) Incidental damages resulting from the seller's breach include expenses reasonably incurred in inspection, receipt, transportation and care and custody of goods rightfully rejected, any commercially reasonable charges, expenses or commissions in connection with effecting cover and any other reasonable expense incident to the delay or other breach.
(2) Consequential damages resulting from the seller's breach include
    (a) any loss resulting from general or particular requirements and needs of which the seller at the time of contracting had reason to know and which could not reasonably be prevented by cover or otherwise; and
    (b) injury to person or property proximately resulting from any breach of warranty.

§ 2–716. Buyer's Right to Specific Performance or Replevin.

(1) Specific performance may be decreed where the goods are unique or in other proper circumstances.

(2) The decree for specific performance may include such terms and conditions as to payment of the price, damages, or other relief as the court may deem just.
(3) The buyer has a right of replevin for goods identified to the contract if after reasonable effort he is unable to effect cover for such goods or the circumstances reasonably indicate that such effort will be unavailing or if the goods have been shipped under reservation and satisfaction of the security interest in them has been made or tendered.

§ 2–717. Deduction of Damages from the Price. The buyer on notifying the seller of his intention to do so may deduct all or any part of the damages resulting from any breach of the contract from any part of the price still due under the same contract.

§ 2–718. Liquidation or Limitation of Damages; Deposits.

(1) Damages for breach by either party may be liquidated in the agreement but only at an amount which is reasonable in the light of the anticipated or actual harm caused by the breach, the difficulties of proof of loss, and the inconvenience or nonfeasibility of otherwise obtaining an adequate remedy. A term fixing unreasonably large liquidated damages is void as a penalty.
(2) Where the seller justifiably withholds delivery of goods because of the buyer's breach, the buyer is entitled to restitution of any amount by which the sum of his payments exceeds
  (a) the amount to which the seller is entitled by virtue of terms liquidating the seller's damages in accordance with subsection (1), or
  (b) in the absence of such terms, twenty percent of the value of the total performance for which the buyer is obligated under the contract or $500, whichever is smaller.
(3) The buyer's right to restitution under subsection (2) is subject to offset to the extent that the seller establishes
  (a) a right to recover damages under the provisions of this Article other than subsection (1), and
  (b) the amount or value of any benefits received by the buyer directly or indirectly by reason of the contract.
(4) Where a seller has received payment in goods their reasonable value or the proceeds of their resale shall be treated as payments for the purposes of subsection (2); but if the seller has notice of the buyer's breach before reselling goods received in part performance, his resale is subject to the conditions laid down in this Article on resale by an aggrieved seller (Section 2–706).

§ 2–719. Contractual Modification or Limitation of Remedy.

(1) Subject to the provisions of subsections (2) and (3) of this section and of the preceding section on liquidation and limitation of damages,
  (a) the agreement may provide for remedies in addition to or in substitution for those provided in this Article and may limit or alter the measure of damages recoverable under this Article, as by limiting the buyer's remedies to return of the goods and repayment of the price or to repair and replacement of non-conforming goods or parts; and
  (b) resort to a remedy as provided is optional unless the remedy is expressly agreed to be exclusive, in which case it is the sole remedy.
(2) Where circumstances cause an exclusive or limited remedy to fail of its essential purpose, remedy may be had as provided in this Act.
(3) Consequential damages may be limited or excluded unless the limitation or exclusion is unconscionable. Limitation of consequential damages for injury to the person in the case of consumer goods is prima facie unconscionable but limitation of damages where the loss is commercial is not.

§ 2–720. Effect of "Cancellation" or "Rescission" on Claims for Antecedent Breach. Unless the contrary intention clearly appears, expressions of "cancellation" or "rescission" of the contract or the like shall not be construed as a renunciation or discharge of any claim in damages for an antecedent breach.

§ 2–721. Remedies for Fraud. Remedies for material misrepresentation or fraud include all remedies available under this Article for non-fraudulent breach. Neither rescission or a claim for rescission of the contract for sale nor rejection or return of the goods shall bar or be deemed inconsistent with a claim for damages or other remedy.

§ 2–722. Who Can Sue Third Parties for Injury to Goods. Where a third party so deals with goods which have been identified to a contract for sale as to cause actionable injury to a party to that contract

(a) a right of action against the third party is in either party to the contract for sale who has title to or a security interest or a special property or an insurable interest in the goods; and if the goods have been destroyed or converted a right of action is also in the party who either bore the risk of loss under the contract for sale or has since the injury assumed that risk as against the other;
(b) if at the time of the injury the party plaintiff did not bear the risk of loss as against the other party to the contract for sale and there is no arrangement between them for disposition of the recovery, his suit or settlement is, subject to his own interest, as a fiduciary for the other party to the contract;
(c) either party may with the consent of the other sue for the benefit of whom it may concern.

§ 2–723. Proof of Market Price: Time and Place.

(1) If an action based on anticipatory repudiation comes to trial before the time for performance with respect to some or all of the goods, any damages based on market price (Section 2–708 or Section 2–713) shall be determined according to the price of such goods prevailing at the time when the aggrieved party learned of the repudiation.
(2) If evidence of a price prevailing at the times or places described in this Article is not readily available the price prevailing within any reasonable time before or after the time described or at any other place which in commercial judgment or under usage of trade would serve as a reasonable substitute for the one described may be used, making any proper allowance for the cost of transporting the goods to or from such other place.
(3) Evidence of a relevant price prevailing at a time or place other than the one described in this Article offered by one party is not admissible unless and until he has given the other party such notice as the court finds sufficient to prevent unfair surprise.

§ 2–724. Admissibility of Market Quotations. Whenever the prevailing price or value of any goods regularly bought and sold in any established commodity market is in issue, reports in official publications or trade journals or in newspapers or periodicals of general circulation published as the reports of such market shall be admissible in evidence. The circumstances of the preparation of such a report may be shown to affect its weight but not its admissibility.

§ 2–725. Statute of Limitations in Contracts for Sale.

(1) An action for breach of any contract for sale must be commenced within four years after the cause of action has accrued. By the original agreement the parties may reduce the period of limitation to not less than one year but may not extend it.

(2) A cause of action accrues when the breach occurs, regardless of the aggrieved party's lack of knowledge of the breach. A breach of warranty occurs when tender of delivery is made, except that where a warranty explicitly extends to future performance of the goods and discovery of the breach must await the time of such performance the cause of action accrues when the breach is or should have been discovered.

(3) Where an action commenced within the time limited by subsection (1) is so terminated as to leave available a remedy by another action for the same breach such other action may be commenced after the expiration of the time limited and within six months after the termination of the first action unless the termination resulted from voluntary discontinuance or from dismissal for failure or neglect to prosecute.

(4) This section does not alter the law on tolling of the statute of limitations nor does it apply to causes of action which have accrued before this Act becomes effective.

Article 2A—Leases

PART 1: GENERAL PROVISIONS

§ 2A–101. Short Title. This Article shall be known and may be cited as the Uniform Commercial Code—Leases.

See Appendix VI [following Amendment 24 therein] for material relating to changes in the Official Comment to conform to the 1990 amendments to various sections of Article 2A.

§ 2A–102. Scope. This Article applies to any transaction, regardless of form, that creates a lease.

§ 2A–103. Definitions and Index of Definitions.

(1) In this Article unless the context otherwise requires:

(a) "Buyer in ordinary course of business" means a person who in good faith and without knowledge that the sale to him [or her] is in violation of the ownership rights or security interest or leasehold interest of a third party in the goods buys in ordinary course from a person in the business of selling goods of that kind but does not include a pawnbroker. "Buying" may be for cash or by exchange of other property or on secured or unsecured credit and includes receiving goods or documents of title under a preexisting contract for sale but does not include a transfer in bulk or as security for or in total or partial satisfaction of a money debt.

(b) "Cancellation" occurs when either party puts an end to the lease contract for default by the other party.

(c) "Commercial unit" means such a unit of goods as by commercial usage is a single whole for purposes of lease and division of which materially impairs its character or value on the market or in use. A commercial unit may be a single article, as a machine, or a set of articles, as a suite of furniture or a line of machinery, or a quantity, as a gross or carload, or any other unit treated in use or in the relevant market as a single whole.

(d) "Conforming" goods or performance under a lease contract means goods or performance that are in accordance with the obligations under the lease contract.

(e) "Consumer lease" means a lease that a lessor regularly engaged in the business of leasing or selling makes to a lessee who is an individual and who takes under the lease primarily for a personal, family, or household purpose [, if the total payments to be made under the lease contract, excluding payments for options to renew or buy, do not exceed $_____].

(f) "Fault" means wrongful act, omission, breach, or default.

(g) "Finance lease" means a lease with respect to which:

(i) the lessor does not select, manufacture, or supply the goods;

(ii) the lessor acquires the goods or the right to possession and use of the goods in connection with the lease; and

(iii) one of the following occurs:

(A) the lessee receives a copy of the contract by which the lessor acquired the goods or the right to possession and use of the goods before signing the lease contract;

(B) the lessee's approval of the contract by which the lessor acquired the goods or the right to possession and use of the goods is a condition to effectiveness of the lease contract;

(C) the lessee, before signing the lease contract, receives an accurate and complete statement designating the promises and warranties, and any disclaimers of warranties, limitations or modifications of remedies, or liquidated damages, including those of a third party, such as the manufacturer of the goods, provided to the lessor by the person supplying the goods in connection with or as part of the contract by which the lessor acquired the goods or the right to possession and use of the goods; or

(D) if the lease is not a consumer lease, the lessor, before the lessee signs the lease contract, informs the lessee in writing (a) of the identity of the person supplying the goods to the lessor, unless the lessee has selected that person and directed the lessor to acquire the goods or the right to possession and use of the goods from that person, (b) that the lessee is entitled under this Article to the promises and warranties, including those of any third party, provided to the lessor by the person supplying the goods in connection with or as part of the contract by which the lessor acquired the goods or the right to possession and use of the goods, and (c) that the lessee may communicate with the person supplying the goods to the lessor and receive an accurate and complete statement of those promises and warranties, including any disclaimers and limitations of them or of remedies.

(h) "Goods" means all things that are movable at the time of identification to the lease contract, or are fixtures (Section 2A–309), but the term does not include money, documents, instruments, accounts, chattel paper, general intangibles, or minerals or the like, including oil and gas, before extraction. The term also includes the unborn young of animals.

(i) "Installment lease contract" means a lease contract that authorizes or requires the delivery of goods in separate lots to be separately accepted, even though the lease contract contains a clause "each delivery is a separate lease" or its equivalent.

(j) "Lease" means a transfer of the right to possession and use of goods for a term in return for consideration, but a sale, including a sale on approval or a sale or return, or retention or creation of a security interest is not a lease. Unless the context clearly indicates otherwise, the term includes a sublease.

(k) "Lease agreement" means the bargain, with respect to the lease, of the lessor and the lessee in fact as found in their language or by implication from other circumstances including course of dealing or usage of trade or course of performance as provided in this Article. Unless the context clearly indicates otherwise, the term includes a sublease agreement.

(l) "Lease contract" means the total legal obligation that results from the lease agreement as affected by this Article and any other applicable rules of law. Unless the context clearly indicates otherwise, the term includes a sublease contract.

(m) "Leasehold interest" means the interest of the lessor or the lessee under a lease contract.

(n) "Lessee" means a person who acquires the right to possession and use of goods under a lease. Unless the context clearly indicates otherwise, the term includes a sublessee.

(o) "Lessee in ordinary course of business" means a person who in good faith and without knowledge that the lease to him [or her] is in violation of the ownership rights or security interest or leasehold interest of a third party in the goods, leases in ordinary course from a person in the business of selling or leasing goods of that kind but does not include a pawnbroker. "Leasing" may be for cash or by exchange of other property or on secured or unsecured credit and includes receiving goods or documents of title under a preexisting lease contract but does not include a transfer in bulk or as security for or in total or partial satisfaction of a money debt.

(p) "Lessor" means a person who transfers the right to possession and use of goods under a lease. Unless the context clearly indicates otherwise, the term includes a sublessor.

(q) "Lessor's residual interest" means the lessor's interest in the goods after expiration, termination, or cancellation of the lease contract.

(r) "Lien" means a charge against or interest in goods to secure payment of a debt or performance of an obligation, but the term does not include a security interest.

(s) "Lot" means a parcel or a single article that is the subject matter of a separate lease or delivery, whether or not it is sufficient to perform the lease contract.

(t) "Merchant lessee" means a lessee that is a merchant with respect to goods of the kind subject to the lease.

(u) "Present value" means the amount as of a date certain of one or more sums payable in the future, discounted to the date certain. The discount is determined by the interest rate specified by the parties if the rate was not manifestly unreasonable at the time the transaction was entered into; otherwise, the discount is determined by a commercially reasonable rate that takes into account the facts and circumstances of each case at the time the transaction was entered into.

(v) "Purchase" includes taking by sale, lease, mortgage, security interest, pledge, gift, or any other voluntary transaction creating an interest in goods.

(w) "Sublease" means a lease of goods the right to possession and use of which was acquired by the lessor as a lessee under an existing lease.

(x) "Supplier" means a person from whom a lessor buys or leases goods to be leased under a finance lease.

(y) "Supply contract" means a contract under which a lessor buys or leases goods to be leased.

(z) "Termination" occurs when either party pursuant to a power created by agreement or law puts an end to the lease contract otherwise than for default.

(2) Other definitions applying to this Article and the sections in which they appear are:

"Accessions"	Section 2A–310(1).
"Construction mortgage"	Section 2A–309(1) (d).
"Encumbrance"	Section 2A–309(1) (e).
"Fixtures"	Section 2A–309(1) (a).
"Fixture filing"	Section 2A–309(1) (b).
"Purchase money lease"	Section 2A–309(1) (c).

(3) The following definitions in other Articles apply to this Article:

"Account"	Section 9–106.
"Between merchants"	Section 2–104(3).
"Buyer"	Section 2–103(1) (a).
"Chattel paper"	Section 9–105(1) (b).
"Consumer goods"	Section 9–109(1).
"Document"	Section 9–105(1) (f).
"Entrusting"	Section 2–403(3).
"General intangibles"	Section 9–106.
"Good faith"	Section 2–103(1) (b).
"Instrument"	Section 9–105(1) (i).
"Merchant"	Section 2–104(1).
"Mortgage"	Section 9–105(1) (j).

"Pursuant to commitment"	Section 9–105(1) (k).
"Receipt"	Section 2–103(1) (c).
"Sale"	Section 2–106(1).
"Sale on approval"	Section 2–326.
"Sale or return"	Section 2–326.
"Seller"	Section 2–103(1) (d).

(4) In addition Article 1 contains general definitions and principles of construction and interpretation applicable throughout this Article.

As amended in 1990.

§ 2A–104. Leases Subject to Other Law.

(1) A lease, although subject to this Article, is also subject to any applicable:
   (a) certificate of title statute of this State: (list any certificate of title statutes covering automobiles, trailers, mobile homes, boats, farm tractors, and the like);
   (b) certificate of title statute of another jurisdiction (Section 2A–105); or
   (c) consumer protection statute of this State, or final consumer protection decision of a court of this State existing on the effective date of this Article.

(2) In case of conflict between this Article, other than Sections 2A–105, 2A–304(3), and 2A–305(3), and a statute or decision referred to in subsection (1), the statute or decision controls.

(3) Failure to comply with an applicable law has only the effect specified therein.

As amended in 1990.

§ 2A–105. Territorial Application of Article to Goods Covered by Certificate of Title. Subject to the provisions of Sections 2A–304(3) and 2A–305(3), with respect to goods covered by a certificate of title issued under a statute of this State or of another jurisdiction, compliance and the effect of compliance or noncompliance with a certificate of title statute are governed by the law (including the conflict of laws rules) of the jurisdiction issuing the certificate until the earlier of (a) surrender of the certificate, or (b) four months after the goods are removed from that jurisdiction and thereafter until a new certificate of title is issued by another jurisdiction.

§ 2A–106. Limitation on Power of Parties to Consumer Lease to Choose Applicable Law and Judicial Forum.

(1) If the law chosen by the parties to a consumer lease is that of a jurisdiction other than a jurisdiction in which the lessee resides at the time the lease agreement becomes enforceable or within 30 days thereafter or in which the goods are to be used, the choice is not enforceable.

(2) If the judicial forum chosen by the parties to a consumer lease is a forum that would not otherwise have jurisdiction over the lessee, the choice is not enforceable.

§ 2A–107. Waiver or Renunciation of Claim or Right After Default. Any claim or right arising out of an alleged default or breach of warranty may be discharged in whole or in part without consideration by a written waiver or renunciation signed and delivered by the aggrieved party.

§ 2A–108. Unconscionability.

(1) If the court as a matter of law finds a lease contract or any clause of a lease contract to have been unconscionable at the time it was made the court may refuse to enforce the lease contract, or it may enforce the remainder of the lease contract without the unconscionable

clause, or it may so limit the application of any unconscionable clause as to avoid any unconscionable result.

(2) With respect to a consumer lease, if the court as a matter of law finds that a lease contract or any clause of a lease contract has been induced by unconscionable conduct or that unconscionable conduct has occurred in the collection of a claim arising from a lease contract, the court may grant appropriate relief.

(3) Before making a finding of unconscionability under subsection (1) or (2), the court, on its own motion or that of a party, shall afford the parties a reasonable opportunity to present evidence as to the setting, purpose, and effect of the lease contract or clause thereof, or of the conduct.

(4) In an action in which the lessee claims unconscionability with respect to a consumer lease:

(a) If the court finds unconscionability under subsection (1) or (2), the court shall award reasonable attorney's fees to the lessee.

(b) If the court does not find unconscionability and the lessee claiming unconscionability has brought or maintained an action he [or she] knew to be groundless, the court shall award reasonable attorney's fees to the party against whom the claim is made.

(c) In determining attorney's fees, the amount of the recovery on behalf of the claimant under subsections (1) and (2) is not controlling.

§ 2A–109. Option to Accelerate at Will.

(1) A term providing that one party or his [or her] successor in interest may accelerate payment or performance or require collateral or additional collateral "at will" or "when he [or she] deems himself [or herself] insecure" or in words of similar import must be construed to mean that he [or she] has power to do so only if he [or she] in good faith believes that the prospect of payment or performance is impaired.

(2) With respect to a consumer lease, the burden of establishing good faith under subsection (1) is on the party who exercised the power; otherwise the burden of establishing lack of good faith is on the party against whom the power has been exercised.

PART 2: FORMATION AND CONSTRUCTION OF LEASE CONTRACT

§ 2A–201. Statute of Frauds.

(1) A lease contract is not enforceable by way of action or defense unless:

(a) the total payments to be made under the lease contract, excluding payments for options to renew or buy, are less than $1,000; or

(b) there is a writing, signed by the party against whom enforcement is sought or by that party's authorized agent, sufficient to indicate that a lease contract has been made between the parties and to describe the goods leased and the lease term.

(2) Any description of leased goods or of the lease term is sufficient and satisfies subsection (1) (b), whether or not it is specific, if it reasonably identifies what is described.

(3) A writing is not insufficient because it omits or incorrectly states a term agreed upon, but the lease contract is not enforceable under subsection (1) (b) beyond the lease term and the quantity of goods shown in the writing.

(4) A lease contract that does not satisfy the requirements of subsection (1), but which is valid in other respects, is enforceable:

(a) if the goods are to be specially manufactured or obtained for the lessee and are not suitable for lease or sale to others in the ordinary course of the lessor's business, and the lessor, before notice of repudiation is received and under circumstances that reasonably indicate that the goods are for the lessee, has made either a substantial beginning of their manufacture or commitments for their procurement;

(b) if the party against whom enforcement is sought admits in that party's pleading, testimony or otherwise in court that a lease contract was made, but the lease contract is not enforceable under this provision beyond the quantity of goods admitted; or

(c) with respect to goods that have been received and accepted by the lessee.

(5) The lease term under a lease contract referred to in subsection (4) is:
   (a) if there is a writing signed by the party against whom enforcement is sought or by that party's authorized agent specifying the lease term, the term so specified;
   (b) if the party against whom enforcement is sought admits in that party's pleading, testimony, or otherwise in court a lease term, the term so admitted; or
   (c) a reasonable lease term.

§ 2A-202. Final Written Expression: Parol or Extrinsic Evidence. Terms with respect to which the confirmatory memoranda of the parties agree or which are otherwise set forth in a writing intended by the parties as a final expression of their agreement with respect to such terms as are included therein may not be contradicted by evidence of any prior agreement or of a contemporaneous oral agreement but may be explained or supplemented:

   (a) by course of dealing or usage of trade or by course of performance; and
   (b) by evidence of consistent additional terms unless the court finds the writing to have been intended also as a complete and exclusive statement of the terms of the agreement.

§ 2A-203. Seals Inoperative. The affixing of a seal to a writing evidencing a lease contract or an offer to enter into a lease contract does not render the writing a sealed instrument and the law with respect to sealed instruments does not apply to the lease contract or offer.

§ 2A-204. Formation in General.

(1) A lease contract may be made in any manner sufficient to show agreement, including conduct by both parties which recognizes the existence of a lease contract.
(2) An agreement sufficient to constitute a lease contract may be found although the moment of its making is undetermined.
(3) Although one or more terms are left open, a lease contract does not fail for indefiniteness if the parties have intended to make a lease contract and there is a reasonably certain basis for giving an appropriate remedy.

§ 2A-205. Firm Offers. An offer by a merchant to lease goods to or from another person in a signed writing that by its terms gives assurance it will be held open is not revocable, for lack of consideration, during the time stated or, if no time is stated, for a reasonable time, but in no event may the period of irrevocability exceed 3 months. Any such term of assurance on a form supplied by the offeree must be separately signed by the offeror.

§ 2A-206. Offer and Acceptance in Formation of Lease Contract.

(1) Unless otherwise unambiguously indicated by the language or circumstances, an offer to make a lease contract must be construed as inviting acceptance in any manner and by any medium reasonable in the circumstances.
(2) If the beginning of a requested performance is a reasonable mode of acceptance, an offeror who is not notified of acceptance within a reasonable time may treat the offer as having lapsed before acceptance.

§ 2A-207. Course of Performance or Practical Construction.

(1) If a lease contract involves repeated occasions for performance by either party with knowledge of the nature of the performance and opportunity for objection to it by the other, any course of performance accepted or acquiesced in without objection is relevant to determine the meaning of the lease agreement.
(2) The express terms of a lease agreement and any course of performance, as well as any course of dealing and usage of trade, must be construed whenever reasonable as consistent with each other; but if that construction is unreasonable, express terms control course of performance, course of performance controls both course of dealing and usage of trade, and course of dealing controls usage of trade.

(3) Subject to the provisions of Section 2A–208 on modification and waiver, course of performance is relevant to show a waiver or modification of any term inconsistent with the course of performance.

§ 2A–208. Modification, Rescission and Waiver.

(1) An agreement modifying a lease contract needs no consideration to be binding.
(2) A signed lease agreement that excludes modification or rescission except by a signed writing may not be otherwise modified or rescinded, but, except as between merchants, such a requirement on a form supplied by a merchant must be separately signed by the other party.
(3) Although an attempt at modification or rescission does not satisfy the requirements of subsection (2), it may operate as a waiver.
(4) A party who has made a waiver affecting an executory portion of a lease contract may retract the waiver by reasonable notification received by the other party that strict performance will be required of any term waived, unless the retraction would be unjust in view of a material change of position in reliance on the waiver.

§ 2A–209. Lessee Under Finance Lease as Beneficiary of Supply Contract.

(1) The benefit of a supplier's promises to the lessor under the supply contract and of all warranties, whether express or implied, including those of any third party provided in connection with or as part of the supply contract, extends to the lessee to the extent of the lessee's leasehold interest under a finance lease related to the supply contract, but is subject to the terms of the warranty and of the supply contract and all defenses or claims arising therefrom.
(2) The extension of the benefit of a supplier's promises and of warranties to the lessee (Section 2A–209(1)) does not: (i) modify the rights and obligations of the parties to the supply contract, whether arising therefrom or otherwise, or (ii) impose any duty or liability under the supply contract on the lessee.
(3) Any modification or rescission of the supply contract by the supplier and the lessor is effective between the supplier and the lessee unless, before the modification or rescission, the supplier has received notice that the lessee has entered into a finance lease related to the supply contract. If the modification or rescission is effective between the supplier and the lessee, the lessor is deemed to have assumed, in addition to the obligations of the lessor to the lessee under the lease contract, promises of the supplier to the lessor and warranties that were so modified or rescinded as they existed and were available to the lessee before modification or rescission.
(4) In addition to the extension of the benefit of the supplier's promises and of warranties to the lessee under subsection (1), the lessee retains all rights that the lessee may have against the supplier which arise from an agreement between the lessee and the supplier or under other law.

As amended in 1990.

§ 2A–210. Express Warranties.

(1) Express warranties by the lessor are created as follows:
    (a) Any affirmation of fact or promise made by the lessor to the lessee which relates to the goods and becomes part of the basis of the bargain creates an express warranty that the goods will conform to the affirmation or promise.
    (b) Any description of the goods which is made part of the basis of the bargain creates an express warranty that the goods will conform to the description.
    (c) Any sample or model that is made part of the basis of the bargain creates an express warranty that the whole of the goods will conform to the sample or model.

(2) It is not necessary to the creation of an express warranty that the lessor use formal words, such as "warrant" or "guarantee," or that the lessor have a specific intention to make a warranty, but an affirmation merely of the value of the goods or a statement purporting to be merely the lessor's opinion or commendation of the goods does not create a warranty.

§ 2A–211. Warranties Against Interference and Against Infringement; Lessee's Obligation Against Infringement.

(1) There is in a lease contract a warranty that for the lease term no person holds a claim to or interest in the goods that arose from an act or omission of the lessor, other than a claim by way of infringement or the like, which will interfere with the lessee's enjoyment of its leasehold interest.

(2) Except in a finance lease there is in a lease contract by a lessor who is a merchant regularly dealing in goods of the kind a warranty that the goods are delivered free of the rightful claim of any person by way of infringement or the like.

(3) A lessee who furnishes specifications to a lessor or a supplier shall hold the lessor and the supplier harmless against any claim by way of infringement or the like that arises out of compliance with the specifications.

§ 2A–212. Implied Warranty of Merchantability.

(1) Except in a finance lease, a warranty that the goods will be merchantable is implied in a lease contract if the lessor is a merchant with respect to goods of that kind.

(2) Goods to be merchantable must be at least such as
   (a) pass without objection in the trade under the description in the lease agreement;
   (b) in the case of fungible goods, are of fair average quality within the description;
   (c) are fit for the ordinary purposes for which goods of that type are used;
   (d) run, within the variation permitted by the lease agreement, of even kind, quality, and quantity within each unit and among all units involved;
   (e) are adequately contained, packaged, and labeled as the lease agreement may require; and
   (f) conform to any promises or affirmations of fact made on the container or label.

(3) Other implied warranties may arise from course of dealing or usage of trade.

§ 2A–213. Implied Warranty of Fitness for Particular Purpose. Except in a finance lease, if the lessor at the time the lease contract is made has reason to know of any particular purpose for which the goods are required and that the lessee is relying on the lessor's skill or judgment to select or furnish suitable goods, there is in the lease contract an implied warranty that the goods will be fit for that purpose.

§ 2A–214. Exclusion or Modification of Warranties.

(1) Words or conduct relevant to the creation of an express warranty and words or conduct tending to negate or limit a warranty must be construed wherever reasonable as consistent with each other; but, subject to the provisions of Section 2A–202 on parol or extrinsic evidence, negation or limitation is inoperative to the extent that the construction is unreasonable.

(2) Subject to subsection (3), to exclude or modify the implied warranty of merchantability or any part of it the language must mention "merchantability", be by a writing, and be conspicuous. Subject to sub-section (3), to exclude or modify any implied warranty of fitness the exclusion must be by a writing and be conspicuous. Language to exclude all implied warranties of fitness is sufficient if it is in writing, is conspicuous and states, for example, "There is no warranty that the goods will be fit for a particular purpose".

(3) Notwithstanding subsection (2), but subject to subsection (4),
   (a) unless the circumstances indicate otherwise, all implied warranties are excluded by expressions like "as is," or "with all faults," or by other language that in common

understanding calls the lessee's attention to the exclusion of warranties and makes plain that there is no implied warranty, if in writing and conspicuous;
(b) if the lessee before entering into the lease contract has examined the goods or the sample or model as fully as desired or has refused to examine the goods, there is no implied warranty with regard to defects that an examination ought in the circumstances to have revealed; and
(c) an implied warranty may also be excluded or modified by course of dealing, course of performance, or usage of trade.

(4) To exclude or modify a warranty against interference or against infringement (Section 2A–211) or any part of it, the language must be specific, be by a writing, and be conspicuous, unless the circumstances, including course of performance, course of dealing, or usage of trade, give the lessee reason to know that the goods are being leased subject to a claim or interest of any person.

§ 2A–215. Cumulation and Conflict of Warranties Express or Implied.

Warranties, whether express or implied, must be construed as consistent with each other and as cumulative, but if that construction is unreasonable, the intention of the parties determines which warranty is dominant. In ascertaining that intention the following rules apply:
(a) Exact or technical specifications displace an inconsistent sample or model or general language of description.
(b) A sample from an existing bulk displaces inconsistent general language of description.
(c) Express warranties displace inconsistent implied warranties other than an implied warranty of fitness for a particular purpose.

§ 2A–216. Third Party Beneficiaries of Express and Implied Warranties.

Alternative A

A warranty to or for the benefit of a lessee under this Article, whether express or implied, extends to any natural person who is in the family or household of the lessee or who is a guest in the lessee's home if it is reasonable to expect that such person may use, consume, or be affected by the goods and who is injured in person by breach of the warranty. This section does not displace principles of law and equity that extend a warranty to or for the benefit of a lessee to other persons. The operation of this section may not be excluded, modified, or limited, but an exclusion, modification, or limitation of the warranty, including any with respect to rights and remedies, effective against the lessee is also effective against any beneficiary designated under this section.

Alternative B

A warranty to or for the benefit of a lessee under this Article, whether express or implied, extends to any natural person who may reasonably be expected to use, consume, or be affected by the goods and who is injured in person by breach of the warranty. This section does not displace principles of law and equity that extend a warranty to or for the benefit of a lessee to other persons. The operation of this section may not be excluded, modified, or limited, but an exclusion, modification, or limitation of the warranty, including any with respect to rights and remedies, effective against the lessee is also effective against the beneficiary designated under this section.

Alternative C

A warranty to or for the benefit of a lessee under this Article, whether express or implied, extends to any person who may reasonably be expected to use, consume, or be affected by the goods and who is injured by breach of the warranty. The operation of this section may not be excluded, modified, or limited with respect to injury to the person of an individual to whom the warranty extends, but an exclusion, modification, or limitation of the warranty, including any with respect to rights and remedies, effective against the lessee is also effective against the beneficiary designated under this section.

§ 2A–217. Identification. Identification of goods as goods to which a lease contract refers may be made at any time and in any manner explicitly agreed to by the parties. In the absence of explicit agreement, identification occurs:

(a) when the lease contract is made if the lease contract is for a lease of goods that are existing and identified;
(b) when the goods are shipped, marked, or otherwise designated by the lessor as goods to which the lease contract refers, if the lease contract is for a lease of goods that are not existing and identified; or
(c) when the young are conceived, if the lease contract is for a lease of unborn young of animals.

§ 2A–218. Insurance and Proceeds.

(1) A lessee obtains an insurable interest when existing goods are identified to the lease contract even though the goods identified are nonconforming and the lessee has an option to reject them.
(2) If a lessee has an insurable interest only by reason of the lessor's identification of the goods, the lessor, until default or insolvency or notification to the lessee that identification is final, may substitute other goods for those identified.
(3) Notwithstanding a lessee's insurable interest under subsections (1) and (2), the lessor retains an insurable interest until an option to buy has been exercised by the lessee and risk of loss has passed to the lessee.
(4) Nothing in this section impairs any insurable interest recognized under any other statute or rule of law.
(5) The parties by agreement may determine that one or more parties have an obligation to obtain and pay for insurance covering the goods and by agreement may determine the beneficiary of the proceeds of the insurance.

§ 2A–219. Risk of Loss.

(1) Except in the case of a finance lease, risk of loss is retained by the lessor and does not pass to the lessee. In the case of a finance lease, risk of loss passes to the lessee.
(2) Subject to the provisions of this Article on the effect of default on risk of loss (Section 2A–220), if risk of loss is to pass to the lessee and the time of passage is not stated, the following rules apply:
    (a) If the lease contract requires or authorizes the goods to be shipped by carrier
        (i) and it does not require delivery at a particular destination, the risk of loss passes to the lessee when the goods are duly delivered to the carrier; but
        (ii) if it does require delivery at a particular destination and the goods are there duly tendered while in the possession of the carrier, the risk of loss passes to the lessee when the goods are there duly so tendered as to enable the lessee to take delivery.
    (b) If the goods are held by a bailee to be delivered without being moved, the risk of loss passes to the lessee on acknowledgment by the bailee of the lessee's right to possession of the goods.
    (c) In any case not within subsection (a) or (b), the risk of loss passes to the lessee on the lessee's receipt of the goods if the lessor, or, in the case of a finance lease, the supplier, is a merchant; otherwise the risk passes to the lessee on tender of delivery.

§ 2A–220. Effect of Default on Risk of Loss.

(1) Where risk of loss is to pass to the lessee and the time of passage is not stated:
    (a) If a tender or delivery of goods so fails to conform to the lease contract as to give a right of rejection, the risk of their loss remains with the lessor, or, in the case of a finance lease, the supplier, until cure or acceptance.

(b) If the lessee rightfully revokes acceptance, he [or she], to the extent of any deficiency in his [or her] effective insurance coverage, may treat the risk of loss as having remained with the lessor from the beginning.

(2) Whether or not risk of loss is to pass to the lessee, if the lessee as to conforming goods already identified to a lease contract repudiates or is otherwise in default under the lease contract, the lessor, or, in the case of a finance lease, the supplier, to the extent of any deficiency in his [or her] effective insurance coverage may treat the risk of loss as resting on the lessee for a commercially reasonable time.

§ 2A–221. Casualty to Identified Goods. If a lease contract requires goods identified when the lease contract is made, and the goods suffer casualty without fault of the lessee, the lessor or the supplier before delivery, or the goods suffer casualty before risk of loss passes to the lessee pursuant to the lease agreement or Section 2A–219, then:

(a) if the loss is total, the lease contract is avoided; and

(b) if the loss is partial or the goods have so deteriorated as to no longer conform to the lease contract, the lessee may nevertheless demand inspection and at his [or her] option either treat the lease contract as avoided or, except in a finance lease that is not a consumer lease, accept the goods with due allowance from the rent payable for the balance of the lease term for the deterioration or the deficiency in quantity but without further right against the lessor.

PART 3: EFFECT OF LEASE CONTRACT

§ 2A–301. Enforceability of Lease Contract. Except as otherwise provided in this Article, a lease contract is effective and enforceable according to its terms between the parties, against purchasers of the goods and against creditors of the parties.

§ 2A–302. Title to and Possession of Goods. Except as otherwise provided in this Article, each provision of this Article applies whether the lessor or a third party has title to the goods, and whether the lessor, the lessee, or a third party has possession of the goods, notwithstanding any statute or rule of law that possession or the absence of possession is fraudulent.

§ 2A–303. Alienability of Party's Interest Under Lease Contract or of Lessor's Residual Interest in Goods; Delegation of Performance; Transfer of Rights.

(1) As used in this section, "creation of a security interest" includes the sale of a lease contract that is subject to Article 9, Secured Transactions, by reason of Section 9–102(1) (b).

(2) Except as provided in subsections (3) and (4), a provision in a lease agreement which (i) prohibits the voluntary or involuntary transfer, including a transfer by sale, sublease, creation or enforcement of a security interest, or attachment, levy, or other judicial process, of an interest of a party under the lease contract or of the lessor's residual interest in the goods, or (ii) makes such a transfer an event of default, gives rise to the rights and remedies provided in subsection (5), but a transfer that is prohibited or is an event of default under the lease agreement is otherwise effective.

(3) A provision in a lease agreement which (i) prohibits the creation or enforcement of a security interest in an interest of a party under the lease contract or in the lessor's residual interest in the goods, or (ii) makes such a transfer an event of default, is not enforceable unless, and then only to the extent that, there is an actual transfer by the lessee of the lessee's right of possession or use of the goods in violation of the provision or an actual delegation of a material performance of either party to the lease contract in violation of the provision. Neither the granting nor the enforcement of a security interest in (i) the lessor's interest under the lease contract or (ii) the lessor's residual interest in the goods is a transfer that materially impairs the prospect of obtaining return performance by, materially changes the

duty of, or materially increases the burden or risk imposed on, the lessee within the purview of subsection (5) unless, and then only to the extent that, there is an actual delegation of a material performance of the lessor.

(4) A provision in a lease agreement which (i) prohibits a transfer of a right to damages for default with respect to the whole lease contract or of a right to payment arising out of the transferor's due performance of the transferor's entire obligation, or (ii) makes such a transfer an event of default, is not enforceable, and such a transfer is not a transfer that materially impairs the prospect of obtaining return performance by, materially changes the duty of, or materially increases the burden or risk imposed on, the other party to the lease contract within the purview of subsection (5).

(5) Subject to subsections (3) and (4):
  (a) if a transfer is made which is made an event of default under a lease agreement, the party to the lease contract not making the transfer, unless that party waives the default or otherwise agrees, has the rights and remedies described in Section 2A–501(2);
  (b) if paragraph (a) is not applicable and if a transfer is made that (i) is prohibited under a lease agreement or (ii) materially impairs the prospect of obtaining return performance by, materially changes the duty of, or materially increases the burden or risk imposed on, the other party to the lease contract, unless the party not making the transfer agrees at any time to the transfer in the lease contract or otherwise, then, except as limited by contract, (i) the transferor is liable to the party not making the transfer for damages caused by the transfer to the extent that the damages could not reasonably be prevented by the party not making the transfer and (ii) a court having jurisdiction may grant other appropriate relief, including cancellation of the lease contract or an injunction against the transfer.

(6) A transfer of "the lease" or of "all my rights under the lease", or a transfer in similar general terms, is a transfer of rights and, unless the language or the circumstances, as in a transfer for security, indicate the contrary, the transfer is a delegation of duties by the transferor to the transferee. Acceptance by the transferee constitutes a promise by the transferee to perform those duties. The promise is enforceable by either the transferor or the other party to the lease contract.

(7) Unless otherwise agreed by the lessor and the lessee, a delegation of performance does not relieve the transferor as against the other party of any duty to perform or of any liability for default.

(8) In a consumer lease, to prohibit the transfer of an interest of a party under the lease contract or to make a transfer an event of default, the language must be specific, by a writing, and conspicuous.

As amended in 1990.

§ 2A–304. Subsequent Lease of Goods by Lessor.

(1) Subject to Section 2A–303, a subsequent lessee from a lessor of goods under an existing lease contract obtains, to the extent of the leasehold interest transferred, the leasehold interest in the goods that the lessor had or had power to transfer, and except as provided in subsection (2) and Section 2A–527(4), takes subject to the existing lease contract. A lessor with voidable title has power to transfer a good leasehold interest to a good faith subsequent lessee for value, but only to the extent set forth in the preceding sentence. If goods have been delivered under a transaction of purchase, the lessor has that power even though:
  (a) the lessor's transferor was deceived as to the identity of the lessor;
  (b) the delivery was in exchange for a check which is later dishonored;
  (c) it was agreed that the transaction was to be a "cash sale"; or
  (d) the delivery was procured through fraud punishable as larcenous under the criminal law.

(2) A subsequent lessee in the ordinary course of business from a lessor who is a merchant dealing in goods of that kind to whom the goods were entrusted by the existing lessee of that lessor before the interest of the subsequent lessee became enforceable against that

lessor obtains, to the extent of the leasehold interest transferred, all of that lessor's and the existing lessee's rights to the goods, and takes free of the existing lease contract.

(3) A subsequent lessee from the lessor of goods that are subject to an existing lease contract and are covered by a certificate of title issued under a statute of this State or of another jurisdiction takes no greater rights than those provided both by this section and by the certificate of title statute.

As amended in 1990.

§ 2A–305. Sale or Sublease of Goods by Lessee.

(1) Subject to the provisions of Section 2A–303, a buyer or sublessee from the lessee of goods under an existing lease contract obtains, to the extent of the interest transferred, the leasehold interest in the goods that the lessee had or had power to transfer, and except as provided in subsection (2) and Section 2A–511(4), takes subject to the existing lease contract. A lessee with a voidable leasehold interest has power to transfer a good leasehold interest to a good faith buyer for value or a good faith sublessee for value, but only to the extent set forth in the preceding sentence. When goods have been delivered under a transaction of lease the lessee has that power even though:
   (a) the lessor was deceived as to the identity of the lessee;
   (b) the delivery was in exchange for a check which is later dishonored; or
   (c) the delivery was procured through fraud punishable as larcenous under the criminal law.

(2) A buyer in the ordinary course of business or a sublessee in the ordinary course of business from a lessee who is a merchant dealing in goods of that kind to whom the goods were entrusted by the lessor obtains, to the extent of the interest transferred, all of the lessor's and lessee's rights to the goods, and takes free of the existing lease contract.

(3) A buyer or sublessee from the lessee of goods that are subject to an existing lease contract and are covered by a certificate of title issued under a statute of this State or of another jurisdiction takes no greater rights than those provided both by this section and by the certificate of title statute.

§ 2A–306. Priority of Certain Liens Arising by Operation of Law. If a person in the ordinary course of his [or her] business furnishes services or materials with respect to goods subject to a lease contract, a lien upon those goods in the possession of that person given by statute or rule of law for those materials or services takes priority over any interest of the lessor or lessee under the lease contract or this Article unless the lien is created by statute and the statute provides otherwise or unless the lien is created by rule of law and the rule of law provides otherwise.

§ 2A–307. Priority of Liens Arising by Attachment or Levy on, Security Interests in, and Other Claims to Goods.

(1) Except as otherwise provided in Section 2A–306, a creditor of a lessee takes subject to the lease contract.

(2) Except as otherwise provided in subsections (3) and (4) and in Sections 2A–306 and 2A–308, a creditor of a lessor takes subject to the lease contract unless:
   (a) the creditor holds a lien that attached to the goods before the lease contract became enforceable;
   (b) the creditor holds a security interest in the goods and the lessee did not give value and receive delivery of the goods without knowledge of the security interest; or
   (c) the creditor holds a security interest in the goods which was perfected (Section 9–303) before the lease contract became enforceable.

(3) A lessee in the ordinary course of business takes the leasehold interest free of a security interest in the goods created by the lessor even though the security interest is perfected (Section 9–303) and the lessee knows of its existence.

(4) A lessee other than a lessee in the ordinary course of business takes the leasehold interest free of a security interest to the extent that it secures future advances made after the secured party acquires knowledge of the lease or more than 45 days after the lease contract becomes enforceable, whichever first occurs, unless the future advances are made pursuant to a commitment entered into without knowledge of the lease and before the expiration of the 45-day period.

As amended in 1990.

§ 2A–308. Special Rights of Creditors.

(1) A creditor of a lessor in possession of goods subject to a lease contract may treat the lease contract as void if as against the creditor retention of possession by the lessor is fraudulent under any statute or rule of law, but retention of possession in good faith and current course of trade by the lessor for a commercially reasonable time after the lease contract becomes enforceable is not fraudulent.
(2) Nothing in this Article impairs the rights of creditors of a lessor if the lease contract (a) becomes enforceable, not in current course of trade but in satisfaction of or as security for a preexisting claim for money, security, or the like, and (b) is made under circumstances which under any statute or rule of law apart from this Article would constitute the transaction a fraudulent transfer or voidable preference.
(3) A creditor of a seller may treat a sale or an identification of goods to a contract for sale as void if as against the creditor retention of possession by the seller is fraudulent under any statute or rule of law, but retention of possession of the goods pursuant to a lease contract entered into by the seller as lessee and the buyer as lessor in connection with the sale or identification of the goods is not fraudulent if the buyer bought for value and in good faith.

§ 2A–309. Lessor's and Lessee's Rights When Goods Become Fixtures.

(1) In this section:
    (a) goods are "fixtures" when they become so related to particular real estate that an interest in them arises under real estate law;
    (b) a "fixture filing" is the filing, in the office where a mortgage on the real estate would be filed or recorded, of a financing statement covering goods that are or are to become fixtures and conforming to the requirements of Section 9–402(5);
    (c) a lease is a "purchase money lease" unless the lessee has possession or use of the goods or the right to possession or use of the goods before the lease agreement is enforceable;
    (d) a mortgage is a "construction mortgage" to the extent it secures an obligation incurred for the construction of an improvement on land including the acquisition cost of the land, if the recorded writing so indicates; and
    (e) "encumbrance" includes real estate mortgages and other liens on real estate and all other rights in real estate that are not ownership interests.
(2) Under this Article a lease may be of goods that are fixtures or may continue in goods that become fixtures, but no lease exists under this Article of ordinary building materials incorporated into an improvement on land.
(3) This Article does not prevent creation of a lease of fixtures pursuant to real estate law.
(4) The perfected interest of a lessor of fixtures has priority over a conflicting interest of an encumbrancer or owner of the real estate if:
    (a) the lease is a purchase money lease, the conflicting interest of the encumbrancer or owner arises before the goods become fixtures, the interest of the lessor is perfected by a fixture filing before the goods become fixtures or within ten days thereafter, and the lessee has an interest of record in the real estate or is in possession of the real estate; or
    (b) the interest of the lessor is perfected by a fixture filing before the interest of the encumbrancer or owner is of record, the lessor's interest has priority over any conflicting interest of a predecessor in title of the encumbrancer or owner, and the lessee has an interest of record in the real estate or is in possession of the real estate.

(5) The interest of a lessor of fixtures, whether or not perfected, has priority over the conflicting interest of an encumbrancer or owner of the real estate if:
  (a) the fixtures are readily removable factory or office machines, readily removable equipment that is not primarily used or leased for use in the operation of the real estate, or readily removable replacements of domestic appliances that are goods subject to a consumer lease, and before the goods become fixtures the lease contract is enforceable; or
  (b) the conflicting interest is a lien on the real estate obtained by legal or equitable proceedings after the lease contract is enforceable; or
  (c) the encumbrancer or owner has consented in writing to the lease or has disclaimed an interest in the goods as fixtures; or
  (d) the lessee has a right to remove the goods as against the encumbrancer or owner. If the lessee's right to remove terminates, the priority of the interest of the lessor continues for a reasonable time.

(6) Notwithstanding subsection (4) (a) but otherwise subject to subsections (4) and (5), the interest of a lessor of fixtures, including the lessor's residual interest, is subordinate to the conflicting interest of an encumbrancer of the real estate under a construction mortgage recorded before the goods become fixtures if the goods become fixtures before the completion of the construction. To the extent given to refinance a construction mortgage, the conflicting interest of an encumbrancer of the real estate under a mortgage has this priority to the same extent as the encumbrancer of the real estate under the construction mortgage.

(7) In cases not within the preceding subsections, priority between the interest of a lessor of fixtures, including the lessor's residual interest, and the conflicting interest of an encumbrancer or owner of the real estate who is not the lessee is determined by the priority rules governing conflicting interests in real estate.

(8) If the interest of a lessor of fixtures, including the lessor's residual interest, has priority over all conflicting interests of all owners and encumbrancers of the real estate, the lessor or the lessee may (i) on default, expiration, termination, or cancellation of the lease agreement but subject to the agreement and this Article, or (ii) if necessary to enforce other rights and remedies of the lessor or lessee under this Article, remove the goods from the real estate, free and clear of all conflicting interests of all owners and encumbrancers of the real estate, but the lessor or lessee must reimburse any encumbrancer or owner of the real estate who is not the lessee and who has not otherwise agreed for the cost of repair of any physical injury, but not for any diminution in value of the real estate caused by the absence of the goods removed or by any necessity of replacing them. A person entitled to reimbursement may refuse permission to remove until the party seeking removal gives adequate security for the performance of this obligation.

(9) Even though the lease agreement does not create a security interest, the interest of a lessor of fixtures, including the lessor's residual interest, is perfected by filing a financing statement as a fixture filing for leased goods that are or are to become fixtures in accordance with the relevant provisions of the Article on Secured Transactions (Article 9).

As amended in 1990.

§ 2A–310. Lessor's and Lessee's Rights When Goods Become Accessions.

(1) Goods are "accessions" when they are installed in or affixed to other goods.

(2) The interest of a lessor or a lessee under a lease contract entered into before the goods became accessions is superior to all interests in the whole except as stated in subsection (4).

(3) The interest of a lessor or a lessee under a lease contract entered into at the time or after the goods became accessions is superior to all subsequently acquired interests in the whole except as stated in subsection (4) but is subordinate to interests in the whole existing at the time the lease contract was made unless the holders of such interests in the whole have in writing consented to the lease or disclaimed an interest in the goods as part of the whole.

(4) The interest of a lessor or a lessee under a lease contract described in subsection (2) or (3) is subordinate to the interest of
  (a) a buyer in the ordinary course of business or a lessee in the ordinary course of business of any interest in the whole acquired after the goods became accessions; or
  (b) a creditor with a security interest in the whole perfected before the lease contract was made to the extent that the creditor makes subsequent advances without knowledge of the lease contract.

(5) When under subsections (2) or (3) and (4) a lessor or a lessee of accessions holds an interest that is superior to all interests in the whole, the lessor or the lessee may (a) on default, expiration, termination, or cancellation of the lease contract by the other party but subject to the provisions of the lease contract and this Article, or (b) if necessary to enforce his [or her] other rights and remedies under this Article, remove the goods from the whole, free and clear of all interests in the whole, but he [or she] must reimburse any holder of an interest in the whole who is not the lessee and who has not otherwise agreed for the cost of repair of any physical injury but not for any diminution in value of the whole caused by the absence of the goods removed or by any necessity for replacing them. A person entitled to reimbursement may refuse permission to remove until the party seeking removal gives adequate security for the performance of this obligation.

§ 2A–311. Priority Subject to Subordination. Nothing in this Article prevents subordination by agreement by any person entitled to priority.

As added in 1990.

PART 4: PERFORMANCE OF LEASE CONTRACT: REPUDIATED, SUBSTITUTED AND EXCUSED

§ 2A–401. Insecurity: Adequate Assurance of Performance.

(1) A lease contract imposes an obligation on each party that the other's expectation of receiving due performance will not be impaired.

(2) If reasonable grounds for insecurity arise with respect to the performance of either party, the insecure party may demand in writing adequate assurance of due performance. Until the insecure party receives that assurance, if commercially reasonable the insecure party may suspend any performance for which he [or she] has not already received the agreed return.

(3) A repudiation of the lease contract occurs if assurance of due performance adequate under the circumstances of the particular case is not provided to the insecure party within a reasonable time, not to exceed 30 days after receipt of a demand by the other party.

(4) Between merchants, the reasonableness of grounds for insecurity and the adequacy of any assurance offered must be determined according to commercial standards.

(5) Acceptance of any nonconforming delivery or payment does not prejudice the aggrieved party's right to demand adequate assurance of future performance.

§ 2A–402. Anticipatory Repudiation. If either party repudiates a lease contract with respect to a performance not yet due under the lease contract, the loss of which performance will substantially impair the value of the lease contract to the other, the aggrieved party may:

  (a) for a commercially reasonable time, await retraction of repudiation and performance by the repudiating party;
  (b) make demand pursuant to Section 2A–401 and await assurance of future performance adequate under the circumstances of the particular case; or
  (c) resort to any right or remedy upon default under the lease contract or this Article, even though the aggrieved party has notified the repudiating party that the aggrieved party would await the repudiating party's performance and assurance and has urged

retraction. In addition, whether or not the aggrieved party is pursuing one of the foregoing remedies, the aggrieved party may suspend performance or, if the aggrieved party is the lessor, proceed in accordance with the provisions of this Article on the lessor's right to identify goods to the lease contract notwithstanding default or to salvage unfinished goods (Section 2A–524).

§ 2A–403. Retraction of Anticipatory Repudiation.

(1) Until the repudiating party's next performance is due, the repudiating party can retract the repudiation unless, since the repudiation, the aggrieved party has cancelled the lease contract or materially changed the aggrieved party's position or otherwise indicated that the aggrieved party considers the repudiation final.
(2) Retraction may be by any method that clearly indicates to the aggrieved party that the repudiating party intends to perform under the lease contract and includes any assurance demanded under Section 2A–401.
(3) Retraction reinstates a repudiating party's rights under a lease contract with due excuse and allowance to the aggrieved party for any delay occasioned by the repudiation.

§ 2A–404. Substituted Performance.

(1) If without fault of the lessee, the lessor and the supplier, the agreed berthing, loading, or unloading facilities fail or the agreed type of carrier becomes unavailable or the agreed manner of delivery otherwise becomes commercially impracticable, but a commercially reasonable substitute is available, the substitute performance must be tendered and accepted.
(2) If the agreed means or manner of payment fails because of domestic or foreign governmental regulation:

(a) the lessor may withhold or stop delivery or cause the supplier to withhold or stop delivery unless the lessee provides a means or manner of payment that is commercially a substantial equivalent; and
(b) if delivery has already been taken, payment by the means or in the manner provided by the regulation discharges the lessee's obligation unless the regulation is discriminatory, oppressive, or predatory.

§ 2A–405. Excused Performance. Subject to Section 2A–404 on substituted performance, the following rules apply:

(a) Delay in delivery or nondelivery in whole or in part by a lessor or a supplier who complies with paragraphs (b) and (c) is not a default under the lease contract if performance as agreed has been made impracticable by the occurrence of a contingency the nonoccurrence of which was a basic assumption on which the lease contract was made or by compliance in good faith with any applicable foreign or domestic governmental regulation or order, whether or not the regulation or order later proves to be invalid.
(b) If the causes mentioned in paragraph (a) affect only part of the lessor's or the supplier's capacity to perform, he [or she] shall allocate production and deliveries among his [or her] customers but at his [or her] option may include regular customers not then under contract for sale or lease as well as his [or her] own requirements for further manufacture. He [or she] may so allocate in any manner that is fair and reasonable.
(c) The lessor seasonably shall notify the lessee and in the case of a finance lease the supplier seasonably shall notify the lessor and the lessee, if known, that there will be delay or nondelivery and, if allocation is required under paragraph (b), of the estimated quota thus made available for the lessee.

§ 2A–406. Procedure on Excused Performance.

(1) If the lessee receives notification of a material or indefinite delay or an allocation justified under Section 2A–405, the lessee may by written notification to the lessor as to any goods involved, and with respect to all of the goods if under an installment lease contract the value of the whole lease contract is substantially impaired (Section 2A–510):
  (a) terminate the lease contract (Section 2A–505(2)); or
  (b) except in a finance lease that is not a consumer lease, modify the lease contract by accepting the available quota in substitution, with due allowance from the rent payable for the balance of the lease term for the deficiency but without further right against the lessor.
(2) If, after receipt of a notification from the lessor under Section 2A–405, the lessee fails so to modify the lease agreement within a reasonable time not exceeding 30 days, the lease contract lapses with respect to any deliveries affected.

§ 2A–407. Irrevocable Promises: Finance Leases.

(1) In the case of a finance lease that is not a consumer lease the lessee's promises under the lease contract become irrevocable and independent upon the lessee's acceptance of the goods.
(2) A promise that has become irrevocable and independent under subsection (1):
  (a) is effective and enforceable between the parties, and by or against third parties including assignees of the parties; and
  (b) is not subject to cancellation, termination, modification, repudiation, excuse, or substitution without the consent of the party to whom the promise runs.
(3) This section does not affect the validity under any other law of a covenant in any lease contract making the lessee's promises irrevocable and independent upon the lessee's acceptance of the goods.

As amended in 1990.

PART 5: DEFAULT

§ 2A–501. Default: Procedure.

(1) Whether the lessor or the lessee is in default under a lease contract is determined by the lease agreement and this Article.
(2) If the lessor or the lessee is in default under the lease contract, the party seeking enforcement has rights and remedies as provided in this Article and, except as limited by this Article, as provided in the lease agreement.
(3) If the lessor or the lessee is in default under the lease contract, the party seeking enforcement may reduce the party's claim to judgment, or otherwise enforce the lease contract by self-help or any available judicial procedure or nonjudicial procedure, including administrative proceeding, arbitration, or the like, in accordance with this Article.
(4) Except as otherwise provided in Section 1–106(1) or this Article or the lease agreement, the rights and remedies referred to in subsections (2) and (3) are cumulative.
(5) If the lease agreement covers both real property and goods, the party seeking enforcement may proceed under this Part as to the goods, or under other applicable law as to both the real property and the goods in accordance with that party's rights and remedies in respect of the real property, in which case this Part does not apply.

As amended in 1990.

§ 2A–502. Notice After Default. Except as otherwise provided in this Article or the lease agreement, the lessor or lessee in default under the lease contract is not entitled to notice of default or notice of enforcement from the other party to the lease agreement.

§ 2A–503. Modification or Impairment of Rights and Remedies.

(1) Except as otherwise provided in this Article, the lease agreement may include rights and remedies for default in addition to or in substitution for those provided in this Article and may limit or alter the measure of damages recoverable under this Article.
(2) Resort to a remedy provided under this Article or in the lease agreement is optional unless the remedy is expressly agreed to be exclusive. If circumstances cause an exclusive or limited remedy to fail of its essential purpose, or provision for an exclusive remedy is unconscionable, remedy may be had as provided in this Article.
(3) Consequential damages may be liquidated under Section 2A–504, or may otherwise be limited, altered, or excluded unless the limitation, alteration, or exclusion is unconscionable. Limitation, alteration, or exclusion of consequential damages for injury to the person in the case of consumer goods is prima facie unconscionable but limitation, alteration, or exclusion of damages where the loss is commercial is not prima facie unconscionable.
(4) Rights and remedies on default by the lessor or the lessee with respect to any obligation or promise collateral or ancillary to the lease contract are not impaired by this Article.

As amended in 1990.

§ 2A–504. Liquidation of Damages.

(1) Damages payable by either party for default, or any other act or omission, including indemnity for loss or diminution of anticipated tax benefits or loss or damage to lessor's residual interest, may be liquidated in the lease agreement but only at an amount or by a formula that is reasonable in light of the then anticipated harm caused by the default or other act or omission.
(2) If the lease agreement provides for liquidation of damages, and such provision does not comply with subsection (1), or such provision is an exclusive or limited remedy that circumstances cause to fail of its essential purpose, remedy may be had as provided in this Article.
(3) If the lessor justifiably withholds or stops delivery of goods because of the lessee's default or insolvency (Section 2A–525 or 2A–526), the lessee is entitled to restitution of any amount by which the sum of his [or her] payments exceeds:
    (a) the amount to which the lessor is entitled by virtue of terms liquidating the lessor's damages in accordance with subsection (1); or
    (b) in the absence of those terms, 20 percent of the then present value of the total rent the lessee was obligated to pay for the balance of the lease term, or, in the case of a consumer lease, the lesser of such amount or $500.
(4) A lessee's right to restitution under subsection (3) is subject to offset to the extent the lessor establishes:
    (a) a right to recover damages under the provisions of this Article other than subsection (1); and
    (b) the amount or value of any benefits received by the lessee directly or indirectly by reason of the lease contract.

§ 2A–505. Cancellation and Termination and Effect of Cancellation, Termination, Rescission, or Fraud on Rights and Remedies.

(1) On cancellation of the lease contract, all obligations that are still executory on both sides are discharged, but any right based on prior default or performance survives, and the cancelling party also retains any remedy for default of the whole lease contract or any unperformed balance.
(2) On termination of the lease contract, all obligations that are still executory on both sides are discharged but any right based on prior default or performance survives.

(3) Unless the contrary intention clearly appears, expressions of "cancellation," "rescission," or the like of the lease contract may not be construed as a renunciation or discharge of any claim in damages for an antecedent default.
(4) Rights and remedies for material misrepresentation or fraud include all rights and remedies available under this Article for default.
(5) Neither rescission nor a claim for rescission of the lease contract nor rejection or return of the goods may bar or be deemed inconsistent with a claim for damages or other right or remedy.

§ 2A–506. Statute of Limitations.

(1) An action for default under a lease contract, including breach of warranty or indemnity, must be commenced within 4 years after the cause of action accrued. By the original lease contract the parties may reduce the period of limitation to not less than one year.
(2) A cause of action for default accrues when the act or omission on which the default or breach of warranty is based is or should have been discovered by the aggrieved party, or when the default occurs, whichever is later. A cause of action for indemnity accrues when the act or omission on which the claim for indemnity is based is or should have been discovered by the indemnified party, whichever is later.
(3) If an action commenced within the time limited by subsection (1) is so terminated as to leave available a remedy by another action for the same default or breach of warranty or indemnity, the other action may be commenced after the expiration of the time limited and within 6 months after the termination of the first action unless the termination resulted from voluntary discontinuance or from dismissal for failure or neglect to prosecute.
(4) This section does not alter the law on tolling of the statute of limitations nor does it apply to causes of action that have accrued before this Article becomes effective.

§ 2A–507. Proof of Market Rent: Time and Place.

(1) Damages based on market rent (Section 2A–519 or 2A–528) are determined according to the rent for the use of the goods concerned for a lease term identical to the remaining lease term of the original lease agreement and prevailing at the times specified in Sections 2A–519 and 2A–528.
(2) If evidence of rent for the use of the goods concerned for a lease term identical to the remaining lease term of the original lease agreement and prevailing at the times or places described in this Article is not readily available, the rent prevailing within any reasonable time before or after the time described or at any other place or for a different lease term which in commercial judgment or under usage of trade would serve as a reasonable substitute for the one described may be used, making any proper allowance for the difference, including the cost of transporting the goods to or from the other place.
(3) Evidence of a relevant rent prevailing at a time or place or for a lease term other than the one described in this Article offered by one party is not admissible unless and until he [or she] has given the other party notice the court finds sufficient to prevent unfair surprise.
(4) If the prevailing rent or value of any goods regularly leased in any established market is in issue, reports in official publications or trade journals or in newspapers or periodicals of general circulation published as the reports of that market are admissible in evidence. The circumstances of the preparation of the report may be shown to affect its weight but not its admissibility.

As amended in 1990.

§ 2A–508. Lessee's Remedies.

(1) If a lessor fails to deliver the goods in conformity to the lease contract (Section 2A–509) or repudiates the lease contract (Section 2A–402), or a lessee rightfully rejects the goods (Section 2A–509) or justifiably revokes acceptance of the goods (Section 2A–517), then

with respect to any goods involved, and with respect to all of the goods if under an installment lease contract the value of the whole lease contract is substantially impaired (Section 2A–510), the lessor is in default under the lease contract and the lessee may:

(a) cancel the lease contract (Section 2A–505(1));

(b) recover so much of the rent and security as has been paid and is just under the circumstances;

(c) cover and recover damages as to all goods affected whether or not they have been identified to the lease contract (Sections 2A–518 and 2A–520), or recover damages for nondelivery (Sections 2A–519 and 2A–520);

(d) exercise any other rights or pursue any other remedies provided in the lease contract.

(2) If a lessor fails to deliver the goods in conformity to the lease contract or repudiates the lease contract, the lessee may also:

(a) if the goods have been identified, recover them (Section 2A–522); or

(b) in a proper case, obtain specific performance or replevy the goods (Section 2A–521).

(3) If a lessor is otherwise in default under a lease contract, the lessee may exercise the rights and pursue the remedies provided in the lease contract, which may include a right to cancel the lease, and in Section 2A–519(3).

(4) If a lessor has breached a warranty, whether express or implied, the lessee may recover damages (Section 2A–519(4)).

(5) On rightful rejection or justifiable revocation of acceptance, a lessee has a security interest in goods in the lessee's possession or control for any rent and security that has been paid and any expenses reasonably incurred in their inspection, receipt, transportation, and care and custody and may hold those goods and dispose of them in good faith and in a commercially reasonable manner, subject to Section 2A–527(5).

(6) Subject to the provisions of Section 2A–407, a lessee, on notifying the lessor of the lessee's intention to do so, may deduct all or any part of the damages resulting from any default under the lease contract from any part of the rent still due under the same lease contract.

As amended in 1990.

§ 2A–509. Lessee's Rights on Improper Delivery; Rightful Rejection.

(1) Subject to the provisions of Section 2A–510 on default in installment lease contracts, if the goods or the tender or delivery fail in any respect to conform to the lease contract, the lessee may reject or accept the goods or accept any commercial unit or units and reject the rest of the goods.

(2) Rejection of goods is ineffective unless it is within a reasonable time after tender or delivery of the goods and the lessee seasonably notifies the lessor.

§ 2A–510. Installment Lease Contracts: Rejection and Default.

(1) Under an installment lease contract a lessee may reject any delivery that is nonconforming if the nonconformity substantially impairs the value of that delivery and cannot be cured or the nonconformity is a defect in the required documents; but if the nonconformity does not fall within subsection (2) and the lessor or the supplier gives adequate assurance of its cure, the lessee must accept that delivery.

(2) Whenever nonconformity or default with respect to one or more deliveries substantially impairs the value of the installment lease contract as a whole there is a default with respect to the whole. But, the aggrieved party reinstates the installment lease contract as a whole if the aggrieved party accepts a nonconforming delivery without seasonably notifying of cancellation or brings an action with respect only to past deliveries or demands performance as to future deliveries.

§ 2A–511. Merchant Lessee's Duties as to Rightfully Rejected Goods.

(1) Subject to any security interest of a lessee (Section 2A–508(5)), if a lessor or a supplier has no agent or place of business at the market of rejection, a merchant lessee, after rejection of goods in his [or her] possession or control, shall follow any reasonable instructions received from the lessor or the supplier with respect to the goods. In the absence of those instructions, a merchant lessee shall make reasonable efforts to sell, lease, or otherwise dispose of the goods for the lessor's account if they threaten to decline in value speedily. Instructions are not reasonable if on demand indemnity for expenses is not forthcoming.

(2) If a merchant lessee (subsection (1)) or any other lessee (Section 2A–512) disposes of goods, he [or she] is entitled to reimbursement either from the lessor or the supplier or out of the proceeds for reasonable expenses of caring for and disposing of the goods and, if the expenses include no disposition commission, to such commission as is usual in the trade, or if there is none, to a reasonable sum not exceeding 10 percent of the gross proceeds.

(3) In complying with this section or Section 2A–512, the lessee is held only to good faith. Good faith conduct hereunder is neither acceptance or conversion nor the basis of an action for damages.

(4) A purchaser who purchases in good faith from a lessee pursuant to this section or Section 2A–512 takes the goods free of any rights of the lessor and the supplier even though the lessee fails to comply with one or more of the requirements of this Article.

§ 2A–512. Lessee's Duties as to Rightfully Rejected Goods.

(1) Except as otherwise provided with respect to goods that threaten to decline in value speedily (Section 2A–511) and subject to any security interest of a lessee (Section 2A–508(5)):
   (a) the lessee, after rejection of goods in the lessee's possession, shall hold them with reasonable care at the lessor's or the supplier's disposition for a reasonable time after the lessee's seasonable notification of rejection;
   (b) if the lessor or the supplier gives no instructions within a reasonable time after notification of rejection, the lessee may store the rejected goods for the lessor's or the supplier's account or ship them to the lessor or the supplier or dispose of them for the lessor's or the supplier's account with reimbursement in the manner provided in Section 2A–511; but
   (c) the lessee has no further obligations with regard to goods rightfully rejected.

(2) Action by the lessee pursuant to subsection (1) is not acceptance or conversion.

§ 2A–513. Cure by Lessor of Improper Tender or Delivery; Replacement.

(1) If any tender or delivery by the lessor or the supplier is rejected because nonconforming and the time for performance has not yet expired, the lessor or the supplier may seasonably notify the lessee of the lessor's or the supplier's intention to cure and may then make a conforming delivery within the time provided in the lease contract.

(2) If the lessee rejects a nonconforming tender that the lessor or the supplier had reasonable grounds to believe would be acceptable with or without money allowance, the lessor or the supplier may have a further reasonable time to substitute a conforming tender if he [or she] seasonably notifies the lessee.

§ 2A–514. Waiver of Lessee's Objections.

(1) In rejecting goods, a lessee's failure to state a particular defect that is ascertainable by reasonable inspection precludes the lessee from relying on the defect to justify rejection or to establish default:
   (a) if, stated seasonably, the lessor or the supplier could have cured it (Section 2A–513); or

(b) between merchants if the lessor or the supplier after rejection has made a request in writing for a full and final written statement of all defects on which the lessee proposes to rely.

(2) A lessee's failure to reserve rights when paying rent or other consideration against documents precludes recovery of the payment for defects apparent on the face of the documents.

§ 2A–515. Acceptance of Goods.

(1) Acceptance of goods occurs after the lessee has had a reasonable opportunity to inspect the goods and
   (a) the lessee signifies or acts with respect to the goods in a manner that signifies to the lessor or the supplier that the goods are conforming or that the lessee will take or retain them in spite of their nonconformity; or
   (b) the lessee fails to make an effective rejection of the goods (Section 2A–509(2)).

(2) Acceptance of a part of any commercial unit is acceptance of that entire unit.

§ 2A–516. Effect of Acceptance of Goods; Notice of Default; Burden of Establishing Default After Acceptance; Notice of Claim or Litigation to Person Answerable Over.

(1) A lessee must pay rent for any goods accepted in accordance with the lease contract, with due allowance for goods rightfully rejected or not delivered.

(2) A lessee's acceptance of goods precludes rejection of the goods accepted. In the case of a finance lease, if made with knowledge of a nonconformity, acceptance cannot be revoked because of it. In any other case, if made with knowledge of a nonconformity, acceptance cannot be revoked because of it unless the acceptance was on the reasonable assumption that the nonconformity would be seasonably cured. Acceptance does not of itself impair any other remedy provided by this Article or the lease agreement for nonconformity.

(3) If a tender has been accepted:
   (a) within a reasonable time after the lessee discovers or should have discovered any default, the lessee shall notify the lessor and the supplier, if any, or be barred from any remedy against the party not notified;
   (b) except in the case of a consumer lease, within a reasonable time after the lessee receives notice of litigation for infringement or the like (Section 2A–211) the lessee shall notify the lessor or be barred from any remedy over for liability established by the litigation; and
   (c) the burden is on the lessee to establish any default.

(4) If a lessee is sued for breach of a warranty or other obligation for which a lessor or a supplier is answerable over the following apply:
   (a) The lessee may give the lessor or the supplier, or both, written notice of the litigation. If the notice states that the person notified may come in and defend and that if the person notified does not do so that person will be bound in any action against that person by the lessee by any determination of fact common to the two litigations, then unless the person notified after seasonable receipt of the notice does come in and defend that person is so bound.
   (b) The lessor or the supplier may demand in writing that the lessee turn over control of the litigation including settlement if the claim is one for infringement or the like (Section 2A–211) or else be barred from any remedy over. If the demand states that the lessor or the supplier agrees to bear all expense and to satisfy any adverse judgment, then unless the lessee after seasonable receipt of the demand does turn over control the lessee is so barred.

(5) Subsections (3) and (4) apply to any obligation of a lessee to hold the lessor or the supplier harmless against infringement or the like (Section 2A–211).

As amended in 1990.

§ 2A–517. Revocation of Acceptance of Goods.

(1) A lessee may revoke acceptance of a lot or commercial unit whose nonconformity substantially impairs its value to the lessee if the lessee has accepted it:
   (a) except in the case of a finance lease, on the reasonable assumption that its nonconformity would be cured and it has not been seasonably cured; or
   (b) without discovery of the nonconformity if the lessee's acceptance was reasonably induced either by the lessor's assurances or, except in the case of a finance lease, by the difficulty of discovery before acceptance.
(2) Except in the case of a finance lease that is not a consumer lease, a lessee may revoke acceptance of a lot or commercial unit if the lessor defaults under the lease contract and the default substantially impairs the value of that lot or commercial unit to the lessee.
(3) If the lease agreement so provides, the lessee may revoke acceptance of a lot or commercial unit because of other defaults by the lessor.
(4) Revocation of acceptance must occur within a reasonable time after the lessee discovers or should have discovered the ground for it and before any substantial change in condition of the goods which is not caused by the nonconformity. Revocation is not effective until the lessee notifies the lessor.
(5) A lessee who so revokes has the same rights and duties with regard to the goods involved as if the lessee had rejected them.

As amended in 1990.

§ 2A–518. Cover; Substitute Goods.

(1) After a default by a lessor under the lease contract of the type described in Section 2A–508(1), or, if agreed, after other default by the lessor, the lessee may cover by making any purchase or lease of or contract to purchase or lease goods in substitution for those due from the lessor.
(2) Except as otherwise provided with respect to damages liquidated in the lease agreement (Section 2A–504) or otherwise determined pursuant to agreement of the parties (Sections 1–102(3) and 2A–503), if a lessee's cover is by a lease agreement substantially similar to the original lease agreement and the new lease agreement is made in good faith and in a commercially reasonable manner, the lessee may recover from the lessor as damages (i) the present value, as of the date of the commencement of the term of the new lease agreement, of the rent under the new lease agreement applicable to that period of the new lease term which is comparable to the then remaining term of the original lease agreement minus the present value as of the same date of the total rent for the then remaining lease term of the original lease agreement, and (ii) any incidental or consequential damages, less expenses saved in consequence of the lessor's default.
(3) If a lessee's cover is by lease agreement that for any reason does not qualify for treatment under subsection (2), or is by purchase or otherwise, the lessee may recover from the lessor as if the lessee had elected not to cover and Section 2A–519 governs.

As amended in 1990.

§ 2A–519. Lessee's Damages for Nondelivery, Repudiation, Default, and Breach of Warranty in Regard to Accepted Goods.

(1) Except as otherwise provided with respect to damages liquidated in the lease agreement (Section 2A–504) or otherwise determined pursuant to agreement of the parties (Sections 1–102(3) and 2A–503), if a lessee elects not to cover or a lessee elects to cover and the cover is by lease agreement that for any reason does not qualify for treatment under Section 2A–518(2), or is by purchase or otherwise, the measure of damages for nondelivery or repudiation by the lessor or for rejection or revocation of acceptance by the lessee is the present value, as of the date of the default, of the then market rent minus the present value as

of the same date of the original rent, computed for the remaining lease term of the original lease agreement, together with incidental and consequential damages, less expenses saved in consequence of the lessor's default.

(2) Market rent is to be determined as of the place for tender or, in cases of rejection after arrival or revocation of acceptance, as of the place of arrival.

(3) Except as otherwise agreed, if the lessee has accepted goods and given notification (Section 2A–516(3)), the measure of damages for nonconforming tender or delivery or other default by a lessor is the loss resulting in the ordinary course of events from the lessor's default as determined in any manner that is reasonable together with incidental and consequential damages, less expenses saved in consequence of the lessor's default.

(4) Except as otherwise agreed, the measure of damages for breach of warranty is the present value at the time and place of acceptance of the difference between the value of the use of the goods accepted and the value if they had been as warranted for the lease term, unless special circumstances show proximate damages of a different amount, together with incidental and consequential damages, less expenses saved in consequence of the lessor's default or breach of warranty.

As amended in 1990.

§ 2A–520. Lessee's Incidental and Consequential Damages.

(1) Incidental damages resulting from a lessor's default include expenses reasonably incurred in inspection, receipt, transportation, and care and custody of goods rightfully rejected or goods the acceptance of which is justifiably revoked, any commercially reasonable charges, expenses or commissions in connection with effecting cover, and any other reasonable expense incident to the default.

(2) Consequential damages resulting from a lessor's default include:

(a) any loss resulting from general or particular requirements and needs of which the lessor at the time of contracting had reason to know and which could not reasonably be prevented by cover or otherwise; and

(b) injury to person or property proximately resulting from any breach of warranty.

§ 2A–521. Lessee's Right to Specific Performance or Replevin.

(1) Specific performance may be decreed if the goods are unique or in other proper circumstances.

(2) A decree for specific performance may include any terms and conditions as to payment of the rent, damages, or other relief that the court deems just.

(3) A lessee has a right of replevin, detinue, sequestration, claim and delivery, or the like for goods identified to the lease contract if after reasonable effort the lessee is unable to effect cover for those goods or the circumstances reasonably indicate that the effort will be unavailing.

§ 2A–522. Lessee's Right to Goods on Lessor's Insolvency.

(1) Subject to subsection (2) and even though the goods have not been shipped, a lessee who has paid a part or all of the rent and security for goods identified to a lease contract (Section 2A–217) on making and keeping good a tender of any unpaid portion of the rent and security due under the lease contract may recover the goods identified from the lessor if the lessor becomes insolvent within 10 days after receipt of the first installment of rent and security.

(2) A lessee acquires the right to recover goods identified to a lease contract only if they conform to the lease contract.

§ 2A–523. Lessor's Remedies.

(1) If a lessee wrongfully rejects or revokes acceptance of goods or fails to make a payment when due or repudiates with respect to a part or the whole, then, with respect to any goods involved, and with respect to all of the goods if under an installment lease contract the

value of the whole lease contract is substantially impaired (Section 2A–510), the lessee is in default under the lease contract and the lessor may:
(a) cancel the lease contract (Section 2A–505(1));
(b) proceed respecting goods not identified to the lease contract (Section 2A–524);
(c) withhold delivery of the goods and take possession of goods previously delivered (Section 2A–525);
(d) stop delivery of the goods by any bailee (Section 2A–526);
(e) dispose of the goods and recover damages (Section 2A–527), or retain the goods and recover damages (Section 2A–528), or in a proper case recover rent (Section 2A–529);
(f) exercise any other rights or pursue any other remedies provided in the lease contract.

(2) If a lessor does not fully exercise a right or obtain a remedy to which the lessor is entitled under subsection (1), the lessor may recover the loss resulting in the ordinary course of events from the lessee's default as determined in any reasonable manner, together with incidental damages, less expenses saved in consequence of the lessee's default.

(3) If a lessee is otherwise in default under a lease contract, the lessor may exercise the rights and pursue the remedies provided in the lease contract, which may include a right to cancel the lease. In addition, unless otherwise provided in the lease contract:
(a) if the default substantially impairs the value of the lease contract to the lessor, the lessor may exercise the rights and pursue the remedies provided in subsections (1) or (2); or
(b) if the default does not substantially impair the value of the lease contract to the lessor, the lessor may recover as provided in subsection (2).

As amended in 1990.

§ 2A–524. Lessor's Right to Identify Goods to Lease Contract.

(1) After default by the lessee under the lease contract of the type described in Section 2A–523(1) or 2A–523(3) (a) or, if agreed, after other default by the lessee, the lessor may:
(a) identify to the lease contract conforming goods not already identified if at the time the lessor learned of the default they were in the lessor's or the supplier's possession or control; and
(b) dispose of goods (Section 2A–527(1)) that demonstrably have been intended for the particular lease contract even though those goods are unfinished.

(2) If the goods are unfinished, in the exercise of reasonable commercial judgment for the purposes of avoiding loss and of effective realization, an aggrieved lessor or the supplier may either complete manufacture and wholly identify the goods to the lease contract or cease manufacture and lease, sell, or otherwise dispose of the goods for scrap or salvage value or proceed in any other reasonable manner.

As amended in 1990.

§ 2A–525. Lessor's Right to Possession of Goods.

(1) If a lessor discovers the lessee to be insolvent, the lessor may refuse to deliver the goods.

(2) After a default by the lessee under the lease contract of the type described in Section 2A–523(1) or 2A–523(3) (a) or, if agreed, after other default by the lessee, the lessor has the right to take possession of the goods. If the lease contract so provides, the lessor may require the lessee to assemble the goods and make them available to the lessor at a place to be designated by the lessor which is reasonably convenient to both parties. Without removal, the lessor may render unusable any goods employed in trade or business, and may dispose of goods on the lessee's premises (Section 2A–527).

(3) The lessor may proceed under subsection (2) without judicial process if it can be done without breach of the peace or the lessor may proceed by action.

As amended in 1990.

§ 2A–526. Lessor's Stoppage of Delivery in Transit or Otherwise.

(1) A lessor may stop delivery of goods in the possession of a carrier or other bailee if the lessor discovers the lessee to be insolvent and may stop delivery of carload, truckload, planeload, or larger shipments of express or freight if the lessee repudiates or fails to make a payment due before delivery, whether for rent, security or otherwise under the lease contract, or for any other reason the lessor has a right to withhold or take possession of the goods.

(2) In pursuing its remedies under subsection (1), the lessor may stop delivery until
  (a) receipt of the goods by the lessee;
  (b) acknowledgment to the lessee by any bailee of the goods, except a carrier, that the bailee holds the goods for the lessee; or
  (c) such an acknowledgment to the lessee by a carrier via reshipment or as warehouseman.

(3) (a) To stop delivery, a lessor shall so notify as to enable the bailee by reasonable diligence to prevent delivery of the goods.
  (b) After notification, the bailee shall hold and deliver the goods according to the directions of the lessor, but the lessor is liable to the bailee for any ensuing charges or damages.
  (c) A carrier who has issued a nonnegotiable bill of lading is not obliged to obey a notification to stop received from a person other than the consignor.

§ 2A–527. Lessor's Rights to Dispose of Goods.

(1) After a default by a lessee under the lease contract of the type described in Section 2A–523(1) or 2A–523(3) (a) or after the lessor refuses to deliver or takes possession of goods (Section 2A–525 or 2A–526), or, if agreed, after other default by a lessee, the lessor may dispose of the goods concerned or the undelivered balance thereof by lease, sale, or otherwise.

(2) Except as otherwise provided with respect to damages liquidated in the lease agreement (Section 2A–504) or otherwise determined pursuant to agreement of the parties (Sections 1–102(3) and 2A–503), if the disposition is by lease agreement substantially similar to the original lease agreement and the new lease agreement is made in good faith and in a commercially reasonable manner, the lessor may recover from the lessee as damages (i) accrued and unpaid rent as of the date of the commencement of the term of the new lease agreement, (ii) the present value, as of the same date, of the total rent for the then remaining lease term of the original lease agreement minus the present value, as of the same date, of the rent under the new lease agreement applicable to that period of the new lease term which is comparable to the then remaining term of the original lease agreement, and (iii) any incidental damages allowed under Section 2A–530, less expenses saved in consequence of the lessee's default.

(3) If the lessor's disposition is by lease agreement that for any reason does not qualify for treatment under subsection (2), or is by sale or otherwise, the lessor may recover from the lessee as if the lessor had elected not to dispose of the goods and Section 2A–528 governs.

(4) A subsequent buyer or lessee who buys or leases from the lessor in good faith for value as a result of a disposition under this section takes the goods free of the original lease contract and any rights of the original lessee even though the lessor fails to comply with one or more of the requirements of this Article.

(5) The lessor is not accountable to the lessee for any profit made on any disposition. A lessee who has rightfully rejected or justifiably revoked acceptance shall account to the lessor for any excess over the amount of the lessee's security interest (Section 2A–508(5)).

As amended in 1990.

§ 2A–528. Lessor's Damages for Nonacceptance, Failure to Pay, Repudiation, or Other Default.

(1) Except as otherwise provided with respect to damages liquidated in the lease agreement (Section 2A–504) or otherwise determined pursuant to agreement of the parties (Sections 1–102(3) and 2A–503), if a lessor elects to retain the goods or a lessor elects to dispose of the goods and the disposition is by lease agreement that for any reason does not qualify for treatment under Section 2A–527(2), or is by sale or otherwise, the lessor may recover from the lessee as damages for a default of the type described in Section 2A–523(1) or 2A–523(3) (a), or, if agreed, for other default of the lessee, (i) accrued and unpaid rent as of the date of default if the lessee has never taken possession of the goods, or, if the lessee has taken possession of the goods, as of the date the lessor repossesses the goods or an earlier date on which the lessee makes a tender of the goods to the lessor, (ii) the present value as of the date determined under clause (i) of the total rent for the then remaining lease term of the original lease agreement minus the present value as of the same date of the market rent at the place where the goods are located computed for the same lease term, and (iii) any incidental damages allowed under Section 2A–530, less expenses saved in consequence of the lessee's default.

(2) If the measure of damages provided in subsection (1) is inadequate to put a lessor in as good a position as performance would have, the measure of damages is the present value of the profit, including reasonable overhead, the lessor would have made from full performance by the lessee, together with any incidental damages allowed under Section 2A–530, due allowance for costs reasonably incurred and due credit for payments or proceeds of disposition.

As amended in 1990.

§ 2A–529. Lessor's Action for the Rent.

(1) After default by the lessee under the lease contract of the type described in Section 2A–523(1) or 2A–523(3) (a) or, if agreed, after other default by the lessee, if the lessor complies with subsection (2), the lessor may recover from the lessee as damages:
   (a) for goods accepted by the lessee and not repossessed by or tendered to the lessor, and for conforming goods lost or damaged within a commercially reasonable time after risk of loss passes to the lessee (Section 2A–219), (i) accrued and unpaid rent as of the date of entry of judgment in favor of the lessor, (ii) the present value as of the same date of the rent for the then remaining lease term of the lease agreement, and (iii) any incidental damages allowed under Section 2A–530, less expenses saved in consequence of the lessee's default; and
   (b) for goods identified to the lease contract if the lessor is unable after reasonable effort to dispose of them at a reasonable price or the circumstances reasonably indicate that effort will be unavailing, (i) accrued and unpaid rent as of the date of entry of judgment in favor of the lessor, (ii) the present value as of the same date of the rent for the then remaining lease term of the lease agreement, and (iii) any incidental damages allowed under Section 2A–530, less expenses saved in consequence of the lessee's default.

(2) Except as provided in subsection (3), the lessor shall hold for the lessee for the remaining lease term of the lease agreement any goods that have been identified to the lease contract and are in the lessor's control.

(3) The lessor may dispose of the goods at any time before collection of the judgment for damages obtained pursuant to subsection (1). If the disposition is before the end of the remaining lease term of the lease agreement, the lessor's recovery against the lessee for damages is governed by Section 2A–527 or Section 2A–528, and the lessor will cause an appropriate credit to be provided against a judgment for damages to the extent that the amount of the judgment exceeds the recovery available pursuant to Section 2A–527 or 2A–528.

(4) Payment of the judgment for damages obtained pursuant to subsection (1) entitles the lessee to the use and possession of the goods not then disposed of for the remaining lease term of and in accordance with the lease agreement.
(5) After default by the lessee under the lease contract of the type described in Section 2A–523(1) or Section 2A–523(3) (a) or, if agreed, after other default by the lessee, a lessor who is held not entitled to rent under this section must nevertheless be awarded damages for nonacceptance under Section 2A–527 or Section 2A–528.

As amended in 1990.

§ 2A–530. Lessor's Incidental Damages. Incidental damages to an aggrieved lessor include any commercially reasonable charges, expenses, or commissions incurred in stopping delivery, in the transportation, care and custody of goods after the lessee's default, in connection with return or disposition of the goods, or otherwise resulting from the default.

§ 2A–531. Standing to Sue Third Parties for Injury to Goods.

(1) If a third party so deals with goods that have been identified to a lease contract as to cause actionable injury to a party to the lease contract (a) the lessor has a right of action against the third party, and (b) the lessee also has a right of action against the third party if the lessee:
    (i) has a security interest in the goods;
    (ii) has an insurable interest in the goods; or
    (iii) bears the risk of loss under the lease contract or has since the injury assumed that risk as against the lessor and the goods have been converted or destroyed.
(2) If at the time of the injury the party plaintiff did not bear the risk of loss as against the other party to the lease contract and there is no arrangement between them for disposition of the recovery, his [or her] suit or settlement, subject to his [or her] own interest, is as a fiduciary for the other party to the lease contract.
(3) Either party with the consent of the other may sue for the benefit of whom it may concern.

§ 2A–532. Lessor's Rights to Residual Interest. In addition to any other recovery permitted by this Article or other law, the lessor may recover from the lessee an amount that will fully compensate the lessor for any loss of or damage to the lessor's residual interest in the goods caused by the default of the lessee.

As added in 1990.

Article 3—Negotiable Instruments

PART 1: GENERAL PROVISIONS AND DEFINITIONS

§ 3–101. Short Title. This Article may be cited as Uniform Commercial Code—Negotiable Instruments.

§ 3–102. Subject Matter.

(a) This Article applies to negotiable instruments. It does not apply to money, to payment orders governed by Article 4A, or to securities governed by Article 8.
(b) If there is conflict between this Article and Article 4 or 9, Articles 4 and 9 govern.
(c) Regulations of the Board of Governors of the Federal Reserve System and operating circulars of the Federal Reserve Banks supersede any inconsistent provision of this Article to the extent of the inconsistency.

§ 3–103. Definitions.

(a) In this Article:

(1) "Acceptor" means a drawee who has accepted a draft.

(2) "Consumer account" means an account established by an individual primarily for personal, family, or household purposes.

(3) "Consumer transaction" means a transaction in which an individual incurs an obligation primarily for personal, family, or household purposes.

(4) "Drawee" means a person ordered in a draft to make payment.

(5) "Drawer" means a person who signs or is identified in a draft as a person ordering payment.

(6) ["Good faith" means honesty in fact and the observance of reasonable commercial standards of fair dealing.]

(7) "Maker" means a person who signs or is identified in a note as a person undertaking to pay.

(8) "Order" means a written instruction to pay money signed by the person giving the instruction. The instruction may be addressed to any person, including the person giving the instruction, or to one or more persons jointly or in the alternative but not in succession. An authorization to pay is not an order unless the person authorized to pay is also instructed to pay.

(9) "Ordinary care" in the case of a person engaged in business means observance of reasonable commercial standards, prevailing in the area in which the person is located, with respect to the business in which the person is engaged. In the case of a bank that takes an instrument for processing for collection or payment by automated means, reasonable commercial standards do not require the bank to examine the instrument if the failure to examine does not violate the bank's prescribed procedures and the bank's procedures do not vary unreasonably from general banking usage not disapproved by this Article or Article 4.

(10) "Party" means a party to an instrument.

(11) "Principal obligor," with respect to an instrument, means the accommodated party or any other party to the instrument against whom a secondary obligor has recourse under this article.

(12) "Promise" means a written undertaking to pay money signed by the person undertaking to pay. An acknowledgment of an obligation by the obligor is not a promise unless the obligor also undertakes to pay the obligation.

(13) "Prove" with respect to a fact means to meet the burden of establishing the fact (Section 1–201(8)).

(14) ["Record" means information that is inscribed on a tangible medium or that is stored in electronic or other medium and is retrievable in perceivable form.]

(15) "Remitter" means a person who purchases an instrument from its issuer if the instrument is payable to an identified person other than the purchaser.

(16) "Remotely-created consumer item" means an item drawn on a consumer account, which is not created by the payor bank and does not bear a handwritten signature purporting to be the signature of the drawer.

(17) "Secondary obligor," with respect to an instrument, means (a) an indorser or an accommodation party, (b) a drawer having the obligation described in Section 3–414(d), or (c) any other party to the instrument that has recourse against another party to the instrument pursuant to Section 3–116(b).

(b) Other definitions applying to this Article and the sections in which they appear are:

"Acceptance"	Section 3–409.
"Accommodated party"	Section 3–419.
"Accommodation party"	Section 3–419.

"Account"	Section 4–104.
"Alteration"	Section 3–407.
"Anomalous indorsement"	Section 3–205.
"Blank indorsement"	Section 3–205.
"Cashier's check"	Section 3–104.
"Certificate of deposit"	Section 3–104.
"Certified check"	Section 3–409.
"Check"	Section 3–104.
"Consideration"	Section 3–303.
"Draft"	Section 3–104.
"Holder in due course"	Section 3–302.
"Incomplete instrument"	Section 3–115.
"Indorsement"	Section 3–204.
"Indorser"	Section 3–204.
"Instrument"	Section 3–104.
"Issue"	Section 3–105.
"Issuer"	Section 3–105.
"Negotiable instrument"	Section 3–104.
"Negotiation"	Section 3–201.
"Note"	Section 3–104.
"Payable at a definite time"	Section 3–108.
"Payable on demand"	Section 3–108.
"Payable to bearer"	Section 3–109.
"Payable to order"	Section 3–109.
"Payment"	Section 3–602.
"Person entitled to enforce"	Section 3–301.
"Presentment"	Section 3–501.
"Reacquisition"	Section 3–207.
"Special indorsement"	Section 3–205.
"Teller's check"	Section 3–104.
"Transfer of instrument"	Section 3–203.
"Traveler's check"	Section 3–104.
"Value"	Section 3–303.

(c) The following definitions in other Articles apply to this Article:

"Banking day"	Section 4–104.
"Clearing house"	Section 4–104.
"Collecting bank"	Section 4–105.
"Depositary bank"	Section 4–105.
"Documentary draft"	Section 4–104.
"Intermediary bank"	Section 4–105.
"Item"	Section 4–104.
"Payor bank"	Section 4–105.
"Suspends payments"	Section 4–104.

(d) In addition, Article 1 contains general definitions and principles of construction and interpretation applicable throughout this Article.

Legislative Note. A jurisdiction that enacts this statute that has not yet enacted the revised version of UCC Article 1 should add to Section 3–103 the definition of "good faith" that appears in the official version of Section 1–201(b)(20) and the definition of "record" that appears in the official version of Section 1–201(b)(31). Sections 3–103(a)(6) and (14) are reserved for that purpose. A jurisdiction that already has adopted or simultaneously adopts the revised Article 1 should not add those definitions, but should leave those numbers "reserved." If jurisdictions follow the numbering suggested here, the subsections will have the same numbering in all jurisdictions that have adopted these amendments (whether they have or have not adopted the revised version of UCC Article 1).

§ 3–104. Negotiable Instrument.

(a) Except as provided in subsections (c) and (d), "negotiable instrument" means an unconditional promise or order to pay a fixed amount of money, with or without interest or other charges described in the promise or order, if it:
   (1) is payable to bearer or to order at the time it is issued or first comes into possession of a holder;
   (2) is payable on demand or at a definite time; and
   (3) does not state any other undertaking or instruction by the person promising or ordering payment to do any act in addition to the payment of money, but the promise or order may contain (i) an undertaking or power to give, maintain, or protect collateral to secure payment, (ii) an authorization or power to the holder to confess judgment or realize on or dispose of collateral, or (iii) a waiver of the benefit of any law intended for the advantage or protection of an obligor.

(b) "Instrument" means a negotiable instrument.

(c) An order that meets all of the requirements of subsection (a), except paragraph (1), and otherwise falls within the definition of "check" in subsection (f) is a negotiable instrument and a check.

(d) A promise or order other than a check is not an instrument if, at the time it is issued or first comes into possession of a holder, it contains a conspicuous statement, however expressed, to the effect that the promise or order is not negotiable or is not an instrument governed by this Article.

(e) An instrument is a "note" if it is a promise and is a "draft" if it is an order. If an instrument falls within the definition of both "note" and "draft," a person entitled to enforce the instrument may treat it as either.

(f) "Check" means (i) a draft, other than a documentary draft, payable on demand and drawn on a bank or (ii) a cashier's check or teller's check. An instrument may be a check even though it is described on its face by another term, such as "money order."

(g) "Cashier's check" means a draft with respect to which the drawer and drawee are the same bank or branches of the same bank.

(h) "Teller's check" means a draft drawn by a bank (i) on another bank, or (ii) payable at or through a bank.

(i) "Traveler's check" means an instrument that (i) is payable on demand, (ii) is drawn on or payable at or through a bank, (iii) is designated by the term "traveler's check" or by a substantially similar term, and (iv) requires, as a condition to payment, a countersignature by a person whose specimen signature appears on the instrument.

(j) "Certificate of deposit" means an instrument containing an acknowledgment by a bank that a sum of money has been received by the bank and a promise by the bank to repay the sum of money. A certificate of deposit is a note of the bank.

§ 3–105. Issue of Instrument.

(a) "Issue" means the first delivery of an instrument by the maker or drawer, whether to a holder or nonholder, for the purpose of giving rights on the instrument to any person.

(b) An unissued instrument, or an unissued incomplete instrument that is completed, is binding on the maker or drawer, but nonissuance is a defense. An instrument that is conditionally issued or is issued for a special purpose is binding on the maker or drawer, but failure of the condition or special purpose to be fulfilled is a defense.
(c) "Issuer" applies to issued and unissued instruments and means a maker or drawer of an instrument.

§ 3–106. Unconditional Promise or Order.

(a) Except as provided in this section, for the purposes of Section 3–104(a), a promise or order is unconditional unless it states (i) an express condition to payment, (ii) that the promise or order is subject to or governed by another record, or (iii) that rights or obligations with respect to the promise or order are stated in another record. A reference to another record does not of itself make the promise or order conditional.
(b) A promise or order is not made conditional (i) by a reference to another record for a statement of rights with respect to collateral, prepayment, or acceleration, or (ii) because payment is limited to resort to a particular fund or source.
(c) If a promise or order requires, as a condition to payment, a countersignature by a person whose specimen signature appears on the promise or order, the condition does not make the promise or order conditional for the purposes of Section 3–104(a). If the person whose specimen signature appears on an instrument fails to countersign the instrument, the failure to countersign is a defense to the obligation of the issuer, but the failure does not prevent a transferee of the instrument from becoming a holder of the instrument.
(d) If a promise or order at the time it is issued or first comes into possession of a holder contains a statement, required by applicable statutory or administrative law, to the effect that the rights of a holder or transferee are subject to claims or defenses that the issuer could assert against the original payee, the promise or order is not thereby made conditional for the purposes of Section 3–104(a); but if the promise or order is an instrument, there cannot be a holder in due course of the instrument.

§ 3–107. Instrument Payable in Foreign Money. Unless the instrument otherwise provides, an instrument that states the amount payable in foreign money may be paid in the foreign money or in an equivalent amount in dollars calculated by using the current bank offered spot rate at the place of payment for the purchase of dollars on the day on which the instrument is paid.

§ 3–108. Payable on Demand or at Definite Time.

(a) A promise or order is "payable on demand" if it (i) states that it is payable on demand or at sight, or otherwise indicates that it is payable at the will of the holder, or (ii) does not state any time of payment.
(b) A promise or order is "payable at a definite time" if it is payable on elapse of a definite period of time after sight or acceptance or at a fixed date or dates or at a time or times readily ascertainable at the time the promise or order is issued, subject to rights of (i) prepayment, (ii) acceleration, (iii) extension at the option of the holder, or (iv) extension to a further definite time at the option of the maker or acceptor or automatically upon or after a specified act or event.
(c) If an instrument, payable at a fixed date, is also payable upon demand made before the fixed date, the instrument is payable on demand until the fixed date and, if demand for payment is not made before that date, becomes payable at a definite time on the fixed date.

§ 3–109. Payable to Bearer or to Order.

(a) A promise or order is payable to bearer if it:
  (1) states that it is payable to bearer or to the order of bearer or otherwise indicates that the person in possession of the promise or order is entitled to payment;
  (2) does not state a payee; or
  (3) states that it is payable to or to the order of cash or otherwise indicates that it is not payable to an identified person.

(b) A promise or order that is not payable to bearer is payable to order if it is payable (i) to the order of an identified person or (ii) to an identified person or order. A promise or order that is payable to order is payable to the identified person.

(c) An instrument payable to bearer may become payable to an identified person if it is specially indorsed pursuant to Section 3–205(a). An instrument payable to an identified person may become payable to bearer if it is indorsed in blank pursuant to Section 3–205(b).

§ 3–110. Identification of Person to Whom Instrument Is Payable.

(a) The person to whom an instrument is initially payable is determined by the intent of the person, whether or not authorized, signing as, or in the name or behalf of, the issuer of the instrument. The instrument is payable to the person intended by the signer even if that person is identified in the instrument by a name or other identification that is not that of the intended person. If more than one person signs in the name or behalf of the issuer of an instrument and all the signers do not intend the same person as payee, the instrument is payable to any person intended by one or more of the signers.

(b) If the signature of the issuer of an instrument is made by automated means, such as a check writing machine, the payee of the instrument is determined by the intent of the person who supplied the name or identification of the payee, whether or not authorized to do so.

(c) A person to whom an instrument is payable may be identified in any way, including by name, identifying number, office, or account number. For the purpose of determining the holder of an instrument, the following rules apply:
  (1) If an instrument is payable to an account and the account is identified only by number, the instrument is payable to the person to whom the account is payable. If an instrument is payable to an account identified by number and by the name of a person, the instrument is payable to the named person, whether or not that person is the owner of the account identified by number.
  (2) If an instrument is payable to:
    (i) a trust, an estate, or a person described as trustee or representative of a trust or estate, the instrument is payable to the trustee, the representative, or a successor of either, whether or not the beneficiary or estate is also named;
    (ii) a person described as agent or similar representative of a named or identified person, the instrument is payable to the represented person, the representative, or a successor of the representative;
    (iii) a fund or organization that is not a legal entity, the instrument is payable to a representative of the members of the fund or organization; or
    (iv) an office or to a person described as holding an office, the instrument is payable to the named person, the incumbent of the office, or a successor to the incumbent.

(d) If an instrument is payable to two or more persons alternatively, it is payable to any of them and may be negotiated, discharged, or enforced by any or all of them in possession of the instrument. If an instrument is payable to two or more persons not alternatively, it is payable to all of them and may be negotiated, discharged, or enforced only by all of them. If an instrument payable to two or more persons is ambiguous as to whether it is payable to the persons alternatively, the instrument is payable to the persons alternatively.

§ 3–111. Place of Payment. Except as otherwise provided for items in Article 4, an instrument is payable at the place of payment stated in the instrument. If no place of payment is stated, an instrument is payable at the address of the drawee or maker stated in the instrument. If no address is stated, the place of payment is the place of business of the drawee or maker. If a drawee or maker has more than one place of business, the place of payment is any place of business of the drawee or maker chosen by the person entitled to enforce the instrument. If the drawee or maker has no place of business, the place of payment is the residence of the drawee or maker.

§ 3–112. Interest.

(a) Unless otherwise provided in the instrument, (i) an instrument is not payable with interest, and (ii) interest on an interest bearing instrument is payable from the date of the instrument.

(b) Interest may be stated in an instrument as a fixed or variable amount of money or it may be expressed as a fixed or variable rate or rates. The amount or rate of interest may be stated or described in the instrument in any manner and may require reference to information not contained in the instrument. If an instrument provides for interest, but the amount of interest payable cannot be ascertained from the description, interest is payable at the judgment rate in effect at the place of payment of the instrument and at the time interest first accrues.

§ 3–113. Date of Instrument.

(a) An instrument may be antedated or postdated. The date stated determines the time of payment if the instrument is payable at a fixed period after date. Except as provided in Section 4–401(c), an instrument payable on demand is not payable before the date of the instrument.

(b) If an instrument is undated, its date is the date of its issue or, in the case of an unissued instrument, the date it first comes into possession of a holder.

§ 3–114. Contradictory Terms of Instrument. If an instrument contains contradictory terms, typewritten terms prevail over printed terms, handwritten terms prevail over both, and words prevail over numbers.

§ 3–115. Incomplete Instrument.

(a) "Incomplete instrument" means a signed writing, whether or not issued by the signer, the contents of which show at the time of signing that it is incomplete but that the signer intended it to be completed by the addition of words or numbers.

(b) Subject to subsection (c), if an incomplete instrument is an instrument under Section 3–104, it may be enforced according to its terms if it is not completed, or according to its terms as augmented by completion. If an incomplete instrument is not an instrument under Section 3–104, but, after completion, the requirements of Section 3–104 are met, the instrument may be enforced according to its terms as augmented by completion.

(c) If words or numbers are added to an incomplete instrument without authority of the signer, there is an alteration of the incomplete instrument under Section 3–407.

(d) The burden of establishing that words or numbers were added to an incomplete instrument without authority of the signer is on the person asserting the lack of authority.

§ 3–116. Joint and Several Liability; Contribution.

(a) Except as otherwise provided in the instrument, two or more persons who have the same liability on an instrument as makers, drawers, acceptors, indorsers who indorse as joint payees, or anomalous indorsers are jointly and severally liable in the capacity in which they sign.

(b) Except as provided in Section 3–419(f) or by agreement of the affected parties, a party having joint and several liability who pays the instrument is entitled to receive from any party having the same joint and several liability contribution in accordance with applicable law.

§ 3–117. Other Agreements Affecting Instrument. Subject to applicable law regarding exclusion of proof of contemporaneous or previous agreements, the obligation of a party to an instrument to pay the instrument may be modified, supplemented, or nullified by a separate agreement of the obligor and a person entitled to enforce the instrument, if the instrument is issued or the obligation is incurred in reliance on the agreement or as part of the same transaction giving rise to the agreement. To the extent an obligation is modified, supplemented, or nullified by an agreement under this section, the agreement is a defense to the obligation.

§ 3–118. Statute of Limitations.

(a) Except as provided in subsection (e), an action to enforce the obligation of a party to pay a note payable at a definite time must be commenced within six years after the due date or dates stated in the note or, if a due date is accelerated, within six years after the accelerated due date.
(b) Except as provided in subsection (d) or (e), if demand for payment is made to the maker of a note payable on demand, an action to enforce the obligation of a party to pay the note must be commenced within six years after the demand. If no demand for payment is made to the maker, an action to enforce the note is barred if neither principal nor interest on the note has been paid for a continuous period of 10 years.
(c) Except as provided in subsection (d), an action to enforce the obligation of a party to an unaccepted draft to pay the draft must be commenced within three years after dishonor of the draft or 10 years after the date of the draft, whichever period expires first.
(d) An action to enforce the obligation of the acceptor of a certified check or the issuer of a teller's check, cashier's check, or traveler's check must be commenced within three years after demand for payment is made to the acceptor or issuer, as the case may be.
(e) An action to enforce the obligation of a party to a certificate of deposit to pay the instrument must be commenced within six years after demand for payment is made to the maker, but if the instrument states a due date and the maker is not required to pay before that date, the six-year period begins when a demand for payment is in effect and the due date has passed.
(f) An action to enforce the obligation of a party to pay an accepted draft, other than a certified check, must be commenced (i) within six years after the due date or dates stated in the draft or acceptance if the obligation of the acceptor is payable at a definite time, or (ii) within six years after the date of the acceptance if the obligation of the acceptor is payable on demand.
(g) Unless governed by other law regarding claims for indemnity or contribution, an action (i) for conversion of an instrument, for money had and received, or like action based on conversion, (ii) for breach of warranty, or (iii) to enforce an obligation, duty, or right arising under this Article and not governed by this section must be commenced within three years after the [cause of action] accrues.

§ 3–119. Notice of Right to Defend Action. In an action for breach of an obligation for which a third person is answerable over pursuant to this Article or Article 4, the defendant may give the third person notice of the litigation in a record, and the person notified may then give similar notice to any other person who is answerable over. If the notice states (i) that the person notified may come in and defend and (ii) that failure to do so will bind the person notified in an action later brought by the person giving the notice as to any determination of fact common to the two litigations, the person notified is so bound unless after seasonable receipt of the notice the person notified does come in and defend.

PART 2: NEGOTIATION, TRANSFER, AND INDORSEMENT

§ 3–201. Negotiation.

(a) "Negotiation" means a transfer of possession, whether voluntary or involuntary, of an instrument by a person other than the issuer to a person who thereby becomes its holder.
(b) Except for negotiation by a remitter, if an instrument is payable to an identified person, negotiation requires transfer of possession of the instrument and its indorsement by the holder. If an instrument is payable to bearer, it may be negotiated by transfer of possession alone.

§ 3–202. Negotiation Subject to Rescission.

(a) Negotiation is effective even if obtained (i) from an infant, a corporation exceeding its powers, or a person without capacity, (ii) by fraud, duress, or mistake, or (iii) in breach of duty or as part of an illegal transaction.
(b) To the extent permitted by other law, negotiation may be rescinded or may be subject to other remedies, but those remedies may not be asserted against a subsequent holder in due course or a person paying the instrument in good faith and without knowledge of facts that are a basis for rescission or other remedy.

§ 3–203. Transfer of Instrument; Rights Acquired by Transfer.

(a) An instrument is transferred when it is delivered by a person other than its issuer for the purpose of giving to the person receiving delivery the right to enforce the instrument.
(b) Transfer of an instrument, whether or not the transfer is a negotiation, vests in the transferee any right of the transferor to enforce the instrument, including any right as a holder in due course, but the transferee cannot acquire rights of a holder in due course by a transfer, directly or indirectly, from a holder in due course if the transferee engaged in fraud or illegality affecting the instrument.
(c) Unless otherwise agreed, if an instrument is transferred for value and the transferee does not become a holder because of lack of indorsement by the transferor, the transferee has a specifically enforceable right to the unqualified indorsement of the transferor, but negotiation of the instrument does not occur until the indorsement is made.
(d) If a transferor purports to transfer less than the entire instrument, negotiation of the instrument does not occur. The transferee obtains no rights under this Article and has only the rights of a partial assignee.

§ 3–204. Indorsement.

(a) "Indorsement" means a signature, other than that of a signer as maker, drawer, or acceptor, that alone or accompanied by other words is made on an instrument for the purpose of (i) negotiating the instrument, (ii) restricting payment of the instrument, or (iii) incurring indorser's liability on the instrument, but regardless of the intent of the signer, a signature and its accompanying words is an indorsement unless the accompanying words, terms of the instrument, place of the signature, or other circumstances unambiguously indicate that the signature was made for a purpose other than indorsement. For the purpose of determining whether a signature is made on an instrument, a paper affixed to the instrument is a part of the instrument.
(b) "Indorser" means a person who makes an indorsement.
(c) For the purpose of determining whether the transferee of an instrument is a holder, an indorsement that transfers a security interest in the instrument is effective as an unqualified indorsement of the instrument.
(d) If an instrument is payable to a holder under a name that is not the name of the holder, indorsement may be made by the holder in the name stated in the instrument or in the holder's name or both, but signature in both names may be required by a person paying or taking the instrument for value or collection.

§ 3-205. Special Indorsement; Blank Indorsement; Anomalous Indorsement.

(a) If an indorsement is made by the holder of an instrument, whether payable to an identified person or payable to bearer, and the indorsement identifies a person to whom it makes the instrument payable, it is a "special indorsement." When specially indorsed, an instrument becomes payable to the identified person and may be negotiated only by the indorsement of that person. The principles stated in Section 3–110 apply to special indorsements.

(b) If an indorsement is made by the holder of an instrument and it is not a special indorsement, it is a "blank indorsement." When indorsed in blank, an instrument becomes payable to bearer and may be negotiated by transfer of possession alone until specially indorsed.

(c) The holder may convert a blank indorsement that consists only of a signature into a special indorsement by writing, above the signature of the indorser, words identifying the person to whom the instrument is made payable.

(d) "Anomalous indorsement" means an indorsement made by a person who is not the holder of the instrument. An anomalous indorsement does not affect the manner in which the instrument may be negotiated.

§ 3-206. Restrictive Indorsement.

(a) An indorsement limiting payment to a particular person or otherwise prohibiting further transfer or negotiation of the instrument is not effective to prevent further transfer or negotiation of the instrument.

(b) An indorsement stating a condition to the right of the indorsee to receive payment does not affect the right of the indorsee to enforce the instrument. A person paying the instrument or taking it for value or collection may disregard the condition, and the rights and liabilities of that person are not affected by whether the condition has been fulfilled.

(c) If an instrument bears an indorsement (i) described in Section 4–201(b), or (ii) in blank or to a particular bank using the words "for deposit," "for collection," or other words indicating a purpose of having the instrument collected by a bank for the indorser or for a particular account, the following rules apply:

   (1) A person, other than a bank, who purchases the instrument when so indorsed converts the instrument unless the amount paid for the instrument is received by the indorser or applied consistently with the indorsement.

   (2) A depositary bank that purchases the instrument or takes it for collection when so indorsed converts the instrument unless the amount paid by the bank with respect to the instrument is received by the indorser or applied consistently with the indorsement.

   (3) A payor bank that is also the depositary bank or that takes the instrument for immediate payment over the counter from a person other than a collecting bank converts the instrument unless the proceeds of the instrument are received by the indorser or applied consistently with the indorsement.

   (4) Except as otherwise provided in paragraph (3), a payor bank or intermediary bank may disregard the indorsement and is not liable if the proceeds of the instrument are not received by the indorser or applied consistently with the indorsement.

(d) Except for an indorsement covered by subsection (c), if an instrument bears an indorsement using words to the effect that payment is to be made to the indorsee as agent, trustee, or other fiduciary for the benefit of the indorser or another person, the following rules apply:

   (1) Unless there is notice of breach of fiduciary duty as provided in Section 3–307, a person who purchases the instrument from the indorsee or takes the instrument from the indorsee for collection or payment may pay the proceeds of payment or the value given for the instrument to the indorsee without regard to whether the indorsee violates a fiduciary duty to the indorser.

(2) A subsequent transferee of the instrument or person who pays the instrument is neither given notice nor otherwise affected by the restriction in the indorsement unless the transferee or payor knows that the fiduciary dealt with the instrument or its proceeds in breach of fiduciary duty.

(e) The presence on an instrument of an indorsement to which this section applies does not prevent a purchaser of the instrument from becoming a holder in due course of the instrument unless the purchaser is a converter under subsection (c) or has notice or knowledge of breach of fiduciary duty as stated in subsection (d).

(f) In an action to enforce the obligation of a party to pay the instrument, the obligor has a defense if payment would violate an indorsement to which this section applies and the payment is not permitted by this section.

§ 3–207. Reacquisition. Reacquisition of an instrument occurs if it is transferred to a former holder, by negotiation or otherwise. A former holder who reacquires the instrument may cancel indorsements made after the reacquirer first became a holder of the instrument. If the cancellation causes the instrument to be payable to the reacquirer or to bearer, the reacquirer may negotiate the instrument. An indorser whose indorsement is canceled is discharged, and the discharge is effective against any subsequent holder.

PART 3: ENFORCEMENT OF INSTRUMENTS

§ 3–301. Person Entitled to Enforce Instrument. "Person entitled to enforce" an instrument means (i) the holder of the instrument, (ii) a nonholder in possession of the instrument who has the rights of a holder, or (iii) a person not in possession of the instrument who is entitled to enforce the instrument pursuant to Section 3–309 or 3–418(d). A person may be a person entitled to enforce the instrument even though the person is not the owner of the instrument or is in wrongful possession of the instrument.

§ 3–302. Holder in Due Course.

(a) Subject to subsection (c) and Section 3–106(d), "holder in due course" means the holder of an instrument if:

(1) the instrument when issued or negotiated to the holder does not bear such apparent evidence of forgery or alteration or is not otherwise so irregular or incomplete as to call into question its authenticity; and

(2) the holder took the instrument (i) for value, (ii) in good faith, (iii) without notice that the instrument is overdue or has been dishonored or that there is an uncured default with respect to payment of another instrument issued as part of the same series, (iv) without notice that the instrument contains an unauthorized signature or has been altered, (v) without notice of any claim to the instrument described in Section 3–306, and (vi) without notice that any party has a defense or claim in recoupment described in Section 3–305(a).

(b) Notice of discharge of a party, other than discharge in an insolvency proceeding, is not notice of a defense under subsection (a), but discharge is effective against a person who became a holder in due course with notice of the discharge. Public filing or recording of a document does not of itself constitute notice of a defense, claim in recoupment, or claim to the instrument.

(c) Except to the extent a transferor or predecessor in interest has rights as a holder in due course, a person does not acquire rights of a holder in due course of an instrument taken (i) by legal process or by purchase in an execution, bankruptcy, or creditor's sale or similar proceeding, (ii) by purchase as part of a bulk transaction not in ordinary course of business of the transferor, or (iii) as the successor in interest to an estate or other organization.

(d) If, under Section 3–303(a)(1), the promise of performance that is the consideration for an instrument has been partially performed, the holder may assert rights as a holder in due course of the instrument only to the fraction of the amount payable under the instrument equal to the value of the partial performance divided by the value of the promised performance.
(e) If (i) the person entitled to enforce an instrument has only a security interest in the instrument and (ii) the person obliged to pay the instrument has a defense, claim in recoupment, or claim to the instrument that may be asserted against the person who granted the security interest, the person entitled to enforce the instrument may assert rights as a holder in due course only to an amount payable under the instrument which, at the time of enforcement of the instrument, does not exceed the amount of the unpaid obligation secured.
(f) To be effective, notice must be received at a time and in a manner that gives a reasonable opportunity to act on it.
(g) This section is subject to any law limiting status as a holder in due course in particular classes of transactions.

§ 3–303. Value and Consideration.

(a) An instrument is issued or transferred for value if:
  (1) the instrument is issued or transferred for a promise of performance, to the extent the promise has been performed;
  (2) the transferee acquires a security interest or other lien in the instrument other than a lien obtained by judicial proceeding;
  (3) the instrument is issued or transferred as payment of, or as security for, an antecedent claim against any person, whether or not the claim is due;
  (4) the instrument is issued or transferred in exchange for a negotiable instrument; or
  (5) the instrument is issued or transferred in exchange for the incurring of an irrevocable obligation to a third party by the person taking the instrument.
(b) "Consideration" means any consideration sufficient to support a simple contract. The drawer or maker of an instrument has a defense if the instrument is issued without consideration. If an instrument is issued for a promise of performance, the issuer has a defense to the extent performance of the promise is due and the promise has not been performed. If an instrument is issued for value as stated in subsection (a), the instrument is also issued for consideration.

§ 3–304. Overdue Instrument.

(a) An instrument payable on demand becomes overdue at the earliest of the following times:
  (1) on the day after the day demand for payment is duly made;
  (2) if the instrument is a check, 90 days after its date; or
  (3) if the instrument is not a check, when the instrument has been outstanding for a period of time after its date which is unreasonably long under the circumstances of the particular case in light of the nature of the instrument and usage of the trade.
(b) With respect to an instrument payable at a definite time the following rules apply:
  (1) If the principal is payable in installments and a due date has not been accelerated, the instrument becomes overdue upon default under the instrument for nonpayment of an installment, and the instrument remains overdue until the default is cured.
  (2) If the principal is not payable in installments and the due date has not been accelerated, the instrument becomes overdue on the day after the due date.
  (3) If a due date with respect to principal has been accelerated, the instrument becomes overdue on the day after the accelerated due date.
(c) Unless the due date of principal has been accelerated, an instrument does not become overdue if there is default in payment of interest but no default in payment of principal.

§ 3–305. Defenses and Claims in Recoupment; Claims in Consumer Transactions.

(a) Except as otherwise provided in this section, the right to enforce the obligation of a party to pay an instrument is subject to the following:
  (1) a defense of the obligor based on (i) infancy of the obligor to the extent it is a defense to a simple contract, (ii) duress, lack of legal capacity, or illegality of the transaction which, under other law, nullifies the obligation of the obligor, (iii) fraud that induced the obligor to sign the instrument with neither knowledge nor reasonable opportunity to learn of its character or its essential terms, or (iv) discharge of the obligor in insolvency proceedings;
  (2) a defense of the obligor stated in another section of this Article or a defense of the obligor that would be available if the person entitled to enforce the instrument were enforcing a right to payment under a simple contract; and
  (3) a claim in recoupment of the obligor against the original payee of the instrument if the claim arose from the transaction that gave rise to the instrument; but the claim of the obligor may be asserted against a transferee of the instrument only to reduce the amount owing on the instrument at the time the action is brought.

(b) The right of a holder in due course to enforce the obligation of a party to pay the instrument is subject to defenses of the obligor stated in subsection (a)(1), but is not subject to defenses of the obligor stated in subsection (a)(2) or claims in recoupment stated in subsection (a)(3) against a person other than the holder.

(c) Except as stated in subsection (d), in an action to enforce the obligation of a party to pay the instrument, the obligor may not assert against the person entitled to enforce the instrument a defense, claim in recoupment, or claim to the instrument (Section 3–306) of another person, but the other person's claim to the instrument may be asserted by the obligor if the other person is joined in the action and personally asserts the claim against the person entitled to enforce the instrument. An obligor is not obliged to pay the instrument if the person seeking enforcement of the instrument does not have rights of a holder in due course and the obligor proves that the instrument is a lost or stolen instrument.

(d) In an action to enforce the obligation of an accommodation party to pay an instrument, the accommodation party may assert against the person entitled to enforce the instrument any defense or claim in recoupment under subsection (a) that the accommodated party could assert against the person entitled to enforce the instrument, except the defenses of discharge in insolvency proceedings, infancy, and lack of legal capacity.

(e) In a consumer transaction, if law other than this article requires that an instrument include a statement to the effect that the rights of a holder or transferee are subject to a claim or defense that the issuer could assert against the original payee, and the instrument does not include such a statement:
  (1) the instrument has the same effect as if the instrument included such a statement;
  (2) the issuer may assert against the holder or transferee all claims and defenses that would have been available if the instrument included such a statement; and
  (3) the extent to which claims may be asserted against the holder or transferee is determined as if the instrument included such a statement.

(f) This section is subject to law other than this article that establishes a different rule for consumer transactions.

Legislative Note: If a consumer protection law in this state addresses the same issue as subsection (g), it should be examined for consistency with subsection (g) and, if inconsistent, should be amended.

§ 3–306. Claims to an Instrument. A person taking an instrument, other than a person having rights of a holder in due course, is subject to a claim of a property or possessory right in the instrument or its proceeds, including a claim to rescind a negotiation and to recover the instrument or its proceeds. A person having rights of a holder in due course takes free of the claim to the instrument.

§ 3–307. Notice of Breach of Fiduciary Duty.

(a) In this section:
  (1) "Fiduciary" means an agent, trustee, partner, corporate officer or director, or other representative owing a fiduciary duty with respect to an instrument.
  (2) "Represented person" means the principal, beneficiary, partnership, corporation, or other person to whom the duty stated in paragraph (1) is owed.

(b) If (i) an instrument is taken from a fiduciary for payment or collection or for value, (ii) the taker has knowledge of the fiduciary status of the fiduciary, and (iii) the represented person makes a claim to the instrument or its proceeds on the basis that the transaction of the fiduciary is a breach of fiduciary duty, the following rules apply:
  (1) Notice of breach of fiduciary duty by the fiduciary is notice of the claim of the represented person.
  (2) In the case of an instrument payable to the represented person or the fiduciary as such, the taker has notice of the breach of fiduciary duty if the instrument is (i) taken in payment of or as security for a debt known by the taker to be the personal debt of the fiduciary, (ii) taken in a transaction known by the taker to be for the personal benefit of the fiduciary, or (iii) deposited to an account other than an account of the fiduciary, as such, or an account of the represented person.
  (3) If an instrument is issued by the represented person or the fiduciary as such, and made payable to the fiduciary personally, the taker does not have notice of the breach of fiduciary duty unless the taker knows of the breach of fiduciary duty.
  (4) If an instrument is issued by the represented person or the fiduciary as such, to the taker as payee, the taker has notice of the breach of fiduciary duty if the instrument is (i) taken in payment of or as security for a debt known by the taker to be the personal debt of the fiduciary, (ii) taken in a transaction known by the taker to be for the personal benefit of the fiduciary, or (iii) deposited to an account other than an account of the fiduciary, as such, or an account of the represented person.

§ 3–308. Proof of Signatures and Status as Holder in Due Course.

(a) In an action with respect to an instrument, the authenticity of, and authority to make, each signature on the instrument is admitted unless specifically denied in the pleadings. If the validity of a signature is denied in the pleadings, the burden of establishing validity is on the person claiming validity, but the signature is presumed to be authentic and authorized unless the action is to enforce the liability of the purported signer and the signer is dead or incompetent at the time of trial of the issue of validity of the signature. If an action to enforce the instrument is brought against a person as the undisclosed principal of a person who signed the instrument as a party to the instrument, the plaintiff has the burden of establishing that the defendant is liable on the instrument as a represented person under Section 3–402(a).

(b) If the validity of signatures is admitted or proved and there is compliance with subsection (a), a plaintiff producing the instrument is entitled to payment if the plaintiff proves entitlement to enforce the instrument under Section 3–301, unless the defendant proves a defense or claim in recoupment. If a defense or claim in recoupment is proved, the right to payment of the plaintiff is subject to the defense or claim, except to the extent the plaintiff proves that the plaintiff has rights of a holder in due course which are not subject to the defense or claim.

§ 3–309. Enforcement of Lost, Destroyed, or Stolen Instrument.

(a) A person not in possession of an instrument is entitled to enforce the instrument if:
  (1) the person seeking to enforce the instrument:
    (i) was entitled to enforce the instrument when loss of possession occurred; or
    (ii) has directly or indirectly acquired ownership of the instrument from a person who was entitled to enforce the instrument when loss of possession occurred.

(2) the loss of possession was not the result of a transfer by the person or a lawful seizure; and

(3) the person cannot reasonably obtain possession of the instrument because the instrument was destroyed, its whereabouts cannot be determined, or it is in the wrongful possession of an unknown person or a person that cannot be found or is not amenable to service of process.

(b) A person seeking enforcement of an instrument under subsection (a) must prove the terms of the instrument and the person's right to enforce the instrument. If that proof is made, Section 3–308 applies to the case as if the person seeking enforcement had produced the instrument. The court may not enter judgment in favor of the person seeking enforcement unless it finds that the person required to pay the instrument is adequately protected against loss that might occur by reason of a claim by another person to enforce the instrument. Adequate protection may be provided by any reasonable means.

§ 3–310. Effect of Instrument on Obligation for Which Taken.

(a) Unless otherwise agreed, if a certified check, cashier's check, or teller's check is taken for an obligation, the obligation is discharged to the same extent discharge would result if an amount of money equal to the amount of the instrument were taken in payment of the obligation. Discharge of the obligation does not affect any liability that the obligor may have as an indorser of the instrument.

(b) Unless otherwise agreed and except as provided in subsection (a), if a note or an uncertified check is taken for an obligation, the obligation is suspended to the same extent the obligation would be discharged if an amount of money equal to the amount of the instrument were taken, and the following rules apply:

(1) In the case of an uncertified check, suspension of the obligation continues until dishonor of the check or until it is paid or certified. Payment or certification of the check results in discharge of the obligation to the extent of the amount of the check.

(2) In the case of a note, suspension of the obligation continues until dishonor of the note or until it is paid. Payment of the note results in discharge of the obligation to the extent of the payment.

(3) Except as provided in paragraph (4), if the check or note is dishonored and the obligee of the obligation for which the instrument was taken is the person entitled to enforce the instrument, the obligee may enforce either the instrument or the obligation. In the case of an instrument of a third person which is negotiated to the obligee by the obligor, discharge of the obligor on the instrument also discharges the obligation.

(4) If the person entitled to enforce the instrument taken for an obligation is a person other than the obligee, the obligee may not enforce the obligation to the extent the obligation is suspended. If the obligee is the person entitled to enforce the instrument but no longer has possession of it because it was lost, stolen, or destroyed, the obligation may not be enforced to the extent of the amount payable on the instrument, and to that extent the obligee's rights against the obligor are limited to enforcement of the instrument.

(c) If an instrument other than one described in subsection (a) or (b) is taken for an obligation, the effect is (i) that stated in subsection (a) if the instrument is one on which a bank is liable as maker or acceptor, or (ii) that stated in subsection (b) in any other case.

§ 3–311. Accord and Satisfaction by Use of Instrument.

(a) If a person against whom a claim is asserted proves that (i) that person in good faith tendered an instrument to the claimant as full satisfaction of the claim, (ii) the amount of the claim was unliquidated or subject to a bona fide dispute, and (iii) the claimant obtained payment of the instrument, the following subsections apply.

(b) Unless subsection (c) applies, the claim is discharged if the person against whom the claim is asserted proves that the instrument or an accompanying written communication contained a conspicuous statement to the effect that the instrument was tendered as full satisfaction of the claim.

(c) Subject to subsection (d), a claim is not discharged under subsection (b) if either of the following applies:
  (1) The claimant, if an organization, proves that (i) within a reasonable time before the tender, the claimant sent a conspicuous statement to the person against whom the claim is asserted that communications concerning disputed debts, including an instrument tendered as full satisfaction of a debt, are to be sent to a designated person, office, or place, and (ii) the instrument or accompanying communication was not received by that designated person, office, or place.
  (2) The claimant, whether or not an organization, proves that within 90 days after payment of the instrument, the claimant tendered repayment of the amount of the instrument to the person against whom the claim is asserted. This paragraph does not apply if the claimant is an organization that sent a statement complying with paragraph (1)(i).

(d) A claim is discharged if the person against whom the claim is asserted proves that within a reasonable time before collection of the instrument was initiated, the claimant, or an agent of the claimant having direct responsibility with respect to the disputed obligation, knew that the instrument was tendered in full satisfaction of the claim.

§ 3–312. Lost, Destroyed, or Stolen Cashier's Check, Teller's Check, or Certified Check.

(a) In this section:
  (1) "Check" means a cashier's check, teller's check, or certified check.
  (2) "Claimant" means a person who claims the right to receive the amount of a cashier's check, teller's check, or certified check that was lost, destroyed, or stolen.
  (3) "Declaration of loss" means a statement, made in a record under penalty of perjury, to the effect that (i) the declarer lost possession of a check, (ii) the declarer is the drawer or payee of the check, in the case of a certified check, or the remitter or payee of the check, in the case of a cashier's check or teller's check, (iii) the loss of possession was not the result of a transfer by the declarer or a lawful seizure, and (iv) the declarer cannot reasonably obtain possession of the check because the check was destroyed, its whereabouts cannot be determined, or it is in the wrongful possession of an unknown person or a person that cannot be found or is not amenable to service of process.
  (4) "Obligated bank" means the issuer of a cashier's check or teller's check or the acceptor of a certified check.

(b) A claimant may assert a claim to the amount of a check by a communication to the obligated bank describing the check with reasonable certainty and requesting payment of the amount of the check, if (i) the claimant is the drawer or payee of a certified check or the remitter or payee of a cashier's check or teller's check, (ii) the communication contains or is accompanied by a declaration of loss of the claimant with respect to the check, (iii) the communication is received at a time and in a manner affording the bank a reasonable time to act on it before the check is paid, and (iv) the claimant provides reasonable identification if requested by the obligated bank. Delivery of a declaration of loss is a warranty of the truth of the statements made in the declaration. If a claim is asserted in compliance with this subsection, the following rules apply:
  (1) The claim becomes enforceable at the later of (i) the time the claim is asserted, or (ii) the 90th day following the date of the check, in the case of a cashier's check or teller's check, or the 90th day following the date of the acceptance, in the case of a certified check.
  (2) Until the claim becomes enforceable, it has no legal effect and the obligated bank may pay the check or, in the case of a teller's check, may permit the drawee to pay the check. Payment to a person entitled to enforce the check discharges all liability of the obligated bank with respect to the check.

(3) If the claim becomes enforceable before the check is presented for payment, the obligated bank is not obliged to pay the check.
(4) When the claim becomes enforceable, the obligated bank becomes obliged to pay the amount of the check to the claimant if payment of the check has not been made to a person entitled to enforce the check. Subject to Section 4–302(a)(1), payment to the claimant discharges all liability of the obligated bank with respect to the check.

(c) If the obligated bank pays the amount of a check to a claimant under subsection (b)(4) and the check is presented for payment by a person having rights of a holder in due course, the claimant is obliged to (i) refund the payment to the obligated bank if the check is paid, or (ii) pay the amount of the check to the person having rights of a holder in due course if the check is dishonored.

(d) If a claimant has the right to assert a claim under subsection (b) and is also a person entitled to enforce a cashier's check, teller's check, or certified check which is lost, destroyed, or stolen, the claimant may assert rights with respect to the check either under this section or Section 3–309.

PART 4: LIABILITY OF PARTIES

§ 3–401. Signature.

(a) A person is not liable on an instrument unless (i) the person signed the instrument, or (ii) the person is represented by an agent or representative who signed the instrument and the signature is binding on the represented person under Section 3–402.

(b) A signature may be made (i) manually or by means of a device or machine, and (ii) by the use of any name, including a trade or assumed name, or by a word, mark, or symbol executed or adopted by a person with present intention to authenticate a writing.

§ 3–402. Signature by Representative.

(a) If a person acting, or purporting to act, as a representative signs an instrument by signing either the name of the represented person or the name of the signer, the represented person is bound by the signature to the same extent the represented person would be bound if the signature were on a simple contract. If the represented person is bound, the signature of the representative is the "authorized signature of the represented person" and the represented person is liable on the instrument, whether or not identified in the instrument.

(b) If a representative signs the name of the representative to an instrument and the signature is an authorized signature of the represented person, the following rules apply:
(1) If the form of the signature shows unambiguously that the signature is made on behalf of the represented person who is identified in the instrument, the representative is not liable on the instrument.
(2) Subject to subsection (c), if (i) the form of the signature does not show unambiguously that the signature is made in a representative capacity or (ii) the represented person is not identified in the instrument, the representative is liable on the instrument to a holder in due course that took the instrument without notice that the representative was not intended to be liable on the instrument. With respect to any other person, the representative is liable on the instrument unless the representative proves that the original parties did not intend the representative to be liable on the instrument.

(c) If a representative signs the name of the representative as drawer of a check without indication of the representative status and the check is payable from an account of the represented person who is identified on the check, the signer is not liable on the check if the signature is an authorized signature of the represented person.

§ 3–403. Unauthorized Signature.

(a) Unless otherwise provided in this Article or Article 4, an unauthorized signature is ineffective except as the signature of the unauthorized signer in favor of a person who in good faith pays the instrument or takes it for value. An unauthorized signature may be ratified for all purposes of this Article.

(b) If the signature of more than one person is required to constitute the authorized signature of an organization, the signature of the organization is unauthorized if one of the required signatures is lacking.

(c) The civil or criminal liability of a person who makes an unauthorized signature is not affected by any provision of this Article which makes the unauthorized signature effective for the purposes of this Article.

§ 3–404. Impostors; Fictitious Payees.

(a) If an impostor, by use of the mails or otherwise, induces the issuer of an instrument to issue the instrument to the impostor, or to a person acting in concert with the impostor, by impersonating the payee of the instrument or a person authorized to act for the payee, an indorsement of the instrument by any person in the name of the payee is effective as the indorsement of the payee in favor of a person who, in good faith, pays the instrument or takes it for value or for collection.

(b) If (i) a person whose intent determines to whom an instrument is payable (Section 3–110(a) or (b)) does not intend the person identified as payee to have any interest in the instrument, or (ii) the person identified as payee of an instrument is a fictitious person, the following rules apply until the instrument is negotiated by special indorsement:

  (1) Any person in possession of the instrument is its holder.

  (2) An indorsement by any person in the name of the payee stated in the instrument is effective as the indorsement of the payee in favor of a person who, in good faith, pays the instrument or takes it for value or for collection.

(c) Under subsection (a) or (b), an indorsement is made in the name of a payee if (i) it is made in a name substantially similar to that of the payee or (ii) the instrument, whether or not indorsed, is deposited in a depositary bank to an account in a name substantially similar to that of the payee.

(d) With respect to an instrument to which subsection (a) or (b) applies, if a person paying the instrument or taking it for value or for collection fails to exercise ordinary care in paying or taking the instrument and that failure substantially contributes to loss resulting from payment of the instrument, the person bearing the loss may recover from the person failing to exercise ordinary care to the extent the failure to exercise ordinary care contributed to the loss.

§ 3–405. Employer's Responsibility for Fraudulent Indorsement by Employee.

(a) In this section:

  (1) "Employee" includes an independent contractor and employee of an independent contractor retained by the employer.

  (2) "Fraudulent indorsement" means (i) in the case of an instrument payable to the employer, a forged indorsement purporting to be that of the employer, or (ii) in the case of an instrument with respect to which the employer is the issuer, a forged indorsement purporting to be that of the person identified as payee.

  (3) "Responsibility" with respect to instruments means authority (i) to sign or indorse instruments on behalf of the employer, (ii) to process instruments received by the employer for bookkeeping purposes, for deposit to an account, or for other disposition, (iii) to prepare or process instruments for issue in the name of the employer,

(iv) to supply information determining the names or addresses of payees of instruments to be issued in the name of the employer, (v) to control the disposition of instruments to be issued in the name of the employer, or (vi) to act otherwise with respect to instruments in a responsible capacity. "Responsibility" does not include authority that merely allows an employee to have access to instruments or blank or incomplete instrument forms that are being stored or transported or are part of incoming or outgoing mail, or similar access.

(b) For the purpose of determining the rights and liabilities of a person who, in good faith, pays an instrument or takes it for value or for collection, if an employer entrusted an employee with responsibility with respect to the instrument and the employee or a person acting in concert with the employee makes a fraudulent indorsement of the instrument, the indorsement is effective as the indorsement of the person to whom the instrument is payable if it is made in the name of that person. If the person paying the instrument or taking it for value or for collection fails to exercise ordinary care in paying or taking the instrument and that failure substantially contributes to loss resulting from the fraud, the person bearing the loss may recover from the person failing to exercise ordinary care to the extent the failure to exercise ordinary care contributed to the loss.

(c) Under subsection (b), an indorsement is made in the name of the person to whom an instrument is payable if (i) it is made in a name substantially similar to the name of that person or (ii) the instrument, whether or not indorsed, is deposited in a depositary bank to an account in a name substantially similar to the name of that person.

§ 3–406. Negligence Contributing to Forged Signature or Alteration of Instrument.

(a) A person whose failure to exercise ordinary care substantially contributes to an alteration of an instrument or to the making of a forged signature on an instrument is precluded from asserting the alteration or the forgery against a person who, in good faith, pays the instrument or takes it for value or for collection.

(b) Under subsection (a), if the person asserting the preclusion fails to exercise ordinary care in paying or taking the instrument and that failure substantially contributes to loss, the loss is allocated between the person precluded and the person asserting the preclusion according to the extent to which the failure of each to exercise ordinary care contributed to the loss.

(c) Under subsection (a), the burden of proving failure to exercise ordinary care is on the person asserting the preclusion. Under subsection (b), the burden of proving failure to exercise ordinary care is on the person precluded.

§ 3–407. Alteration.

(a) "Alteration" means (i) an unauthorized change in an instrument that purports to modify in any respect the obligation of a party, or (ii) an unauthorized addition of words or numbers or other change to an incomplete instrument relating to the obligation of a party.

(b) Except as provided in subsection (c), an alteration fraudulently made discharges a party whose obligation is affected by the alteration unless that party assents or is precluded from asserting the alteration. No other alteration discharges a party, and the instrument may be enforced according to its original terms.

(c) A payor bank or drawee paying a fraudulently altered instrument or a person taking it for value, in good faith and without notice of the alteration, may enforce rights with respect to the instrument (i) according to its original terms, or (ii) in the case of an incomplete instrument altered by unauthorized completion, according to its terms as completed.

§ 3-408. Drawee Not Liable on Unaccepted Draft. A check or other draft does not of itself operate as an assignment of funds in the hands of the drawee available for its payment, and the drawee is not liable on the instrument until the drawee accepts it.

§ 3-409. Acceptance of Draft; Certified Check.

(a) "Acceptance" means the drawee's signed agreement to pay a draft as presented. It must be written on the draft and may consist of the drawee's signature alone. Acceptance may be made at any time and becomes effective when notification pursuant to instructions is given or the accepted draft is delivered for the purpose of giving rights on the acceptance to any person.
(b) A draft may be accepted although it has not been signed by the drawer, is otherwise incomplete, is overdue, or has been dishonored.
(c) If a draft is payable at a fixed period after sight and the acceptor fails to date the acceptance, the holder may complete the acceptance by supplying a date in good faith.
(d) "Certified check" means a check accepted by the bank on which it is drawn. Acceptance may be made as stated in subsection (a) or by a writing on the check which indicates that the check is certified. The drawee of a check has no obligation to certify the check, and refusal to certify is not dishonor of the check.

§ 3-410. Acceptance Varying Draft.

(a) If the terms of a drawee's acceptance vary from the terms of the draft as presented, the holder may refuse the acceptance and treat the draft as dishonored. In that case, the drawee may cancel the acceptance.
(b) The terms of a draft are not varied by an acceptance to pay at a particular bank or place in the United States, unless the acceptance states that the draft is to be paid only at that bank or place.
(c) If the holder assents to an acceptance varying the terms of a draft, the obligation of each drawer and indorser that does not expressly assent to the acceptance is discharged.

§ 3-411. Refusal to Pay Cashier's Checks, Teller's Checks, and Certified Checks.

(a) In this section, "obligated bank" means the acceptor of a certified check or the issuer of a cashier's check or teller's check bought from the issuer.
(b) If the obligated bank wrongfully (i) refuses to pay a cashier's check or certified check, (ii) stops payment of a teller's check, or (iii) refuses to pay a dishonored teller's check, the person asserting the right to enforce the check is entitled to compensation for expenses and loss of interest resulting from the nonpayment and may recover consequential damages if the obligated bank refuses to pay after receiving notice of particular circumstances giving rise to the damages.
(c) Expenses or consequential damages under subsection (b) are not recoverable if the refusal of the obligated bank to pay occurs because (i) the bank suspends payments, (ii) the obligated bank asserts a claim or defense of the bank that it has reasonable grounds to believe is available against the person entitled to enforce the instrument, (iii) the obligated bank has a reasonable doubt whether the person demanding payment is the person entitled to enforce the instrument, or (iv) payment is prohibited by law.

§ 3-412. Obligation of Issuer of Note or Cashier's Check. The issuer of a note or cashier's check or other draft drawn on the drawer is obliged to pay the instrument (i) according to its terms at the time it was issued or, if not issued, at the time it first came into possession of a holder, or (ii) if the issuer signed an incomplete instrument, according to its terms when completed, to the extent stated in Sections 3–115 and 3–407. The obligation is owed to a person entitled to enforce the instrument or to an indorser who paid the instrument under Section 3–415.

§ 3–413. Obligation of Acceptor.

(a) The acceptor of a draft is obliged to pay the draft (i) according to its terms at the time it was accepted, even though the acceptance states that the draft is payable "as originally drawn" or equivalent terms, (ii) if the acceptance varies the terms of the draft, according to the terms of the draft as varied, or (iii) if the acceptance is of a draft that is an incomplete instrument, according to its terms when completed, to the extent stated in Sections 3–115 and 3–407. The obligation is owed to a person entitled to enforce the draft or to the drawer or an indorser who paid the draft under Section 3–414 or 3–415.

(b) If the certification of a check or other acceptance of a draft states the amount certified or accepted, the obligation of the acceptor is that amount. If (i) the certification or acceptance does not state an amount, (ii) the amount of the instrument is subsequently raised, and (iii) the instrument is then negotiated to a holder in due course, the obligation of the acceptor is the amount of the instrument at the time it was taken by the holder in due course.

§ 3–414. Obligation of Drawer.

(a) This section does not apply to cashier's checks or other drafts drawn on the drawer.

(b) If an unaccepted draft is dishonored, the drawer is obliged to pay the draft (i) according to its terms at the time it was issued or, if not issued, at the time it first came into possession of a holder, or (ii) if the drawer signed an incomplete instrument, according to its terms when completed, to the extent stated in Sections 3–115 and 3–407. The obligation is owed to a person entitled to enforce the draft or to an indorser who paid the draft under Section 3–415.

(c) If a draft is accepted by a bank, the drawer is discharged, regardless of when or by whom acceptance was obtained.

(d) If a draft is accepted and the acceptor is not a bank, the obligation of the drawer to pay the draft if the draft is dishonored by the acceptor is the same as the obligation of an indorser under Section 3–415(a) and (c).

(e) If a draft states that it is drawn "without recourse" or otherwise disclaims liability of the drawer to pay the draft, the drawer is not liable under subsection (b) to pay the draft if the draft is not a check. A disclaimer of the liability stated in subsection (b) is not effective if the draft is a check.

(f) If (i) a check is not presented for payment or given to a depositary bank for collection within 30 days after its date, (ii) the drawee suspends payments after expiration of the 30–day period without paying the check, and (iii) because of the suspension of payments, the drawer is deprived of funds maintained with the drawee to cover payment of the check, the drawer to the extent deprived of funds may discharge its obligation to pay the check by assigning to the person entitled to enforce the check the rights of the drawer against the drawee with respect to the funds.

§ 3–415. Obligation of Indorser.

(a) Subject to subsections (b), (c), (d), (e) and to Section 3–419(d), if an instrument is dishonored, an indorser is obliged to pay the amount due on the instrument (i) according to the terms of the instrument at the time it was indorsed, or (ii) if the indorser indorsed an incomplete instrument, according to its terms when completed, to the extent stated in Sections 3–115 and 3–407. The obligation of the indorser is owed to a person entitled to enforce the instrument or to a subsequent indorser who paid the instrument under this section.

(b) If an indorsement states that it is made "without recourse" or otherwise disclaims liability of the indorser, the indorser is not liable under subsection (a) to pay the instrument.

(c) If notice of dishonor of an instrument is required by Section 3–503 and notice of dishonor complying with that section is not given to an indorser, the liability of the indorser under subsection (a) is discharged.
(d) If a draft is accepted by a bank after an indorsement is made, the liability of the indorser under subsection (a) is discharged.
(e) If an indorser of a check is liable under subsection (a) and the check is not presented for payment, or given to a depositary bank for collection, within 30 days after the day the indorsement was made, the liability of the indorser under subsection (a) is discharged.

§ 3–416. Transfer Warranties.

(a) A person who transfers an instrument for consideration warrants to the transferee and, if the transfer is by indorsement, to any subsequent transferee that:
    (1) the warrantor is a person entitled to enforce the instrument;
    (2) all signatures on the instrument are authentic and authorized;
    (3) the instrument has not been altered;
    (4) the instrument is not subject to a defense or claim in recoupment of any party which can be asserted against the warrantor;
    (5) the warrantor has no knowledge of any insolvency proceeding commenced with respect to the maker or acceptor or, in the case of an unaccepted draft, the drawer; and
    (6) with respect to a remotely-created consumer item, that the person on whose account the item is drawn authorized the issuance of the item in the amount for which the item is drawn.
(b) A person to whom the warranties under subsection (a) are made and who took the instrument in good faith may recover from the warrantor as damages for breach of warranty an amount equal to the loss suffered as a result of the breach, but not more than the amount of the instrument plus expenses and loss of interest incurred as a result of the breach.
(c) The warranties stated in subsection (a) cannot be disclaimed with respect to checks. Unless notice of a claim for breach of warranty is given to the warrantor within 30 days after the claimant has reason to know of the breach and the identity of the warrantor, the liability of the warrantor under subsection (b) is discharged to the extent of any loss caused by the delay in giving notice of the claim.
(d) A [cause of action] for breach of warranty under this section accrues when the claimant has reason to know of the breach.

§ 3–417. Presentment Warranties.

(a) If an unaccepted draft is presented to the drawee for payment or acceptance and the drawee pays or accepts the draft, (i) the person obtaining payment or acceptance, at the time of presentment, and (ii) a previous transferor of the draft, at the time of transfer, warrant to the drawee making payment or accepting the draft in good faith that:
    (1) the warrantor is, or was, at the time the warrantor transferred the draft, a person entitled to enforce the draft or authorized to obtain payment or acceptance of the draft on behalf of a person entitled to enforce the draft;
    (2) the draft has not been altered;
    (3) the warrantor has no knowledge that the signature of the drawer of the draft is unauthorized; and
    (4) with respect to any remotely-created consumer item, that the person on whose account the item is drawn authorized the issuance of the item in the amount for which the item is drawn.
(b) A drawee making payment may recover from any warrantor damages for breach of warranty equal to the amount paid by the drawee less the amount the drawee received or is entitled to receive from the drawer because of the payment. In addition, the drawee is entitled to compensation for expenses and loss of interest resulting from the breach. The right of the drawee to recover damages under this subsection is not affected by any failure of the drawee to exercise ordinary care in making payment. If the drawee accepts the draft, breach

of warranty is a defense to the obligation of the acceptor. If the acceptor makes payment with respect to the draft, the acceptor is entitled to recover from any warrantor for breach of warranty the amounts stated in this subsection.

(c) If a drawee asserts a claim for breach of warranty under subsection (a) based on an unauthorized indorsement of the draft or an alteration of the draft, the warrantor may defend by proving that the indorsement is effective under Section 3–404 or 3–405 or the drawer is precluded under Section 3–406 or 4–406 from asserting against the drawee the unauthorized indorsement or alteration.

(d) If (i) a dishonored draft is presented for payment to the drawer or an indorser or (ii) any other instrument is presented for payment to a party obliged to pay the instrument, and (iii) payment is received, the following rules apply:

 (1) The person obtaining payment and a prior transferor of the instrument warrant to the person making payment in good faith that the warrantor is, or was, at the time the warrantor transferred the instrument, a person entitled to enforce the instrument or authorized to obtain payment on behalf of a person entitled to enforce the instrument.

 (2) The person making payment may recover from any warrantor for breach of warranty an amount equal to the amount paid plus expenses and loss of interest resulting from the breach.

(e) The warranties stated in subsections (a) and (d) cannot be disclaimed with respect to checks. Unless notice of a claim for breach of warranty is given to the warrantor within 30 days after the claimant has reason to know of the breach and the identity of the warrantor, the liability of the warrantor under subsection (b) or (d) is discharged to the extent of any loss caused by the delay in giving notice of the claim.

(f) A [cause of action] for breach of warranty under this section accrues when the claimant has reason to know of the breach.

§ 3–418. Payment or Acceptance by Mistake.

(a) Except as provided in subsection (c), if the drawee of a draft pays or accepts the draft and the drawee acted on the mistaken belief that (i) payment of the draft had not been stopped pursuant to Section 4–403 or (ii) the signature of the drawer of the draft was authorized, the drawee may recover the amount of the draft from the person to whom or for whose benefit payment was made or, in the case of acceptance, may revoke the acceptance. Rights of the drawee under this subsection are not affected by failure of the drawee to exercise ordinary care in paying or accepting the draft.

(b) Except as provided in subsection (c), if an instrument has been paid or accepted by mistake and the case is not covered by subsection (a), the person paying or accepting may, to the extent permitted by the law governing mistake and restitution, (i) recover the payment from the person to whom or for whose benefit payment was made or (ii) in the case of acceptance, may revoke the acceptance.

(c) The remedies provided by subsection (a) or (b) may not be asserted against a person who took the instrument in good faith and for value or who in good faith changed position in reliance on the payment or acceptance. This subsection does not limit remedies provided by Section 3–417 or 4–407.

(d) Notwithstanding Section 4–215, if an instrument is paid or accepted by mistake and the payor or acceptor recovers payment or revokes acceptance under subsection (a) or (b), the instrument is deemed not to have been paid or accepted and is treated as dishonored, and the person from whom payment is recovered has rights as a person entitled to enforce the dishonored instrument.

§ 3–419. Instruments Signed for Accommodation.

(a) If an instrument is issued for value given for the benefit of a party to the instrument ("accommodated party") and another party to the instrument ("accommodation party") signs the instrument for the purpose of incurring liability on the instrument without being a direct beneficiary of the value given for the instrument, the instrument is signed by the accommodation party "for accommodation."

(b) An accommodation party may sign the instrument as maker, drawer, acceptor, or indorser and, subject to subsection (d), is obliged to pay the instrument in the capacity in which the accommodation party signs. The obligation of an accommodation party may be enforced notwithstanding any statute of frauds and whether or not the accommodation party receives consideration for the accommodation.

(c) A person signing an instrument is presumed to be an accommodation party and there is notice that the instrument is signed for accommodation if the signature is an anomalous indorsement or is accompanied by words indicating that the signer is acting as surety or guarantor with respect to the obligation of another party to the instrument. Except as provided in Section 3–605, the obligation of an accommodation party to pay the instrument is not affected by the fact that the person enforcing the obligation had notice when the instrument was taken by that person that the accommodation party signed the instrument for accommodation.

(d) If the signature of a party to an instrument is accompanied by words indicating unambiguously that the party is guaranteeing collection rather than payment of the obligation of another party to the instrument, the signer is obliged to pay the amount due on the instrument to a person entitled to enforce the instrument only if (i) execution of judgment against the other party has been returned unsatisfied, (ii) the other party is insolvent or in an insolvency proceeding, (iii) the other party cannot be served with process, or (iv) it is otherwise apparent that payment cannot be obtained from the other party.

(e) If the signature of a party to an instrument is accompanied by words indicating that the party guarantees payment or the signer signs the instrument as an accommodation party in some other manner that does not unambiguously indicate an intention to guarantee collection rather than payment, the signer is obliged to pay the amount due on the instrument to a person entitled to enforce the instrument in the same circumstances as the accommodated party would be obliged, without prior resort to the accommodated party by the person entitled to enforce the instrument.

(f) An accommodation party who pays the instrument is entitled to reimbursement from the accommodated party and is entitled to enforce the instrument against the accommodated party. In proper circumstances, an accommodation party may obtain relief that requires the accommodated party to perform its obligations on the instrument. An accommodated party that pays the instrument has no right of recourse against, and is not entitled to contribution from, an accommodation party.

§ 3–420. Conversion of Instrument.

(a) The law applicable to conversion of personal property applies to instruments. An instrument is also converted if it is taken by transfer, other than a negotiation, from a person not entitled to enforce the instrument or a bank makes or obtains payment with respect to the instrument for a person not entitled to enforce the instrument or receive payment. An action for conversion of an instrument may not be brought by (i) the issuer or acceptor of the instrument or (ii) a payee or indorsee who did not receive delivery of the instrument either directly or through delivery to an agent or a co-payee.

(b) In an action under subsection (a), the measure of liability is presumed to be the amount payable on the instrument, but recovery may not exceed the amount of the plaintiff's interest in the instrument.

(c) A representative, other than a depositary bank, who has in good faith dealt with an instrument or its proceeds on behalf of one who was not the person entitled to enforce the instrument is not liable in conversion to that person beyond the amount of any proceeds that it has not paid out.

PART 5: DISHONOR

§ 3–501. Presentment.

(a) "Presentment" means a demand made by or on behalf of a person entitled to enforce an instrument (i) to pay the instrument made to the drawee or a party obliged to pay the instrument or, in the case of a note or accepted draft payable at a bank, to the bank, or (ii) to accept a draft made to the drawee.

(b) The following rules are subject to Article 4, agreement of the parties, and clearing-house rules and the like:

(1) Presentment may be made at the place of payment of the instrument and must be made at the place of payment if the instrument is payable at a bank in the United States; may be made by any commercially reasonable means, including an oral, written, or electronic communication; is effective when the demand for payment or acceptance is received by the person to whom presentment is made; and is effective if made to any one of two or more makers, acceptors, drawees, or other payors.

(2) Upon demand of the person to whom presentment is made, the person making presentment must (i) exhibit the instrument, (ii) give reasonable identification and, if presentment is made on behalf of another person, reasonable evidence of authority to do so, and (iii) sign a receipt on the instrument for any payment made or surrender the instrument if full payment is made.

(3) Without dishonoring the instrument, the party to whom presentment is made may (i) return the instrument for lack of a necessary indorsement, or (ii) refuse payment or acceptance for failure of the presentment to comply with the terms of the instrument, an agreement of the parties, or other applicable law or rule.

(4) The party to whom presentment is made may treat presentment as occurring on the next business day after the day of presentment if the party to whom presentment is made has established a cut-off hour not earlier than 2 p.m. for the receipt and processing of instruments presented for payment or acceptance and presentment is made after the cut-off hour.

§ 3–502. Dishonor.

(a) Dishonor of a note is governed by the following rules:

(1) If the note is payable on demand, the note is dishonored if presentment is duly made to the maker and the note is not paid on the day of presentment.

(2) If the note is not payable on demand and is payable at or through a bank or the terms of the note require presentment, the note is dishonored if presentment is duly made and the note is not paid on the day it becomes payable or the day of presentment, whichever is later.

(3) If the note is not payable on demand and paragraph (2) does not apply, the note is dishonored if it is not paid on the day it becomes payable.

(b) Dishonor of an unaccepted draft other than a documentary draft is governed by the following rules:

(1) If a check is duly presented for payment to the payor bank otherwise than for immediate payment over the counter, the check is dishonored if the payor bank makes timely return of the check or sends timely notice of dishonor or nonpayment under Section 4–301 or 4–302, or becomes accountable for the amount of the check under Section 4–302.

(2) If a draft is payable on demand and paragraph (1) does not apply, the draft is dishonored if presentment for payment is duly made to the drawee and the draft is not paid on the day of presentment.

(3) If a draft is payable on a date stated in the draft, the draft is dishonored if (i) presentment for payment is duly made to the drawee and payment is not made on the day the draft becomes payable or the day of presentment, whichever is later, or (ii) presentment for acceptance is duly made before the day the draft becomes payable and the draft is not accepted on the day of presentment.

(4) If a draft is payable on elapse of a period of time after sight or acceptance, the draft is dishonored if presentment for acceptance is duly made and the draft is not accepted on the day of presentment.

(c) Dishonor of an unaccepted documentary draft occurs according to the rules stated in subsection (b)(2), (3), and (4), except that payment or acceptance may be delayed without dishonor until no later than the close of the third business day of the drawee following the day on which payment or acceptance is required by those paragraphs.

(d) Dishonor of an accepted draft is governed by the following rules:

(1) If the draft is payable on demand, the draft is dishonored if presentment for payment is duly made to the acceptor and the draft is not paid on the day of presentment.

(2) If the draft is not payable on demand, the draft is dishonored if presentment for payment is duly made to the acceptor and payment is not made on the day it becomes payable or the day of presentment, whichever is later.

(e) In any case in which presentment is otherwise required for dishonor under this section and presentment is excused under Section 3–504, dishonor occurs without presentment if the instrument is not duly accepted or paid.

(f) If a draft is dishonored because timely acceptance of the draft was not made and the person entitled to demand acceptance consents to a late acceptance, from the time of acceptance the draft is treated as never having been dishonored.

§ 3–503. Notice of Dishonor.

(a) The obligation of an indorser stated in Section 3–415(a) and the obligation of a drawer stated in Section 3–414(d) may not be enforced unless (i) the indorser or drawer is given notice of dishonor of the instrument complying with this section or (ii) notice of dishonor is excused under Section 3–504(b).

(b) Notice of dishonor may be given by any person; may be given by any commercially reasonable means, including an oral, written, or electronic communication; and is sufficient if it reasonably identifies the instrument and indicates that the instrument has been dishonored or has not been paid or accepted. Return of an instrument given to a bank for collection is sufficient notice of dishonor.

(c) Subject to Section 3–504(c), with respect to an instrument taken for collection by a collecting bank, notice of dishonor must be given (i) by the bank before midnight of the next banking day following the banking day on which the bank receives notice of dishonor of the instrument, or (ii) by any other person within 30 days following the day on which the person receives notice of dishonor. With respect to any other instrument, notice of dishonor must be given within 30 days following the day on which dishonor occurs.

§ 3–504. Excused Presentment and Notice of Dishonor.

(a) Presentment for payment or acceptance of an instrument is excused if (i) the person entitled to present the instrument cannot with reasonable diligence make presentment, (ii) the maker or acceptor has repudiated an obligation to pay the instrument or is dead or in insolvency proceedings, (iii) by the terms of the instrument presentment is not necessary to enforce the obligation of indorsers or the drawer, (iv) the drawer or indorser whose obligation is being enforced has waived presentment or otherwise has no reason to expect or right to require that the instrument be paid or accepted, or (v) the drawer instructed the drawee not to pay or accept the draft or the drawee was not obligated to the drawer to pay the draft.

(b) Notice of dishonor is excused if (i) by the terms of the instrument notice of dishonor is not necessary to enforce the obligation of a party to pay the instrument, or (ii) the party whose obligation is being enforced waived notice of dishonor. A waiver of presentment is also a waiver of notice of dishonor.

(c) Delay in giving notice of dishonor is excused if the delay was caused by circumstances beyond the control of the person giving the notice and the person giving the notice exercised reasonable diligence after the cause of the delay ceased to operate.

§ 3–505. Evidence of Dishonor.

(a) The following are admissible as evidence and create a presumption of dishonor and of any notice of dishonor stated:
   (1) a document regular in form as provided in subsection (b) which purports to be a protest;
   (2) a purported stamp or writing of the drawee, payor bank, or presenting bank on or accompanying the instrument stating that acceptance or payment has been refused unless reasons for the refusal are stated and the reasons are not consistent with dishonor;
   (3) a book or record of the drawee, payor bank, or collecting bank, kept in the usual course of business which shows dishonor, even if there is no evidence of who made the entry.

(b) A protest is a certificate of dishonor made by a United States consul or vice consul, or a notary public or other person authorized to administer oaths by the law of the place where dishonor occurs. It may be made upon information satisfactory to that person. The protest must identify the instrument and certify either that presentment has been made or, if not made, the reason why it was not made, and that the instrument has been dishonored by non-acceptance or nonpayment. The protest may also certify that notice of dishonor has been given to some or all parties.

PART 6: DISCHARGE AND PAYMENT

§ 3–601. Discharge and Effect of Discharge.

(a) The obligation of a party to pay the instrument is discharged as stated in this Article or by an act or agreement with the party which would discharge an obligation to pay money under a simple contract.

(b) Discharge of the obligation of a party is not effective against a person acquiring rights of a holder in due course of the instrument without notice of the discharge.

§ 3–602. Payment.

(a) Subject to subsection (e), an instrument is paid to the extent payment is made by or on behalf of a party obliged to pay the instrument, and to a person entitled to enforce the instrument.

(b) Subject to subsection (e), a note is paid to the extent payment is made by or on behalf of a party obliged to pay the note to a person that formerly was entitled to enforce the note only if at the time of the payment the party obliged to pay has not received adequate notification that the note has been transferred and that payment is to be made to the transferee. A notification is adequate only if it is signed by the transferor or the transferee; reasonably identifies the transferred note; and provides an address at which payments subsequently are to be made. Upon request, a transferee shall seasonably furnish reasonable proof that the note has been transferred. Unless the transferee complies with the request, a payment to the person that formerly was entitled to enforce the note is effective for purposes of subsection (c) even if the party obliged to pay the note has received a notification under this paragraph.

(c) Subject to subsection (e), to the extent of a payment under subsections (a) and (b), the obligation of the party obliged to pay the instrument is discharged even though payment is made with knowledge of a claim to the instrument under Section 3–306 by another person.

(d) Subject to subsection (e), a transferee, or any party that has acquired rights in the instrument directly or indirectly from a transferee, including any such party that has rights as a holder in due course, is deemed to have notice of any payment that is made under subsection (b) after the date that the note is transferred to the transferee but before the party obliged to pay the note receives adequate notification of the transfer.

(e) The obligation of a party to pay the instrument is not discharged under subsections (a) through (d) if:
   (1) a claim to the instrument under Section 3–306 is enforceable against the party receiving payment and (i) payment is made with knowledge by the payor that payment is prohibited by injunction or similar process of a court of competent jurisdiction, or (ii) in the case of an instrument other than a cashier's check, teller's check, or certified check, the party making payment accepted, from the person having a claim to the instrument, indemnity against loss resulting from refusal to pay the person entitled to enforce the instrument; or
   (2) the person making payment knows that the instrument is a stolen instrument and pays a person it knows is in wrongful possession of the instrument.

(f) As used in this section, "signed," with respect to a record that is not a writing, includes the attachment to or logical association with the record of an electronic symbol, sound, or process with the present intent to adopt or accept the record.

§ 3–603. Tender of Payment.

(a) If tender of payment of an obligation to pay an instrument is made to a person entitled to enforce the instrument, the effect of tender is governed by principles of law applicable to tender of payment under a simple contract.

(b) If tender of payment of an obligation to pay an instrument is made to a person entitled to enforce the instrument and the tender is refused, there is discharge, to the extent of the amount of the tender, of the obligation of an indorser or accommodation party having a right of recourse with respect to the obligation to which the tender relates.

(c) If tender of payment of an amount due on an instrument is made to a person entitled to enforce the instrument, the obligation of the obligor to pay interest after the due date on the amount tendered is discharged. If presentment is required with respect to an instrument and the obligor is able and ready to pay on the due date at every place of payment stated in the instrument, the obligor is deemed to have made tender of payment on the due date to the person entitled to enforce the instrument.

§ 3–604. Discharge by Cancellation or Renunciation.

(a) A person entitled to enforce an instrument, with or without consideration, may discharge the obligation of a party to pay the instrument (i) by an intentional voluntary act, such as surrender of the instrument to the party, destruction, mutilation, or cancellation of the instrument, cancellation or striking out of the partyís signature, or the addition of words to the instrument indicating discharge, or (ii) by agreeing not to sue or otherwise renouncing rights against the party by a signed record.

(b) Cancellation or striking out of an indorsement pursuant to subsection (a) does not affect the status and rights of a party derived from the indorsement.

(c) In this section, "signed," with respect to a record that is not a writing, includes the attachment to or logical association with the record of an electronic symbol, sound, or process with the present intent to adopt or accept the record.

§ 3–605. Discharge of Secondary Obligors.

(a) If a person entitled to enforce an instrument releases the obligation of a principal obligor in whole or in part, and another party to the instrument is a secondary obligor with respect to the obligation of that principal obligor, the following rules apply:
   (1) Any obligations of the principal obligor to the secondary obligor with respect to any previous payment by the secondary obligor are not affected. Unless the terms of the release preserve the secondary obligor's recourse, the principal obligor is discharged, to the extent of the release, from any other duties to the secondary obligor under this article.

(2) Unless the terms of the release provide that the person entitled to enforce the instrument retains the right to enforce the instrument against the secondary obligor, the secondary obligor is discharged to the same extent as the principal obligor from any unperformed portion of its obligation on the instrument. If the instrument is a check and the obligation of the secondary obligor is based on an indorsement of the check, the secondary obligor is discharged without regard to the language or circumstances of the discharge or other release.

(3) If the secondary obligor is not discharged under paragraph (2), the secondary obligor is discharged to the extent of the value of the consideration for the release, and to the extent that the release would otherwise cause the secondary obligor a loss.

(b) If a person entitled to enforce an instrument grants a principal obligor an extension of the time at which one or more payments are due on the instrument and another party to the instrument is a secondary obligor with respect to the obligation of that principal obligor, the following rules apply:

(1) Any obligations of the principal obligor to the secondary obligor with respect to any previous payment by the secondary obligor are not affected. Unless the terms of the extension preserve the secondary obligor's recourse, the extension correspondingly extends the time for performance of any other duties owed to the secondary obligor by the principal obligor under this article.

(2) The secondary obligor is discharged to the extent that the extension would otherwise cause the secondary obligor a loss.

(3) To the extent that the secondary obligor is not discharged under paragraph (2), the secondary obligor may perform its obligations to a person entitled to enforce the instrument as if the time for payment had not been extended or, unless the terms of the extension provide that the person entitled to enforce the instrument retains the right to enforce the instrument against the secondary obligor as if the time for payment had not been extended, treat the time for performance of its obligations as having been extended correspondingly.

(c) If a person entitled to enforce an instrument agrees, with or without consideration, to a modification of the obligation of a principal obligor other than a complete or partial release or an extension of the due date and another party to the instrument is a secondary obligor with respect to the obligation of that principal obligor, the following rules apply:

(1) Any obligations of the principal obligor to the secondary obligor with respect to any previous payment by the secondary obligor are not affected. The modification correspondingly modifies any other duties owed to the secondary obligor by the principal obligor under this article.

(2) The secondary obligor is discharged from any unperformed portion of its obligation to the extent that the modification would otherwise cause the secondary obligor a loss.

(3) To the extent that the secondary obligor is not discharged under paragraph (2), the secondary obligor may satisfy its obligation on the instrument as if the modification had not occurred, or treat its obligation on the instrument as having been modified correspondingly.

(d) If the obligation of a principal obligor is secured by an interest in collateral, another party to the instrument is a secondary obligor with respect to that obligation, and a person entitled to enforce the instrument impairs the value of the interest in collateral, the obligation of the secondary obligor is discharged to the extent of the impairment. The value of an interest in collateral is impaired to the extent the value of the interest is reduced to an amount less than the amount of the recourse of the secondary obligor, or the reduction in value of the interest causes an increase in the amount by which the amount of the recourse exceeds the value of the interest. For purposes of this subsection, impairing the value of an interest in collateral includes failure to obtain or maintain perfection or recordation of the interest in collateral, release of collateral without substitution of collateral of equal value or equivalent reduction of the underlying obligation, failure to perform a duty to preserve the value of collateral owed, under Article 9 or other law, to a debtor or other person secondarily liable, and failure to comply with applicable law in disposing of or otherwise enforcing the interest in collateral.

(e) A secondary obligor is not discharged under subsections (a)(3), (b), (c), or (d) unless the person entitled to enforce the instrument knows that the person is a secondary obligor or has notice under Section 3–419(c) that the instrument was signed for accommodation.

(f) A secondary obligor is not discharged under this section if the secondary obligor consents to the event or conduct that is the basis of the discharge, or the instrument or a separate agreement of the party provides for waiver of discharge under this section specifically or by general language indicating that parties waive defenses based on suretyship or impairment of collateral. Unless the circumstances indicate otherwise, consent by the principal obligor to an act that would lead to a discharge under this section constitutes consent to that act by the secondary obligor if the secondary obligor controls the principal obligor or deals with the person entitled to enforce the instrument on behalf of the principal obligor.

(g) A release or extension preserves a secondary obligorís recourse if the terms of the release or extension provide that:

(1) the person entitled to enforce the instrument retains the right to enforce the instrument against the secondary obligor; and

(2) the recourse of the secondary obligor continues as if the release or extension had not been granted.

(h) Except as otherwise provided in subsection (i), a secondary obligor asserting discharge under this section has the burden of persuasion both with respect to the occurrence of the acts alleged to harm the secondary obligor and loss or prejudice caused by those acts.

(i) If the secondary obligor demonstrates prejudice caused by an impairment of its recourse, and the circumstances of the case indicate that the amount of loss is not reasonably susceptible of calculation or requires proof of facts that are not ascertainable, it is presumed that the act impairing recourse caused a loss or impairment equal to the liability of the secondary obligor on the instrument. In that event, the burden of persuasion as to any lesser amount of the loss is on the person entitled to enforce the instrument.

APPENDIX C

TITLE VII OF THE CIVIL RIGHTS ACT OF 1964

The U.S. Equal Employment Opportunity Commission

An Act

To enforce the constitutional right to vote, to confer jurisdiction upon the district courts of the United States to provide injunctive relief against discrimination in public accommodations, to authorize the attorney General to institute suits to protect constitutional rights in public facilities and public education, to extend the Commission on Civil Rights, to prevent discrimination in federally assisted programs, to establish a Commission on Equal Employment Opportunity, and for other purposes.

Be it enacted by the Senate and House of Representatives of the United States of America in Congress assembled, That this Act may be cited as the "Civil Rights Act of 1964."

***

DEFINITIONS

SEC. 2000e. *[Section 701].* For the purposes of this subchapter-

(a) The term "person" includes one or more individuals, governments, governmental agencies, political subdivisions, labor unions, partnerships, associations, corporations, legal representatives, mutual companies, joint stock companies, trusts, unincorporated organizations, trustees, trustees in cases under title 11 *[bankruptcy],* or receivers.

(b) The term "employer" means a person engaged in an industry affecting commerce who has fifteen or more employees for each working day in each of twenty or more calendar weeks in the current or preceding calendar year, and any agent of such a person, but such term does not include (1) the United States, a corporation wholly owned by the Government of the United States, an Indian tribe, or any department or agency of the District of Columbia subject by statute to procedures of the competitive service (as defined in section 2102 of title 5 *[of the United States Code]*), or (2) a bona fide private membership club (other than a labor organization) which is exempt from taxation under section 501(c) of title 26 *[the Internal Revenue Code of 1954],* except that during the first year after March 24, 1972 *[the date of enactment of the Equal Employment Opportunity Act of 1972],* persons having fewer than twenty five employees (and their agents) shall not be considered employers.

(c) The term "employment agency" means any person regularly undertaking with or without compensation to procure employees for an employer or to procure for employees opportunities to work for an employer and includes an agent of such a person.

(d) The term "labor organization" means a labor organization engaged in an industry affecting commerce, and any agent of such an organization, and includes any organization of any kind, any agency, or employee representation committee, group, association, or plan so engaged in which employees participate and which exists for the purpose, in whole or in part, of dealing with employers concerning grievances, labor disputes, wages, rates of pay, hours, or other terms or conditions of employment, and any conference, general committee, joint or system board, or joint council so engaged which is subordinate to a national or international labor organization.

(e) A labor organization shall be deemed to be engaged in an industry affecting commerce if (1) it maintains or operates a hiring hall or hiring office which procures employees for an employer or procures for employees opportunities to work for an employer, or (2) the number of its members (or, where it is a labor organization composed of other labor organizations or their representatives, if the aggregate number of the members of such other labor organization) is (A) twenty five or more during the first year after March 24, 1972 *[the date of enactment of the Equal Employment Opportunity Act of 1972]*, or (B) fifteen or more thereafter, and such labor organization-

(1) is the certified representative of employees under the provisions of the National Labor Relations Act, as amended *[29 U.S.C. 151 et seq.]*, or the Railway Labor Act, as amended *[45 U.S.C. 151 et seq.]*;

(2) although not certified, is a national or international labor organization or a local labor organization recognized or acting as the representative of employees of an employer or employers engaged in an industry affecting commerce; or

(3) has chartered a local labor organization or subsidiary body which is representing or actively seeking to represent employees of employers within the meaning of paragraph (1) or (2); or

(4) has been chartered by a labor organization representing or actively seeking to represent employees within the meaning of paragraph (1) or (2) as the local or subordinate body through which such employees may enjoy membership or become affiliated with such labor organization; or

(5) is a conference, general committee, joint or system board, or joint council subordinate to a national or international labor organization, which includes a labor organization engaged in an industry affecting commerce within the meaning of any of the preceding paragraphs of this subsection.

(f) The term "employee" means an individual employed by an employer, except that the term "employee" shall not include any person elected to public office in any State or political subdivision of any State by the qualified voters thereof, or any person chosen by such officer to be on such officer's personal staff, or an appointee on the policy making level or an immediate adviser with respect to the exercise of the constitutional or legal powers of the office. The exemption set forth in the preceding sentence shall not include employees subject to the civil service laws of a State government, governmental agency or political subdivision. **With respect to employment in a foreign country, such term includes an individual who is a citizen of the United States.**

(g) The term "commerce" means trade, traffic, commerce, transportation, transmission, or communication among the several States; or between a State and any place outside thereof; or within the District of Columbia, or a possession of the United States; or between points in the same State but through a point outside thereof.

(h) The term "industry affecting commerce" means any activity, business, or industry in commerce or in which a labor dispute would hinder or obstruct commerce or the free flow of commerce and includes any activity or industry "affecting commerce" within the meaning of the Labor Management Reporting and Disclosure Act of 1959 *[29 U.S.C. 401 et seq.]*, and further includes any governmental industry, business, or activity.

(i) The term "State" includes a State of the United States, the District of Columbia, Puerto Rico, the Virgin Islands, American Samoa, Guam, Wake Island, the Canal Zone, and Outer Continental Shelf lands defined in the Outer Continental Shelf Lands Act *[43 U.S.C. 1331 et seq.]*.

(j) The term "religion" includes all aspects of religious observance and practice, as well as belief, unless an employer demonstrates that he is unable to reasonably accommodate to an employee's or prospective employee's religious observance or practice without undue hardship on the conduct of the employer's business.

(k) The terms "because of sex" or "on the basis of sex" include, but are not limited to, because of or on the basis of pregnancy, childbirth, or related medical conditions; and women affected by pregnancy, childbirth, or related medical conditions shall be treated the same for all employment related purposes, including receipt of benefits under fringe benefit programs, as other persons not so affected but similar in their ability or inability to work, and nothing in section 2000e-2(h) of this title *[section 703(h)]* shall be interpreted to permit otherwise. This subsection shall not require an employer to pay for health insurance benefits for abortion, except where the life of the mother would be endangered if the fetus were carried to term, or except where medical complications have arisen from an abortion: Provided, That nothing herein shall preclude an employer from providing abortion benefits or otherwise affect bargaining agreements in regard to abortion.

(l) The term "complaining party" means the Commission, the Attorney General, or a person who may bring an action or proceeding under this subchapter.
(m) The term "demonstrates" means meets the burdens of production and persuasion.
(n) The term "respondent" means an employer, employment agency, labor organization, joint labor management committee controlling apprenticeship or other training or retraining program, including an on the job training program, or Federal entity subject to section 2000e-16 of this title.

EXEMPTION

SEC. 2000e-1. *[Section 702].*

(a) This subchapter shall not apply to an employer with respect to the employment of aliens outside any State, or to a religious corporation, association, educational institution, or society with respect to the employment of individuals of a particular religion to perform work connected with the carrying on by such corporation, association, educational institution, or society of its activities.
(b) It shall not be unlawful under section 2000e-2 or 2000e-3 of this title *[section 703 or 704]* **for an employer (or a corporation controlled by an employer), labor organization, employment agency, or joint labor management committee controlling apprenticeship or other training or retraining (including on the job training programs) to take any action otherwise prohibited by such section, with respect to an employee in a workplace in a foreign country if compliance with such section would cause such employer (or such corporation), such organization, such agency, or such committee to violate the law of the foreign country in which such workplace is located.**
(c) (1) If an employer controls a corporation whose place of incorporation is a foreign country, any practice prohibited by section 2000e-2 or 2000e-3 of this title *[section 703 or 704]* **engaged in by such corporation shall be presumed to be engaged in by such employer.**
(2) Sections 2000e-2 and 2000e-3 of this title *[sections 703 and 704]* **shall not apply with respect to the foreign operations of an employer that is a foreign person not controlled by an American employer.**
(3) For purposes of this subsection, the determination of whether an employer controls a corporation shall be based on-
(A) the interrelation of operations;
(B) the common management;
(C) the centralized control of labor relations; and
(D) the common ownership or financial control, of the employer and the corporation.

UNLAWFUL EMPLOYMENT PRACTICES

SEC. 2000e-2. *[Section 703].*

(a) It shall be an unlawful employment practice for an employer-
(1) to fail or refuse to hire or to discharge any individual, or otherwise to discriminate against any individual with respect to his compensation, terms, conditions, or privileges of employment, because of such individual's race, color, religion, sex, or national origin; or
(2) to limit, segregate, or classify his employees or applicants for employment in any way which would deprive or tend to deprive any individual of employment opportunities or otherwise adversely affect his status as an employee, because of such individual's race, color, religion, sex, or national origin.
(b) It shall be an unlawful employment practice for an employment agency to fail or refuse to refer for employment, or otherwise to discriminate against, any individual because of his race, color, religion, sex, or national origin, or to classify or refer for employment any individual on the basis of his race, color, religion, sex, or national origin.
(c) It shall be an unlawful employment practice for a labor organization-
(1) to exclude or to expel from its membership, or otherwise to discriminate against, any individual because of his race, color, religion, sex, or national origin;

(2) to limit, segregate, or classify its membership or applicants for membership, or to classify or fail or refuse to refer for employment any individual, in any way which would deprive or tend to deprive any individual of employment opportunities, or would limit such employment opportunities or otherwise adversely affect his status as an employee or as an applicant for employment, because of such individual's race, color, religion, sex, or national origin; or

(3) to cause or attempt to cause an employer to discriminate against an individual in violation of this section.

(d) It shall be an unlawful employment practice for any employer, labor organization, or joint labor management committee controlling apprenticeship or other training or retraining, including on the job training programs to discriminate against any individual because of his race, color, religion, sex, or national origin in admission to, or employment in, any program established to provide apprenticeship or other training.

(e) Notwithstanding any other provision of this subchapter, (1) it shall not be an unlawful employment practice for an employer to hire and employ employees, for an employment agency to classify, or refer for employment any individual, for a labor organization to classify its membership or to classify or refer for employment any individual, or for an employer, labor organization, or joint labor management committee controlling apprenticeship or other training or retraining programs to admit or employ any individual in any such program, on the basis of his religion, sex, or national origin in those certain instances where religion, sex, or national origin is a bona fide occupational qualification reasonably necessary to the normal operation of that particular business or enterprise, and (2) it shall not be an unlawful employment practice for a school, college, university, or other educational institution or institution of learning to hire and employ employees of a particular religion if such school, college, university, or other educational institution or institution of learning is, in whole or in substantial part, owned, supported, controlled, or managed by a particular religion or by a particular religious corporation, association, or society, or if the curriculum of such school, college, university, or other educational institution or institution of learning is directed toward the propagation of a particular religion.

(f) As used in this subchapter, the phrase "unlawful employment practice" shall not be deemed to include any action or measure taken by an employer, labor organization, joint labor management committee, or employment agency with respect to an individual who is a member of the Communist Party of the United States or of any other organization required to register as a Communist action or Communist front organization by final order of the Subversive Activities Control Board pursuant to the Subversive Activities Control Act of 1950 *[50 U.S.C. 781 et seq.]*.

(g) Notwithstanding any other provision of this subchapter, it shall not be an unlawful employment practice for an employer to fail or refuse to hire and employ any individual for any position, for an employer to discharge any individual from any position, or for an employment agency to fail or refuse to refer any individual for employment in any position, or for a labor organization to fail or refuse to refer any individual for employment in any position, if-

(1) the occupancy of such position, or access to the premises in or upon which any part of the duties of such position is performed or is to be performed, is subject to any requirement imposed in the interest of the national security of the United States under any security program in effect pursuant to or administered under any statute of the United States or any Executive order of the President; and

(2) such individual has not fulfilled or has ceased to fulfill that requirement.

(h) Notwithstanding any other provision of this subchapter, it shall not be an unlawful employment practice for an employer to apply different standards of compensation, or different terms, conditions, or privileges of employment pursuant to a bona fide seniority or merit system, or a system which measures earnings by quantity or quality of production or to employees who work in different locations, provided that such differences are not the result of an intention to discriminate because of race, color, religion, sex, or national origin, nor shall it be an unlawful employment practice for an employer to give and to act upon the results of any professionally developed ability test provided that such test, its administration or action upon the results is not designed, intended or used to discriminate because of race, color, religion, sex or national origin. It shall not be an unlawful employment practice under this subchapter for any employer to differentiate upon the basis of sex in determining the amount of the wages or compensation paid or to be paid to employees of such employer if such differentiation is authorized by the provisions of section 206(d) of title 29 *[section 6(d) of the Fair Labor Standards Act of 1938, as amended]*.

(i) Nothing contained in this subchapter shall apply to any business or enterprise on or near an Indian reservation with respect to any publicly announced employment practice of such business or enterprise under which a preferential treatment is given to any individual because he is an Indian living on or near a reservation.

(j) Nothing contained in this subchapter shall be interpreted to require any employer, employment agency, labor organization, or joint labor management committee subject to this subchapter to grant preferential treatment to any individual or to any group because of the race, color, religion, sex, or national origin of such individual or group on account of an imbalance which may exist with respect to the total number or percentage of persons of any race, color, religion, sex, or national origin employed by any employer, referred or classified for employment by any employment agency or labor organization, admitted to membership or classified by any labor organization, or admitted to, or employed in, any apprenticeship or other training program, in comparison with the total number or percentage of persons of such race, color, religion, sex, or national origin in any community, State, section, or other area, or in the available work force in any community, State, section, or other area.

(k) (1) (A) An unlawful employment practice based on disparate impact is established under this title only if-

(i) a complaining party demonstrates that a respondent uses a particular employment practice that causes a disparate impact on the basis of race, color, religion, sex, or national origin and the respondent fails to demonstrate that the challenged practice is job related for the position in question and consistent with business necessity; or

(ii) the complaining party makes the demonstration described in subparagraph (C) with respect to an alternative employment practice and the respondent refuses to adopt such alternative employment practice.

(B) (i) With respect to demonstrating that a particular employment practice causes a disparate impact as described in subparagraph (A)(i), the complaining party shall demonstrate that each particular challenged employment practice causes a disparate impact, except that if the complaining party can demonstrate to the court that the elements of a respondent's decision making process are not capable of separation for analysis, the decision making process may be analyzed as one employment practice.

(ii) If the respondent demonstrates that a specific employment practice does not cause the disparate impact, the respondent shall not be required to demonstrate that such practice is required by business necessity.

(C) The demonstration referred to by subparagraph (A)(ii) shall be in accordance with the law as it existed on June 4, 1989, with respect to the concept of "alternative employment practice".

(2) A demonstration that an employment practice is required by business necessity may not be used as a defense against a claim of intentional discrimination under this title.

(3) Notwithstanding any other provision of this title, a rule barring the employment of an individual who currently and knowingly uses or possesses a controlled substance, as defined in schedules I and II of section 102(6) of the Controlled Substances Act (21 U.S.C. 802(6)), other than the use or possession of a drug taken under the supervision of a licensed health care professional, or any other use or possession authorized by the Controlled Substances Act *[21 U.S.C. 801 et seq.]* or any other provision of Federal law, shall be considered an unlawful employment practice under this title only if such rule is adopted or applied with an intent to discriminate because of race, color, religion, sex, or national origin.

(l) It shall be an unlawful employment practice for a respondent, in connection with the selection or referral of applicants or candidates for employment or promotion, to adjust

the scores of, use different cutoff scores for, or otherwise alter the results of, employment related tests on the basis of race, color, religion, sex, or national origin.

(m) Except as otherwise provided in this title, an unlawful employment practice is established when the complaining party demonstrates that race, color, religion, sex, or national origin was a motivating factor for any employment practice, even though other factors also motivated the practice.

(n) (1) (A) Notwithstanding any other provision of law, and except as provided in paragraph (2), an employment practice that implements and is within the scope of a litigated or consent judgment or order that resolves a claim of employment discrimination under the Constitution or Federal civil rights laws may not be challenged under the circumstances described in subparagraph (B).

(B) A practice described in subparagraph (A) may not be challenged in a claim under the Constitution or Federal civil rights laws-

(i) by a person who, prior to the entry of the judgment or order described in subparagraph (A), had-

(I) actual notice of the proposed judgment or order sufficient to apprise such person that such judgment or order might adversely affect the interests and legal rights of such person and that an opportunity was available to present objections to such judgment or order by a future date certain; and

(II) a reasonable opportunity to present objections to such judgment or order; or

(ii) by a person whose interests were adequately represented by another person who had previously challenged the judgment or order on the same legal grounds and with a similar factual situation, unless there has been an intervening change in law or fact.

(2) Nothing in this subsection shall be construed to-

(A) alter the standards for intervention under rule 24 of the Federal Rules of Civil Procedure or apply to the rights of parties who have successfully intervened pursuant to such rule in the proceeding in which the parties intervened;

(B) apply to the rights of parties to the action in which a litigated or consent judgment or order was entered, or of members of a class represented or sought to be represented in such action, or of members of a group on whose behalf relief was sought in such action by the Federal Government;

(C) prevent challenges to a litigated or consent judgment or order on the ground that such judgment or order was obtained through collusion or fraud, or is transparently invalid or was entered by a court lacking subject matter jurisdiction; or

(D) authorize or permit the denial to any person of the due process of law required by the Constitution.

(3) Any action not precluded under this subsection that challenges an employment consent judgment or order described in paragraph (1) shall be brought in the court, and if possible before the judge, that entered such judgment or order. Nothing in this subsection shall preclude a transfer of such action pursuant to section 1404 of title 28, United States Code.

OTHER UNLAWFUL EMPLOYMENT PRACTICES

SEC. 2000e-3. *[Section 704].*

(a) It shall be an unlawful employment practice for an employer to discriminate against any of his employees or applicants for employment, for an employment agency, or joint labor management committee controlling apprenticeship or other training or retraining, including on the job training programs, to discriminate against any individual, or for a labor organization to discriminate against any member thereof or applicant for membership, because he has opposed any practice made an unlawful employment practice by this subchapter, or because he has made a charge, testified, assisted, or participated in any manner in an investigation, proceeding, or hearing under this subchapter.

(b) It shall be an unlawful employment practice for an employer, labor organization, employment agency, or joint labor management committee controlling apprenticeship or other training or retraining, including on the job training programs, to print or publish or cause to be printed or published any notice or advertisement relating to employment by such an employer or membership in or any classification or referral for employment by such a labor organization, or relating to any classification or referral for employment by such an employment agency, or relating to admission to, or employment in, any program established to provide apprenticeship or other training by such a joint labor management committee, indicating any preference, limitation, specification, or discrimination, based on race, color, religion, sex, or national origin, except that such a notice or advertisement may indicate a preference, limitation, specification, or discrimination based on religion, sex, or national origin when religion, sex, or national origin is a bona fide occupational qualification for employment.

EQUAL EMPLOYMENT OPPORTUNITY COMMISSION

SEC. 2000e-4. *[Section 705].*

(a) There is hereby created a Commission to be known as the Equal Employment Opportunity Commission, which shall be composed of five members, not more than three of whom shall be members of the same political party. Members of the Commission shall be appointed by the President by and with the advice and consent of the Senate for a term of five years. Any individual chosen to fill a vacancy shall be appointed only for the unexpired term of the member whom he shall succeed, and all members of the Commission shall continue to serve until their successors are appointed and qualified, except that no such member of the Commission shall continue to serve (1) for more than sixty days when the Congress is in session unless a nomination to fill such vacancy shall have been submitted to the Senate, or (2) after the adjournment sine die of the session of the Senate in which such nomination was submitted. The President shall designate one member to serve as Chairman of the Commission, and one member to serve as Vice Chairman. The Chairman shall be responsible on behalf of the Commission for the administrative operations of the Commission, and, except as provided in subsection (b) of this section, shall appoint, in accordance with the provisions of title 5 *[United States Code]* governing appointments in the competitive service, such officers, agents, attorneys, administrative law judges *[hearing examiners],* and employees as he deems necessary to assist it in the performance of its functions and to fix their compensation in accordance with the provisions of chapter 51 and subchapter III of chapter 53 of title 5 *[United States Code],* relating to classification and General Schedule pay rates: Provided, That assignment, removal, and compensation of administrative law judges *[hearing examiners]* shall be in accordance with sections 3105, 3344, 5372, and 7521 of title 5 *[United States Code].*

(b) (1) There shall be a General Counsel of the Commission appointed by the President, by and with the advice and consent of the Senate, for a term of four years. The General Counsel shall have responsibility for the conduct of litigation as provided in sections 2000e-5 and 2000e-6 of this title *[sections 706 and 707].* The General Counsel shall have such other duties as the Commission may prescribe or as may be provided by law and shall concur with the Chairman of the Commission on the appointment and supervision of regional attorneys. The General Counsel of the Commission on the effective date of this Act shall continue in such position and perform the functions specified in this subsection until a successor is appointed and qualified.

(2) Attorneys appointed under this section may, at the direction of the Commission, appear for and represent the Commission in any case in court, provided that the Attorney General shall conduct all litigation to which the Commission is a party in the Supreme Court pursuant to this subchapter.

(c) A vacancy in the Commission shall not impair the right of the remaining members to exercise all the powers of the Commission and three members thereof shall constitute a quorum.

(d) The Commission shall have an official seal which shall be judicially noticed.

(e) The Commission shall at the close of each fiscal year report to the Congress and to the President concerning the action it has taken *[the names, salaries, and duties of all individuals in its employ]* and the moneys it has disbursed. It shall make such further reports on the cause of and means of eliminating discrimination and such recommendations for further legislation as may appear desirable.

(f) The principal office of the Commission shall be in or near the District of Columbia, but it may meet or exercise any or all its powers at any other place. The Commission may establish such regional or State offices as it deems necessary to accomplish the purpose of this subchapter.

(g) The Commission shall have power-

(1) to cooperate with and, with their consent, utilize regional, State, local, and other agencies, both public and private, and individuals;

(2) to pay to witnesses whose depositions are taken or who are summoned before the Commission or any of its agents the same witness and mileage fees as are paid to witnesses in the courts of the United States;

(3) to furnish to persons subject to this subchapter such technical assistance as they may request to further their compliance with this subchapter or an order issued thereunder;

(4) upon the request of (i) any employer, whose employees or some of them, or (ii) any labor organization, whose members or some of them, refuse or threaten to refuse to cooperate in effectuating the provisions of this subchapter, to assist in such effectuation by conciliation or such other remedial action as is provided by this subchapter;

(5) to make such technical studies as are appropriate to effectuate the purposes and policies of this subchapter and to make the results of such studies available to the public;

(6) to intervene in a civil action brought under section 2000e-5 of this title *[section 706]* by an aggrieved party against a respondent other than a government, governmental agency or political subdivision.

(h) (1) The Commission shall, in any of its educational or promotional activities, cooperate with other departments and agencies in the performance of such educational and promotional activities.

(2) In exercising its powers under this title, the Commission shall carry out educational and outreach activities (including dissemination of information in languages other than English) targeted to-

(A) individuals who historically have been victims of employment discrimination and have not been equitably served by the Commission; and

(B) individuals on whose behalf the Commission has authority to enforce any other law prohibiting employment discrimination, concerning rights and obligations under this title or such law, as the case may be.

(i) All officers, agents, attorneys, and employees of the Commission shall be subject to the provisions of section 7324 of title 5 *[section 9 of the Act of August 2, 1939, as amended (the Hatch Act)],* notwithstanding any exemption contained in such section.

(j) (1) The Commission shall establish a Technical Assistance Training Institute, through which the Commission shall provide technical assistance and training regarding the laws and regulations enforced by the Commission.

(2) An employer or other entity covered under this title shall not be excused from compliance with the requirements of this title because of any failure to receive technical assistance under this subsection.

(3) There are authorized to be appropriated to carry out this subsection such sums as may be necessary for fiscal year 1992.

ENFORCEMENT PROVISIONS

SEC. 2000e-5. *[Section 706].*

(a) The Commission is empowered, as hereinafter provided, to prevent any person from engaging in any unlawful employment practice as set forth in section 2000e-2 or 2000e-3 of this title *[section 703 or 704].*

(b) Whenever a charge is filed by or on behalf of a person claiming to be aggrieved, or by a member of the Commission, alleging that an employer, employment agency, labor organization, or joint labor management committee controlling apprenticeship or other training or retraining, including on the job training programs, has engaged in an unlawful employment practice, the Commission shall serve a notice of the charge (including the date, place and circumstances of the alleged unlawful employment practice) on such employer, employment agency, labor organization, or joint labor management committee (hereinafter referred to as the "respondent") within ten days, and shall make an investigation thereof. Charges shall be in writing under oath or affirmation and shall contain such information and be in such form as the Commission requires. Charges shall not be made public by the Commission. If the Commission determines after such investigation that there is not reasonable cause to believe that the charge is true, it shall dismiss the charge and promptly notify the person claiming to be aggrieved and the respondent of its action. In determining whether reasonable cause exists, the Commission shall accord substantial weight to final findings and orders made by State or local authorities in proceedings commenced under State or local law pursuant to the requirements of subsections (c) and (d) of this section. If the Commission determines after such investigation that there is reasonable cause to believe that the charge is true, the Commission shall endeavor to eliminate any such alleged unlawful employment practice by informal methods of conference, conciliation, and persuasion. Nothing said or done during and as a part of such informal endeavors may be made public by the Commission, its officers or employees, or used as evidence in a subsequent proceeding without the written consent of the persons concerned. Any person who makes public information in violation of this subsection shall be fined not more than $1,000 or imprisoned for not more than one year, or both. The Commission shall make its determination on reasonable cause as promptly as possible and, so far as practicable, not later than one hundred and twenty days from the filing of the charge or, where applicable under subsection (c) or (d) of this section, from the date upon which the Commission is authorized to take action with respect to the charge.

(c) In the case of an alleged unlawful employment practice occurring in a State, or political subdivision of a State, which has a State or local law prohibiting the unlawful employment practice alleged and establishing or authorizing a State or local authority to grant or seek relief from such practice or to institute criminal proceedings with respect thereto upon receiving notice thereof, no charge may be filed under subsection (a) of this section by the person aggrieved before the expiration of sixty days after proceedings have been commenced under the State or local law, unless such proceedings have been earlier terminated, provided that such sixty day period shall be extended to one hundred and twenty days during the first year after the effective date of such State or local law. If any requirement for the commencement of such proceedings is imposed by a State or local authority other than a requirement of the filing of a written and signed statement of the facts upon which the proceeding is based, the proceeding shall be deemed to have been commenced for the purposes of this subsection at the time such statement is sent by registered mail to the appropriate State or local authority.

(d) In the case of any charge filed by a member of the Commission alleging an unlawful employment practice occurring in a State or political subdivision of a State which has a State or local law prohibiting the practice alleged and establishing or authorizing a State or local authority to grant or seek relief from such practice or to institute criminal proceedings with respect thereto upon receiving notice thereof, the Commission shall, before taking any action with respect to such charge, notify the appropriate State or local officials and, upon request, afford them a reasonable time, but not less than sixty days (provided that such sixty day period shall be extended to one hundred and twenty days during the first year after the effective day of such State or local law), unless a shorter period is requested, to act under such State or local law to remedy the practice alleged.

(e) (1) A charge under this section shall be filed within one hundred and eighty days after the alleged unlawful employment practice occurred and notice of the charge (including the date, place and circumstances of the alleged unlawful employment practice) shall be served upon the person against whom such charge is made within ten days thereafter, except that in a case of an unlawful employment practice with respect to which the person aggrieved has initially instituted proceedings with a State or local agency with authority to grant or seek relief from such practice or to institute criminal proceedings with respect thereto upon receiving notice thereof, such charge shall be filed by or on behalf of the person aggrieved within three hundred days after the alleged unlawful employment practice occurred, or within thirty days after receiving notice that the State or local agency has terminated the proceedings under the State or local law, whichever is earlier, and a copy of such charge shall be filed by the Commission with the State or local agency.

(2) For purposes of this section, an unlawful employment practice occurs, with respect to a seniority system that has been adopted for an intentionally discriminatory purpose in violation of this title (whether or not that discriminatory purpose is apparent on the face of the seniority provision), when the seniority system is adopted, when an individual becomes subject to the seniority system, or when a person aggrieved is injured by the application of the seniority system or provision of the system.

(f) (1) If within thirty days after a charge is filed with the Commission or within thirty days after expiration of any period of reference under subsection (c) or (d) of this section, the Commission has been unable to secure from the respondent a conciliation agreement acceptable to the Commission, the Commission may bring a civil action against any respondent not a government, governmental agency, or political subdivision named in the charge. In the case of a respondent which is a government, governmental agency, or political subdivision, if the Commission has been unable to secure from the respondent a conciliation agreement acceptable to the Commission, the Commission shall take no further action and shall refer the case to the Attorney General who may bring a civil action against such respondent in the appropriate United States district court. The person or persons aggrieved shall have the right to intervene in a civil action brought by the Commission or the Attorney General in a case involving a government, governmental agency, or political subdivision. If a charge filed with the Commission pursuant to subsection (b) of this section, is dismissed by the Commission, or if within one hundred and eighty days from the filing of such charge or the expiration of any period of reference under subsection (c) or (d) of this section, whichever is later, the Commission has not filed a civil action under this section or the Attorney General has not filed a civil action in a case involving a government, governmental agency, or political subdivision, or the Commission has not entered into a conciliation agreement to which the person aggrieved is a party, the Commission, or the Attorney General in a case involving a government, governmental agency, or political subdivision, shall so notify the person aggrieved and within ninety days after the giving of such notice a civil action may be brought against the respondent named in the charge (A) by the person claiming to be aggrieved or (B) if such charge was filed by a member of the Commission, by any person whom the charge alleges was aggrieved by the alleged unlawful employment practice. Upon application by the complainant and in such circumstances as the court may deem just, the court may appoint an attorney for such complainant and may authorize the commencement of the action without the payment of fees, costs, or security. Upon timely application, the court may, in its discretion, permit the Commission, or the Attorney General in a case involving a government, governmental agency, or political subdivision, to intervene in such civil action upon certification that the case is of general public importance. Upon request, the court may, in its discretion, stay further proceedings for not more than sixty days pending the termination of State or local proceedings described in subsection (c) or (d) of this section or further efforts of the Commission to obtain voluntary compliance.

(2) Whenever a charge is filed with the Commission and the Commission concludes on the basis of a preliminary investigation that prompt judicial action is necessary to carry out the purposes of this Act, the Commission, or the Attorney General in a case involving a government, governmental agency, or political subdivision, may bring an action for appropriate temporary or preliminary relief pending final disposition of such charge. Any temporary restraining order or other order granting preliminary or temporary relief shall be issued in accordance with rule 65 of the Federal Rules of Civil Procedure. It shall be the duty of a court having jurisdiction over proceedings under this section to assign cases for hearing at the earliest practicable date and to cause such cases to be in every way expedited.

(3) Each United States district court and each United States court of a place subject to the jurisdiction of the United States shall have jurisdiction of actions brought under this subchapter. Such an action may be brought in any judicial district in the State in which the unlawful employment practice is alleged to have been committed, in the judicial district in

which the employment records relevant to such practice are maintained and administered, or in the judicial district in which the aggrieved person would have worked but for the alleged unlawful employment practice, but if the respondent is not found within any such district, such an action may be brought within the judicial district in which the respondent has his principal office. For purposes of sections 1404 and 1406 of title 28 *[of the United States Code]*, the judicial district in which the respondent has his principal office shall in all cases be considered a district in which the action might have been brought.

(4) It shall be the duty of the chief judge of the district (or in his absence, the acting chief judge) in which the case is pending immediately to designate a judge in such district to hear and determine the case. In the event that no judge in the district is available to hear and determine the case, the chief judge of the district, or the acting chief judge, as the case may be, shall certify this fact to the chief judge of the circuit (or in his absence, the acting chief judge) who shall then designate a district or circuit judge of the circuit to hear and determine the case.

(5) It shall be the duty of the judge designated pursuant to this subsection to assign the case for hearing at the earliest practicable date and to cause the case to be in every way expedited. If such judge has not scheduled the case for trial within one hundred and twenty days after issue has been joined, that judge may appoint a master pursuant to rule 53 of the Federal Rules of Civil Procedure.

(g) (1) If the court finds that the respondent has intentionally engaged in or is intentionally engaging in an unlawful employment practice charged in the complaint, the court may enjoin the respondent from engaging in such unlawful employment practice, and order such affirmative action as may be appropriate, which may include, but is not limited to, reinstatement or hiring of employees, with or without back pay (payable by the employer, employment agency, or labor organization, as the case may be, responsible for the unlawful employment practice), or any other equitable relief as the court deems appropriate. Back pay liability shall not accrue from a date more than two years prior to the filing of a charge with the Commission. Interim earnings or amounts earnable with reasonable diligence by the person or persons discriminated against shall operate to reduce the back pay otherwise allowable.

(2) (A) No order of the court shall require the admission or reinstatement of an individual as a member of a union, or the hiring, reinstatement, or promotion of an individual as an employee, or the payment to him of any back pay, if such individual was refused admission, suspended, or expelled, or was refused employment or advancement or was suspended or discharged for any reason other than discrimination on account of race, color, religion, sex, or national origin or in violation of section 2000e-3(a) of this title *[section 704(a)]*.

(B) On a claim in which an individual proves a violation under section 2000e-2(m) of this title *[section 703(m)]* and a respondent demonstrates that the respondent would have taken the same action in the absence of the impermissible motivating factor, the court-

(i) may grant declaratory relief, injunctive relief (except as provided in clause (ii)), and attorney's fees and costs demonstrated to be directly attributable only to the pursuit of a claim under section 2000e-2(m) of this title *[section 703(m)]*; and

(ii) shall not award damages or issue an order requiring any admission, reinstatement, hiring, promotion, or payment, described in subparagraph (A).

(h) The provisions of chapter 6 of title 29 *[the Act entitled "An Act to amend the Judicial Code and to define and limit the jurisdiction of courts sitting in equity, and for other purposes," approved March 23, 1932 (29 U.S.C. 105-115)]* shall not apply with respect to civil actions brought under this section.

(i) In any case in which an employer, employment agency, or labor organization fails to comply with an order of a court issued in a civil action brought under this section, the Commission may commence proceedings to compel compliance with such order.

(j) Any civil action brought under this section and any proceedings brought under subsection (i) of this section shall be subject to appeal as provided in sections 1291 and 1292, title 28 *[United States Code]*.
(k) In any action or proceeding under this subchapter the court, in its discretion, may allow the prevailing party, other than the Commission or the United States, a reasonable attorney's fee **(including expert fees)** as part of the costs, and the Commission and the United States shall be liable for costs the same as a private person.

CIVIL ACTIONS BY THE ATTORNEY GENERAL

SEC. 2000e-6. *[Section 707].*

(a) Whenever the Attorney General has reasonable cause to believe that any person or group of persons is engaged in a pattern or practice of resistance to the full enjoyment of any of the rights secured by this subchapter, and that the pattern or practice is of such a nature and is intended to deny the full exercise of the rights herein described, the Attorney General may bring a civil action in the appropriate district court of the United States by filing with it a complaint (1) signed by him (or in his absence the Acting Attorney General), (2) setting forth facts pertaining to such pattern or practice, and (3) requesting such relief, including an application for a permanent or temporary injunction, restraining order or other order against the person or persons responsible for such pattern or practice, as he deems necessary to insure the full enjoyment of the rights herein described.
(b) The district courts of the United States shall have and shall exercise jurisdiction of proceedings instituted pursuant to this section, and in any such proceeding the Attorney General may file with the clerk of such court a request that a court of three judges be convened to hear and determine the case. Such request by the Attorney General shall be accompanied by a certificate that, in his opinion, the case is of general public importance. A copy of the certificate and request for a three judge court shall be immediately furnished by such clerk to the chief judge of the circuit (or in his absence, the presiding circuit judge of the circuit) in which the case is pending. Upon receipt of such request it shall be the duty of the chief judge of the circuit or the presiding circuit judge, as the case may be, to designate immediately three judges in such circuit, of whom at least one shall be a circuit judge and another of whom shall be a district judge of the court in which the proceeding was instituted, to hear and determine such case, and it shall be the duty of the judges so designated to assign the case for hearing at the earliest practicable date, to participate in the hearing and determination thereof, and to cause the case to be in every way expedited. An appeal from the final judgment of such court will lie to the Supreme Court.

In the event the Attorney General fails to file such a request in any such proceeding, it shall be the duty of the chief judge of the district (or in his absence, the acting chief judge) in which the case is pending immediately to designate a judge in such district to hear and determine the case. In the event that no judge in the district is available to hear and determine the case, the chief judge of the district, or the acting chief judge, as the case may be, shall certify this fact to the chief judge of the circuit (or in his absence, the acting chief judge) who shall then designate a district or circuit judge of the circuit to hear and determine the case.

It shall be the duty of the judge designated pursuant to this section to assign the case for hearing at the earliest practicable date and to cause the case to be in every way expedited.
(c) Effective two years after March 24, 1972 *[the date of enactment of the Equal Employment Opportunity Act of 1972]*, the functions of the Attorney General under this section shall be transferred to the Commission, together with such personnel, property, records, and unexpended balances of appropriations, allocations, and other funds employed, used, held, available, or to be made available in connection with such functions unless the President submits, and neither House of Congress vetoes, a reorganization plan pursuant to chapter 9 of title 5 *[United States Code]*, inconsistent with the provisions of this subsection. The Commission shall carry out such functions in accordance with subsections (d) and (e) of this section.
(d) Upon the transfer of functions provided for in subsection (c) of this section, in all suits commenced pursuant to this section prior to the date of such transfer, proceedings shall continue

without abatement, all court orders and decrees shall remain in effect, and the Commission shall be substituted as a party for the United States of America, the Attorney General, or the Acting Attorney General, as appropriate.
(e) Subsequent to March 24, 1972 *[the date of enactment of the Equal Employment Opportunity Act of 1972],* the Commission shall have authority to investigate and act on a charge of a pattern or practice of discrimination, whether filed by or on behalf of a person claiming to be aggrieved or by a member of the Commission. All such actions shall be conducted in accordance with the procedures set forth in section 2000e-5 of this title *[section 706].*

EFFECT ON STATE LAWS

SEC. 2000e-7. *[Section 708].*

Nothing in this subchapter shall be deemed to exempt or relieve any person from any liability, duty, penalty, or punishment provided by any present or future law of any State or political subdivision of a State, other than any such law which purports to require or permit the doing of any act which would be an unlawful employment practice under this subchapter.

INVESTIGATIONS, INSPECTIONS, RECORDS, STATE AGENCIES

SEC. 2000e-8. *[Section 709].*

(a) In connection with any investigation of a charge filed under section 2000e-5 of this title *[section 706],* the Commission or its designated representative shall at all reasonable times have access to, for the purposes of examination, and the right to copy any evidence of any person being investigated or proceeded against that relates to unlawful employment practices covered by this subchapter and is relevant to the charge under investigation.
(b) The Commission may cooperate with State and local agencies charged with the administration of State fair employment practices laws and, with the consent of such agencies, may, for the purpose of carrying out its functions and duties under this subchapter and within the limitation of funds appropriated specifically for such purpose, engage in and contribute to the cost of research and other projects of mutual interest undertaken by such agencies, and utilize the services of such agencies and their employees, and, notwithstanding any other provision of law, pay by advance or reimbursement such agencies and their employees for services rendered to assist the Commission in carrying out this subchapter. In furtherance of such cooperative efforts, the Commission may enter into written agreements with such State or local agencies and such agreements may include provisions under which the Commission shall refrain from processing a charge in any cases or class of cases specified in such agreements or under which the Commission shall relieve any person or class of persons in such State or locality from requirements imposed under this section. The Commission shall rescind any such agreement whenever it determines that the agreement no longer serves the interest of effective enforcement of this subchapter.
(c) Every employer, employment agency, and labor organization subject to this subchapter shall (1) make and keep such records relevant to the determinations of whether unlawful employment practices have been or are being committed, (2) preserve such records for such periods, and (3) make such reports therefrom as the Commission shall prescribe by regulation or order, after public hearing, as reasonable, necessary, or appropriate for the enforcement of this subchapter or the regulations or orders thereunder. The Commission shall, by regulation, require each employer, labor organization, and joint labor management committee subject to this subchapter which controls an apprenticeship or other training program to maintain such records as are reasonably necessary to carry out the purposes of this subchapter, including, but not limited to, a list of applicants who wish to participate in such program, including the chronological order in which applications were received, and to furnish to the Commission upon request, a detailed description of the manner in which persons are selected to participate in the apprenticeship or other training program. Any employer, employment agency, labor organization, or joint labor management committee which believes that the application to it of any regulation or order issued under this section would result in undue hardship may apply to the Commission for an exemption from the application of such regulation or order, and, if such application for

an exemption is denied, bring a civil action in the United States district court for the district where such records are kept. If the Commission or the court, as the case may be, finds that the application of the regulation or order to the employer, employment agency, or labor organization in question would impose an undue hardship, the Commission or the court, as the case may be, may grant appropriate relief. If any person required to comply with the provisions of this subsection fails or refuses to do so, the United States district court for the district in which such person is found, resides, or transacts business, shall, upon application of the Commission, or the Attorney General in a case involving a government, governmental agency or political subdivision, have jurisdiction to issue to such person an order requiring him to comply.
(d) In prescribing requirements pursuant to subsection (c) of this section, the Commission shall consult with other interested State and Federal agencies and shall endeavor to coordinate its requirements with those adopted by such agencies. The Commission shall furnish upon request and without cost to any State or local agency charged with the administration of a fair employment practice law information obtained pursuant to subsection (c) of this section from any employer, employment agency, labor organization, or joint labor management committee subject to the jurisdiction of such agency. Such information shall be furnished on condition that it not be made public by the recipient agency prior to the institution of a proceeding under State or local law involving such information. If this condition is violated by a recipient agency, the Commission may decline to honor subsequent requests pursuant to this subsection.
(e) It shall be unlawful for any officer or employee of the Commission to make public in any manner whatever any information obtained by the Commission pursuant to its authority under this section prior to the institution of any proceeding under this subchapter involving such information. Any officer or employee of the Commission who shall make public in any manner whatever any information in violation of this subsection shall be guilty, of a misdemeanor and upon conviction thereof, shall be fined not more than $1,000, or imprisoned not more than one year.

INVESTIGATORY POWERS

SEC. 2000e-9. *[Section 710].* For the purpose of all hearings and investigations conducted by the Commission or its duly authorized agents or agencies, section 161 of title 29 *[section 11 of the National Labor Relations Act]* shall apply.

POSTING OF NOTICES; PENALTIES

SEC. 2000e-10. *[Section 711].*
(a) Every employer, employment agency, and labor organization, as the case may be, shall post and keep posted in conspicuous places upon its premises where notices to employees, applicants for employment, and members are customarily posted a notice to be prepared or approved by the Commission setting forth excerpts, from or, summaries of, the pertinent provisions of this subchapter and information pertinent to the filing of a complaint.
(b) A willful violation of this section shall be punishable by a fine of not more than $100 for each separate offense.

VETERANS' SPECIAL RIGHTS OR PREFERENCE

SEC. 2000e-11. *[Section 712].* Nothing contained in this subchapter shall be construed to repeal or modify any Federal, State, territorial, or local law creating special rights or preference for veterans.

RULES AND REGULATIONS

SEC. 2000e-12. *[Section 713].*
(a) The Commission shall have authority from time to time to issue, amend, or rescind suitable procedural regulations to carry out the provisions of this subchapter. Regulations issued under this section shall be in conformity with the standards and limitations of subchapter II of chapter 5 of title 5 *[the Administrative Procedure Act]*.

(b) In any action or proceeding based on any alleged unlawful employment practice, no person shall be subject to any liability or punishment for or on account of (1) the commission by such person of an unlawful employment practice if he pleads and proves that the act or omission complained of was in good faith, in conformity with, and in reliance on any written interpretation or opinion of the Commission, or (2) the failure of such person to publish and file any information required by any provision of this subchapter if he pleads and proves that he failed to publish and file such information in good faith, in conformity with the instructions of the Commission issued under this subchapter regarding the filing of such information. Such a defense, if established, shall be a bar to the action or proceeding, notwithstanding that (A) after such act or omission, such interpretation or opinion is modified or rescinded or is determined by judicial authority to be invalid or of no legal effect, or (B) after publishing or filing the description and annual reports, such publication or filing is determined by judicial authority not to be in conformity with the requirements of this subchapter.

FORCIBLY RESISTING THE COMMISSION OR ITS REPRESENTATIVES

SEC. 2000e-13. *[Section 714].* The provisions of sections 111 and 1114, title 18 *[United States Code],* shall apply to officers, agents, and employees of the Commission in the performance of their official duties. Notwithstanding the provisions of sections 111 and 1114 of title 18 *[United States Code],* whoever in violation of the provisions of section 1114 of such title kills a person while engaged in or on account of the performance of his official functions under this Act shall be punished by imprisonment for any term of years or for life.

TRANSFER OF AUTHORITY

[Administration of the duties of the Equal Employment Opportunity Coordinating Council was transferred to the Equal Employment Opportunity Commission effective July 1, 1978, under the President's Reorganization Plan of 1978.]

EQUAL EMPLOYMENT OPPORTUNITY COORDINATING COUNCIL

SEC. 2000e-14. *[Section 715].* *[There shall be established an Equal Employment Opportunity Coordinating Council (hereinafter referred to in this section as the Council) composed of the Secretary of Labor, the Chairman of the Equal Employment Opportunity Commission, the Attorney General, the Chairman of the United States Civil Service Commission, and the Chairman of the United States Civil Rights Commission, or their respective delegates.]*

The Equal Employment Opportunity Commission *[Council]* shall have the responsibility for developing and implementing agreements, policies and practices designed to maximize effort, promote efficiency, and eliminate conflict, competition, duplication and inconsistency among the operations, functions and jurisdictions of the various departments, agencies and branches of the Federal Government responsible for the implementation and enforcement of equal employment opportunity legislation, orders, and policies. On or before October 1 *[July 1]* of each year, the Equal Employment Opportunity Commission *[Council]* shall transmit to the President and to the Congress a report of its activities, together with such recommendations for legislative or administrative changes as it concludes are desirable to further promote the purposes of this section.

EFFECTIVE DATE

SEC. 2000e-15. *[Section 716].*

[(a) This title shall become effective one year after the date of its enactment.

(b) Notwithstanding subsection (a), sections of this title other than sections 703, 704, 706, and 707 shall become effective immediately.

(c)] The President shall, as soon as feasible after July 2, 1964 *[the enactment of this title]*, convene one or more conferences for the purpose of enabling the leaders of groups whose members will be affected by this subchapter to become familiar with the rights afforded and obligations imposed by its provisions, and for the purpose of making plans which will result in the fair and effective administration of this subchapter when all of its provisions become effective. The President shall invite the participation in such conference or conferences of (1) the members of the President's Committee on Equal Employment Opportunity, (2) the members of the Commission on Civil Rights, (3) representatives of State and local agencies engaged in furthering equal employment opportunity, (4) representatives of private agencies engaged in furthering equal employment opportunity, and (5) representatives of employers, labor organizations, and employment agencies who will be subject to this subchapter.

TRANSFER OF AUTHORITY

[Enforcement of Section 717 was transferred to the Equal Employment Opportunity Commission from the Civil Service Commission (Office of Personnel Management) effective January 1, 1979 under the President's Reorganization Plan No. 1 of 1978.]

EMPLOYMENT BY FEDERAL GOVERNMENT

SEC. 2000e-16. *[Section 717].*

(a) All personnel actions affecting employees or applicants for employment (except with regard to aliens employed outside the limits of the United States) in military departments as defined in section 102 of title 5 *[United States Code]*, in executive agencies *[other than the General Accounting Office]* as defined in section 105 of title 5 *[United States Code]* (including employees and applicants for employment who are paid from nonappropriated funds), in the United States Postal Service and the Postal Rate Commission, in those units of the Government of the District of Columbia having positions in the competitive service, and in those units of the legislative and judicial branches of the Federal Government having positions in the competitive service, and in the Library of Congress shall be made free from any discrimination based on race, color, religion, sex, or national origin.

(b) Except as otherwise provided in this subsection, the Equal Employment Opportunity Commission *[Civil Service Commission]* shall have authority to enforce the provisions of subsection (a) of this section through appropriate remedies, including reinstatement or hiring of employees with or without back pay, as will effectuate the policies of this section, and shall issue such rules, regulations, orders and instructions as it deems necessary and appropriate to carry out its responsibilities under this section. The Equal Employment Opportunity Commission *[Civil Service Commission]* shall-

(1) be responsible for the annual review and approval of a national and regional equal employment opportunity plan which each department and agency and each appropriate unit referred to in subsection (a) of this section shall submit in order to maintain an affirmative program of equal employment opportunity for all such employees and applicants for employment;

(2) be responsible for the review and evaluation of the operation of all agency equal employment opportunity programs, periodically obtaining and publishing (on at least a semiannual basis) progress reports from each such department, agency, or unit; and

(3) consult with and solicit the recommendations of interested individuals, groups, and organizations relating to equal employment opportunity.

The head of each such department, agency, or unit shall comply with such rules, regulations, orders, and instructions which shall include a provision that an employee or applicant for employment shall be notified of any final action taken on any complaint of discrimination filed by him thereunder. The plan submitted by each department, agency, and unit shall include, but not be limited to-

(1) provision for the establishment of training and education programs designed to provide a maximum opportunity for employees to advance so as to perform at their highest potential; and

(2) a description of the qualifications in terms of training and experience relating to equal employment opportunity for the principal and operating officials of each such department, agency, or unit responsible for carrying out the equal employment opportunity program and of the allocation of personnel and resources proposed by such department, agency, or unit to carry out its equal employment opportunity program.

With respect to employment in the Library of Congress, authorities granted in this subsection to the Equal Employment Opportunity Commission *[Civil Service Commission]* shall be exercised by the Librarian of Congress.

(c) Within **90 days** of receipt of notice of final action taken by a department, agency, or unit referred to in subsection (a) of this section, or by the Equal Employment Opportunity Commission *[Civil Service Commission]* upon an appeal from a decision or order of such department, agency, or unit on a complaint of discrimination based on race, color, religion, sex or national origin, brought pursuant to subsection (a) of this section, Executive Order 11478 or any succeeding Executive orders, or after one hundred and eighty days from the filing of the initial charge with the department, agency, or unit or with the Equal Employment Opportunity Commission *[Civil Service Commission]* on appeal from a decision or order of such department, agency, or unit until such time as final action may be taken by a department, agency, or unit, an employee or applicant for employment, if aggrieved by the final disposition of his complaint, or by the failure to take final action on his complaint, may file a civil action as provided in section 2000e-5 of this title *[section 706],* in which civil action the head of the department, agency, or unit, as appropriate, shall be the defendant.

(d) The provisions of section 2000e-5(f) through (k) of this title *[section 706(f) through (k)],* as applicable, shall govern civil actions brought hereunder, **and the same interest to compensate for delay in payment shall be available as in cases involving nonpublic parties.**

(e) Nothing contained in this Act shall relieve any Government agency or official of its or his primary responsibility to assure nondiscrimination in employment as required by the Constitution and statutes or of its or his responsibilities under Executive Order 11478 relating to equal employment opportunity in the Federal Government.

SPECIAL PROVISIONS WITH RESPECT TO DENIAL, TERMINATION, AND SUSPENSION OF GOVERNMENT CONTRACTS

SEC. 2000e-17. *[Section 718].* No Government contract, or portion thereof, with any employer, shall be denied, withheld, terminated, or suspended, by any agency or officer of the United States under any equal employment opportunity law or order, where such employer has an affirmative action plan which has previously been accepted by the Government for the same facility within the past twelve months without first according such employer full hearing and adjudication under the provisions of section 554 of title 5 *[United States Code],* and the following pertinent sections: Provided, That if such employer has deviated substantially from such previously agreed to affirmative action plan, this section shall not apply: Provided further, That for the purposes of this section an affirmative action plan shall be deemed to have been accepted by the Government at the time the appropriate compliance agency has accepted such plan unless within forty five days thereafter the Office of Federal Contract Compliance has disapproved such plan.

APPENDIX D

THE CIVIL RIGHTS ACT OF 1991

The U.S. Equal Employment Opportunity Commission

Title I—Federal Civil Rights Remedies

PROHIBITION AGAINST ALL RACIAL DISCRIMINATION IN THE MAKING AND ENFORCEMENT OF CONTRACTS

SEC. 101. Section 1977 of the Revised Statutes (42 U.S.C. 1981) is amended-

(1) by inserting "(a)" before "All persons within"; and

(2) by adding at the end the following new subsections:

"(b) For purposes of this section, the term 'make and enforce contracts' includes the making, performance, modification, and termination of contracts, and the enjoyment of all benefits, privileges, terms, and conditions of the contractual relationship.

"(c) The rights protected by this section are protected against impairment by nongovernmental discrimination and impairment under color of State law."

DAMAGES IN CASES OF INTENTIONAL DISCRIMINATION

SEC. 102. The Revised Statutes are amended by inserting after section 1977 (42 U.S.C. 1981) the following new section:

"SEC. 1977A. DAMAGES IN CASES OF INTENTIONAL DISCRIMINATION IN EMPLOYMENT. *[42 U.S.C. 1981a]*

"(a) Right of Recovery. -

"(1) Civil Rights. - In an action brought by a complaining party under section 706 or 717 of the Civil Rights Act of 1964 (42 U.S.C. 2000e-5) against a respondent who engaged in unlawful intentional discrimination (not an employment practice that is unlawful because of its disparate impact) prohibited under section 703, 704, or 717 of the Act (42 U.S.C. 2000e-2 or 2000e-3), and provided that the complaining party cannot recover under section 1977 of the Revised Statutes (42 U.S.C. 1981), the complaining party may recover compensatory and punitive damages as allowed in subsection (b), in addition to any relief authorized by section 706(g) of the Civil Rights Act of 1964, from the respondent.

"(2) Disability. - In an action brought by a complaining party under the powers, remedies, and procedures set forth in section 706 or 717 of the Civil Rights Act of 1964 (as provided in section 107(a) of the Americans with Disabilities Act of 1990 (42 U.S.C. 12117 (a)), and section 505(a)(1) of the Rehabilitation Act of 1973 (29 U.S.C. 794a(a)(1)), respectively) against a respondent who engaged in unlawful intentional discrimination (not an employment practice that is unlawful because of its disparate impact) under section 501 of the Rehabilitation Act of 1973 (29 U.S.C. 791) and the regulations implementing section 501, or who violated the requirements of section 501 of the Act or the regulations implementing section 501 concerning the provision of a reasonable accommodation, or section 102 of the Americans with Disabilities Act of 1990 (42 U.S.C. 12112), or committed a violation of section 102(b)(5) of the Act, against an individual, the complaining party may recover compensatory and punitive damages as allowed in subsection (b), in addition to any relief authorized by section 706(g) of the Civil Rights Act of 1964, from the respondent.

"(3) Reasonable Accommodation and Good Faith Effort. - In cases where a discriminatory practice involves the provision of a reasonable accommodation pursuant to section 102(b)(5) of the Americans with Disabilities Act of 1990 or regulations implementing section 501 of the Rehabilitation Act of 1973, damages may not be awarded under this section where the covered entity demonstrates good faith efforts, in consultation with the person with the disability who has informed the covered entity that accommodation is needed, to identify and make a reasonable accommodation that would provide such individual with an equally effective opportunity and would not cause an undue hardship on the operation of the business.

"(b) Compensatory and Punitive Damages. -

"(1) Determination of punitive damages. - A complaining party may recover punitive damages under this section against a respondent (other than a government, government agency or political subdivision) if the complaining party demonstrates that the respondent engaged in a discriminatory practice or discriminatory practices with malice or with reckless indifference to the federally protected rights of an aggrieved individual.

"(2) Exclusions from compensatory damages. - Compensatory damages awarded under this section shall not include back pay, interest on back pay, or any other type of relief authorized under section 706(g) of the Civil Rights Act of 1964.

"(3) Limitations. - The sum of the amount of compensatory damages awarded under this section for future pecuniary losses, emotional pain, suffering, inconvenience, mental anguish, loss of enjoyment of life, and other nonpecuniary losses, and the amount of punitive damages awarded under this section, shall not exceed, for each complaining party -

"(A) in the case of a respondent who has more than 14 and fewer than 101 employees in each of 20 or more calendar weeks in the current or preceding calendar year, $50,000;

"(B) in the case of a respondent who has more than 100 and fewer than 201 employees in each of 20 or more calendar weeks in the current or preceding calendar year, $100,000; and

"(C) in the case of a respondent who has more than 200 and fewer than 501 employees in each of 20 or more calendar weeks in the current or preceding calendar year, $200,000; and

"(D) in the case of a respondent who has more than 500 employees in each of 20 or more calendar weeks in the current or preceding calendar year, $300,000.

"(4) Construction. - Nothing in this section shall be construed to limit the scope of, or the relief available under, section 1977 of the Revised Statutes (42 U.S.C. 1981).

"(c) Jury Trial. - If a complaining party seeks compensatory or punitive damages under this section -

"(1) any party may demand a trial by jury; and

"(2) the court shall not inform the jury of the limitations described in subsection (b)(3).

"(d) Definitions. - As used in this section:

"(1) Complaining party. - The term 'complaining party' means -

"(A) in the case of a person seeking to bring an action under subsection (a)(1), the Equal Employment Opportunity Commission, the Attorney General, or a person who may bring an action or proceeding under title VII of the Civil Rights Act of 1964 (42 U.S.C. 2000e et seq.); or

"(B) in the case of a person seeking to bring an action under subsection (a)(2), the Equal Employment Opportunity Commission, the Attorney General, a person who may bring an action or proceeding under section 505(a)(1) of the Rehabilitation Act of 1973 (29 U.S.C. 794a(a)(1)), or a person who may bring an action or proceeding under title I of the Americans with Disabilities Act of 1990 (42 U.S.C. 12101 et seq.).

"(2) Discriminatory practice. - The term 'discriminatory practice' means the discrimination described in paragraph (1), or the discrimination or the violation described in paragraph (2), of subsection (a)."

ATTORNEY'S FEES

[This section amends section 722 of the Revised Statutes (42 U.S.C. 1988) by adding a reference to section 102 of the Civil Rights Act of 1991 to the list of civil rights actions in which reasonable attorney's fees may be awarded to the prevailing party, other than the United States.]

SEC. 103. The last sentence of section 722 of the Revised Statutes (42 U.S.C. 1988) is amended by inserting ",1977A" after "1977".

DEFINITIONS

SEC. 104. *[This section amends section 701 of the Civil Rights Act of 1964 (42 U.S.C. 2000e) by adding the following new subsections: (l) "complaining party," (m) "demonstrates," and (n) "respondent".]*

BURDEN OF PROOF IN DISPARATE IMPACT CASES

SEC. 105.

(a) *[This subsection amends section 703 of the Civil Rights Act of 1964 (42 U.S.C. 2000e-2) by adding a new subsection (k), on the burden of proof in disparate impact cases.]*

(b) No statements other than the interpretive memorandum appearing at Vol. 137 Congressional Record S 15276 (daily ed. Oct. 25, 1991) shall be considered legislative history of, or relied upon in any way as legislative history in construing or applying, any provision of this Act that relates to Wards Cove - Business necessity/cumulation/alternative business practice. *[42 U.S.C. 1981 note]*

PROHIBITION AGAINST DISCRIMINATORY USE OF TEST SCORES

SEC. 106. *[This section amends section 703 of the Civil Rights Act of 1964 (42 U.S.C. 2000e-2) by adding a new subsection (l), on the prohibition against discriminatory use of test scores.]*

CLARIFYING PROHIBITION AGAINST IMPERMISSIBLE CONSIDERATION OF RACE, COLOR, RELIGION, SEX, OR NATIONAL ORIGIN IN EMPLOYMENT PRACTICES

SEC. 107.

(a) In general. *[This subsection amends section 703 of the Civil Rights Act of 1964 (42 U.S.C. 2000e-2) by adding a new subsection (m), clarifying the prohibition against consideration of race, color, religion, sex, or national origin in employment practices.]*

(b) Enforcement provisions. *[This subsection amends section 706(g) of the Civil Rights Act of 1964 (42 U.S.C. 2000e-5(g)) by renumbering existing subsection (g), and adding at the end a new subparagraph (B) to provide a limitation on available relief in "mixed motive" cases (where the employer demonstrates it would have made the same decision in the absence of discrimination).]*

FACILITATING PROMPT AND ORDERLY RESOLUTION OF CHALLENGES TO EMPLOYMENT PRACTICES IMPLEMENTING LITIGATED OR CONSENT JUDGMENTS OR ORDERS

SEC. 108. *[This section amends section 703 of the Civil Rights Act of 1964 (42 U.S.C. 2000e-2) by adding a new subsection (n), on the resolution of challenges to employment practices implementing litigated or consent judgments or orders.]*

PROTECTION OF EXTRATERRITORIAL EMPLOYMENT

SEC. 109.

(a) Definition of Employee. *[This subsection amends the definition of "employee" in section 701(f) of the Civil Rights Act of 1964 (42 U.S.C. 2000e(f)) and section 101(4) of the Americans with Disabilities Act of 1990 (42 U.S.C. 12111(4)) by adding a sentence to the end of each definition to include U.S. citizens employed abroad within the laws' protections.]*

(b) Exemption. *[This subsection amends section 702 of the Civil Rights Act of 1964 (42 U.S.C. 2000e-1) by adding new subsections (b) (on compliance with the statute if violative of foreign law) and (c) (on the control of a corporation incorporated in a foreign country). This subsection similarly amends section 102 of the Americans with Disabilities Act of 1990 (42 U.S.C. 12112) by relettering the existing subsections and adding a new subsection (c) "Covered Entities in Foreign Countries."]*
(c) Application of Amendments. - The amendments made by this section shall not apply with respect to conduct occurring before the date of the enactment of this Act. *[42 U.S.C. 2000e note]*

TECHNICAL ASSISTANCE TRAINING INSTITUTE

SEC. 110.
(a) Technical Assistance. *[This subsection amends section 705 of the Civil Rights Act of 1964 (42 U.S.C. 2000e-4) by adding a new subsection (j), establishing the Technical Assistance Training Institute.]*
(b) Effective Date. - The amendment made by this section shall take effect on the date of enactment of this Act. *[42 U.S.C. 2000e-4 note]*

EDUCATION AND OUTREACH

SEC. 111. *[This section amends section 705(h) of the Civil Rights Act of 1964 (42 U.S.C. 2000e-4(h)) by renumbering the existing subsection and adding at the end a paragraph requiring the EEOC to engage in certain educational and outreach activities.]*

EXPANSION OF RIGHT TO CHALLENGE DISCRIMINATORY SENIORITY SYSTEMS

SEC. 112. *[This section amends section 706(e) of the Civil Rights Act of 1964 (42 U.S.C. 2000e-5(e)) by renumbering the subsection and adding at the end a paragraph to expand the right of claimants to challenge discriminatory seniority systems.]*

AUTHORIZING AWARD OF EXPERT FEES

SEC. 113.
(a) Revised Statutes. - Section 722 of the Revised Statutes is amended-

(1) by designating the first and second sentences as subsections (a) and (b), respectively, and indenting accordingly; and

(2) by adding at the end the following new subsection:

"(c) In awarding an attorney's fee under subsection (b) in any action or proceeding to enforce a provision of section 1977 or 1977A of the Revised Statutes, the court, in its discretion, may include expert fees as part of the attorney's fee." *[42 U.S.C. 1988]*
(b) Civil Rights Act of 1964. *[This section amends section 706(k) of the Civil Rights Act of 1964 (42 U.S.C. 2000e-5(k)) to provide for recovery of expert fees as part of an attorney's fees award.]*

PROVIDING FOR INTEREST AND EXTENDING THE STATUTE OF LIMITATIONS IN ACTIONS AGAINST THE FEDERAL GOVERNMENT

SEC. 114. *[This section amends section 717 of the Civil Rights Act of 1964 (42 U.S.C. 2000e-16) by extending the time for federal employees or applicants to file a civil action from 30 to 90 days (from receipt of notice of final action taken by a department, agency or unit), and allowing federal employees or applicants the same interest to compensate for delay in payments as is available in cases involving nonpublic parties.]*

NOTICE OF LIMITATIONS PERIOD UNDER THE AGE DISCRIMINATION IN EMPLOYMENT ACT OF 1967

SEC. 115. *[This section amends section 7(e) of the Age Discrimination in Employment Act of 1967 (ADEA) (29 U.S.C. 626(e)) by eliminating the two- and three-year statute of limitations and making ADEA suit-filing requirements the same as those under Title VII, and requiring the EEOC to provide notice to charging parties upon termination of the proceedings.]*

LAWFUL, COURT-ORDERED REMEDIES, AFFIRMATIVE ACTION, AND CONCILIATION AGREEMENTS NOT AFFECTED

SEC. 116 *[42 U.S.C. 1981 note].* Nothing in the amendments made by this title shall be construed to affect court-ordered remedies, affirmative action, or conciliation agreements, that are in accordance with the law.

COVERAGE OF HOUSE OF REPRESENTATIVES AND THE AGENCIES OF THE LEGISLATIVE BRANCH

SEC. 117.

(a) Coverage of the House of Representatives. *[This subsection extends the rights and protections of Title VII of the Civil Rights Act of 1964, as amended, to employees of the U.S. House of Representatives. Procedures for processing discrimination complaints are handled internally by the House, not by the EEOC.] [2 U.S.C. 60l]*

(b) Instrumentalities of Congress. *[This subsection extends the rights and protections of the Civil Rights Act of 1991 and Title VII of the Civil Rights Act of 1964, as amended, to "Instrumentalities of Congress," which are defined to include: the Architect of the Capitol, the Congressional Budget Office, the General Accounting Office, the Government Printing Office, the Office of Technology Assessment, and the United States Botanic Garden. Each agency is to establish its own remedies and procedures for enforcement.]*

ALTERNATIVE MEANS OF DISPUTE RESOLUTION

SEC. 118 *[42 U.S.C. 1981 note].* Where appropriate and to the extent authorized by law, the use of alternative means of dispute resolution, including settlement negotiations, conciliation, facilitation, mediation, fact finding, minitrials, and arbitration, is encouraged to resolve disputes arising under the Acts or provisions of Federal law amended by this title.

Title II—Glass Ceiling

[This title sets up a "Glass Ceiling Commission" to focus attention on, and complete a study relating to, the existence of artificial barriers to the advancement of women and minorities in the workplace, and to make recommendations for overcoming such barriers. The Commission is to be composed of 21 members, with the Secretary of Labor serving as the Chairperson of the Commission. This title does not directly impose any responsibilities or obligations on the EEOC except to provide information and technical assistance as requested by the new Commission.] [42 U.S.C. 2000e note]

Title III—Government Employee Rights

GOVERNMENT EMPLOYEE RIGHTS ACT OF 1991

SEC. 301 *[2 U.S.C. 1201].*

(a) Short title. - This title may be cited as the "Government Employee Rights Act of 1991".

(b) Purpose. - The purpose of this title is to provide procedures to protect the right of Senate and other government employees, with respect to their public employment, to be free of discrimination on the basis of race, color, religion, sex, national origin, age, or disability.

(c) Definitions. - For purposes of this title:

(1) Senate employee. - The term "Senate employee" or "employee" means -

(A) any employee whose pay is disbursed by the Secretary of the Senate;

(B) any employee of the Architect of the Capitol who is assigned to the Senate Restaurants or to the Superintendent of the Senate Office Buildings;

(C) any applicant for a position that will last 90 days or more and that is to be occupied by an individual described in subparagraph (A) or (B); or

(D) any individual who was formerly an employee described in subparagraph (A) or (B) and whose claim of a violation arises out of the individual's Senate employment.

(2) Head of employing office. - The term "head of employing office" means the individual who has final authority to appoint, hire, discharge, and set the terms, conditions or privileges of the Senate employment of an employee.

(3) Violation. - The term "violation" means a practice that violates section 302 of this title.

DISCRIMINATORY PRACTICES PROHIBITED

SEC. 302 [2 U.S.C. 1202]. *[Sections 320 and 321 (which protect Presidential appointees and previously exempt state employees who may file complaints of discrimination with EEOC under this title) refer to the rights, protections and remedies of this section and section 307(h).]*
All personnel actions affecting employees of the Senate shall be made free from any discrimination based on -

(1) race, color, religion, sex, or national origin, within the meaning of section 717 of the Civil Rights Act of 1964 (42 U.S.C. 2000e-16);

(2) age, within the meaning of section 15 of the Age Discrimination in Employment Act of 1967 (29 U.S.C. 633a); or

(3) handicap or disability, within the meaning of section 501 of the Rehabilitation Act of 1973 (29 U.S.C. 791) and sections 102–104 of the Americans with Disabilities Act of 1990 (42 U.S.C. 12112-14).

[SECTIONS 303 THROUGH 306: Section 303 (2 U.S.C. 1203) establishes the Office of Senate Fair Employment Practices, which will administer the procedures set forth in sections 304 through 307. Section 304 (2 U.S.C. 1204) outlines the four-step procedure described in Sections 305 through 309 for consideration of alleged violations. Section 305 (2 U.S.C. 1205) describes the Step I counseling procedures. Section 306 (2 U.S.C. 1206) describes the Step II mediation process. Section 307 (2 U.S.C. 1207), described fully below, sets forth the formal complaint and hearing procedures.]

STEP III: FORMAL COMPLAINT AND HEARING

SEC. 307 [2 U.S.C. 1207]. *[SECTION 307, SUBSECTIONS (a) THROUGH (g), AND (i): Subsections (a) through (g), and (i) of Section 307 describe the process from the formal complaint through the hearing stage.]*

[Sections 320 and 321 (which protect Presidential appointees and previously exempt state employees who may file complaints of discrimination with EEOC under this title) refer to the rights, protections and remedies of section 302 and the following subsection.]

(h) Remedies. - If the hearing board determines that a violation has occurred, it shall order such remedies as would be appropriate if awarded under section 706 (g) and (k) of the Civil Rights Act of 1964 (42 U.S.C. 2000e-5 (g) and (k)), and may also order the award of such compensatory damages as would be appropriate if awarded under section 1977 and section 1977A (a) and (b)(2) of the Revised Statutes (42 U.S.C. 1981 and 1981A (a) and (b)(2)). In the case of a determination that a violation based on age has occurred, the hearing board shall order such remedies as would be appropriate if awarded under section 15(c) of the Age Discrimination in Employment Act of 1967 (29 U.S.C. 633a(c)). Any order requiring the payment of money must be approved by a Senate resolution reported by the Committee on Rules and Administration. The hearing board shall have no authority to award punitive damages.

[SECTIONS 308 THROUGH 313: Section 308 (2 U.S.C. 1208) describes the procedures by which a Senate employee or head of an employing office may request a review by the Select

Committee on Ethics of a decision issued under Section 307. Section 309 (2 U.S.C. 1209) describes the circumstances under which a Senate employee or Member of the Senate may petition for a review by the United States Court of Appeals for the Federal Circuit. Section 310 (2 U.S.C. 1210) describes the procedures by which a complaint may be resolved. Section 311 (2 U.S.C. 1211) enumerates reimbursable costs of attending hearings. Section 312 (2 U.S.C. 1212) prohibits intimidation or reprisal against any employee because of the exercise of a right under this title. Section 313 (2 U.S.C. 1213) outlines confidentiality requirements for counseling, mediation, hearings, final decisions, and records.]

EXERCISE OF RULEMAKING POWER

SEC. 314 *[2 U.S.C. 1214].* The provisions of this title, except for sections 309, 320, 321, and 322, are enacted by the Senate as an exercise of the rulemaking power of the Senate, with full recognition of the right of the Senate to change its rules, in the same manner, and to the same extent, as in the case of any other rule of the Senate. Notwithstanding any other provision of law, except as provided in section 309, enforcement and adjudication with respect to the discriminatory practices prohibited by section 302, and arising out of Senate employment, shall be within the exclusive jurisdiction of the United States Senate.

TECHNICAL AND CONFORMING AMENDMENTS

SEC. 315. *[This section makes technical and conforming amendments to section 509 of the Americans with Disabilities Act of 1990 (ADA) (42 U.S.C. 12209) with respect to Senate employees.]*

[SECTIONS 316 THROUGH 319: Section 316 (2 U.S.C. 1215) states that the consideration of political affiliation, domicile, and political compatibility with the employing office in an employment decision shall not be considered a violation of this title. Section 317 (2 U.S.C. 1216) states that a Senate employee may not commence a judicial proceeding to redress a prohibited discriminatory practice, except as provided in this title. Sec. 318 (2 U.S.C. 1217) expresses the Senate's view that legislation should be enacted to provide the same or comparable rights and remedies as are provided under this title to Congressional employees lacking such rights and remedies. Section 319 (2 U.S.C. 1218) reaffirms the Senate's commitment to Rule XLII of the Standing Rules of the Senate.]

COVERAGE OF PRESIDENTIAL APPOINTEES

SEC. 320 *[2 U.S.C. 1219].*

(a) In General. -

(1) Application. - The rights, protections, and remedies provided pursuant to section 302 and 307(h) of this title shall apply with respect to employment of Presidential appointees.

(2) Enforcement by administrative action. - Any Presidential appointee may file a complaint alleging a violation, not later than 180 days after the occurrence of the alleged violation, with the Equal Employment Opportunity Commission, or such other entity as is designated by the President by Executive Order, which, in accordance with the principles and procedures set forth in sections 554 through 557 of title 5, United States Code, shall determine whether a violation has occurred and shall set forth its determination in a final order. If the Equal Employment Opportunity Commission, or such other entity as is designated by the President pursuant to this section, determines that a violation has occurred, the final order shall also provide for appropriate relief.

(3) Judicial review. -

(A) In general. - Any party aggrieved by a final order under paragraph (2) may petition for review by the United States Court of Appeals for the Federal Circuit.

(B) Law applicable. - Chapter 158 of title 28, United States Code, shall apply to a review under this section except that the Equal Employment Opportunity Commission or such other entity as the President may designate under paragraph (2) shall be an "agency" as that term is used in chapter 158 of title 28, United States Code.

(C) Standard of review. - To the extent necessary to decision and when presented, the reviewing court shall decide all relevant questions of law and interpret constitutional and statutory provisions. The court shall set aside a final order under paragraph (2) if it is determined that the order was -

(i) arbitrary, capricious, an abuse of discretion, or otherwise not consistent with law;
(ii) not made consistent with required procedures; or
(iii) unsupported by substantial evidence.

In making the foregoing determinations, the court shall review the whole record or those parts of it cited by a party, and due account shall be taken of the rule of prejudicial error.

(D) Attorney's fees. - If the presidential appointee is the prevailing party in a proceeding under this section, attorney's fees may be allowed by the court in accordance with the standards prescribed under section 706(k) of the Civil Rights Act of 1964 (42 U.S.C. 2000e-5(k)).

(b) Presidential appointee. - For purposes of this section, the term "Presidential appointee" means any officer or employee, or an applicant seeking to become an officer or employee, in any unit of the Executive Branch, including the Executive Office of the President, whether appointed by the President or by any other appointing authority in the Executive Branch, who is not already entitled to bring an action under any of the statutes referred to in section 302 but does not include any individual -

(1) whose appointment is made by and with the advice and consent of the Senate;
(2) who is appointed to an advisory committee, as defined in section 3(2) of the Federal Advisory Committee Act (5 U.S.C. App.); or
(3) who is a member of the uniformed services.

COVERAGE OF PREVIOUSLY EXEMPT STATE EMPLOYEES

SEC. 321 *[2 U.S.C. 1220].*

(a) Application. - The rights, protections, and remedies provided pursuant to section 302 and 307(h) of this title shall apply with respect to employment of any individual chosen or appointed, by a person elected to public office in any State or political subdivision of any State by the qualified voters thereof -

(1) to be a member of the elected official's personal staff;
(2) to serve the elected official on the policymaking level; or
(3) to serve the elected official as an immediate advisor with respect to the exercise of the constitutional or legal powers of the office.

(b) Enforcement by administrative action. -

(1) In general. - Any individual referred to in subsection (a) may file a complaint alleging a violation, not later than 180 days after the occurrence of the alleged violation, with the Equal Employment Opportunity Commission, which, in accordance with the principles and procedures set forth in sections 554 through 557 of title 5, United States Code, shall determine whether a violation has occurred and shall set forth its determination in a final order. If the Equal Employment Opportunity Commission determines that a violation has occurred, the final order shall also provide for appropriate relief.

(2) Referral to state and local authorities. -

(A) Application. - Section 706(d) of the Civil Rights Act of 1964 (42 U.S.C. 2000e-5(d)) shall apply with respect to any proceeding under this section.

(B) Definition. - For purposes of the application described in subparagraph (A), the term "any charge filed by a member of the Commission alleging an unlawful employment practice" means a complaint filed under this section.

(c) Judicial review. - Any party aggrieved by a final order under subsection (b) may obtain a review of such order under chapter 158 of title 28, United States Code. For the purpose of this review, the Equal Employment Opportunity Commission shall be an "agency" as that term is used in chapter 158 of title 28, United States Code.

(d) Standard of review. - To the extent necessary to decision and when presented, the reviewing court shall decide all relevant questions of law and interpret constitutional and statutory provisions. The court shall set aside a final order under subsection (b) if it is determined that the order was -

(1) arbitrary, capricious, an abuse of discretion, or otherwise not consistent with law;
(2) not made consistent with required procedures; or
(3) unsupported by substantial evidence.

In making the foregoing determinations, the court shall review the whole record or those parts of it cited by a party, and due account shall be taken of the rule of prejudicial error.

(e) Attorney's fees. - If the individual referred to in subsection (a) is the prevailing party in a proceeding under this subsection, attorney's fees may be allowed by the court in accordance with the standards prescribed under section 706(k) of the Civil Rights Act of 1964 (42 U.S.C. 2000e-5(k)).

SEVERABILITY

SEC. 322 *[2 U.S.C. 1221].* Notwithstanding section 401 of this Act, if any provision of section 309 or 320(a)(3) is invalidated, both sections 309 and 320(a)(3) shall have no force and effect.

PAYMENTS BY THE PRESIDENT OR A MEMBER OF THE SENATE

SEC. 323 *[2 U.S.C. 1222].* The President or a Member of the Senate shall reimburse the appropriate Federal account for any payment made on his or her behalf out of such account for a violation committed under the provisions of this title by the President or Member of the Senate not later than 60 days after the payment is made.

REPORTS OF SENATE COMMITTEES

SEC. 324 *[2 U.S.C. 1223].*

(a) Each report accompanying a bill or joint resolution of a public character reported by any committee of the Senate (except the Committee on Appropriations and the Committee on the Budget) shall contain a listing of the provisions of the bill or joint resolution that apply to Congress and an evaluation of the impact of such provisions on Congress.

(b) The provisions of this section are enacted by the Senate as an exercise of the rulemaking power of the Senate, with full recognition of the right of the Senate to change its rules, in the same manner, and to the same extent, as in the case of any other rule of the Senate.

INTERVENTION AND EXPEDITED REVIEW OF CERTAIN APPEALS

SEC. 325 *[2 U.S.C. 1224].*

(a) Intervention. - Because of the constitutional issues that may be raised by section 309 and section 320, any Member of the Senate may intervene as a matter of right in any proceeding under section 309 for the sole purpose of determining the constitutionality of such section.

(b) Threshold Matter. - In any proceeding under section 309 or section 320, the United States Court of Appeals for the Federal Circuit shall determine any issue presented concerning the constitutionality of such section as a threshold matter.

(c) Appeal. -

(1) In general. - An appeal may be taken directly to the Supreme Court of the United States from any interlocutory or final judgment, decree, or order issued by the United States Court of Appeals for the Federal Circuit ruling upon the constitutionality of section 309 or 320.

(2) Jurisdiction. - The Supreme Court shall, if it has not previously ruled on the question, accept jurisdiction over the appeal referred to in paragraph (1), advance the appeal on the docket and expedite the appeal to the greatest extent possible.

Title IV—General Provisions

SEVERABILITY

SEC. 401 *[42 U.S.C. 1981 note].* If any provision of this Act, or an amendment made by this Act, or the application of such provision to any person or circumstances is held to be invalid, the remainder of this Act and the amendments made by this Act, and the application of such provision to other persons and circumstances, shall not be affected.

EFFECTIVE DATE

SEC. 402 *[42 U.S.C. 1981 note].*

(a) In General. - Except as otherwise specifically provided, this Act and the amendments made by this Act shall take effect upon enactment.

(b) Certain Disparate Impact Cases. Notwithstanding any other provision of this Act, nothing in this Act shall apply to any disparate impact case for which a complaint was filed before March 1, 1975, and for which an initial decision was rendered after October 30, 1983.

Approved November 21, 1991.

Glossary

A

abandonment Behavior in which a tenant moves out of a leased premises before the end of the term and discontinues making rent payments.

absolute privilege A special right, immunity, permission, or benefit given to certain individuals that allows them to make any statements about someone without being held liable for defamation for any false statement made, regardless of intent or knowledge of the falsity of the claim.

absolutism A theory of ethics which requires that individuals defer to a set of rules to guide them in the ethical decision-making process. Whether an action is moral depends on whether it conforms to the given set of ethical rules.

abuse of process The malicious and deliberate misuse or perversion of a legal procedure.

acceptance A key factor in the agreement element of a contract; consists of the agreement of one party, the offeree, to the terms of the offer in the contract made by the other party, the offeror.

acceptor A person (drawee) who accepts and signs a draft to agree to pay the draft when it is presented.

accommodation party A party who signs an instrument to provide credit for another party who has also signed the instrument.

accord and satisfaction An arrangement between contracting parties whereby one of the parties substitutes a different performance for his or her original duty under the contract. The promise to perform the new duty is the *accord,* and the actual performance of that new duty is the *satisfaction.*

accountant-client privilege The right of an accountant to not reveal any information given in confidence by a client. The privilege is not granted by every state or by the federal government.

accounting A review and listing of all partnership assets and/or profit.

accredited investor A private investor who is allowed to accept private securities offerings under certain specific guidelines set by the SEC.

act utilitarianism A theory of ethics which requires that individuals examine all the potential actions in each situation and choose the action that yields the greatest amount of pleasure over pain for all involved.

actual cause The determination that the defendant's breach of duty resulted directly in the plaintiff's injury.

actual eviction An eviction in which a landlord physically prevents the lessee from entering the leased premises.

actual malice In defamation, either a person's knowledge that his or her statement or published material is false or the person's reckless disregard for whether it was false.

actual notice Notice of agency termination that is given by directly informing third parties, either orally or in writing.

actus reus Latin for "guilty act"; a wrongful behavior that is associated with the physical act of a declared crime.

ad substantiation An FTC standard requiring that advertisers have a reasonable basis for the claims made in their ads.

adhesion contract A contract created by a party to an agreement that is presented to the other party on a take-it-or-leave-it basis. Such contracts are legal but are sometimes rescinded on the grounds of unconscionability and the absence of one party's free will to enter a contract.

administrative agency Any government body created by the legislative branch (e.g., Congress, a state legislature, or a city council) to carry out specific duties.

administrative law The collection of rules and decisions made by administrative agencies to fill in particular details missing from constitutions and statutes.

administrative law judge (ALJ) A judge who presides over an administrative hearing; may attempt to get the parties to settle but has the power to issue a binding decision.

Administrative Procedures Act (APA) Federal legislation that places limitations on how agencies are run and contains very specific guidelines on rule making by agencies.

admission A statement made in court, under oath, or at some stage during a legal proceeding, in which a party against whom charges have been brought admits that an oral contract existed, even though the contract was required to be in writing.

advance directive A legal instrument in which a person expresses his wishes about efforts to prolong his life.

adversarial negotiation Negotiation in which each party seeks to maximize its own gain.

adverse possession An involuntary property transfer in which a person acquires ownership of property by treating a piece of real property as his or her own, without protest or permission from the owner.

affiliate A business enterprise located in one state that is directly or indirectly owned and controlled by a company located in another state. Also called *foreign subsidiary.*

affirm An appellate court decision that accepts a lower court's judgment in a case that has been appealed.

affirmative defense A defendant's response to a plaintiff's claim in which the defendant attacks the plaintiff's legal right to bring the action rather than attacking the fact of the claim or making excuses for unlawful behavior. Common affirmative defenses are expiration of the statute of limitations, mistake of fact, intoxication, insanity, duress, and entrapment.

after-acquired property Property acquired by a debtor after the security arrangement is made.

Age Discrimination in Employment Act (ADEA) of 1967 Federal law that prohibits employers from refusing to hire, discharging, or discriminating in terms and conditions of employment on the basis of an employee's or applicant's being age 40 or older.

agency The fiduciary relationship that arises when one person consents to have another act on his behalf and subject to his control and the other consents to do so.

agency by estoppel See **apparent agency.**

agency coupled with an interest An agency relationship that is created for the benefit of the agent, not the principal.

agency relationship The association between one party and an agent who acts on behalf of that party.

agent A party who has the authority to act on behalf of and bind another party.

agreement One of the four elements necessary for a contract; consists of an offer made by one party, the offeror, and the acceptance of the offer by another party, the offeree.

alien corporation A business that is incorporated in a foreign country.

allonge Accompanying a negotiable instrument, a piece of paper that provides room for an endorsement if no room is available on the negotiable instrument itself.

alteration (1) An unauthorized change to an instrument that modifies the obligation of a party to the instrument. (2) A change that affects the condition of the premises.

alternative dispute resolution (ADR) The resolution of legal problems through methods other than litigation.

ambulatory A term pertaining to the ability of a will to be changed by a testator.

Americans with Disabilities Act (ADA) Federal law that prohibits discrimination against employees and job applicants with disabilities.

anatomical gift All or part of an individual's body that the individual wishes to donate to a hospital, university, organ bank, etc.

answer The response of the defendant to the plaintiff's complaint.

antidumping duties Special tariffs that are imposed on imported goods in order to offset illegal dumping.

antilapse clause In an insurance policy, a clause which states that the insured has a grace period in which to make an overdue payment.

apparent agency An agency relationship created by operation of law when one party, by her actions, causes a third party to believe someone is her agent even though that person actually has no authority to act as her agent. Also called *agency by estoppel.*

appeal The act or fact of challenging the decision of a trial court after final judgment or some other legal ruling by taking the matter to the appropriate appellate court, and in some cases to the U.S. Supreme Court, in an attempt to reverse the decision.

appellate court A higher court, usually consisting of more than one judge, that reviews the decision and results of a lower court (either a trial court or a lower-level appellate court) when a losing party files for an appeal. Appellate courts do not hold trials but may request additional oral and written arguments from each party; they issue written decisions, which collectively constitute case law or the common law. Also called *court of appellate jurisdiction.*

appraisal clause A part of an insurance contract that calls for an assessment when parties disagree about the value and loss of a specific item.

appraisal right A dissenting shareholder's right to have his or her shares appraised and to receive monetary compensation from the corporation for their value.

appropriation for commercial gain A privacy tort that occurs when someone uses a person's name, likeness, voice, identity, or other identifying characteristics for commercial gain without that person's permission.

arbitration A type of alternative dispute resolution wherein disputes are submitted for resolution to private nonofficial persons selected in a manner provided by law or the agreement of the parties.

arbitration clause A part of an insurance contract that calls for a dispute to be settled by an arbitrator, a neutral third party.

arraignment The first appearance in court by the defendant, at which the defendant is advised of the pending charges, the right to counsel, and the right to trial by jury and he or she enters a plea to the charge.

arrest The action in which the police, or a person acting under the law, seize, hold, or take an individual into custody.

arson The crime of intentionally setting fire to another's property.

articles of incorporation A document that contains basic information about a corporation and is filed with the state.

articles of partnership The written agreement that creates a partnership.

artisan's lien A claim placed on personal property to satisfy a person's debt related to the property.

assault A civil wrong that occurs when one person intentionally and voluntarily places another in fear or apprehension of an immediate, offensive physical harm. Assault does not require actual contact.

assignee In a contract, the party who receives the rights of another party (an assignor) to collect what was contractually agreed on in the original contract.

assignment (1) A contracting party's (an assignor's) transfer of his or her rights to the contract to a third party (an assignee). (2) A transfer of a tenant's entire interest in a leased property.

assignor In a contract, the party who transfers his or her rights to a contract to a third party (an assignee), giving the assignee the right to collect what was contractually agreed on in the original contract.

assumption of the risk A defense whereby the defendant must prove that the plaintiff voluntarily assumed the risk that the defendant caused.

attachment (1) The point at which a creditor becomes the secured party who has a security interest in the collateral. (2) A court order permitting a local court officer to seize a debtor's property.

attempt to monopolize The use of certain business practices with the intent to gain market share by excluding competitors and thereby gain monopoly power.

automated teller machine (ATM) A machine connected to banking computers that enables customers to conduct transactions without having to enter their bank.

automatic stay After bankruptcy has been filed, a moratorium during which creditors cannot bring or continue action against the debtor or his or her property.

B

bail A thing of value, such as a money bail bond or any other form of property, that is given to the court to temporarily allow a person's release from jail and to ensure his or her appearance in court.

bailment (of personal property) A relationship that arises when one party (the bailer) gives possession of personal property to another (the bailee) with an advance agreement on the time period, the compensation, if any, and the bailee's treatment of the property.

bait-and-switch advertising A deceptive practice in which a seller advertises a low-priced item, generally unavailable to the consumer, and then pushes the consumer to buy a more expensive item.

Bankruptcy Abuse Prevention and Consumer Protection Act (BAPCPA) of 2005 Federal law that renovated the bankruptcy system by addressing the increased number of bankruptcy filings, significant losses associated with bankruptcy filings, loopholes and incentives that allowed for abuse, and the financial ability of debtors.

bankruptcy estate The assets that are collected from a debtor who files for bankruptcy.

battery A civil wrong that occurs when one person intentionally and voluntarily brings about a nonconsented harmful or offensive contact with a person or something closely associated with him or her. Battery requires an actual contact.

beachhead acquisition A takeover in which an aggressor gradually accumulates the target company's shares.

bearer instrument An instrument payable to cash or to whoever is in possession of the instrument.

bench trial A trial before a judge, with the judgment decided by the judge rather than a jury; occurs when the defendant has waived his or her right to a jury trial.

beneficiary (1) A person who can expect to benefit from a relationship. (2) A person who receives, or will receive, the proceeds from an insurance policy or a will.

bid rigging An agreement among firms to not bid against one another or to submit a certain level of bid.

bilateral contract A promise exchanged for a promise.

bilateral free trade agreement An international agreement between two nations that relates to trade between them.

bill of lading A document issued by a person engaged in the business of transporting goods that verifies receipt of the goods for shipment.

binder An agreement that gives temporary insurance until the company decides to accept or reject the insurance application.

binding arbitration clause A contract provision mandating that all disputes arising under the contract must be settled by arbitration.

blank endorsement A payee's or last endorsee's signature on a negotiable instrument.

blank qualified endorsement A blank endorsement containing words that limit the enforceability of the check, such as the term *without recourse* (which means the endorser will not be liable).

blue-sky law A law that regulates the offering and sale of purely intrastate securities.

bond See **debt security.**

booking After an individual is arrested, the procedure of recording the name of the defendant and the alleged crime in the investigating agency's or police department's records.

bounty payment A government reward for an act that is beneficial to the public.

boycott A refusal to deal with, purchase goods from, or work for a business.

bribery A corrupt and illegal activity in which a person offers, gives, solicits, or receives money, services, or anything of value in order to gain an illicit advantage.

brief A written legal argument, which a party presents to a court, that explains why that party to the case should prevail. Also called *factum.*

burden of proof To convict a defendant, the duty of the plaintiff or prosecution to establish a claim or allegation by admissible evidence and to prove to the jury or court, beyond any reasonable doubt, that the defendant committed all the essential elements of the crime.

burglary A crime in which someone unlawfully enters a building with intent to commit a felony or theft.

business ethics The use of ethics and ethical principles to solve business dilemmas.

business law The enforceable rules of conduct that govern the actions of buyers and sellers in market exchanges.

business trust A business organization governed by a group of trustees who operate the trust for beneficiaries.

buyer in the ordinary course of business A person who routinely buys goods in good faith from a person who routinely sells those goods.

bylaws Rules and regulations that govern a corporation's internal management.

C

capacity The legal ability to enter into a binding contract.

case law The collection of legal interpretations made by judges. They are considered to be law unless otherwise revoked by a statutory law. Also known as *common law.*

case or controversy A term used in the U.S. Constitution to describe the structure and requirements of conflicting claims of individuals that can be brought before a federal court for resolution. A case or controversy requires an actual dispute between parties over their legal rights that remains in conflict at the time the case is presented and that is a proper matter for judicial determination. Also referred to as *justifiable controversy.*

cash tender offer A type of takeover in which the aggressor corporation offers to pay the target shareholders cash for their stock.

cashier's check A check for which both drawer and drawee are the same bank.

casualty insurance Insurance that protects a party from accidental injury.

categorical imperative The principle that an act is ethical if we want all people to act according to its dictates.

cease-and-desist order An FTC order requiring that a company stop its illegal behavior.

certificate of deposit (CD) A document whereby a bank promises to pay a payee a certain amount of money at a future time.

certificate of incorporation A document certifying that a corporation is incorporated in the state and is authorized to conduct business.

certificate of limited partnership A document signed on the formation of a limited partnership and filed with the secretary of state.

certified check Any check that is accepted by the bank from which the funds are drawn.

chain-style business operation A type of franchise in which the franchise operates under the franchisor's business name and is required to follow the franchisor's standards and methods of business operation.

charging order An order that entitles a creditor to collect a partner's profits.

chattel paper A writing that indicates both a monetary obligation and a security interest in specific goods.

check A special draft that orders a bank (the drawee) to pay a specified sum of money to the payee from the drawer's account.

choice-of-law clause A contractual clause in which the parties specify which state's law will apply to the interpretation of the contract in the event of a dispute.

chose in action After an acquisition, the surviving corporation's right to sue for debt and damages on behalf of the absorbed corporation.

circuit court of appeal A court that hears appeals from the district courts located within its circuit, as well as appeals from decisions of federal administrative agencies. Also called *federal district court of appeal.*

civil law The body of laws that govern the rights and responsibilities either between persons or between persons and their government.

Civil Rights Act (CRA) of 1964—Title VII Federal law (as amended by the Civil Rights Act of 1991) that protects employees against discrimination based on race, color, religion, national origin, and sex; also prohibits harassment based on the same protected categories.

closely held corporation A corporation that does not sell stock to the general public.

closing The meeting at which a transfer of title takes place: The seller signs over the deed, and the buyer gives the seller a check for the amount due.

codicil The document by which a testator changes his or her will.

collateral The property that is subject to a secured interest.

collecting bank Any bank, with the exception of the payor bank, that handles a check during the check collection process.

collective bargaining The process whereby workers organize collectively and bargain with employers regarding the conditions of employment.

commerce clause Clause 3 of Article I, Section 8, of the U.S. Constitution, which authorizes and empowers Congress "[t]o regulate Commerce with foreign Nations, and among the several States, and with the Indian Tribes."

commercial general liability policy A policy that generally provides protection for the insured for bodily injury, as well as for third parties for property injury.

commercial insurance Insurance that covers some type of business risk.

commercial reasonableness Reasonable commercial standards of fair dealing, required of merchants in addition to honesty in fact.

commercial speech Speech made by businesses about commercial matters, such as the sale of goods and services. It is protected by the First Amendment.

common areas Areas that are used by all tenants.

common carrier A carrier that is licensed to provide transportation services to the public.

common-carrier delivery contract A type of contract in which purchased goods are delivered to the buyer via an independent contractor, such as a trucking line.

common law See **case law.**

common stock Corporate stock that does not convey any preference to its holders.

communication In a contract, an offer made to the offeree or the offeree's agent.

comparative law The study of the legal systems of different states.

compensatory damages Money awarded to a plaintiff as reimbursement for her or his losses; based on the amount of actual damage or harm to property, lost wages or profits, pain and suffering, medical expenses, disability, etc.

complaint A formal written document that begins a civil lawsuit; contains the plaintiff's list of allegations against the defendant, along with the damages the plaintiff seeks.

complete performance Contract performance that occurs when all aspects of the parties' duties under the contract are carried out perfectly.

computer crime Crime that is committed using a computer.

concealment The active hiding of the truth about a material fact.

concurrent authority Both the state and federal court systems have the power to render a binding verdict for this type of case.

concurrent conditions In a contract, terms under which each party's performance is conditioned on the performance of the other; occur only when the parties are required to perform for each other simultaneously.

condemnation The legal process by which a transfer of property is made against the protest of the property owner.

condition precedent In a contract, an event that must occur in order for a party's duty to arise.

condition subsequent In a contract, a future event that terminates the obligations of the parties when it occurs.

conditional contract A contract that becomes enforceable only on the happening or termination of a specified condition.

conditional endorsement An endorsement whereby payment can be made only on the fulfillment of a predecided condition, such as painting one's house.

conditional estate An ownership interest in which the holder has the same interest as that in a fee simple absolute except that this interest is subject to a condition.

conditional privilege A special right, immunity, permission, or benefit given to certain individuals that allows them to make any statements about someone without being held liable for defamation for any false statements made without actual malice.

conditional sales contract A type of contract in which the sale itself is contingent on approval; can be either a sale-on-approval contract or a sale-or-return contract.

conforming goods Goods that conform to contract specifications.

conglomerate merger A merger in which a company merges with another company that is not a competitor or a buyer or seller to the company.

consent decree An agreement that binds the violating party to cease his or her illegal behavior.

consent order A statement in which a company agrees to stop disputed behavior but does not admit that it broke the law.

consequential damages In a contract, foreseeable damages that result from special facts and circumstances arising outside the contract itself. The damages must be within the contemplation of the parties at the time the breach occurs. Also called *special damages.*

consequentialism A general approach to ethical dilemmas which requires that we consider the consequences our actions will have on relevant people.

consideration The bargained-for exchange; what each party gets in exchange for his or her promise under a contract.

Consolidated Omnibus Budget Reconciliation Act (COBRA) Federal law which ensures that when employees lose their jobs or have their hours reduced to a level at which they would not be eligible to receive medical, dental, or optical benefits from their employer, the employees will be able to continue receiving benefits under the employer's policy for up to 18 months by paying the premiums for the policy.

consolidations Combinations of two or more corporations where none of the original corporations continue to exist as a legal entity.

constitutional law The general limits and powers of a government as interpreted from its written constitution.

constructive eviction An eviction that occurs when a property has become unsuitable for use due to the unlivable quality of the property.

constructive notice Notice of agency termination that is usually given by publishing an announcement in a newspaper.

constructive trust (1) An implied trust in which a party is named to hold the trust for its rightful owner. (2) An equitable trust imposed on someone who wrongfully obtains or holds legal right to property he or she should not possess.

consumer good A good used or bought for use primarily for personal, family, or household purposes.

consumer lease A lease that has a value of $25,000 or less and exists between a lessor who is regularly engaged in the business of leasing or selling and a lessee who leases the goods primarily for a personal, family, or household purpose.

contract A promise or set of promises for the breach of which the law gives a remedy or the performance of which the law in some way recognizes a duty.

contract clause The clause in the U.S. Constitution that prohibits the government from unreasonably interfering with an existing contract.

contract under seal Contracts simply identified with the word *seal* or the letters *L.S.* (an abbreviation for *locus sigilli,* which means "the place for the seal") at the end.

contractual capacity The legal ability to enter into a binding agreement.

contributory negligence A defense to negligence whereby the defendant can escape all liability by proving that the plaintiff failed to act in a way that would have protected him or her from an unreasonable risk of harm and that the plaintiff's negligent behavior contributed in some way to the plaintiff's accident.

Convention on the International Sale of Goods (CISG) An international agreement applicable to transactions involving the commercial sale of goods.

conversion Permanent interference with another's use and enjoyment of his or her personal property.

cooperative An organization formed by individuals to market new products. Individuals in a cooperative pool their resources together to gain an advantage in the market.

co-ownership A type of ownership in which multiple individuals possess ownership interests in a property.

copyright The protection of the expression of a creative work; i.e., protection of the fixed form that expresses the ideas.

corporation A legal entity formed by issuing stock to investors, who are the owners of the corporation.

corporation by estoppel A defective corporation that has conducted business with a third party and therefore cannot deny its status as a corporation to escape liability.

corrective advertising Advertising in which a company explicitly states that formerly advertised claims were untrue. Also called *counteradvertising.*

cost-benefit analysis An economic school of jurisprudence in which all costs and benefits of a law are given monetary values. Those laws with the highest ratios of benefits to costs are then preferable to those with lower ratios.

counterclaim A claim made by the defendant against the plaintiff that is filed along with the defendant's answer.

counteroffer An offer made by an offeree to the offeror that relates to the same matter as the original offer but proposes a substituted bargain that differs from the one proposed in the original offer.

countervailing duties Special tariffs imposed on subsidized goods to offset the beneficial effect of an illegal subsidy.

course of dealing A history of previous commercial transactions between the same parties.

course of performance The history of dealings between the parties in the particular contract at issue.

court of appellate jurisdiction See **appellate court.**

court of original jurisdiction See **trial court.**

covenant not to compete An agreement not to compete against a party for a set period of time within a designated geographic area.

covenant of quiet enjoyment A promise that a tenant has the right to quietly enjoy the land.

cover A buyer's right to substitute goods for those due under a sales or lease agreement when the seller provides nonconforming goods.

creditor An entity to which a debtor owes money.

creditor beneficiary A third party who benefits from a contract in which the promisor agrees to pay the promisee's debt.

creditors' meeting A meeting of all the creditors listed in the Chapter 7 required schedule for liquidation.

criminal fraud Any crime or offense in which an individual intentionally uses some sort of misrepresentation to gain an advantage over another person.

criminal law A classification of law involving the rights and responsibilities an individual has with respect to the public as a whole.

criteria pollutant Any of the six air pollutants that are subject to the National Ambient Air Quality Standards under the Clean Air Act.

critical-thinking skills The ability to understand the structure and worth of an argument by evaluating the facts, issue, reasons, and conclusion of the argument.

cross-licensing An illegal contractual arrangement in which two or more parties license each other to use their specified intellectual property *only* on the condition that neither licenses anyone else to use the property without the other's consent.

cure A breaching party's right to provide conforming goods when nonconforming goods were initially delivered; subject to a reasonable time test.

customary international law A general and consistent practice by nations that is accepted as binding law.

customs union A free trade area with the additional feature of a common external tariff on products originating outside the union.

cyber terrorist A hacker whose intention is the exploitation of a target computer or network to create a serious impact, such as the crippling of a communications network or the sabotage of a business or organization, which may have an impact on millions of citizens if the terrorist's attack is successful.

cyberlaw A classification of law regulating business activities that are conducted online.

D

***de facto* corporation** Latin for "corporation in fact"; a corporation that has not substantially met the requirements of the state incorporation statutes.

***de jure* corporation** Latin for "lawful corporation"; a corporation that has met the mandatory statutory provisions and thus received its certificate of incorporation.

debt security A security that represents a loan to a corporation. Also called *bond.*

debtor A party that owes money to another party.

deceptive advertising The practice of advertising with claims that mislead or could mislead a reasonable consumer.

defamation A false statement or an action that harms the reputation or character of an individual, business, product, group, government, or nation.

default Failure to make payments on a loan.

default judgment Judgment for the plaintiff that occurs when the defendant fails to respond to the complaint.

defaulted see **default.**

defective corporation A corporation whose incorporation process included an error or omission.

defendant The person, party, or entity against whom a civil or criminal lawsuit is filed in a court of law.

definite and certain (terms) The requirement, under common law, that a contract must include and clearly define all material terms.

definite-term lease A type of lease that expires at the end of a specified term.

delegatee A third party who is not part of the original contract but to whom duties to perform are transferred by one of the contracting parties (a delegator).

delegation A contracting party's (a delegator's) transfer of his or her duty to perform to a third party who is not part of the original contract (a delegatee).

delegator A party in a contract who transfers his or her duties to perform to a third party who is not a part of the original contract (a delegatee).

demand instrument A type of draft that allows the payee to demand payment at any time from a holder.

deontology The ethical theory which states that an action can be determined as ethical on the basis of right and wrong, regardless of its consequences.

depositary bank The first bank that receives a check for payment.

deposition A pretrial sworn and recorded testimony of a witness that is acquired out of court with no judge present.

design defect A defect that is found in all products of a particular design and renders them dangerous.

digital cash Money stored electronically and used in place of physical currency.

direct deposit An electronic process, preauthorized by a customer, that allows funds to be deposited directly into the customer's bank account.

directed verdict A ruling by the judge, after the plaintiff has presented her case but before any evidence is put forward by the defendant, in favor of the defendant because the plaintiff has failed to present the minimum amount of evidence necessary to establish his claim.

discharge A written federal court order signed by a bankruptcy judge which states that the debtor is immune from creditor actions to collect debt; i.e., a release from liability.

discharged Released from liability; term applied to negotiable instrument liability that has terminated.

disclosed principal A principal whose identity is known to a third party. The third party is aware that the agent is making an agreement on behalf of the principal.

discovery The pretrial phase in a lawsuit during which each party requests relevant documents and other evidence from the other side in an attempt to "discover" pertinent facts and to avoid any surprises in the courtroom during the trial. Discovery tools include requests for admissions, interrogatories, depositions, requests for inspection, and document production requests.

dishonored Refused; specifically, a payment that has been refused despite a holder's presenting an instrument in a timely and proper manner.

dishonored instrument An instrument that a party has refused to pay.

disparagement A business tort that occurs when a statement is intentionally used to defame a business product or service.

disparate impact A form of discrimination that arises when an employer's policy or practice appears to apply to everyone equally but its actual effect is that it disproportionately limits employment opportunities for a protected class.

disparate treatment A form of intentional discrimination in which an employee is hired, fired, denied a promotion, or the like, on the basis of membership in a protected class.

Dispute Settlement Understanding An agreement that is part of the WTO system whereby recognized governments of WTO member states may bring an action alleging a violation of GATT by other member states.

dissolution The change in the relation of partners caused by any partner's ceasing to be associated with the carrying on of the partnership's business.

distributor A merchant who purchases goods from a seller for resale in a foreign market.

distributorship A type of franchise in which the franchisor manufactures a product and licenses a dealer to sell the product in an exclusive territory.

district court A trial court in the federal system.

dividend A distribution of corporate profits or income that is ordered by the directors and paid to the shareholders.

document of title A transport document that, when appropriately made out, entitles the bearer to claim the goods from the carrier.

domestic corporation A corporation located in the state in which it is incorporated.

donee beneficiary A third party who benefits from a contract in which a promisor agrees to give a gift to the third party.

dormant commerce clause A restriction on states' authority that is implied in the commerce clause of the U.S. Constitution: The power given to Congress to enact legislation that affects interstate commerce in effect prohibits a state from passing legislation that improperly burdens interstate commerce.

draft An instrument validating an order by a drawer to a drawee to pay a payee.

dram shop act A regulation under which bartenders can be held liable for injuries caused by individuals who become intoxicated in their bars.

drawee The party that must obey an order. In the context of banking, the drawee is the bank that must pay the funds ordered by a customer's check.

drawer The party that writes an order, or the person who writes a check.

due diligence defense A defense in which the defendant argues that he or she applied the appropriate degree of attention, care, and research expected of a party in a given situation and had reasonable grounds to believe that certain facts and statements were accurate and had no omission of material facts.

due process clause A clause in the Fifth Amendment of the U.S. Constitution which provides that the government cannot deprive an individual of life, liberty, or property without a fair and just hearing.

dumping The practice wherein an exporter sells products in a foreign state for less than the price charged for the same or comparable goods in the exporter's home market.

durable power of attorney A document which specifies that an agent's authority is intended to continue beyond the principal's incapacitation.

duress Any unlawful act or threat exercised on a person whereby the person is forced to enter into an agreement or to perform some other act against his or her will.

duty The standard of care a defendant must meet in order to not subject a person in the position of the plaintiff to an unreasonable risk of harm.

duty of loyalty An agent's obligation to act in the interest of the principal.

duty of notification An agent's obligation to inform the principal of the agent's actions on the principal's behalf and of all relevant information.

duty to compensate A principal's obligation to pay an agent for his or her services.

E

easement An irrevocable right to use some part of another's land for a specific purpose, without taking anything from it.

easement by prescription An easement created by state law when certain conditions are met, most frequently by openly using a portion of another's property for a statutory period of time (usually 25 years).

effective date The date on which insurance takes effect.

efficiency The economic principle of getting the most output from the least input.

Electronic Communications Privacy Act (ECPA) of 1986 Federal law that extended employees' privacy rights to electronic forms of communication including e-mail and cell phones; outlaws the intentional interception of electronic communications and the intentional disclosure or use of the information obtained through such interception.

electronic fund transfer (EFT) The transfer of funds by an electronic terminal, telephone, or computer.

embezzlement A wrongful conversion of another's funds or property by one who is lawfully in possession of those funds or that property.

e-money Any electronic, nonphysical form of currency.

Employee Retirement Income Security Act (ERISA) Federal law that sets minimum standards for most voluntarily established pension and health plans in private industry to provide protection for individuals in these plans.

employment-at-will doctrine The doctrine which provides that either the employer or the employee can terminate the employment relationship at any time.

enabling legislation A statute that specifies the name, functions, and specific powers of an administrative agency and grants the agency broad powers for the purpose of serving the "public interest, convenience, and necessity."

endorsee One who receives an endorsement.

endorsement for deposit or collection only The most common type of endorsement, which provides that the instrument can only be deposited into an account.

endorsement to prohibit further endorsement An endorsement that provides increased protection to the endorsee.

endorser One who issues an endorsement.

English rule A rule which states that the first assignee to give notice of assignment to the obligor is the party with rights to the contract.

entrapment A relatively common defense under which the defendant claims that he would not have committed the crime or broken the law if he had not been induced or tricked into doing so by law enforcement officials.

entrustment The transfer of goods to a merchant who ordinarily deals in that type of goods. If the merchant subsequently sells them to a good-faith third-party purchaser, the buyer acquires good title to the goods.

environmental impact statement (EIS) A document that must be filed whenever there is a major federal activity that might have a significant impact on the environment. It details the environmental impact of the proposed action, any adverse environmental effects of implementing the action, and other environmental considerations.

equal dignity rule A rule requiring that contracts that would normally fall under the statute of frauds and need a writing if negotiated by the principal must be in writing even if negotiated by an agent.

Equal Pay Act (EPA) of 1963 Federal law that prohibits an employer from paying workers of one gender less than the wages paid to employees of the opposite gender for work that requires equal skill, effort, and responsibility.

equal protection clause A clause in the Fourteenth Amendment of the U.S. Constitution that prevents states from denying "the equal protection of the laws" to any citizen. This clause implies that all citizens are created equal.

equity security A security that represents ownership in a corporation.

establishment clause One of two provisions in the First Amendment of the U.S. Constitution that protect citizens' freedom of religion. It prohibits (1) the establishment of a national religion by Congress and (2) the preference of one religion over another or of religion over nonreligious philosophies in general.

estate planning The process whereby an individual decides what to do with his or her real and personal property during and after life.

ethical dilemma A question about how a person should behave that requires the person to reflect about the advantages and disadvantages of the optional choices for various stakeholders.

ethical guideline A simple tool to help determine whether an action is moral.

ethical relativism The ethical theory that denies the existence of an ultimate ethical system, holding instead that a decision must be determined as ethical on the basis of its own context.

ethics The study and practice of decisions about what is good or right.

ethics of care The ethical theory that emphasizes human interaction, holding that what makes a decision ethical is how well it builds and promotes human relationships.

European Union A customs union that consists of an association of states, has a basis in international law, and was formed for the purpose of forging closer ties among the peoples of Europe.

exchange tender offer A type of takeover in which the aggressor corporation offers to exchange the target shareholders' current stock for its own stock.

exclusive-dealing contract An agreement in which a seller requires that a buyer buy products supplied only by that seller.

exculpatory clause A clause in a contract that basically frees one party (usually the drafter of the agreement) from all liability arising out of performance of the contract; generally based on factors such as consumer ignorance or a great deal of unexplained fine print that serve to deprive the less powerful party of a meaningful choice.

executed A term applied to a contract whose terms have all been fully performed.

executive agency An agency that is typically located within the executive branch, under one of the cabinet-level departments. The agency head is appointed by the president with the advice and consent of the Senate and may be discharged by the president at any time, for any reason. Also called *cabinet-level agency.*

executive order A directive that has the force of law but is issued by a governor or the president.

executory A term applied to a contract whose terms have not all been fully performed.

exemplary damages See **punitive damages.**

exempted rule making An APA exemption from rule making that allows an agency to decide whether public participation will be allowed. Exemptions include rule-making proceedings with regard to military or foreign affairs, agency management or personnel, and public property, loans, grants, benefits or contracts of an agency.

express condition A condition specifically and explicitly stated in a contract and usually preceded by words such as *conditioned on, if, provided that,* or *when.*

express contract A contract in which all the terms are clearly set forth in either written or spoken words.

express trust A trust created either while the settlor is alive or by will.

express warranty Any description of a good's physical nature or its use, either in general or specific circumstances, that becomes part of a contract.

expressed agency An agency created in a written or oral agreement. Also called *agency by agreement.*

extortion A criminal offense in which a person obtains money, property, and/or services from another by wrongfully threatening or inflicting harm to his or her person, property, or reputation. Also called *blackmail.*

F

failure to provide adequate warnings A defect that arises when a potentially dangerous product is not labeled to indicate that it can be dangerous.

Fair Labor Standards Act (FLSA) Federal law which requires that a minimum wage of a specified amount be paid to all employees in covered industries; also mandates that employees who work more than 40 hours in a week be paid no less than 1½ times their regular wage for all hours beyond 40 worked in a given week.

fair-use doctrine The doctrine which provides for the lawful use of a limited portion of another's work for purposes of criticism, comment, news reporting, teaching, scholarship, or research.

False Claims Act An act that allows employees to sue employers on behalf of the federal government for fraud against the government. The employee retains a share of the recovery as a reward for his or her efforts.

false imprisonment The unlawful restraint of another against the person's will.

false light A privacy tort that occurs when highly offensive information is published about an individual that is not valid or places the person in a false light.

false pretense A materially false representation of an existing fact, with knowledge of the falsity of the representation and with the intent to defraud.

Family and Medical Leave Act (FMLA) Federal act requiring that employers provide all eligible employees with up to 12 weeks of leave during any 12-month period for several family-related occurrences (e.g., birth of a child, care of a sick spouse).

family incentive trust A trust designed to take effect on the completion of a specified behavior.

federal preemption A principle asserting the supremacy of federal legislation over state legislation when both pertain to the same subject matter. Also called *field preemption.*

Federal Register The government publication in which an agency publishes each proposed rule, along with an explanation of the legal authority for issuing the rule and a description of how the public can participate in the rule-making process, and later publishes the final rule.

Federal Unemployment Tax Act (FUTA) Federal law passed in 1935 that created a state system to provide unemployment compensation to qualified employees who lose their jobs.

federalism A system of government in which power is divided between a central authority and constituent political units.

fee simple absolute An ownership interest in which the holder has exclusive rights to ownership and possession of the land to the holder; the most comprehensive type of estate.

felony A serious crime, such as murder, rape, or robbery, that is punishable by imprisonment for more than one year or death.

fictitious payee Someone having no right to payment. Under the UCC fictitious-payee rule, any check made out to a fictitious payee and endorsed must be honored and is not considered a forgery.

finance lease A type of lease in which the lessor does not select, manufacture, or supply the goods but acquires title to the goods or the right to their possession and use in connection with the terms of the lease.

financing statement A document that lists the names and addresses of all the parties involved in the transaction, a description of the collateral, and the signature of the debtor.

fire insurance Insurance that protects against property losses incurred by damage from fire.

firm offer An offer made in writing and containing assurances that it will be irrevocable for a period of time not longer than three months despite a lack of consideration for the irrevocability.

first appearance The initial appearance of an arrested individual before a judge, who determines whether there was probable cause for the arrest. If the judge ascertains that probable cause did not exist, the individual is freed.

first-assignment-in-time rule A rule which states that the first party granted an assignment is the party correctly entitled to the contractual right.

fixture An item that was originally a piece of personal property but becomes part of realty after it is permanently attached to the real property in question.

food disparagement A tort that provides ranchers and farmers with a cause of action when someone spreads false information about the safety of a food product.

for-profit corporation A corporation whose objective is to make a profit.

foreign corporation A corporation that conducts business in a state in which it is not incorporated.

Foreign Corrupt Practices Act (FCPA) Federal law prohibiting U.S. companies from offering or paying bribes to foreign government officials, political parties, and candidates for office for the purpose of obtaining or retaining business.

foreign sales representative An agent who distributes, represents, or sells goods on behalf of a foreign seller, usually in return for the payment of a commission.

foreign subsidiary See **affiliate.**

forfeiture A party's forfeiting of his or her interest in the premises.

forgery The fraudulent making or altering of a writing in a way that changes the legal rights and liabilities of another and with the intent to deceive or defraud.

formal contract A contract that must have a special form or must be created in a specific manner.

formal rule making A type of rule making that is used when legislation requires a formal hearing process with a complete transcript; consists of publication of the proposed rule in the *Federal Register,* a public hearing, publication of formal findings, and publication of the final rule if adopted.

forum selection agreement A contractual clause in which the parties choose the location where disputes between them will be resolved.

franchise A business arrangement between an owner of a trade name or trademark and a person who sells goods or services under the trade name or trademark.

franchise agreement A contract whereby a company (the franchisor) grants permission (a license) to another entity (the franchisee) to use the franchisor's name, trademark, or copyright in the operation of a business and associated sale of goods in return for payment.

franchisee The seller of goods or services under a trade name or trademark in a franchise.

franchisor The owner of the trade name or trademark in a franchise.

fraud (1) An intentional deception that causes harm to another. (2) A basis for contesting a will if the testator relied on false statements when he or she made the will.

fraud in the factum A liability defense available to a party who signs a negotiable instrument without knowing that it is a negotiable instrument.

fraudulent misrepresentation (1) The tort that occurs when a misrepresentation is made with intent to facilitate personal gain and with the knowledge that it is false. (2) In contracts, a false representation of a material fact that is consciously false and is intended to mislead the other party. Also called *intentional misrepresentation.*

fraudulent transfer A transfer of property that is made with intent to defraud creditors or for an amount significantly lower than the property's fair market value and that occurs within two years of filing for bankruptcy.

free-exercise clause A clause in the First Amendment of the U.S. Constitution. which states that government (state and federal) cannot make a law "prohibiting the free exercise" of religion; has been interpreted as including absolute freedom to believe and freedom to act, which may face state restriction.

free trade agreement An international agreement between two or more nations whereby tariffs and other trade barriers are reduced and gradually eliminated.

Freedom of Information Act (FOIA) Federal law passed in 1966 that mandates and facilitates public access to government information and records, including records about oneself. Sensitive information (e.g., on national security) is excluded.

full eviction An eviction in which a landlord physically prevents the lessee from entering the leased premises.

full faith and credit clause A clause in the U.S. Constitution (Article IV, Section 1) mandating that each state must recognize, respect, and enforce the public records, legislative acts, and judicial decisions of the other states.

future interest A person's present right to property ownership and possession in the future.

G

gambling Agreements in which parties pay consideration (money placed during bets) for the chance, or opportunity, to obtain an amount of money or property.

garnishment An order that satisfies a debt by seizing a debtor's property that is being held by a third party.

General Agreement on Tariffs and Trade (GATT) A comprehensive multilateral trading system designed to achieve distortion-free international trade through the minimization of tariffs and removal of artificial barriers.

general partnership A partnership in which the partners divide profits and management responsibility and share unlimited personal liability for the partnership's debts.

general personal jurisdiction A doctrine permitting adjudication of any claims against a defendant regardless of whether the claim has anything to do with the forum.

general power of attorney A type of express authority that allows an agent to conduct all business for the principal.

general warranty deed A deed containing a covenant in which the seller agrees to protect the buyer against being dispossessed because of any adverse claim against the land.

geographic market An area in which a company competes with others in the relevant product market.

gift *causa mortis* A gift that is made in contemplation of one's immediate death.

Golden Rule The idea that we should act in the way that we would like others to act toward us.

good faith Honesty in fact.

Good Samaritan statute A statute that exempts from liability a person, such as a physician passerby, who voluntarily renders aid to an injured person but negligently, but not unreasonably negligently, causes injury while rendering the aid.

good title Title acquired from someone who already owns the goods free and clear.

goods All physically existing things that are movable at the time of identification in the contract for sale.

goods in bailment Purchased goods that are in some kind of storage under the control of a third party, such as a warehouseman.

Government in Sunshine Act Federal law which requires that agency business meetings be open to the public if the agency is headed by a collegiate body (i.e., two or more persons, the majority of whom are appointed by the president with the advice and consent of the Senate); also requires that agencies keep records of closed meetings.

green taxes Taxes imposed on environmentally harmful activities.

gross negligence An act committed with extreme reckless disregard for the property or life of another person.

group boycott A boycott in which two or more competitors agree to refuse to deal with a certain person or company. Also called *refusal to deal.*

group insurance Insurance that is purchased by neither the insured party nor the insurer.

guaranty A type of contract which ensures that a third party is secondarily liable for the debt to be paid; similar to a suretyship.

H

hacker A person who illegally accesses, or enters, another person's or company's computer system to obtain information or steal money.

Hague Evidence Convention A multilateral convention establishing procedures for transnational discovery between private persons in different states.

half-truth Information that is true but is not complete.

health care proxy A document that empowers an agent to make medical decisions for a principal who is unable to make those decisions for himself or herself.

historical school A school of jurisprudence that uses traditions as the model for future laws and behavior. Also called *tradition* or *custom.*

holder A party in possession of a negotiable instrument.

holder in due course (HDC) An individual who acquires a negotiable instrument in good faith.

homestead exemption An exemption that allows a debtor to retain all or a portion of the family home so that the family will retain some form of shelter.

horizontal division of market An agreement between two or more competitors to divide markets among themselves by geography, customers, or products.

horizontal merger A merger between two or more competitors producing the same or similar products.

horizontal restraint of trade An agreement between two competitors in the same market to engage in a practice that restrains trade.

hostile takeover A takeover to which the management of the target corporation objects.

hybrid agency An agency that has characteristics of both executive and independent agencies.

hybrid rule making A type of rule making that combines features of both formal and informal rule making; consists of publication in the *Federal Register,* a written-comment period, and an informal public hearing with restricted cross-examination.

I

identification with the vulnerable The school of jurisprudence of pursuing change on the grounds that some higher law or body of moral principles connects all of us in the human community.

illusory promise A situation in which a party appears to commit to something but really has not committed to anything. It is not a promise and thus not consideration.

implied authority The authority of an agent that arises by inference from the words and actions of the principal.

implied condition A condition that is not specifically and explicitly stated but is inferred from the nature and language of the contract.

implied contract A contract that arises not from words of agreement but from the conduct of the parties.

implied-contract exception An exception to the employment at-will doctrine which provides that an implied employment contract may arise from statements the employer makes in an employment handbook or materials advertising the position.

implied covenant of good faith and fair dealing exception An exception to the employment at-will doctrine that imposes a duty on the employer to treat employees fairly with respect to termination.

implied trust A trust created by a court when (1) an express trust fails and the court can imply the existence of a trust from certain behavior or (2) the law steps in to protect someone from fraud or other wrongdoing.

implied warranty of fitness for a particular purpose An assurance, inferred in any UCC sale, that when a seller/lessor knows or has reason to know (1) why the buyer/lessee is purchasing/leasing the goods and (2) that the buyer/lessee is relying on him or her to make the selection, the buyer/lessee has an enforceable warranty if such assurance is false.

implied warranty of habitability A requirement that the premises be fit for ordinary residential purposes.

implied warranty of merchantability An assurance, inferred in every sale unless clearly disclaimed, that merchantable goods will conform to a reasonable performance expectation. The purchaser must have purchased or leased the good from a merchant.

implied warranty of trade usage An assurance, inferred in the context of certain UCC sales, depending on the circumstances, that can be created through a well-accepted course of dealing or trade usage.

imposter rule A rule which holds that if one party obtains a negotiable instrument by impersonating another party and endorses it with the impersonated party's signature, the loss falls on the drawer of the instrument.

in pari delicto In equal fault.

***in personam* jurisdiction** The power of a court to require that a party (usually the defendant) or a witness come before the court; extends to the state's borders in the state court system and across the court's geographic district in the federal system. Also called *personal jurisdiction* and *jurisdiction in personam.*

***in rem* jurisdiction** The power of a court over the property or status of an out-of-state defendant located within the court's jurisdiction area.

incidental beneficiary One who unintentionally gains a benefit from a contract between other parties.

income beneficiary The recipient of the interest or appreciation generated by a trust.

incontestability clause A part of an insurance contract that precludes an insurance company from challenging statements in an insurance application after a certain period of time.

incorporator An individual who applies for incorporation on behalf of a corporation.

independent agency An agency that is typically not located within a government department. It is governed by a board of commissioners appointed by the president with the advice and consent of the Senate.

indictment A finding by the grand jury that there is evidence to charge the defendant and bring him or her to trial.

individual insurance Insurance in which the insured party is an individual.

indivisible contract A contract that cannot be divided and must be performed in its entirety.

industry guides Interpretations of consumer laws created by the FTC to encourage businesses to stop unlawful behavior.

infant A person who is not legally an adult (in most U.S. localities, a person under 18) and thus is considered to lack the mental capabilities of an adult. Infancy can be used as a partial defense to defuse the guilty-mind requirement of a crime.

informal contract A contract that requires no formalities. Also called *simple contract.*

informal rule making A type of rule making in which an agency publishes a proposed rule in the *Federal Register,* considers public comments, and then publishes the final rule. Also called *notice-and-comment rule making.*

information A finding by a magistrate that there is enough evidence to charge the defendant and bring her or him to trial.

informational picketing Picketing designed to truthfully inform the public of a labor dispute between an employer and the employees.

injunction A court order either forcing a party to do something or prohibiting a party from doing something.

innkeepers Entities that are regularly in the business of making lodging available to the public.

innocent misrepresentation A false statement made about a material fact by a person who believed the statement was true.

insanity An affirmative defense which claims that the defendant had a severe mental illness when the crime was committed that substantially impaired his or her capacity to understand and appreciate the moral wrongfulness of the act.

insider trading Illegal buying or selling of a corporation's securities by corporate insiders, such as officers and directors, on the basis of material, nonpublic information and in breach of a fiduciary duty or some other relationship of trust and confidence.

insolvent debtor A debtor who cannot pay debts in a timely fashion.

instrument Any writing that serves as evidence of the right to payment of money.

insurable interest A party who has an interest in property or life.

insurance A contract in which the insured party makes payments to the insurer in exchange for the insurer's promise to make payment or transfer goods to another party in the event of injury or destruction to the insured party's property or life.

insured party The party who makes a payment in exchange for payment in the event of damage or injury to property or person.

insurer The party who receives payments from the insured party and makes the payment to the beneficiary.

integrated contract A written contract intended to be the complete and final representation of the parties' agreement.

intellectual property Intangible property that is the product of one's mind and not one's hands.

intended beneficiary A third party to a contract whom the contracting parties intended to benefit directly from their contact.

intent The intended purpose or goal of an action, especially in a contract.

intentional infliction of emotional distress The tort that occurs when someone intentionally engages in outrageous conduct that is likely to cause extreme emotional distress to another person.

intentional interference with contract The tort that occurs when someone intentionally takes an action that will cause a person to breach a contract that he or she has with another.

intentional misrepresentation See **fraudulent misrepresentation.**

intentional tort A civil wrong resulting from an intentional act committed on the person, property, or economic interest of another. Intentional torts include assault, battery, conversion, false imprisonment, intentional infliction of emotional distress, trespass to land, and trespass to chattels.

***inter vivos* gift** A gift that is made by a person during his or her lifetime.

intermediary bank Any bank, other than a payor or depositary bank, that transfers a check during the check collection process.

intermediate scrutiny A standard of review under which a law must be necessary to achieve a substantial, or important, government interest and must be narrowly tailored to that interest.

international agreement A written agreement between two or more nations that is governed by international law and relates to international subject matter.

International Labor Organization An international organization operating under the principle that "labor should not be regarded merely as a commodity or article of commerce"; develops labor rights norms that serve as the basis for many international standards.

international law The body of law that governs the conduct of nations and international organizations and their relations with one another and with natural and juridical persons.

interpretive rule A rule that does not create any new rights or duties but is merely a detailed statement of an agency's interpretation of an existing law, including the actions a party must take to be in compliance with the law.

interrogatory A formal set of written questions that one party to a lawsuit asks the opposing party during the pretrial discovery process to clarify matters of evidence and help determine what facts will be presented at a trial in the case. The questions must be answered in writing under oath or under penalty of perjury within a specified time. Also called *request for further information.*

Interstate Commerce Commission (ICC) The first federal administrative agency; created to regulate the anticompetitive conduct of railroads.

intestacy statute A statute that outlines how a person's property will be handled if that person dies without a will.

intestate The state of dying without a will.

intrusion on an individual's affairs or seclusion A physical, electronic, or mechanical intrusion that invades someone's solitude, seclusion, or personal affairs when he or she has the right to expect privacy. The tort occurs at the time of the intrusion; no publication is necessary.

involuntary intoxication An affirmative defense in which the defendant claims that she took the intoxicant without awareness of its likely effect, mistook its identity, or was forced to ingest it and that it left her unable to understand that the act committed was wrong.

Islamic law A legal system based on the fundamental tenet that law is derived from and interpreted in harmony with Shari'a (God's law) and the Koran.

J

joint and several liability A type of liability in which a third party can choose to sue the partners separately or to sue all partners jointly in one action.

joint stock company A partnership agreement in which company members hold transferable shares while all the goods of the company are held in the names of the partners.

joint tenancy A type of co-ownership in which the joint tenants own equal shares of the property and, upon the death of one tenant, the property is divided equally among the surviving joint owners. The tenants may sell their shares without the consent of the other owners, and their interest can be attached by creditors.

joint tenants Parties who hold property in joint tenancy.

joint venture An association between two or more parties wherein the parties share profits and management responsibilities with respect to a specific project.

jointly liable A term applied to partners who share liability for the partnership's debts.

judicial lien A court order that allows a creditor to satisfy a debt by seizing the property of the debtor.

judicial review The power of a court to review legislative and executive actions, such as a law or an official act of a government employee or agent, to determine whether they are constitutional.

jurisdiction The power of a court to hear cases and resolve disputes.

justifiable use of force The use of force that is necessary to prevent imminent death or great bodily harm to oneself or another or to prevent the imminent commission of a forcible felony.

L

lack of genuine assent A defense to the agreement of a contract in which the offeree claims that the offeror secured the agreement through improper means, such as duress, fraud, undue influence, or misrepresentation.

landlord The owner of a property being leased. Also called *lessor.*

landlord's lien A court order that allows a landlord, through a sheriff, to seize a tenant's personal property as security for unpaid rent.

Landrum-Griffin Act Federal law that primarily governs the internal operations of labor unions. It requires financial disclosures by unions, establishes penalties for financial abuses by union officials, and includes "Labor's Bill of Rights" to protect employees from their own unions.

larceny The unlawful taking, attempting to take, carrying, leading, or riding away of another person's property with intent to permanently deprive the rightful owner of the property.

last-clear-chance doctrine A doctrine used by a plaintiff when the defendant establishes contributory negligence. If the plaintiff can establish that the defendant had the last opportunity to avoid the accident, the plaintiff may still recover, despite being contributorily negligent.

lease (1) A transfer of the right to possess and use goods for a period of time in return for consideration. (2) The agreement between a landlord and a tenant that specifies the terms of a property rental.

leasehold A possessory interest, but not an ownership interest, transferred by contract (lease).

leasehold estate The leased property.

legal assent A promise to buy or sell that the courts will require that the parties obey.

legal object The requirement that, to be enforceable, a contract cannot be either illegal or against public policy.

legal positivism The school of jurisprudence which holds that because society requires authority, a legal and authoritarian hierarchy should exist. When a law is made, therefore, obedience is expected because authority created it.

legal realism The school of jurisprudence which dictates that context must be considered as well as law. Context includes factors such as economic conditions and social conditions.

lessee (1) A person who acquires the right to possession and use of goods under a lease. (2) The party who assumes temporary ownership of a rental property. Also called *tenant.*

lessor (1) A person who transfers the right to possession and use of goods under a lease. (2) The owner of a rental property. Also called *landlord.*

letter of credit A binding document that a buyer obtains from his or her bank to guarantee that payment for goods will be made to the seller.

leveraged buyout (LBO) A takeover-resistance strategy in which a group within the target corporation buys all the corporate stock held by the public, thereby turning the company into a privately held corporation.

lex mercatoria The "law of merchants" as defined by customs or trade usages developed by merchants to facilitate business transactions.

liability insurance Insurance that protects a business from tort liability to third parties.

liability without fault See **strict liability.**

license A revocable right to temporarily use another's property.

licensing agreement A contract in which one company (the licensor) grants permission to another company (the licensee) to use the licensor's intellectual property in return for payment.

lien A claim to property.

life estate An ownership interest in which the holder has the right to possess the property until his or her death.

life insurance A contract between a policy owner and an insurance company that requires the insurance company to pay a designated beneficiary a sum of money upon the occurrence of the insured's death.

limited liability company (LLC) An unincorporated business that is taxed like a partnership, with the members paying personal income taxes, but has the limited liability of a corporation.

limited liability partnership (LLP) A partnership in which all the partners assume liability for any partner's professional malpractice to the extent of the partnership's assets.

limited partnership (LP) A partnership consisting of at least one general partner and at least one limited partner in which the general partners assume all liability for the partnerships's debts and the limited partners assume no responsibility beyond their originally invested capital.

liquidated damages Damages specified as a term of the contract before a breach of contract occurs.

liquidated debt Debt for which there is no dispute between the parties about the fact that money is owed and the amount of money owed.

liquidation The process in which a debtor turns over all assets to a trustee.

living trust A trust created by a trustor and administered by another party while the trustor is still alive.

living will A document in which a person expresses his or her advance directives.

long-arm statute A statute that enables a court to obtain jurisdiction against an out-of-state defendant as long as the defendant has sufficient minimum contacts within the state, such as committing a tort or doing business in the state.

M

mailbox rule A rule which holds that an acceptance is valid when it is placed in the mailbox, whereas a revocation is effective only when received by the offeree. In some jurisdictions the mailbox rule has been expanded to faxes.

maker A person who promises to pay a set sum to the holder of a promissory note or certificate of deposit.

malicious prosecution A tort in which one person wrongfully subjects another to criminal or civil litigation for the sole purpose of causing problems for that other person, often in retaliation for previous litigation between the two.

malpractice action A legal action filed against a professional person for failure to act in accordance with prevailing professional standards.

manifest A document that records possession of hazardous waste from inception to disposal.

manufacturing arrangement A type of franchise in which the franchisor provides the franchisee with a formula or ingredient that is necessary to manufacture a product.

manufacturing defect A defect in an individual product that makes the product more dangerous than other, identical products.

marine insurance Insurance that protects against loss of ships and cargo from the "perils of the sea."

market power See **monopoly power.**

market share A firm's fractional share of the relevant market.

market share theory Product liability theory which holds that when it is impossible to identify the manufacturer of a particular product that caused harm, the plaintiff may sue all manufacturers of the product, with liability apportioned among them on the basis of each one's market share.

marketable title Title for property to which the seller has legal title and against which there are no liens or restrictions of which the buyer is not aware.

material breach A substantial breach of a significant term or terms of a contract that excuses the nonbreaching party from further performance under the contract and gives the nonbreaching party the right to recover damages.

material terms In a contract, the terms that allow a court to determine what the damages are in the event that one of the parties breaches the contract; include the subject matter, quantity, price, quality, and parties.

mechanic's lien A claim placed on real property to satisfy the debt a person incurred to have improvements made to that property.

med-arb A type of dispute resolution process in which both parties agree to start out in mediation and, if unsuccessful, to move on to arbitration.

mediation A type of intensive negotiation in which disputing parties select a neutral party to help facilitate communication and suggest ways for the parties to solve their dispute.

meeting-the-competition defense A defense to the Clayton Act in which a firm engages in price discrimination to compete in good faith with another seller's low price.

members Owners of a limited liability company.

mens rea Latin for "guilty mind"; the mental state accompanying a wrongful behavior.

merchant A person who deals in goods of the kind or by his occupation holds himself out as having knowledge or skill peculiar to the practices or goods involved in the transaction, or a person who employs an intermediary who, by her occupation, holds herself out as having such knowledge or skill.

merger A combination of two or more corporations in which only one of the corporations continues to exist.

merger clause A clause in a written agreement within the statute of frauds which states that the written agreement accurately reflects the final, complete version of the agreement.

minitrial A type of conflict resolution in which lawyers for each side present their arguments to a neutral adviser, who then offers an opinion on what the verdict will be if the case goes to trial. This decision is not binding.

minor A person who has not yet reached the age of 18.

Miranda rights The rights that are read to an arrested individual by a law enforcement agent before the individual is questioned about the commission of the crime.

mirror-image rule A principle which holds that the terms of an acceptance must mirror the terms of the offer. If the terms of the acceptance do not mirror the terms of the offer, no contract is formed and the attempted acceptance is a counteroffer.

misappropriation theory A theory of insider trading which holds that if an individual wrongfully acquires (misappropriates) and uses inside information for trading for his or her personal gain, that person is liable for insider trading.

misdemeanor A crime that is less serious than a felony and is punishable by a fine and/or imprisonment for less than one year.

misrepresentation An untruthful assertion by one of the parties about a material fact.

mistake An erroneous belief about the facts of a contract at the time the contract is concluded. When a mistake occurs, legal assent is absent.

mistake of fact (1) A mistake that is not caused by the neglect of a legal duty by the person committing the mistake but, rather, consists of unconscious ignorance of a past or present material event or circumstance. (2) An affirmative defense in which the defendant tries to prove that she or he made an honest and reasonable mistake that negates the guilty-mind element of a crime.

mixed sale A contract that combines one or more goods with one or more services.

mock trial A contrived or imitation trial, recruited by a jury selection firm, that attorneys sometimes use in preparing for a real trial in order to test theories, experiment with arguments, and try to predict the outcome of the real trial.

model law See **uniform law.**

modified comparative negligence In some states, a defense whereby the defendant is not liable for the percentage of harm that he or she proves can be attributed to the plaintiff's own negligence if the plaintiff's negligence is responsible for less than 50 percent of the harm. If the defendant establishes that the plaintiff's negligence caused more than 50 percent of the harm, the defendant has no liability.

modify An appellate court decision that grants an alternative remedy in a case; granted when the court finds that the decision of the lower court was correct but the remedy was not.

monetary damages Money claimed by or ordered paid to a party to compensate for injury or loss caused by the wrong of the opposite party.

money order A signed document indicating that funds are to be paid from the drawee to the drawer.

monopoly power The ability to control price and drive competitors out of the market.

moral hazard The possibility that individuals who are insulated from risk sometimes behave differently than they would if not insulated.

most-favored-nation relations See **normal trade relations.**

motion In a civil case, a request made by either party that asks a judge or a court to issue an order in that party's favor.

motion for judgment on the pleadings In a civil case, a request made by either party, after pleadings have been entered, that asks a judge or a court, to issue a judgment.

motion for summary judgment In a civil case, a request made by either party that asks a judge or a court to promptly and expeditiously dispose of the case without a trial. Any evidence or information that would be admissible at trial may be considered on a motion for summary judgment. The court may hold oral arguments or decide the motion on the basis of the parties' briefs and supporting documentation alone.

motion to dismiss In a civil case, a request by the defendant that asks a judge or a court to dismiss the case because even if all the allegations are true, the plaintiff is not entitled to any legal relief. Also called *demurrer.*

movability The quality of a negotiable instrument that ensures it is mobile and available.

multilateral trade agreement An international agreement between three or more nations that relates to trade between them.

multiple-product order A form of cease-and-desist order issued by the FTC that applies not only to a specified product but also to other products produced by the same firm.

mutual (mistake) The result of an error by both parties about a material fact, i.e., one that is important in the context of a particular contract.

N

National Labor Relations Act Federal labor legislation consisting of the Wagner and Taft-Hartley acts.

National Labor Relations Board (NLRB) An administrative agency created by the Wagner Act to interpret and enforce the National Labor Relations Act (NLRA).

national treatment A GATT principle of trade law that prohibits WTO member states from regulating, taxing, or otherwise treating imported products any differently from domestically produced products.

natural law A school of jurisprudence that recognizes the existence of higher law, or law that is morally superior to human laws.

necessary A basic necessity of life, generally including food, clothing, shelter, and basic medical services.

necessity An affirmative defense in which the defendant tries to prove that he or she was acting to prevent imminent harm and that there was no legal alternative to the action the defendant took.

negligence Behavior that creates an unreasonable risk of harm to others.

negligence per se A doctrine that allows a judge or jury to infer duty and breach of duty from the fact that a defendant violated a statute that was designed to prevent the type of harm that the plaintiff incurred.

negligent misrepresentation A false statement of material fact made by a person who thinks it is true but who would have known the truth about the fact had he or she used reasonable care to discover or reveal it.

negligent tort A civil wrong that occurs when the defendant acts in a way that subjects other people to an unreasonable risk of harm (i.e., the defendant is careless, to someone else's detriment). Negligence claims are usually used to achieve compensation for accidents and injuries.

negotiable instrument A written document signed by a person who makes an unconditional promise to pay a specific sum of money on demand or at a certain time to the holder of the instrument; an acceptable medium for exchanging value from one person to another.

negotiation (1) A bargaining process in which disputing parties interact informally to attempt to resolve their dispute. (2) The transfer of the rights to a negotiable instrument from one party to another.

New York Convention An international agreement governing the use of arbitration as a method of resolving private international disputes.

no-par share A stock share that does not have a par value.

nolo contendere A plea in which the defendant does not admit guilt but agrees not to contest the charges.

nominal damages Monetary damages awarded to a plaintiff in a very small amount, typically $1 to $5, to signify that the plaintiff has been wronged by the defendant even though the plaintiff suffered no compensable harm.

nondisclosure The failure to provide pertinent information about a projected contract.

nonprobate property Property that is not part of a probate estate.

nonprofit corporation A corporation that operates for educational, charitable, social, religious, civic, or humanitarian purposes, rather than to earn a profit.

nontariff barrier Any impediment to international trade other than tariffs.

normal trade relations A GATT principle of trade law which requires that WTO member states treat like goods coming from other member states on an equal basis.

North American Free Trade Agreement (NAFTA) An international agreement between the United States, Canada, and Mexico whereby tariffs and other trade barriers will be reduced and gradually eliminated.

note A promise by the maker of the note to pay the payee of the note.

notice-and-comment rule making See **informal rule making.**

novation In a contract, the substitution of a third party for one of the original parties. The duties remain the same under the contract, but one original party is discharged and the third party takes that original party's place.

nuisance A person's use of her property in a manner that unreasonably interferes with another's use and enjoyment of his land.

O

objective impossibility (of performance) In a contract, a situation in which it is in fact not possible to lawfully carry out one's contractual obligations.

obligee A contractual party who agrees to receive something from the other party.

obligor A contractual party who agrees to do something for the other party.

Occupational Safety and Health Act (OSHA) of 1970 Federal law that established the Occupational Safety and Health Administration, the agency responsible for setting safety standards under the act and for enforcing the act through inspections and the levying of fines against violators.

offer A key factor in the agreement element of a contract; consists of the terms and conditions set by one party, the offeror, and presented to another party, the offeree.

Omnibus Crime Control and Safe Streets Act of 1968 Federal statute that prohibits employers from listening to the private telephone conversations of employees or disclosing the contents of these conversations. Employers may ban personal calls and monitor calls for compliance as long as they discontinue listening to any conversation once they determine it is personal.

option contract An agreement whereby the offeree gives the offeror a piece of consideration in exchange for the offeror's agreement to hold the offer open for a specified period of time.

order (1) An order to appear and bring specified documents. (2) A binding decision issued by an ALJ after a hearing.

order instrument An instrument payable to a specific, named payee.

order of relief An order stating that bankruptcy proceedings can continue.

organ donor card A document that expresses a person's desire to donate organs or tissue.

overdraft A bank's action to pay an amount specified on a check, without there being sufficient funds in its customer's account.

P

par-value share A stock share that has a fixed face value noted on the stock certificate.

parent-subsidiary merger See **short-form merger.**

parol evidence rule A common law rule which states that oral evidence of an agreement made prior to or contemporaneously with a written agreement is inadmissible when the parties intend to have the written agreement be the complete and final version of their agreement.

partial eviction An eviction in which a landlord prevents the tenant from entering part of the leased premises.

partial performance An exception to the statute of frauds in which the performance of portions of an unwritten agreement by one or both parties can constitute proof that an oral contract exists between the parties.

partially disclosed principal A principal whose identity is not known by a third party, although the third party is aware that the agent is making an agreement on behalf of a principal. Also called *unidentified principal.*

partnership A voluntary association between two or more people who co-own a business for profit.

past consideration Something given or done in the past by one party that later prompts a promise by another party. As such, nothing has been given in exchange, and the court will not enforce the promise.

patent Protection that grants the holder the exclusive right to produce, sell, and use the patented object for 20 years; can be obtained for a product, process, invention, or machine or a plant produced by asexual reproduction.

payee The party that receives the benefit of an order (check, etc.).

payor bank The bank responsible for disbursing the funds indicated on a check.

per se violation An action that by its very existence carries with it liability, as opposed to an action that violates a rule of reason.

peremptory challenge In a jury trial, the right of the plaintiff and the defendant in jury selection to reject, without stating a reason, a certain number of potential jurors who appear to have an unfavorable bias.

perfect tender rule The requirement that a seller deliver goods in conformity with the contract, down to the last detail.

perfection The series of legal steps a secured party takes to protect its right in collateral from other creditors that want to have their debts returned through the same collateral.

periodic-tenancy lease A lease created for a recurring term.

personal defense A liability defense that is not applicable to holders in due course.

personal insurance Insurance that covers an individual's health or life.

personal jurisdiction See ***in personam* jurisdiction.**

personal property Any property that is not land or permanently affixed to the land.

personal representative The person designated by a testator to collect the testator's property after he or she dies, pay the debts and taxes, and make sure the remainder of the estate gets distributed.

personal service The process in which an officer of the court hands legal documents, such as a summons or complaint, to the defendant.

petit jury A group of 6 to 12 citizens who are summoned to court and sworn in by the court to hear evidence presented by both sides and render a verdict in a trial.

petty offense A minor crime that is punishable by a small fine and/or imprisonment for less than six months in a jail.

picketing A labor activity in which individuals place themselves outside an employer's place of business for the purpose of informing passersby of the facts of a labor dispute.

plain-meaning rule A rule of interpretation which states that words in a contract should be given their ordinary meaning.

plaintiff The person or party who initiates a lawsuit (an action) before a court by filing a complaint with the clerk of the court against the defendant(s). Also known as *claimant* or *complainant.*

plea bargain An agreement in which the prosecutor agrees to reduce charges, drop charges, or recommend a certain sentence if the defendant pleads guilty.

pledge The transfer of collateral to a secured party.

point-of-sale system An EFT system that enables consumers to directly transfer funds from a bank account to a merchant.

police power The power retained by each state to pass laws that protect the health, safety, and welfare of its citizens.

policy The insurance document signed by the insured party and the insurer.

policy statement A general statement about the directions in which any agency intends to proceed with respect to its rule-making or enforcement activities; has no binding impact on anyone.

political speech Speech that is used to support political candidates or referenda. Compared to other types of speech, it is given a high level of protection by the First Amendment.

posteffective period In securities registration, the period that begins when the SEC declares the registration statement effective and ends when the issuer sells all the securities offered or withdraws them from sale.

posttrial motion A request filed after a trial is over, by either party, to the trial court. Types include a motion for a new trial, a motion for judgment notwithstanding the verdict (JNOV), and a motion to amend or nullify the judgment.

power of attorney A specific type of express authority that grants an agent specific powers.

precedent A tool used by judges to make rulings on cases on the basis of key similarities to previous cases.

predatory pricing The practice in which a company prices one product below normal cost until competitors are eliminated and then it sharply increases the price.

preexisting duty A promise to do something that one is already obligated to do. It is not considered valid consideration.

preferential payment **A** payment made by an insolvent debtor that gives preferential treatment to one creditor over another.

preferred stock Stock that conveys preferences to its holder with respect to assets and dividends.

prefiling period In securities registration, the period that begins when an issuer starts to think about issuing securities and ends when the issuer files the registration statement and prospectus with the SEC.

Pregnancy Discrimination Act (PDA) of 1987 Federal law that amended Title VII of the Civil Rights Act of 1964 by expanding the definition of sex discrimination to include discrimination based on pregnancy.

prejudicial error of law An error of law that is so significant that it affects the outcome of the case.

premium An insurance payment.

prenuptial agreement An agreement two parties enter into before marriage that clearly states the ownership rights each party enjoys in the other party's property. To be enforceable, it must be in writing.

presentment The act of making a demand for the drawee to pay.

presentment warranty A warranty covering the parties accepting an instrument for payment; created to ensure that the accepting or paying party is paying the proper party.

pretrial An event that includes consultation with attorneys, pleadings, the discovery process, and the pretrial conference.

pretrial conference A meeting of the judge and the attorneys for both sides to narrow the issues for trial and identify witnesses for trial.

price discrimination The practice of selling the same goods to different buyers at different prices.

price fixing A restraint of trade in which two or more competitors agree to set prices for a product or service.

prima facie Latin for "at first view"; term applied to evidence that is sufficient to raise a presumption that a wrong occurred.

primarily liable Liable for paying the amount designated on an instrument when it is presented for payment.

primary boycott A boycott against an employer with whom the union is directly engaged in a labor dispute.

primary-line injury Under the Robinson-Patman Act, an injury that occurs when preferential treatment is given to a competitor.

principal The party that an agent's authority can bind or act on behalf of.

principle of rights The principle that judges the morality of a decision on the basis of how it affects the rights of all those involved.

Privacy Act Federal law that mandates that a federal agency may not disclose information about an individual to other agencies or organizations without that individual's written consent.

privacy tort A wrongful act in which invasion of privacy causes damage to an individual and for which a civil action can be brought. The four privacy torts are false light, public disclosure of private facts, appropriation for commercial gain, and intrusion on an individual's affairs or seclusion.

private corporation A corporation that is created by private persons and does not have government duties.

private law Law that involves suits between private individuals or groups.

private nuisance A nuisance that affects only a single individual or a very limited number of individuals.

private placement exemption An exemption from the SEC's securities registration process because the offerings are being made to private accredited investors and will not be advertised to the general public.

private trial An ADR method in which a referee is selected and paid by the disputing parties to offer a legally binding judgment in a dispute.

privileges and immunities clause The clause in the U.S. Constitution which requires that each state grant citizens of other states the same legal benefits that it grants its own citizens.

privity of contract The relationship that exists between parties to a contract.

probable cause Any essential element and/or standard by which a lawful officer may make a valid arrest, conduct a personal or property search, or obtain a warrant.

probate The process of settling an estate.

problem-solving negotiation Negotiation in which the parties seek to achieve joint gain.

procedural due process The requirement that a government must use fair procedures before depriving a person of his or her life, liberty, or property.

procedural unconscionability Unconscionability that derives from the process of making a contract.

proceeds Something that is exchanged for a debtor's sold collateral.

product liability insurance Insurance that protects a company from liability in the event that its customers suffer injury.

product market A market in which all products identical to or substitutes for a company's product are sold.

professional insurance Insurance that protects professionals from suits by third parties who claim negligent job performance.

profit The right to go onto someone's land and take part of the land or a product of it away from the land.

promisee In a third-party beneficiary contract, the party to the contract who owes something to the promisor in exchange for the promise made to the third-party beneficiary.

promisor In a third-party beneficiary contract, the party to the contract who made the promise that benefits the third party.

promissory estoppel The legal enforcement of an otherwise unenforceable contract due to a party's detrimental reliance on the contract.

promoter A person who begins the corporate creation and organization process.

property insurance Insurance that protects property from loss or damages.

prospectus A written document filed with the SEC that contains a description of a security and other financial information regarding the company offering the security; also distributed as an advertising tool to potential investors.

proximate cause The extent to which, as a matter of policy, a defendant may be held liable for the consequences of his or her actions. In the majority of states, proximate cause requires that the plaintiff and the type of injury suffered by the plaintiff were foreseeable at the time of the accident. In the minority of states, proximate cause exists if the defendant's actions led to the plaintiff's harm.

proxy A writing signed by a shareholder that authorizes the individual named in the writing to exercise the shareholder's votes (corresponding to his or her shares of stock) at a shareholders' meeting.

proxy solicitation The process of obtaining authority to vote on behalf of shareholders.

public corporation A corporation that is created by government to help administer law.

public disclosure of private facts A privacy tort that occurs when a person publishes a highly offensive private fact, such as information about one's sex life or failure to pay debts, about someone who did not waive his or her right to privacy.

public disclosure test The ethical guideline that urges us to consider how others may view our actions when making a decision.

public figure privilege A special right, immunity, or permission that allows people to make any statement about public figures, typically politicians and entertainers, without being held liable for defamation as long as false statements were not made with malice.

public law Law that involves suits between private individuals or groups and their governments.

public policy exception An exception to the employment-at-will doctrine that prohibits employers from firing employees for doing something that is consistent with furthering public policy.

publicly held corporation A corporation whose stock is available to the public.

puffing The use of generalities and clear exaggerations.

punitive damages Compensation awarded to a plaintiff that goes beyond reimbursement for actual losses and is imposed to punish the defendant and deter such conduct in the future. Also called *exemplary damages.*

purchase-money security interest (PMSI) A security interest formed when a debtor uses borrowed money from the secured party to buy the collateral.

pure comparative negligence A defense accepted in some states whereby the defendant is not liable for the percentage of harm that he or she can prove can be attributed to the plaintiff's own negligence.

Q

qualified endorsement An endorsement that does not bind the endorser to the negotiable instrument in the event that the creator does not honor that instrument.

quantitative restriction A limit on the importation of certain goods that is imposed on the basis of number of units, weight, or value for national economic reason, or for the protection of domestic industry; prohibited by GATT.

quasi-contract A court-imposed contractual obligation to prevent unjust enrichment.

quasi *in rem* jurisdiction A type of jurisdiction exercised by a court over an out-of-state defendant's property that is within the jurisdictional boundaries of the court; applies to personal suits against a defendant in which the property is not the source of the conflict but is sought as compensation by the plaintiff. Also called *attachment jurisdiction.*

quick-look standard In a restraint of trade case, the standard that allows a defendant to offer justification for his or her per se violation.

quitclaim deed A deed that carries no warranties. The grantor simply conveys whatever interests he or she holds.

R

Racketeer Influenced and Corrupt Organizations (RICO) Act Federal law that provides extended penalties for criminal acts performed as part of an ongoing criminal organization.

ratify To approve an unauthorized agent's signature on an instrument.

rational-basis test The lowest standard of review; requires that a law be designed to protect a legitimate state interest and be rationally related to that interest.

reaffirmation agreement An agreement in which a debtor agrees to pay a debt even though it could have been discharged in bankruptcy.

real defense A liability defense that applies universally to all parties.

real property Land and everything permanently attached to it.

resonable expectation of privacy Under the ECPA, the protection afforded to individuals' communications against unauthorized surveillance or access; applies only minimally to communications via an employer's equipment.

reasonable person standard A measurement of the way members of society expect an individual to act in a given situation.

recognizance An obligation in which a party acknowledges in court that he or she will perform some specified act and/or pay a price on failure to do so.

recording Filing a deed, with any other related documents such as mortgages, with the appropriate county office, thereby giving official notice of the transfer to all interested parties.

red-herring prospectus A prospectus with a warning written in red print at the top of the page telling investors that the registration has been filed with the SEC but not yet approved.

refusal to deal See **group boycott.**

reg-neg A type of rule making in which representatives of concerned interest groups and of the involved government agency participate in mediated bargaining sessions to reach an agreement, which is forwarded to the agency.

registration statement A description, filed with the SEC, of securities being offered for sale; includes an explanation of how proceeds from the sale will be used, information on the registrant's business and properties, and certified financial statements.

rejection Termination of a contract that occurs when an offeree does not accept the offer or terms of the contract.

relative permanence The quality of a negotiable instrument that ensures its longevity.

remainderman The recipient of the trust corpus, the property held in trust, when the trust is terminated.

remand An appellate court decision that returns a case to the trial court for a new trial or for a limited hearing on a specified subject matter; rendered when the court decides that an error was committed that may have affected the outcome of the case.

rent The compensation paid to a landlord for the tenant's right to possession and exclusive use of the premises.

rent escalation clause In a lease, a clause that permits the landlord to increase the rent in association with increases in costs of living, property taxes, or the tenant's commercial business.

reply A response by the plaintiff to the defendant's counterclaim.

request to produce documents In a lawsuit, a discovery tool that forces the opposing party to produce certain information unless it is privileged or irrelevant to the case.

res ipsa loquitur A doctrine that allows a judge or jury to infer that, more likely than not, the defendant's negligence was the cause of the plaintiff's harm even though there is no direct evidence of the defendant's lack of due care.

rescind To cancel a contract.

rescission The termination of a contract.

respondeat superior Latin for "let the superior speak"; the principle by which liability for harm caused by an agent/employee is held by the principal/employer.

Restatements of the Law Summaries of common law rules in a particular area of the law. Restatements do not carry the weight of law but can be used to guide interpretations of particular cases.

restitution The return of any property given up under a contract.

restricted security A security that has limited transferability and is usually issued in a private placement.

restrictive covenant A promise to use or not to use one's land in particular ways.

restrictive endorsement An endorsement that limits the transferability of an instrument or controls the manner of payment under an instrument.

retained earnings Profits that a corporation keeps.

reverse An appellate court decision that overturns the judgment of a lower court, concluding that the lower court was incorrect and its verdict cannot be allowed to stand.

revocation Termination of a contract that occurs when an offeror takes back the initial offer and annuls the opportunity for the offeree to accept the offer.

RICO Act See **Racketeer Influenced and Corrupt Organizations (RICO) Act.**

right of first refusal A method of restricting stock transferability whereby a corporation or its shareholders have the right to purchase any shares of stock offered for resale by a shareholder within a specified time frame.

right of survivorship The right that specific partnership property will pass on to the surviving partner(s).

right to die A person's right to place limits on other people's efforts to prolong her or his life.

rightfully dissolved A term applied to the dissolution of a partnership in a way that does not violate the partnership agreement.

ripeness A measure of the readiness of a case for a decision to be made; designed to prevent premature litigation for a dispute that is insufficiently developed. A claim is not ripe for litigation if it rests on contingent future events that may not occur as anticipated or may not occur at all.

risk A potential loss.

risk management The transfer and distribution of risk.

robbery The unlawful taking or attempted taking of personal property by force or threat of force and/or by putting the victim in fear.

rule-of-reason analysis An inquiry into the competitive effects of a company's anticompetitive behavior to determine whether the benefits of the behavior outweigh the harm.

rule utilitarianism A subset of utilitarianism which holds that general rules that *on balance* produce the greatest amount of pleasure for all involved should be established and followed in each situation.

S

S corporation A corporation that enjoys the tax status of a partnership.

Sabbath law A law that prohibits the performance of certain activities on Sundays.

sale The passing of title from a seller to a buyer for a price.

sale-on-approval contract A contract in which the seller allows the buyer to take possession of the goods before deciding whether to complete the contract by making the purchase.

sale-or-return contract A contract in which the buyer and seller agree that the buyer may return the goods at a later time.

Sarbanes-Oxley Act Federal law that criminalizes specific nonaudit services when they are provided by a registered accounting firm to an audit client; also increases the punishment for a number of white-collar offenses. Also known as the *Public Company Accounting Reform and Investor Protection Act of 2002.*

scienter Deliberately or knowingly.

search warrant A court order that authorizes law enforcement agents to search for or seize items specifically described in the warrant.

secondarily liable Liable for paying the amount designated on an instrument should the primarily liable party default.

secondary boycott An illegal labor action in which unionized employees who have a labor dispute with their employer boycott another company to force it to cease doing business with their employer.

secondary-line injury Under the Robinson-Patman Act, an injury that is created when preferential treatment is granted to specific buyers.

secured interest An interest in personal property or fixtures that secures payment or performance to a creditor.

secured party The party that holds an interest in a secured property.

secured transaction A transaction in which the payment of a debt is guaranteed by personal property owned by the debtor.

security A financial instrument designated as a note, stock, or bond or any other instrument named in the Securities Act of 1933.

security agreement An agreement in which a debtor gives a secured interest to a secured party.

self-dealing Any instance in which directors or officers make decisions that violate their corporate duty of loyalty.

self-tender offer A takeover-resistance strategy in which a target corporation offers to buy its shareholders' stock.

service of process The procedure by which a court delivers a copy of the statement of claim or other legal documents, such as a summons, complaint, or subpoena, to a defendant.

settlor A person who creates a trust.

severable contract A contract whose terms can be divided.

sexual harassment Unwelcome sexual advances, requests for sexual favors, and other verbal or physical conduct of a sexual nature that makes submission a condition of employment or a factor in employment decisions or that creates an intimidating, hostile, or offensive work environment. The two types are hostile environment and quid pro quo.

shadow jury An unofficial jury, hired by a party in a legal case, that watches the actual trial and deliberates at the end of each day to give the attorney an idea of how the real jurors are reacting to the case.

shareholder An investor who holds stock in a corporation, and thus is an owner of the corporation.

shareholder's derivative suit A lawsuit filed by a shareholder on behalf of the corporation.

shelter principle The principle which holds that when an item is transferred, the transferee acquires all the rights the transferor had to the item.

short-form merger A merger in which a parent corporation absorbs a subsidiary corporation. Also called *parent-subsidiary merger.*

short-swing profits Profits made from the sale of company stock within any six-month period by a statutory insider.

signal picketing An unprotected form of picketing in which services and/or deliveries to the employer are cut off.

signature liability Liability that is attributed because of a party's signature on an instrument.

simple contract A contract that is not a formal contract. Also called an *informal contract.*

simple delivery contract A type of contract in which purchased goods are transferred to a buyer from a seller either at the time of the sale or sometime later by the seller's delivery.

situational ethics An ethical theory which holds that to evaluate the morality of an action, we must imagine ourselves in the position of the person facing the ethical dilemma and then, on that basis, determine whether that person's action was ethical.

slander of quality A business tort that occurs when false spoken statements criticize a business product or service and result in a loss of sales.

slander of title A business tort that occurs when false published statements are related to the ownership of the business property.

smart card A plastic card, similar to an ATM card, that contains a microchip for storing data; used to electronically transfer funds.

social responsibility of business The responsibility of firms doing business within a community to meet the expectations that the community imposes on them.

socialist law A legal system based on the premise that the rights of society as a whole outweigh the rights of the individual.

sole proprietor The single person at the head of a sole proprietorship.

sole proprietorship A business in which one person (sole proprietor) controls the management and profits.

special damages See **consequential damages.**

special endorsement An endorser's signature accompanying the name of the endorsee.

special power of attorney A type of express authority that allows an agent to act on behalf of the principal only in regard to specifically outlined acts.

special qualified endorsement A special endorsement containing words that limit the enforceability of the check, such as the term *without recourse* (which means the endorser will not be liable).

special warranty deed A deed which promises only that the seller has not done anything to lessen the value of the estate.

specific performance An order of the court requiring that a nonbreaching party fulfill the terms of the contract.

specific personal jurisdiction A doctrine permitting adjudication of a claim against a defendant only if the defendant purposefully availed himself or herself of the protections of the forum and if the selected forum is reasonable.

stakeholders The groups of people affected by a firm's decisions.

stale check A check that is not presented to a bank within six months of its date.

standing The legal right of a party to bring a lawsuit by demonstrating to the court sufficient connection to and harm from the law or action challenged (i.e., the plaintiff must demonstrate that he or she is harmed or will be harmed). Otherwise, the court will dismiss the case, ruling that the plaintiff "lacks standing" to bring the suit.

stare decisis Latin for "standing by the decision"; a principle stating that rulings made in higher courts are binding precedent for lower courts.

statute of frauds State-level legislation that addresses the enforceability of contracts that fail to meet the requirements set forth in the statute; serves to protect promisors from poorly considered oral contracts by requiring that certain contracts be in writing.

statutory insiders Certain large stockholders, executive officers, and directors who are deemed insiders by the Securities Exchange Act of 1934.

statutory law The assortment of rules and regulations put forth by legislatures.

stock certificate A document that serves as a stockholder's proof of ownership in a corporation.

stock warrant A type of security issued by a corporation (usually together with a bond or preferred stock) that gives the holder the right to purchase a certain amount of common stock at a stated price.

stop-payment order An order by a drawer that instructs the drawee bank not to pay an issued check.

stored-value card A plastic card that contains data regarding the value of the card, thereby allowing EFTs to be made.

strict liability Liability in which responsibility for damages is imposed regardless of the existence of negligence. Also called *liability without fault.*

strict-liability offense An offense for which no *mens rea* is required.

strict-liability tort A civil wrong that occurs when a defendant takes an action that is inherently dangerous and cannot ever be undertaken safely, no matter what precautions the defendant takes. The defendant is liable for the plaintiff's damages without any requirement that the plaintiff prove that the defendant was negligent.

strict product liability Liability under which, courts may hold the manufacturer, distributor, or retailer liable for any reasonably foreseeable injured party.

strict scrutiny The most exacting standard of review used by the courts in determining the constitutionality of a statute; requires a compelling government interest and the least restrictive means of attaining that objective.

strike A temporary, concerted withdrawal of labor.

subject-matter jurisdiction The power of a court over the type of case presented to it.

subjective impossibility (of performance) In a contract, a situation in which it would be very difficult for a party to carry out his or her contractual obligations.

sublease A transfer of less than all of a tenant's interest in a leased property.

submission agreement A contract which provides that a specific dispute will be resolved in arbitration.

subpoena An order to appear at a particular time and place and provide testimony.

subpoena *duces tecum* An order to appear and bring specified documents.

subscriber An investor who agrees to purchase stock in a new corporation.

subscription agreement An agreement between promoters (persons raising capital for a new corporation) and subscribers (investors) in which the subscribers agree to purchase stock in the new corporation.

subsidy A financial contribution by a government that confers a benefit on a specific industry or enterprise.

substantial evidence The type of evidence required by a court to support an agency's fact finding.

substantial impairment A concept, used to modify the perfect tender rule, whereby a buyer can revoke acceptance of goods or a buyer/lessee can reject an installment of a particular item only if the defects substantially impair the value of the goods.

substantial performance Contract performance that occurs when nearly all the terms of the agreement have been met, there has been an honest effort to complete all the terms, and there has been no willful departure from the terms of the agreement.

substantive due process The requirement that laws depriving an individual of life, liberty, or property be fair and not arbitrary.

substantive unconscionability Unconscionability that derives from contract terms that are so one-sided, unjust, or overly harsh that the contract should not be enforced.

summary jury trial An abbreviated trial that leads to a nonbinding jury verdict.

summons A legal document issued by a court and addressed to a defendant that notifies him or her of a lawsuit and specifies how and when to respond to the complaint. A summons may be used in both civil and criminal proceedings.

supremacy clause Article VI, Paragraph 2, of the U.S. Constitution, which states that the Constitution and all laws and treaties of the United States constitute the supreme law of the land. Thus, any state or local law that directly conflicts with the U.S. Constitution or federal laws or treaties is void.

suretyship A contract between a creditor and a third party who agrees to pay another person's debt.

surrender A mutual agreement between a landlord and a tenant in which the lessee returns his or her interest in the premises to the landlord.

syndicate An investment group that comes together for the explicit purpose of financing a specific large project.

T

Taft-Hartley Act Federal legislation designed to curtail some of the powers that unions had acquired under the Wagner Act; designates certain union actions as unfair. Also called *Labor-Management Relations Act.*

takings clause A clause in the Fifth Amendment of the U.S. Constitution requiring that when government uses its power to take private property for public use, it must pay the owner just compensation, or fair market value, for the property. Also called *just-compensation clause.*

tariff A tax levied on imported goods.

teller's check A check for which the drawer and drawee are separate banks.

tenancy-at-sufferance lease A lease that is created when a tenant who was lawfully in possession of a leased property remains in possession of that property unlawfully after the lease ends because the person with the power to evict him failed to do so.

tenancy-at-will lease A lease that may be terminated by the parties at any time.

tenancy by the entirety A type of co-ownership that is available only to married couples. The spouses' shares are equal, and if one owner dies, the surviving spouse assumes full ownership.

tenancy in common A type of co-ownership in which each owner has the right to sell his or her interest without the consent of the other owners, may own an unequal share of the property, and may have a creditor attach his or her interest.

tenant A person who assumes the temporary legal right to possess property. Also called *lessee.*

tender An offer by a contracting party to perform, along with being ready, willing, and able to perform, a duty outlined in the contract.

tender of delivery A requirement that a seller/lessor have and hold conforming goods at the disposal of the buyer/lessee and give the buyer/lessee reasonable notification to enable him or her to take delivery.

tender offer A type of takeover in which an aggressor corporation offers the target shareholders a price above their stock's current market value.

term-life insurance Life insurance that provides coverage for a specified term.

termination In a contract, the point at which an offer can no longer be accepted as part of a binding agreement or an offeree no longer has the power to form a legally binding contract by accepting the offer; can occur through revocation by the offeror, rejection by the offeree, death or incapacity of the offeror, destruction or subsequent illegality of the subject matter of the offer, or lapse of time or failure of another condition stated in the offer.

termination statement An amendment to a financing statement which states that the debtor has no obligation to the secured party.

tertiary-line injury Under the Robinson-Patman Act, an injury that occurs when someone who is given an illegally low price passes his savings on to his customers.

testamentary capacity The minimum age required to write a legal will and be of sound mind.

testamentary trust An express trust created by a will.

testator A person who writes a will.

third-party beneficiary A recipient of contractual benefits who is not one of the contracting parties; created when two parties enter into a contract with the intended purpose of benefiting a third party.

time instrument A type of draft that allows the payee to collect payment only at a specific time in the future.

tippee An individual who receives confidential information from an insider.

tipper An insider who gives inside information to someone.

tipper/tippee theory A theory of insider trading which holds that any individual (tippee) who acquires material inside information as a result of an insider's (tipper's) breach of duty has engaged in insider trading.

Title VII See **Civil Rights Act (CRA) of 1964—Title VII.**

tombstone advertisement A print advertisement that announces a forthcoming sale of securities in a format similar to that of a tombstone.

tort A violation of another person's rights or a civil wrongdoing that does not arise out of a contract or statute; primary types are intentional, negligent, and strict-liability torts.

tortfeasor A person who commits an intentional or through-negligence tort that causes a harm or loss for which a civil remedy may be sought.

trade dress The overall appearance and image of a product.

trade libel A business tort that occurs when false printed statements criticize a business product or service and result in a loss of sales.

trade secret A process, product, method of operation, or compilation of information that gives a businessperson an advantage over his or her competitors.

trademark A distinctive mark, word, design, picture, or arrangement that is used by a producer in conjunction with a product and tends to cause consumers to identify the product with the producer.

trademark dilution The use of a distinctive or famous trademark, such as "McDonald's," in a manner that diminishes the value of the mark.

transfer warranty A warranty regarding a negotiable instrument and its transfer; created by the party who transfers the instrument.

traveler's check An order that is payable on demand, is drawn on or through a bank, is designated by the phrase *traveler's check,* and requires a countersignature by the person whose signature appears on the check.

treaty A binding agreement between two nations or international organizations.

trespass to personalty The temporary interference with a person's use or enjoyment of his or her personal property.

trespass to realty A tort that occurs when someone goes on another's property without permission or places something on another's property without permission.

trial An event in which parties to a dispute present evidence in court, before a judge or a jury, in order to achieve a resolution to their dispute.

trial court A court in which most civil or criminal cases start when they first enter the legal system. The parties present evidence and call witnesses to testify. Trial courts are referred to as *courts of common pleas* or *county courts* in state court systems and *district courts* in the federal system. Also called *court of original jurisdiction* and *court of first instance.*

trust (1) A business arrangement in which stock owners appoint beneficiaries and place their securities with a trustee, who manages the company and pays a share of the earnings to the stockholders. (2) An estate-planning arrangement whereby a person transfers property to another person and the property is used for the benefit of a third person.

trust endorsement An endorsement that is used when the instrument is being transferred to an agent or trustee for the benefit of either the endorser or a third party; gives the endorser the rights of a holder.

trustee (1) In bankruptcy proceeding, an individual who takes over administration of a debtor's estate. (2) A person who operates a business trust for beneficiaries.

tying arrangement Illegal agreement in which the sale of one product is tied to the sale of another.

U

unconscionability Ground for rescinding an unconscionable contract.

unconscionable A term applied to a contract in which one party has so much more bargaining power than the other party that the powerful party dictates the terms of the agreement and eliminates the other party's free will.

underwriter A party who receives payments from an insured party and makes the payment to the beneficiary.

undisclosed principal A principal whose existence is not known by a third party. That is, the third party does not know that an agent is acting on behalf of a principal.

undue influence The situation in which one person takes advantage of his or her dominant position in a relationship to unfairly persuade the other person and interfere with that person's ability to make his or her own decision.

unemployment compensation The state system, created by the Federal Unemployment Tax Act, that provides unemployment compensation to qualified employees who lose their jobs.

unenforceable A term applied to a contract that, because of a law, cannot be enforced by the courts.

unfair competition The act of competing with another not to make a profit but for the sole purpose of driving that other out of business.

unfortunate accident An incident that simply could not be avoided, even with reasonable care.

unidentified principal See **partially disclosed principal.**

Uniform Commercial Code (UCC) A statutory source of contract law in the United States that is applicable to transactions involving the sale of goods. The UCC was created in 1952 and adopted by all 50 states, the District of Columbia, and the Virgin Islands; it may be modified by each state to reflect the wishes of the state legislature.

uniform law A law created to account for the variability of laws among states; serves to standardize the otherwise different interstate laws. Also called *model law.*

Uniform Probate Code A statute that clarifies laws that govern transfers accomplished through wills and trusts.

unilateral A mistake that is the result of an error by one party about a material fact, that is, a fact that is important in the context of the particular contract.

unilateral contract A promise exchanged for an act.

unilateral mistake The result of an error by one party about a material fact, i.e., a fact that is important in the context of a particular contract.

United Nations Convention on Contracts for the International Sale of Goods (CISG) The legal structure for international sales, including business-to-business sales contracts.

universalization test The ethical guideline that urges us to consider, before we act, what the world would be like if everyone acted in that way.

unliquidated debt A debt for which the parties either dispute the fact that any money is owed or agree that some money is owed but dispute the amount.

unprotected speech Speech that is not protected by the First Amendment; includes hate speech, insulting or fighting words, obscenity, and defamation.

unqualified opinion letter A letter issued by an auditor when the financial statements presented are free of material misstatements and are in accordance with GAAP.

usage of trade Any practice that members of an industry expect to be part of their dealings.

usury The lending of money at an exorbitant or unlawful rate of interest.

utilitarianism The ethical principle that urges individuals to act in a way that creates the most happiness for the largest number of people.

V

valid A term applied to a contract that includes all four elements of a contract—agreement (offer and acceptance), consideration, contractual capacity, and legal object—and thus is enforceable.

values Positive abstractions that capture our sense of what is good and desirable.

venue The court with subject-matter and personal jurisdiction that is the most appropriate geographic location for the resolution of a dispute.

vertical merger A merger in which a company at one level of the manufacturing-distribution system acquires a company at another level of the system.

vertical restraint against trade An agreement between two parties at different levels in the manufacturing-distribution system to engage in a practice that restrains trade.

vest To mature, as in the maturing of rights such that a party can legally act on the rights.

vicarious liability The liability or responsibility imposed on a person, a party, or an organization for damages caused by another; most commonly used in relation to employment, with the employer held vicariously liable for the damages caused by its employees.

virtue ethics The ethical system which proposes that a decision is ethical when it promotes positive character traits such as honesty, courage, or fairness.

virus A computer program that rearranges, damages, destroys, or replaces computer data.

void A term applied to a contract that is not valid because its object is illegal or it has a defect that is so serious that it is not a contract.

void title Not true title; e.g., the title held by someone who knowingly or unknowingly purchased stolen goods.

voidable A term applied to a contract that one or both parties have the ability to either withdraw from or enforce.

voidable title Title that occurs when a contract between the original parties would be void but the goods have already been sold to a third party.

voir dire The process of questioning potential jurors to ensure that the jury will be made up of nonbiased individuals.

W

Wagner Act The first major piece of federal legislation adopted explicitly to encourage the formation of labor unions and provide for collective bargaining between employers and unions as a means of obtaining the peaceful settlement of labor disputes.

waiting period In securities registration, the period between the time an issuer files a registration statement and prospectus with the SEC requesting to offer a security and the time the offer is approved by the SEC, which is a minimum of 20 days.

warehouse receipt A receipt issued by one who is engaged in the business of storing goods for compensation.

warranty (1) An assurance, either express or implied, by one party that the other party can rely on its representations of fact. (2) In sales, a binding promise regarding a product in the event that the product does not meet the manufacturer's or seller's promises.

warranty liability Liability that is attributed when the transfer of an instrument breaches a warranty associated with an instrument.

warranty of title An assurance, inferred in every UCC sales transaction, that the seller has good and valid title to the goods and has the right to transfer the title free and clear of any liens, judgments, or infringements of intellectual property rights of which the buyer does not have knowledge.

waste Permanent and substantial injury to a landlord's property.

watered stock Stock that is issued to individuals below its fair market value.

white-collar crime A variety of nonviolent illegal acts against society that occur most frequently in the business context.

whole-life insurance Life insurance that provides protection for the entire life of the insured person.

will A legal document in which a person outlines how she wants her property to be distributed after her death.

winding up The process of completing unfinished partnership business.

workers' compensation law A state law that provides for financial compensation to employees or their dependents when the covered employee is injured on the job.

working papers The various documents used and developed during an audit, including notes, calculations, copies, memorandums, and other papers constituting the accountant's work product.

World Trade Organization (WTO) An international organization that facilitates international cooperation in opening markets and provides a forum for future trade negotiations and the settlement of international trade disputes.

WPH process (of ethical decision making) A set of ethical guidelines that urges us to consider whom an action affects, the purpose of the action, and how we view its morality (whether by utilitarian ethics, deontology, etc.).

writ of certiorari A Supreme Court order, issued after the Court decides to hear an appeal, mandating that the lower court send to the Supreme Court the record of the appealed case.

writ of execution A court order that authorizes a local law officer to seize and sell a debtor's real or personal nonexempt property, within the court's geographic jurisdiction, to enforce a judgment awarded by the court.

writing A type of documentation that shows contractual intent and satisfies the statute of frauds requirement.

wrongful civil proceeding A tort in which one person wrongfully subjects another to criminal or civil litigation that has no justifiable basis.

wrongful dissolution A partnership dissolution that violates the partnership agreement.

Z

zoning The process in which government places restrictions on the use of property to allow for the orderly growth and development of a community and to protect the health, safety, and welfare of its citizens.

Photo Credits

CHAPTER 3

Page 49: © Getty Images, © Mollie Isaacs, Collection of the Supreme Court of the United States, © Robin Reid, Collection of the Supreme Court of the United States, © Getty Images, © Steve Petteway, Colletion of the Supreme Court of the United States, © Steve Petteway, Colletion of the Supreme Court of the United States, © Steve Petteway, Colletion of the Supreme Court of the United States, © Steve Petteway, Colletion of the Supreme Court of the United States, © Steve Petteway, Colletion of the Supreme Court of the United States.

CHAPTER 4

Page 70: © Corbis.

CHAPTER 5

Page 94: © Brand X Pictures/PunchStock, © The McGraw-Hill Companies, Inc./Jill Braaten, photographer, © Hisham F. Ibrahim/Getty Images; p. 106: © Clay Good/Zuma Press.

CHAPTER 7

Page 175: © 2007 Getty Images , Inc.

CHAPTER 10

Page 237: © The McGraw-Hill Companies, Inc./Jack Holtel, photographer.

CHAPTER 12

Page 285: © Brian Jannsen / Alamy; p. 291: © ASSOCIATED PRESS; p. 286:© whiteboxmedia limited/Alamy.

CHAPTER 14

Page 326: © U.S. Army Photo by Mass Communication Specialist 3rd Class Dustin Kelling.

CHAPTER 16

Page 366: © Royalty-Free/Corbis.

CHAPTER 18

Page 405: © Stockbyte/Getty Images.

CHAPTER 31

Page 683: © Brand X/Fotosearch.

CHAPTER 32

Page 702: © Royalty-Free/Corbis.

CHAPTER 35

Page 784: © The McGraw-Hill Companies, Inc./Jill Braaten, photographer.

CHAPTER 41

Page 895: © Anton J. Geisser/Getty Images.

CHAPTER 42

Page 932: © The McGraw-Hill Companies, Inc./Andrew Resek, photographer.

CHAPTER 45

Page 994: © Creatas/Jupiter Images.

CHAPTER 46

Page 1020: © Royalty-Free/Corbis.

CHAPTER 52

Page 1153: © Stockbyte/Getty Images.

APPENDIX B:

Uniform Commercial Code, copyright © by the American Law Institute and the National Conference of Commissioners on Uniform State Laws.

Name Index

T

V

W

X

Y

Z

Subject Index

Page numbers followed by n refer to material in notes.

A

B

D

E

F

G

H

I

K

L

M

O

P

Q

R

S

T

U

V

W

Y

Z